Collectors' Information Bureau

COLLECTIBLES

MARKET GUIDE & PRICE INDEX

Limited Edition: Plates • Figurines • Cottages • Bells • Graphics • Ornaments • Dolls • Steins

Twelfth Edition

Your Complete Source for Information on Limited Edition Collectibles

Collectors' Information Bureau
Barrington, Illinois

Inquiries to the Collectors' Information Bureau
should be mailed to 5065 Shoreline Rd., Suite 200,
Barrington, Illinois 60010
Phone (708) 842-2200

Manufactured in the United States of America

Library of Congress Catalog Card Number: 1068-4808

ISBN 0-930785-18-5 Collectors' Information Bureau

ISBN 0-87069-733-1 Wallace-Homestead

CREDITS

Book Cover Design, Color Section Layout and Photo Styling:
Philip B. Schaafsma Photography, Grand Rapids, Michigan

Book Design and Graphics:
Trade Typographers, Inc., Grand Rapids, Michigan
Wright Design, Grand Rapids, Michigan

By Heio W. Reich

President of COLLECTORS' INFORMATION BUREAU
and
President of RECO INTERNATIONAL CORP.

Foreward

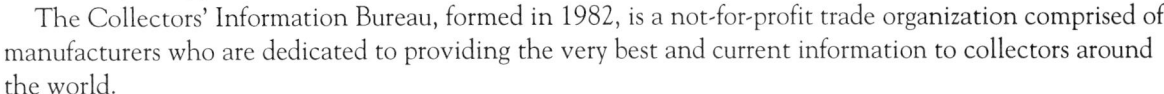

Dear Collector:

As President of the Collectors' Information Bureau, it is my personal pleasure to introduce this updated twelfth edition of the COLLECTIBLES MARKET GUIDE & PRICE INDEX.

With over 675 pages at your fingertips, you will find information on most every aspect of collecting: feature articles, collector clubs, artist biographies, company histories, decorating tips, travel ideas, the secondary market, insuring collections, glossary and reading suggestions. An attractive 36-page color photography chapter highlights the industry's most recent product introductions and all-time favorites.

What's more, the GUIDE showcases over 35,000 values in its 200 page-plus price index, covering limited edition plates, figurines, cottages, crystal, dolls, ornaments, bells, prints and steins.

The Collectors' Information Bureau, formed in 1982, is a not-for-profit trade organization comprised of manufacturers who are dedicated to providing the very best and current information to collectors around the world.

Whether you're reading this book or one of our other fascinating reference books, price guides or newsletters, it is our wish that as you learn more about your hobby, you will enjoy your collectibles to a greater extent. Opportunities abound as you explore your hobby; meeting fellow collectors and forming friendships at conventions and other collectible events enhances your collecting experience.

Please count the Collectors' Information Bureau and its 83 member companies amongst your special friends, as you sit back, relax and open this volume, which includes a wealth of information devoted to you, the collector.

Cordially,

Heio W. Reich

Heio W. Reich
Port Washington, NY
November 1994

P.S. If you discover any unanswered questions in this treasure-trove of collectibles information, please write to our research staff or call the headquarters at (708) 842-2200. The staff welcomes all collectible inquiries!

1. "Golden Conquerors" by Lenox Collections
2. "Four Bears" by Rick Cain Studios
3. "Love Tide" by Marty Bell Fine Art, Inc.
4. "Enduring" by Legends
5. "Fisherman Santa" by Midwest of Cannon Falls
6. *Victorian Springtime* by Shelia's Collectibles
7. "Limited Edition Country Cottage" by Iris Arc Crystal
8. "Ebbets Field" by LCS Products & Services
9. "Pintails Trio" by C.U.I., Inc.
10. "Big Ben" by Fraser International, Inc.
11. "Waldkirchen Father Christmas" by Old World Christmas
12. "Escublar" by Precious Art/Panton International
13. "Teddy Bear Tales" by Reco International Corp.
14. "Flora" by G. Armani
15. "Basket of Love" by Lladro
16. "Prayer for the Wild Things" by The Greenwich Workshop, Inc.
17. "Cabbagetown" by Michael's Limited
18. "Four Seasons Autumn Angel" by Roman, Inc.
19. "Cape Hatteras, Lighthouse" by George Z. Lefton Co.
20. "The Colonial Capitol at Williamsburg, Virginia" by Brandywine Collectibles
21. "Heartbreak Willie" by WACO Products Corporation
22. "Waltz of the Dolphins" by Maruri USA Corporation
23. "A Touch of Magic" by Possible Dreams, Ltd.
24. "Rockwell's Studio" by Hawthorne Architectural Register
25. "USS Enterprise NCC-1701" by The Hamilton Collection
26. "Thomas Jefferson Character Jug" by Royal Doulton
27. "The Gentleman Soldier" by The Lance Corporation

28. "Dedlock Arms" and "Visions of a Christmas Past" Accessories by Department 56, Inc.
29. "Magic Makers" by The Bradford Exchange
30. "Russian Santa" by Duncan Royale
31. "Baroque Angel" by Goebel
32. "Victorian Parlor," "The Owl and the Pussy Cat," "Lunch Wagon," "Bedford County Courthouse" and "U.S. Flag" by F.J. Designs/The Cat's Meow
33. "Becky High" by Ladie and Friends, Inc.
34. "O'Donovan's Castle" by John Hine Studios
35. "Dollmaker's Cottage" by Fitz and Floyd
36. "Osprey Stein" by Anheuser-Busch
37. "The Recital" by Cast Art Industries
38. "Gyr Falcon" by Creart
39. "Pye Corner Cottage" by Lightpost Publishing
40. "All Aboard...Santa's North Pole Express" by June McKenna Collectibles, Inc.
41. "Tiffany" by Seymour Mann, Inc.
42. "Tulu" by Georgetown Collection, Inc.
43. "Little Bo Peep" by The Ashton-Drake Galleries
44. "Danny, The Limited Edition Coca-Cola Heirloom Collector Doll" by The Franklin Mint
45. "Snow White" by The Lawton Doll Company
46. "Catcus Flower" by Artaffects, Ltd.
47. "Kelsey" by Dynasty Dolls
48. "Olde World Santa" by Classic Collectables by Uniquely Yours
49. "18-Inch Old World Reindeer with Bells" by Annalee Mobilitee Dolls, Inc.

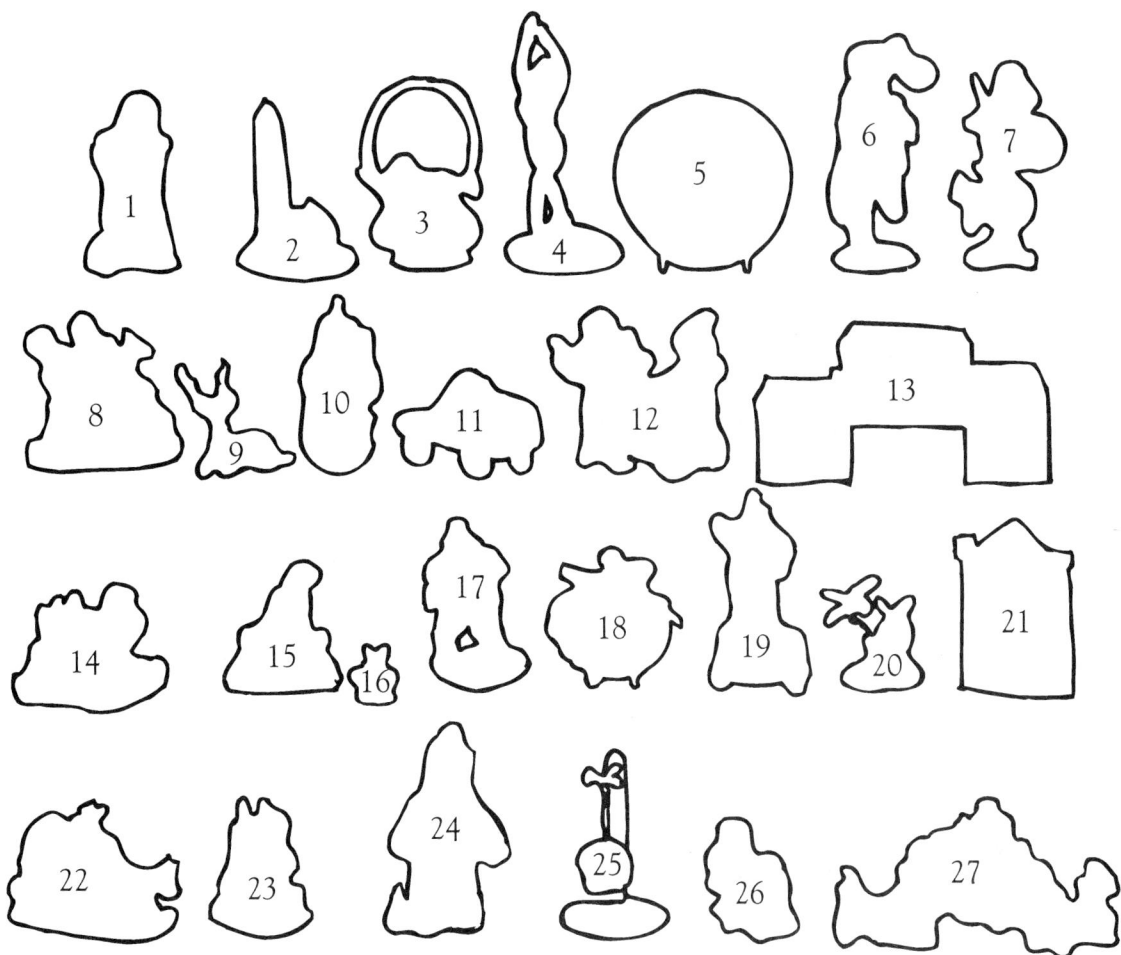

1. "Gift of Love" by Sarah's Attic, Inc.
2. "St. Simons, Georgia" by Harbour Lights
3. "Gold Pansies on Cranberry" by The Fenton Art Glass Company
4. "Kristi Yamaguchi — Gold Medal Grace" by Gartlan USA
5. "A Winter's Day at the Deer Park" — 100th Edition Christmas Plate by Bing & Grondahl
6. "Fritz" by Byers' Choice Ltd.
7. "Aria" by Rawcliffe Corporation
8. "Bayou Boys" by Calabar Creations
9. "Inspiration Africa" — the Kudu by Swarovski America Ltd.
10. "Snow Dancing" by Christopher Radko
11. "Murray® 1955 Red Champion" by Hallmark Galleries
12. "Scrooge in Robe" and "Marley's Ghost" by Kurt S. Adler, Inc.
13. *The Author Collection Series I* by R.R. Creations, Inc.

14. "Watermeadows" by Lilliput Lane
15. "Chantel" by Miss Martha Originals
16. "Winnie-the-Pooh" © Disney by Summerhill Crystal
17. "Cooperstown Collection® Santa" by Flambro Imports
18. "Messiah Angel" by Margaret Furlong Designs
19. "Hot Dog" by Ron Lee's World of Clowns
20. "Magnificent Pair on Trumpet Vine" by United Design Corp.
21. "Rutledge House: Charleston, South Carolina" by Historical Miniatures, Inc.
22. "Texas Lonesteer" by GANZ
23. "Ride Into Christmas" (HUM 396/2/0) M.I. *Hummel* figurine by Goebel
24. "Angus/Scotland" by The Great American Taylor Collectibles Corp.
25. "Peter Rabbit 1994" by Hand & Hammer Silversmiths
26. "Polishing Up" by VickiLane Inc.
27. "Oh Joyful Night Nativity" by BAND Creations

Contents

Contributing Writers

Catherine Bloom
Peter George
Susan K. Jones

Gail Cohen
Katherine Holden
James VanMaanen

Collectors' Information Bureau Staff

Sue Knappen
Carol VanElderen
Deborah Wojtysiak
Cindy Zagumny

Rose Schwager
Peggy Veltri
Barbara Workman

Acknowledgments

The staff of Collectors' Information Bureau wishes to thank the following persons who deserve special recognition for their invaluable contributions to the creation of this book: Catherine Bloom, Gail Cohen, Peter George, Katherine Holden, Susan K. Jones, Ray and Lorrie Kiefer of the National Association of Limited Edition Dealers, Donna Nemmers and John Waters of Wm. C. Brown Communications, Todd Mellema and Philip Schaafsma of Philip B. Schaafsma Photography, James VanMaanen and Kristin Wiley and Mike Policka of Wright Design.

Special thanks goes out to our distinguished panel of over 300 limited edition retailers and secondary market experts whose knowledge and dedication have helped make our Price Index possible. We wish we could recognize them by name, but they have agreed that to be singled out in this manner may hinder their ability to maintain an unbiased view of the marketplace.

We also wish to express our deep appreciation to the following persons whose dedication, hard work and encouragement made the twelfth edition of the *Collectibles Market Guide & Price Index* possible: Karen Feil, Ronald Jedlinski, Ken LeFevre, Heio W. Reich and James P. Smith, Jr.

C.I.B. Members

During its first year of existence, the CIB Membership Roster included fourteen member firms. Today, the roster of member companies numbers eighty-three — an ever-increasing membership!

Kurt S. Adler, Inc.
1107 Broadway
New York, NY 10010

Anheuser-Busch, Inc.
Retail Sales Department
2700 South Broadway
St. Louis, MO 63118

Annalee Mobilitee Dolls, Inc.
Box 708 Reservoir Road
Meredith, NH 03253

Armani
c/o Miller Import Corp.
300 Mac Lane
Keasbey, NJ 08832

Artaffects, Ltd.
Box 98
Staten Island, NY 10307

The Ashton-Drake Galleries
9200 N. Maryland Avenue
Niles, IL 60714

Attic Babies
P.O. Box 912
Drumright, OK 74030

BAND Creations
28427 N. Ballard
Lake Forest, IL 60045

Marty Bell Fine Art, Inc.
9314 Eton Avenue
Chatsworth, CA 91311

The Bradford Exchange
9333 Milwaukee Avenue
Niles, IL 60714

Brandywine Collectibles
2413 Wolftrap Rd.
Yorktown, VA 23692

Byers' Choice Ltd.
P.O. Box 158
Chalfont, PA 18914

Rick Cain Studios
619 S. Main Street
Gainesville, FL 32601

Calabar Creations
1941 S. Vineyard Avenue
Ontario, CA 91761

Cast Art Industries, Inc.
1120 California Avenue
Corona, CA 91719

The Cat's Meow/F.J. Designs
2163 Great Trails Drive
Wooster, OH 44691

Christopher Radko
Planetarium Station
P.O. Box 770
New York, NY 10024

Classic Collectables by Uniquely Yours
P.O. Box 16861
Philadelphia, PA 19142

Creart
209 E. Ben White, Suite 103
Austin, TX 78704

C.U.I., Inc./Classic Carolina Collections/Dram Tree
1502 North 23rd Street
Wilmington, NC 28405

Department 56, Inc.
P.O. Box 44456
Eden Prairie, MN 55344-1456

The Walt Disney Company
500 South Buena Vista Street
Burbank, CA 91521-6876

Duncan Royale
1141 So. Acacia Avenue
Fullerton, CA 92631

Dynasty Dolls
c/o Cardinal Inc.
P.O. Box 99
400 Markley Street
Port Reading, NJ 07064

eggspressions! inc.
1635 Deadwood Avenue
Rapid City, SD 57702

Enesco Corporation
1 Enesco Plaza
Elk Grove Village, IL 60007

The Fenton Art Glass Company
700 Elizabeth Street
Williamstown, WV 26187

Fitz and Floyd/Silvestri
13111 N. Central Expressway
Dallas, TX 75243

Flambro Imports
1530 Ellsworth Industrial Drive
Atlanta, GA 30318

Forma Vitrum
20414 N. Main Street
Cornelius, NC 28031

The Franklin Mint
Franklin Center, PA 19091

Fraser International, Inc.
5990 N. Belt E, Unit 606
Humble, TX 77396

Margaret Furlong Designs
210 State Street
Salem, OR 97301

GANZ
908 Niagara Falls Blvd.
North Tonawanda, NY 14120-2060

Gartlan USA
1951 Old Cuthbert Road
Cherry Hill, NJ 08034

Georgetown Collection
866 Spring Street
Westbrook, ME 04092

Goebel
Goebel Plaza
P.O. Box 10, Rte. 31
Pennington, NJ 08534-0010

Great American Taylor Collectibles Corp.
Dept BIC
P.O. Box 428
Aberdeen, NC 28315

The Greenwich Workshop
One Greenwich Place
Shelton, CT 06484

Hallmark Cards, Inc.
Hallmark Keepsake Ornament Collectors' Club #161
P.O. Box 412734
Kansas City, MO 64141-2734

The Hamilton Collection*
4810 Executive Park Court
Jacksonville, FL 32216-6069

Hand & Hammer Silversmiths
Hand & Hammer Collectors' Club
2610 Morse Lane
Woodbridge, VA 22192

Harbour Lights
8130 La Mesa Blvd.
La Mesa, CA 91941

Hawthorne Architectural Register
9210 N. Maryland Avenue
Niles, IL 60714

John Hine Studios, Inc.
4456 Campbell Road
P.O. Box 800667
Houston, TX 77280-0667

Historical Miniatures
95 Hathaway Street, C-10
Providence, RI 02907

M.I. Hummel Club*
Division of Goebel Art GmbH
Goebel Plaza
P.O. Box 11
Pennington, NJ 08534-0011

Iris Arc Crystal
114 East Haley Street
Santa Barbara, CA 93101

LCS Products & Services Corp.
8240 Ronda Drive
Canton, MI 48187

Ladie and Friends, Inc.
220 North Main Street
Sellersville, PA 18960

The Lance Corporation
321 Central Street
Hudson, MA 01749

The Lawton Doll Company
548 North First
Turlock, CA 95380

Ron Lee's World of Clowns
2180 Agate Court
Simi Valley, CA 93065

George Z. Lefton Co.
3622 S. Morgan Street
Chicago, IL 60609

LEGENDS
2665D Park Center Drive
Simi Valley, CA 93065

Lenox Collections
1170 Wheeler Way
Langhorne, PA 19047

Lightpost Publishing
Ten Almaden Blvd. 9th Floor
San Jose, CA 95113

Lilliput Lane Limited
c/o Lilliput Incorporated
9052 Old Annapolis Road
Columbia, MD 21045

Lladro Collectors Society
43 W. 57th Street
New York, NY 10019

Seymour Mann, Inc.
225 Fifth Avenue,
Showroom #102
New York, NY 10010

Maruri U.S.A.
7541 Woodman Place
Van Nuys, CA 91405

June McKenna Collectibles Inc.
P.O. Box 846
Ashland, VA 23005

Michael's Limited
P.O. Box 217
Redmond, WA 98078-0217

Midwest of Cannon Falls
32057 64th Avenue, P.O. Box 20
Cannon Falls, MN 55009-0020

Miss Martha Originals, Inc.
P.O. Box 5038
Glencoe, AL 35905

Old World Christmas
P.O. Box 8000
Spokane, WA 99203

Pacific Rim Import Corp.
5930 4th Avenue South
Seattle, WA 98108

PenDelfin Sales Inc.
750 Ensminger Road #108
Box 884
Tonawanda, NY 14150

Possible Dreams
6 Perry Drive
Foxboro, MA 02035

Precious Art/Panton
110 E. Ellsworth Road
Ann Arbor, MI 48108

R.R. Creations
P.O. Box 8707
Pratt, KS 67124

Rawcliffe Corporation
155 Public Street
Providence, RI 02903

Reco International Corp.*
150 Haven Avenue
Port Washington, NY 11050

Roman, Inc.*
555 Lawrence Avenue
Roselle, IL 60172-1599

**Royal Copenhagen/
Bing & Grondahl**
27 Holland Avenue
White Plains, NY 10603

Royal Doulton
700 Cottontail Lane
Somerset, NJ 08873

Sarah's Attic
126-1/2 West Broad, P.O. Box 448
Chesaning, MI 48616

Shelia's Inc.
P.O. Box 31028
Charleston, SC 29417

Swarovski America Ltd.
2 Slater Road
Cranston, RI 02920

Today's Creations, Inc.
167 Main Street
Lodi, NJ 07644

United Design Corporation
P.O. Box 1200
Noble, OK 73068

VickiLane
3233 NE Cadet
Portland, OR 97220

WACO Products Corp.
One North Corporate Drive
Riverdale, NJ 07457-0160

*Charter Member

The Joy of Collecting
Collectors from Across the Country Share The Fun and Offer Advice to Fellow Fine Art Enthusiasts

"Robert Louis Stevenson said, 'It is perhaps a more fortunate destiny to have a taste for collecting than to be born a millionaire.' He was right! Collecting makes me happy every day of my life!" With this ringing endorsement, Gwen Schoen of Sacramento, California logs in as one of Collectors' Information Bureau's most enthusiastic recent interview subjects. Like many of her fellow collectors' Ms. Schoen reports spending more than $2,500 per year on her passion for Department 56 cottages and other collectibles.

"An obsession." "A fever." "A never-ending source of joy." These are just a few of the descriptions other collectors gave us for their collecting hobbies. Reporting ownership of as many as 1,500 plates, well over 100 dolls, and similar numbers of other collector's items, our CIB panel truly has caught the collecting spirit. As Gail R. Edwards of Oklahoma City, Oklahoma explains, "Many things

in life you buy, you don't get your money's worth, but with collecting you get a lot more than your money's worth. You get beauty — and great conversation."

How Collections Begin

For many of our respondents, a gift or the purchase of one simple item touched off a veritable fire for collecting. As Jeff J. Jorgens of Lincoln, Nebraska recalls, "My collection started out by receiving steins as Christmas gifts. I now purchase about forty to fifty steins per year!" Frank Schuler of Fullerton, California recalls, "I received an offering from The Bradford Exchange to purchase 'The Toymaker' — Rockwell Heritage #1. From then on my plate collecting escalated to some 1,500 plates!"

Collecting runs in the family for many — either

Transparent, plexiglass shelves make the "plates the stars" in this display of works by Edna Hibel, P. Buckley Moss and other artists provided by Roger Jorn of Lake Worth, Florida.

Edith Phillips of Williams, Arizona favors wildlife works of art. In one corner of her bedroom she groups plates, prints and figurines inspired by owls in this pleasing arrangement.

they "caught the bug" from an older relative, or they plan to hand down their treasures to their children and grandchildren. "The very first collectible I saw belonged to my grandmother," reminisces Ellen Wigginton of Holt, Michigan. "She collected porcelain figurines and I was in awe. I would sit and stare for hours and slowly but surely developed an appreciation for figurines that has currently manifested itself in David Winter cottages." The hereditary interest seems to be continuing, as Ms. Wigginton tells us, "My eleven-year-old son and six-year-old daughter admire (the cottages) and have expressed interest in someday owning them."

One form of collectible may initially attract an enthusiast's attention, then lead to his interest in another medium. This happened to Mel Smith of Seattle, Washington, who advanced from, "Bells — to spoons — to cups and decanters — then to plates. My interest tapered off almost to a stop on everything but plates. They remain constant. I picked up a John Wayne black-and-white plate in a store ten years ago; now I have over 300 plates."

Collectors Reveal Their "All-Time Favorites"

Many collectors admit that a certain particular piece — or a line of collectibles — is especially

near and dear to the heart. For Mary I. Sanchez of Sound Beach, New York, collecting helped her to overcome grief following a tragedy. "My first trip to Spain came after I had lost my only child. My dad thought the change and meeting my relatives might help. Everywhere we went in Spain we saw clowns. I finally asked why and was told the most famous clown was from Spain. He was their mascot. So my first Lladro was a clown, of course."

Bruce Steffensmeier, who resides in Germany, favors Swarovski Silver Crystal because "The glimmer reminds me of the glisten of a freshly fallen snow. It is such an incredibly beautiful collectible or gift — the quality of sparkle portrays all the good of the world."

The historical aspect of Charles Dickens' Village homes is what captivates Christopher Terrasi of York, Pennsylvania. "What life was in that era! It is a very interesting and different feeling when I look at the homes," he exclaims. "It feels like the people are alive!"

Many Wonderful Options for Display

While some collectors feel constrained by the size of their homes and rooms, most are very resourceful in displaying their treasures. Curio cabinets seem to be the favorite display device, while some collectors become more daring and create

their own methods of showing off favorite pieces. As Sal Candela of Elmhurst, New York relates, "I have a very large glass and mirror wall unit in which I display most of my collectibles. They are spotlighted to give a glow effect, especially in the evening."

When asked if she displays her beloved David Winter cottages, Ellen Wigginton answered, "You could say that — I remodeled a room to include built-in curios. Am I crazy or what?" Barbara Ann Hart of LaPorte, Texas also has her own ideas when it comes to display. She uses fish aquariums with plexiglass cut to fit the top. "These are then set into bookcases," she explains. "This gives a neat, dust-free, simple way to show them off."

Christopher Terrasi does not believe in showing collectibles only during one season of the year. When it comes to his Charles Dickens' Village homes, he says, "I display the whole fifty-eight homes the year-round. I have them on shelves on the walls around my beauty shoppe and the customers really enjoy them." On the other hand, many collectors go "all out" when Christmas rolls around. Roberta Jordan of Big Bend, Wisconsin says, "At Christmas my Department 56 decorations come out plus all the hundreds of ornaments on two trees."

Collecting Holds Interest for Years and Years

The collectors we interviewed showed no signs of "slowing down," even though many of them own hundreds of pieces and must rotate them to show them off in their homes. While some tease that "only the Lord knows" why they keep collecting, others have more specific insights. "To finish off sets," Jeff Jorgens says, while Bruce Steffensmeier speaks of "The chase. Will the buy become a sought-after item? I try to be aware of the new and the hot."

Few of our respondents are interested in active secondary market trading; in fact, when asked if they do it, many answered with an exclamatory "No!" However, some collectors do enjoy keeping careful track of buy-sell activity so they will know the current value of their belongings. Barbara A. Pawson of East Windsor, New Jersey, an avid collector of Wee Forest Folk, says "I enjoy tracking the valuation and appreciation as much as the (Folk) themselves. I maintain a database of all public and private sales and auctions all over the country, and have a very complete record of all current values."

Meeting Artists Makes Happy Memories

Collectibles artists win celebrity status among those who cherish their works. Sometimes meeting such an artist compares to the excitement surrounding a rock star's appearance — at least that's how Ellen Wigginton remembers her encounter with David Winter. "I'm afraid I have nothing memorable to report," she says of her meeting with the charming English sculptor, "except that I hyperventilate easily."

Mary I. Sanchez was particularly impressed by Robert Olszewski, a creator of Goebel Miniatures. "He's a remarkable, extremely talented man, what a joy he was," she recalls. "I am now really hooked on his productions. At the end of the day he took off his smock and took great care to neatly fold it up until it was the size of an envelope. This is a man who loves and takes pride in everything he does, and it shows."

Armani collectors Sal and Anna Candela had the pleasure of meeting Giuseppe Armani recently. "It was a long-awaited thrill for both of us to speak to him," Candela reports, "especially since we speak the same language (Italian)." The Candelas purchased three figurines signed and dated by Armani himself, and had photos taken with the artist.

A trip to the Precious Moments Chapel in Missouri became a special memory for Shirley Chretien of Windham, Maine when artist Sam Butcher showed up unexpectedly. "As we were walking through the Visitors Center, we saw Mr. Butcher on his way out. We were so thrilled and couldn't think straight. We hadn't gotten our chapel pieces because we were just on our way in. He stopped and waited while we purchased them and he signed them for us, and waited for pictures to be taken."

Dealers and Collectors Clubs Enhance Enjoyment

Many collectors note the benefits of an ongoing relationship with a good collectibles dealer or mail order firm. One unique example is the help Ellen Wigginton's favorite dealer offers her on holiday occasions. "My dealer, Kean's Hallmark in Mason, Michigan, allows me a 'gift box.' That is, I put all the pieces I want in a box and during the holidays, my family and friends shop out of the box. It's great for me because I always get what I want — and guarantee him lots of business."

Club members-only items are one enticement

for collectors to join clubs sponsored by particular manufacturers. Roberta Jordan belongs to six clubs primarily for this purpose. Collectors also appreciate club newsletters, previews of new editions, and other amenities offered by national and international clubs. On the local level, they most often mention the fun of discussing their "passion" with like-minded individuals.

All in all, our collector's panel agrees that their "addiction" is something for which they want no cure. For the "lure of the chase," the joy of discovery, the comradery with fellow collectors and the pride of home display, collecting is more than a hobby: it's a never-ending source of pleasure.

The Federal Duck Stamp plates of Edith Phillips are enhanced by a three-dimensional duck decoy and an arrangement of dried flowers.

The Art of Decorating with Collectibles
Artistic Decorating Tips Lend Variety and Beauty to Collectors' Homes

Explorations of ancient cultures reveal that people have always surrounded themselves with both priceless and practical objects of beauty. One culture favored simple bowls. Others savored works of gold or porcelain.

Today's collectors seem to have an affinity for objects which provide both comfort and pleasure. In turn, collectibles allow owners to express their personalities and tastes, sometimes in a manner more revealing than their life stories.

Ruth Wolf of The Limited Edition store in Merrick, New York noted: "People who collect limited editions are very fortunate because they can use their collections as part of their life. They can literally surround themselves by the things they enjoy as opposed to keeping their treasures in a safety deposit box."

Doing Your Homework

While few collectors slavishly follow the current fads, they may find it helpful to keep abreast of current decorating, accessory, and lighting trends. There are a number of ways to keep up with innovative ideas. Collectors should read a variety of decorating and collectibles publications — both ads and features can spark new ideas for showcasing

pieces. Manufacturers and store designers also use innovative decorative techniques to enhance in-shop sales. Many of their methods can be adapted by collectors. Visit museums and antique shops for inspiration, keeping a notebook of ideas and a file of clippings or photos for future use.

Decorating is never an exact science, but it is wise to study some of the basic "how-to" books to become familiar with terms like "visual unity," "spatial relationships" and "balance."

Getting Started

Before moving furniture and pounding nails, one should study the ambiance of the room to decide where the focal point should be. Should a single, large piece or a grouping of smaller collectibles be used? The primary arrangement will

This wall unit offers a safe haven for a hand-carved heron and The Hamilton Collections' "Early Spring" plate. The wildlife theme is carried through with a plate and three adorable baby seal figurines.

The effect of Marty Bell's "Laverstoke Lodge" framed lithograph is heightened by this victorian grouping which includes a candelabra, books, violets, tea service, lace napkin and roses.

Goebel Miniatures Nativity by Robert Olszewski consists of three detailed vignettes and a dramatic illustrated display environment. To date, it is the finest example of a unified display showcasing miniatures.

set the general tone for the room and help determine the placement of other collectible arrangements, which frequently include "favorites" like books, plants and flowers and other small objects.

Collectors must select not only the right pieces for each display, but also accessories such as frames, stands, domes, boxes, display cases and bases. Collectible accessories serve two purposes: they display a piece to its best advantage, while also protecting it. Thousands of items are produced for this purpose.

Plate frames, cases and horizontal hangers give plates a more finished appearance. Select only frames which do not rub or damage the rim. Appropriately styled wall brackets can be useful in showcasing figurines in wall groupings. For variety, display objects at differing heights.

When using bases or pedestals in a grouping, bases of the same material (all wood or acrylic) should be selected to avoid a cluttered look. Rotating cases or bases allow collectibles to be viewed from all sides.

Seek out new and innovative lighting accessories to highlight individual items. An art-glow light (a polystyrene bowl with small bulb and diffuser) fits on the back of stained-glass plates so that plates are no longer dependent on adjacent lamps or candles for illumination.

Individual Pieces And Groupings

In the past, decorating an entire wall with plates for a gallery effect was very popular. There is a definite unity and impact with this method, but it frequently detracts from the individual beauty of the plates. Many designers now prefer to work with smaller groupings which display a single plate or figurine as a work of art in its own right. As a collection increases, limiting the number of pieces being displayed becomes both necessary and aesthetically more pleasing.

Planning On Paper

To work out the most attractive wall groupings, many collectors make rough sketches of possible arrangements. If the grouping is quite complex, the collector may prefer to make paper patterns of each item and arrange them on the floor before transferring the mock grouping to a wall. Taping a

paper pattern to a wall is much easier than hanging a ready-to-display print or figurine.

Once a suitable grouping has been decided upon, the proper markings may be transferred to the wall, using a tape measure and level. Hangers and frames should be inspected to ensure that a faulty hanger doesn't create an uneven arrangement.

Dolls

Some of the most charming doll arrangements are created with cribs, rockers and antique furniture. Gigi of Gigi's Dolls and Sherry's Teddy Bears in Chicago, Illinois recalled, "One of our collectors has a talent for creating doll groupings that begin with a painting or print as a backdrop. Depending on the colors and perspective, she then adds a doll in the right proportion and color, some plush animals or accessories. Dolls posed with antique toys under a dome also make a nice presentation. In displaying our dolls and bears, we enjoy using step tables and chairs because they provide a sense of unity."

Collectors are encouraged to experiment with different types of doll stands, bases, domes, glass and Lucite cases or lighted cabinets where dolls can be displayed, spotlighted and protected.

At least two inches of space must be allotted above and around the doll in a dome or case. Even more space may be needed with large dolls. When displaying a doll with other toys, collectors should be sure that the playthings are from the same period as the doll. A 19th-century porcelain doll would certainly look best surrounded by antique accessories.

Ornaments

At one time, the only accepted means of displaying collectible ornaments was the Christmas tree. Today, ornaments are shown in a variety of attractive settings!

In areas where greenery is not available, small shrubs or dried foliage can be gilded or painted and placed in a decorative pot. Ornaments can then be hung or nestled in the branches. Ornaments may also be placed on mantles, or in large greenery-filled bowls in the center of the table.

Condominium dwellers, because of their more confined quarters, frequently opt to display ornaments on wreaths. The ornaments may be old family favorites or current collectibles such as *Snowbabies* combined with white ornaments and glitter. The possibilities for theme wreaths are endless.

Cherished collections of well-polished crystal, gold and silver ornaments take on new life when individually suspended on velvet or satin ribbons in front of mirrors or windows.

Silver and gold ornaments may also be strung on a chain or ribbon and worn as a necklace.

Bells And Steins

In the past, bell collectors have simply placed their collections on a mantle or shelf or in display cases which have been compartmentalized. Now, cases or shelves where the background can be changed by inserting a variety of backdrops covered with materials such as gold foil and red velvet or painted in neutral or pastel shades offer a variety of display options. Collectors can invest in new lighting and blend bells with accessories and collectibles for more interest.

Created by special demand, this display cabinet of solid red oak veneer and moldings, with brass detailing was designed especially for David Winter Cottages. The cabinet has a mirrored back, allowing the cottages to be viewed from back as well as front, two halogen toplights, adjustable glass shelving and keyed lock.

Glass shelves in windows make a marvelous display for colored glass and crystal bells. Miniature lights behind each shelf can add a new dimension to the display on special occasions.

Ann Huver, a novice bell collector, places wind chimes in front of heat and air-conditioning vents. The movement of air produces the gentle sound of the glass chimes and creates the illusion that the rhythmic sounds are coming from her bell collection.

Steins have traditionally evoked images of the old beer halls of Europe where lights were dim and steins were simply placed on shelves. This Old World decor has been repeated all over the world.

Today's stein collectors recognize the historical and artistic significance of steins produced with antique molds, or newer molds with modern themes. They prefer to place stein collections in more formal rooms like libraries and dens.

Gail Cornell of Cornell Importers in St. Paul, Minnesota, a major importer of fine steins, had these suggestions: "Many of our stein collectors collect according to themes like wildlife, trains, Rockwell or even owls. One of our train enthusiasts had a shelf constructed that resembles an old steam engine. All of his train steins are displayed on the shelves behind the engine. Many of our collectors, also amass collectibles by theme. For example, one man displays his buffalo steins with his brass buffalo figurines."

Display steins on rotating bases in lighted glass cases or breakfronts where the full detailing and craftsmanship can be savored.

An ultra-modern display of steins featuring boating themes is the centerpiece of a private yacht club overlooking the Straits of Mackinac and the Mackinac Bridge in northern Michigan. Major groupings of steins are displayed on gleaming glass and mirrored shelves which are constantly in motion. Spotlighted from all angles, the steins are bathed in varying degrees of light.

Figurines

Advances in technology have led manufacturers to use leaded crystal, glass, cold-cast resins, pewter and other alloys in producing figurines. Each material provides unique decorating opportunities.

A representative of the M.I. Hummel Club suggests, "To incorporate your *Hummel* figurines into a room, take them off the shelves and hutches and out of the cases and place them on a table near an overstuffed chair. Mingle favorite figurines with painted folk art, knickknacks, wreaths, baskets of dried flowers or herbs, quilted pillows and old-fashioned keepsakes to create an honest, natural, down-home appearance."

In crystal figurines, the colors created by the prisms, coating materials and light are so subtle that they frequently need a light background to bring out the color. Wood backgrounds seem too harsh, but a mirrored surface or a backdrop paint-

Outdoors, the ground is blanketed with snow. Toasty and inviting in Mr. and Mrs. James Holman's home is their display of the Dickens' Village Collection *from Department 56, Inc.*

This appealing assortment of dolls from Ladie and Friends provides an active cheering section for the cook in Barb Lang's kitchen.

ed a dull black or covered with black velvet is quite effective. Crystal mixes well with brass in many groupings.

A gentle light behind a glass case, or tungsten-halogen lighting, can bring out the highlights in crystal pieces. Rheostats on lighting systems vary the intensity of the light to create different effects. Display environments created by Robert Olszewski remain one of the most innovative methods yet developed for showcasing a collection. Other companies are now introducing bases or dioramas for a variety of arrangements.

Creating A Perfect World

One of the most interesting types of collectibles during the past decade has been miniature cottages and castles. The emergence of these miniatures was followed by the introduction of larger cottages, buildings and accessories, such as the *Dickens' Village* produced by Department 56, Inc. and *Pleasantville 1893* from Flambro Imports. All of these pieces require special decorating expertise.

Miniature cottages and castles are best displayed on tabletops, shelves or in cases where they are protected. Most pieces are enhanced by the addition of an attractive base or a swatch of fabric which picks up accent colors. The proper lighting and accessories can also heighten the effect.

Kim Calhoun of John Hine Studios noted, "Some of our most interesting displays this year incorporated topiary shrubs, heavy lace doilies and antique knickknacks. We have also seen an increase in the use of cottages in floral displays of both dry and fresh flowers."

The construction of a lighted village demands a

number of basic elements. First, a firm base must be selected to safely support the entire display. The electrical system should be installed using safety-approved wiring, while motors and even train systems must be planned and installed before the ground cover (grass or snow) is added. Waterfalls, pumps and ponds should be specially placed in areas where they will not come in contact with wiring or plugs and must always be installed according to safety standards.

Mirrors or foil are frequently used to imitate a frozen pond, while twigs and stones can add a natural touch. To add variety, buildings can be placed at different levels by building papier-maché mountains or by covering boxes with fabric and batting.

The most attractive arrangements frequently incorporate lights and the movement of trains, streams or waterfalls which add vitality to the scene.

Ed Gillies of Ed Gillies Marketing who specializes in the promotion of lighted collectible buildings offered these observations: "The thing we see

Barry Harris, owner of Amanda's Fine Gifts in San Antonio, Texas started a new tradition at his daughter Jackie's wedding by having a "Father Of The Bride" cake displaying ten Lladro figurines.

is the change of seasonality. Most of these collections were started as Christmas displays but now we are finding that people are building additions to their homes to display their collection year-round. One collector added a shelf wider than a plate rail all around one room so her houses can be displayed in the round all year. There is a lot of adult play value involved in decorating with these displays."

"Many collectors now have added flowering shrubs and plants for spring and summer and trees and foliage in gold, scarlet and browns to signify autumn," he continued.

Figurines, plates, dolls, lithographs, ornaments and steins are not simply things to be displayed, but are a very real reflection of a collector's style, sense of humor and outlook on life. With the wide selection of collectibles available today, everyone can decorate with affordable collectible objects, adding variety and beauty to their homes.

The simple joys of childhood are celebrated in this grouping which includes M. I. Hummel figurines, an old-fashioned rose print, vase and antique bottle, a basket filled with potpourri and a handful of fresh cut blades of wheat.

The Secondary Market
What Is It? How Does It Work?...
And Advice From Secondary Market Dealers

One dimension of collecting that seems to capture the interest of collectors more than any other is the secondary market. The first Swarovski club piece, "The Lovebirds," issued for $150 and today commands $2500-$4000 on the secondary market. Also intriguing, The "Field Mouse" from the *Walt Disney Classics Collection* sold for $195; this retired piece is valued at $1400-$1800 as of this printing, and the quote for this little treasure varies weekly. Because most collectors buy what they like, they may or may not end up owning collectibles which have escalated in value.

Many collectors are content just to stay abreast of the market without actually getting involved, much like reading the New York Stock Exchange prices daily, but not owning any stocks. Others enter the market slowly, testing the waters, dabbling their toes. And yet, some prefer to dive right in!

Is it necessary to be aware of the secondary market to enjoy collecting? Not at all. But for those of you who would like to know more about it, whether you plan to deal on the secondary market or not, this article should help answer some questions you may have.

Be certain to realize, however, that there is no right way or wrong way to buy, sell or trade on the secondary market. Though there are various ways to accomplish any of these, you should find the one method that is most comfortable for you.

Supply and Demand

Like most consumer products, the price of a collectible on the secondary market is determined by supply and demand. As the demand for a collectible increases, so does its price. When the demand wanes, the price decreases accordingly. Likewise, the price can have an effect on demand. As the price of a piece reaches a certain point, the demand decreases. This occurs when collectors feel that the piece has reached or exceeded its highest value. Then, of course, as the price decreases, the demand may once again increase as collectors take advantage of the lower prices.

Like water, prices seek their own level. This is

not to say that the prices do not rise higher than where they will "settle" or that there are not any bargains.

Brokers

The first question you must answer, if you are buying or selling, is whether you will handle the transaction yourself or use the services of a secondary market broker. If selling, the advantage of doing it yourself is that you will receive the total amount from the sale of the item(s) and not have to pay a brokerage commission. The advantages of selling through a broker include knowing that you will receive payment for the pieces you send, not having to pay for classified ads and long distance phone calls, and letting the work be done for you. Some brokers offer after-market services through their stores, while others own a business exclusively dedicated to matching up buyers and sellers on the secondary market.

When buying, the advantages of making a purchase through a brokerage are the assurance of receiving a piece for the money you spend, having the piece inspected and the option to return it if you are not completely satisfied.

Commission Rates

When you contact various brokers, you will find that commission rates vary. In most instances, the seller pays the commission. Some brokers charge a commission as low as 10% and others up to as high as 35%. The Collectors' Information Bureau's *Directory to Secondary Market Retailers* features over 200 aftermarket brokers with full-page histories to help collectors learn more about each broker's business practices.

Buying

When making a purchase, you will realize another aspect that varies among brokers: the manner in which they list their items for sale. They are listed, usually, in either of two methods. One method lists the final price that the buyer

will pay for the piece. This is the same manner in which you look at prices when making purchases, be they in a store or in a catalog. The other manner of listing is to show what the seller will receive when the piece is sold, and the buyer must then add the proper commission to determine what the final cost will be. With most brokers using either method, the shipping cost must also be added.

There is no advantage to buying from a broker that uses one method as opposed to the other. As a buyer, though, you want to be aware of which method a broker is using and what your total cost will be for that item. Please remember to use your final price when comparing quotes that you get from brokers.

Surcharges

Surcharges are any added costs that lower the amount of money that you will receive if selling or, in the case of buying, add to your cost. These can include the requirement of subscribing to a newsletter in order to sell, a fee required to actually list with a broker or additional fees for using a credit card.

Advice to Collectors

Collectibles, Etc. Brown Deer, WI; Sandy Forgach
Deal with a reputable firm. There are lots of private individuals on their own. Watch out! I can tell you horror stories.

The Cottage Collector, East Lyme, CT;
Frank Wilson
I advise new collectors to *slow* down. There is a lot of product available. Newly retired pieces often go up fast at first, then settle down in a year, with the price a year after retirement sometimes lower than right after retirement.

Collector's Marketplace, Montrose, PA;
Russ Wood and Renee Tyler
We would strongly recommend that a collector use a reputable secondary market broker. There have been numerous reports to us about abuses by individual sellers or less than reputable dealers — anything from poor merchandise to non-payment.
We would also advise the collectors who are selling their collectibles not to hold out for top dollar. Values decrease as well as increase, and we have seen collectors lose the chance for a nice profit because they were holding out for the last dollar. Conversely, our comment from year to year still applies: don't miss the chance to own something you really want because of a $5 or $10 price differential.

Blevins Plates 'n' Things, Vallejo, CA;
Stella Blevins
Try to buy while a collectible is still on the primary market, as tracking secondary items will be much more difficult in the future. Remember — prices do fluctuate, so don't always assume that there will be a continual increase. Secondary market prices are based strictly on supply and demand.

A Work of Art, Valhalla, NY; Joan Lewis
Read everything you can get your hands on; speak to as many people as you can who seem knowledgeable.
The old tenet still holds: Buy what you like; display it in your favorite rooms and enjoy it. If it happens to go up in value, that is an extra plus. Meanwhile, you have had all that pleasure from it.

The Collectible Source, Warwick, RI;
Peter George
Be aware of two things when dealing on the secondary market. 1. Be certain with whom you are dealing. If at all possible, check the reputation of the person or company. 2. Know what you are purchasing. Too often a collector, thinking that he or she has made a "find," has hastily purchased a piece other than what they thought it was.

Opa's Haus Inc. and the OHI Exchange, New Braunfels, TX; Staff
The advice to buyers: Buy for your own pleasure and needs; avoid buying for speculative investment purposes, especially over a long term. The advice to sellers: Don't be greedy in your price demands; price your items in accordance with the way you would want to buy.

Collections Unlimited, Tarzana, CA; Mickey Kaz
Proceed with care: Don't buy just to resell on the market because you could go broke! Consult the Collectors' Information Bureau or other authorized publications for a price range — not just dealers. If a consumer locates a retired item with a healthy secondary market, then buy, buy, buy if you find it at issue price.
Read collectible publications, just like you would the Wall Street Journal to watch your stocks.

Other Services

Another aspect to consider in doing business with a broker is the cost of any added services such as a toll-free "800" number. No toll-free number is completely cost-free to a buyer or seller, but rather is figured into the cost of doing business by the broker and, thus, figures into his or her commission. Remember, however, that you also pay for every call you make to a broker that does not have a toll-free number.

Value

The one thing that you should be aware of is the value of the piece that you are buying or selling. With this in mind, you can determine if the deal that you are about to make is a fair one. One good source to check for recent price quotes is the Collectors' Information Bureau's Price Index, located in the back of this book. It is the most comprehensive Price Index for limited edition plates, figurines, bells, graphics, ornaments, dolls and steins available on the market today!

Conclusion

Once again, there is no right or wrong way when dealing on the secondary market. Just remember to be aware of the following:
1. The value of the item
2. The broker's method of listing
3. Any additional fees
4. Your final cost
5. Can the item be returned and for what reasons

With these points in mind, you can have a great time trading on the secondary market.

Peter George is the editor of the "Village Chronicle" and the owner of The Collectible Source, Inc. in Warwick, Rhode Island.

How should collectors select a secondary market firm to assist them with their aftermarket transactions?

Collectibles, Etc. Brown Deer, WI; Sandy Forgach

Find a reputable firm and stay with them; don't list your retired collectibles all over so everyone is assisting you at the same time. If you choose to work with multiple brokers, call the brokers to inform them when you have bought or sold the desired retired piece.

The Cottage Locator, East Lyme, CT; Frank Wilson

Select a firm from good experiences had by others (word of mouth), good (fast) service, and honesty and integrity.

Collector's Marketplace, Montrose, PA; Russ Wood and Renee Tyler

Reputation is the bottom line. The collector should use a broker who is knowledgeable, honest and willing to stand behind the merchandise. Use the broker that will go the extra mile to best serve the interests of the collector. Credibility checks can be made through such organizations as the Collectors' Information Bureau, the National Association of Limited Edition Dealers, local collector's clubs, or individuals who have had dealings with any particular secondary market brokers.

Blevins Plates 'n' Things, Vallejo, CA; Stella Blevins

You need to pick a firm that you can trust in all their dealings — a reputable business that has been around long enough to be knowledgeable. Some are better at plates, some dolls, *Precious Moments*, cottages, etc. They should be honest enough to tell you if it's not their strong point, but are willing to put out the effort if the collector is depending on them to find a particular treasure.

A Work of Art, Valhalla, NY; Joan Lewis

I cannot think of a better source than with the Collectors' Information Bureau...Listen to the sound of the person you are speaking to, and use your common sense judgment. Also, avoid 'glowing guarantees' from anyone.

Ellis in Wonderland, Sacramento, CA; Sandie Ellis

Ask for a referral from the manufacturer or distributor — or better yet — the Collectors' Information Bureau.

Collectible Exchange, Inc., New Middletown, OH; Connie Eckman

Buy national magazines and read the classified ads. I think retailers and other publications are dependable. Word of mouth is also important. Buying one-on-one is riskier and places yourself without recourse if a problem occurs. Also, don't order from the first person you talk to without checking around first. This causes more hardship than people realize.

What has been the biggest change in the secondary market over the past two years?

Collectibles, Etc. Brown Deer, WI; Sandy Forgach
We've been in business for fifteen years and have seen the secondary market much more active in recent years. There are more guide books, publications and exchange services available to collectors.

Collector's Marketplace, Montrose, PA;
Russ Wood and Renee Tyler
Four years ago, the secondary market was an unknown concept. It has now developed into a major force in the collectibles industry, so accepted by the collector that the 'secondary market' is now a household word. This has propelled collectors to become more diversified in their collectible interests, moving away from a singular concentration, into a wider variety of potential investment.

Blevins Plates 'n' Things, Vallejo, CA;
Stella Blevins
Collectors in general are much more aware that there is a secondary market. The range of plates sought after on the secondary market is much broader. Norman Rockwell and *Gone With The Wind* have been the main secondary market focus.

There has also been a marked increase in the trading of dolls and figurines. The Ashton-Drake dolls are traded on a daily basis on the secondary market.

A recent move by The Bradford Exchange to suspend trading of many plates on their trading floor has created a challenge to locate many of the sought-after plates.

Collections Unlimited, Tarzana, CA; Mickey Kaz
More manufacturers are recognizing the existence of the secondary market. They are cooperating by providing information to publications, who then secure values for those items. Many are also providing consumers with company literature and information about the market.

Ellis in Wonderland, Sacramento, CA;
Sandie Ellis
We have seen a tremendous increase in the number of collectors looking to sell. Sellers far outnumber buyers today.

Collectible Exchange, Inc., New Middletown, OH;
Connie Eckman
The biggest change in the secondary market that we've seen is the way collectors have become aware and informed about the collectibles they are buying or investing in and, therefore, how they conduct their secondary market transactions.

Insuring Your Collectibles
Establishing the Value of Your Collection and Protecting Your Treasures Against Loss or Theft

Like many people, you may have started collecting by purchasing some items that you thought would look nice in your home. As you bought more of these, a collection developed. The value of this collection, as far as you knew, rested only in the sentiment that you had for it. Soon, however, you realized that many of the pieces had escalated amazingly in value. What was once just a gathering of keepsakes became a collection that would be difficult to replace.

As the value of collectibles has increased dramatically over the past several years, so has the need to insure them against damage or theft. Since most collectibles have a limited production life, it may be difficult or impossible to replace an item, if needed. A collectible that was purchased at a store for a nominal cost may command a much greater dollar amount on the secondary market. To guard against this, you may find it wise to have your collectibles insured as you would any possession of value.

Documentation Is Essential

The first step in the process of insuring your collectibles is documentation. The more information that you have about your collectibles, the easier it will be to substantiate their value in the case of a loss. The single most important item that you can have is a receipt. Be sure to keep all receipts for all the collectibles that you purchase even if you buy them from a neighbor or friend. Next, you should record all pertinent information for each article. Include each of the following, where applicable:

- Name of manufacturer
- Item name or description
- Year of issue
- Artist's name
- Limited edition number
- Series number
- Special markings
- Cost at issue
- Purchase cost, if different
- Place of purchase
- Date of purchase
- Secondary market value
- Any other information you deem necessary

To further document your valuables, photograph them with a camera or, even better, a video camera. Video offers a few advantages over still photography. One is the ease of use, another is the ability to record information on the tape by speaking into the microphone while recording. The first step, with either type of camera, is to photograph your collectibles as they are normally displayed in your home. Next, record them individually. Take close-ups, including any markings such as limited edition numbers, backstamps and signatures. Special care should be taken to record any details that would make the article more valuable.

A video camera is an excellent tool to use for documenting collectibles because the valuables are not only visually represented, but you may also record spoken information on the tape at the same time.

Establishing the Value of Your Collectibles

Another requirement for proper documentation is establishing the value of each collectible. A respected publication such as the Collectors' Information Bureau's *Collectibles Market Guide and Price Index* is accepted by most agents. Be sure to use the latest edition available to ensure that the values are up-to-date.

Should you have a one-of-a-kind or other rare item, you may have to have it appraised in order to establish its worth. Do not overlook the importance of using a qualified appraiser. To locate an appraiser, check in your local yellow pages and/or refer to a museum or your insurance agent for suggestions. Give high consideration to members of the American Society of Appraisers. They have passed rigorous testing and are considered to be highly qualified. Having decided on two or three appraisers, ask for references and check them. Use only appraisers for whom you receive high recommendations; it will be worth the time and cost should the appraised pieces be lost.

When you have completed this procedure, view the photographs or tape to check the quality. If all is well, make duplicate copies and, along with a copy of the written documentation, store them in a safety deposit box or other safe storage area off-premises.

Types of Policies

Insuring your collectibles is not a difficult task, though it should not be taken lightly. If you rely on your homeowners (or renters) insurance to cover your valuables, you may discover, after making a claim, that you are underinsured. For this reason, collectors who wish to insure their valuables should be certain that their particular policy will adequately cover the insured in the event of a loss. Though they vary from one company to another, many homeowners policies cover items in the home at their value at the time they were purchased. The best thing you can do is to make sure you have a replacement-value policy and not a cash-value policy.

A home's contents are normally covered for an amount up to fifty percent of the overall coverage. This coverage, however, reimburses you only at the current market value, which would be much less than its replacement value. Though you may pay more, you would be better protected by obtaining coverage for full replacement cost of your home and its contents. Keep in mind, however, that special coverage may by required to fully insure many of your collectibles.

For many collectibles a floater, or rider, will be required. This is a policy in which you "schedule" each piece individually for its replacement cost. Many companies have a Fine Arts or Personal Articles floater that would pertain to covering collectibles. With this, you will be covered for the full value of the item. Remember, if the item appreciates to a higher value than when it was scheduled, the company is required to reward you only the scheduled value or replace the item. Because of this, you should be certain to reschedule at least once a year, or whenever the collectible takes a drastic jump in value. Also, do not forget to add newly acquired items or those that have recently escalated beyond the initial value. For some collections, those of an extremely high value, an insurance company may require the collector to hold a Special Lines policy. This is a policy designed to cover unusual or relatively expensive items. The premiums on this type of insurance, however, are higher than that of a regular policy.

Meeting With Your Agent

Another important part of the process is meeting with your insurance agent. When you meet with him or her, you should be well-prepared to offer as much information as possible. The more information that you can give, the more accurate the agent can be when determining which policy or policies you should utilize. You should also have a list of questions to ask him. Some of the questions should include:

- Does the floater cover all risks?
- Is there a deductible? If so, what is it?
- Does the policy cover breakage? If not, what is the additional cost?
- What constitutes breakage?
- Are the items covered if they are taken off-premises?

Before meeting with the agent, spend an evening or two jotting down any potential losses you think may arise. Ask the agent if the suggested policies cover you in each instance. If not, look for another policy.

All pertinent information, as listed in this article, should be documented for each collectible you own, using a record book such as this one from "The Antique Trader."

Complete, Accurate Coverage

Keep in mind that every policy is different. Do not rely on past policies or the policy that a friend or relative has. Chances are, the policy offered by your agency will vary from others. And, by all means, even if the agent assures you that all of the circumstances that you have presented will be covered, read the complete policy very carefully. After all, the final responsibility for complete, accurate coverage of your collectibles is yours.

Limited Edition Collectibles: A Brief History
As Plate Collecting Reaches its Centennial, a Lively Market Continues for Bells, Dolls, Ornaments, Graphics, Figurines and Steins

The year 1995 marks the 100th anniversary of a pivotal event for limited edition collectors: the introduction of the first true collector plate series. Harald Bing debuted "Behind the Frozen Window" that year and inaugurated an annual Bing & Grondahl collection of Danish plates that has endured through two World Wars and the Great Depression.

"Behind the Frozen Window" and the plates that followed were originally meant simply as gifts on which the Danes could present special Christmas cookies and other treats. But when American soldiers began bringing Bing & Grondahl Christmas plates home as souvenirs in the 1940s, a thriving U.S. market was born. Also sought after were the Danish plates of Royal Copenhagen, Dutch Royal Delft issues, German Rosenthal plates and other European issues.

Per Jensen, a Danish-American, facilitated the growth of plate collecting when he imported Bing & Grondahl and Royal Copenhagen back issues to sell on the U.S. antique market. William Freudenberg, Jr. of Chicago and Pat Owen of Ft.

Autographed collectibles are a highly sought-after trend in the collectibles industry. For example, this "Carlton Fisk" plate from Gartlan USA is a popular limited edition because it is personally signed by Fisk himself.

Lauderdale, Florida also were early believers in the power of plate collecting. They imported and traded the plates for growing numbers of American enthusiasts.

Plate collecting did not "catch fire," however, until its horizons were broadened past the classic, blue-and-white Christmas issues from the early part of this century. "Deux Oiseaux" debuted in 1965 from the French studio of Lalique: the first non-Christmas, non-blue-and-white, non-porcelain collector plate. This crystal issue let loose a veritable torrent of creativity which yielded many firsts: a jasperware plate from Wedgwood of England, a bas-relief Hummel plate from Goebel of Germany, the first Norman Rockwell plate and many more.

When the late Rod MacArthur launched The Bradford Exchange in the mid-1970s, collectors enjoyed the first readily available "stock market for plates." Now they were able to buy and sell on a nationwide network. Further advancements took

The Walt Disney Classics Collection *is the first collection of limited edition animation sculptures to be produced by The Walt Disney Company, and the company has selected Cinderella, Lucifer and Bruno as its first scene to be honored with retirement. From left are "Meany, Sneaky Roose-A-Fee," "They Can't Stop Me From Dreaming" and "Just Learn To Like Cats."*

In celebrating the history of African Americans, Sarah Schultz of Sarah's Attic has created the Black Heritage Collection, attracting collectors of diverse racial and ethnic backgrounds. This charming group of characters are the "Gospel Singers" produced by Sarah's Attic.

An exciting development in the collectibles realm, in 1993 Kevin Francis Ceramics released the first-ever toby jug to bear the likeness of President Clinton. Here, Kevin Pearson, one of the partners in Kevin Francis Ceramics, poses with the first prototype of President Clinton.

place with the establishment of the National Association of Limited Edition Dealers and the Collectibles and Platemakers Guild.

While secondary market trading for plates today is much less intense than it was in the late 1970s and the early-to-mid 1980s, there are still several million enthusiastic plate collectors. From its simple beginnings in Denmark, plate collecting has become a fascinating pastime over the last century. Today, plates of porcelain, wood, crystal, and many other materials feature the art of some of the world's most celebrated painters and sculptors of the past and present. Themes range from wildlife, holidays and history to children and popular culture. The Price Index at the end of this volume lists thousands of the most actively traded issues in today's diverse and fast-moving plate market.

The Oldest Collectibles: Bells and Dolls

Centuries before Harald Bing unveiled his first limited edition plate, bell creation was considered as much an art as an economic necessity. The first bells of ancient Greece, Rome, Egypt and Asia were used for religious ceremonies, to sound warnings, or to indicate that an area was "all clear" after a military attack. In addition, bells play a part in many of our most delightful memories and historical events: from the old school bell to the wintry sound of sleigh bells to that perennial symbol of freedom, The Liberty Bell.

Early bells were crudely made of iron, bronze or other durable metals. But with the intervention of European monarchs, court artisans began to explore ways to make bells as beautiful to look at

Hallmark introduced an industry first in the form of a voice recordable Christmas ornament, titled "Messages of Christmas." The only product of its kind available nationwide, this battery-powered ornament features an endearing chipmunk perched atop a cassette player, which enables its owner to record a 15-second, personalized message of holiday cheer and good wishes.

as they were to listen to. Thus, pieces crafted of porcelain, bone china, Venetian glass and even full lead crystal became the order of the day. Many fine museums hold the treasures of early collectors, and since 1940, the American Bell Association has served as a source of information and enjoyment for collectors everywhere.

The first known limited edition bells, created

expressly with collectibility in mind, were the Royal Bayreuth "Sunbonnet Babies" unveiled at the turn of the century. Since then, many firms that also make plates, figurines and other collectibles have seen fit to add bells to their lines: notably the classic *M.I. Hummel*, *Precious Moments* and Lladro bells. And while bells are far from the most active secondary market traders, they enjoy sustained popularity.

Dolls are considered by many experts to be the oldest collectibles of all, for there is evidence of their existence as far back as 2000 B.C. What's more, when the ruins of Pompeii and Herculaneum were uncovered centuries after the eruption of Mt. Vesuvius in A.D. 79, the perfectly preserved body of a little girl was found still clutching her doll. In the Middle Ages, boys played with knight dolls on horseback, while girls enjoyed dolls crafted of wood, wax or a paper-like material.

The 19th century was known as a "Golden Age" for dollmaking in Germany and France, with elegant, fashionably dressed dolls crafted of hand-painted porcelain with kid bodies. The post-war era brought a boom in vinyl dolls including Barbie and G.I. Joe. Today, collectors are rediscovering the joys of doll collecting — with everything from replicas of classic "Golden Age" beauties to adorable baby and toddler dolls earning status and attracting bids on the secondary market.

Ornaments Are Not Just for Christmas Anymore

With many collectors owning hundreds or even thousands of ornaments today, it is amazing to contemplate the growth of a hobby that began in

To complement the dated Annual Christmas Bell, Goebel of Germany offered two matching undated angel motif pieces — a figurine and hanging ornament. All three are titled "Celestial Musician," and are the first edition in a series of four M.I. Hummel® groupings.

The "Brave and Free" image was first painted by Gregory Perillo and distributed as a collector plate by Artaffects in 1976. 1993 saw the same image produced by Artaffects in three-dimensional doll form. The "Brave and Free" doll was a success as well — it won the coveted NALED "Doll of the Year" (DOTY) award in 1993.

Germany circa 1820. It was then that German families discovered the beautiful glass balls of Lauscha, a center for glassmaking since the 16th century. Another advancement took place in the 1850s, when Louis Greiner-Schlotfeger perfected the formula for silvering, so that classic ball ornaments could glow with a mirror-like shine.

Americans began to share in these holiday riches when the young dime store magnate, Frank Woolworth, imported his first $25 worth of German glass ornaments in 1880. Since then, glass ornaments have been joined by charming Christmas artworks crafted of wax, paper, tinsel, crystal, porcelain and — an American favorite — shimmering silver.

Hallmark's entry into the dated ornament business in the 1970s foreshadowed the "ornament explosion" of the 1980s and beyond. Prior to this, collectible ornaments had most often been prohibitively expensive sterling silver pieces from Halls or Shreve, Crump and Lowe, or American makers like Reed and Barton, Towle and many more. Now, collectible ornaments emerged from a host of makers — crafted of porcelain, wood or even molded plastic.

Some collectors relegate their ornaments to Christmas display — often placing a tree in each room of the home to accommodate all their trea-

sures. But more and more, collectors find ways to display some of their ornaments year-round — believing that the enjoyment should not be limited to a few short weeks per year.

Graphics and Figurines Bring Fine Art to the American Home

Centuries ago, only royalty and the rich could own most artworks, since original paintings and sculptures were the only pieces available. But over the last few centuries, a number of reproduction techniques — including lithography, woodcuts, engravings and serigraphy — have opened up a whole new world of affordable graphics to collectors. And during the 20th century, some of Europe's most gifted sculptors turned their talents to the creation of originals for molding in limited editions.

Today, collectible prints are more popular than ever before in history. With growing affluence and greater art appreciation, most Americans now consider fine art a "must" to decorate their homes. They enjoy owning graphics that bring both Old Masters and contemporary talents into their living rooms for daily enjoyment. For an overview of today's print market, check the Price Index at the end of this book.

As for figurines, most collectors trace the Dorothy Doughty *Birds Of America*, introduced by Royal Worcester of England in the 1930s, as the earliest limited edition collection of sculpture. Miss Doughty had an exceptional ability to sculpt birds and flowers with absolute fidelity to nature.

To complete each of her sculptures, she supervised the creation of between twenty and forty molds to capture every detail of the original.

Joining Royal Worcester in the figurine market before long were Royal Doulton of England, and Kaiser and Goebel of Germany. In the United

"Old Joe's Beetling Shop: A Veritable Den of Iniquity!" joins past issues of "Ebeneezer Scrooge's Counting House," "Mister Fezziwig's Emporium," "A Christmas Carol," "Fred's Home" and "Scrooge's School" as the Christmas series of David Winter Cottages builds upon the story of Scrooge in Charles Dickens' novel.

In "Paris, City of Lights," artist Thomas Kinkade features his family in a nostalgic street scene bustling with activity. That's the artist himself in the lower left foreground, wearing a red beret. He has even signed his tiny canvas — the smallest Kinkade signature on record.

America's favorite fat cat and his friends are portrayed for the first time in faceted crystal designs by Imal Wagner of Summerhill Crystal. Cat lovers, animal enthusiasts, fans of the comic strip characters and its creator Jim Davis can celebrate Garfield's 15th birthday with the Garfield Collection, featuring "Garfield," "Pookie" and "Odie."

States, 20th-century masters including Edward Marshall Boehm and Boleslaw Cybis established separate studios bearing their names and devoted to crafting the finest three-dimensional porcelain art. Not long after that, the Lladro brothers — Juan, Jose and Vicente — opened their famous Lladro porcelain studio in Valencia, Spain.

While traditional figurines of people, flowers and animals continue to charm many collectors, trends in the field include the proliferation of cottages, fantasy figurines, whimsical animals, and works of three-dimensional art in crystal. These creations now are listed side by side with classic

One of the most widely-recognized symbols around the world, the proud design on this "A & Eagle Trademark Stein" from Anheuser-Busch is an indelible image of Americana. This handcrafted limited edition was so well-liked, it sold out in an amazing eight weeks.

porcelain pieces from Boehm and Cybis, Goebel's timeless *M.I. Hummel* figurines, and scores of other series from around the world.

Drinking Vessels Become Coveted Collectibles

Hundreds of years ago, the earliest steins were designed with very practical considerations in mind. They were made sturdy so that they would hold up under rugged conditions, and they had hinged lids to protect the ale or beer inside from insects and the elements. But because it is human nature to add beauty and decorative value to even the most utilitarian objects, steinmakers soon began to enhance their creations with bas-relief designs, etching, inlays, painting, and other handsome art elements.

For several generations before World War II, Germany was the heart of the steinmaker's art. Several famous studios — most notably the Mettlach manufactory of Villeroy & Boch — earned fame for their etched and cameo-like steins depicting historical figures, stories, and other handsome subjects. Today those century-old steins may command hundreds or even thousands of dollars at auction, and modern-day reproductions are sought after by general collectors and stein aficionados alike. Stein Collectors International serves the traditional stein enthusiast with historical information, advice and fellowship.

Meanwhile, a number of contemporary firms have revived the steinmaker's art — and developed some important innovations of their own. Anheuser-Busch began with beer-related steins, but now offers wildlife, seasonal, sports, and historical steins as well. CUI/Carolina Collections/Dram Tree presents a wide array of subjects in media both traditional and new. And firms such as The Hamilton collection and Norman Rockwell Gallery — known for their creations in other media — have entered the stein realm as well.

This brief survey of the history of collectibles can provide you with only a taste of the diversity and art significance of the many plates, bells, graphics, steins, dolls, ornaments and figurines on the market today. Throughout this volume you will find much more detail on specific creators, producers and marketers of these popular works of contemporary art — and you'll find many of them listed in the extensive Price Index at the back of the book as well.

The lives of these famous people from ancient and recent history pique our interest and imagination. From left to right and top to bottom are: "Heartbreak Hotel" plate by The Bradford Exchange, Kurt S. Adler, Inc.'s "Benjamin Franklin" nutcracker, "Ida B. Wells" figurine by Miss Martha Originals Inc., Royal Doulton's "Napoleon" toby jug, "Yeltzin Doll" nesting dolls from Marina's Russian Collection, Inc., "Rockwell Triple Self Portrait" figurine produced by Goebel United States, Sarah's Attic's "Otis Redding" figurine, "Dollar Doll" nesting dolls by Marina's Russian Collection, Inc., "Elvis Presley Postage Stamp Stein" by C.U.I. Inc./Classic Carolina Collections/ Dram Tree, Sarah's Attic's "George Washington" figurine, "Salvador Dali" and "John F. Kennedy" toby jugs by Kevin Francis, Inc. and "Abraham Lincoln" figurine from Sarah's Attic.

Men and women holding various occupations and coming from every walk of life are portrayed here gracefully, realistically or whimsically. Whether together as lovers or following separate callings, each adult has found a niche in life. On the left page from left to right and top to bottom are: Armani's kneeling "Maternity" and standing "Maternity" figurines, "Morning Glory" plate by Reco International Corp.,

"Bessie and Corkie" figurine from Miss Martha Originals Inc., "Maternity in a Garden" figurine by Armani, the M.I. Hummel Club's "Storybook Time" (HUM 458) figurine, Byers' Choice Ltd.'s "School Boy," "Teacher" and "School Girl" Carolers® figurines, "The Butterfly Net" plate from Roman, Inc. and "Choir Director" Caroler® figurine by Byers' Choice Ltd.

On the right page from left to right and top to bottom are: the Lladro Collectors Society's "Sunday Sermon" and "The Fireman" figurines, Armani's "Girl on Horseback Riding" and "Lovers" figurines, "Family Doll" nesting dolls by Marina's Russian Collection, Inc., "Fair Maiden" figurine by Royal Doulton, "Egg Counting" nesting dolls from Marina's Russian Collection, Inc., "Little Bo Peep" figurine by Artaffects, Ltd., Duncan Royale's "Preacher Man" figurine, "Mazel Tov" by the Lladro Collectors Society and Royal Doulton's "Henley."

The innocence and wonder of childhood is captured on youngsters' open faces and in their carefree activities. As little boys and girls play, talk, sing and reflect, they discover new things about the world. On the left page from left to right and top to bottom are: Hallmark Cards, Inc.'s "Days to Remember" figurine, "Cassie Yocum" doll by Ladie and Friends, Inc., "1993-94 Ice Cream Logo Kid" doll by Annalee® Mobilitee™ Dolls, Inc., "Valerie" figurine from Miss Martha Originals Inc., the Lladro Collectors Society's "Best Friend" figurine, "Simon and Andrew" figurine by Miss Martha Originals Inc., Royal Copenhagen/Bing & Grondahl's "The Christmas Elf" plate, "Annabelle Bowman" doll by Ladie and Friends, Inc., The Hadley Companies' "Innocent View" plate and "Wot's All This Talk About Love?" by the Enesco Corporation.

On the right page from left to right and top to bottom are: "Me and My Pony" plate from Reco International Corp., "Pearl Bowman" doll by Ladie and Friends, Inc., the M.I. Hummel Club's "Adventure Bound" (HUM 347) figurine, "Tulips for Mother" ANRI figurine by Goebel United States, "Sylvia" figurine by Miss Martha Originals Inc., the Enesco Corporation's "Our Friendship is Soda-Licious" figurine, "The Artist" (HUM 304) figurine from the M.I. Hummel Club, "Morning Discovery" miniature lithograph by Pemberton & Oakes, the Lladro Collectors Society's "Sunday's Child" boy and girl figurines and "Dora Valentine" doll by Ladie and Friends, Inc.

A variety of dolls created by renowned artists are styled with authentic outfits and memorable expressions. On the left page from left to right and top to bottom are: Georgetown Collection's "Peaches and Cream," Dynasty Doll's "Jeanette," "Kima" from Timeless Creations, a division of Mattel, Inc., Seymour Mann, Inc.'s "Reilly," "Sweetie" by The Ashton-Drake Galleries, "The Velveteen Rabbit" by The Lawton Doll Company, Dynasty Doll's "Rosemary," "Happy Birthday Amy" by Gorham Inc. and "The Lawton Logo Doll" from The Lawton Doll Company.

On the right page from left to right and top to bottom are: "Alicia" from Goebel United States, the George-town Collection's "Vasilisa," Dynasty Doll's "Tami," "Grace" by the Georgetown Collection, The Franklin Mint's "Jumeau Doll," "Natalia's Matrioshka" by Gorham Inc., "Mommy I'm Sorry" by The Ashton-Drake Galleries, Gorham Inc.'s "Rose," "Jimmy/Sooo Big" by The Ashton-Drake Galleries and The Lawton Doll Company's "Apple Blossom Time."

More endearing and delightful dolls are portrayed here in various poses. From left to right and top to bottom are: The Hamilton Collection's "Amy," "Tuesday's Child" by the Nahrgang Collection, Dynasty Doll's "Antoinette," "Eugenie" by Seymour Mann, Inc., the Nahrgang Collection's "Taylor," "Precious" by Seymour Mann, Inc., Gorham Inc.'s "Chelsea's Bonnet," "Heather" from The Hamilton Collection, "Brandon" by The Ashton-Drake Galleries, Dynasty Doll's "Pon-Pon" and "Spanky" by Seymour Mann, Inc.

Loved by kids and adults alike, clowns and their humorous antics never go out of style. From left to right and top to bottom are: Duncan Royale's "American" figurine, "Dottie" doll from Goebel United States, "Special Occasion" figurine by Ron Lee's World of Clowns, Flambro Imports' "Kittens For Sale?" figurine, "No Vacancy" plate by Ron Lee's World of Clowns, "The Veterinarian" and "Sweeping Up 2" figurines from Flambro Imports, "Katie and Barney" doll by Ladie and Friends, Inc. and Flambro Imports' "After the Parade" figurine.

Here, favorite storybook, cartoon and fantasy characters and places are skillfully represented, their stories told through print or visual arts. On the left page from left to right and top to bottom are: Schmid's "Notch Hall and Village" figurine, The Ashton-Drake Galleries' "Cinderella" doll, Hand & Hammer Silversmiths' "Alice in Wonderland" Christmas ornaments, "Troll Maiden" plate by Reco International Corp., "Darkwing Duck" figurine by Ron Lee's World of Clowns, "Joe Cool T-Bird" from Silver Deer, Ltd., Precious Art/Panton's "His Secret" figurine, *The PenDelfin Story* from PenDelfin Sales Inc., Duncan Royale's "Julenisse" figurine, "Believe in Your Dreams" plate by Reco International Corp. and "Sneakers Apeak" figurine by Precious Art/Panton.

On the right page from left to right and top to bottom are: "Ganymede Stein" by Anheuser-Busch, Inc., Fitz and Floyd's "A Mad Tea Party" plate, "Metropolis" figurine from Ron Lee's World of Clowns, Precious Art/Panton's "Stormslayer" and "All Mine" figurines, "Shiver Me Timbers" shoehouse by John Hine Studios, Inc., Fitz and Floyd's "Realm of Camelot" waterglobe, United Design's "Writing the Legend" figurine, "The Mouse" by The Lance Corporation, Precious Art/Panton's "Spreading His Wings" figurine, "What The…?" by Ron Lee's World of Clowns, "Horatio Pernickety's Amorous Intent" cottage from John Hine Studios, Inc. and The Hamilton Collection's "Captain Jean-Luc Picard" plate.

Brilliantly faceted and glistening cut-crystal figurines reveal the artists' talent in creating characters that sparkle with a life of their own and everyday objects that are anything but ordinary. On the left page from left to right and top to bottom are: "Harp" by Swarovski America Ltd., Iris Arc Crystal's "Country Church," Summerhill Crystal's "Classic Mickey," "Literary Ace Comic Strip" by Silver Deer, Ltd., Iris Arc Crystal's "Basket of Violets," Crystal World's "Victorian House" and "Harbor Lighthouse," "Slot Machine" by Iris Arc Crystal and "Lute" by Swarovski America Ltd.

On the right page from left to right and top to bottom are: "Santa Maria" by Swarovski America Ltd., "Dolphin Paperweight" by Goebel United States, "Three South Sea Fish" and "Sea Horse" by Swarovski America Ltd., Crystal World's "Teddies at Eight" and "Hush Puppy," "The Malt Shop" by Silver Deer, Ltd., Iris Arc Crystal's "Annual Edition Gramophone," "Curious Cat" by Crystal World, Summerhill Crystal's "Odie," "Large Pookie" and "Garfield" and Iris Arc Crystal's "Annual Edition Classic Telephone".

Small in stature but large in appeal, these figurines, plates and ornaments are appreciated for their intricate detail and fine craftsmanship. On the left page from left to right and top to bottom are: "Merry Mousetale Pageant" figurine from Midwest Importers of Cannon Falls, Inc., VickiLane's "Mouse Angel" figurine, Royal Doulton's "Mary," "Joseph" and "Jesus" three-piece nativity set, "Brotherly Love" miniature plate by Pemberton & Oakes, "New World Ahoy" figurine by Hallmark Cards, Inc., Hawthorne Architectural Register's "Olde Porterfield Tea Room" cottage, Hand & Hammer Silversmiths' "Peter Rabbit" ornament, "Forty Winks" figurine by PenDelfin Sales Inc., "Storyteller" figurine from GANZ, "America At Peace" ornament by Hand & Hammer Silversmiths, VickiLane's "Sew Creative" figurine, United Design's "Getting 'Round On My Own" figurine, "Fishing Friends" by Band Creations, "Vanilla" figurine from PenDelfin Sales Inc. and Schmid's *Roosevelt Bears* in Patriotic Suits.

On the right page from left to right and top to bottom are: "Days to Remember" figurine by Sarah's Attic, Schmid's "Home For Christmas" figurine, "The Thinker" miniature plate from Pemberton & Oakes, "Grandma's Favorite" figurine from BAND Creations, "Window of Dreams" miniature plate by Pemberton & Oakes, BAND Creations' "Fish Tales" figurine, VickiLane's "Hank Seated On A Stump" figurine, "Needles" figurine by Band Creations, VickiLane's "Nativity," "Little Truffle Smelling Flower" and "Our First Christmas Together" ornament by GANZ and Russian lacquer box by Marina's Russian Collection, Inc.

Blooming florals in every imaginable color and size are not only for outdoor gardens, but also accents to the interior of any home, when they are portrayed in the form of exquisitely detailed collectibles. From left to right and top to bottom are: The Bradford Exchange's "Home Sweet Home" plate, "Mansard Lady" wall sculpture by Michael's Limited, Napoleon USA, Inc.'s "Typhoon Rose Plant" figurine, "Steiner Street" wall sculpture by Michael's Limited, Lilliput Lane Limited's "Stradling Priory" cottage, "Rose And Bud On Trunk" figurine by Napoleon USA, Inc., "Enchanted Cottage" wall sculpture by Michael's Limited, Lilliput Lane Limited's "Cotman Cottage," "Daisy Days" miniature canvas transfer by Pemberton & Oakes, "May Rose" figurine by Napoleon USA, Inc., The Bradford Exchange's "Garden Discovery" plate and "Iris" figurine by Napoleon USA, Inc.

Animals can be cute and cuddly or enchanting and captivating. Artists have represented some of these little creatures dressed in clothes or performing many human tasks, such as playing the piano, singing or having a picnic. From left to right and top to bottom are: Enesco Corporation's "Friends Come In All Sizes" figurine, "Tulip" doll by Goebel United States, Possible Dreams' "Lady Ashley" figurine, VickiLane's "Tea Time" figurine, Royal Doulton's "Peter Rabbit" figurine, "Sir Mouse" and "Lady Mouse" figurines by John Hine Studios, Inc., "Lily Blossom" figurine by Possible Dreams, "The Big Day" figurine with bases by GANZ, The Franklin Mint's "Teddy Bear Picnic" plate, "M.C. Illions and Sons, circa 1910" musical carousel horse by Hallmark Cards, Inc., Enesco Corporation's "Music Mice-Tro" figurine and Fitz and Floyd's "Bremen Town Musicians" teapot.

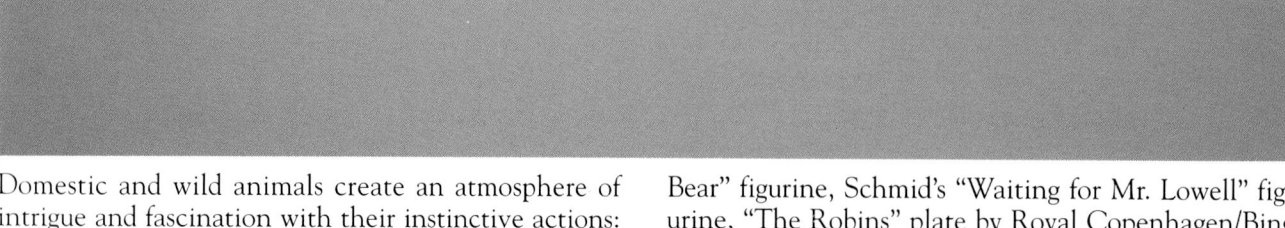

Domestic and wild animals create an atmosphere of intrigue and fascination with their instinctive actions: stalking, howling, mothering or playing. On the left page from left to right and top to bottom are: "Arabian" figurine by Maruri U.S.A., The Hamilton Collection's "A Mother's Love" plate, Creart's "White Blizzard" sculpture, "Wood Duck" and "Ostrich" figurines by Silver Deer, Ltd., BAND Creations' "Brown Bear" figurine, Schmid's "Waiting for Mr. Lowell" figurine, "The Robins" plate by Royal Copenhagen/Bing & Grondahl, Creart's "Eagle Head" sculpture, "Seated Bear" figurine from Hallmark Cards, Inc., "First Breath Dolphin Stein" by C.U.I., Inc./Classic Carolina Collections/Dram Tree and "Thoroughbred" figurine by Maruri U.S.A.

On the right page from left to right and top to bottom are: "Imperial Panda" sculpture from Maruri U.S.A., Creart's "Coyote" sculpture, The Bradford Exchange's "We've Been Spotted" plate, "Baby Elephant Sitting" figurine by Maruri U.S.A., Creart's "Wolf and Pups" figurine, "Elephant Pair Playing" figurine by Maruri U.S.A., The Hadley Companies' "Rosie" plate, "Spectacled Eider, Federal Duck Stamp Stein" by C.U.I., Inc./Classic Carolina Collections/Dram Tree and Creart's "Travieso" sculpture.

Mystery and allure enshroud Native American heritage and Western tradition. Their history is an interesting category on which to reflect and study. On the left page from left to right and top to bottom are: "Stonewall Jackson Stein" by C.U.I., Inc./Classic Carolina Collections/Dram Tree, Georgetown Collection's "Quick Fox" and "Many Stars" dolls, The Hadley Companies' "Navajo Fantasy" and "Young Warrior" plates, "Old West Hotel" wall sculpture by Michael's Limited, "Stonewall Jackson" toby jug by Kevin Francis Inc., "Song of the Sioux" and "Brave and Free" dolls by Artaffects, Ltd. and "Pony Express Rider" by Annalee Mobilitee Dolls, Inc.

On the right page from left to right and top to bottom are: LEGENDS' "Salmon Falls" and "Eminent Crow" sculptures, The Lance Corporation's "Two Eagles" figurine, "Prairie Flower" plate from The Hamilton Collection, Polland Studios' "Blue Bonnets and Yellow Ribbon" and "Mountain Man" figurines, "Hunters Brothers," "Give Us Peace" and "The Noble Heart" figurines by LEGENDS, The Lance Corporation's "J.E.B. Stuart" figurine and "Canyon of the Cat" plate from The Bradford Exchange.

From historic lighthouses and a windmill, to churches and an outdoor gazebo complete with a band, architectural beauty and interest abound in this variety of detailed buildings crafted of several different media. On the left page from left to right and top to bottom are: "Olde Porterfield Tea Room" cottage by Hawthorne Architectural Register, Harbour Lights' "Cape Hatteras" lighthouse, "Doc Mitchell's" house by the Geo. Zoltan Lefton Company, "The White House" teapot by Fitz and Floyd, "Southeast Block Island" lighthouse from Harbour Lights, Lilliput Lane Limited's "Simply Amish" cottage, "Bruton Parish," "Grissell Hay Lodging House," "Raleigh Tavern" and "Governor's Palace" buildings from The Cat's Meow/FJ Designs, Harbour Lights' "Split Rock" lighthouse, "The Stone House" wall sculpture by Michael's Limited, Lilliput Lane Limited's "Cley-next-the-Sea" figurine and Harbour Lights' "Portland Head" lighthouse.

On the right page from left to right and top to bottom are: "Cape Hatteras Lighthouse" and "St. James Cathedral" from the Geo. Zoltan Lefton Company, The Hadley Companies' "Welcome to Paradise" plate, "Toby Inn" from Kevin Francis Inc., The Lance Corporation's "Pumpkin Island Light" figurine, "Arches Thrice" cottage by John Hine Studios, Inc., Harbour Lights' "St. Simons" lighthouse, The Norman Rockwell Gallery's "Evergreen Cottage," "Gazebo and Tully Brothers Band" by The Lance Corporation, "Magnolia Plantation House," "St. Philip's Episcopal Church," "The Rutledge House," "The Col. John Ashe House" and "The Victorian Rose" houses from Shelia's Inc.

Stunning lithographs adorn a room with vibrant or subtle hues. These graphics depict exquisite still-life, building, character and landscape scenes. On the left page from left to right and top to bottom are: "Paris, City of Lights," "Sunday Outing" and "Lamplight Lane" by Lightpost Publishing, "La Balançoire," "Bouquet de Tulipes" and "Jeunes Filles Au Piano" from the Renoir Impressionists Society.

On the right page clockwise from the top are: "Main Street, Stockbridge" and "Springtime in Stockbridge" by The Norman Rockwell Gallery, "Speldhurst Farm," "Umbrella Cottage" and "Byfleet Cottage" from Marty Bell Fine Art, Inc.

"Angels we have heard on high…" The words to a well-known Christmas song come to mind as one views these inspiring angel collectibles. To display these heavenly creations in one's home is just the way to get into the Christmas spirit. From left to right and top to bottom are: "Teeter Tots" figurine by Cast Art Industries, Inc., Roman, Inc.'s "This Way Santa" figurine, "The Finishing Touches" figurine by Cast Art Industries, Inc., "2-inch Miniature Celestial Angel," "3-inch Cross Angel," "4-inch Cross Angel" and "Star of Bethlehem" ornaments by Margaret Furlong Designs, Department 56, Inc.'s "Winken, Blinken and Nod" figurine and accessories, "Love My Teddy," "Love My Puppy" and "Love My Kitty" figurines by Cast Art Industries, "The Annunciation" plate by Roman, Inc., "Angel with Leaves" figurine from United Design and "Wood Angel Duet" figurine from Midwest Importers of Cannon Falls, Inc.

Winter and Christmas are magical times of the year. A mention of the Christmas holiday brings to mind visions of carolers, snow-covered landscapes, nativity scenes and gifts of toys. From left to right and top to bottom are: "Murray® Dump Truck" from Hallmark Cards, Inc., "The Skating Party" plate by Royal Copenhagen/Bing & Grondahl, the Geo. Zoltan Lefton Company's "Mark Hall" house, "Reindeer Stable" by Seymour Mann, Inc., "Good Samaritan Band" and "Victorian Gazebo" by the Geo. Zoltan Lefton Company, the M.I. Hummel Club's "Winter Song" (HUM 476) figurine, "Up to the Housetop" display and figurines by Goebel Miniatures, Department 56, Inc.'s "Airport" and "Airplane," "Nativity Set" by June McKenna Collectibles Inc., "The Pied Bull Inn" and accessories from Department 56, Inc. and Reco International Corp.'s "Candlelight Christmas."

Here, Santa Claus is busy performing a variety of activities: from the traditional list-making and toy-giving to the unexpected golfing and cookie-baking. The figurines on the left page from left to right and top to bottom are: Kurt S. Adler, Inc.'s "Par for the Claus," "Gnome Santa On Deer" by Midwest Importers of Cannon Falls, Inc., Duncan Royale's "Star Man," "Santa's Special Friend" from Possible Dreams, "Grandpa Santa's Piggyback" by Kurt S. Adler, Inc., Possible Dreams' "Rockwell Pepsi Santa" and "Strumming the Lute," "Working Santa" (2nd ed.) from Byers' Choice Ltd., "The Patriot" by June McKenna Collectibles Inc. and United Design's "Loads of Happiness."

On the right page from left to right and top to bottom are: "Santa O'Nicholas" figurine and "Toymaker Santa" nutcracker by Midwest Importers of Cannon Falls, Inc., Duncan Royale's "Kris Kringle" figurine, Sarah's Attic's "Oh My! Santa" figurine, "Baby's First Christmas" figurine by Goebel United States, "Tomorrow's Christmas" figurine by June McKenna Collectibles Inc., "Santa's Workshop" waterglobe by The Norman Rockwell Gallery, "Baking Cookies" by June McKenna Collectibles Inc., Schmid's Belsnickle Bishop Annual Figurine and June McKenna Collectibles Inc.'s "Bedtime Stories."

Visions of snowy scenes, merry carolers and dazzling ornaments dance through the heads of those who love the holiday season. On the left page from left to right and top to bottom are: the M.I. Hummel Club's "Ride Into Christmas" (HUM 396/2/0) figurine, "A Christmas Carol" ornaments from Hand & Hammer Silversmiths, "The Bristol Falls Carolers Society" figurines from Roman, Inc., Fitz and Floyd's "Holiday Hamlet Village Sign," "Santa's Gifts" plate by Royal Copenhagen/Bing & Grondahl, "The Three Kings" figurines by Roman, Inc., "All I Want For Christmas…" figurine and base from GANZ, Christopher Radko's "A Shy Rabbit's Heart," "Tiger," "Russian Santa," "Star Fire," "Wings and a Prayer" and "Ice Bear" Christmas ornaments and Department 56, Inc.'s "St. Luke's Church" and accessories.

On the right page from left to right and top to bottom are: "Rockwell's Studio" by Hawthorne Architectural Register, "Eamont Lodge" by Lilliput Lane Limited, Department 56, Inc.'s "Hembleton Pewterer" cottage and accessories, "The Pleasantville Courthouse," "Mason's Hotel & Saloon" and "The Pleasantville Post Office" from Flambro Imports, "Kelly" and "Joella" doll ornaments and "Carousel Tiger" and "Carousel Horse" ornaments from Kurt S. Adler, Inc., Royal Copenhagen/Bing & Grondahl's "1993 Christmas Plate" and the Geo. Zoltan Lefton Company's "Blacksmith" cottage.

Favorite pastimes almost always include some type of sport. Sports heros are admired, and hobbies are often taken up in hopes of emulating them — that's the American way. From left to right and top to bottom are: Gartlan USA, Inc.'s "The Gallery Series" depicting Wayne Gretsky, "Brooklyn Dodgers Ebbets Field Stein" from C.U.I., Inc./Classic Carolina Collections/Dram Tree, "Brett & Bobby Hull — A Matched Set" figurines by Gartlan USA, Inc., Anheuser-Busch, Inc.'s "Center Ice" stein, The Franklin Mint's "Harley-Davidson Motorcycle," Gartlan USA, Inc.'s "Seattle Thunder" plate depicting Ken Griffey Jr., "Baseball Catcher" from Annalee Mobilitee Dolls, Inc., Gartlan USA, Inc.'s "The Franchise" plate depicting Tom Seaver, "Mickey in the '60s" plate from Enesco Corporation, "1993 Christa MacAuliffe Graduate Skier" by Annalee Mobilitee Dolls, Inc., Anheuser-Busch, Inc.'s "Joe Louis Stein" and "The Man" (Stan Musial) figurine by Gartlan USA, Inc.

Santa Claus is known around the world. Here, Santa and other Christmas characters are featured with an international flair. From left to right and top to bottom are: "European Santa with Little Girl," "Bob Cratchit & Tiny Tim" and "Scrooge" from Classic Collectables by Uniquely Yours, "A Pinch of Advice" figurine by Calabar Creations, "Desmond Claus/ England" from The Great American® Taylor Collectibles Corp., "Nutcracker King" ornament by Old World Christmas, "Wilhelm Claus/Holland" from The Great American® Taylor Collectibles Corp., Old World Christmas' "Santa Above Bell" ornament, "Angus Claus/Scotland" by The Great American® Taylor Collectibles Corp., "Teddy Bear Factory," "Town Christmas Tree" and "Candy Cane Factory" from Brandywine Collectibles, "Matte Santa Head" ornament by Old World Christmas and Great American® Taylor's "Gord Claus/Canada."

Wildlife, sports, architecture and clowns are a few of the popular themes showcased in this wonderfully diversified selection of limited edition collectibles. On the left page from left to right and top to bottom are: "Willie the Collector" figurine by WACO Products Corporation, "Forest Nimble" sculpture from Rick Cain Studios, WACO's "Amazing Willie" figurine, "The Hotel Taft: Miami Beach Deco District" by Historical Miniatures, Inc., "Vita-Veggie Vendor" figurine from Calabar Creations, "The Pink House: Charleston, South Carolina," "Rainbow Row: Green #1 and Blue #1: Charleston, South Carolina" by Historical Miniatures, Inc., "Westminster Abbey" from Fraser International, "Treasured Times Birthday House" with "Elm Tree" by Brandywine Collectibles, and Fraser International's "Foxglove Cottage" and "The Old Anchor Inn."

On the right page from left to right and top to bottom are: "Spirit Totem" sculpture from Rick Cain Studios, "When I Grow Up" figurine from WACO Products Corporation, "Arctic Son" sculpture from Rick Cain Studios, "Prac-Tees" figurine by Calabar Creations, "Ebbets Field" stein by LCS Products & Services, "Candy Box" from The Fenton Art Glass Company, LCS' "Ebbets Field" plate, "USS Enterprise NCC-1701-D" ship from Star Trek®: The Next Generation™ by Rawcliffe Corporation, "Kennedy House," "Betsy Ross House" and "Stone House" by R.R. Creations, Inc., "Ivan Claus/Russia" from The Great American® Taylor Collectibles Corp. and "X-Wing Fighter" ship from Star Wars® by Rawcliffe Corporation.

Today's world of limited edition collectibles encompasses a wide variety of works of art — from fanciful lithographs, ornaments and figurines to practical and beautiful vases and bowls. From left to right and top to bottom are: "Royal Music Barque" lithograph from The Greenwich Workshop, Inc., "Amphora on Stand" Vase, "Cranberry Glass Vase" and "Rolled Rim Bowl" from The Fenton Art Glass Company, Calabar Creations' "Teddy Talks" figurine, "Azure" from the *Rainbow Collection of Bubble Fairies™* by Rawcliffe Corporation, "Ballerina" ornament by Old World Christmas, "Radiant Angel" from The Fenton Art Glass Company, "Petal" from the *Four Seasons Collection of Bubble Fairies™* by Rawcliffe Corporation, Old World Christmas' "Hey Diddle Diddle" ornament and "Little Angelo" figurine by Calabar Creations.

Anheuser-Busch, Inc.

A 500-Year-Old Craft Finds a Superb Modern Interpretation in Collector Steins from the Makers of Budweiser®

Beer making is a form of true artistry to a master brewer — and for centuries, handsome beer steins have been created to contain and protect the delicious results of this careful blending of hops, malt and grain. While the earliest steins were mainly functional, the past hundred years has seen the creation of true works of art. German firms like Villeroy & Boch and Gerz offered steins in the 1800s that today can bring hundreds of thousands of dollars on the auction market. And while these collectible steins may be out of financial reach for many of us, since 1975 Anheuser-Busch's remarkable *Collector Series* has captured the glories of 19th-century steins at affordable prices.

All Anheuser-Busch steins are crafted with the same dedication to perfection that makes Budweiser® and the firm's other beers so honored and renowned. Some feature classic themes, while others boast contemporary topics. The steins of character and celebration are ready for actual use, or they can be preserved in "mint condition" as cherished display pieces.

The Anheuser-Busch Tradition of Leadership

Anheuser-Busch has reigned as the world's largest brewer for nearly four decades with record annual sales of 86.8 million barrels of beer in 1992. Founded in St. Louis, Missouri in 1852, the firm forged an association with several renowned stein manufacturers in the mid-1970s to create its own fine steins. Collaborators included the Ceramarte stein factory in Brazil and classic German stein makers including Gerz, Thewalt and Rastal — making it possible for Anheuser-Busch to offer a greater variety of steins with each passing year.

At first, the concept was to create commemorative pieces and rewards for Anheuser-Busch beer wholesalers. But the steins were so attractive to collectors that Anheuser-Busch was inspired to test the retail sale of steins in 1980. Results were astounding: in the first year alone, 50,000 *Holiday* steins were sold. By 1990, annual sales of the *Holiday* stein had topped the 1,000,000-unit mark!

Collectors Also Seek Examples of "Breweriana"

The attraction of Anheuser-Busch steins has proven so attractive to collectors that some aficionados boast ownership of almost every piece introduced since 1975. In addition to steins, many of these enthusiasts also collect what is known as "breweriana" — such stein accouterments as bottles, cans, labels and signs.

While many Anheuser-Busch steins focus on brewery heritage for their subject matter, others showcase holiday celebrations, or non-profit organizations supported by Anheuser-Busch. The firm also commissions local and national artists based upon their specialties to create "theme" steins. When a new artist earns a first commission, Anheuser-Busch experts counsel him or her on unique stein design and production challenges.

The Gerz Meisterwerke Collection

Recently Anheuser-Busch announced the signing of an exclusive agreement with S.P. Gerz GMBH and Gerz Inc., the largest manufacturer of handcrafted steins in Germany, and its U.S. subsidiaries, for the creation of the *Gerz Meisterwerke Collection*. Gerz, founded in 1897, is well known among collectors for its high-quality, handcrafted steins. The landmark agreement makes Anheuser-Busch — already the world's largest marketer of collectible steins — the exclusive North American distributor and marketing agent of a new line of steins designed and produced by Gerz.

The first in the series of limited edition steins, titled "Santa's Mail Bag," captures the warmth and spirit of giving presents during the holiday season. This premier stein was issued in an edition of 5,000 pieces, and is part of *The Saturday Evening Post* Christmas Collection, featuring designs by Norman Rockwell. The 10¾" tall ceramic deep-relief stein features the Rockwell holiday cover illustration that first appeared on December 21, 1935. Each limited edition stein is handcrafted by Gerz and hand-painted — so no two are exactly alike. The stein sold out within six weeks of introduction.

The second Anheuser-Busch and Gerz stein collaboration, "Golden Retriever," is the premier edition in the *First Hunt* collection. This stein illustrates the special feeling that comes with the first hunt for dog and sportsman alike. Naturalist artist Pat Ford has captured all the rough-hewn beauty and allure of nature in detailed ceramic relief. The 10" tall stein, handcrafted in Germany, features a large handle resembling a dog collar, and a pewter lid. Each limited edition stein comes individually numbered on a "dog tag" hanging from the handle.

An additional three new steins in the *Gerz Meisterwerke Collection* debuted in mid-1993. Especially notable, considering the 30th anniversary of his tragic death, is the first edition of the new Gerz Meisterwerke *American Heritage* collection, entitled "John F. Kennedy." The second edition in the *Saturday Evening Post* collection, "Santa's Helper," also was introduced.

Budweiser Racing Featured on New Specialty Steins

Two recently debuted steins from Anheuser-Busch feature the Budweiser racing team of driver Bill Elliot and car owner Junior Johnson. Handcrafted by Gerz, and measuring 10½" in height, "The Bill Elliot Stein" features a solid pewter lid with a finely detailed figurine saluting Budweiser's

#11 NASCAR on top. Elliot is shown in full-color relief against a backdrop of Car #11 racing to victory amid a sea of checkered racing flags. A real collector's prize for the racing enthusiast, this limited edition stein comes individually numbered and gift boxed with a Certificate of Authenticity. Of the 25,000 in the series, 1,500 will be signed by Bill Elliott. They became available for the first time in July of 1993.

One of the most successful drivers in the sport, Elliot has been racing for nearly ten years, and in that short time, he has won the coveted Daytona 500 title twice and the 1988 Winston Cup Championship. He also has been voted the most popular driver six times in the last eight years. Now teamed with legendary car owner Junior Johnson, Elliot is destined to add to his amazing achievements on the speedway. Johnson began racing more than forty years ago, driving his brother's "whiskey car" to a second-place finish in a race held in Johnson's native Wilkes County, Virginia. As a racing team owner, Johnson has captured six national championships and more than $15,000,000 in winnings.

Both Johnson and Elliot are highlighted on the colorful Budweiser racing team stein. Handcrafted by Ceramarte of Brazil, this 6" tall commemorative stein captures portraits of the famed racing team in bold ceramic relief. Detailed in the background of the Budweiser "Racing Team Stein" are the loyal

This "Golden Retriever" stein is the premier edition in the First Hunt series from Anheuser-Busch's Gerz Meisterwerke Collection. This stein illustrates the thrill of the hunt for both dog and sportsman. The artist is Pat Ford, and the 10" stein features a large handle — resembling a dog collar — as well as a pewter lid adorned by a duck figurine.

Leonard Freeman created this image of "The Labrador" for Anheuser-Busch's Hunter's Companion series. Measuring 8¼" tall, the stein has a pewter lid topped with a unique Labrador figurine.

This specialty stein features Bill Elliot, famed driver for the Budweiser racing team. Handcrafted by Gerz of Germany and measuring 10½" in height, "The Bill Elliot Stein" features a solid pewter lid with a finely detailed figurine saluting Budweiser's #11 NASCAR on top.

pit crew and grandstand crowds cheering the team to victory.

"General Robert E. Lee" and "President Abraham Lincoln" Collectibles Continue Historical Civil War Series

Following up on the successful "General Grant" stein and collector plate — first issues in Anheuser-Busch's *Civil War* series — the firm has announced the introduction of the two final stein/plate combinations in the collection: this time in tribute to "General Robert E. Lee" and "President Abraham Lincoln." Both the "General Lee" stein and plate present the noble Confederate general surrounded by depictions of five scenes from The War Between the States: "Bombardment of Fort Sumter," "Stuart's Peninsula Raid," "Pickett's Charge, Gettysburg," "Storming the Union Breastworks, Chancellorsville," and "Lee and Traveler at Washington College." The Lincoln stein depicts a montage of scenes representative of the tumultuous period in which he served as President of the United States. From the divisive issue of slavery through the reunification and strengthening of the republic, Lincoln shines through history as a humble man of great ability and compassion.

Both Lee and Lincoln stand atop these 12¾" steins, which feature a ceramic body, pewter base, and an intricate pewter lid created in the likeness of the U.S. Capitol building rotunda. Handcrafted by Ceramarte of Brazil, each stein in the 25,000-piece limited edition is individually numbered and gift boxed with a Certificate of Authenticity. The 10¼" diameter porcelain plates are rimmed with platinum bands and are backstamped and hand-numbered with a Letter of Authenticity. Production of the plates will be limited to twenty-five firing days.

"The Labrador" and the "A & Eagle Trademark Stein" Intrigue Anheuser-Busch Collectors

The hunter's loyal Labrador retriever, shown hard at work, adorns, "The Labrador," the first stein in Anheuser-Busch's new *Hunter's Companion* series. Handcrafted by Ceramarte in Brazil, the ceramic relief stein stands 8¼" tall and features a pewter lid topped by a unique Labrador figurine. The various scenes of the noble canine in the field are created by renowned artist Leonard Freeman. Each stein in this limited edition is individually gift boxed and numbered with a Certificate of Authenticity.

As the premier edition in its historical *A & Eagle* series, Anheuser-Busch has unveiled the "A & Eagle Trademark Stein," a 4¾" issue highlighting three early versions of the famous A & Eagle trademark dating from 1872 to 1885. One of the most widely recognized symbols around the world, the proud A & Eagle design is an indelible image of Americana. The uniquely shaped stein is handcrafted by Ceramarte of Brazil, and features richly colored trim and detailed relief. First in a series of four, the limited edition stein comes gift-boxed and individually numbered with a Certificate of Authenticity. This stein sold out in an amazing eight weeks.

1993 Introductions Continue the Anheuser-Busch Tradition

Among the most recent works crafted under Anheuser-Busch's commission are the second-edition "Ganymede" stein and matching plate from the *Archives* series. The *Sports History* series continues with its sixth edition, "Hockey — Center Ice."

A second edition for the *Oktoberfest* stein series and a third and final issue for the *Sports Legends* series, "Joe Louis," also debuted in 1993, while the *Holiday* plate series continued with a fifth edition called "Special Delivery." The fourth *Man's Best Friend* series plate, titled "Outstanding in Their Field," also was unveiled in July, 1993.

Collectors Enjoy Displaying Their Anheuser-Busch Treasures

A great deal of the fun of owning Anheuser-Busch steins resides in the enjoyment of displaying them in home or office — especially *Archives* pieces like "Columbian Exposition." The "Columbian Exposition" stein marks the 400th anniversary of Columbus's travels to the new world, and commemorates the 1893 Columbian Exposition. It also includes a symbolic image of the U.S. toasting Christopher Columbus. Handcrafted in detailed relief with pewter lid and ceramic inlay, the stein measures 6½" in height.

Secondary market price rises as well as prompt sell-outs for many steins bode well for continued growth in the Anheuser-Busch stein market. And with expansion continuing in collector plates, ornaments and figurines, the firm continues to unveil new designs and styles — all aimed at continuing the steinmaking quality and tradition established by Anheuser-Busch almost twenty years ago.

Annalee® Mobilitee Dolls
Annalee Demonstrates New England Charm at Annual Annalee Doll Society Auction Extravaganza

A visit to an Annalee Doll Society Auction Weekend is enough to restore anyone's faith in good old American values — relaxing in the sunshine with friends, historical costumes and crazy getups, wonderful food and drink under festive tents, and the drama of skyrocketing auction prices on the rarest and most coveted of Annalee's collectible dolls, from 50s classics to today's one-of-a-kind "Artist's Proofs."

Annalee Thorndike presides over the event, her ready smile a warm welcome to collectors nationwide who converge on Meredith, New Hampshire, and as always, Annalee's husband Chip — joined by sons Townsend ("Town") and Chuck — are present to make sure all their guests are having the time of their lives.

To the uninitiated, this auction can provide a real awakening. One-of-a-kind pieces may sell for hundreds or thousands of dollars, and Annalee designs from the early years attract furious bidding. The all-time record-breaker, a "Halloween Girl" doll from the 50s, brought $6,600 at the 1992 auction; that same day, a 20" Santa Claus from the same period sold for $3,300. Another highlight of the Summer Auction is the unveiling of the Doll Society's exclusive "Folk Hero™" doll and the auction of its Artist's Proof — one of several one-of-a-kind Proof dolls auctioned yearly for charitable purposes.

Prices are only part of the excitement, however: collectors can choose from a wide range of designs and special products each year, at prices from $5.95 and up. The most recent Annalee catalog and *Collector* magazine features limited-edition pieces based on themes like sports, careers, diverse cultures and more. The rest of the line is drawn largely from seasonal and holiday themes. In an unusual policy, dolls produced as "Limited Issue Premiere" items for the members of the Annalee Doll Society™ are made available — minus collectible tags and features — to the general public after its limited issue has expired.

Brought to life in the form of flowers, human figures, holiday characters, and animals, the line varies widely. All, however, share the same sense of timeless whimsy and — naturally — the same

The "Ice Cream Logo Kid" is the 1993-94 Logo doll for Annalee Doll Society™ members. This charming doll has a retail value of $37.50, but it is just one of the many benefits of annual membership to the Doll Society, for only $27.50.

sunny, crinkly-eyed smile that lights up the face of Annalee Thorndike herself!

Where It All Began

Annalee and Chip Thorndike never suspected that Annalee's whimsical dolls would captivate collectors worldwide: in fact, they began as a hobby for a teenage Annalee, who first made them in the 1930s, "just for fun." When friends saw how special her characters could be, they asked Annalee to create designs for them, too.

Eventually, she began selling her pieces through the League of New Hampshire Craftsmen, to merchants for their holiday displays, and to family and

friends. When she married Chip in 1941, however, she was content to join him on his chicken farm and start a family. The Harvard-educated Chip wanted nothing more than to enjoy the farmer's simple life. Indeed, it was not until 1953, after the chicken industry moved southward, that the Thorndikes "phased out" the chickens and officially transferred their energies to the establishment of Annalee® Mobilitee Dolls, Incorporated.

Despite outside jobs and hard work on the farm, the Thorndikes had realized that providing for their family would require a change, and they decided to commit themselves to doll making, hoping that the public's love of her happy little characters could support them. The young family pitched in, determined to try. The public became entranced by Annalee's dolls, and soon word spread far beyond New Hampshire. Chuck and Town recall that their childhood years were surrounded by their mother's designs; in the early days of Annalee® Mobilitee™ Dolls, the family farmhouse *was* their "Factory in the Woods," and every available space was piled with dolls in various stages of completion. Doll fever seems to have stayed with the Thorndike boys, since today Chuck has joined his mother as an Annalee designer, and Town serves as CEO, President, and Chairman of the Board for the company.

In the early days, Annalee wondered if she could continue to create new designs, but her innovative spirit has never waned. Now, with Chuck involved in the creative process, it seems that the possibilities remain unlimited. Yet no matter how many dolls they create, the Thorndikes remain devoted to the same careful craftsmanship that has served them well since the 1950s.

Each doll begins with a conceptual drawing, which is fine-tuned until it meets with Annalee's approval. Then, a manual for each new doll's design is prepared to ensure that every department performs every detail correctly. Annalee passes judgment on the positioning of every doll that leaves the studio — each is equipped with a flexible frame that allows the utmost in "poseability." While Town sees to the business and Annalee and Chuck work on designs, Chip continues to design accessories — from the wooden skis of the early days to wooden boats for the recently released fishing dolls.

The Thorndike family has chosen to keep the dolls as handcrafted as possible, and make each an individual, with a variety of facial expressions for each "character." To keep the line fresh, the Thorndikes retire dolls and add new dolls or varia-

tions yearly. When a doll retires, it may eventually join the ranks of the "auction successes" that are so actively pursued by collector/investors.

The Annalee Doll Society: Join The Club!

Ever since the Annalee Doll Society was initiated in 1983 to meet the needs of Annalee collectors, it has provided fun and opportunity for these enthusiasts. With a membership in the tens of thousands and growing, the Society offers many benefits. The Membership Kit includes a yearly 7-inch Logo Kid doll, annual pin and membership card, a special-edition Annalee Sun Pin, subscription to *The Collector*, a full-color quarterly magazine devoted to Annalee's dolls and collectors along with a special binder, a Sale List of valuable dolls available through Annalee's Antique and Collectible Doll Shop, and free admission to the Annalee Doll Museum in Meredith. Other benefits include access to Doll Society events and eligibility to purchase exclusive, signed and numbered dolls available only to Doll Society members. In addition, Annalee's has recently allowed Doll Society members access to the occasional surplus of retired limited edition dolls from the catalog line, no longer available to the general public.

While the value of the current Logo Kid alone is $37.50, the Kid and all other benefits are available to Doll Society members for only $27.50 annually. For more information (or to join the Doll Society), contact any Doll Society Sponsor Store or call 1-800-43-DOLLS.

Reaching Out

The Thorndikes participate enthusiastically in philanthropy today as they have all their lives. They believe in using their success to better society — and not simply by making donations. This family gets involved.

The Thorndikes often use the popularity of their dolls to support a variety of causes. By featuring the logo or theme of the group they wish to benefit on an original Annalee creation, the Thorndikes draw attention to that group's needs. By auctioning the Artist's Proof and setting aside a percentage of the proceeds, they are able to address these needs. The dolls are often marketed through the Doll Society, whose members appreciate the value of these extremely limited-run items.

During each annual Annalee Doll Society Auction Weekend, Annalee's auctions several of

Always energetic, upbeat and smiling, Annalee and Chip Thorndike are a familiar sight to visitors at the Factory in the Woods in Meredith, New Hampshire. Chip often creates charming accessories to enhance the dolls designed by his gifted wife, Annalee.

their Artist's Proofs and donates the proceeds to favorite causes including health, education (Annalee's sponsors the Thorndike Scholarship Fund, dedicated to assisting Annalee employees and their families), conservation, homelessness and the arts. To demonstrate their commitment to the environment, Annalee created the "Two-in-a-Tent" mouse, featuring two mice snuggling in a pup tent. Proceeds from this work of art has benefitted the New Hampshire Land Trust.

During Operation Desert Storm in 1991, the Thorndikes met with the Chairman of the Joint Chiefs of Staff General Colin Powell and White House Chief of Staff John Sununu, presenting General Powell with the first seven-inch "Desert Storm Mouse." Annalee's donation of 500 of the mice and 1,500 special "Desert Mouse Head" pins were delivered to American troops in the Gulf. In addition, ten percent of the proceeds from the sale of every "Desert Mouse" and "Desert Mouse Head" pin was donated to the American Red Cross. More

recently, the "Mississippi Levee Mouse" was created to raise funds for flood relief in the wake of the flooding of 1993. Ten percent of its proceeds will be donated to flood relief efforts.

Each year, Annalee's donates dolls as prizes — and auction entries — to benefit the Christa McAuliffe Sabbatical Trust fund at the annual Christa McAuliffe Ski Invitational. Each year's creations, with wooden base, glass dome, plaque, and special certificate, are donated as awards for the members of the top four teams. Ironically, Annalee's team, which competes in the invitational, won the top honors in 1993. Two of the dolls won by Team Annalee were immediately donated by team captain Town Thorndike to the charity auction at the event's awards banquet.

Meet The Artist

While the Annual Auction Weekend draws capacity crowds to Meredith, New Hampshire, the Thorndikes are always delighted to welcome visitors. The Annalee Doll Museum and Town Thorndike's Antique and Classic Car Collection are within walking distance of one another, and convenient to Lake Winnipesaukee's many attractions. But for those who can't make the trek to New Hampshire, Annalee and the family provide another way to "meet the artist" — they travel throughout the country, not only visiting collectible shows, but dropping in on Doll Society Sponsor Stores as well. A visit to one of these nearly 300 sponsors brings out crowds of Annalee admirers and collectors, eager for the chance to meet Annalee or Chuck, talk with them, and have them sign autograph cards or personal items.

Similarly, the realization that many collectors are unable to get all the way to New Hampshire led Annalee's to move the Fall Auction to Hershey, Pennsylvania in 1993. This cooperative effort with Hershey allows the Midwestern and Western collectors a chance to share in the Annalee Auction Experience.

Always cheery and upbeat herself, Annalee Thorndike proclaims her goal as a simple one: she simply wants to "make people smile." With the happy expressions on her dolls' faces to cheer every admirer, this artist meets her goal with grace and enthusiasm. From "Thorndikes' Eggs and Auto Parts" to the delightful world of Annalee® Mobilitee Dolls, the Thorndikes' success story warms the hearts of all who experience the joy of Annalee, her family and her appealing Annalee dolls.

Armani Collection From Miller Import Corporation
Giuseppe Armani Embodies the Classic Art Style of Tuscany in Elegant, Hand-Made Sculptures

"People often ask me how I am able to create new sculptures," says the personable and gifted Giuseppe Armani. "Sculpting comes naturally to me, but the process is not easy to explain. Think about what relaxes you most. Perhaps you enjoy cooking. When you are chopping vegetables, or measuring ingredients, your mind is clear except for the task at hand. You become totally focused on the food: the texture, the smell, the *art* of cooking. When you finally present the meal, and it's a success, you get a wonderful feeling inside. And so it is for me with sculpting."

Armani admits, however, that the artistic path is seldom completely smooth. "When I am creating, I concentrate only on the clay and the figure in my head. But creativity is hard work. Like every good designer, I have to be concerned with more than just the way something looks in my mind. Will we be able to manufacture the mold? What finishes will we use? How many figures need to be produced? I need to answer all of these questions and a hundred more while trying to bring the figurine from my head to your hands. When I finally present a figure to you, I get the same wonderful feeling inside that you do when a meal is *multa bene.*"

Collectors might expect an artist of Armani's stature to be aloof and remote, but as these comments indicate, he is as easy to know as a kindly next-door neighbor. On a recent tour of the United States, Armani charmed thousands of his collectors with his ready smile and friendly ways. And yet his tours must necessarily be limited in length, for the sculptor finds his inspiration — as he always has — in the rich artistic heritage of Italy.

A Lifelong Love Affair With the Renaissance Art Tradition

Today, Giuseppe Armani enjoys worldwide fame and popularity for his romantic sculptural masterworks, yet his heart remains always in Tuscany. If Armani has his way, he will spend the rest of his days here — in the cradle of artistic civilization and home to several centuries worth of artistic masters. Tuscany was the land in which geniuses like Leonardo da Vinci and Michelangelo Buonarroti brought light to the world with their works. What's more, starting as early as 1600, Tuscany has been prominent in the development of ceramic and porcelain manufacture.

Giuseppe Armani was born in Calci Provence of Pisa in 1935. The walls of his medieval village were covered with drawings, and the young boy soon was inspired to design with chalk on any surface that presented itself. Little friends, animals, and tree and fairy tale creatures were his first subjects.

When Armani was fourteen, his family moved to Pisa, site of the world-famous leaning tower. The move was to be the last one Armani would make. Pisa came to be his artistic and spiritual home. And there he undertook a rigorous, ten-year-long curriculum in art and anatomy. Feeling the strong presence of the Renaissance masters around him, Armani immersed himself in the techniques, textures and styles of Michelangelo, da Vinci, Donatello and Pisano. Eventually, he won the right to apprentice himself to a master sculptor at a world-renowned studio. And although Armani had disciplined himself to study painting and other two-dimensional media, he learned that it was only through sculpture that his work was truly to come alive.

Florence Sculture d'Arte Studios Capture the Glory of Armani

At the height of the Renaissance, the city of Florence emerged as Italy's center for artistic genius and expression. Modern-day visitors find themselves overwhelmed by the sheer volume of stunning art mastery. As one visitor expressed, "At the end of each day in Florence, I had to retreat to my hotel room to rest my eyes and my spirit. I truly felt that I had 'overdosed on beauty,' and I needed to rejuvenate myself so that I would have the energy to enjoy each masterpiece to the fullest."

The genius of Michelangelo and Leonardo da Vinci lives on in Florence because their tradition and techniques have been handed down from generation to generation. And nowhere is the glory of

the Renaissance more apparent in the present day than at the studios of Florence Sculture d'Arte. There in the heart of Tuscany, where Florence, Siena, Volterra and S. Gimagnano nestle in the surrounding hills, these classic studios thrive. And it is in the studios of Florence Sculture d'Arte that Master Sculptor Giuseppe Armani's sculptures are carefully reproduced, hand-painted to exacting standards and prepared for shipment around the world.

Down through the ages, art studios have experimented with new techniques and different formulae. The Florence Studio was one of the first to discover a new development, known as "cold cast" porcelain, that has since been used by many of the major figurine factories throughout the world. This new material was the result of many years of experimentation and work by Florence craftsmen. The resulting Armani figurines retain much more detail when this new material is used for production. Older, more "traditional" methods of production have physical limitations that result in much of the artistic content intended by the sculptor being lost.

At Florence Sculture d'Arte, the final hand work is even more exacting than that of many "traditional" factories. The Armani models are carefully built up, then hand-painted to exacting standards with specialized decoration techniques. The Tuscan artists in the Florence Sculture d'Arte Studios are in perfect harmony with these high artistic standards. Therefore, the Armani figurines from these renowned studios reach unparalleled perfection in all details, under Giuseppe Armani's personal direction.

The process of creation begins when Armani creates an original piece in clay. Although the artist began his career chiseling in the classic medium of marble, he considers clay a magical material that allows him to massage and manipulate it into incredibly life-like works of art. The better part of three weeks is required of the artist to sculpt a new figure of medium size and difficulty. Once the original is complete, it is fired in a kiln at very high temperatures and then perfectly smoothed. From this piece, a flexible mold is taken, using a very special technique that allows the faithful reproduction of the original.

The mold is then filled with a liquid compound of kaolin powders and resin, whose formula has been developed through years of experiments. The compound heats through an internal reaction and hardens in two to three hours. By this process the entire artistic content intended for the sculpture is maintained in every piece, whereas with other traditional techniques this is not possible. The piece is taken out of the mold and hand-polished with

Giuseppe Armani has beautifully captured the essence of wedded bliss with this romantic figurine of a couple, perched atop a staircase. Issue price for this hand-painted "Bride and Groom" is $275.

extreme care. Minute pieces are cast separately and mounted to form a solid piece. Finally, every piece is fully hand-painted according to an original paint specimen conceived by Giuseppe Armani himself. There is a wide range of finishes for Armani pieces, including full color, pastel and "flesh" bisque. While the full-color finish is the most labor intensive, each involves an intricate and painstaking process.

Lovely Ladies, Clowns, Christmas and Even Disney Light Armani's World

Giuseppe Armani is most renowned for his incredibly tall, slim, elegant ladies. Yet in recent years, he has expanded his sculptural horizons in many new directions — much to the delight of his collectors. In addition to several new series celebrating feminine beauty, Armani has turned his attention to the Nativity, "underwater adventures," a special commission from Disney and much more.

From bath to boudoir, Armani's new *Vanity Fair* series captures beautiful young women in the midst of primping for a special night out. Attractively dressed in soft colors of seafoam green, lavender, pink and yellow, the *Vanity Fair* ladies will make an alluring addition to any Armani collection.

A special 1992 G. Armani Society feature is the stunning "Ascent" figurine. It portrays a woman who has kicked off her high-heeled shoes to walk alone, along the ocean's edge. The wind tugs at her dress, and the silk ripples as she walks. From nowhere, a dove flutters to her side and almost by

instinct, she reaches out to it. The dove lands gently on her arm — the moment Armani captures forever before the dove flutters softly away. This figurine was retired at the end of 1992.

Also worthy of note is the stunning "Eve" figurine, that has already been retired. Giuseppe Armani completed "Eve" in 1988. He knew instantly that there was something very special about her mysterious beauty, and he decided to take her for his very own. Then, for the first time, "Eve" was offered worldwide in a limited edition of 1,000 at the exceptional price of $250. Its sell-out was almost instant, as collectors delighted in "Eve's" terra cotta beauty.

Images of wedded bliss emerge in Armani's romantic wedding series, and his "A Touch of Spring" portrays a lovely, serene maiden dressed in a flowing print gown. The *Etrusca Art* series portrays beautiful ladies dressed and coiffed to reflect different periods in fashion history. And of course, there are the very popular My *Fair Ladies*™ figurines, noted for their Art Deco look. From this series, the beloved "Lady with Peacock," retired in 1991, and "Lady with Mirror," retired in 1992, are now actively traded on the secondary market. In addition to many other pieces portraying women with fans, children, animals and birds, there are new additions that showcase couples in romantic settings such as "Tango," "Telephone," "Cocktails," "Dancers" and several more.

Clowns have a special meaning for Giuseppe Armani, and thus he was thrilled to add them to The Armani Collection. As he explains, "When sculpting clowns I am reminded of my childhood

The G. Armani Society proudly introduced "Venus" as its 1993 Members-Only Redemption Figurine. This finely crafted, 15¹/₂" Armani original is hand-painted and hand-finished in the studios of Florence Sculture d'Arte in Italy. The price for the lovely "Venus" is $225.

— when I first saw clowns. They inspired a sort of poetry and enhanced feeling for me. Clowns externalize what is normally held inside the human soul — happiness, sadness, mischief and much more." The Armani clowns include the G. Armani Society 1991 "members only" figurine, "Ruffles."

Armani Nativity scenes include pure white bisque kissed with golden accents to reflect the serenity and joy of the holiday season. There are also cherubic Armani angels, both in figurine and Christmas ornament form. Expressing the artist's versatility are his *Etrusca Arte* underwater series, featuring fish in rich, iridescent colors.

A special treat for Giuseppe Armani was the opportunity to participate in the first "Disneyana" Convention sponsored by the Walt Disney Company in September 1992. For the occasion, Armani unveiled a specially commissioned sculpture of "Cinderella." This Convention will be an annual event held at Walt Disney World in Orlando, Florida, or on alternate years, at Disneyland in Anaheim, California.

Armani Enthusiasts May Join the G. Armani Society

By popular demand of Armani fans and collectors, the G. Armani Society was developed. The Society's missions include helping collectors to learn more about the artist, to meet other collectors with similar interests, to go "behind the scenes" with the artist to better understand his perspective in creating individual pieces or series, to learn first about new introductions or pending retirements, to have the opportunity to acquire members-only merchandise, and to participate in other members-only activities. Dues are $37.50 for the first year, with renewal memberships at $25 per year.

Members-only pieces include some of Armani's most inspired works, as unveiled in the quarterly G. Armani Society publication, the "G. Armani Review." The charming and enthusiastic Connie Ribaudo serves as executive director for the Society, and she travels widely — sometimes with the artist himself in attendance — to meet with collectors and dealers.

For his American collectors and Society members, Armani brings an important message of dedication. As he says, "My impression of the American collector is of someone who has great affection for my work. I also feel that they are very selective in their choices, and this represents a challenge to me as I know I have to meet their expectations. They can be assured that I am aware of this and will always make sure not to disappoint them!"

Artaffects: The Sky's The Limit For This Innovative Company
From Remington to Perillo…From Cassatt to Sauber… Artaffects Mixes the Best of Yesterday With Today to Create a Future Filled With Possibilities

Gregory Perillo walked into Artaffects' new building and was mighty impressed. The modern, freshly painted offices were a far cry from the turn-of-the-century dwelling that housed the growing company for a decade. The new "executive offices" of President Richard J. Habeeb featured all the appointments befitting a successful entrepreneur.

But something was missing. The computers and the desks were there…the coffee machine atop a new white table awaited staffers. What seemed out of place? It took a moment, but the missing puzzle piece presented itself: there was no art on the walls.

It wasn't until Perillo strolled into the president's empty office that he caught sight of a familiar painting opposite Habeeb's desk. Even from a distance, Greg could identify his landmark art: "Brave and Free." Feeling flattered, he walked to the painting and touched the canvas, wondering why Habeeb had brought the original from his home. The thought was interrupted as Richard walked briskly into the office.

Perillo smiled, extending his hand: "You brought the painting from home!"

Looking from the art to Greg and back again, Habeeb laughed. "You think so? Look closely." Now it was Perillo's turn to look puzzled.

Habeeb took the art down and showed the artist that the "Brave and Free" painting was actually an ArtCanvas reproduction, recently introduced to the public. Perillo could only utter "Wow."

The "Brave and Free" ArtCanvas, the first piece of art hung in the new Artaffects corporate headquarters, was more than just a representation of a masterpiece. It was, in every sense, the symbol of a company dedicated to innovation. For seventeen years, Artaffects had undergone near meteoric changes in growth and style…changes that founder Habeeb could hardly have imagined twenty years before…

School, Fate and The Wall Street Journal

English teacher Richard Habeeb lived the dream of his childhood. He completed a degree in English education, found a sparkling lifetime companion in wife Geraldine and settled into a domestic life. Like many newlyweds, the Habeebs found limited edition collectible plates an ideal way to bring fine art to their walls at prices they could afford. From Remington's bold western art to Mary Cassatt's Impressionistic magic, much of it (thankfully available on fine porcelain)…found its way to the Habeeb home.

But for Richard Habeeb, art also presented an intellectual challenge. His penchant for studying subjects he loved led to reading an article in the *Wall Street Journal* describing the investment potential of collectibles. This combined with his fascination for fine art led to the acquisition of more plates than he can remember. By 1975, the apartment was filled with them. The Habeeb's decision to sell a few issues literally began a second career for him. By this time, Richard realized he loved the field of collectible art just about as much as he loved teaching.

For the next two years, Habeeb plunged himself

The Simple Wonders *collection has grown to sixty-six adorable figures and wearable angels…even the nativity set has expanded to include "Wisekids" and precious pilgrims.*

into collectible "moonlighting." He taught school by day and ran "Richard's Limited Editions" from his dining room table at night. A post office box handled orders, trades and requests for market information. Eventually, the business grew so strong, Richard was compelled to make a career decision: could he continue to give his "all" to two professions at the same time? The answer was a resounding "no." The school system of New York lost a terrific educator.

Beyond Selling: Collectibles Master Turns Producer

Once free of the constraints of two full-time careers, Richard Habeeb realized he could stretch his vision of the collectible art field further by helping educate collectors and promoting the exchange of collectibles. He wanted to become a producer of limited edition plates; to discover new talent and bring it to the collectors of America. Again, fate intervened. A chance meeting with Native American and wildlife master Gregory Perillo struck a responsive chord between the two.

Perillo's works hung in galleries across America. Awards lined his walls; a testament to his talent and the influence of his teacher-mentor William Leigh. Before long, the two explored their common dream: taking fine art to collectors everywhere. That commitment, sealed in 1977, continues today as a strong personal, professional bond.

With Perillo's art leading the way, Richard Habeeb introduced a powerful collection of porcelain art under the hallmark of Vague Shadows. Then he began to seek other works, establishing The Signature Collection to showcase contemporary masters such as Rob Sauber. Sauber's romantic style proved a perfect counterbalance to Perillo's earthy art. The Sauber-Habeeb partnership launched new ideas beginning with a collection of romantic brides from various cultures that collectors embraced immediately.

Always one to learn from discoveries, Habeeb studied public reaction to Sauber's style and issued commemorative plate art to mark life's special occasions. A personalizable backstamp behind wedding, baby, anniversary and new home issues surprised and delighted collectors. Special boxing and a pen, embellishments with imagination, were the sort of ideas that helped the company grow beyond those first years.

Another division, The Curator Collection, also flourished with its emphasis on porcelain reproductions of classic art from the past. Bessie Pease Gutmann, Claude Monet and Mary Cassatt are three of the greats introduced on plate art by the

The Blue Ribbon Babies *nursery continues to grow with the addition of six newborns. A personal profile card (with rib-tickling details about their private lives) is included with every be-ribboned porcelain figure.*

Curator Collection division. Before long, visions of a small company dedicated to a few collections of limited edition art were just memories. There was a new vision. And with it came the need for a new image; one that started at the top. With a bright, new name.

What's In a Name? A Decade of Success!

Due to the diversity of new artists and styles of art, the names "Signature Collection," "Curator Collection" and "Vague Shadows" were no longer appropriate labels for the burgeoning Habeeb gallery. Time had come to pick a single, powerful name under which all offerings could be marketed. After much research and discussion, the name "Artaffects" was picked. The word was a perfect combination of "art" and "affects," for art truly does affect the most sensitive side of man's nature...and that's exactly what Artaffects aimed to do in the decades ahead.

Artaffects took the next step: an intensive search for the best variety of established and new artist talent available. Within five years, these sculptors and painters joined the Artaffects family:

MaGo: Sensitive painter of children and cherubs. His limited edition art has established trends and gathered followers across the nation; a premier MaGo angel doll with violin personifies

the sacred, gentle MaGo collectible art so highly prized by collectors everywhere.

Carol Roeda: The introduction of Carol Roeda's *Simple Wonders* collection marked an inspirational first for Artaffects. The *Simple Wonders* family has grown by leaps and bounds: pins, figures and nativities...sixty-four adorable pieces...each one, an Artaffects delight.

Lou Marchetti: The late, great painter's legacy includes sacred scenes in the style of the old masters. The Marchetti touch is most beautifully seen in his last series *The Life of Christ*. Eight eloquent scenes from the life of Jesus were painted by Marchetti with grace and elegance.

Adrian Chesterman: Fanciful dinosaurs and gorgeous wildlife now sets Artaffects apart from the rest with the recent discovery of this "fantasy specialist." Chesterman's vivid imagination is sure to become legend.

Martha Leone: Wonderful gingerbread roofs and vivid color may be the first thing you notice about Leone's primitive landscapes, but they won't be the last. This turn-of-the-century plate collection is pure Americana.

Blue Ribbon Babies: Newborn animals sporting blue ribbons and winning personalities have captured hearts and special places on hearths, shelves and tables around the globe.

Ruffles and Rhymes: Candy-kissed colors and sculpted ruffles so real, collectors ask to touch them! Six beloved nursery rhyme figures come in signature boxes...there's even a splendid "Little Bo Peep" collectible doll!

In addition to all of the exciting, new talent joining Artaffects, contemporary Perillo offerings continue to be as stunning and popular as ever. Space doesn't permit the description of all of Greg's recent introductions, but these must be mentioned: *The Village of the Sun* figurine collection and the *Children of the Plains* doll series. Both are indicative of the scope of Artaffects' commitment to new and exciting collectible art.

Village of the Sun, an authentic Navajo village, literally recreates a society with interlocking relationships and compelling tales. It breaks new collectible ground. The *Children of the Plains* doll collection is a true trendsetter; eight issues await eager Perillo fans.

Artaffects could never be described as a company resting on its laurels. The Perillo Collectors Club keeps Artaffects in close touch with the changing desires of the American collecting public. Ongoing efforts to make the Club the most benefit-laden organization in the industry reflect the Artaffects commitment to serve collectors and shops across the U.S.

In the continuing story of Artaffects Ltd., the sky is truly the limit. New horizons...new artists...bold and contemporary subjects deeply rooted in our multi-cultural heritage are in the future. A recent introduction from the brush of Adrian Chesterman shows dinosaurs during the time of King Arthur. Bold colors. Knights and Ladies. Children. A celebration of the life of the imagination. This...and more...is the direction Artaffects plans in the years ahead. Won't you follow our journey skyward?

Children of the Plains *shown clockwise (from the top)* "Bird Song" - doll four (top), "Song of the Sioux" - doll two (right), "Brave and Free" - doll one (front) and "Gentle Shepherd" - doll three (left).

The Ashton-Drake Galleries
Heartwarming Stories of Five of America's Premier Doll Artists

Children bring such joy to our lives! They're loving. They're rambunctious. And just when you think it's time for a fanny pat, they put their arms around your neck and make rainbows appear. That's the magic of childhood...and the magic of dolls created to reflect the sweet looks and adorable personalities of real children. Artists and collectors agree: owning a beautiful doll is like holding close a sweet memory. That's exactly how Ashton-Drake's premier doll designers feel about their tiny creations.

Ashton-Drake doll designs fill special places in the heart. Sometimes they teach history. Or reflect an exotic culture. Examples of this diversity are found in such porcelain treasures as mischievous Stevie, angelic "Florence Nightingale," award-winning "Chen" or "Little Bo Peep." How different! Yet how universal their charm.

What begins as the meticulous process of research and design concludes with the application of Ashton-Drake's prestigious Uniform Grading Standard. During this lengthy process, important questions are asked about artist credentials, sculpting techniques, costume design, poseability and more. Only when these criteria are met is the name of the artist and the designation "Premiere Grade" awarded to the finished doll.

But "quality control" concerns are actually the end of the journey. You want to know that Ashton-Drake designs and crafting are faithfully supervised by the designer; that like your own child's upbringing, each artist has been personally involved from the moment fingers touch the clay that ultimately became "Jason" or "Jennifer," "Jessica" or "Matthew," "Bo Peep" or "Little Sherlock." Let's discover how five of America's top doll designers go about the exciting, challenging, and heartwarming work of creating the dolls you adore for a lifetime...

Kathy Barry-Hippensteel — Her Dolls Have Personality Plus!

It's a good bet you'll find Kathy Barry-Hippensteel's name on every baby magazine subscription list in America! Kathy is inspired by the

Yolanda Bello describes her four Lullaby Babies as "cuddly as my own newborn sons..." A master designer, Bello is a personal favorite of collectors everywhere.

sweet faces and poses she discovers turning pages. She particularly likes to find infants and children with distinct, funny personalities. A silly grin. A missing tooth. A baby caught in the act of discovering fingers and toes.

Kathy's goal to create spontaneous infants in the act of being themselves is more difficult than just "sketching or sculpting a happy, pretty child," she notes. Kathy feels that dolls that do nothing more than 'look good' are too simple. Not one to take the easy route, Kathy Barry-Hippensteel decided to make her dolls look real from the start...but you should know that "being challenged" is what got Kathy into doll design in the first place.

As the mother of a premature baby in need of extra medical attention, Kathy was concerned about affording beautiful dolls for her daughter. When she heard about a dollmaking class given by designer Yolanda Bello, she signed up immediately. Happily, Kathy found more than a way to create doll art for her little girl...she found a wonderful career, too.

Years later, Kathy's delightful doll clan is growing just like her real family. Her daughter can now

play with darling "Molly," "Elizabeth" and irresistible "Christopher." The future is limitless for Kathy and her daughter...all thanks to talent, wisdom...and the challenge of a lifetime.

Yolanda Bello —
Her Designs Have Made Doll History

If it were possible to combine the image of "legend" with personality traits like "vivacious," "creative" and "warm," you'd come up with a near-perfect picture of Yolanda Bello. This dynamic doll artist came to Ashton-Drake with her vision of the ideal doll in 1984: a limited edition she had named "Jason." The rest, as they say, is history.

Yolanda Bello is a wonderful combination of dedicated artist and humanitarian. Her approach to doll design mixes maternal tenderness and love for all human beings with extensive professional training and a keen eye for detail. She has a special talent for envisioning a child's inner soul even before she begins to sculpt.

Study the look on baby "Lisa" as she awakens from her nap. Examine little "Michael" reaching for his ball. These are the delighted expressions we see in our own children and grandchildren — the Bello look of natural joy.

Yolanda's dolls have captured more than sixty awards, but this energetic artist will gladly tell you that letters from fans across America are as precious as all of her trophies. Mail pours into The Ashton-Drake offices weekly describing the emotional pleasure collectors feel each time they hold one of her "children." The love and support she receives have kept Yolanda's designs fresh and new for over a decade.

In a society like ours, rushing and hurrying seems unavoidable, thus time spent with our children is a cherished gift. Perhaps this is why Yolanda Bello fans revere her dolls. In her art, they recognize this artist's gift for capturing the essence of a child forever.

Dianna Effner —
She Makes Fairy Tales Come Alive

Lazy summer days in rural Missouri provide lush backdrops for doll designer Dianna Effner. Dianna's photography is a prelude to her personal style of doll crafting. Armed with lenses, spirited models and a few toys, Dianna may spend an entire day waiting for just the right expression. In an instant, a delighted laugh may set the stage for a one-of-a-kind collector doll. Imagine the sense of adventure she feels each time she sets out!

When the photographs are processed, Dianna combs through the prints to find "that special

First issue in the Joys of Summer *series by Kathy Barry-Hippensteel, "Tickles," comes with a fuzzy caterpillar and a lifetime of smiles.*

"Every Cloud Has a Silver Lining" is the first in a series of four Heavenly Inspirations *from award-winning Cindy M. McClure's divine talent.*

look." Then she begins the actual process of sculpting. Soon, the personality she seeks emerges from the clay. It's a wondrous process that began quite by accident over a decade ago. That's when Dianna discovered that easy-to-make flour and salt dough could be fashioned into figures of her favorite fairy tales.

Other artists admired her work, giving her the supreme compliment: Would she craft doll parts for them? Dianna considered the offers until she

attended a doll show and realized that she had the talent to design her very own dream dolls!

Over the past twelve years, Dianna Effner has come into her own. She's the creator of Ashton-Drake's *Heroines from the Fairytale Forests* series and *Dianna Effner's Mother Goose* collection. It's been a true labor of love. In fact...a fairy tale made real by Dianna Effner's faith and determination.

Cindy M. McClure — *Inspired By Faith And Dreams*

Her angelic dolls are soft and divinely beautiful. Dressed in gauzy white robes, feathered wings peek out behind gorgeous faces. Each little angel sits upon a shimmering pillow: a cloud. A rainbow. A moon. A star. These are the *Heavenly Inspirations* of doll artist Cindy M. McClure.

Cindy's spiritual nature flows from her designs. She sees in the children of our world innocent reminders of the faith and hope for which each of us prays. This vision has won admirers from coast to coast and a divine assortment of earthly awards, as well. Recipient of Doll of the Year Honors from the International Doll Academy two years in a row, Cindy's trust in the direction of her career has never been stronger.

"Very young children are perfect models for heavenly messengers," she says. Cindy McClure doll collectors must agree. McClure dolls have taken meteoric journeys on the secondary market, appreciating substantially once sold out. A continual recipient of awards and lots of media attention, Cindy and her dolls are among the most popular on today's market.

But lest you think the Cindy McClure doll family is too ethereal to be enjoyed by the average collector, think again. Every one of Cindy's dolls is named after a very real child. What a match! A bit of heaven. A bit of realism. Who could ask for a more blessed doll collection?

Mary Tretter — *A Lifetime Passion For Doll Design*

"I'll never forget the day I awoke and found toilet paper all over my house," Mary Tretter chuckles. "I was all set to scold my son, but when I saw the expression on his face and heard his giggle, I couldn't help but laugh."

A memory too priceless to be forgotten is often recounted by a proud parent to friends. But when you're a talented doll artist...well, that delightful image might just become a best-selling doll. That's exactly what happened to Mary Tretter.

Best known for her imaginative illustrations,

Mary Tretter was a favorite of educational textbook publishers for years. Not one to rest on her success as a commercial artist, Mary also took her knowledge and personality into the classroom to teach what she loved. But busy as she was, Mary couldn't turn off the "creative thoughts" when she returned home each day. So in addition to all of her professional and family responsibilities, she began to explore her lifetime passion for doll design.

Mary's heartfelt wish to become a professional doll designer turned out to be a move in the right direction. Her first creation, "Caught in the Act," was a winner from the moment it was introduced to collectors. As Mary began to meet her new fans, she was thrilled to hear stories her little Stevie inspired. This true-to-life doll tickled favorite memories of other boys and girls "decorating" a bathroom with tissue, too. This was just the sort of reaction Mary Tretter had hoped for.

With collector enthusiasm evident, could critical acclaim be far behind? Two top awards for doll sculpture from New York's Doll Artisan Guild have come her way along with a growing list of admiring collectors.

Though Mary Tretter is new to collectible dolls, her adorable work creates a path that's sure to widen with each new design. What makes this success more meaningful is the fact that her first doll began as a personal moment to be treasured forever: the giggly image of her beautiful son filling her home...and her world...with an equal mixture of tissue and love.

Collectors love Stevie's antics! Mary Tretter's "Caught in the Act" hints at a rosy future for this talented artist.

Attic Babies
Marty Maschino's Raggedy Rag Dolls Reveal Delightful Childhood Memories to Collectors

To see Attic Babies is to screech with delight!!! At first glance, the almost obsessive urge to pick them up and examine them closely is overcoming. Touching their hair, poking their bellies, and investigating every square inch of their intricate accessories is an absolute must! Marty Maschino, through her Attic Babies, shows collectors just how wonderful life can be as long as one keeps looking for the hidden humor. Attic Babies, the original tea-stained characters of this kind, have all but tip-toed into the collectibles market. Their rapid rise in popularity is greatly indebted to the human spirit's reluctance to let go of childhood. These childish reminders reassure admirers of how to successfully get only the best out of life, no matter how rough the terrain one must travel to get there. Ragged, old, worn and very much loved, the Attic Babies whisper of mankind's uncanny resilience to life's little fiascoes.

Introducing Attic Babies and Rediscovering Youth

Marty Maschino, designer of Attic Babies, says, "Growing older does not mean one must become tart and boring, but instead it means one has a wiser mind to perfect one's childish tendencies!" Attic Babies are a tribute to a rediscovered childhood. The legend of the Attic Babies tells of a child growing out of his youth and storing his innocence in the attic, along with his childish belongings. While many years of growth and experience affect the child, the tarnished babies hold onto their charm. As a child becomes an adult, he will eventually take a trip back to his own "attic" to discover the child he left long ago... Most people, like Marty Maschino, are happy to discover that the child is still inside, still loving, remembering and anticipating life...maybe even more so the second time around!

Attic Babies are toys for the adult without the guilt. They are easily disguised as decorative items, when placed on shelves, beds, furniture and window sills. Because these babies are rag dolls, concern about breakage is minimal; however, the tea-stain makes them look old and fragile, giving the perfect excuse

A part of Marty Maschino's life is often revealed in the creation of her Attic Babies. "Suttie Sue," Marty's nickname, is a numbered and limited edition.

to tell the children why only adults (being the responsible party) can be trusted to play with them.

The Attic Babies line consists of, not only raggedy babies, but also playful parodies of the ultimate professional, sports, hobby and recreational dolls, as well as zoo animals that will tug at anyone's heartstrings. Not only are these hand-made whimsical dolls practical and functional, they are also entertaining. Each of Marty Maschino's designs come armed with extraordinary, distinctive personalities that are adorned with hysterical names such as: "Fertile Myrtle," "Virtuous Vergie," "Lucious Lulu," "Tubby Timbo," "Fatty Matty," "Fire Fightin' Fergie" and hundreds more. Most of the charismatic designs and names are influenced by people directly related to Marty's life, such as friends, family, and even childhood memories. Several of the dolls Marty has designed have later been revealed as renditions of herself at different times in her life, such as "Fertile Myrtle," "Party Marty" and "Suttie Sue."

The Attic Babies artist also meets people on signings and at shows, and their names or personali-

ties often make their way into the Attic Babies family. People often ask Marty how she could possibly come up with hundreds of unique characters and names without running out on occasion, but to people like Marty, creativity is a part of life that isn't easily ignored. Whether it manifests itself on canvas, in the kitchen, packing the kids' lunch, or even in the vegetable garden, this type of creativity cannot be suppressed, nor cultivated on demand.

Marty Maschino designs her Attic Babies twice yearly. Anywhere between ten and twenty dolls and animals could be designed each season. After a doll has "lived his life with great service and loyalty," Marty may select him to go forth and re-tire. Besides the yearly retirements, some dolls are designed as signed, numbered and limited editions, and will retire after meeting their limited number.

The Prelude to an Artist's Dream Comes True

Marty Maschino, now mother of five, began study-ing commercial art at CSU in Oklahoma City and then ventured into free lance work. Later, Marty worked as an interior designer and also as an artist for a department store chain. Marty, even as a child, was a natural when it came to anything requiring a creative eye. As her young family began to grow, she found it much more beneficial to the children if she worked out of her home. She began exhibiting items at shows, and soon realized that of those items, her rag dolls were an extraordinary hit (not to mention being much easier to carry around for the pregnant artist). In 1986, Attic Babies began as a home-based business.

In July of 1987, the first "magical sixteen" babies were sent to the Dallas Gift Market, where orders came in by the droves. Marty does her best work under pressure, but she realized at this point that she alone could not produce this large of a quantity. To alleviate the demand, she hired home sewers. In the next two years, Attic Babies relocated three times to larger facilities, where it now resides in Drumright, Oklahoma. Attic Babies' new location, half way between Tulsa and Oklahoma City, is in a 15,000 square foot building with approximately one hun-dred employees. The office and factory are open Monday through Friday, and tours are available Monday through Thursday from 8:30 a.m. until 2:30 p.m. As much time as needed is taken to answer visitors' questions and satisfy their curiosity, so it's well worth the time to visit this wild bunch in the steamy Midwest.

Marty Maschino is the designer of Attic Babies — the whimsical, tea-stained rag dolls that are a tribute to a rediscovered childhood.

"Tour Babies" are also available from Attic Babies. They are designed yearly as a special gift for those who take time out of their schedules to visit the factory. These dolls are sold at a wonderful price, exclusively in Drumright, and are only available to visiting patrons. In the beginning, Attic Babies was merely a dream to a creative young woman, but seven years, and well over 400 designs later, her dreams sit atop shelves and warm hearts worldwide.

In 1990, Marty Maschino was chosen as Oklahoma's Small Business Person of the Year. Also that year, Marty was invited to Washington, D.C. where Mrs. Bush was presented with a special edition, "Grammy Bar," designed as a funny rendi-tion of the First Lady. Marty has also designed special babies for *McCalls Patterns* and was invited to the National Governors' Convention in 1993, where she designed dolls commemorating Native Oklahoma for each Governor's spouse.

Attic Babies Collectors' Club — Being a Part of the Craziness

The Attic Babies Collectors' Club began in 1992 and has practically doubled in number every year. This group of chatty collectors has become a close part of office life at Attic Babies. They have their own group on Prodigy and correspond daily. Many have become pen pals, and even great friends, by running into each other while touring the Attic Babies factory.

Club members get all the inside information. Not only do they receive a quarterly newsletter that is both informative and quite humorous, but they also receive memos on signings, collectible shows and behind-the-scenes information on new designs and soon-to-retire dolls. Lots of special offers are given to club members only. In April of 1994, Attic Babies gave members an opportunity to bid on retired dolls dating back to 1987 in the 1994 Attic Babies Silent Auction.

For an initial fee of $30.00 and a $20.00 renewal fee, members receive, in addition to the quarterly newsletter, the Attic Babies Collectors' Club t-shirt and button, both adorned with colorful artwork of the year's Club doll. Club members will also recieve a mug, a folder containing a catalog and other important information, and a membership card entitling them to purchase the year's Attic Babies Club Doll which is hand-signed and numbered. The doll is only manufactured for club members and is not available to the public.

Marty Maschino, as well as Attic Babies employees, feel that their club is special. "Our club members know our names, and we know theirs... that makes it special." What makes the Attic Babies Collectors' Club so successful? Marty's whimsical babies shine with her own carefree and charismatic charm because she designs each doll with a piece of herself entwined within their enchanted hearts. Many collectors relate to the Attic Babies...because they are real!

Attic Babies' Zoo Animals have their own distinctive personalities and names. Pictured from left to right are "Josie Posie-Poo," "Lionel Ryan McDoogle," "Beatrice Bippitibop" and "Lanky Leona."

BAND Creations
Bringing Figurals to Collectors From a Variety of Artists

BAND Creations was established by Dennis Sowka in 1988 to distribute a variety of figurals by different artists to the collectible world. Sowka had fifteen years experience with inspirational, Christmas and collectible items and thus knew many artists in America whose works people would love to collect.

Currently BAND distributes figurines made by Tom Rubel, Teresa Madsen, Patricia Wilson, Jeanette Richards and Sandra Penfield.

The Superb Artistry of Tom Rubel

Tom Rubel knew as a child that art was his future. And from the beginning, working in three-dimensional art beguiled him. A graduate of the American Academy of Art in Chicago, his experiences include designing precious metals for both The Lincoln Mint and The Hamilton Mint, Creative Director for Roman, Inc. and working with Takara, U.S.A. and Silver Deer, and now his work with BAND Creations.

A constant for Rubel is beauty. He says, "The one thing that is always foremost in my mind is to learn to see beauty. The subjects that I draw never really change, but the way I think about them does. My imagination and inner feeling develop the ideas and principles of the art, and shape the form."

Tom Rubel takes his intense focus on beauty to new heights with his new eight-piece Nativity, which was introduced at the International Collectible Exposition in South Bend by BAND Creations in July of 1993. Throughout history, the Nativity has been the subject of reverence by renowned artists — and now Tom Rubel, long known for his artistic collectibles, works with this beloved Christian theme to bring to modern-day collectors his personal interpretation of this cherished theme.

Opening with eight pieces, there will be an additional eight portraits added each year so that collectors can add to their collections.

Rubel's Nativity consists of intricate cold-cast sculptures. Each portrait takes months to complete from drawings to sculpture to production. Each sculpture is painstakingly hand-painted to bring

out both the power and subtlety of Rubel's art. The initial eight portraits in this new collection include The Holy Family, Three Kings, Gloria Angel, Angel and Mandolin and Angel with Lamb. The price of this eight-piece set is $340.

Look to the Future

It is very likely that in 1994 BAND will release Rubel's *A Christmas Treasury* which tentatively will include four old world angels crafted in resin. Each is scheduled to carry an instrument cast in antique brass and collectors may choose between antique white or antique beige. All are to be 10½ inches tall. Rubel doesn't intend to leave animals out of the holiday season, which makes sense because he is such a nature lover, and he intends to include four resin bears, one Christmas puppy

The "November" angel of the month from Jeanette Richards and Sandra Penfield's Best Friends™ series, bears a Thanksgiving pumpkin pie.

and one Christmas kitty, all 4 inches tall. Retail prices for Rubel's Christmas sculptures are scheduled to range from $20 to $285, for his Renaissance Santa.

Rubel also has classical sculptures through BAND including ballerina figurines, both musical and non musical, as well as porcelain little ladies inspired by his own daughter. The diversity of this artist continues to delight collectors near and far — and for good reason.

Best Friends *Introduced in 1992*

Best Friends are small miniatures about 1¹/₂ inches to 3 inches created by Jeanette Richards and Sandra Penfield and introduced to the collectibles field at the International Collectible Exposition at Secaucas, New Jersey, in Spring 1992. *Best Friends* is a series of twelve angels, each one representing a specific month. Each angel has something in her hand to represent her month, such as a heart for February, a flag and drum for July, a pumpkin and mask for October. *Best Friends* also includes a five-piece carolers set, an angel pin which has two angels and an angel necklace with three angels.

These clay miniatures are the creation of two women who are now "best friends" in Wisconsin. Jeanette Richards, from a family of artists in Ohio, studied art in Washington, D.C. Sandra Penfield grew up in Minnesota and studied art at the University of North Dakota. Their mutual interest in art brought them together first as partners in a graphic design business in Wisconsin in 1984. Always experimenting with new ideas, they created their first Christmas angel in 1990, and it portrays the essence of innocence and delight. One angel lead to another and their new creations blossomed as they focused on facets of friendship and family life.

Best Friends has expanded beyond the angels of the month to a series called *First Friends Begin in Childhood*. These groupings emphasize friendship, and this 1993 series includes a bride and groom and three angels, three Santas and a grandpa and grandson fishing on a log. In all, there are sixteen pieces in the *First Friends Begin in Childhood* collection.

All the sculptures by Richards and Penfield are originally made in culpey clay, then reproduced in poly-resin. Richards says, "We really work on the pieces together. Sandra does one and I do another. Even the designs we do together. It goes faster that way. It also reflects what's important to us — the idea of friendship, of people being there for one another."

Although most of their pieces are in open editions, one angel they have is strictly limited to

The friendly and whimsical "Needles" the nurse from the BusyBodies *collection would be a welcome sight to any hospitalized patient.*

fifty pieces. It is called "Angels in the Snow." It shows a boy in a snow suit making an angel outline in the snow and a tiny angel is watching him from behind a pine tree. This angel retails for $100. Each angel of the month retails for $10.

Victorian Santas Made Entirely By Hand

Another artist BAND represents is Pat Wilson who creates Victorian sad-faced Santas. With their long white beards they look as though Father Time were their brother.

Wilson has been a Santa collector for a long time, both old Santas and new. She remembered an old Victorian Santa her Grandmother had, and based her first hand-made Santa on that memory. Wilson has been creating Victorian Santas for fifteen years. She has about twelve Santas now for BAND Creations, and each style is limited to 200 pieces.

Each Santa's face is made from an original clay sculpture, then molds are made. The beard and hair is from raw Michigan Lincoln wool — Wilson is adamant about supporting home-state products in her artwork. Wilson does essentially everything herself, from the designing to the pouring to the hand-painting. She also designs each outfit and now obtains some help with the sewing.

The idea of a sad Santa goes back to Germany in the last century. Wilson updates her Santas by expanding their themes. For example she has a

Seaside Santa who carries shells, driftwood, birch bark and seaweed. Wilson says, "Most collectors keep this particular Santa out all year long." The most popular Santa has the long red velvet robe and long beard made from hand-washed raw wool. Wilson says, "Every year I create new Santas — new themes — right now I'm working on a Highland Santa. My Santas have very original looking old faces and their beards are what catches you eye right away."

Retail prices range from about $170 to $370 and the sizes of the Santas range from 17 inches to 24 inches tall.

New to Collect — BusyBodies

Teresa Madsen created the three-dimensional *BusyBodies* in 1992. These are small (4 inches) poly resin figurines which Madsen created "because I wanted something different but cute, a face that wasn't real, but a caricature." Her first twelve BusyBodies all have a professional or sports theme.

The whimsical characters have unique facial expressions which is truly Teresa's signature. She says, "These facial expressions establish a kind of bond between the figurines and the person, where everyone can relate to the feeling of being expressed. They make you laugh and smile."

Anyone who's ever been in a hospital has known a "Needles" the nurse, and fishermen can relate to "Fish Tales." Madsen's personal favorite is "Slicer" the golfer because "She's impish looking, as though she's saying 'Yea, I'm golfing, I might not be that good, but so what?'"

Each *BusyBody* comes with a giftbox and a hang tag. The dozen in this first series will soon be followed by more. The retail price of each *BusyBody* is $15. One future idea Madsen has is to create clusters of miniatures—little sets where they can be displayed on the same platform. Each miniature will be about 2 inches tall.

Figurals for Nearly Every Taste

BAND has seen to it that figurals are available for nearly every collector's taste or desire. The Nativity, Santas of all kinds, animals, angels in the traditional style or fanciful angels of the month, enchanting figurals that let us recognize the funny side of people we meet every day, artful ballerinas, porcelain girls with parasols and reminders of the role of best friends in our lives. It's a wonderful beginning.

These "Rainbow of Friends" angels from BAND Creations' Best Friends™ series have their hands as well as their hearts joined together.

The Bradford Exchange
World's Largest Trading Center Showcases Classic Themes and Current Trends in Collector's Plates

Since the early 1970s, The Bradford Exchange has demonstrated a unique vision of plate collecting. The firm offers an organized, orderly market where collectors buy and sell plates — and it has become one of the world's most successful marketers of collector's plates as well. Today, The Bradford Exchange operates the world's largest trading center for limited edition collector's plates from its international headquarters in Niles, Illinois, which serves as a coordinating link for Bradford offices around the world.

The Bradford Exchange offers quarterly Market Reports, also known as "Quote Sheets," which provide the "last trade prices" of hundreds of Bradford-recommended plates. Each business day, the computerized Exchange facilitates buying and selling on an international basis, with trading prices fluctuating in response to supply and demand on the secondary market. "Buys" and "sells" are entered by mail and phone.

As for its marketing dimension, Bradford analysts have the pulse of the market: they know what collectors want and how their tastes vary from nation to nation. New plates are introduced to meet these demands, with current popular themes including nature and wildlife, movies and celebrities, landscapes, sports, trains, and what The Bradford Exchange calls "unique medium."

Nature and Wildlife Themes Captivate Collectors

Bradford analysts regularly track the market performance of plates inspired by nature and wildlife — and they note that a few exceptional ones have more than doubled in value in recent years. Picking up on this attractive theme, The Bradford Exchange recently has unveiled works of art by Lena Liu, Lily Chang, Julie Kramer Cole, Thomas Hirata, Charles Fracé, and John Seerey-Lester.

The collector's plates of award-winning artist Lena Liu begin as delicate paintings on fragile silk. What they become are exquisite works on porcelain, enabling Ms. Liu to lead the way in a fast-growing plate market segment. Since Ms. Liu's first plate nearly doubled in value within months of its retirement, collectors are particularly intrigued with issues from her subsequent series.

"The Ruby-Throated Hummingbird" premiers Lena Liu's *Hummingbird Treasury*, in which a tiny bird hovers over a delicate hibiscus, searching for nectar. Surrounding the scene is a spectacular decorative border which re-creates green marble and malachite highlighted with lustrous gold. "Roses" marks the debut of Lena Liu's *Basket Bouquets*, a series in which each plate portrays a romantic, flower-filled basket surrounded by a floral border design and double bands of gold. "Roses" offers a lavish bouquet of pink and white roses complemented by a smattering of green leaves and a handful of purple hydrangea, spilling forth from a hand-woven country basket.

Ms. Liu's *Symphony Of Shimmering Beauty* plate collection begins with "Iris Quartet," in which gold highlights are used to outline the elegant lines of white, blue, maroon and violet irises surrounded by foxglove and spurge.

Lena Liu's "Roses" from the Basket Bouquets series combines a lush assortment of roses with a floral border and a double band of gold. The plate was named Plate of the Year in 1993 by NALED.

Plates Present Dogs and Cats

Lynn Kaatz's *It's A Dog's Life* series appeals to canine lovers, with a plate called "We've Been Spotted" highlighting a pair of Dalmatian pups. As for cat lovers, they're sure to enjoy Frank Paton's "Who's the Fairest of Them All?" from the *Victorian Cat Capers* series. It shows a confident feline calmly surveying herself in the looking glass.

Like Lena Liu, artist Lily Chang enjoys painting flowers. But rather than add wild creatures to her art, Ms. Chang prefers to portray tiny kittens in her first plate series. Her "Garden Discovery" plate premiers the *Petal Pals* series, and features two Persian kittens; one napping, and the other with bright blue eyes awake to the glorious natural wonders around her. A butterfly as colorful as stained glass hovers near a stand of tall, regal irises in stunning hues of cobalt and lapis. Upcoming *Petal Pals* plates will present different types of kittens in other romantic floral settings.

A very different kind of cat — a regal mountain lion — serves as subject for the first plate in Julie Kramer Cole's *The Faces Of Nature* collection. This series is the first to present "hidden image" art in the medium of collector's plates. Each plate contains wildlife partially concealed within majestic landscapes of the American West. The debut issue shows two Sioux scouts riding silently through a snow-laden canyon. Hidden within the canyon walls is the image of a mountain lion.

Wildlife Plates Offer The Works of Award-Winning Artists

Considering the sustained popularity of wildlife plates, The Bradford Exchange wants collectors to have the opportunity to own works from some of today's most renowned living masters.

Thomas Hirata's wildlife portraits are presented in a series entitled *Wild Spirits*, which begins with "Solitary Watch." In Hirata's portrayal of a noble timber wolf, this lord of the northern wilderness gazes intently at his pack as they bound across the snow-shrouded terrain to join him. Like a proud sentinel, he stands before the white and gray mountains, his silver fur blending with nature.

Grand Safari: Images Of Africa offers collectors the opportunity to join art master Charles Fracé on an odyssey to Africa, and share his vision of its turbulent beauty. His plate, "A Moment's Rest," portrays the savage beauty of two cheetahs on Africa's Serengeti Plain. They bask in the morning sun, their rosette-spotted fur glowing like flecked topaz. Exotic facial "tear marks" add to the mystique of this most feline of creatures. This African safari continues with Fracé originals capturing

A close-up of the handsome, brooding young Elvis Presley is blended with a portrait of The King in front of "Heartbreak Hotel" in this first issue from the Elvis Presley Hit Parade *plate collection, one of several Elvis series introduced in recent years by The Bradford Exchange.*

other noble creatures the artist encountered on his own recent safari in Eastern Africa.

John Seerey-Lester unveils the "Denali Family" as the first of his series called *Bear Tracks*. The collection represents the famed artist's attempt to offer each plate collector a memorable encounter with the living symbols of the untouched wilderness: the magnificent grizzly bear. In "Denali Family," a glorious bath of "alpenglow" sweeps over the Alaskan tundra, highlighting the silver-tipped fur of a grizzly mother and her two yearlings as they scan the brush for intruders.

Movie and Celebrity Plates Win Collectors' Hearts

Ever since the 1970s, plate collectors have enjoyed owning porcelain works of art featuring the images of famous people and films. The Bradford Exchange has been a leader in this collecting category, with several recent issues continuing this classic subject area. The *Disney Treasured Moments* plate collection, for example, debuts with "Cinderella," and portrays the most beloved characters from Disney's animated classics. The first plate depicts the moment just before "Cinderella" meets her prince at the Royal Ball. Other Disney Studios collaborations with Bradford include series such as *Snow White And The Seven Dwarfs*, *Mickey's Christmas Carol*, and *Beauty And The Beast*.

Collectors seem to have unlimited passion for

plates related to "Gone With the Wind," with series entitled *The Passions Of Scarlett O'Hara* and *Critics Choice: Gone With The Wind* currently in circulation. The first plate in the latter series, "Marry Me, Scarlett," was named Plate of the Year by the National Association of Limited Edition Dealers in 1992.

The Bradford Exchange has premiered a number of successful Elvis Presley collector's plates in recent years, with more issues expected soon. "Heartbreak Hotel" from *The Elvis Presley Hit Parade* is the first in a series that conveys the mood and message of the entertainer's greatest hits. *Portraits Of The King*, beginning with "Love Me Tender," provides a close-up look at the different facets of Elvis, off-stage. For the on-stage Elvis, collectors need look no further than *Elvis Presley: In Performance*, with the first-issue plate entitled "'68 Comeback Special." Focusing on the Presley film career is the collection called *Elvis On The Big Screen*.

The Marilyn Monroe Collection highlights scenes from the renowned actress' best-known roles in films from Twentieth Century Fox Film Corp. Movies depicted included "The Seven-Year Itch" and "Diamonds Are a Girl's Best Friend." Another Monroe series, called *The Magic Of Marilyn*, portrays some of the most famous of the late actress' live appearances.

Beatles fans will be pleased to know that Apple

Corps Limited and Determined Productions have entered into an alliance with The Bradford Exchange to portray the Fab Four in *The Beatles Collection*. Beginning with "The Beatles, Live in Concert," the series features key moments from the legendary career of John, George, Paul and Ringo. Another group of plates inspired by the renowned quartet is a six-issue series called *The Beatles 1967-1970*. It begins with a plate celebrating the 25th anniversary of Sgt. Pepper's Lonely Hearts Club Band.

Bradford Plates Cover a Wide Range of Popular Subjects

With collectible cottages pleasing many of today's art lovers, The Bradford Exchange has arranged to offer a number of collector's plates on this heartwarming theme. The famed "Painter of Light," Thomas Kinkade, has created series called *Thomas Kinkade's Home Is Where The Heart Is* and *Thomas Kinkade's Yuletide Memories*. Kinkade also has series inspired by *Garden Cottages Of England* and *Home For The Holidays*. What's more, his *Thomas Kinkade's Thomashire* introduces a special place from the artist's imagination, with "Olde Porterfield Tea Room" as the first fanciful image. Also creating artwork for cottage-theme plates from The Bradford Exchange is Impressionist Carl Valente, whose plate debut is "Garden Paths of Oxfordshire" from the *Poetic Cottages* collection.

The Bradford Exchange endeavors to remain on the "cutting edge" of the plate world with unique uses of media such as "Sweet Stander" — the only collector's plate to bring the delightful sound of "The Carousel Waltz" alive for its admirers. A cold-cast porcelain, hand-painted series of plates called *The World Of Beatrix Potter*, and a hand-cast, bas-relief collection entitled *Rockwell's Christmas Legacy*, are three-dimensional interpretations of the heartwarming legacies of two artists whose work has endured for decades.

In the sports realm, *The Legends Of Baseball* series begins with "Babe Ruth: The Called Shot," officially endorsed by the family of Babe Ruth and the Babe Ruth Baseball League, Inc. The plate depicts the fateful day when Babe Ruth knocked a home run out of Wrigley Field in Chicago after pointing toward the centerfield wall.

With its bustling plate exchange as a backdrop for a robust primary plate market, The Bradford Exchange plans to continue its impressive list of achievements, fulfilling the needs and wishes of collectors in North America, and all around the globe.

"Love's First Dance" from the Beauty And The Beast *series depicts Belle and the Beast enjoying their first dance together surrounded by the palace's enchanted objects. A free audio cassette of the movie soundtrack comes with the plate.*

Brandywine Collectibles
"Capturing the Heart of America"

All across the country, people are creating miniature villages in their homes and shops. The charming collections from Brandywine Collectibles and its troupe of artisans in Yorktown, Virginia figure prominently in the current interest in miniature architecture. Reminiscent of another era, Brandywine Collectibles are handmade under the watchful eye of its founder and designer Marlene Whiting and her husband Truman (Tru), President and CEO of Brandywine Woodcrafts, Inc. Marlene's houses and shops capture the heart of historic American architecture, as well as her own recollections of our country's numerous small towns, in a scale easy to incorporate into today's homes.

Meet Marlene Whiting

"Growing up in Pittsburgh, Pennsylvania, my mom taught me to sew, to knit, to crochet, and to cook. I was always encouraged to do all kinds of handwork. 'We can make it ourselves!,' was the key. I just assumed everyone did the same thing," stated Marlene with a smile.

Although winning a few awards for her art in high school should have given her a clue, Marlene pursued her other love, English Literature, in college. In April of her senior year, she and Tru were married. After graduation, they quickly settled into the fast paced existence of the USAF fighter pilot's life. "Frequent moves and many separations were the way of our lives. The separations were, for me, filled with kids, sewing, needlework and crafts. The first four years of our marriage, we were apart better than fifty per cent of every month," Marlene continued.

Their son Truman III was born in 1967, followed in 1970 by daughter Donna. In 1974, Marlene discovered tole and decorative painting. "To afford classes, I designed, made and sold appliqued infant quilts, coordinated with infant seat covers, burp cloths and bibs. The quilting business grew so that I didn't have time to paint!" However, Tru was assigned to Iran, and the entire family moved to its capitol, Tehran. Unable to purchase supplies for quilting, Marlene found other outlets for her creativity. Recognizing that westerners living in

"The Dress Shop" and "The Flower Shop" are two pieces of Marlene Whiting's Hometown Series which were highlighted last summer in American Country Collectibles magazine's feature story on cottages. Collectors can have their Hometown pieces personalized to reflect their favorite local shops, or family names and interests.

Tehran longed for anything western to remind them of home, she taught classes in gingerbread house building, purchasing the ingredients from the local bazaars and sweet shops. She created and sold macrame at the American Women's Club, incorporating cord, ceramic "donkey" beads and handmade copper pots and bells from the Iranian craftspeople, which made her items unique and popular. The profits allowed Marlene to order decorative painting supplies and books from home, enabling her to continue to practice and learn.

Leaving the Mideast in January of '79 in the midst of the Iranian revolution, Tru, Marlene and the children spent six months in Phoenix, Arizona re-establishing their lives in the States. The USAF then moved them to Las Vegas. Here, Marlene, no longer just a student of painting, began teaching decorative painting. For eighteen months she taught, building up to four classes a week at various levels of skill. Then the Air Force intervened again, this time moving the family to Yorktown, Virginia.

Something Borrowed, Something New

Tired of teaching and discouraged by the time it took for an oil painting to dry in Virginia's humid

"Happy Birthday House," from Brandywine Collectibles Treasured Times series, comes with a greeting label to be inscribed by the gift giver. Limited to an edition of 750 and available in two color schemes, the charming facade recognizes our "most popular personal holiday."

climate, Marlene decided to try a new direction for her creative endeavors. Borrowing $50.00 from her husband and investing in acrylic paints and brushes, Marlene created a few little wooden hearts, and cut-outs of barnyard animals. With these nestled in a charming old market basket, she headed to Plantiques, a lovely local gift shop, to show and hope-fully sell her wares. Not wanting to disturb the busy shopkeeper, Marlene set the basket down and wan-dered about the fourteen rooms of country decorating. Much to her surprise, the shopkeeper sought her out, saying that people wanted to buy some of the things in the basket! The shopkeeper bought everything in the basket and Marlene watched, astonished, as her work was sold to pleased customers before her eyes! When Marlene reached home, the phone was ringing — it was the delighted shopkeeper who had sold all the pieces and was ask-ing for more. An auspicious beginning of things to come! The store owner eventually asked Marlene to create some primitive-looking little houses. Tru cut Marlene's designs out of wood, making the pieces look like the charming houses in the historic Hilton Village area surrounding Plantiques.

Encouraged by Fellow Artists to Continue

In 1983, a local celebrity and renowned folk art-ist, Nancy Thomas, suggested that Marlene show her houses to Colonial Williamsburg. Charmed by the detailed, hand cut and hand-painted creations, the Williamsburg buyer commissioned Tru and Marlene to make replicas of the historic houses in the famous town. The first customer was the then Secretary of State George Schultz, who remains an ardent col-lector of Tru and Marlene's work. Today, the Williamsburg Collection has grown to thirty replicas, still painstakingly cut of native Virginian poplar, hand-painted, signed and numbered, and still avail-able in Colonial Williamsburg.

Through Plantiques, Marlene Whiting's first customer, she and Tru had an opportunity to meet Tom Clark of Cairn Studios. Marlene and Tru made a giant jumping jack gnome for Tom when he came to do a signing appearance. It was during this time that Marlene began experimenting with house facades, sculpted in clay. Tom Clark and his team encouraged her and taught Marlene and Tru all about resin casting. "Without their encouragement, I might not have continued," she says. At first she sculpted only replicas of historic architecture: Williamsburg, Hilton Village, Yorktown, Old Salem, etc. But in 1989, Marlene sculpted a tiny shop she called "Stitch & Sew." It was followed by a school, general store and toystore. Each was her own creation, drawn and sculpted with fond thoughts of all the small towns in her home state of Pennsylvania. Designed to be kits for the craftsperson, Marlene soon discov-ered that the customer preferred the already decorated pieces, so the first whimsical designs were released as Hometown Series I. Little did Marlene suspect she was starting down the road to such a popular series! Hometown Series IX was introduced in July 1994! These delightful sets of shops have a unique feature — any customer can have a special name painted on the sign of the shops to create a special village reflecting favorite Hometown locations or family names. All the limited edition Hometown pieces are available for only two years and then re-tired. New series are introduced twice a year. In 1995, Hometown Series X and XI will make their debut.

In January 1994, Brandywine Collectibles intro-duced their new Treasured Times Collection — celebrating all the happy times in our lives. Special celebrations for special occasions have always meant a great deal to the Whiting family, so Treasured Times was a natural outgrowth of Marlene's own experi-ences: "This is something I've been wanting to do for a long time. These special little houses are just another way to say 'I love you' or 'You are special to me' — they are mementos that can be given and displayed on the special days. My hope is that they add to festive occasions and bring a smile to the recipient year round!" Starting with the effervescent "Happy Birthday House" and the feminine "Mother's Day House," the Treasured Times Collection is gradually growing to provide happy commemorative gifts for all the special occasions we treasure.

Complete with a special greeting label to be inscribed by the customer, *Treasured Times* pieces in their special gift boxes are thoughtful and lasting gifts. 1995 will see continued additions — "The Anniversary House" and "Welcome to Your New Home" are two in the planning stages.

North Pole Series

Recognizing the universal love and excitement of the Christmas holiday season, Marlene has interpreted the American legend of Santa Claus' hometown in her *North Pole Collection*. Sized perfectly for a mantle or sideboard display, Marlene's *North Pole Collection* grows in size each year, along with its popularity! In 1994 the "North Pole Town Hall" and "Post Office" were introduced. Each year's additions are a carefully guarded secret until released in June.

Downtown, U.S.A.

In January 1992 Tru and Marlene introduced a new group of economically priced buildings to the gift industry. Called *Downtown U.S.A.*, the series featured twenty-eight of Marlene's imaginative designs of small town shops. Each is a printed reproduction of the original painting, mounted on wood, cut out and finished. "The printing allows me much more flexibility with colors, shading and detail in the original artwork than I would have if we were to use the screen printing technique. It is also very affordable. Tru's phrase for it is 'the hand-painted look without the hand-painted price!'" Sales of *Downtown U.S.A.* have skyrocketed since their introduction. There are currently over fifty-five designs available, each in every day or Christmas versions, available individually or in "street scenes" of five designs per unit. All can be personalized to suit the customer with family members' names or the names of local shops. Plans for 1995 include the introduction of a new series in this line, to be known as *Country Lane*. Look for it!

Today

Brandywine Woodcrafts, Inc. and Brandywine Collectibles offer over 100 different hand cast, hand-painted building facades. In addition to the historic collections, the *North Pole Collection*, and all the current personalized *Hometown* pieces, there is a large selection of accessory pieces to add excitement to the village setting. New pieces are introduced twice a year — there were twenty-one new designs in 1994! Marlene and Tru enjoy watching over the busy enterprise that started at the family kitchen table thirteen years ago. They look forward to the excitement each day brings as Brandywine Woodcrafts, Inc. and Brandywine Collectibles continue to "Capture the Heart of America."

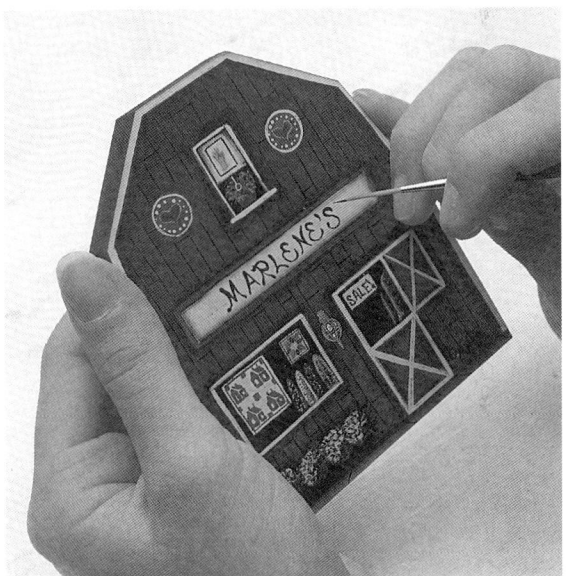

Unique, detailed and affordable, Marlene Whiting's immensely popular Downtown U.S.A. *series currently features over fifty styles of shops. With the added excitement of personalized signs, collectors can build a village reflecting their own names and interests.*

Byers' Choice® Ltd.
A Dickens of an Idea

During a trip to London many years ago, Joyce and Bob Byers found a unique series of porcelain figures in an antique shop. These pieces, which appeared to step right from the pages of a Charles Dickens novel, captured the spirit of 19th century England for Joyce, and she immediately fell in love with them.

Upon returning home, Joyce saw a set of papier-maché choir figures that seemed to capture the true spirit of Christmas. While debating whether or not to purchase these as gifts, she was struck by an idea…she could try to create caroling figures with the feeling of the 19th century.

As an amateur artist with a degree in fashion design, Joyce began working on the project using materials she had at home: plaster, papier-maché, wire, paints, and almost every kind of fabric imag-

In 1993, Byers' Choice introduced The Nutcracker *series with the little girl, "Marie."*

inable. She was already adept at handcrafts and enjoyed seeing her creations come to life; figurines that resulted from this effort were no exception. Joyce fashioned each character with a singing posture and called them "Carolers®" to convey a connection both to Christmas and to Dickens' *A Christmas Carol*. These early figurines were quite different than "The Carolers" as we know them today.

When family members saw the Carolers at Christmastime, they adored them. All of a sudden, Christmas shopping became that much easier, as over the next few years all of the Byers' friends and relatives received the figurines as gifts. A neighbor suggested taking the figurines to craft and antique shows. The first Carolers sold out quickly, but Bob was fortunate enough to be approached by someone from a New York display company who said that his company would be interested in buying the figurines if they could be enlarged and altered according to their customers' needs. Joyce rose to the challenge, thus determining the fate of Byers' Choice.

Over the next years, Joyce, Bob and their two sons spent much of each fall making figurines for friends, craft fairs, a few stores and the display company. As the demand for handcrafts grew, the family found itself even busier. After the Carolers began overwhelming the dining room, the garage was converted to a workshop. In 1981, with the addition of full-time helpers, the family hobby was incorporated, and Bob and Joyce cast their lot with The Carolers. By then the facial features, dress, materials of construction and finish details of the figurines had also evolved into the common features by which the Carolers are now recognized.

Today Byers' Choice Ltd. is still a cottage industry that hires skilled handcrafters and professionally trained artists. In order to meet a growing demand, it was necessary to make significant changes in both the method of manufacture and, to a limited extent, the appearance of the figurines. While today's Carolers are very different from those produced in the early years, almost everyone agrees that they are far better and more attractive. Joyce still sculpts all of the faces and designs most of the clothes for the Carolers.

This family grouping of Carolers® figurines joyously sings under the flickering light of a street lamp. The accessory lamp is a working electrical light.

Meanwhile, Bob takes care of the financial and administrative side of the business, trying to serve the customer in any way possible. In 1987, the job of overseeing each figurine through production fell to son Robert, while son Jeffrey joined the family business in 1990 as marketing manager. Virtually everyone agrees that the family of Carolers figurines gets better each year, and many of the older ones have become valuable collectors' items.

The history of the Carolers is a good old "made in the USA" story. With a lot of hard work and imagination, Bob and Joyce Byers have seen their hobby grow into a family business dedicated to serving the customer. With the boundless energy of the Byers' Choice family, the Carolers should only get better.

Byers' Choice Expands Its Line

In 1978 Byers' Choice crafted only traditional adult caroling figures, an Old World Santa and a New World Santa. Only 100 of each style of the traditional adults were made. In the ensuing years more than 100 special characters have been created. These include many different Santas and musicians and figures representing various occupations and the four seasons. In 1983 Scrooge was unveiled as the first in a series featuring characters from Charles Dickens' *A Christmas Carol*. The positive response to this series led Joyce to begin work on figures from *The Nutcracker*. The first character, the little girl "Marie," was introduced in 1993.

Byers' Choice has further broadened its line with figures inspired by the 100th anniversary of the Salvation Army's red kettle, as well as a series of old-time street vendors known as the *Cries of London*. Children, adult and grandparent skaters

Byers' Choice donates a portion of all proceeds from Salvation Army figures to that charitable organization.

have also become immensely popular. Although the specialty pieces have proven to be sought-after collectibles, the most popular figures continue to be traditional Carolers. Of these, no more than 100 of any one style are made.

The Collectors Speak

From the beginning Byers' Choice received many wonderful letters from fans telling how much the Caroler figurines mean to them. An overwhelming number of questions prompted the firm to publish the "Caroler Chronicle." In this newsletter which is published three times a year, the company responds to the nearly 100,000 collectors who have indicated an interest in learning more about Byers' Choice Caroler figurines. The "Chronicle" highlights various figures, both new and retired, and tells how and why they came to be. Information about signings and other special Caroler happenings are included. A chronological index of Byers' Choice characters and their years of production is also published.

One fan compared collecting Byers' Choice figurines to eating peanuts: once she had one, she couldn't resist going back for another, and another, and another...

Just like the traditional Carolers, only 100 of each child, adult and grandparent Skater is made.

Cain Studios

Rick Cain's "Multi Imagery" Technique Captivates Collectors
Who Are Intrigued by the Natural World

"I work in what I call multi imagery: a wolf might have several other small wolves hidden from immediate view just waiting to be discovered," says Rick Cain, the guiding light behind the Gainesville, Florida-based Cain Studios.

"I am ever changing as a part of the human experience, and so my art follows my changes. Doing wildlife sculpture is one way of communicating with a large audience on common ground," Cain continues.

"Cain Studios was started as a way to get my art to a wider audience by way of cast limited editions. Our company is composed of people from many walks of life who work according to a team philosophy — taking care of their work in a harmonious manner — knowing each piece created is the most important piece they touch, to its ultimate purchaser.

"Through these wildlife sculptures, we celebrate the creation of creatures great and small who share the world with us. When I sculpt, I use nature's abstraction, nature's call for us to identify with her. This comes through in wood shapes, stone fragments of a mountain, or other materials as they present themselves to me."

An Artist from Earliest Childhood

At an age when most boys are set on becoming astronauts or firemen or baseball players, Rick Cain had already determined that he would be an artist. Born in an Air Force Base hospital in Tucson, Arizona, Cain found it necessary to adjust to frequent moves and school changes required of his military family. Young Rick found his security and strength in his artistic ability.

"My parents were bent on my being anything other than an artist," Cain recalls. "All I wanted to be was an artist. At the age of eight I announced, 'I will be a famous artist someday.' Wow! It happened!"

The talented youth would surprise (and sometimes frustrate) his teachers and his parents as he relentlessly pursued his goal. At a tender age, he began teaching himself to be an artist. Every day he would practice, mastering the techniques of pen-

Artist Rick Cain carves all the original wood sculptures from which his limited edition, "multi imagery" works of art are crafted. His Cain Studios now employs over 30 individuals, all of whom are encouraged toward creative teamwork by the sculptor himself. As Rick Cain says, "We are avid believers in the creative spirit and attempt to incorporate this belief into our work."

cil drawing, for instance — sketching forms, giving them depth and dimension — studying human and animal anatomy, and training in matters and precision and detail until it all flowed naturally for him.

At the age of 20, Rick Cain discovered wood as an art medium. Yet he did not limit himself to creating designs in the wood — he soon moved on to releasing the shapes and images inherent in the wood itself. He was living in Florida now, and the gnarled and weathered tropical hardwoods revealed their personalities in his hands as he brought out wizened old men's faces and graceful human and animal forms.

Within months after starting to sculpt in wood, Cain was showing at his first art exhibit. Since then his work has been in hundreds of juried art shows and exhibitions. He has been honored with numerous awards, including a First Place in the Canadian International Woodcarving Exhibition. What's more, Cain was selected to participate in the New York International Sculpture Fair and the Walt Disney Festival of the Masters.

Another important recognition for Cain is his membership in the National Museum and Gallery Registration Association. In addition, Cain's original works, as well as his limited edition sculptures, hold places of prestige in private and public collections throughout the world.

A Philosopher-Artist Shares His World View

Rick Cain is a deeply introspective person who examines his own motivations and feelings as thoroughly as he studies the wood he sculpts. He firmly believes that his talent is a gift that he is charged with using to the fullest. He asks himself, "Why do people buy my art? Do they collect wolves or wildlife, and my work happens to fit that category? Sometimes, of course, yes, but most people buy my work because it speaks to them on a creative level. They recognize and respond to the Creative Force behind the work and, guess what? That's not me!

"Oh, yes, I carve each original myself, but I am not creativity. I am a vehicle, a medium. I believe that I am a caretaker of a talent given to me by the grace of God — that universal principle that orders chaos, and created that, too!"

As for his method of work, Cain explains: "I sit and sit, studying wood — its knots, bends, curves, its color, its smell. All these things are a joy to me — a collection of associated peaceful feelings that get me to the place in me that becomes Zen meditation."

Rick Cain's Goal Is to Serve the Collector

Cain believes he has gained considerable insight into those who love his work by watching them as they discover his art. "Where is the excitement in finding that new collectible," he asks himself. "Is it in that object you see? No, that feeling, that warmth is inside of you. That thing is just an object. Your viewing it is what makes the collectible beautiful.

"What is collectible? Something you hold dear and near...something precious to your heart? Memories of love, friends, good times and some-times objects — things we cherish. So, yes, my art is collectible and is sold in all 50 United States, I'm proud to say, and in several international markets."

An Overview of the Creations from Cain Studios

Sleek shore birds, bold eagles, noble Native Americans and elegant fantasy figures combine with many other natural and imaginative subjects to make up the diverse collections of Cain Studios Inc. While most of Rick Cain's works are meant as decorative sculpture, he sometimes adds a functional touch: pieces like "The Hatchling," "Innerview," and "Box Turtle" serve as boxes for small treasures.

Many of Cain's limited edition pieces already have sold out and are available only on the secondary market. But this prolific artist continues to add new works to his collection on a regular basis.

One particularly popular series has the arctic wolf as its focus. The first piece was the "Arctic Moon." This beautiful white and pastel sculpture sold out in a very short time. Rick Cain has received letters from devoted collectors telling him how the "Arctic Moon" touched them in a special way.

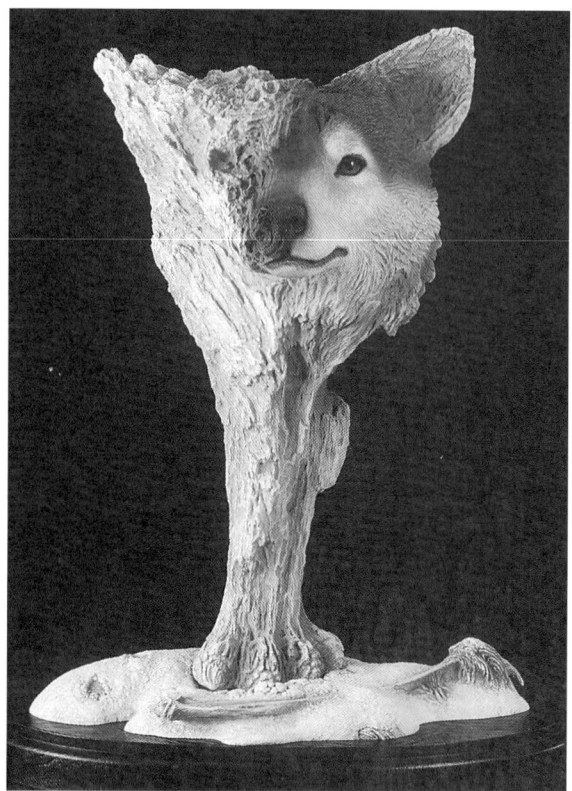

Rick Cain's dramatic "Raven Shadow" measures 23-1/2" x 17" x 13".

Immediately following the sell out of "Arctic Moon," Rick created "Arctic Son." This piece is a beautiful companion piece to the "Arctic Moon." The demand was so great for another arctic wolf that this piece was introduced as a special Christmas sculpture. "Arctic Son" sold out in a record four days.

In January of 1994, Rick Cain Studios introduced their third arctic wolf entitled "Midnight Son." This sculpture is for purchase by Collectors Guild members only. Along with the signature arctic wolf, Rick Cain has sculpted a den of young wolves to the side of the face. The response to this piece has been overwhelming. The membership to the Guild has more than doubled since the "Midnight Son" was introduced. This piece is available throughout 1994. On December 31, 1994, the series will close.

An Opportunity to Join the Rick Cain Studios Collectors Guild

Designed for enthusiasts of Cain's art, the Rick Cain Studios Collectors Guild offers boundless advantages. One of the most valuable benefits of club membership is that Rick Cain will carve a special sculpture that will be offered for purchase to Guild members only.

Upon becoming a Guild member, the collector receives a free sculpture and a quarterly newsletter. The newsletter features information concerning pieces that are soon to retire or sell out, interesting articles by and about Rick Cain and his studio, previews of new pieces, and a Locator Service for buyers and sellers of pieces that are no longer available through Cain Studios.

Additional yearly membership privileges include: exclusive redemption coupons for purchase of sculptures created by Rick Cain for Collectors Guild members; a beautiful membership certificate; free unlimited registration of all the member's Rick Cain sculptures; and a free set of beautiful notecards.

This three-dimensional portrait of a noble Native American is entitled "American Dream," and measures 24-1/2" x 24" x 12".

What's more, members are among the first to get a look at special offers — including the recent *Rick Cain Studios Sculpture Diary*. This full-color book includes information about each Rick Cain sculpture. Another unique offering is the "Portfolio I — Rick Cain Originals" — a custom-bound, limited edition portfolio of rarely seen originals by Cain.

Currently membership dues in the Guild are $25.00 annually. For more information on joining, contact the Rick Cain Studios Collectors Guild at 619 S. Main Street, Gainesville, Florida, 32601; or call 1-800-535-3949.

CALABAR Creations
Welcome to the LAND OF CALABAR: Where Colorful Art Life And Beauty Are Raised

Tony Van, President of Calabar Creations, was already established in the giftware industry with his company, Character Collectibles, when he met artist Pete Apsit. After that meeting, Character Collectibles took on a whole new direction, becoming wildly successful manufacturing "critters" in hydrostone that were characterized by their warm country charm, quality and affordability. In the span of three years, the company tripled the number of items available to the collector. Their lines of character pigs and whimsical cows even earned the "flattery" of imitation by competitors.

Pete Apsit's designs opened new horizons for Character Collectibles. When the proliferation of his work departed from the original country theme of the company, it seemed time to branch out. Thus Calabar Creations was formed.

Pete Apsit's Special Vision of Children and Animals

With a collectibles career spanning two decades and a host of admiring collectors, Pete Apsit is one of today's most honored sculptors. His "new era" of figurines for Calabar Creations dawns with what he and Tony Van call "a tribute to all American children."

Apsit's creations reflect his "California attitude" — the belief that life is a gift to be enjoyed. Apsit believes that through the eyes of children he can bring that message home: the little ones allow us to see life unblemished by stress and complications.

Pete Apsit's children are not "sweet little sophisticated darlings" — impeccably dressed and well-mannered. Instead, they belong to a fresh, free "kid society" where innocence prevails, but misbehavior occurs. It's a place where old clothes sure feel better than Sunday best and where friends (including animal friends) are the most precious gifts on earth. Pete's children are free from class barriers, racial prejudice and adult inhibitions.

The Little Farmers Collection

Pete Apsit's *Little Farmers* was the collector's

"Interference" from Pete Apsit's Yesterday's Friends *Collection for Calabar Creations.*

series that established Calabar Creations in the limited edition market. It captures the joy of rural life through the antics of a group of adorable children.

In "Playful Kittens," we see Martha — whose work at her spinning wheel is distracted by the felines at her feet. "Going Home" introduces Reggie, who is trying to convince a sweet-natured pig and her piglet to make their way back to the barn for the night. Jessie is a "Caring Friend," who is determined to give his pup a bath — no matter how hard the little canine tries to avoid it.

These three "little farmers" and their friends are sure to delight anyone with a place in their heart for life on a farm.

The Charm of Yesterday's Friends

Known as the "landmark collection" of Calabar Creations, the *Yesterday's Friends* series introduces another wonderful troupe of happy, involved youngsters. Again the talents of Pete Apsit gain free expression in these hand-painted figurines.

"Old TEE-mer" from Calabar's Tee Club Collection.

Crotchety Old Men Shine in the Tee Club Collection

A group of grouchy old men can make you smile, <u>if</u> they are Pete Apsit's grouchy old men! He has captured true-to-life expressions in his *Tee Club* Collection — no doubt inspired by his first bad encounter with the serious game of golf.

Pictured is the intrepid "Old TEE-mer." He's enjoying a beautiful day on the green with a trustful little bird riding along. On the other side of the course we see the sour "TEEd-off," who broke his club in an attempt to get the ball from between two rocks. Let's not forget the stubborn "Naugh-TEE." Is he playing golf or digging for oil?

The confident "Certain-TEE" is sure of his shot, and the perfectionist "Prac-TEEs" is intent on becoming the best. Amid all this emotion, the achiever is gently "Putt-TEEing" with a British kind of cool. These are the newest faces on the green, depicting with humor and empathy the strong emotions hidden in the seemingly peaceful game of golf.

SantaVenture Shows a New Side of St. Nick

On a more fantastical view, Pete created *SantaVenture* or the other side of Santa. We see Santa's fun side when he personally tests the toys in "Santa Tested." In "Nuts For You" his soft side is revealed when he makes certain even the least of God's creatures receives a gift during the magical night of Christmas. Embarrassment is uppermost when St. Nick tries in vain to learn what Suzie Goose plans to give him for Christmas.

These moments and more are captured by Pete in a collection designed to open our eyes further to the complex personality that is Santa Claus.

New Releases

Pete is constantly creating. One of his latest series, *Daddy's Girl*, is inspired by the family photo album of Calabar Creations' Art Director, Danielle Aphessetche. As an avid photographer, Danielle's father used his hobby to capture the happy, precious moments of his special little girl's childhood.

"All Aboard!" finds little Danielle sitting in a wash basin. The little tub serves as a boat on her imaginary journey. "Discovery" depicts Danielle's first encounter with hatching chicks. How did the chicks get into the eggs? The rigors of childhood require a confidante to share the troubles or joys of the day. "Teddy Talks" captures little Danielle with her favorite confidante, her teddy bear.

"Free Wheeling" introduces Eli, who worked on his soap box scooter for months before showing it off to envious friends. "Bluester" sings the blues to his indifferent Juliet, his sad heart in his voice. Then meet a most melodious trio of "Bayou Boys": Warren plays the wash board, Tad keeps tempo on the pail, and Vince croons to make the girls swoon. Toby the dog does his best to harmonize.

Suzette of "Strike So Sweet" is so composed and confident after the game, you'd never know she was a "ball of fire" during the contest. As for "Hop-a-long Pete," he gallops on a dream of Wild West adventures. We can even catch a glimpse of an embarrassing situation for a tiny trespasser in "Tug-a-Leg."

Pictured is "Interference" which shows the problem that ensues when the opposing team's mascot takes matters into his own paws.

Among these "Yesterday's Friends" or the others in the collection, you may recognize your own friends and buddies. They are the ones who stood by you in front of a not-so-understanding Mother or after a crushing defeat. They are the ones you want to call and talk to now, to reminisce.

The Works of Richard Myer Shine Bright

Calabar also offers figurines by Richard Myer, a well-known Western artist who has been sculpting for over 20 years. Myer designed *Red Moon Children* exclusively for Calabar Creations, after establishing himself with his bronze artwork, some of which grace the collections of Roy Rogers, Gene Autry and Ronald Reagan.

The *Red Moon Children* centers on memories of when the West was still open, and young Americans of the frontier were blessed with an unclouded view of the world. Their world is filled with harmony. In "Reputable Rainmakers," a young brave is so sure that his rain dance is going to produce a result, that he carries an umbrella. Harmony with the animal kingdom is shown in "Deer Talk" where a very young brave finds a lost deer in the forest and befriends it. Harmony between men is displayed with "Temptations," when a little brave faces a terrible dilemma: owning a beautiful red apple, should he give it to Cordero his trusted pony, or to Laura the fair girl with yellow hair from the settlement by the river?

Pictured is the delightful scene of "Tickle My Fancy" when Little Deer and Pale Moon are playing in the forest. "Come down from your tree Little Deer!" urges Pale Moon, "Let's go find flowers for our mothers. I'll tickle you until you come down my timid little friend." Each piece from this limited edition reflects an atmosphere of peace, calm, and simplicity, and tends to capture your imagination — taking you to your own personal, serene place.

A Painstaking Artistic Process

Each Calabar Creations work begins as a clay original, which serves as the master for mold making at the Calabar art department. Next a master is poured of a hard-cast material — able to withstand the abuse of many mold formings. Several masters are created because a production mold rapidly loses its ability to reproduce intricate details and variety in texture — the Calabar Creations trademarks.

At this stage, unpainted samples, called "whites," are sent to Danielle Aphessetche, the Art Director and colorist. She chooses the colors for the piece and paints the "white" prototype. This painted original is then used by the factory as the model for painting each figurine made. Now the piece is ready to go into production.

The factory pours and cures the figurines. They are then meticulously cleaned and polished. The painter then duplicates the original color scheme. After inspection, each piece receives its brass registration plaque. The piece is now ready to be gift-boxed and shipped to stores for the collector's pleasure.

Calabar Creations Goal

The commitment of Calabar Creations is to offer figurines that will give pleasure both to the eyes and to the soul; works of art that will touch a child's curiosity and awaken the sleeping child in all adults. Calabar Creations strives to portray a world between dreamland and reality...a land where children are wise and adults are allowed to dream... a special corner of the world filled with laughter and rainbows. In the land of CALABAR:

Colorful Art Life And Beauty Are Raised

"Tickle My Fancy" represents Richard Myer's Red Moon Children.

Cast Art Industries Inc.
Building on the Success of *Dreamsicles*™
This Innovative Manufacturer Is Introducing New Artists

Ask the people at California-based Cast Art Industries about their corporate goal, and the response is always the same: that their business is to make people smile. While this may seem to be a simple mission, it is hard to imagine that any company could succeed in producing so many smiles in so short a time.

Cast Art Industries was founded in December 1990 by Scott Sherman, Frank Colapinto and Gary Barsellotti, three friends with more than fifty years of combined experience in the gift industry. Sherman was formerly a Florida corporate president who, despite his youth, had substantial experience in administration and marketing. Colapinto, a long time resident of California, had spent most of his career building a national sales force in the gift industry. Barsellotti, Italian-born and trained, was an expert in the manufacturing of fine quality figurines.

The company began as a manufacturer, securing contracts to produce decorative boxes, figurines, lamps and souvenir items for other companies. Within a few months, Cast Art had signed exclusive contracts with independent artists and was producing and selling its own product lines. The success of the designs, and the consistent high quality of the reproductions, quickly caused the collecting world to take notice and made Cast Art one of the fastest-growing companies in the industry.

The *Dreamsicles*™ Phenomenon

In March 1991, Cast Art introduced the first *Dreamsicles*™, a group of thirty-one adorable cherub and animal figurines designed by artist Kristin Haynes. Kristin's fresh approach to a timeless subject was an instant hit with the gift-buying public, and *Dreamsicles*™ rapidly became one of the most popular new lines in the world of collectibles.

The collection now numbers over 150 pieces and includes storybook animals, holiday pieces and Christmas tree ornaments in addition to a growing variety of cherubs. All are hand-cast and hand-painted, then decorated with dried flowers, to assure that no two are ever exactly alike.

In June 1992, the *Dreamsicles*™ line received national recognition as the Best Selling New

The charming Dreamsicles™ *cherubs have captured the hearts of collectors everywhere.*

Category at the Gift Creations Concepts (GCC) industry show in Minneapolis. GCC is a large gift buying cooperative, with more than 300 member retailers.

In its September 1992 issue, *Giftbeat*, an industry newsletter, published the results of its first survey of gift, collectible, trend and stationery stores representing every region of the country. Based on sales volume the previous month, *Dreamsicles*™ was named the Number One General Gift Line, and also received votes in the collectibles gifts category, offering the first hint that the figurines were gaining acceptance among serious collectors. *Dreamsicles*™ retained the number one ranking in each subsequent monthly survey throughout the last half of the year and into 1993.

Cast Art's first *Dreamsicles*™ Limited Edition piece, a seated cherub, consisted of 10,000 pieces signed and numbered by the artist. It sold out within a few months and was retired in August 1992. With a retail price of less than $50.00, this

hand-cast, hand-painted figurine was quickly recognized by collectors as representing an attractive value.

The 1993 *Dreamsicles*™ Limited Edition received an even stronger reception and sold out within a few weeks of its first offering. Entitled "The Flying Lesson," this piece depicts three of Kristin's cherubs, one of whom is being taught to fly by the others. It was Cast Art's first Limited Edition to be mounted on an oval wooden base bearing an engraved title plaque. Production was limited to 10,000 copies, each accompanied by a Certificate of Authenticity signed and numbered by the artist.

The seemingly overnight success of *Dreamsicles*™ is highly unusual, since most items of this type are not recognized as true collectibles until several years after release. Virtually all pieces in the line have attained a collectible status, and a secondary trading market is beginning to develop.

Old World Folk Arts

Also among Cast Art's early successes was a series of "tree spirits" figures designed by artist Rick Albee. The line has become known as *Enchanted Forest*™ and was recently expanded to include a new group of dragons, witches and sorcerers in addition to Albee's collection of woodsy characters and decorated boxes. Manufactured from the finest artists' resins and hand-painted, the reproductions closely resemble the texture, finish and feel of the carved wood originals.

An accomplished artist, author and storyteller, Albee first searches for pine knots in the western woodlands, and then masterfully hand carves his enchanting forest folk in the old world manner. *Enchanted Forest*™ reproductions offer collectors a new opportunity to participate in a time-honored folk tradition.

New Ideas and Styles

To further expand its product lines, Cast Art searches out promising young artists and helps them develop to their full potential. In 1993, the company introduced the works of Steve and Gigi Hackett, clever young California designers whose humorous *Animal Attraction*™ and *Story Time Treasures*™ figurines have been the gift industry's bright spots.

Animal Attraction™ is a group of offbeat animal characters which includes dancing bears, "flasher" cows, and a variety of hilarious pigs in bikinis, aerobics outfits, "punker" attire and other poses. The tongue-in-cheek, slightly off-color attitudes of the collection represent a substantial departure from Cast Art's other lines, and make *Animal Attraction*™ popular with youthful collectors.

Cast Art's Dreamsicles™ *have become America's number one gift line.*

Mr. and Mrs. Bunny are just two of the popular Dreamsicles™ *animals.*

Steve and Gigi employ a unique approach to the art of sculpture. A Disney-trained artist, Steve first conceives his characters and executes the initial designs. Gigi then helps to refine each piece and selects the subtle pastels which decorate them. The success of their collaboration is further evidenced by *Story Time Treasures*™. This grouping depicts a new approach to six timeless children's classics, from *Peter Rabbit* to *The Frog Prince*. Each sculpture consists of the title character reading the bedtime story to his youngster, and reminds us of the joys of sharing a special moment and a good book with a child. The collection works equally well as a charming series of children's lamps.

Welcome to Cuckoo Corners™

Another recent introduction was *Cuckoo Corners*™, a whimsical group of characters which demonstrates yet another dimension of the many-faceted talents of Kristin Haynes. Over two years in development, this new collection was eagerly awaited by Kristin's fans. The complete line debuted at the January 1993 gift shows and received immediate acclaim.

Cuckoo Corners™ is a mythical place whose citizens include characters of all ages. From screaming babies to silly seniors, they remind us of our own friends and relatives in their best and worst moods. The collection of twenty-six pieces portrays a wide range of emotions, some subtle, some outrageous, yet all with a keen empathy for the human spirit which sets Kristin apart from other artists.

The hand-painted *Cuckoo Corners*™ series is destined to become another favorite among collectors.

Dreamsicles™ *Collectors' Club Offering Charter Memberships*

Introduced in 1993, the *Dreamsicles*™ Collectors' Club is offering Charter Member status. A specially designed membership figurine, entitled "A Star Is Born," will be retired after the end of the year. Members receive a Club binder and printed guides to the collection, a colorful Membership Card and a subscription to the "ClubHouse" newsletter, as well as the opportunity to purchase "members only" pieces. Annual dues of the Club are $27.50 per year.

1994 promises to be another eventful year for Cast Art and its more than 13,000 retailers throughout the U.S. and Canada, as well as for *Dreamsicles*™ fans everywhere. In response to public demand, favorite cherub designs will be appearing as greeting cards, ceramic mugs, plush toys and a variety of childrens' and adults' apparel lines. An aggressive licensing campaign is under way and, with initial response exceeding expectations, look for *Dreamsicles*™ to take the country by storm.

Cast Art has other exciting collectors' programs scheduled in the coming months, including the introduction of its *"World of Whimsy"* by artist Edward Maher. It's just one more in a growing list of "firsts" from one of the most dynamic companies in the collectibles industry.

Christopher Radko
What Looked Like the Loss of a Family Tradition
Turns Out to be a Tradition Renewed

When Christopher Radko was growing up in Scarsdale, New York, the highlight of his family's Christmas was decorating the tree with their astonishing collection of blown-glass ornaments. Three generations of Radkos had collected more than 2,000 of the handcrafted beauties. As a boy, Christopher loved to slide under the fresh tree's lowest branches to play, mesmerized as he was by the reflection of bubble lights, twinkling stars and shimmering spheres.

In 1984, the holidays were unfolding as usual. Christopher was removing sap and needles from the old tree stand, the annual chore that always fell to him, when he decided that a new one was in order. After a bit of shopping around, he bought a stand guaranteed to hold up an eighteen-foot high tree, a good four feet taller than the Radkos' own tree, and the fun of decorating the tree went on as it always did.

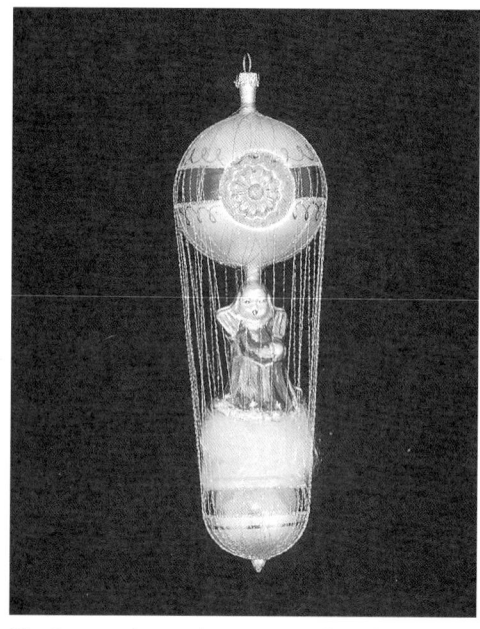

The first members-only ornament of Starlight, Christopher Radko's collectors club, was "Angels We Have Heard On High," limited to 5,000 pieces.

Christopher Radko's sparkling 1993 collection continued the tradition of fine glass ornament making.

One cold December morning, though, the worst happened. Despite its guarantee, the stand buckled and the tree crashed to the floor, shattering more than half of the fragile decorations.

"I was absolutely heartbroken because those ornaments were our family's direct link to the traditions and memories of four generations of Christmas celebrations," Christopher remembers. "Even though I knew there was no way I could replace the ornaments, my great-grandmother and grandmother had handed down, I thought that the least I could do was buy some substitutes so our tree wouldn't look so forlorn." He searched in the stores near his home town, and shopped the grand department stores of New York City. Sadly, he discovered that most ornaments were being made from plastic and other mystery materials. The few glass ornaments that could be found were poorly blown of flimsy glass, and the painted details were frightful. It was a depressing Christmas for the Radko home.

A New Tradition Begins

The following spring, while Christopher was visiting relatives in Poland, a cousin introduced him to a farmer who once made blown-glass ornaments; he said he might be able to make a few new ones. There was only one catch: Christopher had to supply him with detailed drawings of exactly what kinds of ornaments he wanted. Upon seeing the designs, the glassblower said that they were just like the ornaments that his father and grandfather had made before the second World War, and that although he had never made such complicated pieces, he would be happy to try.

After Christopher returned to the States with his newly crafted glass ornaments, family members and friends clamored for glorious glass ornaments of their own. He realized then that he had discovered not just a need but his own knack for fulfilling it.

Today, only eight years later, Christopher busies teams of Polish, German, Czech and Italian glassblowers with limited editions of his ornaments. The 1994 line features over 400 dazzling designs. Ideas come not only from memories of his family's antique ornaments, but also from Christopher's other inspirations: architecture, fabrics, films and museum collections. It takes about a week to make each ornament, which is blown, silvered, lacquered, painted and glittered entirely by hand. Among Christopher's most unusual ornaments are his figural ones: his recent collections have featured a pipe-smoking monkey, a cowboy Santa, a Persian peacock in a gilded cage, and even a Fu Manchu. Some of them reprise molds unused since the turn-of-the-century.

"My company's success has allowed me to revive Christmas crafts and techniques that were all but lost," Christopher explains. "As a Christmas artist, with my annual collection of new designs, I am reviving a tradition of designing that had its heyday at the turn-of-the-century. My glassblowers are uncovering old molds and relearning skills that their cottage industry hasn't used in seventy years. Now, even young apprentice glassblowers are being trained in the traditions of their great-grandfathers, ensuring that fine glass ornament-making will continue into the next century. That's something to celebrate!"

The "Who's Who" of Ornament Collectors

Because about half of the ornaments in the line are retired or changed in some way each year, Christopher's ornaments are highly collectible.

Katherine Hepburn, Bruce Springsteen, Dolly Parton, Mikhail Barishnikov and Hillary Rodham Clinton are all devoted collectors. There's even a Radko ornament club and quarterly newsletter.

For 1993, Christopher launched *Starlight*, his collectors club, and quarterly newsletter. The premier issue was introduced in October, 1992, and is already considered a collector's item. The *Starlight* quarterly is filled with articles and illustrations

Christopher Radko designed "A Shy Rabbit's Heart" as a fundraiser ornament to promote AIDS awareness and to help AIDS-related organizations.

Christopher Radko has created over a thousand dazzling designs. Featured are "Frosty," "Roly Poly Santa," "Winter Tree" and "Starburst."

showing how the ornaments are made, interviews with the craftsmen and stories on Christmas history. Members of *Starlight* purchased the 1993 club ornament "Angels We Have Heard On High." This whimsical angel in a glass balloon was limited to a production of 5,000 pieces and has sold out. Each came with a special hand-numbered story tag with Christopher's name on it.

Christopher Radko Ornaments Benefit Organizations

For 1993, two other unique ornaments introduced in limited quantities were "A Partridge in a Pear Tree" and "A Shy Rabbit's Heart." The story of the Twelve Days of Christmas offered inspiration for an annual series ornament, each limited, with a hand-numbered tag. "A Shy Rabbit's Heart" is Christopher's way of spreading awareness and supporting the fight against AIDS. All his profits were divided equally among five AIDS-related organizations, including a food organization, a hospice and a pediatric AIDS foundation.

The Christopher Radko Collection includes delicately hand-painted, blown-glass ornaments and delightful garlands.

Limited to 5,000 pieces, "A Partridge in a Pear Tree" is first in the Twelve Days of Christmas *series.*

Christopher is also proud of the fact that organizations such as the World Wildlife Fund, the Smithsonian Institution, and the Metropolitan Museum of Art have commissioned limited editions of his ornaments. Christopher's ornaments are bought as gifts as well, and a number of better stores offer them year-round for birthdays, anniversaries, hostess and housewarming gifts, and baby or bridal shower gifts.

But perhaps the most wonderful thing about Christopher's success is that now any of us can decorate a tree with exquisitely old-fashioned blown-glass ornaments. And thanks to Christopher, we don't have to travel to Europe to find them.

Classic Collectables by Uniquely Yours
A Child's Inspiration Leads to Success
for the Gifted Eileen Tisa

"Black Santa on a Trike" is one of the new additions to the Classic Collectables by Uniquely Yours line, making its debut in 1994. Also available in a Caucasian version, the 19" Santa is limited to an edition of 600.

Little did Eileen Tisa know that the seed to a new career was taking root when she sat down one day with her son, Jimmy, and some clay from the local craft shop. Eight-year-old Jimmy was very artistic. He had just had a school painting displayed in the Young Artists of 1978 exhibit at the Philadelphia Civic Center, and Eileen felt compelled to find a challenge for her precocious offspring.

Since Jimmy was an only child, his mother made it a point to join him in his activities. But as they worked with the clay, Jimmy realized that he preferred sketching to sculpting. For Eileen, it was a very different matter. She discovered a talent and

joy in creating human likenesses! Although they were very primitive at first, Eileen's sculpted faces soon found themselves topping bottles and then clay-covered wire armatures. She also developed her sewing skills in order to design clothing for these wonderful little people.

Always inspired by the Christmas season and Charles Dickens' beloved classic, *A Christmas Carol,* Eileen chose Bob Cratchit, Tiny Tim, Ebenezer Scrooge, Marley and the other characters from the story as the subjects for her first creations. She also developed supporting characters including choir boys, children on sleds and carolers. Over the years, most of these sculptures became special gifts for family and friends.

Next, the inventive Ms. Tisa found fascination in flower designing, especially bridal arrangements in silk. In 1989, she began selling her silk flowers and other crafts at mall shows and church bazaars. At these shows she found herself surprised and pleased by the positive response to her handmade figurines, so she began to focus her talents on improving this facet of her craft.

A Valley Forge Show Becomes
a Turning Point

In time — as the faces took on more detail, character and expression — so did her talent at creating new costumes and concepts. All this delighted the small-but-growing number of collectors who avidly followed Eileen's progress. The firm "Classic Collectables by Uniquely Yours" was born, with Eileen introducing various Santa figurines for 1989 as well as "The Little Match Girl" from Hans Christian Andersen's tale. This charming work was retired in 1992.

In 1990, Eileen's husband of 22 years, Jim, passed away at the age of 44. She then found herself at a crossroads. Should she abandon her small (and not yet very profitable) craft business and find other employment, or try to find a way to make a living with her crafts? Ironically, on a whim, Eileen had decided to share a booth with a friend at the Eastern Regional Gift Show at Valley Forge only months

before Jim's death. She had been interested in seeing what kind of response her work would receive from wholesale gift buyers.

Although the show was very difficult since it took place just three months after Jim's death, it proved an overwhelming success for Classic Collectables by Uniquely Yours. With the help of Eileen's parents, an aunt who was adept at sewing, and her son Jimmy, all orders were filled. A primitive but successful production began to take shape!

While still working through the grief process, Eileen had found some relief and comfort in keeping herself immersed in work. She had managed to create "Kris Kringle," a 33" limited edition Santa and "Father Christmas," a 24" limited edition Santa. Both pieces made their debut at that Valley Forge Gift Show, and both have since been retired.

Encouraged by her success in Valley Forge, Eileen decided to develop more works of art to sell to wholesalers. She next created "Jolly Saint Nick," an appealing, pipe-smoking, 19" Santa. "Saint Nicholas," a 19" old-world Santa, also emerged. Both of these pieces are still in the company's line because of their enduring popularity. The mother-and-daughter "Christmas Shoppers" also debuted at that time.

For awhile the company experimented with miniature characters from *A Christmas Carol*, but Eileen found them too tedious and time-consuming to be profitable. The "Victorian Band" became part of the regular Dicken's line for about a year before retiring in 1991. "Lighting the Menorah," a vignette honoring Hanukkah, was also produced and retired in 1991.

As the sales and numbers of collectors continued to grow, so did the line. "Pilgrims" and "Trick or Treaters" (an adorable witch and devil team) were hits for the fall. Valentine's Day inspired a pair of charming childhood sweethearts. Springtime brought "The Girl With the Bunnies" and "The Boy With the Easter Basket," "Bride" and "Groom," a variety of ladies in Victorian garb and men in top hats and tails to accompany them, as well as "The Victorian Girl," and "Boy with a Hoop."

The surge in country crafts inspired "The Country Woman" with her basket of vegetables. And Mother's Day was celebrated with the vignette "Mother and Daughter." Summer saw the creation of "The African Woman" and "The African Man" in their colorful garb.

A Move Toward Nationwide Expansion

Since the Eastern Regional Gift Show brought mostly buyers from the immediate area, Eileen decided to add on the Market Square Gift Show, which she heard attracted more national buyers. With the successful addition of these winter and summer shows, Classic Collectables by Uniquely Yours began to grow well beyond what the Tisa home could accommodate.

What had begun in the kitchen and a small back bedroom had soon overtaken the entire house and garage as well as Eileen's parents' basement and

From the Dickens A Christmas Carol *line comes this family of carolers. Each pair of children, parents and grandparents is mounted on a wooden base and dressed in the Victorian garb of the Dickensian era in England.*

The magnificent "Pere Noel" stands a full 42" (3-1/2 feet) tall and is a vision in light blue velvet and pastels. This French Santa is part of a limited edition of 500.

garage. So in 1993, Eileen began to lease a work-shop/office in nearby Delaware County. With the luxury of space and the help of local crafts people, the business was able to expand quickly with distribution across the United States.

The response from retailers and collectors nation-wide has been overwhelmingly positive. They report that the detailing and quality of Eileen's creations — along with the comparatively low prices — makes this line sell quickly and keeps collectors coming back for more!

While the Dickens line and the smaller Santas are very much in demand by collectors, the larger Santas are by far the "runaway best sellers." These include the 33" "Victorian Santa," the 25" "Renaissance Santa," and the popular 33" "Olde World Santa." These limited edition, signed and dated Santas make an impressive presentation and have become incorporated into many shops' display windows to attract collectors into the stores.

As always, the face of each figurine still is hand-sculpted by Eileen Tisa, who then makes molds of each face. They are next hand-molded of a life-like composition clay and sent to be hand-painted. The clothing and construction of each figurine is completed, with meticulous attention to detail, under the artist's watchful eye. All materials and wooden bases are made in the United States, with the exception of a few accessories.

One-of-a-Kinds and New Additions

Each year, Classic Collectables by Uniquely Yours produces a dozen or so "One-of-a-Kind" Santas that are created and sold at gift shows. Although they are priced quite a bit higher than the limited edition Santas, buyers seek them eagerly, knowing that they will quickly be snatched up by avid collectors who prize these "One-of-a-Kind" pieces. Unique themes are employed for these creations — expressed in their titles such as "Backwoods Santa," "Old West Santa," and "English Countryside Santa." Many of these are purchased by Art and Craft Galleries and some have found their way to such galleries in England, Germany and Ireland.

Among the newer additions to the line is the "Black Santa on a Trike," which also is available in a Caucasian version. "The Victorian Treetop Angel" is a vision in white velvet and gold lamé with pastel accents. Indeed, the company plans to expand each year with appearances at more national gift shows, and by attracting new, potential buyers via the mail.

Although keeping up with such a rapidly growing business has been hectic to say the least, Eileen Tisa wouldn't trade the challenge and excitement of watching her business grow for anything in the world. The expansion of Classic Collectables by Uniquely Yours has helped the local economy as well, by employing homebound mothers and senior citizens who welcome the extra money and the opportunity to work from home.

"We feel assured that the business will continue its rapid progress because of our success at keeping most of our customers even from those early shows," says Eileen. "Adding new accounts has been important to our growth, but nothing makes me happier than hearing from a small shop owner who calls to tell me that she or he 'no sooner got the figurines unpacked — and they were gone.'"

CREART™
Award-Nominated Sculpture Created From Nature's Marvels

"One hundred percent natural" is a phrase often used to describe many of the foods we eat. That phrase also springs to mind as one views the delightful creations of Creart™, the manufacturer of nature-inspired collectibles, whose animal-themed sculptures grow increasingly popular each year.

Several of Creart's recent selections, in fact, have been nominated for *Collector Editions* magazine's "Awards of Excellence." 1990 saw two sculptures accorded the prestigious nominations: "Over the Clouds" and "The Challenge — Rams." In 1991 the magazine chose to honor three of Creart's creations, "Playmates — Sparrows," "White Hunter Polar Bear" and "Breaking Away — Gazelles," while "Puma" and "Soaring Royal Eagle" made the honor roll in 1992.

Considering that all these nominations were lavished on a relative newcomer to the collectibles field, how has the firm managed to achieve such praise for its truthful portraits of animals and birds? "We can credit everything to the talent and persistence of our excellent artists," says Carlos Estevez, president of Creart U.S. Estevez is the gentleman who — with his wife Minerva — first discovered the company's work while vacationing in Mexico City, and subsequently brought that work to the attention of United States collectors.

Creart's Nature's Care Collection *includes, clockwise from left:* "Gorilla and Baby," "Grizzly and Cubs," "Jack Rabbit and Young," "Wolf and Pups" *and* "Lioness and Cubs." *Each is limited to 2,500 and priced at $100 to $120 suggested retail.*

Delineation of Surface Texture

"There are so many different companies producing animal figurines," Estevez explains, "but I can truthfully say that I have not seen anything to equal what Creart achieves — especially in terms of the delineation of an animal's anatomy, proportion, muscle tone and surface texture." That surface texture, in particular, is unusually detailed and totally different from one animal to the next.

From the regal mane of the majestic lion titled "Symbol of Power," to the earthy, leathery hide of the "African Elephant with Leaf," to the exquisite delineation of the coat on the face and neck of the "Horse Head" — all limited to an edition of 2,500 — each animal's surface texture is amazingly realistic.

"What first attracted my wife and me to these sculptures was the incredible reality that the artist had achieved. In fact, I remember very well the actual day we first saw the work. It was 1986 and the two of us were in a famous department store in Mexico City. We were looking for something interesting to buy, when suddenly — there they were, these amazing animal sculptures!"

After some intricate research, the two found the factory where a new process of manufacturing was being used to give these sculptures an unusually consistent high quality. The singular designs, Estevez and his wife discovered, were being done by a group of sculptors working together. Each was a master in his own right. The group was led by a man named Emilio Martinez and included Francisco Contreras, Vicente Perez and Carlos Fernandez.

Martinez and Contreras, lifetime friends, attended Mexico City's National School of Plastic Arts and studied under some of the nation's finest masters. While Martinez went to work for a figurine candleholder company, Contreras worked independently as sculptor and painter. Perez studied at the same school and had made reproductions of archeological pieces in Mexico's Anthropology Museum of Natural History in Mexico City, home of one of the largest collections of pre-Colombian artifacts.

"A Higher Level of Sculpture"

Out of this combination of talents came the company Creart, established in 1979 in order to create a higher level of figurine sculpture and reproduction. It was this "higher level of sculpture," of course, that first attracted Estevez and his wife to begin importing the sculptures in 1987. In 1980 Perez helped Martinez and Contreras solve a particular problem in finishing one of the Creart models and afterwards joined the company permanently. The remainder of the Creart team handles production and management. Working behind the scenes, they are responsible for the overall performance of the company.

One of the most interesting facets of this unusual firm is the way it relies on the tastes and needs of the collectors to dictate which animals it will produce. In fact, Creart's very first step in creating a new piece is to ask collectors which subjects they are interested in seeing, how those subjects should be portrayed, in what size and at what cost. The responses from collectors are given considerable attention, after which a subject, together with its posture and environment, is chosen. Then, a model sketch is developed for anatomy, proportion and muscle tone.

At this point, Creart's sculptors create an original plastiline statue — from which models are made — and the best of these models is trimmed, detailed and photographed from many different angles. Molds are then constructed by skilled artisans, the most delicate parts of which are reinforced with steel or fiberglass rods which are invisible in the finished piece.

The molds are subsequently filled with the material that Estevez says works best in producing the kind of high relief detail needed. This is an exclusive marble compound that offers exceptional reproduction qualities due to its stability, weight, resistance, impermeability, high density and balance. Because this marble/resin compound offers less rigidity than pure marble, Creart pieces can often be repaired to look like new.

Once Closed, Never Reopened

Highly skilled artisans hand-decorate each figure with as many as twenty-four different colors to achieve a natural texture that can't be duplicated on glass or porcelain, and then a lusterless, transparent lacquer is applied to make cleaning the figurine easy with just a damp cloth. An exceptionally thorough Quality Control department checks finished pieces for any flaw, and each

Artist Vicente Perez created "White Blizzard," limited to 1,500 and priced at $275 suggested retail, in Creart's Wild American Edition.

sculpture found acceptable is then numbered as part of a limited edition which, when closed, is never reopened for any reason. The sculpture is mounted on an appropriate stand and individually boxed along with a certificate request card which the collector can mail to Creart to obtain a personalized, limited edition certificate.

What distinguishes the style of the two Creart founders? Estevez explains that Emilio Martinez especially loves to sculpt soft, round animals. Francisco Contreras is an innovator whose models all feature a new approach, while Vicente Perez handles the more heavily detailed pieces. "Every piece goes through Vicente's hands for the final detailing and approval," notes Estevez.

A new artist recently joined the Creart family: Carlos Estevez himself. Creart's U.S. President had the first of his own sculptures produced for collectors in the spring of 1993. "I've always loved art and have been drawing different ideas of my own for some time now," he explains. "I would send them to Mexico and ask the artists there to produce something similar to what I'd drawn. Now, finally, I've sculpted one of my own designs — a pair of sea otters basking on a rock." One of Creart's major retailers, The Nature Company of Berkeley, California, with over 100 stores serving collectors in the U.S. and Canada, chose these sea otters — limited to an edition of 2,500 — for an exclusive contract with its stores.

"Representational Art at Its Best"

Sydni Scott, buyer for The Nature Company, calls Creart one of the most successful and profitable lines sold by her firm. "Each piece of Creart is as biologically accurate as it is beautiful," Ms. Scott says, "because it's representational art at its best, as well as being fine quality, limited edition art."

In fact, she notes, "This firm perfectly represents our mission statement at The Nature Company: *to provide fine quality products devoted to the observation, understanding and appreciation of the natural world.*"

Distinguished by its quality and detail, Creart is considered very affordable. "Ever since we began," explains Estevez, "we've dedicated ourselves to the serious collector. Therefore, we can't make any compromises regarding the complexity or quality of our pieces. Actually, we've discovered that, once collectors understand the value of our sculptures, they don't question the price."

Nonetheless, in 1992, the company decided to offer a wider range of collectors a more affordably priced grouping of animal sculptures via its *Stylus* collection. Instead of the usual price tag of $220 to $800, the selections in the *Stylus* line were priced from $100 to $175 suggested retail. These included an eagle, puma, three horses and a horse's head.

The success of *Stylus* led to another affordably priced series introduced in 1993 entitled *The Nature's Care Collection*. Offering smaller and less detailed sculptures (between four and six inches high) which range from $100 to $120 each, the series' initial pieces include "Jack Rabbit and Young," Estevez' delightful "Otters," "Lioness and Cubs," "Wolf and Pups," "Doe and Fawns," "Gorilla and Baby," "Grizzly and Cubs," "Eagle and Chicks" and "Penguin and Chicks."

1993 also saw a continuation of the *Wild American Edition* of various animal heads, including the "White Blizzard Wolf," limited to 1,500 pieces, and a new Bald Eagle titled "The American Symbol," limited to 1,500. The company's popular *American Wildlife Collection* has had three new '93 additions: "The Red Fox" and "Howling Coyote" — each limited to editions of 1,500 — and "Grizzly Bear," limited to 2,500.

Coming Up? Human and Animal Sculpture

Some of the most exciting news about this fast-growing firm is that, in addition to its famous animal sculpture, which will soon include couples and families of both wild and endangered mammal species, Creart will introduce some new human figures, as well. Human sculpture has been absent from the line for several years now. This is why master sculptor Carlos Fernandez is so important. This highly educated and talented artist stresses the theme of the harmony of man and nature. He particularly loves to create scenes of men and women at peace with animals.

Creart has come quite a distance since Carlos and Minerva first discovered the firm in 1986. Now, one part of Creart remains in Mexico, while the other is here in the U.S. The two parts make up the new Creart, a truly bi-national company committed to producing the highest quality modeling, reproduction and service.

"We will definitely continue to go out to our collectible dealers and ask which animals their customers want to see and exactly how they want these to look," promises Estevez. Happily, collectors aren't simply telling the company what to produce: they're also buying the finished product. Estevez notes that when he and his wife first discovered the sculpture, the firm was making only fifty pieces per week. Currently, Creart creates some 350 pieces per week in order to satisfy the needs of collectors!

"Howling Coyote," from Creart's American Wildlife Collection, *was created by Emilio Martinez in a limited edition of 1,500 retailing for $198 each.*

C.U.I., Inc.
Excellence in Collectible Steins Inspired by Sports and Wildlife

While plate collecting nears its 100th anniversary, stein collecting represents a much older hobby: this enjoyable pursuit can be traced back well over 400 years. In the collectibles circle, that is a very long time. Yet after centuries of history, stein collecting in the United States — and the steins themselves that are sought by enthusiasts — have changed greatly in the last decade.

Prior to the 1980s, American stein collectors were few indeed. Yet today their numbers grow year by year, as each passing season reveals new artistry and designs unlike the expected "looks" that characterized steins for generations. The goal of C.U.I., Inc. has always been the painstaking "Americanization" of these centuries-old collectibles.

The Creation of a C.U.I. Collectible Stein

C.U.I.'s management spends countless hours with their creative staff to focus on meaningful stein themes that are part of our American heritage. Once a theme is selected, they endeavor to develop an intriguing series concept. Next, they consider the make-up of the stein: be it bas-relief, low relief, intricate glazing, or a solid body with no relief. The development of a lid configuration is next, plus the determination of whether or not to use a pewter remarque figurine on the lid.

The most difficult task for C.U.I. is the translation from the art concept to an actual prototype. Generally this requires up to six months, but some steins have taken over a year to develop. Once the product prototype has C.U.I.'s stamp of approval, the firm's representatives search for key components of the stein from around the world.

Only the best manufacturers are used, with stein bodies coming from Brazil, China, Mexico, Germany or the United States. Each manufacturer has particular strengths in specific media. All of C.U.I.'s lids and alloys are lead-free and are imported from Germany. The solid pewter remarque figurines are handcrafted and sometimes hand-painted; these are imported from England.

Whatever their source, all the stein elements are brought together at the C.U.I. factory in North Carolina, where they are assembled. The assembly process includes decorating steins with decals which are manufactured in the C.U.I. plant and applied to the stein by hand. Occasionally platinum or gold bands are hand-brushed onto the steins as an enhancement, and finally each stein is hand-numbered.

The next step is to fire the steins to ensure the permanency of their designs, at temperatures ranging as high as 1400 degrees F. When the steins have cooled, they are put onto a roller-type conveyor belt in the lidding department. Thus begins the lidding process. C.U.I. boasts that they are the only factory in the United States that has automated lidding capabilities. The lidding department can apply lids to 3,000 steins per day. From the lidding department, the steins are taken to the shipping area where they are carefully boxed and set up for shipment.

With a meager beginning of three employees and 1,300 square feet of office space, C.U.I. now can boast of sixty employees and a 45,000-square-foot facility.

A Variety of Steins Earn Awards and Collector Approval

With the stein collecting category moving away from the traditional look and subject matter, the doors have been opened for many new collectors to get involved, especially ardent wildlife and sports enthusiasts. Steins have become "Americanized" and recognized as a collectible art form of increasing value.

During its initial period of growth, C.U.I. was fortunate and proud to be recognized by the Department of the Interior for its efforts with the Federal Duck Stamp program. C.U.I. was also named a "Partner in Excellence" with Miller Brewing Company, a Licensed Vendor of the Year by Adolph Coors Company, and saluted as a major contributor to Ducks Unlimited through the sales of its highly successful stein and plate series.

In conjunction with Coors, C.U.I. has produced six steins in their *Rodeo* series where a portion of each sale is designated to the Cowboy Crisis Fund. When C.U.I. began designing and marketing wildlife collectible steins, they did not realize the overwhelming response that would ensue. Considerable funds have and will continue to be generated for their worthwhile projects. C.U.I. is

proud of these affiliations and the substantial revenue that is being generated for wildlife causes. In C.U.I. literature, each edition supporting wildlife conservation is designated by a special crest.

The fastest growing category for C.U.I. in recent years has been sports collectibles. This is not just a trend in steins: sports memorabilia throughout the United States is in very high demand, bringing incredible prices on the secondary market. C.U.I. offers a wide assortment of team and player-identified steins. All teams are available in the National Football League, Major League Baseball and the National Hockey League. Also, steins have been and will continue to be produced for championship teams within each league. Creative focus has been to capture some of the nostalgia and rich tradition of the sports world. Great moments, team anniversaries and players are subjects C.U.I. will bring to life on its steins.

An Array of Products from Classic Carolina Collections

Collectors who receive the mailings of Classic Carolina Collections have an outstanding host of products to choose from. One outstanding example is the Ducks Unlimited stein series including "Canvasback" and "Mallard." A new Ducks

The miraculous birth of a baby dolphin is followed by a gentle push from his mother to the surface of the water for his very first breath. C.U.I., Inc. introduced the "First Breath" stein and plate portrayals of this endearing event as second editions in the Environmental Series.

Unlimited series, *Waterfowl Of North America,* offers art by Terry Burleson on a first edition entitled "Into the Wind." The *Federal Duck Stamp* stein features the "Spectacled Eider," with art by Jim Hautman. "Tempting Trio" is the fourth-edition *National Wild Turkey Federation* stein, with art by Jim Kasper. The fourth stein in a *Civil War* edition features "Robert E. Lee."

Other new issues from Classic Carolina Collections include "Elvis — '68 Comeback," the *Corvette* series "1963 Corvette," *Oktoberfest, Big Game* series, *Lions* and *Polar Bears,* and the *Lighthouse Preservation Society* series issue, "Split Rock Light."

Miller Brewing Company's latest issue steins are "George Washington Crossing the Delaware," "Lewis and Clark" in the *Birth Of A Nation* series, and the hand-painted *Coopers* series, "Brewmaster's Crew 1889."

Coors *Rocky Mountain Legends* series features the "Fly Fisherman, Mountain Climber" with art by Tim Stortz. The Coors *Rodeo* series boasts six steins in the set, features original art by Marci Haynes Scott and benefits the Cowboy Crisis Fund. Stroh Brewery features a "Bandwagon Street Party" in their *Bavaria* Collection.

The list of themes goes on and on with steins featuring award-winning art by wildlife artists and other celebrated painters. C.U.I. provides a diverse range of selections that will appeal to the many different types of stein collectors.

Dram Tree Steins May Be Acquired at Retail

C.U.I. offers fine collectibles through retail dealers under the trademark name Dram Tree. These works of art are sold nationwide by over one hundred independent manufacturer's representatives and are permanently displayed in nine major showrooms. Dram Tree displays at the New York Gift Show and at the International Collectibles Exposition in South Bend, Indiana.

Dram Tree steins feature all the amenities preferred by collectors. For example, most steins are individually numbered, limited editions with complete bottom stamps and Certificates of Authenticity. The vast array of subject matter, prices and exclusive imagery opens many doors beyond the traditional gift-collectible trade, positively impacting sales. Dram Tree celebrates this classic heritage with a unique offering of commemorative steins establishing a hallmark of quality, collectibility and value. Serious collectors have recognized the beauty and value of Dram Tree products, elevating the firm's position in the collectibles marketplace to that of a leader and trend-setter.

Beautifully crafted and painted, the elegant mallard pair soar in flight on C.U.I., Inc.'s "Into the Wind" stein from the Ducks Unlimited series. Part of each sale from this collection is given to Ducks Unlimited's conservation efforts.

The fourth edition in C.U.I., Inc.'s Federal Duck Stamp series is a representation of a unique 1993 stamp, "Spectacled Eider." A portion of each sale from this series is donated to the conservation efforts of the United States Fish and Wildlife Service.

The name comes from a gnarled, moss-draped oak known as "The Dram Tree." For over 200 years, seafaring vessels passed the Dram Tree as this stately old oak stood sentinel on the banks of the Cape Fear River, several miles south of the bustling port of Wilmington, North Carolina. For sailors, the sight of the famous tree raised a blend of hope and anticipation. Upon the sighting of the Dram Tree, the ship's captain signaled for the traditional round of rum for the thirsty crew: a celebration of safe entry into port. This Dram Tree celebration was a custom of many ports, and remains part of America's nautical heritage.

C.U.I. Positions Itself For Continued Growth

C.U.I.'s exclusive manufacturing capability allows even the smallest microbrewer, brew pub or home brewer the ability to begin the yearly heritage of creating a commemorative stein. Collectors, as well as the beer aficionado, will welcome every new addition.

C.U.I. has found a market niche, secured its position with technology and strong licensed relationships, thus building a reputation as one of the leaders in the world of collectibles. With its leadership role in place, C.U.I. is poised for continued strong growth and success.

Department 56®, Inc.
Just Imagine...Snowladen Trees, Wreaths at the Windows and Welcome Mats Out...The Tradition Begins

"Department 56" may seem a curious name for a firm that designs and manufactures nostalgic, collectible villages. How the name originated is a story that intrigues the firm's many loyal collectors.

Before Department 56, Inc. became an independent corporation, it was part of a large parent company that used a numbering system to identify each of its departments. While Department 21 was administration and Department 54 was the gift warehouse, the name assigned to wholesale gift imports was "Department 56."

Department 56, Inc. originally began by importing fine Italian basketry. However, a new product line introduced in 1977 set the groundwork for the collectible products of today. Little did the company's staff realize that their appealing group of four lighted houses and two churches would pave the way for one of the late 20th-century's most popular collectibles.

These miniature buildings were the beginning of *The Original Snow Village*®. Each design was handcrafted of ceramic, and hand-painted to create all the charming details of an "olden day" village. To create the glow from the windows, a switched cord and bulb assembly was included with each individually boxed piece.

Collectors could see the little lighted buildings as holiday decorations under a Christmas tree or on the mantel. Glowing lights gave the impression of cozy homes and neighborhood buildings with happy, bustling townsfolk in a wintry setting. Sales were encouraging, so Department 56, Inc. decided to develop more *Snow Village* pieces to add to their 1978 line.

Word of mouth and consumer interest helped Department 56 realize *The Original Snow Village* collection would continue. Already there were reports of collectors striving to own each new piece as it was introduced.

By 1979, the Department 56, Inc. staff made an important operational decision. In order to keep *The Original Snow Village* at a reasonable size, buildings would have to be retired from production each year to make room for new designs. Being new to the world of collectibles, they did not realize the full impact of this decision. Collectors who had not

From the Dickens' Village *series comes this quaint piece entitled "The King's Road Post Office." Its issue price is $45.*

yet obtained a retired model would attempt to seek out that piece on the secondary market. This phenomenon has led to reports that early *Snow Village* pieces are valued at considerably more than their original issue price.

Today, as in the past, the Department 56 architects continue to keep the Village alive by bringing collectors new techniques and new materials, all of which result in an exciting array of buildings and charming accessories.

The Heritage Village Collection® From Department 56, Inc.

Love of holiday traditions sparked the original concept of The Heritage Village Collection. When decorating our homes, we are often drawn to objects reminiscent of an earlier time. Holiday memories wait, hidden in a bit of wrinkled tissue or a dusty box, until that time each year, when rediscovered, we unpack our treasures and are magically transported to a beloved time and place.

The first Heritage Village grouping was the *Dickens' Village*® series introduced in 1984. Extensive research, charming details and the fine hand-painting of the seven original porcelain shops and

"Village Church" established them as favorites among collectors.

Other series followed with the introduction of *The New England Village*®, *The Alpine Village*©, *Christmas In The City*® series, the presentation of *The Little Town Of Bethlehem*© in 1987, and the 1991 introduction of *The North Pole*©. Each of these ongoing collectible series has been researched for authenticity and has the same attention to detail as the original *Dickens' Village*.

As each of the villages began to grow, limited edition pieces were added, along with trees, street lamps, and accessory groupings to complete the nostalgic charm of each collection. Each lighted piece is stamped in the bottom with its designated series name, title, year of introduction, and Department 56, Inc. logo to assure authenticity.

Each model is packed in its own individual styrofoam storage carton and illustrated sleeve. A special compartment in the boxing of all lighted pieces holds a UL-approved switched cord and bulb. This method not only protects the pieces during shipping, but also provides a convenient way of repacking and storing your collection for many years.

Each grouping within The Heritage Village Collection captures the holiday spirit of a bygone era. *Dickens' Village*, for instance, portrays the bustling, hearty and joyous atmosphere of the holidays in Victorian England. *New England Village* brings back memories of "over the river and through the woods," with a journey through the countryside.

The *Alpine Village* recreates the charm of a quaint mountain town, where glistening snow and clear lakes fed by icy streams dot the landscape. *Christmas In The City* evokes memories of busy

"Sigmund the Snowshoer," an appealing little monk, is part of The Merrymakers *and carries an issue price of $20.*

sidewalks, street corner Santas, friendly traffic cops and bustling crowds amid cheery shops, townhouses and theaters.

In 1987, Department 56, Inc. introduced *The Little Town Of Bethlehem*. The unique twelve-piece set reproduces the essence of the birthplace of Jesus. This complete village scene continues to inspire and hearten those who celebrate Christmas everywhere.

In 1991, Department 56, Inc. presented *The North Pole* series as a new, ongoing part of The Heritage Village Collection. The brightly lit North Pole buildings and accompanying accessories depict the wonderful Santa Claus legend with charm and details that bring childhood dreams to life for the young and the young-at-heart.

Celebrate Snowbabies© and Other Department 56 Favorites

Another collectible series from Department 56, Inc. is *Snowbabies*©. These adorable, whimsical figurines have bright blue eyes and creamy white snowsuits covered by flakes of new-fallen snow. They sled, make snowballs, ride polar bears and frolic with their friends. Since their introduction, *Snowbabies* have enchanted collectors around the country and have brightened the imagination of all of us who celebrate the gentle play of youthful innocence.

Each of the finely detailed bisque porcelain collectibles, with hand-painted faces and hand-

"Join the Parade" represents the delightful Snowbabies *collection, at an issue price of $37.50.*

applied frosty bisque snow crystals, is complete in its own gold foil-stamped storybook box.

In 1989, a line of pewter miniature *Snowbabies* was introduced, to the great delight of collectors of miniatures. These tiny treasures are made from many of the same designs as their bisque counterparts, and come packaged in little white gift boxes sprinkled with gold stars.

Every year, new *Snowbaby* friends are introduced in these very special collections.

In addition to *Snowbabies* and the Villages, three other series have caught the loyal Department 56 collectors' fancy. They are *Winter Silhouette©*, *Merry Makers©*, and *All Through The House©*.

Winter Silhouette is a collection of highly detailed white porcelain figurines, many with pewter, silver or gold accents. *Winter Silhouette* has an elegant simplicity that brings back Christmas visions of family pleasures in a bygone era.

New in 1991, *Merry Makers* are chubby little monks dressed in dark green robes. Standing just under four inches tall, each of these delightful friars is handcrafted of porcelain, and hand-painted. They work, play and sing together in happy harmony.

The year 1991 also saw the beginning of another new series, *All Through The House*. Featuring backdrops and furniture, as well as figurines, these highly detailed pieces offer warm, nostalgic memories inspired by the activities they portray. Made of cold cast porcelain and beautifully hand-painted, this charming collection celebrates family traditions *All Through The House*.

Collectors Discover the Wide Range of Department 56, Inc. Creations

In addition to the popular collectibles already mentioned, Department 56, Inc. continues to

"Nicholas, Natalie and Spot the Dog" offer a portrait of holiday contentment from the All Through The House *collection. Issue price is $45.*

develop colorful and innovative giftware as well as ongoing lines for Spring and Easter, Christmas trim and many beautiful Christmas ornaments.

Seldom does a firm win the attention and loyalty of collectors as quickly as Department 56, Inc. has done since its first *Original Snow Village* buildings debuted in 1977. As one enthusiast stated, "A company can't make an item collectible. People have to make it collectible, and the people have discovered Department 56."

Duncan Royale
From Classic Santas to African Americans...at Duncan Royale the Stories Never End

Just over a decade ago, Duncan Royale took the collectible gift market by storm with the introduction of the limited edition *History of Santa Claus* collection. Since then — to the delight of collectors worldwide — Duncan Royale has presented many more handsome collections. And under the strong leadership of company founder and President Max Duncan, the firm has become well known for unique art and sculpture that tells a story.

Each Duncan Royale collection emerges as a result of hours of painstaking research and creative production. After the theme for a collection is developed, artists sketch renderings that exemplify the theme, tradition and history of each personality. When final drawings and colors are selected, the sculptor breathes dimension and "stop-frame action" into each character, adding detail and depth.

Molds are cast from the original clay sculpture, and the porcelain figurines are produced by a cold cast process which captures minute and intricate details. Precision hand-painting strokes each piece with vivid, vibrant color. On some pieces, six to seven undercoatings may be used to obtain the desired hues. Each piece receives a limited edition number and its own mini book that tells a brief story about the figure. And all Duncan Royale collectibles are security-packed in their own handsome gift boxes.

Historical Series Got the Duncan Royale Magic Underway

In order to create and develop the original *History of Santa Claus* Collection, Max Duncan traveled extensively, consulting scores of experts and conducting research in libraries and museums throughout the world. Diligent efforts uncovered numerous personalities from history, literature and mythology, who have influenced our present-day notions of Santa Claus. This research appears in published form as a full-color volume entitled *History of Santa*. And the collection itself has been expanded to include thirty-six different Santa personalities.

While early issues paid tribute to well-known Western Santa Claus images from Europe and the United States, the history has continued to unfold with pieces inspired by such diverse, symbolic figures as "Judah Maccabee," who is remembered in the Jewish celebration of Hanukkah. He was the instrument for bringing the gift of freedom and light to the Jews. There is also a figurine inspired by "Hoteiosho of Japan," an old Japanese god known for his amiable and serene nature, who plays the role of Santa Claus for Japan's small Christian population. In addition, the "Saturnalia King" takes us back to ancient Rome, where he reigned over the Winter Solstice celebrations from December 17th to 24th.

In 1987, Duncan Royale introduced the *History of Classic Clowns and Entertainers*. This twenty-four-piece collection chronicles the evolution of clowns and entertainers for 4,000 years, from early

Duncan Royale's "Angel of Peace" represents the studio's touching new Angel collection. Here, in hand-painted splendor, we see a lovely blonde angel with both the lion and the lamb.

Greco-Roman times through the twentieth century. The last character in the series is everybody's favorite, the immortal Bob Hope. A beautifully illustrated, hard-cover collectors book, *History of Classic Clowns and Entertainers*, sets in prose the memorable stories of these endearing champions of comedy.

The Fanciful Charms of Woodland Fairies *and* Calendar Secrets

One of the most delightful Duncan Royale innovations of the late 1980s was the *Woodland Fairies* series: a group of delightful characters capturing the antics of magical forest folk. Each character bears the name of a favorite tree: from "Cherry," "Mulberry" and "Apple" to "Sycamore," "Pine Tree" and "Almond Blossom."

Duncan Royale's *Calendar Secrets* depict the celebrations, traditions and legends of the twelve calendar months. In addition, they illustrate the history of each month of the Roman calendar as the secrets unfold. To complement this magnificent collection, Duncan Royale has introduced a *Calendar Secrets* book, colorfully illustrated and filled with historical information and the lore behind how our calendar was formed, and how the months were named.

The Early Americans *Help Collectors to Step Into the Past*

America is a "new" country at just over 200 years of age. And since professionals of today enjoy learning about their counterparts of the past, Duncan Royale has captured the essence of colonial careers in *The Early Americans*. Each individual who is honored in a figurine was selected for outstanding skills as well as the ability to use imagination and humor to pave the way for others.

For example, the "Fireman" returns us to a turn-of-the-century fire station. We can almost hear the sound of the bell as our eager hero heeds the alarm. He gathers his equipment and courage. Meanwhile, the ever-loyal dalmatian, oblivious to the seriousness of the moment, chews on the fireman's much-needed boot! "Show and Tell" is a day that every child looks forward to, and every adult remembers. Now with "Teacher," we are able to comprehend — through mature eyes — the look our own school teacher may have expressed on that most exciting day.

A good "Lawyer" must always possess the gift of eloquence. Law and oration go hand-in-hand. Our "Lawyer" is getting in a final dress rehearsal before a most critical audience: his beagle. Other occupations profiled in this heart-touching col-

Here's Buckwheat from the classic "Little Rascals" comedies, posed with his friend Petee the dog or in other memorable vignettes! These works of art premier Duncan Royale's Buckwheat collection.

lection include: "Doctor," "Nurse," "Accountant," "Policeman," "Salesman," "Dentist," "Store-keeper," "Banker," "Homemaker," "Chiropractor," "Secretary" and "Pharmacist." The series is limited to 10,000 of each piece and may be purchased individually or as a matched, numbered set.

Ebony *Captures the Rich Culture and Heritage of Black Americans*

Ebony is a rare, tropical hardwood full of texture and richness. And now *Ebony* also is a collection from Duncan Royale — created in tribute to African-American life, accomplishments and culture. This heritage has become one of the strongest building blocks of American society as we know it today. The musical forerunners of Soul, Gospel, Rock and Roll, the Blues and Jazz are deeply imbedded in Black American culture. The *Ebony* collection from Duncan Royale highlights a number of compelling personalities from these diverse musical "roots." Each figurine is individually numbered with an edition limited to 5,000 pieces. These endearing characters are sure to be treasured by collectors for years to come.

After a hard workday, "Harmonica Man" takes joy in relaxation by playing his instrument — both for himself and for the entertainment of those around him. Old "Fiddler Man" always wears a smile and finds himself surrounded by children, passing on his stories to the next generation. "Banjo Man" enjoys sitting on the deck of a Mississippi cargo boat, strumming his banjo to pass away the lonely hours. "Spoons Player" teaches us

that life can be full of joy if we take the time to savor the simple pleasures. "Preacher" and "Gospel Singer" share the spirituality of religion, both through the spoken word and in song. An entire "Jazz Man Set" may be acquired, or collectors may choose individual instrumentalists on "Sax," "Trumpet," "Bass," "Piano" or "Bongo."

The Inspiration of Love...and of Angels

A Duncan Royale collection entitled *The Greatest Gift...Love* was created by artist Peter Apsit in tribute to the "Annunciation," "Nativity" and "Crucifixion." Each piece is available in either an elegant marble version or in painted porcelain, with all editions limited to 5,000 pieces.

New to Duncan Royale is a series entitled *Angels*, including marvelous works of art showing angels in various real-world guises. For example, "Angel of Peace" is portrayed symbolically with both the lion and the lamb, while "Ebony Angel" watches over two sweet African-American youngsters.

The beautiful "Fallana" dances her traditional African dance and smiles as she captures the rhythm of the music. This hand-painted figurine represents Duncan Royale's collection of Jubilee Dancers.

The Buckwheat Collection and Jubilee Dancers *Make Their Duncan Royale Debut*

Inspired by the "Little Rascals" character from the famous "Our Gang" comedies, the *Buckwheat* collection shows the renowned youngster in a wide range of popular poses. Crafted by hand and painted in numerous bright colors, the pieces include: "Petee & Friend," showing Buckwheat, dressed as Farina, with his gang's memorable dog with the bull's-eye marking; "The Painter," with Buckwheat making a mess of his painting chore; "O'tay," with Buckwheat making his trademark O.K. hand sign; and "Smile for the Camera," where Buckwheat stops practicing his drums for a moment in order to flash a happy grin.

Another important new Duncan Royale collection is entitled *Jubilee Dancers*, and it focuses on energetic African dancers in colorful, traditional garb. Two of the initial issues are: "Keshia," in bright orange and gold; and "Fallana," dressed in shades of pink, turquoise, and tan with elegant touches of fringe.

The Duncan Royale Collectors Club *Offers Many Benefits*

For those who revel in the diversity and richness of Duncan Royale offerings, there is no membership more special than that of the Duncan Royale Collectors Club. Members are invited to acquire special "members-only" club pieces, and to buy or sell Duncan Royale back issues on the exclusive Royale Exchange.

The "Royale Courier" is a comprehensive and fun-to-read newsletter that provides collectors with news of product introductions, acquisition opportunities, Duncan Royale history, special opportunities and much more. It also carries the Collectors' Information Bureau's Price Index, which shows many of the retired *History of Santa Claus* issues rising sharply in value over the years.

From the historical delights of Santa Claus to the appeal of Buckwheat himself, Duncan Royale has the pulse of American collectors. And under the direction of Max Duncan, this much-honored firm creates works of art that collectors treasure deeply — both for their detail of sculpture and coloration and for the emotional power of their messages. Most important of all: each Duncan Royale issue has a significant story behind it. And at Duncan Royale, the stories never end.

Dynasty Doll Collection
Collectors Thrill to the Fashionable Costumes and Distinctive Expressions of Elegant Dynasty Dolls

The award-winning studios of Dynasty Dolls have earned a special place in the hearts of American collectors. With their distinct personalities, faces and expressions, these lavishly costumed Dynasty Dolls enjoy an especially loyal following. But few Dynasty collectors know the "inside story" of their favorite studio's origins. For Dynasty began as the dream of three young American men...and the path of their dream took several turns before they discovered their "niche" in today's thriving world of collectible dolls.

Just after World War II ended, three brothers-in-law, Sidney Darwin, Samuel J. Kronman and Charles H. Dengrove, launched a ceramic factory in Carteret, New Jersey. Samuel was a ceramic engineer for Stangl Pottery, and Sidney and Charles were just out of the service. Both Sidney and Charles had business experience before going into the armed forces.

"They tried for quite awhile to develop some items," explains Gary Darwin, son of founder Sidney and today the vice president of sales for Cardinal, Inc. and Dynasty Dolls. "They had many technical problems getting started, due to some innovative ceramic techniques that Samuel pioneered."

The entrepreneurs saw their patience rewarded when they launched their first big item: a Measuring Spoon Holder with spoons, fashioned to look like a flower pot with leaves. "When you put the brightly colored plastic measuring spoons in, it formed what looked like a flower pot," Gary Darwin recalls. "They sold well over three million pieces. That's what got the company off the ground."

In the late 1940s, the American gift industry was relatively small and close-knit, according to Gary Darwin. "That's when they got distribution heavily entrenched," Darwin says of his father and two uncles. "Their line included piggy banks, butter melters, sprinklers for ironing, napkin holders, decorative switch plates, and other useful and attractive decorative items."

A fire in the 1950s forced a move to larger quarters in Carteret. "They set up another pottery with state-of-the-art equipment," Darwin recounts.

"Jamaal" represents Uta Brauser's City Kids, *a collection of handsome Black dolls by Dynasty. Wearing black silk pants, a gray shirt, a black ankle-length "leather" trench coat, gold chains and sunglasses, "Jamaal" is 23½" in height and is offered in a limited edition of 5,000 at an issue price of $220.*

"This included a high-speed and more efficient tunnel kiln. My uncle Samuel was responsible for developing some unique methods in ceramic manufacturing. They employed 150 people, and operated the pottery twenty-four hours a day, seven days a week until 1960."

Importation Broadens the Firm's Horizons

"During the 1950s," continues Darwin, "even with increased capacity and more efficient manufacturing methods, it became more and more difficult to compete as a domestic resource, with imports coming in mainly from Japan." The pottery was closed and the company was transformed into an import concern, with Sidney Darwin mak-

The lovely brown-eyed brunette, "Adelle," is part of Dynasty's Studio Editions collection. The 23" tall "Adelle" wears a cream "silk" dress trimmed with ecru lace, pearls and pink rosettes. Limited to an edition of 2,500, the doll's issue price is $210.

Hazel Tertsakian designed pretty "Rosemary" for Dynasty Dolls: a blonde child with blue eyes and a pink party dress trimmed with ecru lace. The 16" "Rosemary" is offered in a limited edition of 2,500 and carries an issue price of $120. It is part of Dynasty's Studio Editions.

ing his first buying trip to the Far East in 1960. "Importing let us become a multi-media resource, not just a ceramics manufacturer," Darwin says. During the 1960s and 1970s, Sidney selected an impressive array of giftware merchandise that was sold both to shops and to the leading mail order companies.

"In the mid-1970s, we imported six styles of dollhouse furniture and put them into the line," Gary Darwin says. "The six miniatures absolutely took off, even though collectors and dealers told us they were all wrong: wrong size, wrong color, wrong dimensions. We learned very quickly and a new division, Concord Miniature Collection, was born. Today, the Concord line is part of Cardinal, Inc. and it is the largest creator and importer of one-inch to one-foot scale miniature furniture in the world."

Dollhouse Furniture Leads to the Creation of Collectible Dolls

"As Concord grew, we looked for other categories of merchandise to sell to miniature or dollhouse retailers. That's how we got into the doll business," Gary Darwin recalls. "Our best dolls were a couple in Frontier-style costumes, in velvet as well as calico. They took off, but in the giftware trade — not the miniature trade. Talk about backing into a business!", Darwin chuckles.

"At the same time, dolls did very well through our catalog showroom channels of distribution. We were encouraged to build a special identity for our dolls and to package them distinctively," Darwin explains. The resulting Dynasty Dolls concept built rapidly into a recognizable favorite among doll collectors.

After founder Samuel J. Kronman died, and founder Charles Dengrove retired, Cardinal Inc. and Dynasty Dolls' course was charted by Sidney Darwin and his sons, Gary and Allen. The Darwins encouraged a continuation of the development of Dynasty Dolls into a distinctive doll line to fit the desire of collectors. "Dynasty Dolls gives the collector a popular priced collector doll with all the personality, style, costuming and accessories of the higher priced models," Darwin says. "We currently offer between 300 and 350 styles. Some are antique reproductions, but mainly we work with a variety of artists who design their own products," Darwin says.

The design and selection of dolls and costumes is under the direction of Anne L. Dolan and Donna R. Rovner. Ms. Dolan has been associated with the gift and decorative industry for many years, both as a designer and buyer. Ms. Rovner

Here comes the "Annual Bride" from Dynasty Dolls, limited to production during 1993. This beautiful creation represents the Civil War Era, and she wears an ivory satin gown with an overskirt, both generously trimmed with lace. Her shoes and gloves are painted with exquisite detail, and she wears delicate, pearl drop earrings. Her floral cascade bouquet and double veil add final touches to this lovely blue-eyed bride's attire. Issue price for the "1993 Annual Bride" is $190.

has been involved with dolls as a collector, historian and a designer. Both Ms. Dolan and Ms. Rovner collaborate in creating and designing new dolls. In addition, they work closely with the artists who design and sculpt for Dynasty to assure that the new additions to the line are coordinated and in keeping with the Dynasty image.

Artists currently designing for Dynasty include Marci Cohen, Karen Henderson, Hazel Tertsakian, Teena Halbig, Gail Hoyt, Gloria Tepper, Pat Kolesar, and most recently, Uta Brauser.

Award-Winning Dynasty Dolls Looks to the Future

Dynasty was the proud recipient of a 1993 *Dolls* magazine nomination as a candidate for an Award of Excellence for "Jamaal," part of the *Uta Brauser's City Kids* collection. This unique collection consists of five beautifully sculpted black dolls ranging in size from 16½" to 23½".

Leafing through the Dynasty Doll current catalog, the lines' uniqueness becomes evident. The coveted *Dynasty Annual Dolls* will be especially appealing. The 1993 "Annual Bride" is a statuesque 22" beauty, sculpted by Hazel Tertsakian, attired in a Civil War Era gown. "Ariel," Dynasty's

Annual Doll, is an 18" tall blonde, blue-eyed girl dressed in shades of lavender. Both 1993 Annuals are limited to one year of production. The *Annual Christmas Doll*, limited to 5,000 pieces, is "Genevieve." At 19" tall, with upswept blonde curls and green eyes, she is lavishly dressed in green velvet, white and gold. She is musical, playing "Adeste Fidelis" ("Oh Come All Ye Faithful"). brides, babies, ballerinas, little girls, ladies and international as well as Native American themes round out the offerings of the Dynasty Doll Line.

Studio Editions by Dynasty, a relatively new line of gallery dolls available for the advanced collector, features lavishly attired dolls of beautifully sculpted children and ladies that reflect romance and elegance of days gone by.

Dynasty Dolls enjoys a rich history of tradition, positioned for future success. Expansion and growth highlight Dynasty's march into the next century with spectacular plans that will position it among the preeminent doll companies in America. New concepts and designs are always in the making to offer collectors innovative and exciting dolls at affordable prices.

Limited to production during 1993, "Ariel" is a Dynasty Annual Doll with blonde hair and blue eyes. The 18" doll is dressed in shades of lavender and white eyelet. The issue price for this work of art is $120.

eggspressions!® inc.

From the Simple to the *Eggsotic*, Whimsical to the Magical...Enchanting Eggs for Every Colleggting Occasion

Long before the Revolution that overthrew the Czars, Russian jeweler Peter Carl Fabergé earned a series of spectacular royal commissions. He created stunning works of art using the simple, perfect egg as inspiration. Today those Russian Fabergé eggs...adorned with precious gems and gold...sell for hundreds of thousands or even millions of dollars — on the rare occasion that one becomes available at auction.

Now in that same wonderful tradition, South Dakota artist Connie Drew makes *eggsotic*, *eggsquisite* creations from non-endangered finch, quail, chicken, duck, goose, emu, rhea and ostrich eggs — affordable and *eggsceptional* works of art for today's collectors and connoisseurs.

Born more than a half-century ago on Bastille Day, Ms. Drew is as distinctive as the designs which she and her company, ***eggspressions!® inc.***, create for a nationwide market. "There aren't any capital letters in the name," she says with a wink. "I only capitalize God, America, and the name of the bank!"

Besides being the proud owner of her own *eggstensive* decorated egg colleggtion (including "pert'near all" of Theo Fabergé's eggs), Ms. Drew's life is a blend of art, music, folk philosophy, glitter and whimsical delights. For a time, the irrepressible

*The **eggspressions!® inc.** "Butterfly Wings" (left), adorned with both light and dark amethyst crystals, displays spring's new life. "Elegant Choice" (center) is a pearly-white egg, trimmed with golden mesh and decorated with a crystal flower. "Winter Song" (right) reveals a songbird perched upon a nest of golden leaves. A bouquet of acorns and wild flowers rims the egg's frost-covered window.*

Connie collected owls, hoping to gain wisdom. She stopped when she noticed they were keeping her up at night!

Now she surrounds herself with twinkling stars, butterflies, unicorns, a Scarlett O'Hara doll "draped in the drapes," various bronze sculptures, oil paintings, Broadway musical paraphernalia, unique graphic prints, and a bodacious coffee table displaying her growing colleggtion of opulent egg-shaped Judith Leiber purses.

Even though Ms. Drew has a star named after her, is an avid self-taught Macintosh computer user, and paints each nail on her fingers and toes a different color, she insists that she's not *eggscentric*.

Czech Heritage Inspires an Eggsuberant Artist

This energetic lady learned the art of "drop-pull" egg decorating from her mother and grandmother, and she continues to draw upon her Czechoslovakian background for designing and coloring methods. Although she still utilizes many of the same patterns and designs passed down from the generations, more modern procedures and supplies now are used as well.

Having become an *eggspert* on traditional symbols, she finds herself in demand for *leggtures* during the Easter season. Indeed, Lent has always been a particularly busy time of year for Ms. Drew, ever since she began creating egg art originals in her home studio. From Ash Wednesday to Palm Sunday, working from "the crack of noon to pert'near midnight," she would annually turn more than a thousand eggs into miniature works of art.

Today, her long love affair with decorated eggs has grown from her home studio to a 10,000 square foot building complete with *eggsecutive* offices, a gift shop, factory (or "egg plant"), and "brooder" — a think tank where new ideas are "hatched." And she creates eggs all year around because, as she asserts, "eggs aren't just for Easter anymore!"

Located in Rapid City, South Dakota in the beautiful Black Hills, ***eggspressions!*** is not far from the famous Mount Rushmore National Memorial. Here, skilled artists create a dazzling variety of

collectible eggs. Some are hand-painted, some musical, and some are transformed into jewelry boxes, lamps, baskets and elaborately carved and adorned ornaments.

The Creative Process at eggspressions!

Each *eggspressions!* masterpiece begins with nature's purest creation: the egg. Honored by all cultures for centuries, the egg embodies the natural forces of life and vitality. Indeed, historically the decoration of an egg meant harnessing its magical properties. Giving one as a gift was considered an act of love and respect.

Between the simple egg and the *eggspressions!* collectible that will emerge, there are many intricate steps. To begin, the egg must be prepared for decoration. This process includes drilling a tiny hole into the top and bottom of each egg, and blowing air into the egg allowing the insides to be removed. The edible parts are donated to non-profit local charities for their food programs.

After they are sterilized, the eggshells are ready for the artist. "Nature's most perfect package" provides the painter and decorator with the opportunity to create all manner of charming and unique collectibles.

The "Misty Rose" egg (left) is enhanced by an 18K gold-plated butterfly and a crystal "dewdrop," symbolizing budding romance. "Mint Julep" (center) has an ornate rose and a large pearl decorating the mint green keepsake. Multi-colored crystals line the opening. "Lara" (right) plays "Lara's Theme." A scooped rainbow of crystals trims this egg's pink pearly-mist finish.

Eggs Crafted in the Classic Czechoslovakian Style

Czechoslovakian eggs — or Czeggs — are beautifully handcrafted by a style of decoration known as the drop-pull technique. This originated in the former Czechoslovakia and is used in other European countries as well. The method requires the "dropping" of warm wax onto an egg and "pulling" it across the surface. The pattern consists of motifs which have been passed down for generations. Every stroke and color carries strong symbolic overtones, and every Czegg is designed to tell a story.

Once the Czeggs have been stroked, they're taken to a special dipping room, where each egg is covered with a heavy lacquer. The gloss produces a handsome shine and also serves to seal the wax and strengthen the shell. The Czeggs are then left to hang for a full day, and when they are dry, they are creatively decorated with genuine Austrian crystals.

The end product is an irresistible piece of work — each Czegg a finely crafted masterpiece. *The Easter Collection*, which includes eggs representing "The Last Supper," "The Crucifixion," and "The Resurrection," is an *eggsample* of this fine craftsmanship.

Eggs to Decorate the Holiday Tree

The *eggspressions!* Christmas ornament eggs will add a special note to the holiday decor of any home. Each ornament begins with a real eggshell. First a guideline is etched onto the eggshell, then a border print is attached following the guide. When dry, it is

From *eggspressions!® inc.*, "Choo Choo Christmas" (left) has spiraled columns of red Austrian crystals and a miniature wooden train beneath a decorated tree. Victorian "Romantique" (center) features pink frosted hearts, pearls, and a twisted gold filigree. In "Winter Colt" (right), crystallized saplings serve as a sheltered hideaway for this mare and her yearling.

carved with a high-speed air drill to make an opening in the egg. This provides a staging area for the artist to construct a scene. A special adhesive is brushed inside the shell and glitter is swirled inside the egg.

Next, a platform is built and a miniature scene is meticulously created. The oval opening is then decorated with magical icicles deftly created by the artist. A festive trim of sparkle and color adds a finishing touch. A gold cord is attached, and the *eggspressions!* ornament is ready for the Christmas tree.

Elegant Jewel Boxes from eggspressions! inc.

"Lara" is one of the precious jewel boxes from *eggspressions!* It plays the haunting theme from "Dr. Zhivago." To create each jewel box, plain goose eggshells are given a rich paint finish, and then they are marked, hinged and cut. For a musical jewel box, the music box is then inserted.

The eggshell is then filled with a compound designed to add weight to the jewel box. Next, each box is carefully lined with the highest quality material and trim, and then lavished with genuine Austrian crystals. The result is a miniature treasure chest — elegant and breathtaking — a keepsake to hold one's tiniest and best-loved mementos.

Carved Eggs and Cascarones

For carved eggs such as "Dogwood," an intricate pattern is carved out by hand with a high-speed air drill. Then the design is subtly brushed with color to enhance its delicate appearance. With a few finishing touches, the carved egg becomes a showpiece — and comes with "The Legend of the Dogwood" as an *eggstra* bonus!

Cascarones allow friends to have their own "ticker-tape parade" any time they clap their hands. These confetti-filled eggs add a festive flair and make an occasion out of any gathering. For weddings and outdoor occasions, *eggspressions!* offers bird seed filled Cascarones.

The Old World tradition of giving decorated eggs as tokens of love and respect continues with

eggspressions! There are no limits to the design possibilities of this art form, which brings the centuries-old tradition of decorating eggs to the present. Each new product release now is a signed and numbered limited edition, so the coll*egg*tibility of *eggspressions!* eggs is stronger than ever. Thanks to the innovative Connie Drew, each egg becomes an *eggspression* of the unique talent and workmanship of her studio's gifted artists.

The Easter Collection *from eggspressions!® inc. includes eggs representing "The Last Supper," (left) "The Crucifixion" (center) and "The Resurrection" (right). These Czechoslovakian eggs — or Czeggs — are masterfully handcrafted in a style of decoration known as the drop-pull technique which originated in the former Czechoslovokia and is used in other European countries.*

Enesco Corporation
Collectibles For Every Collector

Enesco Corporation, one of the most respected names in the giftware industry, has been regarded as a leader in its field for thirty-five years. Credited with being among the most innovative and trend-setting designers and producers of fine gifts and collectibles, Enesco continues its steady growth and prominence worldwide.

The introduction of the now-famous Enesco *Precious Moments*® Collection catapulted Enesco from being a gift designer to its expanded role as a leading collectibles producer. Today, Enesco has an international following of collectors with such award-winning collections as *Cherished Teddies*®, *Memories of Yesterday*®, *Small World of Music*™, *Maud Humphrey Bogart, Treasury of Christmas Ornaments*® and many others.

Fifteen Years of Love, Caring and Sharing With The Precious Moments *Collection*

It was in 1978 that simple drawings of teardrop-eyed children evolved into The Enesco *Precious Moments* Collection. Under the guidance of Enesco President Eugene Freedman, the children with soulful expressions and inspirational titles soon became a phenomenon in the collectibles industry and are now the number one collectible in the country.

Adapted from the work of artist Sam Butcher, the *Precious Moments* Collection of porcelain bisque figurines has touched collectors with messages of love, caring and sharing. Even with his remarkable vision for the Collection, Freedman could not have foreseen the deep attachment collectors have for these teardrop-eyed figurines.

For collectors to communicate, exchange information and learn more about the Collection, Enesco sponsored the Precious Moments Collectors' Club in 1981. By the end of the charter year, tens of thousands had joined. Today the Enesco *Precious Moments* Collectors' Club is the largest club of its kind in the world and has been honored several times as the Collectors' Club of the Year by the National Association of Limited Edition Dealers (NALED). The Enesco *Precious Moments* Birthday Club was formed in 1985 to introduce children to collectibles. Both clubs have more than 500,000 members.

Christopher sits by his toy chest in "Old Friends Are The Best Friends" from the Cherished Teddies® *Collection. Based on illustrations by artist Priscilla Hillman, the figurine won a 1992 TOBY award from* Teddy Bear and Friends *magazine.*

Memories of Yesterday *Collection Develops Strong Following*

While the *Precious Moments* Collection has flourished for more than fifteen years, other Enesco collectible lines have gained an enthusiastic collector following. Introduced in 1988, the *Memories of Yesterday* Collection is based on the work of famed British artist Mabel Lucie Attwell (1879-1965), regarded as the foremost illustrator of children in England this century.

The Collection portrays chubby-legged children of the '20s and '30s and is ranked among the country's top ten collectibles. In support of the collection, Enesco established the Memories of Yesterday Collector's Society, which officially began in 1991.

Music, Magic and Motion With The Small World of Music *Collection*

The Enesco Musical Society also began its charter year in 1991 and supports the Enesco *Small*

World of Music Collection of deluxe action musicals. More than twelve years ago, Enesco introduced the first of its action musicals — a clown balancing and rotating on a ball. Today, Enesco has become a pioneer in action musicals by combining creativity, new technology, ambitious engineering and fine craftsmanship.

Subjects for the action musicals range from mice dancing on a grand piano to dalmatians frolicking in a fire truck to "The Majestic," an old fashioned ferris wheel with flickering lights, motion and its own cassette deck that plays a tape of calliope music. These action musicals have earned numerous international awards and are highly sought after throughout the world.

Cherished Teddies
Wins Worldwide Recognition

Introduced in 1992, the *Cherished Teddies* Collection has received international recognition from collectors and the collectibles industry. The adorable teddy bear figurines have found a special place in the hearts of collectors with their warm expressions and universal appeal.

Designed by artist and children's author Priscilla Hillman, each cold cast figurine comes with a Certificate of Adoption and its own name so collectors can "adopt" the teddy bear. Hillman's illustrations have also been recreated in the *Calico Kittens*™ Collection. The cat figurines also feature messages of love and friendship.

The Enesco Precious Moments® Collection celebrated its 15th anniversary in 1993 with a commemorative figurine titled "15 Years Together, What A Tweet!" The porcelain bisque figurine features an angel conducting a choir of fifteen birds.

Enesco Treasury of Christmas Ornaments
Starts Collectors' Club

With Christmas ornaments continuing as one of the fastest growing collectibles, the Enesco *Treasury of Christmas Ornaments* Collection has become a year-round collector favorite. Subjects for the extensive collection include classic characters such as Mickey Mouse and GARFIELD as well as recognized licenses, including Disney, Parker Brothers, General Mills, McDonald's and Coca-Cola. Intricate detail, creativity and the use of familiar objects such as eyeglasses, teacups and utensils also characterize the Collection.

The popularity of the Collection resulted in the formation of the Treasury of Christmas Ornaments Collectors' Club, which began its Charter Year on July 1, 1993.

Maud Humphrey Bogart Collection
Celebrates Victoriana

Artist Maud Humphrey Bogart captured the romance, elegance and innocence of the Victorian

There's lots of action, fun and excitement during "The Greatest Show On Earth," a deluxe action musical from the Enesco Small World of Music™ *Collection. The circus comes to life under this illuminated big top featuring everything from swinging trapeze artists to cycling bears. The musical includes a standard cassette deck and comes with a tape of classic circus tunes.*

era in her turn-of-the-century portraits. Long before her son Humphrey Bogart became world famous as an actor, she established herself as one of the country's most gifted artists.

Her beloved artwork lives on today through the *Maud Humphrey Bogart* Collection of limited edition figurines, which were first introduced in 1988. Inspired by the Victorian children in her paintings, the Collection rekindles the beauty and gentle spirit of a bygone era.

Besides finely detailed figurines, the Collection also includes the *Maud Humphrey Bogart Victorian Village* of buildings and miniature figurines recreating the people and places in Rochester, New York, that influenced the artist's life and illustrations. The Collection is supported by the Maud Humphrey Bogart Collectors' Club, founded in 1990.

Sports Impressions: Making A Hit With Sports Collectibles

From Shaquille O'Neal to Nolan Ryan, Sports Impressions has all the bases covered with limited edition collectibles of the most popular athletes from today and yesterday. Founded in 1985 by Long Island retailer Joe Timmerman, Sports Impressions has become a leading designer and producer of collector plates, figurines and other memorabilia. More than 100 prominent personalities and teams in professional baseball, football, basketball, golf, hockey and boxing are featured on a winning lineup of sports collectibles

Top sports artists design each plate with meticulous attention to detail to capture the players in action. Some of the porcelain bisque figurines are even hand-signed by the athletes, including Roger Clemens and Ryne Sandberg.

With the growing popularity of sports memorabilia, Sports Impressions started a collectors' club in 1989. Members of the Sports Impressions Collectors' Club receive a special symbol of membership piece and have the opportunity to purchase members only releases.

Lucy & Me *and Other Enesco Collectibles*

The year Sam Butcher's drawings were transformed into the *Precious Moments* Collection, Enesco discovered another artist. Lucy Rigg had been making teddy bears out of baker's clay for

The Maud Humphrey Bogart Victorian Village portrays the people and places in Rochester, New York, that influenced the artist's life and enchanting illustrations. The first introduction features Maud Humphrey Bogart's childhood home at No. 5 Greenwood, which is limited in edition to 18,840 pieces. The scene can be completed with miniature figurines and accessories.

almost ten years when Freedman decided to turn her creations into porcelain bisque figurines in 1978. The *Lucy & Me®* Collection features teddy bears dressed up as familiar subjects and objects from flowers to pizza. The charming and whimsical appeal of these teddy bears has kept the collection growing in size and popularity over the past fifteen years.

In addition to a talented staff of nearly sixty artists and designers, Enesco also has collectibles from such well-known artists as Martha Holcombe (*Miss Martha's Collection*™), Karen Hahn (*Laura's Attic*™), Bessie Pease Gutmann (*The Gentle World of Bessie Pease Gutmann*™), John Grossman (*The Gifted Line*), Jim Davis (*GARFIELD*), Ellen Williams (*Sisters & Best Friends*™), Jill Barklem (*Brambley Hedge*™), Walt Disney (*Mickey & Co.*), Lesley Anne Ivory (*Ivory Cats*), Kathy Wise and Ruth Morehead, among others.

As collectors discriminately seek new collections for lasting appeal and interest, Enesco always discovers classics and new art to meet the demand. Based on its success with the *Precious Moments* Collection and its other popular collections, Enesco will certainly be a driving force in collectibles in the 1990s and beyond.

Fenton Art Glass
A Family Tradition in Fine Glassmaking Since 1905

In the age of mass production, The Fenton Art Glass Company remains unique: reflecting the charm and graciousness of an earlier, gentler time. Each piece of Fenton glass begins as a fiery gob of molten glass which is then formed with pride by master craftsmen using techniques and tools that are centuries old. As Fenton Art Glass approaches its 90th anniversary, it continues to develop new and unusual colors and treatments to keep the firm in the forefront of the handmade glass industry.

The Fenton Art Glass Company was founded in 1905 by Frank L. Fenton and his brother John, in an old glass factory building in Martins Ferry, Ohio. Here they painted decorations on glass blanks made by other firms. The Fentons found that they had trouble getting the glass they wanted when they wanted it, and soon decided to produce their own. The first glass from the Fenton factory in Williamstown, West Virginia was made on January 2, 1907. The piece was a "deformed cream pitcher" made by "carryover" worker Charles Brand.

Early Innovations from Fenton Art Glass

One of the first colors produced by the new company was called Chocolate Glass, and in late 1907, Fenton began to make iridescent pressed glass. Fifty years later this glass was called Carnival Glass. Iridescent glass was the backbone of the Fenton line for the next ten years, and it helped the company become financially successful in those early years. Iridescent glass was still selling in the 1920s, but it was made in delicate pastel colors with very little pattern in a treatment called "stretch glass." High quality Carnival Glass now sells for as much as $600 to $4,500 a piece. A recent rare piece sold for $22,500.

A Perfume Bottle Cures Depression Doldrums

During the '30s and '40s, Fenton Art Glass struggled to survive the depression and war shortages along with other American manufacturers.

Fenton Art Glass Collectible Eggs feature seven new designs each year. Each egg design is limited to 2,500 pieces. The eggs are designed by Fenton artists Martha Reynolds and Frances Burton.

Fenton switched to producing mixing bowls and orange juice reamers to keep people working, but did not hold back on developing beautiful new colors. Jade, Mandarin Red, Mulberry and Peach Blow from this period are eagerly sought by Fenton collectors today. Fenton recovered after the Depression with the help of a little hobnail perfume bottle designed at the behest of the Allen B. Wrisley Company. The bottle business made Fenton well again and also opened new business for Hobnail glass and antique reproductions of Victorian glass.

The Historical Collection is offered for a period of one year and features shape or color reproductions of antique American glass.

Fenton's Second Generation

Between 1948 and 1949, the top three members of Fenton management died, and brothers Frank M. Fenton, age 33, and Bill Fenton, age 25, took over as President and Vice-President of Sales respectively. The next five years were rough ones, but then milk glass began to sell beautifully all over the country. Fenton's Hobnail milk glass became the company's bread-and-butter line.

The team of Frank and Bill Fenton led the factory through significant growth for the next 30-plus years. Together they continued to develop new designs based on the flexibility and character of handmade glass. Often they have said that Fenton's success depends on crafting items that cannot be made by machine.

New Leadership for the 1980s, 1990s and Beyond

In February, 1986, the leadership of Fenton Art Glass passed to the third generation when George W. Fenton became President. Bill Fenton is Chair-man of the Board and Frank is retired, but both are at work every day as advisors. There are seven third-generation Fentons actively employed in the glass business and gift shop, and a fourth-generation member has just joined the team.

While a number of hand-glass companies have closed their doors over the past 15 years, Fenton has survived and grown by continuing to be flexible — and by offering a constant stream of new products to the market.

A Rainbow of Fenton Glass

Fenton Art Glass is renowned for creating beautiful and unique colors in glass. These include exotic glass varieties such as Carnival, Stretch, Opalescent, Cranberry, Mulberry, Burmese, Rosalene and Favrene.

The Iridescent glass now known as "Carnival" reigned as Fenton's major product from 1907 to 1920. The blue-green treatment has proven most popular, while red Carnival is rarest and most valuable. "Stretch" glass, created in the early 1920s, is made by spraying hot glass with metallic salts and then re-heating to create a satin finish. When flared or crimped, the metallic skin on the glass surface stretches creating a shimmering crackled finish.

Like the fiery opal stone, Opalescent glass creates a wondrous effect through a secret blend of ingredients matched with a skillful balance of chilling and reheating. The result is a gleaming transparent color glass that shades to opaque white. Cranberry glass was developed in England over 100 years ago and has been beloved by American collectors since its first appearance in the market. Fenton Cranberry follows the original formula beginning with a layer of gold ruby which is encased in sparkling crystal and then mouth blown to its final shape.

Mulberry glass also requires the addition of pure gold along with a layer of cobalt blue. A team of 24 skilled craftsmen gather, blow, finish and handle these multi-layered, heirloom-quality pieces for Fenton.

The most collectible glasses from Fenton recreate three beautiful treatments from the "Golden Age of Glass," 1860-1920. The first is Burmese glass made with both gold and uranium. The name was provided when its blushing pink edges on creamy yellow glass reminded Queen Victoria of a Burmese sunset. Rosalene glass is also noted for its deep pink edges but on a white background. Both colors require careful reheating to develop their unique shaded colorations.

The third collectible treatment is Favrene which

first appeared over 100 years ago and was made popular by Louis C. Tiffany. Pure silver in the formula is coaxed to the surface when the glass is reheated.

Special Fenton Offerings Keep Collectors Enthralled

Each year, Fenton Art Glass produces new editions to several popular limited edition series. These include the *Historical Collection, Connoisseur Collection, Collectible Eggs, Christmas Collection, Family Signature* series, and *Valentines.*

Classic molds from the past inspire the *Historical Collection* pieces, all made in special colors and treatments that have never before been used with these shapes. Each year for the *Connoisseur Collection*, Fenton selects a small grouping of art objects — unique in design, made in exotic glass treatments, and limited in number. Seven *Connoisseur* offerings for 1994 included a Favrene piece and a reverse painted lamp.

Fenton offers four editions of beautifully detailed glass *Collectible Eggs,* hand-painted and signed by its artist. Each numbered, gift-boxed egg boasts a 22k-gold plated base. For Christmas, Fenton produces an annual limited edition collection including a plate, bell, fairy light and lamp — all entirely hand-painted. The 1994 theme was "Silent Night," first edition in the *Christmas Star* series. It features a starlight woodland scene in metallic paints on Cobalt Satin glass.

The *Family Signature* series includes a few select pieces which represent the glass worker's and decorator's finest creations, within a very limited time frame. Each bears the signature of a Fenton family member. As for *Valentines*, Fenton introduces three new items each year in a Cranberry Opalescent Heart pattern, as well as one to three items in the Mary Gregory style of painting. Both offerings are limited to a specific selling period.

Fenton Glass Markings

The Handler's Mark, Decorator's Signature, and Fenton Logo represent three markings that "savvy" Fenton collectors should know. The "Handler's Mark" is applied to each Fenton basket by the highly-skilled individual who attaches the handle. The "Decorator's Signature" appears on the bottom of each hand-painted piece, and the "Fenton Logo" is placed on each piece of glass to permanently mark it as authentically Fenton.

Two pieces from the Family Signature Series, a collection available for a limited time each year. The "Autumn Leaves Candy Box" is inscribed with Don Fenton's signature, while the "Autumn Gold Opalescent Basket" includes Frank Fenton's signature.

A Colorful Future for Fenton Collectors

For those who enjoy collecting "all things Fenton," the firm invites collectors to join one or both of the national organizations formed in celebration of Fenton Art Glass. The Fenton Art Glass Collectors of America (FAGCA) was chartered in 1977. With 20 local chapters, the organization has over 5,000 current members.

The National Fenton Glass Society was formed in 1990 and incorporated in Ohio in 1991.

Fenton Art Glass will celebrate its 90th birthday in 1995 by offering a limited edition of art glass pieces. New shapes and decorations will be limited to one-year production. With the firm's 100th birthday just down the road, the Fenton family and their dedicated employees pledge to continue developing exciting glass colors — and unique limited edition shapes — for all those who appreciate the beauty of handmade glass.

Fitz And Floyd
Today's Treasures Becoming Tomorrow's Heirlooms

For those who enjoy decorating their tables with the newest and trendiest fine china, Fitz and Floyd has long been a favorite firm. But in recent years, the artists of this thirty-plus year old company have broken new ground in the creation of three-dimensional works of collectible art.

Fitz and Floyd launched its collectibles division in 1991 with its first annual Christmas ornament. Limited to 7,200 pieces worldwide, the edition sold out in under five months. Two years later, Fitz and Floyd already boasted more than ninety individual items in its collectibles division. Thus the firm is rapidly becoming an important resource for collectors.

The giftware and collectibles of Fitz and Floyd are renowned for their amazing detail work. The firm's artists spare no expense or time in the creation of intricate pieces, even though that means the development of many distinct attachments that are molded, painted, fired separately and then permanently affixed to create a complex, finished figure or decorative work of art.

The unique look of Fitz and Floyd stems from the artistry of innovators like Terry Kerr and Vicky Balcou. Kerr is the creator of the firm's incredibly popular "White House Teapot," as well as its *A Christmas Carol* holiday grouping. Ms. Balcou is the designer of Fitz and Floyd's first porcelain lighted Christmas village, *Holiday Hamlet*™.

Terry Kerr: Sculptor and Collector of Holiday Artwork

Designer and artist Terry Kerr attended Southern Methodist University in the early 1970s where he studied fine arts. He also enrolled in the gifted artists program of the Dallas Museum of Art. After working in advertising, packaging design and visual merchandising/display for several companies, Kerr began his career with Fitz and Floyd in 1977.

Kerr was brought on staff to design Fitz and Floyd's fashionable fine china as well as their unique, whimsical giftware, collectibles and decorative accessories. The artist has designed such well-known china patterns as "Cloisonne Peony" and the ever-popular "St. Nicholas" Christmas pattern. He also designed Fitz and Floyd's first Halloween giftware group.

During the 1980s, Kerr worked as a free-lance design consultant for Fitz and Floyd, Department 56, Inc. and The Franklin Mint, where he designed many collectible lines. In early 1991, he returned to Fitz and Floyd full-time where he undertook the responsibility of designing many of the company's new collectible items. He created most of the new Collector's Series limited edition teapots, as well as the latest collectible Christmas group, *A Christmas Carol*. This collection celebrates the 150th anniversary of Charles Dickens' famous story through a variety of collectibles and unique gift items.

Kerr is a native of Dallas, Texas. His outside interests include collecting Santa Claus figurines, theater and antique collecting.

Designer of Books and Gift Wrap Turns Attention to Collectibles

Artist and designer Vicky Balcou attended the University of Texas, Austin, where she received her Bachelor of Arts degree in Fine Arts. Throughout her early studies and college career, Ms. Balcou also studied privately with internationally known designers and artists.

In 1965, Ms. Balcou moved with her husband, a well-known sculptor, to Mexico City and then to El Paso, Texas where she began free-lancing as a designer and artist on special projects. She designed scholarly texts and other publications for the SMU Press at Southern Methodist University and has also worked for several graphics and advertising agencies.

In 1975, the artist joined Susan Crane, Inc., exclusively as a giftwrap designer. Her specialty was in Christmas themes, and she credits this time in her career as the inspiration for her keen sense of drawing and painting merry elves, Santa Claus and other Christmas-related items.

Vicky Balcou began her distinguished career with Fitz and Floyd as a giftware and decorative accessories designer. Recently, she also has begun to design some of the collectible lines at the company. She is best known for her *Old World Elves* giftware, as well as Fitz and Floyd's unique new lighted Christmas village, *Holiday Hamlet*™.

A native of Ft. Worth, Texas, Ms. Balcou enjoys

From the Holiday Hamlet™ collection of lighted cottages comes this delightful piece entitled "Dr. B. Well, Country Doctor." Richly detailed and hand-painted in vibrant colors, this work of art is the creation of Fitz and Floyd artist Vicky Balcou.

art, painting and mentoring her daughter in her artistic career development.

The Much-Heralded Debut of Holiday Hamlet™

Vicky Balcou's fertile imagination — and her long experience creating Christmas images — combine in her new *Holiday Hamlet™* Collection for Fitz and Floyd. All the friendly characters of this enchanting Christmas town are busily preparing for a season of happiness and merrymaking. You'll see "Dr. B. Well" and "Dr. Quack" at work, and "Mr. and Mrs. Grizzly" with their luggage in tow. And you'll see the "Parson" directing the bell choir in a joyous song. Special details set *Holiday Hamlet™* apart, too: for instance, the "Village Square Clock" features a real, working clock.

There's so much to see and do in *Holiday Hamlet™*, so collectors are invited to hop on board the "Blizzard Express" and explore the magic of Christmas. Fitz and Floyd promises that this is just a first in what will be a series of lighted cottage collections. Others on the drawing board include

Booville for Halloween, and *Candyland* for Christmas. Collectors will have ample opportunity to develop their own collections, as each piece in every series will be sold individually: nothing in sets.

A Diverse Range of Fitz and Floyd Collectibles In Many Media

From *Floppy Folks™* dolls to collector plates, from Christmas ornaments to *Holiday Hamlet™*, many collectibles from Fitz and Floyd have proven popular among collectors. For example, "The Magic of the Nutcracker," the first annual Christmas plate from Fitz and Floyd, sold out rapidly in 1992 with an edition size of 3,600 pieces. In addition, the "Nutcracker Sweets" 1992 annual Christmas ornament, second in the series, was one of the most sought-after ornaments of that year. Only 7,500 lucky collectors were able to obtain one.

Another notable work of art is "Christopher Columbus," the first edition in a series entitled *Figures From History*. It commemorated the 500th anniversary of Columbus' discovery of the Americas. With an edition limit of 7,200 pieces, its edition closed out within months of introduction.

The Charms of Fitz and Floyd Teapots, Cookie Jars and Centerpieces

Long renowned for its whimsical teapots and cookie jars, Fitz and Floyd is taking major strides toward making these categories into bona fide collecting specialties with limited editions and secondary market activity. Fitz and Floyd Marketing

This handsome "White House Teapot" caused collectors to line up for hours when its creator, Terry Kerr, appeared for a department store signing party before President Clinton's inauguration.

Six of the most popular characters from Lewis Carroll's beloved tale of Alice in Wonderland *appear in this collection of hand-painted figurines by Fitz and Floyd.*

Manager Brad Monterio reports that many collectors are creating special display units in their homes — glass shelving and glass cupboards, for example. While all of the Fitz and Floyd teapots and cookie jars are completely functional, some collectors are perceiving them more as works of art to admire rather than serviceable items. Indeed, some admirers already have collected Fitz and Floyd teapots and cookie jars for more than two decades.

Monterio got a taste of the potential for collectible teapots before President Clinton's Inauguration when artist Terry Kerr made a special autographing appearance at a department store. "We flew in several hundred teapots for the occasion, thinking that would surely be adequate. Terry was due to start signing at 11 a.m. The teapots we had were sold out before he got there, so we had to take back orders!" Monterio explained. The 5,000-piece "White House Teapot" edition was nearly sold out by mid-1993.

Fitz and Floyd also has won a place in collectors' and home decorators' hearts with its stunning, seasonal centerpieces for spring, Thanksgiving, Easter, Christmas, and other holidays and times of year. The firm makes spectacular seasonal tureens as well — but they find that many customers buy them for their ornamental value rather than for serving.

Alice in Wonderland *Collectibles Abound*

To retell the Lewis Carroll classic, *Alice in Wonderland*, Fitz and Floyd has introduced a marvelous array of collectibles including everything from collector plates and cookie jars to teapots and toby jugs. There's the "Queen of Hearts Cookie Jar," and the "Mad Hatter Tea Party Teapot" with sugar and creamer featuring the "Hatter" and "Alice in Wonderland" herself.

A set of six collectible *Alice in Wonderland* figurines portray the king and queen, Alice herself, the mad hatter, white rabbit, and Cheshire cat — each masterfully and colorfully hand-painted. There are even "Alice in Wonderland" *Floppy Folks™* collectible bean bag dolls of "White Rabbit," "Cheshire Cat" and "Mad Hatter," each with his own wicker chair.

As one of the brightest new stars on the collectibles horizon, Fitz and Floyd is off to an impressive start with its first few years of innovative designs in a wide range of art and decorative categories. For the future, the sky is the limit — as Fitz and Floyd's gifted artists stretch their imagination both for subject matter and media.

FJ Designs
Faline Jones' Cat's Meow Village:
The Purr-fect Collectibles for Cat Lovers

Just like an architect or city planner, Faline Jones has developed a Master Blueprint for her very successful line of two-dimensional, miniature historical buildings. And true to their name of Cat's Meow *Village*, each appealing little building features a tiny black feline resting on a window ledge or waiting patiently at the door. As sure as paw prints on a freshly washed auto, these marks are the sign that the piece has been touched by the artistry of Faline Jones.

Faline (or "Feline" — as some people pronounce it!) Jones, the originator of the Cat's Meow *Village*, began the business she now runs with her husband, Terry, in the fall of 1982 in the basement of their Wooster, Ohio home. Beginning with a $39 piece of pine and her grandfather's old band saw, she designed, cut, painted and stenciled sets of miniature wooden buildings and sold them as quickly as they could be supplied to local gift shops. Terry Jones helped with buying and cutting the wood, and he devised a way to spraypaint the background colors in their garage. From this modest beginning, their business grew to employ 200 people.

The firm's "cat connection" stems from its owner's great love of felines. "Casper," Ms. Jones' brown and white tabby, inspired her firm's logo, and at times her household has been home to as many as eight cats at once.

Cat's Meow Architecture Takes on Historic Significance and Secondary Market Value

The phenomenal growth of Faline and Terry Jones' business over the next several years reads like a textbook chapter on the triumph of the free enterprise system. Beginning with a display of their *Village* wares at the 1983 Columbus Gift Mart, they were swamped with orders and forced to find a more efficient way to meet the demand for their product.

The Gift Mart success allowed Ms. Jones to move operations out of her basement and into the back room of another business in 1984, only to take over that entire building's space within the year. Two years later, her husband, formerly an

auto parts salesman, officially joined the company, taking over personnel and maintenance operations. By the spring of 1989 the business had once more outgrown its facilities. The reputation of Cat's Meow had spread across the country, and a new building was constructed to house its then 120-member team of employees.

By this time not only the location of the business but also the product itself had undergone a change. In the first two years of her business, Ms. Jones' miniature buildings were personal interpretations. Each might feature elements of architectural detail from buildings that she admired, but none really existed. However, starting the third year, she began to pattern her designs after actual buildings and historic landmarks. From this impulse, the concept of the *Village* developed. Now each January a ten-piece Series is introduced, designated with a Roman numeral corresponding with the number of years FJ Designs has been in business. Each *Village* series of ten buildings faithfully reproduces examples of typical American architecture, chosen with respect for the craftsmanship, commerce, culture and activities that are part of every community.

The Williamsburg *series from FJ Designs pays tribute to these* historic Virginia buildings: front row, "Bruton Parish Church" and "Governor's Palace;" back row, "Raleigh Tavern" and "Grissel Hay Lodging House."

Also in January or June, a four-piece Theme Series is introduced to highlight a particular subject, such as lighthouses or barns, or a cultural pocket of America, such as Nantucket or Washington, D.C. One or two national charitable organizations are selected (based on the theme of the series) to receive a portion of the first year profits from the sale of these Series. Inspired by the restored Colonial village of Williamsburg, Virginia, Faline Jones recently introduced one of these four-piece collections: the *Williamsburg* series. Featured buildings include "Bruton Parish Church," "Grissel Hay Lodging House," "Raleigh Tavern," and "Governor's Palace."

In addition, eight to ten new accessory pieces are added yearly, and the annual *Christmas* series appears every June 1 and is closed on December 31. The *Christmas* series has the shortest issue time of any Cat's Meow Series, thus creating high demand in the primary and retired secondary market sales.

The collectibility of the *Village* pieces began to increase as Ms. Jones devised a system of retiring old patterns as new ones were developed. As new series and accessories are introduced each year, an equivalent amount are retired, so ever-changing street scenes are the result. The normal life span of a *Village* piece is approximately five years, and the regular product line includes roughly one hundred houses and seventy-five accessories at any given time.

Travel and Study Fuel Faline Jones' Creativity

Although today designs are developed by staff designers who use computers to aid in the process, Ms. Jones has final approval over all patterns. She also chooses the buildings that will be reproduced, after extensive library research as well as study of her vast store of literature on historical places and architecture, postcards, newspaper clippings, photographs and books. The artist also garners fresh inspiration from the historic buildings in towns she visits.

To develop a new series, Ms. Jones selects about 100 suitable buildings from her collection and then narrows this group down to just ten. Once her staff develops designs from the ten buildings that meet with her approval, the designers construct a paper pattern with specifications for the work to be done and a black and white design for screen printing. Then, the paper patterns are used to cut the pieces. Each building is sanded smooth and spray painted in one of the soft colonial colors

used for the entire *Village* Series. Crisp touches of black and white are screen printed to highlight structural details such as archways, Palladian windows and clapboard siding. Roofs are finished off either by hand-brushing or dipping.

Every building is designed within a 6" x 6" scale and is cut from a 1/4" thick piece of medium density fiberboard. Each piece is finished both front and back, resulting in a two-dimensional effect, and allowing collectors to display their pieces where they are visible from all angles. A flat finish is used, and since no overcoat varnishes are applied, the buildings must be handled and stored with care. To help collectors identify authentic Cat's Meow *Village* buildings, each is stamped on the bottom with a copyright stamp indicating the year of introduction, and including the Cat's Meow name, the building name and the name of the series to which it belongs.

In addition to the buildings themselves, collectors can people their miniature towns with children building a snowman, a load of kids on the "School of Hard Knox" bus, or a proper Victorian nanny airing the baby. All accessories — which also include trees, old-time street signs and picket fences — are reproduced in the same muted golds, blues, greens and brick reds of the *Village* buildings.

Now Collectors May Experience Chippewa Lake Amusement Park

The oldest amusement park in the United States has been recreated in all its glory by Faline Jones in her collection entitled *Chippewa Lake Amusement Park*. The park was built beginning in 1875 between Akron and Cleveland, along the largest natural lake in Ohio. It was named for the Chippewa Indians who hunted and fished in the area. While the heyday of the amusement park extended from the 1920s to the 1950s, today Chippewa Lake's buildings lay quietly waiting to be revived, and a portion of the profits from this Series' first year sales will be contributed to those revitalization and rebuilding efforts.

The four *Chippewa Lake Amusement Park* buildings include the "Pavilion," "Midway," "Bath House," and "Ball Room." These are the buildings that served as anchors for visitors' fun, and landmarks for the beloved park itself. Ms. Jones explains her reasons for selecting these particular structures: "The pavilion was built out over the lake, where picnickers could enjoy the water while eating. I have portrayed the side where many game and food concessions stands came and went. The heartbeat of any amusement park is the midway. I

have depicted several attractions that were part of Chippewa Lake over the years.

"The Bath House contained boys' dormitory rooms upstairs. Pug Rentner and Cliff (Gip) Battles (Pro Football Hall of Famers) worked a few seasons at the park as lifeguards during the day and Ball Room bouncers at night. In 1937 Lawrence Welk held his first radio broadcast from the Starlight Ball Room. Vaughn Monroe played to a sell-out crowd of 5,400 dancers during the 1940s."

The National Cat's Meow Collector's Club Grows in Popularity and Membership

To accommodate the increasing number of *Village* collectors, FJ Designs formed The National Cat's Meow Collector's Club in June of 1989. By the end of that year, over 4,000 collectors had joined. The club continues to grow today with over 18,000 members nationally. Dealers who belong to the club display a redemption center decal provided by FJ Designs. "That tells us we are definitely in the collector's market at this point, and we are working on our secondary resale market next," Ms. Jones says.

An official membership card is included in the club's $22 membership fee, along with a notebook filled with current collection history sheets (background information on individual buildings), a personal checklist to keep track of collections, a year's subscription to the colorful club newsletter, "The Village Mews," a buying list of all custom designs, a redemption card for that year's four-piece series produced exclusively for members, and a lapel pin or tote bag.

Faline Jones Selects Village Dealers With Extra Care

"In order for our product to sell in a store, you need to know the histories behind the houses and have an interest to pass along to the customers," Faline Jones explains. That is why she primarily selects small to mid-size gift shops to carry the *Village* collectibles. Currently, these pieces are sold in forty-eight states and retail between $8 and $12.

To ensure that her dealers have whimsical stories to tell, Ms. Jones often adds her own imaginative and playful personal touches to her line of miniatures. For example, the *Village VI History* collection features the "Stiffenbody Funeral Home." And an "FJ Realty Company" was included in the *1990 Series VIII* collection. "We joke with local

Issued to recreate the fun of Chippewa Lake Amusement Park, these works of art include: front row, "Chippewa Lake Sign" and "Midway;" second row, "Pavilion," "Bath House" and "Ball Room."

realtors about how many houses we sell in a year," Ms. Jones explains, "so I thought we'd better set up a realty company just to make things legitimate."

Dealers May Request Special Pieces from FJ Designs

FJ Designs responds to customer needs by offering a unique custom service opportunity. Cat's Meow dealers may request a special individual piece or a small special theme series. For a fee, the company will design and produce a minimum of 150 copies for which that store will have exclusive sales rights.

Custom work has become an increasingly large part of FJ Designs' business. In 1992, replicas of 1,000 buildings from across the country were reproduced: more than twice as many as in 1990. Some of the more unusual items in this eclectic collection include the "Big Chicken" Kentucky Fried Chicken building near Atlanta, Georgia, the Lancaster County Prison in Pennsylvania and the Ohio State Football Stadium complete with the OSU band.

The popularity of the Cat's Meow *Village* Collection continues to grow as FJ Designs expands its line of products and works hard to please customers. And for Faline Jones, there is no city limit boundary to inhibit the number of her miniature historical treasures. "Every piece in the Cat's Meow *Village* has a little bit of history," she says. "There is always something new to add about the American way of life. Just as history is never ending, neither is the *Village*.

Flambro Imports Inc.
Popular Art Studio Boasts Successful Alliances With Emmett Kelly, Jr., Joan Berg Victor and Dennis Fairweather

The strength of Flambro Imports always has rested with its wonderful subjects and artists. The "Weary Willie" clowns of Emmett Kelly, Jr....the nostalgic Americana of Joan Berg Victor's *Pleasantville 1893*...and now the delightfully British sculptures of Dennis Fairweather. On the eve of Emmett Kelly, Jr.'s seventieth birthday, Flambro presents its remarkable collection of three-dimensional art for the mid-1990s.

Happy Birthday, Emmett Kelly, Jr.!

He's been a clown for thirty-three years. At sixty-nine, he's an institution — with a line of collectibles bearing his likeness; an animated Christmas special in production; and a legion of fans around the world. Emmett Kelly, Jr. also is one of the few characters ever to be immortalized in porcelain while still alive. And in 1994 — to mark his seventieth birthday — the Emmett Kelly, Jr. Collectors' Society will spend three days (November 4, 5 and 6) celebrating their hero in Atlanta, Georgia.

Kelly was the child of a famous family: born November 13, 1924 in Dyersburg, Tennessee, to the beloved clown Emmett Kelly, Sr. The older Kelly originated the character of "Weary Willie," and Emmett Jr.'s mother, Eva May Moore Kelly, was in an aerial act for the same company — the John Robinson Circus.

While many of his fans suppose that Emmett Jr. was a clown from childhood on, he did not make his debut as "Weary Willie" until 1960. Before then, he had served in the Navy during World War II, and worked as a waiter and railroad man. Encouraged and trained by his father, Emmett Jr. debuted in the 1960 circus festival in Peru, Indiana.

Under the tutelage of both his father and their manager and agent, Leonard Green, Emmett spent the next three years criss-crossing the United States with "Austin's Motor Derby." In 1963, he was the featured performer of the Hagen-Wallace Circus. His biggest break came in 1964 when he spent a year appearing in the Kodak booth of the World's Fair Pavilion in Flushing, New York.

During that time he set two world's records. It was estimated that more than 5,000,000 photos were taken of him, making Emmett the world's most photographed person. He was also the subject of the world's largest photo — a 30' x 36' picture that lit up the side of the Kodak pavilion.

For years after the close of the World's Fair, Emmett continued to act as Kodak's Ambassador of Goodwill — visiting over 2,400 children's and Veteran's hospitals. It was probably the most rewarding time of his clowning career. His most spectacular story is this.

"There was this one little girl...must have been about twelve years old. It was in a hospital in New Orleans," he recalls. Kelly walked to her bedside, but was told the girl had been in a coma for three months: couldn't see, hear, talk, or understand. Kelly autographed one of his postcards and put it

"The Vigilante" Emmett Kelly, Jr. figurine can be purchased only from an authorized EKJ Collectors Center during a Personal Appearance by America's favorite clown. Kelly loves nothing better than to autograph these figurines at the time of purchase. "The Vigilante" shows Kelly living the life of two American folklore characters: half hobo, half cowboy.

These three figurines capture the heartwarming charm of "Weary Willie" as he clowns through life. From left, they are: "The World Traveler," "Kittens for Sale," and "After the Parade."

between her fingers. Then he walked away. As soon as he left the room she opened her eyes, looked up at a priest and asked, "Who was that man?" The priest told her, "Honey, that was an angel in a clown suit."

The story doesn't end there. Years later, Kelly met a girl performing as a mime and twirling batons. She told him that she was the same girl he had awakened that day in the hospital!

Emmett Kelly, Jr. started his own circus after the World's Fair, and named it The All-Star Circus. It was the only circus to appear at the White House and it played there twice: in 1972 for Tricia Nixon Cox, and in 1973 for the White House Easter Egg Hunt.

These days, besides promoting the Flambro collectibles line, Kelly is a resident of Tombstone, Arizona. There he is an active member of a group called the Tombstone Vigilantes — a non-profit civic group that donates eighty percent of its income to charities and other local causes.

Among the many benefits of Society membership is a subscription to the "EKJournal" publication, as well as the opportunity to acquire Members Only figurines. For 1993, the figurine available exclusively to members of the EKJ Collectors' Society was "The Ringmaster," which depicts Emmett and his old friend, Count Nicholas. The Count, now eighty-three, was a famous Ringmaster of Ringling and Cole Brothers circuses and worked with Emmett for many years.

They continue to be close friends.

Also new for 1993 from Flambro and EKJ was a collection entitled *Real Rags*, crafted in a fabric maché medium. The medium combines a resin figurine with a costume in actual stiffened fabric, and it is elaborately accessorized. The initial introduction was five pieces: "Looking Out to See 2," "Sweeping Up 2," "Thinker 2," and "Big Business 2," as well as "Checking His List," a new Christmas design. All of these, except the Christmas design, are re-creations of early EKJ Limited Editions in porcelain, all of which were sold out and retired but are still extremely popular poses of America's Favorite Clown.

On tap for 1994 are several pieces: Limited Edition, Member's Only, and the 1994 dated ornament, all commemorating Emmett's landmark seventieth birthday. The birthday limited edition entitled "Let Him Eat Cake" is one of the most elaborate figurines ever produced by Flambro. The Member's Only figurine, "Birthday Mail," is cleverly designed as well.

From The Imagination of Joan Berg Victor: Pleasantville 1893

Imagine a village that captures all the warmth and simplicity of small-town American life at the turn-of-the-century. Joan Berg Victor has done just that in *Pleasantville 1893*, created exclusively for Flambro Imports. As Ms. Victor explains, "*Pleas-*

antville 1893 invites the reader and collector to be a part of a time a hundred years ago — to learn about life in the make-believe town of Pleasantville, to get to know the townsfolk and their way of life. I welcome young families and individuals to learn, to laugh, and to share in the fun and fantasy of this uniquely charming collection."

Joan Berg Victor's environment, family, education and experience all have been valuable in influencing her to create this wonderful make-believe town. Her interest in collecting antiques is evident in her stories of life at the turn-of-the-century in her village of Pleasantville.

Ms. Victor was brought up in the Midwest and earned her undergraduate degree with honors from Newcomb College, the Women's College of Tulane University. There she not only received academic awards, but also was elected Miss Tulane. At Yale University, she was awarded a Master of Fine Arts degree with honors.

The drawings and paintings of Joan Berg Victor can be found in private and museum collections all over the country, not to mention having appeared in publications such as *Fortune* magazine, "The New York Times," and "The Wall Street Journal."

Through the years, Ms. Victor has written and illustrated over two dozen books. Her first books were created for young children and as her own two children, Daniel and Elizabeth, got older, her books were adapted to suit their level of interest. Her favorite book, of course, is the one about Pleasantville: it deals on a personal level with all ages, and can be enjoyed by most readers.

The year 1993 marked the "Centennial Celebration" for Pleasantville, with a host of vignettes titled "The Storybook Village," "Main Street," "Orchard Street," "Elm Street," "River Road" and "Balcomb's Farm." There are also many appealing "Townsfolk" and "Accessories" to add warmth and realism to the home display. In addition, there are a number of heartwarming ornaments depicting "An 1890s Christmas" in Pleasantville. For 1994, Flambro Imports has previewed the beautiful "Sacred Heart Rectory," "Sacred Heart Catholic Church," as well as assorted choirboys, priests and nuns as "Townsfolk."

To celebrate the Centennial of Pleasantville, the Pleasantville Historical Preservation Society was formed with a wide range of benefits including "free home delivery" of the "Pleasantville Gazette," an exclusive, members-only "Pleasantville Gazette" building and much more.

Flambro Imports added "Balcomb's Farm" to the Pleasantville 1893 collection in 1993. This perfect pastoral scene includes The Balcomb Farmhouse, Barn, Silo, Hen House, Ice House, Outhouse and farm accessories.

Flambro Forms International Strategic Alliance

In 1993, Flambro Imports joined forces with the Bronze Age Company, Ltd. of Galashiels, Scotland, which is headed by internationally acclaimed artist and sculptor, Peter Fagan. In 1985, Fagan expanded the company to include Colour Box Miniatures, Ltd., one of Britain's major giftware companies, and Cavalcade Limited, a multi-theme giftware manufacturing and marketing company.

The Cavalcade "portfolio" includes collections from international artists such as Dennis Fairweather, who has developed a number of collections including *British Blighters*. Fairweather figurines are regarded as the market leaders in their class for original design, quality and lasting, timeless appeal. They are collected worldwide by those who appreciate the craftsmanship behind the *British Blighters* — a motley crew of humorous caricatures. Fairweather also has created the *Mr. Stubbs* line — caricatures of an amusing 19th-century Britisher "born to pursue pleasure."

Cavalcade also hosts American sculptress Martha Carey and United Kingdom humorist Malcom Bowmer, who was the first sculptor to join Cavalcade with his *Eggbert* range of character figurines. Cavalcade also boasts the license for the "Looney Tunes" characters of Warner Brothers. Flambro will be the exclusive U.S.A. distributor for Bronze Age.

Forma Vitrum

Forma Vitrum and Artist Bill Job Create Excitement in Stained Glass Not Seen Since the Days of Louis C. Tiffany

Stained glass artist Bill Job first came to the attention of the worldwide press in May of 1992. The *Wall Street Journal Asia* reported on this artist from Tennessee who had moved his family to China to fulfill a lifelong dream: to integrate the language and customs of China with Western style management in order to build a successful company.

The Chinese government selected Bill Job as one of the first Americans to receive permission to own a company in China. Then it was up to Bill to decide what products his company should create. He decided to focus on stained glass products for two reasons. First, Bill's background in carpentry and woodworking gave him an appreciation for handcrafted products. Second, Bill discovered that most Chinese workers are very patient and talented craftspeople — skills that are necessary when making intricate products.

"Trinity Church," released in the fall of 1994, is a limited edition of 7,000. Made from over 233 pieces of glass, this church is the first to incorporate fusing glass on glass to create a look of stone. The cathedral window is made from tiny chips of glass fused to create this look. Also shown are flowering trees and shrubs and cast bronze figures.

Bill Job's Desire to Make Exquisite Quality Stained Glass Affordable

Stained glass pieces are very time consuming to make and require patience as well as artistic skills. For this reason, most well-made stained glass products are too expensive for the average person to own. Bill Job was convinced that he could change this fact. He attended glass shows in the United States to learn more about glass crafting techniques. In 1989, less than one year after he had been given a license to run his own company, Bill put together a team of talented craftspeople to construct stained glass products.

The basic techniques used in Forma Vitrum's products have not changed since the innovations made by Louis Comfort Tiffany in the 1800s. Each piece of glass is scored and cut into the desired shape, then wrapped in a copper foil tape and soldered together into the pattern desired. Next a patina is used to blacken the solder by causing it to oxidize. A silicon oil is then applied to seal the solder and stop the oxidation process. After a final inspection, the brass signature plate is attached, and the number of the piece is hand-engraved.

The early work done by Bill Job and his employees consisted primarily of creating Tiffany reproduction lampshades for American and European customers. Producing these lamps was wonderful training for Bill Job and his craftspeople, but Bill was still searching for a new way to introduce stained glass into the hearts and homes of more Americans. He began making decorative items for the home: sun catchers, stained glass panels and little houses that were lit from within. His wife Kitty and his daughters, Patti and Christy, fell in love with the little houses and convinced Bill that they might be appreciated as beautiful pieces of art in homes everywhere. Bill soon realized he had found an intriguing way to introduce people to the beauty of stained glass.

Bill Job Meets David MacMahan: A Friendship and Forma Vitrum Are Formed

In January 1993, Bill packed up some of his glass houses and traveled to the Los Angeles Gift Show. He displayed his houses in a small booth hoping to attract the interest of buyers. After a few days at the

"Thompson's Drug Store," a limited edition of 5,000, incorporates 219 pieces of glass and pewter attachments. The cornerstone of Forma Vitrum's Vitreville *collection is shown with a line of pewter signs and accessories and a set of ornamental pines, maple and oak trees.*

show, Bill was disappointed as he had not met anyone who shared his passion for the glass houses.

However, fate has a way of working according to its own plan — the man who would market Bill's products didn't stop at Bill's booth. They met when they shared a table in the cafeteria.

David MacMahan was at the Los Angeles Gift Show promoting products he had invented throughout the 1980s — gadgets and toys that made people laugh and deal with stress. Featured in *Newsweek*, *People Magazine* and other publications, millions of these items, which talked, cheered and made funny noises, had been sold. But as the '90s began, David noticed that people were focusing more on products of quality and lasting value. He had been pondering on the changes in the U.S. market and how he should change his product to reflect these changes, when he decided to take a break from the show in the cafeteria. David sat next to a man who seemed friendly, and the two began a conversation about their experiences at the show.

As the two men talked, they realized how their situations complemented each other — David was searching for a new product line of high quality, and Bill needed someone skilled in the areas of marketing and promotion. David walked with Bill back to his small booth and instantly fell in love with the beautiful stained glass houses. Bill and David spent the rest of the day and evening talking and brainstorming together, and they realized how compatible their business philosophies were. Both men took great pride in building success based on honesty, integrity and innovation. At the end of the show,

Bill and David shook hands and became business partners.

Their new company was named Forma Vitrum, which is Latin for "beautiful glass." The stained glass buildings were divided into two groups: the *Vitreville* collection and *The Woodland Village*. Because each piece of art is handcrafted, it was obvious that only limited quantities of so many designs could be made. It was determined that each piece would have a signature plate and would be sequentially numbered after final inspection. A Certificate of Authenticity and a registration form for a future collectors club would accompany each piece.

The Vitreville Collection Grows Like a Traditional Small Town in America: One Building at a Time

The *Vitreville* collection began with homes for residents of the town. Bill and David decided the town should be built the way small towns grew up in America. Each home had to reflect a traditional style and quality characteristic of people who built houses to last generations. Each house would be named after the profession of the resident living within it. Once the houses were completed, churches, lighthouses and other buildings were added.

Two of the initial buildings in the *Vitreville* collection were retired in January of 1994. "The Bavarian Chapel" and "Pillars of Faith" were retired after approximately 2,400 of each design was produced. By March of 1994, they were completely sold out. These two pieces have simpler lines and less detail than the later introductions.

The Lighthouses Form a Collection Called Coastal Classics

The lighthouses Bill designed for *Vitreville* became so popular that it was decided that they should stand alone as a separate collection. While Bill may be inspired by specific lighthouses he has seen, the designs are not meant to represent any known lighthouses. They are for the enjoyment of those who love nautical themes.

Vitreville's *Limited Editions Showcase Bill Job's Increasing Skill and Creativity*

Three Limited Edition pieces, "The Country Church" (12,500), "Thompson's Drug Store" (5,000) and "The Trinity Church" (7,000) have been introduced in 1993 and 1994. These three buildings represent some of Bill's best designs, and each con-

tains innovative developments in stained glass construction. The fused rooftops and "stone treatment" on the churches along with the cast pewter attachments for window, sign and balcony treatments are all-new innovations in stained glass techniques.

The Woodland Village Series: Because There's a Child's Imagination Within All of Us

The second series of homes is entitled *The Woodland Village*. This collection appeals to the whimsical side of people. The story behind the collection centers on an imaginary village located in a heavily wooded forest. The people of the village are tiny and live happily in the forest, free from illness and crime. They have a true appreciation for nature and all beautiful things as evidenced by the houses they build. Each home is named after the forest animal the family admires most. The houses in this tiny village are so beautiful at night that the tiny residents sleep during the day so they can be awake at night to enjoy the warm, colorful glow from their homes.

The houses in *The Woodland Village* are crafted from ArtGlass, which has even richer and brighter colors than stained glass. These houses have become a favorite for children who light up their cottages at night as comforting night lights.

The Accessories: Carrying Intricate Detail Beyond the Buildings

Once the collections reached stores in the United States, requests came in immediately for accessories. Collectors needed people, trees, signs and fences to make their village beautiful all year. So signs, clocks, lampposts and fences were made of cast pewter. Tremendous energy was spent on creating the most realistic trees and shrubs possible, with different seasons represented by having trees in fall and winter foliage, as well as spring flowering shrubs and trees. *Vitreville* residents were meticulously created out of bronze. The pewter and bronze accessories are hand-painted, and their quality parallels that found in the stained glass buildings.

Vitreville, *The Woodland Village* and *Coastal Classics* were designed to enrich a home all year long. In the same classical style of a Tiffany lamp or a cathedral window, these pieces inspire a feeling of warmth and richness unmatched by other home accessories. As a collector of Forma Vitrum products, the more you know about glass, the skill and time needed to make each structure, and the life of the artist, the more you will value each piece in your collection. To truly fall in love with this classic artform, just darken a room, light your houses and enter a wonderland of color, light and beauty only possible through stained glass.

"Sailor's Knoll," "The Carolina Lighthouse" and "Lookout Point" from Forma Vitrum's Coastal Classics collection are the perfect addition to any decor or nautical setting. They can also be used as a night light. Complementing the collection are the bronze figures of "Luther the Lookout" and "Seaworthy Silas."

The Franklin Mint
A Never-Ending Universe of Personal Treasures for the 21st-Century and Beyond

Although it may have begun with a smooth, shiny stone brought home to a cave to be examined, cherished and displayed, the art of collecting is an ancient joy that has evolved into an enduring source of personal enjoyment and pride.

As the world expanded, so did the need and ability to own and cherish personal treasures. That shining stone became a glittering jewel...taken from the earth and carefully cut and faceted to extraordinary splendor. Or it inspired a sculpture to depict a memory, a milestone, a magic moment in life.

From native folk art to rich oil paintings... exquisite Fabergé eggs created for royalty to beautiful lifelike wooden decoys, created to enhance the hunt and sustain life...in every civilization, every generation, new works of art have risen to take their place in the hearts of humankind.

So, too, has risen a fine art studio dedicated to providing incomparable works of artistic and historic significance that are destined to become the prized heirlooms of tomorrow. The award-winning artists of The Franklin Mint use the skill of their hands and the love in their hearts to create treasures of timeless beauty...and endless fascination.

As the millennium approaches, these gifted artisans commit themselves to providing the world with the most extraordinary personal luxury items for today...tomorrow...and forever.

Ideas Take Flight on Wings of the Imagination

The Franklin Mint is a place where dreams begin. Located deep within the heart of the historic Brandywine River Valley, The Franklin Mint is the home of some of the most talented people in the world. Artists in every discipline — designers, sculptors, jewelers, engravers, medallists, doll and model makers — work together in an environment of unlimited creative freedom...and endless inspiration.

In their quest for perfection, these individuals create works of art to which few can compare. Extraordinary sculpture in porcelain, pewter, crystal and bronze. The world's finest commemorative coins and stamps. Authentic replicas of historic masterpieces. Award-winning heirloom dolls. Books handcrafted in old-world tradition. Collector plates of universal appeal. Furnishings of uncompromising quality and craftsmanship for the home. The ultimate in die-cast automotive classics. Jewelry ablaze with the most precious of gems ...gleaming with the richness of gold and silver. Classic games the whole family can share and enjoy. Acquisitions of taste, beauty and supreme artistry. Personal treasures destined to command attention...and admiration.

"Catherine Rose" is a collector doll that brings to life the splendor of the Victorian era. Designed by doll artist Janet Johnson, Catherine's delicate features are sculpted and hand-painted in fine bisque porcelain. Her hand-set gray-blue eyes sparkle like radiant jewels. Her rose-red lips are a wondrous contrast to her creamy white complexion — as if sweetly kissed to a blush by chilly winter winds. "Catherine Rose" stands 15" and has a custom designed ensemble of luxurious emerald-green velvet. Her coat, hat and muff are richly accented with glittering golden embroidery and golden soutache. Her genuine leather spats of dark brown leather are embroidered with swirling golden accents. This heirloom doll is available for $195.

The Franklin Mint Joins Forces With Prestigious Organizations Worldwide

The achievements of great artists, distinguished organizations and master craftspeople are shared with collectors around the world through the resources of The Franklin Mint. Beautiful showpieces include those from The Vatican in Rome, and masterworks from renowned art museums like the Louvre in Paris and the Victoria and Albert in London. Franklin collectors also share in the majesty of time-honored institutions with the House of Faberge, The House of Coppini, and The Princess Grace Foundation.

Models authorized by Rolls-Royce, Mercedes-Benz, General Motors, Lamborghini and Ferrari grace The Franklin Mint list of offerings, as do works created in collaboration with important environmental causes like the World Wildlife Fund, the Humane Society and Conservation International.

Fabulous fashion classics from Franklin emerge in creative coalition with Bill Blass, Adolpho, Givenchy, Bob Mackie, Hanae Mori and Mary McFadden. The Franklin Mint classics of literature include famed works of Pulitzer Prize-winning authors like Norman Mailer, E. L. Doctrow and John Updike. And inspiring masterpieces, from world-renowned artists including Norman Rockwell, Andrew Wyeth, Erté and Peter Max, also intrigue Franklin collectors.

The Great American Freedom Machine, "The Harley-Davidson Heritage Softail Classic," features the classic "Fat Bob" fuel tank and Softail suspension system. Replicated in 1:10 scale, this is the first and only official die-cast replica of this fabulous motorcycle authorized by Harley-Davidson. "The Harley-Davidson Softail Classic" is available exclusively from Franklin Mint Precision Models and sells for $120.

Franklin Creates International Commemorative Treasures

Much of The Franklin Mint's finest work involves the creation of commemorative art — for governments, major museums, and prestigious organizations on all seven continents. Commemorative partners include the United Nations, the International Olympic Committee, the Royal Geographic Society and the World Wildlife Fund.

Franklin Mint originals honor those who share the spirit of heritage and pride such as The White House Historical Association, the National Historical Society and the Western Heritage Museum. Franklin also shares in the concerns of distinguished environmental organizations as The Kabuki National Theatre, La Scala in Milan and the Royal Shakespeare Theatre.

In search of treasures from the Far East and the Wild West...from the frozen North to the deep South...from the Caribbean to the Gold Coast and from enchanted fairy tale kingdoms to the realms of royalty, The Franklin Mint scans the globe to create works of art to touch the innermost places of the heart.

Discoveries of Art Lost... But Not Forgotten

The Franklin Mint has never forgotten that the traditions of the past inspire the creations of today...and the treasures of tomorrow. Thus, from the ancient civilizations of the Egyptians and Etruscans, come new works to rival those buried for thousands of years.

From the depths of Atlantis to the gods of ancient Greece and Rome come new masterpieces of sculpture to rival those found only in the world's most prestigious museums and private collections. From the dynasties of the Ming to priceless works created for the Czars of Imperial Russia come porcelains of incomparable beauty and splendor.

From the masters of the Renaissance to sparkling reflections of the New Age come treasures that speak of power...and individual achievement. From Asia's mighty warriors to America's legendary heroes come works of history, heritage and pride.

Award-Winning Collector's Treasures of Timeless Beauty...and Universal Appeal

Since its founding, The Franklin Mint has brought pleasure and enjoyment to millions of collectors the world over, with works of art that bring

"Scrabble, The Classic Collector's Edition," fully authorized and authenticated by the Milton Bradley Company, is the first and only classic collector's edition of America's favorite word game. Available only from The Franklin Mint, this edition features a handsome hardwood-framed playing board mounted on a turntable base. All 100 letter tiles are spectacularly minted into ingots and embellished with 24K gold. Complete with a player's dictionary and official score sheets, "The Classic Collector's Edition" of Scrabble sells for $555.

to life the most memorable characters that have touched our hearts.

These include the legendary Scarlett O'Hara and the dashing Rhett Butler from the most romantic love story of all time — *Gone With The Wind*. With Dorothy and Toto, the Tin Man, Scarecrow and the Cowardly Lion from the unforgettable *Wizard Of Oz*. Re-creating the world-famous illustrations of Charles Dana Gibson, whose art set the standard of beauty at the turn-of-the-century with the legendary Gibson Girl.

Franklin also works exclusively with one of America's favorite doll artists, the beloved "Sparkle Queen," Maryse Nicole. And with some of Europe's most famous doll artists, including Sylvia Natterer and Gerda Neubacher.

Collectors enjoy timeless tributes to such legends of the silver screen as The Duke, John Wayne. And with portraits that recapture all the glamour of the one — the only — Marilyn Monroe. All in all, a collection of works of art with a precious heritage...and a never-ending future of beauty.

"Vehicles of the Imagination" For Those Who Dare to Dream

For those driven to new heights of excitement and new levels of achievement, Franklin Mint Precision Models are simply miles ahead. These fine die-cast automotive replicas include classics from the past, like the Rolls-Royce Silver Ghost,

the Mercedes Gullwing, the Ford Model T, the Duesenberg Twenty Grand, and all-American legends like Harley-Davidson, the Petty Nascar, the Cadillac Eldorado and the Chevrolet Bel Air.

Franklin also presents Europe's elite dream machines: the fabulous Ferrari, the Porsche 911 and the Bugatti Royale. Collectors get on the fast track with The Southern Crescent, fly high with Shoo-shoo Baby, and put out fires with the Ahrens-Fox Fire Engine. In addition, there are daring innovations like the Lamborghini Countach, and America's hottest sports car, the Corvette Sting Ray.

Personal Treasures to Touch the Heart of the Child in All of Us

The Franklin Mint works together with those at the forefront of the entertainment industry: Paramount Pictures, Twentieth Century Fox and Turner Home Entertainment. And Franklin shares a partnership with great "families" like Warner Brothers and Parker Brothers to bring to life some of the most lovable characters of all time: the Jetsons, the Flintstones, the Road Runner, and Bugs Bunny, just to name a few.

Franklin creates classic games the whole family will share and enjoy such as the Collector's Edition of "The Looney Tunes Chess Set," and with all-time family favorites like Scrabble and Monopoly.

Creating magic with the one and only Walt Disney Company, Franklin pays tribute to Walt Disney's genius with sculpture and dolls of sheer enchantment like Mickey and Minnie Mouse, the beautiful Snow White and the unforgettable Cinderella.

Stewart and Lynda Rae Resnick Lead The Franklin Mint

The Franklin Mint is guided by Lynda and Stewart Resnick, who serve as Vice Chairman and Chairman. As such, they are committed to preserving and honoring the great artistic and historical traditions of the past — and to creating new works of art for today's collector. They are also community and civic leaders, lending their talents, support and expertise to institutions including The National Gallery of Art, The Metropolitan Museum of Art and The Los Angeles County Museum of Art. As the 21st century approaches, Mr. and Mrs. Resnick lead The Franklin Mint into a future destined for glorious achievement in the fine art field.

Fraser International Inc.

Presenting Souvenirs of British and American History for Your Home

Do you fancy a country cottage, authentic in every detail? Have you dreamed of life in a British castle, complete with soaring towers and centuries of rich history? Find yourself fascinated by momentous buildings like The Tower of London or The White House? Thanks to Ian MacGregor Fraser of Scotland, now you may indulge these "real estate fantasies" without ever leaving your living room. He re-creates all of these renowned sites and more in completely authentic miniature works of art.

When Fraser began creating his cottages, castles and historic landmarks about nine years ago, he had just three helpers. By 1988, he had formed Fraser Creations, was employing 200 people, and Great Britain's Prince Philip had presented him with the Scottish Enterprise Award for the best and most creative new industry in Scotland. Today, close to 300 artisans have a hand in creating Fraser's miniatures, and there are about 150 designs in the line. Most are issued in open editions, although about 100 designs have been retired, seventy of them in December, 1993. Pieces vary in height from about one to ten inches, and in price from $20.00 to $300.

During the late 1980s and early 1990s, some of Fraser's cottages and castles found their way into the United States, primarily via American tourists returning from trips to the United Kingdom. It wasn't until mid-1993 that his work became readily available here, when Fraser International Inc. became the company's exclusive United States distributor.

Enthusiasm in the American Marketplace

Fraser exhibited at both the Long Beach, California and South Bend, Indiana collectible expositions, and collectors' response to his work was enthusiastic.

"What we've done in the American market, sales wise, in such a short time is greater than we've achieved elsewhere," says Fraser. "It's really our biggest success. American collectors are by far the most intelligent and well-versed collectors in the world. In addition, their awareness of the secondary

Fraser International's wonderfully detailed sculptures for the American Heritage collection include two versions of "The White House" (center front and back) as well as models of the "Jefferson Memorial" (left) and "Lincoln Memorial" (right). The larger "White House" piece includes the 32 trees planted by American presidents ranging from John Quincy Adams to George Bush.

market is truly impressive," he adds.

The artistic talent behind these popular pieces was born in a cottage in the Scottish lowlands, currently resides in Edinburgh, and has a deep love for his homeland. "To me," he says, "Scotland is the most beautiful country in the world. I could never live anywhere else." Although never formally trained in art, he has more than thirty years experience working with various media: painting in oil and watercolor, creating silkscreen prints and copper pictures, and sculpting figurines; he's even created sixty-foot murals in fiberglass. He's now settled into designing miniatures, something he likes, as he can do it "sitting down." And his sitting down to miniatures is a bonanza for collectors.

Fraser Creations is family owned and operated. A few of the company's employees assist in the sculpting, but Fraser finishes every piece, has the last word regarding the execution of the sculpture and usually adds a last minute personal touch. His wife, Marion, is head of quality control. Their daughter, Myriam, is in charge of the air-brush department. Their son, Colin, manages the factory and product distribution in all countries except the United States.

From Fraser's the British Heritage *collection come two of England's most memorable landmarks, "Big Ben" (left) and "Westminster Abbey."*

Long Hours in the Studio Produce Wonderfully Detailed Originals

Fraser's employees know him as a quiet man who, in his own words, is a "workaholic." When he sculpts, he keeps his attention on his work. Days merge into nights, holidays get swallowed up, and he stays with a piece until it is done perfectly, to his own impeccable standards. "When I start something new, I get completely involved with it. It absorbs me," he says. This could be frustrating for his family, as it takes him from three days to two weeks to execute a design, depending on its complexity. Only his steadily increasing travel agenda and his golden retriever, Sultan, can get him away from his studio.

Collectors see another side of him, however. He's a fount of knowledge about the buildings he replicates in miniature, and if you ask him about their history, you'll discover an outgoing man whose soft Scottish brogue and enthusiasm for the architectural heritage of the British Isles is sure to charm you.

The Creative Process for Sculptor Fraser

Before starting a sculpture, Fraser prefers to see the building he will be depicting in miniature, although he also refers to his extensive collection of architectural photographs. After he's sculpted a wax model, a master mold is made. Then comes injection molds, which are used for the working models. The pieces are made of either Crystacle, Alpha K or resin. After the pieces are cast, they go to the fettling department, where rough edges are removed and the pieces are checked for errors.

Once approved, the Crystacle and Alpha K pieces go through a paint dip for the base color (the resin

pieces are cast in the color, and so are not dipped). Next, they are painted by hand, with one painter generally staying with a piece until it is finished. Working with a range of sable brushes, the painters spend about two days to complete a small piece; however, they usually work on three or four simultaneously. When the paint is dry, each one is flocked with green felt.

The Honor of Patronage by the British Royal Family

Fraser's historical accuracy and attention to detail caught the interest of Britain's Royal Family, and shops owned by them in various castles and landmarks carry the full range of historical buildings in the artist's *British Heritage* collection. The Queen's own properties, including "Windsor Castle" and "Balmoral Castle," highlight this collection, along with other world-renowned landmarks of London and surrounding areas. "Buckingham Palace" is a particularly imposing piece, featuring surrounding grounds and environs, as well as the enormous palace itself.

The *British Heritage* collection also presents many of England's most revered religious structures, such as "Westminster Abbey," "St. Paul's Cathedral," and "Canterbury Cathedral." In tribute to William Shakespeare, there are "Anne Hathaway's Cottage" and "Shakespeare's Birthplace."

Large trees, bridges and a babbling brook surround "The Red Lion Tavern" in this uplifting work of art from Fraser's Classic Cottage collection. Creator Ian MacGregor Fraser prides himself on creating a 360° perspective for all of his pieces — meaning that they are equally embellished from every angle of view.

That collection now is mirrored on our side of the Atlantic, with the recent introduction of Fraser's *American Heritage* collection. The first pieces in the collection depict "The White House," the "Lincoln Memorial," and the "Jefferson Memorial."

Many pieces in the *Heritage* collections are issued in two sizes. The larger works are up to ten inches high and depict a building and its surrounding area; the ten-inch sculpture of "The White House," for example, includes The President's Park, a road, fountain and flowers. The smaller pieces range from about one to three inches in height and focus on the building. The large pieces sell for about $150 each, while the small ones are available for about $50.00.

As mentioned earlier, Fraser retired some seventy designs in 1993. He did so to make way for more than eighty new designs that were introduced during 1994, with more to come in the near future. These new works are strong on environment, on each building's setting and the plant and animal life surrounding it.

The *German* collection re-creates all the aspects of classic German towns, including two chapels, several elegant homes in various architectural styles, and "Holstein Town Gates," "Alstadter Town Hall," and "Mayor Toppler's Little House."

Fraser plans to continue making frequent visits to United States collectibles expositions, and he enjoys meeting collectors. He has an open-door policy at his factory, located in the town of Penicuik, just four miles from Edinburgh. Collectors may visit his factory, he says, where he'll welcome them and arrange a tour of the facilities.

Portions of this feature are reprinted with permission from an article by Katherine Holden that appeared in Collector Editions *magazine.* Collectors' Information Bureau *thanks Ms. Holden and* Collector Editions *for their generous cooperation.*

From the British Heritage *collection, Fraser presents three historical works of art inspired by renowned sites. They are (clockwise from upper right):* "St. Paul's Cathedral," "The White Tower," *and* "The Tower of London."

GANZ / Little Cheesers
Nostalgic Mice from the "Old World" Colonize North America...And Capture the Hearts of Collectors

"A long time ago, the Little Cheesers lived in the Old World. They made their homes in tree stumps, toadstools and burrows. Very cleverly, they used leaves for umbrellas, blossoms for drinking cups and spider webs for fishing nets.

Then one day, some of the Little Cheesers made a courageous voyage across the Billowing Sea to the New World where they settled and built a new way of life. Instead of living in tree trunks, they learned to make cozy cottages from clapboards and shingles.

Later still, they invented a motorcar which was fueled by a special blend of dingleberries, cow chips, road apples and meadow muffins. This of course, was much kinder to Mother Nature than using oil and gasoline, but still allowed them to travel far and wide.

Indeed, the Little Cheesers always care about the environment because they never forget all the good things that Mother Earth can provide. Especially, they remember all the recipes for scrumptious natural dishes like milkweed omelets, huckleberry shortcake and rosehip soda pop which they prepare every time there's a special occasion in Cheeserville. Since they love to eat all these delicious goodies, the Cheesers find lots of reasons to celebrate..."

— *from* The Historical
Chronicle of Cheeserville©
by Frowzy Roquefort the Third

Admiring fans have followed the chronicles of the *Little Cheesers* ever since these delightful figurines first made their debut in 1991. Costumed in the elegant attire of our great-grandparents' era, the *Little Cheesers* reflect a simpler and gentler time, in the traditions of country families just beginning the transition to city life. So far, the community has developed around four themes — a picnic, a wedding, a Christmas celebration and a springtime collection.

The *Little Cheesers* were born as the result of a trip to the Far East in late 1990 by William R. Dawson, a veteran of the gift and collectibles industries. Dawson was instrumental in the creation of a line of collectible mice figurines, which

he named *Little Cheesers*. Presented and protected as authentic collectibles, the line was introduced with great success in January 1991. In July of that year, the Canadian firm of Ganz purchased *Little Cheesers*.

The company's president, Howard Ganz, selected artist and writer Christine Thammavongsa to take over development and expansion of *Little Cheesers*, creating a community of mice with their own houses, vehicles and fascinating stories. Since then, in consultation with Dawson, Christine has named each individual character and developed the delightful stories of their lives and pastimes. What's more, she designs all new additions to the line and is considered the "muse" for *Little Cheesers* chronicler Frowzy Roquefort the Third. Christine says that her goal is to create a universe that is kinder and more "dreamlike" than the human world — and her works and stories highlight family closeness, caring for others and concern for the environment.

The rousing success of the *Little Cheesers* continues the prominence of Ganz as a creator of popular gifts and collectibles. Founded more than forty years ago by Howard Ganz's grandfather, Samuel Ganz, the business helped begin a new life

The Little Cheesers Christmas Collection *includes a number of heartwarming characters such as (left to right): "Snow Cheeser," "Violet with Snowball," "Jeremy and Teddy" and "Santa Cheeser." Curiously, "Santa Cheeser" bears a striking resemblance to Papa Woodsworth, and Papa isn't anywhere to be found as the Cheeserville Christmas celebration begins. Is this just a coincidence? That's up to* Little Cheesers *collectors to decide!*

As the Little Cheesers *chronicler describes this scene, "It was a glorious day for a picnic. Hickory Harvestmouse was courting Blossom Thistledown under the shade of a dewflower bush. Blossom had brought some fresh apples to go with Hickory's bottle of bubbly gooseberry juice. Meanwhile, all the other Little Cheesers were celebrating National Cheeser Day at the fairground in Mayflower Meadow..." The whimsical "Picnic Base" sets the scene for "Blossom and Hickory in Love," along with some charming miniature accessories: "Basket of Apples," "Wine Glasses" and one of the retired "Bottles" — all from the Cheeserville Picnic Collection. The musical "Picnic Base" plays "Edelweiss."*

for the Ganz family. In 1944, Hitler's Nazi Army occupied the Ganzs' native Rumania, inflicting hardship and suffering. At war's end in 1945, the Ganz family fled to Austria and Germany, and ultimately to Canada. With $100 of their own money and $700 raised from family friends, Howard's father, Sam, and his uncle and grandfather launched Ganz Bros. Toys Limited in 1950. Once the first Ganz teddy bear was handcrafted, the company soon became known for its fine-quality plush animals. Today, under the leadership of Howard Ganz, the firm (now known simply as Ganz) markets its renowned *Little Cheesers* and other gifts, collectibles and plush throughout the United States, Canada and around the world.

Eyecatching Details Enhanced by Quality Craftsmanship

Christine Thammavongsa's process for creating each *Little Cheesers* piece requires numerous care-

ful steps. This complexity is all the more remarkable considering the affordable prices of these collectible pieces: they range from $1.00 to $85.00, with the average figurine costing $14.00 at retail.

To begin, Christine sketches the characters she has in mind, then presents them to a sculptor in the Far East who brings her work to life in three dimensions. Christine and the sculptor work together to perfect each detail before an original model is produced.

Little Cheesers figurines and miniatures are handcrafted of "cold cast porcelain" to enhance the details of each finished piece by retaining surface texture and undercuts of the original sculpture. This addition of porcelain dust to an organic resin also results in a more hand-sculpted appearance than fired porcelain, while increasing the strength and durability of each piece. Finally, the collection is hand-painted with water-based paints, producing a striking watercolor wash finish which beautifully complements the personalities of the *Little Cheesers*.

Little Cheesers Community Continues to Grow

With the publication of a fully illustrated book, *The Historical Chronicle of Cheeserville*, more and more collectors will discover the heartwarming charm of Christine Thammavongsa's mouse personalities. The book features Little Truffle, a mischievous youngster who wanders away from a Cheeserville celebration — later to be rescued by Sweet Cicely, Papa Woodsworth and Grandmama Thistledown.

What's more, Ganz continues to add personalities, poses and support pieces to the collection. New pieces for 1993 included:

"The Storyteller"...depicting Frowzy Roquefort III nestled in an overstuffed armchair reading his Cheeserville chronicles.

"Sunday Drive"...with Mama and Papa Woodsworth motoring in their 1902 Muenster convertible to the Cheeserville Summer picnic.

"Sweet Dreams"...as Little Truffle is tucked into bed after his adventurous day at the Cheeserville picnic.

In addition, 1993 saw the introduction of several other figurines, musicals, ornaments, photo frames and plush pieces as well as the special inspirational pieces:

"For Someone Special"...Cousin Chicory is seated in a wheelchair illustrating the honor of people meeting life's challenges with determination and joy.

"Words of Wisdom"...depicts Grandpa Thistledown strolling with his walking stick as a reminder of the years of valuable experience our elders have and wish to share. This piece is intended as an especially heartwarming gift between generations on birthdays and anniversaries.

"Flex-Collectibility" and Special Markings Enhance Collector Enjoyment

A key enticement for *Little Cheesers* collectors is the flexibility designed into each series of figurines. William R. Dawson named this concept "flex-collectibility" — a concept that intrigues art lovers of all ages. Like the pieces of a doll house, the different *Little Cheesers* figurines and miniatures can be arranged in endless combinations to create scenes on any of the bases. As an added attraction, each *Little Cheesers* trinket box may be used as a figurine base as well. With many of the bases offering musical selections, the collection wonderfully stimulates the sense of hearing as well as the sense of sight.

All *Little Cheesers* figurines are documented for the future with an understamp which is either template printed, or applied with a stick-on label, and all but the earliest productions have item numbers included on their understamps. Ganz has been especially careful to catalogue each new piece in this special way, to ensure the pieces' easy recognition by future generations of collectors.

Little Cheesers *Are Retired Periodically*

Each year, Ganz announces the retirement of selected *Little Cheesers* pieces, making way for new introductions. Once a piece is retired, it may be acquired through dealers until their stocks are sold out, and then it will be available only on the secondary market. As Howard Ganz explains, "When you have a line as popular and successful as *Little Cheesers*, it is very difficult to decide which pieces you will stop manufacturing — hopefully to be replaced by equally successful new designs. Nevertheless, it is the ever-present potential for retirement that keeps collectors collecting, and keeps the collection fresh."

Ten pieces were retired at the end of 1991 after just 1,200 to 4,475 pieces of each were produced. Similar numbers were retired during 1992, and the

A new addition to the Cheeserville Picnic Collection is "Sunday Drive," showing Mama and Papa Woodsworth in their 1902 Muenster automobile on the way to Mayflower Meadow for the National Cheeser Day Picnic.

"Wedding Procession" depicts Blossom Thistledown and Hickory Harvestmouse on their wedding day, accompanied by two of their adorable flower girls. This piece is sold separately from the musical wooden base which plays the "Wedding March" by Wagner. In addition to their collectibility, Little Cheesers pieces like this make captivating wedding cake toppers.

firm pledges to keep collectors and dealers informed as retirement decisions are made.

With the boundless imagination of Christine Thammavongsa and the charm of the *Little Cheesers*, this line of "mouse personalities" has unlimited potential for growth. Collectors are invited to "stay tuned" as the adventures of Cheeserville and all its delightful little characters unfold, year after year.

Gartlan USA, Inc.
The Gartlan USA Signature —
Personal Autographs; Superstars Of Sports

Tom Seaver had been signing Gartlan USA's limited-edition collector plates featuring the New York Mets Hall-of-Famer for more than an hour, when — CRASH — one of the unsigned 10¼" plates careened to its demise.

Unruffled, Seaver looked up from his penmanship and quipped, "Well, there goes the no-hitter."

Magic Johnson, basketball's ethereal ambassador, invited neighbors for lunch during his Gartlan USA signing session. "Are you sure it wouldn't be a bother?" asked his Bel Air cohorts. "Not at all," Magic replied. "We've got service for nineteen hundred."

And Joe Montana's mom, reviewing her son's limited-edition figure, was elated, except for one tiny thing. "His hair is too long," she lamented.

After the original artwork was resculpted, changes in the molds were affected immediately.

Since 1985, Gartlan USA has been the world leader in fine-art, limited edition sports collectibles. Founded by R. H. Gartlan, the company's niche is built on an attention to detail, athletes' personal signatures on premier products, and a focus on the marquee names from the world of sport. Its product mix includes limited edition figures, collector plates, lithographs and ceramic trading cards.

The Gartlan USA line-up includes such sports heroes as Joe DiMaggio, John Wooden, Ted Williams, Stan Musial, Roger Staubach, Yogi Berra, Whitey Ford, George Brett, Gordie Howe, Mike Schmidt and many more.

Quality Attracts Marquee Names

The ability to attract such headline stars speaks to the quality of the Gartlan USA line.

"In the early days, we'd make a presentation to a player. He'd look at artistic renderings and mutter something like 'Is that a big button?'," Gartlan recalls.

Although fine-art sports collecting is still in its infancy, athletes and collectors alike are increasingly cognizant of the value of these pieces.

"Magic Johnson himself mused, after confessing that he would never sign 1,987 plates again, 'I wonder where these will be in ten years, in fifty years?'," Gartlan says.

Carlton Fisk, a shoo-in for baseball's Hall of Fame, says he is approached by companies with household names on a daily basis, but has shied away from most offers. "What attracted me to Gartlan USA was how lifelike the figures appear and the respect to each and every detail the artists maintained," Fisk explains.

The key to that detail is an intimate working relationship with each athlete.

"Wayne Gretzky, evaluating the original artwork for his figure, asked if the right side of his jersey couldn't be sculpted under his hip pad," states Gartlan. "When he was young, his skills were so good that he competed against kids much older. Consequently, the uniforms were much larger. To facilitate his slap shot, he tucked in the right side of his sweater. To this day, superstitiously, he still tucks in his sweater; in fact, he orders his jerseys with Velcro™ to ensure they stay in place."

Similar fine tuning was executed for Joe Montana. Just as she did with Joe's hair, Mrs. Montana pointed out an extension in Montana's left index finger just before releasing the ball. Artist Michael J. Taylor captured it on artwork for the plate and a canvas transfer.

Gartlan USA — Trendsetter Among Sports Collectibles

The Joe Montana canvas transfer was the first execution of this fine-art technique in the sports collecting community.

The canvas transfer wasn't Gartlan USA's first "first."

Its premier piece — a hand-signed porcelain Pete Rose figure — is recognized as the first fine-art, autographed sports figure ever produced. Basketball's Magic Johnson, hockey's Wayne Gretzky, football's Roger Staubach, coaching legend John Wooden and umpire Al Barlick represent the first series of high-end, limited editions in their respective professions.

Moreover, Gartlan USA's *Master Museum Collection* is a collaboration of the greatest names

Gartlan USA president R.H. Gartlan presents Wayne Gretzky a silver figure in appreciation for Gretzky's on- and off-ice accomplishments. The figure is a replica of Gartlan USA's best-selling Wayne Gretzky autographed figure.

in sports and sports art.

Kareem Abdul-Jabbar, Wayne Gretzky, Joe Montana and Ted Williams have been commemorated in museum-grade cast pewter in an autographed, matched-number set.

Limited to an edition of only 500 pieces worldwide, this set took more than two years to coordinate.

A fifth piece has been added to the set and features the immortal baseball Hall-of-Famer Stan "the Man" Musial.

Each collector who owns the initial four pieces is given the right of first refusal on subsequent pieces in the series.

It is these kinds of intricate logistics that add immensely to, and are a trademark of, the Gartlan USA line.

"It is the acute collector who appreciates the labor and scheduling that go into getting an athlete to physically sit down and sign a couple thousand plates," states Gartlan.

It is never an easy process.

When signing with hockey superstar Brett Hull, there was a change in his schedule, and Gartlan had to drive, literally overnight, more than 1,200 plates from Superior, Wisconsin to St. Louis so Hull could sign them the next day.

The plates had already been autographed by his Dad (Hall-of-Famer Bobby Hull) so every shipment was a sensitive exercise.

Baseball Hall-of-Famer Luis Aparicio flew from Venezuela to the United States for four days to sign Gartlan USA plates; Negro League star James "Cool Papa" Bell died before signing the entirety of his nearly 2,000 figures.

It is such challenges and logistics that endear Gartlan USA collectibles to sports fans around the globe.

Collectors' League Sports Polished Collectors

In an effort to acknowledge its collectors' support and reward their loyalty, Gartlan USA established the Gartlan USA Collectors' League in 1989.

Each year, the club caters to sports fans of all ages and collectors of varying media.

A free collector's plate is given away with each new membership or renewal. A membership is founded on an annual subscription basis, while members-only offers, usually figures, extend through a much more limited time frame, e.g., three to six months. The free gift changes with each calendar year, thus enabling members to maintain the integrity of their collection.

Players commemorated on Collectors' League plates have included Pete Rose, umpire Al Barlick, Joe Montana, Ken Griffey Jr. and Gordie Howe.

Figures offered exclusively to members only

Four-time world champion and NFL All-Pro quarterback Joe Montana signs Gartlan USA's limited edition canvas transfers.

"Stan Musial" is the fifth piece in the Master's Museum Collection — an elite collection of limited-edition, personally autographed pewter figures.

have included miniatures featuring Wayne Gretzky, Joe Montana, Kareem Abdul-Jabbar, Mike Schmidt and Hank Aaron.

A signed Hank Aaron figure — featuring Hammerin' Hank in the Atlanta Braves uniform — was offered to League Charter Members. Limited to a worldwide edition of 755 pieces, it commemorated Aaron's position atop the career home-run leaders. The piece included a display case and a ceramic front page, which recreated, in miniature, the front page following the record-setting blast that surpassed Babe Ruth's all-time record.

Collectors' League members receive other benefits in addition to free gifts and pieces reserved solely for members.

A quarterly newsletter identifies new Gartlan USA issues available to members and non-members alike; behind-the-scenes glimpses at the sports collecting hobby; and advice on collecting in general. This periodical is shipped free of charge to Collector League members.

Collector League members are also included on Gartlan USA's dealer mailing list. This ensures that League members receive advance notice on all new issues. Because many issues ship sold out from the Gartlan USA California headquarters, League members are able to reserve such pieces two to three months before national marketing campaigns inform the general collecting public these pieces even exist.

Gartlan USA also hosts many events featuring the Hall-of-Famers it commemorates. League members are always preferred guests to these invitation-only events. At public signings League members enjoy V.I.P. status and head-of-the-line privileges.

For more than 100 years sports enthusiasts have sought such head-of-the-line status when it comes to capturing mementos of their favorite sports moment; similarly, plate and figure collectors have embraced their hobby for nearly as long.

Gartlan USA's bonding of these two pastimes has proven itself in this newest area of fine-art collecting: sports. Meanwhile, Gartlan USA's innovative leadership offers sports collectors products that embody the best of sports, fine-art, limited editions and collecting...fun!

Gartlan USA artist Michael J. Taylor, left, and future Hall-of-Fame catching great Carlton Fisk share a light moment during Fisk's plate signing session for Gartlan USA.

Georgetown Collection
Fine Art and Heartfelt Emotion
From Some of the World's Greatest Doll Artists

From its studios in Portland, Maine, the Georgetown Collection achieves an ambitious and very specific mission: creating the finest collectible dolls for today and tomorrow — in the tradition of the priceless heirloom dolls of yesterday.

Two things are essential in meeting this goal. The first is a small group of distinguished and visionary artists that reads like a veritable "who's who" of top contemporary doll makers. Linda Mason, Brigitte Deval, Ann Timmerman, Jan Galperin and Sissel Skille have all accepted Georgetown's coveted commissions to create collectible dolls. The second part of the equation depends on Georgetown itself and demands a commitment to excellence in every phase of design and production. Neither part can exist without the other, and together, this collaboration of talented artists with a responsive company results in a truly extraordinary product.

Artistic Excellence, Unparalleled Quality Control and Customer Service

"It's true that we do things a little differently here," explains Jeff McKinnon, president of the Georgetown Collection. "To begin with, we give our artists total artistic control over their dolls. They do what they feel is right. Consequently, the end product is *their* design rather than that of some anonymous group — and this is why we're able to attract such superb talent."

McKinnon goes on to say that, as a partner and supporter of great doll artists, Georgetown insists that only top quality components go into each of its dolls. "Among the tradespeople who produce our porcelain, wigs and the material for our costuming, we have a reputation for only accepting the very best quality. And that is what we consistently get."

The Georgetown reputation for excellent customer service is another reason for the firm's continued success. "Good customer service," says McKinnon, "comes down to simply working harder. We treat every customer as an individual, and we *listen*. It's also interesting, I think, that Georgetown has experienced very little turnover since the company first began. We're very proud that we

With her expressive dark eyes, traditional Cheyenne costume and regal bearing, Linda Mason's "Many Stars" has captured the imagination of collectors and doll market watchers alike. This Georgetown original from the America Diary Dolls™ series earned its creators an historic honor when it won both the Dolls magazine Award of Excellence and the Doll Reader Doll of the Year award for 1992. The complete series was also honored with a Concept of the Year nomination from Doll Reader.

have such long-term relationships with our employees, artists, vendors — and most importantly — our customers!"

The Award-Winning Linda Mason

Out of this fruitful partnership has come a number of remarkable nominations and awards — most notably for the delightful creations of doll artist Linda Mason. Already a four-time winner of the prestigious Award of Excellence from *Dolls* magazine, Ms. Mason has earned even more kudos for her doll "Many Stars," whose beautiful face and traditional Native American Cheyenne costume helped her achieve the remarkable dual honor of winning the 1992 Award of Excellence from *Dolls* magazine and the 1992 Doll of the Year Award from *Doll Reader* magazine. What's more, Mason's

entire *American Diary Dolls*™ series was nominated for the *Doll Reader* special award for Concept of the Year!

And what a concept it is! Each doll in this unusual series tells an American girl's story from a different point of view, time and place. Among the dolls included are the aforementioned "Many Stars" from the Great Plains circa 1849; "Bridget Quinn," an Irish-American from Boston circa 1899; "Jenny Cooper," a British-American from Sag Harbor, circa 1905; "Christina Merovina," an Italian-American from Philadelphia, circa 1911; "Rachel Williams," an African-American from Chicago, circa 1893. "Tulu" of the Alaskan Territory (part of the *American Diary Dolls*™ series) and Mason's very first boy doll, a handsome Native American named "Quick Fox" (who happens to be the brother of "Many Stars") are among the artist's new dolls for Georgetown.

Despite their diversity, what the dolls have in common is what Linda Mason's dolls all seem to possess: a special courage, goodness and a sense of wonder. Each doll comes complete with a beautifully illustrated biography, explaining the doll's family background and what it was like to grow up in that particular era. From horse-drawn wagons to oil lamps and baking from scratch, the lives of the children of a century past were more difficult — but in some ways vastly richer — than ours today.

The costumes of these *American Diary Dolls*™ are as authentic as the dolls themselves, and each is crafted by hand to old-fashioned heirloom standards. Most importantly, each doll is issued in a signed *Artist's Edition*™ limited to 100 firing days. This short firing period gives Linda Mason complete control over the quality at every stage of the doll's crafting.

Another of Mason's more recent collections is titled *Sugar and Spice*™, featuring "Little Sweetheart," a doll that is as pretty as a Valentine in her ruffled bonnet and golden heart necklace; "Pepper," in her jumpsuit, skipping rope; and "Little Sunshine" in nightgown and knitted slippers, ready to serve tea to Mother.

The Incredible Art of Brigitte Deval

Perhaps the most prestigious of Georgetown's artists is Brigitte Deval, the first and still the best-known of the wave of European doll artists whose work took America by storm during the 1980s. Deval creates true portrait dolls, as riveting as the finest museum-quality paintings.

Born in Bavaria, the daughter of a famous portrait photographer, Deval crafted her first doll at age six. In her early twenties, she moved to an Italian village in the hills of Tuscany, where she now lives with her husband and two children and creates her magnificent dolls.

It was German artist Peter Wolf who first introduced Deval's work to doll authority John Darcy Noble, curator emeritus of the Toy Collection at the Museum of the City of New York. Noble calls Deval "One of the world's most famous doll makers, and in my opinion, she is among the superlative few." Artist Wolf agrees: "Her dolls are the best," he says, "the very best."

Artists' representative Tom Boland was the man who brought Deval's dolls to the attention of the public. He first saw her work in the windows of Tiffany & Company, loved what he saw, and quickly brought Brigitte into his stable of top doll artists. It was through Boland that the connection with Georgetown came about.

While prices for Deval's one-of-a-kind dolls range from $2,500 to $15,000, her collaborations with the Georgetown Collection offer collectors the opportunity to own this artist's work at a considerably more affordable price. If, that is, the work is still available. Two of Deval's earliest pieces for Georgetown — "Katie" and "Megan" — (from the *Little Loves*™ series) are now sold out, as is the "Faerie Princess," another of Deval's dolls. "Laura's First Day of School" and "Tea Time for Emma," are two of the other dolls from *Little Loves*™. Another popular series titled *Small Wonders*™ offers three dolls — "Abbey the Gardener," "Corey the Beachcomber" and "Sarah the Little Slugger."

New to Georgetown: Sissel Skille

The newest name in the Georgetown stable is Sissel Skille, a Norwegian doll artist whose one-of-a-kind dolls, according to an article in *Contemporary Doll Magazine*, now command prices of $7,000 or more. Ms. Skille is a school teacher who juggles her two careers quite neatly, producing truly beautiful doll children with incredibly lifelike detail. The eyes of these children seem to reflect — not simply an expression — but the kind of depth of character often known as "soul."

The eyes, note Skille, are the feature she completes first whenever she begins a doll. "Once I look deeply into the eyes, this helps me complete the face in the manner I feel the doll wants to be completed."

Because Skille is a true perfectionist, she creates fewer than ten dolls per year. This makes her collaboration with Georgetown of particular note, since collectors can now take delight in a Skille doll of their very own.

Ann Timmerman: The Gaze That Captures the Essence

When you meet Ann Timmerman, the first thing you notice is her penetrating gaze. Her eyes seem to search the face for clues to a person's inner life — the "real" character which is not always shown to the world at large. This unusual gaze may account for the unique ability of this extraordinary artist to "read" features and portray the essence of each particular doll she creates.

Ms. Timmerman's dolls for Georgetown include the popular "Peaches and Cream," whose smooth, creamy complexion; delicate, heart-shaped mouth; and cheeks aglow with blush of childhood all add up to an incredibly beautiful little girl. "Sweet Strawberry," Timmerman's follow-up to "Peaches and Cream" demonstrates again this artist's gift of capturing the fresh, innocent and extraordinarily alluring world of childhood. Complete with wicker basket and seated in a white wicker chair that is included with the doll, "Sweet Strawberry" is the second in the Georgetown/Timmerman series titled *Portraits of Perfection*.

Jan Galperin: From Illustrator to Doll Artist

Jan Galperin, another popular Georgetown artist, has a most unusual history prior to creating her dolls. After graduating from art school where she studied fashion design, this talented woman went to work as a courtroom illustrator in Philadelphia. What at first glance might seem a bit "un-doll-like" proved instead to be very worthwhile. "The courtroom illustrating," notes Galperin, "gave me the chance to carefully study faces, and this led to my eventual interest in sculpture."

Studying under world-famous sculptor Ronald van Ruckeyvelt, whom she credits for her success, Galperin takes her role in creating dolls very seriously. As the mother of two young children, she explains: "I believe that each doll I create should be a positive role model for my children."

Her first doll for Georgetown, "Grace," takes her name from the favorite hymn she loves to sing in church, "Amazing Grace." Her adorable face, complete with chubby cheeks and dimples, lights up as she sings. "Grace" leads off a new Georgetown series titled *Hearts in Song*.

A Continuing Commitment to Excellence

Building on its already strong reputation for award-winning doll art, the Georgetown Collection will continue its devotion to excellence — working, as always, with a small cadre of today's most honored doll artists. New themes and concepts will emerge over the years — including an exciting series of collectors plates, the first of which, "Buffalo Child" in the *Children of the Great Spirit* series, has been created by one of America's most highly praised artists Carol Theroux. The Georgetown mission, however, will remain constant: to create the finest *Artist's Editions* available in the tradition of beautiful heirloom-quality collectibles.

Adorable little "Grace" is the creation of Jan Galperin as the premier issue in her Hearts in Song™ series. "Grace" is dressed in her special choir robe to sing her first solo: the inspiring hymn, "Amazing Grace."

Ann Timmerman's Portraits of Perfection™ series begins with "Peaches and Cream," a delightful little barefoot girl in a peach-trimmed ivory bubble suit.

Another of Linda Mason's designs is "Quick Fox," a young American Indian boy. Standing 15" tall, "Quick Fox" is crafted of fine porcelain and retails for $134.

Goebel United States

Bette Ball and Karen Kennedy Keep Yesterday's Memories Alive Through Their Original Designs of Limited Edition Porcelain Dolls

Bette Ball and Karen Kennedy have not forgotten their childhood memories. In fact, they cherish the innocence and delight so much that they have made it the basis of their careers. These gifted doll designers share their visions of gentle days gone by in a marvelous array of limited edition porcelain dolls, many of which are musical.

Each creation, whether it be from the *Victoria Ashlea Originals®*, Dolly Dingle, Betty Jane Carter, Carol Anne or Charlot Byj series, is a masterpiece of fine detailing, craftsmanship and tasteful design. The goal of Ms. Ball and Ms. Kennedy is to capture the imagination and love of discerning collectors today and for many generations to come.

Like the excitement of finding a treasured collectible in grandmother's attic or a trip down memory lane, each exquisite designer doll is destined to evoke memories of the carefree child in each of us. Those you choose for your collection will become your best friends.

The Success of Dolly Dingle

Goebel United States' award-winning, international designer Bette Ball, upon graduating from Moore College, Philadelphia, worked in advertising art, fine art and table and giftware design. In 1977, Ms. Ball's husband started a new importing company for Wilhelm Goebel. Ms. Ball designed her first doll line, featuring twelve limited edition porcelain dolls, for the company in 1980.

In 1983, Bette and her daughter Ashlea were browsing through an antique shop and happened upon a box of old Dolly Dingle cut-outs. Bette recalled, "As a child, I made an army of paper dolls and supplied them with enormous wardrobes." The cut-out character of Dolly Dingle was destined to win her heart. Goebel bought the rights to this early-twentieth-century cut-out doll originally created by Grace Drayton.

By 1985, Dolly Dingle had become "America's Sweetheart" in the form of lifelike, three-dimensional dolls created by Bette Ball. That year, Ms. Ball earned the prestigious Doll of the Year (DOTY) Award for her creation of a sixteen-inch Dolly Dingle musical doll. This award-winning doll was dressed in a grand party dress blossoming with yards and yards of violets.

Today the Dolly Dingle line continues to win admirers all over the world. Indeed, you can see Bette's creations in over seventeen museums across the globe. Dolly Dingle's family tree grows with new members each year. The branches include the Sweeties, the Blossoms, the Twinkles, the Snooks, the Tingles, the Dumplings, the Bumps, the Quicklys, the Bumbles, the Croissants and their pets.

Dolly Dingle and Company Enter the World of Television

Ms. Ball's first television doll show was in January 1987. She is in her fourth year of appearing on "Doll Collector" on QVC cable television. The program airs the last Sunday of each month with a marvelous selection of her creations. The Dolly Dingle, Betty Jane Carter and Carol Anne dolls featured on the shows are made exclusively for the Quality Value Convenience Network.

Ms. Kennedy now creates Goebel's Charlot Byj dolls for QVC and appears often on "Doll Collector." Both Bette and Karen enter the homes of more than forty-five million people through QVC. Both enjoy meeting and speaking with their fans through live telephone conversations held during the QVC broadcasts.

Exquisitely Dressed Dolls With Musical Flair

While Bette will always reserve a special place in her heart for Dolly Dingle, she and fellow designer Karen Kennedy have made *Victoria Ashlea* famous throughout Europe and the United States.

The *Victoria Ashlea* line, named after Bette's daughter, was created in 1982 by Bette Ball. Karen Kennedy became Ms. Ball's protégé and assistant immediately after graduating from the Philadelphia College of Textiles and Science with a major in fashion design. As an award-winning doll designer herself, Karen shares Bette's great love for fabrics, her eye for detail and her demand for the utmost in quality. Their creativity flourished in an atmosphere of friendship and artistic collabora-

Bette Ball has created a new line of musical porcelain collector dolls with matching children's dresses in sizes 3T to 6. From the smile on her face, it is easy to see that Alicia feels pretty in her beautiful dress of vibrant blue background with bold flowers. Alicia's matching seventeen-inch doll, with no name so you may name her, features the same silken cerise bow and scalloped lace trim around the neckline.

tion. As Ms. Kennedy explained, "Bette and I work really well together. Each of us does her own individual designs. Then, to ensure that each doll is as special as he or she can be, we critique each other's designs."

The two designers also agree that adding a fine musical movement to each doll, twelve inches or larger, provides an additional dimension to their creations. Bette Ball's inspiration for this concept came from an antique German doll she was given as a child. "It had a music box concealed in its cloth body. I will always remember the joy it gave me when I found the hidden music. I made it my special song."

The selection of each doll's name and her musical accompaniment are sources of great pride for Bette, Karen and the entire doll design studio staff. In addition, the artists will often design dolls to represent specific relatives or friends. Ms. Ball reflected, "I feel these have been some of my best creations because of the personal feeling I have for the special person."

Crafting a Bette Ball or Karen Kennedy Original

Each doll begins with a drawing that serves as the basis for costuming and porcelain production. The doll may be a Victorian-style woman at eighteen inches to forty-two inches in height or a tot at twelve to thirty inches in height. The designers are particularly concerned about proportion. As Ms. Ball explained, "If the proportion is correct, the doll appears more lifelike."

The costumes are made from Bette's and Karen's drawings and fabric selections. Patterns are drafted for each outfit and the material is cut and sewn. Each limited edition doll has its own individual pattern. Upon completion, the doll is photographed and sent to the production facility along with a description sheet, fabric, the pattern and photograph.

Craftsmen at the production facility copy the original doll and then return it to the designer along with the completed sample. After the facility's work is approved, the limited edition is authorized. At that time, a description tag for the doll's wrist, a Certificate of Authenticity, a designer gift box and a keepsake tag are printed. The keepsake tag is sewn into the seam of each doll's clothing to allow the collector to record who the doll came from, the date and the occasion for which it was received. This is a unique feature carried by all Goebel dolls.

Bette Ball adds another classic to her series of Betty Jane Carter dolls made exclusively for QVC. "Scarlett" carries her own porcelain doll wearing a dress of rich tapestry that complements her ensemble. The music box hidden in Scarlett's cloth body plays "A Dream Is A Wish Your Heart Makes." The doll stands twenty-four inches tall and is limited in edition to 1,000 worldwide.

Excellent Fabrics Make These Designs Outstanding

The shared interests and educational backgrounds of Bette Ball and Karen Kennedy have given them both a love for fine fabrics. This they joyfully express in the varied costumes of their doll creations.

Bette explained, "Quality fabric has always been a passion of mine. It was never difficult for me to understand why Scarlett O'Hara used the rich, opulent velvet dining room draperies when she wanted to impress and capture a suitor. I've always maintained that it is a waste of time to make anything of inferior fabric." Therefore, fabrics for Goebel dolls are selected four times a year at eight top fabric houses.

Most Bette Ball and Karen Kennedy Dolls are Limited Editions

While there are several ways in which the editions of collectible items are limited, dolls are limited strictly by number. The quantity of the edition is hand-numbered on the back of the doll's neck, on the Certificate of Authenticity, on the hand tag or on a combination of these locations.

For example, "L/E 1000" means that only 1,000 dolls from the original drawing, plus the designer's artist proof, will ever be produced. Most Bette Ball and Karen Kennedy dolls are limited to 500 or 1,000 worldwide. A few small dolls carry editions limited to 2,500.

Doll Designers Keep New Ideas Flowing

Both designers seem to have a never-ending idea bank for creating their dolls. Karen gets many of her ideas from real children, and she is also inspired by magazines and Victorian books. She takes themes, fashion ideas and costuming concepts and uses them to create dolls of exceptional quality and playfulness.

Bette Ball relies on frequent museum visits, window shopping in world capitals and gallery openings for her inspiration. She loves to see what's new — colors in decorating, fashions and other trends keep her designs fresh and unique.

Doll Collectors Take Note

To receive autographed photographs, QVC show information, a Dolly Dingle family tree, museum lists or doll pamphlets, collectors may call the Goebel United States Customer Service line at 1-800-366-4632. They can also visit one of the many doll shops, gift shops, fine department stores or watch QVC shows that feature these dolls to get an up-close feel for the caring and devotion each designer pours into her creations.

Karen Kennedy created "Ginger Muffin" as part of her new series of Charlot Byj dolls. The doll is limited in edition to 500 and her music box plays "Everybody Loves Somebody." She is exclusively available through QVC.

From the timeless Victoria Ashlea Originals® collection comes the introductory series of Tiny Tots Clowns — Karen Kennedy presents gaily-costumed clowns that will inspire your imagination. Each hand-painted, 12" doll is limited in edition to 2,000 worldwide. From left are "Beth," "Julie," "Leslie" and "Kaylee."

The Great American® Taylor Collectibles Corp.
A Rich History of Popular Collectibles from the Sandhills of North Carolina

With their soulful, shoe-button eyes and cuddly good looks, the *Taylor Bears*™ of The Great American® Taylor Collectibles Corp. were born to win collectors' hearts. Indeed, these wonderful folk art bear characters established Great American as an important new force in the world of collecting — soon after the North Carolina company's founding in 1980 by its namesake, Jack Taylor.

Over 100 different designs in *The Taylor Bear Family*™ introduced a marvelous clan of bears dressed in bright clothing and ready for fun and adventure. Favorite characters included "Glyn" and "Marcie," their daughter "Elizabeth," her husband "Beauregard," and the grandchildren "Suzy" and "Sidney."

Although they were cold-cast before hand-painting, these adorable bears boast a hand-carved look reminiscent of the great, classic folk arts of their Carolina roots. The original *Taylor Bear Family*™ retired in 1989, but they were succeeded by another marvelous collection, *The Taylor Bear Professionals*™. Most of these doctors, fire fighters, teachers, nurses and other "hard-working bears" still are available today. Sadly, their creator, Glyn Snow, died in 1989: a tragedy for all those who love the *Taylor Bears*.

These adorable members of The Taylor Bear Family™ *were among the first works of art from* The Great American® Taylor Collectibles Corp. *They include the grandparents "Glyn" and "Marcie," their daughter "Elizabeth" and her husband "Beauregard," and the grandchildren "Suzy" and "Sidney."*

The Taylor Bear Professionals™ *highlight favorite jobs as exhibited by sweet-faced bears.*

Danila Devins Unveils Folk Art Santas

Next in "Great American chronology" came the *House Hangers* and *St. Nicholas* art of sculptor Danila Devins, who has created hundreds of folk art designs and other innovations for the firm in recent years. Ms. Devins lives in scenic Southern Pines, North Carolina on her farm, surrounded by horses and German Shepherds.

Born in Florence, Italy, Ms. Devins studied there at the Regio Istituto d'Arte. Her family moved to the United States where she continued her studies at the Ringling School of Art in Sarasota, Florida. Much honored for her creations, Ms. Devins has received numerous awards. These include First Prize "Racing Art" from The Red Mile in Louisville, Kentucky, and four consecutive first prizes for Professional Sculpture for Commercial Use at the North Carolina State Fair: 1985 through 1988. In Premio, Italy, she was awarded the Gold Plaque in 1986 and 1989, along with other awards too numerous to mention.

Ms. Devins created her first *St. Nicholas* series issue for Great American in 1987, and each year since she has developed a new design. Each of her Santas is offered in an edition limited to 2,500 for worldwide distribution. For 1993, she created a handsome "Environmentalist" Santa, intended to better our awareness of the natural world around us. In this figurine a broadwing hawk peers over St. Nicholas' shoulder as he fondly snuggles a young red

fox. Resting beside him is a playful raccoon ready for a snooze after a long day's hunt.

In addition to her *St. Nicholas* figurines, Dani Devins has developed a large variety of collectibles for Great American. These include the *Great Americans*, such as "Ronald Reagan," "Amelia Earhart," "Robert E. Lee" and more. Her *Jolly Boy Santas* come in a set of eight, retiring in 1994.

Newly introduced are her 1994 *Classic Santas Series 6*, which will remain open until 1996. These Santas are about 6-1/2" tall and retail for $23.00 each. Ms. Devins will sculpt six new Santas each year for this series, and each annual grouping will "live" for three years before retiring.

Old World Santas *Remain Perennially Popular*

Perhaps Great American's most beloved line of all is Lancy Smith's *Old World Santas*, which were introduced in 1988. Each year, five new originals are carved in wood and five from the past are retired. Each year's set "lives" three years before retirement. All are serially numbered, gifted box, and — as is traditional with Great American collectibles — they come with rights to full-color personalized Certificates of Ownership. All the collector needs to do is mail the blue request card enclosed with each figurine to acquire this attractive certificate with its gold seal: a personalized document handsome enough for framing.

Each of the *Old World Santas* is 100% "Made in the U.S.A." of an oak-like cold-cast material, then hand-painted to perfection by skilled artists in North Carolina's Sandhills. Pieces range in height from 6" to 8", and the issue price for active editions is $29.00 each.

The first twenty *Old World Santas* already have been retired, with secondary market trading well underway for most pieces. The 1988 collection, which retired at the end of 1990, featured "Jangle" from

These Old World Santas *for 1994 include, from left to right, Lancy Smith's "Wilhelm," "Ivan," "Angus," "Gord" and "Desmond."*

"Angus Claus" from Scotland poses before the free, full-color brochure that highlights all the Old World Santas. *The brochure is available to collectors "for the asking" from Great American.*

Ireland, "Kris Kringle" from Switzerland, "Ching Chang" from China, "Hans" of Germany and "Jingle," the English Santa. In 1989, five more Santas were unveiled, and their editions closed at the end of 1991. These were: "Yule" of Germany, "Nicholai" of Russia, the French Santa "Pierre," Belgium's "Noel" and "Rudy" of Austria.

For 1990 (retired at the end of 1992), the *Old World Santas* included: "Mario" of Italy, "Matts" from Sweden, "Sven" of Norway, "Vander" from Holland" and the British "Cedric." Retired at the end of 1993 (after original issuance in early 1991) were: "Boris" of Russia, "Samuel" from the U.S.A., "Duncan" of Scotland, "Benjamin" from Israel and "Mitch" of Wales.

Retiring at the end of 1994 are the Santas first unveiled in January, 1992. They are: "Jacques" of France, "Mickey" of Ireland, "Terry" from Denmark, "José" from Spain and "Stu" from Poland. "Stu" has his own special story. It seems he's from Warsaw, and he can't abide clutter or dust. So he carries his straw broom everywhere to keep everything tidy. Those who are neat get more presents from "Stu"!

Still open until the end of 1995 are the editions from the January, 1993 *Old World Santas*. They include: "Franz" of Switzerland, "Bjorn" of Sweden, "Ryan" of Ireland, "Vito" from Italy, and "Otto" of Germany. We know that "Otto" lives in Wiesbaden, Germany. His great-grandfather was a Prussian general who loved to have his men march to drums. Every Christmas "Otto" marches along the Rhine, beating his drum and distributing toys to the delight of girls and boys.

First introduced at the beginning of 1994 and available through 1996 are these wonderful Santas: "Ivan" from Russia, "Desmond" of England, "Gord"

The first-edition Collector's Club piece, "William," is shown here at left along with the second-edition club piece for 1995, "Winston."

from Canada, "Wilhelm" of Holland, and the Scotsman, "Angus." "Angus" hails from Aberdeen, Scotland, where he and his pet Scotty dog, McNeil, raise Aberdeen Angus cattle on a nearby ranch. "Angus" plays checkers with the Lord Mayor of Aberdeen every Tuesday night, and McNeil entertains by dancing on his hind legs when he hears the Lord Mayor's bagpipes played on the CD!

Latest Artist from Great American

The International Collectible Exposition in Secaucus, New Jersey saw the April, 1994 introduction of Jim Clement's *Wood Carving Santas.*

These reproductions capture every detail of Clement's original wood carvings, with fifteen initial designs now available. Five more will be added in 1995, with five retiring on December 31, 1994.

"William" Premiers the Great American Collectors Club

All buyers of the endearing "William," first edition of the Great American Collectors' Guild, will receive a free, one-year membership in the club as well as three newsletters. "William," dressed in red, white and blue and equipped with baseball gear, believes that baseball builds character and promotes peace.

William would rather play baseball than anything else. As he says, "Those who keep their eyes on the ball get ahead in this world." With more and more well-received products introduced each year, that "can-do" philosophy applies to The Great American Taylor Collectibles Corp. as well!

Jim Clement's Wood Carving Santas were introduced to much acclaim at the April, 1994 International Collectible Exposition in Secaucus, New Jersey.

The Greenwich Workshop, Inc.

As Publishers, Artists and Authorized Dealers, The Greenwich Workshop "Family" Believes That Collecting Fine Art Offers the Reward of Discovery

The Greenwich Workshop, Inc., is one of the leading fine art publishers specializing in the burgeoning medium of visual entertainment. The company's principal offerings are signed and numbered limited edition fine art prints, but The Greenwich Workshop also offers open edition posters, quality books, bronze sculptures and Living Canvas® videos.

Greenwich Workshop prints and related art products are distributed through 1,100 art galleries and framers in the United States, Canada and the United Kingdom. In addition, under the name "Big Horn Galleries," the company operates several retail art galleries specializing in original art. They are located in Fairfield, Connecticut; Cody, Wyoming; Aspen, Colorado; and Carmel, California. To serve the Canadian and U.K. markets, the company operates in conjunction with The Greenwich Workshop Ltd., located in Scarborough, Ontario, and The Greenwich Workshop Europe, located in Upton upon Severn, England.

During 1972, its first year of business, The Greenwich Workshop published the limited edition prints of three painters. Today, from its headquarters in Shelton, Connecticut, it publishes high-quality works of art by nearly forty of the world's finest, most-sought artists.

A Pioneer in "The Art of Discovery"

As the company grew over the decades, The Greenwich Workshop has expanded its focus to include new aspects of "The Art of Discovery™." The Greenwich Workshop was among the firms that pioneered the concept of the signed and numbered limited edition print. To bring the pleasure of art to new groups of collectors, the company continues to look for new ways to bring high quality art to every age group and income bracket.

One of the few unchanging aspects of its business is The Greenwich Workshop's commitment to quality. Art has an indefinable, pleasurable effect for consumers; higher quality leads to a greater effect, so the company has dedicated itself to bringing that

"Evening Angels" is the latest limited edition fine art print from renowned fantasy artist James C. Christensen, and the second Greenwich Workshop "Art in Concert" collaboration of artwork with music.

level of quality to all who seek it. The implementation of this philosophy requires innovation, so the company has stayed at the forefront of the industry by finding the best artists and publishing their work in many high-quality formats.

The Greenwich Workshop found long-term success with prints related to particular subject matter. These prints included art of the American West, North American and African wildlife, Americana, and nautical art, aviation, fantasy, nostalgia, U.S. history, and what is now called "concept art."

"Beauty and the Beast" is the newest limited edition fine art print from Thomas Blackshear II, one of today's most respected young artists.
© 1994 The Greenwich Workshop, Inc. All rights reserved.

This latter category is the creation of Bev Doolittle, whose vision and success were instrumental in making The Greenwich Workshop an industry leader. From her very first Greenwich Workshop print in 1979, she has sold out her editions in record time and in record numbers, making her the industry's best-selling artist.

The Greenwich Workshop has been a consistent leader, introducing and establishing Bev Doolittle and artists in each of these art genres. Another successful category the company has showcased is fantasy. Over the years, the company has seen artists like James C. Christensen and James Gurney pass from relative obscurity to industry phenomenon with their respective lands "a little left of reality" and "apart from time."

In its efforts to bring art to an always-growing base, the company works with the top names in the art field, as well as with many successful painters who initially found fame in other areas as well. These include astronaut Alan Bean, best-selling author Robert Fulghum and actor Bill Dee Williams. Their work continues to bring "The Art of Discovery" to new eyes.

A Continuing Commitment to Innovation

Taking each new work of art as an individual challenge, The Greenwich Workshop has developed trade names for various product segments. Some of the company's innovations include the larger-format *MasterWork*™ print, the intimately-sized prints in *The Greenwich Workshop Cameo*™ *Collection*, the *Greenwich Workshop Classics*™ collection based on timeless and beloved fables, fairy tales or myths, and the *Personal Commission*® print. Among their latest innovations is *The Greenwich Workshop Chapbook*™ series, a refinement of a 16th-century tradition combining words and art to tell of an artist's inspiration.

The Greenwich Workshop also markets a line of high-quality, fine art posters, many of which have been published with the cooperation of leading museums and organizations, including the Smithsonian Institution's National Air and Space Museum, the Folger Shakespeare Library, the Cowboy Artists of America and Yosemite National Park. At present, the company is working with the Library of Congress to publish historical treasures from its remarkable collection.

From Walls to Bookshelves to the Television Screen

In the area of books, too, The Greenwich Workshop employs its expertise in art publishing. The company found great success publishing limited edition collector art books for its dealer base and then collaborating with top book publishers in the creation of high-quality, mass-market versions of these books, to bring the work of their artists to the general public.

The Greenwich Workshop's first book, *The Art of Charles Wysocki: An American Celebration*, is now in its fifth printing, with over 100,000 copies in print. Their second, *The Art of Bev Doolittle*, is now in its seventh printing, with more than 270,000 in print. The need for an expanded, full-time book department became clear with the creation, design and publication of *Dinotopia: A Land Apart from Time* by James Gurney. That book has become an international publishing event with more than a million copies in print, a limited edition print and fine art poster program, a plethora of accompanying licensed products, and a sequel set for 1995 publication.

The Greenwich Workshop Press was created with the goal of "selling more books the second year of release than the first." With that dedication to quality and support, the resulting books — featuring the Western art of James Bama, Tom Lovell, Frank C.

McCarthy, and Howard Terpning, the aviation art of William S. Phillips, and *A Journey of the Imagination* by James Christensen — have won awards for excellence, and the imprint is gaining recognition for a quality of conception and design that is unique in the industry.

Another recent innovation The Greenwich Workshop has introduced is *The Living Canvas®* video series. Videos are produced to accompany selected limited edition prints, to promote specific artists, or as stand-alone products. In order to develop this concept throughout its business, the company has established an internal video-operation. These videos enjoy a growing use in telling "the story behind the story" of certain prints. For instance, an aviation print depicting a historic occasion may be accompanied by an original, feature-length video that documents and brings to life the full story behind the artist's print. Greenwich Workshop videos have won awards from industry associations and film festivals, and have been aired on public television stations.

The success of these divisions of the company has opened an entirely new realm in marketing. Now Greenwich Workshop works of art grace many products, from calendars to clothing. The company's standards of high quality are maintained by the Greenwich Workshop Licensing Department. Each artist is carefully matched to each new medium, ensuring that artistic credibility is preserved at all times.

Doing Good While Doing Well

Today, The Greenwich Workshop chooses to publish subjects that enrich people's lives, carry viewers to new worlds, or simply provide the pure satisfaction of a beautifully rendered work of art. From aviation to wildlife, from books to sculptures, The Greenwich Workshop focuses on the pleasure of discovering art in all aspects of life and living. Therefore, both the company and its artists share a concern for the environment, an appreciation of history, and a love of cultural heritage.

Nowhere are these beliefs more clearly evident than in the company's historic practice of using art to contribute to worthwhile causes. In the words of Chairman and Chief Executive Officer David P. Usher, "We want to do good while we are doing well." Throughout its existence, The Greenwich Workshop has donated more than three million dollars to various non-profit organizations related to health, the environment, public-service, history and cultural preservation.

Design for the Future

The next expansion of Greenwich Workshop facilities occurred in 1994, when the company moved from its Trumbull headquarters (30,000 square feet) to a 55,000-square-foot location at One Greenwich Place, Shelton, Connecticut, to accommodate growth in all areas of the business. There the company will continue to explore new horizons in "The Art of Discovery."

"Moonfire" is the latest of wilderness and wildlife artist Stephen Lyman's best-selling limited edition fine art "firelight" prints.

Hallmark Keepsake Ornaments
Twenty Years of Cherished Memories and Prized Collectibles

Since its first collection of Christmas ornaments — six decorated balls and twelve yarn figures — appeared in 1973, Hallmark Keepsake Ornaments have helped revolutionize the way Americans decorate Christmas trees. Today, twenty years later, families can affordably adorn their trees with special remembrances and collector pieces — an array of specially designed and crafted ornaments such as tin locomotives, rocking horses, and ornaments featuring lights, motion and sound.

Before 1973, most Americans decorated their Christmas trees with mass-produced glass balls, along with tinsel and garland, or with expensive limited edition ornaments. But since that time, an ornament collecting phenomenon has swept the country, and many have discovered the collectibility of Keepsake Ornaments.

Twenty Years of "Firsts"

The first edition of Hallmark's *Here Comes Santa* series, now the longest-running Keepsake Ornament series, was introduced in 1979. Special Edition ornaments have been unveiled each year since 1980, beginning with "Heavenly Minstrel" and "Checking It Twice." Artists' Favorites — a selection of ornaments featuring the signature of the designer — have been part of each year's collection since 1987. The first Artists' Favorites included four ornaments by Ed Seale, Bob Siedler and Donna Lee.

In 1984, Lighted Keepsake Ornaments appeared, paving the way for the addition of sound, music, motion and even talking Keepsake Magic Ornaments. Hallmark introduced the field's first complete line of miniature ornaments in 1988 with Keepsake Miniature Ornaments. These miniatures are perfect for those who want or need smaller decorative holiday items and different ways to commemorate the holiday.

As interest in collecting Keepsake Ornaments grew, so did the Hallmark Keepsake Ornament Collector's Club. Formed in 1987, today it is more than 100,000 members strong and is one of the largest and fastest-growing collector organizations in the nation. The first national Hallmark Keepsake Ornament Collector's Club Convention was held in Kansas City, Missouri in 1991. In addition, Keepsake Ornament enthusiasts meet in

One of the first Hallmark Personalized Keepsake Ornaments is this appealing "Mailbox Delivery," featuring a red mailbox that may be personalized. Inside there's a raccoon bearing a letter!

more than 150 local clubs coast to coast, even including Alaska.

Another measure of the ornaments' popularity is the warm reception for the books of Clara Scroggins, one of America's most knowledgeable authorities on ornament collecting. Ms. Scroggins introduced her first Hallmark Keepsake Ornament book in 1983, and the sixth edition, *Keepsake Ornaments: A Collector's Guide 1973-1993*, was published in 1993.

The anniversary year of 1993 also saw three important "firsts" for Hallmark Keepsake Ornaments. The first Personalized Keepsake Ornament line appeared: important because personalization is one of the strongest trends to emerge in the 1990s. Hallmark now offers twelve Keepsake Ornaments that may be personalized with name, date, or even a phrase. For example, "Festive Album Photo Holder" features an album that may be personalized on the cover; "Santa Says" includes a cord that may be pulled to reveal a personalized message; and "Mailbox Delivery" features a red mailbox that may be personalized and that opens to reveal a letter-bearing raccoon.

Hallmark also introduced the first Anniversary Editions in 1993, with four ornaments commemorating the twenty years of Keepsake Ornaments. In addition, the first Keepsake Ornament inspired by a collector appeared. "Look for the Wonder" was designed in honor of the 1991 Keepsake Ornament Convention's costume contest winner, Joanne

Pawelek. The ornament, designed by Donna Lee, reflects Ms. Pawelek's favorite Christmas memories of Ukranian holiday traditions.

Hallmark Keepsake Ornaments: A Contemporary Expression of a Beloved American Tradition

For many people, decorating their homes and Christmas trees with ornaments is one of the most enjoyable ways to capture the magic and excitement of the holidays. Research by Hallmark Cards shows that more than eighty percent of all United States families will put up and decorate a Christmas tree this year, carrying on a centuries-old tradition.

Although Christmas trees first appeared in America in the 1700s, the emergence of the modern Christmas tree actually dates back to fifteenth and sixteenth-century Germany. Evergreens were used first in German church plays at Christmas and were hung with apples to symbolize a Paradise tree. Paradise trees later found their way into German homes, where they were adorned with small white wafers, and later, small pastries cut into stars, angels, hearts and flowers. During the next 200 years, this custom slowly spread throughout Germany and Europe.

Although decorated trees were first brought to America by Hessians — German mercenaries — fighting in the Revolutionary War, decorated trees did not become widely popular until people saw the ornaments brought to America by families emigrating from Germany and England in the 1840s.

In 1880, F.W. Woolworth, of five-and-dime fame, reluctantly stocked his stores with German-made ornaments. But to his surprise, by 1890, he was selling $25 million worth of ornaments at nickel and dime prices. The ornaments available at that time primarily were German hand-cast lead and hand-blown glass decorations. As time passed, the ornaments became more elaborate — and expensive. Silk and wood thread, chenille and tinsel embellished many of them. Stiff spun glass appeared as angel and butterfly wings; tinsel was used on fancy flower baskets, vases, air balloons and egg zeppelins.

Germany faced virtually no competition until 1925. Then Japan began producing ornaments in large quantities for export to this country. Czechoslovakia also entered the field with many fancy ornaments. By 1935, more than 250 million Christmas tree ornaments were being imported to the United States.

Not until 1939 and the outbreak of World War II did an American company significantly enter the ornament business. Using a machine designed to make light bulbs, Corning engineers produced more than 2,000 glass ornament balls a minute.

These glass ball ornaments — along with tinsel and garland — remained the standard American Christmas tree fare until 1973 when Hallmark Cards introduced the first Keepsake Ornaments. Now families could affordably adorn their trees with an array of such specially designed and crafted ornaments as Tin Locomotives, Rocking Horses, Frosty Friends and Clothespin Soldiers.

"Passionate Hobby" Leads to Successful Hallmark Keepsake Ornament Collector's Club

According to Hallmark research, collecting ornaments is one of America's favorite pastimes. Approximately twelve percent of the U.S. population buy at least one quality designed ornament each year. More than half of those individuals consider themselves collectors. And of those who buy Keepsake Ornaments, seven out of ten are collectors.

Thus, it comes as no surprise that there are already more than 100,000 members of the Hallmark Keepsake Collector's Club, with many thousands of new members joining annually. For a $20 membership fee, the Club's exclusive benefits include: an annual Keepsake of Membership Ornament, handcrafted exclusively for Club members; a subscription to "Collector's Courier," the club's quarterly newsletter; a personalized membership card; a sneak preview issue of the *Dream Book*; and an updated Keepsake Ornament Treasury binder.

The 1991 Keepsake Ornament Convention costume design winner, Joanne Pawelek, inspired this "Look for the Wonder" ornament.

One of the Keepsake Ornament Collectors' Club Limited Edition Ornaments for 1993 from Hallmark is "Gentle Tidings." A wood display stand is included at no additional charge.

Members also have the opportunity to order exclusive and limited edition ornaments. In 1993, these included the 1993 Members Only Anniversary Edition ornament "Trimmed With Memories," celebrating the twentieth anniversary of Keepsake Ornaments, as well as the 1993 Limited Edition Ornaments titled "Sharing Christmas" and "Gentle Tidings." (Wood display stands are included with both Limited Edition Ornaments). Only a limited number of these ornaments are produced, so club members' orders are processed on a first-come, first-serve basis.

Each year in June, participating Hallmark stores host an Ornament Premiere to unveil the year's Keepsake Ornaments. This provides the avid collector the chance to view the entire ornament collection early in the year. Hallmark Keepsake Ornament artists and Collector's Club representatives also make special appearances at selected Hallmark stores nationwide to visit with collectors and to autograph ornaments.

The Newest "Crop" of Keepsake Ornaments

During 1993, Hallmark offered a total of 230 ornaments ranging in price from $3 to $35. Keepsake Ornaments included 141 designs divided into six design groups: Anniversary Edition, Collectible Series, For Someone Special, Artists' Favorites, New Attractions and Special Editions.

In recognition of the twentieth anniversary of Keepsake Ornaments, Hallmark issued four Anniversary Edition designs titled "Tannenbaum's

Department Store," "Shopping With Santa," "Frosty Friends," and "Glowing Pewter Wreath." New as part of the Collectible Series in 1993 were three ornament series: "Humpty-Dumpty" premiered the *Mother Goose* series, "U.S. Christmas Stamps" was first in the *U.S. Christmas Stamps* series; and "Peanuts®" was first in *The Peanuts® Gang* series.

Hallmark again offers the Artists' Favorites with a selection of five ornaments, each personalized with its designer's signature. Hallmark also presented two 1993 Special Edition ornaments: "Julianne and Teddy," featuring Julianne, whose dress is made from real fabric; and "Dickens Caroler Bell — Lady Daphne," featuring a Victorian lady created from fine porcelain and painted by hand. This ornament is the fourth and final in the *Dickens Caroler Bell* collection. New Attractions feature six ornaments from the *Winnie the Pooh* collection; three Holiday Fliers (tin ornaments with propellers that really turn); and six ornaments from the *Looney Tunes* collection.

The 1993 Keepsake Magic Ornaments feature nineteen designs incorporating light, motion, music, voice or a combination of these. For example, "Radio News Flash" features voice, sound and light, and plays a recorded news bulletin about Santa's arrival. Another Keepsake Magic Ornament, "Winnie the Pooh," features the well-known voice of Pooh. All of the motion ornaments include on-off switches that stop the ornaments' motion while the light stays on to illuminate the ornaments' holiday scenes. Hallmark was the first to introduce this feature.

The Keepsake Miniature Ornaments line for 1993 offered thirty-six of these tiny ornaments. Two new series of Keepsake Miniature Ornaments are titled *On The Road* and *March Of The Teddy Bears*. The second theme set of ornaments in the Keepsake Miniature line is *Tiny Green Thumbs* — six little mice situated among gardening tools, flower pots and baskets. In addition, the fourth *Precious Edition* ornament, which is part of an ongoing collection of finely crafted ornaments using age-old techniques, is entitled "Crystal Angel" and is full-lead crystal and gold plated.

Considering the level of awareness and trust Americans have for Hallmark Cards, it comes as no surprise that millions became immediate fans of Hallmark Keepsake Ornaments. With twenty years of "ornament innovation" in the past, the artists and designers of Hallmark ornaments look forward with great anticipation. They will continue to innovate — creating "cherished moments and prized collectibles" for families and their Christmas trees across the land.

The Hamilton Collection

Staying One Step Ahead of Collectible Trends Makes The Hamilton Collection a Leading Creator of Porcelain Plates and Dolls

Ever since the elegant "Clara and Nutcracker" made its debut in 1978, The Hamilton Collection has reigned as one of America's most honored purveyors of limited edition plates. Combining fine art expertise with "the pulse of the marketplace," Hamilton's worldwide sources have set the pace for some of the most important plate trends of the past three decades. And in just five years, Hamilton Heritage Dolls has established an exciting new stronghold among collectors as well: an impeccable reputation for elegant dolls on a wide variety of charming themes.

Recent newsmaking plates from Hamilton have showcased the work of renowned Western artists such as David Wright, Chuck DeHaan and Chuck Ren; painters of popular culture subjects like Thomas Blackshear and Susie Morton; the Victorian keepsakes of John Grossman; and the famed "Precious Moments" characters of Sam Butcher. Hamilton Heritage Dolls' star-studded line-up of designers include the renowned Joke Grobben, Phyllis Parkins and Jane Zidjunas, among many others.

Western Art Masters Create Historic Hamilton Collector Plates

Imagine the morning sun as it breaks through the clouds…the roar of the surf as the ocean ebbs and flows…the rhythmic pounding of hooves as a magnificent, chestnut-colored stallion charges down the beach. This is the drama of "Surf Dancer" — the collector plate debut of the award-winning Western art master, Chuck DeHaan. As a former horse trainer and cowboy, DeHaan has a unique ability to portray the raw beauty of the horse and the sea…a breathtaking glimpse of nature's power and splendor. "Surf Dancer" represents just one of a collection of plates from DeHaan, presented exclusively by The Hamilton Collection and entitled *Unbridled Spirits*. Each plate celebrates the beauty and power of horses running free, and each carries the same original issue price of $29.50.

While DeHaan's genius centers around his paintings of horses, The Hamilton Collection also has introduced several remarkable Western art

plate series inspired by the nobility of Native Americans. Artist David Wright recently unveiled "Prairie Flower" as his first *Princesses Of The Plains* offering, as one example. Wright first won fame among Hamilton collectors with his stirring plate portrait of "Sacajawea," the first in a series featuring renowned American Indian heroines. Now with "Prairie Flower," he shares a moment of happy anticipation as an Indian bride contemplates the ceremony that is soon to take place.

Another gifted painter of Native Americans is Chuck Ren, who won the Hamilton commission to create the *Mystic Warriors* plate collection beginning with "Deliverance." A native of the American Southwest, he divides his time between painting and collecting Western artifacts. These artifacts — and the clothing of the Plains Indians which Ren has accumulated — provide the artist with a rich store of authentic props for his work.

In Chuck Ren's "Deliverance," a mighty warrior has traveled far to a place he considers holy, following the paths used by his ancestors for countless generations. "Oh Great Spirit, send me your guidance for the great challenges that await me," he requests. Ren brings this spiritual moment alive in a work of rare significance, presented on fine porcelain.

Popular Culture Plates Bring Honor to Hamilton

In years past, The Hamilton Collection and its artists have earned awards and recognition for collector plates featuring beloved television programs, movies, actors and singers. Thomas Blackshear and Hamilton shared "Plate of the Year" honors for one of the artist's several tributes to *The Wizard Of Oz*, and Hamilton has collaborated with him to produce his very popular and widely renowned *Star Trek*® plates. Most recently, Blackshear has turned his attention to the newest *Star Trek*® series, with a collection of remarkable portraits of *Star Trek: The Next Generation*™ crew.

To many *Star Trek* fans, it seems like only yesterday that Mr. Spock and Captain Kirk first ventured "where no man has ever gone before." But now "Captain Jean-Luc Picard™" and company

Chuck Ren, a renowned painter of Native Americans, created the original painting for this Mystic Warriors *plate entitled "Deliverance."*

The Victorian keepsakes of John Grossman have become extremely popular since The Hamilton Collection unveiled "A Visit from St. Nicholas."

Pretty blonde "Amy" enjoys a ride on her favorite rocking horse, in this appealing work of art from Jane Zidjunas and Hamilton Heritage Dolls.

have been a part of our television life for more than six full years — and thus Hamilton and Blackshear have created a series of plates officially authorized by Paramount Pictures to mark this Anniversary. The mission of *Star Trek: The Next Generation* is to chart "the continuing voyages of *Starship Enterprise™*," and Picard makes a compelling leader for their journeys.

In Blackshear's portrait, Picard is portrayed against a vast and infinitely beautiful backdrop of deep space, ablaze with stars in the brilliance of birth and death. The "Captain Jean-Luc Picard" plate is adorned by a specially designed commemorative 23K gold border. At 8-1/4" in diameter, it is one in a series that will honor other characters from *Star Trek: The Next Generation*.

Susie Morton has been portraying celebrities on porcelain since 1978, and even before that she had established her reputation as an "artist to the stars." Her early plates honoring "Marilyn Monroe," "John Wayne," "Elvis Presley," and other stars of film and music today trade hands at prices high above their original levels. Now in association with Hamilton and Republic Pictures, Ms. Morton draws upon the archives of this renowned movie studio to create *The Republic Pictures Film Library Collection*. The first plate to debut is "Showdown with Laredo" from *Angel And The Badman*, a Republic Picture, starring John Wayne as Quirt Evans. The artwork portrays "The Duke" in two poses from this 1947 hit: a close-up and a longer shot of the actual showdown duel. Other films saluted as the series unfolds include *Rio Grande*, *The Sands Of Iwo Jima* and five other John Wayne classics from Republic Pictures.

The Victorian Ephemera of John Grossman

Artist John Grossman started his career painting contemporary landscapes, but a day spent browsing in an antique store changed his life forever. Grossman happened upon a collection of Victorian paper "ephemera," or keepsakes: elegantly flowered calling cards, romantic notes and other wonderful and colorful snippets. From that moment on, Grossman began building a world-class collection of antique Victorian ephemera. Today, he is a leading authority of Victoriana — and he has developed a unique art style: the Victorian keepsake collage.

Now The Hamilton Collection celebrates the joyous spirit of Victoriana with "Dearest Kiss," the first limited edition collector plate ever to present Grossman's priceless Victorian treasures captured on fine porcelain. Created under Grossman's personal direction, "Dearest Kiss" revolves around an affectionate image of youth. An ardent young suitor kisses the cheek of his sweet beloved. To frame these delicate innocents, Grossman has arranged a myriad of fanciful antique art treasures: tiny roses in blush pink and delicate apricot...pert blue-and-white forget-me-nots...angels and cupids, fairies and cherubs. And "Dearest Kiss" is surrounded by a lavishly elegant border design of 23K gold, making it all the more attractive.

Hamilton Christmas Collectibles Include Both Plates and Dolls

Fresh from the success of "Dearest Kiss," The Hamilton Collection and John Grossman joined

forces once again to select some of the artist's most delightful Christmas ephemera for a holiday plate collection entitled *Victorian Christmas Memories*. The first plate, "A Visit From St. Nicholas," captures the moment when two happy children's fondest wish comes true. Magically, Santa Claus himself appears at their home to wish them a happy holiday!

Another delightful holiday plate, "Come Let Us Adore Him," debuts the *Precious Moments® Bible Story* collection from the world-renowned artist, Sam Butcher. Butcher's famous *Precious Moments* characters act out the story of Jesus' birth in this heartwarming plate, accented with a 23K gold decorative border. Significantly, this is the first plate collection ever to feature the magnificent original art from the *Precious Moments* Chapel in Carthage, Missouri.

Christmas-theme art is a favorite of collectors all year-round, and so Hamilton has extended its offerings on this theme to include elegant porcelain dolls. In collaboration with the master of child-subject art, Donald Zolan, Hamilton offers "A Christmas Prayer": a fine collector doll recreating Zolan's original painting of the same name. Kneeling on a red velvet pillow with her tiny hands clasped reverently and her shining eyes raised, a little girl whispers her evening prayers. Crafted of fine bisque porcelain and hand-painted, "A Christmas Prayer" carries an issue price of $95.00.

Famous Doll Artists Win New Acclaim for Hamilton

Over the years, The Hamilton Collection has made it a point to seek out some of the finest contemporary artists to create its limited edition plates. Now that dolls have become such an important part of the Hamilton "line-up," the firm has forged strong relationships with some of the world's most renowned doll designers as well. One of the best-known examples of this type of alliance is the Hamilton Heritage Dolls/Connie Walser Derek beauty, little "Jessica."

When "Jessica" was introduced in 1989, the market response was unprecedented. "We had never experienced anything like this at Hamilton," Chairman J.P. Smith recalls. Ms. Derek was also surprised. "I knew from the start that she was very appealing, but I had no idea that 'Jessica'

would be as popular as she has been." Collectors were drawn to this porcelain baby doll's wistful expression, sparkling blue eyes and finely detailed costume, but it was her resemblance to a real baby that captured their fascination more than anything else. Letters received by Hamilton Heritage Dolls spoke lovingly about the doll's breathtaking realism, which stimulated memories of grandchildren, nieces, and daughters alike. Then, some months after "Jessica" debuted, Hamilton invited Connie Walser Derek to smash the doll's master mold, signaling a sell-out for the doll and the end of production.

Jane Zidjunas is another renowned doll designer whose "toddlers" have won the hearts of Hamilton collectors. Pretty little "Jennifer" captured the attention of *Doll Reader* magazine as well, winning a recent "Doll of the Year" award in the Direct Purchase Category. "Jennifer" cuddles her new puppy close as she asks sweetly, "Mommy, *Please* can I keep him?" With her big brown eyes and her heartwarming expression, you just know she will get her way. Another Zidjunas charmer is "Amy," who rides on her very own handcrafted rocking horse. "Amy's" baby fine blonde hair is caught up in a cascade of curls with a pretty bow that matches the soft pastels of her peach, blue and yellow romper.

Another little-girl doll from Hamilton Heritage Dolls is Kay McKee's "Shy Violet," whose tender feelings are poignantly expressed in the charming tilt of her head and her downcast violet eyes. "Shy Violet" is especially prized for the intricacy of her costume: even the smocking of her pinafore — stitched by hand in deep violet hues — highlights the color of her eyes.

Like the other Hamilton Heritage Doll designers mentioned above, Virginia Ehrlich Turner has earned the acclaim of collectors, dealers, and the doll media alike. She has won numerous awards, and many of her dolls have sold out almost overnight. Her first collaboration with Hamilton has yielded "Michelle," a golden-haired beauty with enormous blue eyes, dimples, and a delightful hint of mischief in her laughing expression.

With scores more stunning collector plates and heartwarming dolls in development for the years to come, The Hamilton Collection and Hamilton Heritage Dolls stand poised to continue their inspired service to collectors and art connoisseurs on both sides of the Atlantic.

Hand & Hammer Silversmiths
Chip deMatteo Draws on His Family Heritage of Silver Craftsmanship to Create Elegant Collectible Ornaments

The origins of the thriving firm of Hand & Hammer Silversmiths can be found in New York City during the Roaring 1920s. It was there that William deMatteo, Sr., then a sixteen-year-old Italian immigrant, began a career that has inspired three generations of deMatteo silversmiths to excel at their craft. Since then, the deMatteos have shared the mysteries of their art with hundreds of apprentice and journeymen silversmiths as well.

Perfecting his craft in New York City, William deMatteo, Sr. became one of the premier silversmiths of his generation. His son, William (Bill) deMatteo, Jr., in turn became one of the most honored American silversmiths of the twentieth century. The younger deMatteo settled his young family at Colonial Williamsburg, where he became

As a child in the 1950s, little Chip deMatteo helped his mother welcome Bill deMatteo home from his work as Master Silversmith at Colonial Williamsburg. By the time he was ten, Chip became one of his father's most gifted pupils in the fine art of silversmithing.

Master Silversmith during the 1950s and oversaw a workshop of over 100 craftsmen. His two most talented pupils at Williamsburg were Philip Thorp, then a student at William & Mary, and Bill deMatteo's own son, Chip.

At a very early age, Chip showed a remarkable sense for design and talent for silversmithing. From the age of ten onward, he worked doing chores around the shop, and later developed his own style as an artist and silversmith. After college, Chip moved to Washington, D.C., where he played the "starving artist" role for several years. During that time, Chip supplemented his income doing silver work for his father and for Thorp, who was then Bill's foremost journeyman silversmith.

Along with several other silversmiths from Williamsburg, Bill, Phil and Chip moved to Alexandria, Virginia in the late 1970s, and set up their own shop at Hand & Hammer Silversmiths. It was then that the unique designs which define Hand & Hammer's work began to shine. As the studio attracted more craftsmen and purchased more equipment, the small shop in Old Town Alexandria became inadequate. To meet its needs for growth, Hand & Hammer jumped into the twenty-first century with a spacious, high-tech, custom-designed shop in Woodbridge, Virginia. It is from here that all of the beautiful Hand & Hammer pieces are created today.

The Development of a Hand & Hammer Design

Each Hand & Hammer design begins at Chip deMatteo's drawing table, where he turns his quick sketches into finished, scaled drawings. Master modelmaker Greg Villalobos is then called upon to turn those drawings into actual patterns, sculpting them by hand in either wax or metal. Making the pattern is an exacting process, often taking many weeks to complete.

Attention to detail at this stage is critical to the successful outcome of the prototype, from which molds for the casting process will be made. Hand & Hammer's ornaments are cast using the age-old

Today Chip deMatteo (third from left, front row) and Philip Thorp (third from left, back row) enjoy a harmonious working relationship with their highly trained craftspeople and support employees at Hand & Hammer Silversmiths. That's "Danny," the studio mascot, perched atop the work table.

"lost wax" method. This is a difficult, time-consuming process by which a casting model is made and then destroyed as part of the procedure. Lost wax casting is much preferred over machine stamping because it yields a piece with greater detail, and frees the designer in terms of overall form, shape or size.

After it is cast, each piece must be "finished" in the shop in Woodbridge. This is accomplished with a series of abrasives. The first step is usually tumbling: a process in which pieces are placed with abrasives in a rotating barrel for an entire day. The next steps involve progressive hand-polishing with a succession of finer and finer abrasives until the silver surface of the piece is mirror-like. Hand & Hammer's polishers, Tim, Betty Jo, Ron and Art, have been with the company for a long time, as it takes many years to develop the skills needed to make the pieces of raw silver come to life.

The shop is watched over by Gene Sutton, who, like Phil Thorp and Chip deMatteo, was trained by Bill deMatteo in Williamsburg. The pieces all are held to a rigorous quality check at each stage of finishing, so only the finest works of art leave Sutton's shop. Of course, there still is more to be done. Washing, wrapping and packaging takes time and careful effort. Employees Pam and Kathy make sure everything that goes out to the stores is first-rate.

The Inspiration for Hand & Hammer Designs

Chip deMatteo is constantly asked, "Where do you get the ideas for your wonderful designs?" According to him, it's one of the hardest questions to answer. "I've always been creative," he says. "When I was little, the most fun to me was figuring out how to make something, or to find out how something worked. I got into trouble for taking apart the seat of the school bus to see how it was put together," he laughs. "But I can have an idea buzzing around in my head for a long time before I figure out how I want it to look as an ornament or piece of jewelry. Sometimes I'll agonize over a design and sometimes it comes out just

Chip deMatteo relished the opportunity to work from Beatrix Potter's original drawings in the creation of this ornament, designed to honor the 100th anniversary of "The Tale of Peter Rabbit."

right on the first try. It's a whole new process each time. That's why it's always interesting," he says with a smile.

While original designs are the vast majority of Chip's work, he enjoys working from old and famous drawings. The "Alice in Wonderland" set of four ornaments was designed using the original John Tenniel drawings for Lewis Carroll's classic story. "Those were fun to do. Tenneil's drawings are what everyone refers to when they talk about "Alice in Wonderland," and I think ours turned out very well. By contrast, look at our 'Christmas Carol' set of four ornaments. I wanted to illustrate the Dickens book in my own way, and I'm pleased with the result," says Chip deMatteo.

In recent years, Chip has enjoyed designing sterling silver charms for charm bracelets. He did a set of "Alice in Wonderland" charms, "Wizard of Oz" charms, and "Mother Goose" charms, as well as a full contingent of Beatrix Potter's delightful creatures in miniature. "The Beatrix Potter pieces are wonderful, and working from her original drawings in England was a real thrill for me," continues Chip. "People have a wonderful nostalgic response to her little animals." In honor of the 100th anniversary of "The Tale of Peter Rabbit," Chip has designed a special ornament.

Over the years, Chip deMatteo has designed nearly 500 ornaments, some in collaboration with his father. Many of these have been sold through finer department and gift stores. In addition, some of Hand & Hammer's most collectible designs are series produced expressly for particular firms.

Hand & Hammer Enjoys Prestigious Commissions

Since 1963, Shreve, Crump & Low of Boston has commissioned Hand & Hammer to create exclusive ornaments for them. Two series, *Boston Landmarks*, and *Landmarks Of America*, are particularly notable. Also in Boston, the Museum of Fine Arts has commissioned Hand & Hammer's lovely ornaments for their Christmas catalog since 1979. Based on drawings in their collection, the series of Aubrey Beardsley's angels has been very popular. An annual dated ornament is also designed for them based on pieces from their textile collection.

The U.S. Historical Society in Richmond, Virginia has long been an exclusive customer for Hand & Hammer. An annual angel has been commissioned since 1983, with the design usually based on a famous stained glass window. Also for the Historical Society, Chip has designed a series, *Homes Of The Great American Presidents*, a set of nine ornaments fitted in a handsome leather presentation folio.

News From the Hand & Hammer Collectors' Club

Hand & Hammer collectors have long asked for a complete list of collectibles from their favorite studio, and in 1989 this request inspired "Silver Tidings," the newsletter of the Hand & Hammer Collectors' Club. The entire list is updated and published annually, along with occasional newsletters which relate the latest collectibles and where to find them.

Hand & Hammer's Collectors' Club membership is free, and the Club sponsors store and show appearances by Chip deMatteo and Philip Thorp. Collectors may sign up for the Club through participating Collectors' Club retailers or by calling Hand & Hammer at 1-800-SILVERY.

With all the new pieces coming out of the Hand & Hammer workshop, one might think that Chip deMatteo could become tired or burned out. "Not true," he says emphatically, "I have so much to keep me interested. I work with people I like, and I make beautiful things. That's what keeps me going." And Hand & Hammer's devotees hope that he "keeps going" for a long, long time.

Harbour Lights
Capturing the Romance, Drama and Architectural Significance of the World's Most Historic Lighthouses

"There is no structure as altruistic as a lighthouse.
Its only purpose is to serve humanity."
— George Bernard Shaw

For centuries, lighthouses guided our seafaring ancestors away from imminent danger to harbors of refuge and to the safety of the open sea. The graves of many less fortunate ships — and their captains and crews — lie, far beneath the waves, around the world. Now through its growing collection of hand-painted lighthouse miniatures, Harbour Lights reminds us all of the thousands of voyages made safe by these sentinels of the sea.

The saga of Harbour Lights begins with a jolly, bearded American named Bill Younger. Brought up in Washington D.C., and spending several years of his adult life in Scotland and England, Bill thrives on history. As a youth, he was recruited for Chesapeake Bay fishing expeditions with his uncle. The fishing he disliked, but the trips had a positive by-product: they allowed Bill to discover the glories of lighthouses. Later, time spent living with his wife and children in a 500-year-old house in England — and his long-standing enthusiasm for classic architecture — kindled Bill's appreciation for David Winter's delightful English Cottages.

Bill Younger had been the United States Western Regional Manager for David Winter Cottages for some years when he launched his own collectible line, Harbour Lights, in 1990. Chartered to provide "Lighthouses of the World," Harbour Lights began with several groupings of American lighthouses. In the future, the firm plans to design and craft miniature replicas of many more lighthouses from around the globe.

A Brief History of Lighthouses...
and Their Modern Plight

The world's first lighthouse was erected in 260 B.C. in Pharos, a small island off the coast of Egypt. It was the brainchild of Ptolemy I, a Macedonian general under Alexander the Great. Standing more than 400 feet high, it was renowned as one of the Seven Wonders of the Ancient World. Keeping its fires stoked was a formidable job, as its flames needed to be seen for thirty-five miles. The Pharos of Alexandria Light guided mariners until 1300 A.D., when it was destroyed by an earthquake. Various more recent structures can be seen throughout Europe, including the stunning Renaissance structure near Bordeaux, France known as Cordouan Light. Indeed, it is said that Christopher Columbus himself developed his lust for the sea while visiting his grandfather, the keeper of the Genoa Light.

In the United States, the first lighthouse built was on Little Brewster Island in Boston Harbor. It did not survive the Revolutionary War, but in the late 1700s, hundreds of lighthouses popped up on the American coastline. Their widely varied architecture reflected environmental needs, regional differences, geography and scientific experimentation. Some stood alone, while others incorporated homes for their keepers. Some were exceedingly tall, such as the 191-foot "light" at Cape Hatteras,

At 191 feet, "Cape Hatteras" is the tallest lighthouse in the United States. Located on Diamond Shoals in North Carolina, the lighthouse keeps watch over a deadly area known as the "Graveyard of the Atlantic." The barber pole-striped "Cape Hatteras" represents Harbour Lights' Original Collection.

North Carolina. Others were much shorter, sometimes reflecting their locations on rocky cliffs.

A turning point in lighthouse history occurred in 1789, when George Washington signed the Lighthouse Act, transferring a dozen lights from state control to the federal government. By the year 1800, there were over 800 lighthouses in the young American nation. Advances in lighting techniques kept the lighthouses current as decades passed, but by the latter part of the 20th century, many lighthouses were all but obsolete. In the bicentennial year of U.S. lighthouses, 1989, the Coast Guard's lavish celebrations were overshadowed for many lighthouse traditionalists by the fact that the last few lights were to be automated, thus concluding a romantic chapter in history.

We can only imagine what life must have been like for the solitary lighthouse keeper. Often so isolated that he saw other individuals just four times a year when they brought him supplies, he endured a dangerous and lonely job. Yet his service to mariners was undeniable: lighthouse keepers were directly responsible for saving hundreds of sailors each year who would have veered off course without the comforting sentinel of light to guide them.

Today, the saga of lighthouses has entered an era where preservation is paramount. Without the help of architectural buffs, lighthouse enthusiasts and other caring individuals, these dramatic structures may crumble and fade from our view. Luckily, organizations like the U.S. Lighthouse Society, Great Lakes Lighthouse Society and Shore Village Museum are devoted to organizing support for the beloved "lights."

Perhaps the most visible lighthouse promoter in America is Wayne "Mr. Lighthouse" Wheeler, the self-proclaimed "Head Pooh Bah" of the U.S. Lighthouse Society. A former Coast Guard officer,

Both "Southeast Block Island" and "New London Ledge" are lighthouse replicas from the Harbour Lights New England collection.

Wheeler told his wife one day in 1982 that there were so many Americans interested in lighthouses and their preservation that "these people really should get organized." He took on the task himself, and within a few years his work with the U.S. Lighthouse Society became a full-time career. Today, Wheeler travels the country, spreading the word about the romance and beauty of lighthouses and soliciting help for their historic preservation. He even claims dedicated Society members in land-locked North Dakota.

Harbour Lights Feeds the Enthusiasm of Lighthouse Aficionados

One glance through the daily mail at Harbour Lights is enough to illustrate how well this handsome line of limited edition lighthouses has fulfilled the pent-up demand of collectors. Hearing about Harbour Lights through word of mouth, collectors can't wait to put pen to paper and write for catalogs, price lists and historical background.

"These letters really tickle us," says Kim Andrews, Bill Younger's daughter and Managing Director for the Harbour Lights line. "We started with seventeen pieces, then added seven Great Lakes lights and seven from New England, and most recently, the seven *Southern Belles* in spring of 1993. A number of collectors wrote us to say they had all thirty-one pieces (pre-*Southern Belles*). Plus, they've even found the few with 'errors' or unusual features that were made briefly."

Collectors write Ms. Andrews asking about plans for a Harbour Lights Collectors Club, and she and Bill Younger are taking those requests seriously. "We'll start slowly," Ms. Andrews reports. "The first thing we'll offer is a newsletter."

The Original Collection *Highlights Bicentennial Stamp Subjects*

The first four Harbour Lights issues were inspired by lighthouses featured as commemorative stamps for the U.S. Lighthouse Bicentennial in 1989. While supplies last, each piece purchased from this group is accompanied by its respective stamp. In addition, each limited edition lighthouse is hand-made and hand-painted by skilled craftspeople, and each comes with its own history, Certificate of Authenticity and Registration Card. Just for fun, there is a hidden sea horse image on each Harbour Lights piece.

"West Quoddy Head" of Maine was the original lighthouse tower at West Quoddy Head, built in 1808 and used only fifty years. One of the most recognized lights in the nation, "West Quoddy

Head" incorporates a traditional New England house. "Admiralty Head" of Washington is located on Whidbey Island in what is now the Fort Casey State Park. It was first lighted in 1861 and served until 1903. While the lighthouse is open to the public only in the summer, the Harbour Lights "Admiralty Head" replica may be enjoyed all year-round.

"Sandy Hook" of New Jersey is the oldest standing lighthouse in the United States. Dating back to Colonial days, it is surprisingly still in use today. "Cape Hatteras" of North Carolina shows off its distinctive, barber pole stripes just as it has since 1798. "Great Captain Island" of Connecticut has its lighthouse sitting atop a traditional brick structure. Completed in 1838, the lighthouse was purchased in 1973 by the town of Greenwich, Connecticut, which has it open for residents' recreational purposes.

"Old Point Loma" of California was first lighted in 1855 and soared 462 feet above sea level. The Cape Cod-style building has a round, brick tower atop its center. Its vantage point is considered one of the three best harbor views in the world. "Fort Niagara" of New York is constructed of limestone in the Romanesque tradition. During the prohibition years, in addition to their regular maritime duties, Coast Guard personnel at "Fort Niagara" kept on the lookout for "rum runners." "Boston Harbor" of Massachusetts recreates the first lighthouse structure in the United States, which was destroyed by the British during the American Revolution.

"Cape Blanco" of Oregon has burned almost continually since it was first lighted on December 20, 1870. It is the westmost location of any lighthouse on the United States mainland. "North Head" of Washington has withstood gusts of 160 miles per hour while most structures nearby suffered great damage. The white tower is only two miles from Cape Disappointment Light. "Umpqua River" of Oregon was built in what was then known as the Oregon Territory, and it was first lit in 1857.

"Castle Hill" of Rhode Island nestles into a rocky ledge at the west end of Newport, and it is made of heavy, rough, granite blocks in a Richardsonian Romanesque style. "Sand Island" of Wisconsin, first lighted in 1881, is located on the Apostle Islands on Lake Superior. It is a brownstone tower and keeper's dwelling in the Gothic style. "Yaquina Head" of Oregon boasts a light 163 feet above sea level. It often is referred to as Cape Foulweather Station due to a mix-up in its original, planned location.

"Burrows Island" of Washington stands just thirty-four feet in height and is located on Puget Sound. Its light is mounted on the top of a house-type structure which also acts as the fog signal building. "Coquille River" Oregon, affectionately referred to as Bandon Light, went into service in 1896 and out of service in 1939. After years of neglect it was restored recently. "St. George's Reef" of California was one of the most expensive lighthouses ever built, due to its difficult location.

Harbour Lights Unveils New England and Great Lakes Lights

The New England series from Harbour Lights captures the nautical spirit of America's historic beginnings, including "Southeast Block Island" of Rhode Island, "New London Ledge" of Connecticut, "Whaleback" of New Hampshire, "Nauset Beach" and "Minots Ledge" of Massachusetts, and "Portland Head" and "Portland Breakwater" of Maine.

The Great Lakes collection portrays lighthouses that long have withstood the demanding, rigorous winters of the Midwest. Time and again, entire lighthouses have been blanketed with snow and ice, with only the welcoming beacon visible to the mariners. These include "Old Mackinac Point" of Michigan, "Buffalo" of New York, "Split Rock" of Minnesota, "Michigan City" of Indiana, "Cana Island" of Wisconsin, "Marblehead" of Ohio, and "Grosse Point" of Illinois.

The new Southern Belles grouping of lighthouses pays tribute to the gems of the South Atlantic coast, all portrayed — just as previous Harbour Lights presentations have been — with complete commitment to accuracy, authenticity and support of lighthouse preservation.

With more lighthouses from around the world on its drawing board, Harbour Lights invites collectors to join in supporting lighthouse preservation. They suggest that collectors contact Wayne Wheeler of the U.S. Lighthouse Society in San Francisco (244 Kearny St. — 5th Floor, San Francisco, CA 94108), Richard Moehl of the Great Lakes Lighthouse Keepers Association (P.O. Box 580, Allen Park, MI 48101), or Ken Black of the Shore Village Museum (104 Limerock Street, Rockland, ME 04841).

Hawthorne Architectural Register
Miniature Buildings Inspired by the Best of American Architecture Lead to a Housing "Boom" for Collectors

Anyone who reads the business pages knows that housing starts have been down for some time, and the U.S. real estate market is sluggish — especially compared to the "boom years" of the 1980s. But the 1990s are developing a housing sales boom of their own, at least in one segment: miniature buildings that replicate the best of American architecture.

Leading the way in this housing market upswing is Hawthorne Architectural Register: a top marketer of highly detailed architectural sculptures. Although many of these pieces are less than four inches tall, they beautifully capture every aspect of style and detail found in the full-size, original buildings.

Hawthorne's "listings" include houses in styles ranging from 18th-century native stone cottages to antebellum mansions to Victorian "painted ladies." However, no matter what style they are, all Hawthorne buildings must meet standards of excellence which the company has established in the following areas: historical significance of the subject; artists' credentials; quality of sculptural detail at scale; authenticity of architectural detail; period-inspired palette; period building materials depicted; authenticity of environmental details; and

Scarlett O'Hara runs down the porch steps of her beloved Tara while Mammy calls to her from an upstairs window in "Tara...Scarlett's Pride." Hawthorne Architectural Register adds drama to many of its creations with tiny figures strategically placed outside of its miniature buildings.

statement of edition and required documentation.

Most of Hawthorne's miniatures are designed and sculpted by the husband-and-wife team of Kenneth and Hope LeVan. In addition to being accomplished artists and sculptors, the Pennsylvania couple has personally restored twelve historic buildings, including their current residence, built in 1750 as the home of patriot Colonel John Lesher.

"Springbridge Cottage" Features a Tiny Figurine

The LeVans' sculptures showcase authentic details that do more than create an accurate reproduction; they also provide a fascinating glimpse into the everyday lives of earlier Americans. For example, in "Springbridge Cottage," a tiny stairway leads to a Dutch door, half-open in welcome; the walls are covered with colorful roses; and a young girl named Rebecca sits on a small stone bridge. The artists drew inspiration for this series from the many stone structures found around their Pennsylvania hometown, including their own restored home.

"Springbridge Cottage" is the first sculpture in *Stonefield Valley*, a collection based on rural communities constructed of native stone by 18th-Century European settlers. It is also Hawthorne's first cottage to include a human figure — in the form of a tiny, hand-painted figurine less than an inch tall. This appealing innovation was subsequently incorporated into several other series sculpted by Mr. and Mrs. LeVan, including *Gone With The Wind* and *Victoria Grove*.

Scarlett's Beloved Tara is Captured by the LeVans

For many, the grace of the Old South is epitomized by the fictional buildings which formed the backdrop for Scarlett and Rhett's romance in *Gone With The Wind*. Now the elegant lines of Tara, Twelve Oaks and other key structures from this classic American film have been reproduced as architectural miniatures. The *Gone With The Wind* collection begins with "Tara...Scarlett's Pride," an

authentic portrayal of the film's opening scene.

Amid the stately columns and lush grounds of the O'Hara family home, a pewter figurine depicts Scarlett storming away after learning of Ashley's engagement while another figurine in an upstairs window represents Mammy, calling for Scarlett to return.

Victoria Grove Series Combines Buildings and Gardens

A more sedate scene is the subject of "Lilac Cottage," the initial sculpture in *Victoria Grove*, a series blending the charm of Victorian architecture with the classic beauty of that era's lush gardens. A one-and-a-half story Queen Anne Victorian painted salmon, peach and blue, this cottage takes its name from the blooming lilac bushes which surround it.

A delicate pewter figurine of a young girl named Susannah sits on the front steps. Dressed in her Sunday best, Susannah enjoys a few quiet moments with her cat while she waits for the rest of the family to get ready for church. A picket fence and a goldfish pond in the backyard add more charm to this idyllic vignette.

Colonial Buildings Round Out the LeVans' Contributions

The LeVans are also responsible for two other Hawthorne collections: *Strolling In Colonial America*, which recreates key landmarks of a typical American town, circa 1766; and *Concord: Home Of American Literature*, which depicts the homes of famous literary figures who settled in the Massachusetts town during the 1850s.

"Jefferson's Ordinarie," whose edition closed on July 4, 1992, was the first in the *Strolling In Colonial America* series, and it captures the beauty and charm of a Colonial village inn — or "ordinarie" — circa 1776. The village inn was the center of social and political life in Colonial America. "Jefferson's Ordinarie" features a main building connected by a double-arched breezeway to a separate summer kitchen, where food is prepared. It is hand-painted in fourteen colors of the Colonial period.

Another piece from this landmark series is "Millrace Store," the general store where people came to socialize and trade in a typical colonial town. Two semi-detached buildings with cedar shingle roofs — a store and the storekeeper's residence — are depicted in this sculpture. Other sculpted details include a hand-lettered sign, an open Dutch door, and barrels of tea, rum and

A little girl enjoys a quiet moment outdoors with her cat while the rest of her family prepares for church inside their "Lilac Cottage." The picket fence and authentic Victorian paint job add charm to this Hawthorne edition.

Hawthorne Architectural Register recently entered the field of lighted porcelain cottages with handsome creations like "Olde Porterfield Tea Room."

spices stored on the dock. "Millrace Store" is hand-painted in sixteen colors of the Colonial period.

Strolling In Colonial America continues with "Eastbrook Church," the colonial house of worship. Its arched vestibule shelters the main entrance, which has one door open in symbolic welcome. A neat brick wall surrounds the churchyard, and in the small cemetery, three sheep keep the lawn trimmed amid a stone cross and simple stone markers. The building is hand-painted in ten colors of the Colonial period.

As for *Concord: Hometown Of American Literature*, the series celebrates the unique literary heritage of Concord, Massachusetts. The collection begins with the residence that Nathaniel Hawthorne moved into in 1852. It features a unique three-story tower designed by Hawthorne

to provide him with an inspiring view of the countryside while he worked. Trellised climbing roses shade the front door and in back, a comfortable bench with an open book depicts one of the writer's favorite spots for contemplation.

Norman Rockwell Family Trust Authorizes Hawthorne Sculptures

Additional Hawthorne sculptures have been inspired by two other small towns which were also made famous by the talents of a gifted former resident. Norman Rockwell lived and worked in Arlington, Vermont from 1938 to 1953 before moving to Stockbridge, Massachusetts, where he spent the last twenty-five years of his life. His studio and other buildings from his Vermont years are the subject of *Rockwell's Home For The Holidays*, while *Stockbridge At Christmas* consists of important buildings from his Massachusetts hometown. Both are authorized by the Norman Rockwell Family Trust.

The former series begins with "Christmas Eve at the Studio," and represents the first Hawthorne sculpture to feature an exclusive picture window concept. This allows collectors to look inside the studio and see the artist working at his easel. Covered with snow and decorated with evergreens and colored lights, the studio and barn are ready for the holidays.

The latter series represents one of Hawthorne's first entries into the popular illuminated segment of the market. These larger-scale, hollow porcelain houses are being marketed under the name *Hawthorne Porchlight Collections*. They are lit on all four sides by a hidden bulb and cord, inserted from the bottom. *Stockbridge At Christmas* is based on an illustration originally painted by the late artist for the December 1967 issue of *McCalls* magazine.

In addition to the Stockbridge collection, *Thomas Kinkade's Candlelight Cottages*, representing the first three-dimensional translation of artwork by "The Painter of Light," have also been introduced under the Porchlight name.

As the array presented here attests, Hawthorne offers a constantly expanding selection of solid and illuminated houses. The studio plans to continue developing architectural sculptures which offer the collector truly affordable housing for years to come.

This range of Hawthorne buildings shows the many architectural styles depicted: from rustic country structures to the elaborate gingerbread trim of the classic Victorians. Whatever the style, Hawthorne Architectural Register and its artists are devoted to authenticity in every detail of sculpture and coloration.

John Hine Studios, Inc.
Artists' Talents Flourish in John Hine Studios Creative Environment

John Hine has an eye for raw talent. And his restored, seventeenth-century barn, "Eggars Hill," in Hampshire, England is the "heart" of the John Hine Studios' creativity. With its elaborate gardens and visitors' center, the Eggars Hill site attracts admirers from around the world. There they can feel the excitement in the air as John Hine takes new talent under his wing.

While each of his artists enjoys complete creative freedom, Hine works closely with them, one on one. He wins their trust so that they relish his critiques and rely on him to support the creative process by helping them to identify and develop new ideas. Meanwhile, Hine continually seeks out new artisans, while those already on board redouble their efforts to stretch their gifts to the limit.

A Fruitful Partnership: John Hine and David Winter

John Hine and David Winter launched their first collaborative effort in 1979, when the renowned artist Faith Winter recommended her nineteen-year-old son David to Hine for a special project. Hine had an idea for heraldic plaques to be sold in England's market stalls, and he soon realized that young David was possessed of a special ability.

As Hine recalls, "There has never been the slightest doubt in my mind about the talent of David Winter. (At that time) only a handful of people knew him and nobody thought of him as a highly significant sculptor who would one day become a household name. Yet there was, even then, the first glimmering signs of something truly outstanding.

"Instinct has always been my lodestar and the bristling of the hairs on the back of my neck when I watched David at work reinforced that fundamental intuition. It led me to believe that here, in front of my eyes, was the chrysalis of an immense emerging talent."

The plaques Hine and David Winter developed did not prove popular, but a market vendor advised that butter dishes in the shape of cottages would sell well. From this idea, David's first miniature cottage, "The Mill House," was born.

To create their cottages, Hine and Winter set up shop in an old coal shed behind David's parents home, and as the craze for English cottages grew, so did Winter's abilities. Winter utilized a hard sculpting wax and made his own tools from "found objects" such as matchsticks or a bit of lace. The range of cottages began to include pieces that had caves, tunnels, bridges, even Robin Hood's hideaway, with details as miniscule as a mouse.

David Winter continues to challenge the moldmaking engineers as his sculptures become increasingly more sophisticated. Some of his recent pieces have added metal structures such as railings or beams too fragile to be produced in Crystacal, the material that the cottages are cast from.

The current range of David Winter Cottages available now numbers over one hundred, with a similar amount of retired cottages on the "secondary market," appreciating in value. Although Winter now works from his own home studio, he still meets with Hine every Tuesday night at the pub for their weekly brainstorming session.

Maurice Wideman

"Moe" Wideman, as he is fondly known to collectors, was sought out by John Hine to create an American version of the English cottage. Moe, although a Canadian, was perfect for this American task, because he spent his youth traveling everywhere around the United States. His earliest jobs were in the commercial art field, the most memorable being the creation of a lifesize Hereford cow sculpture for the Department of Agriculture. Wideman also created miniature farm buildings such as barns and silos.

Wideman's talent as an artist and his curiosity about America's architectural "melting pot" truly came to life in The American Collection. The sculptor spent a year in the Studios, working with John Hine to conceptualize the pieces. Wideman created his originals in a soft oil clay, just as he still does today. He insists on creating his own master molds, as he did in the early days. Wideman always has worked with Master Paint Originator Kerry Agar in England to determine authentic

London By Gaslight, a series of cottages and buildings lining a bustling street in Victorian London, is a collaborative project between John Hine Studios artists Bob Russell and Andrew Stadden. Russell sculpted the architecture while Stadden created the characters walking along the boulevard.

coloration, and continues to do so. But now Wideman and Hine discuss new concepts in their biannual meetings in England, and by fax and phone.

The American Collection now has retired, but Wideman's affinity for Americana continues in his range titled *Moe's Houses.* Every piece tells a recognizable tale through the hilarious characters that inhabit it, whether it's mischievous trick-or-treaters or the folks from down on the farm.

The Man John Hine Calls "Genius Jon"

Jon Herbert, dubbed "The Genius" by John Hine, studied and created art throughout his youth. He began at John Hine Studios as a mold-maker and caster, knowing that he would gain hands-on experience in a new medium. John Hine had heard of Herbert's talents as a woodworker,

David Winter works outdoors on a pleasant spring day in England, while his cat Budjar looks on.

and asked Herbert to create a special parquetry box. When Hine saw the results, he knew immediately that Jon Herbert possessed many untapped talents.

The first collaboration of Hine and Herbert was the *Shoe Houses*: whimsical cottages that resemble shoes surrounded by elaborate gardens. Next came the *Father Time Clocks*: castles and manor houses with real working clocks in their facades.

The latest from "Genius Jon" is *Animal Antics*: a collection of costumed animals with a twist of fantasy. For example, a dragon is perched on a treasure chest, while a kingly frog rides his turtle mount, and a mouse couple show off their finery. It is anyone's guess what the next collaboration between Hine and Herbert will produce!

A Studio Full of Master Craftsmen and Artists

There are many other success stories from the John Hine Studios. Some of the artisans create on location; others from their own favorite digs. All work closely with John Hine as the masterpieces progress. Prominent, current Hine collaborators include Bob Russell, Andrew Stadden, Janet King, John Hughes, and the craftspeople of the Cameo Guild Studios.

Bob Russell is one of today's John Hine artists: a sculptor whose influences come mainly from the styles of Art Nouveau and medieval fantasy. Russell attended Coventry College of Art and the Liverpool College of Art before John Hine first saw his creations at a 1983 exhibit in Birmingham, England. Immediately, Hine recognized Russell's potential. And since then, many wonderful projects have been the result of their collaboration.

Russell has done several special John Hine Studios commissions for Disney, including castles

for both Cinderella and Sleeping Beauty. His most popular accomplishment to date has been *London By Gaslight*, a series of miniature English buildings with illuminated windows along a Victorian street.

Andrew Stadden grew up around collectible artworks, as his father Charles Stadden is a well-known sculptor of military miniatures. The young artist trained as an electrical engineer, but eventually followed in his father's footsteps. David Winter Cottages collectors may recognize Stadden's work as the miniature Baron and Baroness characters on "Mad Baron Fourthrite's Folly" cottage, or the animals and townspeople added onto the *Shires Collection. London by Gaslight* also features Stadden's miniatures, with recognizable Londoners such as Jack the Ripper, Holmes and Watson, a "bobby" or a street lamp-lighter.

Janet King, trained at the Epsom School of Art and Design and Amersham Art and Design College, is a multi-talented artist. Her sketches and paintings have graced the Guild magazine *Cottage Country*, as well as "The Tale of Pershore Mill." She is equally skilled as a sculptor, however. *Santa's Big Day* is Ms. King's series of twelve figurines that depict Santa waking up, fixing the reindeers' breakfast, and delivering toys, with many humorous occurrences along the way. Her most recent creation is *Family Tree*: heartwarming miniatures of a Victorian family selecting their tree, decorating it and exchanging special gifts.

John Hine and John Hughes share an appreciation and talent for classical music, and it was for this reason that Hine lured Hughes away from the piano department of Harrods in London. Hughes created musical scores for several recordings of John Hine Studios' music division, but was quickly sidetracked into the world of David Winter Cottages. As he is now Guild Chairman and assistant editor of the *Cottage Country* Guild magazine, one might expect Hughes to have his hands too full for other John Hine Studios projects. However, collectors enjoy John Hughes' books, such as *The David Winter Cottages Handbook* and *Inside David Winter Cottages*, too much for him to limit himself to one area of expertise.

David Winter has begun a series of collabora-

Artist "Genius Jon" Herbert claims that Shoe Houses *are created only in the dreams of an old shoemaker named Crispin, but collectors have caught on that it is really Herbert's witty imagination and talent behind these fanciful creations. "Rosie's Cottage" is just one of* The Shoemaker's Dream *collection.*

tive artworks with the artisans of Cameo Guild Studios titled *David Winter Scenes*. Winter's vignette bases form the scenery surrounding some of his most popular cottages, such as the market square in front of "The Bakehouse," or the farmyard for "The Bothy." Cameo Guild has created miniature characters cast in fine bronze that populate these cottages, with amazing hand-painted details. Together, the two media create an entirely new way to display David Winter Cottages.

John Hine continues to search out talent, and to allow imagination to come to fruition in some of the collectibles industry's most exciting artworks. Collectors are always welcome to visit the Studios to see the creative process at work and have a spot of tea: the Studios and Workshops of John Hine are open to the public seven days a week.

Historical Miniatures Inc.

Maude Weisser's American Heritage Buildings Evoke Memories of Our Architectural Past as Seen Through the Eyes of a Talented Miniature Maker

From the day she received her first doll house as a gift from her mother, Maude Weisser has carried on a love affair with buildings in miniature. Influenced by that childhood time, her appreciation for miniatures has inspired Ms. Weisser to design and produce her own delightful versions of American Architecture in miniature — known as the *American Heritage* line.

As a young woman, Maude's natural interests and talents were advanced by an impressive education in the field of Art and Design. She first earned an

The cast metal lamp post and door-railing details of "The Pink House" give this wonderful Historical Miniatures an extra measure of life. This work of art highlights Maude Weisser's Charleston, South Carolina series.

Associate's Degree from George Brown College of Applied Arts in Toronto, Ontario, Canada. Then she ventured to New York City to earn a Bachelor's Degree from the famed Parson's School of Design. A host of international experiences next fed her creativity, as she went on to study art and design in many lands including Africa, Austria, West Germany and Israel. Among her many accomplishments, Ms. Weisser is an artist, jeweler, metals and enamel designer, as well as a theatrical prop maker.

Perhaps the most formative experience of her education, according to the artist, was her stint in Israel as an architectural model maker for the City of Jerusalem. This led to her intensive education in the painstaking process of miniature-making — the art that is her forte today. The municipality of Jerusalem employed Maude as an architectural model maker for two years, and the disciplines she learned there have certainly paid off back in North America.

"Because of the special nature of the City of Jerusalem with its historical and religious significance, as well as all the archaeological ruins there, Jerusalem must be very careful and selective in allowing new structures to be built," Maude Weisser explains. "In fact, it is one of the few cities in the entire world which maintains an up-to-date, 1:500-scale model of the complete city. Proposed new buildings then can be made to scale and placed in their speculative location within the model. Thus the effects of all new structures can be fully studied before building permits are granted.

"It was my experience working as a model maker with this project that led to the creation of my first collectibles line: *The Treasures of the Holy Land* collection," which has gained in popularity among collectors over the past few years, Ms. Weisser continues.

Now this architectural artist is using these same skills and talents to develop her *American Heritage* line, which premiered early in 1994.

These works of art are produced in their entirety at Maude's studio and workshop in Providence, Rhode Island, which today is her home.

The Creation of Historical Miniatures Is a Family Affair

One of the most interesting aspects of Ms. Weisser's Historical Miniatures of the United States is that they combine the art of carving, the skill of metalwork, and the knowledge of mold-making. While Maude is the sole designer/artist for the line, her husband Eyal is the mold maker and production manager.

"This is really a joint effort," Maude explains. "I am the artistic end of the business, and Eyal handles the technical/business end of things. He has designed and built most of our production facilities, including needs such as drying chambers, casting tables, and more. I definitely could not do what I do here without him," she states emphatically.

The selection of design subjects for Ms. Weisser's Historical Miniatures is the first step in her creative process. Ideas may come about from photographs, designs, or architectural plans of historic American buildings — especially those in wonderful "archi-

This pink and green building, "The Chart House," depicts a typical row house in the famous French Quarter of New Orleans. The detailing of the metal "wrought iron" balcony and awning poles make this piece very faithful to its Louisiana roots.

tecture towns" such as New Orleans, Louisiana; Charleston, South Carolina; and Miami, Florida.

Next, the designs are carved in a special blend of clay, wax and wood. "This is a very unique combination which stems from my background as a jeweler as opposed to a sculptor," Maude readily explains. "This is a jewelry-making technique."

Once each model is finished, it is time for Maude's husband Eyal to take over the process. "Eyal was lucky enough to have studied mold-making techniques in England, where they are really pioneers in the field," Maude Weisser notes. Once Eyal gives his final approval to the mold he has crafted, production of the individual pieces can begin.

Individual Finishing Makes Each Miniature a Unique Original

All of the pieces made by Historical Miniatures are cold-cast, and then finished by hand by a staff of trained artists. The application of beautifully designed metalwork is a specialty that truly sets Ms. Weisser's works apart. Miniature buildings whose

Also from the Charleston series, "Rutledge House" shows off the cast-metal detailing on the front porch of this elegant mansion. The metal, which is added on to the piece after casting, ensures authenticity of the period.

full-size originals bear wrought iron decor, stair railings or other details in metal get the type of decoration that brings them to life architecturally.

There are other finishing touches added to the Historical Miniatures that capture the mood and setting of the buildings they replicate. For example, there are tiny benches in front of the Miami art deco buildings — and there's a lamp post outside Charleston's Pink House. These details add an extra dimension of realism to Maude's work.

The same highly trained artist/painter works on each piece from start to finish: no cookie-cutter approaches will do at Historical Miniatures. "All of our painters are highly skilled artists," Maude Weisser asserts. "Each person is trained by me personally in our studio's special techniques. We don't have an assembly-line system here," Maude continues. "Because each painter begins and completes a piece, no two pieces are exactly alike — there are slight stylistic differences, which I enjoy, because each artist is an individual!" At one time, Maude did all the painting herself, she notes, "But now we are too busy. I still try to sneak some painting time in when I can. I also like to demonstrate my painting techniques when I visit collectibles shops and when I attend the International Collectible Shows."

American Series *Now Available from Historical Miniatures Inc.*

Several well-known and historic American cities appear in the series released by Historical Miniatures in 1994. Maude's first introduction for the year was *Charleston, South Carolina.* She explains: "I released Charleston first because it is America's crown jewel of antebellum architecture. It is a perfectly preserved historical city, and it is rich with American history."

The second 1994 release was *The Art Deco Buildings of Miami.* As Maude Weisser comments, "Although I have seen many American cities reproduced in many forms, I had never seen the Miami deco buildings in reproduction at all. That is a very interesting period in art and design, and I really had fun working on these buildings."

The *New Orleans* buildings, featuring a good deal of wrought iron detail, came third. "These were a real challenge because of the metalwork," the artist admits, "and I am very proud of how they look. The collectors really enjoy these buildings because of the ironwork! Of course, I enjoy working on *all* of my designs."

Another popular group — recently introduced — are the pieces inspired by the beautiful seaside resort of Cape May, New Jersey. These works of art feature the gorgeous Victorian homes that have made this little Atlantic coast town famous.

The American Heritage Door series has just debuted, featuring detailed replicas of American doorways from all over the country. This charming series is carved with extreme attention to detail. Like the "Door Posters," which have become popular recently, this collection has true national appeal.

All editions released by Historical Miniatures are limited, with edition numbers to be announced by Maude Weisser upon retirement. Plans are now underway for the release of the firm's first signed and numbered limited edition series, as well as for the establishment of a collector's club. Also to be released soon is the *New England* series.

"It is really difficult choosing which series to release," Maude relates. "Not because of a lack of buildings to do, but because there are so many wonderful buildings in this country! I have a tough time narrowing each series down. The good news is that I always have new ideas for pieces to add to the existing series, and I think the collectors will love building each city in miniature as I release the new pieces!"

Historical Miniatures is also becoming well known for their extensive custom order program. Maude and Eyal work individually with dealers, shop owners, etc., to create pieces of particular interest for local clientele. Naturally this work takes them all over the country, meeting different people and seeing many wonderful and beautiful places — work which both Maude and Eyal feel lucky to do.

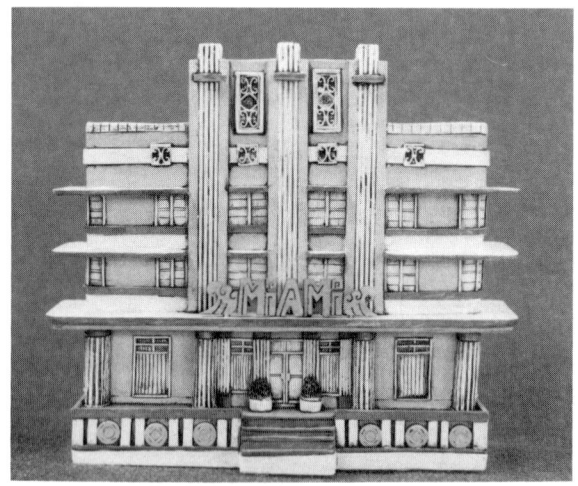

Maude Weisser says of "Hotel Carlisle" and her Miami Beach Art Deco series: "Many American buildings have been reproduced in miniature, but to the best of my knowledge this is a first for the Miami Beach deco buildings."

Iris Arc Crystal
Dazzling Rainbow Crystal® Designs Portray the Innovative and Generous Spirit of Iris Arc

In 1976 Jonathan Wygant and Francesca Patruno embarked on a journey that would shape their future for years to come.

While brainstorming ways to finance a trip to the Pacific Northwest, Ms. Patruno suggested they buy crystal chandelier prisms and sell them as they traveled. The idea turned out to be an inspired one as the couple discovered that people would gladly pay for the fine crystal prisms.

The dazzling rainbow patterns cast by the multi-faceted prisms captivated customers so much that the young partners decided to set up a business upon returning to Santa Barbara.

While discussing a name for their new company, Ms. Patruno told Wygant about the myth of Iris, Greek goddess of messages and the rainbow. Iris' mission was to travel across the heavens and deliver communiques from Zeus to other gods and to mortals. To accomplish her task, she traveled upon the iridescent arc that we know as the rainbow. In fact, before the word "rainbow" existed, English-speakers called this natural phenomenon the "Arc of Iris."

The twosome began selling their crystals from their van, then moved into a two-car garage with an attached workroom. Their first office was their living room. "We had nine employees before our landlord gently asked us to find a business location for our company in 1978," Wygant recalls with a smile.

He continues, "Crystal enthusiasts began to collect the many styles of prisms we offered, and we began to develop paperweights and fashionable jewelry to keep up with their interest. However, it was not until 1979 that we introduced the most significant development in the collectible industry: American-made, faceted crystal figurines."

Iris Arc Infuses Crystal With Dazzling Rainbow Hues

From the beginning of their decision to manufacture figurines, Iris Arc made a commitment to produce original designs using innovation combined with the artistry of meticulously detailed handwork to bring traditional, heartwarming and progressive themes to life.

The limited edition "Country Church" showcases Iris Arc's ability to portray remarkably detailed subjects in shimmering Rainbow Crystal®.

Two feathered friends splash playfully in this limited edition "Birdbath" from Iris Arc Crystal.

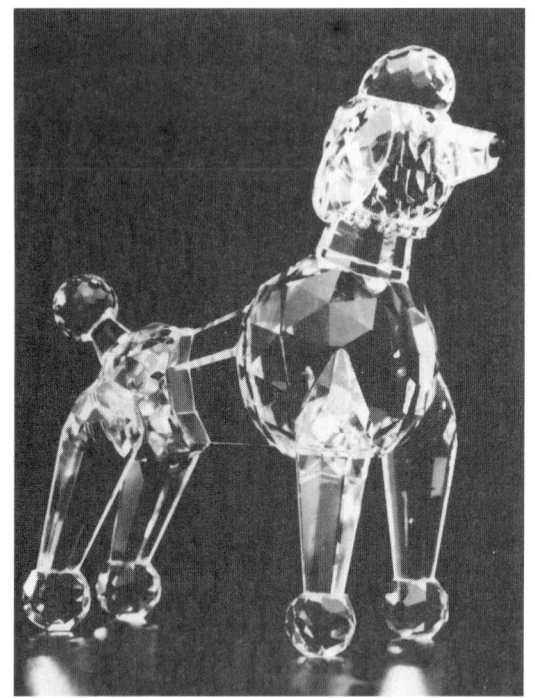

A charming "Poodle" exemplifies the appeal and attention to detail that attract so many collectors to Iris Arc Crystal designs.

The first figurine introduced was a delightful snowman with a colorful scarf. Iris Arc soon evolved into a full-scale, American manufacturing facility with a highly skilled staff of artists and craftspeople, unveiling fifteen to twenty figurines annually.

During the first three years of figurine production, Iris Arc produced only designs of clear crystal. As Wygant recalls, "We considered ourselves purists — only clear crystal was acceptable for our elegant, yet sometimes whimsical, figurines."

Then in 1982, Iris Arc unveiled a "Small Teddy Bear" with a silver heart. The piece was an instant success! Even though it sold well, one of their sales associates said it was hard to see the heart and that it should be changed to red crystal. As "purists," the Iris Arc team resisted the notion, but eventually decided on a pink heart.

"The "Teddy Bear With Pink Heart" immediately went to the top of our best sellers list," Wygant remembers. "It outsold the clear-hearted teddy by three to one! Everyone on our design team was surprised — but pleasantly so!" After a few additional designs with color accents, Iris Arc took the plunge with their all-time best selling "Peacock" in aurora borealis. As Wygant says, "We finally understood that colored crystal was better received than clear crystal in the marketplace.

Starting in 1985, we began to create more and more colored designs."

Over the years, Iris Arc Crystal has led the industry in design and production innovation. Besides being the first company to use color, their artisans have also pioneered lapidary techniques. Cutting, grinding and polishing crystal to very exact tolerances enables Iris Arc to create designs of great detail. An early example of these advanced lapidary techniques is shown in the "Poodle," introduced in 1985. Experimentation with colorful coatings and intricately sculpted cast crystal components, has led to such exquisite designs as the limited edition "Country Cottage" and "Cathedral."

In 1988, Iris Arc Crystal copyrighted the name "Rainbow Crystal®" to describe the addition of various colors to crystal that brings to life the violets in a flower basket or the green boughs of a Christmas tree with twinkling colored lights. Wygant estimates that "Seventy-five percent of Iris Arc's figurines and paperweights are fashioned from Rainbow Crystal® — a testament to the fastest-growing category in faceted crystal today."

Iris Arc Wins Awards for Product Excellence and Commitment to Community

While Iris Arc designs have won top collectible awards — such as "Best Crystal Design" at the Long Beach International Collectible Exposition, "Award of Excellence in Figurine Design" from *Collector Editions* magazine and inclusion in the *New Glass Review* by the Corning Museum of Glass — the founders are equally proud of their firm's honors for community service. Wygant and Ms. Patruno demonstrated their philanthropic philosophies when their business experienced a temporary slow-down in 1982.

Rather than lay off any of their eighty employees, the partners established their "Arc Angel Program." For one day each week with full pay, employees were invited to volunteer at local community organizations. The other option was to take the day off without pay. Most employees jumped right into the volunteer effort, doing cooking and cleaning for elderly people in need or assisting with public works projects. For these efforts, Iris Arc was awarded the Presidential Service Award by President Ronald Reagan for their philanthropic endeavors. In 1983, Iris Arc was back on an expansion track, being named one of the country's fastest-growing companies by *Inc* magazine.

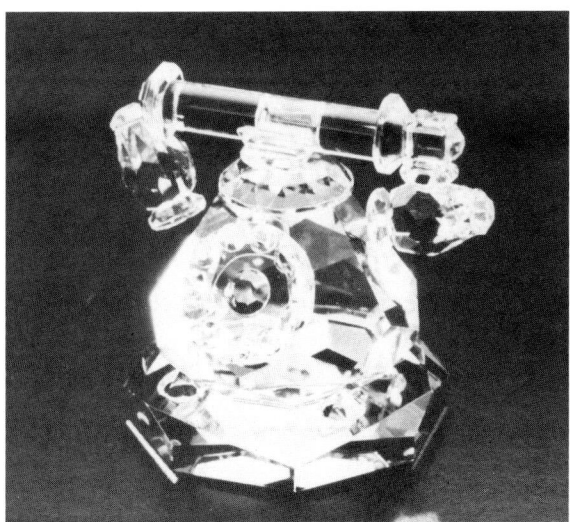

"The Classic Telephone" is the second Annual Edition from the Iris Arc Collectors Society.

Iris Arc's Product Line Combines Fantasy and Romance With Animals, Sports and Garden Themes

For more than fifteen years now, Iris Arc has been delighting collectors with Crystal Kingdom® figurines and tabletop art objects. Iris Arc designs are investments, both in exquisite beauty and in collectible value. One reason for this is that every piece is hand-crafted. Another is that Iris Arc retires designs after the completion of their editions. To ensure authenticity, Iris Arc copyrights their designs and marks all figurines with a distinctive etch.

Iris Arc offers a *Romance Collection* with teddies and bunnies adorned with colored crystal hearts and an *American Spirit Collection*, a collection of designs that are proudly and uniquely American. The *Floral Collection* unveils a rainbow of detailed blooms, while a visit to the *Garden Gazebo* delights with swans and peacocks. The *Fantasy Collection* combines exquisite castles with designs such as the "Dragon" and "Treasure Chest." In the *Sports Collection*, there's a "Tennis Bear" and a "Baseball Bear" and crystal tributes for golfers. A *Child's World* includes a "Toy Chest," the "Red Flyer Wagon" and baby carriages. The *Sea Spirit Collection* and *Wildlife Collection* abound with remarkable accent pieces such as an "Oyster with Pearl" and a "Baby Elephant."

For collectors of miniatures, Iris Arc features a marvelous range of tiny pieces between ³/₄" and 1¹/₄" in height, as well as Tabletop Art Objects in Rainbow Crystal®, crystal prisms in clear, aurora borealis or "Pink Ice" and sparkling crystal post earrings.

Iris Arc Artists Create Designs With The Gift of Light™

Iris Arc has attracted two of the world's most innovative crystal designers: Mark Goena and Christopher Hughes. With a Bachelor's degree in Fine Art, Goena creates designs with a combination of creativity and craftsmanship that have won him widespread popularity. His floral designs have become Iris Arc trademarks and his limited editions, such as the "Country Cottage" and the "Basket of Flowers," have won numerous honors. As the designer says, "I enjoy bringing life and emotion to my creations. I hope my dedication to quality design and craftsmanship endows my figurines with lasting beauty and value."

Iris Arc designer Christopher Hughes says, "I was fortunate enough to grow up in Santa Barbara, and be raised in a very artistic family. My father was a professional artist and guitar maker. I was lucky to inherit his talent for working with solid forms. Crystal is a difficult enough substance to manipulate, but I try to push the limits — to design pieces that are not only aesthetically appealing but detailed to a high degree. The combination seems to be a winning one."

An Invitation to Enjoy the Benefits of the Iris Arc Collectors Society

A wonderful year of privileges awaits collectors the moment they become a member of the Iris Arc Collectors Society. Benefits include a free Enrollment Gift, exclusive members-only annual editions, a subscription to the "Illuminations" newsletter and news about the latest introductions, design retirements, artist appearances and other special events. A one-year membership costs $25 and a two-year membership is $40.

Iris Arc Crystal has attracted a celebrated audience, with pieces being presented as awards to important world personalities including Lech Walesa, Mother Theresa, Bishop Tutu, Jonas Salk, Stevie Wonder and Buckminster Fuller. Yet the firm's founders insist on retaining the same company values that fueled their initial success. The clarity, communication and beauty of the goddess "Iris," and a dedication to give something back to the community combine in a studio that creates many of the most exquisite and unique crystal designs available in today's world of fine art collectibles.

June McKenna® Collectibles, Inc.
June McKenna's Santas Capture the True Spirit of Christmas

Once you've met June McKenna, it doesn't seem surprising that her highly creative "Santa business" began while helping her son research and sculpt a dinosaur for a third grade science project. In skimming through the encyclopedia, June noticed an article that detailed how pioneer women used a mixture of cornstarch and salt to mold dolls. It sounded like an ideal gift for her mother, an avid collector of antique dolls.

June began experimenting with the old cornstarch recipe and eventually sculpted her first old-fashioned Santa. Her mother was delighted by the originality and the results. But, June realized that cornstarch was no longer an adequate medium and began experimenting with other sculpting materials. Most of these early figures, which were based on holiday themes, were given to family and friends who shared her love of Christmas.

Authentic antique Santas were quite rare, so June had to depend on her imagination and what little research material was available. She verified the authenticity of Santa's costumes, walking sticks and packs throughout the centuries, but it was more difficult to identify the proper period toys to be placed in Santa's bag.

From Hobby to Business

An energetic personality, June began making and selling her plump Santa ornaments at area craft shows in 1980. The following year, June placed her first Santa on consignment in a gift shop where a sales manager from Bentwood House of Reston, Virginia, a national gift and accessories firm, saw her work and offered to represent it. The business experienced a second surge when BrassSmith House, a companion company, began marketing the McKenna line.

In 1982, June officially formed June McKenna® Collectibles, Inc. Her first line included thirteen — mostly Santa — Christmas ornaments. The following year, she added her first limited edition, signed and numbered "Father Christmas" figurine which retailed at $95. Recent secondary market sales reveal that this piece now has a market value of $5,500, and in one documented transaction, "Father Christmas" recently sold for $8,500. Although the artist does not receive any profits

from these sales, it was a tremendous boost for her reputation and self-esteem.

The volume of orders for June's fanciful Santas grew so rapidly that her husband, Dan, quit his job to help with the business. Early on, the business moved from the family home into an old firehouse which was destroyed by an arsonist in 1984. Fortunately, the company was able to quickly rebuild on the same site. In two years, the company outgrew the new building and moved into a modern industrial complex on the outskirts of Ashland, Virginia.

June McKenna® Collectibles, Inc. currently employs about seventy-five people throughout the year, with the work force swelling to 110 during September, their peak production period. Dan supervises the production process, while son Scott has joined them as head of the shipping department.

Why Is Her Line So Successful?

"People really do want to buy American, and they believe that we still can produce the best products in the world. Collectors are pleased with

June McKenna is pictured with Peg McCulloh, owner of McCulloh Sampler in Red Bank, New Jersey, during one of June's personal appearances.

the consistent quality of my work. Occasionally, a customer will ask to see a number of different examples of a piece to find the one with the best craftsmanship, but our quality control is so good that they have a hard time choosing the one they want. Fortunately, there is very little difference in quality between pieces," June explained.

"I think that people truly enjoy Christmas and the joy and good will that I'm trying to express with my work. I'm one of only a handful of artists today who actually does all their own design work and sculpting. When your name is on something, you want it to be right.

"One of the first things that people mention about my work is the detail. I want it to be perfect and everytime the collector looks at a piece, I want them to see new details and expressions they haven't noticed before. I hate finishing a piece because there always seems to be something that could be added. Sometimes Dan must remind me of the limitations of the production process. All of our pieces are done in a white-resin material which takes our palette of colors best. Because of all the details, all stages of production must be carefully supervised," June continued.

"One of the nicest things about all of our collectibles is that they can take the wear and tear of active families. Pieces that have been damaged can be returned to the factory for touch-ups. We even fixed one lady's collection that was damaged during Hurricane Hugo in South Carolina."

During her first ten years in business, June created over 225 different original editions; most of them Christmas-motif figurines.

"I deliberately kept the number of pieces produced each year to about twenty, because I have so many faithful collectors who purchase every piece I issue. In 1984, we introduced 'Old Saint Nick,' a signed edition limited to 4,000 pieces and approximately twelve inches high, and the *Flatback Christmas* collectible, 'Tree Topper Angel.' The following year, the *Black Folk Art* figurine series was introduced. I wanted this series to represent ordinary joys of family life. The registered edition of the 'Colonial' Santa was added in 1986."

McKenna's Line

Mindful that not all collectors have the same budgets, June offers a variety of lines and prices so that everyone can afford a McKenna Santa.

Each year, the line includes five new ornaments which are available for two years only. These plump little figures can be hung or stand alone.

Although she hasn't realized her goal every year, June also attempts to offer four limited edition Santas annually.

These Santas differ in both their size and the number of pieces produced in each edition. June's initial edition *Santa Collection* was limited to 4,000 figurines with a few exceptions such as the 2,000-piece "Baking Cookies" special limited edition which shows Santa with his hand on Mrs. Santa's shoulder at work in the kitchen making Christmas cookies.

The *Flatback Santa Collection* is limited to 10,000 pieces. As a special favor to budget-minded collectors, June still maintains a series of flatback pieces which are undecorated on the back and less expensive for beginning collectors.

Santa's costumes may range from sedate "The Christmas Bishop" to the more fanciful "Christmas Wizard" dressed in a blue robe adorned with stars. There are also robes of fur and coarsely woven wools in shades of brown, green and red. His headgear and his gifts vary from century to century. At home, Santa relaxes in shirtsleeves, nightshirt and slippers. Regardless of the costume or the period, Santa's features remain the same. Sometimes his gaze is solemn and thoughtful but most of the time, his expression radiates a cherub-like innocence and the good humor children have come to expect.

While his faithful reindeer are never far away, June's imagination allows the Jolly Old Elf to travel not only by sleigh, but also on foot. One of June's most imaginative pieces is "Santa's Hot Air Balloon" which was limited to 1,500 pieces. At home, he can be found at his workbench, or napping in preparation for his round-the-world journey. One of the most charming of these pieces is "Forty Winks".

Santa's efforts are supported by Mrs. Santa and a cast of Christmas characters like the elves, reindeer, carolers, snowmen, the Holy Family, shepherds, wisemen and angels.

Personal Favorites

When asked what pieces have become her personal favorites, June noted, "I always love the piece I'm working on but there are other figurines I treasure for their memories. I had worked really hard for several days to complete the 'Last Gentle Nudge' which shows Santa napping. I was just finishing it when one of the boys was going up to bed. As he went by, he looked at it for a minute and said, 'Mom, it looks unfinished. It needs a

"Tomorrow's Christmas," a 1993 Registered Edition Santa, pays tribute to the environment by showing Santa's concern for our diminishing forests. For each tree that Santa cuts, he will plant another to take its place so our forests can be enjoyed for many years to come.

The "1993 Santa Name Plaque" is a charming addition to any of June McKenna's collections.

dog.' I knew he was right, and I spent the rest of the night sculpting a Boston terrier just like our dog and placed the sleeping figure at Santa's feet. In the morning, my son took one look at the piece and proudly declared the piece finished," she continued.

"Like millions of other young children I sat on Santa's lap in a department store when I was small and told him secrets and what I wanted for Christmas. Years later, when the store — which was in Richmond, Virginia — went out of business, I saw Santa's big golden chair abandoned and alone. So many happy memories still surround that chair, and it seemed to be perfect as a background piece for 'Bedtime Stories.' To make this piece even more universal, I surrounded Santa with children of all ages and races," she added.

Appearances and Collectors Club

June understands what an important part her collectors played in her success, and she is always eager to meet them. She makes about fifty appearances a year at shows and shops where she signs her artwork and autographs. To make these events even more memorable, June has designed a special figurine which is available only to collectors attending one of her personal appearances.

To maintain contact with collectors between

shows, June currently offers a mini-club for collectors. For $3 a year, collectors receive two editions of her information packed newsletter, "Visions," and her latest catalog.

Although all the details have not yet been worked out, June hopes to offer collectors a number of unique opportunities and "members-only" pieces as members of the June McKenna® Collectors Club which is tentatively slated to begin in April 1994.

The McKenna Touch

All of June McKenna's works have a common thread. Her bubbly personality, good humor and willingness to work hard enough to become successful are all apparent. One of the dealers who has handled the line since it started added these insights.

"There is peace, kindness and thoughtfulness in her work which truly reflect June's personality and concern for others. Her artwork is a gift from the heart. It brings joy to families all year long. Her philosophy of the spirit of Christmas doesn't need mountains of gifts. She knows that joy comes from the small blessings in life. The best gift is being alive and being able to share the holidays with family and friends."

Kurt S. Adler, Inc.

The World's Leading Resource for Christmas Decorative Accessories Evolves Into a Major Supplier of Holiday Collectibles

For many years during the company's forty-year-plus history, Kurt S. Adler has designed and supplied ornaments and other holiday accessories for collectors from around the world. Every year the firm has changed its line of more than 20,000 different items by nearly forty percent, and has provided collectors with a broad array of charming holiday products to add to their private collections.

Recently Kurt S. Adler, Inc. created the KSA Collectibles line that features collectible nutcrackers and smokers, limited edition dolls and Santas, Fabriché™ holiday figurines and ornaments, and Smithsonian antique carousel animal ornaments. To broaden the line's availability to collectors, the firm has developed networks of authorized dealers throughout North America specializing in specific collectible groups.

Collectible Nutcrackers and Smokers Widely Recognized for Tremendous Demand and Soaring Values

In just a few years since it began marketing collectible nutcrackers, the firm has enjoyed a tremendous response to the line. In addition, several nutcrackers have shown an ability to appreciate greatly in a very short period of time.

Kurt S. Adler, Inc. supplied and distributed the first limited edition nutcrackers and smoking figures from the famous Steinbach factory, located in Hohenhameln in the northern region of Germany. For six generations, the Steinbachs have been producing fine nutcrackers and smokers, and today are world-renowned for quality and craftsmanship. Highly skilled artisans, who have trained many years in the fine art of wood-carving, recreate each folklore legend by hand-painting and hand-turning the finest Northern European wood into nutcrackers and smokers with meticulous attention to detail. Outstanding workmanship, unique designs and an intriguing background have made the collection one of the fastest-growing groups of collectibles today. Many pieces have been specially designed for the KSA Collectibles line from Kurt S. Adler, Inc.

The "Merlin the Magician" nutcracker, which was introduced in 1991 at a retail price of $185,

has been reported to have sold for as much as $1500 on the secondary market. Steinbach nutcrackers and smokers are highly sought after by collectors and destined to become cherished heirlooms with tremendous potential to appreciate greatly in value. "Merlin," the premier issue in the *Camelot* series of nutcrackers and smokers, was later followed by "King Arthur" and, most recently, "Sir Lancelot." The *Camelot Series* also includes "Merlin the Magician" and "King Arthur" smoking figures. Several other series of nutcrackers have been introduced, including the *American Presidents* series which features George Washington, Abraham Lincoln and Teddy Roosevelt. More recent groups include *The Famous Chieftains Series* featuring "Chief Sitting Bull," *The American Inventor Series* with its premier issue "Benjamin Franklin," and *The Christmas Legends Series* which debuted "Father Christmas." Steinbach nutcrackers and smokers are available to collectors

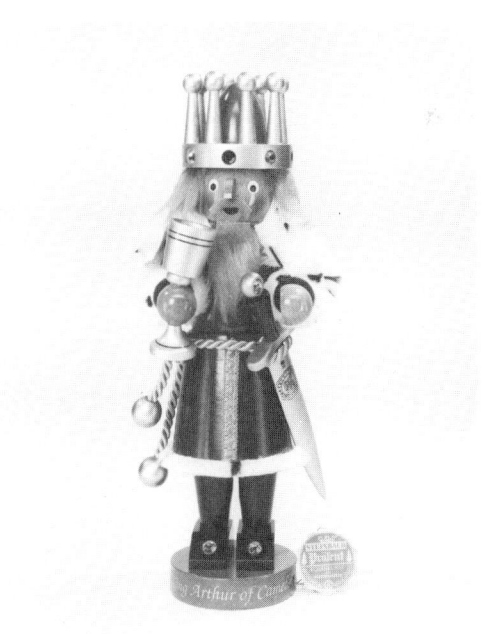

"King Arthur" Steinbach smoking figure from the Camelot Series of nutcrackers and smokers depicts the famous King holding his Excalibur sword and the Holy Grail. He is dressed in full royal regalia including His Majesty's crown. The smoker is limited to 7,500 pieces.

*"Chief Sitting Bull" Steinbach Nutcracker is featured
in* The Famous Chieftains *series from Kurt S. Adler, Inc.
"Chief Sitting Bull," limited to 8,500 pieces, is hand-painted
and hand-turned by Steinbach artisans in Germany. The
nutcracker, which stands 19" high, depicts the famous character
in a colorful headdress and costume, along with authentic-looking tribal weaponry.*

*"Merlin the Magician" Fabriché™ figurine from Kurt S. Adler,
Inc. is limited to 7,500 pieces. It is the premier figurine in the
Camelot Series of Fabriché™ holiday figurines.*

throughout the firm's network of authorized North
American dealers.

Kurt S. Adler, Inc. also has introduced collectible German nutcrackers from the Zuber
Factory. The Zuber group features such delightful
characters as "The Ice Cream Vendor," "Napoleon
Bonaparte," "The Pizzamaker," "Gepetto The Toymaker," "Bronco Billy The Cowboy," "The West
Point Cadet" and "The Nor'Eastern Sea Captain."
Zuber nutcrackers, many of which are limited editions, have developed a strong following among
collectors.

For lovers of Disney films, the firm also offers
several nutcrackers depicting those wonderful animated Disney characters. This group includes
Mickey Mouse, Donald Duck, Goofy and Pinocchio.

Fabulous Sculptures From Top Designers Featured in The Fabriché™ Collection of Holiday Figurines and Ornaments

Over the years, the firm has developed a complete line of Fabriché™ holiday figurines and ornaments featuring wonderful Christmas characters
created with unparalleled design, superior quality
and skillful workmanship. Fabriché™ is a mixed-
media technique based on the Old World art of
papier-maché, combined with modern methods

and materials. This merging of different media
gives the effect of movement and lifelike expressions. The group features the skilled artistry of
some of the nation's top designers who bring wonderful holiday characters to life in intricate detail.

Marjorie Grace Rothenberg, a veteran designer
of holiday ornaments and figurines, recreates masterful pieces from her country studio at the foothills of the Berkshire Mountains. Among her many
designs are "Merry Kissmas" which features Santa
kissing his wife under the mistletoe, "Apron Full
of Love" depicting Mrs. Claus with an apron full of
holiday goodies, "Santa Steals A Kiss And A
Cookie," as well as "Here Kitty" and "Grandpa
Santa's Piggyback." Other highlights of the group
include "Christmas Is In The Air" which shows
Santa in a hot air balloon, a golfing Santa in "Par
For The Claus," "All That Jazz" displaying an
African-American Santa on saxophone and "With
All The Trimmings" which features Santa serving
a turkey feast.

Several Fabriché™ figurines are available in the
Smithsonian Museum Collection portraying Santa
traveling in unique modes of transportation.
"Santa On A Bicycle" features him on a high-
wheeled bicycle; "Holiday Drive" shows him driving in an antique automobile; and "Holiday
Flight" depicts the jolly old fella in an open-cock-

pit airplane. Fabriché™ angels also are included in this series.

Teddy bears and elves star in the *Fabriché™ Bear & Friends* and *Santa's Helpers* groups, respectively.

Fabriché™ ornaments feature many of the collectible figurine designs reduced to a smaller size and designed to decorate a tree. "Par For The Claus," "Not A Creature Was Stirring," "An Apron Full of Love" and "Homeward Bound" are offered in this group, while "Holiday Drive" and "Santa On A Bicycle" are featured in the *Smithsonian Museum Collection.* Fabriché™ figurines and ornaments are available through the firm's network of authorized dealers located across North America.

Cornhusk Mice Highly Sought Out By Collectors

One of Kurt S. Adler Inc.'s popular ornament collections features cornhusk mice portrayed as different human characters in whimsical settings. These unique ornaments have been created by Marjorie Grace Rothenberg for both Christmas and Easter.

Smithsonian Carousel Ornaments Charm Collectors

For the past few years, Kurt S. Adler, Inc. has developed a splendid assortment of antique carousel ornaments in its *Smithsonian Museum Carousel Series.* Every year the firm retires two items and unveils two antique carousel animal ornaments, each available in a genuine Smithsonian gift box. These ornaments are exact replicas which recreate carousel animal figures from turn-of-the-century merry-go-rounds discovered in the Smithsonian Museum Archives. Some that are currently available include "The Elephant," "The Camel," "The Tiger," "The Horse," "The Rooster" and "The Seahorse."

Award-Winning Designer Jocelyn Mostrom Dazzles Collectors With Dolls, Ornaments and Limited Edition Santas

Award-winning doll designer Jocelyn Mostrom has converted many of her popular cornhusk designs and applied them to porcelain. She has created collectible dolls and doll ornaments which are featured in both the *Christmas In Chelsea* and *Royal Heritage Collection.*

Inspired by the famous English gardens, *Christmas In Chelsea* features dolls that have an ethereal quality of turn-of-the-century storybook pictures depicting garden fairies. The *Royal Heritage Collec-*

tion features endearing children in regal turn-of-the-century attire. Each child, named after a member of the Royal Family, has been richly adorned in ivory lace combined with burgundy, forest green and ivory velvet. In addition, a 14-inch, limited edition collectible doll named "Anastasia" has been introduced. A "Medieval King of Christmas" and "Good King Wenceslas" also are offered in this group. Kurt S. Adler, Inc. has developed a network of authorized dealers across North America who carry Jocelyn Mostrom's designs.

Many limited edition Old World Santas have been created by Ms. Mostrom, as well. "Father Christmas," "Black Forest Santa" and "Patriotic Santa" are among the Santas offered in the group.

Snowglobes, Musicals and Miniature Villages To Come

For the past four decades, collectors have been seeking out the firm's snowglobes, musicals and other holiday accessories. Santas, snowmen, carolers and many other Christmas characters have been designed in snowglobes, some in musical versions which play such popular themes as "The Nutcracker Suite" and "Santa Claus Is Coming To Town."

"Par For The Claus" Fabriché™ figurine, features a Santa meticulously handcrafted in a red jacket and trousers with brown and white golf shoes. Standing 9½" tall, "Par For The Claus" shows Santa grabbing an iron from his golfbag as he heads for the links. "Par For The Claus" is also featured in a smaller version as a Fabriché™ Christmas ornament.

LCS Products and Services

Introducing *Early Innings*™ Collector's Plates and Steins Featuring Baseball's Most Beloved Old Ball Parks

The crack of bat against ball...the roar of the crowd...the excitement of a home run or a collision at home plate...all this and more celebrates America's lasting love affair with baseball. Collector interest in baseball nostalgia is greater today than ever before. And now — thanks to LCS Products and Services — the *Early Innings* collection of plates and steins captures the excitement and magic that has made baseball America's national pastime.

These exquisite works of art commemorate the parks and stadiums where America's greatest "sports romance" began. Beginning with "Ebbets Field," "Tiger Stadium" and "Comiskey Park," the series will expand to include legendary fields like "Fenway Park," the "Polo Grounds," "Yankee Stadium," "Forbes Field," and many more. Many of these great stadiums are no longer standing, and others soon will be gone. But thanks to the extensive research and art mastery of illustrator Chuck Wilkinson, **The Old Ball Parks** will always be remembered in this remarkable, limited edition form.

Larry Kinney and Tom Collins Pursue a Sports Lover's Dream

When Tom Collins was with The Stroh Brewery during the 1980s, he developed a variety of collectible steins. He also met Larry Kinney, who was later to establish LCS. Kinney's firm, Datapak Services Corp., was working on stein and memorabilia programs for Stroh's, along with collectors' catalogs, Ernie Harwell lithographs, and the Tiger Stadium Hall of Fame poster. Kinney could see that there was a market for collector steins, plates and other memorabilia. He linked this with his personal love for baseball, nostalgia, and the classic baseball stadiums — the main ingredients that eventually would fuel the creation of the *Early Innings* collection.

When Stroh's discontinued its stein program in 1989, Larry Kinney joined forces with Tom Collins to come out with a stein series of their own. As Collins recalls, "We considered several subjects that would be of interest to our market and found out

two things: most of them had been done before and most of the ones that had been done were not in keeping with our standards. Either the subject was not appropriate for a stein, or they were made to look too American. We thought the image should be classic and very high quality. We also wanted a subject that had some romance.

"Talks were beginning in Detroit to tear down Tiger Stadium. All kinds of protests were forming to try to stop it. The Tiger Stadium Fan Club even got together and hugged the stadium on April 20, 1988! We also began to hear about other cities with old ball parks that were facing similar threats. Baseball is certainly a great sport, rightly called America's pastime. Both Larry and I, like most other American boys, grew up playing baseball morning until night, all summer long. Along with hot dogs and

The "Ebbets Field" stein features bas-relief sculpting, hand-painting, and a pewter lid with ceramic inlay. It showcases the original home of the Brooklyn Dodgers.

"Ebbets Field" inaugurates the Early Innings *plate collection featuring* **The Old Ball Parks.**

apple pie, baseball is one of the things that makes America what it is.

"But even more than the sport, we thought that the old ball parks were closer to the hearts of the fans, whether they lived in the city or not. I've seen and grown to love Yankee Stadium and Fenway Park even though I've never been there. All of the old ball parks, but especially one's home stadium, inspire tremendous emotion and romance. Everyone remembers the first time they walk through the tunnel and enter the ball park. Our artist, Chuck Wilkinson, says that the Tiger Stadium plate is a story about a boy's first time at a Tiger game with his father."

First Up to the Plate: The Ebbets Field Collectibles

Because of their personal fondness for the Tigers and the Detroit area, Collins and Kinney wanted to lead off their series with Tiger Stadium. "But most of the fans we talked with said that Ebbets Field should be the first," Collins recalls. The legendary home of the Brooklyn Dodgers has a history that stretches back to 1908, when Charles Ebbets secretly began to buy four and one-half acres of land-filled marsh in New York. The borders were Bedford Avenue, Sullivan Street, Franklin Avenue and Montgomery Street.

Over the next four years, Ebbets purchased 1,200

individual plots at a total cost of $200,000. To finance construction of his ball park, he sold 50% interest to Edward and Steven McKeever, who were local contractors. Total construction costs would come to $750,000. On April 9, 1913, the Dodgers lost to the Phillies at the first major league game played at Ebbets Field. The ball park brought the Dodgers and the fans of Brooklyn together in one of baseball's greatest love affairs, until their last game there on September 24, 1957. After only forty-six years, on February 23, 1960, Ebbets Field faced the wrecking ball, painted white with stitches to resemble a baseball.

"Ebbets Field" and each upcoming plate in the LCS series is 8-1/4" in diameter and features a 22K gold rim and an edition limited to twenty-five firing days. The matching bas-relief steins each will stand 8-3/4" tall, and will be decorated in full color relief with a genuine pewter lid with ceramic inlay. Both the plates and steins are individually serial numbered and each includes a Certificate of Authenticity.

The Pride of Downtown Detroit: Tiger Stadium

"Batting second" in the LCS line-up is the "Tiger Stadium" plate. Still in use by the modern Tiger Baseball Club, this field enjoys a history that stretches back to 1896 when Detroit's minor league team selected a hay market at Michigan and Trumbull to build Bennett Park. In 1912 the park was reconstructed to hold 23,000 fans of the now American League Tigers and dedicated Navin Field, after Frank Navin who was the president of the club.

In 1938 the new owner-president, Walter O. Briggs, completed another expansion, increasing capacity to 58,000. An upper deck was added including what is still the only double-deck bleachers in the Majors. A giant scoreboard was erected in center field of what was now Briggs Stadium. On January 1, 1961, the park was again renamed to Tiger Stadium, after it was acquired by John Fetzer.

Chuck Wilkinson's Fascination with History, Social Change and Art Shine Through in His Early Innings Creations for LCS

Renowned illustrator Chuck Wilkinson embarked on extensive research for his creation of the art for "Tiger Stadium" and other upcoming *Early Innings* collectibles. Born in Detroit, Wilkinson studied at the famed Pratt Institute in New York. Prior to his

association with LCS, Wilkinson produced four posters for the internationally acclaimed Mobil Masterpiece Theater and has been a regular contributor to *Ladies Home Journal.* His portfolio paintings for the St. Andrew's Country Club in Boca Raton, Florida received awards in the CA Annual, New York City Advertising Club, and the Society of Illustrators. His works have been on exhibit in New York and Detroit.

Wilkinson's "lifestyle" paintings, done in egg tempera, evoke the elegance of an earlier age and have become synonymous with American nostalgia. As the artist notes, "I've always had an interest in the earlier era — the 1930s and 1940s — the style and elegance of that time. I love to do the research (for the *Early Innings* pieces) in the library. I have to keep everything accurate — cars, the way people dress — it all has to correspond to that time."

As a Detroiter himself, Wilkinson especially enjoyed painting Tiger Stadium. "It's always been considered the gem of the old ball parks," he asserts. "It has the most active stadium fan club of all, and its 100th-year celebration is coming up soon. I showed it back in the 1950s when people still arrived at the ball park in the street cars on Trumbull and Michigan.

"Right now as we speak, I'm working on the Comiskey Park artwork. That's the old Chicago White Sox stadium that's been replaced by a new, modern one. I've tried to get everything I could in the way of Comiskey Park memorabilia so that I can portray it the way it appeared in the late 1930s and early 1940s. That was before most of the 'facelifts' and expansions eliminated some of its original beauty. I've learned so much about life back then by doing this research — for instance, Labor Day used to be the last summer day that men would wear their straw hats — called 'boaters.' On Labor Day at the ball park, all the men would throw their 'boaters' onto the field as an end-of-summer ritual! And back then, women wore hats to the ball park just like they did to church."

Wilkinson is impressed by the care Collins and Kinney take in the production of the *Early Innings* plates and steins. He's especially fascinated by the Brazil-made steins. "They use a relief-sculpting process and accommodate my art to the stein," he says. The craftsmanship in Brazil mirrors that in Germany, the original home of steinmaking, according to Wilkinson.

A Bright Future for LCS and Early Innings

There are many more issues to come in **The Old Ball Parks** series, with the entire series to be unveiled during 1995. Collins remains as upbeat about the future of baseball as he is about the LCS plates and steins. "We called our series *Early Innings* because the game is not over; baseball will be around for a long time. We are not completely against change or even new stadiums. We love Tiger Stadium, and the other old ball parks, just as much as the fan clubs do. Of course new isn't always better, but it certainly isn't always bad. We believe that the old ball parks are just the 'early innings' of America's beloved pastime!"

The pride of Detroit baseball fans, "Tiger Stadium" is showcased on this work of art by award-winning illustrator Chuck Wilkinson.

Ladie and Friends™

The Family and Friends of Lizzie High® Star in Delightful Wooden Doll Creations from the Family Trees of Barbara and Peter Wisber

A collaboration...a labor of love. That's what Barbara and Peter Wisber consider their creative efforts on *The Family And Friends Of Lizzie High® Dolls* — works of art that have delighted collectors now for nearly a decade. When Barbara Wisber got the notion that she wanted to add dolls to their already-popular line of two-dimensional folk art, she took her ideas to her husband, who turned her fancy into fact.

The first dolls were very simple. Barbara had picked up a two and one-quarter-inch ball while in a hardware store. She felt compelled to purchase it even though she was unsure of the purpose she would put it to. Reflecting on that simple ball, Barbara brought forth the original concept of a very basic doll, reminiscent of early folk dolls handcrafted by a loving parent for an enthralled child.

Harkening back to these simpler times, Barbara and Peter thought of the universal delights of childhood: games to be played, friends to be made, wonderlands to be explored, adventures to be lived, lessons to be learned. They thought that an accompanying tale would enhance the charm of each doll and that a good old country name would also add to each doll's appeal.

For names they thought of Peter's family Bible in its place of prominence in his parents' living room. On the cover of that Bible is engraved the name of Peter's great-great-grandmother, Lizzie High. Inside the Bible can be found names of many family members. Peter's family has had extensive genealogical research done, and they found scores of other wonderful names as they read through the family history.

Country Children Debut the Doll Collection

The first nine dolls created for introduction at the January 1985 giftware shows were very simple indeed. Six little girls wore simple muslin frocks with a variety of shawls and kerchiefs in country plaids, and three young boys in painted overalls sported checkered neckerchiefs. The tales that accompanied these dolls could have been from simpler times a hundred years ago, or from gentler

Inspired by Barbara Wisber herself is this adorable, artistic youngster named "Barbara Helen."

days a childhood ago. These characters care for a pet goose, a prize-winning pig, and a baby brother. They jump rope, make wreaths, and love to dress up in their Sunday best. They love picnics, gathering fruit for mom's pies and jams, and gathering eggs to earn money for dance lessons and candy.

For the Summer giftware shows of 1985, Barbara and Peter came up with a dozen more characters. A complete *Christmas Pageant*™ became available that first holiday season, complete with Nativity, angels with pennants and wisemen. Little girls were decorating their homes, taking their little sisters to see Santa, baking cookies and hanging their favorite striped stockings on the mantle Christmas Eve. The first of many wonderful Santa Clauses was introduced that first holiday season: "Benjamin Bowman," who "dresses like Santa every year and gives presents to all the little ones...he loves to see their faces."

Bear Families and Bunnies Join Human Images To Broaden the Appeal for Lizzie High Collectors

For introduction in Spring of 1986, a family of rabbits joined the Collection: *The Pawtuckets® Of Sweet Briar Lane*. Nine full-size characters and two

pairs of *Little One Bunnies* delighted in the joys of Spring and of the Easter season. Nineteen full-size child characters also joined the Collection that season. Most of these characters, rabbits and children alike, came dressed in pretty pastels and their tales dealt with a wide variety of activities and delights — domesticity in the hutch and cookie baking after school, picnics and marketing and fishing and gardening. Two of this season's characters have been brought back in Second Edition versions and remain among the top ten most popular dolls available from Ladie and Friends. "Grace Valentine" is very thoughtful and "always remembers her friends with beautiful flowers from her garden…." While "Juliet Valentine" is "always busy doing the most beautiful embroidery…she says it passes the time."

In the Fall of 1986 another family of special characters was introduced to the Lizzie High line. *The Grummels™ Of Log Hollow* brought their own unique magic to the Collection as eleven full-size bears and two *Little One Bears* engaged in such varied activities as teddy bear picnics, beekeeping, candlemaking, concocting herbal brews, reading, laundry, and a bear "dressing up like Santa and handing out all the presents" while "the little ones never let on they know who it is."

The Grummels™ and *The Pawtuckets™* were retired from the Collection in Fall of 1988 and Fall of 1989 respectively. They remain, however, very popular. Scores of Lizzie High collectors contact Ladie and Friends regularly hoping to learn of ways of obtaining the retired bears and bunnies. Collectors who advertise their wish lists for these special dolls in Ladie and Friends' biannual newsletter — "The Lizzie High Notebook" — are having some success obtaining these ever-popular characters.

The Transition to More Sophisticated Dolls

The dolls that were introduced in 1986 brought with them an innovation that begins the evolution of these characters from simply country kids to characters in more sophisticated costumes. Instead of just a muslin shift with a shawl, or a kerchief around their heads, several of the 1986 additions wore dresses with pinafores over them, and some wore shawls as well, but still they would be wearing muslin as either the underdress or the pinafore.

The first characters in costumes for the Halloween holiday also joined the Collection in 1986. Halloween has always been a favorite holiday in

the Wisber house. Barbara and Peter couldn't resist naming the trick-or-treating witch with her accompanying little ghost "Marisa Valentine with little brother Petey" in honor of their own children.

The Evolution Continues

"Amy Bowman" was among the dolls introduced for the Spring of 1987. "Amy" was the first character to wear an underdress and pinafore, neither of which was muslin. And "Amy" and some of the other dolls introduced with her were no longer standing in the usual Lizzie High position: "Amy" sits on a swing, and several other characters introduced in 1987 sit on benches or stools, while still other characters stand in new ways — bent over their tasks or even on one foot (a position especially challenging to designer Peter).

In 1987 the first "professionals" also were added to the Lizzie High Collection. "Margaret Bowman," an aspiring schoolteacher, and "Addie High," who "wants to be a nurse…," are consistently among the top ten best sellers.

The male characters that joined the Collection in 1987 were given coats to wear for the first time, rather than having painted jackets or shirts. The "Groom" (introduced with his "Bride" and "The Flower Girl") looked so nice in his cloth coat that soon all the boy dolls were being produced with actual coats instead of painted ones.

"Jacob High" was introduced in the Spring of 1988 as the first of the boys wearing actual fabric overalls and a fabric shirt. The first little girl to wear overalls, "Janie Valentine," joined the Collection at the same time. An even bigger innovation for 1988 was the positioning of several characters

"Audrey High" (left) was the first members-only doll introduced for Lizzie High Society members only. The 3,000 "Kathryn Bowman" dolls (right) went on the market in June, 1992 and within two weeks, dealers had ordered every one. The piece captures Kathryn and her little sister at their upright piano.

in sitting positions on the floor. With legs spread to either side, three new characters exhibit all the enthusiasm of childhood as they settle into tasks such as coloring, dog bathing or gift opening.

The 1988 issues commemorate many holidays and events. Particularly popular from that year's introductions are the "Pilgrim Boy," "Pilgrim Girl" and "Indian Girl" from "Mrs. Poole's fifth grade class' Thanksgiving Play."

The 1988 characters "Victoria and Johann Bowman" enjoy the magic of Graduation Day, while "Jason and Jessica High" make Mother's Day special. "Lucy Bowman" is a "perfect pumpkin," learning that plumpness is sometimes an advantage. A new "Santa Claus" soaks his feet, attended by "Mrs. Claus."

Highlights of Lizzie High for the Early 1990s

Forest Friends "Marlene" and "Albert Valentine" joined the Collection in 1990, stirring up fond memories of adventures with the troop or pack we met with weekly...the friends with whom we sometimes got to go exploring new worlds. With the introduction of the Forest Friends came another significant innovation — resin critters cast from Peter's sculpted characters.

When Barbara wanted a turtle to accompany "Marlene" and could not find a suitable one from any source she knew, she turned to Peter to solve her problem. Peter sculpted a turtle and then had it made into the mold from which resin reproductions are now cast. Prior to "Marlene's" turtle, the animals that Ladie and Friends created to accompany the dolls were either two-dimensional and cut from boards, or composed from little wooden balls and sliced wooden eggs. Peter's sculpting talents have since produced over a dozen kittens, puppies, bunnies and even a "rubber" duck. These more lifelike additions contribute immensely to the overall charm of the dolls.

For Christmas, 1990 The Little Ones At Christmas were introduced: four different little characters who "love decorating the house, baking cookies, trimming the tree...and opening gifts that rattle." Christmas of 1990 also saw the introduction of the first participant in The Christmas Concert, "Claire Valentine," playing her part on the triangle.

In late 1990, Barbara and Peter had worked out all the details on two characters that would meet the desires of many for dolls celebrating the Fourth of July. But then due to the Gulf War, patriotic demand made for a shortage of red, white and blue fabric. Fortunately, the war was short-lived, and so was the fabric shortage. "Trudy Valentine" and "Michael Bowman" then became widely available in their all-American outfits.

Another new Santa joined the Collection in 1991. "The Department Store Santa," along with his assistant, "Santa's Helper," bring fond memories to all who sat on Santa's lap in the big department store. "Christmas Little Ones," "Esther Dunn" in a second edition with her little sister Naomi, and "Cynthia High" with her little sister Jessica, carried on with their traditional outings to see "The Department Store Santa."

In 1992 twelve new Little Ones were brought into the collection, doing Spring, Summer, Fall and Winter things and celebrating seasonal holidays. Skiers also joined the Collection in 1992, as did a new participant in The Christmas Concert: "Judith High," who plays perfect violin solos. "Barbara Helen," who is named after the creative "ladie" of Ladie and Friends, "dreams of someday becoming a famous artist."

The year 1992 also saw the introduction of Ladie and Friends' first Limited Edition. Three thousand "Kathryn Bowman" dolls were crafted in 1992, and the doll went on the market June 1. Within two weeks, Lizzie High dealers had ordered all 3,000 of Kathryn and her little sister at the upright piano.

The Lizzie High® Society Debuts

As if 1992 were not special enough, Ladie and Friends started a collector's club for dedicated Lizzie High collectors. The Lizzie High Society started signing on Charter Members in September 1992 for the Charter Year that ran until August of 1993. The doll created for Society members only, "Audrey High," has been a great hit since her introduction in January 1993. And now that the Charter Year is over and she can no longer be ordered, she'll likely become a collectible treasure indeed.

The year 1993 has brought more Little Ones, more big ones and more reservoirs of memory and love preserved. Another wonderfully evocative Santa joined the Lizzie High Collection for Christmas 1993: a Mommy kissing a Daddy in a Santa suit while Little Ones peek out from their hiding places is sure to bring special joy to the hearts and homes of all those who have discovered the magic of Barbara and Peter Wisber's Family and Friends of Lizzie High.

The Lance Corporation
Celebrating Twenty-Five Years of Fine American Sculpture From the New England-Based Studios of Chilmark, Hudson and Sebastian

As The Lance Corporation enters its second quarter-century of leadership in the art metal sculpture field, this versatile American firm expresses appreciation to its collectors for their ideas, their loyalty and their inspiration. Grounded in American history and culture, Lance nonetheless prides itself on innovation — both in sculptural subjects and in fine art techniques. Indeed, since 1968, Lance has been recognized as a pacesetter in the field of fine art sculpture.

From its picturesque hometown of Hudson, Massachusetts, Lance offers three renowned lines of fine art sculpture — each with its own personality and following. Some pieces are crafted in fine pewter...others are hand-painted over pewter... while still others are hand-painted over cast porcelain. Yet all the works of Chilmark, Hudson Pewter and Sebastian Miniatures meet Lance's high standards of quality, historical accuracy and detail in every stage of creation and production.

Chilmark: Recent Breakthroughs from an Industry Leader

In 1974, the renowned bronze sculptor Don Polland brought his "Cheyenne" model to Lance for casting in pewter. That began a long and successful collaboration that continues today. Now known as Chilmark, this limited edition line of pewter sculptures features, in addition to Polland, the works of well-known artists such as Anne McGrory, Tim Sullivan, Joseph Slockbower, Francis J. Barnum and Lowell Davis.

Anne McGrory's favorite subjects as an artist are wildlife and western themes. She has previously sculpted designs in both categories for Chilmark, but with "Buffalo Vision," first issue in her collection entitled *The Seekers*, she was able to fuse these into one truly magnificent sculpture. In the process, Ms. McGrory has launched an innovative art form which Chilmark calls "hidden image."

In this design, the art literally embodies the vision sought by the young brave. Throughout the sculpture are hidden images of the buffalo intricately woven into the subject itself. Though successfully duplicated in two-dimensional paintings, the use of hidden images in sculpture is a fresh departure for Chilmark. *The Seekers* combines Ms. McGrory's rich talent, hidden images and Chilmark's special MetalART™ enhancements for a truly unique new series.

The MetalART™ "look" itself represents a radical departure for Chilmark: an advance the firm has undertaken after studying the market for several years, particularly in the area of western bronzes. While the traditional bronze finishes still prevail, a segment of the market has introduced brighter colors and finishes in their work, with enthusiastic collector response.

Enter MetalART™, Chilmark's term for the process that encompasses the entire process of creating art metal sculpture in fine pewter, utilizing the combined talents of the artist, foundry craftspeople and detailers. The last group are "alchemists" that design and assemble the various components, apply the accents of gold, sterling silver, bronze and the colorful flourishes that transform fine pewter sculpture into vibrant art. Their innovations have resulted in a marvelous new array of Chilmark creations, including Tim Sullivan's stunning *To The Great Spirit* collection, Joseph Slockbower's *The Great Chiefs* collection and numerous works by Don Polland.

Many Chilmark collectors specialize in handsome and historically significant Civil War-theme

The Adversaries, *Francis Barnum's successful series, honors the Leaders of the Civil War. This group of four Civil War Generals includes, from left to right, "William Tecumseh Sherman," "Ulysses S. Grant," "Robert E. Lee," and "Stonewall Jackson." Each piece in the series is sold out.*

"Winkin', Blinkin' and Knot" is from The Lance Corporation's new C.P. Smithshire™ collection. The woodland inhabitants of Smithshire™, The Shirelings™, are sculpted by Lance artist, Cindy Smith.

pieces created by Francis J. Barnum: over thirty-five pieces since 1987. So popular are these works that their limited editions often are fully subscribed in a matter of months. One example of this phenomenon is "Parsons' Battery," a Barnum limited edition of 500 created to capture the dramatic events of October 1862 in Perryville, Kentucky. Developed in conjunction with the Cincinnati Civil War Round Table, a portion of the proceeds of the sold-out piece will benefit Civil War Battlefield Preservation.

Described as a landmark series portraying the leaders of the Civil War, Barnum's *The Adversaries* offers compelling figures of "Robert E. Lee," "Ulysses S. Grant," "Thomas J. 'Stonewall' Jackson" and "William Tecumseh Sherman." All four are now sold out in editions of 950. Barnum's *Cavalry Generals* have proven similarly popular, with "J.E.B. Stuart" a sell-out in an edition of 950. Other subjects in this finely crafted collection include "George Armstrong Custer," "Bedford Forrest" and "Philip Sheridan." The "Lincoln Bust," one of Barnum's newest creations, is available in three distinct editions: bronze, limited to 50 and now sold out; MetalART™, limited to 350; and pewter, limited to 500.

Perhaps the most touching of all Francis J. Barnum's Civil War originals is "Dear Mother," a sculpture portraying a very young soldier no more than sixteen years of age. Many young boys joined the ranks of their older brothers and uncles in the armies of both sides of the Civil War. Swept up by the spirit of the times, these youngsters lied about their age and the recruiting officers, eager to provide fresh troops, took them in. Sitting on a tree stump, our young hero seems lost in thought as he prepares the words to send to mother...promising to return home soon, and praying that he will.

The year 1993 saw the first joint venture between Chilmark and the renowned American country artist Lowell Davis with the execution of his "Skedaddlin'." A beautiful plow scene produced in Chilmark fine pewter is enlivened with Davis' well-known humor.

Legions of Disney fans have discovered the beauties of Chilmark originals in collections entitled *Generations Of Mickey* and *Sorcerer's Apprentice Collectors Series*, as well as miscellaneous Disney offerings. In 1990, The Walt Disney Company granted the *Sorcerer's Apprentice Collectors Series* its Best New Product of the Year award. What's more, the *Generations Of Mickey* have proven extremely popular among Disneyana collectors who ordinarily specialize in antique items only.

In addition to all of these collecting riches, Chilmark offers a range of Christmas items and special edition redemption specials, and event pieces. All of these as well as other new introductions are chronicled in "The Chilmark Report" and "The Spotlight," confidential newsletters sent exclusively to registered owners of Chilmark sculptures.

Hudson Debuts Unique New Summer Village Series

Introduced recently by the Hudson division of The Lance Corporation is *The Summer Villagers*... an outing at Tully Park. As we enter the scene, it is a splendid day for a park outing, and *The Summer Villagers* are taking every advantage of the occasion.

Balloon sales are terrific, and "Linda" had a very hard time choosing her favorite color. "Mr. Lawrence" really got carried away and is finally proposing to his long-time acquaintance, "Miss McCorkle." "Stephen" is trying to impress "Mrs. Cutler" with his new kite, but she is only interested in proudly showing off her new offspring. Meanwhile, "Janet" doesn't seem at all impressed

with the antics of "Michael" and "Paul," who are vying for her affection.

These are just a few of the delightful *Summer Villagers* characters, crafted in shining pewter and generously adorned with hand-painting. The focal point for their adventures is the magnificent "Gazebo," the stage for the sometimes off-key, but always entertaining, "Tully Brothers Band." *The Summer Villagers* is an extension of Hudson's Victorian-era favorite, *The Villagers*™, which has a distinct winter theme.

The artists of Hudson pay tribute to *Civil War Leaders* and other Civil War characters in handsome works of art that were first unveiled during 1993. The *Leaders* series includes handsome, head-to-toe figurines approximately 3¹/₂" to 4¹/₈" in height, honoring "Abraham Lincoln," "Robert E. Lee," "Stonewall Jackson," "Ulysses S. Grant," and "Philip Sheridan."

Also offered by Hudson is an authentic-looking "Civil War Battlefield," which enables collectors to position and re-position their favorite pieces as they see fit. Figurines that work well with the battlefield include various soldiers and officers from the Blue and Gray. These pieces may be acquired separately, or as a complete set with the battlefield.

In addition, Hudson crafts a remarkable variety of pewter collectibles and gifts including *Disney*, *Americana* and *Fantasy*.

The Sebastian "Firefighter" is a limited edition which sold out prior to its formal introduction, while "I Know I Left It Here Somewhere" has been introduced in an edition limited to 1,000 pieces.

Sebastian Limited Editions Equals Immediate Sell-out

Ever since the late Prescott W. Baston introduced his first Sebastian Miniatures in 1938, these highly decorated, cast porcelain works of art have been favorites with collectors. Now designed and sculpted by Baston's son, Woody, Sebastian Miniatures are America's oldest continually produced collectible line. They have been manufactured and distributed by Lance since 1975.

Sebastian limited editions are so coveted by collectors that they often sell out remarkably fast: witness the "Firefighter" from Woody Baston's *Professionals* series. This work of art sold out in an edition of 500 within just two hours of its announcement — and that was a full month before its formal introduction.

Members of the Sebastian Miniatures Collectors Society enjoy the opportunity to acquire "members-only" pieces, and these works of art also have a history of rapid sales. One example is the "Leprechaun," which proved so popular that Woody Baston was inspired to create another leprechaun figure recently in an edition of 1,000 pieces. Entitled "I Know I Left It Here Somewhere," it portrays a standing leprechaun scratching his head as he tries to figure out where he has left his pot of gold.

The Shirelings™ of C.P. Smithshire™ Come to The Lance Corporation

C.P. Smithshire™ — a collection of more than thirty lilliputian woodsdwellers called Shirelings™, are new from Lance. The Shirelings, sculpted by artist Cindy Smith and produced in cold-cast "sheramic," are 5¹/₂" to 7" figurines. They include the poets, painters, artisans, musicians, scholars and craftspeople of Smithshire™.

The new *C.P. Smithshire™* collection was introduced in July 1993 at the International Collectible Exposition held in South Bend, Indiana. The Pangaean Society, the organization for Shirelings™ collectors, launched its charter year in September. Like the classic works of Chilmark, Hudson and Sebastian, this new collection bears the unmistakable marks of quality and uniqueness that have won favor for The Lance Corporation among collectors and connoisseurs.

In its second quarter-century, Lance stands to win even more staunch admirers with its diverse line of collectibles inspired by history, heartwarming images, favorite characters and delightful tales.

The Lawton Doll Company
Exquisite Limited Edition Dolls That Tell
a Story as Time Goes By...

For Wendy Lawton, every beloved childhood memory seems highlighted by dolls. Looking back on her youth in San Francisco, this gifted doll sculptor and costumer can't ever recall a time when dolls were not an important part of her life.

"My very first dolls were a pair of two and one-half inch, hard plastic, Renewal joined babies (purchased at Woolworths for five cents each), carefully sewn into a twin bunting made of soft cotton flannel," Ms. Lawton recalls fondly. "My mother understood the importance of having a doll scaled to fit in a tiny pocket or a child-sized hand. I can still remember the comforting feel of the soft flannel bunting as I'd suck my thumb while holding the babies in the other four fingers. Those battered little babies are still a treasured part of my doll collection to this day."

Not long ago, Ms. Lawton went through her family photo album to see if she could find photographs of some of her first dolls. Not surprisingly, she found it difficult to locate a photo of herself *without* a doll in her arms, or close at hand.

"My younger sister, Linda, and I played dolls hour after hour for years, from Tiny Tears through Barbie," Ms. Lawton smiles. "We sewed for them, cooked for them and curled and styled their hair. We even took our dolls along in strollers when we went shopping downtown. We were blessed with a magical childhood, rich with make-believe and 'let's pretend.' My parents believed in the importance of creative play.

"We were provided with the tools of childhood — which for me were dolls — and plenty of time in which to learn to exercise our imaginations. Who would have guessed that all those years of play were actually job training for me!"

Dolls and Beloved Books and Stories Inspire Wendy Lawton's Art

While Wendy Lawton enjoyed work as a graphic artist, kindergarten teacher and daycare administrator after completing her education at San Jose State University, she found her true vocation after the birth of her first child, Rebecca. In the early years of her marriage to her husband, Keith, Ms. Lawton spent lots of time experimenting with doll making. She made many cloth dolls and even experimented with bread dough and plaster as dollmaking media.

Soon after the arrival of Rebecca, the artist began to search out someone who could teach her porcelain dollmaking. "I had a profound desire to somehow capture Rebecca at that moment in time," Ms. Lawton recalls. She found a wonderful teacher who had been making and repairing dolls for nearly fifty years. "She taught me dollmaking from the first clay sculpture all the way through moldmaking to the final china paint. I even learned how to make a hand wefted wig!" Ms. Lawton recalls.

Wendy Lawton began to work in porcelain by doing commissioned portrait dolls. Then a few copies of these portraits were sold in local California shops. From that point on, it seems there were never quite enough Lawton Dolls to go around!

Today Rebecca Lawton is a lovely teenager, and the Lawtons have a handsome young son, Patrick, as well. Keith and Wendy Lawton, along with partners Jim and Linda Smith, are kept busy by the ever-growing demands of Lawtons — now a booming doll making business in Turlock, California. And while The Lawton Doll Company has won fame and numerous awards for beautiful dolls on many subjects, the studio is best known for Wendy Lawton's porcelain characters inspired by the beloved heroes and heroines of favorite children's storybooks.

The Loving Creation of a Lawton Doll

Collectors and dealers praise Lawtons for the uniqueness of its dolls and their costumes — especially the fact that Ms. Lawton sculpts a new head for each and every new edition. Many companies use the same doll sculpture over and over, simply re-dressing the doll. All Lawton dolls are entirely made in the U.S.A., in the firm's own California workshops. Wendy Lawton guides each step of the production process personally.

Each edition of Lawtons' dolls is strictly limited, with most offered in editions of 250, 350 or 500 dolls. The one exception is the firm's licensed doll, "Marcella." This unique work of art features a miniature Raggedy Ann in the arms of a doll who looks

Proud little mama Patricia shows off her beloved Patsy® doll, which is a faithful replica of the popular 1930s doll. "Patricia And Her Patsy" is from Lawton's Classic Playthings™ collection.

The Lawton Doll Company rekindles the magic of the nursery in this endearing version of "The Velveteen Rabbit," complete with shoebutton-eyed rabbit and carrot-topped owner.

just like the real "Marcella" whose father, Johnny Gruelle, created Raggedy Ann at the turn-of-the-century.

Much thought and research goes into the "theming" of each doll. As Louise Fecher of *Dolls* magazine said, "With guides like Heidi, Hans Brinker and Laura Ingalls, (Ms. Lawton) travels through the pages of children's classic literature." Lawton dolls have been inspired by literary characters, holidays, seasons, poetry and memorable childhood events.

Lawtons Step-by-Step Creative Process

Once Wendy Lawton has completed her research for a particular doll, she creates a prototype — a process that can consume an incredible amount of time. That first sculpt is subjected to three different molding stages, with refinements in between each stage. At the same time, initial sketches for costuming give way to fabric selection, pattern drafting and sample garment creation. Meanwhile, wigs are selected and props are designed or sourced. These initial stages require anywhere between three weeks and three months — sometimes longer.

Then the edition of dolls is created, one by one, following the same process for each doll in the edition. The costume is cut and sewn, props or hats are made, greenware is poured, and body parts are soft-fired and then detailed. Next, the body parts are high-fired and the head is detailed, with the eye openings cut and beveled before the head is high-fired.

Once all six porcelain parts are complete, they are sanded before the cheeks are painted and fired. Painting and shading, and highlighting the lips come next, before firing once again. Then the eyelashes and eyebrows are painted on before a final firing.

To put the doll's parts together, Lawton's craftspeople set hooks in the body parts, then string the doll together. The doll's eyes are set and cleaned, and she is dressed in all her finery. Finally, each doll is numbered and registered, her pate is affixed, her wig is added and styled, and she is carefully boxed for shipment.

Not counting the processes involved in making the costume, props, wigs and accessories, there are fifty-six different hand operations required to make a single Lawton doll. Because of Lawton's strict quality control requirements, more than half of all dolls are rejected at one step or another before they win the right to represent the studio in the marketplace. Each doll requires no less than twenty to twenty-five hours of individual attention, including firing time and up to ten hours of hand labor on creation and costuming.

Highlights of the Lawton Doll Line

The Lawton Doll Company issues an entirely new line of dolls each year. Collectors eagerly await the unveiling of the new designs, introduced to the trade at The New York Toy Fair in February, and to the collectors soon after. Because editions are relatively small and available for only a year or so, market appreciation often occurs at issue closure.

The new dolls are usually issued as part of an ongoing series or collection, such as *Childhood Classics*®, *Cherished Customs*®, *Christmas Legends*™, *Folktales and Fairy Stories*™ or *Classic Playthings*™. Among the *Childhood Classics*® collection have been favorites such as "Alice in Wonderland," "Heidi," "Pollyanna," "Little Princess," "Anne of Green Gables," or more recently, "Tom Sawyer" with his bandaged toe and famous paintbrush and "The Velveteen Rabbit," which featured an adorable carrot-topped boy in a smocked romper holding his precious little velveteen rabbit.

The *Cherished Customs*® collection focuses on customs the world over, celebrating the rich cultural patchwork of our world. Often the native peoples help in the creation of the costumes or accessories of these dolls, as with the Navajo weaving on "Cradleboard" or the Javanese costume work and hand-carved wooden mask on "Topeng Klana."

The *Folktales and Fairy Stories*™ collection has highlighted many of our favorite fables, such as "Snow White" dressed in a dirndl dress, just as if she stepped out of the Grimms Brothers fairy tale. "Goldilocks and Baby Bear" are a favorite of collectors as brought to life in Lawton's whimsically unique interpretation.

Lawton Collector's Guild Members May Acquire "Members-Only" Dolls

Each year, members of the Lawton Collector's Guild are afforded a special, no-obligation opportunity to purchase an exclusive doll that Wendy Lawton will design for Guild members only. This is just one of the several benefits of Guild membership, which requires a $15.00 initial fee and a yearly renewal at just $7.50 annually.

Members of the Guild receive a membership card, Lawton logo pin in delicate cloisonne enamel, a subscription to Lawton's Collector's Guild Quarterly newsletter, a vinyl-covered three-ring binder to protect copies of the Quarterly, and a set of postcards featuring the current collections of Lawton dolls. For more information about Guild membership, contact Lawton Collector's Guild at P.O. Box 969, Turlock, California 95381.

The beloved fairy tale, Goldilocks and the Three Bears, is brought to life in Wendy Lawton's unconventional but delightfully whimsical interpretation, "Goldilocks and Baby Bear."

The Javanese court dances flow with an undulating liquidity, weaving timeless tales of the Ramayana. This authentic and exquisitely costumed Lawton doll is named after the dance called "Topeng Klana."

Lefton's Colonial Village
History in Miniature, A Wonderful Place To Be

"I wish I could live in my collection, not just with it," LaVerne Nelson of Schaumburg, Illinois wrote to the editor of "The Colonial Village News." "I like to imagine myself in miniature, walking down the streets of my display and looking in the shop windows and hearing sleigh bells," she mused.

That idea might have been implanted when she read the following from the *Colonial Village Illustrated Collector's Guide & History* book - a must for any collector because of its extraordinary pictures and prose.

"...take your first step into *Colonial Village*. If you open the windows of your mind, you'll be able to sense what you see. You'll feel the nip of the crisp, clean air on your nose and smell the aroma of fresh-baked bread as you approach the bakery and the minty chocolate of the Sweet Shop mingled with hickory smoke from the chimneys. You'll hear the snow crunch under your feet and the jingling of sleigh bells as a horse-drawn cutter glides by with a whinny and a neigh. You'll be in *Colonial Village*...and it's a wonderful place to be."

According to John Lefton, LaVerne's is not an uncommon feeling among *Colonial Village* collectors. "They relate very personally to it," he says, "in an almost metaphysical way."

This strong "sense of place" — of making fantasy reality — is encouraged by the buildings and people that populate the Collection and by the special things that Lefton has done to add to their aura of nostalgia.

Real Estate Tycoons

Colonial Village collectors think of themselves as property owners...and they have Deeds of Title to prove it. Instead of the ubiquitous 'certificates of authenticity,' Lefton created antique deed reproductions for each of the buildings. Along with the 'legal description' of the property is a brief history of when it was built and by or for whom.

The Collection debuted, modestly, in 1986 with the introduction of two assortments of six buildings for a total of twelve, seven of which have since been retired.

Lefton's Colonial Village Deeds of Title are antique reproductions that offer collectors a pleasant and informative change from ordinary certificates of authenticity. Each has a story about the place and the people who lived and worked there.

Response was anything but modest, however, and the Geo. Zoltan Lefton Co. — now in its fifty-second year — knew it had a hit on its hands.

"We resisted the urge to meet demand with too many items," says founder George Z. Lefton. "We didn't want to rush the development at risk of losing the charm and detail that made them special," he says. "We pursued a path of careful, controlled growth."

So, one by one, buildings were researched, sculpted and crafted to standards that exceeded others. "It was important that they not just be 'different' than anything else, I wanted them to be better," Sidney Lebow, Lefton's executive vice-president and product development director added.

In 1991, the first limited edition, "Hillside Church," was introduced, and the 4,000 pieces were eagerly acquired by collectors who antici-

The World's Largest Colonial Village *Panoramic Display is an inspiration to collectors wanting to create their own special scenes.*

pated their rarity would increase their value. They were right. The $60 issue price soon doubled, tripled and quadrupled on the secondary market. Subsequent annual limited editions enjoyed similar success.

The current Collection boasts almost eighty illuminated buildings and well over a hundred 'ceramic citizens,' antique vehicles and scenic accents.

Luxury Homes and Business Opportunities

The structures range from cozy cottages to Victorian mansions complete with 'gingerbread' trim. There are stately, tall-steepled churches and imposing public buildings. Among the most popular are the shops and stores that provide *Colonial Village* 'residents' everything from fresh flowers and produce to antiques and toys.

Their appeal can be explained by these excerpts from the *Deeds and History* book:

"Standing before the forge, wielding a heavy hammer, the blacksmith had to coax red-hot metal into shapes it had never been and would forever be."

"When the first iron horses came whinnying their way into town, reined only by rails, they stopped at the Old Time Station."

It is not surprising that the book has been praised for its literary merit. "I wish all our history and social studies books were as well and fascinatingly written," says Illinois librarian, Leslie Geist.

Setting The Scene

In 1991 Lefton designers and scenic artists created the World's Largest *Colonial Village* Panoramic Display. It covered eight scale acres and was featured in the centerfold of their *Illustrated Collector's Guide & History* book.

"Through their response, we recognized," John Lefton says, "that there was a desire among collectors, for some help in creating both year-round and seasonal displays for their collections. That became a focus of our efforts and the results have been impressive."

Lefton's How-To articles in the "*Colonial Village* News" have been so popular, they've been reprinted so retailers can share the 'ways and means' with their collector-customers. They provide step-by-step instructions along with materials' lists and money-saving tips like this: "Use an inexpensive keyhole saw but a serrated knife will work fine." "Key to the speed, ease and economy is inexpensive insulating foam available from your local lumber yard or home store." "To make a 'stream' put

down a wrinkled-up strip of blue plastic wrap. (Hers came from the morning newspaper)."

Not only are readers informed, they're encouraged to try their hand at it with contests that offer *Colonial Village* cash prizes to winners that they can spend adding to their real estate holdings.

In 1993, at the Long Beach, California International Collectible Exposition, Lefton showed their innovative modular display. Although it looked like a single 5 foot by 16 foot unit, it was actually eight sections that fit together and could be disassembled for shipping or, in the collector's case, storage. "The whole thing could fit in a closet," says *Colonial Village* Coordinator, Steven Lefton Sharp.

Needless to say, collectors were intrigued and Lefton responded by sharing their design secrets.

The heart and soul of the Collection are, of course, the buildings. "They seem to get more special each year," says veteran collector Morgan Ryan of Chicago. "The detail and coloration really set them apart." A good example of what Morgan is talking about is the "Joseph House," a 1993 introduction. The turret and three-story facade create production challenges to assure that as the ceramic building is fired nothing warps, twists or gets out of alignment. And while the house is predominantly mauve, there are no fewer than a dozen different colors and distinctive glazes used to give it a special look and feeling.

Just as the buildings have character, the 'ceramic citizens' that populate *Colonial Village* have personalities. Many of them were named for Lefton friends and family. Mr. and Mrs. Notfel represent — with backwards spelling and period dress — the company's founder George Zoltan Lefton and his wife Magda. Steven and Stacey are Mr. Lefton's grandchildren.

Collectors' Service Bureau

Many new *Colonial Village* real estate owners received their first building as a gift or bought it on vacation. To help them find a local retailer, Lefton publishes a toll-free help-line number (1-800-628-8492) in all their brochures. The Collectors' Service Bureau also answers collectors' questions, provides them with replacements for missing Deeds and tries to maximize their enjoyment in seeking and finding *Colonial Village* items.

Careful attention to detail is one of the reasons collectors are attracted to Lefton's Colonial Village.

The expanded 1993 edition of the Colonial Village Illustrated Collector's Guide & History *book should prove to be even more popular than the sold-out '92 premier edition.*

LEGENDS
The Brilliance of Mixed Media™ Marries Bronze, Pewter and Brass Vermeil With Striking Touches of 24K Gold

When a team of four brothers launched LEGENDS in 1986, they were already renowned for their fine art sculptures for giftware-related companies like American Express and Walt Disney Productions. Since then, LEGENDS has dramatically impacted the world of collectibles with works ranging from small-scale issues to full-sized gallery sculptures.

The studio's subject matter is remarkably broad as well: encompassing authentic Native American figures, Western and Civil War history, and endangered wildlife. Through the everlasting media of sculpture, LEGENDS fine art proudly represents and preserves the proud heritage of the Native American Indian, as well as many other significant American heroes, leaders and legends who grace the annals of our nation's history.

Committed to environmental and wildlife conservation, LEGENDS actively supports the work of various non-profit organizations, such as Defenders of Wildlife, the Grounded Eagle Foundation, the World Wildlife Fund and the National Audubon Society. Additionally, LEGENDS maintains its commitment to the preservation and advancement of today's Native Americans through significant donations that support vital organizations such as the Native American Rights Fund (NARF), Red Cloud Indian School in South Dakota and the American Indian Dance Theatre.

The Creative Process for Mixed Media™

LEGENDS has always remained in the forefront of new concepts and innovations in the collectibles and fine art markets — most notably in the conception and creation of Mixed Media™. This significant and valuable contribution to the world of limited edition fine art sculpture combines multiple brilliant media, including LEGENDS Bronze, Fine Pewter, Brass Vermeil, 24K Gold Vermeil, Lucite®, and many other vibrant metals and hot torched-acid patinas. Also used periodically are Black Nickel, Rose Copper Vermeil, Sunrise Gold Copper Vermeil and Flame Copper Vermeil.

When LEGENDS unveiled their first Mixed Media™ work in 1987, collectors immediately recognized the uniqueness of this stunning new concept in fine art sculpture. And while imitators have surfaced over the years, LEGENDS remains the only studio to create each of its works using the authentic colors of the actual metals to create color on the sculpture — never paints or dyes.

The step-by-step crafting process for a LEGENDS sculpture begins when a LEGENDS artist creates an original work. This sculptural original may require many months — sometimes years — of sculpting and re-sculpting soft clay before the original is finalized in the form of plastiline. From these masters, working models are created.

Each piece is sectioned into many tiny component parts to help LEGENDS create the intricate detail found in all of their sculptures. They are then placed into molds for the creation of individual cavities. Hot molten metal is poured into these cavities and is left until it cools down to room temperature.

Each component part is tirelessly hand-cleaned and refitted by foundry artisans with over two decades of experience. Handwork with fine stainless steel tools recovers detail lost in the soldering process. The finished Mixed Media™ work is oxidized to a deep black patina and then relieved by hand with steel wool and sand to bring back highlights of the original metals. Only then is the piece appointed with the unique characteristics that make LEGENDS sculptures the leaders in today's fine art marketplace.

LEGENDS Artists Pride Themselves on Absolute Authenticity

Since the inception of the studio, the talented artists of LEGENDS have strived to incorporate the highest grade of authenticity in their work. Great attention to detail and thorough research goes into each sculpture to ensure that the subject matter is represented in its truest form. LEGENDS takes great pride in bringing their collectors authentic works of fine art that are untouched by the commercial temptations of mass production. At no time is authenticity sacrificed for beauty. In fact, it is true authenticity that makes a LEGENDS

C. A. Pardell's "Defending the People" offers a dramatic fourth issue for the LEGENDS American West Premier Edition Collection.

Lucite® is married to Mixed Media™ metals in the LEGENDS "Salmon Falls" sculpture by Willy Whitten, the first issue in the Clear Visions collection.

Returning wolves to the wilds of Yellowstone Park is the cause that inspired Kitty D. Cantrell to create her stunning "Yellowstone Bound" sculpture.

fine art sculpture so beautiful and valuable.

One of the foremost qualities of LEGENDS sculptures is their historical accuracy. LEGENDS is extremely proud of the historical accuracy and fidelity to principals of Native American culture that are the hallmarks of their work. LEGENDS is committed to the highest standards of artistic value and historic integrity. Therefore, LEGENDS collectors can be assured that the sculptures they purchase are not just beautiful, but historically accurate as well.

Extensive photographic and ethnographic research goes into the preparation of every LEGENDS sculpture. For example, the sculptures in Chris Pardell's *Legacies Of The West Premier Edition* are derived from actual historical photographs. Pardell studies all known photographs and portraits of his subjects as a critical first step in creating a sculpture. In fact, one of the actual photos of Quanah Parker — a Comanche chief — was used by the artist to create "Defiant Comanche." And one of the actual photos of Chief Joseph (Nez Perce) inspired "No More, Forever."

The LEGENDS Collectors Society

LEGENDS supports its collectors through the LEGENDS Collectors Society (LCS) — an exclusive, free membership program that collectors receive upon the purchase of any LEGENDS limited edition sculpture. As members, collectors acquire a personalized LCS membership card, as well as many other valuable and exclusive benefits.

Among the most coveted of these benefits is the opportunity for collectors to acquire new sculptures before their open market release, combined with valuable and informative monthly full-color materials regarding new and existing LEGENDS releases. LEGENDS also records sculpture titles, insurance, and secondary market activity for safekeeping as a service to LCS members, and provides assistance in sculpture appraisal. What's more, LCS members receive "The LEGENDS Collector," an informative and entertaining quarterly newsletter created especially for them.

The LCS Membership Card provides its own set of benefits, most important of which is that it identifies LEGENDS collectors at the time of their purchases. The card gives LCS members access to any upcoming special collectors-only sculptures, and it serves as the collector's redemption during specific redemption periods on premier sculptures. Finally, it can be used as proof-of-collector during special LEGENDS events.

Chris Pardell Presents "Defending the People"

Chris Pardell was the artist whose sculptures first brought LEGENDS to national prominence. Noted by Collector's World owner Mario Pancino as "the best Western artist now working," Pardell is unique in his ability to capture the essence of the individuals he portrays. The Montrose, California-based Pancino marvels that Pardell's work "just doesn't look like anyone else's. Pardell does his homework. And he pays great attention to detail."

One of Pardell's most dramatic recent works for LEGENDS is called "Defending the People," and portrays Crazy Horse and Moving Robe Woman as they prepare for battle against the troops of the

deadly Bluecoat Cavalry. With the cry of "The chargers are coming! The soldiers are upon us," warriors of the Oglala, Blackfoot Sioux, Minneconjou and Hunkpapa tribes raced south toward the attack using whatever weapons they could grab to defend their village. The women tried to flee to the safety of the north. After long hours of battle, as the last of the soldiers stood against the might of the Indian nations, Moving Robe Woman was among those who rushed in through the thick of battle to fight in hand-to-hand combat.

It was a day of destiny, now portrayed with drama and dignity in a signed and certified limited edition of 950. "Defending the People" marks the fourth masterful issue in Pardell's *American West Premier Edition*.

Willy Whitten's "Salmon Falls" Features Shimmering Lucite®

In its continued quest for innovation in fine sculpture, LEGENDS encouraged art master Willy Whitten to integrate Lucite® into his latest Mixed Media™ design. The result is "Salmon Falls," a stunning depiction of a Huron Indian brave and his sacred fishing ritual. He has said his fishing prayers. He has purified himself and offered the "Salmon People" gifts of tobacco, and he has pledged to treat their sacred red bodies with respect. Indeed, the Huron Indians consider the Salmon fish a brother who is asked to give up his life so that the human Indian may survive.

Early this morning, this young Huron hunter arose quietly while all around him his tribesmen still slept peacefully. He picked up his fishing gear, pushed aside the deerskin covering the door of his longhouse, and swiftly left the village. After a peaceful walk, he reached the waterfall and the fishing pool at its base. He is now ready to use his harpoon to provide sustenance for his fellow tribe members.

All of this is articulated in glorious detail through the brilliance of Mixed Media™ using Lucite® as water, and numerous colors of fine high-quality metals to create the hunter, his clothing, accessories and his natural surroundings. "Salmon Falls" is introduced in a signed, certified limited edition of 950, and is an impressive 14½" high by 7" deep by 6" long.

LEGENDS Commissions Kitty D. Cantrell to Create "Yellowstone Bound"

Through award-winning artist Kitty Cantrell's faithful attitude, hard work and immense talent, she continues to grace the world with her commitment to wildlife and the environment. Her exquisite sense of detail and brilliant perception of balance, tension and form enable her to embody the true beauty of endangered wildlife. Cantrell strives to draw attention to people's perception of what wildlife is for. "Animals should not have to justify their existence. They should be allowed to be, simply because they are."

One of Ms. Cantrell's most recent introductions is a specially commissioned sculpture for LEGENDS, entitled "Yellowstone Bound." Focusing on humankind's adversarial relationship with the wolf, she advocates for this noble creature's return to the wilds of Yellowstone Park. As national wolf expert L. David Mech has said, "Yellowstone is a place that literally begs to have wolves." Recognizing the importance of this vital issue, LEGENDS is proudly donating 5% of its proceeds from the sale of "Yellowstone Bound" to the Yellowstone Wolf Recovery Program.

LEGENDS Discovers a Brilliant Young Artist: Dan Medina

Although he is only in his mid-twenties, Dan Medina's award-winning genius already has proven that he possesses exceptional talent. A self-taught illustrator, painter and sculptor, Medina explains his approach to sculpture: "I envision sculpting as an exciting three-dimensional extension of my illustrations," he says. "The ability to create overpowers me, whether it pertains to science or the arts. The power to encompass human emotion and even dreams in a work of art is what I live for."

Dan Medina has applied his remarkable gift for sculpture to a recent introduction for LEGENDS entitled "Hunter's Quest." This is the second release in his *Mystical Quest* collection, and measures 18" high by 10" long by 8" deep. The edition is certified, signed and limited to 950.

It has only been a few short years since LEGENDS developed the masterful innovation of Mixed Media™ and began creating sculptures using that exquisite media. Since then, this California-based firm has earned a strong — and growing — reputation for integrity, sculptural excellence and innovation. Considering these factors — and the studio's commitment to historical accuracy and old-world craftsmanship in fine metal — the "LEGENDS tradition" stands to flourish and grow for generations to come.

Lenox Collections
"The Lenox Difference" Is a 100-Year-Old Tradition of Excellence Carried Forward in Every Work of Art

It began in 1889. A young artist-potter named Walter Scott Lenox founded a company dedicated to the daring proposition that an American firm could create the finest china in the world. He possessed a zeal for *perfection* that he applied to the relentless pursuit of his artistic goals.

In the years that followed, Lenox china became the first American chinaware ever exhibited at the National Museum of Ceramics, in Sevres, France. In 1918, Lenox received the singular honor of being the first American company to create the official state table service for The White House.

Lenox China has been in use at The White House ever since, commissioned by Presidents and First Ladies of four different eras. Works of Lenox may also be found in more than half our Governors' mansions. They are in United States embassies around the world. And they have been specially commissioned for gifts of state.

Today, in every work of art created by Lenox Collections, the traditions begun by Walter Scott Lenox are carried forward.

The Lenox Tradition

On one occasion in the struggling early days of the firm, Walter Scott Lenox took an eminent guest on a tour through the new workshops. They stopped before a kiln and watched as craftsmen removed chinaware representing an investment of $2,000 (quite a large sum in those days). Lenox looked at the pieces with his usual piercing scrutiny and noticed a tiny flaw in every one, possibly visible only to him. Before Lenox could voice his dismay, the enthusiastic visitor cried out, "This is exhilarating. Such excitement!" "Yes," Lenox replied. Without hesitation, he then ordered everything that had just come out of the kiln to be destroyed.

The Lenox Difference

Lenox Collections today creates works in many mediums. In every case, it maintains an unbending position regarding *quality*. The collector will see this difference in the detail of each Lenox hand-painted

"Neuschwanstein" is the remarkable re-creation of a king's fantasy. The castle's four buildings, two courtyards, seven towers and 293 windows are portrayed with breathtaking detail by master miniaturist Ron Spicer. The sculpture is handcrafted in an artist's blend of resin porcelain and painted entirely by hand. "Neuschwanstein" is 8" long by 6" high, including base.

porcelain sculpture...in the fiery, hand-polished luster of each Lenox crystal bowl, sculpture or vase...and, of course, in the flawless finish of every piece of Lenox china.

This quest for excellence in artistry has earned Lenox the privilege of creating authorized works for famed organizations throughout the world...from the Smithsonian Institution in Washington, D.C. to the famed Palace Museum in Peking's Forbidden City.

Lenox Craftsmanship

From the company's very beginning, Walter Scott Lenox stopped at nothing to locate the most gifted craftsmen both in America and abroad. When he set out to reproduce a special, pearlescent china, nothing would do but to send to Ireland for those potters who knew the craft best. Having served as an apprentice himself, Lenox realized that craftsman-

"Golden Splendor" is the first collector plate by the outstanding nature artist Catherine McClung. This award-winning artist portrays beautiful birds in their glorious natural setting. The 8-1/4" plate is crafted of Lenox ivory china to the quality standard that has made Lenox collector plates prized for generations.

ship is what bridges the gulf between dream and reality.

Now, in our own time, Lenox Collections literally searches the world to find the craftsmen most particularly skilled in producing each special work. And these craftsmen are then challenged to surpass themselves — to apply their gifts to a standard of excellence that is *unique* in all the world.

Lenox Beauty...To Endure Forever

On the subject of beauty, Walter Scott Lenox schooled his company to satisfy only one critic — posterity. His goal was to create art that would live forever.

Today, this goal remains unchanged. Every work of art Lenox Collections creates is a message to collectors, and to the world, about the company's firm commitment to uphold its founder's mission. Lenox works are created today to endure for generations and to be treasured by collectors a hundred years from now.

Lenox and Its Collectors

Throughout its history, Lenox has attracted some of the most exacting customers in the world...from the royal patron who commissioned a service of the most elegant china to set a table for 1,000 guests...to

heads of state and dignitaries from countries throughout the world. From United States Presidents Wilson and Roosevelt to Truman and Reagan, each has turned to Lenox, confident of receiving the very best.

Today, Lenox Collections conducts an ongoing search for great talent and has extended its patronage to gifted artists of many different lands. To earn the Lenox hallmark, the highest standards must be met. Every nature subject must be shown completely true to life. Each historical piece must be authentic in every detail, and all works must be infused with the fire of imagination.

The Lenox Pledge of Satisfaction

Lenox Collections takes pride in offering works of uncompromisingly high standards of quality, crafted with care and dedication by skilled artisans. The Lenox goal, in every case, is to meet the highest expectations of artistry and fine workmanship. Therefore, if a collector is ever less than completely satisfied, Lenox will either replace the work or refund the purchase price.

Similarly, if a work is ever broken or damaged, Lenox will strive to satisfy the collector as well. If the edition is still open and a replacement is available, Lenox will send it to the owner at only one-half the current price of the work.

Lenox Collections invites collectors to share in the Lenox heritage of excellence. And the company pledges to make today's collectors as satisfied as the Presidents, First Ladies and royalty who have gone before.

The Tradition Continues with Lenox Collector Plates

Lenox entered the collectible plate market in 1902 by introducing bone china dinnerware with special-order decorations. It was William Morley, perhaps the most celebrated artist in the company's early history, who set the standard for superior artistry with these original custom order plates. Orchids, first requested in 1906, were among Morley's best subjects. A set of eighteen portrait plates that were created at this time were auctioned in 1979 for $14,000.

Today, Lenox Collections offers fine art plates by some of today's most highly regarded artists.

Catherine McClung, nationally recognized for her paintings of birds, has been awarded Best of Show at the Chicago Art Exhibition, and featured in the Birds in Art Exhibition at the prestigious Leigh

Yawky Woodson Museum. *Nature's Collage* is the artist's first plate collection.

Lynn Bywaters creates Santas robed in regal splendor, adorned in snowy ermine, embroidered in silver and gold. Collectors can acquire *The Magic of Christmas*, a collection of Lynn Bywater's Santas, directly from Lenox Collections.

There are few artists today who enjoy as much critical and collector acclaim as folk artist Warren Kimble. His work is featured in prestigious collections all over the world. Now, collectors can acquire some of Warren Kimble's most sought-after art in his first-ever Lenox plate collection — *The Warren Kimble Barnyard Animals*.

Lenox Supports Conservation Efforts

Because of illegal poaching and shrinking habitats, many of the world's magnificent animals face extinction. To raise awareness of their plight, the artists of Lenox work with wildlife organizations such as the Smithsonian Institution's National Zoological Park in Washington, D.C., the National Foundation to Protect America's Eagles™ and the Rainforest Alliance. Together, Lenox Collections and the specialists of these organizations create works of art to serve as constant reminders that our animals, and their natural habitats, must be preserved to prevent their extinction.

Lenox Porcelain and Crystal

The difference that Lenox demands in quality of workmanship, artistry and imagination may be observed in every one of today's classic porcelain and crystal sculptures.

One stunning example of Lenox hand-painted porcelain wildlife sculpture is the "African Elephant Calf." This work has been sculpted under the supervision of specialists at the Smithsonian Institution's National Zoological Park in Washington, D.C.

With "Prim & Proper," the artists of Lenox have captured feline grace in Lenox Crystal. This elegant pair of crystal cats — one clear, one frosted — can stand alone, or they can nestle together producing an interplay of contours and contrasts.

The grace of the dolphin is portrayed in a work of art in pure white bone china glistening with a touch of gold. Dramatic and elegant, "Dance of the Dolphins" is a true showpiece.

These are but a few of today's best-known Lenox sculptures.

Lenox Looks to the Future

Never a company to rest on its laurels, Lenox Collections actively seeks opportunities to collaborate with prestigious organizations to bring today's collectors fascinating new works of art.

Collectors can watch for exciting creations, authorized by Turner Entertainment, which celebrate the drama and passion of *Gone With the Wind*. And car enthusiasts will be pleased to hear that Lenox Collections, in association with the Chevrolet Motor Division, will be crafting new works to "rev" the engine of the most dedicated collector.

The Tradition Lives On

Walter Scott Lenox died in 1920 at the age of sixty. However, his dream lives on in the work of today's talented Lenox artists, designers and craftsmen, and in the remarkable works of art that are cherished, treasured and enjoyed by generations of collectors across America and around the world.

Fluid feline grace is captured in a work of art that combines the clarity of polished crystal with the luster of frosted crystal. A sleek and sophisticated pair, "Prim and Proper" are etched with the Lenox hallmark, symbol of incomparable quality.

Lightpost Publishing
"Painter of Light"™ Thomas Kinkade Captures the Warm Glow of Art in the Style of the 19th-Century Luminists

"I've been fascinated by the effects of light ever since my days as a painter for the movie business," recalls Thomas Kinkade, the artistic force behind Lightpost Publishing of San Jose, California. "Back then I became known as a 'painter of light' — and I've devoted myself to creating a sense of light as the dominant theme in all of my paintings."

Since 1983, Kinkade has disciplined himself to a rigorous six-day-a-week schedule of research, field work and painting. The artist's favorite subjects are quaint towns, tranquil landscapes and charming cottages — and his concern for accuracy leads him to spend long hours researching historical documents and vintage photographs. He also visits each location as often as necessary to capture its intimate details and its unique patterns of light.

Kinkade's "quest for the light" has led him to study techniques from the Renaissance and the Impressionist periods. "In the Renaissance, the concept was that shadows are transparent. Artists threw everything into a relief of light and shadow," the voluble Kinkade explains. "The Impressionists' goal was to create radiant light effects."

Kinkade's most direct inspiration comes from a group of 19th-century American artists known as The Luminists. In California's Oakland Museum hang the canvases Kinkade admires most: landscapes by Thomas Hill, William Keith, Albert Bierstadt, John F. Kensett and Frederick Edwin Church. As for the effect of The Luminists on his work, Kinkade has several observations. He strives for "depth and mood," while combining a "warm palette, enhancement and softening of the edges, and an overall sense of light" in his unabashedly romantic paintings.

Kinkade sees his art as a way to express his deep faith in daily life. As a devout Christian, he sets aside time for regular church activities — and he considers his artistic abilities to be a special gift from God. "Everyone who is a believer has a ministry," Kinkade asserts. "I try to remember that I am a minister with a paint brush. I simply want to use pigment and canvas and paint brushes to create images that are uplifting to others."

Sometimes the healing power of art becomes especially clear, as in a recent encounter Kinkade enjoyed with one of his collectors. "At a show a

From his studios at the base of the Sierra Mountains and at Carmel by the Sea, Thomas Kinkade continues to perfect his craft as America's "Painter of Light."™ Painstaking research and field work are supplemented by long hours in the studio to create works of art that serve as "a window for the imagination."

lady approached me and told me that her house was one of those destroyed in the big Oakland fire. 'The art collection I inherited from my mother all was burned,' she told me. 'Collecting your work has given me a new start.' She actually felt that these paintings were giving her new hope and meaning," Kinkade recounts with joy.

A Natural-Born Artist Finds His Niche

Thomas Kinkade was born in 1958 and grew up in the foothills of the Sierra Mountains. From the age of four his calling as an artist was evident, and by sixteen he was an accomplished painter in oil. An apprenticeship under the well-known California representational painter Glenn Wessels won Kinkade a world of knowledge as well as a special legacy: Wessels gifted Kinkade with photographer Ansel Adams' paint brushes.

Kinkade next embarked on studies at the University of California, Berkeley and the Art

Center College of Design in Pasadena. His fierce devotion to his craft is evident in that to remain in school, the impoverished young artist often lived only on potatoes for weeks on end. What's more, he had to cook his spuds at a friend's place because Kinkade's modest flat did not include an oven!

The artist's next adventure took place in the summer of 1982, when he and his Berkeley roommate, Jim Gurney, decided to ride the rails and sketch the countryside. In Yuma, Arizona the twosome discovered that they could make plenty of money to pay for their trip by sketching portraits at a cowboy bar for two dollars apiece. Continuing their journey as far as New York City, the pair had another inspiration. They convinced Watson-Guptill Publishing to give them a contract on a book: *The Artist's Guide To Sketching*. The resulting volume became a best-selling art instructional book.

Kinkade's association with the movie industry began at the tender age of twenty-two, when he was commissioned to create over 600 background paintings for the animated feature film, *Fire and Ice*. Constant attention to the effects of light was essential to movie background painting, and this experience fueled Kinkade's fascination with The Luminists. By 1983, Kinkade was ready to leave the film industry to pursue his vision as a painter of light-filled landscapes.

Since then, his career has been documented in a host of magazines, he has become a regular guest on talk shows, and he has won an impressive list of honors. These include two Certificates of Merit from the New York Society of Illustrators, two Founder's Awards from the National Parks Academy for the Arts, a two-man show at the C. M. Russell Museum in Great Falls, Montana, more than ten one-man shows, and countless personal appearances. Other awards are Kinkade's selection as official artist for the 1989 National Parks Collectors' Print, 1990 Commemorative Press Collector's Print honoring Rotary International, 1991 "Plate of the Show" in South Bend, Best New Artist of the Year for NALED in 1992 and Print of the Year for 1993 from NALED and *Collector Editions* magazine.

Kinkade Blends Studio Time With Field Work

Today, Thomas Kinkade lives with his family in the San Francisco Bay area. With his studio only minutes away, he rides his bike to work just as his long-time hero Norman Rockwell did to his studio in Stockbridge, Massachusetts. This leisurely five-minute bike ride provides many painting ideas for Thomas Kinkade's future artistic ventures.

As for his work day, Kinkade considers his two young children as "built-in alarm clocks." He and his wife, Nanette, get the little girls ready for the day and Kinkade attends to his daily three-mile run, breakfast and prayer before arriving at his studio by 9 a.m. He breaks briefly for lunch and continues working until about 6 p.m., six days a week. Sunday is reserved for church and family activities.

To enhance his solitary time in the studio retreat, Kinkade listens to an extensive collection of musical recordings. His taste ranges from symphonic to 40s swing, "with many stops in between." The artist also loves listening to books on tape — especially when the subject matter keys in to what he is painting. "As I work on a painting of, for example, an English scene, I have Charles Dickens in the background describing the countryside!" Kinkade explains.

While the artist spends most of his year in the California studio, he finds location work to be very stimulating. A favorite "studio base" is in the Cotswold district of England. When Kinkade sets out across the Atlantic, he prepares a complete "studio in a suitcase" including canvases, painting materials, a folding easel and a portable drying rack for storing wet paintings.

The Latest Kinkade Offerings Reflect His Travels

From the quaintness of English cottages to the glories of Carmel by the Sea and the romance of Paris, Thomas Kinkade's most recent limited edition graphics showcase some of his favorite places in the world and in his imagination. "Beside Still Waters," for example, feature's Kinkade's vision of

Thomas Kinkade's "Beside Still Waters" offers the artist's vision of the Garden of Eden: a hideaway filled with flowers, bathed in silvery light.

the Garden of Eden — a wonderful hideaway, bathed in a silvery light. Ablaze with flowers of every hue and description, the scene also features a spring of gently rushing waters. "Sweetheart Cottage II, A Tranquil Dusk at Falbrooke Thatch," continues Kinkade's *Sweetheart Cottage Series* with a work of art devoted to Valentine's Day. It pictures a perfect romantic hideaway: Falbrooke Thatch. The quaint cottage is nestled next to a charming little waterfall with an arched footbridge.

"Glory of Morning" and "Glory of Evening" are two new limited edition offerings sold as a pair. Kinkade explains his inspiration by saying, "For me the quality of light is a delight! My 'Glory of Morning' sparkles with warm light filtered through myriad tiny water drops until the colors glisten. You can see that light reflected on the flowers of a fabulous garden that becomes a living rainbow. Flowers, artists — and Kinkade collectors — all delight to the glories of a lovely morning. 'Glory of Evening' is as different from its companion piece as sunset is from sunrise. The dust of a busy day, and its low-lying clouds, reflect the violet of sunset. That radiance colors the garden flowers, deepening their hues. Such evenings as this lay a purple cloak upon the land, and every home becomes a castle."

Kinkade painted "Winter's End" under the influence of a favorite poet. As he says, "We all leave tracks in our passages through life. I like to imagine that the sled which left its trail in the melting snow might be the same one that carried the traveler in Robert Frost's famous poem. Certainly, this evergreen wood is 'lovely, dark and deep.' And it's a comfort to know these sled tracks will never disappear — not as long as you have 'Winter's End' to keep the memory fresh."

As for "Paris, City of Lights," Kinkade confesses: "I've long had a love affair with Paris. The broad boulevards with their flower vendors, the bustle of life lived in the wonderfully civilized cafés…it's a great pleasure to nurse a cappuccino and watch the pageant of Parisian life pass by. My 'Paris, City of Lights' could be titled 'The Kinkades of Paris.' That's me, in the red beret, painting the fabulous Café Nanette. The real Nanette, holding baby Chandler, hails a cab, while our oldest daughter Merritt looks on. I've even signed my tiny canvas — the smallest Kinkade signature on record, and one of the proudest."

In painting "Studio in the Garden," Thomas Kinkade showcases his belief that "An artist's studio is his most important self-portrait. That's certainly true of my second studio, in the town of Carmel by the Sea. On lovely days I paint under the sky, overlooking the blue Pacific. Huge windows satisfy my passion for light; flowers surround me in a charming English garden. And, as you'll undoubtedly notice, I've decorated the bright walls with paintings that are my personal favorites."

Also new from Lightpost Publishing is Kinkade's "Lamplight Lane," which combines quaint English cottages, a lively stream spanned by an ornate Victorian bridge, and sunlight breaking through the clouds. "Sunday Outing" highlights a favorite family tradition of the Kinkades. As Thomas describes, "After church we'll take off in the family car, often driving in California's Apple Hill country, where the neat orchards and charming old farm houses provide a link with days gone by."

Like many of his previous works, the pieces described above are available through Lightpost Publishing as hand-signed and numbered collector's prints in two editions; one edition for each image has been produced on 100% rag paper, and the other on cotton fiber artist's canvas. Additional offerings include 200 artist's proofs, 200 gallery proofs, and 100 publisher's proofs of each image.

An Invitation to Join the Thomas Kinkade Painter of Light™ Collectors' Society

Recently introduced is the opportunity for collectors to join the Thomas Kinkade Collectors' Society, and to enjoy an attractive range of benefits for the annual membership fee of $35 ($45 in Canada). Each year, members will have the opportunity to purchase a "Members Only" Kinkade piece, exclusively created for the Society. These select pieces will be available for purchase only by Society Members through local dealers. Other benefits include a membership card, quarterly newsletter, and advance information about special appearances and events, as well as an Annual Free Gift from the Society.

The Collectors' Society is run by friendly, helpful people dedicated to providing Thomas Kinkade collectors with opportunities to enjoy their membership to the fullest. To access their assistance, or to obtain a membership application, call the Society at 1-800-366-3733.

With subjects ranging from small-town America to landscapes and the English countryside, Thomas Kinkade's oil paintings and reproductions communicate deeply with viewers. Kinkade paints a simpler, idyllic world which seems to radiate an inner light. This is consistent with his goals as an artist. As he puts it, "I try to create paintings that are a window for the imagination. If people look at my work and are reminded of the way things were or perhaps the way they could be, then I've done my job."

Lilliput Lane
Everything We Do, We Strive To Do It More Professionally

No words can describe the lush English countryside with its green meadows and gardens. This idyllic setting is accented by the cottages and castles which can only be found in England. Blessed with tenacity and humor, David Tate, the founder of Lilliput Lane Limited, set out to recreate the freshness of the countryside and authentic English architecture before it disappeared.

Collectors all over the world have come to appreciate Tate's integrity in preserving the rich architectural detailing of both humble cottages and historical landmarks. While the original pieces in the series were award-winning English cottages, the line was expanded to include the cottages, mills and pubs of Ireland, Scotland and Wales. These were followed by collections of German, Dutch, French, Spanish and American buildings.

Tate has an unusual blend of determination and talent. He knows that wanting to do a good job isn't enough. At Lilliput Lane, quality became the byword.

"Our business policy is built on quality," said Roger Fitness, president of Lilliput, Incorporated, the United States operation of Lilliput Lane.

"In everything we do, we strive to do it more professionally," Fitness continued, "from the studio where the flower gardens are painted to the staff who is trained to be of service to collectors by answering questions or expediting requests. We want everything we do to say 'quality'."

David Tate's Story

Born in 1945, in the Yorkshire district of England, Tate was the only son of a small, close-knit family. A bright child, he showed an exceptional talent for drawing and earned an art scholarship at the age of ten.

Tate's art career took a series of detours. At fifteen, he was forced to leave school to help support his mother. He held a series of jobs as a salesman, photographer and public relations executive for the ceramics industry before becoming a senior executive in the British fiberglass industry. In 1982, Tate took an extraordinary gamble when he left the corporate world and formed his own company.

The name for his company, Lilliput Lane, comes from Jonathan Swift's classic, *Gulliver's Travels*. Tate and his wife moved to Penrith in the Lake District of northern England, not far from Tate's birthplace and the Scottish border. They set up shop in an old farmhouse where the first Lilliput Lane cottage was sculpted.

Tate personally supervises the search for unique cottages and buildings. Months of study and hundreds of photos go into the production of a single cottage of particular vernacular styling (this refers to the distinctive style of buildings found only in one small area of the country). All traces of modern improvements will be removed during the sculpting process to make it an authentic representation of its original period.

Once a design has been approved, a silicone mold will be produced. Each figurine will be cast in "amorphite," a strong, hard substance which reproduces all the fine detailing. After being removed from the mold, each sculpture is "fettled" or cleaned to remove any excess material before being dipped in a sealant and dried.

A Renaissance man of many interests, Tate set out to find employees who shared his belief that hard work could be melded with innovation and an enjoyment in one's work. The firm grew from

An impressive example of Suffolk vernacular architecture, "Cotman Cottage" was inspired by the work of John Sell Cotman.

seven employees to about 600. More than 300 painters work in the Lilliput Lane studios. Each painter is responsible for the entire process. Eight separate inspections take place during the crafting and painting to maintain quality control.

The enthusiastic acceptance of the *Lilliput Lane Collection* was not limited to collectors. Imagine Tate's surprise in 1988 when his name was placed on the Honors List which annually salutes British citizens for making a contribution to England's prestige and economy. Soon after, he was invested as an M.B.E. (Member of the Order of the British Empire) by Queen Elizabeth II. The company was twice named one of the United Kingdom's Five Top Companies by the Confederation of British Industry. Tate also accepted the Queen's Award for Export at an audience with former Prime Minister Margaret Thatcher.

Lilliput Lane Comes to America

In 1988, Roger Fitness was selected to head the United States operation under the name Gift Link, Incorporated which is based in Columbia, Maryland. In August 1993, Gift Link, Inc. changed its name to Lilliput, Inc. to reflect the success that the Lilliput Lane brand has enjoyed in the American marketplace.

The Lilliput Lane Collectors' Club was formed in 1988 and soon became one of the fastest-growing organizations with more than 60,000 members worldwide. An annual membership in the Lilliput Lane Collectors Club entitles members to a number of advantages. Members receive a single membership packet which contains the Members-Only cottage ("The Spinney"-1993), an up-to-date catalog, the current copy of the club's quarterly magazine, *Gulliver's World* which provides information on new cottages, history, folklore and traditions that enliven history. The packet also includes the redemption card needed to purchase the Club Special Redemption Piece ("Heaven Lea"-1993) and this year's free gift, Collectors Club stationery.

In 1990, the Lilliput Lane piece, "Convent in the Woods," was chosen at the South Bend Exposition as "Best Collectible of Show." The

The Classics Collection *is a new series of miniature English cottages.* Blaise Hamlet *is the first offering in this nine cottage series.*

same year, *Collector Editions* magazine's "Award of Excellence" was presented to Lilliput Lane for "Periwinkle Cottage."

There are now 175 retired Lilliput Lane figurines and 185 currently available pieces in the line.

The Classics Collection *of Lilliput Lane*

Just as David Tate was a leader in the development of the Cottage Collectibles, he now offers collectors another option, *The Classics* of Lilliput Lane. The term "classic" is defined as being of first rank and acknowledged excellence. To introduce this new series, a miniature *Blaise Hamlet* series has been sculpted. The *Blaise Hamlet* is a "classic" example of English picturesque architecture and is a collection of nine cottages.

Each piece in *The Classics* series exhibits attention to detail and the meticulous hand-painting done in rich, permanent colors: In other words — PERFECTION IN MINIATURE.

Lilliput Lane's 1993 Anniversary Piece "Cotman Cottage"

Introduced at the Long Beach International Exposition in March 1993, "Cotman Cottage" was designed as a replacement for the "Honeysuckle Cottage" which was the 10th anniversary special in recognition of Lilliput Lane's ten years in business. This cottage was available only during 1993. The molds were destroyed, making "Cotman Cottage" a truly limited piece.

The "Cotman Cottage" is an impressive example of Suffolk vernacular architecture. The cottage is a comfortable family home in the countryside. Great pride has been taken in maintaining the thatched roof, dormers and porch. The shrubs are neatly trimmed; its fence mended; and an open gate welcomes collectors into a fragrant English garden filled with an array of wild and cultivated flowers. "Cotman Cottage" was inspired by the works of John Sell Cotman, an English watercolor artist who emerged as a leading painter of landscapes and illustrator of architectural antiques from around Suffolk.

Christmas 1993 At Lilliput Lane

Three new pieces — "Partridge Cottage," "St. Joseph's Church" and "The Gingerbread Shop" — have been added to the *Lilliput Lane Christmas Collection*. All are stone buildings which reflect the pride and craftsmanship of the stonemasons and artisans. Dusted with a light skiff of snow, these

The latest limited edition in Ray Day's American Landmarks series is a Romantic Italianate home owned by Winnie Watson Sweet.

sturdy structures will protect those within their walls from winter winds.

The second ornament in Lilliput Lane's Annual Christmas series is "Robin Cottage". The cottage is accented with a brightly lit Christmas tree and is available only in 1993.

The second work in the series of four Christmas Lodges, is "Eamont Lodge." This 1840 castellated lodge house guards the entrance to Lowther Castle Estate near Penrith.

An American Landmark — Winnie's Place

Americans are a sentimental lot. When Ray Day's *American Landmarks* series was introduced in 1989, Day chose familiar landmarks like the old barns, churches and public buildings scattered throughout the countryside. They were ordinary structures that reminded collectors of our humble past, work ethic and values.

"Winnie's Place," an offering in the *American Landmarks* series, is a Valentine for a truly remarkable woman who played a major role in the world of American collectibles. Done in the architectural style of the Romantic Italianate, "Winnie's Place" was constructed in 1881. Today's resident is Winnie Watson Sweet, owner of Watson's Collectibles and Gifts in New Carlisle, Indiana. For many years, Winnie and her staff were responsible for bringing together artists, manufacturers, distributors of the plate and collectible industries and the collectors. Her show was the South Bend Plate and Collectibles Show Exposition.

Lladro Collectors Society
A Tradition to Treasure

When the famed Spanish porcelain firm of Lladro first announced plans for an international Collectors Society in 1985, few could have predicted the worldwide impact. Today, the Lladro Collectors Society looks back upon nearly a decade of success as a source of inspiration, information and enjoyment for Lladro aficionados in nations spanning the globe.

One of the most cherished membership benefits of the Lladro Collectors Society is the opportunity to acquire exclusive figurines which are introduced annually, and made available to Society members only. In 1985, the first of these charming works of art, "Little Pals," made its debut at an original price of $95.

At a recent Lladro Auction, "Little Pals" commanded $4100 in intense bidding. The next Members-Only figurine, "Little Traveler," brought $1700 at the same fast-paced event. Indeed, each retiring Members-Only figurine has attracted strong secondary market trading as new Society members seek to complete their collections with previous years' issues.

"Best Friend" is the 1993 Lladro Collectors Society "members only" piece, depicting the love of a little girl and her teddy bear. Priced at $195, it is available only to Society members.

Hugh Robinson, Director of the Lladro Collectors Society since its inception, looks back proudly on the Members-Only collection. "Each year we have seen a figurine introduced that combines artistry and individuality," he explains. "From the boyish rogues like 'Little Pals,' 'Little Traveler,' 'My Buddy,' and 'Can I Play,' to the girlishly sweet 'School Days,' 'Spring Bouquets,' 'Summer Stroll,' and now 'Best Friend,' each has enchanted us with a personality all its own."

Yet for most Lladro collectors, the demonstrated investment potential of their beloved figurines plays only a minor part in their enjoyment. For upon the horizon of its Ninth Anniversary, the Lladro Collectors Society offers its members a remarkable array of opportunities and services.

Lladro Expands Membership Benefits

A new offering for collectors who join the Lladro Collectors Society is the "Lladro Antique News."

The "Lladro Antique News" is published four times a year, and is mailed to members along with the *Expressions* magazine. This exciting publication, created by an independent consultant, provides the latest information on Lladro in the secondary market. It also gives insight into the history of Lladro and the making of porcelain figurines.

An Enchanted Serenade

A new benefit for joining the Lladro Collectors Society in 1993 was the opportunity to purchase the beautiful limited edition, "Jesters Serenade." This magnificent sculpture portrays the timeless beauty of love. A seated ballerina holds a bouquet of delicate flowers that she has just received from the Jester who stands behind her in his colorful cloak. As she gazes down at them, lost in her dreams, the jester serenades her. He pours out his love for her through the music he plays on his violin. The details and feelings that this piece evoke can only be the creation of a Lladro artisan.

This limited edition of 3,000 pieces was made available at the beginning of 1993 solely to members of the Lladro Collectors Society. The piece

Lladro Collectors Society members enjoy the privilege of acquiring the stunning "Jesters Serenade," a limited edition of 3,000 with a $1995 issue price.

continued to be sold only to members for the remainder of that year. Any new member joining in 1993 received a reservation card to purchase this special piece.

The Heartwarming Charms of "Best Friend"

The 1993 Members-Only figurine, available since the beginning of 1993, has captured the hearts of loyal members as well as bringing new members to the Lladro Collectors Society. Once again the Lladro sculptors have created a delicate portrayal of youth and innocence, with the introduction of "Best Friend." A young girl seated on a beautiful pedestal gazes lovingly at her confidant, her "Best Friend," her teddy bear. Her dress is detailed with small flowers, and her hair is swept back with a bow. Even her shoes and stockings carry the exquisite details loved by Lladro collectors.

Like all of the finest Lladro figurines, "Best Friend" combines skilled artistry and sublime sensitivity. She was designed and produced by the Lladro family of artisans, exclusively for members of the Lladro Collectors Society. This finely glazed, 6¼" porcelain figurine was introduced in January of 1993 at a suggested retail price of $195. The redemption period ends on June 30, 1994.

A Four-Year Series of Gifts for New and Renewing Members of the Lladro Collectors Society

Each year since its inception, the Lladro Collectors Society has bestowed a special gift upon its members as a token of thanks and appreciation. From 1991 through 1994, that gift is a series of beautiful, annual bells.

Lladro Collectors Society members expressed their preference for a thank-you gift that was an actual Lladro porcelain. Thus the artists of Lladro created a limited edition series of four bells depicting the four seasons. Members will receive the first bell upon joining or renewing their memberships and each additional bell upon subsequent renewals. These renewal gifts are particularly exciting because the value of each of the *Four Seasons Bells* is more than the $35 annual cost of renewing the Society membership.

The bell that was offered for 1993 is the "Autumn Bell." Members who joined the Lladro Collectors Society, or renewed their existing memberships for the 1993 year, received this beautiful bell as a gift. This bell features an autumn scene that was conceived and created by Lladro's master craftsmen, and is set off with an amber accent.

The remaining bell, for 1994, continues the concept of the seasons with a Winter theme. The "Spring Bell" offered in 1991 and the "Summer Bell" offered in 1992 may be purchased, at a suggested retail price of $35 each, by those members who join the Society through 1994 and wish to acquire the entire *Four Seasons* bell series. Each bell comes with a satin-finished ribbon.

Lladro Collectors Society Members Enjoy a Host of Outstanding Benefits

Originally formed to enhance the appreciation of exceptional porcelain figurines, the Lladro Collectors Society is an association of individuals who admire fine craftsmanship, enjoy exclusive opportunities to acquire limited edition figurines, and wish to become more knowledgeable about the fascinating world of Lladro porcelains.

In addition to an annual opportunity to acquire a Members-Only figurine like "Best Friend," members receive a free subscription to Lladro's *Expressions* magazine. This well-written, full-color publication has achieved worldwide recognition and several awards. It is filled with articles and features of special interest to collectors.

One of the most popular columns in *Expressions* notes the current standing of Lladro limited editions' availability. This service alerts collectors when certain pieces are nearing their edition limits, so that they may be sure to acquire the pieces at the original price.

Expressions readers will also be among the first to learn of special U.S. appearances by Juan, Jose and Vicente Lladro as well as other members of the Lladro family and Society Director Hugh Robinson.

Members of the Society receive an attractive binder designed especially to keep their *Expressions* magazines stored and organized.

All new members receive a handsome porcelain membership plaque depicting Don Quixote and bearing the signatures of the Lladro brothers: Juan, Jose and Vicente. Members also are honored with a handsomely embossed membership card. In addition, each Society member becomes an Associate Member of the Lladro Museum in New York City, with full rights to use its research facilities.

A highlight for many Lladro Collectors Society members is the opportunity to join their fellow collectors on a Society tour of Lladro headquarters in Valencia, Spain — the capstone of one of several luxurious journeys throughout Spain available only to Society members. Full details of these memorable tours are made available in *Expressions*.

Each year from 1991 through 1994, Lladro Collectors Society members receive a handsome bell in a series of four as a "thank-you" gift for joining or renewing membership in the Society. This "Autumn Bell" is the third in the series of four.

For more information on the many benefits and opportunities of Lladro Collectors Society membership, contact the organization's United States office at 43 West 57th Street, New York, New York 10019-3498.

Margaret Furlong Designs
Pristine Porcelain Angels and Stars Recapture
Gentle Elegance in Designs Fit for the White House

The first things to notice about Margaret Furlong are her glorious auburn hair and her sunny smile. And although we know that her life as an artist, business owner, wife and mother must be hectic and demanding, we marvel at her serenity and calm. This is a lady who still takes time for a proper cup of tea with friends and family. And because she is an artist, her tea table is always a true work of art, enhanced by her trademark exquisite white porcelains, adorned with lace and ribbons and linens, and finished with flowers and fresh-cut greenery from her own terraced garden.

Indeed, everything about Margaret Furlong and her Salem, Oregon studio evokes images of a gentler, simpler time. The 19,000-square-foot building is an old brick warehouse, lovingly restored and remodeled as the perfect working home for the artist and her staff of forty-eight artisans and craftspeople. Ms. Furlong herself creates each new work of art personally, just as she did years ago when her business was new.

Yet behind the doors of her gleaming production facility, things are bustling all year-round. For it is here that Ms. Furlong's wonderful, snowy-white angels and stars…her golden shell designs and elegant picture frames…come to life through a painstaking process of hand-craftsmanship.

A Desire to "Make Art" Fuels the Growth of a Thriving Enterprise

Fifteen years ago, Margaret Furlong was established in an old carriage house studio in Lincoln, Nebraska. She had earned a Masters Degree in Fine Arts from the University of Nebraska, and taught art there for a time. But her heart belonged in the studio, where she created her own style of appealing Midwestern "snowscapes." Using large, thin slabs of porcelain doctored with nylon fibers, she draped these torn-edged "cloths" of porcelain over forms to create snow-covered furrows, hills and haystacks. After firing, as she explains, "I would arrange these largely unglazed forms like a stack of slightly disarrayed papers and raise them to supposedly ethereal heights on boxes of clear plexi-glass."

"The Star of Bethlehem Angel" is the 1993 limited edition from Margaret Furlong Designs. It represents the current five-year series of limited editions entitled Joyeux Noel. The star on the piece symbolizes the star which guided the Magi to celebrate the birth of Jesus Christ and the enlightenment he came to give to all mankind.

In addition to these landscape pieces, Ms. Furlong was working on a commissioned project using shells as a subject matter. The shell forms which she had cast for this project were strewn all over her studio. It was near holiday time, and it occurred to the artist that she could create something special for Christmas. As she recalls, "I combined several shell forms, a molded face, a textured coil and a tapered trumpet into a 'shell angel' — my first design for the gift trade. This angel design of white-on-white unglazed porcelain satisfied my more purist sculptural tendencies and yet had a sweetness which I felt would have appeal to collectors."

The elegant angel had an even greater significance for its sculptor. "I wanted this to be a celebration piece of my recent personal commitment of faith to Christianity. So it was with this one Christmas ornament design, a commitment to share in all my designs the things I held dear to my heart, and a firm commitment to quality and good design, that I began my business."

The first year for Ms. Furlong was rather slow and laborious, requiring the artist to immerse herself in production techniques, mold making, presenting her works to museum gift shops, and coordinating her multiple roles in designing and producing art.

The Growing Business Faces Challenges and a Cross-Country Move

Marriage to Jerry Alexander marked the beginning of the second year in business for Margaret Furlong, with an almost immediate move to Seattle, Washington as part of the bargain. "With a transplanted studio, this time in a not-so-romantic basement garage of a condo in the suburbs, I started all over," Ms. Furlong recalls with a smile.

It was time for Ms. Furlong to "go national," so she set up a marketing plan and within a few months had sales representatives in all the major metropolitan areas of the United States. With growing demand for her creations, Ms. Furlong faced the challenge of developing sample kits, product catalogs, multiple package designs and bringing additional production artists on staff. At the same time, growing pains led to problems on the production line. But as the artist asserts, every mistake and disappointment for her has been another "stepping stone to success."

The third year in business required another move: this time to Salem, Oregon, where husband Jerry Alexander became a full-time partner in the business. His work on the "numbers side" enabled Ms. Furlong to concentrate her efforts in the areas she loves best: product design, package and catalog design, production and promotion.

Each year since has included steady growth, always tempered with an unwavering focus on quality and good design. But 1983 was surely the most "productive" year of all for Margaret and Jerry, for it was then that their daughter Caitlin was born. Indeed, their happy family life provides the artist with her greatest inspiration. As she says, "I don't do a design to become a commercial success. I do it to reflect my loves. I love my home, my garden, and most of all, I love my family."

It's Christmas All Year-Round at Margaret Furlong's Studio

One of the early successes for Ms. Furlong and her angels came when President and Mrs. Ronald Reagan selected a collection of Margaret Furlong angels to decorate their personal White House Christmas tree in 1981. Interspersed with her children's preschool ornaments and family heirlooms, Nancy Reagan brightened her tree with snow-white, limited edition Furlong angels. And while the Reagans are among the most famous collectors of Margaret Furlong Designs, they have been joined over the years by thousands of enthusiastic families and individuals. In fact, Ms. Furlong's *Musical* series (1980-84) and *Gifts From God* series (1985-89) have become highly sought collectibles.

In addition, Margaret Furlong's designs have been featured in a host of holiday publications, recommended as delightful additions to Christmas home decor. *Victoria, Victorian Homes, Country Home, Traditional Home, Country Living, Gourmet, Redbook, Good Housekeeping* and *Ladies Home Journal* all have showcased Ms. Furlong's angels, stars and other shell designs. The personable artist has appeared in many television features as well, often showing reporters and viewers around her studio to display her process of creation and production.

The Limited Edition Musical and Gifts From God Series

Beginning with that first angel made in Nebraska, Ms. Furlong has created a new limited edition angel every year. Each angel emerges after a creative process of inspiration, and the artist loves to describe what influenced her to design them. The 1980 "The Caroler Angel," for example, premiered the *Musical* series with an angel holding a songbook and singing the praises of the

"The Caroler Angel" was Margaret Furlong's first limited edition angel and the first design in the five-year limited edition Musical *series. It was issued in an edition of 3,000 in 1980. The angel holds a songbook and sings the praises of the Christ child's birth.*

Christ child's birth. It is appropriate that this was the first limited edition angel created by Ms. Furlong, since it is a confirmation of her faith and her desire to express this part of her life through her art. In 1981, "The Lyricist Angel" appealed to Margaret Furlong as an image because of its elegant form and its ability to evoke the beauty of music. The angel holds the harp-like lyre, a musical instrument which is referenced throughout the Bible.

The *Musical* series — with each design offered in an edition of 3,000 — continued in 1982 with "The Lutist Angel," wearing a hat which bears a shell: the image that inspired all of Ms. Furlong's angels. The graceful quality of the lute repeats the form of the angel, while the lute's image and the headdress suggest the depiction of angels during the Renaissance period. "The Concertinist Angel" from 1983 wears a graceful halo, and tiny holly leaves and berries frame her face. The geometric folds of the concertina echo and compliment the soft ripples of the scallop shell body. The final *Musical* series issue, the 1984 "The Herald Angel," wears roses and olive branches in her hair, symbols of Christianity and peace.

Margaret Furlong began her *Gifts From God* series in 1985 with "The Charis Angel," enhanced by the generous use of tiny shells which frame the angel's face and embellish the cross she carries. "Charis" comes from the Greek word meaning "grace gift of God." "The Hallelujah Angel" for 1986 carries a heart wreath of early spring flowers including lily tulips, crocuses and primroses. Named "Hallelujah," which means "Praise the Lord," the angel's wreath symbolizes the work of God's hands. Ms. Furlong's love of gardening and her appreciation of the joyful promise of each spring bloom led her to choose flowers to adorn this angel design.

The "Angel of Light" for 1987 holds a bold image of the sun, a symbol of light and enlightenment. The angel celebrates not only the blessings of God's beautiful light in the physical realm, but also the spiritual enlightenment God offers to everyone. In 1988, Ms. Furlong unveiled "The Celestial Angel," who carries her stars — symbols of eternity — by the armful. More stars encircle her head, shining joyfully through the darkness and reflecting heaven. The final *Gifts From God* design, "The Coronation Angel" from 1989, holds a crown that symbolizes the reign of God's children when God bestows his glory on us in heaven.

The Five-Year Joyeux Noel *Series*

With "The Celebration Angel" as its debut in 1990, Margaret Furlong now is creating a new five-year series entitled *Joyeux Noel*, with each annual issue limited to an edition of 10,000 angels. "Celebration" holds a wreath intricately woven with mistletoe, ribbons and seashells. The wreath is the "circle of eternity" which symbolizes the gift of eternal life through Jesus Christ. In 1991, Ms. Furlong unveiled "The Thanksgiving Angel," which continues the celebration of God's gift of Jesus Christ to mankind. This hand-made angel holds a gift embellished with ribbons and tassels. Stems of ivy are tucked behind the bow and frame her delicate face.

For 1992, "The Joyeux Noel Angel" made her debut as the central angel in the *Joyeux Noel* series. This angel holds a scroll to announce the joyous celebration of Christmas. The scroll is festive with shell and holly accents. Sprigs of holly also surround her delicate face. Most recently, for 1993, Ms. Furlong unveiled "The Star of Bethlehem Angel," celebrating Christ's birth and commemorating how the Magi were guided to the newborn child by the heavenly light of a star.

In addition to the limited edition angels themselves, Ms. Furlong offers a diverse line including angel designs in three additional sizes, wreaths, hearts, treetoppers and many other ornament designs. Her catalogs abound with ideas for marvelous home display, with angels, stars and shells appearing as part of table settings, adding charm to potted plants, serving as party favors, or providing a posh final touch on a stunning gift package. All this, of course, in addition to the ornaments' original function as Christmas tree adornments. Packaging has always been a priority at Margaret Furlong Designs, with the pure white ornaments presented against charming, patterned backgrounds or shadow boxes of white and gold.

From her studio in the Pacific Northwest, Margaret Furlong works each day at a labor of love, turning her ideas into artistic reality. Each handmade design is given great attention to detail and quality — to create lovely keepsakes and treasured gifts for collectors throughout the United States.

Marty Bell
"America's Premier Artist For Heart and Home"

Marty Bell is not your average house painter. She'll expertly cover walls, roofs, doors, shutters and window panes...along with just about every flower in the yard. And she doesn't need to use a ladder — an easel will suit her just fine.

This California native has been charming collectors with her pastoral portrayals of authentic English thatched, tiled and slate roof cottages in limited edition lithograph form for more than a decade now, and she shows no signs of stopping. She has painted well over 2,100-plus original oil paintings with over 100 in progress, introduced a news series of bone-china plates, and recently spent nearly a month on the other side of the Atlantic discovering more wonderful, whimsical dwellings to depict.

Finding Just the Right Place

On her most recent visit to the enchanted isle, Marty kept a watchful eye as she and her husband Steve drove through the English countryside. "I don't make up scenes," states the artist. "People should be able to ask 'Where is that cottage'?" When a particular scene or spot captures Marty's 'artist heart,' the two adventurers stop the car and work as a team. Marty concentrates on basic composition as Steve clicks away using telephoto and wide angle lenses. What do the inhabitants of these houses think? "They are so gracious," smiles the artist. "Many times they'll come out of the cottages and invite us about their homes." They may also offer the couple some good leads, circling

Titled "Old Mother Hubbard's Cottage," Marty Bell's painting of this quaint country cottage, made famous by the children's nursery rhyme, marks the inaugural edition of the first coordinated release from Lilliput Lane Ltd., and Marty Bell Fine Art, Inc.

Marty Bell's "Umbrella Cottage," an old toll house located in the English coastal town of Lyme Regis, is known far and wide for its charming thatched umbrella shaped roof.

towns on the map where they'd be sure to find just the perfect place to paint, truly a Bell family-type treasure hunt!

A Natural Talent

Early in life, Marty discovered her love of art. In high school, she began developing her skills in the arts. After completing high school, Marty attended college where she studied interior and fashion design. While in college, Marty met her husband to be, Steve. They were married in 1950.

Something special happened to Marty in 1966. She discovered she wanted to become and was meant to be an artist. "The shades went up and the lights went on!" Marty says when describing how she felt after completing her first original oil painting. She promptly enrolled in an art class, and within the space of a year, was teaching classes of her own at the request of her fellow classmates.

It took eleven years of teaching and three more years of fine-tuning her talent and selling her original works, combined with the encouragement and support of her husband Steve, to convince Marty to establish her own limited edition publishing business.

Marty Bell Brings the English Countryside to America

Working from a vacation snapshot given to her by a friend, the artist set to canvas her first English country cottage in 1974. After the sale of that first selection, the artist's life and that of her family would never be the same. Many of her English paintings were selling before she could complete them. After painting English scenes from photographs supplied by others, Steve and Marty took their first photo trip to England. They spent a month driving through the country and returned with over 2,000 photographs of cottages, villages and country scenes. Now they make frequent sojourns because they left their hearts there! "I love the country's stable, old-world quality," relates Marty.

You can feel the values of long ago." She expresses similar feelings about her subjects: "the ancient houses." The artist elaborates, "They were made with as much creativity as possible, considering the builder's limitations and the tools they didn't have." Marty recalls her discovery of the cottage depicted in "Upper Chute," an image available as a plate that sold out as a lithograph. Walking down the lane, she was greeted by a wall of flowers that led to a door. "I started to cry, moved by so much beauty," stated Marty. "I thought, 'How can people drive by this, without stopping to enjoy'?"

Contentment You Want To Take Home

But people do stop and take notice of the artist's work, and everyone seems to agree it has a definite soothing effect. "I receive many thank-you notes saying 'I get a lot of peace from your paintings,'" Marty tells us. "Life's wild some days, so what hangs on your walls should be peaceful." Dealer Ruann Bellock of Ruann's Gifts & Collectibles, Orange, California, echoes this sentiment. "Her

subjects calm you down," she explains. "After a stressful day, Marty Bell helps unstress you." Bellock has been selling the artist's prints since 1987, and has only the highest praise for her: "Marty Bell is just pure charm!"

Perhaps her biggest supporters are her family. You could surely describe them as close-knit, after all, they work together at Marty Bell Fine Art, Inc. "We have three sons, and each heads his own department. My husband is the president; I'm the resident artist," she says adding, "and our sons actually asked to join us!" Then there are her nine grandchildren, and Bell's only regret is not having "more time to hug them all!"

Marty's Heart and Home

Artist Marty Bell approaches her life and career with the same relentless energy she shows when playing lively dixieland or soft gospel on the piano in the Great Hall of her new English manor home, Bell Hall.

Marty's exuberance spills over in a variety of ways, almost dizzying to recount. She usually paints until two or three in the morning, seven days a week, and for the past five years she has spent her days supervising the building of the new home she and her husband, Steve, are completing. By necessity, Marty and her husband are on the site every day. The Bell's 11,000-square-foot "proper English house" strikes an impressive image in the northwest San Fernando Valley of Southern California. Designed by the couple to accommodate large groups of friends and business clients, Bell Hall boasts grand wide halls with ornate woodwork throughout.

Unusual details include a minstrel's balcony, a fireplace with an opening so tall that Bell can almost stand inside it, flying buttress beams in the Great Hall and tower rooms and little niches throughout. "England is a great storybook country," says Marty. Her knowledge and love of England have developed through more than a decade of painting English country scenes, so she was able to combine authentic English architectural details with her own dreams. Highlights of her seven-bedroom house include terraces, a slate roof and exterior walls featuring a brick pattern created by Marty in which stone clusters are surrounded by swirls of brick. As for furnishings, Marty says she likes the eclectic look. "One piece from here, another from there. There are lots of tapestries and European rugs. It took years to accumulate all this stuff," she says. Not one to seek overpriced gallery pieces, Marty haunts swap meets and used furniture outlets looking for deals. Many of the English items the Bells collected were placed in storage for several years while the house was under construction.

Shop owners and their employees arrive regularly at the new 22,000-square-foot offices of Marty Bell Fine Art in Chatsworth. Afterward, they visit Bell Hall for dessert and tour her studio. By visiting the artist at home, they get to know her better. Visitors also may view more than 100 paintings in progress, some which may take two or three years to complete.

Marty says she achieves her artistic goal when someone "sees something in my art that gives them a lift, a peace, that they [had] when they bought it in the shop, something that the world doesn't give any more."

She is able to share that peace by finding it in her own life. "I'm a homebody," says Marty. "I love to be home. I just want to make it a happy, joyous place where contentment lives." With Marty Bell's art, people get more than a little help with their decorating, they get contentment that can be taken home.

Abundantly talented, Marty Bell introduced "Speldhurst Farm" earlier this year. The painting successfully expresses the diversity of her images and talent.

Maruri USA
Creators of Fine Porcelain Art and Ceramics Offer Stunning Sculptures of Birds, Flowers and Animals

The art of fine porcelain sculpture requires two things above all else: art masters of exceptional talent, and total devotion to quality. In the entire world, there are no more than a score of studios which have achieved true excellence in porcelain.

Some — like Royal Worcester or Meissen in Europe — earned their reputations centuries ago and retain them today by continued greatness. Others — like Cybis and Boehm in the U.S. — represent 20th-century porcelain masters who learned the secrets discovered in Asia thousands of years ago.

Until a decade ago, American collectors were largely unaware of another contemporary porcelain studio with the potential for a "world class" reputation. Then Maruri — a Japanese firm with roots in the age-old Ceramic Capital of Seto — introduced some magnificent wildlife sculptures.

Maruri's majestic "Wild Wings" American Bald Eagle sculpture combines hand-painted fine porcelain with bronze accents. It marks the fourth issue in the Maruri Studio collection, and measures a full 14" in height. The sculpture comes with a wooden base and Certificate of Authenticity. Its issue price is $395.

Within months, Maruri became a respected name in the U.S. collectibles market. And since then, Maruri's honor and fame have grown with each passing year.

Only a few years after its introduction, the Maruri "American Bald Eagle I," by renowned artist W. D. Gaither, commanded $600 on the secondary market — up from a modest issue price of $165. By 1991 — a decade after its introduction — the piece was selling regularly in the $1150 range. Since then, Maruri has introduced scores of stunning works by Gaither and other superb artists — capturing the glories of nature in hand-painted porcelain.

Maruri Makes Its Home in The Ceramic Capital of the World

Maruri was originally founded generations ago in Seto, the fabled ceramic capital of Japan. At that time, porcelain craftsmanship flourished among family-oriented workshops, one of which was the family business of Mizuno. The Mizuno brothers named their business Maruri, and soon this studio earned a wide reputation for excellent bone china, figurines and true-to-nature bird and animal sculptures.

Maruri prides itself on its studied approach in the creation of limited-edition sculptures. Each piece takes many days to complete, using a multi-step process that has been followed faithfully over the years.

Distinctive Handcrafting Sets The Maruri Process Apart

As their ancestors did centuries ago, Maruri's contemporary craftsmen follow an exacting process to create each of their porcelain masterworks. They begin by crafting as many molds as are needed to capture all of the individual nuances or details of a figure. Then they use the ancient Grand Feu formula for porcelain to create a creamy, feldspar-containing mixture in the form of liquid slip.

Each mold is filled with just the right thickness of porcelain, then allowed to dry slowly until the

"The Arabian" is the oldest purebred horse in the world, renowned for its great stamina, intelligence, and unique love of human companionship. This pair of fleet equines represents the Horses Of The World collection from Maruri USA. At 6¹/₂" in height, the hand-painted porcelain sculpture sells for $175.

exact degree of dryness is achieved and the molds are removed. Then the pieces are assembled, after which all seam lines and points of juncture are smoothed and refined by hand to eliminate creases or other signs of joining.

Support molds are then strategically positioned to assure proper drying and the pieces are placed in a temperature-controlled room for several days to continue the drying process. Each piece is then kiln-fired for at least sixteen hours. The temperature is carefully controlled as it gradually builds to a maximum heat and then is slowly reduced.

After firing, Maruri artisans carefully inspect each piece for flaws, and as many as 35 to 40% may be discarded. Each surviving piece is then sandblasted to achieve a flawless, smooth surface, and again is checked for defects. At this point, the porcelain is brilliant and strong. Once the sandblasting is finished, artists painstakingly hand-paint each piece in many subtly differentiated colors.

A Maruri Studio Limited Edition: "Wild Wings"

From time to time, Maruri introduces a very special work of art that combines numerous figures in a composition of rare delicacy and intricacy. Just such an event has occurred with the unveiling of "Wild Wings," which captures the spirit of America in an exquisite, hand-painted fine porcelain and bronze Bald Eagle. Maruri artisans' attention to detail is reflected throughout, from the sharp talons to the glare of the eyes and the stretch of the wings. Even the tree branches look real.

Individually numbered and limited to only 3,500 pieces for worldwide distribution, the 14" "Wild Wings" combines porcelain and painted bronze to capture the sharp talons of the eagle, the glare of the eyes, the stretch of the wings, and the realism of the tree branches. The sculpture comes complete with its own polished wooden base and Certificate of Authenticity. Its issue price has been set at $395.00.

An earlier limited edition, "Delicate Motion," displays three violet-crowned hummingbirds frolicking amid a spray of morning glories. Individually numbered and limited to only 3,500 pieces for worldwide distribution, "Delicate Motion" is crafted of porcelain and bronze and is accompanied by a polished wooden base and Certificate of Authenticity. Its issue price is $325.00.

Now You May Join Maruri on a Polar Expedition

Few of us will ever be privileged to view polar bears, harp seals, arctic foxes and penguins in the wild. But now Maruri has created a group of amazingly lifelike replicas that can be enjoyed in the comfort of home. The *Polar Expedition* collection offers beautifully crafted reproductions of some of nature's most fascinating creatures in hand-painted porcelain.

From the legendary strength of the mighty Polar Bear...to the delightfully playful Baby Seal...the waddling Emperor Penguin...the gracefully sleek Arctic Fox...these works of art are beautiful to see and wonderful to touch. Each figure in the *Polar*

The charming "Elephant Pair Playing" is one of five sculptures in Maruri's Gentle Giants collection of African elephant fine porcelain figurines. It measures 6¹/₄" in height and carries a price tag of $80.

Expedition collection comes with a Certificate of Authenticity: your assurance that it has been made with all the quality and care for which Maruri is renowned.

Additions to the Maruri Line
Add Depth and Breadth

Maruri offers a wide range of figurines and sculptures inspired by eagles, owls, hummingbirds, doves, and even the animals seen on African safaris. The *Gentle Giants* collection, for instance, features five African elephant fine porcelain figurines. Each piece is hand-painted, and styles consist of a single baby elephant standing, a baby elephant sitting, a pair of elephants playing, a mother and baby together and a large elephant pair.

The African elephant is the largest land mammal in the world. Although they are an endangered species, we can still enjoy the beauty of these magnificent creatures in handsome, fine porcelain figurines from Maruri. Each work of art comes with a wooden base and Certificate of Authenticity.

W. D. Gaither's *African Safari* series resulted from the sculptor's personal experiences on a "photo safari" in Zululand, South Africa. There he sketched and photographed the elephants, rhinos, buffalo, lions, leopards, kudus, impalas and other great beasts that served as inspiration for his masterful sculptures.

Bird sculptures include the owl-subject series, *Eyes Of The Night*; a collection of delicate and elusive hummingbirds called *The Maruri Hummingbirds*, and a group of snow-white doves entitled *Wings Of Love*.

Horses Of The World
Salute Elegant Equines

Relatively new to the Maruri line is a bold collection of equines entitled *Horses Of The World*. From a common prehistoric ancestor, numerous horse breeds have developed over time, each with their own attributes of strength, speed, endurance and beauty — but certain breeds have come to be seen as the most beautiful and characteristic of all horses. It is these breeds that were selected to be portrayed in six fine porcelain horse figurines. Each figurine is hand-painted and comes with an elegant wood base that features the horse breed

name on an engraved, gold-colored plate. Horses included are the Clydesdale, Thoroughbred, Quarter Horse, Camargue, Paint Horse and Arabian, with prices ranging from $145.00 to $175.00.

"The Clydesdale," known for a kindly disposition and great strength, has historically been used for farm work and was once used for transporting coal from Scottish mines. "The Thoroughbred" evolved in England and is the racehorse par excellence as well as one of the most beautiful horses in the world. "The American Quarter Horse" is one of America's most popular breeds. Its intelligence and agility make it an exceptional riding horse. "The Camargue" of France is known as the "White Horse of the Sea." This breed is famous for its striking white coat even though the foals are always born dark.

"The Paint Horse" was a favorite mount in the Old West, since its broken color patterns provided good camouflage. And "The Arabian," the oldest purebred in the world, has great stamina, intelligence, and a unique love of human companionship.

As Maruri broadens and extends its line of brilliant naturalist sculptures, one thing is certain: the firm will continue to craft each work of art individually, with no shortcuts. Maruri's age-old process has yielded lasting works of fine art for generations. Today, Maruri continues this tradition, providing an enduring tribute to some of the world's most enchanting creatures.

These dark-eyed Baby Harp Seals are among the delights of Maruri's Polar Expedition sculpture collection.

Michael's Limited
Brings You That Feeling — You've Been There Before...Through the Beautiful Wall Sculptures From *Brian Baker's Déjà Vu Collection*

Michael O'Connell, President of Michael's Limited, began his career with Walt Disney Productions working for Walt Disney Imagineering, the company that designs and creates theme parks, (i.e. Disneyland and Walt Disney World).

In 1976, Michael left Walt Disney Productions to pursue other interests, including model railroading. As a result, he developed Chooch Enterprises, Inc., a leader in the manufacturing of model railroad hobby products. Chooch Enterprises, Inc., moved to Seattle by 1980 where the company continues to manufacture products for the hobby industry.

For several years, Michael was also interested in doing architectural wall decor. However, it was not until 1987 that Brian Baker, an employee of Chooch Enterprises, Inc., made this possible. Brian asked for a block of clay so he could create a Christmas present for a friend. Michael O'Connell was so impressed by what Brian created that an idea was born. Brian had sculpted the first "Hotel Couronne," launching his career and the creation of Michael's Limited.

Today *Brian Baker's Déjà Vu Collection* is one of the most exciting collectibles and decorative accessories in the gift industry.

Meet Brian Baker

From Europe to Mexico and from Thailand to homeland, Brian Baker's zest for life comes from his fascination for history and the arts. When he is not busy creating a new sculpture, Brian can be found exploring the Pacific Northwest or searching for adventure in a distant land. The culture and architecture of the world intrigues him. Brian's discoveries have inspired him to share the beauty and experience with others through the creation of *Brian Baker's Déjà Vu Collection*.

Brian Baker was born in 1962 and raised in Seattle, Washington's Puget Sound area. He went to work in 1981 for a gift company specializing in framed plaques using calligraphy and strips of decorative European braid. Brian advanced quickly within the company. Over five years he acquired valuable knowledge of the gift industry, as well as developing his craft.

Brian Baker's Déjà Vu Collection makes a wonderful display, especially with flowers and other decorative accessories.

Brian embarked on his most ambitious adventure in 1986 when he began his solo trip around the world. He leisurely toured throughout Asia and then began to explore parts of Europe. In Paris, Brian was enchanted by paintings that captured the character and personality of the charming buildings. This inspired him to delve into the wonderful heritage of Europe and to share these discoveries of history and culture with others. His keen interest in the buildings of Europe quickly spread to a fascination with the varied architecture of the United States.

Over the years, Brian's travels have taken him to over forty countries, including many in the Far East, Middle East, Europe, Mexico and the South Pacific. One of Brian's favorite countries is Thailand. Here he finds the architecture to be some of the most beautiful in the world and the people the most friendly. He likes Bali for its fascinating culture and Germany for its medieval castles and lush landscapes. Brian often visits his friends in Mexico and is intrigued by what it offers as insight into the ancient civilizations. In Sweden, Brian has nearly one hundred distant relatives. He has visited the country three times and enjoys their summer celebrations.

After his travels around the world, Brian returned home to Redmond, Washington in 1986.

At this time, he began working at Michael's Limited. While employed here, he wanted to make a wall-hanging house for a Christmas present. Borrowing some clay, he fashioned his first sculpture. Michael O'Connell, owner of Michael's Limited, liked the work so much he suggested that Brian make a few more. That same year the finished sculptures were shown at the San Francisco Gift Show and the rest, as they say, is history.

Brian creates each new building quite similarly to the way many actual ones are built, including additions and remodeling. He lets the building "create itself." Brian's skillful sculpting of clay is the first in a series of important and often difficult steps leading to the finished work. The second step is forming a mold to be used for casting. All of the designs are hand-cast in fine cast bonded stone. Brian then carefully develops a color scheme suitable for the building and its place in the overall collection. His first proof is reproduced by an artist to establish a sample for the other artisans to duplicate. These artisans are an excellent team who carefully complete dozens of designs, each one faithful to Brian's original.

Brian's trademark in his *Déjà Vu Collection* is his umbrella. There is one hidden in the shadows or quietly tucked away in a corner. Not every building has one. Some people think that the umbrellas represent the well-known rain of Seattle, but Brian has a different story. "On my first building (#1000, the original "Hotel Couronne"), I wanted a hungry French cat sitting by the door. I could not seem to design a cat that pleased me, so I left the cat's tail as the handle and made the body into an umbrella. This result became a souvenir of the rainy day when I first saw the building in Rouen."

This same creativity goes into every sculpture by Brian. He is a detail-oriented man. This is evident as one watches him work at his sculpting table. He takes great care and pride in creating each and every house. Brian tries to become part of the building, imagining the people who would live or work there. This is Brian Baker's way of bringing history to life and making one feel like Déjà Vu — you've been there before...

Brian Baker's *Déjà Vu Collectors' Club*

1993 marked the charter year for Brian Baker's Deja Vu Collectors' Club. The sculpture for the charter year membership kit was inspired by a 19th-century San Francisco house called "City Cottage." However, the collectors'-only redemption house for the charter year was something very special — "Brian's First House." The house was the first that Brian owned and was painted red, similar to the color used in traditional Swedish farmhouses. Most rural buildings in Dalarna, Sweden, where Brian's relatives live, are painted this red with white and sometimes blue trim. Brian's hobby is gardening, and he planted hundreds of plants and flowers that change with the seasons. The car found parked in the garage is his first car, a 1962 Ford Fairlane that he has had since he was fifteen.

Brian Baker's Déjà Vu Collectors' Club membership sculpture for 1994 is a cottage. Even though Brian has traveled around the world, he finds some of the most interesting architecture to be a part of our own colonial history. The 1994 Collectors' Club redemption sculpture, available only to members, is taken from Colonial Williamsburg, Virginia.

Limited Editions

The only Limited Edition sculpture to actually be signed and numbered by Brian Baker was the "Amsterdam Canal." Brian was impressed with Amsterdam. It's 6,700 houses and buildings, under the care of the National Trust, made it the largest historical city in Europe. It was during the 17th century that the city reached its golden age. At the time, canals were dug around the medieval city walls and powerful merchants built richly decorated buildings allowing the merchants to flaunt their wealth. Today over 1,000 bridges cross the city's 160 canals, and the best way to get around may still be by boat. Limited to only 1,000, the "Amsterdam Canal" was sold out in 1993.

Two numbered Limited Editions of 500 each, released in 1993, sold out immediately upon release. "American Classic" is of Victorian architecture, which is representative of the entire country. "James River Plantation" is of Georgian architecture developed from around 1700 until the revolution. The pineapple above the door, as a symbol of hospitality, was a unique feature to this period of architecture.

The Limited Editions for 1994 will not be signed but numbered only. Michael's Limited wants you to be surprised, so all we can tell you is that one of the sculptures was inspired by Brian's latest trip to San Francisco and another from a tour in the Charleston, South Carolina area.

The "American Classic" wall sculpture by artist Brian Baker expertly portrays the beautiful architecture representative of America's Victorian-era building style.

The Georgian architecture most prominently popular from 1700 to the Revolutionary War is displayed in the finely detailed "James River Plantation" wall sculpture by Brian Baker for Michael's Limited.

New Releases For 1994

In 1994 *Brian Baker's Déjà Vu Collection* will release some very interesting new sculptures. Among those to be released are a covered bridge, country mill, barbershop, police station and another lighthouse.

Early Retired Sculptures

Among some of the early sculptures created by Brian Baker was #1100 "Japanese House." This sculpture of a small teahouse was released in June 1987 and retired January 1989. The "Japanese House" was the first and only sculpture to date, inspired by Asian architecture.

Midwest Importers of Cannon Falls, Inc.
Merry Mousetales™ Bring Life to Midwest Importers Collectibles — Celebrating Holidays All Year-Round

Once upon a time...the mouse folk of Hideaway Hall lived hidden from the people of the manor. While scurrying from nooks and crannies to secret cubbyholes, they often stole curious glances at the "Hightowers" (as the family was called). Their fancy dress and fine ways always prompted much discussion — and a lot of daydreams. Tea parties and dances, feasts and games — what a merry life they led!

Now it just so happened one day that the Hightowers left on an extended holiday. Finding themselves alone in the big house, the mouse folk dared to creep out of hiding. Free to scurry about, they marveled at their fine surroundings. Shiny polished wood and velvety soft pillows, curious ticking clocks and fine china — all were theirs to explore! Growing bolder as the days went on, they proceeded to make themselves quite at home.

"Millie Picadilly" led an expedition into the sewing room. Gathering scraps of fabric and fancy trims, they set about creating mouse-sized versions of the fine clothing they'd admired from afar. In no time, stylish coattails and top hats, ruffled caps and pinafores were everywhere.

On a stroll through the parlor, "Maximillian Merriweather" spied a mantle clock. "Now there's a fine location for a cottage!" he exclaimed. Recruiting his nephews for help, in no time Maximillian had the clock sporting cheery windows and a front door. Inspired by such ingenuity, "Tyler and Teddy Tinkertale" turned a teapot into a bustling tearoom. A lovely house in a shoe soon followed for the Picadillys.

Meanwhile the "Tweedlemouses" set off to explore the kitchen. In high spirits, they scurried through cupboards and climbed into cookie jars. Soon they were nibbling on bits of sugar cookies and candies — even an especially delicious wedge of cheese.

The mouse folk grew even merrier as the days passed. Parties and games, pageants and parades — each day brought new celebrations and adventures. It soon became clear that Hideaway Hall and the mouse folk of the manor would never be quite the same. The days of living in hiding were over — and the world of Merry Mousetales™ had begun!

A World of Adorable Mice

With this whimsical story as a backdrop, the Merry Mousetales™ collection makes its debut from Midwest Importers of Cannon Falls, Inc. Their beautifully sculpted mouse characters are offered in a variety of adorable situations, as ornaments, figurines, cut-away houses, and in a number of other gift categories including trinket boxes, a tea set and a door wedge.

Pieces will be added to the collection each season, and pieces will be retired regularly as well. Spring 1994, for example, marks the introduction of springtime situations, and the following season there will be Halloween and Thanksgiving introductions.

Merry Mousetales™ Join a Line of Collectibles from Around the World... With "Roots" in Minnesota

In addition to this appealing new Merry Mousetales™ collection, Midwest Importers of Cannon Falls, Inc. offers the European charm of elegant nutcrackers, handsome German wood-turned figurines, Christmas-theme items and much more. A thriving business has grown from what might have been a tragedy: for the company's founder Ken Althoff envisioned Midwest Importers only after he was diagnosed with multiple sclerosis.

About forty years ago, Althoff received the news that he had MS, and he realized that his work as a Lutheran pastor might soon present problems of stamina and mobility. He and his wife decided to look "for another way to get through the world" — and discovered a whole new life in the process.

Amazingly, Ken Althoff is healthy and active even now. And just as miraculous as his good health is the growth of the little business he and his wife began in Minnesota during the 1950s. From its beginnings as a small-scale importer of traditional European collectibles, today Midwest Importers of Cannon Falls, Inc. has grown to be an industry leader in the business of designing and importing fine-crafted gifts and decorations.

It's a joyous Christmas celebration for these adorable Merry Mousetales" *characters from Midwest Importers of Cannon Falls, Inc.*

From the quaint little town of Cannon Falls, Minnesota (Population: 2,653) Althoff's daughter, Kathleen Brekken, now presides over a line that includes thousands of seasonal gifts and decorations. With charming offerings for Christmas, Easter, Valentine's Day, Halloween, Thanksgiving and more, Ms. Brekken keeps her in-house staff of designers busy all year long.

In addition to its midwestern U.S. headquarters, the firm has a base of operations in the United Kingdom and offices in Manila, Hong Kong and Taipei. Yet even though Midwest Importers of Cannon Falls, Inc. now enjoys a worldwide reach, its roots in European craftsmanship remain an essential focus for the business.

Erzgebirge Nutcrackers Boast Rich Historical Roots

The romance of the Nutcracker Prince from Tchaikovsky's *Nutcracker Fantasy* has inspired many an American collector to seek out handsome wooden nutcrackers from the Erzebirge region of Germany. This area is dense with lavish forests — a natural resource that encouraged villagers to develop many unique wood-crafted items. Over the centuries, the woodworkers of the Erzgebirge have stayed true to their handcrafting tradition and today are known throughout the world for creating items of superb craftsmanship and quality. In honor of the *Nutcracker Fantasy*, which popularized the nutcracker, Midwest Importers introduced a limited edition series beginning in 1993 with the "Mouse King." New for the series in 1994 is the addition of "Herr Drosselmeyer" and the "Prince." All fantasy pieces are numbered limited editions.

In 1993, Midwest Importers commemorated the

150th anniversary of the publication of Charles Dickens' *A Christmas Carol* with a limited edition series of nutcrackers including "Bob Cratchit & Tiny Tim," "Ebenezer Scrooge" and the "Ghost of Christmas Present." For 1994, the "Ghost of Christmas Past," "Ghost of Christmas Yet To Come" and "Marley's Ghost" are being introduced. Each piece in the series is a hand-numbered limited edition featuring the name of the character on the base.

The reunification of Germany has released the creativity of the Erzgebirge woodcrafters, who now are able to travel more, and to enjoy exposure to Western television shows, sports, etc. Though the traditional designs of soldiers and kings are still among their favorites, new nutcrackers representing American football players, skiers and cowboys are quickly becoming popular. Many of the nutcracker factories formerly owned and run by the government of the former East Germany have been purchased by the employees and management, who are now taking renewed pride in their business. These companies are beginning to put their names on the base of their items, enabling collectors to identify studios whose creations they enjoy collecting most.

Christian Ulbricht Nutcrackers Combine Traditional Designs With Personal Themes

In 1992, Christian Ulbricht and Midwest Importers introduced a limited edition Santa series for nutcracker collectors. Every piece in this collection has been hand-signed by Christian himself! The first two introductions of the series were sold out within months of introduction: "Father Christmas" in 1992 and "Toymaker Santa" in 1993. Featured for 1994 is the "Victorian Santa." A new series for 1994 is a tribute to the American Folk Hero introducing limited editions of "Johnny Appleseed" and "Davy Crockett."

Christian Ulbricht runs a family business, with his wife Inge, son Gunther and daughter Ines all actively participating. Midwest Importers sponsored Christian and his son Gunther's first personal appearances in the United States in 1992, and brought them back in 1993 to give more collectors an opportunity to meet the famous family.

Charming Wood Figurines from Grunhainichen

More than seventy-five years have passed since Grete Wendt and her friend Grete Kühn first cre-

ated their little hand-turned wood figurines in the German village of Grunhainichen. The tradition they founded — one of uncompromising quality and commitment to craftsmanship in every detail — continues today under the direction of Grete Wendt's nephew Hans.

As the exclusive United States distributor of these delightful little figurines, Midwest Importers is proud to introduce a limited quantity of the "Angel Music Box," which has not been in production since 1933. The musical angel stands beneath an archway of heavenly stars and as the handle turns, it plays *Silent Night*. Each piece is hand-signed and carries the "Wendt und Kuhn" trademark of eleven dots on each wing.

Spanish Nativity Figures from Belenes Puig

While Midwest Importers brings American collectors many superb items from Germany, the firm also enjoys a strong relationship with fine art studios in other lands. Notable among these is the Old World firm of Belenes Puig (formerly known as J. Puig Llobera), creators of handcrafted nativity figures in Barcelona, Spain.

Each nativity figure is meticulously handcrafted and lovingly detailed. The creative process begins with an original sculpture in chalk, from which molds are made for use with terra-cotta. Clothing is draped upon each figure, using fabric which has been dipped in a liquid that rapidly hardens to create dramatic, flowing costumes. Hand-painting in multi-hued finishes imparts the beautiful rich patina characteristic of the works of Belenes Puig.

Two New Heritage Santas Make Their Debuts

To honor the international tradition of Santa Claus, Midwest Importers has created an exclusive family of Santas inspired by the legend and lore of Christmas around the world, *The Heritage Santa Collection*™. Wonderfully detailed and beautifully crafted, each *Heritage Santa* character comes with his own unique Christmas legend and is available in sizes and product categories to please a variety of collectors.

The newest collection addition is the American Santa, "Santa Claus." With his rosy cheeks and twinkling eyes, he is a tribute to the 'melting pot' of America. *Heritage Santas* that retired in 1993 are "Scanda Klaus" of Scandinavia and "Herr Kristmas" of the Black Forest of Germany. In 1994, "Santa Nykolai," the Slavic Santa, and

"Pere Noel," the French Santa, will be out of production with limited availability.

The Woodcarvings of Leo R. Smith III

Woodcarver Leo R. Smith III believes that "the artist is a reflection of the environment." Smith's home and source of inspiration is the picturesque little town of Fountain City on the Mississippi, in Wisconsin. This area of river and woodlands holds not only beauty, but also a rich trove of the legend and folklore captured in Smith's compelling folk art pieces.

Midwest Importers introduced five new limited edition sculptures into the Leo R. Smith III collection in 1993. There will be six more limited edition pieces introduced in 1994, including a first-ever ornament. In 1992, one of his sculptures — "Witch Riding White Horse" — was the first to be retired. Midwest Importers has arranged for Smith to make a number of in-store appearances to meet collectors and sign sculptures. Beautifully crafted and strikingly unique, each member of *The Leo R. Smith III Collection* is a treasured gift and the delight of serious collectors.

An International View With A Midwestern Base

From their home in Cannon Falls to art studios around the world, the Midwest Importers' family share their vision of excellence with friends across America. For Christmas, Easter, Valentine's Day, Halloween, Thanksgiving and year-round, Midwest Importers offers a marvelous and ever-growing range of items to intrigue art lovers and collectors alike.

From left to right, these handsome Erzgebirge A Christmas Carol nutcrackers are: "Bob Cratchit & Tiny Tim," "Ebenezer Scrooge" and the "Ghost of Christmas Present." They were introduced to help celebrate the 150th anniversary of the publication of Charles Dickens' immortal book.

M. I. Hummel Club®
Loyal Club Members and Collectors Celebrate the Enduring Spirit of Sister M. I. Hummel

She drew and painted them practically from the time she could first hold a pencil: the rosy-cheeked, bright-eyed youngsters who surrounded her during her happy German childhood. Sister Maria Innocentia Hummel delighted in the energy and optimism of little ones — and she captured their charm in hundreds of drawings that brought cheer to all at the Convent of Siessen. As a member of the Sisters of the Third Order of St. Francis, Sister M. I. Hummel came to understand that her finest service to the Lord would be to share her talent for art. But little did she know that this marvelous gift would provide pleasure to collectors all over the world for generations after her death.

The brilliance of this shy German nun might never have been known outside the convent community had it not been for the vision of Franz Goebel. As the fourth-generation family member to head the company bearing his name, Goebel was always on the lookout for promising new artists. In 1879, the Duke of Saxe-Coburg-Gotha first granted permission for the Goebel Company to create kiln-fired porcelain figurines. Originally founded in 1871 to manufacture marbles, slates and slate pencils, Goebel artisans already had spent four decades earning an international reputation for porcelain craftsmanship when Franz Goebel discovered Sister M. I. Hummel in 1934.

While strolling through gift shops in Munich, Goebel happened upon a little store that specialized in religious images. A display of greeting cards captivated him: it was the art of Sister M. I. Hummel! Simple and touching in their innocence, the drawings spoke to Goebel like nothing else he had seen in Munich. It struck him that this would be the perfect basis for a new line of figurines.

Franz Goebel wrote to Sister Hummel, proposing that his artists translate her two-dimensional drawings into three-dimensional figurines. At first, the gentle nun hesitated. But when Goebel arranged a meeting among himself, Sister Hummel, and the Mother Superior of the convent, a historic agreement was reached. Goebel assured the sisters that the figurines would be completely true to the original artwork. He promised that they would be handcrafted to meet the highest quality standards. He

"I Brought You a Gift" (HUM 479) is the new member gift provided to each individual who joins the M. I. Hummel Club for the first time. Crafted with care in Germany, this charming figurine carries on the enduring tradition of Sister M. I. Hummel and her art. It has a retail value of $80 U.S. and $100 Canadian, but it is provided only to new Club members for free.

gave Sister Hummel and the Convent of Siessen final artistic control. Indeed, he stated that once she approved an original figurine, her signature would be incised on the base of each piece. What's more, beginning then and to this very day, part of the proceeds of each figurine is provided to the convent and then sent to charitable organizations throughout the world.

The first *M. I. Hummel* figurines were unveiled at the 1935 Leipzig Fair, where buyers from all over Europe expressed their excitement at the art's uniqueness and fresh charm. The figurines were a tremendous success, and everyone looked forward to long years of happy productivity from the gifted nun of Siessen.

Alas, the hardships of World War II took their toll on the convent and on Sister M. I. Hummel herself. She fell ill and died in 1946 at the age of thirty-seven. Ironically, her fame was spreading quickly across the Atlantic at the time of her

death. American GIs were bringing the adorable child-subject figurines home to America as special gifts for family and friends. When they got the news about the popularity of the "Hummels," American gift sellers and department stores flocked to order them and to share them with a wider audience. And since Sister M. I. Hummel had been prolific in her short life, there were still many drawings to serve as inspiration.

How an M.I. Hummel *Drawing Becomes a Hand-Painted Figurine*

Today, collectors all over the world await each new *M. I. Hummel* presentation, brought to life by the gifted artisans of Goebel. The process of creating an *M. I. Hummel* figurine is long and involved, performed by a team of dedicated masters. Each new artist must serve a three-year apprenticeship under the watchful eye of senior Goebel craftspeople before joining the prestigious ranks of the *M. I. Hummel* "team." This long apprenticeship is necessary because of the exacting, ten-step process required to craft each *M. I. Hummel* work of art. The ten steps are: sculpting, model-cutting, mold-making, casting, assembling, bisque firing, glazing, glaze firing, decorating, and decor firing(s).

To begin, the sculptor creates a clay model using Sister M. I. Hummel's original art as the basis. The Convent of Siessen must approve each model before prototypes are crafted for moldmaking. A single figurine may require as many as forty individual mold pieces! To make the molds, individual parts are embedded in clay. Then plaster of paris is poured over them to make the master mold. The working model is made of acrylic resin, and then a series of working molds are devised — again using plaster of paris. More than one working mold is required because each mold must be rejected as soon as it loses its exactness of detail.

In casting, liquid porcelain "slip" is poured into the working mold. Excess slip is poured out after about twenty minutes, leaving the shell of the figurine. Next, individual pieces of the figurine are assembled, using more slip to join them. After smoothing to remove seams, the assembled figurines dry at room temperature for about one week. Bisque firing at approximately 2100°F follows, during which each figurine shrinks in size and emerges with a powdery white finish. Glaze firing at 1870°F comes next, after figurines are hand-dipped and sprayed with a tinted liquid glaze. At this stage, the Goebel trademark also is fired onto the base.

For decorating, thousands of individual colors have been developed in Goebel's own laboratories.

The goal is to approximate the varied palette used by Sister M. I. Hummel herself. To produce an edition of figurines, highly skilled painters follow a decorated sample which has been approved by the Convent of Siessen. The initials under the base of each figurine indicate a final decorating check before decor firing commences at approximately 1100°F. As many as three decor firings may be necessary to fuse the colors permanently to each porcelain figurine. All in all, an *M. I. Hummel* figurine requires many weeks to produce, including a total of over 700 detailed hand operations. This painstaking process has been the standard of excellence for Goebel ever since the first *M. I. Hummel* figurines were produced nearly sixty years ago.

Members Enjoy the Many Benefits of the M. I. Hummel Club™

Ever since 1977, collectors of *M. I. Hummel* figurines have relished the friendship, the fun, and the special privileges that come with membership in the M. I. Hummel Club. For the affordable annual fee of $40 (U.S.) and $55 (Canadian), a new member may join the oldest collectors' club of its kind. Renewing members pay a smaller fee: currently $32.50 (U.S.) and $45 (Canadian). Each new member receives a special welcome gift, currently a charming *M. I. Hummel* figurine called "I Brought You a Gift." Renewing members also are sent a yearly token of appreciation, such as the 1993-94 piece, "A Sweet Offering." Each of these

Collectors who are celebrating fifteen years of membership in the M. I. Hummel Club are privileged to acquire "Honey Lover" (HUM 312), an exclusive figurine created to mark this special anniversary.

The adorable figurine, "I Didn't Do It" (HUM 626), is the M. I. Hummel Club's Exclusive Edition for 1993-94.

figurines carries a retail value of $80 U.S. or $100 Canadian — at least double the membership or renewal fee.

Members of the Club are privileged also to acquire other special M. I. Hummel works of art created with their pleasure in mind. There is an annual exclusive figurine, available only to Club members. Most recent of these issues is the adorable "I Didn't Do It." There is also a Preview Edition called "Sweet As Can Be," available only to Club members for two years. This piece bears a special M. I. Hummel Club backstamp, but after the preview period ends, it may become an open edition available to everyone — then bearing the non-exclusive regular Goebel backstamp. What's more, the Club celebrates its long-time members by offering them the opportunity to purchase figurines to mark their personal anniversaries as Club members. Five-year Club members are provided with special redemption certificates for "Flower Girl," while ten-year members may acquire "The Little Pair," and fifteen-year veterans are eligible for "Honey Lover."

As one of the most comprehensive collectors' clubs in the world, the M. I. Hummel Club offers a wide range of services and special opportunities to members. These include Collectors' Market, Research Service, Annual Essay Contests, Travel Opportunities and Local Chapters. Collectors' Market is a free service to M. I. Hummel Club members who wish to buy and/or sell any Goebel collectible. The Club endeavors to match poten-

tial buyers with individuals who wish to sell the same item. Then the buyer contacts the potential seller to negotiate a price. Research Service is available to members who wish to authenticate older Goebel pieces they may own. When the Club is sent a clear photograph or drawing of the piece's markings, mold numbers and trademarks, as well as a photograph of the entire piece, such facts as authenticity, identity, age, background and production history can often be provided.

The M. I. Hummel Club sponsors an Annual Essay Contest for members. The recent "Young at Heart" contest asked members to think back to their youth and write about a compelling memory, a tender moment, or a special slice of their past that is reflected in an M. I. Hummel figurine. Then each entrant could elect to sponsor a favorite child to illustrate the essay. Winning entries earned M. I. Hummel figurine awards ranging in retail value from $150 to $1,085.

An annual range of Travel Opportunities afford Club members the opportunity to see the world, spend time with their fellow M.I. Hummel collectors, and tour the legendary W. Goebel Porzellanfabrik. There are tours offering a variety of destinations throughout Europe, and — of course — Sister M. I. Hummel's homeland of Germany.

Members say that one of the most personal pleasures of Club membership is the chance to become active in one of the over 100 Local Club Chapters throughout North America. At no additional cost, Club membership brings each individual a subscription to a Local Chapter newsletter, a Local Chapter patch and membership card sticker and invitations to Regional Conferences. If there is no Local Chapter in a collector's home area, he or she is invited to start one with the help of the Club's Local Chapter Services division.

In addition to all of these benefits, Club members also receive: a subscription to *Insights*, the Club's colorful and informative quarterly magazine; a Membership Card; and a handsome binder filled with a collector's log, price list and facts about M. I. Hummel history and production.

Surely the gentle young Sister M. I. Hummel could never have dreamed that her charming drawings would continue to captivate millions for decades after her death. But today, the delightful and varied M. I. Hummel figurines are considered among the world's most cherished collectibles. And members of the M. I. Hummel Club enjoy the best opportunities of all to share in the delights of Sister Hummel's art and the warm friendship of fellow collectors!

Miss Martha Originals
Black History and Memories of "Way Back When" Please Martha Holcombe's Collectors Across the U.S.A.

Ask Martha Holcombe what she remembers best about her childhood, and she'll tell you a tale of carefree summer days spent on her grandmother's farm. Nestled in the Appalachian foothills of Northeast Alabama, the farm afforded young Martha the opportunity to ride the old mule, pick some cotton, swim in the creek — and never wear shoes until the school bell rang in September! Martha also has vivid memories of hours spent watching the fields be prepared using a "one-horse plow" — and of course, raiding Grandmother's watermelon patch.

A self-taught artist, Ms. Holcombe receives inspiration for her artwork from real-life people, photographs, newspapers and books. She credits God for her artistic gifts. And to this day, many of the situations she depicts in her wonderfully detailed sculptures hearken back to those childhood days on Grandmother's farm.

After completing high school, the Alabama native married and lived as a housewife while she and her husband raised three children: Lisa, Keith and Kim. When her children were in high school, Martha Holcombe enrolled in a nearby community college where she received a degree in Mental Health Technology with professional certificates in Counseling, Bible and Christian Education.

The Origins of Miss Martha Originals

What today is the thriving firm of Miss Martha Originals, Inc. began in 1980 with a simple doll pattern design. Ms. Holcombe had an idea on how to earn money to make repairs at her church: Gadsden First Church of the Nazarene. That initial doll pattern was to be sold by mail, with proceeds to the church. The business was named Miss Martha Originals because the children at the church all called Ms. Holcombe by that affectionate name (Miss Martha).

What started with one box of patterns in "Miss Martha's" living room soon expanded to a renovated garage behind her house. The next move was to a vacant store building, then two store buildings, and finally in 1985 to a brand-new facility in the Gadsden Industrial Park.

The creations that fueled this sensation were the *All God's Children* figurines, first unveiled in a collection of eight in 1985. The name for the series comes from a favorite Bible verse of Miss Martha herself: "See how much the Father has loved us! His love is so great that we are called God's Children." (1 John 3:1).

For the first year in business, Miss Martha Originals worked with several United States companies to produce the pecan shell/resin castings from Martha Holcombe's original sculptures. The quality did not meet with the artist's high standards, so the decision was made to learn to do the entire process "in house." Since the creation of the first eight *All God's Children* pieces, Miss Martha Originals has needed to expand its facilities five more times. The complete *All God's Children* line is crafted with pride in the U.S.A., at the Gadsden, Alabama factory.

All God's Children *Recapture Precious Memories of Childhood for American Collectors*

Over the years, Miss Martha Originals has attracted an enthusiastic and growing cadre of collectors from all over the United States. They warm to the nostalgic visions of times "way back when" that Martha Holcombe captures in her three-dimensional portraits of African-American children.

They travel from far and wide to attend the annual *All God's Children* Family Reunions in Gadsden, Alabama, where they can meet Miss Martha herself and enjoy fellowship with other collectors and their families. And they love to explain their fascination with the works of their beloved Miss Martha.

Collector Priscilla Harris discovered *All God's Children* when her own family had left for a four-month stay in Japan. She loves her figurines so much that now, "Along with carrying pictures of our family, we carry with us a photo album (as a matter of fact, two) to show off our newly acquired family (of Miss Martha Originals)." Her husband Frank enjoys collecting the figurines as well, and

as Mrs. Harris says, "We're both happy in the union of the Harris Family with the Miss Martha Family."

Iva Kernan says, "I was one of nine kids, raised on a farm. And many of the people Martha creates remind me of my young days. You know most of the things in the North were the same as they were in the South during those slim, but good times. Take the hard farm work for example; but then we also had the play. And the fun of going barefoot in the summer. Of course there wasn't much choice in that matter since we only got one pair of shoes a year. Oh yes, *All God's Children* renews my mind on many fond things."

Sandra Jean Hoffman comments that "The figurines are definitely from my generation. We bought block ice when I was a child, so 'Jessie' made me remember going to the ice truck for ice. And I loved RC and Moon Pies, so 'Prissy' with a Moon Pie brings back memories."

When Dr. and Mrs. Herbert Armstrong first came across *All God's Children*, it was love at first sight. "My husband and I are very close," Betty Armstrong explains. "We just happened to be together — because we shop together all the time — when we first saw the pieces. He was very interested in them. I was completely hooked. Right away I joined the *All God's Children* Collector's Club."

Collector's Club Offers Special Opportunities

Many other collectors of Miss Martha Originals also have discovered the joy of membership in the *All God's Children* Collector's Club. The annual fee of just $20 entitles members to the following benefits: a free figurine, a membership card, free subscription to a quarterly magazine, announcements of special appearances by Martha Holcombe, exclusive invitations to special events such as the annual reunion, opportunity to buy exclusive "members only" figurines, and a personal checklist to keep accurate records of your collection.

Martha Holcombe keeps up a busy schedule of personal appearances across the country, with Collector's Club members among the first in line to meet the personable artist and have their collectibles signed. The annual *All God's Children* Family Reunion draws Club members from across the land for a day of food, friendship, meeting Miss Martha, and buying and trading at the swap meet. Southern accents blend with the cadences of the Northeast and Midwest as every visitor enjoys the hospitality of Gadsden, Alabama.

When asked to account for the widespread popularity of Miss Martha Originals and the All God's Children Collector's Club, Jeffrey Dalgliesh of

From the Miss Martha Originals Historical Series, "Frederick Douglass" portrays the leading spokesman for his people in the 19th century. Douglass devoted his life to the abolition of slavery and to the struggle for human rights. "Frederick Douglass" was cited recently by Collectors Mart magazine as one of the best-selling individual figurines on the American market.

Educator, reformer, school builder, presidential advisor and active spokesperson for Black affairs, "Mary Mcleod Bethune" is shown proudly holding the official charter of the Daytona Normal and Industrial Institute for Girls, dated 1905.

An author and lecturer, "Frances Harper" also was the leading black poet of her time. She worked diligently for the abolition of slavery, women's rights and temperance. Her serene beauty shines through in this finely crafted figurine from Miss Martha Originals.

D. King Irwin Company explained, "It's a piece of Americana. It tells the story of America. That's what attracts people to it, because they relate to it. Everybody can see a life experience in it." Dalgliesh also commends Miss Martha's Originals for the figurines' affordable price tags — as low as $16 to $40 for handsome pieces.

Miss Martha Adds Historical Art to Her Nostalgic Works

In addition to her heartwarming visions of youngsters from "way back when," Martha Holcombe has earned widespread praise for her well-researched *African American Historical Series*. Subjects include "Harriet Tubman," "Sojourner Truth," "Frederick Douglass," "Dr. Daniel Hale Williams," "Ida B. Wells," "George Washington Carver," "Mary Bethune" and "Frances E. W. Harper." The staff of Miss Martha Originals is proud to show the contributions that these individuals (and others to follow in the series) have made to American society.

Cited as one of the fastest-selling figurines in the U.S. market, "Frederick Douglass" from the *African American Historical Series* also won its creator a remarkable honor from the Friends of Frederick Douglass Society of Rochester, New York. Martha Holcombe was recognized for her part in helping to perpetuate the memory of Frederick Douglass, a slave who eventually became an influential newspaper publisher and public servant in the North. His publication, "The North Star," fought for equal rights for all Americans and was an early advocate of rights for women. He died in 1895.

Asked why she happened to select Douglass as a subject, Ms. Holcombe said that many people from various parts of the country had written to her, suggesting that she sculpt Douglass. "I did some research," she said, "and decided that Douglass would make a fine addition to my series of Black Americans."

How Miss Martha Originals Are Created

The development of each Miss Martha Original requires an intense period of research, sculpting, and painstaking production. The process begins when Martha Holcombe sculpts the original figurine using soft clay, and delivers the piece to the mold room. Silicone rubber is poured over the original sculpture to make the first master. When the mold is cured, the clay sculpture is removed.

Next the master prototypes are cast, using a polyurethane resin. The first castings are sent back to Martha for approval and any necessary rework. Production molds are then made using the polyurethane prototypes. Each separate mold is marked with a number, and this same number appears on each figurine crafted with that mold. Any one mold can be used only fifty to seventy-five times before it is destroyed to avoid loss of detail. After the molds are made, actual production begins.

Figurines are cast using a special blend of resins and pecan shell flour. They are then washed in a special solution, and the bottoms of the figurine are sanded. Mold seams are removed using air tools, then each piece is inspected for quality. Small holes caused by air bubbles are removed.

Figurines are painted by skilled craftspeople in their homes, with the quality control department inspecting all the painting to do necessary touch-ups and painting of facial features. Antiquing stain is applied next, followed by finishing touches such as hairbows. After a final quality control inspection, figurines are surrounded in protective bubblewrap and then boxed for shipment.

To authenticate each figurine, the signature of M. Holcombe, the name of the piece, and its mold number are etched in. What's more, a Certificate of Authenticity is provided with each figurine at the time of purchase. Each collector is invited to establish a personal number for the *All God's Children* pieces through their retailer. Some of Miss Martha's figurines are retired at the end of each year, and they are then available only on the secondary market.

Demand Grows…and Collectors Have a New Way to Enjoy The Art of Miss Martha

Several years ago, Miss Martha sculpted a new group of originals that required molds more complex than the Gadsden factory could produce. She entered into a licensing agreement with Enesco for this renowned firm to craft the *Miss Martha Collection*. Each piece in this new collection of child-subject figurines is cast from Martha Holcombe's original sculpts, offering collectors another way to acquire and display the works of Miss Martha.

Martha Holcombe's description of her relationship with Enesco helps to sum up her goal in creating all of her heartwarming sculptures: "I feel that *All God's Children* and *Miss Martha's Collection* complement each other as they are all sculpted with the desire that Jesus Christ will be honored through my work."

Old World Christmas®
Old World Christmas Carries On the Tradition of Producing Fine German Mouth-blown Glass Ornaments

Deep in the forests of central Germany, the century-old art of creating glass Christmas ornaments originated and continues much in the same manner today. Though hindered by political strife and war, the art of blown glass ornament making continues to thrive. Many of the original molds have been salvaged and commissioned for exclusive use by Old World Christmas®. These molds are again being used to produce heirloom-quality ornaments, rich with tradition, for importation to the United States.

Indeed, Old World Christmas has access to the most extensive collection of antique molds in the world. According to Tim Merck, the firm's president, going through the Germans' stash of these wonderful old molds is similar to panning for gold. Each year seems to find a greater number of molds that are irresistible, and 1995 proves to be no exception. Old World Christmas, the exclusive importer of old-mold glass Christmas ornaments with the trademark star cap, is pleased to be offering an expanding line of fine holiday collectibles, thanks to the efforts of its founders, Tim and Beth Merck.

Old World Christmas was founded in 1981 when the owners realized a void in the market for high-quality, collectible Christmas ornaments and decorations. When Old World Christmas first introduced its ornaments to the market, glass ornaments from Europe were of very inferior quality and offered little collectible value. Old World Christmas believed that collectors would actively seek exceptional Christmas ornaments, and in 1984, a German family workshop was commissioned to produce the Mercks' design concepts for importation to the United States. These ornaments and collectibles have proved to be extremely popular.

The "Star-Cap" — A Symbol of Quality Craftsmanship

The family-owned glass blowing company was a natural choice for Old World Christmas. Nestled in a mountainous region of Germany, this area is renowned for its glass-blown ornaments handed down through the generations. Each beautiful glass orna-

Old World Christmas offers the exclusive Collectors' Club piece, the "Large Santa in Chimney" glass ornament, to club members throughout 1994. Handcrafted in Germany, this limited edition piece was designed by acclaimed artist E.M. Merck and was nominated for the Award of Excellence for ornaments by Collector Editions magazine.

ment is tediously mouth blown, one at a time, into a finely crafted porcelain mold. Once the ornament has been removed from the mold and cooled, a hot solution of liquid silver is poured inside. Then the ornament is delicately hand-painted with many brightly colored lacquers. Finally, the long stem is cut and the special star-shaped cap is attached.

This star cap guarantees that the ornament is authentic from the Old World Christmas Collection. Developed in 1985, this metal cap design is still being used today. The exclusive star-shaped

255

These three 1994 additions to the E.M. Merck Nutcracker Collection are sure to become treasured family heirlooms. The nutcrackers contain the finest detailing from the feather on the Knight's hat to the toys on the Father Christmas and the vegetables on the Gardener's tray. Using the finest materials and attention to detail, each nutcracker is hand-signed by the artist.

hanger that proudly tops each ornament is a registered trademark that guarantees fine craftsmanship, original design and collectibility. The "star cap" is the symbol collectors seek when acquiring Old World Christmas heirlooms.

The glass Christmas ornaments that are produced today exclusively for Old World Christmas are created in the same century-old art that has been passed down through the ages. Most of the glass ornaments are even made in the original molds used at the turn of the century, preserving the tradition of German glass ornaments for generations to come.

The Old World Christmas Pickle

The most popular of the Old World Christmas glass ornaments is the Christmas pickle. This is due to the Old World Christmas pickle ornament's legendary tradition. The pickle ornament was considered a special tree decoration by many families in Germany. There, the fir tree was decorated on Christmas Eve. The pickle was always the last ornament to be hung on the Christmas tree, with the parents taking great care to hide it deep within the green boughs among the other ornaments. When the children were allowed to view the tree, they would begin gleefully searching for the pickle ornament, for they knew that whoever first found that special ornament would receive an extra little gift left by St. Nicholas for the most observant child. In keeping with the giving spirit of Christmas, the Old World Christmas glass pickle ornament has become a family heirloom and a cherished tradition in many homes throughout America.

Old World Christmas also claimed an industry first in 1984 with the introduction of slip-on glass light covers. The light covers were fashioned after turn-of-the-century Christmas lights and were designed to slip-on over mini-lights. They are produced both in molded glass and bisque porcelain featuring fine detailing and hand-painting.

An Innovative Company with Old World Tradition

The 1990s are proving to be Old World Christmas' decade. New designs, exclusive contracts with German manufacturers, national recognition for design excellence, and the rapid success of the Collectors' Club are setting Old World Christmas into high gear with record sales and product development.

Old World Christmas prides itself in presenting exclusive products of exceptional quality. To accomplish this, Old World Christmas has successfully established long-term contractual agreements with three German companies for sole distribution rights of their glass ornaments and finely-crafted wood products. With the support of these three fine companies, who are known for their traditional designs and quality products, Old World Christmas is able to overcome the stereotype of mass-produced products by offering pieces that receive generous amounts of time and attention to detail that result in very collectible heirlooms.

E.M. Merck, premier designer for Old World Christmas, possesses a strong background in German cultural traditions, art history and graphic designs and holds a degree in fine arts. In 1992, E.M. Merck created a special limited edition glass nutcracker ornament to commemorate the 100th anniversary of Tchaikovsky's ballet the "Nutcracker." This piece was successfully produced in a new mold which was created through a process that was "lost" in the former East Germany for many years. Old World Christmas now has the ability to use either new molds or original antique molds, of which Old World Christmas has access to the largest collection of antique glass ornament molds in the world. With access to the best of both new and old molds, the possibilities are endless for wonderful new collectible creations from Old World Christmas.

Nutcrackers Prove to be Popular

It is yet to be determined if Old World Christmas is more famous for its ornaments or collectible nutcrackers. Using quality materials and exacting

details, Old World Christmas has introduced an innovative collection of nutcrackers also designed by E.M. Merck. Produced in Germany exclusively for Old World Christmas and individually hand-signed by the artist, these nutcrackers are receiving rave reviews by collectors, as well as national awards. These nutcrackers, with their intricate detail, exceptional quality and affordable prices, have made them extremely popular. Tim Merck, President of Old World Christmas, reports: "The finest stores in the country are ordering these new nutcrackers in depth, and this line is one of the best things that has ever happened to our firm."

One of E.M. Merck's latest nutcracker designs is the "Waldkirchen Father Christmas." Continuing in the European tradition, this nutcracker captures the holiday spirit of giving. Attempting to capture the child-like feeling of Christmas, E.M. Merck's attention to detail, exceptional eye for color and intuition about collectibles shine through in the "Waldkirchen Father Christmas." This nutcracker is covered with toys and the finest gifts of the season, and is sure to become a treasured heirloom for collectors.

Collectors' Club Enjoys Phenomenal Success

Due to an overwhelming demand from retail consumers, Old World Christmas founded a collectors' club in August 1992 to bring together collectors and Christmas enthusiasts who are dedicated to the enchantment and collectible value of Old World Christmas. As the supplier who has pioneered the concept of presenting only the highest quality in holiday collectibles and decorations, it is only fitting that Old World Christmas should present the industry with the first collectors' club dedicated to traditional, hand-made holiday products created by skilled European artisans. The Old World Christmas Collectors' Club has become a tremendous

success with thousands of members to date. A $30.00 yearly membership fee to the club entitles members to purchase exclusive collectibles (limited to club members only) redeemable through retailers and to receive free gifts of heirloom ornaments and full-color Collectors' Guides. Members also receive the club newsletter, "The Old World Christmas Star Gazette." The newsletter provides members with up-to-date information regarding new designs, retired items, and general information on the history and traditions of Old World Christmas collectibles.

Old World Christmas has become a leader in the giftware industry. The firm has brought to the industry an unsurpassed level of performance by focusing on exclusive quality products, outstanding service and strong retail sales support. These are the commitments of excellence upon which the company was built and continues to uphold today, to take its rightful place as a significant supplier of holiday collectibles and decorations.

Adding to the Old World Christmas line of beautiful glass ornaments, these six 1994 introductions are produced in the age-old tradition. Each ornament is tediously mouth-blown, one at a time, into a fine porcelain mold. Colored lacquers are applied by skilled artisans, the trademark star cap is attached, and an heirloom is born!

Pacific Rim Import Corp.

Bristol Township & Waterfront Lets Collectors Re-Discover the Life and Architecture in Victorian England

Imagine yourself on a make-believe walk through Bristol, England during the height of the Victorian age. The year is 1860...a genteel era of gaslights, cobblestones, horse-drawn carts, and carriages. New-fallen snow crunches beneath your feet as you stroll past shops and manors with their Christmas trims. You're invited to explore the holiday world of mid-nineteenth century England, as portrayed by artist Pat Sebern for *Bristol Township & Waterfront.*

The main market street through town has been hectic with holiday activity. "George Straith Grocery" has become a real gathering place as shoppers dash in for the traditional dinner goose and trims. Travelers and coaches have been arriving and departing the "Iron Horse Livery" with great excitement all day. For many, the old "Pegglesworth Inn" will be their destination come nightfall. A warm bath and a hearty meal are included with the price of the room. The "Surrey Road Church" nearby will surely be full of holiday travelers.

A sign identifies "Wilkes and Bunsby," the local Barristers, who have hung festive garlands on their tall-timbered building. "Bristol Books" alongside has been doing a brisk business. There are also rooms available across the street above Mr. Beecroft's Shop, where he sells "Maps and Charts."

Down a snowy side street, we glimpse the "Foxdown Manor" and "Chesterfield House." "Trinity Church" is tucked into the winter scene, as well as the "Violin Shop" nearby. Mr. Locke had barely enough time to hang a wreath — he's been so busy with music and singing lessons.

The next sign we see hangs from the stone and thatched roof shop of the "Silversmith." Christmas is a busy season for Mr. Dorrit, who crafts beautiful silver goblets and candlesticks. The cottage where he lives with his family is attached around the side of his shop.

We stretch to see past the "High Gate Mill" and the "Black Swan Millinery" — and just make out the silhouettes of two more churches. It is now that we catch a glimpse of one of the most exciting scenes in all of Bristol — the combination of church spires and ships' masts that characterize the town.

When we round the next corner, we enter a very different-looking street: the *Waterfront.* This section, with its cobbles and historic buildings all perched at water's edge, is the place where Bristol's seafaring past is most evident. We can see the angular-shaped "Customs House" with the "Bristol Post" attached on the right. "Regent Warehouse" appears out of the darkness with the snow piling up between the many barrels out front. The "Bristol Tattler" is the local newspaper which connects to the "Foghorn Inn" with its pier.

Hanging signs on the next building indicate that Mr. Hawke and Mr. Braggs run the import/export business. Built on pilings, the "Rusty Knight Inn" also houses a pub with moorage for boats around the

The "Regent Warehouse" comes alive with busy villagers surrounding the hand-painted building from the Bristol Township & Waterfront.

back. While these buildings are constructed over water, there are also boardwalks for any landlubbers wanting to do business.

A little further down the boardwalk we can see "Admiralty Shipping" and "Lower Quay Chapel," a quaint little waterfront church with a pier for tying up boats. Finally, blinking in its proper place in the harbor is "Bristol Point Lighthouse." The old lighthouse keeper Percy Noggs lives in the attached building and keeps the blinking tower light in working order. Several buildings loom beyond, but the snow and fog make them difficult to see. With the lights reflecting in the water, the hanging signs and Christmas trims, this section of Bristol is truly enchanting!

A Matchless Collection Captures Victorian Bristol in Three Dimensions

You have just experienced a glance at the *Bristol Township & Waterfront* at holiday time. Each individual piece portrays the style and charm of mid-nineteenth century Bristol, England. Located

Two elegantly dressed villagers approach the quaint "Surrey Road Church." This old stone church features a cross atop its tower, stone archways at the windows, and wreaths hung in front to create the appearance of an inviting, wintry church at Christmas.

"Portshead Lighthouse" is beautifully accessorized by the water-like product, Bristol Bay Reflective Film. This lighthouse features a unique, two-light arrangement. The second light extends up inside the "stone" tower and blinks through the cut out windows.

where the Avon and Fromme rivers converge, this British town was a major shipping center for centuries. With its harbor in the heart of the city, the Bristol skyline constantly changed as masted sailing ships moved slowly between the lofty spires of churches and a myriad of smoking chimneys.

The collections' designer, Pat Sebern, first submitted drawings for a waterfront version of Bristol to Pacific Rim Import Corp. in 1991. To research both the Victorian architecture and the characteristics of waterfront buildings, she traveled to England and spent time studying these styles. She concentrated her efforts in the waterfront and harbor areas of Western England.

Photographs and sketches of small-but-important details enabled Ms. Sebern to recapture them in each of her works. Research revealed how Bristol suffered major damage in World War II, and how many wonderful — but damaged — buildings had to be replaced. The artist spent time in the archives of Bristol's main library studying line drawings, descriptions and photographs of old Bristol buildings and landmarks as they were originally built.

She also visited several coastal cities where waterfront architecture exists. Original stone work was still in place on many towers and bridges, and every neighborhood seemed to have a major church. Coaching inns and pubs were also observed in great numbers, with many displaying their founding dates in stone. Another interesting detail seen on many buildings were hanging signs. Almost like book illustrations, these wooden signs displayed information about the business or its name. Unique to the Bristol collections, then, are the hanging signs Ms. Sebern developed. Like the originals in England, they add character and charm to this Victorian style collection.

Upon her return to Seattle, Ms. Sebern's most fascinating challenge was to design the *Bristol Waterfront* buildings so that they appeared to be suspended above water. To do this, she undercut the bottom edge, and added boardwalks and pilings. The hanging signs previously mentioned were developed on wire brackets to fit into small holes in the porcelain buildings.

Also distinctive are the brick streets and cobblestone lanes, remarkably reproduced in a new felt

In addition to the Bristol Township & Waterfront, *Pacific Rim Import Corp. offers the adorable* Bunny Toes *figurines including this charming bunny, "Winifred With Blooms."*

product and available in a host of colors. There are three cobblestone color combinations on gray felt, as well as a gray-beige color scheme on white felt. As for bricks, they are available in a choice of red, brown or green. Each pattern of felt is available in 18" x 36" sizes, and comes complete with suggestions for use and display ideas. In addition, there is a product called Bristol Bay Reflective Film which creates a wonderful, water-like reflective support base for *Waterfront* pieces when used over cardboard or foamboard.

What's more, the *Bristol Township & Waterfront* base-mounted lights allow collectors an unobstructed view of all four sides of each building. The light, bulb and cord are all hidden down below. Cords can then be run under the felt product, creating a neighborhood of cobblestone and brick lanes instead of a maze of electrical cords! Most lighted villages, by contrast, can only be viewed from three sides to avoid "seeing the light works" on the fourth side of the building.

In 1994, four new buildings were added to the *Bristol Township & Waterfront*, while a number of buildings have already been retired since the collection's original 1990 introduction. Also available now are four sets of very small resin figures which inhabit the *Township*. A set of eight musicians stroll around singing carols while two sets of elegantly dressed villagers sell hot cross buns and carry holiday packages. An additional group of *Waterfront* characters is seen with fish and satchels. The *Bristol Township & Waterfront* continues to attract additional admirers with each new introduction and is very agreeably priced from $25.00 to $45.00.

Pacific Rim Also Offers Bunny Toes

Spring of 1994 brought a second group of collectibles into the Pacific Rim product line...*Bunny Toes* made its debut with "Tillie" and "Timothy" in their spring gardens. "Winifred" and "Wendell" meanwhile scooped up arms full of tulips. These precious little characters are about 3" high and created in cold-cast resin. Delicate watercolor detailing graces each piece. While initially available in spring designs, plans are underway to have them leaping into every season and every heart!

Since its beginning about forty years ago, Pacific Rim Import Corp. has undergone many changes. Presently, its product line includes several thousand items — but most impressive of all to American collectors are some of its most recent, decorative artworks: *Bristol Township & Waterfront* and the *Bunny Toes* collection.

PenDelfin Studios
The "Hobby" That Became an Empire

Who but PenDelfin founder Jean Walmsley Heap would begin writing a history of the company by celebrating her childhood diseases? Before you label the British artist-writer-sculptor-designer-entrepreneur "hypochondriac," you should know that childhood illnesses presented idyllic opportunities (with bravely collected gifts of colored pencils and sketch pads) to dream and sketch. As soon as Miss Heap began sketching, symptoms were forgotten. Even now, she fondly remembers those days.

Childhood illnesses disappeared, but Miss Heap's love of art grew stronger. She received a scholarship to study at the Burnley School of Art. At the end of her training, Miss Heap proclaimed a goal of writing and illustrating children's books. She exhibited florals and studies of children at many galleries until artistic plans were put aside when England went to war.

Always one to make the best of any situation, Miss Heap tried to join the Royal Navy but was promptly rejected. So she found work in a leather industry designing everything from military uniforms to stuffed animals. The job proved a terrific training ground and paved the way to a challenging assignment: The Canadian Red Cross commissioned Miss Heap to paint murals on nursery walls housing British children. These enchanting murals led to her recognition by the Royal Society of Arts.

Miss Heap was anxious to return to writing and illustrating children's books when the war ended, but fate intervened. In 1953, Miss Heap's desire to fashion clay models of her book characters lead her away from one-dimensional art. This was the beginning of a new career...and the start of PenDelfin.

Life in The Wooden Hut

The first meeting between Jean Walmsley Heap and her future partner, Jeannie Todd, was so inauspicious, the event was recorded with a single line in the company's forty-year retrospective! The two were introduced at the Burnley Artists' Society Autumn Exhibition and wound up working together at the Burnley Building Society three years later. Miss Heap had been named the Society's part-time "resident artist" and Jeannie Todd walked into her studio one day demanding art lessons! Miss Heap agreed.

As the two set off to sketch, a thunderstorm broke. Dashing back to Jeannie Todd's house, Miss Heap spotted a small hut amid the gardens; a potential studio for doing crafts. How perfect! They would make all sorts of gifts for friends and save a fortune, the two decided.

The place was quickly cleaned and a galvanized tub of China clay was set into place. The "hobby/business" was off and running as soon as they picked a name for their enterprise. After much deliberation, "PenDelfin" was picked. The word combined Pendle (a nearby hill) with elfin (their very first sculptures).

Miss Heap's strengths were designing and modeling. Jeannie Todd would steer the mold-making and casting processes. Friends and relatives helped as unpredictable calamities peppered their first days. Boiling rubber fumes clung to the walls of the Todd house (the molding process was moved to her kitchen since the hut had no electricity). Saucepans burned up with regularity. Each woman "sacrificed a treasured pressure cooker." But they were undaunted. In the end, an 8-inch high "Pendle Witch" emerged from their efforts. The artists had proven themselves ready for a "real" studio!

Move Number Two...
And More Adventures

PenDelfin Studio Two was established in a shop in the village of Harle Syke. Initially, a Jean Walmsley Heap character named "Little Thrifty" was slated for casting. But first efforts were a disaster! The stove was destroyed and the finished product looked like anything *but* Little Thrifty. They turned their attention back to a familiar subject: the Pendle Hill witch.

This sculpture proved to be a charm. Before long, Pendle Hill witches were selling with great vigor at a local inn. Neither Jean Walmsley Heap's nor Jeannie Todd's first wish was to produce figures simply for the money, but business is business, they agreed. Witch production at PenDelfin went into full swing.

By 1954, the studio had become a gathering place for local artisans and job seekers. Doreen Noel Roberts (known as Dorian) wandered in, looking for employment. By the time she left, an unpaid position was hers. She had agreed to work in return for a complete education in the business (and an agreement to allow her pet hen Sylvana accompany her to work). Both were on hand to help with the next move to a local co-operative grocery.

As PenDelfin's staff expanded, a few angels (business-minded visionaries with connections and cash) were also needed. Enter Greta Godbold! When Miss Godbold first saw figures coming out of PenDelfin studios, she asked "Why aren't they in stores?" When no satisfactory answer was forth-coming, Miss Godbold packed a suitcase full of samples and appointed herself the PenDelfin sales staff. Returning with a "real order" a bit later, the entire company pitched in and soon everyone realized the business was expanding; working on deadline would become routine.

Not one to stop with becoming the group's sales staff, Miss Godbold next introduced Rawlins Davenport, another merchandising angel. In short order, he helped move PenDelfin from "craft industry" to corporation. At this critical juncture, Miss Heap's father sat her down and advised her that she must choose between writing books and running the business. Book illustration was put on hold. PenDelfin came first.

Move Number Three...And Number Four! How Big Can We Grow?

New molding methods, state-of-the art equipment, modern management systems and a growing list of new sculptures pushed PenDelfin Studios out of the fifties and into the sixties. How the company grew! Makeshift work stations helped for awhile, but when the seams again began to burst, another move was the only answer. This time, to three floors with a private elevator. PenDelfin had arrived!

Larger quarters heralded international distribution. In 1965, PenDelfin officially entered the North American markets. In the midst of this came yet another move to Brennand Mill where more efficient casting systems were designed, and personnel expansion marked the next twelve years.

By the time PenDelfin's owners celebrated the twentieth anniversary of the move into Jeannie Todd's garden hut, another landmark event had taken place: a permanent home was found. PenDelfin bought half a building called Cameron Mill. The year was 1973. Jean Walmsley Heap and

From a childhood dream to an international company, PenDelfin founder Jean Walmsley Heap enjoys four decades of success.

Jeannie Todd watched in amazement as one hundred forty employees moved into "thirty two thousand square feet of light and space."

The new space was mind-boggling: elegant offices and three elevators moved employees in and out. There was room for a beautiful design studio and space galore for the installation of the company's pride and joy: a special casting machine which quickened production time while still employing handcrafting steps.

In general, the year of the move into Cameron Mill brought a welcome mix of excitement. PenDelfin began to attract attention from the media. Gold-stamped invitations to tea with Queen Elizabeth arrived. Accepting these much-coveted invitations was a culmination of years of hard work. Especially for Jeannie Todd who would die a year later.

In 1976, PenDelfin expanded geographically. Jean Walmsley Heap had found a perfect haven for the design unit in Wales. Miss Heap, staff members and assorted animals relocated belongings to an old Welsh farm on the Lleyn Peninsula. For the next fourteen years, both Cameron Mill and Wales experienced unparalleled success until a phone call on the night of June 11, 1986 announced the unthinkable: Cameron Mill had gone up in flames during the night. Newspapers described it as "the million pound blaze." To some, the end of PenDelfin seemed inevitable.

From the Rubble, A New Beginning

As hopeless as the situation might have seemed on June 11th, a determined PenDelfin family

Doreen Noel Roberts (known as Dorian) arrived at PenDelfin to 'learn the business' in 1954. Forty years later, her designs are 'the heartbeat' of the business.

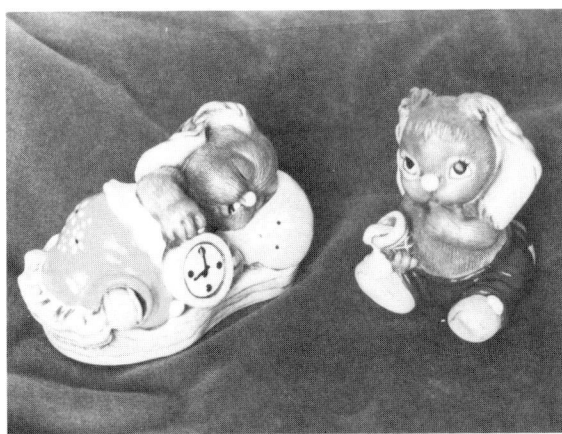

"Forty Winks" and "Vanilla," designed by Doreen Noel Roberts, are recent additions to PenDelfin's adorable Bed Series *and* Picnic Series.

spent little time grieving. One week after the fire, a message arrived in Wales stating: "We are back in production." Miss Heap ignored requests to stay in Wales, arriving at the charred building in hat and boots. She helped move salvageable items to 10,000 square feet of dry flooring at the rear of the building.

Workers brought chairs and tables from home. Meanwhile, negotiations to purchase the other half of the Mill began before the first mop hit the floor. Miraculous as it may seem, holiday decorations were being strung across the refurbished facility by Christmas. Staff members were ready to celebrate more than the Yuletide...and this particular incident describes, more than any other, the "stuff" of which the PenDelfin folks are made.

Collectors not familiar with PenDelfin's cheery rabbits, fairy tale characters, mice, elves, pixies, "real estate," wagons, decorative figures and displays may marvel at how this little company grew from a wooden hut in an English garden to an international company in forty years. But couple PenDelfin's eclectic history with the endearing collectible art coming from individual hearts and minds, and you understand why success was inevitable: The product is timeless and endearing. The staff is made up of a rare mix of dedication, artistic genius, tenacity and loyalty.

And of course "the commitment" is what binds it all together. What began as the vision of a child named Jean Walmsley Heap moved through the spirits of hundreds of people fortunate enough to have walked through the front doors of this extraordinary company. What fortunate surprises will the next forty years bring?

Possible Dreams®
The Santa Claus Network™ Adds an Extra Dimension to Collecting Clothtique® Originals from Possible Dreams

It has often been said that creativity lies in looking at the same old thing and seeing something different. And it was this that inspired Possible Dreams to envision a new line of fine art collectibles. Possible Dreams President Warren Stanley was on one of his frequent international buying trips when he came upon a process that replicated a centuries-old method of stiffening cloth. Originally developed in Europe, this technique was being practiced by only a handful of contemporary artists. Stanley approached some of today's most innovative designers, who jumped at the chance to make truly realistic costumes for their porcelain figurines. And thus the Possible Dreams Clothtique® line was introduced!

Although Clothtique is just a decade old, the Clothtique Originals of Possible Dreams already has grown from seven original pieces to a wideranging collection — featuring some of America's most renowned art masters. Tom Browning, Mark Alvin, Judith Ann Griffith, Lynn Bywaters, Jan Brett, Judi Vaillancourt and Thomas Blackshear all have applied their talents to the Clothtique® range. A line of Pepsi Cola Santas features works from Norman Rockwell and other famed artists, and a number of other Rockwell and J. C. Leyendecker covers from *The Saturday Evening Post* now grace the Clothtique line.

The first Clothtique introductions featured angels and nativities, but since then Santa Claus has become a highly popular subject for Possible Dreams artists and collectors. Indeed, the first three Clothtique Santas sold out to dealers within five months of issue. And when Possible Dreams found they were fielding thousands of pieces of mail from dedicated Clothtique collectors, the firm established a Santa Claus Collectors Club — called The Santa Claus Network™ — as an opportunity to share more information and privileges with admirers of Clothtique Santas.

Mark Alvin's "Strumming the Lute" features Clothtique® design mastery at its best: note the detail work in Santa's costume and the joy in his expression as he plays the traditional Eastern European instrument. ©1993 Sunrise Publications, Inc. Original art by Mark Alvin. Licensee: Possible Dreams, Ltd.

Santa replaces his "Ho, Ho, Ho" with "Fore" in this novel Clothtique® Original from artist Tom Browning. Two elf caddies have shoveled the path for Santa's short putt — and note those snazzy argyle socks on old St. Nick! ©1993 Tom Browning — Santa's Time Off™. Licensee: Possible Dreams, Ltd.

"The Marriage License" is based on the original design of Norman Rockwell from the June 11, 1955 Saturday Evening Post. *©1992 Curtis Publishing Co. Licensee: Possible Dreams, Ltd.*

The Creation of a Clothtique Original

Centuries ago, a process much like today's Clothtique was originated in Southern Europe. Yet for most of today's art masters, the concept was completely fresh and new. Paul Chang — an artist who was already a recognized expert in papier-maché — perfected the technique, and the resulting medium combines charm, beauty, and a special, lifelike "feel" that is unique to Clothtique.

This blend of old-world artistry and modern technology — as well as Chang's special gift for combining porcelain, resin and cloth — makes Clothtique a product that looks as much like "real life" as possible. The textures of fur and rich fabrics...the soft folds of a "woolen" robe or the tilt of a hat...the richness of thick, embroidered tapestry...all come alive in Clothtique.

Meet the Clothtique Santas — And Join The Santa Claus Network™

Alive with details, color and artistry, the Clothtique Santas range from the American traditional St. Nick in many guises and poses to portrayals of the "Jolly Old Elf" in costumes from around the world. In the world of Possible Dreams, we find Santa skiing, sledding, riding a sleigh and engineering a steam train. He also appears in the costumes of many nations and races — and Santa stars in limited edition Clothtique pieces such as "Patriotic Santa," "Father Christmas" and "Tradi-

tional USA Santa and Elf." Each of these special Santas is offered in a sequentially numbered edition of 10,000 pieces, and each stands 17" tall. The limited edition Santas each bear commemorative brass tags, and each comes nestled inside a handsome gift box.

Some of the most recent Santas from Possible Dreams reflect the unique visions of contemporary artists such as Mark Alvin and Judith Ann Griffith. We all know the mileage Santa covers on his annual night flight on Christmas Eve. But it amounts to just a short junket compared to the distance he's travelled through time. "Strumming the Lute" is how artist Mark Alvin turns back the clock to an East European countryside steeped in the folklore of St. Nicholas. Alvin, whose wide range of creative experiences includes ornament design and card illustration, rekindles an authentic past with details like a loose-fitting tunic and trousers with gaily embroidered trim. The fur hat and leggings attest to the fashion and function of that bitterly cold climate in and around December 25. Even the delicate fingers at the neck of the traditional lute adds to the overall charm and expressive qualities of this piece.

Judith Ann Griffith's "Tree Planter" represents a New Age Santa, perfect for the environmentally conscious nineties. His sculpted face, flowing robe and perched dove symbolize the timeless message of "Peace on Earth," and the shovel is used to dig into the soil so that his ready-to-plant Christmas tree can take root. Through the unique Clothtique process that blends stiffened cloth, porcelain and resin, the 10" "Tree Planter" teaches us and future generations the valuable lesson that the Earth must be respected. Other new Santa additions include: Tom Browning's "Ice Capers" with Santa on skates; "Nature's Love" with Mark Alvin portraying St. Nicholas holding a baby seal; and Browning's "Easy Putt" with Santa taking time for a quick round of golf.

Collectors who find themselves caught up in the magic of the Clothtique Santas may well want to invest in membership in The Santa Claus Network™ from Possible Dreams. Each member receives a host of benefits including a free 8" tall Clothtique Santa, available to Network members only. Membership allows for the purchase of another exclusive Santa each year, as well as a subscription to a colorful, quarterly newsletter, a complete directory of Clothtique Santas in the *Collectors Guide Book*, and a personal Membership Card. All this is available for $25 annually (add $5 for memberships outside the Continental U.S.).

Citizens of Londonshire® Charm Clothtique Enthusiasts

Just as famous as the *Clothtique Santa* collections are the characters in the appealing *Londonshire®* series, based on the land "Beyond the Third Rainbow®." Londonshire has become almost real to the subscribers to this country's special newspaper, "The Londonshire Daily Mail," and the thousands of others who receive one of these characters as a gift.

The story of Londonshire begins in the land that we now call Great Britain. There lived a famed nobleman: Lord Rolland Bannister. Lord Bannister was one of the animal kingdom's best friends, and he devoted his life to his animal family since he had no living relatives. It is told that as Lord Bannister lay dying, he clutched a magic jewel which had once belonged to Merlin of King Arthur's Court. The jewel was rumored to contain three rainbows.

"Earl of Hamlett" is 12" high and is one of the Citizens of Londonshire. ©*Possible Dreams, Ltd.*

As Lord Bannister drew his last breath, the crystal started to emit a brilliant light and Lord Bannister uttered his dying wish: "That all animals should enjoy human happiness in a faraway land they could call their own." The animals fulfilled that dying wish by sailing away to a new life in "Londonshire."

The *Londonshire* collection features such lovable characters as the "Earl of Hamlett," a pig who serves as the local restauranteur and chef, and his children, "Walter" and "Wendy." A charming addition to the line is "Tiffany Sorbet," a lady hippo and proprietor of the local ice cream parlor. From the ruddy masculinity of "Officer Kevin" to the delicate grace of "Lady Ashley" and "Lady Margaret," the Citizens of Londonshire are a whimsical link between past and present.

Works of Norman Rockwell and J. C. Leyendecker in Clothtique

Through a licensing agreement with The Curtis Publishing Company, Possible Dreams is especially proud to bring the art of Norman Rockwell and J. C. Leyendecker to life. Inspired by classic *Saturday Evening Post* covers, these Clothtique treasures now may be enjoyed in three dimensions and vivid color.

The Rockwell collection includes Christmas favorites such as "Santa's Helpers," "Gramps at the Reins," "Santa Plotting His Course" and "Balancing the Budget." There are also several pieces marking the seasons, such as "Springtime" and "The Marriage License." And Norman Rockwell's classic "Triple Self Portrait" is now available in Clothtique, with incredible lifelike detailing. Leyendecker's "Hugging Santa" and "Santa on the Ladder" round out this marvelous, historic set of offerings.

The creative eye of Warren Stanley — combined with the innovative spirit of Possible Dreams C.E.O. Leni Miller — ensure that the Clothtique line will continue to expand and prosper. From Londonshire to the North Pole, from Norman Rockwell's classic Americana to the New Age inspiration of Judith Ann Griffith, the artistic mastery of Clothtique will keep making collectible dreams come true through the company called Possible Dreams.

Precious Art/Panton

Krystonia Brings Collectors a Touch of Make-Believe, a Pinch of Fantasy, Lots of Whimsy and a Whole Lot of Fun

From the World of Krystonia comes a cordial invitation for collectors to enter a whimsical land full of mysterious, magical adventures. Since 1987, when the first Krystonian characters exploded onto the scene, many collectors have been so delighted that, for them, collecting will never be the same!

This mystical land of expansive deserts, towering mountains and lush valleys has drawn the interest of young and old alike. Maybe it's because we all grew up with fantasy from the stories that we first read as little ones at Grandma's knee. Or possibly it's the excitement of visiting a new country — far different from any other we've encountered.

Krystonia figures come to life as hand-painted figurines and also in three books where they play starring roles: *Chronicles of Krystonia*, *Krystonia Adventures*, and *Krystonia III*. These delightful books let you experience the many adventures in this whimsical make-believe kingdom. Haphazard as they may seem in some respects, Krystonia's inhabitants are ever resilient — they always spring back for more!

A Visit to Krystonia Means Adventure and Fantasy Delight

There are magical krystals throughout Krystonia, and the search for them is always on. These krystals possess great power: for with them the evil "N'Borg" could cast all of Krystonia into a winter of no end — and all would be at his mercy. From the menacing "Krak N'Borg" castle, he rules his henchmen with an iron fist — with the exception of the beautiful "N'Leila." Even his master of dark arts, "N'Chakk," is constantly exasperated that their attempts at conquest are thwarted. Only one thing is certain, "N'Borg" will never rest until his conquest of Krystonia is compete. The wizards know that they must always be on guard, for if they are not alert, the worst of their nightmares could come true.

The Council of Wizards are a diverse and interesting group of Krystonia characters. It is their wish to live in peace and harmony, and they work daily toward this end. "Rueggan," the tinkerer, works with his Gorphs, or mindless blobs, to bring ancient machines back to life, often with hilarious results. "Gilbran" and "Shepf" are wind wizards of the highest degree, although many still remember "Gilbran" causing the worst storm in Krystonia's history.

"Turfen" casts the most peaceful of dreams and if not for "Azael," it's very possible that the Wizard Council would never have been formed. Sometimes their biggest chore is to keep the practical joking wizard, "Haaph," and the most arrogant of chefs, "Hotpot," from each others' clutches. As most would say, a Krystonian day that goes by without a snag or incident is a very good day indeed. By whispering their charm words through the krystals at the Obelish, the wizards cast the most marvelous of spells, and with only the good will of all of Krystonia on their minds, they go about their daily tasks.

The Dragon Society of Cairn Tor is another matter. Nowhere will you find more colorful personalities. Led by the ever-complaining "Grumblypeg Grunch," they transport goods

These three Krystonian characters look as if they have just come off the pages of their own adventure book. And look: "Pultzr," in the center, is reading about himself and his friends!

This mother tiger watches over her cub in a selection from the highly realistic Precious Art/Panton collection entitled The Safari Kingdom.

throughout the land. Harsh as he seems, his message is good and his goal — for every dragon being able to read — is most admirable. From "Stoope" to "Stupendous," as he calls himself, to the ever-rocking "Spyke," there is always activity in Cairn Tor.

The young dragons of Cairn Tor are guaranteed to steal your heart. Who can forget "Koozl," carrying his best friend, a stuffed bear, or "Tokkel," first emerging from his egg? What about "Jumbly," the "Juggler" and the ever-organized "Shadra"? Then there's "Pultzr" and his enormous appetite for learning — they all join together to keep activity at a very high level. Only "Flayla," who makes the best of nannies, quiets them all when it is storytime.

In Krystonia, you don't have to wander far to encounter amazing sights to behold. "Groc" and the troll bridge builders are fast at work, and "Moplos" is leading "Mos," his pack animal, in with a load of krystals. Looking into the desert, "Shigger's Maj Dron" are riding their Mahouhdas through the scorching heat, hoping they are not attacked by the dreaded "Hagga-Beast." "Tulan" has just arrived from a sea voyage with trunks filled with valuable cloths from other lands.

There is much to tell of this land of Krystonia, and "Kephren" the recorder spends endless hours translating the many scrolls that arrive by dragon transport. This may sound like a tedious existence on the surface, but it's anything but that. "Kephren" works diligently, for he knows this is not the end, but only the beginning of all the stories yet to be told of Krystonia.

The Origins of Krystonia and Its Characters

How Krystonia originated in a tiny, cramped factory in England's Stoke-on-Trent, Chesterton — and grew to its large, modern facility — is quite a story. With its startling initial success in 1987, Krystonia quickly outgrew its humble surroundings, but its creators have never forgotten them. Hard working, quality oriented artisans show great pride in every Krystonia figurine they produce.

Using cold-cast porcelain, every sculpted detail is beautifully apparent. Often you will notice a slight variance from figurine to figurine within an edition, showing that each character is hand-painted with just a light touch of the painter's personality added. Of course, every character must have his or her own sparkling krystal adornment for the finishing touch.

Krystonia's creators chose Stoke-on-Trent as the location for their production studios because of the British tradition of excellence and the wealth of expert painters available there. The intent from the very beginning was to combine high-quality collectibles with whimsical, enjoyable stories and characters.

Indeed, while Krystonia's physical roots are in England, the characters' true roots reside in the minds and hearts of David Lee Woodard and Pat Chandok. This is where each Krystonia personality begins. Woodard and Chandok lead a creative team of artists who breathe life into every Krystonia inhabitant. Working with gifted English sculptors, painters and writers, no character is completed until just the right personality is achieved. Each step is taken cautiously and with great care and love, for in Krystonia there are no ordinary characters.

Storylines fall to David Lee Woodard, Pat Chandok and Mark Scott. While Dave and Pat create many of the plots, it is Mark who develops them in storybook form. This trio creates the delightful personalities and storybook adventures portrayed in the beloved Krystonia books. What happens next only they may know, but it is bound to be loaded with fantasy fun.

Because Dave and Pat had fifteen years of giftware experience before they entered the World of Krystonia, they knew that these characters would be successful if they could infuse each creation with a real, heartwarming feeling. Judging from the reaction people have when they first see a new figurine — everything from a smile to outright laughter — this creative team has met their goal.

Krystonia Collectors Club Prepares for Its Fifth Year

After four years of tremendous growth, in February of 1994 the Krystonia Collectors Club will begin its fifth year. As they willingly admit, Krystonia Collectors can't wait to get their next newsletter, and see what is happening in their favorite kingdom. A different Krystonian introduces each newsletter, and readers learn a bit more about these fascinating characters. These newsletters keep collectors informed of all kinds of Krystonian events. What's more, each year that a collector joins or renews, they receive a free gift that will never again be available to the open market. "Spreading His Wings" was the fourth year members-only figurine, and featured "Owhey," trying to fly.

Realistic detail makes these mischievous Precious Art/Panton mice come to life. They are hand-painted with special care at the firm's fine art studios at Stoke-on-Trent, England.

Precious Art/Panton Presents a Growing Krystonia Line...And More

While Krystonia started with just nineteen figurines, there will be over 130 different pieces introduced to the line by 1994. Krystonia figurines now grace plaques, waterballs and miniatures. The Krystonia accessories of scrolls, bags and signs have pleased collectors, who add them to their displays at home. With the large demand for these items, there are already more on the drawing board.

Before the World of Krystonia emerged from the Precious Art/Panton studios in England, the firm introduced diverse product lines from the Far East, including the stunning metal working of Samuri warriors in plates, music boxes, pictures and more. Many musical items followed, leading to Precious Art's debut of the first up-and-down movement carousel.

Precious Art/Panton proudly presents *The Safari Kingdom*, a beautifully realistic group of African and American animals. In this grouping, river otters flow down a waterfall, bunnies come out to play, brown bears climb trees, and there are even wolves on the prowl. There is also a group of coldcast *Mischievous Mice* who join in the fun as they eat fruit, climb on old boots, sit in moccasins, and live humbly but happily in an old can. The tiniest mice of all are the *Malcolm Merriweather* collection, dancing through the landscaping of Mulberry Park.

What will come next for Precious Art/Panton? Whatever the new direction, the studio's artists and writers vow never to stray from the uniqueness and quality that collectors treasure most. Whether in the fantasy land of Krystonia or the realism of wildlife sculpture, Precious Art/Panton's goal is to bring fun — and pride of ownership — to collector friends everywhere.

R.R. Creations, Inc.
The Open Window Collection®: "Our Miniatures Are Your Memories"

From the architectural masterworks of colonial Williamsburg to a simple Amish buggy shop, each charming work of art from R.R. Creations has one special feature in common. Take a careful look and you'll see that every wooden miniature boasts an open window, the firm's registered trademark.

"The open window symbolizes that God sometimes closes a door, but always opens a window," explains Doreen Ross — one "R" in R.R. Creations along with her husband, Dave Ross. As President and Vice-President respectively, Doreen and Dave provide the guiding spirit for this growing firm from their cherished home town of Pratt, Kansas.

It was their unwillingness to abandon the happy, small-town life of Pratt that led the Rosses to their own "open window" in 1987. Both were unemployed, but they loved the town they had come to live in just one year earlier.

Doreen Ross proposed to her husband that they could develop a line of small, wood miniature building replicas with a Midwestern flair all its own. After much prayer and considerable research, the couple sprung into action. They set up a carpentry shop in the family garage.

"In our garage it was a 'lot of fun' because we could only sand or cut at one time. Everything had to be cleaned up and then we could paint," Doreen remembers fondly. "We started without even knowing what a silk screen looked like."

Classic Collections From R.R. Creations

Early buildings from that "garage period" are called *Grandpa's Farm* — and they are still a part of the R.R. Creations line in an extended series now called *Grandpa's Farm II*. There's a handsome red barn, a big white farm house, an outhouse, windmill and accessories. The inspiration for these heartwarming farm pieces comes from the old Haviland homestead which belonged to Dave Ross' grandfather and from Doreen's parents' farm in Ohio.

Next came *On the Square*, a set of miniature buildings that replicate those most frequently found on a small-town central square. Currently available is *On the Square II*, with its Victorian-style storefronts "selling" antiques, crafts, books, and other merchandise, as well as accessories including street lamps, an American flag on a flagpole and trees.

Another appealing series is entitled *Amish Collection*, which highlights the simple lifestyle of these country folk. Collectors may still acquire pieces from *Amish Collection II*, including a family in traditional attire, several of their buildings and accessories.

An Early Appreciation for People's Customized Choices

In addition to the many buildings that the Rosses develop through their own research and brainstorming, they have been making replicas of "somebody's memories," as Doreen puts it, almost since they opened their doors. Well-known sites they have "miniaturized" include Elvis Presley's home, the Chautauqua Hills Jelly Company in Sedan, Kansas,

Dave and Doreen Ross design and craft their handsome R.R. Creations Open Window Collection of miniature building replicas from the small town of Pratt, Kansas. They began their company in the family garage in 1987, and now preside over a thriving business with an international scope.

the Michigan Victorian House, the Faulkner House and the John Hayes House.

Even more rewarding to the Rosses and their employees, however, are the custom jobs done to capture the memories of someone's own beloved home, their old school house, depot or courthouse.

"Whether or not we like the buildings is never a factor in our efforts to reproduce them well," Doreen Ross assures. "The people just love them because it's their memory. When we paint the buildings, we try to see them through their eyes." She says, "At first, we used to just do the colors ourselves, but now we're getting them to send us color chips. When you see the building, it looks a lot different than a photograph. They all have a little personality."

It's fun for those at R.R. Creations to see unusual orders come in: they've created a Scottish Highlander which was a school mascot, as well as a gazebo for a University. Officials from a town in West Virginia ordered what came to be called the "Roth Rock," a memorial rock in honor of the man who had settled their town.

Doreen Ross believes the possibilities for such creations are endless. "There are many opportunities to do different buildings like insurance companies, real estate offices, banks, or buildings no longer existing. It's something that even a small town can have done affordably. A miniature memory made out of wood means a lot to some people. Some people collect only one kind of building, a firehouse because their father was a fireman or a drugstore because their grandpa had a drugstore. They have good memories," she asserts.

The R.R. Creations Historical Collection: Series II *features these three Early American buildings as well as several appropriate accessory pieces. They may be displayed on a tabletop, in a shadow box or on a door lintel.*

Three historical lighthouse buildings make a handsome addition to the Open Window Collection. *Like the other works of art from R.R. Creations, each is designed on the basis of extensive research and crafted with care in Pratt, Kansas.*

The Creation of The Open Window Collection

The Rosses are adamant about the quality of each wooden miniature replica they make, preferring to use pine instead of fiberboard. To guard against the possibility of sap discoloring the ink they use for painting, they have created a new process that involves a sealer.

When they began their business, Doreen and Dave performed every step in the production process themselves. They developed each design, cut the wood, did the hand-painting, and marketed the finished product. Now they employ a staff of local Pratt workers to share the load.

Dave and his assistants handle the actual production of each piece, while the design work is handled in the office under Doreen's guidance using a computer aided drafting and design system. The program also enables them to complete their color separations, which are transferred to silk screens. Background colors and edges are hand-painted onto the cut wooden forms. Screening takes place color by individual color — with each hue requiring a separate screen.

Every building has the Ross signature, certifying its status as a true "R.R. Creation." Early versions had the company logo burned into the bottom of each piece. Current pieces display a silk screened logo on the reverse with a fifty-word history.

At $22.50 for initial membership and $19.50 for renewal, the Open Window Club House Collectors Club offers a host of benefits and gifts. A selection of club materials and available buildings is shown here.

R.R. Creations "Goes International" at Harrod's

Pieces from *The Open Window Collection* were among just a handful of products selected to represent Kansas at a unique "American Frontier" promotion at Harrod's of London, some months back.

As Doreen Ross explains proudly, "There were 500 booths set up at this special Harrod's buyer's market in Wichita, and many of the booths carried more than one line of products. They selected items from only six booths, and we were fortunate to be one of them."

Sixteen R.R. Creations buildings went on display at Harrod's, inspiring the Rosses to think about enlarging their geographic horizons. "Now that we have our foot in the door over there, we hope to expand our line internationally," Doreen explains. Buildings shown at Harrod's include a couple of beloved Pratt, Kansas landmarks: the Santa Fe Depot and the Barron Theatre.

Limited Editions Dominate the Firm's Current Line

All of the new R.R. Creations pieces introduced since 1994 will be hand-numbered within a limit of 2,500 for each piece. According to the Rosses, this "limited edition decision" was warmly received by dealers and collectors.

Works of art that will remain available until December 31, 1995 include the *Historical Collection II*, *Williamsburg Collection II*, *In the Country Series II* and *Christmas Memories Series II*, in addition to the previously mentioned *Grandpa's Farm Collection Series II*, *On the Square Series II* and *Amish Collection Series II*.

The *Historical Collection II* features three architecturally significant Colonial buildings plus accessories, while the *Williamsburg* series continues R.R. Creations' tribute to some of the most elegant buildings in the renowned Virginia town. *In the Country II* offers typical "down home" buildings, while *Christmas Memories* shows homes and a church "decked out" with wreaths, red bows and other holiday "cheer."

The Open Window Club House Collectors Club

Enthusiasts of R.R. Creations' delightful building replicas now have the opportunity to join The Open Window Club House Collectors Club.

Club membership offers a free gift of any hand-signed building from the collectible line — providing it is still in production — along with a redemption certificate for the first "members-only" piece.

Also included with membership is a hard-bound catalog of all exclusive designs available all over the United States that may be updated twice yearly. Club membership fees are $22.50 for the first year, and $19.50 for renewals. For more information, collectors may contact Debi Gaston at R.R. Creations, Inc., P.O. Box 8707, Pratt, Kansas 67124.

Rawcliffe Corporation
Fine Pewter Collectibles Capture the Magic of Star Wars®, Star Trek® and Popular Fantasy Subjects

"Everybody collects something" notes Peter Brown, the fourth-generation owner of the Providence, Rhode Island-based Rawcliffe Corporation. Judging from the remarkable growth of Rawcliffe over the past two decades, Brown is "right on the money" with his assessment of the current collectibles marketplace.

Brown's great-grandfather began this thriving firm as a manufacturer for the silverware trade. He also made precision industrial parts — a focus that set the stage for the marvelously detailed pewter pieces Rawcliffe makes today. When Peter Brown joined the business in 1971, the Rawcliffe foundry had just two employees in addition to Peter's father, and their main product was bronze plaques. Since then,

Measuring just 4" tall, Wish Fairies, *from original artist Jessica deStefano, are a greeting card and gift in one. Each in the series of twelve* Wish Fairies *comes packaged with a wing-shaped greeting card expressing wishes for "Health," "Fun," "Happiness," "Good Fortune," "Rainbows," "Sunshine," "Friendship," "Love," "Success," "Laughter," "Dreams" and "Good Luck." Suggested retail is $34.95. For each* Wish Fairy *sold, a donation will be made to Amos House in Providence, Rhode Island, a non-profit organization providing food, shelter, social services and hope to needy individuals and families.*

Rawcliffe has expanded greatly through the development of pewter artistry. Today the firm employs 170 people and its giftware and collectible products are available at over 17,000 stores nationwide.

Three years after Peter took over as President, Rawcliffe began manufacturing in pewter, an alloy formulated of 94% tin. Taking advantage of the firm's proximity to the Rhode Island School of Design (RISD), he engaged the artistic expertise of RISD graduate Patsy Davis to create Rawcliffe's first original sculptures. By 1976, Rawcliffe had mastered the process of reproducing sculptures in pewter using the age-old "lost wax" process, and it was time to begin the marketing effort in earnest.

Five years later, Rawcliffe was cited by *Inc. Magazine* as one of America's fastest-growing companies. Brown considers the quality and diversity of his offerings as the key to their great success. Indeed, Rawcliffe's products have become increasingly sophisticated and varied. Today they offer collectible items depicting virtually every wild and domesticated animal, sport, pet, hobby, avocation, pastime, personality type, caricature and market trend. Rawcliffe creates "generic" giftware items for all occasions, as well as specialized items for each person's "passion."

Rawcliffe's Creative Process in Fine Art Pewter

Some manufacturers "water down" their pewter alloy with high levels of lead — so much so that their pewter sculptures can actually be used to write on paper like a lead pencil! However, Rawcliffe prides itself on using a highly pure alloy of 94% tin, which is both lovely to look at and remarkably durable. Indeed, each pewter piece is buffed and finished to a warm patina that highlights its intricate details.

The creation of a Rawcliffe collectible begins with an original artist sculpture. Rawcliffe artists work in a soft wax which is much like modeling clay. They must take into consideration every step of the production process in designing each original piece.

The development of Rawcliffe's pewter products involves a complex series of operations by skilled

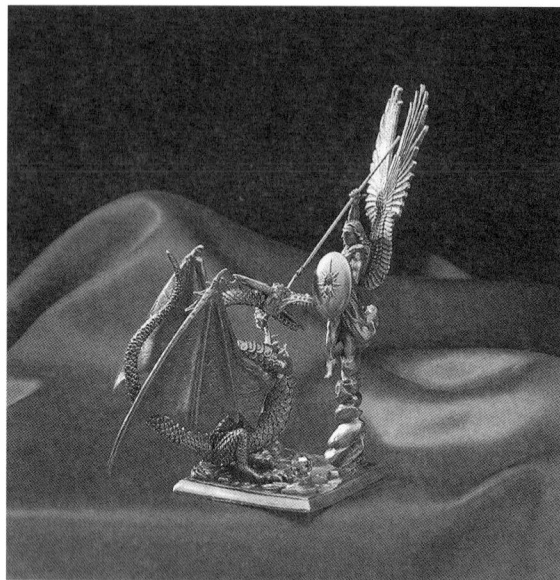

"Archangel Michael" is a highly detailed figurine depicting the victory of good over evil. This fine pewter creation features hand-set crystals — a large blue crystal in the hero's shield and fiery red crystals in the dragon's eyes — and has a suggested retail of $55.00. The overall piece stands 5-1/2" tall, with the Archangel's wings spanning 3-1/2" of that height. As with hundreds of Rawcliffe's handcrafted fantasy figures, this sculpture requires many pieces to be individually cast and assembled to create the final sculpture.

workers. After mold-making and casting, every piece reaches the hands of one of Rawcliffe's competent metal workers. They remove any imperfections and "chase" in any lost details. Next the props and bases are soldered onto the pewter pieces. Some complex figurines may be cast in as many as ten different pieces and must be individually assembled and reworked before the piece is complete.

At the last stage of production, each piece is specially treated and hand-polished, taking care that all details are retained and that the solder joints are smooth and strong, especially on delicate sculptures. The result is a perfect duplicate of the artist's original model — truly a handcrafted artistic reproduction.

Licensed Works Highlight the Rawcliffe Collection

By virtue of its excellent craftsmanship and quality reputation, Rawcliffe has obtained numerous contracts for producing licensed merchandise in handcrafted pewter. Dozens of figures and ships from the popular Star Trek® and Star Wars® series are currently in production, along with numerous Disney and Looney Tunes® characters. For example,

Rawcliffe's Star Wars® offerings include Han Solo's "Millennium Falcon," Luke Skywalker's "X-Wing Fighter," and Darth Vader's "Tie Fighter." Each of these ships is a limited edition of 15,000 pieces and is offered on a custom wood base featuring a pewter name plaque. Also in the collection are the unforgettable characters of "R2D2," "Darth Vader," "Princess Leia," "Han Solo," "Yoda," "Chewbacca," "Luke Skywalker," "Boba Fett" and "Obi Wan Kenobi." The "Imperial Star Destroyer," the "A-Wing" and "B-Wing Fighters" and a "Stormtrooper" complete the action series.

The Rawcliffe Star Trek® line includes characters and ships inspired by the original Star Trek® television series, as well as the more recent syndicated TV shows: "Star Trek®: The Next Generation™," and "Star Trek®: Deep Space Nine™."

Thanks to Rawcliffe, collectors who enjoy the space adventures of any of the Star Trek® series may own characters ranging from "the originals" like "Captain Kirk," "Commander Spock," "Dr. McCoy" and "Scotty" to the more recent Star Trek® favorites: "Captain Jean-Luc Picard," his right-hand man "Commander William T. Riker," and the lovely "Beverly Crusher, M.D." As for the Deep Space Nine™ crew, "Commander Benjamin Sisko" leads off the series depicting all seven main characters.

Star Trek® ships offered in remarkable detail by Rawcliffe range from the original "USS Enterprise" to the updated "USS Enterprise NCC-1701-D" from "Star Trek®: The Next Generation™." A number of enemy ships are depicted as well, so that collectors may re-live the drama of all of their favorite adventures as they admire these handsome replicas.

The newest licensed products depict memorable scenes from Star Trek® Generations, the seventh feature film in the ongoing saga of good and evil in the 23rd and 24th centuries. The Star Trek® line has also grown to include a series of pewter keychains and pewter-decorated mugs featuring the colorful logos, insignias and characters from all the TV shows and films.

Thunderbolt™ and Partha Pewter™ Miniatures

Rawcliffe also has earned a strong reputation for its fantasy-subject figurines, both in pewter and in other fine materials. One important example is the *Thunderbolt Miniatures™* and *Partha Pewter™* series: dragons and knights and beautiful damsels in distress...plus much, much more.

While many of these miniatures stand just a few

inches tall, their detail work is nothing short of superb. There's "Knights of the Air," with two valiant warriors doing battle astride their winged steeds..."Magic Carpet Ride," where a regal pair traverse the skies with the help of their magical genie..."Mother Love," with a maternal dragon guarding her nest. Rawcliffe's genius for pewter artistry makes each piece a remarkable work for display. Collectors marvel at the texture of the dragons' lizard-like skin and the flying creatures' wing feathers...the intricacy of the knights' and ladies' costumes.

To add richness and color to the fantasy figurines and characters, many of the pieces are enhanced with shimmering rhinestones and crystals. For example, "King Arthur of the Britons" has two ruby-colored stones on his shoulder pieces, while "Sir Percivale De Galys" has a sapphire-blue stone set into his shield. Other pieces sit atop agate slices or unique holograms.

Jessica deStefano Creates Fanciful Bubble Fairies™

Also in a fantasy mode — but utilizing a whole different set of materials and colors — are the *Bubble Fairies*™ collection created exclusively for Rawcliffe by artist Jessica deStefano. This sculptor is famous for her meticulously detailed originals and her ability to capture character and emotion. Her sculpture springs to life with a new and fresh "look" all its own. Ms. deStefano notes that the *Bubble Fairies*™ were created to express the spirit and the child that exists in every one of us.

There are several wonderful *Bubble Fairies*™ groupings, including the original *Bubble Fairies*™, *Baby Bubble Fairies*™, *The Four Seasons*™ limited edition collection, *The Rainbow Collection*™, *Garden Fairies*™, *Wish Fairies*™, and the newest limited edition *Angel Fairies of The Seasons*™.

Bubble Fairies™ got their name because they are the only fairies light enough to ride on a bubble without breaking it. *Bubble Fairies*™ never die; they just vanish in thin air like a bubble that is popped. According to Jessica's legend, a new *Bubble Fairy*™ reappears when someone makes a magic wish, though no one knows just how they are born.

Each *Baby Bubble Fairy*™ carries a little pouch with its name on it and fairy dust inside. If ever you are sprinkled with fairy dust, it gives you a good feeling all over. Fairies use it to help settle disagreements among people. They use it to cheer people who are sick and they sprinkle it on each other to keep themselves constantly happy. Cast in artist's resin, beautifully hand-painted, and sitting atop their iridescent bubbles, the *Bubble Fairies*™ are available exclusively from Rawcliffe Corporation.

After more than two decades in the business, Peter Brown's appreciation for the fact that "everyone collects something" remains stronger than ever. His goal is to continue developing special works of art and creations for today's marketplace which fuel that "collecting fire" for Rawcliffe's many loyal collectors.

Rawcliffe is authorized by Lucas Films to manufacture both figurines and ships related to the popular Star Wars® film series. Mounted on hardwood bases and featuring pewter name plates, each finely detailed replica is perched for action and adventure. Shown left to right are Luke Skywalker's "X-Wing Fighter" (2-1/2" tall with a suggested retail of $95.00), Darth Vader's "Tie Fighter Ship" (2-1/2" tall with a suggested retail of $135) and Han Solo's "Millennium Falcon" (2-1/4" tall with a suggested retail of $115). The issue is limited to 15,000 pieces.

Reco International Corp.

Award-Winning Artists Keep Reco International on the Leading Edge of Limited Edition Collectibles for More Than Twenty-Five Years

Congratulations and kudos poured in from all over the world as Reco International Corp. celebrated its Silver Anniversary in 1992. And on this momentous occasion, Reco founder Heio Reich reminisced about the origins of his renowned firm...and its evolution to fulfill the changing desires of collectors. Now with the 1990s well underway, Reich and Reco have pledged to continue their dedication to excellence in producing and marketing the works of some of today's most gifted art masters.

When Heio Reich founded Reco in 1967, his goal was to provide American collectors with a panorama of world-class collectible art. As a native of Berlin, Germany, Reich enjoyed a great many contacts with European art studios. Thus Reco gained fame by introducing plates from some of Europe's most celebrated makers, including Fuerstenberg, Royale, Dresden, Royal Germania Crystal, King's and Moser.

Many of the plates Reco imported to the United States have risen substantially in value since their introduction in the late 1960s and early 1970s. But Heio Reich sensed a golden opportunity in 1977, and he steered his business in a whole new direction. Since then, Reco International has reigned as one of the nation's top producers of limited edition plates by renowned American painters like Sandra Kuck, John McClelland, Jody Bergsma and Dot and Sy Barlowe.

While some studios specialize in only one area such as child-subject art or wildlife, Reco seeks out artists of excellence in many different subjects and styles. Sandra Kuck's and John McClelland's children, wildlife and nature from Dot and Sy Barlowe, and fantasy visions from Jody Bergsma all grace the current Reco line-up. In the past, Clemente Micarelli has painted varied scenes including homages to the ballet, religious events and weddings. Subjects as diverse as Edwardian bears and military art may be found in the Reco archives.

The original Reco series from European art studios often commemorated Christmas, Mother's Day, Father's Day and other holidays — and so

Sandra Kuck's 1993 contributions to Reco's elegant Premier Collection are "La Belle" and "Le Beau," two classic portraits of children with their kitten pets. Each plate is available in an edition of 7,500.

does the contemporary Reco line. Currently, Reco is at the forefront of Mother's Day and Christmas collectibles, with works by Kuck, Bergsma and McClelland. Sandra Kuck and Jody Bergsma both have Mother's Day plate series with annual editions, while Kuck, Bergsma and John McClelland each have their own Reco Christmas plate series. Rounding out the holiday collections are an ornament collection from Sandra Kuck, and ornaments, angels and crèche figurines from the gifted John McClelland.

The Premier Collection Highlights Reco Artists' Ultimate Works

Especially exciting for loyal Reco collectors has been the recent introduction of the Reco Premier Collection, featuring outstanding limited editions of the highest artistic achievement. The first pieces unveiled were "Puppy" and "Kitten" by Sandra Kuck, a set of two plates featuring Ms. Kuck's elegant and nostalgic child-and-pet art and graced with elaborate gold adornments. Both plates promptly sold out in editions of 7,500 each.

The *Premier Collection* continues with another McClelland specialty, a portrait of mother and child entitled "Love." And so popular were "Puppy" and "Kitten" that Sandra Kuck has followed up with a pair of girl-and-boy sequels: "La Belle," and "Le Beau."

Next, John McClelland indulged a lifelong dream of creating a Japanese-style bowl with "Cherry Blossom Viewing." Offered in a stunning gift box and richly decorated, this exquisite porcelain bowl is limited to just 750 pieces.

Home Studio to the Most Honored Plate Artist in History: Sandra Kuck

Since "Sunday Best" was introduced by Reco International and Sandra Kuck in 1983, the Reco-Kuck connection has been renowned as one of the strongest bonds in the limited edition world. When Ms. Kuck met Heio Reich, she was known primarily as a children's portraitist and gallery artist. Reich knew instinctively that Sandra Kuck's combination of Old Master colorations and detail with child subjects would capture the imagination of plate collectors.

"Sunday Best" won multiple honors including the coveted "Plate of the Year" and "Silver Chalice" awards. And it earned Ms. Kuck her very first "Artist of the Year" award from the National Association of Limited Edition Dealers (NALED). When she accepted this singular honor at the 1984 NALED Banquet in South Bend, Indiana, Ms. Kuck had no idea that another FIVE consecutive "Artist of the Year" honors — and many other coveted awards — would follow. This sustained leadership of the plate art field has made Ms. Kuck the "First Lady of Plates" — the most honored artist in collector plate history.

While Ms. Kuck still delights in creating her trademark portraits of children, she has branched

Jody Bergsma's "The Birth of a Dream" exemplifies her delightful fantasy style in a plate from her Castles And Dreams *collection for Reco International.*

out into various media and decorative styles with impressive results. She began a new Christmas series in 1992 entitled *Peace On Earth*, and in 1993, her *Gift Of Love* Mother's Day Collection premiered with "Morning Glory." In addition to its beautiful image, each plate in the *Gift Of Love* series will bear a Sandra Kuck remarque, or special drawing, of burnished gold. The popular *Hearts And Flowers* series of Sandra Kuck plates was completed in 1993, with a brand-new series in the works. What's more, Ms. Kuck's *Precious Memories Of Motherhood* collection of mother-child dolls was completed in 1992, with two issues already sold out.

John McClelland: A Reco Artist for More Than Fifteen Years

As Reco International celebrated its Silver Anniversary in 1992, the firm also marked fifteen years of cordial and productive association with a delightful southern gentleman and gifted American artist: John McClelland. Indeed, it was the art of John McClelland that first inspired Heio Reich to change the direction of Reco International during the 1970s. So impressed was Reich with the charming, child-subject paintings of McClelland that he changed from creating only traditional blue-and-white European-style plates to a full-color plate producer in order to introduce John McClelland originals on porcelain.

A great admirer of classic illustrators like J. C. Leyendecker, Norman Rockwell, Al Parker and Dean Cornwall, McClelland began his New York art career in the later years of the "Golden Age of Illustration." When illustrated magazines gave way to television in the early 1950s, McClelland turned his attention to portraiture, working from his Connecticut home. He also is renowned to millions as the painter of covers for the Miles Kimball catalog.

When John McClelland and Heio Reich introduced their first plate together, "Rainy Day Fun" became an overnight success. Collectors were hungry for paintings of children on porcelain, and they flocked to own this vision of a smiling child in her bright yellow slicker. McClelland's *Mother Goose* plate series, which began with "Mary, Mary," amplified his fame and won the artist a "Plate of the Year" award in 1980. Since then, Reco and McClelland have collaborated on works of art in various media including plates, figurines, dolls, and ornaments as well as the exceptional "Cherry Blossom Viewing" bowl.

Two new McClelland plate series have debuted in recent months through Reco International: *The Wonder Of Christmas* and *The Children's Garden*.

The Christmas series captures the fondest moments of children at holiday time, while the garden series is a must for all who love flowers and children. It captures the abundance of a southern garden in full bloom, as well as the innocent freshness of children.

The Wonderful Fantasy Art World of Jody Bergsma

When Reco plate artist Jody Bergsma was a child, her mother encouraged her to "draw her dreams" to overcome her youthful fears. It was an imaginative solution to a small problem — but it led to great things. Jody soon fell in love with sketching and painting, and she began to develop her unique artistic style. In addition, she found that she had been blessed with a very special gift: the ability to capture the fleeting, magical world which most of us see only in our dreams.

While she began selling paintings at the age of fifteen, Ms. Bergsma did not commit herself wholeheartedly to an art career until she traveled to Europe in 1978. There, drinking in the wonders of the Old Masters and Impressionists in Amsterdam's many galleries and museums, she vowed that she would create paintings to inspire other people. Today, Jody Bergsma works from her own sunny gallery in Bellingham, Washington, creating prints and plates that feature her trademark "little people."

Over the past few years, she has forged a successful association with Reco International to create the *Guardians Of The Kingdom* series, Christmas and Mother's Day plate series with annual issues such as the Mother's Day beauty for 1993: "My Greatest Treasure," and the newly introduced *Castles And Dreams* plate collection. A favorite with collectors, Ms. Bergsma often attends plate shows where her charm and unique perspective win her new admirers.

The Husband-and-Wife Team of Dot and Sy Barlowe

Since the 1940s, Dot and Sy Barlowe have collaborated in their art and in their lives. Equally gifted as artists, the pair have spent their married lives working on individual and dual projects that express their love for and deep understanding of the natural world.

The Barlowes' projects for Reco International include: *Town And Country Dogs*, a series of portraits of favorite breeds in beautiful, natural settings; and *Our Cherished Seas*, depicting the life and natural beauty of our oceans.

A New Artist Joins the Reco Studio: Judy York

Judy York already enjoyed nationwide fame for her very realistic portraits of nostalgic family moments when Reco International commissioned her for collector plates. The first York-Reco collaboration is a series entitled *The Heart Of The Family*. The premier issues, "Sharing Secrets" and "Spinning Dreams," are outstanding images depicting the home and family as the center of activity, in a lovely period setting.

Ms. York creates vignettes which draw you into the world she has created — visually and emotionally. Her work is consistently in high demand in the field of fine art graphic prints for this very reason. Collector response to her first collection of plates has been just as positive.

Versatility Keeps Reco at the Top of the Market

Reco International also enjoys fruitful associations with a number of renowned and talented plate artists including: Clemente Micarelli, creator of *The Nutcracker Ballet* series; Garri Katz, painter for *Great Stories Of The Bible*; and Inge Dreschler, artist for a series of tranquil landscapes called *God's Own Country*.

In addition Reco has produced the beloved works of the late Cicely Mary Barker in a *Flower Fairies Year* plate collection. Special occasion plates, music boxes, and figurines by Sandra Kuck and John McClelland, and the *Sophisticated Ladies* collection of cat plates, figurines and musicals by Aldo Fazio, round out this prolific studio's recent line.

As one of the first American firms to sense the true potential for limited edition plates, Reco International strives to remain on the "cutting edge" of today's art collectibles world. Under the strong guidance of Heio Reich, Reco pledges to remain a versatile and innovative leader among limited edition studios.

Clemente Micarelli's inspiring image of this revered event is the first in his series, The Glory Of Christ.

Roman, Inc.

After Thirty Years...Roman Continues Creating the Makings of Tradition — Tomorrow's Collectibles Today

Thirty years ago, Ronald Jedlinski started his company behind his father's retail giftware store and developed a "game plan" that would make his own business dreams come true. Beginning Roman, Inc. as a wholesaler of religious products, Jedlinski always envisioned a mission for his firm that extended far beyond the Chicago-based enterprise. With his combination of hard work, ambition and vision, Jedlinski soon earned a coveted opportunity: Roman became the exclusive North American source for the creations of the famous House of Fontanini in Tuscany, Italy.

While religious works such as the *Fontanini® Heirloom Nativities* have always played a strong and enduring role in the Roman tradition, Jedlinski and his staff now work with an impressively diverse roster of artists from around the world. Today the Roman line reflects all of life's rich and varied family experiences in its subject matter, including children, marriage, relationships, history and religion.

Renowned as the "home studio" for the beloved collectibles artist, Frances Hook, Roman now works with a wide range of award-winning painters and sculptors including Barbi Sargent, Elio Simonetti, Irene Spencer, Angela Tripi, Abbie Williams, Ellen Williams and Richard Judson Zolan. Their works emerge as figurines, hanging ornaments, plates, dolls and bells crafted in a variety of media.

Celebrated Illustrator Barbi Sargent Creates Tender Expressions

Barbi Sargent's claim to being "one of the most reproduced artists in the world" is bolstered by her impressive credentials after nearly thirty years in the greeting card, children's book and gift fields. Indeed, it seems that nearly everyone has, at one time, given or received a Barbi Sargent greeting card, children's book, figure or toy. Her latest creation, a captivating character named "Sunshine," debuts in Ms. Sargent's delightful new message collection for Roman, Inc.: *Tender Expressions* from the Heart.

"Sunshine" is a sweet child, accompanied by her

Fontanini, the Italian crafter of heirloom nativities, breaks new ground for Roman, Inc. with this Victorian Bristol Falls Carolers Society collection. Here we see "Fountain Square," the gathering site for the charming community's early residents, complete with facades for a church, store, house and town sign.

playmates, animal friends and a bluebird. Together they express special sentiments of friendship and love. And "Sunshine" brings more than brightness and smiles to faces. Ms. Sargent has designated a sculpture of "Sunshine" for dedication to the young patients of the world-famous Cleveland Clinic Foundation Children's Hospital.

"The courageous youngsters in the Cleveland Clinic Children's Hospital motivated me to create the 'Sunshine' character," Ms. Sargent comments. "I will donate all my royalties from sales of the 'Thoughts of You are in My Heart' figure towards the very vital work and programs for children at The Cleveland Clinic Foundation." Roman is supplementing Barbi's wonderful support for The Cleveland Clinic Foundation by matching her donations dollar for dollar.

The Fontanini Tradition Continues With Master Sculptor Elio Simonetti

Since 1908, the Fontaninis of Northern Italy have been renowned for superb nativities. Now Elio Simonetti continues this tradition for Fontanini and Roman with a newly sculpted Three Kings that upholds this celebrated artistic heritage. Simonetti's royal procession is lavished with opulent detail. Skilled artists paint each polymer

figure in dramatic colors accented with gold, while a process of antiquing adds further dimension to each piece.

Simonetti has been the Fontanini master sculptor for over forty years. From the very beginning, his works were lauded for his magical touch for infusing them with lifelike qualities. It was this mastery that first attracted the attention of Mario Fontanini, then head of the Fontanini business. Over the past four decades, Fontanini and Simonetti have collaborated on the creation of stunning Nativity figures in a variety of sizes from the miniature 2¹/₂" figures to the stunning four-foot-tall masterpieces. Their beauty is appreciated throughout the world by critics and collectors alike.

Considered his crowning achievement, Simonetti is especially proud of his life-sized sculptures for the 50" *Fontanini*® *Heirloom Nativity*. When the Fontanini family presented a gift of the life-sized Nativity to Pope John Paul II, the Pontiff expressed his admiration of the exquisite beauty of Simonetti's masterpieces with the statement, "I hope God grants him long life to continue his fantastic sculpting." Today, these figures bring joy to the Pope in his private Vatican quarters.

With skill acquired from years of working in her specialty of clay, Angela Tripi shaped the figures for her first limited-edition Nativity to meet her demanding standards. After firing and painting by hand, she clothes her creations in garments fashioned from real fabric, then fixes the costumes to a hard finish using a secret family formula dating back hundreds of years. Limited to 2,500 sets, this inspirational eight-piece Nativity set carries a suggested retail price of $425. Height of tallest figure is 8".

New from Fontanini is a tribute to turn-of-the-century America with the *Bristol Falls Carolers Society*: a collection of characters ready to serenade their town with holiday carols.

Italian Artist Angela Tripi Creates The Museum Collection

Determination and a lifelong dream have brought Italy's Angela Tripi to her current status as a world-class artist with a growing U.S. collector following. Today, Ms. Tripi fulfills her aspirations by creating masterpiece sculptures in her workshop in Palermo, Sicily. Her works have captivated audiences on both sides of the Atlantic. Her *Museum Collection Of Angela Tripi* earned Collectible of the Show in the sculpture category at a recent Long Beach Collectible Exposition in California.

Before catching Jedlinski's perceptive eye, Ms. Tripi achieved recognition with major exhibitions in Italy, France and Japan. In 1988, her first efforts for Roman were Biblical: Old Testament subjects. Next, Tripi ventured into secular themes including the 500th anniversary of Christopher Columbus' voyage, masterful representations of golf's early days, and — for 1993 and 1994 — early Americana, professionals, collectible Santas, clowns, angels, a limited edition nativity and an annual angel ornament.

Angela Tripi is anything but an overnight success. Indeed, she toiled in an office by day for fifteen years, all the while contemplating working after hours at what she loved best: devoting all her spare time to perfecting her sculpting techniques.

"Faces, expressions, dialogues with people…all my experiences are stored in my soul," Ms. Tripi explains of her figures whose faces she imbues with so much character. "When I create my works, I withdraw from the world around me, looking inwards. I draw on all those feelings, memories, images…working them into my subjects."

Abbie Williams — A Gifted Portrayer of Children

The late Frances Hook's works were already beloved among collectors of plates and figurines when she recommended her protege and friend, Abbie Williams, to Roman. The resulting relationship has inspired a wide range of collectible plates with art by Abbie Williams — featuring her favorite subjects: children.

Ms. Williams' initial collector plate series, *The Magic Of Childhood*, portrayed the special friendships only children and animals enjoy. She fol-

lowed with two Christian-themed series, *The Lord's Prayer* and *Love's Prayer*. Her delightful newest series is entitled *Precious Children*.

Abbie Williams' ability to capture the spontaneity of children in her art extends to a series of sculptured music boxes, *Children Of The Month*; a special March of Dimes fund-raising edition, "A Time to Laugh," in association with The Bradford Exchange; and the "Mary, Mother of the Carpenter" lithograph which was presented to Pope John Paul II at the Vatican.

Williams has also created *Legacy Of Love, Bless This Child* for Black American collectors and gift givers and a captivating plate series devoted to "firsts" in babies' lives, *God Bless You, Little One*. In addition, Ms. Williams has introduced her first collector doll, "Molly," in association with Roman and The Hamilton Collection.

Ellen Williams Captures Hearts With '90s Bridal Editions

Popular bridal artist Ellen Williams has delighted collectors with her eagerly anticipated "Stephanie Helen"—the 1990s Bride, for her award-winning *Classic Brides Of The Century*™ collection. Ms. Williams drew on her interest in historic fashion to create this porcelain bisque series depicting bridal fashion as a reflection of historical and social trends from 1900 though the 1990s.

Limited edition bridal dolls based on *Classic Brides Of The Century* — further demonstrating the artist's signature theme of fashion reflecting social trends — are "Flora" — the 1900s Bride (NALED "Doll of the Year" 2nd Runner-Up), "Jennifer"—the 1980s Bride and "Kathleen"—the 1930s Bride.

A history of wedding traditions also is traced by Ms. Williams' bridal couples collection representing the decades from 1900 to 1990. *Love Everlasting*™ and *Wedding Portraits*, Ms. Williams' unique collections of heirloom portrayals of musical and non-musical bridal couples, captures them in romantic poses.

Foremost American Impressionist Zolan Makes Roman Debut

As one of the nation's exceptional painters, Richard Judson Zolan brings his sterling reputation as an established American Impressionist talent to his commissions for Roman, Inc.

Electricity of color and motion rivets the attention and draws the viewer into Richard Judson Zolan's Victorian garden fantasy, "The Butterfly Net." Shown here is the artwork in a limited edition collector plate, but this same Romantic Impressionist image also has inspired a photo frame, an ornament, framed plaque, vase, mug, music box, bell, mini-plate and print from Roman, Inc.

Strongly influenced by Monet, Renoir, Degas and other nineteenth-century French Impressionists, Zolan describes his work as Romantic American Impressionism.

Roman now brings Zolan's artistry to a wider audience for enjoyment throughout the home, for collecting and for special occasion gift giving. The full range of decorative and functional items splendidly reflects the unsurpassable elegance of Zolan's illustrations of "Summer at the Seashore," "The Butterfly Net," "Best Friends" and "The Antique Doll." There are collector plates, plaques, frames, ornaments, mugs, vases, music boxes, bells, mini-plates, figurines and prints available in this extensive and exquisite new line: a tribute to the genius of Richard Judson Zolan and the enduring glory of the Impressionist style.

With worldwide associations and the strong visionary leadership of Ron Jedlinski, Roman embarks on another thirty years of art mastery. In the decades to come, collectors can look forward to a marvelous array of decorative art from the international resources of Roman, Inc.

Ron Lee's World of Clowns
The Beginnings of a Clown Adventure

As the last vestige of sun slips behind the trees, its final glow filters through the windows focusing on a huge room abundantly decorated with every conceivable clown artifact. Like a spotlight capturing an entertainer, the elongated rays pinpoint an artist intently at work. Concentrating on the mass of clay in one hand, and the small tool in the other, a new clown creation soon emerges from the creative mind and talented fingers of Ron Lee.

In a household filled with active sounds of his family, Hobo Joe was born. So were "Puppy Love," "Snowdrifter," "Heartbroken Harry" and countless numbers of clown characters. Thriving in a room bursting with his energy as well as that of his wife and four children, Ron diligently follows an arduous daily routine that could easily include sculpting a new figurine, sketching a life-size carousel animal, writing a newsletter for his Collector's Club, making a personal appearance at a collectible shop, or helping to raise money for charity. His almost hyper personality is apparent as four, five or even six ideas could be hatching at the same time. While his highly competent staff has difficulty keeping up with such a busy schedule, Ron avows it's the "only way to go." If you ask Ron Lee why he chose sculpting instead of other forms of art, he will tell you, "I need to be able to touch, to feel, to turn, to lift, to know it has dimension, a sense of reality. Even though the figurines I create are, what would you say, fanciful, if I could hold them in my hands, to me they suddenly become alive; they take on life and seem real, almost like children to be cherished and cared for."

Ron Lee Introduces Clowns, Clowns, and More Clowns

Recently establishing himself as the foremost sculptor of classic cartoon character limited edition sculptures, early in 1993 Ron returned to basics, introducing throughout the year more than fifty new clowns focusing on the traditional antics of the circus. "Although I enjoy creating wonderful cartoon characters in three dimensions and in complete scenes, I really felt a need to get back to my 'clowning around' roots," he stated candidly. Presented in a broad spectrum of primary and pastel colors, the clowns range in size from five to

One of Ron Lee's most popular characters, Hobo Joe, can now be enjoyed in a five-part plate series. The first in this series is "No Vacancy," produced in the finest quality porcelain, heavily gold banded, individually numbered and certificated.

eight inches high. There are clowns with cars, clowns with boats, clowns with trains, clowns with planes, and just clowns being clowns. Lollipop colored favorites catch your eye, as balloons and umbrellas are flying high. There's the *High Five* collection, as well as *Step Right Up*, which features the larger more prominent figurines. *Clowns, Clowns and More Clowns* feature a grouping of smaller, but equally detailed sculptures. As spring approached, a collection of *18 Hilarious Par Excellence* sculptures featuring a potpourri of dazzling and cheerful clown sculptures, small in stature but big in design, were introduced. Continuing on through the year, there was a *Trio of Elegance*, three designs based upon a new concept focusing on a more elegantly attired clown, in scenes conceived in a more delicate surrounding. The more traditional clown is viewed in *All Around Clowns*, which features the "Merry go Clown," a beautiful carousel horse and rider, both magnificent in stature and design. All of Ron Lee's sculptures are individually hand-painted by a staff of hand-picked artists, and are limited to very low edition sizes.

Ron Lee Announces Premier Collection Selling Out As Quickly As Offered

The *Ron Lee Premier Collection*, which was first introduced nationwide in October 1992, has reached sold out status with the first four collections. These prestigious designs can only be purchased through bona fide premier dealers who subscribe to the program. This first exclusive series of clowns featuring Ron Lee's alter ego, "Hobo Joe" secured sales and continued requests beyond the expectations of both the creator and his Premier Dealers. The second offering, "Pockets," also sold out almost simultaneously with its introduction, as well as the third and fourth collections. Premier Dealer offerings have limited edition sizes of only 500, thus the demand far exceeds the supply. The program consists of four collections to be introduced each year, and all sculptures bear the distinction of being individually hand-painted, and being reproduced in fine metal and pewter, enhanced by 24k gold plating. Some of the larger figurines are reproduced in a fine quality resin called polyron. The high rate of success of this program ensures its continuance for many years to come.

Meticulously detailed "Metropolis," one of four exciting Superman sculptures by Ron Lee, is mounted on imported charcoal grey onyx lending itself to the stalwart image of our hero as he leaps tall buildings. Colorfully hand-painted, the edition size is a very low 750.

Ron Lee Expands His World To Include Limited Edition Plates

Ron Lee, recognized sculptor of heirloom quality cartoon characters, clown and circus-theme collectibles, introduced his own series of collectors plates focusing on his famous "Hobo Joe" clown character in 1992. "I waited to present this series because I wanted to convey a special feeling in the designs. Whenever I create art, whether a single sculpture or a scene featuring numerous characters, I strive to evoke emotion that will translate to all the viewers of my work," commented Ron Lee. These plates have evolved into vividly colored plates accented and trimmed in gold depicting complete scenes featuring the antics of that lovable hero of the downtrodden, Hobo Joe. Working to deliver the utmost quality in collectible plates, Ron Lee will present a total of five irresistible designs that will certainly complement his collectible Hobo Joe clown sculptures.

"Look! Up In the Sky!" "It's a Bird!" "It's a Plane!" "It's Superman!"

Beside returning to clown characters, Ron Lee, master artist and sculptor, could not resist the temptation to create original limited edition sculptures of the most famous comic book hero of all time, Superman. All the excitement and glory of the Man of Steel is brought to life in this new action line reminding us all of our childhood when heroes were heroes and villains were truly bad guys. Four classic moments in Superman history are meticulously detailed, individually hand-painted, and mounted on imported charcoal-grey onyx. The sculptures are offered in limited editions of 750 each.

A Television Star Is Born

This year Ron Lee made several appearances on QVC, entertaining all those who watched with his outgoing manner, spontaneous wit and candid charm. Presenting some of his finest work to a television audience gave him the opportunity to reach the many thousands of people who have been collecting his sculptures for many years. As Lee explains, "Clowns have been a way of life to me almost my whole life, and to be able to convey this to so many people in such a short span of time is not just a dream but a fantasy come true. How many people get to live their fantasies?" The man, his work, his energy, his life — all of it emerges in the whimsical and good-natured clown characters that could very easily be called Ron Lee.

A trio of "elegant hobos," representing a brand new character designed by Ron Lee, is depicted in three separate poses. From left to right, these delightful clowns are doing an old "Softshoe," presenting a gift for that "Special Occasion," and as "The Wanderer" preparing to hitch a ride. Hand-painted in brilliant colors, the collection has a limited edition size of only 750.

The Ron Lee Premier Collection, introduced a year ago, has met with phenomenal success. The third series featured the character Jake in three different scenes, "Jake-A-Juggling Cylinder," "Jake-A-Juggling Clubs" and "Jake-A-Juggling Balls." Limited to only 500 pieces, these highly specialized sculptures are available through Premier Dealers only.

The Royal Copenhagen Group
Bing & Grondahl and Royal Copenhagen…
and the History of Plate Collecting

Many generations ago, Europe's elite developed a charming Christmas custom. At holiday time they would gift each of their servants with a platter of delicious fruit, cookies, candies and other tasty treats. In the early years of this tradition, it seems that the platters were little more than crude wooden slabs: the food was the focus of attention. The idea was to bring a spark of happiness into the lives of people who had very little, by providing them with the makings of a holiday feast.

The servants were delighted with their Christmas bounty, and they even looked forward to receiving the simple platters on which their treats arrived. So much so that they began to hang the platters on their walls as decorations to enjoy all year long. They called these utilitarian vessels their "Christmas Plates."

When they noticed the servants of one household showing off their Christmas plates to the employees of another, the wealthy realized that a rivalry was developing. Who would receive the most elegant plates? This became a matter of status among the servants, and the employers were quick to add fuel to the fire. They began to take more care in the selection of the platters themselves, so that their gifts could become a lasting symbol of appreciation to their recipients. Platters of shining metal, carved wood and decoratively painted pottery replaced the simple vessels of the earlier days.

Now the wealthy began to try to outdo each other as well, devoting more and more attention to the platters and less and less to their contents. Eventually they started dating each platter so that it could become a special memento of the year of receipt. Thus the custom of making and collecting Christmas Plates began. And central to the "collectibility factor" of Christmas plates was Harald Bing, then president of the famed Danish porcelain firm of Bing & Grondahl.

As Ole Simonsen, Bing & Grondahl's former president, recalled, "When my grandfather, the late Harald Bing, in 1895 conceived the idea of the world's first Christmas plate, he wanted not only to create a Christmas greeting or gift of particular quality and beauty, but also a series of Danish sceneries, historic buildings, etc., that would appeal to collectors all over the world and at the same time make them interested in his beloved mother country." Simonsen stressed that his grandfather's goal was to bring the history and customs of Denmark, "the world's oldest kingdom," to collectors everywhere.

A Brief History of Bing & Grondahl

Bing & Grondahl already was Denmark's well-established National Factory of Porcelain when Harald Bing introduced the concept of collecting plates at Christmastime. Copenhagen was still a small town when the firm was established in 1853.

Frederik Vilhelm Grondahl was a young sculptor for The Royal Copenhagen Porcelain Manufactory in the mid-1850s. When he suggested that figurines created by the renowned sculptor Thorvaldsen be copied in unglazed "biscuit" porcelain, his employers disagreed. Frustrated by what he saw as their lack of foresight, Grondahl took his ambitious ideas to M. H. and J. H. Bing, the owners of a successful store selling stationery, books and art objects. The business expertise of the Bings and the art mastery of Grondahl made a potent combination, and before long, the Bing & Grondahl Porcelain Factory was born.

One of Bing & Grondahl's major discoveries was the secret of underglaze painting. Before 1886, the firm had made many elegant pieces such as dinnerware, figurines and vases, but these had always been crafted of either "biscuit" or overglaze porcelain. After perfecting their unique underglaze technique, Bing & Grondahl created quite a furor at the Paris World Fair in 1889, with its stunning new "Heron" service, designed by Pietro Krohn, and crafted using underglaze painting.

Bing & Grondahl was incorporated in 1895. That same year, Harald Bing conceived his idea for the Christmas plate, using the underglaze technique in blue and white. The introduction of that first plate, "Behind the Frozen Window," marked history's first commercial production of Christmas plates.

"Behind the Frozen Window" was placed on the market shortly before Christmas and bore the inscription "Jule Aften 1895" (Christmas Eve

286

This is the plate that began Christmas plate collecting: Bing & Grøndahl's 1895 "Behind the Frozen Window." Crafted in blue-and-white porcelain underglaze, the plate cost just 50 cents when Harald Bing unveiled it to his Danish public. Today — on the rare occasion that one of the plates becomes available at auction — it would be expected to command as much as $5,500.

1895). Every year since, despite two World Wars and a devastating Depression, a seven-inch, blue-and-white plate has been introduced. Orders for the Christmas Plates are accepted from dealers and distributors only through June 30 of each year. After Christmas all molds are destroyed, preventing any later reproduction, and enhancing value to collectors. Indeed, the first Bing & Grøndahl Christmas Plate, which sold for 50 cents in 1895, today commands a price as high as $5,500 on the secondary market as excitement increases for the 1995 Centennial of Bing & Grøndahl plate collecting.

The Historic Origins of the Royal Copenhagen Porcelain Manufactory

The Chinese secret formula for "white gold," or porcelain, was still a closely guarded secret when members of Denmark's Royal Family vowed to "crack the code" during the 1760s. In competition with the Royal Families of other European nations, the Danes wished to have the most elegant dinnerware and decorative items available, custom-designed to their taste. In a dramatic effort to discover their own porcelain formula, the Danish Royals summoned Louis Fournier, the renowned French sculptor and ceramist. Fournier embarked upon experiment after experiment, but to the frustration of all involved he enjoyed little success.

Finally, triumph arrived at the hand of Franz Heinrich Muller, a Danish pharmacist and chemist, who happened upon the secret of true hardpaste porcelain in 1772.

Muller swiftly submitted samples of his discovery to the Queen Dowager, Juliane Marie. So enthralled was she with Muller's work that she christened his firm "the Danish Porcelain Factory." Founded in January 1775, this organization originally enjoyed several enthusiastic shareholders. By April 1779, however, it fell under the complete control of the Danish Monarchy.

Because of Denmark's international renown as a seafaring nation, the Factory's trademark was developed as three wavy lines, symbolizing the ancient Danish waterways from the Kattegat to the Baltic: the Sound, the Great Belt and the Little Belt. Before long, the trademark and the creations of the Danish Porcelain Factory brought an emotional resurgence of national pride to the people of Denmark.

Arnold Krog, an architect, became art director of Royal Copenhagen in January 1885, and proceeded to develop a fine technique for Danish underglaze painting. This method became the basis for the Royal Copenhagen blue-and-white Christmas Plate series, an annual collection which debuted in 1908 with "Madonna and Child" and continues to this day.

Each Royal Copenhagen Christmas plate bears the date of its year of issue, and is crafted for only one year. When that time period is up, the molds

"Madonna and Child" was the first Royal Copenhagen Christmas Plate, introduced in 1908.

Hand-painting brings the blue-and-white underglaze technique alive. Here, a painter at the Royal Copenhagen factory completes work on a plate.

are destroyed so that the plate can never be made again.

From the series' initiation, Royal Copenhagen Christmas plate subject matter has been selected from suggestions submitted by employees of the manufactory. At first, only a few special underglaze painters were permitted to submit work, but now every employee of Royal Copenhagen is eligible to apply. Prizes as well as worldwide notoriety await the yearly winners.

The Remarkable Process of Danish Underglaze Painting

The technique developed by Arnold Krog remains to this day the method employed by skilled collector plate artists — both at Royal Copenhagen and at Bing & Grondahl. Indeed, plates made using this method are still the only collections in the world produced and finished by hand. One unique aspect of this art style is that the painter utilizes various tones of a single color, originally only blue. Eventually brown and pale green versions were developed as well. The genius of the process lies in the fact that when the artist applies the color, no variations of shade can be discerned.

Shades can be distinguished only by the thickness of the pigment layers, which are brought out in the high-temperature firing process. Copenhagen blue-and-white Christmas Plates, for example, are fired at about 2640 degrees Fahrenheit. When the plates are exposed to this temperature, their glazes fuse and become as transparent as

glass. The color in all its variations — which was not visible before — now appears distinctly under the glaze.

Other Notable Achievements of "B&G"

While Christmas plates were the initial claims to international collectible fame both for Bing & Grondahl and Royal Copenhagen, each firm has enjoyed many other successes as well. Bing & Grondahl, for example, initiated the world's first Mother's Day plate series in 1969 with "Dog and Puppies." The collection continues with popular annual issues to this day. Royal Copenhagen also produced a very popular *Motherhood* plate series from 1982 to 1987.

Although Bing & Grondahl and Royal Copenhagen have exchanged technicians and artists over the years, their Christmas plates and other elegant issues have maintained their distinctive styles, which are obvious to the discerning collector. Even today when Bing & Grondahl and Royal Copenhagen have merged, their plates are decorated by two different methods at two different locations. No other Christmas plates in the world have ever come close to the popularity of the Danish Christmas plates. Part of their strength is due to tradition, part to artistic brilliance. But perhaps most important of all is the fact that these are the only truly hand-decorated plates in the world of collectibles.

In addition to creating the first Christmas plate, Bing & Grondahl initiated the concept of Mother's Day plate collecting with this first issue, "Dog and Puppies," from 1969. Like the Christmas plates, this work of art — and each yearly issue since — has been crafted in blue-and-white underglaze.

Royal Doulton
Prestige Figurines and Classic Character Jugs Pay Tribute to War and Battle Heroes from Many Nations

"We don't play it safe," Eric Griffiths, Royal Doulton's now-retired Art Director for Ceramic Sculpture once said. "The impetus comes from always reaching out for something a little beyond our grasp. Sculpture is ninety-five percent craft. The rules can be learned fairly quickly, but it's what you do that's important, and making it say something people can relate to. Artists are communicators."

For generations, the famed British firm of Royal Doulton has been renowned for its figurines, Character Jugs, and other innovative, three-dimensional works of art. Today, the Royal Doulton Figure Collection is extraordinary in its diversity and scope, yet its international appeal lies in the individuality of each piece.

Each is a character in its own right — caught for a moment in part of its own story. The expressiveness of the face's fine detail and the impression of movement, so skillfully captured in clay, give a convincing window on an intriguing ideal world.

It is a world that has attracted many thousands of collectors, most of whom started off with a solitary figure but were drawn by the myriad of themes into a lifetime's passion. Each new design is eagerly awaited, each withdrawal from the range noted. Yet such a band of loyal cognoscenti has not lulled Royal Doulton's designers into complacency. As Griffiths noted, they always endeavor to approach each project from a fresh point of view.

Most of the artists who design the figures work from their own studios, coming in once a month for discussions with the art director. "It's a creative gossip really," Griffith said. These meetings ensure that the artist stays in touch with the practicalities of production and remains within the general directions decided by the company.

The Studio has an outline of how many figures, in what categories, will be required in the next year or so, but always requests between two and three times as many prototypes to choose from. Many figures get no further than the prototype stage; others are tried in different poses and colors before they capture that special ingredient.

"Ulysses S. Grant" and "Robert E. Lee" are two handsome figurines from Royal Doulton created to commemorate the 130th anniversary of the Battle of Gettysburg.

The "Abraham Lincoln" Character Jug portrays the distinctive features of the 16th President of the United States.

The Royal Doulton War and Battle Heroes

Capturing the imagination of collectors on both sides of the Atlantic recently have been the Royal Doulton *War And Battle Heroes*, with eight subjects introduced to date. All are limited editions, with strict numerical limitations. Considering the enthusiastic response of collectors to the first eight subjects, Royal Doulton promises more heroes in the months and years to come. So far, the figurines and Character Jugs introduced celebrate battles fought and wars won during a span of 140 years, from 1805 to 1945. Here are some descriptions of *War And Battle Heroes* works of art.

"Vice Admiral Lord Horatio Nelson" represents the 1993 Character Jug of the Year. Nelson is considered one of Britain's greatest military heroes, having had spectacular success in battle, combined with humanity as a commander. In 1805, Nelson commanded the British flagship, The Victory, against the French and Spanish fleets at the Battle of Trafalgar off the coast of Spain. He was fatally wounded in the battle, but lived long enough to see that the combined fleets were destroyed. This naval success inspired by Nelson ended Napoleon's control of the sea and played a major role in Napoleon's ultimate defeat.

Royal Doulton's superb jug depicts Nelson in full dress uniform wearing his portfolio of medals and awards. A patch covers his right eye which was lost in battle in 1797. His ship, The Victory, forms the intricate handle. The Vice Admiral Lord Nelson Jug retails for $225.

Napoleon's ultimate defeat came in 1815 at the hands of the "Duke of Wellington" at the Battle of Waterloo. Thus, this new prestige figure is designed as a companion piece to the "Napoleon" figure launched in the Fall of 1992. Waterloo, one of the most famous battles of modern history, took place in Belgium on June 18, 1815. Napoleon's force totalled some 72,000, while Wellington led 68,000 men. By defeating Napoleon at Waterloo, the Duke ended the Napoleonic Wars and became famous as "the conqueror of the world's conqueror."

This handsome, twelve-inch figure features Wellington with a metal sword and scabbard. The design around the base depicts scenes from the battle, as well as Wellington's horse Copenhagen. With a worldwide edition limit of 1,500, the Duke of Wellington figure retails for $1750.

The Battle of Gettysburg, the greatest battle ever fought on American soil, marked the turning point of the Civil War. To commemorate the 130th anniversary of the decisive battle (July 1-3,

1863), companion figurines of "Lieutenant General Ulysses S. Grant" and "General Robert E. Lee" have been introduced as limited editions of 5,000 each.

Prior to the Civil War, Grant and Lee were good friends. In fact, Lee was invited to lead the Northern Army before Grant. Instead, Lee returned home to lead the Southern Army, which was outnumbered four to one. Grant's strength was his ability to organize large numbers of men. While he became the 18th President on March 4, 1869, a position he held until 1887, he never again enjoyed the success of his military years. Lee, a Southerner who did not believe in slavery, rejected warfare as a means to resolve political conflict.

These intricate figures portray Grant and Lee at the Battle of Gettysburg dressed in full military attire. Grant stands in front of a log fence over which a Union flag is draped. He holds a map outlining battle details in his left hand. Lee is shown in front of a broken wagon wheel draped with a Confederate flag. He carries a pair of binoculars in his right hand and holds his hat and gloves in his left. Each figure retails for $1175.

"Abraham Lincoln," the 16th President of the United States, is honored as the first issue in a new United States exclusive collection of large size Character Jugs celebrating U.S. Presidents. On March 4, 1861, Lincoln was inaugurated as President. Just thirty-nine days later, on April 13, the War Between the States began. Lincoln's term of office was during the most desperate years in the history of the United States. His goal was to save the Union because to him the Union was the only important democratic government in the world.

The "Abraham Lincoln" Jug is an excellent likeness of Lincoln, capturing his thin, gaunt features. The handle incorporates the Union flag and the first line from the Gettysburg Address, a literary masterpiece delivered during the dedication of the Soldiers National Cemetery at Gettysburg. The jug retails for $190 and has an edition limit of 2,500 pieces.

Two new "Winston Churchill" pieces represent World War II. The first is a powerful figure with an edition limit of 5,000 pieces. Churchill made frequent appearances and impromptu speeches throughout London during World War II. It was these visits and meetings with the blitz victims that raised the spirit of the British people and banished any thoughts of surrender.

Royal Doulton's newest figure depicts "Winston Churchill" surveying the bomb damage to an East

End London street. A metal walking stick further enhances the pose. The time is 1940 when Churchill was sixty-six years old and installed as Prime Minister for the first time. The retail price is $595.

Following the success of the 1992 Character Jug of the Year depicting "Winston Churchill," a new small size Character Jug of the charismatic wartime leader joins the range. Here, Churchill is shown wearing a characteristic black and white polka dot bow tie and smoking one of his beloved cigars. A reproduction of the now defunct "News Chronicle" newspaper headline from May 8, 1945 proclaiming "Today is V Day" forms the unusual handle. The suggested retail price is $95.

Royal Doulton Combines Tradition and Innovation

The Royal Doulton artists who paint the colorful costumes and subtle skin tones of the Figure Collection are maintaining a tradition that goes back to the 19th century. During the 1890s, one of the company's most distinguished Art Directors, Charles Noke, modeled the earliest examples — "Cardinal Wolsey" and "Queen Catherine." By 1909 Noke was keen to revive the genre of Staffordshire figures and the first productions, based on classical and literary themes, caused a stir among critics.

More extensive production of figure series began in 1920 after Doulton received rave notices at the British Industries Fair. Since then, new additions have constantly been designed, and more than 1,000 different figures have been created. They range from limited editions and the elaborate prestige figures such as "Princess Badoura" to the popular *London Street Sellers*. The "Old Balloon Seller," for example, has remained in production for sixty years.

"Winston Churchill" is presented in the form of a figurine surveying the World War II bomb damage to an East End London street.

The Royal Doulton Figure Collection is now more varied and extensive than ever, with over 240 subjects. Introductions in the last few years have included the stylized *Images* collection, a more abstract concept of the human figure, and most recently, miniature ladies with all the movement and detail of their "big sisters" caught in figures less than four inches tall — a real tribute to the skill, craftsmanship and experience of all those who contribute to their production.

Sarah's Attic

Sarah Schultz Expresses Ideals of Love, Respect and Dignity in Charming Figurines That Capture the Diversity of America

"I couldn't believe it! I cried through the presentation," Sarah Schultz recalls of the big moment she won Michigan's coveted award for Wholesale/Retail Entrepreneur of the Year. "All of the people here have worked very hard for this. I couldn't have won this award without the help of so many people." Featured in *Inc.* magazine for her firm's accomplishments, Schultz and all at Sarah's Attic were honored for their history, their financial growth and their community involvement.

Sarah Schultz never could have imagined that her motherly quest to create funds for her childrens' college education and a new family room couch would result in such a thriving business. But Sarah's Attic began for the mother of five when she realized that the art she created "just for fun" might provide some nice "extras" for the growing Schultz clan.

The year was 1983, and Mrs. Schultz was working in her husband's pharmacy in picturesque Chesaning, Michigan. Her main responsibility was managing the gift department. She observed that the best-selling products were her own original creations: items such as stenciled slates, boards, pictures and a few sweet-faced dolls. Sarah often traveled to gift shows throughout the country looking for unique items for the gift department. In Charlotte, North Carolina, a sales representative complimented her on her tote bag, which Sarah had stenciled herself. He encouraged her to market her works, but at first the thought seemed overwhelming.

Later that evening, Sarah's thoughts drifted home to her husband and children. Her oldest son would be starting college in the fall, with four more young Schultzes to follow. Wouldn't it be nice to bring in a little extra money…and perhaps replace that shabby old couch? The next time the sales rep approached Sarah, she readily agreed.

With the help of her family, friends and a few employees, work on the first Sarah's Attic "Granny's Favorites" designs began on the Schultz dining room table. Because Sarah is a firm believer in Love, Respect and Dignity, a heart was painted on each piece to symbolize her trademark of quality and originality. In 1984, she moved her business to the back room of her husband's pharmacy.

Painting, staining and packing were all done in this 15' x 20' room.

By 1984, the growing studio moved to 1,200 square feet of space directly above the pharmacy: literally "Sarah's Attic." Then by 1986, *Sarah's Gang* was born in the form of child-subject pecan resin figurines, replacing stenciled rulers and slates as the company's top sellers. Sarah's Attic has now grown to over 1,000 figurines and is still growing. Each figurine is carefully researched and planned before it is molded to Sarah's satisfaction. As it comes to life, each is given a name and a title. What's more, many of the figurines have cute stories behind them.

The expansion of Sarah's Attic required several moves during the 1980s, with a "home" for the 1990s consisting of a 10,000 square-foot remodeled former grocery store. The art room, mail room and business offices still remain in the "Attic," however. It comes as no surprise that Sarah Schultz has worked fourteen to fifteen-hour work days for some time, but as she says, "I'm trying to slow down a little. I'm learning to delegate." All of her five children have worked for Sarah's Attic in one way or another, and son Tim is now Sarah's right-hand man, serving as vice-president of the firm. Her daughter Julie is also a part of the Sarah's Attic family, serving as national sales manager.

The golden, heart-filled moments expressed in these "Beary Adorables" from Sarah's Attic include, from left to right: "I Miss You Beary Much," "You're Beary Huggable," "I'm Beary Sorry" and "Your Beary Special." The bears range in size from 2¹/₂" to 3⁷/₈", and each sells for $18.

Childhood Memories Fuel
Sarah Schultz's Creativity

The new home of Sarah's Attic overlooks the same river where Sarah and her father used to fish when she was a young girl. Each time Sarah walks into her thriving studio, with a family of 100 workers creating her designs, her heart still flutters to see how far her beloved business has come in such a very short time. Sarah Schultz is especially proud of the fact that all of her products are made completely in the U.S.A., and that she has been able to provide employment opportunities for so many people of diverse skills and talents. Often, however, her mind drifts back to the 1950s when she was the first paper girl in Chesaning, Michigan history.

Sarah's childhood was not an easy one, however. At a young age, she developed rheumatic fever. In a move to cheer her up, her father began a collection of angels for her. With many prayers, the faith of her father, and her beloved angels, she recovered. Later, as a dedication to her late father, and to everyone who ever lost a loved one, Sarah created the *Angels in the Attic Collection.*

When Sarah was growing up, an African American family lived in a nearby apartment. Sarah delivered the daily paper to this family, and a loving friendship developed. The kindness and warmth that was shared with Sarah inspired her to develop the *Black Heritage Collection.*

On August 17, 1963, Sarah Johnston married her high school sweetheart, Jack (Jack Boy) Schultz. Sarah continued working for Michigan Bell Telephone to put her husband through pharmacy school. After graduation, he began working in his father's pharmacy in Chesaning, and eventually purchased it. As a mother, Sarah felt her five children had grown up overnight, so she brought back the memory of them growing up, along with "Sally Booba" (Sarah) and "Jack Boy" (husband Jack) in the "Daisy Petals" series, which is part of the *Cherished Memories Collection.* The Schultz children's figurine alter-egos are named "Spike" (Mark), "Sparky" (Tim), "Bomber" (Tom), "Jewel" (Julie) and "Stretch" (Mike).

Sarah's Attic Offers a Wide Variety of Collections Led By Best-Selling Black Heritage Designs

Of the many heartwarming collections now available through Sarah's Attic, the *Black Heritage Collection* is the best seller of all. In celebrating the history of African-Americans, Sarah Schultz has created a host of charming characters, attracting collectors of diverse racial and ethnic back-

Sitting in their cozy living room, we meet a group of charmers from Sarah's Gang, and notice their unique accessories. In addition to the figurines themselves, collectors may acquire decorator accents including a "Seasonal Trunk," 11" "Floor Base With Rug," "ABC-123 Blocks," "Toy Horse" and "Lamp."

grounds. Other Sarah's Attic series capture people, holiday spirit, animals, dolls and toys, favorite buildings and even pretty flowers, all in Sarah's unique style.

Included in the *Cherished Memories Collection* is "Tender Moments." This series keeps those special memories alive in all our hearts with figurines designed to reflect those special years from birth to twenty-one. These lovable children make perfect gifts for youngsters. "Classroom Memories," another group in this collection, offers a nostalgic look at yesterday's one-room school, with both students and accessories. "Dreams of Tomorrow" shows adorable children wearing dress-up gear that establishes them as "perfect professionals" — showing off their vocations of the future. This series is topping the Sarah's Attic best-seller list.

The *Heirlooms From the Attic Collection* of beautiful dolls brings Sarah Schultz's own childhood friends to life once again — whether making mischief or enjoying a neighborhood tea party. *Sarah's Gang* began with six members back in 1985, and today represents the friendship and loyalty common to all generations growing up in America. Meanwhile, *Sarah's Neighborhood Friends* can be found caroling in the winter or peddling their goods in the summer. At Christmastime they enjoy putting on a Nativity play for families in their neighborhood.

Speaking of the holidays, Sarah's Attic offers the *Santas of the Month Collection* to show that love can exist all year — not just at Christmas time. These delightful Santas are perfect for anyone who has ever wondered what Santa does "the rest of the year."

In the *Spirit of Christmas Collection,* old-world Santas join with elves, animals and children to

keep the holiday spirit of joy, hope and giving alive all year. In this collection you will find the "Gingerbabies." These creatures are made from a very special recipe which includes lots of ginger, molasses, vanilla, nutmeg, almond, cinnamon and a dash of love. When they're "baked," it's the dash of love that brings them to life.

Sarah Schultz shows her love for whimsical animal characters in her *Cuddly Critter Collection*, which offers a group of animal families, each showing off his or her own distinct personality. Within this grouping is the "Beary Adorables" series. The name says it all — it is a series devoted to the bear lover. Some of these characters from Beary Hollow are young and some are old; they like to quilt and cook and travel, and they enjoy playing and cuddling. The "Cotton Tale" series captures glimpses of the bunnies of Carrot Corner, U.S.A. These bunnies live, work and have fun together, and they're always ready to welcome new friends.

Flowers mean a great deal to Sarah Schultz, and she uses her "Daisy Petals" series to recall those pretty white-and-yellow daisies in all of our childhood meadows. This group features recreations of Sarah's family, and each piece has a raised daisy on it to identify it as a member of this group.

In another of her collections, Sarah has introduced a new concept called *United Hearts*. This helps to bring all of the collections together to show the unity and love that can exist on earth.

Among the many Santas of the Month available through Sarah's Attic are, from left to right: "April Easter Santa," "May Spring Santa," and "June Summertime Santa." The figurines range from 4¹/₂" to 5" in height, and retail for $35 each.

Even though the collections vary from diverse people to an array of animal species, they all have one thing in common: a heart!

A Chance to Join the Forever Friends Collectors' Club

Collectors are invited to become members of the Sarah's Attic Forever Friends Collectors' Club. They will be the only collectors eligible to purchase figurines from this heartwarming collection. Sarah herself invites each collector to join and start a special friendship that will last forever.

The Club figurines have been designed to recapture the Love, Trust and Friendship that bonds adults and children. It recalls those precious childhood hours spent with Mother or a special mentor on the front porch, sharing your hopes and dreams, knowing you could trust each other with your deepest thoughts. Each year's "Members Only" figurines will carry on this delightful theme.

Upon joining the club and paying annual membership dues of $25, new members will receive the free "Love Starts With Children" figurine: a $70 value, as well as redemption certificates for the current "Members Only" figurines. A personalized membership card, subscription to the tri-annual *From the Heart* magazine, a "Collectors' Guide," which features all current products, a folder to keep written materials stored and organized, and a checklist of Sarah's Attic current and retired collectibles, round out the Club's generous array of benefits.

A Dream for the Future: Houses of Love, Respect and Dignity

In a recent interview with Pune Dracker of *Collector Editions* magazine Sarah Schultz outlined her future plans for a Sarah's Attic Theme Park. "Oh, it's just a dream," Ms. Schultz asserts, but she continues with vivid detail. "There'll be a House of Love, a House of Respect, and a House of Dignity, and all the characters from the figurines will be running in and out."

Considering the dream-come-true quality of the overnight success of Sarah's Attic, collectors and friends take Sarah Schultz's future visions very, very seriously. Someday soon, we may all be able to visit *Sarah's Gang* in their very own park...a tribute to a gifted lady and to her devotion to the universal qualities of Love, Respect and Dignity.

Seymour Mann
An Award-Winning Collectible Resource Draws its Uniqueness from Some of the Nation's Most Gifted Designers

Seymour Mann believes that every collectible should be — first and foremost — a work of art. And with each new honor and award his New York firm and its artists receive, it becomes even clearer that collectors and dealers agree. Top artists are impressed with the firm as well, for today Seymour Mann demonstrates the ability to attract some of America's most renowned artists for exclusive designs.

In just one recent month, Seymour Mann was nominated for four Awards of Excellence by *Dolls* magazine. This represents an all-time high for the firm which earned three nominations in 1992 — and an Award of Excellence in 1991 as well as two nominations. The year 1991 saw Seymour Mann earn a nomination for a Doll of the Year (DOTY) Award from *Doll Reader* magazine as well.

While dolls were Seymour Mann's original "claim to fame" in the collectibles world, the firm also has won considerable recognition for works of art in other media. *Collector Editions* magazine bestowed an Award of Excellence on Seymour Mann in 1992 for a light-up cottage, and the firm also has received three nominations in the past three years for its holiday collectibles. What's more, Seymour Mann's honors are not confined to American shores: the firm has attracted numerous honors and citations at international expositions and shows over the years as well.

A Family of Artists Inspires Seymour and Eda Mann

Seymour Mann founded the firm that bears his name in 1965 in New York City — originally as a tableware and giftware company. The firm's showroom still is housed in its original location in the heart of Manhattan: at 225 Fifth Avenue. Eda Mann, an accomplished artist, has been a Master Designer for her husband's company since the very beginning. Eda was born in London and spent her youth studying art under the supervision of two uncles, both of whom were professional artists. Her family came to the United States when Eda was sixteen. Her father became a well-known soci-

Seymour Mann, President, and Master Designer Eda Mann, continue to create and produce quality giftware and collectibles that delight people everywhere. This dynamic husband and wife team give added meaning to the word "success."

ety artist in America during the 1930s and 1940s, and created many movie posters for studios such as MGM and Columbia Pictures.

Eda Mann studied art at the National Academy of Design in New York City, which at that time was a scholarship school. She won many awards for her sculptures and paintings. Recently, her paintings have been accepted by the Metropolitan Museum of Art, and today some of her originals also are on display at the National Academy of Design. Mrs. Mann has worked as a fashion designer as well, which may account for the beautiful costumes that adorn the Seymour Mann dolls.

Mrs. Mann met her husband-to-be while he was working as a professional musician and band leader. After marrying, the Manns combined their talents to form a partnership which began in the 1940s. Eda designed figurines and other decorative accessories while Seymour marketed her creations. Spearheaded by his business savvy and her design talents, they pioneered new designs in tableware and giftware, and Seymour Mann, Inc. grew to be a leader in the gift and collectibles field.

Eda Mann long had enjoyed a hobby creating dolls for her daughters and granddaughters when it occurred to her husband that others might enjoy these delightful creations. By the late 1970s,

Seymour Mann began to transform Eda's dolls into collectibles. Over the years, the Seymour Mann doll line has grown into the *Connoisseur Collection* featuring hundreds of dolls, and the company has become renowned all over the world as a leading resource for affordable, collectible dolls.

Seymour Mann Attracts Outstanding Doll Artists

Now in the 1990s, Seymour Mann has evolved into a doll artists' company, with a "stable" of designers including such honored doll creators as Paulette Aprile, Pat Kolesar, Hal Payne, Michelle Severino, Hanna Kahl-Hyland and June Grammer. But before this could take place, Seymour Mann had to find a way to keep the new *Connoisseur Collection* at an affordable price level.

By 1991, Seymour Mann was known for dolls in the under-$150 retail price range. As founder and president of the company, Mann felt strongly about keeping his customers satisfied by continuing to supply moderately priced collectibles. Yet a large number of Seymour Mann collectors were waiting for something new and different from their favorite firm.

Seymour Mann developed the idea of *Signature Series* dolls, a collection which would offer artists' dolls at affordable prices to doll enthusiasts everywhere. The company sought out some of the nation's finest doll artists who wished to reach a larger audience than their current limited editions afforded them. The *Signature Series* debuted at the International Toy Fair in 1992. At last, artists' dolls were offered to the public at prices that were not prohibitive!

Designer Paulette Aprile explains: "As an artist, I can produce only a very limited number of dolls, and therefore, my dolls are available to only a few collectors. By working with Seymour Mann, I can offer comparable quality at a much more affordable price to a broader range of collectors. Since Seymour Mann is married to a well-known artist, his company is especially attuned to working with designers, and very sensitive to our needs and wishes."

Gideon Oberweger, executive vice-president of Seymour Mann since the 1960s, contributes greatly to the success of the firm and its artists. With his buying, marketing and management expertise, he is able to identify and select overseas manufacturers that can best capture the essence of each artist's distinctive work.

As Oberweger comments, "It is a very compli-

"Pavlova" is a collectible porcelain doll designed by award-winning artist Paulette Aprile for Seymour Mann in the company's award-winning Signature Series. Standing 19" tall, the doll features a ballerina with black hair and blue eyes.

cated business of sourcing and selecting the manufacturer which can provide the best reproductions for each artist's original doll. Each designer has a distinct look and feeling toward his or her artistry. We closely supervise the production of each doll in order to transform the original into acceptable collectible reproductions. Some adjustments have to be made to compensate for the cost and production differences, but these adjustments can be selected and achieved by the artists, not the manufacturer."

Seymour Mann Creates Award-Winning Christmas Collectibles

Seymour Mann works with famous artists for its other creations as well, including holiday figurines, lighted houses, musicals and ornaments. Award-winning designer Lorraine Sciola earned an Award of Excellence for Seymour Mann in 1992 for her "Reindeer Stable." Ms. Sciola also has designed other light-up houses and the *Snow Kids* group of musicals and figurines.

Noted designer Janet Sauerbrey has designed the *Gingerbread Dreams* collection of light-up houses and ornaments depicting gingerbread houses and holiday characters. Mary Alice Byerly has created the *Shoebox Elf* collection, featuring nine-

inch porcelain elf dolls available with wooden beds and other accessories. Also, Kenji has designed the *Christmas Cat* collection featuring cat figurines in holiday settings.

From Cats to Collectible Teapots

Speaking of cats, Seymour Mann has become world-renowned for porcelain cat musicals. Each collectible features cats in whimsical and playful settings, with popular musical tunes. Three years ago, the "Puss 'n Boots" cat musical won an Award of Excellence from *Collector Editions* magazine.

Seymour Mann also has been developing fine tableware and serving accessories for many years, having built the foundation of its business on this type of product. The firm offers a complete line of collectible ceramic teapots in a variety of unique colors and designs, including Oriental elephants and cats, triangular shapes, and fruit and vegetable designs.

With award after award to their credit, Seymour and Eda Mann look forward to even more art innovations in the future. And because they are able to attract some of America's top artists to share their vision of collectibles as works of art, collectors can expect a wide range of affordable creations to come from the house of Seymour Mann.

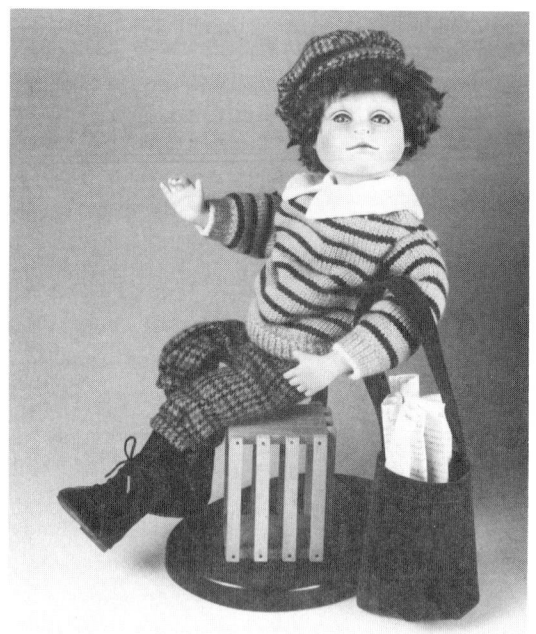

"Spanky" is dressed in a turn-of-the-century newspaper boy outfit. The 17" porcelain doll was designed by Hal Payne for Seymour Mann, Inc in its Signature Series.

Seymour Mann won a 1992 Award of Excellence from Collector Editions *magazine for its "Reindeer Stable" Light-Up House.*

Shelia's Fine Handpainted Collectibles
Shelia Thompson Captures History in Miniature From a Charming Studio and Workshop in Historic Charleston

From the first moment they arrived in Charleston, South Carolina two decades ago, Shelia and Jim Thompson found themselves captivated by the city's historic charm. And because Shelia is an artist, it seemed only natural that she would come to focus her talent and creativity on the city's rich store of antebellum buildings and houses. Today, her early body of work stands as a "miniature monument" to her favorite city's history.

As a self-schooled painter of watercolors, Shelia Thompson is unconstrained by the "do's and don'ts" of art professors. When she envisions a particular medium or method, she sets out to bring it to life. Such was the case with her desire to create miniature collectible houses in wood.

"I am not an educated artist," Ms. Thompson explains, "so when skilled printers told me that it was impossible to screen print on wood, I thought that since most of my techniques were 'wrong' from a schooled artist's point of view, I may as well go ahead and do something else 'wrong' — since that seemed to be what worked for me!" True to her predictions, the "wrong" thing worked again, and Ms. Thompson began producing her first delightful little screen-printed and hand-painted houses.

The "Colonel Ashe House" (left) and the "John Rutledge House" are the latest editions to Shelia's Charleston *series. The intricate detail in the wrought iron is just one of the features that make Shelia's Fine Handpainted Collectibles so sought-after by collectors.*

Family Needs Inspire a Wife and Mother to Perfect Her Art

"My first efforts at producing little houses came out of simple need," Ms. Thompson recalls. "My husband and I were struggling financially, and I wanted some extra money for Christmas presents for my children." So in 1979, with a length of wood and a borrowed saw, Shelia and Jim cut out the first of what would become a highly collectible line of houses.

"My first pieces were entirely hand-painted. I would come home from my job as a dental assistant, and begin painting houses. Jim would spend his weekends cutting them out. Then, I would load up my car and drive to the City Market in downtown Charleston. In order to get a space there, which was 'first come, first served,' I would sometimes sleep in my car with all my little houses. At first light, I would go put my name on the list, and then I would set up in a space and sell my miniature houses all day."

When demand for Shelia's hand-painted houses became so intense that she could no longer keep up, she devised a way to keep the distinctive look of her product in a way that could be produced in editions, rather than one-by-one. "I learned how to hand-print, and I was able to use a combination of printing and hand-painting to get a look that was unique in the market. My business was in my home, and little houses lined our hallways and spare room. My children spent their high school years stepping over them, and eating around them on our table!"

A Part-Time Avocation Becomes a Full-Time Fine Arts Career

With demand for Shelia's Fine Handpainted Collectibles booming, Ms. Thompson decided to turn her part-time project into a full-fledged business. Before long, husband Jim made a similar decision. He realized that his wife needed him to take care of the financial and operational aspects of the business, so that she could devote herself to her art. When even Jim's weekend bookkeeping

The "Anne Peacock House" is Shelia's 1993 Collector's Society "Members Only" piece.

and production work could not satisfy the needs of the business, he gave up his career in sales to join in partnership with Shelia. The couple has not looked back.

"Shelia and I have never thought about failure," recalls Jim Thompson, now Chief Executive Officer of the firm. "Even when times have been tough, we have always looked to the future with a positive attitude. That was how I was able to give up a career with a lot of security and take a risk. I have always believed in Shelia's talent and in her creative abilities, so I wasn't afraid to make the move to give her all the support in her efforts that I could."

Loving Care Makes Each of Shelia's Collectibles a Unique Work of Art

With many successes to their credit after these modest beginnings, Shelia and Jim Thompson maintain their steadfast commitment to hard work and to excellence. "I think it's our passion for quality and our attention to the smallest details that have made our miniatures popular," Ms. Thompson asserts.

While early pieces focused strictly on Charleston's historic homes and buildings, the company's line of collectibles now has expanded to match the growing interest of collectors in every state of the union. Now Shelia and her team of craftspeople have focused their talents on historic landmarks in Williamsburg, Savannah, Philadelphia, New England, Texas, and many other parts of the United States, with over 200 separate items currently in production.

Each piece is produced from original artwork

hand-drawn by Ms. Thompson herself. They are silkscreened and hand-painted on wood using custom-mixed paints and inks to match the colors and features of the original buildings. Indeed, Ms. Thompson herself can often be found on the streets of Charleston and other historic cities, matching paint chips with the actual buildings she is replicating. Even such fine details as scrollwork, shrubbery and cupolas are given loving and careful attention to make sure they are true to the original structure. Each building also contains a description of its history and significance, screen-printed in script on the back. All of Shelia's designs are in correct proportion to the original buildings they represent, reflecting the care and precision that go into their creation.

As is fitting with true collector's items, certain Shelia's Fine Handpainted Collectibles are retired periodically. After the retirement date, the screens are destroyed, and the only sources for finding the piece are other collectors who received it before it was retired or through dealers who specialize in the secondary market. This process guarantees that retirements are legitimate.

Technology Combines With the Personal Touch at Shelia's

The company's owners continue to reinforce their ongoing commitment to quality, even during a period of sustained growth. A new climate-controlled screen-printing facility offers visible evidence of this commitment. In the past, Charleston's high humidity had forced company artists to rework screens for printing, which can be very time consuming. The controlled environment in the new building eliminates this problem, allowing Shelia's to keep pace with collector demand while enhancing quality. As Ms. Thompson explains, "The most important factor in building our business has been our determination to maintain our quality, no matter what it takes."

Collectors and friends may rest assured that Shelia's Fine Handpainted Collectibles will never lose its warm southern hospitality and family atmosphere. Shelia and Jim's daughter, Darlene Miklos, now works as part of her mother's design team. Even the family's black poodle, Suzie, has a role in the business: Ms. Thompson relies heavily on Suzie's judgment about prospective employees! Suzie accompanies her mistress to work every day, and as Ms. Thompson explains, "Every applicant that we have hired in spite of Suzie's growling and barking has lasted less than a week. On the other

hand, if she wags her tail and comes around to be petted by a prospective employee, I know we're getting a good person."

Painted Ladies *Series Pays Tribute to Victorian Homes*

A recent introduction from Shelia's Fine Handpainted Collectibles characterizes the charm and beauty that sets these handsome miniature houses apart. The new *Painted Ladies II and III* series feature replicas of buildings constructed during the Victorian era, with elaborate details such as scrollwork and cupolas. So popular have these buildings been that pieces for the first release dates sold out almost overnight.

"The initial response to the new line has been fantastic," Ms. Thompson reports. "I think much of the success of this series comes from the color and detail in each house. I devote hours to every detail. For instance, if you look at the scrollwork, you will be able to see intricate patterns in every aspect. We produce only historically significant buildings, and we try to match every nuance in color and style. It's especially rewarding when peo-ple see our product line and can pick out buildings that they have visited."

Shelia's Fine Handpainted Collectibles Collector's Society Debuts

In 1993, Shelia's reached a new milestone with the introduction of a Collector's Society and an initial Charter Membership drive limited to 5,000 collectors. Enrollment in the Society is handled only through retailers, with membership benefits including advance notice of new offerings, members-only pieces, a signed and numbered limited edition painted by Shelia, a special collector's piece, a collector's notebook, a subscription to the company's newsletter and access to the retired pieces' directory.

Shelia Thompson's goal in creating her handsome miniature buildings is simple: to ensure that their only true rivals are the original buildings themselves. With her gift for art and devotion to detail, the leadership of her husband, Jim, and the support of her family and staff, Ms. Thompson captures the imagination of collectors across America with her historic and collectible designs.

Shelia's four recent introductions — The Painted Ladies III, debuted in mid-1993. All four houses are from Cape May, New Jersey.

Swarovski America Limited
A Worldwide Passion For Crystal

For many owners of Swarovski Silver Crystal, their figurines are more than just decorative objects: they are a passion. With collections sometimes totalling more than 150 pieces, these enthusiastic collectors are part of a growing international network — the Swarovski Collectors Society (SCS).

Swarovski established SCS in 1987, eleven years after the introduction of its Swarovski Silver Crystal line, in response to the overwhelming number of requests and inquiries flowing in from collectors all over the world. The Society was launched initially in the major English-speaking markets — the United States, United Kingdom, Canada and Australia — where collecting was a well-established tradition. But within months, widespread acceptance made it clear that membership should be extended to include European and Asian markets as well.

Although Swarovski and Swarovski Silver Crystal management were optimistic about how the concept of a society would be received, no one had anticipated the large number of membership applications that subsequently flooded in. The number of SCS members has skyrocketed and today there are no fewer than eighteen branch offices and over 175,000 active members in twenty-one countries around the world — including such far-off places as Singapore, Italy, Germany and Hong Kong.

The Many Benefits of SCS Membership

Swarovski Silver Crystal admirers who join the Society become eligible for a whole range of privileges and advantages. They are informed about Swarovski activities and new products in a twice-yearly, full-color magazine, the *Swarovski Collector*. This magazine — published in seven languages — contains a wealth of articles and information of interest to crystal lovers, while its down-to-earth style adds a human touch that clearly appeals to Society members. They also receive tips on cleaning and caring for their precious collections.

The most important of all Society privileges, however, is the member's exclusive right to purchase the SCS Annual Edition: a spectacular, full-cut crystal design. Each piece bears the SCS logo, the designer's initials and the year of issue, enhancing the value and appreciation to the collector. Some annual editions have risen significantly in value, as evidenced by the appreciation figures shown in this volume's Price Index.

A Distinguished History Sets the Stage for Swarovski Today

Collectors' passion for Swarovski Silver Crystal stems from a century-long commitment to excellence. Swarovski is the world's leading creator and supplier of cut crystal stones used by such industries as fashion, design and lighting. The company also produces a wide range of crystal objects, jewelry and accessory lines.

Through two World Wars and the Great Depression of the 1930s, the Swarovski company endured as one of Europe's most trusted sources for crystal jewelry stones and other decorative products. But it was not until 1976 that Daniel Swarovski's heirs introduced the first piece in the Swarovski Silver Crystal collection. Since then, Swarovski has earned worldwide renown for its shimmering crystal works of art.

This first Inspiration Africa *creation represents the 1993 SCS Annual Edition. "The Elephant" was designed by the gifted Martin Zendron exclusively for SCS members.*

Swarovski Exhibits a Deep Commitment to the Arts

When Daniel Swarovski I founded his company in 1895, he sought to achieve superior technical and artistic standards. A belief in the value of innovation and artistic achievement has guided Swarovski ever since. Now the company is committing itself to making the arts accessible to a wide international audience and to helping educate the public about different cultures. Since 1991, Swarovski has been proud to be the sole sponsor of seven separate museum exhibitions. During 1994, two such exhibitions will be on display in the United States.

Jewels Of Fantasy: Costume Jewelry Of The Twentieth Century represents the first major international exhibition on the development of costume jewelry. One of the main aims of *Jewels Of Fantasy* is to recognize and pay tribute to the talented craftsmen and designers, many of whom are unknown, whose outstanding creations have contributed so greatly to the success of the fashion jewelry industry. The designers represented include Chanel, Dior, Lacroix and many more. As the world's leading manufacturer and supplier of cut crystal stones to the fashion industry, it has been Swarovski's privilege to work closely with these men and women from the early years of the century, when the industry was first developing. *Jewels Of Fantasy* may be seen at The Baltimore Museum of Art, Baltimore, Maryland, from February through April 1994.

Benin: Royal Art Of Africa presents one of the most valuable collections of Benin artwork. It will be on view during 1994 at the Museum of Fine Arts, Houston (February-April); the Cleveland Museum of Art (May-July); The Baltimore Museum of Art (September-October); and the Seattle Art Museum (December 1994-January 1995).

Introducing "Inspiration Africa" — the Elephant

While some collectors associate cut crystal animal figurines with stylized sentimentality, SCS has radically changed the material's image in recent years. The first SCS series of three pairs of birds foretold a new naturalism, while the second — particularly the Dolphins and the Whales — added movement. Together with a number of revolutionary processing techniques developed by Swarovski, these features have turned crystal into an exciting new medium and made it accessible to a much wider audience.

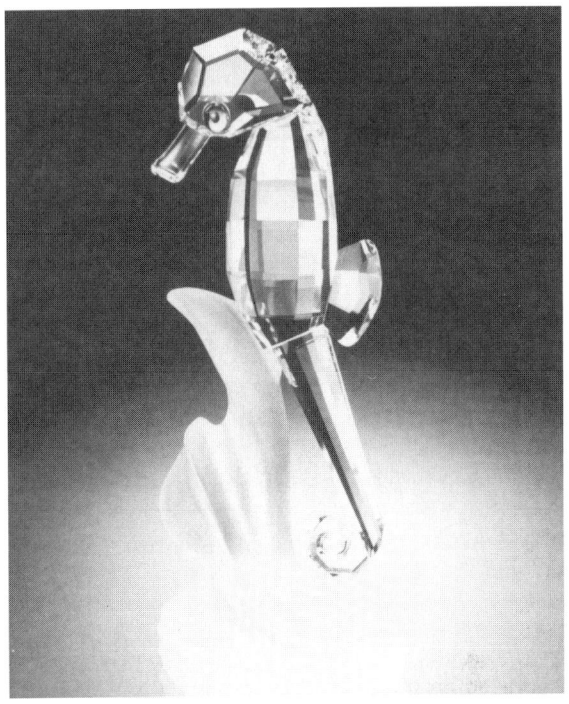

One of the elegant works of art in the Swarovski South Sea series is this shimmering, multi-faceted "Sea Horse."

A prime example of this phenomenon is the Swarovski Collectors Society *Inspiration Africa* premier piece. It offers an uncannily realistic depiction of a full-grown African bull elephant in his natural environment. Radiating physical strength and vigor, he asserts his presence in no uncertain terms. The packaging and logo of the new series were also inspired by the world's second-largest continent. The design is based on an Ashanti ceremonial stool, a symbol of office of the lineage heads of the people who inhabit southern Ghana and the neighboring areas of Togo and the Ivory Coast.

Martin Zendron: The "Elephant's" Creator

Martin Zendron, the designer of the first of the three limited editions in the SCS *Inspiration Africa* series, was born in 1964 in the medieval town of Hall in the Austrian Tyrol. He now lives and works a few kilometers away from his birthplace in historic Wattens, the home of Swarovski Silver Crystal.

Although Zendron enjoyed drawing, painting and modeling at school, he never seriously considered the idea of being a designer. Rather, he just "grew into" it. The link with Swarovski, however, existed from an early age: Zendron's family moved

to Wattens while he was still a boy because of his father's job. He still works for Swarovski's prototype department and makes the first model of each new design. After an education in glassmaking and design, and working for a well-known Tyrolean retailer specializing in glass objects, Zendron joined Swarovski in 1988.

Zendron's first creations for Swarovski were the "Harp" and "Lute," elegant pieces that reveal a rare artistic talent and craftsmanship, and underscore the freshness of his approach to cut crystal design. Then Zendron was assigned to a task much-coveted among Swarovski designers: he was asked to design the "Elephant," the 1993 limited edition for SCS and the first piece in the new *Inspiration Africa* series.

Michael Stamey Takes Collectors on a South Sea Adventure

For Michael Stamey, creator of the newest crystal figurines that join Swarovski Silver Crystal's *South Sea* group, home could not be farther from the tropics. Tucked away in the Austrian Tyrol, his studio, housed in an old farm building, looks out upon snow-capped mountains, pine trees and pastures. It is in this picturesque alpine setting that his imagination is free to dream of such exotic places and inspires him to skillfully craft the creatures that live there in sparkling, multi-faceted crystal.

Designed by Borek Sipek, this "Tableclock" represents the type of bold new, contemporary designs in the Swarovski Selection.

"We selected the 'Three South Sea Fish' and 'Sea Horse' to develop an underwater landscape," Stamey explains. Their shape and composition work well with existing pieces from the *South Sea* group. The tall, slim "Sea Horse" complements the flatness of the "Butterfly Fish," while the "Three South Sea Fish" add movement and energy to the scene as they swim amidst coral.

Stamey is no stranger to marine life. He has created the SCS annual limited edition pieces, "Lead Me" — the Dolphins, "Save Me" — the Seals and "Care For Me" — the Whales for its *Mother and Child* series. Each item artfully captures the essence of these ocean animals with their offspring in full-cut crystal.

An avid snorkeler, Stamey loves to watch the light change under water and witness the abundant sea life when vacationing on the Mediterranean. "Snorkeling is an adventure," he explains. "You never know what to expect next." This same spirit of discovery led him through the year-long development of the "Three South Sea Fish" and "Sea Horse." He drew inspiration from a souvenir sea horse purchased on a trip to Florida, memories of the fish he kept in an aquarium when he was a boy, and books and videotapes on underwater life.

Swarovski Selection Offers Sparkling Accessories

With the introduction of a new collection of artist-designed decorative accessories, Swarovski brings cut crystal into the world of contemporary design. *Swarovski Selection* is a major departure from traditional cut crystal designs. The fourteen-piece collection includes vases, bowls, clocks, a candleholder as well as a pen holder, card holder, jewel box and ashtray — each a design original.

To create this line, Swarovski commissioned seven European designers of international repute. Swarovski set no limits; not even the function was specified. Each designer was free to create whatever he wished, working with Swarovski's highly technical crystal-cutting process.

Swarovski Selection was created as a result of the company's market research, which revealed that consumers of fine home furnishings hold cut crystal in high esteem, but have few choices beyond traditional design.

Today's Creations Inc.

Times to Remember Captures Every Memorable Aspect of the Bridal Experience

A flowing white gown...a bouquet of gorgeous flowers...a towering wedding cake...a romantic first dance with the handsome bridegroom. These are just a few of the memorable aspects that help make a wedding day perfect. And now, thanks to Today's Creations, every bride (or bride-to-be) can experience the emotion and excitement of that wonderful wedding again and again. For this New Jersey-based firm will unveil, in March 1995, a stunning set of contemporary bridal figurines called *Times to Remember*.

In six original works of art, *Times to Remember* portrays the universal feelings of brides, grooms and their happy families. When introduced in order, these elegant figurines tell the story of a wedding day to cherish.

First we see the loving mother, helping her daughter put the finishing touches on her gown, make-up and hairstyle. "Mother and Bride" will bring a happy tear to the eye of many women who recall just such an intimate moment — a few last-minute bits of advice from the doting mother...the nervous bride's need for reassurance that she looks her best...the profession of everlasting love between mother and daughter.

Next we observe "Bride with Bouquet," the classic photographic portrait subject. Fresh and graceful as the flowers she holds near her heart, the bride wears an expression of expectation and love as she prepares for this — the most important commitment of her young life.

"With This Ring" portrays the high point of the marriage ceremony, as the bride says "I do" to her adoring husband. The most dramatic moment of the wedding, this moment seals the covenant of marriage before God and before all the assembled family and guests.

Two wonderful figurines introduce us to the reception festivities, and both involve traditional dances. "The First Dance" symbolizes the beginning of the bride and groom's life together as they dance to their special song. Then "Daddy's Little Girl" saves a dance for that first man in her life, as the loving father embraces his daughter and admires the beau-

Al Gordon, artist for Today's Creations Inc., is putting the final touches on the illustration of "With This Ring." Mr. Gordon's illustrations became the blueprints for Today's Creations' unique bridal figurines.

tiful young woman he and her mother have raised.

The final figurine in this first suite of six is called "Slice of Life." It depicts yet another classic moment from the American wedding scene as the bride and groom slice the first few pieces of wedding cake to feed each other and pose for the camera.

Each of these heart-touching vignettes will be captured in an 8"-tall figurine, cold cast to ensure that every marvelous detail is preserved to perfection. Collectors will have the choice of a hand-painted version of each figurine, or a pristine, all-white style that appears particularly contemporary in display. For those who enjoy musical figurines, "The First Dance" and "Daddy's Little Girl" both will be made available in versions with built-in musical movements.

The *Times to Remember* collection carries a limited edition of 5,000 for each work of art. What's more, an original poem has been composed and included with each figurine — an addition that provides all the more depth and emotional power to this remarkable fine art presentation. All figurines come with a wooden base and brass name plate, and a Certificate of Authenticity will be included in every beautifully designed gift box.

The Creative Minds Behind Times to Remember

Devotion and determination have been the hallmarks of the creative process for *Times to Remember* and Today's Creations. The team at Today's Creations includes Marty Miller and Randy Gordon, each of whom brought unique skills and insights to their association.

Marty Miller directed the research model for the *Times to Remember* project, ensuring that every aspect would be completely reflective of American wedding tradition. Miller's background includes doing research grants for the Federal Government. This professional skill offered the team a unique and insightful way of extracting information and ideas. The question Miller always asked himself and his partner was, "How do we make it better?"

Randy Gordon has a history that is somewhat unique for a "player" in the collectibles industry. His background includes being a player in minor league baseball for the Detroit Tigers. As an athlete, he has always strived for perfection. Indeed as a bowler, he has achieved perfection with five perfect 300 games to his credit! This dedication has carried over to his business career and shows in the excellence of the *Times to Remember* collection.

The initial concept for a bridal series of figurines came from Randy Gordon, who serves as Vice-President of Sales and Marketing for Marty Miller Marketing. The Miller firm is a sales, marketing and design company specializing in the collectibles market. Its namesake, Marty Miller, has twenty years experience in the field, while Gordon brings a decade of experience to the *Times to Remember* creative process.

Using Randy Gordon's concept of a bridal focus, the team conducted extensive research in the bridal market. They learned several facts which indicated that collectors would happily embrace the concept of Times *to Remember*. First and foremost, no manufacturer had ever before sculpted all the significant scenes of a wedding. Most such sculptural works centered only on the bride herself. Second, most bridal figurines were Victorian in style — not representative of the brides of today. Third, the only available contemporary bridal figurines carried very high price tags.

The mission for *Times to Remember* became clear. Today's Creations would develop an entire series of 1990s-style bridal figurines at moderate prices, intended to appeal to the bride and groom of today. The firm's goal would be to achieve a realistic — yet appealing — portrayal of special wedding participants and events.

Artist Al Gordon Brings the Dream to Reality

The illustrator for *Times to Remember*, Al Gordon, has over thirty years of experience in all aspects of the art and collectibles fields. His impressive portfolio includes time spent running his own design group, developing original characters, and working for many major licensing companies. Al Gordon has illustrated Disney and Looney Tunes characters, and he also boasts the unique ability to translate reality into a two-dimensional illustration. These illustrations became the blueprints for the three-dimensional, hand-sculpted figurines you see today.

The inspiration behind Al Gordon's work was Sue, his wife for over forty years. The love, respect and friendship they shared through the years showed in the passion of Al's designs. She was with him throughout his career and remained by his side through the completion of these first six *Times to Remember* designs. Sadly, Sue lost her battle with lung cancer in May, 1994, and did not see the final pieces. Al has dedicated this *Times to Remember* series to the memory of his loving wife.

Production Begins

Bill Berzack, president of Today's Creations, has been importing products to the United States for over twenty years. His knowledge of the production studios in various lands provided the final piece to the creative puzzle. When Bill first showed Al's illustrations to officials at his chosen studio, the sculptor's response was, "These are the best illustrations I've ever seen." Everyone was convinced that Today's Creations had something special — an impression that was further reinforced by the outstanding sculptures that emerged. They far exceeded the creative team's expectations!

Times to Remember *Sets the Stage for Today's Creations*

While the *Times to Remember* figurines are sure to attract brides of all generations, research shows that the current bridal market is booming. In 1991 alone there were almost 2,500,000 marriages in the United States, which generated over $32,000,000,000 in retail sales. With gift and collectible retailers expanding their bridal displays, these marvelous figurines are sure to be showcased in a wide variety of stores. And with almost 70% of all weddings occurring between April and October, the March 1995 introduction of the collection will be timed perfectly for both stores and consumers.

Not content to rest on their laurels, the creators of *Times to Remember* already have a second series of collectibles well underway. Titled *Today's Heroes*, these works of art will be sculpted in a 1990s contemporary and realistic style. Each figurine will portray a much-honored profession, with the first piece inspired by the fireman.

Over 200 photos of firemen in action were taken to ensure accuracy in the final portrayal of pose, uniform and equipment. Depicted in completely authentic detail, the fireman and others in the *Today's Heroes* series will be available in 1995.

As Today's Creations carves out its niche in the gift and collectible field, careful research will remain the firm's hallmark. The creative team's goal is to present contemporary collectibles that break new ground while inspiring and pleasing America's discerning collectors.

Artist Al Gordon, with over thirty years experience in all aspects of the art and collectibles fields, is shown with a small sampling of the characters he has illustrated. His diversified talent enabled Today's Creations to create the Times to Remember *bridal figurine series.*

United Design
A Host of Charming, Collectible Figurines...
Created With Pride in the U.S.A.

Visitors to their stunning, 200,000-square-foot plant and office complex in Noble, Oklahoma find it difficult to believe that Gary and Jeanie Clinton's first art studio was housed in their back-yard chicken coop! The Clintons have come a long way since then, but the husband-and-wife team still share the same values that inspired their business from the beginning. Devotion to creativity, quality, and "hands-on" craftsmanship has set United Design and its appealing products apart.

It all began when the Clintons sold $300 worth of their creations at their very first craft show in 1973. Gary and Jeanie knew they were on to something. "We took half the $300 and made a down payment on two pottery kilns, which we moved and rebuilt in an orchard next to our house. Then we ran electricity to a deserted chicken coop in our backyard and turned it into a studio," the Clintons recall. Since then their business — soon christened United Design — has grown at an astounding rate.

Today during peak periods, the United Design team can produce an average of 25,000 pieces daily. Both Gary and Jeanie remain actively involved in the creative life of United Design — overseeing product development and working with sculptors and artists to guide the overall vision of the firm. The company owes its rapid growth and unparalleled success to its corporate philosophy, which includes an all-encompassing concern for animals and the environment.

United Design Collectors Appreciate the Studio's Limited Edition Craftsmanship

Among the first United Design favorites to capture the attention of collectors were the *Stone Critters*® and *Itty Bitty Critters*®. Since these series were introduced, the company has made large strides in the limited edition collectible field in recent years. Collectors have been intrigued both with the charm of unique lines such as *The Legend Of Santa Claus*™, *Pennibears*™, and *Legend Of The Little People*™, and with the exceptional detail work that United Design's cold-casting techniques allow. Each figurine goes through up to fifteen

"My Forever Love," the third in the Sweetheart series of Pennibears by Penni Jo Jonas, is crafted of bonded porcelain and enhanced with Ms. Jonas' trademark: a copper penny embedded in its base.

steps before it is ready to ship, and each step requires the talents of several dedicated American artisans or craftsmen.

The first step in the process is an original sculpture created by one of the master artists on the United Design team. These include the gifted Ken Memoli, Larry Miller, Dianna Newburn, Donna Kennicutt, Suzan Bradford — and Penni Jo Jonas, creator of the beloved *Pennibears*™. Using a variety of tools and a lot of imagination, the sculptor will create an original from clay, sculpting in all the intricate detail to be molded into the finished piece.

Once the original clay sculpture is complete, the piece is carefully delivered to the mold room. A thin layer of silicon or latex is poured over the sculpture and the mold maker uses an air brush to blow the silicon or latex into all the fine cracks

and crevices that make up the detail of the piece.

From this resin master, a series of production molds are made, again using silicon or latex. Each production mold is prepared with a thick, surrounding "back-up" mold, which ensures the casting process does not stretch the initial mold out of shape.

Following the mold-making process, actual casting begins. At this stage, the production molds are filled with a white liquid gypsum product called hydrostone, a rocklike substance that sets up extremely hard. Other United Design pieces are crafted of cold-cast porcelain, a combination of the dry elements of porcelain with resin substances. In either case, the resulting castings are removed from the molds, then dried and cured by passing through a heat chamber.

Once the pieces are completely dry, a step called "fettling" begins. In this process, craftsmen use knives, dental tools and dental drills to cut away mold flashings and etch any needed detail back into the molded piece. After fettling, the molded pieces are ready for staining and painting.

Staining gives an overall undercoat to the piece, which is then overpainted in oils, acrylics or a combination of each. The artists who hand-paint

Created to help benefit The Starlight Foundation, "The Gift '93" represents an edition of 3,500 figurines and was sculpted by Suzan Bradford.

each piece use both regular brush and airbrush techniques, depending on the effect desired. Once the final touches are added, each piece is adorned by an American flag tag that says "Made in U.S.A.," and packed for shipment in a handsome, protective gift box.

"The artistry and craftsmanship in the figurines we produce is fascinating to watch," says Gary Clinton. "We've had many people ask to visit our facilities and now, with our modern new production lines, we can accommodate several large groups each day." United Design also welcomes tours and visitors to its on-site gift shop, which displays and sells all of the company's items at retail prices.

The Pennibears™ of Penni Jo Jonas Call United Design "Home"

Like Gary and Jeanie Clinton, Penni Jo Jonas began her career in sculpting and figurine making as a "cottage industry." Indeed, Ms. Jonas initially used homey tools such as a food processor and toaster oven to create her highly popular *Pennibears™*. While making items to furnish a doll house one day, she experimented with her first tiny teddy bear.

The *Pennibears* became a part of the United Design family when Ms. Jonas found herself unable to keep up with the growing demand of her "kitchen table" business. "I actually went to United Design to see if they could make some molds so I could cast pieces myself. Gary Clinton, the owner, showed my work to several people on his product development staff. They were all so delighted with the *Pennibears* they asked me to come to work for them. I was so delighted with what I saw at the company that I said okay."

Today's *Pennibears* command the attention and love of collectors nationwide who thrill to each new vignette. The button-eyed bears can be acquired in a wide range of poses and activities, from "Gotta Try Again" and "My Forever Love" to "A Happy Camper" and "May Joy Be Yours."

Santa Claus and Legendary "Little People" Delight United Design Collectors

To honor the legendary figure of Santa Claus and provide cherished Christmas memories for collectors, the artists of United Design have created a series of richly detailed, limited edition figurines called *The Legend Of Santa Claus*. Some of these bright, hand-painted pieces depict Santa as he appears in various cultures, while others pay

These delightful figurines are typical of the whimsical subjects in United Design's Legends Of The Little People™ *Collection.*

tribute to an All-American Santa engaged in his yearly ritual.

While the earlier Santas, beginning in 1986, were sculpted primarily by Larry Miller and Suzan Bradford, the team of Ken Memoli and Penni Jo Jonas got into the act during 1990 with the introduction of "Safe Arrival." Memoli sculpted a grandfatherly Santa with a big empty sack, while Ms. Jonas created six tiny Victorian toys which can be placed in the sack or removed. Two additions to *The Legend Of Santa Claus* series are "Victorian Santa" and "Victorian Santa with Teddy." Created by Suzan Bradford, these designs appeal to the growing interest in all things Victorian.

Sculptor Larry Miller is the force behind *The Legend Of The Little People*, introduced in 1989 in a limited edition. These appealing little characters live deep in the woods with their animal friends. In his mind's eye, Miller has conjured up a world of leprechauns, brownies, menehunes and others, who frolic through the forest with friends such as the turtle, frog, mole and owl, virtually forgotten by the Large Folk. Each figurine, cast in hydrostone, is accompanied by a Certificate of Authenticity and a collector's book.

The Easter Bunny Family *and* The Angel Collection™

Although United Design's *The Easter Bunny Family* was not introduced as a limited edition line, collectors have made these "critters" collectible and much sought after. Created by United Design sculptor Donna Kennicutt, the bunnies boast colorful eggs, ducklings and chicks to help in the celebration of a joyous Easter. United Design introduced seven new Easter Bunny figurines in 1992, and retired six designs in 1993.

In 1991 *The Angel Collection*™ was introduced. There are three versions of "The Gift," limited edition angels created to help support the work of The Starlight Foundation. The 1991 edition of 2,000 figurines, and the 1992 edition of 3,500 figurines, each sold out entirely in their year of introduction. "The Gift '93" is limited to 3,500 figurines and is expected to sell out promptly as well.

Communication Links Keep Collectors Informed

One of the pleasures of collecting United Design's limited edition lines is the opportunity to receive newsletters about *Pennibears*™, *The Legend Of Santa Claus*, and other products, simply by registering one's purchases with the company. This communication link is enhanced by frequent appearances by United Design artists at annual collectibles shows. So while United Design retains its strong roots in Noble, Oklahoma, its owners and artists will continue to expand their horizons by reaching out to collectors all over the nation.

United Design's lush, green atrium, complete with lagoon. Schools of Koi fish populate the lagoon. Guests at United Design's manufacturing, administration and distribution facilities are greeted by a large Galapagos tortoise as they enter the atrium.

VickiLane Creative Design
Art Is a Heartwarming Way of Life for VickiLane Creators
Ron and Vicki Anderson

From her earliest childhood, an artistic atmosphere — and the expression of her abilities and talents — have been an essential part of life for Vicki Anderson. As the daughter of Jack and Viletta West of Viletta China Company, Vicki grew up surrounded by opportunities for education and development in the art fields: first in Roseburg, Oregon and later at the University of Oregon.

By the time she reached high school, young Vicki West had already discovered that she was blessed with marketable art talents. She received strong recognition and achievement awards for her calligraphy, watercolors, china painting and sculptures. Her artistic efforts became a means of financial support for her college education, resulting in the formation of a small business. Since then, Vicki's natural gifts — plus her own hard work and that of her husband, Ron Anderson — have resulted in a blossoming business with two locations employing over fifty people. Today, Vicki Anderson brings her creative imagination to life in her collectible art, affecting others with the same joy and love that are evident in each of her hand-made products.

A Thriving Family Business

Ever since their marriage in 1970, Ron and Vicki Anderson have studied and worked side by side, each contributing their individual strengths and mutual support to all endeavors. In 1983, the couple launched VickiLane Creative Design — at first with just the two of them working at home in the garage. Consistent and continuous growth has marked their path since those humble beginnings. Ron and Vicki believe that the past ten years have been the beginning of an exciting adventure for themselves and their collectors, with a bright future ahead. With great enthusiasm, they predict even more appealing products and more growth in the coming years.

VickiLane sees its service as bringing charming and unique gifts to the nation and the world. Each design is created and entirely hand-made with

Vicki Anderson is truly the heart of VickiLane. This creative lady has a remarkable ability to bring ideas to life through her skills and imagination. With a twinkle in her eyes, she designs one masterpiece of make-believe after another.

pride by craftspeople personally trained by Vicki and Ron Anderson. The resulting pieces become beloved for their combination of appeal, quality and sweetness, as well as collectibility. Basic form and color coordination are top priorities, so that all VickiLane collectibles can be united in display. Each piece becomes a joyous expression of life, having lasting value either as a collectible gift, or a decorative piece for the collector and family to enjoy. And because Vicki Anderson is such a prolific artist, each month provides new creations as she continues to share her imaginative talents.

Enter the Make-Believe World of VickiLane

Imagine for a moment that you have captured a dream, a moment of your pleasant memories, or sweet imaginary thoughts — and that you can hold it in your hand. VickiLane offers such a make-believe world where reality is nearby in each creation, symbolizing life situations. You find yourself recalling happy, meaningful thoughts and emotions, remembering times in your life with warm, fond memories. This world of VickiLane is

filled with innocence and soft expressions, as seen in creations that capture something inside the beholder. Observing the workmanship and artistry, you feel a part of each beautiful piece. It is Vicki's own wish to you that her feelings, thoughts, messages about living, and all life's heartwarming memories become a part of your life through her designs.

For example, contemporary "cow-llectors" will enjoy four new dressed figurines in keeping with the current times. "Jesse" peers beyond the boundaries of his field from the top of the fence, wondering what the big world is like out there. He anticipates the good life that lies ahead, beyond everything he sees or hopes for. "Elsie" is playing with her dolls in the cart, pretending she is already a mommy, as most cowgirls do. "Hank" is pondering his future in a "mooment" of reflection: "When I grow up, I want to be a ...," dreaming the day away. Then, we find "Cow Belle" in a romantic mood, admiring her lovely pasture, smelling the fragrant flowers, tinkling her bell softly as she wanders along in the refreshing summer breeze.

Each New VickiLane Design is Like an Addition to the "Family"

Ron Anderson says that "collectors are always curious to know what Vicki will come up with next." Even her production staff waits in anticipation to see what will unfold each month. Vicki's moldmaker states, "It's like a new birth into the family each time I get something new to work with, and I am always impressed." Mrs. Anderson has been extremely successful in portraying even

"Jesse" the cow leans against the fence post and dreams of far-away adventure in this appealing, hand-painted "cow-llectible" from VickiLane Creative Design.

her most imaginative ideas, much to the delight of her collectors. Very few artists have mastered as many media and fields of the art world as Vicki. Much of that success is attributed to her natural abilities, but also to her many years of study and education, which she constantly continues and improves.

Her little characters come to life with the make-believe that captivates collectors into falling in love with VickiLane creations. Two series that are very popular are the *Sweet Thumpins* bunnies, and *Mice Memories*. Each character is an individual delight, and as "families," these characters fascinate all the more. All seasons of life or times of the year can be found represented in Vicki's full line of sculptures.

Meet the Bunnies of Sweet Thumpin' Land

Living near Blackberry Hill in Vicki Anderson's imagination are six members of the bunny family in *Sweet Thumpin' Land*. The first of Vicki Anderson's limited edition figurines includes "Rachel Rabbit," who is passing through the gate to see her friend "Jessica." Rachel symbolizes each person's entry through the gate leading to the path of VickiLane. Rachel finds Jessica so that they can share tea and tender carrots in the second limited edition, "Tea Time."

"Albert" is working with his son, "Briar," building a toy airplane at his carpentry bench. The moment of amazement watching his father is captured in this limited edition named "Building Memories." For Christmas time, the "Cookie Peddler" shows Grandpa offering two bunnies his fresh tray of cookies for sale at a special price. Then "Violet" and her son "Benjamin" rest and talk on the park bench after spending the day together.

Communication With Collectors Keeps Vicki Anderson Inspired

Ron Anderson encourages collectors to keep in direct contact with him and Vicki, because "We enjoy getting letters. It makes us feel like we have a new friend each time. It is a joy to bring happiness into another person's life through the products we have available. Vicki's work continues to be in demand, even with a change in the times and current trends. When it comes to admiring her charming creatures, young and old enjoy them alike. Vicki has a sixth sense, it seems, for knowing what people will really appreciate."

In a letter to VickiLane, one collector said, "I

Here's "Blossom" at her desk, just after discovering how valuable her studying has been. She wants to be the first to raise her hand for her favorite teacher, Miss April.

Violet and her son Benjamin share a "Special Time" together after a day of shopping.

am always amazed each time I look at a new design, and am always surprised and awed at the detail and personality in the faces (Vicki) creates." Another collector dreamed, "I wish I lived next door, so I could be the first one to see what she is making next. It's a never-ending mystery. This woman really has a lot of creative talent!" Yet

another person expressed, "They (the figurines) are so cute and adorable, they bring back many good memories of my own life, and make me feel good (and younger) all over again."

"A photograph just doesn't do (Vicki's) work justice," another collector asserted, "you have to see for yourself the creativity and the 'message' that you can hear when you look at the expressions on their faces and connect it to what they are doing. You can think up your own story and let your own imagination run while you sit and look at them." Still another collector said simply of Vicki, "I wish I had her talent!"

As these quotes show, there is a sense of anticipation among those closely acquainted with Vicki Anderson's work. Many of the items she created years ago are still in popular demand, yet each new product elevates the level of quality and intricacy, detail and complexity found in her work. Vicki's recent endeavors in watercolor prints have been quickly received with enthusiasm. They help unite characters from some of her most popular sculpted figurines in scenes of great charm and animation.

An Invitation to Enter the World of VickiLane

Ron and Vicki Anderson invite collectors to take a walk down VickiLane with them...and to meet all the delightful personalities created from Vicki's thoughts and imagination. As friends of VickiLane, collectors have the opportunity to read about each design, listen to the heart of the designer, and begin to appreciate the depth of feeling in each wonderful creation. The tales found with these collectible figurines offer a marvelous world of adventure as they open the pathway to VickiLane: a magical land filled with beauty.

With destiny in their hearts, the Andersons have set out to make an impact on the gift and collectible industries. They have chosen a philosophy underlying each step of their journey: "Create an experience of joy and beauty that will delight and uplift every heart, making a positive influence through the products we design, the ideas we stimulate, and the many jobs we provide." Vicki feels fortunate to be able to put her talents to work in this outstanding way. And with her family surrounding her, she loves every minute of it!

WACO Products Corporation
Bringing Magic to Life With WACO'S *Melody In Motion*®

When it comes to music and motion, WACO prides itself on bringing the magic to life! WACO combines fine art and advanced technology to create a line of delightful *Melody In Motion*® figurines. These creations are prized for their fine porcelain characterizations, beautiful studio recorded music, and complex, life-like movements.

The *Melody In Motion* porcelains are molded from sculptures created by the award-winning Japanese master sculptor Seiji Nakane. Handcrafted in Seto, the porcelain capital of Japan, each figurine is faithfully reproduced by highly trained production staff members to match Nakane's original sculptures.

Masterful Craftsmanship and State-of-the-Art Technology Combined

The figurines are formed of the pure clay which is found only in Seto, then fired to a bisque finish. The final touch is performed by skilled artisans who carefully paint each detail by hand. The figurines are then fired for a second time. Each piece is thoroughly inspected to ensure that every one meets the exact specifications of the original artwork.

Precision mechanical technology and solid state sound reproduction inside every *Melody In Motion* figurine create an electro-mechanical device that activates the music and the graceful movement — thus making each and every *Melody In Motion* porcelain unique. A high-quality precision motor drives a gear train that activates a multitude of cams and levers to create the life-like movements of each figurine. Each part of the mechanical device is custom made for that style figurine, with each mechanism designed and engineered to achieve a specific movement.

This advanced technology is truly exceptional, and is comparable to that found in high-quality appliances and camcorders. Combining music to complete the story of each figurine is achieved by selecting the appropriate tune and musical instrument, and then recording the selected tune in a sound studio by professional instrumentalists. The high quality of the music is evident in the

Santa toasts us with his bottle of Coca Cola® and taps his foot to the tune of "Jingle Bell Rock" for this 1994 Melody In Motion® presentation.

Tchaikovsky theme played by a professional concert cellist, or the carousel music recorded from working carousel band organs from around the world.

Combining the art of porcelain with precision technology, each figurine is presented as a tableau that tells a story to spark the imagination of the collector. *Melody In Motion* figurines, which can only be produced in limited quantities due to complex design and painstaking craftsmanship, are exceptional both in beauty and in technology.

A Brief History of "Automata" Sets the Stage for Melody In Motion

Although the *Melody In Motion* figurines are unique in today's collectibles market, the concept of a moving figure in an artistic tableau is very old.

From the Melody In Motion® *clock grouping, Willie is featured in "Low Pressure Job" as a comical fireman whose fire hose has a leak. With his faithful dalmatian at his side, he whistles "There'll Be A Hot Time In The Old Town Tonight."*

In fact, mankind's fascination with "automata" can be traced back for hundreds of years.

As early as the 3rd century B.C., during the Han dynasty in China, a mechanical orchestra was handcrafted for the Emperor. In those days, these entertaining devices were powered by water movement or air pressure. By the mid-15th century, wind-up spring mechanisms were introduced and they became a portable power source for automata. By the end of the 1700s, very intricate automatons in human form were created by master-makers. Those masters were able to produce only a few pieces in their lifetime. All were for wealthy patrons; only a handful of those works survive. Today they can only be found in museums or in private collections.

Melody In Motion: The Willie Collection

The character of "Willie" is at the heart of *Melody In Motion*. This wistful clown tells a timeless story about the human condition. The "Willie" figurines bring back warm memories and evoke satisfying feelings about life. As an anchor in a sea of rapidly changing values, collectors say that they offer a welcome, safe haven.

"Heartbreak Willie" soulfully wails his saxophone to the classic 50s tune: "Heartbreak Hotel." "Willie the Golfer" comes complete with a Japanese quartz clock in his tower, and plays "Oh, What a Beautiful Mornin'." "Lamp Light Willie" features a lamp that turns on and off by a separate switch, and plays "Standing on the Corner." These and many other whimsical figures allow us to enter "Willie's" carefree world for a time...to take it easy and forget our worries.

Melody In Motion: The Carousel Collection

The "Grand Carousel" serves as the showpiece of the *Melody In Motion* line. Standing 22-1/2" tall and weighing twenty-five pounds, it is a wonder of animation and music. The pre-production process took Seiji Nakane more than a year, and the completion of the first Carousel was a project of over two years' time. This combination of "beauty" (porcelain) and "beast" (motor, gears and audio system) has emerged as one of the masterworks in the contemporary collectibles field. It is as magnificent in appearance as it is in technological achievement. It boasts flashing lights and two levels of moving horses. Intricate detailing and brilliant colors create a fantasy crowded with golden lions, purple elephants and legendary griffins. The carousel comes with two audio tapes of authentic band music. What's more, its audio tape player — built into the base — plays all standard cassette tapes.

The *Melody In Motion* collection also boasts three additional carousels of various sizes and features. The "Blue Danube Carousel" has colorful horses moving gracefully up and down their shiny gold-toned poles to the popular tune of the "Blue Danube Waltz." "Victoria Park Carousel" is sculpted in exquisite detail and delicately painted in soft pastels. This grand carousel plays the glorious melody, "Under the Double Eagle." The "King of Clowns Carousel" displays two exquisitely sculpted reliefs crowned with beautifully shaped scallops. Each one displays the artisan's touch — extravagant flourishes and energetic clowns, as well as lively and nostalgic band-organ music.

Melody In Motion: The Heritage Collection

A diverse array of hand-painted porcelains, *The Heritage Collection* features a number of familiar and appealing characters. There's "When I Grow Up," where a little boy admires his hero — a fireman — to the tune of "Wind Beneath My Wings"; and

"South of the Border," with a laid-back Mexican troubadour playing "Cielito Lindo."

"Campfire Cowboy" moves his head, hand and foot to his own rendition of "Mammas, Don't Let Your Babies Grow Up To Be Cowboys," and "Fiddler" stomps his foot and moves his bow and hand as he plays "She'll Be Coming 'Round the Mountain." The "Peanut Vendor," "Balloon Clown" and "Madame Harp Player" round out this *Heritage* tribute, each with its own special movement and music.

Melody In Motion: The Clock Collection

"Willie" and other characters star in the *Melody In Motion* clock grouping: eight hand-made and hand-painted porcelain figurines with handsome built-in, working clocks. In addition, of course, each piece features music and movement. There's "Low Pressure Job," "Day's End," "Willie the Golfer," "The Artist," "Wall St. Willie," and "Clockpost Willie" featuring the collection's "signature character."

In addition, "Grandfather Clock" portrays a distinguished old gent in his rocking chair as he smokes his pipe and rocks back and forth to the rhythmic tune of "The Syncopated Clock." Finally, "Golden Mountain Clock" portrays three gnomes pushing ore cars through a tunnel, while two others work their pickaxes into the Gold Mine Walls to the tune of "Viennese Musical Clock."

Melody In Motion: The Santa Collection and Retired Pieces

Each year since 1986, WACO has introduced an annual Santa, and each year these appealing "St. Nick" sculptures have sold out and retired. For 1994, the official *Melody In Motion* Santa — presented in association with Coca Cola® — is called "Jingle Bell Rock."

In addition, there are over thirty more *Melody In Motion* figurines on a wide range of subjects, whose limited editions have been retired or scheduled for retirement. The success and popularity of the *Melody In Motion* line is evident in the strong interest of collectors for these older editions.

A Personal Invitation to Join the Melody In Motion Collectors Society

WACO cordially invites collectors to participate in the magic by joining the *Melody In Motion* Collectors Society. Dues are $27.50 for the first year, or $50.00 for two years' membership. Collectors will

also have the opportunity to purchase gift memberships for relatives or special friends.

During the first year of membership, a host of exciting benefits will be offered to members. An exclusive figurine for Society members only, "Springtime," will be the gift of sculptor Seiji Nakane to each new member. If "Springtime" were available at retail, it would sell for $45.00 or more. In addition, each member will receive a personal Membership Card, a complimentary annual subscription to the "Melody Notes" newsletter, the latest *Melody In Motion* catalog and a $10.00 members' coupon, which can be applied to the purchase of any *MIM* figurine except the Member's Only issue.

Each member will also receive a Personal Redemption Certificate entitling that individual to purchase the Society's limited edition figurine created exclusively for members. This 9-3/4"-tall work of art, "Willie the Collector," has assembled his own miniature collection for all to marvel at. His head moves, as he whistles the tune, "When The Saints Go Marching In," and the same tune is heard in the background, as if it were played by the miniature "Willie The Trumpeter," which is being held by him.

Willie enjoys a lazy afternoon of fishing and "Smooth Sailing" in this Melody In Motion® *figurine. He whistles "Those Lazy Hazy Days of Summer" in accompaniment to a song on the radio.*

The Walt Disney Classics Collection
Capturing Moments of Beauty and Magic From Classic Disney Animated Films and Short Cartoons

Walt Disney's desire to create the "illusion of life" with real characters and stories that would "ring true" was the impetus behind every technical and creative breakthrough in Disney animation. As Walt and his artists pushed the boundaries of animation art, they developed techniques that became major filmmaking principles and established a philosophy that has become the Disney way — going the extra step, and adding that final special touch to achieve what couldn't previously be accomplished.

Now, the lifelikeness and believability at the heart of every classic animated Disney film has inspired today's gifted group of Disney artists to achieve the same "illusion of life" in fine sculptures for the *Walt Disney Classics Collection*. To capture the living spirit of the original characters and scenes in a three-dimensional art program, Disney artists apply the same exacting animation principles and Disney philosophy.

Going that extra step — or "plussing" as it's called at Disney, occurs at every stage of each figurine's development — even the most basic one of

A dancing Mickey and Minnie Mouse are featured in The Delivery Boy *series, "a black and white" grouping based on a 1931 classic Disney cartoon.*

deciding which film moments are most special and memorable. Disney artists, archivists and collectors view hundreds of hours of animation art, character model sheets and beautiful film background paintings to find the moments that touch people's hearts and memories in a special way. Is it Sorcerer Mickey frolicking with his enchanted broom? Or the Field Mouse lifting his paws to capture a single, trembling dewdrop? These are essential questions, for every decision — from pose to painting — ultimately flows from the desire to capture the magic in each of the chosen moments.

Creating In a New Dimension

Once the character or scene has been selected, the original animation drawings are researched for reference. Working from hundreds of drawings, sketches, and even fully rendered paintings, Disney artists begin to sketch drawings to be used for the sculpture, relying on their own expertise to find a pose or gesture with the most appeal and greatest emotional impact.

As they work, they often answer different questions than those posed in animation: "What does the space between Thumper's ears look like from a top view? How does Lucifer look from behind?" Here too, going that extra step plays a role as hundreds of drawings are created, critiqued and revised until the artists' drawings identifying the exact animation pose to be used are handed over to the sculptor, along with all the animation research materials. As noted, the artists' drawings will sometimes include turn-arounds to help answer the "different questions" posed in translating two-dimensional animation drawings into three-dimensional sculpting.

As with the drawings, sculpts are done — and done again — as animators and sculptors look for ways to more fully capture the piece's emotion. Extensive critiquing is done by numerous animation artists — old and new — to make sure the sculpt works from all angles — a consideration not necessary in original animation, but a judgment about "believability" that Disney animation artists

are trained to make. Here, animation principles play an especially important role. Applied to the sculpts, the principles enhance the characters' believability. Lucifer's paw is extended for more "pounceability." Friend Owl's eyes crinkle up with laughter, and Donald's pesky nephew gets a bit more of a cocky tilt to his head.

Once a final sculpt is approved, Disney again takes that extra special "plussing" step by using many individual molds to fully capture the detail of a single sculpt. Slip, a liquid form of clay, is poured into the molds and allowed to partially air dry. The "greenware" is removed from the molds and the numerous delicate pieces are assembled with more slip. Each piece must then be hand-detailed to add texture and other details, and to remove tiny marks left by the mold. Assembling the pieces from the molds can be as painstaking as the original sculpting itself. A sculpture like "Goofy's Grace Notes" from the 1942 *Symphony Hour* cartoon contains eighteen individual pieces. Even Goofy's bowtie is cast separately to create the dimension and depth of a real bowtie. And "Horace's High Notes," also from the *Symphony Hour*, contains nineteen separate pieces!

Once assembled, the painting and firing process begins. To recreate the mood of the original animation, the Disney Ink and Paint labs strive to duplicate exact animation colors used in the film. As Disney artists translate original Disney animation colors to ceramics, they discover new opportunities to suggest textures and special effects that animation could only hint at. They also discover new challenges since ceramic colors react differ-

ently to heat. Often, the difference between ceramic and animation colors dictates many hours of experimentation to get just the right match. To achieve the correct coloration, multiple firings are often required.

For example, to create Donald's jacket in the "Oh, Boy What a Jitterbug!" piece from the 1940 cartoon, *Mr. Duck Steps Out*, a first firing lays the teal undercolor on the jacket, while a second adds the snappy yellow stripes. And in the sculpture "Meany, Sneaky, Roos-A-Fee" Disney artists have caught Lucifer, the troublemaking feline from *Cinderella* in the act of dabbing his paw in the dustpan, ready to ruin Cinderella's freshly scrubbed floor. With true Disney attention to detail, even the bottom of Lucifer's paw is covered with soot — requiring an additional firing — yet another example of taking that extra step.

But where the Disney concept of "plussing" makes the collection truly special is the final delicate extra touches to the sculptures. Some of them require many additional hours of design as pieces are "plussed" with precious metals, crystal, or blown glass to provide an extra touch of believability.

For example, "A Lovely Dress for Cinderelly," not only features the beautifully hand-painted pink gown itself, but also ³/₄-inch hand-painted bronze miniatures of the mice and blue birds working on the dress. To meet their exact design and modeling specifications, Disney searched worldwide for a studio that could produce these quality miniatures.

Even the scissors, needles, and mice's tails are made of hand-painted cast metal. The ends of the pink bow adorning the dress are also sculpted out of bronze and hand-painted, so that the birds can appear dramatically suspended in mid-air! The ballgown comes with a sculpted attic floor on a walnut wood base, showcased under a crystal-clear glass dome.

Another example of "plussing" involved the design of the *Delivery Boy* sculptures based on Disney's 1931 cartoon classic. Characters in early cartoons had arms and legs that were not anatomically correct. Because their limbs moved more like rubber hoses, the cartooning style became known as "rubber hose" animation.

Disney was determined to capture this old-time look in their animation sculptures, but was told it could not be done, since it required fusing different substances. Refusing to allow production challenges to compromise the look of the pieces, Disney artists and constituents worked for a full year, experimenting with a variety of materials.

From the 1940 cartoon, Mr. Duck Steps Out, *Donald and Daisy Duck are shown jitterbugging in the sold out, limited edition piece, "Oh, Boy What a Jitterbug!". Also included in the collection is Donald's candy-toting nephew, Dewey.*

The Walt Disney Classics Collection *strikes a new high note with animation sculptures from the 1942 cartoon classic,* Symphony Hour. *Featured are Mickey Mouse, Horace Horsecollar, Clarabelle Cow and Goofy.*

Finally, the team found that cast pewter, joined to the porcelain bodies, yielded the desired result. This inventive solution allows Mickey and Minnie to be shown dancing on one foot. This special effect — the thin, fluid look of the arms and legs — could not have been achieved with fragile ceramic material alone. In addition, the sculptures are painted in black and white — showing many variations and gradations of these colors — just like the early film shorts.

Countless other sculptures in the collection have also been "plussed." Goofy's bassoon and Horace Horsecollar's trumpet from the *Symphony Hour* sculptures are both plated with 24 karat gold. When painted porcelain bubbles seemed too heavy in Cinderella's hand in the "They Can't Stop Me From Dreaming," sculpture, a hand-blown glass bubble was used instead. The shining stars on Sorcerer Mickey's hat in the "Mischievous Apprentice" sculpture from *Fantasia* are made from platinum. And in "Little April Shower" from *Bambi*, the woodland mouse takes his morning shower beneath a single, shining cut-glass drop.

In addition to the incredible care and attention to detail that goes into the creation of each sculpture in the *Walt Disney Classics Collection*, each piece bears a backstamp or bottomstamp to increase collectibility. The stamp includes the Walt Disney signature logo, the name of the film represented, and a special symbol to denote the year in which the sculpture was produced. Roy E. Disney, President of Disney Animation and Walt's nephew, endorses each sculpture with a Certificate of Authenticity. "We spent two years developing the *Walt Disney Classics Collection*," explains Susanne Lee, vice president of the *Walt Disney Classics Collection*, "and the culminating proof of our success is that the sculptures have earned the endorsement of Roy E. Disney."

While the development process for sculptures is lengthy, in some ways, the entire process has brought each character even closer to Walt Disney's original vision of lifelikeness and believability. In their own way, the sculpts "plus" the original animation by achieving the ultimate dimensional look — bringing the animation art yet another step closer to "the illusion of life."

New Sculptures

The *Walt Disney Classics Collection* was introduced in 1992 with thirty-two pieces reflecting special moments from films such as *Bambi*, *Cinderella*, and *Fantasia* as well as short cartoons starring Mickey Mouse, Donald Duck and other beloved Disney characters.

On the drawing board from the *Walt Disney Classics Collection*, are several new upcoming sculptures. First is a delightful new grouping of characters from Walt Disney's 1931 cartoon classic, *Three Little Pigs*, celebrating its sixtieth anniversary this year. At the time of its release, *Three Little Pigs* broke all contemporary box office records, becoming a bigger hit than some of the features it was shown with. This remarkably inventive film broke new ground in creating animated personalities and was enriched by attention to detail, music and the imaginative use of color.

Other upcoming sculptures in the Collection include a grouping of characters from Walt Disney's animated classic *Peter Pan*, celebrating its fortieth anniversary this year. The grouping will reflect all the comedy, fantasy and action of the film based on Barrie's classic play. Feature characters include boyish hero Peter Pan, treacherous Captain Hook, and the feisty little coquette, Tinker Bell.

The *Walt Disney Classics Collection* offers a wide range of opportunities for collectors to participate in the program. Open stock prices range in price from $55 to $300 and limited edition sculptures sell from $200 to $800. With the fabled Disney Archives to choose from, and with collectors' desires firmly in mind, the creators of the *Walt Disney Classics Collection* have an unlimited wealth of treasures and tradition to draw from.

Company Summaries
About the Marketers and Manufacturers of
Limited Edition Collectibles

There are several hundred firms actively involved in today's world of limited edition collectibles, with bases of operation in the United States, Canada and in many other countries. This chapter presents some basic background information about some of the more prominent firms in the field. Each company summary provides an address, and in many cases the name of a contact person, which collectors may use when inquiring about a firm's products and services. Also included is a listing of the types of limited edition products each firm makes or markets. This chapter provides an interesting and helpful introduction to many limited edition collectibles manufacturers.

ALASKA PORCELAIN STUDIOS, INC.
P.O. Box 1550
Soldotna, AK 99669
(907) 262-5626

Figurines, Dolls, Bells, Christmas Ornaments

Founded in 1986 by Jonathan Rodgers, artist, and Kay Vernon, ceramist, the studio is devoted to fine porcelain statuary art that reflects Alaska's history, indigenous cultures, wildlife and lifestyles. From humble beginnings in a one-car garage, the studio has grown to occupy an 8,000-square-foot facility just outside Soldotna on Alaska's Kenai Peninsula. It is here, set on the edge of the rivers and ocean, that the concept, design, mold-production, porcelain production and finishing of each piece takes place. Tours of the factory are available Monday through Friday from June 15 through September 15.

The Alaska Porcelain Collectors' Society offers an array of benefits to its members.

ALEXANDER DOLL COMPANY, INCORPORATED
615 West 131 Street
New York, NY 10027
(212) 283-5900

Dolls

One of the first and most successful doll companies in the United States, the Alexander Doll Company was founded in 1923 by Beatrice Alexander Behrman who later became known throughout the world as "Madame Alexander." In the 1920s and 1930s, the demand for Madame Alexander Dolls skyrocketed, and Madame Alexander received the first Doll of the Year (DOTY) Lifetime Achievement Award. Some of the most popular dolls were the Dionne Quintuplets, Scarlett O'Hara, Princess Elizabeth and Princess Margaret Rose.

The Alexander Doll Company has grown in size and popularity; to date, more than 5,000 different styles of dolls have been produced by the company and The Madame Alexander Doll Club currently has over 14,000 members.

AMERICAN ARTIST PORTFOLIO INC.
Pauline Ward
9625 Tetley Drive
Somerset, VA 22972
(800) 842-4445
(703) 672-0286

Graphics

American Artist Portfolio Inc. was founded in 1988 to publish and market the works of realist artist Adolf Sehring. Located in Somerset, Virginia, American Artist Portfolio's first offerings were eight still lifes and landscapes. A year later, two more graphics were added to the edition. Sehring created four serigraghs depicting African wildlife in 1990. In 1993, two new multigraphs were created: "Look What I Got" and "Wildflowers," utilizing a new printing process.

Renowned for his portraits of children and dignitaries, Sehring is the only American artist to be commissioned by the Vatican to paint the official portrait of Pope John Paul II.

Sehring's offset lithographs and mixed-media serigraphs are reproduced from the artist's original oils and are sold through select galleries throughout the continental United States, Alaska, Hawaii and Japan.

AMERICAN ARTISTS/ GRAPHICS BUYING SERVICE
Peter Canzone
925 Sherwood Drive
Lake Bluff, IL 60044
(708) 295-5355
Fax: (708) 295-5491

Plates, Figurines, Graphics

Graphics Buying Service (GBS) originated as a firm devoted to the commissioning and marketing of graphic art, offering quality, limited edition prints by top plate artists, at affordable prices.

GBS artists have included James Auckland, Irene Spencer, Frank Russell and Gertrude Barrer, Donald Zolan, Richard Zolan, Fred Stone, Dave Chapple and Mary Vickers. Currently, American Artists handles only Fred Stone lithographs.

In 1981, GBS began a division called American Artists, dedicated to the creation of the finest in limited edition

collector plates. Today, American Artists/GBS continues to introduce graphics and limited edition plates as well as posters and sculptures. The firm is currently producing plates by the award-winning equine artist Fred Stone, cat plates by Zoe Stokes and Susan Leigh, and works by Donald Zolan.

AMERICAN GREETINGS
10500 American Road
Cleveland, OH 44144
(216) 252-7300

Christmas Ornaments, Plates
American Greetings is the world's largest publicly owned manufacturer and distributor of greeting cards and social expression products, gift wrap and accessories, party goods, stationery, calendars, candles, picture frames and hair accessories.

The firm is also a recognized leader in the creation and licensing of character properties such as Holly Hobbie, Ziggy, Strawberry Shortcake and the Care Bears.

Products are distributed through a global network of 97,000 retail outlets in over fifty countries, and are printed in sixteen languages.

Founded in 1906, American Greetings employs 21,000 and operates thirty-one plants and facilities in the United States, the United Kingdom and Mexico.

ANHEUSER-BUSCH, INC.
2700 South Broadway
St. Louis, MO 63118
(314) 577-7465
Fax: (314) 577-9656

Steins, Plates
Founded in St. Louis, Missouri in 1852, Anheuser-Busch has reigned as the world's largest brewer for over thirty-five years. Since 1975, Anheuser-Busch has created steins of character and celebration, with classic and contemporary themes and styles to please a wide range of collectors. All are crafted with the same dedication to perfection that beer drinkers have come to expect from this renowned American brewer.

Working in close collaboration with the Ceramarte stein manufactory in Brazil, where the majority of Anheuser-Busch steins are crafted, as well as with classic German stein makers like Gerz, Thewalt and Restal, Anheuser-Busch is able to add more steins and greater variety to its offerings each year.

Anheuser-Busch has responded to immense collector demand by producing a number of handsome series, including *Discover America, Sports Series, Clydesdale Series, National Landmark Series, Limited Edition Series, Birds of Prey Series* and *Civil War Series*.

In addition to its famous steins, Anheuser-Busch now has unveiled several series of collector plates measuring 8½" in diameter and featuring 24-karat gold rims. Their topics vary from the 1992 *Olympic Team* to *Man's Best Friend* and a *Holiday Series*.

With the current growth of the stein market, prospects for Anheuser-Busch stein collectors look strong. And with expansion continuing into collector plates, ornaments and figurines, the firm continues to research new designs and styles to continue the stein-making quality and tradition established by Anheuser-Busch.

The fifth and newest edition to the Endangered Species Series, *the "Grizzly Bear Stein" portrays the mighty carnivore roaming his territory as the undisputed ruler of his domain.*

ANNA-PERENNA PORCELAIN, INC.
Klaus D. Vogt or Neil Kugelman
71 Weyman Avenue
New Rochelle, NY 10805
(914) 633-3777
(800) 627-2550
Fax: (914) 633-8727

Plates, Figurines
ANNA-PERENNA Porcelain is an international firm specializing in limited edition art plates made of hard-paste Bavarian porcelain, miniature figurines and limited edition sculptures.

Founded in 1977 by Klaus D. Vogt, the former president of Rosenthal, U.S.A., ANNA-PERENNA has translated the art of Thaddeus Krumeich, Count Bernadotte, Al Hirschfeld and foremost Pat Buckley Moss, into limited edition plates.

ANNA-PERENNA Porcelain also produces a unique collection of limited edition porcelain figurines designed by P. Buckley Moss.

Other ANNA-PERENNA collectible lines include the *Adorables*, handmade and hand-painted miniatures by Scottish artist Peter Fagan. These whimsical pieces have generated thousands of loyal members of the Adorables Collectors Society in Europe and the United States.

ANNA-PERENNA also represents Art Foundation Studios of Spain, and the famous sculptors Joseph Bofill, Jose Luis de Casasola and NICO.

ANNALEE® MOBILITEE DOLLS INC.
Reservoir Road, Box 708
Meredith, NH 03253-0708
(603) 279-3333
Fax: (603) 279-6659

Dolls, Christmas Ornaments
The story of Annalee Thorndike, artist and creator of Annalee Dolls, is as close as one can come to a fairy tale. With humble beginnings in Concord, New Hampshire, Annalee made dolls as a hobby: first for herself and then for friends who kept their requests coming. Always an individual, Annalee spurned "nine-to-five" work after high school and made dollmaking her career, selling her dolls by word-of-mouth and through a craftsmen's league.

Annalee's move to Meredith, New Hampshire came when she married Chip Thorndike. For a time, her dolls became "just a hobby" as the Thorndikes dealt with the demands of chicken farming. When economic times changed and the business failed, Annalee and Chip turned to dollmaking as their main income. Chip's inventive nature proved invaluable as he created the frame that gave the dolls their "Mobilitee." He proved to be a craftsman, creating detailed accessories for the dolls. Over the years, the demand for Annalee's characters, spurred by their exposure in New York City and other urban markets, continued to grow until today, Annalee Mobilitee employs over 400 workers and is known worldwide.

Today the Annalee Doll Society™ has

grown from a grass-roots fan club, founded in 1983, to a collectibles society of over 30,000 members who eagerly await each year's new dolls. The Doll Society's Summer and Fall Auctions give members the opportunity to meet with fellow collectors and seek out the older dolls that have grown phenomenally in value. Annalee and Chip, with assistance from sons Chuck and Town, still lead Annalee Dolls. As the company and its facilities continue to grow, Annalee still designs the dolls with help from Chuck and oversees the operations with Town, now company president and CEO. Annalee Thorndike's presence is reflected in the spark and twinkle that radiates from the face of every doll that she designs.

The 1993 Folk Hero™ doll from Annalee® Mobilitee Dolls is the "Pony Express," a Hero mounted on his horse and in full western attire.

ANRI WOODSCULPTURES

Cheryl Gorski
73 Route 31 North
Pennington, NJ 08534
(609) 737-7010
ANRI Club: (800) YES-ANRI
Fax: (609) 737-1545

Plates, Figurines, Christmas Ornaments

The House of ANRI, located in the South Tyrol, Italy, was founded in 1912 by Anton Riffeser. Since that time, an ANRI Woodsculpture has come to be one of the most sought-after collectible art forms. The hand-painted limited editions include relief plates and figurines by such renowned artists as Juan Ferrandiz and Sarah Kay. The beautiful wood-sculpted nativity sets of Ulrich Bernardi, Professor Karl Loult and Ferrandiz are also world-renowned. ANRI Club, a society for collectors of ANRI, was formed in 1983.

Among the specific benefits offered to members are: a free "Gift of Love" figurine designed by Sarah Kay and valued at $175; the opportunity to purchase

exclusive Club figurines; a subscription to *Reflections*, their Club magazine; unlimited access to their research services; advance notice of special events; and a Members-Only binder filled with the history and production of ANRI figurines, current information and members' very own collector's log.

This adorable collection of hand-sculpted, wooden figurines depicting the four seasons comes from Australian artist Sarah Kay and the master artisans at ANRI. From the left are: "Winter Cheer," "Summer Beauty," "Spring Delight" and "Autumn Magic."

ARMANI COLLECTION

c/o Miller Import Corporation
300 Mac Lane
Keasbey, NJ 08832
(908) 417-0330
Fax: (908) 417-0031

Figurines

The dream of providing American collectors with some of the world's finest collectibles and giftware prompted Herb Miller to found Miller Import Corporation in 1953. Using his savings as capital, Miller began searching the world for quality products.

One of Miller's first real discoveries was high quality, full-lead crystal from Germany. The *Byrdes Crystal Collection*, which contains over 175 pieces of crystal, soon became one of his most popular lines.

But it was Miller's discovery of a small company in Italy that was to make collectibles history. There Miller discovered the work of sculptor Giuseppe Armani and thought his unique style could become popular in the United States. Miller began working closely with Armani to create human and wildlife subjects which would appeal to American collectors. These figurines were to become known as the *Armani Collection*.

Today, Armani's work is known throughout the collectible and art world for its realistic sculpting and elegant painting and detail. Each year, this prolific sculptor delights his audiences with new sculptures presented in the age-old Renaissance tradition, but retaining a contemporary flair that transcends the age.

Armani first executes his sculptural masterworks in clay, and then draws upon the expertise of the Florence Sculture d'Arte studios to recreate his works for collectors. Produced in the finest cold-cast porcelain, Armani's figurines are finished by master painters. Upon completion, Miller Import works closely with Armani to ensure that each and every new sculpture in his collection is presented to the United States marketplace.

Miller Import Corporation is the exclusive U.S. importer and distributor of the *Armani Collection* and is founder of the G. Armani Society, the collector club for fans of Armani's works.

From Armani's Four Seasons collection, "Spring - The Bicycle," is an elegant and graceful portrayal of a breezy spring day.

ART MARKETING GROUP INT'L, LTD.

Jerry Miley
1701 West St. Germain Street
Suite 102,
St. Cloud, MN 56301
(612) 252-3942
Fax: (612) 252-9397

D.H. USSHER LTD. (CANADIAN DIST.)
1132 West 15th Street
North Vancouver, British Columbia
Canada V7P 1M9

Plates, Graphics

Art Marketing Group has been pro-

ducing limited edition collector plates and framed prints since 1983.

Derk Hansen of Woodbury, Minnesota is the artist for all the plates and prints that the company currently sells.

ARTAFFECTS, LTD.
Richard Habeeb
P.O. Box 98
Staten Island, NY 10307
(718) 948-6767
Fax: (718) 967-4521

Plates, Dolls, Figurines, Graphics, Bells, Christmas Ornaments
Richard J. Habeeb, an avid plate collector since 1971, unexpectedly began a business when advertising to sell some of his plates. A family of 20,000 collectors was developed, collectors who listened to Richard's recommendations.

This background as a collector and dealer spurred him on to develop collectibles under his own hallmark. Vague Shadows was formed in 1977 to produce and market the works of Gregory Perillo. Both the *Curator Collection* and *Signature Collection* were formed to feature the works of outstanding artists whose paintings set standards of excellence in their fields. In 1988, all three collections were consolidated under one hallmark, Artaffects.

Gregory Perillo has produced many award-winning collectibles for Artaffects, which range from plates to figurines, lithographs, porcelain collector dolls, pewter belt buckles and sculptures. The Artaffects Perillo Collectors Club has proven very popular with Perillo collectors both old and new.

"Brave & Free," from Artaffects' Children of the Plains series by artist Gregory Perillo, is crafted of special porcelains with beaded clothing and accessory materials that most closely resemble original Native American garments.

Artaffects also represents the work of Carol Roeda and her *Simple Wonders*, Rob Sauber, Sally Maxwell, MaGo (Maurizio Goracci), Lou Marchetti and Adrian Chesterman. New figural collections include the adorable *Blue Ribbon Babies*, the Victorian nursery rhyme grouping entitled *Ruffles and Rhymes* and a striking selection of angels and flowers called *Petals from Heaven*. *Children of the Plains*, Gregory Perillo's newest doll series, is also being produced.

ARTISTS OF THE WORLD
Thomas E. Blachowski
2915 North 67th Place
Scottsdale, AZ 85251
(602) 946-6361
Fax: (602) 941-8918

Figurines, Christmas Ornaments
Artists of the World was founded in 1976 to represent Arizona artist, Ettore (Ted) DeGrazia. However, over the years, they have represented many artists, including Don Ruffin, Larry Toschik and Kee Fun Ng.

To this day, Artists of the World is still primarily focused in reproducing the works of Ted DeGrazia. A variety of products with DeGrazia's unique style is currently available, such as figurines, miniature figurines and collector plates. Artists of the World also represents the Horizonte line of whimsical animal figurines and magnets. These animals are from Uruguay and come in many different sizes and species.

Artists of the World's main showroom is located in Scottsdale, and collectors are welcome to call and make arrangements to visit when they are in Arizona.

THE ASHTON-DRAKE GALLERIES
9200 North Maryland Avenue
Niles, IL 60714
(800) 634-5164

Dolls
The Ashton-Drake Galleries is a leading collectibles company specializing in limited edition dolls. Ashton-Drake uses the Uniform Grading Standards for Dolls to evaluate the dolls it reviews. Only dolls which meet all ten standards and are judged to be of the highest quality, or "premiere" grade, are recommended to collectors.

Its first collection — *Yolanda's*

Picture-Perfect Babies — was designed by popular doll artist Yolanda Bello. Since then, Ashton-Drake has introduced a variety of doll collections by other accomplished artists, including Cindy McClure, Dianna Effner, Kathy Barry-Hippensteel, Michelle Severino, Jeanne Singer, Gabrielle Rademann, Mary Tretter, Julie Good-Krüger and Susan Krey. Baby, children, fashion and character dolls are all represented in the company's product line.

Ashton-Drake dolls are available at dealers throughout the country or by contacting the company directly.

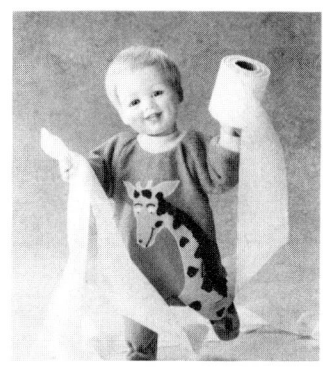

Stevie runs down the hallway with a roll of toilet paper in his hand, leaving a trail behind him. "Catch Me If You Can" is part of The Ashton-Drake Galleries' Caught in the Act series by artist Mary Tretter.

THE B & J COMPANY
P.O. Box 67
Georgetown, TX 78626
(512) 863-8318
Fax: (512) 863-0833

Plates, Dolls, Graphics
The B & J Company was started in 1975 in Tempe, Arizona by Bill and Jan Hagara to produce and market prints of Jan Hagara's work. In 1977, they moved the business to Georgetown, Texas.

Their first offerings were cards and fine art prints, featuring children with an old-fashioned look, which has become Jan's trademark.

Jan's plate series are very successful and have tremendous secondary market activity. Jan's prints are also extremely popular, selling out in a few months, with editions of 1,000 or 2,000.

The popularity of Jan's work also led to the formation of the Jan Hagara Collectors' Club in 1987. In a recent move designed to enhance their marketing effort, the Hagaras purchased the Royal

Orleans Company, which is now known as Jan Hagara Collectables, Inc.

BAND CREATIONS

28427 North Ballard
Lake Forest, IL 60045
(708) 816-0900

Dolls, Figurines

BAND Creations is an importer/distributor of many new and interesting collectibles and giftware lines.

Artist Teresa Madsen created *Busy-Bodies* for BAND Creations, a collection of whimsical and amusing professional and sports figures.

Jeannette Richards and Sandra Penfield created *Best Friends*, a collection of angels of the month, and a second series, *First Friends Begin in Childhood*. Both exciting new series have made a definite impression on the collectibles market.

Well-known artist Tom Rubel created "The Nativity" for BAND Creations from the *Studio Collection*, a dynamic work of art and a lovely collectible.

Just recently, BAND introduced the *Athena Collection* of fine ceramic collectible bottles depicting famous Grecian art.

Artist Pat Wilson's exquisite Santas for BAND Creations are hand-made limited editions, whose faces and hands are sculpted by Pat herself.

The November Angel from BAND Creations' Best Friends™ collection was created by artists Jeannette Richards and Sandra Penfield.

BAREUTHER

c/o Wara Intercontinental Co.
Helga or Ingo Rautenberg
20101 West Eight Mile Road
Detroit, MI 48219
(313) 535-9110
Fax: (313) 535-9112

Plates

The Bareuther & Company porcelain factory of Germany began producing giftware, vases and dinnerware in 1867. Established by Johann Matthaeus Ries, the shop contained a porcelain kiln and an annular brick kiln.

The business later was sold to Oskar Bareuther, who continued to produce quality tableware.

Over the years, the small shop prospered and grew into a well-established undertaking, and today, after celebrating its 125th anniversary in 1992, can be considered one of the leading porcelain factories.

To celebrate the centennial of Bareuther, the company began to issue limited edition Christmas plates in 1967, which are Cobalt blue. Their popular *Mother's Day* series was initiated in 1969.

BEADAZZLED CRYSTAL, INC.

Christine Strand, Sales Manager
1451 Fifth Street
Berkeley, CA 94710
(510) 527-5796

Figurines

Beadazzled Crystal has been in business since 1978, and is dedicated to bringing the customer state-of-the-art design, quality materials and classic crafting in all figurine creations, thus building a reputation for reliability, excellence and great service. Beadazzled Crystal takes pride in offering a wide selection of designs arranged into themes such as *Circus Parade*, *Myth and Magic*, *Playtime* and *Bears on Review*, as well as spectacular artwork from a limited edition collection.

In 1989, Beadazzled Crystal took the opportunity to purchase the rights to reproduce the well-known designs of Black & Paterno Crystal, whose line has recently expanded to include figurines on musical bases or amethyst rock bases, and figurines with genuine gemstones.

Beadazzled also markets prisms, crystal prism hangers and crystal jewelry.

BELLEEK

Dist. by Reed & Barton
Lisa Perry
144 W. Britannia Street
Taunton, MA 02780
(800) 822-1824
(508) 824-6611
Fax: (508) 822-7269

Plates, Figurines, Bells, Christmas Ornaments

Belleek Parian China, coveted and collected worldwide for generations, celebrates a 136-year tradition of hand-crafting the world's most translucent china.

Today, Belleek china is still crafted in the village of Belleek much the same way it was made in the early 19th century. While Belleek is best known for its Shamrock pattern, the company offers a broad selection of giftware, including collectible plates, figurines, bells and Christmas ornaments.

The Belleek Collectors' International Society is an international organization comprised of dedicated Belleek enthusiasts.

The complete line of Belleek products is exclusively distributed in the United States by Reed & Barton. Founded in 1824, Reed & Barton is one of America's oldest silver companies whose tradition of excellence has earned it a reputation that is second to none.

JODY BERGSMA GALLERIES

1344 King Street
Bellingham, WA 98226
(206) 733-1101
Fax: (206) 647-2758

Graphics, Plates

Jody Bergsma Galleries, founded by artist Jody and her husband Rocky in Bellingham, Washington, house Bergsma's studio, offices, a small café and a large selection of her limited edition prints and original paintings. The gallery stands straight off the interstate and next to the tourist bureau, making it easily accessible to out-of-towners.

Bergsma tries to create up to 100 whimsical and fantasy paintings a year featuring the big-eyed children which have become her trademark. About half of them end up as limited edition prints. Equally as popular as her paintings are the plate designs Bergsma creates for Reco International.

BING & GRONDAHL

27 Holland Avenue
White Plains, NY 10603
(914) 428-8222
Fax: (914) 428-8251

Plates, Figurines, Bells, Christmas Ornaments

In 1853 when brothers Meyer and

Jacob Bing joined Frederik Grondahl in starting a new porcelain factory named Bing & Grondahl, their dreams were modest. The company produced figurines in bisque, and dinnerware and porcelain objects that were all replicas of the work of Danish sculptor, Thorvaldsen. In 1895, Bing & Grondahl produced "Behind the Frozen Window." It became the world's first Christmas plate and is also considered to be the plate that began the tradition of plate collecting.

The quality of the firm's collections became well known, and Bing & Grondahl pieces began appearing in museums around the world. The firm also serves by appointment to the courts of Denmark, Sweden and Great Britain.

Bing & Grondahl proudly pays tribute to the world's best-loved baby animals with "Koala Bear," the first edition in a new annual figurine series.

In addition to collector plates and tableware, Bing & Grondahl also introduced a variety of figurines and other porcelain pieces. In 1969, Bing & Grondahl introduced the first Mother's Day plate and in 1985, the first annual Children's Day plate. The *Mother's Day* series also has a hand-painted companion figurine. Selected Bing & Grondahl Annual Figurines were later used as models when Bing & Grondahl entered the doll market with "Mary," their first porcelain doll.

The *Christmas Collectibles* collection currently contains the annual Christmas plate, bell and matching porcelain ornament. The popular *Christmas in America* series contains a plate, matching ornament and bell. Another series from Bing & Grondahl is the *Santa Claus Collection* introduced in 1989. Bing & Grondahl also features the limited edition *Annual Figurine* series.

THE BOEHM STUDIO

Virginia Perry
25 Fairfacts
Trenton, NJ 08638
(609) 392-2207
(800) 257-9410

Figurines

Since Edward Boehm and his wife, Helen, started their studio in 1950, Boehm porcelain art has become renowned for its impeccable quality and detail. Among its famed creations are superb hand-painted sculptures of flowers, animals and birds.

Boehm porcelains can be found in over 130 museums and institutions throughout the world. The last ten U.S. presidents have used Boehm porcelains as gifts to visiting Heads of State.

Recently, the Gregorian Etruscan Museum in the Vatican Museums was named in memory of Edward Boehm, the first time in its 500-year history that a layperson has been so honored.

Boehm company-owned galleries are located in Chicago, Costa Mesa, Dallas, Houston, Trump Tower in New York and Trenton.

J.H. BOONE'S INC.

624A Matthews-Mint Hill Road
Matthews, NC 28105
(704) 847-0404
Fax: (704) 847-0428

Kalyn Imports (Canadian Dist.)
3520 Pharmacy Avenue, 1-C
Scarboro, Ontario M1W 2TB
(416) 497-7984
(416) 490-0298

Figurines

Only three years old, J.H. Boone's quality and innovation have made a good name for the firm. The work of artist Neil Rose shows a very deep understanding of the Old West. His renditions of the Plains Indians — their lives, history and culture — are extremely detailed. Each limited edition sculpture is of cold-cast resin and is an exact reproduction of the original.

The runaway success of Neil Rose led Boone's to begin offering additional artists. *Traces*, wildlife designs by Paul Carrico, are intended to raise awareness of the hundreds of endangered animals and habitats. The carved wood originals in the *Nature Drifts Collection* by Bill Atkinson was introduced in 1993. The

company has also added limited edition wall art by photographer Edward Curtis, hand-painted boxes by Gary Rose and authentic Indian artifacts by Southwest tribes.

MICHAEL BOYETT STUDIO & FOUNDRY

Michael Boyett
P.O. Box 2012
Nacogdoches, TX 75963-2012
(409) 560-4477

Figurines

Michael Boyett Studio and Foundry was founded in 1987. After years of having his work produced by other companies, Michael began production of all his new work. The line currently has twenty sculptures and one print. Subjects for his sculptures are Christian, wildlife, military and Western themes. Small limited editions are a special attraction for collectors and are available in both fine pewter and real bronze. His realistic and moving style has captivated collectors for over seventeen years.

THE BRADFORD EXCHANGE

9333 N. Milwaukee Avenue
Niles, IL 60714
(708) 966-2770

40 Pacific Court
London, Ontario N5V 3K4
(519) 452-1990

Plates

As the world's largest trading center for limited edition collector's plates, The Bradford Exchange provides an organized, orderly market where collectors can buy and sell plates.

The company is also one of the world's most successful marketers of collector's plates and the leading publisher of information on the international collector's plate market.

Over the years, the exchange has recommended to collectors many innovative plate series featuring art from around the world, including *Beauties of the Red Mansion*, the first series of collector's plates from the People's Republic of China and *Russian Legends*, the first series of collector's plates from the U.S.S.R. Bradford plates feature a broad range of subjects by many distinguished artists, including Julie Kramer

Cole, Bruce Emmett, Charles Fracé, Nate Giorgio, Paul Jennis, Thomas Kinkade, Lena Liu, Chris Notarile and Norman Rockwell. Only Bradford-recommended plates are eligible for trading on the exchange.

To help inform collectors about the thousands of different collector's plates on the market, the exchange publishes *The Bradford Book of Collector's Plates*, a reference guide to the international hobby of plate collecting. The quarterly "Bradford Exchange Current Quotations" contains the issue, high bid, low ask, close and estimated market prices for the more than 2,000 plates listed on the exchange.

In addition to its headquarters located in the Chicago suburb of Niles, Illinois, Bradford has offices in eleven other locations around the world. Plates are available directly from the exchange or from authorized gift and collectible dealers.

"Canyon of the Cat" is the first issue in The Faces of Nature *series from The Bradford Exchange.*

BRADLEY COLLECTIBLES

Joanna Hartstein
2400 North Spring Street
Los Angeles, CA 90012
(213) 221-4162
Fax: (213) 221-8272

Dolls

Over forty years ago, Bradley Collectibles was founded with a total of six dolls. Now Bradley offers collectors more than four hundred unique selections.

This company built its early reputation on its now-classic silk-faced doll. Subsequently, Bradley Collectibles brought forth a series of top-quality, exquisitely costumed porcelain dolls and clowns.

Today, president Joanna Hartstein, along with chief designer and artist Beth Ilyssa, has transformed Bradley into one of the premier collectible companies in the country.

The firm also sponsors the Bradley Collectible Doll Club which keeps collectors informed about Bradley Dolls. Also available to members only is a limited edition porcelain doll designed especially for collectors.

Because of their success, Bradley Collectibles presents more news: they have recently begun distributing vinyl dolls manufactured in Croatia, and are currently seeking a Canadian distributor.

BRANDYWINE WOODCRAFTS

Marlene or Truman Whiting
2413 Wolftrap Road
Yorktown, VA 23692
(800) 336-5031
(804) 898-6895

Figurines

In 1981, a shopkeeper asked Marlene Whiting to add replicas of local historic buildings to the hand-painted gift line she was producing from her home. Today her family-run firm, Brandywine Woodcrafts, manufactures three types of miniature collectible houses and accessories. Whether a rendering of an historic American building, or a whimsical product of Marlene's imagination, each piece is designed by her. Many are signed and numbered limited editions, and many can be personalized with family or hometown names. All are sculpted, cast and hand-painted in the United States, with new pieces introduced twice a year.

BUCCELLATI, INC.

46 East 57th Street
New York, NY 10022
(212) 308-2900
Fax: (212) 750-1323

Christmas Ornaments

Mario Buccellati founded the House of Buccellati in Milan in the early 1900s, though the Buccellati tradition began a century earlier. Craftsmen were trained in ancient engraving techniques to create superb gold and silver art.

Demand for Buccellati designs grew, and in 1952, Luca Buccellati, son of the founder, opened the first family store in the United States. Today, the

American operation is headed by the founder's namesake and grandson, Mario Buccellati II.

Buccellati remains one of the few companies that still produces hundreds of entirely handmade pieces annually, using classical and baroque influences. Gold, silver, precious and semi-precious stones and other materials are combined with meticulous attention to detail, to create jewelry and collectibles which are sought by discriminating collectors everywhere.

BYERS' CHOICE LTD.

P.O. Box 158
Chalfont, PA 18914
(215) 822-6700
Fax: (215) 822-3847

Figurines

In 1981 Bob and Joyce Byers incorporated Byers' Choice Ltd., a company which sprang from a hobby begun many years before. An interest in the history of Christmas prompted Joyce to blend her artistic skills into the creation of caroling figurines reminiscent of the 19th century. With wire, paper and assorted fabrics, she fashioned a Christmas decoration which became the first step in the development of this multi-million-dollar handcraft enterprise.

Byers' Choice is a family business. Joyce sculpts the original faces and designs the large variety of costumes. Bob Sr. takes care of the financial and administrative aspects of the business. Bob Jr. oversees production, and son Jeff is involved in the marketing of the product.

Approximately eighty craftsmen and professionally trained artists account for the company's ability to produce this quality handcrafted figurine.

Byers' Choice "Velvet Santa" and assorted children Carolers® figurines make a unique and attractive Christmas decoration.

Byers' Choice Caroler figurines have increased in collectibility since 1983 when "Scrooge" initiated the introduction of their Charles Dickens *A Christmas Carol* series. Other seasonal figures have been produced; however, the overwhelming emphasis has been on Christmas.

The Byers have enjoyed watching their company grow. They receive great satisfaction in listening to and serving their ever-expanding loyal collector base.

C.U.I., INC./CLASSIC CAROLINA COLLECTIONS/ DRAM TREE

1502 North 23rd Street
Wilmington, NC 28405
(919) 251-1110
Fax: (919) 251-3587

Steins

Over six decades ago, Percy K. Hexter purchased a small manufacturing business in New Jersey. The concept was to create and manufacture America's finest quality porcelain products.

Although the enterprise has changed its name since the early days, the same tradition of excellence in quality, service, and guaranteed customer satisfaction remains the driving force of the company.

Today, Peter K. Hexter, Jr., grandson of the founder, is CUI's president. He is quick to point out that CUI's success has been built on a total commitment from management and employees. Collectively, they share a common desire to be the best in the world.

CUI's eye for design and unique approach to maximizing full market potential with its prestigious licenses have earned several "Licensee of the Year" awards. Moreover, serious collectors have recognized the beauty and value of CUI products, elevating its position in the collectibles marketplace to that of a leader and trendsetter.

Commissioned fish and wildlife art from the most highly regarded artists embrace their products. Wildlife art, one of the fastest-growing art categories in America, rises to new levels in CUI's exciting collectibles medium. The combination of producing truly unique and distinctive products, while assisting in the funding of important habitat restoration and conservation projects, is one of their most meaningful achievements.

In years to come, CUI's focus will not change. They will continue to set trends in the market through excellence in products and unconditionally guaranteed customer satisfaction.

Commemorating the Silver Anniversary of Elvis' reappearance in the live entertainment realm, this "1968 Comeback Special Stein" is produced by C.U.I., Inc/Classic Carolina Collections/Dram Tree.

CAITHNESS GLASS INC.

Charlotte Judd
141 Lanza Avenue, Bldg. 12
Garfield, NJ 07026
(201) 340-3330
Fax: (201) 340-9415

Figurines

Caithness Glass is the largest producer of museum-quality paperweights in the world and is the only company that makes the four basic kinds of weights — millefiori, lampwork, sulphide and modern. Caithness also purchased the famous Whitefriars company in 1980 and still offers a range of new Whitefriars designs each year. Paperweights are offered in limited edition and unlimited editions and are handcrafted in Scotland. Their United States Collectors' Club is one of a number of worldwide chapters.

CAPE COLLECTIBLES

Division of Cape Craftsmen
Paige Nelson or Charles Tull
415 Peanut Rd.
P.O. Box 517
Elizabethtown, NC 28337
(800) 262-5447
(919) 862-8121
Fax: (919) 862-4611

Figurines

Cape Collectibles, a new division of Cape Craftsmen, Inc., introduced two 1993 collectible programs.

It's a Wonderful Life Gift Collection, the Original Bedford Falls Village, features seven lighted buildings and twelve accessories, and also two musical waterballs (each with a memorable scene and tune), lovingly re-created from the most viewed Christmas movie of all time.

The first copyrighted carousel horse collection in the world — replicas of fourteen actual carousel horses from a full-scale, working carousel located at the Kentucky Horse Park in Lexington, Kentucky — is Cape Collectibles' second line for 1993. The original carousel is constructed of hand-carved, basswood figures designed by Art Ritchie and Dan Jones. The 1993 introduction featured the first six of these outer-row horses in different styles and sizes, five of them limited editions.

CARLTON CARDS

10500 American Road
Cleveland, OH 44144
(216) 252-4944
Fax: (216) 252-6979

Christmas Ornaments

In 1988, Summit Corporation, an American Greetings subsidiary, produced forty-one Heirloom Collection™ ornaments, sold under their own logo in Summit-owned and operated stores in the United States and Canada.

Carlton Cards, a division of American Greetings, made a grand entrance into the ornament industry in 1989 by offering forty Summit-designed ornaments under the Carlton logo. 1990 marked the beginning of the popular *Collector's Series*.

In 1991, Summit and Carlton ornaments were offered under the Carlton logo exclusively. The assortment included seventy-two ornaments — and the continuation of the *Collector's Series*.

For 1992, Carlton expanded to ninety ornament designs, including captions for "Dad," "Son" and anniversary pieces, while a number of Carlton ornaments gained media attention.

Five of Jim Hensen's Muppets™ ornament designs are new for Carlton in 1993. The line has been expanded to 135 designs, including new captions for brother, godchildren, parents-to-be and sweetheart.

The company also offers three lighted ornaments.

CAST ART INDUSTRIES, INC.

1120 California Avenue
Corona, CA 91719
(909) 371-3025
Fax: (909) 371-0674

Figurines, Christmas Ornaments

Formed the day after Christmas in 1990, Cast Art Industries introduced its first product line just three months later. Known as *Dreamsicles*™, this line of precious collectible cherubs and animals has become a gift industry phenomenon and continues to grow in popularity among collectors.

Dreamsicles™ received national recognition as the "Best Selling New Category" at the Gift Creations Concepts (GCC) industry show in Minneapolis in June of 1992. The line has been consistently named as the number one general gift line in sales and reorders, according to monthly surveys of gift and collectibles retailers conducted by "Giftbeat," an industry newsletter.

Dreamsicles™ have quickly attained status as true collectibles. The line has expanded to a total of more than 150 cherub and animal figurines, all products of the imagination of American artist Kristin Haynes. Like all Cast Art products, they are individually hand-cast and hand-painted, then wreathed with dried flowers, to assure that no two are ever exactly alike.

In response to customer demand, the *Dreamsicles*™ Collectors Club was formed and began offering Charter memberships in 1993. The trademark and characters are also being licensed to manufacturers of plush toys, children's clothing and other merchandise.

"Love My Puppy" is one of Kristin Haynes' best-selling new Dreamsicles™ cherubs introduced during 1993.

Building on its reputation as one of the country's fastest-growing gift manufacturers, Cast Art has expanded its product lines, introducing the works of several talented artists. *Enchanted Forest*™ is a selection of gnomes and wizards reproduced from the woodcarvings of Californian Rick Albee. *Cuckoo Corners*™ is a collection of whimsical characters also designed by Kristin Haynes. *Animal Attraction*™ and *Story Time Treasures*™ are designs from the clever young husband-and-wife team of Steve and Gigi Hackett. Two additional lines are being prepared for introduction in January 1994.

CAZENOVIA ABROAD, LTD.

Glen Trush
67 Albany Street
Cazenovia, NY 13035
(315) 655-3433
Fax: (315) 655-4249

Christmas Ornaments, Figurines

Cazenovia Abroad, Ltd. was established as a retail store for fine gifts in 1967. Its founder, Pat Trush, in the second year of operation, found sterling silver teething rings in Portugal, and adapted them to Christmas ornaments. The small retail operation sold out of the initial six pieces during the first year, so the decision was made to market the ornaments at wholesale, to other fine gift and jewelry stores. Each year, additional ornaments were added to the collection.

The collection now includes over forty full-size ornaments, and almost as many miniature ornaments. In 1991, the first three limited edition carousel figurines were released and three more in 1992.

Cazenovia Abroad offers a full line of sterling and silver-plated collectibles sold through jewelry, fine gift and table-top stores.

CHERYL SPENCER COLLIN STUDIO

24 River Road
Eliot, ME 03903
(207) 439-6016
Fax: (207) 439-5787

Figurines

Since 1984, the Cheryl Spencer Collin Studio has been the innovator in lighthouse collectibles. Cheryl's superb artistry and craftsmanship enables her to reproduce exquisite lighthouse recreations of incredible detail. All of her sculptures incorporate various flora and fauna indigenous to the area in which the lighthouse is found, with whimsical accents such as her dog, Svea, and dwarf rabbit, Willie.

To ensure the quality of her work, Cheryl has located her studio near her home in Eliot, Maine. Before she places her handwritten signature on the base sticker, Cheryl painstakingly oversees the molding, casting and hand-painting of each piece. Collectors have long admired her lighthouse collection, now consisting of over forty-five replicas.

CHIMERA STUDIOS, INC./ THE PIG LADY

3708 E. Hubbard
Mineral Wells, TX 76007
(800) THE-HOGS
Fax: (817) 325-1630

Figurines

Chimera Studios was formed in 1989 when Preston and Kathy Clay combined their two businesses, Clay Castings and The Pig Lady. Since its inception, the firm's aim has been to produce a high-quality, original line of figurines which would charm and amuse collectors. Since 1986, The Pig Lady has developed a loyal following of collectors worldwide who enjoy her slightly off-center sense of humor in the creation of her limited edition pig figures.

In a more serious vein, Kathy recently completed a very important work: "A Promise of Peace." This work, intended to speak to everyone's desire for a better world, portrays a noble sixteen-inch male figure behind a majestic reclining lion, with a lamb nestled securely between his feet.

CHRISTOPHER RADKO DESIGNS

Planetarium Station
P.O. Box 770
New York, NY 10024
(212) 362-5344
Fax: (212) 362-2613

Christmas Ornaments

For almost a decade, Christopher Radko has been the nation's leading designer and importer of fine quality glass Christmas ornaments and traditional German holiday gift containers.

As both the owner and artist, Christopher Radko has built a reputation for unique designs; each year's exciting col-

lection includes over fifty percent new designs, and many are accordingly retired. Precision of painted detail is a hallmark of Christopher Radko Designs.

Christopher started working originally in Poland, with a small factory of four. Today, this satisfying partnership employs almost 200 glassblowers, moldmakers and decorators. Christopher has also recently expanded to work with the last few master glass craftsmen still living today in Italy, Germany and the Czech Republic.

In Germany, Christopher has developed an exclusive relationship with the Schaller family who have been producing hollow gift containers in the shapes of Santas, rabbits, turkeys and witches since 1895. These figures are cast in the molds created by the Schallers' great-grandfather, and are then painted to Christopher's exacting details.

Christopher specializes in reviving and adding a new twist to turn-of-the-century designs, and he is especially successful at annually creating new molds and at ferreting out antique molds and designs which have not been available in this country for over eighty years.

Pictured are several of Christopher Radko's distinctive, iridescent blown-glass Christmas ornaments and garland.

Christopher's decorations are made almost entirely of the same original organic paints, materials and techniques that were used in the 19th century. The success of the company is based on thousands of loyal collectors who recognize the care and extraordinary quality that these decorations represent.

CLAY ART
David Gaines
239 Utah Avenue
South San Francisco, CA 94080
(415) 244-4970
(800) 252-9555
Fax: (415) 244-4979

Figurines
Clay Art was started in 1979 in San Francisco by Michael Zanfagna and Jenny McLain and specializes in collectible giftware and tabletop accessories. These highly collectible items are distributed throughout the United States, Canada and Europe.

Beautiful, collectible ceramic masks are handcrafted in San Francisco, including two or three signed and numbered limited editions every year.

Collectible tabletop accessories, encompassing salt and peppers, cookie jars, teapots, creamers and sugars, mugs, plates and much more are designed with a unique and whimsical nature that give them their high level of collectibility.

SANDY CLOUGH STUDIO
Rick Clough
123 Parkview Drive
Marietta, GA 30060
(404) 428-9406
(800) 447-8409

Graphics
Sandy Clough Studio was formed in 1981 to serve as the publisher of limited edition prints and canvas lithographs by fourth-generation artist Sandy Clough.

Sandy grew up in Mississippi where she received her B.A. in Art and her M.A. in Art Education. She is known for her superbly realistic work and for paintings with a depth of feeling that touch the heart. Her personal commitment to traditional family values is beautifully reflected in her art.

Sandy has won many awards and her work is available in both the United States and Canada.

THE COLLECTABLES, INC.
John Parkins
Rt. 4 Box 503
Rolla, MO 65401
(314) 364-7849
(800) 874-7120
Fax: (314) 364-2448

Dolls, Christmas Ornaments
The Collectables, Inc. was established in 1975 when Phyllis Parkins' hobby became a career, growing out of her love of painting and crafting. Phyllis' line of antique reproduction and originals has expanded to fifty dolls along with treetop angels, cherubs and a line of Victorian jewelry and frames.

Phyllis' Collector Club was formed in

the fall of 1989, with a steady growth each year. The Collectables porcelain dolls have received several major awards including Doll of the Year (DOTY) awards and *Collector Editions'* Awards of Excellence.

THE CONSTANCE COLLECTION
P.O. Box 250
Route 1 Box 538
Midland, VA 22728
(703) 788-4500
Fax: (703) 788-4100

Figurines
Constance A. Guerra formed The Constance Collection five years ago. The company's only designer-sculptor, Constance, is also president of the company. But it is also a family business. Her mother and father work daily at handling the marketing and management of the company. She considers them the company's most valuable assets.

Guerra designs and produces about seventy-five new figurines each year. Some of her most popular collections are the *Golden Americans, State Santas* (fifty Santas representing all fifty states in limited editions), *Santa Claus, Heavenly Angels* and *Kitty Kat Klub*.

To make her figurines as authentic as possible, Guerra consults with different experts and does a great deal of research at the Library of Congress.

M. CORNELL IMPORTERS, INC.
1462 18th Street
St. Paul, MN 55112
(612) 633-8690
Fax: (612) 636-3568

Steins
M. Cornell Importers, Inc. began as a family business in 1959 when Morris and Maria Cornell started importing cuckoo clocks, music boxes and steins. Today, their son Henry and his wife Gail oversee a multi-faceted business encompassing the development, importation and nationwide distribution of collectible steins.

Cornell has worked in very close cooperation with numerous German manufacturers, developing hundreds of new steins over the years. Always focusing on the American market, Cornell has consistently introduced new artists, molds, color combinations, handles and

lids to the stein industry. Their conventional steins are joined by other popular favorites such as miniature steins, character steins and special-theme steins.

Cornell has also introduced a complete selection of collectible teapots made in England by a variety of manufacturers, as well as a complete selection of handcrafted wooden boxes made in Poland.

COUNTRY ARTISTS

c/o Lilliput Incorporated
Oakland Bldg.
9052 Old Annapolis Road
Columbia, MD 21045
(410) 964-2202

Figurines

Country Artists was started in 1987 by Richard Cooper. The brand name "Country Artists" was established to represent products that have a conservation or environmental concern. The firm manufactures detailed wildlife sculptures that are individually hand-painted and hand-finished. They are now the market leaders in the United Kingdom in the field of wildlife. Country Artists exports to the United States, Japan and Europe.

The company's manufacturing units are in Stratford-upon-Avon, famed Shakespeare country. Painting studios are in both Stratford and Stoke-on-Trent, home of the potteries.

Country Artists is expanding its overseas markets and is looking to Lilliput Inc. as their exclusive U.S. distributor.

CREART

Minerva or Carlos Estevez
U.S. Representatives
4517 Manzanillo Drive
Austin, TX 78749
(512) 280-3143
(800) 343-1505
Fax: (512) 280-0695

Figurines

Creart was founded in Mexico in 1979, when five experts in the science of manufacturing realized their dream of forming a company dedicated to producing high-quality, extraordinarily realistic sculptures. In 1986, Creart was introduced in the United States by Minerva and Carlos Estevez and has earned its place in the American collectibles market.

Among the artistic minds and spirits contributing to the Creart legacy today

are Emilio Martinez, Vicente Perez and Francisco "Paco" Contreras. Because the Creart family is dedicated to excellence, they never stop searching for innovative ways to produce even better products. They, along with their talented staff, introduced eighteen new designs in 1993.

Creart's limited edition sculptures are made of a bonded marble, which produces a stable, impermeably hard sculpture to ensure a lifelong treasure. Each piece is individually numbered and the collector is provided with a request card to receive a personalized Certificate of Authenticity.

Each year, limited edition sculptures are offered in depictions of *American Wildlife*, *African Wildlife*, *Equestrian* life, *Man's Best Friend* and the *Nature's Care Collection* with additional series being added.

Creart has been selected for the fourth year in a row as a *Collector Editions Award of Excellence* nominee. This year's nomination goes to "Wolf and Cubs" by Francisco "Paco" Contreras.

The artist for "Sea Otters" is none other than Creart President Carlos Estevez himself, while "Penguins" was created by Vicente Perez for the Nature's Care Collection.

CROSS GALLERY, INC.

Mary Schmidt
P.O. Box 4181
Jackson, WY 83001
(307) 733-2200
Fax: (307) 733-1414

Plates, Figurines, Dolls, Christmas Ornaments, Graphics

Cross Gallery, Inc., located in Jackson Hole, Wyoming, publishes and distributes limited editions, offset reproductions and handpulled originals. Cross Gallery is the exclusive limited publisher of Penni Anne Cross. The Gallery offers her limited edition lithographs, serigraphs, stone lithographs, etchings, plates

and ornaments. They also handle Ms. Cross' original sketches, drawings, paintings and repligraphs, which are high-quality, "close-to-original" reproductions.

Before beginning each portrayal of native Americans, Cross prays to have people see the Creator first in her work, and then the creation. "My inspiration is Jesus Christ," she says.

If art is an expression of an artist's soul, then it is easy to see why Cross's art is characterized by confidence, serenity and love. A strong Christian faith bolstered by the Indian philosophy taught by her friends has enriched both her understanding and portrayal of life.

CRYSTAL REFLECTION

Gregory Lowe
150 Park Lane
Brisbane, CA 94005
(415) 468-2520
Fax: (415) 468-2554

Figurines

Crystal Reflection was established in 1976 and is located in Brisbane, California. A leader in the design and production of 32% Austrian lead crystal collectibles, Crystal Reflection introduced in 1991 "Prestige In Crystal" — *Wildlife Collection* and limited edition *Bald Eagles*. Unsurpassed in quality, workmanship and artistry, the *Wildlife Collection* has set a new standard in the industry.

Artist Som Von's recent introduction of "The King And The Prey" is Crystal Reflection's most recent design.

CRYSTAL WORLD

3 Borinski Drive
Lincoln Park, NJ 07035
(800) 445-4251
(201) 633-0707
Fax: (201) 633-0102

Figurines

Founded in 1983, Crystal World has grown to become one of the most respected names in the world for production of 32% lead crystal collectibles. Their primary focus has always been on quality: quality of design, quality of materials and quality of workmanship. Couple this with their seemingly endless penchant for innovation, and it is easy to see why they are one of the largest crystal collectible producers in America.

Crystal World draws on the talents of an international staff of accomplished

designers: senior designer Ryuju Nakai, Tom Suzuki and Nicolo Mulargia. The uniqueness and originality of their designs have inspired countless collectors and admirers of fine crystal alike.

In 1986, Crystal World introduced the innovative "Rainbow Castle." The "Rainbow Castle" was the first such figurine ever to combine the shimmering beauty of clear faceted crystal with the magical rainbow-colored crystal of its mountain base. The result was an entirely new dimension in fine crystal collectibles which took the industry by storm. Crystal World's *Original Rainbow Castle Collection®* continues to be extremely popular.

Something else that sets this company apart from the others in the crystal figurine market is their finely detailed architectural collectibles. The "Empire State Building," the "Taj Mahal," the "Eiffel Tower" and the "U.S. Capitol Building" are a few of their limited edition works of art, each complete with a signed Certificate of Authenticity by the artist.

New for 1993 are "Victorian House" by Nicolo Mulargia, "Country Gristmill" by Tom Suzuki and "Enchanted Castle" crafted by Ryuju Nakai, the latest addition to the *Original Rainbow Castle Collection®*.

Still among the most popular crystal figurines anywhere are Crystal World's whimsical *Teddyland* collection and endearing *Collectible Kitties* collection, which are widely admired for their noted personality, warmth and charm.

Crystal World's tiny "Ice Cream Teddies" by artist Nicolo Mulargia stands only 1⅛ inches high.

CYBIS

65 Norman Avenue
Trenton, NJ 08618
(609) 392-6074

Figurines, Christmas Ornaments

Cybis is America's oldest porcelain art studio, founded by Boleslaw Cybis, who has been compared to other world-renowned artists, including Leonardo da Vinci.

A gift of Cybis porcelain is still considered one of the highest American honors bestowed upon royalty, heads of government and celebrities. Because of the reputation and quality of Cybis porcelains, American presidents throughout the years have selected Cybis pieces as official gifts of state.

In addition to the homes of discriminating collectors, Cybis pieces adorn the Vatican, Buckingham Palace, the Smithsonian Institute and other major collections throughout the world.

Cybis' sculptures are available in fine gift and collectible stores throughout the United States and at the company's Trenton, New Jersey gallery.

DADDY'S LONG LEGS

c/o KVK, Inc.
300 Bank Street
Southlake, TX 76092
(817) 488-4644

Dolls

KVK, Inc. is the parent company of Daddy's Long Legs dolls. Karen Germany, the designer of Daddy's Long Legs dolls, and her husband Brent, own and operate KVK. The company manufactures the dolls at their home office/warehouse in Southlake, Texas, between Dallas and Fort Worth. Daddy's Long Legs is an entirely American-made product.

Daddy's Long Legs dolls were introduced in January 1990 and a Collector's Club was established in January 1993. For information on becoming a member of the Collector's Club, contact Daddy's Long Legs.

DANFORTH PEWTERERS

Barbara Cunningham
P.O. Box 828
52 Seymour Street
Middlebury, VT 05753
(802) 388-8666
Fax: (802) 388-0099

Christmas Ornaments, Figurines

Fred and Judi Danforth founded Danforth Pewterers in Vermont in 1975. Judi's training as a silversmith at R.I.T.'s School for American Craftsmen inspired her interest in pewtersmithing. Fred is a direct descendant of Thomas Danforth and his family, who were 18th century Connecticut pewtersmiths.

Fred and Judi's career began with an apprenticeship in New Brunswick, Canada. Living in Vermont with their two daughters, they maintain a growing business creating handcrafted pewter hollowware and cast pewter ornaments, buttons and jewelry.

Judi specializes in Christmas ornaments, and each year she designs a new ornament to commemorate that year.

For antique pewter collectors, a piece of original Danforth Pewter hollowware will surely add interest to any collection. Each piece is signed, dated and bears the lion touchmark based upon one that was used by Fred's ancestors in Colonial America.

ANDREW D. DARVAS, INC.

2165 Dwight Way
Berkeley, CA 94704
(510) 843-7838
Fax: (510) 843-1815

Figurines

Andrew D. Darvas, Inc. has been a major importer of Bossons Character Wall Masks from England since 1963 and plays an integral part in their distribution and promotional efforts in the U.S.

Ray Bossons began designing the internationally recognized "Character Wall Masks" in 1958.

These realistic faces portray the various peoples of the world, historic and literary characters. Recent limited editions include dramatic portraits such as "Custer & Sitting Bull" and "Don Quixote & Sancho Panza." Both are limited to 9,500 pieces.

To ensure their lifelike detail and quality, the entire Bosson production process is done by hand.

DEPARTMENT 56, INC.

P.O. Box 44456
Eden Prairie, MN 55344-1456
(800) 548-8696 (LIT-TOWN)
Fax: (612) 943-4500

Figurines

Department 56, Inc. originally began by importing fine Italian basketry. However a new product line introduced in 1977, called *The Original Snow Village®*, set the groundwork for the

collectible products we know today.

1977 sales of these six original buildings were encouraging, so Department 56 decided to develop more Snow Village pieces to add to their 1978 line. By 1979, Department 56 made an important operational decision: in order to keep *The Original Snow Village* at a reasonable size, buildings would have to be retired from production each year to make room for new designs.

The Department 56, Inc. Master Sculptors form the clay models for each building with an emphasis on fine detail. From the original concept to drawings, sculpting, casting, firing, hand-painting and packaging, craftsmanship and quality is evident. Each piece is stamped in the bottom with its designated series name, title, year of introduction, and Department 56, Inc. logo, all assurances of authenticity.

The first introduction of *The Heritage Village Collection* was *The Dickens' Village* series, introduced in 1984. Extensive research, charming details and fine hand-painting of the seven original porcelain shops and "Village Church" established them as a favorite among collectors.

Other series followed with the introduction of *The New England Village* series, *The Alpine Village* series, the *Christmas in the City* series, *The Little Town of Bethlehem* series in 1987, and in 1991, the introduction of *The North Pole* series.

As with *The Original Snow Village*, each piece of *The Heritage Village Collection* is bottom-stamped and packed in an individual styrofoam storage carton with illustrated sleeve. Each year, Department 56, Inc. continues to unveil intriguing new lighted pieces and accessories for their collectors.

The Original Snow Village *sign from* Department 56, Inc. *is titled "Kids Decorating the Village Sign."*

DESIGNS AMERICANA
7400 Boone Avenue N.
Minneapolis, MN 55428
(612) 425-8666
Fax: (612) 425-1653

Figurines

Jim and Jan Shore began Designs Americana in 1989 as a company intended to design, manufacture and market their creative and well-received Santa Claus figurines. Though they began on their own, as independent artists, Designs Americana is now located in two buildings totaling more than 40,000 square feet and employs 165 in-house workers, plus up to 200 outside painters.

Designs Americana makes Santas for every taste, ranging in height from one inch to three and one-half feet tall, and in several styles. While the company is known for its wide variety of Santa figures, animals and other creatures are featured as well.

DIMENSION MINIATURES
2233 Lee Circle Drive
Woodland Park, CO 80863

Figurines

Dimension Miniatures studio creates unique vignette sculptures. Each presents a dramatic moment in time and place in a three-dimensional, holograph-like depiction and is enclosed in a custom glass case or dome. The scene may be viewed in the round, from front and sides, or encased in a lighted shadow box to be installed in a wall or furniture piece.

Subject themes encompass scenes from stage and film dramas, literature, history, sports, fantasy or fairy tales. The vignettes are often purchased by collectors, patrons and interior decorators as objets d'art and accent pieces in homes, offices and public areas.

Crafting a Dimension Miniature vignette entails intricate detail work. Each artisan must be familiar with fine and graphic arts, sculpting, ceramics, metal casting and machining and fine wood cabinetry. Each vignette is a uniquely conceived and executed one-of-a-kind work of art.

THE WALT DISNEY STUDIOS
500 South Buena Vista Street
Burbank, CA 91521-6876
(818) 567-5500

Figurines

Throughout its seventy-year history, The Walt Disney Company has introduced young and old to a host of unforgettable characters through the magic of Disney animation. These beloved Disney characters, recognized around the world, are now captured in three dimensions by *The Walt Disney Classics Collection*, the first line of animation sculptures created by the artists of The Walt Disney Studios.

The sculptures can be displayed singly or grouped together to re-create memorable scenes from classic Disney features and short cartoons. Each piece in the Collection owes its lifelike charm and believability to the same principles that underlie Disney's unique animation process, a discipline never before applied to collectible figurines.

The Walt Disney Classics Collection is created by a talented team of Disney animators and artists, many of whom worked on the original films. The Disney Archives, which contains original animation sketches and other historic materials, is also extensively consulted to ensure that the sculptures remain true to the original films.

Each figurine in *The Walt Disney Classics Collection* features a backstamp including Walt Disney's signature logo, as well as the name of the film and a special symbol to denote the year of production. In addition, sculptures are titled using dialogue from the film where possible, and each comes with a Certificate of Authenticity signed by Roy E. Disney.

These animation sculptures from The Walt Disney Classics Collection *are based on Disney's 1931 black and white cartoon,* The Delivery Boy.

The Walt Disney Classics Collection is sold exclusively at selected fine department, gift and collector stores including locations at Disneyland, The Walt

Disney World Resort and The Disney Store.

DOLLMAKERS ORIGINALS INTERNATIONAL, INC.

Peter Consalvi and Sonja Hartmann
1230 Pottstown Pike
Glenmoore, PA 19343
(215) 458-0277
Fax: (215) 458-7488

Dolls

Dollmakers Originals International, Inc. has been recognized as a three-phase company who manufactures, imports and distributes some of the finest collectible dolls in the industry. They exclusively represent many doll artists from America and Europe.

The company produces five lines of porcelain and vinyl dolls in their Pennsylvania studio. All production is supervised by renowned German doll artist, Sonja Hartmann.

In 1993, Dollmakers Originals International, Inc. won two Doll of the Year (DOTY) awards, four IDEX awards and was nominated four times for Awards of Excellence.

DOLLS BY JERRI

651 Anderson Street
Charlotte, NC 28205
(704) 333-3211
Fax: (704) 333-7706

Dolls

Beginning in 1976 as a cottage industry producing limited editions of Jerri's imaginative all-porcelain dolls, Dolls by Jerri has continued to expand through a combination of Jerri's prolific creative talents and husband Jim McCloud's experienced marketing and management skills.

Jerri's sculpting artistry is clearly defined in the detailed features of her elegant high-fashion dolls and her real-to-life toddlers and babies. Both her porcelain and her vinyl dolls are painted by hand with the "softest" of colorations that have become distinctive hallmarks of a Jerri doll.

Over the years, dolls from this fine company have received many awards including the coveted DOTY from *Doll Reader* magazine and the Award of Excellence from *Dolls* magazine.

DUNCAN ROYALE

1141 South Acacia Avenue
Fullerton, CA 92631
(714) 879-1360
Fax: (714) 879-4611

Figurines, Plates, Ornaments

Duncan Royale was founded more than thirty years ago by its President Max E. Duncan. The company's early years were devoted to importing a variety of figurines and porcelain items. During the last decade, the company has turned to designing and creating limited edition, copyrighted collectibles.

Since 1983, Duncan Royale has introduced several "storytelling" series and collections that are very popular with collectors: *The History of Santa Claus, The History of Classic Entertainers, The Greatest Gift...Love, Woodland Fairies, Calendar Secrets, Ebony, Early Americans, Christmas Images, Jubilee Dancers, Angels* and the *Buckwheat Collection*. All of Duncan Royale's works reveal the excellence of innovation and artistry necessary for success.

Duncan Royale will, in the coming years, continue to introduce collections that relate a story. They allow the collector the chance to enjoy beautiful art as well as experience history and legends that can be shared with others.

"Lottie," from Duncan Royale's Jubilee series, dances into the Ebony Collection.

DYNASTY DOLL COLLECTION

Gary R. Darwin V.P. Sales
P.O. Box 99
Port Reading, NJ 07064
(908) 636-6160
Fax: (908) 636-6215

Dolls

The Dynasty Doll Division of Cardinal Inc. was started in 1980, in response to the demand for high-quality porcelain collector dolls at affordable prices. The line has grown to over 300 styles, including limited editions, annual dolls, reproductions and artist dolls in a variety of costumes.

In 1987, Dynasty received its first "Dolls Award of Excellence" from *Dolls* magazine for "Gayle." In 1989, two dolls were nominated for awards — "Amber," the 1989 Dynasty annual doll, and "Cayala." In 1990 another annual doll, "Marcella," received an award. "Jamaal" from *Uta Brauser's City Kids* collection was the recipient of a 1993 "Dolls Award of Excellence" nomination.

Dynasty continues to meet the public's demand for collector dolls and has licensed many fine artists. These include Marci Cohen, Karen Henderson, Hazel Tertsakian, Teena Halbig, Gail Hoyt, Gloria Tepper, Pat Kolesar and Uta Brauser.

Cardinal Inc., the parent company, was founded in 1946 by its current president, Sidney Darwin and brothers-in-law Samuel J. Kronman and Charles Dengrove. Originally a ceramics manufacturer, Cardinal ceased domestic production in 1960. Its entire line is imported, primarily from the Far East.

"Genevieve," Dynasty Doll's 1993 Annual Christmas Doll, plays a popular holiday favorite, "Adeste Fidelis."

EBELING & REUSS

Ronald D. Rapelje
333 Court St.
P.O. Box 1289
Allentown, PA 18105-1289
(215) 776-7100
Fax: (215) 776-7102

Figurines, Bells, Christmas Ornaments, Steins

Ebeling & Reuss Co., founded in 1886, is a major importer of fine giftware and collectibles.

Ronald D. Rapelje was named president and chief executive officer of Ebeling & Reuss in 1990. He purchased the company August 15, 1992 and is currently the sole shareholder.

Among the many collectible lines that Ebeling & Reuss offers are Goebel annual collectible bells, eggs, ornaments, Domex beer steins, Gerz steins, Duchess China collectible china and figurines from Europe.

ELKE'S ORIGINALS, LTD.
8900 S.W. Burnham F-8
Tigard, OR 97223
(503) 620-1513
Fax: (503) 684-8250

Dolls
Elke's Originals, Ltd. specializes in the production of limited edition porcelain dolls by award-winning artist, Elke Hutchens. Since its founding in 1983, Elke's Originals, Ltd. dolls have been at the vanguard of the new popularity of original artist dolls. Each design is a strict limited edition. The dolls are all handcrafted in the United States and are available through fine doll shops in America, Canada and Europe.

Four of Elke's designs have won the *Dolls* magazine Award of Excellence. In addition, Elke's designs have received six *Doll Reader* magazine Doll of the Year (DOTY) awards, most recently for "Cherie" and "Cecilia" (1992). "Braelyn" received the 1991 Manufacturer's Doll Face of the Year (DOTY) award.

ELLENBROOKE DOLLS, INCORPORATED
1450 Marcy Loop
Grants Pass, OR 97527

Dolls
In 1976, Connie Walser-Derek started Connie's Dolls and Company, a retail and mail-order business that caters to aspiring dollmakers and doll collectors. But Derek's real fame within the doll industry rests on her original dolls produced in porcelain, wax and vinyl.

Derek got started reproducing and repairing antique dolls, but by 1985 her dolls had earned her a reputation as a maker of museum-quality dolls. Derek also signed a contract to do a series of porcelain dolls for The Hamilton Collection.

To meet the demand for a more affordable line, Derek formed Ellenbrooke

Dolls, Inc., which produces dolls in a number of different editions, including a limited production edition, the exclusive signature edition in porcelain or wax and limited artist's proofs.

ENESCO CORPORATION
One Enesco Plaza
Elk Grove Village, IL 60007
(708) 640-5200
Fax: (708) 640-6151

Figurines, Plates, Bells, Dolls, Christmas Ornaments
Founded in 1958, Enesco Corporation firmly established its prominence twenty years later with the introduction of the Enesco *Precious Moments* Collection. Based on the work of inspirational artist Sam Butcher, the collection features teardrop-eyed children who share messages of love, caring and sharing. The award-winning porcelain bisque figurines have touched the lives of millions to become this country's number one collectible.

The overwhelming popularity of the *Precious Moments Collection* led to the formation of the Enesco Precious Moments Collectors' Club℠ in 1981. In 1985, the Enesco Precious Moments Birthday Club℠ was established to attract younger collectors and teach them about the joy of collecting.

Another highly-acclaimed collectible line is the Enesco *Memories of Yesterday®* Collection, based on illustrations by the late British artist Mabel Lucie Attwell and introduced in 1988. The Enesco Memories of Yesterday Collector's Society℠ was formed in 1991.

The Enesco Musical Society℠ also premiered in 1991, in support of the Enesco *Small World of Music™* Collection of deluxe action musicals.

Only introduced in 1992, the *Cherished Teddies®* Collection, designed by artist and children's author Priscilla Hillman, has already won international recognition from collectors and the collectibles industry. Hillman also created the *Calico Kittens™* Collection of cat figurines that premiered in 1993.

Reflecting the gentleness and innocence of the Victorian era, the *Maud Humphrey Bogart Collection* has become a favorite among collectors. The collection is supported by the Maud Humphrey Bogart Collectors' Club℠.

In addition to the growing interest in Victoriana, sports collectibles are also

becoming hot items. Sports Impressions, a division of Enesco, features limited edition plates, figurines and other collectibles portraying the biggest names in professional sports. In response to collector demand, the Sports Impressions Collectors' Club℠ was launched in 1989.

Other notable collections from Enesco include *Lucy & Me®* teddy bears by artist Lucy Rigg; *Miss Martha's Collection™* by sculptress Martha Holcombe; *Laura's Attic™* by Enesco artist Karen Hahn; *North Pole Village®* by Sandi Zimnicki; the Enesco *Treasury of Christmas Ornaments*; *Mickey & Co.* giftware collection featuring favorite Disney characters; and the Enesco *Rose O'Neill Kewpie Collection*.

"Old Friends Are The Best Friends" is a charming addition to Enesco's Cherished Teddies® Collection by artist Priscilla Hillman.

F.J. DESIGNS, INC./ THE CAT'S MEOW
2163 Great Trails Dr., Dept. C
Wooster, OH 44691
(216) 264-1377
Fax: (216) 263-0219

Figurines
In the fall of 1982, The Cat's Meow Village company began in the basement of Terry and Faline Jones' home. Mrs. Jones opened the firm with a $39 piece of pine, a creative concept and a lot of ingenuity. She created the Cat's Meow Village, a product line of two-dimensional miniature historical buildings and accessories. Husband Terry joined the company on a full-time basis in 1986.

During 1983, Mrs. Jones shipped the Village to store owners throughout Ohio and western Pennsylvania. In the spring of 1984, The Cat's Meow moved from the Jones' basement into the back room of a woodworking shop, only to take over the entire building by the spring of

the following year! At this point, Mrs. Jones decided to change the name of the company to the generic FJ Designs name.

Beginning her third year of business, Faline Jones began to pattern her designs after actual buildings and historic landmarks no longer in existence. That's when the concept for the Village was developed. The Village would include faithful reproductions of typical American architecture, chosen with respect for the craftsmanship, commerce, culture and activities that are part of every community.

The collectibility of the Village began to increase as Mrs. Jones devised a system of retiring old patterns as new ones were developed. A Village series retires after five years of production, with the special annual Christmas series retiring each year.

The company formed The National Cat's Meow Collector's Club in June 1989. By the end of that year, over 4,000 collectors had joined. The club is still growing today, with over 15,000 members nationally.

The Williamsburg Series *from FJ Designs/ Cat's Meow includes* "The Bruton Parish Church," "Governor's Palace," "Grissle Hay House" *and* "Raleigh Tavern."

FANTASY CREATIONS

Henry Blumner
1201 Broadway
New York, NY 10001
(212) 679-7644
Fax: (212) 532-0839

Figurines

Fantasy Creations is the exclusive United States distributor for the *Myth and Magic Collection* of Olde English pewter figurines, produced in England by the Tudor Mint. A collectors club, The Myth and Magic Collectors Club, can be joined for $37.50 annually. Each figurine has an artist's signature and incorporates a piece of Swarovski Crystal.

FEDERICA DOLLS OF FINE ART

4501 West Highland Road
Milford, MI 48380
(800) 421-DOLL
(313) 887-9575

Dolls

Federica Kasabasic, pre-school teacher and the owner of two Early Childhood Education Centers in Michigan, has been dedicated to the caring of children for many years. Her involvement and love for children, along with her studies in fine art, inspired her to sculpt and design her dolls.

Federica's dolls are available in the highest quality vinyl and porcelain. Each doll is created with only the finest materials and fabric. The porcelain dolls have hand glass eyes from England. The eyes in the vinyl dolls are glastic — glass covered with plastic for protection. The upper and lower eyelashes, applied by hand, are made of human hair. The eyebrows are hand-painted, and the highest quality human hair and kanekelon wigs adorn each doll. All the clothing is made with 100% natural fabrics.

FENTON ART GLASS COMPANY

700 Elizabeth Street
Williamstown, WV 26187
(304) 375-6122
Fax: (304) 375-6459

Plates, Figurines, Bells

The Fenton Art Glass Company was founded in 1905 by Frank L. Fenton. For over eighty-five years, Fenton has made colored glass, tableware and giftware. In the early years, Fenton was best known for originating Carnival glass, now highly sought by collectors.

In recent years, Fenton has re-created rare glasses from the mid-1800s: Burmese, Rosalene and Favrene, to the delight of two national Fenton Collectors Clubs.

For more information, contact the Fenton Art Glass Collectors of America, P.O. Box 384, Williamstown, WV 26187 or National Fenton Glass Society, P.O. Box 4008, Marietta, OH 45750.

FITZ AND FLOYD

2055-C Luna Road
Carrollton, TX 74006
(214) 484-9494
Fax: (214) 620-7044

Dolls, Figurines, Plates, Christmas Ornaments, Bells

Fitz and Floyd launched its Heirloom Collectibles Division in 1991 with its first annual Christmas ornament, whose edition sold out in under five months. Within the next two years, Fitz and Floyd proudly premiered several new collectors' series items. The company is rapidly becoming an important resource for limited edition pieces and other collectibles.

From *Floppy Folks*™ dolls to collectors' plates, from Christmas ornaments to the *Holiday Hamlet*™ porcelain lighted Christmas-theme village, many collectibles from Fitz and Floyd have proven popular among collectors.

A few exceptionally celebrated pieces are: "The Magic of the Nutcracker," the first annual Christmas plate from Fitz and Floyd, which sold out right away in 1992; the "Nutcracker Sweets" annual Christmas ornament of 1992; and "Christopher Columbus," the first limited edition teapot in the *Figures From History* series, which commemorated the 500th anniversary of Columbus' discovery of the Americas, also sold out soon after its introduction.

Collectors can count on Fitz and Floyd to bring them high-quality collectibles in a wide range of subjects, as the company continues to expand.

The 1993 limited edition "Railroad Station" is from Fitz and Floyd's lighted village entitled Holiday Hamlet™, *part of the* Enchanted Forest™ Collection.

FLAMBRO IMPORTS INCORPORATED

1530 Ellsworth Industrial Drive
Atlanta, GA 30318
(404) 352-1381
Fax: (404) 352-2150

Bells, Christmas Ornaments, Figurines, Plates

While Flambro Imports marked its

beginnings almost three decades ago as a flourishing gift and accessories company, it was President Allan Flamm who expanded the company into the collectibles market. Located in Atlanta, Georgia, Flambro Imports is recognized as a select dealer in fine gifts and collectibles, notably Emmett Kelly, Jr. and *Pleasantville 1893*.

In 1980, Flamm signed Flambro's first licensing agreement for figurines depicting Emmett Kelly, Jr., America's best-known clown. The first Emmett Kelly, Jr. figurines were introduced the following year. The line was greeted with enthusiasm by collectors who appreciated the high quality of the porcelain craftsmanship and the careful attention to details. Joining the limited edition figurines and plates, the miniature Emmett Kelly, Jr. figurines have also become extremely popular with collectors.

An exciting addition to the Flambro collectible line is *Pleasantville 1893*. This lighted bisque porcelain village is based upon the book written by Joan Berg Victor, of the same title. Introduced in 1990, buildings are architecturally and historically correct to the Victorian period, produced in the finest bisque porcelain and completely hand-painted. Each building comes with its own heartwarming story, relating a history about the structure and its residents or owners and employees. Accessories, including prominent town people, round out the collection.

"Vigilante" from Flambro Imports is sold exclusively during special appearances by Emmett Kelly, Jr., commemorating his involvement in the Tombstone, Arizona Old West charity group.

Joining the Emmett Kelly, Jr. Collector's Society and new in 1993 is the formation of the Pleasantville 1893 Historical Preservation Society. During this first year of the Pleasantville collectors' society, members joining the society will be chartered as Centennial Members.

THE FRANKLIN MINT

Jack Wilkie
Franklin Center, PA 19091
(215) 459-7494
Fax: (215) 459-6880

Plates, Figurines, Bells, Graphics, Dolls, Christmas Ornaments

The Franklin Mint is a leading creator of luxury and home decor products and heirloom-quality collectibles. The company offers exclusive, originally designed products, including high-fashion jewelry; upscale home decor and table accessories (from fine porcelain sculpture to exquisite crystal); collector plates; precision-crafted die-cast automobile replicas and porcelain collector dolls; medallics and philatelics; historic weapon replicas; recreations of famous works housed in the world's most prestigious museums; and classic collector books in fine bindings. The company also publishes *ALMANAC*, the world's largest collectors' magazine, with an active circulation of more than one million readers.

The legendary board game "Monopoly — The Collector's Edition" is now available from The Franklin Mint in an exclusive issue fit for a millionaire.

FRASER INTERNATIONAL

Tom Jackson
6900 SW 21st Court, #6
Davie, FL 33317
(305) 370-9204
Fax: (305) 370-9255

Figurines

Located in Penicuik, a small market town just south of Edinburgh, Scotland, Fraser Creations has been handcrafting miniature cottages since the mid-1980s.

Initially occupying converted riding stables, product demand enabled Fraser Creations to relocate into their present facility in 1988. These premises include offices, a showroom/shop, storage and production facilities.

It was from these premises that the highly successful *British Heritage* series and the *Landscape Collection* were launched, and the American marketplace targeted. The *British Heritage* series features miniature reproductions of famous landmarks like Big Ben and Westminster Abbey. The bas-relief landscapes bring the cottage theme and the countryside together to form one remarkable collectible product.

MARGARET FURLONG DESIGNS

210 State Street
Salem, OR 97301
(503) 363-6004
Fax: (503) 371-0676

Christmas Ornaments

An abstract landscape artist with a Master's degree in Fine Arts from the University of Nebraska, Margaret Furlong never thought she'd be hand-crafting porcelain angels.

But sixteen years ago, Margaret had a dream to create a business related to her background in, and love of, sculpture and design. At that time, she was established in a studio, an old carriage house in Lincoln, Nebraska, crafting pottery and ceramic sculpture. In addition, she was working on a commission, using shells as the subject matter. She combined several of the shell forms into a stunning white angel, which was so well-liked, that she continued the enterprise.

Margaret's angels are white-on-white unglazed porcelain, a symbol of purity and her commitment to her Christian faith.

Margaret and her husband, Jerry Alexander, now own Carriage House Studio, Inc., known as Margaret Furlong Designs, employing forty-eight people and producing 125 different designs each year. Although the angels remain the most popular offering in the line, Margaret Furlong Designs also creates shell stars, hearts, snowflakes, wreaths, picture frames and a line of porcelain pins and earrings.

Margaret is involved with every aspect of creating the collection, down

to the design of the boxes for her pieces. Her boxes are adorned with inspirations, hearts and stars. Collectors love everything Margaret designs. Her popular angels have decorated Christmas trees at the White House, governors' mansions and historical properties throughout the United States. Margaret's designs are also featured in national publications each year.

1993 designs from Margaret Furlong Designs are the "Star of Bethlehem" limited edition angel, fourth in the five-year Joyeux Noel series; the three- and four-inch angels holding sunburst crosses, symbolizing Christ and his Light; and a two-inch "Celestial" angel, designed as a celebration of new life.

GAIL LAURA COLLECTABLES, INC.

Gail Laura
302 Rosedale Lane
Bristol, TN 37620
(615) 968-7713

Figurines

Although she had been told by teachers that she was not artistic, Gail Laura never gave up her love for crafts and creativity. When her husband, Pete, suggested that she try sculpting, she readily agreed and a business was born. That was 1987. Today, the company, Gail Laura Collectables, Inc., is growing steadily in response to collector demand for the original artwork that Gail Laura sculpts with pins, needles and her own fingers.

Gail Laura would like to thank all the customers who have loyally carried her figurine line to its present popularity, and wishes much success to all new collectors.

GANZ/LITTLE CHEESERS

908 Niagara Falls Blvd.
North Tonawanda, NY 14120-2060
(800) 724-2950

1 Pearce Road
Woodbridge, Ontario L4L 3T2
(800) 263-2311

Figurines

GANZ began in 1950 as a very small, family owned and operated company called GANZ Bros. Toys Limited, which originally produced stuffed teddy bears. With a lot of hard work and dedication on the part of the Ganz family, the company grew steadily and expanded from Canada to the United States.

With the move into the United States, the company formed an American corporation and correspondingly, a change of name was necessary — hence, GANZ, Inc. In 1991, the company made a conscious decision to expand their product line into gift products beyond toys, including mugs, novelties, figurines, frames and more.

Part of that expansion was the birth of the *Little Cheesers* line of collectible figurines, which were an instant hit at their introduction in 1991. Although GANZ continues to produce a large variety of fun and adorable collectibles, *Little Cheesers* has earned a very prominent place in the company and in collectors' hearts and homes. Artist Christine Thammavongsa is the creative force that has helped these endearing mice become so popular. Collectors can rest assured that she will continue to charm them with her creations in the future.

"Little Truffle Smelling Flower" is an adorable Little Cheeser figurine from the Cheeserville Picnic Collection by GANZ.

MICHAEL GARMAN PRODUCTIONS, INC.

2418 W. Colorado Avenue
Colorado Springs, CO 80904
(719) 471-1600
(800) 874-7144

Figurines

Internationally-known sculptor Michael Garman founded Michael Garman Productions in 1972 to reproduce his unique art form and to make it available to collectors at an affordable price. Included in Michael's unique sculptures are the *American Moments Series* and his *Cityscapes*, which forever preserve a slice of Americana in one-sixth scale, some of which incorporate a combination of lights and mirrors, creating a holographic-type illusion that fascinates viewers of all ages. Individual figures include the following series: *Western, Firefighters, Aviators, Early American, Native American, Sports, Military, Law Enforcement* and more. The international art community has established Garman as one of America's best-loved artists.

GARTLAN USA, INC.

15502 Graham Street
Huntington Beach, CA 92649
(714) 897-0090
Fax: (714) 892-1034

Plates, Figurines, Graphics

The tradition of collecting sports memorabilia has taken on an entirely new dimension since Gartlan USA introduced its extraordinary line of fine-art sports collectibles, ranging from limited edition lithographs, plates and figurines, to open editions of mini-plates and ceramic trading cards.

Headquartered in Huntington Beach, California, Gartlan USA was established in 1985. Robert H. Gartlan envisioned this totally new concept in commemorating the achievements of some of America's leading athletes, including the Hall-of-Fame performances of Joe DiMaggio, Kareem Abdul-Jabbar, Wayne Gretzky, Joe Montana and many more.

The career of each superstar selected for this honor is telescoped into a montage of images by skilled sports artists. This artwork is recreated as a limited edition lithograph or limited edition plate. In some cases, an open edition collector plate is also issued.

The companion figurine of each athlete, coach or official captures the vitality and skill that brought each individual to prominence in his or her field. In most cases, figurines are available in two different sizes. As an added element of collectibility, all limited edition lithographs, plates and figurines are signed by the athlete.

Among the other sports greats honored are: Earvin "Magic" Johnson, Pete Rose, Mike Schmidt, George Brett, Roger

Staubach, Reggie Jackson, Ted Williams, Johnny Bench, Carl Yastrzemski and Hank Aaron.

New additions to the Gartlan USA line include Olympic gold-medalist Kristi Yamaguchi, Hall-of-Famer Tom Seaver, Yogi Berra, umpire Al Barlick and baseball greats Whitey Ford, Darryl Strawberry, Ken Griffey Jr., Rod Carew, Ralph Kiner, Stan Musial and Carlton Fisk. Gartlan USA's foray into hockey also includes Brett and Bobby Hull and Gordie Howe.

In commemorating these players, and then executing such a wide line of high-quality sports collectibles, Gartlan USA has earned the admiration of today's sports fans.

Part of the Joe Montana Collection, *this 10¼" 24-karat personally-signed plate was offered in a worldwide edition of 2,250.*

GEORGETOWN COLLECTION, INC.
866 Spring Street
P.O. Box 9730
Portland, ME 04104-5030
(800) 626-3330

Dolls

From its studios in Portland, Maine, the Georgetown Collection achieves an ambitious and very specific mission: to create the finest porcelain collectible dolls for today and tomorrow — in the tradition of the priceless heirloom dolls of yesterday. A veritable "who's who" of top contemporary dollmakers, Linda Mason, Brigitte Deval, Ann Timmerman, Jan Galperin, Sissel Skille and Carol Theroux have all accepted Georgetown's coveted commission to create collectible dolls, and in doing so have garnered top industry nominations and awards. Together, this collaboration of talented artists with a responsive

company results in truly extraordinary dolls created in *Artist's Editions*™ and available exclusively from the Georgetown Collection.

Georgetown's "Many Stars" by Linda Mason was the winner of both the Award of Excellence and Doll of the Year (DOTY) in 1992, an unprecedented event in the collectible doll world.

GOEBEL MINIATURES
4820 Adohr Lane
Camarillo, CA 93012
(805) 484-4351
Fax: (805) 482-2143

Figurines

Formed in 1978, Goebel Miniatures produces fine collectible miniature figurines and jewelry by using the "lost wax" casting process developed by Egyptian and Chinese artists over 5,000 years ago.

After first embarking on a line of miniature furniture known as the *Butterfly Collection* for the dollhouse market, the company soon discovered that the tiny handcrafted figurines produced by Master Artist Robert Olszewski would be the company's future. The furniture line was discontinued in early years, and the company grew rapidly.

One of the goals of Goebel Miniatures is to reproduce in miniature some of the finest examples of antique and contemporary masterpieces. Goebel Miniatures takes great pride in honoring the companies and artists who produced the full-scale originals.

Although some designs are released as limited editions (usually due to the amount of difficulty involved in reproduction), it is rare for the company to do so. Goebel Miniatures believes that limiting an edition is no guarantee of artistic worth. The real value of a work of art comes from its artistic quality. Goebel Miniatures' first limited edition

"Alice in the Garden," based on the Lewis Carroll works and commissioned in 1981 by *Miniature Collector Magazine*, was released at $60 per figurine and now is independently valued at more than $1,000 per figurine on the secondary market.

Goebel Miniatures figurines range in themes from children, women, wildlife, and history, to the art of Ted DeGrazia, Walt Disney, Norman Rockwell and M.I. Hummel. Each piece is cast in bronze, is no more than one-and-a-half inches tall and has a display environment to accompany the series.

From the Peter Pan series by Goebel Miniatures comes "Peter Pan's London" with "Peter Pan," "Wendy," "John," "Michael" and "Nana."

GOEBEL UNITED STATES
Goebel Plaza
P.O. Box 10 Route 31
Pennington, NJ 08534
(609) 737-8700
Fax: (609) 737-8685

Figurines, Dolls, Plates

Founded in 1871, Goebel Germany has maintained a special relationship with the United States since before the turn-of-the-century. Today, as Goebel products enjoy increasing popularity in nearly ninety countries, its major audience on a worldwide basis is still the American consumer.

While the company's three-dimensional figurines reflect popular collecting and gift-giving trends, Goebel figurines evoke traditional values. They represent a certain timeless quality which spans the years. Dedicated to top-of-the-line craftsmanship, coupled with an upscale family image, Goebel United States' many successful lines include *Victoria Ashlea Originals*® limited edition dolls, ANRI, Goebel Miniatures, Goebel Crystal/Giftware, the *Mark Klaus Kollection*, Norman Rockwell fig-

urines and plates and Steinbach crystal.

This unique product mix reflects original creations designed by Goebel artists as well as licensed two-dimensional art developed outside the Goebel studios.

Limited edition "Cindy" from Goebel United States is a musical doll designed by Bette Ball, playing "Make Someone Happy."

GOOD-KRUGER DOLLS

1842 William Penn Way, Suite A
Lancaster, PA 17601
(717) 399-3602
Fax: (717) 399-3021

Dolls

Good-Kruger Dolls is a family-run business based on the sculpting and design talents of Julie Good-Kruger. In business since 1980, Good-Kruger Dolls produce Julie's doll designs in porcelain and vinyl limited editions. Currently, vinyl dolls range in price from $179 to $250 for editions of 500 to 2,000 pieces, and porcelain dolls sell for $600 to $750 in editions of 100 to 200 pieces. Julie's sculptures are strong in character and quality — the doll faces look as though they could be real children. An emphasis on hand-work in the costuming, the best materials and attention to detail have always been hallmarks of Good-Kruger award-winning dolls.

THE GREENWICH WORKSHOP, INC.

30 Lindeman Drive
Trumbull, CT 06611
(800) 243-4246
(203) 371-6568

THE GREENWICH WORKSHOP, LTD.
3781 Victoria Park Avenue
Unit 6
Scarborough, Ontario M1W 3K5
(800) 263-4001 (Inside Canada)
(416) 490-8342

Graphics

In the early 1970s, The Greenwich Workshop was founded with a clearly expressed dedication and commitment to provide an innovative and quality product to the collector.

The firm pioneered Western, Aviation and Fantasy art in limited edition print form. *The Living Canvas*, brings the art experience to life with award-winning videos produced by The Greenwich Workshop to accompany select prints and to profile individual artists. Their offerings also include Americana, Marine, Wildlife and the art of Bev Doolittle. The Greenwich Workshop also publishes books, including the popular *Dinotopia*®, now with 700,000 in print worldwide.

The Greenwich Workshop employs some of the finest artists at work today, including James Christensen, Howard Terpning, Frank C. McCarthy, Stephen Lyman, Rod Frederick, William S. Phillips and Bev Doolittle among others.

DAVE GROSSMAN CREATIONS, INC.

Flora Spuhl or Dave Grossman
1608 North Warson Road
St. Louis, MO 63132
(314) 423-5600
Fax: (314) 423-7620

Plates, Figurines, Christmas Ornaments

Dave Grossman Designs began producing collectibles in 1975. The company has remained in St. Louis, Missouri since 1968 and is owned and run solely by Dave Grossman. Mr. Grossman originally began his business by creating and marketing metal sculptures and has since expanded into many areas of collectible art.

In 1975, Grossman became the first company to produce a collectible line inspired by the work of Norman Rockwell, doing so under a license from Curtis Publishing Company. The firm has continued to produce Rockwell items for sixteen years.

Grossman also has other licensed lines, including Emmett Kelly, *Gone With The Wind* and *The Wizard of Oz*.

Additionally, Grossman produces many other figurine lines and plans to expand existing lines while marketing new collectibles.

H&G STUDIOS, INC.

Dick Gabbe
8259 North Military Trail
Palm Beach Gardens, FL 33410
(407) 626-4770
(800) 777-1333
Fax: (407) 775-1290

Plates, Figurines, Dolls, Graphics

H&G Studios, Inc. was founded in 1987 by Bill Hibel and Dick Gabbe, who collectively committed over fifty years to the gift and collectibles industry.

Talented artists such as Brenda Burke, Dennis Lewan, Alan Murray and Francois Cloutier create the original art. Then the finest quality producers in Italy, England and the United States are employed to perform the manufacturing functions. The result is a continuing line of artistic, collectible and gift-oriented products that obtain high acceptability by the consuming public.

The company has been recently named as the exclusive distributor of *M.I. Hummel*® music boxes in North America.

THE HADLEY COMPANIES

11001 Hampshire Avenue South
Bloomington, MN 55438
(612) 943-8474
Fax: (612) 943-8098

Plates, Graphics

The Hadley Companies grew from a hobby into an enterprise that includes the country's largest manufacturer of hand-carved decoys, a major publisher of limited edition art, a chain of retail galleries and two of the country's leading galleries of original art.

Ray E. Johnson founded the company in 1975 with the help of two friends. Their original intent was to create wooden decoys on a lathe which replicated a Wisconsin antique. A showroom, opened next to the factory, was so popular that the trio opened the first retail gallery in Rosedale Center the following year. Currently, The Wooden Bird galleries have twenty-seven loca-

tions in Minnesota, Michigan, Ohio, Illinois, Wisconsin and California and are still expanding at a controlled pace.

Today, The Hadley Companies market limited edition collector plates, lithographs and flatware by some of America's most renowned Americana, wildlife, western and figure artists such as Terry Redlin, Steve Hanks, Ozz Franca, Martin Grelle, Les Didier, Ted Blaylock, Jerry Raedeke, Bryan Moon, Olaf Wieghorst, John Clymer, Clark Hulings, Darrell Bush, Kevin T. Daniel, Mike Casper, Jon Van Zyle, Tim Liess, James Kennedy and Judi Kent Pyrah through Hadley House, The Wooden Bird and the Special Markets divisions of the company.

Hadley House's international dealer network spans the United States and Canada, and the Special Markets division is purveyor to major conservation groups and many *Fortune 500* companies.

Known for his nostalgic images of yesteryear, Terry Redlin has created a memorable holiday scene in "Winter Wonderland," third in the Annual Christmas series from The Hadley Companies.

HAILS FINE ART
Robert Hails
Dimensional Aesthetics
18319 Georgia Avenue
Olney, MD 20832
(301) 774-6249

Graphics
Hails Fine Art, division of Dimensional Aesthetics, exclusively represents the internationally-known artist, Barbara Hails. The publisher provides a collection of museum-quality hand-signed and numbered limited edition reproductions from her superb pastel paintings. Her most recent continuing theme, the *Magnificent Gardens Series*, has captured the imagination of collec-

tors, selling out ten images in 1992.

Barbara Hails' limited editions are available through distinctive collector galleries in North America or direct by toll-free call (1-800-451-6411). A color catalog of the complete line is available for $3.

HALLMARK CARDS, INC.
2501 McGee Street
Kansas City, MO 64108

Christmas Ornaments, Figurines
The modest card business started by Joyce C. Hall in 1910 has since grown into a huge corporation, the undisputed leader of its industry. Hallmark Cards, Inc. is a worldwide organization with international headquarters in Kansas City, Missouri, where the company had its beginning. The company produces greeting cards in twenty languages and its products can be found in more than 100 countries around the globe. In addition to cards, Hallmark also produces hundreds of related items such as paper products, candles, puzzles, mugs, home decorations and of course, Keepsake Ornaments and Collectibles.

This corporation had its start in two shoeboxes of postcards, Mr. Joyce C. Hall's entire inventory, which he sold from his small room at the local YMCA. The first departure from greeting cards came in 1922, when the company introduced decorated gift wrap to replace the then-standard, solid-colored tissue paper. Diversification of product and meeting consumer needs became the driving forces of growth at Hallmark, and the physical plant expanded along with the Hallmark product line.

In 1973, Hallmark introduced its Keepsake Ornament line, changing the Christmas decoration industry and America's decorating habits forever. Over the years, Keepsake Ornaments blazed trails that include the introduction of Lighted and Magic Ornaments, miniature ornaments, personalized ornaments and even recordable ones. In 1987, the Keepsake Ornament Collector's Club was introduced, and it continues to exist as the largest of its kind today. Building on the success of the highly collectible Keepsake Ornament line, Hallmark Galleries, a line of beautiful artistically-rendered collectibles, has been introduced, receiving great acclaim from consumers.

Creativity and communication with

consumers are Hallmark's keys to success. "Good taste is good business" was and continues to be, the byword of Hallmark Cards, Inc.

These four designs capture the workmanship and artistry that Keepsake artist Duane Unruh sculpts into each piece in the Hallmark Galleries Days to Remember, the Art of Norman Rockwell collection.

THE HAMILTON COLLECTION
4810 Executive Park Court
P.O. Box 2567
Jacksonville, FL 32232
(800) 228-2945

Plates, Dolls, Figurines, Christmas Ornaments, Bells, Steins
The Hamilton Collection is one of America's most honored purveyors of limited editions with an outstanding reputation for quality. Commissioning only the most talented artists, their collectibles continue to capture the imagination and emotion of collectors. Hamilton's recent line of Heritage Dolls has also carved a well-known niche in the collectible doll industry.

CEO James P. Smith, Jr. nurtured the company from its birth in 1978, and developed it into a strong and successful corporation. Today, with his vision and the creativity of Hamilton's fine artists, the company continues to grow in renown.

The plate artists focus on many themes: Chuck DeHaan, David Wright and Chuck Ren on Western themes; Thomas Blackshear and Susie Morton on entertainment themes; John Grossman's Victorian keepsakes; and Sam Butcher on his famous *Precious Moments* children. Gifted doll artists for Hamilton include Connie Walser-Derek, Jane Zidjunas, Virginia Ehrlich Turner and Joke Grobben among many others. It is no wonder the artwork of

each Hamilton artist finds its way into collectors' hearts.

In the future, The Hamilton Collection and Hamilton Heritage Dolls will continue to provide collectors with the quality service and collectibles they have grown to expect from this very prominent company.

The Hamilton Collection's "Deliverance" plate by artist Chuck Ren is an integral and beautiful part of the Mystic Warriors *series.*

HAND & HAMMER SILVERSMITHS

2610 Morse Lane
Woodbridge, VA 22192
(703) 491-4866
Fax: (703) 491-2031

Christmas Ornaments

The tradition of master silver craftsmanship is rapidly disappearing from the artistic scene. Fortunately, William deMatteo apprenticed with his father, a silversmith who willingly passed on the skill necessary to work in gold and silver.

Once his apprenticeship was completed, deMatteo became the master silversmith at Colonial Williamsburg in Virginia. In 1979, deMatteo, his assistant Philip Thorp and deMatteo's son, Chip, founded Hand & Hammer Silversmiths.

Hand & Hammer Silversmiths serves a number of commercial, corporate and academic society customers. It also has developed ornaments and jewelry for some of the country's most prestigious museums, historical societies, stores and organizations.

Since 1981, Chip deMatteo has created more than 400 ornament designs for organizations such as the U.S. Historical Society, the Boston Museum, Frederick Warne Co. of London, Lord & Taylor, Gump's, Tiffany's, Cartier

and Neiman-Marcus. In 1987, Hand & Hammer introduced its first limited edition dated series, *Bells*. It was soon followed by the equally limited *Santa* and *Carousel* series.

Also of interest to serious collectors is the five-piece *The Night Before Christmas* limited edition ornament collection and the four-piece limited edition *Victorian Village* collection based on Currier & Ives lithographs. Since 1990, Hand & Hammer has had the exclusive license to produce silver ornaments and jewelry based on the popular Beatrix Potter stories and characters.

"Heart Tree" is a sterling silver ornament created by Hand & Hammer Silversmiths, designed by artist Chip deMatteo.

HARBOUR LIGHTS

8130 La Mesa Blvd.
La Mesa, CA 91941
(800) 365-1219

Figurines

For centuries, lighthouses guided our seafaring ancestors away from imminent disaster to harbours of refuge and to the safety of the open sea. Harbour Lights was formed by Bill Younger of Younger and Associates to remind Americans of the thousands of voyages made safe by these sentinels of the sea.

Since the beginning of this company in 1990, several notable series of these authentic models of our nation's historic past have found their way into the collectible market and into the homes of avid collectors. The *Original Collection* contains several pieces that were featured as commemorative stamps for the U.S. Lighthouse Bicentennial in 1989. Other important series include *The Great Lakes Series*, *The New England Series* and *Southern Belles*, totalling Harbour Lights' range at thirty-seven pieces to date.

The lighthouses are made from Hydrostone, a gypsum-based product,

with a great amount of attention to detail; after being cast in molds, the pieces are hand-dipped in lacquer, then hand-painted and numbered. Each comes with a brief history of the lighthouse depicted, a Certificate of Authenticity and a registration card.

Harbour Lights has done well in their attempt to share a glimpse of what our seafaring ancestors knew so well — that the lighthouse stands for beauty and strength in the face of danger.

Harbour Lights' "Key West, Florida" lighthouse is part of the Southern Belles *series.*

HAWTHORNE ARCHITECTURAL REGISTER

9210 N. Maryland Ave.
Niles IL 60714
(708) 966-0070

Figurines

Hawthorne Architectural Register is a leading marketer of highly detailed architectural miniatures with an emphasis on sculptures inspired by traditional American architecture. Colonial, Victorian, antebellum and 18th-century native stone are among the styles represented in its collections. All Hawthorne buildings must meet standards of excellence which the company has established in the following areas: historical significance of subject; artists' credentials; quality of sculptural detail at scale; authenticity of architectural detail; period-inspired palette; period building materials depicted; authenticity of environmental details; statement of edition and required documentation.

Less than four inches high, many of the company's miniatures are sculpted by the husband-and-wife team of Kenneth and Hope LeVan. Hawthorne has also introduced larger-scale, illuminated houses, inspired by the work of

artists such as Norman Rockwell and Thomas Kinkade. Called the *Hawthorne Porchlight Collections*, these hollow porcelain buildings are lit on all four sides.

Hawthorne architectural collectibles are available directly from the company or at gift and collectibles stores across the country.

The Stonefield Valley *series from Hawthorne Architectural Register premiered with the enchanting structure, "Springbridge Cottage."*

HEIRLOOM EDITIONS LTD.

Barbara Ringer
25100-B South Normandie Avenue
Harbor City, CA 90710
(310) 539-5587
(800) 433-4785
Fax: (310) 539-8891

Bells

Heirloom Editions Ltd. was founded by Barbara Ringer in 1977. The original idea was to provide thimbles for collectors of the fourth leading worldwide collectible from one large source. Heirloom manufactures porcelain, pewter and bronze thimbles in their California factory. Heirloom imports exclusive designs of thimbles from Europe. The creative designs are done by Barbara. This company now manufactures and imports over 3,500 different styles of thimbles, making them the world's largest supplier of collectible thimbles.

Heirloom has also manufactured porcelain bells for collectors since 1984, and now produces Viennese Bronze bands and novelties from original molds purchased from the Vienna, Austria Redl Factory in 1983.

In 1991, Heirloom acquired the exclusive rights to import collectible Staffordshire Fine Ceramic teapots.

HEIRLOOM LIMITED

4330 Margaret Circle
Mound, MN 55364
(612) 474-2402

Dolls, Plates, Graphics

Corinne Layton's company, Heirloom Limited, was established after encouragement from her husband, Bill, prompted her to pursue a career in art. Response from the public was so great when she did shows at malls, that the business naturally continued. Corinne uses photographs and live subjects for her paintings of children and lacy Victorian scenes.

Plate series for The Bradford Exchange have been produced from her work, as well as prints on paper or canvas from Heirloom Limited and a doll series for the Ashton-Drake Galleries.

Corinne and Bill Layton manage Heirloom Limited together.

EDNA HIBEL STUDIO

P.O. Box 9967
Riviera Beach, FL 33419
(407) 848-9633
Fax: (407) 848-9640

Plates, Figurines, Graphics, Christmas Ornaments, Dolls

Edna Hibel is among America's foremost artists of international renown. Edna Hibel Studio distributes her limited edition graphics, sculptures, dolls, plates and other collectibles, decorative arts and jewelry.

Since 1940, museums, galleries and private collectors worldwide have recognized Ms. Hibel's talents. Many of her collectibles are displayed alongside her original oil paintings and drawings in the Hibel Museum of Art in Palm Beach, Florida.

Hibel's collectibles have received foreign recognition and numerous awards from the National Association of Limited Edition Dealers, The Bradford Exchange and the International Collectible Exposition, which presented Hibel with the 1992 International Collectible Artist Award.

Hibel's art products are sold by many distributors worldwide, including Canada through Kaiser Porcelain, 5572 Ambler Dr., Mississauga, Ontario L4W 2K9.

JOHN HINE STUDIOS, INC.

4456 Campbell Road
P.O. Box 801207
Houston, TX 77280-1207
(713) 690-4477

Figurines

John Hine and David Winter met in 1979 and quickly discovered that they shared an interest in the past. A sculptor, Winter had fashioned a number of sculptured cottages which Hine found so charming that he suggested that they go into business together. Later that year, they formed John Hine Ltd. Winter designed the cottages, and Hine handled the manufacturing and marketing.

The first cottage was introduced in the spring of 1980. Although the partners had envisioned a small English craft company, the popularity of the cottages soon made the David Winter cottages one of the leading collectibles of the decade. In 1987, the David Winter Cottage Collectors Guild was formed. Currently, there are more than 100 cottages in the line, in addition to approximately fifty-five cottages and buildings now retired.

In 1990, Hine introduced the *American Collection* by Canadian sculptor Maurice Wideman. This more traditional series contains about forty miniature homes and buildings that range from a California winery to a New England town hall.

Maurice, known to his collectors as Moe, has created a humorous collection of miniatures called *Moe Houses*, which depict the "lighter side of life" as only Moe can interpret it!

Fantasy reigns supreme in Jon Herbert's *Shoemaker's Dream*, a series of miniature English buildings that seem to spring from equally astonishing footwear.

In addition to the *Shoemaker's Dream*, Herbert has created *Father Time Clocks*, a whimsical series of castles, manors and cottages, all with working clocks dropped into the facade.

Animal Antics are also a new creation for Jon Herbert, introduced in 1993, sculpted with the same elaborate details as the shoe houses. There are six cleverly-costumed animal figurines in the collection, including "Lucky Dragon," "Tabby Tabitha" and "Sir and Lady Mouse."

A new introduction from John Hine Studios, the *London by Gaslight* collec-

tion of miniature lighted houses, has the aura of a London street at twilight in Victorian times. The cottages are sculpted by artist Bob Russell, and are complemented by metal figures of the Victorian era, created by metalsmith Andrew Stadden.

"On The Riverbank" by David Winter was free to Guild members in 1993.

MARK HOPKINS SCULPTURE, INC.

L. Susan Fife
21 Shorter Industrial Blvd.
Rome, GA 30165-1838
(706) 235-8773
Fax: (706) 235-2814

Figurines

In 1988, Mark Hopkins Sculpture emerged as a company with a dream…to produce and sell fine art bronze sculpture at affordable prices. Today, a staff of trained artists and craftsmen take great pride in their reputation for excellent quality and service, and their ability to produce Mark's works at a price which is bringing bronze into the homes of art lovers from all walks of life. Mark Hopkins has gained widespread recognition as an extraordinary artist. Using his technical expertise in the "lost wax" method of bronze casting, he creates unique designs in a wide variety of subjects ranging from sports to wildlife, sea life, children and Native Americans.

HOPKINS SHOP

Highway 52 South and Resinwood Drive
Moncks Corner, SC 29461
(800) 356-1813 Orders Only
(803) 761-7626
Fax: (803) 761-7634

Figurines

Hopkins Shop was founded in 1973 by John Hopkins Sr., a builder and fur-

niture designer, and his son, John Jr., an art major in college. In 1985 they created the Village Lights, a series of lighted English and turn-of-the-century American style cottages.

Hopkins Shop then produced the *Enchanted Kingdom*, a collection of fantasy castles accented with Swarovski crystals. This grouping includes the original "Enchanted Kingdom" pieces, "Raven-stone Ruins," "Birthstone Castles" and the "Dream Castles."

M.I. HUMMEL CLUB

Division of GmbH Inc.
Goebel Plaza
P.O. Box 11
Pennington, NJ 08534-0011
1-800-666-CLUB

Figurines, Plates, Bells

The M.I. Hummel Club (formerly the Goebel Collector's Club) was formed in 1977. This organization is designed to inform those who enjoy figurines, plates, bells, miniatures and other works based upon the art of Sister M.I. Hummel.

The M.I. Hummel Club offers many benefits to its members, including a free figurine valued at $80, and a four-color quarterly magazine, *Insights*, which is filled with informative articles. The membership kit contains an official membership card, a specially designed binder with inserts detailing the history and the intricacies of the handcrafting of *M.I. Hummel* figurines, and redemption cards to provide members with the opportunity to buy *M.I. Hummel* exclusive collectibles.

The annual exclusive figurine, available only to M.I. Hummel Club members for 1993-1994, is titled "I Didn't Do It."

Another benefit of Club membership is the opportunity to travel on custom-

designed trips with others who share their hobby. European trips always include the behind-the-scenes tour of the factory in Roedental, Bavaria.

Members benefit also from the exclusive Collectors' Market, through which they can buy and sell Goebel collectibles on a confidential basis. Because of the Club's link to the factory archives, members also can have their research questions answered in depth.

Local Chapters give individuals the opportunity to meet one another in small regional groups to expand their *M.I. Hummel* knowledge and friendships.

VICTORIA IMPEX CORPORATION

2150 John Glenn Drive, Ste. 400
Concord, CA 94520
(800) 861-6888
(510) 685-6788
Fax: (510) 685-8839

Dolls, Figurines

Founded in 1979 by Victoria and Paul Chang, Victoria Impex Corp. has made a name for itself in the collectible doll market. They have always maintained high quality, creativity and excellent customer service. That is why *Giftware News* magazine listed Victoria Impex as the number three doll company in 1989.

In the early years, Victoria Impex experimented with a number of different gift products but it was the design of their porcelain dolls, clowns and pierrots that gave them a name in the industry.

In 1988, Victoria Impex expanded its distribution to include the United Kingdom, Canada and Puerto Rico. Yet, their fundamental principle continues to remain: "Quality and customer service."

INCOLAY STUDIOS INC.

445 North Fox Street
P.O. Box 711
San Fernando, CA 91340
(818) 365-2521
Fax: (818) 365-9599

Plates

One of the most ancient forms of art was the detailed carving of cameos from multi-layered gemstones. The figures and scenes were carved on the white layer, while the multi-colored layers formed the background.

The artisans of Incolay Studios Inc.

have revived this lost art, using a totally different medium, handcrafted Incolay Stone. The process for creating Incolay Stone is a closely guarded secret in which various colored minerals and coupling agents are combined in the stratified background to reproduce the same variegated formations and beauty of natural stone.

In 1977, Incolay Studios entered the limited edition collectors plate market with the *Romantic Poet Series*. Incolay has continued with several popular plate series since then, the most recent entitled *Christmas Cameos*.

IRIS ARC CRYSTAL
114 East Haley Street
Santa Barbara, CA 93101
(800) 392-7546 outside CA
(800) 367-3248 inside CA
Fax: (805) 965-2458

Figurines, Christmas Ornaments
Jonathan Wygant and Francesca Patruno founded Iris Arc Crystal in 1976. Initially, Iris Arc marketed faceted crystal in the form of prisms and jewelry. The name for their firm came from the Greek myth of Iris, the goddess of the rainbow who was sent by Zeus to Earth on a rainbow to give a message to mortals. Eventually, they added the tag line "The Gift of Light."

"Light is the essence of what crystal is all about. Consequently, every single piece they feature in their collection is a prism — cut and faceted so the light plays through it, breaking up into rainbows of color," said Wygant.

The hand-sculpted limited edition "Rainbow Cathedral," designed by artist Mark Goena, is a majestic addition to the American Spirit Collection *from Iris Arc Crystal.*

From their early experience selling prisms, Wygant and Patruno graduated in 1979 to become the first American manufacturer of faceted crystal figurines. Using imported full-lead crystal, each figurine is handcrafted at their company in Santa Barbara, California. One of the first companies to promote the halogen lighting of crystal figurines, Iris Arc offers a number of fine limited edition pieces.

Iris Arc's cottages, romance and floral themes are among the most popular to collectors. As part of its commitment to serving collectors' desire for colorful crystal collectibles, the company has trademarked the name "Rainbow Crystal" and founded the Iris Arc Crystal Collectors Society. The society features exclusive, members-only editions, a free enrollment gift, newsletters and grand prize drawings.

JANCO STUDIO
P.O. Box 30012
Lincoln, NE 68503
(402) 435-1430

Figurines, Christmas Ornaments
Janco Studio is a relative newcomer to the collectible industry. Started by sculptor Bert Anderson, Janco made its first appearance at the International Collectible Exposition in Secaucus, New Jersey in April of 1992. Since then, they have been rapidly expanding their lines and their distribution. Their series include *Joymaker Elves, Bearer of Christmas Dreams,* and *Angels & Imps.* Janco strives for exceptional detail and quality. All limited edition pieces are signed and numbered by the artist, and come with a registration card that can be returned to receive a Certificate of Authenticity.

KAISER PORCELAIN (U.S.) INC.
2045 Niagara Falls Blvd. Unit 11 & 12
Niagara Falls, NY 14304
(716) 297-2331
Fax: (716) 297-2749

KAISER PORCELAIN CO. LTD.
5572 Ambler Drive
Mississauga, Ontario L4W 2K9

KAISER PORCELAIN LTD.
Bangors Road North
Iver Heath, Bucks SLO OBL
England

VIKING IMPORT HOUSE
412 S.E. 6th Street
Fort Lauderdale, FL 33301

Plates, Figurines, Bells, Dolls, Christmas Ornaments
In the heart of the Bavarian porcelain-making center, Kaiser Porcelain has been in production for over 120 years. Kaolin clay or "white gold" as it is commonly referred to, adds to the pristine beauty of the porcelain produced there.

August Alboth, artist and craftsman, established the original workshop in Coburg, Germany in 1872. Later joined in business by Georg Kaiser, the company trademark, "Alka-Kunst," was created in 1925. It incorporated the first two letters of the principals' names and the German word for art (*kunst*).

In 1953, the present factory was constructed in Staffelstein, which has increased in size and technology throughout the years. The firm's name was changed to Kaiser Porcelain in 1970.

Hubert Kaiser, chief executive of this family-owned company, strives for continued excellence and quality.

KEIRSTEAD GALLERY LIMITED
Brenda Keirstead
40 Grant Timmins Drive
Kingston, Ontario K7L 4V4
(613) 549-4066
Fax: (613) 549-5783

Graphics
Keirstead Gallery was established in 1977 to distribute the work of James Lorimer Keirstead and Janice Dawn Keirstead. The firm's objective is to create reproductions that look and feel like originals, by capturing mood, texture and vibrant, exciting color.

Lithographic reproductions of Keirstead paintings are produced to the highest standards. Skilled craftspeople are trained to apply clear acrylic varnish on images to create a texture similar to the artist's original oil paintings. Each print is presented in a wooden frame with linen matting.

KEVIN FRANCIS
85 Landcroft Road
East Dulwich, London
England SE22 9JS
011-44-81-081-693-1841
Fax: 011-44-81-299-1513

U.S.A. Office
P.O. Box 1267
Warren, MI 48090
(313) 795-8360
Fax: (313) 795-3884

Figurines

Kevin Francis was formed in 1986 to publish books on popular antiques and collectibles. The two partners, Kevin Pearson and Francis Salmon, met while studying for an economics degree in Leeds, England, in the 1970s. They then went their separate ways into advertising and lecturing, but a chance encounter in a London tube station one day led to their first collaborative venture producing the original United Kingdom price guide for character and toby jugs. The next three years saw a dozen successful titles under the Kevin Francis imprint.

Not content with just writing about toby jugs, Kevin and Francis decided to commission their own. Ceramic artist Peggy Davies created the first, extremely successful toby jug for Kevin Francis, a likeness of Vic Schuler, author of the book, *British Toby Jugs*.

Because of its instant popularity, Kevin Francis continued producing toby characters. All of the new designs that followed proved the success of the winning formula of high quality and low edition sizes. Sadly, Peggy Davies passed away in 1989. However, new artists keeping to the same exacting and demanding artistry are Geoff Blower, Doug Tootle and Andrew Moss.

"Bernard Leach" from the Artist and Potters series and "Sherlock Holmes" are two detailed and expertly crafted toby jugs from Kevin Francis, Inc.

Kevin Francis is dedicated to pleasing collectors with fresh ideas and diverse variations of toby personalities. Since the start, they produced over 120 releases, with sixty of these sold out. The publishing side of Kevin Francis is still alive and well, and 1993 saw its twentieth title released. Neither Kevin Pearson nor Francis Salmon ever envisioned, in their student days, that they would be running a ceramics company producing "the finest toby jugs ever made" — according to their many collectors worldwide.

KIRK STIEFF COMPANY
800 Wyman Park Drive
Baltimore, MD 21211
(410) 338-6000
Fax: (410) 338-6097

Bells, Christmas Ornaments

Since 1815, Kirk Stieff has been known for classic style and timeless elegance. The Roosevelts, the Bonapartes, the Astors — all have treasured the quality, craftsmanship and beauty that are Kirk Stieff traditions.

Pioneering the acclaimed Repousse style of raised hand-chasing, Samuel Kirk crafted magnificent designs of sterling flatware that continue today as some of the firm's most popular patterns. The creativity and exacting standards envisioned by Samuel Kirk and later, Charles Stieff, led to the distinctive selection to create authentic reproductions of historic artifacts bearing the names of Colonial Williamsburg, the Smithsonian Institution and the Monticello Foundation.

The Kirk Stieff difference of unyielding quality and fine American craftsmanship is a tradition that will be carried into the twenty-first century.

KNOBSTONE STUDIO
R.R. 3, Box 168A
Scottsburg, IN 47170
(812) 752-7022
Fax: (812) 752-5222

Dolls

The Knobstone Collection of collectible old world Santas can be described as unique, artistic and of the finest quality available. Every face is an original (not molded or cast) created by artist/owner Bob McAdams. Each facial expression is sculpted to match the theme, whether whimsical, jovial or serene. Bodies are soft sculpture, and several styles, colors and themes are available from this versatile and talented artist. A signed and dated Certificate of Authenticity is included with each doll. Other features of the Knobstone Collection are handcrafted toys and accessories and a Gallery book.

KURT S. ADLER, INC.
1107 Broadway
New York, NY 10010
(212) 942-0900
Fax: (212) 807-0575

Christmas Ornaments, Figurines, Dolls

During the past forty-plus years, Kurt S. Adler, Inc. (KSA) has become known as the world's leading resource of Christmas decorative accessories and a major name in the collectibles industry. With collectors seeking out its products for many years, the company has introduced many groups of collectibles during the past decade.

Available from Kurt S. Adler, Inc. are collectible nutcrackers and smoking figures that have been produced by the famous Steinbach factory in Germany. Steinbach nutcrackers and smokers are painstakingly hand-painted and hand-turned from the finest northern European woods with meticulous attention to detail by highly skilled artisans trained in the fine art of woodcarving. Other exquisite nutcrackers are available from the Zuber factory and the Erzgebirge region, both also located in Germany. In addition, several Disney nutcrackers are highly sought-after by collectors.

The *Fabriché* Collection of holiday figurines and ornaments features collectibles re-created from the Smithsonian Museum Archives and designs from veteran designer Marjorie Grace Rothenberg and the KSA Design Team. Fabriché sculptures are guaranteed by Kurt S. Adler, Inc. for unparalleled design, superior quality and skillful workmanship.

Jocelyn Mostrom has developed two groups of Christmas doll ornaments and accessories called *Christmas In Chelsea*, a series of ethereal garden fairies inspired by the famous English Gardens, and the *Royal Heritage* series featuring endearing children in turn-of-the-century attire.

The firm also developed a splendid assortment of antique carousel orna-

ments in the *Smithsonian Carousel Series*, featuring exact replicas of carousel animal figures found on turn-of-the-century merry-go-rounds in the Smithsonian Museum Archives. Other ornaments that have become highly collectible are cornhusk mice depicting human characters with delightful costumes, each designed by Marjorie Grace Rothenberg.

As a leading supplier of snowglobes, musicals and other holiday accessories, collectors can expect that Kurt S. Adler will develop collectibles in many new areas.

Featured in the Fabriché Holiday Ornament Collection *and as a Fabriché Holiday Figure from Kurt S. Adler, Inc.*, "Homeward Bound" *depicts Santa Claus returning from a long journey of spreading good cheer.*

LADIE AND FRIENDS™

220 North Main St.
Sellersville, PA 18960
(215) 453-8200
Fax: (215) 453-8155

Dolls

In a collaboration of love, Barbara and Peter Wisber created *The Family and Friends of Lizzie High® Dolls* almost a decade ago. Originally, it was Barbara's idea to add dolls to the line of two-dimensional folk art that she and her husband already produced. With Peter's help, the new doll line became a resounding success.

The first few country children made were a hit with collectors, so the Wisbers moved on to create a complete *Christmas Pageant*™ series for the winter holidays. As spring rolled around, a rabbit family, *The Pawtuckets® of Sweet Briar Lane*, multiplied into a series. From there, Barbara and Peter knew that collectors would continue to love and cherish the dolls they made, so they did not

stop. *The Grummels*™ *of Log Hollow*, Halloween characters, a wedding party and several *Little Ones* came into being. *Forest Friends* and more Christmas dolls, including some Santas, were added in the early 1990s.

In 1992, the Lizzie High Society was formed as a collectors club, inviting Charter Members to receive benefits and collectible information from Ladie and Friends. All of the dolls in the *Family and Friends of Lizzie High®* collection are heartwarming collectibles that may be received into collectors' homes with open arms. Rest assured that Ladie and Friends™ will continue to create adorable keepsakes for years to come.

"Margaret Bowman" and "Addie High" are from Ladie and Friends' Lizzie High™ *doll collection.*

LALIQUE

400 Veterans Blvd.
Carlstadt, NJ 07072

Plates

Lalique is a family-owned maker of exceptionally fine crystal products, including one of the most famous plates in the limited edition market: the first-issue, 1965 "Deux Oiseaux." This plate was the first non-traditional collector plate ever introduced.

The founder of the firm in the late nineteenth century was Rene Lalique, a goldsmith and jeweler. Lalique built a reputation for fine, Art Deco-style items including perfume bottles, vases and figurines. After the death of Rene Lalique, his son Marc took over the presidency until his death in 1977. Then Marie-Claude Lalique, Marc's daughter, stepped in to head the firm. She is also its chief designer, and she was the creator of the famous "Deux Oiseaux" and the other plates in the twelve-year annual.

THE LANCE CORPORATION

321 Central Street
Hudson, MA 01749
(508) 568-1401
Fax: (508) 568-8741

Figurines, Plates, Christmas Ornaments, Bells

In the early 1960s, a group of Boston-based foundry experts, working under the name Lance Laboratories, experimented with mold and casting techniques to produce precision metal products. The material and techniques they developed allowed them to cast a variety of metals with amazing accuracy and detail.

In 1976, Don Polland, an established bronze sculptor, brought his "Cheyenne" model to Lance for casting in pewter. This began a long and successful collaboration that continues today. At the same time, Lance, now known as The Lance Corporation, was developing its own Chilmark limited edition line of collectibles. In addition to Polland, Chilmark now produces the works of such famous artists as Francis Barnum, Anne McGrory, David LaRocca, Michael Boyett, Joe Slockbower, Tim Sullivan and Lowell Davis.

In addition, Lance produces a line of whimsical and contemporary pieces under the name of Hudson Pewter. The line has expanded through the years and now includes a wide representation of products and themes including the very successful *Disney*, *Noah's Ark* and *Villagers*™ collections.

"Cruising" is the Lance Corporation's first Disney sculpture in Chilmark MetalArt™.

Since 1975, Lance has also manufactured and distributed Sebastian Miniatures. The highly decorated and colorful bonded porcelain miniatures are America's oldest continually-produced

collectible line. First introduced in 1938 by artist Prescott W. Baston, they are currently designed and sculpted by Baston's son, Woody.

Always adaptable to the changing tastes of collectors, in 1993 Lance introduced *c.p. smithshire*™, a line of colorful and whimsical woodland people, called Shirelings™. The Shirelings are sculpted by Cindy Smith, and The Pangaean Society, a collector club for these lilliputian figures, was launched in September.

THE LANDMARKS CO.
Michael R. Leahy
4997 Bent Oak Drive
Acworth, GA 30101
(404) 590-9621

Figurines
A newcomer to the high-end collectibles marketplace, Landmarks is truly unique in many ways. Some of the world's renowned historic preservation organizations have commissioned Landmarks to create highly detailed, exact replicas of their most famous properties — stately mansions, plantation homes, magnificent churches and grand palaces.

Earlier this year, Landmarks introduced "Isaiah Davenport House - 1820," first issue in their new series, *The Antebellum South Collection*. Commissioned by the Historic Savannah Foundation, this cold-cast porcelain sculpture consists of over 150 hand-painted attachments and is being produced in a limited edition of 750 pieces. The second issue slated for late 1993 is an "Historic Charleston" single house.

THE LAWTON DOLL COMPANY
548 North First Street
Turlock, CA 95380
(209) 632-3655
Fax: (209) 632-6788

Dolls
More than a dozen years ago, Wendy and Keith Lawton formed Lawtons, a company dedicated to the manufacturing and marketing of Wendy's original porcelain dolls. Even from the beginning, it seems they could never make quite enough Lawton dolls to meet the demand. In 1987, they were joined by Jim and Linda Smith of Tide-Rider, a firm which had been importing European toys for over twenty-five years.

The partners have built a strong business based on the high standards that collectors have come to expect from Lawton dolls.

Wendy still sculpts an original face for each new issue. And the skilled artists who work at Lawton take pride in every detail, still meticulously hand-crafting each doll in Lawton's workshops in the San Joaquin Valley of California.

"Patricia And Her Patsy®*," the first issue in The Lawton Doll Company's Classic Playthings* collection, *portrays an all-porcelain Patricia showing off her beloved Patsy doll, a faithful replica of a popular 1930s doll.*

Lawton's goal remains the same as it was in the beginning: to make the finest doll it is possible to produce; to maintain the Lawton "look" — crisp and realistic portraits, with a straightforward American appeal; to work hard to maintain a price that offers real value for each dollar spent on a Lawton doll; and to continue to do the research necessary to create dolls that illustrate the human experience — from beloved literature to the customs and celebrations of people the world over.

Because of Lawton's dedication to excellence, Lawton dolls have been the recipients of more than thirty industry awards and nominations.

THE GEO. ZOLTAN LEFTON COMPANY
3622 South Morgan Street
Chicago, IL 60609
Corp. Headquarters: (312) 254-4344
Collectors' Service Bureau: (800) 628-8492
(800) 938-1800
Fax: (312) 254-4545

Figurines, Plates
Turn back the clock. All the way to

1938. Europe was about to be engulfed in a military conflict that would soon involve the U.S. and escalate into World War II. These were bad times.

As the Nazis overran their neighbors' boundaries, confiscating property and leaving a wake of death and destruction, hundreds of thousands fled, unable to defend themselves.

Many emigrated to the United States. Among them was a thirty-three-year-old Hungarian refugee, George Zoltan Lefton. He brought with him a dream: "Stay with something you know and you will never fail."

One thing he knew well was how to work with ceramics. That knowledge became the foundation of a business that would grow, prosper and, in 1991, celebrate its fiftieth successful year.

Lefton was a pioneer. He was one of the very first to re-establish porcelain trade in Japan after the War. Some of those early pieces, marked "Made in Occupied Japan" are now prized collectors' items.

"Things aren't highly prized just because they're labeled 'collectible'," says John Lefton, the founder's nephew and current vice president of the company. "What makes some of our old things so valuable today is the intrinsic quality and design that my uncle put into them decades ago."

That lesson has not been lost on the present generation. *Colonial Village* began modestly with a dozen assorted buildings. Collector demand caused the collection to grow to more than seventy structures and hundreds of ceramic citizens, antique vehicles and scenic accessories.

The 1993 Colonial Village limited edition, *"St. James Church," is shown next to one of Lefton's first porcelain bisque figurines, imported from Japan almost fifty years ago.*

LEGENDS

Zev Beckerman
2665-D Park Center Drive
Simi Valley, CA 93065
(805) 520-9660
Fax: (805) 520-9670

Figurines

LEGENDS — the 1986 prodigy of its parent, Starlite Originals, Inc., which was founded in 1972 — has dramatically impacted the market with its creation of unique and affordable certified limited edition fine art sculpture. LEGENDS takes great pride in remaining at the forefront of new concepts and innovations, and it is their masterful innovation of their original and exquisite Mixed Media™ concept — the combination of multiple mediums such as LEGENDS' bronze, fine pewter, lucite, brass and 24-karat gold vermeils, and much more — that has established them as the industry leaders while redefining the limitations of the artform. Because of their commitment to authenticity, detail and the use of natural colors, LEGENDS' sculptures are literally unparalleled in the industry. LEGENDS does not use paints or dyes to achieve the beautiful array of colors found in their sculptures. Rather, the colors you see are the actual colors of the metals and acid patinas used.

Proudly made in the U.S.A., LEGENDS' collection of fine art sculptures incorporates a subject range from Native American, Western and Civil War history to the beauty of endangered wildlife. Their entire collection is a unique compilation of the exquisite works of some of America's most highly acclaimed, award-winning artists such as Christopher A. Pardell, Kitty D. Cantrell, Willy Whitten and Dan Medina.

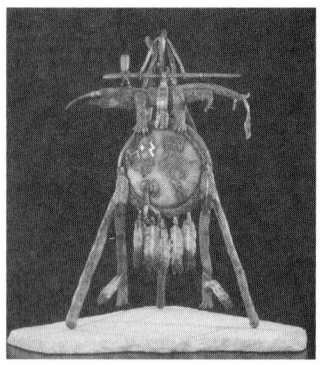

"Dream Medicine," the first release of Willy Whitten's five-piece collection called Relics of the Americas, has been created in LEGENDS' brilliant Mixed Media™.

LEMAX, INC.

Customer Service
50 Oliver Street
North Easton, MA 02356
(800) 972-6162
(508) 230-8967
Fax: (508) 230-9028

Figurines

The enthusiastic reception accorded the Lemax Collection since its introduction in 1991 has resulted in a rapidly expanding series of houses and accessories.

Each Lemax Dickensvale Collectible™ is of the finest handcrafted porcelain workmanship, created exclusively by Lemax. Majestic lighted cathedrals and quaint cottages are carefully hand-painted and have perfect proportional integrity, thereby assuring an authentic display.

A growing number of discerning porcelain collectors recognize the value and artistic quality of a genuine Lemax.

Collectors are welcome to call for a catalog.

LENOX COLLECTIONS/ GORHAM

Jo Ann Snow
P.O. Box 519
Langhorne, PA 19047
(215) 741-7688
Fax: (215) 750-7362

Figurines, Plates, Bells, Christmas Ornaments, Dolls

It began in 1889. A young artist-potter named Walter Scott Lenox founded a company dedicated to the daring proposition that an American firm could create the finest china in the world. He possessed a zeal for perfection that he applied to the relentless pursuit of his artistic goals.

Because of his hard work, Lenox china became the first American chinaware ever exhibited at the National Museum of Ceramics in Sevres, France. In 1918, Lenox received the singular honor of being the first American company to create the official state table service for the White House. Lenox china has been in use at the White House ever since.

Today, in every work of art created by Lenox Collections, the traditions begun by Walter Scott Lenox are carried forward, both in the making of china and many other fine collectibles.

In 1992, Gorham Dolls and Collectibles merged with Lenox Collections to continue the Lenox tradition of excellence in their lines. Lenox also works in a variety of media. In every case, an unbending position regarding quality is maintained. Sculptures are hand-painted, doll costumes are hand-tailored, crystal pieces are hand-polished and, of course, each piece of china retains a flawless finish.

Gifted artists of many different lands now earn the Lenox hallmark for their works only when they satisfy the highest standards. Every nature subject must be shown completely true-to-life and each historical piece must be authentic in every detail.

"Lauren" from Lenox Collections/Gorham stands 15" tall, her wide blue eyes reflecting childhood wonder as she carries her teddy bear in a flower basket.

This quest for excellence in artistry has earned Lenox the privilege of creating authorized works for famed institutions throughout the world, from The Smithsonian Institution in Washington, D.C. to the famed Palace Museum in Peking's Forbidden City.

Lenox Collections invites you to share in this heritage. And it pledges to make you as satisfied as the Presidents, First Ladies and royalty who have preceded you as Lenox collectors.

LEXINGTON HALL LTD.

c/o The Wimbledon Collection
P.O. Box 21948
Lexington, KY 40522-1928

Dolls

The Wimbledon Collection, more widely known as Lexington Hall Dolls, was established by Gustave "Fritz" Wolff in 1974. He had been mass-producing

inexpensive dolls in a factory in Taiwan for four years, as well as teaching at various institutions. The business became his full-time career when he introduced high-quality porcelain dolls, which were an instant hit.

Fritz's daughter, Gretchen, had been interested in her father's work from childhood, and when she began working with him, her artistic expertise was immediately apparent. She is now a full partner with her father.

The father-daughter team took collectors by storm with their *Designer Series Original Sculptures*, a very unique collection of dolls, each with an interesting personality. Collectors can anticipate more wonderful selections from the Lexington Hall Doll duo in the future.

LIGHTPOST PUBLISHING
Ten Almaden Blvd., 9th Floor
San Jose, CA 95113
(408) 279-4777
Fax: (408) 947-4677

Graphics
Lightpost Publishing is most widely known in the limited edition field for its publishing of fine art prints by artist Thomas Kinkade. Kinkade is widely regarded as one of the foremost living painters of light.

Thomas Kinkade began painting seriously at the age of fourteen. After studies at the University of California, Berkeley, and Art Center College of Design in Pasadena, California, Kinkade began work for the motion picture industry at age twenty-two. He personally created over 600 background paintings for the animated feature film, *Fire and Ice*. Also during this period, he and fellow artist James Gurney authored a best selling book entitled *The Artist's Guide to Sketching*.

In 1983, Kinkade left the film industry to pursue his vision as a painter of romantic landscapes and city scenes. Since then, his career has been documented in several magazine feature articles. In addition, Kinkade's painting, "Artist's Point," was chosen from nearly 2,700 entrants nationwide, as the official 1989 National Parks Collector Print and stamp.

To research his paintings, Kinkade regularly transports elaborate painting gear to locations ranging from the glaciers of Alaska to the busy streets of Paris. Kinkade feels that painting on

location lends energy and mood to his compositions.

Thomas Kinkade works in a studio located in the Santa Cruz foothills. In addition to a rigorous six-day week of painting, he and his family are highly involved with a nearby Christian church where Kinkade serves on the board of counsel.

Thomas Kinkade's glowing "Heather's Hutch" was inspired by a real English stone cottage and is part of the Sugar and Spice Cottages *series.*

LILLIPUT LANE LIMITED
Lilliput Incorporated
9052 Old Annapolis Road
Columbia, MD 21045
(410) 964-2202
Fax: (410) 964-5673

Figurines
Lilliput Lane Limited was founded in September 1982 by David J. Tate. From the company's modest beginnings in an old run-down barn, Lilliput Lane has evolved into a leader in the cottage collectibles market. Lilliput Lane is based in Penrith, in the Lake District of Northwest England.

As the founder, David Tate established high standards and new manufacturing techniques essential for the vernacular reproductions of extremely detailed sculptures. David has spent years researching the architecture of England and has a collection of reference books and thousands of photographs that he utilizes for his designs. He and his team of skilled artists and technicians work on new pieces for months at a time to ensure that all of the historical features are accurately portrayed in the finest detail.

Lilliput Lane's collection of architecture includes English, Scottish, Irish, German and French Cottages, *The Blaise Hamlet Village Collection* and *The American Landmarks* series. New sculp-

tures are introduced each and every year to broaden and expand the collectibility of the various ranges.

Lilliput Lane has enjoyed outstanding success and was named one of the top five companies by the Confederation of British Industry in 1987 and 1988. In the USA, Lilliput Lane was voted 'Best Collectible of Show' in South Bend 1990 for the piece "Convent in the Woods." In the same year, *Collector Editions* magazine presented an "Award of Excellence" from their collectors to Lilliput Lane for "Periwinkle Cottage."

Lilliput Lane is distributed exclusively in the United States by Lilliput Incorporated.

Lilliput Lane's 1993 Anniversary piece was "Cotman Cottage," an impressive example of Suffolk vernacular architecture.

LLADRO
1 Lladro Drive
Moonachie, NJ 07074
(201) 807-1177
Fax: (201) 807-1168

Figurines, Bells, Ornaments
In 1951, three brothers named Juan, Jose and Vicente Lladro pooled their talents and finances to start a ceramic-making operation in Valencia, Spain. After building a kiln on the family patio, the brothers began to produce ceramics that made the name Lladro synonymous with superb quality and craftsmanship.

From the very beginning they concentrated almost exclusively on the production of figurines at the expense of the utilitarian wares that commonly provided the backbone of such a company's prosperity. This emphasis, however, reflected the sculptural sympathies of the brothers, and continues even today in the wide range of Lladro figurines.

Many of their first offerings were decorated with miniature, delicately sculpt-

ed porcelain flowers. Their vases were modeled after Dresden and Sevres porcelains. But it wasn't long before the Lladro brothers developed their own highly stylized "signature" figures with their own sense of grace and movement.

In order to create these highly specialized works of art, teams of talented workers of unparalleled experience in porcelain manufacture were assembled. They were to become the cornerstone of the present-day company.

Today, the company sells a wide range of both limited and open-ended edition figurines. The subjects range from flowers and animals to nativity sets and sports activities. In addition, Lladro manufactures vases, lamp bases and miniatures. In a recent effort to expand its scope, the firm founded the Lladro Collectors Society, which is open to those who decorate with or collect Lladro.

The second generation of the Lladro family is now becoming very involved with the company. Each brother has one child on the Board of Directors. They are committed to carrying on the Lladro family name and tradition of fine craftsmanship through the next century.

The exquisite Lladro "Love Story" figurine has an issue price of $2800.

LOIS JEANNE DOLLS, INC.
537 Shearer Street
North Wales, PA 19454
(215) 699-9298

Dolls
Lois Jeanne Dolls, Inc. was founded in the spring of 1991 by artisan Marcy Britton to create limited edition original pressed felt dolls — each edition size nominally twenty-five pieces. Marcy has exhibited her dolls at the New York Toy Fair in 1992 and 1993, and has been nominated by *Dolls* magazine for Doll of

the Year in the cloth doll category for "Karla" (1992) and "Amanda" (1993).

All of Marcy's fourteen current designs are from original molds made by the artist, feature hand-painted facial expressions and original outfits and come with a Certificate of Authenticity. Retail prices range from $300 to $550.

LYNN'S PRINTS
Diane or Ted Graebner
P.O. Box 133
Lodi, OH 44254
(216) 948-4607

Graphics
Lynn's Prints was established in 1986 due to an overwhelming response to Diane Graebner's artistic portrayal of the Amish living near her home.

Phenomenal growth and widespread acclaim of her work has taken place in a very short time. Her paintings are of the simple elegance and peacefulness of spirit within the Amish communities, focusing on family values and interactions. She respects the Amish and their beliefs and therefore does not take photographs or paint facial features, wanting only to share the Amish strength of religion and family.

Among Mrs. Graebner's releases are Graebner Groupings, introduced in July of 1993. These collectible figures on wood are numbered and limited to an edition of only 2,500. There are twenty-five figures in the *Skating* series and twenty-five figures in the *Apple Pickin'* edition.

MCK GIFTS, INC.
P.O. Box 621848
Littleton, CO 80162-1848
(303) 979-1715
Fax: (303) 979-6838

Figurines
MCK Gifts, Inc. was founded by Mike and Marilyn McKeown, who have thirteen years of experience in the giftware industry. The company was formed to promote local artisans and is dedicated to providing high-quality, collectible gifts created by new artists.

Their first collectible line, introduced in 1993, is entitled *The Patchville Bunnies Collection* and is designed by Colorado native Alfred A. Mazzuca, Jr. As a self-taught artist, Mazzuca has been drawing since childhood. Two years ago, he turned his love of art into his profes-

sion, and his prints became remarkably successful. This success motivated him to create the world of Patchville, with whimsical, lop-eared bunnies that are individually cast and delicately hand-painted.

SEYMOUR MANN, INCORPORATED
225 Fifth Avenue
New York, NY 10010
(212) 683-7262

Dolls, Figurines, Christmas Ornaments
A winner of many collectible doll and figurine awards, citations and honors, Seymour Mann has recruited America's top artists and designers and reconfirmed its commitment to transform collectibles into art forms.

Eda and Seymour Mann combined their talents in business enterprises since marrying in the 1940s. Seymour used his marketing savvy and business expertise while Eda tapped her artistry to create figurines and decorative accessories. Later she developed dolls for the award-winning *Connoisseur Collection*.

Recently the firm has developed the *Signature Series* of collectible dolls featuring the works of the nation's top artists, including Paulette Aprile, Hanna Kahl-Hyland, Michelle Severino, Hal Payne, Pat Kolesar and June Grammer.

The lovely blue-eyed ballerina, "Pavlova," was designed by Paulette Aprile as part of Seymour Mann, Inc.'s Signature Series.

With the co-leadership of Gideon Oberweger, Seymour Mann, Inc. has been able to seek out overseas manufacturers who can best capture the essence of each artist's work. Each designer has a distinct ideal for his or her artistry, and the production of each doll must be closely supervised in order to transform the original into accept-

able collectible reproductions.

The company also has become known for its cat musical collection. Each collectible features cats in whimsical settings, accompanied by popular tunes. In addition, Seymour Mann, Inc. has developed unique collectible teapots in its fine tableware collection.

If the past four decades are any indication, Seymour Mann, Inc. can be expected to work with the finest artists in the collectible industry and to continue to win many more awards.

MARINA'S RUSSIAN COLLECTION

507 North Wolf Road
Wheeling, IL 60090
(708) 808-0994
Fax: (708) 808-0997

Figurines

Among Russian folk arts, one of the most beautiful is the intricate art of painting miniatures on papier-maché items. The softly luminescent paintings are lacquered over to preserve their beauty and the collectible treasure on which they are painted. This fine skill originated in Russia in the late 18th century and remains an applied art in villages there today.

Also popular and probably the best known of all Russian folk arts are the brightly painted, wooden Matryoshka Nesting Dolls. Sets of three to seventy painted dolls, nestled within each other, are made in varied shapes and sizes.

Both of these wonderful art forms are produced by Marina's Russian Collection, under the direction of Marina and the creativity of Russian artists S.G. Guseva and U.V. Gusev.

To meet the growing demand for information about Russian Nesting Dolls, Marina Marder, head of Marina's Russian Collection, and Larissa Soloviova have written the Russian Matryoshka book.

From the stunning lacquered boxes to the charming Nesting Dolls, Marina's Russian Collection offers American connoisseurs a marvelous opportunity to sample the rich diversity of Russian Folk Art. Working with some of the most gifted painters and craftspeople of the former Soviet Union, Marina will continue to open international doors through the "universal language" of visual arts.

MARTY BELL FINE ART, INC.

9314 Eton Avenue
Chatsworth, CA 91311
(800) 637-4537
Fax: (818) 709-7668

Graphics, Plates

Marty Bell Fine Art, Inc. established in 1968, today is the publisher of superlative limited edition lithographs for the original oil paintings of "America's Premier Artist for Heart and Home" — Marty Bell.

Acclaimed for thousands of beautiful images captured on canvas, Marty Bell is best known for her renditions of England's country cottages and pastoral portrayals. Her love of the English countryside continues to prompt extended sojourns to this captivating isle where she studies "real life" settings which may become subjects of future paintings.

After receiving an overwhelming response and demand for her original oil paintings, Marty and her husband Steve began reproducing her art in 1981. Marty Bell's works have since been in high demand. Thus, Marty Bell offerings have expanded to include many gift and collectible selections. And the Marty Bell Collector's Society, formed in 1991, has enrolled over 4,000 members in only two years, while continuing to register new members in increasing numbers every month.

1992 marked the introduction of Marty Bell Fine Art, Inc.'s collectible series of plates. Under the brush strokes and artistry of Marty Bell, lovely English images are presented in an enchanting plate series entitled In a Cottage Garden.

Under the able direction of her husband, Steve Bell, and their three sons, Mark, Jeff and Greg, Marty Bell Fine Art, Inc. publishes and distributes her art and collectible selections throughout the United States from Chatsworth, California. Marty plans to produce at least twenty new paintings per year for reproduction, plus one-of-a-kind origi-

nals, while also touring nationwide to make personal signing appearances.

"Coln St. Aldwyn's" by Marty Bell depicts a little village nestled by the river Coln, deep in the Cotswold hills of Gloucester.

MARTY SCULPTURE, INC.

P.O. Box 599
Milton, VT 05468
(800) 654-0478
Fax: (802) 893-1433

Figurines

Martha Carey, trained in fashion illustration, took up clay sculpting in the early 1970s, first creating and marketing clay figures locally. In 1977, she discovered the possibilities of hydrostone, a medium which allowed larger production with the same artistic attributes as clay, and founded Marty Sculpture, Inc. In 1980, her husband Carl left his job with IBM to assume the operational command of this increasingly successful business, Martha (Marty) and Carl Carey still retain sole ownership and operation of Marty Sculpture.

Marty's early success was capped by her series entitled North American Birds. Her first limited edition piece, introduced in 1982, "Silent Vigil," sold out within eleven months.

Today, The Herd, a realistic rendering of thirty elephants in "personality poses," along with the Dragon Keep, Bearfoot and Purrfect Pets collections have given Marty a prestigious position in the collectibles field.

MARURI USA CORPORATION

Ed Purcell
7541 Woodman Place
Van Nuys, CA 91405
(800) 5-MARURI

Figurines

Until 1982, American collectors were largely unaware of a superb porcelain studio in Japan — a firm with roots

in the age-old ceramic capital of Seto. In that year, Maruri introduced its wildlife sculptures by renowned artist W.D. Gaither. Within months, Maruri became a respected name in the United States collectibles market.

The fourth limited edition in the Maruri Studio Collection *is the majestic "Wild Wings," a fourteen-inch American Bald Eagle.*

Less than two years after its introduction, the Maruri-Gaither "American Bald Eagle I" brought $600 on the secondary market — up from its modest issue price of $165. The exceptional quality of Maruri which attracted such attention, is the result of high standards set generations ago, and observed just as strictly today.

Maruri prides itself on its studied approach to the creation of limited edition figurines. The studio's premier master sculptor is Ito, who oversees the Seto operation. Ito's understanding of classic porcelain artistry is evident in every Maruri piece. In addition to Ito's many works, Maruri carries on its association with many great artists, creating a wide variety of superb sculptures.

1993 marks the introduction of one of those unbeatable sculptures — the fourth limited edition in the *Maruri Studio Collection*, titled "Wild Wings," a majestic American Bald Eagle.

MARVART DESIGNS, INC.
Marvin W. Kramer
1490 Florida Street
Farmingdale, NY 11735
(516) 420-9765

Figurines, Plates
The MarvArt artists' studio located on Long Island has been creating fine works of art in cold cast marble and ceramic for over twenty-one years. Life-like realism is achieved in these expertly sculpted figurines by superior artists. Each is handcrafted from a bonded blend of natural Georgian and New England marble. MarvArt only produces figurines and plates of fine, museum quality. Their limited edition hand-painted animal figurines, double etched oval plates, and three-dimensional engravings are thought to be among the best-looking animal portrayals in the world today.

MAYFLOWER GLASS
P.O. Box 1536
625 W. Center Street
Lexington, NC 27292
(704) 249-2752

Figurines
The Mayflower Glass Collection consists of a line of exquisitely artistic glassware, most notably old-style ships in bottles. Each piece is set on a fine wood base, with a brass name plate, making it a true work of art. Also available are glass golfer, golf bag and airplane figurines under glass domes. Variations of most pieces are offered: frosted or gilded glass, personalized name plates or clock bases. These intriguing collections make wonderful gifts and additions to home decor.

Although the head office is located in England, Mayflower Glass also has its own sales office and warehouse in Lexington, North Carolina for distribution in the United States.

In 1992 and 1993, the English Mayflower Glass company received the Queen's Award for Export Achievement.

MCGUFFEY DOLLS, INC.
1300 East Bay Drive, Unit 1
Largo, FL 34641

Dolls
McGuffey Dolls and JoMel Studios is a family-owned business. Joseph McGuffey is president and manager, and Karen McGuffey Miller is sculptress and doll artist. Melva McGuffey is a doll artist and designer. In 1982, Melva began making re-creations. Their doll business began to grow as they attended international gift shows. In 1989, Karen began doing her original porcelain dolls. All are based on real children, and each doll is numbered and signed by Karen and accompanied by a Certificate of Authenticity.

The new venture for the McGuffeys is their line of vinyl dolls which were introduced in 1993 at the New York Toy Fair.

JUNE MCKENNA COLLECTIBLES, INC.
205 Haley Road P.O. Box 846
Ashland, VA 23005
(804) 798-2024

Figurines, Christmas Ornaments
Exquisite attention to detail marked by authentic period clothing and toys, a whimsical face highlighted by an upturned nose and twinkling brown eyes — these are the trademarks of June McKenna's famous Santa Claus figurines as she focuses on the jolly old man as he was known in the 16th through the 19th centuries.

The artist sculpts the figurines in clay, achieving such realism that people are often seen touching the lace collar on one piece or the gold braid on another to see whether they are made of fabric or wood resin. Artists meticulously hand-paint each individual figure and then cover the finished piece with the antique finish which gives the distinctive old world appearance which is such a striking part of June McKenna's work.

There are perhaps two ways in which the success of a collectible line can easily be measured, and June McKenna Collectibles achieves high marks on both counts. Although June McKenna only began carving her Santa Claus figures in 1982, her major limited edition pieces for 1983 through 1989 have already sold out. And the second criterion for success is that June's pieces are designed to be both attractive and affordable to everyone from the young child who loves Santa to the most serious collector.

June McKenna Collectibles, Inc. introduced "The Patriot Santa" as their 1993 Limited Edition Santa.

June McKenna figurines, which range in size from five to seventeen inches, are available in a wide variety of prices, starting at $30 each.

JAN MCLEAN ORIGINALS

255B Hillside Road
South Dunedin, New Zealand
64 (3) 455-6843
Fax: 64 (3) 455-6843

Dolls

Jan McLean designs, sculpts and produces limited edition porcelain art dolls. She signs and numbers each of the highly sought-after dolls that leave her studio. As well as limited editions of twenty-five, thirty or one hundred dolls, she produces a very small number of one-of-a-kind dolls.

She has been invited to exhibit at Disney World, Florida in 1991 and 1993 and is a member of the Original Doll Artist Council of America. Her sold-out *Flowers of the Heart Collection* consists of "Pansy," which won the *Dolls* magazine Award of Excellence in 1991, "Marigold," which was nominated for the *Dolls* magazine Award of Excellence in 1992, and "Poppy," "Primrose," "Fuschia," "Petunia," "Buttercup" and "Daisy."

MICHAEL'S LIMITED

8547 152nd Ave. NE
Redmond, WA 98052
(800) 835-0181
Fax: (206) 861-0608

Figurines

Taking its name from its founder, Michael O'Connell, Michael's Limited offers collectors beautifully hand-made, hand-painted, architecturally-inspired wall sculptures from *Brian Baker's Déjà Vu Collection*.

Brian Baker's Déjà Vu Collection is designed exclusively by artist Brian Baker and sold throughout the United States, Asia, Europe and Mexico.

The name "Déjà Vu" was inspired by the emotions these sculptures evoke. After studying these delightful sculptures, many collectors get the feeling — they've been there before.... Many of the sculptures recreate buildings Brian has seen on his worldwide travels. He enjoys sharing the heritage of these buildings with others.

Michael calls Brian one of the finest self-taught artists he has ever known. Brian's precise detailing and tremendous

sculpting ability exemplify the high standards needed for reproducing these detailed art castings. Brian oversees each sculpture through the entire production process. Each collectible is individually formed and hand-painted by skilled artisans in Michael's Pacific Northwest studios.

The popularity of the Collection led to the formation of the Brian Baker's Déjà Vu Collectors' Club in 1993.

Michael's Limited also produces *The Summer Breeze Collection*, which delightfully enhances *Brian Baker's Déjà Vu Collection*.

"Mansard Lady" by Brian Baker for Michael's Limited is from Brian Baker's Déjà Vu Collection.

LEE MIDDLETON ORIGINAL DOLLS

Mark Putinski
1301 Washington Boulevard
Belpre, OH 45714
(614) 423-1717
Fax: (614) 423-5983

Dolls

A deeply religious person, Lee Middleton, co-founder and artistic force of Lee Middleton Original Dolls, attributes her ability to capture the innocence and wonder of infants and children to God. As a token of "giving credit where credit is due," each of Lee's original dolls leaves the factory accompanied by a tiny Bible.

Lee started Lee Middleton Original Dolls in 1980. By late 1980, Lee had moved her business from her kitchen table to a series of rented locations. Today, a large production plant on the Ohio River in Belpre, Ohio houses this dynamic and ever-growing company.

Although all of her early dolls were handcrafted porcelains, Lee introduced more affordable, porcelain-looking vinyl dolls in 1984.

A Middleton Collectors' Club keeps collectors informed about Lee's newest offerings, and tours of Lee Middleton Original Dolls are conducted on a regular basis for interested collectors.

MIDWEST IMPORTERS OF CANNON FALLS, INC.

Attn: Consumer Inquiries
P.O. Box 20
Cannon Falls, MN 55009
(800) 377-3335

Figurines, Christmas Ornaments

Midwest Importers of Cannon Falls, Inc. was founded in 1955 by Kenneth W. Althoff as a small, family-owned business of importing, retailing and wholesaling handcrafted European products. Since that time, Midwest has grown to be an industry leader in the business of wholesaling and designing seasonal giftware. Since 1985, Kathleen Brekken, daughter of Ken Althoff, has served as president and CEO of Midwest, guiding the company into its present position of unparalleled growth and success.

Midwest Importers now sources and develops products literally around the world, and is proud to offer an exciting collection of exclusively designed collectible nutcrackers, Santas, figurines and ornaments.

As a wholesale distributor, Midwest utilizes wholesale catalogs, gift shows, and a network of independent sales representatives to sell products to the company's primary customer, the independent specialty retailer. Midwest Importers' products are available to consumers at fine gift shops and specialty retail stores throughout the country.

"Santa Claus" and "Mrs. Claus" are limited edition nutcrackers by Christian Ulbricht for Midwest Importers of Cannon Falls, Inc.

Midwest Importers' company headquarters is located in Cannon Falls, Minnesota.

MILL POND PRESS, INC.

310 Center Court
Venice, FL 34292
(813) 497-6020
(800) 237-2233
Fax: (813) 497-6026

Graphics, Sculptures

Mill Pond Press is North America's premier publisher of limited edition art prints. The variety of fabulous art ranges from wildlife to florals, from landscapes to fantasy, from children to the Western experience, representing the works of more than fifty world-class artists. The selection of art includes reproduction prints, original lithographs, serigraphs, glicees, art books and posters. "The Difference is the Quality" is the company's motto, and excellence has been the company's standard for twenty years.

Mill Pond issues a monthly catalog, Art for Collectors, which announces the release of ten to twelve new prints each month. The prints are distributed through a network of dealers in the United States, Canada and the United Kingdom.

MISS MARTHA ORIGINALS, INC.

P.O. Box 5038
Glencoe, AL 35905
(205) 492-0221

Dolls, Figurines, Christmas Ornaments

What is today the thriving firm of Miss Martha Originals, Inc. began in 1980 with a simple doll pattern design. Martha Holcombe had no idea that her mail-order doll business, which she started as a fund-raiser for her church, would turn into a successful, nationally-known company.

The creations that fueled the great expansion of Ms. Holcombe's business were the All God's Children figurines, first introduced in 1985. Over the years, Miss Martha Originals has continued to grow, attracting large numbers of admiring collectors from all over the United States. They warm to the nostalgic visions of times "way back when" that Martha Holcombe captures in her three-dimensional portraits of African-American children.

With the introduction of Harriet Tubman in 1989, Martha began a Black historical series to honor the unsung heroes of African-American history. This series is an open-edition collection, and the latest introductions of "Ida B. Wells" and "Frances Harper" bring the total to eight historical figurines.

Adorable little "Zack," standing 5¹/₂ inches tall and wearing oversized hat and boots, is a charming addition to the All God's Children collection from Miss Martha Originals.

Every figurine in the All God's Children collection is cast from Martha Holcombe's original sculptures. One of Martha's goals in sculpting is to have the figurines express the tenderness, love and beauty of life. But as she states, her primary goal is that "all pieces are sculpted with the desire that Jesus Christ will be honored" through her work.

THE MOSS PORTFOLIO

2878 Hartland Road
Falls Church, VA 22043
(703) 849-0845

Graphics

The Moss Portfolio publishes and distributes the works of P. Buckley Moss to approximately 500 galleries across the country and abroad. Moss' works include watercolors, oils, original prints, limited edition offset reproductions and porcelains. Moss is known for her paintings of the Amish and Mennonites and subjects such as landscapes, architecture and family paintings. Her style, while broadly speaking "Americana," is distinctively her own. Her involvement in raising funds for charities through the sale of her art has generated more than 1.5 million dollars for worthy causes in the last two years. The P. Buckley Moss Society counts 14,000 among its membership and is dedicated to promoting the appreciation of art and aiding Moss in her charitable endeavors.

NAHRGANG COLLECTION

1005 First Avenue
Silvis, IL 61282
(309) 792-9180

Dolls

The Nahrgang Collection evolved from a small family business in Moline, Illinois on the banks of the Mississippi River. Jan Nahrgang, with the help of her husband Larry and daughter Jennifer, started the business in 1980. What began as a hobby, led to a thriving business involving more family members and numerous employees. The business has doubled every year for the past ten years.

Nahrgang dolls are sold in fine doll and gift shops across the country and as far away as Australia. Nahrgang dolls are recognized for their fine detailed sculpture, delicate hand-painting done exclusively by Jan, and exquisitely hand-sewn costumes. All the dolls and costumes are handmade in Illinois and are usually designed from children Jan has had contact with in her teaching position at Franklin Elementary School. In addition to dolls modeled after children, exquisite fashion dolls are also produced. All editions are usually limited to 250.

Nahrgang dolls have received numerous awards and recognition. The most prestigious to date has been the 1990 Doll of The Year award from Doll Reader magazine for "Karissa."

"Tuesday's Child" is a poseable, 24-inch ballerina from the Nahrgang Collection.

Due to the demand and extreme amount of time to produce handcrafted

Nahrgang porcelain dolls, exquisite porcelain-like vinyl dolls are being produced by the Nahrgang Collection in a new factory in Silvis, Illinois (a neighboring town). At this facility, the famous Nahrgang porcelain dolls will continue to be produced in small quantities along with the new limited edition vinyl designs.

The company intends to remain a small business in America's Heartland with the unique feature of producing handmade collectible treasures for doll lovers around the world.

NAPOLEON
Allen Goeldner
P.O. Box 860
Oakes, PA 19456
(215) 666-1650
Fax: (215) 666-1379

Figurines
The name "capodimonte," a type of porcelain figurine, originates from a section of Naples, where the production of ceramic flowers began. That company was founded in 1741 by Charles IV in the Capodimonte Royal Palace and ceased in 1821.

Until 1745, the capodimonte production mainly consisted of small objects like snuff-boxes, covered vases, soup tureens and coffee and tea services. In 1759, during the reign of Ferdinand IV, the company was called Royal Fernandea Factory, and it produced until 1806, adding figurines and landscapes to the production.

The trademark consisted of a royal crown with the letters "F.R.F." interlaced. Since 1763, the mark was represented first by the letter "N" surmounted by the nobility crown. Subsequently, three other marks, differing in shapes, were used, composed of the same letter and crown.

Napoleon's stunning "Red Hybiscus" figurine is hand-painted with specially-mixed colors to achieve a realistic result.

In later years, the mark underwent other changes. Unfortunately, it has now become public property, and it is indiscriminately used by many factories at any quality level.

That is why Napoleon created and registered its own mark, by this time esteemed throughout the world, in order to make its porcelain flowers unique and to avoid any confusion. In fact, the craftsmen of Napoleon continue a tradition acquired through decades of experience and handed down from one generation to the next.

NEW MASTERS PUBLISHING CO., INC.
Constance Hardin
2301 14th Street Suite 105
Gulfport, MS 39501
(601) 863-5145
800 647-9578
Fax: (601) 863-5145

Graphics
Pati Bannister, now a United States citizen, was born in London, England, into a family of accomplished artists. After an early career as an illustrator for children's books and the famous English equestrian publication, Riding, she worked as a special effects artist for the J. Arthur Rankin film studios where she further developed a keen and sensitive eye for detail and color mixing, and their impact on all aspects of design and composition in a work of art.

In 1952, Pati Bannister moved to the United States and later settled on the Mississippi Gulf Coast overlooking a wildlife sanctuary. There she paints for the New Masters Publishing Company.

NOVELINO GIFT COLLECTIONS
12-A Mason
Irvine, CA 92718
(800) 325-4438
Fax: (714) 380-8014

Figurines, Christmas Ornaments, Bells
Novelino Gift Collections is an import gift company that produces and distributes several lines of collectible giftware throughout the United States. The company is a prime producer and distributor of collectible cold cast, poly resin, pewter and wood products in a large range of figurines, bells and Christmas ornaments.

Additionally, Novelino has developed several items exclusively for large U.S. retailers, either producing existing products for them or custom items.

Novelino is proud to exclusively present the National Wildlife Federation Collection and animal figurine collections for the William Holden Wildlife Foundation. A portion of the purchase of each animal in these collections is donated to these worthwhile organizations.

OLD WORLD CHRISTMAS
P.O. Box 8000
Spokane, WA 99203-0030
(509) 534-9000 ext. 160
Fax: (509) 534-9098

Christmas Ornaments, Figurines
Old World Christmas was founded in 1981 when the owners, Tim and Beth Merck, recognized a void in the market for high-quality, collectible Christmas ornaments and decorations. Embracing the century-old art of creating glass Christmas ornaments, Old World Christmas commissioned the German family workshop of Inge-Glas to produce their designs for importation to the United States. These high-quality, traditional ornaments were immediately successful and Old World Christmas expanded their line to include additional Christmas collectibles and giftware. Using the best available materials and exacting details, Old World Christmas recently introduced an innovative collection of nutcrackers designed by E.M. Merck. Produced in Germany by KWO and individually hand-signed by the artist, these nutcrackers are receiving rave reviews by collectors.

OLDENBURG ORIGINALS
Hidden Meadow Farm
W5061 Pheasant Valley Road
Waldo, WI 53093
(414) 528-7127

Dolls
Maryanne Oldenburg's love for children is evident in her work. Trained as a commercial artist, Oldenburg began making dollhouses and miniatures in 1970 before learning to make dolls with polyform clay. By the late 1970s, she had mastered the porcelain and mold-making processes needed to make high-quality porcelain dolls.

Oldenburg's dolls are all based on "real" children and events. Working

from photos and facial measurements, the artist molds a clay model from which all the working molds will be taken.

Oldenburg's limited edition dolls are signed and numbered, with most editions limited from fifteen to fifty dolls, with one-of-a-kind dolls also offered. The artist also designs dolls for the Georgetown Collection and teaches sculpting in traveling seminars, doll conventions and at her home studio. Oldenburg is also a member of ODACA (Original Doll Artist Council of America).

OLDHAM PORCELAINS, LTD.
Victoria L. Oldham
18 Hemlock Road
P.O. Box 545
Lansdowne, PA 19050
(215) 259-4444
Fax: (215) 622-3037

Figurines, Dolls
Since 1974, Charles and Victoria Oldham have created landmark sculptures for world-famous porcelain studios and private collectors.

Today, they collaborate in the creation of a unique line of sculptures in fine, high-fired porcelain with the establishment of their Pennsylvania studio. Unlike larger porcelain houses, the Oldhams personally execute reproductions from their master prototypes so that the finished sculptures remain faithful to their original artistic vision.

Current works include "Newborn Treasure," portraying a mother cradling her newborn, "Cradle by the Sea," featuring baby sea turtles hatching, the "Bluebird of Happiness," and a collection of life-sized kittens and cats.

OMNI MODELS, INC.
Jeff Dutton
106 Southwest Blvd.
Kansas City, MO 64108
(816) 474-9747
Fax: (816) 474-3911

Figurines
Since 1981, Omni Models, Inc. has been producing the finest museum-quality architectural models of building projects located throughout the world. Their success has been largely due to the attention to detail and quality of the finished product.

As a result of developing advanced casting techniques, Omni has focused its experience on *Frontier Expressions*. This effort will be an ongoing series of collectible figures of Indians, trappers, early settlers and period miniatures. Jerry Brown, actively involved in historic re-enactment, or "buckskinning," is the artist who creates these intricately detailed busts, winning many accolades from collectors for the beauty of the beadwork and depictions of furs and feathers that set these sculptures apart.

OPA'S HAUS, INC.
Ken Armke
1600 River Road
New Braunfels, TX 78132
(210) 629-1191
Fax: (210) 629-0153

Steins, Graphics
Opa's Haus is known for its OHI editions — high-quality limited edition steins produced to its specifications in Germany. American wildlife motifs from renowned artists are a specialty.

The company is also the exclusive distributor of the two limited edition "lost" M.I. Hummel® prints of Sieglinde© as a child, and it is the home of the OHI Exchange, a national leader in the offering and sale of secondary market collectibles.

Opa's Haus was founded in 1969 and has been in the same location since 1974.

ORIGINAL APPALACHIAN ARTWORKS, INC.
Diane Cobb
P.O. Box 714
Cleveland, GA 30528
(706) 865-2171
Fax: (706) 865-5862

Dolls
In 1977, a young art student named Xavier Roberts combined an interest in sculpture with age-old quilting skills of the Appalachian Mountains. The results were life-size cloth "babies" whom he called Little People®.

A year later, Roberts and five college friends established "Babyland General® Hospital" in Cleveland, Georgia. A short time later more than 500,000 of these hand-stitched "babies" had been adopted for fees ranging from $150 to $650.

In August 1982, Roberts granted Coleco Industries, Inc. the license to produce a small, mass-market version of the babies, and the name was changed to Cabbage Patch Kids®. In July 1989, Hasbro Inc., one of the world's largest toy companies, assumed the licensing agreement previously held by Coleco.

Collectors will find Cabbage Patch Kids, whether the hand-stitched, limited edition originals or mass-market versions, maintaining an eternal child-like innocence.

ORREFORS OF SWEDEN
Robin Spink
140 Bradford Drive
Berlin, NJ 08009
(609) 768-5400
Fax: (609) 768-9726

Christmas Ornaments
Orrefors, one of the world's leading producers of fine crystal art glass, tableware and accessories, was established in 1726 as a foundry in the forest area of southern Sweden. In 1898, it began manufacturing glass bottles, eau de cologne holders and simple tableware.

Orrefors' direction began changing again in 1916 and 1917 when it became the first glass producer to retain fine artists and designers like Simon Gate, a portrait and landscape painter, and Edward Hald, a former student of Matisse.

In 1925, Orrefors won grand prizes at the Paris Exposition. This was only the first of countless prizes and exhibitions of Orrefors art glass in the leading museums around the world.

In 1993, Orrefors released the tenth in its series of collectible crystal Christmas ornaments by Olle Alberius.

PAST IMPRESSIONS
Caroline Doss
P.O. Box 188
Belvedere, CA 94920
(415) 435-1625 or
(415) 358-9075
Fax: (415) 435-1625

Graphics
Alan Maley, internationally acclaimed artist, is highly regarded for his sensitive interpretation of life at the turn-of-the-century.

Born in England, Maley attended the Reigate College of Art and then took the opportunity to enter the British movie industry. He distinguished himself as one of the foremost artists in the

motion picture industry with his work appearing in many of the best-known and loved movies of our time. Maley's dream to work in Hollywood was achieved in 1964, when he was invited to work at The Walt Disney Studios, where he spent many happy years.

In 1984, Alan Maley formed his own publishing company, Past Impressions, to produce limited editions of his own paintings. All prints produced under his close supervision are of the finest quality. They are a tribute to his unique talent and keen perception in interpreting the style, grace and elegance of a bygone era.

PEMBERTON & OAKES

Mary Hugunin
133 E. Carrillo Street
Santa Barbara, CA 93101
(805) 963-1371

Plates, Figurines, Graphics

Pemberton & Oakes is most widely known in the limited edition field for its fine art collectibles, which feature the works of Donald Zolan, America's beloved painter of children.

The range of Zolan collectibles includes full-size and miniature plates, framed miniature lithographs, full-size lithographs, art samplers, framed canvas transfers and art books. Many companies work with Pemberton & Oakes to license Zolan art and create products including dolls, calendars, prints, Christmas ornaments, greeting cards, figurines and so forth.

Donald Zolan's art focuses on the wonder of early childhood. It has been referred to as "family art" because collectors see, once again, moments from their own early years as well as moments their children have experienced.

"Little Traveler" is the first issue in Donald Zolan's first bone china miniature plate series, Times To Treasure.

The Pemberton & Oakes Gallery in Santa Barbara, California offers original works and displays the wide range of collectibles alongside the original oils. Guests are welcome to visit the gallery Monday through Friday from 8:30-5:00.

The president of Pemberton & Oakes is John Hugunin, former president of The Bradford Exchange.

PENDELFIN SALES INCORPORATED

P.O. Box 884
750 Ensminger Road Suite 108
Tonawanda, NY 14150
(800) 263-4491

Figurines

On the day that Elizabeth the Second was crowned Queen of England, two young English women founded their business. It began as a quiet hobby for Jeannie Todd and Jean Walmsley Heap who enjoyed molding small clay figures as gifts for their friends. Soon their enterprise grew too large for the garden hut where it started and spilled over into Todd's kitchen. Later, they moved their business to a small shop where customers soon began arriving.

Since they lived in the shadow of Pendle Hill (the old Witch Hill of "Mist over Pendle") and were creating elfin characters, the partners selected Pendle and Elfin hence "PenDelfin" for the name of their company. A broomstick was added to their trademark for luck.

Made of a durable stone-based compound, the PenDelfin line includes a collection of cottages, shops and landmarks like the bandstand and jetty. These charming display pieces provide the perfect backdrop for the diverse members of the Rabbit Family who inhabit this magical land.

The PenDelfin Family's little camper, "Scout," is trying to cook his egg without getting out of his nice warm sleeping bag!

In addition to their figurines, PenDelfin also produces limited edition collector plates, books and pictures.

PICKARD, INC.

Henry Pickard
782 Corona Avenue
Antioch, IL 60002
(708) 395-3800
Fax: (708) 395-3827

Plates

Pickard China reached its 100th anniversary in 1993, being founded in 1893 by Wilder Austin Pickard and has the distinction of being the only American china company still owned and operated by its founding family.

In 1937, the studio was moved to Antioch, Illinois where a factory was built and a formula for fine china was developed. The emphasis then switched from hand-painted, one-of-a-kind entertaining pieces and decorative accessories to fine china dinnerware under the direction of Wilder's son, Henry Austin Pickard.

In the 1960s, current President Henry Austin (Pete) Pickard, Jr. began to diversify Pickard's product line. In addition to dinnerware and gifts, Pickard entered the field of limited editions, winning awards for eight consecutive years.

In addition to plates, Pickard has been a catalyst in bringing the bowl into acceptance as a limited edition collectible.

POLLAND STUDIOS

c/o Donald J. Polland
P.O. Box 1146
Prescott, AZ 86302
(602) 778-1900
Fax: (602) 778-4034

Figurines

Donald Polland's early works were ambitious, cast-bronze sculptures, but in the late 1960s he began rethinking his entire concept of art. Gradually, he realized he wanted to create different, miniature "jewels" with the same detailing as his larger works.

In 1972, he established the Polland Studios in Laguna Beach, California, and a short time later, Polland entered the gift and collectibles market. Finding that the cost of casting bronze was too prohibitive, he searched for a suitable, less costly material. The search ended in

January 1974 when Polland's first pewter sculptures were introduced by The Lance Corporation. This remains one of Polland's most successful associations.

In 1979, Polland became affiliated with Border Fine Arts which produced a line of Polland cold-cast porcelains which were distributed by Schmid. A decade later, Polland Studios took over the entire design, manufacturing and marketing of this line in the United States.

The Boston Polland Studios has been moved back to Prescott, Arizona, home of Charolette and Don Polland. The Massachusetts porcelain/pewter factory has also been moved to the Prescott area. Polland's son, Daryl, and his wife manage this facility.

"The Mountain Man," the 1993 Polland Collector Society membership gift, is cast in fine pewter and stands 4½ inches high.

PORSGRUNDS PORSELAENSFABRIK A/S

Porselensvegen.12, P.O. Box 100
N-3901 Porsgrunn/Norway
+47 3 550040
Fax: +47 3 559110

PORSGRUND USA INC.
2920-3000 Wolff Street
Racine, WI 53404
(414) 632-3433
Fax: (414) 632-2529

Plates, Figurines, Bells, Christmas Ornaments

Johan Jeremiassen of Norway was convalescing in Germany after an illness, and he noticed that German porcelain manufacturers imported large quantities of quartz and feldspar from Norway, and wondered why porcelain was not produced in his native land. Upon returning home, he convinced his wife's family, the Knudsen's, that a

porcelain factory would be an excellent investment. The Knudsens' prominent shipping contribution to the company is acknowledged by the anchor in the Porsgrund trademark.

Porsgrund, 108 years old, makes fine porcelain of outstanding design, and has received numerous national and international awards for the past forty years. Porsgrund will also make the official licensed products in porcelain for the XVII Olympic Winter Games in Lillehammer in 1994.

POSSIBLE DREAMS® LIMITED

6 Perry Drive
Foxboro, MA 02035
(508) 543-6667

Figurines, Christmas Ornaments

Possible Dreams has envisioned and given life to a line of fine art collectibles — Clothtique® figurines, made from a centuries-old method of stiffening cloth. That method was originally developed in Europe, and Possible Dreams President Warren Stanley decided to put it to work on the company's collectibles.

At first, the line was made up of angels and nativities and quickly became popular with collectors. When Santas were later introduced, even more collectors and dealers clamored for Possible Dreams' Clothtique line. Popular demand resulted in the establishment of The Santa Claus Network™, a collectors club.

Dedicated and talented artists design innovative Clothtique Santas that never cease to be new and different. Collectors may choose from a wide range of limited edition Santa Claus portrayals, each one unique.

Just as popular is a Clothtique collection of whimsical and lovable animals from the *Londonshire®* series. Londonshire is the land "Beyond the Third Rainbow," and its intelligent and well-dressed animal citizens come to collectors with intricate detail and many accessories. Collectors even receive "The Londonshire Daily Mail," giving them the latest news from this magical land.

Through a licensing agreement, Possible Dreams is also proud to transform the *Saturday Evening Post* art of Norman Rockwell and J.C. Leyendecker into Clothtique characters. Several of the artists' most famous works have thus come to life in three dimensions and vivid color.

The Clothtique line is sure to continue expanding into new realms as the support of thousands of collectors continues to grow in response to Possible Dreams' variety of unique and wonderful offerings.

Possible Dreams introduced "May Your Wishes Come True," part of the Clothtique® Collection.

PRECIOUS ART / PANTON INTERNATIONAL

110 E. Ellsworth
Ann Arbor, MI 48108-2203
(313) 677-3510
Fax: (313) 677-3412

Figurines

Fun is a buzz-word at Precious Art/ Panton. Since 1981, they have been producing fine-quality, limited edition collectibles that have ranged from the first up-and-down carousel to the award-winning *World of Krystonia*.

Precious Art is headquartered in Ann Arbor, Michigan and is owned by Sam and Pat Chandok. Their first entry into the gift industry was a musical one. Their wonderful selection of musical boxes led them in their early days to be considered a music box source for the industry.

Truly realistic cold-cast animals from England are part of the Chandoks' repertoire. The *Safari Kingdom* shows a variety of exotic animals featuring mothers and young ones in their natural habitats. The *Mischievous Mice* appear so real that while looking at them you believe they're about to eat the fruit they are sitting on.

The very popular *World of Krystonia* is an industry leader in collectibles. This make-believe line of wizards, dragons, and more has stolen the heart of many a collector. Collectors may follow the adventures of all the English-made characters by reading the three books entitled *Chronicles of Krystonia*, *Krystonian*

Adventures and *Krystonia III*. The Krystonia Collectors Club is now in its fourth year and continues to grow at an exciting pace.

"Dubious Alliance" was the 1992 issue in Krystonia's Classic Moments series.

PRESTIGE DOLLS
Caroline Kandt-Lloyd
P.O. Box 1081
Gresham, OR 97030
(503) 667-1008

Dolls

Prestige Dolls began in 1989 with a line of original porcelain dolls by Caroline Kandt-Lloyd. These dolls were limited in production and ranged from editions of five to 250. In 1990, one-of-a-kind dolls were also added to the line.

Caroline began her doll career after spending time outside the United States studying tropical medicine and then teaching in a nursing program in Africa. Upon returning, a hobby soon turned into a part-time job and then a career change. Caroline taught classes and seminars before beginning to sculpt her own creations.

Happy children's faces are Caroline's trademark. She knows personally each of the children she has taken from human form to doll form. Caroline and her husband Stewart share the responsibilities of production. Caroline sculpts and designs, while Stewart takes her clay model into the mold stage. Stewart also handles the production and business details. Family members and friends complete the staff who all take special delight in creating these works of love.

Prestige Dolls introduces new faces each year to its selection, taking great pains in putting the best materials into each doll.

R.R. CREATIONS, INC.
Open Window Collection
P.O. Box 8707
209 S. Main Street
Pratt, KS 67124
(800) 779-3610
(316) 672-3610
Fax: (316) 672-5850

Graphics

R.R. Creations, Inc., conceived in the minds of Dave and Doreen Ross, began production of silk-screened wooden replicas in 1987 in Pratt, Kansas. Within six years, they gained a strong foothold in the industry, establishing a solid reputation for reliability and quality. Since they incorporated in 1990, R.R. Creations has hired and currently employs thirty-eight persons.

The Rosses work and live by the belief that while God sometimes closes a door, he always opens a window. They have incorporated that principle into their business, and now every building reproduced displays an open window.

RABBIT RUN ENTERPRISES
Verna Wetherholt Richards
P.O. Box 2304
Decatur, IL 62524
(217) 422-7700

Figurines

Rabbit Run Enterprises, a collectible manufacturer in Decatur, Illinois, presents "Wetherholt's World." Artist Larry D. Wetherholt creates hand-painted wood resin and porcelain sculptures in an *America, America* series. In this collection, Larry sculpts characters from an America of the past, present and future. Each piece in the series comes with its own story printed on an accompanying card. Also available from Rabbit Run are an African-American series, a new *Pals* series and bronzes by Wetherholt.

On the horizon is a Rabbit Run collectors club — interested collectors should contact Rabbit Run Enterprises.

RAWCLIFFE CORPORATION
155 Public Street
Providence, RI 02903
(401) 331-1645
(800) 343-1811

Figurines

Rawcliffe Corporation of Providence,

Rhode Island manufactures giftware and collectibles of fine pewter, including licensed merchandise, decorative glassware and items spanning virtually every sport, pet, hobby, personality type and market trend. All products start as original artist sculptures, which are meticulously hand-cast and hand-finished in the United States. Careful packaging, presentation and merchandising are important enhancements to Rawcliffe's products.

Originally begun as a manufacturer of silverware and precision industrial parts, the foundry had three employees when fourth-generation owner Peter Brown took over in 1971. By 1983, Rawcliffe was cited by *Inc.* magazine as one of the nation's fastest-growing companies. It now employs 170 people and has a national network of representative groups servicing over 17,000 accounts.

RECO INTERNATIONAL CORP.
Marlene Marcus
150 Haven Avenue, P.O. Box 951
Port Washington, NY 11050
(516) 767-2400
Fax: (516) 767-2409

Bells, Christmas Ornaments, Dolls, Figurines, Graphics, Plates

Reco International Corp. was founded in 1967 by Heio Reich, a native of Berlin, Germany. From its inception, Reco has been dedicated to the world of limited editions. Reco's first offerings were collector plates created in association with renowned porcelain manufacturers like Fuerstenberg, Royale, Dresden, Royal Germania Crystal, King's and Moser. All of these series are complete and now available only on the secondary market.

In 1977, Reco discovered John McClelland, a well-known illustrator and artist who specialized in child-subject art. He began with designing collector plates for the company, and soon expanded his creativity to include many other collectibles. Reco later introduced a number of McClelland figurine series, a series of music boxes, and in 1990, McClelland also entered the collectible doll market.

Another noted Reco artist is Sandra Kuck. Ms. Kuck has created a number of popular series for Reco. She was also selected to create plate art for the March of Dimes series, *Our Children, Our Future*. She has won many awards,

including the coveted NALED award for Artist of the Year for six years in a row. Ms. Kuck did not stop at plates, either. In addition to lines of music boxes and Christmas ornaments, she also has successfully entered the doll market with a precious doll series.

Reco continues to add many innovative designs by talented artists to its repertoire of fine collectibles. Various plates, figurines and musicals, in subjects ranging from humorous to religious and from nature to fantasy, have been designed by Aldo Fazio, Dot and Sy Barlowe, Garri Katz, Clemente Micarelli, Jody Bergsma, Inge Drechsler and Cicely Mary Barker.

"Best Friends" plate by Sandra Kuck is the first issue in Reco International Corp.'s Sugar and Spice series

RED MILL MFG., INC.

Karen S. McClung
1023 Arbuckle Road
Summerville, WV 26651
(304) 872-5231
Fax: (304) 872-5234

Figurines

Red Mill Mfg. was established in 1980 as a manufacturer of handcrafted collectibles made from crushed pecan shells. That first year, the line included only twelve different collectibles — the 1993 line consists of over 100 different designs. A number of pieces are retired from the line annually and new designs are added.

Red Mill's limited edition eagles and angels are favorites among collectors, but the company offers a great variety — something for everyone.

REED & BARTON

144 West Britannia Street
Taunton, MA 02780
(800) 822-1824
Fax: (508) 822-7269

Bells, Christmas Ornaments

Reed & Barton has been one of America's leading silversmiths since its founding in 1824. The company has been manufacturing fine sterling silver, silverplate, and stainless flatware and giftware for more than 160 years.

The Reed & Barton *Christmas Ornament Collection* represents one of the finest, most extensive assortment of silver and gold ornaments in the world. Since the introduction of its sterling silver and 24-karat gold-over-sterling *Christmas Crosses* in 1971, Reed & Barton has added a number of highly successful annual series, including the *Holly Bell, The Twelve Days of Christmas* (sterling and lead crystal), *Noel Bell, Tree Castle, Carousel Horse, Colors of Christmas* and *Yuletide Bell.* Also popular with collectors are the golden "Lace Basket," "Snowflake Bell" and Mini-Tree ornaments in silverplate.

THE RENOIR IMPRESSIONISTS SOCIETY

c/o Terry Arts International, Inc.
109 Bushaway Rd.
Wayzata, MN 55391
(612) 473-5266

Graphics

The Renoir Impressionists Society is a new organization which has been formed as a result of Dean Terry recently meeting Paul and Marie-Paule Renoir in Brussels. A friendship and collaboration began, which has since grown into the establishment and growth of the company.

Paul Renoir is the grandson of the great master Impressionist Pierre-Auguste Renoir. Renoir painted over 4,000 paintings in his lifetime. He was a productive artist for almost sixty years, painting right up to his death in 1919. Paul has catalogued over 3,700 of these 4,000-plus paintings. In addition, he has documented voluminous other materials, such as letters and photographs and letters that were exchanged with other famous artists who were his friends, such as Monet, Cezanne, Degas and Matisse, to name but a few.

The Renoir Impressionists Society's

objective is to bring to its members select reproductions of Renoir's works, as well as the work of other Impressionist artists, many of whom were Renoir's friends who painted by his side. In addition, the Society would like to share the wealth of personal experiences and family information from the "era of Renoir," recounted by none other than grandson Paul and his wife, Marie-Paule.

This exquisite, hand-pulled, museum-quality Renoir lithograph, "La Balançoire," is from the Renoir Impressionists Society.

HAROLD RIGSBY GRAPHICS

Patricia Rigsby or Quinna Pedigo
P.O. Box 1761
Glasgow, KY 42142
(800) 892-4984
(502) 678-2608

Graphics

In 1978, Harold Rigsby formed his own graphics company, Harold Rigsby Graphics, Inc., to produce and distribute both his open issues and his limited edition wildlife prints.

Harold Rigsby earned a degree with honors from Herron School of Art at Indiana University and studied at Western Kentucky University, the Louisville School of Art and the Instituto-Allende in Mexico.

After art school, Rigsby worked as a portrait artist at a tourist attraction. He later became the advertising director for a pharmaceutical company. In 1978, Rigsby released his first print which sold out immediately, so he began to paint daily.

Rigsby seeks out and studies his subjects in zoos across the country. Working from a series of sketches and photos, the artist then completes his artwork in his own studio.

RIVER SHORE

Carol Jones
4810 Executive Park Court
P.O. Box 2567
Jacksonville, FL 32232

Plates, Figurines, Bells

River Shore was founded in 1975, and in 1976 introduced its *Famous Americans* series — the first-ever copper collector plates. The plates were based on artwork by Norman Rockwell and sculpted by Roger Brown to create a bas-relief effect.

Other popular collections from River Shore include the *Babies of Endangered Species* and the *Wilderness Babies* by Brown, *Puppy Playtime* and *Delights of Childhood* by Jim Lamb, and *America at Work*, a favorite of collectors, featuring Americans in interesting occupations, as portrayed by the legendary Norman Rockwell on the covers of *The Saturday Evening Post*.

THE NORMAN ROCKWELL GALLERY

9200 Center for the Arts Drive
Niles, IL 60714
(708) 581-8326

Figurines, Christmas Ornaments

The Norman Rockwell Gallery offers a wide variety of handcrafted, hand-painted collectibles — from cottages, Christmas ornaments and figurines, to snow globes, collectible mugs and framed canvas reproductions — all inspired by the life and works of America's best-loved artist.

Each work bears the distinctive seal of The Norman Rockwell Family Trust — the official authorization of the artist's own family — as the discriminating collector's assurance of both quality and value. Additionally, all Rockwell Gallery products are backed by an unconditional, money-back guarantee.

Notable Gallery offerings include a set of seven, 22-karat gold-rimmed porcelain mini-plates depicting Rockwell's classic "Main Street, Stockbridge" painting, as well as a collection of handcrafted snow globes also inspired by the famous illustration. ("Rockwell's Studio" was the premier issue.) Also available are snow globes inspired by two classic Rockwell portrayals of Santa Claus, "Santa's Workshop" and "Around the World," and framed canvas reproductions of the artist's classic paintings

"Springtime in Stockbridge" and "Spring Flowers."

All Rockwell Gallery products are accompanied by individual Certificates of Authenticity, as well as descriptive literature about the artwork.

As a benefit to members, a quarterly newsletter, "The Norman Rockwell Gallery Collector," is distributed free of charge.

One of Norman Rockwell's early Saturday Evening Post cover illustrations comes to life as the "Evergreen Cottage" sculpture authorized by The Norman Rockwell Family Trust.

ROMAN, INC.

555 Lawrence Avenue
Roselle, IL 60172-1599
(708) 529-3000
Fax: (708) 529-1121

Plates, Figurines, Dolls, Christmas Ornaments, Bells, Graphics

Roman, Inc. is proof that the American dream lives. With a family background in giftware retailing, it was inevitable that Ronald Jedlinski would enter some facet of the collectibles and giftware fields. Jedlinski formed Roman, Inc. independently as a wholesaler of religious products in 1963.

Today, Roman is an established leading religious, inspirational, special-occasion and Christmas-trim giftware and collectibles producer with a solid reputation. In over thirty years of operations, Roman has earned a notable niche in the collectibles field with quality, creative collections of significance by leading American and European artists with prestigious reputations in diverse art areas — Barbi Sargent, Irene Spencer, Angela Tripi, Abbie Williams, Ellen Williams and Richard Judson Zolan. The Midwestern firm has developed into an inspirational collectibles leader with superb editions eloquently portraying traditional family values. Meticulously crafted in a variety of media, each collectible faithfully captures the essence of every artist's original artwork.

Roman has brought these and many other artists' fine creativity to a wide audience for enjoyment throughout the home and for collecting. The company will continue to produce distinctive suites of collectibles to an admiring collector audience.

"Sunshine" is the captivating central character of the Message Collection, Tender Expressions From the Heart by artist Barbi Sargent for Roman, Inc.

RON LEE'S WORLD OF CLOWNS

2180 Agate Court
Simi Valley, CA 93065
(805) 520-8460
Fax: (805) 520-8472

Figurines

Recognized as a leading manufacturer and sculptor of clown and circus-theme collectibles, the prolific and mega-talented Ron Lee has created over 1,100 designs in sixteen years. The California-based company, Ron Lee's World of Clowns, is dedicated to creating heirloom-quality collectibles.

The company was born in 1976 when Ron Lee began creating sculptures of his now famous "Hobo Joe" clown character. Ron Lee currently employs many local artisans, casters, mold makers, finishing, shipping and office personnel to staff his company and reproduce his art in limited editions, and to run the collector's club.

Because of Ron Lee's superior craftsmanship and talented staff, a signed Ron Lee limited edition is easily identified when displayed on a shelf. Completely manufactured in the United States, all sculptures are finely detailed and mounted on polished onyx with tiny gold beading at the base of each statue. Each edition is made of fine white metals and pewter, which is then plated in

24-karat gold, individually hand-finished and hand-painted.

Renowned for his clown and circus-theme designs, Ron Lee has also established a reputation as the "king of cartoon" classic character sculptures. Sold nationwide, these endearing collections have secured a tremendous amount of media and collector attention, while also receiving numerous awards and accolades.

Although Ron Lee has enjoyed working with animated characters, 1993 marks his renewed focus on clowns which take him "back to basics" with classic clown antics and humor. Included in that renewed vigor toward clown portrayals is the introduction of the first offering of collector clown plates from Ron Lee.

The limited edition "Merry Go Clown," an individual sculpture by Ron Lee, is the only Ron Lee clown to be portrayed sitting on a horse.

ROSE ART INDUSTRIES, INC.

555 Main Street
Orange, NJ 07050
(201) 414-1313
Rose Art West (Cameo Kewpies©)
(318) 303-3787

Dolls

Founded in 1923, Rose Art Industries, Inc., a third-generation, family-owned company, produces and markets a broad range of toys, games, dolls and stationery products. Rose Art's licensed doll lines include Cameo Kewpies©, Precious Moments™ playable vinyl dolls, Raggedy Ann and Andy™ playable vinyl dolls and porcelain collectibles and Xuxa™ (pronounced "shoo-sha") fashion dolls, based on a popular Brazilian entertainer.

In February 1993, Rose Art obtained the master toy license and all manufac-turing rights from Jesco, Inc. for Cameo Kewpie© dolls worldwide. Based on illustrations by Rose O'Neill, the Cameo Kewpie© was originally sculpted and produced by Joseph Kallus, founder of the Cameo Doll Company. In 1993, Rose Art issued a limited edition fourteen-inch porcelain Kewpie doll and a limited edition porcelain Scootles doll.

PATRICIA ROSE STUDIO

Patricia Rose
509 S. Bay Blvd.
P.O. Box 4070
Anna Maria, FL 34216

Dolls, Figurines, Graphics

The Patricia Rose Studio is in its fourth year of operation. Patricia has been a photo realist portrait artist since 1969. Her love for detail and realistic human proportions has been carried over into her sculpting of her popular lady and children dolls.

Patricia was selected by Walt Disney Studios to be in the Disney World one-of-a-kind show in November 1993. She has also been commissioned to design the Miss America dolls. She and her partner, Sharon Crain, have come out with a line of jewel-adorned miniatures. They have been nominated for an award by *Collector Editions* magazine as well as an award this year by *Dolls* magazine.

ROSENTHAL U.S.A.

66-26 Metropolitan Avenue
Middle Village, NY 11379
(718) 417-3400
Fax: (718) 417-3407

Plates

Rosenthal was founded by Philip Rosenthal in 1879 in Selb, Bavaria. For over a century, Rosenthal has been known for extraordinary design by award-winning artists such as Salvatore Dali, Victor Vasarely, Bjorn Wiinblad, Dorothy Hafner, Raymond Loewy and Roy Lichtenstein. Rosenthal produces porcelain, ceramics, crystal and flatware. Product lines include artist-designed dinnerware, giftware and collectibles. Limited edition offerings include porcelain, crystal and ceramic objets d'art, tableware, artists wall plates and sculptures. The variety of design is diverse, from classic-traditional to contemporary and avante-garde.

ROYAL COPENHAGEN

27 Holland Avenue
White Plains, NY 10603
(914) 428-8222
Fax: (914) 428-8251

Plates, Figurines, Christmas Ornaments

The original Royal Copenhagen Porcelain Manufactory Ltd. is Denmark's oldest porcelain maker. It was established in 1755 by Franz Heinrich Muller, a pharmacist and chemist who was the first to duplicate porcelain in Denmark. He was supported by Denmark's dowager queen, Juliane Marie.

In 1779, "The Danish Porcelain Factory" came under royal control where it remained until 1868, when it passed into private ownership. However, the firm still is a purveyor to the royal court. The royal control is symbolized by a crown in the firm's trademark. Three wavy lines under the crown part of the trademark represent Denmark's three ancient waterways: the Sound, the Great Belt and the Little Belt.

The first Royal Copenhagen commemorative plate was produced in 1888, but it was not until 1908 that Royal Copenhagen introduced its *Christmas* series.

The *Christmas* plates were issued with the text in English, German, French and Czechoslovakian until 1931, when Dutch was added. Two years later, the Dutch edition was dropped. The other foreign texts were dropped in 1945. The Royal Copenhagen *Christmas* series remains one of the most popular series in the world.

The first edition in Royal Copenhagen's plate series, Nature's Children, *is entitled "The Robins," created by Danish artist Jorgen Nielsen.*

The first Royal Copenhagen *Mother's Day* series was added in 1971 and ended in 1982. A second *Motherhood* series by Svend Vestergaard premiered the same year. In 1988, Royal Copenhagen introduced the *American Mother's Day* series.

In 1991, Royal Copenhagen introduced, for the first time since 1908, the first edition of its second Christmas plate series. *Christmas in Denmark* is a brilliantly colorful and romantic Christmas plate series designed by renowned Danish artist Hans Henrik Hansen.

ROYAL COPENHAGEN INC./ BING & GRONDAHL

27 Holland Avenue
White Plains, NY 10603
(914) 428-8222

Plates, Figurines, Bells, Christmas Ornaments

In 1987, two of the world's most respected porcelain companies, Bing & Grondahl and Royal Copenhagen merged under the umbrella of Royal Copenhagen A/S. (Royal Copenhagen Inc. is now owned by Carlsberg A/S, a conglomerate made up of sixty other companies including Holmegaard Glass and Georg Jensen Silver.)

The Royal Copenhagen group of companies is made up of Royal Copenhagen Porcelain and Bing & Grondahl, Georg Jensen Silver and Holmegaard Glass. These companies each retain separate identities and product lines.

ROYAL DOULTON USA, INC.

Hattie Purnell-Burson
700 Cottontail Lane
Somerset, NJ 08873
(908) 356-7880
Fax: (908) 356-9467

ROYAL DOULTON CANADA, INC.
Shona McCleod
850 Progress Avenue
Scarborough, Ontario M1H 3C4

Plates, Figurines, Christmas Ornaments

Royal Doulton, founded in 1815 as Doulton and Company, has developed a fine reputation worldwide for quality and excellence in dinnerware, crystal, figurines and other fine collectibles.

In 1901, the company was awarded a Royal Warrant and the right to incorporate the word Royal into the company name. Founded by John Doulton, the company truly began to flourish under the direction of John Doulton's son, Henry Doulton, who employed some of the finest artists of that time. His commitment and desire for excellence was contagious and was quickly adopted by the fine artists who worked for Royal Doulton.

Charles J. Noke, art director, 1914-1936, also had that same commitment. Noke was responsible for the growth of the range of Royal Doulton figurines and character jugs. By 1920, Noke had succeeded in producing figurines acclaimed by the critics and public alike.

All the talent present in the company's staff and artists has led Royal Doulton to expand its collectible offerings. A wide range of figurines — animals, famous characters and children — is produced to attract and excite collectors of all ages. The Figure of the Year in 1993 was "Patricia," the third issue in the annual series. Various character jugs by Royal Doulton have also been very popular. "Vice Admiral Lord Nelson" was the 1993 Character Jug of the Year. The Royal Doulton Christmas ornament assortment is continuing its expansion as well.

The Classic Heroes Collection *from Royal Doulton consists of four notorious figures. Featured left to right are: "Long John Silver," "Captain Hook," "Robin Hood" and "Dick Turpin."*

ROYAL WORCESTER LIMITED

Ms. Paulette Copps
Severn Street
Worcester, England WR1 2NE
0905 23221
Fax: 0905 23601

Plates, Figurines

Founded in 1751, Royal Worcester is the oldest continuously operating manufacturer of porcelain in the United Kingdom. Following the visit of George III and Queen Charlotte, the company was granted a Royal Warrant in 1789 and warrants have since been granted by every successive Monarch. In 1989 the Company introduced a *200th Anniversary Collection* to commemorate the 1789 event.

Royal Worcester produces tableware and giftware in porcelain and bone china sought by collectors the world over. The company claims the honor of making the first limited edition, in 1935, and this was followed over the years by superb bone china figurines and sculptures by Dorothy Doughty, Doris Lindner, Ruth and Ronald Van Ruyckevelt and others.

SANDICAST, INC.

Edwin Rosenblatt
8480 Miralani Drive
San Diego, CA 92126-4396
(619) 695-9611
Fax: (619) 695-0615

Figurines

Founded in 1981 by world-renowned artist Sandra Brue, Sandicast features extremely realistic sculptural reproductions of favorite dogs, cats and wildlife. Sandra Brue offers two new design introductions each year and has made great efforts to find subjects that represent the epitome of their breed or species. Each reproduction is hand-cast and hand-painted, featuring sparkling glass eyes and fine detail that captures the inner spirit of each animal. Sandra Brue has been commissioned to create sculptures of animals for the San Diego Zoo, The American Kennel Club and many private organizations. Sandicast Collectors Guild members have exclusive access to special Sandra Brue designs and limited editions. For further information, contact the Guild at 1-800-722-3316.

SARAH'S ATTIC

126 ½ West Broad Street
Chesaning, MI 48616
(800) 4-FRIEND
(517) 845-3990
Fax: (517) 845-3477

Christmas Ornaments, Dolls, Figurines, Plates

Sarah Schultz started her own business on the family dining room table in 1983, turning her favorite hobby into a wholesale company.

With the help of her husband, five children, and many friends, Sarah originally began to supply the family pharmacy with unique gifts to complement the country decor. When orders poured in and space ran out, the business moved to the "attic" above the pharmacy in late 1984. By mid-1989, Sarah's Attic had expanded to four times its original size. In the fall of 1991, due to cramped quarters, Sarah's Attic was on the move once again. Sarah purchased and remodeled a former grocery store with 10,000 square feet of work area. The art room and business offices still remain in the "attic."

As business expanded, so did the line, to include collectibles and wood items that complement any decor. Through all this growth and many changes, one thing remained the same — Sarah's devotion to excellent quality. Because of Sarah's devotion and because of her firm belief in love, respect and dignity, a heart was painted on each piece as a symbol and trademark of those characteristics.

Sarah's Attic has turned into an extremely successful company, which is no surprise to Sarah's collectors. They know that once they have purchased a Sarah's Attic collectible, they have purchased a high-quality, original treasure of timeless value which is made with love, respect and dignity.

This Beary Special Collection *from Sarah's Attic portrays golden heart-filled moments.*

SCHMID

Marcie Kanofski
55 Pacella Park
Randolph, MA 02368
(617) 961-3000
Fax: (617) 961-4355

Plates, Figurines, Christmas Ornaments

The name Schmid has been synonymous with the finest gifts and collectibles since 1932. Still family-owned,

the company remains dedicated to the same uncompromising standards of design and workmanship that have made it an industry leader for over sixty years.

Schmid has expanded considerably over the years. Today, the company boasts a number of sought-after licenses, including *Disney Treasures*, inspired by the ever-popular Disney films. Other well-known Schmid licenses include Kitty Cucumber by artist Mary Lillemoe and Beatrix Potter, consisting of musicals, figurines, ornaments and nursery accessories.

In addition to its licenses, Schmid represents some of the most talented artists in the world, including celebrated Americana artist Lowell Davis, fantasy artist David Wenzel, Belsnickle creator Linda Baldwin, folk artist Marge Crunkleton, and TOBY award-winning miniature bear artist April Whitcomb Gustafson.

In 1935, Schmid became the first company to introduce the figurines of M.I. Hummel to American collectors and is the exclusive United States distributor of those collectibles today.

Part of Schmid's Disney Treasures Collection, these three charming figurines are modeled after characters in the Disney movie, *Aladdin.*

SCULPTURE WORKSHOP DESIGNS

William Graham
P.O. Box 420
Blue Bell, PA 19422
(215) 643-7447

Christmas Ornaments

Sculpture Workshop Designs offers silver Christmas ornaments which are noted for their extraordinary detail and high bas-relief. One or two ornament designs are issued each year, designed and sculpted by artist F. Kreitchet,

MFA, University of Pennsylvania.

The company, founded in 1984, has offered special historical commemorative ornaments, issued in small limited editions of only 200 works. Traditional designs are offered in editions of 2,500 works. In 1992, the company created "Forever Santa," the first in a special Santa series.

Sculpture Workshop Designs' ornaments hang upon the Christmas trees of four United States Presidents as well as those of knowledgeable collectors throughout the country.

SECOND NATURE DESIGN

Jesse Bromberg
110 S. Southgate Drive
Bldg. C-4
Chandler, AZ 85226
(602) 961-3963
Fax: (602) 961-4178

Figurines

Second Nature Design is a company whose goal is to assemble an international consortium of artisans who create affordable wildlife collectibles for the peoples of the world. Each artist shares with Second Nature Design the belief that the public should be more aware and actively involved with environmental preservation. The company promotes this by producing several series of realistic, beautiful re-creations of hand-carved and hand-painted wildlife collectibles. Some popular limited editions have been recently retired.

Second Nature Design is developing and providing affordable, lifelike collectibles for the enjoyment of everyone, with the intention that the collector realize and appreciate the delicate balance of nature.

SHADE TREE CREATIONS, INC.

Bill Vernon
6210 NW 124th Place
Gainesville, FL 32606
(800) 327-6923
(904) 462-1830
Fax: (904) 462-1799

Figurines

Shade Tree has been serving the gift industry for nineteen years. *The Cowboys* by sculptor Bill Vernon were introduced in 1980 as simply another gift line. By the late 1980s, popularity of *The*

Cowboys had "snowballed." Suddenly the company was receiving daily requests from collectors for more information on the Western-style figurines. The Cowboy Collector Society was formed in 1990. Membership is free with the purchase of a Shade Tree Cowboy. The purpose of the Collector Society is to keep collectors informed of new releases and developments. The Society also sponsors a complete secondary market trading division for its members wishing to buy or sell retired artwork.

SHELIA'S, INC.
1856 Belgrade Avenue C-1
Charleston, SC 29407
(803) 766-0485
Fax: (803) 556-0040

Figurines
Shelia's, Inc. was founded in 1979 by Charleston artist Shelia Thompson. Shelia is the creator of Shelia's Fine Handpainted Collectibles and limited edition prints. The company has its studio and manufacturing facilities located in Charleston, South Carolina. The company, once located in Shelia's home, now occupies 22,000 square feet in the business park owned by Jim and Shelia Thompson. Shelia's original designs were hand-cut from wood with a jigsaw by her husband Jim, and then entirely hand-painted by Shelia. Although the company now employs sixty people and operates two shifts, Shelia has remained its sole designer and artist. Each of the 200-plus collectibles which have been introduced into the line were taken from Shelia's original artwork. A long-time member of the Charleston Artists Guild, Shelia feels that the unique appearance of each historic house or public building depends on how she interprets the piece, and in order to maintain that unique quality and style, she must continue to create the original artwork. The screen-printing techniques used in creating the line are also unique to Shelia's, Inc., and were developed over the years by Shelia and her staff to adapt to working on wood.

Shelia's Fine Handpainted Collectibles include series from all over the United States, covering such historic cities as Williamsburg, Savannah and Charleston, South Carolina. Each building is researched carefully for historic accuracy, and the histories on the back are created from information gathered by delving into the building's past and its historic significance.

Shelia's, Inc. is marketed exclusively by the company itself, and sales are headquartered in Charleston, South Carolina.

This array of Shelia's latest releases includes "Rainbow Row '93" and "Painted Ladies II and III."

SHENANDOAH DESIGNS INTERNATIONAL, INC.
P.O. Box 911
20 Railroad Avenue
Rural Retreat, VA 24368
(703) 686-6188
Fax: (703) 686-4921

Upper Canada Soap & Candle Makers
1510 Caterpillar Road
Mississauga, Ontario L4X 2W9
(416) 897-1710
Fax: (416) 897-6169

Figurines, Christmas Ornaments
Shenandoah Designs International, Inc. was founded by Jack Weaver in his hometown in the mountains of Southwest Virginia. The company was first known as the home of his *Annie & Jack Bears*®, offering the familiar resin teddy bears in various collections.

The company has additionally offered several collections of exclusive Santas, sculpted by craftsmen especially commissioned by Shenandoah. Among the more popular have been sets of miniature pewter and resin Santas for shadowbox collectors.

Several of Shenandoah's continually best-loved products are made from their own specially formulated blend of non-toxic, durable metals, called Merrymetal®. All Merrymetal® designs are available in antique brass and/or pewter finish.

In 1993, Shenandoah introduced their delightful and highly collectible *Keepers*®, a line of several figures with specific "jobs" assigned to them.

SILVER DEER, LTD.
4824 Sterling Drive
Boulder, CO 80301
(800) 729-3337
(303) 449-6771
Fax: (303) 449-0653

Figurines, Bells, Christmas Ornaments, Snowglobes
Founded over seventeen years ago, Silver Deer, Ltd. was one of the first North American companies to design and manufacture crystal figurines using 32% full-lead Austrian crystal. Comprising over 200 designs, the *Crystal Zoo Collection* has become recognized as a standard of excellence for design innovation, quality and craftsmanship.

Silver Deer also holds the distinction of capturing licensed characters in crystal, such as Walt Disney's Winnie-the-Pooh, Beatrix Potter's Peter Rabbit and Charles Schulz's Snoopy. In January 1993, Silver Deer obtained a license from Paramount Pictures to reproduce *Star Trek* memorabilia in crystal.

Gina Truex is the senior crystal designer and has earned an MFA degree. She is known not only for her designs in crystal but also for those done in other media such as papier-mâché.

"Christmas Cardinal" from Silver Deer's Christmas Animals Collection by artist Tom Rubel stands 3¹/₂ inches high.

Silver Deer is also proud of the *Ark Collection* designed by renowned artist Tom Rubel. This collection includes the ever popular *Christmas Animals Collection* comprised of figurines, Christmas ornaments, musical snowglobes and bells. The newest creations by Tom Rubel for Silver Deer's Ark are *Baby Christmas Animals*, featuring adorable baby animals in holiday attire.

SPORTS COLLECTORS WAREHOUSE

Dist. by Legends in Lithographs
54-510 Avienda Diaz
La Quinta, CA 92253
(800) 548-4671
(619) 564-0504

Graphics

Sports Collectors Warehouse and Legends in Lithographs, publishers and distributors respectively, began producing limited edition, athlete-signed lithographs of America's greatest sports legends in 1986. The overall guiding concept was to tell the story of professional sports through the depiction of its most famous and legendary athletes, to preserve forever a part of Americana that has passed into history.

To date, fifty-one prints of the greatest baseball, football, basketball, boxing and motor racing legends have been published in lithograph form. Also, each print is individually hand-signed by the athlete(s). This unrivaled line makes Sports Collectors Warehouse the premier publisher of sports art in America.

SPORTS IMPRESSIONS

1501 Arthur Avenue
Elk Grove Village, IL 60007
(708) 640-5200
Fax: (708) 290-8322

Plates, Figurines

Sports Impressions is a leading producer and designer of limited edition collector plates, figurines and other sports-related collectibles featuring more than 100 prominent personalities in football, baseball, basketball, boxing, golf and hockey.

Founded in 1985 by sports enthusiast and retailer Joe Timmerman, the company continues building the roster of popular players in its collectibles line-up. Some of the limited edition figurines are even hand-signed by the athletes. With the popularity of sports collectibles, the company introduced the Sports Impressions Collectors' Club in 1989. Sports Impressions is part of the Enesco Worldwide Giftware Group.

SUMMERHILL CRYSTAL

A division of CFL, Ltd.
601 South 23d Street
P.O. Box 1479
Fairfield, IA 52556
(515) 472-8279
Fax: (515) 472-8496

Beginning officially in 1981, Summerhill Crystal evolved from a wholesale/retail crystal company, then known as Crystal Forest Ltd., which created jewelry and prisms. Shortly thereafter, the company began creating crystal figurines to complement their existing line of products. Summerhill Crystal is their consumer brand name and a division of the parent corporation.

Chief Designer and Vice-President Imal Wagner directs, as well as innovates, the company's new crystal concepts and designs to be added to the Summerhill Crystal line of faceted crystal sculptures.

The process of creating faceted crystal art and sculptures requires a tremendous amount of skill and understanding of the properties of crystal and the behavior of light. The most successful designs are executed to maximize the amount of light to be captured, reflected and deflected in the multi-facets of the completed cut-crystal piece. Summerhill's artists are talented and determined enough to achieve the perfect representation of crystal concept and design.

Summerhill established its glass division in 1987, which employs all the same standards and principles as crystal artwork. Influenced by the Art Nouveau period, Imal's newest designs in glass include delicate flowers that appear to glow with a luminescence from within.

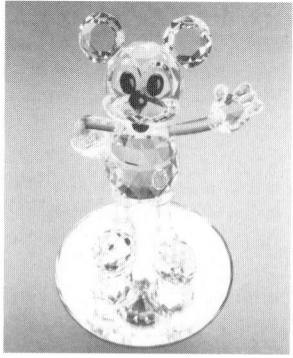

"Mickey Mouse" was created by Summerhill Crystal's chief designer, Imal Wagner, as part of the prestigious and exclusive crystal collection for The Disney Stores.

Synonymous with quality, Summerhill Crystal is sold overseas, in various countries. On the home front, Summerhill continues to receive commissions from The Disney Store to create exclusive art.

Imal has also mastered designs featuring items and characters from a variety of breakthrough, box-office-hit "live action" films. These crystal creations will only be offered through exclusive promotions using a national electronic media network.

Breaking the boundaries of design in crystal and glass figurines and sculptures, the philosophy of the company in Imal's own words is: "Anything is possible."

SWAROVSKI AMERICA LIMITED

2 Slater Road
Cranston, RI 02920
(401) 463-3000
(800) 556-6478
Fax: (401) 463-8459

Figurines

On October 1, 1895, a few weeks before his thirty-fourth birthday, Daniel Swarovski I left his Bohemian homeland with his wife and three sons in pursuit of a dream. His destination was Wattens in the Austrian Tyrol, where he planned to set up a factory for the industrial production of cut crystal jewelry stones. At that time, he could hardly have foreseen that he was laying the foundations of a corporation which, less than a century later, would be the world's leading manufacturer of cut crystal jewelry stones.

Today, Swarovski produces twenty billion stones annually, objects and ornaments in full crystal, chandelier parts, grinding and abrasive tools, optical instruments and glass reflecting elements for road and rail safety.

Swarovski's main production facility is still located in Wattens, Austria. This is also the headquarters for global marketing management. Its company headquarters, including all other domestic and international management functions, is in Feldmeilen, Switzerland, near Zurich.

In the autumn of 1976, four chandelier parts were glued together to create the first member of Swarovski's crystal menagerie — a full-cut crystal mouse. Other pieces followed rapidly, and as one idea bred another, Swarovski tech-

nicians quickly developed the expertise necessary to interpret more complex designs. Swarovski Silver Crystal was born! It was not long before crystal parts were manufactured exclusively for Silver Crystal. Today, the collection comprises over 120 artist-designed pieces.

In response to countless requests and inquiries from crystal lovers and collectors worldwide, the Swarovski Collectors Society was founded in 1987. Benefits include special activities and events organized for members only. Members receive a bi-annual full-color magazine, the *Swarovski Collector*, full of information on new products, collector profiles, how to care for their precious collections and much, much more.

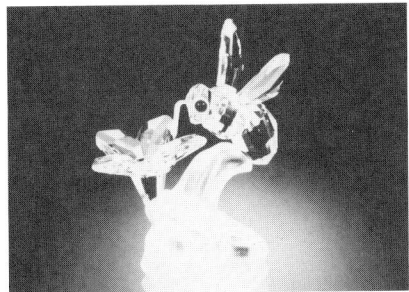

The Swarovski Silver Crystal "Bumble Bee" buzzes among the Flowers and Foliage *series.*

T.S.M. & COMPANY

Teresa Schiavi
98 Rose Hill Avenue
New Rochelle, NY 10804
(914) 235-5675
Fax: (914) 576-6120

Graphics

T.S.M. & Company is a partnership established to produce and sell the artwork of sporting and wildlife artist Adriano Manocchia. The artist's line includes original oil paintings, limited edition offset lithographs and hand-pulled etchings. In the past, Adriano has also created bronzes and porcelain sculptures.

Adriano began as a photojournalist and ran a successful photo and film agency before switching from photography to painting. In 1979, he dedicated most of his time to painting wildlife and later, outdoor sporting art. Adriano has received numerous honors and recognition from various groups for his artwork.

TEXAS STAMPS

P.O. Box 42388
Houston, TX 77242-2388
(800) 779-4100
(713) 266-7007
Fax: (713) 266-7706

United States postage stamps have long been coveted by collectors as some of the most beautiful and most desirable stamps in the world. Many of them, engraved in minute detail, are works of art. The stories surrounding the stamps are equally interesting.

Texas Stamps has gathered many of these authentic, unused United States postage stamps into collections as tributes to different professions and themes. All stamps used in Texas Stamps' products have been acquired from collectors throughout the country and are mounted on beautiful, hand-cut mats, decorated with a foil-stamped emblem of the profession or theme.

TIMELESS CREATIONS™

A Division of Mattel
333 Continental Blvd.
El Segundo, CA 90245-5012
(310) 524-2000

Dolls

Designed especially for the adult collector, Timeless Creations'™ collector dolls have signified superior quality, unique design and authentic detailing since they first made their debut in 1976. In the 1980s, Timeless Creations strengthened its growing reputation as a worldwide quality doll distributor by offering dolls designed by renowned European artist, Annette Himstedt. The '80s also brought the exciting introduction of Timeless Creations' limited edition porcelain Barbie dolls, and the '90s unveiled the first dazzling Barbie doll created by famous Hollywood designer, Bob Mackie.

The company's integral members of the Mattel collector doll family are the incredibly realistic doll children by award-winning designer Annette Himstedt. Ms. Himstedt is a recognized leader in the creation of collector dolls prized for imaginative style and exquisite detailing. All of her "children" have finely sculpted, hand-painted features, soft bodies made of wool and cotton, glass eyes, vinyl heads and limbs, hand-

knotted wigs and eyelashes made of human hair, and clothing of all-natural fabrics. Each comes with a registration card and Certificate of Authenticity.

Annette Himstedt introduced three dolls to her collection in 1993 — "Kima" from Greenland, "Tara" from Germany and "Lona" from California, all distributed by Timeless Creations, a division of Mattel.

TOWLE SILVERSMITHS

Harris Zeltsar
144 Addison St.
Boston, MA 02128
(617) 561-2200
Fax: (617) 569-8484

Christmas Ornaments

Towle represents 303 years of craftsmanship 1690-1993. One of the most important crafts in Colonial America was silversmithing. The Moultons of Newburyport, Massachusetts followed this craft for over 200 years. More members of this family followed the silversmith's profession than any other early American family.

The Towle tradition of craftsmanship is still being carried on today. Many of Towle's present employees are second and third generations of the family to work at Towle. From this unique heritage, comes the understanding and respect that distinguishes their work today.

Towle Silversmiths creates and produces beautiful sterling Christmas ornaments. Some of these ongoing limited edition series include the *Floral Medallion*, *Story of Christmas* and the *Towle Old Master Snowflake* collections.

GLYNDA TURLEY PRINTS, INC.

P.O. Box 112
74 Cleburne Park Road
Heber Springs, AR 72543
(800) 633-7931
Fax: (501) 362-5020

Graphics

Glynda Turley Prints, Inc., established in 1985, is a manufacturer and wholesaler of gift and decorative accessories created by Glynda Turley. The company's primary products, marketed in gift shops, custom frame shops and art galleries, are framed prints, canvas replicas, paper and wooden keepsake boxes, afghans, tapestry pillows, framed tapestries, soaps and frame accessories. The firm manufactures many of their own products, publishes all of their own prints and also licenses many of Glynda's designs to other companies. Their marketing efforts include: advertising in the national trade publications, in-house sales by direct mail or telephone and trade show exhibits.

TURNER ART CO.

306 East Main Street
Marshallville, GA 31057
(800) 554-7146

Graphics

It was in her father's Marshallville, Georgia dry goods store that Louise Turner, who had been an artist from youth, came into contact with the friends who became subjects of her paintings. These friends, white and black, were all surprised and pleased when she asked them to come to her house to sit for a while so she could paint them. The black children and black family life intrigued her most.

Louise's sensitivity and appreciation for the southern spirit of happiness gave her paintings an atmosphere charged with joy.

Founded by Louise's family, Turner Art Co. publishes limited edition lithographs from original works by Louise Taylor Turner (1913-1962).

TURNER DOLLS, INC.

P.O. Box 36
Heltonville, IN 47436
(812) 834-6692
Fax: (812) 834-1501

Dolls

Virginia and Boyce Turner have been producing dolls for thirteen years and reside in Heltonville, Indiana on a small farm where they also have their factory. Turner dolls are known for their lifelike faces and poseable bodies. Virginia has been sculpting these dolls for four years and says that as the oldest of six children, mother of three daughters and grandmother of eight, she has been surrounded by children all of her life and now enjoys creating her porcelain children. Both of her parents were talented artists, and she is grateful to them for the background she received from them.

UNITED DESIGN CORPORATION

Jim Claude
P.O. Box 1200
Noble, OK 73068
(800) 727-4883
Fax: (405) 360-4442

UNITED DESIGN CANADA, LTD.
Allen Hume
Norwich, Ontario N0J 1P0
(800) 361-4438
(519) 86302443

Figurines, Christmas Ornaments

In 1973, Gary and Jean Clinton, both graduates of the University of Oklahoma School of Art, founded a company which was to become United Design Corporation in Noble, Oklahoma. Their goal was to produce figurines with a uniquely American look, a look that would reflect both the vitality and the good humor of the American perspective.

United Design's animal figurines, especially the *Stone Critters®* collection, is the largest line of animal figurines in the world, with over 500 different designs available.

A limited edition line of Santa Claus figurines, *The Legend of Santa Claus™*, was introduced in 1986. In the fall of 1988, the firm also introduced *The Legend of The Little People™* collection of limited edition figurines.

In 1990 United Design introduced *PenniBears™*, a limited edition collection of miniature teddy bears. United Design also sponsors a PenniBears Collectors Club.

The *Easter Bunny Family™* is a collection of bunnies introduced in 1988. Though not produced in limited edi-

tion, this line has become very popular among collectors.

The beautiful *Angels Collection™* of limited edition figurines was introduced in 1991, also well-received by collectors.

All of the products produced by United Design are created by artists and craftsmen who adhere to the philosophy expressed by the company's mission statement: "...to provide giftware creations inspired by the joy and wonder of the world around us, thereby prospering through serving and satisfying customers the world over."

United Design introduced "Madonna," part of the limited edition Angels Collection.

D.H. USSHER LTD.

Des Ussher
1132 West 15th Street
North Vancouver, British Columbia
Canada V7P 1M9
(604) 986-0365
Fax: (604) 986-9984

Plates

D.H. Ussher Ltd. represents a wide range of United States-based collectible firms in Canada. These include Armstrong's, Hollywood Limited Editions, American Artists, Porter & Price Inc. and Artaffects. The firm also distributes brass hangers and plate stands from Decorative Display Products and frames from Lynette Decor Products. In 1985, D.H. Ussher Ltd. began producing for the limited edition market and is currently active with products under the labels Reefton Meadows and Western Authentics.

D.H. Ussher Ltd. became licensed in 1989 with both Major League Baseball and the National Hockey League and has been actively signing athletes to collectible contracts, including a contract with the Blue Jays baseball team for the 1992 World Series plates.

To mark the 40th anniversary of the conquest of Mt. Everest by Sir Edmund Hillary, D.H. Ussher has signed Sir Edmund to a 1993 personal plate contract.

U.S. HISTORICAL SOCIETY

Emily Preston
First and Main Streets
Richmond, VA 23219
(804) 648-4736
Fax: (804) 648-0002

Plates, Figurines, Dolls, Christmas Ornaments

The United States Historical Society is a non-profit educational organization dedicated to historical research and the sponsorship of projects and issuance of objects which are artistically and historically significant. The Society works with museums, educational institutions, foundations and other organizations to create objects for collection that have historic significance, artistic value and a high level of craftsmanship.

The Society has worked with several prestigious organizations and companies to produce collectible treasures. Among the current projects of the Society are: the Canterbury Stained Glass Christmas Plate with Canterbury Cathedral, the Charleton Heston "Will Penny" Revolver, the "One More for Yeager" lithographic print and the American Eagle Colt .45 with the Air Force Association, the *Renoir Doll* series with Sophie Renoir and the Hopalong Cassidy Single Action .45 Revolver.

V.F. FINE ARTS, INC.

Rick McBurney
P.O. Box 246
Lisbon, OH 44432
(216) 424-5231
Fax: (216) 424-5203

Figurines, Graphics

V.F. Fine Arts was founded to promote Sandra Kuck's limited edition prints and original artworks. The company is named in honor of Sandra's father, Vermont Franklin (V.F.).

V.F. Fine Arts is under the direction of Sandra's husband, John, in Boca Raton, Florida and is operated by Sandra's brother and his wife in Ohio.

The company offers through its dealership, some of Sandra's most memorable original oil paintings and also receives inquiries for her personal commissioned portraits.

As always, Sandra Kuck's signature means her collectors are receiving only the best in quality and a real investment for tomorrow.

VAILLANCOURT FOLK ART

Gary Vaillancourt
145 Armsby Road
Sutton, MA 01590
(508) 865-9183
Fax: (508) 865-4140

Figurines, Christmas Ornaments

Vaillancourt Folk Art was founded in 1984 by Judi and Gary Vaillancourt. Vaillancourt Folk Art's main product line is chalkware cast from antique moulds that were originally used to make chocolate or ice cream forms. The moulds date from the mid-1800s to the early 1900s. A plaster-like substance, chalkware first appeared in the mid-1800s and was referred to as "poor man's Staffordshire." It since has developed into a popular collectible.

Each piece of Vaillancourt chalkware is an original — individually hand-painted, signed and numbered.

Vaillancourt products include limited edition chalkware and moulds, hand-painted clocks and special production pieces.

Vaillancourt Folk Art is distributed through folk art dealers, specialty gift stores, art galleries, museum gift shops, leading department stores and fine furniture stores throughout the United States.

VICKILANE INC.

Ron Anderson
3233 NE Cadet
Portland, OR 97220-3601
(800) 678-4254
Fax: (503) 747-1957

Figurines

For Vicki Anderson, art has always been a primary part of life as far back as she can recall. Even as a high school student, Vicki's artwork, calligraphy and watercolors already received acclaim. She began her college education at the University of Oregon in 1970 as an art major, with her husband Ron majoring in computer science and math.

They began marketing figurines at home, and back then the Andersons believed their little business would only be a temporary part of their lives. However, the orders never ceased to come

in, necessitating a major decision to expand and continue designing. Since that time, VickiLane Inc. has been a full-time occupation. Vicki and Ron's first production building in Roseburg, Oregon, employed only ten individuals, but by 1983, an additional shop was built in Springfield, Oregon with more employees. Currently, over fifty people work there and future plans include further growth into a third location.

Vicki is constantly developing her skills and keeping up-to-date. Vicki especially has a deep appreciation for each era of art history, and is aware of its influence on her work, helping to merge current trends with long-standing traditions.

"I have known in my heart through our years together that the areas of sculpting, pastels, calligraphy, watercolor or oils would always be an amazement to me as I watch my wife create. Few artists possess the range of skills as she, and do them well. She has a twinkle in her eye and a smile on her face, which are reflected in her creations," says Ron.

VickiLane's "Mouse Couple On Log," of the Mice Memories *series, portrays Earnest and Sunshine enjoying a sunny afternoon together.*

VIKING IMPORT HOUSE, INC.

Pat Owen
690 NE 13th Street
Ft. Lauderdale, FL 33304-1110
(305) 763-3388
(800) 327-2297
Fax: (305) 462-2317

Plates, Bells, Christmas Ornaments, Figurines, Dolls, Steins

Viking Import House, now in its forty-sixth year in the collectibles market, not only presents the newest offerings from the finest makers in the industry, but is also a source for older, hard-to-find editions. This year, Viking is introducing the *Original Sculptures of*

Largo, a collection of figures from the Old West, in a uniquely-created patina of bronze. Viking Import House has exclusive United States distribution of Memory Lane cottages and Leroy Black Art Figurines from Naturecraft of England. Both lines have active collectors clubs. Viking also distributes Highbank porcelains from Scotland and Kaiser porcelains from Germany.

VILETTA CHINA COMPANY

Mr. Karasci
8000 Harwin Drive, #150
Houston, TX 77036-1891
(713) 785-0761
(800) 231-5762
Fax: (713) 977-4333

Plates, Bells, Christmas Ornaments

Viletta China Company was started in 1959 in Roseberg, Oregon, by Viletta West, who hand-painted china and sold it through stores in the Pacific Northwest. In 1978, Viletta China relocated to Houston, Texas and expanded its distribution throughout the United States and Canada.

The firm is involved in many areas of fine china including commemorative pieces, fine giftware, dinnerware and limited edition collector plates. Recently, the firm has enhanced its offerings with crystal and 24% lead crystal products.

W.T. WILSON / PEWTER PORT

David Hasslinger
185 York Avenue
Pawtucket, NY 02860
(800) 722-0485
(401) 723-0060
Fax: (401) 728-0485

Figurines, Bells, Christmas Ornaments

W.T. Wilson/Pewter Port is an American manufacturer of handcrafted gifts. The many collectibles they produce are always strong in detail, realism and quality craftsmanship.

William T. Wilson founded Pewter Port in 1979 and kept the growing company in the family over the years — in 1993 his son Bill Wilson launched the W.T. Wilson Limited division. Pewter Port manufactures collectible bells and ornaments, as well as a highly popular line of miniature antique toy reproductions called *Timeless Toys*, created by artist Earl Wagner. In the W.T. Wilson

division, charming and endearing children and nature themes are expertly portrayed in the form of limited edition figurines by artist Donna Carter.

WACO PRODUCTS CORPORATION

1 North Corporate Drive
Riverdale, NJ 07457-0160
(201) 616-1660

Figurines

WACO Products Corporation is a leading manufacturer and distributor of collectible figurines, executive games and novelties. In 1984, WACO introduced its first *Melody In Motion* porcelain figurines.

Melody In Motion figurines are based on original sculptures by master sculptor, Seiji Nakane. Nakane's art is faithfully translated into high-quality porcelain figures in Seto, Japan. Concealed within each figurine is a special mechanism which plays an appropriate tune and also allows portions of the figurine to move gracefully. The musical selections are studio-recorded and are superior to most musicals on the market.

In 1985, WACO introduced the first three figures in the *Melody In Motion Variety* series. In 1986, the annual *Santa* series was added. New subjects based on Nakane's sculptures are added on a regular basis.

SUSAN WAKEEN DOLL COMPANY

Tom Wallace
106 Powder Mill Road Box 1007
Canton, CT 06019
(203) 693-1112
Fax: (203) 693-0678

Dolls

Susan Wakeen, a soft-spoken but determined doll artist, began her creative career by making doll reproductions. Though they were popular at doll shows, Susan abandoned that venture in favor of creating her own sculptured dolls. Today, these originals command high prices on the secondary market and are continually sought-after by collectors.

The company's original name was The Littlest Ballet Company, as Susan studied dance and focused on producing mostly ballerina dolls. In 1989, Susan's company's name was changed to The Susan Wakeen Doll Company to reflect the artist's broadening scope — from

babies and play dolls to fairy tale characters and fashion figures.

Collectors will continue to enjoy Susan Wakeen dolls for many years to come.

WALLACE SILVERSMITHS

Janice Crowley
P.O. Box 9114
East Boston, MA 02128

Christmas Ornaments

In 1834, young Robert Wallace established his first spoon factory in Cheshire, Connecticut. In 1854, he formed a partnership with Samuel Simpson. Their firm, Wallace, Simpson & Company Inc., became R. Wallace & Sons Manufacturing Company in 1871.

A few years later, they were producing a complete line of hollowware as well as sterling and silverplated flatware, and by the 1920s were introducing new sterling patterns annually.

In the 1950s, following the purchases of the Watson Company, Tuttle Silversmiths and Smith & Smith Company, the name was changed once more to the current Wallace Silversmiths.

Their first limited edition, the annual "Sleigh Bell," was produced in 1971, with many popular series of ornaments and collectibles offered in the following years.

WATERFORD CRYSTAL

41 Madison Avenue
New York, NY 10010
(212) 532-5950

Bells, Christmas Ornaments

More than 200 years ago, craftsmen in Waterford on the southeastern coast of Ireland began creating a crystal with preeminence of design, clarity and luminescence.

After a hundred-year reign, the Waterford factory closed, and an entire century passed before the priceless Waterford heritage was resumed. The founders of the new Waterford chose to rekindle the ancient Irish art. Old methods of hand manufacturing were revived, and once again, Irish craftsmen fashioned the elegant patterns from white-hot molten crystal.

Waterford Christmas ornaments and bells brilliantly capture the holiday spirit with charming prismatic designs of favorite holiday symbols.

WEDGWOOD

41 Madison Avenue
New York, NY 10010
(212) 532-5950

Bells, Christmas Ornaments, Plates

Josiah Wedgwood founded his own potteryworks in 1759. Less than five years later, he perfected a cream-colored, glazed earthenware which withstood both heat and cold. Queen Charlotte so loved it, that she decreed all creamware to be known as "Queen's Ware."

Thomas Bentley later joined the firm as a partner, bringing with him a knowledge of the arts and valuable social contacts.

In addition to his "useful wares," Wedgwood's Black Basalt became one of the company's most popular products. His most famous invention was Jasper; unglazed, vitreous, fine stoneware which could be stained various colors, providing a suitable background for white relief work.

Wedgwood remains an active member in the collectibles field, producing Christmas plates, thimbles, bells and mugs in its famous Jasper, and several plate series in fine bone china and earthenware.

WILLITTS DESIGNS

Mary Beggs
P.O. Box 750009
Petaluma, CA 94975
(707) 778-7211
Fax: (707) 769-0304

Figurines, Plates, Bells, Christmas Ornaments, Graphics

Willitts Designs was founded in 1961 by William Willitts, Sr. and his wife Elda. Their personal ethics set a standard of business practices that carried the company through rapid growth, an acquisition with Hallmark Cards and to the re-purchase of the company in December of 1992. The family atmosphere remains a vital component of today's Willitts culture, and fundamental to continuing the entrepreneurial traditions of the company.

Today, Willitts is known for their collectible work with licenses such as The Walt Disney Company, World Wildlife Fund, Paramount Pictures (*Star Trek*) and the *American Carousel Collection* by Tobin Fraley.

WINDSTONE EDITIONS, INC.

13012 Saticoy Street #3
North Hollywood, CA 91605
(800) 982-4464
Fax: (818) 982-4674

Figurines

Highly-acclaimed artist Melody Peña and her husband John Alberti formed Windstone Editions, Inc. in 1984 to manufacture and market Melody's popular figurines. Recognized today as one of the outstanding artists of fantasy and natural history figurines, Peña's cast stone sculptures include families of dragons, wizards, unicorns, griffins, dinosaurs and more. Peña's thirty-plus sculpted pieces range in height from about three to thirteen inches and sell for between $20 and $275 each.

Windstone Editions prefers not to call their collectibles "limited editions," believing in the value of art for its inherent quality and superior craftsmanship; however, several editions of their figurines are retired.

WINSTON ROLAND

1909 Oxford Street E.
Unit 17
London, Ontario N5V 2Z7
(519) 659-6601
Fax: (519) 451-1735

4600 Witmar Industrial Estates
Unit 4
Niagara Falls, New York 14305

Plates, Graphics

In 1988, Winston Roland was founded to manufacture and distribute limited edition collector plates and prints by Winston Roland, distribute lithophanes by David Failing and Aztec frames and works by various other artists. President Greg Peppler has furthered the success of the firm, introducing in the summer of 1993 a new giftware line from the company to complement their existing products. The artwork from Winston Roland is displayed at major gift and collectible shows in the United States and Canada.

THE WORLD GALLERY OF DOLLS & COLLECTIBLES

P.O. Box 581
Great Falls, VA 22068
(703) 821-0607
Fax: (703) 759-0408

Dolls

The World Gallery of Dolls & Collectibles is a trademark of the Home Shopping Network.

In less than a decade, shopping at home has become a popular way of seeing and acquiring the latest products in a national marketplace. Collectibles, and especially dolls, have developed a loyal and growing audience for this new and exciting way to shop.

World Gallery dolls are all authentically collectible. Each one is designed by a well-known artist and is manufactured to high-quality standards. Every doll is accompanied by a Certificate of Authenticity and often by additional documentation enhancing its collectibility.

Among the world-class artists designing dolls for The World Gallery are Thelma Resch, Beverly Parker, Patricia Loveless, Val Shelton, Fayzah Spanos, Susan Stone Aiken and Vincent J. De Filippo.

JOHANNES ZOOK ORIGINALS

1519 South Badour
Midland, MI 48640
(517) 835-9388

Dolls

In 1983, Pat and Joanna Secrist began making collectible porcelain dolls to sell in a toy shop that they planned to open. Pat sculpted the faces and Joanna dressed the dolls. The toy shop never opened, but the collectible doll business blossomed. In 1986, they began making their own vinyl dolls. Johannes Zook Originals continues to grow, adding new faces and designs every year.

Zook dolls such as "Patrick," "Sara," "Bonnie," "Stephanie" and "Shalequa" have all either won or have been nominated for the *Dolls* magazine Award of Excellence or the DOTY award. Johannes Zook Originals is a sister company of Apple Valley Doll Works, maker of REAL-EYES®, and is a division of Secrist Toys.

Meet the Artists
Biographies of Some of Today's Most Popular and Talented Limited Edition Artists

Limited edition artists are the subjects of a great deal of interest and admiration on the part of collectors. Many collectors will travel hundreds of miles to attend an open house or convention featuring that special artist or craftsman. The following articles include biographical information about some of the best-known artists in today's world of limited editions. This listing is not comprehensive, but it will provide an introduction to a good number of the talented women and men whose works bring pleasure to collectors all over the world.

SUSAN STONE AIKEN

Susan Stone Aiken, Gorham's first lady of dolls, has designed well over 100 dolls for the company since her original collection of ten dolls was introduced by Gorham in 1981.

Every doll dressed by Ms. Aiken is renowned for its original, heirloom quality. In fact, she has had the distinct honor of seeing many of her dolls appreciate in value far beyond their original issue price.

A native of Massachusetts, Ms. Aiken trained as an artist at the University of Maine and the Rhode Island School of Design. She has taken courses in fashion illustration and pattern making, and her talent as a seamstress is a natural gift. Ms. Aiken gets much of her inspiration from books and photos of turn-of-the-century fashions. But she does have an instinctive feeling for the combinations of materials that are authentic and correct.

"I'm from an old New England family," she says, "and I grew up surrounded by antiques. When I create a costume for a doll, it is like discovering an old friend."

After researching her ideas, she begins with a sketch, then personally selects fabrics, laces and trims to create an original sample. She works with the sculptor so that the face, coloring and hairstyle coordinate with the costume she has designed.

Aiken finds her work especially rewarding because she gets to make artist appearances for Gorham and is able to meet collectors who appreciate the love and effort she puts into each design. The culmination of her talents and efforts can be seen in the *Gorham Doll Collection*.

MARK ALVIN

Growing up in a large family on the shores of Cape Cod, Mark Alvin and his brothers and sisters were constantly encouraged by their parents to be inventive and original. There was no television in the house. Instead, Mark's father, who was not only a house painter but also a sculptor of marble and rare woods, would read to the family *The Wind in the Willows*. Music was played on wooden instruments in the sunlight of the living room, and in winter, everyone gathered about driftwood fires on the beach. Mark's mother created poetry and nurtured the family with love and caring.

After high school, Mark joined a New Age community, played in rock bands, started a greeting card company and began a wandering search for himself.

Into each of his paintings, Mark puts his love of the finely-crafted. As a self-taught artist, having no formal artistic training since high school, Mark paints Santa Claus motifs for greeting cards as well as fine-art wildlife. In fact, he has been a finalist in duck stamp competitions in both South Carolina and in Florida. Mark usually works in gouache to create his illustrations, although he has also recently worked in oils. As Mark says, "I always paint with the viewer in mind by filling my creations with light which we both may share for a fleeting moment."

Mark Alvin's unique vision is reflected in the Clothtique® Santas he designs for Possible Dreams.

VICKI ANDERSON

In the world of VickiLane where make-believe and reality thrive side by side, each precious work of art transmits the feelings, thoughts and blessings of Vicki Elaine Anderson to every collector with love.

Vicki grew up in a household brimming with creativity and has maintained an active interest in art all her

life. As a high school student, Vicki met and fell in love with Ron Anderson, and after attending a community college, the two embarked on a marriage and partnership that has thrived both personally and professionally. The Andersons' artistic collaboration began when they pooled their talents to design and market a line of sculptures and calligraphy prints. Back then, the Andersons believed that their business would only be a temporary part of their lives. They sold it in 1977 after Ron completed his ministerial studies and they were called to pastor a church in a small community.

In 1985, Ron and Vicki began to realize their study, experience and faith had prepared them for a new arena of service. They set out to make a mark in the gift and collectibles business with the founding of VickiLane, Inc.

Vicki Anderson is truly the heart of VickiLane. This creative lady has a remarkable ability to bring ideas to life through her skills and imagination. With a twinkle in her eyes, she designs one masterpiece of make-believe after another and vows to continue sharing the beauty of her magical world for many years to come.

PATRICIA ANDREWS

Hallmark Keepsake Ornament artist Patricia Andrews most enjoys designing ornaments that look as if they could come to life. One of her favorites is "Sugar Plum Fairy," a 1990 Limited Edition Ornament. To get the ornament just right, Patricia said she designed several miniature versions of the ballerina in different poses to see which was the most graceful. Speaking of graceful, her 1992 "Lighting the Way" design is just that. This lighted ornament depicts an angel in a flowing robe holding a lantern that flickers.

The artist also has her whimsical side, as was seen when she created "Two Peas in a Pod" in 1990. That same year she also designed "Elf of the Year," a lighted Keepsake Magic Ornament.

Like many of the other Hallmark ornament designers, Patricia began her career as an engraver some fifteen years ago. She is married to Dill Rhodus, who also designs Keepsake Ornaments.

PAULETTE APRILE

A native of California, Paulette Aprile is a self-taught artist of original dolls. Since childhood, she always loved art and could be found drawing pictures or clothes for her paper dolls, as well as attempting to sew new clothes.

Married with three children, she continued to sew clothes for her daughters' dolls. Paulette then decided to learn all about ceramics and porcelain and applied that knowledge to dollmaking. She experimented with slip, molds and tools, and she proved to be a stern taskmaster.

A member of three doll clubs, she made reproduction dolls which won ribbons in area competitions. After teaching dollmaking courses and mastering the art, Paulette began to create some very popular originals. Her "Father Christmas" doll was ordered by the White House during the Reagan administration. In 1987, her "Cynthia" doll won the Best Sculpture Award and *Dolls* magazine's Award of Excellence. In 1990, she was commissioned to design a life-size bride and ringbearer for the EuroDisney Park in Paris. In 1991, one of her limited edition designs, "Stephanie," was nominated for *Dolls'* Award of Excellence.

Since then, she has been selected by Seymour Mann, Inc. to design dolls for the company's *Signature Series*. Among the dolls that she designed in 1993 was a ballerina doll, "Pavlova," which was nominated for an Award of Excellence.

Paulette also designed many other collectible dolls for Seymour Mann, including a bridal doll named "Alexandria," and "Violetta," which debuted in the *Tragic Heroine Series*.

GIUSEPPE ARMANI

For many years, collectors have been delighted by the elegance and grace of Giuseppe Armani's many fine figurines. The Italian master sculptor has a unique talent for translating both human and animal form, and for capturing the emotion and ambiance of the occasion into each of his works.

Born in Calci, Italy in 1935, Armani began his artistic career as a child in his village. Working with chalk, he sketched his many childhood friends, real and imaginary, on whatever surface he could find.

Armani was about fourteen years old when his family moved to Pisa. There he studied art and anatomy for the next ten years. Although Armani started as a painter, the artist confesses that he always envisioned his art in three-dimensional form. Therefore, he eventually turned to sculpture for expression.

The artist still lives in Pisa where he has a sculpture studio. In addition, he works with the artists and artisans at the Florence Sculture d'Arte Studios where his works are reproduced, painted and prepared for the worldwide market. At the Florence Studios, Armani is the premier designer and sculptor, and it is there that he supervises all aspects of his sculptures which are known as the *Armani Collection*.

Armani has made several trips to the United States, meeting collectors of his works and promoting his newly-formed collectors' club, the G. Armani Society.

The *Armani Collection* is imported to the United States exclusively by Miller Import Corporation of Keasbey, New

Jersey. The G. Armani Society is also managed by this company.

MABEL LUCIE ATTWELL

British artist Mabel Lucie Attwell was born in London, the ninth of ten children. Her father encouraged his family to pursue artistic interests, so Attwell started drawing at an early age.

She sold her first drawing before she was sixteen years old to a London publisher for two pounds (about $4 U.S.). From that humble beginning, Attwell was a working artist. She paid her own way through art school by selling her work.

It was during her studies in art school that Mabel Lucie Attwell met and married a fellow art student, illustrator Harold Earnshaw. They had two sons and a daughter. Her daughter Peggy became the "Attwell child," the adorable toddler with large eyes, a winsome expression and often a large bow in her hair.

Attwell's earliest published illustrations appeared in 1905; she illustrated gift books, children's books and fairy tales. Her distinctive treatment of children as cherubic, chubby-legged and winsome was established early in her career. Throughout her career, her art was always in demand — even by the Royal Family. As a toddler, Prince Charles was presented with a set of nursery china bearing Miss Attwell's illustrations, and Princess Margaret chose Miss Attwell's artwork for personal Christmas cards when she was a child in the 1930s.

Mabel Lucie Attwell died peacefully on November 5, 1964. Enesco continued her legacy in 1987 by licensing the rights to translate her artwork into porcelain bisque figurines through the *Enesco Memories of Yesterday* Collection.

The Collection premiered in 1988 and was soon ranked among the top ten collectibles in the United States. In 1991, Enesco formed the Memories of Yesterday Collectors' Society.

BRIAN BAKER

Brian Baker's zest for life comes from his fascination with history and the arts. When he is not busy creating a new sculpture, Brian can be found exploring the Pacific Northwest or searching for adventure in a distant land. Having visited more than forty different countries, Brian is inspired to share the cultures, beautiful architecture and his travel experiences with others through the creation of his *Déjà Vu Collection*.

Brian Baker was born in 1962 and raised in Seattle, Washington's Puget Sound area. He went to work in 1981 for a gift company specializing in framed plaques. Brian advanced quickly within the company, acquiring valuable knowledge of the gift industry, and developing his craft at the same time.

Brian embarked on his most ambitious adventure in 1986 when he began his solo trip around the world. In Paris, he saw wonderful architecture and paintings of houses that inspired him to delve into the history of Europe's and America's architectural histories.

After his worldwide travels, Brian returned home to Redmond, Washington in 1986. At this time he began working at Michael's Limited. There he made a clay wall-hanging house for a Christmas present. Michael O'Connell, owner of Michael's Limited, liked the work so much he suggested that Brian make a few more. The finished sculptures became popular right away and the rest, as they say, is history.

Brian's trademark in his *Déjà Vu Collection* is an umbrella. On many of his sculptures, one is hidden in the shadows or quietly tucked away in a corner. Brian is a detail-oriented man, which is evident in the great care and pride he takes in creating each house himself. Brian tries to become part of the building, imagining the people who would live or work there. This is his way of bringing history to life and making one feel like "Déjà Vu" — you've been there before…

VICKY BALCOU

Artist and designer Vicky Balcou attended the University of Texas in Austin where she received her Bachelor of Arts degree in Fine Arts. Throughout her early studies and college career, Vicky also studied privately with internationally known designers and artists.

In 1965, Vicky moved with her husband, a well-known sculptor, to Mexico City and then to El Paso, Texas where she began freelancing as a designer and artist on special projects. She designed scholarly texts and other publications for the SMU Press at Southern Methodist University and has also worked for several graphics and advertising agencies.

In 1975, Vicky joined Susan Crane, Inc., exclusively as a giftwrap designer. Her specialty was Christmas themes, and she credits this time in her career when she developed her keen sense of drawing and painting merry elves, Santa Claus and other Christmas-related items.

In 1980, Vicky began her distinguished career with Fitz and Floyd as a giftware and decorative accessories designer. Recently, Vicky began designing some of the collectibles lines at the company. She is most known for her "Old World Elves" giftware, as well as Fitz and Floyd's unique lighted Christmas village called "Holiday Hamlet."

Vicky Balcou is a native of Ft. Worth,

Texas. Her outside interests include art, painting and mentoring her daughter in her artistic career development.

LINDA BALDWIN

Missourian Linda Lindquist Baldwin had no experience in art before creating her first Belsnickle Santa in 1986. What she did have, though, was an intense desire to recreate the antique Santas displayed in a book she had just purchased at a yard sale for five cents.

"I was absolutely fascinated by those Santas," recalls Linda. "But when I learned that the price for each one was as much as $6,000, I decided to try making my own."

After a few attempts, Linda perfected the process for handsculpting and hand-painting her papier maché Belsnickles. Before long, she had an established reputation among Christmas collectors, and found it increasingly difficult to keep up with the demand. That's when she turned to Schmid, whose *Belsnickle Collection* is handcrafted of hollowed cold cast porcelain to mimic the look and feel of Linda's original sculptures.

Like Linda's originals, Schmid's *Belsnickle Collection* is comprised of three distinct Santa figures, all based on Linda's research on the centuries-old history of Santa in different cultures. The "Belsnickle," a long-limbed and stern Santa, is from 19th-century Germany. His counterpart is "Father Christmas," also tall and lean, but bearing fruit, nuts and candy for those who have been good. The "Roly-Poly" is the transitional Santa of early 20th-century America—rotund, red-cheeked and elfish, much like the Santa we know today. Linda intends to continue creating her popular, one-of-a-kind originals in the years to come.

BETTE BALL

Bette Ball is the award-winning designer of the highly acclaimed Betty Jane Carter®, Carol Anne®, Dolly Dingle® and Victoria Ashlea Originals® porcelain dolls. She is known and appreciated by doll collectors for her uncompromising quality of design.

Ms. Ball double-majored in Fine Arts and Costume Design in art school. Her paintings hang in many private collections around the world. She also enjoys an international reputation for her design in fine china and giftware.

She is a member of the International Foundation of Doll Makers, The Society of Professional Doll Makers, as well as a recipient of the prestigious DOTY award and NALED Doll of the Year awards.

Bette's dolls have been honored by acceptance in many museums such as The Yokohama Doll Museum in Japan; The McCurdy Historical Doll Museum, Utah; The White Castle Doll Museum, California; Arizona Toy and Doll Museum, Arizona; Doll Castle Museum, New Jersey; San Francisco Doll Museum, California; and Mary Stoltz Doll & Toy Museum, Pennsylvania.

Bette Ball has endeared herself to countless admirers through personal and television appearances, where she lends her vibrant personality to discussions on designing and collecting dolls.

Bette is director of doll design for Goebel United States.

CICELY MARY BARKER

English artist Cicely Mary Barker, whose Flower Fairies have thrilled generations of children, has won the hearts of yet another generation of collectors of fantasy and romance. Born in Surrey, England in 1895, Ms. Barker demon-

strated her artistic talent at a very early age. A frail child, she was educated at home and spent a considerable amount of time sketching seascapes and children. Although she had no formal training, her talents were developed during her association with artists she met through the local Croydon Art Society.

In 1923, the first volume of her Flower Fairies was published. Whimsical and sensitive in every detail, her Flower Fairies reflected an art nouveau style with the color richness and subtlety of that period. Her *Children's Book of Hymns* was published in 1929 and was re-issued fifty years later. Cicely Mary Barker died in 1973, shortly after the 50th anniversary of her first Flower Fairies book.

W.S. George produced a limited edition plate series based on Ms. Barker's sketches entitled *Beloved Hymns of Childhood*.

Reco International Corp. released the *Flower Fairies Year Plate Collection*. Each plate has a portion of the artist's poems printed on the backstamp.

DOT AND SY BARLOWE

When Dot and Sy Barlowe first collaborated as fellow artists at New York's

Museum of Natural History in the 1940s, they began a harmonious personal and working relationship that has been preserved to this day. Four years after their marriage in 1946, they began working as free-lance illustrators. Since then — together and separately — they have earned national recognition for their historic and naturalist art.

Together, the Barlowes have illustrated nature books for some of the largest publishing houses in America, including Knopf, Random House, Morrow, Follett, American Heritage Press, Putnam, Harper & Row, McGraw-Hill, and Grosset and Dunlap. For the Golden Press alone, they illustrated fifteen books, including such well-known nature identification volumes as *Seashores, Trees of America* and *Amphibians of North America*.

In addition, the Barlowes have contributed illustrations to several Audubon Society guides and to *The Audubon Society Encyclopedia of North American Birds*. They also share their knowledge of nature illustration and botany by teaching at the Parsons School of Design in New York. The artists have done features for publications including *The New York Times* and *Newsday*, and their works have been honored with numerous awards and exhibitions at the Society of Illustrators in New York and Expo '67 in Montreal.

Reco International Corp. has presented an eight-plate *Vanishing Animal Kingdoms* collection by Sy Barlowe, and a *Gardens of Beauty* plate collection by Dorothea Barlowe. The artists also introduced a series of animal figurines through Reco. Other recent introductions include *Town & Country Dogs* and *Our Cherished Seas* plate series.

FRANCIS J. BARNUM

Francis J. Barnum of Loveland, Ohio joined the Chilmark Gallery of artists in the midst of a thirty-year career as a designer, modelmaker and sculptor. His career — from commercial illustrator to serious artist of American subjects — parallels the careers of Frederic Remington, Charles M. Russell and many of today's best artists.

Born and raised in Ohio's Cuyahoga River Valley, the family farm had been the site of countless Shawnee Indian encampments. As a boy he began saving and cataloging Indian artifacts, a hobby

that paved the way for Barnum's lifelong interest in archeological history.

Painstaking research and attention to even the smallest detail is obvious in all of Barnum's work. In addition to bringing a sense of high drama to his scenes, Barnum has the ability to capture the very emotions of his characters. Barnum's sculptures for Lance's Chilmark line are as diverse as his previous experiences, with most spanning the United States' most remembered war, the American Civil War.

Barnum has designed *the* series commemorating the Civil War through depictions of many well-known leaders as well as the anonymous heroes in Chilmark Fine Pewter. Numbering over thirty-five pieces in 1993, Barnum's collection takes us from Gettysburg to Shiloh to Antietam and runs the gamut of emotions from defeat to victory.

PRESCOTT WOODBURY BASTON

Prescott Woodbury Baston was born in Arlington, Massachusetts in 1909 and received his formal art training at the Vesper George School of Art in

Boston in the late 1920s.

Baston began sculpting under his own name in 1938, and in 1940, formed the Sebastian Miniature Company. The success of his tiny figurines prompted him to move his company from the basement of his home to a studio in Marblehead, Massachusetts. He produced over 900 different "Sebastian Miniatures" for his retail line and private commissions. His tiny, hand-painted miniatures were distributed initially through gift shops in New England and later, throughout the nation. He also designed and produced advertising give-away pieces for over 100 corporations.

In 1969, Baston, then over sixty years old, turned his design attention to plates and figurines that were cast in pewter by other gift manufacturers. They included *The Birth of a Nation* and the *Currier & Ives* plate series for Royal Worcester.

In 1976, The Lance Corporation began producing 100 of Baston's most popular designs for national distribution. Paralleled with an explosion of American interest in nostalgic collectibles, Sebastian Miniatures started to attract the attention they had never enjoyed in the previous forty years.

Prescott Woodbury Baston died in May 1984, after seeing his son, Woody, begin sculpting his own Sebastian Miniatures, and the love of the man and his art still continue today.

PRESCOTT "WOODY" BASTON, JR.

In 1981, Sebastian Miniatures reached a landmark when the first Sebastian Miniature sculpted by Prescott "Woody" Baston, Jr., the son of Prescott Baston, was introduced.

A trained artist, Woody had wanted to try his hand at making Sebastian Miniatures from the time he was a boy. He began working part-time in the studio during his junior year in high school and spent summers learning all phases of production. Following four years of study at Boston University, he graduated with a Bachelor's degree in Fine Arts, majoring in sculpture.

After a stint in the Army, Woody joined The Lance Corporation in Hudson, Massachusetts as production manager. In 1968, his father had begun designing miniature figurines to be cast by Lance in Hudson pewter.

In 1975, operations at the Marblehead plant were halted and production continued in the Hudson facility. At the present time, Woody is vice-president of marketing services and the sole sculptor of Sebastian Miniatures since the death of his father in 1984. Woody has sculpted more than 150 miniatures for the Lance Sebastian retail line and private commissions.

MARTY BELL

Acclaimed for thousands of beautiful images captured on canvas, Marty Bell is America's premier artist for the heart and home. Best known for her renditions of England's country cottages, Marty Bell has had a passion for painting since her early thirties.

Enrolling in a group oil painting class, Marty sought aid to develop and establish the style of painting she wanted to produce. Although only a student, she began establishing a following of fellow students anxious to learn her techniques and unique style. One year after Marty's start in oil painting, she opened her own art school at the request of her classmates.

In 1974, Marty painted a few English scenes which promptly sold. After eleven years of teaching and self-development, and with the strong encouragement of her husband/manager, Marty closed her art school to produce the paintings she longed to create.

Her love for the English countryside prompts extended sojourns to this captivating isle. It is during these journeys that she studies "real life" settings which may become the subjects for future paintings.

Marty began reproducing her art in 1981. Today, over 120 of her original oil paintings have been published in limited edition, and thousands of collectors across America have chosen these popular works of art to grace their homes.

Under the direction of her husband Steve Bell, and her three sons, Mark, Jeff and Greg, Marty Bell Fine Art, Inc. continues to publish and distribute Marty's art and collectible selections throughout the United States from her native Chatsworth, California.

YOLANDA BELLO

Award-winning doll artist Yolanda Bello began "restyling" her dolls when she was a young child in Caracas, Venezuela. With each change, Bello's imagination helped transform her ordinary dolls into new and exciting characters.

Bello moved to Chicago, Illinois when she was fourteen, bringing her love of dolls with her. She eventually began working as a figurine sculptor while pursuing her interest in doll design and sculpture in her spare time. In 1981, Ms. Bello created her first porcelain dolls — a pair of Spanish girls — and the reaction was so favorable that within a year, dollmaking had become her full-time profession.

Since then, Yolanda Bello has designed and produced dolls which have earned her critical acclaim and more than fifty prizes in major juried exhibitions, including five Best of Show awards, a prestigious Doll of the Year award in 1985 and First Place in Doll Achievement from the National Association of Limited Edition Dealers in 1987, 1988, 1989 and 1991.

Ms. Bello's designs range from one-of-a-kind dolls portraying the characters in the opera *Carmen* for the New York Metropolitan Galleries, to her most sought-after limited edition dolls. Yolanda's *Picture-Perfect Babies*, her first collection produced by the Edwin M. Knowles China Co. exclusively for the Ashton-Drake Galleries, *Children of Mother Goose*, *Yolanda's Precious Playmates*, *Moments to Remember*, *Yolanda's Lullaby Babies*, *Yolanda's Heaven Scent Babies* and *Yolanda's World of Love Special Edition Dolls* have been enthusiastically received by collectors.

JODY BERGSMA

The whimsical world of Jody Bergsma's "Little People" may be pure fantasy, but its simplicity and beauty has touched the hearts of collectors. Born in 1953 in Bellingham, Washington, Bergsma came from a family of five children where her early artistic efforts were encouraged and prominently displayed. When Bergsma was fifteen, her aunt Eileen Knight invited her to Port Angeles to enter her first art show. She made sixty dollars, which motivated both her artistic and entrepreneurial efforts.

In 1973, Bergsma attended a small college in Vancouver, Canada where she came under the influence of the Canadian impressionists called the "Group of Seven." In 1978, she began a year-long journey through Europe where she visited the museums in Amsterdam,

London and Paris. She painted in southern France, Venice and Florence and ended her studies in Athens and the Greek Islands. Returning home, Bergsma withdrew from her engineering studies and became a serious, full-time artist.

Bergsma has had numerous one-woman shows of her abstract watercolors and has released over 300 different "Little People" prints through the Jody Bergsma Gallery. Jody's first collector plate series for Reco International was *Guardians of the Kingdom*, which is also available through The Hamilton Collection. Reco International introduced the *Jody Bergsma Christmas* series, featuring "I Wish You An Angel" for 1993 and her *Mother's Day* series, featuring "My Greatest Treasure," also in 1993. A new figurine line was also recently introduced.

A new series began in 1993 entitled *Castles and Dreams*. The first three plates are "Birth Of A Dream," "Dreams Come True" and "Believe in Your Dreams." Each Jody Bergsma plate offers a poetic message from the artist on the backstamp.

ULRICH BERNARDI

Known for his designs of religious figures and crèche sets, Ulrich Bernardi, a native of Val Gardena since his birth in 1925, has made a life of modeling and designing.

Following his studies at the Academy of Art in Ortisei and after many years of post-graduate work, which won him the title of "Master of Arts," Bernardi was honored at exhibitions throughout Europe.

Upon graduation from the Academy of Art, Bernardi continued to finely hone his extraordinary talent in drawing, modeling and woodsculpting while

working in his first apprenticeship with a master woodsculptor. It was also during this period that he encountered the area of art that continues to be his deepest passion and greatest joy—the sculpting of nativity scenes.

During his four years of apprenticeship, the distinguishing characteristics and unique style of Bernardi's hand-sculpted works began to emerge more and more clearly—the natural feel for the wood, the flow of the dresses or cloaks, the ruddy complexions indigenous to his region, and the sincere innocent expressions of his subjects. The spirit of his work is embodied in his creation of European folklore.

Within the past years, Bernardi has been the master sculptor for all Sarah Kay figurines, translating the two-dimensional drawings of the Australian artist into three-dimensional master models of wood sculptures. In this role, Bernardi works closely with Sarah Kay in order to develop a deep understanding of her art, exploring styles, techniques and artistic philosophies, the meaning of symbols and the intended implication of the artwork. His sculpting then becomes the master from which other skilled woodsculptors create the individual pieces.

Probably more than any other ANRI master sculptor, Bernardi's contributions, from his two crèche sets, to his Madonnas, to his Sarah Kay portrayals and depictions of young and old Groeners at work and play, truly round out the line of ANRI woodsculptings.

THOMAS BLACKSHEAR

As an admirer of turn-of-the-century art masters like N.C. Wyeth and J.C. Leyendecker, Thomas Blackshear strives

to capture the mood and inherent drama in each of his subjects. Yet Blackshear is very much a man of the present day, and thus he draws upon contemporary techniques and art media to create his true-to-life cinematic masterworks.

Through the use of gouache, acrylics, pastels and oils, Blackshear captures the personality and drama of some of the world's best-loved cinematic characters. His unique talent has been represented on movie posters for *Indiana Jones and the Temple of Doom*, *The Black Cauldron*, *Legend* and *Star Wars* and has earned him the admiration of moviegoers.

Blackshear's talent earned him gold and silver awards from the Kansas City Directors Club in 1982, and many of his works were on display at Society of Illustrators shows during this time.

In 1986, Blackshear created the original art for a popular series of collector plates entitled the *Star Wars* plate collection. On the heels of that success, Blackshear was commissioned to create the first officially authorized plate collection celebrating the 50th anniversary of *The Wizard of Oz* for The Hamilton Collection.

In 1990, Blackshear created a major new commemorative work that won him the prestigious "Plate of the Year" Award. This stunning plate-painting, entitled "Fifty Years of Oz," firmly established Blackshear as one of the most gifted cinematic artists of our time.

In 1991, he created the original art for Hamilton's *Star Trek® 25th Anniversary Collection* as well as the *Star Trek® 25th Anniversary Commemoration* collage plate.

Most recently, Blackshear unveiled his very popular *Star Trek® The Next Generation 5th Anniversary Commemorative* plate collection, which premiered with a dramatic portrait of "Captain Jean-Luc Picard."

TED BLAYLOCK

During his early adult life, Ted Blaylock held a variety of tough, work-a-day jobs, all far removed from the world of fine art. Yet, throughout this period ran one common thread — the love of art. Regardless of the job, his leisure time was spent developing his talent for drawing and painting.

In 1969, Blaylock decided to follow his artistic instincts and opened an art gallery and instruction school in Col-

linsville, Illinois. Three years later, with his wife and four young sons, he left the security of his hometown and headed west — in those years a more accepting market for the work of new artists.

Today, the exciting but often tenuous life of a wandering artist is over for Blaylock. He resides in Mesa, Arizona where his distinctive wildlife and western paintings are avidly sought by a growing body of collectors.

Ted Blaylock is represented by Hadley House.

BARBARA BLYTHE

An accomplished and successful wildlife artist, Barbara Blythe has won numerous awards and honors for her prints and original paintings.

Barbara is a graduate of the University of North Carolina at Charlotte with a Bachelor of Arts degree in Education.

Barbara joined CUI, Inc. in mid-1992 where she works in watercolors and acrylics to create illustrations for steins, plates and other collectibles. She has painted such diverse subjects as lighthouses, Civil War scenes, early American history, wildlife, sports figures, street festivals and Christmas scenes.

In her spare time, Barbara likes to paint and enjoys outdoor activities such as camping and white-water rafting.

MAUD HUMPHREY BOGART

Long before her only son Humphrey Bogart won worldwide fame as an actor, Maud Humphrey established herself as one of the country's most gifted artists.

Maud Humphrey always loved to draw and paint. She left her home in Rochester, New York, to study at the famous Art League in New York City. Her training continued in Paris at the Julian Studios where she worked under several master painters.

Upon returning to New York, Humphrey was hired to produce illustrations for Christmas cards, books, calendars and advertisements. She became one of the country's most sought-after artists as more requests poured in from magazines, book publishers and advertising companies. In several months, the "Maud Humphrey Babies" became the talk of the nation.

When she was thirty-three, Maud Humphrey married Belmont DeForest Bogart, a prominent Manhattan physician. Their son, Humphrey Bogart, first entered the public eye when his mother painted his portrait and sent it to a New York advertising agency. His picture showed up on all the labels and advertisements of a baby food company, and he became famous as the "Original Maud Humphrey Baby." The Bogarts also had two daughters, Frances and Catherine.

Maud Humphrey died in 1940 in Hollywood, but her artwork lives on. Offered by The Balliol Corporation and The Hamilton Collection, original creations inspired by her illustrations are now reaching a wide new audience of collectors — the *Little Ladies* plate collection, the "Playing Bride" and "First Lesson" porcelain collector dolls and an array of fanciful figurines. Also, the *Maud Humphrey Bogart Collection* from Enesco premiered with nine limited edition figurines. Since then, this collection — all inspired by the adorable children in Miss Humphrey's paintings — has won nationwide acclaim.

MICHAEL BOYETT

Texan Michael Boyett is recognized as one of the most important sculptors of the American West. His works are exhibited in Western art galleries and museums throughout the United States. Special invitational exhibitions of his works have included the inauguration of President Jimmy Carter (Washington, D.C.), The George Phippen Memorial Art Show (Prescott, Arizona), Texas Rangers Hall of Fame (Waco, Texas) and the Texas Art Classic (Fort Worth, Texas).

Born in Boise, Idaho in 1943, Boyett began painting and sculpting as a child. He received recognition at the age of twelve when one of his paintings was chosen to hang in the governor's office in Topeka, Kansas. Boyett attended the University of Texas Art School and holds Bachelor and Masters degrees in Fine Arts from the Stephen F. Austin State University.

Boyett worked exclusively in bronze until 1979, when the Chilmark foundry of Hudson, Massachusetts, began casting his miniature scale sculptures in pewter.

SUZAN BRADFORD

Suzan's love of art stemmed from age two, as she watched oil paintings develop at her artist-mother's knee. Her Air Force pilot father supplied the rough carpentry/three-dimensional side of her

life's vantage point and also a catalytic viewing of the Louvre's "Winged Victory of Samothrace" at the age of six. At age ten, she vowed to "be a sculptor like Michelangelo." Though short of that mark, her empathy and striving for life-like forms has remained kindled over the years, as many friends, family, and animal critters have graced her life in Florida, Kansas, Colorado and Oklahoma. The latter included almost a dozen horses, a herd of Holsteins, range ewes at lambing time, barnyard fowl of many types, dogs (some of whom travel well to Santa Fe and beyond), cats, parakeets, turtles and a saucy cockatiel.

Suzan's freelance and commissioned artworks are in private collections across the country and venture into the mediums of drawing, oil painting, watercolor, mixed media, stoneware pottery, terracotta sculptures, bronzes and lithographs.

Ms. Bradford has been with United Design for seven years and is the creator of several lines: *Backyard Birds*™, the original *Fancy Frames*™ and *Candle-lights*™. She has also sculpted many of *The Legend of Santa Claus*™ limited edition figurines, as well as the *Animal Magnetism*™ line.

UTA BRAUSER

Doll artist Uta Brauser has gained international respect for the historical accuracy and socially relevant expression that typify her creations. Her use of vivid colors coupled with her finely drawn characterizations result in unique dolls reflecting fully developed technical and artistic concepts. By personally putting the finishing touches on each doll, Uta causes distinctive personalities to emerge that can best be described as

"portraits of time and place." Cardinal Inc.'s Dynasty Doll Collection™ is proud to exclusively offer Uta's art for discriminating collectors.

Born in Munich, Germany, Brauser was encouraged by her artistic mother and father to develop her artistic gifts. By the age of fifteen, Uta had done portraits, sold sketches and pastels, and made puppets for school.

As a teenager and budding artist, Brauser's independent nature gained momentum through performance and street arts in Munich's central square. Then she went to Italy and the sunny island of Capri. After four years, she moved on to Salerno and Naples and taught German in a state school. Other jobs followed, but all the while she made little dolls.

When she started doing trade fairs and became more immersed in earning a living from sculpting and dollmaking, Brauser moved to Florence. Today, she resides in New York City.

Slowly and steadily, sales of her dolls increased, flowering into a prosperous market that today demands attention from thousands of collectors. The reason could be that no two of her dolls are alike, and buyers seem to be drawn to particular dolls, just as they would be to certain human personalities.

TOM BROWNING

Just a glance at one of Tom Browning's Clothtique® Santas from Possible Dreams brings a whiff of nostalgia for a bygone era. His grasp of composition, style and color are worked with an impressionist's hand to infuse his paintings with an inner light — a light that is refracted into a three dimensional embodiment.

"I always knew what I wanted to do. I had encouragement from my parents and fourth grade teacher," relates Tom. "On Saturday mornings I'd tune into a learn-to-draw program on television and follow the instructions." By the time he was ten years old, there was no doubt in Tom's mind that he was going to be an artist.

Yet it wasn't until he enrolled at the University of Oregon that he began to discover the real talent within. An instructor who was also an illustrator was especially influential. "His specialty was painting figures and heads. Watching another artist work is the best learning tool. Since college, I've gotten most of my learning from working with other artists and taking workshops."

As he talks about his work, Tom becomes very introspective. "Painting is a pretty involved process. When I solve the composition problem and laying in of the colors, then the most exciting part begins — all the technical things needed to finish it up. The ones that just go easily from start to finish move like electricity."

Tom Browning's subject matter has changed over the years from wildlife to landscapes, still life to figure work. "I'm a little more romantic now," he admits. And that romance is evident in every Clothtique Santa Claus he creates.

SAM BUTCHER

Sam Butcher began his artistic career as a "chalk minister" using illustrations to teach young children about God. With the job's low pay and a young family to support, Sam supplemented his income by working as a janitor. From these humble beginnings, Sam Butcher has become one of the most popular artists in the world, and has been honored with various awards.

In the mid-1970s, one of Sam's friends encouraged him to share his artistic ministry: little teardrop-eyed, innocent and soulful-looking children named "Precious Moments." The little messengers would appear on a small line of greeting cards.

The new line was an instant hit at an International Christian Booksellers Association Annual Convention in Anaheim, California. It was the beginning of artistic and financial success for Sam.

While attending the College of Arts and Crafts in Berkeley, he met young Katie Cushman. Two years later, they were married. By 1974, they had seven children who have been a constant inspiration for Sam's *Precious Moments* art. At first, his drawings were only for family and friends, and they touched people with the simple inspirational messages Sam wrote.

It was in 1978 that Sam's cards and posters found their way into the hands of Enesco President and CEO Eugene Freedman, who recognized the potential for fine porcelain bisque figurines. Although Sam feared commercializing the inspirational aspect of his art, he ultimately agreed to allow Enesco to translate the drawings into figurines. Within a short time, the new *Precious Moments® Collection* became the number one collectible in the United States.

JOYCE F. BYERS

Joyce Fritz Byers developed an early sense of creative design. By the age of twelve, her artistic curiosity had expanded from sewing doll costumes to include sculpture and oil painting.

Joyce attended Drexel University, earning a degree in Home Economics. Her creative nature drew her towards fashion design, and upon graduation she took a position designing children's clothing.

By the late 1960s, Joyce had married Bob Byers and was living with their two sons in Bucks County, Pennsylvania.

Never without an artistic project, Joyce began making caroling Christmas figures, first for herself, and then as gifts for her family and friends. For about ten years, Joyce perfected the methods of construction and refined her sculpting skills.

In the late 1970s, the demand for the Carolers® figurines became so great that with Bob's assistance, they turned a Christmas hobby into a business.

Joyce has remained responsible for the creation of each character. She sculpts each original face in clay and designs the costumes for each of the hundreds of different figures they produce each year. She has taught artisans the skills necessary for quantity production, so that each Byers' Choice figurine is completely hand-made. It is this intensive handwork which imparts into each figurine the delightful personality sought by nearly 100,000 collectors.

The incredible success of Byers' Choice figurines has enabled Bob and Joyce to share the joy of giving in the true spirit of Christmas. Each year, they give more than twenty-five percent of their company's profits to charities.

LYNN BYWATERS

Born in Hartford, Connecticut, Lynn Bywaters traces her interest in becoming an illustrator to the time when she began reading fairy tales and fantasy books. The works of turn-of-the-century children's book illustrators such as Edmund Dulac, Kay Nellson, Edward

Detmold and Arthur Rackham were particularly influential to her work. She was also inspired by ancient Egyptian, Japanese, Renaissance and pre-Raphaelite artworks. Lynn studied art and illustration at Syracuse University, where she received a Bachelor of Fine Arts degree.

Whether her subject is an engaging furry animal, a mythological creature or a mother and child, there is an ever-present illusion of realism in each of Lynn's illustrations. Adding to this effect is the meticulous detail with which she portrays all aspects of her subjects and their surroundings. The texture of an animal's fur, the twinkle of an eye or the subtle shadings in a single blade of grass are expertly captured by her brush. Gouache, an opaque watercolor, is the medium she uses most often for her paintings. Clothtique® Santa Claus figurines by Possible Dreams, Ltd. are based on some of Lynn's illustrations.

Lynn now resides in Connecticut with her husband, an Akita dog and a small grey cat. When not working as a freelance illustrator, she enjoys reading science fiction and fantasy novels. Lynn loves animals, empty beaches and hiking in the White Mountains.

KITTY D. CANTRELL

Award-winning artist Kitty D. Cantrell conceives on canvas the visions she sculpturally incarnates for LEGENDS. In a style reminiscent of Remington and James, her work is a narrative of an artistic philosophy linked to the physical composite of the medium in which she creates.

Kitty Cantrell is a realist. Her sculpture is intricately detailed yet impressionistic, the dichotomy of which is realized in the intensity of her work.

Alienated from academia by professors who counselled, "Animals are not

art," Ms. Cantrell reinvested her tuition in supplies. The year was 1972. Since then, the California native has pursued her passion for wildlife through the accomplishment of her art.

Ms. Cantrell's freelance career has culminated in a technical proficiency in chasing, mold making, casting and patinas. She has achieved artistic maturity as a painter, mastering perception, line, depth and color; as a sculptor, volume, balance, tension and form.

Eloquently addressing the endangerment of our wildlife, Kitty Cantrell's discovery and definition of individual personality through the width of a brow and the slant of an eye has distinguished her with many prestigious awards.

A conservationist, she is active in the World Wildlife Fund, National Wildlife Federation, National Audubon Society, American Endangered Species Foundation, Grounded Eagle Foundation, Nature Conservancy and San Diego Zoologist Society. She strives to "draw attention to people's perception of what wildlife is for. Animals should not have to justify their existence. They should be allowed to be simply because they are."

The artist resides in Southern California with her husband, sculptor Eric Fredsti.

MIKE CAPSER

The openness of Mike Capser's art offers an expansive world for imaginations to explore. The graceful beauty of this imagery comes naturally to Capser who lives with his family under the wide and open skies of Montana.

Capser paints, draws and sculpts contemporary, western and wildlife subjects. A critical part of his work is based on painstaking research and inspiration from hunting, studying and sketching in the wild, untouched land of his childhood. He relies on much of his rich, personal experience with the West to get the right "feeling" for his subjects.

He has received numerous awards and honors for his paintings and has been accepted in many shows including the annual C. M. Russell Show in Great Falls, Montana and the prestigious Birds in Art Exhibition in Wausau, Wisconsin.

Several of Capser's images have been used by the National Wildlife Federation for Christmas cards. His artwork can be seen in galleries across the United States.

Mike Capser is represented by Hadley House.

ROBERT CHAD

Robert Chad began sculpting for Hallmark Keepsake Ornaments because he wanted to add another dimension to his drawing. Having worked as a printmaker and animator following college, Chad said, "I reached a point with my work where I felt I needed to do something different." Chad joined the Keepsake Ornament design staff in 1987.

Chad applies his attention to detail to a variety of subjects, including his personal favorites, elves. In 1990, he designed "Holiday Flash," a Keepsake Magic Ornament depicting an elf photographer holding a flashing camera.

Chad also created "Dickens Caroler Bell—Mr. Ashbourne," the 1990 Special Edition, and "Perfect Fit," a Miniature ornament. His 1992 creations include "Elfin Marionette," an Artists' Favorites design.

Above all, Chad strives to bring realism to his designs. "I think the nicest compliment would be for someone to look at one of my ornaments and feel as if (it) could come to life."

PAT CHANDOK AND DAVE WOODARD

From up-and-down carousels to safari animals, Pat Chandok and David Lee Woodard have spent fifteen years originating giftware products. After completing her education in Bombay, Pat moved to the United States and opened her first gift shop in Ann Arbor, Michigan. She relied on her marketing skills and knowledge of foreign cultures to mix different product lines to create a shop of unique flavor. In 1977, David Lee Woodard joined with Pat to expand her shops. David brought years of marketing and sales experience and was a great match for Pat's areas of expertise.

In 1980, Pat and Dave started importing their first quality giftware items. Through their shops, they became more and more interested in the collectibles industry and began to produce limited edition art. This led them to produce limited edition plates, carousels and figurines.

In 1987, they presented the *World of Krystonia* to the market. Pat and Dave have been hard at work creating new characters ever since. This award-winning line of a whimsical kingdom takes constant care, so Pat and Dave make sure it gets plenty of it. Whether they are involved in creating characters or making up a storyline, every step is carefully taken.

They are blessed to be working with a group of talented English artists. Sculptor Bob Worthington, master painter Phil Bryan and accomplished writer Mark Scott work closely with Pat and Dave to bring each *Krystonia* character to life. With three Krystonian books on the market and a fourth in the works, Pat and Dave are ready to take *Krystonia* collectors to the next level in this wonderful world of make-believe.

LILY CHANG

Following in the wake of *Petal Pals*, her first collector's plate series, the new and elegant *Gardens of Paradise* collection should firmly establish Lily Chang as a true plate-market star.

Ms. Chang studied art with several distinguished Chinese watercolor masters when she was very young. Early success, a first prize from Taipei's International Women's Fine Arts Contest in the flowers and birds category, inspired her to paint in her leisure time. Professionally, she pursued a career in the sciences. She received a Master's Degree in Environmental Engineering at the University of New York at Buffalo and taught environmental science and engineering in Taiwan for many years.

After permanently moving to the United States, Lily Chang became a full-time artist. Soon she was winning award after award at juried art exhibitions. Ms. Chang now lives in Gainesville and is a member of the Gainesville Fine Arts Association and the Center of Modern Art.

The artist's early professional interest and great love of nature is evident in all her graceful works, and no artist could work with a better combination of tools than Ms. Chang — her trained scientist's eye and her artist's sensitive hands. Now with her *Gardens of Paradise*

collection, Ms. Chang, for the first time, marries the delicacy of her original painting on silk with the magnificence of a decorative triple border and 22-karat gold overlay translated onto a fine porcelain collector's plate. The Bradford Exchange is proud to present collectors with this important and innovative series.

MARCI COHEN

Doll artist, Marci Cohen works full-time at home in her studio in Freehold, New Jersey, creating original porcelain dolls. Marci began collecting dolls when she was about three, then started making crafts at five or six years of age. She attended the Fashion Institute of Technology in New York City, but did not immediately pursue dollmaking, except as a hobby.

Cohen's growing skills and experience have carried her through stuffed, clay and eventually ceramic dolls. But the ultimate step was to porcelain. She says she started making porcelain dolls a little more than a year ago so that she could add to her collection without spending a fortune. Since then, she has made about eighty, including five dolls for Cardinal Inc.'s Dynasty Doll Collection™ — "Katy," "Poppy," "Poppy Jo," "Tory" and "Tami."

These and all of Marci's creations are very lifelike and crafted to appear similar to antique porcelain dolls. It is no wonder that her works are so popular with doll collectors.

JULIE KRAMER COLE

After graduating from the Colorado Institute of Art, Julie Kramer Cole sketched her way through many years of working as a freelance fashion illustrator

in Denver. And now, after twelve successful years in Western art, she and her husband Mark own their own limited edition print company. Ms. Cole is recognized as one of the foremost Western artists specializing in hidden nature art.

Originally from Ohio and now living in Loveland, Colorado, Ms. Cole is descended from Irish and German stock. But it was her Cherokee stepfather who enriched her life, she says, with his stories of Indian ways.

Subsequent explorations of Native American culture and spirituality led Ms. Cole to the mystical themes she has portrayed in her work over the past decade.

"I've found working in this genre very rewarding, because of the way hidden elements of nature draw the viewer in. There's nothing quite like it to get people involved," says the award-winning Ms. Cole.

This type of art is fun and it sparks conversation — two inviting features certain to charm plate collectors. Add Julie Kramer Cole's fine portraiture skill — her magical depictions of native American life — and you have extraordinary treasures to cherish for years to come! Her two plate collections are *Faces of Nature* and *Touching the Spirit*, available from The Bradford Exchange.

JOSE FCO. "PACO" CONTRERAS

Jose Fco. "Paco" Contreras was born on January 8, 1945 in Pueblà Mexico. Moving to Mexico City, he studied professionally at the National Plastics San Carlos of the National University Autonomy of Mexico, graduating in graphic design.

Having done clay modeling since high school, Paco's first job was related to creating commercial figures. In 1977, he joined other friends and artists to

form Creaciones and Reproduciones Artisticas (Creart). At the same time, Paco studied drawing under Maestro Jose Luis Cuevas and artistic anatomy under Maestro Emilio Castaneda. After ten years, Paco left the company to dedicate his time to ceramics, working with Maestro Soledad Hernandez.

Paco's works have been exhibited in many museums and universities including the Sciences and Humanity College Library, Studio of San Pedro Tlahuac, University Museum, "House of the Dolls," The National Plastics San Carlos of The National University of Autonomy of Mexico and The Bachilleres College.

In 1992, Paco Contreras returned to Creart with a renewed spirit and many new ideas.

DOUGLAS CORSINI

Grandson of an Italian woodcarver, Douglas Corsini has already made a greater impact in the world of art in his early years than most sculptors achieve in a lifetime. He is regularly commissioned to do private works for prominent organizations in Europe and America, including BAND Creations.

In his *Angel of the Month* bell series,

Douglas Corsini captures a wonder and pleasure for individuals to enjoy for a lifetime. Cast in solid pewter and hand-finished, the bells are enriched with a high polished finish. This type of excellent workmanship makes Corsini's bells outstanding art objects for collectors to enjoy and treasure for many years to come.

KEN CROW

Ken Crow recalls the very first glimpse he got of the Hallmark Keepsake Ornament department and remembers that he "got the same chills, the same feelings as a kid going to Disneyland for the first time." His dream of becoming a Hallmark artist came true when he joined the staff of designers who create Keepsake Ornaments.

He has since created some of the line's most fascinating designs. In 1991 he created "Arctic Dome," a Keepsake Magic Ornament depicting a festive football game. Ken, who worked as a cartoonist before joining Hallmark, drew the caricatures of the fans in the stands. His other designs include "Santa's Ho-Ho-Hoedown," "Cool Swing," "Santa's Woody" and "Club Hollow," a Collectors' Club ornament.

Crow's fascination with toys and ornaments with motion shows up in designs like "Hidden Treasure," another Collectors' Club Keepsake design. He is a native of Long Beach, California.

MARGE CRUNKLETON

Marge Crunkleton was well-known as the creator of a distinctive collection of rag dolls when she was struck by an idea for a Christmas collection one holiday season.

"I was watching a young father and his toddler waiting in line to see Santa one day at the local mall, and it

occurred to me that parents are the real Santa's helpers, because they make Santa come alive for their children." Reasoning that all those helpers have to get their training somewhere, she "founded" *The Christmas Academy* for Schmid.

Like her rag dolls, the faces of Marge's "Crunkle Clauses" (as she likes to call them) are modeled after people she has met in her life. "This way, these people become a part of my life, and I become a part of theirs," she says.

When she's not adding to *The Christmas Academy*'s roster with more creations, Marge is absorbed in her duties as proprietor of an authentic General Store in historic Murray's Mill, North Carolina. Built in 1860, this charming site boasts a working grist mill with a 28-foot water wheel, dam and waterfall. Of course, all her dolls and figurines are in her studio. "It's like an imaginary world where kids, young and old, can still come and buy penny candy, only now it costs a nickel," she chuckles. "It doesn't really matter anyway, because it's the fun that counts."

And making life a little more fun is what Marge Crunkleton is all about.

KEVIN DANIEL

Kevin Daniel's artwork spans a wide variety of subjects, as he renders each wildlife scene with his own special blend of realism and impressionism. In the hauntingly beautiful *Treasures of Life Collection*, his art has attracted a wide and growing body of collectors.

Kevin Daniel has been awarded many honors including the 1991 Minnesota Wildlife Heritage Foundation Artist of the Year, 1987 North American Limited Edition Dealers Artist of

the Year for collector plates, winner of the 1990 Minnesota Duck Stamp competition and Best of Show awards at the Kansas City National Wildlife Art Show and the Oklahoma Wildlife Festival.

Daniel was born and raised in Minneapolis, Minnesota. He can be seen, camera in hand, exploring the Minnesota River bottoms near his home, or shopping for antiques to authenticate his *Treasures of Life* paintings.

Kevin Daniel is represented by Hadley House.

LOWELL DAVIS

Painter and sculptor Lowell Davis appreciates the nostalgic search by Americans for the "good ol' days." When the droughts of the 1930s caused his father to lose the family farm in Red Oak, Missouri, the Davis family moved into quarters behind his uncle's general store. There, under the guidance of his grandpa, Lowell learned to draw and whittle.

As a young man, Davis left this peaceful setting for Dallas and a job as art director in a major advertising agency. Yet, he longed for the simple life of his childhood and soon returned home. He restored a 1930s-era house on a ram-

bling farm in Carthage, Missouri, and set to work capturing on canvas, porcelain and bronze, the every-day events of rural life. Lowell's work has always been imbued with old-fashioned values and the good humor of a gentler time. Schmid recognized Davis' talent and began to produce his complete line of figurines, limited edition plates and other collectibles.

Lowell also spent much of his time reconstructing his boyhood town of Red Oak, which had virtually disappeared in his absence. He moved several Red Oak homes and businesses to a huge site near his farm, restoring them to their original beauty. Lowell called the place Red Oak II, and it is now complete with almost all of the buildings and shops of the first Red Oak town.

Explains Lowell: "This place represents the good life. By preserving it, I can keep the solid values of that time alive for future generations."

RAY DAY

Since 1973, Ray Day has painted America's rural landscapes in watercolor and published limited editions of his originals.

From 1986, Ray's watercolors have also been published on limited edition porcelain plates. Enthusiastic collectors responded by presenting him "Best of Show" awards at the International Plate and Collectibles shows both in South Bend and Pasadena.

Today, Ray Day's watercolors continue to bring enjoyment to collectors who find pleasure in the nostalgic and historic. He finds inspiration all over America...from coast to coast...from noted landmarks to hidden treasures.

At the invitation of Lilliput Lane, one of the world's finest makers of collectible cottages, Ray is creating the *American Landmarks* collection. He sculpts each building in wax, then sends

it to the Lilliput Lane Studios in Penrith, England, where molding, casting and painting take place. The finished miniatures, based on actual locations, are available in collectible stores throughout the United States and abroad.

Ray Day has spent thirty-one years teaching high school art and theater. In addition, he and his wife Eileen continue to publish his watercolors from their southern Indiana home. Their daughter, Jennifer, who is a graphic artist, is currently pursuing a career in Art Education.

Ray serves on the Rural Landmarks Council of the Historic Landmarks Foundation in Indiana. He regularly encourages collectors to join protective societies, both local and national. "At least join the National Trust for Historic Preservation," he says, "to be informed of preservation needs and efforts throughout the country."

CHUCK DEHAAN

As a young man in the '60s, Chuck DeHaan was torn between two careers. He loved the outdoor life of a horse trainer, and being a cowboy seemed like second nature to him. But he also recognized his talent for art, and he did not neglect this special gift.

When he was only fourteen, he ran away from home to follow the rodeo circuit, but even in those early horse training days, DeHaan always kept pencils and sketch pads close at hand. Because he never had a formal studio or even a drawing table or easel, he learned to work anywhere. To this day, DeHaan doesn't use photos or models; his art comes "out of his head" just as it did during those rodeo days.

Chuck DeHaan first turned his complete attention to art in 1965. He ini-

tially ran a successful advertising agency specializing in the horse world. But art lovers realized that this painter had something much too special to be relegated to ad illustrations. A cover for *Western Horseman* magazine brought in so many offers, that he couldn't keep up with his commercial art.

In 1979, DeHaan agreed to create his first limited edition prints. He has since risen to the top of his art profession and has been honored with a Golden Spur Award, two "Artist of the Year" awards and the titles of "State Artist of Texas" and "Top Western Artist" in the country.

All the glory and beauty Chuck DeHaan sees in horses were brought together in his first painting for the collector plate medium, "Surf Dancer," created for The Hamilton Collection in 1992.

Recently Hamilton delighted collectors by introducing DeHaan's dramatic new issue titled "Winter Renegade." And once again, this renowned artist exhibits his remarkable ability to capture the majesty and drama of his favorite subject — the powerful and graceful horse.

CHIP DEMATTEO

Chip deMatteo began his apprenticeship when he was still a boy. He grew up in a restored home in Colonial Williamsburg and each morning watched his father, William deMatteo, set off for his silversmith's shop on the grounds of Williamsburg.

As a child, Chip enjoyed spending time in his father's shop, and by the time he was ten, he was actually doing small jobs for his father. Eventually, Chip went to college where he studied art. After completing his education, Chip spent a few years as a "starving artist" in Washington, D.C., all the

while supplementing his income with silver work for his father.

In the late 1970s, Chip, his father and a partner Philip Thorp formed Hand & Hammer Silversmiths in Alexandria, Virginia. Since 1981, Chip has been the sole designer for Hand & Hammer where he has created more than 400 ornament designs.

Using the "lost-wax" technique, Chip has designed a number of highly sought-after series. Especially popular are the *Bell, Santa,* and *Carousel* series, in addition to the *Beatrix Potter, Night Before Christmas* and *Victorian Village* collections.

BRIGITTE DEVAL

Brigitte Deval has been creating dolls since she was six years old. While growing up in Bavaria watching her father, a well-known portrait photographer, she became skilled in many art forms. She became a talented portrait artist and sculptress. Early on, Brigitte chose to focus on the creation of dolls because of their similarity to real life.

Brigitte is truly one of the worlds' best loved doll artists. Collectors will find her works of art displayed at the finest shows and galleries in the United States and Europe. Several of her creations have graced the windows of Tiffany's.

Her vision of childhood portrayed in one-of-a-kind dolls has established a following of collectors willing to pay thousands of dollars to own just one of her original designs.

A master at her craft, Brigitte loves to search the souls of children. In their tiny features, she finds the soft, tender expressions of innocence and love unique to the very young. These are the lines and shadows that she works so skillfully into her wax-over-porcelain creations. The wax gives a wonderful translucent quality to the "skin" and

makes the expression come alive.

Brigitte spends much of her time traveling in the United States and Europe, attending shows and exhibitions. When not on the road, she spends time with her family in her beautiful home outside Sienna, Italy. It is here that she is inspired to create new and beautiful dolls.

WALT DISNEY

© The Walt Disney Company

During a forty-three year Hollywood career, which spanned the development of the motion picture medium as a modern American art, Walter Elias Disney, a modern Aesop, established himself and his product as a genuine part of Americana. David Low, the late British cartoonist, called Disney "the most significant figure in graphic arts since Leonardo."

A pioneer and innovator, and the possessor of one of the most fertile imaginations the world has ever known, Walt Disney, along with members of his staff, received more than 950 honors and citations from every nation in the world, including forty-eight Academy Awards and seven Emmys in his lifetime. Walt Disney's personal awards included honorary degrees from Harvard, Yale, the University of Southern California and UCLA; the Presidential Medal of Freedom; France's Legion of Honor and Officer d'Academie decorations; Thailand's Order of the Crown; Brazil's Order of the Southern Cross; Mexico's Order of the Aztec Eagle; and the Showman of the World Award from the National Association of Theatre Owners.

Walt Disney's worldwide popularity was based upon the ideas which his name represents: imagination, optimism and self-made success in the American tradition. He did more to touch the hearts, minds and emotions of millions

of Americans than any other man in the past century. Through his work, he brought joy, happiness and a universal means of communication to the people of every nation. Certainly, our world shall know but one Walt Disney.

Today, his legend lives on through programs such as the *Walt Disney Classics Collection*, which embodies the same storytelling and entertainment philosophies originally instilled by Walt Disney.

MAX DUNCAN

In recent years, collectors throughout the United States have met the driving force behind the "stories that never end..." — Max Duncan, founder and president of Duncan Royale. Max travels throughout the United States making appearances at Duncan Royale dealer galleries. His itinerary includes television interviews, radio spots, signature sessions, seminars and visits with many collectors. Max enjoys these personal meetings with collectors and has planned several promotional tours.

Born in Indiana, Max moved to California as a toddler and only lightly claims the "Hoosier" status. A Navy veteran from World War II, Max graduated from Woodbury College in Los Angeles in 1952, with a Bachelor of Arts degree in advertising and public relations. After five years with the Sunbeam Corporation, he began his successful career in the visual arts, advertising and giftware industry.

Known for his innovation and creativity, his enthusiasm and a warm personality, Max masterminded and developed the concept of Duncan Royale collections with an eye toward serious collectors everywhere. His subjects are familiar to most of us and often reveal how little we know about some-

thing we know well — but do we? The character and charisma embodied in each Duncan Royale personality — whether Santa Claus, clowns, entertainers, fairies, people of the Scriptures, early Americans or others — challenge us to discover deeper meanings to things we often take for granted.

What is next? Rest assured that Max Duncan has some lofty new ideas. You will be hearing from your favorite storyteller, because the stories "never end!"

DIANNA EFFNER

Dianna Effner brings an unusual sensitivity and depth of emotion to the dollmaking world. By selecting children's characters as the subject of her dolls, Ms. Effner has found the freedom to explore the world of fantasy and inner feelings.

As a child, Ms. Effner made dolls from old socks and papier-mâché. Later, she studied sculpture at Bradley University where she earned her degree in Fine Arts. Ms. Effner then began making her dolls in porcelain because it allowed her more control over the process of creating lifelike features.

Today, Dianna Effner's dolls are part of private collections across the U.S. Her first doll for Knowles China, "Little Red Riding Hood" from the *Heroines of the Fairy Tale Forests*, was nominated for an Award of Excellence by *Dolls* magazine in 1989 and a Doll Achievement Award from The National Association of Limited Edition Dealers in 1990. "The Little Girl With A Curl," from Dianna Effner's latest series, *Mother Goose*, won the 1992 Dolls of Excellence Award from *Dolls* magazine. Both of these collections of limited edition dolls are available from The Ashton-Drake Galleries.

BRUCE EMMETT

Artist Bruce Emmett, who first gained plate-world fame with his *Elvis Presley: Looking at a Legend* series, has since created two additional collections marketed by The Bradford Exchange: *Elvis Presley: In Performance* and *Elvis on the Big Screen*.

He spent hours studying Elvis movies and documentary tapes and thousands of photographs — many of them extremely rare — and listened over and over again to the classic recordings of the music that made Elvis Presley a legend.

Emmett has always been interested in both art and Elvis Presley, buying his first Elvis recording in 1956 when he was seven, and drawing pictures and sketches from his earliest childhood. He received his fine-art training from Syracuse University, and graduated in 1973 with a Bachelor of Fine Arts degree.

As a professional illustrator and portraitist, Emmett has created art for many distinguished clients, including *Reader's Digest*, ABC, NBC, CBS, Ralph Lauren, publishers Harper and Row, Macmillan, Dell, Avon, Berkley, Warner, Zebra and Scholastic Books. He has also created posters for such Broadway hits as "Sugar Babies" and "The Gin Game." His work has been exhibited in several prestigious Society of Illustrators annual shows. Emmett lives and works in New York.

JUAN FERRANDIZ

Born in Barcelona, Spain, Ferrandiz first studied at the Belles Artes School in Barcelona. He continued to refine his artistic style through classes in private art schools and through self-teaching.

Ferrandiz still considers his artistic development unfinished. For the past few years he has followed a career as a Professor of Art at the Industrial University while devoting himself to the

386

design of his special love, youthful themes. His subjects include various small animals, always united as symbols of fraternity in harmony with the innocence of childhood. His style may be expressed as a kind of freshness, almost exploding into a feeling of juvenile tenderness and vitality. The complete works of Ferrandiz are directed to create a world of love, of comprehension and understanding, of poetry, of unity in aspirations, of banishment of hatred, and of peace in the world with an honest message.

Today, Ferrandiz lives simply, yet happily in a villa that overlooks his beloved Barcelona. He is very much the true Renaissance man, the quintessential cultured European — a man for all seasons, who has created a vocabulary of expression, a world within which he lives, that is distinctly his own. Ferrandiz is a poet, a painter, an author and an illustrator of children's books as well.

CHARLES FRACÉ

Surprisingly, the illustrious career of Charles Fracé began by chance. In 1962, photographer Shelley Grossman invited Fracé to work as an assistant on a Florida wildlife assignment. Working alongside Grossman and respected natu-

ralist John Hamlet, Fracé developed a reverence for the wonders of nature. In fact, Fracé recollects that it was the beauty of the outdoor world which had first inspired him to draw as a child on eastern Pennsylvania's Bear Mountain.

Upon his return from Florida, Fracé worked ten-hour days in his studio, and he traveled into the wild to live alongside his subjects. Soon, he was earning recognition as a respected illustrator of wildlife.

Fracé's work has been featured in over 300 one-man shows throughout the United States and Canada. He has been honored by a number of prestigious museums, including the Denver Museum of Natural History and the Leigh Yawkey Woodson Art Museum. Additionally, the artist has spent several weeks each year appearing at exhibits and visiting with collectors.

To commemorate twenty-five years as a wildlife artist, Fracé established the Fracé Fund for Wildlife Preservation in 1987. This organization has made funds available to the Atlanta Zoo, the Carnivore Preservation Trust and other organizations dedicated to preserving the balance of nature. The non-profit fund is subsidized through the sale of Fracé's highly valued Artist's Proofs.

Fracé's work has also been reproduced on six plate series available from The Bradford Exchange. His most recent collections are *Winter's Majesty* and *Grand Safari: Images of Africa*.

Throughout most of the year, Fracé is found hard at work in his studio. There, he is close to his wife and sons — and close to nature. Fracé remains committed to his belief in the power of art, stating, "My goal is to strive to be even better, to push each painting a step further."

OZZ FRANCA

Born in Brazil, Ozz Franca as a young boy displayed precocious artistic talents.

At age fourteen, he won a first prize at the "Spring Salon" show in Sao Paulo, and four years later held his first one-man show. After graduating from art school, he traveled to the United States on a scholarship, and eventually moved to Hollywood, California.

His work has covered many subjects, but he is perhaps best known for his sensitive portraits of both historical and contemporary American Indians. Franca's paintings hang in the collections of many prominent entertainment and political figures, and he was twice honored by his adopted city of Los Angeles for his cultural contributions.

Although an American citizen, Franca drew his inspiration from both cultures, and spent time each year in the United States and Brazil. Ozz Franca died in November, 1991. His works are published by Hadley House.

JOHN FRANCIS

John Francis constantly draws on his love of animals, the outdoors and his native Casper, Wyoming, when designing Hallmark Keepsake Ornaments. That influence shows in the many Keepsake Ornaments he has created.

John designed "Baby Partridge" and "The Animals Speak," a 1989 lighted Keepsake Magic Ornament. That same year he sculpted several of the ornaments in the *Teddy Bear Years Collection*. Two favorite childhood pets inspired John's "Tramp and Laddie," an Artists' Favorites design from 1991. In reality Tramp was a tiny kitten who wandered into John's yard and was protected from a stray dog by his pet Scottish collie named Laddie.

John attended Hastings College in Hastings, Nebraska, where he decided to change his major from engineering to art. He worked in various departments at Hallmark before joining the Keepsake Ornament staff. He signs his

Artists' Favorites and other ornaments with "Collin," his middle name.

MARGARET FURLONG

Margaret Furlong Alexander combines her "commitment to personal values and spiritual values" with her wonderful artistic gifts in producing the beautiful white porcelain angels, stars and other designs for her company, Margaret Furlong Designs.

Margaret's love affair with white began when she started sculpting abstract snowscapes in Nebraska in the '70s. Furlong's first angel ornament appeared in 1979, after she combined several shell forms, a molded face, a textured coil and a tapered trumpet into a "shell angel," rare in its unshaded and unglazed porcelain medium.

Since then she has married, moved to Seattle and then to Salem, Oregon, where her business is now thriving and she and her husband Jerry Alexander are raising their daughter Caitlin. Along the way she has built both a life and a company that reflect her Christian values and spirit of fun.

Margaret divides her time between her home studio and the Carriage House Studio, located five minutes away, though she always works her schedule around her daughter. Her staff of forty-eight now produces over 120 different designs, which are sold throughout the country in collectible, Christmas, fine gift and department stores.

Margaret views each new design as a gift from God that she can enjoy along with all of her collectors. Somehow it seems appropriate that an angel maker would try to share her own happiness with those closest to her. And Margaret Furlong's genuineness, wisdom and joy are worth sharing, both as visions of pure white angels and as an example for others.

W.D. GAITHER

W.D. "Bill" Gaither is a multifaceted artist with thousands of paintings and prints on display in galleries and private collections all over America. In addition to his work in the limited edition art realm, Gaither is actively involved in dozens of environmental and wildlife conservation organizations, reflecting his consuming interest in animals and birds.

As a sculptor and painter, Gaither's special gift stems from his immersion in the world of wildlife. His workshops hold books on a myriad of subjects, mounted specimens, dozens of sketches and partially completed sculptures.

The artist prides himself on creating works which are always active, fluid and alive — never static or frozen. His wildlife studies reflect a living moment in time in the animal's life in the wild — feeding, running, attacking, playing, leaping, soaring or charging.

Gaither's first sculpture in association with the Maruri Studio premiered in 1982. In just two years' time, his "American Bald Eagle II" rose in value from $165 to $600. Since then, wildlife art connoisseurs eagerly await each Maruri introduction — many of which sell out immediately and begin rising in value.

JAN GALPERIN

Jan Galperin began her art career earlier than most people. Her father was an artist, and when she was very small, he would let her hold the paint brush and "paint" on his canvases. Little did he know that his little girl would grow up to be a very talented sculptress and doll artist.

While in art school, Jan focused on

sculpture and fashion design. After graduating, she got the rather unlikely job of courtroom illustrator. This experience was a great opportunity to study faces and expressions.

Jan studied sculpting with the world-renowned sculptor Ronald van Ruyckevelt whose instruction was instrumental to her success. For many years, Jan anonymously sculpted for several major porcelain companies. In 1992 she brought her first doll to the New York Toy Fair, and shortly thereafter, she began working with the Georgetown Collection on a series of reproduction dolls.

In 1992, Georgetown introduced her first doll, "Grace," from the *Hearts in Song*™ collection. "Grace" depicts a little girl singing "Amazing Grace," a song that has great meaning to many people.

In addition to sculpting full-time, Jan is the mother of two children. They now dabble in the arts at her side, just as she did when she was their age. They are her source of inspiration, and she hopes her dolls are positive role models for them and an inspiration to all.

PETER GEE

Peter Gee, the sculptor who has created both the Gainsborough and

Reynolds collections, became a Royal Doulton modeler almost by accident. In 1973, at age seventeen, he applied for a job as caster at Royal Crown Derby, but created a good deal of interest when he showed some models on which he had worked at school. The art director of Royal Doulton was called in to examine the young sculptor's work, and as a result, Peter was apprenticed to the Royal Doulton Design Studios.

Peter has shown his versatility with contributions to most of Royal Doulton's sculptural ranges, including a Figure of the Year piece, a unique collectible representing the Jazz Era, and collections of figurines based on portraits by two famous English artists.

The idea for the *Gainsborough Ladies* collection was originally just one suggestion put forward by Peter for a new "family" of figures in the late 1980s. The decision to follow the successful *Gainsborough Ladies* with a collection of figures based on the work of Reynolds arose from the great rivalry enjoyed by the two artists in the 18th century.

Peter expresses himself as "very pleased" with the results of his ambitious project to reinterpret the art of two of Britain's greatest portraitists. While there are no definite plans for any future collections in this vein, Peter would love to work on further subjects by the two artists. In the meantime, collectors can certainly look forward to more exciting new figures in the years to come from this talented and versatile modeler.

NATE GIORGIO

At age twenty-nine, Nate Giorgio has already made a name for himself in the fine arts arena. He has created commissioned artwork of some of our most famous celebrities, including Michael Jackson, Quincy Jones, Madonna, Prince and Johnny Cash.

While Giorgio never studied art formally, by age twenty-two he already had an agent and was creating illustrations for advertisements, movie posters and book covers. It is no wonder, then, that his work caught the interest of collectibles companies such as The Bradford Exchange. Giorgio's world-tour program cover and 1989 calendar for Michael Jackson was enthusiastically received, and led him to create not only many posters for the movie industry and logos

for entertainment companies, but also numerous pieces for collectors throughout the United States and England.

Working in mixed media, including oils, pastels and watercolors, Mr. Giorgio explores and celebrates the spirit of the entertainer — his favorite subject. Giorgio describes his celebrity paintings as character studies, not portraits. "It's not photographic or realistic. I try to really capture their personalities," says the artist. The results are fantasy-like compositions where faces burst out of sunlit settings or celebrities appear to float over surreal cityscapes. His plate series have also captured some of rock music's legendary entertainers. They are *The Beatles Collection* and *The Elvis Presley Hit Parade*. Both are available from The Bradford Exchange.

MARK GOENA

Mark Goena, a sixth generation Californian, was raised in a talented family of amateur artists. Mr. Goena has been designing figurines for Iris Arc Crystal since 1986. Before specializing in crystal, he worked in ceramic, metal, stone and wood. His work in metal and stone continues.

With a Bachelors degree in Fine Arts from the University of California/Davis and a strong technical background, Mr. Goena combines his skills to create designs with a unique combination of creativity and craftsmanship. From the historical charm of architectural designs to the warm appeal of the *Romance Collection*, the ability of his designs to evoke emotion contributes to their popularity. A sense of movement, as seen in his sports figures, also brings many of his designs to life. His floral designs sparkle with the brilliant color and fine detail which have become Iris Arc trademarks.

Examples of Mr. Goena's greatest

artistic achievements include recognition by the Corning Museum of Glass for his colorful "Country Cottage" and designing the exquisite "Rainbow Crystal Cathedral." This one-of-a-kind masterpiece is comprised of over 2,000 component parts with 24,634 facets, weighs 63½ pounds and required over 500 hours of design time.

From miniatures to limited editions to one-of-a-kind masterpieces, Mark Goena's dedication to quality design and craftsmanship has produced figurines of consistently high value and lasting beauty.

JULIE GOOD-KRÜGER

For Julie Good-Krüger, creating an Amish doll seems perfectly natural. After all, Julie and her husband Tim live in a renovated stone grist mill in Strasburg, Pennsylvania, which is in the very heart of Lancaster County's Amish community.

Julie's interest in dolls goes back to childhood when her grandmother gave her some antique dolls. In high school, she enjoyed reading doll magazines and creating small sculptures on plaques. Her interest in dolls waned during her college years, but in the late 1970s, she began experimenting with dollmaking, hoping to earn extra money for graduate school.

She spent three years learning to make dolls before she allowed anyone to see her work. In 1980, her lifelike child dolls were introduced to the public. Over the past decade, Julie has earned the admiration of her peers and collectors. Her dolls have won numerous awards, and in 1988 and 1989 Ms. Good-Krüger's dolls were nominated for "Doll of the Year" (DOTY) Awards.

Amish Blessings is Julie Good-Krüger's first doll series for The Ashton-Drake

Galleries. "In *Amish Blessings*, I've attempted to capture as authentically as possible the love these special people have for their children and the traditions they hold close to their hearts," the artist said.

JUNE AMOS GRAMMER

Art has always been an integral part of June Amos Grammer's life. Born in New Jersey, her family moved to Texas, where she graduated from the art school of Texas A & M. She married her high school sweetheart, artist George Grammer, and moved to New York City to pursue a career as a fashion illustrator. Her exciting career included modeling and illustrating for fashion magazines such as *Harper's Bazaar*, serving as art director for a Franklin Simon store and teaching at Parson's School of Design in New York.

After a twenty-year career in fashion, she decided it was time for a career change. In 1982, she was asked to illustrate a children's book titled *Mary Anne* by Mary Mapes Dodge. The story, which describes a little girl given a doll without clothing, unfolds with the girl creating a beautiful wardrobe for her favorite charge. This assignment helped June launch her career as a doll designer.

She went on to design dolls for the Lenox Gallery of Gifts, and her illustrations were also used by Lenox to create a set of children's china. She was commissioned by Schmid to create a musical doll series, and she designed a line of giftwrap for the Steven Lawrence Company.

Recently she has signed with Seymour Mann, Inc. to manufacture her doll originals in the firm's *Signature Series*. Among her most recent collectible doll designs is "Nikki," the first in a series of *Tiny Tots*.

JUDITH ANN GRIFFITH

Judith Ann Griffith's home is in the wooded Ozark mountains of Arkansas. The studio and garden where she lives and works are ongoing creations of native stone, wood and flora to which she and her many friends have contributed their imaginations.

Love for nature has always been Judith's inspiration. "I am awed at the exquisite delicacy and power of a bird's wing; at the intensity of the green light within the forest; at how all the elements of nature can reflect aspects within

in ourselves, and at how we reap what we sow within our own cycles," says Judith.

Her artwork celebrates a deep reverence for life and for the beauty and peace which truly exist on earth. She hopes that her art is an inspiration for others to work in love and harmony for the well-being of life on this planet.

Judith Ann Griffith has applied her talents to the Clothtique® Originals from Possible Dreams. Her "Tree Planter" represents a Santa Claus figurine, perfect for the environmentally conscious '90s.

JOKE GROBBEN

Joke Grobben is certainly one of the world's most talented doll artists, creating her amazing "little people" (or Kinderpoppen) from methods that can only be described as inspired. Although she was formally trained in the classical technique familiar to most sculptors, the beautiful dolls which she now produces in her famed studio in Holland have evolved from a technique entirely self-developed and non-traditional.

After studying sculpture at the Vriju (or "Free") Academy on The Hague, Joke gave her first public exhibition in 1978 from the prestigious *Hotel des*

Indes, which proved an immediate success. She completed a doll-like figure of a child on the request of an enthralled collector, thereafter deciding to devote the entirety of her career to this type of "ultimate portraiture."

Since that time, in addition to constantly creating new works for her ongoing European exhibits, she has also established the famed studio from which she conducts lectures and hands-on dollmaking courses in three languages for students from around the world.

As if these accomplishments weren't enough, Joke has also authored several how-to/pattern books on her trend-setting style of dollmaking. Yet she still finds time to approach each of her commissions with true sculptor's zeal, sculpting by hand and sewing the bodies and costumes. Finally, she crowns each completed Kinderpoppen with a wig fashioned from real hair. An original Grobben doll is obviously unique unto itself.

Recently, The Hamilton Collection introduced Joke Grobben's North American premier porcelain doll — the darling "Heather." A stunning collector doll, "Heather's" sweet and thoughtful expression resulted in her nomination for the 1993 DOTY award.

JOHN GROSSMAN

"I feel a tremendous responsibility to conserve and preserve these old images," artist John Grossman says of his 200,000-piece collection of Victorian paper keepsakes. But as an artist, I also love taking an old design and transforming it into something new."

John began drawing at ten, and majored in art at a commercial high school in his native Des Moines. After attending the Minneapolis School of Art on scholarship, Grossman worked as

a lettering artist in San Francisco. Studies at the Cours de la Civilization Francais at the Sorbonne in Paris helped hone his skills further.

Back in San Francisco, Grossman worked as a graphic designer until he embarked on his career as a fine artist. Several major showings led to his appointment to the California Arts Commission as vice-chair, and later as chair. Grossman enjoyed his life as a painter of California landscapes, but he met a turning point nearly twenty years ago when he lost his heart to Victoriana.

With his gift for art and his natural appreciation for "all things Victorian," Grossman has been able to assemble and share his remarkable collection of antique Victorian keepsakes and mementos. Like the Victorians of a century ago, Grossman arranges and rearranges these antiques to create his own appealing collages. Until now, these Victorian keepsake collages had never before been made available to collectors in the form of limited edition plates. But under the commission of The Hamilton Collection, John created collages specifically for the porcelain medium, entitled *Romantic Victorian Keepsakes*.

Then, in joyous celebration of a festive Victorian Christmas, John Grossman created another extraordinary plate series of porcelain collages entitled *Victorian Christmas Memories*. Beginning with "A Visit From St. Nicholas," each collage in the collection is rich in holiday tradition.

EGIDIO GUERRA

From his birth in 1941, Egidio Guerra found himself surrounded by the beauties of Capodimonte. Inspired by the 200-year-old traditions of his ancestors, young Guerra began modeling flowers and other art objects at a very early age. When he was admitted to the Art Institute of Bassano, he concentrated on floral design. Over the years, his genius was cultivated until he was able to achieve a level of realism and beauty that rivals nature's own.

Renowned throughout Italy as a premier floral sculptor, Guerra has been called upon to participate in national and international competitions for more than two decades. He participated in the Floral Art Exhibit in New York in 1970, in Utrecht (Holland) in both 1971 and 1972, in Madrid in 1974 and the National Artisan Exhibits in Milan in 1979. He was awarded top prizes in all of these exhibitions, and has been called upon several times to render exotic flowers for the National Botanical Association.

Egidio Guerra has been the master sculptor of Napoleon S.N.C., Flero, Italy since 1969. All of the floral designs distributed by Napoleon Studios are created by Egidio Guerra and are either made entirely by him or from molds and forms created by him.

S. G. GUSEVA

In 1963, S. G. Guseva was born in the small town of Galich, near Kostroma, in Russia. She very successfully graduated from the nearby School of Art in 1977, thereafter going on to study at the College of Art and Industry in Zagorsk. Guseva knew she was destined to be an artist by occupation. Indeed, she has been working with Marina's Russian Collection in the Studio of Decor and Applied Art as a teacher and artist since 1984.

When she is not busy at Marina's Russian Collection, Guseva is often participating in exhibitions all over the former Soviet Union.

U. V. GUSEV

In Zagorsk City, a town in the Moscow area of Russia, an artist was born in 1959. U.V. Gusev graduated from the School of Art in 1972 and studied at the Abramtsevo Art College from 1974 through 1978.

For two years after his graduation, Gusev served in the Soviet Army, unable for a time to pursue his ambition as an artist. However, he did return in 1980 to work for ten years as an artist in the Science Institute.

Presently, Gusev employs his artistic talents at Marina's Russian Collection, also taking part in shows and exhibitions throughout the former Soviet Union.

APRIL GUSTAFSON

Miniature artist April Whitcomb Gustafson has been attracted to tiny things since childhood. "I was so near-sighted as a kid I couldn't see the squares in the kitchen floor linoleum," she laughs. "As a result, I loved anything that was so small it couldn't be appreciated unless you held it up close. And I was absolutely enchanted with miniature bears."

April has been collecting miniature bears since age six, but high quality miniatures were getting harder and harder to find by the time she graduated from art school in 1979. So, April began sculpting her own bears at night in her Boylston, Massachusetts home, after returning from her full-time job as a graphic artist.

Almost immediately, and largely by word of mouth, April's miniatures became enormously popular with collectors around the world, selling for between $100 and $1500 each. Two have won coveted industry awards and one was recently nominated.

April's interest in creating the *Roosevelt Bear Collection* for Schmid was sparked by the purchase of Seymour Eaton's "Travelling Roosevelt Bear" stories of the early 1900s. Particularly drawn to the exceptionally detailed illustrations, she was determined to capture that detail in sculpture.

April has since added "A Big Top Christmas" to her *Roosevelt Bear Collection* for Schmid, and is looking forward to creating more designs for the company. "I've got an endless list of ideas, and

I want to see each of them brought to life," she says.

STEPHEN AND GIGI HACKETT

Collectors in search of rising young stars will want to familiarize themselves with the works of Steve and Gigi Hackett, a talented husband-and-wife team whose figurines were recently introduced by Cast Art Industries, Inc.

Steve apprenticed with the Disney organization and left to undertake freelance commissions, one-of-a-kind sculptures for the rich and famous, and a soon-to-be-released animated television series. Collaborating with his wife Gigi, a unique team approach and wry sense of humor has resulted in two new collectible series.

Animal Attractions is an assortment of humorous portrayals of favorite four-legged friends, including "flasher" cows, bikini-clad pigs and dancing bears. *Story Time Treasures* are representations of beloved children's stories, from *The Three Little Pigs* to *The Frog Prince*, each depicting a parent animal reading to his youngster.

These delightful works are available as collectible figurines and children's lamps. Like all Cast Art products, the reproductions are painstakingly hand-cast and hand-painted.

Steve and Gigi Hackett represent a fresh new wave of young California artists whose works are beginning to attract nationwide attention.

KAREN HAHN

Artist Karen Hahn has greatly contributed to the giftware industry and Enesco product line over the past several years. As Enesco Art Director, Karen continues developing and designing new products which show her fine

attention to detail and gentle creative touch.

Inspired by her daughter, Karen created an emotional and appealing collection of detailed cold-cast figurines. The *Laura's Attic*™ Collection reflects Karen's memorable childhood activities and those of her little daughter, Laura. Through heartwarming limited edition figurines, the collection celebrates the joy and innocence of childhood.

Karen's work has also been honored by the Francis Hook Scholarship Fund. Her action musical "Wee Wedding Wishes" was a winner in the Fund's 1991 licensed art program. A figurine from *White Lace and Promises*, her collection which captures traditional wedding customs, and her "Rapunzel" jack-in-the-box musical have also won the Fund's licensed art award in previous years.

Karen's other designs include deluxe action musicals for the *Enesco Small World of Music*™ collection, ornaments for the *Enesco Treasury of Christmas Ornaments*® collection, *My American Dream* and *Domino and Dominique*.

Karen also serves as a consultant on every musical in the *Small World of Music*™ collection, renowned for its creativity and fine craftsmanship.

Prior to joining Enesco in 1985, Karen worked as a free-lance illustrator. She holds a degree in illustration from Northern Illinois University.

TEENA HALBIG

Born in Chattanooga, Tennessee, and raised in Evansville, Indiana, artist Teena Robinson Halbig was at first intrigued by the field of scientific work. She attended Indiana University for a couple of years and finished her education at the University of Louisville in

Kentucky, where she was employed in the science field for several years.

Teena was introduced to ceramic crafting by a friend, and experimented with ceramic dollmaking as a hobby. In 1981, Teena enthusiastically began making her first dolls in a kiln that her husband Eddie gave her as a gift.

Her first show was a great success, and Teena's business as an artist took off. In 1986, Dynasty Doll Collection™ commissioned her for design work for original sculptures. She has worked for the company since then, creating "Chia-You," "Shiew Mei," "Claudine" and "Trina," among other dolls.

STEVE HANKS

The work of Steve Hanks, which almost always features people, reflects a mystery of form and an intricate involvement with color. Highly detailed and realistic, his oils and watercolors urge the viewer to become part of the creative process.

An intense and articulate man, Hanks is passionate about life, and passionate about his art. "I try to capture a certain introspective solitude in my figures," he comments, "and deal with a vulnerability that all of us sometimes feel." It has been said that his subjects are so alive they seem to have been caught poised between heartbeats.

With a father in the military service, the young Hanks moved frequently, finally settling in the high desert of Albuquerque, New Mexico, where he finished the last two years of high school. He was a student at Berkeley in the '60s. He then enrolled at the Academy of Art in San Francisco, and subsequently graduated from the California College of Arts and Crafts in Oakland, California.

Steve Hanks is represented by Hadley House.

HANS HENRIK HANSEN

Born in 1952, Hans Henrik Hansen graduated from the Academy of Applied Art in Copenhagen with an emphasis on Graphic Design.

For twelve years, he was the principal decorator at the retail store for the Royal Copenhagen Porcelain Manufactory, where his window decorations were the rage of fashionable Copenhagen.

Since 1987, Hans has been devoted almost exclusively to creating designs and illustrations for the porcelain manufactory. His first Christmas series, *Jingle Bells*, is now a permanent gift series.

With the introduction of the distinctly different *Santa Claus* collection in 1989, Hans became the first artist since 1895 to create a colorful Christmas plate for Bing & Grondahl. The first plate in the series, "Santa's Workshop," is a festive rendition of Santa and his elves preparing Christmas gifts. The *Santa Claus* collection is a series of six annual plates and matching ornaments, which will culminate with the celebration of Christmas Day.

For the first time since 1908, Royal Copenhagen issued a series of six annual Christmas plates and coordinating ornaments titled *Christmas in Denmark*. The original art for this series was created by Hans Henrik Hansen. "Bringing Home the Tree" was the fifth plate in the collection.

WILLIAM K. HARPER

A respected figurine designer for Royal Doulton, William K. Harper spent more than a decade learning his profession. In a recent interview, Harper noted that while a figurine designer employs the same aesthetic elements as a fine artist, the designer must also create a piece which will please collectors and still be profitable. The inspirations for Harper's figures range from his childhood memories of visiting the circus, to historical personalities who are developed only after careful research.

According to Harper, each image selected must be in keeping with the other Doulton characters in style, coloring, size and price. It is the designer's role to create a figure which will evoke an immediate response from collectors while at the same time tell a story and/or reveal the character of the subject through body movements, clothing and a few appropriate props. The figurine designer also must take special care in considering all of the stages of production and as much as possible, avoid designs which would be too difficult to execute.

Harper's figures range from comic figures like the "Clown" and "Punch and Judy Man," to imaginative figures like "St. George and the Dragon," "The Centurion" and "Votes for Women." He is also the designer of the popular eleven-piece *Gilbert and Sullivan* series. Harper also modeled the Henry VIII Jug which received rave reviews from collectors.

KRISTIN HAYNES

About ten years ago, artist Kristin Haynes turned her talents to sculpture and began creating unique, adorable cherubs which became popular with fans in southern California. Demand grew so great that Kristin could no longer make reproductions in sufficient quantities on her own.

Kristin showed her samples to Cast Art Industries, a quality gift manufacturing company, which quickly saw the potential in the artist's fresh style. Cast Art recognized that to be successful, the line must maintain its unique characteristics: reproductions would be handcrafted using the finest natural materials, hand-painted, and offered as collectibles at an affordable price. The line was named *Dreamsicles* and introduced to the public in March 1991. Among the fastest-growing lines in the history of collectibles, *Dreamsicles* have consistently been named America's number one seller in monthly surveys of gift retailers.

Kristin's *Dreamsicles* now include more than 150 cherubs, animals and Christmas pieces. Her 1993 limited edition entitled "The Flying Lesson" sold out within a few short weeks. Kristin continues to create new *Dreamsicles* designs from her farmhouse studio and is presently introducing a new collection of whimsical characters known as the citizens of *Cuckoo Corners*.

JEAN WALMSLEY HEAP

Jean Walmsley Heap has always "taken drawing for granted — like breathing." Jean began modeling and drawing as a child, and by age ten, began selling her pictures with a view to buying a wooden hut "to live and paint in." This idea was discouraged, but per-

mission was granted to use the broom cupboard under the stairs which was now called "Studio One."

Three years later, Jean was awarded a scholarship to the Burnley School of Art where she trained under the guidance of distinguished artist Noel H. Leaver, A.R.C.A. He had great faith in Jean's talents, teaching her clay-modeling as well as painting and composition.

Later Jean began exhibiting child studies and flower paintings regularly in art galleries. During WWII, she was commissioned by the Canadian Red Cross to design large murals for the bare walls of wartime nurseries, as a gift to the children of Britain.

In 1953, Jean and her good friend Jeannie Todd began the hobby that would become their claim to international fame. In a tiny garden hut, Jean designed and modeled their very first piece — a witch, flying against the moon, with a wide-eyed cat on her shoulder. The witch sculpture was crafted in honor of Pendle Hill, known far and wide as the Hill of Witches. Various other models followed, but it was not until Jean modeled "Father Rabbit" that orders began to roll in. The "hobby" grew into what is now the Pen-Delfin Studios with offices in Canada, the United States and England. Today Jean Walmsley Heap is Chairman of PenDelfin.

KAREN HENDERSON

Karen Henderson is an accomplished doll artist who graduated from the California College of Arts with a B.A. degree in Commercial Art and Illustration. She and her sister Kathy founded Kissing Kousins Dolls in 1985, after Karen had been sculpting and making porcelain dolls for a few years. She concentrated especially on designing Black dolls, and she continues to do so.

Karen's doll artistry has received a great deal of recognition, represented by such companies as the Ehler Company of Los Angeles, California and the prestigious Thomas Boland Company of New York. Her major works have been shown at the New York Toy Fair and other large trade shows. Thus, Dynasty Doll Collection™ is proud to feature some of Karen's dolls, including "Annie," "Annie at Play," "Tina" and "Julie."

JON HERBERT

Jon Herbert, creator of The Shoemaker's Dream Shoe Houses, Animal Antics and Father Time Clocks, was born in 1963 and raised in Farnham, Surrey. Herbert had always wanted to be an artist. As a youth, he spent much of his free time modeling such things as clay dinosaurs and gorillas. He attended a local school of Art and Design in pottery and later held various jobs involving woodworking in miniature, modelmaking for cartoons, and eventually mold design for the Studios and Workshops of John Hine in 1987.

Herbert's talent came to the attention of John Hine when Hine saw several of Jon's sketches. Intrigued by his talent, John Hine asked to see some of Herbert's sculpting and woodworking and was amazed by the ambitious projects. Herbert came up with the idea for

Shoe Houses based on the old nursery rhyme "There was an old woman who lived in a shoe…," imagining other sorts of people that might live in shoes. John Hine loved the idea, and the current range of twenty-three Shoe Houses was created. Later, Hine asked Herbert to put clocks into the Shoe Houses, but instead Jon came up with a series of whimsical houses with working clocks built into the facade — the series called Father Time Clocks. John Hine now refers to Herbert as "Genius Jon." Jon's latest creation is Animal Antics, a collection of costumed animals with amusing detail.

LAWRENCE HEYDA

Lawrence Heyda was born in Chicago on February 8, 1944, and grew up in the peaceful suburb of Elmhurst. His college days were spent at the University of Illinois with a dual major in engineering and English, and working during the summer for McDonnell Aircraft on the Gemini Space Capsule. After graduating with honors in 1966, he returned to the University to receive another Bachelor degree with honors in painting in 1969.

After college, he worked with a company producing animated figures and multi-media displays. During that time, Heyda perfected a technique for creating very realistic computer-run human figures. In 1973, he signed with Movieland Wax Museum and produced full figures of Johnny Cash, George C. Scott, Lorne Greene, Ali McGraw and Ryan O'Neal. Following this, he was commissioned by Sports World in Dallas, Texas to sculpt the busts of twenty-four famous athletes.

Heyda continued his foray in the sports industry with several significant

contributions to Gartlan USA, based in Huntington Beach, California. Original sculpture for the company touches several sports and athletes.

His Hall of Fame figurines for Gartlan USA include baseball immortals Joe DiMaggio, Johnny Bench, Carl Yastrzemski, Ted Williams, Steve Carlton and Darryl Srawberry. Basketball figures include Kareem Abdul-Jabbar and coaching great John Wooden. He has also produced the company's best-selling Wayne Gretzky figure and other hockey legends, such as Gordie Howe, Bobby Hull and Brett Hull.

Heyda's DiMaggio, Bench, Yastrzemski, Williams and Gretzky are some of the most sought-after (and valuable) sports pieces on the secondary market.

DOUG HILBURN

Doug Hilburn, a native North Carolinian, began studying art at the University of North Carolina at Chapel Hill. Later, he received his Bachelor of Fine Arts degree in communication arts from East Carolina, concentrating in illustration and design.

Doug started working at CUI, Inc. in 1988 as a free-lance illustrator and product designer. In 1990, he became a full-time employee. He enjoys using oils, watercolors and acrylics to create illustrations, but most often works on a Macintosh computer. In 1992, Doug became Director of Product Design and has recently been directly involved in designing tin products for CUI's newly created division, Metallic Images, Inc.

When Doug can catch time away from work, he can always be found on a local golf course. His motto is: "I only play golf on days that end in 'Y'."

PRISCILLA HILLMAN

Endearing and special childhood memories of sitting with her sister at the

kitchen table with paint brushes and watercolors influenced Priscilla Hillman's charming illustrations and uplifting children's books that have touched the hearts of both young and old.

Art was always a central part of Priscilla's life. Although she loved drawing, Priscilla decided to study botany at the University of Rhode Island. After graduating, she worked for the U.S. Oceanographic Office but continued pursuing her artistic interests.

"Tumpy Rumple," her first effort at illustrating and writing a children's book, took her three years to complete. Priscilla then created "Precious Bears," which appeared on needlecraft and greeting cards.

In the late 1980s, a serious back problem kept Priscilla inactive for several months. During this time, Priscilla "drew in her mind." When she was finally able to move about, Priscilla went straight to her drawing board to put "sketches" of cute and cuddly teddy bears on paper. The *Cherished Teddies® Collection* came to life, and Priscilla's first giftware collection based on her charming illustrations was introduced in 1992. The *Cherished Teddies® Collection* has since received worldwide recognition from collectors and the collectibles industry, as some of the figurines have won prestigious awards of excellence.

With the success of the *Cherished Teddies® Collection*, Enesco introduced another collection by Priscilla Hillman in 1993. The *Calico Kittens™ Collection* features adorable cold cast cat figurines with messages of friendship and love.

ANNETTE HIMSTEDT

Annette Himstedt, award-winning doll designer and president of Kinder Aus Porzellan (Children From Porcelain) of Germany, began her career in

1977 by modeling an exquisitely detailed doll of her daughter. Friends and neighbors immediately began commissioning these portrait dolls of their own children, allowing Annette to develop her craft, and eventually to gain worldwide recognition for her artistry as well as a tremendous international following of serious doll collectors.

Completely self-taught and a perfectionist by nature, Himstedt discovered early on that her dolls would not be truly lifelike if she followed traditional methods of working with porcelain. Himstedt was convinced that in order to get the likeness that she wanted, she would have to form the porcelain with her hands instead of premodel them and use molds for a porcelain founding. Hand-forming porcelain was an idea that was considered impossible by many experts. Nevertheless, she persevered, sculpting dolls whose delicate and expressive faces embody the essence of childhood.

As worldwide demand for her dolls increased, Himstedt began to work in vinyl in addition to porcelain, and she set up a manufacturing facility in Spain. Annette Himstedt's vinyl dolls are designed for Timeless Creations, a division of Mattel, Inc. Her success has not affected her relentless drive for perfection in every detail — she insists on overseeing each stage of the production process.

Universally recognized by collectors and her peers, Himstedt has received many awards for her achievements, and her dolls have been exhibited in galleries and museums in Germany, France, Switzerland, Italy and Japan.

TORI DAWN YOUNGER HINE

As a youngster, Tori Dawn exhibited enormous natural artistic talent. At eight years old, she was already submit-

ting drawings to national publications, and at nine years old, she began studying with a local artist in Orange County, California, who trained her in the use of oil, acrylic and pastels.

In 1985, Tori Dawn's father, Bill Younger, introduced David Winter Cottages in the United States. It seemed obvious that his talented daughter should be trained to paint the cottages. In 1986, Tori Dawn traveled to England where she studied painting techniques under Audrey White, David Winter's original paintress. Tori Dawn became the first painting artist in the United States for John Hine Studios, and she spent much of the next three years traveling throughout the United States as the David Winter promotional painting artist. During this time, Tori Dawn was amazed to discover that she was being acclaimed by many collectors who met her.

During a later visit to England, Tori Dawn met Harry Hine, whom she married in 1990. They spent the next two years in England, working closely with John Hine Limited and later relocated to the San Diego area with their new baby boy.

Since her enormous talent was so obviously admired by collectors, many people were thrilled when she began working with Harbour Lights, a company headed by Tori Dawn's sister, Kimberly Andrews. The figurines she paints depict a series of lighthouses from America's early architecture.

KATHY HIPPENSTEEL

Kathy Hippensteel sculpts only baby dolls, and she has dedicated her career to creating the most lifelike dolls possible. This dedication has earned her awards in virtually every show she has entered, including a top award from the Illinois Doll Makers' Association.

"Chen," the first doll in her *International Festival of Toys & Tots* collection, was nominated for a prestigious 1989 Award of Excellence by *Dolls* magazine and received a 1990 Achievement Award from the National Association of Limited Edition Dealers. Her other collections available from Ashton-Drake are *Born to Be Famous, Baby Book Treasures, Joys of Summer, Growing Young Minds, Sense of Discovery, Happiness Is…*, and *I Want Mommy*.

Today, Ms. Hippensteel's dolls are displayed with the most celebrated dolls of this century in doll museums in Paris, France, and in the United States. Private collectors consider her works to be some of their most valued acquisitions.

MARTHA HOLCOMBE

Martha Holcombe grew up in the Appalachian foothills of northeast Alabama playing barefoot at her grandmother's farm on warm summer days. Her favorite memories include riding an old mule, picking cotton, swimming in the creek, and watching the "one horse plow" furrow the fields. It's these childhood memories in the South that have inspired her art and have made Martha one of America's foremost artisans.

Martha, known to many as Miss Martha, creates from her heart and deep personal faith. Her gentle spirit and soft-spoken manner belie the courageous, determined woman who set out in 1980 to raise funds for a much-needed new roof for her church. To meet her personal pledge for the project, she began a mail order business to sell originally designed doll patterns.

Martha met her pledge, and the business prospered from a small box of patterns in her living room to its own building in her northern Alabama hometown of Gadsden. From soft-sculpture doll patterns, Martha began creating the now famous *All God's Children*™ collection, a special line of handcrafted, signed and numbered figurines.

She now heads Miss Martha Originals, which produces *All God's Children*™ in the Gadsden facility, markets the line and employs several hundred men and women. The popularity of the collection led to the All God's Children Collectors' Club, which also is managed under Martha Holcombe's direction.

A self-taught artist, Martha receives inspiration for her "children" from real life people, photographs, newspapers and books.

In 1991, Enesco Corporation introduced a heartwarming collection of figurines sculpted by Martha. *Miss Martha's Collection*™ captures the simplicity and tenderness of childhood through a series of cold-cast figurines. The children portrayed in each figurine have distinct personalities, names, special stories and lifelike expressions.

Since 1993, each figurine in *Miss Martha's Collection*™ has featured an annual yearmark with a symbol and a scripture reference to encourage collectors to look up the verse.

FRANCES HOOK

The collectibles, art and publishing business communities have saluted the inimitable artistry and spirit of the late Frances Hook with their highest tribute by establishing a foundation in her name to foster young artists' studies. The Frances Hook Scholarship Fund has grown since its inception following Hook's death in 1983, currently awarding over $50,000 in awards and scholarships to art students from first grade to college undergraduates.

Frances Hook served as a wonderful role model for aspiring artists of all ages. Born in Ambler, Pennsylvania, she studied art while in high school. A scholarship at the Pennsylvania Museum of Art led to the development of her style in the exacting pastel discipline and her unique manner of capturing the spirit and vitality of children. That talent is outstanding in her renderings of famous 1960s Northern Tissue children.

Mrs. Hook also illustrated children's books. She joined her husband, Richard, also an artist, in several collaborations of the successful illustration of *The Living Bible* by Tyndale House Publishers.

Following her husband's death, Mrs. Hook entered a new and rewarding stage of her career. Roman, Inc. approached her about designing a collection of limited edition porcelain figurines, which proved to be a resounding collector success nationwide. Her strong relationship with Roman led to the introduction of a series of collector editions by Frances Hook — plates, prints and more figurines.

All releases since Frances Hook's death are issued under the direction of her daughter, Barbara. Mrs. Hook's daughter is sharing her mother's work with the public by converting Mrs. Hook's home in Maine into the Frances Hook Gallery.

GAIL HOYT

Gail Hoyt has been designing dolls for over a dozen years, as a response to requests for doll repairs on antique dolls she sold in a shop she owned. She gave up the antique shop in favor of a doll shop and taught dollmaking classes for several years.

When she decided to turn to creating originals rather than reproductions, Gail sought and found a famous master

dollmaker from Germany to teach her this art. Her first doll, "Nicole," was nominated in 1989 for an award from *Doll Reader* magazine. Gail says, "I knew then I was doing what I always dreamed — to be an original doll artist." In 1990, "Bridget and Mother Goose" was nominated for an "Award of Excellence" from *Dolls* magazine. She has also designed dolls for Dynasty Doll Collection, including "Samantha," "Carley" and "Marlene."

Gail says that the inspiration for her doll designs comes from children she has seen. She captures their innocent qualities by studying their faces before beginning the sculpting process. The artist expresses her creative philosophy in her own words: "I believe that a doll should bring happiness and captivate the heart of any collector."

SISTER MARIA INNOCENTIA HUMMEL

Sister Maria Innocentia Hummel was the creator of hundreds of colorful and charming sketches, drawings and paintings of children. Her work is the basis for scores of appealing, hand-painted fine earthenware figurines, as well as limited edition plates and bells, created and offered exclusively by W. Goebel

Porzellanfabrik of Germany.

She was born Berta Hummel in Bavaria in 1909. Her father had inclinations toward art, and so did Berta from earliest youth. She graduated from the Munich Academy of Applied Art, meanwhile devoting much of her energies toward her religion.

Much to the dismay of her art teachers, Berta Hummel entered a convent upon her graduation, taking the name Sister Maria Innocentia. Because the convent of Siessen, a teaching order, was quite poor, she gained permission to raise money by selling some of her artwork in the form of postcards. In 1934, Franz Goebel, the fourth-generation head of the porcelain-producing firm, discovered her art at a time when he was searching for ideas for a new line of figurines.

The first *M.I. Hummel* figurines debuted at the Leipzig Fair in 1935, and since then have been popular with collectors around the world. Sadly, Sister M.I. Hummel died much too soon, not yet aware of her full triumph as an artist. She died in 1946 at the age of thirty-seven.

PAUL DAVID JACKSON

Paul David Jackson began his sculpting career in 1977 in Sheringham, Norfolk, England concentrating on working in porcelain. He also spent a good deal of time creating fantasy illustrations from short story ideas of his own. Paul has had numerous exhibitions throughout England and has shown his art at the Dolls House Gallery in Portsmouth, New Hampshire.

After marrying in 1978, Paul and his wife Penny, also an artist, set up a studio to create and display their work. While Penny was pregnant with their daughter, Paul, who was a bear collector, began painting the characters Oscar and Bertie. As he continued to paint the bears, the thread of a story began to develop, and the Edwardian bears came to life in Paul's art. The original paintings for Oscar and Bertie were shown at the Birmingham International Gift Fair, and thus began a long list of licenses for products featuring Paul's bears.

Reco International quickly licensed the bears for their collector plate series entitled *Oscar and Bertie's® Edwardian Holiday*. Oscar and Bertie can also be found on stationery, puzzles, sheets and fabrics which are distributed worldwide.

PAUL JENNIS

When you're recreating characters from one of the nation's most-loved movies, it pays to heed the advice of your critics — any critics.

That's what Paul Jennis of Raritan Township, New Jersey, has done for the plates he has created for his first two series from The Bradford Exchange, *Critic's Choice: Gone With the Wind* and *Gone With the Wind: The Passions of Scarlett O'Hara*.

Mr. Jennis, thirty-three, has become so caught up with the *Gone With the Wind* plate series that he says he would like to devote all of his attention to this facet of the art world. Although he really enjoys athletics, model building and piano playing, Jennis says his work is his true hobby. In his work, Jennis strives to capture the likeness and nature of the characters from "Gone With the Wind." That means listening closely when his wife Pauline or someone else outside the art field tells him, "That's not how Scarlett would do that." It also means paying attention to details, like painting Scarlett O'Hara with a slightly raised eyebrow to add a toughness to her.

A perfectionist, Jennis says he has been told not to be so hard on himself. But maybe that's what makes his art so well-liked by collectors.

PENNI JO JONAS

Just a few short years ago, Penni Jo was a homemaker with no idea she would have such a successful artistic career. But the phenomenon of her teddy bear creations has propelled her into the national spotlight among collectible figurine artists.

Penni Jo's first creations were made in her kitchen, using colored clays she mixed in her food processor and baked in her toaster oven. A miniature teddy bear she made for her daughter's dollhouse became the inspiration for a series of similar bears. The little bears were soon sculpted with clothes and accessories and eventually became known as *PenniBears*™. Her local following of collectors blossomed into a national following, and in 1989 Penni Jo joined the staff of United Design, where all the intricate details of *PenniBears*™ are now reproduced by talented production artists and craftsmen.

In addition to *PenniBears*™, Penni Jo designs and sculpts several other collectible figurine editions, including *Fancy Frames*™, (Small) *Nativity*™, *Animal Magnetism*™, Christmas ornaments, Angel ornaments, and *Itty Bitty Critters*™.

Delightfully open and candid about her transition from homemaker to nationally renowned artist, Penni Jo loves to meet collectors and fans as much as they love her and the exquisitely detailed miniatures she sculpts.

FALINE FRY JONES

Born in Wooster, Ohio, Faline Fry Jones took an active interest in art — a talent she traces back to her mother's side of the family. She actively pursued several arts and crafts, including candlemaking, leatherworking, tie dying and macrame. These craft items were taken to a consignment shop, where they were sold on a regular basis.

Always interested in cats, Faline began crafting cat doorstops out of fabric. One day, when she dropped her doorstops at the consignment shop, she noticed a small wooden house for sale. Thinking that she could make a nicer one, Faline sat down and made her very first building.

Thus began Faline Fry Jones' business, which she initially named Cat's Meow. Started in her basement in 1982, Faline patterned her designs after actual buildings and historic landmarks no longer in existence and named these pieces the Cat's Meow Village. By 1989, a new facility was built to house the 130-member team of employees, and the name of the firm was changed to FJ Designs. Today, Faline and her husband, Terry, run a highly successful multi-million dollar international collectibles company.

Faline Jones has won several awards for her business and artistic efforts, including the Small Business Person of the Year Award by the Wooster Chamber of Commerce and the Recognition Award from Ohio Small Business Revitalization, both in 1989. She is active in several local and national organizations, including the International Screen Print Association. Faline's interest also lies with the good education of our nation's youth. Serving this purpose, she is on the board of directors of her local Junior Achievement chapter.

LYNN KAATZ

A native of the Great Lakes Region of northern Ohio, the young Lynn Kaatz learned to know and love the countryside and waterways he would

later come to paint. Mr. Kaatz graduated from Ohio State University and the Cooper School of Art (first in his class) and quickly began a successful freelance art career. Combining his formal art training with an instinctive love for the outdoors, he creates breathtaking landscapes, realistic wildlife paintings and carvings, and touching animal portraits.

A tireless researcher, Mr. Kaatz studies every nuance of his subjects, fusing his observations with personal memories. The results, whether executed in watercolor, acrylics, oils or woodcarving, always reflect a deep appreciation of the outdoors, as well as the sensitivity of an astute artist and a caring man.

His distinguished career is studded with awards, and Ducks Unlimited has repeatedly honored Mr. Kaatz with Best of Artist and Best of Show recognition. In 1988, he was chosen to create the artwork for a limited-edition collector's plate series sponsored by this prestigious organization: *Classic Waterfowl: The Ducks Unlimited Collection*. A different aspect of his talent was showcased in *Waterfowl Legacy*, a series of hand-painted, bas-relief sculptural plates.

In addition to ducks, he is also closely associated with the subject of dogs. Various breeds of hunting dogs were featured in his first series, *Field Puppies*, which was sponsored by the United Kennel Club. He has subsequently created two additional series depicting canines: *Field Trips* and *It's a Dog's Life*. His plates are available from The Bradford Exchange.

HANNA KAHL-HYLAND

Hanna Kahl-Hyland was born and educated in Northern Germany and was raised with a strong interest in and great love for the fine arts. She studied at St. Martin's School of Art in London.

In the early '80s, Hanna and her husband emigrated to the United States, where she began carving wooden fairy tale dolls. Recently, she mastered the art and craft of designing porcelain dolls. Her first porcelain doll was sculpted from a childhood photograph of her sister. Her fairy tale dolls have been exhibited at the Pittsburgh Children's Museum.

Hanna signed with Seymour Mann, Inc. because she was assured that the firm would manufacture fine interpre-

tations of her doll originals. Seymour Mann's international reputation as a high-quality collectible doll supplier with strong marketing capabilities convinced her to develop new designs for the firm's *Signature Series*. One of her doll designs for Seymour Mann was "Reilly," a red-haired, blue-eyed beauty which was nominated for an Award of Excellence by *Dolls* magazine for the best porcelain doll in the $300 and up category.

GARRI KATZ

Garri Katz was born in the Soviet Union when the dark cloud of war spread over all the nations of Europe. As a child he found comfort in drawing and painting on scraps of paper — an activity which helped calm his fears during the difficult days of World War II. After the war, young Katz completed his schooling at the Odessa Institute of Fine Arts, where he studied for four years before launching his career as a painter and illustrator.

In 1973, Katz and his family immigrated to Israel. His paintings of religious and historic subjects and his celebrations of everyday life in Israel soon earned Katz many invitations to display his works in one-man shows in that land. Then in 1984, Katz began a series of shows in the United States sponsored by patrons who had discovered his genius during trips to Israel. Today, art connoisseurs from many different nations purchase Katz paintings and watercolors for as high as $12,000 each. His works are on display in Israel, Belgium, Germany, Canada and the United States. Katz resides in Florida.

Garri Katz's first limited edition collector plate series for Reco represents a commission from Reco International.

Entitled *Great Stories from the Bible*, each of the eight plates portrays a memorable moment from a beloved Bible story.

SARAH KAY

Even with all the international acclaim and recognition Sarah Kay receives for her beautiful designs, she still prefers to work at her home in a quiet suburb of Sydney, Australia, because home is where Sarah Kay began to sketch the playful innocence of her own children years ago.

In 1993, Sarah Kay and ANRI celebrated the tenth anniversary of a creative collaboration that has produced truly unforgettable dolls and figurines. Sarah Kay's touching images were actually conceived out of a mother's loving appreciation of her own children, as she observed her children's special moments.

Because of a rather shy and private demeanor, her talent was usually reserved for her family and close friends. After much encouragement from them, Sarah Kay was finally persuaded to show her unique designs to an Australian greeting card manufacturer who immediately recognized her skillful perception of emotion and mood. The Sarah Kay greeting card line became immensely popular in Australia.

Her beautiful portrayals soon appeared internationally, and Sarah Kay became beloved by a thoroughly delighted European public. Among her admirers in Europe were the designers at ANRI, who envisioned her work transformed into an enchanting series of ANRI figurines. Realizing that her drawings would translate exquisitely into three-dimensional form, ANRI initiated a creative partnership with Sarah Kay.

In 1983, Master Sculptor Ulrich Bernardi, already well known for his

original nativity figurines and other religious pieces, began interpreting Sarah Kay motifs. Using the finest cembra pine anywhere, he began transforming Sarah's designs into three-dimensional woodsculpture.

Ten years later, ANRI's artists still delicately hand-sculpt these treasured figurines at their workshop in St. Christina, Italy. Sarah Kay takes great pride in her artistic achievements and her successes with ANRI. The magic she continues to create for the company is for her a labor of love, performed where she is happiest — at home, embracing those who have provided her with inspiration.

KAREN KENNEDY

A love affair with fashion design and dolls began at an early age for Goebel's talented doll designer Karen Kennedy. In the artistic atmosphere of their atelier, she is free to combine both loves by creating exclusive costumes for *Victoria Ashlea Originals®* and Goebel's other doll lines.

Two of Ms. Kennedy's designs were accepted into museums: The Doll Castle Museum in Washington, New Jersey and the Mary Stolz Doll and Toy Museum in East Stroudsburg, Pennsylvania.

She loves to meet with collectors personally to share her knowledge and thoughts on collecting and has appeared on television many times to promote her appearances.

Karen is a fast rising young star for Goebel United States.

DONNA KENNICUTT

Known best for her bronze sculptures of animal wildlife, Donna Kennicutt's philosophy is simple: "Doing is also learning." A native of Oklahoma, Kennicutt took art classes during her school years. She studied with Robert Burns

Wilson and Irene Bradford. Her artworks are now in private collections across the United States, France and other countries.

During her nine years at United Design Corporation, Ms. Kennicutt has created and sculpted the popular *Easter Bunny Family*™, as well as *Children's Garden of Critters*™ and *Bouquet*™.

TERRY KERR

Designer and artist Terry Kerr attended Southern Methodist University in the early 1970s where he studied fine arts. He also enrolled in the gifted artists program of the Dallas Museum of Art.

After working in advertising, packaging design and visual merchandising/display for several companies, Terry began his illustrious career with Fitz and Floyd in 1977. He was brought on staff to design Fitz and Floyd's fashionable fine china as well as their unique, whimsical giftware and decorative accessories. Terry has designed such well-known china patterns as "Cloisonne Peony" and the ever-popular "St. Nicholas"

Christmas pattern. He also designed Fitz and Floyd's first Halloween giftware group.

During the 1980s, Terry worked as a free-lance design consultant for Fitz and Floyd, Department 56 and The Franklin Mint, where he designed many collectible lines.

In early 1991, Terry returned to Fitz and Floyd full-time where he undertook the responsibility of designing many of the company's new collectible items. He has designed most of the new *Collector's Series* limited edition teapots, as well as the latest Christmas group, *A Christmas Carol*. This collection celebrates the 150th anniversary of Charles Dickens' famous story through a variety of collectibles and unique gift items.

Terry Kerr is a native of Dallas, Texas. His outside interests include collecting Santa Claus figurines, theater and antique collecting.

THOMAS KINKADE

Thomas Kinkade is widely regarded as one of the foremost living painters of light. His complex technique bears great kinship to a group of 19th century painters known as the Luminists, who strove for three visual aspects in their works: soft edges, a warm palette, and an overall sense of light. Kinkade's mastery of these three aspects gives his paintings the warm glow and softness for which he is known.

This internationally published artist was born in 1958, and by the age of sixteen, was an accomplished painter in oil. After studies at the University of California, Berkeley and Art Center College of Design, Kinkade began work for the motion picture industry where he personally created over 600 background paintings for the animated feature film, *Fire & Ice*. In 1983, he left the film industry to pursue his vision as a

painter of light-filled landscapes. Along with the landscape paintings he produces, Kinkade creates plate designs which are distributed by The Bradford Exchange.

Thomas Kinkade is an outgoing man with a sense of humor. A devout Christian, he finds time for church activities, reading, and extensive travel with his family while maintaining a rigorous six-day week painting schedule.

Thomas Kinkade's oil paintings and reproductions communicate deeply with viewers, providing hope and warm nostalgia in a complex and often stressful world. He paints a simpler, idyllic world which seems to radiate an inner light.

PAT KOLESAR

Back in 1979, Pat Kolesar was an avid doll collector who began to notice that all dolls looked the same. At that time, she unleashed her creative talents to design dolls that reflected the various and unpredictable moods of children. Her doll faces are atypically realistic with very distinct looks. Pat's designs are intended to show on the outside what people feel on the inside.

Since her debut, Pat has earned more than forty Blue Ribbons at regional doll shows and national conventions of the United Federation of Doll Clubs (UFDC) held throughout the U.S. In 1991, she received two Awards of Excellence nominations from *Dolls* magazine, one for "Enoc the Eskimo Boy," which was designed for Seymour Mann. In 1992, Ms. Kolesar won first prize at the UFDC Show in San Francisco. In 1993, her designs won two Awards of Excellence from *Dolls* magazine. Also this year, she has designed many collectible dolls for Seymour Mann's *Signature Series*, including three porcelain dolls: "Kissing Kyle," "Kissing Kelly" and "Kissing Casey." Pat has also designed two dolls named "Frick and

Frack" for the Dynasty Doll Collection.

The vivacious artist is an accomplished painter and sculptress who studied with Nat Ramer and other well-known artists. She recently was commissioned to design a portrait doll of William Simon, former Secretary of the Treasury. Several of her dolls currently are on display at museums across the country.

SUSAN KREY

Susan Krey was raised in the countryside of Middlesex, England where her mother, an artist, acquainted her with the basics of color, light and form. Ms. Krey attended a London art school, then emigrated to Melbourne, Australia, where she taught art and worked as a fabric designer.

Ms. Krey later moved to America, and in 1981 decided to combine her artistic talent with her love for children (she has five of her own). She began to create dolls which are noted for their simple, thoughtful design, gentle personalities, and astonishingly realistic sculpt. Her dolls are displayed in museums and private collections across Australia, Canada and the United States and have earned her several blue ribbons.

"One of my goals as a doll artist is to use interaction between dolls to tell a story," says Ms. Krey. "With the little girls in *Polly's Tea Party*, I've not only attempted to create natural, childlike expressions and soft, subtle costumes, but also to bring a favorite playtime tradition to life." *Polly's Tea Party* is available from The Ashton-Drake Galleries.

SANDRA KUCK

Creating several series of plates and an ongoing collection of lithographs,

Sandra Kuck's paintings of children display a rare gift for capturing the true spirit of childhood.

Educated at U.C.L.A., Ms. Kuck moved to New York and entered the Art Students League where she learned to do portraiture and figure drawing. She soon discovered that people, and in particular children, interested her most.

Before long, Ms. Kuck's children's paintings were on display in many New York-area galleries. Reco International President Heio Reich spotted her work and approached her to create a series of plates, *Games Children Play*. Soon she added *The Grandparent Collector's Plates* series and *Little Professionals*.

Ms. Kuck's other collections include *Days Gone By*, *A Childhood Almanac*, annual Christmas and Mother's Day series, and *Barefoot Children*, which are being offered by Reco through The Hamilton Collection. Ms. Kuck has earned the NALED Artist of the Year award six years running — an unprecedented honor. She is also the recipient of numerous awards including Print and Plate of the Year, Plate of the Show, Silver Chalice and Award of Excellence.

Sandra entered a new medium in 1989 with the introduction of "Loving Steps," for which she won Doll of the Year. "Loving Steps" is the first in a series of mother and child porcelain dolls, entitled *The Precious Memories of Motherhood Doll Collection*. "Lullaby" was the second issue followed by "Expectant Moments" and "Bedtime."

Ms. Kuck's beautiful portraits of children from an era gone by, "Puppy" and "Kitten," were introduced in 1991 as part of *The Premier Collection*. The latest additions are "La Belle" and "Le Beau." Also in 1991, Ms. Kuck's *Hearts and Flowers* plate series debuted, and she was honored with a retrospective of her work at the 1991 South Bend

Collectible Exposition.

"Best Friends," the first issue in a new series entitled *Sugar and Spice*, was introduced by Reco in 1993. "Morning Glory," the first issue in the *Gift of Love* Mother's Day collection, and "Rejoice," second in the annual series *Tidings Of Joy*, were also released in 1993.

DAVID LAROCCA

Photo Credit: Nancy DuVergen Smith

Born in May 1954, in Cambridge, Massachusetts, David LaRocca received his formal art education at the Massachusetts College of Art. His early artistic efforts were the result of his attempts to copy in miniature his father's collection of statuary, armor and weapons. Later, he began researching these pieces to improve his accuracy and detailing.

While his teachers stressed abstract forms and texture, LaRocca tended toward perfecting his exacting representational work in miniature. After getting into body building, LaRocca became equally fascinated with the human anatomy and its movements. To ensure accurate body movements, LaRocca does his figures nude and then clothes them in authentic costumes.

Through his exhaustive research, LaRocca verifies the authentic details of every shield, gun and canteen. This fact is most obvious when one studies his sculptures for Chilmark Pewter, which include western, military and historical designs.

In addition to his work for the Chilmark line, LaRocca has sculpted many designs for Lance's Hudson Pewter line. His most recent designs have been for the highly successful *Villagers* and, new in 1993, *Summer Villagers* collections.

WENDY LAWTON

Born in San Francisco in 1950,

Wendy Lawton grew up in a large happy family. When she was ten, her family moved to the East Bay suburb of Union City where she attended grammar and high school. Wendy then enrolled in San Jose State University where she majored in home economics and art. She worked her way through college, scooping ice cream and teaching summer art classes. Later, Wendy worked as a graphic artist, kindergarten teacher and daycare administrator.

In 1971, Wendy married Keith Lawton. Because she had always loved dolls, Wendy began to experiment with cloth, bread dough and even plaster for making dolls. The birth of the Lawtons' daughter Rebecca prompted her to seek out a dollmaker who would teach her the intricate processes needed to make porcelain dolls and hand-wefted wigs.

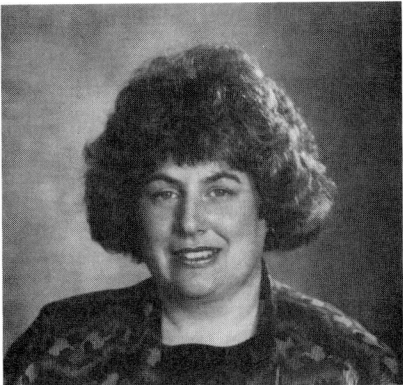

Wendy's first dolls were commissioned portrait dolls, but once retailers saw her work, they immediately began placing orders. Wendy's dolls are recognized for their fresh, all-American look.

In the late 1970s, Wendy and Keith formed Lawtons to produce and market Wendy's dolls, and in 1986 Lawtons produced the first in what would become a distinguished collection of original limited edition porcelain dolls. In 1987, Jim and Linda Smith, whose firm Tide-Rider has been importing toys for over twenty-five years, joined Keith and Wendy Lawton as partners. With this strong company background in place, Lawtons has gone on to receive twenty-seven nominations for *Doll Reader's* Doll of the Year Award (DOTY) and *Dolls* magazine's Dolls of Excellence, winning two Gold Medals and two DOTY's. "The Lawton Logo Doll," designed by Wendy Lawton for her prestigious company, marks the 100th edition.

JULIA LEE

Julia Lee relies on her wide range of interests for ideas for new Hallmark Keepsake Ornaments. When she's not designing ornaments, the Missouri native enjoys the outdoors, hiking, camping, wood carving, skiing and fishing. Many of these pastimes are represented in Julia's designs.

She imagined Santa fishing when she designed "Hooked on Santa," the 1991 ornament which shows Santa catching his trousers on his own fishing hook. That same year Julia created "Ski Lift Bunny," and "Jingle Bells." Animals show up regularly in Julia's ornament designs, as was the case with "Turtle Dreams," which shows a turtle sleeping inside a shell that opens and closes.

Julia said designing Keepsake Ornaments is a constant challenge. "I try to be creative when I design the ornaments. It's always a challenge to create something that hasn't been done before."

RON LEE

A native Californian, Ron Lee has demonstrated his unique abilities since he was a child. At a very early age, he would sit playing with florist clay as he watched his father create exquisite floral

designs for his successful business.

Talented in many areas, Ron wore a number of different career hats before he finally began working with his father who had inspired him as a child. During this time, Ron began designing intricate western scenes, impressing featured Lance Corporation artist Don Polland, who worked with him to develop his talent and skill. It wasn't long before Ron was a working designer for a gift-ware manufacturer in northern California. Determined to pursue his dream, Ron Lee returned to southern California while continuing to design for other manufacturers.

In 1976, Ron Lee began his own business in which he focused his talent, developing and creating classic clown designs. Securing success with the help of a devout following of collectors, Ron's business grew into his present location in Simi Valley, California, which also houses his Collector's Club.

Ron Lee has carved out yet another niche in the collectibles marketplace: limited edition sculptures based on classic cartoon and live-action characters from the golden age of television and movies. Ron also continues to receive ongoing commissions to create exclusive designs for The Disney Stores.

A thousand of Ron's designs are documented in his book of collectibles entitled *Ron Lee's World of Clowns*. Ron and Jill Lee reside with their four children in Chatsworth, California.

MARTHA LEONE

Martha "Marty" Blair was born in Manhattan, grew up in New Jersey and attended Rhode Island School of Design. She spent the early part of her career successfully designing greeting cards. She married artist John Leone in 1970, and in 1974 they moved to rural Roxbury, New York.

Martha Leone's "neo-primitive" paintings compel the viewer's eye to wander, taking in all the rich detail and color. They take the viewer back to a simpler time and trigger a spark of nostalgia.

"My paintings may seem fanciful, but they are very real," she says. "The locale for most of them is within five miles of my home. The activities I portray I know about from either having participated in them, or from talking at length with people that have."

Martha's latest series for Artaffects is titled *Christmas Celebrations of Yesteryear*. The eight plates in the series feature all the happy hustle and bustle of the Christmas season.

KENNETH AND HOPE LE VAN

Pennsylvania natives Kenneth and Hope LeVan have been working together as a team since the mid-'80s.

Hope grew up in Chester County, Pennsylvania. She studied fine arts at the Philadelphia College of Art where she graduated with highest honors in painting.

Ken was raised in Harrisburg, Pennsylvania, and is a graduate of the Pratt Institute in Brooklyn, New York, where he majored in industrial design.

Together, they have worked on a variety of art and design projects, ranging from porcelain dinnerware and crystal to three-dimensional representations of Walt Disney characters. Their work has earned them international awards in product design, graphic design and package design.

The couple has traveled extensively throughout the United States and Europe to study architecture and has amassed an extensive collection of books and photographs on the subject. They have restored twelve historic buildings, including their current home, which was built in 1750 for patriot Colonel John Lesher.

In 1991, the LeVans combined their artistic talents with their expertise in historic structures to create their first series of architectural miniatures: *Strolling Through Colonial America*, available from Hawthorne Architectural Register. Since then, this remarkably gifted duo has designed four additional collections of sculptures for Hawthorne inspired by American architecture: *Stonefield Valley*, *Gone With the Wind Collection*, *Victoria Grove* and *Concord: Home of American Literature*.

DENNIS LIBERTY

Dennis Liberty has been an artist since he was ten years old. He says he was "always making figures" out of clay and wax. Liberty earned his Bachelor of Fine Arts degree from the University of New Mexico in Albuquerque. During this period, he also sandwiched in a four year hitch in the Navy, serving as a photographer on the USS Independence.

His sculptures are on permanent display in several museums and galleries and are part of many private galleries.

Liberty has been making metal objects for many years, ranging from bronze sculptures to pewter figurines. Liberty's fantasy designs helped him make his mark on Lance's Hudson Pewter Line. His subjects for Hudson have recently expanded to include miniatures for the *Circle H Ranch*, *Indian Village*, *Life at the Pole* and *The Civil War* series.

The *Crystals of Zorn* series represents Liberty's first effort in the limited edition fine pewter market. His designs for Chilmark include the eagles "Proud Hunter" and "The Patriot," and in 1993 he sculpted the premier design in Chilmark's *Annual Santa* series,

"St. Nicholas," executed in Chilmark MetalART™.

MARY LILLEMOE

In a way, Kitty Cucumber has been a part of Mary Lillemoe's life since she was a girl growing up in Minneapolis. "Kitty is based on a cat I had as a child," smiles Mary. "She was all grey, just like Kitty, but she had a crooked tail and an unlikely name for a cat — Flub A Dub. I loved her."

It wasn't until her children were in their teens, however, that the idea for Kitty Cucumber actually presented itself. Although she'd earned an art degree from the University of Minnesota, she married soon after college, moved to New York and focused on raising daughter Annie and son Jim. Then one day she sat down and started doing some sketches of a little grey kitten similar to Flub A Dub, dressing her in Victorian costumes. When Mary showed them to her daughter, Annie suggested the name Kitty Cucumber. It worked perfectly.

Excited by her new creation, Mary surrounded Kitty Cucumber with an assortment of feline friends and placed them all in nostalgic, yet playful, settings. This cast of characters made its official debut in a book published by B. Shackman & Co. and soon became so popular that the kittens began appearing on greeting cards and other paper products. In 1985 Schmid began transforming Mary's characters into the *Kitty Cucumber Collection*, a handcrafted and hand-painted line of collectibles. Today, Kitty Cucumber is one of America's top collectibles.

LENA LIU

Lena Liu was born in Tokyo during her father's tour of duty as a liaison officer for the Chinese Nationalist government. Her mother came from a well-to-do family, and her father was trained as a military officer, attending schools in England and the United States. The family later moved to Taipei, Taiwan.

Lena's talent was recognized early, and she began taking Oriental art lessons under Professor Sun Chia-Chin and later under Professor Huang Chun-Pi before coming to the United States with her family.

She graduated from the School of Architecture and Design at the State University of New York/Buffalo in 1974 and later went to graduate school at U.C.L.A. She worked for an architectural firm until 1977 when she began painting full-time.

Lena's art combines traditional Chinese art with today's Western culture. Working on silk canvas, she uses natural dyes and a "wet on wet" technique to obtain her delicate, transparent colors. To guarantee their authenticity, she carefully researches all her subjects. Ms. Liu's first plate series, *On Gossamer Wings*, was sponsored by the Xerxes Society.

Since then, six other series have debuted featuring her artwork, including Lena Liu's *Hummingbird Treasury* and Lena Liu's *Flower Fairies*. Lena Liu's limited edition plates are available through The Bradford Exchange.

JOYCE LYLE

You could say Joyce Lyle took the long way around to becoming a Hallmark Keepsake Ornament artist. She started out studying physical education at Oklahoma State University, but later took up art education in hopes of teaching. She was soon married and raising five children, a daughter and four sons, which kept her and her husband more than busy.

She joined Hallmark for two years in 1979 and then tried her hand as a freelance artist. Joyce joined the Keepsake Ornament staff in 1984. She has since created a variety of unforgettable ornaments. The artist's strong religious beliefs have inspired designs such as "Little Star Bringer" and "Angelic Harpist," both miniature designs, and her *Heavenly Angels* series.

A memory of her father was the basis for the 1990 "Holiday Cardinals" and 1991 "Cardinal Cameo." "They were created with my dad in mind because he loved birds, and there were always cardinals around his feeders," Joyce said.

Joyce was raised in Tulsa, Oklahoma.

TERESA MADSEN

Teresa Madsen, a native Minnesotan, has been interested in art and sculpting since her grade and high school days. During her years as a cosmetologist, she made various figurines as a hobby and always wanted to pursue her creative interests as an artist on a full-time basis. The combination of her

artistic abilities and experiences gave inspiration to the creation of the *Busy-Bodies* collection from BAND Creations/DreamShapes, Inc.

The unique facial expressions for each of the *BusyBodies* figurines are truly a signature of the creations sculpted by Teresa. "These facial expressions establish a kind of bond between the figurines and the person, where everyone can relate to the feeling being expressed. They make you laugh and smile," says Teresa. The ideas are those that most of us can relate to and makes the *BusyBodies* almost human. She says that her poses come from real experiences which are sculpted into life according to its character.

Each of Teresa Madsen's originals are created in her suburban Minneapolis home. These originals are hand-sculpted in molding clay and are finally completed by applying the paint to finish the art work. Teresa admits that she has some obvious benefits working out of her home. "Not only does my husband, Rick, help me out on some of the painting, but I am able to spend time with our young son, Austin."

Teresa Madsen continues to create the *BusyBodies* collection from BAND Creations for all to enjoy, and to laugh with and at.

MAGO

MaGo was born in 1941. Interestingly, his name means "the magician" in Italian; it is a contraction of his first and last given names, Maurizio Goracci. MaGo began to express himself artistically at a very early age, already painting in oils by the age of ten.

During a three-year stint in the Italian Navy, MaGo delighted his fellow shipmates by painting portraits and theatrical sets. Although MaGo continued

to develop his art, he refused to exhibit his work until his early thirties, in order to "be absolutely certain of my unique form of expression." He has since exhibited throughout Europe, North and South America and in the South Pacific.

MaGo moved to the United States in 1982 and has settled in New York City. His daily routine involves rising at approximately 10 a.m. and painting long into the night, often until 5 a.m., with breaks for meals and exercise. He is obviously a dedicated painter, both for himself and for Artaffects in the field of limited editions and gift items.

He finds painting for Artaffects a challenge because for this field, he must work with a relatively smaller image area than he is usually accustomed to. For this, his artwork must be very straightforward and to the point. Working with Artaffects also gives him a chance to collaborate with other craftsmen who will handle the final production of his work, to make sure his art will translate perfectly to porcelain and other media.

MaGo has been called "the musical painter," not only because he paints with classical background music, but also because through his oils he composes symphonies of beauty, color and light. His work combines the best elements of realism and impressionism. MaGo credits his special style of painting to his strongest influences: Van Dyke, Reubens and Velasquez.

MaGo's "music for the eye" and striking use of harmony and light are very much apparent in his *Heavenly Angels* series of eight plates for Artaffects.

MaGo is currently working on a group of special paintings that will reinforce his standing as one of America's greatest contemporary masters.

EDA MANN

Born in London, England, Eda studied art under two uncles and her father, all professional artists. Eda was sixteen when she immigrated to the United States to study at the National Academy of Design in New York. After graduation, Eda began her professional career as a fabric and fashion designer. While vacationing she met Seymour Mann, an accomplished musician. Shortly after their marriage, the Manns formed a professional partnership in which Seymour handled the business affairs and Eda designed figurines and other decorative

accessories for their popular giftware line such as the *Americana Collection.*

In the 1960s, they founded Seymour Mann, Inc. In addition to raising a family and designing their giftware line, Eda continued to paint. Her work was praised by critics, and two of her paintings have been accepted by the Metropolitan Museum of Art in New York.

A doll collector herself for many years, Eda also made dolls for her children and grandchildren. In 1981, Eda's first limited edition dolls were introduced in the *Connoisseur Doll Collection.* In the past decade, Eda has designed more than 1,500 dolls for this collection. Several of Eda's works have received award recognition.

Eda has recently completed a series of doll paintings and plans to put them on public exhibition in Paris. Considering her talent for portraiture, these future works promise to be as exciting as the dolls they portray.

Each year Eda also designs many dolls for the firm's *Signature Series,* which features doll designs of the nation's top artists.

EMILIO MARTINEZ

Emilio Martinez, master sculptor, was born in June of 1947 in Mexico City.

He attended the National School of Plastic Arts of Mexico City, majoring in commercial drafting and publicity art for television, with specialization in displays. He was tutored in paint technique by Maestro Rafael Rodriguez and studied composition and enamel in copper under the tutelage of Maestro Ayaco Tsuru.

But Emilio's heart was in creation and design and, with that in mind, he started working for a company designing pottery and candles. Always striving for independence and development of his own style, Emilio continued his studies in painting and sculpture.

Emilio is one of the founders of Creart, established in 1978, and is in charge of the art department.

Emilio's love for nature and wildlife, combined with his talent, result in the creation of his excellent wildlife sculptures. Originality, realism and superb detailing are the trademarks of his work. In the peaceful surroundings of the Creart studio in Mexico, where life moves at a slow pace, Emilio faces each day by saying, "Today I am working on my masterpiece."

LINDA MASON

Linda Mason, like many doll artists, has been interested in dolls since she was a little girl. She began making reproduction dolls as a hobby in the late '70s, and finished her first sculpture about ten years later. Unlike most other hobbyists, Linda launched a career with that first doll which would bring her to the pinnacle of the doll world.

In the years since, Linda's popularity has steadily risen. Her limited edition porcelain dolls have consistently sold out, forcing her to reduce the size of her editions with each passing year. She has also added a line of limited edition vinyl dolls to her portfolio.

To keep up with all these demands, Linda has hired assistants to handle the behind-the-scenes tasks of pouring and firing and packing. Linda handles all of the sculpting and costume design. And she is the only one who touches the face or styles the hair on every doll that leaves her studio.

For the Georgetown Collection, Linda has designed a line of reproduction dolls. *The American Diary Dolls*™ is her celebration of America's ethnic diversity. Each doll comes from a different time and place in American history and has a special story to tell. Each one is actually shipped with a book telling about her life. Linda's husband, Donnie, plays an integral part, researching and writing the stories about the little girls.

Linda has been honored five times since 1990 with national awards, and in 1992 she received both the Award of Excellence and the Doll Of The Year (DOTY) award for "Many Stars" from the *American Diary Dolls* collection.

Despite the fame, Linda remains as genuine and sincere as ever. She really enjoys meeting the people who collect her dolls and says that is her favorite part of the business.

SALLY MAXWELL

Sally Maxwell is as unique as her art. She has developed her chosen medium to its fullest. With a single cutting tool, some India ink, a No. 2 sable brush and a piece of scratchboard, Maxwell painstakingly creates a unique style of art, earning her a reputation as the foremost exponent of color scratchboard in the United States today.

Sally Maxwell was born in Monmouth, Illinois in 1946. At an early age, she moved with her family to Mystic, Connecticut. Here is where she became interested in art. "I grabbed my mother's oil paints and set up an easel on the

banks of a river. I painted the seaport from across the river — it was very impressionistic, really kind of nice." Some years later she moved back to Illinois, attended Monmouth College and eventually went into the field of graphic arts.

One day she obtained a dusty book written in 1949, called *How to Cut Drawings on Scratchboard*. This started her off on her great passion for color scratchboard art. After months of experimentation, she began perfecting her own special technique of applying color to scratchboard.

Since then, Sally Maxwell has designed several scratchboard series for Artaffects. Each plate in her latest series, *Love Puppies*, depicts a different breed of dog in a variety of humorous situations.

JOHN MCCLELLAND

The life-sized portrait of his daughter, Susan, which John McClelland created some years back may well have been the major turning point of his career. An art director used the portrait for an ad in a trade magazine, and Miles Kimball, the mail order company, spotted it and asked John McClelland to do a Christmas cover for their catalog. That was the beginning of an association which continues today.

Brigitte Moore of Reco International saw McClelland's Miles Kimball art in the mid-1970s, and Reco arranged for the artist to create limited edition plates. McClelland today is one of the field's most celebrated artists, with numerous Plate of the Year and Artist of the Year awards.

He also has designed several figurine series, and is the creator of a number of limited edition lithographs.

In addition to his many limited edi-

tion offerings and his Miles Kimball work, McClelland is a portraitist with a large following. He also has created scores of illustrations for publications including *The Saturday Evening Post*, *Redbook*, *American* and *Readers Digest*.

McClelland has written two "how-to" books for artists and has taught both intermediate and advanced classes in portrait painting.

John is one of the renowned artists who was asked to paint a childhood image for *The March of Dimes* series. The plate is entitled "A Time to Plant."

McClelland added to his long list of achievements by creating *The Children's Circus Doll Collection*, based upon the popular Reco plate series. 1989 marked a tribute to John McClelland with a retrospective of the artist's work at the South Bend Collectible Exposition, where John's greatest work was on display.

The Treasured Songs of Childhood series was completed in 1990 and in 1991, John's first Christmas series, *The Wonder of Christmas*, debuted. In 1992, Reco introduced John's recent plate series, *A Children's Garden*.

John contributed two issues to Reco's *Premier Collection*: "Love," and "Cherry Blossom Viewing," an exquisite fine china, limited edition bowl.

CINDY M. MCCLURE

Cindy M. McClure has the distinction of being one of the few artists in the world to win the prestigious Doll of the Year Award from the International Doll Academy for two consecutive years. In addition to winning the Doll of the Year Award in 1986 and 1987, Ms. McClure has captured more than twenty major awards in her dollmaking career.

Today, Ms. McClure's dolls are eagerly sought by collectors because many of her original artist dolls, even those made only a few years ago, have appreciated significantly in value on the secondary market.

Ms. McClure's dolls are also in demand because of her sensitive portrayal of children. This is not surprising, because her dolls are inspired by real children she has met. Even the names that she selects for her dolls are names that belong to real children. The artist's new series is *Heavenly Inspirations* which is available through The Ashton-Drake Galleries.

DEREK MCDOWELL

Derek McDowell hails from West Virginia, but is happy to call North Carolina home after having lived there for nine years. Derek studied mechanical drafting, computer aided drafting and autocad at Cape Fear Community College.

Since joining CUI, Inc. in 1991 as a technical artist, Derek has handled most of CUI's customer requested stein projects. He works on a Macintosh computer creating artwork which is output to film, and then screen printed in CUI's decorating department. Derek is also called upon to produce technical drawings and specs for product development.

Derek enjoys spending time in his workshop at home and with his wife and young son, Trey.

ANNE TRANSUE MCGRORY

Anne Transue McGrory began drawing at the age of three. Although she was interested in wildlife and nature, her fascination was thwarted because of childhood allergies which prevented her from exploring the outdoors.

Her college major in illustration emphasized wildlife art. McGrory received her bachelor's degree from the Rhode Island School of Design in 1981. After graduation, she did illustrations for the Massachusetts Audubon Society and for the next three years designed jewelry for a manufacturer in Belmont, Massachusetts. From this experience, Anne developed an interest in three-dimensional art.

McGrory began her sculpting career for The Lance Corporation in 1985 and has created several series for the Hudson line. Her designs for the Chilmark line include a series of original sculptures based on the paintings of Frederick Remington. The first three pieces in the highly successful *OffCanvas*™ series sold out within six months of issue.

Chilmark unveiled McGrory's latest innovation, "hidden image" sculpture, in January of 1993 with the introduction of "Buffalo Vision," first issue in *The Seekers*. Though successfully duplicated in two-dimensional paintings, the use of hidden buffalo images throughout McGrory's warrior bust is a unique and fresh departure for Metal-ART™ sculpture.

JUNE MCKENNA

Exquisite attention to detail marked by authentic period clothing and toys, a whimsical face highlighted by an upturned nose and twinkling brown eyes — these are the trademarks of June

McKenna's famous Santa Claus figurines. Focusing on Santa Claus as he was known in the 16th through the 19th centuries, June McKenna works to include just the right touches to make each figurine the highly sought-after collectible that it is.

The artist, using minute dental tools, sculpts the figurine in clay, achieving such realism that people are often seen touching the lace collar on one piece or the gold braid on another to see whether they are made of fabric or wood resin. A mold is formed and wood resin poured into it and allowed to harden. Finally, artisans meticulously hand-paint each individual figurine and then cover the finished product with the antique finish which gives the distinctive old world appearance which is such a striking part of June McKenna's work.

There are, perhaps, two ways in which the success of a collectible line can easily be measured, and June McKenna Collectibles achieves high marks on both counts. Although June McKenna only began carving her Santa Claus figures in 1982, her major limited edition pieces for 1983 through 1989 have already sold out — quite a feat for a collectible line. And the second criterion for success, one set by June McKenna herself, is that her pieces are designed to be both attractive and affordable to everyone, from the young child who loves Santa, to the most serious collector.

DAN MEDINA

Dan Medina's award-winning artistic genius has proven that he possesses genuine God-given talents. A self-taught illustrator, painter and sculptor, Dan has earned numerous awards in a variety of acclaimed state competitions, including the prestigious City of Los Angeles Bicentennial Award.

Before attempting any artwork,

Dan thoroughly researches each subject to maintain authenticity and develop as many concepts as possible. "Some may sculpt to replicate," Dan explains, "whereas I sculpt to capture a moment in time."

Strongly influenced by artists of the Renaissance period, such as Leonardo da Vinci and Michelangelo, Dan's interest in the art world began as a child. Today, he has evolved into an accomplished, critically-acclaimed sculptor. He also contributes some of his artistic influence to his close association with artist C.A. Pardell.

For a number of years, Dan has served as LEGENDS' art director and has provided significant support to the LEGENDS foundry through his invaluable research and development efforts. "I envision sculpting as an exciting three-dimensional extension of my illustrations. The ability to create overpowers me, whether it pertains to science or the arts. The power to encompass human emotion and even dreams in a work of art is what I live for." It is quite apparent that Dan perceives sculpture as a medium through which he can express emotions. Through his work, he strives to create a balance between the worlds of science and art.

A native of southern California, Dan proves with his artistic genius that he is simply an artist beyond his years.

KEN MEMOLI

"I never knew my grandfather, but he was a big influence in my life. His name was Karl Lang and he was one of the sculptors who worked under Gutzon Borglum on the carving of Stone Mountain, Georgia, and the Mount Rushmore Memorial in South Dakota. I guess it must be in the genes, because I'm very

attracted to sculpture. It's just sort of a feeling."

Now a sculptor for United Design, Ken was born in Stamford, Connecticut and studied art at both the University of Hartford and the University of Oklahoma. Eager to learn, he's done landscape designing and limited edition cookie jars for a woman who specialized in Black collectibles. One of his biggest commissions was to carve a Statue of Liberty for Oklahoma City's celebration of the United States' Bicentennial.

In 1970, Memoli began as a freelancer for United Design, and is now a full-time sculptor for the company. One of the first series he was involved in was the *Little Prince and Princess* done in bonded porcelain. His more recent works include several larger *Animal Classics*, *Twigs*, *Large Easter Rabbits*, *Winterlight* and a *Legend of Santa Claus* figurine which was released as a limited edition.

CLEMENTE MICARELLI

The spirited festivities of Christmas Eve and the fairytale-like story of Clara and her nutcracker provided artist Clemente Micarelli with the perfect vehicle for his entry into the collector plate market. Micarelli studied art at both the Pratt Institute and The Art Students League in New York and the Rhode Island School of Design.

His paintings have been exhibited in numerous shows where he has won many awards. Represented nationally by Portraits, Inc. and C.C. Price Gallery in New York, Micarelli has painted the portraits of prominent personalities throughout the United States and Europe.

Micarelli also has done fashion illustrations for Gimbels, Jordan Marsh, Filene's and Anderson Little in Boston. He has taught at the Rhode Island School of Design, the Art Institute of

Boston and the Scituate Arts Association and South Shore Art Center.

In 1991, Reco International introduced the fourth issue in Micarelli's *Nutcracker Ballet Series*, "Dance of the Snow Fairies." Each plate in the series is based on an actual performance from the renowned Boston Ballet.

The talented portraitist has painted a *Wedding Series* of plates and bells, commissioned by Reco International.

Mr. Micarelli has recently applied his exceptional talent to a plate series depicting revered events in the life of Jesus entitled *The Glory of Christ Collection*.

LARRY MILLER

Raised in a small mining town in Arizona, Larry Miller graduated from the University of Arts and Sciences of Oklahoma, and the University of Oklahoma. He spent five years in the U.S. Army Corps of Engineers where he worked as an illustrator.

Miller's experience as a sculptor has undergone a series of transitions. In college, he concentrated on welding sculptures, but his interest later shifted to bronze. Three of his bronzes are in the permanent collection of the Gil Crease Museum in Tulsa, Oklahoma.

A member of United Design's staff for ten years, Miller has sculpted pieces for the *Stone Critters*®, *Animal Classics*™, *The Legend of Santa Claus*™, *The Legend of the Little People*™ and *Jolly Old Elf*™ product lines.

"I love fantasy. That's one of the reasons I like doing the Legends series. I've done leprechauns and little people, and I'm at my best when my sculptures highlight fantasy."

BRYAN MOON

British born Bryan Moon is a versatile wildlife artist with a perceptible individual style. He weaves a tapestry of emotion in each of his paintings, reflecting his commitment to the subject and his own high standards of excellence.

Moon moved to Minnesota from England twenty-three years ago with his wife and two sons. Recently, he retired as vice-president of advertising from Northwest Orient Airlines, when his painting and drawing were done on leisure time only. Today, Moon lives in Old Frontenac, Minnesota and creates art on a full-time basis.

Through his experiences in Africa, China, the South and North Poles and the South Pacific, Moon has created an impressive exhibit of originals and prints.

Bryan Moon is represented by Hadley House.

JASON MORGAN

Jason Morgan began working for CUI, Inc. in 1989. He does illustration for product, creates logos, designs collectors' edition steins and works on the Macintosh to create artwork for film output and screen printing.

Jason is a native Texan and studied

art at Tyler Junior College in Tyler, Texas. He also studied and has experience in various aspects of photography. He uses acrylics and watercolors to create illustrations for use on steins, plates and collectibles.

Jason and his wife devote many hours to the local Humane Society and various environmental organizations.

ANDREW MOSS

Andrew Moss was apprenticed to Peggy Davies for four years and greatly benefited from the teaching of this remarkable lady. It was she who first recognized his talent and encouraged him to start modeling alongside his job as a caster. He was touched to be presented with Peggy's modeling tools and is now demonstrating that her confidence was well placed with recent figures such as "The Last of the Reindeer" and "Charlotte Rhead."

Andrew has modeled a number of toby jugs for Kevin Francis, Inc., including "The Teddy," "Helmut Kohl," "The Golfer" and "President Gorbachev," which have been very well received by collectors.

He has also worked on the Warner Brothers *Looney Tunes* collection.

JOCELYN MOSTROM

Jocelyn Mostrom and her dolls have been featured in several national magazine articles and a book of contemporary Santa dolls. She first came to national recognition as the woman who raised the American craft of cornhusk doll-making into a fine art. With the vision of a true artist, she was able to utilize a primitive Folk Art to design wonderful porcelain dolls that would rival the appeal of priceless antiques.

There was a time when Jocelyn claimed she would never dress her dol-

lies with anything except cornhusk costumes. All this was said before her association with Kurt S. Adler, Inc. Today, Jocelyn happily admits enjoying the challenge of working in many mediums to create her dolls and the freedom to experiment with new subjects.

The first step in her creative process is to select a favorite historical period, immerse herself in research studying the people and their times, and then create lifelike dolls to dramatize their lifestyles. Known for creating dolls with unique personalities, she depicts them with open-mouths, outreached arms and bodies-in-motion. Detailed costumes and accessories, hand-painted and delicately sculptured heads, combined with bodies poised for clearly defined activities are the trademarks of her dolls.

Jocelyn designed an exclusive collection of Christmas doll ornaments titled *Christmas in Chelsea*, as well as a series of limited edition Santas for Kurt S. Adler, Inc. She has also been engaged by the firm to design the *Royal Heritage Collection* of collectible dolls and holiday ornaments featuring endearing children in regal, turn-of-the-century dress.

REAL MUSGRAVE

Real Musgrave is an artist who follows

a whimsical muse. The *Pocket Dragons, Wizards* and other creatures that Real sculpts spring to life from the complex and wonderful world he has created in drawings and paintings for over twenty years. Those finely detailed drawings bespeak the heritage of beautifully illustrated children's books from the turn-of-the-century, but to everything he adds a vision of gentleness and humor which is uniquely his own.

Real and his wife Muff have been married since 1968. They immediately began creating what many call their "Magic Kingdom." In 1978 Muff became Real's business manager and full-time creative partner. Now for days at a time, they can forget that the outside world exists as Real happily works in his studio, immersed in his own creations and surrounded by the animals who provide ideas and inspiration. Days blend into nights and time loses its meaning as new drawings, paintings and sculptures gradually take shape.

His work has been exhibited in shows at the Delaware Art Museum, the New York Society of Illustrators, the Canton Art Institute, the Worcester Science Center and many other galleries and museums. It has attracted collectors from all countries, and today Real is recognized as one of the foremost fantasy artists in the world. The *Pocket Dragons* appear in greeting cards, posters, limited edition prints, jigsaw puzzles and counted cross stitch patterns, as well as the delightful sculptures produced by Collectible World Studios/Land of Legend and distributed by Lilliput Incorporated.

JAN NAHRGANG

As the mother of six and a full-time special education teacher of grade school children, Jan Nahrgang experiences

firsthand all the bliss and the disappointments that fill young children's lives. Over the past ten years, Ms. Nahrgang also has developed a rare gift for translating her love of children into dolls that capture their innocence and charm.

Ms. Nahrgang made her first porcelain doll more than ten years ago to fulfill a Christmas request. One doll led to another, and after a number of sculpting classes and study, she moved from copying reproduction dolls to designing originals.

While she continues to teach full time, her doll business, The Nahrgang Collection, is very much a family-run business in Moline, Illinois. Almost all of her family have become involved in the enterprise. Husband Larry pours the doll heads and keeps the books. Daughter Jennifer is the company's shipping and decorating manager. Jan's son, Ray Monterestelli, is the production manager and marketing director.

Still very much committed to creating original dolls, Ms. Nahrgang spends a great deal of time sculpting her dolls. She designs and makes the first dress and paints all the faces herself, attempting to paint about twenty dolls a night — about equal to the factory's daily production.

Originality and subtle humor are evident in Jan Nahrgang's doll designs. Although she is a newcomer to the industry, the quality of Ms. Nahrgang's dolls was recognized in 1990 when her "Karissa" doll was nominated for *Doll Reader* magazine's 1990 "Doll of the Year" (DOTY) award in the collectible porcelain doll category.

RYUJU NAKAI

Born in Japan, the son of a Buddhist monk, Ryuju Nakai has called America home for over twenty years, living happily in New Jersey with his wife

Cynthia and their three children.

Prior to founding Crystal World in 1983, he worked as a goldsmith, honing his patience, his eye for fine detail and his keen sensitivity to aesthetic beauty and balance. Working in the jewelry industry, he developed an inexplicable fascination for lead crystal art being displayed alongside his fine jewelry. This fascination fostered his change of mediums, and his skills acquired as a goldsmith have since been manifested adeptly in his designs for Crystal World.

There are many differences between the two mediums. "Working in crystal is very different," says Nakai, "because of the way light is reflected by and through the crystal. When you make a crystal figurine, you need one strong point where the viewer can focus attention... Crystal requires extremely precise cutting and you must also grind and polish each piece yourself, which takes much, much time. I think this is why our architectural series stands alone, because we are creating each piece entirely by ourselves."

With numerous of his designs having been nominated for awards, he believes that successful collectibles, like successful lives, depend on proper "give-and-take". In reference to collectibles, he explains: "When we say 'give-and-take', we generally mean telling a story through the use of two characters... The point is that they are interacting with each other, and interacting — this give-and-take — provides the story and theme that catches and then holds the attention of the collector."

If the past is any indication of the future, Ryuju Nakai's designs will continue to hold the attention of countless collectors.

DIANNA NEWBURN

"I love making the children, especially the little girl dolls, because I love dressing them up in all the frilly clothes," says Dianna Newburn.

Being an avid doll collector, Dianna experimented with making miniature clay dolls of her own. "Then, of course, the dolls had to have tiny toys to play with and miniature furniture to sit on," she says. Soon she had a whole doll's room full of clay miniatures.

She went to miniature shows with a friend and soon had a national following of her work, Collectibles by Dianna,

among miniature collectors. Eventually she began making her dolls out of porcelain rather than clay. She called her dolls My Precious.

By 1990, her work had become so popular that it sold out at a miniature show in Kansas City just seven minutes after the show opened. She was exhausted from making all the reproductions, and the demand was exceeding her ability to produce in her home studio.

She joined the staff of artists at United Design where she continues to create original dolls and other figurines. The American craftsmen at United Design reproduce the originals with exact detail.

Currently, she is sculpting figurines for the *Angels Collection*™, *Angel Babies*™, *Fairie Tales*™, *Caroling Children*™, the *Itty Bitty Critters*™ collection, a line of miniature toys and children, and a line of miniature clocks, frames and figurines with a storybook theme.

JORGEN NIELSEN

Born in 1942, Jorgen Nielsen joined the artists and manufacturers at Royal

Copenhagen Porcelain Manufactory at the age of seventeen. Since then he has ambitiously pursued various types of artistry at Royal Copenhagen and abroad.

Although he was originally trained as an overglaze painter, Jorgen began working in 1965 as a painter of unique underglaze vases. Only after four years of study travels in Japan, did he return to overglaze painting for a couple of years.

In 1976, Jorgen took the opportunity to work under the tutelage of ceramic artist Nils Thorsson, using the media of faience, porcelain and stoneware. Proving his ambition, he also worked in Royal Copenhagen's drawing studio at this time, as a draftsman of a diversity of subjects.

Currently, Jorgen Nielsen is employed as a free-lance artist for Royal Copenhagen and manages his own studio. For Royal Copenhagen, he has created the wonderful new series *Nature's Children*.

CHRIS NOTARILE

A native of Brooklyn, New York, Chris Notarile is a graduate of the Parsons School of Design in New York City. He originally dreamt of becoming a comic illustrator and, in fact, was publishing his own comic strip while still a teenager. However, while in school, his interest in realistic art soon took precedence. His work has been seen in numerous magazines, and his portraits have appeared on everything from book covers to movie posters. His celebrity subjects have included Bill Cosby, Clint Eastwood, Kevin Costner and Michael J. Fox.

Notarile, who now lives in New Jersey with his wife and two young children, has also created artwork for two series depicting Marilyn Monroe: *The Marilyn Monroe Collection* and *The*

Magic of Marilyn. They are available from The Bradford Exchange.

ROBERT OLSZEWSKI

Growing up on the edge of a small town near Pittsburgh, Pennsylvania, Robert Olszewski was free to roam the countryside and make drawings of the things that pleased him.

He continued to draw and paint throughout high school and college, but he was enough of a realist to also earn a Bachelor's Degree in Art Education. After graduation, Olszewski and his wife set out for California where he taught during the day and painted at night.

He was propelled into the miniature art form when one of his paintings was stolen from a gallery. He had no photo of the stolen work so he painted a copy for the police. Ironically, he liked the miniature copy better.

Intrigued by miniatures, he began to study and experiment with increasingly smaller works of art. Olszewski eventually began working in the ancient "lost wax" technique, and in 1977 produced his first one-twelfth scale figurine. Two years later, he signed an exclusive contract to produce for and oversee the creative directions for Goebel Miniatures studios in Camarillo, California.

The art form of painted bronze miniatures (Cire Perdue Bronze Poly Chromes) pioneered by Goebel Miniatures with Robert Olszewski as Master Artist, is an established and sought after medium in the field of collecting. Today, Robert Olszewski conducts the artistic course of the world's largest studio producing fine miniatures and objects of art.

Olszewski's dedication to his talent and his art form has earned him international acclaim. At middle age, Olszewski feels his best creative years are still ahead of him.

DON PALMITER

While Don Palmiter's name may seem somewhat new to Keepsake Ornament fans, he's actually been with Hallmark for twenty-five years. A Kansas City native, he joined the company right out of high school and spent several years as an engraver.

After joining the ornament staff, for three years the artist worked solely on collectibles, including the *Hometown America* and *Mary and Friends* groups.

In the two short years Don has been designing Keepsake Ornaments, he has created a number of popular designs. His "'57 Corvette" was among the most sought after designs in 1991. Don, who will design the entire *Classic American Cars* series, has had a lifelong affection for classic automobiles. He has owned a 1962 Covair, 1963 Rolls Royce Silver Cloud and a 1968 Corvette. He also collects glass and crystal.

Other recent designs created by Don include "Good Sledding Ahead" and "Green Thumb Santa," which was inspired by the artist's love of gardening.

CHRISTOPHER A. PARDELL

Christopher A. Pardell, gifted young American sculptor, attributes his international acclaim to a natural passion for art and a five-year apprenticeship study-ing under Italian masters: Gino Bonvi, Aldo Gregory and Vertitio Bonofazi.

Influenced by the work of renowned sculptors Russell, Remington and Rodin, Pardell pursued his passion for realism, a passion unchallenged by the abstraction-obsessed classrooms of ivory-tower academia.

Through pantomimed conversations with accomplished artists and craftsmen whose European dialects he could not understand, Pardell became proficient at the many schools of sculptural design. He achieved a classic style and thereafter, he closed his apprenticeship.

Over the next four years, Pardell explored the potential of his gift as a free-lance sculptor, playing with volume, balance, tension and form in a subject range encompassing wildlife to western, oceanic to equestrian and outdoorsmen to nudes. A master of technique and design, he then joined LEGENDS.

Since that time, his natural talent, dedication and unique artistic vision have culminated in the creation of compositions commended by fellow craftsmen and collectors of fine art.

A conservationist, he works closely with six different wildlife organizations. A humanist, he supports Green Peace and the United Sioux of America in an effort to protect the lifestyles threatened by today's age of technological revolution — something he further preserves through the everlasting quality of his art. An opportunist, Pardell founded "Aesthetic Associates," an organization committed to helping young and gifted artists struggling to realize their artistic identities.

Born in Oakland, Pardell now resides in southern California with his wife, Nancy, and their two sons, P.J. and Sean.

PHYLLIS PARKINS

Phyllis Parkins loved china painting and a variety of craft projects. So it really wasn't very surprising when she began making her first porcelain dolls for her young daughters.

In 1977, Phyllis' husband was transferred to Rolla, Missouri. Shortly after they arrived, a neighbor, Mable Scoville, came to welcome them to the area. Mrs. Scoville also was a crafter and skilled seamstress. After seeing some of Phyllis' dolls, Mable offered to sew dresses for them. That fall, Phyllis' dolls

sold out at a large craft show in St. Louis, and dealers approached her about making dolls for their shops. Phyllis' fledgling doll company, The Collectables, was on its way.

The company continued to grow slowly. In 1982, a new factory was built and in 1984, John Parkins came into the business full-time, freeing Phyllis to devote more time to design work.

Recognizing that original dolls were the next trend, Phyllis taught herself to sculpt. Since 1985, Phyllis and her dolls have won recognition with various prestigious awards and nominations for awards. In 1989, Phyllis' Collectors Club was founded. She was also honored in 1990, with the commission to create fifty spellbinding dolls for the White House Christmas tree, the theme being the magical Nutcracker Suite. A new company, Designs by Phyllis, was formed in 1991 to handle the artist's new vinyl doll line.

HAL PAYNE

Born and raised in El Paso, Texas, Hal Payne is an American artist who currently resides in northern Idaho with his family. Art has held Hal's interest since childhood, and the need to create has led him to explore many art forms, including oils, woodworking, mixed media, sculpting and, of course, designing dolls.

In his late twenties, he moved to Los Angeles, where he founded a company designing and building trade show booths for the men's apparel industry. In 1980, he left L.A. for a more peaceful life in northern Idaho where he decided to put his lifelong love of art to the ultimate test and see if he could provide for his family using his art skills exclusively. With his wife's background as a pattern-maker in the garment industry, it was best for them to focus together on designing dolls.

Their work paid off. Since 1987, Hal has won many awards and nominations for awards from *Dolls* magazine for his dolls. He has recently received two more nominations, including one Award of Excellence for "Spanky," which was created for Seymour Mann in its *Signature Series*. Hal designed several other dolls for Seymour Mann, Inc. in 1993.

Hal sincerely hopes that his unique sculptures bring the same joy to collectors that they have brought to him in their creation. His goal is "to re-create, if just for a moment, that time when we were all children and the world was filled with delightful wonder."

NADA PEDLEY

Nada Pedley was born in Slavania, in a small village near Bled. The daughter of a dressmaker, she fondly remembers being dressed up in pretty lacy outfits for special festivals such as Easter and Christmas. This childhood experience clearly influenced her work as an artist and is reflected in her pretty lady figures for Royal Doulton. Nada still adores frills and ribbons and spends much of her spare time scouring antique shops for old lace and dolls.

Her other delight is children, and this manifests itself in her work. A mother of three, Nada devotes most of her time to looking after her family, but for four hours a day, she retires to her "studio," the front room of her semi-detached house, to model.

Being accepted as a modeler for Royal Doulton was "a dream come true" says Nada. It was also the result of many hours of practice and years of study at evening classes in England and Germany. Two years ago, Nada decided to send photographs of her latest work, at that time, flower children with fairies, to Royal Doulton's art director. Since then she has been busy working on child studies and pretty ladies for the company, regularly visiting the factory to show the progress of her work to family or friends.

For reference nowadays, Nada often turns to her collection of sepia photographs and old postcards of children which she has picked up on her visits to museums of childhood all over Europe. Collectors can look forward to seeing plenty more of Nada's wonderful work in the future.

VICENTE PEREZ

Master sculptor Vicente Perez is the kind of artist and sculptor that is not satisfied just to produce a beautiful sculpture. His concept is to attempt to "give life" to his pieces. In his opinion, "realism is the beauty of our work."

Born in Veracruz, Mexico in August 1940, Vicente studied at the National School of Plastic Arts. His art career began in the studios of the maestros, Humberto Pedraza and well-known sculptor and painter Francisco Zuniga. Vicente then went on to teach clay and plastics modeling for fifteen years at The Technical School of Mexico. He also worked for several years at the National Institute of Anthropology and History making replicas of pre-hispanic sculptures, which gave him experience in molding and casting, as well as sculpting.

In 1978, Vicente Perez co-founded, with Emilio Martinez, Creart, a leading manufacturer of wildlife sculptures.

GREGORY PERILLO

As a child in Staten Island, New York, Gregory Perillo's Italian immigrant father would tell him colorful stories about the Old West. Young Greg would sketch what he envisioned from

those grand tales and dreamed of the day when he would visit the American Indians for himself.

After a stint in the Navy, Perillo had the opportunity to come face-to-face with American Indians he had read and dreamed so much about. Except for his curly hair, they mistook the Italian Perillo for a full-blooded Indian. Being mistaken for a Native American solidified his identification with the people he was to paint for the rest of his life.

Perillo dedicated himself to portraying the American Indian culture with fidelity and respect. He studied under the late western art master, William R. Leigh. In fact, he was Leigh's one and only student.

The artist began a series of one-man shows and gallery exhibitions that continues even today. In addition, his works were chosen for the permanent collections of a number of museums and institutions.

In the late 1970s, Perillo began creating limited edition plates, figurines and graphics for Vague Shadows (Artaffects). Since then he has won numerous awards — both personally, and for his portrayals of American Indian life. In 1991, the Artaffects Perillo Collectors Club began and met with great response.

Perillo's most recent plate series include the mystical *Spirits of Nature* and the delightfully playful *Children of the Prairie*.

"Brave and Free," one of Perillo's most beloved images, is now available as a collectible doll in the new series titled *Children of the Plains*. The little Blackfoot boy is joined by "Song of the Sioux," "Gentle Shepherd," "Bird Song" and four more dolls from various Indian nations.

DON POLLAND

In early childhood, Don Polland carved his own toy cowboys and Indians. Living in Utah, Arizona, Colorado and Nevada, he developed an intense interest in the golden days of the American West, which he has continued to express in three-dimensional art throughout each phase of his life.

Polland's first career was that of an illustrator for space age industries. He became a professional artist in 1959. His goal as an artist is to express his personal thoughts and beliefs as a storyteller. He strives to communicate his ideas visually, without the need for words of explanation.

A self-taught and highly motivated artist, Don Polland considers creativity his way of life. His subject matter ranges from working cowboys, to wild animals, to Indians of the past and present. Because of their great challenge and long history in the world of art, Polland especially enjoys creating miniature sculptures.

Polland's works are displayed in an extensive list of museum showings. His awards and honors include numerous Best of Show and First Place awards at art shows nationwide. He was awarded the 1980 Favell Museum Western Heritage Award for excellence in portraying America's West and wildlife in sculpture. In addition, Polland is listed in a variety of "Who's Who" art publications.

Today, Polland continues to work on his beloved miniature figurines. From the studio which bears his name, he also has introduced more than fifty gallery and museum bronzes as well as works for The Franklin Mint, Chilmark and other fine art firms.

JUDI KENT PYRAH

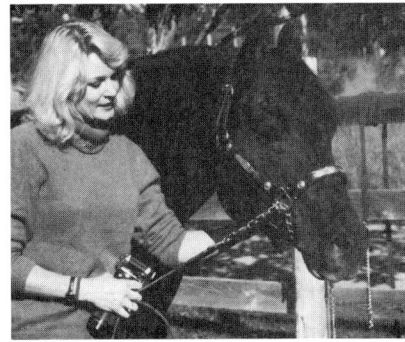

From a child growing up in England who rode unbroken horses "borrowed" from Gypsy encampments, to an adult riding the King of Jordan's well-trained personal stallion on the palace grounds, artist Judi Kent Pyrah has come a long way.

The one constant throughout Ms. Pyrah's life has been horses — riding, grooming, drawing and painting them. Because of her intimate understanding and love of horses, she has mastered translating that knowledge onto canvas.

Ms. Pyrah paints only what she has personally seen or tried. She has played polo, driven four-in-hand, ridden race horses, trotters and pacers. "I've hunted, ridden cross-country, show jumped and worked at race yards and training stables. Everything I've painted, I've been very involved with," she says.

Judi Kent Pyrah currently resides in England with her husband and son. She is represented by Hadley House.

CHRISTOPHER RADKO

Born in New York City, Christopher Radko has traveled extensively, both in the United States, and in Europe. His family background (Polish, Austrian and French) meant that during school vacation he always had a cousin somewhere to visit. These contacts have kept Christopher in good stead when he began his career designing Christmas ornaments.

As a child, Christopher grew up with varied traditions handed down from his faraway relatives. These traditions covered everything from music, art and architecture, to language, literature, food and folk customs.

During December, many of these traditions were combined in Christopher's childhood home. "Christmas was like being at the United Nations for me," Christopher remembers. "We had carols, food, and ornaments from all over Europe." Christopher's family tree towered over fourteen feet, loaded with decorations, some of which dated back to the 1880s.

As a Christmas artist, Christopher draws upon his diverse memories of family celebrations and collections of old

decorations. "All our ornaments were made of glass," Christopher remembers. "I feel strongly about having my designs made by craftsmen in countries that celebrate Christmas. The spirit of the glassblower and decorator is in every ornament I produce."

Each year, more than half of Christopher's collection is changed or retired. This fresh approach carries forth a lost tradition, begun by ornament designers at the turn-of-the-century: that of creating new collections every year. "People get tired of seeing the same old stuff in the stores. Collectors want new designs to add to their tree," Christopher adds.

His desire to create exquisitely blown and intricately decorated ornaments led Christopher to select expert craftsmen only in Italy, the Czech Republic, Germany and Poland. He visits the cottage factories and works with each person on a one-to-one basis, showing them how to revive techniques used at the turn-of-the-century. The results are sparkling ornaments that are every bit as glorious, and often better than those made 100 years ago.

TERRY REDLIN

Over the past fifteen years, Master Artist Terry Redlin has become one of the country's outstanding and most widely collected painters of wildlife and Americana. His signatures — blazing sunrises and sunsets and nostalgic themes — are often cited as the reasons for his immense popularity.

Redlin's interest in the outdoors can be traced to his childhood in Watertown, South Dakota, where he spent as much time as possible fishing and hunting with his uncle. When a motorcycle accident ended his dream of becoming a forest ranger, he opted to pursue a career in the graphic arts. He earned a degree from the St. Paul School of

Associated Arts and spent twenty-five years working in the commercial art field as a layout artist, graphic designer, illustrator and art director. In his leisure hours, he researched wildlife subjects and settings.

In 1977, at the age of forty, Redlin burst onto the wildlife scene and since then, his meteoric rise has been unparalleled in the field of contemporary wildlife art.

Although proud of his artistic achievements, Redlin derives the most satisfaction from his conservation work. Over the past ten years, his donations to Ducks Unlimited alone have raised more than $15 million, setting an all-time record in art sales for wetland preservation projects. By his own estimate, he has donated an additional $4 million to other non-profit conservation groups.

Terry Redlin is a multi-talented artist who brings to life the memories of yesterday and paints to preserve our dreams. He is represented by Hadley House.

CHUCK REN

As a native of the American Southwest, Chuck Ren remembers growing up "surrounded by cowboys and Papago Indians." He also remembers developing an early interest in art, inspired by the dramatic Western themes of Charles Russell and Frederic Remington. His interests led him to the University of Arizona in Tucson, where he received his degree in fine art.

After working several years as a commercial artist, Ren became a free-lance illustrator, serving such prestigious clients as The North American Hockey League, The National Football League, Paramount Pictures and A&M Records.

Ten years ago, the prestigious Gray Stone Press premiered the artist's first limited edition prints, enabling Ren to

trade his free-lance work for a full-time career as a fine artist. He and his family then moved to paradise-like Sedona, Arizona, knowing it was the perfect place for a painter of the West to live and work.

Today, the highly sought-after original paintings of Chuck Ren can be found in galleries and private collections throughout the United States. In 1992, Chuck Ren agreed to make his work available in the popular collector plate medium. His first plate for The Hamilton Collection, titled "Deliverance," was an immediate success among plate collectors. As a result, he began work on a new series of plates titled *The Last Warriors*. Through Ren's devotion to preserving America's rich heritage, his collectors continue to discover the immense natural beauty of the land he calls home, and better appreciate the fascinating traditions of the people who have watched over this land for many years.

PIERRE-AUGUSTE RENOIR

Renoir's love of life and joy in painting shine out of his every work. He was master of many techniques, not only impressionist, and for that reason he is seen as one of the painting masters of all time.

Born in Limoges, France in 1841, Pierre-Auguste Renoir showed a very early gift for drawing. At age thirteen, he was apprenticed to a porcelain factory.

At sixteen Renoir painted his first portrait, of his grandmother, but it was not until 1862 that he enrolled at the Ecole des Beaux-Arts studying under the Swiss Master Gleyre. He was at once drawn into a circle of friends that included Monet, Sisley and Bazille, and came under the influence of Manet and Courbet.

For ten years from 1873, Renoir had his studio in Paris. Although his paintings were frequently rejected by the Salons, Renoir managed to sell work regularly, usually portraits. In 1881 Renoir travelled abroad and on returning to France, spent some time working with Cézanne. From then on, he travelled regularly within France. In 1890 Renoir married Aline Charigot, his mistress of ten years, and together they had three sons.

In his sixties, Renoir was stricken with rheumatoid arthritis. By 1912, both legs were paralyzed and his paintbrush had to be tied to his hand. Renoir always felt that a painting should give pleasure, so neither his own suffering nor that of the world was ever allowed a place in his work. At seventy he began a new career as a sculptor with the help of an assistant.

In 1900 Renoir was awarded the Légion d'Honneur, and in August 1919, he saw one of his portraits hung in the Louvre. Renoir died in December of that year.

DILL RHODUS

"When I'm designing, my goal is to capture the image that I had in my mind when I first imagined the ornament," says artist Dill Rhodus. Dill, who grew up in Kansas City, joined Hallmark about twenty-five years ago as an apprentice engraver. Over the next several years, he honed his skills and became a senior artist engraver.

Dill turned to designing Keepsake Ornaments five years ago. His creations include "Friendship Kitten," the first two editions in the Keepsake Magic Ornament *Peanuts*® series, and "Unicorn Fantasy," the first ornament Dill designed and still his favorite. He has also sculpted a number of Keepsake Miniature Ornament designs, including "Bright Boxers" and "Busy Bear."

The artist spends part of his work day as a quality planner, which involves him in technical and other aspects of producing Keepsake Ornaments. He is married to Patricia Andrews, who is also a Keepsake Ornament artist.

JEANNETTE RICHARDS AND SANDRA PENFIELD

The designers of BAND Creations' *Best Friends*, Jeannette Richards and Sandra Penfield have discovered the excitement of creating a world of clay miniatures. Combining their varied talents, creative abilities and formal education, they have succeeded in capturing the simplicity of the American spirit.

Jeannette, from Rocky River, Ohio, studied art in Washington, D.C. and received her B.A. in English and Art from the University of Dayton, Ohio. Growing up in a family of artists, illustration was her first love.

Sandra grew up in Detroit Lakes, Minnesota and received a B.S. in Art from the University of North Dakota. She taught art and shared her talents through her woodcut prints.

Their mutual interest in art brought them together in Hudson, Wisconsin where they became partners in a graphic design business in 1984.

Always experimenting with new ideas, they created their first Christmas Angel in October, 1990. Portraying the essence of innocence and delight, their new creations blossomed. Using the limitless boundaries of clay, these designs soon evolved to include all the facets of friendship and family life.

LUCY RIGG

Lucy Rigg began making baker's clay teddy bear figurines in 1969 while awaiting the birth of her daughter, Noelle. She decorated the nursery with her first teddy bears, but friends and family were so enchanted with the original creations that Lucy began making

them for others.

Teddy bear collectors bought her hand-painted clay dough bears, known as "Rigglets," at street fairs. To keep up with the growing demand, she imposed a quota on herself to make 100 teddy bears per day and often stayed up until the wee hours of the morning to meet her goal.

As her teddy bears became more popular, Lucy formed her own company. In the late 1970s, Enesco Corporation President Eugene Freedman approached Lucy and proposed turning her handmade teddy bears into a line of porcelain bisque figurines and accessories. Since Enesco introduced the *Lucy & Me*® *Collection* in 1978, it has enjoyed steady support from collectors and teddy bear lovers.

Lucy continues to operate Lucy & Company, designing diaries, baby announcements, calendars and her "teddy bear" version of popular children's books.

Lucy has been a teddy bear collector herself since 1968. Her Seattle home is filled with toys and collector items, which project the warmth and joy of her artwork. She has created a special room to display the *Lucy & Me Collection*, which now includes several hundred figurines, plus many accessory items, including tins, plates, mugs, covered dishes, laminated bags and more — each adorned with her lovable teddy bears.

Lucy is known today as one of the most prolific teddy bear artists in the world.

DOREEN NOEL ROBERTS

Doreen Noel Roberts, poet and painter, was born in Burnley, Lancashire, England and comes from a long line of artists. She spent two years at

college in business training, which was followed by a short instructive spell as an accounting clerk.

In 1954, Doreen joined PenDelfin Studios Ltd., via the Burnley Artists' Society, where her natural talents were developed by Jean Walmsley Heap, chairman of PenDelfin. After absorbing each step of production over the years, Doreen ultimately became a designer and sculptor of the famous PenDelfin rabbits. She now designs and models full-time for PenDelfin and is a member of its board of directors, as well as a partner in the PenDelfin Design Unit.

JIM ROBISON

Wildfowl woodsculptor Jim Robison was born in Pekin, Illinois in 1961. Jim has been carving since he was twelve years old, starting with duck decoys, and over the years, expanding into decorative wildfowl carvings. An avid outdoorsman, Jim's love for wildlife is evident through his work as a self-taught artist, who has also taught woodcarving classes himself.

Jim and his wife Sheri live in a small rural town — Hopedale, Illinois — where they have a fifty-acre farm in which they can enjoy watching wildlife. The inspiration for Jim's work comes

from those surroundings.

Jim's interest in birds has led him into the art of falconry and raptor conservation. He is a director of the Raptor Resource Project in which the goal is to reintroduce the peregrine falcon into the world.

Jim has numerous carving achievements that he has obtained through the years. He is a world-class contender in the wildfowl carving circuit and his sculptures have been selected on three different occasions to be exhibited in the Leigh Yawkey Woodson Art Museum's "Birds In Art" exhibit. His work has been featured in *People* Magazine and in a film produced by Landsburg Productions for NBC's Junior Hall of Fame Show. His carvings have been exhibited in the Illinois State Museum and Jim has been honored by the National Ducks Unlimited Corporation for his generous woodcarving donations.

Creart has provided Jim the opportunity to be a part of the Creart Limited Edition family by commissioning him to create six pieces a year for a very special collection to include "Birds of Prey" and "Tropical Birds." His first introduction under the Creart logo will be a Gray-Phase Gyrfalcon.

NORMAN ROCKWELL

On February 3, 1894, the man who would become the most popular American artist and illustrator of the twentieth century was born in a New York City brownstone.

Norman Rockwell began drawing at the age of five. He sold his first cover illustration to *The Saturday Evening Post* in 1916, and by 1920, he was the *Post's* top illustrator. His trademark style, a realistic technique highlighted by a warm and whimsical sense of humor, was best summed up by the artist himself: "I paint life as I would like it to be."

Through the years, Rockwell would create classic illustrations for such publications as *Life*, *Look*, *McCall's*, and *Boy's Life*, as well as for many prominent advertisers. Among his best-known works are "The Four Freedoms," which would raise more than $130 million in war bond money during the Second World War, and his famous series for the Massachusetts Mutual Life Insurance Company portraying the American family. The latter collection, more than seventy sketches, is now on display in The Norman Rockwell Museum.

Beginning in the 1970s, Rockwell's illustrations became some of the most frequently sought-after subjects for limited edition collectibles. The Norman Rockwell Gallery offers only those collectibles bearing the official authorization seal of The Norman Rockwell Family Trust. Also, The Bradford Exchange distributes limited edition Rockwell plates.

Norman Rockwell continued his productive life as an artist and illustrator in his Stockbridge, Massachusetts studio until his death in November of 1978.

CAROL ROEDA

Each day, Carol Roeda comes into her cheerful studio to sculpt a merry band of inspirational figures. Her colorful angels and sweet children each bear the Carol Roeda hallmark: mouths shaped into big O's as though each figure was in mid-song.

Her sculptures sing to deliver a message, Carol explains, and that message is ageless: "Let all that breathe sing praise to the Lord." It is a theme that is laced throughout her work and her life...a life that is crowded with meaningful work and a loving family.

Carol was born and raised in Grand Rapids, Michigan, graduating from Calvin College with a degree in Special

Education. She taught high school for one year before marrying and turning her attention to caring for her family.

Wanting a creative outlet, Carol turned to pottery. By 1985, she had developed a unique style for portraying children and angels with the trademark singing mouth. Fashioning a delightfully innocent nativity set as a centerpiece for her work at a big craft show, Carol was astonished to find that the nativity set sold immediately...as did every creche scene she placed on her table.

Soon Artaffects, Ltd., a well-known distributor of limited edition art, saw in Carol the magical appeal shoppers had already noted at craft shows. A contract was signed, and Carol Roeda was welcomed into the Artaffects family. Her *Simple Wonders* collection was introduced by Artaffects in 1991. The collection has expanded to over sixty-five figures of winsome children, angels and a nativity grouping. Wearable angel pins and the notable inclusion of African-American, Native American and Asian figures highlight this popular series.

ANITA MARIA ROGERS

It was a case of love at first sight for artist Maria Rogers. "I stepped into this place, looked around and thought, 'This is what I want to do'," said Anita, recalling a tour of the Hallmark Keepsake Ornament department. The tour was given seven years ago by an artist she met through a friend. The only problem was that Anita had never worked with three-dimensional art.

She then set out to teach herself how to sculpt. After completing her portfolio, Anita was hired by Hallmark as a part-time artist. The North Kansas City, Missouri native went on to become a full-time artist in 1987.

She has since designed a number of memorable ornaments, including "Lulu and Family," "Cuddly Lamb" and "Christmas Kitty," all of which reflected her affection for animals. She also sculpted "Secrets for Santa," a 1991 Limited Edition design offered by the Keepsake Ornament Collector's Club.

CINDY MARSCHNER ROLFE

Noted artist Cindy Marschner Rolfe has taken the doll collecting world by storm with her innovative creations and the adorable, breathtakingly lifelike expressions on the faces of her dolls. Still a relative newcomer, her limited edition dolls are already selling for up to $2000 — a delightful surprise for an artist who had to be coaxed by family and friends to market her dolls commercially.

"I make my dolls as lifelike and appealing as possible so that, hopefully, they will remind collectors of their own children and grandchildren," Cindy says.

She gives her father the credit for recognizing and developing her talent. When she was young, she watched for hours while he sketched and carved wood products. That beginning interest in art prompted her many years later to teach herself to sculpt. The resulting clay babies were so much admired by neighbors and family members that Cindy developed her talent further, finally agreeing to sell her dolls to the public.

Cindy's recent endeavor, a doll named "Shannon," was created for Hamilton Heritage Dolls. "Shannon" was inspired by Cindy's young daughter, who loves to pose for pictures and served as a wonderful model for the irresistible doll. Collectors truly have much to anticipate from Cindy Marschner Rolfe in the future.

MARJORIE GRACE ROTHENBERG

Marjorie Grace Rothenberg, also known affectionately in the industry as MGR, has been professionally designing since her teenage years. While still in high school, she received commissions to illustrate children's books as well as magazine and advertising art. A prolific artist, she has been involved in many fields: home furnishings, textile designs, toys and animated display.

In 1970, MGR became art director at Kurt S. Adler, Inc., and for twenty years, she made frequent trips abroad working with talented artisans. Along with Mr. Kurt S. Adler, MGR is one of the early pioneers of the Christmas trade, and under their guidance, she was able to teach a cottage craft industry in the Far East, the fine art of Christmas design.

Now a grandmother, MGR lives and works most of the year with her husband in her country studio at the foothills of the Berkshires, surrounded by barns and charming New England villages. "It is here," says Marjorie, "that I draw constant inspiration..." and it is here that MGR creates her "little people." Her designs start with a detailed drawing, Marjorie then oversees the sculpting, painting, sewing and trimming of each figure, making sure it meets with her standards.

Marjorie Grace Rothenberg designs exclusively for Kurt S. Adler, Inc. and is well-known for the cornhusk mice ornaments that she designed for the company. These mice ornaments depict human characters and were created for both Christmas and Easter holidays. Recently, she has designed many new tabletop Fabriché™ figurines in fine fabric maché. These Fabriché™ sculptures feature Santa, Mrs. Claus, elves and other holiday characters.

TOM RUBEL

Tom Rubel enjoys a long-time association with collectible companies nationwide. Upon college graduation, he
developed strong creative skills at various advertising agencies in Chicago and
eventually entered the collectibles field.

Rubel joined The Lincoln Mint,
utilizing his creative, marketing and
advertising skills. During his tenure, he
developed the first single-struck bas-
relief plate and worked with world
renowned artist Salvador Dali.

Also involved in the development of
The Hamilton Mint, Rubel as vice-pres-
ident-creative, won several awards
including one for a collectibles program
authorized by the National Gallery of
Art in Washington D.C. While with
Hamilton, he also designed a program
for the 1976 Olympics held in Russia.

A resident of Cape Cod, Massachusetts, Rubel has been the sole proprietor of Rubel and Associates since
1984, working as a consultant to the gift
industry. He spends much of his spare
time enjoying nature and researching
his subjects. As a nature lover, Rubel is
fascinated with the opportunity to
observe, study and draw the large and
small creatures of our earth. Mr. Rubel's
comments on his subjects: "I paint subjects as I would like them to be — some
happy, some sad and some humorous —
but all with the joy of life."

Tom Rubel is the creator of Silver
Deer's *Christmas Animals Collection* and
the *Ark Collection* which reflect his love
of nature. For BAND Creations/Dream-
shapes, Inc., he has created the *Studio
Collection* with "The Nativity" as the
collection's initial release.

BARBI SARGENT

Barbi Sargent has earned the title
"one of the most reproduced artists in
the world" because of her thousands of

greeting card designs exchanged around
the world since 1966.

When Sargent began drawing at the
age of two, her artistic mother ensured
that her talents were fully developed. As
a result, Sargent's creative efforts earned
her a scholarship to the Cooper School
of Commercial Art. She embarked on
her greeting card industry career at age
eighteen. Years later, an inspirational
meeting with renowned artist Edna
Hibel encouraged Sargent to form her
own company in 1989, Barbi Sargent
and Company, Inc., producing greeting
cards, fine art prints and licensed
designs.

The creation of characters like
"Gretchen" and "Poppyseed" has
achieved national fame for Sargent as
collectors respond to her skillful and
refreshing approach to portraying children and animals. Her renderings weave
into the tapestry of American gifts and
collectibles, surfacing as popular greeting cards, gift collections, dolls, books
and prints. With licensed products
appearing also on calendars, porcelains,
Christmas ornaments, plates and tins,
Sargent's efforts bring enjoyment to
countless people of all ages.

"Sunshine," Sargent's latest character, stars in the *Tender Expressions*™
From the Heart collection for Roman,
Inc. This captivating character, who
frolics with playmates in this significant
message collection, was developed
because of Sargent's volunteer work
with youngsters at The Cleveland Clinic Foundation. Sargent plans to donate
all royalties from sales of the pledge
figurine, "Thoughts of You Are in My
Heart," to the Tender Expressions
Endowment Fund for vital programs at
The Cleveland Clinic Children's Hospital. Roman contributes a matching
donation.

ROB SAUBER

His lovely ladies are often portrayed
in period attire so it comes as no surprise that Rob Sauber maintains a
romantic view of life. His own story
reads like a tale from a novel, filled with
turns of fortune and lucky coincidences.

Out on his own at age eighteen,
Sauber caught on as a fashion designer
for a department store in Raleigh, North
Carolina. Then he embarked upon a
whirlwind of other occupations, including food service, free-lance photography
and illustration. Saving money along
the way, Sauber eventually accumulated
enough to attend the prestigious Art
Center in Los Angeles.

Stints as a studio artist and freelancer followed his schooling. Then
Sauber left California for New York at
age thirty. Soon a famous artists' agent
signed Sauber, and since then he has
advanced steadily as an illustrator,
watercolor painter and limited edition
plate artist.

Sauber has been working with
Artaffects since 1982. He is widely
known for his *Portraits of American Brides*
series and his *Winter Mindscapes* series
done in the distinctive American Blue.

Rob is currently working on more new
and exciting collectibles for Artaffects.

SARAH SCHULTZ

In 1983, Sarah Schultz was working
in her husband's pharmacy managing
the gift department. Sarah observed
that the best selling products in the gift
department were her own original creations. These originals were items such
as stenciled slates, boards, pictures and
some dolls. Even these first creations
demonstrated the love, respect and dignity that is the foundation of all Sarah's

Attic collectibles.

Many of Sarah's creations come from memories of her past. For example, when Sarah was a little girl, she developed rheumatic fever. In a move to cheer her up, her father began a collection of angels for her. With many prayers, the faith of her father, and the beloved angels, she recovered. Later, as a dedication to her father who passed away, and to everyone who has lost a loved one, Sarah created the collection, *Angels in the Attic*.

When Sarah was growing up, an African-American family lived near her. While delivering the daily paper to them, a loving friendship developed. The kindness and warmth that was shared inspired Sarah to develop the *Black Heritage Collection*.

Because Sarah is a firm believer in love, respect and dignity, a heart is painted on each piece to symbolize these three important words. The signature heart is also Sarah's guarantee that the product is of unmatched quality and truly original.

When a collector buys a Sarah's Attic figurine, he/she can be assured that much love and pride were put into creating, painting and shipping the product. This is why each piece will always bear the signature heart, which is Sarah's trademark of quality and love.

ED SEALE

Ed Seale has always loved crafting beautiful objects with his hands. Ed was born in Toronto and grew up in southern Ontario. He worked as a carpenter in Canada in the summer and as a boat builder in Florida during the winter. His interest turned to art, and in 1968, he joined Hallmark. He has created ornaments for the Keepsake line since 1980.

Among his highly prized series ornaments are "Frosty Friends," "Fabulous Decade" and "Heart of Christmas." The

artist's love of sailing and the sea is evident in "Mouseboat" and "Santa Sailor," which shows Santa in a sailor's suit standing on a lightweight metal anchor.

Ed also has delighted Keepsake Miniature Ornament fans with his "Tiny Tea Party," a set of six ornaments depicting a band of tiny mice in porcelain dishes. Ed was also the creator of the 1992 "Sew, Sew Tiny" and the miniature scenes inside the three "Matchbox Memories" ornaments offered in 1991.

MICHELE SEVERINO

Since she was two years old, Michele Severino has been drawing. During her youth, she spent much time sketching dolls and children as a hobby. She enjoyed it so much that she eventually turned to the fine art of dollmaking, to create the same types of children in three-dimensional, lifelike portrayals. She has made hundreds of dolls to date and is planning to teach sculpting.

Michele is one of several top artists who designs dolls for Seymour Mann in its award-winning *Signature Series*.

Among her most recent awards, Michele Severino has won two Awards of Excellence from *Dolls* magazine for dolls that she designed for Seymour Mann, Inc. In 1992, she designed "Stephi" for Seymour Mann, which was nominated for an award, and in 1993 she designed "Rebecca" for the company, which also was nominated.

In addition, she won the Rolf Ericson Award in 1992 and the 1993 Gold Rosette from the Doll Artisan Guild for outstanding doll sculpture.

LINDA SICKMAN

When artist Linda Sickman first started designing Hallmark Keepsake Ornaments, she feared that only five of her ornaments might sell each year

— one to her parents, her brother, her sister and herself. Now, more than ten years later, her designs are widely collected.

Through ornaments such as the *Rocking Horse* series, *Tin Locomotive* series and the *Jolly Wollies*, Linda evokes fond childhood memories of Christmas in her hometown of Clinton, Missouri.

Linda has contributed several designs to the long-running *Here Comes Santa* series. The prolific artist also conceived the idea for and sculpts the ornaments in the *Peace on Earth* series.

Linda remains as creative as ever after twenty-eight years with Hallmark. "I keep fresh by constantly trying something different — a new medium, such as working with wax, clay, wood or plastic, or new ways to make each new design more interesting, and so far, it seems to be working," she says.

BOB SIEDLER

Bob Siedler became a Hallmark Keepsake Ornament artist through what he calls the "noon doodle" method. "I was working in Hallmark's sales promotion department as a paste-up artist," Bob explains, "and on my lunch hours I started making clay roughs and called them my 'noon doodles'." Those clay roughs landed Bob a spot on the Keepsake Ornament staff in 1980. Bob, who

was raised in Fonda, Iowa, joined Hallmark after graduating from the Spectrum Institute for Advertising Arts.

Bob sculpted the entire 1991 *Winnie-the-Pooh Collection*, which included that Silly Old Bear and several of his friends. Other notable designs created by Bob in recent years are "Chris Mouse Mail," "Beary Artistic" and a group of six 1990 ornaments portraying whimsical penguins. He also designed "Uncle Art's Ice Cream," a 1992 Artists' Favorites ornament.

Since joining the Keepsake Ornament staff, Bob has created more than 125 ornaments.

ELIO SIMONETTI

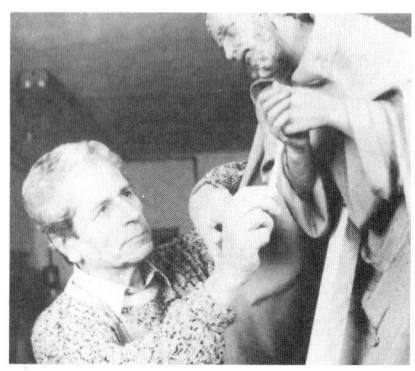

Creating the life-sized Fontanini® Heirloom Nativity sculptures has been the crowning achievement of Elio Simonetti's long and distinguished artistic career and involvement with the renowned House of Fontanini. Receiving the Fontanini family gift of a 50" nativity, Pope John Paul II expressed his admiration of Simonetti's breathtaking masterpiece by stating, "I hope God grants him a long life to continue his fantastic sculpting."

Countless people worldwide share this appreciation for Simonetti's talent and the fine Fontanini craftsmanship when viewing life-sized nativities in a variety of settings. In America, the box office hit movie, *Home Alone*, featured them for millions of viewers. In Europe, the Fontanini Nativities are displayed at Bruxelles, Lucca, Ancona and Palermo cathedrals and were featured in the 1991 Carnevale de Viareggio, Italian equivalent of the Mardi Gras.

For forty years, Simonetti has worked in cooperation with the Fontanini family. As their master sculptor, he continues to prove his talent with his pledge to resculpt all 5" subjects, bringing to them the maturing of his perception and honing of his superlative skills.

Born in Lucca in 1924, Simonetti attended the Liceo for art for a few years; however, he was forced to abandon his studies for full-time work to help support his large family.

His works, lauded for his magical touch that infuses them with lifelike qualities, attracted Mario Fontanini's attention and the relationship was established. The mutual melding of Simonetti and Fontanini talents has resulted in a variety of nativity figures ranging from miniature to life-sized masterpieces.

SISSEL SKILLE

Growing up in the northern part of Norway, Sissel Skille was so intrigued by dolls, that "doll" was her very first word. Sissel became an elementary school teacher, but she still had a strong interest in sculpting and dolls.

In 1980, Sissel set about trying to make a doll. But there were no other dollmakers in Norway, as far as she knew, to ask for advice. Everything she did was trial and error. Also there was no place to buy supplies. She had to make do with plumbing supplies! But she persevered.

Her first dolls were sculpted in clay and finished in porcelain. She was unhappy with the quality of the doll clothes available to her, so Sissel taught herself to design and make her own.

Eventually, she discovered cernit, and switched to that medium. Sissel found that cernit allowed her to quickly see the expression of the doll's face come to life. Each of her creations was one-of-a-kind and was like a child to her. They each had individual personalities that she carried through in the small details of their costuming and hair style.

Sissel's dolls were discovered and introduced in America in the late '80s.

In 1991, she began to work with the Georgetown Collection in the hopes of discovering a way to reproduce her cernit originals. Now Sissel spends her time creating a few very special dolls each year. Some never leave her. They are a part of her family. But a few make the long trip as messengers of joy for collectors to share.

GERHARD SKROBEK

Gerhard Skrobek, a master sculptor of the Goebel company, was born in Silesia, the northernmost part of Germany, subsequently moving with his family to Berlin. There, surrounded by museum art treasures and encouraged by his artist mother, young Skrobek became immersed in the heady climate of artistic tradition. From early childhood, he was fascinated with sculpture and its many artistic forms. He studied at the Reimannschule in Berlin, a renowned private academy of the arts. Later, he continued his studies in Coburg. Through one of his professors, he was introduced to porcelain sculpture at the Goebel studios.

Skrobek joined Goebel in 1951, and soon became one of its leading sculptors and eventually the predominant interpreter of Sister Maria Innocentia Hummel's drawings. Only Skrobek could have created the six-foot replica of the "Merry Wanderer," the famous landmark that stands in front of W. Goebel Porzellanfabrik in Roedental, Germany.

"I am accustomed to creating normal-sized figurines from a lump of modeling clay," says Skrobek, "but here I had to work with a very brittle material, and had to bring many forces into play — I became an architect, mason and sculptor all in one!"

In addition to his world-renowned

ability of capturing the quality of the two-dimensional artwork of Sister Maria Innocentia Hummel into three-dimensional joyous presentations, Mr. Skrobek has contributed his talents to the delightful "The Surprise" and "Hello World" for members of the M.I. Hummel Club. Always delighted to meet with collectors, Mr. Skrobek looks forward to his visits to North America, and opportunities to meet friends, both old and new.

JOSEPH SLOCKBOWER

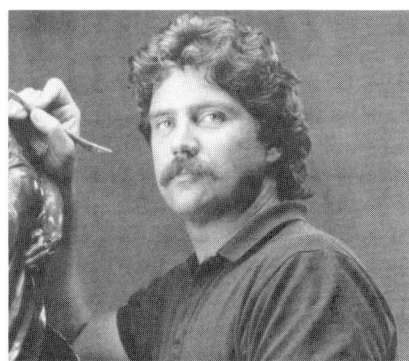

Indians have always held a special fascination for this up-and-coming young artist for Chilmark Pewter. Native Californian Joe Slockbower explains, "I started researching the Indian culture in college in the late '70s. Not only do their physical features tell a story, the Indian way of life fascinates me."

At California State University, Long Beach, where he received his B.A. degree in sculpting, Joe studied life drawing and sculpting. Striving to capture physical features as well as the right expression and the true spirit of his subject is often not an easy undertaking. "I do a lot of research on Indian customs, their beliefs and their costuming. Just as every detail on the person or subject is critical to the finished piece, so is the soul or spiritual aspect of the subject."

His extensive research and genuine interest in the Indian way of life have paid off. Joe recently contracted with The Lance Corporation to do a series entitled *The Great Chiefs* collection. The premier issue, "Chief Joseph," sold out shortly after introduction and was awarded a prestigious *Collector Editions* Award of Excellence in 1992.

Slockbower's *Guardians of the Plains* collection introduced in July 1993 began an ambitious new program for Chilmark MetalART™.

As a contributing artist for Gartlan USA — a leading producer of limited edition sports collectibles —Slockbower created original artwork for figurines featuring such Hall-of-Fame baseball stars as Stan Musial, Rod Carew, Tom Seaver, Ken Griffey Jr., Carlton Fisk and Luis Aparicio. He also sculpted basketball's Isiah Thomas for the company, located in Huntington Beach, California.

LEO R. SMITH III

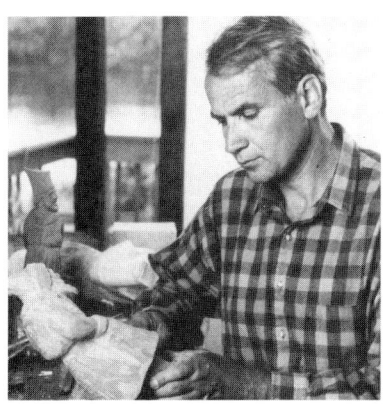

Leo R. Smith III has won many admirers for his intriguing woodcarvings. Largely self-taught, he is known for incorporating elements of the history and folklore of his native Mississippi River Valley into each of his compelling sculptures.

Born and raised in the river town of Winona, Minnesota, Smith began woodcarving over twenty years ago. His marriage to wife Marilyn — a talented artist in her own right — began a lifelong collaboration of carver and painter.

Leo's sculptures, which often take months to complete, are developed as expressions of personal experiences, beliefs and interpretations of the area folklore. Once the carving is completed, Leo and his wife Marilyn develop a color scheme and hand-paint the figure, adding the final touches that bring his characters to life.

Since moving across the river to Fountain City, Wisconsin almost twenty years ago, Leo and Marilyn have garnered national acclaim for their uniquely appealing, original folk art.

It is Midwest Importers' pleasure to offer an exclusive collection of beautifully crafted reproductions of Smith's original carvings, each limited to an edition of 5,000 pieces. Due to overwhelming demand, new sculptures are added to the collection each year. Rich-

ly detailed and imaginatively sculpted, this handsome collection of folk pieces proudly brings the legends of the Mississippi River Valley to life. Collectors and folk art lovers alike will enjoy these folk art treasures.

IRENE SPENCER

One of America's most beloved collectibles artists, Irene Spencer strives to adhere to her philosophy, "My intention in creating is to express, with my best technical ability, a depth of feeling that defies verbal description." Her moving portrayals of that loving and endearing bond between mother and child attest to Mrs. Spencer's achieving this goal with her superb artistry.

Such powerful emotions are aroused by Mrs. Spencer's many collectibles for various noted producers. Roman, Inc. produces plates, sculptures and ornaments based on her celebrated themes of love as well as her penchant for cats' mischievous antics. *Siamese Cats* is Mrs. Spencer's most recent plate collection for Roman.

For Mrs. Spencer, becoming the first female to design a limited edition plate in 1972 stands high on her list of notable achievements. Today, Mrs. Spencer ranks as one of the industry's most popular artists. She has received many honors, including Litho and Plate of the Year, Silver Chalice Award, Artist of the Year and the NALED Award of Devotion.

Mrs. Spencer's childhood dreams of becoming an artist led to nine years of study at the Chicago Art Institute. A subsequent two-year circus tour seasoned the artist for her lifetime career. Mrs. Spencer developed proficiency as an illustrator, designer and cartoonist in commercial art over a period of twenty-two years.

From her impressive credits and the popularity of her artwork, it appears Mrs. Spencer has come a long way towards accomplishing her lifetime goal.

GABRIELE STAMEY

Gabriele Stamey is well known to Swarovski collectors for creating some of the most joyous designs in the *Silver Crystal* collection: the "Silver Crystal City," the "Train" and the "Santa Maria," Swarovski's celebration of the Columbus Quincentennial, to name a few. It is not surprising to hear that many of her designs are drawn from her own very happy childhood.

Gabriele was born in the small town of Worgl, in the Tyrolean lowlands of Austria. The fifth of nine children, her favorite memories are of the feast days and holiday celebrations, particularly birthdays.

So it was only natural that Gabriele was given the assignment of creating an exclusive limited edition for the fifth anniversary of the Swarovski Collectors Society. The result was a charming miniature birthday cake, lovingly crafted.

Gabriele decided at age fourteen to specialize in glass design. After graduation from the College of Glassmaking and Design in Kramsach, Tyrol, she went to work for the Schneegarten factory, producing fine mouth-blown crystal stemware. In 1986, she joined Swarovski.

Gabriele is married to fellow Swarovski crystal designer, Michael Stamey. They live with their two sons, Immanual and Michael, in Angath, Austria.

MICHAEL STAMEY

Crystal designer Michael Stamey was born in Munich, West Germany to an Austrian mother and an American father. His first years were spent in the

U.S.A. in Georgia and North Carolina. Then his parents moved to Austria where Stamey was brought up and educated in the provinces of Styria and Tyrol.

One of his studies was a four year specialist course at the College of Glassmaking and Design in Kramsach, Tyrol. After graduation, he practiced his skills in the local glass industry. He furthered his education in the U.S.A. by studying art and biology in Florence, South Carolina for two years. During this time he also worked as a free-lance textile designer. Upon returning to Austria, he became a designer for D. Swarovski.

Michael's wife, Gabriele, is also a Swarovski crystal designer, having met her husband while studying at the Glass School in Kramsach. The Stameys have two children, Immanuel and Michael. They live in a tiny village called Angath near the market town of Worgl.

Among his designs in the Swarovski *Silver Crystal* collection are the "Butterfly Fish," "Three South Sea Fish," "Sea Horse" and the "Sitting Cat." Stamey is also the designer of the three limited editions in the second Swarovski Collectors Society series, *Mother and Child.*

CHRISTIAN AND KARLA STEINBACH

Herr Christian Steinbach is the president of the Steinbach Factory, the leading producer of collectible nutcrackers and smoking figures in the world. He oversees the entire operation of the world-famous factory which is located in Hohenhameln in the northern region of Germany. Mr. Steinbach, who is the fifth generation to head the company, was instrumental in producing the company's first limited edition nutcrackers and smokers, available from Kurt S. Adler, Inc.

Karla Steinbach is the current Steinbach vice-president overseeing the product development and manufacturing of limited edition nutcrackers and smoking figures. Born November 1957 in the town of Schneeberg in the Erzgebirge Mountains in Germany, Karla is destined to become the sixth generation to head the company when Herr Christian Steinbach retires.

The Steinbach company was founded in 1832 and continues to manufacture nutcrackers, smoking figures, ornaments and music boxes in the Old World tradition. Each piece is handcrafted and hand-painted from the finest northern European woods available.

In 1991, Kurt S. Adler, Inc. introduced the first of a series of limited edition designs from the Steinbach factories. The premier edition "Merlin The Magician" nutcracker is highly sought after by collectors and recently sold for $1500 on the secondary market after its 1991 release at a retail price of $185. The combined talents of KSA Collectibles Group and the Steinbach factory have added many more editions of nutcrackers and smoking figures to tantalize collectors including the *Famous Chieftains, American Presidents, American Inventors, Christmas Legends* and *Camelot* series.

ADI STOCKER

Born in Kizbuhel, Austria, a small town set in the mountains, Adi Stocker was interested in arts and crafts from an early age. He studied at the College of Glassmaking and Design in Kramsach, Tyrol, a specialist school where all the skills of glassmaking are taught, including glassblowing, cutting, engraving, painting and the art of crystal making. He remained there for four years, perfecting his craft.

He first began to practice his skills in the mountains of New Hampshire with Pepi Herrmann Crystal Inc. He stayed

with the company for four years, acquiring extensive knowledge as an all-round glassmaker.

In 1981, Stocker undertook a world trip, visiting such exotic places as Japan, China, Thailand, Nepal and India, before returning to live and work in his native Austria a year later.

In Austria, Stocker pursued both his passions: crystal designing and mountaineering. His favorite "Alpine game" is rock-climbing, which demands constant training to build up the stamina — both mental and physical — required to tackle a rock face. To Stocker, however, it represents the ultimate form of relaxation.

His Swarovski *Silver Crystal* designs include the "Poodle," "Polar Bear," "Field Mouse" and the *African Wildlife* series. For the Swarovski Collectors Society, Stocker's expertise brought the first Annual Edition to fruition, "Togetherness" — the Lovebirds (1987). Stocker has also brought his sensitivities and talents to bear on his own designs: "Sharing" — the Woodpeckers (1988) and "Amour" — the Turtledoves (1989), the second and last Annual Editions in the Swarovski Collectors Society series *Caring and Sharing*, designed exclusively for members of the Swarovski Collectors Society.

TIM SULLIVAN

Western sculptor Tim Sullivan of Missoula, Montana makes the most of his Montana environment whenever he can, in his art and in his lifestyle.

After earning a degree at Carroll College in Helena, Montana, which included a minor in art, he embarked on a two-year stint in the South Pacific as a Peace Corps volunteer. Thereafter, Sullivan returned to Montana. Although

he initially began his career as a painter, he has worked exclusively in bronze sculpture since 1979. In 1992, The Lance Corporation premiered Sullivan's first works in pewter.

A fourth generation Montanan, he had "relatives on both sides who were early cowboys, ranchers, miners." His family always "put an emphasis on heritage," which "led to a sense of pride and love for the life" of the historic West. This love for the West, coupled with the painstaking detail Sullivan puts into his work, made him a perfect candidate for Chilmark MetalART℠.

Sullivan has an eye for detail and sometimes spends months researching the authenticity of costumes and weapons. His premier series for Chilmark, *To The Great Spirit*, is a four-piece collection honoring the individual warrior's quest for the Great Spirit. "Shooting Star" and "Two Eagles" are the first two releases in this series.

ROBERT TABBENOR

Although Robert Tabbenor admits that he was born and bred in the Potter-

ies, he did not set foot in a porcelain factory until 1973 when he began working at Royal Doulton.

Tabbenor was keenly interested in art at school, but learning to use clay was an entirely new experience for him when he began his apprenticeship under Eric Griffiths, director of sculpture at Royal Doulton. It would take him many years to learn human anatomy and to recreate the body and the garments which clothe it. This knowledge was then carefully translated into a workable clay model.

In 1979, Tabbenor's first model, "All Aboard," was accepted for production, and it was soon followed by popular pieces like "Prized Possessions," "Pride and Joy," and the "Auctioneer." All of these sculptures were offered through the Royal Doulton International Collectors Club. Another popular figure, "China Repairer," commemorates the long career of Doulton repairmen in Toronto, Canada.

Through the years, Tabbenor has designed a wide variety of collectibles, ranging from character jugs of an "American Fireman," "Henry V" and "Buffalo Bill," to a miniature collection of jugs based on Dickens' characters like "Oliver Twist," "Fagan" and "Mr. Bumble." Tabbenor also created a series of ladies for the *Vanity Fair Collection* and a number of small animals for the *Little Likeables* which were made in Beswick pottery.

ROBERT TANENBAUM

Renowned for decades as a gifted entertainment-theme artist, Robert Tanenbaum has been commissioned to create numerous portraits of America's most famous personalities, as well as movie posters for many top films. And now — after twenty-five years as a painter of the stars — Tanenbaum has

turned his extraordinary artistic skills towards the All-American sport of baseball. He has captured the game's greatest players of all time in a collection of portraits presented on porcelain, entitled *The Best of Baseball*.

Tanenbaum established himself as a superbly talented portrait artist in 1977. Hughes Aircraft commissioned him to capture the reclusive Howard Hughes at the age of thirty-three in a full-length portrait. Tanenbaum, who extensively researched his subject, completed the portrait and astounded Hughes' associates with its realism, though only a few photographs existed of the eccentric genius at that stage of his life. Word of the artist's remarkable abilities spread quickly, and other coveted Hollywood commissions soon followed.

Although Tanenbaum had little formal artistic training prior to college, he won the All-College Self-Portrait contest in his freshman year at Washington University in St. Louis. Since then the artist has earned a number of honors. Especially noteworthy is the fact that he is one of only twenty-two artists nationwide certified by the American Portrait Society. Now, Tanenbaum enters a new phase of his prolific career with his series of collector plate portraits for The Hamilton Collection, entitled *The Best of Baseball*. Beginning with "The Legendary Mickey Mantle," Tanenbaum portrays these American heroes with incredible realism, creating powerful images of the most beloved and successful players in baseball history, including Babe Ruth, Lou Gehrig and Roberto Clemente.

DAVID J. TATE, M.B.E.

David Tate formed Lilliput Lane in 1982 with family and friends. In only eleven years Lilliput has become the

United Kingdom's leading producer of miniature cottages. Visitors experience a friendliness and an open style of management that has brought David and the company many accolades, one of the most notable being the Queen investing David as a Member of the Order of the British Empire (M.B.E.). This is a title held for life for his contribution towards society and business in Cumbria, where the Lilliput studios can be found.

An artist all his life, David had no formal training, but over the years has successfully painted in oils and watercolors and has worked with some great sculptors.

A highly inventive technician, David acquired his specialist skills in the fiberglass industry. He then set out through Lilliput Lane to create unique and complex models of England's architectural history. He now spends most of his time with his creative team at Penrith as the technical and art director. When David is not in the studio, he is out taking photographs of original medieval cottages either as inspiration for new Lilliput models or to include in his evocative and inspiring audio-visual shows, which he and his wife present around the world.

Always full of fun and laughter, David enjoys his work immensely and draws tremendous energy and inspiration from the staff of Lilliput Lane, and from tens of thousands of Lilliput collectors around the world.

MICHAEL J. TAYLOR

Michael J. Taylor, a shameless Cubs fan, talk radio aficionado and Los Angeles Lakers supporter has fast become one of America's most well-known, if not most popular, sports artist.

A Michigan native, Taylor's popularity spread with his work for Gartlan USA, a leader in limited edition sports collectibles.

Influenced by an artist correspondence course and formal training in college, Taylor worked in commercial and advertising art for more than a dozen years. Meanwhile, Taylor spent much of his spare time creating original paintings for art shows and other exhibitions. With a passion for sports, his moonlighting efforts featured many local heroes, as he was occasionally asked by parents to draw the portrait of a son or daughter student athlete.

He began creating original portraits of more renowned athletes in 1984. Frequently he took these labors of love to professional sports venues to get them autographed. It was during such a trek that he was discovered.

He took the opportunity to create a montage for the Lakers' media guide and then artwork for Kareem Abdul-Jabbar's 1989 retirement tour. At that juncture his work caught R.H. Gartlan's critical eye.

Since that time, he has created original artwork for Gartlan USA's collectors' plates and lithographs of popular sports heroes. Many of these players are also featured on ceramic trading cards. His study of NFL great Joe Montana was reproduced as the first canvas transfer in the sports art world.

GLORIA TEPPER

Gloria Tepper is a self-taught sculptor who has been designing dolls for the past eight years. Her one-of-a-kind doll designs are in limited variations in porcelain, and the dolls' costumes are her own creations. Being a free-lance fabric designer, Gloria pays close attention to the fabric designs of the dolls' costumes.

Gloria, who lives and works in Brooklyn, New York, has been very successful as a doll designer, drawing upon her experience from the National Academy of Fine Arts. Her dolls — such as "Heather" and "Juliet," which have been commissioned by the Dynasty Doll Collection™ — are coveted by collectors throughout the United States.

HAZEL TERTSAKIAN

A native of Yorkshire, England and from a well-known artistic family, Hazel Tertsakian studied art from her earliest years, and embarked on a career as a commercial artist. She made her mark as a fashion illustrator, package designer and art consultant to retail stores both in Britain and the United States.

Hazel worked extensively with children as an art teacher in New York for many years, and also served as a resident artist for the Hearst newspaper.

Always a multi-media artist, moving into the field of ceramics was a natural development for Hazel. Relocating to Florida in 1984, she devoted all her time and talents to doll sculpture. Her creative abilities soon became apparent as her long-legged, high-fashion dolls won awards at doll shows.

Hazel now is a designer for the Dynasty Doll Collection™ from Cardinal Inc. Her lavishly attired *Victorian Ladies* and *Annual Brides* for Dynasty are favorites among collectors.

CHRISTINE THAMMAVONGSA

Gifted artist Christine Thammavongsa employs her diverse talents to create figurines for GANZ that are rich in detail and character. Proof of her talent is the fact that, after only one year of experience with GANZ, Christine was asked to assume creative responsibility for the whole line of *Little Cheesers*®, which GANZ purchased in mid-1991.

Ms. Thammavongsa joined GANZ in 1990 after graduating from the Ontario College of Art and the University of Guelph. She now holds the title of Product Manager and Art Director/Designer for *Little Cheesers*® and several other lines.

Some of the noteworthy projects Ms. Thammavongsa has undertaken for GANZ include contributions to *Pigsville*™, the series of *Featherstone*™ and *Cowtown*™. But *Little Cheesers*® has been the concentration of most of her creative efforts. She not only personally designs the *Springtime in Cheeserville* series and all other new issues, but she also names all the pieces and characters in the entire collection. As if all that weren't enough, Christine is also involved in the writing and illustrating of a storybook about the lovable mice characters of *Little Cheesers*®.

Christine Thammavongsa says she is delighted to bring her imagination to life by creating a rich environmental context for the *Little Cheesers*® to inhabit. Thanks to Christine, life in Cheeserville County is complete with National Cheeser Day celebrations, picnics of honeydew lollipops and sunflower scones, cheese roasts, jamborees, Easter egg hunts and wedding feasts.

CAROL THEROUX

Drawing inspiration and understanding from her own Cherokee Indian ancestry, Carol Theroux combines realism with a spiritual quality that instantly reaches out to the viewer.

"I portray Native Americans in a gentle way, expressing the beauty of the children and young adults," Theroux explains. "I believe that knowledge comes from observation, participation and much research, and so I spend a

great deal of time among contemporary Indians — at reservations and at inter-tribal pow wows. And I always make a genuine effort to present each subject as authentically as possible."

Having devoted a quarter century to studying and painting Native American subjects, Theroux is considered one of the finest artists now working in this increasingly popular field. Her first *Artist's Edition*™ porcelain plate is for the Georgetown Collection and is titled "Buffalo Child," inaugurating Georgetown's first plate series.

The recipient of numerous awards for both her paintings and drawings, Theroux has been an honored exhibitor at America's most prestigious invitational Western Art shows. She is also a member of the Pastel Society of America and is featured in the 1993 *Who's Who in American Art*. In addition, her work is listed in many reference books on Western Art.

SHELIA THOMPSON

Shelia Thompson, who was born in Nashville, Tennessee, has been winning awards for her art since elementary school, when at age eight, she won a blue ribbon for a mural portraying after-school

activities. At age eleven, she won an award for a self-portrait done in pencil.

As a young mother living in Charleston, South Carolina, Shelia taught herself to watercolor from an instruction book. She became a member of the Charleston Artist Guild in 1980 by submitting two watercolors, "Sun Up, Sun Down" and "Ladies Four" which depict people and scenes of the South. Later these works were released in print form as limited editions. Also during this time, Shelia created several miniature prints such as "Rainbow Row" and "Charleston Flower Ladies."

In the 1970s, Shelia began creating her Charleston houses hand-painted on wood. At this time, she individually hand-painted and signed each piece. There are hundreds of one-of-a-kind Shelia's houses in homes across the United States due mostly to the fact that Shelia sold her work originally in the Charleston City Market, a heavily toured area. These items are truly unique and collectible examples of Shelia's early work.

Today, Shelia still remains the sole designer of Shelia's Fine Handpainted Collectibles. For the first time since 1980, Shelia will release a series of limited edition prints taken from her original screen-printed and watercolored works. These prints will include "Magnolia Plantation House," "The Cape May Pink House" and "The Atlanta Queen Anne," plus a new "Rainbow Row" print. Shelia also continues to release new pieces into her line of collectible houses screen-printed and hand-painted on wood.

ANNALEE THORNDIKE

As the oldest of three daughters, Annalee Davis Thorndike was infatuated with dolls from early childhood. Raised in a large Victorian house in a residential section of Concord, New Hampshire, she grew up in a creative environment, her mother an artist and her father a candy maker.

Annalee fondly remembers her childhood activities, particularly her winters spent sledding, skiing and skating, and many of her dolls have been reminiscent of these pastimes. Annalee created her first doll when she was nineteen; it can be seen today at the Annalee Doll Museum.

Annalee married Harvard man Chip Thorndike in 1941 and joined him on his chicken farm in Meredith, New Hampshire. Shortly after the end of World War II, the Thorndike's chicken business folded, and she turned her doll making hobby into a serious business venture involving the whole family. Her husband Chip has contributed over the years by creating accessories for her dolls, and sons Chuck and Townsend have been involved in the business since childhood.

The first dolls she created were used in displays at major department stores. Dioramas featuring dolls involved in recreational activities were also commissioned by the New Hampshire State Park and Recreation Department to promote tourism. As the demand for her dolls grew, so did the variety in her line, and the facilities needed to produce them. Today, the early dolls, made in 1951-54 during the initial years of Annalee Mobilitee Dolls and originally priced at less than $10 in most cases, have soared over 3000% in resale value. In the last seven years, 600 dolls dating from those early years to limited recent editions have been sold at the annual Annalee Doll auction. The actual range of resale value is from $50 to $6000 depending on the doll. These auctions, now in their tenth year, and the nationwide interest and membership in the Annalee Doll Society have established the collectible viability of Annalee dolls.

Today, Annalee creates her dolls at the "Factory in the Woods," nestled among mountains and lakes at the site of the original chicken farm. There are more than 200 dolls in the line, including human, animal, and fantasy figures with Christmas, Thanksgiving, Halloween, Valentine's Day, and St. Patrick's Day themes, as well as a Spring line, a General line, and several series of Limited One-Year Editions, Collector Series, and special Limited Editions available only through the Doll Society.

CHUCK THORNDIKE

Charles "Chuck" Thorndike, older son of Chip and Annalee, has also inherited the family's artistic talents. Long identified with the family business, he has been working along with Annalee in the Design and Art Departments, and recently has continued to expand his artistic pursuits into other areas.

Born March 17, 1945, Chuck attended Paul Smith College and the University of New Hampshire. His education was interrupted by a tour of active duty with the U.S. Navy in Vietnam, and upon his return, he was soon drawn back into the company by the demands of its rapid growth. Over the years, he has been involved in most of the company's departments. At present, his official title at Annalee's is Vice-President of Research and Development.

Chuck is an inventor, having designed and patented a machine to assist in lifting and carrying heavy objects, and has inherited Chip's passion for and talent in photography. He and his family excel in water and snow sports and other varied recreational activities in the Lakes Region of New Hampshire. Their appreciation for the quality of life in this scenic area has led to Chuck's continuing commitment and contributions to a multitude of civic duties and concerns.

Chuck's wife, Karen, is responsible for the establishment of the Annalee Gift Shop, which first opened its doors twenty years ago. They have two sons and a daughter.

Chuck can recall growing up in a household where Rhode Island red hens roamed the premises of the Thorndike Chicken Farm, the tables and beds were piled high with Annalee Dolls, and a

squadron of dollmakers could be found working around the dining room table every day.

TOWN THORNDIKE

Town Thorndike, Chip and Annalee's youngest son, is the President and C.E.O. of Annalee Dolls. Involved in the business most of his life, he has taken on the role of design coordination, contributing ideas, design critiques and final selections for the general and collectible lines. His strength in applying marketing and business strategy to determine design needs has been instrumental to Annalee Dolls' stylistic consistency and commercial success, deferring only to Annalee in the final decision-making process.

Born November 18, 1947, Town attended Bentley College in Boston, graduating with a B.S. in accounting in 1971. He pursued his own business interests, characterizing himself as "jack of all trades, master of none," until joining the company full-time in the late 1970s. He soon took over the Marketing Department, leading the company's move to marketing independence, and his exemplary record of marketing and design decisions — "Dad says I'm the best dart-thrower in the family," he often says — soon led to his appointment as C.E.O. in 1983. In recent years, he has served as an economic adviser to the State of New Hampshire and trustee to the Whittemore Business School of the University of New Hampshire. He was honored in 1992 with the prestigious "Entrepreneur of the Year" award.

Town's family includes three sons, two stepdaughters and one stepson. His wife, Kathie, balances the responsibilities of childrearing, a nursing career and her growing involvement in the family business. They all share the Thorndike love of the outdoors, including such activities as skiing, sailing and water-sports. Town has recently acquired a classic ocean-going schooner, renamed the *William H. Thorndike* in honor of his grandfather, in which he has sailed to and from Hawaii and raced successfully in class competition.

ANN TIMMERMAN

Born and raised in Alabama, Ann Timmerman began creating dolls when she was just a little girl. Whatever she could get her hands on — corn husks, paper, flowers — ended up in a doll. As she grew older, it became apparent that her artistic aptitude would shape her future.

Studying at the University of Alabama, she worked hard at "reading" features and portraying real life in her work. Upon graduation, she made a career as a creative artist in the advertising field, but her heart belonged with her dolls. Her dream was to make doll artistry a full-time career.

Ann juggled work and family, and somehow found time for a hobby making reproduction dolls. But as the collecting world moved towards a preference for artist dolls, she decided to move with it.

Ann made her debut at the 1992 Toy Fair, and her dolls were well received. Soon after Toy Fair, Ann began working with the Georgetown Collection on a line of reproduction dolls. Her first doll for Georgetown, "Peaches and Cream," was introduced in 1993.

Now, Ann devotes herself full-time to her doll business. Fulfilling orders for her limited editions, creating new dolls and designing prototypes for Georgetown keeps her very busy. But she is quick to say that it is all a labor of love.

DOUGLAS TOOTLE

Douglas Tootle is the top modeler for Kevin Francis, Inc. and is responsible for the *Artists and Potters* series and the highly successful standing Churchill toby jugs.

Tootle trained at the Burslem College of Art, graduating with a National Diploma in Design, and then taught for a time before deciding to model full-time on a free-lance basis. During the last twenty years, he has worked for many famous companies, including Wedgwood and Royal Doulton. He has appeared on British TV and his figure portrait of Margaret Thatcher was accepted by the former Prime Minister. He is currently working on the *STAR TREK* Collection.

MARY TRETTER

Mary Tretter is perhaps best known as an illustrator and teacher of commercial art. Her works are eagerly sought by publishers of educational textbooks. In recent years, Ms. Tretter has combined her talent for drawing and sewing with a love of dolls that dates back to her childhood. Two of her original doll designs have won the highest award for sculpture from the Doll Artisans Guild in Oneonta, New York.

For The Ashton-Drake Galleries, Ms. Tretter created a collection titled *Caught in the Act.* "What a pleasure it was to create all these children *Caught*

in the Act," says Ms. Tretter. "So many wonderful, mischievous childhood events came to mind! I finally chose these particular moments because they have a special, fond meaning for me as a parent. I hope you, too, can see something in these dolls that is so familiar, and yet, so much fun."

ANGELA TRIPI

Determination and a lifelong dream have brought Italy's Angela Tripi to her current status as a world-class artist with a growing U.S. collector following. This gifted artist has come a long way since the days when she abandoned formal art study to help with family finances.

Born in 1941, Tripi showed early signs of talent inherited from her father, a well known painter. Tripi painted in her childhood, but soon crossed over to the medium that is second nature to her — sculpting in terra cotta. She fired her initial primitive figures in a makeshift oven. For fifteen years, Tripi worked in an office by day and devoted all her spare time to shaping clay into figures of characters reflecting a people she knows so well — everyday Sicilian peasants.

Before coming to the perceptive eye of Ron Jedlinski, president of Roman, Inc., Tripi's renderings achieved recognition with major exhibitions in Italy, France and Japan in 1986. In 1990, her nativities in Palermo's Villa Niscemi and Sorrento were awarded best sculpture honors.

Today, Tripi fulfills her aspirations by creating masterpieces in her workshop in Palermo, Sicily. Her efforts to expand *The Museum Collection of Angela Tripi*, a distinctive gallery of limited edition sculptures for Roman, Inc., have been increased with the encouragement of being honored with "Collectible of Show," sculpture category, at the 1991 Long Beach Collectible Exposition in California.

The talented sculptor continues to widen her exploration of new themes for *The Museum Collection of Angela Tripi*, creating limited editions on a variety of subjects.

GINA TRUEX

"I love working with the intimate size and jewel-like quality of crystal, a medium that has beauty within itself and yet projects another beauty in colorful shadows," states Gina Truex.

Gina received her B.F.A. degree from the Tyler School of Fine Arts in her hometown of Philadelphia. At the University of Colorado, she completed her M.F.A., specializing in sculpture and drawing.

Gina's designs are varied and countless, including limited editions and licensed pieces. Some of her more prominent designs include the "Bald Eagle," "Bloomer," the *Pinocchio* series, "Bride and Groom" and "Snoopy."

Gina Truex is known nationally not only for her designs in crystal for Silver Deer, but also for her works in other media. Her papier-maché masks and sculptures are exhibited in art galleries and have been featured in the Neiman-Marcus catalog. Silver Deer now offers a series of Gina's masks and sculptures known as *Kindred Spirits*.

CHRISTIAN ULBRICHT

The legend of the nutcracker lives on through the finely handcrafted and loving detailed works of Christian Ulbricht. His delightful nutcrackers and smokers are the culmination of a rich woodcrafting tradition born deep in the heart of Germany's Erzgebirge region.

The history of German woodcrafting dates back more than 200 years, when the mountain forests of the Erzgebirge provided abundant raw materials for local woodturners and carvers. Over the years, these artisans became well-known for their distinctive style and high-quality *Holzkunst*, or woodcraft.

The Ulbricht family began woodcrafting in 1705, and the tradition continues today with Christian Ulbricht's company, *Messrs. Holzkunst Christian Ulbricht*, located in the Bavarian town of Lauingen. Together with his wife Inge, daughter Ines and son Gunther, Ulbricht has built a successful business creating distinctly original designs renowned for their attention to detail and unique sense of humor and whimsy. The Ulbrichts pride themselves on developing only products that are crafted in the finest German woodworking tradition.

For more than twenty years, Midwest Importers of Cannon Falls, Inc. has been bringing the art of Christian Ulbricht to America. To both collectors and admirers, his works are a treasure destined to delight generations to come.

DUANE UNRUH

Fans of Duane Unruh's work know that various sports clearly inspired many

of his ornaments. What many may not know is that Unruh was a high school athletic coach for twenty-four years before joining Hallmark. "When I was in central Kansas, my whole life centered around sports. My father was a high school and college coach, and I followed in his footsteps," the artist said.

Duane joined Hallmark about twelve years ago. He has since created such popular ornaments as the *Mr. and Mrs. Claus* series, "Hot Dogger" and a number of Limited Editions and other Collector's Club ornaments. In addition, he has designed a number of Keepsake Magic Ornaments, including "Bringing Home the Tree" and "Salvation Army Band," both from 1991.

Artistic talent runs in the Unruh family. His twin brother, Arch, is a watercolor artist at Hallmark and has paintings in several Midwest galleries.

JUDI VAILLANCOURT

Judi Vaillancourt, the creative force behind Vaillancourt Folk Art, has been an artistic talent since her youth. A native of Sutton, Massachusetts, Judi became interested in art, antiques and historical homes as a teenager. Around age fourteen she began to refinish antique furniture as a hobby.

Her interest in history and talent in art led to her enrollment in the Massachusetts College of Art in Boston, where she majored in illustration and received a B.A. degree in Fine Arts. "At that time, in the '70s, most of the other students were studying modern art and its abstract forms," relates Judi. "Yet, I was different. I loved the challenge of finding antiques, especially classic pieces that needed restoring."

This drive to conquer new challenges led Judi Vaillancourt to develop her talent in many ways. Over the years she

has designed and made various pieces of colonial furniture; developed a line of antique clocks; painted various scenes and portraits and designed and constructed custom fireplace mantels. In 1984, she began experimenting with antique chocolate molds by filling them with chalkware, a plaster-like substance, and hand-painting each piece. After receiving several orders at a local craft show, Judi's hobby became a business and Vaillancourt Folk Art was born. Today, the company employs forty people and has over 1,000 designs.

Recently, Judi designed several Clothtique® Santas for Possible Dreams. Her inspired Santa Claus figurines include "Father Christmas" and "Out of the Forest," meticulously detailed and accurately colored to rekindle the emotions of a bygone era.

SVEN VESTERGAARD

Sven Vestergaard, born in 1932, became an apprentice at the age of sixteen at the Royal Copenhagen Porcelain Manufactory. Four years later, he was given the highest award — the Silver Medal — and remained at the factory as an overglaze painter until 1959.

He then worked as a designer at Denmark's oldest newspaper, *Berlinske Tidenade*, as well as at various advertising agencies. In 1965, he returned to the factory as a draftsman and became the head of Royal Copenhagen's drawing office in 1976.

Vestergaard has become well-known and respected throughout the world for his designs for Royal Copenhagen Christmas plates, Olympic plates, Hans Christian Andersen plates, National Parks of America plates, American Mother's Day plates and Children's Day series.

Vestergaard lives thirty miles south

of Copenhagen on an estate originally owned by nobility. His 300-year-old thatched cottage provides the setting where the artist creates the many themes for the Royal Copenhagen plates and his oil paintings of peaceful Danish landscapes, animals and nature.

JOAN BERG VICTOR

Joan Berg Victor, artist, designer and author has truly captured a piece of Americana in *Pleasantville 1893*, which was created exclusively for Flambro Imports. Her environment, family, education and experience have all been valuable in influencing her to create this wonderful make-believe town.

Joan was brought up in the Midwest and earned her undergraduate degree with honors from Newcomb College, the Women's College of Tulane University, where she not only received academic honors but also was elected Miss Tulane. At Yale University, Joan was awarded a Master of Fine Arts degree with honors.

Her drawings and paintings can be found in private and museum collections all over the country, not to mention having appeared in publications such as *Fortune* magazine, *The New York Times* and *Wall Street Journal*.

Through the years, Joan has written and illustrated over two dozen books. Her first books were created for young children and as her own two children got older, so too, her books became targeted to an older audience. Her favorite book, of course, is *Pleasantville* because it deals on a personal level with all ages and can be enjoyed by most readers.

Ms. Victor's *Pleasantville 1893* village captures the warmth and simplicity of small town American life at the turn-of-the-century and is evident both in the historically and architecturally

researched pieces and in the beautifully written book about the townspeople of Pleasantville. Families can recapture the nostalgia of years past and live in the memories of stories once told.

LADENE VOTRUBA

Hallmark Keepsake Ornament artist LaDene Votruba doesn't have much trouble generating new designs. She frequents her large home library, scans and collects magazines and always remains alert to new ideas during her travels. These ideas have turned into the many memorable ornaments she has created since joining the Keepsake Ornament staff in 1983.

Among her recent designs were "Greatest Story," second in that series, and "Let It Snow," fifth in the *Collector's Plate* series. She also designed "Folk Art Reindeer," a unique 1991 wooden ornament that is hand-carved and hand-painted.

Outside of her work, the artist enjoys traveling, reading and shopping for antiques.

LaDene grew up on a farm near Wilson, Kansas, and joined Hallmark in 1962 after graduating as an art major from Fort Hays State University in Kansas. She worked in several areas of Hallmark, including process art and greeting card design, before turning her talents to Keepsake Ornaments.

IMAL WAGNER

Imal Wagner is the crystal designer and artist who introduced the techniques and technology that have brought crystal art to a standard never before achieved in the industry. Recognized nationally by the leading trade and collectibles publications as the artist responsible for the evolution of crystal art design, Imal Wagner is cer-

tainly a driving creative force, as well as chief designer at Summerhill Crystal.

Quickly becoming a guiding light in the collectibles industry, Imal Wagner accepted the two coveted and prestigious Awards of Excellence from *Collector Editions* magazine for both of the glass objects categories in 1992.

Early in her career, Imal was a fabric designer and weaver for world famous fashion maven Norma Kamali and celebrated Fiorucci's in New York. Paths eventually led Imal to Fairfield, Iowa, where she met and married Marcus Wagner, president of CFL Ltd., parent company of Summerhill Crystal.

All of Imal's three-dimensional, faceted crystal sculptures entrance collectors with their clarity and beauty as they capture the magic of color and light. At the International Collectible Exposition, Imal introduced "Cherub Wish," the first selection in her limited edition cherub series. These very special angels promise to bring home the luck and magic of the purest "rainbow light." An adorable collection of "itsy-bitsy" creatures sculpted in crystal was also introduced, as well as Imal's miniature "Fairy Blue Coaches."

Imal's collection of Looney Tunes©, the Garfield© family of characters, as well as her Disney© classics, continue to garner attention from the media and collectors nationwide.

Winning awards and breaking the boundaries of design, Summerhill holds the philosophy, in Imal's own words, that "anything is possible."

GRETE WENDT

It has been more than seventy-five years since Grete Wendt created her "crafts of wood" that have become a cherished tradition for many collectors. Her little angel musicians with the brown or blond pony tails and green

and white polka dot wings, are still made today in the Erzgebirge region of Germany — their design unchanged.

Born in 1887 in the Erzgebirge, Grete Wendt attended the Dresden Academy of Handcrafts and later worked designing furniture and creating designs for the toy department at the Workshop for Handcraft. Together with her friend Grete Kühn, Grete Wendt founded the company M. Wendt and M. Kühn in 1915. Miss Wendt specialized in creating wood figurines, and Miss Kühn dedicated her talents to painting a line of woodchip boxes, and trunks. Between 1920 and 1930, Grete Wendt developed the little hand-turned wood figurines that have become known by her name. Grete Kühn's daughter Olly expanded the line with music boxes, the "Pied Piper of Hamelin" and the fish-selling women. Uniquely crafted Santas, charming flower children and other delightful figures were later added to this heartwarming collection.

Today the tradition of fine quality and excellent craftsmanship continues under the ownership and management of Hans Wendt, Grete's nephew. The line is distributed exclusively in the United States by Midwest Importers of Cannon Falls, Inc.

DAVID WENZEL

David Wenzel's love of fantasy was sparked by his mother, who delighted in convincing her children of the existence of elves and other little people — particularly at Christmas. "During the holidays, my mom would sneak outside after dark to tap on the windows and rustle the tree branches," remembers David with a smile. "She had us all believing that the elves were watching our every move."

Considering his childhood, it's not surprising that David was later drawn to the surreal, imaginary worlds created by

J.R.R. Tolkien. Luckily, his interest in fantasy dovetailed perfectly with his talent for illustration, and after graduating from the Hartford Art School, David began his own career in fantasy art. His first job was a dream come true: to illustrate a companion book to Tolkien's *The Hobbit* entitled *Middle Earth: The World of Tolkien Illustrated*. Soon after, he collaborated on *Kingdom of the Dwarfs*, providing the illustrations for this fictional narrative of a fantasy world uncovered in an architectural dig. David has also illustrated many other books, and his work has been exhibited in art shows and galleries nationally.

About five years ago, David and his wife Janice started a greeting card company to introduce his own fantasy world. It is the tiny characters of Hidden Kingdom Cards that provided the inspiration for the *Hidden Kingdom Collection* at Schmid, which includes three separate "worlds": *Kringle Hollow*, *Kingdom of Notch* and *Lady Elizabeth's Garden*.

WILLY WHITTEN

Fluent in an extensive variety of media and techniques, Willy Whitten has the rare distinction of being a self-taught artist who is now acknowledged as a master craftsman. His interest in art began at a very young age — drawing thrilled him, as well as sculpture, which he has studied and worked with since the age of nine.

In his late twenties he viewed an exhibition at the Museum of Art in Los Angeles that caused him to realize that he wanted to sculpt for a living.

Gifted with natural talent and unique vision, Willy acquired extensive modeling and design experience in the demanding field of cinematic special effects. In the last decade, he has been a creative artist on more than two dozen major films, including *The Howling, Baby, Ghostbusters, Aliens* and *The Terminator*. Willy is accomplished as a monumental sculptor, and his sets and animatronic characters can be found in theme parks around the world, including Universal Tours and Disneyland.

His greatest artistic love, and the work for which he is most renowned, is sculpting miniatures. To all his work Willy brings an expressiveness and visuality, demonstrating the rare ability to capture in his sculptures of any size a sense of a person's character and inner identity. He has been able to realize a dream of seeing that work "come alive in the brilliant dimension of metal," he says, when he began working with LEGENDS.

Originally from Indiana, Willy now resides in southern California with his wife, Linda.

MAURICE WIDEMAN

Maurice "Moe" Wideman is the artist and creator behind *The American Collection* from John Hine Studios, a series of American buildings that reflects the diversity of the United States both structurally and culturally. Born in England just a few miles down the road from John Hine Studios, Wideman and his family moved to Canada in his early childhood and spent much time traveling around the United States. His fond memories of these travels are reflected in his art, as many of these recollections come to life in his sculptures. He trained as a sculptor at British Columbia University, and later applied his talents to a wide variety of employment ranging from sculpting life-size cows for the Ministry of Agriculture to creating display settings for fairs. Some early sculptures that he created caught the eye of chairman John Hine, and since that first meeting, the two have collaborated on many projects.

Moe creates his miniature buildings from a soft oil-based clay; using standard modeling tools as well as special instruments he made himself to achieve surface effects. He focuses on a balance of form, texture and color when working. His wife Meg adds input as far as the coloration of the pieces and the training of some of the painters that decorate *The American Collection*.

The American Collection has retired due to the purchase of the Canadian manufacturing facility by another company, but Moe has been hard at work over the past few months, creating a new collection for John Hine Studios, *Moe's Houses*. In this collection, many of the sculpted houses are enhanced by the addition of characters in amusing circumstances. Moe always finds the humor in every situation, and the new collection shows a slice of life through his own point of view.

When Moe isn't busy creating or brainstorming about new additions for *Moe's Houses*, he enjoys relaxing with his two young children or puttering about in the kitchen of their Ontario residence.

ABBIE WILLIAMS

"Doing my best work is about thinking, observing, remembering. Being an artist means learning and growing constantly. The word 'create' means to bring into being…to cause to exist. That's a pretty big assignment!" Abbie Williams says.

This prolific portrait painter, collectibles artist and sculptress has taken on this assignment with zest and great success. Williams studied art and design at Moore College of Fine Arts in Philadelphia. In the 1970s, she relocated to East Boothbay, Maine, to raise her family where her great-grandparents had honeymooned and her family tradition-

ally had spent summer vacations.

Though busy with her children, Williams never abandoned her lifelong love of art, and she painted whenever she could. A chance encounter brought her to meet the well-known artist Frances Hook. They soon became friends and with Hook's encouragement, Williams successfully resumed her career in child portraiture.

Williams developed into a successful portrait and figurative painter in her own right, with her pieces finding their way into homes across the United States and Canada as well as countries as far away as Venezuela and Spain. Hook introduced Williams to Ron Jedlinski of Roman, Inc. As a result, Williams has created a series of collectible and commemorative plates for the company, featuring heartwarming portraits of her favorite subjects — children.

The talented artist's newest efforts for Roman include an eight-plate collection, *Precious Children, Legacy of Love*, a child's commemorative, and the wonderfully conceived *Bless This Child* series. The *God Bless You, Little One* series, devoted to "firsts" in babies' lives, made its debut in 1992. Williams will remember 1991 as a special milestone in her career because it marked the introduction of her first collector doll, "Molly," by The Hamilton Collection in association with Roman, Inc.

ELLEN WILLIAMS

As a foremost giftware artist, Ellen Williams combines her talent for design with seasoned business instinct to create superlative collectibles for several fine companies: Roman, Inc., Enesco Worldwide, Wilton Industries, The Ashton-

Drake Galleries and The San Francisco Music Box Company. She brings to her endeavors the benefit of over twenty years as a giftware industry designer with creations ranging from gifts and dolls to musicals and figurines.

Born in Indiana, Williams subsequently earned a degree in Design and Fine Arts at Indiana University. She then moved to Chicago to embark on her successful career. After twenty years, several of them as vice-president of product development and creative services for Enesco Corporation, Williams formed her own design and licensing company, EHW Enterprises, Inc.

Her bridal collections have reached out to Americans' hearts, making her creations popular nationwide choices. Williams drew on her interest in historic fashion to create the *Classic Brides of the Century*™ collection depicting bridal fashion as a reflection of historical and social trends from 1900 through the 1990s. These enduring sculptures earned 1989 "Collectible of Show" honors at the California International Collectible Exposition. Williams' "Stephanie Helen" — the 1990s bride —garnered the '92 nomination for *Collector Editions* Awards of Excellence for figurines.

Williams continues proving her expertise in bridal collectibles with *Wedding Portraits* from Roman, Inc. — unique heirloom portrayals of bridal couples in loving demonstrative poses like those snapped by photographers.

PAT WILSON

A native Michigan resident, Pat Wilson is the wife of a retired firefighter and the mother of four sons. Yet she still finds the time to feed the fires of her hobby — dollmaking, in which she first became interested in 1977.

Having no formal training or background in art, Pat sought out profession-

al original artists and sculptors who helped perfect her skills. She learned the art as a student and later became an instructor in dollmaking and sculpting. She now works with BAND Creations.

Pat soon perfected her own individual style of realistic sculptures, which she makes into whatever catches her fancy — elfish little people, fairies, realistic Gypsies, sad-faced bag ladies, laughing children and Victorian women. Pat's greatest love is the Victorian style of Father Christmas. All the many variations of the Santas that she creates are inspired by her childhood Christmas memories.

Pat Wilson is involved in the largest part of her dollmaking process, overseeing each step, often doing things herself to ensure authenticity. It's easy to see why Pat's works are so popular with collectors.

DAVID WINTER

The son of an army captain and internationally famous sculptress Faith Winter, David Winter was born in Catterick, Yorkshire, England.

Winter studied sculpture in school and when he met John Hine in 1978, he found a friend and partner who shared his enthusiasm for the buildings and way of life of the past. In 1979, Winter and Hine developed and crafted the first David Winter cottage — "The Millhouse."

Before long, many English shops were requesting the miniature cottages from the fledgling firm. Operating from an old coal shed, Winter did the artwork while Hine concentrated on selling the cottages.

In the studio, Winter becomes completely absorbed in his work, insisting that every window frame, brick and roof tile be completely authentic to the peri-

od. Since many of the buildings are old, Winter includes crooked, old beams, warped roofs and twisted chimneys just as they might be found on a tour of historical Great Britain.

Winter often makes his own tools for sculpting to ensure that he can achieve the effects that he seeks. Once his wax models are complete, the Studios of John Hine cast and trim each cottage according to Winter's own careful instructions. The cottages are hand-painted by "home painters" who have been trained by the Studios. Since the first cottage was introduced, David Winter has created an impressive range of buildings including castles, manor houses, shops, mills, cottages and hamlets of many sizes and styles.

David Winter and John Hine Studios, Inc. have received numerous awards for their contribution to the limited edition collectibles field. In 1988, the firm proudly received The Queen's Award for Export Achievement. Winter has also been honored many times by NALED winning the 1990 Figurine of the Year award for "A Christmas Carol" and First Runner-Up for the Collectible of the Year. The awards continued in 1991 with the "Cottage of the Show" award for the Christmas cottage, "Fred's Home: 'A Merry Christmas, Uncle Ebeneezer,' said Scrooge's nephew Fred, 'and a Happy New Year'." David Winter was also named Artist of the Year in 1991.

BARBARA AND PETER WISBER

Barbara and Peter Wisber have been bringing *The Family and Friends of Lizzie High® Dolls* to delighted collectors for over eight years. It is a collaborative effort and a labor of love.

When Barbara decided to add dolls to their already popular line of folk art,

she took her ideas to Peter who turned her fancy into fact. The evolution to dolls occurred when Barbara came up with the sketch for the first Lizzie High® doll, and Peter cut it out of pine. Each subsequent doll was given a good old-fashioned name borrowed from Peter's family tree, and a "tale" to accompany it, adding to its charm.

Barbara spent her childhood in Philadelphia while Peter grew up in the suburbs. When they married in 1971, their first home was on a large working farm. Those first happy years provided Barbara and Peter with many of the "tales" they have bestowed upon the dolls in the collection.

Eventually they started a family of their own and moved to their present Bucks County farmhouse. Recollections of their own happy childhoods, reminiscent of fun days in the country, and the daily joys of raising their two children shine forth in the regular additions to *The Family and Friends of Lizzie High®* that this talented couple create.

Peter's talents extend to mediums beyond wood as well. He sculpted the models for an array of adorable little animals which enhance the charm of several of the characters in the *Lizzie High® Collection*.

With their natural talent and abundance of love, Barbara and Peter Wisber have parlayed the joys of their partnership into a successful line of lovingly crafted dolls that continue to bring joy to the hearts and homes of an ever-growing number of collectors.

DAVID WRIGHT

While many artists are willing to research the subjects in the relative safety of the library, David Wright prefers to step back in time and travel throughout the West just as the early

pioneers and fur traders must have done more than two centuries ago.

Instead of choosing a well-appointed motor home, Wright and his companions travel by horseback with buckskin clothing and camping gear, just like those used by the trailblazers on their treks across the western frontier. In this way, Wright gains a special understanding for life on the American Frontier.

Born in Kentucky and raised in Tennessee, Wright grew up in the country. His outdoor experiences have provided him with a special feel for nature. After studying art in Europe, Wright spent a number of years as a designer and illustrator. However, Wright turned his full attention to fine art in 1978. Since then his range of subjects has grown to include characters from the Old West — explorers, hunters, trappers, mountain men and Native Americans.

Wright's limited edition prints for Grey Stone Press have done extremely well on the secondary market. One of his print subjects was Sacajawea, the young and beautiful Indian guide for the Lewis and Clark expedition. In 1989, "Sacajawea" premiered Wright's first plate collection, entitled *Noble American Indian Women*, and has since inspired a sculpture collection by the same name.

Now that the edition for "Sacajawea" is closed, Wright has introduced a new plate collection with The Hamilton Collection — his very popular *Princess of the Plains* which debuted with "Prairie Flower."

JUDY YORK

At the ripe old age of twenty-four, Judy York ended years of flirtation with various interests in the arts — painting, music, theatre, writing — and decided to become a professional illustrator.

Judy received a B.A. in Art History from Queens College in New York (earning a Phi Beta Kappa key) and a Master of Arts in Teaching from Wesleyan University. After a year of teaching art to high school students, she returned to the Pratt Institute to follow her calling. Judy put together her book of samples while working as a designer/layout person at Chanticleer Press where she eventually was able to concentrate on illustration full-time. Later, an exclusive contract with Ballantine Books permitted her the financial freedom to do fine arts painting, currently on display at

the Husberg Fine Arts Gallery in Scottsdale, Arizona. This is where Heio Reich of Reco International saw her work and later contacted Judy regarding painting limited edition plates.

Between deadlines, Judy married fellow artist/illustrator Charles Gehm. When not painting, they can be found haunting antique shops and hiking. Judy is a passionate amateur chef and also enjoys making found-object jewelry. Both she and Charles have extensive backgrounds in classical piano.

Judy's first collector plate series for Reco International is entitled *The Heart of the Family*. The first two editions are "Sharing Secrets" and "Spinning Dreams."

MARTIN ZENDRON

Martin Zendron, designer of the first edition in the Swarovski Collectors Society series, *Inspiration Africa*, never seriously thought about becoming a designer. It was something, he says, which he just "grew into."

His link with Swarovski, however, began at an early age when his family moved to Wattens, Austria because of his father's job. His father still works in Swarovski's prototype department and makes the first model of each new design.

Martin attended the College of Glassmaking and Design in Kramsach, Tyrol, a school with an international reputation for excellence. He completed his studies in glass design, with a special course in cutting and engraving.

After graduation, Martin went to work for a well-known Tyrolean retailer, specializing in glass objects. It was there that his work came to the attention of Swarovski. He became a Swarovski Silver Crystal designer in 1988.

Martin's first creations for Swarovski

Silver Crystal were the "Harp" and the "Lute," introduced in 1992, and the "Grand Piano" introduced in 1993. These elegant pieces reveal Martin's fluid artistry and his fresh approach to cut crystal design.

Two years ago, Martin was assigned the coveted task of designing the first annual edition in the new Swarovski Collectors Society series, *Inspiration Africa*. The "Elephant" is the result of his intensive research, consummate craftsmanship and attention to detail.

JANE ZIDJUNAS

Within weeks of attending her first dollmaking class a decade ago, Jane Zidjunas was "hooked." She spent long and rewarding hours striving to reproduce with utmost detail the antique dolls she found in books. Several years later, this gifted sculptor took on the challenge of sculpting her first original doll. After some practice attempts, "Baby Lauren" was born in Ms. Zidjunas' home studio — and the edition of seventy-five sold out to enthusiastic collectors. A thriving doll art career began.

Nationally renowned for her antique reproduction dolls and her contemporary originals, Ms. Zidjunas has won numerous blue ribbons, "Best of Category," and "Best of Show" awards at major doll shows. She was nominated last year for a coveted *Dolls* magazine Award of Excellence.

Jane's toddler doll named "Jennifer," was created for Hamilton Heritage Dolls and continued Ms. Zidjunas' reputation of excellence in doll design. What's more, nominated for the 1993 *Dolls* magazine Award of Excellence is another Zidjunas character, "Amy," a delightful little girl who rides her very own rocking horse. Jane is pleased with the results, especially because toddlers are

her "very favorite subjects."

Today Jane devotes her full-time efforts to doll sculpting from her home studio in Rockford, Michigan, always searching for the finest materials available and always striving to learn the best techniques possible. Since costuming her dolls is one of her greatest pleasures, Ms. Zidjunas designs each doll's outfit and cuts out the pattern, also doing most of the hand sewing. However, in her own words, "The most rewarding aspect of dollmaking for me is the joy dolls bring collectors. It's my fondest hope that dolls like "Jennifer" will be cherished and enjoyed both now, and by future generations!"

SANDI ZIMNICKI

Most young children stay busy playing with a rattle, toys or a teddy bear. But Sandi Zimnicki occupied herself with a stack of papers and a fistful of crayons. Although it didn't take much time for her to run out of paper, it was impossible to exhaust her imagination.

In order to develop her talent for drawing and design, Sandi attended the famous School of the Art Institute of Chicago. In the early 1970s, Sandi began her own design company, Zimnicki Designs, which created annual reports and designs for corporations. Since then, her business has expanded to include the creation of animated display figures. She served as a technical consultant on the movie *Home Alone 2: Lost in New York*, which featured her North Pole Village elves and animated displays.

While maintaining her own company, Zimnicki joined one of the country's premier designers and builders of animated displays for amusement parks and shopping centers. There she developed her talent for visualizing in three

dimension and created wonderfully animated displays for shopping malls.

One particularly productive Christmas, Sandi created The North Pole Village Elves, a whimsical group of Santa's helpers. Ever since that day, these life-sized animated characters have been appearing in malls and store windows throughout the United States and Canada.

Sandi describes her playful, industrious little fellows as "having a special sparkle and special energy all their own." It was this sparkle that captivated Enesco Corporation. In 1986, Enesco started the *North Pole Village Collection* of intricate cold cast figurines and village scenes such as a school, fire station, train station, bakery, post office and toy workshop.

DONALD ZOLAN

Donald Zolan knew by the age of five that he would be an artist. He even focused on his distinctive signature at that early age. Working first with watercolors, Zolan painted his first oil at eight. He won numerous awards and scholarships, culminating in a full scholarship to the American Academy of Art in Chicago.

For the past fifteen years, Zolan has focused exclusively on painting the wonder and joy of early childhood in association with Pemberton & Oakes, his home gallery. From the very beginning, Zolan's collector plates have commanded attention from plate collectors. This is because no one else paints children as Zolan does. Although Zolan's "little people" seem to be doing ordinary things like blowing a dandelion or reading a book, Zolan captures very young children at magic childhood moments of awe —wonder over a new baby, a flower, a butterfly, a pet, a rain puddle or some wild creature. Zolan's children have wonder written all over their faces and bodies.

Zolan's second plate, "Sabina in the Grass," was selected Plate of the Year in 1979. He has been selected as America's favorite living plate artist for six consecutive years, more than any other living artist, and he has received more Individual Artist awards from *Collector Editions* magazine's annual Award of Excellence than any other artist.

RICHARD JUDSON ZOLAN

One of America's exceptional painters, Richard Judson Zolan, has built a sterling reputation as an established American Impressionist talent with an expressive palette and style strongly influenced by Impressionists of yore — Monet, Renoir and Degas. Zolan describes his work as Romantic American Impressionism. Admirers refer to his works as "an extraordinary synergy...a triumphant marriage of modern art with its Renaissance ancestry."

At age eighteen, the Chicago native earned a scholarship to the prestigious Chicago Art Institute. There, under the tutelage of Louis Rittman, who painted in Giverny, France near Monet's villa, Zolan developed his keen interest in the Impressionists. He studied their techniques of conveying light, atmosphere and color, using impasto, a higher-keyed palette and subtle underglazes. Zolan eventually melded these into his unique style. With meticulous brushwork and extraordinary bravura, Zolan has taken this art form to its present-day mode of Romantic American Impressionism.

Reflecting on his career, Zolan comments, "When you go into the arts, you go into the field for the love of creating. Recognition that develops from it is a gift." Zolan's paintings and prints enjoy widespread popularity as a result of exhibits as far away as Japan and in collections throughout the world. A long and distinguished list of persons for whom Zolan has painted commissioned portraits includes President Gerald R. and Betty Ford.

His exclusive giftware for Roman, Inc., *The Richard Judson Zolan Collection*, faithfully translates the breathtaking beauty of six of Zolan's most admired subjects, bringing his superlative artistry to a wider audience for enjoyment.

Collector Clubs
Artists and Companies Invite Collectors to Add An Extra Dimension of Pleasure to Their Hobby

Most collectors want to learn more about their favorite artists and companies, and collector clubs offer one of the best ways to educate them and enhance their enjoyment of collecting. Nearly every club welcomes its members with a beautiful membership kit and the opportunity to purchase exclusive "members-only" collectibles. A listing follows of several nationally-sponsored collector clubs. The Collectors' Information Bureau is always seeking new clubs as this listing is updated, and would appreciate any information on clubs not included here.

Adorables Collectors Society
71-73 Weyman Avenue
New Rochelle, NY 10805
(914) 633-3777
Annual membership fee: $7.50

Collectors can enjoy the whimsically sculpted cats and teddy bear collection by creator Peter Fagan. Club members receive newsletters, a club pin and the opportunity to purchase collector club exclusive pieces.

Alaska Porcelain Collector's Society
P.O. Box 1550
Soldotna, AK 99669
Mile 91.6 North Sterling Hwy.
(907) 262-5626
Annual membership fee: $40

Founded in 1992, the Alaska Porcelain Collector's Society offers members-only selections and a quarterly newsletter, "The Alaska Porcelain Review."

All God's Children Collector's Club
P.O. Box 5038
Glencoe, AL 35905
(205) 492-0221
Annual membership fee: $20

This collector club offers its members a free figurine for joining, a subscription to its quarterly magazine, *All God's Children Collectors' Edition*, an opportunity to purchase collector club-exclusive figurines, a personal checklist, a membership card and an invitation to the annual All God's Children Open House and Fellowship Dinner.

American Bell Association International, Inc.
P.O. Box 19443
Indianapolis, IN 46219
(317) 359-1138
Annual membership fee: Single: $22;
Couple: $25;
International: add $7 postage

Bell collectors will enjoy membership in the American Bell Association. Members receive a year's subscription to *Bell Tower* magazine which includes six 50 to 60-page issues, invitation to an annual bell convention, notices of regional bell meetings in all parts of the country, information on local chapters and their events, and a directory of members. Also available are slide programs and videotapes on all types of bells, for use at local chapter meetings, advertising opportunities and ABA stationery, decals and jewelry items to purchase.

Angel Collectors' Club of America
2706 Greenacre Drive
Sebring, FL 33872
(813) 385-8426
Annual membership fee: $12

This national organization's aim is to promote love and appreciation for angels and to bring about friendship among collectors of angels. Upon joining, collectors may study and appreciate the various angel collections worldwide. Members receive a membership card, a quarterly newsletter "Halo Everybody!,"

an invitation to the biannual convention and the opportunity to participate in several additional activities.

Annalee Doll Society
P.O. Box 1137
Meredith, NH 03253-1137
(800) 433-6557
In NH: (603) 279-3333
Annual membership fee: $27.50

Members receive a 7-inch Logo Kid Doll, one-year subscription to the full-color quarterly magazine, *The Collector*, and the Antique and Collectible Doll Shoppe *Sale List*, plus a Doll Society three-ring binder. In addition, members receive a membership card that entitles the holder to purchase member-exclusive dolls, a lapel pin and a special Annalee Sun Pin. Other benefits include free admission to the Annalee Doll Museum and invitations to the members-only summer Auction Weekend at the Meredith factory and the annual Fall Auction.

Annalee signs the tee shirt of a collector at the Annual Auction Weekend in Meredith, New Hampshire.

ANRI Club

73 Route 31 North
Pennington, NJ 08534
(609) 737-7010
(800) YES-ANRI
Annual membership fee: $50

Members' benefits include a free gift figurine designed by Sarah Kay and valued at $175, the opportunity to purchase Club exclusive figurines, a subscription to *Reflections*, the Club magazine, unlimited access to the company's research services, advance notice of special events, a members-only binder filled with information about the history and production of ANRI figurines, current information and the member's own collector's log.

G. Armani Society

300 Mac Lane
Keasbey, NJ 08832
(800) 3-ARMANI
Annual membership fee: Initial: $37.50;
Renewal: $25

Members receive a membership card, subscription to the G. *Armani Review*, binder, membership plaque and free figurine. Members also have the opportunity to purchase members-only figurines sculpted by Master Sculptor Giuseppe Armani.

This graceful "Venus" sculpture is the 1993 members-only Redemption Figurine for the G. Armani Society, available to members with a redemption certificate.

Artaffects® Perillo Collectors Club™

Box 98
Staten Island, NY 10307
(718) 948-6767
Annual membership fee: $35

Collectors who enjoy award-winning artist Gregory Perillo's portrayal of Native Americans will appreciate the quality of his collectors club as well.

Member benefits include a full-color catalog, three-ring binder, membership card, invitations to personal appearances, a subscription to "Drumbeats," the official Perillo newsletter, secondary market fact sheet, "ArtaQuote" and a free membership gift. Members also have the exclusive opportunity to purchase members-only offerings and receive advance notice of new introductions.

Brian Baker's Déjà Vu Collectors' Club

Department PRDV
P.O. Box 217
Redmond, WA 98073-0217
(800) 835-0181 to inquire about a local registered dealer
Annual membership fee: $35

Begun in February of 1993, this club invites collectors to enhance their enjoyment of collecting *Brian Baker's Déjà Vu Collection.* Charter members receive as part of their membership kit a special sculpture titled "City Cottage." Also included in the member's kit is a certificate of authenticity, signed photograph of Brian Baker and a letter of welcome. Each member will be mailed a personal identification card with membership number and a redemption certificate to purchase the members-only redemption sculpture, "Brian's First House." Twice a year, members will receive a copy of the interesting and informative club newsletter, "Brian's Backyard."

The Marty Bell Collector's Society

9314 Eton Avenue
Chatsworth, CA 91311
(818) 700-0754
Annual membership fee: $30

Established in 1991 for kindred spirits to "America's Premier Artist for Heart and Home," Marty Bell, this collector's club is geared to those who are touched by the joy and peace in her artwork. Members receive a free signed and numbered lithograph, the quarterly newsletter, "The Sound of Bells," a Society cloisonné pin and a map of England indicating the location of Marty's cottages. Members also receive information on new releases, exclusive members-only limited edition offerings, a membership card and private tours of the Marty Bell corporate offices and "originals" gallery.

The Belleek Collectors' International Society

144 W. Britannia Street
Taunton, MA 02780
1-800-822-1824
Annual membership fee: $25

Members receive a membership certificate, full-color catalog, information on all local Belleek Collectors' International Society chapter meetings and local dealers and a subscription to "The Belleek Collector." Members also receive an invitation to visit the Pottery and take the yearly Belleek Collectors' Tour — a twelve-day tour of Ireland.

The Boehm Porcelain Society

P.O. Box 5051
Trenton, NJ 08638
1-800-257-9410
Annual membership fee: $15;
With gift: $150

Club members receive the "Advisory" newsletter, catalogs, literature about Boehm porcelains, invitations to upcoming activities and an opportunity to purchase a collector society-exclusive porcelain sculpture.

Maud Humphrey Bogart Collectors' Club

P.O. Box 245
Elk Grove Village, IL 60009-0245
(708) 956-5401
Annual membership fee: $37.50

The Maud Humphrey Bogart Collectors' Club kit.

As members of this organization, collectors receive a very special benefit package, as well as the opportunity to acquire exclusive limited edition figurines available only to members. The

membership kit includes an exclusive club figurine, a year's subscription to the quarterly "Victorian Times" newsletter, a beautiful binder to hold club materials, a full-color catalog featuring the complete Maud Humphrey Bogart collection, a personalized membership card with a permanent membership number and a *Collection Gift Registry* book featuring illustrations of each figurine in the Collection with blank spaces to record personal notes.

International Bossons Collectors Society, Inc.
21-C John Maddox Drive
Rome, GA 30165
(706) 232-1266
Annual membership fee: $35

The International Bossons Collectors Society (endorsed by the W.H. Bossons Co., Ltd.) is a member-sponsored organization founded in 1981. New members receive a certificate of membership and a quarterly newsletter, "Bossons Briefs," which includes a "shop-and-swap" section for members to swap discontinued items. A members-only piece, "Winston Churchill," is available for a shipping and handling fee, and all members are invited to attend an annual educational conference.

Michael Boyett Collectors Registry
P.O. Box 632012
Nacogdoches, TX 75963-2012
(409) 560-4477
Membership fee: Free lifetime membership upon purchase of a sculpture

Members receive "The Boyett Collectors' Registry" newsletter twice a year and advance notification of new releases.

The Bradley Collectibles Doll Club
1400 North Spring Street
Los Angeles, CA 90012
(213) 221-4162
Annual membership fee: $7

Members receive a quarterly news bulletin, membership card, catalog, list of club headquarter stores and the opportunity to purchase a Club-exclusive doll.

Cabbage Patch Kids® Collectors Club
P.O. Box 714
Cleveland, GA 30528
(706) 865-2171
Annual membership fee: $25

Collectors who join this club will receive a year's subscription to "Limited Edition," the bimonthly newsletter, membership card, pin and customized binder. Members also have the opportunity to purchase special club offerings.

Cain Studios Collectors Guild
619 South Main Street
Gainesville, FL 32601
Annual membership fee: $25

This Collectors Guild is a club designed for fans of artist Rick Cain, and the advantages of joining this club are boundless. Members receive a free wood sculpture, exclusive redemption coupons entitling the holder to purchase Cain Studios members-only sculptures, a subscription to the company's members-only newsletter, a beautiful charter membership certificate and an identification card. Members also receive the privilege of free unlimited registration for all Rick Cain sculptures, previews of new releases and retiring pieces, and a secondary market matching service for buyers and sellers of Cain Studios collectibles.

Caithness Collector's Club
Caithness Glass Inc.
141 Lanza Avenue, Building 12
Garfield, NJ 07026
(201) 340-3330
Annual membership fee: U.S.: $35;
Canada: $40

This club was created to serve all admirers and collectors of Caithness Paperweights. Upon enrolling, members receive a paperweight, a Caithness millefiori lapel pin, a membership card, regular Club newsletters and a full-color annual review. Members also may purchase a paperweight designed annually for club members only.

The Caroler Chronicle
c/o Byers' Choice, Ltd.
P.O. Box 158
Chalfont, PA 18914
(215) 822-6700
Annual membership fee: Complimentary

Members of this Byers' Choice collectors' club receive special, members-only figurines from the *Kids of the World* collection as well as advance information about new introductions and retired pieces.

Cat's Meow Collectors Club
2163 Great Trails Dr. Dept. C
Wooster, OH 44691-3738
(216) 264-1377
Annual membership fee: Initial: $25;
Renewal: $22

New members receive an official Club notebook with color brochure, an identification card with membership number, the Collectors Buying List and subscriptions to the Club newsletter, "The Village Mews" and the Club's secondary market guide, "The Village Exchange." Members also receive exclusive members-only Cat's Meow pieces and a redemption form for the annual series.

The Cat's Meow Collectors Club kit.

The Chilmark Gallery
The Lance Corporation
321 Central Street
Hudson, MA 01749-1398
(508) 568-1401
Annual membership fee: Free upon registering a piece of Chilmark sculpture

As an owner of Chilmark sculpture, collectors will enjoy not only the sculptures themselves, but also all the collector services the foundry provides at no charge. These benefits include a subscription to *The Chilmark Report*, which offers information about new releases, artist appearances and industry news of interest to Chilmark collectors; subscription to *The Observer*, keeping collectors abreast of the ever-growing secondary market; *The Chilmark Collection Price Guide Update*; Certificates of Registration for each sculpture, invaluable when insuring collections; and

Redemption Certificates for annual American West and Civil War registered collector-only sculptures.

The Christopher Radko Family of Collectors

Planetarium Station
P.O. Box 770
New York, NY 10024
(212) 362-5344
Annual membership fee: $20

To be part of a family, not just a club, is the feeling Christopher Radko wants to convey both to people who have collected his ornaments for years, and also to those who are just beginning the adventure.

As members of the Christopher Radko Family, collectors receive a membership card and a year's subscription to the new quarterly newsletter, "Starlight," filled with informative articles and illustrations about the collection. They also receive a voucher entitling them to purchase the current members-only collectible ornament. Each year a new collector's ornament will be issued and other collectibles will be offered.

As a bonus to collectors, each year Christopher Radko tours the country, visiting key accounts and Starlight stores. At these personal appearances, he visits with the local family of collectors, to sign and date their new purchases.

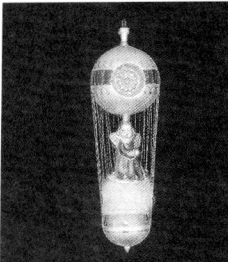

"Angels We Have Heard On High" was the first members-only ornament offered by the Christopher Radko Family of Collectors, with an edition limit of 5,000.

Crystal World Collector's Society

3 Borinski Drive
Lincoln Park, NJ 07035
(201) 633-0707
Annual membership fee: To be established

Crystal World is planning to establish a Collector's Society in 1994. Benefits will include the annual issue of a members-only piece, informative newsletters, notices of retirements and announce-

ments about opportunities to meet the artists at various Artist Shows held at Authorized Crystal World Collectible stores throughout the country.

The Crystal Zoo® Collectors' Club

4824 Sterling Drive
Boulder, CO 80301
(303) 449-6771
Annual membership fee: $25

Silver Deer, Ltd. invites collectors to revel in brilliantly sparkling crystal artwork by joining The Crystal Zoo Collectors' Club. Each membership kit includes an exclusive members-only limited edition valued at over $50, a membership card, a beautiful Member Certificate, copies of the official club newsletter, "Facets," a registry of the complete Crystal Zoo Collection, Redemption Coupons for exclusive figurine offerings and an invitation to special Club activities and promotions.

Daddy's Long Legs Collector's Club

KVK, Inc.
300 Bank Street
Southlake, TX 76092-9972
(817) 488-4644
Annual membership fee: One year: $20;
Two years: $35

Club members may take advantage of the opportunities available to them as part of the elite group of those who collect the continually-growing family of Daddy's Long Legs dolls. Members are entitled to purchase members-only dolls at extremely affordable prices, a full-color catalog of the most currently available dolls, a list of Star Dealers in the member's local area, a personalized club membership identification card, newsletters containing the latest information about Daddy's Long Legs, the opportunity to place locator ads in the newsletter and notification of signings in the member's home area.

Lowell Davis Farm Club

55 Pacella Park Drive
Randolph, MA 02368-1795
(617) 961-3000
Annual membership fee: Initial: $25;
Renewal: $20

Members receive a members-only figurine, official Club cap, membership card, Lowell Davis Collector's Guide and Dealer's Listing, a subscription to

the Lowell Davis "Farm Club Gazette," and a coloring book written and illustrated by Davis himself. Members also have the opportunity to acquire exclusive members-only figurines, and members receive a special invitation to visit Davis at his farm and announcements of his in-store appearances.

The Walt Disney Collectors Society

P.O. Box 11090
Des Moines, IA 50336-1090
Annual membership fee: U.S.: $52;
Canada: $54

The Walt Disney Collectors Society is the first company-sponsored membership organization for all generations of Disney-lovers, developed as an outgrowth of the recently-introduced *Walt Disney Classics Collection*. However, the new program goes beyond the Collection to offer members a unique look at the creative processes, entertainment philosophies and current goings-on that comprise the Disney Magic. Jiminy Cricket, with his wonderful image of conscience, teacher and friend, is the Society's symbol.

Membership benefits include: a free gift sculpture each year, a subscription to *Sketches*, a bound folio designed to hold the full-color magazine and other Society materials, the opportunity to purchase an annual members-only piece, advance notice of new releases, figurine retirement programs and special events, a charter member cloisonné pin and membership card.

The much-loved character Jiminy Cricket is the first gift sculpture offered exclusively to charter members of the new Walt Disney Collectors Society.

Dreamsicles Collectors' Club

1120 California Avenue
Corona, CA 91719
(800) 437-5818
Annual membership fee: $27.50

Members receive a free membership

figurine, a notebook and collectors guide, the "Clubhouse" quarterly newsletter, a membership card and the opportunity to purchase members-only pieces.

Duncan Royale Collectors Club

1141 S. Acacia Ave.
Fullerton, CA 92631
(714) 879-1360
Membership fee: Lifetime membership for $30

Members receive a porcelain bell ornament, an attractive cloisonné lapel pin, a subscription to the quarterly newsletter, "Royale Courier," an elegant binder, a membership card, a Charter Member Certificate and a catalog of Duncan Royale Limited Editions. Members also have the opportunity to purchase exclusive members-only figurines and are extended an invitation to travel with the Club to the "lands behind the stories."

EKJ Collectors Society

P.O. Box 93507
Atlanta, GA 30377-0507
(404) 352-1381
Annual membership fee: Initial: $30;
Renewal: $15.

Members receive an EKJ Society collector's plaque, an annual subscription to the quarterly published newsletter, the "EKJournal," a binder for the Journals, an EKJ lapel pin, membership card, free registration of figurines, an annual full-color EKJ catalog and a toll-free collectors' services "hotline" — 1-800-EKJ-CLUB. Society members also have the opportunity to purchase exclusive members-only figurines through an annual redemption coupon. Invitation to special club-sponsored events is also one of the many benefits offered.

The Enchanted Kingdom Collector's Club

1522 Highway 52
Moncks Corner, SC 29461
(803) 761-7626
Annual membership fee: $20

Fantasy and castle enthusiasts will receive quarterly issues of the "Enchanted Times," the official newsletter of the Enchanted Kingdom Collector's Club. Club members also receive a free copy of a thirty-five-page color booklet featur-

ing all the castles, an official membership card and two redemption certificates, allowing collectors to purchase members-only collectible castles in natural and fantasy colors. A members-only club plaque is included, as well as opportunities to place free ads in the Swap 'n' Sell section of the newsletters.

Enchantica Collectors Club

Munro Collectibles
P.O. Box 200
Waterville, OH 43566
(419) 878-0034
Annual membership fee: $25

This club is for adventurers who decide to embark on a journey deeper into the realms of Enchantica. Club members receive a special figurine along with a membership card and a Redemption Certificate for the purchase of an additional members-only figurine. Color newsletters packed with news, views, photos and illustrations are sent to members periodically.

The Enesco Memories of Yesterday Collectors' Society

One Enesco Plaza
P.O. Box 245
Elk Grove Village, IL 60009-0245
(708) 228-3738
Annual membership fee: $20

Collectors are invited to learn more about the exquisite porcelain bisque collection inspired by the drawings of famous British artist, Mabel Lucie Attwell.
The Welcome Kit includes a Society porcelain bisque figurine, a complete Gift Registry featuring every subject in the Memories of Yesterday collection, the "Sharing Memories" quarterly publication, a membership card and the opportunity to purchase a members-only offering.

The Enesco Memories of Yesterday Collectors' Society kit.

The Enesco Musical Society

One Enesco Plaza
P.O. Box 245
Elk Grove Village, IL 60009-0245
(708) 640-3956
Annual membership fee: $15

Collectors can expand their knowledge of the history and development of music through the ages and become better acquainted with the Enesco Small World of Music™ collection. Upon joining, members will receive an official Enesco Musical Society Membership Certificate, a subscription to the quarterly newsletter, periodic news bulletins sent only to members and the opportunity to purchase a members-only musical offering, a pocket folder and a collector's guide calendar.

The Enesco Precious Moments Birthday Club

One Enesco Plaza
P.O. Box 1529
Elk Grove Village, IL 60009-1529
(708) 640-3045
Annual membership fee: $16.50 for renewing members, $17.50 for new members

Collectors are invited to celebrate a special birthday in an extra special way.
Birthday Club members receive a symbol of membership figurine, a personalized, ready-to-frame Certificate of Membership, a year's subscription to the "Good News Parade," a Happy Birthday card mailed directly from club headquarters, and the invitation to acquire limited edition Birthday Club members-only porcelain bisque subjects. This is a wonderful way to share the joys of collecting with children.

The Enesco Precious Moments Collectors' Club

One Enesco Plaza
P.O. Box 1466
Elk Grove Village, IL 60009-1466
(708) 640-5228
Annual membership fee: $25

Upon joining, collectors will learn more about the Precious Moments Collection and its talented creator, Sam Butcher. Club members receive a symbol of membership figurine, the Club's full-color quarterly publication, "Goodnewsletter," a Club binder, a personal copy of the full color Pocket Guide to

the Enesco Precious Moments Collection, the official Gift Registry, a Club membership card and the privilege of acquiring two members only figurines.

The Enesco Precious Moments Collectors' Club kit.

The Enesco Treasury of Christmas Ornaments Collectors' Club
P.O. Box 773
Elk Grove Village, IL 60009-0773
Annual membership fee: $17.50

A charter year membership includes an exclusive gift Symbol of Membership, "The Treasury Card," a year's subscription to the official club newsletter, "Treasury Times," a membership card, the Treasury Collector's Guide and the opportunity to purchase exclusive members-only Treasury Ornaments.

Fenton Art Glass Collectors of America, Inc. (FAGCA)
P.O. Box 384
Williamstown, WV 26187
(304) 375-6196
Annual membership fee: $15
($2 Associate — for each additional membership in the same household)

For collectors of Fenton Art Glass this club offers the chance to learn more about one of America's great heritages, the glass-making industry, and Fenton Art Glass in particular. Members enjoy annual conventions usually in the first week of August which are held in Williamstown and Parkersburg, West Virginia. The week-long gala includes a private guided tour of the Fenton factory, seminars, special sales and a banquet and auction of unusual glass created especially for FAGCA members.

The Fontanini Collectors' Club
c/o Roman, Inc., Dept. 596
555 Lawrence Avenue
Roselle, IL 60172-1599
(708) 529-3000
Annual membership fee: Initial: $19.50;
Renewal: $15

Members receive an exclusive gift figurine, a subscription to "The Fontanini Collector" quarterly newsletter, a special Fontanini Collectors' Club pin created exclusively for Club members, advance notice of nationwide tour appearances by Fontanini family members, a portfolio organizer for Club information, a membership card and prior announcement of figure retirements and introductions. Members also have the opportunity to acquire a first-year members-only figure and an annual members-only edition.

Tobin Fraley Collector's Society
P.O. Box 419664
Kansas City, MO 64141-6664
(816) 274-7174
Annual membership fee: $35

Membership benefits include: a free carousel horse figurine for members only, the opportunity to purchase other exclusive carousel figures, the *Tobin Fraley Collector's Society Collector's Guide*, the quarterly "Carousel Collector" newsletter, personalized membership card and invitations to Tobin Fraley appearances.

The Kevin Francis Toby Jug Collectors Guild
P.O. Box 1267
Warren, MI 48090
(800) 634-0431
Annual membership fee: One year: $70;
Two years: $120

Collectors of Kevin Francis toby jugs have the option of joining a distinctive collectors club which affords its members several benefits. Members receive a free Guild miniature toby jug, three Guild magazines per year, including free advertising service, exclusive Guild issue editions, a Charter Member's Scroll and membership card with registration number. Members are also offered invitations to the yearly Collectors Guild Dinner, a 10% discount on all Kevin Francis publications, free valuation and dating services, pottery tours, character and toby jug price guide updates and a free enamel Members Badge.

Franklin Mint Collectors Society
The Franklin Mint
Franklin Center, PA 19091
(215) 459-6553
Annual membership fee: Complimentary;
modest fee for minted card

Founded in 1970, The Franklin Mint Collectors Society has grown to be one of the largest organized groups of collectors in the world. Members receive a number of exciting benefits at no cost. Every Collectors Society member receives biannual issues of The Franklin Mint's own publication, *Almanac*. The Society offers an annual minted membership card for members to purchase, and each year, collectors are offered the opportunity to join fellow Society members on an exciting vacation trip designed especially for the Collectors Society.

Gartlan USA's Collectors' League
15502 Graham St.
Huntington Beach, CA 92649
(714) 897-0090
Annual membership fee: $30

Sports enthusiasts will learn more about their favorite sports heroes from Gartlan USA. Members receive a certificate of membership; a one-year subscription to the "Collectors' Illustrated" newsletter; a *free* collector plate featuring the top names in sports; and notification of new Gartlan USA issues before the open market. Collectors may also purchase exclusive members-only figurines.

Diane Graebner Collector's Club
P.O. Box 13493
Fairlawn, OH 44334
(800) 626-4306
Annual membership fee: $20

Club members who enjoy Diane's simple but elegant portrayal of family love will receive a small print, a Certifi-

cate of Membership, a notebook and a quarterly newsletter. Members also have the option to buy member-only prints.

Gutmann Collectors Club

1353 Elm Avenue
Lancaster, PA 17603
(717) 293-2780
Annual membership fee: Initial: $28.50;
Renewal: $19.50

Members receive a permanent membership card, a members-only gift of a solid pewter medallion, a free quarterly newsletter and artist information services. Members may also purchase an exclusive, members-only figurine.

The Jan Hagara Collectors' Club

40114 Industrial Park North
Georgetown, TX 78626
Phone: (512) 863-9499
Annual membership fee: Initial: $22.50;
Renewal: $17.50

Members are offered a free "Audrey" cloisonné membership pin, an identification card entitling the holder to purchase members-only collectibles, a subscription to the club's quarterly newsletter providing the latest club information, and an elegant three-ring logo binder to hold the newsletters. Also extended to members is an invitation to attend the Fourth National Meeting in May of 1994, an opportunity to enter the "Decorate With Jan Hagara" contest and an opportunity to participate in a new membership drive — a free miniature figurine goes to those who sign up four new members.

Hallmark Keepsake Ornament Collector's Club

P.O. Box 412734
Kansas City, MO 64141-2734
Annual membership fee: $20

Ornament collectors will enjoy an array of club benefits within this club's membership kit. Benefits include a members-only Keepsake of Membership Ornament, as well as a miniature Keepsake of Membership Ornament, a subscription to "Collector's Courier" newsletter, a personalized membership card, a preview issue of the *Dream Book*, a Keepsake Ornament Treasury binder

and the opportunity to order exclusive and limited edition ornaments only available to members of the club.

Hand & Hammer Collectors Club

2610 Morse Lane
Woodbridge, VA 22192
1-800-SILVERY or (703) 491-4866
Annual membership fee: Complimentary

Members receive the quarterly newsletter, "Silver Tidings," and an ornament collectors guide. Members also have the opportunity to purchase special releases.

Harbour Lights Collectors' Club

8130 La Mesa Blvd.
La Mesa, CA 91941
(800) 365-1219
Annual membership fee: To be established

Coming soon…for more information, collectors may contact the company at the phone number listed above.

Edna Hibel Society

P.O. Box 9721
Coral Springs, FL 33075
(407) 848-9663
Annual membership fee: One year: $20;
Two years: $35

The Edna Hibel Society is the world's oldest artist fellowship. Admirers of Edna Hibel honor her humanitarian achievements, and enjoy her art in many media, including paintings, drawings, lithographs, serigraphs and sculptures. Society members will receive a free Hibel commemorative poster, personalized membership card, "Hibeletter" newsletter, invitations to cultural events, society tours, private tour of the Hibel Museum of Art, advance previews of Hibel artworks and the exclusive opportunity to acquire members-only limited edition Society collectibles.

The Mark Hopkins Bronze Guild

21 Shorter Industrial Blvd.
Rome, GA 30165-1838
(800) 678-6564
Annual membership fee: Free upon purchase of any Mark Hopkins Sculpture

This Guild's purpose is to enhance each member's enjoyment of collecting

bronze sculptures, with particular emphasis on Mark Hopkins' work. The Guild provides members with interesting facts about the artists and their works, education on bronze casting, information on new products as they are introduced, activities at the foundry, dealer listings and secondary market information. Membership benefits also include opportunities to obtain works that are made expressly for members and advance notification of artist appearances. Gradually, a locator service will be added for those members who want to buy or sell a retired piece.

M.I. Hummel Club

Goebel Plaza, P.O. Box 11
Pennington, NJ 08534-0011
1-800-666-CLUB
Annual membership fee: U.S.: $40;
Canada: $55

Members receive a gift figurine, a year's subscription to *Insights*, the Club's colorful quarterly magazine, membership card, information on Local Chapters of the M.I. Hummel Club and Club services such as the Research Department and Collectors' Market to match buyers and sellers of Goebel collectibles. Members also have the opportunity to purchase Club-exclusive figurines and participate in Club trips to Europe with a members-only tour of the Goebel factory in Roedental, Germany.

Iris Arc Crystal Collectors Society

114 East Haley Street
Santa Barbara, CA 93101
(805) 963-3661
Annual membership fee: $25

Members receive a free crystal ornament as an enrollment gift, including a membership card, a subscription to the Society's semi-annual newsletter, "Illuminations," a full-color catalog and free brochures of the latest figurine introductions. Members also receive the opportunity to purchase exclusive Collectors Society editions.

Jerri Collector's Society

651 Anderson St.
Charlotte, NC 28205
(704) 333-3211
Annual membership fee: $10

Members receive a Collector's Society pin, membership card and the quarterly newsletter. Members also have the opportunity to purchase an annual members-only doll. Other membership benefits include early mail-ins on new dolls and an invitation to the annual convention of the Collector's Society which is a weekend event including factory tours, a banquet and an auction.

Thomas Kinkade Collectors' Society

c/o Lightpost Publishing
P.O. Box 90267
San Jose, CA 95109
(800) 366-3733
Annual membership fee: $35

Lightpost Publishing welcomes collectors to peek behind the scenes into the realm of Thomas Kinkade, the "Painter of Light," through membership in his Collectors' Society. Members receive a free gift of a luminous archival paper print valued at $150, a quarterly newsletter and the opportunity to purchase a 9"x12" members-only framed canvas lithograph.

The Kronberg Collectors' Guild

3150 State Line Road
North Bend, OH 45052
(513) 353-3390
Annual membership fee: $25

Charter members of the Guild receive many special benefits: the option to purchase the first members-only statue for $100 (valued at $125), the Guild newsletter featuring articles about the artist and new product releases, a membership card and the "Kronberg Collection Register," future members-only offerings, announcements of shows and exhibitions, a list of authorized dealers carrying Kronberg Miniature Bronze Statuary and advance notification of the retirement or discontinuance of certain pieces.

Krystonia Collector's Club

110 E. Ellsworth
Ann Arbor, MI 48108
(313) 677-3510
Annual membership fee: $25

The make-believe world of Krystonia gives collectors a special gift each year

they join the club. Members receive newsletters explaining this award-winning fantasy line and announcing artist events. A members-only figurine is produced each year.

"Spreading His Wings" was Krystonia's 1993 club redemption piece.

Lalique Society of America

400 Veterans Blvd.
Carlstadt, NJ 07072
1-800-CRISTAL
Annual membership fee: $40

Connoisseurs of fine crystal will appreciate the special benefits afforded Lalique Society members. They include a subscription to the quarterly *Lalique* magazine, an enrollment gift — an embossed print of a Rene Lalique jewelry design signed by Madame Lalique — invitations to exclusive Society events and chartered trips, as well as access to annual limited edition, members-only crystal designs and special prices on museum and exhibition catalogs, books and other Lalique-related publications. The Society also annually hosts one of the few all-Lalique auctions in the world.

The Landmarks/Antebellum South Collectors Society

4997 Bent Oak Drive
Acworth, GA 30101
(404) 590-9621
Annual membership fee: Free lifetime membership included with purchase of a collectible

Members receive members-only discounts on new releases prior to general availability, a newsletter, invitations to historic tours and yearly pilgrimages to Charleston, Savannah and Natchez.

Lawton Collector's Guild

P.O. Box 969
Turlock, CA 95381
(209) 632-3655
Annual membership fee: Initial: $15;
Renewal: $7.50

Members receive a membership card, cloisonné Lawton logo pin, a year's subscription to "Lawtons Collector's Guild Quarterly," three-ring logo binder and a set of postcards featuring the current collection of Lawton Dolls. Members also have the opportunity to purchase a special doll designed for Guild members only.

Ron Lee's Greatest Clown Collector's Club

2180 Agate Court
Simi Valley, CA 93065
(805) 520-8460
Annual membership fee: $28.50

Known for his outstanding renderings of clowns, Ron Lee makes available to clown enthusiasts the opportunity to join his six-year-old club. Each enrollee receives a free sculpture gift valued at $65, coupons to purchase members-only offerings, a certificate of membership, a club identification card, a periodical newsletter, special club novelty items, advance notice of personal appearances along with information and color pictures of new product introductions.

Lefton Collector Service Bureau

P.O. Box 09178
Chicago, IL 60609-9970
(800) 628-8492

While a club has not yet been formed, Lefton's Collectors' Service Bureau serves as an information center and assists collectors in the pursuit of *Colonial Village* buildings and accessories through Lefton's network of dealers.

LEGENDS Collectors Society

2665-D Park Center Drive
Simi Valley, CA 93065
(800) 726-9660 or
(805) 520-9660
Annual membership fee: Free upon purchase of sculpture

Collectors who enjoy exceptional fine art sculptures will want to learn

more about LEGENDS and their masterworks sculpted in Mixed Media™, of a brilliant array of genuine metals such as bronze, fine pewter, brass vermeil, 24-karat gold vermeil, and lucite. Member benefits include a personalized membership card, a personal LCS membership number, informative monthly mailers, a copy of the quarterly newsletter created specifically for LEGENDS collectors and access to secondary market information. Among several other benefits are first-purchase opportunities on all new LEGENDS releases and a personalized certificate of ownership for each sculpture purchased.

Leroy's World Collector Society

690 NE 13th Street
Ft. Lauderdale, FL 33304-1110
(800) 327-2297
Annual membership fee: $10

Collectors of Black figurines will love Leroy, the mischievous Black lad who has been amusing his fans in twenty-two countries for nineteen years. In addition to a Redemption Card entitling purchase of one of the newest figurines at fifty percent off issue price, each member receives a membership card, full-color brochures of Leroy and all Black figurines brought out by Naturecraft. Members also receive a current price list, all newsletters coming out during the year and the opportunity to buy any Special Editions made for club members only.

Lilliput Lane Collectors' Club

c/o Lilliput Incorporated
The Oakland Building
9052 Old Annapolis Road
Columbia, MD 21045
(410) 964-2043
Annual membership fee: One year: $30;
Two years: $50

The Lilliput Lane Collectors' Club boasts a friendly, efficient staff who provide excellent service. Collectors joining the Club will receive a free cottage, a complimentary bonus gift, a full-color catalog and price list, a membership card as well as a subscription to the colorful, quarterly club magazine, *Gullivers World*. Members may also participate in competitions, receive invitations to

exclusive events and take the opportunity to purchase Special Edition Club pieces.

Little Cheesers® Collectors' Club

GANZ
908 Niagara Falls Blvd.
North Tonawanda, NY 14120-2060
(800) 724-2950
Annual membership fee: To be established

Coming soon...membership benefits to be established.

The Lizzie High® Society

220 North Main Street
Sellersville, PA 18960
(215) 453-8200
Annual membership fee: U.S. — Initial: $20;
Renewal: $15; International — Initial: $25;
Renewal: $18

Members receive a very special Collector's Catalog in a leather-grained binder, a subscription to the biannual newsletter, "The Lizzie High® Notebook," a personalized identification card, a pewter pin and the opportunity to purchase a limited edition doll created exclusively for Society members.
Among the items in the renewal packet are: a new identification card with the member's charter year number, updates of the Collector's Catalog for fall and spring, a continuing subscription to "The Lizzie High® Notebook" and a Redemption Certificate with which to purchase the limited edition members-only doll.

Lladro Collectors Society

43 West 57th Street
New York, NY 10019-3498
(201) 807-0018
Annual membership fee: One year: $35;
Two years: $60

Upon joining, members receive an exclusive Lladro fine porcelain bell, a subscription to *Expressions* magazine, a binder to store the magazines, a bas-relief porcelain plaque bearing the signatures of the three Lladro brothers, a personalized membership card, an opportunity to acquire a members-only figurine and an associate membership to the Lladro Museum in New York City.

The Lladro Collectors Society kit.

The Seymour Mann Collectible Doll Club

P.O. Box 2046
Madison Square Station
New York, NY 10159
Annual membership fee: $5 introductory membership fee, but special membership offer with the purchase of the "Tatiana" doll through an authorized Seymour Mann dealer.

Members receive a membership card, a 20" x 24" full-color doll poster and a Club newsletter. Members also have the opportunity to purchase limited edition dolls available only to Club members, participate in contests and take advantage of special offers.

Melody In Motion Collectors Society

c/o WACO Products Corporation
1 N. Corporate Drive
Riverdale, NJ 07457
(201) 616-1660
Annual membership fee: One year: $27.50;
Two years: $50

Members will receive an exclusive porcelain figurine, an opportunity to purchase a members-only edition figurine, a complimentary subscription to the "Melody In Motion Collectors Society" newsletter, discount coupons to purchase *Melody In Motion* figurines, and a *Melody In Motion* folder containing a four-color catalog. Members also get a personalized membership card entitling the holder to all club benefits and upcoming events and a Redemption Certificate, which allows the purchase of members-only figurines.

Memory Lane Collector's Society

690 NE 13th Street
Ft. Lauderdale, FL 33304-1110
(800) 327-2297
Annual membership fee: $25

In addition to a cottage valued at much more than the membership fee, each member receives the following: a membership card with registration number, full-color brochures showing the Memory Lane Cottages together with current price list, newsletters from time to time and the opportunity to order Special Edition pieces made exclusively for Society members.

"The Kentish Oast" is the first Memory Lane club-exclusive item offered to Society members. The oast is a kiln, usually conical in shape, in which hops, malt or tobacco are dried. This reproduction of an oast found in the green countryside of Kent was modeled by artist Peter Tomlins specifically for the Memory Lane Collector's Society.

Lee Middleton Collectors' Club

1301 Washington Boulevard
Belpre, OH 45714
1-800-843-9572
Membership fee: $150 for charter members
(limited to 500)

Members receive a Certificate of Membership, a photograph personally signed by Lee Middleton, "Lee's Dolls Today" newsletter, an updated catalog and an exclusive Lee Middleton doll.

P. Buckley Moss Society

601 Shenandoah Village Drive, Box 1C
Waynesboro, VA 22980
(703) 943-5678
Annual membership fee: U.S.: $25;
International: $30

New Society members are given a pewter geese membership pin, a membership certificate and card, the "Sentinel" newsletter issued three times a year and a logo binder. Also available exclusively for members are members-only P. Buckley Moss prints. Renewing members receive a porcelain pin, "Friendship."

Myth & Magic Collectors Club

1201 Broadway, Suite 309
New York, NY 10001-5405
(212) 679-7644
Annual membership fee: $37.50

Members receive a free figure valued at $45. The 1993 piece was "The Dragon of Methtindour." Members also receive a subscription to the newsletter, "Methtindour Times," a full-color catalog of the *Myth & Magic* collection, a membership card, the availability to purchase at least two exclusive members-only pieces and the opportunity to travel to England on a special Myth & Magic Collectors Club tour.

Old World Christmas® Collectors' Club

P.O. Box 8000, Dept. C
Spokane, WA 99203-0030
(800) 962-7669, ext. 160
Annual membership fee: One year: $30;
Two years: $57; Three years: $83

Club membership entitles collectors to purchase exclusive collectibles, to receive periodic "Old World Christmas Star Gazette" newsletters, a free *Collectors' Guide* featuring 100 full-color pages of holiday treasures and an heirloom-quality gift.

The Pangaean Society

cp smithshire™
c/o The Lance Corporation
321 Central Street
Hudson, MA 01749-1398
(508) 568-1401
Annual membership fee: $25

Upon joining, members receive a membership card, a free cp smithshire™ 1993-94 Charter Member figure, "Fellowship Inn," a free collector pin and copy of the "cp smithshire" catalog. Membership also includes a subscription to "Shirespeak™," the official collector newsletter announcing new Shirelings™ and those who are "Going Home to the Forest™" (being retired), news of collector events and more. Members receive the opportunity to purchase exclusive members-only sculptures and to receive six free names in the Aftermarket Facilitation™ program.

The cp smithshire™ Pangaean Society club kit.

PenDelfin Family Circle

1250 Terwillegar Avenue
Oshawa, Ontario L1J 7A5 (Canada)
Annual membership fee: U.S.: $30;
Canada: $40

As members of PenDelfin's collectors' club, collectors are invited to become part of a growing family with others who want to share the joy of collecting PenDelfin. A free gift, an exclusive members-only figurine, placement in a drawing for collectibles, "The PenDelfin Times" newsletter, free tours of the studio in England and a membership card and certificate are available to all PenDelfin Family Circle friends.

PenniBears Collectors Club

P.O. Box 1200
Noble, OK 73068
1-800-727-4883
Annual membership fee: $5

Penni Jo Jonas creates delightful figurines in miniature. Miniature enthusiasts who join this club will receive a personalized membership card, a membership packet and a subscription to the newsletter, "PenniBears Post." Members also have the opportunity to purchase annual members-only PenniBears pieces.

Phyllis' Collectors Club

RR 4 Box 503
Rolla, MO 65401
(314) 364-7849
Annual membership fee: Initial: $20;
Renewal: $15; Three years: $45

Collectors are invited to become part of a network of discerning collectors who recognize the beauty and value of Phyllis Parkins' dolls. Annual club members receive an exclusive membership card, a cloisonné lapel pin, a color

catalog and the triannual club newsletter, which features behind-the-scenes articles, previews of new dolls in The Collectables line, Phyllis' personal appearance calendar and a classified secondary market section. Members also receive an attractive padded club album to organize and protect the newsletters, the right to purchase an exclusive membership doll marked with the member's own personal membership number, the opportunity to purchase other members-only items and an invitation to "An Evening With Phyllis" and tour of the factory the first weekend in May.

PJ's Carousel Collection

P.O. Box 532
Newbern, VA 24126
(703) 674-4300
Annual membership fee: U.S.: $40;
Canada: $52

This club is dedicated to preserving the American Carousel and making general information of carousel history available to collectors. Upon joining, members will receive a distinctive members-only PJ Club plaque, a tape of carousel music recorded from an authentic carousel band organ, PJ's color catalog, club newsletter containing information on retired pieces and new additions, a membership card and the right to purchase an exclusive members-only carousel animal.

Pleasantville 1893 Historical Preservation Society

P.O. Box 93507
Atlanta, GA 30377-0507
(404) 352-1381
Annual membership fee: Initial: $30;
One-year renewal: $15; Four-year renewal: $70

Members receive the lighted "Pleasantville Gazette" building, a $40 value, an annual subscription to the quarterly "Pleasantville Gazette" newsletter, a collectible lapel pin, a membership card, an annual full-color Pleasantville catalog and a bisque Christmas ornament from the Pleasantville collection.

Pocket Dragons and Friends Collectors' Club

Land of Legend Limited
41 Regent Road
Hanley, Stoke-on-Trent ST1 3BT (England)
Annual membership fee: One year: $35;
Two years: $56

The Pocket Dragons and Friends Collectors' Club is designed to cater to the needs of collectors of the adorable, whimsical dragons from artist Real Musgrave. Members receive a complimentary figurine entitled "Key To My Heart" and the opportunity to purchase special edition pieces and limited edition prints. Members also receive a quarterly magazine, the *Pocket Dragon Gazette*, invitations to factory tours and special appearances or events, inclusion in competitions to win Pocket Dragons, the Club hotline number and a membership card.

Polland Collectors Society

P.O. Box 2468
Prescott, AZ 86302
(602) 778-1900
Annual membership fee: $35

The American West comes alive in Don Polland's three-dimensional figurines. Members receive newsletters, an annual gift figurine and information on the secondary market on all Polland sculptures. Members also have the opportunity to purchase members-only figurines and receive the dates of special appearances by Don Polland.

Red Mill Collectors Society

One Hunters Ridge
Summersville, WV 26651
(304) 872-5237
Annual membership fee: $15

Upon joining, collectors will receive a membership card, the Society's newsletter published three times annually, advance information on new products and soon-to-be-retired pieces and secondary market information.

The Renoir Impressionists Society

109 Bushaway Road
Wayzata, MN 55391
(800) 358-8995
Annual membership fee: $25

The Renoir Impressionists Society was created to share appreciation for the Impressionist Era and especially the art of Renoir at that time. Members are allowed the opportunity to acquire museum-quality numbered lithographs of Impressionist art, with First Purchase Privileges as new works become available. Also offered members is "The Renoir Society Journal" quarterly publication, a complimentary copy of the book *Renoir My Father* by Jean Renoir and a membership card.

Royal Doulton International Collectors Club

700 Cottontail Lane
Somerset, NJ 08873
(800) 582-2102
Annual membership fee: $25

Members receive a year's subscription to the Club's quarterly magazine, *Gallery*, announcements of special events featuring Michael Doulton and company artisans, access to the historical research information service on Royal Doulton products and information on local chapters of the Club. Members also have the opportunity to purchase specially-commissioned pieces and are able to participate in the "Sell and Swap" column of the U.S. newsletter. Another benefit is the exclusive guided tours for club members to the Royal Doulton Potteries in Stoke-on-Trent, England.

Sandicast® Collectors Guild™

P.O. Box 910079
San Diego, CA 92191
(800) 722-3316
Annual membership fee: U.S.: $25;
International: $30

Each year, world-renowned artist Sandra Brue sculpts an exclusive members-only sculpture for Sandicast collectors. Guild members receive the annual membership gift sculpture, a *Sandicast - The Creations of Sandra Brue* video, a full-color catalog and an identification card. Members are kept informed of new releases, limited editions and retirement of sculptures with a subscription to the new "Paw Press®" newsletter, published twice yearly. In addition, Guild members have the opportunity to purchase Annual Edition members-only designs.

Santa Claus Network™

c/o Possible Dreams
6 Perry Drive
Foxboro, MA 02035
(508) 543-6667
Annual membership fee: U.S.: $25;
International: $30

Members receive a free Possible Dreams® Clothtique® Santa, an informative quarterly newsletter, a colorful and

complete directory of all Clothtique Santas, a membership card and the opportunity to acquire exclusive club offerings.

Possible Dreams' Santa Claus Network™ club kit.

Sarah's Attic Forever Friends Collectors' Club
126 ½ West Broad Street
P.O. Box 448
Chesaning, MI 48616
(800) 4-FRIEND (437-4363)
(517) 845-3990
Annual membership fee: $25

Forever Friends Club members receive a free figurine, a membership card, a subscription to the triannual magazine, *From the Heart*, a color catalog, a nationwide dealer listing, a checklist of Sarah's Attic collectibles dating back to 1983 and redemption certificates to purchase members-only figurines. Members also receive a folder to keep printed matter stored for easy reference.

The Sarah's Attic Forever Friends Collectors' Club kit.

Sebastian Miniatures Collectors' Society
The Lance Corporation
321 Central Street
Hudson, MA 01749-1398
(508) 568-1401
Annual membership fee: $20

Upon joining, members receive a free Sebastian Miniature and a copy of the most recent *Value Register for Sebastian Miniatures*. Membership also includes a subscription to "The Sebastian Collectors Society News" covering new releases, both retail and private commissions, artist events and general collecting information and a subscription to "The Sebastian Exchange," which reports on all Sebastian secondary market activity and auctions. Annual updates of the *Value Register* and Redemption Certificates for members-only miniatures are also member benefits.

In addition to an auction held at the annual Sebastian Miniatures Festival in Massachusetts, Society members may participate in a Look-Alike Contest. Here, a group of Sebastian collectors dress as their favorite Sebastian Miniature figurine.

Shade Tree Cowboy Collector Society
6210 NW 124th Place
Gainesville, FL 32606-1071
(800) 327-6923
Membership fee: Collectors become members by purchasing and registering a Shade Tree Cowboy figurine.

Members receive a certificate that entitles them to purchase collectors-only pieces at twenty percent off retail price, computerized registration of their Cowboy figurines at no charge and a subscription to the biannual newsletter, "Shade Tree Cowboy Collector Society News," which includes a national value guide of current bid prices. The club's main function and benefit is the operation of a secondary market exchange service, which entitles members to free listings and bids, with a nominal fee charged for actual transactions. Members also receive advance notice of retiring figurines as well as preview information and access to new cowboy figurines prior to their general public release dates. The latter allows members to acquire new releases with the lowest serial/registration numbers.

Shelia's Collectors' Society
P.O. Box 31028
Charleston, SC 29417
(803) 766-0485
Annual membership fee: Initial: $25; Renewal: $20

Upon joining, members receive a collectors' club notebook, a membership card, a directory of retired pieces, the "Our House" quarterly newsletter, color flyers of Shelia's Houses, special gifts and a redemption voucher for members-only collectibles.

Silver Deer's Ark Collectors' Club
4824 Sterling Drive
Boulder, CO 80301
(303) 449-6771
Annual membership fee: $25

Artist Tom Rubel has expanded his menagerie of creatures, large and small, as collectors joining this club will see first-hand. Membership kits include a members-only figurine, a membership card, a beautiful Charter Membership Certificate, a copy of "The Peaceable Kingdom" newsletter, a registry of the complete *Ark Collection*, Redemption Coupons for exclusive limited edition offerings and an invitation to special club activities and promotions.

Sports Impressions Collectors' Club
P.O. Box 633
Elk Grove Village, IL 60007-0633
(708) 956-5400
Annual membership fee: $25

Collectors can bring today's and yesterday's hottest NBA, NFL and Major League Baseball stars, as well as other professional sports stars, into their homes through exclusive collectors' plates and figurines. Upon joining, Club members receive a symbol of membership piece, a folder for Club literature, the Sports Impressions catalog, a collector's guide, a membership card, "The Lineup" newsletter and the opportunity to purchase members-only offerings.

Steinbach/KSA Collectible Nutcracker Club
1107 Broadway
New York, NY 10010
(800) 243-9627
Annual membership fee: To be established

Members' privileges include special offers and promotions. Details are to be announced at a later date. Any questions are welcome: please contact the club at the number listed above.

Fred Stone Collectors Club

P.O Box 8005
Lake Bluff, IL 60044
(800) 828-0086
(708) 295-5355
Annual membership fee: $35

Equestrian enthusiasts will appreciate this club, featuring the artwork of award-winning artist Fred Stone. Club members receive a free Fred Stone poster, a free video, monthly newsletters and an opportunity to acquire secondary market prints prior to general availability.

Summerhill Collectors Club

601 S. 23rd Street
P.O. Box 1479
Fairfield, IA 52556
Annual membership fee: $25

Founded in 1992, Summerhill Collectors Club affords its members several benefits: a free, glistening crystal paperweight gift, a personalized certificate of membership, vouchers for members-only exclusive offerings signed and numbered by Imal Wagner, a periodical newsletter, a membership card and advance notice and information about new product introductions and personal appearance signings.

Swarovski Collectors Society

2 Slater Road
Cranston, RI 02920
1-800-426-3088
Annual membership fee: Initial: $30;
One-year renewal: $20; Three-year renewal: $50

Upon joining, members receive a certificate of membership in the form of a 40mm faceted Swarovski crystal paperweight, a personalized membership card, a Society lapel pin, exclusive access to annual and limited editions and a subscription to the biannual *Swarovski Collector* magazine. Also, special events and activities are organized for members only, which include European tours through the Austrian Alps to the home of Swarovski.

VickiLane Collectors Club

3233 NE Cadet Avenue
Portland, OR 97220
(800) 456-4259
Annual membership fee: $30

Membership includes a members-only limited edition figurine, a quarterly newsletter, a membership card and club logo pin. The newsletters contain stories from Cinnamon, Spice, Miss April and other celebrities of VickiLane. It contains news of retiring pieces, preview information on new items, articles about collectors, profiles of collectible stores that feature VickiLane, letters from collectors and continuing articles on artist/designer Vicki Anderson and others at VickiLane.

"Sweet Secrets," designed for VickiLane Collectors Club charter members, portrays Cinnamon whispering to Spice.

"Wetherholt's World" Collectors' Club

c/o Rabbit Run Enterprises
P.O. Box 2304
Decatur, IL 62524
(217) 422-7700
Annual membership fee: $35

Larry Wetherholt is an internationally-known artist and sculptor with sculptures in Japan, England, India, China and Russia as well as throughout the United States.

The "Wetherholt's World" Club, which is currently being formed, will consist of a collectors card, subscription to a biannual newsletter and a special sculpture available each year to club members only. The first club piece will be "The Mechanic," which portrays a boy working on a soap box car.

Questions are welcome — collectors may contact Rabbit Run at the telephone number listed above.

David Winter Cottages Collectors Guild

4456 Campbell Road
P.O. Box 800 667
Houston, TX 77280-0667
(713) 690-4490 or (713) 690-4489
Annual membership fee: $40

Members receive a year's subscription to the quarterly magazine, *Cottage Country*, a complimentary members-only piece, two redemption certificates for special Guild pieces, official notification of news, events and information regarding John Hine Studios and the opportunity to buy a leather magazine binder.

"Swan Upping Cottage" (left) and "Thameside Cottage" (right) were the David Winter Cottages Collectors Guild redemption pieces for 1993.

The Donald Zolan Collector's Society

c/o Pemberton & Oakes
133 E. Carrillo Street
Santa Barbara, CA 93101
(805) 963-1371
Annual membership fee: $17

Known for his award-winning portrayals of children, Donald Zolan invites collectors to join his Society. Benefits include a choice of a free miniature plate or framed miniature lithograph, members-only limited edition collectibles, a quarterly newsletter including product and artist information, the opportunity to purchase Zolan originals and limited-edition collectibles at special prices for Society members only and chances to win one of several exciting prizes in Society contests.

Travel for Collectors

Collectors Gain New Appreciation for Collectibles by Visiting Museums and Touring Manufacturing Facilities

Collectors who vacation in the United States, Canada and abroad are invited to browse through this chapter to discover the locations of exciting collectible tours and museums offered throughout the world by manufacturers and other firms.

There are restaurants, afternoon teas and a circus to attend, blooming gardens to enjoy, art-filled museums and gift shops to visit, an auction in which to participate and favorite collectible factories to tour and gain new appreciation and understanding of their step-by-step production processes. Both veteran collectors and those new to the collectibles industry who take the opportunity to experience their hobby first-hand are certain to gain a deeper appreciation of the fascinating artwork they collect.

United States Museums and Tours

Alaska Porcelain Studio Tour
P.O. Box 1550
Mile 91.6 Sterling Highway
Soldotna, AK 99669
907/262-5626

Facility tours are available Monday through Friday, June 15th through September 15th. Please call for a schedule and other information.

Annalee Doll Museum
50 Reservoir Road
Meredith, NH 03253
800/433-6557

The museum is open from Memorial Day to Columbus Day, 9 a.m.-5 p.m. daily.

Admission is free to Doll Society members, senior citizens and children under 12 years old; fifty cents for all others.

Collectors may call 1-800-433-6557 for directions to the museum. The museum's new Victorian facade is a replica of Annalee Thorndike's childhood home in Concord, New Hampshire.

This exciting museum contains rare and older Annalee Dolls, as well as a videotaped presentation featuring the history of the company and interviews with Annalee. The museum also showcases historic memorabilia related to Annalee and the rest of the Thorndike family.

Annalee Doll Society™ members get a chance to bid on out-of-production dolls for their collections at the Annual Annalee Auction weekend.

Babyland General® Hospital
19 Underwood St.
Cleveland, GA 30528
706/865-2171

Hospital hours are Monday through Saturday, 9 a.m.-5 p.m. and Sunday, 1-5 p.m.

Visitors will see Licensed Patch Nurses performing deliveries of original Cabbage Patch Kids® under the Magic Crystal Tree, which grows within the

early 1900s medical clinic. The gift shop is open during tour hours, and guided tours are available. Cabbage Patch Kids® are available for adoption at the hospital, as well as everything needed to care for them at the gift shop.

Marty Bell Fine Art, Inc.
CORPORATE OFFICES & PUBLISHING FACILITIES
9314 Eton Avenue
Chatsworth, CA 91311
800/637-4537

Marty Bell Fine Art, Inc., home of "America's Premier Artist for Heart and Home" — Marty Bell, opens its doors to countless visitors Monday through Friday each week. All guests are treated to a guided tour throughout the 22,000-square-foot facilities.

Visitors will learn about the complexities of reproducing original art into limited edition lithographs using the canvas transfer process. Guests also visit the gallery of limited edition lithographs which displays the current selections offered by the company.

The favorite stop of all who take the tour is the visit to the "private" gallery of Marty Bell original paintings. Lucky visitors may also have an opportunity to see, and perhaps meet, Marty Bell as she personally signs her artwork at the facilities.

No admission fee. Free guided tours by appointment only. Reservations requested for all groups. Please call for information.

Bell Haven

c/o Iva Mae Long
R.D. #4 Box 54
Tarentum, PA 15084
412/265-2872

Tours are by appointment only.

Admission is $4.

Bell Haven is located on one acre of wooded grounds with bells displayed inside and out of the workshop. Collectors will marvel at the 30,000 bells that have been gathered through the years, beginning in the late 1950s.

Bell Haven is associated with the American Bell Association International, Inc. Collectors are invited to an annual bell collectors convention. For more information, please contact:

The American Bell
Association Int., Inc.
P.O. Box 19443
Indianapolis, IN 46219

The Bell Museum Of Natural History

University of Minnesota
10 Church Street SE
Minneapolis, MN 55455
612/624-1852

The 1994 *Wildlife Art in America* exhibit will showcase over 100 works by North American artists depicting American wildlife. The exhibition is based on the recently combined collections of the American Museum of Wildlife Art and the Bell Museum of Natural History.

Over 100 original works from other museums, collectors and artists are also on display, forming one of the most comprehensive exhibitions of wildlife art ever! The works of historical masters, modern figures and the finest of the current generation are presented, tracing the development of wildlife art from the early naturalists to the modern emphasis on environmental awareness.

The museum itself is open Tuesday through Friday, 9 a.m.-5 p.m.; Saturdays, 10 a.m.-5 p.m.; Sundays, noon-5 p.m.; closed Mondays.

Admission is $2 for adults, $1 for seniors and children, free to children 2 years and under. Thursdays, free admission for all.

Bellingrath Gardens And Home/Boehm Gallery

12401 Bellingrath Garden Road
Theodore, AL 36582
205/973-2217

Open daily 7 a.m.-dusk.

Located twenty miles southwest of Mobile off Interstate 10, Exit 15A to Theodore.

Reservations recommended for group tours and for groups of twenty or more.

Admission for the Gardens is $6.50 for adults; $3.25 for children ages 6-11; free to children under 6 years. Gardens and Home tour fee is $14 for adults; $11 for children ages 6-11; $8.15 for children under 6 years (except babies in arms). Delchamps Gallery of Boehm Porcelain and chapel are included in Gardens tour.

The Boehm Porcelain Gallery is the largest public display of works by Edward Marshall Boehm. Over 233 porcelains are exhibited in lighted cases.

The Bellingrath Home has a large collection of antique porcelains, crystal, silver, paintings and furniture from around the world. Hostesses conduct tours of the home. The Bellingrath Gardens consist of sixty-five acres on the 900-acre grounds, including a bird sanctuary. The Gardens' greenery is planned so that it is in bloom all year-round.

A new gift shop is open, offering Boehm porcelain and specialty items.

The Bradford Museum Of Collector's Plates

9333 Milwaukee Avenue
Niles, IL 60714
708/966-2770

The Bradford Museum of Collector's Plates, located in the Chicago suburb of Niles, Illinois, contains 300 historically significant limited edition plates from producers around the world.

In the center of the museum is The Bradford Exchange Trading Floor where brokers help clients buy and sell plates over the telephone. The trading floor is the heart of the dynamic international collector's plate market.

The museum is open Monday through Friday, 9 a.m.-4 p.m.; Saturday and Sunday, 10 a.m.-4 p.m.

Admission is free. Tours are not available.

Circus World Museum

426 Water St.
Baraboo, WI 53913-2597
608/356-8341
608/356-0800 — 24-hour Information Line

Fifty-acre grounds, featuring live shows, attractions, exhibits, demonstrations and rides are open early May through mid-September, 9 a.m.-6 p.m. (open until 10 p.m. mid-July through mid-August).

The Irvin Feld Exhibit Hall & Visitor Center is open all year, and is located in south-central Wisconsin, fifteen minutes from the Wisconsin Dells.

1993 summer season admission charge was $10.95 for adults, $9.95 for seniors, $5.95 for children ages 3 to 12 and free to children under 3 years old. 1994 prices have not yet been determined. Admission includes all shows, exhibits and demonstrations.

The world's largest facility

devoted to the circus, Circus World Museum is located at the birthplace of the Ringling Bros. Circus and site of the show's original winter quarters (1884-1918). This is also the world's largest repository of antique circus wagons, posters and other artifacts and archival items and is therefore listed as a National Historic Site, owned by the State Historical Society of Wisconsin.

Collectors of Flambro's *Clown Alley Collectibles Series* will find this museum especially interesting.

The Circus World Museum in Baraboo, Wisconsin possesses the world's largest collection of circus wagons. Museum visitors can tour a football field-sized pavilion that houses massive, gilded and carved parade wagons. Above, the Twin Lions Tableau Wagon towers over spectators. The vehicle measures seventeen feet tall and dates back to the 1860s, when it was built in England.

Lowell Davis' Red Oak II
Rt. 1
Carthage, MO 64836
417/358-1943

Open Monday through Saturday, 10 a.m.-6 p.m.; closed December 25th through March 25th.

Bus and group tours by reservation only — call (417) 358-9018.

The tour of this unique, rebuilt 1930s town includes a Reception Center, Belle Starr Museum, Gas Station, Blacksmith Shop, Elmira School, Salem Country Church, Parsonage, General Store/Gift Shop, Feed and Seed Store, School Marm's B & B, Mother-in-Law House, The Bird Song, Frank Yant House B & B, Garfield Wyulie B & B, Sawmill and,

coming soon, Red Oak Inn B & B (B & B stands for Bed and Baskets).

DeGrazia Gallery In The Sun
6300 N. Swan Road
Tucson, AZ 85718
602/299-9191

Open 10 a.m.-4 p.m. daily.
No admission charge.
Reservations are needed for free guided tours.
Located in the foothills of the Santa Catalina Mountains, the Gallery showcases an unrivaled display of DeGrazia art housed in unique adobe structures.
A gift shop is also available.

Department 56 Tour Of One Village Place
6436 City West Parkway
Eden Prairie, MN 55344
1-800/LIT-TOWN (548-8696)

Tour hours are June through September, Fridays 1-4 p.m. (not including holidays). By appointment only; reservations must be made at least one week in advance. Special arrangements can be made for groups of more than twenty.

No admission fee.

The tour includes displays of *The Original Snow Village*, *The Heritage Village Collection* and *Snowbabies*. Original, retired and limited editions, as well as current Department 56 Christmas, Easter and giftware products are featured.

Dollmakers Originals International, Inc.
1230 Pottstown Pike
Glenmoore, PA 19343
215/458-0277
610/458-0277 (after Jan. 1, 1994)

The studio is open Monday through Friday, 9 a.m.-5 p.m.
Tours are by appointment only. Bus groups are welcome.
Visitors will see the production of porcelain and vinyl dolls,

from the pouring of porcelain into the molds, to the dressing and hair styling of the charming dolls.

Admission is free.

FJ Designs/Cats Meow Factory
2163 Great Trails Drive
Wooster, OH 44691
216/264-1377

Tours are given Monday through Friday at 10 a.m. and 1 p.m.

Admission is free. Reservations required with groups of more than six persons. No bus tours are available.

The tour is forty-five minutes long and begins in the lobby area, which displays all new and retired products from FJ Designs, beginning in 1982 to the present. During the tour through the factory, the production processes of five different departments are observed. These processes include sanding, spray painting, screen printing, and the finishing of the Cat's Meow Village pieces.

Pictured is the "Great Trails Building" of FJ Designs/The Cat's Meow that collectors are welcome to visit.

Favell Museum Of Western Art And Indian Artifacts
125 West Main Street
Klamath Falls, OR 97601
503/882-9996

Monday through Saturday, 9:30 a.m.-5:30 p.m.; closed Sundays.

Admission: $4 adults, $3 seniors, $2 children 6 to 16.

The museum overlooks the outlet of the largest natural lake in Oregon, and its 17,000 square feet of display space is laid out

like the spokes of a wagon wheel. Includes works by renowned western artists such as Donald Polland, John Clymer, Joe Beeler, Frank McCarthy, and Mort Kunstler, as well as more than eighty collections of artifacts, including miniature firearms. A gift shop and art gallery are located on the premises.

The Favell Museum was founded by a family with a real western heritage; one which has collected Indian artifacts for many years, enhancing the collection with the works of western artists. This museum is intended to help preserve western artifacts and share them with those interested.

Fenton Art Glass Company
420 Caroline Avenue
Williamstown, WV 26187
304/375-7772

Fenton Art Glass Company offers free forty-minute factory tours, which are given Monday through Friday, 8:30 a.m.-2:30 p.m. The factory is closed on national holidays and during an annual two-week vacation (around the first two weeks in July). Call or write for exact vacation dates!

Admission is free and no reservations are necessary for groups under twenty individuals; reservations are highly recommended for larger groups.

The tour of the plant allows visitors to watch highly skilled craftsmen create handmade glass from its molten state to the finished product. The majority of the factory tour is handicap-accessible.

Also located on the premises are a museum and gift shop which are open all year, Monday

through Saturday, 8 a.m.-5 p.m. and Sundays, noon-5 p.m. Closed Easter, Thanksgiving, Christmas and New Years Day; all other holidays, hours are 10 a.m.-5 p.m. Extended seasonal hours are June through August, 8 a.m.-8 p.m. weekdays; in April, May and September through December, 8 a.m.-8 p.m. on Tuesdays and Thursdays only.

The museum offers examples of Ohio Valley glass with major emphasis on Fenton glass made from 1905 to 1955. Representative glass of other Ohio Valley companies is displayed along with items of historical interest. A thirty-minute movie on the making of Fenton glass is shown at regular times throughout the day.

Admission fees are $1 for adults, fifty cents for children ages 10 to 16, free to children under 10 years; a 20% discount is offered for groups of twenty or more.

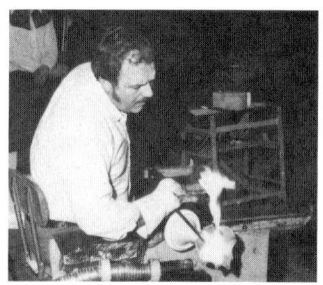

A "finisher" in the glassmaking process demonstrates his skill for collectors participating in the Fenton Art Glass Company's factory tour.

Franklin Mint Museum
U.S. Route 1
Franklin Center, PA 19091
215/459-6168

Open Monday through Saturday 9:30 a.m.-4:30 p.m., Sunday 1-4:30 p.m.

No reservations or admission fee required.

The Franklin Mint Museum houses original masterpieces by such world-famous American artists as Andrew Wyeth and

Norman Rockwell, as well as recreations of works commissioned by the National Wildlife Federation, the Royal Shakespeare Theatre, the Louvre and The White House. On display are the finest works created by the world-famous artists of The Franklin Mint, including extraordinary sculptures in porcelain, crystal, pewter and bronze, award-winning collector dolls, die-cast automotive classics, uniquely designed and minted coins and Philatelics of historic significance. Handicap facilities are provided. Special events are scheduled, and a gallery store and free parking are available.

Frankoma Pottery Tour
P.O. Box 789
2400 Frankoma Road
Sapulpa, OK 74067
800/331-3650 or 918/224-5511

The gift shop is open Monday through Saturday, 9:30 a.m.-6 p.m.; Sundays, 12:30-5 p.m. Tours are given Monday through Friday, 9 a.m.-3 p.m.

Admission is free. Reservations are highly recommended for large groups, to ensure that not too many groups arrive at one time. Tours are every thirty minutes.

The Frankoma Pottery factory is located four miles southwest of Tulsa on Frankoma Road in Sapulpa, Oklahoma. Young and old alike can enjoy this interesting tour. On exhibit are 175 pieces of pottery made in thirteen colors, which Frankoma has been producing for sixty years. Gift items are also displayed.

Margaret Furlong Designs
210 State Street
Salem, OR 97301
800/225-3114

Studio tours available upon request. Arrangements can be made by contacting the studio at the telephone number listed above.

Goebel Miniatures Studios/Factory

4820 Adohr Lane
Camarillo, CA 93012
805/484-4351

All tours must be booked in advance by contacting Travis Tokuyama at the studio to make arrangements. The most common time for tours is Thursdays at 10 a.m.

No admission fee is charged.

Visitors will see a brief film about the production of the miniature figurines and then walk through the studios/factory to see closely the developmental and decorative processes. The tour takes approximately one hour.

Hallmark Visitors Center

P.O. Box 419580
Mail Drop 132
Kansas City, MO 64141-6580
816/274-5672

The Hallmark Visitors Center is open Monday through Friday, 9 a.m.-5 p.m.; Saturdays 9:30 a.m.-4:30 p.m. and open most holidays.

Reservations are required for groups of ten or more, and should be made in advance by calling (816) 274-3613.

The Hallmark Visitors Center, located in Kansas City's Crown Center, presents a lively overview of the world's largest greeting card company. Twelve exhibits are showcased at the Center, including several educational, historical and public interest exhibits and artwork. The center appeals to all ages and people from near and far.

Hibel Museum Of Art

150 Royal Poinciana Plaza
Palm Beach, FL 33480
407/833-6870

Tours are Tuesday through Saturday, 10 a.m.-5 p.m; Sunday, 1-5 p.m.

Admission is free. Reservations are requested for groups of ten or more. Bus tours are invited.

The museum opened in January 1977 as a tribute to artist Edna Hibel by the late Ethelbelle and Clayton B. Craig. It is the world's only public museum dedicated to the art of a living American woman.

The Hibel Museum of Art has an extensive collection of Edna Hibel oil paintings, drawings, sculptures, original graphics, porcelain collectibles and dolls. Visitors will see antique snuff bottles, dolls and a paperweight collection. The museum has a collection of rare art books and antique Oriental, English and Italian furniture.

The museum shop is open during tour hours.

The M.I. Hummel Museum, Inc.

199 Main Plaza
New Braunfels, TX 78131-1100
210/625-5636
800/456-4866

Museum is open Monday through Saturday, 10 a.m.-5 p.m.; Sundays, noon-5 p.m.

Admission is $5 for adults, $4.50 for seniors and groups, $3 for students ages 6 to 18, free to children 5 years and under.

The M.I. Hummel Museum houses the world's largest collection of original drawings by Sister M.I. Hummel, and also includes re-creations of Sister Hummel's studio, schoolroom, chapel and bedroom, with a video film of her life. In addition, the museum offers a children's drawing room and gift shop.

The beautiful M.I. Hummel Museum is located in New Braunfels, Texas.

Incolay Studios Museum

445 North Fox Street
San Fernando, CA 91340
818/365-2521

The tour is available by invitation only and examines the history of twenty-eight years of wonderful reproductions of antiquity handcrafted in Incolay Stone, proudly made in the United States. The actual antiques are on display — the Private Collection as well as the Incolay Collection.

Jerri Doll's Collection Room

Dolls by Jerri Factory
651 Anderson St.
Charlotte, NC 28205
704/333-3211

The factory is open Monday through Friday, 9 a.m.-4 p.m.

No admission is charged. Tours are by appointment only and group size is limited to twenty visitors.

Visitors will see the showroom with a complete collection of every Jerri doll, plate, ornament and figurine created by Jerri since 1976. The steps in creating a Jerri doll can be seen on the tour, from the creative beginnings, to the shipping of the product from the factory.

Landmarks Co./Antebellum South Collectors Society Tours And Pilgrimages

4997 Bent Oak Drive
Acworth, GA 30101
404/590-9621

Society members from across the country may experience the elegance of the Old South while touring plantation homes and grand mansions in all their splendor.

Dates and times to be established. Admission fee varies.

Lawtons' Workshop

548 North First St.
Turlock, CA 95380
209/632-3655

Tours are by special arrangement to groups only.

No admission charge.

Guests are treated to a step-by-step demonstration of Lawtons' actual doll production. Guests will see the process, from the first pour of porcelain slip, to the final inspection and packaging.

The Lizzie High® Museum
A Country Gift Shoppe
Rt. 313, Dublin Pike
Dublin, PA 18917
215/249-9877

Open Monday through Saturday, 10 a.m.-5 p.m.; Sundays, noon-4 p.m. between Thanksgiving and Christmas only.

Admission is free at the museum, which features a complete collection of all the retired Lizzie High® dolls.

The Lizzie High® Museum offers displays of the complete collection of Lizzie High® dolls.

Lee Middleton Original Dolls, Inc.
1301 Washington Boulevard
Belpre, Ohio 45714
800/233-7479

There is no charge for tours of the factory.

Lee Middleton Original Dolls opens its doors to countless visitors from around the world. A larger-than-life doll house in every way, Lee's new manufacturing facility is discreetly hidden behind a beautiful pastel "gingerbread" facade which fronts her 37,000 square foot state-of-the-art production plant. Each tour provides a clear understanding of the creative process behind Lee's porcelain

and vinyl collectible dolls. Visitors will see the mixing and pouring of liquid porcelain, the vinyl molding and curing process and the hand-painting of each doll's face.

The company schedules tours daily, Monday through Friday, 9 a.m.-3 p.m. (Summer tours are given Tuesday through Saturday), and is always pleased to host large group tours at requested times with adequate advance notice.

Lladro Museum And Galleries
43 West 57th Street
New York, NY 10019
212/838-9341

Open Tuesday through Saturday 10 a.m.-5:30 p.m.

Free admission. Reservations required for large groups.

The museum houses the largest collection of retired Lladro porcelains. This display features approximately 1,000 pieces, and the museum occupies three floors of the building.

Also available at the gallery is an in-house theater, where the video *Clay Color and Fire* is shown. This video highlights the process of creating a Lladro figurine, from the original designs for a sculpture to the finished work of art.

Pemberton & Oakes Gallery
133 East Carrillo Street
Santa Barbara, CA 93101
805/963-1371

Pemberton & Oakes Gallery is Donald Zolan's home gallery, located ninety miles north of Los Angeles, along the coast. Collectors are welcome to visit Monday through Friday, 8:30 a.m.-4:30 p.m. Many Zolan originals are on display as well as samples of current Zolan limited edition collectibles.

For further information or exact directions, collectors may

call Pemberton & Oakes at the telephone number listed above.

Precious Moments Chapel & Visitors Center
480 Chapel Road
Carthage, MO 64836
800/543-7975

The Precious Moments Chapel welcomes visitors to the beautiful meadows of the Missouri Ozarks. Located near Carthage, a beautiful Civil War town, the Chapel is the realization of one of America's favorite artists, Samuel J. Butcher.

Experience the warmth and inspiration of the Chapel which contains over 5,000 square feet of murals lining the walls and ceiling. Each of the murals depicts favorite Bible stories of the Old and New Testaments. The fifteen stained glass windows are among the most exquisite treasures in the Chapel. The windows, some containing over 1,200 individually cut pieces of glass, were painstakingly hand-leaded by the artist and his family.

During the Chapel visit, enjoy the numerous displays in the Gallery that change frequently. From the history of *Precious Moments* to the private collection of Sam Butcher's art and memorabilia, stroll down memory lane and catch a glimpse of the personal life of the artist.

In the Visitors' Center, walk through a European village featuring storybook cottages and a castle complete with moat and waterfall. Each cottage houses a gift shoppe. Be charmed by the variety of *Precious Moments* gift items offered, including the many pieces available at the Chapel only.

While visiting, don't miss Tiffany's Family Style Restaurant with its generous portions of salads, sandwiches, lunch entrees and special meals served by a friendly staff.

Musical shows feature the talented Chapelaires performing a variety of favorite gospel and blue-grass hits as well as original songs written and composed by members of the group.

No admission fee. Free guided tours of the Chapel are given daily. Reservations requested for groups of ten or more. The Chapel and Visitors' Center are open daily excluding Thanksgiving, Christmas and New Year's Day. Please call for further information, reservations or operating hours.

Norman Rockwell Center/ Frances Hook Museum

315 Elizabeth Street
P.O. Box 91
Mishicot, WI 54228
414/755-4014

Open Monday through Saturday, 10 a.m.-4 p.m.; Sunday, 1-4 p.m.; evenings by appointment.

Located in the fifteen-room Old School in the Village of Mishicot, Wisconsin.

Reservations requested for groups. Bus groups are welcome. (Contact Carol Anderson.)

One of the largest Norman Rockwell collections in the world, free slide shows, shop displays of art, limited edition prints and collectibles. The Frances Hook Museum/Art Gallery features the artist's limited edition issues and sponsors an annual Frances Hook Celebration in June, complete with a Frances Hook Look-Alike Contest. The Old School also features handcrafted, American-made items by over 800 local artists.

When visiting Dorr County, don't miss Mishicot!

Norman Rockwell Museum

601 Walnut Street
Philadelphia, PA 19106
215/922-4345

Open Monday through Satur-

day, 10 a.m.-4 p.m.; Sundays, 11 a.m.-4 p.m.

Open every day of the year except Christmas, New Year's, Thanksgiving and Easter.

Located at 601 Walnut Street, lower level.

Reservations are necessary for groups of ten or more. Admission charge: $2 for adults, $1.50 for seniors over 62 and AAA members, free to children 12 and under. Group rates are also available.

Exhibits include one of three complete sets of *Saturday Evening Post* covers (324 pieces), over 600 pieces of additional art including the original art for Rockwell's famous War Bond Poster, a replica of his studio and the Four Freedoms Theater which has an eight minute video. Extensive gift shop. Tour should take thirty to forty-five minutes.

The Norman Rockwell Museum

Route 183
Stockbridge, MA 01262
413/298-4100

From May through October the museum is open daily 10 a.m.-5 p.m. From November through April, it is open 11 a.m.-4 p.m. weekdays and 10 a.m.-5 p.m. weekends and holidays. Norman Rockwell Studio open May through October, 10 a.m.-5 p.m. daily. Closed Thanksgiving, Christmas and New Year's Day.

Located on Rt. 183, Stockbridge, Massachusetts.

The museum contains the largest collection in the world of original paintings, drawings and sketches by Norman Rockwell. Exhibitions focus on different aspects of Rockwell's Art and the field of illustrations. It offers the public the opportunity to see original art that is so familiar in prints.

Ron Lee's World Of Clowns Tour

2180 Agate Court
Simi Valley, CA 93065
805/520-8460

Clown lovers the world over visit Ron Lee's World of Clowns in Simi Valley, California. Covering over 20,000 square feet, the guided tour takes visitors through the process of creating limited edition figurines from beginning to end. Visitors have an opportunity to see the original sculptures in their clay form and how they are transformed, through many hand processes, into the finished metal figurines that are completely 24-karat gold plated and hand-painted. Guests are always delighted with the visit to the main painting room where over fifty talented artisans meticulously paint Ron Lee limited edition sculptures. Some lucky tour guests may have an opportunity to see and meet Ron Lee at the factory, as well as see his private "play" room.

No admission fee. Free guided tours are by appointment only. Reservations requested for all groups.

The Ron Lee Gallery and the Collector's Club are also located on the premises.

The Official Sebastian Miniatures Museum

Stacy's Gifts and Collectibles
Route One
Walpole Mall
East Walpole, MA 02032
508/668-4212

Open Monday through Saturday, 10 a.m.-9:30 p.m.; Sundays, 1 p.m.-6 p.m.

Admission is free.

Located in the center of Stacy's Gifts and Collectibles in the Walpole Mall in East Walpole, Massachusetts. The original museum was dedicated on October 29, 1983 by Sebastian creator Prescott W. Baston.

After a complete store renovation in 1989, the museum was rededicated by Woody Baston, son of Prescott and now sole sculptor of Sebastian Miniatures.

The museum is comprised of over 1,000 Sebastian Miniatures from the personal collection of the store owners, the late Sherman Edwards and Doris Edwards. It also contains scrapbooks of some early drawings and advertisements that were used as models for many of the original figurines. In the museum are videos that feature the annual Sebastian Festivals and interviews with both Prescott and Woody Baston.

Shelia's, Inc. Studio Tour
1856 Belgrade, C-1
Charleston, SC 29407
803/766-0485

Tours are available by appointment only, with advance notice.

Collectors may tour the art studio and manufacturing facilities at Shelia's Inc.

United Design Plant
1600 North Main
Noble, OK 73068
800/727-4883

Plant tours are given Monday through Friday, 10 a.m. and 1 p.m.

Admission is free. Reservations for large groups are requested.

Visitors will see the manufacturing process of United Design figurines. All are produced in Noble, Oklahoma by American artists and craftsmen. The plant covers 230,000 square feet and includes the manufacturing, distribution and administration facilities.

The gift shop, open 9 a.m.-5 p.m., has one of every design manufactured on display and many are available for purchase by tourists.

A tour group listens to their guide before beginning a tour of United Design's 230,000-square-foot manufacturing facility. The tour participants are standing outside the company Gift Shop.

Vaillancourt Folk Art
145 Armsby Rd.
Sutton, MA 01590
508/865-9183

The studio is open Monday through Saturday, 9 a.m.-5 p.m.; Sunday, 11 a.m.-5 p.m. Tours are Monday through Friday at 11 a.m.

Admission is free. Reservations are required for groups larger than ten people.

Vaillancourt Folk Art is located in an 1820 New England farmhouse surrounded by stone walls.

The complete tour of the painting studios begins in the moulding room with the viewing of the antique chocolate moulds. The visitors then proceed through the painting rooms and finally to the finishing process. The tour shows the creation of the chalkware originals from beginning to end.

Foreign Museums and Tours

The House Of ANRI
1-39047 St. Christina
Val Gardena, Italy
609/737-7010 ANRI Headquarters

To participate in a tour of the ANRI workshop, collectors must be a Club member. Tours require advance reservations with ANRI Club to ensure an English-speaking guide. All tours take place on Thursdays from 2:00-3:30

p.m. No admission fee is charged; however, a membership card is required.

The House of ANRI is located in Northern Italy in the Dolomite Mountains near the Austrian border. Club members visiting the workshops view the artisans at work. They also witness the step-by-step process of creating an ANRI woodsculpture and possibly have the chance to meet Ernst Riffeser, grandson of **AN**ton **RI**ffeser!

Please call ANRI Club for reservations and directions.

Belleek Pottery
Belleek Co. Fermanagh
Northern Ireland
Phone 011-44-365-658-501 ask for Patricia McCauley

Tour Ireland's oldest and most historic pottery and see how this world-famous china is handcrafted. Belleek Pottery was the winner of the 1990 British Airways tourism award for the best tourist facility in Northern Ireland. The complex hosts a fine museum and audio visual theatre. Pottery tours run every twenty minutes Monday through Friday. After the tour, relax in the restaurant and enjoy a meal served on Belleek tableware. Please call ahead for tour times, as tour times are seasonal.

Belleek Parian China, coveted and collected worldwide for generations, celebrates a 136-year tradition of handcrafting the world's most translucent china.

Today, Belleek Parian China is crafted in the village of Belleek in much the same way it was made in the early 19th century. While Belleek is best known for its famous Shamrock pattern, the pottery offers a broad selection of giftware, including collectible plates, figurines, bells and Christmas ornaments.

The Enesco Precious Moments Collectors' Club Trip To The Orient

P.O. Box 1466
Elk Grove Village, IL 60009-1466
Julia Kirkwood
708/640-3195

This tour is offered annually every Spring for club members, family and friends.

Precious Moments Collectors' Club members can enjoy a memorable 12-day tour to the Orient. The trip includes stops in Japan, Thailand and Hong Kong. Members tour the Precious Moments Design Studio in Nagoya, Japan, where they will meet Master Sculptor Yasuhei Fujioka, who personally oversees the original sculpting of each figurine. Participants also visit the Precious Moments production facilities in Bangkok, Thailand.

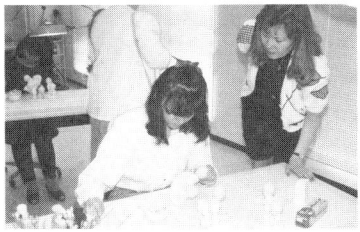

While touring the Precious Moments Design Studio in Nagoya, Japan, collectors watched artisans carefully paint and craft the popular porcelain bisque figurines.

W. Goebel Porzellanfabrik Factory

Coburger Strasse 7
96472 Roedental, Germany
From U.S.: 01149/9563920
From Germany: 09536/92303

The factory is located in Roedental, just a few kilometers from the city of Coburg.

Demonstration room is open Monday through Thursday, 9 a.m.-4 p.m.; Fridays, 9 a.m.-noon; closed Saturdays. Information Center and Goebel Store are open Monday through Friday, 9 a.m.-5 p.m.; Saturdays, 9 a.m.-noon.

Visitors see a film, view a special demonstration and shop in the factory store. Members of the M.I. Hummel Club may also be the factory's guest for lunch Monday through Thursday (but must be there by 11:30 a.m., and advise the receptionist as soon as they arrive); non-members traveling with them pay a nominal amount.

The Studios And Workshops Of John Hine Limited

2 Hillside Road
Eggars Hill
Aldershot, Hampshire GU11 3NB
England
Phone 0252/334672
Fax 0252/313263

The studios and workshops tours are at 2 p.m. daily; tours take an hour and a half.

Admission is free. Reservations are required and can be made by phone or by writing in advance, c/o Keith MacKenzie.

Tours of the John Hine Studios include demonstrations given by craftsmen and women in the fascinating setting of a restored 16th-century barn. Visitors may browse around the award-winning courtyard gardens or relax over a cup of tea. The complete collection of David Winter Cottages are on display as well as exciting new works from John Hine's talented artists, to the setting of a medieval street scene.

The Studios are 35 minutes from London by car or 55 minutes by train (Waterloo Station to Aldershot).

The John Hine Studios at Eggars Hill, Aldershot are set in the lovely English countryside.

Kaiser Porzellan Factory Tour

Alboth & Kaiser GmbH & Co. KG —
Postfach 1160
8623 Staffelstein — Germany
Phone 09573/336-0

Tours can be arranged through Kaiser Porcelain in Niagara Falls. Contact Betsy Braun at (716) 297-2331. No admission charge.

Collectors tour the Kaiser factory in Staffelstein, Germany — the heart of Bavarian porcelain making.

The World Of Krystonia Factory

1-3 Winpenny Road
Parkhouse Industrial Estate
Newcastle-Under-Lyme, Staffordshire
England
Phone 0782/566-636

Tours are by appointment only, Monday through Friday. All tour requests should be submitted in writing.

No admission fee is charged.

The factory, which opened in late 1990, has a guided one-hour tour. Visitors will see the step-by-step process of how a Krystonia figure comes to life. The painters, moldmakers and fettlers can be seen creating the mystical creatures of the Krystonia collection.

Lilliput Lane Studio Tour

Penrith, England
Lilliput Lane Collectors' Club
c/o Lilliput Incorporated
410/964-2202

The Studios of Lilliput Lane are open only to members of the Lilliput Lane Collectors' Club, who are asked to book ahead with membership number if they require a tour. Admission is free.

Open Monday through Friday, tour times are 9:15 a.m., 10:15 a.m., 11:15 a.m., 1:30 p.m. and 2:30 p.m. No 2:30 tour on Fridays.

A maximum of ten to fourteen people per tour.

The tour takes collectors on a

journey through moldmaking, casting and all steps to painting. A history of the company is included during the tour.

A special studio-only piece called "Rose Cottage" is available.

Lladro: A Collector's Odyssey

Lladro Collectors Society
43 West 57th Street
New York, NY 10019-3498

Several tours are available for Collector Society members — ten-day to two-week tours of sights in Spain, as well as a tour of the Lladro factory in Valencia. If traveling on your own, contact the Lladro Collectors Society for information on factory tours.

PenDelfin Studios Limited

Cameron Mill
Howsin Street
Burnley, Lancashire B1O 1PP
England
Phone 011/4428/232301

Tour reservations must be made in advance, by contacting the studio at the address or phone number listed above. After making reservations, a map will be sent to interested collectors, to help them find the studio.

No admission fee is charged.

At PenDelfin Studios, visitors can see the step-by-step processes of the making of PenDelfin figurines, from preliminary molding and painting to the finished product.

Pocket Dragons & Friends Collectors' Club Tour

Collectible World Studios
41 Regent Road
Hanley, Stoke-on-Trent ST1 3BT
England
Phone 0782/212885

The tour must be pre-booked by telephoning the Club secretary to make arrangements.

Admission is free to club members and family, with membership card and proof of identity.

Royal Copenhagen Porcelain Factory

Smallegade 45
2000 Frederikberg, Copenhagen
Denmark
Phone 31 86 48 48

The factory is open from May 15th to September 14th: tours are held Monday through Friday, 9 a.m.-2 p.m. on the hour.

From September 15th to May 14th, tours are held Monday through Friday, 9-11 a.m. on the hour.

Reservations are recommended. For groups of more than five persons, other times for tours can be arranged by prior agreement.

During the tour of the factory, visitors will be told what porcelain is and shown an impressive assortment of porcelain. Visitors will also have the opportunity of seeing porcelain painters at work.

The talk during the one-hour tour is given in Danish, English, German and French.

Royal Doulton Factory

Nile Street
Burslem, Stoke-on-Trent
England ST6 2AJ
800/582-2102
Phone 0782/575454

The guided tour at Stoke-on-Trent is free to club members. Non-members must pay a £2.00 admission fee. Visits for parties of students or senior citizens can be pre-booked at reduced rates.

Tours are given Monday through Friday at 10:30 a.m. and 2 p.m. and can be pre-arranged by calling the Collectors Club or the factory. Tours are not available to children under 14 years old.

Visitors will be guided through working departments, following the creation of tableware, giftware and figures by skilled artisans. The Sir Henry Doulton

Gallery is also open to visitors, featuring examples of Royal Doulton products spanning over 170 years, including the figure collection. The tour is completed with a visit to the gift shop/tea room, which is open Monday through Saturday, 9 a.m.-5:30 p.m.

The Gallery itself is open Monday through Friday, 9 a.m.-12:30 p.m. and 1:30-4:15 p.m.; closed during factory holidays.

Royal Worcester — Dyson Perrins Museum

Severn Street
Worcester WR1 2NE
England
Phone 0905/23221

Open Monday through Friday, 9:30 a.m.-5:00 p.m.; Saturday 10 a.m.-5 p.m. Modest admission fee.

Collectors are invited to view the largest collection of Royal Worcester porcelain in the world.

Royal Worcester Factory Tours

Severn Street
Worcester WR1 2NE
England
Phone 0905/23221

Factory tours are arranged through the Dyson Perrins Museum. It is preferable that tours be booked in advance by phoning Pam Savage at (0905) 23221.

Two tours are offered:

A standard guided tour of the factory takes in all stages of the making and decorating processes. Tours last approximately one hour and leave from the Museum at ten-minute intervals between 10:25 a.m. and 11:25 a.m. and 1:15 p.m. and 3:15 p.m. Maximum group size is twelve. Cost £3.00 (children 11 to 16 years old £2.00).

The Connoisseurs tour is a more detailed tour for those with more specialized interest. Includes visits to departments not

usually open to the general public. Tours last two hours. Two tours a day only — leaving the Museum at 10:15 a.m. and 1:30 p.m. Maximum group size ten (but normally two or four — very personal!) Cost £9.50 per person includes full color guide book plus morning coffee or afternoon tea.

Note — Safety regulations preclude children less than 11 years old. These tours are also unsuitable for very elderly or disabled persons, due to the number of flights of stairs.

Swarovski Collectors Society European Tour

2 Slater Road
Cranston, RI 02920
800/426-3088

Tours offered twice a year in the Fall and Spring and limited to members of the Swarovski Collectors Society.

The first part of the tour is spent in Austrian Tyrol, then moves on to the Lake Geneva region of Switzerland. In the Austrian Tyrol, a special visit will be made to Wattens, the home of the Swarovski Company. In Wattens, special exhibits are constructed and members are able to meet Swarovski craftsmen, designers and technical experts. A private members-only shopping experience at the Swarovski Crystal Shop is arranged.

Swarovski Crystal Shop

A-6112 Wattens
Innstrasse 1
Austria
Phone 05224/5886

From May through September, the shop is open Monday through Saturday, 8 a.m.-6 p.m., Sundays, 8 a.m.-noon; from October through April, open Monday through Friday, 8 a.m.-6 p.m., Saturdays, 8 a.m.- noon.

From the Autobahn, take the Wattens exit between Innsbruck and Salzburg/Munich onto Swarovski Strasse.

Visitors can see Swarovski crystal products and visit the gift shop and cafe. Tours highlight artisans cutting, engraving, painting and blowing glass.

Information On Other Tours

Factories and museums not listed here may also welcome collectors, even if they do not post specific visiting hours. See addresses in "Company Summaries" to contact any firms that you especially want to visit.

Conventions/Special Events/Reading Suggestions
Enrich Your Collecting Experience By Attending a Convention or Special Event and Through Additional Reading Sources

National Collector Conventions

A world of excitement, anticipation and fun-filled education opens to collectors who attend the two national, manufacturer-sponsored collector conventions. Both novice and experienced collectors are invited to visit several hundred booths, where new products are on display and where artists are often on hand to meet the public and sign autographs. Collectors may further enhance their visit by attending seminars on a vast array of topics or by participating in the "Swap and Sell," where they may sell retired collectibles to interested parties. For more information on the conventions, please contact the exposition management at McRand International, Ltd., One Westminster Place, Lake Forest, Illinois 60045.

Heio Reich, president of Reco International Corp., was the recipient of the 1993 International Collectible Achievement Award, presented at "Memories" in South Bend, Indiana. Left to right: Michal McClure, president of the International Collectible Exposition, with Heio Reich, and Eugene Freedman of Enesco Corporation, the 1992 recipient, presenting the award.

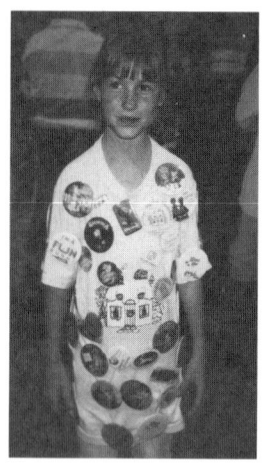

Young and old alike can enjoy collector conventions, as this little girl enthusiastically shows by the many buttons and pins she has gathered throughout the day from several manufacturer's booths.

Three exhibit halls featuring 328 exhibits from 123 manufacturers of limited edition collectibles were packed full during public days at the International Collectible Exposition in South Bend, Indiana. The show played host to over 15,500 retailers and collectors, setting a new attendance record for the exposition.

1995 Show Schedule:
Long Beach, California, April 20-23
Long Beach Convention Center
April 20-21: Dealer days
April 22-23: Open to the public

South Bend, Indiana: July 12-16
South Bend Century Center
July 12-13: Dealer days
July 14-15: Open to the public
July 16: Swap and Sell

Harbour Lights, winner of the double booth award at the South Bend International Collectible Exposition, attractively showcased their lighthouses in this nautical-themed booth.

Special Events

Special events within the collectibles industry come in many different forms — an award, artist appearances, collectible conventions, friendships — all help to shape the industry. The next two pages help tell the "story behind the story," picturing several special activities and some of the collectors who love to participate in these events.

An enthusiastic collector, Evelyn Francour of South Bend, Indiana, got into the spirit of the South Bend Collectibles Exposition. Standing in the Collectors' Information Bureau's booth, she happily sported a vest-full of pins she gathered at the show.

Recovering just in time for the holidays, young Andres Diaz of Aurora, Illinois, enjoyed a talk with Ronald T. Jedlinski, owner and CEO of Roman, Inc. Thousands of playthings and trinkets from Roman, Inc. were delivered at Christmastime to children in twenty Shriner's hospitals across the country.

Annalee® doll artist Chuck Thorndike greeted collector Lynn Castellani at the Annual Auction Weekend held by Annalee® Mobilitee Dolls at Meredith, New Hampshire.

Hockey legend Gordie Howe, the sport's greatest ambassador, cheerfully autographed plates bearing his likeness, during a Gartlan USA plate-signing session.

Jim Swiezynski, Director of Marketing for The Lance Corporation, left, presented a "Parsons' Battery" sculpture to Kurt Holman, Perryville Battlefield Park Manager. Looking on, from left, are Tom Breiner, President of the Cincinatti Civil War Round Table, sculptor Francis Barnum and Jerry Raiser, Chairman of the Round Table's Preservation Committee. Full proceeds from the sale of twenty-five sculptures were earmarked for the Perryville Preservation project, and Lance also made a generous donation to the General Preservation Fund of the Round Table, who used the money to support other restoration projects in 1993.

At a Swarovski Collectors Society (SCS) designer tour event in Secaucus, New Jersey, Swarovski crystal designer Michael Stamey signed his 1992 limited edition piece, "Care For Me — The Whales," for collectors.

Brian Baker, artist of Brian Baker's Déjà Vu Collection for Michael's Limited, at his first personal appearance, happily signed one of his sculptures for collector Milly Del Costillo of Miami, Florida.

A record number of collectors gathered for the opening ceremonies of the Annual International Collectible Exposition at the Century Center in South Bend, Indiana. More than 15,500 attended the exposition.

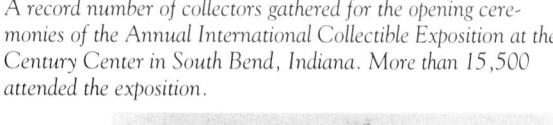

Magazines and Newsletters

The following are independent periodicals about the limited editions field. Many firms also publish newsletters and magazines which they provide free or at nominal cost to their collectors or preferred customers. For subscription information on the publications listed here, write them directly.

AMERICAN ARTIST
1 Color Court
Marion, Ohio 43302
1-800-347-6969

ANTIQUE & COLLECTING HOBBIES
1006 S. Michigan Avenue
Chicago, Illinois 60605
(312) 939-4767

THE ANTIQUE TRADER
P.O. Box 1050
Dubuque, Iowa 52004
(319) 588-2073

CANADIAN ART SALES INDEX
1683 Chestnut Street
Vancouver, B.C.
V6J 4M6
(604) 734-4944

COLLECTOR EDITIONS
170 Fifth Avenue
New York, New York 10010
(212) 989-8700

COLLECTOR'S MART
650 Westdale Drive. Ste. 100
Wichita, Kansas 67209
(316) 946-0600

COLLECTORS NEWS
P.O. Box 156
Grundy Center, Iowa 50638
(319) 824-6981

CONTEMPORARY DOLL MAGAZINE
30595 8 Mile
Livonia, Michigan 48152-1798
(313) 477-6650

DOLL CRAFTER
30595 8 Mile
Livonia, Michigan 48152-1798
(313) 477-6650

DOLLS MAGAZINE
170 Fifth Avenue, 12th Floor
New York, New York 10010
(212) 989-8700

THE DOLL READER
900 Frederick Street
Cumberland, Maryland 21502
(301) 759-5853

DOLL WORLD
P.O. Box 420077
Palm Coast, Florida 32142-9895

INSIGHT ON COLLECTIBLES
103 Lakeshore Road, Suite 202
St. Catherines, Ontario
L2N 2T6
(416) 646-7744

KOVELS ON ANTIQUES AND COLLECTIBLES
P.O. Box 22200
Beachwood, Ohio 44122
(800) 829-9158

KOVELS ON SPORTS COLLECTIBLES
P.O. Box 22200
Beachwood, Ohio 44122
(800) 829-9158

ROCKWELL SOCIETY NEWS
597 Saw Mill River Road
Ardsley, New York 10502
(914) 693-8800

SOUTHWEST ART
5444 Westheimer, Ste. 1440
Houston, Texas 77056
(713) 850-0990

U.S. ART COLLECTIBLES
220 S. 6th Street, Ste. 500
Minneapolis, Minnesota 55402
(612) 339-7571

WILDLIFE ART NEWS
4725 Highway 7
St. Louis Park, Minnesota 55416
(612) 927-9056

NALED
National Association of Limited Edition Dealers

Here is the 1993 roster of the limited edition dealers who are members of NALED, a national group of retail and wholesale merchants who are in the specialized market of selling limited edition plates, dolls, figurines and other collectible items. The group was formed in 1976. This list will help collectors to locate limited edition dealers in various areas of the United States. The National Headquarters for NALED is located at 508 Harlan Road, Mansfield, Ohio 44903.

ALABAMA
CHRISTMAS TOWN, Mobile, AL, 205-661-3608
COLLECTIBLE COTTAGE, Birmingham, AL, 205-988-8551
COLLECTIBLE COTTAGE, Gardendale, AL, 205-631-2413
LIBERTY LANE, Huntsville, AL, 205-837-7012
LIBERTY LANE, Huntsville, AL, 205-880-9033
OLD COUNTRY STORE, Gadsen, AL, 205-492-7659
OLDE POST OFFICE, Trussville, AL, 205-655-7292
TREASURE CHEST, Brewton, AL, 205-867-9757

ARIZONA
BONA'S CHRISTMAS ETC, Tucson, AZ, 602-885-3755
CAROUSEL GIFTS, Phoenix, AZ, 602-997-6488
CROWN SHOP, Little Rock, AZ, 501-227-8442
FOX'S GIFTS & COLLECTABLES, Scottsdale, AZ, 602-947-0560
LAWTON'S GIFTS & COLLECTIBLES, Chandler, AZ, 602-899-7977
MARYLYN'S COLLECTIBLES, Tucson, AZ, 602-742-1501
MUSIC BOX & CLOCK SHOP, Mesa, AZ, 602-833-6943
RUTH'S HALLMARK SHOP, Cottonwood, AZ, 602-634-8050

CALIFORNIA
BLEVINS PLATES 'N THINGS, Vallejo, CA, 707-642-7505
CAMEO GIFTS & COLLECTIBLES, Temecula, CA, 909-676-1635
CARDTOWNE HALLMARK, Garden Grove, CA, 714-537-5240
CAROL'S GIFT SHOP, Artesia, CA, 310-924-6335
COLLECTIBLE CORNER, Placentia, CA, 714-528-3079
COLLECTIBLES UNLIMITED, Tarzana, CA, 818-757-7250
COLLECTOR'S WORLD, Montrose, CA, 818-248-9451
CRYSTAL AERIE, Fremont, CA, 510-820-9133
DE WITTS GIFTS OF ELEGANCE, Oceanside, CA, 619-722-3084
DODIE'S FINE GIFTS, Woodland, CA, 916-668-1909
EASTERN ART, Victorville, CA, 619-241-0166
ELEGANT TOUCH, Arcadia, CA, 818-445-8868
ENCORE CARDS & GIFTS, Cypress, CA, 714-761-1266
EVA MARIE DRY GROCER, Redondo Beach, CA, 310-375-8422
FORTE OLIVIA GIFTS, West Covina, CA, 818-962-2588
FRAME GALLERY, THE, Chula Vista, CA, 619-422-1700
FRIENDS COLLECTIBLES, Canyon Country, CA, 805-298-2232
GALLERIA GIFTS, Reedley, CA, 209-638-4060
KENNEDY'S COLLECTIBLES & GIFTS, Sacramento, CA, 916-973-8754
LENA'S GIFT GALLERY, San Mateo, CA, 415-342-1304
LIEBERG'S, Alhambra, CA, 818-282-8454
LOU'S HALLMARK, Ridgecrest, CA, 619-446-5100
LOUISE MARIE'S FINE GIFTS, Livermore, CA, 510-449-5757
MAC KINNONS STATIONARY, La Habra, CA, 310-691-9322
MARGIE'S GIFTS & COLLECTIBLES, Torrance, CA, 310-378-2526
MARY ANN'S CARDS, GIFTS & COL, Yorba Linda, CA, 714-777-0999

MUSICAL MOMENTS & COLLECTIBLES, Shingle Spgs, CA, 916-677-2221
NORTHERN LIGHTS, San Rafael, CA, 415-457-2884
NYBORG CASTLE GIFTS & COLLECTIBLES, Martinez, CA, 510-930-0200
P M COLLECTABLES, Cupertino, CA, 408-725-8858
REFLECTIONS AT BLACKHAWK, Danville, CA, 510-736-9050
RUMMEL'S VILLAGE GUILD, Montebello, CA, 213-722-2691
RYSTAD'S LIMITED EDITIONS, San Jose, CA, 408-279-1960
SUTTER STREET EMPORIUM, Folsom, CA, 916-985-4647
TOMORROW'S TREASURES, Riverside, CA, 909-354-5731
TOWNEND'S CARD ATTACK, Moreno Valley, CA, 909-788-3989
VILLAGE PEDDLER, La Habra, CA, 310-694-6111
WEE HOUSE FINE COLLECTIBLES, Irvine, CA, 714-552-3228
WILSON GALLERIES, Fresno, CA, 209-224-2223
KENT COLLECTION, Englewood, CO, 303-761-0059

COLORADO
KING'S GALLERY OF COLLECTABLES, Colorado Springs, CO, 719-636-2228
NOEL - THE CHRISTMAS SHOP, Vail, CO, 303-476-6544
PLATES ETC, Arvada, CO, 303-420-0752
QUALITY GIFTS & COLLECTIBLES, Colorado Springs, CO, 719-599-0051
SWISS MISS SHOP, Cascade, CO, 719-684-9679
TOBACCO LEAF, Lakewood, CO, 303-274-8720

CONNECTICUT
CARDS & GIFTS ETC, Danbury, CT, 203-743-6515
CELIA'S HALLMARK, Riverside, CT, 203-698-2509
CRICKET'S HALLMARK, North Haven, CT, 203-239-0135
FIFTH AVENUE, Trumbull, CT, 203-261-7592
J B'S COLLECTIBLES, Danbury, CT, 203-790-1011
MAURICE NASSER, New London, CT, 203-443-6523
PERIWINKLE, Vernon, CT, 203-872-2904
REVAY'S GARDERNS & GIFT SHOP, East Windsor, CT, 203-623-9068
THE TAYLOR'D TOUCH, Marlborough, CT, 203-295-9377
THREE CHEERS HALLMARK, Meriden, CT, 203-634-7509
UTOPIA COLLECTIBLES, Oxford, CT, 203-264-0419
WINDSOR SHOPPE, North Haven, CT, 203-239-4644

DELAWARE
GIFT DESIGN GALLERIES, Dover, DE, 302-734-3002
PEREGOY'S GIFTS, Wilmington, DE, 302-999-1155
TULL BROTHERS, Seaford, DE, 302-629-3071

FLORIDA
CAROL'S HALLMARK SHOP, Tampa, FL, 813-960-8807
CHRISTMAS COLLECTION, Altamonte Springs, FL, 407-862-5383
CHRISTMAS COTTAGE & GIFT SHOPPE, Melbourne, FL, 407-725-0270

CHRISTMAS SHOPPE, Miami, FL, 305-255-5414
CLASSIC CARGO, Destin, FL, 904-837-8171
CORNER GIFTS, Pembroke Pines, FL, 305-432-3739
ENTERTAINER, THE, Jacksonville, FL, 904-725-1166
GAIL'S HALLMARK, Miami, FL, 305-666-6038
HEIRLOOMS OF TOMORROW, North Miami, FL, 305-899-0920
HUNT'S COLLECTIBLES, Satellite Beach, FL, 407-777-1313
METHODIST FOUNDATION GIFT SHOPS, Jacksonville, FL, 904-798-8210
PAPER MOON, West Palm Beach, FL, 407-684-2668
SUN ROSE GIFTS, Indian Harbor Beach, FL, 407-773-0550
VILLAGE PLATE COLLECTOR, Cocoa, FL, 407-636-6914

GEORGIA
BECKY'S SMALL WONDERS, Helen, GA, 706-878-3108
CHAMBERHOUSE, Canton, GA, 404-479-9115
COTTAGE GARDEN, Macon, GA, 912-743-9897
CREATIVE GIFTS, Augusta, GA, 706-796-8794
GALLERY II, Atlanta, GA, 404-872-7272
GIFTS & SUCH, Augusta, GA, 706-738-4574
GLASS ETC, Atlanta, GA, 404-493-7936
IMPRESSIONS, Brunswick, GA, 912-265-1624
MARTHA JANE'S, Cave Springs, GA, 706-777-3608
MTN CHRISTMAS-MTN MEMORIES, Dahlonega, GA, 706-864-9115
PAM'S HALLMARK SHOP, Fayetteville, GA, 404-461-3041
PARSONS, Cumming, GA, 404-887-9991
PIKE'S PICKS FINE GIFTS, Roswell, GA, 404-998-7828
PLUM TREE, Tucker, GA, 404-491-9433
SPECIAL EFFECTS GIFTS & COL, Blue Ridge, GA, 706-632-6950
SWAN GALLERIES, Stone Mountain, GA, 404-498-1324
TINDER BOX AT LENOX, Atlanta, GA, 404-231-9853
WESSON'S, Helen, GA, 706-878-3544
WHIMSEY MANOR, Warner Robins, GA, 912-328-2500

HAWAII
OUR HOUSE COLLECTIBLE GIFT GALLERY, Honolulu, HI, 808-593-1999

ILLINOIS
BITS OF GOLD JEWELRY & GIFTS, Nashville, IL, 618-327-4261
C A JENSEN, LaSalle, IL, 815-223-0377
CHRYSLER BOUTIQUE, Effingham, IL, 217-342-4864
CLASS ACT, Lake Zurich, IL, 708-540-7700
COLLECTOR'S PARADISE, Monmouth, IL, 309-734-3690
COUNTRY OAK COLLECTABLES, Schaumburg, IL, 708-529-0290
COVE GIFTS, Bloomingdale, IL, 708-980-9020
CROWN CARD & GIFT SHOP, Chicago, IL, 312-282-6771
DORIS COLLECTIBLES, St Peter, IL, 618-349-8780
EUROPEAN IMPORTS & GIFTS, Niles, IL, 708-967-5253
GATZ COLLECTABLES, Wheeling, IL, 708-541-4033
GIFTIQUE ONE OF LONG GROVE, Long Grove, IL, 708-634-9171
GRIMM'S HALLMARK, St Charles, IL, 708-513-7008

GUZZARDO'S HALLMARK, Kewanee, IL, 309-852-5621
HALL JEWELERS & GIFTS LTD, Moweaqua, IL, 217-768-4990
HAWK HOLLOW, Galena, IL, 815-777-3616
JBJ THE COLLECTORS SHOP, Champaign, IL, 217-352-9610
KIEFER'S GALLERIES LTD, LaGrange, IL, 708-354-1888
KIEFER'S GALLERY OF CREST HILL, Plainfield, IL, 815-436-5444
KRIS KRINGLE HAUS, Geneva, IL, 708-208-0400
LYNN'S & COMPANY, Arlington Heights, IL, 708-870-1188
MAY HALLMARK SHOP, Woodridge, IL, 708-985-1008
MC HUGH'S GIFTS & COLLECTIBLES, Rock Island, IL, 309-788-9525
PAINTED PLATE LTD EDITION, O'Fallon IL, 618-624-6987
RANDALL DRUG & GIFTS, Aurora, IL, 708-907-8700
ROYALE IMPORTS, Lisle, IL, 708-357-7002
RUTH'S HALLMARK, Bloomingdale, IL, 708-894-7890
SANDY'S DOLLS & COLLECTABLES INC, Palos Hills, IL, 708-423-0070
SOMETHING SO SPECIAL, Rockford, IL, 815-226-1331
STONE'S HALLMARK SHOPS, Rockford, IL, 815-399-4481
STONE'S ON THE SQUARE, Woodstock, IL, 815-338-0072
STRAWBERRY HOUSE, Libertyville, IL, 708-816-6129
STROHL'S LIMITED EDITIONS, Shelbyville, IL, 217-774-5222
TOWER SHOP, Riverside, IL, 708-447-5258
TRICIA'S TREASURES, Fairview Hgts, IL, 618-624-6334
WHYDE'S HAUS, Canton, IL, 309-647-8823

INDIANA
BEA'S HALLMARK, Indianapolis, IN, 317-888-8408
BEAS'S HALLMARK, Rushville, IN, 317-932-3328
CAROL'S CRAFTS, Nashville, IN, 812-988-6388
CURIO SHOPPE, Greensburg, IN, 812-663-6914
GNOME CROSSING, Carmel, IN, 317-846-5577
LANDMARK GIFTS & ANTIQUES, Kokomo, IN, 317-456-3488
NANA'S STICHIN STATION, Butler, IN, 219-868-5634
ROSE MARIE'S, Evansville, IN, 812-423-7557
ROSIE'S CARD & GIFT SHOP, Newburgh, IN, 812-853-3059
SMUCKER DRUGS, Middlebury, IN, 219-825-2485
STUNTZ & HOCH PINES, Walkerton, IN, 219-586-2663
TEMPTATIONS GIFTS, Valparaiso, IN, 219-462-1000
TOMORROW'S TREASURES, Muncie, IN, 317-284-6355
WALTER'S COLLECTIBLES, Princeton, IN, 812-386-3992
WATSON'S *, New Carlisle, IN, 219-654-8600

IOWA
COLLECTION CONNECTION, Des Moines, IA, 515-276-7766
DAVE & JANELLE'S, Mason City, IA, 515-423-6377
DAVIS COLLECTIBLES, Waterloo, IA, 319-232-0050
HAWK HOLLOW, Bellevue, IA, 319-872-5467
HEIRLOOM JEWELERS, Centerville, IA, 515-856-5715
VAN DEN BERG'S, Pella, IA, 515-628-3266

KANSAS
HOURGLASS, Wichita, KS, 316-942-0562

KENTUCKY
ANN'S HALLMARK, Lexington, KY, 606-266-9101
KAREN'S GIFTS, Louisville, KY, 502-425-3310
SCHWAB'S COLLECTIBLES, Lexington, KY, 606-266-2433
STORY BOOK KIDS, Florence, KY, 606-525-7743

LOUISIANA
AD LIB GIFTS, Metairie, LA, 504-835-8755
GALILEAN, THE, Leesville, LA, 318-239-6248
LA TIENDA, Lafayette, LA, 318-984-5920
PARTRIDGE CHRISTMAS SHOPS, Covington, LA, 504-892-4477
PLATES AND THINGS, Baton Rouge, LA, 504-753-2885
PONTALBA COLLECTIBLES, New Orleans, LA, 504-524-8068

MAINE
CHRISTMAS SHOPPE, Bangor, ME, 207-945-0805
GIMBEL & SONS COUNTRY STORE, Boothbay Harbor, ME, 207-633-5088
HERITAGE GIFTS, Oakland, ME, 207-465-3910

MARYLAND
BODZER'S COLLECTIBLES, Baltimore, MD, 410-931-9222
CALICO MOUSE, Annapolis, MD, 301-261-2441

CALICO MOUSE, Glen Burnie, MD, 410-760-2757
CHERRY TREE CARDS & GIFTS, Laurel, MD, 301-498-8528
EDWARDS STORES, Ocean City, MD, 410-289-7000
FIGURINE WORLD, Gaithersburg, MD, 301-977-3997
GREETINGS & READINGS, Towson, MD, 410-825-4225
KEEPSAKES & COLLECTIBLES, Baltimore, MD, 410-727-0444
PENN DEN, Bowie, MD, 301-262-2430
PLATE NICHE, Davidsonville, MD, 410-798-5864
PRECIOUS GIFTS, Ellicott City, MD, 410-461-6813
TIARA GIFTS, Wheaton, MD, 301-949-0210
TOMORROW'S TREASURES, Bel Air, MD, 410-893-7965
WANG'S GIFTS & COLLECTIBLE, Bel Air, MD, 410-838-2626
WANG'S GIFTS & COLLECTIBLES, White Marsh, MD, 410-931-7388

MASSACHUSSETTS
GIFT BARN, North Eastham, MA, 508-255-7000
GIFT GALLERY, Webster, MA, 508-943-4402
HONEYCOMB GIFT SHOPPE, Wakefield, MA, 617-245-2448
LEONARD GALLERY, Springfield, MA, 413-733-9492
LINDA'S ORIGINALS, Brewster. MA, 508-385-4758
MERRY CHRISTMAS SHOPPE, Whitman, MA, 617-447-6677
SHROPSHIRE CURIOSITY SHOP II, Shrewsbury, MA, 508-799-7200
SHROPSHIRE CURIOSITY SHOP II, Shrewsbury, MA, 508-842-5001
SHROPSHIRE CURIOSITY SHOP I, Shrewsbury, MA, 508-842-4202
STACY'S GIFTS & COLLECTIBLES, East Walpole, MA, 508-668-4212
WARD'S, Medford, MA, 617-395-2420

MICHIGAN
CARAVAN GIFTS & COLLECTIBLES, Fenton, MI, 313-629-4212
COPPER CRICKET, Westland, MI, 313-425-6977
COUNTRY CLASSIC COLLECTIBLES, Lapeer, MI, 313-667-4080
CURIO CABINET COL & XMAS COTTAGE, Lexington, MI, 313-359-5040
DEE'S HALLMARK, Clinton Twp, MI, 313-792-5510
ELLE STEVENS JEWELERS, Ironwood, MI, 906-932-5679
ELSIE'S HALLMARK SHOP, Petoskey, MI, 616-347-5270
EMILY'S GIFTS, DOLLS, COLLECTIBLES, St Clair Shores, MI, 313-777-5250
FOUR SEASONS GIFT SHOP, Grand Ledge, MI, 517-627-7469
FRITZ CHINA & GIFTS, Monroe, MI, 313-241-6760
GEORGIA'S GIFT GALLERY, Plymouth, MI, 313-453-7733
HARPOLD'S, South Haven, MI, 616-637-3522
HAUG'S JEWELRY & COLLECTIBLES, Houghton, MI, 906-482-3430
HOUSE OF CARDS & COLLECTIBLES, Macomb, MI, 313-247-2000
HOUSE OF CARDS & COLLECTIBLES, Rochester Hills, MI, 313-375-5600
JACQUELYNS GIFTS, Warren, MI, 313-296-9211
KEEPSAKE GIFTS, Kimball, MI, 313-985-5855
KNIBLOE GIFT CORNER, Jackson, MI, 517-782-6846
LAKEVIEW CARD & GIFT SHOP, Battle Creek, MI, 616-962-0650
MARION'S COLLECTIBLES, Livonia, MI, 313-522-8620
MOMBER PHARMACY & GIFTS, Sparta, MI, 616-887-7323
PAST & PRESENT SHOP, Wyoming, MI, 616-532-7848
PINOCCHIO'S INC, Frankenmuth, MI, 517-652-2751
PLATE LADY, Livonia, MI, 313-261-5220
RAY'S MART, Clinton Twp, MI, 313-791-2265
ROSEMARY'S COLLECTIBLES, Riverview, MI, 313-479-0494
SALLY ANN'S COLLECTIBLES, Waterford, MI, 313-623-6441
SCHULTZ GIFT GALLERY, Pinconning, MI, 517-879-3110
SPECIAL THINGS, Sterling Heights, MI, 313-739-4030
THEN & NOW GIFT SHOP, Union Lake, MI, 313-363-1360
TROY STAMP & COIN EXCHANGE, Troy, MI, 313-528-1181
YOUNG'S CHRISTMAS FANTASY, Warren, MI, 313-573-0230

MINNESOTA
ANDERSEN HALLMARK, Albert Lea, MN, 507-373-0996

BJORNSON IMPORTS, Mound, MN, 612-474-3957
COLLECTIBLES SHOWCASE, Bloomington, MN, 612-854-1668
COMMEMORATIVE IMPORTS, Stillwater, MN, 612-439-8772
GUSTAF'S, Lindstrom, MN, 612-257-6688
HELGA'S HALLMARK, Cambridge, MN, 612-689-5000
HUNT HALLMARK CARD & GIFT, Rochester, MN, 507-289-5152
HUNT SILVER LAKE DRUG & GIFT, Rochester, MN, 507-289-0749
KOPPEN KOLLECTIBLES & DRUG, Pine City, MN, 612-629-6708
MARY D'S DOLLS & BEARS & SUCH, Minneapolis, MN, 612-424-4375
ODYSSEY, Rochester, MN, 507-288-6629
ODYSSEY, Mankato, MN, 507-388-2004
SEEFELDT'S GALLERY, Roseville, MN, 612-631-1397

MISSISSIPPI
CHRISTMAS WORLD, Gulfport, MS, 601-896-9080
DOLL FANTASY & COLLECTIBLES, Hattiesburg, MS, 601-545-3655

MISSOURI
DICKENS GIFT SHOPPE, Branson, MO, 417-334-2992
ELLY'S, Kimmswick, MO, 314-467-5019
EMILY'S HALLMARK, Ballwin, MO, 314-391-8755
HELEN'S GIFTS & ACCESSORIES, Rolla, MO, 314-341-2300
JOHNNIE BROCK'S, St Louis, MO, 314-481-8900
JOHNNIE BROCK'S, St Louis, MO, 314-481-5252
K C COLLECTIBLES & GIFTS, Kansas City, MO, 816-741-2448
OAK LEAF GIFTS, Osage Beach, MO, 314-348-0190
SHIRLOCK II, Joplin, MO, 314-651-3414
TOBACCO LANE, Cape Girardeau, MO, 314-651-3414
UNIQUE GIFT SHOPPE, Springfield, MO, 417-887-5476
YE COBBLESTONE SHOPPE, Sikeston, MO, 314-471-8683

MONTANA
TRADITIONS, Missoula, MT, 406-543-3177

NEBRASKA
GERBER'S FINE COLLECTIBLES, Kearney, NE, 308-237-5139
L & L GIFTS, Fremont, NE, 402-727-7275
MARIANNE K FESTERSEN, Omaha, NE, 402-393-4454
SHARRON SHOP, Omaha, NE, 402-393-8311

NEW HAMPSHIRE
STAINED GLASS FANTASY, Bedford, NH, 603-625-2314
STRAW CELLAR, Wolfeboro, NH, 603-569-1516

NEW JERSEY
CHINA ROYALE INC, Englewood, NJ, 201-568-1005
CHRISTMAS CAROL, Flemington, NJ, 908-782-0700
CLASSIC COLLECTIONS, Livingston, NJ, 201-992-8605
COLLECTORS CELLAR, Pine Beach, NJ, 908-341-4107
COLLECTORS EMPORIUM, Secaucus, NJ, 201-863-2977
CRAFT EMPORIUM, Waldwick, NJ, 201-670-0022
EMJAY SHOP, Stone Harbor, NJ, 609-368-1227
EXTRA SPECIAL TOUCH INC, Pompton Lakes, NJ, 201-835-5441
GIFT CARAVAN, North Arlington, NJ, 201-997-1055
GIFT GALLERY, Paramus, NJ, 201-845-0940
GIFT WORLD, Pennsauken, NJ, 609-663-2000
J C'S HALLMARK, Old Bridge, NJ, 908-826-8208
JIANA, Union, NJ, 201-492-1728
KATHE LUCEY GIFTS & COLLECTIBLES, Kenvil, NJ, 201-584-3848
LIL BIT OF COUNTRY GIFT SHOP, Richwood, NJ, 608-256-0099
LITTLE TREASURES, Rutherford, NJ, 201-460-9353
MEMORY LANE, Union, NJ, 908-687-2071
MOLK BROS, Elmwood Park, NJ, 201-796-8377
NOTES-A-PLENTY GIFT SHOPPE, Flemington, NJ, 908-782-0700
OAKWOOD CARD & GIFT SHOP, Edison, NJ, 908-549-9494
OLD WAGON GIFTS, Colts Neck, NJ, 908-780-6656
SOMEONE SPECIAL, Cherry Hill, NJ, 609-424-1914
SOMEONE SPECIAL, W Berlin, NJ, 609-768-7171
STATION GIFT EMPORIUM, Whitehouse Station, NJ, 908-534-1212
TOM'S GARDEN WORLD, McKee City, NJ, 609-641-4522
WESTON'S LIMITED EDITIONS, Eatontown, NJ, 908-542-3550
ZASLOW'S FINE COLLECTIBLES, Middletown, NJ, 908-957-9560

ZASLOW'S FINE COLLECTIBLES, *Matawan, NJ,*
908-583-1499

NEW MEXICO
LORRIE'S COLLECTIBLES, *Albuquerque, NM,*
505-292-0020

NEW YORK
A LITTLE BIT OF CAMELOT, *Warwick, NY,*
914-986-4438
ALBERT'S ATTIC, *Clarence, NY, 716-759-2231*
ANN'S HALLMARK CARDS & GIFTS, *Newburgh, NY,*
914-564-5585
ANN'S HALLMARK SHOPPE, *Newburgh, NY,*
914-562-3149
CANAL TOWN COUNTRY STORE, *Irondequoit, NY,*
716-338-3670
CANAL TOWN COUNTRY STORE, *Rochester, NY,*
716-225-5070
CANAL TOWN COUNTRY STORE, *Rochester, NY,*
716-424-4120
CERAMICA GIFT GALLERY, *New York, NY,*
212-354-9216
CLASSIC GIFT GALLERY, *Centereach, NY,*
516-467-4813
CLIFTON PARK COUNTRY STORE, *Clifton Park, NY,*
518-371-0585
CLOCK MAN GALLERY, *Poughkeepsie, NY,*
914-473-9055
COLLECTIBLY YOURS, *Spring Valley, NY, 914-425-9244*
CORNER COLLECTIONS, *Hunter, NY, 518-263-4141*
COUNTRY GALLERY, *Fishkill, NY, 914-897-2008*
CROMPOND COUNTRY STORE, *Crompond, NY,*
914-737-4937
ELLIE'S LTD ED & COLLECTIBLES, *Miller Place, NY,*
516-744-5606
ELLIE'S LTD ED & COLLECTIBLES, *Selden, NY,*
516-698-3467
ISLAND TREASURES, *Staten Island, NY, 718-698-1234*
J B'S COLLECTIBLES, *Poughkeepsie, NY, 914-298-0226*
JOY'S LAMPLIGHT SHOPPE, *Avon, NY, 716-226-3341*
LIMITED COLLECTOR, *Corning, NY, 607-936-6195*
LIMITED EDITION, THE, *Merrick, NY, 516-623-4400*
MARESA'S CANDLELIGHT GIFT SHOPPE, *Port
Jefferson, NY, 516-331-6245*
PAUL'S ECONOMY PHARMACY, *Staten Island, NY,*
718-442-2924
PLATE COTTAGE, *St James, NY, 516-862-7171*
PORTS OF THE ORIENT, *Cheektowaga, NY,*
716-681-3020
PRECIOUS GIFT GALLERY, *Levitlawn, NY,*
516-579-3562
PRECIOUS GIFT GALLERY, *Franklin Square, NY,*
516-352-8900
PREMIO, *Massapequa, NY, 516-795-3050*
SIX SIXTEEN GIFT SHOPS, *Bellmore, NY, 516-221-5829*
TODAY'S PLEASURE TOMORROW'S TREASURE,
Jeffersonville, NY, 914-482-3690
VILLAGE GIFT SHOP, *Tonawanda, NY, 716-695-6589*

NORTH CAROLINA
GIFT ATTIC, *Raleigh, NC, 919-781-1822*
MC NAMARA'S, *Highlands, NC, 704-526-5551*
OLDE WORLD CHRISTMAS SHOPPE, *Asheville, NC,*
704-274-4819
TINDER BOX, *Charlotte, NC, 704-366-5164*
TINDER BOX OF WINSTON-SALEM, *Winston-Salem,
NC, 919-765-9511*

NORTH DAKOTA
BJORNSON IMPORTS, *Grand Forks, ND, 701-775-2618*
HATCH'S COLLECTORS GALLERY, *Minot, ND,*
701-852-4666
HATCH'S COLLECTORS GALLERY, *Fargo, ND,*
701-282-4457
HATCH'S COLLECTORS GALLERY, *Bismarck, ND,*
701-255-4821
JUNIQUE'S, *Bismarck, ND, 701-258-3542*

OHIO
ALADDIN LAMP, *Lima, OH, 419-224-5612*
ANN'S HALLMARK, *Cincinnati, OH, 513-662-2021*
BELLFAIR COUNTRY STORES, *Dayton, OH,*
513-426-3921
CABBAGES & KINGS, *Grand Rapids, OH, 419-832-2709*
CELLAR CACHE, *Put-in-Bay, OH, 419-285-2738*
CHRISTMAS TREASURE CHEST, *Ashland, OH,*
419-289-2831
COLLECTION CONNECTION, *Piqua, OH,*
513-773-6788
COLLECTOR'S GALLERY, *Marion, OH, 614-387-0602*
COLLECTOR'S OUTLET, *Mentor On The Lake, OH,*
216-257-1141

COMSTOCK'S COLLECTIBLES, *Medina, OH,*
216-725-4656
CURIO CABINET, *Worthington, OH, 614-885-1986*
EASTERN ART, *Parma, OH, 216-888-6277*
EXCALIBUR GIFT, *Sandusky, OH, 216-572-1322*
GIFT GARDEN, *No Olmsted, OH, 216-777-0116*
GIFT GARDEN, *Euclid, OH, 216-289-0116*
GIFTS & TREASURES, *North Canton, OH,*
216-494-5511
GINGERBREAD HOUSE GIFTS & COL, *West Milton,
OH, 513-698-3477*
HARTVILLE COLLECTIBLES, *Hartville, OH,*
216-877-2172
HIDDEN TREASURES, *Huron, OH, 419-433-2585*
HOUSE OF TRADITION, *Perrysburg, OH, 419-874-1151*
KATHRYN'S GALLERY OF GIFTS, *Solon, OH,*
216-498-0234
LAKESHORE LTD, *Huron, OH, 419-433-6168*
LITTLE RED GIFT HOUSE, *Birmingham, OH,*
216-965-5420
LITTLE SHOP ON THE PORTAGE, *Woodville, OH,*
419-849-3742
LOLA & DALE GIFTS & COLLECTIBLES, *Parma
Heights, OH, 216-885-0444*
MC KENZIE SQUARE, *Hubbard, OH, 216-534-1166*
MUSIK BOX HAUS, *Vermilion, OH, 216-967-4744*
NORTH HILL GIFT SHOP, *Akron, OH, 216-535-4811*
OLDE TYME CLOCKS, *Cincinnati, OH, 513-741-9188*
PORCELLANA LTD, *Hamilton, OH, 513-868-1511*
ROCHELLE'S FINE GIFTS, *Toledo, OH, 419-472-7673*
SANDY'S FAMILY COLLECTIBLES & GIFTS, *Elyria,
OH, 216-365-9999*
SAXONY IMPORTS, *Cincinnati, OH, 513-621-7800*
SCHUMM PHARMACY HALLMARK & GIFTS,
Rockford, OH, 419-363-3630
SETTLER'S FARM, *Middlefield, OH, 216-632-1009*
STORY BOOK KIDS, *Cincinnati, OH, 513-769-5437*
STRAWBERRY PATCH, *Brunswick, OH, 216-225-7796*
STRUBLE'S DRUG INC OF SHELBY, *Shelby, OH,*
419-342-2136
STUHLDREHER FLORAL CO, *Mansfield, OH,*
419-524-5911
TOWNE CENTRE SHOPPE, *Streetsboro, OH,*
216-626-3106

OKLAHOMA
COLONIAL FLORISTS, *Stillwater, OK, 405-372-9166*
DODY'S HALLMARK, *Lawton, OK, 405-353-8379*
NORTH POLE CITY, *Oklahoma City, OK, 405-685-6635*
RATHBONES FLAIR FLOWERS, *Tulsa, OK,*
918-747-8491
SHIRLEY'S GIFTS, *Ardmore, OK, 405-223-2116*
SUZANNE'S COLLECTORS GALLERY*, *Miami, OK,*
918-542-3808
W D GIFTS, *Okmulgee, OK, 918-756-2229*

OREGON
ACCENT ON COLLECTIBLES, *Portland, OR,*
503-253-0841
CROWN SHOWCASE ≠ 2, *Portland, OR, 503-280-0669*
DAS HAUS-AM-BERG, *Salem, OR, 503-363-0669*
MANCKE'S COLLECTIBLES, *Salem, OR, 503-371-3157*
PRESENT PEDDLER, *Portland, OR, 503-639-2325*
TREASURE CHEST GIFT SHOP, *Gresham, OR,*
503-667-2999

PENNSYLVANIA
BANKUS GIFTS, *Pocono Lake, PA, 717-646-9528*
BOB'S CARDS & GIFTS, *Southampton, PA,*
215-364-2872
CARGO WEST CHRISTMAS BARN, *Scotrun, PA,*
717-629-3122
COLLECTOR'S CHOICE, *Pittsburgh, PA, 412-366-4477*
COLLECTOR'S MARKETPLACE, *Montrose, PA,*
717-278-4094
DEN, THE, *Lahaska, PA, 215-794-8493*
DUTCH INDOOR VILLGE, *Lancaster, PA, 717-299-2348*
EMPORIUM COLLECTIBLES GALLERY, *Erie, PA,*
814-833-2895
EUROPEAN TREASURES, *Pittsburgh, PA, 412-421-8660*
GIFT DESIGN GALLERIES, *Strouesburg, PA,*
717-424-7530
GIFT DESIGN GALLERIES, *Whitehall, PA,*
215-266-1266
GIFT DESIGN GALLERIES, *Wilkes-Barre, PA,*
717-822-6704
GILLESPIE JEWELER COLLECTORS GALLERY,
Northampton, PA, 215-261-0882
LAUCHNOR'S GIFTS & COLLECTABLES,
Trexlertown, PA, 215-398-3008
LE COLLECTION, *Belle Vernon, PA, 412-483-5330*
LIMITED EDITIONS, *Forty Fort, PA, 717-288-0940*
LIMITED PLATES, *Collegeville, PA, 215-489-7799*

LINDENBAUM'S COLLECTORS SHOWCASE,
Pittsburgh, PA, 412-367-1980
MOLE HOLE OF PEDDLERS VILLAGE, *Lahaska, PA,*
215-794-7572
PICCADILLY CENTRE, *Duncanville, PA, 814-695-6297*
RED CARDINAL, THE, *Ambler, PA, 215-628-2524*
ROBERTS GALLERY, *Pittsburgh, PA, 412-279-4223*
SAVILLE'S LIMITED EDITIONS, *Pittsburgh, PA,*
412-366-5458
SIDE DOOR, *McMurray, PA, 412-941-3750*
SOMEONE SPECIAL, *Bensalem, PA, 215-245-0919*
SPECIAL ATTRACTIONS, *Sayre, PA, 717-888-9433*
TODAY'S COLLECTABLES, *Philadelphia, PA,*
215-331-3993
TODAY'S TREASURES, *Pittsburgh, PA, 412-341-5233*
VILLAGE OF COLONIAL PEDDLERS, *Carlisle, PA,*
717-243-9350
WISHING WELL, *Reading, PA, 215-921-2566*
YEAGLE'S, *Lahaska, PA, 215-794-7756*

RHODE ISLAND
GOLDEN GOOSE, *Smithfield, RI, 401-232-2310*

SOUTH CAROLINA
ABRAMS DOLLS & COLLECTIBLES, *Conway, SC,*
803-248-9198
CHRISTMAS CELEBRATION, *Mauldin, SC,*
803-277-7373
CURIOSITY SHOP, *Florence, SC, 803-665-8686*
DUANE'S HALLMARK CARD & GIFT SHOP,
Columbia, SC, 803-772-2624

SOUTH DAKOTA
AKERS GIFTS & COLLECTIBLES, *Sioux Falls, SD,*
605-339-1325
GIFT GALLERY, *Brookings, SD, 605-692-9405*

TENNESSEE
BARBARA'S ELEGANTS, *Gatlinburg, TN,*
615-436-3454
CALICO BUTTERFLY, *Memphis, TN, 901-362-8121*
COX'S BAZAAR, *Maryville, TN, 615-982-0421*
HOUR GLASS II, *Chattanooga, TN, 615-877-2328*
LEMON TREE, *Gatlinburg, TN, 615-436-4602*
OLD COUNTRY STORE, *Jackson, TN, 901-668-1223*
ORANGE BLOSSOM, *Martin, TN, 901-587-5091*
PAPILLON INC, *Chatanooga, TN, 615-499-2997*
PATTY'S HALLMARK, *Murfreesboro, TN, 615-890-8310*
PIANO'S FLOWERS & GIFTS, *Memphis, TN,*
901-345-7670
STAGE CROSSING GIFTS & COLLECTIBLES, *Bartlett,
TN, 901-372-4438*

TEXAS
BETTY'S COLLECTABLES LTD, *Harlingen, TX,*
210-423-8234
CHRISTMAS TREASURES, *Baytown, TX,*
713-421-1581
COLLECTIBLE HEIRLOOMS, *Friendswood, TX,*
713-486-5023
COLLECTOR'S COVE, *Greenville, TX, 903-454-2572*
ELOISE'S COLLECTIBLES, *Houston, TX, 713-783-3611*
ELOISE'S COLLECTIBLES, *Katy, TX, 713-578-6655*
ELOISE'S GIFTS & ANTIQUES, *Rockwall, TX,*
214-771-6371
GIFTS CARTOONS COLLECTIBLES, *Hurst, TX,*
817-590-0324
HOLIDAY HOUSE, *Huntsville, TX, 409-295-7338*
KEEPSAKES & KOLLECTIBLES, *Spring, TX,*
713-353-9233
LADYBUG LANE, *Dallas, TX, 214-661-3692*
LOUJON'S GIFTS, *Sugar Land, TX, 713-980-1245*
MR C COLLECTIBLE CENTER, *Carrollton, TX,*
214-242-5100
OPA'S HAUS, *New Braunfels, TX, 512-629-1191*
SHEPHERD'S SHOPPE, THE, *San Antonio, TX,*
210-342-4811
SUNSHINE HOUSE GALLERY, *Plano, TX,*
214-424-5015
TIS THE SEASON, *Ft Worth, TX, 817-877-5244*

VERMONT
CHRISTMAS LOFT, *Jay, VT, 802-988-4358*

VIRGINIA
BIGGS LIMITED EDITIONS, *Richmond, VA,*
804-266-7744
CREEKSIDE COLLECTIBLES & GIFTS, *Winchester, VA,*
703-662-0270
GAZEBO GIFTS, *Newport News, VA, 804-595-0331*

WASHINGTON
CHALET COLLECTORS GALLERY, *Tacoma, WA,*
206-564-0326

GOLD SHOPPE, *Tacoma, WA, 206-473-4653*
JANSEN FLOWERS INC, *Longview, WA, 206-423-0450*
NATALIA'S COLLECTIBLES, *Woodinville, WA,
   206-481-4575*
SLUYS GIFTS, *Poulsbo, WA, 206-779-7171*
STEFAN'S EUROPEAN GIFTS, *Yakima, WA,
   509-457-5503*
TANNENBAUM SHOPPE, *Leavenworth, WA,
   509-548-7014*

WEST VIRGINIA
ARACOMA DRUG GIFT GALLERY, *Logan, WV,
   304-752-3812*
EASTERN ART, *Charleston, WV, 304-345-4786*
FENTON GIFT SHOP, *Williamstown, WV, 304-375-7772*

WISCONSIN
A COUNTRY MOUSE, *Milwaukee, WI, 414-281-4210*
BEAUCHENE'S LTD ED, *Thiensville, WI, 414-242-0170*
BOOK & GIFT COLLECTIBLES, *Manitowoc, WI,
   414-684-4300*
CENTURY COIN SERVICE, *Green Bay, WI,
   414-494-2719*

COLLECTIBLES ETC INC, *Brown Deer, WI,
   414-355-4545*
KIE'S PHARMACY, *Racine, WI, 414-886-8160*
KRIEGER JEWELERS INC, *Green Bay, WI,
   414-468-7071*
KRISTMAS KRINGLE SHOPPE, *Fond Du Lac, WI,
   414-923-8210*
MAXINE'S CARD'S & GIFTS, *Beaver Dam, WI,
   414-887-8289*
NUTCRACKER GIFT HOUSE, *Delavan, WI,
   414-728-8447*
P J'S COLLECTIBLES, *Green Bay, WI, 414-437-3443*
P J'S HALLMARK SHOP, *Marinette, WI, 715-735-3940*
SANSONE DRUGS & GIFTS, *Hubertus, WI,
   414-628-3550*
SANSONE·DRUGS & GIFTS, *Slinger, WI, 414-644-5246*
SANSONE GIFT & CARD, *Mequon, WI, 414-241-3633*
TIVOLI IMPORTS, *Milwaukee, WI, 414-774-7590*

INTERNATIONAL MEMBERS

AUSTRALIA
LIBERTY LANE, *Sydney, NSW Aust, 011-61-2-261-3595*

CANADA
BAKEROSA COLLECTIBLES & BOOKS, *London, Ont,
   519-472-0827*
CHARLES' HOUSE OF PLATES, *Bloomfield, Ont,
   613-393-2249*
CHORNYJS' - HADKE, *Sault St Marie, Ont,
   705-253-0315*
DURAND'S LIMITED EDITIONS, *Calgary, Alb,
   403-277-0008*
HAPPINESS IS, *Durham, Ont, 519-369-2115*
HOMESTEAD GIFT SHOP, *Lennoxville, Quebec,
   819-569-2671*
MIDDAUGH'S COLLECTIBLES, *Goderich, Ont,
   519-524-5540*
OVER THE RAINBOW GALLERY, *Streetsville, Ont,
   416-821-2131*
THE PLATE CONNECTION, *Sherwood Park, Alb,
   403-467-0008*
PLATEFINDERS, *Edmonton, Alb, 403-435-3603*
TOMORROW'S TREASURES, *Bobcaygeon, Ont,
   705-738-2147*

Glossary

You can better appreciate your hobby by acquainting yourself with commonly used terms referred to by collectors and dealers to describe limited edition collectibles. This list is not all-inclusive, but it will provide a good starting point for approaching the collectibles field. When a term you don't understand is used, chances are you can find it here. If not, write the COLLECTORS' INFORMATION BUREAU and we'll do our best to define the term for you — and add it to next year's list.

ALABASTER. A compact, fine-textured gypsum which is usually white and translucent. Some collector plates are made of a material called ivory alabaster, which is not translucent, but has the look and patina of old ivory.

ALLOTMENT. The number within a limited edition which a manufacturer allows to a given dealer, direct marketer or collector.

ANNUAL. The term commonly used to describe a plate or other limited edition which is issued yearly, i.e. the Goebel Hummel *annual* plate. Many *annual* plates commemorate holidays or anniversaries, but they are commonly named by that special date, i.e. the Bing & Grondahl *Christmas* plate, issued annually to commemorate Christmas.

ARTIST PROOF. Originally, the first few in an edition of lithographs or prints created for the artist's approval. Now, many editions contain a small number of prints which are marked A/P instead of numbering — basically as a means of increasing the number in the edition.

BABY DOLL. A doll with the proportions of a baby, with lips parted to take a nipple, and chubby, short-limbed body.

BACKSTAMP. The information on the back of a plate or other limited edition, which serves to document it as part of its limited edition. This information may be hand-painted onto the plate, or it may be incised, or applied by means of a transfer (decal). Typical information which may appear on the backstamp includes the name of the series, name of the item, year of issue, some information about the subject, the artist's name and/or signature, the edition limit, the item's number within that edition, initials of firing master or other production supervisor, etc.

BAND. Also known as a rim, as in "24K gold banded, or rimmed." A typical method of finishing or decorating a plate or bell is to band it in gold, platinum or silver. The firing process allows the precious material to adhere to the piece.

BAS-RELIEF. A technique in which the collectible has a raised design. This design may be achieved by pouring liq-

Studio Dante di Volteradici introduced "Silent Night, Holy Night" from the Christmas Creche Series. The bas-relief plate is made of ivory alabaster.

uid material into a mold before firing, or by applying material to the flat surface of a plate, figurine, or other "blank" piece.

BAVARIA. A section of Germany known as one of the world's richest sources of kaolin clay — an essential component for fine porcelain production. Bavaria is home to a number of renowned porcelain factories.

BEDROOM DEALER. Slang term for an individual who functions as a small scale seller of limited edition collectibles, usually from his or her home. Often unable to purchase at wholesale direct from manufacturers, these dealers may buy items at a discount from a larger dealer and then resell at a small profit.

BISQUE OR BISCUIT. A fired ware which has neither a glaze nor enamel applied to it. Bisque may be white or colored. It gets its name from its biscuit-like, matte texture.

BLUE CHIP. Slang for a well-established series that some believe represents a safe and sound collectibles investment. An interesting play on words in that many of the plate series that fall into this category are Copenhagen or Cobalt blue.

BODY. The basic form of a plate, figurine, bell or other item, or its component materials.

BONE ASH. By means of heat, animal bones are reduced to powder as an ingredient for bone china or porcelain. The name of the resulting powder is calcium phosphate, or bone ash.

BONE CHINA/BONE PORCELAIN. Bone porcelain is similar to hard porcelain in its ingredients, except that calcined bone ash comprises a large percentage of the mix and is the primary contributor to the vitrification and translucency. Bone clay allows for extreme thinness and translucency without the sacrifice of strength and durability.

BOTTOMSTAMP. Same idea as the backstamp, but usually refers to documentation material which appears on the bottom of a figurine. On a bell, such information may appear on the inside.

BYE-LO BABY. Grace Storey Putnam copyrighted this life-sized baby (three days old) in 1922. This style of baby doll is much in fashion today among limited edition collectors.

CAMEO. Relief decoration with a flat surface around it, similar to the look of a jeweler's cameo. A technique used by Wedgwood, Incolay and Avondale among others.

CAST. When liquid clay, or slip, is poured into a mold and hardened. Most often used for figurines, bells, and many other forms.

CERAMIC. The generic term for a piece which is made of some form of clay and finished by firing at high temperatures.

CERTIFICATE/CERTIFICATE OF AUTHENTICITY. A document which accompanies a limited edition item to establish its place within the limited edition. Such a Certificate may include information such as the series' name, item title, artist's name and/or signature, brief description of the item and its subject, signatures of sponsoring and marketing organization representatives, and other documentation material along with the item's individual number or a statement of the edition limit.

The Christmas Cameos *collection from Incolay Studios began in 1990 with "Home with the Tree."*

CHARACTER DOLLS. Usually made of bisque or composition, these dolls are created to resemble a real person, usually an actor or other celebrity.

CHASING. A sculpting process in which tiny hammers and punches are used to create decorative details on ornaments.

CHINA. Originally "china" referred to all wares which came from China. Now this term means products which are fired at a high temperature. China usually is comprised of varying percentages of kaolin clay, feldspar and quartz. Also known as "porcelain."

CHRISTMAS SERIES. Plates, figurines, bells, and other collectible items which are issued to commemorate this yearly holiday, but which normally are sold and displayed all year.

CINNABAR. A red mineral found in volcanic regions, and a principal ingredient in mercury. This material is frequently used to create collectors' items.

CIRE PERDUE. See lost wax.

CLAY. A general term for the materials used to make ceramic items. Malleable when moist, clay becomes hard and strong when fired. It may be composed of any number of earthen materials.

CLOISONNE. An enameling process in which thin metal strips are soldered in place on a base to create a pattern, and then enamel is poured in to provide the color.

CLOSED-END SERIES. A group of limited edition plates, figurines or other collectibles which comprise a specific number — be it 2, 4, 6, 8, 12 or more. This number normally is disclosed when the series begins.

COBALT BLUE. Also known as Copenhagen blue, this rich color is a favorite of ceramicists because it can withstand high firing temperatures. Cobalt oxide is a black powder when applied, but fires to a deep blue.

COLD CAST. A metal powder and a binder are forced into a mold or die under high pressure, and thus a forging process occurs. Allows for exceptional detail and creates pieces which take well to handpainting.

COLLECTOR PLATE. A limited edition plate which is created with the expressed intent that it be collected.

COMMEMORATIVE. An item created to mark a special date, holiday or event.

DEALER. The individual or store from whom a collector purchases plates, bells, and other items at retail.

DECAL. Also known as a transfer, this is a lithographic or silkscreen rendering or a piece of artwork, which is applied to a ceramic, metal, glass or other material and then fired on to fuse it to the surface.

DELFTWARE. Heavy earthenware with a tin glaze. First developed in Delft, Holland in the 16th century.

DIE CUTTING. Process by which a design or pattern is cut out of a piece of steel to form a die.

DISTRIBUTOR. A person in the collectibles market who buys from a manufacturer and sells to dealers, who in turn sell to individual collectors.

DRAFTING. Process of drawing metal into a shape with a plunger and die for making holloware.

EARTHENWARE. A non-vitrified ceramic, composed of ball clay, kaolin, and pegmatite. Most often glazed and fired.

EDITION. The term which refers to the number of items created with the same name and decoration.

EMBOSSED DESIGN. Raised ornamentation produced by the mold or by stamping a design into the body of the item.

ETCHED DESIGN. Decoration produced by cutting into the surface with acid. The object is first covered with an acid resistant paint or wax, and the design is carved through this coating. When immersed in acid, the acid "bites" into the surface in the shape of the design.

FAIENCE. Named after an Italian town called Faenza, faience is similar to Delftware in that it is a tin-glazed earthenware. Also similar to Majolica.

FELDSPAR. When decomposed, this mineral becomes kaolin, which is the essential ingredient in china and porcelain. When left in its undercomposed form, feldspar adds hardness to a ware.

FIRE. To heat, and thus harden, a ceramic ware in a kiln.

FIRING PERIOD. A time period — usually 10 to 100 days — which serves to limit an edition, usually of plates. The number of items made is limited to the capacity of the manufacturer over that 10-to-100 day period.

FIRST ISSUE. The premier item in a series, whether closed-ended or open-ended.

FRENCH BRONZE. Also known as "spelter," this is zinc refined to 99.97% purity. This material has been used as an alternate to bronze for casting for more than a century.

GLAZE. The liquid material which is applied to a ware to serve various purposes: cosmetically, it provides shine and decorative value. It also makes the item more durable. Decorations may be applied before or after glaze is applied.

GRAPHIC. A print produced by one of the "original" print processes such as etchings, engravings, woodblocks, lithographs and serigraphs.

HALLMARK. The mark or logo of the manufacturer of an item.

HARD PASTE PORCELAIN. The hardest porcelain made, this material uses feldspar to enhance vitrification and translucency, and is fired at about 2642 degrees Fahrenheit.

INCISED. Writing or design which is cut into the piece — may provide a backstamp or a decorative purpose.

INCOLAY STONE. A man-made material combining minerals including carnelian and crystal quartz. Used to make cameo-style plates by Incolay Studios.

INLAY. To fill an etched or incised design with another material such as enamel, metal or jewels.

IN STOCK. Refers to prints in a given edition which are still available from the publisher's inventory.

ISSUE. As a verb, to introduce. As a noun, this term means an item within a series or edition.

ISSUE PRICE. The original price upon introduction of a limited edition, established by its manufacturer or principle marketer.

JASPER WARE. Josiah Wedgwood's unglazed stoneware material, first introduced in the 1770s. Although Jasper is white in its original form, it can be stained throughout in various colors. Wedgwood typically offers Jasper in the medium blue called "Wedgwood Blue," as well as darker blue, black, green, lilac, yellow, brown and grey. Some other colors have resulted through continued experimentation. Colored Wedgwood "bodies" often are decorated with white bas-relief, or vice-versa.

KAOLIN. The essential ingredient in china and porcelain, this special clay is found in quantity at several spots throughout the world — and it is there that many famous porcelain houses have developed. These areas include Bavaria in Germany, and the Limoges region of France.

LEAD CRYSTAL. Lead oxide gives this glass its weight and brilliance, as well as its clear ring. Lead crystal has a lead oxide content of 24%, while "full" lead crystal contains more than 30%.

LIMITED EDITION. An item produced only in a certain quantity or only during a certain time period. The typical ways in which collectibles editions are limited include: limited by number; limited by year; limited by specific time period; limited by firing period.

LIMOGES. A town in France which boasts a large deposit of kaolin clay, the essential ingredient in china and porcelain. Home of a number of top porcelain manufacturers.

LOST WAX. A wax "positive" is created by a sculptor, and used to create a ceramic "negative" shell. Then the ceramic shell becomes the original mold — basis for working molds used in the creation of an edition. A classic method of creating three-dimensional pieces.

LOW INVENTORY. The classification given an edition which has been 85% or more sold out by the publisher.

MAJOLICA. Similar to Delftware and Faience, this is a glazed earthenware first made on the Spanish island, Majorca.

MARKET. The buy-sell medium for collectibles.

MARKS OR MARKINGS. The logo or insignia which certifies that an item is made by a particular firm.

MINT CONDITION. A term originally related to the coin collecting hobby, this means that a limited edition item is still in its original, like-new condition, with all accompanying documents.

M.I. Hummel Exclusive New Backstamp

W. Goebel Porzellanfabrik, the producer of M.I. Hummel, introduced this backstamp in 1991. This prestigious crown mark with the intertwined WG monogram, (initials of Goebel company founder William Goebel), appeared on the first figurines introduced at the Leipzig Fair in 1925.

MOLD. The form which supplies the shape of a plate, figurine, bell, doll or other item.

OPEN-ENDED SERIES. A collection of plates or other limited editions which appear at intervals, usually annually, with no limit as to the number of years in which they will be produced. As an example, the Bing & Grondahl Christmas series has been produced annually since 1895, with no end in sight.

OVERGLAZE. A decoration which is applied to an item after its original glazing and firing.

PASTE. The raw material of porcelain before shaping and firing.

PEWTER. An alloy consisting of at least 85% tin.

PORCELAIN. Made of kaolin, quartz and feldspar, porcelain is fired at up to 1450 degrees Centigrade. Porcelain is noted for its translucency and its true ring. Also called "china."

POTTERY. Ceramic ware, more specifically that which is earthen ware or non-vitrified. Also a term for the manufacturing plant where such objects are made and fired.

PRIMARY MARKET. The buy-sell arrangement whereby individuals purchase collectibles direct from their manufacturer, or through a dealer, at issue price.

PRINTED REMARQUE. A hand drawn image by the artist that is photomechanically reproduced in the margin of a print.

PRINT. A photomechanical reproduction process such as offset lithography, collotypes and letterpress.

QUEEN'S WARE. Cream-colored earthenware developed by Josiah Wedgwood, now used as a generic term for similar materials.

QUOTE. The average selling price of a collectible at any given time — may be at issue, or above or below.

RELEASE PRICE. The price for which each print in the edition is sold until the edition is Sold Out and a secondary market (collector price) is established.

RELIEF. A raised design in various levels above a background.

REMARQUE. A hand drawn original image by the artist, either pencil, pen and ink, watercolor or oil that is drawn in the margin of a limited edition print.

SECOND. An item which is not first quality, and should not be included in the limited edition. Normally such items should be destroyed or at least marked on the backstamp or bottomstamp to indicate that they are not first quality.

SECONDARY MARKET PRICE. The retail price that a customer is willing to sell/buy a collectible that is no longer available on the primary market. These prices will vary from one territory to another depending upon the popularity and demand for the subject in each particular area.

SERIGRAPHY. A direct printing process whereby the artist designs, makes and prints his own stencils. A serigraph differs from other prints in that its images are created with paint films instead of printing inks.

SIGNED & NUMBERED. Each individual print is signed and consecutively numbered by the artist, in pencil, either in the image area or in the margin. Edition size is limited.

SIGNED IN THE PLATE. The only signature on the print is printed from the artist's original signature. Not necessarily limited in edition size.

SIGNED ONLY. Usually refers to a print that is signed without consecutive numbers. Not limited in edition size.

SILVERPLATE. A process of manufacturing ornaments in which pure silver is electroplated onto a base metal, usually brass or pewter.

SOLD OUT. The classification given an edition which has been 100% sold out by the publisher.

SPIN CASTING. A process of casting multiple ornaments from rubber molds; most commonly used for low temperature metals such as pewter.

STERLING SILVER. An alloy of $92^1/_2$% pure silver and $7^1/_2$% copper.

STONEWARE. A vitrified ceramic material, usually a silicate clay that is very hard, rather heavy and impervious to liquids and most stains.

TERRA COTTA. A reddish earthenware, or a general term for any fired clay.

TIN GLAZE. The glaze used on Delftware, Faience or Majolica, this material allows for a heavy, white and opaque surface after firing.

TRANSFER. See Decal.

TRANSLUCENCY. Allowing light to shine through a non-transparent object. A positive quality of fine porcelain or china.

TRIPTYCH. A three-panel art piece, often of religious significance.

UNDERGLAZE. A decoration which is applied before the final glazing and firing of a plate or other item. Most often, such a decoration is painted by hand.

VITRIFICATION. The process by which a ceramic body becomes vitrified, or totally non-porous, at high temperatures.

Collectors' Information Bureau

PRICE INDEX·1995

Limited Edition: Plates • Figurines • Cottages • Bells • Graphics • Ornaments • Dolls • Steins

This index includes thousands of the most widely traded limited editions in today's collectibles market. It is based on interviews with over 300 of the most experienced and informed limited edition dealers in the United States, as well as several independent market advisors.

HOW TO USE THIS INDEX

Listings are set up using the following format:

①
Enesco Corporation
79-04-019   Praise the Lord Anyhow-E1374B
③ ④ ⑤   **⑥**

②
Precious Moments Figurines
S. Butcher   Retrd.   8.00   75-95.00
⑦   **⑧**   **⑨**   **⑩**

① Enesco Corporation = Company Name

② Precious Moments Figurines = Series Name

③ 79 = 1979 (year of issue)

④ 04 = Series Number for Enesco Corporation. This number indicates that this series is the 4th listed for this particular company within this index. Each series is assigned a series number.

⑤ 019 = Item Number within series. For example, this is the 19th listing within the series. Each item has a sequential number within its series.

⑥ Praise the Lord Anyhow-E1374B = Proper title of the collectible. Many titles also include the model number for further identification purposes.

⑦ S. Butcher = Artist's Name. The first initial and last name is indicated most often, however a studio name may also be designated in this lot. (Example: Walt Disney).

⑧ Retrd. = Edition Limit. In this case, the collectible is no longer available. The edition limit category generally refers to the number of items created with the same name and decoration. Edition limits may indicate a specific number (i.e. 10,000) or the number of firing days for plates (i.e. 100-day, the capacity of the manufacturer to produce collectibles during a given firing period). Refer to "Open," "Suspd.," "Annual," and "Yr. Iss." under "Terms and Abbreviations" below.

⑨ 8.00 = Issue Price in U.S. Dollars

⑩ 75-95.00 = Current Quote Price reflected may show a price or price range. Quotes are based on interviews with retailers across the country, who provide their actual sales transactions.

How to Read Quote Ranges:

5-25.00	= 5.00-25.00	500-1000	= 500.00-1,000.00
50-75.00	= 50.00-75.00	1-1500.	= 1,000.00-1,500.00
75-100.	= 75.00-100.00	15-2000.	= 1,500.00-2,000.00
100-500.	= 100.00-500.00	15-20000	= 15,000.00-20,000.00

A Special Note to All Precious Moments Collectors: *Each ENESCO Precious Moments subject is engraved with a special annual mark. This emblem changes with each production year. The Collector value for each piece varies because of these distinctive yearly markings. Our pricing reflects an average for all years.*

A Special Note to All Hallmark Keepsake Ornament Collectors: *All quotes in this section are for ornaments in mint condition in their original box.*

A Special Note to All Department 56 Collectors: *Year of Introduction indicates the year in which the piece was designed, sculpted and copyrighted. It is possible these pieces may not be available to the collectors until the following calendar year.*

TERMS AND ABBREVIATIONS

Annual = Issued once a year
Closed = An item or series no longer in production
N/A = Not Available
Open = Not limited by number or time, available until manufacturer stops production, "retires" or "closes" the item or series

Retrd. = Retired
S/O = Sold Out
Set = Refers to two or more items issued together for a single price
Suspd. = Suspended (not currently being produced: may be produced in the future)
Undis. = Undisclosed

Unkn. = Unknown
Yr. Iss. = Year of issue (limited to a calendar year) 28-day, 10-day, etc., limited to this number of production (or firing) days, usually not consecutive

BELLS

		ARTIST	EDITION	ISSUE	QUOTE
ANRI	**ANRI Wooden Christmas Bells**				
76-01-001	Christmas	J. Ferrandiz	Yr.Iss.	6.00	50.00
77-01-002	Christmas	J. Ferrandiz	Yr.Iss.	7.00	40.00
78-01-003	Christmas	J. Ferrandiz	Yr.Iss.	10.00	40.00
79-01-004	Christmas	J. Ferrandiz	Yr.Iss.	13.00	25-30.00
80-01-005	The Christmas King	J. Ferrandiz	Yr.Iss.	18.00	18.50
81-01-006	Lighting The Way	J. Ferrandiz	Yr.Iss.	19.00	18.50
82-01-007	Caring	J. Ferrandiz	Yr.Iss.	19.00	18.50
83-01-008	Behold	J. Ferrandiz	Yr.Iss.	19.00	18.50
85-01-009	Nature's Dream	J. Ferrandiz	Yr.Iss.	19.00	18.50
ANRI	**Juan Ferrandiz Musical Christmas Bells**				
76-02-001	Christmas	J. Ferrandiz	Yr.Iss.	25.00	80.00
77-02-002	Christmas	J. Ferrandiz	Yr.Iss.	25.00	80.00
78-02-003	Christmas	J. Ferrandiz	Yr.Iss.	35.00	75.00
79-02-004	Christmas	J. Ferrandiz	Yr.Iss.	48.00	60.00
80-02-005	Little Drummer Boy	J. Ferrandiz	Yr.Iss.	60.00	63.00
81-02-006	The Good Shepherd Boy	J. Ferrandiz	Yr.Iss.	63.00	63.00
82-02-007	Spreading the Word	J. Ferrandiz	Yr.Iss.	63.00	63.00
83-02-008	Companions	J. Ferrandiz	Yr.Iss.	63.00	63.00
84-02-009	With Love	J. Ferrandiz	Yr.Iss.	55.00	55.00
Artaffects	**Bells**				
87-01-001	Newborn Bell	R. Sauber	Unkn.	25.00	25.00
87-01-002	Motherhood Bell	R. Sauber	Unkn.	25.00	25.00
87-01-003	Sweet Sixteen Bell	R. Sauber	Unkn.	25.00	25.00
87-01-004	The Wedding Bell (White)	R. Sauber	Unkn.	25.00	25.00
87-01-005	The Wedding Bell (Silver)	R. Sauber	Unkn.	25.00	25.00
87-01-006	The Wedding Bell (Gold)	R. Sauber	Unkn.	25.00	25.00
Artaffects	**Bride Belles Figurine Bells**				
88-02-001	Caroline	R. Sauber	Unkn.	27.50	27.50
88-02-002	Jacqueline	R. Sauber	Unkn.	27.50	27.50
88-02-003	Elizabeth	R. Sauber	Unkn.	27.50	27.50
88-02-004	Emily	R. Sauber	Unkn.	27.50	27.50
88-02-005	Meredith	R. Sauber	Unkn.	27.50	27.50
88-02-006	Laura	R. Sauber	Unkn.	27.50	27.50
88-02-007	Sarah	R. Sauber	Unkn.	27.50	27.50
88-02-008	Rebecca	R. Sauber	Unkn.	27.50	27.50
88-02-009	Groom	R. Sauber	Unkn.	22.50	22.50
Artaffects	**Indian Brave Annual Bell**				
89-03-001	Christmas Pow-Pow	G. Perillo	Closed	25.00	30.00
90-03-002	Christmas Bells	G. Perillo	Closed	24.50	24.50
Artaffects	**Indian Princess Annual Bell**				
89-04-001	The Little Princess	G. Perillo	Closed	25.00	30.00
90-04-002	Little Madonna	G. Perillo	Closed	24.50	24.50
Artists of the World	**DeGrazia Bells**				
80-01-001	Los Ninos	T. DeGrazia	7,500	40.00	95.00
80-01-002	Festival of Lights	T. DeGrazia	5,000	40.00	85.00
Belleek	**Belleek**				
88-01-001	Bell, 1st Edition	Belleek	Yr.Iss.	38.00	38.00
89-01-002	Tower, 2nd Edition	Belleek	Yr.Iss.	35.00	35.00
90-01-003	Leprechaun, 3rd Edition	Belleek	Yr.Iss.	30.00	30.00
91-01-004	Church, 4th Edition	Belleek	Yr.Iss.	32.00	32.00
92-01-005	Cottage, 5th Edition	Belleek	Yr.Iss.	30.00	30.00
93-01-006	Pub, 6th Edition	Belleek	Yr.Iss.	30.00	30.00
Belleek	**Twelve Days of Christmas**				
91-02-001	A Partridge in a Pear Tree	Belleek	Yr.Iss.	30.00	30.00
92-02-002	Two Turtle Doves	Belleek	Yr.Iss.	30.00	30.00
93-02-003	Three French Hens	Belleek	Yr.Iss.	30.00	30.00
94-02-004	Four Calling Birds	Belleek	Yr.Iss.	30.00	30.00
Bing & Grondahl	**Annual Christmas Bell**				
80-01-001	Christmas in the Woods	H. Thelander	Yr.Iss.	39.50	39.50
81-01-002	Christmas Peace	H. Thelander	Yr.Iss.	42.50	42.50
82-01-003	The Christmas Tree	H. Thelander	Yr.Iss.	45.00	45.00
83-01-004	Christmas in the Old Town	E. Jensen	Yr.Iss.	45.00	45.00
84-01-005	The Christmas Letter	E. Jensen	Yr.Iss.	45.00	45.00
85-01-006	Christmas Eve at the Farmhouse	E. Jensen	Yr.Iss.	45.00	45.00
86-01-007	Silent Night, Holy Night	E. Jensen	Yr.Iss.	45.00	45.00
87-01-008	The Snowman's Christmas Eve	E. Jensen	Yr.Iss.	47.50	47.50
88-01-009	The Old Poet's Christmas	E. Jensen	Yr.Iss.	49.50	49.50
89-01-010	Christmas Anchorage	E. Jensen	Yr.Iss.	52.00	52.00
90-01-011	Changing of the Guards	E. Jensen	Yr.Iss.	55.00	55.00
91-01-012	The Copenhagen Stock Exchange at Christmas	E. Jensen	Yr.Iss.	59.50	59.50
92-01-013	Christmas At the Rectory	J. Steensen	Yr.Iss.	62.50	62.50
93-01-014	Father Christmas in Copenhagen	J. Steensen	Yr.Iss.	62.50	62.50
94-01-015	A Day At The Deer Park	J. Nielsen	Yr.Iss.	62.50	62.50
95-01-016	The Towers of Copenhagen	J. Nielsen	Yr.Iss.	62.50	62.50
Bing & Grondahl	**Christmas in America Bell**				
88-02-001	Christmas Eve in Williamsburg	J. Woodson	Yr.Iss.	28.00	100.00
89-02-002	Christmas Eve at the White House	J. Woodson	Yr.Iss.	29.00	75.00
90-02-003	Christmas Eve at the Capitol	J. Woodson	Yr.Iss.	30.00	30.00
91-02-004	Independence Hall	J. Woodson	Yr.Iss.	35.00	35.00
92-02-005	Christmas in San Francisco	J. Woodson	Yr.Iss.	37.50	37.50
93-02-006	Coming Home For Christmas	J. Woodson	Yr.Iss.	37.50	37.50
94-02-007	Christmas Eve in Alaska	J. Woodson	Yr.Iss.	37.50	37.50
C.U.I./Carolina Collection/Dram Tree	**Sterling Classic**				
91-01-001	Small Tortoiseshell	J. Harris	Retrd.	100.00	100.00
91-01-002	Swallowtail	J. Harris	Retrd.	100.00	100.00
91-01-003	Camberwell Beauty	J. Harris	Retrd.	100.00	100.00
91-01-004	Large Blue	J. Harris	Retrd.	100.00	100.00
91-01-005	Peacock	J. Harris	Retrd.	100.00	100.00
91-01-006	Clouded Yellow	J. Harris	Retrd.	100.00	100.00
91-01-007	Mouse	J. Harris	Retrd.	100.00	100.00
91-01-008	Kingfisher	J. Harris	Retrd.	100.00	100.00
91-01-009	Barn Owl	J. Harris	Retrd.	100.00	100.00
Enesco Corporation	**Precious Moments Annual Bells**				
83-01-001	Surrounded With Joy-E-0522	S. Butcher	Retrd.	18.00	54-75.00
82-01-002	I'll Play My Drum for Him-E-2358	S. Butcher	Retrd.	17.00	60-85.00
84-01-003	Wishing You a Merry Christmas-E-5393	S. Butcher	Retrd.	19.00	41-55.00
81-01-004	Let the Heavens Rejoice-E-5622	S. Butcher	Retrd.	15.00	180.00
85-01-005	God Sent His Love-15873	S. Butcher	Retrd.	19.00	38-43.00
86-01-006	Wishing You a Cozy Christmas-102318	S. Butcher	Retrd.	20.00	40.00
87-01-007	Love is the Best Gift of All-109835	S. Butcher	Retrd.	22.50	30-44.00
88-01-008	Time To Wish You a Merry Christmas-115304	S. Butcher	Retrd.	25.00	40-45.00
89-01-009	Oh Holy Night-522821	S. Butcher	Retrd.	25.00	39-45.00
90-01-010	Once Upon A Holy Night-523828	S. Butcher	Retrd.	25.00	30-35.00
91-01-011	May Your Christmas Be Merry-524182	S. Butcher	Retrd.	25.00	39.00
92-01-012	But The Greatest Of These Is Love-527726	S. Butcher	Retrd.	25.00	25-35.00
93-01-013	Wishing You The Sweetest Christmas-530174	S. Butcher	Retrd.	25.00	25.00
94-01-014	Your're As Pretty as a Christmas Tree-604216	S. Butcher	Yr.Iss.	27.50	27.50
Enesco Corporation	**Precious Moments Various Bells**				
81-02-001	Jesus Loves Me-E-5208	S. Butcher	Suspd.	15.00	40-50.00
81-02-002	Jesus Loves Me-E-5209	S. Butcher	Suspd.	15.00	40-60.00
81-02-003	Prayer Changes Things-E-5210	S. Butcher	Suspd.	15.00	40-60.00
81-02-004	God Understands-E-5211	S. Butcher	Retrd.	15.00	40-78.00
81-02-005	We Have Seen His Star-E-5620	S. Butcher	Suspd.	15.00	40-50.00
81-02-006	Jesus Is Born-E-5623	S. Butcher	Suspd.	15.00	40-55.00
82-02-007	The Lord Bless You and Keep You-E-7175	S. Butcher	Suspd.	17.00	35-38.00
82-02-008	The Lord Bless You and Keep You-E-7176	S. Butcher	Suspd.	17.00	40-55.00
82-02-009	The Lord Bless You and Keep You- E-7179	S. Butcher	Suspd.	22.50	34-59.00
82-02-010	Mother Sew Dear-E-7181	S. Butcher	Suspd.	17.00	35-50.00
82-02-011	The Purr-fect Grandma-E-7183	S. Butcher	Suspd.	17.00	35-54.00
Enesco Corporation	**Memories of Yesterday Bell**				
90-03-001	Here Comes the Bride-God Bless Her-523100	M. Attwell	Suspd.	25.00	25.00
94-03-002	Time For Bed-525243	M. Attwell	Open	25.00	25.00
Enesco Corporation	**Cherished Teddies**				
92-04-001	Angel Bell-906530	P. Hillman	Open	20.00	20.00
Enesco Corporation	**Bells**				
92-05-001	Susanna 999377	M. Humphrey	Open	22.50	22.50
92-05-002	Sarah 999385	M. Humphrey	Open	22.50	22.50
92-05-003	Hollies For You 996095	M. Humphrey	Open	22.50	22.50
Fenton Art Glass Company	**Connoisseur Bell**				
83-01-001	Bell, Burmese Handpainted	Fenton	Closed	50.00	50.00
83-01-002	Craftsman Bell, White Satin Carnival	Fenton	Closed	25.00	25.00
84-01-003	Bell, Famous Women's Ruby Satin Irid.	Fenton	Closed	25.00	25.00
85-01-004	Bell, 6 1/2" Burmese, Handpainted	Fenton	Closed	55.00	55.00
86-01-005	Bell, Burmese-Shells	Fenton	Closed	60.00	60.00
88-01-006	Bell, 7" Wisteria	Fenton	Closed	45.00	45.00
89-01-007	Bell, Handpainted Rosalene Satin	Fenton	Closed	50.00	50.00
91-01-008	Bell, 7" Roses on Rosalene	Fenton	Closed	50.00	50.00
Fenton Art Glass Company	**Fenton Christmas Bells**				
94-02-001	Magnolia on Gold Bell	M. Reynolds	1,000	35.00	35.00
94-02-002	Angel on Ivory Satin Bell	M. Reynolds	1,000	39.50	39.50
94-02-003	Partridge on Ruby Musical Bell	M. Reynolds	1,000	48.50	48.50
Fenton Art Glass Company	**Christmas Star**				
94-03-001	"Silent Night" Bell-Edition#1 of series	F. Burton	2,500	45.00	45.00
Fitz and Floyd, Inc.	**Annual Christmas Bell**				
94-01-001	Night Before Christmas	V. Balcou	Yr.Iss.	25.00	25.00
Fitz and Floyd, Inc.	**Heirloom Collection**				
94-02-001	Reindeer	R. Havins	Yr.Iss.	25.00	25.00
Goebel/Schmid	**M.I. Hummel Collectibles Annual Bells**				
78-01-001	Let's Sing 700	M. I. Hummel	Closed	50.00	30-55.00
79-01-002	Farewell 701	M. I. Hummel	Closed	70.00	25-70.00
80-01-003	Thoughtful 702	M. I. Hummel	Closed	85.00	30-85.00
81-01-004	In Tune 703	M. I. Hummel	Closed	85.00	60-150.
82-01-005	She Loves Me, She Loves Me Not 704	M. I. Hummel	Closed	90.00	55-80.00
83-01-006	Knit One 705	M. I. Hummel	Closed	90.00	60-85.00
84-01-007	Mountaineer 706	M. I. Hummel	Closed	90.00	50-80.00
85-01-008	Sweet Song 707	M. I. Hummel	Closed	90.00	72-90.00
86-01-009	Sing Along 708	M. I. Hummel	Closed	100.00	72-108.
87-01-010	With Loving Greetings 709	M. I. Hummel	Closed	110.00	160.00
88-01-011	Busy Student 710	M. I. Hummel	Closed	120.00	72-120.
89-01-012	Latest News 711	M. I. Hummel	Closed	135.00	135-150.
90-01-013	What's New? 712	M. I. Hummel	Closed	140.00	140-200.
91-01-014	Favorite Pet 713	M. I. Hummel	Closed	150.00	165-200.
92-01-015	Whistler's Duet 714	M. I. Hummel	Closed	160.00	149-160.
Gorham	**Various**				
75-01-001	Sweet Song So Young	N. Rockwell	Annual	19.50	50.00
75-01-002	Santa's Helpers	N. Rockwell	Annual	19.50	30.00
75-01-003	Tavern Sign Painter	N. Rockwell	Annual	19.50	30.00
76-01-004	Flowers in Tender Bloom	N. Rockwell	Annual	19.50	40.00
76-01-005	Snow Sculpture	N. Rockwell	Annual	19.50	45.00
77-01-006	Fondly Do We Remember	N. Rockwell	Annual	19.50	55.00
77-01-007	Chilling Chore (Christmas)	N. Rockwell	Annual	19.50	35.00
78-01-008	Gaily Sharing Vintage Times	N. Rockwell	Annual	22.50	22.50
78-01-009	Gay Blades (Christmas)	N. Rockwell	Annual	22.50	22.50
79-01-010	Beguiling Buttercup	N. Rockwell	Annual	24.50	26.50
79-01-011	A Boy Meets His Dog (Christmas)	N. Rockwell	Annual	24.50	30.00
80-01-012	Flying High	N. Rockwell	Annual	27.50	27.50
80-01-013	Chilly Reception (Christmas)	N. Rockwell	Annual	27.50	27.50
81-01-014	Sweet Serenade	N. Rockwell	Annual	27.50	27.50
81-01-015	Ski Skills (Christmas)	N. Rockwell	Annual	27.50	27.50
82-01-016	Young Mans Fancy	N. Rockwell	Annual	29.50	29.50
82-01-017	Coal Season's Coming	N. Rockwell	Annual	29.50	29.50
83-01-018	Christmas Medley	N. Rockwell	Annual	29.50	29.50
83-01-019	The Milkmaid	N. Rockwell	Annual	29.50	29.50
84-01-020	Tiny Tim	N. Rockwell	Annual	29.50	29.50
84-01-021	Young Love	N. Rockwell	Annual	29.50	29.50
84-01-022	Marriage License	N. Rockwell	Annual	32.50	32.50
84-01-023	Yarn Spinner	N. Rockwell	5,000	32.50	32.50
85-01-024	Yuletide Reflections	N. Rockwell	5,000	32.50	32.50
86-01-025	Home For The Holidays	N. Rockwell	5,000	32.50	32.50
86-01-026	On Top of the World	N. Rockwell	5,000	32.50	32.50
87-01-027	Merry Christmas Grandma	N. Rockwell	5,000	32.50	32.50
87-01-028	The Artist	N. Rockwell	5,000	32.50	32.50
88-01-029	The Homecoming	N. Rockwell	15,000	37.50	37.50
Gorham	**Currier & Ives - Mini Bells**				
76-02-001	Christmas Sleigh Ride	Currier & Ives	Annual	9.95	35.00
77-02-002	American Homestead	Currier & Ives	Annual	9.95	25.00
78-02-003	Yule Logs	Currier & Ives	Annual	12.95	20.00
79-02-004	Sleigh Ride	Currier & Ives	Annual	14.95	20.00
80-02-005	Christmas in the Country	Currier & Ives	Annual	14.95	20.00
81-02-006	Christmas Tree	Currier & Ives	Annual	14.95	17.50

		ARTIST	EDITION	ISSUE	QUOTE
82-02-007	Christmas Visitation	Currier & Ives	Annual	16.50	17.50
83-02-008	Winter Wonderland	Currier & Ives	Annual	16.50	17.50
84-02-009	Hitching Up	Currier & Ives	Annual	16.50	17.50
85-02-010	Skaters Holiday	Currier & Ives	Annual	17.50	17.50
86-02-011	Central Park in Winter	Currier & Ives	Annual	17.50	17.50
87-02-012	Early Winter	Currier & Ives	Annual	19.00	19.00
Gorham		**Mini Bells**			
81-03-001	Tiny Tim	N. Rockwell	Annual	19.75	19.75
82-03-002	Planning Christmas Visit	N. Rockwell	Annual	20.00	20.00
Dave Grossman Designs		**Norman Rockwell Collection**			
75-01-001	Faces of Christmas NRB-75	Rockwell-Inspired	Retrd.	12.50	35.00
76-01-002	Drum for Tommy NRB-76	Rockwell-Inspired	Retrd.	12.00	30.00
76-01-003	Ben Franklin (Bicentennial)	Rockwell-Inspired	Retrd.	12.50	25.00
80-01-004	Leapfrog NRB-80	Rockwell-Inspired	Retrd.	50.00	60.00
Hallmark Galleries		**Enchanted Garden**			
92-01-001	Fairy Bunny (porcelain) 3500QHG3012	E. Richardson	Retrd.	35.00	35.00
Kirk Stieff		**Musical Bells**			
77-01-001	Annual Bell 1977	Kirk Stieff	Closed	17.95	40-120.
78-01-002	Annual Bell 1978	Kirk Stieff	Closed	17.95	80.00
79-01-003	Annual Bell 1979	Kirk Stieff	Closed	17.95	50.00
80-01-004	Annual Bell 1980	Kirk Stieff	Closed	19.95	50.00
81-01-005	Annual Bell 1981	Kirk Stieff	Closed	19.95	75.00
82-01-006	Annual Bell 1982	Kirk Stieff	Closed	19.95	60-120.
83-01-007	Annual Bell 1983	Kirk Stieff	Closed	19.95	50-60.00
84-01-008	Annual Bell 1984	Kirk Stieff	Closed	19.95	40.00
85-01-009	Annual Bell 1985	Kirk Stieff	Closed	19.95	40.00
86-01-010	Annual Bell 1986	Kirk Stieff	Closed	19.95	55.00
87-01-011	Annual Bell 1987	Kirk Stieff	Closed	19.95	30.00
88-01-012	Annual Bell 1988	Kirk Stieff	Closed	22.50	35-45.00
89-01-013	Annual Bell 1989	Kirk Stieff	Closed	25.00	25.00
90-01-014	Annual Bell 1990	Kirk Stieff	Closed	27.00	27.00
91-01-015	Annual Bell 1991	Kirk Stieff	Closed	28.00	28.00
92-01-016	Annual Bell 1992	Kirk Stieff	Closed	30.00	30.00
93-01-017	Annual Bell 1993	Kirk Stieff	Closed	30.00	30.00
94-01-018	Annual Bell 1994	Kirk Stieff	Open	30.00	30.00
Kirk Stieff		**Bell**			
92-02-001	Santa's Workshop Christmas Bell	Kirk Stieff	3,000	40.00	40.00
93-02-002	Santa's Reindeer Bell	Kirk Stieff	Closed	30.00	30.00
Lance Corporation		**Hudson Pewter Bicentennial Bells**			
74-01-001	Benjamin Franklin	P.W. Baston	Closed	Unkn.	75-100.
74-01-002	Thomas Jefferson	P.W. Baston	Closed	Unkn.	75-100.
74-01-003	George Washington	P.W. Baston	Closed	Unkn.	75-100.
74-01-004	John Adams	P.W. Baston	Closed	Unkn.	75-100.
74-01-005	James Madison	P.W. Baston	Closed	Unkn.	75-100.
Lenox China		**Songs of Christmas**			
91-01-001	We Wish You a Merry Christmas	Unknown	Yr.Iss.	49.00	49.00
92-01-002	Deck the Halls	Unknown	Yr.Iss.	53.00	53.00
93-01-003	Jingle Bells	Unknown	Yr.Iss.	57.00	57.00
94-01-004	Silver Bells	Unknown	Yr.Iss.	62.00	62.00
Lenox Collections		**Crystal Christmas Bell**			
81-01-001	Partridge in a Pear Tree	Lenox	15,000	55.00	55.00
82-01-002	Holy Family Bell	Lenox	15,000	55.00	55.00
83-01-003	Three Wise Men .	Lenox	15,000	55.00	55.00
84-01-004	Dove Bell	Lenox	15,000	57.00	57.00
85-01-005	Santa Claus Bell	Lenox	15,000	57.00	57.00
86-01-006	Dashing Through the Snow Bell	Lenox	15,000	64.00	64.00
87-01-007	Heralding Angel Bell	Lenox	15,000	76.00	76.00
91-01-008	Celestial Harpist	Lenox	15,000	75.00	75.00
Lenox Collections		**Bird Bells**			
91-02-001	Bluebird	Unknown	Open	57.00	57.00
91-02-002	Hummingbird	Unknown	Open	57.00	57.00
91-02-003	Chickadee	Unknown	Open	57.00	57.00
92-02-004	Robin Bell	Unknown	Open	57.00	57.00
Lenox Collections		**Carousel Bell**			
92-03-001	Carousel Horse	Unknown	Open	45.00	45.00
Lladro		**Lladro Christmas Bell**			
87-01-001	Christmas Bell - L5458M	Lladro	Annual	29.50	40-130.
88-01-002	Christmas Bell - L5525M	Lladro	Annual	32.50	23-35.00
89-01-003	Christmas Bell - L5616M	Lladro	Annual	32.50	70-125.
90-01-004	Christmas Bell - L5641M	Lladro	Annual	34.50	30-75.00
91-01-005	Christmas Bell - L5803M	Lladro	Annual	37.50	37.50
92-01-006	Christmas Bell - L5913M	Lladro	Annual	37.50	35-55.00
93-01-007	Christmas Bell - L6010M	Lladro	Annual	37.50	40.00
94-01-008	Christmas Bell - L6139M	Lladro	Annual	39.50	39.50
Lladro		**Lladro Limited Edition Bell**			
94-02-001	Eternal Love 7542M	Lladro	Annual	95.00	95.00
Midwest of Cannon Falls		**The Littlest Angel Collection**			
94-01-001	Angel with Wreath Bell 11632-6	Midwest	Open	12.50	12.50
Old World Christmas		**Porcelain Christmas**			
88-01-001	First Edition Santa Bell	E.M. Merck	Retrd.	10.00	10.00
89-01-002	Second Edition Santa Bell	E.M. Merck	Retrd.	10.00	10.00
Reco International		**Special Occasions**			
89-01-001	The Wedding	S. Kuck	Retrd.	15.00	15.00
Reco International		**Special Occasions-Wedding**			
91-02-001	From This Day Forward	C. Micarelli	Open	15.00	15.00
91-02-002	To Have And To Hold	C. Micarelli	Open	15.00	15.00
Reed & Barton		**Noel Musical Bells**			
80-01-001	1980 Bell	Reed & Barton	Closed	20.00	50.00
81-01-002	1981 Bell	Reed & Barton	Closed	22.50	45.00
82-01-003	1982 Bell	Reed & Barton	Closed	22.50	40.00
83-01-004	1983 Bell	Reed & Barton	Closed	22.50	50.00
84-01-005	1984 Bell	Reed & Barton	Closed	22.50	50.00
85-01-006	1985 Bell	Reed & Barton	Closed	25.00	40.00
86-01-007	1986 Bell	Reed & Barton	Closed	25.00	50.00
87-01-008	1987 Bell	Reed & Barton	Closed	25.00	50.00
88-01-009	1988 Bell	Reed & Barton	Closed	25.00	28-40.00
89-01-010	1989 Bell	Reed & Barton	Closed	25.00	40.00
90-01-011	1990 Bell	Reed & Barton	Closed	27.50	30.00
91-01-012	1991 Bell	Reed & Barton	Closed	30.00	30.00
92-01-013	1992 Bell	Reed & Barton	Closed	30.00	35.00
93-01-014	1993 Bell	Reed & Barton	Yr.Iss.	30.00	30.00

		ARTIST	EDITION	ISSUE	QUOTE
94-01-015	1994 Bell	Reed & Barton	Yr.Iss.	30.00	30.00
Reed & Barton		**Yuletide Bell**			
81-02-001	Yuletide Holiday	Reed & Barton	Closed	14.00	14.00
82-02-002	Little Shepherd	Reed & Barton	Closed	14.00	14.00
83-02-003	Perfect Angel	Reed & Barton	Closed	15.00	15.00
84-02-004	Drummer Boy	Reed & Barton	Closed	15.00	15.00
85-02-005	Caroler	Reed & Barton	Closed	16.50	16.50
86-02-006	Night Before Christmas	Reed & Barton	Closed	16.50	16.50
87-02-007	Jolly St. Nick	Reed & Barton	Closed	16.50	16.50
88-02-008	Christmas Morning	Reed & Barton	Closed	16.50	16.50
89-02-009	The Bell Ringer	Reed & Barton	Closed	16.50	16.50
90-02-010	The Wreath Bearer	Reed & Barton	Closed	18.50	18.50
91-02-011	A Special Gift	Reed & Barton	Closed	22.50	22.50
92-02-012	My Special Friend	Reed & Barton	Closed	22.50	22.50
93-02-013	My Christmas Present	Reed & Barton	Yr.Iss.	22.50	22.50
94-02-014	1994 Yuletide Bell	Reed & Barton	Yr.Iss.	22.50	22.50
River Shore		**Rockwell Children Series I**			
77-01-001	School Play	N. Rockwell	7,500	30.00	75.00
77-01-002	First Day of School	N. Rockwell	7,500	30.00	75.00
77-01-003	Football Hero	N. Rockwell	7,500	30.00	75.00
77-01-004	Flowers for Mother	N. Rockwell	7,500	30.00	60.00
River Shore		**Rockwell Children Series II**			
78-02-001	Dressing Up	N. Rockwell	15,000	35.00	50.00
78-02-002	Future All American	N. Rockwell	15,000	35.00	52.00
78-02-003	Garden Girl	N. Rockwell	15,000	35.00	40.00
78-02-004	Five Cents A Glass	N. Rockwell	15,000	35.00	40.00
River Shore		**Norman Rockwell Single Issues**			
81-03-001	Looking Out to Sea	N. Rockwell	7,000	45.00	95.00
81-03-002	Spring Flowers	N. Rockwell	347	175.00	175.00
81-03-003	Grandpa's Guardian	N. Rockwell	7,000	45.00	45.00
Roman, Inc.		**The Masterpiece Collection**			
79-01-001	Adoration	F. Lippe	Open	20.00	20.00
80-01-002	Madonna with Grapes	P. Mignard	Open	25.00	25.00
81-01-003	The Holy Family	G. Notti	Open	25.00	25.00
82-01-004	Madonna of the Streets	R. Ferruzzi	Open	25.00	25.00
Roman, Inc.		**F. Hook Bells**			
85-02-001	Beach Buddies	F. Hook	15,000	25.00	27.50
86-02-002	Sounds of the Sea	F. Hook	15,000	25.00	27.50
87-02-003	Bear Hug	F. Hook	15,000	25.00	27.50
Roman, Inc.		**Annual Fontanini Christmas Crystal Bell**			
91-03-001	1991 Bell	E. Simonetti	Closed	30.00	30.00
92-03-002	1992 Bell	E. Simonetti	Closed	30.00	30.00
93-03-003	1993 Bell	E. Simonetti	Closed	30.00	30.00
Roman, Inc.		**Annual Nativity Bell**			
90-04-001	Nativity	I. Spencer	Closed	15.00	15.00
91-04-002	Flight Into Egypt	I. Spencer	Closed	15.00	15.00
92-04-003	Gloria in Excelsis Deo	I. Spencer	Closed	15.00	15.00
93-04-004	Three Kings of Orient	I. Spencer	Closed	15.00	15.00
Royal Copenhagen		**Christmas**			
92-01-001	The Queen's Carriage	S. Vestergaard	Closed	69.50	69.50
93-01-002	Christmas Guests	S. Vestergaard	Yr.Iss.	62.50	62.50
94-01-003	Christmas Shopping	S. Vestergaard	Yr.Iss.	62.50	62.50
95-01-004	Christmas at the Manor House	S. Vestergaard	Yr.Iss.	62.50	62.50
Schmid		**Berta Hummel Christmas Bells**			
72-01-001	Angel with Flute	B. Hummel	Yr.Iss.	20.00	75.00
73-01-002	Nativity	B. Hummel	Yr.Iss.	15.00	80.00
74-01-003	The Guardian Angel	B. Hummel	Yr.Iss.	17.50	45.00
75-01-004	The Christmas Child	B. Hummel	Yr.Iss.	22.50	45.00
76-01-005	Sacred Journey	B. Hummel	Yr.Iss.	22.50	25.00
77-01-006	Herald Angel	B. Hummel	Yr.Iss.	22.50	50.00
78-01-007	Heavenly Trio	B. Hummel	Yr.Iss.	27.50	40.00
79-01-008	Starlight Angel	B. Hummel	Yr.Iss.	38.00	45.00
80-01-009	Parade into Toyland	B. Hummel	Yr.Iss.	45.00	55.00
81-01-010	A Time to Remember	B. Hummel	Yr.Iss.	45.00	55.00
82-01-011	Angelic Procession	B. Hummel	Yr.Iss.	45.00	50.00
83-01-012	Angelic Messenger	B. Hummel	Yr.Iss.	45.00	55.00
84-01-013	A Gift from Heaven	B. Hummel	Yr.Iss.	45.00	75.00
85-01-014	Heavenly Light	B. Hummel	Yr.Iss.	45.00	75.00
86-01-015	Tell the Heavens	B. Hummel	Yr.Iss.	45.00	45.00
87-01-016	Angelic Gifts	B. Hummel	Yr.Iss.	47.50	47.50
88-01-017	Cheerful Cherubs	B. Hummel	Yr.Iss.	52.50	55.00
89-01-018	Angelic Musician	B. Hummel	Yr.Iss.	53.00	55.00
90-01-019	Angel's Light	B. Hummel	Yr.Iss.	53.00	53.00
91-01-020	Message From Above	B. Hummel	5,000	58.00	58.00
92-01-021	Sweet Blessings	B. Hummel	5,000	65.00	65.00
93-01-022	Silent Wonder	B. Hummel	5,000	58.00	58.00
Schmid		**Berta Hummel Mother's Day Bells**			
76-02-001	Devotion for Mothers	B. Hummel	Yr.Iss.	22.50	55.00
77-02-002	Moonlight Return	B. Hummel	Yr.Iss.	22.50	45.00
78-02-003	Afternoon Stroll	B. Hummel	Yr.Iss.	27.50	45.00
79-02-004	Cherub's Gift	B. Hummel	Yr.Iss.	38.00	45.00
80-02-005	Mother's Little Helper	B. Hummel	Yr.Iss.	45.00	45.00
81-02-006	Playtime	B. Hummel	Yr.Iss.	45.00	45.00
82-02-007	The Flower Basket	B. Hummel	Yr.Iss.	45.00	45.00
83-02-008	Spring Bouquet	B. Hummel	Yr.Iss.	45.00	45.00
84-02-009	A Joy to Share	B. Hummel	Yr.Iss.	45.00	45.00
Schmid		**The Littlest Light**			
93-03-001	The Littlest Light	B. Hummel	Open	15.00	15.00
Schmid		**Disney Annuals**			
85-04-001	Snow Biz	Disney Studios	10,000	16.50	16.50
86-04-002	Tree for Two	Disney Studios	10,000	16.50	16.50
87-04-003	Merry Mouse Medley	Disney Studios	10,000	17.50	17.50
88-04-004	Warm Winter Ride	Disney Studios	10,000	19.50	19.50
89-04-005	Merry Mickey Claus	Disney Studios	10,000	23.00	23.00
90-04-006	Holly Jolly Christmas	Disney Studios	10,000	26.50	26.50
91-04-007	Mickey & Minnie's Rockin' Christmas	Disney Studios	10,000	26.50	26.50
Schmid/B.F.A.		**RFD Bell**			
79-01-001	Blossom	L. Davis	Closed	65.00	300-400.
79-01-002	Kate	L. Davis	Closed	65.00	300-400.
79-01-003	Willy	L. Davis	Closed	65.00	400.00
79-01-004	Caruso	L. Davis	Closed	65.00	300.00
79-01-005	Wilbur	L. Davis	Closed	65.00	300-350.

		ARTIST	EDITION	ISSUE	QUOTE
79-01-006	Old Blue Lead	L. Davis	Closed	65.00	275-300.
80-01-007	Cow Bell "Blossom"	L. Davis	Closed	65.00	65.00
80-01-008	Mule Bell "Kate"	L. Davis	Closed	65.00	65.00
80-01-009	Goat Bell "Willy"	L. Davis	Closed	65.00	65.00
80-01-010	Rooster Bell "Caruso"	L. Davis	Closed	65.00	65.00
80-01-011	Pig Bell "Wilbur"	L. Davis	Closed	65.00	65.00
80-01-012	Dog Bell "Old Blue and Lead"	L. Davis	Closed	65.00	65.00

CHRISTMAS ORNAMENTS

		ARTIST	EDITION	ISSUE	QUOTE
Kurt S. Adler Inc.	**Fabriché™ Ornament Series**				
92-01-001	Hugs And Kisses W1560	KS. Adler	Open	22.00	22.00
92-01-002	Hello Little One! W1561	KS. Adler	Open	22.00	22.00
92-01-003	Not a Creature Was Stirring W1563	KS. Adler	Open	22.00	22.00
92-01-004	Merry Chrismouse W1565	KS. Adler	Open	10.00	10.00
92-01-005	Christmas in the Air W1593	KS. Adler	Open	35.50	35.50
92-01-006	An Apron Full of Love W1594	M. Rothenberg	Open	27.00	27.00
93-01-007	Master Toymaker W1595	KS. Adler	Open	27.00	27.00
93-01-008	Homeward Bound W1596	KS. Adler	Open	27.00	27.00
93-01-009	Par For the Claus W1625	KS. Adler	Open	27.00	27.00
93-01-010	Santa With List W1510	KS. Adler	Open	20.00	20.00
94-01-011	Cookies For Santa W1639	KS. Adler	Open	28.00	28.00
94-01-012	All Star Santa W1665	KS. Adler	Open	27.00	27.00
94-01-011	Santa's Fishtales W1666	KS. Adler	Open	29.00	29.00
94-01-012	Firefighting Friends W1668	KS. Adler	Open	28.00	28.00
94-01-013	Checking His List W1634	KS. Adler	Open	23.50	23.50
94-01-014	Holiday Flight W1637	Smithsonian	Open	45.00	45.00
Kurt S. Adler Inc.	**Smithsonian Museum Fabriché™ Ornament Series**				
92-02-001	Holiday Drive W1580	KSA/Smithsonian	Open	38.00	38.00
92-02-002	Santa On a Bicycle W1547	KSA/Smithsonian	Open	31.00	31.00
Kurt S. Adler Inc.	**Steinbach Ornament Series**				
92-03-001	The King's Guards ES300	KS. Adler	Retrd.	27.00	27.00
Kurt S. Adler Inc.	**Christmas in Chelsea Collection**				
92-04-001	Allison Sitting in Chair W2812	J. Mostrom	Open	25.50	25.50
92-04-002	Christina W2812	J. Mostrom	Open	25.50	25.50
92-04-003	Holly W2709	J. Mostrom	Retrd.	21.00	21.00
92-04-004	Christopher W2709	J. Mostrom	Retrd.	21.00	21.00
92-04-005	Amanda W2709	J. Mostrom	Retrd.	21.00	21.00
92-04-006	Peony W2728	J. Mostrom	Open	20.00	20.00
92-04-007	Delphinium W2728	J. Mostrom	Open	20.00	20.00
92-04-008	Rose W2728	J. Mostrom	Open	20.00	20.00
92-04-009	Holly Hock W2728	J. Mostrom	Open	20.00	20.00
92-04-010	Amy W2729	J. Mostrom	Retrd.	21.00	21.00
92-04-011	Allison W2729	J. Mostrom	Retrd.	21.00	21.00
94-04-012	Alice, Marguerite W2973	J. Mostrom	Open	28.00	28.00
94-04-013	Guardian Angel With Baby W2974	J. Mostrom	Open	31.00	31.00
Kurt S. Adler Inc.	**Royal Heritage Collection**				
93-05-001	Nicholas W2923	J. Mostrom	Open	25.50	25.50
93-05-002	Patina W2923	J. Mostrom	Open	25.50	25.50
93-05-003	Sasha W2923	J. Mostrom	Open	25.50	25.50
93-05-004	Anastasia W2922	J. Mostrom	Retrd.	28.00	28.00
93-05-005	Elizabeth W2924	J. Mostrom	Open	25.50	25.50
93-05-006	Charles W2924	J. Mostrom	Open	25.50	25.50
93-05-007	Caroline W2924	J. Mostrom	Open	25.50	25.50
93-05-008	Joella W2979	J. Mostrom	Retrd.	27.00	27.00
93-05-009	Kelly W2979	J. Mostrom	Retrd.	27.00	27.00
94-05-010	Snow Princess W2971	J. Mostrom	Open	28.00	28.00
94-05-011	Ice Fairy, Winter Fairy W2972	J. Mostrom	Open	25.50	25.50
Kurt S. Adler Inc.	**Cornhusk Mice Ornament Series**				
93-06-001	Nutcracker Suite Fantasy Cornhusk Mice W2885	M. Rothenberg	Open	15.50	15.50
93-06-002	Ballerina Cornhusk Mice W2700	M. Rothenberg	Open	13.50	13.50
94-06-003	Little Pocahontas, Indian Brave W2950	M. Rothenberg	Open	18.00	18.00
94-06-004	Cowboy W2951	M. Rothenberg	Open	18.00	18.00
94-06-005	Drosselmeir Fairy, Mouse King W2949	M. Rothenberg	Open	16.00	16.00
94-06-006	Clara, Prince W2948	M. Rothenberg	Open	16.00	16.00
94-06-007	3" Father Christmas Ornament W2976	M. Rothenberg	Open	18.00	18.00
94-06-008	9" Father Christmas Ornament W2982	M. Rothenberg	Open	25.00	25.00
Kurt S. Adler Inc.	**Smithsonian Museum Carousel Ornament Series**				
87-07-001	The Antique Carousel Goat S3027/1	KSA/Smithsonian	Retrd.	14.50	14.50
87-07-002	The Antique Carousel Bunny S3027/2	KSA/Smithsonian	Retrd.	14.50	14.50
88-07-003	The Antique Carousel Horse S3027/3	KSA/Smithsonian	Retrd.	14.50	14.50
88-07-004	The Antique Carousel Giraffe S3027/4	KSA/Smithsonian	Retrd.	14.50	14.50
89-07-005	The Antique Carousel Lion S3027/5	KSA/Smithsonian	Retrd.	14.50	15.00
89-07-006	The Antique Carousel Cat S3027/6	KSA/Smithsonian	Retrd.	14.50	15.00
90-07-007	The Antique Carousel Zebra S3027/7	KSA/Smithsonian	Open	14.50	15.00
90-07-008	The Antique Carousel Seahorse S3027/8	KSA/Smithsonian	Open	14.50	15.00
91-07-009	The Antique Carousel Rooster S3027/9	KSA/Smithsonian	Retrd.	14.50	15.00
91-07-010	The Antique Carousel Horse S3027/10	KSA/Smithsonian	Open	14.50	15.00
92-07-011	The Antique Carousel Elephant S3027/11	KSA/Smithsonian	Open	14.50	14.50
92-07-012	The Antique Carousel Camel S3027/12	KSA/Smithsonian	Open	15.00	15.00
93-07-013	The Antique Carousel Tiger S3027/13	KSA/Smithsonian	Open	15.00	15.00
93-07-014	The Antique Carousel Horse S3027/14	KSA/Smithsonian	Open	15.00	15.00
94-07-013	The Antique Carousel Reindeer S3027/15	KSA/Smithsonian	Open	15.50	15.50
94-07-014	The Antique Carousel Pig S3027/16	KSA/Smithsonian	Open	15.50	15.50
Kurt S. Adler Inc.	**Little Dickens**				
94-08-001	Little Scrooge in Bathrobe W2959	J. Mostrom	Open	30.00	30.00
94-08-002	Little Scrooge in Overcoat W2960	J. Mostrom	Open	30.00	30.00
94-08-003	Little Bob Crachit W2961	J. Mostrom	Open	30.00	30.00
94-08-004	Little Mrs. Crachit W2962	J. Mostrom	Open	27.00	27.00
94-08-005	Little Tiny Tim W2963	J. Mostrom	Open	22.50	22.50
94-08-006	Little Marley's Ghost W2964	J. Mostrom	Open	33.50	33.50
Kurt S. Adler Inc.	**International Christmas**				
94-09-001	Poland-Marissa, Hedwig W2965	J. Mostrom	Open	27.00	27.00
94-09-002	Scotland-Bonnie, Douglas W2966	J. Mostrom	Open	27.00	27.00
94-09-003	Eskimo-Atom, Ukpik W2967	J. Mostrom	Open	28.00	28.00
94-09-004	Spain-Maria, Miguel W2968	J. Mostrom	Open	27.00	27.00
94-09-005	Germany-Katerina, Hans W2969	J. Mostrom	Open	27.00	27.00
94-09-006	Native American-White Dove, Little Wolf W2970	J. Mostrom	Open	28.00	28.00
Kurt S. Adler Inc.	**Night Before Christmas**				
94-10-001	Cathy, Johnny	J. Mostrom	Open	24.00	24.00
All God's Children	**Christmas Ornaments**				
87-01-001	Cameo Ornaments (set of 12)- D1912	M. Holcombe	Retrd.	144.00	2000.00
87-01-002	Doll Ornaments (set of 24) - D1924	M. Holcombe	Retrd.	336.00	3000.00

		ARTIST	EDITION	ISSUE	QUOTE
93-01-003	Santa with Scooty-1571	M. Holcombe	Retrd.	22.50	22.50
All God's Children	**Angel Dumpling**				
93-02-001	Eric-1570	M. Holcombe	Retrd.	22.50	22.50
94-02-002	Erica-1578	M. Holcombe	Yr.Iss.	22.50	22.50
Anheuser-Busch, Inc.	**A & Eagle Collector Ornament Series**				
91-01-001	Budweiser Girl-Circa 1890's N3178	A.-Busch, Inc.	Open	15.00	15.00
92-01-002	1893 Columbian Exposition N3649	A.-Busch, Inc.	Open	15.00	15.00
93-01-003	Greatest Triumph N4089	A.-Busch, Inc.	Open	15.00	15.00
Anheuser-Busch, Inc.	**Christmas Ornaments**				
92-02-001	Clydesdales Mini Plate Ornaments N3650	S. Sampson	Open	23.00	23.00
93-02-002	Budweiser Six-Pack Mini Plate Ornaments N4220	M. Urdahl	Open	10.00	10.00
Annalee Mobilitee	**Christmas Ornaments**				
85-01-001	Clown Head	A. Thorndike	5,701	6.95	175.00
92-01-002	3" Skier	A. Thorndike	8,332	14.45	175.00
93-01-003	Pepi Herman Crystal Ornament (artist proof)	A. Thorndike	1	N/A	750.00
93-01-004	Tree Top Star w/ 3" Angel (artist proof)	A. Thorndike	1	N/A	300.00
94-01-005	Annalee Crystal Ornament (prototype)	A. Thorndike	1	N/A	200.00
ANRI	**Ferrandiz Message Collection**				
89-01-001	Let the Heavens Ring	J. Ferrandiz	1,000	215.00	215.00
90-01-002	Hear The Angels Sing	J. Ferrandiz	1,000	225.00	225.00
ANRI	**Ferrandiz Woodcarvings**				
88-02-001	Heavenly Drummer	J. Ferrandiz	1,000	175.00	225.00
89-02-002	Heavenly Strings	J. Ferrandiz	1,000	190.00	190.00
ANRI	**Disney Four Star Collection**				
89-03-001	Maestro Mickey	Disney Studios	Yr.Iss.	25.00	25.00
90-03-002	Minnie Mouse	Disney Studios	Yr.Iss.	25.00	25.00
ANRI	**Christmas Firsts**				
94-04-001	Sarah Kay's First Christmas	S. Kay	500	140.00	140.00
Armani	**Christmas**				
91-01-001	1991 Christmas Ornament 799A	G. Armani	Retrd.	11.50	11.50
92-01-002	1992 Christmas Ornament 788F	G. Armani	Retrd.	23.50	23.50
93-01-003	1993 Christmas Ornament 892P	G. Armani	Retrd.	25.00	25.00
94-01-004	1994 Christmas Ornament 801P	G. Armani	Yr.Iss.	25.00	25.00
Artaffects	**Annual Christmas Ornaments**				
85-01-001	Papoose Ornament	G. Perillo	Unkn.	14.00	65.00
86-01-002	Christmas Cactus	G. Perillo	Unkn.	15.00	50.00
87-01-003	Annual Ornament	G. Perillo	Unkn.	15.00	35.00
88-01-004	Annual Ornament	G. Perillo	Yr.Iss.	18.00	25.00
89-01-005	Annual Ornament	G. Perillo	Yr.Iss.	18.00	25.00
90-01-006	Annual Ornament	G. Perillo	Yr.Iss.	19.50	19.50
91-01-007	Annual Ornament	G. Perillo	Yr.Iss.	19.50	19.50
Artaffects	**Annual Bell Ornaments**				
85-02-001	Home Sweet Wigwam	G. Perillo	Yr.Iss.	14.00	14.00
86-02-002	Peek-A-Boo	G. Perillo	Yr.Iss.	15.00	15.00
87-02-003	Annual Bell Ornament	G. Perillo	Yr.Iss.	15.00	15.00
88-02-004	Annual Bell Ornament	G. Perillo	Yr.Iss.	17.50	17.50
89-02-005	Annual Bell Ornament	G. Perillo	Yr.Iss.	17.50	17.50
90-02-006	Annual Bell Ornament	G. Perillo	Yr.Iss.	17.50	17.50
91-02-007	Annual Bell Ornament	G. Perillo	Yr.Iss.	19.50	19.50
Artaffects	**Sagebrush Kids Bell Ornaments**				
87-03-001	The Fiddler	G. Perillo	Open	9.00	9.00
87-03-002	The Harpist	G. Perillo	Open	9.00	9.00
87-03-003	Christmas Horn	G. Perillo	Open	9.00	9.00
87-03-004	The Gift	G. Perillo	Open	9.00	9.00
87-03-005	Christmas Candle	G. Perillo	Open	9.00	9.00
87-03-006	The Carolers	G. Perillo	Open	9.00	9.00
Artaffects	**Kachina Ornaments**				
91-04-001	Sun Kachina	G. Perillo	Open	17.50	17.50
91-04-002	Old Kachina	G. Perillo	Open	17.50	17.50
91-04-003	Snow Kachina	G. Perillo	Open	17.50	17.50
91-04-004	Dawn Kachina	G. Perillo	Open	17.50	17.50
91-04-005	Kachina Mother	G. Perillo	Open	17.50	17.50
91-04-006	Totem Kachina	G. Perillo	Open	17.50	17.50
Artaffects	**Sagebrush Kids Collection**				
91-05-001	Tee-Pee Ornament	G. Perillo	Open	15.00	15.00
91-05-002	Tee-Pee Ornament	G. Perillo	Open	15.00	15.00
91-05-003	Shield Ornament	G. Perillo	Open	15.00	15.00
91-05-004	Moccasin Ornament	G. Perillo	Open	15.00	15.00
Artaffects	**Simple Wonders**				
91-06-001	Kim	C. Roeda	Open	22.50	22.50
91-06-002	Brittany	C. Roeda	Open	22.50	22.50
91-06-003	Nicole	C. Roeda	Open	22.50	22.50
91-06-004	Megan	C. Roeda	Open	22.50	22.50
91-06-005	Little Feather	C. Roeda	Open	22.50	22.50
91-06-006	Ashley	C. Roeda	Open	22.50	22.50
92-06-007	Sweet Surprise	C. Roeda	Retrd.	15.00	15.00
94-06-008	Deck the Halls (White)	C. Roeda	Yr.Iss.	15.00	15.00
94-06-009	Deck the Halls (Black)	C. Roeda	Yr.Iss.	15.00	15.00
Artists of the World	**De Grazia Annual Ornaments**				
86-01-001	Pima. Indian Drummer Boy	T. De Grazia	Yr.Iss.	28.00	400-500.
87-01-002	White Dove	T. De Grazia	Yr.Iss.	30.00	90-250.
88-01-003	Flower Girl	T. De Grazia	Yr.Iss.	33.00	90-150.
89-01-004	Flower Boy	T. De Grazia	Yr.Iss.	35.00	90-150.
90-01-005	Pink Papoose	T. De Grazia	Yr.Iss.	35.00	95.00
90-01-006	Merry Little Indian	T. De Grazia	10,000	88.00	75-95.00
91-01-007	Christmas Prayer	T. De Grazia	Yr.Iss.	50.00	95.00
92-01-008	Bearing Gift	T. De Grazia	Yr.Iss.	55.00	67.50
93-01-009	Lighting the Way	T. De Grazia	Yr.Iss.	58.00	67.50
94-01-010	Warm Wishes	T. De Grazia	Yr.Iss.	65.00	65.00
95-01-011	Little Prayer	T. De Grazia	Yr.Iss.	49.50	49.50
Attic Babies	**Wooden Ornaments**				
93-01-001	Snowman	M. Maschino	12/94	17.95	17.95
93-01-001	Angel	M. Maschino	12/94	21.95	21.95
93-01-001	Stocking	M. Maschino	12/94	25.95	25.95
Band Creations	**Best Friends-Winter Wonderland**				
94-01-001	4 Assorted Angel Ornaments	Richards/Penfield	Open	5.00	5.00
Band Creations	**Best Friends-Trick or Treat Pals**				
94-01-002	Witch	Richards/Penfield	Open	10.00	10.00

		ARTIST	EDITION	ISSUE	QUOTE
Bing & Grondahl	**Christmas**				
85-01-001	Christmas Eve at the Farmhouse	E. Jensen	Closed	19.50	19.50
86-01-002	Silent Night, Holy Night	E. Jensen	Closed	19.50	25.00
87-01-003	The Snowman's Chrismtas Eve	E. Jensen	Closed	22.50	22.50
88-01-004	In the King's Garden	E. Jensen	Closed	25.00	25.00
89-01-005	Christmas Anchorage	E. Jensen	Closed	27.00	27.00
90-01-006	Changing of the Guards	E. Jensen	Closed	32.50	35.00
91-01-007	Copenhagen Stock Exchange	E. Jensen	Closed	34.50	34.50
92-01-008	Christmas at the Rectory	J. Steensen	Closed	36.50	36.50
93-01-009	Father Christmas in Copenhagen	J. Nielson	Closed	36.50	36.50
94-01-010	A Day at the Deer Park	J. Nielson	Yr.Iss.	36.50	36.50
95-01-011	The Towers of Copenhagen	J. Nielson	Yr.Iss.	36.50	36.50
Bing & Grondahl	**Christmas In America**				
86-02-001	Christmas Eve in Williamsburg	J. Woodson	Closed	12.50	90-150.
87-02-002	Christmas Eve at the White House	J. Woodson	Closed	15.00	15-60.00
88-02-003	Christmas Eve at Rockefeller Center	J. Woodson	Closed	18.50	18.50
89-02-004	Christmas in New England	J. Woodson	Closed	20.00	20-35.00
90-02-005	Christmas Eve at the Capitol	J. Woodson	Closed	20.00	25-45.00
91-02-006	Independence Hall	J. Woodson	Closed	23.50	23.50
92-02-007	Christmas in San Francisco	J. Woodson	Closed	25.00	25.00
93-02-008	Coming Home For Christmas	J. Woodson	Closed	25.00	25.00
94-02-009	Christmas Eve in Alaska	J. Woodson	Yr.Iss.	25.00	25.00
Bing & Grondahl	**Santa Claus**				
89-03-001	Santa's Workshop	H. Hansen	Yr.Iss.	20.00	22.00
90-03-002	Santa's Sleigh	H. Hansen	Yr.Iss.	20.00	22.00
91-03-003	The Journey	H. Hansen	Yr.Iss.	24.00	26.00
92-03-004	Santa's Arrival	H. Hansen	Yr.Iss.	25.00	25.00
93-03-005	Santa's Gifts	H. Hansen	Yr.Iss.	25.00	25.00
94-03-006	Christmas Stories	H. Hansen	Yr.Iss.	25.00	25.00
Boyds Collection Ltd.	**The Bearstone Collection™**				
94-01-001	Faith'-Angel Bear with Trumpet 2500	G. M. Lowenthal	Open	9.45	9.45
94-01-002	Hope'-Angel Bear with Wreath 2501	G. M. Lowenthal	Open	9.45	9.45
94-01-003	Charity'-Angel Bear with Star 2502	G. M. Lowenthal	Open	9.45	9.45
Brandywine Collectibles	**Williamsburg Ornaments**				
88-01-001	Bootmaker	M. Whiting	Closed	9.00	9.00
88-01-002	Apothocary	M. Whiting	Closed	9.00	9.00
88-01-003	Wigmaker	M. Whiting	Closed	9.00	9.00
88-01-004	Nicolson Shop	M. Whiting	Closed	9.00	9.00
88-01-005	Tarpley's Store	M. Whiting	Closed	9.00	9.00
88-01-006	Finnie Quarter	M. Whiting	Closed	9.00	9.00
89-01-004	Cole Shop	M. Whiting	Closed	9.00	9.00
89-01-005	Gunsmith	M. Whiting	Closed	9.00	9.00
89-01-006	Windmill	M. Whiting	Closed	9.00	9.00
89-01-007	Music Teacher	M. Whiting	Closed	9.00	9.00
Brandywine Collectibles	**Custom Collection**				
89-02-001	Lorain Lighthouse	M. Whiting	Closed	9.00	9.00
91-02-002	Smithfield VA. Courthouse	M. Whiting	Closed	9.00	9.00
94-02-003	Smithfield Clerk's Office	M. Whiting	Closed	9.00	9.00
Cast Art Industries	**Dreamsicles Ornaments**				
92-01-001	Cherub With Moon-DX260	K. Haynes	Closed	6.00	6.00
92-01-002	Praying Cherub-DX261	K. Haynes	Closed	6.00	6.00
92-01-003	Cherub With Star-DX262	K. Haynes	Closed	6.00	6.00
92-01-004	Cherub On Cloud-DX263	K. Haynes	Closed	6.00	6.00
92-01-005	Bunny-DX270	K. Haynes	Closed	6.00	6.00
92-01-006	Piggy-DX271	K. Haynes	Closed	6.00	6.00
92-01-007	Raccoon-DX272	K. Haynes	Closed	6.00	6.00
92-01-008	Squirrel-DX273	K. Haynes	Closed	6.00	6.00
92-01-009	Bear-DX274	K. Haynes	Closed	6.00	6.00
92-01-010	Lamb-DX275	K. Haynes	Closed	6.00	6.00
The Cat's Meow	**Christmas Ornaments**				
85-01-001	Rutledge House	F. Jones	Retrd.	4.00	75.00
85-01-002	Bancroft House	F. Jones	Retrd.	4.00	N/A
85-01-003	Grayling House	F. Jones	Retrd.	4.00	N/A
85-01-004	School	F. Jones	Retrd.	4.00	N/A
85-01-005	Chapel	F. Jones	Retrd.	4.00	N/A
85-01-006	Morton House	F. Jones	Retrd.	4.00	N/A
87-01-007	Globe Corner Bookstore	F. Jones	Retrd.	5.00	50.00
87-01-008	District #17 School	F. Jones	Retrd.	5.00	50.00
87-01-009	Kennedy Birthplace	F. Jones	Retrd.	5.00	26-75.00
87-01-010	Blacksmith Shop	F. Jones	Retrd.	5.00	50.00
87-01-011	Set/4	F. Jones	Retrd.	20.00	175-200.
95-01-012	Yaquina Bay Light	F. Jones	12/96	8.75	8.75
95-01-013	Holly Hill Farmhouse	F. Jones	12/96	8.75	8.75
95-01-014	Carnegie Library	F. Jones	12/96	8.75	8.75
95-01-015	Unitarian Church	F. Jones	12/96	8.75	8.75
95-01-016	St. James General Store	F. Jones	12/96	8.75	8.75
95-03-017	North Central School	F. Jones	12/96	8.75	8.75
Cazenovia Abroad	**Christmas Ornaments**				
68-01-001	Teddy Bear-P101TB	Unknown	Unkn.	9.00	34-45.00
68-01-002	Elephant-P102E	Unknown	Unkn.	9.00	34-45.00
68-01-003	Duck-P103D	Unknown	Unkn.	9.00	34-45.00
68-01-004	Bunny-P104B	Unknown	Unkn.	9.00	34-45.00
68-01-005	Cat-P105C	Unknown	Unkn.	9.00	34-45.00
68-01-006	Rooster-P106R	Unknown	Unkn.	10.00	34-45.00
68-01-007	Standing Angel-P107SA	Unknown	Unkn.	9.00	39-52.50
68-01-008	Tiptoe Angel-P108TTA	Unknown	Unkn.	10.00	34-45.00
69-01-009	Fawn-P109F	Unknown	Unkn.	12.00	45.00
70-01-010	Snow Man-P110SM	Unknown	Unkn.	12.00	45.00
70-01-011	Peace-P111P	Unknown	Unkn.	12.00	45.00
70-01-012	Porky-P112PK	Unknown	Unkn.	15.00	45.00
71-01-013	Kneeling Angel-P113KA	Unknown	Unkn.	15.00	48-65.00
72-01-014	Rocking Horse-P114RH	Unknown	Unkn.	15.00	48-65.00
73-01-015	Treetop Angel-P115TOP	Unknown	Unkn.	10.00	37-50.00
74-01-016	Owl-P116O	Unknown	Unkn.	15.00	45.00
75-01-017	Star-P117ST	Unknown	Unkn.	15.00	45.00
76-01-018	Hatching Chick-P118CH	Unknown	Unkn.	15.00	45.00
77-01-019	Raggedy Ann-P119RA	Unknown	Unkn.	18.00	39-52.50
78-01-020	Shell-P120SH	Unknown	Unkn.	20.00	34-45.00
79-01-021	Toy Soldier-P121TS	Unknown	Unkn.	20.00	34-45.00
80-01-022	Burro-P122BU	Unknown	Unkn.	20.00	34-45.00
81-01-023	Clown-P123CL	Unknown	Unkn.	25.00	34-45.00
82-01-024	Rebecca-P124RE	Unknown	Unkn.	25.00	34-45.00
83-01-025	Raggedy Andy-P125AND	Unknown	Unkn.	28.00	39-52.50
83-01-026	Mouse-P126MO	Unknown	Unkn.	28.00	39-52.50
84-01-027	Cherub-P127CB	Unknown	Unkn.	30.00	39-52.50
85-01-028	Shaggy Dog-P132SD	Unknown	Unkn.	45.00	50.00

		ARTIST	EDITION	ISSUE	QUOTE
86-01-029	Peter Rabbit-P133PR	Unknown	Unkn.	50.00	50.00
86-01-030	Big Sister-P134BS	Unknown	Unkn.	60.00	60.00
86-01-031	Little Brother-P135LB	Unknown	Unkn.	55.00	55.00
87-01-032	Lamb-P136LA	Unknown	Unkn.	60.00	60.00
87-01-033	Sea Horse-P137SE	Unknown	Unkn.	35.00	26-35.00
88-01-034	Partridge-P138PA	Unknown	Unkn.	70.00	70.00
88-01-035	Squirrel-P139SQ	Unknown	Unkn.	70.00	70.00
84-01-036	Reindeer & Sleigh-H100	Unknown	Unkn.	1250.00	1500.00
89-01-037	Swan-P140SW	Unknown	Open	45.00	45.00
90-01-038	Moravian Star-P141PS	Unknown	Open	65.00	65.00
91-01-039	Hedgehog-P142HH	Unknown	Open	65.00	65.00
91-01-040	Bunny Rabbit-P143BR	Unknown	Open	65.00	65.00
91-01-041	Angel-P144A	Unknown	Open	63.00	63.00
92-01-042	Humpty Dumpty-P145HD	Unknown	Open	70.00	70.00
Cazenovia Abroad	**Carousel**				
91-02-001	Flag Horse-A301CFH	Herschell-Spillman	2,649	75.00	75.00
91-02-002	Fishing Cat-A302CFH	Cernigliaro	2,649	75.00	75.00
91-02-003	Flirting Rabbit-A303CFH	Cernigliaro	2,649	75.00	75.00
92-02-004	Sneaky Tiger-A304LST	C. Looff	2,649	82.50	82.50
92-02-005	Spillman Polar Bear-A305HPB	Herschell-Spillman	2,649	82.50	82.50
92-02-006	Rose Horse-A306PRH	C.W. Parker	2,649	82.50	82.50
94-02-007	Flying Mane Jumping-A307LFM	Illions	2,649	82.50	82.50
94-02-008	Pig-A308DP	Cernigliaro	2,649	82.50	82.50
94-02-009	Zebra-A309DZ	Cernigliaro	2,649	82.50	82.50
Cazenovia Abroad	**Twelve Days of Christmas**				
94-03-001	Partridge in a Pear Tree A401PP	J. Kall	Open	85.00	85.00
94-03-002	Two Turtle Doves A402TT	J. Kall	Open	85.00	85.00
94-03-003	Three French Hens A403TF	J. Kall	Open	85.00	85.00
Christopher Radko	**1987 Holiday Collection**				
87-01-001	Circle of Santas 8811	C. Radko	Retrd.	16.95	48.00
87-01-002	Royal Porcelain 8812	C. Radko	Retrd.	16.95	48.00
87-01-003	Simply Cartiere 8817	C. Radko	Retrd.	16.95	48.00
87-01-004	Baby Balloon 8832	C. Radko	Retrd.	7.95	25.00
87-01-005	Grecian Column 8842	C. Radko	Retrd.	9.95	30.00
87-01-006	Ripples on Oval 8844	C. Radko	Retrd.	6.00	15.00
87-01-007	Satin Scepter 8847	C. Radko	Retrd.	8.95	30.00
87-01-008	Double Royal Drop 8856	C. Radko	Retrd.	25.00	70.00
87-01-009	Royal Diadem 8860	C. Radko	Retrd.	25.00	70.00
87-01-010	Mushroom in Winter 8862	C. Radko	Retrd.	12.00	40.00
87-01-011	Birdhouse 8873	C. Radko	Retrd.	10.00	30.00
87-01-012	Striped Balloon 8877	C. Radko	Retrd.	16.95	60.00
Christopher Radko	**1988 Holiday Collection**				
88-02-001	Faberge Oval 3	C. Radko	Retrd.	15.00	30.00
88-02-002	Celestial 4	C. Radko	Retrd.	15.00	35.00
88-02-003	Royal Porcelain 12	C. Radko	Retrd.	16.00	35.00
88-02-004	Gilded Leaves 13	C. Radko	Retrd.	16.00	30.00
88-02-005	Stained Glass 16	C. Radko	Retrd.	16.00	32.00
88-02-006	Alpine Flowers 22	C. Radko	Retrd.	16.00	30.00
88-02-007	Christmas Fanfare 50	C. Radko	Retrd.	15.00	35.00
88-02-008	Double Royal Star 56	C. Radko	Retrd.	23.00	60.00
88-02-009	Mushroom Winter 62	C. Radko	Retrd.	10.00	30.00
88-02-010	Crown Jewels 74	C. Radko	Retrd.	15.00	30.00
Christopher Radko	**1989 Holiday Collection**				
89-03-001	Lilac Sparkle 9-7	C. Radko	Retrd.	17.00	30.00
89-03-002	Alpine Flowers 9-43	C. Radko	Retrd.	17.00	30.00
89-03-003	Seahorse 9-54	C. Radko	Retrd.	10.00	30-45.00
89-03-004	Charlie Chaplin 9-55	C. Radko	Retrd.	8.50	45.00
89-03-005	Kim Ono 9-57	C. Radko	Retrd.	6.50	30.00
89-03-006	Joey Clown (light pink) 9-58	C. Radko	Retrd.	9.00	50.00
89-03-007	Smiling Sun 9-59	C. Radko	Retrd.	7.00	45.00
89-03-008	Shy Rabbit 9-61	C. Radko	Retrd.	7.00	50.00
89-03-009	Elf on Ball (matte) 9-62	C. Radko	Retrd.	9.50	45.00
89-03-010	Walrus 9-63	C. Radko	Retrd.	8.00	45.00
89-03-011	Fisher Frog 9-65	C. Radko	Retrd.	7.00	40.00
89-03-012	Shy Kitten 9-66	C. Radko	Retrd.	7.00	20.00
89-03-013	Hurricane Lamp 9-67	C. Radko	Retrd.	7.00	45.00
89-03-014	Parachute 9-68	C. Radko	Retrd.	6.50	20.00
89-03-015	Grecian Urn 9-69	C. Radko	Retrd.	9.00	35.00
89-03-016	Double Top 9-71	C. Radko	Retrd.	7.00	23.00
89-03-017	Serpent 9-72	C. Radko	Retrd.	7.00	17.50
89-03-018	Small Reflector 9-76	C. Radko	Retrd.	7.50	32.00
89-03-019	King Arthur (Lt. Blue) 9-103	C. Radko	Retrd.	12.00	45.00
Christopher Radko	**1990 Holiday Collection**				
90-04-001	Yarn Fight 23	C. Radko	Retrd.	17.00	35.00
90-04-002	Early Winter 24	C. Radko	Retrd.	10.00	29.95
90-04-003	Fat Lady 35	C. Radko	Retrd.	7.00	20.00
90-04-004	Nativity 36	C. Radko	Retrd.	6.00	25.00
90-04-005	Calla Lilly 38	C. Radko	Retrd.	7.00	23.00
90-04-006	Dublin Pipe 40	C. Radko	Retrd.	14.00	50.00
90-04-007	Goggle Eyes 44	C. Radko	Retrd.	9.00	45.00
90-04-008	Snowman on Ball 45	C. Radko	Retrd.	14.00	24.00
90-04-009	Angel on Harp 46	C. Radko	Retrd.	9.00	35.00
90-04-010	Lullaby 47	C. Radko	Retrd.	9.00	35.00
90-04-011	Mother Goose (blue bonnet/pink shawl) 52	C. Radko	Retrd.	10.00	45.00
90-04-012	Golden Puppy 53	C. Radko	Retrd.	8.00	45.00
90-04-013	Joey Clown (red striped) 55	C. Radko	Retrd.	14.00	35.00
90-04-014	Crowned Prince 56	C. Radko	Retrd.	14.00	45.00
90-04-015	Frog Under Balloon 58	C. Radko	Retrd.	14.00	45.00
90-04-016	Tuxedo Penquin 57	C. Radko	Retrd.	8.00	N/A
90-04-017	Walrus 59	C. Radko	Retrd.	8.50	45.00
90-04-018	Smiling Kite 63	C. Radko	Retrd.	14.00	45.00
90-04-019	Conch Shell 65	C. Radko	Retrd.	9.00	25.00
90-04-020	Eagle Medallion 67	C. Radko	Retrd.	9.00	40.00
90-04-021	Sunburst Fish (green/yellow) 68	C. Radko	Retrd.	13.00	28.00
90-04-022	Roly Poly Santa (Red bottom) 69	C. Radko	Retrd.	13.00	45.00
90-04-023	King Arthur (Red) 72	C. Radko	Retrd.	16.00	N/A
90-04-024	Peacock (on snowball) 74	C. Radko	Retrd.	18.00	50.00
90-04-025	Silent Movie (black hat) 75	C. Radko	Retrd.	8.50	45.00
90-04-026	Father Christmas 76	C. Radko	Retrd.	7.00	15.00
90-04-027	Happy Gnome 77	C. Radko	Retrd.	8.00	40.00
90-04-028	Small Nautilus Shell 78	C. Radko	Retrd.	7.00	22.00
90-04-029	Kim Ono 79	C. Radko	Retrd.	6.00	25.00
90-04-030	Santa on Ball 80	C. Radko	Retrd.	16.00	40.00
90-04-031	Ballooning Santa 85	C. Radko	Retrd.	20.00	60.00
90-04-032	Spin Top 90	C. Radko	Retrd.	11.00	35.00
90-04-033	Emerald City 92	C. Radko	Retrd.	7.50	40.00
90-04-034	Maracca 94	C. Radko	Retrd.	9.00	45.00

		ARTIST	EDITION	ISSUE	QUOTE
90-04-035	Rose Lamp 96	C. Radko	Retrd.	14.00	50.00

Christopher Radko — **1991 Holiday Collection**

		ARTIST	EDITION	ISSUE	QUOTE
91-05-001	Shy Elf 1	C. Radko	Retrd.	10.00	40.00
91-05-002	Pierre Le Berry 2	C. Radko	Retrd.	14.00	45.00
91-05-003	Harvest 3	C. Radko	Retrd.	13.50	24.50
91-05-004	Tiger 5	C. Radko	Retrd.	15.00	35.00
91-05-005	Irish Laddie 10	C. Radko	Retrd.	12.00	45.00
91-05-006	Chimney Santa 12	C. Radko	Retrd.	14.50	25.00
91-05-007	Shirley 15	C. Radko	Retrd.	16.00	50.00
91-05-008	Cosette 16	C. Radko	Retrd.	16.00	25.00
91-05-009	Altar Boy 18	C. Radko	Retrd.	16.00	31.00
91-05-010	Prince Umbrella 21	C. Radko	Retrd.	15.00	40.00
91-05-011	Dutch Boy 27	C. Radko	Retrd.	11.00	30.00
91-05-012	Dutch Girl 28	C. Radko	Retrd.	11.00	30.00
91-05-013	Lion's Head 31	C. Radko	Retrd.	16.00	35.00
91-05-014	Dawn & Dust 34	C. Radko	Retrd.	14.00	24.50
91-05-015	Hatching Duck 35	C. Radko	Retrd.	14.00	50.00
91-05-016	Proud Peacock 37	C. Radko	Retrd.	23.00	36.40
91-05-017	Woodland Santa 38	C. Radko	Retrd.	14.00	29.00
91-05-018	Fruit in Balloon 40	C. Radko	Retrd.	22.00	45.00
91-05-019	Aztec Bird 41	C. Radko	Retrd.	20.00	60.00
91-05-020	Apache 42	C. Radko	Retrd.	8.50	24.50
91-05-021	Sally Ann 43	C. Radko	Retrd.	8.00	25.00
91-05-022	Fisher Frog 44	C. Radko	Retrd.	11.00	45.00
91-05-023	Tabby 46	C. Radko	Retrd.	8.00	30-50.00
91-05-024	Bowery Kid 50	C. Radko	Retrd.	14.50	25.00
91-05-025	Prince on Ball (pink/blue/green) 51	C. Radko	Retrd.	15.00	45.00
91-05-026	Sleepy Time Santa 52	C. Radko	Retrd.	15.00	50.00
91-05-027	Pipe Smoking Monkey 54	C. Radko	Retrd.	11.00	32-45.00
91-05-028	Barnum Clown 56	C. Radko	Retrd.	15.00	32-45.00
91-05-029	Mother Goose 57	C. Radko	Retrd.	11.00	35.00
91-05-030	Comet 62	C. Radko	Retrd.	9.00	35.00
91-05-031	Tulip Fairy 63	C. Radko	Retrd.	16.00	N/A
91-05-032	Anchor America 65	C. Radko	Retrd.	21.50	38.00
91-05-033	Sunshine 67	C. Radko	Retrd.	22.00	39.95
91-05-034	Aspen 76	C. Radko	Retrd.	20.50	N/A
91-05-035	Edwardian Lace 82	C. Radko	Retrd.	21.50	50.00
91-05-036	Florentine 83	C. Radko	Retrd.	22.00	39.95
91-05-037	Villandry 87	C. Radko	Retrd.	21.00	45.00
91-05-038	Her Purse 88	C. Radko	Retrd.	10.00	26.50
91-05-039	Dapper Shoe 89	C. Radko	Retrd.	10.00	23-35.00
91-05-040	Flower Child 90	C. Radko	Retrd.	13.00	40.00
91-05-041	Rainbow Bird 92	C. Radko	Retrd.	16.00	25.00
91-05-042	King Arthur (Blue) 95	C. Radko	Retrd.	18.50	N/A
91-05-043	Raspberry & Lime 96	C. Radko	Retrd.	12.00	50.00
91-05-044	Einstein Kite 98	C. Radko	Retrd.	20.00	32.00
91-05-045	Melon Slice 99	C. Radko	Retrd.	18.00	30.40
91-05-046	Trumpet Man 100	C. Radko	Retrd.	21.00	35.00
91-05-047	Madonna & Child 103	C. Radko	Retrd.	15.00	35.00
91-05-048	Chance Encounter 104	C. Radko	Retrd.	13.50	N/A
91-05-049	Sitting Bull 107	C. Radko	Retrd.	16.00	34.00
91-05-050	Sunburst Fish 108	C. Radko	Retrd.	15.00	28.00
91-05-051	Ballooning Santa 110	C. Radko	Retrd.	23.00	60.00
91-05-052	Jemima's Child 111	C. Radko	Retrd.	16.00	35-45.00
91-05-053	Polish Folk Art 116	C. Radko	Retrd.	20.50	45.00
91-05-054	By the Nile 124	C. Radko	Retrd.	21.50	39.50
91-05-055	Olympiad 125	C. Radko	Retrd.	22.00	39.50
91-05-056	Vienna 1901 127	C. Radko	Retrd.	21.50	N/A
91-05-057	Red Star 129	C. Radko	Retrd.	21.50	39.95
91-05-058	Blue Rainbow 136	C. Radko	Retrd.	21.50	39.95
91-05-059	All Weather Santa 137	C. Radko	Retrd.	32.00	69.95
91-05-060	Star Quilt 139	C. Radko	Retrd.	21.50	39.95
91-05-061	Aztec 141	C. Radko	Retrd.	21.50	39.95

Christopher Radko — **1992 Holiday Collection**

		ARTIST	EDITION	ISSUE	QUOTE
92-06-001	Mother Goose 37	C. Radko	Retrd.	15.00	25.00
92-06-002	Virgin Mary 46	C. Radko	Retrd.	20.00	29.00
92-06-003	Cheerful Sun 50	C. Radko	Retrd.	18.00	24.50
92-06-004	Little League 53	C. Radko	Retrd.	20.00	25-35.00
92-06-005	Circus lady 54	C. Radko	Retrd.	12.00	15.00
92-06-006	Her Slipper 56	C. Radko	Retrd.	17.00	22.00
92-06-007	Tulip Fairy 57	C. Radko	Retrd.	18.00	23-30.00
92-06-008	Clown Snake 62	C. Radko	Retrd.	22.00	27.00
92-06-009	Pierre Winterberry 64	C. Radko	Retrd.	17.00	25.00
92-06-010	Barbie's Mom 69	C. Radko	Retrd.	18.00	26.00
92-06-011	Diva 73	C. Radko	Retrd.	17.00	21-25.00
92-06-012	Harlequin Tier Drop 74	C. Radko	Retrd.	36.00	45.00
92-06-013	Downhill Racer 76	C. Radko	Retrd.	34.00	42.00
92-06-014	Royal Scepter 77	C. Radko	Retrd.	36.00	50.00
92-06-015	Sleepytime Santa (pink) 81	C. Radko	Retrd.	18.00	40.00
92-06-016	Fruit in Balloon 83	C. Radko	Retrd.	28.00	60.00
92-06-017	Tuxedo Santa 88	C. Radko	Retrd.	22.00	35.00
92-06-018	Rainbow Parasol 90	C. Radko	Retrd.	30.00	N/A
92-06-019	Seahorse 92	C. Radko	Retrd.	20.00	45.00
92-06-020	Sitting Bull 93	C. Radko	Retrd.	26.00	45.00
92-06-021	Cowboy Santa 94	C. Radko	Retrd.	24.00	N/A
92-06-022	Folk Art Set 95	C. Radko	Retrd.	10.00	13.00
92-06-023	Serpents of Paradise 97	C. Radko	Retrd.	13.00	16-19.00
92-06-024	Candy Trumpet man (red) 98	C. Radko	Retrd.	27.00	45.00
92-06-025	Jumbo 99	C. Radko	Retrd.	31.00	35.30
92-06-026	Two Sided Santa Reflector 102	C. Radko	Retrd.	28.00	35.00
92-06-027	Forest Friends 103	C. Radko	Retrd.	14.00	17.50
92-06-028	Talking Pipe (black stem) 104	C. Radko	Retrd.	26.00	40.00
92-06-029	Santa in Winter White 106	C. Radko	Retrd.	28.00	60.00
92-06-030	St. Nickcicle 107	C. Radko	Retrd.	26.00	33.00
92-06-031	Primary Colors 108	C. Radko	Retrd.	30.00	42.50
92-06-032	Tropical Fish 109	C. Radko	Retrd.	17.00	17.00
92-06-033	Stardust Joey 110	C. Radko	Retrd.	16.00	25.00
92-06-034	Woodland Santa 111	C. Radko	Retrd.	20.00	29.00
92-06-035	Russian Imperial 112	C. Radko	Retrd.	25.00	31.50
92-06-036	Choir Boy 114	C. Radko	Retrd.	24.00	30.00
92-06-037	Dolly Madison 115	C. Radko	Retrd.	17.00	21.00
92-06-038	Butterfly Bouquet 119	C. Radko	Retrd.	26.50	33.00
92-06-039	Aspen 120	C. Radko	Retrd.	26.00	33.00
92-06-040	Victorian Santa & Angel Balloon 122	C. Radko	Retrd.	68.00	91.00
92-06-041	Christmas Cardinals 123	C. Radko	Retrd.	26.00	33.00
92-06-042	Delft Design 124	C. Radko	Retrd.	26.50	35.00
92-06-043	Ziegfeld Follies 126	C. Radko	Retrd.	27.00	40.00
92-06-044	Ice Poppies 127	C. Radko	Retrd.	26.00	32.00
92-06-045	Vienna 1901 128	C. Radko	Retrd.	27.00	40.00
92-06-046	Celestial 129	C. Radko	Retrd.	26.00	40.00
92-06-047	Russian Star 130	C. Radko	Retrd.	26.00	32-40.00
92-06-048	Florentine 131	C. Radko	Retrd.	27.00	40.00
92-06-049	Water Lilies 133	C. Radko	Retrd.	26.00	45.00
92-06-050	Sputniks 134	C. Radko	Retrd.	25.50	32.00
92-06-051	Elf Reflectors 136	C. Radko	Retrd.	28.00	36.00
92-06-052	Merry Christmas Maiden 137	C. Radko	Retrd.	26.00	N/A
92-06-053	By the Nile 139	C. Radko	Retrd.	27.00	33-40.00
92-06-054	Elephant on Parade 141	C. Radko	Retrd.	26.00	33-35.00
92-06-055	Christmas Rose 143	C. Radko	Retrd.	25.50	55.00
92-06-056	King of Prussia 149	C. Radko	Retrd.	27.00	33-35.00
92-06-057	Neopolitan Angels 152	C. Radko	Retrd.	27.00	55.00
92-06-058	Winter Wonderland 156	C. Radko	Retrd.	26.00	33.00
92-06-059	Pink Lace 158	C. Radko	Retrd.	28.00	36.00
92-06-060	Chevron 160	C. Radko	Retrd.	28.00	35.00
92-06-061	Tiffany Bright 161	C. Radko	Retrd.	28.00	N/A
92-06-062	Alpine Flowers 162	C. Radko	Retrd.	28.00	36.00
92-06-063	Kitty Rattle 166	C. Radko	Retrd.	18.00	70.00
92-06-064	Norweigian Princess 170	C. Radko	Retrd.	15.00	22.00
92-06-065	Floral Cascade Tier Drop 175	C. Radko	Retrd.	32.00	41-45.00
92-06-066	Star of Wonder 177	C. Radko	Retrd.	27.00	35.00
92-06-067	Thunderbolt 178	C. Radko	Retrd.	60.00	59.95
92-06-068	Elephant Reflector 181	C. Radko	Retrd.	17.00	25.00
92-06-069	Faith, Hope & Love 183	C. Radko	Retrd.	12.00	N/A
92-06-070	Gabriel's Trumpets 188	C. Radko	Retrd.	20.00	25.00
92-06-071	Holly Finial 200	C. Radko	Retrd.	70.00	83.00
92-06-072	Harold Lloyd Reflector 218	C. Radko	Retrd.	70.00	100.00
92-06-073	To Grandma's House 239	C. Radko	Retrd.	20.00	N/A
92-06-074	Ice Pear 241	C. Radko	Retrd.	20.00	26.00

Christopher Radko — **1993 Holiday Collection**

		ARTIST	EDITION	ISSUE	QUOTE
93-07-001	Tweeter 94	C. Radko	Retrd.	3.20	6.00
93-07-002	Waddles 95	C. Radko	Retrd.	3.80	11.00
93-07-003	Monkey Man 97	C. Radko	Retrd.	16.00	16.00
93-07-004	Snowday Santa 98	C. Radko	Retrd.	20.00	27.00
93-07-005	Beyond the Stars 108	C. Radko	Retrd.	18.50	20.00
93-07-006	Polar Bears 112A	C. Radko	Retrd.	15.50	14.50
93-07-007	Blue Top 114	C. Radko	Retrd.	16.00	16.00
93-07-008	Tuxedo Santa 117	C. Radko	Retrd.	21.90	29.00
93-07-009	Mr. & Mrs. Claus 121	C. Radko	Retrd.	17.90	18.00
93-07-010	Angel of Peace 132	C. Radko	Retrd.	17.00	24.00
93-07-011	Saraband 140	C. Radko	Retrd.	27.80	35.00
93-07-012	Cinderella's Bluebirds 145	C. Radko	Retrd.	25.90	26.00
93-07-013	Pennsylvania Dutch 146	C. Radko	Retrd.	26.80	33.00
93-07-014	Deco Snowfall 147	C. Radko	Retrd.	26.80	33.00
93-07-015	French Rose 152	C. Radko	Retrd.	26.60	27-33.00
93-07-016	Rainbow Reflector 154	C. Radko	Retrd.	26.60	35.00
93-07-017	Serenade Pink 157	C. Radko	Retrd.	26.80	35.00
93-07-018	Cold Fish 158	C. Radko	Retrd.	25.80	26.00
93-07-019	Winterbirds 164	C. Radko	Retrd.	26.80	27.00
93-07-020	Copenhagen 166	C. Radko	Retrd.	26.80	55.00
93-07-021	Little Doggie 180	C. Radko	Retrd.	7.00	15.00
93-07-022	Center Ring (Exclusive) 192	C. Radko	Retrd.	30.80	38.00
93-07-023	Downhill Racer 195	C. Radko	Retrd.	30.00	36.00
93-07-024	Sweetheart 202	C. Radko	Retrd.	16.00	18.00
93-07-025	Star Children 208	C. Radko	Retrd.	18.00	25.00
93-07-026	Monterey 209	C. Radko	Retrd.	27.90	22.00
93-07-027	One Small Leap 222	C. Radko	Retrd.	26.00	33.00
93-07-028	Centurian 224	C. Radko	Retrd.	25.50	30.50
93-07-029	Nellie (Italian ornament) 225	C. Radko	Retrd.	27.50	65.00
93-07-030	Light in the Windows 229	C. Radko	Retrd.	24.50	29.50
93-07-031	V.I.P. 230	C. Radko	Retrd.	23.00	23.00
93-07-032	Grecian Urn 231	C. Radko	Retrd.	23.00	23.00
93-07-033	English Kitchen 234	C. Radko	Retrd.	26.00	28.00
93-07-034	Stocking Stuffers 236	C. Radko	Retrd.	16.00	23.00
93-07-035	Aladdin's Lamp 237	C. Radko	Retrd.	20.00	27.00
93-07-036	Auld Lang Syne 246	C. Radko	Retrd.	15.00	22.00
93-07-037	SnowDance 247	C. Radko	Retrd.	29.00	36.00
93-07-038	Circus Seal 249	C. Radko	Retrd.	28.00	35.00
93-07-039	Forest Friends 250	C. Radko	Retrd.	28.00	35.00
93-07-040	Emperor's Pet 253	C. Radko	Retrd.	22.00	29.00
93-07-041	Pagoda 258	C. Radko	Retrd.	8.00	15.00
93-07-042	Grandpa Bear 260	C. Radko	Retrd.	12.80	13-20.00
93-07-043	Geisha Girls 261	C. Radko	Retrd.	11.90	12-19.00
93-07-044	Mushroom Elf 267	C. Radko	Retrd.	17.90	25.00
93-07-045	Rainbow Shark 277	C. Radko	Retrd.	18.00	40.00
93-07-046	Shy Rabbit 280	C. Radko	Retrd.	14.00	21.00
93-07-047	Monterey 290	C. Radko	Retrd.	15.00	15-22.00
93-07-048	Bell House Boy 291	C. Radko	Retrd.	21.00	28.00
93-07-049	Chimney Sweep Bell 294	C. Radko	Retrd.	26.00	28.00
93-07-050	Majestic Reflector 312	C. Radko	Retrd.	70.00	70.00
93-07-051	Calla Lilly 314	C. Radko	Retrd.	12.90	20.00
93-07-052	Rose Pointe Finial 323	C. Radko	Retrd.	34.00	34.00
93-07-053	Bishop of Myra 327	C. Radko	Retrd.	19.90	27.00
93-07-054	Sloopy Snowman 328	C. Radko	Retrd.	19.90	27.00
93-07-055	Texas Star 338	C. Radko	Retrd.	7.50	8.00
93-07-056	Sail by Starlight 339	C. Radko	Retrd.	11.80	14-19.00
93-07-057	Enchanted Gardens 341	C. Radko	Retrd.	5.50	13.00
93-07-058	Christmas Stars 342	C. Radko	Retrd.	14.00	21.00
93-07-059	Pompadour 344	C. Radko	Retrd.	8.80	11.00
93-07-060	Starlight Santa 348	C. Radko	Retrd.	11.90	19.00
93-07-061	Honey Bear 352	C. Radko	Retrd.	13.90	21.00
93-07-062	U-Boat 353	C. Radko	Retrd.	15.50	23.00
93-07-063	Little Eskimo 355	C. Radko	Retrd.	13.90	21.00
93-07-064	Confucius 363	C. Radko	Retrd.	19.00	28.00
93-07-065	Apache 357	C. Radko	Retrd.	13.90	14-21.00
93-07-066	Gypsy Girl 371	C. Radko	Retrd.	16.00	18-23.00
93-07-067	Kitty Rattle 374	C. Radko	Retrd.	17.80	25.00
93-07-068	Smithy 378	C. Radko	Retrd.	17.90	25.00
93-07-069	Purse 389	C. Radko	Retrd.	15.60	16.00
93-07-070	Quartet 392	C. Radko	Retrd.	3.60	11.00
93-07-071	Spider & the Fly 393	C. Radko	Retrd.	6.40	14.00
93-07-072	Christmas Express 394 (Garland)	C. Radko	Retrd.	58.00	58-125.
93-07-073	Ice Star Santa 405	C. Radko	Retrd.	38.00	47.00
93-07-074	Evening Star Santa 409	C. Radko	Retrd.	59.00	85.00
93-07-075	Alpine Village 420	C. Radko	Retrd.	23.80	35.00
93-07-076	Holiday Spice 422	C. Radko	Retrd.	24.00	24.00

Christopher Radko — **Christopher Radko Family of Collectors**

		ARTIST	EDITION	ISSUE	QUOTE
93-08-001	Angels We Have Heard on High SP1	C. Radko	Retrd.	50.00	155.00
94-08-002	Starbuck Santa SP3	C. Radko	Yr.Iss.	75.00	75.00

Christopher Radko — **Twelve Days of Christmas**

		ARTIST	EDITION	ISSUE	QUOTE
93-09-001	Partridge in a Pear Tree SP2	C. Radko	5,000	35.00	110-300.

		ARTIST	EDITION	ISSUE	QUOTE
94-09-002	Two Turtle Doves SP4	C. Radko	10,000	28.00	28.00
Christopher Radko	**Aids Awareness**				
93-10-001	A Shy Rabbit's Heart 462	C. Radko	Retrd.	15.00	27-75.00
94-10-002	Frosty Cares SP5	C. Radko	Yr.Iss.	25.00	25.00
Christopher Radko	**Pediatrics Cancer Research**				
94-11-001	A Gifted Santa 70	C. Radko	Yr.Iss.	25.00	25.00
Christopher Radko	**Event Only**				
93-12-001	Littlest Snowman 347S	C. Radko	Retrd.	15.00	22.00
94-12-002	Roly Poly 94125E	C. Radko	Yr.Iss.	22.00	22.00
Cybis	**Christmas Collection**				
83-01-001	1983 Holiday Bell	Cybis	Yr.Iss.	145.00	1000.00
84-01-002	1984 Holiday Ball	Cybis	Yr.Iss.	145.00	700.00
85-01-003	1985 Holiday Angel	Cybis	Yr.Iss.	75.00	500.00
86-01-004	1986 Holiday Cherub Ornament	Cybis	Yr.Iss.	75.00	500.00
87-01-005	1987 Heavenly Angels	Cybis	Yr.Iss.	95.00	400.00
88-01-006	1988 Holiday Ornament	Cybis	Yr.Iss.	95.00	375.00
Department 56	**Snowbabies Ornaments**				
86-01-001	Sitting, Lite-Up, Clip-On, 7952-9	Department 56	Closed	7.00	25-35.00
86-01-002	Crawling, Lite-Up, Clip-On, 7953-7	Department 56	Closed	7.00	15-28.00
86-01-003	Winged, Lite-Up, Clip-On, 7954-5	Department 56	Closed	7.00	35-44.00
86-01-004	Snowbaby on Brass Ribbon, 7961-8	Department 56	Closed	8.00	50-100.
87-01-005	Moon Beams, 7951-0	Department 56	Open	7.50	7.50
87-01-006	Snowbaby Adrift Lite-Up, Clip-On, 7969-3	Department 56	Closed	8.50	80-100.
87-01-007	Mini, Winged Pair, Lite-Up, Clip-On, 7976-6	Department 56	Open	9.00	9.00
88-01-008	Twinkle Little Star, 7980-4	Department 56	Closed	7.00	60-81.00
89-01-009	Noel, 7988-0	Department 56	Open	7.50	7.50
89-01-010	Surprise, 7989-8	Department 56	Open	12.00	12.00
89-01-011	Star Bright, 7990-1	Department 56	Open	7.50	7.50
90-01-012	Rock-A-Bye Baby, 7939-1	Department 56	Open	7.00	7.00
90-01-013	Penguin, Lite-Up, Clip-On, 7940-5	Department 56	Closed	5.00	12-25.00
90-01-014	Polar Bear, Lite-Up, Clip-On, 7941-3	Department 56	Closed	5.00	12-25.00
91-01-015	Swinging On a Star, 6810-1	Department 56	Open	9.50	9.50
91-01-016	My First Star, 6811-0	Department 56	Open	7.00	7.00
92-01-017	Snowbabies Icicle With Star, 6825-0	Department 56	Open	16.00	16.00
92-01-018	Starry, Starry Night, 6830-6	Department 56	Open	12.50	12.50
93-01-019	Wee...This is Fun!, 6847-0	Department 56	Open	13.50	13.50
93-01-020	Sprinkling Stars in the Sky, 6848-9	Department 56	Open	12.50	12.50
94-01-021	Gathering Stars in the Sky, 6855-1	Department 56	Open	12.50	12.50
94-01-022	First Star Jinglebaby, 6858-6	Department 56	Open	10.00	10.00
94-01-023	Little Drummer Jinglebaby, 6859-4	Department 56	Open	10.00	10.00
Department 56	**CCP Ornaments-Flat**				
86-02-001	Christmas Carol Houses, set of 3 (6504-8)	Department 56	Closed	13.00	45-90.00
86-02-002	Fezziwig's Warehouse	Department 56	Closed	4.35	N/A
86-02-003	Scrooge and Marley Countinghouse	Department 56	Closed	4.35	N/A
86-02-004	The Cottage of Bob Cratchit & Tiny Tim	Department 56	Closed	4.35	N/A
86-02-005	New England Village, set of 7 (6536-6)	Department 56	Closed	25.00	275-325.
86-02-006	Apothecary Shop	Department 56	Closed	3.50	18-25.00
86-02-007	General Store	Department 56	Closed	3.50	32-45.00
86-02-008	Nathaniel Bingham Fabrics	Department 56	Closed	3.50	20.00
86-02-009	Livery Stable & Boot Shop	Department 56	Closed	3.50	15.00
86-02-010	Steeple Church	Department 56	Closed	3.50	70-115.
86-02-011	Brick Town Hall	Department 56	Closed	3.50	30-50.00
86-02-012	Red Schoolhouse	Department 56	Closed	3.50	60.00
Department 56	**Christmas Carol Character Ornaments-Flat**				
86-03-001	Christmas Carol Characters, set of 3 (6505-6)	Department 56	Closed	13.00	42-80.00
86-03-002	Bob Cratchit & Tiny Tim	Department 56	Closed	4.35	30-75.00
86-03-003	Scrooge	Department 56	Closed	4.35	30.00
86-03-004	Poulterer	Department 56	Closed	4.35	30.00
Department 56	**Village Light-Up Ornaments**				
85-04-001	Dickens' Village, set of 8 (6521-8)	Department 56	Closed	48.00	180-195.
85-04-002	Crowntree Inn	Department 56	Closed	6.00	140.00
85-04-003	Candle Shop	Department 56	Closed	6.00	25-35.00
85-04-004	Green Grocer	Department 56	Closed	6.00	25-35.00
85-04-005	Golden Swan Baker	Department 56	Closed	6.00	17-30.00
85-04-006	Bean and Son Smithy Shop	Department 56	Closed	6.00	25.00
85-04-007	Abel Beesley Butcher	Department 56	Closed	6.00	17-25.00
85-04-008	Jones & Co. Brush & Basket Shop	Department 56	Closed	6.00	30-40.00
85-04-009	Dickens' Village Church	Department 56	Closed	6.00	48.00
87-04-010	Dickens' Village, set of 6 (6520-0)	Department 56	Closed	36.00	100-165.
87-04-011	Blythe Pond Mill House	Department 56	Closed	6.00	30-55.00
87-04-012	Barley Bree Farmhouse	Department 56	Closed	6.00	20-30.00
87-04-013	The Old Curiosity Shop	Department 56	Closed	6.00	35-42.00
87-04-014	Kenilworth Castle	Department 56	Closed	6.00	56-82.00
87-04-015	Brick Abbey	Department 56	Closed	6.00	80-110.
87-04-016	Chesterton Manor House	Department 56	Closed	6.00	40-60.00
87-04-017	Dickens' Village, set of 14 (6521-8, 6520-0)	Department 56	Closed	84.00	325-350.
87-04-018	Christmas Carol Cottages, set of 3 (6513-7)	Department 56	Closed	17.00	80.00
87-04-019	Fezziwig's Warehouse	Department 56	Closed	6.00	25-30.00
87-04-020	Scrooge & Marley Countinghouse	Department 56	Closed	6.00	15-25.00
87-04-021	The Cottage of Bob Cratchit & Tiny Tim	Department 56	Closed	6.00	15-25.00
86-04-022	New England Village, set of 7 (6533-1)	Department 56	Closed	42.00	325.00
86-04-023	Apothecary Shop	Department 56	Closed	6.00	18-25.00
86-04-024	General Store	Department 56	Closed	6.00	35-60.00
86-04-025	Nathaniel Bingham Fabrics	Department 56	Closed	6.00	30-40.00
86-04-026	Livery Stable & Boot Shop	Department 56	Closed	6.00	20-35.00
86-04-027	Steeple Church	Department 56	Closed	6.00	125-150.
86-04-028	Brick Town Hall	Department 56	Closed	6.00	35-50.00
86-04-029	Red Schoolhouse	Department 56	Closed	6.00	65-78.00
87-04-030	New England Village, set of 6 (6534-0)	Department 56	Closed	36.00	200-275.
87-04-031	Timber Knoll Log Cabin	Department 56	Closed	6.00	108-135.
87-04-032	Smythe Woolen Mill	Department 56	Closed	6.00	150-168.
87-04-033	Jacob Adams Farmhouse	Department 56	Closed	6.00	58.00
87-04-034	Jacob Adams Barn	Department 56	Closed	6.00	55-78.00
87-04-035	Craggy Cove Lighthouse	Department 56	Closed	6.00	100-140.
87-04-036	Weston Train Station	Department 56	Closed	6.00	50.00
87-04-037	New England Village, set of 13 (6533-1, 6534-0)	Department 56	Closed	78.00	495-775.
Department 56	**Miscellaneous Ornaments**				
83-05-001	Snow Village Wood Ornaments, set of 6, 5099-7	Department 56	Closed	30.00	N/A
83-05-002	Gabled House	Department 56	Closed	5.00	50-75.00
83-05-003	Swiss Chalet	Department 56	Closed	5.00	50.00
83-05-004	Countryside Church	Department 56	Closed	5.00	50-150.

		ARTIST	EDITION	ISSUE	QUOTE
83-05-005	Carriage House	Department 56	Closed	5.00	50.00
83-05-006	Centennial House	Department 56	Closed	5.00	50-150.
83-05-007	Pioneer Church	Department 56	Closed	5.00	50.00
84-05-008	Dickens 2-sided Tin Ornaments, set of 6, 6522-6	Department 56	Closed	12.00	165-260.
84-05-009	Crowntree Inn	Department 56	Closed	2.00	45.00
84-05-010	Green Grocer	Department 56	Closed	2.00	45.00
84-05-011	Golden Swan Baker	Department 56	Closed	2.00	45.00
84-05-012	Bean and Son Smithy Shop	Department 56	Closed	2.00	45.00
84-05-013	Abel Beesley Butcher	Department 56	Closed	2.00	45.00
84-05-014	Jones & Co. Brush & Basket Shop	Department 56	Closed	2.00	45.00
88-05-015	Christmas Carol- Scrooge's Head, 5912-9	Department 56	Closed	13.00	30-35.00
88-05-016	Christmas Carol- Tiny Tim's Head, 5913-7	Department 56	Closed	10.00	25-40.00
88-05-017	Christmas Carol- Bob & Mrs. Cratchit, 5914-5	Department 56	Closed	18.00	20-44.00
88-05-018	Balsam Bell Brass Dickens' Candlestick, 6244-8	Department 56	Closed	3.00	15.00
88-05-019	Cherub on Brass Ribbon, 8248-1	Department 56	Closed	8.00	50.00
88-05-020	Teddy Bear on Brass Ribbon, 8263-5	Department 56	Closed	7.00	65.00
94-05-021	Dickens Village Dedlock Arms Ornament, 9872-8, (porcelain, gift boxed)	Department 56	Open	12.50	12.50
Duncan Royale	**History Of Santa Claus**				
92-01-001	Santa I (set of 12)	Duncan Royale	Open	144.00	144.00
92-01-002	Santa II (set of 12)	Duncan Royale	Open	144.00	144.00
Enesco Corporation	**Precious Moments Ornaments**				
83-01-001	Surround Us With Joy-E-0513	S. Butcher	Yr.Iss.	9.00	60-65.00
83-01-002	Mother Sew Dear-E-0514	S. Butcher	Open	9.00	16-25.00
83-01-003	To A Special Dad-E-0515	S. Butcher	Suspd.	9.00	30.00
83-01-004	The Purr-fect Grandma-E-0516	S. Butcher	Open	9.00	16-25.00
83-01-005	The Perfect Grandpa-E-0517	S. Butcher	Suspd.	9.00	25-40.00
83-01-006	Blessed Are The Pure In Heart -E-0518	S. Butcher	Yr.Iss.	9.00	40-55.00
83-01-007	O Come All Ye Faithful-E-0531	S. Butcher	Suspd.	10.00	45-60.00
83-01-008	Let Heaven And Nature Sing-E-0532	S. Butcher	Retrd.	9.00	35-45.50
83-01-009	Tell Me The Story Of Jesus-E-0533	S. Butcher	Suspd.	9.00	35-55.00
83-01-010	To Thee With Love-E-0534	S. Butcher	Retrd.	9.00	40-65.00
83-01-011	Love Is Patient-E-0535	S. Butcher	Suspd.	9.00	40-55.00
83-01-012	Love Is Patient-E-0536	S. Butcher	Suspd.	9.00	35-70.00
83-01-013	Jesus Is The Light That Shines- E-0537	S. Butcher	Suspd.	9.00	45-60.00
82-01-014	Joy To The World-E-2343	S. Butcher	Suspd.	9.00	35-66.00
82-01-015	I'll Play My Drum For Him-E-2359	S. Butcher	Yr.Iss.	9.00	100-170.
82-01-016	Baby's First Christmas-E-2362	S. Butcher	Suspd.	9.00	25-70.00
82-01-017	The First Noel-E-2367	S. Butcher	Suspd.	9.00	45-66.00
82-01-018	The First Noel-E-2368	S. Butcher	Retrd.	9.00	40-60.00
82-01-019	Dropping In For Christmas-E-2369	S. Butcher	Retrd.	9.00	36-70.00
82-01-020	Unicorn-E-2371	S. Butcher	Retrd.	10.00	45-75.00
82-01-021	Baby's First Christmas-E-2372	S. Butcher	Suspd.	9.00	35-45.00
82-01-022	Dropping Over For Christmas-E-2376	S. Butcher	Retrd.	9.00	45-59.00
82-01-023	Mouse With Cheese-E-2381	S. Butcher	Suspd.	9.00	75-125.
82-01-024	Our First Christmas Together-E-2385	S. Butcher	Suspd.	10.00	15-55.00
82-01-025	Camel, Donkey & Cow (3 pc. set)-E2386	S. Butcher	Suspd.	25.00	55-90.00
84-01-026	Wishing You A Merry Christmas-E-5387	S. Butcher	Yr.Iss.	10.00	30-45.00
84-01-027	Joy To The World-E-5388	S. Butcher	Retrd.	10.00	40-55.00
84-01-028	Peace On Earth-E-5389	S. Butcher	Suspd.	10.00	30-45.00
84-01-029	May God Bless You With A Perfect Holiday Season-E-5390	S. Butcher	Suspd.	10.00	25-30.00
84-01-030	Love Is Kind-E-5391	S. Butcher	Suspd.	10.00	30-50.00
84-01-031	Blessed Are The Pure In Heart-E-5392	S. Butcher	Yr.Iss.	10.00	40.00
81-01-032	But Love Goes On Forever-E-5627	S. Butcher	Suspd.	6.00	70-135.
81-01-033	But Love Goes On Forever-E-5628	S. Butcher	Suspd.	6.00	60-150.
81-01-034	Let The Heavens Rejoice-E-5629	S. Butcher	Yr.Iss.	6.00	200-250.
81-01-035	Unto Us A Child Is Born-E-5630	S. Butcher	Suspd.	6.00	40-65.00
81-01-036	Baby's First Christmas-E-5631	S. Butcher	Suspd.	6.00	45-60.00
81-01-037	Baby's First Christmas-E-5632	S. Butcher	Suspd.	6.00	45-70.00
81-01-038	Come Let Us Adore Him (4pc. set)-E-5633	S. Butcher	Suspd.	22.00	75-115.
81-01-039	Wee Three Kings (3pc. set)-E-5634	S. Butcher	Suspd.	19.00	100-129.
81-01-040	We Have Seen His Star-E-6120	S. Butcher	Retrd.	6.00	55-80.00
85-01-041	Have A Heavenly Christmas-12416	S. Butcher	Open	12.00	17.50-30.
85-01-042	God Sent His Love-15768	S. Butcher	Yr.Iss.	10.00	30-75.00
85-01-043	May Your Christmas Be Happy-15822	S. Butcher	Suspd.	10.00	30-48.00
85-01-044	Happiness Is The Lord-15830	S. Butcher	Suspd.	10.00	20-37.00
85-01-045	May Your Christmas Be Delightful-15849	S. Butcher	Suspd.	10.00	15-35.00
85-01-046	Honk If You Love Jesus-15857	S. Butcher	Suspd.	10.00	15-27.00
85-01-047	Baby's First Christmas-15903	S. Butcher	Yr.Iss.	10.00	42.00
85-01-048	Baby's First Christmas-15911	S. Butcher	Yr.Iss.	10.00	30-45.00
86-01-049	Shepherd of Love-102288	S. Butcher	Suspd.	10.00	20-40.00
86-01-050	Wishing You A Cozy Christmas-102326	S. Butcher	Yr.Iss.	10.00	30-40.00
86-01-051	Our First Christmas Together-102350	S. Butcher	Yr.Iss.	10.00	15-39.00
86-01-052	Trust And Obey-102377	S. Butcher	Open	10.00	16-35.00
86-01-053	Love Rescued Me-102385	S. Butcher	Open	10.00	16-35.00
86-01-054	Angel Of Mercy-102407	S. Butcher	Open	10.00	15-35.00
86-01-055	It's A Perfect Boy-102415	S. Butcher	Suspd.	10.00	25-40.00
86-01-056	Lord Keep Me On My Toes-102423	S. Butcher	Retrd.	10.00	35-40.00
86-01-057	Serve With A Smile-102431	S. Butcher	Suspd.	10.00	20-35.00
86-01-058	Serve With A Smile-102458	S. Butcher	Suspd.	10.00	25-30.00
86-01-059	Reindeer-102466	S. Butcher	Yr.Iss.	11.00	190-275.
86-01-060	Rocking Horse-102474	S. Butcher	Suspd.	10.00	19-29.00
86-01-061	Baby's First Christmas-102504	S. Butcher	Yr.Iss.	10.00	25-40.00
86-01-062	Baby's First Christmas-102512	S. Butcher	Yr.Iss.	10.00	25-35.00
87-01-063	Bear The Good News Of Christmas-104515	S. Butcher	Yr.Iss.	12.50	25-35.00
87-01-064	Baby's First Christmas-109401	S. Butcher	Yr.Iss.	12.00	35-55.00
87-01-065	Baby's First Christmas-109428	S. Butcher	Yr.Iss.	12.00	35-45.00
87-01-066	Love Is The Best Gift Of All-109770	S. Butcher	Yr.Iss.	11.00	35-50.00
87-01-067	I'm A Possibility-111120	S. Butcher	Suspd.	11.00	30-49.00
87-01-068	You Have Touched So Many Hearts-112356	S. Butcher	Open	11.00	16-30.00
87-01-069	Waddle I Do Without You-112364	S. Butcher	Open	11.00	16-39.00
87-01-070	I'm Sending You A White Christmas-112372	S. Butcher	Suspd.	11.00	20-25.00
87-01-071	He Cleansed My Soul-112380	S. Butcher	Open	12.00	16-25.00
87-01-072	Our First Christmas Together-112399	S. Butcher	Yr.Iss.	11.00	25-35.00
88-01-073	To My Forever Friend-113956	S. Butcher	Open	16.00	20-35.00
88-01-074	Smile Along The Way-113964	S. Butcher	Suspd.	15.00	10-25.00
88-01-075	God Sent You Just In Time-113972	S. Butcher	Suspd.	13.50	25-35.00
88-01-076	Rejoice O Earth-113980	S. Butcher	Retrd.	13.50	25-50.00
88-01-077	Cheers To The Leader-113999	S. Butcher	Suspd.	13.50	25-35.00
88-01-078	My Love Will Never Let You Go-114006	S. Butcher	Suspd.	13.50	25-35.00
88-01-079	Baby's First Christmas-115282	S. Butcher	Yr.Iss.	15.00	25-35.00
88-01-080	Time To Wish You A Merry Christmas-115320	S. Butcher	Yr.Iss.	13.00	45-60.00
88-01-081	Our First Christmas Together-520233	S. Butcher	Yr.Iss.	13.00	20-35.00

		ARTIST	EDITION	ISSUE	QUOTE
88-01-082	Baby's First Christmas-520241	S. Butcher	Yr.Iss.	15.00	22-40.00
88-01-083	You Are My Gift Come True-520276	S. Butcher	Yr.Iss.	12.50	25-50.00
88-01-084	Hang On For The Holly Days-520292	S. Butcher	Yr.Iss.	13.00	25-45.00
91-01-085	Sno-Bunny Falls For You Like I Do-520438	S. Butcher	Yr.Iss.	15.00	25-30.00
89-01-086	Christmas is Ruff Without You-520462	S. Butcher	Yr.Iss.	13.00	13-35.00
89-01-087	May All Your Christmases Be White-521302 (dated)	S. Butcher	Suspd.	15.00	16.00
90-01-088	Glide Through the Holidays-521566	S. Butcher	Retrd.	13.50	30-40.00
90-01-089	Dashing Through the Snow-521574	S. Butcher	Suspd.	15.00	16.00
89-01-090	Our First Christmas Together-521588	S. Butcher	Yr.Iss.	17.50	35.00
90-01-091	Don't Let the Holidays Get You Down-521590	S. Butcher	Suspd.	15.00	16-25.00
89-01-092	Oh Holy Night-522848	S. Butcher	Yr.Iss.	13.50	35.00
89-01-093	Make A Joyful Noise-522910	S. Butcher	Open	15.00	16.00
89-01-094	Love One Another-522929	S. Butcher	Open	17.50	20-25.00
89-01-095	I Believe In The Old Rugged Cross-522953	S. Butcher	Suspd.	15.00	30.00
89-01-096	Peace On Earth-523062	S. Butcher	Yr.Iss.	25.00	65-75.00
89-01-097	Baby's First Christmas-523194	S. Butcher	Yr.Iss.	15.00	30.00
89-01-098	Baby's First Christmas-523208	S. Butcher	Yr.Iss.	15.00	30.00
90-01-099	Dashing Through The Snow-521574	S. Butcher	Open	15.00	15-18.00
90-01-100	Baby's First Christmas-523798	S. Butcher	Yr.Iss.	15.00	25.00
90-01-101	Baby's First Christmas-523771	S. Butcher	Yr.Iss.	15.00	25.00
90-01-102	Once Upon A Holy Night-523852	S. Butcher	Yr.Iss.	15.00	24-30.00
90-01-103	Don't Let the Holidays Get You Down-521590	S. Butcher	Open	15.00	15.00
90-01-104	Wishing You A Purr-fect Holiday-520497	S. Butcher	Yr.Iss.	15.00	20-35.00
90-01-105	Friends Never Drift Apart-522937	S. Butcher	Open	17.50	17.50
90-01-106	Bundles of Joy-525057	S. Butcher	Yr.Iss.	15.00	25-35.00
90-01-107	Our First Christmas Together-525324	S. Butcher	Yr.Iss.	17.50	17.50-25.
90-01-108	May Your Christmas Be A Happy Home-523704	S. Butcher	Yr.Iss.	27.50	35-75.00
91-01-109	Our First Christmas Together-522945	S. Butcher	Yr.Iss.	17.50	17.50-25.
91-01-110	Happy Trails Is Trusting Jesus-523224	S. Butcher	Suspd.	15.00	16.00
91-01-111	Baby's First Christmas (Girl)-527092	S. Butcher	Yr.Iss.	15.00	20.00
91-01-112	Baby's First Christmas (Boy)-527084	S. Butcher	Yr.Iss.	15.00	16-25.00
91-01-113	May Your Christmas Be Merry (Ornament On Base)-526940	S. Butcher	Yr.Iss.	30.00	30-45.00
91-01-114	May Your Christmas Be Merry-524174	S. Butcher	Yr.Iss.	15.00	25.00
91-01-115	The Good Lord Always Delivers-527165	S. Butcher	Suspd.	15.00	18-20.00
92-01-115	Baby's First Christmas-527475	S. Butcher	Yr.Iss.	15.00	15.00
92-01-116	Baby's First Christmas-527483	S. Butcher	Yr.Iss.	15.00	15.00
92-01-117	But The Greatest of These Is Love-527696	S. Butcher	Yr.Iss.	15.00	15-25.00
92-01-118	Our First Christmas-528870	S. Butcher	Yr.Iss.	17.50	17.50
92-01-119	But The Greatest of These Is Love-527734 (Ornament on Base)	S. Butcher	Yr.Iss.	30.00	30-40.00
92-01-120	Good Friends Are For Always-524131	S. Butcher	Open	15.00	16.00
92-01-121	Lord, Keep Me On My Toes-525332	S. Butcher	Open	15.00	16-18.00
92-01-122	I'm Nuts About You-520411	S. Butcher	Yr.Iss.	15.00	15-25.00
93-01-123	Wishing You the Sweetest Christmas-530190	S. Butcher	Yr.Iss.	30.00	30.00
93-01-124	Wishing You the Sweetest Christmas-530212	S. Butcher	Yr.Iss.	15.00	15.00
93-01-125	Loving, Caring And Sharing Along The Way-PM040 (Club Appreciation Members Only)	S. Butcher	Yr.Iss.	12.50	12.50
93-01-126	15 Years Tweet Music Together-530840 (15th Anniversary Commemorative Ornament)	S. Butcher	Yr.Iss.	15.00	18-50.00
93-01-127	Our First Christmas Together-530506	S. Butcher	Yr.Iss.	17.50	17.50
93-01-128	Share in The Warmth of Christmas-527211	S. Butcher	Open	15.00	16.00
93-01-129	It's So Uplifting to Have a Friend Like You-528846	S. Butcher	Open	16.00	16.00
93-01-130	Slow Down & Enjoy The Holidays-520489	S. Butcher	Yr.Iss.	16.00	16.00
93-01-131	Baby's First Christmas-530859	S. Butcher	Yr.Iss.	15.00	15.00
93-01-132	Baby's First Christmas-530867	S. Butcher	Yr.Iss.	15.00	15.00
93-01-133	Sugartown Chapel Ornament-530484	S. Butcher	Yr.Iss.	17.50	17.50
94-01-134	Sam's House - 530468	S. Butcher	Yr.Iss.	17.50	17.50
94-01-135	Our 1st Christmas Together - 529206	S. Butcher	Yr.Iss.	18.50	18.50
94-01-136	Baby's 1st Christmas - 530263	S. Butcher	Yr.Iss.	16.00	16.00
94-01-137	Baby's 1st Christmas - 530255	S. Butcher	Yr.Iss.	16.00	16.00
94-01-138	Bringing You A Merry Christmas - 528226	S. Butcher	Open	16.00	16.00
94-01-139	Onward Christmas Soldiers - 527327	S. Butcher	Open	16.00	16.00
94-01-140	Sending You A White Christmas - 528218	S. Butcher	Open	16.00	16.00
94-01-141	You Are Always In My Heart - 530972	S. Butcher	Yr.Iss.	16.00	16.00
94-01-142	You're As Pretty As A Christmas Tree - 530395	S. Butcher	Yr.Iss.	16.00	16.00

Enesco Corporation — **Precious Moments DSR Open House Weekend Ornaments**

92-02-001	1992 -The Magic Starts With You-529648	S. Butcher	Retrd.	16.00	20-25.00
93-02-002	1993 -An Event For All Seasons-529974	S. Butcher	Retrd.	15.00	20.00
94-02-003	Take A Bow Cuz You're My Christmas Star - 520470	S. Butcher	Yr.Iss.	16.00	16.00

Enesco Corporation — **Precious Moments Easter Seal Commemorative Ornaments**

94-03-001	It's No Secret What God Can Do-244570	S. Butcher	Yr.Iss.	6.50	6.50
95-03-002	Take Time To Smell The Flowers - 128899	S. Butcher	Yr.Iss.	7.50	7.50

Enesco Corporation — **Precious Moments Special Edition**

94-04-001	Caring - PM941	S. Butcher	Yr.Iss.	35.00	35.00

Enesco Corporation — **Memories of Yesterday Ornaments**

88-05-001	Baby's First Christmas 1988-520373	M. Attwell	Yr.Iss.	13.50	20-30.00
88-05-002	Special Delivery! 1988-520381	M. Attwell	Yr.Iss.	13.50	25-38.00
89-05-003	Baby's First Christmas-522465	M. Attwell	Open	15.00	15-20.00
89-05-004	Christmas Together-522562	M. Attwell	Open	15.00	15-25.00
89-05-005	A Surprise for Santa-522473 (1989)	M. Attwell	Yr.Iss.	13.50	20-30.00
90-05-006	Time For Bed-524638	M. Attwell	Yr.Iss.	15.00	15-30.00
90-05-007	New Moon-524646	M. Attwell	Suspd.	15.00	15-25.00
90-05-008	Moonstruck-524794	M. Attwell	Retrd.	15.00	15-25.00
91-05-009	Just Watchin' Over You-525421	M. Attwell	Retrd.	17.50	17.50
91-05-010	Lucky Me-525448	M. Attwell	Retrd.	16.00	20.00
91-05-011	Lucky You-525847	M. Attwell	Retrd.	16.00	20.00
91-05-012	Star Fishin'-525820	M. Attwell	Open	16.00	16.00
91-05-013	S'no Use Lookin' Back Now!-527181(dated)	M. Attwell	Yr.Iss.	17.50	28.00
92-05-014	Merry Christmas, Little Boo-Boo-528803	M. Attwell	Open	37.50	37.50
92-05-015	I'll Fly Along To See You Soon-525804 (1992 Dated Bisque)	M. Attwell	Yr.Iss.	16.00	18.00
92-05-016	Mommy, I Teared It-527041(Five Year Anniversary Limited Edition)	M. Attwell	Yr.Iss.	15.00	20.00
92-05-017	Star Light, Star Bright-528838	M. Attwell	Open	16.00	16.00
92-05-018	Swinging Together-580481(1992 Dated Artplas)	M. Attwell	Yr.Iss.	17.50	22.00
92-05-019	Sailin' With My Friends-587575 (Artplas)	M. Attwell	Open	25.00	25.00
93-05-020	Wish I Could Fly To You-525790 (dated)	M. Attwell	Yr.Iss.	16.00	16.00
93-05-021	May All Your Finest Dreams Come True-528811	M. Attwell	Open	16.00	16.00
93-05-022	Bringing Good Wishes Your Way-592846 (Artplas)	M. Attwell	Open	25.00	25.00
94-05-023	Give Yourself a Hug From Me!-529109 ('94 Dated)	M. Attwell	Yr. Iss.	17.50	17.50
94-05-024	Just Dreaming of You-524786	M. Attwell	Open	16.00	16.00
94-05-025	Bout Time I Came Along to See You-592854 (Artplas)	M. Attwell	Open	8.75	8.75

Enesco Corporation — **Memories of Yesterday Society Member's Only Ornament**

92-06-001	With Luck And A Friend, I's In Heaven-MY922 M. Attwell	M. Attwell	Yr.Iss.	16.00	32.00
93-06-002	I'm Bringing Good Luck-Wherever You Are	M. Attwell	Yr.Iss.	16.00	22.00

Enesco Corporation — **Memories of Yesterday Event Item Only**

93-07-001	How 'Bout A Little Kiss?-527068	Enesco	Yr.Iss.	16.50	50.00

Enesco Corporation — **Enesco Treasury of Christmas Ornaments**

83-08-001	Wide Open Throttle-E-0242	Enesco	3-Yr.	12.00	35.00
83-08-002	Baby's First Christmas-E-0271	Enesco	Yr.Iss.	6.00	N/A
83-08-003	Grandchild's First Christmas-E-0272	Enesco	Yr.Iss.	5.00	N/A
83-08-004	Baby's First Christmas-E-0273	Enesco	3-Yr.	9.00	N/A
83-08-005	Toy Drum Teddy-E-0274	Enesco	4-Yr.	9.00	N/A
83-08-006	Watching At The Window-E-0275	Enesco	3-Yr.	13.00	N/A
83-08-007	To A Special Teacher-E-0276	Enesco	7-Yr.	5.00	15.00
83-08-008	Toy Shop-E-0277	Enesco	7-Yr.	8.00	50.00
83-08-009	Carousel Horse-E-0278	Enesco	7-Yr.	9.00	20.00
81-08-010	Look Out Below-E-6135	Enesco	2-Yr.	6.00	N/A
82-08-011	Flyin' Santa Christmas Special 1982-E-6136	Enesco	Yr.Iss.	9.00	75.00
81-08-012	Flyin' Santa Christmas Special 1981-E-6136	Enesco	Yr.Iss.	9.00	N/A
81-08-013	Sawin' Elf Helper-E-6138	Enesco	2-Yr.	6.00	40.00
81-08-014	Snow Shoe-In Santa-E-6139	Enesco	2-Yr.	6.00	35.00
81-08-015	Baby's First Christmas 1981-E-6145	Enesco	Yr.Iss.	6.00	N/A
81-08-016	Our Hero-E-6146	Enesco	2-Yr.	4.00	N/A
81-08-017	Whoops-E-6147	Enesco	2-Yr.	3.50	N/A
81-08-018	Whoops, It's 1981-E-6148	Enesco	Yr.Iss.	7.50	75.00
81-08-019	Not A Creature Was Stirring-E-6149	Enesco	2-Yr.	4.00	25.00
84-08-020	Joy To The World-E-6209	Enesco	2-Yr.	9.00	35.00
84-08-021	Letter To Santa-E-6210	Enesco	2-Yr.	5.00	30.00
84-08-022	Lucy & Me Photo Frames-E-6211	Enesco	3-Yr.	5.00	N/A
84-08-023	Lucy & Me Photo Frames-E-6211	Enesco	3-Yr.	5.00	N/A
84-08-024	Lucy & Me Photo Frames-E-6211	Enesco	3-Yr.	5.00	N/A
84-08-025	Lucy & Me Photo Frames-E-6211	Enesco	3-Yr.	5.00	N/A
84-08-026	Lucy & Me Photo Frames-E-6211	Enesco	3-Yr.	5.00	N/A
84-08-027	Lucy & Me Photo Frames-E-6211	Enesco	3-Yr.	5.00	N/A
84-08-028	Baby's First Christmas 1984-E-6212	Gilmore	Yr.Iss.	10.00	30.00
84-08-029	Merry Christmas Mother-E-6213	Enesco	3-Yr.	10.00	30.00
84-08-030	Baby's First Christmas 1984-E-6215	Enesco	Yr.Iss.	6.00	N/A
84-08-031	Ferris Wheel Mice-E-6216	Enesco	2-Yr.	9.00	30.00
84-08-032	Cuckoo Clock-E-6217	Enesco	2-Yr.	8.00	40.00
84-08-033	Muppet Babies Baby's First Christmas-E6222	J. Henson	Yr.Iss.	10.00	45.00
84-08-034	Muppet Babies Baby's First Christmas-E6223	J. Henson	Yr.Iss.	10.00	45.00
84-08-035	Garfield Hark! The Herald Angel-E-6224	J. Davis	2-Yr.	7.50	35.00
84-08-036	Fun in Santa's Sleigh-E-6225	J. Davis	2-Yr.	12.00	35.00
84-08-037	Deer! Odie-E-6226	J. Davis	2-Yr.	6.00	30.00
84-08-038	Garfield The Snow Cat-E-6227	J. Davis	2-Yr.	12.00	35.00
84-08-039	Peek-A-Bear Baby's First Christmas-E-6228	Enesco	3-Yr.	10.00	N/A
84-08-040	Peek-A-Bear Baby's First Christmas-E-6229	Enesco	3-Yr.	9.00	N/A
84-08-041	Owl Be Home For Christmas-E-6230	Enesco	2-Yr.	10.00	23.00
84-08-042	Santa's Trolley-E-6231	Enesco	3-Yr.	11.00	50.00
84-08-043	Holiday Penguin-E-6240	Enesco	3-Yr.	1.50	15-20.00
84-08-044	Little Drummer-E-6241	Enesco	5-Yr.	2.00	N/A
84-08-045	Happy Holidays-E-6248	Enesco	2-Yr.	2.00	N/A
84-08-046	Christmas Nest-E-6249	Enesco	2-Yr.	3.00	25.00
84-08-047	Bunny's Christmas Stocking-E-6251	Enesco	Yr.Iss.	2.00	15.00
84-08-048	Santa On Ice-E-6252	Enesco	3-Yr.	2.50	25.00
84-08-049	Treasured Memories The New Sled-E-6256	Enesco	2-Yr.	7.00	N/A
84-08-050	Up On The House Top-E-6280	Enesco	6-Yr.	9.00	N/A
84-08-051	Penguins On Ice-E-6280	Enesco	2-Yr.	7.50	N/A
84-08-052	Grandchild's First Christmas 1984-E-6286	Enesco	Yr.Iss.	5.00	N/A
84-08-053	Grandchild's First Christmas1984-E-6286	Enesco	Yr.Iss.	5.00	N/A
84-08-054	Godchild's First Christmas-E-6287	Enesco	3-Yr.	7.00	N/A
84-08-055	Santa In The Box-E-6292	Enesco	2-Yr.	6.00	N/A
84-08-056	Carousel Horse-E-6913	Enesco	2-Yr.	1.50	N/A
83-08-057	Arctic Charmer-E-6945	Enesco	2-Yr.	7.00	N/A
82-08-058	Victorian Sleigh-E-6946	Enesco	4-Yr.	9.00	15.00
83-08-059	Wing-A-Ding Angel-E-6948	Enesco	3-Yr.	7.00	50.00
82-08-060	A Saviour Is Born This Day-E-6949	Enesco	8-Yr.	4.00	12-20.00
82-08-061	Crescent Santa-E-6950	Gilmore	4-Yr.	10.00	50.00
82-08-062	Baby's First Christmas 1982-E-6952	Enesco	Yr.Iss.	10.00	N/A
82-08-063	Polar Bear Fun Whoops,It's 1982-E-6953	Enesco	Yr.Iss.	10.00	75.00
82-08-064	Holiday Skier-E-6954	J. Davis	5-Yr.	7.00	N/A
82-08-065	Toy Soldier 1982-E-6957	Enesco	Yr.Iss.	6.50	N/A
82-08-066	Merry Christmas Grandma-E-6975	Enesco	3-Yr.	5.00	N/A
82-08-067	Carousel Horses-E-6958	Enesco	3-Yr.	8.00	20-40.00
82-08-068	Dear Santa-E-6959	Gilmore	8-Yr.	10.00	27.00
82-08-069	Penguin Power-E-6977	Enesco	2-Yr.	6.00	15.00
82-08-070	Bunny Winter Playground 1982-E-6978	Enesco	Yr.Iss.	10.00	N/A
82-08-071	Baby's First Christmas 1982-E-6979	Enesco	Yr.Iss.	10.00	N/A
83-08-072	Carousel Horses-E-6980	Enesco	4-Yr.	8.00	N/A
82-08-073	Grandchild's First Christmas 1982-E-6983	Enesco	Yr.Iss.	5.00	73.00
82-08-074	Merry Christmas Teacher-E-6984	Enesco	4-Yr.	7.00	N/A
83-08-075	Garfield Cuts The Ice-E-8771	J. Davis	3-Yr.	6.00	45.00
84-08-076	A Stocking Full For 1984-E-8773	J. Davis	Yr.Iss.	6.00	N/A
83-08-077	Stocking Full For 1983-E-8773	J. Davis	Yr.Iss.	6.00	N/A
85-08-078	Santa Claus Balloon-55794	Enesco	Yr.Iss.	8.50	20.00
85-08-079	Carousel Reindeer-55808	Enesco	4-Yr.	12.00	35-40.00
85-08-080	Angel In Flight-55816	Enesco	4-Yr.	8.00	20.00
85-08-081	Christmas Penguin-55824	Enesco	4-Yr.	7.50	35.00
85-08-082	Merry Christmas Godchild-55832	Gilmore	5-Yr.	8.00	N/A
85-08-083	Baby's First Christmas-55840	Enesco	2-Yr.	15.00	N/A
85-08-084	Old Fashioned Rocking Horse-55859	Enesco	2-Yr.	10.00	15.00
85-08-085	Child's Second Christmas-55867	Enesco	5-Yr.	11.00	N/A
85-08-086	Fishing For Stars-55875	Enesco	5-Yr.	9.00	20.00
85-08-087	Baby Blocks-55883	Enesco	2-Yr.	12.00	N/A
85-08-088	Christmas Toy Chest-55891	Enesco	5-Yr.	10.00	N/A

		ARTIST	EDITION	ISSUE	QUOTE
85-08-089	Grandchild's First Ornament-55921	Enesco	5-Yr.	7.00	8.00
85-08-090	Joy Photo Frame-55956	Enesco	Yr.Iss.	6.00	N/A
85-08-091	We Three Kings-55964	Enesco	Yr.Iss.	4.50	20.00
85-08-092	The Night Before Christmas-55972	Enesco	2-Yr.	5.00	N/A
85-08-093	Baby's First Christmas 1985-55980	Enesco	Yr.Iss.	6.00	N/A
85-08-094	Baby Rattle Photo Frame-56006	Enesco	2-Yr.	5.00	N/A
85-08-095	Baby's First Christmas 1985-56014	Gilmore	Yr.Iss.	10.00	N/A
85-08-096	Christmas Plane Ride-56049	L. Rigg	6-Yr.	10.00	N/A
85-08-097	Scottie Celebrating Christmas-56065	Enesco	5-Yr.	7.50	25.00
85-08-098	North Pole Native-56073	Enesco	2-Yr.	9.00	N/A
85-08-099	Skating Walrus-56081	Enesco	2-Yr.	9.00	20.00
85-08-100	Ski Time-56111	J. Davis	Yr.Iss.	13.00	N/A
85-08-101	North Pole Express-56138	J. Davis	Yr.Iss.	12.00	N/A
85-08-102	Merry Christmas Mother-56146	J. Davis	Yr.Iss.	8.50	N/A
85-08-103	Hoppy Christmas-56154	J. Davis	Yr.Iss.	8.50	N/A
85-08-104	Merry Christmas Teacher-56170	J. Davis	Yr.Iss.	6.00	N/A
85-08-105	Garfield-In-The-Box-56189	J. Davis	Yr.Iss.	6.50	25.00
85-08-106	Merry Christmas Grandma-56197	Enesco	Yr.Iss.	7.00	N/A
85-08-107	Christmas Lights-56200	Enesco	2-Yr.	8.00	N/A
85-08-108	Victorian Doll House-56251	Enesco	Yr.Iss.	13.00	40.00
85-08-109	Tobaoggan Ride-56286	Enesco	4-Yr.	6.00	N/A
85-08-110	Look Out Below-56375	Enesco	Yr.Iss.	8.50	40.00
85-08-111	Flying Santa Christmas Special-56383	Enesco	2-Yr.	10.00	N/A
85-08-112	Sawin Elf Helper-56391	Enesco	Yr.Iss.	8.00	N/A
85-08-113	Snow Shoe-In Santa-56405	Enesco	Yr.Iss.	8.00	50.00
85-08-114	Our Hero-56413	Enesco	Yr.Iss.	5.50	N/A
85-08-115	Not A Creaturxe Was Stirring-56421	Enesco	2-Yr.	4.00	N/A
85-08-116	Merry Christmas Teacher-56448	Enesco	Yr.Iss.	9.00	N/A
85-08-117	A Stocking Full For 1985-56464	J. Davis	Yr.Iss.	6.00	25.00
85-08-118	St. Nicholas Circa 1910-56659	Enesco	5-Yr.	6.00	15.00
85-08-119	Christmas Tree Photo Frame-56871	Enesco	4-Yr.	10.00	N/A
90-08-120	Deck The Halls-566063	Enesco	3-Yr.	12.50	N/A
88-08-121	Making A Point-489212	G.G. Santiago	3-Yr.	10.00	N/A
88-08-122	Mouse Upon A Pipe-489220	G.G. Santiago	2-Yr.	10.00	12.00
88-08-123	North Pole Deadline-489387	Enesco	3-Yr.	13.50	N/A
88-08-124	Christmas Pin-Up-489409	Enesco	2-Yr.	11.00	18.00
88-08-125	Airmail For Teacher-489425	Gilmore	3-Yr.	13.50	N/A
86-08-126	1st Christmas Together 1986-551171	Enesco	Yr.Iss.	9.00	15-35.00
86-08-127	Elf Stringing Popcorn-551198	Enesco	4-Yr.	10.00	20-30.00
86-08-128	Christmas Scottie-551201	Enesco	4-Yr.	7.00	15-30.00
86-08-129	Santa and Child-551236	Enesco	4-Yr.	13.50	25-50.00
86-08-130	The Christmas Angel-551244	Enesco	4-Yr.	22.50	40-50.00
86-08-131	Carousel Unicorn-551252	Gilmore	4-Yr.	12.00	30-40.00
86-08-132	Have a Heavenly Holiday-551260	Enesco	4-Yr.	9.00	N/A
86-08-133	Siamese Kitten-551279	Enesco	4-Yr.	9.00	40.00
86-08-134	Old Fashioned Doll House-551287	Enesco	4-Yr.	15.00	N/A
86-08-135	Holiday Fisherman-551309	Enesco	3-Yr.	8.00	40.00
86-08-136	Antique Toy-551317	Enesco	3-Yr.	9.00	N/A
86-08-137	Time For Christmas-551325	Gilmore	4-Yr.	13.00	N/A
86-08-138	Christmas Calendar-551333	Enesco	2-Yr.	7.00	N/A
86-08-139	Merry Christmas-551341	Gilmore	3-Yr.	8.00	95.00
86-08-140	The Santa Claus Shoppe Circa1905-551562	J. Grossman	4-Yr.	8.00	15.00
86-08-141	Baby Bear Sleigh-551651	Gilmore	3-Yr.	9.00	30.00
86-08-142	Baby's First Christmas 1986-551678	Gilmore	Yr.Iss.	10.00	20.00
86-08-143	First Christmas Together-551708	Enesco	3-Yr.	6.00	10.00
86-08-144	Baby's First Christmas-551716	Enesco	3-Yr.	5.50	10.00
86-08-145	Baby's First Christmas 1986-551724	Enesco	Yr.Iss.	6.50	30.00
86-08-146	Peek-A-Bear Grandchild's First Christmas-	Enesco	Yr.Iss.	6.00	23.00
86-08-147	Peek-A-Bear Present-552089	Enesco	4-Yr.	2.50	N/A
86-08-148	Peek-A-Bear Present-552089	Enesco	4-Yr.	2.50	N/A
86-08-149	Peek-A-Bear Present-552089	Enesco	4-Yr.	2.50	N/A
86-08-150	Peek-A-Bear Present-552089	Enesco	4-Yr.	2.50	N/A
86-08-151	Merry Christmas 1986-552186	L. Rigg	Yr.Iss.	8.00	N/A
86-08-152	Merry Christmas 1986-552534	L. Rigg	Yr.Iss.	8.00	N/A
86-08-153	Lucy & Me Christmas Tree-552542	L. Rigg	3-Yr.	7.00	25.00
86-08-154	Santa's Helpers-552607	Enesco	3-Yr.	2.50	N/A
86-08-155	My Special Friend-552615	Enesco	3-Yr.	6.00	N/A
86-08-156	Christmas Wishes From Panda-552623	Enesco	3-Yr.	6.00	N/A
86-08-157	Lucy & Me Ski Time-552658	L. Rigg	2-Yr.	6.50	30.00
86-08-158	Merry Christmas Teacher-552666	Enesco	3-Yr.	6.50	N/A
86-08-159	Country Cousins Merry Christmas, Mom-	Enesco	3-Yr.	7.00	23.00
86-08-160	Country Cousins Merry Christmas, Dad-	Enesco	3-Yr.	7.00	23.00
86-08-161	Country Cousins Merry Christmas, Mom-552712	Enesco	4-Yr.	7.00	23.00
86-08-162	Country Cousins Merry Christmas, Dad-552712	Enesco	4-Yr.	7.00	25.00
86-08-163	Grandmother's Little Angel-552747	Enesco	4-Yr.	8.00	N/A
87-08-164	Puppy's 1st Christmas-552909	Enesco	2-Yr.	4.00	N/A
87-08-165	Kitty's 1st Christmas-552917	Enesco	2-Yr.	4.00	25.00
87-08-166	Merry Christmas Puppy-552925	Enesco	2-Yr.	3.50	N/A
87-08-167	Merry Christmas Kitty-552933	Enesco	2-Yr.	3.50	N/A
86-08-168	I Love My Grandparents-553263	Enesco	Yr.Iss.	6.00	N/A
86-08-169	Merry Christmas Mom & Dad-553271	Enesco	Yr.Iss.	6.00	N/A
86-08-170	S. Claus Hollycopter-553344	Enesco	4-Yr.	13.50	35.00
86-08-171	From Our House To Your House-553360	Enesco	3-Yr.	15.00	40.00
86-08-172	Christmas Rattle-553379	Enesco	3-Yr.	8.00	35.00
86-08-173	Bah, Humbug!-553387	Enesco	4-Yr.	9.00	N/A
86-08-174	God Bless Us Everyone-553395	Enesco	4-Yr.	10.00	15.00
87-08-175	Carousel Mobile-553409	Enesco	3-Yr.	15.00	50.00
86-08-176	Holiday Train-553417	Enesco	4-Yr.	10.00	N/A
86-08-177	Lighten Up!-553603	J. Davis	5-Yr.	10.00	N/A
86-08-178	Gift Wrap Odie-553611	J. Davis	Yr.Iss.	7.00	20.00
86-08-179	Merry Christmas-553646	Enesco	4-Yr.	8.00	N/A
87-08-180	M.V.B. (Most Valuable Bear)-554219	Enesco	2-Yr.	3.00	N/A
87-08-181	M.V.B. (Most Valuable Bear)-554219	Enesco	2-Yr.	3.00	N/A
87-08-182	M.V.B. (Most Valuable Bear)-554219	Enesco	2-Yr.	3.00	N/A
87-08-183	M.V.B. (Most Valuable Bear)-554219	Enesco	2-Yr.	3.00	N/A
88-08-184	1st Christmas Together-554537	Gilmore	3-Yr.	15.00	N/A
88-08-185	An Eye On Christmas-554545	Gilmore	3-Yr.	22.50	50.00
88-08-186	A Mouse Check-554553	Gilmore	3-Yr.	13.50	45.00
88-08-187	Merry Christmas Engine-554561	Enesco	2-Yr.	22.50	35.00
89-08-188	Sardine Express-554588	Gilmore	2-Yr.	17.50	30.00
88-08-189	1st Christmas Together 1988-554596	Enesco	Yr.Iss.	10.00	N/A
88-08-190	Forever Friends-554626	Gilmore	2-Yr.	12.00	27.00
88-08-191	Santa's Survey-554642	Enesco	2-Yr.	35.00	75-100.
89-08-192	Old Town's Church-554871	Gilmore	2-Yr.	17.50	20.00
88-08-193	A Chipmunk Holiday-554898	Gilmore	3-Yr.	11.00	25.00
88-08-194	Christmas Is Coming-554901	Enesco	3-Yr.	12.00	12.00
88-08-195	Baby's First Christmas 1988-554928	Enesco	Yr.Iss.	7.50	N/A
88-08-196	Baby's First Christmas 1988-554936	Gilmore	Yr.Iss.	10.00	25.00
88-08-197	The Christmas Train-554944	Enesco	3-Yr.	15.00	N/A
88-08-198	Li'l Drummer Bear-554952	Gilmore	3-Yr.	12.00	12.00
87-08-199	Baby's First Christmas-555061	Enesco	3-Yr.	12.00	N/A
87-08-200	Baby's First Christmas-555088	Enesco	3-Yr.	7.50	N/A
87-08-201	Baby's First Christmas-555118	Enesco	3-Yr.	6.00	N/A
87-08-202	Sugar Plum Bearies-555193	Enesco	2-Yr.	4.50	N/A
87-08-203	Garfield Merry Kissmas-555215	J. Davis	3-Yr.	8.50	30.00
87-08-204	Sleigh Away-555401	Enesco	3-Yr.	12.00	N/A
87-08-205	Merry Christmas 1987-555428	L. Rigg	Yr.Iss.	8.00	N/A
87-08-206	Merry Christmas 1987-555436	L. Rigg	Yr.Iss.	8.00	N/A
87-08-207	Lucy & Me Storybook Bear-555444	L. Rigg	3-Yr.	6.50	N/A
87-08-208	Time For Christmas-555452	L. Rigg	3-Yr.	12.00	20.00
87-08-209	Lucy & Me Angel On A Cloud-555487	L. Rigg	3-Yr.	8.00	35.00
87-08-210	Teddy's Stocking-555940	Gilmore	3-Yr.	10.00	N/A
87-08-211	Kitty's Jack-In-The-Box-555959	Enesco	3-Yr.	11.00	30.00
87-08-212	Merry Christmas Teacher-555967	Enesco	3-Yr.	7.50	N/A
87-08-213	Mouse In A Mitten-555975	Enesco	3-Yr.	7.50	N/A
87-08-214	Boy On A Rocking Horse-555983	Enesco	3-Yr.	12.00	18.00
87-08-215	Peek-A-Bear Letter To Santa-555991	Enesco	2-Yr.	8.00	30.00
87-08-216	Garfield Sugar Plum Fairy-556009	J. Davis	3-Yr.	8.50	20.00
87-08-217	Garfield The Nutcracker-556017	J. Davis	4-Yr.	8.50	35.00
87-08-218	Home Sweet Home-556033	M. Gilmore	3-Yr.	15.00	40.00
87-08-219	Baby's First Christmas-556041	Enesco	4-Yr.	10.00	20.00
87-08-220	Little Sailor Elf-556068	Enesco	3-Yr.	10.00	28.00
87-08-221	Carousel Goose-556076	Enesco	3-Yr.	17.00	40.00
87-08-222	Night Caps-556084	Enesco	2-Yr.	5.50	N/A
87-08-223	Night Caps-556084	Enesco	2-Yr.	5.50	N/A
87-08-224	Night Caps-556084	Enesco	2-Yr.	5.50	N/A
87-08-225	Night Caps-556084	Enesco	2-Yr.	5.50	N/A
87-08-226	Rocking Horse Past Joys-556157	Enesco	3-Yr.	10.00	20.00
87-08-227	Partridge In A Pear Tree-556173	Gilmore	3-Yr.	9.00	35.00
87-08-228	Carousel Lion-556025	M. Gilmore	3-Yr.	12.00	25.00
87-08-229	Skating Santa 1987-556211	Enesco	Yr.Iss.	13.50	75.00
87-08-230	Baby's First Christmas 1987-556238	Gilmore	Yr.Iss.	10.00	25.00
87-08-231	Baby's First Christmas 1987-556254	Enesco	Yr.Iss.	7.00	25.00
87-08-232	Teddy's Suspenders-556262	Enesco	4-Yr.	8.50	22.00
87-08-233	Baby's First Christmas 1987-556297	Enesco	Yr.Iss.	2.00	N/A
87-08-234	Baby's First Christmas 1987-556297	Enesco	Yr.Iss.	2.00	N/A
87-08-235	Beary Christmas Family-556300	Enesco	2-Yr.	2.00	N/A
87-08-236	Beary Christmas Family-556300	Enesco	2-Yr.	2.00	N/A
87-08-237	Beary Christmas Family-556300	Enesco	2-Yr.	2.00	N/A
87-08-238	Beary Christmas Family-556300	Enesco	2-Yr.	2.00	N/A
87-08-239	Beary Christmas Family-556300	Enesco	2-Yr.	2.00	N/A
87-08-240	Beary Christmas Family-556300	Enesco	2-Yr.	2.00	N/A
87-08-241	Merry ChristmasTeacher-556319	Enesco	2-Yr.	2.00	N/A
87-08-242	Merry ChristmasTeacher-556319	Enesco	2-Yr.	2.00	N/A
87-08-243	Merry ChristmasTeacher-556319	Enesco	2-Yr.	2.00	N/A
87-08-244	Merry ChristmasTeacher-556319	Enesco	2-Yr.	2.00	N/A
87-08-245	1st ChristmasTogether 1987-556335	Enesco	Yr.Iss.	9.00	18.00
87-08-246	Country Cousins Katie Goes Ice Skating-	Enesco	3-Yr.	8.00	30.00
87-08-247	Country Cousins Scooter Snowman-556386	Enesco	3-Yr.	8.00	30.00
87-08-248	Santa's List-556394	Enesco	3-Yr.	7.00	23.00
87-08-249	Kitty's Bed-556408	Enesco	3-Yr.	12.00	30.00
87-08-250	Grandchild's First Christmas-556416	Enesco	3-Yr.	10.00	N/A
87-08-251	Two Turtledoves-556432	Gilmore	3-Yr.	9.00	30.00
87-08-252	Three French Hens-556440	Gilmore	3-Yr.	9.00	30.00
88-08-253	Four Calling Birds-556459	Gilmore	3-Yr.	11.00	30.00
87-08-254	Teddy Takes A Spin-556467	Enesco	4-Yr.	13.00	35.00
87-08-255	Tiny Toy Thimble Mobile-556475	Enesco	2-Yr.	12.00	35.00
87-08-256	Bucket O'Love-556491	Enesco	2-Yr.	2.50	N/A
87-08-257	Bucket O'Love-556491	Enesco	2-Yr.	2.50	N/A
87-08-258	Puppy Love-556505	Enesco	3-Yr.	6.00	N/A
87-08-259	Peek-A-Bear My Special Friend-556513	Enesco	4-Yr.	6.00	30.00
87-08-260	Our First Christmas Together-556548	Enesco	3-Yr.	13.00	20.00
87-08-261	Three Little Bears-556556	Enesco	3-Yr.	7.50	15.00
87-08-262	Lucy & Me Mailbox Bear-556564	L. Rigg	4-Yr.	3.00	N/A
87-08-263	Twinkle Bear-556572	Gilmore	3-Yr.	8.00	N/A
87-08-264	I'm Dreaming Of A Bright Christmas-556602	Enesco	2-Yr.	2.50	N/A
87-08-265	I'm Dreaming Of A Bright Christmas-556602	Enesco	2-Yr.	2.50	N/A
87-08-266	Christmas Train-557196	Enesco	3-Yr.	10.00	N/A
88-08-267	Dairy Christmas-557501	M. Cook	2-Yr.	10.00	30.00
88-08-268	Merry Christmas 1988-557595	L. Rigg	Yr.Iss.	10.00	N/A
88-08-269	Merry Christmas 1988-557609	L. Rigg	Yr.Iss.	10.00	N/A
88-08-270	Toy Chest Keepsake-558206	L. Rigg	3-Yr.	12.50	30.00
88-08-271	Teddy Bear Greetings-558214	L. Rigg	3-Yr.	8.00	30.00
88-08-272	Jester Bear-558222	L. Rigg	2-Yr.	8.00	N/A
88-08-273	Night-Watch Cat-558362	J. Davis	3-Yr.	13.00	35.00
88-08-274	Christmas Thim-bell-558389	Enesco	Yr.Iss.	4.00	30.00
88-08-275	Christmas Thim-bell-558389	Enesco	Yr.Iss.	4.00	N/A
88-08-276	Christmas Thim-bell-558389	Enesco	Yr.Iss.	4.00	N/A
88-08-277	Christmas Thim-bell-558389	Enesco	Yr.Iss.	4.00	N/A
88-08-278	Baby's First Christmas-558397	D. Parker	3-Yr.	16.00	30.00
88-08-279	Christmas Tradition-558400	Gilmore	2-Yr.	10.00	25.00
88-08-280	Stocking Story-558419	G.G. Santiago	3-Yr.	10.00	23.00
88-08-281	Winter Tale-558427	G.G. Santiago	2-Yr.	6.00	N/A
88-08-282	Party Mouse-558435	G.G. Santiago	3-Yr.	12.00	30.00
88-08-283	Christmas Watch-558443	G.G. Santiago	2-Yr.	11.00	32.00
88-08-284	Christmas Vacation-558451	G.G. Santiago	3-Yr.	8.00	23.00
88-08-285	Sweet Cherub-558478	G.G. Santiago	3-Yr.	7.00	8.00
88-08-286	Time Out-558486	G.G. Santiago	2-Yr.	11.00	N/A
88-08-287	The Ice Fairy-558516	G.G. Santiago	3-Yr.	23.00	45-55.00
88-08-288	Santa Turtle-558559	Enesco	2-Yr.	10.00	35.00
88-08-289	The Teddy Bear Ball-558567	Enesco	3-Yr.	10.00	25.00
88-08-290	Turtle Greetings-558583	Enesco	2-Yr.	8.50	25.00
88-08-291	Happy Howladays-558605	Enesco	Yr.Iss.	7.00	15.00
88-08-292	Special Delivery-558699	J. Davis	3-Yr.	9.00	30.00
88-08-293	Deer Garfield-558702	J. Davis	3-Yr.	12.00	30.00
88-08-294	Garfield Bags O' Fun-558761	J. Davis	Yr.Iss.	3.30	N/A
88-08-298	Gramophone Keepsake-558818	Enesco	2-Yr.	13.00	20.00
88-08-299	North Pole Lineman-558834	Gilmore	2-Yr.	10.00	50.00
88-08-300	Five Golden Rings-559121	Gilmore	3-Yr.	11.00	25.00
88-08-301	Six Geese A-Laying-559148	Gilmore	3-Yr.	11.00	25.00
88-08-302	Pretty Baby-559156	R. Morehead	3-Yr.	12.50	25.00
88-08-303	Old Fashioned Angel-559164	R. Morehead	3-Yr.	12.50	20.00
88-08-304	Two For Tea-559776	Gilmore	3-Yr.	20.00	35-40.00
88-08-305	Merry Christmas Grandpa-560065	Enesco	3-Yr.	8.00	N/A
90-08-306	Reeling In The Holidays-560405	M. Cook	2-Yr.	8.00	15.00
91-08-307	Walkin' With My Baby-561029	M. Cook	2-Yr.	10.00	N/A
89-08-308	Scrub-A-Dub Chipmunk-561037	M. Cook	2-Yr.	8.00	20.00

		ARTIST	EDITION	ISSUE	QUOTE
89-08-309	Christmas Cook-Out-561045	M. Cook	2-Yr.	9.00	20.00
89-08-310	Sparkles-561843	S. Zimnicki	3-Yr.	17.50	25-27.50
89-08-311	Bunkie-561835	S. Zimnicki	3-Yr.	22.50	30.00
89-08-312	Popper-561878	S. Zimnicki	3-Yr.	12.00	25.00
89-08-313	Seven Swans A-Swimming-562742	Gilmore	3-Yr.	12.00	23.00
89-08-314	Eight Maids A-Milking-562750	Gilmore	3-Yr.	12.00	23.00
89-08-315	Nine Dancers Dancing-562769	Gilmore	3-Yr.	15.00	23.00
89-08-316	Baby's First Christmas 1989-562807	Enesco	Yr.Iss.	8.00	20.00
89-08-317	Baby's First Christmas 1989-562815	Gilmore	Yr.Iss.	10.00	N/A
89-08-318	First Christmas Together 1989-562823	Enesco	Yr.Iss.	11.00	N/A
89-08-319	Travelin' Trike-562882	Gilmore	3-Yr.	15.00	15.00
89-08-320	Victorian Sleigh Ride-562890	Enesco	3-Yr.	22.50	22.50
91-08-321	Santa Delivers Love-562904	Gilmore	2-Yr.	17.50	17.50
89-08-322	Chestnut Roastin'-562912	Gilmore	2-Yr.	13.00	13.00
90-08-323	Th-Ink-In' Of You-562920	Gilmore	2-Yr.	20.00	30.00
89-08-324	Ye Olde Puppet Show-562939	Enesco	2-Yr.	17.50	34.00
89-08-325	Static In The Attic-562947	Enesco	2-Yr.	13.00	25.00
89-08-326	Mistle-Toast 1989-562963	Gilmore	Yr.Iss.	15.00	25.00
89-08-327	Merry Christmas Pops-562971	Gilmore	3-Yr.	12.00	12.00
90-08-328	North Pole Or Bust-562998	Gilmore	2-Yr.	25.00	25.00
89-08-329	By The Light Of The Moon-563005	Gilmore	3-Yr.	12.00	24.00
89-08-330	Stickin' To It-563013	Gilmore	2-Yr.	10.00	12.00
89-08-331	Christmas Cookin'-563048	Gilmore	3-Yr.	22.50	25.00
89-08-332	All Set For Santa-563080	Gilmore	3-Yr.	17.50	25.00
90-08-333	Santa's Sweets-563196	Gilmore	2-Yr.	20.00	20.00
90-08-334	Purr-Fect Pals-563218	Enesco	2-Yr.	8.00	8.00
90-08-335	The Pause That Refreshes-563226	Enesco	3-Yr.	15.00	N/A
89-08-336	Ho-Ho Holiday Scrooge-563234	J. Davis	3-Yr.	13.50	30.00
89-08-337	God Bless Us Everyone-563242	J. Davis	3-Yr.	13.50	30.00
89-08-338	Scrooge With The Spirit-563250	J. Davis	3-Yr.	13.50	30.00
89-08-339	A Chains Of Pace For Odie-563269	J. Davis	3-Yr.	12.00	25.00
90-08-340	Jingle Bell Rock 1990-563390	G. Armgardt	Yr.Iss.	13.50	30.00
89-08-341	Joy Ridin'-563463	J. Davis	2-Yr.	15.00	30.00
89-08-342	Just What I Wanted-563668	M. Peters	3-Yr.	13.50	13.50
90-08-343	Pucker Up!-563676	M. Peters	3-Yr.	11.00	11.00
89-08-344	What's The Bright Idea-563684	M. Peters	3-Yr.	13.50	13.50
90-08-345	Fleas Navidad-563978	M. Peters	3-Yr.	13.50	25.00
90-08-346	Tweet Greetings-564044	J. Davis	2-Yr.	15.00	30.00
90-08-347	Trouble On 3 Wheels-564052	J. Davis	3-Yr.	20.00	35.00
89-08-348	Mine, All Mine!-564079	J. Davis	Yr.Iss.	15.00	40.00
90-08-349	Star of Stars-564389	J. Jonik	3-Yr.	9.00	15.00
90-08-350	Hang Onto Your Hat-564397	J. Jonik	3-Yr.	8.00	15.00
90-08-351	Fireplace Frolic-564435	N. Teiber	2-Yr.	25.00	32.00
89-08-352	Hoe! Hoe! Hoe!-564761	Enesco	Yr.Iss.	20.00	35.00
91-08-353	Double Scoop Snowmouse-564796	M. Cook	3-Yr.	13.50	13.50
90-08-354	Christmas Is Magic-564826	M. Cook	2-Yr.	10.00	10.00
90-08-355	Lighting Up Christmas-564834	M. Cook	2-Yr.	10.00	10.00
89-08-356	Feliz Navidad! 1989-564842	M. Cook	Yr.Iss.	11.00	40.00
89-08-357	Spreading Christmas Joy-564850	M. Cook	3-Yr.	10.00	10.00
89-08-358	Yuletide Tree House-564915	J. Jonik	3-Yr.	20.00	20.00
90-08-359	Brewnig Warm Wishes-564974	Enesco	2-Yr.	10.00	10.00
90-08-360	Yippie-I-Yuletide-564982	K. Hahn	3-Yr.	15.00	15.00
90-08-361	Coffee Break-564990	K. Hahn	3-Yr.	15.00	15.00
90-08-362	You're Sew Special-565008	K. Hahn	Yr.Iss.	20.00	35.00
89-08-363	Full House Mouse-565016	K. Hahn	2-Yr.	13.50	25.00
89-08-364	I Feel Pretty-565024	K. Hahn	3-Yr.	20.00	30.00
90-08-365	Warmest Wishes-565032	K. Hahn	3-Yr.	15.00	15.00
90-08-366	Baby's Christmas Feast-565040	K. Hahn	3-Yr.	13.50	13.50
90-08-367	Bumper Car Santa-565083	G.G. Santiago	Yr.Iss.	20.00	40.00
89-08-368	Special Delivery(Proof Ed.)-565091	G.G. Santiago	Yr.Iss.	12.00	15.00
90-08-369	Ho! Ho! Yo-Yo!(Proof Ed.)-565105	G.G. Santiago	Yr.Iss.	12.00	15.00
89-08-370	Weightin' For Santa-565148	G.G. Santiago	3-Yr.	7.50	7.50
89-08-371	Holly Fairy-565199	C.M. Baker	Yr.Iss.	15.00	45.00
90-08-372	The Christmas Tree Fairy-565202	C.M. Baker	Yr.Iss.	15.00	40.00
89-08-373	Christmas 1989-565210	L. Rigg	Yr.Iss.	12.00	38.00
89-08-374	Top Of The Class-565237	L. Rigg	3-Yr.	11.00	11.00
89-08-375	Deck The Hogs-565490	M. Cook	2-Yr.	12.00	14.00
89-08-376	Pinata Ridin'-565504	M. Cook	2-Yr.	11.00	N/A
89-08-377	Hangin' In There 1989-565598	K. Wise	Yr.Iss.	10.00	19.50
90-08-378	Meow-y Christmas 1990-565601	K. Wise	Yr.Iss.	10.00	25.00
90-08-379	Seaman's Greetings-566047	Enesco	2-Yr.	11.00	24.00
90-08-380	Hang In There-566055	Enesco	3-Yr.	13.50	13.50
91-08-381	Pedal Pushin' Santa-566071	Enesco	Yr.Iss.	20.00	30.00
90-08-382	Merry Christmas Teacher-566098	Enesco	2-Yr.	11.00	11.00
90-08-383	Festive Flight-566101	Enesco	2-Yr.	11.00	11.00
90-08-384	Santa's Suitcase-566160	Enesco	3-Yr.	25.00	25.00
89-08-385	The Purr-Fect Fit!-566462	Enesco	3-Yr.	15.00	35.00
90-08-386	Tumbles 1990-566519	S. Zimnicki	Yr.Iss.	16.00	25.00
90-08-387	Twiddles-566551	S. Zimnicki	3-Yr.	15.00	30.00
91-08-388	Snuffy-566578	S. Zimnicki	3-Yr.	17.50	17.50
90-08-389	All Aboard-567671	Gilmore	2-Yr.	17.50	17.50
89-08-390	Gone With The Wind-567698	Enesco	Yr.Iss.	13.50	30.00
89-08-391	Dorothy-567760	Enesco	Yr.Iss.	12.00	35.00
89-08-392	The Tin Man-567779	Enesco	Yr.Iss.	12.00	25.00
89-08-393	The Cowardly Lion-567787	Enesco	Yr.Iss.	12.00	25.00
89-08-394	The Scarecrow-567795	Enesco	Yr.Iss.	12.00	25.00
90-08-395	Happy Holiday Readings-568104	Enesco	2-Yr.	8.00	8.00
89-08-396	Christmas 1989-568325	L. Rigg	Yr.Iss.	12.00	N/A
91-08-397	Holiday Ahoy-568368	Enesco	2-Yr.	12.50	12.50
91-08-398	Christmas Countdown-568376	Enesco	3-Yr.	20.00	20.00
89-08-399	Clara-568406	Enesco	Yr.Iss.	12.50	20.00
90-08-400	The Nutcracker-568414	Enesco	Yr.Iss.	12.50	30.00
91-08-401	Clara's Prince-568422	Enesco	Yr.Iss.	12.50	18.00
89-08-402	Santa's Little Reindear-568430	Enesco	2-Yr.	15.00	25.00
91-08-403	Tuba Totin' Teddy-568449	Enesco	3-Yr.	15.00	15.00
90-08-404	A Calling Home At Christmas-568457	Enesco	2-Yr.	15.00	15.00
91-08-405	Love Is The Secret Ingredient-568562	L. Rigg	2-Yr.	15.00	15.00
90-08-406	A Spoonful of Love-568570	L. Rigg	2-Yr.	10.00	10.00
90-08-407	Christmas Swingtime 1990-568597	L. Rigg	Yr.Iss.	13.00	N/A
90-08-408	Christmas Swingtime 1990-568600	L. Rigg	Yr.Iss.	13.00	N/A
90-08-409	Bearing Holiday Wishes-568619	L. Rigg	3-Yr.	22.50	22.50
90-08-410	Smitch-570184	S. Zimnicki	3-Yr.	22.50	22.50
91-08-411	Twinkle & Sprinkle-570206	S. Zimnicki	3-Yr.	22.50	22.50
90-08-412	Blinkie-570214	S. Zimnicki	3-Yr.	15.00	15.00
90-08-413	Have A Coke And A Smile-571512	Enesco	3-Yr.	15.00	25.00
90-08-414	Fleece Navidad-571903	M. Cook	2-Yr.	13.50	25.00
90-08-415	Have a Navaho-Ho-Ho 1990-571970	M. Cook	Yr.Iss.	15.00	35.00
90-08-416	Cheers 1990-572411	T. Wilson	Yr.Iss.	13.50	22.00
90-08-417	A Night Before Christmas-572438	T. Wilson	2-Yr.	17.50	17.50
90-08-418	Merry Kissmas-572446	T. Wilson	2-Yr.	10.00	30.00
91-08-419	Here Comes Santa Paws-572535	J. Davis	3-Yr.	20.00	20.00
90-08-420	Frosty Garfield 1990-572551	J. Davis	Yr.Iss.	13.50	35.00
90-08-421	Pop Goes The Odie-572578	J. Davis	2-Yr.	15.00	30.00
91-08-422	Sweet Beams-572586	J. Davis	2-Yr.	13.50	13.50
90-08-423	An Apple A Day-572594	J. Davis	2-Yr.	12.00	12.00
90-08-424	Dear Santa-572608	J. Davis	3-Yr.	17.00	17.00
91-08-425	Have A Ball This Christmas-572616	J. Davis	Yr.Iss.	15.00	15.00
90-08-426	Oh Shoosh!-572624	J. Davis	3-Yr.	17.00	17.00
90-08-427	Little Red Riding Cat-572632	J. Davis	Yr.Iss.	13.50	33.00
91-08-428	All Decked Out-572659	J. Davis	2-Yr.	13.50	13.50
90-08-429	Over The Rooftops-572721	J. Davis	2-Yr.	17.50	28-35.00
90-08-430	Garfield NFL Los Angeles Rams-572764	J. Davis	2-Yr.	12.50	12.50
90-08-431	Garfield NFLCincinnati Bengals-573,000	J. Davis	2-Yr.	12.50	12.50
90-08-432	Garfield NFLCleveland Browns-573019	J. Davis	2-Yr.	12.50	12.50
90-08-433	Garfield NFL Houston Oiliers-573027	J. Davis	2-Yr.	12.50	12.50
90-08-434	Garfield NFL Pittsburg Steelers-573035	J. Davis	2-Yr.	12.50	12.50
90-08-435	Garfield NFL Denver Broncos-573043	J. Davis	2-Yr.	12.50	12.50
90-08-436	Garfield NFLKansas City Chiefs-573051	J. Davis	2-Yr.	12.50	12.50
90-08-437	Garfield NFL Los Angeles Raiders-573078	J. Davis	2-Yr.	12.50	12.50
90-08-438	Garfield NFL San Diego Chargers-573086	J. Davis	2-Yr.	12.50	12.50
90-08-439	Garfield NFL Seattle Seahawks-573094	J. Davis	2-Yr.	12.50	12.50
90-08-440	Garfield NFL Buffalo Bills-573108	J. Davis	2-Yr.	12.50	12.50
90-08-441	Garfield NFL Indianapolis Colts-573116	J. Davis	2-Yr.	12.50	12.50
90-08-442	Garfield NFL Miami Dolphins-573124	J. Davis	2-Yr.	12.50	12.50
90-08-443	Garfield NFL New England Patriots-573132	J. Davis	2-Yr.	12.50	12.50
90-08-444	Garfield NFL New York Jets-573140	J. Davis	2-Yr.	12.50	12.50
90-08-445	Garfield NFL Atlanta Falcons-573159	J. Davis	2-Yr.	12.50	12.50
90-08-446	Garfield NFL New Orleans Saints-573167	J. Davis	2-Yr.	12.50	12.50
90-08-447	Garfield NFL San Francisco 49ers-573175	J. Davis	2-Yr.	12.50	12.50
90-08-448	Garfield NFL Dallas Cowboys-573183	J. Davis	2-Yr.	12.50	12.50
90-08-449	Garfield NFL New York Giants-573191	J. Davis	2-Yr.	12.50	12.50
90-08-450	Garfield NFL Philadelphia Eagles-573205	J. Davis	2-Yr.	12.50	12.50
90-08-451	Garfield NFL Phoenix Cardinals-573213	J. Davis	2-Yr.	12.50	12.50
90-08-452	Garfield NFL Washington Redskins-573221	J. Davis	2-Yr.	12.50	12.50
90-08-453	Garfield NFL Chicago Bears-573248	J. Davis	2-Yr.	12.50	12.50
90-08-454	Garfield NFL Detroit Lions-573256	J. Davis	2-Yr.	12.50	12.50
90-08-455	Garfield NFL Green Bay Packers-573264	J. Davis	2-Yr.	12.50	12.50
90-08-456	Garfield NFLMinnesota Vikings-573272	J. Davis	2-Yr.	12.50	12.50
90-08-457	Garfield NFL Tampa Bay Buccaneers-573280	J. Davis	2-Yr.	12.50	12.50
91-08-458	Tea For Two-573299	K. Hahn	3-Yr.	30.00	50.00
91-08-459	Hot Stuff Santa-573523	Enesco	Yr.Iss.	25.00	30.00
90-08-460	Merry Moustronauts-573558	M. Cook	3-Yr.	20.00	40.00
91-08-461	Santa Wings It-573612	J. Jonik	3-Yr.	13.00	13.00
90-08-462	All Eye Want For Christmas-573647	Gilmore	3-Yr.	27.50	32.00
90-08-463	Stuck On You-573655	Gilmore	2-Yr.	12.50	12.50
90-08-464	Professor Michael Bear, The One Bear Band-573663	Gilmore	3-Yr.	22.50	28.00
90-08-465	A Caroling Wee Go-573671	Gilmore	3-Yr.	12.00	12.00
90-08-466	Merry Mailman-573698	Gilmore	2-Yr.	15.00	30.00
90-08-467	Deck The Halls-573701	Gilmore	3-Yr.	22.50	30.00
90-08-468	You're Wheel Special-573728	Gilmore	3-Yr.	15.00	15.00
91-08-469	Come Let Us Adore Him-573736	Gilmore	2-Yr.	9.00	9.00
91-08-470	Moon Beam Dreams-573760	Gilmore	3-Yr.	12.00	12.00
91-08-471	A Song For Santa-573779	Gilmore	3-Yr.	25.00	25.00
90-08-472	Warmest Wishes-573825	Gilmore	Yr.Iss.	17.50	24.50
91-08-473	Kurious Kitty-573868	Gilmore	3-Yr.	17.50	17.50
90-08-474	Old Mother Mouse-573922	Gilmore	2-Yr.	17.50	20-32.00
90-08-475	Railroad Repairs-573930	Gilmore	2-Yr.	12.50	25.00
90-08-476	Ten Lords A-Leaping-573949	Gilmore	3-Yr.	15.00	25.00
90-08-477	Eleven Drummers Drumming-573957	Gilmore	3-Yr.	15.00	25.00
90-08-478	Twelve Pipers Piping-573965	Gilmore	3-Yr.	15.00	25.00
90-08-479	Baby's First Christmas 1990-573973	Gilmore	Yr.Iss.	10.00	N/A
90-08-480	Baby's First Christmas 1990-573981	Gilmore	Yr.Iss.	12.00	N/A
91-08-481	Peter, Peter Pumpkin Eater-574015	Gilmore	2-Yr.	20.00	30.00
90-08-482	Little Jack Horner-574058	Gilmore	2-Yr.	17.50	35.00
91-08-483	Mary, Mary Quite Contrary-574066	Gilmore	2-Yr.	22.50	32.50
91-08-484	Through The Years-574252	Gilmore	Yr.Iss.	17.50	17.50
91-08-485	Holiday Wing Ding-574333	Enesco	3-Yr.	22.50	22.50
91-08-486	North Pole Here I Come-574597	Enesco	3-Yr.	10.00	10.00
91-08-487	Christmas Caboose-574856	Gilmore	2-Yr.	25.00	30.00
90-08-488	Bubble Trouble-575038	K. Hahn	3-Yr.	20.00	35.00
91-08-489	Merry Mother-To-Be-575046	K. Hahn	3-Yr.	13.50	13.50
90-08-490	A Holiday 'Scent' Sation-575054	K. Hahn	3-Yr.	15.00	30.00
90-08-491	Catch Of The Day-575070	K. Hahn	3-Yr.	25.00	25.00
90-08-492	Don't Open 'Til Christmas-575089	K. Hahn	3-Yr.	17.50	17.50
90-08-493	I Can't Weight 'Til Christmas-575119	K. Hahn	3-Yr.	16.50	30.00
91-08-494	Deck The Halls-575127	K. Hahn	2-Yr.	15.00	25.00
90-08-495	Mouse House-575186	Enesco	3-Yr.	16.00	16.00
91-08-496	Dream A Little Dream-575593	Enesco	2-Yr.	17.50	17.50
91-08-497	Christmas Two-gether-575615	L. Rigg	3-Yr.	22.50	22.50
91-08-498	Christmas Trimmings-575631	Gilmore	2-Yr.	17.00	17.00
91-08-499	Gumball Wizard-575658	Gilmore	2-Yr.	13.00	13.00
91-08-500	Crystal Ball Christmas-575666	Gilmore	2-Yr.	22.50	22.50
90-08-501	Old King Cole-575682	Gilmore	2-Yr.	20.00	28.50
91-08-502	Tom, Tom The Piper's Son-575690	Gilmore	2-Yr.	15.00	33.00
91-08-503	Tire-d Little Bear-575852	L. Rigg	Yr.Iss.	12.50	12.50
90-08-504	Baby Bear Christmas 1990-575860	L. Rigg	Yr.Iss.	12.00	28.00
91-08-505	Crank Up The Carols-575887	L. Rigg	2-Yr.	17.50	17.50
90-08-506	Beary Christmas 1990-576158	L. Rigg	Yr.Iss.	12.00	12.00
91-08-507	Christmas Swingtime 1991-576166	L. Rigg	Yr.Iss.	13.00	13.00
91-08-508	Christmas Swingtime 1991-576174	L. Rigg	Yr.Iss.	13.00	13.00
91-08-509	Christmas Cutie-576182	Enesco	3-Yr.	13.50	13.50
91-08-510	Meow Mates-576220	Enesco	3-Yr.	12.00	12.00
91-08-511	Frosty The Snowmant-576425	Enesco	3-Yr.	15.00	15.00
91-08-512	Ris-ski Business-576719	T. Wilson	2-Yr.	10.00	10.00
91-08-513	Pinocchio-577391	J. Davis	3-Yr.	15.00	15.00
90-08-514	Yuletide Ride 1990-577502	Gilmore	Yr.Iss.	13.50	50.00
90-08-515	Tons of Toys-577510	Enesco	Yr.Iss.	13.00	30.00
90-08-516	McHappy Holidays-577529	Enesco	2-Yr.	17.50	24.50
90-08-517	Heading For Happy Holidays-577537	Enesco	3-Yr.	17.50	17.50
90-08-518	'Twas The Night Before Christmas-577545	Enesco	3-Yr.	17.50	17.50
90-08-519	Over One Million Holiday Wishes!-577553	Enesco	Yr.Iss.	17.50	30.00
90-08-520	You Malt My Heart-577596	Enesco	2-Yr.	25.00	25.00
91-08-521	All I Want For Christmas-577618	Enesco	2-Yr.	20.00	20.00
91-08-522	Things Go Better With Coket-580597	Enesco	3-Yr.	17.00	17.00
91-08-523	Christmas To Go-580600	M. Cook	Yr.Iss.	22.50	22.50
91-08-524	Have A Mariachi Christmas-580619	M. Cook	2-Yr.	13.50	13.50
91-08-525	Christmas Is In The Air-581453	Enesco	Yr.Iss.	15.00	15.00
91-08-526	Holiday Treats-581542	Enesco	Yr.Iss.	17.50	17.50
91-08-527	Christmas Is My Goal-581550	Enesco	2-Yr.	17.50	17.50

		ARTIST	EDITION	ISSUE	QUOTE
91-08-528	A Quarter Pounder With Cheer®-581569	Enesco	3-Yr.	20.00	20.00
91-08-529	From The Same Mold-581798	Gilmore	3-Yr.	17.00	17.00
91-08-530	The Glow Of Christmas-581801	Enesco	2-Yr.	20.00	20.00
91-08-531	All Caught Up In Christmas-583537	Enesco	2-Yr.	10.00	10.00
91-08-532	Lights..Camera..Kissmas!-583626	Gilmore	Yr.Iss.	15.00	15.00
91-08-533	Sweet Steed-583634	Gilmore	3-Yr.	15.00	15.00
91-08-534	Dreamin' Of A White Christmas-583669	Gilmore	2-Yr.	15.00	15.00
91-08-535	Merry Millimeters-583677	Gilmore	3-Yr.	17.00	17.00
91-08-536	Here's The Scoop-583693	Enesco	2-Yr.	13.50	20.00
91-08-537	Happy Mealr On Wheels-583715	Enesco	3-Yr.	22.50	22.50
91-08-538	Christmas Kayak-583723	Enesco	2-Yr.	13.50	13.50
91-08-539	Marilyn Monroe-583774	Enesco	Yr.Iss.	20.00	20.00
91-08-540	A Christmas Carol-583928	Gilmore	3-Yr.	22.50	22.50
91-08-541	Checking It Twice-583936	Enesco	2-Yr.	25.00	25.00
91-08-542	Merry Christmas Go-Round-585203	J. Davis	3-Yr.	20.00	20.00
91-08-543	Holiday Hideout-585270	J. Davis	2-Yr.	15.00	15.00
91-08-544	Our Most Precious Gift-585726	Enesco	Yr.Iss.	17.50	17.50
91-08-545	Christmas Cheer-585769	Enesco	2-Yr.	13.50	13.50
91-08-546	Fired Up For Christmas-586587	Gilmore	2-Yr.	32.50	32.50
91-08-547	One Foggy Christmas Eve-586625	Gilmore	3-Yr.	30.00	30.00
91-08-548	For A Purr-fect Mom-586641	Gilmore	Yr.Iss.	12.00	12.00
91-08-549	For A Special Dad-586668	Gilmore	Yr.Iss.	17.50	17.50
91-08-550	With Love-586676	Gilmore	Yr.Iss.	13.00	13.00
91-08-551	For A Purr-fect Aunt-586692	Gilmore	Yr.Iss.	12.00	12.00
91-08-552	For A Dog-Gone Great Uncle-586706	Gilmore	Yr.Iss.	12.00	12.00
91-08-553	Peddling Fun-586714	Gilmore	Yr.Iss.	16.00	16.00
91-08-554	Special Keepsakes-586722	Gilmore	Yr.Iss.	13.50	13.50
91-08-555	Hats Off To Christmas-586757	K. Hahn	Yr.Iss.	22.50	22.50
91-08-556	Baby's First Christmas 1991-586935	Enesco	Yr.Iss.	12.50	12.50
91-08-557	Jugglin' The Holidays-587028	Enesco	2-Yr.	13.00	13.00
91-08-558	Santa's Steed-587044	Enesco	Yr.Iss.	15.00	15.00
91-08-559	A Decade of Treasures-587052	Gilmore	Yr.Iss.	37.50	75.00
91-08-560	Mr. Mailmouse-587109	Gilmore	2-Yr.	17.00	17.00
91-08-561	Starry Eyed Santa-587176	Enesco	2-Yr.	15.00	15.00
91-08-562	Lighting The Way-588776	Enesco	2-Yr.	20.00	20.00
91-08-563	Rudolph-588784	Enesco	2-Yr.	17.50	17.50
89-08-564	Tea For Two-693758	N. Teiber	2-Yr.	12.50	30.00
90-08-565	Holiday Tea Toast-694770	N. Teiber	2-Yr.	13.50	13.50
91-08-566	It's Tea-lightful-694789	Enesco	2-Yr.	13.50	13.50
89-08-567	Tea Time-694797	N. Teiber	2-Yr.	12.50	30.00
89-08-568	Bottom's Up 1989-830003	Enesco	Yr.Iss.	11.00	32.00
90-08-569	Sweetest Greetings 1990-830011	Gilmore	Yr.Iss.	10.00	27.00
90-08-570	First Class Christmas-830038	Gilmore	3-Yr.	10.00	10.00
89-08-571	Caught In The Act-830046	Gilmore	3-Yr.	12.50	12.50
89-08-572	Readin' & Ridin'-830054	Gilmore	3-Yr.	13.50	34.00
91-08-573	Beary Merry Mailman-830151	L. Rigg	3-Yr.	13.50	13.50
90-08-574	Here's Looking at You!-830259	Gilmore	2-Yr.	17.50	17.50
91-08-575	Stamper-830267	S. Zimnicki	Yr.Iss.	13.50	13.50
91-08-576	Santa's Key Man-830461	Gilmore	2-Yr.	11.00	11.00
91-08-577	Tie-dings Of Joy-830488	Gilmore	Yr.Iss.	12.00	12.00
90-08-578	Have a Cool Yule-830496	Gilmore	3-Yr.	12.00	27.00
90-08-579	Slots of Luck-830518	K. Hahn	2-Yr.	13.50	45-60.00
91-08-580	Straight To Santa-830534	J. Davis	2-Yr.	13.50	13.50
91-08-581	Letters To Santa-830925	Gilmore	2-Yr.	15.00	15.00
91-08-582	Sneaking Santa's Snack-830933	Gilmore	3-Yr.	13.00	13.00
91-08-583	Aiming For The Holidays-830941	Gilmore	2-Yr.	12.00	12.00
91-08-584	Ode To Joy-830968	Gilmore	3-Yr.	10.00	10.00
91-08-585	Fittin' Mittens-830976	Gilmore	3-Yr.	12.00	12.00
91-08-586	The Finishing Touch-831530	Gilmore	Yr.Iss.	10.00	10.00
91-08-587	A Real Classic-831603	Gilmore	Yr.Iss.	10.00	10.00
91-08-588	Christmas Fills The Air-831921	Gilmore	3-Yr.	12.00	12.00
91-08-589	Deck The Halls-860573	M. Peters	3-Yr.	12.00	12.00
91-08-590	Bathing Beauty-860581	K. Hahn	3-Yr.	13.50	35.00
92-08-591	Sparky & Buffer-561851	S. Zimnicki	3-Yr.	25.00	25.00
92-08-592	Moonlight Swing-568627	L. Rigg	3-Yr.	15.00	15.00
92-08-593	Carver-570192	S. Zimnicki	Yr.Iss.	17.50	17.50
92-08-594	A Rockin' GARFIELD Christmas-572527	J. Davis	2-Yr.	17.50	17.50
92-08-595	The Nutcracker-574023	Gilmore	3-Yr.	25.00	25.00
92-08-596	Humpty Dumpty-574244	Gilmore	2-Yr.	25.00	25.00
92-08-597	Music Mice-Tro!-575143	Enesco	2-Yr.	12.00	12.00
92-08-598	On Target Two-Gether-575623	Enesco	Yr.Iss.	17.00	17.00
92-08-599	Rock-A-Bye Baby-575704	Gilmore	2-Yr.	13.50	13.50
92-08-600	Queen of Hearts-575712	Gilmore	2-Yr.	17.50	17.50
92-08-601	Tasty Tidings-575836	L. Rigg	Yr.Iss.	13.50	13.50
92-08-602	Bearly Sleepy-578029	Gilmore	Yr.Iss.	17.50	17.50
92-08-603	Spreading Sweet Joy-580465	Enesco	Yr.Iss.	13.50	13.50
92-08-604	Ring My Bell-580740	J. Davis	Yr.Iss.	13.50	13.50
92-08-605	4 x 4 Holiday Fun-580783	J. Davis	2-Yr.	20.00	20.00
92-08-606	The Holidays Are A Hit-581577	Enesco	2-Yr.	17.50	17.50
92-08-607	Tip Top Tidings-581828	Enesco	2-Yr.	13.00	13.00
92-08-608	Christmas Lifts The Spirits-582018	Enesco	2-Yr.	25.00	25.00
92-08-609	A Pound Of Good Cheers-582034	Enesco	2-Yr.	17.50	17.50
92-08-610	Sweet as Cane Be-583642	Gilmore	3-Yr.	15.00	15.00
92-08-611	Sundae Ride-583707	Enesco	2-Yr.	20.00	20.00
92-08-612	The Cold, Crisp Taste Of Coket-583766	Enesco	3-Yr.	17.00	17.00
92-08-613	Sew Christmasy-583820	Enesco	3-Yr.	25.00	25.00
92-08-614	Catch A Falling Star-583944	Gilmore	2-Yr.	15.00	15.00
92-08-615	Swingin' Christmas-584096	Enesco	2-Yr.	15.00	15.00
92-08-616	Mc Ho, Ho, Ho-585181	Enesco	3-Yr.	22.50	22.50
92-08-617	Holiday On Ice-585254	J. Davis	3-Yr.	17.50	17.50
92-08-618	Fast Track Cat-585289	J. Davis	3-Yr.	17.50	17.50
92-08-619	Holiday Cat Napping-585319	J. Davis	2-Yr.	20.00	20.00
92-08-620	The Finishing Touches-585610	T. Wilson	2-Yr.	17.50	17.50
92-08-621	Jolly Ol' Gent-585645	J. Jonik	3-Yr.	13.50	13.50
92-08-622	A Child's Christmas-586358	Enesco	3-Yr.	25.00	25.00
92-08-623	Festive Fiddlers-586501	Enesco	Yr.Iss.	20.00	25.00
92-08-624	La Luminaria-586579	M. Cook	2-Yr.	13.50	13.50
92-08-625	Cozy Chrismas Carriage-586730	Gilmore	2-Yr.	22.50	22.50
92-08-626	Small Fry's First Christmas-586749	Enesco	2-Yr.	17.00	17.00
92-08-627	Friendships Preserved-586765	K. Hahn	Yr.Iss.	22.50	22.50
92-08-628	Window Wish List-586854	Gilmore	2-Yr.	30.00	30.00
92-08-629	Through The Years-586862	Gilmore	Yr.Iss.	17.50	17.50
92-08-630	Baby's First Christmas 1992-586943	Enesco	Yr.Iss.	12.50	12.50
92-08-631	Firehouse Friends-586951	Gilmore	Yr.Iss.	22.50	22.50
92-08-632	Bubble Buddy-586978	Gilmore	2-Yr	13.50	13.50
92-08-633	The Warmth Of The Season-586994	Enesco	2-Yr.	20.00	20.00
92-08-634	It's A Go For Christmas-587095	Gilmore	2-Yr.	15.00	15.00
92-08-635	Post-Mouster General-587117	Gilmore	2-Yr.	20.00	20.00
92-08-636	To A Deer Baby-587168	Enesco	Yr.Iss.	18.50	18.50
92-08-637	Moon Watch-587184	Enesco	2-Yr.	20.00	20.00
92-08-638	Guten Cheers-587192	Enesco	Yr.Iss.	22.50	22.50
92-08-639	Put On A Happy Face-588237	Enesco	2-Yr.	15.00	15.00
92-08-640	Beginning To Look A Lot Like Christmas-588253	Enesco	2-Yr.	15.00	15.00
92-08-641	A Christmas Toast-588261	Enesco	2-Yr.	20.00	20.00
92-08-642	Merry Mistle-Toad-588288	Enesco	2-Yr.	15.00	15.00
92-08-643	Tic-Tac-Mistle-Toe-588296	Enesco	3-Yr.	23.00	23.00
92-08-644	Heaven Sent-588423	J. Penchoff	2-Yr.	12.50	12.50
92-08-645	Holiday Happenings-588555	Gilmore	3-Yr.	30.00	30.00
92-08-646	Seed-son's Greetings-588571	Gilmore	3-Yr.	27.00	27.00
92-08-647	Santa's Midnight Snack-588598	Gilmore	2-Yr.	20.00	20.00
92-08-648	Trunk Of Treasures-588636	Enesco	Yr.Iss.	30.00	30.00
92-08-649	Festive Newsflash-588792	Enesco	2-Yr.	17.50	17.50
92-08-650	A-B-C-Son's Greetings-588806	Enesco	2-Yr.	16.50	16.50
92-08-651	Hoppy Holidays-588814	Enesco	Yr.Iss.	13.50	13.50
92-08-652	Fireside Friends-588830	Enesco	2-Yr.	20.00	20.00
92-08-653	Christmas Eve-mergency-588849	Enesco	2-Yr.	27.00	27.00
92-08-654	A Sure Sign Of Christmas-588857	Enesco	2-Yr.	22.50	22.50
92-08-655	Holidays Give Me A Lift-588865	Enesco	2-Yr.	30.00	30.00
92-08-656	Yule Tide Together-588903	Enesco	2-Yr.	20.00	20.00
92-08-657	Have A Soup-er Christmas-588911	Enesco	2-Yr.	17.50	17.50
92-08-658	Christmas Cure-Alls-588938	Enesco	2-Yr.	20.00	20.00
92-08-659	Dial 'S' For Santa-589373	Enesco	2-Yr.	25.00	25.00
92-08-660	Joy To The Whirled-589551	K. Hahn	2-Yr.	20.00	20.00
92-08-661	Merry Make-Over-589586	K. Hahn	3-Yr.	20.00	20.00
92-08-662	Campin' Companions-590282	K. Hahn	3-Yr.	20.00	20.00
92-08-663	Fur-Ever Friends-590797	Gilmore	2-Yr.	13.50	13.50
92-08-664	Tee-rific Holidays-590827	Enesco	3-Yr.	25.00	25.00
92-08-665	Spinning Christmas Dreams-590908	K. Hahn	3-Yr.	22.50	22.50
92-08-666	Christmas Trimmin'-590932	Enesco	3-Yr.	17.00	17.00
92-08-667	Wrappin' Up Warm Wishes-593141	Enesco	Yr.Iss.	17.50	17.50
92-08-668	Christmas Biz-593168	Enesco	2-Yr.	22.50	22.50
92-08-669	Holiday Take-Out-593508	Enesco	Yr.Iss.	17.50	17.50
92-08-670	A Christmas Yarn-593516	Gilmore	Yr.Iss.	20.00	20.00
92-08-671	Treasure The Earth-593826	K. Hahn	2-Yr.	25.00	25.00
92-08-672	Toyful' Rudolph-593982	Enesco	2-Yr.	22.50	22.50
92-08-673	Take A Chance On The Holidays-594075	Enesco	3-Yr.	20.00	20.00
92-08-674	Lights..Camera..Christmas!-594369	Enesco	3-Yr.	20.00	20.00
92-08-675	Spirited Stallion-594407	Enesco	Yr.Iss.	15.00	15.00
92-08-676	A Watchful Eye-595713	Enesco	Yr.Iss.	15.00	15.00
92-08-677	Good Catch-595721	Enesco	Yr.Iss.	12.50	12.50
92-08-678	Squirrelin' It Away-595748	K. Hahn	Yr.Iss.	12.00	12.00
92-08-679	Checkin' His List-595756	Enesco	Yr.Iss.	12.50	12.50
92-08-680	Christmas Cat Nappin'	Enesco	Yr.Iss.	12.00	12.00
92-08-681	Bless Our Home-595772	Enesco	Yr.Iss.	12.00	12.00
92-08-682	Salute the Season-595780	K. Hahn	Yr.Iss.	12.00	12.00
92-08-683	Fired Up For Christmas-595799	Enesco	Yr.Iss.	12.00	12.00
92-08-684	Speedin' Mr. Snowman-595802	M. Rhyner	Yr.Iss.	12.00	12.00
92-08-685	Merry Christmas Mother Earth-595810	K. Hahn	Yr.Iss.	11.00	11.00
92-08-686	Wear The Season With A Smile-595829	Enesco	Yr.Iss.	10.00	10.00
92-08-687	Jesus Loves Me-595837	K. Hahn	Yr.Iss.	10.00	10.00
92-08-688	Merry Kisses-831166	Enesco	2-Yr.	17.50	17.50
92-08-689	Christmas Is In The Air-831174	Enesco	2-Yr.	25.00	25.00
92-08-690	To The Point-831182	Gilmore	2-Yr.	13.50	13.50
92-08-691	Poppin' Hoppin' Holidays-831263	Gilmore	Yr.Iss.	25.00	25.00
92-08-692	Tankful Tidings-831271	Gilmore	2-Yr.	30.00	30.00
92-08-693	Ginger-Bred Greetings-831581	Gilmore	Yr.Iss.	12.00	12.00
92-08-694	A Gold Star For Teacher-831948	Gilmore	3-Yr.	15.00	15.00
92-08-695	A Tall Order-832758	Gilmore	3-Yr.	12.00	12.00
92-08-696	Candlelight Serenade-832766	Gilmore	2-Yr.	12.00	12.00
92-08-697	Holiday Glow Puppet Show-832774	Gilmore	3-Yr.	15.00	15.00
92-08-698	Christopher Columouse-832782	Gilmore	Yr.Iss.	12.00	12.00
92-08-699	Cartin' Home Holiday Treats-832790	Enesco	2-Yr.	13.50	13.50
92-08-700	Making Tracks To Santa-832804	Gilmore	2-Yr.	15.00	15.00
92-08-701	Special Delivery-832812	Enesco	2-Yr.	12.00	12.00
92-08-702	A Mug Full Of Love-832928	Gilmore	Yr.Iss.	13.50	13.50
92-08-703	Have A Cool Christmas-832944	Gilmore	Yr.Iss.	13.50	13.50
92-08-704	Knitten' Kittens-832952	Gilmore	Yr.Iss.	17.50	17.50
92-08-705	Holiday Honors-833029	Gilmore	Yr.Iss.	15.00	15.00
92-08-706	Christmas Nite Cap-834424	Gilmore	3-Yr.	13.50	13.50
92-08-707	North Pole Peppermint Patrol-840157	Gilmore	2-Yr.	25.00	25.00
92-08-708	A Boot-iful Christmas-840165	Gilmore	Yr.Iss.	20.00	20.00
92-08-709	Watching For Santa-840432	Enesco	2-Yr.	25.00	25.00
92-08-710	Special Delivery-840440	Enesco	Yr.Iss.	22.50	22.50
93-08-711	I'm Dreaming of a White-Out Christmas-566144	Enesco	2-Yr.	22.50	22.50
93-08-712	Born To Shop-572942	Enesco	Yr.Iss.	26.50	26.50
93-08-713	Toy To The World-575763	Enesco	2-Yr.	25.00	25.00
93-08-714	Bearly Balanced-580724	Enesco	Yr.Iss.	15.00	15.00
93-08-715	Joyeux Noel-582026	Enesco	2-Yr.	24.50	24.50
93-08-716	Holiday Mew-Sic-582107	Enesco	2-Yr.	20.00	20.00
93-08-717	Santa's Magic Ride-582115	Enesco	2-Yr.	24.00	24.00
93-08-718	Warm And Hearty Wishes-582344	Enesco	Yr.Iss.	17.50	17.50
93-08-719	Cool Yule-582352	Enesco	Yr.Iss.	12.00	12.00
93-08-720	Have A Holly Jell-O Christmas-582387	Enesco	Yr.Iss.	45.00	45.00
93-08-721	Festive Firemen-582565	Gilmore	2-Yr.	17.00	17.00
93-08-722	Light Up Your Holidays With Coke-583758	Enesco	Yr.Iss.	27.50	27.50
93-08-723	Pool Hall-idays-584851	Enesco	2-Yr.	19.90	19.90
93-08-724	Bah Humbug-585394	Davis	Yr.Iss.	15.00	15.00
93-08-725	Chimer-585777	Zimnicki	Yr.Iss.	25.00	25.00
93-08-726	Sweet Whiskered Wishes-585807	Enesco	Yr.Iss.	17.00	17.00
93-08-727	Grade "A" Wishes From Garfield -585823	Davis	2-Yr.	20.00	20.00
93-08-728	Tree For Two-586781	Gilmore	2-Yr.	17.50	17.50
93-08-729	A Bright Idea-586803	Gilmore	2-Yr.	22.50	22.50
93-08-730	Baby's First Christmas 1993-585823	Gilmore	Yr.Iss.	17.50	17.50
93-08-731	My Special Christmas-586900	Gilmore	Yr.Iss.	17.50	17.50
93-08-732	Baby's First Christmas Dinner-587001	Enesco	Yr.Iss.	12.00	12.00
93-08-733	A Pause For Claus-588318	Enesco	2-Yr.	22.50	22.50
93-08-734	Not A Creature Was Stirring...-588663	Gilmore	2-Yr.	27.50	27.50
93-08-735	Terrific Toys-588644	Enesco	Yr.Iss.	20.00	20.00
93-08-736	Christmas Dancer-588652	Enesco	Yr.Iss.	15.00	15.00
93-08-737	Countin' On A Merry Christmas-588954	Enesco	2-Yr.	22.50	22.50
93-08-738	To My Gem-589004	Enesco	Yr.Iss.	27.50	27.50
93-08-739	Christmas Mall Call-589012	Enesco	2-Yr.	20.00	20.00
93-08-740	Spreading Joy-589047	Enesco	2-Yr.	27.50	27.50
93-08-741	Pitter-Patter Post Office-589055	Enesco	2-Yr.	20.00	20.00
93-08-742	Happy Haul-idays-589098	Enesco	2-Yr.	30.00	30.00
93-08-743	Hot Off ThePress-589292	Enesco	2-Yr.	27.50	27.50
93-08-744	Designed With You In Mind-589306	Enesco	2-Yr.	16.00	16.00
93-08-745	Seeing Is Believing-589381	Gilmore	2-Yr.	20.00	20.00
93-08-746	Roundin' Up Christmas Together-590800	Enesco	Yr.Iss.	25.00	25.00
93-08-747	Toasty Tidings-590940	Enesco	2-Yr.	20.00	20.00
93-08-748	Focusing On Christmas-590983	Gilmore	2-Yr.	27.50	27.50

		ARTIST	EDITION	ISSUE	QUOTE
93-08-749	Dunk The Halls-591009	Enesco	2-Yr.	18.50	18.50
93-08-750	Mice Capades-591386	Hahn	2-Yr.	26.50	26.50
93-08-751	25 Points For Christmas-591750	Enesco	Yr.Iss.	25.00	25.00
93-08-752	Carving Christmas Wishes-592625	Gilmore	2-Yr.	25.00	25.00
93-08-753	Celebrating With A Splash-592692	Enesco	Yr.Iss.	17.00	17.00
93-08-754	Slimmin' Santa-592722	Enesco	Yr.Iss.	18.50	18.50
93-08-755	Plane Ol' Holiday Fun-592773	Enesco	Yr.Iss.	27.50	27.50
93-08-756	Smooth Move, Mom-593176	Enesco	Yr.Iss.	20.00	20.00
93-08-757	Tool TIme, Yule TIme-593192	Enesco	Yr.Iss.	18.50	18.50
93-08-758	Speedy-593370	Zimnicki	2-Yr.	25.00	25.00
93-08-759	On Your Mark, Set, Is That To Go?-593524	Enesco	Yr.Iss.	13.50	13.50
93-08-760	Do Not Open 'Til Christmas-593737	Hahn	2-Yr.	15.00	15.00
93-08-761	Greetings In Stereo-593745	Hahn	Yr.Iss.	19.50	19.50
93-08-762	Tangled Up For Christmas-593974	Enesco	2-Yr.	14.50	14.50
93-08-763	Sweet Season's Eatings-594202	Enesco	Yr.Iss.	22.50	22.50
93-08-764	Have A Darn Good Christmas-594229	Gilmore	2-Yr.	21.00	21.00
93-08-765	The Sweetest Ride-594253	Gilmore	2-Yr.	18.50	18.50
93-08-766	Lights...Camera...Christmas-594369	Enesco	Yr.Iss.	20.00	20.00
93-08-767	Have A Cheery Christmas, Sister-594687	Enesco	Yr.Iss.	13.50	13.50
93-08-768	Say Cheese-594962	Gilmore	2-Yr.	13.50	13.50
93-08-769	Christmas Kicks-594989	Enesco	Yr.Iss.	17.50	17.50
93-08-770	Time For Santa-594997	Gilmore	2-Yr.	17.50	17.50
93-08-771	Holiday Orders-595004	Enesco	Yr.Iss.	20.00	20.00
93-08-772	T'Was The Night Before Christmas-595012	Enesco	Yr.Iss.	22.50	22.50
93-08-773	Sugar Chef Shoppe-595055	Gilmore	2-Yr.	23.50	23.50
93-08-774	Merry Mc-Choo-Choo-595063	Enesco	Yr.Iss.	30.00	30.00
93-08-775	Basketful Of Friendship-595098	Enesco	Yr.Iss.	20.00	20.00
93-08-776	Rockin' With Santa-595195	Enesco	2-Yr.	13.50	13.50
93-08-777	Christmas-To-Go-595217	Enesco	Yr.Iss.	25.50	25.50
93-08-778	Sleddin' Mr. Snowman-595275	Enesco	2-Yr.	13.00	13.00
93-08-779	A Kick Out Of Christmas-595373	Enesco	2-Yr.	10.00	10.00
93-08-780	Friends Through Thick And Thin-595381	Enesco	2-Yr.	10.00	10.00
93-08-781	See-Saw Sweethearts-595403	Enesco	2-Yr.	10.00	10.00
93-08-782	Special Delivery For Santa-595411	Enesco	2-Yr.	10.00	10.00
93-08-783	Top Marks For Teacher-595438	Enesco	2-Yr.	10.00	10.00
93-08-784	Home Tweet Home-595446	Enesco	2-Yr.	10.00	10.00
93-08-785	Clownin' Around-595454	Enesco	2-Yr.	10.00	10.00
93-08-786	Heart Filled Dreams-595462	Enesco	2-Yr.	10.00	10.00
93-08-787	Merry Christmas Baby-595470	Enesco	2-Yr.	10.00	10.00
93-08-788	Your A Hit With Me, Brother-595535	Hahn	Yr.Iss.	10.00	10.00
93-08-789	For A Sharp Uncle-595543	Enesco	Yr.Iss.	10.00	10.00
93-08-790	Paint Your Holidays Bright-595551	Hahn	2-Yr.	10.00	10.00
93-08-791	Goofy "Goals" For It-596019	Enesco	Yr.Iss.	15.00	15.00
93-08-792	Goofy Slam Dunk'-598027	Enesco	Yr.Iss.	15.00	15.00
93-08-793	Goofy Scores Again-598035	Enesco	Yr.Iss.	15.00	15.00
93-08-794	Goofy About Football'-596043	Enesco	Yr.Iss.	15.00	15.00
93-08-795	You Got To Treasure The Holidays, Man'-596051	Enesco	Yr.Iss.	22.50	22.50
93-08-796	Ariel's Under-The-Sea Tree-596078	Enesco	Yr.Iss.	20.00	20.00
93-08-797	Here Comes Santa Claws-596086	Enesco	Yr.Iss.	22.50	22.50
93-08-798	You're Tea-Lighting, Mom!-596094	Enesco	Yr.Iss.	17.50	17.50
93-08-799	Hearts A Glow-596108	Enesco	Yr.Iss.	18.50	18.50
93-08-800	Love's Sweet Dance-596116	Enesco	Yr.Iss.	25.00	25.00
93-08-801	Holiday Wishes-596124	Enesco	Yr.Iss.	15.00	15.00
93-08-802	Hangin Out For The Holidays-596132	Enesco	Yr.Iss.	15.00	15.00
93-08-803	Magic Carpet Ride-596140	Enesco	Yr.Iss.	20.00	20.00
93-08-804	Holiday Treasures-596159	Enesco	Yr.Iss.	18.50	35.00
93-08-805	Happily Ever After-596167	Enesco	Yr.Iss.	22.50	22.50
93-08-806	The Fairest Of Them All-596175	Enesco	Yr.Iss.	18.50	18.50
93-08-807	December 25...Dear Diary-596809	Hahn	2-Yr.	10.00	10.00
93-08-808	Wheel Merry Wishes-596930	Hahn	2-Yr.	15.00	15.00
93-08-809	Good Grounds For Christmas-596957	Hahn	Yr.Iss.	24.50	24.50
93-08-810	Ducking The Season's Rush-597597	Enesco	Yr.Iss.	17.50	17.50
93-08-811	Here Comes Rudolphr-597686	Enesco	2-Yr.	17.50	17.50
93-08-812	It's Beginning To Look A Lot Like Christmas-597694	Enesco	Yr.Iss.	22.50	22.50
93-08-813	Christmas In The Making-597716	Enesco	Yr.Iss.	20.00	20.00
93-08-814	Mickey's Holiday Treasure-597759	Enesco	Yr.Iss.	12.00	12.00
93-08-815	Dream Wheels-597856	Enesco	Yr.Iss.	29.50	50.00
93-08-816	All You Add Is Love-598429	Enesco	Yr.Iss.	18.50	18.50
93-08-817	Goofy About Skiing-598631	Enesco	Yr.Iss.	22.50	22.50
93-08-818	A Toast Ladled With Love-830828	Hahn	2-Yr.	15.00	15.00
93-08-819	Christmas Is In The Air-831174	Enesco	2-Yr.	25.00	25.00
93-08-820	Delivered to The Nick In Time-831808	Gilmore	2-Yr.	13.50	13.50
93-08-821	Sneaking A Peek-831840	Gilmore	2-Yr.	10.00	10.00
93-08-822	Jewel Box Ballet-831859	Hahn	2-Yr.	20.00	20.00
93-08-823	A Mistle-Tow-831867	Gilmore	2-Yr.	15.00	15.00
93-08-824	Grandma's Liddle Griddle-832936	Gilmore	Yr.Iss.	10.00	10.00
93-08-825	To A Grade "A" Teacher-833037	Gilmore	2-Yr.	10.00	10.00
93-08-826	Have A Cool Christmas-834467	Gilmore	2-Yr.	10.00	10.00
93-08-827	For A Star Aunt-834556	Gilmore	Yr.Iss.	12.00	12.00
93-08-828	Watching For Santa-840432	Enesco	2-Yr.	25.00	25.00
93-08-829	The Treasury Card (Club) - T,0001	Gilmore	Yr.Iss.	20.00	20.00
93-08-830	Together We Can Shoot For The Stars (Club) - TR931	Hahn	Yr.Iss.	17.50	17.50
93-08-831	Can't Weights For The Holidays (Club) - TR932	Enesco	Yr.Iss.	18.50	18.50
94-08-832	Seedlings Greetings (Club) - TR933	Hahn	Yr.Iss.	22.50	22.50
94-08-833	Spry Fry (Club) - TR934	Enesco	Yr.Iss.	15.00	15.00
94-08-834	Sending You A Season's Greetings - 550140	Butcher	Yr.Iss.	25.00	25.00
94-08-835	Goofy Delivery - 550639	Enesco	Yr.Iss.	22.50	22.50
94-08-836	Happy Howl-idays - 550647	Enesco	Yr.Iss.	22.50	22.50
94-08-837	Christmas Crusin' - 550655	Enesco	Yr.Iss.	22.50	22.50
94-08-838	Holiday Honeys - 550663	Enesco	Yr.Iss.	20.00	20.00
94-08-839	May Your Holiday Be Brightened With Love - 550698	Butcher	Yr.Iss.	15.00	15.00
94-08-840	May All Your Wishes Come True - 550701	Butcher	Yr.Iss.	20.00	20.00
94-08-841	Baby's First Christmas - 550728	Butcher	Yr.Iss.	20.00	20.00
94-08-842	Baby's First Christmas- 550736	Butcher	Yr.Iss.	20.00	20.00
94-08-843	Our First Christmas Together - 550744	Butcher	Yr.Iss.	25.00	25.00
94-08-844	Drumming Up A Season Of Joy- 550752	Butcher	Yr.Iss.	18.50	18.50
94-08-845	Friendships Warm The Holidays - 550760	Butcher	Yr.Iss.	20.00	20.00
94-08-846	Dropping In For The Holidays - 550779	Butcher	Yr.Iss.	20.00	20.00
94-08-847	Ringing Up Holiday Wishes - 550787	Butcher	Yr.Iss.	18.50	18.50
94-08-848	A Child Is Born - 550795	Butcher	Yr.Iss.	25.00	25.00
94-08-849	Tis The Season To Go Shopping - 550817	Butcher	Yr.Iss.	22.50	22.50
94-08-850	The Way To A Mouse's Heart - 550922	Enesco	Yr.Iss.	15.00	15.00
94-08-851	Teed-Off Donald - 550930	Enesco	Yr.Iss.	15.00	15.00
94-08-852	Holiday Show-Stopper - 550949	Enesco	Yr.Iss.	15.00	15.00
94-08-853	Answering Christmas Wishes - 551023	Enesco	Yr.Iss.	17.50	17.50
94-08-854	Pure Christmas Pleasure - 551066	Enesco	Yr.Iss.	20.00	20.00

		ARTIST	EDITION	ISSUE	QUOTE
94-08-855	Good Tidings, Tidings, Tidings, Tidings - 551333	Enesco	Yr.Iss.	20.00	20.00
94-08-856	From Our House To Yours - 551384	Gilmore	Yr.Iss.	25.00	25.00
94-08-857	Sugar 'N' Spice For Someone Nice - 551406	Gilmore	Yr.Iss.	30.00	30.00
94-08-858	Picture Perfect Christmas - 551465	Enesco	Yr.Iss.	15.00	15.00
94-08-859	Toodles - 551503	Zimnicki	Yr.Iss.	25.00	25.00
94-08-860	A Bough For Belle! - 551554	Enesco	Yr.Iss.	18.50	18.50
94-08-861	Ariel's Christmas Surprise! - 551570	Enesco	Yr.Iss.	20.00	20.00
94-08-862	Merry Little Two-Step - 551589	Enesco	Yr.Iss.	12.50	12.50
94-08-863	Sweets For My Sweetie - 551600	Enesco	Yr.Iss.	15.00	15.00
94-08-864	Friends Are The Spice of Life - 551619	Hahn	Yr.Iss.	20.00	20.00
94-08-865	Cool Cruise - 551635	Enesco	Yr.Iss.	20.00	20.00
94-08-866	A Christmas Tail - 551759	Enesco	Yr.Iss.	20.00	20.00
94-08-867	Merry Mischief- 551767	Enesco	Yr.Iss.	15.00	15.00
94-08-868	L'il Stocking Stuffer - 551791	Enesco	Yr.Iss.	17.50	17.50
94-08-869	Once Upon A Time - 551805	Enesco	Yr.Iss.	15.00	15.00
94-08-870	Wishing Upon A Star - 551813	Enesco	Yr.Iss.	18.50	18.50
94-08-871	A Real Boy For Christmas - 551821	Enesco	Yr.Iss.	15.00	15.00
94-08-872	Minnie's Holiday Treasure - 552216	Enesco	Yr.Iss.	12.00	12.00
94-08-873	Sweet Holidays - 552259	Butcher	Yr.Iss.	11.00	11.00
94-08-874	Special Delivery - 561657	Enesco	Yr.Iss.	20.00	20.00
94-08-875	Merry Miss Merry - 564508	Hahn	Yr.Iss.	12.00	12.00
94-08-876	Santa Delivers - 564567	Enesco	Yr.Iss.	12.00	12.00
94-08-877	Buttons 'N' Bow Boutique - 578363	Gilmore	Yr.Iss.	22.50	22.50
94-08-878	A Sign of Peace - 581992	Enesco	Yr.Iss.	18.50	18.50
94-08-879	Wishing You Well At Christmas - 582050	Enesco	Yr.Iss.	25.00	25.00
94-08-880	Ahoy Joy! - 582085	Enesco	Yr.Iss.	20.00	20.00
94-08-881	Santa...Phone Home - 582166	Enesco	Yr.Iss.	25.00	25.00
94-08-882	Christmas Swishes - 582379	Enesco	Yr.Iss.	17.50	17.50
94-08-883	The Latest Scoop From Santa - 582395	Gilmore	Yr.Iss.	18.50	18.50
94-08-884	Chiminy Cheer - 582409	Gilmore	Yr.Iss.	22.50	22.50
94-08-885	Cozy Candlelight Dinner - 582417	Gilmore	Yr.Iss.	25.00	25.00
94-08-886	Fine Feathered Festivities - 582425	Gilmore	Yr.Iss.	22.50	22.50
94-08-887	Joy From Head To Hose - 582433	Gilmore	Yr.Iss.	15.00	15.00
94-08-888	Yuletide Yummies - 584835	Gilmore	Yr.Iss.	20.00	20.00
94-08-889	Merry Christmas Tool You, Dad - 584886	Enesco	Yr.Iss.	22.50	22.50
94-08-890	Exercising Good Taste - 584967	Enesco	Yr.Iss.	17.50	17.50
94-08-891	Holiday Chew-Chew - 584983	Gilmore	Yr.Iss.	22.50	22.50
94-08-892	Mine, Mine, Mine - 585815	Davis	Yr.Iss.	20.00	20.00
94-08-893	To The Sweetest Baby - 588725	Gilmore	Yr.Iss.	18.50	18.50
94-08-894	Rockin' Ranger - 588970	Enesco	Yr.Iss.	25.00	25.00
94-08-895	Peace On Earthworm - 588989	Enesco	Yr.Iss.	20.00	20.00
94-08-896	Good Things Crop Up At Christmas - 589071	Enesco	Yr.Iss.	25.00	25.00
94-08-897	Christmas Crossroads - 589128	Enesco	Yr.Iss.	20.00	20.00
94-08-898	Have A Ball At Christmas - 590673	Enesco	Yr.Iss.	15.00	15.00
94-08-899	Have A Totem-ly Terrific Christmas - 590819	Enesco	Yr.Iss.	30.00	30.00
94-08-900	Cocoa 'N' Kisses For Santa- 591939	Enesco	Yr.Iss.	22.50	22.50
94-08-901	On The Road With Coke™ - 592528	Enesco	Yr.Iss.	25.00	25.00
94-08-902	What's Shakin' For Christmas - 592668	Enesco	Yr.Iss.	18.50	18.50
94-08-903	"A" For Santa - 592676	Enesco	Yr.Iss.	17.50	17.50
94-08-904	Christmas Fly-By - 592714	Enesco	Yr.Iss.	15.00	15.00
94-08-905	Santa...You're The Pops! - 593761	Enesco	Yr.Iss.	22.50	22.50
94-08-906	Purdy Packages, Pardner! - 593834	Enesco	Yr.Iss.	20.00	20.00
94-08-907	Handle With Care - 593842	Enesco	Yr.Iss.	20.00	20.00
94-08-908	To Coin A Phrase, Merry Christmas - 593877	Enesco	Yr.Iss.	20.00	20.00
94-08-909	Featured Presentation - 593885	Enesco	Yr.Iss.	20.00	20.00
94-08-910	Christmas Fishes From Santa Paws - 593893	Enesco	Yr.Iss.	18.50	18.50
94-08-911	Melted My Heart - 594237	Gilmore	Yr.Iss.	15.00	15.00
94-08-912	Finishing First - 594342	Gilmore	Yr.Iss.	20.00	20.00
94-08-913	Yule Fuel - 594385	Enesco	Yr.Iss.	20.00	20.00
94-08-914	Toy Tinker Topper - 595047	Gilmore	Yr.Iss.	20.00	20.00
94-08-915	Santa Claus Is Comin' - 595209	Enesco	Yr.Iss.	20.00	20.00
94-08-916	Seasoned With Love - 595268	Enesco	Yr.Iss.	22.50	22.50
94-08-917	Sweet Dreams - 595489	Enesco	Yr.Iss.	12.50	12.50
94-08-918	Peace On Earth - 595497	Enesco	Yr.Iss.	12.50	12.50
94-08-919	Christmas Two-gether - 595500	Enesco	Yr.Iss.	12.50	12.50
94-08-920	Santa's L'il Helper - 595519	Enesco	Yr.Iss.	12.50	12.50
94-08-921	Expecting Joy - 595527	Hahn	Yr.Iss.	12.50	12.50
94-08-922	Sweet Greetings - 595578	Enesco	Yr.Iss.	12.50	12.50
94-08-923	Ring In The Holidays - 595586	Hahn	Yr.Iss.	12.50	12.50
94-08-924	Grandmas Are Sew Special - 595594	Enesco	Yr.Iss.	12.50	12.50
94-08-925	Holiday Catch - 595608	Hahn	Yr.Iss.	12.50	12.50
94-08-926	Bubblin' with Joy - 595616	Enesco	Yr.Iss.	12.50	12.50
94-08-927	Good Friends Are Forever - 595950	Gilmore	Yr.Iss.	13.50	13.50
94-08-928	Christmas Tee Time - 596256	Enesco	Yr.Iss.	25.00	25.00
94-08-929	Have a Merry Dairy Christmas - 596264	Enesco	Yr.Iss.	22.50	22.50
94-08-930	Happy Holi-date - 596272	Hahn	Yr.Iss.	22.50	22.50
94-08-931	O' Come All Ye Faithful - 596280	Hahn	Yr.Iss.	15.00	15.00
94-08-932	One Small Step... - 596299	Hahn	Yr.Iss.	30.00	30.00
94-08-933	To My Favorite V.I.P. - 596698	Enesco	Yr.Iss.	20.00	20.00
94-08-934	Building Memories - 596876	Hahn	Yr.Iss.	25.00	25.00
94-08-935	Open For Business - 596906	Hahn	Yr.Iss.	17.50	17.50
94-08-936	Twas The Nite Before Christmas - 597643	Gilmore	Yr.Iss.	18.50	18.50
94-08-937	I Can Bear-ly Wait For A Coke™ - 597724	Enesco	Yr.Iss.	18.50	18.50
94-08-938	Gallant Greeting- 598313	Enesco	Yr.Iss.	20.00	20.00
94-08-939	Merry Menage - 598321	Enesco	Yr.Iss.	20.00	20.00
94-08-940	Bundle Of Joy - 598992	Enesco	Yr.Iss.	10.00	10.00
94-08-941	Bundle Of Joy - 599018	Enesco	Yr.Iss.	10.00	10.00
94-08-942	Have A Dino-mite Christmas - 599026	Hahn	Yr.Iss.	18.50	18.50
94-08-943	Good Fortune To You - 599034	Enesco	Yr.Iss.	25.00	25.00
94-08-944	Building a Sew-man - 599042	Enesco	Yr.Iss.	18.50	18.50
94-08-945	Merry Memo-ries - 599050	Enesco	Yr.Iss.	22.50	22.50
94-08-946	Ski-son's Greetings - 599069	Enesco	Yr.Iss.	20.00	20.00
94-08-947	Holiday Freezer Teaser - 59908525.00	Gilmore	Yr.Iss.	25.00	25.00
94-08-948	Almost Time For Santa - 599093	Gilmore	Yr.Iss.	25.00	25.00
94-08-949	Santa's Secret Test Drive - 599107	Gilmore	Yr.Iss.	20.00	20.00
94-08-950	You're A Wheel Cool Brother - 599115	Gilmore	Yr.Iss.	22.50	22.50
94-08-951	Hand-Tossed Tidings - 599166	Enesco	Yr.Iss.	17.50	17.50
94-08-952	Tasty Take Off - 599174	Enesco	Yr.Iss.	20.00	20.00
94-08-953	Formula For Love - 599530	Olsen	Yr.Iss.	10.00	10.00
94-08-954	Santa's Ginger-bred Doe - 599697	Gilmore	Yr.Iss.	15.00	15.00
94-08-955	Nutcracker Sweetheart - 599700	Enesco	Yr.Iss.	15.00	15.00
94-08-956	Merry Reindeer Ride - 599719	Enesco	Yr.Iss.	20.00	20.00
94-08-957	Santa's Sing-A-Long - 599727	Gilmore	Yr.Iss.	20.00	20.00
94-08-958	A Holiday Opportunity - 599735	Enesco	Yr.Iss.	20.00	20.00
94-08-959	Holiday Stars - 599743	Enesco	Yr.Iss.	20.00	20.00
94-08-960	The Latest Mews From Home - 653977	Enesco	Yr.Iss.	16.00	16.00

		ARTIST	EDITION	ISSUE	QUOTE
94-08-961	You're A Winner Son! - 834564	Gilmore	Yr.Iss.	18.50	18.50
94-08-962	Especially For You - 834580	Gilmore	Yr.Iss.	27.50	27.50
Enesco Corporation		**Cherished Teddies**			
92-09-001	Angel - 950777	P. Hillman	Open	12.50	12.50
92-09-002	Bear In Stocking, dated 1992-950653	P. Hillman	Yr.Iss.	16.00	24-36.00
92-09-003	Bear On Rocking Horse - 950793	P. Hillman	Open	20.00	20.00
92-09-004	3 Asst. Christmas Bear - 951226	P. Hillman	Open	12.50	12.50
93-09-005	Girl w/Muff Dated 1993 - 912832	P. Hillman	Yr.Iss.	13.50	20.00
93-09-006	Baby Boy Dated 1993 - 913014	P. Hillman	Yr.Iss.	12.50	12.50
93-09-007	Baby Girl Dated 1993 - 913006	P. Hillman	Yr.Iss.	12.50	12.50
93-09-008	Jointed Teddy Bear -914894	P. Hillman	Open	12.50	12.50
93-09-009	3 Asst. Angel - 912980	P. Hillman	Open	12.50	12.50
94-09-010	I'll Play My Drum For You Dated 1994 - 912891	P. Hillman	Yr.Iss.	10.00	10.00
94-09-011	Beary Christmas Dated 1994 -617253	P. Hillman	Yr.Iss.	15.00	15.00
94-09-012	Bundled Up For The Holidays -617229	P. Hillman	Open	15.00	15.00
Enesco Corporation		**Maud Humphrey Bogart Ornaments**			
89-10-001	Sarah H1367	M. Humphrey	19,500	35.00	38.00
90-10-002	Victoria H1365	M. Humphrey	19,500	35.00	38.00
90-10-003	Michelle H1370	M. Humphrey	19,500	35.00	38.00
90-10-004	Catherine H1366	M. Humphrey	19,500	35.00	38.00
90-10-005	Gretchen H1369	M. Humphrey	19,500	35.00	38.00
90-10-006	Rebecca H5513	M. Humphrey	19,500	35.00	38.00
91-10-007	Cleaning House-915084	M. Humphrey	Open	24.00	24.00
91-10-008	Gift of Love-915092	M. Humphrey	Open	24.00	24.00
91-10-009	My First Dance-915106	M. Humphrey	Open	24.00	24.00
91-10-010	Special Friends-915114	M. Humphrey	Open	24.00	24.00
91-10-011	Susanna-915122	M. Humphrey	Open	24.00	24.00
91-10-012	Sarah-915165	M. Humphrey	Open	24.00	24.00
92-10-013	Hollies For You-915726	M. Humphrey	Closed	24.00	24.00
93-10-014	Tidings of Joy-915483	M. Humphrey	Open	27.50	27.50
Fitz and Floyd, Inc.		**Fitz and Floyd Annual Christmas Ornaments**			
91-01-001	Plaid Teddy	M. Collins	Closed	15.00	15.00
92-01-002	Nutcracker Sweets	R. Havins	Closed	18.00	18.00
93-01-003	A Christmas Carol, Dickens	T. Kerr	7,500	18.00	18.00
94-01-004	Night Before Christmas	V. Balcou	7,500	18.00	18.00
Fitz and Floyd, Inc.		**Fitz and Floyd's Baby First Christmas**			
92-02-001	Rock-A-Bye Teddy	M. Collins	Closed	18.00	18.00
93-02-002	Li'l Angel	M. Collins	Closed	18.00	18.00
94-02-003	Bundles of Joy	M. Collins	Yr.Iss.	18.00	18.00
Fitz and Floyd, Inc.		**Our First Christmas**			
93-03-001	Christmas at Our House	M. Collins	Closed	18.00	18.00
93-03-002	The Honey Bunnies	M. Collins	Closed	18.00	18.00
94-03-003	Home for the Holidays	M. Collins	Yr.Iss.	18.00	18.00
94-03-004	Bear Huggs	M. Collins	Yr.Iss.	18.00	18.00
Fitz and Floyd, Inc.		**Heirloom Collection**			
92-04-001	Plaid Teddy with Star	M. Collins	Retrd.	15.00	15.00
92-04-002	Plaid Teddy with Gift	M. Collins	Retrd.	15.00	15.00
92-04-003	Partridge and Pear Tree	Averitt	Retrd.	15.00	15.00
92-04-004	Elf with Teddy Bear	V. Balcou	Retrd.	15.00	15.00
92-04-005	St. Nicholas Medallion, large	T. Kerr	Retrd.	18.00	18.00
92-04-006	St. Nicholas Medallion, small	T. Kerr	Retrd.	14.00	14.00
92-04-007	Holiday Cat	V. Balcou	Retrd.	15.00	15.00
92-04-008	Merry Christmas Elf	V. Balcou	Open	15.00	15.00
92-04-009	Elf with Candy Cane	V. Balcou	Open	15.00	15.00
92-04-010	Plaid Teddy in Wagon	M. Collins	Open	15.00	15.00
93-04-011	Christmas Quilt	M. Collins	Open	15.00	15.00
94-04-012	Kris Kringle	R. Havins	Open	15.00	15.00
94-04-013	Reindeer	R. Havins	Open	15.00	15.00
Flambro Imports		**Emmett Kelly Jr. Christmas Ornaments**			
89-01-001	65th Birthday	Undis.	Closed	24.00	50-120.
90-01-002	30 Years Of Clowning	Undis.	Closed	30.00	70-150.
91-01-003	EKJ With Stocking And Toys	Undis.	Closed	30.00	40-50.00
92-01-004	Home For Christmas	Undis.	Closed	24.00	30-45.00
93-01-005	Christmas Mail	Undis.	Closed	25.00	50.00
94-01-006	'70 Birthday Commemorative	Undis.	Yr.Iss.	24.00	24.00
Flambro Imports		**Little Emmetts**			
95-02-001	Little Emmett Wreath	Undis.	Open	11.50	11.50
95-02-002	Little Emmett Bulb Garland	Undis.	Open	11.50	11.50
Margaret Furlong Designs		**Musical Series**			
80-01-001	The Caroler	M. Furlong	Closed	50.00	100-125.
81-01-002	The Lyrist	M. Furlong	Closed	45.00	75-100.
82-01-003	The Lutist	M. Furlong	Closed	45.00	75-100.
83-01-004	The Concertinist	M. Furlong	Closed	45.00	75.00
84-01-005	The Herald Angel	M. Furlong	Closed	45.00	75-100.
Margaret Furlong Designs		**Annual Ornaments**			
80-02-001	3" Trumpeter Angel	M. Furlong	Closed	12.00	12.00
80-02-002	4" Trumpeter Angel	M. Furlong	Closed	21.00	21.00
82-02-003	3" Star Angel	M. Furlong	Closed	12.00	12.00
82-02-004	4" Star Angel	M. Furlong	Closed	21.00	21.00
Margaret Furlong Designs		**Gifts from God**			
85-03-001	The Charis Angel	M. Furlong	Closed	45.00	250.00
86-03-002	The Hallelujah Angel	M. Furlong	Closed	45.00	250-500.
87-03-003	The Angel of Light	M. Furlong	Closed	45.00	100.00
88-03-004	The Celestial Angel	M. Furlong	Closed	45.00	100-150.
89-03-005	Coronation Angel	M. Furlong	Closed	45.00	75-125.
Margaret Furlong Designs		**Joyeux Noel**			
90-04-001	Celebration Angel	M. Furlong	10,000	45.00	45-55.00
91-04-002	Thanksgiving Angel	M. Furlong	10,000	45.00	45.00
92-04-003	Joyeux Noel Angel	M. Furlong	10,000	45.00	45.00
93-04-004	Star of Bethlehem Angel	M. Furlong	10,000	45.00	45.00
94-04-005	Messiah Angel	M. Furlong	10,000	45.00	45.00
Ganz		**Little Cheesers/The Christmas Collection**			
92-01-001	Santa Cheeser Ornament	GDA/Thammavongsa	Open	14.00	14.00
92-01-002	Jenny Butterfield Ornament	GDA/Thammavongsa	Open	17.00	17.00
92-01-003	Myrtle Meadowmouse Ornament	GDA/Thammavongsa	Open	15.00	15.00
92-01-004	Little Truffle Ornament	GDA/Thammavongsa	Open	9.50	9.50
92-01-005	Jeremy With Teddy Bear Ornament	GDA/Thammavongsa	Open	13.00	13.00
92-01-006	Abner Appleton Ornament	GDA/Thammavongsa	Open	15.00	15.00
93-01-007	Baby's First X'mas Ornament	C. Thammavongsa	Open	12.50	12.50
93-01-008	Little Stocking Stuffer Ornament	C. Thammavongsa	Open	10.50	10.50
93-01-009	Our First Christmas Together Ornament	C. Thammavongsa	Open	18.50	18.50
93-01-010	Dashing Through the Snow Ornament	C. Thammavongsa	Open	11.00	11.00
93-01-011	Santa's Little Helper Ornament	C. Thammavongsa	Open	11.00	11.00
93-01-012	Skating Into Your Heart Ornament	C. Thammavongsa	Open	10.00	10.00
93-01-013	Medley Meadowmouse X'mas Bell Ornament	C. Thammavongsa	Open	17.00	17.00
94-01-014	Swinging Into the Season	C. Thammavongsa	Open	11.00	11.00
94-01-015	Peace on Earth	C. Thammavongsa	Open	8.00	8.00
94-01-016	Santa's Workshop	C. Thammavongsa	Open	10.00	10.00
94-01-017	Chelsea's Stocking Bell	C. Thammavongsa	Open	15.50	15.50
94-01-018	Candy Cane Caper	C. Thammavongsa	Open	9.00	9.00
94-01-019	Sleigh Ride	C. Thammavongsa	Closed	9.00	9.00
94-01-020	All I Want For Christmas	C. Thammavongsa	Closed	13.50	13.50
94-01-021	Medley Playing Drum	C. Thammavongsa	Closed	5.50	5.50
94-01-022	Cheeser Showman	C. Thammavongsa	Closed	5.00	5.00
94-01-023	Violet With Snowball	C. Thammavongsa	Closed	5.50	5.50
94-01-024	Hickory Playing Cello	C. Thammavongsa	Closed	10.00	10.00
94-01-025	Grandpa Blowing Horn	C. Thammavongsa	Closed	10.00	10.00
94-01-026	Cousin Woody Playing Flute	C. Thammavongsa	Closed	10.00	10.00
94-01-027	Angel	C. Thammavongsa	Open	8.00	8.00
Ganz		**Cowtown/The Christmas Collection**			
94-02-001	Jingle Bull	C. Thammavongsa	Open	15.50	15.50
94-02-002	Bronco Bully	C. Thammavongsa	Open	13.00	13.00
94-02-003	Christmoos Eve	C. Thammavongsa	Open	12.00	12.00
94-02-004	Hallemooah	C. Thammavongsa	Open	12.00	12.00
94-02-005	Calf-in-the Box	C. Thammavongsa	Open	12.50	12.50
94-02-006	Li'l Red Gliding Hoof	C. Thammavongsa	Open	12.00	12.00
94-02-007	Downhill Dare Debull	C. Thammavongsa	Open	12.00	12.00
94-02-008	Little Drummer Calf	C. Thammavongsa	Open	12.00	12.00
Ganz		**Pigsville/The Christmas Collection**			
94-03-001	Joy to the World	C. Thammavongsa	Open	10.00	10.00
94-03-002	Santa Pig	C. Thammavongsa	Open	11.00	11.00
94-03-003	Caroler	C. Thammavongsa	Open	10.00	10.00
94-03-004	Wheeeeee! Piggy	C. Thammavongsa	Open	9.00	9.00
94-03-005	Drummer Pig	C. Thammavongsa	Open	10.00	10.00
94-03-006	Christmas Treats	C. Thammavongsa	Open	9.00	9.00
Ganz		**Pigsville/The Valentine Collection**			
94-04-001	Lovestruck	C. Thammavongsa	Open	10.50	10.50
Ganz		**Little Cheesers/The Silverwoods**			
94-05-001	Santa Silverwood	C. Thammavongsa	Open	9.00	9.00
94-05-002	Mrs. Claus	C. Thammavongsa	Open	9.00	9.00
94-05-003	Xmas Express	C. Thammavongsa	Open	8.50	8.50
94-05-004	Giddy Up!	C. Thammavongsa	Open	8.50	8.50
94-05-005	Christmas Surprise	C. Thammavongsa	Open	8.50	8.50
94-05-006	Hickory Dickory Dock	C. Thammavongsa	Open	9.50	9.50
94-05-007	Deck the Halls	C. Thammavongsa	Open	9.50	9.50
94-05-008	Comfort and Joy	C. Thammavongsa	Open	6.00	6.00
Goebel		**Co-Boy Annual Ornaments**			
86-01-001	Coboy with Wreath	G. Skrobek	Closed	18.00	25.00
87-01-002	Coboy with Candy Cane	G. Skrobek	Closed	25.00	25.00
88-01-003	Coboy with Tree	G. Skrobek	Closed	30.00	30.00
Goebel		**Charlot Byj Annual Ornaments**			
86-02-001	Santa Lucia Angel	Charlot Byj	Closed	18.00	25.00
87-02-002	Christmas Pageant	Charlot Byj	Closed	20.00	20.00
88-02-003	Angel with Sheet Music	Charlot Byj	Closed	22.00	22.00
Goebel		**Charlot Byj Baby Ornaments**			
86-03-001	Baby Ornament	Charlot Byj	Closed	18.00	18.00
87-03-002	Baby Snow	Charlot Byj	Closed	20.00	20.00
88-03-003	Baby's 1st Stocking	Charlot Byj	Closed	27.50	27.50
Goebel		**Annual Ornaments**			
78-04-001	Santa (white)	Goebel	Closed	7.50	12.00
78-04-002	Santa (color)	Goebel	Closed	15.00	17-50.00
79-04-003	Angel/Tree (white)	Goebel	Closed	8.00	13.00
79-04-004	Angel/Tree (color)	Goebel	Closed	16.00	18-45.00
80-04-005	Mrs. Santa (white)	Goebel	Closed	9.00	14.00
80-04-006	Mrs. Santa (color)	Goebel	Closed	17.00	17-40.00
81-04-007	The Nutcracker (white)	Goebel	Closed	10.00	10.00
81-04-008	The Nutcracker (color)	Goebel	Closed	18.00	18-35.00
82-04-009	Santa in Chimney (white)	Goebel	Closed	10.00	10.00
82-04-010	Santa in Chimney (color)	Goebel	Closed	18.00	18.00
83-04-011	Clown (white)	Goebel	Closed	10.00	10.00
83-04-012	Clown (color)	Goebel	Closed	18.00	18-35.00
84-04-013	Snowman (white)	Goebel	Closed	10.00	10.00
84-04-014	Snowman (color)	Goebel	Closed	18.00	18-35.00
85-04-015	Angel (white)	Goebel	Closed	9.00	9.00
85-04-016	Angel (color)	Goebel	Closed	18.00	18-35.00
86-04-017	Drummer Boy (white)	Goebel	Closed	9.00	9.00
86-04-018	Drummer Boy (color)	Goebel	Closed	18.00	18.00
87-04-019	Rocking Horse (white)	Goebel	Closed	10.00	10.00
87-04-020	Rocking Horse (color)	Goebel	Closed	20.00	20.00
88-04-021	Doll (white)	Goebel	Closed	13.00	12.50
88-04-022	Doll (color)	Goebel	Closed	23.00	22.50
89-04-023	Dove (white)	Goebel	Closed	13.00	12.50
89-04-024	Dove (color)	Goebel	Closed	20.00	20.00
90-04-025	Girl In Sleigh	Goebel	Closed	30.00	30.00
91-04-026	Baby On Moon	Goebel	Closed	35.00	35.00
Goebel		**Christmas Ornaments**			
87-05-001	Three Angels with Toys-(Set)	Goebel	Open	30.00	30.00
87-05-002	Three Angels with Instruments-(Set)	Goebel	Open	30.00	30.00
88-05-003	Snowman	Goebel	Open	10.00	10.00
88-05-004	Santa's Boot	Goebel	Open	7.50	7.50
88-05-005	Saint Nick	Goebel	Open	15.00	15.00
88-05-006	Nutcracker	Goebel	Open	15.00	15.00
86-05-007	Teddy Bear - Red Hat	Goebel	Open	5.00	5.00
86-05-008	Teddy Bear - Red Scarf	Goebel	Open	5.00	5.00
86-05-009	Teddy Bear - Red Boots	Goebel	Open	5.00	5.00
86-05-010	Angel - Red with Song	Goebel	Open	6.00	6.00
86-05-011	Angel - Red with Book	Goebel	Open	6.00	6.00
86-05-012	Angel - Red with Bell	Goebel	Open	6.00	6.00
86-05-013	Angel with Lantern (color)	Goebel	Open	8.00	8.00
86-05-014	Angel with Lantern (white)	Goebel	Open	6.00	6.00
86-05-015	Angel with Horn (color)	Goebel	Open	8.00	8.00
86-05-016	Angel with Horn (white)	Goebel	Open	6.00	6.00
86-05-017	Angel with Lute (color)	Goebel	Open	8.00	8.00
86-05-018	Angel with Lute (white)	Goebel	Open	6.00	6.00
88-05-019	Angel with Toy Teddy Bear	Goebel	Open	10.00	10.00
88-05-020	Angel with Toy Rocking Horse	Goebel	Open	10.00	10.00

		ARTIST	EDITION	ISSUE	QUOTE
88-05-021	Angel with Toy Train	Goebel	Open	10.00	10.00
88-05-022	Angel with Toys-(Set of three)	Goebel	Open	30.00	30.00
88-05-023	Angel with Banjo	Goebel	Open	10.00	10.00
88-05-024	Angel with Accordian	Goebel	Open	10.00	10.00
88-05-025	Angel with Violin	Goebel	Open	10.00	10.00
88-05-026	Angel with Music Set	Goebel	Open	30.00	30.00

Goebel/M.I. Hummel — **M.I. Hummel Annual Figurine Ornaments**

88-01-001	Flying High 452	M.I. Hummel	Closed	75.00	125-135.
89-01-002	Love From Above 481	M.I. Hummel	Closed	75.00	80-135.
90-01-003	Peace on Earth 484	M.I. Hummel	Closed	80.00	85-105.
91-01-004	Angelic Guide 571	M.I. Hummel	Closed	95.00	95-195.
92-01-005	Light Up The Night 622	M.I. Hummel	Closed	100.00	100.00
93-01-006	Herald on High 623	M.I. Hummel	Closed	155.00	155.00

Goebel/M.I. Hummel — **M.I. Hummel Collectibles Christmas Bell Ornaments**

89-02-001	Ride Into Christmas 775	M.I. Hummel	Closed	35.00	35-85.00
90-02-002	Letter to Santa Claus 776	M.I. Hummel	Closed	37.50	38-50.00
91-02-003	Hear Ye, Hear Ye 777	M.I. Hummel	Closed	40.00	39.50
92-02-004	Harmony in Four Parts 778	M.I. Hummel	Closed	50.00	50.00
93-02-005	Celestial Musician 779	M.I. Hummel	Closed	50.00	50.00
94-02-006	Festival Harmony w/Mandolin 780	M.I. Hummel	Yr.Iss.	50.00	50.00

Goebel/M.I. Hummel — **M.I. Hummel Collectibles Miniature Ornaments**

93-03-001	Celestial Musician 646	M.I. Hummel	Open	90.00	90.00
94-03-002	Festival Harmony w/Mandolin 647	M.I. Hummel	Open	95.00	95.00

Gorham — **Archive Collectible**

88-01-001	Victorian Heart	Gorham	Closed	50.00	65.00
89-01-002	Victorian Wreath	Gorham	Closed	50.00	50.00
90-01-003	Elizabethan Cupid	Gorham	Closed	60.00	60.00
91-01-004	Baroque Angels	Gorham	Closed	55.00	55.00
92-01-005	Madonna and Child	Gorham	Closed	50.00	50.00
93-01-006	Angel With Mandolin	Gorham	Closed	50.00	50.00

Gorham — **Annual Snowflake Ornaments**

70-02-001	Sterling Snowflake	Gorham	Closed	10.00	300.00
71-02-002	Sterling Snowflake	Gorham	Closed	10.00	55.00
72-02-003	Sterling Snowflake	Gorham	Closed	10.00	55.00
73-02-004	Sterling Snowflake	Gorham	Closed	11.00	75.00
74-02-005	Sterling Snowflake	Gorham	Closed	18.00	50.00
75-02-006	Sterling Snowflake	Gorham	Closed	18.00	30-75.00
76-02-007	Sterling Snowflake	Gorham	Closed	20.00	85.00
77-02-008	Sterling Snowflake	Gorham	Closed	23.00	30-70.00
78-02-009	Sterling Snowflake	Gorham	Closed	23.00	40-70.00
79-02-010	Sterling Snowflake	Gorham	Closed	33.00	85.00
80-02-011	Silverplated Snowflake	Gorham	Closed	15.00	90.00
81-02-012	Sterling Snowflake	Gorham	Closed	50.00	225.00
82-02-013	Sterling Snowflake	Gorham	Closed	38.00	55-85.00
83-02-014	Sterling Snowflake	Gorham	Closed	45.00	55-90.00
84-02-015	Sterling Snowflake	Gorham	Closed	45.00	55-85.00
85-02-016	Sterling Snowflake	Gorham	Closed	45.00	55-75.00
86-02-017	Sterling Snowflake	Gorham	Closed	45.00	55-65.00
87-02-018	Sterling Snowflake	Gorham	Closed	50.00	55-65.00
88-02-019	Sterling Snowflake	Gorham	Closed	50.00	50.00
89-02-020	Sterling Snowflake	Gorham	Closed	50.00	50.00
90-02-021	Sterling Snowflake	Gorham	Closed	50.00	60.00
91-02-022	Sterling Snowflake	Gorham	Closed	55.00	55.00
92-02-023	Sterling Snowflake	Gorham	Closed	50.00	60.00
93-02-024	Sterling Snowflake	Gorham	Yr.Iss.	50.00	50.00

Gorham — **Annual Crystal Ornaments**

85-03-001	Crystal Ornament	Gorham	Closed	22.00	22.00
86-03-002	Crystal Ornament	Gorham	Closed	25.00	25.00
87-03-003	Crystal Ornament	Gorham	Closed	25.00	25.00
88-03-004	Crystal Ornament	Gorham	Closed	28.00	28.00
89-03-005	Crystal Ornament	Gorham	Closed	28.00	28.00
90-03-006	Crystal Ornament	Gorham	Closed	30.00	30.00
91-03-007	Crystal Ornament	Gorham	Closed	35.00	35.00
92-03-008	Crystal Ornament	Gorham	Closed	32.50	32.50
93-03-009	Crystal Ornament	Gorham	Yr.Iss.	32.50	32.50

Gorham — **Baby's First Christmas Crystal**

91-04-001	Baby's First Rocking Horse	Gorham	Open	35.00	35.00

Dave Grossman Creations — **Gone With the Wind Ornaments**

87-01-001	Tara	D. Geenty	Closed	15.00	45.00
87-01-002	Rhett	D. Geenty	Closed	15.00	45.00
87-01-003	Scarlett	D. Geenty	Closed	15.00	45.00
87-01-004	Ashley	D. Geenty	Closed	15.00	45.00
88-01-005	Rhett and Scarlett	D. Geenty	Closed	20.00	40.00
89-01-006	Mammy	D. Geenty	Closed	20.00	20.00
90-01-007	Scarlett (Red Dress)	D. Geenty	Closed	20.00	20.00
91-01-008	Prissy	Unknown	Closed	20.00	20.00
92-01-009	Scarlett (Green Dress)	Unknown	Closed	20.00	20.00
93-01-010	Rhett (White Suit) GWO-93	Unknown	Closed	20.00	20.00
94-01-011	Scarlett GWO-94	Unknown	Yr.Iss.	20.00	20.00
94-01-012	Gold Plated GWO-00	Unknown	Open	13.00	13.00
94-01-013	Limited Edition GWO-94	Unknown	Yr.Iss.	25.00	25.00

Dave Grossman Creations — **Norman Rockwell Collection-Annual Rockwell Figurine Ornaments**

78-02-001	Caroler NRX-03	Rockwell-Inspired	Retrd.	15.00	45.00
79-02-002	Drum for Tommy NRX-24	Rockwell-Inspired	Retrd.	20.00	30.00
80-02-003	Santa's Good Boys NRX-37	Rockwell-Inspired	Retrd.	20.00	30.00
81-02-004	Letters to Santa NRX-39	Rockwell-Inspired	Retrd.	20.00	30.00
82-02-005	Cornettist NRX-32	Rockwell-Inspired	Retrd.	20.00	30.00
83-02-006	Fiddler NRX-83	Rockwell-Inspired	Retrd.	20.00	30.00
84-02-007	Christmas Bounty NRX-84	Rockwell-Inspired	Retrd.	20.00	30.00
85-02-008	Jolly Coachman NRX-85	Rockwell-Inspired	Retrd.	20.00	30.00
86-02-009	Grandpa on Rocking Horse NRX-86	Rockwell-Inspired	Retrd.	20.00	30.00
87-02-010	Skating Lesson NRX-87	Rockwell-Inspired	Retrd.	20.00	30.00
88-02-011	Big Moment NRX-88	Rockwell-Inspired	Retrd.	20.00	25.00
89-02-012	Discovery NRX-89	Rockwell-Inspired	Retrd.	20.00	20.00
90-02-013	Bringing Home The Tree NRX-90	Rockwell-Inspired	Retrd.	20.00	20.00
91-02-014	Downhill Daring B NRX-91	Rockwell-Inspired	Retrd.	20.00	20.00
92-02-015	On The Ice	Rockwell-Inspired	Retrd.	20.00	20.00
93-02-016	Granps NRX-93	Rockwell-Inspired	Retrd.	24.00	24.00
93-02-017	Marriage License First Christmas Together NRX-m1	Rockwell-Inspired	Retrd.	30.00	30.00
94-02-018	Merry Christmas NRX-94	Rockwell-Inspired	Yr.Iss.	24.00	24.00

Dave Grossman Creations — **Norman Rockwell Collection-Annual Rockwell Ball Ornaments**

75-03-001	Santa with Feather Quill NRO-01	Rockwell-Inspired	Retrd.	3.50	25.00
76-03-002	Santa at Globe NRO-02	Rockwell-Inspired	Retrd.	4.00	25.00
77-03-003	Grandpa on Rocking Horse NRO-03	Rockwell-Inspired	Retrd.	4.00	12.00
78-03-004	Santa with Map NRO-04	Rockwell-Inspired	Retrd.	4.50	12.00
79-03-005	Santa at Desk with Mail Bag NRO-05	Rockwell-Inspired	Retrd.	5.00	12.00
80-03-006	Santa Asleep with Toys NRO-06	Rockwell-Inspired	Retrd.	5.00	10.00
81-03-007	Santa with Boy on Finger NRO-07	Rockwell-Inspired	Retrd.	5.00	10.00
82-03-008	Santa Face on Winter Scene NRO-08	Rockwell-Inspired	Retrd.	5.00	10.00
83-03-009	Coachman with Whip NRO-9	Rockwell-Inspired	Retrd.	5.00	10.00
84-03-010	Christmas Bounty Man NRO-10	Rockwell-Inspired	Retrd.	5.00	10.00
85-03-011	Old English Trio NRO-11	Rockwell-Inspired	Retrd.	5.00	10.00
86-03-012	Tiny Tim on Shoulder NRO-12	Rockwell-Inspired	Retrd.	5.00	10.00
87-03-013	Skating Lesson NRO-13	Rockwell-Inspired	Retrd.	5.00	10.00
88-03-014	Big Moment NRO-14	Rockwell-Inspired	Retrd.	5.50	6.00
89-03-015	Discovery NRO-15	Rockwell-Inspired	Retrd.	6.00	6.00
90-03-016	Bringing Home The Tree NRO-16	Rockwell-Inspired	Retrd.	6.00	6.00
91-03-017	Downhill Daring NRO-17	Rockwell-Inspired	Retrd.	6.00	6.00
92-03-018	On The Ice NRO-18	Rockwell-Inspired	Retrd.	6.00	6.00
93-03-019	Granps NRO-19	Rockwell-Inspired	Retrd.	6.00	6.00
94-03-020	Triple Self Portrait-Commemorative NRO-20	Rockwell-Inspired	Yr.Iss.	6.00	6.00

Dave Grossman Creations — **Norman Rockwell Collection-Character Doll Ornaments**

83-04-001	Doctor and Doll NRD-01	Rockwell-Inspired	Retrd.	20.00	30.00
83-04-002	Lovers NRD-02	Rockwell-Inspired	Retrd.	20.00	30.00
83-04-003	Samplers NRD-03	Rockwell-Inspired	Retrd.	20.00	30.00

Hallmark Galleries — **Enchanted Garden**

92-01-001	Neighborhood Dreamer 1500QHG3014	E. Richardson	19,500	15.00	15.00

Hallmark Keepsake Ornaments — **1973 Hallmark Keepsake Collection**

73-01-001	Betsey Clark 250XHD100-2	Keepsake	Yr.Iss.	2.50	65-85.00
73-01-002	Betsey Clark-First Edition 250XHD 110-2	Keepsake	Yr.Iss.	2.50	75.00
73-01-003	Manger Scene 250XHD102-2	Keepsake	Yr.Iss.	2.50	75.00
73-01-004	Christmas Is Love 250XHD106-2	Keepsake	Yr.Iss.	2.50	80.00
73-01-005	Santa with Elves 250XHD101-5	Keepsake	Yr.Iss.	2.50	75-85.00
73-01-006	Elves 250XHD103-5	Keepsake	Yr.Iss.	2.50	75.00

Hallmark Keepsake Ornaments — **1973 Keepsake Yarn Ornaments**

73-02-001	Mr. Santa 125XHD74-5	Keepsake	Yr.Iss.	1.25	24.50
73-02-002	Mrs. Santa 125XHD75-2	Keepsake	Yr.Iss.	1.25	22.50
73-02-003	Mr. Snowman 125XHD76-5	Keepsake	Yr.Iss.	1.25	24.50
73-02-004	Mrs. Snowman 125XHD77-2	Keepsake	Yr.Iss.	1.25	22.50
73-02-005	Angel 125XHD78-5	Keepsake	Yr.Iss.	1.25	22.50
73-02-006	Elf 125XHD79-2	Keepsake	Yr.Iss.	1.25	21.50
73-02-007	Choir Boy 125XHD80-5	Keepsake	Yr.Iss.	1.25	27.50
73-02-008	Soldier 100XHD81-2	Keepsake	Yr.Iss.	1.00	22.00
73-02-009	Little Girl 125XHD82-5	Keepsake	Yr.Iss.	1.25	22.50
73-02-010	Boy Caroler 125XHD83-2	Keepsake	Yr.Iss.	1.25	29.50
73-02-011	Green Girl 125XHD84-5	Keepsake	Yr.Iss.	1.25	22.50
73-02-012	Blue Girl 125XHD85-2	Keepsake	Yr.Iss.	1.25	22.50

Hallmark Keepsake Ornaments — **1974 Hallmark Keepsake Collection**

74-03-001	Norman Rockwell 250QX111-1	Keepsake	Yr.Iss.	2.50	80.00
74-03-002	Norman Rockwell 250QX106-1	Keepsake	Yr.Iss.	2.50	45-75.00
74-03-003	Betsey Clark-Second Edition 250QX 108-1	Keepsake	Yr.Iss.	2.50	45-75.00
74-03-004	Charmers 250QX109-1	Keepsake	Yr.Iss.	2.50	25.00
74-03-005	Snowgoose 250QX107-1	Keepsake	Yr.Iss.	2.50	75.00
74-03-006	Angel 250QX110-1	Keepsake	Yr.Iss.	2.50	65.00
74-03-007	Raggedy Ann and Andy(4/set) 450QX114-1	Keepsake	Yr.Iss.	4.50	75.00
74-03-008	Little Miracles (Set of 4) 450QX115-1	Keepsake	Yr.Iss.	4.50	55.00
74-03-009	Buttons & Bo (Set of 2) 350QX113-1	Keepsake	Yr.Iss.	3.50	50.00
74-03-010	Currier & Ives (Set of 2) 350QX112-1	Keepsake	Yr.Iss.	3.50	42-55.00

Hallmark Keepsake Ornaments — **1974 Keepsake Yarn Ornaments**

74-04-001	Mrs. Santa 150QX100-1	Keepsake	Yr.Iss.	1.50	22.50
74-04-002	Elf 150QX101-1	Keepsake	Yr.Iss.	1.50	22.50
74-04-003	Soldier 150QX102-1	Keepsake	Yr.Iss.	1.50	21.50
74-04-004	Angel 150QX103-1	Keepsake	Yr.Iss.	1.50	27.50
74-04-005	Snowman 150QX104-1	Keepsake	Yr.Iss.	1.50	22.50
74-04-006	Santa 150QX105-1	Keepsake	Yr.Iss.	1.50	23.50

Hallmark Keepsake Ornaments — **1975 Keepsake Property Ornaments**

75-05-001	Betsey Clark (Set of 4) 450QX168-1	Keepsake	Yr.Iss.	4.50	50.00
75-05-002	Betsey Clark (Set of 2) 350QX167-1	Keepsake	Yr.Iss.	3.50	25-40.00
75-05-003	Betsey Clark 250QX163-1	Keepsake	Yr.Iss.	2.50	36-40.00
75-05-004	Betsey Clark-Third Ed. 300QX133-1	Keepsake	Yr.Iss.	3.00	30-75.00
75-05-005	Currier & Ives (Set of 2) 250QX164-1	Keepsake	Yr.Iss.	2.50	40.00
75-05-006	Currier & Ives (Set of 2) 400QX137-1	Keepsake	Yr.Iss.	4.00	35-40.00
75-05-007	Raggedy Ann and Andy(2/set) 400QX138-1	Keepsake	Yr.Iss.	4.00	65.00
75-05-008	Raggedy Ann 250QX165-1	Keepsake	Yr.Iss.	2.50	50.00
75-05-009	Norman Rockwell 250QX166-1	Keepsake	Yr.Iss.	2.50	55-75.00
75-05-010	Norman Rockwell 300QX134-1	Keepsake	Yr.Iss.	3.00	35.00
75-05-011	Charmers 300QX135-1	Keepsake	Yr.Iss.	3.00	30.00
75-05-012	Marty Links 300QX136-1	Keepsake	Yr.Iss.	3.00	35.00
75-05-013	Buttons & Bo (Set of 4) 500QX139-1	Keepsake	Yr.Iss.	5.00	30-45.00
75-05-014	Little Miracles (Set of 4) 500QX140-1	Keepsake	Yr.Iss.	5.00	25-40.00

Hallmark Keepsake Ornaments — **1975 Keepsake Yarn Ornaments**

75-06-001	Raggedy Ann 175QX121-1	Keepsake	Yr.Iss.	1.75	35.00
75-06-002	Raggedy Andy 175QX122-1	Keepsake	Yr.Iss.	1.75	39.50
75-06-003	Drummer Boy 175QX123-1	Keepsake	Yr.Iss.	1.75	24.50
75-06-004	Santa 175QX124-1	Keepsake	Yr.Iss.	1.75	22.00
75-06-005	Mrs. Santa 175QX125-1	Keepsake	Yr.Iss.	1.75	21.50
75-06-006	Little Girl 175QX126-1	Keepsake	Yr.Iss.	1.75	19.50

Hallmark Keepsake Ornaments — **1975 Handcrafted Ornaments: Nostalgia**

75-07-001	Locomotive (dated) 350QX127-1	Keepsake	Yr.Iss.	3.50	110-175.
75-07-002	Rocking Horse 350QX128-1	Keepsake	Yr.Iss.	3.50	110-175.
75-07-003	Santa & Sleigh 350QX129-1	Keepsake	Yr.Iss.	3.50	200.00
75-07-004	Drummer Boy 350QX130-1	Keepsake	Yr.Iss.	3.50	150.00
75-07-005	Peace on Earth (dated) 350QX131-1	Keepsake	Yr.Iss.	3.50	100-160.
75-07-006	Joy 350QX132-1	Keepsake	Yr.Iss.	3.50	125-200.

Hallmark Keepsake Ornaments — **1975 Handcrafted Ornaments: Adorable**

75-08-001	Santa 250QX155-1	Keepsake	Yr.Iss.	2.50	250.00
75-08-002	Mrs. Santa 250QX156-1	Keepsake	Yr.Iss.	2.50	275.00
75-08-003	Betsey Clark 250QX157-1	Keepsake	Yr.Iss.	2.50	225.00
75-08-004	Raggedy Ann 250QX159-1	Keepsake	Yr.Iss.	2.50	295.00
75-08-005	Raggedy Andy 250QX160-1	Keepsake	Yr.Iss.	2.50	375.00
75-08-006	Drummer Boy 250QX161-1	Keepsake	Yr.Iss.	2.50	325.00

Hallmark Keepsake Ornaments — **1976 First Commemorative Ornament**

76-09-001	Baby's First Christmas 250QX211-1	Keepsake	Yr.Iss.	2.50	75-95.00

Hallmark Keepsake Ornaments — **1976 Bicentennial Commemoratives**

76-10-001	Bicentennial '76 Commemorative 250QX211-1	Keepsake	Yr.Iss.	2.50	60.00

		ARTIST	EDITION	ISSUE	QUOTE
76-10-002	Bicentennial Charmers 300QX198-1	Keepsake	Yr.Iss.	3.00	60.00
76-10-003	Colonial Children (Set of 2) 4 400QX208-1	Keepsake	Yr.Iss.	4.00	40-65.00
Hallmark Keepsake Ornaments	**1976 Property Ornaments**				
76-11-001	Betsey Clark-Fourth Ed.300QX 195-1	Keepsake	Yr.Iss.	3.00	175.00
76-11-002	Betsey Clark 250QX210-1	Keepsake	Yr.Iss.	2.50	38-42.00
76-11-003	Betsey Clark (Set of 3) 450QX218-1	Keepsake	Yr.Iss.	4.50	50.00
76-11-004	Currier & Ives 250QX209-1	Keepsake	Yr.Iss.	2.50	40.00
76-11-005	Currier & Ives 300QX197-1	Keepsake	Yr.Iss.	3.00	42.00
76-11-006	Norman Rockwell 300QX196-1	Keepsake	Yr.Iss.	3.00	55-65.00
76-11-007	Rudolph and Santa 250QX213-1	Keepsake	Yr.Iss.	2.50	65.00
76-11-008	Raggedy Ann 250QX212-1	Keepsake	Yr.Iss.	2.50	65.00
76-11-009	Marty Links (Set of 2) 400QX207-1	Keepsake	Yr.Iss.	4.00	45.00
76-11-010	Happy the Snowman (Set of 2) 350QX216-1	Keepsake	Yr.Iss.	3.50	55.00
76-11-011	Charmers (Set of 2) 350QX215-1	Keepsake	Yr.Iss.	3.50	45.00
Hallmark Keepsake Ornaments	**1976 Decorative Ball Ornaments**				
76-12-001	Chickadees 225QX204-1	Keepsake	Yr.Iss.	2.30	50.00
76-12-002	Cardinals 225QX205-1	Keepsake	Yr.Iss.	2.30	55.00
Hallmark Keepsake Ornaments	**1976 Handcrafted Ornaments: Yesteryears**				
76-13-001	Train 500QX181-1	Keepsake	Yr.Iss.	5.00	135-160.
76-13-002	Santa 500QX182-1	Keepsake	Yr.Iss.	5.00	155.00
76-13-003	Partridge 500QX183-1	Keepsake	Yr.Iss.	5.00	115.00
76-13-004	Drummer Boy 500QX184-1	Keepsake	Yr.Iss.	5.00	135.00
Hallmark Keepsake Ornaments	**1976 Handcrafted Ornaments: Twirl-Abouts**				
76-14-001	Angel 450QX171-1	Keepsake	Yr.Iss.	4.50	130-150.
76-14-002	Santa 450QX172-1	Keepsake	Yr.Iss.	4.50	110-115.
76-14-003	Soldier 450QX173-1	Keepsake	Yr.Iss.	4.50	95.00
76-14-004	Partridge 450QX174-1	Keepsake	Yr.Iss.	4.50	195.00
Hallmark Keepsake Ornaments	**1976 Handcrafted Ornaments: Tree Treats**				
76-15-001	Shepherd 300QX175-1	Keepsake	Yr.Iss.	3.00	115.00
76-15-002	Angel 300QX176-1	Keepsake	Yr.Iss.	3.00	140-195.
76-15-003	Santa 300QX177-1	Keepsake	Yr.Iss.	3.00	150-225.
76-15-004	Reindeer 300QX 178-1	Keepsake	Yr.Iss.	3.00	150.00
Hallmark Keepsake Ornaments	**1976 Handcrafted Ornaments: Nostalgia**				
76-16-001	Rocking Horse 400QX128-1	Keepsake	Yr.Iss.	3.50	160.00
76-16-002	Drummer Boy 400QX130-1	Keepsake	Yr.Iss.	3.50	155.00
76-16-003	Locomotive 400QX222-1	Keepsake	Yr.Iss.	3.50	185.00
76-16-004	Peace on Earth 400QX223-1	Keepsake	Yr.Iss.	3.50	195.00
Hallmark Keepsake Ornaments	**1976 Yarn Ornaments**				
76-17-001	Raggedy Ann 175QX121-1	Keepsake	Yr.Iss.	1.75	35.00
76-17-002	Raggedy Andy 175QX122-1	Keepsake	Yr.Iss.	1.75	39.50
76-17-003	Drummer Boy 175QX123-1	Keepsake	Yr.Iss.	1.75	22.50
76-17-004	Santa 175QX124-1	Keepsake	Yr.Iss.	1.75	23.50
76-17-005	Mrs. Santa 175QX125-1	Keepsake	Yr.Iss.	1.75	21.50
76-17-006	Caroler 175QX126-1	Keepsake	Yr.Iss.	1.75	27.50
Hallmark Keepsake Ornaments	**1977 Commemoratives**				
77-18-001	Baby's First Christmas 350QX131-5	Keepsake	Yr.Iss.	3.50	45.00
77-18-002	Granddaughter 350QX208-2	Keepsake	Yr.Iss.	3.50	150.00
77-18-003	Grandson 350QX209-5	Keepsake	Yr.Iss.	3.50	150.00
77-18-004	Mother 350QX261-5	Keepsake	Yr.Iss.	3.50	75.00
77-18-005	Grandmother 350QX260-2	Keepsake	Yr.Iss.	3.50	150.00
77-18-006	First Christmas Together 350QX132-2	Keepsake	Yr.Iss.	3.50	75.00
77-18-007	Love 350QX262-2	Keepsake	Yr.Iss.	3.50	95.00
77-18-008	For Your New Home 350QX263-5	Keepsake	Yr.Iss.	3.50	120.00
Hallmark Keepsake Ornaments	**1977 Property Ornaments**				
77-19-001	Charmers 350QX153-5	Keepsake	Yr.Iss.	3.50	50.00
77-19-002	Currier & Ives 350QX130-2	Keepsake	Yr.Iss.	3.50	55.00
77-19-003	Norman Rockwell 350QX151-5	Keepsake	Yr.Iss.	3.50	70.00
77-19-004	Disney 350QX133-5	Keepsake	Yr.Iss.	3.50	45.00
77-19-005	Disney (Set of 2) 400QX137-5	Keepsake	Yr.Iss.	4.00	75.00
77-19-006	Betsey Clark -Fifth Ed. 350QX264-2	Keepsake	Yr.Iss.	3.50	485.00
77-19-007	Grandma Moses 350QX150-2	Keepsake	Yr.Iss.	3.50	175.00
Hallmark Keepsake Ornaments	**1977 Peanuts Collection**				
77-20-001	Peanuts 250QX162-2	Keepsake	Yr.Iss.	2.50	65.00
77-20-002	Peanuts 350QX135-5	Keepsake	Yr.Iss.	3.50	55.00
77-20-003	Peanuts (Set of 2) 400QX163-5	Keepsake	Yr.Iss.	4.00	65.00
Hallmark Keepsake Ornaments	**1977 Christmas Expressions Collection**				
77-21-001	Bell 350QX154-2	Keepsake	Yr.Iss.	3.50	65.00
77-21-002	Ornaments 350QX155-5	Keepsake	Yr.Iss.	3.50	65.00
77-21-003	Mandolin 350QX157-5	Keepsake	Yr.Iss.	3.50	65.00
77-21-004	Wreath 350QX156-2	Keepsake	Yr.Iss.	3.50	65.00
Hallmark Keepsake Ornaments	**1977 The Beauty of America Collection**				
77-22-001	Mountains 250QX158-2	Keepsake	Yr.Iss.	2.50	15.00
77-22-002	Desert 250QX159-5	Keepsake	Yr.Iss.	2.50	25.00
77-22-003	Seashore 250QX160-2	Keepsake	Yr.Iss.	2.50	25.00
77-22-004	Wharf 250QX161-5	Keepsake	Yr.Iss.	2.50	30-50.00
Hallmark Keepsake Ornaments	**1977 Decorative Ball Ornaments**				
77-23-001	Rabbit 250QX139-5	Keepsake	Yr.Iss.	2.50	95.00
77-23-002	Squirrel 250QX138-2	Keepsake	Yr.Iss.	2.50	115.00
77-23-003	Christmas Mouse 250QX134-2	Keepsake	Yr.Iss.	3.50	65.00
77-23-004	Stained Glass 250QX152-2	Keepsake	Yr.Iss.	3.50	65.00
Hallmark Keepsake Ornaments	**1977 Colors of Christmas**				
77-24-001	Bell 350QX200-2	Keepsake	Yr.Iss.	3.50	35-45.00
77-24-002	Joy 350QX201-5	Keepsake	Yr.Iss.	3.50	45.00
77-24-003	Wreath 350QX202-2	Keepsake	Yr.Iss.	3.50	25-45.00
77-24-004	Candle 350QX203-5	Keepsake	Yr.Iss.	3.50	55.00
Hallmark Keepsake Ornaments	**1977 Holiday Highlights**				
77-25-001	Joy 350QX310-2	Keepsake	Yr.Iss.	3.50	25-40.00
77-25-002	Peace on Earth 350QX311-5	Keepsake	Yr.Iss.	3.50	45-60.00
77-25-003	Drummer Boy 350QX312-2	Keepsake	Yr.Iss.	3.50	35-60.00
77-25-004	Star 350QX313-5	Keepsake	Yr.Iss.	3.50	50.00
Hallmark Keepsake Ornaments	**1977 Twirl-About Collection**				
77-26-001	Snowman 450QX190-2	Keepsake	Yr.Iss.	4.50	55-65.00
77-26-002	Weather House 600QX191-5	Keepsake	Yr.Iss.	6.00	85-95.00
77-26-003	Bellringer 600QX192-2	Keepsake	Yr.Iss.	6.00	45-65.00
77-26-004	Della Robia Wreath 450QX193-5	Keepsake	Yr.Iss.	4.50	90-115.
Hallmark Keepsake Ornaments	**1977 Metal Ornaments**				
77-27-001	Snowflake Collection (Set of 4) 500QX 210-2	Keepsake	Yr.Iss.	5.00	95.00
Hallmark Keepsake Ornaments	**1977 Nostalgia Collection**				
77-28-001	Angel 500QX182-2	Keepsake	Yr.Iss.	5.00	75-115.
77-28-002	Toys 500QX183-5	Keepsake	Yr.Iss.	5.00	85-145.
77-28-003	Antique Car 500QX180-2	Keepsake	Yr.Iss.	5.00	65.00
77-28-004	Nativity 500QX181-5	Keepsake	Yr.Iss.	5.00	80-125.
Hallmark Keepsake Ornaments	**1977 Yesteryears Collection**				
77-29-001	Angel 600QX172-2	Keepsake	Yr.Iss.	6.00	85-100.
77-29-002	Reindeer 600QX173-5	Keepsake	Yr.Iss.	6.00	100-135.
77-29-003	Jack-in-the-Box 600QX171-5	Keepsake	Yr.Iss.	6.00	100-120.
77-29-004	House 600QX170-2	Keepsake	Yr.Iss.	6.00	100-115.
Hallmark Keepsake Ornaments	**1977 Cloth Doll Ornaments**				
77-30-001	Angel 175QX220-2	Keepsake	Yr.Iss.	1.75	40-50.00
77-30-002	Santa 175QX221-5	Keepsake	Yr.Iss.	1.75	40-60.00
Hallmark Keepsake Ornaments	**1978 Commemoratives**				
78-31-001	Baby's First Christmas 350QX200-3	Keepsake	Yr.Iss.	3.50	75.00
78-31-002	Granddaughter 350QX216-3	Keepsake	Yr.Iss.	3.50	50.00
78-31-003	Grandson 350QX215-6	Keepsake	Yr.Iss.	3.50	50.00
78-31-004	First Christmas Together 350QX218-3	Keepsake	Yr.Iss.	3.50	35.00
78-31-005	25th Christmas Together 350QX269-3	Keepsake	Yr.Iss.	3.50	10-25.00
78-31-006	Love 350QX268-3	Keepsake	Yr.Iss.	3.50	50.00
78-31-007	Grandmother 350QX267-6	Keepsake	Yr.Iss.	3.50	18-25.00
78-31-008	Mother 350QX266-3	Keepsake	Yr.Iss.	3.50	10-25.00
78-31-009	For Your New Home 350QX217-6	Keepsake	Yr.Iss.	3.50	75.00
Hallmark Keepsake Ornaments	**1978 Peanuts Collection**				
78-32-001	Peanuts 250QX204-3	Keepsake	Yr.Iss.	2.50	50.00
78-32-002	Peanuts 350QX205-6	Keepsake	Yr.Iss.	3.50	50-65.00
78-32-003	Peanuts 350QX206-3	Keepsake	Yr.Iss.	3.50	50.00
78-32-004	Peanuts 250QX203-6	Keepsake	Yr.Iss.	2.50	50.00
Hallmark Keepsake Ornaments	**1978 Property Ornaments**				
78-33-001	Betsey Clark-Sixth Edition 350QX 201-6	Keepsake	Yr.Iss.	3.50	55.00
78-33-002	Joan Walsh Anglund 350QX221-6	Keepsake	Yr.Iss.	3.50	75.00
78-33-003	Spencer Sparrow 350QX219-6	Keepsake	Yr.Iss.	3.50	50.00
78-33-004	Disney 350QX207-6	Keepsake	Yr.Iss.	3.50	75.00
Hallmark Keepsake Ornaments	**1978 Decorative Ball Ornaments**				
78-34-001	Merry Christmas (Santa) 350QX202-3	Keepsake	Yr.Iss.	3.50	45.00
78-34-002	Hallmark's Antique Card Collection Design 350QX220-3	Keepsake	Yr.Iss.	3.50	40.00
78-34-003	Yesterday's Toys 350QX250-3	Keepsake	Yr.Iss.	3.50	55.00
78-34-004	Nativity 350QX253-6	Keepsake	Yr.Iss.	3.50	150.00
78-34-005	The Quail 350QX251-6	Keepsake	Yr.Iss.	3.50	40.00
78-34-006	Drummer Boy 350QX252-3	Keepsake	Yr.Iss.	3.50	55.00
78-34-007	Joy 350QX254-3	Keepsake	Yr.Iss.	3.50	15-25.00
Hallmark Keepsake Ornaments	**1978 Holiday Highlights**				
78-35-001	Santa 350QX307-6	Keepsake	Yr.Iss.	3.50	95.00
78-35-002	Snowflake 350QX308-3	Keepsake	Yr.Iss.	3.50	50.00
78-35-003	Nativity 350QX309-6	Keepsake	Yr.Iss.	3.50	80.00
78-35-004	Dove 350QX310-3	Keepsake	Yr.Iss.	3.50	125.00
Hallmark Keepsake Ornaments	**1978 Holiday Chimes**				
78-36-001	Reindeer Chimes 450QX320-3	Keepsake	Yr.Iss.	4.50	60.00
Hallmark Keepsake Ornaments	**1978 Little Trimmers**				
78-37-001	Thimble Series (Mouse)-First Ed. 250QX133-6	Keepsake	Yr.Iss.	2.50	250-300.
78-37-002	Santa 250QX135-6	Keepsake	Yr.Iss.	2.50	55-65.00
78-37-003	Praying Angel 250QX134-3	Keepsake	Yr.Iss.	2.50	95.00
78-37-004	Drummer Boy 250QX136-3	Keepsake	Yr.Iss.	2.50	55-75.00
78-37-005	Set of 4 - 250QX355-6	Keepsake	Yr.Iss.	10.00	400-425.
Hallmark Keepsake Ornaments	**1978 Colors of Christmas**				
78-38-001	Merry Christmas 350QX355-6	Keepsake	Yr.Iss.	3.50	50.00
78-38-002	Locomotive 350QX356-3	Keepsake	Yr.Iss.	3.50	40-50.00
78-38-003	Angel 350QX354-3	Keepsake	Yr.Iss.	3.50	35.00
78-38-004	Candle 350QX357-6	Keepsake	Yr.Iss.	3.50	85.00
Hallmark Keepsake Ornaments	**1978 Handcrafted Ornaments**				
78-39-001	Dove 450QX190-3	Keepsake	Yr.Iss.	4.50	85.00
78-39-002	Holly and Poinsettia Ball 600QX147-6	Keepsake	Yr.Iss.	6.00	85.00
78-39-003	Schneeberg Bell 800QX152-3	Keepsake	Yr.Iss.	8.00	135-199.
78-39-004	Angels 800QX150-3	Keepsake	Yr.Iss.	8.00	345-400.
78-39-005	Carrousel Series-First Edition 600QX146-3	Keepsake	Yr.Iss.	6.00	345-400.
78-39-006	Joy 450QX138-3	Keepsake	Yr.Iss.	4.50	70-80.00
78-39-007	Angel 400QX139-6	Keepsake	Yr.Iss.	4.50	85.00
78-39-008	Calico Mouse 450QX137-6	Keepsake	Yr.Iss.	4.50	145-175.
78-39-009	Red Cardinal 450QX144-3	Keepsake	Yr.Iss.	4.50	150-175.
78-39-010	Panorama Ball 600QX145-6	Keepsake	Yr.Iss.	6.00	135-150.
78-39-011	Skating Raccoon 600QX142-3	Keepsake	Yr.Iss.	6.00	65-85.00
78-39-012	Rocking Horse 600QX148-3	Keepsake	Yr.Iss.	6.00	65-95.00
78-39-013	Animal Home 600QX149-6	Keepsake	Yr.Iss.	6.00	150-175.
Hallmark Keepsake Ornaments	**1978 Yarn Collection**				
78-40-001	Green Boy 200QX123-1	Keepsake	Yr.Iss.	2.00	20.00
78-40-002	Mrs. Claus 200QX125-1	Keepsake	Yr.Iss.	2.00	19.50
78-40-003	Green Girl 200QX126-1	Keepsake	Yr.Iss.	2.00	17.50
78-40-004	Mr. Claus 200QX340-3	Keepsake	Yr.Iss.	2.00	20.00
Hallmark Keepsake Ornaments	**1979 Commemoratives**				
79-41-001	Baby's First Christmas 350QX208-7	Keepsake	Yr.Iss.	3.50	20.00
79-41-002	Baby's First Christmas 800QX154-7	Keepsake	Yr.Iss.	8.00	135-175.
79-41-003	Grandson 350QX210-7	Keepsake	Yr.Iss.	3.50	20-30.00
79-41-004	Granddaughter 350QX211-9	Keepsake	Yr.Iss.	3.50	28.00
79-41-005	Mother 350QX251-9	Keepsake	Yr.Iss.	3.50	10-20.00
79-41-006	Grandmother 350QX252-7	Keepsake	Yr.Iss.	3.50	10.00
79-41-007	Our First Christmas Together 350QX209-9	Keepsake	Yr.Iss.	3.50	45.00
79-41-008	Our Twenty-Fifth Anniversary350QX 250-7	Keepsake	Yr.Iss.	3.50	10-20.00
79-41-009	Love 350QX258-7	Keepsake	Yr.Iss.	3.50	15-30.00
79-41-010	Friendship 350QX203-9	Keepsake	Yr.Iss.	3.50	17.50
79-41-011	Teacher 350QX213-9	Keepsake	Yr.Iss.	3.50	5-15.00
79-41-012	New Home 350QX212-7	Keepsake	Yr.Iss.	3.50	35.00
Hallmark Keepsake Ornaments	**1979 Property Ornaments**				
79-42-001	Betsey Clark-Seventh Edition 350QX 201-9	Keepsake	Yr.Iss.	3.50	30.00
79-42-002	Peanuts (Time to Trim) 350QX202-7	Keepsake	Yr.Iss.	3.50	25.00
79-42-003	Spencer Sparrow 350QX200-7	Keepsake	Yr.Iss.	3.50	25.00
79-42-004	Joan Walsh Anglund 350QX205-9	Keepsake	Yr.Iss.	3.50	25-35.00
79-42-005	Winnie-the-Pooh 350QX206-7	Keepsake	Yr.Iss.	3.50	30.00
79-42-006	Mary Hamilton 350QX254-7	Keepsake	Yr.Iss.	3.50	20-30.00

		ARTIST	EDITION	ISSUE	QUOTE
Hallmark Keepsake Ornaments	**1979 Decorative Ball Ornaments**				
79-43-001	Night Before Christmas 350QX214-7	Keepsake	Yr.Iss.	3.50	40.00
79-43-002	Christmas Chickadees 350QX204-7	Keepsake	Yr.Iss.	3.50	30.00
79-43-003	Behold the Star 350QX255-9	Keepsake	Yr.Iss.	3.50	35.00
79-43-004	Christmas Traditions 350QX253-9	Keepsake	Yr.Iss.	3.50	32.50
79-43-005	Christmas Collage 350QX257-9	Keepsake	Yr.Iss.	3.50	20.00
79-43-006	Black Angel 350QX207-9	Keepsake	Yr.Iss.	3.50	15.00
79-43-007	The Light of Christmas 350QX256-7	Keepsake	Yr.Iss.	3.50	20.00
Hallmark Keepsake Ornaments	**1979 Holiday Highlights**				
79-44-001	Christmas Angel 350QX300-7	Keepsake	Yr.Iss.	3.50	85.00
79-44-002	Snowflake 350QX301-9	Keepsake	Yr.Iss.	3.50	40.00
79-44-003	Christmas Tree 350QX302-7	Keepsake	Yr.Iss.	3.50	75.00
79-44-004	Christmas Cheer 350QX303-9	Keepsake	Yr.Iss.	3.50	30-55.00
79-44-005	Love 350QX304-7	Keepsake	Yr.Iss.	3.50	85.00
Hallmark Keepsake Ornaments	**1979 Colors of Christmas**				
79-45-001	Words of Christmas 350QX350-7	Keepsake	Yr.Iss.	3.50	85.00
79-45-002	Holiday Wreath 350QX353-9	Keepsake	Yr.Iss.	3.50	39.50
79-45-003	Partridge in a Pear Tree 350QX351-9	Keepsake	Yr.Iss.	3.50	40.00
79-45-004	Star Over Bethlehem 350QX352-7	Keepsake	Yr.Iss.	3.50	65.00
Hallmark Keepsake Ornaments	**1979 Little Trimmer Collection**				
79-46-001	Thimble Series-Mouse 300QX133-6	Keepsake	Yr.Iss.	3.00	150-225.
79-46-002	Santa 300QX135-6	Keepsake	Yr.Iss.	3.00	55.00
79-46-003	A Matchless Christmas 400QX132-7	Keepsake	Yr.Iss.	4.00	65-75.00
79-46-004	Angel Delight 300QX130-7	Keepsake	Yr.Iss.	3.00	80-90.00
Hallmark Keepsake Ornaments	**1979 Handcrafted Ornaments**				
79-47-001	Holiday Scrimshaw 400QX152-7	Keepsake	Yr.Iss.	4.00	205-235.
79-47-002	Christmas Heart 650QX140-7	Keepsake	Yr.Iss.	6.50	100-115.
79-47-003	Christmas Eve Surprise 650QX157-9	Keepsake	Yr.Iss.	6.50	65.00
79-47-004	Santa's Here 500QX138-7	Keepsake	Yr.Iss.	5.00	55-75.00
79-47-005	Raccoon 650QX142-3	Keepsake	Yr.Iss.	6.50	85.00
79-47-006	The Downhill Run 650QX145-9	Keepsake	Yr.Iss.	6.50	135-150.
79-47-007	The Drummer Boy 800QX143-9	Keepsake	Yr.Iss.	8.00	90-125.
79-47-008	Outdoor Fun 800QX150-7	Keepsake	Yr.Iss.	8.00	135-150.
79-47-009	A Christmas Treat 500QX134-7	Keepsake	Yr.Iss.	5.00	80.00
79-47-010	The Skating Snowman 500QX139-9	Keepsake	Yr.Iss.	5.00	65-75.00
79-47-011	Christmas is for Children 500QX135-9	Keepsake	Yr.Iss.	5.00	95.00
79-47-012	Ready for Christmas 650QX133-9	Keepsake	Yr.Iss.	6.50	95-150.
Hallmark Keepsake Ornaments	**1979 Collectible Series**				
79-48-001	Carousel-Second Edition 650QX146-7	Keepsake	Yr.Iss.	6.50	160-185.
79-48-002	Thimble-Second Edition 300QX131-9	Keepsake	Yr.Iss.	3.00	145-160.
79-48-003	Snoopy and Friends 800QX141-9	Keepsake	Yr.Iss.	8.00	110.00
79-48-004	Here Comes Santa-First Edition 900QX155-9	Keepsake	Yr.Iss.	9.00	400.00
79-48-005	Bellringer-First Edition 10QX147-9	Keepsake	Yr.Iss.	10.00	400.00
Hallmark Keepsake Ornaments	**1979 Holiday Chimes**				
79-49-001	Reindeer Chimes 450QX320-3	Keepsake	Yr.Iss.	4.50	75.00
79-49-002	Star Chimes 450QX137-9	Keepsake	Yr.Iss.	4.50	55-85.00
Hallmark Keepsake Ornaments	**1979 Sewn Trimmers**				
79-50-001	The Rocking Horse 200QX340-7	Keepsake	Yr.Iss.	2.00	20.00
79-50-002	Merry Santa 200QX342-7	Keepsake	Yr.Iss.	2.00	20.00
79-50-003	Stuffed Full Stocking 200QX341-9	Keepsake	Yr.Iss.	2.00	10-20.00
79-50-004	Angel Music 200QX343-9	Keepsake	Yr.Iss.	2.00	20.00
Hallmark Keepsake Ornaments	**1980 Commemoratives**				
80-51-001	Baby's First Christmas 400QX200-1	Keepsake	Yr.Iss.	4.00	17-35.00
80-51-002	Black Baby's First Christmas 400QX 229-4	Keepsake	Yr.Iss.	4.00	20.00
80-51-003	Baby's First Christmas 12QX156-1	Keepsake	Yr.Iss.	12.00	35-45.00
80-51-004	Grandson 400QX201-4	Keepsake	Yr.Iss.	4.00	15-30.00
80-51-005	Granddaughter 400QX202-1	Keepsake	Yr.Iss.	4.00	12-30.00
80-51-006	Son 400QX211-4	Keepsake	Yr.Iss.	4.00	17-32.00
80-51-007	Daughter 400QX212-1	Keepsake	Yr.Iss.	4.00	15-35.00
80-51-008	Dad 400QX214-1	Keepsake	Yr.Iss.	4.00	8-16.00
80-51-009	Mother 400QX203-4	Keepsake	Yr.Iss.	4.00	7-16.00
80-51-010	Mother and Dad 400QX230-1	Keepsake	Yr.Iss.	4.00	7-15.00
80-51-011	Grandmother 400QX204-1	Keepsake	Yr.Iss.	4.00	15.00
80-51-012	Grandfather 400QX231-4	Keepsake	Yr.Iss.	4.00	7-15.00
80-51-013	Grandparents 400QX213-4	Keepsake	Yr.Iss.	4.00	40.00
80-51-014	25th Christmas Together 400QX206-1	Keepsake	Yr.Iss.	4.00	7-16.00
80-51-015	First Christmas Together 400QX205-4	Keepsake	Yr.Iss.	4.00	30.00
80-51-016	Christmas Love 400QX207-4	Keepsake	Yr.Iss.	4.00	32.00
80-51-017	Friendship 400QX208-1	Keepsake	Yr.Iss.	4.00	9-19.00
80-51-018	Christmas at Home 400QX210-1	Keepsake	Yr.Iss.	4.00	29-37.00
80-51-019	Teacher 400QX209-4	Keepsake	Yr.Iss.	4.00	6-14.00
80-51-020	Love 400QX302-1	Keepsake	Yr.Iss.	4.00	50.00
80-51-021	Beauty of Friendship 400QX303-4	Keepsake	Yr.Iss.	4.00	55.00
80-51-022	First Christmas Together 400QX305-4	Keepsake	Yr.Iss.	4.00	30-55.00
80-51-023	Mother 400QX304-1	Keepsake	Yr.Iss.	4.00	35.00
Hallmark Keepsake Ornaments	**1980 Property Ornaments**				
80-52-001	Betsey Clark-Eighth Edition 400QX 215-4	Keepsake	Yr.Iss.	4.00	29.50
80-52-002	Betsey Clark 650QX307-4	Keepsake	Yr.Iss.	6.50	50-60.00
80-52-003	Betsey Clark's Christmas 750QX194-4	Keepsake	Yr.Iss.	7.50	25.00
80-52-004	Peanuts 400QX216-1	Keepsake	Yr.Iss.	4.00	30.00
80-52-005	Joan Walsh Anglund 400QX217-4	Keepsake	Yr.Iss.	4.00	11-22.00
80-52-006	Disney 400QX218-1	Keepsake	Yr.Iss.	4.00	25.00
80-52-007	Mary Hamilton 400QX219-4	Keepsake	Yr.Iss.	4.00	20.00
80-52-008	Muppets 400QX220-1	Keepsake	Yr.Iss.	4.00	25-37.50
80-52-009	Marty Links 400QX221-4	Keepsake	Yr.Iss.	4.00	10-20.00
Hallmark Keepsake Ornaments	**1980 Decorative Ball Ornaments**				
80-53-001	Christmas Choir 400QX228-1	Keepsake	Yr.Iss.	4.00	150.00
80-53-002	Nativity 400QX225-4	Keepsake	Yr.Iss.	4.00	125.00
80-53-003	Christmas Time 400QX226-1	Keepsake	Yr.Iss.	4.00	17-25.00
80-53-004	Santa's Workshop 400QX223-4	Keepsake	Yr.Iss.	4.00	10-20.00
80-53-005	Happy Christmas 400QX222-1	Keepsake	Yr.Iss.	4.00	30.00
80-53-006	Jolly Santa 400QX227-4	Keepsake	Yr.Iss.	4.00	30.00
80-53-007	Christmas Cardinals 400QX224-1	Keepsake	Yr.Iss.	4.00	35.00
Hallmark Keepsake Ornaments	**1980 Holiday Highlights**				
80-54-001	Three Wise Men 400QX300-1	Keepsake	Yr.Iss.	4.00	22.50
80-54-002	Wreath 400QX301-4	Keepsake	Yr.Iss.	4.00	85.00
Hallmark Keepsake Ornaments	**1980 Colors of Christmas**				
80-55-001	Joy 400QX350-1	Keepsake	Yr.Iss.	4.00	20.00
Hallmark Keepsake Ornaments	**1980 Frosted Images**				
80-56-001	Drummer Boy 400QX309-4	Keepsake	Yr.Iss.	4.00	20.00
80-56-002	Santa 400QX310-1	Keepsake	Yr.Iss.	4.00	20.00
80-56-003	Dove 400QX308-1	Keepsake	Yr.Iss.	4.00	25-40.00

		ARTIST	EDITION	ISSUE	QUOTE
Hallmark Keepsake Ornaments	**1980 Little Trimmers**				
80-57-001	Clothespin Soldier 350QX134-1	Keepsake	Yr.Iss.	3.50	25-40.00
80-57-002	Christmas Teddy 250QX135-4	Keepsake	Yr.Iss.	2.50	80-135.
80-57-003	Merry Redbird 350QX160-1	Keepsake	Yr.Iss.	3.50	50-65.00
80-57-004	Swingin' on a Star 400QX130-1	Keepsake	Yr.Iss.	4.00	65-85.00
80-57-005	Christmas Owl 400QX131-4	Keepsake	Yr.Iss.	4.00	45.00
80-57-006	Thimble Series-A Christmas Salute 400QX131-9	Keepsake	Yr.Iss.	4.00	150.00
Hallmark Keepsake Ornaments	**1980 Handcrafted Ornaments**				
80-58-001	The Snowflake Swing 400QX133-4	Keepsake	Yr.Iss.	4.00	25-45.00
80-58-002	Santa 1980 550QX146-1	Keepsake	Yr.Iss.	5.50	80-95.00
80-58-003	Drummer Boy 550QX147-4	Keepsake	Yr.Iss.	5.50	60-95.00
80-58-004	Christmas is for Children 550QX135-9	Keepsake	Yr.Iss.	5.50	95.00
80-58-005	A Christmas Treat 550QX134-7	Keepsake	Yr.Iss.	5.50	75.00
80-58-006	Skating Snowman 550QX139-9	Keepsake	Yr.Iss.	5.50	75.00
80-58-007	A Heavenly Nap 650QX139-4	Keepsake	Yr.Iss.	6.50	45-55.00
80-58-008	Heavenly Sounds 750QX152-1	Keepsake	Yr.Iss.	7.50	70-95.00
80-58-009	Caroling Bear 750QX140-1	Keepsake	Yr.Iss.	7.50	105-150.
80-58-010	Santa's Flight 550QX138-1	Keepsake	Yr.Iss.	5.50	95-115.
80-58-011	The Animals' Christmas 800QX150-1	Keepsake	Yr.Iss.	8.00	40-65.00
80-58-012	A Spot of Christmas Cheer 800QX153-4	Keepsake	Yr.Iss.	8.00	145.00
80-58-013	Elfin Antics 900QX142-1	Keepsake	Yr.Iss.	9.00	225.00
80-58-014	A Christmas Vigil 900QX144-1	Keepsake	Yr.Iss.	9.00	185.00
Hallmark Keepsake Ornaments	**1980 Special Editions**				
80-59-001	Heavenly Minstrel 15QX156-7	Keepsake	Yr.Iss.	15.00	345-450.
80-59-002	Checking it Twice 20QX158-4	Keepsake	Yr.Iss.	20.00	168-195.
Hallmark Keepsake Ornaments	**1980 Holiday Chimes**				
80-60-001	Snowflake Chimes 550QX165-4	Keepsake	Yr.Iss.	5.50	20.00
80-60-002	Reindeer Chimes 550QX320-3	Keepsake	Yr.Iss.	5.50	25.00
80-60-003	Santa Mobile 550QX136-1	Keepsake	Yr.Iss.	5.50	25.00
Hallmark Keepsake Ornaments	**1980 Collectible Series**				
80-61-001	Norman Rockwell-First Edition 650QX306-1	Keepsake	Yr.Iss.	6.50	180-225.
80-61-002	Frosty Friends-First Edition650QX 137-4	Keepsake	Yr.Iss.	6.50	600.00
80-61-003	Snoopy & Friends-Second Edition 900QX154-1	Keepsake	Yr.Iss.	9.00	100.00
80-61-004	Carrousel-Third Edition 750QX141-4	Keepsake	Yr.Iss.	7.50	140-155.
80-61-005	Thimble-Third Edition 400QX132-1	Keepsake	Yr.Iss.	4.00	175.00
80-61-006	Here Comes Santa-Second Ed.12QX 143-4	Keepsake	Yr.Iss.	12.00	95-225.
80-61-007	The Bellringers-Second Edition15QX157-4	Keepsake	Yr.Iss.	15.00	60-85.00
Hallmark Keepsake Ornaments	**1980 Yarn Ornaments**				
80-62-001	Santa 300QX161-4	Keepsake	Yr.Iss.	3.00	8.00
80-62-002	Angel 300QX162-1	Keepsake	Yr.Iss.	3.00	8.00
80-62-003	Snowman 300QX163-4	Keepsake	Yr.Iss.	3.00	8.00
80-62-004	Soldier 300QX164-1	Keepsake	Yr.Iss.	3.00	7.00
Hallmark Keepsake Ornaments	**1981 Commemoratives**				
81-63-001	Baby's First Christmas-Girl450QX 600-2	Keepsake	Yr.Iss.	4.50	15-30.00
81-63-002	Baby's First Christmas-Boy450QX 601-5	Keepsake	Yr.Iss.	4.50	20.00
81-63-003	Baby's First Christmas-Black 450QX602-2	Keepsake	Yr.Iss.	4.50	19.00
81-63-004	Baby's First Christmas 550QX516-2	Keepsake	Yr.Iss.	5.50	29.50
81-63-005	Baby's First Christmas 850QX513-5	Keepsake	Yr.Iss.	8.50	10.00
81-63-006	Baby's First Christmas 1300QX440-2	Keepsake	Yr.Iss.	13.00	35-50.00
81-63-007	Godchild 450QX603-5	Keepsake	Yr.Iss.	4.50	10-17.00
81-63-008	Grandson 450QX604-2	Keepsake	Yr.Iss.	4.50	10-24.00
81-63-009	Granddaughter 450QX605-5	Keepsake	Yr.Iss.	4.50	12-30.00
81-63-010	Daughter 450QX607-5	Keepsake	Yr.Iss.	4.50	10-35.00
81-63-011	Son 450QX606-2	Keepsake	Yr.Iss.	4.50	13-30.00
81-63-012	Mother 450QX608-2	Keepsake	Yr.Iss.	4.50	5-15.00
81-63-013	Father 450QX609-5	Keepsake	Yr.Iss.	4.50	5-15.00
81-63-014	Mother and Dad 450QX700-2	Keepsake	Yr.Iss.	4.50	10-15.00
81-63-015	Friendship 450QX704-2	Keepsake	Yr.Iss.	4.50	12.00
81-63-016	The Gift of Love 450QX705-5	Keepsake	Yr.Iss.	4.50	15-22.00
81-63-017	Home 450QX709-5	Keepsake	Yr.Iss.	4.50	20.00
81-63-018	Teacher 450QX800-2	Keepsake	Yr.Iss.	4.50	6-13.00
81-63-019	Grandfather 450QX701-5	Keepsake	Yr.Iss.	4.50	15.00
81-63-020	Grandmother 450QX702-2	Keepsake	Yr.Iss.	4.50	5-15.00
81-63-021	Grandparents 450QX703-5	Keepsake	Yr.Iss.	4.50	10-17.00
81-63-022	First Christmas Together 450QX706-2	Keepsake	Yr.Iss.	4.50	10-30.00
81-63-023	25th Christmas Together 450QX707-5	Keepsake	Yr.Iss.	4.50	6-20.00
81-63-024	50th Christmas 450QX708-2	Keepsake	Yr.Iss.	4.50	6-15.00
81-63-025	Love 550QX502-2	Keepsake	Yr.Iss.	5.50	45.00
81-63-026	Friendship 550QX503-5	Keepsake	Yr.Iss.	5.50	15.00
81-63-027	First Christmas Together 550QX505-5	Keepsake	Yr.Iss.	5.50	22-35.00
81-63-028	25th Christmas Together 550QX504-2	Keepsake	Yr.Iss.	5.50	22.00
Hallmark Keepsake Ornaments	**1981 Property Ornaments**				
81-65-001	Betsey Clark Cameo 850QX512-2	Keepsake	Yr.Iss.	8.50	20-30.00
81-65-002	Betsey Clark 900QX423-5	Keepsake	Yr.Iss.	9.00	50-80.00
81-65-003	Betsey Clark-Ninth Edition450QX 802-2	Keepsake	Yr.Iss.	4.50	20-30.00
81-65-004	Muppets 450QX807-5	Keepsake	Yr.Iss.	4.50	15-35.00
81-65-005	Kermit the Frog 900QX424-2	Keepsake	Yr.Iss.	9.00	80-95.00
81-65-006	The Divine Miss Piggy 1200QX425-5	Keepsake	Yr.Iss.	12.00	80-95.00
81-65-007	Mary Hamilton 450QX806-2	Keepsake	Yr.Iss.	4.50	10-23.00
81-65-008	Marty Links 450QX808-2	Keepsake	Yr.Iss.	4.50	7-20.00
81-65-009	Peanuts 450QX803-5	Keepsake	Yr.Iss.	4.50	12-30.00
81-65-010	Joan Walsh Anglund 450QX804-2	Keepsake	Yr.Iss.	4.50	8-20.00
81-65-011	Disney 450QX805-5	Keepsake	Yr.Iss.	4.50	10-30.00
Hallmark Keepsake Ornaments	**1981 Decorative Ball Ornaments**				
81-66-001	Christmas 1981 450QX809-5	Keepsake	Yr.Iss.	4.50	25.00
81-66-002	Christmas Magic 450QX810-2	Keepsake	Yr.Iss.	4.50	19.50
81-66-003	Traditional (Black Santa) 450QX801-5	Keepsake	Yr.Iss.	4.50	40-95.00
81-66-004	Let Us Adore Him 450QX811-5	Keepsake	Yr.Iss.	4.50	25-55.00
81-66-005	Santa's Coming 450QX812-2	Keepsake	Yr.Iss.	4.50	10-25.00
81-66-006	Christmas in the Forest 450QX813-5	Keepsake	Yr.Iss.	4.50	145.00
81-66-007	Merry Christmas 450QX814-2	Keepsake	Yr.Iss.	4.50	10-23.00
81-66-008	Santa's Surprise 450QX815-5	Keepsake	Yr.Iss.	4.50	20.00
Hallmark Keepsake Ornaments	**1981 Crown Classics**				
81-67-001	Angel 450QX507-5	Keepsake	Yr.Iss.	4.50	10-25.00
81-67-002	Tree Photoholder 550QX515-5	Keepsake	Yr.Iss.	5.50	10-15.00
81-67-003	Unicorn 850QX516-5	Keepsake	Yr.Iss.	8.50	13-23.00
Hallmark Keepsake Ornaments	**1981 Frosted Images**				
81-68-001	Mouse 400QX508-2	Keepsake	Yr.Iss.	4.00	20.00
81-68-002	Angel 400QX509-5	Keepsake	Yr.Iss.	4.00	33.00
81-68-003	Snowman 400QX510-2	Keepsake	Yr.Iss.	4.00	22.00

	ARTIST	EDITION	ISSUE	QUOTE
Hallmark Keepsake Ornaments 1981 Holiday Highlights				
81-69-001 Shepherd Scene 550QX500-2	Keepsake	Yr.Iss.	5.50	11-22.00
81-69-002 Christmas Star 550QX501-5	Keepsake	Yr.Iss.	5.50	10-22.00
Hallmark Keepsake Ornaments 1981 Little Trimmers				
81-70-001 Puppy Love 350QX406-2	Keepsake	Yr.Iss.	3.50	25-40.00
81-70-002 Jolly Snowman 350QX407-5	Keepsake	Yr.Iss.	3.50	35-57.00
81-70-003 Perky Penguin 350QX409-5	Keepsake	Yr.Iss.	3.50	45-60.00
81-70-004 Clothespin Drummer Boy 450QX408-2	Keepsake	Yr.Iss.	4.50	25-45.00
81-70-005 The Stocking Mouse 450QX412-2	Keepsake	Yr.Iss.	4.50	80-115.
Hallmark Keepsake Ornaments 1981 Hand Crafted Ornaments				
81-71-001 Space Santa 650QX430-2	Keepsake	Yr.Iss.	6.50	65-110.
81-71-002 Candyville Express 750QX418-2	Keepsake	Yr.Iss.	7.50	80-125.
81-71-003 Ice Fairy 650QX431-5	Keepsake	Yr.Iss.	6.50	75-95.00
81-71-004 Star Swing 550QX421-5	Keepsake	Yr.Iss.	5.50	60.00
81-71-005 A Heavenly Nap 650QX139-4	Keepsake	Yr.Iss.	6.50	49.50
81-71-006 Dough Angel 550QX139-6	Keepsake	Yr.Iss.	5.50	80.00
81-71-007 Topsy-Turvy Tunes 750QX429-5	Keepsake	Yr.Iss.	7.50	65-80.00
81-71-008 A Well-Stocked Stocking 900QX154-7	Keepsake	Yr.Iss.	9.00	65-75.00
81-71-009 The Friendly Fiddler 800QX434-2	Keepsake	Yr.Iss.	8.00	75.00
81-71-010 The Ice Sculptor 800QX432-2	Keepsake	Yr.Iss.	8.00	85-95.00
81-71-011 Christmas Dreams 1200QX437-5	Keepsake	Yr.Iss.	12.00	200-225.
81-71-012 Christmas Fantasy 1300QX155-4	Keepsake	Yr.Iss.	13.00	40-65.00
81-71-013 Sailing Santa 1300QX439-5	Keepsake	Yr.Iss.	13.00	175-225.
81-71-014 Love and Joy 900QX425-2	Keepsake	Yr.Iss.	9.00	95.00
81-71-015 Drummer Boy 250QX148-1	Keepsake	Yr.Iss.	2.50	45.00
81-71-016 St. Nicholas 550QX446-2	Keepsake	Yr.Iss.	5.50	40-50.00
81-71-017 Mr. & Mrs. Claus 1200QX448-5	Keepsake	Yr.Iss.	12.00	115-125.
81-71-018 Checking It Twice 2250QX158-4	Keepsake	Yr.Iss.	23.00	195.00
Hallmark Keepsake Ornaments 1981 Holiday Chimes				
81-72-001 Snowman Chimes 550QX445-5	Keepsake	Yr.Iss.	5.50	25.00
81-72-002 Santa Mobile 550QX136-1	Keepsake	Yr.Iss.	5.50	40.00
81-72-003 Snowflake Chimes 550QX165-4	Keepsake	Yr.Iss.	5.50	25.00
Hallmark Keepsake Ornaments 1981 Collectible Series				
81-73-001 Rocking Horse - 1st Edition900QX 422-2	Keepsake	Yr.Iss.	9.00	575-625.
81-73-002 Bellringer - 3rd Edition 1500QX441-5	Keepsake	Yr.Iss.	15.00	70-95.00
81-73-003 Norman Rockwell - 2nd Edition 850QX 511-5	Keepsake	Yr.Iss.	8.50	30-45.00
81-73-004 Here Comes Santa - 3rd Ed.1300QX438-2	Keepsake	Yr.Iss.	13.00	200-295.
81-73-005 Carrousel - 4th Edition 900QX427-5	Keepsake	Yr.Iss.	9.00	60-85.00
81-73-006 Snoopy and Friends - 3rd Ed. 1200QX436-2	Keepsake	Yr.Iss.	12.00	75-85.00
81-73-007 Thimble - 4th Edition 450QX413-5	Keepsake	Yr.Iss.	4.50	125.00
81-73-008 Frosty Friends - 2nd Edition800QX433-5	Keepsake	Yr.Iss.	8.00	275-350.
Hallmark Keepsake Ornaments 1981 Fabric Ornaments				
81-74-001 Cardinal Cutie 300QX400-2	Keepsake	Yr.Iss.	3.00	10-20.00
81-74-002 Peppermint Mouse 300QX401-5	Keepsake	Yr.Iss.	3.00	32.50
81-74-003 Gingham Dog 300QX402-2	Keepsake	Yr.Iss.	3.00	18.00
81-74-004 Calico Kitty 300QX403-5	Keepsake	Yr.Iss.	3.00	18.00
Hallmark Keepsake Ornaments 1981 Plush Animals				
81-75-001 Christmas Teddy 500QX404-2	Keepsake	Yr.Iss.	5.50	22.00
81-75-002 Raccoon Tunes 550QX405-5	Keepsake	Yr.Iss.	5.50	15.00
Hallmark Keepsake Ornaments 1982 Commemoratives				
82-76-001 Baby's First Christmas-Photoholder 650QX312-6	Keepsake	Yr.Iss.	6.50	15-30.00
82-76-002 Baby's First Christmas 1300QX455-3	Keepsake	Yr.Iss.	13.00	32-42.00
82-76-003 Baby's First Christmas (Boy)450QX 216-3	Keepsake	Yr.Iss.	4.50	22.00
82-76-004 Baby's First Christmas (Girl)450QX 207-3	Keepsake	Yr.Iss.	4.50	20.00
82-76-005 Godchild 450QX222-6	Keepsake	Yr.Iss.	4.50	10-20.00
82-76-006 Grandson 450QX224-6	Keepsake	Yr.Iss.	4.50	10-25.00
82-76-007 Granddaughter 450QX224-3	Keepsake	Yr.Iss.	4.50	10-30.00
82-76-008 Son 450QX204-3	Keepsake	Yr.Iss.	4.50	10-30.00
82-76-009 Daughter 450QX204-6	Keepsake	Yr.Iss.	4.50	13-32.00
82-76-010 Father 450QX205-6	Keepsake	Yr.Iss.	4.50	17.00
82-76-011 Mother 450QX205-3	Keepsake	Yr.Iss.	4.50	5-17.00
82-78-012 Mother and Dad 450QX222-3	Keepsake	Yr.Iss.	4.50	5-17.00
82-76-013 Sister 450QX208-3	Keepsake	Yr.Iss.	4.50	11-30.00
82-76-014 Grandmother 450QX200-3	Keepsake	Yr.Iss.	4.50	4-15.00
82-76-015 Grandfather 450QX207-6	Keepsake	Yr.Iss.	4.50	5-15.00
82-76-016 Grandparents 450QX214-6	Keepsake	Yr.Iss.	4.50	7-15.00
82-76-017 First Christmas Together 850QX306-6	Keepsake	Yr.Iss.	8.50	35.00
82-76-018 First Christmas Together 450QX211-3	Keepsake	Yr.Iss.	4.50	20.00
82-76-019 FirstChristmas Together-Locket 1500QX456-3	Keepsake	Yr.Iss.	15.00	25-40.00
82-76-020 Christmas Memories 650QX311-6	Keepsake	Yr.Iss.	6.50	19.50
82-76-021 Teacher 450QX214-3	Keepsake	Yr.Iss.	4.50	3-12.00
82-76-022 New Home 450QX212-6	Keepsake	Yr.Iss.	4.50	6-17.00
82-76-023 Teacher 650QX312-3	Keepsake	Yr.Iss.	6.50	15.00
82-76-024 25th Christmas Together 450QX211-6	Keepsake	Yr.Iss.	4.50	6-20.00
82-76-025 50th Christmas Together 450QX212-3	Keepsake	Yr.Iss.	4.50	6-20.00
82-76-026 Moments of Love 450QX209-3	Keepsake	Yr.Iss.	4.50	6-15.00
82-76-027 Love 450QX209-6	Keepsake	Yr.Iss.	4.50	7-17.00
82-76-028 Friendship 450QX208-6	Keepsake	Yr.Iss.	4.50	7-20.00
82-76-029 Teacher-Apple 550QX301-6	Keepsake	Yr.Iss.	5.50	5-13.00
82-76-030 Baby's First Christmas 550QX302-3	Keepsake	Yr.Iss.	5.50	40.00
82-76-031 First Christmas Together 550QX302-6	Keepsake	Yr.Iss.	5.50	8-20.00
82-76-032 Love 550QX304-3	Keepsake	Yr.Iss.	5.50	30.00
82-76-033 Friendship 550QX304-6	Keepsake	Yr.Iss.	5.50	15-25.00
Hallmark Keepsake Ornaments 1982 Property Ornaments				
82-77-001 Miss Piggy and Kermit 450QX218-3	Keepsake	Yr.Iss.	4.50	28-40.00
82-77-002 Muppets Party 450QX218-6	Keepsake	Yr.Iss.	4.50	28-37.00
82-77-003 Kermit the Frog 1100QX495-6	Keepsake	Yr.Iss.	11.00	60-85.00
82-77-004 The Divine Miss Piggy 1200QX425-5	Keepsake	Yr.Iss.	12.00	125.00
82-77-005 Betsey Clark 850QX305-6	Keepsake	Yr.Iss.	8.50	24.50
82-77-006 Norman Rockwell-3rd ed.850QX305-3	Keepsake	Yr.Iss.	8.50	10-30.00
82-77-007 Betsey Clark-10th edition450QX215-6	Keepsake	Yr.Iss.	4.50	15.00
82-77-008 Norman Rockwell 450QX202-3	Keepsake	Yr.Iss.	4.50	16-29.50
82-77-009 Peanuts 450QX200-6	Keepsake	Yr.Iss.	4.50	13-33.00
82-77-010 Disney 450QX217-3	Keepsake	Yr.Iss.	4.50	20-35.00
82-77-011 Mary Hamilton 450QX217-6	Keepsake	Yr.Iss.	4.50	10-20.00
82-77-012 Joan Walsh Anglund 450QX219-3	Keepsake	Yr.Iss.	4.50	7-18.00
Hallmark Keepsake Ornaments 1982 Designer Keepsakes				
82-78-001 Old World Angels 450QX226-3	Keepsake	Yr.Iss.	4.50	22.00
82-78-002 Patterns of Christmas 450QX226-6	Keepsake	Yr.Iss.	4.50	22.50
82-78-003 Old Fashioned Christmas 450QX227-6	Keepsake	Yr.Iss.	4.50	39.50
82-78-004 Stained Glass 450QX228-3	Keepsake	Yr.Iss.	4.50	12-22.00
82-78-005 Merry Christmas 450QX225-6	Keepsake	Yr.Iss.	4.50	7-19.00
82-78-006 Twelve Days of Christmas 450QX203-6	Keepsake	Yr.Iss.	4.50	30.00
Hallmark Keepsake Ornaments 1982 Decorative Ball Ornaments				
82-79-001 Christmas Angel 450QX220-6	Keepsake	Yr.Iss.	4.50	7-19.00
82-79-002 Santa 450QX221-6	Keepsake	Yr.Iss.	4.50	19.00
82-79-003 Currier & Ives 450QX201-3	Keepsake	Yr.Iss.	4.50	6-17.00
82-79-004 Season for Caring 450QX221-3	Keepsake	Yr.Iss.	4.50	20.00
Hallmark Keepsake Ornaments 1982 Colors of Christmas				
82-80-001 Nativity 450QX308-3	Keepsake	Yr.Iss.	4.50	40.00
82-80-002 Santa's Flight 450QX308-6	Keepsake	Yr.Iss.	4.50	40.00
Hallmark Keepsake Ornaments 1982 Ice Sculptures				
82-81-001 Snowy Seal 400QX300-6	Keepsake	Yr.Iss.	4.00	12-19.00
82-81-002 Arctic Penguin 400QX300-3	Keepsake	Yr.Iss.	4.00	7-19.00
Hallmark Keepsake Ornaments 1982 Holiday Highlights				
82-82-001 Christmas Sleigh 550QX309-3	Keepsake	Yr.Iss.	5.50	75.00
82-82-002 Angel 550QX309-6	Keepsake	Yr.Iss.	5.50	25.00
82-82-003 Christmas Magic 550QX311-3	Keepsake	Yr.Iss.	5.50	22-29.00
Hallmark Keepsake Ornaments 1982 Handcrafted Ornaments				
82-83-001 Three Kings 850QX307-3	Keepsake	Yr.Iss.	8.50	20.00
82-83-002 Baroque Angel 1500QX456-6	Keepsake	Yr.Iss.	15.00	150.00
82-83-003 Cloisonne Angel 1200QX145-4	Keepsake	Yr.Iss.	12.00	95.00
Hallmark Keepsake Ornaments 1982 Brass Ornaments				
82-84-001 Santa and Reindeer 900QX467-6	Keepsake	Yr.Iss.	9.00	40-50.00
82-84-002 Brass Bell 1200QX460-6	Keepsake	Yr.Iss.	12.00	20.00
82-84-003 Santa's Sleigh 900QX478-6	Keepsake	Yr.Iss.	9.00	14-35.00
Hallmark Keepsake Ornaments 1982 Handcrafted Ornaments				
82-85-001 The Spirit of Christmas 1,000QX452-6	Keepsake	Yr.Iss.	10.00	105-125.
82-85-002 Jogging Santa 800QX457-6	Keepsake	Yr.Iss.	8.00	30-45.00
82-85-003 Santa Bell 1500QX148-7	Keepsake	Yr.Iss.	15.00	40-60.00
82-85-004 Santa's Workshop 1,000QX450-3	Keepsake	Yr.Iss.	10.00	60-75.00
82-85-005 Cycling Santa 2,000QX435-5	Keepsake	Yr.Iss.	20.00	110-150.
82-85-006 Christmas Fantasy 1300QX155-4	Keepsake	Yr.Iss.	13.00	59.00
82-85-007 Cowboy Snowman 800QX480-6	Keepsake	Yr.Iss.	8.00	50.00
82-85-008 Pinecone Home 800QX461-3	Keepsake	Yr.Iss.	8.00	110-175.
82-85-009 Raccoon Surprises 900QX479-3	Keepsake	Yr.Iss.	9.00	125-145.
82-85-010 Elfin Artist 900QX457-3	Keepsake	Yr.Iss.	9.00	25-47.00
82-85-011 Ice Sculptor 800QX432-2	Keepsake	Yr.Iss.	8.00	75.00
82-85-012 Tin Soldier 650QX483-6	Keepsake	Yr.Iss.	6.50	25-40.00
82-85-013 Peeking Elf 650QX419-5	Keepsake	Yr.Iss.	6.50	25-40.00
82-85-014 Jolly Christmas Tree 650QX465-3	Keepsake	Yr.Iss.	6.50	50-75.00
82-85-015 Embroidered Tree - 650QX494-6	Keepsake	Yr.Iss.	6.50	40.00
Hallmark Keepsake Ornaments 1982 Little Trimmers				
82-86-001 Cookie Mouse 450QX454-6	Keepsake	Yr.Iss.	4.50	48-60.00
82-86-002 Musical Angel 550QX459-6	Keepsake	Yr.Iss.	5.50	110-125.
82-86-003 Merry Moose 550QX415-5	Keepsake	Yr.Iss.	5.50	30-55.00
82-86-004 Christmas Owl 450QX131-4	Keepsake	Yr.Iss.	4.50	35.00
82-86-005 Dove Love 450QX462-3	Keepsake	Yr.Iss.	4.50	30-55.00
82-86-006 Perky Penguin 400QX409-5	Keepsake	Yr.Iss.	4.00	35.00
82-86-007 Christmas Kitten 400QX454-3	Keepsake	Yr.Iss.	4.00	32-35.00
82-86-008 Jingling Teddy 400QX477-6	Keepsake	Yr.Iss.	4.00	25.00
Hallmark Keepsake Ornaments 1982 Collectible Series				
82-87-001 Holiday Wildlife-1st Ed. 700QX313-3	Keepsake	Yr.Iss.	7.00	340-375.
82-87-002 Tin Locomotive-1st Ed. 1300QX460-3	Keepsake	Yr.Iss.	13.00	400-595.
82-87-003 Clothespin Soldier-1st Ed. 500QX458-3	Keepsake	Yr.Iss.	5.00	100-135.
82-87-004 The Bellringer-4th Ed. 1500QX455-6	Keepsake	Yr.Iss.	15.00	80-100.
82-87-005 Carrousel Series-5th Ed. 1000QX478-3	Keepsake	Yr.Iss.	10.00	90-100.
82-87-006 Snoopy and Friends-4th Ed. 1000QX478-3	Keepsake	Yr.Iss.	13.00	75-85.00
82-87-007 Here Comes Santa-4th Edition 1500QX464-3	Keepsake	Yr.Iss.	15.00	70-130.
82-87-008 Rocking Horse-2nd Ed. 1000QX 502-3	Keepsake	Yr.Iss.	10.00	325-375.
82-87-009 Thimble-5th Edition 500QX451-3	Keepsake	Yr.Iss.	5.00	60-75.00
82-87-010 Frosty Friends-3rd Ed. 800QX 452-3	Keepsake	Yr.Iss.	8.00	135-270.
Hallmark Keepsake Ornaments 1982 Holiday Chimes				
82-88-001 Tree Chimes 550QX484-6	Keepsake	Yr.Iss.	5.50	49.00
82-88-002 Bell Chimes 550QX494-3	Keepsake	Yr.Iss.	5.50	25.00
Hallmark Keepsake Ornaments 1983 Commemoratives				
83-89-001 Baby's First Christmas 750QX301-9	Keepsake	Yr.Iss.	7.50	5-20.00
83-89-002 Baby's First Christmas 1400QX402-7	Keepsake	Yr.Iss.	14.00	28-40.00
83-89-003 Baby's First Christmas 450QX200-7	Keepsake	Yr.Iss.	4.50	12-24.00
83-89-004 Baby's First Christmas 450QX200-9	Keepsake	Yr.Iss.	4.50	12-24.00
83-89-005 Baby's First Christmas 700QX302-9	Keepsake	Yr.Iss.	7.00	25.00
83-89-006 Grandchild's First Christmas400QX430-9	Keepsake	Yr.Iss.	14.00	10-35.00
83-89-007 Child's Third Christmas 450QX226-9	Keepsake	Yr.Iss.	4.50	20.00
83-89-008 Grandchild's First Christmas 600QX 312-9	Keepsake	Yr.Iss.	6.00	20.00
83-89-009 Baby's Second Christmas 450QX226-7	Keepsake	Yr.Iss.	4.50	25.00
83-89-010 Granddaughter 450QX202-7	Keepsake	Yr.Iss.	4.50	30.00
83-89-011 Grandson 450QX201-9	Keepsake	Yr.Iss.	4.50	12-30.00
83-89-012 Son 450QX202-9	Keepsake	Yr.Iss.	4.50	20.00
83-89-013 Daughter 450QX203-7	Keepsake	Yr.Iss.	4.50	20-42.00
83-89-014 Godchild 450QX201-7	Keepsake	Yr.Iss.	4.50	14.00
83-89-015 Grandmother 450QX205-7	Keepsake	Yr.Iss.	4.50	10-20.00
83-89-016 Mom and Dad 650QX429-7	Keepsake	Yr.Iss.	6.50	8-23.00
83-89-017 Sister 450QX206-9	Keepsake	Yr.Iss.	4.50	17.00
83-89-018 Grandparents 650QX429-9	Keepsake	Yr.Iss.	6.50	10-22.00
83-89-019 First Christmas Together 450QX208-9	Keepsake	Yr.Iss.	4.50	30.00
83-89-020 First Christmas Together 600QX310-7	Keepsake	Yr.Iss.	6.00	15-40.00
83-89-021 First Christmas Together 750QX301-7	Keepsake	Yr.Iss.	7.50	10-20.00
83-89-022 First Christmas Together-Brass Locket 1500QX 432-9	Keepsake	Yr.Iss.	15.00	15-45.00
83-89-023 Love Is a Song 450QX223-9	Keepsake	Yr.Iss.	4.50	20-25.00
83-89-024 Love 1300QX422-7	Keepsake	Yr.Iss.	13.00	40.00
83-89-025 Love 600QX310-9	Keepsake	Yr.Iss.	6.00	40.00
83-89-026 Love 450QX207-9	Keepsake	Yr.Iss.	4.50	25.00
83-89-027 Teacher 600QX304-9	Keepsake	Yr.Iss.	6.00	10.00
83-89-028 First Christmas Together 600QX306-9	Keepsake	Yr.Iss.	6.00	10-22.00
83-89-029 Friendship 600QX305-9	Keepsake	Yr.Iss.	6.00	14.50
83-89-030 Love 600QX305-7	Keepsake	Yr.Iss.	6.00	10-20.00
83-89-031 Mother 600Qx306-7	Keepsake	Yr.Iss.	6.00	20.00
83-89-032 25th Christmas Together 450QX224-7	Keepsake	Yr.Iss.	4.50	17.00
83-89-033 Teacher 450QX224-9	Keepsake	Yr.Iss.	4.50	6-15.00
83-89-034 Friendship 450QX207-7	Keepsake	Yr.Iss.	4.50	7-17.00
83-89-035 New Home 450QX210-7	Keepsake	Yr.Iss.	4.50	8-32.00
83-89-036 Tenth Christmas Together 650QX430-7	Keepsake	Yr.Iss.	6.50	10-20.00

Hallmark Keepsake Ornaments — 1983 Property Ornaments

		ARTIST	EDITION	ISSUE	QUOTE
83-90-001	Betsey Clark 650QX404-7	Keepsake	Yr.Iss.	6.50	35.00
83-90-002	Betsey Clark 900QX440-1	Keepsake	Yr.Iss.	9.00	20-32.00
83-90-003	Betsey Clark-11th Edition 450QX211-9	Keepsake	Yr.Iss.	4.50	30.00
83-90-004	Peanuts 450QX212-7	Keepsake	Yr.Iss.	4.50	11-27.00
83-90-005	Disney 450QX212-9	Keepsake	Yr.Iss.	4.50	50.00
83-90-006	Shirt Tales 450QX214-9	Keepsake	Yr.Iss.	4.50	22.50
83-90-007	Mary Hamilton 450QX213-7	Keepsake	Yr.Iss.	4.50	39.50
83-90-008	Miss Piggy 1300QX405-7	Keepsake	Yr.Iss.	13.00	225.00
83-90-009	The Muppets 450QX214-7	Keepsake	Yr.Iss.	4.50	30-40.00
83-90-010	Kermit the Frog 1100QX495-6	Keepsake	Yr.Iss.	11.00	35.00
83-90-011	Norman Rockwell-4th Ed. 750QX 300-7	Keepsake	Yr.Iss.	7.50	35.00
83-90-012	Norman Rockwell 450QX215-7	Keepsake	Yr.Iss.	4.50	30-50.00

Hallmark Keepsake Ornaments — 1983 Decorative Ball Ornaments

83-91-001	Currier & Ives 450QX215-9	Keepsake	Yr.Iss.	4.50	8-19.00
83-91-002	Christmas Joy 450QX216-9	Keepsake	Yr.Iss.	4.50	10-30.00
83-91-003	Here Comes Santa 450QX217-7	Keepsake	Yr.Iss.	4.50	40.00
83-91-004	Oriental Butterflies 450QX218-7	Keepsake	Yr.Iss.	4.50	25.00
83-91-005	Angels 500QX219-7	Keepsake	Yr.Iss.	5.00	22.00
83-91-006	Season's Greeting 450QX219-9	Keepsake	Yr.Iss.	4.50	10-22.00
83-91-007	1983 450QX220-9	Keepsake	Yr.Iss.	4.50	17-30.00
83-91-008	The Wise Men 450QX220-7	Keepsake	Yr.Iss.	4.50	30-39.50
83-91-009	Christmas Wonderland 450QX221-9	Keepsake	Yr.Iss.	4.50	95.00
83-91-010	An Old Fashioned Christmas 450QX2217-9	Keepsake	Yr.Iss.	4.50	25.00
83-91-011	The Annunciation 450QX216-7	Keepsake	Yr.Iss.	4.50	22.50

Hallmark Keepsake Ornaments — 1983 Holiday Highlights

83-92-001	Christmas Stocking 600Qx303-9	Keepsake	Yr.Iss.	6.00	15-40.00
83-92-002	Star of Peace 600QX304-7	Keepsake	Yr.Iss.	6.00	6-15.00
83-92-003	Time for Sharing 600QX307-7	Keepsake	Yr.Iss.	6.00	40.00

Hallmark Keepsake Ornaments — 1983 Crown Classics

83-93-001	Enameled Christmas Wreath 900QX 311-9	Keepsake	Yr.Iss.	9.00	5-13.00
83-93-002	Memories to Treasure 700QX303-7	Keepsake	Yr.Iss.	7.00	22.00
83-93-003	Mother and Child 750QX302-7	Keepsake	Yr.Iss.	7.50	12-35.00

Hallmark Keepsake Ornaments — 1983 Holiday Sculptures

83-94-001	Santa 400QX308-7	Keepsake	Yr.Iss.	4.00	33.00
83-94-002	Heart 400QX307-9	Keepsake	Yr.Iss.	4.00	45.00

Hallmark Keepsake Ornaments — 1983 Handcrafted Ornaments

83-95-001	Embroidered Stocking 650QX479-6	Keepsake	Yr.Iss.	6.50	10-22.00
83-95-002	Embroidered Heart 650QX421-7	Keepsake	Yr.Iss.	6.50	19.50
83-95-003	Scrimshaw Reindeer 800QX424-9	Keepsake	Yr.Iss.	8.00	16-33.00
83-95-004	Jack Frost 900QX407-9	Keepsake	Yr.Iss.	9.00	60.00
83-95-005	Unicorn 1000QX426-7	Keepsake	Yr.Iss.	10.00	35-65.00
83-95-006	Porcelain Doll, Diana 900QX423-7	Keepsake	Yr.Iss.	9.00	10-30.00
83-95-007	Brass Santa 900QX423-9	Keepsake	Yr.Iss.	9.00	19.00
83-95-008	Santa's on His Way 1,000QX426-9	Keepsake	Yr.Iss.	10.00	32.00
83-95-009	Old-Fashioned Santa 1100QX409-9	Keepsake	Yr.Iss.	11.00	38-53.00
83-95-010	Cycling Santa 2000QX435-5	Keepsake	Yr.Iss.	20.00	195.00
83-95-011	Santa's Workshop 1000QX450-3	Keepsake	Yr.Iss.	10.00	60.00
83-95-012	Ski Lift Santa 800QX418-7	Keepsake	Yr.Iss.	8.00	50-75.00
83-95-013	Hitchhiking Santa 800QX424-7	Keepsake	Yr.Iss.	8.00	39.50
83-95-014	Mountain Climbing Santa 650QX407-7	Keepsake	Yr.Iss.	6.50	21-40.00
83-95-015	Jolly Santa 350QX425-9	Keepsake	Yr.Iss.	3.50	20-35.00
83-95-016	Santa's Many Faces 600QX311-6	Keepsake	Yr.Iss.	6.00	30.00
83-95-017	Baroque Angels 1300QX422-9	Keepsake	Yr.Iss.	13.00	58.00
83-95-018	Madonna and Child 1200QX428-7	Keepsake	Yr.Iss.	12.00	22-42.00
83-95-019	Mouse on Cheese 650QX413-7	Keepsake	Yr.Iss.	6.50	30-50.00
83-95-020	Peppermint Penguin 650QX408-9	Keepsake	Yr.Iss.	6.50	28-50.00
83-95-021	Skating Rabbit 800QX409-7	Keepsake	Yr.Iss.	8.00	47-55.00
83-95-022	Skiing Fox 800QX420-7	Keepsake	Yr.Iss.	8.00	30-38.00
83-95-023	Mouse in Bell 1,000QX419-7	Keepsake	Yr.Iss.	10.00	65.00
83-95-024	Mailbox Kitten 650QX415-7	Keepsake	Yr.Iss.	6.50	40-60.00
83-95-025	Tin Rocking Horse 650QX414-9	Keepsake	Yr.Iss.	6.50	45.00
83-95-026	Bell Wreath 650QX420-9	Keepsake	Yr.Iss.	6.50	32.00
83-95-027	Angel Messenger 650QX408-7	Keepsake	Yr.Iss.	6.50	95.00
83-95-028	Holiday Puppy 350QX412-7	Keepsake	Yr.Iss.	3.50	15-30.00
83-95-029	Rainbow Angel 550QX416-7	Keepsake	Yr.Iss.	5.50	112-125.
83-95-030	Sneaker Mouse 450QX400-9	Keepsake	Yr.Iss.	4.50	22-40.00
83-95-031	Christmas Koala 400QX419-9	Keepsake	Yr.Iss.	4.00	20-32.00
83-95-032	Caroling Owl 450QX411-7	Keepsake	Yr.Iss.	4.50	20-40.00
83-95-033	Christmas Kitten 400QX454-3	Keepsake	Yr.Iss.	4.00	35.00

Hallmark Keepsake Ornaments — 1983 Collectible Series

83-96-001	The Bellringer-5th Edition1500QX 403-9	Keepsake	Yr.Iss.	15.00	85-135.
83-96-002	Holiday Wildlife-2nd Edition 700QX 309-9	Keepsake	Yr.Iss.	7.00	40-75.00
83-96-003	Here Comes Santa-5th Edition 1300QX 403-7	Keepsake	Yr.Iss.	13.00	200-250.
83-96-004	Snoopy and Friends-5th Ed.1300QX416-9	Keepsake	Yr.Iss.	13.00	75-85.00
83-96-005	Carrousel-6th Edition 1100QX401-9	Keepsake	Yr.Iss.	11.00	33-50.00
83-96-006	Porcelain Bear-1st Edition700QX428-9	Keepsake	Yr.Iss.	7.00	72-85.00
83-96-007	Clothespin Soldier-2nd Edition 500QX402-9	Keepsake	Yr.Iss.	5.00	20-45.00
83-96-008	Rocking Horse-3rd Edition1000QX417-7	Keepsake	Yr.Iss.	10.00	220-295.
83-96-009	Frosty Friends-4th Edition800QX400-7	Keepsake	Yr.Iss.	8.00	210-285.
83-96-010	Thimble - 6th Edition 500QX401-7	Keepsake	Yr.Iss.	5.00	28-39.00
83-96-011	Tin Locomotive - 2nd Edition 1300QX404-9	Keepsake	Yr.Iss.	13.00	220-275.

Hallmark Keepsake Ornaments — 1984 Commemoratives

84-97-001	Baby's First Christmas 1600QX904-1	Keepsake	Yr.Iss.	16.00	40-50.00
84-97-002	Baby's First Christmas 1400QX438-1	Keepsake	Yr.Iss.	14.00	30-45.00
84-97-003	Baby's First Christmas 700QX300-1	Keepsake	Yr.Iss.	7.00	7-17.00
84-97-004	Baby's First Christmas 600QX340-1	Keepsake	Yr.Iss.	6.00	10-40.00
84-97-005	Baby's First Christmas-Boy 450QX 240-4	Keepsake	Yr.Iss.	4.50	15-25.00
84-97-006	Baby's First Christmas-Girl 450QX 340-1	Keepsake	Yr.Iss.	4.50	15-25.00
84-97-007	Baby's Second Christmas 450QX241-1	Keepsake	Yr.Iss.	4.50	20-37.00
84-97-008	Child's Third Christmas 450QX261-1	Keepsake	Yr.Iss.	4.50	20.00
84-97-009	Grandchild's First Christmas110QX460-1	Keepsake	Yr.Iss.	11.00	6-25.00
84-97-010	Grandchild's First Christmas450QX257-4	Keepsake	Yr.Iss.	4.50	17.00
84-97-011	Godchild 450QX242-1	Keepsake	Yr.Iss.	4.50	20.00
84-97-012	Grandson 450QX242-4	Keepsake	Yr.Iss.	4.50	12-28.00
84-97-013	Granddaughter 450QX243-1	Keepsake	Yr.Iss.	4.50	28.00
84-97-014	Grandparents 450QX256-1	Keepsake	Yr.Iss.	4.50	15.00
84-97-015	Grandmother 450QX244-1	Keepsake	Yr.Iss.	4.50	8-15.00
84-97-016	Father 600QX257-1	Keepsake	Yr.Iss.	6.00	17.00
84-97-017	Mother 600QX343-4	Keepsake	Yr.Iss.	6.00	16.00
84-97-018	Mother and Dad 650QX258-1	Keepsake	Yr.Iss.	6.50	7-22.00
84-97-019	Sister 650QX259-4	Keepsake	Yr.Iss.	6.50	18.00
84-97-020	Daughter 450QX244-4	Keepsake	Yr.Iss.	4.50	20-30.00
84-97-021	Son 450QX243-4	Keepsake	Yr.Iss.	4.50	10-30.00
84-97-022	The Miracle of Love 600QX342-4	Keepsake	Yr.Iss.	6.00	29.50
84-97-023	First Christmas Together 600QX342-1	Keepsake	Yr.Iss.	6.00	7-22.00
84-97-024	First Christmas Together 1600QX904-4	Keepsake	Yr.Iss.	16.00	30-40.00
84-97-025	First Christmas Together 1500QX436-4	Keepsake	Yr.Iss.	15.00	10-35.00
84-97-026	First Christmas Together 750QX340-4	Keepsake	Yr.Iss.	7.50	8-23.00
84-97-027	First Christmas Together 450QX245-1	Keepsake	Yr.Iss.	4.50	15-20.00
84-97-028	Heartful of Love 1000QX443-4	Keepsake	Yr.Iss.	10.00	45.00
84-97-029	Love...the Spirit of Christmas450QX247-4	Keepsake	Yr.Iss.	4.50	8-32.00
84-97-030	Love 450QX255-4	Keepsake	Yr.Iss.	4.50	11-22.00
84-97-031	Ten Years Together 650QX258-4	Keepsake	Yr.Iss.	6.50	7-22.00
84-97-032	Twenty-Five Years Together650QX259-1	Keepsake	Yr.Iss.	6.50	19.50
84-97-033	Gratitude 600QX344-4	Keepsake	Yr.Iss.	6.00	10.00
84-97-034	The Fun of Friendship 600QX343-1	Keepsake	Yr.Iss.	6.00	10-34.00
84-97-035	Friendship 450QX248-1	Keepsake	Yr.Iss.	4.50	15.00
84-97-036	A Gift of Friendship 450QX260-4	Keepsake	Yr.Iss.	4.50	25.00
84-97-037	New Home 450QX245-4	Keepsake	Yr.Iss.	4.50	60-107.
84-97-038	From Our Home to Yours 450QX248-4	Keepsake	Yr.Iss.	4.50	50.00
84-97-039	Teacher 450QX249-1	Keepsake	Yr.Iss.	4.50	5-15.00
84-97-040	Baby-sitter 450QX253-1	Keepsake	Yr.Iss.	4.50	4-12.00

Hallmark Keepsake Ornaments — 1984 Property Ornaments

84-98-001	Betsey Clark Angel 900QX462-4	Keepsake	Yr.Iss.	9.00	15-32.00
84-98-002	Katybeth 900QX463-1	Keepsake	Yr.Iss.	9.00	11-30.00
84-98-003	Peanuts 450QX252-1	Keepsake	Yr.Iss.	4.50	10-35.00
84-98-004	Disney 450QX250-4	Keepsake	Yr.Iss.	4.50	22-30.00
84-98-005	The Muppets 450QX251-4	Keepsake	Yr.Iss.	4.50	8-24.00
84-98-006	Norman Rockwell 450QX251-4	Keepsake	Yr.Iss.	4.50	8-22.00
84-98-007	Currier & Ives 450QX250-1	Keepsake	Yr.Iss.	4.50	20.00
84-98-008	Shirt Tales 450QX252-4	Keepsake	Yr.Iss.	4.50	20-25.00
84-98-009	Snoopy and Woodstock 750QX439-1	Keepsake	Yr.Iss.	7.50	30.00
84-98-010	Muffin 550QX442-1	Keepsake	Yr.Iss.	5.50	28.00
84-98-011	Kit 550QX453-4	Keepsake	Yr.Iss.	5.50	20-30.00

Hallmark Keepsake Ornaments — 1984 Traditional Ornaments

84-99-001	White Christmas 1600QX905-1	Keepsake	Yr.Iss.	16.00	70-95.00
84-99-002	Twelve Days of Christmas1500QX 415-9	Keepsake	Yr.Iss.	15.00	70.00
84-99-003	Gift of Music 1500QX451-1	Keepsake	Yr.Iss.	15.00	50-95.00
84-99-004	Amanda 900QX432-1	Keepsake	Yr.Iss.	9.00	10-30.00
84-99-005	Holiday Jester 1100QX437-4	Keepsake	Yr.Iss.	11.00	20-40.00
84-99-006	Uncle Sam 600QX449-1	Keepsake	Yr.Iss.	6.00	45.00
84-99-007	Chickadee 600QX451-4	Keepsake	Yr.Iss.	6.00	35.00
84-99-008	Cuckoo Clock 1,000QX455-1	Keepsake	Yr.Iss.	10.00	45.00
84-99-009	Alpine Elf 600QX452-1	Keepsake	Yr.Iss.	6.00	37.50
84-99-010	Nostalgic Sled 600QX442-4	Keepsake	Yr.Iss.	6.00	12-30.00
84-99-011	Santa Sulky Driver 900QX436-1	Keepsake	Yr.Iss.	9.00	13-32.00
84-99-012	Old Fashioned Rocking Horse 750QX346-4	Keepsake	Yr.Iss.	7.50	8-17.50
84-99-013	Madonna and Child 600QX344-1	Keepsake	Yr.Iss.	6.00	10-40.00
84-99-014	Holiday Friendship 1300QX445-1	Keepsake	Yr.Iss.	13.00	24.50
84-99-015	Peace on Earth 750QX341-4	Keepsake	Yr.Iss.	7.50	10-25.00
84-99-016	A Savior is Born 450X254-1	Keepsake	Yr.Iss.	4.50	10-20.00
84-99-017	Holiday Starburst 500QX253-4	Keepsake	Yr.Iss.	5.00	20.00
84-99-018	Santa 750QX458-4	Keepsake	Yr.Iss.	7.50	9-19.00
84-99-019	Needlepoint Wreath 650QX459-4	Keepsake	Yr.Iss.	6.50	7-15.00
84-99-020	Christmas Memories Photoholder 650QX300-4	Keepsake	Yr.Iss.	6.50	13.00

Hallmark Keepsake Ornaments — 1984 Holiday Humor

84-100-001	Bell Ringer Squirrel 1,000QX443-1	Keepsake	Yr.Iss.	10.00	20-40.00
84-100-002	Raccoon's Christmas 900QX447-7	Keepsake	Yr.Iss.	9.00	34-55.00
84-100-003	Three Kittens in a Mitten 800QX431-1	Keepsake	Yr.Iss.	8.00	30-50.00
84-100-004	Marathon Santa 800QX456-4	Keepsake	Yr.Iss.	8.00	40.00
84-100-005	Santa Star 550QX450-4	Keepsake	Yr.Iss.	5.50	40.00
84-100-006	Snowmobile Santa 650QX431-4	Keepsake	Yr.Iss.	6.50	35.00
84-100-007	Snowshoe Penguin 650QX453-1	Keepsake	Yr.Iss.	6.50	50-60.00
84-100-008	Christmas Owl 600QX444-1	Keepsake	Yr.Iss.	6.00	20-32.00
84-100-009	Musical Angel 550QX434-4	Keepsake	Yr.Iss.	5.50	60.00
84-100-010	Napping Mouse 550QX435-1	Keepsake	Yr.Iss.	5.50	35-50.00
84-100-011	Roller Skating Rabbit 500QX457-1	Keepsake	Yr.Iss.	5.00	15-32.00
84-100-012	Frisbee Puppy 500QX444-4	Keepsake	Yr.Iss.	5.00	40-48.00
84-100-013	Reindeer Racetrack 450QX254-4	Keepsake	Yr.Iss.	4.50	20.00
84-100-014	A Christmas Prayer 450QX246-1	Keepsake	Yr.Iss.	4.50	10-17.00
84-100-015	Flights of Fantasy 450QX256-4	Keepsake	Yr.Iss.	4.50	20.00
84-100-016	Polar Bear Drummer 450QX430-1	Keepsake	Yr.Iss.	4.50	30.00
84-100-017	Santa Mouse 450QX433-4	Keepsake	Yr.Iss.	4.50	40-45.00
84-100-018	Snowy Seal 400QX450-1	Keepsake	Yr.Iss.	4.00	12-24.00
84-100-019	Fortune Cookie Elf 450Q452-4	Keepsake	Yr.Iss.	4.50	39.50
84-100-020	Peppermint 1984 450Q452-1	Keepsake	Yr.Iss.	4.50	50.00
84-100-021	Mountain Climbing Santa 650QX407-7	Keepsake	Yr.Iss.	6.50	34.50

Hallmark Keepsake Ornaments — 1984 Limited Edition

84-101-001	Classical Angel 2750QX459-1	Keepsake	Yr.Iss.	28.00	65-105.

Hallmark Keepsake Ornaments — 1984 Collectible Series

84-102-001	Nostalgic Houses and Shops-1st Edition 1300QX 448-1	Keepsake	Yr.Iss.	13.00	150-210.
84-102-002	Wood Childhood Ornaments- 1st Edition 650QX 439-4	Keepsake	Yr.Iss.	6.50	45.00
84-102-003	The Twelve Days of Christmas- 1st Edition 600QX 3484	Keepsake	Yr.Iss.	6.00	235-275.
84-102-004	Art Masterpiece- 1st Edition650QX349-4	Keepsake	Yr.Iss.	6.50	15.00
84-102-005	Porcelain Bear- 2nd Edition700QX454-1	Keepsake	Yr.Iss.	7.00	26-39.00
84-102-006	Tin Locomotive- 3rd Edition 1400QX440-4	Keepsake	Yr.Iss.	14.00	60-85.00
84-102-007	Clothespin Soldier -3rd Edition 500QX447-1	Keepsake	Yr.Iss.	5.00	16-24.00
84-102-008	Holiday Wildlife - 3rd Edition 725QX 347-4	Keepsake	Yr.Iss.	7.25	20-30.00
84-102-009	Rocking Horse - 4th Edition 1000QX435-4	Keepsake	Yr.Iss.	10.00	50-75.50
84-102-010	Frosty Friends -5th Edition 800QX 437-1	Keepsake	Yr.Iss.	8.00	55-80.00
84-102-011	Norman Rockwell - 5th Edition 750QX341-1	Keepsake	Yr.Iss.	7.50	22-33.00
84-102-012	Here Comes Santa -6th Edition 1300QX438-4	Keepsake	Yr.Iss.	13.00	58-85.00
84-102-013	The Bellringer - 6th & Final Edition 1500QX 438-4	Keepsake	Yr.Iss.	15.00	30-45.00
84-102-014	Thimble - 7th Edition 500QX430-4	Keepsake	Yr.Iss.	5.00	33-50.00
84-102-015	Betsey Clark - 12th Edition 500QX 249-4	Keepsake	Yr.Iss.	5.00	25-35.00

Hallmark Keepsake Ornaments — 1984 Keepsake Magic Ornaments

84-103-001	Village Church 1500QLX702-1	Keepsake	Yr.Iss.	15.00	35-50.00
84-103-002	Sugarplum Cottage 1100QLX701-1	Keepsake	Yr.Iss.	11.00	45.00
84-103-003	City Lights 1,000QLX701-4	Keepsake	Yr.Iss.	10.00	50.00
84-103-004	Santa's Workshop 1300QLX700-4	Keepsake	Yr.Iss.	13.00	45-62.50

	ARTIST	EDITION	ISSUE	QUOTE
84-103-005 Santa's Arrival 1300QLX702-4	Keepsake	Yr.Iss.	13.00	45-65.00
84-103-006 Nativity 1200 QLX700-1	Keepsake	Yr.Iss.	12.00	18-28.00
84-103-007 Stained Glass 800QLX703-1	Keepsake	Yr.Iss.	8.00	20.00
84-103-008 Christmas in the Forest 800QLX703-4	Keepsake	Yr.Iss.	8.00	11-25.00
84-103-009 Brass Carrousel 900QLX707-1	Keepsake	Yr.Iss.	9.00	95.00
84-103-010 All Are Precious 800QLX704-1	Keepsake	Yr.Iss.	8.00	12-25.00
Hallmark Keepsake Ornaments 1985 Commemoratives				
85-104-001 Baby's First Christmas 1600QX499-5	Keepsake	Yr.Iss.	16.00	22.00
85-104-002 Baby's First Christmas 1500QX499-2	Keepsake	Yr.Iss.	15.00	40.00
85-104-003 Baby Locket 1600QX401-2	Keepsake	Yr.Iss.	16.00	35-38.00
85-104-004 Baby's First Christmas 575QX370-2	Keepsake	Yr.Iss.	5.75	20.00
85-104-005 Baby's First Christmas 700QX478-2	Keepsake	Yr.Iss.	7.00	14.50
85-104-006 Baby's First Christmas 500QX260-2	Keepsake	Yr.Iss.	5.00	15.00
85-104-007 Baby's Second Christmas 600QX478-5	Keepsake	Yr.Iss.	6.00	20.00
85-104-008 Child's Third Christmas 600QX475-5	Keepsake	Yr.Iss.	6.00	25.00
85-104-009 Grandchild's First Christmas500QX260-5	Keepsake	Yr.Iss.	5.00	15.00
85-104-010 Grandchild's First Christmas 1100QX495-5	Keepsake	Yr.Iss.	11.00	11-24.00
85-104-011 Grandparents 700QX380-5	Keepsake	Yr.Iss.	7.00	10.00
85-104-012 Niece 575QX520-5	Keepsake	Yr.Iss.	5.75	10.50
85-104-013 Mother 675QX372-2	Keepsake	Yr.Iss.	6.75	10.00
85-104-014 Mother and Dad 775QX509-2	Keepsake	Yr.Iss.	7.75	18.50
85-104-015 Father 650QX376-2	Keepsake	Yr.Iss.	6.50	11.00
85-104-016 Sister 725QX506-5	Keepsake	Yr.Iss.	7.25	10.00
85-104-017 Daughter 550QX503-2	Keepsake	Yr.Iss.	5.50	20.00
85-104-018 Godchild 675QX380-2	Keepsake	Yr.Iss.	6.75	20.00
85-104-019 Son 550QX502-5	Keepsake	Yr.Iss.	5.50	42.50
85-104-020 Grandmother 475QX262-5	Keepsake	Yr.Iss.	4.75	12.00
85-104-021 Grandson 475QX262-2	Keepsake	Yr.Iss.	4.75	13.00
85-104-022 Granddaughter 475QX263-5	Keepsake	Yr.Iss.	4.75	11-25.00
85-104-023 First Christmas Together 1675QX400-5	Keepsake	Yr.Iss.	16.75	30.00
85-104-024 Love at Christmas 575QX371-5	Keepsake	Yr.Iss.	5.75	37.50
85-104-025 First Christmas Together 675QX370-5	Keepsake	Yr.Iss.	6.75	10.00
85-104-026 First Christmas Together 1300QX493-5	Keepsake	Yr.Iss.	13.00	17.00
85-104-027 Holiday Heart 800QX498-2	Keepsake	Yr.Iss.	8.00	25.00
85-104-028 First Christmas Together 800QX507-2	Keepsake	Yr.Iss.	8.00	8.00
85-104-029 Heart Full of Love 675QX378-2	Keepsake	Yr.Iss.	6.75	8-10.00
85-104-030 First Christmas Together 475QX261-2	Keepsake	Yr.Iss.	4.75	10.00
85-104-031 Twenty-Five Years Together800QX500-5	Keepsake	Yr.Iss.	8.00	8.00
85-104-032 Friendship 775QX506-2	Keepsake	Yr.Iss.	7.75	7.75
85-104-033 Friendship 675QX378-5	Keepsake	Yr.Iss.	6.75	12.00
85-104-034 From Our House to Yours 775QX520-2	Keepsake	Yr.Iss.	7.75	7.75
85-104-035 Teacher 600QX505-2	Keepsake	Yr.Iss.	6.00	10-19.50
85-104-036 With Appreciation 675QX375-2	Keepsake	Yr.Iss.	6.75	9.50
85-104-037 Special Friends 575QX372-5	Keepsake	Yr.Iss.	5.75	10.00
85-104-038 New Home 475QX269-5	Keepsake	Yr.Iss.	4.75	25.00
85-104-039 Baby-sitter 475QX264-2	Keepsake	Yr.Iss.	4.75	4.75
85-104-040 Good Friends 475QX265-2	Keepsake	Yr.Iss.	4.75	11.00
Hallmark Keepsake Ornaments 1985 Property Ornaments				
85-105-001 Snoopy and Woodstock 750QX491-5	Keepsake	Yr.Iss.	7.50	31.50-55
85-105-002 Muffin the Angel 575QX483-5	Keepsake	Yr.Iss.	5.75	24.00
85-105-003 Kit the Shepherd 575QX484-5	Keepsake	Yr.Iss.	5.75	24.00
85-105-004 Betsey Clark 850QX508-5	Keepsake	Yr.Iss.	8.50	22.50
85-105-005 Hugga Bunch 500QX271-5	Keepsake	Yr.Iss.	5.00	19.50
85-105-006 Fraggle Rock Holiday 475QX265-5	Keepsake	Yr.Iss.	4.75	10.00
85-105-007 Peanuts 475QX266-5	Keepsake	Yr.Iss.	4.75	20-25.00
85-105-008 Norman Rockwell 475QX266-2	Keepsake	Yr.Iss.	4.75	20-23.00
85-105-009 Rainbow Brite and Friends 475QX 268-2	Keepsake	Yr.Iss.	4.75	20.00
85-105-010 A Disney Christmas 475QX271-2	Keepsake	Yr.Iss.	4.75	25.00
85-105-011 Merry Shirt Tales 475QX267-2	Keepsake	Yr.Iss.	4.75	19.00
Hallmark Keepsake Ornaments 1985 Traditional Ornaments				
85-106-001 Porcelain Bird 650QX479-5	Keepsake	Yr.Iss.	6.50	30-40.00
85-106-002 Sewn Photoholder 700QX379-5	Keepsake	Yr.Iss.	7.00	22.50
85-106-003 Candle Cameo 675QX374-2	Keepsake	Yr.Iss.	6.75	10-15.00
85-106-004 Santa Pipe 950QX494-2	Keepsake	Yr.Iss.	9.50	22.50
85-106-005 Old-Fashioned Wreath 750QX373-5	Keepsake	Yr.Iss.	7.50	19.50
85-106-006 Peaceful Kingdom 575QX373-2	Keepsake	Yr.Iss.	5.75	15-18.00
85-106-007 Christmas Treats 550QX507-5	Keepsake	Yr.Iss.	5.50	15-24.00
85-106-008 The Spirit of Santa Claus -Special Ed. 2250QX 498-5	Keepsake	Yr.Iss.	23.00	85.00
85-106-009 Nostalgic Sled 600QX442-4	Keepsake	Yr.Iss.	6.00	19.50
Hallmark Keepsake Ornaments 1985 Holiday Humor				
85-107-001 Night Before Christmas 1300QX449-4	Keepsake	Yr.Iss.	13.00	13-32.00
85-107-002 Nativity Scene 475QX264-5	Keepsake	Yr.Iss.	4.75	25.00
85-107-003 Santa's Ski Trip 1200QX496-2	Keepsake	Yr.Iss.	12.00	40.00
85-107-004 Mouse Wagon 575QX476-2	Keepsake	Yr.Iss.	5.75	37.00
85-107-005 Children in the Shoe 950QX490-5	Keepsake	Yr.Iss.	9.50	30-40.00
85-107-006 Do Not Disturb Bear 775QX481-2	Keepsake	Yr.Iss.	7.75	20.00
85-107-007 Sun and Fun Santa 775QX492-2	Keepsake	Yr.Iss.	7.75	35.00
85-107-008 Bottlecap Fun Bunnies 775QX481-5	Keepsake	Yr.Iss.	7.75	33-45.00
85-107-009 Lamb in Legwarmers 700QX480-2	Keepsake	Yr.Iss.	7.00	18.00
85-107-010 Candy Apple Mouse 750QX470-5	Keepsake	Yr.Iss.	6.50	45.00
85-107-011 Skateboard Raccoon 650QX473-2	Keepsake	Yr.Iss.	6.50	22.00
85-107-012 Stardust Angel 575QX475-2	Keepsake	Yr.Iss.	5.75	22-35.00
85-107-013 Soccer Beaver 650QX477-5	Keepsake	Yr.Iss.	6.50	15-25.00
85-107-014 Beary Smooth Ride 650QX480-5	Keepsake	Yr.Iss.	6.50	15.00
85-107-015 Swinging Angel Bell 1100QX492-5	Keepsake	Yr.Iss.	11.00	25-37.00
85-107-016 Doggy in a Stocking 550QX474-2	Keepsake	Yr.Iss.	5.50	27.00
85-107-017 Engineering Mouse 550QX473-5	Keepsake	Yr.Iss.	5.50	15.00
85-107-018 Kitty Mischief 500QX474-5	Keepsake	Yr.Iss.	5.00	12-20.00
85-107-019 Baker Elf 575QX491-2	Keepsake	Yr.Iss.	5.75	20.00
85-107-020 Ice-Skating Owl 500QX476-5	Keepsake	Yr.Iss.	5.00	16.00
85-107-021 Dapper Penguin 500QX477-2	Keepsake	Yr.Iss.	5.00	20.00
85-107-022 Trumpet Panda 450QX471-2	Keepsake	Yr.Iss.	4.50	13-22.00
85-107-023 Merry Mouse 450QX403-2	Keepsake	Yr.Iss.	4.50	18-22.00
85-107-024 Snow-Pitching Snowman 450QX470-2	Keepsake	Yr.Iss.	4.50	20-32.00
85-107-025 Three Kittens in a Mitten 800QX431-1	Keepsake	Yr.Iss.	8.00	34.50
85-107-026 Roller Skating Rabbit 500QX457-1	Keepsake	Yr.Iss.	5.00	19.00
85-107-027 Snowy Seal 400QX450-1	Keepsake	Yr.Iss.	4.00	16.00
Hallmark Keepsake Ornaments 1985 Country Christmas Collection				
85-108-001 Old-Fashioned Doll 1450QX519-5	Keepsake	Yr.Iss.	15.00	30-35.00
85-108-002 Country Goose 775QX518-5	Keepsake	Yr.Iss.	7.75	7.75-15.
85-108-003 Rocking Horse Memories 1000QX518-2	Keepsake	Yr.Iss.	10.00	10.00
85-108-004 Whirligig Santa 1250QX519-2	Keepsake	Yr.Iss.	13.00	13-20.00
85-108-005 Sheep at Christmas 825QX517-5	Keepsake	Yr.Iss.	8.25	13-20.00
Hallmark Keepsake Ornaments 1985 Heirloom Christmas Collection				
85-109-001 Keepsake Basket 1500QX514-5	Keepsake	Yr.Iss.	15.00	15-20.00
85-109-002 Victorian Lady 950QX513-2	Keepsake	Yr.Iss.	9.50	20-25.00

	ARTIST	EDITION	ISSUE	QUOTE
85-109-003 Charming Angel 975QX512-5	Keepsake	Yr.Iss.	9.75	9.75-24.
85-109-004 Lacy Heart 875QX511-2	Keepsake	Yr.Iss.	8.75	8.75-28.
85-109-005 Snowflake 650QX510-5	Keepsake	Yr.Iss.	6.50	6.50-20.
Hallmark 1985 Limited Edition				
85-110-001 Heavenly Trumpeter 2750QX405-2	Keepsake	Yr.Iss.	28.00	70-95.00
Hallmark Keepsake Ornaments 1985 Collectible Series				
85-111-001 Windows of the World-1st Ed.975QX490-2	Keepsake	Yr.Iss.	9.75	80.00
85-111-002 Miniature Creche-1st Ed.875QX482-5	Keepsake	Yr.Iss.	8.75	31.00
85-111-003 Nostalgic Houses and Shops-Second Ed.- 1375QX497-5	Keepsake	Yr.Iss.	13.75	50-95.00
85-111-004 Art Masterpiece-2nd Ed.675QX377-2	Keepsake	Yr.Iss.	6.75	11-20.00
85-111-005 Wood Childhood Ornaments-2nd Ed. 700QX472-2	Keepsake	Yr.Iss.	7.00	31-45.00
85-111-006 Twelve Days of Christmas-2nd Ed. 650QX371-2	Keepsake	Yr.Iss.	6.50	40-75.00
85-111-007 Porcelain Bear-3rd Ed.750QX479-2	Keepsake	Yr.Iss.	7.50	35-46.00
85-111-008 Tin Locomotive-4th Ed.1475QX497-2	Keepsake	Yr.Iss.	14.75	50.00
85-111-009 Holiday Wildlife-4th Ed.750QX376-5	Keepsake	Yr.Iss.	7.50	20.00
85-111-010 Clothespin Soldier-4th Ed.550QX471-5	Keepsake	Yr.Iss.	5.50	20-25.00
85-111-011 Rocking Horse-5th Ed.1075QX493-2	Keepsake	Yr.Iss.	10.75	50.00
85-111-012 Norman Rockwell-6th Ed.750QX374-5	Keepsake	Yr.Iss.	7.50	22-30.00
85-111-013 Here Comes Santa-6th Ed.1400QX496-5	Keepsake	Yr.Iss.	14.00	40-65.00
85-111-014 Frosty Friends-6th Ed.850QX482-2	Keepsake	Yr.Iss.	8.50	45-50.00
85-111-015 Betsey Clark-13th & final Ed.500QX263-2	Keepsake	Yr.Iss.	5.00	23-30.00
85-111-016 Thimble-8th Ed.550QX472-5	Keepsake	Yr.Iss.	5.50	23-37.00
Hallmark Keepsake Ornaments 1985 Keepsake Magic Ornaments				
85-112-001 Baby's First Christmas 1650QLX700-5	Keepsake	Yr.Iss.	17.00	30-40.00
85-112-002 Katybeth 1075QLX710-2	Keepsake	Yr.Iss.	10.75	30.00
85-112-003 Chris Mouse-1st edition1250QLX703-2	Keepsake	Yr.Iss.	13.00	70.00
85-112-004 Swiss Cheese Lane 1300QLX706-5	Keepsake	Yr.Iss.	13.00	33-45.00
85-112-005 Mr. and Mrs. Santa 1450QLX705-2	Keepsake	Yr.Iss.	15.00	73.00
85-112-006 Little Red Schoolhouse 1575QLX711-2	Keepsake	Yr.Iss.	15.75	70.00
85-112-007 Love Wreath 850QLX702-5	Keepsake	Yr.Iss.	8.50	18-30.00
85-112-008 Christmas Eve Visit 1200QLX710-5	Keepsake	Yr.Iss.	12.00	25-27.50
85-112-009 Season of Beauty 800QLX712-2	Keepsake	Yr.Iss.	8.00	20-30.00
Hallmark Keepsake Ornaments 1986 Commemoratives				
86-113-001 Baby's First Christmas 900QX412-6	Keepsake	Yr.Iss.	9.00	32-38.00
86-113-002 Baby's First Christmas Photoholder 800QX379-2	Keepsake	Yr.Iss.	8.00	15.00
86-113-003 Baby's First Christmas 600QX380-3	Keepsake	Yr.Iss.	6.00	11-25.00
86-113-004 Baby's First Christmas 550QX271-3	Keepsake	Yr.Iss.	5.50	15.00
86-113-005 Grandchild's First Christmas1000QX411-6	Keepsake	Yr.Iss.	10.00	10.00
86-113-006 Baby's Second Christmas 650QX413-3	Keepsake	Yr.Iss.	6.50	22-27.50
86-113-007 Child's Third Christmas 650QX413-6	Keepsake	Yr.Iss.	6.50	15-20.00
86-113-008 Baby Locket 1600QX412-3	Keepsake	Yr.Iss.	16.00	18-30.00
86-113-009 Husband 800QX383-6	Keepsake	Yr.Iss.	8.00	7-15.00
86-113-010 Sister 675QX380-6	Keepsake	Yr.Iss.	6.75	13.00
86-113-011 Mother and Dad 750QX431-6	Keepsake	Yr.Iss.	7.50	7.50-17.
86-113-012 Mother 700QX382-6	Keepsake	Yr.Iss.	7.00	7-15.00
86-113-013 Father 650QX431-3	Keepsake	Yr.Iss.	6.50	6.50-13.
86-113-014 Daughter 575QX430-6	Keepsake	Yr.Iss.	5.75	30.00
86-113-015 Son 575QX430-3	Keepsake	Yr.Iss.	5.75	26.00
86-113-016 Niece 600QX426-6	Keepsake	Yr.Iss.	6.00	10.00
86-113-017 Nephew 675QX381-3	Keepsake	Yr.Iss.	6.25	6.25-12.
86-113-018 Grandmother 475QX274-3	Keepsake	Yr.Iss.	4.75	8-18.00
86-113-019 Grandparents 750QX432-3	Keepsake	Yr.Iss.	7.50	17.00
86-113-020 Granddaughter 475QX273-6	Keepsake	Yr.Iss.	4.75	15-22.50
86-113-021 Grandson 475QX273-3	Keepsake	Yr.Iss.	4.75	20.00
86-113-022 Godchild 475QX271-6	Keepsake	Yr.Iss.	4.75	10-14.50
86-113-023 First Christmas Together 1600QX400-3	Keepsake	Yr.Iss.	16.00	27.50
86-113-024 First Christmas Together 1200QX409-6	Keepsake	Yr.Iss.	12.00	30.00
86-113-025 First Christmas Together 7,000QX379-3	Keepsake	Yr.Iss.	7.00	7-20.00
86-113-026 First Christmas Together 475QX270-3	Keepsake	Yr.Iss.	4.75	16.00
86-113-027 Ten Years Together 750QX401-3	Keepsake	Yr.Iss.	7.50	24.50
86-113-028 Twenty-Five Years Together800QX410-3	Keepsake	Yr.Iss.	8.00	24.50
86-113-029 Fifty Years Together 1000QX400-6	Keepsake	Yr.Iss.	10.00	10-18.00
86-113-030 Loving Memories 900QX409-3	Keepsake	Yr.Iss.	9.00	13-34.50
86-113-031 Timeless Love 600QX379-6	Keepsake	Yr.Iss.	6.00	24.50
86-113-032 Sweetheart 1100QX408-6	Keepsake	Yr.Iss.	11.00	27-50.00
86-113-033 Season of the Heart 4750QX270-6	Keepsake	Yr.Iss.	4.75	12.50
86-113-034 Friendship Greeting 800QX427-3	Keepsake	Yr.Iss.	8.00	8-15.00
86-113-035 Joy of Friends 675QX382-3	Keepsake	Yr.Iss.	6.75	12.50
86-113-036 Friendship's Gift 600QX381-6	Keepsake	Yr.Iss.	6.00	12.00
86-113-037 From Our Home to Yours 600QX383-3	Keepsake	Yr.Iss.	6.00	6-12.00
86-113-038 Gratitude 600QX432-6	Keepsake	Yr.Iss.	6.00	9.50
86-113-039 Friends Are Fun 475QX272-3	Keepsake	Yr.Iss.	4.75	30.00
86-113-040 New Home 475QX274-6	Keepsake	Yr.Iss.	4.75	20.00
86-113-041 Teacher 475QX275-3	Keepsake	Yr.Iss.	4.75	4.75-12.
86-113-042 Baby-Sitter 475QX275-6	Keepsake	Yr.Iss.	4.75	10.00
Hallmark Keepsake Ornaments 1986 Property Ornaments				
86-114-001 The Statue of Liberty 600QX384-3	Keepsake	Yr.Iss.	6.00	7-15.00
86-114-002 Snoopy and Woodstock 800QX434-6	Keepsake	Yr.Iss.	8.00	30-38.00
86-114-003 Heathcliff 750QX436-3	Keepsake	Yr.Iss.	7.50	21-31.00
86-114-004 Katybeth 700QX435-3	Keepsake	Yr.Iss.	7.00	22.50
86-114-005 Paddington Bear 600QX435-6	Keepsake	Yr.Iss.	6.00	22.00
86-114-006 Norman Rockwell 475QX276-3	Keepsake	Yr.Iss.	4.75	10-20.00
86-114-007 Peanuts 475QX276-6	Keepsake	Yr.Iss.	4.75	18.00
86-114-008 Shirt Tales Parade 475QX277-3	Keepsake	Yr.Iss.	4.75	14.50
Hallmark Keepsake Ornaments 1986 Holiday Humor				
86-115-001 Santa's Hot Tub 1200QX426-3	Keepsake	Yr.Iss.	12.00	35-53.00
86-115-002 Playful Possum 1100QX425-3	Keepsake	Yr.Iss.	11.00	35.00
86-115-003 Treetop Trio 975QX424-6	Keepsake	Yr.Iss.	11.00	16-29.50
86-115-004 Wynken, Blynken and Nod 975QX424-6	Keepsake	Yr.Iss.	9.75	32-42.00
86-115-005 Acorn Inn 850QX424-3	Keepsake	Yr.Iss.	8.50	23-30.00
86-115-006 Touchdown Santa 800QX423-3	Keepsake	Yr.Iss.	8.00	26-40.00
86-115-007 Snow Buddies 800QX423-6	Keepsake	Yr.Iss.	8.00	32.50
86-115-008 Open Me First 725QX422-6	Keepsake	Yr.Iss.	7.25	20.00
86-115-009 Rah Rah Rabbit 700QX421-6	Keepsake	Yr.Iss.	7.00	20-40.00
86-115-010 Tipping the Scales 675QX418-6	Keepsake	Yr.Iss.	6.75	15-27.50
86-115-011 Li'l Jingler 675QX419-3	Keepsake	Yr.Iss.	6.75	22-35.50
86-115-012 Ski Tripper 675QX420-6	Keepsake	Yr.Iss.	6.75	12-27.00
86-115-013 Popcorn Mouse 675QX421-3	Keepsake	Yr.Iss.	6.75	35.00
86-115-014 Puppy's Best Friend 650QX420-3	Keepsake	Yr.Iss.	6.50	17-27.50
86-115-015 Happy Christmas to Owl 600QX418-3	Keepsake	Yr.Iss.	6.00	14-25.00
86-115-016 Walnut Shell Rider 600QX419-6	Keepsake	Yr.Iss.	6.00	15.00
86-115-017 Heavenly Dreamer 575QX417-3	Keepsake	Yr.Iss.	5.75	21-35.00
86-115-018 Mouse in the Moon 550QX416-6	Keepsake	Yr.Iss.	5.50	15-28.00

	ARTIST	EDITION	ISSUE	QUOTE
86-115-019 Merry Koala 500QX415-3	Keepsake	Yr.Iss.	5.00	18.00
86-115-020 Chatty Penguin 575QX417-6	Keepsake	Yr.Iss.	5.75	13-19.00
86-115-021 Special Delivery 500QX415-6	Keepsake	Yr.Iss.	5.00	15-24.00
86-115-022 Jolly Hiker 500QX483-2	Keepsake	Yr.Iss.	5.00	15-30.00
86-115-023 Cookies for Santa 450QX414-6	Keepsake	Yr.Iss.	4.50	15-25.00
86-115-024 Merry Mouse 450QX403-2	Keepsake	Yr.Iss.	4.50	22.00
86-115-025 Skateboard Raccoon 650QX473-2	Keepsake	Yr.Iss.	6.50	39.50
86-115-026 Beary Smooth Ride 650QX480-5	Keepsake	Yr.Iss.	6.50	19.50
86-115-027 Snow-Pitching Snowman 450QX470-2	Keepsake	Yr.Iss.	4.50	22.50
86-115-028 Kitty Mischief 500QX474-5	Keepsake	Yr.Iss.	5.00	24.50
86-115-029 Soccer Beaver 650QX477-5	Keepsake	Yr.Iss.	6.50	24.50
86-115-030 Do Not Disturb Bear 775QX481-2	Keepsake	Yr.Iss.	7.75	15-25.00

Hallmark Keepsake Ornaments — 1986 Special Edition

86-116-001 Jolly St. Nick 2250QX429-6	Keepsake	Yr.Iss.	22.50	50-75.00

Hallmark Keepsake Ornaments — 1986 Limited Edition

86-117-001 Magical Unicorn 2750QX429-3	Keepsake	Yr.Iss.	27.50	110.00

Hallmark Keepsake Ornaments — 1986 Christmas Medley Collection

86-118-001 Joyful Carolers 975QX513-6	Keepsake	Yr.Iss.	9.75	35.00
86-118-002 Festive Treble Clef 875QX513-3	Keepsake	Yr.Iss.	8.75	10-28.00
86-118-003 Favorite Tin Drum 850QX514-3	Keepsake	Yr.Iss.	8.50	30.00
86-118-004 Christmas Guitar 700QX512-6	Keepsake	Yr.Iss.	7.00	18-25.00
86-118-005 Holiday Horn 800QX514-6	Keepsake	Yr.Iss.	8.00	17-29.00

Hallmark Keepsake Ornaments — 1986 Country Treasures Collection

86-119-001 Country Sleigh 1,000QX511-3	Keepsake	Yr.Iss.	10.00	23-30.00
86-119-002 Remembering Christmas 865QX510-6	Keepsake	Yr.Iss.	8.75	20-30.00
86-119-003 Little Drummers 1250QX511-6	Keepsake	Yr.Iss.	12.50	17-28.00
86-119-004 Nutcracker Santa 1,000QX512-3	Keepsake	Yr.Iss.	10.00	38-45.00
86-119-005 Welcome, Christmas 825QX510-3	Keepsake	Yr.Iss.	8.25	18-30.00

Hallmark Keepsake Ornaments — 1986 Traditional Ornaments

86-120-001 Holiday Jingle Bell 1600QX404-6	Keepsake	Yr.Iss.	16.00	25-43.00
86-120-002 Memories to Cherish 750QX427-6	Keepsake	Yr.Iss.	7.50	24.50
86-120-003 Bluebird 725QX428-3	Keepsake	Yr.Iss.	7.25	45-50.00
86-120-004 Glowing Christmas Tree 700QX428-6	Keepsake	Yr.Iss.	7.00	12.75
86-120-005 Heirloom Snowflake 675QX515-3	Keepsake	Yr.Iss.	6.75	10-22.00
86-120-006 Christmas Beauty 600QX322-3	Keepsake	Yr.Iss.	6.00	10.00
86-120-007 Star Brighteners 600QX322-6	Keepsake	Yr.Iss.	6.00	16.50
86-120-008 The Magi 475QX272-6	Keepsake	Yr.Iss.	4.75	8-13.00
86-120-009 Mary Emmerling: American Country Collection 795QX275-2	Keepsake	Yr.Iss.	7.95	25.00

Hallmark Keepsake Ornaments — 1986 Collectible Series

86-121-001 Mr. and Mrs. Claus-1st Edition1300QX402-6	Keepsake	Yr.Iss.	13.00	83.00
86-121-002 Reindeer Champs-1st Edition750QX422-3	Keepsake	Yr.Iss.	7.50	125-150.
86-121-003 Betsey Clark: Home for Christmas-1st Edition 500QX277-6	Keepsake	Yr.Iss.	5.00	30.00
86-121-004 Windows of the World-2nd Edition 1000QX408-3	Keepsake	Yr.Iss.	10.00	40-65.00
86-121-005 Miniature Creche-2nd Edition900QX407-6	Keepsake	Yr.Iss.	9.00	48.00
86-121-006 Nostalgic Houses and Shops-3rd Edition 1375QX403-3	Keepsake	Yr.Iss.	13.75	220-260.
86-121-007 Wood Childhood Ornaments-3rd Edition 750QX407-3	Keepsake	Yr.Iss.	7.50	21-33.00
86-121-008 Twelve Days of Christmas-3rd Edition 650QX378-6	Keepsake	Yr.Iss.	6.50	33.00
86-121-009 Art Masterpiece-3rd & Final Ed. 675QX350-6	Keepsake	Yr.Iss.	6.75	20-25.00
86-121-010 Porcelain Bear-4th Edition 775QX405-6	Keepsake	Yr.Iss.	7.75	25-41.00
86-121-011 Tin Locomotive-5th Edition 1475QX403-6	Keepsake	Yr.Iss.	14.75	47-55.00
86-121-012 Holiday Wildlife-5th Edition 750QX321-6	Keepsake	Yr.Iss.	7.50	20.00
86-121-013 Clothespin Soldier-5th Edition 550QX406-3	Keepsake	Yr.Iss.	5.50	20-30.00
86-121-014 Rocking Horse-6th Edition 1075QX401-6	Keepsake	Yr.Iss.	10.75	50-57.00
86-121-015 Norman Rockwell-7th Edition 775QX321-3	Keepsake	Yr.Iss.	7.75	18-26.00
86-121-016 Frosty Friends-7th Edition 850QX405-3	Keepsake	Yr.Iss.	8.50	47-70.00
86-121-017 Here Comes Santa-8th Edition 1400QX404-3	Keepsake	Yr.Iss.	14.00	42-54.00
86-121-018 Thimble-9th Edition 575QX406-6	Keepsake	Yr.Iss.	5.75	20-33.00

Hallmark Keepsake Ornaments — 1986 Lighted Ornament Collection

86-122-001 Baby's First Christmas1950QLX710-3	Keepsake	Yr.Iss.	19.50	35-40.00
86-122-002 First Christmas Together2200QLX707-3	Keepsake	Yr.Iss.	14.00	39.50
86-122-003 Santa and Sparky-1st Edition 2200QLX703-3	Keepsake	Yr.Iss.	22.00	75-125.
86-122-004 Christmas Classics-1st Edition 1750QLX704-3	Keepsake	Yr.Iss.	17.50	55-85.00
86-122-005 Chris Mouse-2nd Edition1300QLX705-6	Keepsake	Yr.Iss.	13.00	75-85.00
86-122-006 Village Express 2450QLX707-2	Keepsake	Yr.Iss.	24.50	87-120.
86-122-007 Christmas Sleigh Ride 2450QLX701-2	Keepsake	Yr.Iss.	24.50	115-145.
86-122-008 Santa's On His Way 1500QLX711-5	Keepsake	Yr.Iss.	15.00	63-70.00
86-122-009 General Store 1575QLX705-3	Keepsake	Yr.Iss.	15.75	43-60.00
86-122-010 Gentle Blessings 1500QLX708-3	Keepsake	Yr.Iss.	15.00	110-175.
86-122-011 Keep on Glowin' 1,000QLX707-6	Keepsake	Yr.Iss.	10.00	37-50.00
86-122-012 Santa's Snack 1,000QLX706-6	Keepsake	Yr.Iss.	10.00	40-56.00
86-122-013 Merry Christmas Bell 850QLX709-3	Keepsake	Yr.Iss.	8.50	15-25.00
86-122-014 Sharing Friendship 850QLX706-3	Keepsake	Yr.Iss.	8.50	15-25.00
86-122-015 Mr. and Mrs. Santa 1450QLX705-2	Keepsake	Yr.Iss.	14.50	65-95.00
86-122-016 Sugarplum Cottage 1100QLX701-1	Keepsake	Yr.Iss.	11.00	45.00

Hallmark Keepsake Ornaments — 1987 Commemoratives

87-123-001 Baby's First Christmas 975QX411-3	Keepsake	Yr.Iss.	9.75	25.00
87-123-002 Baby's First Christmas Photoholder 750QX4661-9	Keepsake	Yr.Iss.	7.50	29.50
87-123-003 Baby's First Christmas 600QX372-9	Keepsake	Yr.Iss.	6.00	20.00
87-123-004 Baby's First Christmas-Baby Girl 475QX274-7	Keepsake	Yr.Iss.	4.75	15.00
87-123-005 Baby's First Christmas-Baby Boy475QX274-9	Keepsake	Yr.Iss.	4.75	15.00
87-123-006 Grandchild's First Christmas900QX460-9	Keepsake	Yr.Iss.	9.00	9-24.00
87-123-007 Baby's Second Christmas 575QX460-7	Keepsake	Yr.Iss.	5.75	25.00
87-123-008 Child's Third Christmas 575QX459-9	Keepsake	Yr.Iss.	5.75	28.00
87-123-009 Baby Locket 1500QX461-7	Keepsake	Yr.Iss.	15.00	25-30.00
87-123-010 Mother and Dad 700QX462-7	Keepsake	Yr.Iss.	7.00	18.00
87-123-011 Mother 650QX373-7	Keepsake	Yr.Iss.	6.50	8.00
87-123-012 Dad 600QX462-9	Keepsake	Yr.Iss.	6.00	40-46.00
87-123-013 Husband 700QX373-9	Keepsake	Yr.Iss.	7.00	12.00
87-123-014 Sister 600QX474-7	Keepsake	Yr.Iss.	6.00	15.00
87-123-015 Daughter 575QX463-7	Keepsake	Yr.Iss.	5.75	35.00
87-123-016 Son 575QX463-9	Keepsake	Yr.Iss.	5.75	35-50.00
87-123-017 Niece 475QX275-9	Keepsake	Yr.Iss.	4.75	12.50
87-123-018 Grandmother 475QX277-9	Keepsake	Yr.Iss.	4.75	5-13.00
87-123-019 Grandparents 475QX277-7	Keepsake	Yr.Iss.	4.75	8-18.00
87-123-020 Grandson 475QX276-9	Keepsake	Yr.Iss.	4.75	15.00
87-123-021 Granddaughter 600QX374-7	Keepsake	Yr.Iss.	6.00	18.00
87-123-022 Godchild 475QX276-7	Keepsake	Yr.Iss.	4.75	10-15.00
87-123-023 First Christmas Together 1500QX446-9	Keepsake	Yr.Iss.	15.00	30.00
87-123-024 First Christmas Together 950QX446-7	Keepsake	Yr.Iss.	9.50	16-30.00
87-123-025 First Christmas Together 800QX445-9	Keepsake	Yr.Iss.	8.00	18-28.00
87-123-026 First Christmas Together 650QX371-9	Keepsake	Yr.Iss.	6.50	7-20.00
87-123-027 First Christmas Together 475QX272-9	Keepsake	Yr.Iss.	4.75	9-20.00
87-123-028 Ten Years Together 700QX444-7	Keepsake	Yr.Iss.	7.00	24.50
87-123-029 Twenty-Five Years Together750QX443-9	Keepsake	Yr.Iss.	7.50	8-24.00
87-123-030 Fifty Years Together 800QX443-7	Keepsake	Yr.Iss.	8.00	22.50
87-123-031 Word of Love 800QX447-7	Keepsake	Yr.Iss.	8.00	20-30.00
87-123-032 Heart in Blossom 600QX372-7	Keepsake	Yr.Iss.	6.00	24.50
87-123-033 Sweetheart 1100QX447-9	Keepsake	Yr.Iss.	11.00	20-30.00
87-123-034 Love is Everywhere 475QX278-7	Keepsake	Yr.Iss.	4.75	19.50
87-123-035 Holiday Greetings 600QX375-7	Keepsake	Yr.Iss.	6.00	12.75
87-123-036 Warmth of Friendship 600QX375-9	Keepsake	Yr.Iss.	6.00	12.00
87-123-037 Time for Friends 475QX280-7	Keepsake	Yr.Iss.	4.75	17.00
87-123-038 From Our Home to Yours 475QX279-9	Keepsake	Yr.Iss.	4.75	6-12.00
87-123-039 New Home 600QX376-7	Keepsake	Yr.Iss.	6.00	29.50
87-123-040 Babysitter 475QX279-7	Keepsake	Yr.Iss.	4.75	12.00
87-123-041 Teacher 575QX466-7	Keepsake	Yr.Iss.	5.75	19.50

Hallmark Keepsake Ornaments — 1987 Holiday Humor

87-124-001 Snoopy and Woodstock 725QX472-9	Keepsake	Yr.Iss.	7.25	20-25.00
87-124-002 Bright Christmas Dreams 725QX440-7	Keepsake	Yr.Iss.	7.25	78.00
87-124-003 Joy Ride 1150QX440-7	Keepsake	Yr.Iss.	11.50	40.00
87-124-004 Pretty Kitten 1100QX448-9	Keepsake	Yr.Iss.	11.00	34.50
87-124-005 Santa at the Bat 775QX457-9	Keepsake	Yr.Iss.	7.75	16-30.00
87-124-006 Jogging Through the Snow725QX457-7	Keepsake	Yr.Iss.	7.25	18-24.00
87-124-007 Jack Frosting 700QX449-9	Keepsake	Yr.Iss.	7.00	30.00
87-124-008 Raccoon Biker 700QX458-7	Keepsake	Yr.Iss.	7.00	14-25.00
87-124-009 Treetop Dreams 675QX459-7	Keepsake	Yr.Iss.	6.75	15-25.00
87-124-010 Night Before Christmas 650QX451-7	Keepsake	Yr.Iss.	6.50	18-33.00
87-124-011 Owliday Wish 650QX455-9	Keepsake	Yr.Iss.	6.50	14-25.00
87-124-012 Let It Snow 650QX458-9	Keepsake	Yr.Iss.	6.50	12-22.00
87-124-013 Hot Dogger 650QX471-9	Keepsake	Yr.Iss.	6.50	24.00
87-124-014 Spots 'n Stripes 550QX452-9	Keepsake	Yr.Iss.	5.50	13-27.00
87-124-015 Seasoned Greetings 625QX454-9	Keepsake	Yr.Iss.	6.25	15-33.00
87-124-016 Chocolate Chipmunk 600QX456-7	Keepsake	Yr.Iss.	6.00	45.00
87-124-017 Fudge Forever 500QX449-7	Keepsake	Yr.Iss.	5.00	25-35.00
87-124-018 Sleepy Santa 625QX450-7	Keepsake	Yr.Iss.	6.25	30-33.00
87-124-019 Reindoggy 575QX452-7	Keepsake	Yr.Iss.	5.75	20-25.00
87-124-020 Christmas Cuddle 575QX453-7	Keepsake	Yr.Iss.	5.75	18-35.00
87-124-021 Paddington Bear 550QX472-7	Keepsake	Yr.Iss.	5.50	19-25.00
87-124-022 Nature's Decorations 475QX273-9	Keepsake	Yr.Iss.	4.75	25-33.00
87-124-023 Dr. Seuss: The Grinch's Christmas 475QX278-3	Keepsake	Yr.Iss.	4.75	30.00
87-124-024 Jammie Pies 475QX283-9	Keepsake	Yr.Iss.	4.75	14.50
87-124-025 Peanuts 475QX281-9	Keepsake	Yr.Iss.	4.75	24-30.00
87-124-026 Happy Santa 475QX456-9	Keepsake	Yr.Iss.	4.75	29.50
87-124-027 Icy Treat 450QX450-9	Keepsake	Yr.Iss.	4.50	20-25.00
87-124-028 Mouse in the Moon 550QX416-6	Keepsake	Yr.Iss.	5.50	21.00
87-124-029 L'il Jingler 675QX419-3	Keepsake	Yr.Iss.	6.75	27.50
87-124-030 Walnut Shell Rider 600QX419-6	Keepsake	Yr.Iss.	6.00	18.00
87-124-031 Treetop Trio 1100QX425-6	Keepsake	Yr.Iss.	11.00	25.00
87-124-032 Jolly Hiker 500QX483-2	Keepsake	Yr.Iss.	5.00	17.50
87-124-033 Merry Koala 500QX415-3	Keepsake	Yr.Iss.	5.00	17.00

Hallmark Keepsake Ornaments — 1987 Old-Fashioned Christmas Collection

87-125-001 Nostalgic Rocker 650QX468-9	Keepsake	Yr.Iss.	6.50	29.50
87-125-002 Little Whittler 600QX469-9	Keepsake	Yr.Iss.	6.00	25-33.00
87-125-003 Country Wreath 575QX470-9	Keepsake	Yr.Iss.	5.75	25-30.00
87-125-004 In a Nutshell 550QX469-7	Keepsake	Yr.Iss.	5.50	24-33.00
87-125-005 Folk Art Santa 525QX474-9	Keepsake	Yr.Iss.	5.25	19-35.00

Hallmark Keepsake Ornaments — 1987 Christmas Pizzazz Collection

87-126-001 Doc Holiday 800QX467-7	Keepsake	Yr.Iss.	8.00	40.00
87-126-002 Christmas Fun Puzzle 800QX467-9	Keepsake	Yr.Iss.	8.00	16-25.00
87-126-003 Jolly Follies 850QX466-9	Keepsake	Yr.Iss.	8.50	20-30.00
87-126-004 St. Louie Nick 775QX453-9	Keepsake	Yr.Iss.	7.75	15-22.00
87-126-005 Holiday Hourglass 800QX470-7	Keepsake	Yr.Iss.	8.00	17-23.00
87-126-006 Mistletoad 700QX468-7	Keepsake	Yr.Iss.	7.00	20-30.00
87-126-007 Happy Holidata 650QX471-7	Keepsake	Yr.Iss.	6.50	15-30.00

Hallmark Keepsake Ornaments — 1987 Traditional Ornaments

87-127-001 Goldfinch 700QX464-9	Keepsake	Yr.Iss.	7.00	45.00
87-127-002 Heavenly Harmony 1500QX465-9	Keepsake	Yr.Iss.	15.00	18-35.00
87-127-003 Special Memories Photoholder 675QX464-7	Keepsake	Yr.Iss.	6.75	15-23.00
87-127-004 Joyous Angels 775QX465-7	Keepsake	Yr.Iss.	7.75	15-30.00
87-127-005 Promise of Peace 650QX374-9	Keepsake	Yr.Iss.	6.50	17-25.00
87-127-006 Christmas Keys 575QX473-9	Keepsake	Yr.Iss.	5.75	20-29.00
87-127-007 I Remember Santa 475QX278-9	Keepsake	Yr.Iss.	4.75	22-25.00
87-127-008 Norman Rockwell: Christmas Scenes 475QX282-7	Keepsake	Yr.Iss.	4.75	25.00
87-127-009 Currier & Ives: American Farm Scene 475QX282-9	Keepsake	Yr.Iss.	4.75	15-23.00

Hallmark Keepsake Ornaments — 1987 Limited Edition

87-128-001 Christmas Time Mime 2750QX442-9	Keepsake	Yr.Iss.	27.50	46-60.00
87-128-002 Christmas is Gentle 1750QX444-9	Keepsake	Yr.Iss.	17.50	58-75.00

Hallmark Keepsake Ornaments — 1987 Special Edition

87-129-001 Favorite Santa 2250QX445-7	Keepsake	Yr.Iss.	22.50	47.00

Hallmark Keepsake Ornaments — 1987 Artists' Favorites

87-130-001 Three Men in a Tub 800QX454-7	Keepsake	Yr.Iss.	8.00	20.00
87-130-002 Wee Chimney Sweep 625QX451-9	Keepsake	Yr.Iss.	6.25	15-25.00
87-130-003 December Showers 550QX448-7	Keepsake	Yr.Iss.	5.50	21-35.00
87-130-004 Beary Special 475QX455-7	Keepsake	Yr.Iss.	4.75	17.50

Hallmark Keepsake Ornaments — 1987 Collectible Series

87-131-001 Holiday Heirloom-1st Ed./limited ed. 2500QX485-7	Keepsake	Yr.Iss.	25.00	45-50.00
87-131-002 Collector's Plate-1st Edition 800QX481-7	Keepsake	Yr.Iss.	8.00	30-60.00
87-131-003 Mr. and Mrs. Claus-2nd Edition 2nd Edition 132QX483-7	Keepsake	Yr.Iss.	13.25	40-45.00
87-131-004 Reindeer Champs-2nd Edition 750QX480-9	Keepsake	Yr.Iss.	7.50	35-40.00
87-131-005 Betsey Clark: Home for Christmas-2nd Edition 500QX272-7	Keepsake	Yr.Iss.	5.00	15-25.00
87-131-006 Windows of the World-3rd Edition 1000QX482-7	Keepsake	Yr.Iss.	10.00	20-25.00
87-131-007 Miniature Creche -3rd Edition 900QX481-9	Keepsake	Yr.Iss.	9.00	24-30.00

	ARTIST	EDITION	ISSUE	QUOTE
87-131-008 Nostalgic Houses and Shops-4th Edition 483QX483-9	Keepsake	Yr.Iss.	14.00	50-65.00
87-131-009 Twelve Days of Christmas-4th Edition 650QX370-9	Keepsake	Yr.Iss.	6.50	25.00
87-131-010 Wood Childhood Ornaments-4th Edition 750QX441-7	Keepsake	Yr.Iss.	7.50	16-24.50
87-131-011 Porcelain Bear-5th Edition 775QX442-7	Keepsake	Yr.Iss.	7.75	24-30.00
87-131-012 Tin Locomotive-6th Edition 1475QX484-9	Keepsake	Yr.Iss.	14.75	43-58.00
87-131-013 Holiday Wildlife -6th Edition 750QX371-7	Keepsake	Yr.Iss.	7.50	15.00
87-131-014 Clothespin Soldier-6th & Final Ed. 550QX480-7	Keepsake	Yr.Iss.	5.50	19.00
87-131-015 Frosty Friends -8th Edition 850QX440-9	Keepsake	Yr.Iss.	8.50	40-55.00
87-131-016 Rocking Horse-7th Edition1075QX482-9	Keepsake	Yr.Iss.	10.75	40-45.00
87-131-017 Norman Rockwell-8th Edition775QX370-7	Keepsake	Yr.Iss.	7.75	15-30.00
87-131-018 Here Comes Santa-9th Edition 1400QX484-7	Keepsake	Yr.Iss.	14.00	38-45.00
87-131-019 Thimble-10th Edition 575QX441-9	Keepsake	Yr.Iss.	5.75	20-29.50
Hallmark Keepsake Ornaments	**1987 Keepsake Magic Ornaments**			
87-132-001 Baby's First Christmas 1350QLX704-9	Keepsake	Yr.Iss.	13.50	30-35.00
87-132-002 First Christmas Together 1150QLX708-7	Keepsake	Yr.Iss.	11.50	40.00
87-132-003 Santa and Sparky-2nd Edition1950QLX701-9	Keepsake	Yr.Iss.	19.50	65-75.00
87-132-004 Christmas Classics-2nd Ed.1600ZLX702-9	Keepsake	Yr.Iss.	16.00	55-75.00
87-132-005 Chris Mouse-3rd Edition1100QLX705-7	Keepsake	Yr.Iss.	11.00	45-50.00
87-132-006 Christmas Morning 2450QLX701-3	Keepsake	Yr.Iss.	24.50	33-50.00
87-132-007 Loving Holiday 2200QLX701-6	Keepsake	Yr.Iss.	22.00	38-52.50
87-132-008 Angelic Messengers 1875QLX711-3	Keepsake	Yr.Iss.	18.75	53-68.00
87-132-009 Good Cheer Blimp 1600QLX704-6	Keepsake	Yr.Iss.	16.00	37-52.00
87-132-010 Train Station 1275QLX703-9	Keepsake	Yr.Iss.	12.75	50-60.00
87-132-011 Keeping Cozy 1175QLX704-7	Keepsake	Yr.Iss.	11.75	30-35.00
87-132-012 Lacy Brass Snowflake 1150QLX709-7	Keepsake	Yr.Iss.	11.50	16-25.00
87-132-013 Meowy Christmas I 1,000QLX708-9	Keepsake	Yr.Iss.	10.00	62.50
87-132-014 Memories are Forever Photoholder 850QLX706-7	Keepsake	Yr.Iss.	8.50	27.50
87-132-015 Season for Friendship 850QLX706-9	Keepsake	Yr.Iss.	8.50	11-20.00
87-132-016 Bright Noel 700QLX705-9	Keepsake	Yr.Iss.	7.00	18-30.00
Hallmark Keepsake Ornaments	**1987 Keepsake Collector's Club**			
87-133-001 Wreath of Memories QXC580-9	Keepsake	Yr.Iss.	Unkn.	48-75.00
87-133-002 Carrousel Reindeer QXC580-7	Keepsake	Yr.Iss.	Unkn.	55-65.00
Hallmark Keepsake Ornaments	**1988 Commemoratives**			
88-134-001 Baby's First Christmas 975QX470-1	Keepsake	Yr.Iss.	9.75	30.00
88-134-002 Baby's First Christmas 750QX470-4	Keepsake	Yr.Iss.	7.50	22.00
88-134-003 Baby's First Christmas 600QX372-1	Keepsake	Yr.Iss.	6.00	17.00
88-134-004 Baby's Second Christmas 600QX471-1	Keepsake	Yr.Iss.	6.00	20-30.00
88-134-005 Child's Third Christmas 600QX471-4	Keepsake	Yr.Iss.	6.00	20.00
88-134-006 Baby's First Christmas (Boy)475QX272-1	Keepsake	Yr.Iss.	4.75	15.00
88-134-007 Baby's First Christmas (Girl)475QX272-4	Keepsake	Yr.Iss.	4.75	15-26.00
88-134-008 Mother and Dad 800QX414-4	Keepsake	Yr.Iss.	8.00	20.00
88-134-009 Sister 800QX499-4	Keepsake	Yr.Iss.	8.00	10.00
88-134-010 Dad 700QX414-1	Keepsake	Yr.Iss.	7.00	15-26.00
88-134-011 Mother 650QX375-1	Keepsake	Yr.Iss.	6.50	10-13.00
88-134-012 Daughter 575QX415-1	Keepsake	Yr.Iss.	5.75	45-50.00
88-134-013 Son 575QX415-4	Keepsake	Yr.Iss.	5.75	31.00
88-134-014 Grandmother 475QX276-4	Keepsake	Yr.Iss.	4.75	15.00
88-134-015 Grandparents 475QX277-1	Keepsake	Yr.Iss.	4.75	15.00
88-134-016 Granddaughter 475QX277-4	Keepsake	Yr.Iss.	4.75	10-20.00
88-134-017 Grandson 475QX278-1	Keepsake	Yr.Iss.	4.75	15-19.50
88-134-018 Godchild 475QX278-4	Keepsake	Yr.Iss.	4.75	6-22.50
88-134-019 Sweetheart 975QX490-1	Keepsake	Yr.Iss.	9.75	20-27.00
88-134-020 First Christmas Together 900QX489-4	Keepsake	Yr.Iss.	9.00	28.00
88-134-021 First Christmas Together 675QX373-1	Keepsake	Yr.Iss.	6.75	16-20.00
88-134-022 Twenty-Five Years Together 675QX373-4	Keepsake	Yr.Iss.	6.75	7-14.00
88-134-023 Fifty Years Together 675QX374-1	Keepsake	Yr.Iss.	6.75	8-19.00
88-134-024 Love Fills the Heart 600QX374-4	Keepsake	Yr.Iss.	6.00	19.50
88-134-025 First Christmas Together 475QX274-1	Keepsake	Yr.Iss.	4.75	25.00
88-134-026 Five Years Together 475QX274-4	Keepsake	Yr.Iss.	4.75	6-19.50
88-134-027 Ten Years Together 475QX275-1	Keepsake	Yr.Iss.	4.75	5-15.00
88-134-028 Love Grows 475QX275-4	Keepsake	Yr.Iss.	4.75	19.00
88-134-029 Spirit of Christmas 475QX276-1	Keepsake	Yr.Iss.	4.75	15.50
88-134-030 Year to Remember 700QX416-4	Keepsake	Yr.Iss.	7.00	14.50
88-134-031 Teacher 625QX417-1	Keepsake	Yr.Iss.	6.25	16.50
88-134-032 Gratitude 600QX375-4	Keepsake	Yr.Iss.	6.00	12.00
88-134-033 New Home 600QX376-1	Keepsake	Yr.Iss.	6.00	19.50
88-134-034 Babysitter 475QX279-1	Keepsake	Yr.Iss.	4.75	5-10.50
88-134-035 From Our Home to Yours 475QX279-4	Keepsake	Yr.Iss.	4.75	12.00
Hallmark Keepsake Ornaments	**1988 Hallmark Handcrafted Ornaments**			
88-135-001 Peanuts 475QX280-1	Keepsake	Yr.Iss.	4.75	28.00
88-135-002 Jingle Bell Clown 1500QX477-4	Keepsake	Yr.Iss.	15.00	27.50
88-135-003 Travels with Santa 1,000QX477-1	Keepsake	Yr.Iss.	10.00	25-32.50
88-135-004 Goin' Cross-Country 850QX476-4	Keepsake	Yr.Iss.	8.50	14-29.00
88-135-005 Winter Fun 850QX478-1	Keepsake	Yr.Iss.	8.50	16-25.00
88-135-006 Go For The Gold 800QX417-4	Keepsake	Yr.Iss.	8.00	16-35.50
88-135-007 Party Line 875QX476-1	Keepsake	Yr.Iss.	8.75	20-27.00
88-135-008 Soft Landing 700QX475-1	Keepsake	Yr.Iss.	7.00	12-18.00
88-135-009 Feliz Navidad 675QX416-1	Keepsake	Yr.Iss.	6.75	18-30.00
88-135-010 Squeaky Clean 675QX475-4	Keepsake	Yr.Iss.	6.75	13-27.00
88-135-011 Christmas Memories 650QX372-4	Keepsake	Yr.Iss.	6.50	19.50
88-135-012 Purrfect Snuggle 625QX474-4	Keepsake	Yr.Iss.	6.25	15-25.00
88-135-013 Snoopy and Woodstock 600QX474-1	Keepsake	Yr.Iss.	6.00	25-30.00
88-135-014 The Town Crier 550QX473-4	Keepsake	Yr.Iss.	5.50	13-25.00
88-135-015 Christmas Scenes 475QX273-1	Keepsake	Yr.Iss.	4.75	17.50
88-135-016 Jolly Walrus 450QX473-1	Keepsake	Yr.Iss.	4.50	18-22.50
88-135-017 Slipper Spaniel 450QX472-4	Keepsake	Yr.Iss.	4.50	10-20.00
88-135-018 Arctic Tenor 400QX472-1	Keepsake	Yr.Iss.	4.00	17.00
88-135-019 Christmas Cuckoo 800QX480-1	Keepsake	Yr.Iss.	8.00	22.50
88-135-020 Peek-a-boo Kittens 750QX487-1	Keepsake	Yr.Iss.	7.50	21.00
88-135-021 Cool Juggler 650QX487-4	Keepsake	Yr.Iss.	6.50	17.00
88-135-022 Sweet Star 500QX418-4	Keepsake	Yr.Iss.	5.00	18-27.00
88-135-023 Hoe-Hoe-Hoel 500QX422-1	Keepsake	Yr.Iss.	5.00	11-23.00
88-135-024 Nick the Kick 500QX422-4	Keepsake	Yr.Iss.	5.00	18.00
88-135-025 Holiday Hero 500QX423-1	Keepsake	Yr.Iss.	5.00	15.50
88-135-026 Polar Bowler 500QX478-1	Keepsake	Yr.Iss.	5.00	10-17.00
88-135-027 Par for Santa 500QX479-1	Keepsake	Yr.Iss.	5.00	17.00
88-135-028 Gone Fishing 500QX479-4	Keepsake	Yr.Iss.	5.00	14.00
88-135-029 Kiss the Claus 500QX486-1	Keepsake	Yr.Iss.	5.00	10-17.00
88-135-030 Love Santa 500QX486-4	Keepsake	Yr.Iss.	5.00	17.00
88-135-031 Teeny Taster 475QX418-1	Keepsake	Yr.Iss.	4.75	22-35.00
88-135-032 Filled with Fudge 475QX419-1	Keepsake	Yr.Iss.	4.75	20.00
88-135-033 Santa Flamingo 475QX483-4	Keepsake	Yr.Iss.	4.75	16-30.00
88-135-034 Kiss from Santa 450QX482-1	Keepsake	Yr.Iss.	4.50	18-25.00

	ARTIST	EDITION	ISSUE	QUOTE
88-135-035 Oreo 400QX481-4	Keepsake	Yr.Iss.	4.00	11-25.00
88-135-036 Noah's Ark 850QX490-4	Keepsake	Yr.Iss.	8.50	20.00
88-135-037 Sailing! Sailing! 850QX491-1	Keepsake	Yr.Iss.	8.50	28.00
88-135-038 Americana Drum 775QX488-1	Keepsake	Yr.Iss.	7.75	14-24.00
88-135-039 Kringle Portrait 750QX496-1	Keepsake	Yr.Iss.	7.50	17-30.00
88-135-040 Uncle Sam Nutcracker 700QX488-4	Keepsake	Yr.Iss.	7.00	20.00
88-135-041 Kringle Tree 650QX495-4	Keepsake	Yr.Iss.	6.50	20-35.00
88-135-042 Glowing Wreath 600QX492-1	Keepsake	Yr.Iss.	6.00	14.50
88-135-043 Sparkling Tree 600QX483-1	Keepsake	Yr.Iss.	6.00	8-15.00
88-135-044 Shiny Sleigh 575QX492-4	Keepsake	Yr.Iss.	5.75	15.00
88-135-045 Kringle Moon 550QX495-1	Keepsake	Yr.Iss.	5.00	17-27.50
88-135-046 Loving Bear 475QX493-4	Keepsake	Yr.Iss.	4.75	10-20.00
88-135-047 Christmas Cardinal 475QX494-1	Keepsake	Yr.Iss.	4.75	9-20.00
88-135-048 Starry Angel 475494-4	Keepsake	Yr.Iss.	4.75	14.50
88-135-049 Old-Fashioned School House 400QX497-1	Keepsake	Yr.Iss.	4.00	16.50
88-135-050 Old-Fashioned Church 400QX498-1	Keepsake	Yr.Iss.	4.00	16.50
Hallmark Keepsake Ornaments	**1988 Special Edition**			
88-136-001 The Wonderful Santacycle 2250QX411-4	Keepsake	Yr.Iss.	22.50	34-40.00
Hallmark Keepsake Ornaments	**1988 Artist Favorites**			
88-137-001 Little Jack Horner 800QX408-1	Keepsake	Yr.Iss.	8.00	14-20.00
88-137-002 Merry-Mint Unicorn 850QX423-4	Keepsake	Yr.Iss.	8.50	12-20.00
88-137-003 Midnight Snack 600QX410-4	Keepsake	Yr.Iss.	6.00	16-26.00
88-137-004 Cymbals of Christmas 550QX411-1	Keepsake	Yr.Iss.	5.50	15-28.00
88-137-005 Baby Redbird 500QX410-1	Keepsake	Yr.Iss.	5.00	15-20.00
88-137-006 Very Strawbeary 475QX409-1	Keepsake	Yr.Iss.	4.75	14-25.00
Hallmark Keepsake Ornaments	**1988 Collectible Series**			
88-138-001 Holiday Heirloom-Second Ed. 2500QX406-4	Keepsake	Yr.Iss.	25.00	24-50.00
88-138-002 Tin Locomotive-Seventh Ed.1475QX400-4	Keepsake	Yr.Iss.	14.75	38-53.00
88-138-003 Nostalgic Houses and Shops-Fifth Edition 1450QX401-4	Keepsake	Yr.Iss.	14.50	35.00
88-138-004 Here Comes Santa-Tenth Ed.1400QX400-1	Keepsake	Yr.Iss.	14.00	31-46.00
88-138-005 Mr. and Mrs. Claus-Third Ed.1300QX401-1	Keepsake	Yr.Iss.	13.00	35-45.00
88-138-006 Rocking Horse-Eighth Ed.1075QX402-4	Keepsake	Yr.Iss.	10.75	35-40.00
88-138-007 Windows of the World-Fourth Edition 1,000QX402-1	Keepsake	Yr.Iss.	10.00	24.00
88-138-008 Frosty Friends-Ninth Ed.875QX403-1	Keepsake	Yr.Iss.	8.75	41-65.00
88-138-009 Miniature Creche-Fourth Ed.850QX403-4	Keepsake	Yr.Iss.	8.50	25.00
88-138-010 Porcelain Bear-Sixth Ed.800QX404-4	Keepsake	Yr.Iss.	8.00	25-40.00
88-138-011 Collector's Plate-Second Ed.800QX406-1	Keepsake	Yr.Iss.	8.00	24-35.00
88-138-012 Norman Rockwell-Ninth Ed.775QX370-4	Keepsake	Yr.Iss.	7.75	14-24.00
88-138-013 Holiday Wildlife-Seventh Ed.775QX371-1	Keepsake	Yr.Iss.	7.75	16.00
88-138-014 Wood Childhood-Fifth Ed.750QX404-1	Keepsake	Yr.Iss.	7.50	24.50
88-138-015 Reindeer Champs-Third Ed.750QX405-1	Keepsake	Yr.Iss.	7.50	24-35.00
88-138-016 Five Golden Rings-Fifth Ed.650QX371-4	Keepsake	Yr.Iss.	6.50	18-23.00
88-138-017 Thimble-Eleventh Ed.575QX405-4	Keepsake	Yr.Iss.	5.75	15.00
88-138-018 Mary's Angels-First Ed.500QX407-4	Keepsake	Yr.Iss.	5.00	42.00
88-138-019 Betsey Clark: Home for Christmas-Third Edition 500QX271-4	Keepsake	Yr.Iss.	5.00	17-23.00
Hallmark Keepsake Ornaments	**1988 Keepsake Magic Ornaments**			
88-139-001 Baby's First Christmas 2400QLX718-4	Keepsake	Yr.Iss.	24.00	45.00
88-139-002 First Christmas Together 1200QLX702-7	Keepsake	Yr.Iss.	12.00	20-35.00
88-139-003 Santa and Sparky-Third Ed.1950QLX719-1	Keepsake	Yr.Iss.	19.50	30-50.00
88-139-004 Christmas Classics-Third Edition 1500QLX716-1	Keepsake	Yr.Iss.	15.00	30-50.00
88-139-005 Chris Mouse-Fourth Ed.875QLX715-4	Keepsake	Yr.Iss.	8.75	40-50.00
88-139-006 Country Express 2450QLX721-1	Keepsake	Yr.Iss.	24.50	67-77.00
88-139-007 Kringle's Toy Shop 2450QLX701-7	Keepsake	Yr.Iss.	25.00	35-55.00
88-139-008 Parade of the Toys 2200QLX719-4	Keepsake	Yr.Iss.	22.00	35-50.00
88-139-009 Last-Minute Hug 1950QLX718-1	Keepsake	Yr.Iss.	19.50	42-58.00
88-139-010 Skater's Waltz 1950QLX720-1	Keepsake	Yr.Iss.	19.50	36-49.50
88-139-011 Kitty Capers 1300QLX716-4	Keepsake	Yr.Iss.	13.00	43.00
88-139-012 Christmas is Magic 1200QLX717-1	Keepsake	Yr.Iss.	12.00	35-49.50
88-139-013 Heavenly Glow 1175QLX711-4	Keepsake	Yr.Iss.	11.75	19-29.00
88-139-014 Radiant Tree 1175QLX712-1	Keepsake	Yr.Iss.	11.75	22-25.00
88-139-015 Festive Feeder 1150QLX720-4	Keepsake	Yr.Iss.	11.50	44.50
88-139-016 Circling the Globe 1050QLX712-4	Keepsake	Yr.Iss.	10.50	46.00
88-139-017 Bearly Reaching 950QLX715-1	Keepsake	Yr.Iss.	9.50	40.00
88-139-018 Moonlit Nap 875QLX713-4	Keepsake	Yr.Iss.	8.75	20-24.50
88-139-019 Tree of Friendship 850QLX710-4	Keepsake	Yr.Iss.	8.50	22.50
88-139-020 Song of Christmas 850QLX711-1	Keepsake	Yr.Iss.	8.50	13-23.00
Hallmark Keepsake Ornaments	**1988 Keepsake Miniature Ornaments**			
88-140-001 Baby's First Christmas	Keepsake	Yr.Iss.	6.00	11.00
88-140-002 First Christmas Together	Keepsake	Yr.Iss.	4.00	9-20.00
88-140-003 Mother	Keepsake	Yr.Iss.	3.00	12.00
88-140-004 Friends Share Joy	Keepsake	Yr.Iss.	2.00	15.00
88-140-005 Love is Forever	Keepsake	Yr.Iss.	2.00	15.00
88-140-006 Holy Family	Keepsake	Yr.Iss.	8.50	11-21.00
88-140-007 Sweet Dreams	Keepsake	Yr.Iss.	7.00	16-26.00
88-140-008 Skater's Waltz	Keepsake	Yr.Iss.	7.00	14-22.00
88-140-009 Little Drummer Boy	Keepsake	Yr.Iss.	4.50	20-26.50
88-140-010 Three Little Kitties	Keepsake	Yr.Iss.	6.00	13-18.50
88-140-011 Snuggly Skater	Keepsake	Yr.Iss.	4.50	27.50
88-140-012 Happy Santa	Keepsake	Yr.Iss.	4.50	20.00
88-140-013 Sneaker Mouse	Keepsake	Yr.Iss.	4.00	14-22.00
88-140-014 Country Wreath	Keepsake	Yr.Iss.	4.00	12.00
88-140-015 Joyous Heart	Keepsake	Yr.Iss.	3.50	22-30.00
88-140-016 Candy Cane Elf	Keepsake	Yr.Iss.	3.00	22.00
88-140-017 Folk Art Lamb	Keepsake	Yr.Iss.	2.50	14-19.50
88-140-018 Folk Art Reindeer	Keepsake	Yr.Iss.	2.50	13-19.50
88-140-019 Gentle Angel	Keepsake	Yr.Iss.	2.00	14-19.50
88-140-020 Brass Star	Keepsake	Yr.Iss.	1.50	20-28.00
88-140-021 Brass Angel	Keepsake	Yr.Iss.	1.50	19.50
88-140-022 Brass Tree	Keepsake	Yr.Iss.	1.50	19.50
88-140-023 Jolly St. Nick	Keepsake	Yr.Iss.	8.00	30-37.00
88-140-024 Family Home-First Edition	Keepsake	Yr.Iss.	8.50	30-45.00
88-140-025 Kittens in Toyland-First Edition	Keepsake	Yr.Iss.	5.00	25.00
88-140-026 Rocking Horse-First Edition	Keepsake	Yr.Iss.	4.50	22-38.00
88-140-027 Penguin Pal-First Edition	Keepsake	Yr.Iss.	3.75	25-30.00
Hallmark Keepsake Ornaments	**1988 Hallmark Keepsake Ornament Collector's Club**			
88-141-001 Our Clubhouse QXC580-4	Keepsake	Yr.Iss.	Unkn.	33-50.00
88-141-002 Sleighful of Dreams 800QC580-1	Keepsake	Yr.Iss.	8.00	48-75.00
88-141-003 Holiday Heirloom-Second Edition 2500QXC406-4	Keepsake	Yr.Iss.	25.00	24-30.00
88-141-004 Christmas is Sharing 1750QXC407-1	Keepsake	Yr.Iss.	17.50	37.50
88-141-005 Angelic Minstrel 2750QXC408-4	Keepsake	Yr.Iss.	27.50	27-35.00
88-141-006 Hold on Tight QXC570-4	Keepsake	Yr.Iss.	Unkn.	80.00

Hallmark Keepsake Ornaments — 1989 Commemoratives

	ARTIST	EDITION	ISSUE	QUOTE
89-142-001 Baby's First Christmas Photoholder 625QX468-2	Keepsake	Yr.Iss.	6.25	25.00
89-142-002 Baby's First Christmas-Baby Girl475QX272-2	Keepsake	Yr.Iss.	4.75	12.50
89-142-003 Baby's First Christmas-Baby Boy475QX272-5	Keepsake	Yr.Iss.	4.75	16.00
89-142-004 Baby's First Christmas 675QX381-5	Keepsake	Yr.Iss.	6.75	10.00
89-142-005 Granddaughter's First Christmas 675QX382-2	Keepsake	Yr.Iss.	6.75	9-15.00
89-142-006 Grandson's First Christmas 675QX382-5	Keepsake	Yr.Iss.	6.75	15.00
89-142-007 Baby's First Christmas 725QX449-2	Keepsake	Yr.Iss.	7.25	55.00
89-142-008 Baby's Second Christmas 675QX449-5	Keepsake	Yr.Iss.	6.75	25.00
89-142-009 Baby's Third Christmas 675QX469-5	Keepsake	Yr.Iss.	6.75	18.00
89-142-010 Baby's Fourth Christmas 675QX543-2	Keepsake	Yr.Iss.	6.75	14-20.00
89-142-011 Baby's Fifth Christmas 675QX543-5	Keepsake	Yr.Iss.	6.75	14-20.00
89-142-012 Mother 975QX440-5	Keepsake	Yr.Iss.	9.75	20.00
89-142-013 Mom and Dad 975QX442-5	Keepsake	Yr.Iss.	9.75	15.00
89-142-014 Dad 725QX442-5	Keepsake	Yr.Iss.	7.25	11-20.00
89-142-015 Sister 475QX279-2	Keepsake	Yr.Iss.	4.75	8-15.00
89-142-016 Grandparents 475QX277-2	Keepsake	Yr.Iss.	4.75	12.00
89-142-017 Grandmother 475QX277-5	Keepsake	Yr.Iss.	4.75	12.00
89-142-018 Granddaughter 475QX278	Keepsake	Yr.Iss.	4.75	15.00
89-142-019 Grandson 475QX278-5	Keepsake	Yr.Iss.	4.75	14-24.00
89-142-020 Godchild 625QX311-2	Keepsake	Yr.Iss.	6.25	13.00
89-142-021 Sweetheart 975QX486-5	Keepsake	Yr.Iss.	9.75	33.00
89-142-022 First Christmas Together 675QX485-2	Keepsake	Yr.Iss.	9.75	15-19.50
89-142-023 First Christmas Together 675QX383-2	Keepsake	Yr.Iss.	6.75	13-20.00
89-142-024 First Christmas Together 475QX273-2	Keepsake	Yr.Iss.	4.75	15.00
89-142-025 Five Years Together 475QX273-5	Keepsake	Yr.Iss.	4.75	14-20.00
89-142-026 Ten Years Together 475QX274-2	Keepsake	Yr.Iss.	4.75	19.50
89-142-027 Twenty-five Years Together Photoholder 875QX485-5	Keepsake	Yr.Iss.	8.75	12-17.50
89-142-028 FortyYears Together Photoholder 875QX545-2	Keepsake	Yr.Iss.	8.75	12-17.50
89-142-029 Fifty Years Together Photoholder 875QX486-2	Keepsake	Yr.Iss.	8.75	12-17.50
89-142-030 Language of Love 625QX383-5	Keepsake	Yr.Iss.	6.25	16.50
89-142-031 World of Love 475QX274-5	Keepsake	Yr.Iss.	4.75	16.50
89-142-032 Friendship Time 975QX413-2	Keepsake	Yr.Iss.	9.75	25.00
89-142-033 Teacher 575QX412-5	Keepsake	Yr.Iss.	5.75	14-25.00
89-142-034 New Home 475QX275-5	Keepsake	Yr.Iss.	4.75	15.00
89-142-035 Festive Year 775QX384-2	Keepsake	Yr.Iss.	7.75	15.00
89-142-036 Gratitude 675QX385-2	Keepsake	Yr.Iss.	6.75	13.50
89-142-037 From Our Home to Yours 625QX384-5	Keepsake	Yr.Iss.	6.25	8-13.00
89-142-038 Daughter 625QX443-2	Keepsake	Yr.Iss.	6.25	15-30.00
89-142-039 Son 625QX444-5	Keepsake	Yr.Iss.	6.25	18-33.00
89-142-040 Brother 625QX445-2	Keepsake	Yr.Iss.	6.25	15.00

Hallmark Keepsake Ornaments — 1989 Holiday Traditions

	ARTIST	EDITION	ISSUE	QUOTE
89-143-001 Joyful Trio 975QX437-2	Keepsake	Yr.Iss.	9.75	12-26.00
89-143-002 Old-World Gnome 775QX434-5	Keepsake	Yr.Iss.	7.75	17.50
89-143-003 Hoppy Holidays 775QX469-2	Keepsake	Yr.Iss.	7.75	13-17.50
89-143-004 The First Christmas 775QX547-5	Keepsake	Yr.Iss.	7.75	15.50
89-143-005 Gentle Fawn 775QX548-5	Keepsake	Yr.Iss.	7.75	15.00
89-143-006 Spencer Sparrow, Esq. 675QX431-2	Keepsake	Yr.Iss.	6.75	15.00
89-143-007 Snoopy and Woodstock 675QX433-2	Keepsake	Yr.Iss.	6.75	15-30.00
89-143-008 Sweet Memories Photoholder 675QX438-5	Keepsake	Yr.Iss.	6.75	19.00
89-143-009 Stocking Kitten 675QX456-5	Keepsake	Yr.Iss.	6.75	11-15.00
89-143-010 George Washington Bicentennial 625QX386-2	Keepsake	Yr.Iss.	6.75	8-15.00
89-143-011 Feliz Navidad 675QX439-2	Keepsake	Yr.Iss.	6.75	17.50
89-143-012 Cranberry Bunny 575QX426-2	Keepsake	Yr.Iss.	5.75	14.50
89-143-013 Deer Disguise 575QX426-5	Keepsake	Yr.Iss.	5.75	15-24.50
89-143-014 Paddington Bear 575QX429-2	Keepsake	Yr.Iss.	5.75	12-20.00
89-143-015 Snowplow Santa 575QX420-5	Keepsake	Yr.Iss.	5.75	15.50
89-143-016 Kristy Claus 575QX424-5	Keepsake	Yr.Iss.	5.75	11.50
89-143-017 Here's the Pitch 575QX545-5	Keepsake	Yr.Iss.	5.75	13.50
89-143-018 North Pole Jogger 575QX546-2	Keepsake	Yr.Iss.	5.75	13.50
89-143-019 Camera Claus 575QX546-5	Keepsake	Yr.Iss.	5.75	11-15.50
89-143-020 Sea Santa 575QX415-2	Keepsake	Yr.Iss.	5.75	13.50
89-143-021 Gym Dandy 575QX418-5	Keepsake	Yr.Iss.	5.75	10-15.50
89-143-022 On the Links 575QX419-2	Keepsake	Yr.Iss.	5.75	14.50
89-143-023 Special Delivery 525QX432-5	Keepsake	Yr.Iss.	5.25	15.00
89-143-024 Hang in There 525QX430-5	Keepsake	Yr.Iss.	5.25	27-35.00
89-143-025 Owliday Greetings 400QX436-5	Keepsake	Yr.Iss.	4.00	15.00
89-143-026 Norman Rockwell 475QX276-2	Keepsake	Yr.Iss.	4.75	13-19.50
89-143-027 A Charlie Brown Christmas 475QX276-5	Keepsake	Yr.Iss.	4.75	30.00
89-143-028 Party Line 875QX476-1	Keepsake	Yr.Iss.	8.75	26.50
89-143-029 Peek-a-Boo Kitties 750QX487-1	Keepsake	Yr.Iss.	7.50	16-22.00
89-143-030 Polar Bowler 575QX478-4	Keepsake	Yr.Iss.	5.75	17.00
89-143-031 Gone Fishing 575QX479-4	Keepsake	Yr.Iss.	5.75	17.00
89-143-032 Teeny Taster 475QX418-1	Keepsake	Yr.Iss.	4.75	17.00
89-143-033 A Kiss™ From Santa 450QX482-1	Keepsake	Yr.Iss.	4.50	19.50
89-143-034 Oreo®Chocolate Sandwich Cookies 400QX481-4	Keepsake	Yr.Iss.	4.00	15.00

Hallmark Keepsake Ornaments — 1989 New Attractions

	ARTIST	EDITION	ISSUE	QUOTE
89-144-001 Sparkling Snowflake 775QX547-2	Keepsake	Yr.Iss.	7.75	22-25.00
89-144-002 Festive Angel 675QX463-5	Keepsake	Yr.Iss.	6.75	18-22.00
89-144-003 Graceful Swan 675QX464-2	Keepsake	Yr.Iss.	6.75	18-22.00
89-144-004 Nostalgic Lamb 675QX466-5	Keepsake	Yr.Iss.	6.75	9-13.50
89-144-005 Horse Weathervane 575QX463-2	Keepsake	Yr.Iss.	5.75	15-23.00
89-144-006 Rooster Weathervane 575QX467-5	Keepsake	Yr.Iss.	5.75	10-14.00
89-144-007 Country Cat 625QX467-2	Keepsake	Yr.Iss.	6.25	15-17.00
89-144-008 Nutshell Holiday 575QX465-2	Keepsake	Yr.Iss.	5.75	17-27.50
89-144-009 Nutshell Dreams 575QX465-5	Keepsake	Yr.Iss.	5.75	13-27.50
89-144-010 Nutshell Workshop 575QX487-2	Keepsake	Yr.Iss.	5.75	15-27.50
89-144-011 Claus Construction 775QX488-5	Keepsake	Yr.Iss.	7.75	15-20.00
89-144-012 Cactus Cowboy 675QX411-2	Keepsake	Yr.Iss.	6.75	33-44.00
89-144-013 Rodney Reindeer 675QX407-2	Keepsake	Yr.Iss.	6.75	10-13.50
89-144-014 Let's Play 725QX488-2	Keepsake	Yr.Iss.	7.25	25.00
89-144-015 TV Break 625QX409-2	Keepsake	Yr.Iss.	6.25	15.50
89-144-016 Balancing Elf 675QX489-5	Keepsake	Yr.Iss.	6.75	22.50
89-144-017 Wiggly Snowman 675QX489-2	Keepsake	Yr.Iss.	6.75	20-24.50
89-144-018 Cool Swing 625QX487-5	Keepsake	Yr.Iss.	6.25	30.00
89-144-019 Goin' South 425QX410-5	Keepsake	Yr.Iss.	4.25	17-30.00
89-144-020 Peppermint Clown 2475QX450-5	Keepsake	Yr.Iss.	24.75	23-35.00

Hallmark Keepsake Ornaments — 1989 Artists' Favorites

	ARTIST	EDITION	ISSUE	QUOTE
89-145-001 Merry-Go-Round Unicorn 1075QX447-2	Keepsake	Yr.Iss.	10.75	15-20.00
89-145-002 Carousel Zebra 925QX451-5	Keepsake	Yr.Iss.	9.25	16-31.00
89-145-003 Mail Call 875QX452-2	Keepsake	Yr.Iss.	8.75	15-30.00
89-145-004 Baby Partridge 675QX452-5	Keepsake	Yr.Iss.	6.75	10-18.00
89-145-005 Playful Angel 675QX453-5	Keepsake	Yr.Iss.	6.75	15-22.00
89-145-006 Cherry Jubilee 500QX453-2	Keepsake	Yr.Iss.	5.00	15-18.00
89-145-007 Bear-i-Tone 475QX454-2	Keepsake	Yr.Iss.	4.75	9-14.50

Hallmark Keepsake Ornaments — 1989 Special Edition

	ARTIST	EDITION	ISSUE	QUOTE
89-146-001 The Ornament Express 2200QX580-5	Keepsake	Yr.Iss.	22.00	35-53.00

Hallmark Keepsake Ornaments — 1989 Collectible Series

	ARTIST	EDITION	ISSUE	QUOTE
89-147-001 Christmas Kitty-First Ed.1475QX544-5	Keepsake	Yr.Iss.	14.75	20-26.00
89-147-002 Winter Surprise-First Ed.1075QX427-2	Keepsake	Yr.Iss.	10.75	25.00
89-147-003 Hark! It's Herald-First Ed.675QX455-5	Keepsake	Yr.Iss.	6.75	18-25.00
89-147-004 Crayola Crayon-First Ed.875QX435-2	Keepsake	Yr.Iss.	8.75	40.00
89-147-005 The Gift Bringers-First Ed.500QX279-5	Keepsake	Yr.Iss.	5.00	20-30.00
89-147-006 Mary's Angels-Second Ed.575QX454-5	Keepsake	Yr.Iss.	5.75	43-55.00
89-147-007 Collector's Plate-Third Ed.825QX461-2	Keepsake	Yr.Iss.	8.25	20-30.00
89-147-008 Mr. and Mrs. Claus-Fourth Ed. 1325QX 457-5	Keepsake	Yr.Iss.	13.25	30-40.00
89-147-009 Reindeer Champs-Fourth Ed.775QX456-2	Keepsake	Yr.Iss.	7.75	15-30.00
89-147-010 Betsey Clark: Home for Christmas-Fourth Edition 500QX230-2	Keepsake	Yr.Iss.	5.00	13-17.00
89-147-011 Windows of the World-Fifth Ed.1075QX462-5	Keepsake	Yr.Iss.	10.75	20.00
89-147-012 Miniature Creche-Fifth Ed.925QX459-2	Keepsake	Yr.Iss.	9.25	15-20.00
89-147-013 Nostalgic Houses and Shops-Sixth Edition 1425QX458-2	Keepsake	Yr.Iss.	14.25	35-39.00
89-147-014 Wood Childhood Ornaments-Sixth Edition 775QX459-5	Keepsake	Yr.Iss.	7.75	14-22.00
89-147-015 Twelve Days of Christmas-Sixth Ed. 675QX381-2	Keepsake	Yr.Iss.	6.75	15-20.00
89-147-016 Porcelain Bear-Seventh Ed.875QX461-5	Keepsake	Yr.Iss.	8.75	20.00
89-147-017 Tin Locomotive-Eighth Ed.1475QX460-2	Keepsake	Yr.Iss.	14.75	37-52.00
89-147-018 Rocking Horse-Ninth Ed.1075QX462-2	Keepsake	Yr.Iss.	10.75	31.00
89-147-019 Frosty Friends-Tenth Ed.925QX457-2	Keepsake	Yr.Iss.	9.25	27-43.00
89-147-020 Here Comes Santa Eleventh Ed 1475QX458-5	Keepsake	Yr.Iss.	14.75	29-44.00
89-147-021 Thimble-Twelfth Edition 575QX455-2	Keepsake	Yr.Iss.	5.75	12-18.00

Hallmark Keepsake Ornaments — 1989 Keepsake Magic Collection

	ARTIST	EDITION	ISSUE	QUOTE
89-148-001 Baby's First Christmas 3,000QLX727-2	Keepsake	Yr.Iss.	30.00	47-65.00
89-148-002 First Christmas Together1750QLX734-2	Keepsake	Yr.Iss.	17.50	33-45.00
89-148-003 Forest Frolics-First Edition2450QLX728-2	Keepsake	Yr.Iss.	24.50	85.00
89-148-004 Christmas Classics-Fourth Edition 1350QLX724-2	Keepsake	Yr.Iss.	13.50	25-30.00
89-148-005 Chris Mouse-Fifth Edition 950QLX722-5	Keepsake	Yr.Iss.	9.50	50.00
89-148-006 Joyous Carolers 3,000QLX729-5	Keepsake	Yr.Iss.	30.00	47-60.00
89-148-007 Tiny Tinker 1950QLX717-4	Keepsake	Yr.Iss.	19.50	50-65.00
89-148-008 Rudolph the Red-Nosed Reindeer 1950QLX725-2	Keepsake	Yr.Iss.	19.50	50.00
89-148-009 Loving Spoonful 1950QLX726-2	Keepsake	Yr.Iss.	19.50	32.50
89-148-010 Holiday Bell 1750QLX722-2	Keepsake	Yr.Iss.	17.50	29-35.00
89-148-011 Busy Beaver 1750QLX724-5	Keepsake	Yr.Iss.	17.50	35-40.00
89-148-012 Backstage Bear 1350QLX721-5	Keepsake	Yr.Iss.	13.50	27-38.00
89-148-013 The Animals Speak 1350QLX723-2	Keepsake	Yr.Iss.	13.50	78.00
89-148-014 Angel Melody 950QLX720-2	Keepsake	Yr.Iss.	9.50	15-17.00
89-148-015 Unicorn Fantasy 950QLX723-5	Keepsake	Yr.Iss.	9.50	16-19.00
89-148-016 Moonlit Nap 875QLX713-4	Keepsake	Yr.Iss.	8.75	22.50
89-148-017 Kringle's Toy Shop 2450QLX701-7	Keepsake	Yr.Iss.	24.50	40-60.00
89-148-018 Metro Express 2800QLX727-5	Keepsake	Yr.Iss.	28.00	72-80.00
89-148-019 Spirit of St. Nick 2450QLX728-5	Keepsake	Yr.Iss.	24.50	65.00

Hallmark Keepsake Ornaments — 1989 Keepsake Miniature Ornaments

	ARTIST	EDITION	ISSUE	QUOTE
89-149-001 Baby's First Christmas 600QXM573-2	Keepsake	Yr.Iss.	6.00	12.00
89-149-002 Mother 600QXM564-5	Keepsake	Yr.Iss.	6.00	10.00
89-149-003 First Christmas Together 850QXM564-2	Keepsake	Yr.Iss.	8.50	10.00
89-149-004 Lovebirds 600QXM563-5	Keepsake	Yr.Iss.	6.00	9-14.50
89-149-005 Special Friend 450QXM565-2	Keepsake	Yr.Iss.	4.50	11-14.00
89-149-006 Sharing a Ride 850QXM576-5	Keepsake	Yr.Iss.	8.50	10-15.00
89-149-007 Little Star Bringer 600QXM562-2	Keepsake	Yr.Iss.	6.00	17-32.00
89-149-008 Santa's Roadster 600QXM566-5	Keepsake	Yr.Iss.	6.00	15-25.00
89-149-009 Load of Cheer 600QXM574-5	Keepsake	Yr.Iss.	6.00	12-20.00
89-149-010 Slow Motion 600QXM575-2	Keepsake	Yr.Iss.	6.00	11-16.50
89-149-011 Merry Seal 600QXM575-5	Keepsake	Yr.Iss.	6.00	11-15.00
89-149-012 Starlit Mouse 450QXM565-5	Keepsake	Yr.Iss.	4.50	12-22.00
89-149-013 Little Soldier 450QXM567-5	Keepsake	Yr.Iss.	4.50	9-24.00
89-149-014 Acorn Squirrel 450QXM568-2	Keepsake	Yr.Iss.	4.50	8-12.00
89-149-015 Happy Bluebird 450QXM566-2	Keepsake	Yr.Iss.	4.50	11-21.00
89-149-016 Stocking Pal 450QXM567-2	Keepsake	Yr.Iss.	4.50	10-15.00
89-149-017 Scrimshaw Reindeer 450QXM568-5	Keepsake	Yr.Iss.	4.50	6-10.00
89-149-018 Folk Art Bunny 450QXM569-2	Keepsake	Yr.Iss.	4.50	12.00
89-149-019 Brass Snowflake 450QXM570-2	Keepsake	Yr.Iss.	4.50	12-14.00
89-149-020 Pinecone Basket 450QXM573-4	Keepsake	Yr.Iss.	4.50	6-9.00
89-149-021 Strollin' Snowman 450QXM574-2	Keepsake	Yr.Iss.	4.50	10.00
89-149-022 Brass Partridge 300QXM572-5	Keepsake	Yr.Iss.	3.00	9-12.00
89-149-023 Cozy Skater 450QXM573-5	Keepsake	Yr.Iss.	4.50	10-20.00
89-149-024 Old-World Santa 300QXM569-5	Keepsake	Yr.Iss.	3.00	6.00
89-149-025 Roly-Poly Ram 300QXM570-5	Keepsake	Yr.Iss.	3.00	12-15.00
89-149-026 Roly-Poly Pig 300QXM571-2	Keepsake	Yr.Iss.	3.00	12.00
89-149-027 Puppy Cart 300QXM571-5	Keepsake	Yr.Iss.	3.00	7-22.00
89-149-028 Kitty Cart 300QXM572-2	Keepsake	Yr.Iss.	3.00	6-15.00
89-149-029 Holiday Deer 300QXM577-2	Keepsake	Yr.Iss.	3.00	12.00
89-149-030 Bunny Hug 300QXM577-5	Keepsake	Yr.Iss.	3.00	7-11.00
89-149-031 Rejoice 300QXM578-2	Keepsake	Yr.Iss.	3.00	10.00
89-149-032 Holy Family 850QXM561-1	Keepsake	Yr.Iss.	8.50	14.50
89-149-033 Three Little Kitties 600QXM569-4	Keepsake	Yr.Iss.	6.00	18.50
89-149-034 Country Wreath 450QXM573-1	Keepsake	Yr.Iss.	4.50	12.00
89-149-035 Noel R.R.-First Edition 850QXM576-2	Keepsake	Yr.Iss.	8.50	9-20.00
89-149-036 The Kringles-First Edition600QXM562-2	Keepsake	Yr.Iss.	6.00	26.00
89-149-037 Old English Village-Second Edition 850QXM561-5	Keepsake	Yr.Iss.	8.50	22.00
89-149-038 Penguin Pal-Second Ed.450QXM560-2	Keepsake	Yr.Iss.	4.50	16-37.00
89-149-039 Rocking Horse-Second Ed. 450QXM560-5	Keepsake	Yr.Iss.	4.50	22.00
89-149-040 Kittens in Toyland-Second Edition 450QXM561-2	Keepsake	Yr.Iss.	4.50	15-20.00
89-149-041 Santa's Magic Ride 850QXM563-2	Keepsake	Yr.Iss.	8.50	15-20.00

Hallmark Keepsake Ornaments — 1989 Hallmark Keepsake Ornament Collector's Club

	ARTIST	EDITION	ISSUE	QUOTE
89-150-001 Visit from Santa QXC580-2	Keepsake	Yr.Iss.	Unkn.	39-50.00
89-150-002 Collect a Dream 900QXC428-5	Keepsake	Yr.Iss.	9.00	43-65.00
89-150-003 Christmas is Peaceful 1850QXC451-2	Keepsake	Yr.Iss.	18.50	29-45.00
89-150-004 Noelle 1975QXC448-3	Keepsake	Yr.Iss.	19.75	49.00
89-150-005 Holiday Heirloom-Third Ed.2500QXC460-5	Keepsake	Yr.Iss.	25.00	29-44.00
89-150-006 Sitting Purrty QXC581-2	Keepsake	Yr.Iss.	Unkn.	45-54.00

	ARTIST	EDITION	ISSUE	QUOTE
Hallmark Keepsake Ornaments 1990 Commemoratives				
90-151-001 Baby's First Christmas 975QX4853	Keepsake	Yr.Iss.	9.75	14-17.00
90-151-002 Baby's First Christmas 675QX3036	Keepsake	Yr.Iss.	6.75	10.00
90-151-003 Baby's First Christmas-Baby Boy 475QX2063	Keepsake	Yr.Iss.	4.75	17-24.00
90-151-004 Baby's First Christmas-Baby Girl 475QX2066	Keepsake	Yr.Iss.	4.75	15.00
90-151-005 Baby's First Christmas-Photo Holder 775QX4843	Keepsake	Yr.Iss.	7.75	23.00
90-151-006 Granddaughter's First Christmas 675QX3106	Keepsake	Yr.Iss.	6.75	13.50
90-151-007 Mom-to-Be 575QX4916	Keepsake	Yr.Iss.	5.75	25.00
90-151-008 Grandson's First Christmas 675QX3063	Keepsake	Yr.Iss.	6.75	13.50
90-151-009 Dad-to-Be 575QX4913	Keepsake	Yr.Iss.	5.75	17-22.00
90-151-010 Baby's First Christmas 775QX4856	Keepsake	Yr.Iss.	7.75	25.00
90-151-011 Baby's Second Christmas 675QX4683	Keepsake	Yr.Iss.	6.75	32.00
90-151-012 Child's Third Christmas 675QX4866	Keepsake	Yr.Iss.	6.75	17.00
90-151-013 Child's Fourth Christmas 675QX4873	Keepsake	Yr.Iss.	6.75	15.00
90-151-014 Child's Fifth Christmas 675QX4876	Keepsake	Yr.Iss.	6.75	15.00
90-151-015 Sweetheart 1175QX4893	Keepsake	Yr.Iss.	11.75	18-23.00
90-151-016 Our First Christmas Together 975QX4883	Keepsake	Yr.Iss.	9.75	16.00
90-151-017 Our First Christmas Together-Photo Holder Ornament 775QX4886	Keepsake	Yr.Iss.	7.75	15.50
90-151-018 Our First Christmas Together 675QX3146	Keepsake	Yr.Iss.	6.75	15-20.00
90-151-019 Our First Christmas Together 475QX2136	Keepsake	Yr.Iss.	4.75	12-15.00
90-151-020 Time for Love 475QX2133	Keepsake	Yr.Iss.	4.75	16.00
90-151-021 Peaceful Kingdom 475QX2106	Keepsake	Yr.Iss.	4.75	12.00
90-151-022 Jesus Loves Me 675QX3156	Keepsake	Yr.Iss.	6.75	13.50
90-151-023 Five Years Together 475QX2103	Keepsake	Yr.Iss.	4.75	18.00
90-151-024 Ten Years Together 475QX2153	Keepsake	Yr.Iss.	4.75	13-18.00
90-151-025 Twenty-Five Years Together 975QX4896	Keepsake	Yr.Iss.	9.75	17-19.50
90-151-026 Forty Years Together 975QX4903	Keepsake	Yr.Iss.	9.75	27.00
90-151-027 Fifty Years Together 975QX4906	Keepsake	Yr.Iss.	9.75	17-19.50
90-151-028 Mother 875QX4536	Keepsake	Yr.Iss.	8.75	15.50
90-151-029 Dad 675QX4533	Keepsake	Yr.Iss.	6.75	11-18.00
90-151-030 Mom and Dad 875QX4593	Keepsake	Yr.Iss.	8.75	15-20.00
90-151-031 Grandmother 475QX2236	Keepsake	Yr.Iss.	4.75	18.00
90-151-032 Grandparents 475QX2253	Keepsake	Yr.Iss.	4.75	14.00
90-151-033 Godchild 675QX3167	Keepsake	Yr.Iss.	6.75	11-21.00
90-151-034 Son 575QX4516	Keepsake	Yr.Iss.	5.75	15.00
90-151-035 Daughter 575QX4496	Keepsake	Yr.Iss.	5.75	15.00
90-151-036 Brother 575QX4493	Keepsake	Yr.Iss.	5.75	10.00
90-151-037 Sister 475QX2273	Keepsake	Yr.Iss.	4.75	13-17.50
90-151-038 Grandson 475QX2293	Keepsake	Yr.Iss.	4.75	18.00
90-151-039 Granddaughter 475QX2286	Keepsake	Yr.Iss.	4.75	17-29.00
90-151-040 Friendship Kitten 675QX4142	Keepsake	Yr.Iss.	6.75	16-22.00
90-151-041 New Home 675QX4343	Keepsake	Yr.Iss.	6.75	25.00
90-151-042 Across The Miles 675QX3173	Keepsake	Yr.Iss.	6.75	13-17.00
90-151-043 From Our Home to Yours 475QX2166	Keepsake	Yr.Iss.	4.75	13.00
90-151-044 Teacher 775QX4483	Keepsake	Yr.Iss.	7.75	12-15.50
90-151-045 Copy of Cheer 775QX4486	Keepsake	Yr.Iss.	7.75	15.50
90-151-046 Child Care Giver 675QX3166	Keepsake	Yr.Iss.	6.75	13.50
Hallmark Keepsake Ornaments 1990 New Attractions				
90-152-001 S. Claus Taxi 1175QX4686	Keepsake	Yr.Iss.	11.75	25-30.00
90-152-002 Coyote Carols 875QX4993	Keepsake	Yr.Iss.	8.75	16-19.50
90-152-003 King Klaus 775QX4106	Keepsake	Yr.Iss.	7.75	12-28.00
90-152-004 Hot Dogger 775QX4976	Keepsake	Yr.Iss.	7.75	14-29.00
90-152-005 Poolside Walrus 775QX4986	Keepsake	Yr.Iss.	7.75	12-15.50
90-152-006 Three Little Piggies 775QX4996	Keepsake	Yr.Iss.	7.75	14-28.00
90-152-007 Billboard Bunny 775QX5196	Keepsake	Yr.Iss.	7.75	13-15.50
90-152-008 Mooy Christmas 675QX4933	Keepsake	Yr.Iss.	6.75	20-25.00
90-152-009 Pepperoni Mouse 675QX4973	Keepsake	Yr.Iss.	6.75	13-20.00
90-152-010 Santa Schnoz 675QX4983	Keepsake	Yr.Iss.	6.75	17-28.00
90-152-011 Cozy Goose 575QX4966	Keepsake	Yr.Iss.	5.75	13.50
90-152-012 Two Peas in a Pod 475QX4926	Keepsake	Yr.Iss.	4.75	19-25.00
90-152-013 Chiming In 975QX4366	Keepsake	Yr.Iss.	9.75	15-30.00
90-152-014 Christmas Croc 775QX4373	Keepsake	Yr.Iss.	7.75	12-15.50
90-152-015 Born to Dance 775QX5043	Keepsake	Yr.Iss.	7.75	14-24.00
90-152-016 Stocking Pals 1075QX5493	Keepsake	Yr.Iss.	10.75	22.00
90-152-017 Home for the Owlidays 675QX5183	Keepsake	Yr.Iss.	6.75	11-21.00
90-152-018 Baby Unicorn 975QX5486	Keepsake	Yr.Iss.	9.75	10-19.50
90-152-019 Spoon Rider 975QX5496	Keepsake	Yr.Iss.	9.75	14-24.00
90-152-020 Lovable Dears 875QX5476	Keepsake	Yr.Iss.	8.75	13-17.50
90-152-021 Meow Mart 775QX4446	Keepsake	Yr.Iss.	7.75	15-20.00
90-152-022 Perfect Catch 775QX4693	Keepsake	Yr.Iss.	7.75	11-26.00
90-152-023 Nutshell Chat 675QX5193	Keepsake	Yr.Iss.	6.75	14-21.00
90-152-024 Gingerbread Elf 575QX5033	Keepsake	Yr.Iss.	5.75	10.00
90-152-025 Stitches of Joy 775QX5186	Keepsake	Yr.Iss.	7.75	14.50
90-152-026 Little Drummer Boy 775QX5233	Keepsake	Yr.Iss.	7.75	18-29.00
90-152-027 Goose Cart 775QX5236	Keepsake	Yr.Iss.	7.75	13-23.00
90-152-028 Holiday Cardinals 775QX5243	Keepsake	Yr.Iss.	7.75	13-18.00
90-152-029 Christmas Partridge 775QX5246	Keepsake	Yr.Iss.	7.75	15.50
90-152-030 Joy is in the Air 775QX5503	Keepsake	Yr.Iss.	7.75	19-30.00
90-152-031 Happy Voices 675QX4645	Keepsake	Yr.Iss.	6.75	14.50
90-152-032 Jolly Dolphin 675QX4683	Keepsake	Yr.Iss.	6.75	19-35.00
90-152-033 Long Winter's Nap 675QX4703	Keepsake	Yr.Iss.	6.75	13-17.50
90-152-034 Hang in There 675QX4713	Keepsake	Yr.Iss.	6.75	14-24.00
90-152-035 Kitty's Best Pal 675QX4716	Keepsake	Yr.Iss.	6.75	12.50-20.
90-152-036 SNOOPY and WOODSTOCK 675QX4723	Keepsake	Yr.Iss.	6.75	15-30.00
90-152-037 Beary Good Deal 675QX4733	Keepsake	Yr.Iss.	6.75	10-13.50
90-152-038 Country Angel 675QX5046	Keepsake	Yr.Iss.	6.75	175-195.
90-152-039 Feliz Navidad 675QX5173	Keepsake	Yr.Iss.	6.75	13-32.00
90-152-040 Bearback Rider 975QX5483	Keepsake	Yr.Iss.	9.75	17-30.00
90-152-041 Polar Sport 775QX5156	Keepsake	Yr.Iss.	7.75	12-15.50
90-152-042 Polar Pair 575QX4626	Keepsake	Yr.Iss.	5.75	15.00
90-152-043 Polar Video 575QX4633	Keepsake	Yr.Iss.	5.75	9-19.00
90-152-044 Polar V.I.P. 575QX4663	Keepsake	Yr.Iss.	5.75	11.50
90-152-045 Polar TV 775QX5166	Keepsake	Yr.Iss.	7.75	12-15.00
90-152-046 Polar Jogger 575QX4666	Keepsake	Yr.Iss.	5.75	9-19.00
90-152-047 Garfield 475QX2303	Keepsake	Yr.Iss.	4.75	18-20.00
90-152-048 Peanuts 475QX2233	Keepsake	Yr.Iss.	4.75	10-20.00
90-152-049 Norman Rockwell Art 475QX2296	Keepsake	Yr.Iss.	4.75	15.00
Hallmark Keepsake Ornaments 1990 Artists' Favorites				
90-153-001 Donder's Diner 1375QX4823	Keepsake	Yr.Iss.	13.75	23-39.00
90-153-002 Welcome, Santa 1175QX4773	Keepsake	Yr.Iss.	11.75	19-23.00
90-153-003 Happy Woodcutter 975QX4763	Keepsake	Yr.Iss.	9.75	17-26.00
90-153-004 Angel Kitty 875QX4746	Keepsake	Yr.Iss.	8.75	13-20.00
90-153-005 Gentle Dreamers 875QX4756	Keepsake	Yr.Iss.	8.75	17-30.00
90-153-006 Mouseboat 775QX4753	Keepsake	Yr.Iss.	7.75	10-23.00

	ARTIST	EDITION	ISSUE	QUOTE
Hallmark Keepsake Ornaments 1990 Special Edition				
90-154-001 Dickens Caroler Bell-Mr. Ashbourne 2175QX5056	Keepsake	Yr.Iss.	21.75	41-45.00
Hallmark Keepsake Ornaments 1990 Collectible Series				
90-155-001 Merry Olde Santa-First Edition 1475QX4736	Keepsake	Yr.Iss.	14.75	68-75.00
90-155-002 Greatest Story-First Edition 1275QX4656	Keepsake	Yr.Iss.	12.75	26.00
90-155-003 Heart of Christmas-First Edition 1375QX4726	Keepsake	Yr.Iss.	13.75	55-60.00
90-155-004 Fabulous Decade-First Edition 775QX4466	Keepsake	Yr.Iss.	7.75	36-44.00
90-155-005 Christmas Kitty-Second Edition 1475QX4506	Keepsake	Yr.Iss.	14.75	20-32.00
90-155-006 Winter Surprise-Second Edition 1075QX4443	Keepsake	Yr.Iss.	10.75	19-33.00
90-155-007 CRAYOLA Crayon-Bright Moving Colors-Second Edition 875QX4586	Keepsake	Yr.Iss.	8.75	22-49.00
90-155-008 Hark! It's Herald-Second Edition 675QX4463	Keepsake	Yr.Iss.	6.75	17-20.00
90-155-009 The Gift Bringers-St. Lucia-Second Edition 500QX2803	Keepsake	Yr.Iss.	5.00	12-20.00
90-155-010 Mary's Angels-Rosebud-Third Edition 575QX4423	Keepsake	Yr.Iss.	5.75	25-37.00
90-155-011 Cookies for Santa-Fourth Edition 875QX4436	Keepsake	Yr.Iss.	8.75	25.00
90-155-012 Popcorn Party-Fifth Edition 1375QX4393	Keepsake	Yr.Iss.	13.75	19-40.00
90-155-013 Reindeer Champs-Comet-Fifth Edition 775QX4433	Keepsake	Yr.Iss.	7.75	19.00
90-155-014 Betsey Clark: Home for Christmas-Fifth Edition 500QX2033	Keepsake	Yr.Iss.	5.00	15-17.50
90-155-015 Holiday Home-Seventh Edition 1475QX4696	Keepsake	Yr.Iss.	14.75	51.00
90-155-016 Seven Swans A-Swimming-Seventh Edition 675QX3033	Keepsake	Yr.Iss.	6.75	19.00
90-155-017 Rocking Horse-Tenth Edition 1075QX4646	Keepsake	Yr.Iss.	10.75	50-57.50
90-155-018 Frosty Friends-Eleventh Edition 975QX4396	Keepsake	Yr.Iss.	9.75	20-32.00
90-155-019 Festive Surrey-Twelfth Edition 1475QX4923	Keepsake	Yr.Iss.	14.75	10-34.50
90-155-020 Irish-Sixth Edition 1075QX4636	Keepsake	Yr.Iss.	10.75	15-22.00
90-155-021 Cinnamon Bear-Eighth Edition 875QX4426	Keepsake	Yr.Iss.	8.75	20-32.00
Hallmark Keepsake Ornaments 1990 Keepsake Magic Ornaments				
90-156-001 Children's Express 2800QLX7243	Keepsake	Yr.Iss.	28.00	57-75.00
90-156-002 Hop 'N Pop Popper 2,000QLX7353	Keepsake	Yr.Iss.	20.00	65-90.00
90-156-003 Baby's First Christmas 2800QLX7246	Keepsake	Yr.Iss.	28.00	41-60.00
90-156-004 Christmas Memories 2500QLX7276	Keepsake	Yr.Iss.	25.00	44-47.00
90-156-005 Forest Frolics 2500QLX7236	Keepsake	Yr.Iss.	25.00	54-75.00
90-156-006 Santa's Ho-Ho-Hoedown 2500QLX7256	Keepsake	Yr.Iss.	25.00	80.00
90-156-007 Mrs. Santa's Kitchen 2500QLX7263	Keepsake	Yr.Iss.	25.00	50-60.00
90-156-008 Song and Dance 2,000QLX7253	Keepsake	Yr.Iss.	20.00	59-65.00
90-156-009 Elfin Whittler 2,000QLX7265	Keepsake	Yr.Iss.	20.00	35-45.00
90-156-010 Deer Crossing 1800QLX7213	Keepsake	Yr.Iss.	18.00	40-45.00
90-156-011 Our First Christmas Together 1800QLX7255	Keepsake	Yr.Iss.	18.00	27-47.00
90-156-012 Holiday Flash 1800QLX7333	Keepsake	Yr.Iss.	18.00	25-36.00
90-156-013 Starship Christmas 1800QLX7336	Keepsake	Yr.Iss.	18.00	33-53.00
90-156-014 Partridges in a Pear 1400QLX7212	Keepsake	Yr.Iss.	14.00	25-30.00
90-156-015 Letter to Santa 1400QLX7226	Keepsake	Yr.Iss.	14.00	28-34.00
90-156-016 Starlight Angel 1400QLX7306	Keepsake	Yr.Iss.	14.00	22-28.00
90-156-017 The Littlest Angel 1400QLX7303	Keepsake	Yr.Iss.	14.00	24-28.00
90-156-018 Blessings of Love 1400QLX7363	Keepsake	Yr.Iss.	14.00	44-54.00
90-156-019 Chris Mouse Wreath 1000QLX7296	Keepsake	Yr.Iss.	10.00	27-39.00
90-156-020 Beary Short Nap 1000QLX7326	Keepsake	Yr.Iss.	10.00	20-23.00
90-156-021 Elf of the Year 1000QLX7356	Keepsake	Yr.Iss.	10.00	14-26.00
Hallmark Keepsake Ornaments 1990 Keepsake Miniature Ornaments				
90-157-001 Thimble Bells 600QXM5543	Keepsake	Yr.Iss.	6.00	19-30.00
90-157-002 Nature's Angels 450QMX5733	Keepsake	Yr.Iss.	4.50	26.00
90-157-003 Cloisonne Poinsettia 1050QMX5533	Keepsake	Yr.Iss.	10.75	20-25.00
90-157-004 Coal Car 850QXM5756	Keepsake	Yr.Iss.	8.50	20-25.00
90-157-005 School 850QXM5763	Keepsake	Yr.Iss.	8.50	16-30.00
90-157-006 The Kringles 600QXM5753	Keepsake	Yr.Iss.	6.00	24-30.00
90-157-007 Kittens in Toyland 450QXM5736	Keepsake	Yr.Iss.	4.50	16-30.00
90-157-008 Rocking Horse 450QXM5743	Keepsake	Yr.Iss.	4.50	17-20.00
90-157-009 Penguin Pal 450QXM5746	Keepsake	Yr.Iss.	4.50	14.00
90-157-010 Santa's Streetcar 850QQXM5766	Keepsake	Yr.Iss.	8.50	13-17.00
90-157-011 Snow Angel 600QXM5773	Keepsake	Yr.Iss.	6.00	13.00
90-157-012 Baby's First Christmas 850QXM5703	Keepsake	Yr.Iss.	8.50	15.00
90-157-013 Grandchild's First Christmas 600QXM5723	Keepsake	Yr.Iss.	6.00	10.00
90-157-014 Special Friends 600QXM5726	Keepsake	Yr.Iss.	6.00	11-14.00
90-157-015 Mother 450QXM5716	Keepsake	Yr.Iss.	4.50	12-19.00
90-157-016 Warm Memories 450QXM5713	Keepsake	Yr.Iss.	4.50	10-19.00
90-157-017 First Christmas Together 600QXM5536	Keepsake	Yr.Iss.	6.00	11.00
90-157-018 Loving Hearts 300QXM5523	Keepsake	Yr.Iss.	3.00	6-14.00
90-157-019 Stringing Along 850QXM5606	Keepsake	Yr.Iss.	8.50	17.00
90-157-020 Santa's Journey 850QXM5826	Keepsake	Yr.Iss.	8.50	18-25.00
90-157-021 Wee Nutcracker 850QXM5843	Keepsake	Yr.Iss.	8.50	14-20.00
90-157-022 Bear Hug 600QXM5633	Keepsake	Yr.Iss.	6.00	10-20.00
90-157-023 Acorn Wreath 600QXM5686	Keepsake	Yr.Iss.	6.00	8-12.00
90-157-024 Puppy Love 600QXM5666	Keepsake	Yr.Iss.	6.00	9-12.00
90-157-025 Madonna and Child 600QXM5643	Keepsake	Yr.Iss.	6.00	9-12.00
90-157-026 Basket Buddy 600QXM5696	Keepsake	Yr.Iss.	6.00	8-12.00
90-157-027 Ruby Reindeer 600QXM5816	Keepsake	Yr.Iss.	6.00	9-12.00
90-157-028 Perfect Fit 450QXM5516	Keepsake	Yr.Iss.	4.50	8-18.00
90-157-029 Panda's Surprise 450QXM5616	Keepsake	Yr.Iss.	4.50	9-13.50
90-157-030 Stamp Collector 450QXM5623	Keepsake	Yr.Iss.	4.50	7-10.00
90-157-031 Christmas Dove 450QXM5636	Keepsake	Yr.Iss.	4.50	10-19.00
90-157-032 Type of Joy 450QXM5646	Keepsake	Yr.Iss.	4.50	7-17.00
90-157-033 Teacher 450QXM5653	Keepsake	Yr.Iss.	4.50	7-17.00
90-157-034 Air Santa 450QXM5656	Keepsake	Yr.Iss.	4.50	9-13.00
90-157-035 Sweet Slumber 450QXM5663	Keepsake	Yr.Iss.	4.50	10-15.00
90-157-036 Busy Carver 450QXM5673	Keepsake	Yr.Iss.	4.50	10.00
90-157-037 Lion and Lamb 450QXM5676	Keepsake	Yr.Iss.	4.50	6.50-41.
90-157-038 Going Sledding 450QXM5683	Keepsake	Yr.Iss.	4.50	10.00
90-157-039 Country Heart 450QXM5693	Keepsake	Yr.Iss.	4.50	9-19.00
90-157-040 Nativity 450QXM5706	Keepsake	Yr.Iss.	4.50	10-13.00
90-157-041 Holiday Cardinal 300QXM5526	Keepsake	Yr.Iss.	3.00	9-12.00
90-157-042 Brass Bouquet 600QMX5776	Keepsake	Yr.Iss.	6.00	9.50
90-157-043 Brass Santa 300QXM5786	Keepsake	Yr.Iss.	3.00	6-15.00
90-157-044 Brass Horn 300QXM5793	Keepsake	Yr.Iss.	3.00	9-12.00
90-157-045 Brass Peace 300QXM5796	Keepsake	Yr.Iss.	3.00	8.50
90-157-046 Brass Year 300QXM5833	Keepsake	Yr.Iss.	3.00	8.00

Hallmark Keepsake Ornaments — 1990 Limited Edition

	ARTIST	EDITION	ISSUE	QUOTE
90-158-001 Dove of Peace 2475QXC447-6	Keepsake	25400	24.75	49-55.00
90-158-002 Christmas Limited1975 QXC476-6	Keepsake	38700	19.75	70-85.00
90-158-003 Sugar Plum Fairy 2775QXC447-3	Keepsake	25400	27.75	49-60.00

Hallmark Keepsake Ornaments — 1990 Keepsake Collector's Club

	ARTIST	EDITION	ISSUE	QUOTE
90-159-001 Club Hollow QXC445-6	Keepsake	Yr.Iss.	Unkn.	36-46.00
90-159-002 Crown Prince QXC560-3	Keepsake	Yr.Iss.	Unkn.	40.00
90-159-003 Armful of Joy 800QXC445-3	Keepsake	Yr.Iss.	8.00	40-50.00

Hallmark Keepsake Ornaments — 1991 Commemoratives

	ARTIST	EDITION	ISSUE	QUOTE
91-160-001 Baby's First Christmas 1775QX5107	Keepsake	Yr.Iss.	17.75	23-42.50
91-160-002 Baby's First Christmas-Baby Boy475QX2217	Keepsake	Yr.Iss.	4.75	15-18.00
91-160-003 Baby's First Christmas-Baby Girl475QX2227	Keepsake	Yr.Iss.	4.75	10-15.00
91-160-004 Baby's First Christmas-Photo Holder 775QX4869	Keepsake	Yr.Iss.	7.75	12-22.00
91-160-005 Mom-to-Be 575QX4877	Keepsake	Yr.Iss.	5.75	13-15.00
91-160-006 Dad-to-Be 575QX4879	Keepsake	Yr.Iss.	5.75	15.00
91-160-007 Grandson's First Christmas 675QX5117	Keepsake	Yr.Iss.	6.75	10.00
91-160-008 Granddaughter's First Christmas 675QX5119	Keepsake	Yr.Iss.	6.75	10.00
91-160-009 A Child's Christmas 975QX4887	Keepsake	Yr.Iss.	9.75	12-15.50
91-160-010 Baby's First Christmas 775QX4889	Keepsake	Yr.Iss.	7.75	18-29.50
91-160-011 Baby's Second Christmas 675QX4897	Keepsake	Yr.Iss.	6.75	15-24.00
91-160-012 Child's Third Christmas 675QX4899	Keepsake	Yr.Iss.	6.75	21.00
91-160-013 Child's Fourth Christmas 675QX4907	Keepsake	Yr.Iss.	6.75	15.00
91-160-014 Child's Fifth Christmas 675QX4909	Keepsake	Yr.Iss.	6.75	13-15.00
91-160-015 Sweetheart 975QX4957	Keepsake	Yr.Iss.	9.75	17.50
91-160-016 Our First Christmas Together-Photo Holder 875QX4917	Keepsake	Yr.Iss.	8.75	15-30.00
91-160-017 Our First Christmas Together 875QX4919	Keepsake	Yr.Iss.	8.75	20.00
91-160-018 Our First Christmas Together 675QX3139	Keepsake	Yr.Iss.	6.75	15.00
91-160-019 Our First Christmas Together 475QX2229	Keepsake	Yr.Iss.	4.75	15-20.00
91-160-020 Under the Mistletoe 875QX4949	Keepsake	Yr.Iss.	8.75	20.00
91-160-021 Jesus Loves Me 775QX3147	Keepsake	Yr.Iss.	7.75	15.50
91-160-022 Five Years Together 775QX4927	Keepsake	Yr.Iss.	7.75	15.50
91-160-023 Ten Years Together 775QX4929	Keepsake	Yr.Iss.	7.75	15.50
91-160-024 Twenty -Five Years Together 875QX4937	Keepsake	Yr.Iss.	8.75	16-19.50
91-160-025 Forty Years Together 775QX4939	Keepsake	Yr.Iss.	7.75	19.50
91-160-026 Fifty Years Together 875QX4947	Keepsake	Yr.Iss.	8.75	16-20.00
91-160-027 Mother 975QX5457	Keepsake	Yr.Iss.	9.75	16.00
91-160-028 Dad 775QX5127	Keepsake	Yr.Iss.	7.75	19.50
91-160-029 Mom and Dad 975QX5467	Keepsake	Yr.Iss.	9.75	22.00
91-160-030 Grandmother 475QX2307	Keepsake	Yr.Iss.	4.75	10-15.50
91-160-031 Grandparents 475QX2309	Keepsake	Yr.Iss.	4.75	14.00
91-160-032 Godchild 675QX5489	Keepsake	Yr.Iss.	6.75	15.50
91-160-033 Son 575QX5469	Keepsake	Yr.Iss.	5.75	12.00
91-160-034 Daughter 575QX5477	Keepsake	Yr.Iss.	5.75	14.00
91-160-035 Brother 675QX5479	Keepsake	Yr.Iss.	6.75	17.00
91-160-036 Sister 675QX5487	Keepsake	Yr.Iss.	6.75	16-20.00
91-160-037 Grandson 475QX2297	Keepsake	Yr.Iss.	4.75	13-15.50
91-160-038 Granddaughter 475QX2299	Keepsake	Yr.Iss.	4.75	17-22.00
91-160-039 Friends Are Fun 975QX5289	Keepsake	Yr.Iss.	9.75	17-32.00
91-160-040 Extra-Special Friends 475QX2279	Keepsake	Yr.Iss.	4.75	15.50
91-160-041 New Home 675QX5449	Keepsake	Yr.Iss.	6.75	16.00
91-160-042 Across the Miles 675QX3157	Keepsake	Yr.Iss.	6.75	13.00
91-160-043 From Our Home to Yours 475QX2287	Keepsake	Yr.Iss.	4.75	14.00
91-160-044 Terrific Teacher 675QX5309	Keepsake	Yr.Iss.	6.75	13.50
91-160-045 Teacher 475QX2289	Keepsake	Yr.Iss.	4.75	12-25.00
91-160-046 Gift of Joy 875QX5319	Keepsake	Yr.Iss.	8.75	17-19.50
91-160-047 The Big Cheese 675QX5327	Keepsake	Yr.Iss.	6.75	18.00

Hallmark Keepsake Ornaments — 1991 New Attractions

	ARTIST	EDITION	ISSUE	QUOTE
91-161-001 Winnie-the Pooh 975QX5569	Keepsake	Yr.Iss.	9.75	34-50.00
91-161-002 Piglet and Eeyore 975QX5577	Keepsake	Yr.Iss.	9.75	40-48.00
91-161-003 Christopher Robin 975QX5579	Keepsake	Yr.Iss.	9.75	35-40.00
91-161-004 Rabbit 975QX5607	Keepsake	Yr.Iss.	9.75	30.00
91-161-005 Tigger 975QX5609	Keepsake	Yr.Iss.	9.75	95-100.
91-161-006 Kanga and Roo 975QX5617	Keepsake	Yr.Iss.	9.75	40-50.00
91-161-007 Look Out Below 875QX4959	Keepsake	Yr.Iss.	8.75	18-22.00
91-161-008 Yule Logger 875QX4967	Keepsake	Yr.Iss.	8.75	17-22.00
91-161-009 Glee Club Bears 87566QX4969	Keepsake	Yr.Iss.	8.75	13-24.00
91-161-010 Plum Delightful 875QX4977	Keepsake	Yr.Iss.	8.75	17-20.00
91-161-011 Snow Twins 875QX4979	Keepsake	Yr.Iss.	8.75	15-25.00
91-161-012 Loving Stitches 875QX4987	Keepsake	Yr.Iss.	8.75	18-28.00
91-161-013 Fanfare Bear 875QX5337	Keepsake	Yr.Iss.	8.75	14-25.00
91-161-014 Mrs. Cratchit 1375QX4999	Keepsake	Yr.Iss.	13.75	26-38.00
91-161-015 Merry Carolers 2975QX4799	Keepsake	Yr.Iss.	29.75	38-95.00
91-161-016 Ebenezer Scrooge 1375QX4989	Keepsake	Yr.Iss.	13.75	27.50
91-161-017 Bob Cratchit 1375QX4997	Keepsake	Yr.Iss.	13.75	22.50
91-161-018 Tiny Tim 1075QX5037	Keepsake	Yr.Iss.	10.75	23-33.00
91-161-019 Evergreen Inn 875QX5389	Keepsake	Yr.Iss.	8.75	12-15.50
91-161-020 Santa's Studio 875QX5397	Keepsake	Yr.Iss.	8.75	15.50
91-161-021 Holiday Cafe 875QX5399	Keepsake	Yr.Iss.	8.75	15.50
91-161-022 Jolly Wolly Santa 775QX5419	Keepsake	Yr.Iss.	7.75	17-26.50
91-161-023 Jolly Wolly Snowman 775QX5427	Keepsake	Yr.Iss.	7.75	15-22.50
91-161-024 Jolly Wolly Soldier 775QX5429'	Keepsake	Yr.Iss.	7.75	12-22.50
91-161-025 Partridge in a Pear Tree 975QX5297	Keepsake	Yr.Iss.	9.75	19.50
91-161-026 Christmas Welcome 975QX5299	Keepsake	Yr.Iss.	9.75	19.50
91-161-027 Night Before Christmas 975QX5307	Keepsake	Yr.Iss.	9.75	20-25.00
91-161-028 SNOOPY and WOODSTOCK 675QX5197	Keepsake	Yr.Iss.	6.75	12-33.00
91-161-029 PEANUTS 500QX2257	Keepsake	Yr.Iss.	5.00	10-22.50
91-161-030 GARFIELD 775QX5177	Keepsake	Yr.Iss.	7.75	20.00
91-161-031 Norman Rockwell Art 500QX2259	Keepsake	Yr.Iss.	5.00	16.00
91-161-032 Mary Engelbreit 475QX2237	Keepsake	Yr.Iss.	4.75	19.50
91-161-033 Up 'N'Down Journey 975QX5047	Keepsake	Yr.Iss.	9.75	12-25.00
91-161-034 Old-Fashioned Sled 875QX4317	Keepsake	Yr.Iss.	8.75	16-26.00
91-161-035 Folk Art Reindeer 875QX5359	Keepsake	Yr.Iss.	8.75	12-15.50
91-161-036 Sweet Talk 875QX5367	Keepsake	Yr.Iss.	8.75	17.00
91-161-037 Snowy Owl 775QX5269	Keepsake	Yr.Iss.	7.75	17-20.00
91-161-038 Dinoclaus 775QX5277	Keepsake	Yr.Iss.	7.75	16-19.50
91-161-039 Basket Bell Players 775QX5377	Keepsake	Yr.Iss.	7.75	16-25.00
91-161-040 Nutshell Nativity 675QX5176	Keepsake	Yr.Iss.	6.75	20-28.00
91-161-041 Cuddly Lamb 675QX5199	Keepsake	Yr.Iss.	6.75	20.00
91-161-042 Feliz Navidad 675QX5279	Keepsake	Yr.Iss.	6.75	11-13.50
91-161-043 Polar Classic 675QX5287	Keepsake	Yr.Iss.	6.75	25.00
91-161-044 All-Star 675QX5329	Keepsake	Yr.Iss.	6.75	17-26.00
91-161-045 Chilly Chap 675QX5339	Keepsake	Yr.Iss.	6.75	13-20.00
91-161-046 On a Roll 675QX5347	Keepsake	Yr.Iss.	6.75	16-26.00
91-161-047 Joyous Memories-Photoholder 675QX5369	Keepsake	Yr.Iss.	6.75	17.50
91-161-048 Ski Lift Bunny 675QX5447	Keepsake	Yr.Iss.	6.75	15.50
91-161-049 Nutty Squirrel 575QX4833	Keepsake	Yr.Iss.	5.75	13-15.50
91-161-050 Notes of Cheer 575QX5357	Keepsake	Yr.Iss.	5.75	13-15.50

Hallmark Keepsake Ornaments — 1991 Artists' Favorites

	ARTIST	EDITION	ISSUE	QUOTE
91-162-001 Polar Circus Wagon 1375QX4399	Keepsake	Yr.Iss.	13.75	30-35.00
91-162-002 Noah's Ark 1375QX4867	Keepsake	Yr.Iss.	13.75	25-39.50
91-162-003 Santa Sailor 975QX4389	Keepsake	Yr.Iss.	9.75	18-22.00
91-162-004 Hooked on Santa 775QX4109	Keepsake	Yr.Iss.	7.75	16-28.00
91-162-005 Fiddlin' Around 775QX4387	Keepsake	Yr.Iss.	7.75	18.00
91-162-006 Tramp and Laddie 775QX4397	Keepsake	Yr.Iss.	7.75	17.50

Hallmark Keepsake Ornaments — 1991 Special Edition

	ARTIST	EDITION	ISSUE	QUOTE
91-163-001 Dickens Caroler Bell-Mrs. Beaumont-2175QX5039	Keepsake	Yr.Iss.	21.75	40-50.00

Hallmark Keepsake Ornaments — 1991 Collectible Series

	ARTIST	EDITION	ISSUE	QUOTE
91-164-001 1957 Corvette-First Edition1275QX4319	Keepsake	Yr.Iss.	12.75	110-175.
91-164-002 Peace on Earth-Italy First Ed.1175QX5129	Keepsake	Yr.Iss.	11.75	20-26.00
91-164-003 Heavenly Angels-First Edition 775QX4367	Keepsake	Yr.Iss.	7.75	30.00
91-164-004 Puppy Love-First Edition 775QX5379	Keepsake	Yr.Iss.	7.75	30-55.00
91-164-005 Merry Olde Santa-Second Ed. 1475QX4359	Keepsake	Yr.Iss.	14.75	41-70.00
91-164-006 Heart of Christmas-Second Ed. 1375QX4357	Keepsake	Yr.Iss.	13.75	26.00
91-164-007 Greatest Story-Second Edition 1275QX4129	Keepsake	Yr.Iss.	12.75	25.50
91-164-008 Fabulous Decade-Second Ed. 775QX4119	Keepsake	Yr.Iss.	7.75	25.00
91-164-009 Winter Surprise-Third Ed. 1075QX4277	Keepsake	Yr.Iss.	10.75	22.00
91-164-010 CRAYOLA CRAYON-Bright Vibrant Carols-Third Edition 975QX4219	Keepsake	Yr.Iss.	9.75	18-25.00
91-164-011 Hark! It's Herald Third Edition 675QX4379	Keepsake	Yr.Iss.	6.75	19-32.00
91-164-012 The Gift Bringers-Christkind Third Edition 500QX2117	Keepsake	Yr.Iss.	5.00	15.00
91-164-013 Mary's Angels-Iris Fourth Ed. 675QX4279	Keepsake	Yr.Iss.	6.75	20-40.00
91-164-014 Let It Snow! Fifth Ediiton 875QX4369	Keepsake	Yr.Iss.	8.75	20-25.00
91-164-015 Checking His List Sixth Edition 1375QX4339	Keepsake	Yr.Iss.	13.75	25-30.00
91-164-016 Reindeer Champ-Cupid Sixth Ed. 775QX4347	Keepsake	Yr.Iss.	7.75	18-33.00
91-164-017 Fire Station-Eigth Edition 1475QX4139	Keepsake	Yr.Iss.	14.75	31-35.00
91-164-018 Eight Maids A-Milking-Eigth Ed. 675QX3089	Keepsake	Yr.Iss.	6.75	19.00
91-164-019 Rocking Horse-11th Ed. 1075QX4147	Keepsake	Yr.Iss.	10.75	23.00
91-164-020 Frosty Friends-Twelfth Edition 975QX4327	Keepsake	Yr.Iss.	9.75	18-25.00
91-164-021 Santa's Antique Car-13th Ed. 1475QX4349	Keepsake	Yr.Iss.	14.75	28-33.00
91-164-022 Christmas Kitty-Third Edition 1475QX4377	Keepsake	Yr.Iss.	14.75	27-32.00
91-164-023 Betsey Clark: Home for Christmas Sixth Edition 500QX2109	Keepsake	Yr.Iss.	5.00	14.00

Hallmark Keepsake Ornaments — 1991 Keepsake Magic Ornaments

	ARTIST	EDITION	ISSUE	QUOTE
91-165-001 PEANUTS 1800QLX7229	Keepsake	Yr.Iss.	18.00	50-55.00
91-165-002 Santa Special 4,000QLX7167	Keepsake	Yr.Iss.	40.00	54-65.00
91-165-003 Salvation Army Band 3,000QLX7273	Keepsake	Yr.Iss.	30.00	55-77.50
91-165-004 Forest Frolics 2500QLX7219	Keepsake	Yr.Iss.	25.00	55-69.50
91-165-005 Chris Mouse Mail 1,000QLX7207	Keepsake	Yr.Iss.	10.00	25-39.50
91-165-006 Arctic Dome 2500QLX7117	Keepsake	Yr.Iss.	25.00	59.90
91-165-007 Baby's First Christmas 3,000QLX7247	Keepsake	Yr.Iss.	30.00	55-90.00
91-165-008 Bringing Home the Tree-2800QLX7249	Keepsake	Yr.Iss.	28.00	51-65.00
91-165-009 Ski Trip 2800QLX7266	Keepsake	Yr.Iss.	28.00	50-60.00
91-165-010 Kringles's Bumper Cars-2500QLX7119	Keepsake	Yr.Iss.	25.00	45-49.50
91-165-011 Our First Christmas Together-2500QXL7137	Keepsake	Yr.Iss.	25.00	48-60.00
91-165-012 Jingle Bears 2500QLX7323	Keepsake	Yr.Iss.	25.00	45-58.00
91-165-013 Toyland Tower 2000QLX7129	Keepsake	Yr.Iss.	20.00	35-49.50
91-165-014 Mole Family Home 2000QLX7149	Keepsake	Yr.Iss.	20.00	35-46.00
91-165-015 Starship Enterprise 2000QLX7199	Keepsake	Yr.Iss.	20.00	180-300.
91-165-016 It's A Wonderful Life 2000QLX7237	Keepsake	Yr.Iss.	20.00	50-75.00
91-165-017 Sparkling Angel 1800QLX7157	Keepsake	Yr.Iss.	18.00	29.50
91-165-018 Santa's Hot Line 1800QLX7159	Keepsake	Yr.Iss.	18.00	32-42.50
91-165-019 Father Christmas 1400QLX7147	Keepsake	Yr.Iss.	14.00	30.00
91-165-020 Holiday Glow 1400QLX7177	Keepsake	Yr.Iss.	14.00	30-35.00
91-165-021 Festive Brass Church 1400QLX7179	Keepsake	Yr.Iss.	14.00	21-24.50
91-165-022 Friendship Tree 1000QLX7169	Keepsake	Yr.Iss.	10.00	25-33.00
91-165-023 Elfin Engineer 1000QLX7209	Keepsake	Yr.Iss.	10.00	20.50
91-165-024 Angel of Light 3000QLT7239	Keepsake	Yr.Iss.	30.00	59.50

Hallmark Keepsake Ornaments — 1991 Keepsake Miniature Ornaments

	ARTIST	EDITION	ISSUE	QUOTE
91-166-001 Woodland Babies 600QXM5667	Keepsake	Yr.Iss.	6.00	21.50
91-166-002 Thimble Bells-Second Edition 600QXM5659	Keepsake	Yr.Iss.	6.00	18.50
91-166-003 Nature's Angels-Second Ed. 450QXM5657	Keepsake	Yr.Iss.	4.50	19.00
91-166-004 Passenger Car-Third Ed. 850QXM5649	Keepsake	Yr.Iss.	8.50	21.50
91-166-005 The Kringles-Third Edition 6,000QXM5647	Keepsake	Yr.Iss.	6.00	19-25.00
91-166-006 Inn-Fourth Edition 850QXM5627	Keepsake	Yr.Iss.	8.50	14-21.00
91-166-007 Rocking Horse-Fourth Ed. 450QXM5637	Keepsake	Yr.Iss.	4.50	21.00
91-166-008 Kittens in Toyland-Fourth Ed. 450QXM5639	Keepsake	Yr.Iss.	4.50	14-24.00
91-166-009 Penquin Pal-Fourth Ed. 450QXM5629	Keepsake	Yr.Iss.	4.50	15-17.50
91-166-010 Ring-A-Ding Elf 850QXM5669	Keepsake	Yr.Iss.	8.50	18-28.00
91-166-011 Lulu & Family 600QXM5677	Keepsake	Yr.Iss.	6.00	20.00
91-166-012 Silvery Santa 975QXM5679	Keepsake	Yr.Iss.	9.75	20-23.00
91-166-013 Heavenly Minstrel 975QXM5687	Keepsake	Yr.Iss.	9.75	21-31.00
91-166-014 Tiny Tea Party Set of 6 2900QXM5827	Keepsake	Yr.Iss.	29.00	140.00
91-166-015 Special Friends 850QXM5797	Keepsake	Yr.Iss.	8.50	15-19.50
91-166-016 Mom 600QXM5699	Keepsake	Yr.Iss.	6.00	16-27.00
91-166-017 Baby's First Christmas 600QXM5799	Keepsake	Yr.Iss.	6.00	17.00
91-166-018 Our First Christmas Together 600QXM5819	Keepsake	Yr.Iss.	6.00	16.50
91-166-019 Key to Love 450QXM5689	Keepsake	Yr.Iss.	4.50	16-19.50
91-166-020 Grandchild's First Christmas 450QXM5697	Keepsake	Yr.Iss.	4.50	11.00
91-166-021 Treeland Trio 850QXM5899	Keepsake	Yr.Iss.	8.50	16-19.50
91-166-022 Wee Toymaker 850QXM5967	Keepsake	Yr.Iss.	8.50	17.50
91-166-023 Feliz Navidad 600QXM5887	Keepsake	Yr.Iss.	6.00	13-23.00
91-166-024 Top Hatter 600QXM5889	Keepsake	Yr.Iss.	6.00	16-26.00
91-166-025 Upbeat Bear 600QXM5907	Keepsake	Yr.Iss.	6.00	15-20.00
91-166-026 Friendly Fawn 600QXM5947	Keepsake	Yr.Iss.	6.00	17-20.00
91-166-027 Caring Shepherd 600QXM5949	Keepsake	Yr.Iss.	6.00	16-19.50
91-166-028 Cardinal Cameo 600QXM5957	Keepsake	Yr.Iss.	6.00	16-26.00
91-166-029 Courier Turtle 450QXM5857	Keepsake	Yr.Iss.	4.50	13-17.50
91-166-030 Fly By 450QXM5859	Keepsake	Yr.Iss.	4.50	16-19.50
91-166-031 Love Is Born 600QXM5959	Keepsake	Yr.Iss.	6.00	17-19.50
91-166-032 Cool 'n' Sweet 450QXM5867	Keepsake	Yr.Iss.	4.50	15-23.00
91-166-033 All Aboard 450QXM5869	Keepsake	Yr.Iss.	4.50	16-19.50
91-166-034 Bright Boxers 450QXM5877	Keepsake	Yr.Iss.	4.50	17.50

	ARTIST	EDITION	ISSUE	QUOTE
91-166-035 Li'l Popper 450QXM5897	Keepsake	Yr.Iss.	4.50	15-20.00
91-166-036 Kitty in a Mitty 450QXM5879	Keepsake	Yr.Iss.	4.50	14.50
91-166-037 Seaside Otter 450QXM5909	Keepsake	Yr.Iss.	4.50	11-14.50
91-166-038 Fancy Wreath 450QXM5917	Keepsake	Yr.Iss.	4.50	13-17.50
91-166-039 N. Pole Buddy 450QXM5927	Keepsake	Yr.Iss.	4.50	17-22.50
91-166-040 Vision of Santa 450QXM5937	Keepsake	Yr.Iss.	4.50	13-23.00
91-166-041 Busy Bear 450QXM5939	Keepsake	Yr.Iss.	4.50	12.50
91-166-042 Country Sleigh 450QXM5999	Keepsake	Yr.Iss.	4.50	10-15.00
91-166-043 Brass Church 300QXM5979	Keepsake	Yr.Iss.	3.00	9-19.00
91-166-044 Brass Soldier 300QXM5987	Keepsake	Yr.Iss.	3.00	9.50
91-166-045 Noel 300QXM5989	Keepsake	Yr.Iss.	3.00	12.50
91-166-046 Holiday Snowflake 300QXM5997	Keepsake	Yr.Iss.	3.00	12.50

Hallmark Keepsake Ornaments 1991 Club Limited Editions

91-167-001 Secrets for Santa 2375QXC4797	Keepsake	28,700	23.75	50.00
91-167-002 Galloping Into Christmas 1975QXC4779	Keepsake	28,400	19.75	58.00

Hallmark Keepsake Ornaments 1991 Keepsake Collector's Club

91-168-001 Hidden Treasure/Li'l Keeper 1500QXC4769	Keepsake	Yr.Iss.	15.00	36.00
91-168-002 Beary Artistic 1000QXC7259	Keepsake	Yr.Iss.	10.00	31.00

Hallmark Keepsake Ornaments 1992 Collectible Series

92-169-001 Tobin Fraley Carousel-First Ed. 2800QX4891	Keepsake	Yr.Iss.	28.00	30-75.00
92-169-002 Owliver-First Ed. 775QX4544	Keepsake	Yr.Iss.	7.75	15-19.50
92-169-003 Betsey's Country Christmas-First Ed. 500QX2104	Keepsake	Yr.Iss.	5.00	12-30.00
92-169-004 1966 Mustang-Second Ed. 1275QX4284	Keepsake	Yr.Iss.	12.75	25-45.00
92-169-005 Peace On Earth-Spain Second Ed. 1175QX5174	Keepsake	Yr.Iss.	11.75	20-25.00
92-169-006 Heavenly Angels-Second Ed.775QX4454	Keepsake	Yr.Iss.	7.75	17.50
92-169-007 Puppy Love-Second Ed. 775QX4484	Keepsake	Yr.Iss.	7.75	42.00
92-169-008 Merry Olde Santa-Third Ed. 1475QX4414	Keepsake	Yr.Iss.	14.75	35.00
92-169-009 Heart of Christmas-Third Ed. 1375QX4411	Keepsake	Yr.Iss.	13.75	18-31.00
92-169-010 Fabulous Decade-Third Ed. 775QX4244	Keepsake	Yr.Iss.	7.75	35.00
92-169-011 CRAYOLA CRAYON-Bright Colors Fourth Ed. 975QX4264	Keepsake	Yr.Iss.	9.75	27.00
92-169-012 The Gift Bringers-Kolyada Fourth Ed. 500QX2124	Keepsake	Yr.Iss.	5.00	13.00
92-169-013 Mary's Angels-Lily Fifth Ed. 675QX4274	Keepsake	Yr.Iss.	6.75	45-49.50
92-169-014 Gift Exchange Seventh Ed. 1475QX4294	Keepsake	Yr.Iss.	14.75	30.00
92-169-015 Reindeer Champs-Donder Seventh Ed. 875QX5284	Keepsake	Yr.Iss.	8.75	15-25.00
92-169-016 Five-and-Ten-Cent Store Ninth Ed. 1475QX4254	Keepsake	Yr.Iss.	14.75	27.00
92-169-017 Nine Ladies Dancing Ninth Ed. 675QX3031	Keepsake	Yr.Iss.	6.75	18.00
92-169-018 Rocking Horse Twelfth Ed. 1075QX4261	Keepsake	Yr.Iss.	10.75	23.00
92-169-019 Frosty Friends Thirteenth Ed. 975QX4291	Keepsake	Yr.Iss.	9.75	21.00
92-169-020 Kringle Tours Fourteenth Ed. 1475QX4341	Keepsake	Yr.Iss.	14.75	20-27.00
92-169-021 Greatest Story Third Ed. 1275QX4251	Keepsake	Yr.Iss.	12.75	24.00
92-169-022 Winter Surprise Fourth Ed. 1175QX4271	Keepsake	Yr.Iss.	11.75	27-33.00
92-169-023 Hark! It's Herald Fourth Ed. 775QX4464	Keepsake	Yr.Iss.	7.75	17.50
92-169-024 Sweet Holiday Harmony Sixth Ed. 875QX4461	Keepsake	Yr.Iss.	8.75	18.50

Hallmark Keepsake Ornaments 1992 Artists' Favorites

92-170-001 Mother Goose 1375QX4984	Keepsake	Yr.Iss.	13.75	30.00
92-170-002 Elfin Marionette1175QX5931	Keepsake	Yr.Iss.	11.75	11.75
92-170-003 Polar Post 875QX4914	Keepsake	Yr.Iss.	8.75	8.75
92-170-004 Turtle Dreams 875QX4991	Keepsake	Yr.Iss.	8.75	13.50
92-170-005 Uncle Art's Ice Cream 875QX5001	Keepsake	Yr.Iss.	8.75	8.75
92-170-006 Stocked With Joy 775QX5934	Keepsake	Yr.Iss.	7.75	7.75

Hallmark Keepsake Ornaments 1992 Special Edition

92-171-001 Dickens Caroler Bell-Lord Chadwick Third Ed. 2175QX4554	Keepsake	Yr.Iss.	21.75	44.00

Hallmark Keepsake Ornaments 1992 Commemoratives

92-172-001 Baby's First Christmas1875QX4581	Keepsake	Yr.Iss.	18.75	32-40.00
92-172-002 Baby's First Christmas 775QX4641	Keepsake	Yr.Iss.	7.75	15-18.00
92-172-003 Baby's First Christmas-Baby Girl 475QX2204	Keepsake	Yr.Iss.	4.75	9-12.00
92-172-004 Baby's First Christmas-Baby Boy 475QX2191	Keepsake	Yr.Iss.	4.75	12.00
92-172-005 For My Grandma 775QX5184	Keepsake	Yr.Iss.	7.75	14.00
92-172-006 A Child's Christmas 975QX4574	Keepsake	Yr.Iss.	9.75	15-18.00
92-172-007 Grandson's First Christmas 675QX4621	Keepsake	Yr.Iss.	6.75	6.75
92-172-008 Grandaughter's First Christmas 675QX4634	Keepsake	Yr.Iss.	6.75	6.75
92-172-009 Mom-to-Be 675QX4614	Keepsake	Yr.Iss.	6.75	16.00
92-172-010 Dad-to-Be 675QX4611	Keepsake	Yr.Iss.	6.75	16.00
92-172-011 Baby's First Christmas 775QX4644	Keepsake	Yr.Iss.	7.75	17.00
92-172-012 Baby's Second Christmas 675QX4651	Keepsake	Yr.Iss.	6.75	15.00
92-172-013 Child's Third Christmas 675QX4654	Keepsake	Yr.Iss.	6.75	13-18.00
92-172-014 Child's Fourth Christmas 675QX4661	Keepsake	Yr.Iss.	6.75	19.00
92-172-015 Child's Fifth Christmas 675QX4664	Keepsake	Yr.Iss.	6.75	14.00
92-172-016 For The One I Love 975QX4884	Keepsake	Yr.Iss.	9.75	9.75
92-172-017 Our First Christmas Together 975QX5061	Keepsake	Yr.Iss.	9.75	22.00
92-172-018 Out First Christmas Together 875QX4694	Keepsake	Yr.Iss.	8.75	17.50
92-172-019 Our First Christmas Together 675QX3011	Keepsake	Yr.Iss.	6.75	17.50
92-172-020 Love To Skate 875QX4841	Keepsake	Yr.Iss.	8.75	16.00
92-172-021 Anniversary Year 975QX4851	Keepsake	Yr.Iss.	9.75	17.50
92-172-022 Dad 775QX4674	Keepsake	Yr.Iss.	7.75	16.50
92-172-023 Mom 775QX5164	Keepsake	Yr.Iss.	7.75	17.50
92-172-024 Brother 675QX4684	Keepsake	Yr.Iss.	6.75	13-15.00
92-172-025 Sister 675QX4681	Keepsake	Yr.Iss.	6.75	10-15.00
92-172-026 Son 675QX5024	Keepsake	Yr.Iss.	6.75	10-15.00
92-172-027 Daughter 675QX5031	Keepsake	Yr.Iss.	6.75	12-16.00
92-172-028 Mom and Dad 975QX4671	Keepsake	Yr.Iss.	9.75	33-36.00
92-172-029 Grandparents 475QX2004	Keepsake	Yr.Iss.	4.75	4.75
92-172-030 Grandmother 475QX2011	Keepsake	Yr.Iss.	4.75	4.75
92-172-031 Godchild 675QX5941	Keepsake	Yr.Iss.	6.75	17.50
92-172-032 Grandaughter 675QX5604	Keepsake	Yr.Iss.	6.75	13.00
92-172-033 Grandson 675QX5611	Keepsake	Yr.Iss.	6.75	15.00
92-172-034 Friendship Line 975QX5034	Keepsake	Yr.Iss.	9.75	26.50
92-172-035 Friendly Greetings 775QX5041	Keepsake	Yr.Iss.	7.75	7.75
92-172-036 New Home 875QX5191	Keepsake	Yr.Iss.	8.75	15-19.50
92-172-037 Across the Miles 675QX3044	Keepsake	Yr.Iss.	6.75	6.75
92-172-038 From Our Home To yours 475QX2131	Keepsake	Yr.Iss.	4.75	4.75
92-172-039 Secret Pal 775QX5424	Keepsake	Yr.Iss.	7.75	8.00
92-172-040 Teacher 475QX2264	Keepsake	Yr.Iss.	4.75	4.75
92-172-041 World-Class Teacher 775QX5054	Keepsake	Yr.Iss.	7.75	7.75
92-172-042 V. P. of Important Stuff 675QX5051	Keepsake	Yr.Iss.	6.75	12.00

	ARTIST	EDITION	ISSUE	QUOTE
92-172-043 Holiday Memo 775QX5044	Keepsake	Yr.Iss.	7.75	14.00
92-172-044 Special Dog 775QX5421	Keepsake	Yr.Iss.	7.75	27.50
92-172-045 Special Cat 775QX5414	Keepsake	Yr.Iss.	7.75	14-27.50

Hallmark Keepsake Ornaments 1992 New Attractions

92-173-001 Eric the Baker 875QX5244	Keepsake	Yr.Iss.	8.75	8.75
92-173-002 Otto the Carpenter 875QX5254	Keepsake	Yr.Iss.	8.75	8.75
92-173-003 Max the Tailor 875QX5251	Keepsake	Yr.Iss.	8.75	8.75
92-173-004 Franz the Artist 875QX5261	Keepsake	Yr.Iss.	8.75	8.75
92-173-005 Freida the Animals' Friend 875QX5264	Keepsake	Yr.Iss.	8.75	8.75
92-173-006 Ludwig the Musician 875QX5281	Keepsake	Yr.Iss.	8.75	8.75
92-173-007 Silver Star 2800QX5324	Keepsake	Yr.Iss.	28.00	48-59.50
92-173-008 Locomotive 975QX5311	Keepsake	Yr.Iss.	9.75	58.00
92-173-009 Coal Car 975QX5401	Keepsake	Yr.Iss.	9.75	18.00
92-173-010 Stock Car 975QX5314	Keepsake	Yr.Iss.	9.75	18.00
92-173-011 Caboose 975QX5321	Keepsake	Yr.Iss.	9.75	18.00
92-173-012 Gone Wishin' 875QX5171	Keepsake	Yr.Iss.	8.75	18-22.00
92-173-013 Skiing 'Round 875QX5214	Keepsake	Yr.Iss.	8.75	17.50
92-173-014 North Pole Fire Fighter 975QX5104	Keepsake	Yr.Iss.	9.75	20-30.00
92-173-015 Rapid Delivery 875QX5094	Keepsake	Yr.Iss.	8.75	19.50
92-173-016 Green Thumb Santa 775QX5101	Keepsake	Yr.Iss.	7.75	15.00
92-173-017 Golf's a Ball 675QX5984	Keepsake	Yr.Iss.	6.75	26.50
92-173-018 A Santa-Full! 975QX5991	Keepsake	Yr.Iss.	9.75	28-40.00
92-173-019 Tasty Christmas 975QX5994	Keepsake	Yr.Iss.	9.75	15-18.50
92-173-020 Santa's Roundup 875QX5084	Keepsake	Yr.Iss.	8.75	8.75-19
92-173-021 Deck the Hogs 875QX5204	Keepsake	Yr.Iss.	8.75	21.50
92-173-022 Patridge In a Pear Tree 875QX5234	Keepsake	Yr.Iss.	8.75	17.50
92-173-023 Spirit of Christmas Stress 875QX5231	Keepsake	Yr.Iss.	8.75	12-20.00
92-173-024 Please Pause Here 1475QX5291	Keepsake	Yr.Iss.	14.75	30-35.00
92-173-025 SNOOPYr and WOODSTOCK 875QX5954	Keepsake	Yr.Iss.	8.75	18.50
92-173-026 Mary Engelbreit Santa Jolly Wolly 775QX5224	Keepsake	Yr.Iss.	7.75	7.75
92-173-027 GARFIELD 775QX5374	Keepsake	Yr.Iss.	7.75	16.50
92-173-028 Norman Rockwell Art 500QX2224	Keepsake	Yr.Iss.	5.00	16.00
92-173-029 PEANUTSr 500QX2244	Keepsake	Yr.Iss.	5.00	30.00
92-173-030 Owl 975QX5614	Keepsake	Yr.Iss.	9.75	25-30.00
92-173-031 Santa Maria 1275QX5074	Keepsake	Yr.Iss.	12.75	27.00
92-173-032 Fun on a Big Scale 1075QX5134	Keepsake	Yr.Iss.	10.75	21.00
92-173-033 Genius at Work 1075QX5371	Keepsake	Yr.Iss.	10.75	20.00
92-173-034 Hello-Ho-Ho 975QX5141	Keepsake	Yr.Iss.	9.75	14.50
92-173-035 Cheerful Santa 975QX5154	Keepsake	Yr.Iss.	9.75	25-35.00
92-173-036 Memories to Cherish 1075QX5161	Keepsake	Yr.Iss.	10.75	20.00
92-173-037 Tread Bear 875QX5091	Keepsake	Yr.Iss.	8.75	22.00
92-173-038 Merry "Swiss" Mouse 775QX5114	Keepsake	Yr.Iss.	7.75	14.00
92-173-039 Honest George 775QX5064	Keepsake	Yr.Iss.	7.75	16.00
92-173-040 Bear Bell Champ 775QX5071	Keepsake	Yr.Iss.	7.75	14.00
92-173-041 Egg Nog Nest 775QX5121	Keepsake	Yr.Iss.	7.75	14.00
92-173-042 Jesus Loves Me 775QX3024	Keepsake	Yr.Iss.	7.75	14.00
92-173-043 Loving Shepherd 775QX5151	Keepsake	Yr.Iss.	7.75	14.00
92-173-044 Toboggan Tail 775QX5459	Keepsake	Yr.Iss.	7.75	15.00
92-173-045 Down-Under Holiday 775QX5144	Keepsake	Yr.Iss.	7.75	18.00
92-173-046 Holiday Wishes 775QX5131	Keepsake	Yr.Iss.	7.75	16.00
92-173-047 Feliz Navidad 675QX5181	Keepsake	Yr.Iss.	6.75	9-16.00
92-173-048 Holiday Teatime 1475QX5431	Keepsake	Yr.Iss.	14.75	29.50
92-173-049 Santa's Hook Shot 1275QX5434	Keepsake	Yr.Iss.	12.75	29.50
92-173-050 Cool Fliers 1075QX5474	Keepsake	Yr.Iss.	10.75	19.50
92-173-051 Elvis 1495QX562-4	Keepsake	Yr.Iss.	14.95	30.00

Hallmark Keepsake Ornaments 1992 Magic Ornaments

92-174-001 PEANUTS-Second Ed. 1800QLX7214	Keepsake	Yr.Iss.	18.00	51-55.00
92-174-002 Forest Frolics-Fourth Ed. 2800QLX7254	Keepsake	Yr.Iss.	28.00	50-60.00
92-174-003 Chris Mouse Tales-Eighth Ed. 1200QLX7074	Keepsake	Yr.Iss.	12.00	25.00
92-174-004 Santa Special 4,000QLX7167	Keepsake	Yr.Iss.	40.00	80.00
92-174-005 Continental Express 3200QLX7264	Keepsake	Yr.Iss.	32.00	58.50
92-174-006 Look! It's Santa 1400QLX7094	Keepsake	Yr.Iss.	14.00	32.00
92-174-007 The Dancing Nutcracker 3,000QLX7261	Keepsake	Yr.Iss.	30.00	52-60.00
92-174-008 Enchanted Clock 3,000QLX7274	Keepsake	Yr.Iss.	30.00	55.00
92-174-009 Christmas Parade 3,000QLX7271	Keepsake	Yr.Iss.	30.00	54.00
92-174-010 Good Sledding Ahead 2800QLX7244	Keepsake	Yr.Iss.	28.00	52-57.50
92-174-011 Yuletide Rider 2800QLX7314	Keepsake	Yr.Iss.	28.00	52-58.00
92-174-012 Santa's Answering Machine 2200QLX7241	Keepsake	Yr.Iss.	22.00	40.50
92-174-013 Baby's First Christmas 2200QLX7281	Keepsake	Yr.Iss.	22.00	85-95.00
92-174-014 Out First Christmas Together 2000QLX7221	Keepsake	Yr.Iss.	20.00	38-50.00
92-174-015 Santa Sub 1800QLX7321	Keepsake	Yr.Iss.	18.00	34-40.00
92-174-016 Lighting the Way 1800QLX7231	Keepsake	Yr.Iss.	18.00	38.00
92-174-017 Under Construction 1800QLX7324	Keepsake	Yr.Iss.	18.00	36-42.00
92-174-018 Feathered Friends 1400QLX7091	Keepsake	Yr.Iss.	14.00	24.00
92-174-019 Watch Owls 1200QLX7084	Keepsake	Yr.Iss.	12.00	24.00
92-174-020 Nut Sweet Nut 1000QLX7081	Keepsake	Yr.Iss.	10.00	21.00
92-174-021 Angel Of Light 3000QLT7239	Keepsake	Yr.Iss.	30.00	30.00
92-174-022 Shuttlecraft Galileo 2400QLX733-1	Keepsake	Yr.Iss.	24.00	25-42.50

Hallmark Keepsake Ornaments 1992 Miniature Ornaments

92-175-001 The Night Before Christmas 1375QXM5541	Keepsake	Yr.Iss.	13.75	25-34.50
92-175-002 The Bearymores-First Ed. 575QXM5544	Keepsake	Yr.Iss.	5.75	16.50
92-175-003 Woodland Babies-Second Ed. 600QXM5444	Keepsake	Yr.Iss.	6.00	13.50
92-175-004 Thimble Bells-Third Ed. 600QXM5461	Keepsake	Yr.Iss.	6.00	17.50
92-175-005 Nature's Angels-Third Ed. 450QXM5451	Keepsake	Yr.Iss.	4.50	18.00
92-175-006 Box Car-Fourth Ed/Noel R.R. 700QXM5441	Keepsake	Yr.Iss.	7.00	18.00
92-175-007 The Kringles-Fourth Ed. 600QXM5381	Keepsake	Yr.Iss.	6.00	16.00
92-175-008 Church-Fifth Ed./Old English V. 700QXM5384	Keepsake	Yr.Iss.	7.00	20.50
92-175-009 Rocking Horse-Fifth Ed. 450QXM5454	Keepsake	Yr.Iss.	4.50	13.50
92-175-010 Kittens in Toyland-Fifth Ed. 450QXM5391	Keepsake	Yr.Iss.	4.50	14.00
92-175-011 Feeding Time 575QXM5481	Keepsake	Yr.Iss.	5.75	16.00
92-175-012 Black-Capped Chickadee 300QXM5484	Keepsake	Yr.Iss.	3.00	6.00
92-175-013 Holiday Holly 975QXM5364	Keepsake	Yr.Iss.	9.75	19.00
92-175-014 Harmony Trio-Set of Three 1175QXM5471	Keepsake	Yr.Iss.	11.75	23.75
92-175-015 Grandchild's First Christmas 575QXM5501	Keepsake	Yr.Iss.	5.75	12.00
92-175-016 Baby's First Christmas 450QXM5494	Keepsake	Yr.Iss.	4.50	16.00
92-175-017 Mom 450QXM5504	Keepsake	Yr.Iss.	4.50	12.00
92-175-018 Grandma 450QXM5514	Keepsake	Yr.Iss.	4.50	4.50
92-175-019 Friends Are Tops 450QXM5521	Keepsake	Yr.Iss.	4.50	9.00
92-175-020 A+ Teacher 375QXM5511	Keepsake	Yr.Iss.	3.75	3.75
92-175-021 Inside Story 725QXM5881	Keepsake	Yr.Iss.	7.30	14.50
92-175-022 Holiday Splash 575QXM5834	Keepsake	Yr.Iss.	5.75	11.50
92-175-023 Christmas Copter 575QXM5844	Keepsake	Yr.Iss.	5.75	14.00
92-175-024 Coca-Cola Santa 575QXM5884	Keepsake	Yr.Iss.	5.75	10-15.00

	ARTIST	EDITION	ISSUE	QUOTE
92-175-025 Wee Three Kings 575QXM5531	Keepsake	Yr.Iss.	5.75	13.00
92-175-026 Angelic Harpist 450QXM5524	Keepsake	Yr.Iss.	4.50	12.00
92-175-027 Polar Polka 450QXM5534	Keepsake	Yr.Iss.	4.50	13.50
92-175-028 Buck-A-Roo 450QXM5814	Keepsake	Yr.Iss.	4.50	9.50
92-175-029 Ski For Two 450QXM5821	Keepsake	Yr.Iss.	4.50	4.50
92-175-030 Hoop It Up 450QXM5831	Keepsake	Yr.Iss.	4.50	10.00
92-175-031 Visions Of Acorns 450QXM5851	Keepsake	Yr.Iss.	4.50	4.50
92-175-032 Friendly Tin Soldier 450QXM5874	Keepsake	Yr.Iss.	4.50	10.00
92-175-033 Bright Stringers 375QXM5841	Keepsake	Yr.Iss.	3.75	13.00
92-175-034 Fast Finish 375QXM5301	Keepsake	Yr.Iss.	3.75	11.50
92-175-035 Cozy Kayak 375QXM5551	Keepsake	Yr.Iss.	3.75	6.00
92-175-036 Snug Kitty 375QXM5554	Keepsake	Yr.Iss.	3.75	13.00
92-175-037 Snowshoe Bunny 375QXM5564	Keepsake	Yr.Iss.	3.75	3.75
92-175-038 Gerbil Inc. 375QXM5924	Keepsake	Yr.Iss.	3.75	3.75
92-175-039 Hickory, Dickory, Dock 375QXM5861	Keepsake	Yr.Iss.	3.75	12.00
92-175-040 Going Places 375QXM5871	Keepsake	Yr.Iss.	3.75	9.00
92-175-041 Minted For Santa 375QXM5854	Keepsake	Yr.Iss.	3.75	13.00
92-175-042 Cool Uncle Sam 300QXM5561	Keepsake	Yr.Iss.	3.00	13.50
92-175-043 Perfect Balance 300QXM5571	Keepsake	Yr.Iss.	3.00	12.50
92-175-044 Puppet Show 300QXM5574	Keepsake	Yr.Iss.	3.00	3.00
92-175-045 Christmas Bonus 300QXM5811	Keepsake	Yr.Iss.	3.00	7.00
92-175-046 Spunky Monkey 300QXM5921	Keepsake	Yr.Iss.	3.00	12.00
92-175-047 Little Town of Bethlehem 300QXM5864	Keepsake	Yr.Iss.	3.00	15.00
92-175-048 Sew Sew Tiny (set of 6) 2900QXM5794	Keepsake	Yr.Iss.	29.00	49.50
Hallmark Keepsake Ornaments 1992 Easter Ornaments				
92-176-001 Easter Parade-First Ed. 675QEO8301	Keepsake	Yr.Iss.	6.75	24.00
92-176-002 Egg in Sports-First Ed. 675QEO9341	Keepsake	Yr.Iss.	6.75	28.50
Hallmark Keepsake Ornaments 1992 Collectors' Club				
92-176-001 Santa's Club List 1500QXC7291	Keepsake	Yr.Iss.	15.00	35.50
92-176-002 Rodney Takes Flight 975QXC5081	Keepsake	Yr.Iss.	9.75	22.00
92-176-003 Chipmunk Parcel Service 675QXC5194	Keepsake	Yr.Iss.	6.75	20.50
Hallmark Keepsake Ornaments 1992 Limited Edition Ornaments				
92-177-001 Victorian Skater (w/ base) 2500QXC4067	Keepsake	14,700	25.00	35.00
92-177-002 Christmas Treasures 2200QXC5464	Keepsake	15,500	22.00	22.00
Hallmark Keepsake Ornaments 1993 Anniversary Edition				
93-178-001 Tannenbaum's Dept. Store 2600QX5612	Keepsake	Yr.Iss.	26.00	54-60.00
93-178-002 Shopping With Santa 2400QX5675	Keepsake	Yr.Iss.	24.00	45-50.00
93-178-003 Frosty Friends 2,000QX5682	Keepsake	Yr.Iss.	20.00	40-50.00
93-178-004 Glowing Pewter Wreath 1875QX5302	Keepsake	Yr.Iss.	18.75	35.50
Hallmark Keepsake Ornaments 1993 Collectible Series				
93-179-001 Humpty-Dumpty-First Ed. 1375QX5282	Keepsake	Yr.Iss.	13.75	27.50
93-179-002 U.S. Christmas Stamps-First Ed. 1075QX5292	Keepsake	Yr.Iss.	10.75	20.00
93-179-003 Peanuts-First Ed. 975QX5315	Keepsake	Yr.Iss.	9.75	35-47.00
93-179-004 Tobin Fraley Carousel-Second Ed. 2800QX5502	Keepsake	Yr.Iss.	28.00	40.50
93-179-005 Owliver-Second Ed. 775QX5425	Keepsake	Yr.Iss.	7.75	16.00
93-179-006 Betsey's Country Christmas-Second Ed. 500QX2062	Keepsake	Yr.Iss.	5.00	10.00
93-179-007 1956 Ford Thunderbird-Third Ed. 1275QX5275	Keepsake	Yr.Iss.	12.75	25.00
93-179-008 Puppy Love-Third Ed. 775QX5045	Keepsake	Yr.Iss.	7.75	23-28.00
93-179-009 Heart Of Christmas-Fourth Ed. 1475QX4482	Keepsake	Yr.Iss.	14.75	26.50
93-179-010 Merry Olde Santa-Fourth Ed. 1475QX4842	Keepsake	Yr.Iss.	14.75	30.00
93-179-011 Fabulous Decade-Fouth Ed. 775QX4475	Keepsake	Yr.Iss.	7.75	16.50
93-179-012 CRAYOLA CRAYON-Bright Shining Castle Fifth Ed. 1075QX4422	Keepsake	Yr.Iss.	11.00	18-26.00
93-179-013 Mary's Angels-Ivy-Sixth Ed. 675QX4282	Keepsake	Yr.Iss.	6.75	15.00
93-179-014 A Fitting Moment-Eighth Ed. 1475QX4202	Keepsake	Yr.Iss.	14.75	26.50
93-179-015 Cozy Home-Tenth Ed. 1475QX4175	Keepsake	Yr.Iss.	14.75	18-35.00
93-179-016 Ten Lords A-Leaping-Tenth Ed. 675QX3012	Keepsake	Yr.Iss.	6.75	15.00
93-179-017 Rocking Horse-13th Ed. 1075QX4162	Keepsake	Yr.Iss.	10.75	26.50
93-179-018 Frosty Friends-14th Ed. 975QX4142	Keepsake	Yr.Iss.	9.75	25.00
93-179-019 Happy Haul-idays-15th Ed. 1475QX4102	Keepsake	Yr.Iss.	14.75	26-30.00
93-179-020 Peace On Earth-Poland-Third Ed. 1175QX5242	Keepsake	Yr.Iss.	11.75	20.50
93-179-021 Heavenly Angels-Third Ed. 775QX4945	Keepsake	Yr.Iss.	7.75	10-18.00
93-179-022 The Gift Bringers-The Magi-Fifth Ed. 500QX2065	Keepsake	Yr.Iss.	5.00	16.00
93-179-023 Reindeer Champs-Blitzen-Eighth Ed. 875QX4331	Keepsake	Yr.Iss.	8.75	20.50
93-179-024 Barbie 1475QX5725	Keepsake	Yr.Iss.	14.75	40-80.00
Hallmark Keepsake Ornaments 1993 Artists' Favorites				
93-180-001 On Her Toes 875QX5265	Keepsake	Yr.Iss.	8.75	15-18.00
93-180-002 Wake-Up Call 875QX5262	Keepsake	Yr.Iss.	8.75	18.00
93-180-003 Howling Good Time 975QX5255	Keepsake	Yr.Iss.	9.75	15-18.00
93-180-004 Bird Watcher 975QX5252	Keepsake	Yr.Iss.	9.75	15.00
93-180-005 Peek-a-Boo Tree 1075QX5245	Keepsake	Yr.Iss.	10.75	21.50
Hallmark Keepsake Ornaments 1993 Special Editions				
93-181-001 Julianne and Teddy 2175QX5295	Keepsake	Yr.Iss.	21.75	35.00
93-181-002 Dickens Caroler Bell-Lady Daphne-Fourth Ed. 2175QX5505	Keepsake	Yr.Iss.	21.75	21.75
Hallmark Keepsake Ornaments 1993 Commemoratives				
93-182-001 Baby's First Christmas 1875QX5512	Keepsake	Yr.Iss.	18.75	27-40.00
93-182-002 Baby's First Christmas 1075QX5515	Keepsake	Yr.Iss.	10.75	17.50
93-182-003 Baby's First Christmas-Baby Girl 475QX2092	Keepsake	Yr.Iss.	4.75	4.75
93-182-004 Baby's First Christmas-Baby Boy 475QX2105	Keepsake	Yr.Iss.	4.75	4.75
93-182-005 Baby's First Christmas 775QX5522	Keepsake	Yr.Iss.	7.75	17.50
93-182-006 A Child's Christmas 975QX5882	Keepsake	Yr.Iss.	9.75	20.00
93-182-007 Grandchild's First Christmas 675QX5552	Keepsake	Yr.Iss.	6.75	13.00
93-182-008 To My Grandma 775QX5555	Keepsake	Yr.Iss.	7.75	7.75
93-182-009 Mom-to-Be 675QX5535	Keepsake	Yr.Iss.	6.75	14.00
93-182-010 Dad-to-Be 675QX5532	Keepsake	Yr.Iss.	6.75	10-16.00
93-182-011 Baby's First Christmas 775QX5525	Keepsake	Yr.Iss.	7.75	15.00
93-182-012 Baby's Second Christmas 675QX5992	Keepsake	Yr.Iss.	6.75	15.00
93-182-013 Child's Third Christmas 675QX5995	Keepsake	Yr.Iss.	6.75	10-15.00
93-182-014 Child's Fourth Christmas 675QX5215	Keepsake	Yr.Iss.	6.75	10-15.00
93-182-015 Child's Fifth Christmas 675QX5222	Keepsake	Yr.Iss.	6.75	10-16.00
93-182-016 Our First Christmas Together 1875QX5955	Keepsake	Yr.Iss.	18.75	30-34.00
93-182-017 Our First Christmas Together 975QX5642	Keepsake	Yr.Iss.	9.75	17.00
93-182-018 Our First Christmas Together 875QX5952	Keepsake	Yr.Iss.	8.75	15.00
93-182-019 Our First Christmas Together 675QX3015	Keepsake	Yr.Iss.	6.75	12.00
93-182-020 Our Christmas Together 1075QX5942	Keepsake	Yr.Iss.	10.75	20.50

	ARTIST	EDITION	ISSUE	QUOTE
93-182-021 Strange and Wonderful Love 875QX5965	Keepsake	Yr.Iss.	8.75	16.00
93-182-022 Anniversary Year 975QX5972	Keepsake	Yr.Iss.	9.75	17.50
93-182-023 Mom and Dad 975QX5845	Keepsake	Yr.Iss.	9.75	17.50
93-182-024 Dad 775QX5855	Keepsake	Yr.Iss.	7.75	10-17.00
93-182-025 Mom 775QX5852	Keepsake	Yr.Iss.	7.75	16.00
93-182-026 Son 675QX5865	Keepsake	Yr.Iss.	6.75	14.00
93-182-027 Daughter 675QX5872	Keepsake	Yr.Iss.	6.75	13.00
93-182-028 Brother 675QX5542	Keepsake	Yr.Iss.	6.75	13.00
93-182-029 Sister 675QX5545	Keepsake	Yr.Iss.	6.75	17.00
93-182-030 Sister to Sister 975QX5885	Keepsake	Yr.Iss.	9.75	25-50.00
93-182-031 Our Family 775QX5892	Keepsake	Yr.Iss.	7.75	16.00
93-182-032 Niece 675QX5732	Keepsake	Yr.Iss.	6.75	13.00
93-182-033 Nephew 675QX5735	Keepsake	Yr.Iss.	6.75	11.00
93-182-034 Grandparents 475QX2085	Keepsake	Yr.Iss.	4.75	4.75
93-182-035 Grandmother 675QX5665	Keepsake	Yr.Iss.	6.75	6.75
93-182-036 Granddaughter 675QX5635	Keepsake	Yr.Iss.	6.75	13.00
93-182-037 Grandson 675QX5632	Keepsake	Yr.Iss.	6.75	11.00
93-182-038 Godchild 875QX5875	Keepsake	Yr.Iss.	8.75	17.50
93-182-039 Special Cat 775QX5235	Keepsake	Yr.Iss.	7.75	14.00
93-182-040 Special Dog 775QX5962	Keepsake	Yr.Iss.	7.75	15.00
93-182-041 Warm and Special Friends 1075QX5895	Keepsake	Yr.Iss.	10.75	20.50
93-182-042 Across the Miles 875QX5912	Keepsake	Yr.Iss.	8.75	17.50
93-182-043 New Home 775QX5905	Keepsake	Yr.Iss.	7.75	30-35.00
93-182-044 Apple for Teacher 775QX5902	Keepsake	Yr.Iss.	7.75	7.75
93-182-045 Star Teacher 575QX5645	Keepsake	Yr.Iss.	5.75	13.00
93-182-046 Coach 675QX5935	Keepsake	Yr.Iss.	6.75	14.00
93-182-047 People Friendly 875QX5932	Keepsake	Yr.Iss.	8.75	16.00
93-182-048 Top Banana 775QX5925	Keepsake	Yr.Iss.	7.75	17.50
Hallmark Keepsake Ornaments 1993 New Attractions				
93-183-001 Sylvester and Tweety 975QX5405	Keepsake	Yr.Iss.	9.75	30.50
93-183-002 Bugs Bunny 875QX5412	Keepsake	Yr.Iss.	8.75	21.00
93-183-003 Elmer Fudd 875QX5495	Keepsake	Yr.Iss.	8.75	16.00
93-183-004 Porky Pig 875QX5652	Keepsake	Yr.Iss.	8.75	17.50
93-183-005 Winnie the Pooh 975QX5715	Keepsake	Yr.Iss.	9.75	20-26.00
93-183-006 Kanga and Roo 975QX5672	Keepsake	Yr.Iss.	9.75	17-20.00
93-183-007 Owl 975QX5695	Keepsake	Yr.Iss.	9.75	17.00
93-183-008 Rabbit 975QX5702	Keepsake	Yr.Iss.	9.75	17.00
93-183-009 Tigger and Piglet 975QX5705	Keepsake	Yr.Iss.	9.75	25-35.00
93-183-010 Eeyore 975QX5712	Keepsake	Yr.Iss.	9.75	17.50
93-183-011 Tin Hot Air Balloon 775QX5615	Keepsake	Yr.Iss.	7.75	15.00
93-183-012 Tin Airplane 775QX5622	Keepsake	Yr.Iss.	7.75	18-26.00
93-183-013 Tin Blimp 775QX5625	Keepsake	Yr.Iss.	7.75	15.00
93-183-014 Making Waves 975QX5775	Keepsake	Yr.Iss.	9.75	22.00
93-183-015 Putt-Putt Penguin 975QX5795	Keepsake	Yr.Iss.	9.75	17.50
93-183-016 Icicle Bicycle 975QX5835	Keepsake	Yr.Iss.	9.75	17.50
93-183-017 Big on Gardening 975QX5842	Keepsake	Yr.Iss.	9.75	17.50
93-183-018 Fills the Bill 875QX5572	Keepsake	Yr.Iss.	8.75	16.00
93-183-019 Perfect Match 875QX5772	Keepsake	Yr.Iss.	8.75	17.50
93-183-020 Home For Christmas 775QX5562	Keepsake	Yr.Iss.	7.75	15.00
93-183-021 Bowling For ZZZ's 775QX5565	Keepsake	Yr.Iss.	7.75	17.50
93-183-022 Dunkin' Roo 775QX5575	Keepsake	Yr.Iss.	7.75	15.00
93-183-023 Beary Gifted 775QX5762	Keepsake	Yr.Iss.	7.75	17.50
93-183-024 Snowbird 775QX5765	Keepsake	Yr.Iss.	7.75	7.75
93-183-025 Christmas Break 775QX5825	Keepsake	Yr.Iss.	7.75	15.50
93-183-026 Quick As A Fox 875QX5792	Keepsake	Yr.Iss.	8.75	16.00
93-183-027 Faithful Fire Fighter 775QX5782	Keepsake	Yr.Iss.	7.75	17.50
93-183-028 Caring Nurse 675QX5785	Keepsake	Yr.Iss.	6.75	17.50
93-183-029 Star Of Wonder 675QX5982	Keepsake	Yr.Iss.	6.75	35.00
93-183-030 He Is Born 975QX5362	Keepsake	Yr.Iss.	9.75	35.00
93-183-031 Water Bed Snooze 975QX5375	Keepsake	Yr.Iss.	9.75	20.50
93-183-032 Room For One More 875QX5382	Keepsake	Yr.Iss.	8.75	35-45.00
93-183-033 Maxine 875QX5385	Keepsake	Yr.Iss.	8.75	8.75
93-183-034 Superman 1275QX5752	Keepsake	Yr.Iss.	12.75	36-48.00
93-183-035 The Pink Panther 1275QX5755	Keepsake	Yr.Iss.	12.75	24.50
93-183-036 PEANUTS 500QX2072	Keepsake	Yr.Iss.	5.00	13.00
93-183-037 One-Elf Marching Band 1275QX5342	Keepsake	Yr.Iss.	12.75	25.00
93-183-038 Curly 'n' Kingly 1075QX5285	Keepsake	Yr.Iss.	10.75	18.50
93-183-039 That's Entertainment 875QX5345	Keepsake	Yr.Iss.	8.75	15.50
93-183-040 Big Roller 875QX5352	Keepsake	Yr.Iss.	8.75	16.00
93-183-041 Snow Bear Angel 775QX5355	Keepsake	Yr.Iss.	7.75	16.00
93-183-042 Playful Pals 1475QX5742	Keepsake	Yr.Iss.	14.75	27-30.00
93-183-043 Lou Rankin Polar Bear 975QX5745	Keepsake	Yr.Iss.	9.75	20.50
93-183-044 Mary Engelbreit 500QX2075	Keepsake	Yr.Iss.	5.00	9-13.00
93-183-045 Look For Wonder 1275QX5685	Keepsake	Yr.Iss.	12.75	25.00
93-183-046 Peep Inside 1375QX5322	Keepsake	Yr.Iss.	13.75	25.00
93-183-047 Silvery Noel 1275QX5305	Keepsake	Yr.Iss.	12.75	20.50
93-183-048 Snowy Hideaway 975QX5312	Keepsake	Yr.Iss.	9.75	15.50
93-183-049 Makin' Music 975QX5325	Keepsake	Yr.Iss.	9.75	17.50
93-183-050 Smile! It's Christmas 975QX5335	Keepsake	Yr.Iss.	9.75	17.50
93-183-051 High Top-Purr 875QX5332	Keepsake	Yr.Iss.	8.75	22.00
93-183-052 Feliz Navidad 875QX5365	Keepsake	Yr.Iss.	9.75	16.00
93-183-053 Ready For Fun 775QX5124	Keepsake	Yr.Iss.	7.75	16.00
93-183-054 Clever Cookie 775QX5662	Keepsake	Yr.Iss.	7.75	16.00
93-183-055 Little Drummer Boy 875QX5372	Keepsake	Yr.Iss.	8.75	17.50
93-183-056 Popping Good Times 1475QX5392	Keepsake	Yr.Iss.	14.75	26.50
93-183-057 The Swat Team 1275QX5395	Keepsake	Yr.Iss.	12.75	26.50
93-183-058 Great Connections 1075QX5402	Keepsake	Yr.Iss.	10.75	22.50
Hallmark Keepsake Ornaments 1993 Keepsake Magic Ornaments				
93-184-001 PEANUTS-Third Ed. 1800QLX7155	Keepsake	Yr.Iss.	18.00	36.00
93-184-002 Forest Frolics-Fifth Ed. 2500QLX7165	Keepsake	Yr.Iss.	25.00	48-53.00
93-184-003 Chris Mouse Flight-Ninth Ed. 1200QLX7152	Keepsake	Yr.Iss.	12.00	24-30.00
93-184-004 Road Runner and Wile E. Coyote 3000QLX7415	Keepsake	Yr.Iss.	30.00	68-75.00
93-184-005 Winnie The Pooh 2400QLX7422	Keepsake	Yr.Iss.	24.00	50.00
93-184-006 Home On The Range 3200QLX7395	Keepsake	Yr.Iss.	32.00	63.00
93-184-007 Santa's Workshop 2800QLX7375	Keepsake	Yr.Iss.	28.00	54.00
93-184-008 Last-Minute Shopping 2800QLX7385	Keepsake	Yr.Iss.	28.00	55.00
93-184-009 Bells Are Ringing 2800QLX7402	Keepsake	Yr.Iss.	28.00	40-60.00
93-184-010 Baby's First Christmas 2200QLX7365	Keepsake	Yr.Iss.	22.00	40.00
93-184-011 Our First Christmas Together 2,000QLX7355	Keepsake	Yr.Iss.	20.00	38.50
93-184-012 North Pole Merrython 2500QLX7392	Keepsake	Yr.Iss.	25.00	45-50.00
93-184-013 Song Of The Chimes 2500QLX7405	Keepsake	Yr.Iss.	25.00	50-55.00
93-184-014 Radio News Flash 2200QLX7362	Keepsake	Yr.Iss.	22.00	40.50
93-184-015 Dollhouse Dreams 2200QLX7372	Keepsake	Yr.Iss.	22.00	30-44.50
93-184-016 The Lamplighter 1800QLX7192	Keepsake	Yr.Iss.	18.00	36.00
93-184-017 Dog's Best Friend 1200QLX7172	Keepsake	Yr.Iss.	12.00	21.50
93-184-018 Santa's Snow-Getter 1800QLX7352	Keepsake	Yr.Iss.	18.00	36.00
93-184-019 Raiding The Fridge1600QLX7185	Keepsake	Yr.Iss.	16.00	31.50

	ARTIST	EDITION	ISSUE	QUOTE
Hallmark Keepsake Ornaments — 1993 Miniature Ornaments				
93-185-001 On The Road-First Ed. 575QXM4002	Keepsake	Yr.Iss.	5.75	13.00
93-185-002 March Of The Teddy Bears-First Ed. 500QX2403	Keepsake	Yr.Iss.	4.50	13.00
93-185-003 The Bearymores-Second Ed. 575QXM5125	Keepsake	Yr.Iss.	5.75	16.50
93-185-004 The Night Before Christmas-Second Ed. 4505QXM5115	Keepsake	Yr.Iss.	4.50	15.00
93-185-005 Nature's Angels-Fourth Ed. 450QXM5122	Keepsake	Yr.Iss.	4.50	11.50
93-185-006 Flatbed Car-Fifth Ed.700QXM5105	Keepsake	Yr.Iss.	7.00	14.50
93-185-007 Toy Shop-Sixth Ed. 700QXM5132	Keepsake	Yr.Iss.	7.00	14.50
93-185-008 Rocking Horse-Sixth Ed. 450QXM5112	Keepsake	Yr.Iss.	4.50	10.00
93-185-009 Woodland Babies-Third Ed. 575QXM5102	Keepsake	Yr.Iss.	5.75	13.00
93-185-010 The Kringles-Fifth Ed. 575QXM5135	Keepsake	Yr.Iss.	5.75	13.50
93-185-011 Thimble Bells-Fourth Ed. 575QXM5142	Keepsake	Yr.Iss.	5.75	13.50
93-185-012 Baby's First Christmas 575QXM5145	Keepsake	Yr.Iss.	5.75	15.00
93-185-013 Snuggle Birds 575QXM5182	Keepsake	Yr.Iss.	5.75	13.00
93-185-014 Mom 450QXM5155	Keepsake	Yr.Iss.	4.50	10.00
93-185-015 Grandma 450QXM5162	Keepsake	Yr.Iss.	4.50	11.50
93-185-016 Special Friends 450QXM5165	Keepsake	Yr.Iss.	4.50	9.00
93-185-017 Secret Pals 375QXM5172	Keepsake	Yr.Iss.	3.75	7.00
93-185-018 Tiny Green Thumbs, Set of 6, 2900QXM4032	Keepsake	Yr.Iss.	29.00	36.00
93-185-019 'Round The Mountain 725QXM4025	Keepsake	Yr.Iss.	7.25	16.00
93-185-020 Christmas Castle 575QXM4085	Keepsake	Yr.Iss.	5.75	12.50
93-185-021 Cloisonne Snowflake 975QXM4012	Keepsake	Yr.Iss.	9.75	17.50
93-185-022 Visions Of Sugarplums 725QXM4022	Keepsake	Yr.Iss.	7.25	15.00
93-185-023 Monkey Melody 575QXM4092	Keepsake	Yr.Iss.	5.75	12.00
93-185-024 Crystal Angel 975QXM4015	Keepsake	Yr.Iss.	9.75	52.00
93-185-025 Pull Out A Plum 575QXM4095	Keepsake	Yr.Iss.	5.75	11.50
93-185-026 Refreshing Flight 575QXM4112	Keepsake	Yr.Iss.	5.75	13.00
93-185-027 North Pole Fire Truck 475QXM4105	Keepsake	Yr.Iss.	4.75	10.00
93-185-028 Merry Mascot 375QXM4042	Keepsake	Yr.Iss.	3.75	8.50
93-185-029 Pear-Shaped Tones 375QXM4052	Keepsake	Yr.Iss.	3.75	7.00
93-185-030 I Dream Of Santa 375QXM4055	Keepsake	Yr.Iss.	3.75	9.00
93-185-031 Country Fiddling 375QXM4062	Keepsake	Yr.Iss.	3.75	9.00
93-185-032 Cheese Please 375QXM4072	Keepsake	Yr.Iss.	3.75	7.00
93-185-033 Ears To Pals 375QXM4075	Keepsake	Yr.Iss.	3.75	8.00
93-185-034 Into The Woods 375QXM4045	Keepsake	Yr.Iss.	3.75	7.00
93-185-035 Learning To Skate 300QXM4122	Keepsake	Yr.Iss.	3.00	8.00
93-185-036 Lighting A Path 300QXM4115	Keepsake	Yr.Iss.	3.00	8.00
Hallmark Keepsake Ornaments — 1993 Easter Ornaments				
93-186-001 Springtime Bonnets-First Ed. 775QEO8322	Keepsake	Yr.Iss.	7.75	18.00
93-186-002 Easter Parade-Second Ed. 675QEO8325	Keepsake	Yr.Iss.	6.75	16.00
93-186-003 Egg in Sports-Second Ed. 675QEO8332	Keepsake	Yr.Iss.	6.75	17.50
Hallmark Keepsake Ornaments — 1993 Keepsake Collector's Club				
93-186-001 Trimmed With Memories 1200QXC5432	Keepsake	Yr.Iss.	12.00	36.00
93-186-002 It's In The Mail 1000QXC5272	Keepsake	Yr.Iss.	10.00	20.00
Hallmark Keepsake Ornaments — 1993 Limited Edition Ornaments				
93-187-001 Sharing Christmas 2000QXC5435	Keepsake	16,500	20.00	41.00
93-187-002 Gentle Tidings 2500QXC5442	Keepsake	17,500	25.00	45.00
Hallmark Keepsake Ornaments — Showcase 1993 Portraits in Bisque				
93-188-001 Joy of Sharing1575QK1142	Keepsake	Yr.Iss.	15.75	15.75
93-188-002 Mistletoe Kiss1575QK1145	Keepsake	Yr.Iss.	15.75	15.75
93-188-003 Christmas Feast 1575QK1152	Keepsake	Yr.Iss.	15.75	15.75
93-188-004 Norman Rockwell-Filling the Stockings 1575QK1155	Keepsake	Yr.Iss.	15.75	15.75
93-188-005 Norman Rockwell-Jolly Postman 1575QK1142	Keepsake	Yr.Iss.	15.75	15.75
Hallmark Keepsake Ornaments — Showcase 1993 Folk Art Americana				
93-189-001 Riding the Wind 1575QK1045	Keepsake	Yr.Iss.	15.75	15.75
93-189-002 Angel in Flight 1575QK1052	Keepsake	Yr.Iss.	15.75	15.75
93-189-003 Polar Bear Adventure 1500QK1055	Keepsake	Yr.Iss.	15.00	15.00
93-189-004 Riding in the Woods 1575QK1065	Keepsake	Yr.Iss.	15.75	15.75
93-189-005 Santa Claus 1675QK1072	Keepsake	Yr.Iss.	16.75	16.75
Hallmark Keepsake Ornaments — Showcase 1993 Old-World Silver				
93-190-001 Silver Dove of Peace 2475QK1075	Keepsake	Yr.Iss.	24.75	24.75
93-190-002 Silver Sleigh 2475QK1082	Keepsake	Yr.Iss.	24.75	24.75
93-190-003 Silver Stars and Holly 2475QK1085	Keepsake	Yr.Iss.	24.75	24.75
93-190-004 Silver Santa 2475QK1092	Keepsake	Yr.Iss.	24.75	24.75
Hallmark Keepsake Ornaments — Showcase 1993 Holiday Enchantment				
93-191-001 Visions of Sugarplums 1375QK1005	Keepsake	Yr.Iss.	13.75	13.75
93-191-002 Journey to the Forest 1375QK1012	Keepsake	Yr.Iss.	13.75	13.75
93-191-003 The Magi 1375QK1025	Keepsake	Yr.Iss.	13.75	13.75
93-191-004 Bringing Home the Tree 1375QK1042	Keepsake	Yr.Iss.	13.75	13.75
93-191-005 Angelic Messengers 1375QK1032	Keepsake	Yr.Iss.	13.75	13.75
Hallmark Keepsake Ornaments — 1994 Collectible Series				
94-192-001 Betsey's Country Christmas-Third Ed. 500QX2403	Keepsake	Yr.Iss.	5.00	5.00
94-192-002 Pipers Piping-Eleventh Ed. 695QX3183	Keepsake	Yr.Iss.	6.95	6.95
94-192-003 Rocking Horse-Fourteenth Ed. 1095QX5016	Keepsake	Yr.Iss.	10.95	10.95
94-192-004 PEANUTS-Lucy-Second Ed. 995QX5203	Keepsake	Yr.Iss.	9.95	9.95
94-192-005 Xmas Stamp-Second Ed. 1095QX5206	Keepsake	Yr.Iss.	10.95	10.95
94-192-006 Hey Diddle Diddle-Second Ed. 1395QX5213	Keepsake	Yr.Iss.	13.95	13.95
94-192-007 Tobin Fraley Carousel-Third Ed. 2800QX5223	Keepsake	Yr.Iss.	28.00	28.00
94-192-008 Owliver-Third Ed. 795QX5226	Keepsake	Yr.Iss.	7.95	7.95
94-192-009 Puppy Love-Fourth Ed. 795QX5253	Keepsake	Yr.Iss.	7.95	7.95
94-192-010 Merry Olde Santa-Fifth Ed. 1495QX5256	Keepsake	Yr.Iss.	14.95	14.95
94-192-011 Fabulous Decade-Fifth Ed. 795QX5263	Keepsake	Yr.Iss.	7.95	7.95
94-192-012 Heart of Christmas-Fifth Ed. 1495QX5266	Keepsake	Yr.Iss.	14.95	14.95
94-192-013 CRAYOLA CRAYON-Bright Playful Colors-Sixth Ed. 1095QX5273	Keepsake	Yr.Iss.	10.95	10.95
94-192-014 Mary's Angels-Jasmine -Seventh Ed. 695QX5276	Keepsake	Yr.Iss.	6.95	6.95
94-192-015 Handwarming Present-Ninth Ed. 1495QX5283	Keepsake	Yr.Iss.	14.95	14.95
94-192-016 Neighborhood Drugstore-Eleventh Ed. 1495QX5286	Keepsake	Yr.Iss.	14.95	14.95
94-192-017 Frosty Friends-Fifteenth Ed. 995QX5293	Keepsake	Yr.Iss.	9.95	9.95
94-192-018 Makin' Tractor Tracks-Sixteenth Ed. 1495QX5296	Keepsake	Yr.Iss.	14.95	14.95
94-192-019 Cat Naps-First Ed. 795QX5313	Keepsake	Yr.Iss.	7.95	7.95
94-192-020 Yuletide Central-First Ed. 1895QX5316	Keepsake	Yr.Iss.	18.95	18.95
94-192-021 Baseball Heroes-Babe Ruth-First Ed. 1295QX5323	Keepsake	Yr.Iss.	12.95	12.95
94-192-022 1957 Chevy-Fourth Ed. 1295QX5422	Keepsake	Yr.Iss.	12.95	12.95
94-192-023 Kiddie Car Classics-First Ed. 1395QX5426	Keepsake	Yr.Iss.	13.95	13.95
Hallmark Keepsake Ornaments — 1994 Artists' Favorites				
94-193-001 Cock-a-Doodle Christmas 895QX5396	Keepsake	Yr.Iss.	8.95	8.95
94-193-002 Making It Bright 895QX5403	Keepsake	Yr.Iss.	8.95	8.95
94-193-003 Keep on Mowin' 895QX5413	Keepsake	Yr.Iss.	8.95	8.95
94-193-004 Kitty's Catamaran 1095QX5416	Keepsake	Yr.Iss.	10.95	10.95
94-193-005 Happy Birthday Jesus 1295QX5423	Keepsake	Yr.Iss.	12.95	12.95
Hallmark Keepsake Ornaments — 1994 Special Edition				
94-194-001 Lucinda and Teddy 2175QX4813	Keepsake	Yr.Iss.	21.75	21.75
Hallmark Keepsake Ornaments — 1994 Commemoratives				
94-195-001 Baby's First Christmas 1895QX5633	Keepsake	Yr.Iss.	18.95	18.95
94-195-002 Baby's First Christmas 1295QX5743	Keepsake	Yr.Iss.	12.95	12.95
94-195-003 Baby's First Christmas-Baby Girl 500QX2433	Keepsake	Yr.Iss.	5.00	5.00
94-195-004 Baby's First Christmas-Baby Boy 500QX2436	Keepsake	Yr.Iss.	5.00	5.00
94-195-005 Baby's First Christmas Photo 795QX5636	Keepsake	Yr.Iss.	7.95	7.95
94-195-006 Baby's First Christmas 795QX5713	Keepsake	Yr.Iss.	7.95	7.95
94-195-007 Baby's Second Christmas 795QX5716	Keepsake	Yr.Iss.	7.95	7.95
94-195-008 Child's Third Christmas 695QX5723	Keepsake	Yr.Iss.	6.95	6.95
94-195-009 Child's Fourth Christmas 695QX5726	Keepsake	Yr.Iss.	6.95	6.95
94-195-010 Child's Fifth Christmas 695QX5733	Keepsake	Yr.Iss.	6.95	6.95
94-195-011 Grandchild's First Christmas 795QX5676	Keepsake	Yr.Iss.	7.95	7.95
94-195-012 Dad-To-Be 795QX5473	Keepsake	Yr.Iss.	7.95	7.95
94-195-013 Mom-To-Be 795QX5506	Keepsake	Yr.Iss.	7.95	7.95
94-195-014 Grandma Photo 695QX5613	Keepsake	Yr.Iss.	6.95	6.95
94-195-015 Our First Christmas Together 695QX3186	Keepsake	Yr.Iss.	6.95	6.95
94-195-016 Our First Christmas Together 995QX4816	Keepsake	Yr.Iss.	9.95	9.95
94-195-017 Our First Christmas Together 995QX5643	Keepsake	Yr.Iss.	9.95	9.95
94-195-018 Our First Christmas Together 1895QX5706	Keepsake	Yr.Iss.	18.95	18.95
94-195-019 Our First Christmas Together Photo 895QX5653	Keepsake	Yr.Iss.	8.95	8.95
94-195-020 Tou Can Love 895QX5646	Keepsake	Yr.Iss.	8.95	8.95
94-195-021 Anniversary Year 1095QX5683	Keepsake	Yr.Iss.	10.95	10.95
94-195-022 Godparents 500QX2423	Keepsake	Yr.Iss.	5.00	5.00
94-195-023 Grandparents 500QX2426	Keepsake	Yr.Iss.	5.00	5.00
94-195-024 Godchild 895QX4453	Keepsake	Yr.Iss.	8.95	8.95
94-195-025 Dad 795QX5463	Keepsake	Yr.Iss.	7.95	7.95
94-195-026 Mom 795QX5466	Keepsake	Yr.Iss.	7.95	7.95
94-195-027 Sister 695QX5513	Keepsake	Yr.Iss.	6.95	6.95
94-195-028 Brother 695QX5516	Keepsake	Yr.Iss.	6.95	6.95
94-195-029 Granddaughter 695QX5523	Keepsake	Yr.Iss.	6.95	6.95
94-195-030 Grandson 695QX5526	Keepsake	Yr.Iss.	6.95	6.95
94-195-031 Sister to Sister 995QX5533	Keepsake	Yr.Iss.	9.95	9.95
94-195-032 Niece 795QX5543	Keepsake	Yr.Iss.	7.95	7.95
94-195-033 Nephew 795QX5546	Keepsake	Yr.Iss.	7.95	7.95
94-195-034 Our Family 795QX5576	Keepsake	Yr.Iss.	7.95	7.95
94-195-035 Special Dog 795QX5603	Keepsake	Yr.Iss.	7.95	7.95
94-195-036 Special Cat 795QX5606	Keepsake	Yr.Iss.	7.95	7.95
94-195-037 Grandpa 795QX5616	Keepsake	Yr.Iss.	7.95	7.95
94-195-038 Daughter 695QX5623	Keepsake	Yr.Iss.	6.95	6.95
94-195-039 Son 695QX5626	Keepsake	Yr.Iss.	6.95	6.95
94-195-040 Mom and Dad 995QX5666	Keepsake	Yr.Iss.	9.95	9.95
94-195-041 Grandmother 795QX5673	Keepsake	Yr.Iss.	7.95	7.95
94-195-042 Across the Miles 895QX5656	Keepsake	Yr.Iss.	8.95	8.95
94-195-043 New Home 895QX5663	Keepsake	Yr.Iss.	8.95	8.95
94-195-044 Friendly Push 895QX5686	Keepsake	Yr.Iss.	8.95	8.95
94-195-045 Thick 'N' Thin 1095QX5693	Keepsake	Yr.Iss.	10.95	10.95
94-195-046 Secret Santa 795QX5736	Keepsake	Yr.Iss.	7.95	7.95
Hallmark Keepsake Ornaments — 1994 New Attractions				
94-196-001 Norman Rockwell 500QX2413	Keepsake	Yr.Iss.	5.00	5.00
94-196-002 Mary Engelbreit 500QX2416	Keepsake	Yr.Iss.	5.00	5.00
94-196-003 BEATRIX POTTER The Tale of Peter Rabbit 500QX2443	Keepsake	Yr.Iss.	5.00	5.00
94-196-004 Friendship Sundae 1095QX4766	Keepsake	Yr.Iss.	10.95	10.95
94-196-005 Fred and Barney 1495QX5003	Keepsake	Yr.Iss.	14.95	14.95
94-196-006 Speedy Gonzales 895QX5343	Keepsake	Yr.Iss.	8.95	8.95
94-196-007 Yosemite Sam 895QX5346	Keepsake	Yr.Iss.	8.95	8.95
94-196-008 Relaxing Moment 1495QX5356	Keepsake	Yr.Iss.	14.95	14.95
94-196-009 Beatles Gift Set 4800QX5373	Keepsake	Yr.Iss.	48.00	48.00
94-196-010 Daffy Duck 895QX5415	Keepsake	Yr.Iss.	8.95	8.95
94-196-011 Dorothy and Toto 1095QX5433	Keepsake	Yr.Iss.	10.95	10.95
94-196-012 Scarecrow 995QX5436	Keepsake	Yr.Iss.	9.95	9.95
94-196-013 Tin Man 995QX5443	Keepsake	Yr.Iss.	9.95	9.95
94-196-014 Cowardly Lion 995QX5446	Keepsake	Yr.Iss.	9.95	9.95
94-196-015 LEGO'S 1095QX5453	Keepsake	Yr.Iss.	10.95	10.95
94-196-016 Lou Rankin Seal 995QX5456	Keepsake	Yr.Iss.	9.95	9.95
94-196-017 Road Runner and Wile E. Coyote 1295QX5602	Keepsake	Yr.Iss.	12.95	12.95
94-196-018 Tasmanian Devil 895QX5605	Keepsake	Yr.Iss.	8.95	8.95
94-196-019 Winnie the Pooh/Tigger 1295QX5746	Keepsake	Yr.Iss.	12.95	12.95
94-196-020 GARFIELD 1295QX5753	Keepsake	Yr.Iss.	12.95	12.95
94-196-021 Batman 1295QX5853	Keepsake	Yr.Iss.	12.95	12.95
94-196-022 A Sharp Flat 1095QX5773	Keepsake	Yr.Iss.	10.95	10.95
94-196-023 Follow the Sun 895QX5846	Keepsake	Yr.Iss.	8.95	8.95
94-196-024 It's a Strike 895QX5856	Keepsake	Yr.Iss.	8.95	8.95
94-196-025 Practice Makes Perfect 795QX5863	Keepsake	Yr.Iss.	7.95	7.95
94-196-026 Thrill a Minute 895QX5866	Keepsake	Yr.Iss.	8.95	8.95
94-196-027 Big Shot 795QX5873	Keepsake	Yr.Iss.	7.95	7.95
94-196-028 Busy Batter 795QX5876	Keepsake	Yr.Iss.	7.95	7.95
94-196-029 Kringle's Kayak 795QX5886	Keepsake	Yr.Iss.	7.95	7.95
94-196-030 Colors of Joy 795QX5893	Keepsake	Yr.Iss.	7.95	7.95
94-196-031 Merry Fishmas 895QX5913	Keepsake	Yr.Iss.	8.95	8.95
94-196-032 Kickin' Roo 795QX5916	Keepsake	Yr.Iss.	7.95	7.95
94-196-033 All Pumped Up 895QX5923	Keepsake	Yr.Iss.	8.95	8.95
94-196-034 Reindeer Pro 795QX5926	Keepsake	Yr.Iss.	7.95	7.95
94-196-035 Open-and-Shut Holiday 995QX5696	Keepsake	Yr.Iss.	9.95	9.95
94-196-036 Stamp of Approval 795QX5703	Keepsake	Yr.Iss.	7.95	7.95
94-196-037 Out of This World Teacher 795QX5766	Keepsake	Yr.Iss.	7.95	7.95
94-196-038 Caring Doctor 895QX5823	Keepsake	Yr.Iss.	8.95	8.95
94-196-039 Holiday Patrol 895QX5826	Keepsake	Yr.Iss.	8.95	8.95
94-196-040 Extra-Special Delivery 795QX5833	Keepsake	Yr.Iss.	7.95	7.95
94-196-041 Red Hot Holiday 795QX5843	Keepsake	Yr.Iss.	7.95	7.95
94-196-042 Champion Teacher 695QX5836	Keepsake	Yr.Iss.	6.95	6.95
94-196-043 Child Care Giver 795QX5906	Keepsake	Yr.Iss.	7.95	7.95
94-196-044 Coach 795QX5933	Keepsake	Yr.Iss.	7.95	7.95
94-196-045 Gentle Nurse 695QX5973	Keepsake	Yr.Iss.	6.95	6.95
94-196-046 Yuletide Cheer 995QX5976	Keepsake	Yr.Iss.	9.95	9.95

	ARTIST	EDITION	ISSUE	QUOTE
94-196-047 Tulip Time 995QX5983	Keepsake	Yr.Iss.	9.95	9.95
94-196-048 Daisy Days 995QX5986	Keepsake	Yr.Iss.	9.95	9.95
94-196-049 Harvest Joy 995QX5993	Keepsake	Yr.Iss.	9.95	9.95
94-196-050 A Feline of Christmas 895QX5816	Keepsake	Yr.Iss.	8.95	8.95
94-196-051 Angel Hare 895QX5896	Keepsake	Yr.Iss.	8.95	8.95
94-196-052 Feelin' Groovy 795QX5953	Keepsake	Yr.Iss.	7.95	7.95
94-196-053 Hearts in Harmony 1095QX4406	Keepsake	Yr.Iss.	10.95	10.95
94-196-054 Joyous Song 895QX4473	Keepsake	Yr.Iss.	8.95	8.95
94-196-055 Feliz Navidad 895QX5793	Keepsake	Yr.Iss.	8.95	8.95
94-196-056 Cheers to You! 1095QX5796	Keepsake	Yr.Iss.	10.95	10.95
94-196-057 Jump-along Jackalope 895QX5756	Keepsake	Yr.Iss.	8.95	8.95
94-196-058 In the Pink 995QX5763	Keepsake	Yr.Iss.	9.95	9.95
94-196-059 Helpful Shepherd 895QX5536	Keepsake	Yr.Iss.	8.95	8.95
94-196-060 Time of Peace 795QX5813	Keepsake	Yr.Iss.	7.95	7.95
94-196-061 Sweet Greeting (2) 1095QX5803	Keepsake	Yr.Iss.	10.95	10.95
94-196-062 Deer Santa Mouse (2) 1495QX5806	Keepsake	Yr.Iss.	14.95	14.95
94-196-063 Mistletoe Surprise (2)1295QX5996	Keepsake	Yr.Iss.	12.95	12.95
94-196-064 Candy Caper 895QX5776	Keepsake	Yr.Iss.	8.95	8.95
94-196-065 Jingle Bell Band 1095QX5783	Keepsake	Yr.Iss.	10.95	10.95
94-196-066 Cheery Cyclists 1295QX5786	Keepsake	Yr.Iss.	12.95	12.95
94-196-067 Magic Carpet Ride 795QX5883	Keepsake	Yr.Iss.	7.95	7.95
94-196-068 Ice Show 795QX5946	Keepsake	Yr.Iss.	7.95	7.95
Hallmark Keepsake Ornaments	**1994 Keepsake Magic Ornaments**			
94-197-001 Away in a Manager 1600QLX7383	Keepsake	Yr.Iss.	16.00	16.00
94-197-002 Chris Mouse Jelly-Tenth Ed. 1200QLX7393	Keepsake	Yr.Iss.	12.00	12.00
94-197-003 Kringle Trolley 2,000QLX7413	Keepsake	Yr.Iss.	20.00	20.00
94-197-004 Candy Cane Lookout 1800QLX7376	Keepsake	Yr.Iss.	18.00	18.00
94-197-005 Rock Candy Miner 2000QLX7403	Keepsake	Yr.Iss.	20.00	20.00
94-197-006 PEANUTS-Fourth Ed. 2000QLX7406	Keepsake	Yr.Iss.	20.00	20.00
94-197-007 Maxine 2,000QLX7503	Keepsake	Yr.Iss.	20.00	20.00
94-197-008 Peekaboo Pup 2000QLX7423	Keepsake	Yr.Iss.	20.00	20.00
94-197-009 Conversations With Santa 2800QLX7426	Keepsake	Yr.Iss.	28.00	28.00
94-197-010 Feliz Navidad 2800QLX7433	Keepsake	Yr.Iss.	28.00	28.00
94-197-011 Winnie the Pooh Parade 3200QLX7493	Keepsake	Yr.Iss.	32.00	32.00
94-197-012 Forest Frolics-6th Ed. 2800QLX7436	Keepsake	Yr.Iss.	28.00	28.00
94-197-013 Country Showtime 2200QLX7416	Keepsake	Yr.Iss.	22.00	22.00
94-197-014 Very Merry Minutes 2400QLX7443	Keepsake	Yr.Iss.	24.00	24.00
94-197-015 Gingerbread Fantasy-Special Edition 4400QLX7382	Keepsake	Yr.Iss.	44.00	44.00
94-197-016 White Christmas 2800QLX7463	Keepsake	Yr.Iss.	28.00	28.00
94-197-017 Baby's First Christmas 2000QLX7466	Keepsake	Yr.Iss.	20.00	20.00
94-197-018 Santa's Sing-Along 2400QLX7473	Keepsake	Yr.Iss.	24.00	24.00
94-197-019 The Eagle Has Landed 2400QLX7486	Keepsake	Yr.Iss.	24.00	24.00
94-197-020 Tobin Fraley-First Ed. 3200QLX7496	Keepsake	Yr.Iss.	32.00	32.00
Hallmark Keepsake Ornaments	**1994 Miniature Ornaments**			
94-198-001 On the Road-Second Ed. 575QXM5103	Keepsake	Yr.Iss.	5.75	5.75
94-198-002 March of the Teddy Bears-Second Ed. 450QXM5106	Keepsake	Yr.Iss.	4.50	4.50
94-198-003 Stock Car-Sixth Ed. 700QXM5113	Keepsake	Yr.Iss.	7.00	7.00
94-198-004 Rocking Horse-Seventh Ed. 450QXM5116	Keepsake	Yr.Iss.	4.50	4.50
94-198-005 Night Before Christmas-Third Ed. 450QXM5123	Keepsake	Yr.Iss.	4.56	4.56
94-198-006 Nature's Angels-Fifth Ed. 450QXM5126	Keepsake	Yr.Iss.	4.50	4.50
94-198-007 The Bearymores-Third Ed. 575QXM5133	Keepsake	Yr.Iss.	5.75	5.75
94-198-008 Hat Shop-Seventh Ed. 700QXM5143	Keepsake	Yr.Iss.	7.00	7.00
94-198-009 Nutcracker Guild-First Ed. 575QXM5146	Keepsake	Yr.Iss.	5.75	5.75
94-198-010 Centuries of Santa-First Ed. 600QXM5153	Keepsake	Yr.Iss.	6.00	6.00
94-198-011 Have a Cookie 575QXM5166	Keepsake	Yr.Iss.	5.75	5.75
94-198-012 Scooting Along 675QXM5173	Keepsake	Yr.Iss.	6.75	6.75
94-198-013 Noah's Ark (special edition) 2450QXM4106	Keepsake	Yr.Iss.	24.50	24.50
94-198-014 Dazzling Reindeer-Pr. Ed. 975QXM4026	Keepsake	Yr.Iss.	9.75	9.75
94-198-015 Baking Tiny Treats, set/6 2900QXM4033	Keepsake	Yr.Iss.	29.00	29.00
94-198-016 Babs Bunny 575QXM4116	Keepsake	Yr.Iss.	5.75	5.75
94-198-017 Plucky Duck 575QXM4123	Keepsake	Yr.Iss.	5.75	5.75
94-198-018 Hamton 575QXM4126	Keepsake	Yr.Iss.	5.75	5.75
94-198-019 Dizzy Devil 575QXM4133	Keepsake	Yr.Iss.	5.75	5.75
94-198-020 Pour Some More 575QXM5156	Keepsake	Yr.Iss.	5.75	5.75
94-198-021 Buster Bunny 575QXM5163	Keepsake	Yr.Iss.	5.75	5.75
94-198-022 Baby's First Christmas 575QXM4003	Keepsake	Yr.Iss.	5.75	5.75
94-198-023 Hearts A-Sail 575QXM4006	Keepsake	Yr.Iss.	5.75	5.75
94-198-024 Mom 450QXM4013	Keepsake	Yr.Iss.	4.50	4.50
94-198-025 Friends Need Hugs 450QXM4016	Keepsake	Yr.Iss.	4.50	4.50
94-198-026 Journey to Bethlehem 575QXM4036	Keepsake	Yr.Iss.	5.75	5.75
94-198-027 Love Was Born 450QXM4043	Keepsake	Yr.Iss.	4.50	4.50
94-198-028 Tea With Teddy 725QXM4046	Keepsake	Yr.Iss.	7.25	7.25
94-198-029 Jolly Visitor 575QXM4053	Keepsake	Yr.Iss.	5.75	5.75
94-198-030 Graceful Carousel 75QXM4056	Keepsake	Yr.Iss.	7.75	7.75
94-198-031 Corny Elf 450QXM4063	Keepsake	Yr.Iss.	4.50	4.50
94-198-032 Melodic Cherub 375QXM4066	Keepsake	Yr.Iss.	3.75	3.75
94-198-033 A Merry Flight 575QXM4073	Keepsake	Yr.Iss.	5.75	5.75
94-198-034 Beary Perfect Tree 475QXM4076	Keepsake	Yr.Iss.	4.75	4.75
94-198-035 Just My Size 375QXM4086	Keepsake	Yr.Iss.	3.75	3.75
94-198-036 Jolly Wolly Snowman 375QXM4093	Keepsake	Yr.Iss.	3.75	3.75
94-198-037 Sweet Dreams 300QXM4096	Keepsake	Yr.Iss.	3.00	3.00
94-198-038 Cute as a Button 375QXM4103	Keepsake	Yr.Iss.	3.75	3.75
Hallmark Keepsake Ornaments	**1994 Easter Ornaments**			
94-199-001 Sweet as Sugar 875QE08086	A. Rogers	Yr.Iss.	8.75	8.75
94-199-002 Egg Car-First Ed. 775QE08093	K. Crow	Yr.Iss.	7.75	7.75
94-199-003 Springtime Bonnets-Second Ed. 775QE08096	R. Bishop	Yr.Iss.	7.75	7.75
94-199-004 Golf-Third Ed. 675QE08133	B. Seidler	Yr.Iss.	6.75	6.75
94-199-005 Horn-Third Ed. 675QE08136	D. Rhodus	Yr.Iss.	6.75	6.75
94-199-006 Yummy Recipe 775QE08143	A. Rogers	Yr.Iss.	7.75	7.75
94-199-007 Sunny Bunny Garden, set/3 1500QE08146	E. Seale	Yr.Iss.	15.00	15.00
94-199-008 Baby's First Easter 675QE08153	J. Francis	Yr.Iss.	6.75	6.75
94-199-009 Daughter 575QE08156	T. Andrews	Yr.Iss.	5.75	5.75
94-199-010 Son 575QE08163	T. Andrews	Yr.Iss.	5.75	5.75
94-199-011 CRAYOLA CRAYON-Colorful Spring 775QE08166	K. Crow	Yr.Iss.	7.75	7.75
94-199-012 PEANUTS 775QE08176	D. Unruh	Yr.Iss.	7.75	7.75
94-199-013 Divine Duet 675QE08183	L. Votruba	Yr.Iss.	6.75	6.75
94-199-014 Treetop Cottage 975QE08186	L. Sickman	Yr.Iss.	9.75	9.75
94-199-015 Easter Art Show 775QE08193	L. Votruba	Yr.Iss.	7.75	7.75
94-199-016 Sweet Easter Wishes Tender Touches 875QE08196	L. Votruba	Yr.Iss.	8.75	8.75
94-199-017 Peeping Out 675QE08203	D. Unruh	Yr.Iss.	6.75	6.75
94-199-018 Joyful Lamb 575QE08206	D. Unruh	Yr.Iss.	5.75	5.75
94-199-019 Riding a Breeze 575QE08213	D. Palmiter	Yr.Iss.	5.75	5.75

	ARTIST	EDITION	ISSUE	QUOTE
94-199-020 Carrot Trimmers 500QE08226	Hallmark	Yr.Iss.	5.00	5.00
Hallmark Keepsake Ornaments	**1994 Personalized Ornaments**			
94-200-001 Etch-A-Sketch® 1295QP6006	Keepsake	Yr.Iss.	12.95	12.95
94-200-002 Goin' Fishin' 1495QP6023	Keepsake	Yr.Iss.	14.95	14.95
94-200-003 From the Heart 1495QP6036	Keepsake	Yr.Iss.	14.95	14.95
94-200-004 Computer Cat 'N' Mouse 1295QP6046	Keepsake	Yr.Iss.	12.95	12.95
94-200-005 Reindeer Rooters 1295QP6056	Keepsake	Yr.Iss.	12.95	12.95
94-200-006 Novel Idea 1295QP6066	Keepsake	Yr.Iss.	12.95	12.95
94-200-007 Cookie Time 1295QP6073	Keepsake	Yr.Iss.	12.95	12.95
94-200-008 Holiday Hello 2495QXR6116	Keepsake	Yr.Iss.	24.95	24.95
94-200-009 Santa Says 1495QP6005	Keepsake	Yr.Iss.	14.95	14.95
94-200-010 Goin' Golfin' 1295QP6012	Keepsake	Yr.Iss.	12.95	12.95
94-200-011 Mailbox Delivery 1495QP6015	Keepsake	Yr.Iss.	14.95	14.95
94-200-012 On the Billboard 1295QP6022	Keepsake	Yr.Iss.	12.95	12.95
94-200-013 Festive Album 1295QP6025	Keepsake	Yr.Iss.	12.95	12.95
94-200-014 Playing Ball 1295QP6032	Keepsake	Yr.Iss.	12.95	12.95
94-200-015 Baby Block 1495QP6035	Keepsake	Yr.Iss.	14.95	14.95
Hallmark Keepsake Ornaments	**1994 Special Issues**			
94-201-001 Holiday Barbie #2 1495QX5216	Keepsake	Yr.Iss.	14.95	14.95
94-201-002 Barbie #1-Nostalgic 1495QX5006	Keepsake	Yr.Iss.	14.95	14.95
94-201-003 Simba/Nala-Lion King (2) 1295QX5303	Keepsake	Yr.Iss.	12.95	12.95
94-201-004 Timon/Pumbaa-Lion King 895QX5366	Keepsake	Yr.Iss.	8.95	8.95
94-201-005 Mufasa/Simba-Lion King 1495QX5406	Keepsake	Yr.Iss.	14.95	14.95
94-201-006 Barney 995QX5966	Keepsake	Yr.Iss.	9.95	9.95
94-201-007 Barney 2400QLX7506	Keepsake	Yr.Iss.	24.00	24.00
94-201-008 Simba/Sarabi/Mufasa the Lion King 3200QLX7513	Keepsake	Yr.Iss.	32.00	32.00
94-201-009 Klingon Bird of Prey™ 2400QLX7386	Keepsake	Yr.Iss.	24.00	24.00
Hallmark Keepsake Ornaments	**1994 Premiere Event**			
94-202-001 Eager for Christmas 1500QX5336	Keepsake	Yr.Iss.	15.00	15.00
Hallmark Keepsake Ornaments	**1994 Keepsake Collector's Club**			
94-203-001 Happy Collecting 300QXC4803	Keepsake	Yr.Iss.	3.00	3.00
94-203-002 Sweet Bouquet 850QXC4806	Keepsake	Yr.Iss.	8.50	8.50
94-203-003 Holiday Pursuit 1175QXC4823	Keepsake	Yr.Iss.	11.75	11.75
94-203-004 First Hello 500QXC4846	Keepsake	Yr.Iss.	5.00	5.00
94-203-005 On Cloud Nine 1200QXC4853	Keepsake	Yr.Iss.	12.00	12.00
94-203-006 Mrs. Claus' Cupboard 5500QXC4843	Keepsake	Yr.Iss.	55.00	55.00
94-203-007 Tilling Time 500QXC8256	Keepsake	Yr.Iss.	5.00	5.00
Hallmark Keepsake Ornaments	**1994 Limited Editions**			
94-204-001 Jolly Holly Santa 2200QXC4833	Keepsake	N/A	22.00	22.00
94-204-002 Majestic Deer 2500QXC4836	Keepsake	N/A	25.00	25.00
Hallmark Keepsake Showcase Ornaments	**Showcase 1994 Old World Silver Collection**			
94-205-001 Silver Poinsettias 2475QK1006	Keepsake	Yr.Iss.	24.75	24.75
94-205-002 Silver Snowflakes 2475QK1016	Keepsake	Yr.Iss.	24.75	24.75
94-205-003 Silver Bows 2475QK1023	Keepsake	Yr.Iss.	24.75	24.75
94-205-004 Silver Bells 2475QK1026	Keepsake	Yr.Iss.	24.75	24.75
Hallmark Keepsake Showcase Ornaments	**Showcase 1994 Folk Art Americana Collection**			
94-206-001 Catching 40 Winks 1675QK1183	Keepsake	Yr.Iss.	16.75	16.75
94-206-002 Rarin' to Go 1575QK1193	Keepsake	Yr.Iss.	15.75	15.75
94-206-003 Going to Town 1575QK1166	Keepsake	Yr.Iss.	15.75	15.75
94-206-004 Racing Through the Snow 1575QK1173	Keepsake	Yr.Iss.	15.75	15.75
94-206-005 Roundup Time 1675QK1176	Keepsake	Yr.Iss.	16.75	16.75
Hallmark Keepsake Showcase Ornaments	**Showcase 1994 Christmas Lights**			
94-207-001 Peaceful Village 1575QK1106	Keepsake	Yr.Iss.	15.75	15.75
94-207-002 Moonbeams 1575QK1116	Keepsake	Yr.Iss.	15.75	15.75
94-207-003 Mother and Child 1575QK1126	Keepsake	Yr.Iss.	15.75	15.75
94-207-004 Home for the Holidays 1575QK1123	Keepsake	Yr.Iss.	15.75	15.75
Hallmark Keepsake Showcase Ornaments	**Showcase 1994 Holiday Favorites**			
94-208-001 Graceful Fawn 1175QK1033	Keepsake	Yr.Iss.	11.75	11.75
94-208-002 Joyful Lamb 1175QK1036	Keepsake	Yr.Iss.	11.75	11.75
94-208-003 Peaceful Dove 1175QK1043	Keepsake	Yr.Iss.	11.75	11.75
94-208-004 Jolly Santa 1375QK1046	Keepsake	Yr.Iss.	13.75	13.75
94-208-005 Dapper Snowman 1375QK1053	Keepsake	Yr.Iss.	13.75	13.75
Hamilton Collection	**Christmas Angels**			
94-01-001 Angel of Charity	S. Kuck	Open	19.50	19.50
Hand & Hammer	**Hand & Hammer Ornaments**			
80-01-001 Icicle 009	De Matteo	490	25.00	50.00
81-01-002 Roundel 109	De Matteo	220	25.00	45.00
81-01-003 Gabriel with Liberty Cap 301	De Matteo	275	25.00	60.00
81-01-004 Gabriel 320	De Matteo	Suspd.	25.00	32.00
82-01-005 Fleur de Lys Angel 343	De Matteo	320	28.00	35.00
82-01-006 Madonna & Child 388	De Matteo	175	28.00	50.00
84-01-007 Beardsley Angel 398	De Matteo	Open	28.00	48.00
82-01-008 Carved Heart 425	De Matteo	Suspd.	29.00	65.00
82-01-009 Straw Star 448	De Matteo	590	25.00	40.00
83-01-010 Fire Angel 473	De Matteo	315	25.00	28-36.00
83-01-011 Indian 494	De Matteo	190	29.00	50.00
83-01-012 Pollock Angel 502	De Matteo	Suspd.	35.00	90.00
83-01-013 Calligraphic Deer 511	De Matteo	Suspd.	25.00	29.00
83-01-014 Egyptian Cat 521	De Matteo	Unkn.	13.00	13.00
83-01-015 Dove 522	De Matteo	Unkn.	13.00	13.00
83-01-016 Sargent Angel 523	De Matteo	690	29.00	34.00
83-01-017 Cherub 528	De Matteo	295	29.00	50.00
83-01-018 Japanese Snowflake 534	De Matteo	350	29.00	35.00
83-01-019 Sunburst 543	De Matteo	Unkn.	13.00	50.00
83-01-020 Wise Man 549	De Matteo	Suspd.	29.00	36.00
84-01-021 Freer Star 553	De Matteo	Unkn.	13.00	30.00
84-01-022 Pineapple 558	De Matteo	Suspd.	30.00	38.00
84-01-023 Crescent Angel 559	De Matteo	Suspd.	30.00	32.00
84-01-024 Rosette 571	De Matteo	220	32.00	50.00
84-01-025 Nine Hearts 572	De Matteo	275	34.00	50.00
84-01-026 USHS 1984 Angel 574	De Matteo	Suspd.	35.00	95.00
84-01-027 Wreath 575	De Matteo	Unkn.	13.00	30.00
84-01-028 Praying Angel 576	De Matteo	Suspd.	29.00	30.00
84-01-029 Rocking Horse 581	De Matteo	Unkn.	13.00	13.00
84-01-030 Bunny 582	De Matteo	Unkn.	13.00	30.00
84-01-031 Ibex 584	De Matteo	400	29.00	50.00
84-01-032 Bird & Cherub 588	De Matteo	Unkn.	13.00	30.00
84-01-033 Wild Swan 592	De Matteo	Suspd.	35.00	50.00
84-01-034 Moravian Star 595	De Matteo	Open	38.00	50.00
84-01-035 Manger 601	De Matteo	Suspd.	29.00	32.00
84-01-036 Mt. Vernon Weathervane 602	De Matteo	Suspd.	32.00	39.00
85-01-037 Peacock 603	De Matteo	470	34.00	37.00
85-01-038 Model A Ford 604	De Matteo	Unkn.	13.00	30.00
85-01-039 Crane 606	De Matteo	150	38.00	50.00

		ARTIST	EDITION	ISSUE	QUOTE
85-01-040	Angel 607	De Matteo	225	36.00	50.00
85-01-041	Militiaman 608	De Matteo	460	25.00	30.00
85-01-042	Nutcracker 609	De Matteo	510	30.00	50.00
85-01-043	Liberty Bell 611	De Matteo	Suspd.	32.00	40.00
85-01-044	Angel 612	De Matteo	217	32.00	50.00
85-01-045	Abigail 613	De Matteo	500	32.00	50.00
85-01-046	Audubon Swallow 614	De Matteo	Suspd.	48.00	100.00
85-01-047	Audubon Bluebird 615	De Matteo	Suspd.	48.00	100.00
85-01-048	Guardian Angel 616	De Matteo	1340	35.00	39.00
85-01-049	Shepherd 617	De Matteo	1770	35.00	39.00
85-01-050	Carousel Pony 618	De Matteo	Unkn.	13.00	13.00
85-01-051	Art Deco Deer 620	De Matteo	Suspd.	34.00	38.00
85-01-052	Halley's Comet 621	De Matteo	432	35.00	50.00
85-01-053	Mermaid 622	De Matteo	Suspd.	35.00	39.00
85-01-054	George Washington 629	De Matteo	Suspd.	35.00	39.00
85-01-055	USHS Madonna 630	De Matteo	Suspd.	35.00	50.00
85-01-056	USHS Bluebird 631	De Matteo	Suspd.	29.00	50.00
85-01-057	USHS Swallow 632	De Matteo	Suspd.	29.00	50.00
85-01-058	Grasshopper 634	De Matteo	Open	32.00	39.00
85-01-059	Hosanna 635	De Matteo	715	32.00	50.00
85-01-060	Teddy 637	De Matteo	Suspd.	37.00	40.00
85-01-061	Herald Angel 641	De Matteo	Suspd.	36.00	40.00
85-01-062	Cherub 642	De Matteo	815	37.00	37.00
85-01-063	Butterfly 646	De Matteo	Suspd.	39.00	39.00
85-01-064	French Quarter Heart 647	De Matteo	Open	37.00	36.00
85-01-065	Samantha 648	De Matteo	Suspd.	35.00	36.00
85-01-066	Eagle 652	De Matteo	375	30.00	50.00
85-01-067	Piazza 653	De Matteo	Suspd.	32.00	50.00
85-01-068	Camel 655	De Matteo	Unkn.	13.00	30.00
85-01-069	Reindeer 656	De Matteo	Unkn.	13.00	30.00
85-01-070	Lafarge Angel 658	De Matteo	Suspd.	32.00	50.00
85-01-071	Family 659	De Matteo	915	32.00	40.00
85-01-072	Unicorn 660	De Matteo	Suspd.	37.00	37.00
85-01-073	Old North Church 661	De Matteo	Open	35.00	39.00
85-01-074	Madonna 666	De Matteo	227	35.00	50.00
85-01-075	Bicycle 669	De Matteo	Unkn.	13.00	30.00
85-01-076	St. Nicholas 670	De Matteo	Unkn.	13.00	30.00
86-01-077	Nativity 679	De Matteo	Suspd.	36.00	38.00
86-01-078	Winged Dove 680	De Matteo	Suspd.	35.00	36.00
86-01-079	Nutcracker 681	De Matteo	1,356	37.00	37.00
86-01-080	Phaeton 683	De Matteo	Unkn.	13.00	13.00
86-01-081	Archangel 684	De Matteo	Suspd.	29.00	30.00
86-01-082	Teddy Bear 685	De Matteo	Suspd.	38.00	40.00
86-01-083	Hallelujah 686	De Matteo	Unkn.	38.00	42.00
86-01-084	Bear Claus 692	De Matteo	Unkn.	13.00	13.00
86-01-085	Prancer 698	De Matteo	Open	38.00	38.00
86-01-086	USHS Angel 703	De Matteo	Suspd.	35.00	50.00
86-01-087	Teddy 707	De Matteo	Unkn.	13.00	30.00
86-01-088	Christmas Tree 708	De Matteo	Unkn.	13.00	13.00
86-01-089	Lafarge Angel 710	De Matteo	Suspd.	31.00	50.00
86-01-090	Salem Lamb 712	De Matteo	Suspd.	32.00	50.00
86-01-091	Snowflake 713	De Matteo	Suspd.	36.00	40.00
86-01-092	Wreath 714	De Matteo	Suspd.	36.00	38.00
86-01-093	Santa Skates 715	De Matteo	Suspd.	36.00	36.00
86-01-094	Nightingale 716	De Matteo	Suspd.	35.00	50.00
86-01-095	Mother Goose 719	De Matteo	Open	34.00	40.00
86-01-096	Kringle Bear 723	De Matteo	Unkn.	13.00	30.00
86-01-097	Victorian Santa 724	De Matteo	250	32.00	38.00
87-01-098	Noel 731	De Matteo	Open	38.00	38.00
87-01-099	Naptime 732	J. Walpole	Suspd.	32.00	32.00
87-01-100	Hunting Horn 738	De Matteo	Open	37.00	37.00
87-01-101	Santa Star 739	J. Walpole	Suspd.	32.00	32.00
87-01-102	Sweetheart Star 740	De Matteo	Suspd.	39.50	39.50
87-01-103	Santa 741	De Matteo	Unkn.	13.00	13.00
87-01-104	Pegasus 745	De Matteo	Unkn.	13.00	13.00
87-01-105	Snow Queen 746	De Matteo	Suspd.	35.00	39.00
87-01-106	Dove 747	De Matteo	Unkn.	13.00	13.00
87-01-107	USHS Gloria Angel 748	De Matteo	Suspd.	39.00	50.00
87-01-108	Angel with Lyre 750	De Matteo	Suspd.	32.00	40.00
87-01-109	Santa and Sleigh 751	De Matteo	Suspd.	32.00	40.00
87-01-110	Reindeer 752	De Matteo	Open	38.00	38.00
87-01-111	Snowman 753	De Matteo	825	38.00	38.00
87-01-112	Cat 754	De Matteo	Open	37.00	37.00
87-01-113	Clipper Ship 756	De Matteo	Suspd.	35.00	35.00
87-01-114	Ride a Cock Horse 757	De Matteo	Suspd.	34.00	39.00
87-01-115	Art Deco Angel 765	De Matteo	Suspd.	38.00	40.00
87-01-116	Old Ironsides 767	De Matteo	Open	35.00	39.00
87-01-117	First Christmas 771	De Matteo	Unkn.	13.00	13.00
87-01-118	Stocking 772	De Matteo	Unkn.	13.00	13.00
88-01-119	Drummer Bear 773	De Matteo	Unkn.	13.00	13.00
88-01-120	Stocking 774	De Matteo	Unkn.	13.00	13.00
87-01-121	Minuteman 776	De Matteo	Suspd.	35.00	40.00
87-01-122	Buffalo 777	De Matteo	Suspd.	36.00	36.00
88-01-123	Star of the East 785	De Matteo	Suspd.	35.00	35.00
88-01-124	Dove 786	De Matteo	112	36.00	50.00
88-01-125	Madonna 787	De Matteo	600	35.00	35.00
88-01-126	Magi 788	De Matteo	Suspd.	39.50	39.50
88-01-127	Jack in the Box 789	De Matteo	Suspd.	39.50	39.50
88-01-128	Skaters 790	De Matteo	Suspd.	39.50	39.50
88-01-129	Angel 797	De Matteo	Unkn.	13.00	13.00
88-01-130	Christmas Tree 798	De Matteo	Unkn.	13.00	13.00
88-01-131	Thumbelina 803	De Matteo	Suspd.	35.00	40.00
88-01-132	Star 806	De Matteo	311	50.00	150.00
88-01-133	Madonna 809	De Matteo	15	39.00	50.00
89-01-134	Carousel Horse 811	De Matteo	2,150	34.00	34.00
88-01-135	Bank 812	De Matteo	400	40.00	40.00
88-01-136	Santa with Scroll 814	De Matteo	250	34.00	37.00
88-01-137	Madonna 815	De Matteo	Suspd.	39.00	50.00
88-01-138	Rabbit 816	De Matteo	Unkn.	13.00	13.00
88-01-139	Buggy 817	De Matteo	Unkn.	13.00	13.00
88-01-140	Angel 818	De Matteo	Suspd.	32.00	40.00
88-01-141	Boston State House 819	De Matteo	Open	34.00	40.00
88-01-142	US Capitol 820	De Matteo	Open	38.00	40.00
88-01-143	Nativity 821	De Matteo	Suspd.	32.00	39.00
88-01-144	Old King Cole 824	De Matteo	Suspd.	34.00	39.00
88-01-145	Stocking 827	De Matteo	Unkn.	13.00	13.00
88-01-146	Conn. State House 833	De Matteo	Open	38.00	38.00
88-01-147	Sleigh 834	De Matteo	Open	34.00	38.00
89-01-148	Stocking Bear 835	De Matteo	Unkn.	13.00	13.00
88-01-149	Night Before Xmas Col. 841	De Matteo	10,000	160.00	160.00
89-01-150	First Christmas 842	De Matteo	Unkn.	13.00	13.00
89-01-151	Locket Bear 844	De Matteo	Unkn.	25.00	25.00

		ARTIST	EDITION	ISSUE	QUOTE
88-01-152	Cable Car 848	De Matteo	Open	38.00	38.00
88-01-153	Star 854	De Matteo	275	32.00	35.00
89-01-154	Santa 1989 856	De Matteo	1,715	35.00	35.00
89-01-155	Goose 857	De Matteo	650	37.00	37.00
89-01-156	Presidential Seal 858	De Matteo	500	39.00	65.00
88-01-157	Eiffel Tower 861	De Matteo	225	38.00	40.00
88-01-158	Coronado 864	De Matteo	Suspd.	38.00	38.00
90-01-159	Carousel Horse 866	De Matteo	1,915	38.00	38.00
90-01-160	Joy 867	De Matteo	1,140	36.00	36.00
90-01-161	Goose & Wreath 868	De Matteo	Open	37.00	37.00
90-01-162	1990 Santa 869	De Matteo	2,250	38.00	38.00
90-01-163	Cardinals 870	De Matteo	Open	39.00	39.00
90-01-164	Angel with Star 871	De Matteo	Open	38.00	38.00
89-01-165	Nutcracker 1989 872	De Matteo	1,790	38.00	50.00
89-01-166	USHS Angel 1989 901	De Matteo	Suspd.	38.00	50.00
89-01-167	Swan Boat 904	De Matteo	Open	38.00	38.00
89-01-168	MFA Noel 905	De Matteo	Suspd.	36.00	42.00
89-01-169	MFA Angel w/Tree 906	De Matteo	Suspd.	36.00	42.00
89-01-170	MFA Durer Snowflake 907	De Matteo	2,000	36.00	42.00
89-01-171	Independence Hall 908	De Matteo	Open	38.00	38.00
90-01-172	Cat on Pillow 915	De Matteo	Unkn.	13.00	13.00
90-01-173	Mouse w/Candy Cane 916	De Matteo	Unkn.	13.00	13.00
89-01-174	L&T Ugly Duckling 917	De Matteo	Suspd.	38.00	38.00
90-01-175	Farmhouse 919	De Matteo	Suspd.	37.00	37.00
90-01-176	Covered Bridge 920	De Matteo	Suspd.	37.00	37.00
90-01-177	Church 921	De Matteo	Suspd.	37.00	37.00
90-01-178	Mill 922	De Matteo	Suspd.	37.00	37.00
90-01-179	Currier & Ives Set -Victorian Village 923	De Matteo	2,000	140.00	140.00
90-01-180	Santa & Reindeer 929	De Matteo	395	39.00	43.00
90-01-181	Christmas Seal 931	De Matteo	Unkn.	25.00	25.00
89-01-182	Bugle Bear 935	De Matteo	Unkn.	12.00	12.00
89-01-183	Jack in the Box Bear 936	De Matteo	Unkn.	12.00	12.00
89-01-184	MFA LaFarge Angel set 937	De Matteo	Suspd.	98.00	98.00
90-01-185	First Christmas Bear 940	De Matteo	Suspd.	35.00	35.00
90-01-186	Santa in the Moon 941	De Matteo	Suspd.	38.00	38.00
90-01-187	Mole & Rat Wind in Will 944	De Matteo	Open	36.00	36.00
90-01-188	Toad Wind in Willows 945	De Matteo	Open	38.00	38.00
90-01-189	Merry Christmas Locket 948	De Matteo	Unkn.	25.00	25.00
90-01-190	Teddy Bear Locket 949	De Matteo	Unkn.	25.00	25.00
89-01-191	Barnesville Buggy 1989 950	De Matteo	Unkn.	13.00	13.00
89-01-192	Victorian Heart 954	De Matteo	Unkn.	13.00	13.00
89-01-193	Stocking Bear 955	De Matteo	Unkn.	12.00	12.00
89-01-194	Stocking w/Toys 956	De Matteo	Unkn.	12.00	12.00
90-01-195	Teddy Bear w/Heart 957	De Matteo	Unkn.	13.00	13.00
90-01-196	Clown w/Dog 958	De Matteo	Unkn.	13.00	13.00
90-01-197	Heart Angel 959	De Matteo	Suspd.	39.00	39.00
90-01-198	Carriage 960	De Matteo	Unkn.	13.00	13.00
90-01-199	Blake Angel 961	De Matteo	Unkn.	36.00	36.00
90-01-200	Colonial Capitol 965	De Matteo	Open	39.00	39.00
90-01-201	Governor's Palace 966	De Matteo	Open	39.00	39.00
90-01-202	Cockatoo 969	De Matteo	Unkn.	13.00	13.00
90-01-203	Father Christmas 970	De Matteo	Suspd.	36.00	36.00
90-01-204	Old Fashioned Santa 971	De Matteo	Suspd.	36.00	36.00
90-01-205	Patriotic Santa 972	De Matteo	Suspd.	36.00	36.00
90-01-206	Santa in Balloon 973	De Matteo	Suspd.	36.00	36.00
90-01-207	Santa on Reindeer 974	De Matteo	Suspd.	36.00	36.00
90-01-208	Santa UpTo Date 975	De Matteo	Suspd.	36.00	36.00
90-01-209	Presidential Homes 990	De Matteo	Open	350.00	475.00
90-01-210	Mrs. Rabbit 991	De Matteo	Open	39.50	39.50
90-01-211	Jeremy Fisher 992	De Matteo	Open	39.50	39.50
90-01-212	Peter Rabbit 993	De Matteo	Open	39.50	39.50
90-01-213	Peter's First Christmas 994	De Matteo	Suspd.	39.50	39.50
90-01-214	Flopsy Bunnies 995	De Matteo	Suspd.	39.50	39.50
90-01-215	First Baptist Angel 997	De Matteo	200	35.00	35.00
91-01-216	I Love Santa 998	De Matteo	Open	36.00	36.00
90-01-217	1990 Peter Rabbit 1018	De Matteo	4,315	39.50	65.00
90-01-218	Peter Rabbit Locket Ornament 1019	De Matteo	Unkn.	30.00	30.00
90-01-219	Jemima Puddleduck 1020	De Matteo	Unkn.	30.00	30.00
90-01-220	Landing Duck 1021	De Matteo	Unkn.	13.00	13.00
90-01-221	White Tail Deer 1022	De Matteo	Unkn.	13.00	13.00
90-01-222	Elk 1023	De Matteo	Unkn.	13.00	13.00
90-01-223	Angel With Violin 1024	De Matteo	Suspd.	39.00	39.00
91-01-224	Carousel Horse 1025	De Matteo	Open	38.00	38.00
91-01-225	Angel With Horn 1026	De Matteo	Open	32.00	32.00
90-01-226	Conestoga Wagon 1027	De Matteo	Open	38.00	38.00
90-01-227	Liberty Bell 1028	De Matteo	Open	38.00	38.00
90-01-228	The Boston Light 1032	De Matteo	Open	39.50	39.50
90-01-229	1990 Snowflake 1033	De Matteo	1,415	36.00	45.00
90-01-230	Pegasus 1037	De Matteo	Suspd.	35.00	35.00
90-01-231	Angels 1039	De Matteo	Suspd.	36.00	36.00
90-01-232	Beardsley Angel 1040	De Matteo	Suspd.	34.00	34.00
90-01-233	Georgia State Capitol 1042	De Matteo	2,000	39.50	39.50
90-01-234	N. Carolina State Capitol 1043	De Matteo	2,000	39.50	39.50
90-01-235	Florida State Capitol 1044	De Matteo	2,000	39.50	39.50
90-01-236	S. Carolina State Capitol 1045	De Matteo	2,000	39.50	39.50
90-01-237	Joy 1047	De Matteo	Suspd.	39.00	39.00
90-01-238	Steadfast Tin Soldier 1050	De Matteo	Suspd.	36.00	36.00
91-01-239	Cow Jumped Over The Moon 1055	De Matteo	Suspd.	38.00	38.00
91-01-240	1991 Santa 1056	De Matteo	3,750	38.00	38.00
90-01-241	USHS Angel 1990 1061	De Matteo	Suspd.	39.00	39.00
90-01-242	San Francisco Row House 1071	De Matteo	Open	39.50	39.50
91-01-243	Mommy & Baby Seal 1075	De Matteo	Suspd.	36.00	36.00
91-01-244	Mommy & Baby Wolves 1076	De Matteo	Suspd.	36.00	36.00
91-01-245	Mommy & Baby Koala Bear 1077	De Matteo	Suspd.	36.00	36.00
91-01-246	Mommy & Baby Kangaroo 1078	De Matteo	Suspd.	36.00	36.00
91-01-247	Mommy & Baby Panda Bear 1079	De Matteo	Suspd.	36.00	36.00
91-01-248	Large Jemima Puddleduck 1083	De Matteo	Open	49.50	49.50
90-01-249	Ferrel's Angel 1990 1084	De Matteo	Unkn.	15.00	15.00
91-01-250	Olivers Rocking Horse 1085	De Matteo	Open	37.00	37.00
91-01-251	Mrs. Rabbit 1991 1086	De Matteo	Suspd.	39.50	39.50
91-01-252	Tailor of Gloucester 1087	De Matteo	Open	39.50	39.50
91-01-253	Pig Robinson 1090	De Matteo	Open	39.50	39.50
91-01-254	Appley Dapply 1091	De Matteo	Open	39.50	39.50
91-01-255	Peter Rabbit With Book 1093	De Matteo	Open	39.50	39.50
90-01-256	Koala San Diego Zoo 1095	De Matteo	Open	36.00	36.00
90-01-257	Locomotive 1100	De Matteo	Suspd.	39.00	39.00
90-01-258	Montpelier 1113	De Matteo	Open	36.00	36.00
90-01-259	Ducklings 1114	De Matteo	Open	38.00	38.00
91-01-260	Large Peter Rabbit 1116	De Matteo	Open	49.50	49.50
91-01-261	Large Tailor of Gloucester 1117	De Matteo	Open	49.50	49.50
91-01-262	Nativity 1118	De Matteo	Open	38.00	38.00

		ARTIST	EDITION	ISSUE	QUOTE
91-01-263	Alice 1119	De Matteo	Open	39.00	39.00
91-01-264	Mad Tea Party 1120	De Matteo	Open	39.00	39.00
91-01-265	White Rabbit 1121	De Matteo	Open	39.00	39.00
91-01-266	Queen of Hearts 1122	De Matteo	Open	39.00	39.00
91-01-267	Waiting For Santa 1123	De Matteo	Open	38.00	38.00
90-01-268	Ember 1124	De Matteo	120	N/A	N/A
91-01-269	USHS Angel 1991 1139	De Matteo	Suspd.	38.00	38.00
91-01-270	Columbus 1140	De Matteo	1,500	39.00	39.00
91-01-271	The Voyages Of Columbus 1141	De Matteo	1,500	39.00	39.00
91-01-272	Precious Planet 1142	De Matteo	2,000	120.00	120.00
91-01-273	MFA Snowflake 1991 1143	De Matteo	Suspd.	36.00	36.00
91-01-274	Fir Tree 1145	De Matteo	Open	39.00	39.00
91-01-275	Nutcracker 1151	De Matteo	Open	49.50	49.50
91-01-276	Paul Revere 1158	De Matteo	Open	39.00	39.00
91-01-277	Alice in Wonderland 1159	De Matteo	Open	140.00	140.00
91-01-278	Nutcracker 1183	De Matteo	Open	38.00	38.00
91-01-279	Nutrcracker Suite 1184	De Matteo	Open	38.00	38.00
91-01-280	Gus 1195	De Matteo	200	N/A	N/A
91-01-281	San Francisco Heart 1196	De Matteo	Open	39.00	39.00
92-01-282	Xmas Tree & Heart 1162	De Matteo	Suspd.	36.00	36.00
92-01-283	Andrea 1163	De Matteo	Suspd.	36.00	36.00
92-01-284	Joy 1164	De Matteo	Open	39.50	39.50
92-01-285	Unicorn 1165	De Matteo	Suspd.	36.00	36.00
92-01-286	Noah's Ark 1166	De Matteo	Open	36.00	36.00
92-01-287	Jemima Puddleduck 1992 1167	De Matteo	Suspd.	39.50	39.50
92-01-288	Mrs. Rabbit 1181	De Matteo	Open	39.50	39.50
92-01-289	Round Teapot 1206	De Matteo	Open	49.50	49.50
92-01-290	Revere Teapot 1207	De Matteo	Open	49.50	49.50
92-01-291	Chocolate Pot 1208	De Matteo	Open	49.50	49.50
92-01-292	Angel W/ Double Horn 1212	De Matteo	2,000	39.00	39.00
92-01-293	Angel 1213	De Matteo	2,000	39.00	39.00
92-01-294	Della Robbia Ornament 1219	De Matteo	Open	39.00	39.00
92-01-295	Fairy Tale Angel 1222	De Matteo	Open	36.00	36.00
92-01-296	Parrot 1233	De Matteo	Open	37.00	37.00
92-01-297	St. John Lion 1235	De Matteo	10,000	39.00	39.00
92-01-298	St. John Angel 1236	De Matteo	10,000	39.00	39.00
92-01-299	Scrooge 1241	De Matteo	Open	36.00	36.00
92-01-300	Bob & Tiny Tim 1242	De Matteo	Open	36.00	36.00
92-01-301	Marley's Ghost 1243	De Matteo	Open	36.00	36.00
92-01-302	Mrs. Cratchit 1244	De Matteo	Open	36.00	36.00
92-01-303	America At Peace 1245	De Matteo	2000	85.00	85.00
92-01-304	MFA Snowflake 1246	De Matteo	Open	39.00	39.00
92-01-305	Princess & The Pea 1247	De Matteo	Open	39.00	39.00
92-01-306	Dorothy 1284	De Matteo	Open	36.00	36.00
92-01-307	Tin Man 1285	De Matteo	Open	36.00	36.00
92-01-308	Scarecrow 1286	De Matteo	Open	36.00	36.00
92-01-309	Cowardly Lion 1287	De Matteo	Open	36.00	36.00
92-01-310	Heart of Christmas 1301	De Matteo	500	39.00	39.00
93-01-311	Angel Bell 1312	De Matteo	Open	38.00	38.00
93-01-312	Clara with Nutcracker 1316	De Matteo	Open	38.00	38.00
93-01-313	Carousel Horse 1993 1321	De Matteo	Yr.Iss.	38.00	38.00
93-01-314	Lion and Lamb 1322	De Matteo	Open	38.00	38.00
93-01-315	Mrs. Rabbit 1993 1325	De Matteo	Yr.Iss	39.50	39.50
93-01-316	Peace 1327	De Matteo	Open	36.00	36.00
93-01-317	Partridge & Pear 1328	De Matteo	Open	38.00	38.00
93-01-318	Violin 1340	De Matteo	Unkn.	39.50	39.50
93-01-319	Angel 1342	De Matteo	Open	38.00	38.00
93-01-320	Zig Zag Tree 1343	De Matteo	Open	39.00	39.00
93-01-321	Beantown 1344	De Matteo	Open	38.00	38.00
93-01-322	Creche 1351	De Matteo	Open	38.00	38.00
93-01-323	Celebrate America 1352	De Matteo	Open	38.00	38.00
93-01-324	Cheer Mouse 1359	De Matteo	Open	39.00	39.00
93-01-325	Window 1360	De Matteo	Open	38.00	38.00
93-01-326	Cable Car to the Stars 1363	De Matteo	Open	39.00	39.00
93-01-327	Public Garden 1370	De Matteo	Open	38.00	38.00
93-01-328	Peter Rabit 100th 1383	De Matteo	Yr.Iss.	39.50	39.50
93-01-329	Snowflake 1993 1394	De Matteo	Yr.Iss.	40.00	40.00
93-01-330	Xmas Tree 1395	De Matteo	Open	40.00	40.00
93-01-331	Puss In Boots 1396	De Matteo	Open	40.00	40.00
93-01-332	Gurgling Cod 1397	De Matteo	Open	50.00	50.00
93-01-333	Mouse King 1398	De Matteo	Open	38.00	38.00
93-01-334	Faneuil Hall 1399	De Matteo	Open	39.00	39.00
93-01-335	Angel 1993 1405	De Matteo	Yr.Iss.	45.00	45.00
93-01-336	Faneuil Hall 1412	De Matteo	Open	39.50	39.50
94-01-337	Golden Gate Bridge 1429	De Matteo	Open	39.50	39.50
94-01-338	Beatrix Potter Noel 1438	De Matteo	Open	39.50	39.50
94-01-339	Emperor 1439	De Matteo	Open	38.00	38.00
94-01-340	Heart of Christmas 1440	De Matteo	500	39.00	39.00
94-01-341	Canterbury Star 1441	De Matteo	Open	35.00	35.00
94-01-342	Marmion Angels 1443	De Matteo	Open	50.00	50.00
94-01-343	1994 Peter Rabbit 1444	De Matteo	Yr.Iss.	39.50	39.50
94-01-344	Cardinal & Holly 1445	De Matteo	Open	38.00	38.00
94-01-345	R.E. Lee Monument 1446	De Matteo	Open	39.00	39.00
94-01-346	Weld Boathouse 1447	De Matteo	Open	39.00	39.00
94-01-347	1994 Star 1462	De Matteo	Yr.Iss.	39.50	39.50
94-01-348	Holly 1472	De Matteo	Open	38.00	38.00
94-01-349	Noel 1477	De Matteo	Open	38.00	38.00
94-01-350	Two Turtle Doves 1478	De Matteo	Open	38.00	38.00
94-01-351	Angel With Star 1480	De Matteo	Open	38.00	38.00
94-01-352	Heralding Angel 1481	De Matteo	Open	39.00	39.00
94-01-353	Marengo 1482	De Matteo	Yr.Iss.	39.00	39.00
94-01-354	1994 Snowflake 1486	De Matteo	Yr.Iss.	39.00	39.00
94-01-355	Trumpet 1504	De Matteo	Open	39.00	39.00
94-01-356	Lyre 1505	De Matteo	Open	39.00	39.00
94-01-357	Mandoline 1506	De Matteo	Open	39.00	39.00
94-01-358	USHS Dove 1521	De Matteo	Open	39.00	39.00
94-01-359	Palace of Fine Arts 1522	De Matteo	Open	39.50	39.50
94-01-360	Esplanade 1523	De Matteo	Open	39.00	39.00
94-01-361	Smithsonian Angel 1534	De Matteo	Yr.Iss.	39.00	39.00
94-01-362	Heart of Christmas 1537	De Matteo	Open	39.00	39.00
94-01-363	Mass State House 1540	De Matteo	Open	39.00	39.00
94-01-364	Paul Revere Lantern 1541	De Matteo	Open	39.00	39.00
94-01-365	Quatrefoil 1542	De Matteo	Open	50.00	50.00
94-01-366	Snowman 1572	De Matteo	Open	39.00	39.00
94-01-367	Jefferson Hotel 1594	De Matteo	Open	39.00	39.00
95-01-368	Peter Rabbit & B Bunny 1492	De Matteo	Open	39.50	39.50
95-01-369	Hart 1501	De Matteo	Open	38.00	38.00
95-01-370	Bird Swirl 1502	De Matteo	Open	39.00	39.00
95-01-371	Peace on Earth 1503	De Matteo	Open	36.00	36.00
95-01-372	Kate Greenaway Noel 1515	De Matteo	Open	39.00	39.00
95-01-373	Snowflake 1574	De Matteo	Open	38.00	38.00
95-01-374	Star 1591	De Matteo	Open	40.00	40.00
95-01-375	Kermit Joy 1596	De Matteo	Open	36.00	36.00
95-01-376	Peter Rabbit 1995 1598	De Matteo	Yr.Iss.	39.50	39.50
95-01-377	Night Before Christmas 1600	De Matteo	Open	160.00	160.00
Hand & Hammer		**Annual Ornaments**			
87-02-001	Silver Bells 737	De Matteo	2,700	38.00	55.00
88-02-002	Silver Bells 792	De Matteo	3,150	39.50	50.00
89-02-003	Silver Bells 843	De Matteo	3,150	39.50	55.00
90-02-004	Silver Bells 865	De Matteo	3,615	39.00	50.00
90-02-005	Silver Bells Rev. 964	De Matteo	4,490	39.00	39.00
91-02-006	Silver Bells 1080	De Matteo	4,100	39.50	39.50
92-02-007	Silver Bells 1148	De Matteo	4,100	39.50	39.50
93-02-008	Silver Bells 1311	De Matteo	Yr.Iss.	39.50	39.50
94-02-009	Silver Bells 1463	De Matteo	Yr.Iss.	39.50	39.50
95-02-010	Silver Bells 1597	De Matteo	Yr.Iss.	39.50	39.50
John Hine N.A. Ltd.		**David Winter Ornaments**			
91-01-001	Scrooge's Counting House	D. Winter	Closed	15.00	15.00
91-01-002	Hogmanay	D. Winter	Closed	15.00	15.00
91-01-003	A Christmas Carol	D. Winter	Closed	15.00	15.00
91-01-004	Mister Fezziwig's Emporium	D. Winter	Closed	15.00	15.00
91-01-005	Set	D. Winter	Closed	60.00	60.00
92-01-006	Fairytale Castle	D. Winter	Closed	15.00	15.00
92-01-007	Fred's Home	D. Winter	Closed	15.00	15.00
92-01-008	Suffolk House	D. Winter	Closed	15.00	15.00
92-01-009	Tudor Manor	D. Winter	Closed	15.00	15.00
92-01-010	Set	D. Winter	Closed	60.00	30-40.00
93-01-011	Scrooge's School	J. Hine Studios	Closed	15.00	15.00
93-01-012	Will O The Wisp	J. Hine Studios	Closed	15.00	15.00
93-01-013	The Grange	J. Hine Studios	Closed	15.00	15.00
93-01-014	Tom Fool's	J. Hine Studios	Closed	15.00	15.00
93-01-015	Set	J. Hine Studios	Closed	60.00	60.00
94-01-016	What Cottage	J. Hine Studios	12/94	17.50	17.50
94-01-017	Old Joe's	J. Hine Studios	12/94	17.50	17.50
94-01-018	Scrooge's Family Home	J. Hine Studios	12/94	17.50	17.50
Iris Arc Crystal		**Christmas Ornaments**			
84-01-001	1984 Merry Christmas Ornament	P. Hale	Retrd.	28.00	28.00
85-01-002	1985 Noel Ornament	P. Hale	Retrd.	28.00	28.00
86-01-003	1986 Noel Christmas Ornament	P. Hale	Retrd.	30.00	30.00
87-01-004	1987 Angel Christmas Ornament	P. Hale	Retrd.	30.00	30.00
88-01-005	1988 Merry Christmas Ornament	P. Hale	Retrd.	30.00	30.00
89-01-006	1989 Christmas Ornament	P. Hale	Retrd.	30.00	30.00
90-01-007	1990 Reindeer Christmas Ornament	M. Goena	Retrd.	30.00	30.00
91-01-008	1991 Santa Christmas Ornament	M. Goena	Retrd.	35.00	35.00
92-01-009	1992 Angel Christmas Ornament	M. Goena	Retrd.	30.00	30.00
93-01-010	1993 Dove Christmas Ornament	M. Goena	Retrd.	35.00	35.00
Kirk Stieff		**Colonial Williamsburg**			
83-01-001	Tree Top Star, silverplate	D. Bacorn	Closed	29.50	29.50
87-01-002	Rocking Horse, silverplate	D. Bacorn	Closed	20.00	30.00
87-01-003	Tin Drum, silverplate	D. Bacorn	Closed	20.00	30.00
88-01-004	Lamb, silverplate	D. Bacorn	Closed	20.00	22.00
88-01-005	Unicorn, silverplate	D. Bacorn	Closed	22.00	22.00
89-01-006	Doll ornament, silverplate	D. Bacorn	Closed	22.00	22.00
92-01-007	Court House	D. Bacorn	Open	10.00	10.00
92-01-008	Prentis Store	D. Bacorn	Open	10.00	10.00
92-01-009	Wythe House	D. Bacorn	Open	10.00	10.00
93-01-010	Governors Palace	D. Bacorn	Open	10.00	10.00
Kirk Stieff		**Kirk Stieff Ornaments**			
84-02-001	Unicorn	D. Bacorn	Closed	18.00	19.95
83-02-002	Charleston Locomotive	D. Bacorn	Closed	18.00	19.95
86-02-003	Icicle, sterling silver	D. Bacorn	Closed	35.00	50.00
89-02-004	Smithsonian Carousel Horse	Kirk Stieff	Closed	50.00	50.00
89-02-005	Smithsonian Carousel Seahorse	Kirk Stieff	Closed	50.00	50.00
90-02-006	Toy Ship	Kirk Stieff	Closed	23.00	23.00
92-02-007	Repoussé Wreath	J. Ferraioli	Open	13.00	13.00
92-02-008	Repoussé Angel	J. Ferraioli	Open	13.00	13.00
92-02-009	Cat and Ornament	D. Bacorn	Closed	10.00	10.00
92-02-020	Guardian Angel	J. Ferraioli	Closed	13.00	13.00
93-02-021	Cat with Ribbon	D. Bacorn	Open	12.00	12.00
93-02-022	Bell with Ribbon	D. Bacorn	Open	12.00	12.00
93-02-023	Wreath with Ribbon	D. Bacorn	Open	12.00	12.00
93-02-024	Baby's Christmas	D. Bacorn	Open	12.00	12.00
93-02-025	French Horn	D. Bacorn	Closed	12.00	12.00
93-02-026	Mouse and Ornament	D. Bacorn	Closed	10.00	10.00
93-02-027	First Christmas Together	D. Bacorn	Closed	10.00	10.00
94-02-028	Unicorn	D. Bacorn	Open	8.00	8.00
94-02-029	Victorian Skaters	D. Bacorn	Open	8.00	8.00
94-02-030	Angel with Star	J. Ferraioli	Open	8.00	8.00
94-02-031	Teddy Bear	D. Bacorn	Open	8.00	8.00
94-02-032	Kitten with Tassel	J. Ferraioli	Open	12.00	12.00
94-02-033	Santa with Tassel	J. Ferraioli	Open	12.00	12.00
94-02-034	Williamsburg Wreath	D. Bacorn	Open	15.00	15.00
Lance Corporation		**Sebastian Christmas Ornaments**			
43-01-001	Madonna of the Chair	P.W. Baston	Closed	2.00	150-200.
81-01-002	Santa Claus	P.W. Baston	Closed	28.50	30.00
82-01-003	Madonna of the Chair (Reissue of '43)	P.W. Baston	Closed	15.00	30-45.00
85-01-004	Home for the Holidays	P.W. Baston Jr.	Closed	10.00	13.00
86-01-005	Holiday Sleigh Ride	P.W. Baston Jr.	Closed	10.00	12.50
87-01-006	Santa	P.W. Baston Jr.	Closed	10.00	12.50
88-01-007	Decorating the Tree	P.W. Baston Jr.	Closed	12.50	12.50
89-01-008	Final Preparations for Christmas	P.W. Baston Jr.	Closed	13.90	13.90
90-01-009	Stuffing the Stockings	P.W. Baston Jr.	Closed	14.00	14.00
91-01-010	Merry Christmas	P.W. Baston Jr.	Closed	14.50	14.50
92-01-011	Final Check	P.W. Baston Jr.	Closed	14.50	14.50
93-01-012	Ethnic Santa	P.W. Baston Jr.	Closed	12.50	12.50
93-01-013	Caroling With Santa	P.W. Baston Jr.	Closed	15.00	15.00
94-01-014	Victorian Christmas Skaters	P.W. Baston Jr.	Annual	17.00	17.00
Lenox China		**Annual Ornaments**			
82-01-001	1982 Ornament	Lenox	Yr.Iss.	30.00	50-90.00
83-01-002	1983 Ornament	Lenox	Yr.Iss.	35.00	75.00
84-01-003	1984 Ornament	Lenox	Yr.Iss.	38.00	65.00
85-01-004	1985 Ornament	Lenox	Yr.Iss.	37.50	60.00
86-01-005	1986 Ornament	Lenox	Yr.Iss.	38.50	50.00
87-01-006	1987 Ornament	Lenox	Yr.Iss.	39.00	45.00
88-01-007	1988 Ornament	Lenox	Yr.Iss.	39.00	45.00
89-01-008	1989 Ornament	Lenox	Yr.Iss.	39.00	39.00
90-01-009	1990 Ornament	Lenox	Yr.Iss.	42.00	42.00
91-01-010	1991 Ornament	Lenox	Yr.Iss.	39.00	39.00

		ARTIST	EDITION	ISSUE	QUOTE
92-01-011	1992 Ornament	Lenox	Yr.Iss.	42.00	42.00
93-01-012	1993 Ornament	Lenox	Yr.Iss.	45.00	45.00
94-01-013	1994 Ornament	Lenox	Yr.Iss.	39.00	39.00
Lenox China	**Days of Christmas**				
87-02-001	Partridge	Lenox	Open	22.50	22.50
88-02-002	Two Turtle Doves	Lenox	Open	22.50	22.50
89-02-003	Three French Hens	Lenox	Open	22.50	22.50
90-02-004	Four Calling Birds	Lenox	Open	25.00	25.00
91-02-005	Five Golden Rings	Lenox	Open	25.00	25.00
92-02-006	Six Geese a-Laying	Lenox	Open	25.00	25.00
93-02-007	Seven Swans	Lenox	Open	26.00	26.00
94-02-008	Eight Maids Milking	Lenox	Open	26.00	26.00
Lenox China	**Yuletide**				
85-03-001	Teddy Bear	Lenox	Closed	18.00	18.00
85-03-002	Christmas Tree	Lenox	Open	18.00	18.00
89-03-003	Santa with Tree	Lenox	Closed	18.00	18.00
89-03-004	Angel with Horn	Lenox	Open	18.00	18.00
90-03-005	Dove	Lenox	Open	19.50	19.50
91-03-006	Snowman	Lenox	Open	19.50	19.50
92-03-007	Goose	Lenox	Open	19.50	19.50
93-03-008	Cardinal	Lenox	Open	19.50	19.50
94-03-009	Cat	Lenox	Open	19.50	19.50
Lenox China	**Holiday Homecoming**				
88-04-001	Hearth	Lenox	Closed	22.50	22.50
89-04-002	Door (Dated)	Lenox	Closed	22.50	22.50
90-04-003	Hutch	Lenox	Open	25.00	25.00
91-04-004	Window (Dated)	Lenox	Yr.Iss.	25.00	25.00
92-04-005	Stove (Dated)	Lenox	Yr.Iss.	25.00	25.00
93-04-006	Clock	Lenox	Yr.Iss.	26.00	26.00
94-04-007	Lamp	Lenox	Yr.Iss.	26.00	26.00
Lenox China	**Santa's Portraits**				
89-05-001	Santa's Visit	Lenox	Open	27.00	27.00
90-05-002	Santa With Garland	Lenox	Open	29.00	29.00
90-05-003	Santa's Ride	Lenox	Open	29.00	29.00
91-05-004	Santa And Child	Lenox	Open	29.00	29.00
92-05-005	Santa in Chimney	Lenox	Open	29.00	29.00
93-05-006	Santa Filling Stocking	Lenox	Open	29.00	29.00
Lenox Collections	**The Christmas Carousel**				
89-01-001	White Horse	Lenox	Open	19.50	19.50
89-01-002	Zebra	Lenox	Open	19.50	19.50
89-01-003	Lion	Lenox	Open	19.50	19.50
89-01-004	Sea Horse	Lenox	Open	19.50	19.50
89-01-005	Pinto	Lenox	Open	19.50	19.50
89-01-006	Goat	Lenox	Open	19.50	19.50
89-01-007	Reindeer	Lenox	Open	19.50	19.50
89-01-008	Polar Bear	Lenox	Open	19.50	19.50
89-01-009	Hare	Lenox	Open	19.50	19.50
89-01-010	Elephant	Lenox	Open	19.50	19.50
89-01-011	Swan	Lenox	Open	19.50	19.50
89-01-012	Unicorn	Lenox	Open	19.50	19.50
89-01-013	Palomino	Lenox	Open	19.50	19.50
89-01-014	Black Horse	Lenox	Open	19.50	19.50
89-01-015	Cat	Lenox	Open	19.50	19.50
89-01-016	Tiger	Lenox	Open	19.50	19.50
90-01-017	Camel	Lenox	Open	19.50	19.50
90-01-018	Rooster	Lenox	Open	19.50	19.50
90-01-019	Giraffe	Lenox	Open	19.50	19.50
90-01-020	Panda	Lenox	Open	19.50	19.50
90-01-021	Frog	Lenox	Open	19.50	19.50
90-01-022	Pig	Lenox	Open	19.50	19.50
90-01-023	St. Bernard	Lenox	Open	19.50	19.50
90-01-024	Medieval Horse	Lenox	Open	19.50	19.50
90-01-025	Set of 24	Lenox	Open	468.00	468.00
Lenox Crystal	**Annual Bell Series**				
87-01-001	Partridge Bell	Lenox	Yr.Iss.	45.00	45.00
88-01-002	Angel Bell	Lenox	Open	45.00	45.00
89-01-003	St. Nicholas Bell	Lenox	Open	45.00	45.00
90-01-004	Christmas Tree Bell	Lenox	Open	49.00	49.00
91-01-005	Teddy Bear Bell	Lenox	Yr.Iss.	49.00	49.00
92-01-006	Snowman Bell	Lenox	Yr.Iss.	49.00	49.00
93-01-007	Nutcracker Bell	Lenox	Yr.Iss.	49.00	49.00
94-01-008	Candle Bell	Lenox	Yr.Iss.	49.00	49.00
Lilliput Lane Ltd.	**Christmas Ornaments**				
92-01-001	Mistletoe Cottage	Lilliput Lane	Closed	27.50	27.50
93-01-002	Robin Cottage	Lilliput Lane	Closed	35.00	35.00
94-01-003	Ivy House	Lilliput Lane	Yr.Iss.	35.00	35.00
Lladro	**Miniature Ornaments**				
88-01-001	Miniature Angels-L1604G (Set of 3)	Lladro	Yr.Iss.	75.00	110-125.
89-01-002	Holy Family-L5657G (Set of 3)	Lladro	Yr.Iss.	79.50	79.50
90-01-003	Three Kings-L5729G (Set of 3)	Lladro	Yr Iss.	87.50	150.00
91-01-004	Holy Shepherds-L5809G	Lladro	Yr.Iss.	97.50	90-108.
93-01-005	Nativity Trio-L6095G	Lladro	Yr.Iss.	115.00	115.00
Lladro	**Annual Ornaments**				
88-02-001	Christmas Ball-L1603M	Lladro	Yr.Iss.	60.00	65.00
89-02-002	Christmas Ball-L5656M	Lladro	Yr.Iss.	65.00	65.00
90-02-003	Christmas Ball-L5730M	Lladro	Yr Iss.	70.00	75-90.00
91-02-004	Christmas Ball-L5829M	Lladro	Yr.Iss.	52.00	52-90.00
92-02-005	Christmas Ball-L5914M	Lladro	Yr.Iss.	52.00	52-90.00
93-02-006	Christmas Ball-L6009M	Lladro	Yr.Iss.	54.00	54.00
94-02-007	Christmas Ball-L6105M	Lladro	Yr.Iss.	55.00	55.00
Lladro	**Tree Topper Ornaments**				
90-03-001	Angel Tree Topper-L5719G-Blue	Lladro	Yr.Iss.	115.00	180-350.
91-03-002	Angel Tree Topper-L5831G-Pink	Lladro	Yr.Iss.	115.00	200.00
92-03-003	Angel Tree Topper-L5875G-Green	Lladro	Yr.Iss.	120.00	200.00
93-03-004	Angel Tree Topper-L5962G-Lavender	Lladro	Yr.Iss.	125.00	200.00
Lladro	**Ornaments**				
92-04-001	Snowman-L5841G	Lladro	Yr.Iss.	50.00	52.00
92-04-002	Santa-L5842G	Lladro	Yr.Iss.	55.00	57.00
92-04-003	Baby's First-1992-L5922G	Lladro	Yr.Iss.	55.00	55.00
92-04-004	Our First-1992-L5923G	Lladro	Yr.Iss.	50.00	50.00
92-04-005	Elf Ornament-L5938G	Lladro	Yr.Iss.	50.00	50.00
92-04-006	Mrs. Claus-L5939G	Lladro	Yr.Iss.	55.00	57.00
92-04-007	Christmas Morning-L5940G	Lladro	Yr.Iss.	97.50	108.00
93-04-008	Nativity Lamb-L5969G	Lladro	Yr.Iss.	85.00	85.00
93-04-009	Baby's First 1993-L6037G	Lladro	Yr.Iss.	57.00	57.00

		ARTIST	EDITION	ISSUE	QUOTE
93-04-010	Our First-L6038G	Lladro	Yr.Iss.	52.00	52.00
Lladro	**Angel Orchestra**				
91-05-001	Heavenly Harpist-15830	Lladro	Yr.Iss.	135.00	144-162.
92-05-002	Angelic Cymbalist-5876	Lladro	Yr.Iss.	140.00	225.00
93-05-003	Angelic Melody-L5963G	Lladro	Yr.Iss.	145.00	168.00
94-05-004	Angelic Violinist-L6126G	Lladro	Yr.Iss.	150.00	150.00
Lladro	**Angels**				
94-06-001	Joyful Offering L6125G	Lladro	Yr.Iss.	245.00	245.00
Seymour Mann Inc.	**Christmas Collection**				
85-01-001	Angel Wall XMAS-523	J. White	Closed	12.00	12.00
86-01-002	Cupid Head XMAS-53	J. White	Open	25.00	25.00
86-01-003	Santa XMAS-384	J. White	Closed	7.50	7.50
89-01-004	Christmas Cat in Teacup XMAS-660	J. White	Closed	13.50	13.50
91-01-005	Floral Plaque XMAS-911	J. White	Closed	10.00	10.00
91-01-006	Flower Basket XMAS-912	J. White	Closed	10.00	10.00
90-01-007	Cupid CPD-5	J. White	Open	13.50	13.50
90-01-008	Cupid CPD-6	J. White	Open	13.50	13.50
90-01-009	Doll Tree Topper OM-124	J. White	Closed	85.00	85.00
90-01-010	Hat w/ Streamers OM-116	J. White	Closed	20.00	20.00
90-01-011	Heartlace OM-119	J. White	Closed	12.00	12.00
90-01-012	Lace Ball OM-120	J. White	Closed	10.00	10.00
90-01-013	Tassel OM-118	J. White	Closed	7.50	7.50
91-01-014	Elf w/ Reindeer CJ-422	Jaimy	Closed	9.00	9.00
91-01-015	Elves w/ Mail CJ-464	J. White	Closed	30.00	30.00
91-01-016	Flat Red Santa CJ-115R	Jaimy	Closed	2.88	2.88
91-01-017	Flat Santa CJ-115	Jaimy	Closed	7.50	7.50
91-01-018	Santas, set of 6 CJ-12	Jaimy	Closed	60.00	60.00
94-01-020	Santa w/ Candle CBU-300	J. White	Open	40.00	40.00
94-01-021	Santa w/ Lamb CBU-301	J. White	Open	40.00	40.00
94-01-022	Santa w/ Stick CBU-302	J. White	Open	40.00	40.00
94-01-023	Santa w/ Lantern CBU-303	J. White	Open	40.00	40.00
94-01-024	Santa w/ Children CBU-304	J. White	Open	40.00	40.00
94-01-025	Santa w/ Child CBU-305	J. White	Open	40.00	40.00
94-01-026	Santa w/ Sled CBU-306	J. White	Open	40.00	40.00
94-01-027	Santa w/ List CBU-307	J. White	Open	40.00	40.00
Seymour Mann Inc.	**Gingerbread Christmas Collection**				
91-02-001	Gingerbread Angel CJ-411	J. Sauerbrey	Closed	7.50	7.50
91-02-002	Gingerbread House CJ-416	J. Sauerbrey	Closed	7.50	7.50
91-02-003	Gingerbread Man CJ-415	J. Sauerbrey	Closed	7.50	7.50
91-02-004	Gingerbread Mouse/Boot CJ-409	J. Sauerbrey	Closed	7.50	7.50
91-02-005	Gingerbread Mrs. Claus CJ-414	J. Sauerbrey	Closed	7.50	7.50
91-02-006	Gingerbread Reindeer CJ-410	J. Sauerbrey	Closed	7.50	7.50
91-02-007	Gingerbread Santa CJ-408	J. Sauerbrey	Closed	7.50	7.50
91-02-008	Gingerbread Sleigh CJ-406	J. Sauerbrey	Closed	7.50	7.50
91-02-009	Gingerbread Snowman CJ-412	J. Sauerbrey	Closed	7.50	7.50
91-02-010	Gingerbread Tree CJ-407	J. Sauerbrey	Closed	7.50	7.50
Seymour Mann Inc.	**Victorian Christmas Collection**				
91-03-001	Couple Against Wind CJ-420	Jaimy	Closed	15.00	15.00
Seymour Mann Inc.	**Christmas Lite-Up Houses**				
94-04-001	Set/10 Lite-up Houses XMR-10	L. Sciola	Open	95.00	95.00
94-04-002	Set/10 Lite-up Houses XMR-11	L. Sciola	Open	95.00	95.00
94-04-003	Lite-up Restaurant XMR-20	L. Sciola	Open	30.00	30.00
94-04-004	Lite-up Church XMR-21	L. Sciola	Open	30.00	30.00
94-04-005	Lite-up Mansion XMR-23	L. Sciola	Open	30.00	30.00
94-04-006	Lite-up Library XMR-24	L. Sciola	Open	30.00	30.00
94-04-007	Lite-up Country House	L. Sciola	Open	30.00	30.00
June McKenna Collectibles, Inc.	**Flatback Ornaments**				
82-01-001	Santa With Toys	J. McKenna	Closed	14.00	80-110.
82-01-002	Mama Bear, Blue Cape	J. McKenna	Closed	12.00	75.00
82-01-003	Papa Bear, Red Cape	J. McKenna	Closed	12.00	85.00
82-01-004	Baby Bear, Teeshirt	J. McKenna	Closed	11.00	85.00
82-01-005	Candy Cane	J. McKenna	Closed	10.00	250-405.
82-01-006	Colonial Man, available in 2 colors	J. McKenna	Closed	12.00	75.00
82-01-007	Colonial Woman, available in 2 colors	J. McKenna	Closed	12.00	65.00
82-01-008	Kate Greenaway Boy	J. McKenna	Closed	12.00	155.00
82-01-009	Kate Greenaway Girl	J. McKenna	Closed	12.00	150.00
82-01-010	Angel With Toys	J. McKenna	Closed	14.00	110.00
83-01-011	Grandma, available in 4 colors	J. McKenna	Closed	12.00	60.00
83-01-012	Grandpa, available in 4 colors	J. McKenna	Closed	12.00	60.00
83-01-013	Mother Bear in Dress, available in 2 colors	J. McKenna	Closed	12.00	50-70.00
83-01-014	Father Bear in Suit, available in 2 colors	J. McKenna	Closed	12.00	50-70.00
83-01-015	Baby Bear in Vest, available in 2 colors	J. McKenna	Closed	11.00	80.00
83-01-016	Raggedy Ann	J. McKenna	Closed	12.00	175-315.
83-01-017	Raggedy Andy	J. McKenna	Closed	12.00	100.00
83-01-018	St. Nick With Lantern	J. McKenna	Closed	14.00	50-75.00
83-01-019	Gloria Angel	J. McKenna	Closed	14.00	350-550.
83-01-020	Baby, blue trim	J. McKenna	Closed	11.00	85.00
83-01-021	Baby, pink trim	J. McKenna	Closed	11.00	75.00
84-01-022	Angel with Horn	J. McKenna	Closed	14.00	150.00
84-01-023	Mr. Claus	J. McKenna	Closed	14.00	65-120.
84-01-024	Mrs. Claus	J. McKenna	Closed	14.00	65-85.00
84-01-025	Country Boy, available in 2 colors	J. McKenna	Closed	12.00	65.00
84-01-026	Country Girl, available in 2 colors	J. McKenna	Closed	12.00	60.00
84-01-027	Old World Santa, available in 3 colors	J. McKenna	Closed	14.00	50-95.00
84-01-028	Old World Santa, gold	J. McKenna	Closed	14.00	225.00
85-01-029	Baby Pig	J. McKenna	Closed	11.00	65-100.
85-01-030	Father Pig	J. McKenna	Closed	12.00	50.00
85-01-031	Mother Pig	J. McKenna	Closed	12.00	50-70.00
85-01-032	Amish Man	J. McKenna	Closed	13.00	50-275.
85-01-033	Amish Woman	J. McKenna	Closed	13.00	50-275.
85-01-034	Primitive Santa	J. McKenna	Closed	17.00	150-200.
86-01-035	Amish Boy	J. McKenna	Closed	13.00	65-275.
86-01-036	Amish Girl	J. McKenna	Closed	13.00	275-360.
86-01-037	Santa with Bells, green	J. McKenna	Closed	14.00	425.00
86-01-038	Santa with Bells, blue	J. McKenna	Closed	14.00	55.00
86-01-039	Santa with Bear	J. McKenna	Closed	14.00	40.00
86-01-040	Santa with Bag	J. McKenna	Closed	16.00	30-40.00
88-01-041	Elizabeth, sill sitter	J. McKenna	Closed	20.00	200-300.
88-01-042	Guardian Angel	J. McKenna	Closed	16.00	40.00
88-01-043	1776 Santa	J. McKenna	Closed	17.00	40.00
88-01-044	Santa With Book (blue & red)	J. McKenna	Closed	17.00	110-175.
88-01-045	Santa With Toys	J. McKenna	Closed	17.00	40.00
88-01-046	Santa With Wreath	J. McKenna	Closed	17.00	40.00
89-01-047	Glorious Angel	J. McKenna	Open	17.00	17.00
89-01-048	Santa With Staff	J. McKenna	Closed	17.00	40.00
89-01-049	Santa With Tree	J. McKenna	Closed	17.00	40.00
89-01-050	Winking Santa	J. McKenna	Closed	17.00	40.00

		ARTIST	EDITION	ISSUE	QUOTE
90-01-051	Ho Ho Ho	J. McKenna	Closed	17.00	40.00
90-01-052	Elf Jeffrey	J. McKenna	Closed	17.00	40.00
90-01-052	Harvest Santa	J. McKenna	Closed	17.00	40.00
91-01-053	Santa With Lights, black or white	J. McKenna	Closed	20.00	45.00
91-01-054	Santa With Banner	J. McKenna	Closed	20.00	20.00
91-01-055	Elf Joey	J. McKenna	Closed	20.00	20.00
91-01-056	Boy Angel	J. McKenna	Closed	20.00	20.00
91-01-057	Girl Angel	J. McKenna	Closed	20.00	30.00
92-01-058	Santa With Basket	J. McKenna	Closed	25.00	30.00
92-01-059	Santa With Sack	J. McKenna	Closed	25.00	30.00
92-01-060	Northpole News	J. McKenna	Closed	25.00	30.00
92-01-061	Elf Scotty	J. McKenna	Closed	25.00	30.00
92-01-062	Praying Angel	J. McKenna	Closed	25.00	30.00
93-01-063	Old Lamplighter	J. McKenna	Open	30.00	30.00
93-01-064	Christmas Treat	J. McKenna	Open	30.00	30.00
93-01-065	Final Notes	J. McKenna	Open	30.00	30.00
93-01-066	Elf Bernie	J. McKenna	Open	30.00	30.00
93-01-067	Angel of Peace- white or pink	J. McKenna	Open	30.00	30.00
94-01-068	Elf-Ricky	J. McKenna	Open	30.00	30.00
94-01-069	Snow Showers	J. McKenna	Open	30.00	30.00
94-01-070	Nutcracker	J. McKenna	Open	30.00	30.00
94-01-071	Ringing in Christmas	J. McKenna	Open	30.00	30.00
94-01-072	Santa with Pipe	J. McKenna	Open	30.00	30.00
94-01-073	Elf-Tammy	J. McKenna	Open	30.00	30.00
94-01-074	Mrs. Klaus	J. McKenna	Open	30.00	30.00
94-01-075	Santa with Skis	J. McKenna	Open	30.00	30.00
94-01-076	Angel, Guiding Light-green, pink & white	J. McKenna	Open	30.00	30.00
Midwest of Cannon Falls		**Wendt und Kuhn Ornaments**			
78-01-001	Angel Clip-on Ornament 07296	Wendt/Kuhn	Open	20.00	21.00
89-01-002	Trumpeting Angel Ornament,2 asst. 94029	Wendt/Kuhn	Open	14.00	15.00
91-01-003	Angel in Ring Ornament 12089	Wendt/Kuhn	Open	12.00	12.50
94-01-004	Angel on Moon, Star, 12 asst. 12945-6	Wendt/Kuhn	Open	20.00	20.00
Midwest of Cannon Falls		**Heritage Santa Collection Ornaments**			
90-02-001	Scanda Klaus Fabric Mache 05208	Midwest	Retrd.	18.00	18.00
90-02-002	Herr Kristmas Fabric Mache 05216	Midwest	Retrd.	18.00	18.00
90-02-003	MacNicholas Fabric Mache 05224	Midwest	Retrd.	18.00	18.00
90-02-004	Papa Frost Fabric Mache 05232	Midwest	Retrd.	18.00	18.00
91-02-005	Scanda Klaus Dimensional 29414	Midwest	Open	11.50	11.50
91-02-006	Herr Kristmas Dimensional 29422	Midwest	Open	11.50	11.50
91-02-007	MacNicholas Dimensional 29430	Midwest	Open	11.50	11.50
91-02-008	Papa Frost Dimensional 29448	Midwest	Retrd.	11.50	11.50
91-02-009	Father Christmas Dimensional 29456	Midwest	Open	11.50	11.50
91-02-010	Santa Niccolo Dimensional 29464	Midwest	Open	11.50	11.50
92-02-011	Santa Nykolai Dimensional 67745	Midwest	Open	11.50	11.50
92-02-012	Pere Noel Dimensional 67739	Midwest	Open	11.50	11.50
93-02-013	Santa España Dimensional 73766	Midwest	Open	11.50	11.50
93-02-014	Santa O'Nicholas Dimensional 73773	Midwest	Open	11.50	11.50
Midwest of Cannon Falls		**Leo R. Smith III Collection**			
94-03-001	Flying Woodsman Santa 11921-1	L.R. Smith	Retrd.	35.00	35.00
Old World Christmas		**Angel & Female**			
86-01-001	Little Red Riding Hood 1001	E.M. Merck	Retrd.	9.90	11.75
86-01-002	Pink Angel with Wings 1002	E.M. Merck	Retrd.	8.90	11.00
86-01-003	Mrs. Santa Claus 1003	E.M. Merck	Retrd.	8.90	10.25
86-01-004	Clip-on Angel with Wings 1004	E.M. Merck	Open	10.00	10.25
87-01-005	Large Burgundy Angel with Wings 1005	E.M. Merck	Open	13.00	12.95
87-01-006	Mushroom Girl 1006	E.M. Merck	Open	9.25	9.25
87-01-007	Girl on Snowball with Teddy 1007	E.M. Merck	Open	9.25	9.25
87-01-008	Pastel Angel with Horn (A) 1008	E.M. Merck	Open	7.00	7.00
87-01-009	Girl in Grapes 1010	E.M. Merck	Retrd.	8.45	11.00
85-01-010	Small Girl with Tree 101029	E.M. Merck	Open	5.85	5.85
85-01-011	Gold Girl with Tree 1010306	E.M. Merck	Open	8.25	8.25
85-01-012	Red Girl with Tree 1010309	E.M. Merck	Open	8.25	8.25
85-01-013	Victorian Girl 101035	E.M. Merck	Retrd.	5.30	8.00
85-01-014	Light Blue Angel with Wings 101052	E.M. Merck	Retrd.	9.25	9.25
85-01-015	Caroling Girl 101062	E.M. Merck	Retrd.	6.65	6.65
85-01-016	Girl with Flowers 101069	E.M. Merck	Retrd.	7.50	9.00
88-01-017	Miss Liberty 1011	E.M. Merck	Open	10.35	10.35
88-01-018	Large Blue Angel 1012	E.M. Merck	Open	13.40	13.40
88-01-019	Large Doll Head 1013	E.M. Merck	Open	11.60	11.60
88-01-020	Girl Under Tree 1014	E.M. Merck	Open	7.80	7.80
88-01-021	Baby in Bunting 1015	E.M. Merck	Retrd.	7.70	13.95
88-01-022	Madonna with Child 1016	E.M. Merck	Open	12.75	12.75
88-01-023	Nativity 1017	E.M. Merck	Open	10.50	10.50
88-01-024	Victorian Angel 1018	E.M. Merck	Open	8.35	8.35
88-01-025	Pilgrim Girl 1019	E.M. Merck	Open	9.25	9.25
88-01-026	Little Witch 1020	E.M. Merck	Open	8.35	8.35
89-01-027	Irish Lassie 1021	E.M. Merck	Open	8.35	8.35
90-01-028	Small Girl Head 1022	E.M. Merck	Open	7.00	7.00
90-01-029	Angel Holding Star 1023	E.M. Merck	Open	7.80	7.80
90-01-030	Girl with Black Cat 1024	E.M. Merck	Open	9.25	9.25
90-01-031	Praying Girl 1025	E.M. Merck	Retrd.	7.80	7.80
90-01-032	Antique Style Doll Head 1026	E.M. Merck	Open	8.45	8.45
90-01-033	Miniature Mrs. Claus 1027	E.M. Merck	Open	4.95	4.95
90-01-034	Angel on Disc 1028	E.M. Merck	Retrd.	11.70	13.00
90-01-035	Heralding Angel 1029	E.M. Merck	Open	7.80	7.80
90-01-036	Girl in Polka Dot Dress 1030	E.M. Merck	Open	12.60	12.60
91-01-037	Baroque Angel 1031	E.M. Merck	Open	12.95	12.95
91-01-038	Praying Angel with Wings 1032	E.M. Merck	Open	8.55	8.55
85-01-039	Doll Head 103209	E.M. Merck	Retrd.	6.40	6.40
91-01-040	Angel of Peace 1033	E.M. Merck	Open	9.25	9.25
91-01-041	Cherub 1034	E.M. Merck	Open	8.80	8.80
91-01-042	Blue Praying Angel With Wings 1035	E.M. Merck	Open	8.25	8.25
91-01-043	Baby Jesus 1036	E.M. Merck	Open	9.25	9.25
91-01-044	Little Tyrolean Girl 1037	E.M. Merck	Open	7.00	7.00
92-01-045	Madonna 1038	E.M. Merck	Open	7.55	7.55
92-01-046	Shy Girl 1039	E.M. Merck	Open	9.90	9.90
92-01-047	Garden Girl 1040	E.M. Merck	Open	8.25	8.25
92-01-048	Thumbelina 1041	E.M. Merck	Open	10.25	10.25
92-01-049	Honey Child 1042	E.M. Merck	Open	7.45	7.45
85-01-050	Girl in Blue Dress 1042227	E.M. Merck	Open	7.00	7.00
92-01-051	Guardian Angel 1043	E.M. Merck	Open	8.25	8.25
92-01-052	Angel on Form 1044	E.M. Merck	Open	9.70	9.70
92-01-053	Girl with White Kitty 1045	E.M. Merck	Open	9.25	9.25
93-01-054	Small Blue Angel 1046	E.M. Merck	Open	6.65	6.65
93-01-055	Triplets in Bed 1051	E.M. Merck	Open	6.65	6.65
93-01-056	Red Riding Hood 1053	E.M. Merck	Open	7.55	7.55
93-01-057	Christmas Girl 1054	E.M. Merck	Open	6.55	6.55
93-01-058	Girl on Bell 1055	E.M. Merck	Open	8.75	8.75
93-01-059	Madonna & Child on Form 1056	E.M. Merck	Open	9.80	9.80
93-01-060	Chubby Mushroom Girl 1057	E.M. Merck	Open	8.00	8.00
93-01-061	Purple Angel with Star 1058	E.M. Merck	Open	8.70	8.70
93-01-062	Frau Schneemann 1059	E.M. Merck	Open	16.90	16.90
93-01-063	Angel Above Celestial Ball 1060	E.M. Merck	Open	41.00	41.00
93-01-064	Ballerina 1061	E.M. Merck	Open	14.50	14.50
94-01-065	Mermaid 1062	E.M. Merck	Open	38.90	38.90
94-01-066	Water Baby 1063	E.M. Merck	Open	8.25	8.25
94-01-067	Heidi and Peter 1064	E.M. Merck	Open	11.90	11.90
94-01-068	Nuremberg Angel 1065	E.M. Merck	Open	8.25	8.25
94-01-069	Mary 1066	E.M. Merck	Open	8.25	8.25
94-01-070	Oma 1067	E.M. Merck	Open	11.45	11.45
94-01-071	Heavenly Angel 1068	E.M. Merck	Open	11.00	11.00
94-01-072	Christmas Cutie 1069	E.M. Merck	Open	6.50	6.50
94-01-073	Double-Sided Egg Baby 1070	E.M. Merck	Open	7.25	7.25
94-01-074	Heidi 1071	E.M. Merck	Open	9.50	9.50
Old World Christmas		**Animals**			
86-02-001	Hungry Rabbit 1201	E.M. Merck	Open	8.55	8.55
86-02-002	Playing Cat 1202	E.M. Merck	Open	8.80	8.80
86-02-003	Bear in Crib 1203	E.M. Merck	Open	9.00	9.00
86-02-004	Cat in Bag 1204	E.M. Merck	Open	9.00	9.00
86-02-005	Monkey 1205	E.M. Merck	Open	5.85	5.85
86-02-006	Sitting Dog with Pipe 1206	E.M. Merck	Open	7.80	7.80
86-02-007	Smiling Dog 1207	E.M. Merck	Open	7.80	7.80
86-02-008	Honey Bear (A) 1208	E.M. Merck	Open	5.20	5.20
86-02-009	Cinnamon Bear 1209	E.M. Merck	Open	5.20	5.20
84-02-010	Kitten 121004	E.M. Merck	Open	7.00	7.00
84-02-011	Three-Sided: Owl, Dog, Cat 121009	E.M. Merck	Open	8.55	8.55
84-02-012	Puppy 121010	E.M. Merck	Open	7.00	7.00
84-02-013	Black Cat 121016	E.M. Merck	Open	9.00	9.00
84-02-014	Circus Dog 121021	E.M. Merck	Open	9.00	9.00
85-02-015	Snail 121041	E.M. Merck	Retrd.	6.70	10.00
85-02-016	Pink Pig 121042	E.M. Merck	Open	7.80	7.80
85-02-017	Frog 121068	E.M. Merck	Open	5.85	5.85
85-02-018	Rainbow Trout 121070	E.M. Merck	Open	6.75	6.75
85-02-019	Large Three-Sided Head 121088	E.M. Merck	Open	12.95	12.95
85-02-020	Large Teddy Bear 121089	E.M. Merck	Retrd.	13.00	15.95
85-02-021	Small Bunny 121090	E.M. Merck	Open	5.20	5.20
87-02-022	Mouse 1211	E.M. Merck	Open	9.90	9.90
85-02-023	Cat in Show 121103	E.M. Merck	Open	7.80	7.80
88-02-024	Lucky Pig 1212	E.M. Merck	Open	8.80	8.80
88-02-025	Jumbo Elephant 1213	E.M. Merck	Open	9.25	9.25
89-02-026	Large Fish 1214	E.M. Merck	Retrd.	6.70	7.25
89-02-027	Lady Bug 1215	E.M. Merck	Open	7.65	7.65
89-02-028	Calico Kitten 1217	E.M. Merck	Open	9.90	9.90
89-02-029	Teddy Bear with Bow 1218	E.M. Merck	Retrd.	6.65	6.65
89-02-030	Rabbit in Tree 1219	E.M. Merck	Open	8.35	8.35
89-02-031	White Kitty 1220	E.M. Merck	Retrd.	7.45	7.45
89-02-032	Cat and the Fiddle 1221	E.M. Merck	Open	7.80	7.80
89-02-033	King Charles Spaniel 1222	E.M. Merck	Open	9.90	9.90
89-02-034	Fat Fish 1223	E.M. Merck	Open	5.85	5.85
89-02-035	Small Goldfish 1224	E.M. Merck	Open	2.25	2.25
90-02-036	Small Squirrel 1225	E.M. Merck	Open	5.75	5.75
90-02-037	Teddy Bear with Bow 1226	E.M. Merck	Open	5.75	5.75
90-02-038	Pink Poodle 1227	E.M. Merck	Open	8.80	8.80
90-02-039	Sitting Black Cat 1228	E.M. Merck	Open	7.00	7.00
90-02-040	Assorted Tropical Fish 1229	E.M. Merck	Open	6.75	6.75
90-02-041	Two Kittens in Basket 1230	E.M. Merck	Open	8.10	8.10
90-02-042	Red Butterfly on Form 1231	E.M. Merck	Open	8.55	8.55
90-02-043	West Highland Terrrier 1232	E.M. Merck	Retrd.	7.45	9.00
90-02-044	Weather Frog 1233	E.M. Merck	Open	8.80	8.80
90-02-045	Pastel Fish 1234	E.M. Merck	Open	6.65	6.65
85-02-046	Grey Elephant 123420	E.M. Merck	Open	7.00	7.00
85-02-047	Matte Gold Bear with Heart 1234356	E.M. Merck	Open	7.00	7.00
90-02-048	Baby Bear with Milk Bottle 1235	E.M. Merck	Open	4.95	4.95
90-02-049	Mama Bear 1236	E.M. Merck	Open	9.90	9.90
90-02-050	Papa Bear 1237	E.M. Merck	Open	10.35	10.35
85-02-051	Butterfly on Form 1237447	E.M. Merck	Open	7.80	7.80
91-02-052	Kitten in Slipper 1240	E.M. Merck	Open	9.25	9.25
91-02-053	Large Puppy with Basket 1241	E.M. Merck	Retrd.	13.25	13.25
91-02-054	Panda Bear 1242	E.M. Merck	Open	9.25	9.25
91-02-055	Crocodile 1243	E.M. Merck	Open	7.35	7.35
91-02-056	Rabbit on Heart 1244	E.M. Merck	Open	8.00	8.00
91-02-057	Lobster 1245	E.M. Merck	Open	7.35	7.35
91-02-058	Sitting Puppy 1246	E.M. Merck	Open	6.75	6.75
91-02-059	Christmas Butterfly 1247	E.M. Merck	Open	7.00	7.00
91-02-060	Christmas Carp 1248	E.M. Merck	Open	7.00	7.00
91-02-061	Goldfish 1249	E.M. Merck	Open	7.00	7.00
92-02-062	Proud Pug 1250	E.M. Merck	Open	9.25	9.25
92-02-063	Lion 1251	E.M. Merck	Open	6.45	6.45
92-02-064	Frog on Lily Pad 1252	E.M. Merck	Open	6.65	6.65
92-02-065	Dog with Trumpet 1253	E.M. Merck	Open	9.25	9.25
92-02-066	Large Lady Bug 1254	E.M. Merck	Open	9.25	9.25
92-02-067	Salmon with Tail 1255	E.M. Merck	Open	9.25	9.25
93-02-068	Velveteen Rabbit 1256	E.M. Merck	Open	5.75	5.75
93-02-069	Sugar Bear 1257	E.M. Merck	Open	8.25	8.25
93-02-070	Monkey with Apple 1258	E.M. Merck	Open	8.80	8.80
93-02-071	Miniature Frog 1259	E.M. Merck	Open	3.50	3.50
93-02-072	Cat in House 1260	E.M. Merck	Open	7.65	7.65
93-02-073	Large Teddy Bear 1261	E.M. Merck	Open	15.65	15.65
93-02-074	Large Frog 1262	E.M. Merck	Open	7.90	7.90
93-02-075	Grizzly Bear 1265	E.M. Merck	Open	8.35	8.35
93-02-076	Buster 1266	E.M. Merck	Open	8.35	8.35
93-02-077	Brilliant Butterfly 1267	E.M. Merck	Open	10.70	10.70
93-02-078	Pastel Butterfly 1268	E.M. Merck	Open	8.45	8.45
93-02-079	Brilliant Butterfly on Form 1271	E.M. Merck	Open	7.25	7.25
93-02-080	Specked Trout 1272	E.M. Merck	Open	7.00	7.00
93-02-081	Sea Serpent 1273	E.M. Merck	Open	14.65	14.65
93-02-082	Frog with Banjo on Ball 1274	E.M. Merck	Open	18.50	18.50
93-02-083	Polar Bear on Icicle 1275	E.M. Merck	Open	18.50	18.50
93-02-084	My Darling 1276	E.M. Merck	Open	6.30	6.30
93-02-085	Circus Elephant on Ball 1277	E.M. Merck	Open	12.00	12.00
93-02-086	Circus Dog On Ball 1278	E.M. Merck	Open	13.20	13.20
93-02-087	Bear Above Reflector 1279	E.M. Merck	Open	33.75	33.75
93-02-088	Very Large Christmas Mouse 1280	E.M. Merck	Open	72.50	72.50
93-02-089	Very Large Christmas Bear 1281	E.M. Merck	Open	72.50	72.50
94-02-090	Sea Horse 1282	E.M. Merck	Open	14.50	14.50
94-02-091	Seal on Ball 1283	E.M. Merck	Open	24.50	24.50
94-02-092	Cow Jumping Over the Moon 1284	E.M. Merck	Open	27.75	27.75
94-02-093	Large Lion 1285	E.M. Merck	Open	19.85	19.85
94-02-094	Large Christmas Mouse 1286	E.M. Merck	Open	44.40	44.40

		ARTIST	EDITION	ISSUE	QUOTE
94-02-095	Large Christmas Bear 1287	E.M. Merck	Open	44.40	44.40
94-02-096	Frog Prince 1288	E.M. Merck	Open	8.10	8.10
94-02-097	Grasshopper 1289	E.M. Merck	Open	10.00	10.00
94-02-098	Ted 1290	E.M. Merck	Open	7.65	7.65
94-02-099	Woodland Squirrel 1291	E.M. Merck	Open	21.00	21.00
94-02-100	Spark Plug 1292	E.M. Merck	Open	14.00	14.00
94-02-101	Tony 1293	E.M. Merck	Open	17.65	17.65

Old World Christmas — Bead Garlands

		ARTIST	EDITION	ISSUE	QUOTE
93-03-001	Clown & Drum Garland 1301	E.M. Merck	Open	55.00	55.00
93-03-002	Fruit Garland 1302	E.M. Merck	Open	55.00	55.00
93-03-003	Celestial Garland 1303	E.M. Merck	Open	55.00	55.00
93-03-004	Pickle Garland 1304	E.M. Merck	Open	55.00	55.00
93-03-005	Frog and Fish Garland 1305	E.M. Merck	Yr.Iss.	55.00	70.00
93-03-006	Angel Garland 1306	E.M. Merck	Open	55.00	55.00
93-03-007	Teddy Bear & Heart Garland 1307	E.M. Merck	Open	55.00	55.00
93-03-008	Santa Garland 1308	E.M. Merck	Yr.Iss.	55.00	73.00
94-03-009	Stars and Stripes Garland 1309	E.M. Merck	Open	55.00	55.00
94-03-010	Christmas Train 1310	E.M. Merck	Open	45.00	45.00
94-03-011	Woodland Christmas Garland 1311	E.M. Merck	Open	65.00	65.00
94-03-012	Floral Garland 1312	E.M. Merck	Open	65.00	65.00
94-03-013	North Pole Garland 1313	E.M. Merck	Open	65.00	65.00

Old World Christmas — Assortment Ornaments

		ARTIST	EDITION	ISSUE	QUOTE
89-04-001	Twelve Assorted Miniature Forms 1402	E.M. Merck	Open	37.00	37.00
89-04-002	Set of 12 Assorted Small Forms 1403	E.M. Merck	Open	42.50	42.50
90-04-003	Assorted Shiny Miniature Forms 1404	E.M. Merck	Open	37.50	37.50
90-04-004	Assorted Miniature Figurals 1405	E.M. Merck	Open	60.00	60.00
92-04-005	Assorted Floral Miniatures 1406	E.M. Merck	Open	55.00	55.00
85-04-006	6 pc Display set, Santa 141039	E.M. Merck	Open	32.50	32.50
86-04-007	Replica of Antique Mold 1411	E.M. Merck	Open	40.00	40.00

Old World Christmas — Collector's Editions

		ARTIST	EDITION	ISSUE	QUOTE
90-05-001	Night Before Christmas Ball 1501	E.M. Merck	500	72.50	72.50
91-05-002	Santa's Visit 1502	E.M. Merck	500	72.50	72.50
92-05-003	Santa's Departure 1503	E.M. Merck	500	72.50	72.50
92-05-004	Nutcracker Ornament 1510	E.M. Merck	Retrd.	33.75	56-110.
93-05-005	Hansel and Gretal 1511	E.M. Merck	2,400	45.00	49.95-75.
92-05-006	Santa with Tinsel Wire 1521	E.M. Merck	Retrd.	55.00	55.00
92-05-007	Angel with Tinsel Wire 1522	E.M. Merck	Retrd.	55.00	55.00
92-05-008	Snowman with Tinsel Wire 1523	E.M. Merck	Retrd.	32.50	32.50
92-05-009	Dresden Santa with Tinsel Wire 1525	E.M. Merck	Open	21.50	21.50
92-05-010	Angel on Swan with Tinsel Wire 1526	E.M. Merck	Open	21.50	21.50
92-05-011	Angel on Balloon 1527	E.M. Merck	Open	22.50	22.50
92-05-012	Cherub Above Ball 1528	E.M. Merck	Open	23.65	23.65
92-05-013	Father Christmas on Balloon 1529	E.M. Merck	Open	22.50	22.50
92-05-014	Very Large Mushroom with Flower 1530	E.M. Merck	Open	59.50	59.50
92-05-015	Very Large Ball with Reflectors 1531	E.M. Merck	Open	59.50	59.50
92-05-016	Very Large Ball with Icicle Drop 1532	E.M. Merck	Open	59.50	59.50
92-05-017	Very Large Drop with Reflectors 1533	E.M. Merck	Open	59.50	59.50
87-05-018	Very Large Icicle 1534	E.M. Merck	Open	59.50	59.50
92-05-019	Flying Peacock with Wings 1550	E.M. Merck	Open	22.50	22.50
92-05-020	Flying Songbird with Wings 1551	E.M. Merck	Open	21.75	21.75
92-05-021	Brilliant Peacock with Wings 1552	E.M. Merck	Open	23.00	23.00
92-05-022	Nightingale with Wings 1553	E.M. Merck	Open	21.00	21.00
93-05-023	Angel with Wings 1556	E.M. Merck	Retrd.	12.50	20.00
93-05-024	Guardian Angel with Wire 1562	E.M. Merck	Open	20.00	20.00
93-05-025	Heavenly Angel 1563	E.M. Merck	Open	20.00	20.00
93-05-026	Victorian Santa on Heart 1564	E.M. Merck	Open	12.95	12.95
93-05-027	Scrap Victorian Santa on Balloon 1565	E.M. Merck	Open	50.00	50.00
93-05-028	Scrap Victorian Angel on Balloon 1566	E.M. Merck	Open	50.00	50.00
93-05-029	Santa with Hot Air Balloon 1570	E.M. Merck	Open	38.85	38.85
93-05-030	Christmas Heart 1593	E.M. Merck	Yr.Iss.	10.00	14.00
94-05-031	Assorted Pumpkin People 1580	E.M. Merck	Open	19.75	19.75

Old World Christmas — Hanging Birds

		ARTIST	EDITION	ISSUE	QUOTE
86-06-001	Owl on Form 1601	E.M. Merck	Open	11.00	11.00
86-06-002	Songbirds on Ball 1602	E.M. Merck	Open	9.25	9.25
86-06-003	Rooster on Form 1603	E.M. Merck	Retrd.	6.65	6.65
86-06-004	Large Owl with Stein 1604	E.M. Merck	Retrd.	10.00	20.00
86-06-005	Swan on Form 1605	E.M. Merck	Open	8.35	8.35
86-06-006	Parrot in Cage 1606	E.M. Merck	Open	7.45	7.45
86-06-007	Small Owl 1607	E.M. Merck	Open	5.75	5.75
86-06-008	Standing Owl 1608	E.M. Merck	Open	8.90	8.90
87-06-009	Fat Rooster 1610	E.M. Merck	Open	10.35	10.35
84-06-010	Cock Robin 161012	E.M. Merck	Open	7.00	7.00
84-06-011	Chick in Egg 161013	E.M. Merck	Open	8.25	8.25
85-06-012	Turkey 161058	E.M. Merck	Retrd.	8.00	8.00
85-06-013	Fancy Peacock 161066	E.M. Merck	Open	9.25	9.25
85-06-014	Cardinal with Wings 161098	E.M. Merck	Open	10.95	10.95
88-06-015	Bird House 1611	E.M. Merck	Open	10.35	10.35
85-06-016	Blue Bird with Wings 161100	E.M. Merck	Retrd.	7.65	7.65
88-06-017	Swans on Lake 1612	E.M. Merck	Open	7.80	7.80
90-06-018	Duck 1613	E.M. Merck	Open	6.20	6.20
90-06-019	Songbird on Form 1614	E.M. Merck	Open	8.80	8.80
90-06-020	Turkey 1615	E.M. Merck	Open	9.00	9.00
90-06-021	Wise Owl 1616	E.M. Merck	Open	8.35	8.35
91-06-022	Large Parrot on Ball 1617	E.M. Merck	Open	11.00	11.00
91-06-023	Songbird on Heart (A) 1618	E.M. Merck	Retrd.	8.25	8.25
91-06-024	Chick on Form 1619	E.M. Merck	Retrd.	8.00	8.00
92-06-025	Birdie 1620	E.M. Merck	Open	8.80	8.80
92-06-026	Gentleman Chick 1621	E.M. Merck	Open	7.65	7.65
92-06-027	Snowy Owl 1622	E.M. Merck	Open	6.00	6.00
92-06-028	Exotic Bird 1623	E.M. Merck	Open	10.35	10.35
92-06-029	Large German Songbird 1624	E.M. Merck	Open	11.25	11.25
92-06-030	Brilliant Hanging Snowbird 1625	E.M. Merck	Open	9.80	9.80
92-06-031	Messenger Bird 1626	E.M. Merck	Open	6.75	6.75
93-06-032	Cardinal on Form 1627	E.M. Merck	Open	7.55	7.55
93-06-024	Stork with Baby 1628	E.M. Merck	Open	9.60	9.60
93-06-025	Rooster at Hen House 1629	E.M. Merck	Open	10.25	10.25
93-06-026	Hanging Pastel Bird 1630	E.M. Merck	Open	10.50	10.50
93-06-027	Hanging Parrot 1631	E.M. Merck	Open	9.60	9.60
93-06-028	Parrot on Reflector 1632	E.M. Merck	Open	12.25	12.25
94-06-029	Royal Swan 1633	E.M. Merck	Open	27.75	27.75
94-06-030	Bird in Nest 1634	E.M. Merck	Open	19.90	19.90

Old World Christmas — Clip-On Birds

		ARTIST	EDITION	ISSUE	QUOTE
86-07-001	Bird in Nest 1801	E.M. Merck	Open	10.35	10.35
86-07-002	Clip-On Rooster 1802	E.M. Merck	Retrd.	8.00	15.00
86-07-003	Gold Bird with Tinsel Tail 1803	E.M. Merck	Open	7.45	7.45
86-07-004	Parrot 1804	E.M. Merck	Open	8.35	8.35
87-07-005	White Cockatoo 1805	E.M. Merck	Open	7.80	7.80
87-07-006	Red Bird with Medallion 1806	E.M. Merck	Open	7.80	7.80
87-07-007	Shiny Gold Bird 1807	E.M. Merck	Open	5.55	5.55
87-07-008	Goldfinch 1808	E.M. Merck	Open	8.55	8.55
87-07-009	Small Purple Bird 1809	E.M. Merck	Open	7.00	7.00
87-07-010	Red Snowbird 1810	E.M. Merck	Retrd.	8.70	8.70
84-07-011	Large Cockatoo 181025	E.M. Merck	Open	13.95	13.95
85-07-012	Fancy Peacock 181073	E.M. Merck	Retrd.	13.50	13.50
85-07-013	Fat Songbird 181074	E.M. Merck	Open	7.80	7.80
85-07-014	Fantasy Bird with Tinsel Tail 181075	E.M. Merck	Open	8.00	8.00
85-07-015	Nuthatch 181076	E.M. Merck	Open	7.00	7.00
85-07-016	Cockatoo 181077	E.M. Merck	Open	8.55	8.55
85-07-017	Blue Bird 181078	E.M. Merck	Open	6.65	6.65
85-07-018	Snowbird 181080	E.M. Merck	Retrd.	8.00	8.00
85-07-019	Shiny Red Songbird 181081	E.M. Merck	Open	5.75	5.75
85-07-020	Pink Bird with Blue Wings 181082	E.M. Merck	Open	5.55	5.55
85-07-021	Nightingale 181083	E.M. Merck	Open	5.55	5.55
85-07-022	Large Goldfinch 181085	E.M. Merck	Open	9.25	9.25
85-07-023	Magnificent Songbird 181086	E.M. Merck	Open	13.95	13.95
85-07-024	Fancy Pink Peacock 181096	E.M. Merck	Open	13.95	13.95
85-07-025	Songbird with Topnotch 181099	E.M. Merck	Open	10.35	10.35
87-07-026	Lilac Bird 1811	E.M. Merck	Open	8.70	8.70
85-07-027	Bird of Pradise 181101	E.M. Merck	Open	7.80	7.80
87-07-028	Red Breasted Songbird 1812	E.M. Merck	Open	9.25	9.25
87-07-029	Fat Burgundy Bird 1813	E.M. Merck	Open	7.80	7.80
87-07-030	Partridge 1814	E.M. Merck	Open	8.80	8.80
87-07-031	Royal Songbird 1815	E.M. Merck	Open	12.75	12.75
87-07-032	Snow Owl 1816	E.M. Merck	Open	9.90	9.90
87-07-033	Robin 1819	E.M. Merck	Retrd.	8.80	10.25
89-07-034	Rainbow Parrot 1820	E.M. Merck	Open	12.60	12.60
90-07-035	Large Robin 1821	E.M. Merck	Open	10.35	10.35
90-07-036	Cardinal 1822	E.M. Merck	Open	9.90	9.90
90-07-037	Small Red-Headed Songbird 1823	E.M. Merck	Open	7.00	7.00
90-07-038	Christmas Bird 1824	E.M. Merck	Open	7.00	7.00
90-07-039	Miniature Peacock 1825	E.M. Merck	Open	8.35	8.35
90-07-040	Tropical Parrot 1826	E.M. Merck	Open	10.35	10.35
90-07-041	Large Pastel Bird 1827	E.M. Merck	Open	10.70	10.70
90-07-042	Miniature Parrot 1828	E.M. Merck	Open	8.45	8.45
90-07-043	Barn Owl 1829	E.M. Merck	Open	9.00	9.00
91-07-044	Large Peacock with Crown 1830	E.M. Merck	Open	13.95	13.95
91-07-045	Rooster 1831	E.M. Merck	Open	10.50	10.50
91-07-046	Festive Bird 1832	E.M. Merck	Open	7.00	7.00
91-07-047	Silly Bird 1833	E.M. Merck	Open	6.75	6.75
91-07-048	Canary 1834	E.M. Merck	Open	7.35	7.35
91-07-049	Bavarian Finch 1835	E.M. Merck	Open	9.25	9.25
91-07-050	Brilliant Snowbird 1836	E.M. Merck	Open	12.95	12.95
91-07-051	Advent Bird 1837	E.M. Merck	Open	8.00	8.00
91-07-052	Cockatiel 1838	E.M. Merck	Open	9.25	9.25
91-07-053	Alpine Bird 1839	E.M. Merck	Open	7.35	7.35
92-07-054	Forest Finch 1840	E.M. Merck	Open	8.00	8.00
92-07-055	Brilliant Songbird 1841	E.M. Merck	Open	7.35	7.35
92-07-056	Large Nightingale 1842	E.M. Merck	Open	8.00	8.00
92-07-057	Christmas Finch 1843	E.M. Merck	Open	7.65	7.65
92-07-058	Small Gull 1844	E.M. Merck	Open	4.95	4.95
92-07-059	Blue Bird with Topnotch 1845	E.M. Merck	Open	9.45	9.45
92-07-060	Large Woodpecker 1846	E.M. Merck	Open	11.15	11.15
92-07-061	Pastel Canary 1847	E.M. Merck	Open	7.65	7.65
92-07-062	Merry Songbird 1848	E.M. Merck	Open	7.90	7.90
93-07-063	Holiday Finch 1849	E.M. Merck	Open	10.60	10.60
93-07-064	King Fisher 1850	E.M. Merck	Open	10.00	10.00
93-07-065	Woodland Finch 1851	E.M. Merck	Open	7.55	7.55
93-07-066	Carnival Canary 1852	E.M. Merck	Open	9.45	9.45
93-07-067	Festive Sparrow 1853	E.M. Merck	Open	6.00	6.00
93-07-068	Tropical Songbird 1854	E.M. Merck	Open	7.55	7.55
93-07-069	Woodland Songbird 1855	E.M. Merck	Open	7.55	7.55
93-07-070	Love Birds 1856	E.M. Merck	Open	10.25	10.25
94-07-071	Regal Peacock 1857	E.M. Merck	Open	17.75	17.75
94-07-072	Woodland Peacock 1858	E.M. Merck	Open	12.00	12.00
94-07-073	Assorted Miniature Songbird 1859	E.M. Merck	Open	4.00	4.00
94-07-074	Magnificent Peacock 1860	E.M. Merck	Open	17.75	17.75
85-07-075	Gold Peacock, Tinsel Tail 1872016	E.M. Merck	Open	8.25	8.25
85-07-076	Large Peacock 187206	E.M. Merck	Open	10.35	10.35
85-07-077	Medium Peacock with Tinsel Tail 187215	E.M. Merck	Open	9.00	9.00

Old World Christmas — Butterflies

		ARTIST	EDITION	ISSUE	QUOTE
87-08-001	Butterfly, White with Red 1901	E.M. Merck	Retrd.	20.95	26.75
87-08-002	Butterfly, White with Blue 1902	E.M. Merck	Retrd.	20.95	25.00
87-08-003	Butterfly, Red with Cream 1903	E.M. Merck	Retrd.	20.95	26.75
87-08-004	Butterfly, Orange with Orange 1904	E.M. Merck	Retrd.	20.95	26.75
87-08-005	Butterfly, Blue with Blue 1905	E.M. Merck	Retrd.	20.95	25.00
87-08-006	Butterfly, Gold with Gold 1906	E.M. Merck	Retrd.	20.95	25.00

Old World Christmas — Churches & Houses

		ARTIST	EDITION	ISSUE	QUOTE
86-09-001	Gingerbread House (A) 2001	E.M. Merck	Retrd.	6.55	9.75
86-09-002	Farm House 2003	E.M. Merck	Open	8.45	8.45
86-09-003	House with Peacock 2004	E.M. Merck	Retrd.	7.45	7.45
86-09-004	House with Blue Roof 2005	E.M. Merck	Open	7.65	7.65
86-09-005	Windmill on Form 2006	E.M. Merck	Retrd.	7.45	15.00
88-09-006	Large Cathedral 2007	E.M. Merck	Open	9.80	9.80
88-09-007	Church/Tree on Form 2008	E.M. Merck	Open	8.35	8.35
88-09-008	Gingerbread House 2009	E.M. Merck	Open	9.00	9.00
88-09-009	Santa's House 2010	E.M. Merck	Open	8.00	8.00
85-09-010	Square House 201040	E.M. Merck	Open	7.80	7.80
85-09-011	Rathaus 201051	E.M. Merck	Retrd.	7.00	7.00
85-09-012	Bavarian House 201059	E.M. Merck	Open	8.00	8.00
85-09-013	Mill 201094	E.M. Merck	Retrd.	9.45	15.95
90-09-014	Garden House with Gnome 2011	E.M. Merck	Retrd.	7.80	10.00
90-09-015	Miniature House 2012	E.M. Merck	Open	4.95	4.95
90-09-016	Lighthouse 2013	E.M. Merck	Open	7.90	7.90
90-09-017	Christmas Chalet 2014	E.M. Merck	Open	8.00	8.00
90-09-018	Small Cathedral 2015	E.M. Merck	Open	8.00	8.00
90-09-019	Fairy Tale House 2016	E.M. Merck	Open	9.25	9.25
90-09-020	Matte Cream Church 2017	E.M. Merck	Open	8.00	8.00
90-09-021	Church on Disc 2018	E.M. Merck	Open	12.50	12.50
91-09-022	Thatched Cottage 2019	E.M. Merck	Open	7.35	7.35
91-09-023	Christmas Shop 2020	E.M. Merck	Open	9.45	9.45
91-09-024	Old Town Scene 2021	E.M. Merck	Open	9.25	9.25
91-09-025	Farm Cottage 2022	E.M. Merck	Open	8.55	8.55
91-09-026	Large Lighthouse/Mill 2023	E.M. Merck	Open	11.00	11.00
91-09-027	Mission with Sea Gull 2024	E.M. Merck	Open	9.45	9.45
91-09-028	Country Cottage 2025	E.M. Merck	Open	8.80	8.80
92-09-029	Mill House 2026	E.M. Merck	Open	8.35	8.35
92-09-030	Watch Tower 2027	E.M. Merck	Open	9.25	9.25
92-09-031	Rose Cottage 2028	E.M. Merck	Open	7.00	7.00

		ARTIST	EDITION	ISSUE	QUOTE
93-09-032	Castle Tower 2029	E.M. Merck	Open	9.45	9.45
93-09-033	Church on Bell 2030	E.M. Merck	Open	11.00	11.00
88-09-034	Matte White Church 203010	E.M. Merck	Open	7.80	7.80
93-09-035	Turkish Tea House 2031	E.M. Merck	Open	6.75	6.75
93-09-036	Bunny House 2032	E.M. Merck	Open	8.45	8.45
93-09-037	Barn 2033	E.M. Merck	Open	9.80	9.80
93-09-038	Large Windmill 2034	E.M. Merck	Open	13.20	13.20
94-09-039	Victorian Windmill 2035	E.M. Merck	Open	12.25	12.25
85-09-040	Matte Cream Church 206790-2	E.M. Merck	Retrd.	6.45	6.45

Old World Christmas — Celestial Figures

		ARTIST	EDITION	ISSUE	QUOTE
86-10-001	Shooting Star on Ball 2201	E.M. Merck	Retrd.	6.65	10.25
87-10-002	Blue Man in the Moon 2203	E.M. Merck	Open	8.45	8.45
90-10-003	Shining Sun 2204	E.M. Merck	Open	7.00	7.00
91-10-004	Shining Star (A) 2205	E.M. Merck	Open	7.00	7.00
92-10-005	Blue Moon 2206	E.M. Merck	Open	7.00	7.00
92-10-006	Old Sol 2207	E.M. Merck	Open	7.55	7.55
92-10-007	Confetti Star 2208	E.M. Merck	Open	8.00	8.00
93-10-008	Comet on Form 2209	E.M. Merck	Open	7.65	7.65
93-10-009	Brilliant Star on Form 2210	E.M. Merck	Open	8.70	8.70
85-10-010	Sun/Moon 221027	E.M. Merck	Retrd.	7.00	7.00
85-10-011	Man in the Moon 221062	E.M. Merck	Open	7.00	7.00
93-10-012	High Noon 2211	E.M. Merck	Open	5.65	5.65
94-10-013	Assorted Shiny Stars 2212	E.M. Merck	Open	4.85	4.85
94-10-014	Midnight Moon 2213	E.M. Merck	Open	8.25	8.25
85-10-015	Large Gold Star with Glitter 2237139	E.M. Merck	Retrd.	7.00	7.00

Old World Christmas — Clowns & Male Figures

		ARTIST	EDITION	ISSUE	QUOTE
86-11-001	Indian in Canoe 2401	E.M. Merck	Open	10.95	10.95
86-11-002	Aviator 2402	E.M. Merck	Open	7.80	7.80
86-11-003	500,000 Clown 2403	E.M. Merck	Open	10.80	10.80
86-11-004	Sailor Head 2404	E.M. Merck	Retrd.	7.45	15.00
86-11-005	Baby 2405	E.M. Merck	Retrd.	6.75	6.75
86-11-006	Pixie with Accordion 2406	E.M. Merck	Retrd.	4.95	4.95
86-11-007	Clown with Banjo 2407	E.M. Merck	Open	7.00	7.00
86-11-008	Clown with Drum 2408	E.M. Merck	Open	10.35	10.35
86-11-009	Clown with Accordion 2409	E.M. Merck	Open	10.35	10.35
86-11-010	Clown with Saxophone 2410	E.M. Merck	Open	10.35	10.35
84-11-011	Keystone Cop 241003	E.M. Merck	Open	9.90	9.90
84-11-012	Clown Playing Bass Fiddle 241005	E.M. Merck	Open	7.80	7.80
84-11-013	Clown in Stocking 241006	E.M. Merck	Retrd.	6.65	9.00
84-11-014	Indian Chief with Peace Pipe 241008	E.M. Merck	Open	7.45	7.45
84-11-015	'Shorty Clown' 241011	E.M. Merck	Retrd.	5.65	5.65
84-11-016	Roly-Poly Keystone Cop 241015	E.M. Merck	Retrd.	9.90	14.95
84-11-017	Scotsman 241017	E.M. Merck	Retrd.	6.20	13.95
84-11-018	'Stop' Keystone Cop 241019	E.M. Merck	Retrd.	6.65	16.95
84-11-019	Large Roly-Poly Clown 241024	E.M. Merck	Open	10.95	10.95
85-11-020	Small Fat Boy 241028	E.M. Merck	Open	5.55	5.55
85-11-021	Boy on Toy Car 241031	E.M. Merck	Open	8.45	8.45
85-11-022	Boy in Yellow Sweater 241032	E.M. Merck	Retrd.	7.00	10.00
85-11-023	Waiter in Tuxedo 241047	E.M. Merck	Retrd.	7.00	18.00
86-11-024	Boy Head with Stocking Cap 2411	E.M. Merck	Retrd.	5.30	7.25
86-11-025	Clown Head in Drum 2412	E.M. Merck	Open	10.25	10.25
86-11-026	Uncle Sam 2413	E.M. Merck	Open	10.80	10.80
86-11-027	Farm Boy 2414	E.M. Merck	Retrd.	4.95	6.50
86-11-028	School Boy 2415	E.M. Merck	Retrd.	4.95	7.25
86-11-029	Clip-on Boy Head 2416	E.M. Merck	Retrd.	6.45	6.45
86-11-030	Gnome Under Mushroom 2417	E.M. Merck	Retrd.	7.00	10.00
86-11-031	Clown Head with Burgundy Hat 2418	E.M. Merck	Open	7.00	7.00
86-11-032	Jester 2419	E.M. Merck	Open	7.45	7.45
87-11-033	Jolly Snowman 2420	E.M. Merck	Open	8.00	8.00
87-11-034	King 2421	E.M. Merck	Open	10.60	10.60
87-11-035	Clown in Red Stocking 2423	E.M. Merck	Open	8.00	8.00
87-11-036	Punch 2424	E.M. Merck	Open	8.70	8.70
87-11-037	Mr. Big Nose 2426	E.M. Merck	Retrd.	8.00	11.00
87-11-038	Scrooge 2427	E.M. Merck	Open	8.55	8.55
87-11-039	Bavarian with Hat 2428	E.M. Merck	Open	12.60	12.60
87-11-040	Jolly Clown Head 2429	E.M. Merck	Open	12.95	12.95
88-11-041	Mushroom Gnome 2430	E.M. Merck	Retrd.	6.20	6.20
88-11-042	Gnome in Tree 2431	E.M. Merck	Open	7.80	7.80
88-11-043	Harpo 2432	E.M. Merck	Retrd.	6.20	17.00
89-11-044	Dwarf with Shovel 2433	E.M. Merck	Open	7.00	7.00
85-11-045	Dutch Boy 243321	E.M. Merck	Retrd.	7.55	11.50
89-11-046	Frosty 2434	E.M. Merck	Open	7.00	7.00
89-11-047	Leprechaun 2435	E.M. Merck	Open	7.65	7.65
89-11-048	Small Clown Head 2436	E.M. Merck	Retrd.	6.65	6.65
89-11-049	Snowman with Broom 2437	E.M. Merck	Open	6.45	6.45
90-11-050	Devil Head 2438	E.M. Merck	Open	8.80	8.80
90-11-051	Black Boy 2439	E.M. Merck	Open	9.00	9.00
90-11-052	Scout 2440	E.M. Merck	Open	9.25	9.25
90-11-053	Dwarf 2441	E.M. Merck	Open	7.00	7.00
90-11-054	English Bobby 2442	E.M. Merck	Open	8.80	8.80
85-11-055	Fat Boy with Sweater & Cap 2442265	E.M. Merck	Open	5.85	5.85
90-11-056	Jolly Accordion Player 2443	E.M. Merck	Open	8.25	8.25
90-11-057	Clown on Ball 2444	E.M. Merck	Open	8.25	8.25
90-11-058	Snowman on Reflector 2445	E.M. Merck	Retrd.	10.35	12.00
90-11-059	Merry Wanderer 2446	E.M. Merck	Open	12.30	12.30
92-11-060	Snowman in Chimney 2447	E.M. Merck	Open	10.50	10.50
92-11-061	Garden Gnome 2448	E.M. Merck	Open	10.50	10.50
92-11-062	Baker 2449	E.M. Merck	Open	8.35	8.35
92-11-063	Bavarian 2450	E.M. Merck	Open	9.25	9.25
92-11-064	Pirate 2451	E.M. Merck	Open	7.45	7.45
92-11-065	Circus Clown 2452	E.M. Merck	Open	7.90	7.90
93-11-066	Winking Leprechaun 2453	E.M. Merck	Open	6.55	6.55
93-11-067	Boxer 2454	E.M. Merck	Open	7.20	7.20
93-11-068	Chimney Sweep 2455	E.M. Merck	Open	7.55	7.55
93-11-069	Santa's Helper 2456	E.M. Merck	Open	6.00	6.00
93-11-070	Sailor 2457	E.M. Merck	Open	7.55	7.55
93-11-071	Bacchus 2458	E.M. Merck	Open	6.65	6.65
93-11-072	Pinocchio 2459	E.M. Merck	Open	9.90	9.90
93-11-073	Jesus 2460	E.M. Merck	Open	7.65	7.65
93-11-074	Turquoise Clown 2461	E.M. Merck	Open	6.45	6.45
93-11-075	Small Snowman 2462	E.M. Merck	Open	6.00	6.00
93-11-076	Small Jester 2463	E.M. Merck	Open	7.35	7.35
93-11-077	Miniature Clown 2464	E.M. Merck	Open	6.00	6.00
93-11-078	Humpty Dumpty 2465	E.M. Merck	Open	8.55	8.55
93-11-079	Large Sad Clown 2466	E.M. Merck	Open	13.40	13.40
93-11-080	Monk 2467	E.M. Merck	Open	7.90	7.90
85-11-081	Fat Standing Clown 246852	E.M. Merck	Open	6.55	6.55
93-11-082	Snowman on Icicle 2469	E.M. Merck	Open	15.45	15.45
93-11-083	Clown Above Ball 2470	E.M. Merck	Open	42.00	42.00
94-11-084	Jack Horner 2471	E.M. Merck	Open	6.50	6.50
94-11-085	Child in Manger 2472	E.M. Merck	Open	7.75	7.75
94-11-086	Hot Shot 2473	E.M. Merck	Open	11.00	11.00
94-11-087	My Buddy 2474	E.M. Merck	Open	7.75	7.75
94-11-088	Jesus on Form 2475	E.M. Merck	Open	17.65	17.65
94-11-089	Merlin 2476	E.M. Merck	Open	17.65	17.65
94-11-090	Joseph 2477	E.M. Merck	Open	8.25	8.25
94-11-091	Roly-Poly 2478	E.M. Merck	Open	24.00	24.00
94-11-092	Razzle-Dazzle 2479	E.M. Merck	Open	17.65	17.65
94-11-093	Show Time 2480	E.M. Merck	Open	18.90	18.90
94-11-094	John Bull 2481	E.M. Merck	Open	9.35	9.35
94-11-095	King Ludwig 2482	E.M. Merck	Open	12.75	12.75
94-11-096	Marley 2483	E.M. Merck	Open	7.75	7.75

Old World Christmas — Fruits & Vegetables

		ARTIST	EDITION	ISSUE	QUOTE
86-12-001	Pumpkin Head 2801	E.M. Merck	Open	7.35	7.35
86-12-002	Carrot with Leaf 2802	E.M. Merck	Open	7.35	7.35
86-12-003	Large Acorn 2803	E.M. Merck	Open	6.65	6.65
86-12-004	Large Walnut 2804	E.M. Merck	Open	3.60	3.60
86-12-005	Pear with Face 2805	E.M. Merck	Open	7.00	7.00
86-12-006	Strawberry 2806	E.M. Merck	Open	4.75	4.75
86-12-007	Grapes with Green Glitter 2807	E.M. Merck	Open	4.75	4.75
86-12-008	Small Pear with Leaf 2808	E.M. Merck	Open	4.75	4.75
86-12-009	Pear with Leaf 2809	E.M. Merck	Open	5.55	5.55
87-12-010	Onion 2810	E.M. Merck	Retrd.	8.25	25.00
84-12-011	Pickle 281018	E.M. Merck	Open	7.00	7.00
84-12-012	Banana 281020	E.M. Merck	Open	8.00	8.00
84-12-013	Mr. Pear 281023	E.M. Merck	Retrd.	6.75	6.75
84-12-014	Large Matte Corn 281033	E.M. Merck	Open	9.25	9.25
85-12-015	Grapes on Form 281038	E.M. Merck	Retrd.	7.00	7.00
85-12-016	Very Large Strawberry 281050	E.M. Merck	Open	9.25	9.25
85-12-017	Large Basket of Grapes 281053	E.M. Merck	Open	10.35	10.35
85-12-018	Mr. Apple 281071	E.M. Merck	Retrd.	6.20	11.00
85-12-019	Large Pear with Leaf 281072	E.M. Merck	Open	7.35	7.35
87-12-020	Potato 2811	E.M. Merck	Open	8.45	8.45
87-12-021	Green Pepper 2812	E.M. Merck	Open	8.00	8.00
87-12-022	Plum With Leaf 2813	E.M. Merck	Open	7.35	7.35
87-12-023	Small Apple With Leaf 2814	E.M. Merck	Open	5.75	5.75
88-12-024	Small Tomato 2815	E.M. Merck	Open	4.00	4.00
88-12-025	Miniature Grapes 2816	E.M. Merck	Open	3.00	3.00
88-12-026	Gold Walnut 2817	E.M. Merck	Open	2.00	2.00
89-12-027	Shiny Corn 2818	E.M. Merck	Open	5.50	5.50
89-12-028	Small Matte Corn 2819	E.M. Merck	Open	4.50	4.50
89-12-029	Cucumber 2820	E.M. Merck	Retrd.	6.65	6.65
89-12-030	Large Frosted Strawberry 2821	E.M. Merck	Open	6.00	6.00
89-12-031	Berry 2822	E.M. Merck	Open	2.70	2.70
89-12-032	Gurken 2823	E.M. Merck	Open	2.70	2.70
90-12-033	Cherries on Form 2825	E.M. Merck	Retrd.	9.00	9.50
90-12-034	Large Red Apple 2828	E.M. Merck	Open	8.55	8.55
90-12-035	Large Golden Apple 2829	E.M. Merck	Open	8.55	8.55
90-12-036	Apricot 2831	E.M. Merck	Open	6.55	6.55
90-12-037	Sweet Pickle 2833	E.M. Merck	Open	4.50	4.50
90-12-038	White Grapes 2834	E.M. Merck	Open	6.75	6.75
90-12-039	Raspberry 2835	E.M. Merck	Retrd.	6.20	6.20
90-12-040	Strawberry Cluster 2836	E.M. Merck	Open	5.20	5.20
90-12-041	Apples on Form 2837	E.M. Merck	Open	9.00	9.00
85-12-042	Purple Grapes 283765	E.M. Merck	Open	5.75	5.75
90-12-043	Fruit Basket 2838	E.M. Merck	Open	7.80	7.80
90-12-044	Lime 2839	E.M. Merck	Open	3.50	3.50
90-12-045	Gold Grapes 2840	E.M. Merck	Open	6.75	6.75
90-12-046	Large Strawberry with Flower 2841	E.M. Merck	Retrd.	10.50	14.00
85-12-047	Small Purple Grapes 2841047	E.M. Merck	Open	4.00	4.00
85-12-048	Large Strawberry 2841432	E.M. Merck	Retrd.	4.20	4.20
90-12-049	Fruits on Form 2842	E.M. Merck	Open	10.35	10.35
90-12-050	Watermelon Slice 2844	E.M. Merck	Open	11.00	11.00
90-12-051	Fancy Strawberry 2845	E.M. Merck	Open	5.55	5.55
90-12-052	Peach 2846	E.M. Merck	Open	7.65	7.65
91-12-053	Very Large Pear 2847	E.M. Merck	Retrd.	10.60	10.60
91-12-054	Very Large Apple 2848	E.M. Merck	Retrd.	10.60	10.60
91-12-055	Large Fruit Basket 2849	E.M. Merck	Open	12.50	12.50
91-12-056	Double Mushroom 2850	E.M. Merck	Open	6.65	6.65
91-12-057	Strawberries/Flower on Form 2851	E.M. Merck	Open	8.55	8.55
91-12-058	Large Purple Grapes with Leaves 2852	E.M. Merck	Open	6.75	6.75
91-12-059	Red Pepper 2853	E.M. Merck	Open	9.45	9.45
91-12-060	Harvest Grapes 2854	E.M. Merck	Open	9.25	9.25
91-12-061	Large Raspberry 2855	E.M. Merck	Open	7.90	7.90
92-12-062	Shiny Red Apple 2856	E.M. Merck	Open	6.55	6.55
92-12-063	Orange 2857	E.M. Merck	Open	7.00	7.00
92-12-064	Large Tomato 2858	E.M. Merck	Open	7.45	7.45
92-12-065	Fruit Basket on Form 2859	E.M. Merck	Open	9.25	9.25
92-12-066	Candied Apple 2860	E.M. Merck	Open	8.70	8.70
92-12-067	Sugar Plum 2861	E.M. Merck	Open	7.55	7.55
92-12-068	Sugar Lemon 2862	E.M. Merck	Open	7.45	7.45
92-12-069	Sugar Pear 2863	E.M. Merck	Open	7.00	7.00
92-12-070	Sugar Strawberry 2864	E.M. Merck	Open	7.65	7.65
92-12-071	Sugar Grapes 2865	E.M. Merck	Open	7.45	7.45
93-12-072	Sugar Harvest Grapes 2866	E.M. Merck	Open	9.70	9.70
93-12-073	Sugar Raspberry 2867	E.M. Merck	Open	8.55	8.55
93-12-074	Chestnut 2869	E.M. Merck	Open	6.00	6.00
93-12-075	Pear Face 2871	E.M. Merck	Open	8.35	8.35
85-12-076	Large Strawberry with Glitter 287282	E.M. Merck	Open	6.45	6.45
93-12-077	Mushroom Face 2873	E.M. Merck	Open	5.85	5.85
93-12-078	Apple Tree 2874	E.M. Merck	Open	8.90	8.90
93-12-079	Pea Pod 2875	E.M. Merck	Open	9.60	9.60
93-12-080	Asparagus 2876	E.M. Merck	Open	10.60	10.60
93-12-081	Large Cornucopia 2877	E.M. Merck	Open	25.00	25.00
93-12-082	Garlic 2878	E.M. Merck	Open	7.00	7.00
93-12-083	Translucent Grapes with 18KT Gold 2879	E.M. Merck	Open	7.25	7.25
93-12-084	Miniature Mushrooms 2880	E.M. Merck	Open	4.00	4.00
93-12-085	Large Sugar Pear 2881	E.M. Merck	Open	12.95	12.95
93-12-086	Large Candied Apple 2882	E.M. Merck	Open	12.95	12.95
94-12-087	New Potato 2883	E.M. Merck	Open	5.80	5.80
94-12-088	Apple Slice 2884	E.M. Merck	Open	9.45	9.45
94-12-089	Orange Slice 2885	E.M. Merck	Open	9.45	9.45
94-12-090	French Carrot 2886	E.M. Merck	Open	4.45	4.45
94-12-091	Grapes with Butterfly 2887	E.M. Merck	Open	9.50	9.50

Old World Christmas — Hearts

		ARTIST	EDITION	ISSUE	QUOTE
86-13-001	Small Gold Heart with Star 3001	E.M. Merck	Retrd.	2.85	4.25
86-13-002	Small Red Heart with Star 3002	E.M. Merck	Open	2.95	2.95
87-13-003	Heart with Ribbon 3003	E.M. Merck	Open	8.45	8.45
87-13-004	Burgundy Heart with Glitter 3004	E.M. Merck	Open	6.75	6.75
88-13-005	Valentine 3005	E.M. Merck	Open	5.75	5.75

		ARTIST	EDITION	ISSUE	QUOTE
88-13-006	Large Red Glitter Heart 3006	E.M. Merck	Open	8.45	8.45
89-13-007	Strawberry Heart 3007	E.M. Merck	Open	3.00	3.00
89-13-008	Double Heart 3008	E.M. Merck	Open	3.00	3.00
89-13-009	Smooth Heart 3009	E.M. Merck	Open	2.25	2.25
92-13-010	Heart with Flowers 3010	E.M. Merck	Retrd.	9.50	9.50
92-13-011	Scrap Angel on Heart (A) 3011	E.M. Merck	Open	8.35	8.35
93-13-012	Frost Red Translucent Heart 3012	E.M. Merck	Open	6.45	6.45
93-13-013	Merry Christmas Heart 3013	E.M. Merck	Open	7.20	7.20
85-13-014	Pink Heart with Glitter 306767	E.M. Merck	Open	6.75	6.75
85-13-015	Large Matte Red Heart 306925	E.M. Merck	Open	5.30	5.30

Old World Christmas — Household Items

		ARTIST	EDITION	ISSUE	QUOTE
86-14-001	Red Stocking 3201	E.M. Merck	Retrd.	9.00	13.00
86-14-002	Cuckoo Clock 3202	E.M. Merck	Open	9.25	9.25
86-14-003	Black Stocking 3203	E.M. Merck	Retrd.	9.45	19.00
88-14-004	Wine Barrel 3204	E.M. Merck	Retrd.	7.00	9.75
88-14-005	Baby's Shoe 3205	E.M. Merck	Open	7.35	7.35
91-14-006	Money Bag 3206	E.M. Merck	Open	7.00	7.00
91-14-007	Pipe (A) 3207	E.M. Merck	Open	9.00	9.00
91-14-008	Small Cuckoo Clock 3209	E.M. Merck	Open	7.00	7.00
91-14-009	Small Wine Barrel 3210	E.M. Merck	Retrd.	6.30	6.30
85-14-010	Wall Clock 321060	E.M. Merck	Open	11.00	11.00
85-14-011	Clip-On Candle 321063	E.M. Merck	Open	12.95	12.95
85-14-012	Pastel Umbrella (A) 321091	E.M. Merck	Retrd.	11.00	11.00
85-14-013	Fancy Coffee Pot 321092	E.M. Merck	Open	13.95	13.95
85-14-014	Lady's Fan 321093	E.M. Merck	Open	6.65	6.65
85-14-015	Large Purse 321095	E.M. Merck	Open	7.00	7.00
92-14-016	Flapper Purse 3211	E.M. Merck	Open	9.25	9.25
85-14-017	Very Large Pink Umbrella 321103	E.M. Merck	Retrd.	29.50	35.00
93-14-018	Christmas Shoe 3212	E.M. Merck	Open	8.25	8.25
93-14-019	Fancy Teapot 3213	E.M. Merck	Open	8.75	8.75
93-14-020	Beer Stein 3214	E.M. Merck	Open	10.95	10.95
93-14-021	Fancy Purse 3215	E.M. Merck	Open	6.00	6.00
93-14-022	Elegant Chocolate Pot 3216	E.M. Merck	Open	12.85	12.85
85-14-023	Pocket Watch 326729	E.M. Merck	Open	5.85	5.85

Old World Christmas — Icicles

		ARTIST	EDITION	ISSUE	QUOTE
88-15-001	Long Champagne Icicle 3401	E.M. Merck	Retrd.	7.25	7.25
85-15-002	Long Silver Icicle 3450380	E.M. Merck	Open.	7.00	7.00

Old World Christmas — Miscellaneous Forms

		ARTIST	EDITION	ISSUE	QUOTE
86-15-001	Flower Basket 3601	E.M. Merck	Open	10.25	10.25
87-15-002	Stars on Form (A) 3602	E.M. Merck	Open	12.95	12.95
88-15-003	Ice Cream Cone with Glitter 3604	E.M. Merck	Open	13.40	13.40
88-15-004	Clip-On Tulip (A) 3605	E.M. Merck	Open	8.70	8.70
88-15-005	Skull 3606	E.M. Merck	Open	7.35	7.35
89-15-006	Red Rose on Form 3607	E.M. Merck	Open	5.85	5.85
89-15-007	Morning Glories 3608	E.M. Merck	Open	8.90	8.90
89-15-008	Flower with Butterfly 3609	E.M. Merck	Retrd.	9.75	10.95
89-15-009	Flower Bouquet in Basket 3610	E.M. Merck	Open	9.45	9.45
89-15-010	Christmas Lantern 3611	E.M. Merck	Open	7.80	7.80
89-15-011	Mr. Sunflower 3612	E.M. Merck	Open	7.80	7.80
89-15-012	Victorian Keepsake 3613	E.M. Merck	Open	9.25	9.25
89-15-013	Edelweiss 3614	E.M. Merck	Open	3.00	3.00
89-15-014	Ribbed Ball with Roses 3615	E.M. Merck	Open	3.00	3.00
89-15-015	Rose 3616	E.M. Merck	Open	2.40	2.40
89-15-016	Shiny Red Clip-On Tulip 3617	E.M. Merck	Retrd.	7.45	7.45
90-15-017	Edelweiss on Form 3618	E.M. Merck	Open	8.25	8.25
90-15-018	Poinsettias 3619	E.M. Merck	Open	9.90	9.90
90-15-019	Assorted Christmas Stars 3620	E.M. Merck	Open	7.00	7.00
90-15-020	Shamrock on Form 3621	E.M. Merck	Open	5.55	5.55
90-15-021	Large Snowflake 3622	E.M. Merck	Open	13.00	13.00
90-15-022	Pink Sea Shell 3623	E.M. Merck	Open	7.00	7.00
90-15-023	Sunburst 3624	E.M. Merck	Retrd.	8.00	8.00
90-15-024	Large Sea Shell 3625	E.M. Merck	Open	8.35	8.35
90-15-025	Assorted Christmas Flowers 3626	E.M. Merck	Open	8.00	8.00
90-15-026	Assorted Pastel Fantasy Forms 3627	E.M. Merck	Open	6.25	6.25
90-15-027	Clip-On Pink Rose 3628	E.M. Merck	Open	9.25	9.25
90-15-028	Large Conical Shell 3629	E.M. Merck	Retrd.	8.70	9.50
90-15-029	Poinsettia Blossom 3630	E.M. Merck	Open	11.60	11.60
92-15-030	Poinsettia on Form 3631	E.M. Merck	Open	7.35	7.35
92-15-031	Christmas Shamrock 3632	E.M. Merck	Open	9.25	9.25
92-15-032	Large Ribbed Ball with Roses 3633	E.M. Merck	Open	7.00	7.00
92-15-033	Christmas Ball with Roses 3634	E.M. Merck	Open	9.45	9.45
92-15-034	Fantasy Christmas Form 3635	E.M. Merck	Open	9.00	9.00
92-15-035	Assorted Spirals 3636	E.M. Merck	Open	8.25	8.25
92-15-036	Pansy 3637	E.M. Merck	Open	7.35	7.35
85-15-037	Ice Cream Cone 3637164	E.M. Merck	Retrd.	14.50	14.50
92-15-038	Basket of Roses 3638	E.M. Merck	Open	11.00	11.00
92-15-039	Garden Flowers 3639	E.M. Merck	Open	9.00	9.00
92-15-040	Assorted Northern Stars 3640	E.M. Merck	Open	6.20	6.20
92-15-041	Snowflake on Form 3641	E.M. Merck	Open	6.75	6.75
93-15-042	Crown 3642	E.M. Merck	Open	8.90	8.90
93-15-043	Lucky Shamrock 3643	E.M. Merck	Retrd.	7.80	12.00
93-15-044	Merry Christmas Ball 3645	E.M. Merck	Open	7.45	7.45
93-15-045	Large Conical Shell 3646	E.M. Merck	Open	7.35	7.35
93-15-046	Assorted Fantasy Form with Wire 3650	E.M. Merck	Open	20.00	20.00
85-15-047	Pink Rose with Glitter 366828	E.M. Merck	Open	4.95	4.95

Old World Christmas — Musical Instruments

		ARTIST	EDITION	ISSUE	QUOTE
86-16-001	Cello 3801	E.M. Merck	Open	6.65	6.65
87-16-002	Guitar 3802	E.M. Merck	Open	6.65	6.65
88-16-003	Large Drum 3803	E.M. Merck	Open	10.35	10.35
88-16-004	Large Bell with Acorns 3804	E.M. Merck	Open	9.00	9.00
89-16-005	Bell with Flowers 3805	E.M. Merck	Open	5.85	5.85
89-16-006	Christmas Bells on From 3806	E.M. Merck	Open	8.35	8.35
90-16-007	Large Christmas Bell 3808	E.M. Merck	Open	10.35	10.35
90-16-008	Lyre 3809	E.M. Merck	Open	8.35	8.35
90-16-009	Zither 3810	E.M. Merck	Open	8.35	8.35
90-16-010	Large Cello 3811	E.M. Merck	Open	8.35	8.35
90-16-011	Large Banjo 3812	E.M. Merck	Open	8.35	8.35
90-16-012	Large Mandolin 3813	E.M. Merck	Open	8.35	8.35
90-16-013	Accordion 3814	E.M. Merck	Open	8.35	8.35
90-16-014	Small Fancy Drum 3815	E.M. Merck	Open	7.80	7.80
90-16-015	Assorted Snow Bells 3816	E.M. Merck	Open	6.65	6.65
90-16-016	Toy Drum 3817	E.M. Merck	Open	9.25	9.25
93-16-017	Large Bell with Holly 3819	E.M. Merck	Open	50.00	50.00
88-16-018	Clip-On Drum 383534	E.M. Merck	Open	8.00	8.00

Old World Christmas — Santas

		ARTIST	EDITION	ISSUE	QUOTE
86-17-001	Santa Under Tree 4001	E.M. Merck	Open	10.35	10.35
86-17-002	Santa On Cone 4002	E.M. Merck	Retrd.	7.90	12.00
86-17-003	Santa On Carriage 4003	E.M. Merck	Retrd.	10.00	16.00
86-17-004	Santa In Chimney 4005	E.M. Merck	Open	8.70	8.70
86-17-005	Father Christmas Head 4006	E.M. Merck	Open	7.80	7.80
86-17-006	Green Clip-On Santa 4007	E.M. Merck	Open	7.80	7.80
86-17-007	St. Nicholas Head 4008	E.M. Merck	Open	6.65	6.65
86-17-008	Santa with Glued-On Tree 4009	E.M. Merck	Open	9.00	9.00
86-17-009	Small Blue Santa 4010	E.M. Merck	Open	5.40	5.40
84-17-010	Large Santa In Basket 401001	E.M. Merck	Open	12.95	12.95
84-17-011	Roly-Poly Santa 401002	E.M. Merck	Open	7.90	7.90
84-17-012	Old Father Christmas Head 401007	E.M. Merck	Open	7.00	7.00
84-17-013	Small Old-Fashioned Santa 401022	E.M. Merck	Open	6.65	6.65
85-17-014	Santa and Tree on Form 401026	E.M. Merck	Open	9.25	9.25
85-17-015	Father Christmas with Tree 401039	E.M. Merck	Open	8.00	8.00
85-17-016	Jolly Father Christmas 401043	E.M. Merck	Open	7.00	7.00
85-17-017	Gold Father Christmas 401045	E.M. Merck	Open	7.45	7.45
85-17-018	Blue Father Christmas 4010498	E.M. Merck	Open	8.00	8.00
85-17-019	Pink Father Christmas 4010499	E.M. Merck	Open	8.00	8.00
85-17-020	Santa in Tree 401054	E.M. Merck	Open	7.45	7.45
85-17-021	Large Santa with Tree 401055	E.M. Merck	Open	12.60	12.60
85-17-022	Parachuting Santa 401056	E.M. Merck	Open	8.00	8.00
85-17-023	Standing Santa 401057	E.M. Merck	Open	11.00	11.00
85-17-024	St. Nicholas on Horse 401064	E.M. Merck	Open	13.95	13.95
85-17-025	Small Santa with Pack 401065	E.M. Merck	Open	5.40	5.40
85-17-026	Matte Santa Head 401087	E.M. Merck	Open	8.00	8.00
86-17-027	Pink Clip-On Santa 4011	E.M. Merck	Open	8.35	8.35
85-17-028	Small Santa in Basket 401105	E.M. Merck	Open	9.25	9.25
87-17-029	Matte Red Roly-Poly Santa 4012	E.M. Merck	Open	7.90	7.90
87-17-030	Burgundy Father Christmas 4013	E.M. Merck	Open	7.80	7.80
87-17-031	Burgundy Santa Claus 4014	E.M. Merck	Open	13.95	13.95
87-17-032	Very Large Santa Head 4015	E.M. Merck	Open	13.95	13.95
87-17-033	Jolly Santa Head 4016	E.M. Merck	Open	8.80	8.80
87-17-034	Santa in Airplane 4017	E.M. Merck	Open	13.95	13.95
87-17-035	Santa Above Ball 4018	E.M. Merck	Open	13.95	13.95
89-17-036	Old-Fashioned Santa (A) 4019	E.M. Merck	Open	5.75	5.75
89-17-037	St Nicholas 4020	E.M. Merck	Open	10.00	10.00
89-17-038	Victorian Santa 4021	E.M. Merck	Open	8.45	8.45
89-17-039	Victorian Santa Head 4022	E.M. Merck	Open	8.35	8.35
89-17-040	Santa Hiding in Tree 4023	E.M. Merck	Open	11.00	11.00
89-17-041	Father Christmas 4024	E.M. Merck	Open	4.25	4.25
89-17-042	Santa 4025	E.M. Merck	Open	4.50	4.50
90-17-043	White Clip-On Santa 4026	E.M. Merck	Open	7.35	7.35
90-17-044	Small Victorian Santa Head 4027	E.M. Merck	Open	7.35	7.35
90-17-045	Blue Victorian St. Nick 4028	E.M. Merck	Retrd.	9.95	9.95
90-17-046	Light Blue St. Nicholas 4029	E.M. Merck	Open	6.45	6.45
90-17-047	Clip-On Victorian St. Nick 4030	E.M. Merck	Open	11.00	11.00
90-17-048	Weihnachtsmann with Tree 4031	E.M. Merck	Open	10.50	10.50
90-17-049	Miniature Santa 4032	E.M. Merck	Open	4.95	4.95
85-17-050	Father Christmas Head 403223	E.M. Merck	Open	7.80	7.80
85-17-051	Father Christmas with Basket 403224	E.M. Merck	Open	7.80	7.80
90-17-052	Snowy Santa 4033	E.M. Merck	Open	10.95	10.95
90-17-053	Weihnachtsmann 4034	E.M. Merck	Open	9.00	9.00
90-17-054	Round Jolly Santa Head 4035	E.M. Merck	Open	11.00	11.00
90-17-055	Father Christmas with Toys 4036	E.M. Merck	Open	13.95	13.95
90-17-056	Very Large Belznickel 4037	E.M. Merck	Open	22.50	22.50
90-17-057	Very Large St. Nick Head 4038	E.M. Merck	Open	22.50	22.50
90-17-058	Festive Santa Head 4039	E.M. Merck	Open	11.00	11.00
90-17-059	Old-Fashioned St. Nicholas 4040	E.M. Merck	Open	11.00	11.00
90-17-060	Old St. Nick with Toys 4041	E.M. Merck	Open	13.95	13.95
90-17-061	Large Weihnachtsmann 4042	E.M. Merck	Open	10.25	10.25
90-17-062	Victorian Scrap Santa 4043	E.M. Merck	Retrd.	9.70	9.70
90-17-063	Old Bavarian Santa 4044	E.M. Merck	Open	12.50	12.50
90-17-064	Victorian Father Christmas 4045	E.M. Merck	Open	10.00	10.00
90-17-065	Father Christmas on Form 4046	E.M. Merck	Open	11.00	11.00
91-17-066	Alpine Santa 4047	E.M. Merck	Open	7.00	7.00
91-17-067	Santa in Mushroom 4048	E.M. Merck	Open	8.70	8.70
92-17-068	Small Santa on Form 4049	E.M. Merck	Open	8.00	8.00
92-17-069	Roaring 20s Santa 4050	E.M. Merck	Open	10.00	10.00
92-17-070	Frontier Santa with Tree 4051	E.M. Merck	Open	11.00	11.00
92-17-071	Gold Weihnachtsmann 4052	E.M. Merck	Open	9.80	9.80
92-17-072	Old Swiss Santa 4053	E.M. Merck	Open	12.50	12.50
92-17-073	Round Santa Head 4054	E.M. Merck	Open	9.00	9.00
92-17-074	Belznickel 4055	E.M. Merck	Open	12.50	12.50
93-17-075	Snowy Purple Santa 4056	E.M. Merck	Open	7.35	7.35
93-17-076	Santa in Sleigh 4057	E.M. Merck	Open	14.65	14.65
93-17-077	Santa in Walnut 4058	E.M. Merck	Open	7.00	7.00
93-17-078	Santa in Chimney 4059	E.M. Merck	Open	12.50	12.50
93-17-079	Purple Belznickel 4060	E.M. Merck	Open	12.50	12.50
93-17-080	Frosty Santa 4061	E.M. Merck	Open	10.25	10.25
93-17-081	Woodland Santa 4062	E.M. Merck	Open	9.35	9.35
93-17-082	Purple Father Christmas 4063	E.M. Merck	Open	8.35	8.35
93-17-083	Large Father Christmas Head 4066	E.M. Merck	Open	22.50	22.50
93-17-084	Blue St. Nick 4067	E.M. Merck	Open	10.00	10.00
93-17-085	Old World Santa 4068	E.M. Merck	Open	11.00	11.00
93-17-086	Santa Above Reflector 4069	E.M. Merck	Open	40.00	40.00
85-17-087	Santa in Chimney 406912	E.M. Merck	Retrd.	11.00	11.00
93-17-088	Santa with Staff 4070	E.M. Merck	Open	10.95	10.95
93-17-089	Very Large Roly-Poly Santa 4071	E.M. Merck	Open	50.00	50.00
93-17-090	Santa Above Bell 4072	E.M. Merck	Open	36.00	36.00
94-17-091	Old World Santa Head 4074	E.M. Merck	Open	6.50	6.50
94-17-092	Double-Sided Santa Head 4075	E.M. Merck	Open	8.00	8.00
94-17-093	Very Merry Santa 4076	E.M. Merck	Open	7.35	7.35
94-17-094	Old-Fashioned St. Nick 4077	E.M. Merck	Open	9.25	9.25
94-17-095	Victorian Father Christmas 4078	E.M. Merck	Open	7.35	7.35
94-17-096	Santa's Shop 4079	E.M. Merck	Open	13.25	13.25
94-17-097	Father Christmas with Chenile 4080	E.M. Merck	Open	10.80	10.80

Old World Christmas — Reflectors

		ARTIST	EDITION	ISSUE	QUOTE
86-18-001	Star Pattern Reflector (A) 4201	E.M. Merck	Open	9.25	9.25
86-18-002	Pink Reflector 4202	E.M. Merck	Open	9.50	9.50
86-18-003	Houseshoe Reflector 4203	E.M. Merck	Retrd.	7.80	7.80
87-18-004	Large Drop with Indents (A) 4204	E.M. Merck	Open	12.85	12.85
90-18-005	Strawberry in Reflector 4205	E.M. Merck	Open	9.25	9.25
90-18-006	Assorted Reflectors with Diamonds 4206	E.M. Merck	Open	9.95	9.95
90-18-007	Assorted 6 cm Reflectors 4207	E.M. Merck	Open	7.00	7.00
91-18-008	Peacock in Reflector 4208	E.M. Merck	Open	9.25	9.25
91-18-009	Pears in Reflector 4209	E.M. Merck	Open	9.25	9.25
92-18-010	Shining Sun Reflector 4210	E.M. Merck	Open	9.00	9.00
92-18-011	Poinsettia in Reflector 4211	E.M. Merck	Open	9.00	9.00
92-18-012	Flower in Reflector 4212	E.M. Merck	Open	9.25	9.25
92-18-013	Mushrooms in Reflector (A) 4213	E.M. Merck	Open	9.90	9.90
92-18-014	Scrap Santa in Reflector 4214	E.M. Merck	Retrd.	8.80	11.00
93-18-015	Reflector with Tinsel Wire 4215	E.M. Merck	Open	20.00	20.00

	ARTIST	EDITION	ISSUE	QUOTE
94-18-016 Small Fantasy Form 4216	E.M. Merck	Open	22.00	22.00
94-18-017 Reflector on Icicle 4217	E.M. Merck	Open	27.75	27.75

Old World Christmas — **Toys**

	ARTIST	EDITION	ISSUE	QUOTE
86-19-001 Large Nutcracker 4401	E.M. Merck	Open	13.50	13.50
86-19-002 Small Nutcracker 4402	E.M. Merck	Open	10.00	10.00
86-19-003 Dumb-Dumb 4403	E.M. Merck	Retrd.	6.45	15.00
86-19-004 Soccer Ball 4404	E.M. Merck	Open	7.00	7.00
88-19-005 Nutcracker Guard 4405	E.M. Merck	Open	8.50	8.50
90-19-006 Lucky Dice 4406	E.M. Merck	Open	7.00	7.00
90-19-007 Large Fancy Carousel 4407	E.M. Merck	Open	12.75	12.75
90-19-008 Rocking Horse/Tree on Form 4408	E.M. Merck	Open	12.95	12.95
90-19-009 Large Doll Buggy with Doll 4409	E.M. Merck	Open	11.50	11.50
93-19-010 Stocking with Toys 4410	E.M. Merck	Open	13.50	13.50
93-19-011 Cornucopia of Toys 4411	E.M. Merck	Open	9.50	9.50
85-19-012 Doll Buggy with Doll 4437138	E.M. Merck	Open	7.00	7.00
85-19-013 Small Carousel 446836	E.M. Merck	Open	7.00	7.00

Old World Christmas — **Transportation**

	ARTIST	EDITION	ISSUE	QUOTE
86-20-001 Rolls Royce 4601	E.M. Merck	Retrd.	7.90	15.95
88-20-002 Cable Car 4602	E.M. Merck	Retrd.	8.45	14.95
90-20-003 Fire Truck 4603	E.M. Merck	Open	8.25	8.25
90-20-004 Old-Time Limousine 4604	E.M. Merck	Open	9.00	9.00
90-20-005 Large Zeppelin 4605	E.M. Merck	Open	8.25	8.25
90-20-006 Fancy Steam Locomotive 4606	E.M. Merck	Open	10.35	10.35
92-20-007 Commemorative Airship 4607	E.M. Merck	Open	9.25	9.25
92-20-008 Locomotive/Tree on Form 4608	E.M. Merck	Open	12.95	12.95
92-20-009 Race Car 4609	E.M. Merck	Open	7.00	7.00
93-20-010 Gold Car 4610	E.M. Merck	Open	9.80	9.80
85-20-011 Cable Car 461067	E.M. Merck	Retrd.	14.95	14.95
85-20-012 Locomotive 461069	E.M. Merck	Retrd.	7.00	13.00
93-20-013 Ocean Liner 4611	E.M. Merck	Open	9.45	9.45
93-20-014 Small Locomotive 4612	E.M. Merck	Open	9.80	9.80
93-20-015 Gray Zeppelin 4613	E.M. Merck	Open	6.75	6.75
85-20-016 Old-Fashioned Car 463747	E.M. Merck	Retrd.	6.25	9.00
85-20-017 Zeppelin 467265	E.M. Merck	Open	7.00	7.00

Old World Christmas — **Trees & Cones**

	ARTIST	EDITION	ISSUE	QUOTE
86-21-001 Small Red & Gold Cones (A) 4801	E.M. Merck	Open	3.75	3.75
88-21-002 Large Mauve & Champagne Cone 4802	E.M. Merck	Retrd.	11.85	11.85
88-21-003 Smal Fir Cone (A) 4803	E.M. Merck	Open	4.50	4.50
89-21-004 Assorted Pearl Cones 4804	E.M. Merck	Open	3.85	3.85
89-21-005 Pine Cone Santa 4805	E.M. Merck	Open	4.75	4.75
90-21-006 Small Pine Cones with Leaves (A) 4806	E.M. Merck	Open	5.25	5.25
90-21-007 Assorted Shiny Cones 4807	E.M. Merck	Open	6.55	6.55
90-21-008 Assorted Pine Cones with Leaves 4809	E.M. Merck	Open	6.75	6.75
90-21-009 Multi-Colored Cone 4810	E.M. Merck	Open	7.00	7.00
85-21-010 Green Tree with Glitter 481044	E.M. Merck	Open	4.50	4.50
85-21-011 Fir Cone With Glitter 481046	E.M. Merck	Open	6.45	6.45
90-21-012 Pine Cone Man 4811	E.M. Merck	Open	8.25	8.25
90-21-013 Multi-Colored Tree 4812	E.M. Merck	Open	5.55	5.55
90-21-014 Fir Tree 4813	E.M. Merck	Open	7.00	7.00
90-21-015 Small Christmas Tree 4814	E.M. Merck	Open	4.95	4.95
90-21-016 Large Christmas Tree 4815	E.M. Merck	Open	8.00	8.00
92-21-017 Tree With Eagle 4816	E.M. Merck	Open	7.00	7.00
93-21-018 Sugar Cone 4817	E.M. Merck	Open	7.55	7.55
85-21-019 Very Large Red & Gold Cones 483612	E.M. Merck	Open	7.00	7.00
85-21-020 Medium Gold Cone w/Glitter 486712-5	E.M. Merck	Open	3.85	3.85
94-21-021 Matte Gold Cone with Snow 486866	E.M. Merck	Open	4.85	4.85

Old World Christmas — **Tree Tops**

	ARTIST	EDITION	ISSUE	QUOTE
86-22-001 Red Santa 5001	E.M. Merck	Open	37.50	37.50
86-22-002 Blue Santa 5002	E.M. Merck	Open	37.50	37.50
86-22-003 Burgundy Angel 5003	E.M. Merck	Open	47.50	47.50
86-22-004 Blue Angel 5004	E.M. Merck	Open	47.50	47.50
86-22-005 Two Angels 5005	E.M. Merck	Open	47.50	47.50
87-22-006 Angel w/Crown 5007	E.M. Merck	Retrd.	50.00	50.00
87-22-007 Santa in Indent 5008	E.M. Merck	Open	25.00	25.00
87-22-008 Star Reflector 5010	E.M. Merck	Open	25.00	25.00
87-22-009 Heart Reflector 5011	E.M. Merck	Open	25.00	25.00
92-22-010 Large Tree Top w/Cherubs 5012	E.M. Merck	Open	57.50	57.50
92-22-011 Miniature Reflector 5013	E.M. Merck	Open	15.00	15.00
92-22-012 Large Spire w/Reflectors 5014	E.M. Merck	Open	69.50	69.50
92-22-013 Large Tree Top w/Roses 5015	E.M. Merck	Open	47.50	47.50
92-22-014 Fancy Spiral Tree Top 5016	E.M. Merck	Open	47.50	47.50
93-22-015 Very Large Reflector 5017	E.M. Merck	Open	65.00	65.00
85-22-016 Fancy Gold Spire w/Bells 5062-66	E.M. Merck	Retrd.	32.00	32.00
85-22-017 Fancy Red Spire w/Bells 5062-69	E.M. Merck	Retrd.	32.00	32.00
85-22-018 Santa Head Tree Top 506345	E.M. Merck	Open	19.35	19.35

Old World Christmas — **Light Covers**

	ARTIST	EDITION	ISSUE	QUOTE
93-23-001 Doll Head 5202	E.M. Merck	Open	5.65	5.65
93-23-002 Peacock 5203	E.M. Merck	Open	5.65	5.65
93-23-003 Sugar Strawberry 5251	E.M. Merck	Open	5.65	5.65
93-23-004 Sugar Plum 5253	E.M. Merck	Open	5.65	5.65
93-23-005 Sugar Fruit Basket 5256	E.M. Merck	Open	5.65	5.65
93-23-006 Frosty Snowman 5270	E.M. Merck	Open	5.65	5.65
93-23-007 Frosty Cone 5271	E.M. Merck	Open	5.65	5.65
93-23-008 Frosty Icicle 5272	E.M. Merck	Open	5.65	5.65
93-23-009 Frosty Tree 5273	E.M. Merck	Open	5.65	5.65
93-23-010 Assorted Frosty Bell 5275	E.M. Merck	Open	5.65	5.65
93-23-011 Frosty Acorn 5276	E.M. Merck	Open	5.65	5.65
93-23-012 Frosty Red Rose 5277	E.M. Merck	Open	5.65	5.65
84-23-013 Gnome 529001-1	E.M. Merck	Retrd.	1.60	6.50
84-23-014 Snowman 519001-2	E.M. Merck	Retrd.	2.50	6.50
84-23-015 Standing Santa 529001-3	E.M. Merck	Retrd.	3.00	6.50
84-23-016 Mrs. Claus 529001-4	E.M. Merck	Retrd.	1.60	6.50
84-23-017 Clown 529001-5	E.M. Merck	Retrd.	1.60	6.50
84-23-018 Assorted Animals, set of 6 529003	E.M. Merck	Retrd.	10.35	39.00
84-23-019 Owl 529003-2	E.M. Merck	Retrd.	1.60	6.50
84-23-020 Bear 519003-3	E.M. Merck	Retrd.	2.50	6.50
84-23-021 Elephant 529003-4	E.M. Merck	Retrd.	1.60	6.50
84-23-022 Hedgehog 529003-5	E.M. Merck	Retrd.	1.60	6.50
84-23-023 Peacock 519003-6	E.M. Merck	Retrd.	2.70	6.50
84-23-024 Assorted Figurals, set of 6 529005	E.M. Merck	Retrd.	10.35	39.00
84-23-025 Flower Basket 529005-1	E.M. Merck	Retrd.	1.60	6.50
84-23-026 House 529005-2	E.M. Merck	Retrd.	1.60	6.50
84-23-027 Carousel 529005-3	E.M. Merck	Retrd.	2.70	6.50
84-23-028 Santa Head 529005-4	E.M. Merck	Retrd.	2.70	6.50
84-23-029 Santa on Heart 529005-5	E.M. Merck	Retrd.	3.00	6.50
84-23-030 Church on Ball 529005-6	E.M. Merck	Retrd.	2.50	6.50
84-23-031 3 Men in a Tub 529007-1	E.M. Merck	Retrd.	1.60	6.50
84-23-032 Queen of Heart 529007-3	E.M. Merck	Retrd.	2.70	6.50
84-23-033 Lil' Boy Blue 529007-5	E.M. Merck	Retrd.	1.60	6.50
85-23-034 Assorted Heads, set of 6 529009	E.M. Merck	Retrd.	10.35	39.00
85-23-035 Clown Head 529009-1	E.M. Merck	Retrd.	1.60	6.50
85-23-036 Red Riding Hood 529009-2	E.M. Merck	Retrd.	1.60	6.50
85-23-037 Santa Head 529009-3	E.M. Merck	Retrd.	3.00	6.50
85-23-038 Doll Head 529009-4	E.M. Merck	Retrd.	1.60	6.50
85-23-039 Father Christmas 529009-5	E.M. Merck	Retrd.	3.00	6.50
85-23-040 Lil' Rascal Head 529009-6	E.M. Merck	Retrd.	1.60	6.50
85-23-041 Assorted Fruit, set of 6 529011	E.M. Merck	Retrd.	20.00	39.00
85-23-042 Pear 529011-1	E.M. Merck	Retrd.	3.00	6.50
85-23-043 Strawberry 529011-2	E.M. Merck	Retrd.	3.00	6.50
85-23-044 Grapes 529011-3	E.M. Merck	Retrd.	3.00	6.50
85-23-045 Pineapple 529011-4	E.M. Merck	Retrd.	3.00	6.50
85-23-046 Apple 529011-5	E.M. Merck	Retrd.	3.00	6.50
85-23-047 Orange 529011-6	E.M. Merck	Open	3.00	3.00
85-23-048 Soldiers, set of 6 529013	E.M. Merck	Retrd.	17.95	39.00
85-23-049 Soldier with Drum 529013-1	E.M. Merck	Retrd.	2.70	6.50
85-23-050 Soldier with Gun 529013-2	E.M. Merck	Retrd.	2.70	6.50
85-23-051 King 529013-3	E.M. Merck	Retrd.	2.70	6.50
85-23-052 Assorted Santas, set of 6 529015	E.M. Merck	Retrd.	20.00	39.00
85-23-053 Santa with Tree 529015-3	E.M. Merck	Retrd.	3.00	6.50
85-23-054 Roly-Poly Santa 529015-6	E.M. Merck	Retrd.	3.00	6.50
85-23-055 Nutcracker Suite Figures, set of 6 529017	E.M. Merck	Retrd.	19.00	39.00
85-23-056 Clara-The Doll 529017-1	E.M. Merck	Retrd.	2.70	6.50
85-23-057 Marie-The Girl 529017-3	E.M. Merck	Retrd.	2.70	6.50
85-23-058 Nutcracker 529017-4	E.M. Merck	Retrd.	2.70	6.50
85-23-059 Mouse King 529017-5	E.M. Merck	Retrd.	2.70	6.50
85-23-060 Sugar Plum Fairy 529017-6	E.M. Merck	Retrd.	2.70	6.50
85-23-061 Transportation Set 529019	E.M. Merck	Retrd.	17.90	39.00
85-23-062 Tug Boat 529019-1	E.M. Merck	Retrd.	2.70	6.50
85-23-063 Balloon 529019-2	E.M. Merck	Retrd.	2.70	6.50
85-23-064 Automobile 529019-3	E.M. Merck	Retrd.	2.70	6.50
85-23-065 Locomotive 529019-4	E.M. Merck	Retrd.	2.70	6.50
85-23-066 Cable Car 529019-5	E.M. Merck	Retrd.	2.70	6.50
85-23-067 School Bus 529019-6	E.M. Merck	Retrd.	2.70	6.50
86-23-068 Assorted Bells, set of 6 529023	E.M. Merck	Retrd.	22.50	39.00
86-23-069 Tree on Bell 529023-1	E.M. Merck	Retrd.	3.95	6.50
86-23-070 Teddy Bear 529023-2	E.M. Merck	Retrd.	3.95	6.50
86-23-071 Santa on Bell 529023-3	E.M. Merck	Retrd.	3.95	6.50
86-23-072 Rocking Horse on Bell 529023-4	E.M. Merck	Retrd.	3.95	6.50
86-23-073 Angel on Bell 529023-5	E.M. Merck	Retrd.	3.95	6.50
86-23-074 Nutcracker on Bell 529023-6	E.M. Merck	Retrd.	3.95	6.50
86-23-075 Assorted Easter Eggs 529031-1	E.M. Merck	Retrd.	3.00	6.50
86-23-076 Hen in Basket 529033-1	E.M. Merck	Retrd.	3.60	6.50
86-23-077 Rabbit in Egg 529033-2	E.M. Merck	Retrd.	3.60	6.50
86-23-078 Chick 529033-3	E.M. Merck	Retrd.	3.60	6.50
86-23-079 Bunny 529033-4	E.M. Merck	Retrd.	3.60	6.50
86-23-080 Chick in Egg 529033-5	E.M. Merck	Retrd.	3.60	6.50
86-23-081 Bunny in Basket 529033-6	E.M. Merck	Retrd.	3.60	6.50
86-23-082 Teddy Bears, set of 6 529041	E.M. Merck	Retrd.	25.00	39.00
86-23-083 Teddy Bear with Candy Cane 529041-1	E.M. Merck	Retrd.	3.95	6.50
86-23-084 Teddy Bear with Red Heart 529041-2	E.M. Merck	Retrd.	3.95	6.50
86-23-085 Teddy Bear with Tree 529041-3	E.M. Merck	Retrd.	3.95	6.50
86-23-086 Teddy Bear with Nightshirt 529041-4	E.M. Merck	Open	3.95	3.95
86-23-087 Teddy Bear with Ball 529041-5	E.M. Merck	Open	3.95	3.95
86-23-088 Teddy Bear with Vest 529041-6	E.M. Merck	Open	3.95	3.95
86-23-089 Assorted Alphabet Blocks 529043-1	E.M. Merck	Retrd.	4.50	6.50
86-23-090 Assorted Roses, set of 6 529045	E.M. Merck	Retrd.	22.50	39.00
86-23-091 Assorted Red Roses 529045-1	E.M. Merck	Retrd.	3.95	6.50
86-23-092 Assorted Yellow Roses 529045-2	E.M. Merck	Retrd.	3.95	6.50
86-23-093 Assorted Pink Roses 529045-3	E.M. Merck	Retrd.	3.95	6.50
86-23-094 Assorted Peach Roses 529045-4	E.M. Merck	Retrd.	3.95	6.50
86-23-095 Father Christmas Set 529047	E.M. Merck	Retrd.	25.00	39.00
86-23-096 Red Father Christmas 529047-1	E.M. Merck	Retrd.	3.95	6.50
86-23-097 Green Father Christmas 529047-2	E.M. Merck	Retrd.	3.95	6.50
86-23-098 Blue Father Christmas 529047-3	E.M. Merck	Retrd.	3.95	6.50
86-23-099 Red Father Christmas 529047-4	E.M. Merck	Retrd.	3.95	6.50
86-23-100 White Father Christmas 529047-5	E.M. Merck	Retrd.	3.95	6.50
86-23-101 Purple Father Christmas 529047-6	E.M. Merck	Retrd.	3.95	6.50
88-23-102 Thanksgiving, set of 6 529049	E.M. Merck	Retrd.	25.00	39.00
88-23-103 Cornucopia 529049-1	E.M. Merck	Retrd.	3.95	6.50
88-23-104 Turkey 529049-2	E.M. Merck	Retrd.	3.95	6.50
88-23-105 Pilgrim Boy 529049-3	E.M. Merck	Retrd.	3.95	6.50
88-23-106 Pilgrim Girl 529049-4	E.M. Merck	Retrd.	3.95	6.50
88-23-107 Indian 529049-5	E.M. Merck	Retrd.	3.95	6.50
88-23-108 Ear of Corn 529049-6	E.M. Merck	Retrd.	3.95	6.50
88-23-109 Toy, set of 6 529051	E.M. Merck	Retrd.	25.00	39.00
88-23-110 Drum 529051-1	E.M. Merck	Retrd.	3.95	6.50
88-23-111 Doll 529051-2	E.M. Merck	Open	3.95	3.95
88-23-112 Stocking 529051-3	E.M. Merck	Retrd.	3.95	6.50
88-23-113 Christmas Tree 529051-4	E.M. Merck	Retrd.	3.95	6.50
88-23-114 Teddy Bear 529051-5	E.M. Merck	Retrd.	3.95	6.50
88-23-115 Clown 529051-6	E.M. Merck	Retrd.	3.95	6.50
88-23-116 Christmas Carol 529053	E.M. Merck	Retrd.	25.00	39.00
88-23-117 Assorted Fast Food 529055-1	E.M. Merck	Retrd.	3.95	6.50
88-23-118 Assorted Birds 529057-1	E.M. Merck	Retrd.	3.95	6.50
85-23-119 Six Red & White Hearts 529201	E.M. Merck	Retrd.	15.00	15.00
85-23-120 Red Heart 529201-1	E.M. Merck	Retrd.	2.85	6.50
85-23-121 White Heart 529201-2	E.M. Merck	Retrd.	2.85	6.50
85-23-122 Pink Heart 529201-3	E.M. Merck	Retrd.	2.85	6.50
85-23-123 Clear Icicles, set of 6 529205	E.M. Merck	Retrd.	20.00	39.00
85-23-124 Clear Icicle 529205-1	E.M. Merck	Retrd.	3.50	6.50
85-23-125 Pastel Icicles 529207	E.M. Merck	Retrd.	N/A	N/A
89-23-126 Assorted Fir Cone 529209-1	E.M. Merck	Retrd.	2.85	6.50
91-23-127 Assorted Spun Glass Globe 529213-1	E.M. Merck	Retrd.	3.50	6.50
89-23-128 Assorted Sea Shells 529301-4	E.M. Merck	Retrd.	3.50	6.50
89-23-129 Panda 529303-1	E.M. Merck	Open	6.45	6.45
89-23-130 Squirrel 529303-2	E.M. Merck	Open	6.45	6.45
89-23-131 Kitten 529303-3	E.M. Merck	Retrd.	6.45	7.25
89-23-132 Puppy 529303-4	E.M. Merck	Open	6.45	7.25
89-23-133 Swan 529303-5	E.M. Merck	Open	6.45	7.25
89-23-134 Frog 529303-6	E.M. Merck	Retrd.	6.45	7.25
92-23-135 Six Snowmen 529305	E.M. Merck	Retrd.	29.00	39.00
91-23-136 Assorted Snowmen 529305-1	E.M. Merck	Retrd.	5.55	7.25

Old World Christmas — **Halloween Light Covers**

	ARTIST	EDITION	ISSUE	QUOTE
87-24-001 Six Halloween Light Covers 9221	E.M. Merck	Open	25.00	25.00
87-24-002 Jack O'Lantern 9221-1	E.M. Merck	Retrd.	3.95	4.50
87-24-003 Ghost w/Pumpkin 9221-2	E.M. Merck	Open	3.95	3.95
87-24-004 Scarecrow 9221-3	E.M. Merck	Retrd.	3.95	4.50
87-24-005 Witch Head 9221-4	E.M. Merck	Retrd.	3.95	4.50
87-24-006 Sad Pumpkin 9221-5	E.M. Merck	Retrd.	3.95	4.50

	ARTIST	EDITION	ISSUE	QUOTE
87-24-007 Skull 9221-6	E.M. Merck	Open	3.95	3.95
87-24-008 Six Halloween Light Covers 9223	E.M. Merck	Retrd.	25.90	27.00
87-24-009 Haunted House 9223-1	E.M. Merck	Open	3.95	3.95
87-24-010 Smiling Cat 9223-2	E.M. Merck	Retrd.	3.95	4.50
87-24-011 Standing Witch 9223-3	E.M. Merck	Open	3.95	3.95
87-24-012 Smiling Ghost 9223-4	E.M. Merck	Open	3.95	3.95
87-24-013 Devil 9223-5	E.M. Merck	Retrd.	3.95	3.95
87-24-014 Pumpkin w/Top Hat 9223-6	E.M. Merck	Open	3.95	3.95
89-24-015 Spider 9241-1	E.M. Merck	Open	7.65	7.65
89-24-016 Witch Head 9241-2	E.M. Merck	Open	7.65	7.65
89-24-017 Dancing Scarecrow 9241-3	E.M. Merck	Open	7.65	7.65
89-24-018 Wizard 9241-4	E.M. Merck	Retrd.	7.65	12.50
89-24-019 Man in the Moon 9241-5	E.M. Merck	Retrd.	7.65	11.95
89-24-020 Pumpkin Face 9241-6	E.M. Merck	Open	7.65	7.65
Old World Christmas	**Easter**			
88-25-001 Gentleman Rabbit 9301	E.M. Merck	Retrd.	25.00	25.00
88-25-002 Gentleman Chick 9311	E.M. Merck	Retrd.	22.50	22.50
88-25-003 Lady Chick 9312	E.M. Merck	Retrd.	22.50	22.50
Old World Christmas	**Easter Light Covers**			
88-26-001 Assorted Easter Egg 9331-1	E.M. Merck	Retrd.	3.95	6.50
88-26-002 Hen in Basket 9333-1	E.M. Merck	Open	4.20	4.20
88-26-003 Rabbit in Egg 9333-2	E.M. Merck	Open	4.20	4.20
88-26-004 Chick 9333-3	E.M. Merck	Open	4.20	4.20
88-26-005 Bunny 9333-4	E.M. Merck	Open	4.20	4.20
88-26-006 Chick in Egg 9333-5	E.M. Merck	Open	4.20	4.20
88-26-007 Bunny in Basket 9333-6	E.M. Merck	Open	4.20	4.20
88-26-008 Assorted Pastel Egg 9335-1	E.M. Merck	Open	2.95	2.95
Old World Christmas	**Porcelain Christmas**			
87-27-001 Father Christmas (A) 9404	E.M. Merck	Retrd.	11.00	11.00
87-27-002 Father Christmas w/Cape 9405	E.M. Merck	Retrd.	11.00	11.00
87-27-003 Father Christmas w/Toys 9406	E.M. Merck	Retrd.	11.00	11.00
87-27-004 Santa Head 9410	E.M. Merck	Retrd.	6.55	6.55
87-27-005 Lighted Angel Tree Top 9420	E.M. Merck	Retrd.	29.50	29.50
89-27-006 Rocking Horse 9431	E.M. Merck	Open	6.65	6.65
89-27-007 Santa 9432	E.M. Merck	Open	6.65	6.65
89-27-008 Hummingbird 9433	E.M. Merck	Open	6.65	6.65
89-27-009 Teddy Bear 9434	E.M. Merck	Open	6.65	6.65
89-27-010 Angel 9435	E.M. Merck	Open	6.65	6.65
89-27-011 Nutcracker 9436	E.M. Merck	Open	6.65	6.65
87-27-012 Roly-Poly Santa 9441	E.M. Merck	Retrd.	6.75	8.65
88-27-013 Bunnies on Skies 9494	E.M. Merck	Retrd.	10.00	10.00
88-27-014 Bear on Skates 9495	E.M. Merck	Retrd.	10.00	10.00
88-27-015 Penguin w/Gifts 9496	E.M. Merck	Retrd.	10.00	10.00
Old World Christmas	**Collector Club**			
92-28-001 Mr. & Mrs. Claus set 1490	E.M. Merck	Retrd.	Gift	N/A
92-28-002 Glass Christmas Maidens, set of 4, 1491	E.M. Merck	Retrd.	35.00	42.00
92-28-003 Dresdener Drummer Nutcracker 7258	E.M. Merck	Retrd.	110.00	125.00
94-28-004 Santa in Moon 1492	E.M. Merck	12/94	Gift	N/A
94-28-005 Large Santa in Chimney 1493	E.M. Merck	12.94	42.50	42.50
Orrefors	**Christmas Ornaments**			
84-01-001 Dove	O. Alberius	Yr.Iss.	30.00	45.00
85-01-002 Angel	O. Alberius	Yr.Iss.	30.00	40.00
86-01-003 Reindeer	O. Alberius	Yr.Iss.	30.00	40.00
87-01-004 Snowman	O. Alberius	Yr.Iss.	30.00	40.00
88-01-005 Sleigh	O. Alberius	Yr.Iss.	30.00	40.00
89-01-006 Christmas Tree "1989"	O. Alberius	Yr.Iss.	35.00	40.00
90-01-007 Holly Leaves And Berries	O. Alberius	Yr.Iss.	35.00	40.00
91-01-008 Stocking	O. Alberius	Yr.Iss.	40.00	40.00
92-01-009 Star	O. Alberius	Yr.Iss.	35.00	40.00
93-01-010 Bell	O. Alberius	Yr.Iss.	35.00	40.00
93-01-011 Baby's1st Christmas	O. Alberius	Yr.Iss.	40.00	40.00
94-01-012 Rocking Horse	O. Alberius	Yr.Iss.	40.00	40.00
Rawcliffe Corporation	**Bubble Fairy™Ornaments**			
93-01-001 Joy Hanging Baby Bubble Fairy RF156	J. deStefano	Open	40.00	40.00
93-01-002 Blessing Hanging Baby Bubble Fairy RF157	J. deStefano	Open	40.00	40.00
93-01-003 Wonder Hanging Baby Bubble Fairy RF158	J. deStefano	Open	40.00	40.00
93-01-004 Sweetness Hanging Baby Bubble Fairy RF159	J. deStefano	Open	40.00	40.00
92-01-005 Holly Hanging Baby Bubble Fairy RF160	J. deStefano	Open	40.00	40.00
Reco International	**The Reco Angel Collection Hang-Ups**			
87-01-001 Innocence	J. McClelland	Open	7.50	7.50
87-01-002 Harmony	J. McClelland	Open	7.50	7.50
87-01-003 Love	J. McClelland	Open	7.50	7.50
87-01-004 Gloria	J. McClelland	Open	7.50	7.50
87-01-005 Devotion	J. McClelland	Open	7.50	7.50
87-01-006 Joy	J. McClelland	Open	7.50	7.50
87-01-007 Adoration	J. McClelland	Open	10.00	10.00
87-01-008 Peace	J. McClelland	Open	10.00	10.00
87-01-009 Serenity	J. McClelland	Open	10.00	10.00
87-01-010 Hope	J. McClelland	Open	10.00	10.00
Reco International	**The Reco Ornament Collection**			
88-02-001 Billy	S. Kuck	Yr.Iss.	15.00	15.00
88-02-002 Lisa	S. Kuck	Yr.Iss.	15.00	15.00
89-02-003 Heather	S. Kuck	Yr.Iss.	15.00	15.00
89-02-004 Timothy	S. Kuck	Yr.Iss.	15.00	15.00
90-02-005 Amy	S. Kuck	Yr.Iss.	15.00	15.00
90-02-006 Johnny	S. Kuck	Yr.Iss.	15.00	15.00
90-02-007 Peace On Earth	S. Kuck	17,500	17.50	17.50
Reed & Barton	**Christmas Cross**			
71-01-001 Sterling Silver-1971	Reed & Barton	Closed	10.00	140.00
71-01-002 24Kt. Gold over Sterling-V1971	Reed & Barton	Closed	17.50	225.00
72-01-003 Sterling Silver-1972	Reed & Barton	Closed	10.00	55-60.00
72-01-004 24Kt. Gold over Sterling-V1972	Reed & Barton	Closed	17.50	65-105.
73-01-005 Sterling Silver-1973	Reed & Barton	Closed	10.00	60.00
73-01-006 24Kt. Gold over Sterling-V1973	Reed & Barton	Closed	17.50	55-65.00
74-01-007 Sterling Silver-1974	Reed & Barton	Closed	12.95	40-60.00
74-01-008 24Kt. Gold over Sterling-V1974	Reed & Barton	Closed	20.00	50-60.00
75-01-009 Sterling Silver-1975	Reed & Barton	Closed	12.95	35-55.00
75-01-010 24Kt. Gold over Sterling-V1975	Reed & Barton	Closed	20.00	45-50.00
76-01-011 Sterling Silver-1976	Reed & Barton	Closed	13.95	45-55.00
76-01-012 24Kt. Gold over Sterling-V1976	Reed & Barton	Closed	19.95	45-50.00
77-01-013 Sterling Silver-1977	Reed & Barton	Closed	15.00	35-55.00
77-01-014 24Kt. Gold over Sterling-V1977	Reed & Barton	Closed	18.50	45-50.00
78-01-015 Sterling Silver-1978	Reed & Barton	Closed	16.00	40-65.00
78-01-016 24Kt. Gold over Sterling-V1978	Reed & Barton	Closed	20.00	45-55.00

	ARTIST	EDITION	ISSUE	QUOTE
79-01-017 Sterling Silver-1979	Reed & Barton	Closed	20.00	70.00
79-01-018 24Kt. Gold over Sterling-V1979	Reed & Barton	Closed	24.00	32-57.00
80-01-019 Sterling Silver-1980	Reed & Barton	Closed	35.00	55.00
80-01-020 24Kt. Gold over Sterling-V1980	Reed & Barton	Closed	40.00	45-50.00
81-01-021 Sterling Silver-1981	Reed & Barton	Closed	35.00	60-80.00
81-01-022 24Kt. Gold over Sterling-V1981	Reed & Barton	Closed	40.00	45.00
82-01-023 Sterling Silver-1982	Reed & Barton	Closed	35.00	75.00
82-01-024 24Kt. Gold over Sterling-V1982	Reed & Barton	Closed	40.00	45.00
83-01-025 Sterling Silver-1983	Reed & Barton	Closed	35.00	75.00
83-01-026 24Kt. Gold over Sterling-V1983	Reed & Barton	Closed	40.00	40-45.00
84-01-027 Sterling Silver-1984	Reed & Barton	Closed	35.00	55.00
84-01-028 24Kt. Gold over Sterling-V1984	Reed & Barton	Closed	45.00	45.00
85-01-029 Sterling Silver-1985	Reed & Barton	Closed	35.00	40-65.00
85-01-030 24Kt. Gold over Sterling-V1985	Reed & Barton	Closed	40.00	40.00
86-01-031 Sterling Silver-1986	Reed & Barton	Closed	38.50	50-65.00
86-01-032 24Kt. Gold over Sterling-V1986	Reed & Barton	Closed	40.00	40.00
87-01-033 Sterling Silver-1987	Reed & Barton	Closed	35.00	50.00
87-01-034 24Kt. Gold over Sterling-V1987	Reed & Barton	Closed	40.00	40.00
88-01-035 Sterling Silver-1988	Reed & Barton	Closed	35.00	50-60.00
88-01-036 24Kt. Gold over Sterling-V1988	Reed & Barton	Closed	40.00	40.00
89-01-037 Sterling Silver-1989	Reed & Barton	Closed	35.00	50.00
89-01-038 24Kt. Gold over Sterling-V1989	Reed & Barton	Closed	40.00	40.00
90-01-039 Sterling Silver-1990	Reed & Barton	Closed	40.00	45.00
90-01-040 24Kt. Gold over Sterling-1990	Reed & Barton	Closed	45.00	45.00
91-01-041 Sterling Silver-1991	Reed & Barton	Closed	40.00	35.00
91-01-042 24Kt. Gold over Sterling-1991	Reed & Barton	Closed	45.00	45.00
92-01-043 Sterling Silver-1992	Reed & Barton	Closed	40.00	40.00
92-01-044 24Kt. Gold over Sterling-1992	Reed & Barton	Closed	45.00	45.00
93-01-045 Sterling Silver-1993	Reed & Barton	Yr.Iss.	40.00	40.00
93-01-046 24Kt. Gold over Sterling-1993	Reed & Barton	Yr.Iss.	45.00	45.00
94-01-047 Sterling Silver-1994	Reed & Barton	Yr.Iss.	40.00	40.00
94-01-048 24Kt. Gold over Sterling-1994	Reed & Barton	Yr.Iss.	45.00	45.00
Reed & Barton	**Holly Ball**			
76-02-001 1976 Silver plated	Reed & Barton	Closed	14.00	50.00
77-02-002 1977 Silver plated	Reed & Barton	Closed	15.00	35.00
78-02-003 1978 Silver plated	Reed & Barton	Closed	15.00	40.00
79-02-004 1979 Silver plated	Reed & Barton	Closed	15.00	35.00
Reed & Barton	**Holly Bell**			
80-03-001 1980 Bell	Reed & Barton	Closed	22.50	40.00
80-03-002 Bell, gold plate, V1980	Reed & Barton	Closed	25.00	45.00
81-03-003 1981 Bell	Reed & Barton	Closed	22.50	35.00
81-03-004 Bell, gold plate, V1981	Reed & Barton	Closed	27.50	35.00
82-03-005 1982 Bell	Reed & Barton	Closed	22.50	35.00
82-03-006 Bell, gold plate, V1982	Reed & Barton	Closed	27.50	35.00
83-03-007 1983 Bell	Reed & Barton	Closed	23.50	50.00
83-03-008 Bell, gold plate, V1983	Reed & Barton	Closed	30.00	35.00
84-03-009 1984 Bell	Reed & Barton	Closed	25.00	30.00
84-03-010 Bell, gold plate, V1984	Reed & Barton	Closed	28.50	35.00
85-03-011 1985 Bell	Reed & Barton	Closed	25.00	35.00
85-03-012 Bell, gold plate, V1985	Reed & Barton	Closed	28.50	28.50
86-03-013 1986 Bell	Reed & Barton	Closed	25.00	35.00
86-03-014 Bell, gold plate, V1986	Reed & Barton	Closed	28.50	32.50
87-03-015 1987 Bell	Reed & Barton	Closed	27.50	30.00
87-03-016 Bell, gold plate, V1987	Reed & Barton	Closed	30.00	30.00
88-03-017 1988 Bell	Reed & Barton	Closed	27.50	30-40.00
88-03-018 Bell, gold plate, V1988	Reed & Barton	Closed	30.00	30.00
89-03-019 1989 Bell	Reed & Barton	Closed	27.50	35.00
89-03-020 Bell, gold plate, V1989	Reed & Barton	Closed	30.00	30.00
90-03-021 Bell, gold plate, V1990	Reed & Barton	Closed	30.00	30.00
90-03-022 1990 Bell	Reed & Barton	Closed	27.50	45.00
91-03-023 Bell, gold plate, V1991	Reed & Barton	Closed	30.00	30.00
91-03-024 1991 Bell	Reed & Barton	Closed	27.50	27.50
92-03-025 Bell, gold plate, V1992	Reed & Barton	Closed	30.00	30.00
92-03-026 Bell, silver plate, 1992	Reed & Barton	Closed	27.50	27.50
93-03-027 Bell, gold plate, V1993	Reed & Barton	Yr.Iss.	27.50	27.50
93-03-028 Bell, silver plate, 1993	Reed & Barton	Yr.Iss.	30.00	30.00
94-03-029 Bell, gold plate, 1994	Reed & Barton	Yr.Iss.	30.00	30.00
94-03-030 Bell, silver plate, 1994	Reed & Barton	Yr.Iss.	27.50	27.50
Reed & Barton	**12 Days of Christmas Sterling and Lead Crystal**			
88-04-001 Partridge in a Pear Tree	Reed & Barton	Closed	25.00	27.50
89-04-002 Two Turtle Doves	Reed & Barton	Closed	25.00	27.50
90-04-003 French Hens	Reed & Barton	Closed	27.50	27.50
91-04-004 Colly birds	Reed & Barton	Closed	27.50	27.50
92-04-005 Five Golden Rings	Reed & Barton	Closed	27.50	27.50
93-04-006 Six French Hens	Reed & Barton	Yr.Iss.	27.50	27.50
94-04-007 Swans A 'Swimming	Reed & Barton	Yr.Iss.	27.50	27.50
94-04-008 Eight Maids A Milking	Reed & Barton	Yr.Iss.	27.50	27.50
Reed & Barton	**Carousel Horse**			
88-05-001 Silverplate-1988	Reed & Barton	Closed	13.50	13.50
88-05-002 Gold-covered-1988	Reed & Barton	Closed	15.00	15.00
89-05-003 Silverplate-1989	Reed & Barton	Closed	13.50	13.50
89-05-004 Gold-covered-1989	Reed & Barton	Closed	15.00	15.00
90-05-005 Silverplate-1990	Reed & Barton	Closed	13.50	13.50
90-05-006 Gold-covered-1990	Reed & Barton	Closed	15.00	15.00
91-05-007 Silverplate-1991	Reed & Barton	Closed	13.50	13.50
91-05-008 Gold-covered-1991	Reed & Barton	Closed	15.00	15.00
92-05-009 Silverplate-1992	Reed & Barton	Closed	13.50	13.50
92-05-010 Gold-covered-1992	Reed & Barton	Closed	15.00	15.00
93-05-011 Silverplate-1993	Reed & Barton	Closed	13.50	13.50
93-05-012 Gold-covered-1993	Reed & Barton	Closed	15.00	15.00
94-05-013 Silverplate-1994	Reed & Barton	Yr.Iss.	13.50	13.50
94-05-014 Gold-covered-1994	Reed & Barton	Yr.Iss.	15.00	15.00
Roman, Inc.	**The Discovery of America**			
91-01-001 Kitstopher Kolumbus	I. Spencer	1,992	15.00	15.00
91-01-002 Queen Kitsabella	I. Spencer	1,992	15.00	15.00
Roman, Inc.	**Fontanini Annual Christmas Ornaments**			
91-02-001 1991 Annual (Girl)	E. Simonetti	Yr.Iss.	8.50	8.50
91-02-002 1991 Annual (Boy)	E. Simonetti	Yr.Iss.	8.50	8.50
92-02-003 1992 Annual (Girl)	E. Simonetti	Yr.Iss.	8.50	8.50
92-02-004 1992 Annual (Boy)	E. Simonetti	Yr.Iss.	8.50	8.50
93-02-005 1993 Annual (Girl)	E. Simonetti	Yr.Iss.	8.50	8.50
93-02-006 1993 Annual (Boy)	E. Simonetti	Yr.Iss.	8.50	8.50
Roman, Inc.	**Museum Collection of Angela Tripi**			
94-03-001 1994 Annual Angel Ornament	A. Tripi	2,500	49.50	49.50
Roman, Inc.	**Catnippers**			
88-04-001 Christmas Mourning	I. Spencer	Open	15.00	15.00

		ARTIST	EDITION	ISSUE	QUOTE
88-04-002	Ring A Ding-Ding	I. Spencer	Open	15.00	15.00
88-04-003	Puss in Berries	I. Spencer	Open	15.00	15.00
89-04-004	Bow Brummel	I. Spencer	Open	15.00	15.00
89-04-005	Happy Holidaze	I. Spencer	Open	15.00	15.00
89-04-006	Sandy Claws	I. Spencer	Open	15.00	15.00
90-04-007	Sock It to Me Santa	I. Spencer	Open	15.00	15.00
90-04-008	Stuck on Christmas	I. Spencer	Open	15.00	15.00
90-04-009	Felix Navidad	I. Spencer	Open	15.00	15.00
91-04-010	Meowy Christmas	I. Spencer	Open	15.00	15.00
91-04-011	Christmas Knight	I. Spencer	Open	15.00	15.00
91-04-012	Faux Paw	I. Spencer	Open	15.00	15.00
91-04-013	Snow Biz	I. Spencer	Open	15.00	15.00
91-04-014	Holly Days Are Happy Days	I. Spencer	Open	15.00	15.00
91-04-015	Pawtridge in a Purr Tree	I. Spencer	Open	15.00	15.00
Roman, Inc.		**Millenium Ornament**			
93-05-001	Silent Night	M. Lucchesi	20,000	20.00	20.00
93-05-002	The Annunciation	M. Lucchesi	20,000	20.00	20.00
93-05-003	Peace On Earth	M. Lucchesi	20,000	20.00	20.00
95-05-004	Cause of Our Joy	M. Lucchesi	20,000	20.00	20.00
Royal Copenhagen		**Christmas**			
80-01-001	Bringing Home the Tree	K. Lange	Annual	19.50	19.50
81-01-002	Admiring Christmas Tree	K. Lange	Annual	19.50	19.50
82-01-003	Waiting For Christmas	K. Lange	Annual	19.50	19.50
83-01-004	Merry Christmas	K. Lange	Annual	19.50	19.50
84-01-005	Jingle Bells	K. Lange	Annual	19.50	19.50
85-01-006	Snowman	K. Lange	Annual	19.50	19.50
86-01-007	Christmas Vacation	K. Lange	Annual	19.50	19.50
87-01-008	Winter Birds	S. Vestergaard	Annual	19.50	19.50
88-01-009	Christmas Eve in Copenhagen	S. Vestergaard	Annual	19.50	19.50
89-01-010	The Old Skating Pond	S. Vestergaard	Annual	19.50	19.50
90-01-011	Christmas in Tivoli	S. Vestergaard	Annual	19.50	19.50
91-01-012	The Festival of Santa Lucia	S. Vestergaard	Annual	39.50	39.50
92-01-013	The Queen's Carriage	S. Vestergaard	Annual	36.50	36.50
93-01-014	Christmas Guests	S. Vestergaard	Annual	36.50	36.50
94-01-015	Christmas Shopping	S. Vestergaard	Annual	36.50	36.50
95-01-016	Christmas at the Manor House	S. Vestergaard	Annual	36.50	36.50
Royal Copenhagen		**Christmas in Denmark**			
91-02-001	Bringing Home the Tree	H. Hansen	Annual	25.00	25.00
92-02-002	Christmas Shopping	H. Hansen	Annual	25.00	25.00
93-02-003	The Skating Party	H. Hansen	Annual	25.00	25.00
94-02-004	The Sleigh Ride	H. Hansen	Annual	25.00	25.00
Royal Copenhagen		**Georg Jensen Gold-Plated Ornament**			
84-03-001	Christmas Bell	G. Jensen	Annual	30.00	50.00
85-03-002	Jingle Bell	G. Jensen	Annual	35.00	50.00
86-03-003	Christmas of Heart	G. Jensen	Annual	35.00	50.00
87-03-004	Snowflakes	G. Jensen	Annual	39.50	50.00
88-03-005	Holly	G. Jensen	Annual	39.50	50.00
89-03-006	Angel Bright	G. Jensen	Annual	42.50	50.00
90-03-007	Christmas Basket	G. Jensen	Annual	49.50	50.00
91-03-008	Christmas Deer	G. Jensen	Annual	49.50	50.00
92-03-009	The Robin's Nest	G. Jensen	Annual	65.00	65.00
93-03-010	Christmas Star	G. Jensen	Annual	65.00	65.00
94-03-011	Mistletoe	G. Jensen	Annual	65.00	65.00
Royal Copenhagen		**Crystal Ball Ornaments**			
93-04-001	N/A	A. Sofi-Romme	Annual	19.50	19.50
94-04-002	Holly	A. Sofi-Romme	Annual	19.50	19.50
Royal Doulton		**Bunnykins**			
91-01-001	Santa Bunny	Unknown	N/A	19.00	19.00
92-01-002	Caroling	Unknown	N/A	19.00	19.00
94-01-003	Merry Midwinter	Unknown	N/A	20.00	20.00
Royal Doulton		**Christmas Ornaments**			
93-02-001	Together for Christmas	Unknown	N/A	20.00	20.00
94-02-002	Home For Christmas	Unknown	N/A	20.00	20.00
Sarah's Attic, Inc.		**Holiday Ornaments**			
87-01-001	Bare Bottom Baby 2061	Sarah's Attic	Closed	10.00	10.00
87-01-002	Goose w/Wreath 3010	Sarah's Attic	Closed	8.00	8.00
87-01-003	Reba Rabbit w/Bonnet 3011	Sarah's Attic	Closed	8.00	8.00
87-01-004	Rayburn Rabbit w/Carrot 3012	Sarah's Attic	Closed	8.00	8.00
87-01-005	Reggie Rabbit w/Scarf 3013	Sarah's Attic	Closed	8.00	8.00
87-01-006	Girl Angel with Fur/Muff 3014	Sarah's Attic	Closed	8.00	8.00
87-01-007	Boy Angel with Fur/Muff 3015	Sarah's Attic	Closed	8.00	8.00
87-01-008	Angel Head/Wings 3016	Sarah's Attic	Closed	8.00	8.00
87-01-009	Angel Head Hands 3017	Sarah's Attic	Closed	8.00	8.00
87-01-010	Santa Head 3/4 View 3018	Sarah's Attic	Closed	8.00	8.00
87-01-011	Santa Head Full View 3019	Sarah's Attic	Closed	8.00	8.00
87-01-012	Santa with Basket 3020	Sarah's Attic	Closed	9.00	9.00
87-01-013	Ruthie Rabbit 3021	Sarah's Attic	Closed	8.00	8.00
87-01-014	Clown 5404	Sarah's Attic	Closed	10.00	10.00
87-01-015	Mini Santa 5406	Sarah's Attic	Closed	9.00	9.00
87-01-016	Corky 5409	Sarah's Attic	Closed	12.00	12.00
87-01-017	Clementine 5410	Sarah's Attic	Closed	12.00	12.00
87-01-018	Amber 5411	Sarah's Attic	Closed	12.00	12.00
87-01-019	Archie 5412	Sarah's Attic	Closed	12.00	12.00
87-01-020	Blondie 5413	Sarah's Attic	Closed	14.00	14.00
87-01-021	Butch 5414	Sarah's Attic	Closed	14.00	14.00
87-01-022	Stocking 5800	Sarah's Attic	Closed	8.00	8.00
88-01-023	Alex Bear 2062	Sarah's Attic	Closed	11.00	11.00
88-01-024	Amelia Bear 2063	Sarah's Attic	Closed	9.00	9.00
88-01-025	Abbee Bear 2064	Sarah's Attic	Closed	8.00	8.00
88-01-026	Ashbee Bear 2065	Sarah's Attic	Closed	8.00	8.00
88-01-027	Sitting Matt 2066	Sarah's Attic	Closed	12.00	12.00
88-01-028	Sitting Maggie 2067	Sarah's Attic	Closed	12.00	12.00
88-01-029	Benni Bear 2078	Sarah's Attic	Closed	8.00	8.00
88-01-030	Mini Matt 2107	Sarah's Attic	Closed	10.00	10.00
88-01-031	Mini Maggie 2108	Sarah's Attic	Closed	10.00	10.00
88-01-032	White Rabbit 2273	Sarah's Attic	Closed	9.00	9.00
88-01-033	Brown Rabbit 2275	Sarah's Attic	Closed	9.00	9.00
88-01-034	Cocker w/Pup-White 2277	Sarah's Attic	Closed	8.00	8.00
88-01-035	Cocker w/Pup-Brown 2278	Sarah's Attic	Closed	8.00	8.00
88-01-036	Kitten Diaper-White 2279	Sarah's Attic	Closed	8.00	8.00
88-01-037	Kitten Diaper-Brown 2280	Sarah's Attic	Closed	8.00	8.00
88-01-038	Bunny w/Wreath-Brown 2282	Sarah's Attic	Closed	6.00	6.00
88-01-039	Matt w/Puppy 3055	Sarah's Attic	Closed	12.00	12.00
88-01-040	Maggie w/Bunny 3056	Sarah's Attic	Closed	12.00	12.00
88-01-041	Cow w/Wreath 3057	Sarah's Attic	Closed	10.00	10.00
88-01-042	Pig 3058	Sarah's Attic	Closed	12.00	12.00
88-01-043	Cat w/Bonnet 3060	Sarah's Attic	Closed	10.00	10.00
88-01-044	Santa Mouse 3062	Sarah's Attic	Closed	10.00	10.00
88-01-045	Hooded Santa 3064	Sarah's Attic	Closed	8.00	8.00
88-01-046	Santa w/Pouch 3065	Sarah's Attic	Closed	8.00	8.00
88-01-047	Daisy Angel 3066	Sarah's Attic	Closed	8.00	8.00
88-01-048	Victorian Angel 3067	Sarah's Attic	Closed	7.00	7.00
88-01-049	Cat 6261	Sarah's Attic	Closed	6.00	6.00
88-01-050	Bunny w/Wreath 6262	Sarah's Attic	Closed	8.00	8.00
88-01-051	Sheep 6263	Sarah's Attic	Closed	8.00	8.00
89-01-052	Brown Cow 2222	Sarah's Attic	Closed	10.00	10.00
89-01-053	Jolly 3206	Sarah's Attic	Closed	15.00	15.00
89-01-054	Christmas Wonder 3207	Sarah's Attic	Closed	20.00	20.00
90-01-055	Toby-Christmas 3279	Sarah's Attic	Closed	20.00	20.00
90-01-056	Star of Christmas 3280	Sarah's Attic	Closed	20.00	20.00
90-01-057	Packy-Bear on Package 3281	Sarah's Attic	Closed	20.00	20.00
90-01-058	Heavenly Family 3282	Sarah's Attic	Closed	32.00	32.00
90-01-059	Gala Angel w/Wreath 3283	Sarah's Attic	Closed	25.00	25.00
90-01-060	Burr Snowman 3284	Sarah's Attic	Closed	18.00	18.00
90-01-061	Abner Rabbit 3285	Sarah's Attic	Closed	17.00	17.00
90-01-062	Blessed Christmas 3286	Sarah's Attic	Closed	23.00	23.00
90-01-063	Spirit of Christmas 3287	Sarah's Attic	Closed	21.00	21.00
90-01-064	Peter Angel 3288	Sarah's Attic	Closed	25.00	25.00
90-01-065	Nutmeg Skates 3289	Sarah's Attic	Closed	17.00	17.00
90-01-066	Rosalee 3290	Sarah's Attic	Closed	27.00	27.00
93-01-067	Peace-Christmas '93 3851	Sarah's Attic	Closed	12.00	12.00
94-01-068	Jolly Santa 4165	Sarah's Attic	12/94	14.50	14.50
94-01-069	America 4166	Sarah's Attic	12/94	14.50	14.50
94-01-070	Tillie 4167	Sarah's Attic	12/94	14.50	14.50
94-01-071	Bear 4168	Sarah's Attic	12/94	14.50	14.50
94-01-072	Snowball Rabbit 4169	Sarah's Attic	12/94	14.50	14.50
94-01-073	Love 4170	Sarah's Attic	12/94	14.50	14.50
94-01-074	Merry Santa 4171	Sarah's Attic	12/94	14.50	14.50
94-01-075	Angelle 4172	Sarah's Attic	12/94	14.50	14.50
94-01-076	School Days 4173	Sarah's Attic	12/94	14.50	14.50
94-01-077	Willie 4174	Sarah's Attic	12/94	14.50	14.50
94-01-078	Kiah 4175	Sarah's Attic	12/94	14.50	14.50
94-01-079	Chilly 4176	Sarah's Attic	12/94	14.50	14.50
94-01-080	Kiah (Gold) 4182	Sarah's Attic	12/94	14.50	14.50
94-01-081	Angelle (Gold) 4183	Sarah's Attic	12/94	14.50	14.50
Sarah's Attic, Inc.		**Santas Of The Month Ornaments**			
88-02-001	Jan. Mini Santa 2200	Sarah's Attic	Closed	16.00	21.00
88-02-002	Feb. Mini Santa 2201	Sarah's Attic	Closed	16.00	21.00
88-02-003	March Mini Santa 2202	Sarah's Attic	Closed	16.00	21.00
88-02-004	April Mini Santa 2203	Sarah's Attic	Closed	16.00	21.00
88-02-005	May Mini Santa 2204	Sarah's Attic	Closed	16.00	21.00
88-02-006	June Mini Santa 2205	Sarah's Attic	Closed	16.00	21.00
88-02-007	July Mini Santa 2206	Sarah's Attic	Closed	16.00	21.00
88-02-008	Aug. Mini Santa 2207	Sarah's Attic	Closed	16.00	21.00
88-02-009	Sept. Mini Santa 2208	Sarah's Attic	Closed	16.00	21.00
88-02-010	Oct. Mini Santa 2209	Sarah's Attic	Closed	16.00	21.00
88-02-011	Nov. Mini Santa 2210	Sarah's Attic	Closed	16.00	21.00
88-02-012	Dec.Mini Santa 2211	Sarah's Attic	Closed	16.00	21.00
Schmid		**Lowell Davis Country Christmas**			
83-01-001	Mailbox	L. Davis	Yr.Iss.	17.50	45-75.00
84-01-002	Cat in Boot	L. Davis	Yr.Iss.	17.50	60-65.00
85-01-003	Pig in Trough	L. Davis	Yr.Iss.	17.50	50-75.00
86-01-004	Church	L. Davis	Yr.Iss.	17.50	35-55.00
87-01-005	Blossom	L. Davis	Yr.Iss.	19.50	25-60.00
88-01-006	Wisteria	L. Davis	Yr.Iss.	19.50	25-50.00
89-01-007	Wren	L. Davis	Yr.Iss.	19.50	30-47.50
90-01-008	Wintering Deer	L. Davis	Yr.Iss.	19.50	30.00
91-01-009	Church at Red Oak II	L. Davis	Yr.Iss.	25.00	25.00
92-01-010	Born On A Starry Night	L. Davis	Yr.Iss.	25.00	25.00
93-01-011	Waiting for Mr. Lowell	L. Davis	Yr.Iss.	20.00	20.00
Schmid		**Lowell Davis Glass Ornaments**			
86-02-001	Christmas at Red Oak	L. Davis	Yr.Iss.	5.00	7-10.00
87-02-002	Blossom's Gift	L. Davis	Yr.Iss.	5.50	9.00
88-02-003	Hope Mom Likes It	L. Davis	Yr.Iss.	5.00	10.00
89-02-004	Peter and the Wren	L. Davis	Yr.Iss.	6.50	8.00
90-02-005	Wintering Deer	L. Davis	Yr.Iss.	6.50	6.50
91-02-006	Christmas at Red Oak II	L. Davis	Yr.Iss.	7.50	7.50
92-02-007	Born On A Starry Night Ball	L. Davis	Yr.Iss.	7.50	7.50
93-02-008	Waiting for Mr. Lowell	L. Davis	Yr.Iss.	7.50	7.50
Schmid		**Disney Annual**			
85-03-001	Snow Biz	Disney Studios	Yr.Iss.	8.50	20.00
86-03-002	Tree for Two	Disney Studios	Yr.Iss.	8.50	15.00
87-03-003	Merry Mouse Medley	Disney Studios	Yr.Iss.	8.50	10.00
88-03-004	Warm Winter Ride	Disney Studios	Yr.Iss.	11.00	45.00
89-04-005	Merry Mickey Claus	Disney Studios	Yr.Iss.	11.00	11.00
90-04-006	Holly Jolly Christmas	Disney Studios	Yr.Iss.	14.00	30.00
91-04-007	Mickey & Minnie's Rockin' Christmas	Disney Studios	Yr.Iss.	14.00	13.50
Swarovski America Ltd.		**Holiday Ornaments**			
86-01-001	Small Angel/Noel	Unknown	Yr.Iss.	18.00	18.00
86-01-002	Small Bell/Merry Christmas	Unknown	Yr.Iss.	18.00	18.00
86-01-003	Small Dove/Peace	Unknown	Yr.Iss.	18.00	18.00
86-01-004	Small Holly/Merry Christmas	Unknown	Yr.Iss.	18.00	18.00
86-01-005	Small Snowflake	Unknown	Yr.Iss.	18.00	18.00
86-01-006	Medium Snowflake	Unknown	Yr.Iss.	22.50	22.50
86-01-007	Medium Bell/Merry Christmas	Unknown	Yr.Iss.	22.50	22.50
86-01-008	Medium Angel/Joyeux Noel	Unknown	Yr.Iss.	22.50	22.50
86-01-009	Large Angel/Noel	Unknown	Yr.Iss.	35.00	35.00
86-01-010	Large Partridge/Merry Christmas	Unknown	Yr.Iss.	35.00	35.00
87-01-011	1987 Holiday Etching-Candle	Unknown	Yr.Iss.	20.00	130.00
88-01-012	1988 Holiday Etching-Wreath	Unknown	Yr.Iss.	25.00	50-85.00
89-01-013	1989 Holiday Etching-Dove	Unknown	Yr.Iss.	35.00	65-100.
90-01-014	1990 Holiday Etching	Unknown	Yr.Iss.	25.00	100.00
91-01-015	1991 Holiday Ornament	Unknown	Yr.Iss.	35.00	46-65.00
92-01-016	1992 Holiday Ornament	Unknown	Yr.Iss.	37.50	150-250.
93-01-017	1993 Holiday Ornament	Unknown	Yr.Iss.	37.50	37.50
94-01-018	1994 Holiday Ornament	Unknown	Yr.Iss.	37.50	37.50
Towle Silversmiths		**Sterling Twelve Days of Christmas Medallions**			
71-01-001	Partridge in Pear Tree	Towle	Closed	20.00	240.00
72-01-002	Two Turtle Doves	Towle	Closed	20.00	75.00
73-01-003	Three French Hens	Towle	Closed	20.00	30-100.
74-01-004	Four Mockingbirds	Towle	Closed	30.00	30-100.
75-01-005	Five Golden Rings	Towle	Closed	30.00	35-65.00
76-01-006	Six Geese-a-Laying	Towle	Closed	30.00	45-90.00
77-01-007	Seven Swans-a-Swimming	Towle	Closed	35.00	30-50.00

		ARTIST	EDITION	ISSUE	QUOTE
78-01-008	Eight Maids-a-Milking	Towle	Closed	37.00	45-75.00
79-01-009	Nine Ladies Dancing	Towle	Closed	Unkn.	40-60.00
80-01-010	Ten Lords-a-Leaping	Towle	Closed	76.00	65.00
81-01-011	Eleven Pipers Piping	Towle	Closed	50.00	65.00
82-01-012	Twelve Drummers Drumming	Towle	Closed	35.00	60.00
Towle Silversmiths		**Songs of Christmas Medallions**			
78-02-001	Silent Night Medallion	Towle	Closed	35.00	65.00
79-02-002	Deck The Halls	Towle	Closed	Unkn.	55.00
80-02-003	Jingle Bells	Towle	Closed	53.00	60.00
81-02-004	Hark the Hearld Angels Sing	Towle	Closed	53.00	60.00
82-02-005	O Christmas Tree	Towle	Closed	35.00	50.00
83-02-006	Silver Bells	Towle	Closed	40.00	60.00
84-02-007	Let It Snow	Towle	Closed	30.00	55.00
85-02-008	Chestnuts Roasting on Open Fire	Towle	Closed	35.00	55.00
86-02-009	It Came Upon a Midnight Clear	Towle	Closed	35.00	45.00
87-02-010	White Christmas	Towle	Closed	35.00	45.00
Towle Silversmiths		**Sterling Floral Medallions**			
83-03-001	Christmas Rose	Towle	Closed	40.00	50.00
84-03-002	Hawthorne/Glastonbury Thorn	Towle	Closed	40.00	45.00
85-03-003	Poinsettia	Towle	Closed	35.00	50.00
86-03-004	Laurel Bay	Towle	Closed	35.00	50.00
87-03-005	Mistletoe	Towle	Closed	35.00	55.00
88-03-006	Holly	Towle	Closed	40.00	55.00
89-03-007	Ivy	Towle	Closed	35.00	50.00
90-03-008	Christmas Cactus	Towle	Closed	40.00	45.00
91-03-009	Chrysanthemum	Towle	Closed	40.00	45.00
92-03-010	Star of Bethlehem	Towle	Closed	40.00	40.00
Towle Silversmiths		**Sterling Nativity Medallions**			
88-04-001	Angel Gabriel	Towle	Closed	40.00	50-60.00
89-04-002	The Journey	Towle	Closed	40.00	55.00
90-04-003	No Room at the Inn	Towle	Closed	40.00	45.00
91-04-004	Tidings of Joy	Towle	Closed	40.00	45.00
92-04-005	Star of Bethlehem	Towle	Closed	40.00	40.00
93-04-006	Mother and Child	Towle	Closed	40.00	40.00
94-04-007	Three Wisemen	Towle	N/A	40.00	40.00
Towle Silversmiths		**Remembrance Collection**			
90-05-001	Old Master Snowflake -1990	Towle	Closed	40.00	55.00
91-05-002	Old Master Snowflake-1991	Towle	Closed	40.00	55.00
92-05-003	Old Master Snowflake-1992	Towle	Closed	40.00	45.00
93-05-004	Old Master Snowflake-1993	Towle	Closed	40.00	45.00
94-05-005	Old Master Snowflake-1994	Towle	N/A	40.00	50.00
Towle Silversmiths		**Christmas AngelMedallions**			
91-06-001	1991 Angel	Towle	Closed	45.00	60.00
92-06-002	1992 Angel	Towle	Closed	45.00	50.00
93-06-003	1993 Angel	Towle	Closed	45.00	45.00
94-06-004	1994 Angel	Towle	N/A	45.00	50.00
United Design Corporation		**Angels Collection-Tree Ornaments™**			
90-01-001	Crystal Angel IBO-401	P.J. Jonas	Retrd.	20.00	20.00
90-01-002	Rose of Sharon IBO-402	P.J. Jonas	Retrd.	20.00	20.00
90-01-003	Star Glory IBO-403	P.J. Jonas	Retrd.	15.00	15.00
90-01-004	Victorian Angel IBO-404	P.J. Jonas	Retrd.	15.00	15.00
90-01-005	Crystal Angel, ivory IBO-405	P.J. Jonas	Open	20.00	20.00
90-01-006	Rose of Sharon, ivory IBO-406	P.J. Jonas	Open	20.00	20.00
90-01-007	Star Glory, ivory IBO-407	P.J. Jonas	Open	15.00	20.00
90-01-008	Victorian Angel, ivory IBO-408	P.J. Jonas	Open	15.00	20.00
91-01-009	Victorian Cupid, ivory IBO-409	P.J. Jonas	Open	15.00	20.00
91-01-010	Rosetti Angel, ivory IBO-410	P.J. Jonas	Open	20.00	24.00
91-01-011	Angel Waif, ivory IBO-411	P.J. Jonas	Open	15.00	20.00
91-01-012	Peace Descending, ivory IBO-412	P.J. Jonas	Open	20.00	20.00
91-01-013	Girl Cupid w/Rose, ivory IBO-413	S. Bradford	Open	15.00	20.00
91-01-014	Fra Angelico Drummer, blue IBO-414	S. Bradford	Open	20.00	20.00
91-01-015	Fra Angelico Drummer, ivory IBO-420	S. Bradford	Open	20.00	20.00
92-01-016	Angel and Tambourine IBO-422	S. Bradford	Open	20.00	20.00
92-01-017	St. Francis and Critters IBO-423	S. Bradford	Open	20.00	20.00
92-01-018	Mary and Dove IBO-424	S. Bradford	Open	20.00	20.00
92-01-019	Angel and Tambourine, ivory IBO-425	S. Bradford	Open	20.00	20.00
93-01-020	Angel Baby w/ Bunny IBO-426	D. Newburn	Open	23.00	24.00
93-01-021	Stars & Lace IBO-427	P.J. Jonas	Open	18.00	20.00
93-01-022	Heavenly Harmony IBO-428	P.J. Jonas	Open	25.00	30.00
93-01-023	Renaissance Angel IBO-429	P.J. Jonas	Open	24.00	24.00
93-01-024	Little Angel IBO-430	D. Newburn	Open	18.00	20.00
93-01-025	Renaissance Angel, crimson IBO-431	P.J. Jonas	Open	24.00	24.00
93-01-026	Stars & Lace, Emerald IBO-432	P.J. Jonas	Open	18.00	20.00
93-01-027	Heavenly Harmony, crimson IBO-433	P.J. Jonas	Open	22.00	30.00
93-01-028	Rosetti Angel, crimson IBO-434	P.J. Jonas	Open	20.00	24.00
93-01-029	Victorian Angel, plum IBO-435	P.J. Jonas	Open	18.00	20.00
93-01-030	Peace Descending, crimson IBO-436	P.J. Jonas	Open	20.00	20.00
93-01-031	Angle Waif, plum IBO-437	P.J. Jonas	Open	20.00	20.00
93-01-032	Star Glory, crimson IBO-438	P.J. Jonas	Open	20.00	20.00
93-01-033	Rose of Sharon, crimson IBO-439	P.J. Jonas	Open	20.00	20.00
93-01-034	Victorian Cupid, crimson IBO-440	P.J. Jonas	Open	15.00	20.00
93-01-035	Little Angel, crimson IBO-445	D. Newburn	Open	18.00	20.00
93-01-036	Crystal Angel, emerald IBO-446	P.J. Jonas	Open	20.00	20.00
94-01-037	Star Flight IBO-447	P.J. Jonas	Open	10.00	10.00
94-01-038	Music and Grace IBO-448	P.J. Jonas	Open	12.00	12.00
94-01-039	Music and Grace, crimson IBO-449	P.J. Jonas	Open	12.00	12.00
94-01-040	Musical Flight IBO-450	P.J. Jonas	Open	14.00	13.50
94-01-041	Musical Flight, crimson IBO-451	P.J. Jonas	Open	14.00	13.50
VickiLane		**Sweet Thumpkins**			
94-01-001	Secrets Out	V. Anderson	Yr.Iss.	15.00	14.50
Wallace Silversmiths		**Annual Silverplated Bells**			
71-01-001	1st Edition Sleigh Bell	Wallace	Closed	12.95	1050.00
72-01-002	2nd Edition Sleigh Bell	Wallace	Closed	12.95	500.00
73-01-003	3rd Edition Sleigh Bell	Wallace	Closed	12.95	500.00
74-01-004	4th Edition Sleigh Bell	Wallace	Closed	13.95	300.00
75-01-005	5th Edition Sleigh Bell	Wallace	Closed	13.95	250.00
76-01-006	6th Edition Sleigh Bell	Wallace	Closed	13.95	300.00
77-01-007	7th Edition Sleigh Bell	Wallace	Closed	14.95	150.00
78-01-008	8th Edition Sleigh Bell	Wallace	Closed	14.95	85.00
79-01-009	9th Edition Sleigh Bell	Wallace	Closed	15.95	110.00
80-01-010	10th Edition Sleigh Bell	Wallace	Closed	18.95	50.00
81-01-011	11th Edition Sleigh Bell	Wallace	Closed	18.95	60.00
82-01-012	12th Edition Sleigh Bell	Wallace	Closed	19.95	90.00
83-01-013	13th Edition Sleigh Bell	Wallace	Closed	19.95	90.00
84-01-014	14th Edition Sleigh Bell	Wallace	Closed	21.95	75.00
85-01-015	15th Edition Sleigh Bell	Wallace	Closed	21.95	90.00
86-01-016	16th Edition Sleigh Bell	Wallace	Closed	21.95	35.00

		ARTIST	EDITION	ISSUE	QUOTE
87-01-017	17th Edition Sleigh Bell	Wallace	Closed	21.99	30.00
88-01-018	18th Edition Sleigh Bell	Wallace	Closed	21.99	30.00
89-01-019	19th Edition Sleigh Bell	Wallace	Closed	24.99	25.00
90-01-020	20th Edition Sleigh Bell	Wallace	Closed	25.00	25.00
90-01-021	Special Edition Sleigh Bell, gold	Wallace	Closed	35.00	35-50.00
92-01-022	22th Edition Sleigh Bell	Wallace	Closed	25.00	25.00
93-01-023	23rd Edition Sleigh Bell	Wallace	Closed	25.00	25.00
94-01-024	24th Edition Sleigh Bell	Wallace	Open	25.00	25.00
94-01-025	Sleigh Bell, gold	Wallace	Open	35.00	35.00
93-01-026	Santa Bel	Wallace	Closed	25.00	25.00
94-01-027	Santa Bell (Holding Toy Sack)	Wallace	Open	25.00	25.00
Wallace Silversmiths		**Candy Canes**			
81-02-001	Peppermint	Wallace	Closed	8.95	225.00
82-02-002	Wintergreen	Wallace	Closed	9.95	60.00
83-02-003	Cinnamon	Wallace	Closed	10.95	50.00
84-02-004	Clove	Wallace	Closed	10.95	50.00
85-02-005	Dove Motif	Wallace	Closed	11.95	50.00
86-02-006	Bell Motif	Wallace	Closed	11.95	80.00
87-02-007	Teddy Bear Motif	Wallace	Closed	12.95	50.00
88-02-008	Christmas Rose	Wallace	Closed	13.99	25- 45.00
89-02-009	Christmas Candle	Wallace	Closed	14.99	35.00
90-02-010	Reindeer	Wallace	Closed	16.00	20.00
91-02-011	Christmas Goose	Wallace	Closed	16.00	20.00
92-02-012	Angel	Wallace	Closed	16.00	16.00
93-02-013	Snowmen	Wallace	Closed	16.00	16.00
94-02-014	Canes	Wallace	Open	17.00	17.00
Wallace Silversmiths		**Grande Baroque 12 Day Series**			
88-03-001	Partridge	Wallace	Closed	39.99	55.00
89-03-002	Two Turtle Doves	Wallace	Closed	39.99	50.00
90-03-003	Three French Hens	Wallace	Closed	40.00	40.00
91-03-004	Four Colly Birds	Wallace	Closed	40.00	40.00
92-03-005	Five Golden Rings	Wallace	Closed	40.00	40.00
93-03-006	Six Geese-A-Laying	Wallace	Closed	40.00	40.00
94-03-007	Seven Swans A Swimming	Wallace	Open	40.00	40.00
Wallace Silversmiths		**Cathedral Ornaments**			
88-04-001	1988-1st Edition	Wallace	Closed	24.99	60.00
89-04-002	1989-2nd Edition	Wallace	Closed	24.99	55.00
90-04-003	1990-3rd Edition	Wallace	Closed	25.00	50.00
Wallace Silversmiths		**24K Goldplate Sculptures**			
88-05-001	Dove	Wallace	Closed	15.99	15.99
88-05-002	Candy Cane	Wallace	Closed	15.99	15.99
88-05-003	Christmas Tree	Wallace	Closed	15.99	15.99
88-05-004	Angel	Wallace	Closed	15.99	15.99
88-05-005	Nativity Scene	Wallace	Closed	15.99	15.99
88-05-006	Snowflake	Wallace	Closed	15.99	15.99
93-05-007	Ringing Bells	Wallace	Closed	10.00	10.00
93-05-008	Carousel	Wallace	Closed	10.00	10.00
93-05-009	Stocking	Wallace	Closed	10.00	10.00
93-05-010	Wreath	Wallace	Closed	10.00	10.00
93-05-011	Tree	Wallace	Closed	10.00	10.00
93-05-012	Dove	Wallace	Closed	10.00	10.00
94-05-013	Mother & Child	Wallace	Open	16.00	16.00
94-05-014	Peace Dove	Wallace	Open	16.00	16.00
Wallace Silversmiths		**Annual Pewter Bells**			
92-06-001	Angel	Wallace	Closed	25.00	25.00
93-06-002	Santa Holding List	Wallace	Yr.Iss.	25.00	25.00
Wallace Silversmiths		**Pewter Ornaments**			
XX-07-001	Toy Soldier	Wallace	Closed	9.99	9.99
XX-07-002	Gingerbread House	Wallace	Closed	9.99	9.99
XX-07-003	Teddy Bear	Wallace	Closed	9.99	9.99
XX-07-004	Rocking Horse	Wallace	Closed	9.99	9.99
XX-07-005	Dove	Wallace	Closed	9.99	9.99
XX-07-006	Candy Cane	Wallace	Closed	9.99	9.99
89-07-007	Wreath	Wallace	Closed	9.99	9.99
89-07-008	Angel with Candles	Wallace	Closed	9.99	9.99
89-07-009	Teddy Bear	Wallace	Closed	9.99	9.99
89-07-010	Cherub with Horn	Wallace	Closed	9.99	9.99
89-07-011	Santa	Wallace	Closed	9.99	9.99
93-07-012	Stocking	Wallace	Open	10.00	10.00
93-07-013	Wreath	Wallace	Open	10.00	10.00
93-07-014	Christmas Tree	Wallace	Open	10.00	10.00
94-07-015	Santa	Wallace	Open	10.00	10.00
94-07-016	Teddy Bear	Wallace	Open	10.00	10.00
94-07-017	Train	Wallace	Open	10.00	10.00
94-07-018	Toy Soldier	Wallace	Open	10.00	10.00
94-07-019	Snowman	Wallace	Open	10.00	10.00
Waterford Wedgwood U.S.A.		**Waterford Crystal Christmas Ornaments**			
78-01-001	1978 Ornament	Waterford	Annual	25.00	105.00
79-01-002	1979 Ornament	Waterford	Annual	28.00	80.00
80-01-003	1980 Ornament	Waterford	Annual	28.00	60.00
81-01-004	1981 Ornament	Waterford	Annual	28.00	44.50
82-01-005	1982 Ornament	Waterford	Annual	28.00	50.00
83-01-006	1983 Ornament	Waterford	Annual	28.00	50.00
84-01-007	1984 Ornament	Waterford	Annual	28.00	50.00
85-01-008	1985 Ornament	Waterford	Annual	28.00	80.00
86-01-009	1986 Ornament	Waterford	Annual	28.00	50.00
87-01-010	1987 Ornament	Waterford	Annual	29.00	40.00
88-01-011	1988 Ornament	Waterford	Annual	30.00	40.00
89-01-012	1989 Ornament	Waterford	Annual	32.00	40.00

DOLLS

Kurt S. Adler Inc.		**Royal Heritage Collection**			
93-01-001	Anastasia J5746	J. Mostrom	3,000	125.00	125.00
93-01-002	Medieval King of Christmas W2981	J. Mostrom	2,000	390.00	390.00
93-01-003	Good King Wenceslas W2928	J. Mostrom	2,000	130.00	130.00
94-01-004	Sasha on Skates J5749	J. Mostrom	3,000	130.00	130.00
94-01-005	Nicholas on Skates J5750	J. Mostrom	3,000	120.00	120.00
Annalee Mobilitee Dolls		**Assorted Dolls**			
50-01-001	10" Boy Building Boat	A. Thorndike	N/A	9.95	1200.00
50-01-002	Cellist	A. Thorndike	N/A	N/A	5250.00
50-01-003	10" Christmas Girl	A. Thorndike	N/A	N/A	2350.00
50-01-004	10" Elf	A. Thorndike	N/A	N/A	900.00
50-01-005	12" Santa on Water Skis	A. Thorndike	1	N/A	3050.00
50-01-006	10" Square Dancers (Boy and Girl)	A. Thorndike	N/A	9.95	2100.00
54-01-007	10" Spring Girl	A. Thorndike	N/A	N/A	2350.00

		ARTIST	EDITION	ISSUE	QUOTE
54-01-008	12" Santa (Bean Nose)	A. Thorndike	N/A	19.95	1000.00
54-01-009	26" Elf	A. Thorndike	N/A	9.95	550.00
55-01-010	14" Fireman	A. Thorndike	N/A	N/A	4750.00
56-01-011	10" Boy Building Boat	A. Thorndike	N/A	N/A	1550.00
57-01-012	10" Halloween Girl	A. Thorndike	N/A	9.95	3200.00
57-01-013	10" Square Dancer (Girl)	A. Thorndike	N/A	9.95	900.00
57-01-014	10" Baby Angel	A. Thorndike	N/A	8.95	525.00
59-01-015	10" Girl and Boy on Tandem Bike	A. Thorndike	N/A	20.95	2200.00
59-01-016	10" Wood Sprite	A. Thorndike	N/A	N/A	750.00
60-01-017	Man Head Pin-on	A. Thorndike	N/A	N/A	800.00
60-01-018	Mouse Head Pin-On	A. Thorndike	N/A	1.00	250.00
60-01-019	Head Pin	A. Thorndike	N/A	N/A	200.00
60-01-020	Girl Head	A. Thorndike	1	N/A	700-2400.
60-01-021	Boy Head	A. Thorndike	1	N/A	650-800.
60-01-022	5" Wee Skis	A. Thorndike	N/A	3.95	325.00
60-01-023	7" Baby Angel (yellow feather hair)	A. Thorndike	N/A	N/A	350.00
60-01-024	7" Angel w/ Paper Wings	A. Thorndike	N/A	N/A	400.00
60-01-025	10" Elf	A. Thorndike	N/A	N/A	400.00
60-01-026	10" Impski	A. Thorndike	N/A	3.95	500.00
60-01-027	10" Impski (white)	A. Thorndike	N/A	3.95	350.00
60-01-028	10" Impski (red)	A. Thorndike	N/A	3.95	325.00
60-01-029	29" Fur Trim Santa	A. Thorndike	N/A	N/A	1000.00
62-01-030	7" Furcapped Baby	A. Thorndike	N/A	2.45	400.00
62-01-031	7" Baby Angel on Cloud	A. Thorndike	N/A	2.45	400-675.
63-01-032	Baby Angel Head w/ Santa Hat	A. Thorndike	N/A	1.00	350.00
63-01-033	Bath Puff (yellow)	A. Thorndike	N/A	1.95	325.00
63-01-034	5" Elf (Lilac)	A. Thorndike	N/A	2.50	325.00
63-01-035	7" Santa w/ Fur Trimmed Suit	A. Thorndike	N/A	2.95	400.00
63-01-036	10" Ballerina	A. Thorndike	N/A	5.95	1350.00
63-01-037	10" Elf	A. Thorndike	N/A	N/A	350.00
63-01-038	10" Friar	A. Thorndike	N/A	2.95	500.00
63-01-039	26" Friar	A. Thorndike	N/A	14.95	2500.00
64-01-040	7" Angel in a Blanket	A. Thorndike	N/A	2.45	325.00
64-01-041	7" Boudoir Puff Baby Angel	A. Thorndike	N/A	3.95	400.00
64-01-042	18" Santa Kid	A. Thorndike	N/A	6.95	450.00
65-01-043	7" Singing Mouse	A. Thorndike	N/A	3.95	450.00
65-01-044	7" Christmas Dumb Bunny	A. Thorndike	N/A	3.95	775.00
65-01-045	7" Gnome w/ Vest	A. Thorndike	N/A	2.45	675.00
65-01-046	7" Colored Mouse (Peek)	A. Thorndike	N/A	3.95	550.00
65-01-047	7" Hangover Mouse	A. Thorndike	N/A	3.95	375.00
65-01-048	7" M/M Indoor Santa	A. Thorndike	N/A	5.95	500.00
65-01-049	10" Golfer Boy Doll	A. Thorndike	N/A	9.95	700.00
65-01-050	10" Monk w/ Christmas Tree Planting	A. Thorndike	N/A	2.95	450.00
65-01-051	10" Reindeer	A. Thorndike	N/A	4.95	425.00
65-01-052	12" Christmas Bonnet Lady Mouse	A. Thorndike	N/A	9.95	400.00
66-01-053	7" Bride & Groom Mice	A. Thorndike	N/A	3.95	600.00
66-01-054	10" Boy & Girl on Tandem Bike	A. Thorndike	N/A	20.95	1350.00
66-01-055	10" Bathersome Chick w/Flippers	A. Thorndike	N/A	5.95	650.00
66-01-056	10" Golfer-Girl Putter	A. Thorndike	N/A	5.95	925.00
66-01-057	10" Go-Go Boy	A. Thorndike	N/A	3.95	350.00
66-01-058	10" Workshop Elf	A. Thorndike	N/A	N/A	425.00
67-01-059	7" Mrs. Santa w/Fur-Trimmed Cape	A. Thorndike	N/A	2.95	450.00
67-01-060	7" Mrs. Holly Mouse	A. Thorndike	N/A	3.95	350.00
67-01-061	7" Garden Club Baby	A. Thorndike	N/A	2.95	575.00
67-01-062	7" Tuckered Mr. & Mrs. Santa Water Bottle	A. Thorndike	N/A	5.95	400.00
67-01-063	7" Gnome w/Pajama Suit	A. Thorndike	N/A	2.95	375.00
67-01-064	7" Ballerina Mouse	A. Thorndike	N/A	3.95	450.00
67-01-065	10" Carnaby Street Boy	A. Thorndike	N/A	3.95	400.00
67-01-066	10" Elf w/ Skis and Poles	A. Thorndike	48	2.95	425-900.
67-01-067	10" Golfer Boy	A. Thorndike	N/A	5.95	925.00
67-01-068	10" Surfer Girl	A. Thorndike	N/A	5.95	625.00
67-01-069	12" Yum-Yum Bunny	A. Thorndike	N/A	9.95	850.00
68-01-070	7" Baby in Christmas Bag	A. Thorndike	N/A	2.95	350.00
68-01-071	7" Patches Pam	A. Thorndike	N/A	2.95	850.00
68-01-072	12" Laura May Cat	A. Thorndike	N/A	7.95	900.00
68-01-073	12" Myrtle Turtle	A. Thorndike	N/A	6.95	260.00
68-01-074	12" Gnome w/ Gay Apron	A. Thorndike	N/A	5.95	900.00
68-01-075	18" Mrs. Santa w/Boudoir Cap & Apron	A. Thorndike	N/A	7.45	250.00
68-01-076	29" Mrs. Indoor Santa	A. Thorndike	N/A	16.95	475.00
68-01-077	Hippy Head (Girl)	A. Thorndike	N/A	1.00	350.00
68-01-078	Hippy Head (Boy)	A. Thorndike	N/A	1.00	350.00
69-01-079	7" Santa w/ Oversized Bag	A. Thorndike	N/A	3.95	350.00
69-01-080	10" Clown (pink w/green polka dots)	A. Thorndike	N/A	3.95	525.00
69-01-081	10" Clown (bright stripes)	A. Thorndike	N/A	3.95	350.00
69-01-082	12" Nightshirt Boy Mouse	A. Thorndike	N/A	9.95	550.00
70-01-083	Monkey Head Pin-on (boy)	A. Thorndike	153	1.00	275.00
70-01-084	Monkey Head Pin-on (girl)	A. Thorndike	153	1.00	275.00
70-01-085	7" Artist Mouse	A. Thorndike	298	3.95	400.00
70-01-086	7" Bartender Mouse	A. Thorndike	289	3.95	400.00
70-01-087	7" Bunny (yellow)	A. Thorndike	3,215	3.95	375.00
70-01-088	7" Christmas Baby on Hat Box	A. Thorndike	1,894	2.95	350.00
70-01-089	7" Sherriff Mouse	A. Thorndike	11	3.95	650.00
70-01-090	10" Mushroom w/7" Santa	A. Thorndike	1,535	7.95	250.00
70-01-091	10" Casualty Ski Elf w/ Crutch & Leg in Cast	A. Thorndike	2,818	4.50	600.00
70-01-092	10" Monk w/ Skis and Poles	A. Thorndike	1,386	3.95	350.00
70-01-093	16" Christmas Wreath w/ Santa Head	A. Thorndike	1,662	9.95	375.00
70-01-094	18" Bride and Groom Frogs	A. Thorndike	1	23.95	1400.00
70-01-095	22" Monkey (chartreuse)	A. Thorndike	70	10.95	725.00
71-01-096	Monkey Head Pin-on (hot pink)	A. Thorndike	N/A	1.00	450.00
71-01-097	Snowman Head Pin-on	A. Thorndike	4,040	1.00	200.00
71-01-098	Snowman Kid	A. Thorndike	1,374	3.95	450.00
71-01-099	3" Reindeer Head	A. Thorndike	N/A	1.00	200.00
71-01-100	7" Naughty Angel	A. Thorndike	12,359	10.95	275.00
71-01-101	7" Swimmer Mouse w/ Inner Tube	A. Thorndike	267	3.95	325.00
71-01-102	7" Santa w/ Skis and Poles	A. Thorndike	N/A	5.45	300.00
71-01-103	7" Santa Mailman	A. Thorndike	8,296	5.50	375.00
71-01-104	10" Ski Elf	A. Thorndike	1,262	3.95	275.00
71-01-105	10" Clown (black & white)	A. Thorndike	N/A	2.00	300.00
72-01-106	7" Football Mouse	A. Thorndike	744	3.95	300.00
72-01-107	7" Santa on Ski-Bob w/ Oversized Bag	A. Thorndike	7,590	7.95	400.00
72-01-108	7" Secretary Mouse	A. Thorndike	727	3.95	500.00
72-01-109	10" Democratic Donkey	A. Thorndike	861	3.95	450.00
72-01-110	16" Democratic Donkey	A. Thorndike	219	12.95	1600.00
72-01-111	16" Elephant (Republican)	A. Thorndike	230	12.95	800.00
72-01-112	18" Candy Kid Boy	A. Thorndike	4,350	11.95	775.00
72-01-113	18" Candy Kid Girl	A. Thorndike	4,350	11.95	775.00
72-01-114	29" Mrs. Snow Woman w/ Cardholder Skirt	A. Thorndike	331	19.95	700.00
73-01-115	18" Christmas Panda	A. Thorndike	437	10.50	600.00
74-01-116	7" Black Santa w/Oversized Bag	A. Thorndike	1,638	5.45	550.00
74-01-117	7" Camper in Tent Mouse	A. Thorndike	468	5.45	325.00
74-01-118	7" Carpenter Mouse	A. Thorndike	2,687	5.45	275.00
74-01-119	7" Gardener Mouse	A. Thorndike	485	5.45	400.00
74-01-120	7" Hunter Mouse w/ Bird	A. Thorndike	690	5.45	325.00
74-01-121	7" Sloppy Painter Mouse	A. Thorndike	349	5.45	550.00
74-01-122	10" Leprechaun w/ Sack	A. Thorndike	8,834	5.45	350.00
74-01-123	22" Leprchaun	A. Thorndike	199	11.45	650.00
74-01-124	29" Bell Hop (special order)	A. Thorndike	3	29.00	1200.00
74-01-125	29" Motorized See-Saw Bunny Set	A. Thorndike	43	250.00	1600.00
75-01-126	7" Colonial Boy Mouse	A. Thorndike	12,739	5.45	350.00
75-01-127	7" Colonial Girl Mouse	A. Thorndike	9,338	5.45	350.00
75-01-128	8" Lamb	A. Thorndike	234	8.95	450.00
75-01-129	10" Colonial Drummer Boy	A. Thorndike	1,846	5.95	375.00
75-01-130	18" Horse	A. Thorndike	221	16.95	375.00
75-01-131	18" Yankee Doodle Dandy w/ 18" Horse	A. Thorndike	437	28.95	900.00
76-01-132	7" Needlework Mouse	A. Thorndike	3,566	6.95	400.00
76-01-133	7" Ski Mouse	A. Thorndike	10,375	6.95	225.00
76-01-134	10" Boy in Tire Swing	A. Thorndike	358	6.95	350.00
76-01-135	10" Uncle Sam	A. Thorndike	1,095	5.95	500.00
76-01-136	12" Angel	A. Thorndike	13,338	10.95	350.00
76-01-137	18" Elephant "Vote '76"	A. Thorndike	806	8.50	500.00
76-01-138	18" Uncle Sam	A. Thorndike	345	16.95	500.00
76-01-139	29" Clown (blue w/white polka dots)	A. Thorndike	466	29.95	925.00
77-01-140	7" Christmas Mouse in Santa's Mitten	A. Thorndike	15,916	7.95	175.00
77-01-141	7" Hobo Mouse	A. Thorndike	1,004	5.95	275.00
77-01-142	8" Rooster	A. Thorndike	1,642	5.95	350.00
77-01-143	18" Boy Bunny w/Carrot	A. Thorndike	1,159	13.50	250.00
77-01-144	29" Mr. Santa Mouse w/Sack	A. Thorndike	704	49.95	800.00
77-01-145	29" Mrs. Santa Mouse w/Muff	A. Thorndike	571	49.95	800.00
77-01-146	42" Scarecrow	A. Thorndike	365	61.95	2050.00
78-01-147	7" Santa w/ 10" Reindeer Trimming Christmas Tree	A. Thorndike	1,621	18.45	425.00
78-01-148	7" Airplane Pilot Mouse	A. Thorndike	2,308	6.95	425.00
78-01-149	7" Carpenter Mouse	A. Thorndike	1,494	6.95	350.00
78-01-150	10" Elf w/ Planter	A. Thorndike	1,978	6.95	275.00
78-01-151	18" Pilgrim Boy	A. Thorndike	1,213	14.95	275.00
78-01-152	29" Caroller Mouse	A. Thorndike	658	49.95	775.00
79-01-153	7" Ballerina	A. Thorndike	4,700	7.45	275.00
79-01-154	7" Gardener Mouse	A. Thorndike	1,939	7.95	325.00
79-01-155	7" Quilting Mouse	A. Thorndike	213	N/A	375.00
79-01-156	7" Skateboard Mouse	A. Thorndike	1,821	7.95	275.00
79-01-157	18" Gnome	A. Thorndike	15,851	19.95	200.00
79-01-158	18" Ballerina Bunny	A. Thorndike	2,315	15.95	450.00
79-01-159	29" Artist Bunny w/Brush & Palette	A. Thorndike	179	42.95	350.00
80-01-160	7" Hockey Mouse	A. Thorndike	2,477	9.95	300.00
80-01-161	8" Girl BBQ Pig	A. Thorndike	3,854	9.95	175.00
80-01-162	10" Balloon w/ Two 10" Frogs	A. Thorndike	837	49.95	850.00
80-01-163	10" Boy on Raft	A. Thorndike	1,087	28.95	325.00
80-01-164	14" Dragon w/Bush Boy	A. Thorndike	2,130	32.95	300.00
80-01-165	18" Ballerina Bunny	A. Thorndike	7,069	27.95	425.00
80-01-166	42" Clown	A. Thorndike	224	74.95	700.00
81-01-167	7" I'm Late Bunny	A. Thorndike	100	N/A	475.00
81-01-168	10" Jack Frost Elf w/ 5" Snowflake (artist proof)	A. Thorndike	5,950	31.95	325.00
81-01-169	18" Butterfly w/ 10" Elf	A. Thorndike	2,507	27.95	500.00
81-01-170	22" Christmas Giraffe w/ 10" Elf	A. Thorndike	1,377	36.95	500.00
81-01-171	22" Sun Mobile	A. Thorndike	3,003	36.95	475.00
82-01-172	7" Cowboy Mouse	A. Thorndike	3,776	12.95	300.00
82-01-173	7" Cowgirl Mouse	A. Thorndike	3,116	12.95	300.00
82-01-174	10" Cyrano de Bergerac	A. Thorndike	35	N/A	2300.00
82-01-175	7" Wood Chopper Mouse	A. Thorndike	1,910	11.95	375.00
83-01-176	5" Easter Parade Girl Bunny w/ Music Box	A. Thorndike	1,167	29.95	400.00
83-01-177	7" Angel w/ Musical Instrument on Music Box	A. Thorndike	N/A	29.95	425.00
84-01-178	5" E.P. Boy Bunny	A. Thorndike	2,583	11.95	200.00
84-01-179	5" E.P. Girl Bunny	A. Thorndike	2,790	11.95	200.00
84-01-180	7" Dentist Mouse	A. Thorndike	2,362	14.95	400.00
84-01-181	7" Angel on Star	A. Thorndike	772	32.95	475.00
84-01-182	7" Boy w/ Firecracker	A. Thorndike	1,893	19.95	400.00
84-01-183	10" Shriner (special order)	A. Thorndike	1,000	N/A	875.00
84-01-184	18" Aerobic Girl	A. Thorndike	622	35.95	375.00
84-01-185	18" E.P. Girl Bunny	A. Thorndike	2,952	35.95	350.00
84-01-186	18" Fawn w/ Wreath	A. Thorndike	2,080	32.95	375.00
84-01-187	30" Santa in Chair w/2 18" Kids	A. Thorndike	940	169.95	1200.00
85-01-188	7" Penguin & Chick #2095	A. Thorndike	3,000	29.95	225.00
85-01-189	7" Cookie Boy Logo Doll	A. Thorndike	3,562	15.00	675.00
85-01-190	7" Dress-Up Boy	A. Thorndike	1,174	18.95	225.00
85-01-191	7" Dress-Up Girl	A. Thorndike	1,536	18.95	225.00
85-01-192	7" Hockey Player Kid	A. Thorndike	1,578	18.95	400.00
85-01-193	7" Kid w/ Kite	A. Thorndike	1,084	17.95	300.00
85-01-194	18" Ballerina Bear	A. Thorndike	918	39.95	275.00
86-01-195	7" Witch Mouse w/ Pumpkin Balloon	A. Thorndike	868	59.95	300.00
86-01-196	48" Velour Santa	A. Thorndike	410	269.95	750.00
87-01-197	3" Baby Witch	A. Thorndike	3,645	13.95	275.00
87-01-198	3" Bride and Groom	A. Thorndike	1,053	38.95	375.00
87-01-200	7" BBQ Mouse	A. Thorndike	1,798	17.95	300.00
87-01-201	7" Bunny in 10" Carrot Balloon	A. Thorndike	624	49.95	375.00
87-01-202	7" Hangover Mouse	A. Thorndike	1,548	13.95	175.00
87-01-203	10" Ski Elf	A. Thorndike	N/A	19.95	350.00
87-01-204	10" Huck Finn (#62)	A. Thorndike	800	102.95	700.00
87-01-205	10" State Trooper (#642)	A. Thorndike	511	134.00	500.00
87-01-206	18" Special Mrs. Santa (special order)	A. Thorndike	341	N/A	400.00
87-01-207	18" Workshop Santa (special order)	A. Thorndike	1,001	N/A	450.00
89-01-208	7" Polar Bear Cub (artist proof)	A. Thorndike	1	N/A	350.00
89-01-209	7" Polar Bear Cub	A. Thorndike	3,000	37.50	300.00
89-01-210	7" Science Center Mouse	A. Thorndike	500	75.00	525.00
89-01-211	7" Robin Hood Mouse (artist proof)	A. Thorndike	1	N/A	350.00
89-01-212	10" Abraham Lincoln (artist proof)	A. Thorndike	1	N/A	1200.00
89-01-213	10" Three Bunnies w/ Maypole	A. Thorndike	647	190.00	600.00
89-01-214	10" BBQ Pig	A. Thorndike	2,471	27.95	325.00
90-01-215	7" Friar Tuck Mouse (artist proof)	A. Thorndike	1	N/A	350.00
90-01-216	7" Maid Marion Mouse (artist proof)	A. Thorndike	1	N/A	350.00
90-01-217	10" Spirit of '76	A. Thorndike	1,080	175.00	550.00
90-01-218	10" Nativity Set (artist proof)	A. Thorndike	1	N/A	700.00
90-01-219	10" Wise Men w/ Camel (artist proof)	A. Thorndike	1	N/A	600.00
90-01-220	12" Santa Duck	A. Thorndike	506	49.95	300.00
90-01-221	15" Christmas Dragon	A. Thorndike	448	49.95	400.00
90-01-222	18" Leopard Kid (design reject)	A. Thorndike	1	N/A	950.00
90-01-223	18" Santa Playing w/Electric Train	A. Thorndike	168	119.00	350.00
90-01-224	18" Naughty Kid	A. Thorndike	1,454	69.95	525.00
91-01-225	3" Water Baby in Pond Lily	A. Thorndike	3,720	14.95	175.00
91-01-226	7" Marine Mouse	A. Thorndike	1	N/A	500.00

		ARTIST	EDITION	ISSUE	QUOTE
91-01-227	7" Fun in the Sun Kid	A. Thorndike	300	80.00	300.00
91-01-228	7" Santa in Tub w/ Rubber Duckie	A. Thorndike	5,373	33.95	200.00
91-01-229	7" Sheriff Mouse (artist proof)	A. Thorndike	1	N/A	650.00
91-01-230	10" Tennesee Mt. Man (design reject)	A. Thorndike	1	N/A	625.00
91-01-231	10" Summer Santa #1663	A. Thorndike	1,926	59.95	425.00
91-01-232	10" Aviator Frog WW II (artist proof)	A. Thorndike	1	N/A	350.00
91-01-233	10" Victory Ski Doll	A. Thorndike	1,192	49.50	350.00
91-01-234	10" Wise Men (artist proof)	A. Thorndike	1	N/A	550.00
92-01-235	7" Disney Kid	A. Thorndike	300	59.95	400.00
92-01-236	7" Hot Shot Businessman Kid (artist proof)	A. Thorndike	1	N/A	800.00
92-01-237	10" Baseball Player (artist proof)	A. Thorndike	1	N/A	425.00
92-01-238	10" Baseball Pitcher (artist proof)	A. Thorndike	1	N/A	425.00
93-01-239	5" Old World Caroler Boy (artist proof)	A. Thorndike	1	N/A	350-400.
93-01-240	5" Old World Caroler Girl (artist proof)	A. Thorndike	1	N/A	350-400.
93-01-241	7" Snowboard Kid (artist proof)	A. Thorndike	1	N/A	450.00
93-01-242	7"Airplane Boy (one of a kind)	A. Thorndike	1	N/A	900.00
93-01-243	7" Baby Bunny w/ Baby Bottle (artist proof)	A. Thorndike	1	N/A	450.00
93-01-244	7" Boy Cutting His Hair (one of a kind)	A. Thorndike	1	N/A	1000.00
93-01-245	7" Bride Mouse (artist proof)	A. Thorndike	1	N/A	400.00
93-01-246	7" Flying Angel (artist proof)	A. Thorndike	1	N/A	400.00
93-01-247	7" Girl Building Snowman (artist proof)	A. Thorndike	1	N/A	500.00
93-01-248	7" Groom Mouse (artist proof)	A. Thorndike	1	N/A	400.00
93-01-249	7" Habitat Mouse (artist proof)	A. Thorndike	1	N/A	500.00
93-01-250	7" Hershey Kid (artist proof)	A. Thorndike	1	N/A	1,000.00
93-01-251	7" Hot Shot Business Girl (artist proof)	A. Thorndike	1	N/A	450.00
93-01-252	7" Ice Cream Logo Kid (white, artist proof)	A. Thorndike	1	N/A	650.00
93-01-253	7" Ice Cream Logo Kid (yellow, artist proof)	A. Thorndike	1	N/A	750.00
93-01-254	7" Mississippi Levee Mouse (artist proof)	A. Thorndike	341	N/A	400.00
93-01-255	7" Mr. Old World Santa (artist proof)	A. Thorndike	1	N/A	425.00
93-01-256	7" Mrs. Old World Santa (artist proof)	A. Thorndike	1	N/A	425.00
93-01-257	7" Naughty Angel w/ Black Eye (artist proof)	A. Thorndike	1	N/A	500.00
93-01-258	7" Scuba Diving Mouse (one of a kind)	A. Thorndike	1	N/A	1000.00
93-01-259	7" Thanksgiving Boy (artist proof)	A. Thorndike	1	N/A	650.00
93-01-260	7" Eric & Shane Boating in Hawaii	A. Thorndike	100	105.00	750.00
93-01-261	10" Baseball Catcher (artist proof)	A. Thorndike	1	N/A	425.00
93-01-262	10" Pony Express (artist proof)	A. Thorndike	1	N/A	1800.00
93-01-263	10" Nun (one of a kind)	A. Thorndike	1	N/A	900.00
93-01-264	10" Hobo Clown (artist proof)	A. Thorndike	1	N/A	550.00
93-01-265	10" E.P. Shopping Ostrich (artist proof)	A. Thorndike	1	N/A	450.00
93-01-266	10" Farmer w/ Rooster (artist proof)	A. Thorndike	1	N/A	1000.00
93-01-267	10" Window Shopper Ostrich (artist proof)	A. Thorndike	1	N/A	500.00
93-01-268	10" Christa McAuliffe Skier (artist proof)	A. Thorndike	1	N/A	625.00
93-01-269	10" Soccer Player (artist proof)	A. Thorndike	1	N/A	500.00
93-01-270	12" Girl Scarecrow (artist proof)	A. Thorndike	1	N/A	650.00
93-01-271	12" Witch Kid (one of a kind)	A. Thorndike	1	N/A	900.00
93-01-272	18" Old World Reindeer w/ Bells (artist proof)	A. Thorndike	1	N/A	450.00
93-01-273	30" Country Girl Bunny w/ Basket (artist proof)	A. Thorndike	1	N/A	700.00
94-01-274	Bang Hat (artist proof)	A. Thorndike	1	N/A	200.00
94-01-275	Musical Ballooning 3" Kids (artist proof)	A. Thorndike	1	N/A	450.00
94-01-276	5" Butterfly Kid (design reject)	A. Thorndike	1	N/A	475.00
94-01-277	7" Dress Up Santa Logo (artist proof)	A. Thorndike	1	N/A	775.00
94-01-278	7" Bunny Kid (artist proof)	A. Thorndike	1	N/A	500.00
94-01-279	7" South American Girl (artist proof)	A. Thorndike	1	N/A	500.00
94-01-280	7" "Tall Ships" Duck (artist proof)	A. Thorndike	1	N/A	450.00
94-01-281	7" Marbles Kid (artist proof)	A. Thorndike	1	N/A	500.00
94-01-282	7"Gypsy Girl (artist proof)	A. Thorndike	1	N/A	500.00
94-01-283	7" Beach Bunny (design reject)	A. Thorndike	1	N/A	700.00
94-01-284	7" Motorcycle Mouse (artist proof)	A. Thorndike	1	N/A	750.00
94-01-285	7" Swiss Alps Boy (artist proof)	A. Thorndike	1	N/A	450.00
94-01-286	7" Auction Mouse (artist proof)	A. Thorndike	1	N/A	750.00
94-01-287	7" Candy Kiss Kid (one of a kind)	A. Thorndike	1	N/A	2250.00
94-01-288	7" Cheerleader Girl (artist proof)	A. Thorndike	1	N/A	650.00
94-01-289	7" Clown Mouse (one of a kind)	A. Thorndike	1	N/A	1050.00
94-01-290	7" Cocktail Mouse (one of a kind)	A. Thorndike	1	N/A	1100.00
94-01-291	7" Football Mouse (artist proof)	A. Thorndike	1	N/A	750.00
94-01-292	7" Girl w/ Teddy Bear (artist proof)	A. Thorndike	1	N/A	650.00
94-01-293	7" Hot Shot Business Girl (artist proof)	A. Thorndike	1	N/A	700.00
94-01-294	7" Jail House Mouse (artist proof)	A. Thorndike	1	N/A	650.00
94-01-295	7" Policeman Mouse (artist proof)	A. Thorndike	1	N/A	750.00
94-01-296	7" Santa w/ Dove (one of a kind)	A. Thorndike	1	N/A	1250.00
94-01-297	7" Scottish Lad (artist proof)	A. Thorndike	1	N/A	675.00
94-01-298	7" House Wife Mouse (artist proof)	A. Thorndike	1	N/A	650.00
94-01-299	7" Valentine Girl w/ Card (artist proof)	A. Thorndike	1	N/A	750.00
94-01-300	7" Hockey Kid (artist proof)	A. Thorndike	1	N/A	1300.00
94-01-301	7" Teacher Mouse (design reject)	A. Thorndike	1	N/A	700.00
94-01-302	10" Ballerina Bear (one of a kind)	A. Thorndike	1	N/A	1100.00
94-01-303	10" Basketball Player (black, artist proof)	A. Thorndike	1	N/A	550.00
94-01-304	10" Basketball Player (white, artist proof)	A. Thorndike	1	N/A	550.00
94-01-305	10" Country Girl Bear (one of a kind)	A. Thorndike	1	N/A	925.00
94-01-306	10" White St. Nicholas (artist proof)	A. Thorndike	1	N/A	650.00
94-01-307	10" Collector Mrs. Nashville (artist proof)	A. Thorndike	1	N/A	350.00
94-01-308	10" Collector Mr. Nashville (artist proof)	A. Thorndike	1	N/A	350.00
94-01-309	10" Collector "Old Salty" (artist proof)	A. Thorndike	1	N/A	750.00
94-01-310	10" Collector Mr. Santa w/ 3 10" Elves (artist proof)	A. Thorndike	1	N/A	650.00
94-01-311	10" M/M Santa Skating Music Box (artist proof)	A. Thorndike	1	N/A	900.00
94-01-312	10" Mrs. Santa "Last Minute Mending" (artist proof)	A. Thorndike	1	N/A	650.00
94-01-313	10" Old World Santa w/ Skis (artist proof)	A. Thorndike	1	N/A	800.00
94-01-314	18" Christmas Panda (design reject)	A. Thorndike	1	N/A	825.00
94-01-315	12" Bean Nose Santa Folk Hero	A. Thorndike	1	N/A	1150.00
94-01-316	12" Carousel Horse (artist proof)	A. Thorndike	1	N/A	1200.00
94-01-317	30" Country Boy Bunny w/Apples (artist proof)	A. Thorndike	1	N/A	400.00

Annalee Mobilitee Dolls — **Doll Society-Logo Kids**

		ARTIST	EDITION	ISSUE	QUOTE
85-02-001	Christmas Logo w/Cookie	A. Thorndike	3,562	N/A	675.00
86-02-002	Sweetheart Logo	A. Thorndike	6,271	N/A	275.00
87-02-003	Naughty Logo	A. Thorndike	1,100	N/A	425.00
88-02-004	Raincoat Logo	A. Thorndike	13,646	N/A	200.00
89-02-005	Christmas Morning Logo	A. Thorndike	16,641	N/A	150.00
90-02-006	Clown	A. Thorndike	20,049	N/A	150.00
91-02-007	Reading Logo	A. Thorndike	26,516	N/A	125.00
92-02-008	Back to School Logo	A. Thorndike	17,524	N/A	90.00
93-02-009	Ice Cream Logo	A. Thorndike	Yr.Iss.	N/A	N/A
94-02-010	Dress Up Santa Logo	A. Thorndike	Yr.Iss	N/A	N/A

Annalee Mobilitee Dolls — **Doll Society-Folk Heroes**

		ARTIST	EDITION	ISSUE	QUOTE
84-03-001	10" Johnny Appleseed	A. Thorndike	1,500	N/A	1000.00
84-03-002	10" Robin Hood	A. Thorndike	1,500	N/A	850.00
85-03-003	10" Annie Oakley	A. Thorndike	1,500	N/A	700.00
86-03-004	10" Mark Twain	A. Thorndike	2,500	N/A	500.00
87-03-005	10" Ben Franklin	A. Thorndike	2,500	N/A	525.00
88-03-006	10" Sherlock Holmes	A. Thorndike	2,500	N/A	500.00
89-03-007	10" Abraham Lincoln	A. Thorndike	2,500	N/A	500.00
90-03-008	10" Betsy Ross	A. Thorndike	2,500	N/A	450.00
91-03-009	10" Christopher Columbus	A. Thorndike	1,132	N/A	300.00
92-03-010	10" Uncle Sam	A. Thorndike	1,034	N/A	N/A
93-03-011	10" Pony Express Rider	A. Thorndike	Yr.Iss.	N/A	N/A
94-03-012	10" Bean Nose Santa	A. Thorndike	Yr.Iss.	N/A	N/A

Annalee Mobilitee Dolls — **Doll Society-Animals**

		ARTIST	EDITION	ISSUE	QUOTE
85-04-001	10" Penguin and Chick	A. Thorndike	3,000	N/A	225.00
86-04-002	10" Unicorn	A. Thorndike	3,000	N/A	350.00
87-04-003	7" Kangaroo	A. Thorndike	3,000	N/A	450.00
88-04-004	5" Owl	A. Thorndike	3,000	N/A	300.00
89-04-005	7" Polar Bear	A. Thorndike	3,000	N/A	300.00
90-04-006	10" Thorndike Chicken	A. Thorndike	3,000	N/A	275.00

ANRI — **Disney Dolls**

		ARTIST	EDITION	ISSUE	QUOTE
89-01-001	Mickey Mouse, 14"	Disney Studios	Closed	850.00	895.00
89-01-002	Minnie Mouse, 14"	Disney Studios	Closed	850.00	895.00
89-01-003	Pinocchio, 14"	Disney Studios	Closed	850.00	895.00
90-01-004	Donald Duck, 14"	Disney Studios	Closed	895.00	895.00
90-01-005	Daisy Duck, 14"	Disney Studios	Closed	895.00	895.00

ANRI — **Sarah Kay Dolls**

		ARTIST	EDITION	ISSUE	QUOTE
88-02-001	Jennifer, 14"	S. Kay	Closed	500.00	500.00
88-02-002	Rebecca, 14"	S. Kay	Closed	500.00	500.00
88-02-003	Sarah, 14"	S. Kay	Closed	500.00	500.00
88-02-004	Katherine, 14"	S. Kay	Closed	500.00	500.00
88-02-005	Martha, 14"	S. Kay	Closed	500.00	500.00
88-02-006	Emily, 14"	S. Kay	Closed	500.00	500.00
88-02-007	Rachael, 14"	S. Kay	Closed	500.00	500.00
88-02-008	Victoria, 14"	S. Kay	Closed	500.00	500.00
89-02-009	Bride to Love And To Cherish	S. Kay	Closed	750.00	790.00
89-02-010	Groom With This Ring Doll	S. Kay	Closed	550.00	730.00
89-02-011	Charlotte (Blue)	S. Kay	Closed	550.00	575.00
89-02-012	Henry	S. Kay	Closed	550.00	575.00
89-02-013	Elizabeth (Patchwork)	S. Kay	Closed	550.00	575.00
89-02-014	Helen (Brown)	S. Kay	Closed	550.00	575.00
89-02-015	Eleanor (Floral)	S. Kay	Closed	550.00	575.00
89-02-016	Mary (Red)	S. Kay	Closed	550.00	575.00
90-02-017	Polly, 14"	S. Kay	Closed	575.00	680.00
90-02-018	Christina, 14"	S. Kay	Closed	575.00	730.00
90-02-019	Faith, 14"	S. Kay	Closed	575.00	685.00
90-02-020	Sophie, 14"	S. Kay	Closed	575.00	660.00
91-02-021	Jessica, 7"	S. Kay	Closed	300.00	300.00
91-02-022	Michelle, 7"	S. Kay	Closed	300.00	300.00
91-02-023	Peggy, 7"	S. Kay	Closed	300.00	300.00
91-02-024	Annie, 7"	S. Kay	Closed	300.00	300.00
91-02-025	Susan, 7"	S. Kay	Closed	300.00	300.00
91-02-026	Julie, 7"	S. Kay	Closed	300.00	300.00
91-02-027	Janine, 14"	S. Kay	Closed	750.00	750.00
91-02-028	Patricia, 14"	S. Kay	Closed	730.00	730.00

ANRI — **Ferrandiz Dolls**

		ARTIST	EDITION	ISSUE	QUOTE
89-03-001	Gabriel, 14"	J. Ferrandiz	Closed	550.00	575.00
89-03-002	Maria, 14"	J. Ferrandiz	Closed	550.00	575.00
90-03-003	Margarite, 14"	J. Ferrandiz	Closed	575.00	730.00
90-03-004	Philipe, 14"	J. Ferrandiz	Closed	575.00	680.00
91-03-005	Carmen, 14"	J. Ferrandiz	Closed	730.00	730.00
91-03-006	Fernando, 14"	J. Ferrandiz	Closed	730.00	730.00
91-03-007	Miguel, 7"	J. Ferrandiz	Closed	300.00	300.00
91-03-008	Juanita, 7"	J. Ferrandiz	Closed	300.00	300.00

Artaffects — **Perillo Doll Collection**

		ARTIST	EDITION	ISSUE	QUOTE
86-01-001	Morning Star (17-1/2")	G. Perillo	1000	250.00	250.00
88-01-002	Sunflower (12")	G. Perillo	2500	175.00	175.00

Artaffects — **Art Doll Collection**

		ARTIST	EDITION	ISSUE	QUOTE
90-02-001	Little Dove (12")	G. Perillo	5000	175.00	175.00
90-02-002	Straight Arrow (12")	G. Perillo	5000	175.00	175.00

Artaffects — **Children of the Plains**

		ARTIST	EDITION	ISSUE	QUOTE
92-03-001	Brave and Free (10" seated)	G. Perillo	Open	111.00	111.00
93-03-002	Song of Sioux (10" seated)	G. Perillo	Open	111.00	111.00
93-03-003	Gentle Shepherd (13" standing)	G. Perillo	Open	111.00	111.00
93-03-004	Bird Song (13" standing)	G. Perillo	Open	111.00	111.00
94-03-005	Cactus Flower	G. Perillo	Open	111.00	111.00
94-03-006	Pathfinder	G. Perillo	Open	111.00	111.00
94-03-007	Princess of the Sun	G. Perillo	Open	111.00	111.00
94-03-008	Little Friend	G. Perillo	Open	111.00	111.00

Artaffects — **Ruffles and Rhymes Doll Collection**

		ARTIST	EDITION	ISSUE	QUOTE
93-04-001	Little Bo Peep (15" High)	Artaffects Studio	Open	89.00	89.00
94-04-002	Little Bo Peep	Artaffects Studio	Open	106.80	106.80

Artaffects — **Country Musicians Collection**

		ARTIST	EDITION	ISSUE	QUOTE
94-05-001	Danny	Artaffects Studio	Open	118.00	118.00

Artaffects — **Single Issue**

		ARTIST	EDITION	ISSUE	QUOTE
94-06-001	Little Breeze	G. Perillo	Open	114.00	114.00

Ashton-Drake Galleries — **Yolanda's Picture - Perfect Babies**

		ARTIST	EDITION	ISSUE	QUOTE
85-01-001	Jason	Y. Bello	Closed	48.00	600-900.
86-01-002	Heather	Y. Bello	Closed	48.00	200-375.
87-01-003	Jennifer	Y. Bello	Closed	58.00	295-350.
87-01-004	Matthew	Y. Bello	Closed	58.00	195-295.
87-01-005	Sarah	Y. Bello	Closed	58.00	95-190.
88-01-006	Amanda	Y. Bello	Closed	63.00	125-195.
89-01-007	Jessica	Y. Bello	Closed	63.00	63-195.
90-01-008	Michael	Y. Bello	Closed	63.00	125-185.
90-01-009	Lisa	Y. Bello	Closed	63.00	125.00
91-01-010	Emily	Y. Bello	Closed	63.00	100-125.
91-01-011	Danielle	Y. Bello	Closed	69.00	100-175.

Ashton-Drake Galleries — **Children of Mother Goose**

		ARTIST	EDITION	ISSUE	QUOTE
87-02-001	Little Bo Peep	Y. Bello	Closed	58.00	200-225.
87-02-002	Mary Had a Little Lamb	Y. Bello	Closed	58.00	145-200.
88-02-003	Little Jack Horner	Y. Bello	Closed	63.00	115-125.
89-02-004	Miss Muffet	Y. Bello	Closed	63.00	63.00

	ARTIST	EDITION	ISSUE	QUOTE
Ashton-Drake Galleries	**Yolanda's Lullaby Babies**			
91-03-001 Christy (Rock-a-Bye)	Y. Bello	Closed	69.00	125.00
92-03-002 Joey (Twinkle, Twinkle)	Y. Bello	Closed	69.00	95.00
93-03-003 Amy (Brahms Lullaby)	Y. Bello	Closed	75.00	75.00
93-03-004 Eddie (Teddy Bear Lullaby)	Y. Bello	Closed	75.00	75.00
93-03-005 Jacob (Silent Night)	Y. Bello	Closed	75.00	75.00
94-03-006 Bonnie (You Are My Sunshine)	Y. Bello	Closed	80.00	80.00
Ashton-Drake Galleries	**Moments To Remember**			
91-04-001 Justin	Y. Bello	Closed	75.00	75.00
92-04-002 Jill	Y. Bello	Closed	75.00	100-125.
93-04-003 Brandon (Ring Bearer)	Y. Bello	Closed	79.95	79.95
93-04-004 Suzanne (Flower Girl)	Y. Bello	Closed	79.95	79.95
Ashton-Drake Galleries	**Yolanda's Precious Playmates**			
92-05-001 David	Y. Bello	Closed	69.95	90-145.
93-05-002 Paul	Y. Bello	Closed	69.95	125-145.
94-05-003 Johnny	Y. Bello	Closed	69.95	69.95
Ashton-Drake Galleries	**Parade of American Fashion**			
87-06-001 The Glamour of the Gibson Girl	Stevens/Siegel	Closed	77.00	200.00
88-06-002 The Southern Belle	Stevens/Siegel	Closed	77.00	200.00
90-06-003 Victorian Lady	Stevens/Siegel	Closed	82.00	82.00
91-06-004 Romantic Lady	Stevens/Siegel	Closed	85.00	85.00
Ashton-Drake Galleries	**Heroines from the Fairy Tale Forests**			
88-07-001 Little Red Riding Hood	D. Effner	Closed	68.00	225-300.
89-07-002 Goldilocks	D. Effner	Closed	68.00	51-125.
90-07-003 Snow White	D. Effner	Closed	73.00	150-175.
91-07-004 Rapunzel	D. Effner	Closed	79.00	85-145.
92-07-005 Cinderella	D. Effner	Closed	79.00	150-295.
93-07-006 Cinderella (Ballgown)	D. Effner	Closed	79.95	125-295.
Ashton-Drake Galleries	**International Festival of Toys and Tots**			
89-08-001 Chen, a Little Boy of China	K. Hippensteel	Closed	78.00	95-197.
89-08-002 Natasha	K. Hippensteel	Closed	78.00	54-78.00
90-08-003 Molly	K. Hippensteel	Closed	83.00	83.00
91-08-004 Hans	K. Hippensteel	Closed	88.00	61-88.00
92-08-005 Miki, Eskimo	K. Hippensteel	Closed	88.00	88.00
Ashton-Drake Galleries	**Born To Be Famous**			
89-09-001 Little Sherlock	K. Hippensteel	Closed	87.00	60-100.
90-09-002 Little Florence Nightingale	K. Hippensteel	Closed	87.00	87.00
91-09-003 Little Davey Crockett	K. Hippensteel	Closed	92.00	92.00
92-09-004 Little Christopher Columbus	K. Hippensteel	Closed	95.00	125.00
Ashton-Drake Galleries	**Baby Book Treasures**			
90-10-001 Elizabeth's Homecoming	K. Hippensteel	Closed	58.00	80.00
91-10-002 Catherine's Christening	K. Hippensteel	Closed	58.00	58.00
91-10-003 Christopher's First Smile	K. Hippensteel	Closed	63.00	100.00
Ashton-Drake Galleries	**Growing Young Minds**			
91-11-001 Alex	K. Hippensteel	Closed	79.00	79-99.00
Ashton-Drake Galleries	**Happiness Is...**			
91-12-001 Patricia (My First Tooth)	K. Hippensteel	Closed	69.00	125-145.
92-12-002 Crystal (Feeding Myself)	K. Hippensteel	Closed	69.95	100.00
93-12-003 Brittany (Blowing Kisses)	K. Hippensteel	Closed	69.95	100.00
93-12-004 Joy (My First Christmas)	K. Hippensteel	Closed	69.95	100.00
94-12-005 Candy Cane (Holly)	K. Hippensteel	Closed	69.95	125.00
94-12-006 Patrick (My First Playmate)	K. Hippensteel	Closed	69.95	80-100.
Ashton-Drake Galleries	**Cindy's Playhouse Pals**			
89-13-001 Meagan	C. McClure	Closed	87.00	125-200.
89-13-002 Shelly	C. McClure	Closed	87.00	87-150.
90-13-003 Ryan	C. McClure	Closed	89.00	89-125.
91-13-004 Samantha	C. McClure	Closed	89.00	89-100.
Ashton-Drake Galleries	**A Children's Circus**			
90-14-001 Tommy The Clown	J. McClelland	Closed	78.00	78-100.
91-14-002 Katie The Tightrope Walker	J. McClelland	Closed	78.00	78.00
91-14-003 Johnnie The Strongman	J. McClelland	Closed	83.00	83.00
92-14-004 Maggie The Animal Trainer	J. McClelland	Closed	83.00	83.00
Ashton-Drake Galleries	**Maude Fangel's Cover Babies**			
91-15-001 Peek-A-Boo Peter	Fangel-Inspired	Closed	73.00	73-150.
91-15-002 Benjamin's Ball	Fangel-Inspired	Closed	73.00	73.00
Ashton-Drake Galleries	**Amish Blessings**			
90-16-001 Rebeccah	J. Good-Kruger	Closed	68.00	100-150.
91-16-002 Rachel	J. Good-Kruger	Closed	69.00	100-175.
91-16-003 Adam	J. Good-Kruger	Closed	75.00	95-225.
92-16-004 Ruth	J. Good-Kruger	Closed	75.00	100-145.
92-16-005 Eli	J. Good-Kruger	Closed	79.95	100-130.
93-16-006 Sarah	J. Good-Kruger	Closed	79.95	100-175.
Ashton-Drake Galleries	**Polly's Tea Party**			
90-17-001 Polly	S. Krey	Closed	78.00	125.00
91-17-002 Lizzie	S. Krey	Closed	79.00	79.00
92-17-003 Annie	S. Krey	Closed	83.00	95.00
Ashton-Drake Galleries	**Yesterday's Dreams**			
90-18-001 Andy	M. Oldenburg	Closed	68.00	68-85.00
91-18-002 Janey	M. Oldenburg	Closed	69.00	69.00
Ashton-Drake Galleries	**My Closest Friend**			
91-19-001 Boo Bear 'N Me	J. Goodyear	Closed	78.00	145-225.
91-19-002 Me and My Blankie	J. Goodyear	Closed	79.00	95-165.
92-19-003 My Secret Pal (Robbie)	J. Goodyear	Closed	85.00	85.00
92-19-004 My Beary Best Friend	J. Goodyear	Closed	79.95	79.95
Ashton-Drake Galleries	**The Littlest Clowns**			
91-20-001 Sparkles	M. Tretter	Closed	63.00	80-100.
91-20-002 Bubbles	M. Tretter	Closed	65.00	65-125.
91-20-003 Smooch	M. Tretter	Closed	69.00	69-125.
92-20-004 Daisy	M. Tretter	Closed	69.95	69.95
Ashton-Drake Galleries	**Romantic Flower Maidens**			
88-21-001 Rose, Who is Love	M. Roderick	Closed	87.00	125-175.
89-21-002 Daisy	M. Roderick	Closed	87.00	125-150.
90-21-003 Violet	M. Roderick	Closed	92.00	125-150.
90-21-004 Lily	M. Roderick	Closed	92.00	104-175.
Ashton-Drake Galleries	**Precious Memories of Motherhood**			
89-22-001 Loving Steps	S. Kuck	Closed	125.00	100-175.
90-22-002 Lullaby	S. Kuck	Closed	125.00	100-125.
91-22-003 Expectant Moments	S. Kuck	Closed	149.00	195-245.
92-22-004 Bedtime	S. Kuck	Closed	150.00	150-175.

	ARTIST	EDITION	ISSUE	QUOTE
Ashton-Drake Galleries	**Classic Brides of The Century**			
90-23-001 Flora, The 1900s Bride	E. Williams	Closed	145.00	145.00
91-23-002 Jennifer, The 1980s Bride	E. Williams	Closed	149.00	149.00
93-23-003 Kathleen, The 1930s Bride	E. Williams	Closed	149.95	149.95
Ashton-Drake Galleries	**My Fair Lady**			
91-24-001 Eliza at Ascot	P. Ryan Brooks	Closed	125.00	185-350.
Ashton-Drake Galleries	**The King & I**			
91-25-001 Shall We Dance?	P. Ryan Brooks	Closed	175.00	275-295.
Ashton-Drake Galleries	**Stepping Out**			
91-26-001 Millie	Akers/Girardi	Closed	99.00	125.00
Ashton-Drake Galleries	**Year Book Memories**			
91-27-001 Peggy Sue	Akers/Girardi	Closed	87.00	129.00
93-27-002 Going Steady (Patty Jo)	Akers/Girardi	Closed	89.95	89.95
93-27-003 Prom Queen (Betty Jean)	Akers/Girardi	Closed	92.00	92.00
Ashton-Drake Galleries	**Winterfest**			
91-28-001 Brian	S. Sherwood	Closed	89.00	110-145.
92-28-002 Michelle	S. Sherwood	Closed	89.95	125-195.
93-28-003 Bradley	S. Sherwood	Closed	89.95	89.95
Ashton-Drake Galleries	**Dianna Effner's Mother Goose**			
90-29-001 Mary, Mary, Quite Contrary	D. Effner	Closed	78.00	125-250.
91-29-002 The Little Girl With The Curl (Horrid)	D. Effner	Closed	79.00	150-195.
91-29-003 The Little Girl With The Curl (Good)	D. Effner	Closed	79.00	80-150.
92-29-004 Little Boy Blue	D. Effner	Closed	85.00	85.00
93-29-005 Snips & Snails	D. Effner	Closed	85.00	110-145.
93-29-006 Sugar & Spice	D. Effner	Closed	89.95	110-125.
93-29-007 Curly Locks	D. Effner	12/95	89.95	89.95
Ashton-Drake Galleries	**A Child's Garden of Verses**			
91-30-001 Nathan (The Land of Nod)	J. Singer	Closed	79.00	79-100.
93-30-002 My Toy Soldiers	J. Singer	Closed	79.95	79.95
93-30-003 Picture Books in Winter	J. Singer	Closed	85.00	85.00
93-30-004 My Ship & I	J. Singer	Closed	85.00	85.00
Ashton-Drake Galleries	**Down The Garden Path**			
91-31-001 Rosemary	P. Coffer	Closed	79.00	79.00
91-31-002 Angelica	P. Coffer	Closed	85.00	85.00
93-31-003 Amanda by the Shore	P. Coffer	Closed	89.95	89.95
Ashton-Drake Galleries	**Beautiful Dreamers**			
92-32-001 Katrina	G. Rademann	Closed	89.00	115-135.
92-32-002 Nicolette	G. Rademann	Closed	89.95	89.95
93-32-003 Brigitte	G. Rademann	Closed	94.00	94.00
93-32-004 Isabella	G. Rademann	Closed	94.00	94.00
93-32-005 Gabrielle	G. Rademann	Closed	94.00	94.00
Ashton-Drake Galleries	**Great Moments From Hollywood**			
91-33-001 Shall We Dance?	P. Brooks	Closed	175.00	275-325.
Ashton-Drake Galleries	**International Spirit Of Christmas**			
89-34-001 American Santa	F. Wick	Closed	125.00	125.00
Ashton-Drake Galleries	**From The Heart**			
92-35-001 Carolin	T. Menzenbach	Closed	79.95	97-125.
92-35-002 Erik	T. Menzenbach	Closed	79.95	125.00
Ashton-Drake Galleries	**Little House On The Prairie**			
92-36-001 Laura	J. Ibarolle	Closed	79.95	125.00
93-36-002 Mary Ingalls	J. Ibarolle	Closed	79.95	100-125.
93-36-003 Nellie Olson	J. Ibarolle	Closed	85.00	100.00
93-36-004 Almanzo	J. Ibarolle	Closed	85.00	85.00
94-36-005 Carrie	J. Ibarolle	12/94	85.00	85.00
94-36-006 Ma Ingalls	J. Ibarolle	12/95	90.00	90.00
94-36-007 Pa Ingalls	J. Ibarolle	12/95	90.00	90.00
Ashton-Drake Galleries	**Rockwell Christmas**			
90-37-001 Scotty Plays Santa	Rockwell-Inspired	Closed	48.00	48.00
91-37-002 Scotty Gets His Tree	Rockwell-Inspired	Closed	59.00	59.00
93-37-003 Merry Christmas Grandma	Rockwell-Inspired	Closed	59.95	59.95
Ashton-Drake Galleries	**Holly Hunt's Bonnet Babies**			
91-38-001 Missy (Grandma's Little Girl)	H. Hunt	Closed	69.00	69.00
92-38-002 Susie (Somebody Loves Me)	H. Hunt	Closed	69.00	95.00
Ashton-Drake Galleries	**Heavenly Inspirations**			
92-39-001 Every Cloud Has a Silver Lining	C. McClure	Closed	59.95	59.95
93-39-002 Wish Upon A Star	C. McClure	Closed	59.95	60-95.00
94-39-003 Sweet Dreams	C. McClure	12/94	65.00	65.00
94-39-004 Luck at the End of Rainbow	C. McClure	12/94	65.00	65.00
94-39-005 Sunshine	C. McClure	12/94	69.95	69.95
94-39-006 Pennies From Heaven	C. McClure	12/95	69.95	69.95
Ashton-Drake Galleries	**Elvis: Lifetime Of A Legend**			
92-40-001 '68 Comeback Special	L. Di Leo	Closed	99.95	99.95
94-40-002 King of Las Vegas	L. Di Leo	Closed	99.95	99.95
Ashton-Drake Galleries	**Caught In The Act**			
92-41-001 Stevie, Catch Me If You Can	M. Tretter	Closed	49.95	55-125.
93-41-002 Kelly, Don't I Look Pretty?	M. Tretter	Closed	49.95	50-75.00
94-41-003 Mikey (Look It Floats)	M. Tretter	12/94	55.00	55.00
94-41-004 Nickie (Cookie Jar)	M. Tretter	12/95	59.95	59.95
94-41-005 Becky (Kleenex Box)	M. Tretter	12/95	59.95	59.95
94-41-006 Sandy	M. Tretter	12/95	59.95	59.95
Ashton-Drake Galleries	**Your Heart's Desire**			
91-42-001 Julia	M. Stauber	Closed	99.00	125.00
Ashton-Drake Galleries	**My Heart Belongs To Daddy**			
92-43-001 Peanut	J. Singer	Closed	49.95	75-100.
92-43-002 Pumpkin	J. Singer	Closed	49.95	49.95
94-43-003 Princess	J. Singer	12/94	59.95	59.95
Ashton-Drake Galleries	**Yolanda's Playtime Babies**			
93-44-001 Todd	Y. Bello	Closed	59.95	59.95
93-44-002 Lindsey	Y. Bello	12/94	59.95	59.95
93-44-003 Shawna	Y. Bello	12/94	59.95	59.95
Ashton-Drake Galleries	**Little Bits**			
93-45-001 Lil Bit of Sunshine	G. Rademann	Closed	39.95	39.95
93-45-002 Lil Bit of Love	G. Rademann	Closed	39.95	39.95
94-45-003 Lil Bit of Tenderness	G. Rademann	Closed	39.95	39.95
94-45-004 Lil Bit of Innocence	G. Rademann	Closed	39.95	39.95
Ashton-Drake Galleries	**Victorian Lace**			
93-46-001 Alicia	C. Layton	Closed	79.95	125-145.

	ARTIST	EDITION	ISSUE	QUOTE
94-46-002 Colleen	C. Layton	12/95	79.95	79.95
94-46-003 Olivia	C. Layton	12/95	79.95	79.95
Ashton-Drake Galleries	**Father's Touch**			
93-47-001 2 A.M. Feeding	L. Di Leo	Closed	99.95	99.95
94-47-002 Come To Daddy	W. Hanson	12/95	99.95	99.95
Ashton-Drake Galleries	**Boys Will Be Boys**			
93-48-001 Fire's Out	J. Singer	Closed	69.95	69.95
93-48-002 Say Ah!	J. Singer	12/94	69.95	69.95
Ashton-Drake Galleries	**Lasting Traditions**			
93-49-001 Something Old	W. Hanson	Closed	69.95	69.95
93-49-002 Finishing Touch	W. Hanson	Closed	69.95	69.95
94-49-003 Mother's Pearls	W. Hanson	Closed	85.00	85.00
94-49-004 Her Traditional Garter	W. Hanson	12/95	85.00	85.00
Ashton-Drake Galleries	**Joys of Summer**			
93-50-001 Tickles	K. Hippensteel	12/94	49.95	49.95
93-50-002 Little Squirt	K. Hippensteel	12/94	49.95	49.95
94-50-003 Yummy	K. Hippensteel	12/94	55.00	55.00
94-50-004 Havin' A Ball	K. Hippensteel	12/94	55.00	55.00
94-50-005 Lil' Scoop	K. Hippensteel	12/94	55.00	55.00
Ashton-Drake Galleries	**A Sense of Discovery**			
93-51-001 Sweetie (Sense of Discovery)	K. Hippensteel	Closed	59.95	59.95
Ashton-Drake Galleries	**I Want Mommy**			
93-52-001 Timmy (Mommy I'm Sleepy)	K. Hippensteel	Closed	59.95	145-195.
93-52-002 Tommy (Mommy I'm Sorry)	K. Hippensteel	12/94	59.95	60-95.00
94-52-003 Up Mommy (Tammy)	K. Hippensteel	12/94	65.00	65.00
Ashton-Drake Galleries	**Lots Of Love**			
93-53-001 Hannah Needs A Hug	T. Menzenbach	12/94	49.95	49.95
93-53-002 Kaitlyn	T. Menzenbach	12/94	49.95	49.95
94-53-003 Nicole	T. Menzenbach	12/95	49.95	49.95
Ashton-Drake Galleries	**Peek A Boo**			
93-54-001 Where's Jamie?	J. Goodyear	Closed	69.95	69.95
Ashton-Drake Galleries	**Look At Me**			
93-55-001 Rose Marie	L. Di Leo	12/94	49.95	49.95
94-55-002 Ann Marie	L. Di Leo	12/94	49.95	49.95
94-55-003 Lisa Marie	L. Di Leo	12/95	55.00	55.00
Ashton-Drake Galleries	**Wishful Thinking**			
93-56-001 Danny (Pet Shop)	M. Tretter	Closed	79.95	79.95
Ashton-Drake Galleries	**Children Of The Sun**			
93-57-001 Little Flower	M. Severino	12/94	69.95	69.95
93-57-002 Desert Star	M. Severino	12/95	69.95	69.95
Ashton-Drake Galleries	**Sooo Big**			
93-58-001 Jimmy	M. Tretter	12/94	59.95	59.95
94-58-002 Kimmy	M. Tretter	12/95	59.95	59.95
Ashton-Drake Galleries	**Two Much To Handle**			
93-59-001 Julie (Flowers For Mommy)	K. Hippensteel	12/94	59.95	59.95
93-59-002 Kevin (Clean Hands)	K. Hippensteel	12/95	59.95	59.95
Ashton-Drake Galleries	**Little Handfuls**			
93-60-001 Ricky	M. Severino	12/94	39.95	39.95
93-60-002 Abby	M. Severino	12/95	39.95	39.95
93-60-003 Josie	M. Severino	12/95	39.95	39.95
Ashton-Drake Galleries	**Yolanda's Heaven Scent Babies**			
93-61-001 Meagan Rose	Y. Bello	12/94	49.95	49.95
93-61-002 Daisy Anne	Y. Bello	12/94	49.95	49.95
93-61-003 Morning Glory	Y. Bello	12/95	49.95	49.95
93-61-004 Sweet Carnation	Y. Bello	12/95	54.95	54.95
93-61-005 Lily	Y. Bello	12/95	54.95	54.95
93-61-006 Cherry Blossom	Y. Bello	12/95	54.95	54.95
Ashton-Drake Galleries	**As Cute As Can Be**			
93-62-001 Sugar Plum	D. Effner	12/94	49.95	49.95
94-62-002 Puppy Love	D. Effner	12/95	49.95	49.95
94-62-003 Angel Face	D. Effner	12/95	49.95	49.95
Ashton-Drake Galleries	**1993 Special Edition Tour**			
93-63-001 Miguel	Y. Bello	Closed	69.95	69.95
93-63-002 Rosa	Y. Bello	Closed	69.95	69.95
Ashton-Drake Galleries	**Tumbling Tots**			
93-64-001 Roly Poly Polly	K. Hippensteel	Closed	69.95	69.95
94-64-002 Handstand Harry	K. Hippensteel	12/95	69.95	69.95
Ashton-Drake Galleries	**Young Love**			
93-65-001 First Kiss	J.W. Smith	Closed	118.00	118.00
93-65-002 Buttercups	J.W. Smith	12/94	Set	Set
Ashton-Drake Galleries	**Gustafson's Fairy Tales**			
93-66-001 Goldilocks and Three Bears	S. Gustafson	Closed	130.00	129.95
Ashton-Drake Galleries	**Barely Yours**			
94-67-001 Cute as a Button	T. Tomescu	12/94	69.95	69.95
94-67-002 Snug as a Bug in a Rug	T. Tomescu	12/95	75.00	75.00
Ashton-Drake Galleries	**Baby Talk**			
94-68-001 All Gone	Good-Krueger	12/95	49.95	49.95
94-68-002 Bye-Bye	Good-Krueger	12/95	49.95	49.95
94-68-003 Night, Night	Good-Krueger	12/95	49.95	49.95
Ashton-Drake Galleries	**Lawton's Nursery Rhymes**			
94-69-001 Little Bo Peep	W. Lawton	12/95	79.95	79.95
94-69-002 Little Miss Muffet	W. Lawton	12/95	79.95	79.95
94-69-003 Mary, Mary	W. Lawton	12/95	85.00	85.00
94-69-004 Mary/Lamb	W. Lawton	12/95	85.00	85.00
Ashton-Drake Galleries	**Rockwell Friend For Life**			
94-70-001 Wrapped Up in Xmas	N. Rockwell	12/95	69.95	69.95
Ashton-Drake Galleries	**In the Good 'Ol Summertime**			
94-71-001 Along the Boardwalk (Ella)	W. Lawton	12/95	69.95	69.95
94-71-002 Meet Me at the Fair	W. Lawton	12/95	69.95	69.95
Ashton-Drake Galleries	**The American Dream**			
94-72-001 Patience	J. Kovacik	12/95	79.95	79.95
94-72-002 Hope	J. Kovacik	12/95	79.95	79.95
Ashton-Drake Galleries	**Season of Dreams**			
94-73-001 Autumn Breeze	G. Rademann	12/95	79.95	79.95

	ARTIST	EDITION	ISSUE	QUOTE
Ashton-Drake Galleries	**Oh Holy Night**			
94-74-001 The Holy Family (Jesus, Mary, Joseph)	Good-Krueger	12/95	129.95	129.95
Ashton-Drake Galleries	**Nursery Newborns**			
94-75-001 It's A Boy	J. Wolf	12/95	79.95	79.95
94-75-002 It's A Girl	J. Wolf	12/95	79.95	79.95
Ashton-Drake Galleries	**Let's Play Mother Goose**			
94-76-001 Cow Jumped Over the Moon	K. Hippensteel	12/95	69.95	69.95
94-76-002 Hickory, Dickory, Dock	K. Hippensteel	12/95	69.95	69.95
Ashton-Drake Galleries	**Happy Thoughts**			
94-77-001 Laughter is the Best Medicine	K. Hippensteel	12/95	59.95	59.95
Ashton-Drake Galleries	**Memories of Yesterday**			
94-78-001 A Friend in Need	M. Attwell	12/95	59.95	59.95
94-78-002 Tomorrow is Another Day	M. Attwell	12/95	59.95	59.95
Ashton-Drake Galleries	**What Little Girls Are Made Of**			
94-79-001 Peaches and Cream	D. Effner	12/95	69.95	69.95
Ashton-Drake Galleries	**Together Forever**			
94-80-001 Kirsten	S. Krey	12/95	59.95	59.95
94-80-002 Courtney	S. Krey	12/95	59.95	59.95
94-80-003 Kim	S. Krey	12/95	59.95	59.95
Ashton-Drake Galleries	**Amish Inspirations**			
94-81-001 Ethan	J. Ibarolle	12/95	69.95	69.95
Ashton-Drake Galleries	**Winter Wonderland**			
94-82-001 Annie	K. Barry-Hippensteel	12/95	59.95	59.95
94-82-002 Bobby	K. Barry-Hippensteel	12/95	59.95	59.95
Ashton-Drake Galleries	**Someone to Watch Over Me**			
94-83-001 Sweet Dreams	K. Barry-Hippensteel	12/95	69.95	69.95
Ashton-Drake Galleries	**Christmas Memories**			
94-84-001 Christopher	Y. Bello	12/95	59.95	59.95
94-84-002 Joshua	Y. Bello	12/95	59.95	59.95
94-84-003 Stephanie	Y. Bello	12/95	59.95	59.95
Ashton-Drake Galleries	**Little Women**			
94-85-001 Jo	W. Lawton	12/95	59.95	59.95
94-85-002 Meg	W. Lawton	12/95	59.95	59.95
94-85-003 Beth	W. Lawton	12/96	59.95	59.95
94-85-004 Amy	W. Lawton	12/96	59.95	59.95
Ashton-Drake Galleries	**The Wonderful Wizard of Oz**			
94-86-001 Dorothy	M. Tretter	12/95	79.95	79.95
94-86-002 Scarecrow	M. Tretter	12/95	79.95	79.95
94-86-003 Tin Man	M. Tretter	12/95	79.95	79.95
94-86-004 The Cowardly Lion	M. Tretter	12/96	79.95	79.95
Ashton-Drake Galleries	**The Legends of Baseball**			
94-87-001 Babe Ruth	T. Tomescu	12/95	79.95	79.95
Ashton-Drake Galleries	**Treasured Togetherness**			
94-88-001 Tender Touch	M. Tretter	12/95	99.95	99.95
94-88-002 Touch of Love	M. Tretter	12/95	99.95	99.95
Ashton-Drake Galleries	**Garden of Inspirations**			
94-89-001 Gathering Violets	B. Hanson	12/95	69.95	69.95
94-89-002 Daisy Chain	B. Hanson	12/95	69.95	69.95
Ashton-Drake Galleries	**Victorian Nursery Heirloom**			
94-90-001 Victorian Lullaby	C. McClure	12/95	79.95	79.95
Ashton-Drake Galleries	**Pretty in Pastels**			
94-91-001 Precious in Pink	J. Goodyear	12/95	79.95	79.95
Ashton-Drake Galleries	**Rainbow of Love**			
94-92-001 Blue Sky	Y. Bello	12/95	59.95	59.95
94-92-002 Yellow Sunshine	Y. Bello	12/95	59.95	59.95
94-92-003 Green Earth	Y. Bello	12/95	59.95	59.95
94-92-004 Pink Flower	Y. Bello	12/96	59.95	59.95
94-92-005 Purple Mountain	Y. Bello	12/96	59.95	59.95
94-92-006 Orange Sunset	Y. Bello	12/96	59.95	59.95
Ashton-Drake Galleries	**Children of Christmas**			
94-93-001 The Little Drummer Boy	M. Sirko	12/95	79.95	79.95
94-93-002 My Little Ballerina	K. Barry-Hippensteel	12/95	59.95	59.95
Attic Babies	**Attic Babies' Retired Dolls**			
92-01-001 Americana Raggedy Santa 1st edition, SNL	M. Maschino	Retrd.	85.95	150.00
92-01-002 Americana Raggedy Santa 2nd edition, SNL	M. Maschino	Retrd.	89.95	89.95
89-01-003 Annie Fannie	M. Maschino	Retrd.	43.95	112.00
87-01-004 Bessie Jo	M. Maschino	Retrd.	31.95	98.00
87-01-005 Beth Sue	M. Maschino	Retrd.	27.95	75.00
88-01-006 Bunnifer	M. Maschino	Retrd.	39.95	82.00
88-01-007 Buttons	M. Maschino	Retrd.	27.95	27.95
92-01-008 Candy Applebee	M. Maschino	12/94	15.95	15.95
92-01-009 Christopher Columbus SNL	M. Maschino	12/94	79.95	79.95
89-01-010 Cotton Pickin' Ninny	M. Maschino	Retrd.	47.95	100.00
87-01-011 Country Clyde	M. Maschino	Retrd.	27.95	27.95
87-01-012 Dirty Harry	M. Maschino	Retrd.	27.95	102.00
90-01-013 Duckie Dinkle	M. Maschino	Retrd.	95.95	95.95
88-01-014 Fester Chester	M. Maschino	12/94	39.95	39.95
90-01-015 Frannie Farkle	M. Maschino	Retrd.	129.95	129.95
90-01-016 Frizzy Lizzy	M. Maschino	Retrd.	95.95	161.00
88-01-017 Hannah Lou	M. Maschino	12/94	39.95	39.95
90-01-018 Happy Huck	M. Maschino	Retrd.	47.95	102.00
93-01-019 Happy Pappy Claus SNL	M. Maschino	Retrd.	73.95	73.95
87-01-020 Harold	M. Maschino	Retrd.	27.95	80.00
89-01-021 Heavenly Heather	M. Maschino	Retrd.	59.95	100.00
89-01-022 Heffy Cheffy	M. Maschino	12/94	75.95	75.95
93-01-023 Ity Bity Santa	M. Maschino	Retrd.	5.95	5.95
90-01-024 Ivan Ivie	M. Maschino	Retrd.	129.95	230.00
87-01-025 Jacob	M. Maschino	Retrd.	27.95	100.00
93-01-026 Jammy Mammy Claus SNL	M. Maschino	Retrd.	67.95	67.95
87-01-027 Jenny Lou	M. Maschino	Retrd.	35.95	35.95
89-01-028 Jolly Jim	M. Maschino	Retrd.	31.95	31.95
90-01-029 Lampsie Divie Ivie	M. Maschino	Retrd.	129.95	230.00
88-01-030 Lazy Daisy	M. Maschino	Retrd.	39.95	39.95
88-01-031 Lazy Liza Jane	M. Maschino	Retrd.	47.95	47.95
88-01-032 Little Dove	M. Maschino	Retrd.	39.95	39.95
87-01-033 Maggie Mae	M. Maschino	Retrd.	27.95	27.95

		ARTIST	EDITION	ISSUE	QUOTE
91-01-034	Maizie Mae	M. Maschino	12/94	27.95	27.95
91-01-035	Mandi Mae	M. Maschino	12/94	27.95	27.95
91-01-036	Memsie Mae	M. Maschino	12/94	27.95	27.95
93-01-037	Merry Ole Farley Fagan Dooberry, SNL	M. Maschino	12/94	131.95	131.95
87-01-038	Miss Pitty Pat	M. Maschino	Retrd.	27.95	100.00
88-01-039	Molly Bea	M. Maschino	Retrd.	39.95	82.00
88-01-040	Moosey Matilda	M. Maschino	Retrd.	39.95	80.00
93-01-041	Mr. Kno Mo Sno, SNL	M. Maschino	Retrd.	51.95	51.95
91-01-042	Mr. Raggedy Claus, SNL	M. Maschino	Retrd.	69.95	120.00
91-01-043	Mrs. Raggedy Claus, SNL	M. Maschino	Retrd.	69.95	120.00
89-01-044	Ms. Waddles	M. Maschino	Retrd.	47.95	47.95
87-01-045	Muslin Bunny	M. Maschino	Retrd.	7.95	7.95
87-01-046	Muslin Teddy	M. Maschino	Retrd.	7.95	7.95
94-01-047	Nattie Fae Tucker, SNL	M. Maschino	Retrd.	64.95	64.95
88-01-048	Naughty Nellie	M. Maschino	Retrd.	31.95	85.00
93-01-049	Old St. Knickerbocker, SNL	M. Maschino	Retrd.	79.95	79.95
92-01-050	Old St. Nick, SNL	M. Maschino	Retrd.	95.95	130.00
89-01-051	Old Tyme Santy	M. Maschino	Retrd.	79.95	79.95
90-01-052	Phylbert Farkle	M. Maschino	Retrd.	129.95	225.00
91-01-053	Pippy Pat	M. Maschino	12/94	47.95	47.95
89-01-054	Prissy Missy	M. Maschino	Retrd.	31.95	31.95
92-01-055	Pumpkin Patty, SNL	M. Maschino	Retrd.	79.95	79.95
87-01-056	Rachel	M. Maschino	Retrd.	29.95	29.95
87-01-057	Raggedy Kitty	M. Maschino	Retrd.	29.95	29.95
90-01-058	Raggedy Ole Chris Cringle 1st edition	M. Maschino	Retrd.	189.95	262.00
90-01-059	Raggedy Ole Chris Cringle 2nd edition	M. Maschino	Retrd.	189.95	189.95
88-01-060	Raggedy Sam	M. Maschino	Retrd.	55.95	115.00
87-01-061	Raggedy Santy 1st edtion	M. Maschino	Retrd.	75.95	200.00
88-01-062	Raggedy Santy 2nd edtion	M. Maschino	Retrd.	89.95	89.95
89-01-063	Rammy Sammy	M. Maschino	Retrd.	43.95	43.95
87-01-064	Rose Ann	M. Maschino	Retrd.	39.95	39.95
88-01-065	Rotten Wilber	M. Maschino	Retrd.	35.95	140.00
88-01-066	Rufus	M. Maschino	Retrd.	35.95	82.00
90-01-067	Salie Ollie Otis	M. Maschino	Retrd.	129.95	129.95
87-01-068	Sally Francis	M. Maschino	Retrd.	35.95	62.00
87-01-069	Sara	M. Maschino	Retrd.	39.95	86.00
92-01-070	Scary Larry Scarecrow, SNL	M. Maschino	Retrd.	79.95	79.95
88-01-071	Silly Willie	M. Maschino	Retrd.	39.95	76.00
89-01-072	Skitty Kitty	M. Maschino	Retrd.	43.95	140.00
88-01-073	Spring Santy	M. Maschino	Retrd.	47.95	47.95
88-01-074	Sweet William	M. Maschino	Retrd.	35.95	152.00
92-01-075	Teeny Weeny Angel	M. Maschino	12/94	9.95	9.95
87-01-076	Toddy Sue	M. Maschino	Retrd.	27.95	87.00
88-01-077	Wacky Jackie	M. Maschino	Retrd.	39.95	39.95
91-01-078	Winkie Binkie	M. Maschino	Retrd.	53.95	53.95
92-01-079	Witchy Wanda, SNL	M. Maschino	Retrd.	79.95	79.95
89-01-080	Wood Doll-small	M. Maschino	Retrd.	23.95	23.95
89-01-081	Wood Doll-medium	M. Maschino	Retrd.	31.95	31.95
90-01-082	Yankee Doodle Debbie	M. Maschino	Retrd.	95.95	150.00
90-01-083	Zitty Zelda, SNL	M. Maschino	Retrd.	89.95	176.00
Attic Babies		**Baggie Collection**			
91-02-001	Country Baggie Rabbit	M. Maschino	Retrd.	19.95	19.95
91-02-002	Christmas Baggie Rabbit	M. Maschino	Retrd.	19.95	19.95
91-02-003	Americana Baggie Rabbit	M. Maschino	Retrd.	19.95	19.95
91-02-004	Christmas Baggie Santa	M. Maschino	Retrd.	19.95	19.95
91-02-005	Americana Baggie Santa	M. Maschino	Retrd.	19.95	19.95
91-02-006	Country Baggie Girl	M. Maschino	Retrd.	19.95	19.95
91-02-007	Christmas Baggie Girl	M. Maschino	Retrd.	19.95	19.95
91-02-008	Americana Baggie Girl	M. Maschino	Retrd.	19.95	19.95
91-02-009	Country Baggie Bear	M. Maschino	Retrd.	19.95	19.95
91-02-010	Christmas Baggie Bear	M. Maschino	Retrd.	19.95	19.95
91-02-011	Americana Baggie Bear	M. Maschino	Retrd.	19.95	19.95
Attic Babies		**Valentine Collection**			
93-03-001	Valentine Bear-Girl	M. Maschino	Retrd.	39.95	39.95
93-03-002	Valentine Bear-Boy	M. Maschino	Retrd.	39.95	39.95
94-03-003	Herwin Heaps-O Hugs	M. Maschino	Retrd.	39.95	39.95
94-03-004	Lottie Lots-A-Love	M. Maschino	Retrd.	39.95	39.95
Attic Babies		**Tour Babies**			
93-04-083	Tour Baby 1993	M. Maschino	Retrd.	19.95	19.95
94-04-084	Tour Baby 1994	M. Maschino	12/94	24.95	24.95
Attic Babies		**Attic Babies' Collector Club**			
92-05-001	Burtie Buzbee, SNL	M. Maschino	Retrd.	40.00	40.00
93-05-002	Izzie B. Ruebottom, SNL	M. Maschino	Retrd.	35.00	35.00
94-05-003	Sunflower Flossie, SNL	M. Maschino	12/94	42.00	42.00
The Collectables Inc.		**The Collectibles Inc. Dolls**			
86-01-001	Tatiana	P. Parkins	Closed	270.00	675.00
87-01-002	Tasha	P. Parkins	Closed	290.00	1400.00
87-01-003	Storytime By Sarah Jane	P. Parkins	Closed	330.00	475-525.
89-01-004	Michelle	P. Parkins	250	270.00	400-450.
89-01-005	Welcome Home	D. Effner	1000	330.00	475-675.
90-01-006	Lizbeth Ann	D. Effner	1000	420.00	420.00
90-01-007	Bassinet Baby	P. Parkins	2000	130.00	375-425.
90-01-008	Danielle	P. Parkins	1000	400.00	475.00
90-01-009	In Your Easter Bonnet	P. Parkins	1000	350.00	350.00
91-01-010	Yvette	P. Parkins	300	580.00	580.00
91-01-011	Lauren	P. Parkins	S/O	490.00	490.00
91-01-012	Bethany	P. Parkins	Closed	450.00	450.00
91-01-013	Natasha	P. Parkins	Closed	510.00	510.00
91-01-014	Adrianna	P. Parkins	Closed	1350.00	1350.00
91-01-015	Kelsie	P. Parkins	500	320.00	320.00
92-01-016	Karlie	P. Parkins	500	380.00	380.00
92-01-017	Marissa	P. Parkins	300	350.00	350.00
92-01-018	Shelley	P. Parkins	300	450.00	450.00
92-01-019	Angel on My Shoulder (Lillianne w/CeCe)	P. Parkins	500	530.00	530.00
92-01-020	Molly	P. Parkins	450	350.00	350.00
92-01-021	Matia	P. Parkins	250	190.00	190.00
92-01-022	Marty	P. Parkins	250	190.00	190.00
92-01-023	Missy	P. Parkins	Open	59.00	59.00
93-01-024	Haley	P. Parkins	500	330.00	330.00
93-01-025	Maggie	P. Parkins	500	330.00	330.00
93-01-026	Amber	P. Parkins	500	330.00	330.00
93-01-027	Little Dumpling (Black)	P. Parkins	500	190.00	190.00
93-01-028	Little Dumpling (White)	P. Parkins	500	190.00	190.00
94-01-029	Madison Sailor	P. Parkins	250	370.00	370.00
94-01-030	Madison	P. Parkins	250	350.00	350.00
94-01-031	Morgan	P. Parkins	250	390.00	390.00
94-01-032	Morgan in Red	P. Parkins	250	390.00	390.00
94-01-033	Amber Hispanic	P. Parkins	500	340.00	340.00
94-01-034	Afternoon Delight	P. Parkins	500	410.00	410.00
94-01-035	Earth Angel	P. Parkins	500	195.00	195.00
94-01-036	Sugar Plum Fairy	P. Parkins	500	250.00	250.00
The Collectables Inc.		**Mother's Little Treasures**			
85-02-001	1st Edition	D. Effner	Closed	380.00	700.00
90-02-002	2nd Edition	D. Effner	Closed	440.00	475-595.
The Collectables Inc.		**Yesterday's Child**			
82-03-001	Jason And Jessica	D. Effner	Closed	150.00	300.00
82-03-002	Cleo	D. Effner	Closed	180.00	250.00
82-03-003	Columbine	D. Effner	Closed	180.00	250.00
83-03-004	Chad And Charity	D. Effner	Closed	190.00	190.00
83-03-005	Noel	D. Effner	Closed	190.00	240.00
84-03-006	Kevin And Karissa	D. Effner	Closed	190.00	250-300.
84-03-007	Rebecca	D. Effner	Closed	250.00	250-300.
86-03-008	Todd And Tiffany	D. Effner	Closed	220.00	250.00
86-03-009	Ashley	P. Parkins	Closed	220.00	275.00
The Collectables Inc.		**Cherished Memories**			
86-04-001	Amy and Andrew	P. Parkins	Closed	220.00	325.00
88-04-002	Jennifer	P. Parkins	Closed	380.00	500-600.
88-04-003	Brittany	P. Parkins	Closed	240.00	300.00
88-04-004	Heather	P. Parkins	Closed	280.00	300-350.
88-04-005	Leigh Ann And Leland	P. Parkins	Closed	250.00	250-300.
88-04-006	Tea Time	D. Effner	Closed	380.00	450.00
90-04-007	Cassandra	P. Parkins	Closed	500.00	550.00
89-04-008	Generations	P. Parkins	Closed	480.00	500.00
90-04-009	Twinkles	P. Parkins	Closed	170.00	275.00
The Collectables Inc.		**Fairy**			
88-05-001	Tabatha	P. Parkins	1500	370.00	400-450.
The Collectables Inc.		**Butterfly Babies**			
89-06-001	Belinda	P. Parkins	Closed	270.00	375.00
90-06-002	Willow	P. Parkins	Closed	240.00	375.00
92-06-003	Laticia	P. Parkins	Closed	320.00	320.00
The Collectables Inc.		**Enchanted Children**			
90-07-001	Kristin	P. Parkins	S/O	550.00	650.00
90-07-002	Tiffy	P. Parkins	S/O	370.00	500.00
90-07-003	Kara	P. Parkins	Closed	550.00	550.00
90-07-004	Katlin	P. Parkins	Closed	550.00	550.00
The Collectables Inc.		**Collector's Club Doll**			
91-08-001	Mandy	P. Parkins	Closed	360.00	360.00
92-08-002	Kallie	P. Parkins	Closed	410.00	410.00
93-08-003	Mommy and Me	P. Parkins	Closed	810.00	810.00
94-08-004	Krystal	P. Parkins	Yr.Iss.	380.00	380.00
The Collectables Inc.		**Angel Series**			
92-09-001	Angel on My Shoulder	P. Parkins	Closed	530.00	530.00
93-09-002	My Guardian Angel	P. Parkins	500	590.00	590.00
94-09-003	Guarding the Way	P. Parkins	500	950.00	950.00
Department 56		**Heritage Village Doll Collection**			
87-01-001	Christmas Carol Dolls1000-6 4/set (Tiny Tim, Bob Crachet, Mrs. Crachet, Scrooge)	Department 56	250	1500.00	1500.00
87-01-002	Christmas Carol Dolls 5907-2 4/set (Tiny Tim, Bob Crachet, Mrs. Crachet, Scrooge)	Department 56	Open	250.00	250.00
88-01-003	Christmas Carol Dolls1001-4 4/set (Tiny Tim, Bob Crachet, Mrs. Crachet, Scrooge)	Department 56	350	1600.00	1600.00
88-01-004	Mr. & Mrs. Fezziwig 5594-8-Set of 2	Department 56	Open	172.00	172.00
Department 56		**Snowbabies Dolls**			
88-02-001	Department 56	Department 56	Closed	200.00	660-695.
Dolls by Jerri		**Dolls by Jerri**			
84-01-001	Clara	J. McCloud	1,000	320.00	12-1500.
84-01-002	Emily	J. McCloud	1,000	330.00	1200.00
85-01-003	Scotty	J. McCloud	1,000	340.00	12-2000.
85-01-004	Uncle Joe	J. McCloud	1,000	160.00	250-300.
85-01-005	Miss Nanny	J. McCloud	1,000	160.00	250-300.
85-01-006	Bride	J. McCloud	1,000	350.00	350-400.
86-01-007	David-2 Years Old	J. McCloud	1,000	330.00	550.00
86-01-008	Princess and the Unicorn	J. McCloud	1,000	370.00	370.00
86-01-009	Charlotte	J. McCloud	1,000	330.00	450-500.
86-01-010	Cane	J. McCloud	1,000	350.00	1200.00
86-01-011	Clown-David 3 Yrs. Old	J. McCloud	1,000	340.00	450.00
86-01-012	Tammy	J. McCloud	1,000	350.00	900.00
86-01-013	Samantha	J. McCloud	1,000	350.00	500.00
86-01-014	Elizabeth	J. McCloud	1,000	340.00	340.00
86-01-015	Audrey	J. McCloud	300	550.00	550.00
86-01-016	Yvonne	J. McCloud	300	500.00	500.00
86-01-017	Annabelle	J. McCloud	300	600.00	600.00
86-01-018	Ashley	J. McCloud	1,000	350.00	450-500.
86-01-019	Allison	J. McCloud	1,000	350.00	450-500.
86-01-020	Nobody	J. McCloud	1,000	350.00	550.00
86-01-021	Somebody	J. McCloud	1,000	350.00	550.00
86-01-022	Danielle	J. McCloud	1,000	350.00	500.00
86-01-023	Helenjean	J. McCloud	1,000	350.00	500-550.
86-01-024	David-Magician	J. McCloud	1,000	350.00	350-500.
86-01-025	Amber	J. McCloud	1,000	350.00	875.00
86-01-026	Joy	J. McCloud	1,000	350.00	350.00
86-01-027	Mary Beth	J. McCloud	1,000	350.00	350.00
86-01-028	Jacqueline	J. McCloud	300	500.00	500.00
86-01-029	Lucianna	J. McCloud	300	500.00	500.00
86-01-030	Bridgette	J. McCloud	300	500.00	500.00
86-01-031	The Fool	J. McCloud	1,000	350.00	350.00
86-01-032	Alfalfa	J. McCloud	1,000	350.00	350.00
85-01-033	Candy	J. McCloud	1,000	340.00	2000.00
82-01-034	Baby David	J. McCloud	538	290.00	2000.00
88-01-035	Holly	J. McCloud	1,000	370.00	750-825.
89-01-036	Laura Lee	J. McCloud	1,000	370.00	575.00
XX-01-037	Boy	J. McCloud	1,000	350.00	425.00
XX-01-038	Uncle Remus	J. McCloud	500	290.00	400-450.
XX-01-039	Gina	J. McCloud	1,000	350.00	475.00
XX-01-040	Laura	J. McCloud	1,000	350.00	425-500.
89-01-041	Goose Girl, Guild	J. McCloud	Closed	300.00	700-875.
XX-01-042	Little Bo Peep	J. McCloud	1,000	340.00	395-450.
XX-01-043	Little Miss Muffet	J. McCloud	1,000	340.00	395-450.
XX-01-044	Megan	J. McCloud	750	420.00	550.00
XX-01-045	Denise	J. McCloud	1,000	380.00	550.00
XX-01-046	Meredith	J. McCloud	750	430.00	600.00
XX-01-047	Goldilocks	J. McCloud	1,000	370.00	450-600.
XX-01-048	Jamie	J. McCloud	800	380.00	450.00

		ARTIST	EDITION	ISSUE	QUOTE
Dynasty Doll	**Annual**				
89-01-001	Amber	Unknown	Retrd.	90.00	90.00
90-01-002	Marcella	Unknown	Retrd.	90.00	90.00
91-01-003	Butterfly Princess	Unknown	Retrd.	110.00	110.00
93-01-004	Annual Bride	H. Tertsakian	Retrd.	190.00	190.00
93-01-005	Ariel	Unknown	Retrd.	120.00	120.00
94-01-006	Annual Bride	H. Tertsakian	Yr.Iss.	200.00	200.00
94-01-007	Janie '94	Unknown	Yr.Iss.	120.00	120.00
Dynasty Doll	**Christmas**				
87-02-001	Merrie	Unknown	Retrd.	60.00	60.00
88-02-002	Noel	Unknown	Retrd.	80.00	80.00
90-02-003	Faith	Unknown	Retrd.	110.00	110.00
91-02-004	Joy	Unknown	Retrd.	125.00	125.00
93-02-005	Genevieve	Unknown	Retrd.	164.00	164.00
94-02-006	Gloria '94	Unknown	5,000	170.00	170.00
Dynasty Doll	**Ballerina Series**				
91-03-001	Masha-Nutcracker	Lee Po Nan	Retrd.	190.00	190.00
93-03-002	Tina Ballerina	K. Henderson	Retrd.	175.00	175.00
Dynasty Doll	**Anna Collection**				
92-04-001	Communion Girl	G. Hoyt	Retrd.	125.00	125.00
Dynasty Doll	**Dynasty Collection**				
91-05-001	Lana	Unknown	Open	85.00	85.00
93-05-002	Tami	M. Cohen	7,500	190.00	190.00
93-05-003	Tory	M. Cohen	7,500	190.00	190.00
93-05-004	Juliet	G. Tepper	Retrd.	160.00	160.00
93-05-005	Heather	G. Tepper	Retrd.	160.00	160.00
93-05-006	Antoinette	H. Tertsakian	5,000	190.00	190.00
93-05-007	Catherine	H. Tertsakian	5,000	190.00	190.00
93-05-008	Katy	M. Cohen	Retrd.	135.00	135.00
93-05-009	Nicole	Unknown	Retrd.	135.00	135.00
93-05-010	Carley	G. Hoyt	Open	120.00	120.00
93-05-011	Megan	Unknown	3,500	150.00	150.00
93-05-012	Julie	K. Henderson	Retrd.	175.00	175.00
93-05-013	Angela	Unknown	1,500	195.00	195.00
93-05-014	Shannon	Unknown	1,500	195.00	195.00
93-05-015	Amanda	Unknown	3,000	195.00	195.00
93-05-016	Kadyrose	M. Cohen	Open	145.00	145.00
93-05-017	Patricia	Unknown	Open	160.00	160.00
94-05-018	Christina	Unknown	3,500	200.00	200.00
94-05-019	Kelsey	S. Kelsey	1,500	225.00	225.00
94-05-020	Rebecca	Unknown	1,500	175.00	175.00
94-05-021	Amy	Unknown	1,500	175.00	175.00
94-05-022	Amelia	G. Hoyt	1,500	170.00	170.00
94-05-023	Laurelyn	Unknown	2,000	180.00	180.00
94-05-024	Gabrielle	S. Kelsey	1,500	180.00	180.00
Dynasty Doll	**Indian Collection**				
92-06-001	Pocahontas	Unknown	Retrd.	95.00	105.00
93-06-002	Sitting Cloud	Unknown	Open	100.00	100.00
94-06-003	Chief Eagle's Wing	Unknown	3,500	165.00	165.00
94-06-004	Spring Winds and Little Wolf	Unknown	3,500	120.00	120.00
Dynasty Doll	**Uta Brauser's City Kids**				
93-07-001	Jamaal	U. Brauser	5,000	220.00	220.00
93-07-002	Kadeem	U. Brauser	3,500	195.00	195.00
93-07-003	Mirambi	U. Brauser	5,000	190.00	190.00
93-07-004	Rickia	U. Brauser	3,500	170.00	170.00
93-07-005	Tisha	U. Brauser	3,500	170.00	170.00
Dynasty Doll	**Victorians**				
94-08-001	Danielle	H. Tertsakian	2,500	195.00	195.00
94-08-002	Beverly	H. Tertsakian	1,500	195.00	195.00
94-08-003	Margaret	H. Tertsakian	1,500	195.00	195.00
94-08-004	Winifred	H. Tertsakian	1,500	195.00	195.00
Dynasty Doll	**Clowns**				
94-09-001	Reginald	R. Lee	5,000	95.00	95.00
94-09-002	Munchie	R. Lee	5,000	95.00	95.00
94-09-003	Boo-Boo	R. Lee	5,000	95.00	95.00
94-09-004	Prissy	R. Lee	5,000	95.00	95.00
94-09-005	Dandy	R. Lee	5,000	95.00	95.00
Elke's Originals, Ltd.	**Elke Hutchens**				
89-01-001	Annabelle	E. Hutchens	250	575.00	1500.00
90-01-002	Aubra	E. Hutchens	250	575.00	900.00
90-01-003	Aurora	E. Hutchens	250	595.00	900.00
91-01-004	Alicia	E. Hutchens	250	595.00	600.00
91-01-005	Braelyn	E. Hutchens	400	595.00	11-1500.
91-01-006	Bellinda	E. Hutchens	400	595.00	750-800.
91-01-007	Brianna	E. Hutchens	400	595.00	1000.00
92-01-008	Bethany	E. Hutchens	400	595.00	700-800.
92-01-009	Cecilia	E. Hutchens	435	635.00	750.00
92-01-010	Cherie	E. Hutchens	435	635.00	900.00
92-01-011	Charles	E. Hutchens	435	635.00	500-600.
92-01-012	Clarissa	E. Hutchens	435	635.00	800-900.
93-01-013	Daphne	E. Hutchens	435	675.00	600.00
93-01-014	Deidre	E. Hutchens	435	675.00	600.00
93-01-015	Desir,e	E. Hutchens	435	675.00	600.00
90-01-016	Kricket	E. Hutchens	500	575.00	500.00
92-01-017	Laurakaye	E. Hutchens	435	550.00	550.00
90-01-018	Little Liebchen	E. Hutchens	250	475.00	1000.00
90-01-019	Victoria	E. Hutchens	500	645.00	645.00
Enesco Corporation	**Precious Moments Dolls**				
81-01-001	Mikey, 18"- E-6214B	S. Butcher	Suspd.	150.00	225.00
81-01-002	Debbie, 18"- E-6214G	S. Butcher	Suspd.	150.00	235.00
82-01-003	Cubby, 18"- E-7267B	S. Butcher	5,000	200.00	540.00
82-01-004	Tammy, 18"- E-7267G	S. Butcher	5,000	300.00	540.00
83-01-005	Katie Lynne, 16"- E-0539	S. Butcher	Suspd.	165.00	175-185.
84-01-006	Mother Sew Dear, 18"- E-2850	S. Butcher	Retrd.	350.00	350-375.
84-01-007	Kristy, 12"- E-2851	S. Butcher	Suspd.	150.00	185.00
84-01-008	Timmy, 12"- E-5397	S. Butcher	Open	125.00	150-175.
85-01-009	Aaron, 12"- 12424	S. Butcher	Suspd.	135.00	150.00
85-01-010	Bethany, 12"- 12432	S. Butcher	Suspd.	135.00	150.00
85-01-011	P.D., 7"- 12475	S. Butcher	Suspd.	50.00	54-75.00
85-01-012	Trish, 7" - 12483	S. Butcher	Suspd.	50.00	54.00
86-01-013	Bong Bong, 13" - 100455	S. Butcher	12,000	150.00	198-250.
86-01-014	Candy, 13" - 100463	S. Butcher	12,000	150.00	350.00
86-01-015	Connie, 12" - 102253	S. Butcher	7,500	160.00	240.00
87-01-016	Angie, The Angel of Mercy - 12491	S. Butcher	12,500	160.00	250.00
90-01-017	The Voice of Spring - 408786	S. Butcher	2-Yr.	150.00	150.00
90-01-018	Summer's Joy - 408794	S. Butcher	2-Yr.	150.00	150.00
90-01-019	Autumn's Praise - 408808	S. Butcher	2-Yr.	150.00	150.00
90-01-020	Winter's Song - 408816	S. Butcher	2-Yr.	150.00	150.00
91-01-021	You Have Touched So Many Hearts-427527	S. Butcher	2-Yr.	90.00	90.00
91-01-022	May You Have An Old Fashioned Christmas - 417785	S. Butcher	2-Yr.	150.00	150.00
91-01-023	The Eyes Of The Lord Are Upon You (Boy Action Muscial) - 429570	S. Butcher	Suspd.	65.00	65.00
91-01-024	The Eyes Of The Lord Are Upon You (Girl Action Musical) - 429589	S. Butcher	Suspd.	65.00	65.00
Enesco Corporation	**Precious Moments-Jack-In-The-Boxes**				
91-02-001	You Have Touched So Many Hearts-422282	S. Butcher	2-Yr.	175.00	175.00
91-02-002	May You Have An Old Fashioned Christmas-417777	S. Butcher	2-Yr.	200.00	200.00
Enesco Corporation	**Jack-In-The-Boxes-4 Seasons**				
90-03-001	Voice of Spring-408735	S. Butcher	2-Yr.	200.00	200.00
90-03-002	Summer's Joy-408743	S. Butcher	2-Yr.	200.00	200.00
90-03-003	Autumn's Praise-408751	S. Butcher	2-Yr.	200.00	200.00
90-03-004	Winter's Song-408778	S. Butcher	2-Yr.	200.00	200.00
Enesco Corporation	**Maud Humphrey Bogart Porcelain Dolls**				
91-04-001	Sarah H5617	M. Humphrey	Open	37.00	37.00
91-04-002	Susanna H5648	M. Humphrey	Open	37.00	37.00
91-04-003	My First Party H5686	M. Humphrey	Open	135.00	135.00
91-04-004	Playing Bride H5618	M. Humphrey	Open	135.00	135.00
Fitz and Floyd, Inc.	**Bloomers Floppy Folks™**				
92-01-001	Peony	M. Collins	Open	50.00	50.00
92-01-002	Bloomer	M. Collins	Open	50.00	50.00
Fitz and Floyd, Inc.	**Halloween Hoedown Floppy Folks ™**				
92-02-002	Wanda Witch	R. Havins	Open	50.00	50.00
92-02-002	Hazel Witch	R. Havins	Open	50.00	50.00
92-02-003	Pumpkin Patch	R. Havins	Open	50.00	50.00
92-02-004	Halloween Kat	R. Havins	Open	50.00	50.00
92-02-005	Drac-in-the-Box	R. Havins	Retrd.	60.00	60.00
Fitz and Floyd, Inc.	**Wonderland Floppy Folks™**				
93-03-001	The Mad Hatter	R. Havins	3,000	60.00	60.00
93-03-002	The Cheshire Cat	R. Havins	3,000	60.00	60.00
93-03-003	The White Rabbit	R. Havins	3,000	60.00	60.00
Fitz and Floyd, Inc.	**Christmas Floppy Folks™**				
93-04-001	Santa Claus	V. Balcou	Open	65.00	65.00
93-04-002	Santa's Reindeer	V. Balcou	Open	65.00	65.00
93-04-003	Santa's Helper	V. Balcou	Open	65.00	65.00
Fitz and Floyd, Inc.	**Dinosaur Floppy Folks™**				
94-05-001	Mama Saurus	R. Havins	Open	55.00	55.00
94-05-002	Papa Saurus	R. Havins	Open	55.00	55.00
94-05-003	Junior Saurus	R. Havins	Open	55.00	55.00
Ganz	**Little Cheesers/Cheeserville Picnic Collection**				
92-01-001	Sweet Cicely Musical Doll In Basket	G.D.A. Group	Open	85.00	85.00
Ganz	**Cowtown**				
94-02-001	Buffalo Bull Cody	C. Thammavongsa	Open	20.00	20.00
94-02-002	Old MooDonald	C. Thammavongsa	Open	20.00	20.00
94-02-003	Santa Cows	C. Thammavongsa	Open	25.00	25.00
Georgetown Collection, Inc.	**Nursery Babies**				
90-01-001	Baby Bunting	T. DeHetre	Closed	118.20	150.00
90-01-002	Patty Cake	T. DeHetre	Closed	118.20	118.20
91-01-003	Diddle, Diddle	T. DeHetre	Closed	118.20	118.20
91-01-004	Little Girl	T. DeHetre	100-day	118.20	118.20
91-01-005	This Little Piggy	T. DeHetre	100-day	118.20	118.20
91-01-006	Rock-A-Bye Baby	T. DeHetre	100-day	118.20	118.20
Georgetown Collection, Inc.	**Baby Kisses**				
92-02-001	Michelle	T. DeHetre	100-day	118.60	118.60
Georgetown Collection, Inc.	**Let's Play**				
92-03-001	Peek-A-Boo Beckie	T. DeHetre	100-day	118.60	118.60
92-03-002	Eentsy Weentsy Willie	T. DeHetre	100-day	118.60	118.60
Georgetown Collection, Inc.	**Sugar & Spice**				
91-04-001	Little Sweetheart	L. Mason	100-day	118.25	118.25
91-04-002	Red Hot Pepper	L. Mason	100-day	118.25	118.25
92-04-003	Little Sunshine	L. Mason	100-day	141.10	141.10
Georgetown Collection, Inc.	**American Diary Dolls**				
90-05-001	Jennie Cooper	L. Mason	100-day	129.25	129.25
91-05-002	Bridget Quinn	L. Mason	100-day	129.25	129.25
91-05-003	Christina Merovina	L. Mason	100-day	129.25	129.25
91-05-004	Many Stars	L. Mason	100-day	129.25	129.25
92-05-005	Rachel Williams	L. Mason	100-day	129.25	129.25
92-05-006	Tulu	L. Mason	100-day	129.25	129.25
93-05-007	Sarah Turner	L. Mason	100-day	130.00	130.00
Georgetown Collection, Inc.	**Little Loves**				
90-06-001	Laura	B. Deval	Closed	139.20	139.20
89-06-002	Katie	B. Deval	Closed	139.20	139.20
88-06-003	Emma	B. Deval	Closed	139.20	139.20
89-06-004	Megan	B. Deval	Closed	138.00	160.00
Georgetown Collection, Inc.	**Small Wonders**				
90-07-001	Corey	B. Deval	100-day	97.60	97.60
91-07-002	Abbey	B. Deval	100-day	97.60	97.60
92-07-003	Sarah	B. Deval	100-day	97.60	97.60
Georgetown Collection, Inc.	**Faerie Princess**				
89-08-001	Faerie Princess	B. Deval	Closed	248.00	248.00
Georgetown Collection, Inc.	**Miss Ashley**				
89-09-001	Miss Ashley	P. Thompson	Closed	228.00	228.00
Georgetown Collection, Inc.	**Tansie**				
88-10-001	Tansie	P. Coffer	Closed	81.00	81.00
Georgetown Collection, Inc.	**Kindergarten Kids**				
92-11-001	Nikki	V. Walker	100-day	129.60	129.60
Georgetown Collection, Inc.	**Portraits of Perfection**				
93-12-001	Peaches & Cream	A. Timmerman	100-day	149.60	149.60
93-12-002	Sweet Strawberry	A. Timmerman	100-day	149.60	149.60
93-12-003	Apple Dumpling	A. Timmerman	100-day	149.60	149.60

		ARTIST	EDITION	ISSUE	QUOTE
94-12-004	Blackberry Blossom	A. Timmerman	100-day	149.60	149.60
Georgetown Collection, Inc.		**Hearts in Song**			
92-13-001	Grace	J. Galperin	100-day	149.60	149.60
93-13-001	Michael	J. Galperin	100-day	150.00	150.00
Georgetown Collection, Inc.		**Children of the Great Spirit**			
93-14-001	Buffalo Child	C. Theroux	100-day	140.00	140.00
93-14-002	Winter Baby	C. Theroux	100-day	160.00	160.00
94-14-003	Golden Flower	C. Theroux	100-day	130.00	130.00
Georgetown Collection, Inc.		**Russian Fairy Tales Dolls**			
93-15-001	Vasilisa	B. Deval	100-day	190.00	190.00
Georgetown Collection, Inc.		**Linda's Little Ladies**			
93-16-001	Shannon's Holiday	L. Mason	100-day	169.95	169.95
Georgetown Collection, Inc.		**Faraway Friends**			
93-17-001	Kristin	S. Skille	100-day	140.00	140.00
94-17-002	Dara	S. Skille	100-day	140.00	140.00
Georgetown Collection, Inc.		**Georgetown Collection**			
93-18-001	Quick Fox	L. Mason	100-day	138.95	138.95
Georgetown Collection, Inc.		**Victorian Innocence**			
94-19-001	Annabelle	L. Mason	100-day	130.00	130.00
Goebel		**Victoria Ashlea® Originals**			
88-01-001	Campbell Kid-Girl-758700	B. Ball	Closed	13.80	13.80
88-01-002	Campbell Kid-Boy-758701	B. Ball	Closed	13.80	13.80
84-01-003	Claude-901032	B. Ball	Closed	110.00	225.00
84-01-004	Claudette-901033	B. Ball	Closed	110.00	225.00
84-01-005	Henri-901035	B. Ball	Closed	100.00	200.00
84-01-006	Henrietta-901036	B. Ball	Closed	100.00	200.00
84-01-007	Jeannie-901062	B. Ball	Closed	200.00	550.00
84-01-008	Victoria-901068	B. Ball	Closed	200.00	1500.00
84-01-009	Laura-901106	B. Ball	Closed	300.00	575.00
83-01-010	Deborah-901107	B. Ball	Closed	220.00	400.00
84-01-011	Barbara-901108	B. Ball	Closed	57.00	110.00
84-01-012	Diana-901119	B. Ball	Closed	55.00	135.00
84-01-013	Clown-901136	B. Ball	Closed	90.00	120.00
84-01-014	Sabina-901155	B. Ball	Closed	75.00	N/A
85-01-015	Dorothy-901157	B. Ball	Closed	130.00	275.00
85-01-016	Claire-901158	B. Ball	Closed	115.00	160.00
85-01-017	Adele-901172	B. Ball	Closed	145.00	275.00
85-01-018	Roxanne-901174	B. Ball	Closed	155.00	275.00
86-01-019	Gina-901176	B. Ball	Closed	300.00	300.00
86-01-020	Cat/Kitty Cheerful Gr Dr-901179	B. Ball	Closed	60.00	60.00
85-01-021	Garnet-901183	B. Ball	Closed	160.00	295.00
86-01-022	Pepper Rust Dr/Appr-901184	B. Ball	Closed	125.00	200.00
86-01-023	Patty Artic Flower Print-901185	B. Ball	Closed	140.00	140.00
87-01-024	Lillian-901199	B. Ball	Closed	85.00	100.00
87-01-025	Suzanne-901200	B. Ball	Closed	85.00	100.00
87-01-026	Kitty Cuddles-901201	B. Ball	Closed	65.00	65.00
87-01-027	Bonnie Pouty-901207	B. Ball	Closed	100.00	100.00
87-01-028	Amanda Pouty-901209	B. Ball	Closed	150.00	215.00
87-01-029	Tiffany Pouty-901211	B. Ball	Closed	120.00	160.00
87-01-030	Alice-901212	B. Ball	Closed	95.00	135.00
88-01-031	Elizabeth-901214	B. Ball	Closed	90.00	90.00
87-01-032	Bride Allison-901218	B. Ball	Closed	180.00	180.00
87-01-033	Dominique-901219	B. Ball	Closed	170.00	225.00
87-01-034	Sarah-901220	B. Ball	Closed	350.00	350.00
87-01-035	Tasha-901221	B. Ball	Closed	115.00	130.00
87-01-036	Michelle-901222	B. Ball	Closed	90.00	90.00
87-01-037	Nicole-901225	B. Ball	Closed	575.00	575.00
87-01-038	Clementine-901226	B. Ball	Closed	75.00	75.00
87-01-039	Catanova-901227	B. Ball	Closed	75.00	75.00
87-01-040	Caitlin-901228	B. Ball	Closed	260.00	260.00
88-01-041	Christina-901229	B. Ball	Closed	350.00	400.00
88-01-042	Melissa-901230	B. Ball	Closed	110.00	110.00
82-01-043	Marie-901231	B. Ball	Closed	95.00	95.00
82-01-044	Trudy-901232	B. Ball	Closed	100.00	100.00
82-01-045	Holly-901233	B. Ball	Closed	160.00	200.00
88-01-046	Brandon-901234	B. Ball	Closed	90.00	90.00
88-01-047	Ashley-901235	B. Ball	Closed	110.00	110.00
88-01-048	April-901239	B. Ball	Closed	225.00	225.00
88-01-049	Sandy-901240	K. Kennedy	Closed	115.00	115.00
88-01-050	Erin-901241	B. Ball	Closed	170.00	170.00
88-01-051	Catherine-901242	B. Ball	Closed	240.00	240.00
88-01-052	Susan-901243	B. Ball	Closed	100.00	100.00
88-01-053	Paulette-901244	B. Ball	Closed	90.00	90.00
88-01-054	Bernice-901245	B. Ball	Closed	90.00	90.00
88-01-055	Ellen-901246	B. Ball	Closed	100.00	100.00
88-01-056	Cat Maude-901247	B. Ball	Closed	85.00	85.00
88-01-057	Jennifer-901248	B. Ball	Closed	150.00	150.00
90-01-058	Helene-901249	K. Kennedy	Closed	160.00	160.00
89-01-059	Ashlea-901250	B. Ball	Closed	550.00	550.00
90-01-060	Matthew-901251	B. Ball	Closed	100.00	100.00
89-01-061	Marissa-901252	K. Kennedy	Closed	225.00	225.00
89-01-062	Holly-901254	B. Ball	Closed	180.00	180.00
89-01-063	Valerie-901255	B. Ball	Closed	175.00	175.00
90-01-064	Justine-901256	B. Ball	Closed	200.00	200.00
89-01-065	Claudia-901257	K. Kennedy	Closed	225.00	225.00
90-01-066	Rebecca-901258	B. Ball	Closed	250.00	250.00
89-01-067	Megan-901260	B. Ball	Closed	120.00	120.00
90-01-068	Carolyn-901261	K. Kennedy	Closed	200.00	200.00
90-01-069	Amy-901262	B. Ball	Closed	110.00	110.00
89-01-070	Lindsey-901263	B. Ball	Closed	100.00	100.00
90-01-071	Heidi-901266	B. Ball	2000	150.00	150.00
84-01-072	Tobie-912023	B. Ball	Closed	30.00	30.00
84-01-073	Sheila-912060	B. Ball	Closed	75.00	135.00
84-01-074	Jamie-912061	B. Ball	Closed	65.00	100.00
85-01-075	Michelle-912066	B. Ball	Closed	100.00	225.00
85-01-076	Phyllis-912067	B. Ball	Closed	60.00	60.00
85-01-077	Clown Casey-912078	B. Ball	Closed	40.00	40.00
85-01-078	Clown Jody-912079	B. Ball	Closed	100.00	150.00
85-01-079	Clown Christie-912084	B. Ball	Closed	60.00	90.00
85-01-080	Chauncey-912085	B. Ball	Closed	75.00	110.00
86-01-081	Baby Lauren Pink-912086	B. Ball	Closed	120.00	120.00
85-01-082	Rosalind-912087	B. Ball	Closed	145.00	225.00
86-01-083	Clown Cyd-912093	B. Ball	Closed	70.00	70.00
82-01-084	Charleen-912094	B. Ball	Closed	65.00	65.00
86-01-085	Clown Christabel-912095	B. Ball	Closed	100.00	150.00
86-01-086	Clown Clarabella-912096	B. Ball	Closed	80.00	80.00

		ARTIST	EDITION	ISSUE	QUOTE
86-01-087	Baby Brock Beige Dress-912103	B. Ball	Closed	60.00	60.00
86-01-088	Clown Calypso-912104	B. Ball	Closed	70.00	70.00
86-01-089	Girl Frog Freda-912105	B. Ball	Closed	20.00	20.00
86-01-090	Googley German Astrid-912109	B. Ball	Closed	60.00	60.00
86-01-091	Clown Clarissa-912123	B. Ball	Closed	75.00	110.00
86-01-092	Baby Courtney-912124	B. Ball	Closed	120.00	120.00
85-01-093	Mary-912126	B. Ball	Closed	60.00	90.00
86-01-094	Clown Lollipop-912127	B. Ball	Closed	125.00	225.00
86-01-095	Clown Cat Cadwalader-912132	B. Ball	Closed	55.00	55.00
86-01-096	Clown Kitten-Cleo-912133	B. Ball	Closed	50.00	50.00
85-01-097	Millie-912135	B. Ball	Closed	70.00	125.00
85-01-098	Lynn-912144	B. Ball	Closed	90.00	135.00
86-01-099	Ashley-912147	B. Ball	Closed	125.00	125.00
87-01-100	Megan-912148	B. Ball	Closed	70.00	70.00
87-01-101	Joy-912155	B. Ball	Closed	50.00	50.00
87-01-102	Kittle Cat-912167	B. Ball	Closed	55.00	55.00
87-01-103	Christine-912168	B. Ball	Closed	75.00	75.00
87-01-104	Noel-912170	B. Ball	Closed	125.00	125.00
87-01-105	Sophia-912173	B. Ball	Closed	40.00	40.00
87-01-106	Julia-912174	B. Ball	Closed	80.00	80.00
87-01-107	Clown Champagne-912180	B. Ball	Closed	95.00	95.00
82-01-108	Clown Jolly-912181	B. Ball	Closed	70.00	70.00
87-01-109	Baby Doll-912184	B. Ball	Closed	75.00	75.00
87-01-110	Baby Lindsay-912190	B. Ball	Closed	80.00	80.00
87-01-111	Caroline-912191	B. Ball	Closed	80.00	80.00
87-01-112	Jacqueline-912192	B. Ball	Closed	80.00	80.00
87-01-113	Jessica-912195	B. Ball	Closed	120.00	135.00
87-01-114	Doreen-912198	B. Ball	Closed	75.00	75.00
88-01-115	Clown Cotton Candy-912199	B. Ball	Closed	67.00	67.00
88-01-116	Baby Daryl-912200	B. Ball	Closed	85.00	85.00
88-01-117	Angelica-912204	B. Ball	Closed	150.00	150.00
88-01-118	Karen-912205	B. Ball	Closed	200.00	250.00
88-01-119	Polly-912206	B. Ball	Closed	100.00	125.00
88-01-120	Brittany-912207	B. Ball	Closed	130.00	145.00
88-01-121	Melissa-912208	B. Ball	Closed	125.00	125.00
88-01-122	Baby Jennifer-912210	B. Ball	Closed	75.00	75.00
88-01-123	Molly-912211	K. Kennedy	Closed	75.00	75.00
88-01-124	Lauren-912212	B. Ball	Closed	110.00	110.00
88-01-125	Anne-912213	B. Ball	Closed	130.00	150.00
89-01-126	Alexa-912214	B. Ball	Closed	195.00	195.00
88-01-127	Diana-912218	B. Ball	Closed	270.00	270.00
88-01-128	Sarah w/Pillow-912219	B. Ball	Closed	105.00	105.00
88-01-129	Betty Doll-912220	B. Ball	Closed	90.00	90.00
88-01-130	Jennifer-912221	B. Ball	Closed	80.00	80.00
88-01-131	Baby Katie-912222	B. Ball	Closed	70.00	70.00
88-01-132	Maritta Spanish-912224	B. Ball	Closed	140.00	140.00
88-01-133	Laura-912225	B. Ball	Closed	135.00	135.00
88-01-134	Crystal-912226	B. Ball	Closed	75.00	75.00
88-01-135	Jesse-912231	B. Ball	Closed	110.00	115.00
88-01-136	Whitney Blk-912232	B. Ball	Closed	62.50	65.00
88-01-137	Goldilocks-912234	K. Kennedy	Closed	65.00	65.00
88-01-138	Snow White-912235	K. Kennedy	Closed	65.00	65.00
88-01-139	Stephanie-912238	B. Ball	Closed	200.00	200.00
88-01-140	Morgan-912239	K. Kennedy	Closed	75.00	75.00
XX-01-141	Charity-912244	B. Ball	Closed	70.00	70.00
88-01-142	Renae-912245	B. Ball	Closed	120.00	120.00
88-01-143	Amanda-912246	B. Ball	Closed	180.00	180.00
88-01-144	Heather-912247	B. Ball	Closed	135.00	150.00
89-01-145	Merry-912249	B. Ball	Closed	200.00	200.00
89-01-146	Tammy-912264	B. Ball	Closed	110.00	110.00
89-01-147	Maria-912265	B. Ball	Closed	90.00	90.00
89-01-148	Nancy-912266	B. Ball	Closed	110.00	110.00
89-01-149	Pinky Clown-912268	K. Kennedy	Closed	70.00	75.00
89-01-150	Margot-912269	B. Ball	Closed	110.00	110.00
89-01-151	Jingles-912271	B. Ball	Closed	60.00	60.00
89-01-152	Vanessa-912272	B. Ball	Closed	110.00	110.00
89-01-153	Alexandria-912273	B. Ball	Closed	275.00	275.00
89-01-154	Lisa-912275	B. Ball	Closed	160.00	160.00
89-01-155	Loni-912276	B. Ball	Closed	125.00	130.00
89-01-156	Diana Bride-912277	B. Ball	Closed	180.00	180.00
90-01-157	Annabelle-912278	B. Ball	Closed	200.00	200.00
89-01-158	Sara-912279	B. Ball	Closed	175.00	175.00
89-01-159	Terry-912281	B. Ball	Closed	125.00	130.00
89-01-160	Sigrid-912282	B. Ball	Closed	145.00	145.00
89-01-161	Missy-912283	B. Ball	Closed	110.00	115.00
89-01-162	Melanie-912284	K. Kennedy	Closed	135.00	135.00
89-01-163	Kristin-912285	K. Kennedy	Closed	90.00	95.00
89-01-164	Suzanne-912286	B. Ball	Closed	120.00	120.00
89-01-165	Ginny-912287	K. Kennedy	Closed	140.00	140.00
89-01-166	Candace-912288	K. Kennedy	Closed	70.00	70.00
89-01-167	Joy-912289	K. Kennedy	Closed	110.00	110.00
89-01-168	Licorice-912290	B. Ball	Closed	75.00	75.00
89-01-169	Jimmy Baby w/ Pillow-912291	K. Kennedy	Closed	165.00	165.00
89-01-170	Hope Baby w/ Pillow-912292	B. Ball	Closed	110.00	110.00
90-01-171	Fluffer-912293	B. Ball	Closed	135.00	140.00
90-01-172	Marshmallow-912294	K. Kennedy	Closed	75.00	75.00
89-01-173	Suzy-912295	B. Ball	Closed	110.00	110.00
90-01-174	Alice-912296	K. Kennedy	Closed	65.00	65.00
90-01-175	Baryshnicat-912298	K. Kennedy	Closed	25.00	25.00
90-01-176	Tasha-912299	K. Kennedy	Closed	25.00	25.00
90-01-177	Priscilla-912300	B. Ball	Closed	185.00	190.00
90-01-178	Mrs. Katz-912301	B. Ball	Closed	140.00	145.00
90-01-179	Pamela-912302	B. Ball	Closed	95.00	95.00
90-01-180	Emily-912303	B. Ball	Closed	150.00	150.00
90-01-181	Brandy-912304	K. Kennedy	Closed	150.00	150.00
90-01-182	Sheri-912305	K. Kennedy	Closed	115.00	115.00
90-01-183	Gigi-912306	K. Kennedy	Closed	150.00	150.00
90-01-184	Joanne-912307	K. Kennedy	Closed	165.00	165.00
90-01-185	Melinda-912309	K. Kennedy	Closed	70.00	70.00
90-01-186	Bettina-912310	B. Ball	Closed	100.00	105.00
90-01-187	Stephanie-912312	B. Ball	Closed	150.00	150.00
90-01-188	Amie-912313	K. Kennedy	Closed	150.00	150.00
90-01-189	Samantha-912314	B. Ball	Closed	185.00	190.00
90-01-190	Tracie-912315	B. Ball	Closed	125.00	125.00
90-01-191	Paula-912316	B. Ball	Closed	100.00	100.00
90-01-192	Debra-912319	K. Kennedy	Closed	120.00	120.00
90-01-193	Robin-912321	B. Ball	Closed	160.00	165.00
90-01-194	Heather-912322	B. Ball	Closed	150.00	150.00
90-01-195	Jillian-912323	B. Ball	Closed	150.00	150.00
90-01-196	Angela-912324	K. Kennedy	Closed	130.00	135.00
90-01-197	Penny-912325	K. Kennedy	Closed	130.00	130.00
90-01-198	Tiffany-912326	K. Kennedy	Closed	180.00	180.00

		ARTIST	EDITION	ISSUE	QUOTE
90-01-199	Susie-912328	B. Ball	Closed	115.00	120.00
90-01-200	Jacqueline-912329	K. Kennedy	Closed	136.00	140.00
90-01-201	Kelly-912331	B. Ball	Closed	95.00	95.00
90-01-202	Annette-912333	K. Kennedy	Closed	85.00	85.00
90-01-203	Julia-912334	K. Kennedy	Closed	85.00	85.00
90-01-204	Monique-912335	K. Kennedy	Closed	85.00	85.00
90-01-205	Monica-912336	K. Kennedy	Closed	100.00	105.00
90-01-206	Helga-912337	B. Ball	Closed	325.00	325.00
90-01-207	Sheena-912338	B. Ball	Closed	115.00	115.00
90-01-208	Kimberly-912341	B. Ball	1,000	140.00	145.00
84-01-209	Amelia-933006	B. Ball	Closed	100.00	100.00
84-01-210	Stephanie-933012	B. Ball	Closed	115.00	115.00
92-01-211	Wendy-912330	K. Kennedy	1,000	125.00	130.00
92-01-212	Margaret-912354	K. Kennedy	1,000	150.00	150.00
92-01-213	Cassandra-912355	K. Kennedy	1,000	165.00	165.00
92-01-214	Noelle-912360	K. Kennedy	1,000	165.00	170.00
92-01-215	Kelli-912361	B. Ball	1,000	160.00	165.00
92-01-216	Ashley-911004	B. Ball	Closed	99.00	105.00
92-01-217	Lauren-912363	K. Kennedy	1,000	190.00	195.00
92-01-218	Denise-912362	K. Kennedy	1,000	145.00	150.00
92-01-219	Kris-912345	K. Kennedy	Closed	160.00	160.00
92-01-220	Hilary-912353	B. Ball	Closed	130.00	135.00
92-01-221	Toni-912367	K. Kennedy	Closed	120.00	120.00
92-01-222	Angelica-912339	B. Ball	1,000	145.00	145.00
92-01-223	Marjorie-912357	B. Ball	Closed	135.00	135.00
92-01-224	Brittany-912365	K. Kennedy	Closed	140.00	145.00
92-01-225	Allison-912358	B. Ball	Closed	160.00	165.00
92-01-226	Jenny-912374	K. Kennedy	Closed	150.00	150.00
92-01-227	Holly Belle-912380	B. Ball	500	125.00	125.00
92-01-228	Michelle-912381	K. Kennedy	Closed	175.00	175.00
92-01-229	Tamika-912382	B. Ball	500	185.00	185.00
92-01-230	Sherise-912383	K. Kennedy	Closed	145.00	145.00
92-01-231	Cindy-912384	B. Ball	1,000	185.00	190.00
92-01-232	Tulip-912385	K. Kennedy	500	145.00	145.00
92-01-233	Carol-912387	K. Kennedy	1,000	140.00	140.00
92-01-234	Alicia-912388	B. Ball	500	135.00	135.00
92-01-235	Iris-912389	K. Kennedy	500	165.00	165.00
92-01-236	Betsy-912390	B. Ball	500	150.00	150.00
92-01-237	Trudie-912391	B. Ball	500	135.00	135.00
92-01-238	Dottie-912393	K. Kennedy	1,000	160.00	160.00
93-01-239	Sarah-912408	B. Ball	2,000	40.00	40.00
93-01-240	Amanda-912409	B. Ball	2,000	40.00	40.00
93-01-241	Jessica-912410	B. Ball	2,000	40.00	40.00
93-01-242	Nicole-912411	B. Ball	2,000	40.00	40.00
93-01-243	Katie-912412	B. Ball	2,000	40.00	40.00
93-01-244	Lauren-912413	B. Ball	2,000	40.00	40.00
93-01-245	Beth-912430	K. Kennedy	2,000	45.00	45.00
93-01-246	Nadine-912431	K. Kennedy	2,000	45.00	45.00
93-01-247	Leslie-912432	K. Kennedy	2,000	45.00	45.00
93-01-248	Kaylee-912433	K. Kennedy	2,000	45.00	45.00
93-01-249	Shannon-912434	K. Kennedy	2,000	45.00	45.00
93-01-250	Julie-912435	K. Kennedy	2,000	45.00	45.00
Goebel		**Victoria Ashlea® Originals-Tiny Tot School Girls**			
94-02-001	Shawna- 912449	K. Kennedy	2,000	47.50	47.50
94-02-002	Christin- 912450	K. Kennedy	2,000	47.50	47.50
94-02-003	Patricia- 912453	K. Kennedy	2,000	47.50	47.50
94-02-004	Monique- 912455	K. Kennedy	2,000	47.50	47.50
94-02-005	Andrea- 12456	K. Kennedy	2,000	47.50	47.50
94-02-006	Susan- 12457	K. Kennedy	2,000	47.50	47.50
Goebel		**Victoria Ashlea® Originals-Tiny Tot Clowns**			
94-03-001	Lisa	K. Kennedy	2,000	45.00	45.00
94-03-002	Stacy	K. Kennedy	2,000	45.00	45.00
94-03-003	Megan	K. Kennedy	2,000	45.00	45.00
94-03-004	Danielle	K. Kennedy	2,000	45.00	45.00
94-03-005	Marie	K. Kennedy	2,000	45.00	45.00
94-03-006	Lindsey	K. Kennedy	2,000	45.00	45.00
Goebel		**Victoria Ashlea® Birthstone Dolls**			
90-04-001	January Birthstone Doll-912250	K. Kennedy	Closed	25.00	25.00
90-04-002	February Birthstone Doll-912251	K. Kennedy	Closed	25.00	25.00
90-04-003	March Birthstone Doll-912252	K. Kennedy	Closed	25.00	25.00
90-04-004	April Birthstone Doll-912253	K. Kennedy	Closed	25.00	25.00
90-04-005	May Birthstone Doll-912254	K. Kennedy	Closed	25.00	25.00
90-04-006	June Birthstone Doll-912255	K. Kennedy	Closed	25.00	25.00
90-04-007	July Birthstone Doll-912256	K. Kennedy	Closed	25.00	25.00
90-04-008	August Birthstone Doll-912257	K. Kennedy	Closed	25.00	25.00
90-04-009	September Birthstone Doll-912258	K. Kennedy	Closed	25.00	25.00
90-04-010	October Birthstone Doll-912259	K. Kennedy	Closed	25.00	25.00
90-04-011	November Birthstone Doll-912260	K. Kennedy	Closed	25.00	25.00
90-04-012	December Birthstone Doll-912261	K. Kennedy	Closed	25.00	25.00
93-04-013	January-Garnet-912394	K. Kennedy	2,500	29.50	29.50
93-04-014	February-Amethyst-912395	K. Kennedy	2,500	29.50	29.50
93-04-015	March-Aquamarine-912396	K. Kennedy	2,500	29.50	29.50
93-04-016	April-Diamond-912397	K. Kennedy	2,500	29.50	29.50
93-04-017	May-Emerald-912398	K. Kennedy	2,500	29.50	29.50
93-04-018	June-Lt. Amethyst-912399	K. Kennedy	2,500	29.50	29.50
93-04-019	July-Ruby-912400	K. Kennedy	2,500	29.50	29.50
93-04-020	August-Peridot-912401	K. Kennedy	2,500	29.50	29.50
93-04-021	September-Sapphire-912402	K. Kennedy	2,500	29.50	29.50
93-04-022	October-Rose Stone-912403	K. Kennedy	2,500	29.50	29.50
93-04-023	November-Topaz-912404	K. Kennedy	2,500	29.50	29.50
93-04-024	December-Zircon-912405	K. Kennedy	2,500	29.50	29.50
95-04-025	January-Garnet-912471	K. Kennedy	2,500	29.50	29.50
95-04-026	February-Amethyst-912472	K. Kennedy	2,500	29.50	29.50
95-04-027	March-Aquamarine-912473	K. Kennedy	2,500	29.50	29.50
95-04-028	April-Diamond-912474	K. Kennedy	2,500	29.50	29.50
95-04-029	May-Emerald-912475	K. Kennedy	2,500	29.50	29.50
95-04-030	June -Lt. Amethyst-912476	K. Kennedy	2,500	29.50	29.50
95-04-031	July-Ruby-912477	K. Kennedy	2,500	29.50	29.50
95-04-032	August-Peridot-912478	K. Kennedy	2,500	29.50	29.50
95-04-033	September-Sapphire-912479	K. Kennedy	2,500	29.50	29.50
95-04-034	October-Rosestone-912480	K. Kennedy	2,500	29.50	29.50
95-04-035	November-Topaz-912481	K. Kennedy	2,500	29.50	29.50
95-04-036	December-Zircon-912482	K. Kennedy	2,500	29.50	29.50
Goebel/M.I. Hummel		**M. I. Hummel Collectible Dolls**			
64-01-001	Gretel 1901	M. I. Hummel	Closed	55.00	125.00
64-01-002	Hansel 1902	M. I. Hummel	Closed	55.00	110.00
64-01-003	Rosa-Blue Baby 1904/B	M. I. Hummel	Closed	45.00	85.00
64-01-004	Rosa-Pink Baby 1904/P	M. I. Hummel	Closed	45.00	75.00
64-01-005	Little Knitter 1905	M. I. Hummel	Closed	55.00	75.00

		ARTIST	EDITION	ISSUE	QUOTE
64-01-006	Merry Wanderer 1906	M. I. Hummel	Closed	55.00	90.00
64-01-007	Chimney Sweep 1908	M. I. Hummel	Closed	55.00	110.00
64-01-008	School Girl 1909	M. I. Hummel	Closed	55.00	75.00
64-01-009	School Boy 1910	M. I. Hummel	Closed	55.00	80.00
64-01-010	Goose Girl 1914	M. I. Hummel	Closed	55.00	80.00
64-01-011	For Father 1917	M. I. Hummel	Closed	55.00	90.00
64-01-012	Merry Wanderer 1925	M. I. Hummel	Closed	55.00	110.00
64-01-013	Lost Stocking 1926	M. I. Hummel	Closed	55.00	75.00
64-01-014	Visiting and Invalid 1927	M. I. Hummel	Closed	55.00	75.00
64-01-015	On Secret Path 1928	M. I. Hummel	Closed	55.00	80.00
Goebel/M.I. Hummel		**M. I. Hummel Porcelain Dolls**			
84-02-001	Birthday Serenade/Boy	M. I. Hummel	Closed	225.00	250-300.
84-02-002	Birthday Serenade/Girl	M. I. Hummel	Closed	225.00	250-300.
84-02-003	On Holiday	M. I. Hummel	Closed	225.00	250-300.
84-02-004	Postman	M. I. Hummel	Closed	225.00	250-300.
85-02-005	Carnival	M. I. Hummel	Closed	225.00	250-300.
85-02-006	Easter Greetings	M. I. Hummel	Closed	225.00	250-300.
85-02-007	Lost Sheep	M. I. Hummel	Closed	225.00	250-300.
85-02-008	Signs of Spring	M. I. Hummel	Closed	225.00	250-300.
Good-Kruger		**Limited Edition**			
90-01-001	Daydream	J. Good-Kruger	Retrd.	199.00	350.00
90-01-002	Annie-Rose	J. Good-Kruger	Retrd.	219.00	450.00
90-01-003	Cozy	J. Good-Kruger	Retrd.	179.00	275-375.
90-01-004	Alice	J. Good-Kruger	Retrd.	250.00	250.00
90-01-005	Christmas Cookie	J. Good-Kruger	Retrd.	199.00	199.00
90-01-006	Sue-Lynn	J. Good-Kruger	Retrd.	240.00	300.00
91-01-007	Teachers Pet	J. Good-Kruger	Retrd.	199.00	250.00
91-01-008	Moppett	J. Good-Kruger	Retrd.	179.00	275.00
91-01-009	Victorian Christmas	J. Good-Kruger	Retrd.	219.00	275.00
91-01-010	Johnny-Lynn	J. Good-Kruger	Retrd.	240.00	500.00
92-01-011	Jeepers Creepers (Porcelain)	J. Good-Kruger	Retrd.	725.00	800.00
92-01-012	Anne	J. Good-Kruger	Retrd.	240.00	500.00
Gorham		**Gorham Dolls**			
81-01-001	Jillian, 16"	S. Stone Aiken	Closed	200.00	350-475.
81-01-002	Alexandria, 18"	S. Stone Aiken	Closed	250.00	550-575.
81-01-003	Christopher, 19"	S. Stone Aiken	Closed	250.00	750-950.
81-01-004	Stephanie, 18"	S. Stone Aiken	Closed	250.00	16-2100.
81-01-005	Cecile, 16"	S. Stone Aiken	Closed	200.00	700-950.
81-01-006	Christina, 16"	S. Stone Aiken	Closed	200.00	400-475.
81-01-007	Danielle, 14"	S. Stone Aiken	Closed	150.00	300-375.
81-01-008	Melinda, 14"	S. Stone Aiken	Closed	150.00	300-375.
81-01-009	Elena, 14"	S. Stone Aiken	Closed	150.00	600-750.
81-01-010	Rosemond, 18"	S. Stone Aiken	Closed	250.00	650-750.
82-01-011	Mlle. Monique, 12"	S. Stone Aiken	Closed	125.00	300.00
82-01-012	Mlle. Jeanette, 12"	S. Stone Aiken	Closed	125.00	175-225.
82-01-013	Mlle. Lucille, 12"	S. Stone Aiken	Closed	125.00	275-475.
82-01-014	Benjamin, 18"	S. Stone Aiken	Closed	200.00	550-600.
82-01-015	Ellice, 18"	S. Stone Aiken	Closed	200.00	550-600.
82-01-016	Corrine, 21"	S. Stone Aiken	Closed	250.00	400-600.
82-01-017	Baby in Blue Dress, 12"	S. Stone Aiken	Closed	150.00	350-375.
82-01-018	Baby in Apricot Dress, 16"	S. Stone Aiken	Closed	175.00	375.00
82-01-019	Baby in White Dress, 18"	Gorham	Closed	250.00	395.00
82-01-020	Melanie, 23"	S. Stone Aiken	Closed	300.00	650-725.
82-01-021	Jeremy, 23"	S. Stone Aiken	Closed	300.00	750-800.
82-01-022	Mlle. Yvonne, 12"	Unknown	Closed	125.00	275-450.
82-01-023	M. Anton, 12"	Unknown	Closed	125.00	195.00
82-01-024	Mlle. Marsella, 12"	Unknown	Closed	125.00	295.00
82-01-025	Kristin, 23"	S. Stone Aiken	Closed	300.00	550-700.
83-01-026	Jennifer, 19" Bridal Doll	S. Stone Aiken	Closed	325.00	700-825.
85-01-027	Linda, 19"	S. Stone Aiken	Closed	275.00	400-475.
85-01-028	Odette, 19"	S. Stone Aiken	Closed	250.00	450-475.
85-01-029	Amelia, 19"	S. Stone Aiken	Closed	275.00	325-400.
85-01-030	Nanette, 19"	S. Stone Aiken	Closed	275.00	325-400.
85-01-031	Alexander, 19"	S. Stone Aiken	Closed	275.00	400-500.
85-01-032	Gabrielle, 19"	S. Stone Aiken	Closed	225.00	400-450.
86-01-033	Julia, 16"	S. Stone Aiken	Closed	225.00	375-425.
86-01-034	Lauren, 14"	S. Stone Aiken	Closed	175.00	375-450.
86-01-035	Emily, 14"	S. Stone Aiken	Closed	175.00	375-450.
86-01-036	Fleur, 19"	S. Stone Aiken	Closed	300.00	400-500.
87-01-037	Juliet	S. Stone Aiken	Closed	325.00	400-450.
86-01-038	Meredith	S. Stone Aiken	Closed	295.00	350-400.
86-01-039	Alissa	S. Stone Aiken	Closed	245.00	300-375.
86-01-040	Jessica	S. Stone Aiken	Closed	195.00	275-350.
Gorham		**Limited Edition Dolls**			
82-02-001	Allison, 19"	S. Stone Aiken	Closed	300.00	4500.00
83-02-002	Ashley, 19"	S. Stone Aiken	Closed	350.00	1200.00
84-02-003	Nicole, 19"	S. Stone Aiken	Closed	350.00	1000.00
84-02-004	Holly (Christmas), 19"	S. Stone Aiken	Closed	300.00	750-900.
85-02-005	Lydia,19"	S. Stone Aiken	Closed	550.00	1800.00
85-02-006	Joy (Christmas), 19"	S. Stone Aiken	Closed	350.00	500-725.
86-02-007	Noel (Christmas), 19"	S. Stone Aiken	Closed	400.00	700-800.
87-02-008	Jacqueline, 19"	S. Stone Aiken	Closed	500.00	600-850.
87-02-009	Merrie (Christmas), 19"	S. Stone Aiken	Closed	500.00	795.00
88-02-010	Andrew, 19"	S. Stone Aiken	Closed	475.00	625-850.
88-02-011	Christa (Christmas), 19"	S. Stone Aiken	Closed	550.00	1500.00
90-02-012	Amey (10th Anniversary Edition)	S. Stone Aiken	Closed	650.00	750-1100
Gorham		**Gorham Holly Hobbie Childhood Memories**			
85-03-001	Mother's Helper	Holly Hobbie	Closed	45.00	125.00
85-03-002	Best Friends	Holly Hobbie	Closed	45.00	125.00
85-03-003	First Day of School	Holly Hobbie	Closed	45.00	125.00
85-03-004	Christmas Wishes	Holly Hobbie	Closed	45.00	125.00
Gorham		**Gorham Holly Hobbie For All Seasons**			
84-04-001	Summer Holly 12"	Holly Hobbie	Closed	42.50	195.00
84-04-002	Fall Holly 12"	Holly Hobbie	Closed	42.50	195.00
84-04-003	Winter Holly 12"	Holly Hobbie	Closed	42.50	195.00
84-04-004	Spring Holly 12"	Holly Hobbie	Closed	42.50	195.00
Gorham		**Holly Hobbie**			
83-05-001	Blue Girl, 14"	Holly Hobbie	Closed	80.00	325.00
83-05-002	Christmas Morning, 14"	Holly Hobbie	Closed	80.00	275.00
83-05-003	Heather, 14"	Holly Hobbie	Closed	80.00	275.00
83-05-004	Little Amy, 14"	Holly Hobbie	Closed	80.00	275.00
83-05-005	Robbie, 14"	Holly Hobbie	Closed	80.00	275.00
83-05-006	Sweet Valentine, 16"	Holly Hobbie	Closed	100.00	350.00
83-05-007	Yesterday's Memories, 18"	Holly Hobbie	Closed	125.00	450.00
83-05-008	Sunday Best, 18"	Holly Hobbie	Closed	115.00	350.00
83-05-009	Blue Girl, 18"	Holly Hobbie	Closed	115.00	395.00

	ARTIST	EDITION	ISSUE	QUOTE
Gorham	**Little Women**			
83-06-001 Beth, 16"	S. Stone Aiken	Closed	225.00	575.00
83-06-002 Amy, 16"	S. Stone Aiken	Closed	225.00	575.00
83-06-003 Meg, 19"	S. Stone Aiken	Closed	275.00	695.00
83-06-004 Jo, 19"	S. Stone Aiken	Closed	275.00	675.00
Gorham	**Kezi Doll For All Seasons**			
85-07-001 Ariel 16"	Kezi	Closed	135.00	500.00
85-07-002 Aubrey 16"	Kezi	Closed	135.00	500.00
85-07-003 Amber 16"	Kezi	Closed	135.00	500.00
85-07-004 Adrienne 16"	Kezi	Closed	135.00	500-525.
Gorham	**Kezi Golden Gifts**			
84-08-001 Faith 18"	Kezi	Closed	95.00	195-225.
84-08-002 Felicity 18"	Kezi	Closed	95.00	195.00
84-08-003 Patience 18"	Kezi	Closed	95.00	195.00
84-08-004 Prudence 18"	Kezi	Closed	85.00	195.00
84-08-005 Hope 16"	Kezi	Closed	85.00	175-225.
84-08-006 Grace 16"	Kezi	Closed	85.00	175.00
84-08-007 Charity 16"	Kezi	Closed	85.00	175-195.
84-08-008 Merrie 16"	Kezi	Closed	85.00	175-195.
Gorham	**Limited Edition Sister Set**			
88-09-001 Kathleen	S. Stone Aiken	Closed	550.00	750-950.
88-09-002 Katelin	S. Stone Aiken	Set	Set	Set
Gorham	**Southern Belles**			
85-10-001 Amanda, 19"	S. Stone Aiken	Closed	300.00	950.00
86-10-002 Veronica, 19"	S. Stone Aiken	Closed	325.00	750.00
87-10-003 Rachel, 19"	S. Stone Aiken	Closed	375.00	825.00
88-10-004 Cassie, 19"	S. Stone Aiken	Closed	500.00	700.00
Gorham	**Valentine Ladies**			
87-11-001 Jane	P. Valentine	Closed	145.00	350-400.
87-11-002 Lee Ann	P. Valentine	Closed	145.00	325.00
87-11-003 Elizabeth	P. Valentine	Closed	145.00	450.00
87-11-004 Rebecca	P. Valentine	Closed	145.00	325.00
87-11-005 Patrice	P. Valentine	Closed	145.00	325.00
87-11-006 Anabella	P. Valentine	Closed	145.00	395-425.
87-11-007 Sylvia	P. Valentine	Closed	160.00	350.00
87-11-008 Rosanne	P. Valentine	Closed	145.00	325.00
87-11-009 Marianna	P. Valentine	Closed	160.00	400.00
88-11-010 Maria Theresa	P. Valentine	Closed	225.00	350.00
88-11-011 Priscilla	P. Valentine	Closed	195.00	325.00
88-11-012 Judith Anne	P. Valentine	Closed	195.00	325.00
88-11-013 Felicia	P. Valentine	Closed	225.00	400.00
89-11-014 Julianna	P. Valentine	Closed	225.00	275-325.
89-11-015 Rose	P. Valentine	Closed	225.00	275-325.
Gorham	**Precious as Pearls**			
86-12-001 Colette	S. Stone Aiken	Closed	400.00	1500.00
87-12-002 Charlotte	S. Stone Aiken	Closed	425.00	800.00
88-12-003 Chloe	S. Stone Aiken	Closed	525.00	900.00
89-12-004 Cassandra	S. Stone Aiken	Closed	525.00	1200.00
XX-12-005 Set	S. Stone Aiken	Closed	1875.00	4000.00
Gorham	**Gorham Baby Doll Collection**			
87-13-001 Christening Day	Aiken/Matthews	Closed	245.00	295.00
87-13-002 Leslie	Aiken/Matthews	Closed	245.00	325.00
87-13-003 Matthew	Aiken/Matthews	Closed	245.00	285.00
Gorham	**Beverly Port Designer Collection**			
87-14-001 Silver Bell 17"	B. Port	Closed	175.00	750.00
87-14-002 Kristobear Kringle 17"	B. Port	Closed	200.00	450.00
87-14-003 Tedwina Kimelina Bearkin 10"	B. Port	Closed	95.00	300.00
87-14-004 Christopher Paul Bearkin 10"	B. Port	Closed	95.00	500.00
87-14-005 Molly Melinda Bearkin 10"	B. Port	Closed	95.00	300.00
87-14-006 Tedward Jonathan Bearkin 10"	B. Port	Closed	95.00	300.00
88-14-007 Baery Mab 9-1/2"	B. Port	Closed	110.00	300.00
88-14-008 Miss Emily 18"	B. Port	Closed	350.00	600.00
88-14-009 T.R. 28-1/2"	B. Port	Closed	400.00	550.00
88-14-010 The Amazing Calliope Merriweather 17"	B. Port	Closed	275.00	1200.00
88-14-011 Hollybeary Kringle 15"	B. Port	Closed	350.00	450.00
88-14-012 Theodore B. Bear 14"	B. Port	Closed	175.00	550.00
Gorham	**Bonnets & Bows**			
88-15-001 Belinda	B. Gerardi	Closed	195.00	450.00
88-15-002 Annemarie	B. Gerardi	Closed	195.00	450.00
88-15-003 Allessandra	B. Gerardi	Closed	195.00	395-550.
88-15-004 Lisette	B. Gerardi	Closed	285.00	495-550.
88-15-005 Bettina	B. Gerardi	Closed	285.00	495-550.
88-15-006 Ellie	B. Gerardi	Closed	285.00	495-550.
88-15-007 Alicia	B. Gerardi	Closed	385.00	800-975.
88-15-008 Bethany	B. Gerardi	Closed	385.00	13-1500.
88-15-009 Jesse	B. Gerardi	Closed	525.00	800-850.
88-15-010 Francie	B. Gerardi	Closed	625.00	895-975.
Gorham	**Small Wonders**			
88-16-001 Patina	B. Gerardi	Closed	265.00	265.00
88-16-002 Madeline	B. Gerardi	Closed	365.00	365.00
88-16-003 Marguerite	B. Gerardi	Closed	425.00	425.00
Gorham	**Joyful Years**			
89-17-001 William	B. Gerardi	Closed	295.00	375.00
89-17-002 Katrina	B. Gerardi	Closed	295.00	375.00
Gorham	**Victorian Cameo Collection**			
90-18-001 Victoria	B. Gerardi	1,500	375.00	375.00
91-18-002 Alexandra	B. Gerardi	Closed	375.00	375.00
Gorham	**Children Of Christmas**			
89-19-001 Clara, 16"	S. Stone Aiken	Closed	325.00	650.00
90-19-002 Natalie, 16"	S. Stone Aiken	1,500	350.00	395-450.
91-19-003 Emily	S. Stone Aiken	1,500	375.00	375-475.
92-19-004 Virginia	S. Stone Aiken	1,500	375.00	375-475.
Gorham	**Les Belles Bebes Collection**			
91-20-001 Cherie	S. Stone Aiken	Closed	375.00	500.00
91-20-002 Desiree	S. Stone Aiken	1,500	375.00	375-475.
93-20-003 Camille	S. Stone Aiken	1,500	375.00	375-475.
Gorham	**Childhood Memories**			
91-21-001 Amanda	D. Valenza	Closed	98.00	98-150.
91-21-002 Kimberly	D. Valenza	Closed	98.00	98-150.
91-21-003 Jessica Anne's Playtime	D. Valenza	Closed	98.00	98-150.
91-21-004 Jennifer	D. Valenza	Closed	98.00	98-150.

	ARTIST	EDITION	ISSUE	QUOTE
Gorham	**Gifts of the Garden**			
91-22-001 Priscilla	S. Stone Aiken	Closed	125.00	200.00
91-22-002 Lauren	S. Stone Aiken	Closed	125.00	200.00
91-22-003 Irene	S. Stone Aiken	Closed	125.00	200.00
91-22-004 Valerie	S. Stone Aiken	Closed	125.00	200.00
91-22-005 Deborah	S. Stone Aiken	Closed	125.00	200.00
91-22-006 Alisa	S. Stone Aiken	Closed	125.00	200.00
91-22-007 Maria	S. Stone Aiken	Closed	125.00	200.00
91-22-008 Joelle (Christmas)	S. Stone Aiken	Closed	150.00	200.00
91-22-009 Holly (Christmas)	S. Stone Aiken	Closed	150.00	200.00
Gorham	**Dolls of the Month**			
91-23-001 Miss January	Gorham	Closed	79.00	125.00
91-23-002 Miss February	Gorham	Closed	79.00	125.00
91-23-003 Miss March	Gorham	Closed	79.00	125.00
91-23-004 Miss April	Gorham	Closed	79.00	125.00
91-23-005 Miss May	Gorham	Closed	79.00	125.00
91-23-006 Miss June	Gorham	Closed	79.00	125.00
91-23-007 Miss July	Gorham	Closed	79.00	125.00
91-23-008 Miss August	Gorham	Closed	79.00	125.00
91-23-009 Miss September	Gorham	Closed	79.00	125.00
91-23-010 Miss October	Gorham	Closed	79.00	125.00
91-23-011 Miss November	Gorham	Closed	79.00	125.00
91-23-012 Miss December	Gorham	Closed	79.00	125.00
Gorham	**Legendary Heroines**			
91-24-001 Jane Eyre	S. Stone Aiken	1,500	245.00	245.00
91-24-002 Guinevere	S. Stone Aiken	1,500	245.00	245.00
91-24-003 Juliet	S. Stone Aiken	1,500	245.00	245.00
91-24-004 Lara	S. Stone Aiken	1,500	245.00	245.00
Gorham	**Gift of Dreams**			
91-25-001 Samantha	Young/Gerardi	Closed	495.00	495.00
91-25-002 Katherine	Young/Gerardi	Closed	495.00	495.00
91-25-003 Melissa	Young/Gerardi	Closed	495.00	495.00
91-25-004 Elizabeth	Young/Gerardi	Closed	495.00	495.00
91-25-005 Christina (Christmas)	Young/Gerardi	Closed	695.00	695.00
Gorham	**The Friendship Dolls**			
91-26-001 Peggy-The American Traveler	P. Seaman	Closed	98.00	98.00
91-26-002 Meagan-The Irish Traveler	L. O'Connor	Closed	98.00	98.00
91-26-003 Angela-The Italian Traveler	S. Nappo	Closed	98.00	98.00
91-26-004 Kinuko-The Japanese Traveler	S. Ueki	Closed	98.00	98.00
Gorham	**Special Moments**			
91-27-001 Baby's First Christmas	E. Worrell	Closed	135.00	135-275.
92-27-002 Baby's First Steps	E. Worrell	Closed	135.00	135-225.
Gorham	**Dollie And Me**			
91-28-001 Dollie's First Steps	J. Pilallis	Closed	160.00	160.00
Gorham	**The Victorian Collection**			
92-29-001 Victoria's Jubilee	E. Woodhouse	Yr.Iss.	295.00	295.00
Gorham	**Days Of The Week**			
92-30-001 Monday's Child	R./L. Schrubbe	Closed	98.00	98.00
92-30-002 Tuesday's Child	R./L. Schrubbe	Closed	98.00	98.00
92-30-003 Wednesday's Child	R./L. Schrubbe	Closed	98.00	98.00
92-30-004 Thurday's Child	R./L. Schrubbe	Closed	98.00	98.00
92-30-005 Friday's Child	R./L. Schrubbe	Closed	98.00	98.00
92-30-006 Saturday's Child	R./L. Schrubbe	Closed	98.00	98.00
92-30-007 Sunday's Child	R./L. Schrubbe	Closed	98.00	98.00
Gorham	**Times To Treasure**			
90-31-001 Storytime	L. Di Leo	Closed	195.00	195.00
91-31-002 Bedtime	L. Di Leo	Closed	195.00	195.00
93-31-003 Playtime	L. Di Leo	Closed	195.00	195.00
Gorham	**Victorian Children**			
92-32-001 Sara's Tea Time	S. Stone Aiken	1,000	495.00	650.00
93-32-002 Catching Butterflies	S. Stone Aiken	1,000	495.00	495.00
Gorham	**Bride Dolls**			
93-33-001 Susannah's Wedding Day	D. Valenza	9,500	295.00	295.00
Gorham	**Carousel Dolls**			
93-34-001 Ribbons And Roses	C. Shafer	Closed	119.00	119.00
Gorham	**Pillow Baby Dolls**			
93-35-001 Sitting Pretty	L. Gordon	Closed	39.00	39.00
93-35-002 Tickling Toes	L. Gordon	Closed	39.00	39.00
93-35-003 On the Move	L. Gordon	Closed	39.00	39.00
Gorham	**Victorian Flower Girls**			
93-36-001 Rose	J. Pilallis	Closed	95.00	95.00
Gorham	**Celebrations Of Childhood**			
92-37-001 Happy Birthday Amy	L. Di Leo	Closed	160.00	160.00
Gorham	**Littlest Angel Dolls**			
92-38-001 Merriel	L. Di Leo	Closed	49.50	49.50
Gorham	**Puppy Love Dolls**			
92-39-001 Katie And Kyle	R./ L. Schrubbe	Closed	119.00	119.00
Gorham	**Daydreamer Dolls**			
92-40-001 Heather's Daydream	S. Stone Aiken	Closed	119.00	119.00
Gorham	**Bonnet Babies**			
93-41-001 Chelsea's Bonnet	M. Sirko	Closed	95.00	95.00
Gorham	**Imaginary People**			
93-42-001 Melinda, The Tooth Fairy	R. Tonner	2,900	95.00	95.00
Gorham	**International Babies**			
93-43-001 Natalia's Matrioshka	R. Tonner	Closed	95.00	95.00
Gorham	**Nature's Bounty**			
93-44-001 Jamie's Fruitful Harvest	R. Tonner	Closed	95.00	95.00
Gorham	**Portrait Perfect Victorian Dolls**			
93-45-001 Pretty in Peach	R. Tonner	2,900	119.00	119.00
Gorham	**Sporting Kids**			
93-46-001 Up At Bat	R. Schrubbe	Closed	49.50	49.50
Gorham	**Tender Hearts**			
93-47-001 Saying Grace	M. Murphy	Closed	119.00	119.00
Gorham	**Christmas Traditions**			
93-48-001 Trimming the Tree	S. Stone Aiken	2,500	295.00	295.00

	ARTIST	EDITION	ISSUE	QUOTE
Gorham	**Christmas Treasures**			
93-49-001 Chrissy	S. Stone Aiken	Closed	150.00	150.00
H & G Studios, Inc.	**Brenda Burke Dolls**			
89-01-001 Arabelle	B. Burke	500	695.00	1400.00
89-01-002 Angelica	B. Burke	50	1495.00	3000.00
89-01-003 Adelaine	B. Burke	25	1795.00	3600.00
89-01-004 Amanda	B. Burke	25	1995.00	6000.00
89-01-005 Alicia	B. Burke	125	895.00	1800.00
89-01-006 Alexandra	B. Burke	125	995.00	2000.00
89-01-007 Bethany	B. Burke	45	2995.00	2995.00
89-01-008 Beatrice	B. Burke	85	2395.00	2395.00
89-01-009 Brittany	B. Burke	75	2695.00	2695.00
90-01-010 Belinda	B. Burke	12	3695.00	3695.00
91-01-011 Tender Love	B. Burke	25	3295.00	3295.00
91-01-012 Sleigh Ride	B. Burke	20	3695.00	3695.00
91-01-013 Charlotte	B. Burke	20	2395.00	2395.00
91-01-014 Clarissa	B. Burke	15	3595.00	3595.00
92-01-015 Dorothea	B. Burke	500	395.00	395.00
93-01-016 Melissa	B. Burke	1	7750.00	7750.00
93-01-017 Giovanna	B. Burke	1	7800.00	7800.00
Hallmark Galleries	**Victorian Memories**			
92-01-001 Seth-plush bear 4000QHG1007	J. Greene	9,500	40.00	40.00
92-01-002 Teddy -plush bear 4500QHG1008	J. Greene	9,500	45.00	45.00
92-01-003 Daisy -plush bear 8500QHG1009	J. Greene	2,500	85.00	85.00
92-01-004 Bear-plush bear 3500QHG1011	J. Greene	9,500	35.00	35.00
92-01-005 Bunny B-plush rabbit 3500QHG1012	J. Greene	9,500	35.00	35.00
92-01-006 Emma/miniature doll 2500QHG1016	J. Greene	9,500	25.00	25.00
92-01-007 Katherine 1QHG1017	J. Greene	1,200	150.00	150.00
92-01-008 Abner 1QHG1018	J. Greene	4,500	110.00	110.00
92-01-009 Abigail 1QHG1019	J. Greene	4,500	125.00	125.00
92-01-010 Alice 1QHG1020	J. Greene	4,500	125.00	125.00
92-01-011 Olivia 1QHG1021	J. Greene	4,500	125.00	125.00
93-01-012 Baby Doll Beatrice 2000QHG1029	J. Greene	Retrd.	20.00	20.00
93-01-013 Hannah 1QHG1030	J. Greene	2,500	130.00	130.00
94-01-014 Mini Jointed Bear Jesse 1200QHG1037	J. Greene	9,500	12.00	12.00
Hallmark Galleries	**Mary Engelbreit's Friendship Garden**			
93-02-001 Porcelain Doll-Margaret 6000QHG5001	M. Engelbreit	12,500	60.00	60.00
93-02-002 Porcelain Doll-Louisa 6500QHG5002	M. Engelbreit	12,500	65.00	65.00
93-02-003 Porcelain Doll-Josephine 6000QHG5003	M. Engelbreit	12,500	60.00	60.00
Hamilton Collection	**Songs of the Seasons Hakata Doll Collection**			
85-01-001 Winter Song Maiden	T. Murakami	9,800	75.00	75.00
85-01-002 Spring Song Maiden	T. Murakami	9,800	75.00	75.00
85-01-003 Summer Song Maiden	T. Murakami	9,800	75.00	75.00
85-01-004 Autumn Song Maiden	T. Murakami	9,800	75.00	75.00
Hamilton Collection	**Dolls of America's Colonial Heritage**			
86-02-001 Katrina	A. Elekfy	Open	55.00	55.00
86-02-002 Nicole	A. Elekfy	Open	55.00	55.00
87-02-003 Maria	A. Elekfy	Open	55.00	55.00
87-02-004 Priscilla	A. Elekfy	Open	55.00	55.00
87-02-005 Colleen	A. Elekfy	Open	55.00	55.00
88-02-006 Gretchen	A. Elekfy	Open	55.00	55.00
Hamilton Collection	**Star Trek Doll Collection**			
88-03-001 Mr. Spock	E. Daub	Closed	75.00	150.00
88-03-002 Captain Kirk	E. Daub	Closed	75.00	120.00
89-03-003 Dr. Mc Coy	E. Daub	Closed	75.00	120.00
89-03-004 Scotty	E. Daub	Closed	75.00	120.00
90-03-005 Sulu	E. Daub	Closed	75.00	120.00
90-03-006 Chekov	E. Daub	Closed	75.00	120.00
91-03-007 Uhura	E. Daub	Closed	75.00	120.00
Hamilton Collection	**The Antique Doll Collection**			
89-04-001 Nicole	Unknown	Closed	195.00	195.00
90-04-002 Colette	Unknown	Open	195.00	195.00
91-04-003 Lisette	Unknown	Open	195.00	225.00
91-04-004 Katrina	Unknown	Open	195.00	195.00
Hamilton Collection	**The Bessie Pease Gutmann Doll Collection**			
89-05-001 Love is Blind	B.P. Gutmann	Closed	135.00	135-225.
89-05-002 He Won't Bite	B.P. Gutmann	Closed	135.00	135.00
91-05-003 Virginia	B.P. Gutmann	Open	135.00	135.00
91-05-004 First Dancing Lesson	B.P. Gutmann	Open	195.00	195.00
91-05-005 Good Morning	B.P. Gutmann	Open	195.00	195.00
91-05-006 Love At First Sight	B.P. Gutmann	Open	195.00	195.00
Hamilton Collection	**The Maud Humphrey Bogart Doll Collection**			
89-06-001 Playing Bride	M.H. Bogart	Closed	135.00	135-175.
90-06-002 First Party	M.H. Bogart	Closed	135.00	135.00
90-06-003 The First Lesson	M.H. Bogart	Closed	135.00	149.00
91-06-004 Seamstress	M.H. Bogart	Closed	135.00	149.00
91-06-005 Little Captive	M.H. Bogart	Open	135.00	135.00
92-06-006 Kitty's Bath	M.H. Bogart	Open	135.00	135.00
Hamilton Collection	**Connie Walser Derek Baby Doll**			
90-07-001 Jessica	C.W. Derek	Closed	155.00	300-320.
91-07-002 Sara	C.W. Derek	Closed	155.00	155-225.
91-07-003 Andrew	C.W. Derek	Open	155.00	155.00
91-07-004 Amanda	C.W. Derek	Open	155.00	155.00
92-07-005 Samantha	C.W. Derek	Open	155.00	155.00
Hamilton Collection	**I Love Lucy (Vinyl)**			
88-08-001 Ethel	Unknown	Closed	40.00	160-210.
88-08-002 Fred	Unknown	Closed	40.00	139.00
90-08-003 Lucy	Unknown	Closed	40.00	135.00
91-08-004 Ricky	Unknown	Closed	40.00	135-210.
92-08-005 Queen of the Gypsies	Unknown	Open	40.00	40.00
92-08-006 Vitameatavegamin	Unknown	Open	40.00	40.00
Hamilton Collection	**I Love Lucy (Porcelain)**			
90-09-001 Lucy	Unknown	Closed	95.00	195-250.
91-09-002 Ricky	Unknown	Closed	95.00	350.00
92-09-003 Queen of the Gypsies	Unknown	Closed	95.00	245.00
92-09-004 Vitameatavegamin	Unknown	Closed	95.00	195.00
Hamilton Collection	**Russian Czarra Dolls**			
91-10-001 Alexandra	Unknown	Closed	295.00	350.00
Hamilton Collection	**Storybook Dolls**			
91-11-001 Alice in Wonderland	L. Di Leo	Open	75.00	75.00
Hamilton Collection	**International Children**			
91-12-001 Miko	C. Woodie	Closed	49.50	80-88.00

	ARTIST	EDITION	ISSUE	QUOTE
91-12-002 Anastasia	C. Woodie	Open	49.50	49.50
91-12-003 Angelina	C. Woodie	Open	49.50	49.50
92-12-004 Lian	C. Woodie	Open	49.50	49.50
92-12-005 Monique	C. Woodie	Open	49.50	49.50
92-12-006 Lisa	C. Woodie	Open	49.50	49.50
Hamilton Collection	**Central Park Skaters**			
91-13-001 Central Park Skaters	Unknown	Open	245.00	245.00
Hamilton Collection	**Jane Zidjunas Toddler Dolls**			
91-14-001 Jennifer	J. Zidjunas	Open	135.00	135.00
91-14-002 Megan	J. Zidjunas	Open	135.00	160.00
92-14-003 Kimberly	J. Zidjunas	Open	135.00	135.00
92-14-004 Amy	J. Zidjunas	Open	135.00	135.00
Hamilton Collection	**Jane Zidjunas Party Dolls**			
91-15-001 Kelly	J. Zidjunas	Open	135.00	135.00
92-15-002 Katie	J. Zidjunas	Open	135.00	135.00
93-15-003 Meredith	J. Zidjunas	Open	135.00	135.00
Hamilton Collection	**The Royal Beauty Dolls**			
91-16-001 Chen Mai	Unknown	Open	195.00	195.00
Hamilton Collection	**Abbie Williams Doll Collection**			
92-17-001 Molly	A. Williams	Closed	155.00	200.00
Hamilton Collection	**Zolan Dolls**			
91-18-001 A Christmas Prayer	D. Zolan	Closed	95.00	250.00
92-18-002 Winter Angel	D. Zolan	Open	95.00	95.00
92-18-003 Rainy Day Pals	D. Zolan	Open	95.00	95.00
92-18-004 Quiet Time	D. Zolan	Open	95.00	95.00
93-18-005 For You	D. Zolan	Open	95.00	95.00
93-18-006 The Thinker	D. Zolan	Open	95.00	95.00
Hamilton Collection	**Baby Portrait Dolls**			
91-19-001 Melissa	B. Parker	Closed	135.00	175.00
92-19-002 Jenna	B. Parker	Closed	135.00	195.00
92-19-003 Bethany	B. Parker	Open	135.00	135.00
93-19-004 Mindy	B. Parker	Open	135.00	135.00
Hamilton Collection	**Just Like Mom**			
91-20-001 Ashley	H. Kish	Closed	135.00	225.00
92-20-002 Elizabeth	H. Kish	Open	135.00	135.00
92-20-003 Hannah	H. Kish	Open	135.00	135.00
93-20-004 Margaret	H. Kish	Open	135.00	135.00
Hamilton Collection	**Helen Kish II Dolls**			
92-21-001 Vanessa	H. Kish	Open	135.00	135.00
Hamilton Collection	**Helen Kish III Dolls**			
94-22-001 Jordan	H. Kish	Open	95.00	95.00
Hamilton Collection	**Picnic In The Park**			
91-23-001 Rebecca	J. Esteban	Open	155.00	155.00
92-23-002 Emily	J. Esteban	Open	155.00	155.00
92-23-003 Victoria	J. Esteban	Open	155.00	155.00
93-23-004 Benjamin	J. Esteban	Open	155.00	155.00
Hamilton Collection	**Bride Dolls**			
91-24-001 Portrait of Innocence	Unknown	Open	195.00	195.00
92-24-002 Portrait of Loveliness	Unknown	Open	195.00	195.00
Hamilton Collection	**Maud Humphrey Bogart Dolls**			
92-25-001 Playing Bridesmaid	Unknown	Closed	195.00	225.00
Hamilton Collection	**Year Round Fun**			
92-26-001 Allison	D. Schurig	Open	95.00	95.00
93-26-002 Christy	D. Schurig	Open	95.00	95.00
93-26-003 Paula	D. Schurig	Open	95.00	95.00
94-26-004 Kaylie	D. Schurig	Open	95.00	95.00
Hamilton Collection	**Laura Cobabe Dolls**			
92-27-001 Amber	L. Cobabe	Open	195.00	195.00
92-27-002 Brooke	L. Cobabe	Open	195.00	195.00
Hamilton Collection	**Belles of the Countryside**			
92-28-001 Erin	C. Heath Orange	Open	135.00	135.00
92-28-002 Rose	C. Heath Orange	Open	135.00	135.00
93-28-003 Lorna	C. Heath Orange	Open	135.00	135.00
94-28-004 Gwyn	C. Heath Orange	Open	135.00	135.00
Hamilton Collection	**Dolls By Kay McKee**			
92-29-001 Shy Violet	K. McKee	Closed	135.00	200.00
92-29-002 Robin	K. McKee	Open	135.00	135.00
93-29-003 Katie Did It!	K. McKee	Open	135.00	135.00
93-29-004 Ryan	K. McKee	Open	135.00	135.00
Hamilton Collection	**Parker-Levi Toddlers**			
92-30-001 Courtney	B. Parker	Open	135.00	135.00
92-30-002 Melody	B. Parker	Open	135.00	135.00
Hamilton Collection	**Parkins Treasures**			
92-31-001 Tiffany	P. Parkins	Closed	55.00	55.00
92-31-002 Dorothy	P. Parkins	Closed	55.00	55.00
93-31-003 Charlotte	P. Parkins	Open	55.00	55.00
93-31-004 Cynthia	P. Parkins	Open	55.00	55.00
Hamilton Collection	**I'm So Proud Doll Collection**			
92-32-001 Christina	L. Cobabe	Open	95.00	95.00
93-32-002 Jill	L. Cobabe	Open	95.00	95.00
94-32-003 Tammy	L. Cobabe	Open	95.00	95.00
94-32-004 Shelly	L. Cobabe	Open	95.00	95.00
Hamilton Collection	**Through The Eyes of Virginia Turner**			
92-33-001 Michelle	V. Turner	Closed	95.00	125.00
92-33-002 Danielle	V. Turner	Open	95.00	95.00
93-33-003 Wendy	V. Turner	Open	95.00	95.00
94-33-004 Dawn	V. Turner	Open	95.00	95.00
Hamilton Collection	**Santa's Little Helpers**			
92-34-001 Nicholas	C.W. Derek	Open	155.00	155.00
93-34-002 Hope	C.W. Derek	Open	155.00	155.00
Hamilton Collection	**Victorian Treasures**			
92-35-001 Katherine	C.W. Derek	Open	155.00	155.00
93-35-002 Madeline	C.W. Derek	Open	155.00	155.00
Hamilton Collection	**Daddy's Little Girls**			
92-36-001 Lindsay	M. Snyder	Open	95.00	95.00
93-36-002 Cassie	M. Snyder	Open	95.00	95.00

	ARTIST	EDITION	ISSUE	QUOTE
93-36-003 Dana	M. Snyder	Open	95.00	95.00
Hamilton Collection	**Proud Indian Nation**			
92-37-001 Navajo Little One	N/A	Closed	95.00	180.00
93-37-002 Dressed Up For The Pow Wow	N/A	Open	95.00	95.00
93-37-003 Autumn Treat	N/A	Open	95.00	95.00
94-37-004 Out with Mama's Flock	N/A	Open	95.00	95.00
Hamilton Collection	**Holiday Carollers**			
92-38-001 Joy	U. Lepp	Open	155.00	155.00
93-38-002 Noel	U. Lepp	Open	155.00	155.00
Hamilton Collection	**Joke Grobben Dolls**			
92-39-001 Heather	J. Grobben	Open	69.00	69.00
93-39-002 Kathleen	J. Grobben	Open	69.00	69.00
93-39-003 Brianna	J. Grobben	Open	69.00	69.00
94-39-004 Bridget	J. Grobben	Open	69.00	69.00
Hamilton Collection	**Treasured Toddlers**			
92-40-001 Whitney	V. Turner	Open	95.00	95.00
93-40-002 Natalie	V. Turner	Open	95.00	95.00
Hamilton Collection	**Children To Cherish**			
91-41-001 A Gift of Innocence	N/A	Yr.Iss.	135.00	135.00
91-41-002 A Gift of Beauty	N/A	Open	135.00	135.00
Hamilton Collection	**Wooden Dolls**			
91-42-001 Gretchen	N/A	9,850	225.00	280.00
91-42-002 Heidi	N/A	9,850	225.00	200-250.
Hamilton Collection	**Little Rascals ™**			
92-43-001 Spanky	S./J. Hoffman	Open	75.00	75.00
93-43-002 Alfalfa	S./J. Hoffman	Open	75.00	75.00
94-43-003 Darla	S./J. Hoffman	Open	75.00	75.00
94-43-004 Buckwheat	S./J. Hoffman	Open	75.00	75.00
94-43-005 Stymie	S./J. Hoffman	Open	75.00	75.00
Hamilton Collection	**Littlest Members of the Wedding**			
93-44-001 Matthew & Melanie	J. Esteban	Open	195.00	195.00
Hamilton Collection	**Toddler Days Doll Collection**			
92-45-001 Erica	D. Schurig	Open	95.00	95.00
93-45-002 Darlene	D. Schurig	Open	95.00	95.00
94-45-003 Karen	D. Schurig	Open	95.00	95.00
Hamilton Collection	**Cindy Marschner Rolfe Dolls**			
93-46-001 Shannon	C. M. Rolfe	Open	95.00	95.00
93-46-002 Julie	C. M. Rolfe	Open	95.00	95.00
93-46-003 Kayla	C. M. Rolfe	Open	95.00	95.00
94-46-004 Janey	C. M. Rolfe	Open	95.00	95.00
Hamilton Collection	**Dolls by Autumn Berwick**			
93-47-001 Laura	A. Berwick	Open	135.00	135.00
Hamilton Collection	**Laura Cobabe Dolls II**			
93-48-001 Kristen	L. Cobabe	Open	75.00	75.00
Hamilton Collection	**Brooks Wooden Dolls**			
93-49-001 Waiting For Santa	P. Ryan Brooks	15,000	135.00	135.00
93-49-002 Are You the Easter Bunny?	P. Ryan Brooks	15,000	135.00	135.00
94-49-003 Be My Valentine	P. Ryan Brooks	Open	135.00	135.00
Hamilton Collection	**Zolan Double Dolls**			
93-50-001 First Kiss	N/A	Open	135.00	135.00
Hamilton Collection	**Parkins Portraits**			
93-51-001 Lauren	P. Parkins	Open	79.00	79.00
93-51-002 Kelsey	P. Parkins	Open	79.00	79.00
94-51-003 Morgan	P. Parkins	Open	79.00	79.00
94-51-004 Cassidy	P. Parkins	Open	79.00	79.00
Hamilton Collection	**First Recital**			
93-52-001 Hillary	N/A	Open	135.00	135.00
94-52-002 Olivia	N/A	Open	135.00	135.00
Hamilton Collection	**Join The Parade**			
92-53-001 Betsy	N/A	Open	49.50	49.50
94-53-002 Peggy	N/A	Open	55.00	55.00
94-53-003 Sandy	N/A	Open	55.00	55.00
Hamilton Collection	**Catherine Mather Dolls**			
93-54-001 Justine	C. Mather	15,000	155.00	155.00
Hamilton Collection	**Phyllis Parkins Dolls**			
92-55-001 Swan Princess	P. Parkins	9,850	195.00	195.00
Hamilton Collection	**Annual Connossieur Doll**			
92-56-001 Lara	N/A	7,450	295.00	295.00
Hamilton Collection	**A Child's Menagerie**			
93-57-001 Becky	B. Van Boxel	Open	69.00	69.00
93-57-002 Carrie	B. Van Boxel	Open	69.00	69.00
94-57-003 Mandy	B. Van Boxel	Open	69.00	69.00
Hamilton Collection	**Connie Walser Derek Dolls**			
92-58-001 Baby Jessica	C. W. Derek	Open	75.00	75.00
93-58-002 Baby Sara	C. W. Derek	Open	75.00	75.00
Hamilton Collection	**Connie Walser Derek Baby Dolls II**			
92-59-001 Stephanie	C.W. Derek	Open	95.00	95.00
92-59-002 Beth	C.W. Derek	Open	95.00	95.00
Hamilton Collection	**Kay McKee Klowns**			
93-60-001 The Dreamer	K. McKee	15,000	155.00	155.00
Hamilton Collection	**Sandra Kuck Dolls**			
93-61-001 A Kiss Goodnight	S. Kuck	Open	79.00	79.00
94-61-002 Teaching Teddy	S. Kuck	Open	79.00	79.00
Hamilton Collection	**Jeanne Wilson Dolls**			
94-62-001 Priscilla	J. Wilson	Open	155.00	155.00
Hamilton Collection	**Bridal Elegance**			
94-63-001 Camille	Boehm	Open	195.00	195.00
Hamilton Collection	**Johnston Cowgirls**			
94-64-001 Savannah	C. Johnston	Open	79.00	79.00
Hamilton Collection	**Kuck Fairy**			
94-65-001 Tooth Fairy	S. Kuck	Open	135.00	135.00

	ARTIST	EDITION	ISSUE	QUOTE
Hamilton Collection	**Derek Toddlers**			
94-66-001 Jessie	C. W. Derek	Open	79.00	79.00
Hamilton Collection	**Boehm Dolls**			
94-67-001 Elena	N/A	Open	155.00	155.00
Hamilton Collection	**Best Buddies**			
94-68-001 Jodie	C. Marschner	Open	69.00	69.00
Hamilton Collection	**Laura Cobabe Tall Dolls**			
94-69-001 Cassandra	L. Cobabe	Open	195.00	195.00
94-69-002 Taylor	L. Cobabe	Open	195.00	195.00
Hamilton Collection	**Elaine Campbell Dolls**			
94-70-001 Emma	E. Campbell	Open	95.00	95.00
Edna Hibel Studios	**Child's Fancy**			
85-01-001 Jennie's Lady Jennifer	E. Hibel	Closed	395.00	2,000.00
87-01-002 Wendy's Lady Gwenolyn	E. Hibel	Closed	495.00	900.00
88-01-003 Sami's Lady Samantha	E. Hibel	Closed	495.00	625.00
89-01-004 Sassee's Lady Sarah	E. Hibel	Closed	495.00	635.00
Edna Hibel Studios	**Grandma's Attic**			
87-02-001 Alice	E. Hibel	Closed	129.00	375.00
88-02-002 Martha	E. Hibel	Closed	139.00	400.00
89-02-003 Melanie	E. Hibel	Closed	139.00	180.00
91-02-004 Katie	E. Hibel	Closed	139.00	145.00
Ladie and Friends ™	**The Family and Friends of Lizzie High®**			
85-01-001 Lizzie High®-1100	B.K. Wisber	Open	30.00	37.00
85-01-002 Sabina Valentine (First Edition)-1101	B.K. Wisber	Closed	30.00	100.00
88-01-003 Sabina Valentine (Second Edition)-1101	B.K. Wisber	Open	40.00	42.00
85-01-004 Nettie Brown (First Edition)-1102	B.K. Wisber	Closed	30.00	100.00
88-01-005 Nettie Brown (Second Edition)-1102	B.K. Wisber	Open	36.00	38.00
85-01-006 Emma High-1103	B.K. Wisber	Closed	30.00	100.00
85-01-007 Rebecca Bowman (First Edition)-1104	B.K. Wisber	Closed	30.00	100.00
89-01-008 Rebecca Bowman (Second Edition)-1104	B.K. Wisber	Open	56.00	59.00
85-01-009 Mary Valentine-1105	B.K. Wisber	Closed	30.00	100.00
85-01-010 Wendel Bowman (First Edition)-1106	B.K. Wisber	Closed	30.00	100.00
92-01-011 Wendel Bowman (Second Edition)-1106	B.K. Wisber	Open	60.00	61.00
85-01-012 Russell Dunn-1107	B.K. Wisber	Closed	30.00	100.00
85-01-013 Luther Bowman (First Edition)-1108	B.K. Wisber	Closed	30.00	100.00
93-01-014 Luther Bowman (Second Edition)-1108	B.K. Wisber	Open	60.00	60.00
85-01-015 Elizabeth Sweetland (First Edition)-1109	B.K. Wisber	Closed	30.00	100.00
91-01-016 Elizabeth Sweetland (Second Edition)-1109	B.K. Wisber	Open	56.00	57.00
85-01-017 Christian Bowman-1110	B.K. Wisber	Closed	30.00	100.00
85-01-018 Amanda High (First Edition)-1111	B.K. Wisber	Closed	30.00	100.00
90-01-019 Amanda High (Second Edition)-1111	B.K. Wisber	Open	54.00	57.00
85-01-020 Louella Valentine-1112	B.K. Wisber	Closed	30.00	100.00
85-01-021 Peter Valentine-1113	B.K. Wisber	Closed	30.00	85.00
85-01-022 Nettie Brown (Christmas)-1114	B.K. Wisber	Closed	30.00	100.00
85-01-023 Cora High-1115	B.K. Wisber	Closed	30.00	100.00
85-01-024 Ida Valentine-1116	B.K. Wisber	Closed	30.00	100.00
85-01-025 Martin Bowman-1117	B.K. Wisber	Closed	30.00	43-85.00
85-01-026 Esther Dunn (First Edition)-1127	B.K. Wisber	Closed	45.00	N/A
91-01-027 Esther Dunn (SecondEdition)-1127	B.K. Wisber	Open	60.00	61.00
91-01-028 Cynthia High-1127A	B.K. Wisber	Open	60.00	61.00
85-01-029 Benjamin Bowman-1129	B.K. Wisber	Closed	30.00	100.00
85-01-030 Flossie High (First Edition)-1128	B.K. Wisber	Closed	45.00	125.00
89-01-031 Flossie High (Second Edition)-1128	B.K. Wisber	Open	54.00	56.00
85-01-032 Hannah Brown-1131	B.K. Wisber	Closed	45.00	125.00
85-01-033 Benjamin Bowman (Santa)-1134	B.K. Wisber	Open	34.00	40.00
85-01-034 Katrina Valentine-1135	B.K. Wisber	Closed	30.00	100.00
86-01-035 Grace Valentine (First Edition)-1146	B.K. Wisber	Closed	32.00	100.00
90-01-036 Grace Valentine (Second Edition)-1146	B.K. Wisber	Open	48.00	49.00
86-01-037 Juliet Valentine (First Edition)-1147	B.K. Wisber	Closed	32.00	100.00
90-01-038 Juliet Valentine (Second Edition)-1147	B.K. Wisber	Open	48.00	50.00
86-01-039 Alice Valentine-1148	B.K. Wisber	Closed	32.00	100.00
86-01-040 Susanna Bowman-1149	B.K. Wisber	Closed	45.00	125.00
86-01-041 Annie Bowman (First Edition)-1150	B.K. Wisber	Closed	32.00	100.00
93-01-042 Annie Bowman (Second Edition)-1150	B.K. Wisber	Open	68.00	68.00
86-01-043 Martha High-1151	B.K. Wisber	Closed	32.00	100.00
86-01-044 Dora High (First Edition)-1152	B.K. Wisber	Closed	30.00	100.00
92-01-045 Dora High (Second Edition)-1152	B.K. Wisber	Closed	48.00	48.00
86-01-046 Delia Valentine-1153	B.K. Wisber	Closed	32.00	100.00
86-01-047 Sara Valentine-1154	B.K. Wisber	Closed	32.00	38-76.00
86-01-048 Sally Bowman-1155	B.K. Wisber	Closed	32.00	110.00
86-01-049 Tillie Brown-1156	B.K. Wisber	Closed	32.00	100.00
86-01-050 Andrew Brown-1157	B.K. Wisber	Closed	45.00	125.00
86-01-051 Edward Bowman (First Edition)-1158	B.K. Wisber	Closed	45.00	125.00
94-01-052 Edward Bowman (Second Edition)-1158	B.K. Wisber	Open	76.00	76.00
86-01-053 Thomas Bowman-1159	B.K. Wisber	Closed	30.00	100.00
86-01-054 Maggie High-1160	B.K. Wisber	Closed	30.00	100.00
86-01-055 Karl Valentine (First Edition)-1161	B.K. Wisber	Closed	30.00	100.00
94-01-056 Karl Valentine (Second Edition)-1161	B.K. Wisber	Open	54.00	54.00
86-01-057 Willie Bowman-1162	B.K. Wisber	Closed	30.00	41.00
86-01-058 Sadie Valentine-1163	B.K. Wisber	Open	45.00	48.00
86-01-059 Sophie Valentine-1164	B.K. Wisber	Closed	45.00	125.00
86-01-060 Katie Bowman-1178	B.K. Wisber	Closed	36.00	82.00
86-01-061 Cassie Yocum (First Edition)-1179	B.K. Wisber	Closed	36.00	100.00
92-01-062 Cassie Yocum (Second Edition)-1179	B.K. Wisber	Open	80.00	80.00
86-01-063 Jillian Bowman-1180	B.K. Wisber	Closed	34.00	110.00
86-01-064 Jenny Valentine-1181	B.K. Wisber	Closed	34.00	110.00
86-01-065 Christopher High-1182	B.K. Wisber	Closed	34.00	42.00
86-01-066 Marland Valentine-1183	B.K. Wisber	Closed	33.00	100.00
86-01-067 Marie Valentine (First Edition)-1184	B.K. Wisber	Closed	47.00	125.00
92-01-068 Marie Valentine (Second Edition)-1184	B.K. Wisber	Open	68.00	69.00
86-01-069 Emily Bowman (First Edition)-1185	B.K. Wisber	Closed	34.00	100.00
90-01-070 Emily Bowman (Second Edition)-1185	B.K. Wisber	Open	48.00	49.00
86-01-071 Matthew Yocum-1186	B.K. Wisber	Closed	33.00	100.00
86-01-072 Madaleine Valentine (First Edition)-1187	B.K. Wisber	Closed	34.00	90.00
89-01-073 Madaleine Valentine (Second Edition)-1187	B.K. Wisber	Open	37.00	80.00
86-01-074 Rachel Bowman (First Edition)-1188	B.K. Wisber	Closed	34.00	100.00
89-01-075 Rachel Bowman (Second Edition)-1188	B.K. Wisber	Open	34.00	37.00
86-01-076 Molly Yocum (First Edition)-1189	B.K. Wisber	Closed	34.00	100.00
89-01-077 Molly Yocum (Second Edition)-1189	B.K. Wisber	Open	39.00	41.00
86-01-078 Carrie High (First Edition)-1190	B.K. Wisber	Closed	45.00	100.00
89-01-079 Carrie High (Second Edition)-1190	B.K. Wisber	Open	46.00	72.00
86-01-080 William Valentine-1191	B.K. Wisber	Closed	36.00	80.00
86-01-081 Jeremy Bowman-1192	B.K. Wisber	Closed	36.00	44.00
86-01-082 Marisa Valentine (w/ Brother Petey)-1194	B.K. Wisber	Open	45.00	49.00
86-01-083 Marisa Valentine (alone)-1194A	B.K. Wisber	Open	33.00	38.00

		ARTIST	EDITION	ISSUE	QUOTE
86-01-084	David Yocum-1195	B.K. Wisber	Open	33.00	36.00
86-01-085	Little Ghosts-1197	B.K. Wisber	Open	15.00	18.00
87-01-086	Johanna Valentine-1198	B.K. Wisber	Closed	37.00	100.00
87-01-087	Abigail Bowman-1199	B.K. Wisber	Closed	40.00	90.00
87-01-088	Naomi Valentine-1200	B.K. Wisber	Closed	40.00	88.00
87-01-089	Amy Bowman-1201	B.K. Wisber	Closed	37.00	82.00
87-01-090	Addie High-1202	B.K. Wisber	Open	37.00	41.00
87-01-091	The Wedding (Bride)-1203	B.K. Wisber	Open	37.00	40.00
87-01-092	The Wedding (Groom)-1203A	B.K. Wisber	Open	34.00	36.00
87-01-093	The Flower Girl-1204	B.K. Wisber	Open	17.00	23.00
87-01-094	Olivia High-1205	B.K. Wisber	Open	37.00	41.00
87-01-095	Imogene Bowman-1206	B.K. Wisber	Closed	37.00	40.00
87-01-096	Rebecca's Mother-1207	B.K. Wisber	Open	37.00	42.00
87-01-097	Penelope High-1208	B.K. Wisber	Closed	40.00	100.00
87-01-098	Margaret Bowman-1213	B.K. Wisber	Open	35.00	41.00
87-01-099	Patsy Bowman-1214	B.K. Wisber	Open	50.00	52.00
87-01-100	Ramona Brown-1215	B.K. Wisber	Closed	40.00	50.00
87-01-101	Gretchen High-1216	B.K. Wisber	Closed	40.00	44.00
87-01-102	Cat on Chair-1217	B.K. Wisber	Closed	16.00	35.00
87-01-103	Katie and Barney-1219	B.K. Wisber	Open	38.00	41.00
87-01-104	Melanie Bowman (First Edition)-1220	B.K. Wisber	Closed	36.00	125.00
92-01-105	Melanie Bowman (Second Edition)-1220	B.K. Wisber	Open	46.00	47.00
87-01-106	Charles Bowman (First Edition)-1221	B.K. Wisber	Closed	34.00	100.00
92-01-107	Charles Bowman (Second Edition)-1221	B.K. Wisber	Open	46.00	47.00
87-01-108	Bridget Bowman-1222	B.K. Wisber	Closed	40.00	92.00
87-01-109	Laura Valentine-1223	B.K. Wisber	Closed	36.00	39.00
87-01-110	Santa Claus (sitting)-1224	B.K. Wisber	Closed	50.00	61.00
87-01-111	Little Witch-1225	B.K. Wisber	Open	17.00	22.00
87-01-112	Priscilla High-1226	B.K. Wisber	Open	56.00	61.00
88-01-113	Megan Valentine-1227	B.K. Wisber	Closed	44.00	94.00
87-01-114	Pauline Bowman-1228	B.K. Wisber	Open	44.00	48.00
88-01-115	Allison Bowman-1229	B.K. Wisber	Open	56.00	59.00
88-01-116	Jacob High-1230	B.K. Wisber	Closed	44.00	46.00
88-01-117	Janie Valentine-1231	B.K. Wisber	Open	37.00	41.00
88-01-118	Ruth Anne Bowman-1232	B.K. Wisber	Closed	44.00	46.00
88-01-119	Daphne Bowman-1235	B.K. Wisber	Closed	38.00	40.00
88-01-120	Mary Ellen Valentine-1236	B.K. Wisber	Open	40.00	43.00
88-01-121	Kinch Bowman-1237	B.K. Wisber	Open	47.00	49.00
88-01-122	Samantha Bowman-1238	B.K. Wisber	Open	47.00	49.00
88-01-123	Hattie Bowman-1239	B.K. Wisber	Open	40.00	44.00
88-01-124	Eunice High-1240	B.K. Wisber	Closed	56.00	58.00
88-01-125	Bess High-1241	B.K. Wisber	Open	45.00	48.00
88-01-126	Betsy Valentine-1245	B.K. Wisber	Open	42.00	43.00
88-01-127	Phoebe High-1246	B.K. Wisber	Closed	48.00	59.00
89-01-128	Vanessa High-1247	B.K. Wisber	Open	45.00	48.00
89-01-129	Amelia High-1248	B.K. Wisber	Open	45.00	48.00
89-01-130	Victoria Bowman-1249	B.K. Wisber	Open	40.00	42.00
89-01-131	Johann Bowman-1250	B.K. Wisber	Open	40.00	42.00
89-01-132	Emmy Lou Valentine-1251	B.K. Wisber	Open	45.00	47.00
89-01-133	Peggy Bowman-1252	B.K. Wisber	Open	58.00	60.00
89-01-134	Jessica High (with Mother)-1253	B.K. Wisber	Open	58.00	60.00
89-01-135	Jessica High (alone)-1253A	B.K. Wisber	Open	20.00	23.00
89-01-136	Jason High (with Mother)-1254	B.K. Wisber	Open	58.00	60.00
89-01-137	Jason High (alone)-1254A	B.K. Wisber	Open	20.00	23.00
89-01-138	Lucy Bowman-1255	B.K. Wisber	Open	45.00	47.00
89-01-139	Miriam High-1256	B.K. Wisber	Open	46.00	48.00
89-01-140	Santa (with Tub)-1257	B.K. Wisber	Open	58.00	61.00
89-01-141	Mrs. Claus-1258	B.K. Wisber	Open	42.00	44.00
90-01-142	Marlene Valentine-1259	B.K. Wisber	Open	48.00	50.00
90-01-143	Albert Valentine-1260	B.K. Wisber	Open	42.00	44.00
90-01-144	Nancy Bowman-1261	B.K. Wisber	Open	48.00	50.00
91-01-145	Annabelle Bowman-1267	B.K. Wisber	Open	68.00	69.00
91-01-146	Michael Bowman-1268	B.K. Wisber	Open	52.00	53.00
91-01-147	Trudy Valentine-1269	B.K. Wisber	Open	64.00	65.00
91-01-148	The Department Store Santa-1270	B.K. Wisber	Open	76.00	77.00
91-01-149	Santa's Helper-1271	B.K. Wisber	Open	52.00	53.00
91-01-150	Barbara Helen-1274	B.K. Wisber	Open	58.00	59.00
92-01-151	Edwin Bowman-1281	B.K. Wisber	Closed	70.00	71.00
92-01-152	Carol Anne Bowman-1282	B.K. Wisber	Closed	70.00	71.00
92-01-153	Joseph Valentine-1283	B.K. Wisber	Open	62.00	63.00
92-01-154	Natalie Valentine-1284	B.K. Wisber	Open	62.00	63.00
92-01-155	Kathryn Bowman (Limited Edition)-1285	B.K. Wisber	Closed	140.00	300.00
92-01-156	Wendy Bowman-1293	B.K. Wisber	Open	78.00	79.00
93-01-157	Christmas Tree w/Cats-1293A	B.K. Wisber	Open	42.00	42.00
92-01-158	Timothy Bowman-1294	B.K. Wisber	Open	56.00	57.00
92-01-159	Joanie Valentine-1295	B.K. Wisber	Open	48.00	49.00
93-01-160	Justine Valentine-1302	B.K. Wisber	Open	84.00	84.00
93-01-161	Pearl Bowman-1303	B.K. Wisber	Open	56.00	56.00
92-01-162	Ashley Bowman-1304	B.K. Wisber	Open	48.00	48.00
92-01-163	Francis Bowman-1305	B.K. Wisber	Open	48.00	48.00
93-01-164	Penny Valentine-1308	B.K. Wisber	Open	60.00	60.00
93-01-165	Santa Claus-1311	B.K. Wisber	Open	48.00	48.00
93-01-166	Mommy-1312	B.K. Wisber	Open	48.00	48.00
94-01-167	Josie Valentine-1322	B.K. Wisber	Open	76.00	76.00
94-01-168	Bonnie Valentine-1323	B.K. Wisber	Open	35.00	35.00
94-01-169	Jamie Bowman-1324	B.K. Wisber	Open	35.00	35.00
94-01-170	Elsie Bowman-1325	B.K. Wisber	Open	64.00	64.00
94-01-171	Prudence Valentine-1331	B.K. Wisber	Closed	180.00	180.00
94-01-172	Christine Bowman-1332	B.K. Wisber	Open	62.00	62.00
94-01-173	Marisa Valentine-1333	B.K. Wisber	Open	58.00	58.00
94-01-174	Shirley Bowman-1334	B.K. Wisber	Open	63.00	63.00
94-01-175	Gilbert High-1335	B.K. Wisber	Open	65.00	65.00
94-01-176	Minnie Valentine-1336	B.K. Wisber	Open	64.00	64.00
94-01-177	Gwendolyn High-1342	B.K. Wisber	Open	56.00	56.00

Ladie and Friends ™ — The Little Ones™

		ARTIST	EDITION	ISSUE	QUOTE
85-02-001	White Girl (First Edition)-1130	B.K. Wisber	Closed	15.00	45-65.00
85-02-002	Black Girl (First Edition)-1130	B.K. Wisber	Closed	15.00	45-65.00
85-02-003	White Boy (First Edition)-1130	B.K. Wisber	Closed	15.00	45-65.00
85-02-004	Black Boy (First Edition)-1130	B.K. Wisber	Closed	15.00	45-65.00
89-02-005	White Girl-pastels (Second Edition)-1130D	B.K. Wisber	Closed	20.00	23.00
89-02-006	Black Girl-pastels (Second Edition)-1130E	B.K. Wisber	Closed	20.00	23.00
89-02-007	White Girl-country color (2nd Edition)-1130F	B.K. Wisber	Closed	20.00	23.00
89-02-008	Black Girl-country color(2nd Edition)-1130G	B.K. Wisber	Closed	20.00	23.00
89-02-009	White Boy (Second Edition)-1130H	B.K. Wisber	Closed	20.00	23.00
89-02-010	Black Boy (Second Edition)-1130I	B.K. Wisber	Closed	20.00	23.00
92-02-011	Little One w/Beach Bucket-1275	B.K. Wisber	Open	26.00	27.00
92-02-012	Little One w/Easter Eggs-1276	B.K. Wisber	Open	26.00	27.00
92-02-013	Little One wApples-1277	B.K. Wisber	Open	26.00	27.00
92-02-014	Little One w/Kitten and Yarn-1278	B.K. Wisber	Open	34.00	35.00
92-02-015	Little One w/Birthday Gift-1279	B.K. Wisber	Open	26.00	27.00
92-02-016	Little One w/Kitten and Milk-1280	B.K. Wisber	Open	32.00	33.00
92-02-017	Little One Reading-1286	B.K. Wisber	Open	36.00	37.00
92-02-018	Little One w/Christmas Lights-1287	B.K. Wisber	Open	34.00	35.00
92-02-019	Little One w/Snowman-1288	B.K. Wisber	Open	36.00	37.00
92-02-020	Little One w/Sled-1289	B.K. Wisber	Open	30.00	31.00
92-02-021	Little One Clown-1290	B.K. Wisber	Open	32.00	33.00
92-02-022	Little One w/Valentine-1291	B.K. Wisber	Open	30.00	31.00
92-02-023	Little One Girl w/Easter Flowers-1296	B.K. Wisber	Open	34.00	34.00
93-02-024	Little One Bunny-1297	B.K. Wisber	Open	36.00	36.00
93-02-025	Little One 4th of July Girl-1298	B.K. Wisber	Open	30.00	30.00
93-02-026	Little One w/Spinning Wheel-1299	B.K. Wisber	Open	36.00	36.00
93-02-027	Little One w/Mop-1300	B.K. Wisber	Open	36.00	36.00
92-02-028	Little One Boy w/Easter Flowers-1306	B.K. Wisber	Open	30.00	30.00
93-02-029	Little One 4th of July Boy-1307	B.K. Wisber	Open	28.00	28.00
93-02-030	Little One w/Violin-1319	B.K. Wisber	Open	28.00	28.00
93-02-031	Little One Picnicking-1320	B.K. Wisber	Open	34.00	34.00
93-02-032	Little One Ballerina-1321	B.K. Wisber	Open	40.00	40.00
94-02-033	Little One Girl Dyeing Eggs-1326	B.K. Wisber	Open	30.00	30.00
94-02-034	Little One Boy Dyeing Eggs-1327	B.K. Wisber	Open	30.00	30.00
94-02-035	Little One Nurse-1328	B.K. Wisber	Open	40.00	40.00
94-02-036	Little One Teacher-1329	B.K. Wisber	Open	38.00	38.00
94-02-037	Little One w/Laundry Basket-1338	B.K. Wisber	Open	38.00	38.00
94-02-038	Little w/Puppy in Tub-1339	B.K. Wisber	Open	43.00	43.00
94-02-039	Little One Girl w/Wagon-1340	B.K. Wisber	Open	42.00	42.00
94-02-040	Little One Boy w/Pumpkin-1341	B.K. Wisber	Open	29.00	29.00

Ladie and Friends ™ — The Little Ones at Christmas™

		ARTIST	EDITION	ISSUE	QUOTE
90-03-001	Little One w/Basket of Greens-1263	B.K. Wisber	Open	22.00	25.00
90-03-002	Little One w/Cookie-1264	B.K. Wisber	Open	22.00	25.00
90-03-003	Little One w/Tree Garland-1265	B.K. Wisber	Open	22.00	25.00
90-03-004	Little One w/Gift-1266	B.K. Wisber	Open	22.00	25.00
91-03-005	White Girl w/Santa Photo-1272	B.K. Wisber	Open	24.00	27.00
91-03-006	Black Girl w/Santa Photo-1272A	B.K. Wisber	Open	24.00	27.00
91-03-007	White Boy w/Santa Photo-1273	B.K. Wisber	Open	24.00	27.00
91-03-008	Black Boy w/Santa Photo-1273A	B.K. Wisber	Open	24.00	27.00
93-03-009	Boy Peeking w/Tree-1313	B.K. Wisber	Open	60.00	60.00
93-03-010	Boy Peeking (Alone)-1314	B.K. Wisber	Open	22.00	22.00
93-03-011	Girl Peeking w/Tree-1315	B.K. Wisber	Open	60.00	60.00
93-03-012	Girl Peeking (Alone)-1316	B.K. Wisber	Open	22.00	22.00
93-03-013	Little One w/Baking Table-1317	B.K. Wisber	Open	38.00	38.00
93-03-014	Little One w/Note for Santa-1318	B.K. Wisber	Open	36.00	36.00
94-03-015	Little One w/Greens on Table-1337	B.K. Wisber	Open	46.00	46.00

Ladie and Friends ™ — The Pawtuckets of Sweet Briar Lane™

		ARTIST	EDITION	ISSUE	QUOTE
86-04-001	Aunt Minnie Pawtucket™ (First Edition)-1136	B.K. Wisber	Closed	45.00	110.00
93-04-002	Aunt Minnie Pawtucket™ Second Edition)-1136	B.K. Wisber	Open	72.00	72.00
93-04-003	Flossie Pawtucket™-1136A	B.K. Wisber	Open	33.00	33.00
86-04-004	Grammy Pawtucket™ (First Edition)-1137	B.K. Wisber	Closed	32.00	110.00
94-04-005	Grammy Pawtucket™ Second Edition)-1137	B.K. Wisber	Open	68.00	68.00
86-04-006	Uncle Harley Pawtucket™ (First Edition)-1138	B.K. Wisber	Closed	32.00	110.00
94-04-007	Uncle Harley Pawtucket™ (Second Edition)-1138	B.K. Wisber	Open	74.00	74.00
86-04-008	Sister Flora Pawtucket™-1139	B.K. Wisber	Closed	32.00	110.00
86-04-009	Brother Noah Pawtucket™-1140	B.K. Wisber	Closed	32.00	110.00
86-04-010	Aunt Lillian Pawtucket™ (First Edition)-1141	B.K. Wisber	Closed	32.00	110.00
94-04-011	Aunt Lillian Pawtucket™ (Second Edition)-1141	B.K. Wisber	Open	58.00	58.00
94-04-013	Pawtucket™ Bunny Hutch-1141A	B.K. Wisber	Open	38.00	38.00
86-04-014	Mama Pawtucket™ (First Edition)-1142	B.K. Wisber	Closed	34.00	110.00
94-04-015	Mama Pawtucket™ Second Edition)-1142	B.K. Wisber	Open	86.00	86.00
86-04-016	Pappy Pawtucket™-1143	B.K. Wisber	Closed	32.00	110.00
86-04-017	Cousin Clara Pawtucket™ (First Edition)-1144	B.K. Wisber	Closed	32.00	110.00
86-04-018	The Little One Bunnies-girl (First Edition)-1145	B.K. Wisber	Closed	15.00	50.00
94-04-019	The Little One Bunnies-girl (Second Edition)-1145	B.K. Wisber	Open	33.00	33.00
86-04-020	The Little One Bunnies-boy (First Edition)-1145	B.K. Wisber	Closed	15.00	20.00
94-04-021	The Little One Bunnies-boy (Second Edition)-1145A	B.K. Wisber	Open	33.00	33.00
87-04-022	Cousin Isabel Pawtucket™-1209	B.K. Wisber	Closed	36.00	110.00
87-04-023	Cousin Alberta Pawtucket™-1210	B.K. Wisber	Closed	36.00	110.00
87-04-024	Sister Clemmie Pawtucket™-1211	B.K. Wisber	Closed	34.00	110.00
87-04-025	Aunt Mabel Pawtucket™-212	B.K. Wisber	Closed	45.00	130.00
87-04-026	Bunny Bed-1218	B.K. Wisber	Closed	16.00	110.00
88-04-027	Cousin Winnie Pawtucket™-1233	B.K. Wisber	Closed	49.00	110.00
88-04-028	Cousin Jed Pawtucket™-1234	B.K. Wisber	Closed	34.00	110.00

Ladie and Friends ™ — The Grummels of Log Hollow™

		ARTIST	EDITION	ISSUE	QUOTE
86-05-001	Cousin Miranda Grummel™-1165	B.K. Wisber	Closed	47.00	70-110.
86-05-002	Uncle Hollis Grummel™-1166	B.K. Wisber	Closed	34.00	70-110.
86-05-003	Ma Grummel™-1167	B.K. Wisber	Closed	36.00	70-110.
86-05-004	Teddy Bear Bed-1168	B.K. Wisber	Closed	15.00	70-100.
86-05-005	Aunt Polly Grummel™-1169	B.K. Wisber	Closed	34.00	70-110.
86-05-006	Cousin Lottie Grummel™-1170	B.K. Wisber	Closed	36.00	70-110.
86-05-007	Aunt Gertie Grummel™ 1171	B.K. Wisber	Closed	34.00	70-110.
86-05-008	Pa Grummel™-1172	B.K. Wisber	Closed	34.00	70-110.
86-05-009	Grandma Grummel™-1173	B.K. Wisber	Closed	45.00	70-110.
86-05-010	Aunt Hilda Grummel™-1174	B.K. Wisber	Closed	34.00	70-110.
86-05-011	Washline-1175	B.K. Wisber	Closed	15.00	70-100.
86-05-012	Grandpa Grummel™-1176	B.K. Wisber	Closed	36.00	180.00
86-05-013	Sister Nora Grummel™-1177	B.K. Wisber	Closed	34.00	70-110.
86-05-014	The Little Ones-Grummels™ (boy/girl)-1196	B.K. Wisber	Closed	15.00	40.00

Ladie and Friends ™ — The Thanksgiving Play

		ARTIST	EDITION	ISSUE	QUOTE
88-06-001	Pilgrim Boy-1242	B.K. Wisber	Open	40.00	42.00
88-06-002	Pilgrim Girl-1243	B.K. Wisber	Open	48.00	50.00
88-06-003	Indian Squaw-1244	B.K. Wisber	Open	36.00	38.00

Ladie and Friends ™ — The Christmas Pageant™

		ARTIST	EDITION	ISSUE	QUOTE
85-07-001	Mary and Baby Jesus-1118	B.K. Wisber	Open	30.00	37.00
85-07-002	Joseph and Donkey-1119	B.K. Wisber	Open	30.00	37.00
85-07-003	"Peace" Angel(First Edition)-1120	B.K. Wisber	Closed	30.00	100.00
89-07-004	"Peace" Angel (Second Edition)-1120	B.K. Wisber	Open	48.00	50.00
85-07-005	"On" Angel-1121	B.K. Wisber	Closed	30.00	100.00
85-07-006	"Earth" Angel-1122	B.K. Wisber	Closed	30.00	100.00

		ARTIST	EDITION	ISSUE	QUOTE
85-07-007	"Noel" Angel (First Edition)-1126	B.K. Wisber	Closed	30.00	100.00
89-07-008	"Noel" Angel (Second Edition)-1126	B.K. Wisber	Open	48.00	50.00
85-07-009	Wiseman #1-1123	B.K. Wisber	Open	30.00	37.00
85-07-010	Wiseman #2-1124	B.K. Wisber	Open	30.00	37.00
85-07-011	Wiseman #3-1125	B.K. Wisber	Open	30.00	37.00
85-07-012	Wooden Creche-1132	B.K. Wisber	Open	28.00	31.00
85-07-013	Christmas Wooly Lamb-1133	B.K. Wisber	Closed	11.00	35.00
86-07-014	Shepherd-1193	B.K. Wisber	Open	32.00	37.00
Ladie and Friends™	**The Christmas Concert**				
90-08-001	Claire Valentine-1262	B.K. Wisber	Open	56.00	57.00
92-08-002	Judith High-1292	B.K. Wisber	Open	70.00	71.00
93-08-003	Stephanie Bowman-1309	B.K. Wisber	Open	74.00	74.00
93-08-004	James Valentine-1310	B.K. Wisber	Open	60.00	60.00
Ladie and Friends™	**Lizzie High® Society™ Members-Only Dolls**				
93-09-001	Audrey High-1301	B.K. Wisber	Closed	59.00	59.00
93-09-002	Becky High-1330	B.K. Wisber	Closed	96.00	96.00
94-09-003	Chloe Valentine	B.K. Wisber	8/95	79.00	79.00
Lawtons	**Childhood Classics®**				
83-01-001	Alice In Wonderland	W. Lawton	Closed	225.00	2-3000.
84-01-002	Heidi	W. Lawton	Closed	325.00	650-850.
85-01-003	Hans Brinker	W. Lawton	Closed	325.00	1-1800.
86-01-004	Anne Of Green Gables	W. Lawton	Closed	325.00	2-2400.
86-01-005	Pollyanna	W. Lawton	Closed	325.00	1-1600.
86-01-006	Laura Ingals	W. Lawton	Closed	325.00	500-900.
87-01-007	Mary Lennox	W. Lawton	Closed	325.00	500-900.
87-01-008	Just David	W. Lawton	Closed	325.00	700-1100
87-01-009	Polly Pepper	W. Lawton	Closed	325.00	450-700.
88-01-010	Rebecca	W. Lawton	Closed	350.00	500-850.
88-01-011	Little Eva	W. Lawton	Closed	350.00	500-1000
88-01-012	Topsy	W. Lawton	Closed	350.00	750-1200
89-01-013	Little Princess	W. Lawton	Closed	395.00	650-950.
89-01-014	Honey Bunch	W. Lawton	Closed	350.00	550-800.
90-01-015	Mary Frances	W. Lawton	Closed	350.00	425.00
90-01-016	Poor Little Match Girl	W. Lawton	Closed	350.00	475.00
91-01-017	The Bobbsey Twins: Freddie	W. Lawton	Closed	364.50	364.50
91-01-018	The Bobbsey Twins: Flossie	W. Lawton	Closed	364.50	364.50
91-01-019	Hiawatha	W. Lawton	Closed	395.00	500.00
91-01-020	Little Black Sambo	W. Lawton	Closed	395.00	595.00
Lawtons	**Childhood Classics® II**				
92-02-001	Peter And The Wolf	W. Lawton	Closed	495.00	495.00
92-02-002	Marigold Garden	W. Lawton	Closed	450.00	450.00
92-02-003	Oliver Twist	W. Lawton	Closed	450.00	450.00
93-02-004	Tom Sawyer	W. Lawton	Closed	395.00	395.00
93-02-005	The Velveteen Rabbit	W. Lawton	Closed	395.00	395.00
94-02-006	Girl of the Limberlost	W. Lawton	500	425.00	425.00
Lawtons	**Sugar 'n' Spice**				
86-03-001	Kimberly	W. Lawton	Closed	250.00	550-800.
86-03-002	Kersten	W. Lawton	Closed	250.00	550-800.
86-03-003	Jason	W. Lawton	Closed	250.00	800-1700
86-03-004	Jessica	W. Lawton	Closed	250.00	800-1700
87-03-005	Marie	W. Lawton	Closed	275.00	450.00
87-03-006	Ginger	W. Lawton	Closed	275.00	395-550.
Lawtons	**Newcomer Collection**				
87-04-001	Ellin Elizabeth, Eyes Closed	W. Lawton	Closed	335.00	750-1000
87-04-002	Ellin Elizabeth, Eyes Open	W. Lawton	Closed	335.00	900-1200
Lawtons	**Timeless Ballads®**				
87-05-001	Highland Mary	W. Lawton	Closed	550.00	600-875.
87-05-002	Annabel Lee	W. Lawton	Closed	550.00	600-695.
87-05-003	Young Charlotte	W. Lawton	Closed	550.00	850-900.
88-05-004	She Walks In Beauty	W. Lawton	Closed	550.00	600.00
Lawtons	**One-Of-A Kind Issues**				
89-06-001	Amelia	W. Lawton	1	N/A	N/A
90-06-002	Goldilocks And Baby Bear	W. Lawton	1	N/A	4250.00
91-06-003	Felicity Minds The Quints	W. Lawton	1	N/A	N/A
92-06-004	Little Miss Muffet	W. Lawton	1	3900.00	3900.00
93-06-005	Jack And The Beanstalk	W. Lawton	1	2500.00	2500.00
93-06-006	Curly Locks, Curly Locks	W. Lawton	1	5700.00	5700.00
94-06-007	Sara Crewe Arrives at Miss Minchin's(Disneyworld Auction-FL)	W. Lawton	1	N/A	N/A
Lawtons	**Special Edition**				
88-07-001	Marcella And Raggedy Ann	W. Lawton	Closed	395.00	550-595.
93-07-002	Flora McFlimsey	W. Lawton	Closed	895.00	895.00
94-07-003	Mary Chilton	W. Lawton	350	395.00	395.00
Lawtons	**Christmas Dolls**				
88-08-001	Christmas Joy	W. Lawton	Closed	325.00	750-1200
89-08-002	Noel	W. Lawton	Closed	325.00	325-750.
90-08-003	Christmas Angel	W. Lawton	Closed	325.00	325.00
91-08-004	Yuletide Carole	W. Lawton	Closed	395.00	395.00
Lawtons	**Special Occasion**				
88-09-001	Nanthy	W. Lawton	Closed	325.00	450-525.
89-09-002	First Day Of School	W. Lawton	Closed	325.00	450-550.
90-09-003	First Birthday	W. Lawton	Closed	295.00	350.00
Lawtons	**Seasons**				
88-10-001	Amber Autumn	W. Lawton	Closed	325.00	300.00
89-10-002	Summer Rose	W. Lawton	Closed	325.00	375-475.
90-10-003	Crystal Winter	W. Lawton	Closed	325.00	325.00
91-10-004	Spring Blossom	W. Lawton	Closed	350.00	350.00
Lawtons	**Wee Bits**				
88-11-001	Wee Bit O'Heaven	W. Lawton	Closed	295.00	450-600.
88-11-002	Wee Bit O'Woe	W. Lawton	Closed	295.00	450-700.
88-11-003	Wee Bit O'Sunshine	W. Lawton	Closed	295.00	450-600.
89-11-004	Wee Bit O'Bliss	W. Lawton	Closed	295.00	350.00
89-11-005	Wee Bit O'Wonder	W. Lawton	Closed	295.00	395.00
Lawtons	**Playthings Past**				
89-12-001	Victoria And Teddy	W. Lawton	Closed	395.00	395.00
89-12-002	Edward And Dobbin	W. Lawton	Closed	395.00	495-600.
89-12-003	Elizabeth And Baby	W. Lawton	Closed	395.00	495-650.
Lawtons	**Cherished Customs**				
90-13-001	The Blessing/Mexico	W. Lawton	Closed	395.00	850.00
90-13-002	Midsommar/Sweden	W. Lawton	Closed	395.00	395.00
90-13-003	Girl's Day/Japan	W. Lawton	Closed	395.00	450-600.
90-13-004	High Tea/Great Britain	W. Lawton	Closed	395.00	450-550.

		ARTIST	EDITION	ISSUE	QUOTE
91-13-005	Ndeko/Zaire	W. Lawton	Closed	395.00	550-750.
91-13-006	Frolic/Amish	W. Lawton	Closed	395.00	395.00
92-13-007	Pascha/Ukraine	W. Lawton	Closed	495.00	495.00
92-13-008	Carnival/Brazil	W. Lawton	Closed	425.00	425.00
92-13-009	Cradleboard/Navajo	W. Lawton	Closed	425.00	425.00
93-13-010	Nalauqataq-Eskimo	W. Lawton	Closed	395.00	395.00
93-13-011	Topeng Klana-Java	W. Lawton	Closed	495.00	495.00
94-13-012	Kwanzaa/Africa	W. Lawton	500	425.00	425.00
Lawtons	**Guild Dolls**				
89-14-001	Baa Baa Black Sheep	W. Lawton	Closed	395.00	650.00
90-14-002	Lavender Blue	W. Lawton	Closed	395.00	450-600.
91-14-003	To Market, To Market	W. Lawton	Closed	495.00	495.00
92-14-004	Little Boy Blue	W. Lawton	Closed	395.00	395.00
93-14-005	Lawton Logo Doll	W. Lawton	Closed	350.00	350.00
94-14-006	Wee Handful	W. Lawton	Open	250.00	250.00
Lawtons	**The Children's Hour**				
91-15-001	Grave Alice	W. Lawton	Closed	395.00	475.00
91-15-002	Laughing Allegra	W. Lawton	Closed	395.00	475.00
91-15-003	Edith With Golden Hair	W. Lawton	Closed	395.00	475.00
Lawtons	**Store Exclusives**				
89-16-001	Main Street, USA (Disney World, Lake Buena Vista, FL)	W. Lawton	Closed	350.00	350.00
90-16-002	Liberty Square (Disney World, Lake Buena Vista, FL)	W. Lawton	Closed	350.00	395.00
90-16-003	Little Colonel (Dolly Dears, Birmingham, AL)	W. Lawton	Closed	395.00	395.00
90-16-004	Garden Song Marta (Toy Village, Lansing, MI)	W. Lawton	Closed	335.00	335.00
91-16-005	Tish (Disney World, Lake Buena Vista, FL)	W. Lawton	Closed	395.00	395.00
92-16-006	Karen (Disney World, Lake Buena Vista, FL)	W. Lawton	Closed	395.00	395.00
93-16-007	Brita/Tea Party (Toy Village, Lansing, MI)	W. Lawton	Closed	395.00	395.00
93-16-008	Kellyn (Disneyland, Anaheim, CA)	W. Lawton	Closed	395.00	395.00
93-16-009	A Goofy Little Kid (Disney World, Lake Buena Vista, FL)	W. Lawton	Closed	395.00	395.00
94-16-010	Morgan (Toy Village, Lansing MI)	W. Lawton	100	425.00	425.00
94-16-011	Melissa and her Mickey (Disney World, Lake Buena Vista, FL)	W. Lawton	100	495.00	495.00
Lawtons	**Christmas Legends™**				
91-17-001	The Legend Of The Poinsettia	W. Lawton	Closed	395.00	395.00
93-17-002	The Little Drummer Boy	W. Lawton	Closed	595.00	595.00
94-17-003	Santa Lucia	W. Lawton	350	425.00	425.00
Lawtons	**Folk Tales And Fairy Stories**				
92-18-001	Little Red Riding Hood	W. Lawton	Closed	450.00	450.00
92-18-002	The Little Emperor's Nightingale	W. Lawton	Closed	425.00	425.00
92-18-003	William Tell, The Younger	W. Lawton	Closed	395.00	395.00
92-18-004	Swan Princess	W. Lawton	Closed	495.00	495.00
93-18-005	Snow White	W. Lawton	Closed	395.00	395.00
93-18-006	Goldilocks And Baby Bear	W. Lawton	Closed	595.00	595.00
94-18-007	Little Gretel	W. Lawton	500	395.00	395.00
Lawtons	**Small Wonders**				
93-19-001	Michael	W. Lawton	Closed	149.95	149.95
93-19-002	Meghan	W. Lawton	Closed	149.95	149.95
93-19-003	Jafry	W. Lawton	Closed	149.95	149.95
93-19-004	Jamilla	W. Lawton	Closed	149.95	149.95
Lawtons	**Memories And Melodies™**				
93-20-001	Lyda Rose	W. Lawton	Closed	295.00	295.00
93-20-002	Apple Blossom Time	W. Lawton	Closed	295.00	295.00
93-20-003	Scarlet Ribbons	W. Lawton	Closed	295.00	295.00
93-20-004	In The Good Ol' Summertime	W. Lawton	Closed	295.00	295.00
94-20-005	Let Me Call You Sweetheart	W. Lawton	250	295.00	295.00
Lawtons	**Classic Playthings™**				
93-21-001	Patricia and Her Patsy®	W. Lawton	Closed	595.00	595.00
94-21-002	Katie and Her Kewpie	W. Lawton	750	595.00	595.00
Lawtons	**Centerpieces**				
92-22-001	Lotta On Stage (First Lawton Collectors Guild Convention)	W. Lawton	Closed	N/A	N/A
93-22-002	Little Colonel II (Dolly Dears, Birmingham, AL)	W. Lawton	Closed	N/A	N/A
Lawtons	**Early American Portrait**				
94-23-001	Abigail and Jane Augusta	W. Lawton	250	995.00	995.00
Lawtons	**Gentle Pursuits**				
94-24-001	Emily and Her Diary	W. Lawton	350	795.00	795.00
Lawtons	**Once Upon A Rhyme™**				
94-25-001	At Aunty's House	W. Lawton	350	795.00	795.00
Lawtons	**Grand Tour™**				
94-26-001	Springtime in Paris	W. Lawton	250	895.00	895.00
Lawtons	**Treasured Tales**				
94-27-001	The Dreamer	W. Lawton	500	395.00	395.00
Lenox Collections	**Lenox China Dolls**				
84-01-001	Maryanne, 20"	J. Grammer	Closed	425.00	N/A
84-01-002	Abigail, 20"	J. Grammer	Closed	425.00	N/A
84-01-003	Jessica, 20"	J. Grammer	Closed	450.00	N/A
84-01-004	Rebecca, 16"	J. Grammer	Closed	375.00	N/A
84-01-005	Amanda, 16"	J. Grammer	Closed	385.00	N/A
84-01-006	Maggie, 16"	J. Grammer	Closed	375.00	N/A
84-01-007	Melissa, 16"	J. Grammer	Closed	450.00	N/A
84-01-008	Samantha, 16"	J. Grammer	Closed	500.00	N/A
Lenox Collections	**China Dolls - Cloth Bodies**				
85-02-001	Amy, 14"	J. Grammer	Closed	250.00	N/A
85-02-002	Elizabeth, 14"	J. Grammer	Closed	250.00	N/A
85-02-003	Sarah, 14"	J. Grammer	Closed	250.00	N/A
85-02-004	Annabelle, 14"	J. Grammer	Closed	250.00	N/A
85-02-005	Miranda, 14"	J. Grammer	Closed	250.00	N/A
85-02-006	Jennifer, 14"	J. Grammer	Closed	250.00	N/A
Lenox Collections	**Lenox Victorian Dolls**				
89-03-001	The Victorian Bride	Unknown	Open	295.00	295.00
90-03-002	Christmas Doll, Elizabeth	Unknown	Open	195.00	195.00
91-03-003	Victorian Christening Doll	Unknown	Open	295.00	295.00
92-03-004	Lady at Gala	Unknown	Open	295.00	295.00

	ARTIST	EDITION	ISSUE	QUOTE
Lenox Collections	**Children of the World**			
89-04-001 Hannah, The Little Dutch Maiden	Unknown	Open	119.00	119.00
90-04-002 Heather, Little Highlander	Unknown	Open	119.00	119.00
91-04-003 Amma-The African Girl	Unknown	Open	119.00	119.00
91-04-004 Sakura-The Japanese Girl	Unknown	Open	119.00	119.00
92-04-005 Gretchen, German Doll	Unknown	Open	119.00	119.00
Lenox Collections	**Sibling Dolls**			
91-05-001 Skating Lesson	A. Lester	Open	195.00	195.00
Lenox Collections	**Ellis Island Dolls**			
91-06-001 Megan	P. Thompson	Closed	150.00	150.00
91-06-002 Stefan	P. Thompson	Closed	150.00	150.00
92-06-003 Angelina	P. Thompson	Closed	150.00	150.00
92-06-004 Catherine	P. Thompson	Closed	152.00	152.00
92-06-005 Anna	P. Thompson	Closed	152.00	152.00
Lenox Collections	**Musical Baby Dolls**			
91-07-001 Patrick's Lullabye	Unknown	Open	95.00	95.00
Lenox Collections	**Bolshoi Nutcracker Dolls**			
91-08-001 Clara	Unknown	Open	195.00	195.00
Lenox Collections	**Country Decor Dolls**			
91-09-001 Molly	Unknown	Open	150.00	150.00
Lenox Collections	**Children With Toys Dolls**			
91-10-001 Tea For Teddy	Unknown	Open	136.00	136.00
Lenox Collections	**Little Women**			
92-11-001 Amy, The Inspiring Artist	Unknown	Open	152.00	152.00
Lenox Collections	**First Collector Doll**			
92-12-001 Lauren	Unknown	Open	152.00	152.00
Lenox Collections	**Inspirational Doll**			
92-13-001 Blessed Are The Peacemakers	Unknown	Open	119.00	119.00
Lenox Collections	**International Baby Doll**			
92-14-001 Natalia, Russian Baby	Unknown	Open	119.00	119.00
Lenox Collections	**Nutcracker Dolls**			
92-15-001 Sugarplum	Unknown	Open	195.00	195.00
93-15-002 Nutcracker	Unknown	Open	195.00	195.00
Lenox Collections	**Prima Ballerina Collection**			
92-16-001 Odette, Queen of the Swans	Unknown	Closed	195.00	195.00
Seymour Mann Inc.	**Connossieur Doll Collection**			
84-01-001 Miss Debutante Debi	E. Mann	Closed	75.00	180.00
85-01-002 Christmas Cheer-125	E. Mann	Closed	40.00	100.00
85-01-003 Wendy-C120	E. Mann	Closed	45.00	150.00
86-01-004 Camelot Fairy-C-84	E. Mann	Closed	75.00	225.00
87-01-005 Audrina-YK-200	E. Mann	Closed	85.00	140.00
87-01-006 Cynthia-DOM-211	E. Mann	Closed	85.00	85.00
87-01-006 Dawn-C185	E. Mann	Closed	75.00	175.00
87-01-007 Linda-C190	E. Mann	Closed	60.00	120.00
87-01-008 Marcy-YK122	E. Mann	Closed	55.00	100.00
87-01-009 Nirmala-YK-210	E. Mann	Closed	50.00	50.00
87-01-010 Rapunzel-C158	E. Mann	Closed	95.00	165.00
87-01-011 Sabrina-C208	E. Mann	Closed	65.00	95.00
87-01-012 Sailorette-DOM217	E. Mann	Closed	70.00	150.00
87-01-013 Vivian-C-201P	E. Mann	Closed	80.00	80.00
88-01-014 Ashley-C-278	E. Mann	Closed	80.00	80.00
88-01-015 Brittany-TK-5	E. Mann	Closed	120.00	120.00
88-01-016 Cissie-DOM263	E. Mann	Closed	65.00	135.00
88-01-017 Crying Courtney-PS75	E. Mann	Closed	115.00	115.00
88-01-018 Cynthia-DOM-211	E. Mann	3,500	85.00	85.00
88-01-019 Doll Oliver-FH392	E. Mann	Closed	100.00	100.00
88-01-020 Giselle on Goose-FH176	E. Mann	Closed	105.00	225.00
88-01-021 Emily-YK-243V	E. Mann	Closed	70.00	70.00
88-01-022 Frances-C-233	E. Mann	Closed	80.00	125.00
88-01-023 Jessica-DOM-267	E. Mann	Closed	90.00	90.00
88-01-024 Joanne Cry Baby-PS-50	E. Mann	Closed	100.00	100.00
88-01-025 Jolie-C231	E. Mann	Closed	65.00	150.00
88-01-026 Julie-C245A	E. Mann	Closed	65.00	160.00
88-01-027 Juliette Bride Musical-C246LTM	E. Mann	Closed	150.00	200.00
88-01-028 Kirsten-PS-40G	E. Mann	Closed	70.00	70.00
88-01-029 Lionel-FH206B	E. Mann	Closed	50.00	120.00
88-01-030 Lucinda-DOM-293	E. Mann	Closed	90.00	90.00
88-01-031 Michelle & Marcel-YK176	E. Mann	Closed	70.00	150.00
88-01-032 Pauline-YK-230	E. Mann	Closed	90.00	90.00
88-01-033 Sabrina -C-208	E. Mann	Closed	65.00	95.00
88-01-034 Sister Agnes 14"-C250	E. Mann	Closed	75.00	75.00
88-01-035 Sister Ignatius Notre Dame-FH184	E. Mann	Closed	75.00	75.00
88-01-036 Sister Teresa-FH187	E. Mann	Closed	80.00	80.00
88-01-037 Tracy-C-3006	E. Mann	Closed	95.00	150.00
88-01-038 Vivian-C201P	E. Mann	Closed	80.00	80.00
89-01-039 Ashley-C-278	E. Mann	Closed	80.00	80.00
89-01-040 Amber-DOM-281A	E. Mann	Closed	85.00	85.00
89-01-041 Betty-PS27G	E. Mann	Closed	65.00	125.00
89-01-042 Brett-PS27B	E. Mann	Closed	65.00	125.00
89-01-043 Brittany-TK-4	E. Mann	Closed	150.00	150.00
89-01-044 Baby John-PS-49B	E. Mann	Closed	85.00	85.00
89-01-045 Crying Courtney-PS-75	E. Mann	Closed	115.00	115.00
89-01-046 Daphne Ecru/Mint Green-C3025	E. Mann	Closed	85.00	85.00
89-01-047 Elisabeth-OM-32	E. Mann	Closed	120.00	120.00
89-01-048 Elizabeth-C-246P	E. Mann	Closed	150.00	200.00
89-01-049 Emily-PS-48	E. Mann	Closed	110.00	110.00
89-01-050 Frances-C233	E. Mann	Closed	80.00	125.00
89-01-051 Happy Birthday-C3012	E. Mann	Closed	80.00	125.00
89-01-052 Heidi-260	E. Mann	Closed	50.00	95.00
89-01-053 Jaqueline-DOLL-254M	E. Mann	Closed	85.00	85.00
89-01-054 Joanne Cry Baby-PS-50	E. Mann	2,500	100.00	100.00
89-01-055 Kayoko-PS-24	E. Mann	Closed	75.00	175.00
89-01-056 Kirsten-PS-40G	E. Mann	Closed	70.00	70.00
89-01-057 Ling-Ling-PS-87G	E. Mann	Closed	90.00	90.00
89-01-058 Liz -YK-269	E. Mann	Closed	70.00	100.00
89-01-059 Lucinda -DOM-293	E. Mann	Closed	90.00	90.00
89-01-060 Mai-Ling-PS-79	E. Mann	2,500	100.00	100.00
89-01-061 Marcey-YK-4005	E. Mann	3,500	90.00	90.00
89-01-062 Margaret-245	E. Mann	Closed	100.00	150.00
89-01-063 Maureen-PS-84	E. Mann	Closed	90.00	90.00
89-01-064 Meimei-PS22	E. Mann	Closed	75.00	225.00
89-01-065 Melissa-LL-794	E. Mann	Closed	95.00	95.00
89-01-066 Miss Kim-PS-25	E. Mann	Closed	75.00	175.00

	ARTIST	EDITION	ISSUE	QUOTE
89-01-067 Patricia/Patrick-215GBB	E. Mann	Closed	105.00	135.00
89-01-068 Paula-PS-56	E. Mann	Closed	75.00	75.00
89-01-069 Pauline Bonaparte-OM68	E. Mann	Closed	120.00	120.00
89-01-070 Ramona-PS-31B	E. Mann	Closed	80.00	80.00
89-01-071 Rebecca-PS-34V	E. Mann	Closed	45.00	45.00
89-01-072 Rosie-290M	E. Mann	Closed	55.00	85.00
89-01-073 Sister Mary-C-249	E. Mann	Closed	75.00	125.00
89-01-074 Sunny-PS-59V	E. Mann	Closed	71.00	71.00
89-01-075 Suzie-PS-32	E. Mann	Closed	80.00	80.00
89-01-076 Tatiana Pink Ballerina-OM-60	E. Mann	Closed	120.00	175.00
89-01-077 Terri-PS-104	E. Mann	Closed	85.00	85.00
89-01-078 Wendy-PS-51	E. Mann	Closed	105.00	105.00
90-01-079 Anabelle-C-3080	E. Mann	Closed	85.00	85.00
90-01-080 Angel-DOM-335	E. Mann	Closed	105.00	105.00
90-01-081 Angela-C-3084	E. Mann	Closed	105.00	105.00
90-01-082 Angela-C-3084M	E. Mann	Closed	115.00	115.00
90-01-083 Anita-FH-277G	E. Mann	Closed	65.00	65.00
90-01-084 Ashley-FH-325	E. Mann	Closed	75.00	75.00
90-01-085 Audrey-YK-4089	E. Mann	Closed	125.00	125.00
90-01-086 Baby Betty-YK-4087	E. Mann	Closed	125.00	125.00
90-01-087 Baby Bonnie-SP-341	E. Mann	Closed	55.00	55.00
90-01-088 Baby Brent-EP-15	E. Mann	Closed	85.00	85.00
90-01-089 Baby Ecru-WB-17	E. Mann	Closed	65.00	65.00
90-01-090 Baby Kate-WB-19	E. Mann	Closed	85.00	85.00
90-01-091 Baby Nelly-PS-163	E. Mann	Closed	95.00	95.00
90-01-092 Baby Sue-DOLL-402B	E. Mann	Closed	27.50	27.50
90-01-093 Baby Sunshine-C-3055	E. Mann	Closed	90.00	90.00
90-01-094 Beth-YK-4099A/B	E. Mann	Closed	125.00	125.00
90-01-095 Bettina-TR-4	E. Mann	Closed	125.00	125.00
90-01-096 Beverly-DOLL-335	E. Mann	Closed	110.00	110.00
90-01-097 Billie-YK-4056V	E. Mann	Closed	65.00	65.00
90-01-098 Caillin-DOLL-11PH	E. Mann	Closed	60.00	60.00
90-01-099 Caitlin-YK-4051V	E. Mann	Closed	90.00	90.00
90-01-100 Carole-YK-4085W	E. Mann	Closed	125.00	125.00
90-01-101 Charlene-YK-4112	E. Mann	Closed	90.00	90.00
90-01-102 Chin Fa-C-3061	E. Mann	Closed	95.00	95.00
90-01-103 Chinook-WB-24	E. Mann	Closed	85.00	85.00
90-01-104 Chrissie-WB-2	E. Mann	Closed	75.00	75.00
90-01-105 Daisy-EP-6	E. Mann	Closed	90.00	90.00
90-01-106 Daphne Ecru-C-3025	E. Mann	Closed	85.00	85.00
90-01-107 Dianna-TK-31	E. Mann	Closed	175.00	175.00
90-01-108 Diane-FH-275	E. Mann	Closed	90.00	90.00
90-01-109 Domino-C-3050	E. Mann	Closed	145.00	200.00
90-01-110 Dorri-DOLL-16PH	E. Mann	Closed	85.00	85.00
90-01-111 Dorothy-TR-10	E. Mann	Closed	135.00	150.00
90-01-112 Eileen-FH-367	E. Mann	Closed	100.00	100.00
90-01-113 Felicia-TR-9	E. Mann	Closed	115.00	115.00
90-01-114 Francesca-C-3021	E. Mann	Closed	100.00	175.00
90-01-115 Gerri Beige-YK4094	E. Mann	Closed	95.00	140.00
90-01-116 Ginny-YK-4119	E. Mann	Closed	100.00	100.00
90-01-117 Hope-YK-4118	E. Mann	Closed	90.00	90.00
90-01-118 Hyacinth-DOLL-15PH	E. Mann	Closed	85.00	85.00
90-01-119 Indian Doll-FH-295	E. Mann	Closed	60.00	60.00
90-01-120 Janette-DOLL-385	E. Mann	Closed	85.00	85.00
90-01-121 Jillian-DOLL-41PH	E. Mann	Closed	90.00	90.00
90-01-122 Joanne-TR-12	E. Mann	Closed	175.00	175.00
90-01-123 Julie-WB-35	E. Mann	Closed	70.00	70.00
90-01-124 Karen-PS-198	E. Mann	Closed	150.00	150.00
90-01-125 Kate-C-3060	E. Mann	Closed	95.00	95.00
90-01-126 Kathy w/Bear-TE1	E. Mann	Closed	70.00	70.00
90-01-127 Kiku-EP-4	E. Mann	Closed	100.00	100.00
90-01-128 Laura-DOLL-25PH	E. Mann	Closed	55.00	55.00
90-01-129 Lauren-SP-300	E. Mann	Closed	85.00	85.00
90-01-130 Lavender Blue-YK-4024	E. Mann	Closed	95.00	135.00
90-01-131 Lien Wha-YK-4092	E. Mann	Closed	100.00	100.00
90-01-132 Ling-Ling-DOLL	E. Mann	Closed	50.00	50.00
90-01-133 Lisa-FH-379	E. Mann	Closed	100.00	100.00
90-01-134 Lisa Beige Accordion Pleat-YK4093	E. Mann	Closed	125.00	125.00
90-01-135 Liza-C-3053	E. Mann	Closed	100.00	100.00
90-01-136 Lola-SP-79	E. Mann	Closed	105.00	105.00
90-01-137 Loretta-FH-321	E. Mann	Closed	90.00	90.00
90-01-138 Lori-WB-72BM	E. Mann	Closed	75.00	75.00
90-01-139 Madame De Pompadour-C-3088	E. Mann	Closed	250.00	250.00
90-01-140 Maggie-PS-151P	E. Mann	Closed	90.00	90.00
90-01-141 Maggie-WB-51	E. Mann	Closed	105.00	105.00
90-01-142 Maria-YK-4116	E. Mann	Closed	85.00	85.00
90-01-143 Melanie-YK-4115	E. Mann	Closed	80.00	80.00
90-01-144 Melissa-DOLL-390	E. Mann	Closed	75.00	75.00
90-01-145 Merry Widow-C-3040	E. Mann	Closed	145.00	145.00
90-01-146 Merry Widow 20"-C-3040M	E. Mann	Closed	140.00	140.00
90-01-147 Nanook-WB-23	E. Mann	Closed	75.00	75.00
90-01-148 Natasha-PS-102	E. Mann	Closed	100.00	100.00
90-01-149 Odessa-FH-362	E. Mann	Closed	65.00	65.00
90-01-150 Ping-Ling-DOLL-363RV	E. Mann	Closed	50.00	50.00
90-01-151 Polly-DOLL-22PH	E. Mann	Closed	90.00	90.00
90-01-152 Princess Fair Skies-FH-268B	E. Mann	Closed	75.00	75.00
90-01-153 Princess Red Feather-PS-189	E. Mann	Closed	90.00	90.00
90-01-154 Priscilla-WB-50	E. Mann	Closed	105.00	105.00
90-01-155 Sabrina-C3050	E. Mann	Closed	105.00	105.00
90-01-156 Sally-WB-20	E. Mann	Closed	95.00	95.00
90-01-157 Shirley-WB-37	E. Mann	Closed	65.00	65.00
90-01-158 Sister Mary-WB-15	E. Mann	Closed	70.00	70.00
90-01-159 Sophie-OM-1	E. Mann	Closed	65.00	65.00
90-01-160 Stacy-TR-5	E. Mann	Closed	105.00	105.00
90-01-161 Sue Chuen-C-3061G	E. Mann	Closed	95.00	95.00
90-01-162 Sunny-FH-331	E. Mann	Closed	70.00	70.00
90-01-163 Susan-DOLL-364MC	E. Mann	Closed	75.00	75.00
90-01-164 Tania-DOLL-376P	E. Mann	Closed	65.00	65.00
90-01-165 Tina-DOLL-371	E. Mann	Closed	85.00	85.00
90-01-166 Tina-WB-32	E. Mann	Closed	65.00	65.00
90-01-167 Tommy-C-3064	E. Mann	Closed	75.00	75.00
90-01-168 Wendy-TE-3	E. Mann	Closed	75.00	75.00
90-01-169 Wilma-PS-174	E. Mann	Closed	75.00	75.00
90-01-170 Yen Yen-YK-4091	E. Mann	Closed	95.00	95.00
91-01-171 Abigail-EP-3	E. Mann	Closed	100.00	100.00
91-01-172 Abigal-WB-72WM	E. Mann	Closed	75.00	75.00
91-01-173 Abby 16" Pink Dress-C3145	E. Mann	Closed	100.00	100.00
91-01-174 Alexis 24" Beige Lace-EP32	E. Mann	Closed	220.00	220.00
91-01-175 Alicia-YK-4215	E. Mann	Closed	90.00	90.00
91-01-176 Amanda Toast-OM-182	E. Mann	Closed	260.00	260.00
91-01-177 Amelia-TR-47	E. Mann	Closed	105.00	105.00

		ARTIST	EDITION	ISSUE	QUOTE
91-01-178	Amy-C-3147	E. Mann	Closed	135.00	135.00
91-01-179	Ann-TR-52	E. Mann	Closed	135.00	135.00
91-01-180	Annette-TR-59	E. Mann	Closed	130.00	130.00
91-01-181	Annie-YK-4214	E. Mann	Closed	145.00	145.00
91-01-182	Antoinette-FH-452	E. Mann	Closed	100.00	100.00
91-01-183	Arabella-C-3163	E. Mann	Closed	135.00	135.00
91-01-184	Ariel 34" Blue/White-EP-33	E. Mann	Closed	175.00	175.00
91-01-185	Audrey-FH-455	E. Mann	2,500	125.00	125.00
91-01-186	Aurora Gold 22"-OM-181	E. Mann	2,500	260.00	260.00
91-01-187	Azure-AM-15	E. Mann	2,500	175.00	175.00
91-01-188	Baby Beth-DOLL-406P	E. Mann	2,500	27.50	27.50
91-01-189	Baby Bonnie w/Walker Music-DOLL-409	E. Mann	2,500	40.00	40.00
91-01-190	Baby Bonnie-SP-341	E. Mann	Closed	55.00	55.00
91-01-191	Baby Brent-EP-15	E. Mann	Closed	85.00	85.00
91-01-192	Baby Carrie-DOLL-402P	E. Mann	2,500	27.50	27.50
91-01-193	Baby Ecru-WB-17	E. Mann	Closed	65.00	65.00
91-01-194	Baby Ellie Ecru Musical-DOLL-402E	E. Mann	2,500	27.50	27.50
91-01-195	Baby Gloria Black Baby-PS-289	E. Mann	Closed	75.00	75.00
91-01-196	Baby John-PS-498	E. Mann	Closed	85.00	85.00
91-01-197	Baby Linda-DOLL-406E	E. Mann	2,500	27.50	27.50
91-01-198	Baby Sue-DOLL-402B	E. Mann	2,500	27.50	27.50
91-01-199	Belinda-C-3164	E. Mann	Closed	150.00	150.00
91-01-200	Bernetta-EP-40	E. Mann	Closed	115.00	115.00
91-01-201	Betsy-AM-6	E. Mann	Closed	105.00	105.00
91-01-202	Bettina-YK-4144	E. Mann	Closed	105.00	105.00
91-01-203	Blaine-TR-61	E. Mann	Closed	115.00	115.00
91-01-204	Blythe-CH-15V	E. Mann	Closed	135.00	135.00
91-01-205	Bo-Peep w/Lamb-C-3128	E. Mann	Closed	105.00	105.00
91-01-206	Bridget-SP-379	E. Mann	2,500	105.00	105.00
91-01-207	Brooke-FH-461	E. Mann	2,500	115.00	115.00
91-01-208	Bryna-AM-100B	E. Mann	2,500	70.00	70.00
91-01-209	Camellia-FH-457	E. Mann	2,500	100.00	100.00
91-01-210	Caroline-LL-838	E. Mann	2,500	110.00	110.00
91-01-211	Caroline-LL-905	E. Mann	2,500	110.00	110.00
91-01-212	Cheryl-TR-49	E. Mann	2,500	120.00	120.00
91-01-213	Chin Chin-YK-4211	E. Mann	Closed	85.00	85.00
91-01-214	Christina-PS-261	E. Mann	Closed	115.00	115.00
91-01-215	Cindy Lou-FH-464	E. Mann	2,500	85.00	85.00
91-01-216	Cissy-EP-56	E. Mann	2,500	95.00	95.00
91-01-217	Clare-DOLL-465	E. Mann	Open	100.00	100.00
91-01-218	Claudine-C-3146	E. Mann	Closed	95.00	95.00
91-01-219	Colette-WB-7	E. Mann	Closed	65.00	65.00
91-01-220	Colleen-YK-4163	E. Mann	Closed	120.00	120.00
91-01-221	Cookie-GU-6	E. Mann	2,500	110.00	110.00
91-01-222	Courtney-LL-859	E. Mann	2,500	150.00	150.00
91-01-223	Creole-AM-17	E. Mann	2,500	160.00	160.00
91-01-224	Crystal-YK-4237	E. Mann	3,500	125.00	125.00
91-01-225	Danielle-AM-5	E. Mann	Closed	125.00	125.00
91-01-226	Darcy-EP-47	E. Mann	Closed	110.00	110.00
91-01-227	Darcy-FH-451	E. Mann	2,500	105.00	105.00
91-01-228	Daria-C-3122	E. Mann	Closed	110.00	110.00
91-01-229	Darlene-DOLL-444	E. Mann	2,500	75.00	75.00
91-01-230	Dawn-C-3135	E. Mann	Closed	130.00	130.00
91-01-231	Denise-LL-852	E. Mann	2,500	105.00	105.00
91-01-232	Dephine-SP-308	E. Mann	Closed	135.00	135.00
91-01-233	Desiree-LL-898	E. Mann	2,500	120.00	120.00
91-01-234	Duanane-SP-366	E. Mann	Closed	85.00	85.00
91-01-235	Dulcie-YK-4131V	E. Mann	Closed	100.00	100.00
91-01-236	Dwayne-C-3123	E. Mann	Closed	120.00	120.00
91-01-237	Edie -YK-4177	E. Mann	Closed	115.00	115.00
91-01-238	Elisabeth and Lisa-C-3095	E. Mann	2,500	195.00	195.00
91-01-239	Elise -PS-259	E. Mann	Closed	105.00	105.00
91-01-240	Elizabeth-AM-32	E. Mann	2,500	105.00	105.00
91-01-241	Emmaline-OM-191	E. Mann	2,500	300.00	300.00
91-01-242	Emmaline Beige/Lilac-OM-197	E. Mann	Closed	300.00	300.00
91-01-243	Emmy-C-3099	E. Mann	Closed	125.00	125.00
91-01-244	Erin-DOLL-4PH	E. Mann	Closed	60.00	60.00
91-01-245	Evalina-C-3124	E. Mann	Closed	135.00	135.00
91-01-246	Fifi-AM-100F	E. Mann	Closed	70.00	70.00
91-01-247	Fleurette-PS-286	E. Mann	2,500	75.00	75.00
91-01-248	Flora-TR-46	E. Mann	Closed	125.00	125.00
91-01-249	Francesca-AM-14	E. Mann	2,500	175.00	175.00
91-01-250	Georgia-YK-4131	E. Mann	Closed	100.00	100.00
91-01-251	Georgia-YK-4143	E. Mann	Closed	150.00	150.00
91-01-252	Gigi-C-3107	E. Mann	Closed	135.00	135.00
91-01-253	Ginger-LL-907	E. Mann	Closed	115.00	115.00
91-01-254	Gloria-AM-100G	E. Mann	2,500	70.00	70.00
91-01-255	Gloria-YK-4166	E. Mann	Closed	105.00	105.00
91-01-256	Gretchen-DOLL-446	E. Mann	Open	45.00	45.00
91-01-257	Gretel-DOLL-434	E. Mann	Closed	60.00	60.00
91-01-258	Hansel and Gretel-DOLL-448V	E. Mann	Closed	60.00	60.00
91-01-259	Helene-AM-29	E. Mann	2,500	150.00	150.00
91-01-260	Holly-CH-6	E. Mann	Closed	100.00	100.00
91-01-261	Honey-FH-401	E. Mann	Closed	100.00	100.00
91-01-262	Honey Bunny-WB-9	E. Mann	Closed	70.00	70.00
91-01-263	Hope-FH-434	E. Mann	2,500	90.00	90.00
91-01-264	Indira-AM-4	E. Mann	2,500	125.00	125.00
91-01-265	Iris-TR-58	E. Mann	Closed	120.00	120.00
91-01-266	Ivy-PS-307	E. Mann	Closed	75.00	75.00
91-01-267	Jane-PS-243L	E. Mann	Closed	115.00	115.00
91-01-268	Janice-OM-194	E. Mann	2,500	300.00	300.00
91-01-269	Jessica-FH-423	E. Mann	2,500	95.00	95.00
91-01-270	Joy-EP-23V	E. Mann	Closed	130.00	130.00
91-01-271	Joyce-AM-100J	E. Mann	2,500	35.00	35.00
91-01-272	Julia-C-3102	E. Mann	Closed	135.00	135.00
91-01-273	Juliette-OM-192	E. Mann	2,500	300.00	300.00
91-01-274	Karen-EP-24	E. Mann	Closed	115.00	115.00
91-01-275	Karmela-EP-57	E. Mann	2,500	120.00	120.00
91-01-276	Kelly-AM-8	E. Mann	Closed	125.00	125.00
91-01-277	Kerry-FH-396	E. Mann	Closed	100.00	100.00
91-01-278	Kim-AM-100K	E. Mann	2,500	70.00	70.00
91-01-279	Kinesha-SP-402	E. Mann	2,500	110.00	110.00
91-01-280	Kristi-FH-402	E. Mann	Closed	100.00	100.00
91-01-281	Kyla-YK-4137	E. Mann	Closed	95.00	95.00
91-01-282	Laura-WB-110P	E. Mann	Closed	85.00	85.00
91-01-283	Leigh-DOLL-457	E. Mann	2,500	95.00	95.00
91-01-284	Leila-AM-2	E. Mann	Closed	125.00	125.00
91-01-285	Lenore-LL-911	E. Mann	2,500	105.00	105.00
91-01-286	Lenore-YK-4218	E. Mann	3,500	135.00	135.00
91-01-287	Libby-EP-18	E. Mann	Closed	85.00	85.00
91-01-288	Lila-AM-10	E. Mann	2,500	125.00	125.00
91-01-289	Lila-FH-404	E. Mann	2,500	100.00	100.00
91-01-290	Lindsey-C-3127	E. Mann	Closed	135.00	135.00
91-01-291	Linetta-C-3166	E. Mann	Closed	135.00	135.00
91-01-292	Lisa-AM-100L	E. Mann	2,500	70.00	70.00
91-01-293	Little Boy Blue-C-3159	E. Mann	Closed	100.00	100.00
91-01-294	Liz-C-3150	E. Mann	2,500	100.00	100.00
91-01-295	Liza-YK-4226	E. Mann	3,500	35.00	35.00
91-01-296	Lola-SP-363	E. Mann	2,500	90.00	90.00
91-01-297	Loni-FH-448	E. Mann	2,500	100.00	100.00
91-01-298	Lori-EP-52	E. Mann	2,500	95.00	95.00
91-01-299	Louise-LL-908	E. Mann	2,500	105.00	105.00
91-01-300	Lucy-LL-853	E. Mann	Closed	80.00	80.00
91-01-301	Madeleine-C-3106	E. Mann	Closed	95.00	95.00
91-01-302	Marcy-TR-55	E. Mann	Closed	135.00	135.00
91-01-303	Mariel 18" Ivory-C-3119	E. Mann	Closed	125.00	125.00
91-01-304	Maude-AM-100M	E. Mann	2,500	70.00	70.00
91-01-305	Melissa-AM-9	E. Mann	Closed	120.00	120.00
91-01-306	Melissa-CH-3	E. Mann	Closed	110.00	110.00
91-01-307	Melissa-LL-901	E. Mann	Closed	135.00	135.00
91-01-308	Meredith-FH-391-P	E. Mann	Closed	95.00	95.00
91-01-309	Meryl-FH-463	E. Mann	2,500	95.00	95.00
91-01-310	Michael w/School Books-FH-439B	E. Mann	2,500	95.00	95.00
91-01-311	Michelle Lilac/Green-EP36	E. Mann	Closed	95.00	95.00
91-01-312	Michelle w/School Books-FH-439G	E. Mann	Closed	95.00	95.00
91-01-313	Miranda-DOLL-9PH	E. Mann	Closed	75.00	75.00
91-01-314	Missy-DOLL-464	E. Mann	Closed	70.00	70.00
91-01-315	Missy-PS-258	E. Mann	Closed	90.00	90.00
91-01-316	Mon Yun w/Parasol-TR33	E. Mann	2,500	115.00	115.00
91-01-317	Nancy 21" Pink w/Rabbit-EP-31	E. Mann	Closed	165.00	165.00
91-01-318	Nancy -WB-73	E. Mann	2,500	65.00	65.00
91-01-319	Nellie-EP-1B	E. Mann	Closed	75.00	75.00
91-01-320	Nicole-AM-12	E. Mann	Closed	135.00	135.00
91-01-321	Noelle-PS-239V	E. Mann	Closed	95.00	95.00
91-01-322	Patti-DOLL-440	E. Mann	2,500	65.00	65.00
91-01-323	Patty-YK-4221	E. Mann	3,500	125.00	125.00
91-01-324	Pepper-PS-277	E. Mann	Closed	130.00	130.00
91-01-325	Pia-PS-246L	E. Mann	Closed	115.00	115.00
91-01-326	Princess Summer Winds-FH-427	E. Mann	2,500	120.00	120.00
91-01-327	Prissy White/Blue-C-3140	E. Mann	Closed	100.00	100.00
91-01-328	Rapunzel-C-3157	E. Mann	2,500	150.00	150.00
91-01-329	Red Wing-AM-30	E. Mann	2,500	165.00	165.00
91-01-330	Robin-AM-22	E. Mann	Closed	120.00	120.00
91-01-331	Rosalind-C-3090	E. Mann	Closed	150.00	150.00
91-01-332	Samantha-GU-3	E. Mann	Closed	100.00	100.00
91-01-333	Sandra-DOLL-6-PHE	E. Mann	2,500	65.00	65.00
91-01-334	Scarlett-FH-399	E. Mann	2,500	100.00	100.00
91-01-335	Scarlett-FH-436	E. Mann	2,500	135.00	135.00
91-01-336	Shaka-SP-401	E. Mann	2,500	110.00	110.00
91-01-337	Sharon 21" Blue-EP-34	E. Mann	Closed	120.00	120.00
91-01-338	Shau Chen-GU-2	E. Mann	2,500	85.00	85.00
91-01-339	Shelley-CH-1	E. Mann	2,500	110.00	110.00
91-01-340	Sophie-TR-53	E. Mann	2,500	135.00	135.00
91-01-341	Stacy-DOLL-6PH	E. Mann	Closed	65.00	65.00
91-01-342	Stephanie-AM-11	E. Mann	Closed	105.00	105.00
91-01-343	Stephanie-FH-467	E. Mann	Closed	95.00	95.00
91-01-344	Stephanie Pink & White-OM-196	E. Mann	Closed	300.00	300.00
91-01-345	Summer-AM-33	E. Mann	Closed	200.00	200.00
91-01-346	Sybil 20" Beige-C-3131	E. Mann	Closed	135.00	135.00
91-01-347	Sybil Pink-DOLL-12PHMC	E. Mann	2,500	75.00	75.00
91-01-348	Tamara-OM-187	E. Mann	Closed	135.00	135.00
91-01-349	Terri-TR-62	E. Mann	Closed	75.00	75.00
91-01-350	Tessa-AM-19	E. Mann	Closed	135.00	135.00
91-01-351	Tina-AM-16	E. Mann	Closed	130.00	130.00
91-01-352	Vanessa-AM-34	E. Mann	Closed	90.00	90.00
91-01-353	Vicki-C-3101	E. Mann	Closed	200.00	200.00
91-01-345	Violet-EP-41	E. Mann	Closed	135.00	135.00
91-01-355	Violet-OM-186	E. Mann	2,500	270.00	270.00
91-01-356	Virginia-SP-359	E. Mann	Closed	120.00	120.00
91-01-357	Wah-Ching Watching Oriental Toddler YK-4175	E. Mann	Closed	110.00	110.00
92-01-358	Alice-JNC-4013	E. Mann	Open	90.00	90.00
92-01-359	Amy-OM-06	E. Mann	2,500	150.00	150.00
92-01-360	Beth-OM-05	E. Mann	Closed	135.00	135.00
92-01-361	Bette-OM-01	E. Mann	2,500	115.00	115.00
92-01-362	Charlotte-FH-484	E. Mann	2,500	115.00	115.00
92-01-363	Chelsea-IND-397	E. Mann	Open	85.00	85.00
92-01-364	Cordelia-OM-009	E. Mann	2,500	250.00	250.00
92-01-365	Cordelia-OM-09	E. Mann	2,500	250.00	250.00
92-01-366	Debbie-JNC-4006	E. Mann	Open	90.00	90.00
92-01-367	Deidre-FH-473	E. Mann	2,500	115.00	115.00
92-01-368	Deidre-YK-4083	E. Mann	Closed	95.00	95.00
92-01-369	Dona-FH-494	E. Mann	2,500	100.00	100.00
92-01-370	Eugenie-OM-225	E. Mann	2,500	300.00	300.00
92-01-371	Giselle-OM-02	E. Mann	Closed	90.00	90.00
92-01-372	Jan-OM-012	E. Mann	9,200	135.00	135.00
92-01-373	Janet-FH-496	E. Mann	2,500	120.00	120.00
92-01-374	Jet-FH-478	E. Mann	2,500	115.00	115.00
92-01-375	Jodie-FH-495	E. Mann	2,500	115.00	115.00
92-01-376	Juliette-OM-08	E. Mann	2,500	175.00	175.00
92-01-377	Laura-OM-010	E. Mann	2,500	250.00	250.00
92-01-378	Laurie-JNC-4004	E. Mann	Open	90.00	90.00
92-01-379	Lydia-OM-226	E. Mann	2,500	250.00	250.00
92-01-380	Maggie-FH-505	E. Mann	Closed	125.00	125.00
92-01-381	Melissa-OM-03	E. Mann	2,500	135.00	135.00
92-01-382	Nancy-JNC-4001	E. Mann	Open	90.00	90.00
92-01-383	Sally-FH-492	E. Mann	2,500	105.00	105.00
92-01-384	Sapphires-OM-223	E. Mann	2,500	250.00	250.00
92-01-385	Sara Ann-FH-474	E. Mann	2,500	115.00	115.00
92-01-386	Scarlett-FH-471	E. Mann	2,500	120.00	120.00
92-01-387	Sonja-FH-486	E. Mann	2,500	125.00	125.00
92-01-388	Sue-JNC-4003	E. Mann	Open	90.00	90.00
92-01-389	Tiffany-OM-014	E. Mann	2,500	150.00	150.00
92-01-390	Trina-OM-011	E. Mann	Closed	165.00	165.00
92-01-391	Violette-FH-503	E. Mann	2,500	120.00	120.00
92-01-392	Yvette-OM-015	E. Mann	2,500	150.00	150.00
93-01-393	Adrienne C-3162	E. Mann	Closed	135.00	135.00
93-01-394	Antonia OM-227	E. Mann	2,500	350.00	350.00
93-01-395	Arlene SP-421	E. Mann	Closed	100.00	100.00
93-01-396	Blaine C-3167	E. Mann	Closed	100.00	100.00
93-01-397	Camille OM-230	E. Mann	2,500	250.00	250.00
93-01-398	Cinnamon JNC-4014	E. Mann	Closed	90.00	90.00
93-01-399	Clare FH-497	E. Mann	2,500	100.00	100.00

		ARTIST	EDITION	ISSUE	QUOTE
93-01-400	Clothilde FH-469	E. Mann	2,500	125.00	125.00
93-01-401	Donna DOLL-447	E. Mann	2,500	85.00	85.00
93-01-402	Ellen YK-4223	E. Mann	3,500	150.00	150.00
93-01-403	Gena OM-229	E. Mann	Closed	250.00	250.00
93-01-404	Happy FH-479	E. Mann	2,500	105.00	105.00
93-01-405	Hedy FH-449	E. Mann	Closed	95.00	95.00
93-01-406	Iris FH-483	E. Mann	2,500	95.00	95.00
93-01-407	Jan Dress-Up OM-12	E. Mann	2,500	135.00	135.00
93-01-408	Jillian SP-428	E. Mann	Closed	165.00	165.00
93-01-409	Juliette OM-8	E. Mann	2,500	175.00	175.00
93-01-410	Kendra FH-481	E. Mann	2,500	115.00	115.00
93-01-411	Kit SP-426	E. Mann	Closed	55.00	55.00
93-01-412	Linda SP-435	E. Mann	Closed	95.00	95.00
93-01-413	Lynn FH-498	E. Mann	2,500	120.00	120.00
93-01-414	Mariah LL-909	E. Mann	Closed	135.00	135.00
93-01-415	Nina YK-4232	E. Mann	3,500	135.00	135.00
93-01-416	Oona TR-57	E. Mann	Closed	135.00	135.00
93-01-417	Rebecca C-3177	E. Mann	2,500	135.00	135.00
93-01-418	Saretta SP-423	E. Mann	2,500	100.00	100.00
93-01-419	Shaka TR-45	E. Mann	2,500	100.00	100.00
93-01-420	Suzie SP-422	E. Mann	2,500	164.00	164.00
94-01-421	Abby YK-4533	E. Mann	3,500	135.00	135.00
94-01-422	Adak PS-412	E. Mann	2,500	150.00	150.00
94-01-423	Alice GU-32	E. Mann	2,500	150.00	150.00
94-01-424	Alice IND-508	E. Mann	2,500	115.00	115.00
94-01-425	Ally FH-556	E. Mann	2,500	115.00	115.00
94-01-426	Alyssa C-3201	E. Mann	2,500	110.00	110.00
94-01-427	Alyssa PP-1	E. Mann	2,500	275.00	275.00
94-01-428	Amy OC-43M	E. Mann	2,500	115.00	115.00
94-01-429	Angel LL-956	E. Mann	2,500	90.00	90.00
94-01-430	Angel SP-460	E. Mann	2,500	140.00	140.00
94-01-431	Angelica FH-291E	E. Mann	2,500	85.00	85.00
94-01-432	Angelina FH-291S	E. Mann	2,500	85.00	85.00
94-01-433	Angeline FH-291WG	E. Mann	2,500	85.00	85.00
94-01-434	Angelita FH-291G	E. Mann	2,500	85.00	85.00
94-01-435	Angelo OC-57	E. Mann	2,500	135.00	135.00
94-01-436	Antonia OM-42	E. Mann	2,500	150.00	150.00
94-01-437	Arilene LL-940	E. Mann	2,500	90.00	90.00
94-01-438	Atanak PS-414	E. Mann	2,500	150.00	150.00
94-01-439	Baby Belle C-3193	E. Mann	2,500	150.00	150.00
94-01-440	Baby Scarlet C-3194	E. Mann	2,500	115.00	115.00
94-01-441	Blair YK-4532	E. Mann	3,500	150.00	150.00
94-01-442	Bobbi NM-30	E. Mann	2,500	135.00	135.00
94-01-443	Brandy YK-4537	E. Mann	3,500	165.00	165.00
94-01-444	Bronwyn IND-517	E. Mann	2,500	140.00	140.00
94-01-445	Cactus Flower Indian LL-944	E. Mann	2,500	105.00	105.00
94-01-446	Callie TR-76	E. Mann	2,500	140.00	140.00
94-01-447	Calypso LL-942	E. Mann	2,500	150.00	150.00
94-01-448	Carmen PS-408	E. Mann	2,500	150.00	150.00
94-01-449	Casey C-3197	E. Mann	2,500	140.00	140.00
94-01-450	Cathy GU-41	E. Mann	2,500	140.00	140.00
94-01-451	Chris FH-561	E. Mann	2,500	85.00	85.00
94-01-452	Chrissie FH-562	E. Mann	2,500	85.00	85.00
94-01-453	Cindy OC-58	E. Mann	2,500	140.00	140.00
94-01-454	Clara IND-518	E. Mann	2,500	140.00	140.00
94-01-455	Clara IND-524	E. Mann	2,500	150.00	150.00
94-01-456	Claudette TR-81	E. Mann	2,500	150.00	150.00
94-01-457	Copper YK-4546C	E. Mann	3,500	150.00	150.00
94-01-458	Cora FH-565	E. Mann	2,500	140.00	140.00
94-01-459	Cory FH-564	E. Mann	2,500	115.00	115.00
94-01-460	Dallas PS-403	E. Mann	2,500	150.00	150.00
94-01-461	Daryl LL-947	E. Mann	2,500	150.00	150.00
94-01-462	Dee LL-948	E. Mann	2,500	110.00	110.00
94-01-463	Delilah C-3195	E. Mann	2,500	150.00	150.00
94-01-464	Faith IND-522	E. Mann	2,500	135.00	135.00
94-01-465	Faith OC-60	E. Mann	2,500	115.00	115.00
94-01-466	Flora FH-583	E. Mann	2,500	115.00	115.00
94-01-467	Florette IND-519	E. Mann	2,500	140.00	140.00
94-01-468	Gardiner PS-405	E. Mann	2,500	150.00	150.00
94-01-469	Georgia IND-510	E. Mann	2,500	220.00	220.00
94-01-470	Georgia SP-456	E. Mann	2,500	115.00	115.00
94-01-471	Hatty/Matty IND-514	E. Mann	2,500	165.00	165.00
94-01-472	Heather YK-4531	E. Mann	3,500	165.00	165.00
94-01-473	Honey LL-945	E. Mann	2,500	150.00	150.00
94-01-474	Hyacinth LL-941	E. Mann	2,500	90.00	90.00
94-01-475	Indian IND-520	E. Mann	2,500	115.00	115.00
94-01-476	Ivy C-3203	E. Mann	2,500	85.00	85.00
94-01-477	Jacqueline C-3202	E. Mann	2,500	150.00	150.00
94-01-478	Jan FH-584R	E. Mann	2,500	115.00	115.00
94-01-479	Janis FH-584B	E. Mann	2,500	115.00	115.00
94-01-480	Jenny OC-36M	E. Mann	2,500	115.00	115.00
94-01-481	Jillian C-3196	E. Mann	2,500	150.00	150.00
94-01-482	Jo YK-4539	E. Mann	3,500	150.00	150.00
94-01-483	Jordan SP-455	E. Mann	2,500	150.00	150.00
94-01-484	Kate OC-55	E. Mann	2,500	150.00	150.00
94-01-485	Katie IND-511	E. Mann	2,500	110.00	110.00
94-01-486	Kelly YK-4536	E. Mann	3,500	150.00	150.00
94-01-487	Kevin MS-25	E. Mann	2,500	150.00	150.00
94-01-488	Kevin YK-4543	E. Mann	3,500	140.00	140.00
94-01-489	Kit YK-4547	E. Mann	3,500	115.00	115.00
94-01-490	Kitten IND-512	E. Mann	2,500	110.00	110.00
94-01-491	Lady Caroline LL-938	E. Mann	2,500	120.00	120.00
94-01-492	Lady Caroline LL-939	E. Mann	2,500	120.00	120.00
94-01-493	Laughing Waters PS-410	E. Mann	2,500	150.00	150.00
94-01-494	Lauren SP-458	E. Mann	2,500	125.00	125.00
94-01-495	Lindsay SP-462	E. Mann	2,500	150.00	150.00
94-01-496	Little Red Riding Hood FH-557	E. Mann	2,500	140.00	140.00
94-01-497	Loretta SP-457	E. Mann	2,500	140.00	140.00
94-01-498	Lucinda PS-406	E. Mann	2,500	150.00	150.00
94-01-499	Magnolia FH-558	E. Mann	2,500	150.00	150.00
94-01-500	Maiden PS-409	E. Mann	2,500	150.00	150.00
94-01-501	Mandy YK-4548	E. Mann	3,500	115.00	115.00
94-01-502	Margaret C-3204	E. Mann	2,500	150.00	150.00
94-01-503	Maria GU-35	E. Mann	2,500	115.00	115.00
94-01-504	Mary OC-56	E. Mann	2,500	135.00	135.00
94-01-505	Mary Ann TR-79	E. Mann	2,500	125.00	125.00
94-01-506	Mary Jo FH-552	E. Mann	2,500	150.00	150.00
94-01-507	Mary Lou FH-565	E. Mann	2,500	135.00	135.00
94-01-508	Megan C-3192	E. Mann	2,500	150.00	150.00
94-01-509	Miss Elizabeth SP-459	E. Mann	2,500	150.00	150.00
94-01-510	Missy FH-567	E. Mann	2,500	140.00	140.00
94-01-511	Morning Dew Indian PS-404	E. Mann	2,500	150.00	150.00
94-01-512	Musical Doll OC-45M	E. Mann	2,500	140.00	140.00
94-01-513	Natalie PP-2	E. Mann	2,500	275.00	275.00
94-01-514	Nikki PS-401	E. Mann	2,500	150.00	150.00
94-01-515	Nikki SP-461	E. Mann	2,500	150.00	150.00
94-01-516	Noel MS-27	E. Mann	2,500	150.00	150.00
94-01-517	Noelle C-3199	E. Mann	2,500	195.00	195.00
94-01-518	Noelle MS-28	E. Mann	2,500	150.00	150.00
94-01-519	Odetta IND-521	E. Mann	2,500	140.00	140.00
94-01-520	Oriana IND-515	E. Mann	2,500	140.00	140.00
94-01-521	Paige GU-33	E. Mann	2,500	150.00	150.00
94-01-522	Pamela LL-949	E. Mann	2500	115.00	115.00
94-01-523	Panama OM-43	E. Mann	2,500	195.00	195.00
94-01-524	Patty GU-34	E. Mann	2,500	115.00	115.00
94-01-525	Payson YK-4541	E. Mann	3,500	135.00	135.00
94-01-526	Payton PS-407	E. Mann	2,500	150.00	150.00
94-01-527	Pearl IND-523	E. Mann	2,500	275.00	275.00
94-01-528	Petula C-3191	E. Mann	2,500	140.00	140.00
94-01-529	Pegeen C-3205	E. Mann	2,500	150.00	150.00
94-01-530	Peggy TR-75	E. Mann	2,500	185.00	185.00
94-01-531	Princess Foxfire PS-411	E. Mann	2,500	150.00	150.00
94-01-532	Princess Moonrise YK-4542	E. Mann	3,500	140.00	140.00
94-01-533	Princess Snow Flower PS-402	E. Mann	2,500	150.00	150.00
94-01-534	Priscilla YK-4538	E. Mann	3,500	135.00	135.00
94-01-535	Rebecca C-3177	E. Mann	2,500	135.00	135.00
94-01-536	Regina OM-41	E. Mann	2,500	150.00	150.00
94-01-537	Rita FH-553	E. Mann	2,500	115.00	115.00
94-01-538	Robby NM-29	E. Mann	2,500	135.00	135.00
94-01-539	Saretta SP-423	E. Mann	2,500	100.00	100.00
94-01-540	Shaka TR-45	E. Mann	2,500	100.00	100.00
94-01-541	Sister Suzie IND-509	E. Mann	2,500	95.00	95.00
94-01-542	Southern Belle FH-570	E. Mann	2,500	140.00	140.00
94-01-543	Sparkle OM-40	E. Mann	2,500	150.00	150.00
94-01-544	Stephie OC-41M	E. Mann	2,500	115.00	115.00
94-01-545	Sue Kwei TR-73	E. Mann	2,500	110.00	110.00
94-01-546	Sugar Plum Fairy OM-39	E. Mann	2,500	150.00	150.00
94-01-547	Suzanne LL-943	E. Mann	2,500	105.00	105.00
94-01-548	Suzie GU-38	E. Mann	2,500	135.00	135.00
94-01-549	Suzie SP-422	E. Mann	2,500	164.00	164.00
94-01-550	Taffey TR-80	E. Mann	2,500	150.00	150.00
94-01-551	Tallulah OM-44	E. Mann	2,500	275.00	275.00
94-01-552	Teresa C-3198	E. Mann	2,500	110.00	110.00
94-01-553	Tiffany OC-44M	E. Mann	2,500	140.00	140.00
94-01-554	Tippi LL-946	E. Mann	2,500	110.00	110.00
94-01-555	Todd YK-4540	E. Mann	3,500	45.00	45.00
94-01-556	Topaz TR-74	E. Mann	2,500	195.00	195.00
94-01-557	Trixie TR-77	E. Mann	2,500	110.00	110.00
94-01-558	Virginia TR-78	E. Mann	2,500	195.00	195.00
94-01-559	Wendy MS-26	E. Mann	2,500	150.00	150.00

Seymour Mann Inc. Signature Doll Series

		ARTIST	EDITION	ISSUE	QUOTE
91-02-001	Amber-MS-1	M. Severino	Closed	95.00	95.00
91-02-002	Becky-MS-2	M. Severino	5,000	95.00	95.00
91-02-003	Bianca-PK-101	P. Kolesar	Closed	120.00	120.00
91-02-004	Bridgette-PK-104	P. Kolesar	Closed	120.00	120.00
91-02-005	Clair-Ann-PK-252	P. Kolesar	5,000	100.00	100.00
91-02-006	Daddy's Little Darling-MS-8	M. Severino	5,000	165.00	165.00
91-02-007	Dozy Elf w/ Featherbed-MAB-100	M.A. Byerly	Closed	110.00	110.00
91-02-008	Duby Elf w/ Featherbed-MAB-103	M.A. Byerly	Closed	110.00	110.00
91-02-009	Dudley Elf w/ Featherbed-MAB-101	M.A. Byerly	Closed	110.00	110.00
91-02-010	Duffy Elf w/ Featherbed-MAB-102	M.A. Byerly	Closed	110.00	110.00
91-02-011	Enoc-PK-100	P. Kolesar	5,000	100.00	100.00
91-02-012	Mikey-MS-3	M. Severino	5,000	95.00	95.00
91-02-013	Mommy's Rays of Sunshine-MS-9	M. Severino	5,000	165.00	165.00
91-02-014	Paulette-PAC-2	P. Aprile	5,000	250.00	250.00
91-02-015	Paulette-PAC-4	P. Aprile	5,000	250.00	250.00
91-02-016	Precious Baby-SB-100	S. Bilotto	5,000	250.00	250.00
91-02-017	Precious Pary Time-SB-102	S. Bilotto	5,000	250.00	250.00
91-02-018	Precious Spring Time-SB-104	S. Bilotto	Closed	250.00	250.00
91-02-019	Shun Lee-PK-102	P. Kolesar	Closed	120.00	120.00
91-02-020	Sparkle-PK-250	P. Kolesar	5,000	100.00	100.00
91-02-021	Stephie-MS-6	M. Severino	Closed	125.00	125.00
91-02-022	Alice-MS-7	M. Severino	5,000	120.00	120.00
91-02-023	Su Lin-MS-5	M. Severino	5,000	105.00	105.00
91-02-024	Susan Marie-PK-103	P. Kolesar	Closed	120.00	120.00
91-02-025	Sweet Pea-PK-251	P. Kolesar	Closed	100.00	100.00
91-02-026	Yawning Kate-MS-4	M. Severino	Closed	105.00	105.00
92-02-027	Abigail-MS-11	M. Severino	5,000	125.00	125.00
92-02-028	Adora-MS-14	M. Severino	5,000	185.00	185.00
92-02-029	Alexandria-PAC-19	P. Aprile	5,000	300.00	300.00
92-02-030	Baby Cakes Crumbs-PK-CRUMBS	P. Kolesar	5,000	17.50	17.50
92-02-031	Baby Cakes Crumbs/Black-PK-CRUMBS/B	P. Kolesar	5,000	17.50	17.50
92-02-032	Bride & Flower Girl-PAC-6	P. Aprile	5,000	600.00	600.00
92-02-033	Cassandra-PAC-8	P. Aprile	Closed	450.00	450.00
92-02-034	Cassie Flower Girl-PAC-9	P. Aprile	Closed	175.00	175.00
92-02-035	Celine-PAC-11	P. Aprile	5,000	165.00	165.00
92-02-036	Clarissa-PAC-3	P. Aprile	5,000	165.00	165.00
92-02-037	Cody-MS-19	M. Severino	Closed	120.00	120.00
92-02-038	Creole Black-HP-202	H. Payne	Closed	250.00	250.00
92-02-039	Cynthia-PAC-10	P. Aprile	Closed	165.00	165.00
92-02-040	Darla-HP-204	H. Payne	5,000	250.00	250.00
92-02-041	Dulcie-HP-200	H. Payne	Closed	250.00	250.00
92-02-042	Dustin-HP-201	H. Payne	5,000	250.00	250.00
92-02-043	Eugenie Bride-PAC-1	P. Aprile	5,000	165.00	165.00
92-02-044	Evening Star-PAC-5	P. Aprile	Closed	500.00	500.00
92-02-045	Kate-MS-15	M. Severino	Closed	190.00	190.00
92-02-046	Little Match Girl-HP-205	H. Payne	Closed	150.00	150.00
92-02-047	Little Turtle Indian-PK-110	P. Kolesar	Closed	150.00	150.00
92-02-048	Megan-MS-12	M. Severino	5,000	125.00	125.00
92-02-049	Melanie-PAC-14	P. Aprile	Closed	300.00	300.00
92-02-050	Nadia-PAC-18	P. Aprile	Closed	175.00	175.00
92-02-051	Olivia-PAC-12	P. Aprile	Closed	300.00	300.00
92-02-052	Pavlova-PAC-17	P. Aprile	5,000	145.00	145.00
92-02-053	Polly-HP-206	H. Payne	5,000	120.00	120.00
92-02-054	Raven Eskimo-PK-106	P. Kolesar	Closed	130.00	130.00
92-02-055	Rebecca Beige Bonnet-MS-17B	M. Severino	5,000	175.00	175.00
92-02-056	Ruby-MS-18	M. Severino	5,000	135.00	135.00
92-02-057	Sally-MS-25	M. Severino	5,000	110.00	110.00
92-02-058	Spanky-HP-25	H. Payne	5,000	250.00	250.00
92-02-059	Stacy-MS-24	M. Severino	Closed	110.00	110.00
92-02-060	Vanessa-PAC-15	P. Aprile	Closed	300.00	300.00
92-02-061	Victoria w/Blanket-MS-10	M. Severino	Closed	110.00	110.00

		ARTIST	EDITION	ISSUE	QUOTE
92-02-062	Violetta-PAC-16	P. Aprile	5,000	165.00	165.00
93-02-063	Bonnett Baby MS-17W	M. Severino	5,000	175.00	175.00
93-02-064	Grace HKH-2	H. Kahl-Hyland	5,000	250.00	250.00
93-02-065	Helene HKH-1	H. Kahl-Hyland	5,000	250.00	250.00
93-02-066	Reilly HKH-3	H. Kahl-Hyland	5,000	260.00	260.00
94-02-067	Sis JAG-110	J. Grammer	5,000	110.00	110.00
94-02-068	Tex JAG-114	J. Grammer	5,000	110.00	110.00
94-02-069	Tracy JAG-111	J. Grammer	5,000	150.00	150.00
94-02-070	Trevor JAG-112	J. Grammer	5,000	115.00	115.00

Mattel — **Bob Mackie Barbie Dolls**

90-01-001	Gold Barbie 5405	B. Mackie	Retrd.	144.00	550-695.
91-01-002	Platinum Barbie 2703	B. Mackie	Retrd.	153.00	350-595.
91-01-003	Starlight Splendor Barbie 2704	B. Mackie	Retrd.	135.00	200-500.
92-01-004	Neptune Fantasy Barbie 4248	B. Mackie	Retrd.	160.00	200-500.
92-01-005	Empress Bride Barbie 4247	B. Mackie	Retrd.	232.00	300-550.
93-01-006	Masquerade	B. Mackie	Retrd.	N/A	200-250.

Mattel — **Nostalgic Porcelain Barbie Dolls**

89-02-001	Wedding Day Barbie 2641	Mattel	Retrd.	198.00	450-600.
90-02-002	Sophisticated Lady 5313	Mattel	Retrd.	198.00	200-215.
90-02-003	Solo in the Spotlight 7613	Mattel	Retrd.	198.00	200-295.

Mattel — **35th Anniversary Dolls by Mattel**

94-03-001	Blonde	Mattel	Retrd.	39.99	39.99
94-03-002	Brunette	Mattel	Retrd.	39.99	95-100.
94-03-003	Gift Pack	Mattel	Retrd.	79.97	100-200.

Mattel — **Golden Jubilee**

94-04-001	Golden Jubliee	C. Spencer	Retrd.	325.00	650-995.

Mattel — **The Winter Princess Collection**

93-05-001	Winter Princess	Mattel	Retrd.	59.95	125-150.
94-05-002	Evergreen Princess	Mattel	Open	59.95	59.95

Jan McLean Originals — **Flowers of the Heart Collection**

90-01-001	Pansy	J. McLean	100	2200.00	2700.00
90-01-002	Poppy	J. McLean	100	2200.00	2800.00
91-01-003	Primrose	J. McLean	100	2500.00	28-3000.
91-01-004	Marigold	J. McLean	100	2400.00	2700.00

Jan McLean Originals — **Jan McLean Originals**

90-02-001	Phoebe I	J. McLean	25	2700.00	3600.00
91-02-002	Lucrezia	J. McLean	15	6000.00	6000.00

Middleton Doll Company — **Porcelain Limited Edition Series**

88-01-001	Cherish-1st Edition	L. Middleton	Retrd.	350.00	500.00
88-01-002	Sincerity -1st Edition-Nettie/Simplicity	L. Middleton	Retrd.	330.00	350-600.
89-01-003	My Lee	L. Middleton	Retrd.	500.00	500.00
89-01-004	Devan	L. Middleton	Retrd.	500.00	500.00
90-01-005	Baby Grace	L. Middleton	Retrd.	500.00	500.00
90-01-006	Johanna	L. Middleton	Retrd.	500.00	500.00
91-01-007	Molly Rose	L. Middleton	Retrd.	500.00	500.00
94-01-008	Bride	L. Middleton	Retrd.	1390.00	1390.00
94-01-009	Tenderness-Petite Pierrot	L. Middleton	Retrd.	500.00	500.00
94-01-010	Blossom	L. Middleton	250	500.00	500.00

Middleton Doll Company — **Limited Edition Vinyl**

81-02-001	Little Angel-Kingdom (Hand Painted)	L. Middleton	Retrd.	40.00	300.00
85-02-002	Little Angel-King-2 (Hand Painted)	L. Middleton	Retrd.	40.00	200.00
89-02-003	Angel Fancy	L. Middleton	Retrd.	120.00	150.00
90-02-004	Baby Grace	L. Middleton	Retrd.	190.00	250.00
90-02-005	Sincerity-Apricots n' Cream	L. Middleton	Retrd.	250.00	250.00
90-02-006	Sincerity-Apples n' Spice	L. Middleton	Retrd.	250.00	250.00
90-02-007	Forever Cherish	L. Middleton	Retrd.	170.00	200.00
90-02-008	First Moments-Twin Boy	L. Middleton	Retrd.	180.00	180.00
90-02-009	First Moments-Twin Girl	L. Middleton	Retrd.	180.00	180.00
90-02-010	Angel Locks	L. Middleton	Retrd.	140.00	150.00
90-02-011	Missy- Buttercup	L. Middleton	5,000	160.00	180.00
90-02-012	Dear One-Sunday Best	L. Middleton	Retrd.	140.00	140.00
91-02-013	Bubba Batboy	L. Middleton	Retrd.	190.00	190.00
91-02-014	My Lee Candy Cane	L. Middleton	Retrd.	170.00	170.00
91-02-015	Devan Delightful	L. Middleton	Retrd.	170.00	170.00
91-02-016	Gracie Mae	L. Middleton	5,000	250.00	250.00
92-02-017	Johanna	L. Middleton	Retrd.	190.00	200.00
92-02-018	Cottontop Cherish	L. Middleton	Retrd.	180.00	180.00
92-02-019	Molly Rose	L. Middleton	5,000	196.00	196.00
92-02-020	Gracie Mae (Brown Hair)	L. Middleton	Retrd.	250.00	250.00
92-02-021	Gracie Mae (Blond Hair)	L. Middleton	Open	250.00	250.00
92-02-022	Serenity Berries & Bows	L. Middleton	Retrd.	250.00	250.00
92-02-023	Sincerity Petals & Plums	L. Middleton	Retrd.	250.00	250.00
93-02-024	Amanda Springtime	L. Middleton	2,000	180.00	180.00
94-02-025	Johanna-Newborn	L. Middleton	2,000	180.00	180.00
94-02-026	Joey-Newborn	L. Middleton	1,000	180.00	180.00
94-02-027	The Bride	L. Middleton	1,000	250.00	250.00
94-02-028	Beloved-Happy Birthday (Pink)	L. Middleton	1,000	220.00	220.00
94-02-029	Beloved-Happy Birthday (Blue)	L. Middleton	1,000	220.00	220.00

Middleton Doll Company — **First Moments Series**

84-03-001	First Moments (Sleeping)	L. Middleton	Retrd.	69.00	150.00
86-03-002	First Moments Blue Eyes	L. Middleton	Retrd.	120.00	150.00
86-03-003	First Moments Brown Eyes	L. Middleton	Retrd.	120.00	150.00
87-03-004	First Moments Boy	L. Middleton	Retrd.	130.00	160.00
87-03-005	First Moments Christening (Asleep)	L. Middleton	Retrd.	160.00	180.00
87-03-006	First Moments Christening (Awake)	L. Middleton	Retrd.	160.00	180.00
90-03-007	First Moments Sweetness	L. Middleton	Open	180.00	180.00
92-03-008	First Moments Awake in Pink	L. Middleton	Retrd.	170.00	170.00
92-03-009	First Moments Awake in Blue	L. Middleton	Retrd.	170.00	170.00
93-03-010	First Moments Heirloom	L. Middleton	Open	190.00	190.00
94-03-011	Sweetness-Newborn	L. Middleton	Open	190.00	190.00

Middleton Doll Company — **Vinyl Collectors Series**

86-04-001	Bubba Chubbs	L. Middleton	Retrd.	100.00	150-200.
88-04-002	Bubba Chubbs Railroader	L. Middleton	Retrd.	140.00	170.00
86-04-003	Little Angel - 3rd Edition	L. Middleton	Retrd.	90.00	110.00
85-04-004	Angel Face	L. Middleton	Retrd.	90.00	150.00
87-04-005	Missy	L. Middleton	Retrd.	100.00	120.00
87-04-006	Amanda - 1st Edition	L. Middleton	Retrd.	140.00	160.00
86-04-007	Dear One - 1st Edition	L. Middleton	Retrd.	90.00	250.00
88-04-008	Cherish	L. Middleton	Retrd.	160.00	250.00
88-04-009	Sincerity - Limited 1st Ed. - Nettie/Simplicity	L. Middleton	Retrd.	160.00	200-250.
89-04-010	My Lee	L. Middleton	Retrd.	170.00	170.00
89-04-011	Devan	L. Middleton	Retrd.	170.00	170.00
89-04-012	Sincerity-Schoolgirl	L. Middleton	Retrd.	180.00	200.00
92-04-013	Little Angel Girl	L. Middleton	Open	130.00	130.00
92-04-014	Little Angel Boy	L. Middleton	Open	130.00	130.00
92-04-015	Beth	L. Middleton	Open	160.00	160.00
92-04-016	Polly Esther	L. Middleton	Open	160.00	160.00
93-04-017	Echo	L. Middleton	Open	180.00	180.00
94-04-018	Angel Kisses Girl	L. Middleton	Open	98.00	98.00
94-04-019	Angel Kisses Boy	L. Middleton	Open	98.00	98.00
94-04-020	Country Girl	L. Middleton	Open	118.00	118.00
94-04-021	Country Boy	L. Middleton	Open	118.00	118.00
94-04-022	Town Girl	L. Middleton	Open	118.00	118.00
94-04-023	Town Boy	L. Middleton	Open	118.00	118.00
94-04-024	Country Girl (Dark Flesh)	L. Middleton	Open	118.00	118.00
94-04-025	Country Boy (Dark Flesh)	L. Middleton	Open	118.00	118.00
94-04-026	Town Girl (Dark Flesh)	L. Middleton	Open	118.00	118.00
94-04-027	Town Boy (Dark Flesh)	L. Middleton	Open	118.00	118.00

Middleton Doll Company — **First Collectibles**

90-05-001	Sweetest Little Dreamer (Asleep)	L. Middleton	Retrd.	40.00	40.00
90-05-002	Day Dreamer (Awake)	L. Middleton	Retrd.	42.00	42.00
91-05-003	Day Dreamer Sunshine	L. Middleton	Retrd.	49.00	49.00
91-05-004	Teenie	L. Middleton	Retrd.	59.00	59.00

Middleton Doll Company — **Birthday Babies**

92-06-001	Winter	L. Middleton	Retrd.	180.00	180.00
92-06-002	Fall	L. Middleton	Retrd.	170.00	170.00
92-06-003	Summer	L. Middleton	Retrd.	160.00	160.00
92-06-004	Spring	L. Middleton	3,000	170.00	170.00

Middleton Doll Company — **Wise Penny Collection**

93-07-001	Jennifer (Peach Dress)	L. Middleton	Retrd.	140.00	140.00
93-07-002	Jennifer (Print Dress)	L. Middleton	Retrd.	140.00	140.00
93-07-003	Molly Jo	L. Middleton	Retrd.	140.00	140.00
93-07-004	Gordon	L. Middleton	Retrd.	140.00	140.00
93-07-005	Ashley (Brown Hair)	L. Middleton	Retrd.	120.00	120.00
93-07-006	Merry	L. Middleton	Retrd.	140.00	140.00
93-07-007	Grace	L. Middleton	Retrd.	140.00	140.00
93-07-007	Ashley (Blond Hair)	L. Middleton	Retrd.	120.00	120.00
93-07-008	Baby Devan	L. Middleton	Retrd.	140.00	140.00

Middleton Doll Company — **Porcelain Collector Series**

92-08-001	Beloved & Bé Bé	L. Middleton	Retrd.	590.00	590.00
92-08-002	Sencerity II - Country Fair	L. Middleton	Retrd.	500.00	500.00
93-08-003	Cherish - Lilac & Lace	L. Middleton	Retrd.	500.00	500.00

Middleton Doll Company — **Porcelain Bears & Bunny**

93-09-001	Buster Bear	L. Middleton	Retrd.	250.00	250.00
93-09-002	Baby Buster	L. Middleton	Retrd.	230.00	230.00
93-09-003	Bye Baby Bunting	L. Middleton	Open	270.00	270.00

Middleton Doll Company — **Christmas Angel Collection**

87-10-001	Christmas Angel 1987	L. Middleton	Retrd.	130.00	400-500.
88-10-002	Christmas Angel 1988	L. Middleton	Retrd.	130.00	200-250.
89-10-003	Christmas Angel 1989	L. Middleton	Retrd.	150.00	190.00
90-10-004	Christmas Angel 1990	L. Middleton	Retrd.	150.00	190.00
91-10-005	Christmas Angel 1991	L. Middleton	Retrd.	180.00	200.00
92-10-006	Christmas Angel 1992	L. Middleton	5,000	190.00	190.00
93-10-007	Christmas Angel 1993-Girl	L. Middleton	4,000	190.00	190.00
93-10-008	Christmas Angel 1993 (set)	L. Middleton	Retrd.	390.00	500.00
94-10-009	Christmas Angel 1994	L. Middleton	5,000	190.00	190.00

Midwest of Cannon Falls — **Folk Art Gallery Collection**

94-01-001	Heartfelt Angel 11422-3	S. Hale	Open	37.00	37.00
94-01-002	Heartfelt Angel 11423-0	S. Hale	Open	20.00	20.00
94-01-003	Sitting Santa 11424-7	S. Hale	Open	30.00	30.00
94-01-004	Santa of Christmas Past 12057-6	S. Hale	Open	130.00	130.00
94-01-005	Gardening Girl 11426-1	S. Hale	Open	45.00	45.00
94-01-006	Bewitching Belinda 11425-4	S. Hale	Open	40.00	40.00
94-01-007	Santa Gone Fishing 12029-3	S. Hale	Open	65.00	65.00

Original Appalachian Artworks — **Little People**

78-01-001	Helen Blue	X. Roberts	Closed	150.00	6-7000.
78-01-002	"A" Blue	X. Roberts	Closed	125.00	4000.00
78-01-003	"B" Red	X. Roberts	Closed	100.00	32-5000.
78-01-004	"C" Burgundy	X. Roberts	Closed	100.00	18-3500.
79-01-005	"D" Purple	X. Roberts	Closed	100.00	16-3000.
78-01-006	"E" Bronze	X. Roberts	Closed	125.00	750-1000
80-01-007	"SP" Preemie	X. Roberts	Closed	100.00	400-700.
80-01-008	Celebrity	X. Roberts	Closed	200.00	400-700.
80-01-009	Grand Edition	X. Roberts	Closed	1000.00	1000.00
80-01-010	"U" Unsigned	X. Roberts	Closed	125.00	350-450.
81-01-011	New 'Ears	X. Roberts	Closed	125.00	200.00
81-01-012	"PR II" Preemie	X. Roberts	Closed	130.00	250.00
81-01-013	Standing Edition	X. Roberts	Closed	300.00	300-400.
82-01-014	"PE" New 'Ears Preemie	X. Roberts	Closed	140.00	300.00
82-01-015	"U" Unsigned	X. Roberts	Closed	125.00	450.00

Original Appalachian Artworks — **Cabbage Patch Kids International**

83-02-001	Oriental/Pair	X. Roberts	Closed	300.00	14-1500.
83-02-002	American Indian/Pair	X. Roberts	Closed	300.00	1850.00
83-02-003	Hispanic/Pair	X. Roberts	Closed	300.00	650.00
84-02-004	Bavarian/Pair	X. Roberts	Closed	300.00	950.00
83-02-005	Irish/Pair	X. Roberts	Closed	320.00	400.00

Original Appalachian Artworks — **Cabbage Patch Kids**

82-03-001	Amy	X. Roberts	Closed	125.00	700.00
82-03-002	Bobbie	X. Roberts	Closed	125.00	700.00
82-03-003	Billie	X. Roberts	Closed	125.00	700.00
82-03-004	Gilda	X. Roberts	Closed	125.00	700-2500
82-03-005	Tyler	X. Roberts	Closed	125.00	3-4000.
82-03-006	Sybil	X. Roberts	Closed	125.00	700.00
82-03-007	Marilyn	X. Roberts	Closed	125.00	700.00
82-03-008	Otis	X. Roberts	Closed	125.00	700.00
82-03-009	Rebecca	X. Roberts	Closed	125.00	700.00
82-03-010	Dorothy	X. Roberts	Closed	125.00	700.00
83-03-011	Andre/Madeira	X. Roberts	Closed	250.00	1-1200.
84-03-012	Daddy's Darlins' Pun'kin	X. Roberts	Closed	300.00	400-500.
84-03-013	Daddy's Darlins' Tootsie	X. Roberts	Closed	300.00	400-500.
84-03-014	Daddy's Darlins' Princess	X. Roberts	Closed	300.00	400-500.
84-03-015	Daddy's Darlins' Kitten	X. Roberts	Closed	300.00	400-500.
84-03-016	Daddy's Darlins', set of 4	X. Roberts	Closed	1600.00	2-2500.
88-03-017	Tiger's Eye-Valentine's Day	X. Roberts	Closed	150.00	300.00
89-03-018	Tiger's Eye-Mother's Day	X. Roberts	Closed	150.00	250-300.
93-03-019	Unicoi Edition	X. Roberts	Closed	210.00	210-350.
93-03-020	Little People Edition 27" (standing)	X. Roberts	Closed	300.00	450.00
93-03-021	Little People 27" (Girl)	X. Roberts	Closed	325.00	600-1000

	ARTIST	EDITION	ISSUE	QUOTE
94-03-022 Little People 27" (Boy)	X. Roberts	Closed	325.00	325-600.
Original Appalachian Artworks	**Cabbage Patch Kids Circus Parade**			
87-04-001 Big Top Clown-Baby Cakes	X. Roberts	2000	180.00	500-550.
89-04-002 Happy Hobo-Bashful Billy	X. Roberts	1000	180.00	350-450.
91-04-003 Mitzi	X. Roberts	1000	220.00	220-250.
Original Appalachian Artworks	**Collectors Club Editions**			
87-05-001 Baby Otis	X. Roberts	Closed	250.00	550.00
89-05-002 Anna Ruby	X. Roberts	Closed	250.00	350-500.
90-05-003 Lee Ann	X. Roberts	Closed	250.00	350-450.
91-05-004 Richard Russell	X. Roberts	Closed	250.00	350-500.
92-05-005 Baby Dodd	X. Roberts	Closed	250.00	250-450.
93-05-006 Patti w/ Cabbage Bud Boutonnier	X. Roberts	Closed	280.00	300.00
Original Appalachian Artworks	**Convention Baby**			
89-06-001 Ashley	X. Roberts	Closed	150.00	500-700.
90-06-002 Bradley	X. Roberts	Closed	175.00	350-500.
91-06-003 Caroline	X. Roberts	Closed	200.00	300-500.
92-06-004 Duke	X. Roberts	Closed	225.00	300-400.
93-06-005 Ellen	X. Roberts	Closed	225.00	250-350.
94-06-006 Justin	X. Roberts	Closed	238.50	238.50
Original Appalachian Artworks	**Happily Ever After**			
93-07-001 Bride	X. Roberts	Closed	230.00	275.00
93-07-002 Groom	X. Roberts	Closed	230.00	275.00
Original Appalachian Artworks	**Christmas Collection**			
79-08-001 X Christmas/Pair	X. Roberts	Closed	300.00	5500.00
80-08-002 Christmas-Nicholas/Noel	X. Roberts	Closed	400.00	25-3500.
82-08-003 Christmas-Baby Rudy/Christy Nicole	X. Roberts	Closed	400.00	16-2500.
83-08-004 Christmas-Holly/Berry	X. Roberts	Closed	400.00	800-1800
84-08-005 Christmas-Carole/Chris	X. Roberts	Closed	400.00	600-1250
85-08-006 Christmas-Baby Sandy/Claude	X. Roberts	Closed	400.00	400-800.
86-08-007 Christmas-Hilliary/Nigel	X. Roberts	Closed	400.00	400.00
87-08-008 Christmas-Katrina/Misha	X. Roberts	Closed	500.00	500.00
88-08-009 Christmas-Kelly/Kane	X. Roberts	Closed	500.00	500.00
89-08-010 Christmas-Joy	X. Roberts	Closed	250.00	550-650.
90-08-011 Christmas-Krystina	X. Roberts	Closed	250.00	250.00
91-08-012 Christmas-Nick	X. Roberts	Closed	275.00	275.00
92-08-013 Christmas-Christy Claus	X. Roberts	Closed	285.00	285.00
93-08-014 Christmas-Rudolph	X. Roberts	Closed	275.00	275.00
94-08-015 Christmas-Natalie	X. Roberts	500	275.00	275.00
Princeton Gallery	**Little Ladies of Victorian England**			
90-01-001 Victoria Anne	Unknown	Open	59.00	59.00
91-01-002 Abigail	Unknown	Open	59.00	59.00
91-01-003 Valerie	Unknown	Open	58.50	58.50
92-01-004 Caroline	Unknown	Open	58.50	58.50
92-01-005 Heather	Unknown	Open	58.50	58.50
93-01-006 Beverly	Unknown	Open	58.50	58.50
Princeton Gallery	**Best Friend Dolls**			
91-02-001 Sharing Secrets	Unknown	Open	78.00	78.00
Princeton Gallery	**Childhood Songs Dolls**			
91-03-001 It's Raining, It's Pouring	Unknown	Open	78.00	78.00
Princeton Gallery	**Dress Up Dolls**			
91-04-001 Grandma's Attic	Unknown	Open	95.00	95.00
Princeton Gallery	**Fabrique Santa**			
91-05-001 Christmas Dream	Unknown	Open	76.00	76.00
Princeton Gallery	**Santa Doll**			
91-06-001 Checking His List	Unknown	Open	119.00	119.00
Princeton Gallery	**Rock-N-Roll Dolls**			
91-07-001 Cindy at the Hop	M. Sirko	Open	95.00	95.00
92-07-002 Chantilly Lace	M. Sirko	Open	95.00	95.00
93-07-003 Yellow Dot Bikini	Unknown	Open	95.00	95.00
Princeton Gallery	**Terrible Twos Dolls**			
91-08-001 One Man Band	M. Sirko	Open	95.00	95.00
Princeton Gallery	**Imaginary People**			
92-09-001 Melinda, Tooth Fairy	Unknown	Open	95.00	95.00
Reco International	**Precious Memories of Motherhood**			
90-01-001 Loving Steps	S. Kuck	Retrd.	125.00	150-195.
91-01-002 Lullaby	S. Kuck	Yr.Iss.	125.00	125.00
92-01-003 Expectant Moments	S. Kuck	Retrd.	149.00	149.00
93-01-004 Bedtime	S. Kuck	Retrd.	149.00	149.00
Reco International	**Childhood Doll Collection**			
94-02-001 A Kiss Goodnight	S. Kuck	Open	79.00	79.00
94-02-002 Teaching Teddy His Prayers	S. Kuck	Open	79.00	79.00
Reco International	**Children's Circus Doll Collection**			
91-03-001 Tommy The Clown	J. McClelland	Yr.Iss.	78.00	78.00
91-03-002 Katie The Tightrope Walker	J. McClelland	Yr.Iss.	78.00	78.00
91-03-003 Johnny The Strongman	J. McClelland	Yr.Iss.	83.00	83.00
92-03-004 Maggie The Animal Trainer	J. McClelland	Yr.Iss.	83.00	83.00
Roman, Inc.	**Ellen Williams Doll**			
89-01-001 Noelle	E. Williams	5,000	125.00	125.00
89-01-002 Rebecca 999	E. Williams	7,500	195.00	195.00
Roman, Inc.	**A Christmas Dream**			
90-02-001 Chelsea	E. Williams	5,000	125.00	125.00
90-02-002 Carole	E. Williams	5,000	125.00	125.00
Roman, Inc.	**Tyrolean Treasures: Wood Body, Moveable Joint**			
90-03-001 Nadia	Unkn.	2,000	650.00	650.00
90-03-002 Susie	Unkn.	2,000	650.00	650.00
90-03-003 Verena	Unkn.	2,000	650.00	650.00
90-03-004 Monica	Unkn.	2,000	650.00	650.00
90-03-005 Melissa	Unkn.	2,000	650.00	650.00
90-03-006 Karin	Unkn.	2,000	650.00	650.00
90-03-007 Tina	Unkn.	2,000	650.00	650.00
90-03-008 Ann	Unkn.	2,000	650.00	650.00
90-03-009 Lisa	Unkn.	2,000	650.00	650.00
90-03-010 David	Unkn.	2,000	650.00	650.00
Roman, Inc.	**Tyrolean Treasures: Soft Body, Human Hair**			
90-04-001 Erika	Unkn.	2,000	575.00	575.00
90-04-002 Ellan	Unkn.	2,000	575.00	575.00
90-04-003 Marisa	Unkn.	2,000	575.00	575.00
90-04-004 Sarah	Unkn.	2,000	575.00	575.00

	ARTIST	EDITION	ISSUE	QUOTE
90-04-005 Andrew	Unkn.	2,000	575.00	575.00
90-04-006 Matthew	Unkn.	2,000	575.00	575.00
Roman, Inc.	**Classic Brides of the Century**			
91-05-001 Flora-The 1900's Bride	E. Williams	Yr.Iss.	145.00	145.00
92-05-002 Jennifer-The 1980's Bride	E. Williams	Yr.Iss.	149.00	149.00
93-05-003 Kathleen-The 1930's Bride	E. Williams	Yr.Iss.	149.00	149.00
Roman, Inc.	**Abbie Williams Collection**			
91-06-001 Molly	E. Williams	5,000	155.00	155.00
Sarah's Attic, Inc.	**Heirlooms from the Attic**			
86-01-001 Brownie Bear 0001	Sarah's Attic	Closed	36.00	36.00
86-01-002 Amie Amish Doll 0002	Sarah's Attic	Closed	40.00	40.00
86-01-003 Buffy Bear 0003	Sarah's Attic	Closed	80.00	80.00
86-01-004 Billy Bear 0004	Sarah's Attic	Closed	80.00	80.00
86-01-005 Betsy Boo Doll 0005	Sarah's Attic	Closed	40.00	40.00
86-01-006 Jennie White Doll 0006	Sarah's Attic	Closed	44.00	44.00
86-01-007 Hope Black Angel 0007	Sarah's Attic	Closed	34.00	34.00
86-01-008 Charity White Angel 0008	Sarah's Attic	Closed	34.00	34.00
86-01-009 Judith Ann Black Doll 0010	Sarah's Attic	Closed	34.00	34.00
86-01-010 Matt Cloth Doll 0011	Sarah's Attic	Closed	70.00	120.00
86-01-011 Maggie Cloth Doll 0012	Sarah's Attic	Closed	70.00	120.00
86-01-012 Sadie Black Doll 0014	Sarah's Attic	Closed	90.00	90.00
86-01-013 Louisa May Black Cloth Doll 0018	Sarah's Attic	Closed	120.00	120.00
86-01-014 Priscilla Doll 0030	Sarah's Attic	Closed	140.00	300.00
86-01-015 Peter Doll 0031	Sarah's Attic	Closed	140.00	140.00
86-01-016 Jennie White Angel Doll 0074	Sarah's Attic	Closed	52.00	52.00
86-01-017 Twinkie Doll 0039A	Sarah's Attic	Closed	32.00	32.00
86-01-018 Cupcake Doll 0039B	Sarah's Attic	Closed	32.00	32.00
86-01-019 Matt Cloth Doll 0039 C	Sarah's Attic	Closed	32.00	32.00
86-01-020 Maggie Cloth Doll 0039 D	Sarah's Attic	Closed	32.00	32.00
86-01-021 Whimpy Doll 0039E	Sarah's Attic	Closed	32.00	32.00
86-01-022 Katie Doll 0039F	Sarah's Attic	Closed	32.00	32.00
86-01-023 Spike Doll 0039G	Sarah's Attic	Closed	32.00	32.00
86-01-024 Nellie Doll 0039H	Sarah's Attic	Closed	32.00	32.00
86-01-025 Willie Doll 0039I	Sarah's Attic	Closed	32.00	32.00
86-01-026 Tillie Doll 0039J	Sarah's Attic	Closed	32.00	32.00
86-01-027 Holly Black Angel 0410	Sarah's Attic	Closed	34.00	34.00
86-01-028 Trapp the Cat Doll 0740	Sarah's Attic	Closed	36.00	36.00
87-01-029 Tess Rag Doll 0083	Sarah's Attic	Closed	140.00	140.00
87-01-030 Roxie Rabbit Doll 0084	Sarah's Attic	Closed	32.00	32.00
87-01-031 Benji Bear 0089	Sarah's Attic	Closed	25.00	25.00
87-01-032 Leroy Black Rag Doll 0105	Sarah's Attic	Closed	54.00	54.00
87-01-033 Lucy Black Rag Doll 0106	Sarah's Attic	Closed	54.00	54.00
87-01-034 Patches White Rag Doll 0110	Sarah's Attic	Closed	54.00	54.00
87-01-035 Polly White Rag Doll 0111	Sarah's Attic	Closed	54.00	54.00
87-01-036 Willie Rag Doll 0343	Sarah's Attic	Closed	32.00	32.00
87-01-037 Tillie Rag Doll 0344	Sarah's Attic	Closed	32.00	32.00
87-01-038 Molly Doll 2053	Sarah's Attic	Closed	44.00	44.00
87-01-039 Sunshine Doll 3003	Sarah's Attic	Closed	118.00	118.00
88-01-040 Melville Cloth Bunny 1104	Sarah's Attic	Closed	46.00	46.00
88-01-041 Maybelle Cloth Bunny 1105	Sarah's Attic	Closed	46.00	46.00
88-01-042 Country Girl Doll 1190	Sarah's Attic	Closed	26.00	26.00
88-01-043 Victorian Girl Doll 1191	Sarah's Attic	Closed	24.00	24.00
88-01-044 Victorian Boy Doll 1192	Sarah's Attic	Closed	24.00	24.00
88-01-045 Ashlee Doll 1193	Sarah's Attic	Closed	20.00	20.00
88-01-046 Albert Doll 1194	Sarah's Attic	Closed	20.00	20.00
88-01-047 Daisy Doll 1195	Sarah's Attic	Closed	20.00	20.00
88-01-048 David Doll 1196	Sarah's Attic	Closed	20.00	20.00
88-01-049 Smiley Clown Doll 3050	Sarah's Attic	Closed	126.00	126.00
88-01-050 Mrs. Claus Doll 6284	Sarah's Attic	Closed	120.00	120.00
88-01-051 Santa Claus Doll 6337	Sarah's Attic	Closed	120.00	120.00
88-01-052 Lily-Black Doll 2221	Sarah's Attic	Closed	90.00	90.00
88-01-053 Michael Doll 4015	Sarah's Attic	Closed	44.00	44.00
89-01-054 Joy Angel 1459	Sarah's Attic	Closed	50.00	55.00
89-01-055 Holly Angel 1460	Sarah's Attic	Closed	50.00	55.00
89-01-056 Becky Doll 1461	Sarah's Attic	Closed	120.00	120.00
89-01-057 Bobby Doll 1462	Sarah's Attic	Closed	120.00	120.00
89-01-058 Harmony-Victorian Clown 1464	Sarah's Attic	Closed	120.00	120.00
89-01-059 Peace Angel 1465	Sarah's Attic	Closed	50.00	55.00
89-01-060 Hope Angel 1466	Sarah's Attic	Closed	50.00	55.00
89-01-061 Victoria Doll 1467	Sarah's Attic	Closed	120.00	120.00
89-01-062 Victor Doll 1468	Sarah's Attic	Closed	120.00	120.00
89-01-063 Noel-Christmas Clown 1469	Sarah's Attic	Closed	120.00	120.00
89-01-064 Liberty Angel 1470	Sarah's Attic	Closed	50.00	55.00
89-01-065 Glory Angel 1471	Sarah's Attic	Closed	50.00	55.00
89-01-066 Freedom-Americana Clown 1472	Sarah's Attic	Closed	120.00	120.00
89-01-067 Spirit of America Santa 1476	Sarah's Attic	Closed	150.00	150.00
89-01-068 Beverly Jane-Black Dress 1496	Sarah's Attic	Closed	160.00	160.00
89-01-069 Beverly Jane-Sunday's Best 1666	Sarah's Attic	Closed	160.00	160.00
89-01-070 Beverly Jane-Green Dress 1693	Sarah's Attic	Closed	160.00	160.00
89-01-071 Beverly Jane-Red Dress 1694	Sarah's Attic	Closed	160.00	160.00
89-01-072 Megan Doll 1752	Sarah's Attic	Closed	70.00	70.00
89-01-073 Scott Doll 1753	Sarah's Attic	Closed	70.00	70.00
89-01-074 Sassafras-School Days 1680	Sarah's Attic	Closed	140.00	195.00
90-01-075 Sassafras-Sweet Dreams 1681	Sarah's Attic	Closed	140.00	195.00
90-01-076 Sassafras-Playtime 1682	Sarah's Attic	Closed	140.00	150-175.
90-01-077 Sassafras-Beachtime 1683	Sarah's Attic	Closed	140.00	150-175.
90-01-078 Sassafras-Sunday's Best 1684	Sarah's Attic	Closed	150.00	195.00
90-01-079 Sassafra-Americana 1685	Sarah's Attic	Closed	150.00	150-175.
90-01-080 Hickory-School Days 1766	Sarah's Attic	Closed	140.00	195.00
90-01-081 Hickory-Sweet Dreams 1767	Sarah's Attic	Closed	140.00	150-175.
90-01-082 Hickory-Playtime 1768	Sarah's Attic	Closed	140.00	150-175.
90-01-083 Hickory-Beachtime 1769	Sarah's Attic	Closed	140.00	150-175.
90-01-084 Hickory-Sunday's Best 1770	Sarah's Attic	Closed	150.00	195.00
90-01-085 Hickory-Americana 1771	Sarah's Attic	Closed	150.00	150-175.
90-01-086 Betty Bear-Sunday's Best 1772	Sarah's Attic	Closed	160.00	160.00
90-01-087 Teddy Bear-Sunday's Best 1773	Sarah's Attic	Closed	160.00	160.00
90-01-088 Teddy Bear-School Days 1774	Sarah's Attic	Closed	160.00	160.00
90-01-089 Teddy Bear-Americana 1775	Sarah's Attic	Closed	160.00	160.00
90-01-090 Betty Bear-Christmas 1815	Sarah's Attic	Closed	160.00	160.00
90-01-091 Teddy Bear-Christmas 1816	Sarah's Attic	Closed	160.00	160.00
91-01-092 All Cloth Opie White Doll 1818	Sarah's Attic	Closed	90.00	90.00
91-01-093 All Cloth Polly White Doll 1819	Sarah's Attic	Closed	90.00	90.00
91-01-094 All Cloth Muffin Black Doll 1820	Sarah's Attic	Closed	90.00	90.00
91-01-095 All Cloth Puffin Black Doll 1821	Sarah's Attic	Closed	90.00	90.00
91-01-096 Enos 1822	Sarah's Attic	Closed	90.00	90.00
91-01-097 Adora 1823	Sarah's Attic	Closed	90.00	90.00
91-01-098 Sassafras-Christmas 1809	Sarah's Attic	Closed	150.00	150-175.
91-01-099 Hickory-Christmas 1810	Sarah's Attic	Closed	150.00	150-175.
91-01-100 Sassafras-Springtime 1813	Sarah's Attic	Closed	150.00	195.00

		ARTIST	EDITION	ISSUE	QUOTE
91-01-101	Hickory-Springtime 1814	Sarah's Attic	Closed	150.00	195.00
92-01-102	Betty Bear-Springtime 1826	Sarah's Attic	Closed	160.00	160.00
92-01-103	Teddy Bear-Springtime 1827	Sarah's Attic	Closed	160.00	160.00
92-01-104	Emily-Victorian 1829	Sarah's Attic	Closed	250.00	250.00
92-01-105	Emily-Country 1830	Sarah's Attic	Closed	250.00	250.00
92-01-106	Hilary-Victorian 1831	Sarah's Attic	Closed	200.00	200.00
92-01-107	Hilary-Country 1832	Sarah's Attic	Closed	200.00	200.00
92-01-108	Edie-Victorian 1833	Sarah's Attic	Closed	170.00	170.00
92-01-109	Edie-Country 1834	Sarah's Attic	Closed	170.00	170.00
92-01-110	Edie-Playtime 1835	Sarah's Attic	Closed	170.00	170.00
92-01-111	Emma-Victorian 1836	Sarah's Attic	Closed	160.00	160.00
92-01-112	Emma-Country 1837	Sarah's Attic	Closed	160.00	160.00
92-01-113	Emma-Playtime 1838	Sarah's Attic	Closed	160.00	160.00
92-01-114	Peace on Earth Santa 3564	Sarah's Attic	Closed	175.00	350.00
92-01-115	Angelle Guardian Angel 3569	Sarah's Attic	Closed	170.00	170.00
92-01-116	Kiah Guardian Angel 3570	Sarah's Attic	Closed	170.00	170.00
92-01-117	Harpster w/Banjo 3591	Sarah's Attic	Closed	250.00	250.00
92-01-118	Whoopie 3597	Sarah's Attic	Closed	200.00	200.00
92-01-119	Wooster 3602	Sarah's Attic	Closed	160.00	160.00
93-01-120	Granny Quilting Lady Doll 3576	Sarah's Attic	Closed	130.00	130.00
93-01-121	Lilla Quilting Lady Doll 3581	Sarah's Attic	Closed	130.00	130.00
93-01-122	Millie Quilting Lady Doll 3586	Sarah's Attic	Closed	130.00	130.00
93-01-123	Sally Booba Doll 3890	Sarah's Attic	500	130.00	130.00
93-01-124	Jack Boy Doll 3893	Sarah's Attic	500	130.00	130.00
94-01-125	Star Black Angel 4107	Sarah's Attic	500	120.00	120.00
94-01-126	Twinkle-White Angel 4108	Sarah's Attic	500	120.00	120.00
94-01-127	Tillie-Clown 9601	Sarah's Attic	1,000	120.00	120.00
94-01-128	Willie-Clown Doll 9601	Sarah's Attic	1,000	120.00	120.00
Timeless Creations		**Barefoot Children**			
87-01-001	Fatou	A. Himstedt	Closed	329.00	850-1200
87-01-002	Fatou (Cornroll)	A. Himstedt	Closed	329.00	1-1300.
87-01-003	Bastian	A. Himstedt	Closed	329.00	700-995.
87-01-004	Ellen	A. Himstedt	Closed	329.00	750-950.
87-01-005	Paula	A. Himstedt	Closed	329.00	700-950.
87-01-006	Lisa	A. Himstedt	Closed	329.00	700-950.
87-01-007	Kathe	A. Himstedt	Closed	329.00	700-950.
87-01-008	Beckus	A. Himstedt	Closed	329.00	950-1400
Timeless Creations		**Heartland Series**			
88-02-001	Timi	A. Himstedt	Closed	329.00	375-500.
88-02-002	Toni	A. Himstedt	Closed	329.00	375-550.
Timeless Creations		**Blessed Are The Children**			
88-03-001	Friederike	A. Himstedt	Closed	499.00	12-1600.
88-03-002	Makimura	A. Himstedt	Closed	499.00	800-1000
88-03-003	Kasimir	A. Himstedt	Closed	499.00	13-1600.
88-03-004	Michiko	A. Himstedt	Closed	499.00	900-1200
88-03-005	Malin	A. Himstedt	Closed	499.00	12-1600.
Timeless Creations		**Reflection of Youth**			
89-04-001	Adrienne (France)	A. Himstedt	Closed	558.00	600-900.
89-04-002	Kai (German)	A. Himstedt	Closed	558.00	600-700.
89-04-003	Janka (Hungry)	A. Himstedt	Closed	558.00	650-950.
89-04-004	Ayoka (Africa)	A. Himstedt	Closed	558.00	850-1200
Timeless Creations		**Fiene And The Barefoot Babies**			
90-05-001	Annchen-German Baby Girl	A. Himstedt	2-Yr.	498.00	500-650.
90-05-002	Taki-Japanese Baby Girl	A. Himstedt	2-Yr.	498.00	650-850.
90-05-003	Mo-American Baby Boy	A. Himstedt	2-Yr.	498.00	450-550.
90-05-004	Fiene-Belgian Girl	A. Himstedt	2-Yr.	598.00	600-800.
Timeless Creations		**Faces of Friendship**			
91-06-001	Liliane (Netherlands)	A. Himstedt	2-Yr.	598.00	500-650.
91-06-002	Shireem (Bali)	A. Himstedt	2-Yr.	598.00	400-500.
91-06-003	Neblina (Switzerland)	A. Himstedt	2-Yr.	598.00	450-600.
Timeless Creations		**Summer Dreams**			
92-07-001	Sanga	A. Himstedt	2-Yr.	599.00	599-650.
92-07-002	Pemba	A. Himstedt	2-Yr.	599.00	599.00
92-07-003	Jule	A. Himstedt	2-Yr.	599.00	475-600.
92-07-004	Enzo	A. Himstedt	2-Yr.	599.00	599.00
Timeless Creations		**Images of Childhood**			
93-08-001	Lona (California)	A. Himstedt	2-Yr.	599.00	599.00
93-08-002	Tara (Germany)	A. Himstedt	2-Yr.	599.00	599.00
93-08-003	Kima (Greenland)	A. Himstedt	2-Yr.	599.00	599.00
Susan Wakeen Doll Co. Inc.		**The Littlest Ballet Company**			
85-01-001	Jeanne	S. Wakeen	375	198.00	800.00
85-01-002	Patty	S. Wakeen	375	198.00	400-500.
85-01-003	Cynthia	S. Wakeen	375	198.00	350.00
85-01-004	Jennifer	S. Wakeen	250	750.00	750.00
87-01-005	Elizabeth	S. Wakeen	250	425.00	1000.00
87-01-006	Marie Ann	S. Wakeen	50	1000.00	1000.00

FIGURINES/COTTAGES

		ARTIST	EDITION	ISSUE	QUOTE
Kurt S. Adler Inc.		**Camelot Steinbach Nutcracker Series**			
91-01-001	Merlin The Magician ES610	KSA/Steinbach	Retrd.	185.00	13-2000.
92-01-002	King Arthur ES621	KSA/Steinbach	Retrd.	195.00	225-350.
93-01-003	Sir Lancelot ES638	KSA/Steinbach	12,000	225.00	225.00
94-01-004	Sir Galahad ES862	KSA/Steinbach	12,000	225.00	225.00
94-01-005	Sir Lancelot Smoker ES833	KSA/Steinbach	7,500	150.00	150.00
Kurt S. Adler Inc.		**American Presidents Steinbach Nutcracker Series**			
92-02-001	Abraham Lincoln ES622	KSA/Steinbach	12,000	195.00	225.00
92-02-002	George Washington ES623	KSA/Steinbach	12,000	195.00	225.00
93-02-003	Teddy Roosevelt ES644	KSA/Steinbach	10,000	225.00	225.00
Kurt S. Adler Inc.		**American Inventors Steinbach Nutcracker Series**			
93-03-001	Ben Franklin ES622	KSA/Steinbach	12,000	225.00	225.00
Kurt S. Adler Inc.		**Famous Chieftans Steinbach Nutcracker Series**			
93-04-001	Chief Sitting Bull ES637	KSA/Steinbach	8,500	225.00	225.00
94-04-002	Red Cloud ES864	KSA/Steinbach	8,500	225.00	225.00
94-04-003	Chief Sitting Bull Smoker ES834	KSA/Steinbach	7,500	150.00	150.00
Kurt S. Adler Inc.		**Christmas Legends Steinbach Nutcracker Series**			
93-05-001	Father Christmas ES645	KSA/Steinbach	7,500	225.00	225.00
94-05-002	St. Nicholas, The Bishop ES865	KSA/Steinbach	7,500	225.00	225.00
Kurt S. Adler Inc.		**Camelot Steinbach Smoking Figure Series**			
92-06-001	Merlin The Magician ES830	KSA/Steinbach	7,500	150.00	150.00
93-06-002	King Arthur ES832	KSA/Steinbach	7,500	175.00	175.00
Kurt S. Adler Inc.		**Steinbach Nutcracker Collection**			
84-07-001	Oil Sheik	KSA/Steinbach	Retrd.	100.00	500.00
91-07-002	Columbus ES697	KSA/Steinbach	Retrd.	194.00	225.00
92-07-003	Happy Santa ES601	KSA/Steinbach	Open	190.00	220.00
Kurt S. Adler Inc.		**Tales of Sherwood Forest**			
92-08-001	Robin Hood ES863	KSA/Steinbach	7,500	225.00	225.00
Kurt S. Adler Inc.		**Zuber Nutcracker Series**			
92-09-001	Bronco Billy The Cowboy EK1	KSA/Zuber	5,000	125.00	125.00
92-09-002	Paul Bunyan The Lumberjack EK2	KSA/Zuber	5,000	125.00	125.00
92-09-003	The Nor' Easter Sea Captain EK3	KSA/Zuber	5,000	125.00	125.00
92-09-004	TheTyrolean EK4	KSA/Zuber	5,000	125.00	125.00
92-09-005	The Golfer EK5	KSA/Zuber	5,000	125.00	125.00
92-09-006	The Chimney Sweep EK6	KSA/Zuber	5,000	125.00	125.00
92-09-007	The Annapolis Midshipman EK7	KSA/Zuber	5,000	125.00	125.00
92-09-008	The West Point Cadet With Canon EK8	KSA/Zuber	5,000	130.00	130.00
92-09-009	Gepetto, The Toymaker EK9	KSA/Zuber	5,000	125.00	125.00
92-09-010	The Pilgrim EK14	KSA/Zuber	5,000	125.00	125.00
92-09-011	The Indian EK15	KSA/Zuber	5,000	135.00	135.00
92-09-012	The Bavarian EK16	KSA/Zuber	5,000	130.00	130.00
92-09-013	The Fisherman EK17	KSA/Zuber	5,000	125.00	125.00
92-09-014	The Gold Prospector EK18	KSA/Zuber	5,000	125.00	125.00
92-09-015	The Country Singer EK19	KSA/Zuber	5,000	125.00	125.00
93-09-016	Herr Drosselmeir Nutcracker EK21	KSA/Zuber	5,000	150.00	150.00
93-09-017	The Pizzamaker EK22	KSA/Zuber	5,000	150.00	150.00
93-09-018	Napoleon Bonaparte EK23	KSA/Zuber	5,000	150.00	150.00
93-09-019	The Ice Cream Vendor EK24	KSA/Zuber	5,000	150.00	150.00
94-09-020	Jazz Player EK25	KSA/Zuber	2,500	145.00	145.00
94-09-021	The Gardner EK26	KSA/Zuber	2,500	150.00	150.00
94-09-022	Scuba Diver EK27	KSA/Zuber	2,500	150.00	150.00
94-09-023	Kurt the Traveling Salesman EK28	KSA/Zuber	2,500	155.00	155.00
94-09-024	Peter Pan EK28	KSA/Zuber	2,500	145.00	145.00
94-09-025	Soccer Player EK30	KSA/Zuber	2,500	145.00	145.00
94-09-026	Mouse King EK31	KSA/Zuber	2,500	150.00	150.00
Kurt S. Adler Inc.		**Mickey Unlimited**			
92-10-001	Goofy H1216	KSA/Disney	Open	78.00	78.00
92-10-002	Mickey Mouse Sorcerer H1221	KSA/Disney	Open	100.00	100.00
92-10-003	Mickey Mouse Soldier H1194	KSA/Disney	Open	72.00	72.00
93-10-004	Pinnochio H1222	KSA/Disney	Open	110.00	110.00
93-10-005	Donald Duck H1235	KSA/Disney	Open	90.00	90.00
93-10-006	Mickey Mouse With Gift Boxes W1608	KSA/Disney	Open	78.00	78.00
94-10-007	Mickey Santa Nutcracker H1237	KSA/Disney	Open	90.00	90.00
94-10-008	Minnie Mouse Soldier Nutcrackers H1236	KSA/Disney	Open	90.00	90.00
94-10-009	Mickey Bandleader W1669	KSA/Disney	Open	45.00	45.00
94-10-010	Minnie With Cymbals W1670	KSA/Disney	Open	45.00	45.00
94-10-011	Donald Duck Drummer W1671	KSA/Disney	Open	45.00	45.00
Kurt S. Adler Inc.		**Jim Henson's Muppet Nutcrackers**			
93-11-001	Kermit The Frog H1223	KSA/JHP	Open	90.00	90.00
Kurt S. Adler Inc.		**Fabriché™ Holiday Figurines**			
91-12-001	Santa Fiddler W1549	M. Rothenberg	Retrd.	100.00	100.00
92-12-002	Bringin in the Yule Log W1589	M. Rothenberg	5,000	200.00	200.00
92-12-003	Santa's Ice Capades W1588	M. Rothenberg	Open	110.00	110.00
92-12-004	Santa Steals A Kiss & A Cookie W1581	M. Rothenberg	Open	150.00	150.00
92-12-005	An Apron Full of Love W1582	M. Rothenberg	Open	75.00	75.00
92-12-006	Christmas is in the Air W1590	K.S. Adler	Open	110.00	110.00
92-12-007	Bundles of Joy W1578	K.S. Adler	Open	78.00	78.00
92-12-008	Homeward Bound W1568	K.S. Adler	Open	61.00	61.00
92-12-009	Merry Kissmas W1548	M. Rothenberg	Retrd.	140.00	140.00
92-12-010	Santa's Cat Nap W1504	M. Rothenberg	Retrd.	98.00	98.00
92-12-011	St. Nicholas The Bishop W1532	K.S. Adler	Open	78.00	78.00
92-12-012	Hugs and Kisses W1531	K.S. Adler	Open	67.00	67.00
92-12-013	I'm Late, I'm Late J7947	T. Rubel	Open	100.00	100.00
92-12-014	It's Time To Go J7943	T. Rubel	Open	150.00	150.00
92-12-015	He Did It Again J7944	T. Rubel	Open	160.00	160.00
93-12-016	Par For The Claus W1603	K.S. Adler	Open	60.00	60.00
93-12-017	Checking It Twice W1604	K.S. Adler	Open	56.00	56.00
93-12-018	Bringing the Gifts W1605	K.S. Adler	Open	60.00	60.00
93-12-019	Forever Green W1607	K.S. Adler	Open	56.00	56.00
93-12-020	With All The Trimmings W1616	K.S. Adler	Open	76.00	76.00
93-12-021	Playtime For Santa W1619	K.S. Adler	Open	67.00	67.00
93-12-022	All That Jazz W1620	K.S. Adler	Open	67.00	67.00
93-12-023	Here Kitty W1618	M. Rothenberg	Open	90.00	90.00
93-12-024	Stocking Stuffer W1622	K.S. Adler	Open	56.00	56.00
93-12-025	Top Brass W1630	K.S. Adler	Open	67.00	67.00
94-12-026	Schussing Claus W1651	K.S. Adler	Open	78.00	78.00
94-12-027	All Star Santa W1652	K.S. Adler	Open	56.00	56.00
94-12-028	Firefighting Friends W1654	K.S. Adler	Open	72.00	72.00
94-12-029	Star Gazing Santa W1656	M. Rothenberg	Open	120.00	120.00
94-12-030	Checking His List W1643	K.S. Adler	Open	60.00	60.00
94-12-031	Holiday Express W1636	K.S. Adler	Open	100.00	100.00
94-12-032	Santa's Fishtales W1640	K.S. Adler	Open	60.00	60.00
94-12-033	Merry St. Nick W1641	Giordano	Open	100.00	100.00
94-12-034	Mail Must Go Through W1667	KSA/WRG	Open	110.00	110.00
94-12-035	Peace Santa W1631	K.S. Adler	Open	60.00	60.00
94-12-036	Ho, Ho, Ho Santa W1632	K.S. Adler	Open	56.00	56.00
94-12-037	Basket of Goodies W1650	K.S. Adler	Open	60.00	60.00
94-12-038	Friendship W1642	K.S. Adler	Open	65.00	65.00
Kurt S. Adler Inc.		**Fabriché™ Thomas Nast Figurines**			
91-13-001	Hello! Little One W1552	K.S. Adler	12,000	90.00	90.00
92-13-002	Christmas Sing-A-Long W1576	K.S. Adler	12,000	110.00	110.00
92-13-003	Caught in the Act W1577	K.S. Adler	Retrd.	133.00	133.00
93-13-004	Dear Santa W1602	K.S. Adler	Retrd.	110.00	110.00
Kurt S. Adler Inc.		**Smithsonian Museum Fabriché™ Series**			
91-14-001	Santa On A Bicycle W1527	KSA/Smithsonian	Open	150.00	150.00
92-14-002	Holiday Drive W1556	KSA/Smithsonian	Open	155.00	155.00
92-14-003	Peace on Earth Angel Treetop W1583	KSA/Smithsonian	Open	52.00	52.00
92-14-004	Peace on Earth Flying Angel W1585	KSA/Smithsonian	Open	49.00	49.00
93-14-005	Holiday Flight W1617	KSA/Smithsonian	Open	144.00	144.00
Kurt S. Adler Inc.		**Fabriché™ Angel Series**			
92-15-001	Heavenly Messenger W1584	K.S. Adler	Open	41.00	41.00
Kurt S. Adler Inc.		**Camelot Fabriché™ Figure Series**			
93-16-001	Merlin the Magician J7966	P. Mauk	7,500	120.00	120.00
93-16-002	Young Arthur J7967	P. Mauk	7,500	120.00	120.00
94-16-003	King Arthur J3372	P. Mauk	7,500	110.00	110.00
93-17-001	Grandpa Santa's Piggyback Ride W1621	M. Rothenberg	7,500	84.00	84.00
94-17-002	The Christmas Waltz 1635	M. Rothenberg	Open	135.00	135.00
94-17-003	Santa's New Friend W1655	M. Rothenberg	Open	110.00	110.00

		ARTIST	EDITION	ISSUE	QUOTE
Kurt S. Adler Inc.	**Fabriché™ Santa's Helpers Series**				
92-18-001	A Stitch in Time W1591	M. Rothenberg	5,000	135.00	135.00
93-18-002	Little Olde Clockmaker W1629	M. Rothenberg	5,000	134.00	134.00
Kurt S. Adler Inc.	**Old World Santa Series**				
92-19-001	Large Black Forest Santa W2717	J. Mostrom	Retrd.	110.00	110.00
92-19-002	Small Grandfather Frost W2718	J. Mostrom	Retrd.	106.00	106.00
92-19-003	Large Father Christmas W2719	J. Mostrom	Retrd.	106.00	106.00
92-19-004	Patriotic Santa W2720	J. Mostrom	3,000	128.00	128.00
92-19-005	Chelsea Garden Santa W2721	J. Mostrom	Retrd.	33.50	33.50
92-19-006	Small Father Christmas W2712	J. Mostrom	Retrd.	33.50	33.50
92-19-007	Pere Noel W2723	J. Mostrom	Retrd.	33.50	33.50
92-19-008	Small Black Forest Santa W2712	J. Mostrom	Retrd.	40.00	40.00
92-19-009	St. Nicholas W2713	J. Mostrom	Retrd.	30.00	30.00
92-19-010	Mrs. Claus W2714	J. Mostrom	5,000	37.00	37.00
92-19-011	Workshop Santa W2715	J. Mostrom	5,000	43.00	43.00
92-19-012	Small Father Frost W2716	J. Mostrom	Retrd.	43.00	43.00
93-19-013	Medieval King of Christmas W2881	J. Mostrom	3,000	390.00	390.00
93-19-014	Good King Wenceslas W2928	J. Mostrom	3,000	134.00	134.00
Kurt S. Adler Inc.	**Visions Of Santa Series**				
92-20-001	Workshop Santa J825	K.S. Adler	7,500	27.00	27.00
92-20-002	Santa Holding Child J826	K.S. Adler	Retrd.	24.50	24.50
92-20-003	Santa With Sack Holding Toy J827	K.S. Adler	7,500	24.50	24.50
92-20-004	Santa Spilling Bag Of Toys J1022	K.S. Adler	7,500	25.50	25.50
92-20-005	Santa Coming Out Of Fireplace J1023	K.S. Adler	Retrd.	29.00	29.00
92-20-006	Santa With Little Girls On Lap J1024	K.S. Adler	7,500	24.50	24.50
Kurt S. Adler Inc.	**The Fabriché™ Bear & Friends Series**				
92-21-001	Not A Creature Was Stirring W1534	K.S. Adler	Open	67.00	67.00
92-21-002	Laughing All The Way J1567	K.S. Adler	Open	83.00	83.00
93-21-003	Teddy Bear Parade W1601	K.S. Adler	Open	73.00	73.00
Kurt S. Adler Inc.	**Sesame Street Series**				
93-22-001	Big Bird Fabrich, Figurine J7928	KSA/JHP	Open	60.00	60.00
93-22-002	Big Bird Nutcracker H1199	KSA/JHP	Open	60.00	60.00
Kurt S. Adler Inc.	**Ho Ho Ho Gang**				
94-23-001	Holy Mackerel J8202	P.F. Bounger	Open	25.00	25.00
94-23-002	Santa Cob J8203	P.F. Bounger	Open	28.00	28.00
94-23-003	Christmas Goose J8201	P.F. Bounger	Open	25.00	25.00
94-23-004	Surprise J8201	P.F. Bounger	Open	25.00	25.00
94-23-005	Will He Make It? J8203	P.F. Bounger	Open	28.00	28.00
Kurt S. Adler Inc.	**Gallery of Angels**				
94-24-001	Guardian Angel M1099	K.S. Adler	2,000	150.00	150.00
94-24-002	Unspoken Word M1100	K.S. Adler	2,000	150.00	150.00
Kurt S. Adler Inc.	**Christmas Legends**				
94-25-001	Aldwyn of the Greenwood J8196	B.F. Bounger	Open	145.00	145.00
94-25-002	Silvanus the Cheerful J8197	B.F. Bounger	Open	165.00	165.00
94-25-003	Berwyn the Grand J8198	B.F. Bounger	Open	175.00	175.00
94-25-004	Caradoc the Kind J8199	B.F. Bounger	Open	70.00	70.00
94-25-005	Florian of the Berry Bush J8199	B.F. Bounger	Open	70.00	70.00
94-25-006	Gustave the Gutsy J8199	B.F. Bounger	Open	70.00	70.00
All God's Children	**All God's Children**				
85-01-001	Abe -1357	M. Holcombe	Retrd.	25.00	1300.00
89-01-002	Adam - 1526	M. Holcombe	Open	36.00	37.00
86-01-003	Amy - 1405W	M. Holcombe	Open	22.00	27.00
86-01-004	Angel - 1401W	M. Holcombe	Open	20.00	26.00
86-01-005	Annie Mae 8 1/2" -1310	M. Holcombe	Retrd.	27.00	90-200.
86-01-006	Annie Mae 6" -1311	M. Holcombe	Retrd.	19.00	120-175.
87-01-007	Aunt Sarah - blue -1440	M. Holcombe	Retrd.	45.00	130-225.
87-01-008	Aunt Sarah - red-1440	M. Holcombe	Retrd.	45.00	350.00
92-01-009	Barney - 1557	M. Holcombe	Open	32.00	33.00
88-01-010	Bean (Clear Water)-1521	M. Holcombe	Retrd.	36.00	120-275.
92-01-011	Bean (Painted Water)-1521	M. Holcombe	Retrd.	36.00	85-120.
87-01-012	Becky with Patch - 1402W	M. Holcombe	Retrd.	19.00	200.00
86-01-013	Becky - 1402W	M. Holcombe	Open	22.00	27.00
87-01-014	Ben - 1504	M. Holcombe	Retrd.	22.00	340-385.
91-01-015	Bessie & Corkie - 1547	M. Holcombe	Open	70.00	70.00
92-01-016	Beth - 1558	M. Holcombe	Open	32.00	33.00
88-01-017	Betsy (Clear Water)- 1513	M. Holcombe	Retrd.	36.00	150-275.
92-01-018	Betsy (Painted Water)- 1513	M. Holcombe	Retrd.	36.00	75-120.
89-01-019	Beverly - 1525	M. Holcombe	Retrd.	50.00	200-500.
91-01-020	Billy - 1545	M. Holcombe	Retrd.	36.00	85-120.
87-01-021	Blossom - blue - 1500	M. Holcombe	Retrd.	60.00	175-325.
87-01-022	Blossom - red- 1500	M. Holcombe	Retrd.	60.00	700-750.
89-01-023	Bo - 1530	M. Holcombe	Retrd.	22.00	44.00
85-01-024	Booker T - 1320	M. Holcombe	Retrd.	19.00	13-1400.
88-01-025	Boone - 1510	M. Holcombe	Retrd.	16.00	75-125.
89-01-026	Bootsie - 1529	M. Holcombe	Retrd.	22.00	36-44.00
87-01-027	Bonnie & Buttons - 1502	M. Holcombe	Retrd.	24.00	65-95.00
92-01-028	Caitlin - 1554	M. Holcombe	Retrd.	36.00	36.00
85-01-029	Callie 4 1/2" - 1361	M. Holcombe	Retrd.	19.00	425-450.
85-01-030	Callie 2 1/4" - 1362	M. Holcombe	Retrd.	12.00	240-250.
88-01-031	Calvin - 777	M. Holcombe	Retrd.	200.00	18-1860.
87-01-032	Cassie - 1503	M. Holcombe	Retrd.	22.00	125-135.
94-01-033	Chantel 1573	M. Holcombe	Open	39.00	39.00
87-01-034	Charity - 1408	M. Holcombe	Retrd.	28.00	30-60.00
94-01-035	Cheri 1574	M. Holcombe	Open	38.00	38.00
89-01-036	David - 1528	M. Holcombe	Open	28.00	30.00
91-01-037	Dori (green dress) - 1544	M. Holcombe	Retrd.	30.00	230-375.
91-01-038	Dori (peach dress) - 1544	M. Holcombe	Open	28.00	30.00
86-01-039	Eli - 1403W	M. Holcombe	Open	26.00	28.00
85-01-040	Emma - 1322	M. Holcombe	Retrd.	27.00	18-1900.
92-01-041	Faith - 1555	M. Holcombe	Retrd.	32.00	60-75.00
87-01-042	Ginnie - 1508	M. Holcombe	Retrd.	22.00	375-400.
86-01-043	Grandma - 1323	M. Holcombe	Retrd.	30.00	3560.00
88-01-044	Hannah - 1515	M. Holcombe	Open	36.00	37.00
88-01-045	Hope - 1519	M. Holcombe	Open	36.00	37.00
86-01-046	Jacob - 1407W	M. Holcombe	Open	26.00	28.00
90-01-047	Jerome - 1532	M. Holcombe	Open	30.00	32.00
89-01-048	Jessica and Jeremy -1522-1523	M. Holcombe	Retrd.	195.00	16-1685.
89-01-049	Jessie - 1501	M. Holcombe	Open	30.00	32.00
87-01-050	Jessie (no base) -1501W	M. Holcombe	Retrd.	19.00	400.00
88-01-051	John -1514	M. Holcombe	Retrd.	30.00	100-175.
90-01-052	Joseph - 1537	M. Holcombe	Open	30.00	30.00
92-01-053	Joy - 1548	M. Holcombe	Open	30.00	30.00
94-01-054	Justin - 1576	M. Holcombe	Open	37.00	37.00
90-01-055	Kacie - 1533	M. Holcombe	Open	38.00	38.00
88-01-056	Kezia - 1518	M. Holcombe	Open	36.00	37.00
86-01-057	Lil' Emmie 4 1/2" -1344	M. Holcombe	Retrd.	18.00	110-140.

		ARTIST	EDITION	ISSUE	QUOTE
86-01-058	Lil' Emmie 3 1/2"-1345	M. Holcombe	Retrd.	14.00	95-125.
88-01-059	Lisa-1512	M. Holcombe	Retrd.	36.00	100-175.
90-01-060	Mary - 1536	M. Holcombe	Open	30.00	30.00
88-01-061	Maya - 1520	M. Holcombe	Retrd.	36.00	375-390.
88-01-062	Meg (blue dress, long hair) -1505	M. Holcombe	Retrd.	21.00	350.00
88-01-063	Meg (blue dress, short hair) -1505	M. Holcombe	Retrd.	21.00	850-875.
88-01-064	Meg (beige dress) -1505	M. Holcombe	Retrd.	21.00	1050.00
92-01-065	Melissa - 1556	M. Holcombe	Open	32.00	32.00
92-01-066	Merci - 1559	M. Holcombe	Open	36.00	37.00
88-01-067	Michael & Kim - 1517	M. Holcombe	Open	36.00	38.00
88-01-068	Moe & Pokey - 1552	M. Holcombe	Retrd.	16.00	35-50.00
87-01-069	Moses - 1506	M. Holcombe	Retrd.	30.00	50-120.
93-01-070	Nathaniel-11569	M. Holcombe	Open	36.00	36.00
91-01-071	Nellie - 1546	M. Holcombe	Retrd.	36.00	60-120.
94-01-072	Niambi- 1577	M. Holcombe	Open	34.00	34.00
87-01-073	Paddy Paw & Luke - 1551	M. Holcombe	Open	24.00	26.00
87-01-074	Paddy Paw & Lucy - 1553	M. Holcombe	Open	24.00	26.00
88-01-075	Peanut -1509	M. Holcombe	Retrd.	16.00	75-130.
90-01-076	Preshus - 1538	M. Holcombe	Open	24.00	24.00
87-01-077	Primas Jones -1377	M. Holcombe	Retrd.	40.00	525-750.
87-01-078	Primas Jones (w/base) -1377	M. Holcombe	Retrd.	40.00	775.00
87-01-079	Prissy with Yarn Hair (6 strands) -1343	M. Holcombe	Retrd.	19.00	115-225.
87-01-080	Prissy with Yarn Hair (9 strands) -1343	M. Holcombe	Retrd.	19.00	500.00
87-01-081	Prissy with Basket -1346	M. Holcombe	Retrd.	16.00	90-125.
86-01-082	Prissy (Moon Pie) - 1557	M. Holcombe	Open	20.00	32.00
86-01-083	Prissy (Bear) - 1558	M. Holcombe	Open	18.00	25.00
87-01-084	Pud - 1550	M. Holcombe	Retrd.	11.00	780-1350
86-01-085	Rachel - 1404W	M. Holcombe	Open	20.00	28.00
92-01-086	Rakiya - 1561	M. Holcombe	Open	36.00	36.00
88-01-087	Sally -1507	M. Holcombe	Retrd.	19.00	125-145.
91-01-088	Samantha - 1542	M. Holcombe	Retrd.	38.00	38-76.00
91-01-089	Samuel - 1541	M. Holcombe	Retrd.	32.00	32.00
89-01-090	Sasha - 1531	M. Holcombe	Open	30.00	32.00
86-01-091	Selina Jane (6 strands) -1338	M. Holcombe	Retrd.	21.95	125-225.
86-01-092	Selina Jane (9 strands) -1338	M. Holcombe	Retrd.	21.95	500.00
93-01-093	Simon & Andrew - 1565	M. Holcombe	Open	45.00	45.00
86-01-094	St. Nicholas-W -1315	M. Holcombe	Retrd.	30.00	115-130.
86-01-095	St. Nicholas-B -1316	M. Holcombe	Retrd.	30.00	125-130.
92-01-096	Stephen (Nativity Shepherd) - 1563	M. Holcombe	Open	36.00	36.00
90-01-097	Sunshine - 1535	M. Holcombe	Open	38.00	38.00
93-01-098	Sylvia - 1564	M. Holcombe	Open	36.00	37.00
88-01-099	Tansi & Tedi (green socks, collar, cuffs)- 1516	M. Holcombe	Retrd.	30.00	260-275.
88-01-100	Tansy & Tedi - 1516	M. Holcombe	Open	N/A	37.00
89-01-101	Tara - 1527	M. Holcombe	Open	36.00	37.00
90-01-102	Tess - 1534	M. Holcombe	Open	30.00	32.00
90-01-103	Thaliyah- 778	M. Holcombe	Retrd.	200.00	17-1800.
92-01-104	Thomas - 1549	M. Holcombe	Open	30.00	30.00
87-01-105	Tiffany - 1511	M. Holcombe	Open	32.00	32.00
94-01-106	Tish 1572	M. Holcombe	Open	38.00	38.00
86-01-107	Toby 4 1/2"- 1331	M. Holcombe	Retrd.	16.00	125-135.
86-01-108	Toby 3 1/2"- 1332	M. Holcombe	Retrd.	13.00	100-120.
85-01-109	Tom- 1353	M. Holcombe	Retrd.	16.00	350-375.
86-01-110	Uncle Bud 8 1/2"- 1303	M. Holcombe	Retrd.	27.00	150-285.
86-01-111	Uncle Bud 6"- 1304	M. Holcombe	Retrd.	19.00	75-150.
92-01-112	Valerie - 1560	M. Holcombe	Open	36.00	37.00
87-01-113	Willie - 1406W	M. Holcombe	Open	22.00	28.00
93-01-114	Zack - 1566	M. Holcombe	Open	34.00	34.00
All God's Children	**Christmas**				
87-02-001	1987 Father Christmas-W -1750	M. Holcombe	Retrd.	145.00	650-675.
87-02-002	1987 Father Christmas-B -1751	M. Holcombe	Retrd.	145.00	650-675.
88-02-003	1988 Father Christmas-W -1757	M. Holcombe	Retrd.	195.00	325-550.
88-02-004	1988 Father Christmas-B -1758	M. Holcombe	Retrd.	195.00	325-550.
88-02-005	Santa Claus-W -1767	M. Holcombe	Retrd.	185.00	550-565.
88-02-006	Santa Claus-B -1768	M. Holcombe	Retrd.	185.00	550-565.
89-02-007	1989 Father Christmas-W -1769	M. Holcombe	Retrd.	195.00	300-600.
89-02-008	1989 Father Christmas-B -1770	M. Holcombe	Retrd.	195.00	300-600.
91-02-009	1990-91 Father Christmas-W -1771	M. Holcombe	Retrd.	195.00	400-550.
91-02-010	1990-91 Father Christmas-B -1772	M. Holcombe	Retrd.	195.00	350-550.
92-02-011	1991-92 Father Christmas-W -1773	M. Holcombe	Retrd.	195.00	275-400.
92-02-012	1991-92 Father Christmas-B -1774	M. Holcombe	Retrd.	195.00	275-400.
92-02-013	Father Christmas Bust-W -1775	M. Holcombe	Retrd.	145.00	300.00
92-02-014	Father Christmas Bust-B -1776	M. Holcombe	Retrd.	145.00	300.00
All God's Children	**Sugar And Spice**				
87-03-001	God is Love (Angel) -1401	M. Holcombe	Retrd.	22.00	515-525.
87-03-002	Friend Show Love (Becky) -1402	M. Holcombe	Retrd.	22.00	515-525.
87-03-003	Blessed are the Peacemakers (Eli) -1403	M. Holcombe	Retrd.	22.00	515-525.
87-03-004	Old Friends are Best (Rachel) -1404	M. Holcombe	Retrd.	22.00	515-525.
87-03-005	Jesus Loves Me (Amy) -1405	M. Holcombe	Retrd.	22.00	515-525.
87-03-006	Sharing with Friends (Willie) -1406	M. Holcombe	Retrd.	22.00	400-525.
87-03-007	Friendship Warms the Heart (Jacob) -1407	M. Holcombe	Retrd.	22.00	515-525.
All God's Children	**International Series**				
88-04-001	Juan - 1807	M. Holcombe	Retrd.	26.00	75-90.00
87-04-002	Kameko - 1802	M. Holcombe	Open.	26.00	28.00
87-04-003	Karl - 1808	M. Holcombe	Open.	26.00	28.00
88-04-004	Katrina - 1803	M. Holcombe	Retrd.	26.00	68-90.00
87-04-005	Kelli - 1805	M. Holcombe	Open	30.00	30.00
87-04-006	Little Chief - 1804	M. Holcombe	Open	32.00	32.00
93-04-007	Minnie - 1568	M. Holcombe	Open	36.00	36.00
87-04-008	Pike - 1806	M. Holcombe	Open	30.00	32.00
87-04-009	Tat - 1801	M. Holcombe	Open	30.00	32.00
All God's Children	**Historical Series**				
89-05-001	Harriet Tubman - 1900	M. Holcombe	Retrd.	65.00	100-175.
90-05-002	Sojourner Truth - 1901	M. Holcombe	Open	65.00	65.00
91-05-003	Frederick Douglass - 1902	M. Holcombe	Open	70.00	70.00
92-05-004	Dr. Daniel Williams - 1903	M. Holcombe	Open	70.00	70.00
92-05-005	Mary Bethune - 1904	M. Holcombe	Open	70.00	70.00
92-05-006	Mary Bethune - 1904 (misspelled)	M. Holcombe	Closed	70.00	135-200.
92-05-007	Frances Harper - 1905	M. Holcombe	Open	70.00	70.00
92-05-008	Ida B. Wells - 1906	M. Holcombe	Open	70.00	70.00
92-05-009	George Washington Carver - 1907	M. Holcombe	Open	70.00	70.00
94-05-010	Augustus Walley (Buffalo Soldier) - 1908	M. Holcombe	Retrd.	95.00	95.00
94-05-011	Bessie Smith- 1909	M. Holcombe	Open	70.00	70.00
All God's Children	**Angelic Messengers**				
94-06-001	Cieara 2500	M. Holcombe	Open	38.00	38.00
94-06-002	Mariah 2501	M. Holcombe	Open	38.00	38.00

	ARTIST	EDITION	ISSUE	QUOTE
All God's Children	**Little Missionary Series**			
94-07-001 Nakia 3500	M. Holcombe	9/95	40.00	40.00
All God's Children	**Collectors' Club**			
89-08-001 Molly -1524	M. Holcombe	Retrd.	38.00	240-500.
90-08-002 Joey -1539	M. Holcombe	Retrd.	32.00	220-350.
91-08-003 Mandy -1540	M. Holcombe	Retrd.	36.00	180-225.
92-08-004 Olivia -1562	M. Holcombe	Retrd.	36.00	100-150.
93-08-005 Garrett -1567	M. Holcombe	Retrd.	36.00	72-85.00
93-08-006 Peek-a-Boo	M. Holcombe	Retrd.	N/A	25-75.00
94-08-007 Alexandria -1575	M. Holcombe	5/95	36.00	36.00
94-08-008 Lindy	M. Holcombe	5/95	Gift	N/A
All God's Children	**Event Piece**			
94-09-001 Uriel 2000	M. Holcombe	Yr.Iss.	45.00	45.00
American Artists	**Fred Stone Figurines**			
85-01-001 The Black Stallion, porcelain	F. Stone	2,500	125.00	260.00
85-01-002 The Black Stallion, bronze	F. Stone	1,500	150.00	175.00
86-01-003 Arab Mare & Foal	F. Stone	2,500	150.00	225.00
86-01-004 Tranquility	F. Stone	2,500	175.00	275.00
87-01-005 Rearing Black Stallion (Porcelain)	F. Stone	3,500	150.00	175.00
87-01-006 Rearing Black Stallion (Bronze)	F. Stone	1,250	175.00	195.00
Anheuser-Busch, Inc.	**Anheuser-Busch Collectible Figurines**			
94-01-001 Buddies N4575	M. Urdahl	7,500	65.00	65.00
ANRI	**Ferrandiz Shepherds of the Year**			
77-01-001 Friendships, 6"	J. Ferrandiz	Annual	110.00	500-675.
77-01-002 Friendships, 3"	J. Ferrandiz	Annual	53.50	330.00
78-01-003 Spreading the Word, 6"	J. Ferrandiz	Annual	270.50	500.00
78-01-004 Spreading the Word, 3"	J. Ferrandiz	Annual	115.00	250-275.
79-01-005 Drummer Boy, 6"	J. Ferrandiz	Annual	220.00	400-425.
79-01-006 Drummer Boy, 3"	J. Ferrandiz	Annual	80.00	250.00
80-01-007 Freedom Bound, 6"	J. Ferrandiz	Annual	225.00	400.00
80-01-008 Freedom Bound, 3"	J. Ferrandiz	Annual	90.00	225.00
81-01-009 Jolly Piper, 6"	J. Ferrandiz	Closed	225.00	375.00
82-01-010 Companions, 6"	J. Ferrandiz	Closed	220.00	275-300.
83-01-011 Good Samaritan, 6"	J. Ferrandiz	Closed	220.00	300-320.
84-01-012 Devotion, 6"	J. Ferrandiz	Closed	180.00	200-250.
84-01-013 Devotion, 3"	J. Ferrandiz	Closed	82.50	125.00
ANRI	**Ferrandiz Matching Number Woodcarvings**			
88-02-001 Dear Sweetheart, 6"	J. Ferrandiz	Closed	525.00	900.00
88-02-002 For My Sweetheart, 6"	J. Ferrandiz	Set	Set	Set
88-02-003 Dear Sweetheart, 3"	J. Ferrandiz	Closed	285.00	495.00
88-02-004 For My Sweetheart, 3"	J. Ferrandiz	Set	Set	Set
88-02-005 Extra, Extra!, 6"	J. Ferrandiz	Closed	665.00	665.00
88-02-006 Sunny Skies, 6"	J. Ferrandiz	Set	Set	Set
88-02-007 Extra, Extra!, 3"	J. Ferrandiz	Closed	315.00	315.00
88-02-008 Sunny Skies, 3"	J. Ferrandiz	Set	Set	Set
88-02-009 Picnic for Two, 6"	J. Ferrandiz	Closed	845.00	845.00
88-02-010 Bon Appetit, 6"	J. Ferrandiz	Set	Set	Set
88-02-011 Picnic for Two, 3"	J. Ferrandiz	Closed	390.00	390.00
88-02-012 Bon Appetit, 3"	J. Ferrandiz	Set	Set	Set
89-02-013 Baker / Pastry, 6"	J. Ferrandiz	Closed	680.00	680.00
89-02-014 Baker / Pastry, 3"	J. Ferrandiz	Closed	340.00	340.00
90-02-015 Alpine Music / Friend, 6"	J. Ferrandiz	Closed	900.00	900.00
90-02-016 Alpine Music / Friend, 3"	J. Ferrandiz	Closed	450.00	450.00
91-02-017 Catalonian Boy/Girl, 6"	J. Ferrandiz	Closed	1000.00	1000.00
91-02-018 Catalonian Boy/Girl, 3"	J. Ferrandiz	Closed	455.00	455.00
ANRI	**Ferrandiz Boy and Girl**			
76-03-001 Cowboy, 6"	J. Ferrandiz	Closed	75.00	500-600.
76-03-002 Harvest Girl, 6"	J. Ferrandiz	Closed	75.00	400-800.
77-03-003 Tracker, 6"	J. Ferrandiz	Closed	100.00	400.00
77-03-004 Leading the Way, 6"	J. Ferrandiz	Closed	100.00	300-375.
78-03-005 Peace Pipe, 6"	J. Ferrandiz	Closed	140.00	325-450.
78-03-006 Basket of Joy, 6"	J. Ferrandiz	Closed	140.00	350-450.
79-03-007 Happy Strummer, 6"	J. Ferrandiz	Closed	160.00	395.00
79-03-008 First Blossom, 6"	J. Ferrandiz	Closed	135.00	345-375.
80-03-009 Friends, 6"	J. Ferrandiz	Closed	200.00	300-350.
80-03-010 Melody for Two, 6"	J. Ferrandiz	Closed	200.00	350.00
81-03-011 Merry Melody, 6"	J. Ferrandiz	Closed	210.00	300-350.
81-03-012 Tiny Sounds, 6"	J. Ferrandiz	Closed	210.00	300-350.
82-03-013 Guiding Light, 6"	J. Ferrandiz	Closed	225.00	275-350.
82-03-014 To Market, 6"	J. Ferrandiz	Closed	220.00	295.00
83-03-015 Bewildered, 6"	J. Ferrandiz	Closed	196.00	295.00
83-03-016 Admiration, 6"	J. Ferrandiz	Closed	220.00	295.00
84-03-017 Wanderer's Return, 6"	J. Ferrandiz	Closed	196.00	250.00
84-03-018 Wanderer's Return, 3"	J. Ferrandiz	Closed	93.00	135.00
84-03-019 Friendly Faces, 6"	J. Ferrandiz	Closed	210.00	225-295.
84-03-020 Friendly Faces, 3"	J. Ferrandiz	Closed	93.00	110.00
85-03-021 Tender Love, 6"	J. Ferrandiz	Closed	225.00	250.00
85-03-022 Tender Love, 3"	J. Ferrandiz	Closed	100.00	125.00
85-03-023 Peaceful Friends, 6"	J. Ferrandiz	Closed	250.00	295.00
85-03-024 Peaceful Friends, 3"	J. Ferrandiz	Closed	120.00	120.00
86-03-025 Season's Bounty, 6"	J. Ferrandiz	Closed	245.00	245.00
86-03-026 Season's Bounty, 3"	J. Ferrandiz	Closed	125.00	125.00
86-03-027 Golden Sheaves, 6"	J. Ferrandiz	Closed	245.00	245.00
86-03-028 Golden Sheaves, 3"	J. Ferrandiz	Closed	125.00	125.00
87-03-029 Dear Sweetheart, 6"	J. Ferrandiz	Closed	250.00	250.00
87-03-030 Dear Sweetheart, 3"	J. Ferrandiz	Closed	130.00	130.00
87-03-031 For My Sweetheart, 6"	J. Ferrandiz	Closed	250.00	250.00
87-03-032 For My Sweetheart, 3"	J. Ferrandiz	Closed	130.00	130.00
88-03-033 Extra, Extra!, 6"	J. Ferrandiz	Closed	320.00	320.00
88-03-034 Extra, Extra!, 3"	J. Ferrandiz	Closed	145.00	145.00
88-03-035 Sunny Skies, 6"	J. Ferrandiz	Closed	320.00	320.00
88-03-036 Sunny Skies, 3"	J. Ferrandiz	Closed	145.00	145.00
89-03-037 Baker Boy, 6"	J. Ferrandiz	Closed	340.00	340.00
89-03-038 Baker Boy, 3"	J. Ferrandiz	Closed	170.00	170.00
89-03-039 Pastry Girl, 6"	J. Ferrandiz	Closed	340.00	340.00
89-03-040 Pastry Girl, 3"	J. Ferrandiz	Closed	170.00	170.00
89-03-041 Swiss Girl, 6"	J. Ferrandiz	Closed	470.00	470.00
89-03-042 Swiss Girl, 3"	J. Ferrandiz	Closed	200.00	200.00
89-03-043 Swiss Boy, 6"	J. Ferrandiz	Closed	380.00	380.00
89-03-044 Swiss Boy, 3"	J. Ferrandiz	Closed	180.00	180.00
90-03-045 Alpine Music, 6"	J. Ferrandiz	1500	450.00	580.00
90-03-046 Alpine Music, 3"	J. Ferrandiz	Closed	225.00	225.00
90-03-047 Alpine Friend, 6"	J. Ferrandiz	1,500	450.00	610.00
90-03-048 Alpine Friend, 3"	J. Ferrandiz	1,500	225.00	365.00
91-03-049 Catalonian Boy, 6"	J. Ferrandiz	Closed	500.00	500.00
91-03-050 Catalonian Boy, 3"	J. Ferrandiz	Closed	227.50	227.50

	ARTIST	EDITION	ISSUE	QUOTE
91-03-051 Catalonian Girl, 6"	J. Ferrandiz	Closed	500.00	500.00
91-03-052 Catalonian Girl, 3"	J. Ferrandiz	Closed	228.00	227.50
92-03-053 Waste Not, Want Not, 6"	J. Ferrandiz	1,000	430.00	430.00
92-03-054 Waste Not, Want Not, 3"	J. Ferrandiz	1,000	190.00	200.00
92-03-055 May I, Too?, 6"	J. Ferrandiz	1,000	440.00	440.00
92-03-056 May I, Too?, 3"	J. Ferrandiz	1,000	230.00	230.00
92-03-057 Madonna With Child, 6"	J. Ferrandiz	1,000	370.00	370.00
92-03-058 Madonna With Child, 3"	J. Ferrandiz	1,000	190.00	190.00
92-03-059 Pascal Lamb, 6"	J. Ferrandiz	1,000	460.00	460.00
92-03-060 Pascal Lamb, 3"	J. Ferrandiz	1,000	210.00	210.00
ANRI	**Ferrandiz Woodcarvings**			
69-04-001 Sugar Heart, 6"	J. Ferrandiz	Closed	25.00	525.00
69-04-002 Sugar Heart, 3"	J. Ferrandiz	Closed	12.50	450.00
69-04-003 Angel Sugar Heart, 6"	J. Ferrandiz	Closed	25.00	2500.00
69-04-004 Heavenly Quintet, 6"	J. Ferrandiz	Closed	25.00	2000.00
69-04-005 Heavenly Gardener, 6"	J. Ferrandiz	Closed	25.00	2000.00
69-04-006 Love's Messenger, 6"	J. Ferrandiz	Closed	25.00	2000.00
74-04-007 Greetings, 6"	J. Ferrandiz	Closed	55.00	475.00
74-04-008 Greetings, 3"	J. Ferrandiz	Closed	30.00	300.00
74-04-009 New Friends, 6"	J. Ferrandiz	Closed	55.00	550.00
74-04-010 New Friends, 3"	J. Ferrandiz	Closed	30.00	275.00
74-04-011 Tender Moments, 6"	J. Ferrandiz	Closed	55.00	575.00
74-04-012 Tender Moments, 3"	J. Ferrandiz	Closed	30.00	375.00
74-04-013 Helping Hands, 6"	J. Ferrandiz	Closed	55.00	700.00
74-04-014 Helping Hands, 3"	J. Ferrandiz	Closed	30.00	350.00
74-04-015 Spring Outing, 6"	J. Ferrandiz	Closed	55.00	900.00
74-04-016 Spring Outing, 3"	J. Ferrandiz	Closed	30.00	625.00
73-04-017 Sweeper, 6"	J. Ferrandiz	Closed	75.00	425.00
73-04-018 Sweeper, 3"	J. Ferrandiz	Closed	35.00	130.00
74-04-019 The Bouquet, 6"	J. Ferrandiz	Closed	75.00	325.00
74-04-020 The Bouquet, 3"	J. Ferrandiz	Closed	35.00	175.00
70-04-021 Artist, 6"	J. Ferrandiz	Closed	25.00	350.00
74-04-022 Artist, 3"	J. Ferrandiz	Closed	30.00	195.00
74-04-023 Little Mother, 6"	J. Ferrandiz	Closed	85.00	285.00
74-04-024 Little Mother, 3"	J. Ferrandiz	Closed	136.00	290.00
74-04-025 Romeo, 6"	J. Ferrandiz	Closed	85.00	395.00
74-04-026 Romeo, 3"	J. Ferrandiz	Closed	50.00	250.00
75-04-027 Inspector, 6"	J. Ferrandiz	Closed	80.00	395.00
75-04-028 Inspector, 3"	J. Ferrandiz	Closed	40.00	250.00
76-04-029 Girl with Rooster, 6"	J. Ferrandiz	Closed	60.00	275.00
76-04-030 Girl with Rooster, 3"	J. Ferrandiz	Closed	32.50	175.00
75-04-031 The Gift, 6"	J. Ferrandiz	Closed	70.00	295.00
75-04-032 The Gift, 3"	J. Ferrandiz	Closed	40.00	195.00
75-04-033 Love Gift, 6"	J. Ferrandiz	Closed	70.00	295.00
75-04-034 Love Gift, 3"	J. Ferrandiz	Closed	40.00	175.00
77-04-035 The Blessing, 6"	J. Ferrandiz	Closed	125.00	250.00
77-04-036 The Blessing, 3"	J. Ferrandiz	Closed	45.00	150.00
69-04-037 Love Letter, 6"	J. Ferrandiz	Closed	25.00	250.00
69-04-038 Love Letter, 3"	J. Ferrandiz	Closed	12.50	150.00
75-04-039 Courting, 6"	J. Ferrandiz	Closed	150.00	450.00
75-04-040 Courting, 3"	J. Ferrandiz	Closed	70.00	235.00
75-04-041 Wanderlust, 6"	J. Ferrandiz	Closed	70.00	450.00
76-04-042 Wanderlust, 3"	J. Ferrandiz	Closed	32.50	125.00
76-04-043 Catch a Falling Star, 6"	J. Ferrandiz	Closed	75.00	250.00
76-04-044 Catch a Falling Star, 3"	J. Ferrandiz	Closed	35.00	150.00
75-04-045 Mother and Child, 6"	J. Ferrandiz	Closed	90.00	295.00
75-04-046 Mother and Child, 3"	J. Ferrandiz	Closed	45.00	150.00
77-04-047 Journey, 6"	J. Ferrandiz	Closed	120.00	400.00
77-04-048 Journey, 3"	J. Ferrandiz	Closed	67.50	175.00
77-04-049 Night Night, 6"	J. Ferrandiz	Closed	67.50	250-315.
77-04-050 Night Night, 3"	J. Ferrandiz	Closed	45.00	120.00
76-04-051 Sharing, 6"	J. Ferrandiz	Closed	32.50	225-275.
76-04-052 Sharing, 3"	J. Ferrandiz	Closed	32.50	130.00
82-04-053 Clarinet, 6"	J. Ferrandiz	Closed	175.00	200.00
82-04-054 Clarinet, 3"	J. Ferrandiz	Closed	80.00	100.00
82-04-055 Violin, 6"	J. Ferrandiz	Closed	175.00	195.00
82-04-056 Violin, 3"	J. Ferrandiz	Closed	80.00	95.00
82-04-057 Bagpipe, 6"	J. Ferrandiz	Closed	175.00	190.00
82-04-058 Bagpipe, 3"	J. Ferrandiz	Closed	80.00	95.00
82-04-059 Flute, 6"	J. Ferrandiz	Closed	175.00	190.00
82-04-060 Flute, 3"	J. Ferrandiz	Closed	80.00	95.00
82-04-061 Guitar, 6"	J. Ferrandiz	Closed	175.00	190.00
82-04-062 Guitar, 3"	J. Ferrandiz	Closed	80.00	95.00
82-04-063 Harmonica, 6"	J. Ferrandiz	Closed	175.00	190.00
82-04-064 Harmonica, 3"	J. Ferrandiz	Closed	80.00	95.00
82-04-065 Harmonica, 3"	J. Ferrandiz	Closed	80.00	95.00
82-04-066 Lighting the Way, 6"	J. Ferrandiz	Closed	225.00	295.00
82-04-067 Lighting the Way, 3"	J. Ferrandiz	Closed	105.00	150.00
81-04-068 Musical Basket, 6"	J. Ferrandiz	Closed	200.00	225.00
81-04-069 Musical Basket, 3"	J. Ferrandiz	Closed	90.00	115.00
82-04-070 The Good Life, 6"	J. Ferrandiz	Closed	225.00	295.00
82-04-071 The Good Life, 3"	J. Ferrandiz	Closed	100.00	200.00
82-04-072 Star Bright, 6"	J. Ferrandiz	Closed	250.00	295.00
82-04-073 Star Bright, 3"	J. Ferrandiz	Closed	110.00	125.00
82-04-074 Encore, 6"	J. Ferrandiz	Closed	225.00	235.00
82-04-075 Encore, 3"	J. Ferrandiz	Closed	100.00	115.00
82-04-076 Play It Again, 6"	J. Ferrandiz	Closed	250.00	255.00
82-04-077 Play It Again, 3"	J. Ferrandiz	Closed	100.00	120.00
73-04-078 Girl with Dove, 6"	J. Ferrandiz	Closed	50.00	175-200.
73-04-079 Girl with Dove, 3"	J. Ferrandiz	Closed	30.00	110.00
79-04-080 Stitch in Time, 6"	J. Ferrandiz	Closed	150.00	235.00
79-04-081 Stitch in Time, 3"	J. Ferrandiz	Closed	75.00	125.00
79-04-082 He's My Brother, 6"	J. Ferrandiz	Closed	155.00	240.00
79-04-083 He's My Brother, 3"	J. Ferrandiz	Closed	70.00	130.00
81-04-084 Stepping Out, 6"	J. Ferrandiz	Closed	220.00	275.00
81-04-085 Stepping Out, 3"	J. Ferrandiz	Closed	95.00	110-145.
79-04-086 High Riding, 6"	J. Ferrandiz	Closed	340.00	475.00
79-04-087 High Riding, 3"	J. Ferrandiz	Closed	145.00	200.00
80-04-088 Umpapa, 4"	J. Ferrandiz	Closed	125.00	140.00
81-04-089 Jolly Piper, 3"	J. Ferrandiz	Closed	100.00	120.00
77-04-090 Tracker, 3"	J. Ferrandiz	Closed	70.00	120-200.
81-04-091 Merry Melody, 3"	J. Ferrandiz	Closed	90.00	115.00
82-04-092 Guiding Light, 3"	J. Ferrandiz	Closed	100.00	115-140.
82-04-093 Companions, 3"	J. Ferrandiz	Closed	95.00	115.00
77-04-094 Leading the Way, 3"	J. Ferrandiz	Closed	62.50	120.00
82-04-095 To Market, 3"	J. Ferrandiz	Closed	95.00	115.00
78-04-096 Basket of Joy, 3"	J. Ferrandiz	Closed	65.00	120.00
81-04-097 Tiny Sounds, 3"	J. Ferrandiz	Closed	90.00	105.00
78-04-098 Spring Dance, 12"	J. Ferrandiz	Closed	950.00	1750.00
78-04-099 Spring Dance, 24"	J. Ferrandiz	Closed	4750.00	6200.00
76-04-100 Gardener, 3"	J. Ferrandiz	Closed	32.00	195.00

		ARTIST	EDITION	ISSUE	QUOTE
76-04-101	Gardener, 6"	J. Ferrandiz	Closed	65.00	275-350.
79-04-102	First Blossom, 3"	J. Ferrandiz	Closed	70.00	110.00
81-04-103	Sweet Arrival Pink, 6"	J. Ferrandiz	Closed	225.00	225.00
81-04-104	Sweet Arrival Pink, 3"	J. Ferrandiz	Closed	105.00	110.00
81-04-105	Sweet Arrival Blue, 6"	J. Ferrandiz	Closed	225.00	255.00
81-04-106	Sweet Arrival Blue, 3"	J. Ferrandiz	Closed	105.00	110.00
82-04-107	The Champion, 6"	J. Ferrandiz	Closed	225.00	250.00
82-04-108	The Champion, 3"	J. Ferrandiz	Closed	98.00	110.00
82-04-109	Sweet Melody, 6"	J. Ferrandiz	Closed	198.00	210.00
82-04-110	Sweet Melody, 3"	J. Ferrandiz	Closed	80.00	90.00
73-04-111	Trumpeter, 6"	J. Ferrandiz	Closed	120.00	240.00
73-04-112	Trumpeter, 3"	J. Ferrandiz	Closed	69.00	115.00
80-04-113	Trumpeter, 10"	J. Ferrandiz	Closed	500.00	500.00
84-04-114	Trumpeter, 20"	J. Ferrandiz	Closed	2350.00	3050.00
79-04-115	Peace Pipe, 3"	J. Ferrandiz	Closed	85.00	120.00
83-04-116	Peace Pipe, 10"	J. Ferrandiz	Closed	460.00	495.00
84-04-117	Peace Pipe, 20"	J. Ferrandiz	Closed	2200.00	3500.00
74-04-118	Happy Wanderer, 6"	J. Ferrandiz	Closed	70.00	200.00
74-04-119	Happy Wanderer, 3"	J. Ferrandiz	Closed	40.00	105.00
73-04-120	Happy Wanderer, 10"	J. Ferrandiz	Closed	120.00	500.00
74-04-121	Flight Into Egypt, 6"	J. Ferrandiz	Closed	70.00	500.00
74-04-122	Flight Into Egypt, 3"	J. Ferrandiz	Closed	35.00	125.00
77-04-123	Poor Boy, 6"	J. Ferrandiz	Closed	125.00	215.00
77-04-124	Poor Boy, 3"	J. Ferrandiz	Closed	50.00	110.00
79-04-125	Happy Strummer, 3"	J. Ferrandiz	Closed	75.00	110.00
78-04-126	Harvest Girl, 3"	J. Ferrandiz	Closed	75.00	110-140.
82-04-127	Hitchhiker, 6"	J. Ferrandiz	Closed	125.00	230.00
82-04-128	Hitchhiker, 3"	J. Ferrandiz	Closed	98.00	85-110.
84-04-129	High Hopes, 6"	J. Ferrandiz	Closed	170.00	255.00
84-04-130	High Hopes, 3"	J. Ferrandiz	Closed	81.00	81-100.
88-04-131	Abracadabra, 6"	J. Ferrandiz	Closed	315.00	345.00
88-04-132	Abracadabra, 3"	J. Ferrandiz	Closed	145.00	165.00
88-04-133	Peace Maker, 6"	J. Ferrandiz	Closed	360.00	395.00
88-04-134	Peace Maker, 3"	J. Ferrandiz	Closed	180.00	200.00
88-04-135	Picnic for Two, 6"	J. Ferrandiz	Closed	425.00	465.00
88-04-136	Picnic for Two, 3"	J. Ferrandiz	Closed	190.00	210.00
88-04-137	Bon Appetit, 6"	J. Ferrandiz	Closed	395.00	440.00
88-04-138	Bon Appetit, 3"	J. Ferrandiz	Closed	175.00	195.00
69-04-139	The Good Sheperd, 3"	J. Ferrandiz	Closed	12.50	120.50
69-04-140	The Good Shepherd, 6"	J. Ferrandiz	Closed	25.00	236.50
71-04-141	The Good Shepherd, 10"	J. Ferrandiz	Closed	90.00	90.00
75-04-142	Going Home, 3"	J. Ferrandiz	Closed	40.00	110.00
75-04-143	Going Home, 6"	J. Ferrandiz	Closed	70.00	240.00
75-04-144	Holy Family, 3"	J. Ferrandiz	Closed	75.00	250.00
75-04-145	Holy Family, 6"	J. Ferrandiz	Closed	200.00	670.00
73-04-146	Nature Girl, 3"	J. Ferrandiz	Closed	30.00	30.00
73-04-147	Nature Girl, 6"	J. Ferrandiz	Closed	60.00	272.00
73-04-148	Girl in the Egg, 3"	J. Ferrandiz	Closed	30.00	127.00
73-04-149	Girl in the Egg, 6"	J. Ferrandiz	Closed	60.00	272.00
76-04-150	Flower Girl, 3"	J. Ferrandiz	Closed	40.00	40.00
76-04-151	Flower Girl, 6"	J. Ferrandiz	Closed	90.00	310.00
76-04-152	The Letter, 3"	J. Ferrandiz	Closed	40.00	40.00
76-04-153	The Letter, 6"	J. Ferrandiz	Closed	90.00	600.00
69-04-154	Talking to the Animals, 3"	J. Ferrandiz	Closed	12.50	125.00
69-04-155	Talking to the Animals, 6"	J. Ferrandiz	Closed	45.00	45.00
71-04-156	Talking to the Animals, 10"	J. Ferrandiz	Closed	90.00	300.00
71-04-157	Talking to Animals, 20"	J. Ferrandiz	Closed	Unkn.	3,000.00
70-04-158	Duet, 3"	J. Ferrandiz	Closed	36.00	165.00
70-04-159	Duet, 6"	J. Ferrandiz	Closed	Unkn.	355.00
73-04-160	Spring Arrivals, 3"	J. Ferrandiz	Open	30.00	160.00
73-04-161	Spring Arrivals, 6"	J. Ferrandiz	Open	50.00	350.00
80-04-162	Spring Arrivals, 10"	J. Ferrandiz	Open	435.00	770.00
80-04-163	Spring Arrivals, 20"	J. Ferrandiz	250	2000.00	3360.00
75-04-164	Summertime, 3"	J. Ferrandiz	Closed	35.00	35.00
75-04-165	Summertime, 6"	J. Ferrandiz	Closed	70.00	258.00
76-04-166	Cowboy, 3"	J. Ferrandiz	Closed	35.00	140-160.
84-04-167	Cowboy, 10"	J. Ferrandiz	Closed	370.00	500.00
83-04-168	Cowboy, 20"	J. Ferrandiz	Closed	2100.00	2100.00
87-04-169	Serenity, 3"	J. Ferrandiz	Closed	125.00	150.50
84-04-170	Bird's Eye View, 3"	J. Ferrandiz	Closed	88.00	129.00
84-04-171	Bird's Eye View, 6"	J. Ferrandiz	Closed	216.00	700.00
86-04-172	God's Little Helper, 2"	J. Ferrandiz	Closed	170.00	255.00
86-04-173	God's Little Helper, 4"	J. Ferrandiz	Closed	425.00	550.00
85-04-174	Butterfly Boy, 3"	J. Ferrandiz	Closed	95.00	140.00
85-04-175	Butterfly Boy, 6"	J. Ferrandiz	Closed	220.00	322.00
84-04-176	Shipmates, 3"	J. Ferrandiz	Closed	81.00	118.50
84-04-177	Shipmates, 6"	J. Ferrandiz	Closed	170.00	247.50
78-04-178	Spreading the Word, 3"	J. Ferrandiz	Closed	115.00	193.50
78-04-179	Spreading the Word, 6"	J. Ferrandiz	Closed	270.00	494.50
82-04-180	Bundle of Joy, 3"	J. Ferrandiz	Closed	100.00	300.00
82-04-181	Bundle of Joy, 6"	J. Ferrandiz	Closed	225.00	322.50
77-04-182	Riding Thru the Rain, 5"	J. Ferrandiz	Open	145.00	450.00
77-04-183	Riding Thru the Rain, 10"	J. Ferrandiz	Open	400.00	1150.00
81-04-184	Sweet Dreams, 3"	J. Ferrandiz	Closed	100.00	140.00
77-04-185	Hurdy Gurdy, 3"	J. Ferrandiz	Closed	53.00	150.00
77-04-186	Hurdy Gurdy, 6"	J. Ferrandiz	Closed	112.00	390.00
77-04-187	Proud Mother, 3"	J. Ferrandiz	Closed	52.50	150.00
77-04-188	Proud Mother, 6"	J. Ferrandiz	Closed	130.00	350.00
80-04-189	Drummer Boy, 3"	J. Ferrandiz	Closed	130.00	200.00
80-04-190	Drummer Boy, 6"	J. Ferrandiz	Closed	300.00	400.00
82-04-191	Circus Serenade, 3"	J. Ferrandiz	Closed	100.00	160.00
82-04-192	Circus Serenade, 6"	J. Ferrandiz	Closed	220.00	220.00
82-04-193	Surprise, 3"	J. Ferrandiz	Closed	100.00	150.00
82-04-194	Surprise, 6"	J. Ferrandiz	Closed	225.00	325.00
75-04-195	Cherub, 2"	J. Ferrandiz	Closed	32.00	90.00
75-04-196	Cherub, 4"	J. Ferrandiz	Closed	32.00	275.00
69-04-197	The Quintet, 3"	J. Ferrandiz	Closed	12.50	140.00
69-04-198	The Quintet, 6"	J. Ferrandiz	Closed	25.00	340.00
71-04-199	The Quintet, 10"	J. Ferrandiz	Closed	100.00	600.00
71-04-200	The Quintet, 20"	J. Ferrandiz	Closed	Unkn.	3000.00
87-04-201	Serenity, 6"	J. Ferrandiz	Closed	245.00	290.50
87-04-202	Nature's Wonder, 3"	J. Ferrandiz	Closed	125.00	150.50
87-04-203	Nature's Wonder, 6"	J. Ferrandiz	Closed	245.00	290.50
87-04-204	Black Forest Boy, 3"	J. Ferrandiz	Closed	125.00	150.50
87-04-205	Black Forest Boy, 6"	J. Ferrandiz	Closed	250.00	301.00
87-04-206	Black Forest Girl, 3"	J. Ferrandiz	Closed	125.00	150.50
87-04-207	Black Forest Girl, 6"	J. Ferrandiz	Closed	250.00	300-350.
87-04-208	Heavenly Concert, 2"	J. Ferrandiz	Closed	200.00	200.00
87-04-209	Heavenly Concert, 4"	J. Ferrandiz	Closed	450.00	550.00
86-04-210	Swiss Girl, 3"	J. Ferrandiz	Closed	122.00	122.00
86-04-211	Swiss Girl, 6"	J. Ferrandiz	Closed	245.00	303.50
86-04-212	Swiss Boy, 3"	J. Ferrandiz	Closed	122.00	161.50

		ARTIST	EDITION	ISSUE	QUOTE
86-04-213	Swiss Boy, 6"	J. Ferrandiz	Closed	245.00	323.50
86-04-214	A Musical Ride, 4"	J. Ferrandiz	Closed	165.00	236.50
86-04-215	A Musical Ride, 8"	J. Ferrandiz	Closed	395.00	559.00
82-04-216	Sweet Dreams, 6"	J. Ferrandiz	Closed	225.00	330.00
83-04-217	Love Message, 3"	J. Ferrandiz	Closed	105.00	150.50
83-04-218	Love Message, 6"	J. Ferrandiz	Closed	240.00	365.50
83-04-219	Edelweiss, 3"	J. Ferrandiz	Open	95.00	190.00
83-04-220	Edelweiss, 6"	J. Ferrandiz	Open	220.00	450.00
86-04-221	Edelweiss, 10"	J. Ferrandiz	Open	500.00	1000.00
86-04-222	Edelweiss, 20"	J. Ferrandiz	250	3300.00	5420.00
83-04-223	Golden Blossom, 3"	J. Ferrandiz	Open	95.00	190.00
83-04-224	Golden Blossom, 6"	J. Ferrandiz	Open	220.00	450.00
86-04-225	Golden Blossom, 10"	J. Ferrandiz	Open	500.00	1000.00
86-04-226	Golden Blossom, 20"	J. Ferrandiz	250	3300.00	5420.00
86-04-227	Golden Blossom, 40"	J. Ferrandiz	Closed	8300.00	12950.00
88-04-228	Winter Memories, 3"	J. Ferrandiz	Closed	180.00	195.00
88-04-229	Winter Memories, 6"	J. Ferrandiz	Closed	398.00	440.00
87-04-230	Among Friends, 3"	J. Ferrandiz	Closed	125.00	150.50
87-04-231	Among Friends, 6"	J. Ferrandiz	Closed	245.00	290.50
89-04-232	Mexican Girl, 3"	J. Ferrandiz	Closed	170.00	175.00
89-04-233	Mexican Girl, 6"	J. Ferrandiz	Closed	340.00	350.00
89-04-234	Mexican Boy, 3"	J. Ferrandiz	Closed	170.00	175.00
89-04-235	Mexican Boy, 6"	J. Ferrandiz	Closed	340.00	350.00
93-04-236	Santa and Teddy, 5"	J. Ferrandiz	750	360.00	380.00
93-04-237	Christmas Time, 5"	J. Ferrandiz	750	360.00	380.00
93-04-238	Holiday Greetings, 3"	J. Ferrandiz	1,000	200.00	200.00
93-04-239	Holiday Greetings, 6"	J. Ferrandiz	1,000	450.00	450.00
93-04-240	Lots of Gifts, 3"	J. Ferrandiz	1,000	200.00	200.00
93-04-241	Lots of Gifts, 6"	J. Ferrandiz	1,000	450.00	450.00
94-04-242	Santa Resting on Bag 5"	J. Ferrandiz	Open	400.00	400.00
94-04-243	Donkey, 3"	J. Ferrandiz	Open	200.00	200.00
94-04-244	Donkey, 6"	J. Ferrandiz	Open	450.00	450.00
94-04-245	Donkey Driver, 3"	J. Ferrandiz	Open	160.00	160.00
94-04-245	Donkey Driver, 6"	J. Ferrandiz	Open	360.00	360.00

ANRI **Ferrandiz Message Collection**

89-05-001	He is the Light, 4 1/2"	J. Ferrandiz	Closed	300.00	300.00
89-05-002	Heaven Sent, 4 1/2"	J. Ferrandiz	Closed	300.00	300.00
89-05-003	God's Precious Gift, 4 1/2"	J. Ferrandiz	Closed	300.00	300.00
89-05-004	Love Knows No Bounds, 4 1/2"	J. Ferrandiz	Closed	300.00	300.00
89-05-005	Love So Powerful, 4 1/2"	J. Ferrandiz	Closed	300.00	300.00
89-05-006	Light From Within, 4 1/2"	J. Ferrandiz	Closed	300.00	300.00
89-05-007	He Guides Us, 4 1/2"	J. Ferrandiz	Closed	300.00	300.00
89-05-008	God's Miracle, 4 1/2"	J. Ferrandiz	Closed	300.00	300.00
89-05-009	He is the Light, 9"	J. Ferrandiz	Closed	600.00	600.00
90-05-010	God's Creation 4 1/2"	J. Ferrandiz	Closed	300.00	300.00
90-05-011	Count Your Blessings, 4 1/2"	J. Ferrandiz	Closed	300.00	300.00
90-05-012	Christmas Carillon, 4 1/2"	J. Ferrandiz	Closed	299.00	299.00

ANRI **Ferrandiz Mini Nativity Set**

84-06-001	Mary, 1 1/2"	J. Ferrandiz	Closed	300.00	540.00
84-06-002	Joseph, 1 1/2"	J. Ferrandiz	Closed	Set	Set
84-06-003	Infant, 1 1/2"	J. Ferrandiz	Closed	Set	Set
84-06-004	Leading the Way, 1 1/2"	J. Ferrandiz	Closed	Set	Set
84-06-005	Ox Donkey, 1 1/2"	J. Ferrandiz	Closed	Set	Set
84-06-006	Sheep Standing, 1 1/2"	J. Ferrandiz	Closed	Set	Set
84-06-007	Sheep Kneeling, 1 1/2"	J. Ferrandiz	Closed	Set	Set
85-06-008	Reverence, 1 1/2"	J. Ferrandiz	Closed	45.00	53.00
85-06-009	Harmony, 1 1/2"	J. Ferrandiz	Closed	45.00	53.00
85-06-010	Rest, 1 1/2"	J. Ferrandiz	Closed	45.00	53.00
85-06-011	Thanksgiving, 1 1/2"	J. Ferrandiz	Closed	45.00	53.00
85-06-012	Small Talk, 1 1/2"	J. Ferrandiz	Closed	45.00	53.00
85-06-013	Camel, 1 1/2"	J. Ferrandiz	Closed	45.00	53.00
85-06-014	Camel Guide, 1 1/2"	J. Ferrandiz	Closed	45.00	53.00
85-06-015	Baby Camel, 1 1/2"	J. Ferrandiz	Closed	45.00	53.00
86-06-016	Mini Melchoir, 1 1/2"	J. Ferrandiz	Closed	45.00	53.00
86-06-017	Mini Caspar, 1 1/2"	J. Ferrandiz	Closed	45.00	53.00
86-06-018	Mini Balthasar, 1 1/2"	J. Ferrandiz	Closed	45.00	53.00
86-06-019	Mini Angel, 1 1/2"	J. Ferrandiz	Closed	45.00	53.00
86-06-020	Mini Free Ride, plus Mini Lamb, 1 1/2"	J. Ferrandiz	Closed	45.00	53.00
86-06-021	Mini Weary Traveller, 1 1/2"	J. Ferrandiz	Closed	45.00	53.00
86-06-022	Mini The Stray, 1 1/2"	J. Ferrandiz	Closed	45.00	53.00
86-06-023	Mini The Hiker, 1 1/2"	J. Ferrandiz	Closed	45.00	53.00
86-06-024	Mini Star Struck, 1 1/2"	J. Ferrandiz	Closed	45.00	53.00
88-06-025	Jolly Gift, 1 1/2"	J. Ferrandiz	Closed	53.00	53.00
88-06-026	Sweet Inspiration, 1 1/2"	J. Ferrandiz	Closed	53.00	53.00
88-06-027	Sweet Dreams, 1 1/2"	J. Ferrandiz	Closed	53.00	53.00
88-06-028	Long Journey, 1 1/2"	J. Ferrandiz	Closed	53.00	53.00
88-06-029	Devotion, 1 1/2"	J. Ferrandiz	Closed	53.00	53.00

ANRI **Limited Edition Couples**

85-07-001	Springtime Stroll, 8"	J. Ferrandiz	Closed	590.00	950.00
85-07-002	First Kiss, 8"	J. Ferrandiz	Closed	590.00	950.00
86-07-003	A Tender Touch, 8"	J. Ferrandiz	Closed	590.00	850.00
86-07-004	My Heart Is Yours, 8"	J. Ferrandiz	Closed	590.00	850.00
87-07-005	Heart to Heart, 8"	J. Ferrandiz	Closed	590.00	850.00
88-07-006	A Loving Hand, 8"	J. Ferrandiz	Closed	795.00	850.00

ANRI **Sarah Kay Figurines**

83-08-001	Morning Chores,6"	S. Kay	Closed	210.00	550.00
83-08-002	Morning Chores, 4"	S. Kay	Closed	95.00	300.00
83-08-003	Morning Chores, 1 1/2"	S. Kay	Closed	45.00	110.00
83-08-004	Helping Mother, 6"	S. Kay	Closed	210.00	495.00
83-08-005	Helping Mother, 4"	S. Kay	Closed	95.00	300.00
83-08-006	Helping Mother, 1 1/2"	S. Kay	Closed	45.00	110.00
83-08-007	Sweeping, 6"	S. Kay	Closed	195.00	435.00
83-08-008	Sweeping, 4"	S. Kay	Closed	95.00	230.00
83-08-009	Sweeping, 1 1/2"	S. Kay	Closed	45.00	110.00
83-08-010	Playtime, 6"	S. Kay	Closed	195.00	495.00
83-08-011	Playtime, 4"	S. Kay	Closed	95.00	250.00
83-08-012	Playtime, 1 1/2"	S. Kay	Closed	45.00	110.00
83-08-013	Feeding the Chickens, 6"	S. Kay	Closed	195.00	450.00
83-08-014	Feeding the Chickens, 4"	S. Kay	Closed	95.00	250.00
83-08-015	Feeding the Chickens, 1 1/2"	S. Kay	Closed	45.00	110.00
83-08-016	Waiting for Mother, 6"	S. Kay	Closed	195.00	445.00
83-08-017	Waiting for Mother, 4"	S. Kay	Closed	95.00	230.00
83-08-018	Waiting for Mother, 1 1/2"	S. Kay	Closed	45.00	110.00
83-08-019	Waiting for Mother, 11"	S. Kay	Closed	495.00	795.00
83-08-020	Bedtime, 6"	S. Kay	Closed	195.00	435.00
83-08-021	Bedtime, 4"	S. Kay	Closed	95.00	230.00
83-08-022	Bedtime, 1 1/2"	S. Kay	Closed	45.00	110.00
83-08-023	From the Garden, 6"	S. Kay	Closed	195.00	450.00

	ARTIST	EDITION	ISSUE	QUOTE
83-08-024 From the Garden, 4"	S. Kay	Closed	95.00	235.00
83-08-025 From the Garden, 1 1/2"	S. Kay	Closed	45.00	110.00
83-08-026 Wake Up Kiss, 6"	S. Kay	Closed	210.00	550.00
84-08-027 Wake Up Kiss, 4"	S. Kay	Closed	95.00	195.00
84-08-028 Wake Up Kiss, 1 1/2"	S. Kay	Closed	45.00	550.00
84-08-029 Finding R Way, 6"	S. Kay	Closed	210.00	495.00
84-08-030 Finding R Way, 4"	S. Kay	Closed	95.00	245.00
84-08-031 Finding R Way, 1 1/2"	S. Kay	Closed	45.00	135.00
84-08-032 Daydreaming, 6"	S. Kay	Closed	195.00	445.00
84-08-033 Daydreaming, 4"	S. Kay	Closed	95.00	235.00
84-08-034 Daydreaming, 1 1/2"	S. Kay	Closed	45.00	125.00
84-08-035 Off to School, 6"	S. Kay	4,000	195.00	450.00
84-08-036 Off to School, 4"	S. Kay	4,000	95.00	240.00
84-08-037 Off to School, 1 1/2"	S. Kay	Closed	45.00	125.00
84-08-038 Off to School, 11"	S. Kay	750	Unkn.	880.00
84-08-039 Off to School, 20"	S. Kay	100	Unkn.	4200.00
84-08-040 Flowers for You, 6"	S. Kay	Closed	195.00	450.00
84-08-041 Flowers for You, 4"	S. Kay	Closed	95.00	250.00
84-08-042 Flowers for You, 1 1/2"	S. Kay	Closed	45.00	125.00
84-08-043 Watchful Eye, 6"	S. Kay	Closed	195.00	445.00
84-08-044 Watchful Eye, 4"	S. Kay	Closed	95.00	235.00
84-08-045 Watchful Eye, 1 1/2"	S. Kay	Closed	45.00	125.00
84-08-046 Special Delivery, 6"	S. Kay	Closed	195.00	312-350.
84-08-047 Special Delivery, 4"	S. Kay	Closed	95.00	187.00
84-08-048 Special Delivery, 1 1/2"	S. Kay	Closed	45.00	125.00
84-08-049 Tag Along, 6"	S. Kay	Closed	195.00	290.00
84-08-050 Tag Along, 4"	S. Kay	Closed	95.00	225.00
84-08-051 Tag Along, 1 1/2"	S. Kay	Closed	45.00	130.00
85-08-052 A Special Day, 6"	S. Kay	Closed	195.00	325.00
85-08-053 A Special Day, 4"	S. Kay	Closed	95.00	195.00
85-08-054 Afternoon Tea, 6"	S. Kay	Closed	195.00	325-365.
85-08-055 Afternoon Tea, 4"	S. Kay	Closed	95.00	185.00
85-08-056 Afternoon Tea, 11"	S. Kay	Closed	Unkn.	770.00
85-08-057 Afternoon Tea, 20"	S. Kay	Closed	Unkn.	3500.00
85-08-058 Nightie Night, 6"	S. Kay	Closed	195.00	325.00
85-08-059 Nightie Night, 4"	S. Kay	Closed	95.00	185.00
85-08-060 Yuletide Cheer, 6"	S. Kay	Closed	210.00	435.00
85-08-061 Yuletide Cheer, 4"	S. Kay	Closed	95.00	250.00
85-08-062 'Tis the Season, 6"	S. Kay	Closed	210.00	425.00
85-08-063 'Tis the Season, 4"	S. Kay	Closed	95.00	250.00
85-08-064 Giddyap!, 6"	S. Kay	Closed	195.00	325.00
85-08-065 Giddyap!, 4"	S. Kay	Closed	95.00	250.00
86-08-066 Our Puppy, 6"	S. Kay	Closed	210.00	355.00
86-08-067 Our Puppy, 4"	S. Kay	Closed	95.00	185.00
86-08-068 Our Puppy, 1 1/2"	S. Kay	Closed	45.00	90.00
86-08-069 Always By My Side, 6"	S. Kay	Closed	195.00	375.00
86-08-070 Always By My Side, 4"	S. Kay	Closed	95.00	195.00
86-08-071 Always By My Side, 1 1/2"	S. Kay	Closed	45.00	95.00
86-08-072 Finishing Touch, 6"	S. Kay	Closed	195.00	312.00
86-08-073 Finishing Touch, 4"	S. Kay	Closed	95.00	172.00
86-08-074 Finishing Touch, 1 1/2"	S. Kay	Closed	45.00	85.00
86-08-075 Good As New, 6"	S. Kay	4,000	195.00	500.00
86-08-076 Good As New, 4"	S. Kay	4,000	95.00	290.00
86-08-077 Good As New, 1 1/2"	S. Kay	Closed	45.00	90.00
86-08-078 Bunny Hug, 6"	S. Kay	Closed	210.00	395.00
86-08-079 Bunny Hug, 4"	S. Kay	Closed	95.00	172.00
86-08-080 Bunny Hug, 1 1/2"	S. Kay	Closed	45.00	85.00
86-08-081 Sweet Treat, 6"	S. Kay	Closed	195.00	312.00
86-08-082 Sweet Treat, 4"	S. Kay	Closed	95.00	172.00
86-08-083 Sweet Treat, 1 1/2"	S. Kay	Closed	45.00	85.00
86-08-084 To Love And To Cherish, 6"	S. Kay	Closed	195.00	312.00
86-08-085 To Love And To Cherish, 4"	S. Kay	Closed	95.00	172.00
86-08-086 To Love And To Cherish, 1 1/2"	S. Kay	Closed	45.00	85.00
86-08-087 To Love and To Cherish, 11"	S. Kay	Closed	Unkn.	667.00
86-08-088 To Love and To Cherish, 20"	S. Kay	Closed	Unkn.	3600.00
86-08-089 With This Ring, 6"	S. Kay	Closed	195.00	312.00
86-08-090 With This Ring, 4"	S. Kay	Closed	95.00	172.00
86-08-091 With This Ring, 1 1/2"	S. Kay	Closed	45.00	85.00
86-08-092 With This Ring, 11"	S. Kay	Closed	Unkn.	667.50
86-08-093 With This Ring, 20"	S. Kay	Closed	Unkn.	3600.00
87-08-094 All Aboard, 6"	S. Kay	Closed	265.00	355.00
87-08-095 All Aboard, 4"	S. Kay	Closed	130.00	185.00
87-08-096 All Aboard, 1 1/2"	S. Kay	Closed	50.00	90.00
87-08-097 Let's Play, 6"	S. Kay	Closed	265.00	355.00
87-08-098 Let's Play, 4"	S. Kay	Closed	130.00	185.00
87-08-099 Let's Play, 1 1/2"	S. Kay	Closed	49.50	90.00
87-08-100 A Loving Spoonful, 6"	S. Kay	4,000	295.00	550.00
87-08-101 A Loving Spoonful, 4"	S. Kay	4,000	150.00	290.00
87-08-102 A Loving Spoonful, 1 1/2"	S. Kay	Closed	49.50	90.00
87-08-103 Little Nanny, 6"	S. Kay	Closed	295.00	400.00
87-08-104 Little Nanny, 4"	S. Kay	Closed	150.00	200.00
87-08-105 Little Nanny, 1 1/2"	S. Kay	Closed	49.50	90.00
87-08-106 All Mine, 6"	S. Kay	Closed	245.00	465.00
87-08-107 All Mine, 4"	S. Kay	Closed	130.00	225.00
87-08-108 All Mine, 1 1/2"	S. Kay	Closed	49.50	95.00
87-08-109 Cuddles, 6"	S. Kay	Closed	245.00	465.00
87-08-110 Cuddles, 4"	S. Kay	Closed	130.00	225.00
87-08-111 Cuddles, 1 1/2"	S. Kay	Closed	49.50	95.00
88-08-112 My Little Brother, 6"	S. Kay	Closed	375.00	450.00
88-08-113 My Little Brother, 4"	S. Kay	Closed	195.00	225.00
88-08-114 My Little Brother, 1 1/2"	S. Kay	Closed	70.00	90.00
88-08-115 Purrfect Day, 6"	S. Kay	Closed	265.00	455.00
88-08-116 Purrfect Day, 4"	S. Kay	Closed	184.00	215.00
88-08-117 Purrfect Day, 1 1/2"	S. Kay	Closed	70.00	90.00
88-08-118 Penny for Your Thoughts, 6"	S. Kay	Closed	365.00	455.00
88-08-119 Penny for Your Thoughts, 4"	S. Kay	Closed	185.00	215.00
88-08-120 Penny for Your Thoughts, 1 1/2"	S. Kay	Closed	70.00	90.00
88-08-121 New Home, 6"	S. Kay	Closed	365.00	500.00
88-08-122 New Home, 4"	S. Kay	Closed	185.00	240.00
88-08-123 New Home, 1 1/2"	S. Kay	Closed	70.00	90.00
88-08-124 Ginger Snap, 6"	S. Kay	Closed	300.00	355.00
88-08-125 Ginger Snap, 4"	S. Kay	Closed	150.00	185.00
88-08-126 Ginger Snap, 1 1/2"	S. Kay	Closed	70.00	90.00
88-08-127 Hidden Treasures, 6"	S. Kay	Closed	300.00	355.00
88-08-128 Hidden Treasures, 4"	S. Kay	Closed	150.00	185.00
88-08-129 Hidden Treasures, 1 1/2"	S. Kay	Closed	70.00	90.00
89-08-130 First School Day, 6"	S. Kay	2,000	550.00	650.00
89-08-131 First School Day, 4"	S. Kay	2,000	290.00	350.00
89-08-132 First School Day, 1 1/2"	S. Kay	Closed	85.00	95.00
89-08-133 Yearly Check-Up, 6"	S. Kay	Closed	390.00	390.00
89-08-134 Yearly Check-Up, 4"	S. Kay	Closed	190.00	195.00
89-08-135 Yearly Check-Up, 1 1/2"	S. Kay	Closed	85.00	95.00
89-08-136 House Call, 6"	S. Kay	Closed	390.00	390.00
89-08-137 House Call, 4"	S. Kay	Closed	190.00	195.00
89-08-138 House Call, 1 1/2"	S. Kay	Closed	85.00	95.00
89-08-139 Take Me Along, 6"	S. Kay	1,000	440.00	525.00
89-08-140 Take Me Along, 4"	S. Kay	2,000	220.00	285.00
89-08-141 Take Me Along, 1 1/2"	S. Kay	Closed	85.00	95.00
89-08-142 Garden Party, 6"	S. Kay	Closed	440.00	475.00
89-08-143 Garden Party, 4"	S. Kay	2,000	220.00	240.00
89-08-144 Garden Party, 1 1/2"	S. Kay	Closed	85.00	95.00
89-08-145 Fisherboy, 6"	S. Kay	Closed	440.00	475.00
89-08-146 Fisherboy, 4"	S. Kay	2,000	220.00	240.00
89-08-147 Fisherboy, 1 1/2"	S. Kay	Closed	85.00	95.00
89-08-148 Cherish, 6"	S. Kay	2,000	398.00	560.00
89-08-149 Cherish, 4"	S. Kay	2,000	199.00	290.00
89-08-150 Cherish, 1 1/2"	S. Kay	Closed	80.00	95.00
90-08-151 Holiday Cheer, 6"	S. Kay	1,000	450.00	610.00
90-08-152 Holiday Cheer, 4"	S. Kay	2,000	225.00	305.00
90-08-153 Holiday Cheer, 1 1/2"	S. Kay	Closed	90.00	95.00
90-08-154 Tender Loving Care, 6"	S. Kay	Closed	440.00	475.00
90-08-155 Tender Loving Care, 4"	S. Kay	Closed	220.00	240.00
90-08-156 Tender Loving Care, 1 1/2"	S. Kay	Closed	90.00	95.00
90-08-157 Spring Fever, 6"	S. Kay	2,000	450.00	610.00
90-08-158 Spring Fever, 4"	S. Kay	2,000	225.00	305.00
90-08-159 Spring Fever, 1 1/2"	S. Kay	Closed	90.00	95.00
90-08-160 Batter Up, 6"	S. Kay	2,000	440.00	505.00
90-08-161 Batter Up, 4"	S. Kay	2,000	220.00	265.00
90-08-162 Batter Up, 1 1/2"	S. Kay	Closed	90.00	95.00
90-08-163 Seasons Greetings, 6"	S. Kay	1,000	450.00	610.00
90-08-164 Seasons Greetings, 4"	S. Kay	2,000	225.00	305.00
90-08-165 Seasons Greetings, 1 1/2"	S. Kay	Closed	90.00	95.00
90-08-166 Shootin' Hoops, 6"	S. Kay	2,000	440.00	450.00
90-08-167 Shootin' Hoops, 4"	S. Kay	2,000	220.00	225.00
90-08-168 Shootin' Hoops, 1 1/2"	S. Kay	Closed	90.00	95.00
91-08-169 Figure Eight, 6"	S. Kay	2,000	550.00	660.00
91-08-170 Figure Eight, 4"	S. Kay	2,000	270.00	365.00
91-08-171 Figure Eight, 1 1/2"	S. Kay	3,750	110.00	110.00
91-08-172 Season's Joy, 6"	S. Kay	1,000	550.00	620.00
91-08-173 Season's Joy, 4"	S. Kay	2,000	270.00	305.00
91-08-174 Season's Joy, 1 1/2"	S. Kay	3,750	110.00	115.00
91-08-175 Winter Surprise, 6"	S. Kay	1,000	550.00	550.00
91-08-176 Winter Surprise, 4"	S. Kay	2,000	270.00	270.00
91-08-177 Winter Surprise, 1 1/2"	S. Kay	3,750	110.00	110.00
91-08-178 Dress Up, 6"	S. Kay	2,000	550.00	550.00
91-08-179 Dress Up, 4"	S. Kay	2,000	270.00	270.00
91-08-180 Dress Up, 1 1/2"	S. Kay	3,750	110.00	110.00
91-08-181 Touch Down, 6"	S. Kay	2,000	550.00	550.00
91-08-182 Touch Down, 4"	S. Kay	2,000	270.00	270.00
91-08-183 Touch Down, 1 1/2"	S. Kay	3,750	110.00	110.00
91-08-184 Fore!!, 6"	S. Kay	2,000	550.00	580.00
91-08-185 Fore!!, 4"	S. Kay	2,000	270.00	325.00
91-08-186 Fore!!, 1 1/2"	S. Kay	3,750	110.00	115.00
92-08-187 Raindrops, 6"	S. Kay	1,000	640.00	640.00
92-08-188 Raindrops, 4"	S. Kay	1,000	350.00	350.00
92-08-189 Raindrops, 1 1/2"	S. Kay	3,750	110.00	110.00
92-08-190 Free Skating, 6"	S. Kay	1,000	590.00	620.00
92-08-191 Free Skating, 4"	S. Kay	1,000	310.00	325.00
92-08-192 Free Skating, 1 1/2"	S. Kay	3,750	110.00	115.00
92-08-193 Merry Christmas, 6"	S. Kay	1,000	580.00	580.00
92-08-194 Merry Christmas, 4"	S. Kay	1,000	350.00	350.00
92-08-195 Merry Christmas, 1 1/2"	S. Kay	3,750	110.00	115.00
92-08-196 Tulips For Mother, 6"	S. Kay	1,000	590.00	620.00
92-08-197 Tulips For Mother, 4"	S. Kay	1,000	310.00	325.00
92-08-198 Tulips For Mother, 1 1/2"	S. Kay	3,750	110.00	115.00
92-08-199 Winter Cheer, 6"	S. Kay	1,000	580.00	580.00
92-08-200 Winter Cheer, 4"	S. Kay	2,000	300.00	300.00
94-08-201 Christmas Wonder, 6"	S. Kay	1,000	700.00	700.00
94-08-202 Christmas Wonder, 4"	S. Kay	1,000	370.00	370.00
94-08-203 Little Chimney Sweep, 6"	S. Kay	1,000	600.00	600.00
94-08-204 Little Chimney Sweep, 4"	S. Kay	1,000	300.00	300.00
94-08-205 Bubbles & Bows, 6"	S. Kay	1,000	600.00	600.00
94-08-206 Bubbles & Bows, 4"	S. Kay	1,000	300.00	300.00
94-08-203 Clowning Around, 6"	S. Kay	1,000	550.00	550.00
94-08-204 Clowning Around, 4"	S. Kay	1,000	300.00	300.00
94-08-205 Jolly Pair, 6"	S. Kay	1,000	650.00	650.00
94-08-206 Jolly Pair, 4"	S. Kay	1,000	350.00	350.00
ANRI		**Sarah Kay Santas**		
88-09-001 Jolly St. Nick, 6"	S. Kay	Closed	398.00	850.00
88-09-002 Jolly St. Nick, 4"	S. Kay	Closed	199.00	300-550.
88-09-003 Jolly Santa, 6"	S. Kay	Closed	480.00	600.00
88-09-004 Jolly Santa, 4"	S. Kay	Closed	235.00	300-350.
89-09-005 Jolly Santa, 12"	S. Kay	Closed	1300.00	1300.00
89-09-006 Santa, 6"	S. Kay	Closed	480.00	480.00
89-09-007 Santa, 4"	S. Kay	Closed	235.00	350.00
90-09-008 Kris Kringle Santa, 6"	S. Kay	Closed	550.00	550.00
90-09-009 Kris Kringle Santa, 4"	S. Kay	Closed	275.00	350.00
91-09-010 A Friend To All, 6"	S. Kay	750	590.00	590.00
91-09-011 A Friend To All, 4"	S. Kay	750	300.00	300.00
92-09-012 Father Christmas, 6"	S. Kay	750	590.00	590.00
92-09-013 Father Christmas, 4"	S. Kay	750	350.00	350.00
ANRI		**Sarah Kay Mini Santas**		
91-10-001 Jolly St. Nick, 1 1/2"	S. Kay	Closed	110.00	110.00
91-10-002 Jolly Santa, 1 1/2"	S. Kay	Closed	110.00	110.00
91-10-003 Sarah Kay Santa, 1 1/2"	S. Kay	Closed	110.00	110.00
91-10-004 Kris Kringle, 1 1/2"	S. Kay	Closed	110.00	110.00
ANRI		**Sarah Kay 10th Anniversary**		
93-11-001 Mr. Santa, 4"	S. Kay	750	375.00	390.00
93-11-002 Mr. Santa, 6"	S. Kay	750	695.00	730.00
93-11-003 Mrs. Santa, 4"	S. Kay	750	375.00	390.00
93-11-004 Mrs. Santa, 6"	S. Kay	750	695.00	730.00
93-11-005 Joy to the World, 4"	S. Kay	1,000	310.00	290.00
93-11-006 Joy to the World, 6"	S. Kay	1,000	600.00	580.00
93-11-007 Christmas Basket, 4"	S. Kay	1,000	310.00	290.00
93-11-008 Christmas Basket, 6"	S. Kay	1,000	600.00	580.00
93-11-009 Innocence, 4"	S. Kay	1,000	345.00	315.00
93-11-010 Innocence, 6"	S. Kay	1,000	630.00	630.00
93-11-011 My Favorite Doll, 4"	S. Kay	1,000	315.00	315.00
93-11-012 My Favorite Doll, 6"	S. Kay	1,000	630.00	630.00

FIGURINES/COTTAGES

ANRI **Christmas Firsts**

		ARTIST	EDITION	ISSUE	QUOTE
94-12-001	Sarah Kay's First Christmas,4"	S. Kay	500	350.00	350.00
94-12-002	Sarah Kay's First Christmas, 6"	S. Kay	250	600.00	600.00

ANRI **Club ANRI**

		ARTIST	EDITION	ISSUE	QUOTE
83-13-001	Welcome 4"	J. Ferrandiz	Closed	110.00	395.00
84-13-002	My Friend 4"	J. Ferrandiz	Closed	110.00	400.00
84-13-003	Apple of My Eye 4 1/2"	S. Kay	Closed	135.00	385.00
85-13-004	Harvest Time 4"	J. Ferrandiz	Closed	125.00	175-385.
85-13-005	Dad's Helper 4 1/2"	S. Kay	Closed	135.00	150-375.
86-13-006	Harvest's Helper 4"	J. Ferrandiz	Closed	135.00	175-335.
86-13-007	Romantic Notions 4"	S. Kay	Closed	135.00	175-310.
86-13-008	Celebration March 5"	J. Ferrandiz	Closed	165.00	225-295.
87-13-009	Will You Be Mine 4"	J. Ferrandiz	Closed	135.00	175-310.
86-13-010	Make A Wish 4"	S. Kay	Closed	165.00	215-325.
87-13-011	A Young Man's Fancy 4"	S. Kay	Closed	135.00	165-265.
88-13-012	Forever Yours 4"	J. Ferrandiz	Closed	170.00	250.00
88-13-013	I've Got a Secret 4"	S. Kay	Closed	170.00	205.00
88-13-014	Maestro Mickey 4 1/2"	Disney Studio	Closed	170.00	200-215.
89-13-015	Diva Minnie 4 1/2"	Disney Studio	Closed	190.00	190.00
89-13-016	I'll Never Tell 4"	S. Kay	Closed	190.00	190.00
89-13-017	Twenty Years of Love 4"	J. Ferrandiz	Closed	190.00	190.00
90-13-018	You Are My Sunshine 4"	J. Ferrandiz	Yr.Iss.	220.00	220.00
90-13-019	A Little Bashful 4"	S. Kay	Yr.Iss.	220.00	220.00
90-13-020	Dapper Donald 4"	Disney Studio	Closed	199.00	199.00
91-13-021	With All My Heart 4"	J. Ferrandiz	N/A	250.00	250.00
91-13-022	Kiss Me 4"	S.Kay	N/A	250.00	250.00
91-13-023	Daisy Duck 4 1/2"	Disney Studio	N/A	250.00	250.00
92-13-024	You Are My All 4"	J. Ferrandiz	N/A	260.00	260.00
92-13-025	My Present For You 4"	S. Kay	N/A	270.00	270.00

ANRI **Disney Woodcarving**

		ARTIST	EDITION	ISSUE	QUOTE
87-14-001	Mickey Mouse, 4"	Disney Studio	Closed	150.00	210.00
87-14-002	Minnie Mouse, 4"	Disney Studio	Closed	150.00	210.00
87-14-003	Pinocchio, 4"	Disney Studio	Closed	150.00	195.00
87-14-004	Donald Duck, 4"	Disney Studio	Closed	150.00	195.00
87-14-005	Goofy, 4"	Disney Studio	Closed	150.00	195.00
87-14-006	Mickey & Minnie, 6" (matching numbers)	Disney Studio	Closed	625.00	1650.00
88-14-007	Donald Duck, 6"	Disney Studio	Closed	350.00	700.00
88-14-008	Goofy, 6"	Disney Studio	Closed	380.00	700.00
88-14-009	Mickey Mouse, 4"	Disney Studio	Closed	180.00	199.00
88-14-010	Pluto, 4"	Disney Studio	Closed	180.00	199.00
88-14-011	Pinocchio, 4"	Disney Studio	Closed	180.00	199.00
88-14-012	Donald Duck, 4"	Disney Studio	Closed	180.00	199.00
88-14-013	Goofy, 4"	Disney Studio	Closed	180.00	199.00
88-14-014	Mickey Mouse, 1 3/4"	Disney Studio	Closed	80.00	100.00
88-14-015	Pluto, 1-3/4"	Disney Studio	Closed	80.00	100.00
88-14-016	Pinocchio, 1 3/4"	Disney Studio	Closed	80.00	140.00
88-14-017	Donald Duck, 1 3/4"	Disney Studio	Closed	80.00	100.00
88-14-018	Goofy, 1 3/4"	Disney Studio	Closed	80.00	100.00
89-14-019	Pluto, 4"	Disney Studio	Closed	190.00	205.00
88-14-020	Pluto, 6"	Disney Studio	Closed	350.00	350.00
88-14-021	Goofy, 6"	Disney Studio	Closed	350.00	350.00
89-14-022	Mickey, 4"	Disney Studio	Closed	190.00	205.00
89-14-023	Minnie, 4"	Disney Studio	Closed	190.00	205.00
89-14-024	Donald, 4"	Disney Studio	Closed	190.00	205.00
89-14-025	Daisy, 4"	Disney Studio	Closed	190.00	205.00
89-14-026	Goofy, 4"	Disney Studio	Closed	190.00	205.00
89-14-027	Mini Mickey, 2"	Disney Studio	Closed	85.00	100.00
89-14-028	Mini Minnie, 2"	Disney Studio	Closed	85.00	100.00
89-14-029	Mini Donald, 2"	Disney Studio	Closed	85.00	100.00
89-14-030	Minnie Daisy, 2"	Disney Studio	Closed	85.00	100.00
89-14-031	Mini Goofy, 2"	Disney Studio	Closed	85.00	100.00
89-14-032	Mini Pluto, 2"	Disney Studio	Closed	85.00	100.00
89-14-033	Mickey, 10"	Disney Studio	Closed	700.00	750.00
89-14-034	Minnie, 10"	Disney Studio	Closed	700.00	750.00
89-14-035	Mickey, 20"	Disney Studio	Closed	3500.00	3500.00
89-14-036	Minnie, 20"	Disney Studio	Closed	3500.00	3500.00
89-14-037	Mickey & Minnie, 20" matched set	Disney Studio	Closed	7000.00	7000.00
89-14-038	Mickey & Minnie Set, 6"	Disney Studio	Closed	700.00	700.00
88-14-039	Mickey Sorcerer's Apprentice, 6"	Disney Studio	Closed	350.00	500.00
88-14-040	Mickey Sorcerer's Apprentice, 4"	Disney Studio	Closed	180.00	199.00
88-14-041	Mickey Sorcerer's Apprentice, 2"	Disney Studio	Closed	80.00	100.00
89-14-042	Pinocchio, 6"	Disney Studio	Closed	350.00	350.00
89-14-043	Pinocchio, 4"	Disney Studio	Closed	190.00	199.00
89-14-044	Pinocchio, 2"	Disney Studio	Closed	85.00	100.00
89-14-045	Pinocchio, 10"	Disney Studio	Closed	700.00	700.00
89-14-046	Pinocchio, 20"	Disney Studio	Closed	3500.00	3500.00
90-14-047	Mickey Mouse, 4"	Disney Studio	Closed	199.00	205.00
90-14-045	Mickey Mouse, 2"	Disney Studio	Closed	100.00	100.00
90-14-049	Minnie Mouse, 4"	Disney Studio	Closed	199.00	205.00
90-14-050	Minnie Mouse, 2"	Disney Studio	Closed	100.00	100.00
90-14-051	Chef Goofy, 5"	Disney Studio	Closed	265.00	265.00
90-14-052	Chef Goofy, 2 1/2"	Disney Studio	Closed	125.00	125.00
90-14-053	Donald & Daisy, 6" (Matched Set)	Disney Studio	Closed	700.00	750.00
91-14-054	Mickey Skating, 4"	Disney Studio	Closed	250.00	350.00
91-14-055	Minnie Skating, 4"	Disney Studio	Closed	250.00	350.00
91-14-056	Mickey Skating, 2"	Disney Studio	Closed	120.00	160.00
91-14-057	Minnie Skating, 2"	Disney Studio	Closed	120.00	120.00
91-14-058	Bell Boy Donald, 6"	Disney Studio	Closed	400.00	400.00
91-14-059	Bell Boy Donald, 4"	Disney Studio	Closed	250.00	250.00

ANRI **Mickey Mouse Thru The Ages**

		ARTIST	EDITION	ISSUE	QUOTE
90-15-001	Steam Boat Willie, 4"	Disney Studio	Closed	295.00	300.00
91-15-002	The Mad Dog, 4"	Disney Studio	Closed	500.00	600.00

ANRI **Bernardi Reflections**

		ARTIST	EDITION	ISSUE	QUOTE
94-16-001	Master Carver, 4"	U. Bernardi	500	350.00	350.00
94-16-002	Master Carver, 6"	U. Bernardi	250	600.00	600.00

Armani **Wildlife**

		ARTIST	EDITION	ISSUE	QUOTE
83-01-001	Eagle Bird of Prey 3213	G. Armani	Open	210.00	425.00
83-01-002	Royal Eagle with Babies 3553	G. Armani	Open	215.00	400.00
82-01-003	Snow Bird 5548	G. Armani	Open	100.00	180.00
88-01-004	Peacock 455S	G. Armani	5,000	600.00	675.00
88-01-005	Peacock 458S	G. Armani	5,000	630.00	700.00
88-01-006	Bird Of Paradise 454S	G. Armani	5,000	475.00	500.00
90-01-007	Three Doves 996S	G. Armani	5,000	670.00	750.00
90-01-008	Soaring Eagle 970S	G. Armani	5,000	620.00	700.00
90-01-009	Bird of Paradise 718S	G. Armani	5,000	550.00	575.00
91-01-010	Flamingo 713S	G. Armani	5,000	420.00	420.00
91-01-011	Swan 714S	G. Armani	5,000	550.00	550.00
91-01-012	Great Argus Pheasant 717S	G. Armani	3,000	600.00	600.00
91-01-013	Flying Duck 839S	G. Armani	5,000	470.00	470.00
91-01-014	Large Owl 842S	G. Armani	5,000	520.00	520.00
93-01-015	Parrot With Vase 736S	G. Armani	3,000	460.00	460.00
93-01-016	Doves With Vase 204S	G. Armani	3,000	375.00	375.00
93-01-017	Peacock With Vase 735S	G. Armani	3,000	375.00	375.00
93-01-018	Horse Head 205S	G. Armani	Open	140.00	140.00
93-01-019	Galloping Horse 905S	G. Armani	7,500	465.00	465.00
93-01-020	Show Horse 907S	G. Armani	7,500	550.00	550.00
93-01-021	Rearing Horse 909S	G. Armani	7,500	515.00	515.00

Armani **My Fair Ladies™**

		ARTIST	EDITION	ISSUE	QUOTE
87-02-001	Lady With Peacock 385C	G. Armani	Retrd.	380.00	15-1680.
87-02-002	Lady with Compact 386C	G. Armani	Retrd.	300.00	500.00
87-02-003	Lady with Muff 388C	G. Armani	5,000	250.00	450.00
87-02-004	Lady With Fan 387C	G. Armani	5,000	300.00	400.00
87-02-005	Flamenco Dancer 389C	G. Armani	5,000	400.00	500.00
87-02-006	Lady With Book 384C	G. Armani	5,000	300.00	450.00
87-02-007	Lady With Great Dane 429C	G. Armani	5,000	365.00	475.00
87-02-008	Mother & Child 405C	G. Armani	5,000	410.00	550.00
89-02-009	Lady With Parrot 616C	G. Armani	5,000	400.00	500.00
93-02-010	Fascination 192C	G. Armani	5,000	500.00	500.00
93-02-011	Fascination 192F	G. Armani	Open	250.00	250.00
93-02-012	Morning Rose 193C	G. Armani	5,000	450.00	450.00
93-02-013	Morning Rose 193F	G. Armani	Open	225.00	225.00
93-02-014	Elegance 195C	G. Armani	5,000	525.00	525.00
93-02-015	Elegance 195F	G. Armani	Open	300.00	300.00
93-02-016	Mahogany 194C	G. Armani	5,000	500.00	500.00
93-02-016	Mahogany 194F	G. Armani	Open	360.00	360.00
94-02-017	Lady w/Umbrella 196C	G. Armani	5,000	335.00	335.00
94-02-017	Lady w/Umbrella 196F	G. Armani	Open	200.00	200.00

Armani **Wedding**

		ARTIST	EDITION	ISSUE	QUOTE
82-03-001	Wedding Couple 5132	G. Armani	Open	110.00	190.00
87-03-002	Wedding Couple 407C	G. Armani	Open	525.00	550.00
88-03-003	Bride & Groom Wedding 475P	G. Armani	Open	270.00	285.00
89-03-004	Just Married 827C	G. Armani	5,000	950.00	1000.00
91-03-005	Wedding Couple At Threshold 813C	G. Armani	7,500	400.00	400.00
91-03-006	Wedding Couple With Bicycle 814C	G. Armani	7,500	600.00	600.00
91-03-007	Wedding Couple Kissing 815C	G. Armani	7,500	500.00	500.00
92-03-008	Bride With Doves 885C	G. Armani	Open	280.00	280.00
92-03-009	Bride With Doves 885F	G. Armani	Open	220.00	220.00
93-03-010	Carriage Wedding902C	G. Armani	2,500	1000.00	1000.00
93-03-011	Carriage Wedding 902F	G. Armani	Open	500.00	500.00
93-03-012	Garden Wedding 189F	G. Armani	Open	120.00	120.00
93-03-013	Garden Wedding 189C	G. Armani	Open	225.00	225.00
93-03-014	Wedding Flowers To Mary 187C	G. Armani	Open	225.00	225.00
93-03-015	Wedding Flowers To Mary 187F	G. Armani	Open	115.00	115.00
93-03-016	Wedding Couple At Wall 201C	G. Armani	Open	225.00	225.00
93-03-017	Wedding Couple At Wall 201F	G. Armani	Open	115.00	115.00
93-03-018	Wedding Couple Forever 791F	G. Armani	Open	250.00	250.00
94-03-019	Bride With Column & Vase 488C	G. Armani	Open	260.00	260.00
94-03-020	Bride With Column & Vase 488F	G. Armani	Open	200.00	200.00
94-03-021	Bride With Flower Vase 489C	G. Armani	Open	135.00	135.00
94-03-022	Bride With Flower Vase 489F	G. Armani	Open	90.00	90.00
94-03-023	Black Wedding Waltz 501C	G. Armani	3,000	750.00	750.00
94-03-024	Black Wedding Waltz 501F	G. Armani	Open	450.00	450.00
94-03-025	Wedding Waltz 493C	G. Armani	3,000	750.00	750.00
94-03-026	Wedding Waltz 493F	G. Armani	Open	450.00	450.00
94-03-027	Black Bride 500C	G. Armani	Open	170.00	170.00
94-03-028	Black Bride 500F	G. Armani	Open	115.00	115.00

Armani **Special Times**

		ARTIST	EDITION	ISSUE	QUOTE
82-04-001	Sledding 5111E	G. Armani	Retrd.	115.00	250.00
82-04-002	Girl with Sheep Dog 5117E	G. Armani	Retrd.	100.00	210.00
82-04-003	Girl with Chicks 5122E	G. Armani	Suspd.	95.00	165.00
82-04-004	Shy Kiss 5138E	G. Armani	Retrd.	125.00	285.00
82-04-005	Soccer Boy 5109	G. Armani	Open	75.00	180.00
82-04-006	Card Players (Cheaters) 3280	G. Armani	Open	400.00	1200.00
91-04-007	Couple in Car 862C	G. Armani	5,000	1000.00	1000.00
91-04-008	Lady with Car 861C	G. Armani	3,000	900.00	900.00
91-04-009	Doctor in Car 848C	G. Armani	2,000	800.00	800.00
94-04-010	The Fairy Tale 219C	G. Armani	Open	335.00	335.00
94-04-011	The Fairy Tale 219F	G. Armani	Open	175.00	175.00
94-04-012	Story Time 250C	G. Armani	Open	275.00	275.00
94-04-013	Grandpa's Nap 251C	G. Armani	Open	225.00	225.00
94-04-014	Old Acquaintance 252C	G. Armani	Open	275.00	275.00
94-04-015	Lady Doctor 249C	G. Armani	Open	200.00	200.00
94-04-016	Lady Doctor 249F	G. Armani	Open	105.00	105.00
94-04-017	Lady Graduate-Lawyer 253C	G. Armani	Open	225.00	225.00
94-04-018	Lady Graduate-Lawyer 253F	G. Armani	Open	120.00	120.00
94-04-019	The Encounter 472F	G. Armani	Open	315.00	315.00

Armani **Premiere Ballerina**

		ARTIST	EDITION	ISSUE	QUOTE
88-05-001	Ballerina Group in Flight 518C	G. Armani	Retrd.	810.00	900.00
88-05-002	Ballerina with Drape 504C	G. Armani	Retrd.	450.00	550.00
88-05-003	Ballerina 508C	G. Armani	Retrd.	430.00	530.00
88-05-004	Two Ballerinas 515C	G. Armani	Retrd.	620.00	775.00
88-05-005	Ballerina in Flight 503C	G. Armani	Retrd.	420.00	500.00
88-05-006	Ballerina 517C	G. Armani	Retrd.	325.00	530.00

Armani **Religious**

		ARTIST	EDITION	ISSUE	QUOTE
87-06-001	Choir Boys 900	G. Armani	5,000	350.00	620.00
88-06-002	Crucifix 1158C	G. Armani	10,000	155.00	420.00
90-06-003	Crucifix Plaque 711C	G. Armani	15,000	265.00	265.00
91-06-004	Crucifix 790C	G. Armani	15,000	180.00	180.00
92-06-005	Madonna With Child 787C	G. Armani	Open	425.00	425.00
92-06-006	Madonna With Child 787F	G. Armani	Open	265.00	265.00
92-06-007	Madonna With Child 787B	G. Armani	Open	260.00	260.00
93-06-008	Crucifix 786C	G. Armani	7,500	250.00	250.00
94-06-009	La Pieta 802C	G. Armani	5,000	950.00	950.00
94-06-010	La Pieta 802F	G. Armani	Open	550.00	550.00
94-06-011	Moses 812C	G. Armani	Open	220.00	220.00
94-06-012	Moses 812F	G. Armani	Open	115.00	115.00

Armani **Pearls Of The Orient**

		ARTIST	EDITION	ISSUE	QUOTE
89-07-001	Madame Butterfly 610C	G. Armani	Retrd.	450.00	500.00
89-07-002	Turnadot 611C	G. Armani	Retrd.	475.00	500.00
89-07-003	Chu Chu San 612C	G. Armani	Retrd.	500.00	550.00
89-07-004	Lotus Blossom 613C	G. Armani	Retrd.	450.00	475.00

Armani **Moonlight Masquerade**

		ARTIST	EDITION	ISSUE	QUOTE
90-08-001	Harlequin Lady 740C	G. Armani	Retrd.	450.00	450.00
90-08-002	Lady Pierrot 741C	G. Armani	Retrd.	390.00	390.00
90-08-003	Lady Clown with Cane 742C	G. Armani	Retrd.	390.00	390.00

		ARTIST	EDITION	ISSUE	QUOTE
90-08-004	Lady Clown with Doll 743C	G. Armani	Retrd.	410.00	410.00
90-08-005	Queen of Hearts 744C	G. Armani	Retrd.	450.00	450.00
Armani	**Renaissance**				
91-09-001	Bust of Eve 590T	G. Armani	Closed	250.00	600-1200
92-09-002	Abundance 870C	G. Armani	5,000	600.00	600.00
92-09-003	Vanity 871C	G. Armani	5,000	585.00	585.00
92-09-004	Twilight 872C	G. Armani	5,000	560.00	560.00
92-09-005	Dawn 874C	G. Armani	5,000	500.00	500.00
92-09-006	Lilac & Roses-Girl w/Flowers 882C	G. Armani	7,500	410.00	410.00
92-09-007	Lilac & Roses-Girl w/Flowers 882B	G. Armani	Open	220.00	220.00
92-09-008	Aurora-Girl With Doves 884C	G. Armani	7,500	370.00	370.00
92-09-009	Aurora-Girl With Doves 884B	G. Armani	Open	220.00	220.00
92-09-010	Liberty-Girl On Horse 903C	G. Armani	5,000	750.00	750.00
92-09-011	Liberty-Girl On Horse 903B	G. Armani	Open	450.00	450.00
93-09-012	Freedom-Man And Horse 906C	G. Armani	3,000	850.00	850.00
93-09-013	Wind Song-Girl With Sail 904C	G. Armani	5,000	520.00	520.00
94-09-014	Ambrosia 482C	G. Armani	5,000	435.00	435.00
94-09-015	Angelica 484C	G. Armani	5,000	575.00	575.00
Armani	**Special Issues**				
91-10-001	Discovery of America Plaque 867C	G. Armani	Closed	400.00	400.00
93-10-002	Mother's Day Plaque 899C	G. Armani	Closed	100.00	100.00
94-10-003	Mother's Day Plaque-The Swing 254C	G. Armani	Yr. Iss.	120.00	120.00
Armani	**G. Armani Society Members Only Figurine**				
90-11-001	Awakening 591C	G. Armani	Closed	137.50	800-1200
91-11-002	Ruffles 745E	G. Armani	Closed	139.00	358-384.
92-11-003	Ascent 866C	G. Armani	Closed	195.00	250-325.
93-11-004	Venus 881C	G. Armani	Closed	225.00	300-450.
93-11-005	Lady Rose (Bonus) 197C	G. Armani	Closed	125.00	125.00
93-11-006	Julie (Bonus) 293P	G. Armani	Closed	90.00	225.00
93-11-007	Juliette (Bonus) 294P	G. Armani	Closed	90.00	125.00
94-11-008	Flora 212C	G. Armani	Yr. Iss.	225.00	225.00
94-11-009	Aquarius (Bonus) 248C	G. Armani	Yr. Iss.	125.00	125.00
94-11-010	Harlequin (Bonus) 490C	G. Armani	Yr. Iss.	300.00	300.00
Armani	**G. Armani Society Members Only Event**				
90-12-001	My Fine Feathered Friends (Bonus)122S	G. Armani	Closed	175.00	175.00
91-12-002	Peace & Harmony (Bonus) 824C	G. Armani	Closed	300.00	250-400.
92-12-003	Springtime 961C	G. Armani	Closed	250.00	500.00
92-12-004	Boy with Dog (Bonus) 407S	G. Armani	Closed	200.00	200.00
93-12-005	Loving Arms 880E	G. Armani	Closed	250.00	250.00
94-12-006	Daisy 202E	G. Armani	Yr. Iss.	250.00	250.00
Armani	**Garden Series**				
91-13-001	Lady with Cornucopie 870C	G. Armani	10,000	600.00	600.00
91-13-002	Lady with Peacock 871C	G. Armani	10,000	585.00	1560.00
91-13-003	Lady with Violin 872C	G. Armani	10,000	560.00	560.00
91-13-004	Lady with Harp 874C	G. Armani	10,000	500.00	500.00
94-13-005	Lady At Well 222C	G. Armani	Open	275.00	275.00
94-13-006	Lady At Well 222F	G. Armani	Open	150.00	150.00
Armani	**Can-Can Dancers**				
89-14-001	Two Can-Can Dancers 516C	G. Armani	Open	820.00	975.00
Armani	**Four Seasons**				
90-15-001	Lady With Bicycle (Spring) 539C	G. Armani	Open	550.00	550.00
90-15-002	Lady With Umbrella (Fall) 541C	G. Armani	Open	475.00	475.00
90-15-003	Lady With Ice Skates (Winter) 542C	G. Armani	Open	400.00	400.00
90-15-004	Lady on Seashore (Summer) 540C	G. Armani	Open	440.00	440.00
92-15-005	Lady With Roses (Spring)181C	G. Armani	Open	275.00	275.00
92-15-006	Lady With Roses (Spring)181B	G. Armani	Open	135.00	135.00
92-15-007	Lady With Fruit (Summer) 182C	G. Armani	Open	275.00	275.00
92-15-008	Lady With Fruit (Summer) 182B	G. Armani	Open	135.00	135.00
92-15-009	Lady With Grapes (Fall) 183C	G. Armani	Open	275.00	275.00
92-15-010	Lady With Grapes (Fall)182B	G. Armani	Open	135.00	135.00
92-15-011	Lady With Vegetables (Winter)183C	G. Armani	Open	275.00	275.00
92-15-012	Lady With Vegetables (Winter)183B	G. Armani	Open	135.00	135.00
Armani	**Special Walt Disney Production**				
92-16-001	Cinderella	G. Armani	Retrd.	500.00	4-4500.
93-16-002	Snow White 199C	G. Armani	Retrd.	750.00	800-1400
93-16-003	Dopey	G. Armani	Retrd.	125.00	125.00
94-16-004	Ariel (Little Mermaid) 505C	G. Armani	1,500	750.00	750.00
Armani	**Motherhood**				
92-17-001	Mother With Child (Mother's Day) 185C	G. Armani	Open	400.00	400.00
92-17-002	Mother With Child (Mother's Day) 185B	G. Armani	Open	235.00	235.00
93-17-003	Garden Maternity 188C	G. Armani	Open	210.00	210.00
93-17-004	Garden Maternity 188F	G. Armani	Open	115.00	115.00
93-17-005	Maternity Embracing 190C	G. Armani	Open	250.00	250.00
93-17-006	Maternity Embracing 190F	G. Armani	Open	160.00	160.00
93-17-007	Mother/Child 792C	G. Armani	Open	385.00	385.00
93-17-008	Mother/Child 792F	G. Armani	Open	250.00	250.00
94-17-009	Kneeling Maternity 216C	G. Armani	Open	275.00	275.00
94-17-010	Kneeling Maternity 216F	G. Armani	Open	135.00	135.00
94-17-011	Mother & Child 470F	G. Armani	Open	150.00	150.00
94-17-012	Mother's Hand 479F	G. Armani	Open	215.00	215.00
94-17-013	Black Maternity 502C	G. Armani	5,000	500.00	500.00
94-17-014	Black Maternity 502F	G. Armani	Open	335.00	335.00
Armani	**Sports**				
92-18-001	Lady Equestrian 910C	G. Armani	Open	315.00	315.00
92-18-002	Lady Equestrian 910F	G. Armani	Open	155.00	155.00
92-18-003	Lady Golfer 911C	G. Armani	Open	325.00	325.00
92-18-004	Lady Golfer 911F	G. Armani	Open	170.00	170.00
92-18-005	Lady Tennis 912C	G. Armani	Open	275.00	275.00
92-18-006	Lady Tennis 912F	G. Armani	Open	175.00	175.00
92-18-007	Lady Skater 913C	G. Armani	Open	300.00	300.00
92-18-008	Lady Skater 913F	G. Armani	Open	170.00	170.00
Armani	**Yesteryears**				
93-19-001	Country Doctor In Car 848C	G. Armani	2,000	800.00	800.00
94-19-002	Summertime-Lady on Swing 485C	G. Armani	5,000	650.00	650.00
94-19-003	Summertime-Lady on Swing 485F	G. Armani	Open	450.00	450.00
Armani	**Romantic**				
92-20-001	Lady with Doves 858E	G. Armani	Retrd.	250.00	450.00
93-20-002	Lovers 191C	G. Armani	3,000	450.00	450.00
93-20-003	Lovers 879C	G. Armani	3,000	570.00	570.00
93-20-004	Lovers 879F	G. Armani	Open	325.00	325.00
93-20-005	Girl With Ducks 887C	G. Armani	Open	320.00	320.00
93-20-006	Girl With Ducks 887F	G. Armani	Open	160.00	160.00
93-20-007	Lovers With Wheelbarrow 891C	G. Armani	Open	370.00	370.00
93-20-008	Lovers With Wheelbarrow 891F	G. Armani	Open	190.00	190.00
93-20-009	Girl w/Dog At Fence 886C	G. Armani	Open	350.00	350.00
93-20-010	Girl w/Dog At Fence 886F	G. Armani	Open	175.00	175.00
93-20-011	Lovers On A Swing 942C	G. Armani	Open	410.00	410.00
93-20-012	Lovers On A Swing 942F	G. Armani	Open	265.00	265.00
93-20-013	Lovers With Roses 888C	G. Armani	Open	300.00	300.00
93-20-014	Lovers With Roses 888F	G. Armani	Open	155.00	155.00
94-20-015	The Embrace 480C	G. Armani	3,000	1450.00	1450.00
Armani	**Romantic Motherhood**				
93-21-001	Maternity On Swing 941C	G. Armani	Open	360.00	360.00
93-21-002	Maternity On Swing 941F	G. Armani	Open	220.00	220.00
Armani	**Country Series**				
93-22-001	Boy With Flute 890C	G. Armani	Open	175.00	175.00
93-22-002	Boy With Flute 890F	G. Armani	Open	90.00	90.00
93-22-003	Girl With Chicks 889C	G. Armani	Open	155.00	155.00
93-22-004	Girl With Chicks 889F	G. Armani	Open	75.00	75.00
93-22-005	Girl With Wheelbarrow /Flowers 468C	G. Armani	Open	240.00	240.00
93-22-006	Girl Tending Flowers 466C	G. Armani	Open	210.00	210.00
93-22-007	Girl With Sheep 178C	G. Armani	Open	150.00	150.00
93-22-008	Girl With Sheep 178F	G. Armani	Open	65.00	65.00
93-22-009	Boy With Accordion 177C	G. Armani	Open	170.00	170.00
93-22-010	Boy With Accordion 177F	G. Armani	Open	75.00	75.00
94-22-011	Laundry Girl 214C	G. Armani	Open	230.00	230.00
94-22-012	Laundry Girl 214F	G. Armani	Open	120.00	120.00
94-22-013	Country Girl with Grapes 215C	G. Armani	Open	230.00	230.00
94-22-014	Country Girl with Grapes 215F	G. Armani	Open	120.00	120.00
94-22-015	Fresh Fruits 471F	G. Armani	Open	250.00	250.00
94-22-016	Back From the Fields 473F	G. Armani	Open	360.00	360.00
Armani	**Gypsy Series**				
94-23-001	Esmeralda-Gypsy Girl 198C	G. Armani	Open	400.00	400.00
94-23-002	Esmeralda-Gypsy Girl 198F	G. Armani	Open	215.00	215.00
Armani	**Clown Series**				
91-24-001	Bust of Clown 725E	G. Armani	5,000	500.00	500.00
94-24-002	Sound the Trumpet 476C	G. Armani	Open	300.00	300.00
94-24-003	The Happy Fiddler 478C	G. Armani	Open	360.00	360.00
Armani	**Terra Cotta**				
94-25-001	The Embrace 1011T	G. Armani	Open	930.00	930.00
94-25-002	Ambrosia 1013T	G. Armani	Open	275.00	275.00
94-25-003	Country Boy With Mushrooms 1014T	G. Armani	2,500	135.00	135.00
94-25-004	La Pieta 1015T	G. Armani	Open	550.00	550.00
94-25-005	Angelica 1016T	G. Armani	Open	450.00	450.00
Armani	**The Galleria Collection: Distinguished Dealers**				
93-26-001	The Sea Wave 1006T	G. Armani	1,500	500.00	500.00
93-26-002	Spring Water 1007T	G. Armani	1,500	500.00	500.00
93-26-003	Spring Herald 1009T	G. Armani	1,500	500.00	500.00
93-26-004	Zephyr 1010T	G. Armani	1,500	500.00	500.00
94-26-005	Leda & The Swan 1012T	G. Armani	1,500	500.00	500.00
94-26-006	The Falconer 224S	G. Armani	3,000	1000.00	1000.00
Armani	**Siena Collection**				
93-27-001	Soft Kiss 1000T	G. Armani	2,500	155.00	155.00
93-27-002	Fresh Fruit 1001T	G. Armani	2,500	155.00	155.00
93-27-003	Back From The Fields 1002T	G. Armani	1,000	400.00	400.00
93-27-004	Encountering 1003T	G. Armani	1,000	350.00	350.00
93-27-005	Sound The Trumpet 1004T	G. Armani	1,000	225.00	225.00
93-27-006	Happy Fiddler 1005T	G. Armani	1,000	225.00	225.00
93-27-007	Mother's Hand 1008T	G. Armani	2,500	250.00	250.00
94-27-008	Country Boy 1014T	G. Armani	2,500	135.00	135.00
Armani	**Gulliver's World**				
94-28-001	Cowboy 657T	G. Armani	1,000	125.00	125.00
94-28-002	Ray of Moon 658T	G. Armani	1,000	100.00	100.00
94-28-003	The Barrel 659T	G. Armani	1,000	225.00	225.00
94-28-004	Seranade 660T	G. Armani	1,000	200.00	200.00
94-28-005	Getting Clean 661T	G. Armani	1,000	130.00	130.00
Armstrong's	**The Red Skelton Collection**				
81-01-001	Freddie in the Bathtub	R. Skelton	7,500	80.00	100.00
81-01-002	Freddie on the Green	R. Skelton	7,500	80.00	100.00
81-01-003	Freddie the Freeloader	R. Skelton	7,500	70.00	150.00
81-01-004	Sheriff Deadeye	R. Skelton	7,500	75.00	150.00
81-01-005	Clem Kadiddlehopper	R. Skelton	7,500	75.00	150.00
81-01-006	Jr., The Mean Widdle Kid	R. Skelton	7,500	75.00	150.00
81-01-007	San Fernando Red	R. Skelton	7,500	75.00	150.00
Armstrong's	**The Red Skelton Porcelain Plaque**				
91-02-001	All American	R. Skelton	1,500	495.00	12-2000.
92-02-002	Independance Day?	R. Skelton	1,500	525.00	525-650.
93-02-003	Red & Freddie Both Turned 80	R. Skelton	1,993	595.00	995-1500
94-02-004	Another Day	R. Skelton	1,994	675.00	675.00
Armstrong's	**Armstrong's/Ron Lee**				
84-03-001	Captain Freddie	R. Skelton	7,500	85.00	425.00
84-03-002	Freddie the Torchbearer	R. Skelton	7,500	110.00	475.00
Armstrong's	**Happy Art**				
82-04-001	Woody's Triple Self-Portrait	W. Lantz	5,000	95.00	300.00
Armstrong's	**Pro Autographed Ceramic Baseball Card Plaque**				
85-07-001	Brett, Garvey, Jackson, Rose, Seaver, auto, 3-1/4X5	Unknown	1,000	150.00	300.00
Artaffects	**Heavenly Blessings**				
85-01-001	First Step	Unknown	Open	15.00	19.00
85-01-002	Heaven Scent	Unknown	Open	15.00	19.00
85-01-003	Bubbles	Unknown	Open	15.00	19.00
85-01-004	So Soft	Unknown	Open	15.00	19.00
85-01-005	See!	Unknown	Open	15.00	19.00
85-01-006	Listen!	Unknown	Open	15.00	19.00
85-01-007	Happy Birthday	Unknown	Open	15.00	19.00
85-01-008	Day Dreams	Unknown	Open	15.00	19.00
85-01-009	Just Up	Unknown	Open	15.00	19.00
85-01-010	Beddy Bye	Unknown	Open	15.00	19.00
85-01-011	Race You!	Unknown	Open	15.00	19.00
85-01-012	Yum, Yum!	Unknown	Open	15.00	19.00
Artaffects	**Musical Figurines**				
84-02-001	The Wedding	R. Sauber	Open	65.00	70.00
86-02-002	The Anniversary	R. Sauber	Open	65.00	70.00
87-02-003	Home Sweet Home	R. Sauber	Open	65.00	70.00
87-02-004	Newborn	R. Sauber	Open	65.00	70.00

		ARTIST	EDITION	ISSUE	QUOTE
87-02-005	Motherhood	R. Sauber	Open	65.00	70.00
87-02-006	Fatherhood	R. Sauber	Open	65.00	70.00
87-02-007	Sweet Sixteen	R. Sauber	Open	65.00	70.00
Artaffects		**Christian Collection**			
87-03-001	Bring To Me the Children	A. Tobey	Open	65.00	100.00
88-03-002	The Healer	A. Tobey	Open	65.00	65.00
Artaffects		**Reflections of Youth**			
88-04-001	Julia	MaGo	N/A	29.50	70.00
89-04-002	Jessica	MaGo	14-day	29.50	60.00
89-04-003	Sebastian	MaGo	14-day	29.50	40.00
Artaffects		**Single Issue**			
82-05-001	Babysitter Musical	G. Perillo	2,500	65.00	90.00
Artaffects		**The Professionals**			
80-06-001	The Big Leaguer	G. Perillo	10,000	65.00	150.00
80-06-002	Ballerina's Dilemma	G. Perillo	10,000	65.00	75.00
81-06-003	The Quarterback	G. Perillo	10,000	65.00	75.00
82-06-004	Rodeo Joe	G. Perillo	10,000	80.00	80.00
82-06-005	Major Leaguer	G. Perillo	10,000	65.00	175.00
83-06-006	Hockey Player	G. Perillo	10,000	65.00	125.00
Artaffects		**The Storybook Collection**			
80-07-001	Little Red Ridinghood	G. Perillo	10,000	65.00	95.00
81-07-002	Cinderella	G. Perillo	10,000	65.00	95.00
82-07-003	Hansel and Gretel	G. Perillo	10,000	80.00	110.00
82-07-004	Goldilocks & 3 Bears	G. Perillo	10,000	80.00	110.00
Artaffects		**The Princesses**			
84-08-001	Lily of the Mohawks	G. Perillo	1,500	65.00	155.00
84-08-002	Pocahontas	G. Perillo	1,500	65.00	125.00
84-08-003	Minnehaha	G. Perillo	1,500	65.00	125.00
84-08-004	Sacajawea	G. Perillo	1,500	65.00	125.00
Artaffects		**The Chieftains**			
83-09-001	Sitting Bull	G. Perillo	5,000	65.00	500.00
83-09-002	Joseph	G. Perillo	5,000	65.00	250.00
83-09-003	Red Cloud	G. Perillo	5,000	65.00	275.00
83-09-004	Geronimo	G. Perillo	5,000	65.00	135.00
83-09-005	Crazy Horse	G. Perillo	5,000	65.00	200.00
Artaffects		**Child Life**			
83-10-001	Siesta	G. Perillo	2,500	65.00	75.00
83-10-002	Sweet Dreams	G. Perillo	1,500	65.00	75.00
Artaffects		**Members Only Limited Edition Redemption Offerings**			
83-11-001	Apache Brave (Bust)	G. Perillo	Open	50.00	150.00
86-11-002	Painted Pony	G. Perillo	Open	125.00	125.00
91-11-003	Chief Crazy Horse	G. Perillo	Open	195.00	195.00
Artaffects		**Limited Edition Free Gifts to Members**			
86-12-001	Dolls	G. Perillo	Open	Gift	N/A
91-12-002	Sunbeam	G. Perillo	Open	Gift	N/A
92-12-003	Little Shadow	G. Perillo	Open	Gift	N/A
Artaffects		**The Little Indians**			
82-13-001	Blue Spruce	G. Perillo	10,000	50.00	75.00
82-13-002	White Rabbit	G. Perillo	10,000	50.00	75.00
82-13-003	Tender Love	G. Perillo	10,000	65.00	65.00
90-13-004	Babysitter	G. Perillo	10,000	65.00	65.00
Artaffects		**Special Issue**			
82-14-001	The Peaceable Kingdom	G. Perillo	950	750.00	1500.00
84-14-001	Papoose	G. Perillo	325	500.00	500-975.
84-14-001	Apache Boy Bust	G. Perillo	Open	40.00	75.00
84-14-002	Apache Girl Bust	G. Perillo	Open	40.00	75.00
85-14-001	Lovers	G. Perillo	Open	70.00	125.00
Artaffects		**The War Pony**			
83-15-001	Sioux War Pony	G. Perillo	495	150.00	250.00
83-15-002	Nez Perce War Pony	G. Perillo	495	150.00	250.00
83-15-003	Apache War Pony	G. Perillo	495	150.00	250.00
Artaffects		**The Tribal Ponies**			
84-16-001	Arapaho	G. Perillo	1,500	65.00	200.00
84-16-002	Comanche	G. Perillo	1,500	65.00	200.00
84-16-003	Crow	G. Perillo	1,500	65.00	250.00
Artaffects		**Pride of America's Indians**			
88-17-001	Brave and Free	G. Perillo	10-day	50.00	150.00
89-17-002	Dark Eyed Friends	G. Perillo	10-day	45.00	75.00
89-17-003	Noble Companions	G. Perillo	10-day	45.00	50.00
89-17-004	Kindred Spirits	G. Perillo	10-day	45.00	50.00
89-17-005	Loyal Alliance	G. Perillo	10-day	45.00	75.00
89-17-006	Small & Wise	G. Perillo	10-day	45.00	50.00
89-17-007	Winter Scouts	G. Perillo	10-day	45.00	50.00
89-17-008	Peaceful Comrades	G. Perillo	10-day	45.00	50.00
Artaffects		**Sagebrush Kids**			
85-18-001	Hail to the Chief	G. Perillo	Closed	19.50	52.00
85-18-002	Dressing Up	G. Perillo	Closed	19.50	52.00
85-18-003	Favorite Kachina	G. Perillo	Closed	19.50	52.00
85-18-004	Message of Joy	G. Perillo	Closed	19.50	52.00
85-18-005	Boots	G. Perillo	Closed	19.50	52.00
85-18-006	Stay Awhile	G. Perillo	Closed	19.50	52.00
85-18-007	Room for Two?	G. Perillo	Closed	19.50	52.00
85-18-008	Blue Bird	G. Perillo	Closed	19.50	52.00
85-18-009	Ouch!	G. Perillo	Closed	19.50	52.00
85-18-010	Take One	G. Perillo	Closed	19.50	52.00
86-18-011	The Long Wait	G. Perillo	Closed	19.50	52.00
86-18-012	Westward Ho!	G. Perillo	Closed	19.50	52.00
86-18-013	Finishing Touches	G. Perillo	Closed	19.50	52.00
86-18-014	Deputies	G. Perillo	Closed	19.50	52.00
86-18-015	Country Music	G. Perillo	Closed	19.50	52.00
86-18-016	Practice Makes Perfect	G. Perillo	Closed	19.50	52.00
86-18-017	The Hiding Place	G. Perillo	Closed	19.50	52.00
86-18-018	Prarie Prayers	G. Perillo	Closed	19.50	52.00
87-18-019	Just Picked	G. Perillo	Closed	19.50	52.00
87-18-020	Row, Row	G. Perillo	Closed	19.50	52.00
87-18-021	My Papoose	G. Perillo	Closed	19.50	52.00
87-18-022	Playing House	G. Perillo	Closed	19.50	52.00
87-18-023	Wagon Train	G. Perillo	Closed	19.50	52.00
87-18-024	Small Talk	G. Perillo	Closed	19.50	52.00
90-18-025	How! Do I Love Thee?	G. Perillo	Closed	39.50	50.00
90-18-026	Easter Offering	G. Perillo	Closed	27.50	50.00

		ARTIST	EDITION	ISSUE	QUOTE
90-18-027	Just Married	G. Perillo	Closed	45.00	45.00
91-18-028	Baby Bronc	G. Perillo	Closed	27.50	80.00
91-18-029	Little Warriors	G. Perillo	Closed	27.50	35.00
91-18-030	Toy Totem	G. Perillo	Closed	27.50	35.00
91-18-031	Just Baked	G. Perillo	Closed	27.50	35.00
91-18-032	Lovin Spoonful	G. Perillo	Closed	27.50	35.00
91-18-033	Teddy Too??	G. Perillo	Closed	27.50	35.00
Artaffects		**Sagebrush Kids-Christmas Caravan**			
87-19-001	Leading the Way	G. Perillo	Open	90.00	120.00
87-19-002	Sleepy Sentinels	G. Perillo	Open	45.00	50.00
87-19-003	Singing Praises	G. Perillo	Open	45.00	50.00
87-19-004	Gold, Frankincense & Gifts	G. Perillo	Open	35.00	35.00
87-19-005	4-Piece Set (Above)	G. Perillo	Open	185.00	255.00
Artaffects		**Sagebrush Kids-Nativity**			
86-20-001	Christ Child	G. Perillo	Open	12.50	13.50
86-20-002	Mary	G. Perillo	Open	17.50	19.50
86-20-003	Joseph	G. Perillo	Open	17.50	19.50
86-20-004	Teepee	G. Perillo	Open	17.50	22.50
86-20-005	4-pc. Set (Above)	G. Perillo	Open	50.00	65.00
86-20-006	King with Corn	G. Perillo	Open	17.50	22.50
86-20-007	King with Pottery	G. Perillo	Open	17.50	22.50
86-20-008	King with Jewelry	G. Perillo	Open	17.50	22.50
86-20-009	Shepherd with Lamb	G. Perillo	Open	17.50	22.50
86-20-010	Shepherd Kneeling	G. Perillo	Open	17.50	22.50
86-20-011	Cow	G. Perillo	Open	12.00	13.50
86-20-012	Donkey	G. Perillo	Open	12.00	13.50
86-20-013	Lamb	G. Perillo	Open	6.00	8.00
86-20-014	Goat	G. Perillo	Open	8.00	9.50
86-20-015	Backdrop Dove	G. Perillo	Open	17.50	21.50
86-20-016	Backdrop Pottery	G. Perillo	Open	17.50	21.50
86-20-017	15 piece Set (Above)	G. Perillo	Open	225.00	245.00
89-20-018	Pig	G. Perillo	Open	15.00	15.00
89-20-019	Racoon	G. Perillo	Open	12.50	12.50
89-20-020	Cactus	G. Perillo	Open	24.50	24.50
89-20-021	Buffalo	G. Perillo	Open	17.50	17.50
90-20-022	Harmony Angel	G. Perillo	Open	37.50	37.50
90-20-023	Melody Angel	G. Perillo	Open	37.50	37.50
91-20-024	Peace Angel	G. Perillo	Open	27.50	27.50
91-20-025	Joy Angel	G. Perillo	Open	27.50	27.50
Artaffects		**Sagebrush Kids-Christmas Treasury**			
90-21-001	Santa's Lullaby	G. Perillo	Open	45.00	45.00
90-21-002	3/Set:Flight Into Egypt (Holy Family /Donkey)	G. Perillo	Open	65.00	65.00
Artaffects		**Sagebrush Kids-Banks**			
90-22-001	Perillo's Piggy Bank	G. Perillo	Open	39.50	39.50
90-22-002	Buckaroo Bank	G. Perillo	Open	39.50	39.50
90-22-003	Wampum Wig-Wam Bank	G. Perillo	Open	39.50	39.50
Artaffects		**Sagebrush Kids-Wedding Party**			
90-23-001	Bride	G. Perillo	Open	24.50	24.50
90-23-002	Groom	G. Perillo	Open	24.50	24.50
90-23-003	Flower Girl	G. Perillo	Open	22.50	22.50
90-23-004	Ring Bearer	G. Perillo	Open	22.50	22.50
90-23-005	Donkey	G. Perillo	Open	22.50	22.50
90-23-006	Chief	G. Perillo	Open	24.50	24.50
90-23-007	Wedding Backdrop	G. Perillo	Open	27.50	27.50
90-23-008	7 Piece Set (Above)	G. Perillo	Open	165.00	165.00
Artaffects		**Perillo Limited Edition Porcelain Figurines**			
91-24-001	One Nation Under God	G. Perillo	5,000	195.00	195.00
91-24-002	Safe And Dry (Umbrella Boy)	G. Perillo	5,000	95.00	95.00
91-24-003	Out Of The Rain (Umbrella Girl)	G. Perillo	5,000	95.00	95.00
91-24-004	Angel of the Plains	G. Perillo	5,000	75.00	75.00
91-24-005	The Sioux Carousel Horse	G. Perillo	5,000	95.00	95.00
91-24-006	The Cheyenne Carousel Horse	G. Perillo	5,000	95.00	95.00
Artaffects		**Musical Figurines**			
89-25-001	A Boy's Prayer	G. Perillo	Open	45.00	65.00
89-25-002	A Girl's Prayer	G. Perillo	Open	45.00	65.00
Artaffects		**Wildlife Figurines**			
90-26-001	Mustang	G. Perillo	Open	85.00	85.00
90-26-002	White-Tailed Deer	G. Perillo	Open	95.00	95.00
90-26-003	Mountain Lion	G. Perillo	Open	75.00	75.00
90-26-004	Bald Eagle	G. Perillo	Open	65.00	65.00
93-26-005	Buffalo	G. Perillo	Open	75.00	75.00
93-26-006	Timber Wolf	G. Perillo	Open	85.00	85.00
93-26-007	Polar Bear	G. Perillo	Open	65.00	65.00
93-26-008	Bighorn Sheep	G. Perillo	Open	75.00	75.00
Artaffects		**The Great Chieftains**			
91-27-001	Crazy Horse (Club Piece)	G. Perillo	Open	195.00	195.00
91-27-002	Sitting Bull	G. Perillo	S/O	195.00	195.00
91-27-003	Red Cloud	G. Perillo	S/O	195.00	195.00
91-27-004	Chief Joseph	G. Perillo	S/O	195.00	195.00
91-27-005	Cochise	G. Perillo	S/O	195.00	195.00
91-27-006	Geronimo	G. Perillo	S/O	195.00	195.00
Artaffects		**The Young Chieftains**			
85-28-001	Young Sitting Bull	G. Perillo	5,000	50.00	50.00
85-28-002	Young Joseph	G. Perillo	5,000	50.00	50.00
85-28-003	Young Red Cloud	G. Perillo	5,000	50.00	50.00
85-28-004	Young Geronimo	G. Perillo	5,000	50.00	50.00
85-28-005	Young Crazy Horse	G. Perillo	5,000	50.00	50.00
Artaffects		**Grand Bronze Collection**			
88-29-001	Free Spirit	G. Perillo	21-day	175.00	175.00
88-29-002	Fresh Waters	G. Perillo	21-day	350.00	350.00
88-29-003	Silhouette	G. Perillo	2,500	300.00	300.00
88-29-004	Partners	G. Perillo	2,500	200.00	200.00
88-29-005	Chief Red Cloud	G. Perillo	2,500	500.00	500.00
88-29-006	Discovery	G. Perillo	2,500	150.00	150.00
88-29-007	Peacemaker	G. Perillo	2,500	300.00	300.00
Artaffects		**American Indian Heritage**			
91-30-001	Cheyenne Nation (bust)	G. Perillo	10-day	55.00	55.00
Artaffects		**Village of the Sun**			
91-31-001	Sunbeam (Club Only)	G. Perillo	Open	Gift	N/A
92-31-002	Little Shadow (Club Renewal Only)	G. Perillo	Open	Gift	N/A
92-31-003	Rolling Thunder (Medicine Man)	G. Perillo	Open	24.00	24.00
92-31-004	Cloud Catcher (Boy with Dog)	G. Perillo	Open	24.00	24.00

		ARTIST	EDITION	ISSUE	QUOTE
92-31-005	Smiling Eyes (Baby with Lamb)	G. Perillo	Open	19.50	19.50
92-31-006	Many Bears (Farmer)	G. Perillo	Open	27.50	27.50
92-31-007	Cactus Flower (Weaver)	G. Perillo	Open	39.50	39.50
92-31-008	Dancing Waters (Tortilla Maker)	G. Perillo	Open	27.50	27.50
92-31-009	Red Bird (Jewelry Maker)	G. Perillo	Open	27.50	27.50
92-31-010	Bright Sky (Cook)	G. Perillo	Open	27.50	27.50
92-31-011	Summer Breeze (Maiden)	G. Perillo	Open	24.00	24.00
92-31-012	Standing Deer (Brave)	G. Perillo	Open	27.50	27.50
92-31-013	Noble Guardian (Horse)	G. Perillo	Open	39.50	39.50
92-31-014	Lambs	G. Perillo	Open	10.00	10.00
92-31-015	Small Cactus (Yellow Flowers)	G. Perillo	Open	7.50	7.50
92-31-016	Small Cactus (Pink Flowers)	G. Perillo	Open	7.50	7.50
92-31-017	Medium Cactus	G. Perillo	Open	10.00	10.00
92-31-018	Large Cactus	G. Perillo	Open	15.00	15.00
92-31-019	Hogan	G. Perillo	Open	59.00	59.00
Artaffects		**The Spirit Dancers**			
94-32-001	Eagle Dancer	G. Perillo	N/A	195.00	195.00
94-32-002	Buffalo Dancer	G. Perillo	N/A	195.00	195.00
Artaffects		**Simple Wonders**			
91-33-001	Joseph	C. Roeda	N/A	45.00	45.00
91-33-002	Joseph (Black)	C. Roeda	N/A	45.00	45.00
91-33-003	Mary	C. Roeda	N/A	40.00	40.00
91-33-004	Mary (Black)	C. Roeda	N/A	40.00	40.00
91-33-005	Baby Jesus	C. Roeda	N/A	35.00	35.00
91-33-006	Baby Jesus (Black)	C. Roeda	N/A	35.00	35.00
91-33-007	Sheep Dog	C. Roeda	N/A	15.00	15.00
91-33-008	Off To School	C. Roeda	N/A	49.50	49.50
91-33-009	Playing Hookey	C. Roeda	N/A	49.50	49.50
91-33-010	Mommy's Best	C. Roeda	N/A	49.50	49.50
91-33-011	Made With Love	C. Roeda	Retrd.	49.50	49.50
91-33-012	Bride	C. Roeda	N/A	55.00	55.00
91-33-013	Groom	C. Roeda	N/A	45.00	45.00
91-33-014	The Littlest Angel	C. Roeda	N/A	29.50	29.50
91-33-015	Star Light, Star Bright	C. Roeda	N/A	35.00	35.00
91-33-016	Lighting the Way	C. Roeda	N/A	39.50	39.50
91-33-017	Forever Friends	C. Roeda	N/A	39.50	39.50
91-33-018	Song of Joy	C. Roeda	N/A	39.50	39.50
91-33-019	I Love Ewe	C. Roeda	Retrd.	37.50	37.50
91-33-020	The Littlest Angel (Black)	C. Roeda	N/A	29.50	29.50
92-33-021	Ten Penny Serenade	C. Roeda	N/A	45.00	45.00
92-33-022	Ten Penny Serenade (Black)	C. Roeda	N/A	45.00	45.00
92-33-023	Rainbow Patrol	C. Roeda	N/A	39.50	39.50
92-33-024	The Three Bears	C. Roeda	N/A	45.00	45.00
92-33-025	Trick or Treat	C. Roeda	N/A	39.50	39.50
92-33-026	A Perfect Fit	C. Roeda	N/A	45.00	45.00
92-33-027	Pocketful of Love	C. Roeda	N/A	35.00	35.00
92-33-028	Pocketful of Love (Black)	C. Roeda	N/A	35.00	35.00
92-33-029	This Too Shall Pass	C. Roeda	N/A	35.00	35.00
92-33-030	Fallen Angel	C. Roeda	N/A	35.00	35.00
92-33-031	Lil' Dumplin	C. Roeda	N/A	25.00	25.00
92-33-032	Lil' Dumplin (Black)	C. Roeda	N/A	25.00	25.00
92-33-033	Little Big Shot	C. Roeda	N/A	35.00	35.00
92-33-034	With Open Arms (Wisechild)	C. Roeda	N/A	39.50	39.50
92-33-035	Following the Star (Wisechild)	C. Roeda	N/A	45.00	45.00
92-33-036	Catch the Spirit (Wisechild)	C. Roeda	N/A	35.00	35.00
93-33-037	Toad Taxi (Black)	C. Roeda	N/A	35.00	35.00
93-33-038	Toad Taxi	C. Roeda	N/A	35.00	35.00
93-33-039	Thumbs Up (Black)	C. Roeda	N/A	29.50	29.50
93-33-040	Thumbs Up	C. Roeda	N/A	29.50	29.50
93-33-041	Catch A Falling Star	C. Roeda	N/A	29.50	29.50
93-33-042	Snuggles (Black)	C. Roeda	N/A	22.50	22.50
93-33-043	Snuggles	C. Roeda	N/A	22.50	22.50
93-33-044	Devine K-9	C. Roeda	N/A	35.00	35.00
93-33-045	Prayer For Peace (Black)	C. Roeda	N/A	35.00	35.00
93-33-046	Prayer For Peace	C. Roeda	N/A	35.00	35.00
93-33-047	Heavenly Lullaby (Black)	C. Roeda	N/A	39.50	39.50
93-33-048	Heavenly Lullaby	C. Roeda	N/A	39.50	39.50
93-33-049	Manna From Heaven (Black)	C. Roeda	N/A	39.50	39.50
93-33-050	Manna From Heaven	C. Roeda	N/A	39.50	39.50
93-33-051	Teamwork	C. Roeda	N/A	29.50	29.50
93-33-052	Lambs Of God	C. Roeda	N/A	29.50	29.50
93-33-053	Francis and Friends	C. Roeda	N/A	37.50	37.50
93-33-054	Multi-Faced Pin	C. Roeda	N/A	12.50	12.50
93-33-055	Asian Angel Pin	C. Roeda	N/A	7.50	7.50
93-33-056	Black Angel Pin	C. Roeda	N/A	7.50	7.50
93-33-057	Angel w/ Blue Ribbon Pin	C. Roeda	N/A	7.50	7.50
93-33-058	Angel w/ Blond Hair Pin	C. Roeda	N/A	7.50	7.50
93-33-059	Angel w/ Brown Hair Pin	C. Roeda	N/A	7.50	7.50
93-33-060	I Love Ewe	C. Roeda	Retrd.	7.50	7.50
93-33-061	Made With Love	C. Roeda	Retrd.	7.50	7.50
93-33-062	Sweet Surprise	C. Roeda	Retrd.	7.50	7.50
94-33-063	Tea For Two (Black)	C. Roeda	N/A	22.50	22.50
94-33-064	Tea For Two	C. Roeda	N/A	22.50	22.50
94-33-065	Pals (Black)	C. Roeda	N/A	20.00	20.00
94-33-066	Pals	C. Roeda	N/A	20.00	20.00
94-33-067	Purrfect Prayer (Black)	C. Roeda	N/A	20.00	20.00
94-33-068	Purrfect Prayer	C. Roeda	N/A	20.00	20.00
94-33-069	What A Catch (Black)	C. Roeda	N/A	20.00	20.00
94-33-070	What A Catch	C. Roeda	N/A	20.00	20.00
94-33-071	Teachers Pet (Black)	C. Roeda	N/A	22.50	22.50
94-33-072	Teachers Pet	C. Roeda	N/A	22.50	22.50
94-33-073	Ewe & Me	C. Roeda	N/A	20.00	20.00
94-33-074	Evergreen Express	C. Roeda	N/A	22.50	22.50
94-33-075	Sunday Best	C. Roeda	N/A	22.50	22.50
Artaffects		**Blue Ribbon Babies**			
92-34-001	Petunia Penguin	Artaffects Studio	Open	19.50	19.50
92-34-002	Penelope Pig	Artaffects Studio	Open	19.50	19.50
92-34-003	Chauncey Camel	Artaffects Studio	Open	19.50	19.50
92-34-004	Siegfried Seal	Artaffects Studio	Open	19.50	19.50
92-34-005	Hortense Hippo	Artaffects Studio	Open	19.50	19.50
92-34-006	Elmont Elephant	Artaffects Studio	Open	19.50	19.50
93-34-007	Mollie Mouse	Artaffects Studio	Open	19.50	19.50
93-34-008	Prescott Panda	Artaffects Studio	Open	19.50	19.50
93-34-009	Oliver Owl	Artaffects Studio	Open	19.50	19.50
93-34-010	Reba Rabbit	Artaffects Studio	Open	19.50	19.50
93-34-011	Clementine Cow	Artaffects Studio	Open	19.50	19.50
93-34-012	Reginald Rhino	Artaffects Studio	Open	19.50	19.50

		ARTIST	EDITION	ISSUE	QUOTE
Artaffects		**Dino Babies**			
94-35-001	Tiny Triceratops	Artaffects Studio	N/A	20.00	20.00
94-35-002	April Apatosaurus	Artaffects Studio	N/A	20.00	20.00
94-35-003	Pickles Pachycephalosaurus	Artaffects Studio	N/A	20.00	20.00
94-35-004	Stanley Stegosaurus	Artaffects Studio	N/A	20.00	20.00
94-35-005	Patti Parasaurolophus	Artaffects Studio	N/A	20.00	20.00
94-35-006	Tyrone Tyrannosaurus	Artaffects Studio	N/A	20.00	20.00
94-35-007	Iggy Iguanadon	Artaffects Studio	N/A	20.00	20.00
94-35-008	Speedy Spinosaurus	Artaffects Studio	N/A	20.00	20.00
94-35-009	Hank Anklysaurus	Artaffects Studio	N/A	20.00	20.00
94-35-010	Alvin Allosaurus	Artaffects Studio	N/A	20.00	20.00
94-35-011	Priscilla Protoceratops	Artaffects Studio	N/A	20.00	20.00
94-35-012	Terri Pterodactyl	Artaffects Studio	N/A	20.00	20.00
Artaffects		**Legacy of the Lands**			
94-36-001	The Tracker (Blackfoot)	Artaffects Studio	N/A	35.00	35.00
94-36-002	Keeping Watch (Pawnee)	Artaffects Studio	N/A	35.00	35.00
94-36-003	The Lookout (Shoshoni)	Artaffects Studio	N/A	35.00	35.00
94-36-004	Thunder in the Ground (Crow)	Artaffects Studio	N/A	35.00	35.00
94-36-005	Hero in the Sun (Comanche)	Artaffects Studio	N/A	35.00	35.00
94-36-006	Moment of Victory (Arapaho)	Artaffects Studio	N/A	35.00	35.00
Artaffects		**Celebrations**			
94-37-001	Russian Celebrations	Artaffects Studio	N/A	35.00	35.00
94-37-002	African American Celebrations	Artaffects Studio	N/A	35.00	35.00
94-37-003	Scandinavian Celebrations	Artaffects Studio	N/A	35.00	35.00
94-37-004	North American Celebrations	Artaffects Studio	N/A	35.00	35.00
94-37-005	Persian Celebrations	Artaffects Studio	N/A	35.00	35.00
Artaffects		**Artaffects Tepee Ornament Collection**			
94-38-001	Buffalo Tepee	Artaffects Studio	N/A	6.00	6.00
94-38-002	Elk Tepee	Artaffects Studio	N/A	6.00	6.00
94-38-003	Eagle Tepee	Artaffects Studio	N/A	6.00	6.00
94-38-004	Dragonfly Tepee	Artaffects Studio	N/A	6.00	6.00
94-38-005	Bear Tepee	Artaffects Studio	N/A	6.00	6.00
94-38-006	Turtle Tepee	Artaffects Studio	N/A	6.00	6.00
94-38-007	Horse Tepee	Artaffects Studio	N/A	6.00	6.00
94-38-008	Wolf Tepee	Artaffects Studio	N/A	6.00	6.00
Artaffects		**Love Bugs**			
94-39-001	Peaches	Artaffects Studio	N/A	30.00	30.00
94-39-002	Blackberry	Artaffects Studio	N/A	30.00	30.00
94-39-003	Blueberry	Artaffects Studio	N/A	30.00	30.00
94-39-004	Raspberry	Artaffects Studio	N/A	30.00	30.00
94-39-005	Cherry	Artaffects Studio	N/A	30.00	30.00
94-39-006	Strawberry	Artaffects Studio	N/A	30.00	30.00
Artaffects		**Petals From Heaven**			
94-40-001	Love Roses	Artaffects Studio	Open	39.50	39.50
94-40-002	Remembrance Pansies	Artaffects Studio	Open	39.50	39.50
94-40-003	Goodness Lilies	Artaffects Studio	Open	39.50	39.50
94-40-004	Friendship Geraniums	Artaffects Studio	Open	39.50	39.50
94-40-005	Devotion Violets	Artaffects Studio	Open	39.50	39.50
94-40-006	Peace Poppies	Artaffects Studio	Open	39.50	39.50
Artists of the World		**DeGrazia Figurine**			
84-01-001	Flower Girl	T. DeGrazia	Susp.	65.00	165-195.
84-01-002	Flower Boy	T. DeGrazia	Closed	65.00	185-250.
84-01-003	Sunflower Boy	T. DeGrazia	Closed	65.00	195-275.
84-01-004	My First Horse	T. DeGrazia	Closed	65.00	250-395.
84-01-005	White Dove	T. DeGrazia	Closed	45.00	110-145.
84-01-006	Wondering	T. DeGrazia	Closed	85.00	200-295.
84-01-007	Flower Girl Plaque	T. DeGrazia	Closed	45.00	85-100.
85-01-008	Little Madonna	T. DeGrazia	Closed	80.00	200-295.
86-01-009	The Blue Boy	T. DeGrazia	Open	70.00	110.00
86-01-010	Festival Lights	T. DeGrazia	Open	75.00	110.00
86-01-011	Merry Little Indian	T. DeGrazia	S/O	175.00	275-325.
85-01-012	Pima Drummer Boy	T. DeGrazia	Closed	65.00	200-395.
87-01-013	Love Me	T. DeGrazia	Closed	95.00	165-395.
87-01-014	Wee Three	T. DeGrazia	Closed	180.00	195-250.
88-01-015	Christmas Prayer Angel	T. DeGrazia	Closed	70.00	175-295.
88-01-016	Los Ni¥os	T. DeGrazia	S/O	595.00	800-1200
88-01-017	Beautiful Burden	T. DeGrazia	Closed	175.00	195-295.
88-01-018	Merrily, Merrily, Merrily	T. DeGrazia	Closed	95.00	220-295.
88-01-019	Flower Boy Plaque	T. DeGrazia	Closed	80.00	85-100.
89-01-020	Two Little Lambs	T. DeGrazia	Closed	70.00	225.00
89-01-021	My First Arrow	T. DeGrazia	Closed	95.00	175-395.
89-01-022	My Beautiful Rocking Horse	T. DeGrazia	Open	225.00	275.00
89-01-023	Los Ninos (Artist's Edition)	T. DeGrazia	S/O	695.00	1500.00
90-01-024	Alone	T. DeGrazia	Open	395.00	495.00
90-01-025	El Burrito	T. DeGrazia	Open	60.00	90.00
90-01-026	Sunflower Girl	T. DeGrazia	Closed	95.00	125-195.
90-01-027	Crucifixion	T. DeGrazia	Yr.Iss.	295.00	295.00
90-01-028	Navajo Boy	T. DeGrazia	Yr.Iss.	110.00	138.00
90-01-029	Desert Harvest	T. DeGrazia	S/O	135.00	145.00
90-01-030	Biggest Drum	T. DeGrazia	Yr.Iss.	110.00	145.00
90-01-031	Little Prayer	T. DeGrazia	Closed	85.00	250-395.
91-01-032	Navajo Mother	T. DeGrazia	3,500	295.00	325.00
91-01-033	Shepherd Boy	T. DeGrazia	Open	95.00	125.00
92-01-034	Sun Showers	T. DeGrazia	5,000	195.00	225.00
92-01-035	Navajo Madonna	T. DeGrazia	Closed	135.00	200-295.
92-01-036	Coming Home	T. DeGrazia	3,500	165.00	175.00
92-01-037	Telling Tales	T. DeGrazia	Closed	48.00	48-75.00
92-01-038	The Listener	T. DeGrazia	Closed	48.00	48-75.00
93-01-039	Saddle Up	T. DeGrazia	5,000	195.00	215.00
93-01-040	El Toro	T. DeGrazia	Open	95.00	97.50
93-01-041	Little Medicine Man	T. DeGrazia	Open	175.00	185.00
93-01-042	Flowers For Mother	T. DeGrazia	Open	145.00	145.00
93-01-043	Mother Silently Prays	T. DeGrazia	3,500	345.00	345.00
93-01-044	Water Wagon	T. DeGrazia	Open	295.00	295.00
94-01-045	Fiesta Flowers	T. DeGrazia	3,500	197.50	197.50
94-01-046	Bearing Gifts	T. DeGrazia	Open	145.00	145.00
94-01-047	Pedro	T. DeGrazia	Open	145.00	145.00
94-01-048	Rio Grande Dance	T. DeGrazia	Open	97.50	97.50
94-01-049	Saguaro Dance	T. DeGrazia	5,000	495.00	495.00
Artists of the World		**DeGrazia Nativity Collection**			
85-02-001	Mary	T. DeGrazia	Open	90.00	100.00
85-02-002	Joseph	T. DeGrazia	Open	100.00	110.00
85-02-003	Jesus	T. DeGrazia	Open	55.00	65.00
85-02-004	Nativity Set-3 pc. (Mary, Joseph, Jesus)	T. DeGrazia	Open	275.00	275.00
93-02-005	Gaspar	T. DeGrazia	Open	135.00	135.00
93-02-006	Balthasar	T. DeGrazia	Open	135.00	135.00
93-02-007	Melchoir	T. DeGrazia	Open	135.00	135.00

		ARTIST	EDITION	ISSUE	QUOTE
Artists of the World	**DeGrazia Annual Christmas Collection**				
92-03-001	Feliz Navidad	T. DeGrazia	1,992	195.00	225.00
93-03-002	Fiesta Angels	T. DeGrazia	1,993	295.00	295.00
94-03-003	Littlest Angel	T. DeGrazia	1,994	165.00	165.00
Artists of the World	**DeGrazia Village Collection**				
93-04-001	Peace Pipe	T. DeGrazia	Open	65.00	65.00
93-04-002	Three Feathers	T. DeGrazia	Open	65.00	65.00
93-04-003	Let's Compromise	T. DeGrazia	Open	65.00	65.00
Artists of the World	**Goebel Miniatures: DeGrazia**				
85-05-001	Flower Girl 501-P	R. Olszewski	Suspd.	85.00	145-200.
85-05-002	Flower Boy 502-P	R. Olszewski	Suspd.	85.00	145-200.
85-05-003	My First Horse 503-P	R. Olszewski	Suspd.	85.00	100-165.
85-05-004	Sunflower Boy 551- P	R. Olszewski	Suspd.	93.00	100-165.
85-05-005	White Dove 504-P	R. Olszewski	Suspd.	80.00	100-125.
85-05-006	Wondering 505-P	R. Olszewski	Suspd.	93.00	100-175.
86-05-007	Little Madonna 552-P	R. Olszewski	Suspd.	93.00	100-225.
86-05-008	Pima Drummer Boy 506-P	R. Olszewski	Suspd.	85.00	155-350.
86-05-009	Festival of Lights 507-P	R. Olszewski	Suspd.	85.00	100-350.
87-05-010	Merry Little Indian 508-P	R. Olszewski	Suspd.	95.00	110-200.
88-05-011	Adobe Display 948D	R. Olszewski	Suspd.	45.00	59.00
89-05-012	Beautiful Burden 554-P	R. Olszewski	Suspd.	110.00	115-200.
90-05-013	Adobe Hacienda (large) Display 958-D	R. Olszewski	Suspd.	85.00	95.00
90-05-014	Chapel Display 971-D	R. Olszewski	Suspd.	95.00	125.00
91-05-015	My Beautiful Rocking Horse 555-P	R. Olszewski	Suspd.	110.00	125-250.
Artists of the World	**DeGrazia Pendants**				
85-06-001	Flower Girl Pendant 561-P	R. Olszewski	Open	125.00	150.00
87-06-002	Festival of Lights 562-P	R. Olszewski	Open	90.00	195.00
Band Creations, Inc.	**Best Friends**				
93-01-001	Sharing Is Caring 300425	Richards/Penfield	Open	12.00	12.00
93-01-002	Oh So Pretty 300426	Richards/Penfield	Open	14.00	14.00
93-01-003	Grandma's Favorite 300427	Richards/Penfield	Open	15.00	15.00
93-01-004	Quiet Time 300428	Richards/Penfield	Open	15.00	15.00
93-01-005	Purr-Fit Friends 300429	Richards/Penfield	Open	12.00	12.00
93-01-006	Fishing Friends 300430	Richards/Penfield	Open	18.00	18.00
93-01-007	Feathered Friends 300431	Richards/Penfield	Open	13.00	13.00
93-01-008	Dad's Best Pal 300432	Richards/Penfield	Open	15.00	15.00
93-01-009	My Beary Best Friend 300433	Richards/Penfield	Open	12.00	12.00
93-01-010	Castles In The Sand 300434	Richards/Penfield	Open	16.00	16.00
93-01-011	A Wagon Full Of Fun 300435	Richards/Penfield	Open	15.00	15.00
93-01-012	Rainbow Of Friends 300436	Richards/Penfield	Open	24.00	24.00
93-01-013	My Best Friend 300437	Richards/Penfield	Open	24.00	24.00
93-01-014	Santa's First Visit 300438	Richards/Penfield	Open	15.00	15.00
93-01-015	Santa's Surprise 300439	Richards/Penfield	Open	14.00	14.00
93-01-016	Checking It Twice 300440	Richards/Penfield	Open	15.00	15.00
Band Creations, Inc.	**Best Friends-Angels Of The Month**				
93-02-001	January UF1	Richards/Penfield	Open	10.00	10.00
93-02-002	February UF2	Richards/Penfield	Open	10.00	10.00
93-02-003	March UF3	Richards/Penfield	Open	10.00	10.00
93-02-004	April UF4	Richards/Penfield	Open	10.00	10.00
93-02-005	May UF5	Richards/Penfield	Open	10.00	10.00
93-02-006	June UF6	Richards/Penfield	Open	10.00	10.00
93-02-007	July UF7	Richards/Penfield	Open	10.00	10.00
93-02-008	August UF8	Richards/Penfield	Open	10.00	10.00
93-02-009	September UF9	Richards/Penfield	Open	10.00	10.00
93-02-010	October UF10	Richards/Penfield	Open	10.00	10.00
93-02-011	November UF11	Richards/Penfield	Open	10.00	10.00
93-02-012	December UF12	Richards/Penfield	Open	10.00	10.00
93-02-013	5pc. Carolers Set UF14 (3 carolers, 1 lamp post, 1 dog)	Richards/Penfield	Open	24.00	24.00
Band Creations, Inc.	**Best Friends-Trick or Treat Pals**				
94-03-001	Halloween Table	Richards/Penfield	Open	14.00	14.00
94-03-002	Boy with Ghost	Richards/Penfield	Open	10.00	10.00
94-03-003	Witch with Ghost	Richards/Penfield	Open	10.00	10.00
94-03-004	Witch Pin	Richards/Penfield	Open	6.00	6.00
94-03-005	Ghost Necklace	Richards/Penfield	Open	6.00	6.00
94-03-006	Witch Earrings	Richards/Penfield	Open	6.00	6.00
94-03-007	Ghost Earrings	Richards/Penfield	Open	6.00	6.00
Band Creations, Inc.	**Best Friends-O Joyful Night Nativity**				
94-04-001	Holy Family (Joseph, Mary & Jesus)	Richards/Penfield	Open	16.00	16.00
94-04-002	Angel on Stable (wall)	Richards/Penfield	Open	16.00	16.00
94-04-003	3 Kings	Richards/Penfield	Open	8.00	8.00
94-04-004	Shepard Boy	Richards/Penfield	Open	8.00	8.00
94-04-005	Camel and Donkey	Richards/Penfield	Open	4.00	4.00
Band Creations, Inc.	**Best Friends-P.S. I Love You Angels**				
94-05-001	Congratulations	Richards/Penfield	Open	12.00	12.00
94-05-002	Good Luck	Richards/Penfield	Open	12.00	12.00
94-05-003	New Baby	Richards/Penfield	Open	12.00	12.00
94-05-004	Anniversary	Richards/Penfield	Open	12.00	12.00
94-05-005	Bride and Groom	Richards/Penfield	Open	12.00	12.00
94-05-006	Get Well	Richards/Penfield	Open	12.00	12.00
94-05-007	Best Wishes	Richards/Penfield	Open	12.00	12.00
94-05-008	Customize Your own message	Richards/Penfield	Open	12.00	12.00
94-05-009	Inspirational	Richards/Penfield	Open	12.00	12.00
94-05-010	Happy Birthday	Richards/Penfield	Open	12.00	12.00
Band Creations, Inc.	**Best Friends-Winter Wonderland**				
94-06-001	Mr. & Mrs. Santa	Richards/Penfield	Open	10.00	10.00
94-06-001	3 Assorted Carolers	Richards/Penfield	Open	11.00	11.00
94-06-001	Reindeer (1 standing, 1 sitting)	Richards/Penfield	Open	8.00	8.00
94-06-001	3 Assorted White Trees & 3 presents	Richards/Penfield	Open	10.00	10.00
94-06-001	Green Tree	Richards/Penfield	Open	3.50	3.50
94-06-001	Angel Earrings	Richards/Penfield	Open	3.50	3.50
Boehm Studios	**Bird Sculptures**				
80-01-001	American Avocet 40134	Boehm	300	1400.00	1655.00
81-01-002	American Bald Eagle 40185	Boehm	655	1200.00	1330.00
82-01-003	American Eagle (Commemorative) 40215	Boehm	250	950.00	1150.00
57-01-004	American Eagle, large 428A	Boehm	31	225.00	11200.00
57-01-005	American Eagle, small 428B	Boehm	76	225.00	9200.00
82-01-006	American Eagle (Symbol of Freedom) 40200	Boehm	35	16500.00	18560.00
58-01-007	American Redstarts 447	Boehm	500	350.00	2010.00
80-01-008	American Redstart 40138	Boehm	225	850.00	1090.00
80-01-009	American Wild Turkey 40154	Boehm	75	1800.00	2020.00
80-01-010	American Wild Turkey (life-size) 40115	Boehm	25	15000.00	16940.00
83-01-011	Anna's Hummingbird 10048	Boehm	300	1100.00	1940.00
80-01-012	Arctic Tern 40135	Boehm	350	1400.00	2060.00

		ARTIST	EDITION	ISSUE	QUOTE
79-01-013	Avocet 100-27	Boehm	175	1200.00	1345.00
72-01-014	Barn Owl 1005	Boehm	350	3600.00	5400.00
72-01-015	Black Grouse 1006	Boehm	175	2800.00	3100.00
73-01-016	Blackbirds, pair 100-13	Boehm	75	5400.00	6470.00
84-01-017	Blackburnian Warbler 40253	Boehm	125	925.00	965.00
82-01-018	Black-eared Bushtit (female) 10038	Boehm	100	975.00	1045.00
82-01-019	Black-eared Bushtit (male) 10039	Boehm	100	975.00	1045.00
69-01-020	Black-headed Grosbeak 400-03	Boehm	675	1250.00	1535.00
56-01-021	Black-tailed Bantams, pair 423	Boehm	57	350.00	4800.00
58-01-022	Black-throated Blue Warbler 441	Boehm	500	400.00	1780.00
76-01-023	Black-throated Blue Warbler 400-60	Boehm	200	900.00	1165.00
67-01-024	Blue Grosbeak 489	Boehm	750	1050.00	1530.00
82-01-025	Blue Jay (with Morning Glories) 40218	Boehm	300	975.00	1190.00
81-01-026	Blue Jay (with Wild Raspberries) 40190	Boehm	350	1950.00	2405.00
62-01-027	Blue Jays, pair 466	Boehm	250	2000.00	12300.00
73-01-028	Blue Tits 1008	Boehm	300	3000.00	3250.00
82-01-029	Blue-throated Hummingbird 10040	Boehm	300	1100.00	1440.00
64-01-030	Bobolink 475	Boehm	500	550.00	1520.00
53-01-031	Bob White Quail, pair 407	Boehm	750	400.00	2500.00
81-01-032	Boreal Owl 40172	Boehm	200	1750.00	1875.00
72-01-033	Brown Pelican 400-22	Boehm	100	10500.00	14400.00
80-01-034	Brown Pelican 40161	Boehm	90	2800.00	2860.00
73-01-035	Brown Thrasher 400-26	Boehm	260	1850.00	1930.00
72-01-036	Cactus Wren 400-17	Boehm	225	3000.00	3410.00
57-01-037	California Quail, pair 433	Boehm	500	400.00	2730.00
79-01-038	Calliope Hummingbird 40104	Boehm	200	900.00	1115.00
87-01-039	Calliope Hummingbird 40319	Boehm	500	575.00	595.00
78-01-040	Canada Geese, pair 400-71	Boehm	100	4200.00	4200.00
77-01-041	Cape May Warbler 400-45	Boehm	400	825.00	990.00
55-01-042	Cardinals, pair 415	Boehm	500	550.00	3650.00
77-01-043	Cardinals 400-53	Boehm	200	3500.00	4095.00
57-01-044	Carolina Wrens 422	Boehm	100	750.00	5400.00
65-01-045	Catbird 483	Boehm	500	900.00	2080.00
83-01-046	Catbird 40246	Boehm	111	1250.00	1250.00
80-01-047	Cedar Waxwing 40117	Boehm	325	950.00	1040.00
56-01-048	Cedar Waxwings, pair 418	Boehm	100	600.00	7835.00
57-01-049	Cerulean Warblers 424	Boehm	100	800.00	4935.00
74-01-050	Chaffinch 100-20	Boehm	125	2000.00	2525.00
76-01-051	Chickadees 400-61	Boehm	400	1450.00	1550.00
68-01-052	Common Tern 497	Boehm	500	1400.00	6040.00
85-01-053	Condor 10057	Boehm	2	75000.00	87710.00
79-01-054	Costa's Hummingbird 40103	Boehm	200	1050.00	1200.00
67-01-055	Crested Flycatcher 488	Boehm	500	1650.00	3,005.00
74-01-056	Crested Tit 100-18	Boehm	400	1150.00	1310.00
80-01-057	Crimson Topaz Hummingbird 40113	Boehm	310	1400.00	1640.00
83-01-058	Dove of Peace 40236	Boehm	709	750.00	1480.00
83-01-059	Doves with Cherry Blossoms, pair 10049	Boehm	150	7500.00	10600.00
79-01-060	Downy Woodpecker 40116	Boehm	300	950.00	1000.00
57-01-061	Downy Woodpeckers 427	Boehm	500	450.00	1760.00
76-01-062	Eagle of Freedom I 400-50	Boehm	15	35000.00	51375.00
76-01-063	Eagle of Freedom II 400-70	Boehm	200	7200.00	7370.00
77-01-064	Eastern Bluebird 400-51	Boehm	300	2300.00	2625.00
59-01-065	Eastern Bluebirds, pair 451	Boehm	100	1800.00	12210.00
75-01-066	Eastern Kingbird 400-42	Boehm	100	3500.00	4275.00
83-01-067	Egret (National Audubon Society) 40221	Boehm	1,029	1200.00	1580.00
75-01-068	European Goldfinch 100-22	Boehm	250	1150.00	1400.00
73-01-069	Everglades Kites 400-24	Boehm	50	5800.00	7340.00
87-01-070	Flamingo w/ Young (National Audubon Society) 40316	Boehm	225	1500.00	1525.00
77-01-071	Fledgling Brown Thrashers 400-72A	Boehm	400	500.00	680.00
67-01-072	Fledgling Canada Warbler 491	Boehm	750	550.00	2205.00
65-01-073	Fledgling Great Horned Owl 479	Boehm	750	350.00	1590.00
71-01-074	Flicker 400-16	Boehm	250	2400.00	2770.00
83-01-075	Forster's Tern (Cresting) 40224	Boehm	300	1850.00	2080.00
83-01-076	Forster's Tern (on the Wing) 40223	Boehm	300	1850.00	2080.00
86-01-077	Gannet 40287	Boehm	30	4300.00	4300.00
72-01-078	Goldcrest 1004	Boehm	500	650.00	1210.00
83-01-079	Golden Eagle 10046	Boehm	25	32000.00	36085.00
54-01-080	Golden Pheasant, decorated 414A	Boehm	7	350.00	19235.00
54-01-081	Golden Pheasant, bisque 414B	Boehm	7	200.00	11375.00
56-01-082	Golden-crowned Kinglets 419	Boehm	500	400.00	2320.00
83-01-083	Goldfinch 40245	Boehm	136	1200.00	1200.00
61-01-084	Goldfinches 457	Boehm	500	400.00	1830.00
82-01-085	Great White Egret 40214	Boehm	50	11500.00	15055.00
66-01-086	Green Jays, pair 486	Boehm	400	1850.00	4120.00
82-01-087	Green Jays, pair 40198	Boehm	65	3900.00	3900.00
73-01-088	Green Woodpeckers 100-15	Boehm	50	4200.00	4890.00
79-01-089	Grey Wagtail 100-26	Boehm	150	1050.00	1385.00
74-01-090	Hooded Warbler 400-30	Boehm	100	2400.00	3020.00
73-01-091	Horned Larks 400-25	Boehm	200	3800.00	4435.00
64-01-092	Ivory-billed Woodpeckers 474	Boehm	4	N/A	N/A
68-01-093	Kestrels, pair 492	Boehm	460	2300.00	3160.00
82-01-094	Killdeer 40213	Boehm	125	1075.00	1090.00
64-01-095	Killdeer, pair 473	Boehm	300	1750.00	5160.00
76-01-096	Kingfishers 100-24	Boehm	200	1900.00	2205.00
80-01-097	Kirtland's Warble 40169	Boehm	130	750.00	890.00
73-01-098	Lapwing 100-14	Boehm	100	2600.00	3000.00
74-01-099	Lark Sparrow 400-35	Boehm	150	2100.00	2340.00
73-01-100	Lazuli Buntings 400-23	Boehm	250	1800.00	2455.00
81-01-101	Least Sandpipers 40136	Boehm	350	2100.00	2540.00
79-01-102	Least Tern 40102	Boehm	350	1275.00	3045.00
62-01-103	Lesser Prairie Chickens, pair 464	Boehm	300	1200.00	2390.00
71-01-104	Little Owl 1002	Boehm	350	700.00	1390.00
84-01-105	Long-eared Owl 10052	Boehm	12	6000.00	6260.00
73-01-106	Long Tail Tits 100-11	Boehm	200	2600.00	3000.00
84-01-107	Magnolia Warbler 40258	Boehm	246	1100.00	1100.00
52-01-108	Mallards, pair 406	Boehm	500	650.00	1745.00
57-01-109	Meadowlark 435	Boehm	750	350.00	3180.00
63-01-110	Mearn's Quail, pair 467	Boehm	350	950.00	3635.00
68-01-111	Mergansers, pair 496	Boehm	440	2200.00	2985.00
78-01-112	Mockingbirds 400-52	Boehm	350	2200.00	3045.00
61-01-113	Mockingbirds, pair 459	Boehm	500	650.00	3970.00
81-01-114	Mockingbird's Nest with Bluebonnet 10033	Boehm	55	1300.00	1365.00
63-01-115	Mountain Bluebirds 470	Boehm	300	1900.00	5480.00
81-01-116	Mourning Dove 40189	Boehm	300	2200.00	2325.00
58-01-117	Mourning Doves 443	Boehm	500	550.00	1490.00
82-01-118	Mute Swans, pair 40219	Boehm	115	5800.00	6350.00
71-01-119	Mute Swans, life-size, pair 400-14A	Boehm	3	N/A	N/A
71-01-120	Mute Swans, small size, pair 400-14B	Boehm	400	4000.00	7820.00
74-01-121	Myrtle Warblers 400-28	Boehm	210	1850.00	2105.00

		ARTIST	EDITION	ISSUE	QUOTE
58-01-122	Nonpareil Buntings 446	Boehm	750	250.00	1165.00
81-01-123	Northern Oriole 40194	Boehm	100	1750.00	1900.00
67-01-124	Northern Water Thrush 490	Boehm	500	800.00	1420.00
71-01-125	Nuthatch 1001	Boehm	350	650.00	1130.00
70-01-126	Orchard Orioles 400-11	Boehm	550	1750.00	2305.00
81-01-127	Osprey 10037	Boehm	100	4350.00	4710.00
81-01-128	Osprey 10031	Boehm	25	17000.00	21070.00
70-01-129	Oven-bird 400-04	Boehm	450	1400.00	1790.00
65-01-130	Parula Warblers 484	Boehm	400	1500.00	3370.00
85-01-131	Parula Warblers 40270	Boehm	100	2450.00	2465.00
75-01-132	Pekin Robins 400-37	Boehm	100	7000.00	9680.00
84-01-133	Pelican 40259	Boehm	93	1200.00	1235.00
73-01-134	Peregrine Falcon 100-12	Boehm	350	4400.00	5470.00
81-01-135	Peregrine Falcon with Young 40171	Boehm	105	1850.00	2020.00
80-01-136	Pheasant 40133	Boehm	100	2100.00	2175.00
84-01-137	Pileated Woodpeckers 40250	Boehm	50	2900.00	2925.00
79-01-138	Prince Rudolph's Blue Bird of Paradise 40101	Boehm	10	35000.00	37200.00
62-01-139	Ptarmigans, pair 463	Boehm	350	800.00	3465.00
74-01-140	Purple Martins 400-32	Boehm	50	6700.00	9150.00
79-01-141	Racquet-tail Hummingbird 40105	Boehm	310	1500.00	1965.00
85-01-142	Racquet-tailed Hummingbird 10053	Boehm	350	2100.00	2500.00
75-01-143	Red-billed Blue Magpie 400-44	Boehm	100	4600.00	6230.00
79-01-144	Red-breasted Nuthatch 40118	Boehm	200	800.00	925.00
57-01-145	Red-winged Blackbirds, pair 426	Boehm	100	700.00	5,590.00
54-01-146	Ringed-necked Pheasants, pair 409	Boehm	500	650.00	1,810.00
76-01-147	Rivoli's Hummingbird 100-23	Boehm	350	950.00	1,535.00
68-01-148	Roadrunner 493	Boehm	500	2600.00	3680.00
82-01-149	Roadrunner 40199	Boehm	150	2100.00	2325.00
64-01-150	Robin (Daffodils) 472	Boehm	500	600.00	5650.00
77-01-151	Robin (Nest) 400-65	Boehm	350	1650.00	2080.00
81-01-152	Robin's Nest with Wild Rose 10030	Boehm	90	1300.00	1380.00
81-01-153	Rose-breasted Grosbeak 10032	Boehm	165	1850.00	1880.00
83-01-154	Royal Terns 10047	Boehm	75	4300.00	4845.00
74-01-155	Ruby-throated Hummingbird 100-21	Boehm	200	1900.00	2825.00
60-01-156	Ruffed Grouse, pair 456	Boehm	250	950.00	5080.00
77-01-157	Ruffed Grouse, pair 400-65	Boehm	100	4400.00	4485.00
66-01-158	Rufous Hummingbirds 487	Boehm	500	850.00	2360.00
86-01-159	Sandhill Crane 40286 (National Audubon Society)	Boehm	205	1650.00	1665.00
77-01-160	Scarlet Tanager 400-41	Boehm	4	1800.00	4275.00
85-01-161	Scarlet Tanager 40267	Boehm	125	2100.00	2125.00
77-01-162	Scissor-tailed Flycatcher 400-48	Boehm	100	3200.00	3650.00
79-01-163	Scops Owl 40114	Boehm	300	975.00	1415.00
73-01-164	Screech Owl 100-10	Boehm	500	850.00	1495.00
80-01-165	Screech Owl 40132	Boehm	350	2100.00	3125.00
78-01-166	Siskens 100-25	Boehm	250	2100.00	2405.00
70-01-167	Slate-colored Junco 400-12	Boehm	500	1600.00	2240.00
72-01-168	Snow Buntings 400-21	Boehm	350	2400.00	2700.00
85-01-169	Soaring Eagle (bisque) 40276B	Boehm	304	950.00	960.00
85-01-170	Soaring Eagle (gilded) 40276G	Boehm	35	5000.00	5290.00
56-01-171	Song Sparrows, pair 421	Boehm	50	2000.00	38450.00
74-01-172	Song Thrushes 100-16	Boehm	100	2800.00	3590.00
74-01-173	Stonechats 100-17	Boehm	150	2200.00	2560.00
61-01-174	Sugarbirds 460	Boehm	100	2500.00	14910.00
74-01-175	Swallows 100-19	Boehm	125	3400.00	4320.00
63-01-176	Towhee 471	Boehm	500	350.00	2430.00
83-01-177	Towhee 40244	Boehm	75	975.00	1045.00
72-01-178	Tree Creepers 1007	Boehm	200	3200.00	3200.00
85-01-179	Trumpeter Swan 40266 (National Audubon Society)	Boehm	500	1500.00	1625.00
65-01-180	Tufted Titmice 482	Boehm	500	600.00	2040.00
65-01-181	Varied Buntings 481	Boehm	300	2200.00	4935.00
74-01-182	Varied Thrush 400-29	Boehm	300	2500.00	3115.00
69-01-183	Verdins 400-02	Boehm	575	1150.00	1565.00
69-01-184	Western Bluebirds 400-01	Boehm	300	5500.00	7020.00
71-01-185	Western Meadowlark 400-15	Boehm	350	1425.00	1735.00
84-01-186	Whooping Crane 40254 (National Audubon Society)	Boehm	647	1800.00	2025.00
71-01-187	Winter Robin 1003	Boehm	225	1150.00	1420.00
81-01-188	Wood Ducks 40192	Boehm	90	3400.00	3560.00
51-01-189	Wood Thrush 400	Boehm	2	375.00	N/A
66-01-190	Wood Thrushes, pair 485	Boehm	400	4200.00	8285.00
54-01-191	Woodcock 413	Boehm	500	300.00	2060.00
82-01-192	Wren 10036	Boehm	50	1700.00	1950.00
72-01-193	Yellow-bellied Sapsucker 400-18	Boehm	250	2700.00	3200.00
74-01-194	Yellow-billed Cuckoo 400-31	Boehm	150	2800.00	3055.00
74-01-195	Yellow-headed Blackbird 400-34	Boehm	75	3200.00	3600.00
82-01-196	Yellow-shafted Flicker 40220	Boehm	175	1450.00	1500.00
73-01-197	Yellowhammers 1009	Boehm	350	3300.00	4180.00
80-01-198	Yellow Warbler 40137	Boehm	200	950.00	1070.00
69-01-199	Young American Eagle 498B	Boehm	850	700.00	1520.00
73-01-200	Young American Eagle, Inaugural 498A	Boehm	100	1500.00	2125.00
75-01-201	Young & Spirited 1976 400-49	Boehm	1,121	950.00	1610.00
Boehm Studios	**Animal Sculptures**				
69-02-001	Adios 400-05	Boehm	130	1500.00	1900.00
77-02-002	African Elephant 5006	Boehm	50	9500.00	14630.00
76-02-003	American Mustangs 5005	Boehm	75	3700.00	5665.00
81-02-004	Appaloosa Horse 40193	Boehm	75	975.00	1070.00
80-02-005	Arabian Oryx, pair 50015	Boehm	60	3800.00	4135.00
83-02-006	Arabian Stallion (Prancing) 55007	Boehm	200	1500.00	1565.00
83-02-007	Arabian Stallion (Rearing) 55006	Boehm	200	1500.00	1565.00
80-02-008	Asian Lion 50017	Boehm	100	1500.00	1645.00
79-02-009	Bengel Tiger 500-13	Boehm	12	25000.00	26540.00
78-02-010	Black Rhinoceros 500-11	Boehm	50	9500.00	9920.00
71-02-011	Bobcats 4001	Boehm	200	1600.00	1990.00
82-02-012	Buffalo 50022	Boehm	100	1625.00	1625.00
78-02-013	Camel & Calf 5009	Boehm	50	3500.00	3700.00
80-02-014	Cheetah 50016	Boehm	100	2700.00	3000.00
85-02-015	Elephant (white bisque) 200-44B	Boehm	200	495.00	575.00
79-02-016	Fallow Deer 500-12	Boehm	30	7500.00	7500.00
71-02-017	Foxes 4003	Boehm	200	1800.00	2360.00
75-02-018	Giant Panda 5003	Boehm	100	3800.00	6890.00
78-02-019	Gorilla 5008	Boehm	50	3800.00	4550.00
82-02-020	Greater Kudu 50023	Boehm	75	7500.00	7500.00
79-02-021	Hunter Chase 55001	Boehm	20	4000.00	4085.00
52-02-022	Hunter 203	Boehm	250	600.00	1400.00
81-02-023	Jaguar 50020	Boehm	100	2900.00	3310.00
73-02-024	Nyala Antelope 5001	Boehm	100	4700.00	6560.00
76-02-025	Otter 5004	Boehm	75	1100.00	1505.00
81-02-026	Polar Bear with Cubs 40188	Boehm	65	1800.00	1875.00
57-02-027	Polo Player 206	Boehm	100	850.00	4610.00
82-02-028	Polo Player on Pinto 55005	Boehm	50	3500.00	3500.00
75-02-029	Puma 5002	Boehm	50	5700.00	6560.00
71-02-030	Raccoons 4002	Boehm	200	1600.00	2105.00
72-02-031	Red Squirrels 4004	Boehm	100	2600.00	2770.00
78-02-032	Snow Leopard 5007	Boehm	75	3500.00	4670.00
78-02-033	Thoroughbred with Jockey 400-85	Boehm	25	2600.00	2785.00
84-02-034	White-tailed Buck 50026	Boehm	200	1375.00	1660.00
79-02-035	Young & Free Fawns 50014	Boehm	160	1875.00	2055.00
Boehm Studios	**Floral Sculptures**				
80-03-001	Begonia (pink) 30041	Boehm	500	1250.00	1470.00
80-03-002	Bluebonnets 30050	Boehm	160	650.00	775.00
79-03-003	Cactus Dahlia 300-33	Boehm	300	800.00	970.00
80-03-004	Caprice Iris (pink) 30049	Boehm	235	650.00	725.00
86-03-005	Cherries Jubilee Camellia 10388	Boehm	250	625.00	625.00
83-03-006	Chrysanthemum 30105	Boehm	75	1250.00	1464.00
85-03-007	Chrysanthemum Petal Camellia 30125	Boehm	500	575.00	600.00
72-03-008	Chrysanthemums 3005	Boehm	350	1100.00	2030.00
71-03-009	Daisies 3002	Boehm	350	600.00	1045.00
81-03-010	Daisy (white) 30056	Boehm	75	975.00	995.00
74-03-011	Debutante Camellia 3008	Boehm	500	625.00	865.00
73-03-012	Dogwood 3003	Boehm	250	625.00	1035.00
81-03-013	Dogwood 30045	Boehm	510	875.00	955.00
78-03-014	Double Clematis Centerpiece 300-27	Boehm	150	1500.00	1780.00
74-03-015	Double Peony 3007	Boehm	275	575.00	995.00
82-03-016	Double Peony 30078	Boehm	110	1525.00	1640.00
78-03-017	Edward Boehm Camellia 300-23	Boehm	500	850.00	960.00
75-03-018	Emmett Barnes Camellia 300-11	Boehm	425	550.00	770.00
85-03-019	Emmett Barnes Camellia 30120	Boehm	275	625.00	630.00
83-03-020	Empress Camellia (white) 30109	Boehm	350	1025.00	1050.00
74-03-021	Gentians 3009	Boehm	350	425.00	730.00
86-03-022	Globe of Light Peony 10372	Boehm	125	475.00	505.00
79-03-023	Grand Floral Centerpiece 300-35	Boehm	15	7500.00	8755.00
78-03-024	Helen Boehm Camellia 300-25	Boehm	500	600.00	1110.00
78-03-025	Helen Boehm Daylily 300-20	Boehm	175	975.00	1140.00
78-03-026	Helen Boehm Iris 300-19	Boehm	175	975.00	1190.00
79-03-027	Honeysuckle 300-34	Boehm	200	900.00	1055.00
86-03-028	Icarian Peony Centerpiece 30119	Boehm	33	2800.00	2865.00
81-03-029	Julia Hamiter Camellia 30061	Boehm	300	675.00	745.00
85-03-030	Kama Pua Hibiscus (orange) 30128	Boehm	122	1600.00	1615.00
84-03-031	Lady's Slipper Orchid 30112	Boehm	76	575.00	575.00
82-03-032	Magnolia Centerpiece 30101	Boehm	15	6800.00	6985.00
75-03-033	Magnolia Grandiflora 300-12	Boehm	750	650.00	1525.00
80-03-034	Magnolia Grandiflora 300-47	Boehm	350	1650.00	1935.00
82-03-035	Marigolds 30072	Boehm	150	1275.00	1275.00
84-03-036	Mary Heatley Begonia 30111	Boehm	200	1100.00	1125.00
80-03-037	Miss Indiana Iris (blue) 30049	Boehm	235	650.00	710.00
81-03-038	Nancy Reagan Camellia 30076	Boehm	600	650.00	830.00
80-03-039	Orchid (pink) 30036	Boehm	175	725.00	780.00
80-03-040	Orchid (yellow) 30037	Boehm	130	725.00	780.00
76-03-041	Orchid Cactus 300-15	Boehm	100	650.00	1030.00
84-03-042	Orchid Centerpiece (assorted) 30016	Boehm	150	2600.00	2650.00
84-03-043	Orchid Centerpiece (pink) 30115	Boehm	350	2100.00	2490.00
84-03-044	Orchid, Cymbidium 30114	Boehm	160	575.00	625.00
84-03-045	Orchid, Odontoglossum 30113	Boehm	100	575.00	610.00
80-03-046	Parrot Tulips 30042	Boehm	300	850.00	1000.00
85-03-047	Peonies (white) 30118	Boehm	100	1650.00	1650.00
78-03-048	Pink Lotus 300-21	Boehm	175	975.00	1055.00
81-03-049	Poinsettia 30055	Boehm	200	1100.00	1230.00
82-03-050	Pontiff Iris 30097	Boehm	200	3000.00	3830.00
81-03-051	Poppies 30058	Boehm	325	1150.00	1265.00
76-03-052	Queen of the Night Cactus 300-14	Boehm	125	650.00	895.00
81-03-053	Rhododendron 30064	Boehm	275	825.00	825.00
85-03-054	Rhododendron (pink, yellow) 30122	Boehm	125	1850.00	1895.00
78-03-055	Rhododendron Centerpiece 300-30	Boehm	350	1150.00	1900.00
81-03-056	Rose (yellow in shell) 30059	Boehm	300	1100.00	1160.00
80-03-057	Rose, Alec's Red 30039	Boehm	500	1050.00	1390.00
81-03-058	Rose, Annenberg 30051	Boehm	200	1450.00	1495.00
78-03-059	Rose, Blue Moon 300-28	Boehm	500	650.00	915.00
85-03-060	Rose, Duet 30130	Boehm	200	1525.00	1550.00
80-03-061	Rose, Elizabeth of Glamis 30046	Boehm	500	1650.00	1970.00
81-03-062	Rose Grace de Monaco 30071	Boehm	350	1650.00	1940.00
81-03-063	Rose, Grandpa Dickson 30069	Boehm	225	1200.00	1430.00
85-03-064	Rose, Helen Boehm 30121	Boehm	360	1475.00	1480.00
82-03-065	Rose, Jehan Sadat 30080	Boehm	200	875.00	1030.00
81-03-066	Rose, Just Joey 30052	Boehm	240	1050.00	1050.00
81-03-067	Rose, Lady Helen 30070	Boehm	325	1350.00	1520.00
82-03-068	Rose, Mountbatten 30094	Boehm	50	1525.00	1665.00
81-03-069	Rose, Nancy Reagan 35027	Boehm	1,200	800.00	920.00
78-04-070	Rose, Pascali 300-24	Boehm	500	950.00	1520.00
82-03-071	Rose, Pascali 30093	Boehm	250	1500.00	1710.00
80-03-072	Rose, Peach 30038	Boehm	350	1800.00	2070.00
81-03-073	Rose, Prince Charles & Lady Diana Centerpiece 30065/6	Boehm	100	4800.00	6330.00
81-03-074	Rose, Prince Charles & Lady Diana Floral 30068	Boehm	600	750.00	850.00
82-03-075	Rose, Princess Margaret 30095	Boehm	350	950.00	1170.00
82-03-076	Rose, Queen Elizabeth 30091	Boehm	350	1450.00	1790.00
82-03-077	Rose, Royal Blessing 30099	Boehm	500	1350.00	1715.00
76-03-078	Rose, Supreme Peace 300-16	Boehm	250	850.00	1745.00
76-03-079	Rose, Supreme Yellow 300-17	Boehm	250	850.00	1735.00
78-03-080	Rose, Tropicana 300-22	Boehm	500	475.00	1075.00
81-03-081	Rose, Tropicana in Conch Shell 30060	Boehm	150	1100.00	1100.00
83-03-082	Rose, Yankee Doodle 30108	Boehm	450	650.00	700.00
86-03-083	Rose Centerpiece (yellow) 10370	Boehm	25	5500.00	5625.00
82-03-084	Royal Bouquet 30092	Boehm	125	1500.00	1690.00
82-03-085	Scabious with Japonica 30090	Boehm	50	1550.00	1575.00
85-03-086	Seminole Hibiscus (pink) 30129	Boehm	100	1800.00	1815.00
78-03-087	Spanish Iris 300-29	Boehm	500	600.00	760.00
83-03-088	Spring Centerpiece 30110	Boehm	100	1125.00	1200.00
82-03-089	Stewart's Supreme Camellia 30084	Boehm	350	675.00	710.00
73-03-090	Streptocalyx Poeppigii 3006	Boehm	50	3400.00	4485.00
71-03-091	Swan Centerpiece 3001	Boehm	135	1950.00	2930.00
76-03-092	Swan Lake Camellia 300-13	Boehm	750	825.00	1790.00
71-03-093	Sweet Viburnum 3004	Boehm	35	650.00	1395.00
82-03-094	Tiger Lilies (orange) 30077	Boehm	350	1225.00	1270.00
80-03-095	Tree Peony 30043	Boehm	325	1400.00	1485.00
82-03-096	Tulips 30089	Boehm	180	1050.00	1090.00
74-03-097	Waterlily 300-10	Boehm	350	400.00	725.00
78-03-098	Watsonii Magnolia 300-31	Boehm	250	575.00	680.00

		ARTIST	EDITION	ISSUE	QUOTE
Boehm Studios		**Figurines**			
86-04-001	Amanda with Parasol 10269	Boehm	27	750.00	750.00
86-04-002	Aria 67003	Boehm	100	875.00	875.00
86-04-003	Aurora 67001	Boehm	100	875.00	875.00
77-04-004	Beverly Sills 7006	Boehm	100	950.00	1010.00
86-04-005	Celeste 67002	Boehm	100	875.00	875.00
86-04-006	Devina 67000	Boehm	100	875.00	875.00
77-04-007	Jerome Hines 7007	Boehm	12	825.00	1000.00
86-04-008	Jo, Skating 10267	Boehm	26	750.00	750.00
86-04-009	Mattina 67004	Boehm	100	875.00	875.00
86-04-010	Meg with Basket 10268	Boehm	26	625.00	625.00
Boyds Collection Ltd.		**The Bearstone Collection™**			
93-01-001	Bailey Bear with Suitcase(old version) 2000	G.M. Lowenthal	Retrd.	14.20	N/A
93-01-002	Bailey Bear with Suitcase(revised version) 2000	G.M. Lowenthal	Open	14.20	14.20-45.
93-01-003	Bailey Bear with Suitcase (prototype) 2000	G.M. Lowenthal	Retrd.	14.20	75.00
93-01-004	Simone De Bearvoire and Her Mom 2001	G.M. Lowenthal	Open	14.20	14.20-47.
93-01-005	Neville...The 'Bedtime Bear' 2002	G.M. Lowenthal	Open	14.20	14.20-49.
93-01-006	Arthur...with Red Scarf 2003-03	G.M. Lowenthal	12/94	10.50	10.50-36.
93-01-007	Grenville...with Green Scarf 2003-04	G.M. Lowenthal	Retrd.	10.50	100.00
93-01-008	Grenville...with Red Scarf 2003-08	G.M. Lowenthal	Open	10.50	10.50
93-01-009	Victoria...'The Lady' 2004	G.M. Lowenthal	Open	18.40	18.40-57.
93-01-010	Moriarty-'The Bear in the Cat Suit' 2005	G.M. Lowenthal	Open	13.75	13.75-44.
93-01-011	Bailey...in the Orchard 2006	G.M. Lowenthal	Open	14.20	14.20-49.
93-01-012	Wilson with Love Sonnets 2007	G.M. Lowenthal	Open	12.60	12.60-60.
93-01-013	Father Chrisbear and Son 2008	G.M. Lowenthal	Retrd.	15.00	100.00
93-01-014	Byron & Chedda w/Catmint 2010	G.M. Lowenthal	12/94	14.20	14.20-45.
93-01-015	Daphne Hare & Maisey Ewe 2011	G.M. Lowenthal	Open	14.20	14.20-45.
93-01-016	Christian by the Sea 2012	G.M. Lowenthal	Open	14.20	14.20-45.
94-01-017	Bailey's Birthday 2014	G.M. Lowenthal	Open	15.95	15.95
94-01-018	Justina & M. Harrison...'Sweetie Pie' 2015	G.M. Lowenthal	Open	26.25	26.25
94-01-019	Grenville & Beatrice...'Best Friends' 2016	G.M. Lowenthal	Open	26.25	26.25
94-01-020	Bailey & Wixie 'To Have and To Hold' 2017	G.M. Lowenthal	Open	15.75	15.75
94-01-021	Bailey & Emily...'Forever Friends'	G.M. Lowenthal	Open	34.00	34.00
94-01-022	Sherlock & Watson-In Disguise 2019	G.M. Lowenthal	Open	15.75	15.75
94-01-023	Wilson at the Beach 2020-06	G.M. Lowenthal	Open	15.75	15.75
94-01-024	Bailey at the Beach 2020-09	G.M. Lowenthal	Open	15.75	15.75
94-01-025	Juliette Angel Bear (ivory) 2029-10	G.M. Lowenthal	Open	12.60	12.60
94-01-026	Clarence Angel Bear (rust) 2029-11	G.M. Lowenthal	Open	12.60	12.60
94-01-027	Grenville the Santabear 2030	G.M. Lowenthal	Open	14.20	14.20
93-01-028	Grenville & Neville...'The Sign' 2099	G.M. Lowenthal	Open	15.75	15.75
93-01-029	Grenville & Neville...'The Sign' (prototype) 2099	G.M. Lowenthal	Retrd.	15.75	65.00
94-01-030	Wilson the "Perfesser" 2222	G.M. Lowenthal	Open	16.25	16.25
94-01-031	Ted & Teddy 2223	G.M. Lowenthal	Open	15.75	15.75
94-01-032	Homer on the Plate 2225	G.M. Lowenthal	Open	15.75	15.75
94-01-033	Daphne...The Reader Hare 2226	G.M. Lowenthal	Open	14.20	14.20
94-01-034	Sebastian's Prayer 2227	G.M. Lowenthal	Open	16.25	16.25
94-01-035	Charlotte & Bebe...'The Gardeners' 2229	G.M. Lowenthal	Open	15.75	15.75
94-01-036	Celeste...'The Angel Rabbit' 2230	G.M. Lowenthal	Open	16.25	16.25
94-01-037	Clara...'The Nurse' 2231	G.M. Lowenthal	Open	16.25	16.25
94-01-038	Grenville...'The Graduate' 2233	G.M. Lowenthal	Open	16.25	16.25
94-01-039	Kringle & Bailey with List 2235	G.M. Lowenthal	Open	14.20	14.20
94-01-040	Elgin the Elf Bear 2236	G.M. Lowenthal	Open	14.20	14.20
94-01-041	Cookie the Santa Cat 2237	G.M. Lowenthal	Open	15.25	15.25
94-01-042	Maynard the Santa Moose 2238	G.M. Lowenthal	Open	15.25	15.25
94-01-043	Bessie the Santa Cow 2239	G.M. Lowenthal	Open	15.75	15.75
94-01-044	Edmond & Bailey...'Gathering Holly' 2240	G.M. Lowenthal	Open	24.25	24.25
94-01-045	Elliot & The Tree 2241	G.M. Lowenthal	Open	16.25	16.25
94-01-046	Elliot & Snowbeary 2242	G.M. Lowenthal	Open	15.25	15.25
94-01-047	Manheim the 'Eco-Moose' 2243	G.M. Lowenthal	Open	15.25	15.25
94-01-048	Knute & The Gridiron 2245	G.M. Lowenthal	Open	16.25	16.25
94-01-049	Agatha & Shelly-'Scardy Cat' 2246	G.M. Lowenthal	Open	16.25	16.25
95-01-050	Hop-a-Long...'The Deputy' 2247	G.M. Lowenthal	Open	14.20	14.20
95-01-051	Otis...'The Fisherman' 2249-06	G.M. Lowenthal	Open	15.75	15.75
95-01-052	Cookie Catberg...'Knittin' Kitten' 2250	G.M. Lowenthal	Open	18.40	18.40
95-01-053	Daphne and Eloise...'Women's Work' 2251	G.M. Lowenthal	Open	15.75	15.75
95-01-054	Lefty...'On the Mound' 2253	G.M. Lowenthal	Open	13.75	13.75
95-01-055	Bailey...'The Baker with Sweetie Pie' 2254	G.M. Lowenthal	Open	12.60	12.60
95-01-056	Amelia's Enterprise 'Carrot Juice' 2258	G.M. Lowenthal	Open	15.75	15.75
95-01-057	Miss Bruin & Bailey 'The Lesson' 2259	G.M. Lowenthal	Open	16.25	16.25
95-01-058	Bailey...'The Honeybear' 2260	G.M. Lowenthal	Open	16.25	16.25
95-01-059	Otis...'Taxtime' 2262	G.M. Lowenthal	Open	16.25	16.25
94-01-060	'Grenville the Santabear' Musical Waterball 2700	G.M. Lowenthal	Open	35.75	35.75
Brandywine Collectibles		**Hilton Village**			
87-01-001	Georgian House	M. Whiting	Closed	8.50	8.50
87-01-002	Gwen's House	M. Whiting	Closed	8.50	8.50
87-01-003	Dutch House	M. Whiting	Closed	8.50	8.50
87-01-004	English House	M. Whiting	Closed	8.50	8.50
87-01-005	Hilton Firehouse	M. Whiting	Closed	8.50	8.50
Brandywine Collectibles		**Yorktown Collection**			
87-02-001	Custom House	M. Whiting	Open	17.50	17.50
87-02-002	Pate House	M. Whiting	Open	19.00	19.00
87-02-003	Moore House	M. Whiting	Open	22.00	22.00
87-02-004	Nelson House	M. Whiting	Open	22.00	22.00
87-02-005	Grace Church	M. Whiting	Open	19.00	19.00
87-02-006	Medical Shop	M. Whiting	Open	13.00	13.00
87-02-007	Swan Tavern	M. Whiting	Open	22.00	22.00
93-02-008	Digges House	M. Whiting	Open	22.00	22.00
Brandywine Collectibles		**Old Salem Collection**			
87-03-001	Schultz Shoemaker	M. Whiting	Open	10.50	10.50
87-03-002	Miksch Tobacco Shop	M. Whiting	Closed	12.00	12.00
87-03-003	First House	M. Whiting	Open	12.80	12.80
87-03-004	Home Moravian Church	M. Whiting	Open	18.50	18.50
87-03-005	Boys School	M. Whiting	Open	18.50	18.50
87-03-006	Winkler Bakery	M. Whiting	Open	20.50	20.50
87-03-007	Vogler House	M. Whiting	Open	20.50	20.50
87-03-008	Salem Tavern	M. Whiting	Open	20.50	20.50
Brandywine Collectibles		**Williamsburg Collection**			
88-04-001	The Magazine	M. Whiting	Open	23.50	23.50
88-04-002	Governor's Palace	M. Whiting	Open	37.50	37.50
88-04-003	Court House of 1770	M. Whiting	Open	26.50	26.50
88-04-004	Wythe House	M. Whiting	Open	25.00	25.00
88-04-005	Colonial Capitol	M. Whiting	Open	43.50	43.50
93-04-006	Kings Arms Tavern	M. Whiting	Open	25.00	25.00
93-04-007	Campbell's Tavern	M. Whiting	Open	28.00	28.00

		ARTIST	EDITION	ISSUE	QUOTE
Brandywine Collectibles		**Custom Collection**			
88-05-001	Burgess Museum	M. Whiting	Open	15.50	15.50
88-05-002	Princetown Monument	M. Whiting	Closed	9.70	9.70
89-05-003	Yankee Candle Co.	M. Whiting	Closed	13.50	13.50
89-05-004	Lorain Lighthouse	M. Whiting	Closed	11.00	11.00
90-05-005	Jared Coffin House	M. Whiting	Open	32.00	32.00
90-05-006	Doylestown Public School	M. Whiting	Open	32.00	32.00
91-05-007	Smithfield VA. Courthouse	M. Whiting	Closed	12.00	12.00
91-05-008	Jamestown Tower	M. Whiting	Closed	9.00	9.00
92-05-009	Loudon County Courthouse	M. Whiting	Open	15.00	15.00
92-05-010	Cumberland County Courthouse	M. Whiting	Open	15.00	15.00
Brandywine Collectibles		**Victorian Collection**			
89-06-001	Seabreeze Cottage	M. Whiting	Closed	15.30	15.30
89-06-002	Serenity Cottage	M. Whiting	Closed	15.30	15.30
89-06-003	Hearts Ease Cottage	M. Whiting	Closed	15.30	15.30
89-06-004	Broadway House	M. Whiting	Closed	22.00	22.00
89-06-005	Peachtree House	M. Whiting	Closed	22.50	22.50
89-06-006	Skippack School	M. Whiting	Closed	22.50	22.50
89-06-007	Fairplay Church	M. Whiting	Closed	19.50	19.50
89-06-008	Elm House	M. Whiting	Closed	25.00	25.00
89-06-009	Old Star Hook & Ladder	M. Whiting	Closed	23.00	23.00
Brandywine Collectibles		**Barnsville Collection**			
90-07-001	Candace Bruce House	M. Whiting	Open	30.00	30.00
90-07-002	Thompson House	M. Whiting	Open	32.00	32.00
90-07-003	Treat-Smith House	M. Whiting	Open	32.00	32.00
90-07-004	Gay 90's Mansion	M. Whiting	Open	32.00	32.00
91-07-005	Bradfield House	M. Whiting	Open	32.00	32.00
91-07-006	B & O Station	M. Whiting	Open	28.00	28.00
91-07-007	Whiteley House	M. Whiting	Open	32.00	32.00
92-07-008	Barnesville Church	M. Whiting	Open	44.00	44.00
92-07-009	Plumtree Bed & Breakfast	M. Whiting	Open	44.00	44.00
Brandywine Collectibles		**North Pole Collection**			
91-08-001	Gingerbread House	D. Whiting	Open	24.00	24.00
91-08-002	Claus House	M. Whiting	Open	24.00	24.00
91-08-003	Reindeer Barn	M. Whiting	Open	24.00	24.00
92-08-004	Elves Workshop	M. Whiting	Open	24.00	24.00
92-08-005	Sugarplum Bakery	M. Whiting	Open	24.00	24.00
92-08-006	Snowflake Lodge	M. Whiting	Open	24.00	24.00
92-08-007	3 Winter Trees	D. Whiting	Open	10.50	10.50
92-08-008	Snowman with St. Sign	M. Whiting	Open	11.50	11.50
93-08-009	Teddybear Factory	M. Whiting	Open	24.00	24.00
93-08-010	Elf Club	M. Whiting	Open	24.00	24.00
93-08-011	Candy Cane Factory	M. Whiting	Open	24.00	24.00
93-08-012	Town Christmas Tree	M. Whiting	Open	20.00	20.00
94-08-013	Town Hall	M. Whiting	Open	25.00	25.00
94-08-014	Post Office	M. Whiting	Open	25.00	25.00
Brandywine Collectibles		**Seymour Collection**			
91-09-001	Seymour Church	M. Whiting	Open	19.00	19.00
91-09-002	Seymour Library	M. Whiting	Open	20.00	20.00
91-09-003	Blish Home	M. Whiting	Open	20.00	20.00
91-09-004	Anderson House	M. Whiting	Open	20.00	20.00
92-09-005	Majestic Theater	M. Whiting	Open	22.00	22.00
Brandywine Collectibles		**Patriots Collection**			
92-10-001	Washingtons Headquarters	M. Whiting	Open	24.00	24.00
92-10-002	Betsy Ross House	M. Whiting	Open	17.50	17.50
Brandywine Collectibles		**Treasured Times**			
94-11-001	Mother's Day House	M. Whiting	750	32.00	32.00
94-11-002	Birthday House	M. Whiting	750	32.00	32.00
94-11-003	New Baby Boy House	M. Whiting	750	32.00	32.00
94-11-004	New Baby Girl House	M. Whiting	750	32.00	32.00
94-11-005	Halloween House	M. Whiting	750	32.00	32.00
94-11-006	Valentine House	M. Whiting	750	32.00	32.00
Brandywine Collectibles		**Hometown I**			
90-12-001	School	M. Whiting	Closed	14.00	14.00
90-12-002	General Store	M. Whiting	Closed	14.00	14.00
90-12-003	Barber Shop	M. Whiting	Closed	14.00	14.00
90-12-004	Toy Store	M. Whiting	Closed	14.00	14.00
Brandywine Collectibles		**Hometown II**			
91-13-001	Church	M. Whiting	Closed	14.00	14.00
91-13-002	Dentist	M. Whiting	Closed	14.00	14.00
91-13-003	Ice Cream Shop	M. Whiting	Closed	14.00	14.00
91-13-004	Stitch-N-Sew	M. Whiting	Closed	14.00	14.00
Brandywine Collectibles		**Hometown III**			
91-14-001	Dairy	M. Whiting	Closed	15.50	15.50
91-14-002	Library	M. Whiting	Closed	15.50	15.50
91-14-003	Firehouse	M. Whiting	Closed	15.50	15.50
91-14-004	Basket Shop	M. Whiting	Closed	15.50	15.50
Brandywine Collectibles		**Hometown IV**			
92-15-001	Country Inn	M. Whiting	Closed	21.50	21.50
92-15-002	Courthouse	M. Whiting	Closed	21.50	21.50
92-15-003	Gas Station	M. Whiting	Closed	21.00	21.00
92-15-004	Bakery	M. Whiting	Closed	21.00	21.00
Brandywine Collectibles		**Hometown V**			
92-16-001	Pharmacy	M. Whiting	12/94	22.00	22.00
92-16-002	Sporting Goods	M. Whiting	12/94	22.00	22.00
92-16-003	Tea Room	M. Whiting	12/94	22.00	22.00
92-16-004	Antiques Shop	M. Whiting	12/94	22.00	22.00
92-16-005	Gift Shop	M. Whiting	12/94	22.00	22.00
Brandywine Collectibles		**Hometown VI**			
93-17-001	School	M. Whiting	Open	24.00	24.00
93-17-002	Church	M. Whiting	Open	24.00	24.00
93-17-003	General Store	M. Whiting	Open	24.00	24.00
93-17-004	Train Station	M. Whiting	Open	24.00	24.00
93-17-005	Diner	M. Whiting	Open	24.00	24.00
Brandywine Collectibles		**Hometown VII**			
93-18-001	Flower Shop	M. Whiting	Open	24.00	24.00
93-18-002	Dress Shop	M. Whiting	Open	24.00	24.00
93-18-003	Candy Shop	M. Whiting	Open	24.00	24.00
93-18-004	Pet Shop	M. Whiting	Open	24.00	24.00
93-18-005	Post Office	M. Whiting	Open	24.00	24.00
93-18-006	Quilt Shop	M. Whiting	Open	24.00	24.00

		ARTIST	EDITION	ISSUE	QUOTE
Brandywine Collectibles		**Hometown VIII**			
94-19-001	Sewing Shop	M. Whiting	Open	26.00	26.00
94-19-002	Country Store	M. Whiting	Open	28.00	28.00
94-19-003	Professional Building	M. Whiting	Open	28.00	28.00
94-19-004	Barber Shop	M. Whiting	Open	28.00	28.00
94-19-005	Fire Company	M. Whiting	Open	28.00	28.00
Brandywine Collectibles		**Hometown IX**			
94-20-001	Bed & Breakfast	M. Whiting	Open	29.00	29.00
94-20-002	Teddys & Toys	M. Whiting	Open	29.00	29.00
94-20-003	Cafe/Deli	M. Whiting	Open	29.00	29.00
94-20-004	Hometown Gazette	M. Whiting	Open	29.00	29.00
94-20-005	Hometown Bank	M. Whiting	Open	29.00	29.00
Brandywine Collectibles		**Accessories**			
87-21-001	Summer Tree with Fence	M. Whiting	Open	7.00	7.00
88-21-002	Flag	M. Whiting	Open	10.00	10.00
88-21-003	Lampost, Wall & Fence	M. Whiting	Open	11.00	11.00
89-21-004	Mailbox, Tree & Fence	M. Whiting	Open	10.00	10.00
89-21-005	Victorian Gas Light	M. Whiting	Open	6.50	6.50
89-21-006	Horse & Carriage	M. Whiting	Open	13.00	13.00
89-21-007	Pumpkin Wagon	M. Whiting	Open	11.50	11.50
90-21-008	Flower Cart	M. Whiting	Open	13.00	13.00
90-21-009	Wishing Well	M. Whiting	Open	10.00	10.00
90-21-010	Bandstand	M. Whiting	Closed	10.50	10.50
90-21-011	Gate & Arbor	M. Whiting	Closed	9.00	9.00
90-21-012	Gooseneck Lamp	M. Whiting	Open	7.50	7.50
91-21-013	Town Clock	M. Whiting	Open	7.50	7.50
91-21-014	Baggage Cart	M. Whiting	Open	10.50	10.50
91-21-015	Street Sign	M. Whiting	Open	8.00	8.00
92-21-016	Apple Tree/Tire Swing	M. Whiting	Open	10.00	10.00
92-21-017	Tree with Birdhouse	M. Whiting	Open	10.00	10.00
94-21-018	Elm Tree with Benches	M. Whiting	Open	16.00	16.00
94-21-019	Lamp with Barber Pole	M. Whiting	Open	10.50	10.50
Byers' Choice Ltd.		**Carolers**			
78-01-001	Traditional Man Caroler	J. Byers	Closed	N/A	300.00
78-01-002	Traditional Lady Caroler (w/ hands)	J. Byers	Closed	N/A	1500.00
82-01-003	Victorian Adult Caroler (1st Version)	J. Byers	Closed	32.00	300.00
82-01-004	Victorian Child Caroler (1st Version)	J. Byers	Closed	32.00	300.00
83-01-005	Victorian Adult Caroler (2nd Version)	J. Byers	Open	35.00	46.00
83-01-006	Victorian Child Caroler (2nd Version)	J. Byers	Open	33.00	46.00
86-01-007	Traditional Grandparents	J. Byers	Open	35.00	42.00
86-01-008	Singing Dogs	J. Byers	Open	13.00	15.00
88-01-009	Victorian Grand Parent Carolers	J. Byers	Open	40.00	45.00
88-01-010	Children with Skates	J. Byers	Open	40.00	47.00
88-01-011	Singing Cats	J. Byers	Open	13.50	15.00
Byers' Choice Ltd.		**Special Characters**			
81-02-001	Thanksgiving Man (Clay Hands)	J. Byers	Closed	Unkn.	2000.00
81-02-002	Thanksgiving Lady (Clay Hands)	J. Byers	Closed	Unkn.	2000.00
82-02-003	Icabod	J. Byers	Closed	32.00	1150.00
82-02-004	Choir Children, boy and girl set	J. Byers	Closed	32.00	450-600.
82-02-005	Valentine Boy	J. Byers	Closed	32.00	450-550.
82-02-006	Valentine Girl	J. Byers	Closed	32.00	450-550.
82-02-007	Easter Boy	J. Byers	Closed	32.00	450-550.
82-02-008	Easter Girl	J. Byers	Closed	32.00	450-550.
82-02-009	Leprechauns	J. Byers	Closed	34.00	12-1500.
82-02-010	Conductor	J. Byers	Closed	32.00	110-170.
82-02-011	Drummer Boy	J. Byers	Closed	34.00	95-210.
83-02-012	Boy on Rocking Horse	J. Byers	300	85.00	15-1800.
84-02-013	Chimney Sweep (Adult)	J. Byers	Closed	36.00	825-1500
85-02-014	Pajama Children	J. Byers	Closed	35.00	200-370.
87-02-015	Boy on Sled	J. Byers	Closed	50.00	180-325.
87-02-016	Caroler with Lamp	J. Byers	Closed	40.00	110-150.
87-02-017	Mother's Day	J. Byers	225	125.00	350-420.
88-02-018	Mother's Day (Son)	J. Byers	Closed	125.00	225-450.
88-02-019	Mother's Day (Daughter)	J. Byers	Closed	125.00	325-400.
88-02-020	Angel Tree Top	J. Byers	100	Unkn.	160-200.
88-02-021	Mother Holding Baby	J. Byers	Closed	40.00	90.00
89-02-022	Newsboy with Bike	J. Byers	Closed	78.00	110-195.
89-02-023	Girl with Hoop	J. Byers	Closed	44.00	85-170.
89-02-024	Mother's Day (with Carriage)	J. Byers	3,000	75.00	250-425.
90-02-025	Postman	J. Byers	Closed	45.00	80-170.
90-02-026	Parson	J. Byers	Closed	44.00	75-100.
90-02-027	Victorian Girl On Rocking Horse(blonde)	J. Byers	Closed	70.00	325.00
90-02-028	Victorian Girl On Rocking Horse(brunette)	J. Byers	Closed	70.00	120-225.
91-02-029	Chimney Sweep- Child	J. Byers	Open	50.00	50.00
91-02-030	Chimney Sweep - Child (1991 version)	J. Byers	Closed	50.00	90.00
91-02-031	Boy w/Apple	J. Byers	Closed	41.00	100-250.
91-02-032	Girl w/Apple	J. Byers	Closed	41.00	150.00
91-02-033	Boy W/Tree	J. Byers	Open	49.00	49.00
92-02-034	Schoolteacher	J. Byers	Open	48.00	48.00
92-02-035	Schoolteacher (1992 version)	J. Byers	Closed	48.00	75.00
92-02-036	Victorian Mother With Toddler (Spr/Sum)	J. Byers	Closed	60.00	90-115.
92-02-037	Victorian Mother With Toddler (Fall/Win)	J. Byers	Closed	60.00	115-125.
93-02-038	Victorian Mother With Toddler (Spr/Sum)	J. Byers	Closed	61.00	115-125.
93-02-039	Choir Director	J. Byers	Open	56.00	56.00
93-02-040	Choir Director (1993 version)	J. Byers	Closed	56.00	75.00
93-02-041	School Kids	J. Byers	Open	48.00	48.00
93-02-042	School Kids (1993 version)	J. Byers	Closed	48.00	125.00
93-02-043	Lamplighter	J. Byers	Open	48.00	48.00
93-02-044	Lamplighter (1993 version)	J. Byers	Closed	48.00	80-125.
94-02-045	Constable	J. Byers	Open	53.00	53.00
94-02-046	Sandwich Board Man	J. Byers	Open	52.00	52.00
94-02-047	Nanny	J. Byers	Open	66.00	66.00
94-02-048	Boy With Goose	J. Byers	Open	49.50	49.50
94-02-049	Baby in Basket	J. Byers	Open	7.50	7.50
94-02-050	Treetop Angel	J. Byers	Open	50.00	50.00
Byers' Choice Ltd.		**Santas**			
78-03-001	Old World Santa	J. Byers	Closed	33.00	250-350.
78-03-002	Velvet Santa	J. Byers	Open	Unkn.	50.00
82-03-003	Santa in a Sleigh (1st Version)	J. Byers	Closed	46.00	800.00
83-03-004	Working Santa	J. Byers	Closed	38.00	120-150.
83-03-005	Velvet Santa w/Tree	J. Byers	Closed	N/A	250.00
84-03-006	Santa in Sleigh (2nd Version)	J. Byers	Closed	70.00	750-795.
84-03-007	Mrs. Claus	J. Byers	Closed	38.00	150-325.
86-03-008	Mrs. Claus on Rocker	J. Byers	Closed	73.00	350-650.
86-03-009	Victorian Santa	J. Byers	Closed	39.00	125-300.
87-03-010	Velvet Mrs. Claus	J. Byers	Open	44.00	44.00
87-03-011	Velvet Mrs. Claus (1987 version)	J. Byers	Closed	44.00	115.00
88-03-012	Saint Nicholas	J. Byers	Closed	44.00	105-190.
88-03-013	Knecht Ruprecht (Black Peter)	J. Byers	Closed	38.00	115-155.
89-03-014	Russian Santa	J. Byers	Closed	85.00	200-500.
90-03-015	Weihnachtsmann (German Santa)	J. Byers	Closed	56.00	130-225.
91-03-016	Father Christmas	J. Byers	Closed	48.00	60-190.
92-03-017	Mrs. Claus (2nd Version)	J. Byers	Closed	50.00	70-150.
92-03-018	Working Santa (2nd Version)	J. Byers	Open	52.00	52.00
92-03-019	Working Santa (2nd Version)('92 version)	J. Byers	Closed	52.00	95.00
93-03-020	Skating Santa	J. Byers	Closed	60.00	80-135.
94-03-021	Old Befana	J. Byers	Open	53.00	53.00
Byers' Choice Ltd.		**Dickens Series**			
83-04-001	Scrooge (1st Edition)	J. Byers	Closed	36.00	12-2000.
84-04-002	Mrs. Cratchit (1st Edition)	J. Byers	Closed	38.00	675-1100
84-04-003	Scrooge (2nd Edition)	J. Byers	Open	38.00	38.00
85-04-004	Mrs. Fezziwig (1st Edition)	J. Byers	Closed	43.00	400-900.
85-04-005	Mr. Fezziwig (1st Edition)	J. Byers	Closed	43.00	385-725.
85-04-006	Mrs. Cratchit (2nd Edition)	J. Byers	Open	39.00	39.00
86-04-007	Marley's Ghost (1st Edition)	J. Byers	Closed	40.00	250-400.
86-04-008	Mrs. Fezziwig (2nd Edition)	J. Byers	Closed	43.00	225-500.
86-04-009	Mr. Fezziwig (2nd Edition)	J. Byers	Closed	43.00	225-500.
87-04-010	Spirit of Christmas Past (1st Edition)	J. Byers	Closed	42.00	250-400.
87-04-011	Marley's Ghost (2nd Edition)	J. Byers	Closed	42.00	100-200.
88-04-012	Spirit of Christmas Present (1st Edition)	J. Byers	Closed	44.00	256-365.
88-04-013	Spirit of Christmas Past (2nd Edition)	J. Byers	Closed	46.00	150-325.
89-04-014	Spirit of Christmas Future (1st Edition)	J. Byers	Closed	46.00	150-250.
89-04-015	Spirit of Christmas Present (2nd Edition)	J. Byers	Closed	48.00	125-325.
90-04-016	Bob Cratchit & Tiny Tim (1st Edition)	J. Byers	Closed	84.00	120-275.
90-04-017	Spirit of Christmas Future (2nd Edition)	J. Byers	Closed	48.00	150-325.
91-04-018	Happy Scrooge (1st Edition)	J. Byers	Closed	50.00	100-200.
91-04-019	Bob Cratchit & Tiny Tim (2nd Edition)	J. Byers	Open	86.00	86.00
91-04-020	Bob Cratchit & Tiny Tim (2nd Edition) (1991 version)	J. Byers	Closed	86.00	100-125.
92-04-021	Happy Scrooge (2nd Edition)	J. Byers	Closed	50.00	90-150.
Byers' Choice Ltd.		**Musicians**			
83-05-001	Violin Player Man (1st Version)	J. Byers	Closed	38.00	800.00
84-05-002	Violin Player Man (2nd Version)	J. Byers	Closed	38.00	1500.00
85-05-003	Horn Player, chubby face	J. Byers	Closed	37.00	700-900.
85-05-004	Horn Player	J. Byers	Closed	38.00	300-400.
86-05-005	Victorian Girl with Violin	J. Byers	Closed	39.00	260-350.
89-05-006	Musician with Clarinet	J. Byers	Closed	44.00	450-650.
90-05-007	Musician With Mandolin	J. Byers	Closed	46.00	120-275.
91-05-008	Musician With Accordian	J. Byers	Closed	48.00	120-250.
91-05-009	Boy With Mandolin	J. Byers	Closed	48.00	200-290.
92-05-010	Musician With French Horn	J. Byers	Closed	52.00	75-150.
Byers' Choice Ltd.		**Nativity**			
87-06-001	Black Angel	J. Byers	Closed	36.00	80-190.
87-06-002	Angel-Great Star (Blonde)	J. Byers	Closed	40.00	125-200.
87-06-003	Angel-Great Star (Brunette)	J. Byers	Closed	40.00	100-200.
87-06-004	Angel-Great Star (Red Head)	J. Byers	Closed	40.00	140-200.
88-06-005	Shepherds	J. Byers	Closed	37.00	80-95.00
89-06-006	King Gasper	J. Byers	Closed	40.00	80-100.
89-06-007	King Melchior	J. Byers	Closed	40.00	80-120.
89-06-008	King Balthasar	J. Byers	Closed	40.00	80-120.
89-06-009	Angel Gabriel	J. Byers	Closed	37.00	90-125.
90-06-010	Holy Family w/stable	J. Byers	Closed	119.00	200-300.
Byers' Choice Ltd.		**Display Figures**			
81-07-001	Display Man	J. Byers	Closed	N/A	2000.00
81-07-002	Display Lady	J. Byers	Closed	N/A	2000.00
82-07-003	Display Drummer Boy-1st	J. Byers	Closed	96.00	600.00
85-07-004	Display Drummer Boy-2nd	J. Byers	Closed	160.00	300.00
82-07-005	Display Santa	J. Byers	Closed	96.00	600.00
83-07-006	Display Carolers	J. Byers	Closed	200.00	500.00
84-07-007	Display Working Santa	J. Byers	Closed	260.00	500.00
85-07-008	Display Old World Santa	J. Byers	Closed	260.00	500.00
85-07-009	Display Children	J. Byers	Closed	140.00	500.00
86-07-010	Display Adults	J. Byers	Closed	170.00	500.00
87-07-011	Mechanical Boy W/ Drum	J. Byers	Closed	N/A	550.00
90-07-012	Display Santa-red	J. Byers	Closed	250.00	450-550.
90-07-013	Display Santa-bayberry	J. Byers	Closed	250.00	450-550.
Byers' Choice Ltd.		**Cries Of London**			
91-08-001	Apple Lady	J. Byers	Closed	80.00	500-1200
92-08-002	Baker	J. Byers	Closed	62.00	80-150.
93-08-003	Chestnut Roaster	J. Byers	Closed	64.00	85-200.
94-08-004	Flower Vendor	J. Byers	Yr. Iss.	64.00	64.00
Byers' Choice Ltd.		**Skaters**			
91-09-001	Adult Skaters	J. Byers	Open	50.00	50.00
91-09-002	Adult Skaters (1991 version)	J. Byers	Closed	50.00	130.00
92-09-003	Children Skaters	J. Byers	Open	50.00	50.00
92-09-004	Children Skaters (1992 version)	J. Byers	Closed	50.00	130.00
93-09-005	Grandparent Skaters	J. Byers	Open	50.00	50.00
93-09-006	Grandparent Skaters (1993 version)	J. Byers	Closed	50.00	145.00
93-09-007	Boy Skater on Log	J. Byers	Closed	55.00	100-125.
Byers' Choice Ltd.		**Toddlers**			
91-10-001	Sled with Dog	J. Byers	Closed	30.00	70-95.00
92-10-002	Shovel	J. Byers	Closed	17.00	35.00
92-10-003	Snowball (lg.)	J. Byers	Open	17.00	19.00
92-10-004	Snowball (lg.) (1992 version)	J. Byers	Closed	17.00	29.00
92-10-005	Sled	J. Byers	Open	17.00	19.00
93-10-006	Package	J. Byers	Closed	18.50	35.00
93-10-007	Gingerbread Boy	J. Byers	Open	18.50	18.50
93-10-008	Teddy Bear	J. Byers	Closed	18.50	40.00
94-10-009	Skis	J. Byers	Open	19.00	19.00
94-10-010	Tree	J. Byers	Open	18.00	18.00
94-10-011	Snowflake	J. Byers	Open	18.00	18.00
Byers' Choice Ltd.		**Salvation Army Band**			
92-11-001	Woman With Kettle	J. Byers	Open	64.00	64.00
92-11-002	Woman With Kettle (1992 version)	J. Byers	Closed	64.00	90-150.
93-11-003	Man With Cornet	J. Byers	Open	54.00	54.00
93-11-004	Woman With Tambourine	J. Byers	Open	58.00	58.00
Byers' Choice Ltd.		**The Nutcracker**			
93-12-001	Marie (1st Edition)	J. Byers	Closed	52.00	80-175.
94-12-002	Fritz (1st Edition)	J. Byers	Yr.Iss.	56.00	56.00
94-12-003	Marie (2nd Edition)	J. Byers	Yr.Iss.	53.00	53.00
Byers' Choice Ltd.		**Children of The World**			
92-13-001	Dutch Boy	J. Byers	Closed	50.00	105-300.
92-13-002	Dutch Girl	J. Byers	Closed	50.00	105-300.

	ARTIST	EDITION	ISSUE	QUOTE
93-13-003 Bavarian Boy	J. Byers	Closed	50.00	90-175.
94-13-004 Irish Girl	J. Byers	Yr.Iss.	50.00	50.00
Byers' Choice Ltd.	**Wayside Country Store Exclusives**			
86-14-001 Colonial Lamplighter s/n	J. Byers	600	46.00	500-750.
87-14-002 Colonial Watchman s/n	J. Byers	600	49.00	400-500.
88-14-003 Colonial Lady s/n	J. Byers	600	49.00	275-350.
Byers' Choice Ltd.	**Snow Goose Exclusive**			
88-15-001 Man with Goose	J. Byers	600	60.00	300.00
Byers' Choice Ltd.	**Country Christmas Store Exclusive**			
88-16-001 Toymaker	J. Byers	600	59.00	750-975.
Byers' Choice Ltd.	**Woodstock Inn Exclusives**			
87-17-001 Skier Boy	J. Byers	200	40.00	250-350.
87-17-002 Skier Girl	J. Byers	200	40.00	250-350.
88-17-003 Woodstock Lady	J. Byers	N/A	41.00	250.00
88-17-004 Woodstock Man	J. Byers	N/A	41.00	250.00
88-17-005 Sugarin Kids (Woodstock)	J. Byers	N/A	41.00	300.00
Byers' Choice Ltd.	**Stacy's Gifts & Collectibles Exclusives**			
87-18-001 Santa in Rocking Chair with Boy	J. Byers	100	130.00	550.00
87-18-002 Santa in Rocking Chair with Girl	J. Byers	100	130.00	450.00
Byers' Choice Ltd.	**Port-O-Call Exclusives**			
87-19-001 Cherub Angel-pink	J. Byers	Closed	N/A	125.00
87-19-002 Cherub Angel-rose	J. Byers	Closed	N/A	125.00
87-19-003 Cherub Angel-blue	J. Byers	Closed	N/A	225.00
87-19-004 Cherub Angel-cream	J. Byers	Closed	N/A	400.00
Rick Cain Studios	**Master Series**			
85-01-001 Box Turtle	R. Cain	5,000	66.00	66.00
85-01-002 Woodland Spirit	R. Cain	5,000	165.00	165.00
85-01-003 Featherview	R. Cain	Retrd.	151.80	151.80
85-01-004 Catchmaster	R. Cain	Retrd.	184.80	184.80
85-01-005 Nightmaster	R. Cain	Retrd.	184.80	184.80
85-01-006 Tidemaster	R. Cain	5,000	242.00	242.00
85-01-007 Sea View	R. Cain	S/O	70.40	70.40
86-01-008 Wind Horse	R. Cain	S/O	70.00	70.00
86-01-009 African Youth	R. Cain	5,000	137.00	137.00
86-01-010 Marshkeeper	R. Cain	5,000	231.00	231.00
86-01-011 Tropical Flame	R. Cain	Retrd.	209.00	209.00
86-01-012 Dragon Sprout	R. Cain	S/O	92.50	92.50
86-01-013 Elder	R. Cain	S/O	550.00	550.00
86-01-014 Aerial Hunter	R. Cain	S/O	70.40	70.40
86-01-015 Sandmaster	R. Cain	5,000	93.00	93.00
87-01-016 Habitat	R. Cain	5,000	93.00	93.00
87-01-017 Liquid Universe	R. Cain	5,000	540.00	540.00
87-01-018 Winged Fortress	R. Cain	5,000	363.00	363.00
87-01-019 Sentinel Crest	R. Cain	S/O	121.00	121.00
87-01-020 Teller	R. Cain	Retrd.	308.00	308.00
87-01-021 Yore Castle	R. Cain	Retrd.	165.00	165.00
87-01-022 Dragonflies Dance	R. Cain	Retrd.	55.00	55.00
87-01-023 Dragon Sprout II	R. Cain	5,000	159.00	159.00
88-01-024 Paradise Found	R. Cain	Retrd.	308.00	308.00
88-01-025 Watercourse Way	R. Cain	5,000	99.00	99.00
88-01-026 Old Man of the Forest	R. Cain	Retrd.	132.00	132.00
88-01-027 Orbist	R. Cain	Retrd.	108.00	108.00
88-01-028 Heron Pass	R. Cain	5,000	231.00	231.00
88-01-029 Lady Reflecting	R. Cain	5,000	93.00	93.00
88-01-030 Fair Atlantis	R. Cain	Retrd.	319.00	319.00
88-01-031 Guardian	R. Cain	Retrd.	325.00	325.00
88-01-032 The Balance	R. Cain	Retrd.	374.00	374.00
88-01-033 Blackberry Summer	R. Cain	Retrd.	165.00	165.00
89-01-034 Encompass	R. Cain	5,000	104.00	104.00
89-01-035 Innerview	R. Cain	5,000	84.00	84.00
89-01-036 Universes	R. Cain	5,000	115.00	115.00
89-01-037 Domain	R. Cain	Retrd.	187.00	187.00
89-01-038 Hatchling	R. Cain	Retrd.	85.00	85.00
90-01-039 Wood Flight	R. Cain	S/O	105.50	105.50
90-01-040 Pathfinder	R. Cain	S/O	101.00	101.00
90-01-041 Scarlett Wing	R. Cain	Retrd.	101.00	101.00
90-01-042 Tropic Array	R. Cain	2,000	100.00	100.00
90-01-043 Falcon Lore	R. Cain	S/O	86.00	86.00
90-01-044 Pondering	R. Cain	2,000	108.00	108.00
90-01-045 Rising Shadow	R. Cain	2,000	187.00	187.00
90-01-046 Dark Feather	R. Cain	S/O	86.00	86.00
90-01-047 Searchers	R. Cain	2,000	174.00	174.00
90-01-048 Dual Motion	R. Cain	2,000	185.00	185.00
90-01-049 Aquarian	R. Cain	2,000	203.00	203.00
90-01-050 Majestic Cradle	R. Cain	900	440.00	440.00
91-01-051 Cain Sign	R. Cain	Open	55.00	55.00
91-01-052 Alpha Sprout	R. Cain	2,000	99.00	99.00
91-01-053 Pride	R. Cain	2,000	105.00	105.00
91-01-054 Cheetah	R. Cain	2,000	105.00	105.00
91-01-055 Soft Wave	R. Cain	2,000	121.00	121.00
91-01-056 Cameo	R. Cain	2,000	154.00	154.00
91-01-057 La Kimono	R. Cain	2,000	176.00	176.00
91-01-058 Spirit Dog	R. Cain	S/O	198.00	198.00
91-01-059 Thunderbowl	R. Cain	2,000	242.00	242.00
91-01-060 Blossom	R. Cain	2,000	99.00	99.00
91-01-061 Jungle Graces	R. Cain	2,000	110.00	110.00
91-01-062 Aerial Victor	R. Cain	2,000	115.00	115.00
92-01-063 Bathing Hole	R. Cain	2,000	102.00	102.00
92-01-064 The Pack	R. Cain	S/O	105.50	105.50
92-01-065 Prairie Thunder	R. Cain	2,000	110.00	110.00
92-01-066 Leading Wolf	R. Cain	S/O	143.00	143.00
92-01-067 Medicine Hawk	R. Cain	2,000	187.00	187.00
92-01-068 Spirit Eagle	R. Cain	S/O	121.00	121.00
92-01-069 Three Bears	R. Cain	2,000	187.00	187.00
92-01-070 Seven Bears	R. Cain	S/O	231.00	231.00
92-01-071 Power of One	R. Cain	2,000	77.00	77.00
92-01-072 Radiance	R. Cain	2,000	132.00	132.00
93-01-073 Wood Song	R. Cain	S/O	143.00	143.00
93-01-074 Wolf Crossing	R. Cain	2,000	715.00	715.00
93-01-075 Fountain of Youth	R. Cain	2,000	132.00	132.00
93-01-076 Rites of Passage	R. Cain	2,000	165.00	165.00
93-01-077 Arctic Moon	R. Cain	S/O	231.00	231.00
93-01-078 Dark Shadow	R. Cain	900	1650.00	1650.00
93-01-079 Wolf Trail	R. Cain	S/O	121.00	121.00
93-01-080 Medicine Bowl	R. Cain	2,000	220.00	220.00
93-01-081 Little Bears	R. Cain	2,000	220.00	220.00
93-01-082 Spirit Totem	R. Cain	S/O	286.00	286.00

	ARTIST	EDITION	ISSUE	QUOTE
93-01-083 Speaks to Strangers	R. Cain	2,000	132.00	132.00
93-01-084 Buffalo's Son	R. Cain	2,000	143.00	143.00
93-01-085 Steppin' Wolf	R. Cain	S/O	210.00	210.00
93-01-086 Where Bear	R. Cain	2,000	253.00	253.00
93-01-087 Arctic Son	R. Cain	S/O	275.00	275.00
94-01-088 Rebirth	R. Cain	2,000	180.00	180.00
94-01-089 Waiting Wolf	R. Cain	S/O	198.00	198.00
94-01-090 Moon Walk	R. Cain	S/O	198.00	198.00
94-01-091 Forest Nimble	R. Cain	2,000	218.00	218.00
94-01-092 Wolf Prince	R. Cain	2,000	325.00	325.00
94-01-093 Four Bears	R. Cain	2,000	1100.00	1100.00
94-01-094 Bear Rising	R. Cain	2,000	180.00	180.00
94-01-095 Vision Bear	R. Cain	2,000	250.00	250.00
94-01-096 Flight Feathers	R. Cain	1,500	180.00	180.00
94-01-097 Mountain Pass	R. Cain	2,000	180.00	180.00
94-01-098 Ivory Hunter	R. Cain	2,500	210.00	210.00
94-01-099 Dragon's Dream	R. Cain	1,500	240.00	240.00
94-01-100 Spirit of the Mountain	R. Cain	2,000	350.00	350.00
Rick Cain Studios	**Vision Quest**			
91-02-001 Silver Shadow	R. Cain	2,000	176.00	176.00
92-02-002 Alphascape	R. Cain	S/O	210.00	210.00
93-02-003 White Vision	R. Cain	2,000	242.00	242.00
Rick Cain Studios	**Eco-Sculpture**			
91-03-001 Highland Voyager	R. Cain	2,000	132.00	132.00
91-03-002 Orchestration	R. Cain	2,000	132.00	132.00
92-03-003 Polar Eclipse	R. Cain	2,000	110.00	110.00
Rick Cain Studios	**Gallery I**			
92-04-001 Wind Spirit	R. Cain	1,500	1650.00	1650.00
92-04-002 American Dream	R. Cain	500	3300.00	3300.00
93-04-003 Raven Shadow	R. Cain	900	2200.00	2200.00
Rick Cain Studios	**Birds of Prey (Miniatures)**			
92-05-001 Bald Eagle	R. Cain	3,000	49.50	49.50
92-05-002 Golden Eagle	R. Cain	3,000	49.50	49.50
92-05-003 Kestrel Hawk	R. Cain	3,000	49.50	49.50
92-05-004 Night Owl	R. Cain	3,000	49.50	49.50
92-05-005 Peregrine Falcon	R. Cain	3,000	49.50	49.50
92-05-006 Red Tail Hawk	R. Cain	3,000	49.50	49.50
Rick Cain Studios	**Path of the Sacred Journey**			
94-06-001 Tales of Old	R. Cain	2,500	250.00	250.00
Rick Cain Studios	**Wolf Fragments**			
94-07-001 Devining Wolf	R. Cain	3,000	110.00	110.00
94-07-002 Pinnacle	R. Cain	3,000	110.00	110.00
Rick Cain Studios	**Collectors Guild**			
92-08-001 High Point	R. Cain	S/O	82.00	82.00
92-08-002 Visor	R. Cain	Retrd.	Gift	N/A
93-08-003 Strider	R. Cain	S/O	82.00	82.00
93-08-004 Star Shadow	R. Cain	Retrd.	Gift	N/A
94-08-005 Midnight Son	R. Cain	Yr.Iss.	297.00	297.00
94-08-006 Arctic Moon II	R. Cain	Yr.Iss.	Gift	N/A
Calabar Creations	**Little Farmers**			
93-01-001 Playful Kittens LF73016	P. Apsit	5,000	64.00	64.00
93-01-002 Going Home LF73027	P. Apsit	5,000	64.00	64.00
93-01-003 It's Not For You LF73038	P. Apsit	5,000	64.00	64.00
93-01-004 Surprise! LF73046	P. Apsit	5,000	60.00	60.00
93-01-005 Oops! LF73058	P. Apsit	5,000	64.00	64.00
93-01-006 Caring Friend LF73066	P. Apsit	5,000	57.00	57.00
93-01-007 Little Lumber Joe LF73077	P. Apsit	5,000	64.00	64.00
93-01-008 True Love LF73087	P. Apsit	5,000	45.00	45.00
93-01-009 Piggy Ride LF73097	P. Apsit	5,000	45.00	45.00
93-01-010 Between Chores LF73105	P. Apsit	5,000	40.00	40.00
93-01-011 Lunch Express LF73117	P. Apsit	5,000	76.00	76.00
93-01-012 Apple Delivery LF73127	P. Apsit	5,000	54.00	54.00
93-01-013 Vita-Veggie Vendor LF73137	P. Apsit	5,000	62.00	62.00
93-01-014 LF Signature Piece LF73147	P. Apsit	Open	40.00	40.00
Calabar Creations	**Red Moon Children**			
93-02-001 Bashful Brave RM67415	R. Myer	5,000	35.00	35.00
93-02-002 Temptations RM67426	R. Myer	5,000	40.00	40.00
93-02-003 I Said Forward! RM67438	R. Myer	5,000	35.00	35.00
93-02-004 Sunset Duet RM67445	R. Myer	5,000	35.00	35.00
93-02-005 Practice Makes Perfect RM67465	R. Myer	5,000	30.00	30.00
93-02-006 Tickle My Fancy RM67475	R. Myer	5,000	37.00	37.00
93-02-007 Reputable Rainmakers RM67486	R. Myer	5,000	30.00	30.00
93-02-008 I Saw It First RM67496	R. Myer	5,000	35.00	35.00
93-02-009 Tying the Knot RM67506	R. Myer	5,000	35.00	35.00
93-02-010 Deer Talk RM67516	R. Myer	5,000	30.00	30.00
93-02-011 Puzzled RM67525	R. Myer	5,000	35.00	35.00
93-02-012 Big Sister RM67535	R. Myer	5,000	35.00	35.00
Calabar Creations	**Santaventure**			
93-03-001 Cart O' Plenty SV73737	P. Apsit	5,000	66.00	66.00
93-03-002 Pilgrim Santa SV73748	P. Apsit	5,000	59.00	59.00
93-03-003 Hooray For Santa SV73757	P. Apsit	5,000	59.00	59.00
93-03-004 A Pinch of Advice SV73768	P. Apsit	5,000	68.00	68.00
93-03-005 Santa Tested SV73778	P. Apsit	5,000	68.00	68.00
93-03-006 Nuts For You SV73787	P. Apsit	5,000	59.00	59.00
93-03-007 Santa's Sack Attack SV73796	P. Apsit	5,000	60.00	60.00
94-03-008 The Last Mile SV73806	P. Apsit	5,000	54.00	54.00
94-03-009 In His Dream SV73816	P. Apsit	5,000	78.00	78.00
94-03-010 Reindeer's Strike SV73827	P. Apsit	5,000	54.00	54.00
94-03-011 Almost Done SV73836	P. Apsit	5,000	50.00	50.00
94-03-012 Viola! SV73847	P. Apsit	5,000	50.00	50.00
94-03-013 Signature Piece SV73577	P. Apsit	5,000	60.00	60.00
Calabar Creations	**Tee Club**			
93-04-001 Prac-Tees TC73858	P. Apsit	5,000	66.00	66.00
93-04-002 Putt-Teeing TC73868	P. Apsit	5,000	66.00	66.00
93-04-003 Teed-Off TC73877	P. Apsit	5,000	60.00	60.00
93-04-004 Old Tee-Mer TC73887	P. Apsit	5,000	78.00	78.00
93-04-005 Certain-Tee TC73898	P. Apsit	5,000	100.00	100.00
93-04-006 Naugh-Tee TC73908	P. Apsit	5,000	56.00	56.00
Calabar Creations	**Yesterday's Friends**			
93-05-001 Freewheeling RW74436	P. Apsit	7,500	48.00	48.00
93-05-002 Bluester RW74446	P. Apsit	7,500	44.00	44.00
93-05-003 Bayou Boys RW74456	P. Apsit	3,500	80.00	80.00
93-05-004 Buddies RW74466	P. Apsit	7,500	50.00	50.00

	ARTIST	EDITION	ISSUE	QUOTE
93-05-005 Mike's Magic RW74475	P. Apsit	7,500	37.00	37.00
93-05-006 Jazzy Bubble RW74486	P. Apsit	7,500	37.00	37.00
93-05-007 Dinner For Two RW74496	P. Apsit	7,500	38.00	38.00
93-05-008 Interference RW74506	P. Apsit	7,500	42.00	42.00
93-05-009 Strike So Sweet RW74517	P. Apsit	7,500	42.00	42.00
94-05-010 Caddle Chris RW74527	P. Apsit	7,500	34.00	34.00
93-05-011 Hop-a-Long Pete RW74539	P. Apsit	3,500	80.00	80.00
93-05-012 Me Big Chief RW74548	P. Apsit	7,500	56.00	56.00
93-05-013 Tug-a-Leg RW74557	P. Apsit	7,500	56.00	56.00
94-05-014 Equipment Manager RW74596	P. Apsit	7,500	56.00	56.00
94-05-015 Scrub-a-Swine RW74606	P. Apsit	7,500	56.00	56.00
94-05-016 Read All About It RW74616	P. Apsit	7,500	56.00	56.00
94-05-017 What A Smile RW74626	P. Apsit	7,500	56.00	56.00
94-05-018 Goose Loose RW74635	P. Apsit	7,500	56.00	56.00
94-05-019 Tuba Notes RW74688	P. Apsit	7,500	56.00	56.00
94-05-020 Read-A-Thon RW74694	P. Apsit	7,500	56.00	56.00
94-05-021 Cornered RW74707	P. Apsit	7,500	56.00	56.00
94-05-022 Parade RW74716	P. Apsit	7,500	56.00	56.00
94-05-023 Excess RW74726	P. Apsit	7,500	56.00	56.00
94-05-024 Funny Frog RW74745	P. Apsit	7,500	56.00	56.00
94-05-025 Signature Piece RW74737	P. Apsit	Open	54.00	54.00
Calabar Creations	**Daddy's Girl**			
94-06-001 All Aboard! DA74804	P. Apsit	5,000	20.00	20.00
94-06-002 Discovery DA74816	P. Apsit	5,000	28.00	28.00
94-06-003 Teddy Talks DA74826	P. Apsit	5,000	40.00	40.00
94-06-004 Moil DA74834	P. Apsit	5,000	20.00	20.00
94-06-005 Peek-A-Boo DA74843	P. Apsit	5,000	20.00	20.00
94-06-006 Spring Harvest DA74856	P. Apsit	5,000	28.00	28.00
Calabar Creations	**Little Professionals**			
94-07-001 Little Miss Market LP75046	P. Apsit	5,000	40.00	40.00
94-07-002 Little Angelo LP75057	P. Apsit	5,000	38.00	38.00
94-07-003 Little Florence LP75065	P. Apsit	5,000	44.00	44.00
Calabar Creations	**Angelic Pigasus**			
94-08-001 Angelica AP75315	P. Apsit	Open	24.00	24.00
94-08-002 Anna AP75324	P. Apsit	Open	22.00	22.00
94-08-003 Angelo AP75335	P. Apsit	Open	24.00	24.00
94-08-004 Aria AP75343	P. Apsit	Open	12.00	12.00
94-08-005 Alba AP75353	P. Apsit	Open	12.00	12.00
Calabar Creations	**Pig Hollow**			
94-09-001 Just Cute PH75442	P. Apsit	Open	9.00	9.00
94-09-002 Pillow Talk PH75453	P. Apsit	Open	12.00	12.00
94-09-003 Move Please PH75462	P. Apsit	Open	11.00	11.00
94-09-004 Barn Fun PH75474	P. Apsit	Open	15.00	15.00
94-09-005 Time For School PH75484	P. Apsit	Open	15.00	15.00
94-09-006 Nap Time PH75492	P. Apsit	Open	11.00	11.00
94-09-007 Sweet Corn PH75503	P. Apsit	Open	9.00	9.00
94-09-008 Old McPig PH75513	P. Apsit	Open	11.00	11.00
94-09-009 Mary Pig PH75524	P. Apsit	Open	11.00	11.00
94-09-010 Going South PH75533	P. Apsit	Open	11.00	11.00
94-09-011 The After Picture PH75544	P. Apsit	Open	12.00	12.00
94-09-012 Reddie PH75554	P. Apsit	Open	12.00	12.00
94-09-013 Signature Piece PH75565	P. Apsit	Open	19.00	19.00
Cast Art Industries	**Dreamsicles**			
92-01-001 Limited Edtion Cherub-DC111	K. Haynes	Retrd.	50.00	50.00
92-01-002 Limited Edition Cherub-DC112	K. Haynes	Retrd.	50.00	50.00
92-01-003 My Funny Valentine-DC201	K. Haynes	Suspd.	17.00	17.00
92-01-004 Cupid's Bow-DC202	K. Haynes	Suspd.	27.00	27.00
92-01-005 Flying Lesson Limited Edition-DC251	K. Haynes	Retrd.	80.00	125-150.
93-01-006 Teeter Tots Limited Edition-DC252	K. Haynes	Retrd.	100.00	100.00
93-01-007 By the Silvery Moon-Limited Edition DC253	K. Haynes	Retrd.	100.00	175.00
94-01-008 The Recital-Limited Editon DC254	K. Haynes	Retrd.	135.00	150.00
91-01-009 Small Cherub with Hanging Ribbon-5104	K. Haynes	Suspd.	10.00	10.00
92-01-010 Bunny Wall Plaque-5018	K. Haynes	Suspd.	22.00	22.00
92-01-011 Bunny Wall Plaque-5019	K. Haynes	Suspd.	22.00	22.00
91-01-012 Cherub Wall Plaque-5130	K. Haynes	Suspd.	15.00	15.00
91-01-013 Cherub Wall Plaque-5131	K. Haynes	Suspd.	15.00	15.00
91-01-014 Musician w/Trumpet-5151	K. Haynes	Suspd.	22.00	22.00
91-01-015 Musician w/Drums-5152	K. Haynes	Suspd.	22.00	22.00
91-01-016 Musician w/Flute-5153	K. Haynes	Suspd.	22.00	22.00
91-01-017 Musician w/Cymbals-5154	K. Haynes	Suspd.	22.00	22.00
91-01-018 Octagonal Ballerina Box-5700	K. Haynes	Suspd.	9.00	9.00
91-01-019 Small Heart "I Love You" Box-5701	K. Haynes	Suspd.	9.00	9.00
91-01-020 Small Square Dinosaur Box-5702	K. Haynes	Suspd.	9.00	9.00
91-01-021 Small Rectangle "Dicky Duck" Box-5703	K. Haynes	Suspd.	9.00	9.00
91-01-022 Speed Racer Box-5750	K. Haynes	Suspd.	14.00	14.00
91-01-023 Medium Heart Cherub Box-5751	K. Haynes	Suspd.	14.00	14.00
91-01-024 Queen Rectangle Cat Box-5800	K. Haynes	Suspd.	28.75	28.75
91-01-025 Queen Round Bears Box-5801	K. Haynes	Suspd.	28.75	28.75
91-01-026 "You're Special" Box-5802	K. Haynes	Suspd.	28.75	28.75
91-01-027 Train Box-5803	K. Haynes	Suspd.	28.75	28.75
91-01-028 Queen Octagonal Cherub Box-5804	K. Haynes	Suspd.	26.00	26.00
91-01-029 King Heart "I Love You" Box-5850	K. Haynes	Suspd.	37.50	37.50
91-01-030 King Oval Cow Box-5860	K. Haynes	Suspd.	55.00	55.00
93-01-031 Lg. Candle Holder Boy-DC138	K. Haynes	12/94	20.00	20.00
93-01-032 Lg. Candle Holder Girl-DC139	K. Haynes	12/94	20.00	20.00
Cast Art Industries	**Dreamsicles Christmas**			
91-02-001 Santa Bunny-DX203	K. Haynes	Yr.Iss.	32.00	32.00
92-02-002 Santa In Dreamsicle Land-DX247	K. Haynes	Yr.Iss.	85.00	85.00
93-02-003 The Finishing Touches-DX248	K. Haynes	Yr.Iss.	85.00	85.00
94-02-004 Holiday on Ice-DX249	K. Haynes	Yr.Iss.	85.00	85.00
Cast Art Industries	**Dreamsicles Animals**			
91-03-001 Hippity Hop- DA106	K. Haynes	12/94	31.00	31.00
91-03-002 Mr. Bunny- DA107	K. Haynes	12/94	27.00	27.00
91-03-003 Mrs. Bunny- DA108	K. Haynes	12/94	27.00	27.00
91-03-004 King Rabbit-DA124	K. Haynes	12/94	66.00	66.00
92-03-005 St. Peter Rabbit-DA243	K. Haynes	12/94	29.00	29.00
92-03-006 Pumpkin Harvest-DA322	K. Haynes	12/94	19.00	19.00
91-03-007 Mutton Chops-DA326	K. Haynes	12/94	7.50	7.50
91-03-008 Wooly Bully-DA327	K. Haynes	12/94	9.00	9.00
91-03-009 Lambie Pie-DA328	K. Haynes	12/94	9.00	9.00
91-03-010 Buddy Bear-DA451	K. Haynes	12/94	7.50	7.50
91-03-011 Mama Bear-DA452	K. Haynes	12/94	9.00	9.00
92-03-012 Winter's Comin'-DA471	K. Haynes	Suspd.	10.00	10.00
91-03-013 Mouse on Skis-DA475	K. Haynes	Suspd.	17.00	17.00
91-03-014 P.J. Mouse-DA476	K. Haynes	12/94	10.00	10.00
91-03-015 Mother Mouse-DA477	K. Haynes	12/94	10.00	10.00

	ARTIST	EDITION	ISSUE	QUOTE
92-03-016 Dino-DA480	K. Haynes	12/94	14.00	14.00
92-03-017 Rhino-DA481	K. Haynes	12/94	14.00	14.00
92-03-018 Dodo-DA482	K. Haynes	12/94	9.00	9.00
92-03-019 Fat Cat-DA555	K. Haynes	12/94	26.00	26.00
92-03-020 Man's Best Friend-DA560	K. Haynes	12/94	11.00	11.00
92-03-021 Puppy Love-DA562	K. Haynes	12/94	12.00	12.00
92-03-022 Red Rover-DA566	K. Haynes	12/94	17.00	17.00
92-03-023 Scooter-DA567	K. Haynes	12/94	11.00	11.00
92-03-024 Hound Dog-DA568	K. Haynes	12/94	11.00	11.00
92-03-025 Lazy Bones-DA605	K. Haynes	Suspd.	14.00	14.00
92-03-026 Papa Pelican-DA602	K. Haynes	12/94	22.00	22.00
92-03-027 Octopus' Garden-DA606	K. Haynes	Suspd.	10.00	10.00
92-03-028 Crabby-DA607	K. Haynes	Suspd.	8.00	8.00
92-03-029 Blowfish-DA608	K. Haynes	Suspd.	10.00	10.00
92-03-030 Largemouth-DA609	K. Haynes	Suspd.	8.00	8.00
92-03-031 Needlenose-DA610	K. Haynes	Suspd.	8.00	8.00
92-03-032 Double fish-DA611	K. Haynes	Suspd.	8.00	8.00
92-03-033 Beach Baby-DA615	K. Haynes	12/94	26.00	26.00
92-03-034 Splash-DA616	K. Haynes	12/94	26.00	26.00
91-03-035 Socrates the Sheep-5029	K. Haynes	Suspd.	18.00	18.00
91-03-036 Ricky Raccoon-5170	K. Haynes	Suspd.	27.00	27.00
91-03-037 Armadillo-5176	K. Haynes	Suspd.	14.00	14.00
Cast Art Industries	**Cuckoo Corners**			
93-04-001 Dolly House-CC061	K. Haynes	12/94	22.00	22.00
93-04-002 Faith Flower Power-CC062	K. Haynes	12/94	27.00	27.00
93-04-003 Beth Friend-CC063	K. Haynes	12/94	22.00	22.00
93-04-004 Heidi Hoedown-CC064	K. Haynes	12/94	27.00	27.00
Cast Art Industries	**Animal Attractions**			
93-05-001 Udderly Ridiculous-AA002	S.&G. Hackett	12/94	28.00	28.00
93-05-002 Undelivered Mail-AA015	S.&G. Hackett	12/94	15.00	15.00
93-05-003 Feeding Time-AA016	S.&G. Hackett	12/94	10.00	10.00
93-05-004 Cat Dancing-AA026	S.&G. Hackett	12/94	21.00	21.00
Cast Art Industries	**Dreamsicles Collectors Club**			
93-06-001 A Star is Born-CD001	K. Haynes	Retrd.	Gift	N/A
94-06-002 Daydream Believer-CD100	K. Haynes	Yr.Iss.	29.95	29.95
94-06-003 Join The Fun-CD002	K. Haynes	Yr.Iss.	Gift	N/A
94-06-004 Makin' A List-CD101	K. Haynes	Yr.Iss.	47.95	47.95
The Cat's Meow	**Series I**			
83-01-001 Federal House	F. Jones	Retrd.	8.00	60-135.
83-01-002 Inn	F. Jones	Retrd.	8.00	450.00
83-01-003 Garrison House	F. Jones	Retrd.	8.00	60-100.
83-01-004 Victorian House	F. Jones	Retrd.	8.00	60-100.
83-01-005 School	F. Jones	Retrd.	8.00	60-100.
83-01-006 Barbershop	F. Jones	Retrd.	8.00	60-135.
83-01-007 Sweetshop	F. Jones	Retrd.	8.00	100-135.
83-01-008 Book Store	F. Jones	Retrd.	8.00	60-100.
83-01-009 Antique Shop	F. Jones	Retrd.	8.00	60-150.
83-01-010 Florist Shop	F. Jones	Retrd.	8.00	60-150.
83-01-011 Toy Shoppe	F. Jones	Retrd.	8.00	100-600.
83-01-012 Apothecary	F. Jones	Retrd.	8.00	125-135.
83-01-013 Set	F. Jones	Retrd.	96.00	13-3200.
The Cat's Meow	**Series II**			
84-02-001 Grandinere House	F. Jones	Retrd.	8.00	75-80.00
84-02-002 Brocke House	F. Jones	Retrd.	8.00	35-95.00
84-02-003 Eaton House	F. Jones	Retrd.	8.00	80-150.
84-02-004 Church	F. Jones	Retrd.	8.00	60-175.
84-02-005 Town Hall	F. Jones	Retrd.	8.00	150.00
84-02-006 Music Shop	F. Jones	Retrd.	8.00	60-200.
84-02-007 Attorney/Bank	F. Jones	Retrd.	8.00	40-125.
84-02-008 S&T Clothiers	F. Jones	Retrd.	8.00	60.00
84-02-009 Millinery/Quilt	F. Jones	Retrd.	8.00	35-95.00
84-02-010 Tobacconist/Shoemaker	F. Jones	Retrd.	8.00	90-100.
84-02-011 Set	F. Jones	Retrd.	96.00	15-2500.
The Cat's Meow	**Series III**			
85-03-001 Hobart-Harley House	F. Jones	Retrd.	8.00	26-50.00
85-03-002 Kalorama Guest House	F. Jones	Retrd.	8.00	26-50.00
85-03-003 Allen-Coe House	F. Jones	Retrd.	8.00	26-50.00
85-03-004 Opera House	F. Jones	Retrd.	8.00	26-50.00
85-03-005 Connecticut Ave. FireHouse	F. Jones	Retrd.	8.00	26-50.00
85-03-006 Dry Goods Store	F. Jones	Retrd.	8.00	26-50.00
85-03-007 Fine Jewelers	F. Jones	Retrd.	8.00	26-50.00
85-03-008 Edinburgh Times	F. Jones	Retrd.	8.00	26-50.00
85-03-009 Main St. Carriage Shop	F. Jones	Retrd.	8.00	26-50.00
85-03-010 Ristorante	F. Jones	Retrd.	8.00	26-50.00
85-03-011 Set	F. Jones	Retrd.	80.00	330-475.
The Cat's Meow	**Series IV**			
86-04-001 John Belville House	F. Jones	Retrd.	8.00	20-40.00
86-04-002 Westbrook House	F. Jones	Retrd.	8.00	20-40.00
86-04-003 Bennington-Hull House	F. Jones	Retrd.	8.00	20-40.00
86-04-004 Vandenberg House	F. Jones	Retrd.	8.00	20-40.00
86-04-005 Chepachet Union Church	F. Jones	Retrd.	8.00	20-40.00
86-04-006 Chagrin Falls Popcorn Shop	F. Jones	Retrd.	8.00	20-40.00
86-04-007 O'Malley's Livery Stable	F. Jones	Retrd.	8.00	20-40.00
86-04-008 The Little House Giftables	F. Jones	Retrd.	8.00	20-40.00
86-04-009 Jones Bros. Tea Co.	F. Jones	Retrd.	8.00	20-40.00
86-04-010 Village Clock Shop	F. Jones	Retrd.	8.00	20-40.00
86-04-011 Set	F. Jones	Retrd.	80.00	200-275.
The Cat's Meow	**Series V**			
87-05-001 Murray Hotel	F. Jones	Retrd.	8.00	14-27.00
87-05-002 Congruity Tavern	F. Jones	Retrd.	8.00	14-27.00
87-05-003 M. Washington House	F. Jones	Retrd.	8.00	14-27.00
87-05-004 Creole House	F. Jones	Retrd.	8.00	14-27.00
87-05-005 Police Department	F. Jones	Retrd.	8.00	14-27.00
87-05-006 Markethouse	F. Jones	Retrd.	8.00	14-27.00
87-05-007 Southport Bank	F. Jones	Retrd.	8.00	14-27.00
87-05-008 Amish Oak/Dixie Shoe	F. Jones	Retrd.	8.00	14-27.00
87-05-009 Dentist/Physician	F. Jones	Retrd.	8.00	14-27.00
87-05-010 Architect/Tailor	F. Jones	Retrd.	8.00	14-27.00
87-05-011 Set	F. Jones	Retrd.	80.00	180-230.
The Cat's Meow	**Series VI**			
88-06-001 Burton Lancaster House	F. Jones	Retrd.	8.00	12-19.00
88-06-002 Ohliger House	F. Jones	Retrd.	8.00	12-19.00
88-06-003 Stiffenbody Funeral Home	F. Jones	Retrd.	8.00	12-19.00
88-06-004 Pruyn House	F. Jones	Retrd.	8.00	12-19.00
88-06-005 First Baptist Church	F. Jones	Retrd.	8.00	12-19.00
88-06-006 City Hospital	F. Jones	Retrd.	8.00	12-19.00

	ARTIST	EDITION	ISSUE	QUOTE
88-06-007 Lincoln School	F. Jones	Retrd.	8.00	12-19.00
88-06-008 Fish/Meat Market	F. Jones	Retrd.	8.00	12-19.00
88-06-009 New Masters Gallery	F. Jones	Retrd.	8.00	12-19.00
88-06-010 Williams & Sons	F. Jones	Retrd.	8.00	12-19.00
88-06-011 Set	F. Jones	Retrd.	80.00	100-150.
The Cat's Meow	**Series VII**			
89-07-001 Thorpe House Bed & Breakfast	F. Jones	12/94	8.00	10.00
89-07-002 Justice of the Peace	F. Jones	12/94	8.00	10.00
89-07-003 Old Franklin Book Shop	F. Jones	12/94	8.00	10.00
89-07-004 Octagonal School	F. Jones	12/94	8.00	10.00
89-07-005 Winkler Bakery	F. Jones	12/94	8.00	10.00
89-07-006 Black Cat Antiques	F. Jones	12/94	8.00	10.00
89-07-007 Village Tinsmith	F. Jones	12/94	8.00	10.00
89-07-008 Williams Apothecary	F. Jones	12/94	8.00	10.00
89-07-009 Handcrafted Toys	F. Jones	12/94	8.00	10.00
89-07-010 Hairdressing Parlor	F. Jones	12/94	8.00	10.00
The Cat's Meow	**Series VIII**			
90-08-001 Puritan House	F. Jones	5-Yr.	8.00	10.00
90-08-002 Haberdashers	F. Jones	5-Yr.	8.00	10.00
90-08-003 Walldorff Furniture	F. Jones	5-Yr.	8.00	10.00
90-08-004 Victoria's Parlour	F. Jones	5-Yr.	8.00	10.00
90-08-005 Globe Corner Bookstore	F. Jones	5-Yr.	8.00	10.00
90-08-006 Medina Fire Department	F. Jones	5-Yr.	8.00	10.00
90-08-007 Piccadilli Pipe & Tobacco	F. Jones	5-Yr.	8.00	10.00
90-08-008 Noah's Ark Veterinary	F. Jones	5-Yr.	8.00	10.00
90-08-009 F.J. Realty Company	F. Jones	5-Yr.	8.00	10.00
90-08-010 Nell's Stems & Stitches	F. Jones	5-Yr.	8.00	10.00
The Cat's Meow	**Series IX**			
91-09-001 Central City Opera House	F. Jones	5-Yr.	8.00	10.00
91-09-002 All Saints Chapel	F. Jones	5-Yr.	8.00	10.00
91-09-003 City Hall	F. Jones	5-Yr.	8.00	10.00
91-09-004 Gov. Snyder Mansion	F. Jones	5-Yr.	8.00	10.00
91-09-005 American Red Cross	F. Jones	5-Yr.	8.00	10.00
91-09-006 The Treble Clef	F. Jones	5-Yr.	8.00	10.00
91-09-007 Osbahr's Upholstery	F. Jones	5-Yr.	8.00	10.00
91-09-008 Spanky's Hardware Co.	F. Jones	5-Yr.	8.00	10.00
91-09-009 CPA/Law Office	F. Jones	5-Yr.	8.00	10.00
91-09-010 Jeweler/Optometrist	F. Jones	5-Yr.	8.00	10.00
The Cat's Meow	**Series X**			
92-10-001 Henyan's Athletic Shop	F. Jones	5-Yr.	8.50	10.00
92-10-002 Grand Haven	F. Jones	5-Yr.	8.50	10.00
92-10-003 Fudge Kitchen	F. Jones	5-Yr.	8.50	10.00
92-10-004 United Church of Acworth	F. Jones	5-Yr.	8.50	10.00
92-10-005 City News	F. Jones	5-Yr.	8.50	10.00
92-10-006 Pure Gas Station	F. Jones	5-Yr.	8.50	10.00
92-10-007 Pickles Pub	F. Jones	5-Yr.	8.50	10.00
92-10-008 Madeline's Dress Shop	F. Jones	5-Yr.	8.50	10.00
92-10-009 Owl And The Pussycat	F. Jones	5-Yr.	8.50	10.00
92-10-010 Leppert's 5 &10	F. Jones	5-Yr.	8.50	10.00
The Cat's Meow	**Series XI**			
93-11-001 Shrimplin & Jones Produce	F. Jones	5-Yr.	9.00	10.00
93-11-002 Johann Singer Boots & Shoes	F. Jones	5-Yr.	9.00	10.00
93-11-003 Haddonfield Bank	F. Jones	5-Yr.	9.00	10.00
93-11-004 Stone's Restaurant	F. Jones	5-Yr.	9.00	10.00
93-11-005 U.S. Post Office	F. Jones	5-Yr.	9.00	10.00
93-11-006 Police-Troop C	F. Jones	5-Yr.	9.00	10.00
93-11-007 Immanuel Church	F. Jones	5-Yr.	9.00	10.00
93-11-008 Barbershop/Gallery	F. Jones	5-Yr.	9.00	10.00
93-11-009 U.S. Armed Forces	F. Jones	5-Yr.	9.00	10.00
93-11-010 Pet Shop/Gift Shop	F. Jones	5-Yr.	9.00	10.00
The Cat's Meow	**Series XII**			
94-12-001 Spread Eagle Tavern	F. Jones	5-Yr.	10.00	10.00
94-12-002 Historical Society	F. Jones	5-Yr.	10.00	10.00
94-12-003 Haddon Hts. Train Depot	F. Jones	5-Yr.	10.00	10.00
94-12-004 Arnold-Lynch Funeral Home	F. Jones	5-Yr.	10.00	10.00
94-12-005 Boyd's Drug Strore	F. Jones	5-Yr.	10.00	10.00
94-12-006 Christmas Tree Hill Gifts	F. Jones	5-Yr.	10.00	10.00
94-12-007 Bedford County Courthouse	F. Jones	5-Yr.	10.00	10.00
94-12-008 Foorman-Morrison House	F. Jones	5-Yr.	10.00	10.00
94-12-009 Masonic Temple	F. Jones	5-Yr.	10.00	10.00
94-12-010 Ritz Theater	F. Jones	5-Yr.	10.00	10.00
The Cat's Meow	**Series XIII**			
95-13-001 Hospital	F. Jones	5-Yr.	10.00	10.00
95-13-002 Alvanas & Coe Barbers	F. Jones	5-Yr.	10.00	10.00
95-13-003 Schneider's Bakery	F. Jones	5-Yr.	10.00	10.00
95-13-004 YMCA	F. Jones	5-Yr.	10.00	10.00
95-13-005 Cedar School	F. Jones	5-Yr.	10.00	10.00
95-13-006 Public Library	F. Jones	5-Yr.	10.00	10.00
95-13-007 Needleworker	F. Jones	5-Yr.	10.00	10.00
95-13-008 Susquehanna Antiques	F. Jones	5-Yr.	10.00	10.00
The Cat's Meow	**Roscoe Village**			
86-14-001 Roscoe General Store	F. Jones	Retrd.	8.00	20-50.00
86-14-002 Jackson Twp. Hall	F. Jones	Retrd.	8.00	20-50.00
86-14-003 Old Warehouse Rest.	F. Jones	Retrd.	8.00	20-50.00
86-14-004 Canal Company	F. Jones	Retrd.	8.00	20-50.00
86-14-005 Set	F. Jones	Retrd.	32.00	100.00
The Cat's Meow	**Fall**			
86-15-001 Mail Pouch Barn	F. Jones	Retrd.	8.00	40-95.00
86-15-002 Vollant Mills	F. Jones	Retrd.	8.00	20-50.00
86-15-003 Grimm's Farmhouse	F. Jones	Retrd.	8.00	20-50.00
86-15-004 Golden Lamb Buttery	F. Jones	Retrd.	8.00	25-35.
86-15-005 Set	F. Jones	Retrd.	32.00	80-160.
The Cat's Meow	**Nautical**			
87-16-001 Monhegan Boat Landing	F. Jones	Retrd.	8.00	18-50.00
87-16-002 Lorain Lighthouse	F. Jones	Retrd.	8.00	18-50.00
87-16-003 Yacht Club	F. Jones	Retrd.	8.00	18-50.00
87-16-004 H & E Ships Chandlery	F. Jones	Retrd.	8.00	18-50.00
87-16-005 Set	F. Jones	Retrd.	32.00	70-75.00
The Cat's Meow	**Main St.**			
87-17-001 Historical Museum	F. Jones	Retrd.	8.00	18-50.00
87-17-002 Franklin Library	F. Jones	Retrd.	8.00	18-50.00
87-17-003 Garden Theatre	F. Jones	Retrd.	8.00	18-50.00
87-17-004 Telegraph/Post Office	F. Jones	Retrd.	8.00	18-50.00
87-17-005 Set	F. Jones	Retrd.	32.00	70-80.00

	ARTIST	EDITION	ISSUE	QUOTE
The Cat's Meow	**Nantucket**			
87-18-001 Nantucket Atheneum	F. Jones	Retrd.	8.00	18-40.00
87-18-002 Unitarian Church	F. Jones	Retrd.	8.00	18-27.00
87-18-003 Maria Mitchell House	F. Jones	Retrd.	8.00	18-27.00
87-18-004 Jared Coffin House	F. Jones	Retrd.	8.00	18-27.00
87-18-005 Set	F. Jones	Retrd.	32.00	70.00
The Cat's Meow	**Hagerstown**			
88-19-001 The Yule Cupboard	F. Jones	Retrd.	8.00	12-18.00
88-19-002 J Hager House	F. Jones	Retrd.	8.00	12-18.00
88-19-003 Miller House	F. Jones	Retrd.	8.00	12-18.00
88-19-004 Woman's Club	F. Jones	Retrd.	8.00	12-18.00
88-19-004 Set	F. Jones	Retrd.	32.00	45-50.00
The Cat's Meow	**Tradesman**			
88-20-001 Hermannhof Winery	F. Jones	Retrd.	8.00	12-24.00
88-20-002 Jenney Grist Mill	F. Jones	Retrd.	8.00	12-24.00
88-20-003 Buckeye Candy & Tobacco	F. Jones	Retrd.	8.00	12-24.00
88-20-004 C.O. Wheel Company	F. Jones	Retrd.	8.00	12-24.00
The Cat's Meow	**Liberty St.**			
88-21-001 County Courthouse	F. Jones	Retrd.	8.00	12-20.00
88-21-002 Wilton Railway Depot	F. Jones	Retrd.	8.00	12-20.00
88-21-003 Graf Printing Co.	F. Jones	Retrd.	8.00	12-20.00
88-21-004 Z. Jones Basketmaker	F. Jones	Retrd.	8.00	12-20.00
The Cat's Meow	**Painted Ladies**			
88-22-001 Lady Elizabeth	F. Jones	Retrd.	8.00	12-18.00
88-22-002 Lady Iris	F. Jones	Retrd.	8.00	12-18.00
88-22-003 Lady Amanda	F. Jones	Retrd.	8.00	12-18.00
88-22-004 Andrews Hotel	F. Jones	Retrd.	8.00	12-18.00
The Cat's Meow	**Wild West**			
89-23-001 F.C. Zimmermann's Gun Shop	F. Jones	Retrd.	8.00	12-18.00
89-23-002 Drink 'em up Saloon	F. Jones	Retrd.	8.00	12-18.00
89-23-003 Wells, Fargo & Co.	F. Jones	Retrd.	8.00	12-18.00
89-23-004 Marshal's Office	F. Jones	Retrd.	8.00	12-18.00
The Cat's Meow	**Market St.**			
89-24-001 Schumacher Mills	F. Jones	Retrd.	8.00	12-18.00
89-24-002 Seville Hardware Store	F. Jones	Retrd.	8.00	12-18.00
89-24-003 West India Goods Store	F. Jones	Retrd.	8.00	12-18.00
89-24-004 Yankee Candle Company	F. Jones	Retrd.	8.00	12-18.00
The Cat's Meow	**Lighthouse**			
90-25-001 Split Rock Lighthouse	F. Jones	5-Yr.	8.00	10.00
90-25-002 Cape Hatteras Lighthouse	F. Jones	5-Yr.	8.00	10.00
90-25-003 Sandy Hook Lighthouse	F. Jones	5-Yr.	8.00	10.00
90-25-004 Admiralty Head	F. Jones	5-Yr.	8.00	10.00
The Cat's Meow	**Ohio Amish**			
91-26-001 Jonas Troyer Home	F. Jones	5-Yr.	8.00	10.00
91-26-002 Ada Mae's Quilt Barn	F. Jones	5-Yr.	8.00	10.00
91-26-003 Eli's Harness Shop	F. Jones	5-Yr.	8.00	10.00
91-26-004 Brown School	F. Jones	5-Yr.	8.00	10.00
The Cat's Meow	**Washington, D.C.**			
91-27-001 U.S. Capitol	F. Jones	5-Yr.	8.00	10.00
91-27-002 White House	F. Jones	5-Yr.	8.00	10.00
91-27-003 National Archives	F. Jones	5-Yr.	8.00	10.00
91-27-004 U.S. Supreme Court	F. Jones	5-Yr.	8.00	10.00
The Cat's Meow	**American Barns**			
92-28-001 Ohio Barn	F. Jones	5-Yr.	8.50	10.00
92-28-002 Bank Barn	F. Jones	5-Yr.	8.50	10.00
92-28-003 Crib Barn	F. Jones	5-Yr.	8.50	10.00
92-28-004 Vermont Barn	F. Jones	5-Yr.	8.50	10.00
The Cat's Meow	**Chippewa Amusement Park**			
93-29-001 Pavilion	F. Jones	5-Yr.	9.00	10.00
93-29-002 Midway	F. Jones	5-Yr.	9.00	10.00
93-29-003 Bath House	F. Jones	5-Yr.	9.00	10.00
93-29-004 Ballroom	F. Jones	5-Yr.	9.00	10.00
The Cat's Meow	**General Store Series**			
93-30-001 Davoll's General Store	F. Jones	5-Yr.	10.00	10.00
93-30-002 Calef's Country Store	F. Jones	5-Yr.	10.00	10.00
93-30-003 S. Woodstock Country Store	F. Jones	5-Yr.	10.00	10.00
93-30-004 Peltier's Market	F. Jones	5-Yr.	10.00	10.00
The Cat's Meow	**Williamsburg Series**			
93-31-001 Bruton Parish	F. Jones	5-Yr.	10.00	10.00
93-31-002 Raleigh Tavern	F. Jones	5-Yr.	10.00	10.00
93-31-003 Grissell Hay Lodging House	F. Jones	5-Yr.	10.00	10.00
93-31-004 Governor's Palace	F. Jones	5-Yr.	10.00	10.00
The Cat's Meow	**West Coast Lighthouse Series**			
94-32-001 Mukilteo Light	F. Jones	5-Yr.	10.00	10.00
94-32-002 East Brother Lighthouse	F. Jones	5-Yr.	10.00	10.00
94-32-003 Heceta Head Light	F. Jones	5-Yr.	10.00	10.00
94-32-004 Point Pinos Light	F. Jones	5-Yr.	10.00	10.00
The Cat's Meow	**Nursery Rhyme Series**			
94-33-001 Crooked House	F. Jones	5-Yr.	10.00	10.00
94-33-002 Peter, Peter Pumpkin Eater	F. Jones	5-Yr.	10.00	10.00
94-33-003 House That Jack Built	F. Jones	5-Yr.	10.00	10.00
94-33-004 Old Woman in the Shoe	F. Jones	5-Yr.	10.00	10.00
The Cat's Meow	**Firehouse Series**			
94-34-001 Denver No. 1	F. Jones	5-Yr.	10.00	10.00
94-34-002 David Crockett No. 1	F. Jones	5-Yr.	10.00	10.00
94-34-003 Toledo No. 18	F. Jones	5-Yr.	10.00	10.00
94-34-004 Vigilant 1891	F. Jones	5-Yr.	10.00	10.00
The Cat's Meow	**Waterfront Series**			
94-35-001 Seaside Market	F. Jones	5-Yr.	10.00	10.00
94-35-002 Arnold Transit Company	F. Jones	5-Yr.	10.00	10.00
94-35-003 Lowell's Boat Shop	F. Jones	5-Yr.	10.00	10.00
94-35-004 Sand Island Lighthouse	F. Jones	5-Yr.	10.00	10.00
The Cat's Meow	**Elm Street Series**			
94-36-001 Blumenthal's	F. Jones	5-Yr.	10.00	10.00
94-36-002 Jim's Hunting & Fishing	F. Jones	5-Yr.	10.00	10.00
94-36-003 Clyde's Shoe Repair	F. Jones	5-Yr.	10.00	10.00
94-36-004 First Congregational Church	F. Jones	5-Yr.	10.00	10.00
The Cat's Meow	**Duke of Gloucester Series**			
94-37-001 Pasteur & Galt Apothecary	F. Jones	5-Yr.	10.00	10.00

	ARTIST	EDITION	ISSUE	QUOTE
94-37-002 Prentis Shop	F. Jones	5-Yr.	10.00	10.00
94-37-003 Nicolson Store	F. Jones	5-Yr.	10.00	10.00
94-37-004 Cole Shop	F. Jones	5-Yr.	10.00	10.00
The Cat's Meow	**Bed & Breakfast Series**			
95-38-001 Kinter House Inn	F. Jones	5-Yr.	10.00	10.00
95-38-002 Southmoreland	F. Jones	5-Yr.	10.00	10.00
95-38-003 Victorian Mansion	F. Jones	5-Yr.	10.00	10.00
95-38-004 Glen Iris	F. Jones	5-Yr.	10.00	10.00
The Cat's Meow	**Shaker Village Series**			
95-39-001 Great Stone Dwelling	F. Jones	5-Yr.	10.00	10.00
95-39-002 Meetinghouse	F. Jones	5-Yr.	10.00	10.00
95-39-003 Trustees Office	F. Jones	5-Yr.	10.00	10.00
95-39-004 Round Barn	F. Jones	5-Yr.	10.00	10.00
The Cat's Meow	**Historic Nauvoo Series**			
95-40-001 Cultural Hall	F. Jones	5-Yr.	10.00	10.00
95-40-002 J. Browning Gunsmith	F. Jones	5-Yr.	10.00	10.00
95-40-003 Printing Office	F. Jones	5-Yr.	10.00	10.00
95-40-004 Stoddard Home & Tinsmith	F. Jones	5-Yr.	10.00	10.00
The Cat's Meow	**Daughters of the Painted Lady Series**			
95-41-001 Barber Cottage	F. Jones	5-Yr.	10.00	10.00
95-41-002 Hall Cottage	F. Jones	5-Yr.	10.00	10.00
95-41-003 The Painted Lady	F. Jones	5-Yr.	10.00	10.00
95-41-004 The Fan House	F. Jones	5-Yr.	10.00	10.00
The Cat's Meow	**California Mission Series**			
95-42-001 Mission San Luis Rey	F. Jones	5-Yr.	10.00	10.00
95-42-002 Mission San Buenaventura	F. Jones	5-Yr.	10.00	10.00
95-42-003 Mission Dolores	F. Jones	5-Yr.	10.00	10.00
95-42-004 Mission San Juan Bautista	F. Jones	5-Yr.	10.00	10.00
The Cat's Meow	**Williamsburg Christmas**			
83-43-001 Christmas Church	F. Jones	Retrd.	6.00	N/A
83-43-002 Garrison House	F. Jones	Retrd.	6.00	N/A
83-43-003 Federal House	F. Jones	Retrd.	6.00	N/A
83-43-004 Georgian House	F. Jones	Retrd.	6.00	450.00
83-43-005 Set	F. Jones	Retrd.	24.00	N/A
The Cat's Meow	**Nantucket Christmas**			
84-44-001 Powell House	F. Jones	Retrd.	6.50	350.00
84-44-002 Shaw House	F. Jones	Retrd.	6.50	350.00
84-44-003 Wintrop House	F. Jones	Retrd.	6.50	N/A
84-44-004 Christmas Shop	F. Jones	Retrd.	6.50	N/A
84-44-005 Set	F. Jones	Retrd.	26.00	1350.00
The Cat's Meow	**Ohio Western Reserve Christmas**			
85-45-001 Western Reserve Academy	F. Jones	Retrd.	7.00	175.00
85-45-002 Olmstead House	F. Jones	Retrd.	7.00	175.00
85-45-003 Bellevue House	F. Jones	Retrd.	7.00	175.00
85-45-004 Gates Mills Church	F. Jones	Retrd.	7.00	175.00
85-45-005 Set	F. Jones	Retrd.	27.00	1250.00
The Cat's Meow	**Savannah Christmas**			
86-46-001 J.J. Dale Row House	F. Jones	Retrd.	7.25	150.00
86-46-002 Liberty Inn	F. Jones	Retrd.	7.25	150.00
86-46-003 Lafayette Square House	F. Jones	Retrd.	7.25	140-150.
86-46-004 Simon Mirault Cottage	F. Jones	Retrd.	7.25	150-300.
86-46-005 Set	F. Jones	Retrd.	29.00	1200.00
The Cat's Meow	**Maine Christmas**			
87-47-001 Damariscotta Church	F. Jones	Retrd.	7.75	150-300.
87-47-002 Portland Head Lighthouse	F. Jones	Retrd.	7.75	200-250.
87-47-003 Cappy's Chowder House	F. Jones	Retrd.	7.75	200-250.
87-47-004 Captain's House	F. Jones	Retrd.	7.75	200-250.
87-47-005 Set	F. Jones	Retrd.	31.00	13-1500.
The Cat's Meow	**Philadelphia Christmas**			
88-48-001 Graff House	F. Jones	Retrd.	7.75	100-200.
88-48-002 Hill-Physick-Keith House	F. Jones	Retrd.	7.75	75-200.
88-48-003 Elfreth's Alley	F. Jones	Retrd.	7.75	75-200.
88-48-004 The Head House	F. Jones	Retrd.	7.75	75-200.
88-48-005 Set	F. Jones	Retrd.	31.00	450-750.
The Cat's Meow	**Christmas In New England**			
89-49-001 The Old South Meeting House	F. Jones	Retrd.	8.00	75-125.
89-49-002 Hunter House	F. Jones	Retrd.	8.00	50-125.
89-49-003 Sheldon's Tavern	F. Jones	Retrd.	8.00	75-125.
89-49-004 The Vermont Country Store	F. Jones	Retrd.	8.00	50-125.
89-49-005 Set	F. Jones	Retrd.	32.00	250-450.
The Cat's Meow	**Colonial Virginia Christmas**			
90-50-001 Rising Sun Tavern	F. Jones	Retrd.	8.00	N/A
90-50-002 St. John's Church	F. Jones	Retrd.	8.00	70-100.
90-50-003 St. John's Church (blue)	F. Jones	Retrd.	8.00	200.00
90-50-003 Dulany House	F. Jones	Retrd.	8.00	35-70.00
90-50-004 Shirley Plantation	F. Jones	Retrd.	8.00	70.00
90-50-005 Set	F. Jones	Retrd.	32.00	150-325.
The Cat's Meow	**Rocky Mountain Christmas**			
91-51-001 First Presbyterian Church	F. Jones	Retrd.	8.20	28-40.00
91-51-002 Tabor House	F. Jones	Retrd.	8.20	28-100.
91-51-003 Western Hotel	F. Jones	Retrd.	8.20	28-60.00
91-51-004 Wheller-Stallard House	F. Jones	Retrd.	8.20	20-40.00
91-51-005 Set	F. Jones	Retrd.	32.80	150-200.
The Cat's Meow	**Hometown Christmas**			
92-52-001 Wayne Co. Courthouse	F. Jones	Retrd.	8.50	19-27.00
92-52-002 Overholt House	F. Jones	Retrd.	8.50	19-27.00
92-52-003 August Imgard House	F. Jones	Retrd.	8.50	19-27.00
92-52-004 Howey House	F. Jones	Retrd.	8.50	19-27.00
92-52-005 Set	F. Jones	Retrd.	34.00	40-108.
The Cat's Meow	**St. Charles Christmas**			
93-53-001 Newbill-McElhiney House	F. Jones	Retrd.	9.00	12-18.00
93-53-002 St. Peter's Catholic Church	F. Jones	Retrd.	9.00	12-18.00
93-53-003 Lewis & Clark Center	F. Jones	Retrd.	9.00	12-18.00
93-53-004 Stone Row	F. Jones	Retrd.	9.00	12-18.00
93-53-005 Set	F. Jones	Retrd.	36.00	30-45.00
The Cat's Meow	**New Orleans Christmas Series**			
94-54-001 Gallier House	F. Jones	12/94	10.00	10.00
94-54-002 St. Patrick's Church	F. Jones	12/94	10.00	10.00
94-54-003 Beauregard-Keyes House	F. Jones	12/94	10.00	10.00
94-54-004 Hermann-Grima House	F. Jones	12/94	10.00	10.00

	ARTIST	EDITION	ISSUE	QUOTE
The Cat's Meow	**New York Christmas Series**			
95-55-001 Clement C. Moore House	F. Jones	12/95	10.00	10.00
95-55-002 Fulton Market	F. Jones	12/95	10.00	10.00
95-55-003 St. Marks-In-the Bowery	F. Jones	12/95	10.00	10.00
95-55-004 Fraunces Taver	F. Jones	12/95	10.00	10.00
The Cat's Meow	**Collector Club Gift - Houses**			
89-56-001 Betsy Ross House	F. Jones	Retrd.	Gift	150-250.
90-56-002 Amelia Earhart	F. Jones	Retrd.	Gift	60-150.
91-56-003 Limberlost Cabin	F. Jones	Retrd.	Gift	40.00
92-56-004 Abigail Adams Birthplace	F. Jones	Retrd.	Gift	N/A
93-56-005 Pearl S. Buck House	F. Jones	Retrd.	Gift	N/A
93-56-006 Set of '89-'93	F. Jones	Retrd.	Gift	450.00
94-56-007 Lillian Gish	F. Jones	12/94	Gift	N/A
95-56-008 Eleanor Roosevelt	F. Jones	Yr.Iss.	Gift	N/A
The Cat's Meow	**Collector Club Pieces - Famous Authors**			
89-57-001 Harriet Beecher Stowe	F. Jones	Retrd.	8.75	N/A
89-57-002 Orchard House	F. Jones	Retrd.	8.75	N/A
89-57-003 Longfellow House	F. Jones	Retrd.	8.75	N/A
89-57-004 Herman Melville's Arrowhead	F. Jones	Retrd.	8.75	N/A
89-57-005 Set	F. Jones	Retrd.	35.00	850.00
The Cat's Meow	**Collector Club Pieces - Great Inventors**			
90-58-001 Thomas Edison	F. Jones	Retrd.	9.25	N/A
90-58-002 Ford Motor Co.	F. Jones	Retrd.	9.25	N/A
90-58-003 Seth Thomas Clock Co.	F. Jones	Retrd.	9.25	75.00
90-58-004 Wright Cycle Co.	F. Jones	Retrd.	9.25	N/A
90-58-005 Set	F. Jones	Retrd.	37.00	275-500.
The Cat's Meow	**Collector Club Pieces - American Songwriters**			
91-59-001 Benjamin R. Hanby House	F. Jones	Retrd.	9.25	N/A
91-59-002 Anna Warner House	F. Jones	Retrd.	9.25	N/A
91-59-003 Stephen Foster Home	F. Jones	Retrd.	9.25	N/A
91-59-004 Oscar Hammerstein House	F. Jones	Retrd.	9.25	N/A
91-59-005 Set	F. Jones	Retrd.	37.00	100.00
The Cat's Meow	**Collector Club Pieces - Signers of the Declaration**			
92-60-001 Josiah Bartlett Home	F. Jones	Retrd.	9.75	N/A
92-60-002 George Clymer Home	F. Jones	Retrd.	9.75	N/A
92-60-003 Stephen Hopkins Home	F. Jones	Retrd.	9.75	N/A
92-60-004 John Witherspoon Home	F. Jones	Retrd.	9.75	N/A
92-60-005 Set	F. Jones	Retrd.	39.00	250.00
The Cat's Meow	**Collector Club Pieces -19th Century Master Builders**			
93-61-001 Henry Hobson Richardson	F. Jones	Retrd.	10.25	N/A
93-61-002 Samuel Sloan	F. Jones	Retrd.	10.25	N/A
93-61-003 Alexander Jackson Davis	F. Jones	Retrd.	10.25	N/A
93-61-004 Andrew Jackson Downing	F. Jones	Retrd.	10.25	N/A
93-61-005 Set	F. Jones	Retrd.	41.00	75.00
The Cat's Meow	**Collector Club Pieces - Williamsburg Merchants**			
94-62-001 East Carlton Wigmaker	F. Jones	12/94	11.15	11.15
94-62-002 J. Geddy Silversmith	F. Jones	12/94	11.15	11.15
94-62-003 Craig Jeweler	F. Jones	12/94	11.15	11.15
94-62-004 M. Hunter Millinery	F. Jones	12/94	11.15	11.15
The Cat's Meow	**Mt. Rushmore Presidential Series**			
95-63-001 Tuckahoe Plantation	F. Jones	12/95	12.00	12.00
95-63-002 Theodore Roosevelt Birthplace	F. Jones	12/95	12.00	12.00
95-63-003 Metamora Courthouse	F. Jones	12/95	12.00	12.00
95-63-004 George Washington Birthplace	F. Jones	12/95	12.00	12.00
95-63-005 Set	F. Jones	12/95	48.00	48.00
The Cat's Meow	**Miscellaneous**			
85-64-001 Pencil Holder	F. Jones	Retrd.	3.95	210.00
85-64-002 Recipe Holder	F. Jones	Retrd.	3.95	250.00
The Cat's Meow	**Limited Edition Promotional Items**			
90-65-001 Frycrest Farm Homestead	F. Jones	Retrd.	10.00	10.00
92-65-002 Glen Pine	F. Jones	Retrd.	10.00	10.00
93-65-003 F.J. Factory	F. Jones	Open	12.95	12.95
93-65-004 F.J. Factory/Gold Cat Edition	F. Jones	Retrd.	12.95	12.95
93-65-005 Convention Museum	F. Jones	Retrd.	12.95	12.95
93-65-006 Nativity Cat on the Fence	F. Jones	Retrd.	19.95	19.95
The Cat's Meow	**Mark Twain's Hannibal Series**			
95-66-001 Becky Thatcher House	F. Jones	12/95	10.00	10.00
The Cat's Meow	**Covered Bridge Series**			
95-67-001 Creamery Bridge	F. Jones	12/95	10.00	10.00
The Cat's Meow	**Circus Series**			
95-68-001 Sideshow	F. Jones	12/95	10.00	10.00
The Cat's Meow	**Martha's Vineyard Series**			
95-69-001 John Coffin House	F. Jones	12/95	10.00	10.00
The Cat's Meow	**Special Item**			
95-70-001 Smokey Bear	F. Jones	8/95	8.95	8.95
The Cat's Meow	**Accessories**			
83-71-001 8" Picket Fence	F. Jones	Retrd.	3.25	10-44.00
83-71-002 5" Hedge	F. Jones	Retrd.	3.00	30-44.00
83-71-003 8" Hedge	F. Jones	Retrd.	3.25	50-60.00
83-71-004 Lilac Bushes	F. Jones	Retrd.	3.00	100-150.
83-71-005 5" Iron Fence	F. Jones	Retrd.	3.00	40-60.00
83-71-006 8" Iron Fence	F. Jones	Retrd.	3.25	50-60.00
83-71-007 Iron Gate	F. Jones	Retrd.	3.00	65.00
85-71-008 Summer Tree	F. Jones	Retrd.	4.00	26-40.00
85-71-009 Fall Tree	F. Jones	Retrd.	4.00	22-40.00
85-71-010 Cherry Tree	F. Jones	Retrd.	4.00	30.00
85-71-011 Pine Tree	F. Jones	Retrd.	4.00	26-35.00
85-71-012 Xmas Pine Tree	F. Jones	Retrd.	4.00	30-35.00
85-71-013 Xmas Pine Tree w/Red Bows	F. Jones	Retrd.	3.00	175-220.
85-71-014 Poplar Tree	F. Jones	Retrd.	4.00	20-50.00
86-71-015 Touring Car	F. Jones	Retrd.	4.00	9-15.00
86-71-016 Dairy Wagon	F. Jones	Retrd.	4.00	9-16.00
86-71-017 Horse & Carriage	F. Jones	Retrd.	4.00	9-16.00
86-71-018 FJ Real Estate Sign	F. Jones	Retrd.	3.00	10-25.00
86-71-019 Chickens	F. Jones	Retrd.	3.25	9-13.00
86-71-020 Ducks	F. Jones	Retrd.	3.25	9-13.00
86-71-021 Cows	F. Jones	Retrd.	4.00	12-16.00
86-71-022 Wells, Fargo Wagon	F. Jones	Retrd.	4.00	12-16.00
86-71-023 Market St. Sign	F. Jones	Retrd.	3.25	8-13.00
86-71-024 Carolers	F. Jones	Retrd.	4.00	9-16.00
86-71-025 Wishing Well	F. Jones	Retrd.	3.25	10-16.00

		ARTIST	EDITION	ISSUE	QUOTE
86-71-026	Ice Wagon	F. Jones	Retrd.	4.00	9-15.00
86-71-027	Liberty St. Sign	F. Jones	Retrd.	3.25	12.00
86-71-028	Cable Car	F. Jones	Retrd.	4.00	9-13.00
87-71-029	Wooden Gate (two-sided)	F. Jones	Retrd.	3.00	6-25.00
87-71-030	Band Stand	F. Jones	Retrd.	6.50	13-18.00
87-71-031	Horse & Sleigh	F. Jones	Retrd.	4.00	6-13.00
87-71-032	5" Picket Fence	F. Jones	Retrd.	3.00	10-30.00
87-71-033	FJ Express	F. Jones	Retrd.	4.00	10-12.00
87-71-034	Railroad Sign	F. Jones	Retrd.	3.00	10.00
87-71-035	Windmill	F. Jones	Retrd.	3.25	10.00
87-71-036	Butch & T.J.	F. Jones	Retrd.	4.00	6-12.00
87-71-037	Charlie & Co.	F. Jones	Retrd.	4.00	10-12.00
87-71-038	Nanny	F. Jones	Retrd.	4.00	6-12.00
88-71-039	Main St. Sign	F. Jones	Retrd.	3.25	6-8.00
88-71-040	Colonial Bread Wagon	F. Jones	Retrd.	4.00	6-9.00
88-71-041	Gas Light	F. Jones	Retrd.	4.00	7.00
88-71-042	Telephone Booth	F. Jones	Retrd.	4.00	6-8.00
88-71-043	U.S. Flag	F. Jones	Retrd.	4.00	6-8.00
88-71-044	Flower Pots	F. Jones	Retrd.	4.00	7.00
88-71-045	Skipjack	F. Jones	Retrd.	6.50	9-13.00
88-71-046	Mail Wagon	F. Jones	Retrd.	4.00	6-9.00
88-71-047	Street Clock	F. Jones	Retrd.	4.00	6-9.00
88-71-048	Pony Express Rider	F. Jones	Retrd.	4.00	6-9.00
89-71-049	Ada Belle	F. Jones	12/94	4.00	4.50
89-71-050	Passenger Train Car	F. Jones	12/94	4.00	4.50
89-71-051	Harry's Hotdogs	F. Jones	12/94	4.00	4.50
89-71-052	Clothesline	F. Jones	12/94	4.00	4.50
89-71-053	Pumpkin Wagon	F. Jones	12/94	3.25	4.50
89-71-054	Rudy & Aldine	F. Jones	12/94	4.00	4.50
89-71-055	Tad & Toni	F. Jones	12/94	4.00	4.50
89-71-056	Snowmen	F. Jones	12/94	4.00	4.50
89-71-057	Rose Trellis	F. Jones	12/94	3.25	4.50
89-71-058	Quaker Oats Train Car	F. Jones	12/94	4.00	4.50
90-71-059	Gerstenslager Buggy	F. Jones	5-Yr.	4.00	4.50
90-71-060	1914 Fire Pumper	F. Jones	5-Yr.	4.00	4.50
90-71-061	1913 Peerless Touring Car	F. Jones	5-Yr.	4.00	4.50
90-71-062	1909 Franklin Limousine	F. Jones	5-Yr.	4.00	4.50
90-71-063	Watkins Wagon	F. Jones	5-Yr.	4.00	4.50
90-71-064	Veterinary Wagon	F. Jones	5-Yr.	4.00	4.50
90-71-065	Amish Buggy	F. Jones	5-Yr.	4.00	4.50
90-71-066	Victorian Outhouse	F. Jones	5-Yr.	4.00	4.50
90-71-067	Bus Stop	F. Jones	5-Yr.	4.00	4.50
90-71-068	Eugene	F. Jones	5-Yr.	4.00	4.50
90-71-069	Christmas Tree Lot	F. Jones	5-Yr.	4.00	4.50
90-71-070	Santa & Reindeer	F. Jones	5-Yr.	4.00	4.50
90-71-071	5" Wrought Iron Fence	F. Jones	5-Yr.	3.00	4.50
90-71-072	Little Red Caboose	F. Jones	5-Yr.	4.00	4.50
90-71-073	Red Maple Tree	F. Jones	5-Yr.	4.00	4.50
90-71-074	Tulip Tree	F. Jones	5-Yr.	4.00	4.50
90-71-075	Blue Spruce	F. Jones	5-Yr.	4.00	4.50
90-71-076	Xmas Spruce	F. Jones	5-Yr.	4.00	4.50
91-71-077	School Bus	F. Jones	5-Yr.	4.00	4.50
91-71-078	Popcorn Wagon	F. Jones	5-Yr.	4.00	4.50
91-71-079	Scarey Harry (Scarecrow)	F. Jones	5-Yr.	4.00	4.50
91-71-080	Amish Garden	F. Jones	5-Yr.	4.00	4.50
91-71-081	Chessie Hopper Car	F. Jones	5-Yr.	4.00	4.50
91-71-082	USMC War Memorial	F. Jones	5-Yr.	6.50	6.50
91-71-083	Village Entrance Sigh	F. Jones	5-Yr.	6.50	6.50
91-71-084	Concert in the Park	F. Jones	5-Yr.	4.00	4.50
91-71-085	Martin House	F. Jones	5-Yr.	3.25	4.50
91-71-086	Marble Game	F. Jones	5-Yr.	4.00	4.50
91-71-087	Barnyard	F. Jones	5-Yr.	4.00	4.50
91-71-088	Ski Party	F. Jones	5-Yr.	4.00	4.50
91-71-089	On Vacation	F. Jones	5-Yr.	4.00	4.50
91-71-090	Jack The Postman	F. Jones	5-Yr.	3.25	4.50
92-71-091	Forsythia Bush	F. Jones	5-Yr.	4.00	4.50
92-71-092	Police Car	F. Jones	5-Yr.	4.00	4.50
92-71-093	Delivery Truck	F. Jones	5-Yr.	4.00	4.50
92-71-094	School Crossing	F. Jones	5-Yr.	4.00	4.50
92-71-095	Mr. Softee Truck	F. Jones	5-Yr.	4.00	4.50
92-71-096	Silo	F. Jones	5-Yr.	4.00	4.50
92-71-097	Springhouse	F. Jones	5-Yr.	3.25	4.50
92-71-098	Nutcracker Billboard	F. Jones	5-Yr.	4.00	4.50
93-71-099	Jennie & George's Wedding	F. Jones	5-Yr.	4.00	4.50
93-71-100	Market Wagon	F. Jones	5-Yr.	4.00	4.50
93-71-101	Chippewa Lake Billboard	F. Jones	5-Yr.	4.00	4.50
93-71-102	Garden House	F. Jones	5-Yr.	3.25	4.50
93-71-103	Johnny Appleseed Statue	F. Jones	5-Yr.	4.00	4.50
93-71-104	Getting Directions	F. Jones	5-Yr.	4.00	4.50
93-71-105	Grape Arbor	F. Jones	5-Yr.	4.00	4.50
93-71-106	Rustic Fence	F. Jones	5-Yr.	4.00	4.50
93-71-107	Cannonball Express	F. Jones	5-Yr.	4.00	4.50
93-71-108	Little Marine	F. Jones	5-Yr.	4.00	4.50
94-71-109	Nativity	F. Jones	5-Yr.	15.00	17.00
94-71-110	Weeping Willow Tree	F. Jones	5-Yr.	4.50	4.50
94-71-111	U.S. Flag	F. Jones	5-Yr.	4.50	4.50
94-71-112	Garden Wall	F. Jones	5-Yr.	4.50	4.50
94-71-113	Lemonade Stand	F. Jones	5-Yr.	4.50	4.50
94-71-114	Street Lamp	F. Jones	5-Yr.	4.50	4.50
94-71-115	Lunch Wagon	F. Jones	5-Yr.	4.50	4.50
94-71-116	Moving Truck	F. Jones	5-Yr.	4.50	4.50
94-71-117	Salvation Army Band	F. Jones	5-Yr.	4.50	4.50
94-71-118	Stock Train Car	F. Jones	5-Yr.	4.50	4.50
94-71-119	Light Ship	F. Jones	5-Yr.	4.50	4.50
94-71-120	Cat & The Fiddle S/2	F. Jones	5-Yr.	4.50	4.50
94-71-121	Apple Tree	F. Jones	5-Yr.	4.50	4.50
94-71-122	Kearsarge Fire Pumper	F. Jones	5-Yr.	4.50	4.50
94-71-123	Wharf	F. Jones	5-Yr.	4.50	4.50
94-71-124	Moving Truck	F. Jones	5-Yr.	4.50	4.50
94-71-125	Yule Tree S/2	F. Jones	5-Yr.	4.50	4.50
94-71-126	Good Humor Man	F. Jones	5-Yr.	4.50	4.50
94-71-127	Gracie (in carriage)	F. Jones	5-Yr.	4.50	4.50
94-71-128	Daily Business (wlbg. people)	F. Jones	5-Yr.	4.50	4.50
94-71-129	Amish Milk Wagon	F. Jones	5-Yr.	4.50	4.50
94-71-130	Berries & Sheep	F. Jones	5-Yr.	4.50	4.50
94-71-131	Deer	F. Jones	5-Yr.	4.50	4.50
94-71-132	Jacob, Atlee & Noah	F. Jones	5-Yr.	4.50	4.50
94-71-133	Amish Produce Wagon	F. Jones	5-Yr.	4.50	4.50
94-71-134	Trick or Treat	F. Jones	5-Yr.	4.50	4.50
94-71-135	Booker T. Washington Monument	F. Jones	5-Yr.	4.50	4.50
94-71-136	Cornstalks & Turkeys	F. Jones	5-Yr.	4.50	4.50
94-71-137	Nativity Visitors Trio Set	F. Jones	5-Yr.	19.00	19.00
95-71-138	Humpty Dumpty	F. Jones	5-Yr.	9.00	9.00
95-71-139	Central Park Skaters	F. Jones	5-Yr.	4.50	4.50
95-71-140	Vineyard Fence	F. Jones	5-Yr.	4.50	4.50
95-71-141	Magnolia Tree	F. Jones	5-Yr.	4.50	4.50
95-71-142	Watermelon Wagon	F. Jones	5-Yr.	4.50	4.50
95-71-143	Hearse	F. Jones	5-Yr.	4.50	4.50
95-71-144	Winter Tree	F. Jones	5-Yr.	4.50	4.50
95-71-145	Charles & Lady	F. Jones	5-Yr.	4.50	4.50
95-71-146	Noah's Ark Trio Set	F. Jones	5-Yr.	21.00	21.00
95-71-147	Father Serra & Indians	F. Jones	5-Yr.	4.50	4.50
95-71-148	San Juan Capistrano Bells	F. Jones	5-Yr.	9.00	9.00
95-71-149	Palm Trees	F. Jones	5-Yr.	9.00	9.00
95-71-150	Rose Arbor	F. Jones	5-Yr.	4.50	4.50
95-71-151	Bennington Flag	F. Jones	5-Yr.	4.50	4.50
95-71-152	Mt. Rushmore	F. Jones	5-Yr.	9.00	9.00
95-71-153	Rubbermaid Train Car	F. Jones	5-Yr.	4.50	4.50
95-71-154	Beech & Cherry Tree Row	F. Jones	5-Yr.	4.50	4.50
95-71-155	Dancing Cat & Clipper Ship	F. Jones	5-Yr.	9.00	9.00
95-71-156	Burma-Shave Signs	F. Jones	5-Yr.	4.50	4.50
95-71-157	Knickerbockers Ball Team	F. Jones	5-Yr.	4.50	4.50
95-71-158	Lion Circus Wagon	F. Jones	5-Yr.	4.50	4.50

Classic Collectibles by Uniquely Yours **Limited Edition Santas**

		ARTIST	EDITION	ISSUE	QUOTE
89-01-001	Kris Kringle	E. Tisa	Closed	178.00	230.00
89-01-002	Father Christmas	E. Tisa	Closed	138.00	190.00
89-01-003	Father Christmas-sm.	E. Tisa	Closed	48.00	56.00
89-01-004	Olde World Santa	E. Tisa	Closed	48.00	56.00
90-01-005	Jolly St. Nick	E. Tisa	250	104.00	130.00
91-01-006	Victorian Santa	E. Tisa	1,500	196.00	230.00
91-01-007	European Santa w/Little Girl	E. Tisa	1,000	118.00	150.00
93-01-008	Olde World Santa	E. Tisa	300	270.00	270.00
93-01-009	Traditional Santa in Sleigh	E. Tisa	400	160.00	170.00
93-01-010	Renaissance Santa	E. Tisa	450	210.00	230.00
93-01-011	Pere Noel	E. Tisa	500	350.00	350.00
94-01-012	Black Santa on Tricycle	E. Tisa	600	160.00	160.00
94-01-013	Santa on Tricycle	E. Tisa	600	160.00	160.00

Classic Collectibles by Uniquely Yours **Additional Santas**

		ARTIST	EDITION	ISSUE	QUOTE
89-02-001	Santa at Work	E. Tisa	Open	68.00	98.00
90-02-002	St. Nicholas	E. Tisa	Open	76.00	94.00
91-02-003	Mrs. Claus	E. Tisa	Open	36.00	48.00
93-02-004	Russian Santa	E. Tisa	Open	72.00	72.00
93-02-005	Olde English Santa	E. Tisa	Open	66.00	66.00

Classic Collectibles by Uniquely Yours **Dicken's-A Christmas Carol**

		ARTIST	EDITION	ISSUE	QUOTE
86-03-001	Single Woman Caroler	E. Tisa	Closed	N/A	N/A
86-03-002	Single Man Caroler	E. Tisa	Closed	N/A	N/A
86-03-003	Single Girl Caroler	E. Tisa	Closed	N/A	N/A
86-03-004	Single Boy Caroler	E. Tisa	Closed	N/A	N/A
88-03-005	Bob Cratchit and Tiny Tim	E. Tisa	Open	68.00	86.00
88-03-006	Marley's Ghost	E. Tisa	Open	36.00	54.00
88-03-007	Ghost of Christmas Past	E. Tisa	Open	36.00	48.00
88-03-008	Ghost of Christmas Present	E. Tisa	Open	68.00	86.00
88-03-009	Ghost of Christmas Yet To Be	E. Tisa	Open	48.00	72.00
88-03-010	Mr. & Mrs. Fezziwig	E. Tisa	Open	78.00	88.00
88-03-011	Mrs. Crachit	E. Tisa	Open	36.00	48.00
88-03-012	Scrooge	E. Tisa	Open	36.00	48.00
88-03-013	Boy on Sled	E. Tisa	Open	32.00	44.00
88-03-014	Girl in a Sleigh	E. Tisa	Open	36.00	52.00
89-03-015	Adult Carolers	E. Tisa	Open	78.00	88.00
89-03-016	Senior Carolers	E. Tisa	Open	78.00	88.00
89-03-017	Children Carolers	E. Tisa	Open	68.00	84.00
88-03-018	Match Girl	E. Tisa	Closed	68.00	68.00
89-03-019	Victorian Band	E. Tisa	Closed	144.00	144.00
89-03-020	Scrooge & Marley	E. Tisa	Closed	78.00	78.00
89-03-021	Christmas Present (vingette w/feast)	E. Tisa	Closed	90.00	90.00
90-03-022	Lighting the Menorrah	E. Tisa	Closed	96.00	96.00

Classic Collectibles by Uniquely Yours **Dicken's-A Christmas Carol (Miniatures)**

		ARTIST	EDITION	ISSUE	QUOTE
87-04-001	Tiny Tim & Bob	E. Tisa	Closed	60.00	60.00
87-04-002	Marley's Ghost	E. Tisa	Closed	40.00	40.00
87-04-003	Christmas Past	E. Tisa	Closed	40.00	40.00
87-04-004	Christmas Present	E. Tisa	Closed	40.00	40.00
87-04-005	Christmas Yet to Be	E. Tisa	Closed	32.00	32.00
87-04-006	Mrs. Fezziwig	E. Tisa	Closed	40.00	40.00
87-04-007	Mr. Fezzziwig	E. Tisa	Closed	40.00	40.00
87-04-008	Scrooge	E. Tisa	Closed	40.00	40.00
87-04-009	Mrs. Cratchit	E. Tisa	Closed	42.00	42.00
87-04-010	Belle	E. Tisa	Closed	40.00	40.00
87-04-011	Father Christmas	E. Tisa	Closed	40.00	40.00

Classic Collectibles by Uniquely Yours **Victorian**

		ARTIST	EDITION	ISSUE	QUOTE
89-05-001	Victorian Woman	E. Tisa	Closed	36.00	36.00
89-05-002	Victorian Man	E. Tisa	Closed	40.00	40.00
89-05-003	Victorian Girl	E. Tisa	Closed	36.00	36.00
89-05-004	Victorian Boy w/Hoop	E. Tisa	Closed	36.00	36.00
89-05-005	Victorian Treetop Angel	E. Tisa	Open	80.00	80.00

Classic Collectibles by Uniquely Yours **Thanksgiving**

		ARTIST	EDITION	ISSUE	QUOTE
88-06-001	Pilgrim-Woman	E. Tisa	Closed	38.00	38.00
88-06-002	Pilgrim-Man	E. Tisa	Closed	40.00	40.00

Classic Collectibles by Uniquely Yours **Halloween**

		ARTIST	EDITION	ISSUE	QUOTE
89-07-001	Trick or Treat-Devil	E. Tisa	Closed	36.00	36.00
89-07-002	Trick or Treat-Witch	E. Tisa	Closed	32.00	32.00
89-07-003	Ghoul	E. Tisa	Closed	38.00	38.00

Classic Collectibles by Uniquely Yours **Easter**

		ARTIST	EDITION	ISSUE	QUOTE
89-08-001	Boy w/Easter Basket	E. Tisa	Closed	36.00	36.00
89-08-002	Girl w/Bunnies	E. Tisa	Closed	36.00	36.00

Classic Collectibles by Uniquely Yours **Valentine's Day**

		ARTIST	EDITION	ISSUE	QUOTE
90-09-001	Valentine-Girl	E. Tisa	Closed	36.00	36.00
90-09-002	Valentine-Boy	E. Tisa	Closed	36.00	36.00

Classic Collectibles by Uniquely Yours **Miscellaneous**

		ARTIST	EDITION	ISSUE	QUOTE
88-10-001	Bride	E. Tisa	Closed	40.00	40.00
88-10-002	Groom	E. Tisa	Closed	40.00	40.00
89-10-003	Mother & Daughter	E. Tisa	Closed	68.00	68.00
89-10-004	African Woman	E. Tisa	Closed	36.00	36.00
89-10-005	African Man	E. Tisa	Closed	40.00	40.00
89-10-006	Christmas Child	E. Tisa	Closed	22.00	22.00
89-10-007	Christmas Shopper	E. Tisa	Closed	26.00	26.00

		ARTIST	EDITION	ISSUE	QUOTE
Creart		**African Wildlife**			
86-01-001	Running Elephant -73	Perez	2,500	260.00	338.00
87-01-002	African Elephant -10	Perez	S/O	410.00	575.00
87-01-003	African Elephant With Leaf -22	Martinez	2,500	230.00	298.00
87-01-004	Giraffe -43	Perez	2,500	250.00	338.00
87-01-005	Cob Antelope -46	Perez	2,500	310.00	398.00
87-01-006	African Lion -61	Martinez	2,500	260.00	338.00
87-01-007	Zebra -67	Perez	2,500	305.00	398.00
87-01-008	White Rhinoceros -136	Perez	2,500	330.00	438.00
90-01-009	Symbol of Power Lion -40	Quesada	2,500	450.00	478.00
90-01-010	Hippopotamus -55	Quesada	2,500	420.00	438.00
91-01-011	Breaking Away Gazelles -256	Quesada	1,500	650.00	698.00
91-01-012	Sound of Warning Elephant -268	Perez	2,500	500.00	518.00
92-01-013	Small African Elephant- 271	Perez	Closed	320.00	320.00
93-01-014	Travieso-358	Perez	1,500	198.00	218.00
93-01-015	Cape Buffalo-412	Contreras	1,500	418.00	418.00
94-01-016	Numa Lion's Head-433	Contreras	2,500	418.00	418.00
94-01-017	Love For Ever Elephant-436	Contreras	2,500	N/A	N/A
94-01-018	Grumbler Cape Buffalo-451	Martinez	1,500	498.00	498.00
Creart		**American Wildlife**			
85-02-001	Pigeons- 64	Perez	Closed	265.00	265.00
86-02-002	Polar Bear- 58	Martinez	2,500	200.00	258.00
86-02-003	Bald Eagle- 70	Martinez	Susp.	730.00	900.00
86-02-004	American Bison- 121	Perez	Susp.	400.00	490.00
87-02-005	Grizzley Bear- 31	Perez	2,500	210.00	278.00
87-02-006	Royal Eagle- 49	Martinez	Closed	545.00	598.00
87-02-007	Puma- 130	Perez	S/O	370.00	470.00
88-02-008	Mammoth-112	Martinez	2,500	450.00	578.00
88-02-009	Flamingo Upright-169	Perez	2,500	230.00	298.00
88-02-010	Flamingo Head Down-172	Perez	2,500	230.00	298.00
88-02-011	Flamingo Flapping-175	Perez	2,500	230.00	298.00
89-02-012	Jaguar- 79	Gonzalez	500	700.00	750.00
89-02-013	Rooster- R40	Martinez	Closed	290.00	290.00
89-02-014	Penguins- R76	Del Valle	Closed	175.00	175.00
90-02-015	The Challenge, Rams- 82	Gonzalez	1,500	698.00	738.00
90-02-016	Over the Clouds Falcon- 85	Martinez	2,500	520.00	538.00
90-02-017	Gray Wolf- 88	Quesada	2,500	365.00	378.00
90-02-018	Dolphin, Front- 142	Perez	2,500	210.00	250.00
90-02-019	Dolphin, Middle- 145	Perez	2,500	210.00	250.00
90-02-020	Dolphin, Back- 148	Perez	2,500	210.00	250.00
90-02-021	White Tail Deer- 151	Martinez	2,500	380.00	478.00
90-02-022	White Tail Doe- 154	Martinez	2,500	330.00	418.00
90-02-023	White Tail Fawn- 157	Martinez	2,500	220.00	290.00
91-02-024	White Hunter Polar Bear- 250	Gonzalez	2,500	380.00	398.00
91-02-025	Royal Eagle With Snake- 259	Martinez	2,500	700.00	738.00
91-02-026	Mischievous Raccoon- 262	Quesada	2,500	370.00	318.00
91-02-027	Playmates Sparrows- 265	Martinez	2,500	500.00	518.00
92-02-028	Soaring Royal Eagle- 52	Martinez	2,500	580.00	598.00
92-02-029	Standing Whitetail Deer- 109	Martinez	2,500	364.00	378.00
92-02-030	California Grizzly- 238	Perez	2,500	270.00	278.00
93-02-031	The Red Fox- 220	Contreras	1,500	199.00	218.00
93-02-032	Howling Coyote- 217	Martinez	1,500	199.00	218.00
93-02-033	Scent of Honey Bear-223	Perez	1,500	398.00	398.00
93-02-034	Buenos Dias Jack Rabbit-229	Martinez	1,500	218.00	218.00
94-02-035	Freedom Eagle-430	Martinez	1,500	500.00	500.00
94-02-036	Singing to the Moon I Wolf-439	Perez	1,500	398.00	398.00
94-02-037	Singing to the Moon II Wolf-442	Perez	1,500	358.00	358.00
94-02-038	Ambushing Puma-508	Nelson	1,950	150.00	150.00
94-02-039	Catamountain-505	Estevez	2,500	118.00	118.00
94-02-040	Puffins-511	Estevez	1,500	258.00	258.00
94-02-041	Out of the Den Puma-523	Estevez	1,500	130.00	130.00
94-02-042	Over the Top Puma-445	Perez	1,500	398.00	398.00
94-02-043	Red Tail Hawk-520	Nelson	1,950	130.00	130.00
94-02-044	Briefly Rest Pumas-526	Nelson	1,950	250.00	250.00
Creart		**Wild America Edition**			
92-03-001	Puma Head- 334	Perez	900	320.00	338.00
92-03-002	Twelve Pointer Deer- 337	Perez	900	472.00	490.00
93-03-003	White Blizzard- 331	Perez	1,500	275.00	278.00
93-03-004	American Symbol- 328	Contreras	1,500	246.00	258.00
93-03-005	Wild America Bison-409	Contreras	1,500	338.00	338.00
Creart		**Horses And Cattle**			
85-04-001	Running Horse- 7	Martinez	2,500	360.00	458.00
85-04-002	Arabian Horse- 34	Martinez	2,500	230.00	298.00
85-04-003	Bull- 28	Martinez	Susp.	285.00	285.00
87-04-004	Horse In Passage- 127	Martinez	2,500	500.00	558.00
88-04-005	Horse Head- 139	Martinez	2,500	440.00	498.00
89-04-006	Quarter Horse Recoil- 1	Gonzalez	Closed	310.00	310.00
89-04-007	Brahma Bull- 13	Gonzalez	2,500	420.00	498.00
89-04-008	Arabian Horse- 91	Perez	2,500	260.00	278.00
89-04-009	Lippizzan Horse- 94	Perez	2,500	260.00	278.00
89-04-010	Thoroughbred Horse-97	Perez	2,500	260.00	278.00
89-04-011	Apaloosa Horse- 100	Martinez	2,500	260.00	278.00
89-04-012	Quarter Horse II- 103	Perez	2,500	260.00	278.00
92-04-013	Pegasus- 106	Perez	2,500	420.00	438.00
93-04-014	Rosie Bella-421	Martinez	950	758.00	758.00
Creart		**From Asia & Europe**			
85-05-001	Indian Elephant Mother- 25	Perez	Suspd.	485.00	490.00
85-05-002	Marco Polo Sheep- 37	Martinez	2,500	270.00	318.00
85-05-003	Tiger- R55	Martinez	Closed	200.00	200.00
86-05-004	Deer- 4	Martinez	Closed	560.00	600.00
86-05-005	Indian Elephant Baby- 16	Perez	Suspd.	200.00	200.00
87-05-006	Drover of Camels- 124	Martinez	2,500	650.00	718.00
87-05-007	Royal Owl- 133	Perez	Closed	340.00	370.00
88-05-008	Bengal Tiger- 115	Perez	Suspd.	440.00	520.00
90-05-009	Giant Panda- 244	Martinez	2,500	280.00	298.00
Creart		**Pets**			
87-06-001	Labrador Retriever- 19	Martinez	2,500	300.00	378.00
89-06-002	Cocker Spaniel American- 184	Martinez	Suspd.	100.00	100.00
89-06-003	Boxer- 187	Martinez	Suspd.	135.00	135.00
89-06-004	Schnauzer Miniature- 190	Perez	Suspd.	110.00	110.00
89-06-005	Great Dane, Brown- 193	Martinez	Suspd.	140.00	140.00
89-06-006	Great Dane, Harlequi- 196	Martinez	Suspd.	140.00	140.00
89-06-007	Pointer, Brown- 199	Perez	Suspd.	132.00	132.00
89-06-008	Pointer, Black- 202	Perez	Suspd.	132.00	132.00
89-06-009	Poodle- 205	Perez	Suspd.	120.00	120.00
89-06-010	Saint Bernard- 208	Perez	Suspd.	130.00	130.00
89-06-011	Labrador, Golden- 211	Martinez	Suspd.	130.00	130.00
89-06-012	Labrador, Black- 214	Martinez	Suspd.	130.00	130.00
91-06-013	German Shepherd Dog- 253	Martinez	2,500	360.00	388.00
Creart		**Nature's Care Collection**			
93-07-001	Penguin and Chicks- 76	Perez	2,500	99.00	132.00
93-07-002	Otters- 325	Estevez	2,500	99.95	99.95
93-07-003	Grizzly and Cubs- 340	Perez	2,500	99.00	118.00
93-07-004	Jack Rabbit and Young- 343	Martinez	2,500	99.95	99.95
93-07-005	Lioness and Cubs- 346	Contreras	2,500	99.00	118.00
93-07-006	Wolf and Pups- 349	Contreras	2,500	99.00	150.00
93-07-007	Doe and Fawns- 355	Contreras	2,500	99.00	138.00
93-07-008	Gorilla and Baby- 394	Contreras	2,500	99.00	110.00
93-07-009	Eagle and Eaglets-352	Contreras	2,500	120.00	130.00
Creart		**Birds of Prey**			
94-08-001	Gyrfalcon-502	Robison	450	1300.00	1300.00
94-08-002	Vigilant Eagle-517	Robison	650	780.00	780.00
94-08-003	Urban Release Peregrine Falcon-514	Robison	650	N/A	N/A
Crystal World		**Limited Edition Series**			
85-01-001	Extra Large-Empire State Building	R. Nakai	Closed	1000.00	1300.00
86-01-002	The Eiffel Tower	T. Suzuki	2,000	1000.00	1300.00
86-01-003	Airplane	T. Suzuki	Closed	400.00	500.00
86-01-004	Crucifix	N. Mulargia	Closed	300.00	400.00
87-01-005	Taj Mahal	T. Suzuki	2,000	2000.00	2100.00
87-01-006	Large Empire State	R. Nakai	2,000	650.00	700.00
87-01-007	Large US Capitol Building	T. Suzuki	Closed	1000.00	1100.00
87-01-008	Manhattanscape	G. Veith	Closed	1000.00	1100.00
88-01-009	Small Eiffel Tower	T. Suzuki	2,000	500.00	600.00
89-01-010	Grand Castle	R. Nakai	1,500	2500.00	2500.00
89-01-011	Dream Castle	R. Nakai	500	9000.00	10000.00
89-01-012	Space Shuttle Launch	T. Suzuki	Closed	900.00	1000.00
90-01-013	Tower Bridge	T. Suzuki	Closed	600.00	650.00
91-01-014	Cruise Ship	T. Suzuki	1,000	2000.00	2100.00
91-01-015	Ellis Island	R. Nakai	Closed	450.00	500.00
92-01-016	Santa Maria	N. Mulargia	Closed	1000.00	1050.00
92-01-017	The White House	R. Nakai	Closed	3000.00	3000.00
93-01-018	Country Gristmill	T. Suzuki	1,250	320.00	320.00
93-01-019	Victorian House	N. Mulargia	2,000	190.00	190.00
93-01-020	Enchanted Castle	R. Nakai	750	800.00	800.00
93-01-021	Riverboat	N. Mulargia	350	570.00	570.00
Crystal World		**Bird Collection**			
83-02-001	Large Owl	R. Nakai	Closed	44.00	75.00
83-02-002	Small Owl	R. Nakai	Closed	22.00	36.00
83-02-003	Owl Standing	R. Nakai	Closed	40.00	70.00
84-02-004	Love Bird	R. Nakai	Closed	44.00	65.00
84-02-005	Bird Family	R. Nakai	Closed	22.00	35.00
85-02-006	Extra Large Parrot	R. Nakai	Closed	300.00	450.00
85-02-007	Large Parrot	R. Nakai	Closed	100.00	150.00
85-02-008	Small Parrot	R. Nakai	Closed	30.00	45.00
86-02-009	Love Birds	N. Mulargia	Closed	54.00	75.00
86-02-010	Bird Bath	N. Mulargia	Closed	54.00	75.00
87-02-011	Small Parrot	R. Nakai	Closed	96.00	110.00
87-02-012	Large Parrot	R. Nakai	Closed	130.00	170.00
90-02-013	Tree Top Owls	T. Suzuki	Closed	55.00	75.00
90-02-014	Wise Owl	T. Suzuki	Closed	55.00	65.00
90-02-015	Small Wise Owl	T. Suzuki	Closed	40.00	45.00
90-02-016	Ollie Owl	T. Suzuki	Closed	32.00	40.00
91-02-017	Parrot Couple	R. Nakai	Closed	90.00	100.00
CUI/Carolina Collection/Dram Tree		**Legends of Santa Claus**			
91-01-001	Checkin' it Twice	Christjohn	Retrd.	60.00	60.00
91-01-002	Have You Been a Good Little Boy	Christjohn	Retrd.	60.00	60.00
91-01-003	Have You Been a Good Little Girl	Christjohn	Retrd.	60.00	60.00
91-01-004	Mrs. Claus	Christjohn	Retrd.	60.00	60.00
91-01-005	Won't You Guide My Sleigh Tonight	Christjohn	Retrd.	60.00	60.00
91-01-006	With A Finger Aside His Nose	Christjohn	Retrd.	60.00	60.00
CUI/Carolina Collection/Dram Tree		**Texaco Fire Chief Pups**			
92-02-001	Christmas Dalmations	Unknown	Open	49.50	49.50
93-02-002	Glide Away Starts	Unknown	Open	49.50	49.50
CUI/Carolina Collection/Dram Tree		**First Encounter Series**			
93-03-001	Stand Off	R. Cruwys	Open	49.50	49.50
Cybis		**Animal Kingdom**			
71-01-001	American Bullfrog	Cybis	Closed	250.00	600.00
75-01-002	American White Buffalo	Cybis	250	1250.00	4000.00
71-01-003	Appaloosa Colt	Cybis	Closed	150.00	300.00
80-01-004	Arctic White Fox	Cybis	100	4500.00	4700.00
84-01-005	Australian Greater Sulpher Crested Cockatoo	Cybis	25	9850.00	9850.00
85-01-006	Baxter and Doyle	Cybis	400	450.00	450.00
68-01-007	Bear	Cybis	Closed	85.00	400.00
85-01-008	Beagles, Branigan and Clancy	Cybis	Open	375.00	625.00
81-01-009	Beavers, Egbert and Brewster	Cybis	400	285.00	335.00
68-01-010	Buffalo	Cybis	Closed	115.00	185.00
XX-01-011	Bull	Cybis	100	150.00	4500.00
76-01-012	Bunny, Muffet	Cybis	Closed	85.00	150.00
77-01-013	Bunny Pat-a-Cake	Cybis	Closed	90.00	150.00
85-01-014	Bunny, Snowflake	Cybis	Open	65.00	75.00
84-01-015	Chantilly, Kitten	Cybis	Open	175.00	210.00
76-01-016	Chipmunk w/Bloodroot	Cybis	225	625.00	675.00
69-01-017	Colts, Darby and Joan	Cybis	Closed	295.00	475.00
82-01-018	Dall Sheep	Cybis	50	Unkn.	4250.00
86-01-019	Dapple Grey Foal	Cybis	Open	195.00	250.00
70-01-020	Deer Mouse in Clover	Cybis	Closed	65.00	160.00
78-01-021	Dormouse, Maximillian	Cybis	Closed	250.00	285.00
78-01-022	Dormouse, Maxine	Cybis	Closed	195.00	225.00
68-01-023	Elephant	Cybis	100	600.00	5000.00
85-01-024	Elephant, Willoughby	Cybis	Open	195.00	245.00
61-01-025	Horse	Cybis	100	150.00	2000.00
86-01-026	Huey, the Harmonious Hare	Cybis	Open	175.00	275.00
67-01-027	Kitten, Blue Ribbon	Cybis	Closed	95.00	500.00
75-01-028	Kitten, Tabitha	Cybis	Closed	90.00	150.00
75-01-029	Kitten, Topaz	Cybis	Closed	90.00	150.00
86-01-030	Mick, The Melodious Mutt	Cybis	Open	175.00	275.00
85-01-031	Monday, Rhinoceros	Cybis	Open	85.00	150.00
71-01-032	Nashua	Cybis	100	2000.00	3000.00
78-01-033	Pinky Bunny/Carrot	Cybis	200	200.00	265.00
72-01-034	Pinto Colt	Cybis	Closed	175.00	250.00
76-01-035	Prairie Dog	Cybis	Closed	245.00	345.00
65-01-036	Raccoon, Raffles	Cybis	Closed	110.00	365.00
68-01-038	Snail, Sir Escargot	Cybis	Closed	50.00	300.00
65-01-039	Squirrel, Mr. Fluffy Tail	Cybis	Closed	90.00	350.00

		ARTIST	EDITION	ISSUE	QUOTE
80-01-040	Squirrel, Highrise	Cybis	400	475.00	525.00
68-01-041	Stallion	Cybis	350	475.00	850.00
66-01-042	Thoroughbred	Cybis	350	425.00	1500.00
86-01-043	White Tailed Deer	Cybis	50	9500.00	11500.00
Cybis	**Biblical**				
60-02-001	Exodus	Cybis	50	350.00	2600.00
60-02-002	Flight Into Egypt	Cybis	50	175.00	2500.00
56-02-003	Holy Child of Prague	Cybis	10	1500.00	N/A
XX-02-004	Holywater Font "Holy Ghost"	Cybis	Closed	15.00	145.00
57-02-005	Madonna, House of Gold	Cybis	8	125.00	4000.00
60-02-006	Madonna Lace & Rose	Cybis	Open	15.00	295.00
63-02-007	Moses, The Great Lawgiver	Cybis	750	250.00	5500.00
84-02-008	Nativity, Mary	Cybis	Open	Unkn.	325.00
84-02-009	Nativity, Joseph	Cybis	Open	Unkn.	325.00
84-02-010	Christ Child with Lamb	Cybis	Open	Unkn.	290.00
84-02-011	Nativity, Angel, Color	Cybis	Open	395.00	575.00
84-02-012	Nativity, Camel, Color	Cybis	Open	625.00	825.00
85-02-013	Nativity, Cow, Color	Cybis	Open	175.00	195.00
85-02-014	Nativity, Cow, White	Cybis	Open	125.00	225.00
85-02-015	Nativity, Donkey, Color	Cybis	Open	195.00	225.00
85-02-016	Nativity, Donkey, White	Cybis	Open	130.00	150.00
85-02-017	Nativity, Lamb, Color	Cybis	Open	150.00	195.00
85-02-018	Nativity, Lamb, White	Cybis	Open	115.00	125.00
84-02-019	Nativity, Shepherd, Color	Cybis	Open	395.00	475.00
76-02-020	Noah	Cybis	500	975.00	2800.00
64-02-021	St. Peter	Cybis	500	Unkn.	1250.00
60-02-022	The Prophet	Cybis	50	250.00	3500.00
Cybis	**Birds & Flowers**				
85-03-001	American Bald Eagle	Cybis	300	2900.00	3595.00
72-03-002	American Crested Iris	Cybis	400	975.00	1150.00
76-03-003	American White Turkey	Cybis	75	1450.00	1600.00
76-03-004	American Wild Turkey	Cybis	75	1950.00	2200.00
77-03-005	Apple Blossoms	Cybis	400	350.00	550.00
72-03-006	Autumn Dogwood w/Chickadees	Cybis	350	1100.00	1200.00
XX-03-007	Birds & Flowers	Cybis	250	500.00	4500.00
61-03-008	Blue-Grey Gnatcatchers, pair	Cybis	200	400.00	2500.00
60-03-009	Blue Headed Virio Building Nest	Cybis	Closed	60.00	1100.00
60-03-010	Blue Headed Virio with Lilac	Cybis	275	1200.00	2200.00
XX-03-011	Butterfly w/Dogwood	Cybis	200	Unkn.	350.00
68-03-012	Calla Lily	Cybis	500	750.00	1750.00
65-03-013	Christmas Rose	Cybis	500	250.00	750.00
77-03-014	Clematis	Cybis	Closed	210.00	315.00
69-03-015	Clematis with House Wren	Cybis	350	1300.00	1400.00
76-03-016	Colonial Basket	Cybis	100	2750.00	5500.00
76-03-017	Constancy Flower Basket	Cybis	Closed	345.00	400.00
64-03-018	Dahlia, Yellow	Cybis	350	450.00	1800.00
76-03-019	Devotion Flower Basket	Cybis	Closed	345.00	400.00
62-03-020	Duckling "Baby Brother"	Cybis	Closed	35.00	140.00
77-03-021	Duckling "Buttercup & Daffodil"	Cybis	Closed	165.00	295.00
70-03-022	Dutch Crocus	Cybis	350	550.00	750.00
76-03-023	Felicity Flower Basket	Cybis	Closed	325.00	345.00
61-03-024	Golden Clarion Lily	Cybis	100	250.00	4500.00
74-03-025	Golden Winged Warbler	Cybis	200	1075.00	1150.00
75-03-026	Great Horned Owl, Color	Cybis	50	3250.00	7500.00
75-03-027	Great Horned Owl, White	Cybis	150	1950.00	4500.00
64-03-028	Great White Heron	Cybis	350	850.00	3750.00
77-03-029	Hermit Thrush	Cybis	150	1450.00	1450.00
59-03-030	Hummingbird	Cybis	Closed	95.00	950.00
63-03-031	Iris	Cybis	250	500.00	4500.00
77-03-032	Krestrel	Cybis	175	1875.00	1925.00
78-03-033	Kinglets on Pyracantha	Cybis	175	900.00	1100.00
71-03-034	Little Blue Heron	Cybis	500	425.00	1500.00
63-03-035	Magnolia	Cybis	Closed	350.00	450-1500
76-03-036	Majesty Flower Basket	Cybis	Closed	345.00	400.00
70-03-037	Mushroom with Butterfly	Cybis	Closed	225.00	450.00
68-03-038	Narcissus	Cybis	500	350.00	550.00
78-03-039	Nestling Bluebirds	Cybis	Closed	235.00	250.00
72-03-040	Pansies, China Maid	Cybis	1,000	275.00	350.00
75-03-041	Pansies, Chinolina Lady	Cybis	750	295.00	400.00
60-03-042	Pheasant	Cybis	150	750.00	5000.00
XX-03-043	Sandpipers	Cybis	400	700.00	1500.00
85-03-044	Screech Owl & Siblings	Cybis	100	3250.00	3925.00
XX-03-045	Skylarks	Cybis	350	330.00	1800.00
62-03-046	Sparrow on a Log	Cybis	Closed	35.00	450.00
82-03-047	Spring Bouquet	Cybis	200	750.00	750.00
57-03-048	Turtle Doves	Cybis	500	350.00	5000.00
68-03-049	Wood Duck	Cybis	500	325.00	800.00
80-03-050	Yellow Rose	Cybis	Closed	80.00	450.00
80-03-051	Yellow Condesa Rose	Cybis	Closed	Unkn.	255.00
Cybis	**Children to Cherish**				
64-04-001	Alice in Wonderland	Cybis	Closed	50.00	850.00
78-04-002	Alice (Seated)	Cybis	Closed	350.00	550.00
78-04-003	Allegra	Cybis	Closed	310.00	350.00
63-04-004	Ballerina on Cue	Cybis	Closed	150.00	700.00
68-04-005	Ballerina, Little Princess	Cybis	Closed	125.00	750.00
85-04-006	Ballerina, Recital	Cybis	Open	275.00	275.00
60-04-007	Ballerina Red Shoes	Cybis	Closed	75.00	1200.00
85-04-008	Ballerina, Swanilda	Cybis	Open	450.00	725.00
68-04-009	Baby Bust	Cybis	239	375.00	1000.00
85-04-010	Beth	Cybis	Open	235.00	275.00
77-04-011	Boys Playing Marbles	Cybis	Closed	285.00	425.00
84-04-012	The Choirboy	Cybis	Open	325.00	345.00
85-04-013	Clara	Cybis	Open	395.00	395.00
86-04-014	Clarissa	Cybis	Open	165.00	195.00
78-04-015	Edith	Cybis	Closed	310.00	325.00
76-04-016	Elizabeth Ann	Cybis	Closed	195.00	275.00
85-04-017	Felicia	Cybis	Open	425.00	525.00
86-04-018	Encore Figure Skater	Cybis	750	625.00	675.00
85-04-019	Figure Eight	Cybis	750	625.00	750.00
XX-04-020	First Bouquet	Cybis	250	150.00	300.00
66-04-021	First Flight	Cybis	Closed	50.00	475.00
81-04-022	Fleurette	Cybis	1,000	725.00	1075.00
73-04-023	Goldilocks	Cybis	Closed	145.00	525.00
74-04-024	Gretel	Cybis	Closed	260.00	425.00
74-04-025	Hansel	Cybis	Closed	270.00	550.00
62-04-026	Heide, White	Cybis	Closed	165.00	550.00
62-04-027	Heide, Color	Cybis	Closed	165.00	550.00
84-04-028	Jack in the Beanstalk	Cybis	750	575.00	575.00
85-04-029	Jody	Cybis	Open	235.00	275.00
86-04-030	Kitri	Cybis	Open	450.00	550.00
78-04-031	Lisa and Lynette	Cybis	Closed	395.00	475.00
78-04-032	Little Boy Blue	Cybis	Closed	425.00	500.00
84-04-033	Little Champ	Cybis	Open	325.00	375.00
80-04-034	Little Miss Muffet	Cybis	Closed	335.00	365.00
73-04-035	Little Red Riding Hood	Cybis	Closed	110.00	475.00
86-04-036	Lullaby, Pink	Cybis	Open	125.00	160.00
86-04-037	Lullaby, Blue	Cybis	Open	125.00	160.00
86-04-038	Lullaby, Ivory	Cybis	Open	125.00	160.00
85-04-039	Marguerite	Cybis	Open	425.00	525.00
74-04-040	Mary, Mary	Cybis	500	475.00	750.00
76-04-041	Melissa	Cybis	Closed	285.00	425.00
84-04-042	Michael	Cybis	Open	235.00	350.00
67-04-043	Pandora Blue	Cybis	Closed	265.00	325.00
58-04-044	Peter Pan	Cybis	Closed	80.00	1000.00
71-04-045	Polyanna	Cybis	Closed	195.00	550.00
75-04-046	Rapunzel, Apricot	Cybis	1,500	475.00	1200.00
78-04-047	Rapunzel, Lilac	Cybis	1,000	675.00	1000.00
72-04-048	Rapunzel, Pink	Cybis	1,000	425.00	1100.00
64-04-049	Rebecca	Cybis	Closed	110.00	360.00
85-04-050	Recital	Cybis	Open	275.00	275.00
82-04-051	Robin	Cybis	1,000	475.00	850.00
82-04-052	Sleeping Beauty	Cybis	750	695.00	1475.00
63-04-053	Springtime	Cybis	Closed	45.00	775.00
57-04-054	Thumbelina	Cybis	Closed	45.00	525.00
59-04-055	Tinkerbell	Cybis	Closed	95.00	1500.00
85-04-056	Vanessa	Cybis	Open	425.00	525.00
75-04-057	Wendy with Flowers	Cybis	Unkn.	250.00	450.00
75-04-058	Yankee Doodle Dandy	Cybis	Closed	275.00	325.00
Cybis	**Commemoratives**				
81-05-001	Arion, Dolphin Rider	Cybis	1,000	575.00	1150.00
69-05-002	Apollo II Moon Mission	Cybis	111	1500.00	2500.00
72-05-003	Chess Set	Cybis	10	30000.00	60000.00
67-05-004	Columbia	Cybis	200	1000.00	2500.00
86-05-005	1986 Commemorative Egg	Cybis	Open	365.00	365.00
67-05-006	Conductor's Hands	Cybis	250	250.00	1500.00
71-05-007	Cree Indian	Cybis	100	2500.00	5500.00
84-05-008	Cree Indian "Magic Boy"	Cybis	200	4250.00	4995.00
75-05-009	George Washington Bust	Cybis	Closed	275.00	350.00
85-05-010	Holiday Ornament	Cybis	Open	75.00	75.00
81-05-011	Kateri Takakwitha	Cybis	100	2875.00	2975.00
86-05-012	Little Miss Liberty	Cybis	Open	295.00	350.00
77-05-013	Oceania	Cybis	200	1250.00	975-1550.
81-05-014	Phoenix	Cybis	100	950.00	950.00
80-05-015	The Bride	Cybis	100	6500.00	10500.00
84-05-016	1984 Cybis Holiday	Cybis	Open	145.00	145.00
85-05-017	Liberty	Cybis	100	1875.00	4000.00
Cybis	**Fantasia**				
74-06-001	Cybele	Cybis	500	675.00	800.00
81-06-002	Desiree, White Deer	Cybis	400	575.00	595.00
84-06-003	Flight and Fancy	Cybis	1,000	975.00	1175.00
80-06-004	Pegasus	Cybis	500	1450.00	750.00
80-06-005	Pegaus, Free Spirit	Cybis	1,000	675.00	775.00
81-06-006	Prince Brocade Unicorn	Cybis	500	2200.00	2600.00
78-06-007	Satin Horse Head	Cybis	500	1100.00	2800.00
77-06-008	Sea King's Steed "Oceania"	Cybis	200	1250.00	1450.00
78-06-009	Sharmaine Sea Nymph	Cybis	250	1450.00	1650.00
82-06-010	Theron	Cybis	350	675.00	850.00
69-06-011	Unicorn	Cybis	500	1250.00	3750.00
77-06-012	Unicorns, Gambol and Frolic	Cybis	1,000	425.00	2300.00
85-06-013	Dore'	Cybis	1,000	575.00	1075.00
Cybis	**Land of Chemeric**				
77-07-001	Marigold	Cybis	Closed	185.00	550.00
81-07-002	Melody	Cybis	1,000	725.00	800.00
79-07-003	Pip, Elfin Player	Cybis	1,000	450.00	665.00
77-07-004	Queen Titania	Cybis	750	725.00	2500.00
77-07-005	Tiffin	Cybis	Closed	175.00	550.00
85-07-006	Oberon	Cybis	750	825.00	825.00
Cybis	**North American Indian**				
74-08-001	Apache, "Chato"	Cybis	350	1950.00	3300.00
69-08-002	Blackfeet "Beaverhead Medicine Man"	Cybis	500	2000.00	2775.00
82-08-003	Choctaw "Tasculusa"	Cybis	200	2475.00	4050.00
77-08-004	Crow Dancer	Cybis	200	3875.00	8500.00
69-08-005	Dakota "Minnehaha Laughing Water"	Cybis	500	1500.00	2500.00
73-08-006	Eskimo Mother	Cybis	200	1875.00	2650.00
79-08-007	Great Spirit "Wankan Tanka"	Cybis	200	3500.00	4150.00
73-08-008	Iriquois "At the Council Fire"	Cybis	500	4250.00	4975.00
69-08-009	Onondaga "Haiwatha"	Cybis	500	1500.00	2450.00
71-08-010	Shoshone "Sacajawea"	Cybis	500	2250.00	2775.00
85-08-011	Yaqui "Deer Dancer"	Cybis	200	2095.00	2850.00
Cybis	**Portraits in Porcelain**				
76-09-001	Abigail Adams	Cybis	600	875.00	1300.00
73-09-002	Ballet-Princess Aurora	Cybis	200	1125.00	1500.00
73-09-003	Ballet-Prince Florimond	Cybis	200	975.00	1100.00
84-09-004	Bathsheba	Cybis	500	1975.00	3250.00
65-09-005	Beatrice	Cybis	700	225.00	1800.00
79-09-006	Berengaria	Cybis	500	1450.00	2-4700.
86-09-007	Carmen	Cybis	500	1675.00	1975.00
82-09-008	Desdemona	Cybis	500	1850.00	4000.00
71-09-009	Eleanor of Aquitaine	Cybis	750	875.00	4250.00
67-09-010	Folk Singer	Cybis	283	300.00	850.00
78-09-011	Good Queen Anne	Cybis	350	975.00	1500.00
67-09-012	Guinevere	Cybis	800	250.00	2400.00
68-09-013	Hamlet	Cybis	500	350.00	2000.00
81-09-014	Jane Eyre	Cybis	500	975.00	1500.00
65-09-015	Juliet	Cybis	800	175.00	4000.00
85-09-016	King Arthur	Cybis	350	2350.00	3450.00
85-09-017	King David	Cybis	350	1475.00	2175.00
72-09-018	Kwan Yin	Cybis	350	1250.00	2000.00
82-09-019	Lady Godiva	Cybis	200	1875.00	3250.00
75-09-020	Lady Macbeth	Cybis	750	850.00	1350.00
79-09-021	Nefertiti	Cybis	500	2100.00	3000.00
69-09-022	Ophelia	Cybis	800	750.00	4500.00
85-09-023	Pagliacci	Cybis	Open	325.00	325.00
82-09-024	Persephone	Cybis	200	3250.00	5250.00
73-09-025	Portia	Cybis	750	825.00	3750.00
76-09-026	Priscilla	Cybis	500	825.00	1500.00
74-09-027	Queen Esther	Cybis	750	925.00	1800.00
85-09-028	Romeo and Juliet	Cybis	500	2200.00	3400.00

		ARTIST	EDITION	ISSUE	QUOTE
68-09-029	Scarlett	Cybis	500	450.00	32-3500.
85-09-030	Tristan and Isolde	Cybis	200	2200.00	2200.00
Cybis	**Theatre of Porcelain**				
81-10-001	Columbine	Cybis	250	2250.00	2250.00
78-10-002	Court Jester	Cybis	250	1450.00	1750.00
80-10-003	Harlequin	Cybis	250	1575.00	1875.00
81-10-004	Puck	Cybis	250	2300.00	2450.00
Cybis	**Carousel-Circus**				
75-11-001	Barnaby Bear	Cybis	Closed	165.00	325.00
81-11-002	Bear, "Bernhard"	Cybis	325	1125.00	1150.00
75-11-003	Bicentennial Horse Ticonderoga	Cybis	350	925.00	4000.00
75-11-004	Bosun Monkey	Cybis	Closed	195.00	425.00
81-11-005	Bull, Plutus	Cybis	325	1125.00	2050.00
85-11-006	Carousel Unicorn	Cybis	325	1275.00	2750.00
79-11-007	Circus Rider "Equestrienne Extraordinaire"	Cybis	150	2275.00	3500.00
77-11-008	Dandy Dancing Dog	Cybis	Closed	145.00	295.00
81-11-009	Frollo	Cybis	1,000	750.00	825.00
76-11-010	Funny Face Child Head/Holly	Cybis	Closed	325.00	750.00
82-11-011	Giraffe	Cybis	750	Unkn.	1750.00
73-11-012	Carousel Goat	Cybis	325	875.00	1750.00
73-11-013	Carousel Horse	Cybis	325	925.00	7500.00
74-11-014	Lion	Cybis	325	1025.00	1350.00
76-11-015	Performing Pony "Poppy"	Cybis	1,000	325.00	1200.00
84-11-016	Phineas, Circus Elephant	Cybis	Open	325.00	425.00
86-11-017	Pierre, the Performing Poodle	Cybis	Open	225.00	275.00
81-11-018	Pony	Cybis	750	975.00	975.00
76-11-019	Sebastian Seal	Cybis	Closed	195.00	200.00
74-11-020	Tiger	Cybis	325	925.00	1500.00
85-11-021	Jumbles and Friend	Cybis	750	675.00	725.00
85-11-022	Valentine	Cybis	Open	335.00	375.00
Cybis	**Children of the World**				
72-12-001	Eskimo Child Head	Cybis	Closed	165.00	400.00
75-12-002	Indian Girl Head	Cybis	Closed	325.00	900.00
75-12-003	Indian Boy Head	Cybis	Closed	425.00	900.00
78-12-004	Jason	Cybis	Closed	285.00	375.00
78-12-005	Jennifer	Cybis	Closed	325.00	375.00
77-12-006	Jeremy	Cybis	Closed	315.00	475.00
79-12-007	Jessica	Cybis	Closed	325.00	475.00
Cybis	**Sport Scenes**				
80-13-001	Jogger, Female	Cybis	Closed	345.00	425.00
80-13-002	Jogger, Male	Cybis	Closed	395.00	475.00
Cybis	**Everyone's Fun Time (Limnettes)**				
72-14-001	Country Fair	Cybis	500	125.00	200.00
72-14-002	Windy Day	Cybis	500	125.00	200.00
72-14-003	The Pond	Cybis	500	125.00	200.00
72-14-004	The Seashore	Cybis	500	125.00	200.00
Cybis	**The Wonderful Seasons (Limnettes)**				
72-15-001	Autumn	Cybis	500	125.00	200.00
72-15-002	Spring	Cybis	500	125.00	200.00
72-15-003	Summer	Cybis	500	125.00	200.00
72-15-004	Winter	Cybis	500	125.00	200.00
Cybis	**When Bells are Ringing (Limnettes)**				
72-16-001	Easter Egg Hunt	Cybis	500	125.00	200.00
72-16-002	Independence Celebration	Cybis	500	125.00	200.00
72-16-003	Merry Christmas	Cybis	500	125.00	200.00
72-16-004	Sabbath Morning	Cybis	500	125.00	200.00
Department 56	**Dickens' Village Series**				
84-01-001	The Original Shops of Dickens' Village, 6515-3, Set of 7	Department 56	Closed	175.00	12-1500.
84-01-002	Crowntree Inn 6515-3	Department 56	Closed	25.00	250-430.
84-01-003	Candle Shop 6515-3	Department 56	Closed	25.00	180-275.
84-01-004	Green Grocer 6515-3	Department 56	Closed	25.00	140-230.
84-01-005	Golden Swan Baker 6515-3	Department 56	Closed	25.00	110-215.
84-01-006	Bean And Son Smithy Shop 6515-3	Department 56	Closed	25.00	165-250.
84-01-007	Abel Beesley Butcher 6515-3	Department 56	Closed	25.00	100-150.
84-01-008	Jones & Co. Brush & Basket Shop 6515-3	Department 56	Closed	25.00	280-425.
84-01-009	Dickens' Village Church (cream) 6516-1	Department 56	Closed	35.00	210-440.
85-01-010	Dickens' Village Church(tan) 6516-1	Department 56	Closed	35.00	150-255.
85-01-011	Dickens' Village Church(green) 6516-1	Department 56	Closed	35.00	190-440.
85-01-012	Dickens' Village Church(dark) 6516-1	Department 56	Closed	35.00	140-150.
85-01-012	Dickens' Cottages 6518-8 Set of 3	Department 56	Closed	75.00	700-1050.
85-01-013	Thatched Cottage 6518-8	Department 56	Closed	25.00	165-300.
85-01-014	Stone Cottage 6518-8	Department 56	Closed	25.00	355-450.
85-01-015	Tudor Cottage 6518-8	Department 56	Closed	25.00	250-500.
85-01-016	Dickens' Village Mill 6519-6	Department 56	2,500	35.00	42-6500.
86-01-017	Christmas Carol Cottages 6500-5, Set of 3 (Fezziwig's Warehouse, Scrooge and Marley Counting House, The Cottage of Bob Cratchit & Tiny Tim)	Department 56	Open	75.00	90.00
86-01-018	Norman Church 6502-1	Department 56	3,500	40.00	22-3500.
86-01-019	Dickens' Lane Shops 6507-2, Set of 3	Department 56	Closed	80.00	450-690.
86-01-020	Thomas Kersey Coffee House 6507-2	Department 56	Closed	27.00	110-230.
86-01-021	Cottage Toy Shop 6507-2	Department 56	Closed	27.00	170-280.
86-01-022	Tuttle's Pub 6507-2	Department 56	Closed	27.00	170-270.
86-01-023	Blythe Pond Mill House 6508-0	Department 56	Closed	37.00	130-300.
86-01-024	By The Pond Mill House 6508-0	Department 56	Closed	37.00	110-240.
86-01-025	Chadbury Station and Train 6528-5	Department 56	Closed	65.00	290-460.
87-01-026	Barley Bree 5900-5, Set of 2 (Farmhouse, Barn)	Department 56	Closed	60.00	330-500.
87-01-027	The Old Curiosity Shop 5905-6	Department 56	Open	32.00	37.50
87-01-028	Kenilworth Castle 5916-1	Department 56	Closed	70.00	400-500.
87-01-029	Brick Abbey 6549-8	Department 56	Closed	33.00	375-475.
87-01-030	Chesterton Manor House 6568-4	Department 56	7,500	45.00	14-1900.
88-01-031	Counting House & Silas Thimbleton Barrister 5902-1	Department 56	Closed	32.00	80-140.
88-01-032	C. Fletcher Public House 5904-8	Department 56	12,500	35.00	540-675.
88-01-033	Cobblestone Shops 5924-2, Set of 3	Department 56	Closed	95.00	300-400.
88-01-034	The Wool Shop 5924-2	Department 56	Closed	32.00	150-250
88-01-035	Booter and Cobbler 5924-2	Department 56	Closed	32.00	90-132.
88-01-036	T. Wells Fruit & Spice Shop 5924-2	Department 56	Closed	32.00	85-124.
88-01-037	Nicholas Nickleby 5925-0, Set of 2	Department 56	Closed	72.00	145-180.
88-01-038	Nicholas Nickleby Cottage 5925-0	Department 56	Closed	36.00	75-100.
88-01-039	Wackford Squeers Boarding School 5925-0	Department 56	Closed	36.00	78-115.
88-01-040	Nickolas Nickleby Cottage 5925-0-misspelled	Department 56	Closed	36.00	85-100.
88-01-041	Nickolas Nickleby set of 2, 5925-0-misspelled	Department 56	Closed	36.00	210-260.
88-01-042	Merchant Shops 5926-9, 5/set,	Department 56	Closed	150.00	225-285.
88-01-043	Poulterer 5926-9	Department 56	Closed	30.00	56-125.
88-01-044	Geo. Weeton Watchmaker 5926-9	Department 56	Closed	30.00	50-80.00
88-01-045	The Mermaid Fish Shoppe 5926-9	Department 56	Closed	30.00	55-125.
88-01-046	White Horse Bakery 5926-9	Department 56	Closed	30.00	55-125.
88-01-047	Walpole Tailors 5926-9	Department 56	Closed	30.00	50-85.00
88-01-048	Ivy Glen Church 5927-7	Department 56	Closed	35.00	75-132.
89-01-049	David Copperfield 5550-6, Set of 3	Department 56	Closed	125.00	162-281.
89-01-050	Mr. Wickfield Solicitor 5550-6	Department 56	Closed	42.50	75-100.
89-01-051	Betsy Trotwood's Cottage 5550-6	Department 56	Closed	42.50	45-97.00
89-01-052	Peggotty's Seaside Cottage 5550-6 (green boat)	Department 56	Closed	42.50	50-86.00
89-01-053	David Copperfield 5550-6, Set of 3 with tan boat	Department 56	Closed	125.00	220-373.
89-01-054	Peggotty's Seaside Cottage 5550-6 (tan boat)	Department 56	Closed	42.50	115-185.
89-01-055	Victoria Station 5574-3	Department 56	Open	100.00	100.00
89-01-056	Knottinghill Church 5582-4	Department 56	Open	50.00	50.00
89-01-057	Cobles Police Station 5583-2	Department 56	Closed	37.50	80-125.
89-01-058	Theatre Royal 5584-0	Department 56	Closed	45.00	60-100.
89-01-059	Ruth Marion Scotch Woolens 5585-9	Department 56	17,500	65.00	300-425.
89-01-060	Green Gate Cottage 5586-7	Department 56	22,500	65.00	235-350.
89-01-061	The Flat of Ebenezer Scrooge 5587-5	Department 56	Open	37.50	37.50
90-01-062	Bishops Oast House 5567-0	Department 56	Closed	45.00	60-125.
90-01-063	Kings Road 5568-9, Set of 2 (Tutbury Printer, C.H. Watt Physician)	Department 56	Open	72.00	72.00
91-01-064	Fagin's Hide-A-Way 5552-2	Department 56	Open	68.00	68.00
91-01-065	Oliver Twist 5553-0 Set of 2	Department 56	Closed	75.00	100-145.
91-01-066	Brownlow House 5553-0	Department 56	Closed	38.00	55-100.
91-01-067	Maylie Cottage	Department 56	Closed	38.00	50-95.00
91-01-068	Ashbury Inn 5555-7	Department 56	Open	55.00	55.00
91-01-069	Nephew Fred's Flat 5557-3	Department 56	Open	35.00	35.00
92-01-070	Crown & Cricket Inn (Charles Dickens' Signature Series), 5750-9	Department 56	Closed	100.00	140-220.
92-01-071	Old Michaelchurch, 5562-0	Department 56	Open	42.00	42.00
92-01-072	Hembleton Pewterer, 5800-9	Department 56	Open	72.00	72.00
92-01-073	King's Road Post Office, 5801-7	Department 56	Open	45.00	45.00
93-01-074	The Pied Bull Inn (Charles Dickens' Signature Series), 5751-7	Department 56	Closed	100.00	135-200.
93-01-075	Boarding and Lodging School, 5809-2 (Christmas Carol Commemorative Piece)	Department 56	Closed	48.00	170-250.
93-01-076	Pump Lane Shoppes,5808-4 set of 3 (Bumpstead Nye Cloaks & Canes, Lomas Ltd. Molasses, W.M. Wheat Cakes & Puddings)	Department 56	Open	112.00	112.00
93-01-077	Kingford's Brewhouse, 5811-4	Department 56	Open	45.00	45.00
93-01-078	Great Denton Mill, 5812-2	Department 56	Open	50.00	50.00
94-01-079	Dedlock Arms, 5752-5 (Charles Dickens' Signature Series)	Department 56	Yr.Iss.	100.00	100-160.
94-01-080	Boarding & Lodging School, 5810-6	Department 56	Open	48.00	48.00
94-01-081	Whittlesbourne Church, 5821-1	Department 56	Open	85.00	85.00
94-01-082	Giggelswick Mutton & Ham, 5822-0	Department 56	Open	48.00	48.00
94-01-083	Dickens' Postern, 9871-0, (Dickens' Village Ten Year Accessory Anniversary Piece)	Department 56	Open	17.50	17.50
Department 56	**New England Village Series**				
86-02-001	New England Village 6530-7, Set of 7	Department 56	Closed	170.00	1100.00
86-02-002	Apothecary Shop 6530-7	Department 56	Closed	25.00	90-130.
86-02-003	General Store 6530-7	Department 56	Closed	25.00	275-300.
86-02-004	Nathaniel Bingham Fabrics 6530-7	Department 56	Closed	25.00	140-170.
86-02-005	Livery Stable & Boot Shop 6530-7	Department 56	Closed	25.00	125-160.
86-02-006	Steeple Church (Original) 6530-7	Department 56	Closed	25.00	175-185.
86-02-007	Brick Town Hall 6530-7	Department 56	Closed	25.00	210-375.
86-02-008	Red Schoolhouse 6530-7	Department 56	Closed	25.00	220-350.
86-02-009	Jacob Adams Farmhouse and Barn 6538-2	Department 56	Closed	65.00	450-550.
86-02-010	Steeple Church (Second Version) 6539-0	Department 56	Closed	30.00	85-125.
87-02-011	Craggy Cove Lighthouse 5930-7	Department 56	Open	35.00	44.00
87-02-012	Weston Train Station 5931-5	Department 56	Closed	42.00	235-300.
87-02-013	Smythe Woolen Mill 6543-9	Department 56	7,500	42.00	1050-13.
87-02-014	Timber Knoll Log Cabin 6544-7	Department 56	Closed	28.00	125-145.
88-02-015	Old North Church 5932-3	Department 56	Open	40.00	42.00
88-02-016	Cherry Lane Shops 5939-0, Set of 3	Department 56	Closed	80.00	250-325.
88-02-017	Ben's Barbershop 5939-0	Department 56	Closed	27.00	75-90.00
88-02-018	Otis Hayes Butcher Shop 5939-0	Department 56	Closed	27.00	60-90.00
88-02-019	Anne Shaw Toys 5939-0	Department 56	Closed	27.00	120-150.
88-02-020	Ada's Bed and Boarding House (lemon yellow) 5940-4	Department 56	Closed	36.00	200-300.
88-02-021	Ada's Bed and Boarding House (pale yellow) 5940-4	Department 56	Closed	36.00	90-125.
89-02-022	Berkshire House (medium blue) 5942-0	Department 56	Closed	40.00	100-156.
89-02-023	Berkshire House (teal) 5942-0	Department 56	Closed	40.00	85-110.
89-02-024	Jannes Mullet Amish Farm House 5943-9	Department 56	Closed	32.00	85-140.
89-02-025	Jannes Mullet Amish Barn 5944-7	Department 56	Closed	48.00	75-120.
90-02-026	Shingle Creek House 5946-3	Department 56	Open	37.50	37.50
90-02-027	Captain's Cottage 5947-1	Department 56	Open	40.00	40.00
90-02-028	Sleepy Hollow 5954-4, Set of 3	Department 56	Closed	96.00	140-165.
90-02-029	Sleepy Hollow School 5954-4	Department 56	Closed	32.00	60-80.00
90-02-030	Van Tassel Manor 5954-4	Department 56	Closed	32.00	50-80.00
90-02-031	Ichabod Crane's Cottage 5954-4	Department 56	Closed	32.00	50-80.00
90-02-032	Sleepy Hollow Church 5955-2	Department 56	Closed	36.00	50-75.00
91-02-033	McGrebe-Cutters & Sleighs 5640-5	Department 56	Open	45.00	45.00
92-02-034	Bluebird Seed and Bulb, 5642-1	Department 56	Open	48.00	48.00
92-02-035	Yankee Jud Bell Casting 5643-0	Department 56	Open	44.00	44.00
92-02-036	Stoney Brook Town Hall 5644-8	Department 56	Open	42.00	42.00
93-02-037	Blue Star Ice Co., 5647-2	Department 56	Open	45.00	45.00
93-02-038	A. Bieler Farm 5648-0, set of 2 (Pennsylvania Dutch Farmhouse, Pennsylvania Dutch Barn)	Department 56	Open	92.00	92.00
94-02-038	Arlington Falls Church, 5651-0	Department 56	Open	40.00	40.00
Department 56	**Alpine Village Series**				
86-03-001	Alpine Village 6540-4, 5/set (Bessor Bierkeller, Gasthof Eisl, Apotheke, E. Staubr Backer, Milch-Kase)	Department 56	Open	150.00	185.00
87-03-002	Josef Engel Farmhouse 5952-8	Department 56	Closed	33.00	625-850.
87-03-003	Alpine Church 6541-2	Department 56	Closed	32.00	95-160.
88-03-004	Grist Mill 5953-6	Department 56	Open	42.00	44.00
90-03-005	Bahnhof 5615-4	Department 56	Closed	42.00	60-90.00
91-03-006	St. Nikolaus Kirche 5617-0	Department 56	Open	37.50	37.50
92-03-007	Alpine Shops 5618-9,2/set (Metterniche Wurst, Kukuck Uhren)	Department 56	Open	75.00	75.00
93-03-008	Sport Laden, 5612-0	Department 56	Open	50.00	50.00

Department 56 — Christmas In the City Series

		ARTIST	EDITION	ISSUE	QUOTE
87-04-001	Sutton Place Brownstones 5961-7	Department 56	Closed	80.00	700-1000.
87-04-002	The Cathedral 5962-5	Department 56	Closed	60.00	250-350.
87-04-003	Palace Theatre 5963-3	Department 56	Closed	45.00	850-1200
87-04-004	Christmas In The City 6512-9, Set of 3	Department 56	Closed	112.00	330-400.
87-04-005	Toy Shop and Pet Store 6512-9	Department 56	Closed	37.50	125-180.
87-04-006	Bakery 6512-9	Department 56	Closed	37.50	70-100.
87-04-007	Tower Restaurant 6512-9	Department 56	Closed	37.50	140-200.
88-04-008	Chocolate Shoppe 5968-4	Department 56	Closed	40.00	80-150.
88-04-009	City Hall (standard) 5969-2	Department 56	Closed	65.00	125-230.
88-04-010	City Hall (small) 5969-2	Department 56	Closed	65.00	125-175.
88-04-011	Hank's Market 5970-6	Department 56	Closed	40.00	60-110.
88-04-012	Variety Store 5972-2	Department 56	Closed	45.00	115-155.
89-04-013	Ritz Hotel 5973-0	Department 56	Open	55.00	55.00
89-04-014	Dorothy's Dress Shop 5974-9	Department 56	12,500	70.00	330-400.
89-04-015	Dorothy's Dress Shop (proof) 5974-9	Department 56	12,500	70.00	325-350.
89-04-016	5607 Park Avenue Townhouse 5977-3	Department 56	Closed	48.00	60-110.
89-04-017	5609 Park Avenue Townhouse 5978-1	Department 56	Closed	48.00	60-110.
90-04-018	Red Brick Fire Station 5536-0	Department 56	Open	55.00	55.00
90-04-019	Wong's In Chinatown 5537-9	Department 56	Open	55.00	55.00
91-04-020	Hollydale's Department Store 5534-4	Department 56	Open	75.00	75.00
91-04-021	Little Italy Ristorante 5538-7	Department 56	Open	50.00	50.00
91-04-022	All Saints Corner Church 5542-5	Department 56	Open	96.00	96.00
91-04-023	Arts Academy 5543-3	Department 56	Closed	45.00	60-100.
90-04-024	The Doctor's Office 5544-1	Department 56	Open	60.00	60.00
92-04-025	Cathedral Church of St. Mark 5549-2	Department 56	3,024	120.00	2-3200.
92-04-026	Uptown Shoppes 5531-0, Set of 3 (Haberdashery, City Clockworks, Music Emporium)	Department 56	Open	150.00	150.00
93-04-027	West Village Shops 5880-7, set of 2 (Potters' Tea Seller, Spring St. Coffee House)	Department 56	Open	90.00	90.00
94-04-028	Brokerage House, 5881-5	Department 56	Open	48.00	48.00

Department 56 — Little Town of Bethlehem Series

		ARTIST	EDITION	ISSUE	QUOTE
87-05-001	Little Town of Bethlehem 5975-7, Set of 12	Department 56	Open	150.00	150.00

Department 56 — Disney Parks Village Series

		ARTIST	EDITION	ISSUE	QUOTE
94-05-001	Mickey's Christmas Shop, set of 2 5350-3 Disney World, FL	Department 56	Open	144.00	144.00
94-05-002	Olde World Antiques, set of 2 5351-1 Disney World, FL	Department 56	Open	90.00	90.00
94-05-003	Fire Station 5352-0 Disneyland, CA	Department 56	Open	45.00	45.00
94-05-004	Mickey and Minnie (Accessory), set of 2 5353-8	Department 56	Open	22.50	22.50
94-05-005	Disney Parks Family (Accessory), set of 3 5354-6	Department 56	Open	32.50	32.50
94-05-006	Olde World Antiques Gate 5355-4	Department 56	Open	15.00	15.00

Department 56 — The Original Snow Village Collection

		ARTIST	EDITION	ISSUE	QUOTE
76-06-001	Mountain Lodge 5001-3	Department 56	Closed	20.00	300-450.
76-06-002	Gabled Cottage 5002-1	Department 56	Closed	20.00	340-450.
76-06-003	The Inn 5003-9	Department 56	Closed	20.00	450-650.
76-06-004	Country Church 5004-7	Department 56	Closed	18.00	320-385.
76-06-005	Steepled Church 5005-4	Department 56	Closed	25.00	775-795.
76-06-006	Small Chalet 5006-2	Department 56	Closed	15.00	325-500.
77-06-007	Victorian House 5007-0	Department 56	Closed	30.00	400-460.
77-06-008	Mansion 5008-8	Department 56	Closed	30.00	500-600.
77-06-009	Stone Church (10") 5009-6	Department 56	Closed	35.00	400-600.
78-06-010	Homestead 5011-2	Department 56	Closed	30.00	225-260.
78-06-011	General Store (white) 5012-0	Department 56	Closed	25.00	435.00
78-06-012	General Store (tan) 5012-0	Department 56	Closed	25.00	660.00
78-06-013	Cape Cod 5013-8	Department 56	Closed	20.00	375-500.
78-06-014	Nantucket 5014-6	Department 56	Closed	25.00	210-290.
78-06-015	Skating Rink, Duck Pond (Set) 5015-3	Department 56	Closed	16.00	1330.00
78-06-016	Small Double Trees w/ red birds 5016-1	Department 56	Closed	13.50	40-69.00
78-06-017	Small Double Trees w/ blue birds 5016-1	Department 56	Closed	13.50	150-165.
79-06-018	Thatched Cottage 5050-0 Meadowland Series	Department 56	Closed	30.00	600.00
79-06-019	Countryside Church 5051-8 Meadowland Series	Department 56	Closed	25.00	700.00
79-06-020	Victorian 5054-2	Department 56	Closed	30.00	270-400.
79-06-021	Knob Hill 5055-9	Department 56	Closed	30.00	330.00
79-06-022	Knob Hill (gold) 5055-9	Department 56	Closed	30.00	325-400.
79-06-023	Brownstone 5056-7	Department 56	Closed	36.00	300-550.
79-06-024	Log Cabin 5057-5	Department 56	Closed	22.00	440-520.
79-06-025	Countryside Church 5058-3	Department 56	Closed	27.50	260-360.
79-06-026	Stone Church (8") 5059-1	Department 56	Closed	32.00	980.00
79-06-027	School House 5060-9	Department 56	Closed	30.00	300-400.
79-06-028	Tudor House 5061-7	Department 56	Closed	25.00	305-415.
79-06-029	Mission Church 5062-5	Department 56	Closed	30.00	1000.00
79-06-030	Mobile Home 5063-3	Department 56	Closed	18.00	16-2750.
79-06-031	Giant Trees 5065-8	Department 56	Closed	20.00	200-380.
79-06-032	Adobe House 5066-6	Department 56	Closed	18.00	2-2700.
80-06-033	Cathedral Church 5067-4	Department 56	Closed	36.00	17-2750.
80-06-034	Stone Mill House 5068-2	Department 56	Closed	30.00	525-600.
80-06-035	Colonial Farm House 5070-9	Department 56	Closed	30.00	340-355.
80-06-036	Town Church 5071-7	Department 56	Closed	33.00	360-515.
80-06-037	Train Station with 3 Train Cars 5085-6	Department 56	Closed	100.00	350-420.
81-06-038	Wooden Clapboard 5072-5	Department 56	Closed	32.00	240-285.
81-06-039	English Cottage 5073-3	Department 56	Closed	25.00	265-395.
81-06-040	Barn 5074-1	Department 56	Closed	32.00	300-490.
81-06-041	Corner Store 5076-8	Department 56	Closed	30.00	230-275.
81-06-042	Bakery 5077-6	Department 56	Closed	30.00	250-325.
81-06-043	English Church 5078-4	Department 56	Closed	30.00	340-365.
81-06-044	Large Single Tree 5080-6	Department 56	Closed	17.00	35-50.00
82-06-045	Skating Pond 5017-2	Department 56	Closed	25.00	210-300.
82-06-046	Street Car 5019-9	Department 56	Closed	16.00	210-400.
82-06-047	Centennial House 5020-2	Department 56	Closed	32.00	285-400.
82-06-048	Carriage House 5021-0	Department 56	Closed	28.00	300-360.
82-06-049	Pioneer Church 5022-9	Department 56	Closed	30.00	240-310.
82-06-050	Swiss Chalet 5023-7	Department 56	Closed	28.00	345-400.
82-06-051	Bank 5024-5	Department 56	Closed	32.00	495-650.
82-06-052	Gabled House 5081-4	Department 56	Closed	30.00	330-400.
82-06-053	Flower Shop 5082-2	Department 56	Closed	25.00	380-410.
82-06-054	New Stone Church 5083-0	Department 56	Closed	32.00	275-375.
83-06-055	Town Hall 5000-8	Department 56	Closed	32.00	245-325.
83-06-056	Grocery 5001-6	Department 56	Closed	35.00	275-335.
83-06-057	Victorian Cottage 5002-4	Department 56	Closed	35.00	260-360.
83-06-058	Governor's Mansion 5003-2	Department 56	Closed	32.00	200-360.
83-06-059	Turn of the Century 5004-0	Department 56	Closed	36.00	200-240.
83-06-060	Gingerbread HouseBank (Non-lighted) 5025-3	Department 56	Closed	24.00	300-400.
83-06-061	Village Church 5026-1	Department 56	Closed	30.00	260-385.
83-06-062	Gothic Church 5028-8	Department 56	Closed	36.00	270-330.
83-06-063	Parsonage 5029-6	Department 56	Closed	35.00	325-360.
83-06-064	Wooden Church 5031-8	Department 56	Closed	30.00	310-330.
83-06-065	Fire Station 5032-6	Department 56	Closed	32.00	550-690.
83-06-066	English Tudor 5033-4	Department 56	Closed	30.00	275-450.
83-06-067	Chateau 5084-9	Department 56	Closed	35.00	390-460.
84-06-068	Main Street House 5005-9	Department 56	Closed	27.00	160-250.
84-06-069	Stratford House 5007-5	Department 56	Closed	28.00	180-220.
84-06-070	Haversham House 5008-3	Department 56	Closed	37.00	205-340.
84-06-071	Galena House 5009-1	Department 56	Closed	32.00	300-325.
84-06-072	River Road House 5010-5	Department 56	Closed	36.00	195-255.
84-06-073	Delta House 5012-1	Department 56	Closed	32.00	265-400.
84-06-074	Bayport 5015-6	Department 56	Closed	30.00	210-310.
84-06-075	Congregational Church 5034-2	Department 45	Closed	28.00	395-550.
84-06-076	Trinity Church 5035-0	Department 56	Closed	32.00	180-320.
84-06-077	Summit House 5036-9	Department 56	Closed	28.00	370-385.
84-06-078	New School House 5037-7	Department 56	Closed	35.00	260-315.
84-06-079	Parish Church 5039-3	Department 56	Closed	32.00	260-400.
85-06-080	Stucco Bungalow 5045-8	Department 56	Closed	30.00	380.00
85-06-081	Williamsburg House 5046-6	Department 56	Closed	37.00	105-148.
85-06-082	Plantation House 5047-4	Department 56	Closed	37.00	90-105.
85-06-083	Church of the Open Door 5048-2	Department 56	Closed	34.00	80-130.
85-06-084	Spruce Place 5049-0	Department 56	Closed	33.00	280-300.
85-06-085	Duplex 5050-4	Department 56	Closed	35.00	90-140.
85-06-086	Depot and Train with 2 Train Cars 5051-2	Department 56	Closed	65.00	100-140.
85-06-087	Ridgewood 5052-0	Department 56	Closed	35.00	120-165.
86-06-088	Waverly Place 5041-5	Department 56	Closed	35.00	300-365.
86-06-089	Twin Peaks 5042-3	Department 56	Closed	32.00	300-445.
86-06-090	2101 Maple 5043-1	Department 56	Closed	32.00	340-385.
86-06-091	Lincoln Park Duplex 5060-1	Department 56	Closed	33.00	90-125.
86-06-092	Sonoma House 5062-8	Department 56	Closed	33.00	75-120.
86-06-093	Highland Park House 5063-6	Department 56	Closed	35.00	100-140.
86-06-094	Beacon Hill House 5065-2	Department 56	Closed	31.00	100-150.
86-06-095	Pacific Heights House 5066-0	Department 56	Closed	33.00	75-100.
86-06-096	Ramsey Hill House 5067-9	Department 56	Closed	36.00	75-140.
86-06-097	Saint James Church 5068-7	Department 56	Closed	37.00	125-150.
86-06-098	All Saints Church 5070-9	Department 56	Open	38.00	45.00
86-06-099	Carriage House 5071-7	Department 56	Closed	29.00	60-110.
86-06-100	Toy Shop 5073-3	Department 56	Closed	36.00	60-105.
86-06-101	Apothecary 5076-8	Department 56	Closed	34.00	75-126.
86-06-102	Bakery 5077-6	Department 56	Closed	35.00	60-100.
86-06-103	Mickey's Diner 5078-4	Department 56	Closed	22.00	415-510.
87-06-104	St. Anthony Hotel & Post Office 5006-7	Department 56	Closed	40.00	85-138.
87-06-105	Snow Village Factory 5013-0	Department 56	Closed	45.00	85-125.
87-06-106	Cathedral Church 5019-9	Department 56	Closed	50.00	90-110.
87-06-107	Cumberland House 5024-5	Department 56	Open	42.00	44.00
87-06-108	Springfield House 5027-0	Department 56	Closed	40.00	60-100.
87-06-109	Lighthouse 5030-0	Department 56	Closed	36.00	330-575.
87-06-110	Red Barn 5081-4	Department 56	Closed	38.00	65-100.
87-06-111	Jefferson School 5082-2	Department 56	Closed	36.00	100-135.
87-06-112	Farm House 5089-0	Department 56	Closed	40.00	50-97.00
87-06-113	Fire Station No. 2 5091-1	Department 56	Closed	40.00	120-150.
87-06-114	Snow Village Resort Lodge 5092-0	Department 56	Closed	55.00	105-150.
88-06-115	Village Market 5044-0	Department 56	Closed	39.00	60-115.
88-06-116	Kenwood House 5054-7	Department 56	Closed	50.00	95-125.
88-06-117	Maple Ridge Inn 5121-7	Department 56	Closed	55.00	60-150.
88-06-118	Village Station and Train 5122-5	Department 56	Closed	65.00	70-100.
88-06-119	Cobblestone Antique Shop 5123-3	Department 56	Closed	36.00	50-97.00
88-06-120	Corner Cafe 5124-1	Department 56	Closed	37.00	50-100.
88-06-121	Single Car Garage 5125-0	Department 56	Closed	22.00	35-100.
88-06-122	Home Sweet Home/House & Windmill 5126-8	Department 56	Closed	60.00	90-126.
88-06-123	Redeemer Church 5127-6	Department 56	Closed	42.00	50-97.00
88-06-124	Service Station 5128-4	Department 56	Closed	37.50	110-165.
88-06-125	Stonehurst House 5140-3	Department 56	Open	37.50	37.50
88-06-126	Palos Verdes 5141-1	Department 56	Closed	37.50	60-90.00
89-06-127	Jingle Belle Houseboat 5114-4	Department 56	Closed	42.00	75-120.
89-06-128	Colonial Church 5119-5	Department 56	Closed	60.00	60-115.
89-06-129	North Creek Cottage 5120-9	Department 56	Closed	45.00	55-90.00
89-06-130	Paramount Theater 5142-0	Department 56	Closed	42.00	65-110.
89-06-131	Doctor's House 5143-8	Department 56	Closed	56.00	80-115.
89-06-132	Courthouse 5144-6	Department 56	Closed	65.00	95-150.
89-06-133	Village Warming House 5145-4	Department 56	Closed	42.00	55-100.
89-06-134	J. Young's Granary 5149-7	Department 56	Closed	45.00	60-100.
89-06-135	Pinewood Log Cabin 5150-0	Department 56	Open	37.50	37.50
90-06-136	56 Flavors Ice Cream Parlor 5151-9	Department 56	Closed	42.00	70-135.
90-06-137	Morningside House 5152-7	Department 56	Closed	45.00	45-100.
90-06-138	Mainstreet Hardware Store 5153-5	Department 56	Closed	42.00	55-100.
90-06-139	Village Realty 5154-3	Department 56	Closed	42.00	55-100.
90-06-140	Spanish Mission Church 5155-1	Department 56	Closed	42.00	42-100.
90-06-141	Prairie House (American Architecture Series), 5156-0	Department 56	Closed	42.00	50-100.
90-06-142	Queen Anne Victorian (American Architecture Series), 5157-8	Department 56	Open	48.00	48.00
91-06-143	Oak Grove Tudor 5400-3	Department 56	Open	42.00	42.00
91-06-144	Honeymooner Motel 5401-1	Department 56	Closed	42.00	65-100.
91-06-145	The Christmas Shop 5097-0	Department 56	Open	37.50	37.50
91-06-146	Village Greenhouse 5402-0	Department 56	Open	35.00	35.00
91-06-147	Southern Colonial (American Architecture Series), 5403-8	Department 56	Open	48.00	48.00
91-06-148	Gothic Farmhouse (American Architecture Series), 5404-6	Department 56	Open	48.00	48.00
91-06-149	Finklea's Finery: Costume Shop 5405-4	Department 56	Closed	45.00	45-90.00
91-06-150	Jack's Corner Barber Shop 5406-2	Department 56	Open	42.00	42.00
91-06-151	Double Bungalow, 5407-0	Department 56	Open	45.00	45.00
92-06-152	Post Office 5422-4	Department 56	Open	35.00	35.00
92-06-153	Grandma's Cottage 5420-8	Department 56	Open	42.00	42.00
92-06-154	St. Luke's Church 5421-6	Department 56	Open	45.00	45.00
92-06-155	Al's TV Shop 5423-2	Department 56	Open	40.00	40.00
92-06-156	Good Shepherd Chapel & Church School Set of 2 5424-0	Department 56	Open	72.00	72.00
92-06-157	Print Shop & Village News 5425-9	Department 56	Open	37.50	37.50
92-06-158	Hartford House 5426-7	Department 56	Open	55.00	55.00
92-06-159	Village Vet and Pet Shop 5427-5	Department 56	Open	32.00	32.00
92-06-160	Craftsman Cottage (American Architecture Series), 5437-2	Department 56	Open	55.00	55.00
92-06-161	Village Station 5438-0	Department 56	Open	65.00	65.00
92-06-162	Airport 5439-9	Department 56	Open	60.00	60.00
93-06-163	Nantucket Renovation 5441-0	Department 56	Closed	55.00	90-140.
93-06-164	Mount Olivet Church, 5442-9	Department 56	Open	65.00	65.00
93-06-165	Village Public Library, 5443-7	Department 56	Open	55.00	55.00
93-06-166	Woodbury House, 5444-5	Department 56	Open	45.00	45.00

		ARTIST	EDITION	ISSUE	QUOTE
93-06-167	Hunting Lodge, 5445-3	Department 56	Open	50.00	50.00
93-06-168	Dairy Barn, 5446-1	Department 56	Open	55.00	55.00
93-06-169	Dinah's Drive-In, 5447-0	Department 56	Open	45.00	45.00
93-06-170	Snowy Hills Hospital, 5448-8	Department 56	Open	48.00	48.00
94-06-171	Fisherman's Nook Resort, 5460-7	Department 56	Open	75.00	75.00
94-06-172	Fisherman's Nook Cabins, set of 2, 5461-5, (Fisherman's Nook Bass Cabin, Fisherman's Nook Trout Cabin)	Department 56	Open	50.00	50.00
94-06-174	The Original Snow Village Starter Set, 5462-3 (Shady Oak Church, Sunday School Serenade Accessory, 3 assorted Sisal Trees, 1.5 oz. bag of real plastic snow)	Department 56	Open	50.00	50.00

Department 56 — North Pole Series

		ARTIST	EDITION	ISSUE	QUOTE
90-07-001	Santa's Workshop 5600-6	Department 56	Closed	72.00	125-175.
90-07-002	North Pole 5601-4 Set of 2 (Reindeer Barn, Elf Bunkhouse)	Department 56	Open	70.00	70.00
91-07-003	Neenee's Dolls & Toys 5620-0	Department 56	Open	37.50	36.00
91-07-004	North Pole Shops, Set of 2 5621-9 (Orly's Bell & Harness Supply, Rimpy's Bakery)	Department 56	Open	75.00	75.00
91-07-005	Tassy's Mittens & Hassel's Woolies 5622-7	Department 56	Open	50.00	50.00
92-07-006	North Pole Post Office 5623-5	Department 56	Open	45.00	45.00
92-07-007	Obbie's Books & Letrinka's Candy 5624-3	Department 56	Open	70.00	70.00
92-07-008	Elfie's Sleds & Skates 5625-1	Department 56	Open	48.00	48.00
93-07-009	North Pole Chapel 5626-0	Department 56	Open	45.00	45.00
93-07-010	Express Depot 5627-8	Department 56	Open	48.00	48.00
93-07-011	Santa's Woodworks 5628-6	Department 56	Open	42.00	42.00
93-07-012	Santa's Lookout Tower 5629-4	Department 56	Open	45.00	45.00

Department 56 — Event Piece - Heritage Village Collection Accessory

		ARTIST	EDITION	ISSUE	QUOTE
92-08-001	Gate House 5530-1	Department 56	Closed	22.50	50-100.

Department 56 — Retired Heritage Village Collection Accessories

		ARTIST	EDITION	ISSUE	QUOTE
84-09-001	Carolers 6526-9, set of 3 w/ Lamppost(wh)	Department 56	Closed	10.00	85-170.
84-09-002	Carolers 6526-9, set of 3 w/ Lamppost(bl)	Department 56	Closed	10.00	25-50.00
85-09-003	Village Train Brighton 6527-7, set of 3	Department 56	Closed	12.00	360-415.
86-09-004	Christmas Carol Figures 6501-3, set of 3	Department 56	Closed	12.50	45-80.00
86-09-005	Lighted Tree With Children & Ladder 6510-2	Department 56	Closed	35.00	300-330.
86-09-006	Sleighride 6511-0	Department 56	Closed	19.50	45-70.00
86-09-007	Covered Wooden Bridge 6531-5	Department 56	Closed	10.00	30-46.00
86-09-008	New England Winter Set 6532-3, set of 5	Department 56	Closed	18.00	40-58.00
86-09-009	Porcelain Trees, 6537-4, set of 2	Department 56	Closed	14.00	25-36.00
86-09-010	Alpine Villagers 6542-0, set of 3	Department 56	Closed	13.00	30-46.00
87-09-011	Farm People And Animals 5901-3, set of 5	Department 56	Closed	24.00	65-95.00
87-09-012	Blacksmith 5934-0, set of 3	Department 56	Closed	20.00	50-75.00
87-09-013	City People 5965-0, set of 5	Department 56	Closed	27.50	42-58.00
87-09-014	Silo And Hay Shed 5950-1	Department 56	Closed	18.00	125-180.
87-09-015	Ox Sled (tan pants) 5951-0	Department 56	Closed	20.00	145-240.
87-09-016	Ox Sled (blue pants) 5951-0	Department 56	Closed	20.00	115-170.
87-09-017	Shopkeepers 5966-8, set of 4	Department 56	Closed	15.00	25-35.00
87-09-018	City Workers 5967-6, set of 4	Department 56	Closed	15.00	30-46.00
87-09-019	Skating Pond 6545-5	Department 56	Closed	24.00	60-90.00
87-09-020	Stone Bridge 6546-3	Department 56	Closed	12.00	65-105.
87-09-021	Village Well And Holy Cross 6547-1, set /2	Department 56	Closed	13.00	125-155.
87-09-022	Maple Sugaring Shed 6589-7, set of 3	Department 56	Closed	19.00	150-220.
87-09-023	Dover Coach 6590-0	Department 56	Closed	18.00	50-86.00
87-09-024	Dover Coach w/o Mustache 6590-0	Department 56	Closed	18.00	90-120.
87-09-025	Village Express Train (electric, black),5997-8	Department 56	Closed	89.95	285-345.
87-09-026	Christmas in the City Sign, 5960-9	Department 56	Closed	6.00	12-20.00
87-09-027	Dickens' Village Sign 6569-2	Department 56	Closed	6.00	7-28.00
87-09-028	New England Village Sign 6570-6	Department 56	Closed	6.00	9-20.00
87-09-029	Alpine Village Sign 6571-4	Department 56	Closed	6.00	15-20.00
88-09-030	Fezziwig and Friends 5928-5, set of 3	Department 56	Closed	12.50	40-60.00
88-09-031	Village Train Trestle 5981-1	Department 56	Closed	17.00	50-70.00
88-09-032	Woodcutter And Son 5986-2, set of 2	Department 56	Closed	10.00	25-46.00
88-09-033	Childe Pond and Skaters 5903-0, set of 4	Department 56	Closed	30.00	65-110.
88-09-034	Nicholas Nickleby Characters 5929-3, set of 4	Department 56	Closed	20.00	25-50.00
88-09-035	Village Harvest People 5941-2 set of 4	Department 56	Closed	27.50	30-60.00
88-09-036	City Newsstand 5971-4, set of 4	Department 56	Closed	25.00	35-50.00
88-09-037	City Bus & Milk Truck 5983-8, set of 2	Department 56	Closed	15.00	20-50.00
88-09-038	Salvation Army Band 5985-4, set of 6	Department 56	Closed	24.00	45-60.00
88-09-039	One Horse Open Sleigh 5982-0	Department 56	Closed	20.00	35-57.00
88-09-040	Village Blvd., Set of 14 5516-6	Department 56	Closed	25.00	25-57.00
89-09-041	Constables 5579-4, set of 3	Department 56	Closed	17.50	42-65.00
89-09-042	Farm Animals 5945-5, set of 4	Department 56	Closed	15.00	30-55.00
89-09-043	Organ Grinder 5957-9, set of 3	Department 56	Closed	21.00	25-45.00
89-09-044	River Street Ice House Cart 5959-5	Department 56	Closed	20.00	40-50.00
89-09-045	David Copperfield Characters, set of 5 5551-4	Department 56	Closed	32.50	35-50.00
89-09-046	Royal Coach 5578-6	Department 56	Closed	55.00	60-90.00
89-09-047	Violet Vendor/Carolers/Chestnut Vendor set of 3 5580-8	Department 56	Closed	23.00	30-50.00
89-09-048	Popcorn Vendor, set of 3 5958-7	Department 56	Closed	22.00	22-45.00
89-09-049	U.S. Mail Box and Fire Hydrant, 5517-4	Department 56	Closed	5.00	15-20.00
89-09-050	Heritage Village Sign, 9953-8	Department 56	Closed	10.00	15-28.00
90-09-051	Busy Sidewalks, set of 4 5535-2	Department 56	Closed	28.00	35-60.00
90-09-052	Amish Family, set of 3 5948-0	Department 56	Closed	20.00	30-46.00
90-09-053	Amish Family, set of 3 5948-0 w/Moustache	Department 56	Closed	20.00	40-60.00
90-09-054	Amish Buggy 5949-8	Department 56	Closed	22.00	40-57.00
90-09-055	Sleepy Hollow Characters, set/3 5956-0	Department 56	Closed	27.50	36-55.00
90-09-056	Carolers on the Doorstep, set of 4 5570-0	Department 56	Closed	25.00	36-48.00
90-09-057	Trimming the North Pole 5608-1	Department 56	Closed	10.00	18-35.00
90-09-058	Santa's Little Helpers, set of 3 5610-3	Department 56	Closed	28.00	35-59.00
91-09-059	Market Day, set of 3 5641-3	Department 56	Closed	35.00	36-60.00
91-09-060	All Around the Town, set of 2 5545-0	Department 56	Closed	18.00	25-46.00
91-09-061	Oliver Twist Characters, set of 3, 5554-9	Department 56	Closed	35.00	36-60.00
92-09-062	Churchyard Gate and Fence, 5563-8, set of 3	Department 56	Closed	15.00	40.00
93-09-063	Express Van (black), 9951-1	Department 56	Closed	25.00	120-150.
93-09-064	Express Van (gold), 9951-1	Department 56	Closed	25.00	625-935.

Department 56 — The Original Snow Village Collection Accessories Retired

		ARTIST	EDITION	ISSUE	QUOTE
79-10-001	Aspen Trees 5052-6, Meadowland Series	Department 56	Closed	16.00	450.00
79-10-002	Sheep, 9 White, 3 Black 5053-4 Meadowland Series	Department 56	Closed	12.00	N/A
79-10-003	Carolers 5064-1	Department 56	Closed	12.00	90-100.
80-10-004	Ceramic Car 5069-0	Department 56	Closed	5.00	35-55.00
81-10-005	Ceramic Sleigh 5079-2	Department 56	Closed	5.00	30-55.00
82-10-006	Snowman With Broom 5018-0	Department 56	Closed	3.00	9-22.00
83-10-007	Monks-A-Caroling (butterscotch) 6459-9	Department 56	Closed	6.00	54-75.00
84-10-008	Scottie With Tree 5038-5	Department 56	Closed	3.00	108-140.
84-10-009	Monks-A-Caroling (brown) 5040-7	Department 56	Closed	6.00	22-46.00
85-10-010	Singing Nuns 5053-9	Department 56	Closed	6.00	54-116.
85-10-011	Snow Kids Sled, Skis 5056-3	Department 56	Closed	11.00	36-50.00
85-10-012	Family Mom/Kids, Goose/Girl 5057-1	Department 56	Closed	11.00	20-46.00
85-10-013	Santa/Mailbox 5059-8	Department 56	Closed	11.00	28-50.00
86-10-014	Girl/Snowman, Boy 5095-4	Department 56	Closed	11.00	36-65.00
86-10-015	Shopping Girls w/Packages (small) 5096-2	Department 56	Closed	11.00	20-58.00
86-10-016	Shopping Girls w/Packages (large) 5096-2	Department 56	Closed	11.00	27-46.00
86-10-017	Kids Around The Tree (small) 5094-6	Department 56	Closed	15.00	26-58.00
86-10-018	Kids Around The Tree (large) 5094-6	Department 56	Closed	15.00	72-95.00
87-10-019	3 Nuns With Songbooks 5102-0	Department 56	Closed	6.00	90-115.
87-10-020	Praying Monks 5103-9	Department 56	Closed	6.00	30-70.00
87-10-021	Children In Band 5104-7	Department 56	Closed	15.00	18-35.00
87-10-022	Caroling Family 5105-5, set of 3	Department 56	Closed	20.00	22.00
87-10-023	Christmas Children 5107-1, set of 4	Department 56	Closed	20.00	22-46.00
87-10-024	Snow Kids 5113-6, set of 4	Department 56	Closed	20.00	42-60.00
88-10-025	Hayride 5117-9	Department 56	Closed	30.00	46-75.00
88-10-026	School Children 5118-7, set of 3	Department 56	Closed	15.00	12-35.00
88-10-027	Apple Girl/Newspaper Boy 5129-2, set of 2	Department 56	Closed	11.00	12-30.00
88-10-028	Woodsman and Boy 5130-6, set of 2	Department 56	Closed	13.00	18-35.00
88-10-029	Woody Station Wagon 5136-5	Department 56	Closed	6.50	20-40.00
88-10-030	Water Tower 5133-0	Department 56	Closed	20.00	45-70.00
88-10-031	School Bus, Snow Plow 5137-3, set of 2	Department 56	Closed	16.00	30-46.00
88-10-032	Sisal Tree Lot 8183-3	Department 56	Closed	45.00	61-97.00
88-10-033	Man On Ladder Hanging Garland 5116-0	Department 56	Closed	7.50	11-20.00
88-10-034	Doghouse/Cat In Garbage Can,set/2 5131-4	Department 56	Closed	15.00	20-50.00
89-10-035	Water Tower-John Deer 568-0	Department 56	Closed	20.00	375-500.
89-10-036	US Special Delivery 5148-9 set of 2	Department 56	Closed	16.00	35.00
89-10-037	US Mailbox 5179-9	Department 56	Closed	3.50	10-17.00
89-10-038	Kids Tree House 5168-3	Department 56	Closed	25.00	30-69.00
89-10-039	Skate Faster Mom 5170-5	Department 56	Closed	13.00	17-46.00
89-10-040	Through the Woods 5172-1, set of 2	Department 56	Closed	18.00	18-46.00
89-10-041	Statue of Mark Twain 5173-0	Department 56	Closed	15.00	20-46.00
89-10-042	Calling All Cars 5174-8, set of 2	Department 56	Closed	15.00	22-40.00
89-10-043	Choir Kids 5147-0	Department 56	Closed	15.00	18-29.00
89-10-044	Bringing Home The Tree 5169-1	Department 56	Closed	15.00	20-35.00
90-10-045	Sleighride 5160-8	Department 56	Closed	30.00	36-69.00
90-10-046	Here We Come A Caroling, set/3 5161-6	Department 56	Closed	18.00	18-35.00
90-10-047	Home Delivery, set of 2 5162-4	Department 56	Closed	16.00	22-46.00
90-10-048	SV Special Delivery, set of 2 5197-7	Department 56	Closed	16.00	24-50.00
90-10-049	Kids Decorating the Village Sign, 5134-9	Department 56	Closed	13.00	12-15.00
90-10-050	Down the Chimney He Goes, 5158-6	Department 56	Closed	6.50	10-14.00
90-10-051	Sno-Jet Snowmobile, 5159-4	Department 56	Closed	15.00	15-25.00
90-10-052	Fresh Frozen Fish 5163-2, set of 2	Department 56	Closed	20.00	24-46.00
91-10-053	Come Join The Parade 5411-9	Department 56	Closed	13.00	17-28.00
91-10-054	Village Marching Band, set of 3 5412-7	Department 56	Closed	30.00	42-60.00
91-10-055	Winter Fountain, 5409-7	Department 56	Closed	25.00	30-57.00
91-10-056	Snowball Fort 5414-3, set of 3	Department 56	Closed	28.00	30-57.00
91-10-057	Country Harvest, 5415-1	Department 56	Closed	13.00	13.00

Department 56 — Snowbabies

		ARTIST	EDITION	ISSUE	QUOTE
86-11-001	Give Me A Push 7955-3	Department 56	Closed	12.00	45-65.00
86-11-002	Hold On Tight 7956-1	Department 56	Open	12.00	12.00
86-11-003	Best Friends 7958-8	Department 56	Closed	12.00	100-160.
86-11-004	Snowbaby Nite-Lite 7959-6	Department 56	Closed	15.00	220-310.
86-11-005	I'm Making Snowballs 7962-6	Department 56	Closed	12.00	25-50.00
86-11-006	Snowbaby Standing, waterglobe 7964-2	Department 56	Closed	7.50	440.00
86-11-007	Climbing on Snowball, Bisque Votive w/Candle 7965-0	Department 56	Closed	15.00	85-100.
86-11-008	Hanging Pair 7966-9	Department 56	Closed	15.00	110.00
86-11-009	Catch a Falling Star, waterglobe 7967-7	Department 56	Closed	18.00	540.00
86-11-010	Snowbaby Holding Picture Frame, set of 2 7970-7	Department 56	Closed	15.00	360-550.
86-11-011	Forest Accessory "Frosty Forest", set of 2 7963-4	Department 56	Open	15.00	15.00
87-11-012	Tumbling In the Snow, set of 5 7957-0	Department 56	Closed	35.00	55-75.00
87-11-013	Down The Hill We Go 7960-0	Department 56	Open	20.00	20.00
87-11-014	Don't Fall Off 7968-5	Department 56	Closed	12.50	50-85.00
87-11-015	Climbing On Tree, set of 2 7971-5	Department 56	Closed	25.00	400-600.
87-11-016	When You Wish Upon a Star, music box 7972-3	Department 56	Closed	30.00	37.00
87-11-017	Snowbaby with Wings, waterglobe 7973-1	Department 56	Closed	20.00	390.00
87-11-018	Winter Surprise 7974-0	Department 56	Closed	15.00	30-46.00
87-11-019	Snowbabies Riding Sleds, waterglobe 7975-8	Department 56	Closed	40.00	850.00
88-11-020	Are All These Mine? 7977-4	Department 56	Open	10.00	10.00
88-11-021	Polar Express 7978-2	Department 56	Closed	22.00	45-85.00
88-11-022	Tiny Trio, set of 3 7979-0	Department 56	Closed	20.00	90-150.
88-11-023	Frosty Frolic 7981-2	Department 56	4,800	35.00	500-770.
89-11-024	Helpful Friends 7982-0	Department 56	Closed	30.00	44-75.00
89-11-025	Frosty Fun 7983-9	Department 56	Closed	27.50	40-85.00
89-11-026	All Fall Down, set of 4 7984-7	Department 56	Closed	36.00	50-90.00
89-11-027	Finding Fallen Stars 7985-5	Department 56	6,000	32.50	143-148.
89-11-028	Penguin Parade 7986-3	Department 56	Closed	25.00	33-70.00
89-11-029	Icy Igloo 7987-1	Department 56	Open	37.50	37.50
89-11-030	Let It Snow, waterglobe 7992-8	Department 56	Closed	25.00	34.00
90-11-031	All Tired Out, waterglobe 7937-5	Department 56	Closed	55.00	55-98.00
90-11-032	Twinkle Little Stars 7942-1, set of 2	Department 56	Closed	37.50	38-42.00
90-11-033	Wishing on a Star 7943-0	Department 56	Open	20.00	20.00
90-11-034	Read Me a Story 7945-6	Department 56	Open	25.00	25.00
90-11-035	We Will Make it Shine 7946-4	Department 56	Closed	45.00	55-98.00
90-11-036	Playing Games Is Fun 7947-2	Department 56	Closed	30.00	45-50.00
90-11-037	A Special Delivery 7948-0	Department 56	Open	13.50	13.50
90-11-038	Who Are You? 7949-9	Department 56	12,500	32.50	100-150.
91-11-039	I'll Put Up The Tree 6800-4	Department 56	Open	24.00	24.00
91-11-040	Why Don't You Talk To Me 6801-2	Department 56	Open	24.00	24.00
91-11-041	I Made This Just For You 6802-0	Department 56	Open	15.00	15.00
91-11-042	Is That For Me 6803-9, set of 2	Department 56	Closed	32.50	40-75.00
91-11-043	Snowbaby Polar Sign 6804-7	Department 56	Open	20.00	20.00
91-11-044	This Is Where We Live 6805-5	Department 56	Open	60.00	60.00
91-11-045	Waiting For Christmas 6807-1	Department 56	Closed	27.50	36-60.00
91-11-046	Dancing To a Tune 6808-0, set of 3	Department 56	Open	30.00	30.00
91-11-047	Fishing For Dreams 6809-8	Department 56	Open	28.00	28.00
91-11-048	Play Me a Tune, waterglobe 7936-7	Department 56	Closed	50.00	78.00
91-11-049	Peek-A-Boo, waterglobe 7938-3	Department 56	Closed	50.00	70.00
92-11-050	Can I Help, Too? 6806-3	Department 56	18,500	48.00	65-150.
92-11-051	I Need A Hug 6813-6	Department 56	Open	20.00	20.00
92-11-052	Let's Go Skiing 6815-2	Department 56	Open	15.00	15.00

		ARTIST	EDITION	ISSUE	QUOTE
92-11-053	Wait For Me 6812-8	Department 56	Open	48.00	48.00
92-11-054	Winken, Blinken, and Nod 6814-4	Department 56	Open	60.00	60.00
92-11-055	This Willl Cheer You Up 6816-0	Department 56	Open	30.00	30.00
92-11-056	Help Me, I'm Stuck 6817-9	Department 56	Open	32.50	32.50
92-11-057	You Can't Find Me! 6818-7	Department 56	Open	45.00	45.00
92-11-058	Look What I Can Do! 6819-5	Department 56	Open	16.50	16.50
92-11-059	Shall I Play For You? 6820-9	Department 56	Open	16.50	16.50
92-11-060	You Didn't Forget Me 6821-7	Department 56	Open	32.50	32.50
92-11-061	Stars-In-A-Row, Tic-Tac-Toe 6822-5	Department 56	Open	32.50	32.50
92-11-062	Just One Little Candle 6823-3	Department 56	Open	15.00	15.00
92-11-063	Join The Parade 6824-1	Department 56	Open	37.50	37.50
92-11-064	Snowbabies Bridge "Over the Milky Way" 6828-4	Department 56	Open	32.00	32.00
92-11-065	Snowbabies Trees "Starry Pines" set of 2, 6829-2	Department 56	Open	17.50	17.50
92-11-066	Read Me a Story, waterglobe 6831-4	Department 56	Open	32.50	32.50
92-11-067	Fishing For Dreams, waterglobe 6832-2	Department 56	Open	32.50	32.50
93-11-068	Look What I Found 6833-0	Department 56	Open	45.00	45.00
93-11-069	Crossing Starry Skies 6834-9	Department 56	Open	35.00	35.00
93-11-070	I'll Teach You A Trick 6835-7	Department 56	Open	24.00	24.00
93-11-071	I Found Your Mittens, Set of 2, 6836-5	Department 56	Open	30.00	30.00
93-11-072	So Much Work To Do 6837-3	Department 56	Open	18.00	18.00
93-11-073	Can I Open it Now? 6838-1 (Event Piece)	Department 56	Closed	15.00	30-60.00
93-11-074	Now I Lay Me Down to Sleep 6839-0	Department 56	Open	13.50	13.50
93-11-075	Somewhere in Dreamland 6840-3	Department 56	Open	85.00	85.00
93-11-076	Where Did He Go? 6841-1	Department 56	Open	35.00	35.00
93-11-077	I'm Making an Ice Sculpture 6842-0	Department 56	Open	30.00	30.00
93-11-078	We Make a Great Pair 6843-8	Department 56	Open	30.00	30.00
93-11-079	Will it Snow Today? 6844-6	Department 56	Open	45.00	45.00
93-11-080	Let's All Chime In! 6845-4, set of 2	Department 56	Open	37.50	37.50
93-11-081	Snowbabies Picture Frame, Baby's First Smile 6846-2	Department 56	Open	30.00	30.00
94-11-082	I'm Right Behind You!, 6852-7	Department 56	Open	60.00	60.00
94-11-083	There's Another One!, 6853-5	Department 56	Open	24.00	24.00
94-11-084	Jack Frost...A Touch of Winter's Magic, 6854-3	Department 56	Open	90.00	90.00
94-11-085	Where Did You Come From?, 6856-0	Department 56	Open	40.00	40.00

Department 56 — Snowbabies Pewter Miniatures

		ARTIST	EDITION	ISSUE	QUOTE
89-12-001	Are All These Mine? 7605-8	Department 56	Closed	7.00	19-21.00
89-12-002	Helpful Friends, set of 4 7608-2	Department 56	Closed	13.50	20-24.00
89-12-003	Polar Express, set of 2, 7609-0	Department 56	Closed	13.50	20-29.00
89-12-004	Icy Igloo, w/tree, set of 2 7610-4	Department 56	Closed	7.50	14-26.00
89-12-005	Tumbling in the Snow!, set of 5, 7614-7	Department 56	Closed	30.00	48-70.00
89-12-006	Finding Fallen Stars, set of 2, 7618-0	Department 56	Closed	12.50	20-40.00
89-12-007	Frosty Frolic, set of 4, 7613-9	Department 56	Closed	24.00	20-37.00
89-12-008	Tiny Trio, set of 3, 7615-5	Department 56	Closed	18.00	25-37.00
89-12-009	Penguin Parade, set of 4, 7616-3	Department 56	Closed	12.50	27.00
89-12-010	All Fall Down, set of 4, 7617-1	Department 56	Closed	25.00	32-35.00
90-12-011	Twinkle Little Stars, set of 2, 7621-0	Department 56	Closed	15.00	25-28.00
90-12-012	Playing Games is Fun!, set of 2, 7623-6	Department 56	Closed	13.50	20.00
90-12-013	A Special Delivery 7624-4	Department 56	Closed	7.00	10-23.00
91-12-014	Waiting for Christmas, 7629-5	Department 56	Closed	13.00	18.00
91-12-015	Dancing to a Tune, set of 3, 7630-9	Department 56	Closed	18.00	25-35.00
91-12-016	Is That For Me?, set of 2, 7631-7	Department 56	Closed	12.50	15-17.00

Department 56 — Village CCP Miniatures

		ARTIST	EDITION	ISSUE	QUOTE
87-13-001	Dickens' Village Original, set of 7 6558-7	Department 56	Closed	72.00	200-250.
87-13-002	Crowntree Inn 6558-7	Department 56	Closed	12.00	42-50.00
87-13-003	Candle Shop 6558-7	Department 56	Closed	12.00	27-40.00
87-13-004	Green Grocer 6558-7	Department 56	Closed	12.00	49.00
87-13-005	Golden Swan Baker 6558-7	Department 56	Closed	12.00	30-49.00
87-13-006	Bean and Son Smithy Shop 6558-7	Department 56	Closed	12.00	37.00
87-13-007	Abel Beesley Butcher 6558-7	Department 56	Closed	12.00	22-30.00
87-13-008	Jones & Co Brush & Basket Shop 6558-7	Department 56	Closed	12.00	52.00
87-13-009	Dickens' Cottages, set of 3 6559-5	Department 56	Closed	30.00	150-200.
87-13-010	Thatched Cottage 6559-5	Department 56	Closed	10.00	98.00
87-13-011	Stone Cottage 6559-5	Department 56	Closed	10.00	118.00
87-13-012	Tudor Cottage 6559-5	Department 56	Closed	10.00	85-105.
87-13-013	Dickens' Village Assorted, set of 3 6560-9	Department 56	Closed	48.00	N/A
87-13-014	Dickens Village Church 6560-9	Department 56	Closed	16.00	42-50.00
87-13-015	Norman Church 6560-9	Department 56	Closed	16.00	83-100.
87-13-016	Blythe Pond Mill House 6560-9	Department 56	Closed	16.00	33-50.00
87-13-017	Christmas Carol Cottages, set of 3 6561-7	Department 56	Closed	30.00	85.00
87-13-018	Fezziwig's Warehouse 6561-7	Department 56	Closed	10.00	21-28.00
87-13-019	Scrooge/ Marley Countinghouse 6561-7	Department 56	Closed	10.00	24-33.00
87-13-020	The Cottage of Bob Cratchit & Tiny Tim 6561-7	Department 56	Closed	10.00	28-36.00
87-13-021	Dickens' Village Assorted, set of 4 6562-5	Department 56	Closed	60.00	N/A
87-13-022	The Old Curiosity Shop 6562-5	Department 56	Closed	15.00	48-58.00
87-13-023	Brick Abbey 6562-5	Department 56	Closed	15.00	60-75.00
87-13-024	Chesterton Manor House 6562-5	Department 56	Closed	15.00	60-75.00
87-13-025	Barley Bree Farmhouse 6562-5	Department 56	Closed	15.00	35-37.00
88-13-026	Dickens' Kenilworth Castle 6565-0	Department 56	Closed	30.00	72-112.
87-13-027	Dickens' Lane Shops, set of 3 6591-9	Department 56	Closed	30.00	100-150.
87-13-028	Thomas Kersey Coffee House 6591-9	Department 56	Closed	10.00	60-65.00
87-13-029	Cottage Toy Shop 6591-9	Department 56	Closed	10.00	37.00
87-13-030	Tuttle's Pub 6591-9	Department 56	Closed	10.00	20-49.00
87-13-031	Dickens' Chadbury Station & Train 6592-7	Department 56	Closed	27.50	65-93.00
88-13-032	New England Village Original, set of 7 5935-8	Department 56	Closed	72.00	250-425.
88-13-033	Apothecary Shop 5935-8	Department 56	Closed	10.50	30-45.00
88-13-034	General Store 5935-8	Department 56	Closed	10.50	50-60.00
88-13-035	Nathaniel Bingham Fabrics 5935-8	Department 56	Closed	10.50	50.00
88-13-036	Livery Stable & Boot Shop 5935-8	Department 56	Closed	10.50	30-50.00
88-13-037	Steeple Church 5935-8	Department 56	Closed	10.50	138-300.
88-13-038	Brick Town Hall 5935-8	Department 56	Closed	10.50	46-55.00
88-13-039	Red Schoolhouse 5935-8	Department 56	Closed	10.50	65-67.00
88-13-040	New England Village Assorted, set of 6 5937-4	Department 56	Closed	85.00	225.00
88-13-041	Timber Knoll Log Cabin 5937-4	Department 56	Closed	14.50	43.00
88-13-042	Smythe Wollen Mill 5937-4	Department 56	Closed	14.50	65-82.00
88-13-043	Jacob Adams Farmhouse 5937-4	Department 56	Closed	14.50	20-40.00
88-13-044	Jacob Adams Barn 5937-4	Department 56	Closed	14.50	20-60.00
88-13-045	Craggy Cove Lighthouse 5937-4	Department 56	Closed	14.50	90-105.
88-13-046	Maple Sugaring Shed 5937-4	Department 56	Closed	14.50	48.00
87-13-047	Little Town of Bethlehem, set of 12 5976-5	Department 56	Closed	85.00	144-180.
86-13-048	Victorian Miniatures, set of 5 6563-3	Department 56	Closed	65.00	N/A
86-13-049	Victorian Miniatures, set of 2 6564-1	Department 56	Closed	45.00	300.00
86-13-050	Estate 6564-1	Department 56	Closed	22.50	N/A
86-13-051	Church 6564-1	Department 56	Closed	22.50	N/A
86-13-052	Williamsburg Snowhouse Series, set of 6	Department 56	Closed	60.00	500-575.
86-13-053	Williamsburg Church, White 6566-8	Department 56	Closed	10.00	40.00
86-13-054	Williamsburg House, Blue 6566-8	Department 56	Closed	10.00	60.00
86-13-055	Williamsburg House Brown Brick 6566-8	Department 56	Closed	10.00	40.00
86-13-056	Williamsburg House, Brown Clapboard	Department 56	Closed	10.00	40.00
86-13-057	Williamsburg House, Red 6566-8	Department 56	Closed	10.00	60.00
86-13-058	Williamsburg House, White 6566-8	Department 56	Closed	10.00	75.00

Department 56 — Easter Collectibles

		ARTIST	EDITION	ISSUE	QUOTE
91-14-001	Bisque Lamb, Large 4" 7392-0	Department 56	Closed	7.50	23-39.00
91-14-002	Bisque Lamb, Small 2.5" 7393-8	Department 56	Closed	5.00	16-28.00
91-14-003	Bisque Lamb, set	Department 56	Closed	12.50	42-50.00
92-14-004	Bisque Rabbit, Large 5" 7498-5	Department 56	Closed	8.00	18-33.00
92-14-005	Bisque Rabbit, Small 4" 7499-3	Department 56	Closed	6.00	12-22.00
92-14-006	Bisque Rabbit, set	Department 56	Closed	14.00	30.00
93-14-007	Bisque Duckling, Large 3.5" 7282-6	Department 56	Closed	8.50	9-18.00
93-14-008	Bisque Duckling, Small 2.75" 7281-8	Department 56	Closed	6.50	8-15.00
93-14-009	Bisque Duckling, set	Department 56	Closed	15.00	22-26.00
94-14-010	Bisque Fledgling in Nest, Large 2.75" 2400-7	Department 56	Open	6.00	6.00
94-14-011	Bisque Fledgling in Nest, Small 2.5" 2401-5	Department 56	Open	5.00	5.00
95-14-012	Bisque Chick, Large 2464-3	Department 56	Open	8.50	8.50
95-14-013	Bisque Chick, Small, 2465-1	Department 56	Open	6.50	6.50

Walt Disney — Classics Collection-Cinderella

		ARTIST	EDITION	ISSUE	QUOTE
92-01-001	Cinderella 6" 41000/w	Disney Studios	Retrd.	195.00	305-405.
92-01-002	Cinderella 6" 41000/c	Disney Studios	Retrd.	195.00	295-395.
92-01-003	Lucifer 2 3/5" 41001	Disney Studios	Retrd.	69.00	95-150.
92-01-004	Bruno 4 2/5" 41002	Disney Studios	Retrd.	69.00	95-150.
92-01-005	Cinderella, Lucifer, Bruno, set of 3	Disney Studios	Retrd.	333.00	475-590.
92-01-006	Sewing Book 41003	Disney Studios	Retrd.	69.00	70-83.00
92-01-007	Sewing Book 41003/no mark	Disney Studios	Retrd.	69.00	83-100.
92-01-008	Needle Mouse 5 4/5" 41004	Disney Studios	Retrd.	69.00	75-80.00
92-01-009	Birds With Sash 6 2/5" 41005	Disney Studios	Retrd.	149.00	149-200.
92-01-010	Chalk Mouse 3 2/5" 41006	Disney Studios	Retrd.	65.00	75-110.
92-01-011	Gus 3 2/5" 41007	Disney Studios	Retrd.	65.00	75-102.
92-01-012	Jaq 4 1/5" 41008	Disney Studios	Retrd.	65.00	75-114.
92-01-013	Cinderella-Opening Title 41009	Disney Studios	Open	29.00	29.00
92-01-014	Cinderella-Opening Title-Technicolor 41009	Disney Studios	Retrd.	29.00	40-48.00
93-01-015	A Dress For Cinderelly 41030	Disney Studios	Retrd.	800.00	17-2300.

Walt Disney — Classics Collection-Bambi

		ARTIST	EDITION	ISSUE	QUOTE
92-02-001	Bambi & Flower 6" 41010	Disney Studios	Retrd.	298.00	440-500.
92-02-002	Friend Owl 8 3/5" 41011	Disney Studios	Open	195.00	195.00
92-02-003	Friend Owl 8 3/5" 41011/w	Disney Studios	Retrd.	195.00	215-220.
92-02-004	Field Mouse-touching 5 3/5" 41012	Disney Studios	Retrd.	195.00	14-1650.
92-02-005	Field Mouse-not touching 5 3/5" 41012	Disney Studios	Retrd.	195.00	16-1850.
92-02-006	Thumper 3" 41013	Disney Studios	Open	55.00	55.00
92-02-007	Thumper 3" 41013/w	Disney Studios	Retrd.	55.00	55-66.00
92-02-008	Thumper's Sisters 3 3/5" 41014	Disney Studios	Open	69.00	69.00
92-02-009	Thumper's Sisters 3 3/5" 41014/w	Disney Studios	Retrd.	69.00	75-90.00
92-02-010	Bambi 41033	Disney Studios	Open	195.00	195.00
92-02-011	Bambi 41033/w	Disney Studios	Retrd.	195.00	245-265.
92-02-012	Flower 41034	Disney Studios	Open	78.00	78.00
92-02-013	Flower 41034/w	Disney Studios	Retrd.	78.00	145-175.
92-02-014	Bambi-Opening Title 41015	Disney Studios	Open	29.00	29.00
92-02-015	Bambi-Opening Title 41015/w	Disney Studios	Retrd.	29.00	35-56.00

Walt Disney — Classics Collection-Fantasia

		ARTIST	EDITION	ISSUE	QUOTE
92-03-001	Sorcerer Mickey 5 1/5" 41016	Disney Studios	Open	195.00	195.00
92-03-002	Sorcerer Mickey 5 1/5" 41016/w	Disney Studios	Retrd.	195.00	250.00
92-03-003	Brooms, set of 2 5 4/5" 41017	Disney Studios	Open	150.00	150.00
92-03-004	Brooms, set of 2 5 4/5" 41017/w	Disney Studios	Retrd.	150.00	235.00
92-03-005	Brooms, w/water spots, set of 2 5 4/5" 41017/w	Disney Studios	Retrd.	75.00	280-305.
92-03-006	Broom, 5 4/5" 41017	Disney Studios	Open	75.00	75.00
92-03-007	Broom, 5 4/5" 41017/w	Disney Studios	Retrd.	75.00	85.00
92-03-008	Broom, w/water spots 5 4/5" 41017/w	Disney Studios	Retrd.	75.00	155.00
93-03-009	Romantic Reflections-Pink Centaurette 41040	Disney Studios	Open	175.00	175.00
93-03-010	Beauty in Bloom-Blue Centaurette 41041	Disney Studios	Open	195.00	215.00
93-03-011	Love's Little Helpers 41042	Disney Studios	Open	290.00	290.00
94-03-012	Hop Lo	Disney Studios	Open	35.00	35.00
94-03-013	Medium Dancer	Disney Studios	Open	50.00	50.00
94-03-014	Tall Mushroom Dancer	Disney Studios	Open	60.00	60.00
92-03-015	Fantasia-Opening Title 41018	Disney Studios	Open	29.00	29.00
92-03-016	Fantasia-Opening Title-Technicolor 41018	Disney Studios	Retrd.	29.00	45-54.00
92-03-017	Fantasia-Opening Title-blank 41018	Disney Studios	Retrd.	29.00	55.00

Walt Disney — Classics Collection-The Delivery Boy

		ARTIST	EDITION	ISSUE	QUOTE
92-04-001	Mickey 6" 41020	Disney Studios	Open	125.00	135.00
92-04-002	Mickey 6" 41020/w	Disney Studios	Retrd.	125.00	216-225.
92-04-003	Minnie 6" 41021	Disney Studios	Open	125.00	135.00
92-04-004	Minnie 6" 41021/w	Disney Studios	Retrd.	125.00	195-225.
92-04-005	Pluto 3 3/5" 41022	Disney Studios	Open	125.00	125.00
92-04-006	Pluto 3 3/5" 41022/w	Disney Studios	Retrd.	125.00	280-360.
92-04-007	Pluto (raised letters) 3 3/5" 41022/w	Disney Studios	Retrd.	125.00	200-225.
92-04-008	Delivery Boy-Opening Title 41019	Disney Studios	Open	29.00	29.00
92-04-009	Delivery Boy-Opening Title 41019/c	Disney Studios	Retrd.	29.00	40.00

Walt Disney — Classics Collection-Mr. Duck

		ARTIST	EDITION	ISSUE	QUOTE
93-05-001	Donald & Daisy 41024/w	Disney Studios	Retrd.	295.00	800-1200
93-05-002	Donald & Daisy 41024/c	Disney Studios	Retrd.	295.00	600-995.
93-05-003	Nephew Duck-Dewey 41025	Disney Studios	Open	65.00	65.00
93-05-004	Nephew Duck-Dewey 41025/w	Disney Studios	Retrd.	65.00	85-90.00
93-05-005	Nephew Duck-Huey 41049	Disney Studios	Open	65.00	65.00
93-05-006	Nephew Duck-Huey 41049/c	Disney Studios	Retrd.	65.00	85.00
93-05-007	Nephew Duck-Louie 41050	Disney Studios	Open	65.00	65.00
93-05-008	Nephew Duck-Louie 41050/c	Disney Studios	Retrd.	65.00	85.00
94-05-009	With Love From Daisy	Disney Studios	Open	180.00	180.00
93-05-010	Mr. Duck Steps Out-Opening Title 41032	Disney Studios	Open	29.00	29.00
93-05-011	Mr. Duck Steps Out-Opening Title 41032/c	Disney Studios	Retrd.	29.00	40.00

Walt Disney — Classics Collection-Symphony Hour

		ARTIST	EDITION	ISSUE	QUOTE
93-06-001	Goofy 41026	Disney Studios	Open	198.00	198.00
93-06-002	Goofy 41026/w	Disney Studios	Retrd.	198.00	1650.00
93-06-003	Goofy 41026/c	Disney Studios	Open	198.00	198.00
93-06-004	Clarabelle 41027	Disney Studios	Open	198.00	198.00
93-06-005	Clarabelle 41027/w	Disney Studios	Retrd.	198.00	250.00
93-06-006	Horace 41028	Disney Studios	Open	198.00	198.00
93-06-007	Horace 41028/w	Disney Studios	Retrd.	198.00	250-285.
93-06-008	Mickey Conductor 41029	Disney Studios	Open	185.00	185.00
93-06-009	Mickey Conductor 41029/w	Disney Studios	Retrd.	185.00	250-285.

		ARTIST	EDITION	ISSUE	QUOTE
93-06-010	Symphony Hour-Opening Title 41031	Disney Studios	Open	29.00	29.00
93-06-011	Symphony Hour-Opening Title 41031/c	Disney Studios	Retrd.	29.00	29-45.00
Walt Disney		**Classics Collection-Three Little Pigs**			
93-07-001	Practical Pig 41036	Disney Studios	Open	75.00	75.00
93-07-002	Practical Pig 41036/c	Disney Studios	Retrd.	75.00	75.00
93-07-003	Fifer Pig 41037	Disney Studios	Open	75.00	75.00
93-07-004	Fifer Pig 41037/c	Disney Studios	Retrd.	75.00	75.00
93-07-005	Fiddler Pig 41038	Disney Studios	Open	75.00	75.00
93-07-006	Fiddler Pig 41038/c	Disney Studios	Retrd.	75.00	75.00
93-07-007	Big Bad Wolf (short tooth) 41039 1st version	Disney Studios	Retrd.	295.00	1100.00
93-07-008	Big Bad Wolf 41039	Disney Studios	Retrd.	295.00	690-995.
93-07-009	Three Little Pigs-Opening Title 41046	Disney Studios	Open	29.00	29.00
93-07-010	Three Little Pigs-Opening Title 41046/c	Disney Studios	Retrd.	29.00	29-50.00
Walt Disney		**Classics Collection-Peter Pan**			
93-08-001	Peter Pan 41043	Disney Studios	Open	165.00	165.00
93-08-002	Peter Pan 41043/c	Disney Studios	Retrd.	165.00	260-275.
93-08-003	Captain Hook 41044	Disney Studios	Open	275.00	275.00
93-08-004	Captain Hook 41044/c	Disney Studios	Retrd.	275.00	800-880.
93-08-005	The Crocodile 41054	Disney Studios	Open	315.00	315.00
93-08-006	The Crocodile 41054/c	Disney Studios	Retrd.	315.00	315.00
93-08-007	Tinkerbell 41045/c	Disney Studios	Retrd.	215.00	770.00
93-08-008	Tinkerbell 41045/f	Disney Studios	Retrd.	215.00	450-550.
93-08-009	Peter Pan-Opening Title 41047	Disney Studios	Open	29.00	29.00
Walt Disney		**Classics Collection-Special Event**			
93-09-001	Flight of Fancy 41051	Disney Studios	Retrd.	35.00	35-75.00
94-09-002	Mr. Smee	Disney Studios	Open	90.00	90.00
Walt Disney		**Walt Disney Collectors Society**			
93-10-001	Jiminy Cricket/w	Disney Studios	Retrd.	Gift	155-200.
93-10-002	Jiminy Cricket/c	Disney Studios	Retrd.	Gift	110-200.
93-10-003	Brave Little Tailor	Disney Studios	Retrd.	160.00	200-320.
94-10-004	Cheshire Cat	Disney Studios	Yr.Iss.	Gift	N/A
94-10-005	Pecos Bill	Disney Studios	Retrd.	650.00	650.00
94-10-006	Admiral Duck	Disney Studios	3/95	165.00	165.00
Disneyana		**Disneyana Conventions**			
92-01-001	Tinker Bell 022075	Lladro	1,500	350.00	19-2800.
92-01-002	Two Merry Wanderers 022074	Goebel	1,500	250.00	600-1000
92-01-003	Big Thunder Mountain A26648	R. Lee	100	1650.00	3000.00
92-01-004	Nifty-Nineties Mickey & Minnie 022503	House of Laurenz	250	650.00	800-1100
92-01-005	Carousel Horse 022482	PJ's	250	125.00	300-500.
92-01-006	1947 Mickey Mouse Plush J20967	Gund	1,000	50.00	150-250.
92-01-007	Carousel Horse Poster (Lithograph)-A26318	R. Souders	2,000	25.00	150.00
92-01-008	Cinderella 022076	Armani	500	500.00	4-4500.
92-01-009	Serigraph Diptych Collage (set of 2)-22073	M. Graves	1,000	900.00	N/A
92-01-010	Cruella DeVill Doll-porcelain 22554	J. Wolf	25	3000.00	4000.00
92-01-011	Cinderella Castle 022077	John Hine Studio	500	250.00	1-2000.
92-01-012	Pinocchio	R. Wright	250	750.00	1750.00
92-01-013	Walt's Convertible (Cel)	Disney Art Ed.	500	950.00	1100.00
93-01-014	Snow White	Armani	2,000	750.00	800-1400
93-01-015	Dopey	Armani	Retrd.	125.00	125.00
93-01-016	The Band Concert-Bronze	B. Toma	25	650.00	55-6000.
93-01-017	Alice in Wonderland	Malvern	10	8000.00	N/A
93-01-018	Barbershop Quartet (Lithograph)	C. Boyer	1,000	350.00	N/A
93-01-019	Family Dinner Figurine	C. Boyer	1,000	600.00	N/A
93-01-020	Two Little Drummers	Goebel	1,500	325.00	475-700.
93-01-021	1947 Minnie Mouse Plush	Gund	1,000	50.00	150.00
93-01-022	Sleeping Beauty Castle	John Hine Studio	500	250.00	520-800.
93-01-023	Peter Pan	Lladro	2,000	400.00	1-1500.
93-01-024	Jumper from King Arthur Carousel	PJ's	250	125.00	155-245.
93-01-025	Mickey's Dreams	R. Lee	250	400.00	660-800.
93-01-026	Disneyland Bandstand Poster	R. Souders	2,000	25.00	N/A
93-01-027	Annette Doll	Alexander Doll	1,000	400.00	600-850.
93-01-038	Mickey Mouse, the Bandleader	Arribas Brothers	25	700.00	3-5000.
93-01-029	Walt's Train Celebration	Disney Art Ed.	950	950.00	1650.00
93-01-030	The Band Concert "Maestro Mickey"	Disney Art Ed.	275	2950.00	N/A
94-01-031	Cinderella/Godmother	Lladro	2,500	875.00	1400.00
94-01-032	Cinderella's Slipper	Waterford	1,200	250.00	600.00
94-01-033	Sleeping Beauty	Malvern	10	5500.00	N/A
94-01-034	Euro Disney Castle	John Hine Studio	750	250.00	600.00
94-01-035	Minnie Be Patient	Goebel	1,500	395.00	660.00
94-01-036	Mickey Self Portrait	Goebel Miniatures	500	295.00	N/A
94-01-037	Scrooge in Money Bin/Bronze	Carl Barks	100	1800.00	3950.00
94-01-038	Sorcerer Mickey-Bronze	B. Toma	100	1000.00	1800.00
94-01-039	Sorcerer Mickey-Crystal	Arribas Brothers	50	1700.00	3100.00
94-01-040	MM/MN/Goofy Limo	Ron Lee	500	500.00	850-1000
94-01-041	Ariel	Armani	1,500	750.00	750.00
94-01-042	Studio Poster	R. Souders	1,000	25.00	N/A
94-01-043	MM/MN w/House Kinetic	F. Prescott	10	4000.00	N/A
Duncan Royale		**History of Santa Claus I**			
83-01-001	St. Nicholas	P. Apsit	Retrd.	175.00	500-1200
83-01-002	Dedt Moroz	P. Apsit	Retrd.	145.00	450-650.
83-01-003	Black Peter	P. Apsit	Retrd.	145.00	350-400.
83-01-004	Victorian	P. Apsit	Retrd.	120.00	300-600.
83-01-005	Medieval	P. Apsit	Retrd.	220.00	15-1650.
83-01-006	Russian	P. Apsit	Retrd.	145.00	300-850.
83-01-007	Wassail	P. Apsit	Retrd.	90.00	155-300.
83-01-008	Kris Kringle	P. Apsit	Retrd.	165.00	12-1400.
83-01-009	Soda Pop	P. Apsit	Retrd.	145.00	10-1500.
83-01-010	Pioneer	P. Apsit	Retrd.	145.00	350.00
83-01-011	Civil War	P. Apsit	10000	145.00	300-350.
83-01-012	Nast	P. Apsit	Retrd.	90.00	25-3700.
Duncan Royale		**History of Santa Claus II**			
86-02-001	Odin	P. Apsit	10,000	200.00	250.00
86-02-002	Lord of Misrule	P. Apsit	10,000	160.00	200.00
86-02-003	Mongolian/Asian	P. Apsit	10,000	240.00	300.00
86-02-004	The Magi	P. Apsit	10,000	350.00	400.00
86-02-005	St. Lucia	P. Apsit	10,000	180.00	225.00
86-02-006	Befana	P. Apsit	10,000	200.00	250.00
86-02-007	Babouska	P. Apsit	10,000	170.00	200.00
86-02-008	Bavarian	P. Apsit	10,000	250.00	300.00
86-02-009	Alsace Angel	P. Apsit	10,000	250.00	300.00
86-02-010	Frau Holda	P. Apsit	10,000	160.00	180.00
86-02-011	Sir Christmas	P. Apsit	10,000	150.00	175.00
86-02-012	The Pixie	P. Apsit	10,000	140.00	175.00

		ARTIST	EDITION	ISSUE	QUOTE
Duncan Royale		**History of Santa Claus III**			
90-03-001	St. Basil	Duncan Royale	10,000	300.00	300.00
90-03-002	Star Man	Duncan Royale	10,000	300.00	300.00
90-03-003	Julenisse	Duncan Royale	10,000	200.00	200.00
90-03-004	Ukko	Duncan Royale	10,000	250.00	250.00
90-03-005	Druid	Duncan Royale	10,000	250.00	250.00
91-03-006	Saturnalia King	Duncan Royale	10,000	200.00	200.00
91-03-007	Judah Maccabee	Duncan Royale	10,000	300.00	300.00
91-03-008	King Wenceslas	Duncan Royale	10,000	300.00	300.00
91-03-009	Hoteisho	Duncan Royale	10,000	200.00	200.00
91-03-010	Knickerbocker	Duncan Royale	10,000	300.00	300.00
91-03-011	Samichlaus	Duncan Royale	10,000	350.00	350.00
91-03-012	Grandfather Frost & Snow Maiden	Duncan Royale	10,000	400.00	400.00
Duncan Royale		**History Of Santa Claus-Special Releases**			
91-04-001	Signature Piece	Duncan Royale	Open	50.00	50.00
92-04-002	Nast & Sleigh	Duncan Royale	5,000	500.00	500.00
Duncan Royale		**History of Santa Claus I -Wood**			
87-05-001	St. Nicholas-8" wood	P. Apsit	500	450.00	450.00
87-05-002	Dedt Moroz-8" wood	P. Apsit	Retrd.	450.00	450.00
87-05-003	Black Peter-8" wood	P. Apsit	Retrd.	450.00	450.00
87-05-004	Victorian-8" wood	P. Apsit	Retrd.	450.00	450.00
87-05-005	Medieval-8" wood	P. Apsit	500	450.00	450.00
87-05-006	Russian-8" wood	P. Apsit	Retrd.	450.00	450.00
87-05-007	Wassail-8" wood	P. Apsit	Retrd.	450.00	450.00
87-05-008	Kris Kringle-8" wood	P. Apsit	500	450.00	450.00
87-05-009	Soda Pop-8" wood	P. Apsit	Retrd.	450.00	450.00
87-05-010	Pioneer-8" wood	P. Apsit	Retrd.	450.00	450.00
87-05-011	Civil War-8" wood	P. Apsit	500	450.00	450.00
87-05-012	Nast-8" wood	P. Apsit	Retrd.	450.00	450.00
Duncan Royale		**History of Santa Claus (18")**			
89-06-001	St. Nicholas-18"	P. Apsit	1,000	1500.00	1500.00
89-06-002	Medieval-18"	P. Apsit	1,000	1500.00	1500.00
89-06-003	Russian-18"	P. Apsit	1,000	1500.00	1500.00
89-06-004	Kris Kringle-18"	P. Apsit	1,000	1500.00	1500.00
89-06-005	Soda Pop-18"	P. Apsit	1,000	1500.00	1500.00
89-06-006	Nast-18"	P. Apsit	1,000	1500.00	1500.00
Duncan Royale		**History of Santa Claus I (6")**			
88-07-001	St. Nicholas-6" porcelain	P. Apsit	6,000/yr	70.00	80.00
88-07-002	Dedt Moroz -6" porcelain	P. Apsit	6,000/yr	70.00	80.00
88-07-003	Black Peter-6" porcelain	P. Apsit	6,000/yr	70.00	80.00
88-07-004	Victorian-6" porcelain	P. Apsit	6,000/yr	60.00	80.00
88-07-005	Medieval-6" porcelain	P. Apsit	6,000/yr	70.00	80.00
88-07-006	Russian-6" porcelain	P. Apsit	6,000/yr	70.00	80.00
88-07-007	Wassail-6" porcelain	P. Apsit	6,000/yr	60.00	80.00
88-07-008	Kris Kringle-6" porcelain	P. Apsit	6,000/yr	60.00	80.00
88-07-009	Soda Pop-6" porcelain	P. Apsit	6,000/yr	60.00	80.00
88-07-010	Pioneer-6" porcelain	P. Apsit	6,000/yr	60.00	80.00
88-07-011	Civil War-6" porcelain	P. Apsit	6,000/yr	60.00	80.00
88-07-012	Nast-6" porcelain	P. Apsit	6,000/yr	60.00	80.00
Duncan Royale		**History of Santa Claus II (6")**			
88-08-001	Odin-6" porcelain	P. Apsit	6,000/yr	80.00	90.00
88-08-002	Lord of Misrule-6" porcelain	P. Apsit	6,000/yr	60.00	80.00
88-08-003	Mongolian/Asian-6" porcelain	P. Apsit	6,000/yr	80.00	90.00
88-08-004	Magi-6" porcelain	P. Apsit	6,000/yr	130.00	150.00
88-08-005	St. Lucia-6" porcelain	P. Apsit	6,000/yr	70.00	80.00
88-08-006	Befana-6" porcelain	P. Apsit	6,000/yr	70.00	80.00
88-08-007	Babouska-6" porcelain	P. Apsit	6,000/yr	70.00	80.00
88-08-008	Bavarian-6" porcelain	P. Apsit	6,000/yr	90.00	100.00
88-08-009	Alsace Angel-6" porcelain	P. Apsit	6,000/yr	80.00	90.00
88-08-010	Frau Holda-6" porcelain	P. Apsit	6,000/yr	50.00	80.00
88-08-011	Sir Christmas-6" porcelain	P. Apsit	6,000/yr	60.00	80.00
88-08-012	Pixie-6" porcelain	P. Apsit	6,000/yr	50.00	80.00
90-08-013	Bob Hope-6" porcelain	P. Apsit	6,000/yr	130.00	130.00
Duncan Royale		**History of Classic Entertainers**			
87-09-001	Greco-Roman	P. Apsit	Retrd.	180.00	350.00
87-09-002	Jester	P. Apsit	Retrd.	410.00	600-850.
87-09-003	Pierrot	P. Apsit	Retrd.	180.00	180-350.
87-09-004	Harlequin	P. Apsit	Retrd.	250.00	350.00
87-09-005	Grotesque	P. Apsit	Retrd.	230.00	350.00
87-09-006	Pantalone	P. Apsit	Retrd.	270.00	350.00
87-09-007	Pulcinella	P. Apsit	Retrd.	220.00	350.00
87-09-008	Russian	P. Apsit	Retrd.	190.00	350.00
87-09-009	Auguste	P. Apsit	Retrd.	220.00	350.00
87-09-010	Slapstick	P. Apsit	Retrd.	250.00	350.00
87-09-011	Uncle Sam	P. Apsit	Retrd.	160.00	250-350.
87-09-012	American	P. Apsit	Retrd.	160.00	350.00
Duncan Royale		**History of Classic Entertainers II**			
88-10-001	Goliard	P. Apsit	Retrd.	200.00	200-350.
88-10-002	Touchstone	P. Apsit	Retrd.	200.00	200-350.
88-10-003	Feste	P. Apsit	Retrd.	250.00	200-350.
88-10-004	Tartaglia	P. Apsit	Retrd.	200.00	200-350.
88-10-005	Zanni	P. Apsit	Retrd.	200.00	200-350.
88-10-006	Mountebank	P. Apsit	Retrd.	270.00	200-350.
88-10-007	Pedrolino	P. Apsit	Retrd.	200.00	200-350.
88-10-008	Thomassi	P. Apsit	Retrd.	200.00	200-350.
88-10-009	Tramp	P. Apsit	Retrd.	200.00	200-350.
88-10-010	White Face	P. Apsit	Retrd.	250.00	200-350.
88-10-011	Mime	P. Apsit	Retrd.	200.00	200-350.
88-10-012	Bob Hope	P. Apsit	Retrd.	250.00	200-350.
Duncan Royale		**History of Classic Entertainers-Special Releases**			
88-11-001	Signature Piece	P. Apsit	Retrd.	50.00	50.00
90-11-002	Mime-18"	P. Apsit	Retrd.	1500.00	1500.00
90-11-003	Bob Hope-18"	P. Apsit	Retrd.	1500.00	15-2000.
Duncan Royale		**Greatest Gift...Love**			
88-12-001	Annunciation, marble	P. Apsit	5,000	270.00	270.00
88-12-002	Annunciation, painted porcelain	P. Apsit	5,000	270.00	270.00
88-12-003	Nativity, marble	P. Apsit	5,000	500.00	500.00
88-12-004	Nativity, painted porcelain	P. Apsit	5,000	500.00	500.00
88-12-005	Crucifixion, marble	P. Apsit	5,000	300.00	300.00
88-12-006	Crucifixion, painted porcelain	P. Apsit	5,000	300.00	300.00
Duncan Royale		**Woodland Fairies**			
88-13-001	Cherry	Duncan Royale	10,000	70.00	70.00
88-13-002	Mulberry	Duncan Royale	10,000	70.00	70.00
88-13-003	Apple	Duncan Royale	Retrd.	70.00	70.00
88-13-004	Poplar	Duncan Royale	10,000	70.00	70.00

	ARTIST	EDITION	ISSUE	QUOTE
88-13-005 Elm	Duncan Royale	10,000	70.00	70.00
88-13-006 Chestnut	Duncan Royale	10,000	70.00	70.00
88-13-007 Calla Lily	Duncan Royale	10,000	70.00	70.00
88-13-008 Pear Blossom	Duncan Royale	Retrd.	70.00	70.00
88-13-009 Lime Tree	Duncan Royale	Retrd.	70.00	70.00
88-13-010 Christmas Tree	Duncan Royale	Retrd.	70.00	70.00
88-13-011 Sycamore	Duncan Royale	Retrd.	70.00	70.00
88-13-012 Pine Tree	Duncan Royale	10,000	70.00	70.00
88-13-013 Almond Blossom	Duncan Royale	Retrd.	70.00	70.00
88-13-014 Guilder Rose	Duncan Royale	Retrd.	70.00	70.00
Duncan Royale	**Calendar Secrets (12")**			
90-14-001 January	D. Aphessetche	5,000	260.00	260.00
90-14-002 February	D. Aphessetche	5,000	370.00	370.00
90-14-003 March	D. Aphessetche	5,000	350.00	350.00
90-14-004 April	D. Aphessetche	5,000	370.00	370.00
90-14-005 May	D. Aphessetche	5,000	390.00	390.00
90-14-006 June	D. Aphessetche	5,000	410.00	410.00
90-14-007 July	D. Aphessetche	5,000	280.00	280.00
90-14-008 August	D. Aphessetche	5,000	300.00	300.00
90-14-009 September	D. Aphessetche	5,000	300.00	300.00
90-14-010 October	D. Aphessetche	5,000	350.00	350.00
90-14-011 November	D. Aphessetche	5,000	410.00	410.00
90-14-012 December	D. Aphessetche	5,000	410.00	410.00
Duncan Royale	**Ebony Collection**			
90-15-001 The Fiddler	Duncan Royale	5,000	90.00	90.00
90-15-002 Harmonica Man	Duncan Royale	5,000	80.00	80.00
90-15-003 Banjo Man	Duncan Royale	5,000	80.00	80.00
91-15-004 Spoons	Duncan Royale	5,000	90.00	90.00
91-15-005 Preacher	Duncan Royale	5,000	90.00	90.00
91-15-006 Female Gospel Singer	Duncan Royale	5,000	90.00	90.00
91-15-007 Male Gospel Singer	Duncan Royale	5,000	90.00	90.00
91-15-008 Jug Man	Duncan Royale	5,000	90.00	90.00
92-15-009 Jug Tooter	Duncan Royale	5,000	90.00	90.00
92-15-010 A Little Magic	Duncan Royale	5,000	80.00	80.00
93-15-011 Ebony Angel	Duncan Royale	5,000	170.00	170.00
Duncan Royale	**Ebony Collection-Jazzman**			
92-16-001 Jazz Man Set	Duncan Royale	5,000	500.00	500.00
92-16-002 Sax	Duncan Royale	5,000	90.00	90.00
92-16-003 Trumpet	Duncan Royale	5,000	90.00	90.00
92-16-004 Bass	Duncan Royale	5,000	90.00	90.00
92-16-005 Piano	Duncan Royale	5,000	130.00	130.00
92-16-006 Bongo	Duncan Royale	5,000	90.00	90.00
Duncan Royale	**Ebony Collection-Jubilee Dancers**			
93-17-001 Fallana	Duncan Royale	5,000	100.00	100.00
93-17-002 Keshia	Duncan Royale	5,000	100.00	100.00
93-17-003 Lottie	Duncan Royale	5,000	100.00	100.00
93-17-004 Wilfred	Duncan Royale	5,000	100.00	100.00
93-17-005 Bliss	Duncan Royale	5,000	100.00	100.00
93-17-006 Lamar	Duncan Royale	5,000	100.00	100.00
Duncan Royale	**Ebony Collection-Friends & Family**			
94-18-001 Daddy	Duncan Royale	5,000	120.00	120.00
94-18-002 Lunchtime	Duncan Royale	5,000	100.00	100.00
94-18-003 Mommie & Me	Duncan Royale	5,000	125.00	125.00
94-18-004 Millie	Duncan Royale	5,000	100.00	100.00
94-18-005 Agnes	Duncan Royale	5,000	100.00	100.00
Duncan Royale	**Ebony Collection-Special Releases**			
91-19-001 Signature Piece	Duncan Royale	Open	50.00	50.00
Duncan Royale	**Ebony Collection-Buckwheat Collection**			
92-20-001 Petee & Friend	Duncan Royale	5,000	90.00	90.00
92-20-002 Painter	Duncan Royale	5,000	80.00	90.00
92-20-003 O'Tay	Duncan Royale	5,000	70.00	90.00
92-20-004 Smile For The Camera	Duncan Royale	5,000	80.00	90.00
Duncan Royale	**Early American (12")**			
91-21-001 Doctor	Duncan Royale	10,000	150.00	150.00
91-21-002 Accountant	Duncan Royale	10,000	170.00	170.00
91-21-003 Lawyer	Duncan Royale	10,000	170.00	170.00
91-21-004 Nurse	Duncan Royale	10,000	150.00	150.00
91-21-005 Fireman	Duncan Royale	10,000	150.00	150.00
91-21-006 Policeman	Duncan Royale	10,000	150.00	150.00
91-21-007 Dentist	Duncan Royale	10,000	150.00	150.00
91-21-008 Pharmacist	Duncan Royale	10,000	150.00	150.00
91-21-009 Teacher	Duncan Royale	10,000	150.00	150.00
91-21-010 Banker	Duncan Royale	10,000	150.00	150.00
91-21-011 Secretary	Duncan Royale	10,000	150.00	150.00
91-21-012 Chiropractor	Duncan Royale	10,000	150.00	150.00
91-21-013 Set of 12	Duncan Royale	10,000	2290.00	2290.00
Duncan Royale	**Early American (6")**			
93-22-001 6" Set of 12	Duncan Royale	6,000	960.00	960.00
93-22-002 Doctor	Duncan Royale	6,000	80.00	80.00
93-22-003 Accountant	Duncan Royale	6,000	80.00	80.00
93-22-004 Lawyer	Duncan Royale	6,000	80.00	80.00
93-22-005 Nurse	Duncan Royale	6,000	80.00	80.00
93-22-006 Fireman	Duncan Royale	6,000	80.00	80.00
93-22-007 Policeman	Duncan Royale	6,000	80.00	80.00
93-22-008 Dentist	Duncan Royale	6,000	80.00	80.00
93-22-009 Pharmacist	Duncan Royale	6,000	80.00	80.00
93-22-010 Teacher	Duncan Royale	6,000	80.00	80.00
93-22-011 Banker	Duncan Royale	6,000	80.00	80.00
93-22-012 Secretary	Duncan Royale	6,000	80.00	80.00
93-22-013 Chiropractor	Duncan Royale	6,000	80.00	80.00
Duncan Royale	**Christmas Images**			
91-23-001 The Carolers	Duncan Royale	10,000	120.00	120.00
91-23-002 The Christmas Pageant	Duncan Royale	10,000	175.00	175.00
92-23-003 Are You Really Santa?	Duncan Royale	10,000	N/A	N/A
92-23-004 The Midnight Watch	Duncan Royale	10,000	N/A	N/A
92-23-005 The Christmas Angel	Duncan Royale	10,000	110.00	110.00
92-23-006 Sneaking A Peek	Duncan Royale	10,000	N/A	N/A
Duncan Royale	**Painted Pewter Miniatures-Santa 1st Series**			
86-24-001 St. Nicholas	Duncan Royale	500	30.00	30.00
86-24-002 Dedt Moroz	Duncan Royale	500	30.00	30.00
86-24-003 Black Peter	Duncan Royale	500	30.00	30.00
86-24-004 Victorian	Duncan Royale	500	30.00	30.00
86-24-005 Medieval	Duncan Royale	500	30.00	30.00
86-24-006 Russian	Duncan Royale	500	30.00	30.00
86-24-007 Wassail	Duncan Royale	500	30.00	30.00

	ARTIST	EDITION	ISSUE	QUOTE
86-24-008 Kris Kringle	Duncan Royale	500	30.00	30.00
86-24-009 Soda Pop	Duncan Royale	500	30.00	30.00
86-24-010 Pioneer	Duncan Royale	500	30.00	30.00
86-24-011 Civil War	Duncan Royale	500	30.00	30.00
86-24-012 Nast	Duncan Royale	500	30.00	30.00
86-24-013 Set of 12	Duncan Royale	500	360.00	360-495.
Duncan Royale	**Painted Pewter Miniatures-Santa 2nd Series**			
88-25-001 Odin	Duncan Royale	500	30.00	30.00
88-25-002 Lord of Misrule	Duncan Royale	500	30.00	30.00
88-25-003 Mongolian	Duncan Royale	500	30.00	30.00
88-25-004 Magi	Duncan Royale	500	30.00	30.00
88-25-005 St. Lucia	Duncan Royale	500	30.00	30.00
88-25-006 Befana	Duncan Royale	500	30.00	30.00
88-25-007 Babouska	Duncan Royale	500	30.00	30.00
88-25-008 Bavarian	Duncan Royale	500	30.00	30.00
88-25-009 Alsace Angel	Duncan Royale	500	30.00	30.00
88-25-010 Frau Holda	Duncan Royale	500	30.00	30.00
88-25-011 Sir Christmas	Duncan Royale	500	30.00	30.00
88-25-012 Pixie	Duncan Royale	500	30.00	30.00
88-25-013 Set of 12	Duncan Royale	500	360.00	360-495.
Duncan Royale	**Collector Club**			
91-26-001 Today's Nast	Duncan Royale	Retrd.	80.00	100-125.
94-26-002 Winter Santa	Duncan Royale	Yr.Iss.	125.00	125.00
Duncan Royale	**1990 & 1991 Special Event Piece**			
XX-27-001 Nast & Music	Duncan Royale	Retrd.	79.95	79.95
eggspressions! inc.	**Hand Painted**			
92-01-001 Warrior's Pride	eggspressions	Open	85.00	85.00
92-01-002 Lobo	eggspressions	Open	85.00	85.00
92-01-003 Buttercup	eggspressions	Open	85.00	85.00
92-01-004 Slumbering Steggy	eggspressions	Open	85.00	85.00
92-01-005 Tryke	eggspressions	Open	90.00	90.00
92-01-006 America's Pride	eggspressions	Open	139.00	139.00
92-01-007 Serena	eggspressions	Open	139.00	139.00
92-01-008 Brrr Rabbit	eggspressions	Open	139.00	139.00
92-01-009 Star Prancer	eggspressions	Open	139.00	139.00
eggspressions! inc.	**Treasure Chests**			
92-02-001 Pearl	eggspressions	Open	98.00	98.00
92-02-002 Ebony	eggspressions	Open	105.00	105.00
92-02-003 Midas	eggspressions	Open	105.00	105.00
92-02-004 Silver Jewels	eggspressions	Open	105.00	105.00
92-02-005 Mint Julep	eggspressions	Open	98.00	98.00
92-02-006 Blush	eggspressions	Open	105.00	105.00
92-02-007 Skye	eggspressions	Open	98.00	98.00
92-02-008 Yellow Rose	eggspressions	Open	105.00	105.00
92-02-009 Velvet Princess	eggspressions	Open	170.00	170.00
92-02-010 Elegant Choice	eggspressions	Open	167.00	167.00
92-02-011 Secret Garden	eggspressions	Open	158.00	158.00
eggspressions! inc.	**Musical Treasure Chests**			
92-03-001 Maria	eggspressions	Open	115.00	115.00
92-03-002 Laura	eggspressions	Open	115.00	115.00
eggspressions! inc.	**Hanging Collectibles**			
92-04-001 Love in Flight	eggspressions	Open	95.00	95.00
92-04-002 McGregor's Garden	eggspressions	Open	98.00	98.00
92-04-003 Tsadora	eggspressions	Open	110.00	110.00
92-04-004 Love Duet	eggspressions	Open	125.00	125.00
92-04-005 Kewpie Doll	eggspressions	Open	99.00	99.00
92-04-006 Apple Blossom Bouquet	eggspressions	Open	62.00	62.00
92-04-007 Winter Colt	eggspressions	Open	104.00	104.00
92-04-008 Golden Crystal	eggspressions	Open	145.00	145.00
92-04-009 Romantique	eggspressions	Open	66.00	66.00
92-04-010 Blue Birds of Happiness	eggspressions	Open	79.00	79.00
eggspressions! inc.	**Wilderness Collection**			
92-05-001 Dear One	eggspressions	Open	98.00	98.00
92-05-002 Togetherness	eggspressions	Open	95.00	95.00
92-05-003 Oh, Nuts	eggspressions	Open	98.00	98.00
92-05-004 Daytime Den	eggspressions	Open	124.00	124.00
92-05-005 Family Outing	eggspressions	Open	98.00	98.00
eggspressions! inc.	**Whimsical**			
92-06-001 Petunia	eggspressions	Open	38.00	38.00
92-06-002 Miss Ellie	eggspressions	Open	38.00	38.00
92-06-003 Kris Kringle	eggspressions	Open	38.00	38.00
92-06-004 Peter	eggspressions	Open	38.00	38.00
92-06-005 Marcella	eggspressions	Open	38.00	38.00
92-06-006 Colours	eggspressions	Open	45.00	45.00
eggspressions! inc.	**Hand Carved**			
92-07-001 Fantasia	eggspressions	Open	55.00	55.00
92-07-002 Misty Rose	eggspressions	Open	50.00	50.00
92-07-003 Snowflake	eggspressions	Open	54.00	54.00
92-07-004 Summer Rose	eggspressions	Open	51.00	51.00
92-07-005 Dogwood	eggspressions	Open	56.00	56.00
92-07-006 Poinsettia	eggspressions	Open	65.00	65.00
92-07-007 Tannenbaum	eggspressions	Open	62.00	62.00
92-07-008 Bells	eggspressions	Open	60.00	60.00
92-07-009 Gabriela	eggspressions	Open	48.00	48.00
92-07-010 Angelica	eggspressions	Open	50.00	50.00
92-07-011 Tabitha	eggspressions	Open	48.00	48.00
92-07-012 Welcome Candle	eggspressions	Open	64.00	64.00
92-07-013 Butterfly Wings	eggspressions	Open	59.00	59.00
92-07-014 Birth Day! - January	eggspressions	Open	48.00	48.00
92-07-015 Birth Day! - February	eggspressions	Open	48.00	48.00
92-07-016 Birth Day! - March	eggspressions	Open	48.00	48.00
92-07-017 Birth Day! - April	eggspressions	Open	48.00	48.00
92-07-018 Birth Day! - May	eggspressions	Open	48.00	48.00
92-07-019 Birth Day! - June	eggspressions	Open	48.00	48.00
92-07-020 Birth Day! - July	eggspressions	Open	48.00	48.00
92-07-021 Birth Day! - August	eggspressions	Open	48.00	48.00
92-07-022 Birth Day! - September	eggspressions	Open	48.00	48.00
92-07-023 Birth Day! - October	eggspressions	Open	48.00	48.00
92-07-024 Birth Day! - November	eggspressions	Open	48.00	48.00
92-07-025 Birth Day! - December	eggspressions	Open	48.00	48.00
eggspressions! inc.	**Hanging Christmas**			
92-08-001 Bill & Coo	eggspressions	Open	53.00	53.00
92-08-002 Candyland	eggspressions	Open	94.00	94.00
92-08-003 Drummer Bear	eggspressions	Open	97.00	97.00

		ARTIST	EDITION	ISSUE	QUOTE
92-08-004	In Tune	eggspressions	Open	120.00	120.00
92-08-005	Winter Wonderland	eggspressions	Open	98.00	98.00
92-08-006	Tiny Treasures	eggspressions	Open	100.00	100.00
92-08-007	Christmas Curiosity	eggspressions	Open	104.00	104.00
92-08-008	Santa's Workshop	eggspressions	125	150.00	150.00
92-08-009	Waiting	eggspressions	Open	92.00	92.00
92-08-010	Winter Haven	eggspressions	Open	98.00	98.00
92-08-011	Cardinals	eggspressions	Open	58.00	58.00
92-08-012	Choo Choo Christmas	eggspressions	Open	124.00	124.00
eggspressions! inc.		**Southwesten Collection**			
92-09-001	Kachina	eggspressions	Open	112.00	112.00
92-09-002	Storyteller	eggspressions	Open	112.00	112.00
eggspressions! inc.		**Curio Collection**			
92-10-001	Winter Song	eggspressions	Open	99.00	99.00
92-10-002	Winter Colt (Stand)	eggspressions	Open	104.00	104.00
eggspressions! inc.		**Easter Collection**			
94-11-001	Sweet Dreams	eggspressions	Open	99.00	99.00
94-11-002	Grandmas Goodies	eggspressions	Open	99.00	99.00
94-11-003	Grandpas Tricks	eggspressions	Open	90.00	90.00
94-11-004	Chicks & Bunnies	eggspressions	Open	88.00	88.00
94-11-005	Playing Grown-Up	eggspressions	Open	84.00	84.00
94-11-006	Easter Preparation	eggspressions	Open	84.00	84.00
94-11-007	Dinner for Six	eggspressions	Open	98.00	98.00
94-11-008	Pre-School Play	eggspressions	Open	108.00	108.00
94-11-009	Home Sweet Home	eggspressions	Open	120.00	120.00
eggspressions! inc.		**Clown Collection**			
94-12-001	Spring Frolic	eggspressions	Open	64.00	64.00
94-12-002	Happy Thoughts	eggspressions	Open	78.00	78.00
eggspressions! inc.		**Jeweled Baskets**			
94-13-001	Absolutely Amethyst	eggspressions	Open	98.00	98.00
94-13-002	Pastels & Pearls	eggspressions	Open	112.00	112.00
94-13-003	Pristine Pearls	eggspressions	Open	118.00	118.00
94-13-004	Rose Marie	eggspressions	Open	98.00	98.00
94-13-005	Black Tie	eggspressions	Open	178.00	178.00
94-13-006	Jaded Jealousy	eggspressions	Open	158.00	158.00
eggspressions! inc.		**Christmas Collection**			
94-14-001	Angel of Love	eggspressions	250	110.00	110.00
94-14-002	Angel of Hope	eggspressions	250	130.00	130.00
94-14-003	O' Holy Night	eggspressions	250	160.00	160.00
94-14-004	Beary Pink Christmas	eggspressions	250	98.00	98.00
94-14-005	Beary Blue Christmas	eggspressions	250	98.00	98.00
94-14-006	Caroling Mice	eggspressions	250	120.00	120.00
94-14-007	Christmas Joy	eggspressions	250	104.00	104.00
94-14-008	Santas Little Sweetheart	eggspressions	100	98.00	98.00
94-14-009	Santas Little Elves	eggspressions	250	130.00	130.00
94-14-010	Frosty's Cheer	eggspressions	500	64.00	64.00
94-14-011	Old St. Nicholas	eggspressions	500	64.00	64.00
eggspressions! inc.		**Music Boxes**			
94-15-001	Holiday Memories	eggspressions	250	190.00	190.00
94-15-002	Making Spirits Bright	eggspressions	25	300.00	300.00
eggspressions!inc.		**Natures Collection**			
94-16-001	Spring Melody	eggspressions	250	130.00	130.00
94-16-002	Love Birds	eggspressions	250	118.00	118.00
94-16-003	Mother's Pride	eggspressions	250	120.00	120.00
eggspressions! inc.		**Romance Collection**			
94-17-001	Lavender Love	eggspressions	250	130.00	130.00
94-17-002	Wedding in White	eggspressions	250	160.00	160.00
94-17-003	Serenity	eggspressions	250	114.00	114.00
94-17-004	Serenade	eggspressions	250	120.00	120.00
eggspressions! inc.		**Childrens Collection**			
94-18-001	Skip A Long	eggspressions	250	118.00	118.00
94-18-002	Jessica	eggspressions	125	240.00	240.00
94-18-003	Purr-fect Hug	eggspressions	250	150.00	150.00
94-18-004	Teddy Bear Sing Along	eggspressions	250	114.00	114.00
eggspressions! inc.		**Keepsake Collection**			
94-19-001	Golden Harmony	eggspressions	250	160.00	160.00
94-19-002	Eternity	eggspressions	250	170.00	170.00
94-19-003	Passion	eggspressions	25	500.00	500.00
Enchantica		**Retired Enchantica Collection**			
88-01-001	Rattajack - Please-2000	A. Bill	Retrd.	40.00	50-60.00
88-01-002	Rattajack - My Ball-2001	A. Bill	Retrd.	40.00	60.00
88-01-003	Rattajack - Terragon Dreams-2002	A. Bill	Retrd.	40.00	58-69.00
88-01-004	Rattajack - Circles-2003	A. Bill	Retrd.	40.00	68-95.00
88-01-005	Anquil- Dragons Footprint-2004	A. Bill	Retrd.	55.00	110-115.
88-01-006	Snappa Hatches Out-2006	A. Bill	Retrd.	25.00	40-75.00
88-01-007	Snappa's First Feast-2007	A. Bill	Retrd.	25.00	36-50.00
88-01-008	Snappa Climbs High-2008	A. Bill	Retrd.	25.00	39-50.00
88-01-009	Snappa Finds a Collar-2009	A. Bill	Retrd.	25.00	39-70.00
88-01-010	Snappa Plays Ball-2010	A. Bill	Retrd.	25.00	39-50.00
88-01-011	Snappa Dozes Off-2011	A. Bill	Retrd.	25.00	39-50.00
88-01-012	Tarbet with Sack-2012	A. Bill	Retrd.	47.00	50-60.00
88-01-013	Hest Checks Crystals-2013	A. Bill	Retrd.	47.00	N/A
88-01-014	Hepna Pushes Truck-2014	A. Bill	Retrd.	47.00	N/A
88-01-015	Blick Scoops Crystals-2015	A. Bill	Retrd.	47.00	50.00
88-01-016	Fantazar- Spring Wizard-2016	A. Bill	Retrd.	132.50	220-275.
88-01-017	Gorgoyle - Spring Dragon-2017	A. Bill	Retrd.	132.50	350-370.
89-01-018	Vrorst - The Ice Sorcerer-2018	A. Bill	Retrd.	155.00	400-700.
89-01-019	Grawlfang - Winter Dragon-2019	A. Bill	Retrd.	132.50	500-750.
89-01-020	Old Yargle-2020	A. Bill	Retrd.	55.00	N/A
89-01-021	Chuckwalla-2021	A. Bill	Retrd.	43.00	N/A
89-01-022	Hobba, Hellbenders Twin Son-2023	A. Bill	Retrd.	69.00	73-105.
90-01-023	Orolan-Summer Wizard-2025	A. Bill	Retrd.	165.00	205.00
90-01-024	Arangast - Summer Dragon-2026	K. Fallon	Retrd.	165.00	350.00
90-01-025	The Swamp Demon-2028	K. Fallon	Retrd.	69.00	90.00
90-01-026	Cellandia-Summer Fairy-2029	K. Fallon	Retrd.	115.00	150.00
90-01-027	Fossfex - Autumn Fairy-2030	K. Fallon	Retrd.	115.00	150.00
91-01-028	Okra, Goblin Princess-2031	K. Fallon	Retrd.	105.00	N/A
91-01-029	Waxifrade - Autumn Wizard-2033	K. Fallon	Retrd.	265.00	300-350.
91-01-030	Snarlgard - Autumn Dragon-2034	K. Fallon	Retrd.	337.00	350-380.
91-01-031	Flight to Danger-2044	K. Fallon	Retrd.	3000.00	6000.00
91-01-032	Bledderag, Goblin Twin-2048	K. Fallon	Retrd.	115.00	140.00
91-01-033	Furza - Carrier Dragon-2050	K. Fallon	Retrd.	137.50	165-170.
92-01-034	Breen - Carrier Dragon-2053	K. Fallon	Retrd.	156.00	155-160.

		ARTIST	EDITION	ISSUE	QUOTE
92-01-035	Sorren & Gart-2054	K. Fallon	Retrd.	220.00	N/A
92-01-036	Olm & Sylphen, Mer-King & Queen-2059	A. Bill	Retrd.	350.00	N/A
92-01-037	Spring Wizard and Yim-2060	A. Bill	Retrd.	410.00	410.00
92-01-038	Thrace-Gladiator-2061	K. Fallon	Retrd.	280.00	280.00
92-01-039	Manu Manu-Peeper-2105	A. Bill	Retrd.	40.00	50.00
93-01-040	Ice Dragon-2109	A. Bill	Retrd.	95.00	N/A
94-01-041	Escape (5th Anniversary)-2110	A. Bill	Retrd.	250.00	250.00
Enchantica		**Enchantica Collectors Club**			
91-02-001	Snappa on Mushroom-2101	A. Bill	Retrd.	Gift	65.00
91-02-002	Rattajack with Snail-2102	A. Bill	Retrd.	60.00	60-105.
92-02-003	Jonquil-2103	A. Hull	Retrd.	Gift	60.00
92-02-004	Ice Demon-2104	K. Fallon	Retrd.	85.00	125.00
92-02-005	Sea Dragon-2106	A. Bill	Retrd.	99.00	200.00
93-02-006	White Dragon-2107	A. Bill	Retrd.	Gift	N/A
93-02-007	Jonquil's Flight-2108	A. Bill	Retrd.	140.00	140.00
94-02-008	Verratus-2111	A. Bill	Yr.Iss.	Gift	N/A
94-02-009	Mimmer-Spring Fairy-2112	A. Bill	Yr.Iss.	100.00	100.00
94-02-010	Gorgoyle Cameo piece-2113	K. Fallon	Yr.Iss.	Gift	N/A
Enesco Corporation		**Precious Moments Special Edition**			
81-01-001	Hello, Lord, It's Me Again-PM-811	S. Butcher	Retrd.	25.00	375-450.
82-01-002	Smile, God Loves You-PM-821	S. Butcher	Retrd.	25.00	210-250.
83-01-003	Put on a Happy Face-PM-822	S. Butcher	Retrd.	25.00	185-205.
83-01-004	Dawn's Early Light-PM-831	S. Butcher	Retrd.	27.50	70-95.00
84-01-005	God's Ray of Mercy-PM-841	S. Butcher	Retrd.	25.00	40-85.00
84-01-006	Trust in the Lord to the Finish-PM-842	S. Butcher	Retrd.	25.00	65-75.00
85-01-007	The Lord is My Shepherd-PM-851	S. Butcher	Retrd.	25.00	60-95.00
85-01-008	I Love to Tell the Story-PM-852	S. Butcher	Retrd.	27.50	60-70.00
86-01-009	Grandma's Prayer-PM-861	S. Butcher	Retrd.	25.00	75-95.00
86-01-010	I'm Following Jesus-PM-862	S. Butcher	Retrd.	25.00	80-95.00
87-01-011	Feed My Sheep-PM-871	S. Butcher	Retrd.	25.00	45-75.00
87-01-012	In His Time-PM-872	S. Butcher	Retrd.	25.00	50-60.00
87-01-013	Loving You Dear Valentine-PM-873	S. Butcher	Retrd.	25.00	35-45.00
87-01-014	Loving You Dear Valentine-PM-874	S. Butcher	Retrd.	25.00	45-50.00
88-01-015	God Bless You for Touching My Life-PM-881	S. Butcher	Retrd.	27.50	48-70.00
88-01-016	You Just Can't Chuck A Good Friendship-PM-882	S. Butcher	Retrd.	27.50	38-50.00
89-01-017	You Will Always Be My Choice- PM-891	S. Butcher	Retrd.	27.50	35-50.00
89-01-018	Mow Power To Ya-PM-892	S. Butcher	Retrd.	27.50	40-53.00
90-01-019	Ten Years And Still Going Strong-PM-901	S. Butcher	Retrd.	30.00	45-60.00
90-01-020	You Are A Blessing To Me-PM-902	S. Butcher	Retrd.	30.00	32-50.00
91-01-021	One Step At A Time-PM-911	S. Butcher	Retrd.	33.00	45-50.00
91-01-022	Lord, Keep Me In TeePee Top Shape-PM-912	S. Butcher	Retrd.	33.00	39-45.00
92-01-023	Only Love Can Make A Home-PM-921	S. Butcher	Retrd.	30.00	30-36.00
92-01-024	Sowing The Seeds of Love-PM-922	S. Butcher	Retrd.	30.00	30-40.00
93-01-025	His Little Treasure-PM-931	S. Butcher	Retrd.	30.00	30-50.00
93-01-026	Loving PM-932	S. Butcher	Retrd.	30.00	30.00
94-01-027	Caring PM-941	S. Butcher	Yr.Iss.	35.00	35.00
Enesco Corporation		**Precious Moments Collectors Club Welcome Gift**			
82-02-001	But Love Goes On Forever-Plaque-E-0202	S. Butcher	Yr.Iss.	Unkn.	65-100.
83-02-002	Let Us Call the Club to Order-E-0303	S. Butcher	Yr.Iss.	Unkn.	50-60.00
84-02-003	Join in on the Blessings-E-0404	S. Butcher	Yr.Iss.	Unkn.	45-55.00
85-02-004	Seek and Ye Shall Find-E-0005	S. Butcher	Yr.Iss.	Unkn.	40-60.00
86-02-005	Birds of a Feather Collect Together-E-0006	S. Butcher	Yr.Iss.	Unkn.	35-55.00
87-02-006	Sharing Is Universal-E-0007	S. Butcher	Yr.Iss.	Unkn.	30-40.00
88-02-007	A Growing Love-E-0008	S. Butcher	Yr.Iss.	Unkn.	30-45.00
89-02-008	Always Room For One More-C-0009	S. Butcher	Yr.Iss.	Unkn.	35-45.00
90-02-009	My Happiness-C-0010	S. Butcher	Yr.Iss.	Unkn.	25-45.00
91-02-010	Sharing the Good News Together-C-0011	S. Butcher	Yr.Iss.	Unkn.	35-55.00
92-02-011	The Club That's Out Of This World-C-0012	S. Butcher	Yr.Iss.	Unkn.	35-55.00
93-02-012	Loving, Caring, and Sharing Along the Way-C-0013	S. Butcher	Yr.Iss.	Unkn.	30-45.00
94-02-013	You Are the End of My Rainbow-C-0014	S. Butcher	Yr.Iss.	Unkn.	Unkn.
Enesco Corporation		**Precious Moments Inscribed Charter Member Renewal Gift**			
81-03-001	But Love Goes on Forever-E-0001	S. Butcher	Yr.Iss.	Unkn.	165-190.
82-03-002	But Love Goes on Forever-Plaque-E-0102	S. Butcher	Yr.Iss.	Unkn.	70-100.
83-03-003	Let Us Call the Club to Order-E-0103	S. Butcher	Yr.Iss.	25.00	55-65.00
84-03-004	Join in on the Blessings-E-0104	S. Butcher	Yr.Iss.	25.00	50-60.00
85-03-005	Seek and Ye Shall Find-E-0105	S. Butcher	Yr.Iss.	25.00	45-55.00
86-03-006	Birds of a Feather Collect Together-E-0106	S. Butcher	Yr.Iss.	25.00	45-50.00
87-03-007	Sharing Is Universal -E-0107	S. Butcher	Yr.Iss.	25.00	40-50.00
88-03-008	A Growing Love-E-0108	S. Butcher	Yr.Iss.	25.00	42-55.00
89-03-009	Always Room For One More-C-0109	S. Butcher	Yr.Iss.	35.00	40-55.00
90-03-010	My Happiness-C-0110	S. Butcher	Yr.Iss.	Unkn.	40-45.00
91-03-011	Sharing The Good News Together-C-0111	S. Butcher	Yr.Iss.	Unkn.	40-45.00
92-03-012	The Club That's Out Of This World-C-0112	S. Butcher	Yr.Iss.	Unkn.	35-40.00
93-03-013	Loving, Caring, and Sharing Along the Way-C-0113	S. Butcher	Yr.Iss.	Unkn.	40-50.00
94-03-014	You Are the End of My Rainbow-C-0114	S. Butcher	Yr.Iss.	Unkn.	Unkn.
Enesco Corporation		**Precious Moments Figurines**			
83-04-001	Sharing Our Season Together-E-0501	S. Butcher	Suspd.	50.00	110-150.
83-04-002	Jesus is the Light that Shines-E-0502	S. Butcher	Suspd.	23.00	36-50.00
83-04-003	Blessings from My House to Yours-E-0503	S. Butcher	Suspd.	27.00	60-80.00
83-04-004	Christmastime Is for Sharing-E-0504	S. Butcher	Retrd.	37.00	70-100.
83-04-005	Surrounded with Joy-E-0506	S. Butcher	Retrd.	21.00	50-85.00
83-04-006	God Sent His Son-E-0507	S. Butcher	Suspd.	32.50	65-90.00
83-04-007	Prepare Ye the Way of the Lord-E-0508	S. Butcher	Suspd.	75.00	100-130.
83-04-008	Bringing God's Blessing to You-E-0509	S. Butcher	Suspd.	35.00	70-100.
83-04-009	Tubby's First Christmas-E-0511	S. Butcher	Suspd.	12.00	17-40.00
83-04-010	It's a Perfect Boy-E-0512	S. Butcher	Suspd.	18.50	42-60.00
83-04-011	Onward Christian Soldiers-E-0523	S. Butcher	Open	24.00	35-95.00
83-04-012	You Can't Run Away from God-E-0525	S. Butcher	Retrd.	28.50	75-155.
83-04-013	He Upholdeth Those Who Fall-E-0526	S. Butcher	Suspd.	35.00	65-120.
87-04-014	His Eye Is On The Sparrow-E-0530	S. Butcher	Retrd.	28.50	85-125.
79-04-015	Jesus Loves Me-E-1372B	S. Butcher	Open	7.00	28-90.00
79-04-016	Jesus Loves Me-E-1372G	S. Butcher	Open	7.00	25-115.
79-04-017	Smile, God Loves You-E-1373B	S. Butcher	Retrd.	7.00	60-107.
79-04-018	Jesus is the Light-E-1373G	S. Butcher	Retrd.	7.00	50-125.
79-04-019	Praise the Lord Anyhow-E-1374B	S. Butcher	Retrd.	8.00	70-95.00
79-04-020	Make a Joyful Noise-E-1374G	S. Butcher	Open	8.00	28-125.
79-04-021	Love Lifted Me-E-1375A	S. Butcher	Retrd.	11.00	55-120.
79-04-022	Prayer Changes Things-E-1375B	S. Butcher	Suspd.	11.00	126-200.
79-04-023	Love One Another-E-1376	S. Butcher	Open	10.00	48-110.
79-04-024	He Leadeth Me-E-1377A	S. Butcher	Suspd.	9.00	80-120.
79-04-025	He Careth For You-E-1377B	S. Butcher	Suspd.	9.00	90-102.
79-04-026	God Loveth a Cheerful Giver-E-1378	S. Butcher	Retrd.	11.00	700-995.
79-04-027	Love is Kind-E-1379A	S. Butcher	Suspd.	8.00	66-130.
79-04-028	God Understands-E-1379B	S. Butcher	Suspd.	8.00	84-135.

		ARTIST	EDITION	ISSUE	QUOTE
79-04-029	O, How I Love Jesus-E-1380B	S. Butcher	Retrd.	8.00	75-130.
79-04-030	His Burden Is Light-E-1380G	S. Butcher	Retrd.	8.00	85-130.
79-04-031	Jesus is the Answer-E-1381	S. Butcher	Suspd.	11.50	120-150.
79-04-032	We Have Seen His Star-E-2010	S. Butcher	Suspd.	8.00	66-144.
79-04-033	Come Let Us Adore Him-E-2011	S. Butcher	Retrd.	10.00	300-350.
79-04-034	Jesus is Born-E-2012	S. Butcher	Suspd.	12.00	90-95.00
79-04-035	Unto Us a Child is Born-E-2013	S. Butcher	Suspd.	12.00	85-105.
82-04-036	May Your Christmas Be Cozy-E-2345	S. Butcher	Suspd.	23.00	60-80.00
82-04-037	May Your Christmas Be Warm-E-2348	S. Butcher	Suspd.	30.00	90-115.
82-04-038	Tell Me the Story of Jesus-E-2349	S. Butcher	Suspd.	30.00	75-100.
82-04-039	Dropping in for Christmas-E-2350	S. Butcher	Suspd.	18.00	70-85.00
87-04-040	Holy Smokes-E-2351	S. Butcher	Retrd.	27.00	80-135.
82-04-041	O Come All Ye Faithful-E-2353	S. Butcher	Retrd.	27.50	75-90.00
82-04-042	I'll Play My Drum for Him-E-2356	S. Butcher	Suspd.	30.00	55-72.00
82-04-043	I'll Play My Drum for Him-E-2360	S. Butcher	Open	16.00	60-70.00
82-04-044	Christmas Joy from Head to Toe-E-2361	S. Butcher	Suspd.	25.00	55-80.00
82-04-045	Camel Figurine-E-2363	S. Butcher	Open	20.00	33-50.00
82-04-046	Goat Figurine-E-2364	S. Butcher	Suspd.	10.00	35-55.00
82-04-047	The First Noel-E-2365	S. Butcher	Suspd.	16.00	35-72.00
82-04-048	The First Noel-E-2366	S. Butcher	Suspd.	16.00	35-69.00
82-04-049	Bundles of Joy-E-2374	S. Butcher	Retrd.	27.50	45-90.00
82-04-050	Dropping Over for Christmas-E-2375	S. Butcher	Retrd.	30.00	48-78.00
82-04-051	Our First Christmas Together-E-2377	S. Butcher	Suspd.	35.00	60-95.00
82-04-052	3 Mini Nativity Houses & Palm Tree E-2387	S. Butcher	Open	45.00	75-110.
82-04-053	Come Let Us Adore Him-E-2395(11pc. set)	S. Butcher	Open	80.00	120-175.
80-04-054	Come Let Us Adore Him-E2800(9 pc. set)	S. Butcher	Open	70.00	125-175.
80-04-055	Jesus is Born-E-2801	S. Butcher	Suspd.	37.00	100-240.
80-04-056	Christmas is a Time to Share-E-2802	S. Butcher	Suspd.	20.00	60-100.
80-04-057	Crown Him Lord of All-E-2803	S. Butcher	Suspd.	20.00	60-95.00
80-04-058	Peace on Earth-E-2804	S. Butcher	Suspd.	20.00	115-140.
80-04-059	Wishing You a Season Filled w/ Joy E-2805	S. Butcher	Retrd.	20.00	95-125.
84-04-060	You Have Touched So Many Hearts E-2821	S. Butcher	Open	25.00	37.50-50.
84-04-061	This is Your Day to Shine-E-2822	S. Butcher	Retrd.	37.50	84-155.
84-04-062	To God Be the Glory-E-2823	S. Butcher	Suspd.	40.00	75-85.00
84-04-063	To a Very Special Mom-E-2824	S. Butcher	Open	27.50	37.50-55.
84-04-064	To a Very Special Sister-E-2825	S. Butcher	Open	37.50	55-65.00
84-04-065	May Your Birthday Be a Blessing-E-2826	S. Butcher	Suspd.	37.50	70-99.00
84-04-066	I Get a Kick Out of You-E-2827	S. Butcher	Suspd.	50.00	120-150.
84-04-067	Precious Memories-E-2828	S. Butcher	Open	45.00	60-75.00
84-04-068	I'm Sending You a White Christmas E-2829	S. Butcher	Open	37.50	50-70.00
84-04-069	God Bless the Bride-E-2832	S. Butcher	Open	35.00	50-60.00
86-04-070	Sharing Our Joy Together-E-2834	S. Butcher	Suspd.	30.00	54-65.00
84-04-071	Baby Figurines (set of 6)-E-2852	S. Butcher	Open	12.00	105-168.
80-04-072	Blessed Are the Pure in Heart-E-3104	S. Butcher	Suspd.	9.00	25-55.00
80-04-073	He Watches Over Us All-E-3105	S. Butcher	Suspd.	11.00	50-110.
80-04-074	Mother Sew Dear-E-3106	S. Butcher	Open	13.00	27.50-80.
80-04-075	Blessed are the Peacemakers-E-3107	S. Butcher	Retrd.	13.00	80-85.00
80-04-076	The Hand that Rocks the Future-E-3108	S. Butcher	Suspd.	13.00	60-95.00
80-04-077	The Purr-fect Grandma-E-3109	S. Butcher	Open	13.00	27.50-75.
80-04-078	Loving is Sharing-E-3110B	S. Butcher	Retrd.	13.00	65-120.
80-04-079	Loving is Sharing-E-3110G	S. Butcher	Open	13.00	30-85.00
80-04-080	Be Not Weary In Well Doing-E-3111	S. Butcher	Retrd.	14.00	78-120.
80-04-081	God's Speed-E-3112	S. Butcher	Retrd.	14.00	60-100.
80-04-082	Thou Art Mine-E-3113	S. Butcher	Open	16.00	35-65.00
80-04-083	The Lord Bless You and Keep You-E-3114	S. Butcher	Open	16.00	37.50-85.
80-04-084	But Love Goes on Forever-E-3115	S. Butcher	Open	16.50	35-115.
80-04-085	Thee I Love-E-3116	S. Butcher	Retrd.	16.50	38-114.
80-04-086	Walking By Faith-E-3117	S. Butcher	Open	35.00	70-125.
80-04-087	Eggs Over Easy-E-3118	S. Butcher	Retrd.	12.00	65-115.
80-04-088	It's What's Inside that Counts-E-3119	S. Butcher	Suspd.	13.00	70-130.
80-04-089	To Thee With Love-E-3120	S. Butcher	Suspd.	13.00	50-95.00
81-04-090	The Lord Bless You and Keep You-E-4720	S. Butcher	Suspd.	14.00	32-48.00
81-04-091	The Lord Bless You and Keep You-E-4721	S. Butcher	Open	14.00	30-80.00
81-04-092	Love Cannot Break a True Friendship E-4722	S. Butcher	Suspd.	22.50	90-140.
81-04-093	Peace Amid the Storm-E-4723	S. Butcher	Suspd.	22.50	59-105.
81-04-094	Rejoicing with You-E-4724	S. Butcher	Open	25.00	45-99.00
81-04-095	Peace on Earth-E-4725	S. Butcher	Suspd.	25.00	60-90.00
81-04-096	Bear Ye One Another's Burdens-E-5200	S. Butcher	Suspd.	20.00	80-105.
81-04-097	Love Lifted Me-E-5201	S. Butcher	Suspd.	25.00	60-97.00
81-04-098	Thank You for Coming to My Ade-E-5202	S. Butcher	Suspd.	22.50	96-140.
81-04-099	Let Not the Sun Go Down Upon Your Wrath-E-5203	S. Butcher	Suspd.	22.50	100-160.
81-04-100	To A Special Dad-E-5212	S. Butcher	Open	20.00	35-79.00
81-04-101	God is Love-E-5213	S. Butcher	Suspd.	17.00	50-105.
81-04-102	Prayer Changes Things-E-5214	S. Butcher	Suspd.	35.00	85-150.
84-04-103	May Your Christmas Be Blessed-E-5376	S. Butcher	Suspd.	37.50	59-75.00
87-04-104	Love is Kind-E-5377	S. Butcher	Retrd.	27.50	78-100.
84-04-105	Joy to the World-E-5378	S. Butcher	Suspd.	18.00	30-45.00
84-04-106	Isn't He Precious?-E-5379	S. Butcher	Open	20.00	30-45.00
84-04-107	A Monarch is Born-E-5380	S. Butcher	Suspd.	33.00	60-75.00
84-04-108	His Name is Jesus-E-5381	S. Butcher	Suspd.	45.00	70-120.
84-04-109	For God So Loved the World-E-5382	S. Butcher	Suspd.	70.00	110-135.
84-04-110	Wishing You a Merry Christmas-E-5383	S. Butcher	Yr.Iss.	17.00	42.00
84-04-111	I'll Play My Drum for Him-E-5384	S. Butcher	Open	10.00	16-30.00
84-04-112	Oh Worship the Lord-E-5385	S. Butcher	Suspd.	10.00	34-45.00
84-04-113	Oh Worship the Lord-E-5386	S. Butcher	Suspd.	10.00	34-45.00
81-04-114	Come Let Us Adore Him-E-5619	S. Butcher	Suspd.	10.00	30-50.00
81-04-115	Donkey Figurine-E-5621	S. Butcher	Open	6.00	15-35.00
81-04-116	They Followed the Star-E-5624	S. Butcher	Open	130.00	200-270.
81-04-117	Wee Three Kings-E-5635	S. Butcher	Open	40.00	75-125.
81-04-118	Rejoice O Earth-E-5636	S. Butcher	Open	15.00	30-65.00
81-04-119	The Heavenly Light-E-5637	S. Butcher	Open	15.00	27.50-60.
81-04-120	Cow with Bell Figurine-E-5638	S. Butcher	Open	16.00	30-50.00
81-04-121	Isn't He Wonderful-E-5639	S. Butcher	Suspd.	12.00	40-72.00
81-04-122	Isn't He Wonderful-E-5640	S. Butcher	Suspd.	12.00	40-72.00
81-04-123	They Followed the Star-E-5641	S. Butcher	Suspd.	75.00	165-185.
81-04-124	Nativity Wall (2 pc. set)-E-5644	S. Butcher	Open	60.00	120-145.
84-04-125	God Sends the Gift of His Love-E-6613	S. Butcher	Suspd.	22.50	60-90.00
82-04-126	God is Love, Dear Valentine-E-7153	S. Butcher	Suspd.	16.00	30-59.00
82-04-127	God is Love, Dear Valentine-E-7154	S. Butcher	Suspd.	16.00	35-65.00
82-04-128	Thanking Him for You-E-7155	S. Butcher	Suspd.	16.00	60-65.00
82-04-129	I Believe in Miracles-E-7156	S. Butcher	Retrd.	17.00	75-115.
87-04-130	I Believe In Miracles-E-7156R	S. Butcher	Retrd.	22.50	65-75.00
82-04-131	There is Joy in Serving Jesus-E-7157	S. Butcher	Retrd.	17.00	35-80.00
82-04-132	Love Beareth All Things-E-7158	S. Butcher	Open	25.00	37.50-70.
82-04-133	Lord Give Me Patience-E-7159	S. Butcher	Suspd.	25.00	45-55.00

		ARTIST	EDITION	ISSUE	QUOTE
82-04-134	The Perfect Grandpa-E-7160	S. Butcher	Suspd.	25.00	45-70.00
82-04-135	His Sheep Am I-E-7161	S. Butcher	Suspd.	25.00	52-55.00
82-04-136	Love is Sharing-E-7162	S. Butcher	Suspd.	25.00	100-162.
82-04-137	God is Watching Over You-E-7163	S. Butcher	Suspd.	27.50	65-85.00
82-04-138	Bless This House-E-7164	S. Butcher	Suspd.	45.00	145-200.
82-04-139	Let the Whole World Know-E-7165	S. Butcher	Suspd.	45.00	75-120.
83-04-140	If God Be for Us, Who Can Be Against Us-E-9239	S. Butcher	Suspd.	27.50	55-70.00
83-04-141	Love is Patient-E-9251	S. Butcher	Suspd.	35.00	75-85.00
83-04-142	Forgiving is Forgetting-E-9252	S. Butcher	Suspd.	37.50	60-85.00
83-04-143	The End is in Sight-E-9253	S. Butcher	Suspd.	25.00	60-140.
83-04-144	Praise the Lord Anyhow-E-9254	S. Butcher	Retrd.	35.00	50-80.00
83-04-145	Bless You Two-E-9255	S. Butcher	Open	21.00	37.50-44.
83-04-146	We are God's Workmanship-E-9258	S. Butcher	Open	19.00	30-55.00
83-04-147	We're In It Together-E-9259	S. Butcher	Suspd.	24.00	45-75.00
83-04-148	God's Promises are Sure-E-9260	S. Butcher	Suspd.	30.00	55-75.00
83-04-149	Seek Ye the Lord-E-9261	S. Butcher	Suspd.	21.00	37-54.00
83-04-150	Seek Ye the Lord-E-9262	S. Butcher	Suspd.	21.00	45-55.00
83-04-151	How Can Two Walk Together Except They Agree-E-9263	S. Butcher	Suspd.	35.00	115-150.
63-04-152	Press On-E-9265	S. Butcher	Open	40.00	55-87.00
73-04-153	Animal Collection, Teddy Bear-E-9267A	S. Butcher	Suspd.	6.50	18-24.30
83-04-154	Animal Collection, Dog W/ Slippers E-9267B	S. Butcher	Suspd.	6.50	18-24.30
83-04-155	Animal Collection, Bunny W/ Carrot E-9267C	S. Butcher	Suspd.	6.50	18-24.30
83-04-156	Animal Collection, Kitty With Bow E-9267D	S. Butcher	Suspd.	6.50	18-24.30
83-04-157	Animal Collection, Lamb With Bird E-9267E	S. Butcher	Suspd.	6.50	18-24.30
83-04-158	Animal Collection, Pig W/ Patches E-9267F	S. Butcher	Suspd.	6.50	18-24.30
83-04-159	Nobody's Perfect-E-9268	S. Butcher	Retrd.	21.00	50-85.00
87-04-160	Let Love Reign-E-9273	S. Butcher	Retrd.	27.50	60-90.00
83-04-161	Taste and See that the Lord is Good E-9274	S. Butcher	Retrd.	22.50	45-80.00
83-04-162	Jesus Loves Me-E-9278	S. Butcher	Open	9.00	16-27.00
83-04-163	Jesus Loves Me-E-9279	S. Butcher	Open	9.00	16-32.00
83-04-164	To Some Bunny Special-E-9282A	S. Butcher	Suspd.	8.00	18-40.00
83-04-165	You're Worth Your Weight In Gold-E-9282B	S. Butcher	Suspd.	8.00	21-40.00
83-04-166	Especially For Ewe-E-9282C	S. Butcher	Suspd.	8.00	20-37.00
83-04-167	Peace on Earth-E-9287	S. Butcher	Suspd.	37.50	85-125.
83-04-168	Sending You a Rainbow-E-9288	S. Butcher	Suspd.	22.50	55-90.00
83-04-169	Trust in the Lord-E-9289	S. Butcher	Suspd.	21.00	45-65.00
85-04-170	Love Covers All-12009	S. Butcher	Suspd.	27.50	48-65.00
85-04-171	Part of Me Wants to be Good-12149	S. Butcher	Suspd.	19.00	45-65.00
87-04-172	This Is The Day Which The Lord Has Made-12157	S. Butcher	Suspd.	20.00	45-80.00
85-04-173	Get into the Habit of Prayer-12203	S. Butcher	Suspd.	19.00	40-45.00
85-04-174	Miniature Clown-12238A	S. Butcher	Open	13.50	19-29.00
85-04-175	Miniature Clown-12238B	S. Butcher	Open	13.50	19-29.00
85-04-176	Miniature Clown-12238C	S. Butcher	Open	13.50	19-29.00
85-04-177	Miniature Clown-12238D	S. Butcher	Open	13.50	19-29.00
85-04-178	It is Better to Give than to Receive-12297	S. Butcher	Suspd.	19.00	65-85.00
85-04-179	Love Never Fails-12300	S. Butcher	Open	25.00	35-49.00
85-04-180	God Bless Our Home-12319	S. Butcher	Open	40.00	55-65.00
86-04-181	You Can Fly-12335	S. Butcher	Suspd.	25.00	55-80.00
85-04-182	Jesus is Coming Soon-12343	S. Butcher	Suspd.	22.50	40-70.00
85-04-183	Halo, and Merry Christmas-12351	S. Butcher	Suspd.	40.00	125-145.
85-04-184	May Your Christmas Be Delightful-15482	S. Butcher	Suspd.	25.00	35-50.00
85-04-185	Honk if You Love Jesus-15490	S. Butcher	Open	13.00	20-35.00
85-04-186	Baby's First Christmas-15539	S. Butcher	Yr.Iss.	13.00	42-45.00
85-04-187	Baby's First Christmas-15547	S. Butcher	Yr.Iss.	13.00	45.00
85-04-188	God Sent His Love-15881	S. Butcher	Yr.Iss.	17.00	30-39.00
86-04-189	To My Favorite Paw-100021	S. Butcher	Suspd.	22.50	50-65.00
87-04-190	To My Deer Friend-100048	S. Butcher	Open	33.00	50-92.00
86-04-191	Sending My Love-100056	S. Butcher	Suspd.	22.50	40-60.00
86-04-192	O Worship the Lord-100064	S. Butcher	Open	24.00	35-49.00
86-04-193	To My Forever Friend-100072	S. Butcher	Open	33.00	50-90.00
87-04-194	He's The Healer Of Broken Hearts-100080	S. Butcher	Open	33.00	50-59.00
87-04-195	Make Me A Blessing-100102	S. Butcher	Retrd.	35.00	70-135.
86-04-196	Lord I'm Coming Home-100110	S. Butcher	Open	22.50	32.50-72.
86-04-197	Lord, Keep Me On My Toes-100129	S. Butcher	Retrd.	22.50	75-100.
86-04-198	The Joy of the Lord is My Strength-100137	S. Butcher	Open	35.00	50-89.00
86-04-199	God Bless the Day We Found You-100145	S. Butcher	Suspd.	37.50	85-120.
95-04-200	God Bless the Day We Found You(Girl)-100145R	S. Butcher	Suspd.	60.00	75-120.
86-04-201	God Bless the Day We Found You-100153	S. Butcher	Open	37.50	45-90.00
95-04-202	God Bless the Day We Found You(Boy)-100153R	S. Butcher	Open	60.00	45-60.00
86-04-203	Serving the Lord-100161	S. Butcher	Suspd.	19.00	44-65.00
86-04-204	I'm a Possibility-100188	S. Butcher	Retrd.	21.00	35-95.00
87-04-205	The Spirit Is Willing But The Flesh Is Weak-100196	S. Butcher	Retrd.	19.00	60-85.00
87-04-206	The Lord Giveth & the Lord Taketh Away-100226	S. Butcher	Open	33.50	40-49.00
86-04-207	Friends Never Drift Apart-100250	S. Butcher	Open	35.00	55-75.00
86-04-208	Help, Lord, I'm In a Spot-100269	S. Butcher	Retrd.	18.50	55-70.00
86-04-209	He Cleansed My Soul-100277	S. Butcher	Open	24.00	37.50-60.
86-04-210	Serving the Lord-100293	S. Butcher	Suspd.	19.00	30-50.00
87-04-211	Scent From Above-100528	S. Butcher	Retrd.	19.00	60-80.00
86-04-212	Brotherly Love-100544	S. Butcher	Suspd.	37.00	60-75.00
87-04-213	No Tears Past The Gate-101826	S. Butcher	Open	40.00	60-67.00
87-04-214	Smile Along The Way-101842	S. Butcher	Retrd.	30.00	145-175.
87-04-215	Lord, Help Us Keep Our Act Together-101850	S. Butcher	Retrd.	35.00	115-165.
86-04-216	O Worship the Lord-102229	S. Butcher	Open	24.00	35-42.00
86-04-217	Shepherd of Love-102261	S. Butcher	Open	10.00	16-24.00
86-04-218	Three Mini Animals-102296	S. Butcher	Open	13.50	19-30.00
86-04-219	Wishing You a Cozy Christmas-102342	S. Butcher	Yr.Iss.	17.00	39-45.00
86-04-220	Love Rescued Me-102393	S. Butcher	Open	21.00	32.50-34.
86-04-221	Angel of Mercy-102482	S. Butcher	Open	19.00	30-39.00
86-04-222	Sharing our Christmas Together-102490	S. Butcher	Suspd.	35.00	65-70.00
87-04-223	We Are All Precious In His Sight-102903	S. Butcher	Yr.Iss.	30.00	75-125.
86-04-224	God Bless America-102938	S. Butcher	Yr.Iss.	30.00	65-70.00
86-04-225	It's the Birthday of a King-102962	S. Butcher	Suspd.	18.50	35-50.00
87-04-226	I Would Be Sunk Without You-102970	S. Butcher	Open	15.00	19-30.00
87-04-227	My Love Will Never Let You Go-103497	S. Butcher	Open	25.00	35-45.00
86-04-228	I Believe in the Old Rugged Cross-103632	S. Butcher	Open	25.00	35-47.00
86-04-229	Come Let Us Adore Him-104000 (9 pc. set w/cassette)	S. Butcher	Open	95.00	125.00

		ARTIST	EDITION	ISSUE	QUOTE
87-04-230	With this Ring I...-104019	S. Butcher	Open	40.00	55-65.00
87-04-231	Love Is The Glue That Mends-104027	S. Butcher	Suspd.	33.50	50-75.00
87-04-232	Cheers To The Leader-104035	S. Butcher	Open	22.50	30-39.00
87-04-233	Happy Days Are Here Again-104396	S. Butcher	Suspd.	25.00	50-60.00
87-04-234	A Tub Full of Love-104817	S. Butcher	Open	22.50	30-42.00
87-04-235	Sitting Pretty-104825	S. Butcher	Suspd.	22.50	43-60.00
87-04-236	Have I Got News For You-105635	S. Butcher	Suspd.	22.50	30-50.00
88-04-237	Something's Missing When You're Not Around -105643	S. Butcher	Suspd.	32.50	37.50
87-04-238	To Tell The Tooth You're Special-105813	S. Butcher	Suspd.	38.50	65-85.00
88-04-239	Hallelujah Country-105821	S. Butcher	Open	35.00	45-54.00
87-04-240	We're Pulling For You-106151	S. Butcher	Suspd.	40.00	60-75.00
87-04-241	God Bless You Graduate-106194	S. Butcher	Open	20.00	30-35.00
87-04-242	Congratulations Princess-106208	S. Butcher	Open	20.00	30-35.00
87-04-243	Lord Help Me Make the Grade-106216	S. Butcher	Suspd.	25.00	48-70.00
88-04-244	Heaven Bless Your Togetherness-106755	S. Butcher	Open	65.00	80-87.00
88-04-245	Precious Memories-106763	S. Butcher	Open	37.50	50-55.00
88-04-246	Puppy Love Is From Above-106798	S. Butcher	Open	45.00	55-63.00
88-04-247	Happy Birthday Poppy-106836	S. Butcher	Suspd.	27.50	39-49.00
88-04-248	Sew In Love-106844	S. Butcher	Open	45.00	55-60.00
87-04-249	They Followed The Star-108243	S. Butcher	Open	75.00	100-115.
87-04-250	The Greatest Gift Is A Friend-109231	S. Butcher	Open	30.00	37.50-49.
88-04-251	Believe the Impossible-109487	S. Butcher	Suspd.	35.00	50-110.
88-04-252	Happiness Divine-109584	S. Butcher	Retrd.	25.00	50-75.00
87-04-253	Wishing You A Yummy Christmas-109754	S. Butcher	Suspd.	35.00	45-55.00
87-04-254	We Gather Together To Ask The Lord's Blessing-109762	S. Butcher	Open	130.00	150-169.
88-04-255	Meowie Christmas-109800	S. Butcher	Open	30.00	40-65.00
87-04-256	Oh What Fun It Is To Ride-109819	S. Butcher	Open	85.00	110-120.
88-04-257	Wishing You A Happy Easter-109886	S. Butcher	Open	23.00	27.50-34.
88-04-258	Wishing You A Basket Full Of Blessings-109924	S. Butcher	Open	23.00	27.50-33.
88-04-259	Sending You My Love-109967	S. Butcher	Open	35.00	45-65.00
88-04-260	Mommy, I Love You-109975	S. Butcher	Open	22.50	27.50-34.
87-04-261	Love Is The Best Gift of All-110930	S. Butcher	Yr.Iss.	22.50	45-39.00
88-04-262	Faith Takes The Plunge-111155	S. Butcher	Open	27.50	34-125.
88-04-263	Tis the Season-111163	S. Butcher	Open	27.50	35-45.00
87-04-264	O Come Let Us Adore Him (4 pc. 9" Nativity)-111333	S. Butcher	Suspd.	200.00	225-275.
88-04-265	Mommy, I Love You-112143	S. Butcher	Open	22.50	27.50-32.
87-04-266	A Tub Full of Love-112313	S. Butcher	Open	22.50	30-33.00
88-04-267	This Too Shall Pass-114014	S. Butcher	Open	23.00	27.50-37.
88-04-268	Some Bunny's Sleeping-115274	S. Butcher	Open	15.00	25-40.00
88-04-269	Our First Christmas Together-115290	S. Butcher	Suspd.	50.00	60-80.00
88-04-270	Time to Wish You a Merry Christmas-115339	S. Butcher	Yr.Iss.	24.00	35-48.00
95-04-271	Love Blooms Eternal - 127019	S. Butcher	Yr.Iss.	35.00	35.00
88-04-272	Rejoice O Earth-520268	S. Butcher	Open	13.00	16-22.00
88-04-273	Jesus the Savior Is Born-520357	S. Butcher	Suspd.	25.00	32.50-50.
92-04-274	The Lord Turned My Life Around-520535	S. Butcher	Open	35.00	35.00
91-04-275	In The Spotlight Of His Grace-520543	S. Butcher	Open	35.00	35.00
90-04-276	Lord, Turn My Life Around-520551	S. Butcher	Open	35.00	35-49.00
92-04-277	You Deserve An Ovation-520578	S. Butcher	Open	35.00	35.00
89-04-278	My Heart Is Exposed With Love-520624	S. Butcher	Open	45.00	50-60.00
89-04-279	A Friend Is Someone Who Cares-520632	S. Butcher	Open	30.00	35-45.00
89-04-280	I'm So Glad You Fluttered Into My Life-520640	S. Butcher	Retrd.	40.00	250-400.
89-04-281	Eggspecially For You-520667	S. Butcher	Open	45.00	50-60.00
89-04-282	Your Love Is So Uplifting-520675	S. Butcher	Open	60.00	65-79.00
89-04-283	Sending You Showers Of Blessings-520683	S. Butcher	Retrd.	32.50	50-75.00
89-04-284	Just A LineTo Wish You A Happy Day-520721	S. Butcher	Open	65.00	70-79.00
89-04-285	Friendship Hits The Spot-520748	S. Butcher	Open	55.00	60-68.00
89-04-286	Jesus Is The Only Way-520756	S. Butcher	Suspd.	40.00	45-50.00
89-04-287	Puppy Love-520764	S. Butcher	Open	12.50	16-22.00
89-04-288	Many Moons In Same Canoe, Blessum You-520772	S. Butcher	Retrd.	50.00	200-240.
89-04-289	Wishing You Roads Of Happiness-520780	S. Butcher	Open	60.00	75.00
89-04-290	Someday My Love-520799	S. Butcher	Retrd.	40.00	70-150.
89-04-291	My Days Are Blue Without You-520802	S. Butcher	Suspd.	65.00	75-125.
89-04-292	We Need A Good Friend Through The Ruff Times-520810	S. Butcher	Suspd.	35.00	50-70.00
89-04-293	You Are My Number One-520829	S. Butcher	Open	25.00	27.50-30.
89-04-294	The Lord Is Your Light To Happiness-520837	S. Bucher	Open	50.00	55-62.00
89-04-295	Wishing You A Perfect Choice-520845	S.Butcher	Open	55.00	60-67.00
89-04-296	I Belong To The Lord-520853	S. Butcher	Suspd.	25.00	35-50.00
90-04-297	Heaven Bless You-520934	S. Butcher	Open	35.00	30-150.
93-04-298	There Is No Greater Treasure Than To Have A Friend Like You -521000	S. Butcher	Open	30.00	30.00
89-04-299	Hello World-521175	S. Butcher	Open	15.00	16.00
90-04-300	That's What Friends Are For-521183	S. Butcher	Open	45.00	45-49.00
90-04-301	Hope You're Up And OnThe Trail Again-521205	S. Butcher	Suspd.	35.00	35-45.00
93-04-302	The Fruit of the Spirit is Love-521213	S. Butcher	Yr.Iss.	30.00	30.00
91-04-303	Take Heed When You Stand-521272	S. Butcher	Suspd.	55.00	55.00
90-04-304	Happy Trip-521280	S. Butcher	Suspd.	35.00	35-73.00
91-04-305	Hug One Another-521299	S. Butcher	Retrd.	45.00	130-150.
90-04-306	Yield Not To Temptation-521310	S. Butcher	Suspd.	27.50	27.50-40.
90-04-307	Faith Is A Victory-521396	S. Butcher	Retrd.	25.00	75-115.
90-04-308	I'll Never Stop Loving You-521418	S. Butcher	Open	37.50	37.50-49.
91-04-309	To A Very Special Mom & Dad-521434	S. Butcher	Suspd.	35.00	35.00
90-04-310	Lord, Help Me Stick To My Job-521450	S. Butcher	Open	30.00	30-40.00
89-04-311	Tell It To Jesus-521477	S. Butcher	Open	35.00	37.50-49.
91-04-312	There's A Light At The End Of The Tunnel-521485	S. Butcher	Open	55.00	55.00
91-04-313	A Special Delivery-521493	S. Butcher	Open	30.00	30.00
91-04-314	Thumb-body Loves You-521698	S. Butcher	Open	55.00	50-59.00
90-04-315	Sweep All Your Worries Away-521779	S. Butcher	Open	40.00	40-130.
90-04-316	Good Friends Are Forever-521817	S. Butcher	Open	50.00	50-57.00
90-04-317	Love Is From Above-521841	S. Butcher	Open	45.00	45-59.00
89-04-318	The Greatest of These Is Love-521868	S. Butcher	Suspd.	27.50	40-54.00
90-04-319	Easter's On Its Way-521892	S. Butcher	Open	60.00	65-75.00
94-04-320	Hoppy Easter Friend-521906	S. Butcher	Open	40.00	40-43.00
91-04-321	Perfect Harmony - 521914	S. Butcher	Open	55.00	55.00
93-04-322	Safe In The Arms Of Jesus-521922	S. Butcher	Open	30.00	30.00
89-04-323	Wishing You A Cozy Season-521949	S. Butcher	Suspd.	42.50	45-53.00
90-04-324	High Hopes-521957	S. Butcher	Suspd.	30.00	35-45.00
91-04-325	To A Special Mum-521965	S. Butcher	Open	30.00	30-33.00
93-04-326	To The Apple Of God's Eye-522015	S. Butcher	Yr.Iss.	32.50	32.50
79-04-327	May Your Life Be Blessed With Touchdowns-522023	S. Butcher	Open	45.00	50-58.00

		ARTIST	EDITION	ISSUE	QUOTE
89-04-328	Thank You Lord For Everything-522031	S. Butcher	Suspd.	55.00	65-75.00
94-04-329	Now I Lay Me Down To Sleep - 522058	S. Butcher	Open	30.00	30.00
91-04-330	May Your World Be Trimmed With Joy-522082	S. Butcher	Open	55.00	55.00
90-04-331	There Shall Be Showers Of Blessings-522090	S. Butcher	Open	60.00	70.00
92-04-332	It's No Yolk When I Say I Love You-522104	S. Butcher	Suspd.	60.00	65.00
89-04-333	Don't Let the Holidays Get You Down-522112	S. Butcher	Retrd.	42.50	50-75.00
89-04-334	Wishing You A Very Successful Season-522120	S. Butcher	Open	60.00	65-70.00
89-04-335	Bon Voyage!-522201	S. Butcher	Open	75.00	80-99.00
89-04-336	He Is The Star Of The Morning-522252	S. Butcher	Suspd.	55.00	60-65.00
89-04-337	To Be With You Is Uplifting-522260	S. Butcher	Retrd.	20.00	22-45.00.
91-04-338	A Reflection Of His Love-522279	S. Butcher	Open	50.00	50.00
90-04-339	Thinking Of You Is What I Really Like To Do-522287	S. Butcher	Open	30.00	30-35.00
89-04-340	Merry Christmas Deer-522317	S. Butcher	Open	50.00	55-65.00
89-04-341	Isn't He Precious-522988	S. Butcher	Suspd.	15.00	16.50-20.
90-04-342	Some Bunny's Sleeping-522996	S. Butcher	Suspd.	12.00	12-19.00
89-04-343	Jesus Is The Sweetest Name I Know-523097	S. Butcher	Suspd.	22.50	25-29.00
91-04-344	Joy On Arrival-523178	S. Butcher	Open	50.00	50.00
90-04-345	The Good Lord Always Delivers- 523453	S. Butcher	Open	27.50	27.50-35.
90-04-346	This Day Has Been Made In Heaven-523496	S. Butcher	Open	30.00	30-45.00
90-04-347	God Is Love Dear Valentine-523518	S. Butcher	Open	27.50	27.50-42.
91-04-348	I Will Cherish The Old Rugged Cross-523534	S. Butcher	Yr.Iss.	27.50	40-45.00
92-04-349	You Are The Type I Love-523542	S. Butcher	Open	40.00	40.00
93-04-350	The Lord Will Provide-523593	S. Butcher	Yr.Iss.	40.00	40.00
91-04-351	Good News Is So Uplifting-523615	S. Butcher	Open	60.00	65.00
94-04-352	I Will Always Be Thinking Of You-523631	S. Butcher	Open	45.00	45.00
90-04-353	Time Heals-523739	S. Butcher	Open	37.50	37.50-40.
90-04-354	Blessings From Above-523747	S. Butcher	Retrd.	45.00	50.00
94-04-355	Just Poppin' In To Say Halo - 523755	S. Butcher	Open	45.00	45.00
91-04-356	I Can't Spell Success Without You-523763	S. Butcher	Suspd.	40.00	45-50.00
90-04-357	Once Upon A Holy Night-523836	S. Butcher	Yr.Iss.	25.00	45.00
92-04-358	My Warmest Thoughts Are You-524085	S. Butcher	Open	55.00	60.00
91-04-359	Good Friends Are For Always-524123	S. Butcher	Open	27.50	27.50
94-04-360	Lord Teach Us to Pray-524158	S. Butcher	Yr.Iss.	35.00	35.00
91-04-361	May Your Christmas Be Merry-524166	S. Butcher	Yr.Iss.	27.50	30-40.00
91-04-362	He Loves Me -524263	S. Butcher	Yr.Iss.	35.00	35-65.00
92-04-363	Friendship Grows When You Plant A Seed-524271	S. Butcher	Retrd.	40.00	40.00
93-04-364	May Your Every Wish Come True-524298	S. Butcher	Open	50.00	50.00
91-04-365	May Your Birthday Be A Blessing-524301	S. Butcher	Open	30.00	30-35.00
92-04-366	What The World Needs Now-524352	S. Butcher	Open	50.00	50.00
91-04-367	May Only Good Things Come Your Way-524425	S. Butcher	Open	30.00	30-35.00
93-04-368	Sealed With A Kiss-524441	S. Butcher	Open	50.00	50.00
93-04-369	A Special Chime For Jesus-524468	S. Butcher	Yr.Iss.	32.50	32.50
94-04-370	God Cared Enough To Send His Best - 524476	S. Butcher	Open	50.00	50.00
90-04-371	Happy Birthday Dear Jesus-524875	S. Butcher	Suspd.	13.50	13.50-16.
92-04-372	It's So Uplifting To Have A Friend Like You-524905	S. Butcher	Open	40.00	40.00
90-04-373	We're Going To Miss You-524913	S. Butcher	Open	50.00	50-55.00
91-04-374	Angels We Have Heard On High-524921	S. Butcher	Open	60.00	60.00
92-04-375	Tubby's First Christmas-525278	S. Butcher	Open	10.00	10.00
91-04-376	It's A Perfect Boy-525286	S. Butcher	Open	16.50	17.00
93-04-377	May Your Future Be Blessed-525316	S. Butcher	Open	35.00	35.00
92-04-378	Going Home-525979	S. Butcher	Open	60.00	60.00
92-04-379	I Would Be Lost Without You-526142	S. Butcher	Open	27.50	27.50
94-04-380	Friends 'Til The Very End-526150	S. Butcher	Open	40.00	40.00
92-04-381	You Are My Happiness-526185	S. Butcher	Yr.Iss.	37.50	45-55.00
94-04-382	You Suit Me to a Tee-526193	S. Butcher	Open	35.00	35.00
94-04-383	Sharing Sweet Moments Together-526487	S. Butcher	Open	45.00	45.00
91-04-384	How Could I Ever Forget You-526924	S. Butcher	Open	15.00	16.00
91-04-385	We Have Come From Afar-526959	S. Butcher	Suspd.	17.50	17.50
92-04-386	Let's Be Friends 527270	S. Butcher	Open	15.00	16.00
93-04-387	Bless-Um You-527335	S. Butcher	Open	35.00	35.00
92-04-388	You Are My Favorite Star-527378	S. Butcher	Open	55.00	55.00
92-04-389	Bring The Little Ones To Jesus-527556	S. Butcher	Open	90.00	90.00
92-04-390	God Bless The U.S.A.-527564	S. Butcher	Yr.Iss.	32.50	35-40.00
93-04-391	Tied Up For The Holidays-527580	S. Butcher	Yr.Iss.	40.00	40.00
93-04-392	Bringing You A Merry Christmas-527599	S. Butcher	Yr.Iss.	45.00	45.00
92-04-393	Wishing You A Ho Ho Ho-527629	S. Butcher	Open	40.00	40.00
92-04-394	But The Greatest of These Is Love-527688	S. Butcher	Yr.Iss.	27.50	27.50
92-04-395	Wishing You A Comfy Christmas-527750	S. Butcher	Open	30.00	30.00
93-04-396	I Only Have Arms For You-527769	S. Butcher	Open	15.00	16.00
92-04-397	This Land Is Our Land-527777	S. Butcher	Yr.Iss.	35.00	40.00
94-04-398	Nativity Cart - 528072	S. Butcher	Open	16.00	16.00
94-04-399	Have I Got News For You - 528137	S. Butcher	Open	16.00	16.00
94-04-400	To a Very Special Sister-528633	S. Butcher	Open	60.00	60.00
93-04-401	America You're Beautiful-528862	S. Butcher	Yr.Iss.	35.00	35.00
93-04-402	Ring Out The Good News-529966	S. Butcher	Yr.Iss.	27.50	27.50
95-04-403	What The World Needs Is Love - 531065	S. Butcher	Open	45.00	45.00
93-04-404	Wishing You the Sweetest Christmas-530166	S. Butcher	Yr.Iss.	27.50	27.50
94-04-405	You're As Pretty As A Christmas Tree - 530425	S. Butcher	Yr.Iss.	27.50	27.50
94-04-406	Serenity Prayer Girl-530697	S. Butcher	Open	35.00	35.00
94-04-407	Serenity Prayer Boy-530700	S. Butcher	Open	35.00	35.00
95-04-408	Vaya Con Dios (To Go With God) - 531146	S. Butcher	Open	32.50	32.50
94-04-409	The Lord is Counting on You-531707	S. Butcher	Open	32.50	32.50
94-04-410	Dropping In For The Holidays - 531952	S. Butcher	Open	40.00	40.00
95-04-411	Hallelujah For The Cross - 532002	S. Butcher	Open	35.00	35.00
95-04-412	Sending You Oceans Of Love - 532010	S. Butcher	Open	35.00	35.00
95-04-413	I Can't Bear To Let You Go - 532037	S. Butcher	Open	50.00	50.00
94-04-414	The Lord Bless You and Keep You-532118	S. Butcher	Open	40.00	40.00
94-04-415	The Lord Bless You and Keep You-532126	S. Butcher	Open	30.00	30.00
94-04-416	The Lord Bless You and Keep You-532134	S. Butcher	Open	30.00	30.00
94-04-417	Luke 2:10-11 - 532916	S. Butcher	Open	35.00	35.00
94-04-418	Nothing Can Dampen The Spirit of Caring-603865	S. Butcher	Open	35.00	35.00
95-04-419	A Poppy For You - 640208	S. Butcher	Open	35.00	35.00

Enesco Corporation **Precious Moments Bridal Party**

84-05-001	Bridesmaid-E-2831	S. Butcher	Open	13.50	22.50-30.
85-05-002	Ringbearer-E-2833	S. Butcher	Open	11.00	17-30.00
85-05-003	Flower Girl-E-2835	S. Butcher	Open	11.00	17-25.00

		ARTIST	EDITION	ISSUE	QUOTE
84-05-004	Groomsman-E-2836	S. Butcher	Open	13.50	22.50-30.
86-05-005	Groom-E-2837	S. Butcher	Open	13.50	20-40.00
85-05-006	Junior Bridesmaid-E-2845	S. Butcher	Open	12.50	20-30.00
87-05-007	Bride-E-2846	S. Butcher	Open	18.00	25-30.00
87-05-008	God Bless Our Family (Parents of the Groom)-100498	S. Butcher	Open	35.00	50-55.00
87-05-009	God Bless Our Family (Parents of the Bride)-100501	S. Butcher	Open	35.00	50-60.00
87-05-010	Wedding Arch-102369	S. Butcher	Suspd.	22.50	45-65.00

Enesco Corporation — Precious Moments Baby's First

		ARTIST	EDITION	ISSUE	QUOTE
84-06-001	Baby's First Step-E-2840	S. Butcher	Suspd.	35.00	65-90.00
84-06-002	Baby's First Picture-E-2841	S. Butcher	Retrd.	45.00	140-190.
85-06-003	Baby's First Haircut-12211	S. Butcher	Suspd.	32.50	90-130.
86-06-004	Baby's First Trip-16012	S. Butcher	Suspd.	32.50	90-174.
89-06-005	Baby's First Pet-520705	S. Butcher	Suspd.	45.00	50-78.00
90-06-006	Baby's First Meal-524077	S. Butcher	Open	35.00	35-45.00
90-06-007	Baby's First Word-527238	S. Butcher	Open	24.00	24-28.00
93-06-008	Baby's First Birthday-524069	S. Butcher	Open	25.00	25.00

Enesco Corporation — Precious Moments Anniversary Figurines

		ARTIST	EDITION	ISSUE	QUOTE
84-07-001	God Blessed Our Years Together With So Much Love And Happiness-E-2853	S. Butcher	Open	35.00	50-60.00
84-07-002	God Blessed Our Year Together With So Much Love And Happiness (1st)-E-2854	S. Butcher	Open	35.00	50-60.00
84-07-003	God Blessed Our Years Together With So Much Love And Happiness (5th)-E-2855	S. Butcher	Open	35.00	50-55.00
84-07-004	God Blessed Our Years Together With So Much Love And Happiness (10th)-E-2856	S. Butcher	Open	35.00	50-55.00
84-07-005	God Blessed Our Years Together With So Much Love And Happiness (25th)-E-2857	S. Butcher	Open	35.00	50-65.00
84-07-006	God Blessed Our Years Together With So Much Love And Happiness (40th)-E-2859	S. Butcher	Open	35.00	50-65.00
84-07-007	God Blessed Our Years Together With So Much Love And Happiness (50th)-E-2860	S. Butcher	Open	35.00	50-65.00
94-07-008	I Still Do-530999	S. Butcher	Open	30.00	30.00
94-07-009	I Still Do-531006	S. Butcher	Open	30.00	30.00

Enesco Corporation — Precious Moments The Four Seasons

		ARTIST	EDITION	ISSUE	QUOTE
85-08-001	The Voice of Spring-12068	S. Butcher	Yr.Iss.	30.00	270-350.
85-08-002	Summer's Joy-12076	S. Butcher	Yr.Iss.	30.00	90-115.
86-08-003	Autumn's Praise-12084	S. Butcher	Yr.Iss.	30.00	55-85.00
86-08-004	Winter's Song-12092	S. Butcher	Yr.Iss.	30.00	100-140.
86-08-005	Set	S. Butcher	Yr.Iss.	120.00	550.00

Enesco Corporation — Precious Moments Rejoice in the Lord

		ARTIST	EDITION	ISSUE	QUOTE
87-09-001	Lord Keep My Life In Tune - 12165	S. Butcher	Suspd.	37.50	80-100.
85-09-002	There's a Song in My Heart-12173	S. Butcher	Suspd.	11.00	25-45.00
85-09-003	Happiness is the Lord-12378	S. Butcher	Suspd.	15.00	30-60.00
85-09-004	Lord Give Me a Song-12386	S. Butcher	Suspd.	15.00	30-50.00
85-09-005	He is My Song-12394	S. Butcher	Suspd.	17.50	35-60.00

Enesco Corporation — Precious Moments Clown

		ARTIST	EDITION	ISSUE	QUOTE
XX-10-001	I Get a Bang Out of You-12262	S. Butcher	Open	30.00	45-55.00
86-10-002	Lord Keep Me On the Ball-12270	S. Butcher	Open	30.00	45-55.00
85-10-003	Waddle I Do Without You-12459	S. Butcher	Retrd.	30.00	75-110.
86-10-004	The Lord Will Carry You Through-12467	S. Butcher	Retrd.	30.00	78-110.

Enesco Corporation — Precious Moments Club 5th Anniversary Commemorative Edition

		ARTIST	EDITION	ISSUE	QUOTE
85-11-001	God Bless Our Years Together-12440	S. Butcher	Retrd.	175.00	240-300.

Enesco Corporation — Precious Moments Family Christmas Scene

		ARTIST	EDITION	ISSUE	QUOTE
85-12-001	May You Have the Sweetest Christmas-15776	S. Butcher	Suspd.	17.00	37-55.00
85-12-002	The Story of God's Love-15784	S. Butcher	Suspd.	22.50	40-59.00
85-12-003	Tell Me a Story-15792	S. Butcher	Suspd.	10.00	25-40.00
85-12-004	God Gave His Best-15806	S. Butcher	Suspd.	13.00	30-45.00
85-12-005	Silent Night-15814	S. Butcher	Suspd.	37.50	75-120.
86-12-006	Sharing Our Christmas Together-102490	S. Butcher	Suspd.	40.00	55-80.00
89-12-007	Have A Beary Merry Christmas-522856	S. Butcher	Suspd.	15.00	30-45.00
90-12-008	Christmas Fireplace-524883	S. Butcher	Suspd.	37.50	85-125.

Enesco Corporation — Precious Moments Club 10th Anniv. Commemorative Edition

		ARTIST	EDITION	ISSUE	QUOTE
88-13-001	The Good Lord has Blessed Us Tenfold-114022	S. Butcher	Yr.Iss.	90.00	135-250.

Enesco Corporation — Precious Moments Birthday Train Figurines

		ARTIST	EDITION	ISSUE	QUOTE
88-14-001	Isn't Eight Just Great-109460	S. Butcher	Open	18.50	22.50-30.
88-14-002	Wishing You Grr-eatness-109479	S. Butcher	Open	18.50	22.50-30.
86-14-003	May Your Birthday Be Warm-15938	S. Butcher	Open	10.00	15-40.00
86-14-004	Happy Birthday Little Lamb-15946	S. Butcher	Open	10.00	15-39.00
86-14-005	Heaven Bless Your Special Day-15954	S. Butcher	Open	11.00	16.50-30.
86-14-006	God Bless You On Your Birthday-15962	S. Butcher	Open	11.00	16.50-40.
86-14-007	May Your Birthday Be Gigantic -15970	S. Butcher	Open	12.50	18.50-40.
86-14-008	This Day Is Something To Roar About-15989	S. Butcher	Open	13.50	20-40.00
86-14-009	Keep Looking Up-15997	S. Butcher	Open	13.50	20-43.00
86-14-010	Bless The Days Of Our Youth-16004	S. Butcher	Open	15.00	22.50-45.
92-14-011	May Your Birthday Be Mammoth-521825	S. Butcher	Open	25.00	25-40.00
92-14-012	Being Nine Is Just Divine-521833	S. Butcher	Open	25.00	25-40.00

Enesco Corporation — Precious Moments Birthday Club Figurines

		ARTIST	EDITION	ISSUE	QUOTE
86-15-001	Fishing For Friends-BC-861	S. Butcher	Yr.Iss.	10.00	108-195.
87-15-002	Hi Sugar-BC-871	S. Butcher	Yr.Iss.	11.00	92-140.
88-15-003	Somebunny Cares-BC-881	S. Butcher	Yr.Iss.	13.50	55-100.
89-15-004	Can't Bee Hive Myself Without You-BC-891	S. Butcher	Yr.Iss.	13.50	35-80.00
90-15-005	Collecting Makes Good Scents-BC-901	S. Butcher	Yr.Iss.	15.00	30-45.00
90-15-006	I'm Nuts Over My Collection-BC-902	S. Butcher	Yr.Iss.	15.00	30-40.00
91-15-007	Love Pacifies-BC-911	S. Butcher	Yr.Iss.	15.00	28-45.00
91-15-008	True Blue Friends-BC-912	S. Butcher	Yr.Iss.	15.00	28-38.00
92-15-009	Every Man's House Is His Castle-BC-921	S. Butcher	Yr.Iss.	16.50	20-25.00
93-15-010	I Got You Under My Skin-BC-922	S. Butcher	Yr.Iss.	16.00	16-20.00
94-15-011	Put a Little Punch In Your Birthday-BC-931	S. Butcher	Yr.Iss.	15.00	15.00
94-15-012	Owl Always Be Your Friend-BC-932	S. Butcher	Yr.Iss.	16.00	16.00
94-15-013	God Bless Our Home-BC-941	S. Butcher	Yr.Iss.	16.00	16.00

Enesco Corporation — Precious Moments Birthday Club Welcome Gift

		ARTIST	EDITION	ISSUE	QUOTE
86-16-001	Our Club Can't Be Beat-B-0001	S. Butcher	Yr.Iss.	Unkn.	70-100.
87-16-002	A Smile's The Cymbal of Joy-B-0002	S. Butcher	Yr.Iss.	Unkn.	55-85.00
88-16-003	The Sweetest Club Around-B-0003	S. Butcher	Yr.Iss.	Unkn.	45-70.00
89-16-004	Have A Beary Special Birthday- B-0004	S. Butcher	Yr.Iss.	Unkn.	32-55.00
90-16-005	Our Club Is A Tough Act To Follow-B-0005	S. Butcher	Yr.Iss.	Unkn.	32-40-00
91-16-006	Jest To Let You Know You're Tops-B-0006	S. Butcher	Yr.Iss.	Unkn.	30-35.00
92-16-007	All Aboard For Birthday Club Fun-B-0007	S. Butcher	Yr.Iss.	Unkn.	25.00
94-16-008	Happiness Is Belonging-B-0008	S. Butcher	Yr.Iss.	Unkn.	Unkn.
94-16-009	Can't Get Enough of Our Club-B-0009	S. Butcher	Yr.Iss.	Unkn.	Unkn.

Enesco Corporation — Birthday Club Inscribed Charter Member Renewal Gift

		ARTIST	EDITION	ISSUE	QUOTE
87-17-001	A Smile's the Cymbal of Joy-B-0102	S. Butcher	Yr.Iss.	Unkn.	60-70.00
88-17-002	The Sweetest Club Around-B-0103	S. Butcher	Yr.Iss.	Unkn.	45-55.00
89-17-003	Have A Beary Special Birthday- B-0104	S. Butcher	Yr.Iss.	Unkn.	45-55.00
90-17-004	Our Club Is A Tough Act To Follow-B-0105	S. Butcher	Yr.Iss.	Unkn.	35-40.00
91-17-005	Jest To Let You Know You're Tops-B-0106	S. Butcher	Yr.Iss.	Unkn.	30-40.00
92-17-006	All Aboard For Birthday Club Fun-B-0107	S. Butcher	Yr.Iss.	Unkn.	25.00
94-17-007	Happines is Belonging-B-0108	S. Butcher	Yr.Iss.	Unkn.	Unkn.
94-17-008	Can't Get Enough of Our Club-B-0109	S. Butcher	Yr.Iss.	Unkn.	Unkn.

Enesco Corporation — Birthday Series

		ARTIST	EDITION	ISSUE	QUOTE
88-18-001	Friends To The End-104418	S. Butcher	Suspd.	15.00	20-35.00
87-18-002	Showers Of Blessings-105945	S. Butcher	Retrd.	16.00	35-60.00
88-18-003	Brighten Someone's Day-105953	S. Butcher	Suspd.	12.50	15-30.00
90-18-004	To My Favorite Fan-521043	S. Butcher	Suspd.	16.00	25-50.00
89-18-005	Hello World!-521175	S. Butcher	Open	13.50	15-30.00
93-18-006	Hope You're Over The Hump-521671	S. Butcher	Open	16.00	16.00
90-18-007	Not A Creature Was Stirring-524484	S. Butcher	Suspd.	17.00	17-25.00
91-18-008	Can't Be Without You-524492	S. Butcher	Open	16.00	16-29.00
91-18-009	How Can I Ever Forget You-526924	S. Butcher	Open	15.00	15.00
92-18-010	Let's Be Friends-527270	S. Butcher	Open	15.00	15.00
92-18-011	Happy Birdie-527343	S. Butcher	Open	8.00	8.00
93-18-012	Happy Birthday Jesus-530492	S. Butcher	Open	20.00	20.00
94-18-013	Oinky Birthday-524506	S. Butcher	Open	13.50	13.50
95-18-014	Wishing You A Happy Bear Hug - 520659	S. Butcher	Open	27.50	27.50

Enesco Corporation — Precious Moments Events Figurines

		ARTIST	EDITION	ISSUE	QUOTE
88-19-001	You Are My Main Event-115231	S. Butcher	Yr.Iss.	30.00	40-70.00
89-19-002	Sharing Begins In The Heart-520861	S. Butcher	Yr.Iss.	25.00	40-80.00
90-19-003	I'm A Precious Moments Fan-523526	S. Butcher	Yr.Iss.	25.00	40-50.00
90-19-004	Good Friends Are Forever-525049	S. Butcher	Yr.Iss.	25.00	N/A
91-19-005	You Can Always Bring A Friend-527122	S. Butcher	Yr.Iss.	27.50	45-65.00
92-19-006	An Event Worth Wading For-527319	S. Butcher	Yr.Iss.	32.50	38-50.00
93-19-007	An Event For All Seasons-530158	S. Butcher	Yr.Iss.	30.00	45.00
94-19-008	Memories Are Made of This-529982	S. Butcher	Yr.Iss.	30.00	30.00
95-19-009	Take Time To Smell The Flowers - 524387	S. Butcher	Yr.Iss.	30.00	30.00

Enesco Corporation — Precious Moments Commemorative Easter Seal Figurines

		ARTIST	EDITION	ISSUE	QUOTE
88-20-001	Jesus Loves Me-9" Fig.-104531	S. Butcher	1,000	N/A	18-2000.
87-20-002	He Walks With Me-107999	S. Butcher	Yr.Iss.	25.00	45-75.00
88-20-003	Blessed Are They That Overcome-115479	S. Butcher	Yr.Iss.	27.50	38-75.00
89-20-004	Make A Joyful Noise-9" Fig.-520322	S. Butcher	1,500	N/A	900-950.
89-20-005	His Love Will Shine On You-522376	S. Butcher	Yr.Iss.	30.00	45-55.00
90-20-006	You Have Touched So Many Hearts-9" fig.-523283	S. Butcher	2,000	N/A	675-775.
91-20-007	We Are God's Workmanship-9" fig.-523879	S. Butcher	2,000	N/A	650-725.
90-20-008	Always In His Care-524522	S. Butcher	Yr.Iss.	30.00	35-45.00
92-20-009	You Are Such A Purr-fect Friend 9" fig.-526010	S. Butcher	2,000	N/A	600-700.
91-20-010	Sharing A Gift Of Love-527114	S. Butcher	Yr.Iss.	30.00	35-65.00
92-20-011	A Universal Love-527173	S. Butcher	Yr.Iss.	32.50	35-55.00
93-20-012	Gather Your Dreams-9" fig.-529680	S. Butcher	2,000	N/A	N/A
93-20-013	You're My Number One Friend-530026	S. Butcher	Yr.Iss.	30.00	30.00
94-20-014	It's No Secret What God Can Do-531111	S. Butcher	Yr.Iss.	30.00	30.00
95-20-015	Take Time To Smell the Flowers-524387	S. Butcher	Yr.Iss.	30.00	30.00

Enesco Corporation — Precious Moments Musical Figurines

		ARTIST	EDITION	ISSUE	QUOTE
83-21-001	Sharing Our Season Together-E-0519	S. Butcher	Retrd.	70.00	115-140.
83-21-002	Wee Three Kings-E-0520	S. Butcher	Suspd.	60.00	90-110.
83-21-003	Let Heaven And Nature Sing-E-2346	S. Butcher	Suspd.	55.00	115-130.
93-21-004	O Come All Ye Faithful-E-2352	S. Butcher	Open	50.00	50.00
82-21-005	I'll Play My Drum For Him-E-2355	S. Butcher	Suspd.	45.00	110-140.
79-21-006	Christmas Is A Time To Share-E-2806	S. Butcher	Retrd.	35.00	140-170.
79-21-007	Crown Him Lord Of All-E-2807	S. Butcher	Suspd.	35.00	75-110.
79-21-008	Unto Us A Child Is Born-E-2808	S. Butcher	Suspd.	35.00	95-125.
80-21-009	Jesus Is Born-E-2809	S. Butcher	Suspd.	35.00	105-135.
80-21-010	Come Let Us Adore Him-E-2810	S. Butcher	Suspd.	45.00	85-150.
80-21-011	Peace On Earth-E-4726	S. Butcher	Suspd.	45.00	95-120.
80-21-012	The Hand That Rocks The Future-E-5204	S. Butcher	Open	30.00	55-85.00
80-21-013	My Guardian Angel-E-5205	S. Butcher	Suspd.	22.50	100.00
81-21-014	My Guardian Angel-E-5206	S. Butcher	Suspd.	22.50	95.00
84-21-015	Wishing You A Merry Christmas-E-5394	S. Butcher	Suspd.	55.00	80-100.
80-21-016	Silent Knight-E-5642	S. Butcher	Suspd.	45.00	125-150.
81-21-017	Rejoice O Earth-E-5645	S. Butcher	Retrd.	35.00	80-125.
81-21-018	The Lord Bless You And Keep You-E-7180	S. Butcher	Open	55.00	80-100.
81-21-019	Mother Sew Dear-E-7182	S. Butcher	Open	35.00	55-75.00
81-21-020	The Purr-fect Grandma-E-7184	S. Butcher	Suspd.	35.00	55-80.00
81-21-021	Love Is Sharing-E-7185	S. Butcher	Retrd.	40.00	125-165.
81-21-022	Let the Whole World Know-E-7186	S. Butcher	Suspd.	60.00	135.00
93-21-023	Lord Keep My Life In Tune (2/set)-12165	S. Butcher	Open	50.00	50.00
84-21-024	We Saw A Star-12408	S. Butcher	Suspd.	50.00	65-80.00
93-21-025	Lord Keep My Life In Tune (2/set)-12580	S. Butcher	Open	50.00	50.00
93-21-026	God Sent You Just In Time-15504	S. Butcher	Retrd.	60.00	90-100.
93-21-027	Silent Night-15814	S. Butcher	Open	55.00	55-75.00
85-21-028	Heaven Bless You-100285	S. Butcher	Suspd.	45.00	69-89.00
86-21-029	Our 1st Christmas Together-101702	S. Butcher	Retrd.	50.00	110-125.
93-21-030	Let's Keep In Touch-102520	S. Butcher	Open	85.00	85.00
93-21-031	Peace On Earth-109746	S. Butcher	Suspd.	120.00	130-155.
87-21-032	I'm Sending You A White Christmas-112402	S. Butcher	Retrd.	55.00	75-110.
87-21-033	You Have Touched So Many Hearts-112577	S. Butcher	Open	50.00	50-60.00
91-21-034	Lord Keep My Life In Balance-520691	S. Butcher	Suspd.	60.00	68.00
93-21-035	The Light Of The World Is Jesus-521507	S. Butcher	Open	65.00	65.00
92-21-036	Do Not Open Till Christmas-522244	S. Butcher	Suspd.	75.00	75.00
92-21-037	This Day Has Been Made In Heaven-523682	S. Butcher	Open	60.00	60.00
93-21-038	Wishing You Were Here-526916	S. Butcher	Open	100.00	100.00

Enesco Corporation — Precious Moments Calendar Girl

		ARTIST	EDITION	ISSUE	QUOTE
88-22-001	January-109983	S. Butcher	Open	37.50	45-67.00
88-22-002	February-109991	S. Butcher	Open	27.50	33.50-67.
88-22-003	March-110019	S. Butcher	Open	27.50	33.50-64.
88-22-004	April-110027	S. Butcher	Open	30.00	35-118.
88-22-005	May -110035	S. Butcher	Open	25.00	30-150.
88-22-006	June-110043	S. Butcher	Open	40.00	50-112.
88-22-007	July-110051	S. Butcher	Open	35.00	45-58.00
88-22-008	August-110078	S. Butcher	Open	40.00	50-57.00
88-22-009	September-110086	S. Butcher	Open	27.50	33.50-49.
88-22-010	October-110094	S. Butcher	Open	35.00	45-59.00
88-22-011	November-110108	S. Butcher	Open	32.50	37.50-50.
88-22-012	December-110116	S. Butcher	Open	27.50	35-75.00

		ARTIST	EDITION	ISSUE	QUOTE
Enesco Corporation	**Precious Moments CLUB 15th Anniv. Commemorative Edition**				
93-23-001	15 Happy Years Together: What A Tweet-530786	S. Butcher	Yr.Iss.	100.00	100-115.
Enesco Corporation	**Precious Moments Beauty of Christmas**				
94-24-001	You're As Pretty As A Christmas Tree	S. Butcher	Yr.Iss.	50.00	50.00
Enesco Corporation	**Commemorative 500th Columbus Anniversary**				
92-25-001	This Land Is Our Land-527386	S. Butcher	Retrd.	350.00	400-500.
Enesco Corporation	**Bless Those Who Serve Their Country**				
91-25-001	Bless Those Who Serve Their Country (Navy) 526568	S. Butcher	Suspd.	32.50	40-48.00
91-25-002	Bless Those Who Serve Their Country (Army) 526576	S. Butcher	Suspd.	32.50	32.50
91-25-003	Bless Those Who Serve Their Country (Air Force) 526584	S. Butcher	Suspd.	32.50	35.00
91-25-004	Bless Those Who Serve Their Country (Girl Soldier) 527289	S. Butcher	Suspd.	32.50	35.00
91-25-005	Bless Those Who Serve Their Country (Soldier) 527297	S. Butcher	Suspd.	32.50	32.50
91-25-006	Bless Those Who Serve Their Country (Marine) 527521	S. Butcher	Suspd.	32.50	45.00
Enesco Corporation	**Sugartown**				
94-26-001	Free Christmas Puppies - 528064	S. Butcher	Open	18.50	18.50
93-26-002	Sammy-528668	S. Butcher	Open	17.00	17.00
92-26-003	Christmas Tree-528684	S. Butcher	Open	15.00	15.00
94-26-004	7 pc. Doctor's Office Collectors Set - 529281	S. Butcher	Yr.Iss.	189.00	189.00
93-26-005	Dusty-529435	S. Butcher	Open	17.00	17.00
93-26-006	Car-529443	S. Butcher	Open	22.50	22.50
92-26-007	Aunt Ruth & Aunt Dorothy-529486	S. Butcher	Open	20.00	20.00
92-26-008	Philip-529494	S. Butcher	Open	17.00	17.00
92-26-009	Nativity-529508	S. Butcher	Open	20.00	20.00
92-26-010	Grandfather-529516	S. Butcher	Open	15.00	15.00
93-26-011	Katy Lynne-529524	S. Butcher	Open	20.00	20.00
92-26-012	Sam Butcher-529567	S. Butcher	Yr.Iss.	22.50	45-60.00
93-26-013	House Night Light 529605	S. Butcher	Open	80.00	80.00
92-26-014	Chapel-529621	S. Butcher	Open	85.00	85.00
94-26-015	Stork With Baby Sam - 529788	S. Butcher	Yr.Iss.	22.50	22.50
93-26-016	Fence-529796	S. Butcher	Open	10.00	10.00
94-26-017	Leon & Evelyn Mae - 529818	S. Butcher	Open	20.00	20.00
94-26-018	Jan - 529826	S. Butcher	Open	17.00	17.00
93-26-019	Sam Butcher-529842	S. Butcher	Yr.Iss.	22.50	22.50
94-26-020	Dr. Sam Sugar - 530850	S. Butcher	Open	17.00	17.00
93-26-021	Collector's Set/7-531774	S. Butcher	Open	189.00	189.00
94-26-022	Sugar & Her Dog House - 533165	S. Butcher	Open	20.00	20.00
Enesco Corporation	**Sugartown Enhancements**				
94-27-001	Lamp Post - 529559	S. Butcher	Open	8.00	8.00
94-27-002	Mailbox - 531847	S. Butcher	Open	5.00	5.00
94-27-003	Curved Road - 533149	S. Butcher	Open	10.00	10.00
94-27-004	Straight Sidewalk - 533157	S. Butcher	Open	10.00	10.00
94-27-005	Single Tree - 533173	S. Butcher	Open	10.00	10.00
94-27-006	Double Tree - 533181	S. Butcher	Open	10.00	10.00
94-27-007	Cobble Stone Bridge - 533203	S. Butcher	Open	17.00	17.00
Enesco Corporation	**Spring Catalog Figurine**				
93-28-001	Happiness Is At Our Fingertips-529931	S. Butcher	Retrd.	35.00	40-75.00
94-28-002	So Glad I Picked You As A Friend-524379	S. Butcher	Yr.Iss.	40.00	40.00
Enesco Corporation	**Two By Two**				
93-29-001	Noah, Noah's Wife, & Noah's Ark (lighted)-530042	S. Butcher	Open	125.00	125.00
93-29-002	Sheep (mini double fig.) -530077	S. Butcher	Open	10.00	10.00
93-29-003	Pigs (mini double fig.) -530085	S. Butcher	Open	12.00	12.00
93-29-004	Giraffes (mini double fig.) -530115	S. Butcher	Open	16.00	16.00
93-29-005	Bunnies (mini double fig.) -530123	S. Butcher	Open	9.00	9.00
93-29-006	Elephants (mini double fig.) -530131	S. Butcher	Open	18.00	18.00
93-29-007	Eight Piece Collector's Set -530948	S. Butcher	Open	190.00	190.00
94-29-008	Llamas-531375	S. Butcher	Open	15.00	15.00
Enesco Corporation	**Sammy's Circus**				
94-30-001	Markie-528099	S. Butcher	Open	18.50	18.50
94-30-002	Dusty-529176	S. Butcher	Open	22.50	22.50
94-30-003	Katie-529184	S. Butcher	Open	17.00	17.00
94-30-004	Tippy-529192	S. Butcher	Open	12.00	12.00
94-30-005	Collin-529214	S. Butcher	Open	20.00	20.00
94-30-006	Sammy-529222	S. Butcher	Yr.Iss.	20.00	20.00
94-30-007	Circus Ten-528196 (Nite-Lite)	S. Butcher	Open	90.00	90.00
Enesco Corporation	**Memories of Yesterday Special Edition**				
88-31-001	Mommy, I Teared It-523488	M. Attwell	10,000	25.00	175-325.
89-31-002	As Good As His Mother Ever Made-522392	M. Attwell	9,600	32.50	114-150.
90-31-003	A Lapful of Luck -525014	M. Attwell	5,000	30.00	114-180.
90-31-004	Set of Three	M. Attwell	N/A	87.50	735.00
Enesco Corporation	**Memories of Yesterday -Charter 1988**				
88-32-001	Mommy, I Teared It-114480	M. Attwell	Open	25.00	40-143.
88-32-002	Now I Lay Me Down To Sleep-114499	M. Attwell	Open	20.00	25-65.00
88-32-003	We's Happy! How's Yourself?-114502	M. Attwell	Open	40.00	45-60.00
88-32-004	Hang On To Your Luck!-114510	M. Attwell	Open	25.00	27-70.00
88-32-005	How Do You Spell S-O-R-R-Y?-114529	M. Attwell	Retrd.	25.00	50-95.00
88-32-006	What Will I Grow Up To Be?-114537	M. Attwell	Suspd.	40.00	45-72.00
88-32-007	Can I Keep Her Mommy?-114545	M. Attwell	Open	25.00	27-70.00
88-32-008	Hush!-114553	M. Attwell	Retrd.	45.00	75-125.
88-32-009	It Hurts When Fido Hurts-114561	M. Attwell	Retrd.	30.00	32-75.00
88-32-010	Anyway, Fido Loves Me-114588	M. Attwell	Suspd.	30.00	32-75.00
88-32-011	If You Can't Be Good, Be Careful-114596	M. Attwell	Retrd.	50.00	55-90.00
88-32-012	Mommy, I Teared It, 9"-115924	M. Attwell	Retrd.	85.00	140-195.
88-32-013	Welcome Santa-114960	M. Attwell	Open	45.00	50-100.
88-32-014	Special Delivery-114979	M. Attwell	Retrd.	30.00	32-70.00
88-32-015	How 'bout A Little Kiss?-114987	M. Attwell	Open	25.00	27-85.00
88-32-016	Waiting For Santa-114995	M. Attwell	Open	40.00	40-50.00
88-32-017	Dear Santa. . .-115002	M. Attwell	Suspd.	50.00	55-65.00
88-32-018	I Hope Santa Is Home . . .-115010	M. Attwell	Open	30.00	33-45.00
88-32-019	It's The Thought That Counts-115029	M. Attwell	Suspd.	25.00	29-75.00
88-32-020	Is It Really Santa?-115347	M. Attwell	Open	50.00	55-60.00
88-32-021	He Knows IF You've Been Bad Or Good-115355	M. Attwell	Open	40.00	45-75.00
88-32-022	Now He Can Be Your Friend, Too!-115363	M. Attwell	Open	45.00	50-70.00
88-32-023	We Wish You A Merry Christmas-115371 (musical)	M. Attwell	Suspd.	70.00	70-125.
88-32-024	Good Morning Mr. Snowman-115401	M. Attwell	Retrd.	75.00	80-170.

		ARTIST	EDITION	ISSUE	QUOTE
Enesco Corporation	**Memories of Yesterday Figurines**				
89-33-001	Blow Wind, Blow-520012	M. Attwell	Open	40.00	40.00
89-33-002	Let's Be Nice Like We Was Before-520047	M. Attwell	Suspd.	50.00	50.00
89-33-003	I'se Spoken For-520071	M. Attwell	Retrd.	30.00	30-50.00
89-33-004	Daddy, I Can Never Fill Your Shoes-520187	M. Attwell	Open	30.00	30.00
89-33-005	This One's For You, Dear-520195	M. Attwell	Suspd.	50.00	50.00
89-33-006	Should I . . . ?-520209	M. Attwell	Suspd.	50.00	50.00
89-33-007	Here Comes The Bride-God Bless Her! -9"-5205272	M. Attwell	Retrd.	95.00	95-100.
89-33-008	We's Happy! How's Yourself?-520616	M. Attwell	Retrd.	70.00	85-150.
89-33-009	Here Comes The Bride & Groom (musical) God Bless 'Em-520896	M. Attwell	Open	50.00	50.00
89-33-010	The Long and Short of It-522384	M. Attwell	Retrd.	32.50	32.50
89-33-011	As Good As His Mother Ever Made-522392	M. Attwell	Open	32.50	32-40.00
89-33-012	Must Feed Them Over Christmas-522406	M. Attwell	Open	38.50	38.50
89-33-013	Knitting You A Warm & Cozy Winter-522414	M. Attwell	Open	37.50	37.50
89-33-014	Joy To You At Christmas-522449	M. Attwell	Open	45.00	45.00
89-33-015	For Fido And Me-522457	M. Attwell	Open	70.00	70.00
90-33-016	Hold It! You're Just Swell-520020	M. Attwell	Suspd.	50.00	50.00
90-33-017	Kiss The Place And Make It Well-520039	M. Attwell	Suspd.	50.00	50.00
90-33-018	Where's Muvver?-520101	M. Attwell	Retrd.	30.00	30.00
90-33-019	Here Comes The Bride And Groom God Bless 'Em!-520136 (musical)	M. Attwell	Suspd.	80.00	80.00
90-33-020	Luck At Last! He Loves Me-520217	M. Attwell	Retrd.	35.00	36-58.00
90-33-021	I'm Not As Backwards As I Looks-523240	M. Attwell	Open	32.50	32.50
90-33-022	I Pray The Lord My Soul To Keep-523259	M. Attwell	Open	25.00	25.00
90-33-023	He Hasn't Forgotten Me-523267	M. Attwell	Suspd.	30.00	30.00
90-33-024	Time For Bed 9"-523275	M. Attwell	Retrd.	95.00	95-125.
90-33-025	Got To Get Home For The Holidays-524751(musical)	M. Attwell	Retrd.	100.00	100.00
90-33-026	Hush-A-Bye Baby-524778	M. Attwell	Open	80.00	80.00
90-33-027	Let Me Be Your Guardian Angel-524670	M. Attwell	Open	32.50	32.50
90-33-028	I'se Been Painting-524700	M. Attwell	Suspd.	37.50	37.50
90-33-029	A Lapful Of Luck-524689	M. Attwell	Open	15.00	15.00
90-33-030	The Greatest Treasure The World Can Hold-524808	M. Attwell	Open	50.00	50.00
90-33-031	Hoping To See You Soon-524824	M. Attwell	Suspd.	30.00	30.00
90-33-032	A Dash of Something With Something For the Pot-524727	M. Attwell	Open	55.00	55.00
90-33-033	Not A Creature Was Stirrin'-524697	M. Attwell	Suspd.	45.00	45.00
90-33-034	Collection Sign-513156	M. Attwell	Retrd.	7.00	7.00
91-33-035	He Loves Me -9" -525022	M. Attwell	Retrd.	100.00	100.00
91-33-036	Give It Your Best Shot-525561	M. Attwell	Open	35.00	35.00
91-33-037	Wishful Thinking-522597	M. Attwell	Open	45.00	45.00
91-33-038	Them Dishes Nearly Done-524611	M. Attwell	Open	50.00	50.00
91-33-039	Just Thinking 'bout You-523461 (musical)	M. Attwell	Suspd.	70.00	70.00
91-33-040	Who Ever Told Mother To Order Twins?-520063	M. Attwell	Open	33.50	33.50
91-33-041	Tying The Knot-522678	M. Attwell	Open	60.00	60.00
91-33-042	Pull Yourselves Together Girls, Waists Are In-522783	M. Attwell	Open	30.00	30.00
91-33-043	I Must Be Somebody's Darling-524832	M. Attwell	Retrd.	30.00	30.00
91-33-044	We All Loves A Cuddle-524832	M. Attwell	Retrd.	30.00	35.00
91-33-045	Sitting Pretty-522708	M. Attwell	Retrd.	40.00	40.00
91-33-046	Why Don't You Sing Along?-522600	M. Attwell	Open	55.00	55.00
91-33-047	Wherever I Am, I'm Dreaming of You-	M. Attwell	Suspd.	40.00	40.00
91-33-048	Opening Presents Is Much Fun!-524735	M. Attwell	Suspd.	37.50	37.50
91-33-049	I'm As Comfy As Can Be-525480	M. Attwell	Suspd.	50.00	50.00
91-33-050	Friendship Has No Boundaries (Special Understamp)-525545	M. Attwell	Yr.Iss.	30.00	30-50.00
91-33-051	Could You Love Me For Myself Alone?-525618	M. Attwell	Retrd.	30.00	30.00
91-33-052	Good Morning, Little Boo-Boo-525766	M. Attwell	Open	40.00	40.00
91-33-053	S'no Use Lookin' Back Now!-527203	M. Attwell	Open	75.00	75.00
92-33-054	I Pray the Lord My Soul To Keep (musical)-525596	M. Attwell	Suspd.	65.00	65.00
92-33-055	Time For Bed-527076	M. Attwell	Open	30.00	30.00
92-33-056	Now Be A Good Dog Fido-524581	M. Attwell	Open	45.00	45.00
92-33-057	A Kiss From Fido-523119	M. Attwell	Suspd.	35.00	35.00
92-33-058	I'se Such A Good Little Girl Sometimes-522759	M. Attwell	Suspd.	30.00	30.00
92-33-059	Send All Life's Little Worries Skipping-527505	M. Attwell	Open	30.00	30.00
92-33-060	A Whole Bunch of Love For You-522732	M. Attwell	Open	40.00	40.00
92-33-061	Hurry Up For the Last Train to Fairyland-525863	M. Attwell	Suspd.	40.00	40.00
92-33-062	I'se So Happy You Called-526401	M. Attwell	2-Yr.	100.00	100.00
92-33-063	I'm Hopin' You're Missing Me Too-525499	M. Attwell	Suspd.	55.00	55.00
92-33-064	You'll Always Be My Hero-524743	M. Attwell	Open	50.00	50.00
92-33-065	Things Are Rather Upside Down-522775	M. Attwell	Suspd.	30.00	30.00
92-33-066	The Future-God Bless 'Em!-524719	M. Attwell	Open	37.50	37.50
92-33-067	Making Something Special For You-525472	M. Attwell	Open	45.00	45.00
92-33-068	Home's A Grand Place To Get Back To Musical-525553	M. Attwell	Open	100.00	100.00
92-33-069	Five Years Of Memories-525669 (Five Year Anniversary Figurine)	M. Attwell	Yr.Iss.	50.00	65.00
92-33-070	Good Night and God Bless You In Every Way!-525634	M. Attwell	Suspd.	50.00	50.00
92-33-071	Collection Sign-527300	M. Attwell	Open	30.00	30.00
92-33-072	Merry Christmas, Little Boo-Boo-528803	M. Attwell	Open	37.50	37.50
92-33-073	Five Years Of Memories Celebrating Our Five Years1992-525669A	M. Attwell	500	N/A	N/A
93-33-074	You Do Make Me Happy-520098	M. Attwell	Open	27.50	27.50
93-33-075	Will You Be Mine?-522694	M. Attwell	Open	30.00	30.00
93-33-076	Here's A Little Song From Me To You Musical-522716	M. Attwell	Open	70.00	70.00
93-33-077	Bringing Good Luck To You-522791	M. Attwell	Open	30.00	30.00
93-33-078	With A Heart That's True, I'll Wait For You-524816	M. Attwell	Open	50.00	50.00
93-33-079	Now I Lay Me Down To Sleep-525413 (musical)	M. Attwell	Suspd.	65.00	65.00
93-33-080	The Jolly Ole Sun Will Shine Again-525502	M. Attwell	Retrd.	55.00	55.00
93-33-081	May Your Flowers Be Even Better Than The Pictures On The Packets-525685	M. Attwell	Open	37.50	37.50
93-33-082	You Won't Catch Me Being A Golf Widow-525715	M. Attwell	Open	30.00	30.00
93-33-083	Having A Wash And Brush Up-527424	M. Attwell	Open	35.00	35.00
93-33-084	A Bit Tied Up Just Now-But Cheerio-527467	M. Attwell	Open	45.00	45.00

		ARTIST	EDITION	ISSUE	QUOTE
93-33-085	Hullo! Did You Come By Underground?-527653	M. Attwell	Yr.Iss.	40.00	40.00
93-33-086	Hullo! Did You Come By Underground? Commemorative Issue: 1913-1993 - 527653A	M. Attwell	500	N/A	N/A
93-33-087	Look Out-Something Good Is Coming Your Way!-528781	M. Attwell	Suspd.	37.50	37.50
93-33-088	Strikes Me, I'm Your Match-529656	M. Attwell	Open	27.50	27.50
93-33-089	Wot's All This Talk About Love?-529737	M. Attwell	2-Yr.	100.00	100.00
93-33-090	Do You Know The Way To Fairyland?-530379	M. Attwell	Open	50.00	50.00
94-33-091	Too Shy For Words-525758	M. Attwell	Open	50.00	50.00
94-33-092	Pleasant Dreams and Sweet Repose-(musical)-526592	M. Attwell	Open	80.00	80.00
94-33-093	Bless 'Em!-523127	M. Attwell	Open	35.00	35.00
94-33-094	Bless 'Em!-523232	M. Attwell	Open	35.00	35.00
94-33-095	Don't Wait For Wishes to Come True-Go Get Them!-527645	M. Attwell	Open	37.50	37.50
94-33-096	Making the Right Connection-529907	M. Attwell	Yr.Iss.	30.00	30.00
94-33-097	The Nativity Pageant-602949	M. Attwell	Open	90.00	90.00
94-33-098	Taking After Mother-525731	M. Attwell	Open	40.00	40.00
94-33-099	Bobbed-526991	M. Attwell	Open	32.50	32.50
94-33-100	Having a Good Ole Laugh-527432	M. Attwell	Open	50.00	50.00
94-33-101	Do Be Friends With Me-529117	M. Attwell	Open	40.00	40.00
94-33-102	Good Morning From One Cheery Soul To Another-529141	M. Attwell	Open	30.00	30.00
94-33-103	May Your Birthday Be Bright And Happy-529575	M. Attwell	Open	35.00	35.00
94-33-104	Thank God For Fido-529753	M. Attwell	2-Yr.	100.00	100.00
94-33-105	Still Going Strong-530344	M. Attwell	Open	27.50	27.50
94-33-106	Comforting Thoughts-531367	M. Attwell	Open	32.50	32.50
95-33-107	Love Begins With Friendship - 602914	M. Attwell	Open	50.00	50.00
95-33-108	A Helping Hand For You - 101192	M. Attwell	Open	40.00	40.00
95-33-109	Wherever You Go, I'll Keep In Touch - 602760	M. Attwell	Open	30.00	30.00
95-33-110	Good Friends Are Great Gifts - 525723	M. Attwell	Open	50.00	50.00
95-33-111	Let's Sail Away Together - 525707	M. Attwell	Open	32.50	32.50
95-33-112	A Friend Like You Is Hard To Find - 101176	M. Attwell	Open	45.00	45.00
95-33-113	You Brighten My Day With A Smile - 522627	M. Attwell	Open	30.00	30.00
95-33-114	Love To You Always - 602752	M. Attwell	Open	30.00	30.00
95-33-115	May You Have A Big Smile For A Long While - 602965	M. Attwell	Open	30.00	30.00
95-33-116	Love To You Today - 602973	M. Attwell	Open	30.00	30.00

Enesco Corporation — **Once Upon A Fairy Tale™...**

92-34-001	Mother Goose-526428	M. Attwell	18000	50.00	50.00
92-34-002	Mary Had A Little Lamb-526479	M. Attwell	18000	45.00	45.00
92-34-003	Simple Simon-526452	M. Attwell	18000	35.00	35.00
93-34-004	Mary, Mary Quite Contrary-526436	M. Attwell	18000	45.00	45.00
93-34-005	Little Miss Muffett-526444	M. Attwell	18000	50.00	50.00
94-34-006	Tweedle Dum & Tweedle Dee-526460	M. Attwell	10000	50.00	50.00

Enesco Corporation — **Memories of Yesterday-Exclusive Membership Figurine**

91-35-001	We Belong Together-S0001	M. Attwell	Yr.Iss.	Gift	35-80.00
92-35-002	Waiting For The Sunshine-S0002	M. Attwell	Yr.Iss.	Gift	60.00
93-35-003	I'm The Girl For You-S0003	M. Attwell	Yr.Iss.	Gift	40.00
94-35-004	Blowing a Kiss to a Dear I Miss-S0004	M. Attwell	Yr.Iss.	Gift	N/A

Enesco Corporation — **Memories of Yesterday-Exclusive Charter Membership Figurine**

92-36-001	Waiting For The Sunshine-S0102	M. Attwell	Yr.Iss.	Gift	N/A
93-36-002	I'm The Girl For You-S0103	M. Attwell	Yr.Iss.	Gift	N/A
94-36-003	Blowing a Kiss to a Dear I Miss-S0104	M. Attwell	Yr.Iss.	Gift	N/A

Enesco Corporation — **Memories of Yesterday-Society Figurines**

91-37-001	Welcome To Your New Home-MY911	M. Attwell	Yr.Iss.	30.00	46-85.00
91-37-002	I Love My Friends-MY921	M. Attwell	Yr.Iss.	32.50	60.00
93-37-003	Now I'm The Fairest Of Them All-MY931	M. Attwell	Yr.Iss.	35.00	35.00
93-37-004	A Little Love Song for You-MY941	M. Attwell	Yr.Iss.	35.00	35.00
94-37-005	Wot's All This Talk About Love- MY942	M. Attwell	Yr.Iss.	27.50	27.50

Enesco Corporation — **Memories of Yesterday-Exclusive Heritage Dealer Figurine**

91-38-001	A Friendly Chat and a Cup of Tea-525510	M. Attwell	Yr.Iss.	50.00	100.00
93-38-002	I'm Always Looking Out For You-527440	M. Attwell	Yr.Iss.	55.00	55.00
94-38-003	Loving Each Other Is The Nicest Thing We've Got- 522430	M. Attwell	Yr.Iss.	60.00	60.00
94-38-004	With A Heart That's True, I'll Wait For You 524816	M. Attwell	Open	50.00	50.00

Enesco Corporation — **Memories of Yesterday-Event Item Only**

94-39-001	I'll Always Be Your Truly Friend-525693	M. Attwell	Yr.Iss.	30.00	30.00

Enesco Corporation — **Memories of Yesterday-Memories Of A Special Day**

94-40-001	Monday's Child...-531421	M. Attwell	Open	35.00	35.00
94-40-002	Tuesday's Child...-531448	M. Attwell	Open	35.00	35.00
94-40-003	Wednesday's Child...-531405	M. Attwell	Open	35.00	35.00
94-40-004	Thursday's Child...-531413	M. Attwell	Open	35.00	35.00
94-40-005	Friday's Child...-531391	M. Attwell	Open	35.00	35.00
94-40-006	Saturday's Child...-531383	M. Attwell	Open	35.00	35.00
94-40-007	Sunday's Child...-531480	M. Attwell	Open	35.00	35.00
94-40-008	Collector's Commemorative Edition Set of 7, Hand-numbered-528056	M. Attwell	1994	250.00	250.00

Enesco Corporation — **Memories of Yesterday-When I Grow Up**

95-41-001	When I Grow Up, I Want To Be A Doctor - 102997	M. Attwell	Open	25.00	25.00
95-41-002	When I Grow Up, I Want To Be A Mother - 103195	M. Attwell	Open	25.00	25.00
95-41-003	When I Grow Up, I Want To Be A Fireman - 103462	M. Attwell	Open	25.00	25.00
95-41-004	When I Grow Up, I Want To Be A Ballerina- 103209	M. Attwell	Open	25.00	25.00
95-41-005	When I Grow Up, I Want To Be A Teacher - 103357	M. Attwell	Open	25.00	25.00
95-41-006	When I Grow Up, I Want To Be A Nurse - 103535	M. Attwell	Open	25.00	25.00

Enesco Corporation — **Memories of Yesterday-A Loving Wish For You**

95-42-001	Wishing You A Bright Future - 135194	M. Attwell	Open	25.00	25.00
95-42-002	An Anniversary Is Love - 135208	M. Attwell	Open	25.00	25.00
95-42-003	Bless You, Little One - 135224	M. Attwell	Open	25.00	25.00
95-42-004	Happiness Is Our Wedding Wish - 135178	M. Attwell	Open	25.00	25.00
95-42-005	A Blessed Day For You - 135186	M. Attwell	Open	25.00	25.00
95-42-006	A Birthday Wish For You - 135216	M. Attwell	Open	25.00	25.00

Enesco Corporation — **Cherished Teddies**

		ARTIST	EDITION	ISSUE	QUOTE
92-43-001	Signage Plaque - 951005	P. Hillman	Open	15.00	15.00
92-43-002	Nathaniel & Nellie "It's Twice As Nice With You" - 950513	P. Hillman	Open	30.00	30.00
92-43-003	Camille "I'd Be Lost Without You" - 950424	P. Hillman	Open	20.00	20.00
92-43-004	Jasmine " You Have Touched My Heart" - 950475	P. Hillman	Open	22.50	22.50
92-43-005	Blossom & Beth "Friends Are Never Far Apart" Musical - 950645	P. Hillman	Open	60.00	60.00
92-43-006	Christopher "Ol Friends Are The Best Friends" 950483	P. Hillman	Open	50.00	50.00
92-43-007	Jeremy "Friends Like You Are Precious And Few" - 950521	P. Hillman	Open	15.00	15.00
92-43-008	Zachary "Yesterday's Memories Are Today's Treasures" - 950491	P. Hillman	Open	30.00	30.00
92-43-009	Mandy "I Love You Just The Way You Are" - 950572	P. Hillman	Open	15.00	15.00
92-43-010	Benji "Life Is Sweet, Enjoy" - 950548	P. Hillman	Open	13.50	13.50
92-43-011	Anna "Hooray For You" - 950459	P. Hillman	Open	22.50	22.50
92-43-012	Beth "Bear Hugs" - 950637	P. Hillman	Open	17.50	17.50
92-43-013	Sara "Lov Ya", Jacki "Hugs & Kisses", Karen "Best Buddy" - 950432	P. Hillman	Open	10.00	10.00
92-43-014	Joshua "Love Repairs All" - 950556	P. Hillman	Open	20.00	20.00
92-43-015	Katie "A Friend Always Knows When You Need A Hug" - 950440	P. Hillman	Open	20.00	20.00
92-43-016	Theodore, Samantha & Tyler "Friends Come In All Sizes" - 950505	P. Hillman	Open	20.00	20.00
92-43-017	Blossom & Beth "Friends Are Never Far Apart" - 950564	P. Hillman	Open	50.00	50.00
92-43-018	Theodore, Samantha & Tyler (9") "Friends Come In All Sizes" - 951196	P. Hillman	Open	130.00	130.00
92-43-019	Marie, Baby & Josh "A Baby Is God's Gift of Love" - 950688	P. Hillman	Open	35.00	35.00
92-43-020	Creche & Quilt - 951218	P. Hillman	Open	50.00	50.00
92-43-021	Richard "My Gift Is Love", Edward "My Gift Is Caring", Wilbur"My Gift Is Sharing" - 950718	P. Hillman	Open	55.00	55.00
92-43-022	Angie "I Brought The Star" 951137	P. Hillman	Open	15.00	15.00
92-43-023	Sammy "Little Lambs Are In My Care" - 950726	P. Hillman	Open	17.50	17.50
92-43-024	Beth "Happy Holidays, Deer Friend" - 950807	P. Hillman	Open	22.50	22.50
92-43-025	Beth "Happy Holidays, Deer Friend" (Musical) - 950815	P. Hillman	Open	60.00	60.00
92-43-026	Charlie "The Spirit of Friendshiip Warms The Heart" - 950742	P. Hillman	Open	22.50	22.50
92-43-027	Jacob "Wishing For Love" - 950734	P. Hillman	Open	22.50	22.50
92-43-028	Theordore, Samantha & Tyler "Friendship Weathers All Storms" - 950769	P. Hillman	Open	20.00	20.00
92-43-029	Steven "A Season Filled With Sweetness" - 951129	P. Hillman	Open	20.00	20.00
92-43-030	Douglas "Let's Be Friends" - 950661	P. Hillman	Open	20.00	20.00
93-43-031	Marie "Friendship Is A Special Treat" - 910767	P. Hillman	Open	20.00	20.00
93-43-032	Priscilla "Love Surrounds Our Friendship" - 910724	P. Hillman	Open	15.00	15.00
93-43-033	Timothy "A Friend Is Forever" - 910740	P. Hillman	Open	15.00	15.00
93-43-034	Amy "Quilted With Love" - 910732	P. Hillman	Open	13.50	13.50
93-43-035	Michael & Michelle "Friendship Is A Cozy Feeling" - 910775	P. Hillman	Open	30.00	30.00
93-43-036	Abigail "Inside We're All The Same" - 900632	P. Hillman	Open	16.00	16.00
93-43-037	Henrietta "A Basketful of Wings" - 910686	P. Hillman	Open	22.00	35-65.00
93-43-038	Molly "Friendship Softens A Bumpy Ride" - 910759	P. Hillman	Open	30.00	30.00
93-43-039	Charity "I Found A Friend In Ewe" - 910678	P. Hillman	Open	20.00	32-48.00
93-43-043	Daisy "Friendship Blossoms With Love" - 910651	P. Hillman	Open	15.00	36-120.
93-43-041	Heidi & David "Special Friends" - 910708	P. Hillman	Open	25.00	25.00
93-43-042	Chelsea "Good Friends Are A Blessing" - 910694	P. Hillman	Open	15.00	24-45.00
93-43-043	Baby Blocks - CRT004	P. Hillman	Open	40.00	40.00
93-43-044	"Cradled With Love" Baby - 911356	P. Hillman	Open	16.50	16.50
93-43-045	"Beary Special One" Age 1 - 911348	P. Hillman	Open	13.50	13.50
93-43-046	"Two Sweet Two Bear" Age 2 - 911321	P. Hillman	Open	13.50	13.50
93-43-047	"Three Cheers For You" Age 3 - 911313	P. Hillman	Open	15.00	15.00
93-43-048	"Unfolding Happy Wishes For You" Age 4 - 911305	P. Hillman	Open	15.00	15.00
93-43-049	"Color Me Five" Age 5 - 911291	P. Hillman	Open	15.00	15.00
93-43-050	"Chalking Up Six Wishes" Age 6 - 911283	P. Hillman	Open	16.50	16.50
93-43-051	Patrick "Thank You For A Friend That's True" - 911410	P. Hillman	Open	18.50	18.50
93-43-052	Patrice "Thank You For The Sky So Blue" - 911420	P. Hillman	Open	18.50	18.50
93-43-053	"Thank You For A Friend That's True" ((Musical) - 914304	P. Hillman	Open	37.50	37.50
93-43-054	"Thank You For The Sky So Blue" (Musical) - 914312	P. Hillman	Open	37.50	37.50
93-43-055	Thomas "Chuggin' Along", Jonathon "Sail With Me", Harrison "We're Going Places" - 911739	P. Hillman	Open	15.00	15.00
93-43-056	Tracie & Nicole "Side By Side With Friends " - 911372	P. Hillman	Open	35.00	35.00
93-43-057	Freda & Tina "Our Friendship Is A Perfect Blend" - 911747	P. Hillman	Open	35.00	35.00
93-43-058	Robbie & Rachel "Love Bears All Things" - 911402	P. Hillman	Open	27.50	27.50
93-43-059	"Cradled With Love" (Musical) - 914320	P. Hillman	Open	60.00	60.00
93-43-060	Alice "Cozy Warm Wishes Coming Your Way" Dated 1993 - 912875	P. Hillman	Yr.Iss.	17.50	26-45.00
93-43-061	Alice "Cozy Warm Wishes Coming Your Way" (9") - 903620	P. Hillman	Open	100.00	100.00
93-43-062	"Sharing The Season Together" (Musical) - 912964	P. Hillman	Open	40.00	40.00
93-43-063	Hans "Friends In Toyland" - 912956	P. Hillman	Open	20.00	20.00
93-43-064	Carolyn "Wishing You All Good Things" - 912921	P. Hillman	Open	22.50	22.50
93-43-065	"Our Friendship Weathers All Storms" (Musical) - 903337	P. Hillman	Open	60.00	60.00
93-43-066	Theodore, Samantha & Tyler "Friendship Weathers All Storms (9") - 912883	P. Hillman	Open	160.00	160.00
93-43-067	Theodore, Samantha & Tyler "Friendship Weathers All Storms" (musical) - 904546	P. Hillman	Open	170.00	170.00
93-43-068	Mary "A Special Friend Warms The Season" - 912840	P. Hillman	Open	25.00	25.00
93-43-069	"Friends Like You Are Precious And Few" - 904309	P. Hillman	Open	30.00	30.00
93-43-070	"Friendship Pulls Us Through" & "Ewe Make Being Friends Special" - 912867	P. Hillman	Open	13.50	13.50

		ARTIST	EDITION	ISSUE	QUOTE
93-43-071	"Cherish The King" (Musical) - 912859	P. Hillman	Open	60.00	60.00
93-43-072	Gretel "We Make Magic, Me And You" - 912778	P. Hillman	Open	18.50	18.50
93-43-073	Gary "True Friendships Are Scarce" - 912786	P. Hillman	Open	18.50	18.50
93-43-074	Connie "You're A Sweet Treat" - 912794	P. Hillman	Open	15.00	15.00
93-43-075	Miles "I'm Thankful For A Friend Like You" - 912751	P. Hillman	Open	17.00	17.00
93-43-076	Prudence "A Friend To Be Thankful For" - 912808	P. Hillman	Open	17.00	17.00
93-43-077	Bucky & Brenda "How I Love Being Friends With You" - 912816	P. Hillman	Open	15.00	15.00
94-43-078	Victoria "From My Heart To Yours" - 916293	P. Hillman	Open	16.50	16.50
94-43-079	Nancy "Your Friendship Makes My Heart Sing" - 916315	P. Hillman	Open	15.00	15.00
94-43-080	Kelly "You're My One And Only" -916307	P. Hillman	Open	15.00	15.00
94-43-081	Oliver & Olivia "Will You Be Mine?" - 916641	P. Hillman	Open	25.00	25.00
94-43-082	Elizabeth & Ashley "My Beary Best Friend" - 916277	P. Hillman	Open	25.00	25.00
94-43-083	"Friendship Is Love That Lasts" (Musical) - 916323	P. Hillman	Open	45.00	45.00
94-43-084	Kathleen "Luck Found Me A Friend In You" - 916447	P. Hillman	Open	12.50	12.50
94-43-085	Sean "Luck Found Me A Friend In You" - 916439	P. Hillman	Open	12.50	12.50
94-43-086	"Some Bunny Loves You" (Musical) - 625302	P. Hillman	Open	60.00	60.00
94-43-087	Becky "Springtime Happiness" - 916331	P. Hillman	Open	20.00	20.00
94-43-088	Faith "There's No Bunny Like You" - 916412	P. Hillman	Open	20.00	20.00
94-43-089	Henry "Celebrating Spring With You" - 916420	P. Hillman	Open	20.00	20.00
94-43-090	Bessie "Some Bunny Loves You" - 916404	P. Hillman	Open	15.00	35-55.00
94-43-091	Courtney "Springtime Is A Blessing From Above" - 916390	P. Hillman	Open	15.00	15.00
94-43-092	Mother "A Mother's Love Bears All Things" - 624861	P. Hillman	Open	20.00	20.00
94-43-094	Father "A Father Is The Bearer Of Strength" - 624888	P. Hillman	Open	13.50	13.50
94-43-094	Older Daughter "Child Of Love" - 624845	P. Hillman	Open	10.00	10.00
94-43-095	Older Son "Child Of Pride" - 624829	P. Hillman	Open	10.00	10.00
94-43-096	Young Daughter "Child Of Kindness" - 624853	P. Hillman	Open	9.00	9.00
94-43-097	Young Son "Child of Hope" - 624837	P. Hillman	Open	9.00	9.00
94-43-098	Jack & Jill "Our Friendship Will Never Tumble" - 624772	P. Hillman	Open	30.00	30.00
94-43-099	Mary, Mary Quite Contrary "Friendship Blooms With Loving Care" - 626074	P. Hillman	Open	22.50	22.50
94-43-100	Tom, Tom The Piper's Son "Wherever You Go I'll Follow" - 624810	P. Hillman	Open	20.00	20.00
94-43-101	Little Jack Horner "I'm Plum Happy You're My Friend" - 624780	P. Hillman	Open	20.00	20.00
94-43-102	Little Miss Muffet "I'm Never Afraid With You At My Side" - 624799	P. Hillman	Open	20.00	20.00
94-43-103	Little Bo Peep "Looking For A Friend Like You" - 624802	P. Hillman	Open	22.50	22.50
94-43-104	"Cuddle Me With Love" (Musical) - 699322	P. Hillman	Open	60.00	60.00
94-43-105	"A Playful Friend" (Musical) - 699314	P. Hillman	Open	60.00	60.00
94-43-106	Betty "Bubblin' Over With Love" - 626066	P. Hillman	Open	18.50	18.50
94-43-107	Billy "Everyone Needs A Cuddle", Betsey "First Step To Love" Bobbie "A Little Friendship To Share" - 624896	P. Hillman	Open	12.50	12.50
94-43-108	Robbie & Rachel "Love Bears All Things" (Musical) - 699349	P. Hillman	Open	50.00	50.00
94-43-109	Christopher "Old Friends Are The Best Friends" (Musical) - 627445	P. Hillman	Open	60.00	60.00
94-43-110	Katie "A Friend Always Knows When You Need A Hug" (Musical) -627445	P. Hillman	Open	45.00	45.00
94-43-111	Nursery Rhyme Books - CRT013	P. Hillman	Open	40.00	40.00
94-43-112	"My Favorite Things - A Cuddle And You" - 628565	P. Hillman	Open	150.00	150.00
94-43-113	"Smooth Sailing" (Musical) - 624926	P. Hillman	Open	60.00	60.00
94-43-114	Taylor "Sail The Seas With Me" - 617156	P. Hillman	Open	15.00	15.00
94-43-115	Breanna "Pumpkin Patch Pals" - 617180	P. Hillman	Open	15.00	15.00
94-43-116	Stacie "You Lift My Spirit" - 617148	P. Hillman	Open	18.50	18.50
94-43-117	Patience "Happiness Is Homemade" - 617105	P. Hillman	Open	17.50	17.50
94-43-118	Wyatt "I'm Called Little Runnig Bear" - 629707	P. Hillman	Open	15.00	15.00
94-43-119	Jededia "Giving Thanks For Friends" - 617091	P. Hillman	Open	17.50	17.50
94-43-120	Thanksgiving Quilt -617075	P. Hillman	Open	12.00	12.00
94-43-121	Phoebe "A Little Friendship Is A Big Blessing" - 617113	P. Hillman	Open	13.50	13.50
94-43-122	Wylie "I'm Called Little Friend" - 617121	P. Hillman	Open	15.00	15.00
94-43-123	Winona "Fair Feather Friends" - 617172	P. Hillman	Open	15.00	15.00
94-43-124	Willie "Bears Of A Feather Stay Together" - 617164	P. Hillman	Open	15.00	15.00
94-43-125	Gloria "Ghost of Christmas Past, " Garland "Ghost Of Christmas Present", Gabriel "Ghost of Christmas Yet To Come" - 614807	P. Hillman	Open	55.00	55.00
94-43-126	Mrs. Cratchit "A Beary Christmas And Happy New Year!" - 617318	P. Hillman	Open	18.50	18.50
94-43-127	Tiny Ted-Bear "God Bless Us Every One" - 614777	P. Hillman	Open	10.00	10.00
94-43-128	Jacob Bearly "You Will Be Haunted By Three Spirits" - 614785	P. Hillman	Open	17.50	17.50
94-43-129	Bear Cratchit "And A Very Merry Christmas Mr. Scrooge" - 617326	P. Hillman	Open	17.50	17.50
94-43-130	Ebearneezer Scrooge "Bah Humbug!" - 617296	P. Hillman	Open	17.50	17.50
94-43-131	Cratchit's House - 651362	P. Hillman	Open	75.00	75.00
94-43-132	Counting House - 622788	P. Hillman	Open	75.00	75.00
94-43-133	Sonja "Holiday Cuddles" - 622818	P. Hillman	Open	20.00	20.00
94-43-134	Nils "Near And Dear For Christmas" - 617245	P. Hillman	Open	22.50	22.50
94-43-135	Eric "Bear Tidings Of Joy" - 622796	P. Hillman	Open	22.50	22.50
94-43-136	Ingrid "Bundled Up With Warm Wishes" Dated 1994 - 617237	P. Hillman	Yr.Iss.	20.00	20.00
94-43-137	"Tis The Season For Deer Friends" (Musical) - 629618	P. Hillman	Open	165.00	165.00
94-43-138	"Bundled Up For The Holidays" (Musical) - 651435	P. Hillman	Open	100.00	100.00
94-43-139	"That's What Friends Are For" - 651095	P. Hillman	Open	22.50	22.50
94-43-143	Ronnie "I'll Play My Drum For You" - 912905	P. Hillman	Open	13.50	13.50

Enesco Corporation **Special Limited Edition Cherished Teddies**

		ARTIST	EDITION	ISSUE	QUOTE
93-44-001	Teddy & Roosevelt "The Book of Teddies 1903-1993" - 624918	P. Hillman	Yr.Iss.	20.00	42-75.00
93-44-002	Holding On To Someone Special-Collector Appreciation Fig.-916285	P. Hillman	Yr.Iss.	20.00	36-60.00
94-44-003	Priscilla Ann "There's No One Like Hue" Collectible Exposition Exclusive available only at Secaucus and South Bend in 1994 and at Long Beach in 1995	P. Hillman	Yr.Iss.	24.00	24-125.

Enesco Corporation **Cherished Teddies Club**

		ARTIST	EDITION	ISSUE	QUOTE
95-45-001	Cub E. Bear CT001	P. Hillman	Yr.Iss.	Gift	N/A
95-45-002	Major Wilson T.Beary CT951	P. Hillman	Yr.Iss.	20.00	20.00
95-45-003	Hilary Hugabear CT952	P. Hillman	Yr.Iss.	17.50	17.50

Enesco Corporation **Maud Humphrey Bogart Figurines**

		ARTIST	EDITION	ISSUE	QUOTE
88-46-001	Tea And Gossip H1301	M. Humphrey	Retrd.	65.00	65-156.
88-46-002	Cleaning House H1303	M. Humphrey	Retrd.	60.00	57-175.
88-46-003	Susanna H 1305	M. Humphrey	Retrd.	60.00	161-375.
88-46-004	Little Chickadees H1306	M. Humphrey	Retrd.	65.00	57-108.
88-46-005	The Magic Kitten H1308	M. Humphrey	Retrd.	66.00	53-120.
88-46-006	Seamstress H1309	M. Humphrey	Retrd.	66.00	90-150.
88-46-007	A Pleasure To Meet You H1310	M. Humphrey	Retrd.	65.00	60-178.
88-46-008	My First Dance H1311	M. Humphrey	Retrd.	60.00	143-176.
88-46-009	Sarah H1312	M. Humphrey	Retrd.	60.00	192-384.
88-46-010	The Bride H1313	M. Humphrey	19,500	90.00	65-90.00
88-46-011	Sealed With A Kiss H1316	M. Humphrey	Retrd.	45.00	60-105.
88-46-012	Special Friends H1317	M. Humphrey	Retrd.	66.00	40-160.
88-46-013	School Days H1318	M. Humphrey	Retrd.	42.50	48-85.00
88-46-014	Gift Of Love H1319	M. Humphrey	Retrd.	65.00	36-60.00
88-46-015	My 1st Birthday H1320	M. Humphrey	Retrd.	47.00	100.00
90-46-016	A Little Robin H1347	M. Humphrey	19,500	55.00	55.00
90-46-017	Autumn Days H1348	M. Humphrey	24,500	45.00	45.00
90-46-018	Little Playmates H1349	M. Humphrey	19,500	48.00	48.00
89-46-019	No More Tears H1351	M. Humphrey	24,500	44.00	44.00
89-46-020	Winter Fun H1354	M. Humphrey	Retrd.	46.00	72-92.00
89-46-021	Kitty's Lunch H1355	M. Humphrey	19,500	60.00	48-60.00
90-46-022	School Lesson H1356	M. Humphrey	19,500	77.00	70-77.00
89-46-023	In The Orchard H1373	M. Humphrey	24,500	33.00	33.00
89-46-024	The Little Captive H1374	M. Humphrey	19,500	55.00	55.00
89-46-025	Little Red Riding Hood H1381	M. Humphrey	24,500	42.50	42.50
89-46-026	Little Bo Peep H1382	M. Humphrey	24,500	45.00	45.00
90-46-027	Playtime H1383	M. Humphrey	19,500	60.00	66.00
90-46-028	Kitty's Bath H1384	M. Humphrey	19,500	103.00	103.00
89-46-029	Springtime Gathering H1385	M. Humphrey	7,500	295.00	295.00
89-46-030	A Sunday Outing H1386	M. Humphrey	15,000	135.00	135.00
89-46-031	Spring Beauties H1387	M. Humphrey	15,000	135.00	135.00
89-46-032	The Bride-Porcelain H1388	M. Humphrey	15,000	125.00	128.00
89-46-033	Little Chickadees-Porcelain H1389	M. Humphrey	15,000	125.00	125.00
89-46-034	Special Friends-Porcelain H1390	M. Humphrey	15,000	125.00	128.00
89-46-035	Playing Bridesmaid H5500	M. Humphrey	19,500	125.00	125.00
89-46-036	The Magic Kitten-Porcelain H5543	M. Humphrey	15,000	125.00	125.00
90-46-037	A Special Gift H5550	M. Humphrey	19,500	70.00	90.00
90-46-038	Holiday Surprise H5551	M. Humphrey	24,500	50.00	50.00
90-46-039	Winter Friends H5552	M. Humphrey	19,500	64.00	64.00
90-46-040	Winter Days H5553	M. Humphrey	24,500	50.00	50.00
90-46-041	My Winter Hat H5554	M. Humphrey	24,500	40.00	40.00
91-46-042	The Graduate H5559	M. Humphrey	19,500	75.00	75.00
90-46-043	A Chance Acquaintance H5589	M. Humphrey	19,500	70.00	135.00
91-46-044	Spring Frolic H5590	M. Humphrey	15,000	170.00	170.00
90-46-045	Sarah (Waterball) H5594	M. Humphrey	19,500	75.00	79.00
90-46-046	Susanna (Waterball) H5595	M. Humphrey	19,500	75.00	79.00
91-46-047	Spring Bouquet H5598	M. Humphrey	24,500	44.00	44.00
91-46-048	The Pinwheel H5600	M. Humphrey	24,500	45.00	45.00
91-46-049	Little Boy Blue H5612	M. Humphrey	19,500	55.00	55.00
91-46-050	Little Miss Muffet H5621	M. Humphrey	24,500	75.00	75.00
91-46-051	My First Dance-Porcelain H5650	M. Humphrey	15,000	110.00	110.00
91-46-052	Sarah-Porcelain H5651	M. Humphrey	15,000	110.00	110.00
91-46-053	Susanna-Porcelain H5652	M. Humphrey	15,000	110.00	110.00
91-46-054	Tea And Gossip-Porcelain H5653	M. Humphrey	15,000	132.00	132.00
91-46-055	Cleaning House (Waterball) H5654	M. Humphrey	19,500	75.00	75.00
91-46-056	My First Dance (Waterball) H5655	M. Humphrey	19,500	75.00	75.00
91-46-057	Hush A Bye Baby H5695	M. Humphrey	19,500	62.00	62.00
91-46-058	All Bundled Up -910015	M. Humphrey	19,500	85.00	85.00
91-46-059	Doubles -910023	M. Humphrey	19,500	70.00	70.00
91-46-060	Melissa -910031	M. Humphrey	24,500	55.00	55.00
91-46-061	My Snow Shovel -910058	M. Humphrey	19,500	70.00	70.00
91-46-062	Winter Ride -910066	M. Humphrey	19,500	60.00	60.00
91-46-063	Melissa (Waterball) -910074	M. Humphrey	19,500	40.00	40.00
91-46-064	Winter Days (Waterball) -915130	M. Humphrey	19,500	75.00	75.00
91-46-065	Winter Friends (Waterball) -915149	M. Humphrey	19,500	75.00	75.00
91-46-066	My Winter Hat -921017	M. Humphrey	15,000	80.00	80.00
91-46-067	Winter Fun -921025	M. Humphrey	15,000	90.00	90.00
92-46-068	Spring's Child 910244	M. Humphrey	24,500	50.00	50.00
92-46-069	Summer's Child 910252	M. Humphrey	24,500	50.00	50.00
92-46-070	Autumn's Child 910260	M. Humphrey	24,500	50.00	50.00
92-46-071	Winter's Child 910279	M. Humphrey	24,500	50.00	50.00
92-46-072	Jack and Jill 910155	M. Humphrey	19,500	75.00	75.00
92-46-073	The Young Artist 910228	M. Humphrey	19,500	75.00	75.00
92-46-074	Stars and Stripes Forever 910201	M. Humphrey	Closed	75.00	150.00
92-46-075	New Friends 910171	M. Humphrey	15,000	125.00	125.00
92-46-076	Under The Mistletoe 910309	M. Humphrey	19,500	75.00	75.00
92-46-077	Hollies For You 910317	M. Humphrey	24,500	55.00	55.00
92-46-078	Hush! Santa's Coming 915378	M. Humphrey	19,500	50.00	50.00
92-46-079	A Melody For You 915432	M. Humphrey	Open	60.00	60.00
92-46-080	The Christmas Carol 915823	M. Humphrey	24,500	75.00	50-75.00
92-46-081	Susanna (Musical) 921084	M. Humphrey	7,500	125.00	125.00
92-46-082	Sarah (Musical) 921076	M. Humphrey	7,500	125.00	125.00
92-46-083	Hollies For You (Musical) 921092	M. Humphrey	5,000	125.00	125.00
93-46-084	Tee Time 915386	M. Humphrey	10,000	50.00	50.00
93-46-085	The Entertainer 910562	M. Humphrey	19,500	60.00	60.00
93-46-086	A Basket Full of Blessings 910147	M. Humphrey	15,000	55.00	55.00
93-46-087	Love's First Bloom 910120	M. Humphrey	15,000	50.00	50.00
93-46-088	Bedtime Blessings 910236	M. Humphrey	10,000	60.00	60.00
93-46-089	Flying Lessons 910139	M. Humphrey	15,000	50.00	50.00
93-46-090	Playing Mama 5th Anniv. Figurine 915963	M. Humphrey	Retrd.	80.00	80.00
93-46-091	Playing Mama Event Figurine 915963R	M. Humphrey	Retrd.	80.00	80.00
94-46-092	Marie-Childhood Memories 869619	M. Humphrey	5,000	35.00	35.00
94-46-093	Good As New 914924	M. Humphrey	5,000	100.00	100.00

		ARTIST	EDITION	ISSUE	QUOTE
94-46-094	Poetry Recital 914959	M. Humphrey	5,000	80.00	80.00
94-46-095	Loving Care 914932	M. Humphrey	5,000	60.00	60.00
94-46-096	Love To Last A Lifetime - 655627	M. Humphrey	5,000	45.00	45.00
94-46-097	Love To Last A Lifetime (Event Only Fig.) - 655627E	M. Humphrey	2,500	45.00	45.00
94-46-098	Care To Accompany Me? - 655619	M. Humphrey	5,000	50.00	50.00
94-46-099	A Hidden Treasure - 914940	M. Humphrey	5,000	60.00	60.00
94-46-100	Gifts Of Happiness - 771015	M. Humphrey	5,000	50.00	50.00

Enesco Corporation — Maud Humphrey Bogart Gallery Figurines

		ARTIST	EDITION	ISSUE	QUOTE
91-47-001	Mother's Treasures H5619	M. Humphrey	15,000	118.00	118.00
91-47-002	Sharing Secrets-910007	M. Humphrey	15,000	120.00	120.00
92-47-003	New Friends-910171	M. Humphrey	15,000	125.00	125.00
92-47-004	A Little Bird Told Me So-910570	M. Humphrey	7,500	120.00	120.00
93-47-005	May I Have This Dance?-915750	M. Humphrey	Yr.Iss.	110.00	110.00

Enesco Corporation — Maud Humphrey Bogart Symbol Of Membership Figurines

		ARTIST	EDITION	ISSUE	QUOTE
91-48-001	A Flower For You H5596	M. Humphrey	Closed	Unkn.	36.00
92-48-002	Sunday Best M0002	M. Humphrey	Closed	Unkn.	53-60.00
93-48-003	Playful Companions M0003	M. Humphrey	Yr.Iss.	Unkn.	Unkn.

Enesco Corporation — Maud Humphrey Bogart Collectors' Club Members Only

		ARTIST	EDITION	ISSUE	QUOTE
91-49-001	Friends For Life MH911	M. Humphrey	Closed	60.00	85-110.
92-49-002	Nature's Little Helper MH921	M. Humphrey	Closed	65.00	78.00
93-49-003	Sitting Pretty MH931	M. Humphrey	Yr.Iss.	60.00	60.00

Enesco Corporation — Maud Humphrey Bogart Victorian Village

		ARTIST	EDITION	ISSUE	QUOTE
93-50-001	No.5 Greenwood-9 11569	M. Humphrey	18,840	50.00	50.00
93-50-002	Village Sign-911542	M. Humphrey	Open	12.00	12.00
93-50-003	No.5 Greenwood Accessories-911534	M. Humphrey	Open	20.00	20.00
93-50-004	A.J. Warner-911518	M. Humphrey	Open	12.00	12.00
93-50-005	Maud Humphrey-911496	M. Humphrey	Open	12.00	12.00
93-50-006	Mabel Humphrey-911933	M. Humphrey	Open	12.00	12.00
93-50-007	No.5 Greenwood Collectors' Proof Set-913804	M. Humphrey	1,868	120.00	120.00
94-50-008	Country School - 911585	M. Humphrey	18,740	50.00	50.00
94-50-009	Humphrey - 911461	M. Humphrey	Open	12.00	12.00
94-50-010	Catherine - 911925	M. Humphrey	Open	12.00	12.00
94-50-011	Francis 911488	M. Humphrey	Open	12.00	12.00
94-50-012	School Accessories - 914223	M. Humphrey	Open	25.00	25.00
94-50-013	Country School Collectors Proof Set - 913790	M. Humphrey	1,868	125.00	125.00
94-50-014	Amazing Grace Church - 911577	M. Humphrey	18,360	55.00	55.00
94-50-015	James - 911445	M. Humphrey	Open	12.00	12.00
94-50-016	Sarah - 911437	M. Humphrey	Open	12.00	12.00
94-50-017	Elizabeth - 911453	M. Humphrey	Open	12.00	12.00
94-50-018	Church Accessories - 914231	M. Humphrey	Open	18.50	18.50
94-50-019	Amazing Grace Collectors Proof Set-913782	M. Humphrey	1,868	125.00	125.00
94-50-020	Maud - 654892	M. Humphrey	Open	12.00	12.00
94-50-021	Mabel - 654884	M. Humphrey	Open	12.00	12.00
94-50-022	A.J. - 654906	M. Humphrey	Open	12.00	12.00
94-50-023	Christmas Accesssories - 654914	M. Humphrey	Open	20.00	20.00
94-50-024	Christmas Scene Collectors Proof Set - 654876	M. Humphrey	Open	120.00	120.00
94-50-025	Chirstmas Scene - 655457	M. Humphrey	Open	50.00	50.00

Enesco Corporation — Linen and Lace

		ARTIST	EDITION	ISSUE	QUOTE
94-51-001	Capture the Moment 912654	M. Humphrey	2,500	125.00	125.00
94-51-002	A Dream Come True 916048	M. Humphrey	2,500	65.00	65.00
94-51-003	Artist of Her Time 916722	M. Humphrey	2,500	60.00	60.00
94-51-004	We Shall Come Rejoicing - 770981	M. Humphrey	2,500	60.00	60.00

Fenton Art Glass Company — 1983 Connoisseur Collection

		ARTIST	EDITION	ISSUE	QUOTE
83-01-001	5 pc. Burmese Epergne Set	Fenton	Closed	200.00	200.00
83-01-002	Vase, 4 1/2" Sculptured Rose Quartz	Fenton	Closed	32.50	32.50
83-01-003	Vase, 7" Sculptured Rose Quartz	Fenton	Closed	50.00	50.00
83-01-004	Basket, 9" Vasa Murrhina	Fenton	Closed	75.00	75.00
83-01-005	Cruet/Stopper Vasa Murrhina	Fenton	Closed	75.00	75.00
83-01-006	Vase, 9" Sculptured Rose Quartz	Fenton	Closed	75.00	75.00
83-01-007	Craftsman Stein, White Satin Carnival	Fenton	Closed	35.00	35.00

Fenton Art Glass Company — 1984 Connoisseur Collection

		ARTIST	EDITION	ISSUE	QUOTE
84-02-001	Basket, 10" Plated Amberina Velvet	Fenton	Closed	85.00	85.00
84-02-002	Top Hat, 8" Plated Amberina Velvet	Fenton	Closed	65.00	65.00
84-02-003	Cane, 18" Plated Amerina Velvet	Fenton	Closed	35.00	35.00
84-02-004	Vase, 9" Rose Velvet-Mother/Child	Fenton	Closed	125.00	125.00
84-02-005	3 pc. Covered Candy Box, Blue Burmese	Fenton	Closed	75.00	75.00
84-02-006	Vase, Swan, 8" Gold Azure	Fenton	Closed	65.00	65.00
84-02-007	Vase, 9" Rose Velvet-Floral	Fenton	Closed	75.00	75.00

Fenton Art Glass Company — 1985 Connoisseur Collection

		ARTIST	EDITION	ISSUE	QUOTE
85-03-001	14 pc. Punch Set Green Opalescent	Fenton	Closed	250.00	250.00
85-03-002	4 pc. Diamond Lace Epergne, Green Opal.	Fenton	Closed	95.00	95.00
85-03-003	Lamp, 22" Burmese-Butterfly/Branch	Fenton	Closed	300.00	300.00
85-03-004	Basket, 8 1/2" Buremese, Handpainted	Fenton	Closed	95.00	95.00
85-03-005	Vase, 12" "Garielle" Scul. French Blue	Fenton	Closed	150.00	150.00
85-03-006	Vase, 7 1/2" Chrysanthemums & Circlet	Fenton	Closed	125.00	125.00
85-03-007	Vase, 7 1/2" Burmese-Shell	Fenton	Closed	135.00	135.00

Fenton Art Glass Company — 1986 Connoisseur Collection

		ARTIST	EDITION	ISSUE	QUOTE
86-04-001	4 pc. Vanity Set, Blue Ridge	Fenton	Closed	125.00	125.00
86-04-002	Handled Vase, 7" French Royale	Fenton	Closed	100.00	100.00
86-04-003	Handled Urn, 13" Cranberry Satin	Fenton	Closed	185.00	185.00
86-04-004	Lamp, 20" Burmese-Shells	Fenton	Closed	350.00	350.00
86-04-005	Basket, Top hat Wild Rose/Teal Overlay	Fenton	Closed	49.00	49.00
86-04-006	Boudoir Lamp Cranberry Pearl	Fenton	Closed	145.00	145.00
86-04-007	Cruet/Stopper Cranberry Pearl	Fenton	Closed	75.00	75.00
86-04-008	Vase, 10 1/2" "Misty Morn", Handpainted	Fenton	Closed	95.00	95.00
86-04-009	Vase 7 1/2", "Danielle" Sandcarved	Fenton	Closed	95.00	95.00

Fenton Art Glass Company — 1987 Connoisseur Collection

		ARTIST	EDITION	ISSUE	QUOTE
87-05-001	Vase, 7 1/4" Blossom/Bows on Cranberry	Fenton	Closed	95.00	95.00
87-05-002	Pitcher, 8" Enameled Azure	Fenton	Closed	85.00	85.00

Fenton Art Glass Company — 1988 Connoisseur Collection

		ARTIST	EDITION	ISSUE	QUOTE
88-06-001	Pitcher, Cased Cranberry/ Opal Teal Ring	Fenton	Closed	60.00	60.00
88-06-002	Vase, 6" Cased Cranberry/Opal Teal/Irid.	Fenton	Closed	50.00	50.00
88-06-003	Basket, Irid. Teal Cased Vasa Murrhina	Fenton	Closed	65.00	65.00
88-06-004	Candy, Wave Crest, Cranberry	Fenton	Closed	95.00	95.00

Fenton Art Glass Company — 1989 Connoisseur Collection

		ARTIST	EDITION	ISSUE	QUOTE
89-07-001	Basket, 7" Cranberry w/Crystal Ring	Fenton	Closed	85.00	85.00
89-07-002	Covered candy, Cranberry, Handpainted	Fenton	Closed	85.00	85.00
89-07-003	Vase, Pinch, 8" Vasa Murrhina	Fenton	Closed	65.00	65.00
89-07-004	Pitcher, Diamond Optic, Rosalene	Fenton	Closed	55.00	55.00
89-07-005	5 pc. Epergne, Rosalene	Fenton	Closed	250.00	250.00
89-07-006	Vase, Basketweave, Rosalene	Fenton	Closed	45.00	45.00
89-07-007	Lamp, 21" Handpainted Rosalene Satin	Fenton	Closed	250.00	250.00

Fenton Art Glass Company — 1990-85th Anniversary Collection

		ARTIST	EDITION	ISSUE	QUOTE
90-08-001	Basket, 5 1/2" Trees on Burmese	Fenton	Closed	57.50	57.50
90-08-002	Vase, 9" Trees on Burmese	Fenton	Closed	75.00	75.00
90-08-003	Lamp, 21" Raspberry on Burmese	Fenton	Closed	295.00	295.00
90-08-004	7 pc. Water Set Raspberry on Burmese	Fenton	Closed	275.00	275.00
90-08-005	Basket, 7" Raspberry on Burmese	Fenton	Closed	75.00	75.00
90-08-006	2 pc. Epergne Petite Floral on Burmese	Fenton	Closed	125.00	125.00
90-08-007	Cruet/Stopper Petite Floral on Burmese	Fenton	Closed	85.00	85.00
90-08-008	Vase, Fan, 6" Rose Burmese	Fenton	Closed	49.50	49.50
90-08-009	Vase, 6 1/2" Rose Burmese	Fenton	Closed	45.00	45.00
90-08-010	Lamp, 20" Rose Burmese	Fenton	Closed	250.00	250.00

Fenton Art Glass Company — 1991 Connoisseur Collection

		ARTIST	EDITION	ISSUE	QUOTE
91-09-001	Vase, Floral on Favrene	Fenton	Closed	125.00	125.00
91-09-002	3 pc. Candy Box, Favrene	Fenton	Closed	90.00	90.00
91-09-003	Vase, Fruit on Favrene	Fenton	Closed	125.00	125.00
91-09-004	Basket, Floral on Rosalene	Fenton	Closed	64.00	64.00
91-09-005	Fish, Paperweight, Rosalene	Fenton	Closed	30.00	30.00
91-09-006	Lamp, 20" Roses on Burmese	Fenton	Closed	275.00	275.00
91-09-007	Vase, 7 1/2" Raspberry Burmese	Fenton	Closed	65.00	65.00

Fenton Art Glass Company — 1992 Connoisseur Collection

		ARTIST	EDITION	ISSUE	QUOTE
92-10-001	Vase, 6 1/2" Rasberry Burmese	Fenton	Closed	45.00	45.00
92-10-002	Pitcher, 4 1/2" Berries/Leaves Burmese	Fenton	Closed	65.00	65.00
92-10-003	Vase, 8" "Seascape"	Fenton	Closed	150.00	150.00
92-10-004	Covered Box "Poppy and Daisy"	Fenton	Closed	95.00	95.00
92-10-005	Vase, "Twining Floral" Rosalene Satin	Fenton	Closed	110.00	110.00
92-10-006	Pitcher, 9" Empire on Cranberry	Fenton	Closed	110.00	110.00

Fenton Art Glass Company — 1993 Connoisseur Collection

		ARTIST	EDITION	ISSUE	QUOTE
93-11-001	Owl Figurine, 6" Favrene	Fenton	Closed	95.00	95.00
93-11-002	Amphora w/Stand Favrene	Fenton	Closed	285.00	285.00
93-11-003	Perfume/Stopper "Rose Trellis" Rosalene	Fenton	Closed	95.00	95.00
93-11-004	Vase "Victorian Roses" Persian Blue Opal.	Fenton	Closed	125.00	125.00
93-11-005	Bowl, Ruby Stretch w/Gold Scrolls	Fenton	Closed	95.00	95.00
93-11-006	Vase, 9" "Leaves of Gold" Plum Irid.	Fenton	Closed	175.00	175.00
93-11-007	Lamp, "Spring Woods" Reverse Painted	Fenton	Closed	590.00	590.00

Fenton Art Glass Company — 1993 Family Signature Collection

		ARTIST	EDITION	ISSUE	QUOTE
93-12-001	Vase, 11" Cranberry Dec.	G. Fenton	Closed	110.00	110.00
93-12-002	Basket, "Lilacs"	B. Fenton	Closed	65.00	65.00
93-12-003	Vase, "Vintage" on Plum	D. Fenton	Closed	80.00	80.00
93-12-004	Vase, Al. Thistle/Ruby Carnival	F. Fenton	Closed	105.00	105.00
93-12-005	Vase, "Cottage Scene"	S. Fenton	Closed	90.00	90.00

Fenton Art Glass Company — 1994 Family Signature Collection

		ARTIST	EDITION	ISSUE	QUOTE
94-13-001	Covered Candy "Autumn Leaves"	D. Fenton	Yr.Iss.	60.00	60.00
94-13-002	Vase, Fuschia	G. Fenton	Yr.Iss.	95.00	95.00
94-13-003	Basket "Lilacs"	S. Fenton	Yr.Iss.	65.00	65.00
94-13-004	Vase "Pansies" on Cranberry	B. Fenton	Yr.Iss.	95.00	95.00
94-13-005	Basket, Autumn Gold Opal	F. Fenton	Yr.Iss.	70.00	70.00
94-13-006	Basket, Ruby Carnival	T. Fenton	Yr.Iss.	65.00	65.00
94-13-007	"Gold Pansies" on Cranberry Pitcher	F. Burton	12/94	85.00	85.00
94-13-008	"Windflowers" on Stiegel Green Stretch Basket	M. Reynolds	12/94	65.00	65.00

Fenton Art Glass Company — 1994 Connoisseur Collection

		ARTIST	EDITION	ISSUE	QUOTE
94-14-001	Gold Amberina Vase	M. Reynolds	750	175.00	175.00
94-14-002	"Lattice Rose" Burmese Pitcher	F. Burton	750	165.00	165.00
94-14-003	Cameo Cranberry Bowl	M. Reynolds	500	390.00	390.00
94-14-004	Plum Opalescent Vase	M. Reynolds	750	165.00	165.00
94-14-005	Favrene 7" Vase	M. Reynolds	850	185.00	185.00
94-14-006	Favrene Clock	F. Burton	850	150.00	150.00
94-14-007	Reverse Painted Lamp, Hummingbirds	F. Burton	300	590.00	590.00

Fenton Art Glass Company — Christmas Star Series

		ARTIST	EDITION	ISSUE	QUOTE
94-15-001	"Silent Night" Fairy Light-Ed. #1	F. Burton	1,500	45.00	45.00
94-15-002	"Silent Night" Lamp Light-Ed. #1	F. Burton	500	275.00	275.00
94-15-003	"Silent Night" Egg on Stand-Ed.#1	F. Burton	1,500	45.00	45.00

Fenton Art Glass Company — Christmas Limited Edition Eggs

		ARTIST	EDITION	ISSUE	QUOTE
94-16-001	Magnolia on Gold Egg on Stand	M. Reynolds	1,500	35.00	35.00
94-16-002	Partridge on Ruby Egg on Stand	M. Reynolds	1,500	35.00	35.00

Fenton Art Glass Company — Collectors Club

		ARTIST	EDITION	ISSUE	QUOTE
78-17-001	Cranberry Opalescent Baskets w/variety of spot moulds	Fenton	Closed	20.00	20.00
79-17-002	Vasa Murrhina Vases (Variety of colors)	Fenton	Closed	25.00	25.00
80-17-003	Velva Rose Bubble Optic "Melon" Vases	Fenton	Closed	30.00	30.00
81-17-004	Amethyst w/White Hanging Hearts Vases	Fenton	Closed	37.50	37.50
82-17-005	Overlay Baskets in pastel shades (Swirl Optic)	Fenton	Closed	40.00	40.00
83-17-006	Cranberry Opalescent 1 pc. Fairy Lights	Fenton	Closed	40.00	40.00
84-17-007	Blue Burmese w/peloton Treatment Vases	Fenton	Closed	25.00	25.00
85-17-008	Overlay Vases in Dusty Rose w/Mica Flecks	Fenton	Closed	25.00	25.00
86-17-009	Ruby Iridized Art Glass Vase	Fenton	Closed	30.00	30.00
87-17-010	Dusty Rose Overlay/Peach Blow Interior w/dark blue Crest Vase	Fenton	Closed	38.00	38.00
88-17-011	Teal Green and Milk marble Basket	Fenton	Closed	30.00	30.00
89-17-012	Mulberry Opalescent Basket w/Coin Dot Optic	Fenton	Closed	37.50	37.50
90-17-013	Sea Mist Green Opalescent Fern Optic Basket	Fenton	Closed	40.00	40.00
91-17-014	Rosalene Leaf Basket and Peacock & Dahlia Basket	Fenton	Closed	65.00	65.00
92-17-015	Blue Bubble Optic Vases	Fenton	Closed	35.00	35.00
93-17-016	Cranberry Opalescent "Jonquil" Basket	Fenton	Closed	35.00	35.00
94-17-017	Cranberry Opalescent Jacqueline Pitcher	Fenton	Yr.Iss.	55.00	55.00
94-17-018	Rosalene Tulip Vase-1994 Convention Pc.	Fenton	Yr.Iss.	45.00	45.00

Fitz And Floyd, Inc. — Wonderland Collection

		ARTIST	EDITION	ISSUE	QUOTE
93-01-001	Wonderland Characters, set of 6	R. Havins	3,000	100.00	100.00
93-01-002	A Mad Tea Party, waterglobe	R. Havins	Open	75.00	75.00
93-01-003	Queen's Croquet Game, waterglobe	R. Havins	Open	45.00	45.00

Fitz And Floyd, Inc. — Nutcracker Sweets Collection

		ARTIST	EDITION	ISSUE	QUOTE
93-02-001	Nutcracker Figurines, set of 6	R. Havins	2,500	135.00	135.00
93-02-002	Nutcracker Sweets, waterglobe	R. Havins	Retrd.	45.00	45.00

Fitz And Floyd, Inc. — A Christmas Carol Collection

		ARTIST	EDITION	ISSUE	QUOTE
93-03-001	Christmas Carol Figurines, set of 11	T. Kerr	2,500	175.00	175.00

		ARTIST	EDITION	ISSUE	QUOTE
Fitz And Floyd, Inc.	**Holiday Hamlet®-Lighted Houses**				
93-04-001	Stocking Stuffer's Workshop	V. Balcou	Open	45.00	45.00
93-04-002	Toymaker's Workshop	V. Balcou	Open	45.00	45.00
93-04-003	Doctor's Office	V. Balcou	Open	75.00	75.00
93-04-004	Holiday Manor	V. Balcou	Open	75.00	75.00
93-04-005	Holiday Hamlet Chapel	V. Balcou	Open	75.00	75.00
93-04-006	Dollmaker's Cottage	V. Balcou	Open	125.00	125.00
93-04-007	Tavern in the Woods	V. Balcou	Open	125.00	125.00
93-04-008	Railroad Station	V. Balcou	Closed	125.00	125.00
94-04-009	Christmas Pageant Stage	V. Balcou	Open	75.00	75.00
94-04-010	Snowman Supply Hut	V. Balcou	Open	65.00	65.00
94-04-011	World's Best Snowman	V. Balcou	Open	55.00	55.00
94-04-012	Whistlestop Junction Train Stop	V. Balcou	Open	65.00	65.00
94-04-013	Mr. Winterberry's Pie Shop	V. Balcou	2,500	100.00	100.00
Fitz And Floyd, Inc.	**Holiday Hamlet®-Accessories**				
93-05-001	Christmas Tree, small	V. Balcou	Open	30.00	30.00
93-05-002	Christmas Tree, large	V. Balcou	Open	45.00	45.00
93-05-003	Village Sign	V. Balcou	Open	40.00	40.00
93-05-004	Village Square Clock	V. Balcou	Open	50.00	50.00
93-05-005	Silent Night Singers	V. Balcou	Open	30.00	30.00
93-05-006	Carols in the Snow	V. Balcou	Open	30.00	30.00
93-05-007	Blizzard Express Train	V. Balcou	Open	95.00	95.00
94-05-008	Hand Car	V. Balcou	Open	35.00	35.00
Fitz And Floyd, Inc.	**Holiday Hamlet®-Figurines**				
93-06-001	Gathering Pine Boughs	V. Balcou	Open	10.00	10.00
93-06-002	Pastry Vendor	V. Balcou	Open	10.00	10.00
93-06-003	Baby Squirrel	V. Balcou	Open	15.00	15.00
93-06-004	Dollmaker's Apprentice	V. Balcou	Open	15.00	15.00
93-06-005	Bell Choir Fox	V. Balcou	Open	10.00	10.00
93-06-006	The Parson	V. Balcou	Open	10.00	10.00
93-06-007	The Conductor	V. Balcou	Open	10.00	10.00
94-06-008	The Porter	V. Balcou	Open	25.00	25.00
93-06-009	Dr. B. Well	V. Balcou	Open	15.00	15.00
93-06-010	Dollmaker	V. Balcou	Open	15.00	15.00
93-06-011	Dr. Quack & Patient	V. Balcou	Open	15.00	15.00
93-06-012	Christmas Treats	V. Balcou	Open	15.00	15.00
93-06-013	Gathering Apples	V. Balcou	Open	15.00	15.00
93-06-014	Bell Choir Bunny	V. Balcou	Open	15.00	15.00
93-06-015	Squirrel Family	V. Balcou	Open	15.00	15.00
93-06-016	Skaters	V. Balcou	Open	20.00	20.00
93-06-017	Welcome Banner	V. Balcou	Open	20.00	20.00
93-06-018	Christmas Carolers	V. Balcou	Open	20.00	20.00
93-06-019	Tying the Christmas Garland	V. Balcou	Open	20.00	20.00
93-06-020	Nanny Rabbit & Bunnies	V. Balcou	Open	20.00	20.00
93-06-021	Delivering Gifts	V. Balcou	Open	20.00	20.00
93-06-022	Old Royal Elf	V. Balcou	Open	20.00	20.00
93-06-023	Santa Claus	V. Balcou	Open	25.00	25.00
93-06-024	Waving Elf	V. Balcou	Open	10.00	10.00
93-06-025	Mrs. Grizzly	V. Balcou	Open	20.00	20.00
93-06-027	Mr. Grizzly	V. Balcou	Open	20.00	20.00
93-06-028	Welcoming Elf	V. Balcou	Open	10.00	10.00
94-06-029	Little Angels	V. Balcou	Open	30.00	30.00
94-06-030	Poor Shepherds	V. Balcou	Open	15.00	15.00
94-06-031	Three Wisemen	V. Balcou	Open	20.00	20.00
94-06-032	Blessed Mother/Joseph Players	V. Balcou	Open	25.00	25.00
94-06-033	Proud Mother/Father	V. Balcou	Open	20.00	20.00
94-06-034	Mr. Winterberry, Pie Vendor	V. Balcou	2,500	25.00	25.00
93-06-035	Christmas Carolers, waterglobe	V. Balcou	Open	45.00	45.00
94-06-036	Holiday Hamlet, waterglobe	V. Balcou	Open	75.00	75.00
Fitz And Floyd, Inc.	**Important Women**				
93-07-001	Betsy Ross, teapot	T. Kerr	1,777	75.00	75.00
94-07-002	Queen Victoria, teapot	T. Kerr	1,750	75.00	75.00
95-07-003	Cleopatra, teapot	T. Kerr	1,750	75.00	75.00
Fitz And Floyd, Inc.	**Figures From History**				
92-08-001	Christopher Columbus, teapot	T. Kerr	7,500	60.00	60.00
93-08-002	George Washington, teapot	T. Kerr	5,000	75.00	75.00
94-08-003	Napoleon Boneparte, teapot	T. Kerr	2,250	75.00	75.00
95-08-004	Winston Churchill, teapot	T. Kerr	2,500	75.00	75.00
Fitz And Floyd, Inc.	**Famous Landmarks of the World**				
93-09-001	The White House, teapot	T. Kerr	5,000	75.00	75.00
94-09-002	St. Basil's Cathedral, teapot	T. Kerr	5,000	75.00	75.00
95-09-003	Taj Mahal, teapot	T. Kerr	3,500	75.00	75.00
Fitz And Floyd, Inc.	**Fables & Fairytales**				
93-10-001	Bremen Town Musicians, teapot	V. Balcou	1,500	75.00	75.00
94-10-002	Three Little Pigs, teapot	T. Kerr	1,500	75.00	75.00
95-10-003	Old Woman in the Shoe, teapot	T. Kerr	1,500	75.00	75.00
Fitz And Floyd, Inc.	**Musical Maestros**				
93-11-001	Wolfgang Amadeus Mozart, teapot	T. Kerr	5,000	75.00	75.00
94-11-002	Ludwig Van Beethoven, teapot	T. Kerr	2,500	75.00	75.00
95-11-003	Johann Sebastian Bach, teapot	T. Kerr	2,500	75.00	75.00
Fitz And Floyd, Inc.	**Literary Masters**				
94-12-001	William Shakespeare, teapot	T. Kerr	5,000	75.00	75.00
95-12-002	Edgar Allen Poe, teapot	T. Kerr	3,500	75.00	75.00
Fitz And Floyd, Inc.	**Famous American Landmarks**				
94-13-001	Statue of Liberty, teapot	T. Kerr	5,000	75.00	75.00
Fitz And Floyd, Inc.	**Places of Worship**				
95-14-001	Notre Dame Cathedral, teapot	T. Kerr	7,500	95.00	95.00
Fitz And Floyd, Inc.	**Woodland Santa Collection**				
91-15-001	Woodland Santa, waterglobe	V. Balcou	Open	75.00	75.00
Fitz And Floyd, Inc.	**Night Before Christmas**				
94-16-001	Night Before Christmas, waterglobe	V. Balcou	Open	85.00	85.00
Flambro Imports	**Emmett Kelly, Jr. Figurines**				
81-01-001	Looking Out To See	Undis.	12,000	75.00	12-2900.
81-01-002	Sweeping Up	Undis.	12,000	75.00	700-1700
82-01-003	Wet Paint	Undis.	15,000	80.00	480-600.
82-01-004	The Thinker	Undis.	15,000	60.00	900-1800
82-01-005	Why Me?	Undis.	15,000	65.00	358-800.
83-01-006	The Balancing Act	Undis.	10,000	75.00	550-900.
83-01-007	Wishful Thinking	Undis.	10,000	65.00	500-700.
83-01-008	Hole In The Sole	Undis.	10,000	75.00	500-650.
83-01-009	Balloons For Sale	Undis.	10,000	75.00	230-700.
83-01-010	Spirit of Christmas I	Undis.	3,500	125.00	14-3600.
84-01-011	Eating Cabbage	Undis.	12,000	75.00	450.00

		ARTIST	EDITION	ISSUE	QUOTE
84-01-012	Big Business	Undis.	9,500	110.00	850.00
84-01-013	Piano Player	Undis.	9,500	160.00	400-750.
84-01-014	Spirit of Christmas II	Undis.	3,500	270.00	390-685.
85-01-015	Man's Best Friend	Undis.	9,500	98.00	550.00
85-01-016	No Strings Attached	Undis.	9,500	98.00	220-375.
85-01-017	In The Spotlight	Undis.	12,000	103.00	150-375.
85-01-018	Emmett's Fan	Undis.	12,000	80.00	550.00
85-01-019	Spirit of Christmas III	Undis.	3,500	220.00	240-700.
86-01-020	The Entertainers	Undis.	12,000	120.00	180-200.
86-01-021	Cotton Candy	Undis.	12,000	98.00	275-700.
86-01-022	Bedtime	Undis.	12,000	98.00	110-225.
86-01-023	Making New Friends	Undis.	9,500	140.00	210-275.
86-01-024	Fair Game	Undis.	2,500	450.00	14-1600.
86-01-025	Spirit of Christmas IV	Undis.	3,500	150.00	220-280.
87-01-026	On The Road Again	Undis.	9,500	109.00	400.00
87-01-027	My Favorite Things	Undis.	9,500	109.00	350-700.
87-01-028	Saturday Night	Undis.	7,500	153.00	290-600.
87-01-029	Toothache	Undis.	12,000	98.00	98.00
87-01-030	Spirit of Christmas V	Undis.	2,400	170.00	220-280.
88-01-031	Over a Barrel	Undis.	9,500	130.00	300-400.
88-01-032	Wheeler Dealer	Undis.	7,500	160.00	160.00
88-01-033	Dining Out	Undis.	12,000	120.00	300-400.
88-01-034	Amen	Undis.	12,000	120.00	120-400.
88-01-035	Spirit of Christmas VI	Undis.	2,400	194.00	200-700.
89-01-036	Making Up	Undis.	7,500	200.00	250.00
89-01-037	No Loitering	Undis	7,500	200.00	264.00
89-01-038	Hurdy-Gurdy Man	Undis.	9,500	150.00	175-250.
89-01-039	65th Birthday Commemorative	Undis.	1,989	275.00	905-2700
90-01-040	Watch the Birdie	Undis.	9,500	200.00	225.00
90-01-041	Convention-Bound	Undis.	7,500	225.00	242-300.
90-01-042	Balloons for Sale II	Undis.	7,500	250.00	250-300.
90-01-043	Misfortune?	Undis.	3,500	400.00	363-400.
90-01-044	Spirit Of Christmas VII	Undis.	3,500	275.00	242-350.
91-01-045	Finishing Touch	Undis.	7,500	245.00	245.00
91-01-046	Artist At Work	Undis.	7,500	295.00	295.00
91-01-047	Follow The Leader	Undis.	7,500	200.00	200.00
91-01-048	Spirit Of Christmas VIII	Undis.	3,500	250.00	310.00
92-01-049	No Use Crying	Undis.	7,500	200.00	200.00
92-01-050	Ready-Set-Go	Undis.	7,500	200.00	200.00
92-01-051	Peanut Butter?	Undis.	7,500	200.00	200.00
93-01-052	Kittens For Sale	Undis.	7,500	190.00	190.00
93-01-053	World Traveler	Undis.	7,500	190.00	190.00
93-01-054	After The Parade	Undis.	7,500	190.00	190.00
93-01-055	Spirit of Christmas IX	Undis.	3,500	200.00	200.00
93-01-056	Spirit of Christmas X	Undis.	3,500	200.00	200.00
94-01-057	Spirit of Christmas XI	Undis.	3,500	200.00	200.00
94-01-058	Forest Friends	Undis.	7,500	190.00	190.00
94-01-059	The Lion Tamer	Undis.	7,500	190.00	190.00
94-01-060	Let Him Eat Cake	Undis.	Retrd.	300.00	300-500.
Flambro Imports	**Circus World Museum Clowns**				
85-02-001	Paul Jerome (Hobo)	Undis.	9,500	80.00	80-150.
85-02-002	Paul Jung (Neat)	Undis.	9,500	80.00	110-120.
85-02-003	Felix Adler (Grotesque)	Undis.	9,500	80.00	80-110.
87-02-004	Paul Jerome with Dog	Undis.	7,500	90.00	90.00
87-02-005	Paul Jung, Sitting	Undis.	7,500	90.00	90.00
87-02-006	Felix Adler with Balloon	Undis.	7,500	90.00	90.00
87-02-007	Abe Goldstein, Keystone Kop	Undis.	7,500	90.00	90.00
Flambro Imports	**Emmett Kelly, Jr. Miniatures**				
86-03-001	Looking Out To See	Undis.	Retrd.	25.00	60-175.
86-03-002	Sweeping Up	Undis.	Retrd.	25.00	50-125.
86-03-003	Wet Paint	Undis.	Retrd.	25.00	50-75.00
86-03-004	Why Me?	Undis.	Retrd.	25.00	54-65.00
86-03-005	The Thinker	Undis.	Retrd.	25.00	42-70.00
86-03-006	Balancing Act	Undis.	Retrd.	25.00	50-100.
86-03-007	Hole in the Sole	Undis.	Retrd.	25.00	66-125.
86-03-008	Balloons for Sale	Undis.	Retrd.	25.00	50-55.00
86-03-009	Wishful Thinking	Undis.	Retrd.	25.00	55.00
87-03-010	Emmett's Fan	Undis.	Retrd.	30.00	40-50.00
87-03-011	Eating Cabbage	Undis.	Retrd.	30.00	40-65.00
88-03-012	Spirit of Christmas I	Undis.	Retrd.	40.00	90-125.
88-03-013	Big Business	Undis.	Numbrd	35.00	38.50
90-03-014	Saturday Night	Undis.	Numbrd	50.00	50.00
90-03-015	My Favorite Things	Undis.	Numbrd	45.00	45.00
90-03-016	Spirit Of Christmas III	Undis.	Retrd.	50.00	90.00
89-03-017	Man's Best Friend?	Undis.	Numbrd	35.00	35.00
89-03-018	Cotton Candy	Undis.	Retrd.	30.00	50.00
91-03-019	In The Spotlight	Undis.	Numbrd	35.00	35.00
91-03-020	No Strings Attached	Undis.	Numbrd	35.00	35.00
92-03-021	Spirit of Christmas II	Undis.	Numbrd	50.00	50.00
92-03-022	Making New Friends	Undis.	Numbrd	40.00	40.00
92-03-023	Piano Player	Undis.	Numbrd	50.00	50.00
92-03-024	On the Road Again	Undis.	Numbrd	35.00	35.00
93-03-025	Spirit of Christmas IV	Undis.	Numbrd	40.00	40.00
Flambro Imports	**Annual Emmett Kelly Jr. Nutcracker**				
90-04-001	1990 Nutcracker	Undis.	Retrd.	50.00	100.00
Flambro Imports	**Emmett Kelly Jr. Metal Sculptures**				
91-05-001	Carousel Rider	Undis.	5,000	125.00	125.00
91-05-002	The Magician	Undis.	5,000	125.00	125.00
91-05-003	Emmett's Pooches	Undis.	5,000	125.00	125.00
91-05-004	Balancing Act, Too	Undis.	5,000	125.00	125.00
Flambro Imports	**Emmett Kelly Jr. A Day At The Fair**				
90-06-001	Step Right Up	Undis.	Retrd.	65.00	65.00
90-06-002	Three For A Dime	Undis.	Retrd.	65.00	65.00
90-06-003	Look At You	Undis.	Retrd.	65.00	65.00
90-06-004	75 Please	Undis.	Retrd.	65.00	65.00
90-06-005	The Stilt Man	Undis.	Retrd.	65.00	65.00
90-06-006	Ride The Wild Mouse	Undis.	Retrd.	65.00	65.00
90-06-007	You Can Do It, Emmett	Undis.	Retrd.	65.00	65.00
90-06-008	Thanks Emmett	Undis.	Retrd.	65.00	65.00
90-06-009	You Go First, Emmett	Undis.	Retrd.	65.00	65.00
91-06-010	The Trouble With Hot Dogs	Undis.	Retrd.	65.00	65.00
91-06-011	Popcorn!	Undis.	Retrd.	65.00	65.00
91-06-012	Coin Toss	Undis.	Retrd.	65.00	65.00
92-06-013	Stilt Man	Undis.	Retrd.	65.00	65.00
Flambro Imports	**Emmett Kelly Jr. Appearance Figurine**				
92-07-001	Now Appearing	Undis.	Open	100.00	100.00
93-07-002	The Vigilante	Undis.	Open	75.00	75.00

		ARTIST	EDITION	ISSUE	QUOTE
Flambro Imports		**Emmett Kelly Jr. Members Only Figurine**			
90-08-001	Merry-Go-Round	Undis.	Closed	125.00	450.00
91-08-002	10 Years Of Collecting	Undis.	Closed	100.00	100-180.
92-08-003	All Aboard	Undis.	Closed	75.00	120.00
93-08-004	Ringmaster	Undis.	Closed	125.00	125.00
94-08-005	Birthday Mail	Undis.	Yr.Iss.	100.00	100.00
Flambro Imports		**Emmett Kelly Jr. Real Rags Collection**			
93-09-001	Checking His List	Undis.	Open	100.00	100.00
93-09-002	Thinker II	Undis.	Open	120.00	120.00
93-09-003	Sweeping Up II	Undis.	Open	100.00	100.00
93-09-004	Looking Out To See II	Undis.	Open	100.00	100.00
93-09-005	Big Business II	Undis.	Open	140.00	140.00
94-09-006	A Good Likeness	Undis.	3,000	120.00	120.00
94-09-007	Eating Cabbage 2	Undis.	3,000	100.00	100.00
94-09-008	On in Two	Undis.	3,000	100.00	100.00
94-09-009	Rudolph Has A Red Nose, Too	Undis.	3,000	135.00	135.00
Flambro Imports		**EKJ Professionals**			
87-10-001	Dentist	Undis.	Open	50.00	50.00
87-10-002	Doctor	Undis.	Open	50.00	50.00
87-10-003	Executive	Undis.	Open	50.00	50.00
87-10-004	Accountant	Undis.	Retrd.	50.00	50.00
87-10-005	Teacher	Undis.	Open	50.00	50.00
87-10-006	Engineer	Undis.	Open	50.00	50.00
87-10-007	Lawyer	Undis.	Open	50.00	50.00
87-10-008	Stockbrocker	Undis.	Open	50.00	50.00
88-10-010	Bowler	Undis.	Retrd.	50.00	50.00
88-10-010	Skier	Undis.	Retrd.	50.00	50.00
88-10-011	Golfer	Undis.	Open	50.00	50.00
88-10-012	Policeman	Undis.	Retrd.	50.00	50.00
88-10-013	Fireman	Undis.	Retrd.	50.00	50.00
88-10-014	Mailman	Undis.	Open	50.00	50.00
90-10-015	The Putt	Undis.	Open	50.00	50.00
90-10-016	Fisherman	Undis.	Open	50.00	50.00
90-10-017	Hunter	Undis.	Open	50.00	50.00
90-10-018	Computer Whiz	Undis.	Open	50.00	50.00
90-10-019	Photographer	Undis.	Open	50.00	50.00
91-10-020	Pharmacist	Undis.	Open	50.00	50.00
91-10-021	The Chef	Undis.	Retrd.	50.00	50.00
91-10-022	Barber	Undis.	Open	50.00	50.00
91-10-023	Painter	Undis.	Open	50.00	50.00
91-10-024	Plumber	Undis.	Retrd.	50.00	50.00
91-10-025	Carpenter	Undis.	Open	50.00	50.00
93-10-026	On Maneuvers	Undis.	Open	50.00	50.00
93-10-027	Pilot	Undis.	Open	50.00	50.00
93-10-028	Realtor	Undis.	Open	50.00	50.00
93-10-029	Veterinarian	Undis.	Open	50.00	50.00
Flambro Imports		**Little Emmetts**			
94-11-001	EKJ, Age 1	Undis.	Open	9.00	9.00
94-11-002	EKJ, Age2	Undis.	Open	9.50	9.50
94-11-003	EKJ, Age 3	Undis.	Open	12.00	12.00
94-11-004	EKJ, Age 4	Undis.	Open	12.00	12.00
94-11-005	EKJ, Age 5	Undis.	Open	15.00	15.00
94-11-006	EKJ, Age 6	Undis.	Open	15.00	15.00
94-11-007	EKJ, Age 7	Undis.	Open	17.00	17.00
94-11-008	EKJ, Age 8	Undis.	Open	21.00	21.00
94-11-009	EKJ, Age 9	Undis.	Open	22.00	22.00
94-11-010	EKJ, Age 10	Undis.	Open	25.00	25.00
94-11-011	Little Emmett, Counting Lession (Musical)	Undis.	Open	30.00	30.00
94-11-012	Little Emmett, You've Got a Friend (Musical)	Undis.	Open	33.00	33.00
94-11-013	Little Emmett, Country Road (Musical)	Undis.	Open	35.00	35.00
94-11-014	Little Emmett, Raindrops (Musical)	Undis.	Open	35.00	35.00
94-11-015	Playful Bookends	Undis.	Open	40.00	40.00
94-11-016	Little Artist Picture Frame	Undis.	Open	22.00	22.00
94-11-017	Little Emmett w/Blackboard	Undis.	Open	30.00	30.00
94-11-018	Little Emmett Fishing	Undis.	Open	35.00	35.00
94-11-019	Little Emmett Shadow Show	Undis.	Open	40.00	40.00
95-11-020	Little Emmett Clown Show	Undis.	Open	50.00	50.00
95-11-021	Little Emmett Carolling	Undis.	Open	40.00	40.00
Flambro Imports		**Pleasantville 1893**			
90-12-001	Sweet Shoppe & Bakery	J. Berg Victor	Open	40.00	40.00
90-12-002	Toy Store	J. Berg Victor	Open	30.00	30.00
90-12-003	1st Church Of Pleasantville	J. Berg Victor	Retrd.	35.00	35.00
90-12-004	Department Store	J. Berg Victor	Retrd.	25.00	25.00
90-12-005	Pleasantville Library	J. Berg Victor	Open	32.00	32.00
90-12-006	The Band Stand	J. Berg Victor	Retrd.	12.00	12.00
90-12-007	The Gerber House	J. Berg Victor	Retrd.	30.00	30.00
90-12-008	Reverend Littlefield's House	J. Berg Victor	Open	34.00	34.00
90-12-009	Mason's Hotel and Saloon	J. Berg Victor	Open	35.00	35.00
91-12-010	Methodist Church	J. Berg Victor	Open	40.00	40.00
91-12-012	Fire House	J. Berg Victor	Open	40.00	40.00
91-12-012	Court House	J. Berg Victor	Open	36.00	36.00
91-12-013	School Houe	J. Berg Victor	Open	36.00	36.00
92-12-014	Railroad Station	J. Berg Victor	Open	40.00	40.00
92-12-015	Bank/Real Estate Office	J. Berg Victor	Open	36.00	36.00
92-12-016	Apothecary/Ice Cream Shop	J. Berg Victor	Open	36.00	36.00
92-12-017	Tubbs, Jr. House	J. Berg Victor	Open	40.00	40.00
92-12-018	Miss Fountains Boarding House	J. Berg Victor	Open	48.00	48.00
92-12-019	Covered Bridge	J. Berg Victor	Open	36.00	36.00
92-12-020	Library	J. Berg Victor	Open	32.00	32.00
92-12-021	Post Office	J. Berg Victor	Open	40.00	40.00
92-12-022	Ashbey House	J. Berg Victor	Open	40.00	40.00
93-12-023	Balcomb's Farm (out buildings)	J. Berg Victor	Open	40.00	40.00
93-12-024	Balcomb's Barn	J. Berg Victor	Open	40.00	40.00
93-12-025	Balcomb's Farmhouse	J. Berg Victor	Open	40.00	40.00
93-12-026	Blacksmith Shop	J. Berg Victor	Open	40.00	40.00
93-12-027	Livery Stable and Residence	J. Berg Victor	Open	40.00	40.00
94-12-028	Gazebo/Bandstand	J. Berg Victor	Open	25.00	25.00
94-12-029	Sacred Heart Catholic Church	J. Berg Victor	Open	40.00	40.00
94-12-030	Sacred Heart Rectory	J. Berg Victor	Open	40.00	40.00
Flambro Imports		**Pleasantville 1893 Members Only**			
92-13-001	Pleasantville Gazette Building	J. Berg Victor	Open	30.00	30.00
Flambro		**Pocket Dragons**			
93-14-001	A Big Hug	R. Musgrave	Open	35.00	35.00
94-14-002	A Book My Size	R. Musgrave	Open	30.00	30.00
92-14-003	A Different Drummer	R. Musgrave	Retrd.	32.50	32.50
89-14-004	A Good Egg	R. Musgrave	Retrd.	36.50	101.00
91-14-005	A Joyful Noise	R. Musgrave	Open	16.50	16.50
94-14-006	A Little Security	R. Musgrave	Open	N/A	N/A
89-14-007	Attack	R. Musgrave	Retrd.	45.00	65-70.00
89-14-008	Baby Brother	R. Musgrave	Retrd.	19.50	35.00
93-14-009	Bath Time	R. Musgrave	Open	90.00	90.00
92-14-010	Bubbles	R. Musgrave	Open	55.00	55.00
94-14-011	Butterfly Kissess	R. Musgrave	Open	N/A	N/A
94-14-012	Candy Cane	R. Musgrave	Open	55.00	55.00
94-14-013	Coffee Please	R. Musgrave	Open	N/A	N/A
94-14-014	Dance Partner	R. Musgrave	Open	N/A	N/A
89-14-015	Do I Have To?	R. Musgrave	Open	45.00	45.00
91-14-016	Dragons in the Attic	R. Musgrave	Open	120.00	120.00
89-14-017	Drowsy Dragon	R. Musgrave	Open	27.50	27.50
89-14-018	Flowers For You	R. Musgrave	Retrd.	42.50	65.00
91-14-019	Friends	R. Musgrave	Open	55.00	55.00
93-14-020	Fuzzy Ears	R. Musgrave	Open	16.50	16.50
89-14-021	Gargoyle Hoping For Raspberry Teacakes	R. Musgrave	Retrd.	139.50	425-485.
94-14-022	Gargoyles Just Wanna Have Fun	R. Musgrave	Open	30.00	30.00
93-14-023	I Ate the Whole Thing	R. Musgrave	Open	32.50	32.50
91-14-024	I Didn't Mean To	R. Musgrave	Open	32.50	32.50
91-14-025	I'm A Kitty	R. Musgrave	Retrd.	37.50	55.00
94-14-026	In Trouble Again	R. Musgrave	Open	35.00	35.00
94-14-027	It's Dark Out There	R. Musgrave	Open	45.00	45.00
94-14-028	It's Magic	R. Musgrave	Open	N/A	N/A
93-14-029	Let's Make Cookies	R. Musgrave	Open	90.00	90.00
93-14-030	Little Bit (lapel pin)	R. Musgrave	Open	16.50	16.50
93-14-031	Little Jewel (brooch)	R. Musgrave	Retrd.	19.50	19.50
89-14-032	Look at Me	R. Musgrave	Retrd.	42.50	75-115.
92-14-033	Mitten Toes	R. Musgrave	Open	16.50	16.50
94-14-034	My Big Cookie	R. Musgrave	Open	35.00	35.00
92-14-035	Nap Time	R. Musgrave	Open	15.00	15.00
89-14-036	New Bunny Shoes	R. Musgrave	Retrd.	28.50	60.00
89-14-037	No Ugly Monsters Allowed	R. Musgrave	Retrd.	47.50	80.00
93-14-038	Oh Goody!	R. Musgrave	Open	16.50	16.50
90-14-039	One-Size-Fits-All	R. Musgrave	Retrd.	16.50	35.00
92-14-040	Oops!	R. Musgrave	Open	16.50	16.50
89-14-041	Opera Gargoyle	R. Musgrave	Retrd.	85.00	125-185.
92-14-042	Percy	R. Musgrave	Open	70.00	70.00
91-14-043	Pick Me Up	R. Musgrave	Open	16.50	16.50
89-14-044	Pink 'n' Pretty	R. Musgrave	Retrd.	23.90	40.00
94-14-045	Playing Dress Up	R. Musgrave	Open	30.00	30.00
91-14-046	Playing Footsie	R. Musgrave	Retrd.	16.50	16.50
89-14-047	Pocket Dragon Countersign	R. Musgrave	Retrd.	50.00	100-150.
92-14-048	Pocket Posey	R. Musgrave	Open	16.50	16.50
93-14-049	Pocket Rider (brooch)	R. Musgrave	Open	19.50	19.50
91-14-050	Practice Makes Perfect	R. Musgrave	Retrd.	32.50	55.00
91-14-051	Putt Putt	R. Musgrave	Retrd.	37.50	55.00
94-14-052	Raiding the Cookie Jar	R. Musgrave	Open	200.00	200.00
93-14-053	Reading the Good Parts	R. Musgrave	Open	70.00	70.00
91-14-054	Scales of Injustice	R. Musgrave	Open	45.00	45.00
89-14-055	Scribbles	R. Musgrave	Retrd.	32.50	45.00
89-14-056	Sea Dragon	R. Musgrave	Retrd.	45.00	75-150.
89-14-057	Sir Nigel Smythebe-Smoke	R. Musgrave	Retrd.	120.00	120-160.
91-14-058	Sleepy Head	R. Musgrave	Open	37.50	37.50
89-14-059	Stalking the Cookie Jar	R. Musgrave	Open	27.50	27.50
89-14-060	Storytime at Wizard's House	R. Musgrave	Retrd.	375.00	450-475.
94-14-061	Snuggles	R. Musgrave	Open	N/A	N/A
90-14-062	Tag-A-Long	R. Musgrave	Retrd.	15.00	35-50.00
89-14-063	Teddy Magic	R. Musgrave	Retrd.	85.00	130.00
90-14-064	The Apprentice	R. Musgrave	Retrd.	22.50	22.50
93-14-065	The Book End	R. Musgrave	Open	90.00	90.00
89-14-066	The Gallant Defender	R. Musgrave	Retrd.	36.50	75-80.00
92-14-067	The Juggler	R. Musgrave	Open	32.50	32.50
92-14-068	The Library Cat	R. Musgrave	Open	38.50	38.50
89-14-069	The Pocket Minstrel	R. Musgrave	Retrd.	36.50	75.00
91-14-070	Thimble Foot	R. Musgrave	Retrd.	38.50	38.50
91-14-071	Tickle	R. Musgrave	Open	27.50	27.50
89-14-072	Toady Goldtrayler	R. Musgrave	Retrd.	55.00	90.00
93-14-073	Treasure	R. Musgrave	Open	90.00	90.00
91-14-074	Twinkle Toes	R. Musgrave	Open	16.50	16.50
92-14-075	Under the Bed	R. Musgrave	2500	450.00	450.00
89-14-076	Walkies	R. Musgrave	Retrd.	65.00	135.00
93-14-077	We're Very Brave	R. Musgrave	Open	37.50	37.50
89-14-078	What Cookie?	R. Musgrave	Open	38.50	38.50
89-14-079	Wizardry for Fun and Profit	R. Musgrave	Retrd.	375.00	450-475.
93-14-080	You Can't Make Me	R. Musgrave	Open	15.00	15.00
89-14-081	Your Paint is Stirred	R. Musgrave	Retrd.	42.50	95.00
92-14-082	Zoom Zoom	R. Musgrave	Open	37.50	37.50
Flambro		**Christmas Editions**			
92-15-001	A Pocket-Sized Tree	R. Musgrave	Retrd.	18.95	65-90.00
93-15-002	Christmas Angel	R. Musgrave	Retrd.	45.00	65.00
91-15-003	I've Been Very Good	R. Musgrave	Open	37.50	65-88.00
89-15-004	Putting Me on the Tree	R. Musgrave	Retrd.	52.50	75.00
94-15-005	Dear Santa	R. Musgrave	Retrd.	50.00	50.00
Flambro		**Pocket Dragon Members Only Pieces**			
91-16-001	A Spot of Tea Won't You Join Us (set)	R. Musgrave	Retrd.	75.00	200-250.
91-16-002	Wizard's House Print	R. Musgrave	Retrd.	39.95	65.00
92-16-003	Book Nook	R. Musgrave	Retrd.	140.00	195.00
93-16-004	Pen Pals	R. Musgrave	Retrd.	90.00	135.00
94-16-005	The Best Seat in the House	R. Musgrave	5/95	75.00	75.00
Flambro		**Pocket Dragon Collector Club**			
91-17-001	Collecting Butterflies	R. Musgrave	Retrd.	Gift	85.00
92-17-002	The Key to My Heart	R. Musgrave	Retrd.	Gift	40-95.00
93-17-003	Want A Bite?	R. Musgrave	Retrd.	Gift	50.00
93-17-004	Bitsy	R. Musgrave	Retrd.	Gift	N/A
94-17-005	Friendship Pin	R. Musgrave	5/95	Gift	N/A
94-17-006	Blue Ribbon Dragon	R. Musgrave	5/95	Gift	N/A
Forma Vitrum™		**Vitreville™**			
93-01-001	Pastor's Place 11101	B. Job	Open	65.00	65.00
93-01-002	Candymaker's Cottage 11102	B. Job	Open	65.00	65.00
93-01-003	Doctor's Domain 11201	B. Job	Open	70.00	70.00
93-01-004	Painter's Place 11202	B. Job	Open	70.00	70.00
93-01-005	Roofer's Roost 11203	B. Job	12/94	70.00	70.00
93-01-006	Tailor's Townhouse 11204	B. Job	Open	70.00	70.00
93-01-007	Tiny Town Church 11501	B. Job	Open	95.00	95.00
93-01-008	Country Church 11502	B. Job	12,500	100.00	100.00
93-01-009	Candlemaker's Delight 11801	B. Job	Open	60.00	60.00
93-01-010	Breadman's Bakery 11301	B. Job	Open	70.00	70.00
94-01-011	Thompson's Drug 11302	B. Job	5,000	140.00	140.00

		ARTIST	EDITION	ISSUE	QUOTE
94-01-012	Maplewood Elementary School 11401	B. Job	Open	100.00	100.00
94-01-013	"Vitreville" Post Office 11402	B. Job	Open	90.00	90.00
94-01-014	"Trinity Church" 11511	B. Job	7,000	130.00	130.00
Forma Vitrum™	**Coastal Classics**				
93-02-001	Michigan Lighthouse 21001	B. Job	Open	50.00	50.00
93-02-002	Maine Lighthouse 21002	B. Job	Open	50.00	50.00
93-02-003	Carolina Lighthouse 21003	B. Job	Open	65.00	65.00
94-02-004	Sailor's Knoll Lighthouse 21011	B. Job	Open	65.00	65.00
94-02-005	Lookout Point Lighthouse 21012	B. Job	Open	60.00	60.00
Forma Vitrum™	**Woodland Village™**				
93-03-001	Rabbit House 31001	B. Job	Open	90.00	90.00
93-03-002	Racoon House 31002	B. Job	Open	80.00	80.00
93-03-003	Badger House 31003	B. Job	Open	80.00	80.00
93-03-004	Owl House 31004	B. Job	Open	80.00	80.00
93-03-005	Chipmunk House 31005	B. Job	Open	80.00	80.00
Forma Vitrum™	**Special Production**				
93-04-001	The Bavarian Church 11503	B. Job	Retrd.	90.00	90.00
93-04-002	Pillars of Faith Church 11504	B. Job	Retrd.	90.00	90.00
Franklin Mint	**Joys of Childhood**				
76-01-001	Hopscotch	N. Rockwell	3,700	120.00	175.00
76-01-002	The Fishing Hole	N. Rockwell	3,700	120.00	175.00
76-01-003	Dressing Up	N. Rockwell	3,700	120.00	175.00
76-01-004	The Stilt Walker	N. Rockwell	3,700	120.00	175.00
76-01-005	Trick or Treat	N. Rockwell	3,700	120.00	175.00
76-01-006	Time Out	N. Rockwell	3,700	120.00	175.00
76-01-007	The Marble Champ	N. Rockwell	3,700	120.00	175.00
76-01-008	The Nurse	N. Rockwell	3,700	120.00	175.00
76-01-009	Ride 'Em Cowboy	N. Rockwell	3,700	120.00	175.00
76-01-010	Coasting Along	N. Rockwell	3,700	120.00	175.00
Fraser International	**Countryside in Miniature Collection**				
88-01-001	Hawthorn Cottage 01	I. Fraser	Retrd.	21.00	21.00
88-01-002	Irish Cottage 03	I. Fraser	Retrd.	25.00	25.00
88-01-003	Bluebell Cottage 04	I. Fraser	Retrd.	27.00	27.00
88-01-004	Smugglers Cove 05	I. Fraser	Retrd.	25.00	25.00
88-01-005	The Mill 06	I. Fraser	Retrd.	25.00	25.00
88-01-006	Sweet Hope 07	I. Fraser	Retrd.	32.00	32.00
88-01-007	Myrtle Cottage 08	I. Fraser	Retrd.	28.00	28.00
88-01-008	The Blacksmith 09	I. Fraser	Retrd.	28.00	28.00
88-01-009	St. Andrews Church 10 mold #1	I. Fraser	Retrd.	32.00	32.00
90-01-010	St. Andrews Church mold #2	I. Fraser	Retrd.	32.00	32.00
88-01-011	Lake View 11	I. Fraser	Retrd.	28.00	28.00
88-01-012	Highland Croft 12 mold #1	I. Fraser	Retrd.	32.00	32.00
90-01-013	Highland Croft mold #2	I. Fraser	Retrd.	32.00	32.00
88-01-014	Lilac Cottage 13	I. Fraser	Retrd.	34.00	34.00
88-01-015	Rose Cottage 14	I. Fraser	Retrd.	35.75	35.75
88-01-016	Acorn Cottage 15	I. Fraser	Retrd.	34.00	25.00
88-01-017	Sheep Farm 16	I. Fraser	Retrd.	34.00	34.00
88-01-018	Lighthouse 17	I. Fraser	Retrd.	32.00	32.00
88-01-019	Cornish-Tin-Mine 18	I. Fraser	Retrd.	35.75	35.75
88-01-020	Green Gables 19	I. Fraser	Retrd.	39.00	39.00
88-01-021	Cotswold Cottage 20	I. Fraser	Retrd.	39.00	39.00
88-01-022	Old Market 21	I. Fraser	Retrd.	39.00	39.00
88-01-023	Swan Inn 22	I. Fraser	Retrd.	39.00	39.00
88-01-024	Camelot 23 (white)	I. Fraser	Retrd.	44.75	44.75
88-01-025	Camelot 23 (gray)	I. Fraser	Retrd.	44.75	44.75
88-01-026	Camelot 23 (beige)	I. Fraser	Retrd.	44.75	44.75
88-01-027	Lavender Lane 24	I. Fraser	Retrd.	42.00	42.00
88-01-028	Riverside 25	I. Fraser	Retrd.	42.00	42.00
88-01-029	Robert Burns Cottage 26	I. Fraser	Retrd.	45.00	45.00
88-01-030	Preston Mill 27	I. Fraser	Retrd.	45.00	45.00
89-01-031	Sea View 29	I. Fraser	Retrd.	49.50	49.50
89-01-032	Fisherman's Cottage 30	I. Fraser	Retrd.	49.50	49.50
88-01-033	The Chandlery 31 mold #1	I. Fraser	Retrd.	54.00	54.00
89-01-034	The Chandlery 31 mold #2	I. Fraser	Retrd.	54.00	54.00
88-01-035	The Homestead 34	I. Fraser	Retrd.	57.00	57.00
88-01-036	Cornish Cottage 35	I. Fraser	Retrd.	57.00	57.00
88-01-037	Milton Manor 36	I. Fraser	Retrd.	57.00	57.00
88-01-038	Snow Church 37	I. Fraser	Retrd.	59.75	59.75
88-01-039	Oak Tree Inn 39	I. Fraser	Retrd.	69.50	69.50
88-01-040	Kent Oast House 41	I. Fraser	Retrd.	75.00	75.00
88-01-041	The Wedding 45 mold #1	I. Fraser	Retrd.	115.00	115.00
90-01-042	The Wedding 45 mold #2	I. Fraser	Retrd.	115.00	115.00
88-01-043	The Wedding on Plinth 46 mold #1	I. Fraser	Retrd.	135.00	135.00
90-01-044	The Wedding on Plinth 46 mold #2	I. Fraser	Retrd.	135.00	135.00
88-01-045	The Forge 47 mold #1	I. Fraser	Retrd.	115.00	115.00
88-01-046	The Forge 47 mold #2	I. Fraser	Retrd.	115.00	115.00
88-01-047	The Forge on Plinth 48	I. Fraser	Retrd.	135.00	135.00
88-01-048	The Millers 49	I. Fraser	Retrd.	129.00	129.00
88-01-049	The Millers on Plinth 50	I. Fraser	Retrd.	159.00	159.00
88-01-050	The Thatchers 51 mold #1	I. Fraser	Retrd.	124.00	124.00
88-01-051	The Thatchers 51 mold #2	I. Fraser	Retrd.	124.00	124.00
88-01-052	The Thatchers on Plinth 52	I. Fraser	Retrd.	149.50	149.50
88-01-053	Tudor Court 53 mold #1	I. Fraser	Retrd.	129.00	129.00
88-01-054	Tudor Court 53 mold #2	I. Fraser	Retrd.	129.00	129.00
88-01-055	Tudor Court on Plinth 54 mold #1	I. Fraser	Retrd.	149.50	149.50
88-01-056	Tudor Court on Plinth 54 mold #2	I. Fraser	Retrd.	149.50	149.50
88-01-057	Staging Post 55	I. Fraser	Retrd.	389.75	389.75
88-01-058	Hillview Base 56	I. Fraser	Retrd.	137.80	137.80
88-01-059	Harbor Base 57	I. Fraser	Retrd.	140.00	140.00
88-01-060	The Barge's Base 58	I. Fraser	Retrd.	270.00	270.00
88-01-061	Highbury House 59	I. Fraser	Retrd.	101.75	101.75
88-01-062	Ivy Mews 60	I. Fraser	Retrd.	45.00	45.00
88-01-063	Old Antique Shop 61	I. Fraser	Retrd.	42.00	42.00
88-01-064	Summerside 62	I. Fraser	Retrd.	45.00	45.00
88-01-065	Woodcutters Cottage 63	I. Fraser	Retrd.	45.00	45.00
88-01-066	Devon Cottage 64	I. Fraser	Retrd.	34.00	34.00
88-01-067	Springbank 65	I. Fraser	Retrd.	41.75	41.75
88-01-068	Fisherman's Wharf 66	I. Fraser	Retrd.	89.75	89.75
88-01-069	Bridge House 67	I. Fraser	Retrd.	27.00	27.00
88-01-070	Primrose Cottage 68	I. Fraser	Retrd.	33.00	33.00
88-01-071	Rowan Cottage 69	I. Fraser	Retrd.	21.00	21.00
88-01-072	Fern Cottage 70	I. Fraser	Retrd.	21.00	21.00
88-01-073	Shepherd's Cottage 71	I. Fraser	Retrd.	99.50	99.50
88-01-074	Shepherd's Cottage on Plinth 73	I. Fraser	Retrd.	119.50	119.50
88-01-075	Ploughman's Cottage 72	I. Fraser	Retrd.	99.50	99.50
88-01-076	Ploughman's Cottage on Plinth 74	I. Fraser	Retrd.	119.50	119.50
88-01-077	Old Brig Inn 79	I. Fraser	Retrd.	63.50	63.50
88-01-078	Morningside 80	I. Fraser	Retrd.	300.00	300.00
88-01-079	Highland House 81	I. Fraser	Retrd.	63.50	63.50
88-01-080	Cove Cottage 82	I. Fraser	Retrd.	32.00	32.00
88-01-081	Creel Cottage 83	I. Fraser	Retrd.	37.00	37.00
88-01-082	Chester House 84	I. Fraser	Retrd.	75.00	75.00
88-01-083	Drover Cottage 85	I. Fraser	Retrd.	22.50	22.50
88-01-084	Yeoman's Cottage 86	I. Fraser	Retrd.	25.00	25.00
88-01-085	Honeymoon Cottage 87	I. Fraser	Retrd.	25.00	25.00
88-01-086	Somerset Cottage 88	I. Fraser	Retrd.	32.75	32.75
88-01-087	Tweedale Cottage 89	I. Fraser	Retrd.	38.75	38.75
88-01-088	Old Leonach Cottage 90	I. Fraser	Retrd.	41.75	41.75
88-01-089	Boatman's House 91	I. Fraser	Retrd.	39.00	39.00
88-01-090	Greystone Manor 92	I. Fraser	Retrd.	54.00	54.00
88-01-091	Merchant's Court 95	I. Fraser	Retrd.	291.00	291.00
90-01-092	Killarney Cottage 96	I. Fraser	Retrd.	63.50	63.50
90-01-093	Heather Lea 97	I. Fraser	Retrd.	21.00	21.00
90-01-094	Linden Lea 98	I. Fraser	Retrd.	32.00	32.00
90-01-095	Bull & Bush 100	I. Fraser	Retrd.	54.00	54.00
90-01-096	Castle of Monte Crisco 101	I. Fraser	Retrd.	149.75	149.75
90-01-097	St. Georges Church 102	I. Fraser	Retrd.	32.00	32.00
91-01-098	But 'N' Ben 104	I. Fraser	Retrd.	17.00	17.00
91-01-099	Pebble Cottage 105	I. Fraser	Retrd.	17.00	17.00
91-01-100	Belle Cottage 106	I. Fraser	Retrd.	17.00	17.00
91-01-101	Rock Cliff 107	I. Fraser	Retrd.	17.00	17.00
91-01-102	Grannie's Heiland Home 108	I. Fraser	Retrd.	21.00	21.00
91-01-103	Fishers Wynd 110	I. Fraser	Retrd.	32.00	32.00
91-01-104	Follyfoot 112	I. Fraser	Retrd.	37.00	37.00
91-01-105	Village Post Office 114	I. Fraser	Retrd.	37.00	37.00
91-01-106	Horseshoe Inn 115	I. Fraser	Retrd.	39.00	39.00
91-01-107	Meadowsweet Farm 116	I. Fraser	Retrd.	39.00	39.00
91-01-108	St. David's Church 117	I. Fraser	Retrd.	42.00	42.00
91-01-109	Lifeboat House 118	I. Fraser	Retrd.	54.00	54.00
91-01-110	The Parsonage 119	I. Fraser	Retrd.	63.50	63.50
88-01-111	Black Isle Cottage 121	I. Fraser	Retrd.	32.00	32.00
91-01-112	Tintagel Post Office 122	I. Fraser	Retrd.	42.00	42.00
91-01-113	Kent Oast House 123	I. Fraser	Retrd.	37.00	37.00
88-01-114	Crooked House 171	I. Fraser	Retrd.	37.00	37.00
Fraser International	**The British Heritage Collection**				
87-02-001	Robert Burn's Cottage 02	I. Fraser	Open	23.50	25.00
87-02-002	John Knox House 28	I. Fraser	Open	39.50	47.50
88-02-003	Anne Hathaway's Cottage 32 mold #1	I. Fraser	Retrd.	53.00	53.00
94-02-004	Anne Hathaway's Cottage 32 mold #2	I. Fraser	Open	53.00	59.50
88-02-005	Shakespeare's Birthplace 33 mold #1	I. Fraser	Retrd.	53.00	53.00
94-02-006	Shakespeare's Birthplace 33 mold #2	I. Fraser	Open	53.00	59.50
87-02-007	Holyrood Palace 42	I. Fraser	Open	85.00	95.00
87-02-008	Edinburgh Castle 43	I. Fraser	Open	85.00	95.00
87-02-009	Royal & Ancient Clubhouse 44	I. Fraser	Open	85.00	95.00
87-02-010	The Giant's Causway 75	I. Fraser	Open	19.50	22.50
87-02-010	The Scott Monument 76	I. Fraser	Open	49.50	55.00
88-02-011	The Tower of London 78	I. Fraser	Open	99.50	115.00
87-02-012	Eilean Donan Castle 93	I. Fraser	Open	85.00	95.00
88-02-013	Craigievar Castle 94	I. Fraser	Open	59.50	75.00
88-02-014	Dove Cottage 99	I. Fraser	Open	45.00	49.50
89-02-015	York Minster 103	I. Fraser	Open	99.50	115.00
89-02-016	Cliffords Tower 109	I. Fraser	Open	31.50	35.00
89-02-017	Micklegate Bar 111	I. Fraser	Open	39.50	45.00
89-02-018	Windsor Castle 120	I. Fraser	Open	99.50	115.00
90-02-019	Culzean Castle 124	I. Fraser	Open	115.00	125.00
91-02-020	Caernarfon Castle 125	I. Fraser	Open	85.00	95.00
91-02-021	Leeds Castle 126	I. Fraser	Open	85.00	95.00
90-02-022	Stirling Castle 127	I. Fraser	Open	115.00	125.00
91-02-023	Balmoral Castle 128	I. Fraser	Open	115.00	125.00
91-02-024	Warwick Castle 131	I. Fraser	Open	99.50	115.00
91-02-025	Buckingham Palace 132	I. Fraser	Open	159.50	175.00
91-02-026	Kings College Chapel 133	I. Fraser	Open	115.00	125.00
92-02-027	St. Pauls Cathedral 134	I. Fraser	Open	149.50	165.00
92-02-028	Westminster Abbey 135	I. Fraser	Open	149.50	165.00
92-02-029	The White Tower 151	I. Fraser	Open	59.50	75.00
91-02-030	Cardiff Castle Keep 152	I. Fraser	Open	49.50	55.00
92-02-031	Canterbury Cathedral 153	I. Fraser	Open	149.50	165.00
92-02-032	Big Ben 154	I. Fraser	Open	57.50	65.00
91-02-033	Nelson's Column 156	I. Fraser	Open	39.50	45.00
91-02-034	St. Margaret's Church 157	I. Fraser	Open	39.50	45.00
92-02-035	The Round Tower 158	I. Fraser	Open	59.50	75.00
92-02-036	The Cenotaph 172	I. Fraser	Open	35.00	37.50
92-02-037	The Royal Albert Hall 174	I. Fraser	Open	59.50	75.00
87-02-038	Old Leonach Cottage 178	I. Fraser	Open	35.00	37.50
Fraser International	**The British Heritage Miniature Collection**				
92-03-001	Edinburgh Castle 159	I. Fraser	Open	39.00	45.00
92-03-002	York Minster 160	I. Fraser	Open	48.00	55.00
92-03-003	Stirling Castle 161	I. Fraser	Open	45.00	49.50
92-03-004	Westminister Abbey 162	I. Fraser	Open	45.00	49.50
92-03-005	St. Pauls Cathedral 163	I. Fraser	Open	45.00	49.50
92-03-006	Windsor Castle 164	I. Fraser	Open	42.00	45.00
92-03-007	Balmoral Castle 165	I. Fraser	Open	42.00	45.00
92-03-008	The Tower of London 166	I. Fraser	Open	42.00	45.00
92-03-009	Warwick Castle 167	I. Fraser	Open	42.00	45.00
92-03-010	Holyrood Palace 168	I. Fraser	Open	42.00	45.00
92-03-011	Buckingham Palace 169	I. Fraser	Open	48.00	55.00
92-03-012	Leeds Castle 170	I. Fraser	Open	42.00	45.00
92-03-013	Ely Cathedral 175	I. Fraser	Open	51.00	55.00
92-03-014	Durham Cathedral 176	I. Fraser	Open	59.50	65.00
92-03-015	Norwich Cathedral 177	I. Fraser	Open	48.00	55.00
92-03-016	Drum Castle 180	I. Fraser	Open	45.00	49.50
92-03-017	Fyvie Castle 182	I. Fraser	Open	48.00	55.00
92-03-018	Castle Fraser 183	I. Fraser	Open	48.00	55.00
92-03-019	Braemar Castle 184	I. Fraser	Open	48.00	55.00
92-03-020	Urquhart Castle 185	I. Fraser	Open	48.00	55.00
92-03-021	Cawdor Castle 186	I. Fraser	Open	54.00	65.00
92-03-022	Crathes Castle 187	I. Fraser	Open	42.00	45.00
93-03-023	Stonehenge 189	I. Fraser	Open	39.50	43.00
93-03-024	Glamis Castle 193	I. Fraser	Open	57.50	65.00
93-03-025	Claypotts 194	I. Fraser	Open	48.00	49.50
Fraser International	**German Collection**				
90-04-001	Schless Neuschwanstein 113	I. Fraser	Open	145.00	165.00
91-04-002	Schloss Linderhof 129	I. Fraser	Open	155.00	175.00
92-04-003	Schloss Heidelberg 136	I. Fraser	Open	155.00	175.00
92-04-004	St. Coloman Chapel 138	I. Fraser	Open	39.50	45.00
92-04-005	St. Wilhelm Chapel 139	I. Fraser	Open	39.50	45.00
92-04-006	Altstadter Town Hall 140	I. Fraser	Open	79.50	90.00
92-04-007	Holstein Town Gates 141	I. Fraser	Open	119.50	130.00

		ARTIST	EDITION	ISSUE	QUOTE
92-04-008	Schloss Badinghagen 142	I. Fraser	Open	79.50	90.00
92-04-009	Mayor Toppler's Little House 143	I. Fraser	Open	39.50	45.00
92-04-010	Schloss Heidelburg (with snow) 188	I. Fraser	Open	165.00	185.00

Fraser International — **Classic Cottage Collection**

94-05-001	Perriwinkle Cottage C01	I. Fraser	Open	29.50	29.50
94-05-002	Fyne View C02	I. Fraser	Open	35.00	35.00
94-05-003	Clover Cottage C03	I. Fraser	Open	37.50	75.00
94-05-004	Saxmund Smithy C04	I. Fraser	Open	39.50	39.50
94-05-005	Buttermere Tearooms C05	I. Fraser	Open	39.50	39.50
94-05-006	Rock Cliff C06	I. Fraser	Open	39.50	39.50
94-05-007	Ennerdale Farm C07	I. Fraser	Open	47.50	47.50
94-05-008	The Old Curiosity Shop C08	I. Fraser	Open	47.50	47.50
94-05-009	St. Mary's Chapel C09	I. Fraser	Open	47.50	47.50
94-05-010	Ranworth View C10	I. Fraser	Open	47.50	47.50
94-05-011	Rosebank C11	I. Fraser	Open	47.50	47.50
94-05-012	Ivy Cottage C12	I. Fraser	Open	49.50	49.50
94-05-013	Heatherlea Cottage C13	I. Fraser	Open	49.50	49.50
94-05-014	Cheddar View C14	I. Fraser	Open	49.50	49.50
94-05-015	Grannie's Hieland Hame C15	I. Fraser	Open	52.50	52.50
94-05-016	Honeymoon Hideaway C16	I. Fraser	Open	52.50	52.50
94-05-017	The Rose & Crown C17	I. Fraser	Open	52.50	52.50
94-05-018	Birch Cottage C18	I. Fraser	Open	59.50	59.50
94-05-019	Foxglove Cottage C19	I. Fraser	Open	59.50	59.50
94-05-020	Duck Cottage C20	I. Fraser	Open	59.50	59.50
94-05-021	Crail Cottage C21	I. Fraser	Open	62.50	62.50
94-05-022	The Old Anchor Inn C22	I. Fraser	Open	65.00	65.00
94-05-023	Inverbeg Gatehouse C23	I. Fraser	Open	69.50	69.50
94-05-024	Benmore Croft C24	I. Fraser	Open	69.50	69.50
94-05-025	Cullin Croft C25	I. Fraser	Open	69.50	69.50
94-05-026	Langdale Farm C26	I. Fraser	Open	69.50	69.50
94-05-027	The Kings Arms C27	I. Fraser	Open	75.00	75.00
94-05-028	Polperro Cottage C28	I. Fraser	Open	75.00	75.00
94-05-029	Follyfoot Farm C29	I. Fraser	Open	75.00	75.00
94-05-030	Puffin Lighthouse C30	I. Fraser	Open	75.00	75.00
94-05-031	Kilrea Cottage C31	I. Fraser	Open	75.00	75.00
94-05-032	Smugglers Hideaway C32	I. Fraser	Open	75.00	75.00
94-05-033	Whitesand Lighthouse C33	I. Fraser	Open	80.00	80.00
94-05-034	Horseshoe Inn C34	I. Fraser	Open	80.00	80.00
94-05-035	Lomond View C35	I. Fraser	Open	80.00	80.00
94-05-036	Coniston House C36	I. Fraser	Open	87.50	87.50
94-05-037	Gamekeepers Lodge C37	I. Fraser	Open	95.00	95.00
94-05-038	Laurel Bank C38	I. Fraser	Open	95.00	95.00
94-05-039	Crathie Church C39	I. Fraser	Open	95.00	95.00
94-05-040	Lavender Lane C40	I. Fraser	Open	95.00	95.00
94-05-041	Windrush Lane C41	I. Fraser	Open	99.50	99.50
94-05-042	The Wine Merchant C42	I. Fraser	Open	99.50	99.50
94-05-043	Dale Farm C43	I. Fraser	Open	135.00	135.00
94-05-044	Strathmore Loged C44	I. Fraser	Open	135.00	135.00
94-05-045	Glengarry Homestead C45	I. Fraser	Open	175.00	175.00
94-05-046	Northborough Manor C46	I. Fraser	Open	225.00	225.00
94-05-047	St. Andrews Kirk C47	I. Fraser	Open	69.50	69.50
94-05-048	The Red Lion Tavern C48	I. Fraser	Open	495.00	495.00
94-05-049	The Village Post Office C49	I. Fraser	Open	75.00	75.00
94-05-050	Honey Cottage C50	I. Fraser	Open	59.50	59.50
94-05-051	Daisy Cottage C51	I. Fraser	Open	29.50	29.50
94-05-052	Swallow Mill C52	I. Fraser	Open	52.50	52.50
94-05-053	Merchant's Manor C53	I. Fraser	Open	52.50	52.50
94-05-054	Carbis View C54	I. Fraser	Open	29.50	29.50
94-05-055	Coombe Cottage C55	I. Fraser	Open	69.50	69.50

Fraser International — **Washington D.C. Collection**

94-06-001	White House A01	I. Fraser	Open	49.50	49.50
94-06-001	Lincoln Memorial A02	I. Fraser	Open	49.50	49.50
94-06-001	Jefferson Memorial A03	I. Fraser	Open	49.50	49.50
94-06-001	White House on Base A06	I. Fraser	Open	225.00	225.00

Fraser International — **Collectors' Society**

93-07-001	Granny Smith's Cottage	I. Fraser	Retrd.	25.00	25.00
94-07-002	Granny Mac Gregor's Cottage	I. Fraser	Yr.Iss.	25.00	25.00

Ganz — **Little Cheesers/Cheeserville Picnic Collection**

91-01-001	Papa Woodsworth	G.D.A. Group	Open	13.00	13.00
91-01-002	Auntie Marigold Eating Cookie	G.D.A. Group	Open	13.00	13.00
91-01-003	Baby Cicely	G.D.A. Group	Open	8.00	8.00
91-01-004	Medley Meadowmouse With Bouquet	G.D.A. Group	Open	13.00	13.00
91-01-005	Violet With Peaches	G.D.A. Group	Open	13.00	13.00
91-01-006	Baby Truffle	G.D.A. Group	Open	8.00	8.00
91-01-007	Harriet Harvestmouse	G.D.A. Group	Retrd.	13.00	13.00
91-01-008	Grandpapa Thistledown Carrying Basket	G.D.A. Group	Open	13.00	13.00
91-01-009	Jenny Butterfield Kneeling	G.D.A. Group	Open	13.00	13.00
91-01-010	Mama With Rolling Pin	G.D.A. Group	Open	13.00	13.00
91-01-011	Grandmama Thistledown Holding Bread	G.D.A. Group	Open	14.00	14.00
91-01-012	Harley Harvestmouse Waving	G.D.A. Group	Open	13.00	13.00
91-01-013	Cousin Woody With Bread and Fruit	G.D.A. Group	Open	14.00	14.00
91-01-014	Marigold Thistledown Picking Up Jar	G.D.A. Group	Open	14.00	14.00
91-01-015	Little Truffle Eating Grapes	G.D.A. Group	Open	8.00	8.00
91-01-016	Jeremy Butterfield	G.D.A. Group	Open	13.00	13.00
91-01-017	Mama Fixing Sweet Cicely's Hair	G.D.A. Group	Retrd.	16.50	16.50
91-01-018	Picnic Buddies	G.D.A. Group	Open	19.00	19.00
91-01-019	Blossom & Hickory In Love	G.D.A. Group	Open	19.00	19.00
91-01-020	Little Truffle Smelling Flowers	G.D.A. Group	Open	16.50	16.50
91-01-021	Fellow With Picnic Hamper	G.D.A. Group	Retrd.	13.00	13.00
91-01-022	Fellow With Plate Of Cookies	G.D.A. Group	Retrd.	13.00	13.00
91-01-023	Lady With Grapes	G.D.A. Group	Retrd.	14.00	14.00
91-01-024	Mama Woodsworth With Crate	G.D.A. Group	Retrd.	14.00	14.00
93-01-025	Sunday Drive	C.Thammavongsa	Open	40.00	40.00
93-01-026	Sweet Dreams	C.Thammavongsa	Open	27.50	27.50
93-01-027	Willy's Toe-Tappin' Tunes	C.Thammavongsa	Open	15.00	15.00
93-01-028	The Storyteller	C.Thammavongsa	10,000	25.00	25.00
93-01-029	For Someone Special	C.Thammavongsa	Open	13.50	13.50
93-01-030	Words Of Wisdom	C.Thammavongsa	Open	14.00	14.00
93-01-031	Clownin' Around	C.Thammavongsa	Open	10.50	10.50
93-01-032	Chuckles The Clown	C.Thammavongsa	Open	16.00	16.00
93-01-033	Little Cheesers Display Plaque	C.Thammavongsa	Open	25.00	25.00
94-01-034	Strummin' Away	C.Thammavongsa	Open	13.00	13.00
94-01-035	Fiddle-Dee-Dee	C.Thammavongsa	Open	13.00	13.00
94-01-036	Swingin' Sax	C.Thammavongsa	Open	13.00	13.00
94-01-037	What a Hoot!	C.Thammavongsa	Open	13.00	13.00
94-01-038	Washboard Blues	C.Thammavongsa	Open	13.00	13.00
94-01-039	Ooom-Pah-Pah	C.Thammavongsa	Open	13.00	13.00
94-01-040	Melody Maker	C.Thammavongsa	Open	17.00	17.00

		ARTIST	EDITION	ISSUE	QUOTE

Ganz — **Little Cheesers/Cheeserville Picnic Collection Mini-Food Acces**

91-02-001	Food Trolley	G.D.A. Group	Retrd.	12.00	12.00
91-02-002	Set Of Four Bottles	G.D.A. Group	Retrd.	10.00	10.00
91-02-003	Napkin In Can	G.D.A. Group	Retrd.	2.00	2.00
91-02-004	Honey Jar	G.D.A. Group	Retrd.	2.00	2.00
91-02-005	Wine Glass	G.D.A. Group	Open	1.25	1.25
91-02-006	Ice Cream Cup	G.D.A. Group	Open	2.00	2.00
91-02-007	Candy	G.D.A. Group	Open	2.00	2.00
91-02-008	Sundae	G.D.A. Group	Open	2.00	2.00
91-02-009	Egg Tart	G.D.A. Group	Open	1.00	1.00
91-02-010	Hot Dog	G.D.A. Group	Open	2.25	2.25
91-02-011	Basket Of Peaches	G.D.A. Group	Open	2.00	2.00
91-02-012	Cherry Mousse	G.D.A. Group	Open	2.00	2.00
91-02-013	Blueberry Cake	G.D.A. Group	Retrd.	2.50	2.50
91-02-014	Chocolate Cake	G.D.A. Group	Open	2.50	2.50
91-02-015	Chocolate Cheesecake	G.D.A. Group	Open	2.00	2.00
91-02-016	Strawberry Cake	G.D.A. Group	Open	2.00	2.00
91-02-017	Doughnut Basket	G.D.A. Group	Open	2.50	2.50
91-02-018	Bread Basket	G.D.A. Group	Open	2.50	2.50
91-02-019	Basket Of Apples	G.D.A. Group	Open	2.25	2.25
91-02-020	Hazelnut Roll	G.D.A. Group	Retrd.	2.00	2.00
91-02-021	Lemon Cake	G.D.A. Group	Retrd.	2.00	2.00
91-02-022	Cherry Pie	G.D.A. Group	Retrd.	2.00	2.00
91-02-023	Food Basket With Blue Cloth	G.D.A. Group	Retrd.	6.50	6.50
91-02-024	Food Basket With Pink Cloth	G.D.A. Group	Retrd.	6.00	6.00
91-02-025	Food Basket With Green Cloth	G.D.A. Group	Open	7.50	7.50
91-02-026	Food Basket With Purple Cloth	G.D.A. Group	Open	6.00	6.00

Ganz — **Little Cheesers/Cheeserville Picnic Collection Musicals**

91-03-001	Musical Sunflower Base	G.D.A. Group	Retrd.	65.00	65.00
91-03-002	Musical Picnic Base	G.D.A. Group	Open	60.00	60.00
91-03-003	Musical Violet Woodsworth Cookie Jar	G.D.A. Group	Retrd.	75.00	75.00
91-03-004	Musical Medley Meadowmouse Cookie Jar	G.D.A. Group	Retrd.	75.00	75.00
91-03-005	Mama & Sweet Cicely Waterglobe	G.D.A. Group	Retrd.	55.00	55.00
91-03-006	Medley Meadowmouse Waterglobe	G.D.A. Group	Open	47.00	47.00
92-03-007	Sweet Cicely Musical Doll Basket	G.D.A. Group	Open	85.00	85.00
91-03-008	Blossom & HIckory Musical Jewelry Box	G.D.A. Group	Retrd.	65.00	65.00
91-03-009	Musical Basket Trinket Box	G.D.A. Group	Open	30.00	30.00
91-03-010	Musical Floral Trinket Box	G.D.A. Group	Open	32.00	32.00
93-03-011	Musical "Secret Treasures" Trinket Box	C.Thammavongsa	Open	36.00	36.00
93-03-012	Wishing Well Musical	C.Thammavongsa	Open	50.00	50.00
94-03-013	The Bandstand Base	C.Thammavongsa	Open	48.50	48.50

Ganz — **Little Cheesers/Cheeserville Picnic Collection Accessories**

94-04-001	Mayflower Meadow Base	C.Thammavongsa	Open	50.00	50.00

Ganz — **Little Cheesers/The Wedding Collection**

92-05-001	Harley & Harriet Harvestmouse	GDA/Thammavongsa	Open	20.00	20.00
92-05-002	Jenny Butterfield/Sweet Cicely (bridesmaids)	GDA/Thammavongsa	Open	20.00	20.00
92-05-003	Blossom Thistledown (bride)	GDA/Thammavongsa	Open	16.00	16.00
92-05-004	Hickory Harvestmouse (groom)	GDA/Thammavongsa	Open	16.00	16.00
92-05-005	Cousin Woody & Little Truffle	GDA/Thammavongsa	Open	20.00	20.00
92-05-006	Grandmama & Grandpapa Thistledown	GDA/Thammavongsa	Retrd.	20.00	20.00
92-05-007	Pastor Smallwood	GDA/Thammavongsa	Open	16.00	16.00
92-05-008	Little Truffle (ringbearer)	GDA/Thammavongsa	Open	10.00	10.00
92-05-009	Myrtle Meadowmouse With Medley	GDA/Thammavongsa	Retrd.	20.00	20.00
92-05-010	Frowzy Roquefort III With Gramophone	GDA/Thammavongsa	Open	20.00	20.00
92-05-011	Marigold Thistledown & Oscar Bobbins	GDA/Thammavongsa	Open	20.00	20.00
92-05-012	Great Aunt Rose Beside Table	GDA/Thammavongsa	Open	20.00	20.00
92-05-013	Mama & Papa Woodsworth Dancing	GDA/Thammavongsa	Open	20.00	20.00
92-05-014	Wedding Procession	GDA/Thammavongsa	Open	40.00	40.00
93-05-015	The Big Day	C. Thammavongsa	Open	20.00	20.00

Ganz — **Little Cheesers/The Wedding Collection Mini-Food Accessories**

92-06-001	Flour Bag	G.D.A. Group	Retrd.	2.00	2.00
92-06-002	Salt Can	G.D.A. Group	Retrd.	2.00	2.00
92-06-003	Chocolate Pastry	G.D.A. Group	Retrd.	2.00	2.00
92-06-004	Souffle	G.D.A. Group	Retrd.	2.50	2.50
92-06-005	Teddy Mouse	G.D.A. Group	Retrd.	2.00	2.00
92-06-006	Chocolate Pudding	G.D.A. Group	Open	2.50	2.50
92-06-007	Tea Pot Set	G.D.A. Group	Retrd.	3.00	3.00
92-06-008	Honey Pot	G.D.A. Group	Open	2.00	2.00
92-06-009	Candles	G.D.A. Group	Open	3.00	3.00
92-06-010	Big Chocolate Cake	G.D.A. Group	Retrd.	4.50	4.50
92-06-011	Fruit Salad	G.D.A. Group	Open	3.00	3.00
92-06-012	Cherry Jello	G.D.A. Group	Open	3.00	3.00
92-06-013	Ring Cake	G.D.A. Group	Open	3.00	3.00
92-06-014	Soup Pot	G.D.A. Group	Open	3.00	3.00
92-06-015	Flower Vase	G.D.A. Group	Retrd.	3.00	3.00
92-06-016	Groom Candleholder	GDA/Thammavongsa	Open	20.00	20.00
92-06-017	Bride Candleholder	GDA/Thammavongsa	Open	20.00	20.00
92-06-018	Cake Trinket Box	GDA/Thammavongsa	Open	14.00	14.00
92-06-019	Bible Trinket Box	GDA/Thammavongsa	Open	16.50	16.50
92-06-020	Grass Base	GDA/Thammavongsa	Retrd.	3.50	3.50
93-06-021	Wedding Cake	C. Thammavongsa	Open	4.50	4.50
93-06-022	Gooseberry Champagne	C. Thammavongsa	Open	3.00	3.00

Ganz — **Little Cheesers/The Wedding Collection Accesories**

93-07-001	Gazebo Base	C. Thammavongsa	Open	42.00	42.00
93-07-002	Banquet Table	C. Thammavongsa	Open	14.00	14.00

Ganz — **Little Cheesers/The Wedding Collection Musicals**

92-08-001	Musical Wooden Base For Wedding Processional	G.D.A. Group	Open	25.00	25.00
92-08-002	Musical Wedding Base	GDA/Thammavongsa	Open	32.00	32.00
92-08-003	Musical Blossom & Hickory Wedding Waterglobe	GDA/Thammavongsa	Open	55.00	55.00
93-08-004	Blossom & Hickory Musical	C. Thammavongsa	Retrd.	50.00	50.00
93-08-005	White Musical Wood Base For Gazebo Base "Evergreen"	C. Thammavongsa	Open	25.00	25.00

Ganz — **Little Cheesers/The Christmas Collection**

91-09-001	Cheeser Snowman	G.D.A. Group	Open	7.50	7.50
91-09-002	Violet With Snowball	G.D.A. Group	Open	8.00	8.00
91-09-003	Medley Playing Drum	G.D.A. Group	Open	8.00	8.00
91-09-004	Little Truffle With Stocking	G.D.A. Group	Open	8.00	8.00
91-09-005	Jeremy With Teddy Bear	G.D.A. Group	Open	12.00	12.00
91-09-006	Santa Cheeser	G.D.A. Group	Open	13.00	13.00
91-09-007	Frowzy Roquefort III Skating	G.D.A. Group	Retrd.	14.00	14.00
91-09-008	Jenny On Sleigh	G.D.A. Group	Open	16.00	16.00
91-09-009	Auntie Blossom With Ornaments	G.D.A. Group	Open	14.00	14.00
91-09-010	Mama Pouring Tea	G.D.A. Group	Retrd.	14.00	14.00
91-09-011	Great Aunt Rose With Tray	G.D.A. Group	Open	14.00	14.00

		ARTIST	EDITION	ISSUE	QUOTE
91-09-012	Abner Appleton Ringing Bell	G.D.A. Group	Retrd.	14.00	14.00
91-09-013	Grandpapa Blowing Horn	G.D.A. Group	Open	14.00	14.00
91-09-014	Hickory Playing Cello	G.D.A. Group	Open	14.00	14.00
91-09-015	Myrtle Meadowmouse With Book	G.D.A. Group	Retrd.	14.00	14.00
91-09-016	Cousin Woody Playing Flute	G.D.A. Group	Open	14.00	14.00
91-09-017	Harley & Harriet Dancing	G.D.A. Group	Retrd.	19.00	19.00
91-09-018	Grandpapa & Sweet Cicely	G.D.A. Group	Open	19.00	19.00
91-09-019	Grandmama & Little Truffle	G.D.A..Group	Retrd.	19.00	19.00
91-09-020	Marigold&Oscar Stealing A Christmas Kiss	G.D.A. Group	Open	19.00	19.00
93-09-021	All I Want For Christmas	C.Thammavongsa	Open	18.00	18.00
93-09-022	Christmas Greetings	C.Thammavongsa	Open	16.50	16.50
93-09-023	Sleigh Ride	C.Thammavongsa	Open	11.00	11.00
94-09-024	Santa's Sleigh	C.Thammavongsa	10,000	22.00	22.00

Ganz — **Little Cheesers/The Christmas Collection Accessories**

91-10-001	Christmas Tree	G.D.A. Group	Open	9.00	9.00
91-10-002	Lamp Post	G.D.A. Group	Open	8.50	8.50
91-10-003	Parlor Scene Base	G.D.A. Group	Open	37.50	37.50
91-10-004	Outdoor Scene Base	G.D.A. Group	Retrd.	35.00	35.00
93-10-005	Candleholder-Santa Cheeser	C.Thammavongsa	Open	19.00	19.00
93-10-006	Ice Pond Base	C.Thammavongsa	Open	5.50	5.50
93-10-007	Gingerbread House	C.Thammavongsa	Open	3.00	3.00
93-10-008	Toy Train	C.Thammavongsa	Open	3.00	3.00
93-10-009	Christmas Gift	C.Thammavongsa	Open	3.00	3.00
93-10-010	Christmas Stocking	C.Thammavongsa	Open	3.00	3.00
93-10-011	Candy Cane	C.Thammavongsa	Open	2.00	2.00
93-10-012	Toy Soldier	C.Thammavongsa	Open	3.00	3.00
94-10-013	Christmas Collection Base	C.Thammavongsa	Open	50.00	50.00

Ganz — **Little Cheesers/The Christmas Collection Musicals**

92-11-001	Musical Santa Cheeser Roly-Poly	G.D.A. Group	Suspd.	55.00	55.00
92-11-002	Little Truffle Christmas Waterglobe	G.D.A. Group	Open	45.00	45.00
92-11-003	Jenny Butterfield Christmas Waterglobe	GDA/Thammavongsa	Retrd.	55.00	55.00
93-11-004	Round Wood Base "We Wish You a Merry X'mas"	C.Thammavongsa	Open	25.00	25.00
93-11-005	Rotating Round Wood Base "I'll be Home for X'mas"	C.Thammavongsa	Open	30.00	30.00

Ganz — **Little Cheesers/Springtime In Cheeserville Collection**

92-12-001	Hippity-Hop. It's Eastertime!	C.Thammavongsa	Open	16.00	16.00
92-12-002	A Wheelbarrow Of Sunshine	C.Thammavongsa	Open	17.00	17.00
92-12-003	Springtime Delights	C.Thammavongsa	Open	12.00	12.00
92-12-004	A Basket Full Of Joy	C.Thammavongsa	Open	16.00	16.00
93-12-005	Gift From Heaven	C.Thammavongsa	Open	10.00	10.00
93-12-006	Blossom Has A Little lamb	C.Thammavongsa	Open	16.50	16.50
93-12-007	Ballerina Sweetheart	C.Thammavongsa	Open	10.00	10.00
93-12-008	Playing Cupid	C.Thammavongsa	Open	10.00	10.00
93-12-009	Hugs & Kisses	C.Thammavongsa	Open	11.00	11.00
93-12-010	Gently Down The Stream	C.Thammavongsa	10,000	27.00	27.00
93-12-011	First Kiss	C.Thammavongsa	Open	24.00	24.00
93-12-012	Sunday Stroll	C.Thammavongsa	Open	22.00	22.00
93-12-013	Sugar & Spice	C.Thammavongsa	Open	24.00	24.00
93-12-014	For My Sweatheart	C.Thammavongsa	Open	22.00	22.00
93-12-015	I Love You	C.Thammavongsa	Open	22.00	22.00
93-12-016	Friends Forever	C.Thammavongsa	Open	22.00	22.00
94-12-017	Birthday Party	C.Thammavongsa	Open	22.00	22.00
94-12-018	Hip Hip Hooray	C.Thammavongsa	Open	22.00	22.00
94-12-019	Get Well	C.Thammavongsa	Open	22.00	22.00

Ganz — **Little Cheesers/Springtime In Cheeserville Accessories**

92-13-001	Decorated With Love	C.Thammavongsa	Open	7.50	7.50
92-13-002	April Showers Bring May Flowers	C.Thammavongsa	Open	7.50	7.50
92-13-003	For Somebunny Special	C.Thammavongsa	Open	7.50	7.50

Ganz — **Little Cheesers/Springtime In Cheeserville Musicals**

92-14-001	Tulips & Ribbons Musical Trinket Box	GDA/Thammavongsa	Suspd.	28.00	28.00

Ganz — **Little Cheesers/The Little Hoppers Collection**

94-15-001	Sweet Nothings	C.Thammavongsa	Open	15.00	15.00
94-15-002	Tricycle Built for Two	C.Thammavongsa	Open	16.00	16.00
94-15-003	Somebunny Loves You	C.Thammavongsa	Open	7.50	7.50
94-15-004	Tender Loving Care	C.Thammavongsa	Open	10.00	10.00
94-15-005	Let's Play Ball	C.Thammavongsa	Open	7.00	7.00
94-15-006	Bubble Bath	C.Thammavongsa	Open	7.50	7.50

Ganz — **The Cowtown Collection**

93-16-001	Old MooDonald	C.Thammavongsa	Open	13.50	13.50
93-16-002	Buffalo Bull Cody	C.Thammavongsa	Open	15.00	15.00
93-16-003	Cowlamity Jane	C.Thammavongsa	Open	15.00	15.00
93-16-004	Moo West	C.Thammavongsa	Open	15.00	15.00
93-16-005	Gloria Bovine & Rudolph Bullentino	C.Thammavongsa	Open	20.00	20.00
93-16-006	Daisy Moo	C.Thammavongsa	Open	11.00	11.00
93-16-007	Jethro Bovine	C.Thammavongsa	Retrd.	15.00	15.00
93-16-008	Bull Rogers	C.Thammavongsa	Open	17.00	17.00
93-16-009	Lil' Orphan Angus	C.Thammavongsa	Open	11.00	11.00
93-16-010	Buttermilk & Buttercup	C.Thammavongsa	Open	16.00	16.00
93-16-011	Bull Ruth	C.Thammavongsa	Retrd.	13.00	13.00
93-16-012	Bull Masterson	C.Thammavongsa	Open	15.00	15.00
94-16-013	Tchaicowsky	C.Thammavongsa	Open	19.00	19.00
94-16-014	Ma & Pa Cattle	C.Thammavongsa	Open	23.50	23.50
94-16-015	Heiferella	C.Thammavongsa	Open	16.50	16.50
94-16-016	Pocowhantis	C.Thammavongsa	Open	16.50	16.50
94-16-017	King Cowmooamooa	C.Thammavongsa	Open	16.50	16.50
94-16-018	Cowsey Jones & The Cannonbull Express	C.Thammavongsa	Open	26.50	26.50
94-16-019	Texas Lonesteer	C.Thammavongsa	10,000	50.00	50.00
94-16-020	Set of Three Cacti	C.Thammavongsa	Open	17.00	17.00
94-16-021	Geronimoo	C.Thammavongsa	Open	17.00	17.00
94-16-022	Amoolia Steerheart	C.Thammavongsa	Open	25.00	25.00

Ganz — **Cowtown/The Valentine Collection**

94-17-001	I Love Moo	C.Thammavongsa	Open	15.00	15.00
94-17-002	Wanted: A Sweetheart	C.Thammavongsa	Open	16.00	16.00
94-17-003	Romecow & Mooliet	C.Thammavongsa	Open	22.00	22.00
94-17-004	Robin Hoof & Maid Mooian	C.Thammavongsa	Open	23.00	23.00

Ganz — **Cowtown/The Christmas Collection**

94-18-001	Christmas Cactus	C.Thammavongsa	Open	13.50	13.50
94-18-002	Saint Nicowlas	C.Thammavongsa	Open	16.00	16.00
94-18-003	Santa Cows	C.Thammavongsa	Open	18.00	18.00
94-18-004	Santa's Little Heifer	C.Thammavongsa	Open	12.50	12.50
94-18-005	Billy the Calf	C.Thammavongsa	Open	14.00	14.00

Ganz — **The Pigsville Collection**

		ARTIST	EDITION	ISSUE	QUOTE
93-19-001	Pig at the Beach	G.D.A. Group	Open	9.00	9.00
93-19-002	Ice Cream Anyone?	G.D.A. Group	Open	9.00	9.00
93-19-003	Tipsy	G.D.A. Group	Open	9.00	9.00
93-19-004	Squeaky Clean	G.D.A. Group	Open	11.00	11.00
93-19-005	Soap Suds	G.D.A. Group	Open	12.00	12.00
93-19-006	Nap Time	G.D.A. Group	Open	11.00	11.00
93-19-007	Mother Love	G.D.A. Group	Open	13.00	13.00
93-19-008	Me & My Ice Cream	G.D.A. Group	Retrd.	17.00	17.00
93-19-009	Prima Ballerina	C.Thammavongsa	Open	11.00	11.00
93-19-010	True Love	C.Thammavongsa	Open	12.00	12.00
93-19-011	Bakin' at the Beach	C.Thammavongsa	Open	11.00	11.00
93-19-012	Wee Little Piggy	C.Thammavongsa	Open	8.00	8.00
93-19-013	P.O.P Display Sign	C.Thammavongsa	Open	8.00	8.00
94-19-014	Pretty Piglet	C.Thammavongsa	Open	8.00	8.00
94-19-019	Bedtime	C.Thammavongsa	Open	9.50	9.50
94-19-016	Birthday Surprise	C.Thammavongsa	Open	9.50	9.50
94-19-017	Sandcastle	C.Thammavongsa	Open	12.00	12.00
94-19-018	Snacktime	C.Thammavongsa	Open	11.50	11.50
94-19-019	Play Ball	C.Thammavongsa	Open	11.50	11.50
94-19-020	Special Treat	C.Thammavongsa	Open	11.50	11.50
94-19-021	Storytime	C.Thammavongsa	Open	13.00	13.00
94-19-022	Wedded Bliss	C.Thammavongsa	Open	16.00	16.00
94-19-023	Ole Fishing Hole	C.Thammavongsa	Open	16.00	16.00

Ganz — **The Pigsville Accessories**

94-20-001	Barn	C.Thammavongsa	Open	35.00	35.00
94-20-002	Silo	C.Thammavongsa	Open	15.00	15.00

Ganz — **Pigsville/The Christmas Collection**

94-21-001	Joy to the World	C.Thammavongsa	Open	10.00	10.00
94-21-002	Santa Pig	C.Thammavongsa	Open	11.00	11.00
94-21-003	Mistletoe Magic	C.Thammavongsa	Open	14.00	14.00
94-21-004	Let It Snow	C.Thammavongsa	Open	12.00	12.00
94-21-005	Christmas Trimmings	C.Thammavongsa	10,000	24.00	24.00
94-21-006	Yuletide Carols	C.Thammavongsa	Open	19.00	19.00

Ganz — **Pigsville/The Valentine Collection**

94-22-001	Together Forever	C.Thammavongsa	Open	15.00	15.00
94-22-002	Champagne & Roses	C.Thammavongsa	Open	14.00	14.00
94-22-003	Sweetheart Pig	C.Thammavongsa	Open	8.00	8.00
94-22-004	I Love You	C.Thammavongsa	Open	9.50	9.50
94-22-005	Lovestruck	C.Thammavongsa	Open	10.00	10.00
94-22-006	I'm All Yours	C.Thammavongsa	Open	11.50	11.50

Gartlan USA — **Plaques**

85-01-001	Pete Rose-"Desire to Win", signed	T. Sizemore	4,192	75.00	300.00
86-01-002	George Brett-"Royalty in Motion", signed	J. Martin	2,000	85.00	250-275.
86-01-003	Reggie Jackson-"The Roundtripper",signed	J. Martin	500	150.00	325.00
86-01-004	Reggie Jackson Artist Proof-The Roundtripper, signed	J. Martin	44	175.00	250-475.
87-01-005	Roger Staubach, signed	C. Soileau	1,979	85.00	250.00

Gartlan USA — **Baseball/Football/Hockey Card Series**

85-02-001	Pete Rose Ceramic Baseball Card	T. Sizemore	Open	9.95	18.00
85-02-002	Pete Rose Ceramic Baseball Card, signed	T. Sizemore	4,192	39.00	50.00
86-02-003	George Brett Baseball Rounder	J. Martin	Open	9.95	14.00
86-02-004	George Brett Baseball Rounder, signed	J. Martin	2,000	30.00	50.00
86-02-005	George Brett Ceramic Baseball	J. Martin	Open	20.00	20.00
86-02-006	George Brett Ceramic Baseball, signed	J. Martin	2,000	39.75	95-125.
87-02-007	Roger Staubach Ceramic Football Card	C. Soileau	Open	10.00	18.00
87-02-008	Roger Staubach Ceramic Football Card, signed	C. Soileau	1,979	39.00	39.00
90-02-009	Wayne Gretzky Ceramic Hockey Card	M. Taylor	Open	16.00	18.00
91-02-010	Joe Montana Ceramic Football Card	M. Taylor	Open	18.00	18.00
92-02-011	Carlton Fisk Ceramic Baseball Card	M. Taylor	Open	18.00	18.00
92-02-012	Tom Seaver Ceramic Baseball Card	M. Taylor	Open	18.00	18.00
92-02-013	Gordon Howe Ceramic Hockey Card	M. Taylor	Open	18.00	18.00
92-02-014	Phil Esposito Ceramic Hockey Card	M. Taylor	Open	18.00	18.00
94-02-015	Troy Aikman Ceramic Football Card	M. Taylor	Open	11.95	11.95
94-02-016	Shaquille O'Neal Ceramic Basketball Card	M. Taylor	Open	11.95	11.95
94-02-017	Frank Thomas Ceramic Baseball Card	M. Taylor	Open	11.95	11.95
94-02-018	Patrick Ewing Ceramic Basketball Card	M. Taylor	Open	11.95	11.95
94-02-019	Dave Earnhardt Ceramic Racing Card	M. Taylor	Open	11.95	11.95
94-02-020	Joe Montana Ceramic Football Card (K.C. Chiefs)	M. Taylor	Open	11.95	11.95
94-02-021	Ken Griffey Jr. Ceramic Baseball Card (1994 Seattle Mariners' Uniform)	M. Taylor	Open	11.95	11.95

Gartlan USA — **Shaquille O'Neal**

94-03-001	Ceramiques™ Five-Card Set	M. Taylor	10,000	79.95	79.95
94-03-002	Ceramiques™ Five-Card A.P. Set, signed	M. Taylor	1,000	249.95	249.95

Gartlan USA — **Troy Aikman**

94-04-001	Classic™ 3-Card Set	M. Taylor	Open	49.95	49.95

Gartlan USA — **Shaquille O'Neal**

94-05-001	Classic™ 3-Card Set	M. Taylor	Open	49.95	49.95

Gartlan USA — **Magic Johnson Gold Rim Collection**

88-06-001	Magic Johnson Artist Proof-"Magic in Motion", signed	Roger	250	175.00	2500.00
88-06-002	Magic Johnson-"Magic in Motion"	Roger	1,737	125.00	450-500.
88-06-003	Magic Johnson Commemorative	Roger	32	275.00	4500.00

Gartlan USA — **Mike Schmidt "500th" Home Run Edition**

87-07-001	Figurine-signed	Roger	1,987	150.00	750-850.
87-07-002	Figurine-signed, Artist Proof	Roger	20	275.00	12-1700.
87-07-003	Plaque-"Only Perfect", signed	Paluso	500	150.00	225.00
87-07-004	Plaque-"Only Perfect", Artist Proof	Paluso	20	200.00	550.00

Gartlan USA — **Pete Rose Diamond Collection**

88-08-001	Farewell Ceramic Baseball Card, signed	Forbes	4,256	39.00	50.00
88-08-002	Farewell Ceramic Baseball Card	Forbes	Open	9.95	18.00

Gartlan USA — **Reggie Jackson "500th" Home Run Edition**

86-09-001	Ceramic Baseball Card, signed	J. Martin	1,986	39.00	50.00
86-09-002	Ceramic Baseball Card	J. Martin	Open	9.95	18.00

Gartlan USA — **Kareem Abdul-Jabbar Sky-Hook Collection**

89-10-001	Kareem Abdul-Jabbar "The Captain"-signed	L. Heyda	1,989	175.00	330.00
89-10-002	Kareem Abdul-Jabbar, Artist Proof	L. Heyda	100	200.00	550.00
89-10-003	Kareem Abdul-Jabbar, Commemorative	L. Heyda	33	275.00	4-6000.

Gartlan USA — **Signed Figurines**

85-11-001	Pete Rose-"For the Record", signed	H. Reed	4,192	125.00	1000.00
89-11-002	Carl Yastrzemski-"Yaz"	L. Heyda	1,989	150.00	300.00
89-11-003	Carl Yastrzemski-"Yaz", Artist Proof	L. Heyda	250	150.00	450-495.
89-11-004	Johnny Bench	L. Heyda	1,989	150.00	300-375.
89-11-005	Johnny Bench, Artist Proof	L. Heyda	250	150.00	425-495.

		ARTIST	EDITION	ISSUE	QUOTE
89-11-006	Joe DiMaggio	L. Heyda	2,214	275.00	895-950.
90-11-007	Joe DiMaggio- Pinstripe Yankee Clipper	L. Heyda	325	695.00	18-2250.
89-11-008	John Wooden-Coaching Classics	L. Heyda	1,975	175.00	175.00
89-11-009	John Wooden-Coaching Classics, Artist Proof	L. Heyda	250	350.00	350.00
89-11-010	Ted Williams	L. Heyda	2,654	295.00	575-675.
89-11-011	Ted Williams, Artist Proof	L. Heyda	250	650.00	650.00
89-11-012	Wayne Gretzky	L. Heyda	1,851	225.00	575-795.
89-11-013	Wayne Gretzky, Artist Proof	L. Heyda	300	695.00	1700.00
89-11-014	Yogi Berra	F. Barnum	2,150	225.00	225.00
89-11-015	Yogi Berra, Artist Proof	F. Barnum	250	350.00	350.00
89-11-016	Steve Carlton	L. Heyda	3,290	175.00	175-225.
89-11-017	Steve Carlton, Artist Proof	L. Heyda	300	350.00	350.00
90-11-018	Whitey Ford	S. Barnum	2,360	125-225.	125-225.
90-11-019	Whitey Ford, Artist Proof	S. Barnum	250	350.00	350.00
90-11-020	Luis Aparicio	J. Slockbower	1,984	125-225.	125-225.
90-11-021	Darryl Strawberry	L. Heyda	2,500	100-225.	100-225.
90-11-022	George Brett	F. Barnum	2,250	225.00	225.00
91-11-023	Ken Griffey, Jr	J. Slockbower	1,989	200-225.	200-225.
91-11-024	Warren Spahn	J. Slockbower	1,973	125-225.	125-225.
91-11-025	Rod Carew - Hitting Splendor	J. Slockbower	1,991	125-225.	125-225.
91-11-026	Brett Hull - The Golden Brett	L. Heyda	1,986	150-250	150-250.
92-11-027	Brett Hull, Artist Proof	L. Heyda	300	350.00	350.00
91-11-028	Bobby Hull - The Golden Jet	L. Heyda	1,983	150-250.	150-250.
92-11-029	Bobby Hull, Artist Proof	L. Heyda	300	350.00	350.00
91-11-030	Hull Matched Figurines	L. Heyda	950	500.00	500.00
91-11-031	Al Barlick	V. Bova	1,989	125-175.	125-175.
91-11-032	Monte Irvin	V. Bova	1,973	100-225.	100-225.
91-11-033	Joe Montana	F. Barnum	2,250	325.00	325-375.
91-11-034	Joe Montana, Artist Proof	F. Barnum	250	500.00	650.00
92-11-035	Isiah Thomas	J. Slockbower	1,990	225.00	225.00
92-11-036	Hank Aaron	F. Barnum	1,982	150-225.	150-225.
92-11-037	Carlton Fisk	J. Slockbower	1,972	150-225.	150-225.
92-11-038	Carlton Fisk, Artist Proof	J. Slockbower	300	350.00	350.00
92-11-039	Gordie Howe	L. Heyda	2,358	150-225.	150-225.
92-11-040	Gordie Howe, Artist Proof	L. Heyda	250	295-500.	295-500.
92-11-043	Hank Aaron Commemorative w/displ. case	F. Barnum	755	275.00	275.00
92-11-044	Hank Aaron, Artist Proof	F. Barnum	300	325.00	350.00
92-11-045	Stan Musial	J. Slockbower	1,969	200-325.	200-325.
92-11-046	Stan Musial, Artist Proof	J. Slockbower	300	300-500.	300-500.
92-11-047	Ralph Kiner	J. Slockbower	1,975	100-225.	100-225.
92-11-048	Tom Seaver	J. Slockbower	1,992	125-225.	125-225.
93-11-049	Kristi Yamaguchi	K. Ling Sun	950	125-195.	125-195.
93-11-050	Bob Cousy	L. Heyda	950	150-225.	150-225.
94-11-051	Sam Snead	L. Cella	950	150-225.	150-225.
94-11-052	Shaquille O'Neal	R. Sun	1,992	225-275.	225-275.
94-11-053	Troy Aikman	V. Davila	1,993	225.00	225.00
94-11-054	Eddie Matthews	R. Sun	950	195.00	195.00
94-11-055	Frank Thomas	D. Carroll	1,993	225.00	225.00
95-11-056	Patrick Ewing	L. Hanna	1,994	225.00	225.00
95-11-057	Dale Earnhardt	L. Hanna	1,994	225.00	225.00
94-11-058	Ken Griffey Jr., signed artist proof	J. Slockbower	300	395.00	395.00
94-11-059	Gordie Howe, signed artist proof	L. Heyda	300	395.00	395.00

Gartlan USA — **Score Board Marquee™**

		ARTIST	EDITION	ISSUE	QUOTE
94-12-001	Troy Aikman	V. Davila	10,000	79.95	79.95
94-12-002	Shaquille O'Neal	R. Sun	10,000	79.95	79.95
94-12-003	Frank Thomas	D. Carroll	10,000	79.95	79.95
94-12-004	Patrick Ewing	L. Hanna	10,000	79.95	79.95
94-12-005	Dale Earnhardt	L. Hanna	10,000	79.95	79.95
95-12-006	Joe Montana (K. C. Chiefs)	F. Barnum	10,000	79.95	79.95

Gartlan USA — **All-Star Gems Miniature Figurines**

		ARTIST	EDITION	ISSUE	QUOTE
89-13-001	Carl Yastrzemski	L. Heyda	10,000	39.95-79.	40-79.00
89-13-002	Johnny Bench	L. Heyda	10,000	39.95-79.	40-79.00
89-13-003	Ted Williams	L. Heyda	10,000	39.95-79.	40-79.00
89-13-004	Steve Carlton	L. Heyda	10,000	39.95-79.	40-79.00
90-13-005	John Wooden	L. Heyda	10,000	39.95-79.	40-79.00
90-13-006	Wayne Gretzky	L. Heyda	10,000	39.95-79.	40-79.00
90-13-007	Pete Rose	F. Barnum	10,000	75.00	79.00
90-13-008	Mike Schmidt	Roger	10,000	39.95-79.	40-79.00
90-13-009	Yogi Berra	F. Barnum	10,000	39.95-79.	40-79.00
90-13-010	George Brett	F. Barnum	10,000	39.95-79.	40-79.00
90-13-011	Whitey Ford	F. Barnum	10,000	39.95-79.	40-79.00
90-13-012	Luis Aparicio	J. Slockbower	10,000	39.95-79.	40-79.00
90-13-013	Darryl Strawberry	L. Heyda	10,000	39.95-79.	40-79.00
90-13-014	Kareem Abdul-Jabbar	L. Heyda	10,000	75.00	75.00
91-13-015	Ken Griffey, Jr.	J. Slockbower	10,000	39.95-79.	40-79.00
91-13-016	Warren Spahn	J. Slockbower	10,000	39.95-79.	40-79.00
91-13-017	Rod Carew	J. Slockbower	10,000	39.95-79.	40-79.00
91-13-018	Brett Hull	L. Heyda	10,000	39.95-79.	40-79.00
91-13-019	Bobby Hull	L. Heyda	10,000	39.95-79.	40-79.00
91-13-020	Monte Irvin	V. Bova	10,000	39.95-79.	40-79.00
91-13-021	Joe Montana	F. Barnum	10,000	39.95-79.	95.00
92-13-022	Isiah Thomas	J. Slockbower	10,000	39.95-79.	40-79.00
92-13-023	Hank Aaron	F. Barnum	10,000	39.95-79.	40-79.00
92-13-024	Carlton Fisk	J. Slockbower	10,000	39.95-79.	40-79.00
92-13-025	Phil Esposito	L. Heyda	10,000	39.95-79.	40-79.00
92-13-026	Stan Musial	J. Slockbower	2,269	99.00	99.00
92-13-027	Tom Seaver	J. Slockbower	10,000	39.95-79.	40-79.00
92-13-028	Ralph Kiner	J. Slockbower	10,000	39.95-79.	40-79.00
92-13-029	Gordie Howe	L. Heyda	10,000	39.95-79.	40-79.00
93-13-030	Kristi Yamaguchi	K. Ling Sun	5,000	39.95-79.	40-79.00
94-13-031	Bob Cousy	L. Heyda	5,000	39.95-79.	40-79.00
94-13-032	Sam Snead	L. Cella	5,000	39.95-79.	40-79.00
94-13-033	Shaquille O'Neal	R. Sun	10,000	39.95-79.	40-79.00
94-13-034	Carl Ripken, Jr.	L. Heyda	10,000	39.95-79.	40-79.00
94-13-035	Troy Aikman	V. Davila	10,000	39.95-79.	40-79.00
94-13-036	Brian Boitano	R. Sun	5,000	39.95-79.	40-79.00
94-13-037	Steve Young	L. Cella	5,000	39.95-79.	40-79.00
94-13-038	Eddie Matthews	R. Sun	5,000	39.95-79.	40-79.00
94-13-039	Frank Thomas	D. Carroll	10,000	39.95	39.95
95-13-040	Patrick Ewing	L. Hanna	10,000	39.95	39.95
95-13-041	Dale Earnhardt	L. Hanna	10,000	39.95	39.95
95-13-042	Joe Montana (K.C. Chiefs)	F. Barnum	10,000	39.95	39.95

Gartlan USA — **Members Only Figurine**

		ARTIST	EDITION	ISSUE	QUOTE
90-14-001	Wayne Gretzky-Home Uniform	L. Heyda	N/A	75.00	225-350.
91-14-002	Joe Montana-Road Uniform	F. Barnum	N/A	75.00	175-195.
91-14-003	Kareem Abdul-Jabbar	L. Heyda	N/A	75.00	100-125.
92-14-004	Mike Schmidt	J. Slockbower	N/A	79.00	100.00
93-14-005	Hank Aaron	J. Slockbower	N/A	79.00	79.00
94-14-006	Shaquille O'Neal	L. Cella	N/A	39.95	39.95

Gartlan USA — **Club Gift**

		ARTIST	EDITION	ISSUE	QUOTE
89-15-001	Pete Rose, Plate (8 1/2")	B. Forbes	Closed	Gift	100.00
90-15-002	Al Barlick, Plate (8 1/2")	M. Taylor	Closed	Gift	49.00
91-15-003	Joe Montana (8 1/2")	M. Taylor	Closed	Gift	125.00
92-15-004	Ken Griffey Jr., Plate (8 1/2")	M. Taylor	Closed	30.00	49.00
93-15-005	Gordie Howe, Plate (8 1/2")	M. Taylor	Closed	30.00	30.00
94-15-006	Shaquille O'Neal, Plate (8 1/2")	M. Taylor	Closed	30.00	30.00
95-15-007	Troy Aikman, Plate (8 1/2")	M. Taylor	Yr.Iss.	30.00	30.00

Gartlan USA — **Master's Museum Collection**

		ARTIST	EDITION	ISSUE	QUOTE
91-16-001	Kareem Abdul-Jabbar	L. Heyda	500	3000.00	3000.00
91-16-002	Wayne Gretzky	L. Heyda	500	set	set
91-16-003	Joe Montana	F. Barnum	500	set	set
91-16-004	Ted Williams	L. Heyda	500	set	set
93-16-005	Stan Musial	J. Slockbower	500	850.00	850.00

Gartlan USA — **Negro League Series**

		ARTIST	EDITION	ISSUE	QUOTE
91-17-001	James "Cool Papa" Bell	V. Bova	1,499	195.00	195.00
91-17-002	Ray Dandridge	V. Bova	1,987	195.00	195.00
91-17-003	Buck Leonard	V. Bova	1,972	195.00	195.00
91-17-004	Matched-Number set #1-950	V. Bova	950	500.00	500.00

Genesis — **Aquatics Collection**

		ARTIST	EDITION	ISSUE	QUOTE
94-01-001	Sea Wolves (Killer Whales)	K. Cantrell	950	950.00	950.00
94-01-002	Old Men of the Sea (Sea Otters)	K. Cantrell	950	990.00	990.00
94-01-003	Ancient Mariner (Sea Turtles)	K. Cantrell	950	950.00	950.00
94-01-004	Bringing Up Baby (Humpback Whales)	K. Cantrell	950	950.00	950.00
94-01-005	Splish Splash (Dolphins)	K. Cantrell	950	950.00	950.00

Genesis — **River Dwellers**

		ARTIST	EDITION	ISSUE	QUOTE
94-02-001	Construction Crew (Beavers)	K. Cantrell	950	990.00	990.00
94-02-002	Ice Follies	K. Cantrell	950	890.00	890.00
94-02-003	Salmon Supper	K. Cantrell	950	990.00	990.00

Genesis — **Ocean Realm**

		ARTIST	EDITION	ISSUE	QUOTE
94-03-001	Dophins (Dolphins in Lucite)	K. Cantrell	1,250	240.00	240.00
94-03-002	Otters	K. Cantrell	1,250	240.00	240.00
94-03-003	Marlins	K. Cantrell	1,250	240.00	240.00
94-03-004	Humpback Whales	K. Cantrell	1,250	240.00	240.00
94-03-005	Manta Rays	K. Cantrell	1,250	240.00	240.00

Genesis — **Special Commission**

		ARTIST	EDITION	ISSUE	QUOTE
94-04-001	Fragile Planet	K. Cantrell	950	N/A	N/A

Goebel — **Goebel Figurines**

		ARTIST	EDITION	ISSUE	QUOTE
63-01-001	Little Veterinarian (Mysterious Malady)201	N. Rockwell	Closed	15.00	500.00
63-01-002	Boyhood Dreams (Adventurers between Adventures) 202	N. Rockwell	Closed	12.00	500.00
63-01-003	Mother's Helper (Pride of Parenthood) 203	N. Rockwell	Closed	15.00	500.00
63-01-004	His First Smoke 204	N. Rockwell	Closed	9.00	500.00
63-01-005	My New Pal (A Boy Meets His Dog) 205	N. Rockwell	Closed	12.00	500.00
63-01-006	Home Cure 206	N. Rockwell	Closed	16.00	500.00
63-01-007	Timely Assistance (Love Aid) 207	N. Rockwell	Closed	16.00	500.00
63-01-008	She Loves Me (Day Dreamer) 208	N. Rockwell	Closed	8.00	500.00
63-01-009	Buttercup Test (Beguiling Buttercup) 209	N. Rockwell	Closed	10.00	500.00
63-01-010	First Love (A Scholarly Pace) 210	N. Rockwell	Closed	30.00	500.00
63-01-011	Patient Anglers (Fisherman's Paradise)211	N. Rockwell	Closed	18.00	500.00
63-01-012	Advertising Plaque 212	N. Rockwell	Closed	Unkn.	750.00

Goebel — **Betsey Clark Figurines**

		ARTIST	EDITION	ISSUE	QUOTE
72-02-001	Bless You	G. Bochmann	Closed	18.00	275.00
72-02-002	Friends	G. Bochmann	Closed	21.00	400.00
72-02-003	So Much Beauty	G. Bochmann	Closed	25.00	350.00
72-02-004	Little Miracle	G. Bochmann	Closed	25.00	350.00

Goebel — **Co-Boy**

		ARTIST	EDITION	ISSUE	QUOTE
71-03-001	Robby the Vegetarian	G. Skrobek	Closed	16.00	80.00
71-03-002	Mike the Jam Maker	G. Skrobek	Closed	16.00	72.00
71-03-003	Bit the Bachelor	G. Skrobek	Closed	16.00	28-80.00
71-03-004	Tom the Honey Lover	G. Skrobek	Closed	16.00	28.00
71-03-005	Sam the Gourmet	G. Skrobek	Closed	16.00	28.00
71-03-006	Plum the Pastry Chef	G. Skrobek	Closed	16.00	28-60.00
71-03-007	Wim the Court Supplier	G. Skrobek	Closed	16.00	28.00
71-03-008	Fips the Foxy Fisherman	G. Skrobek	Closed	16.00	80-90.00
72-03-009	Porz the Mushroom Muncher	G. Skrobek	Closed	20.00	28.00
72-03-010	Sepp the Beer Buddy	G. Skrobek	Closed	20.00	72.00
72-03-011	Kuni the Big Dipper	G. Skrobek	Closed	20.00	60-65.00
71-03-012	Fritz the Happy Boozer	G. Skrobek	Closed	16.00	42-50.00
72-03-013	Bob the Bookworm	G. Skrobek	Closed	20.00	42-50.00
72-03-014	Brum the Lawyer	G. Skrobek	Closed	20.00	72.00
72-03-015	Utz the Banker	G. Skrobek	Closed	20.00	80.00
72-03-016	Co-Boy Plaque	G. Skrobek	Closed	20.00	72.00
XX-03-017	Jack the Village Pharmacist	G. Skrobek	Closed	Unkn.	42-50.00
XX-03-018	John the Hawkeye Hunter	G. Skrobek	Closed	Unkn.	72.00
XX-03-019	Petrl the Village Angler	G. Skrobek	Closed	Unkn.	72.00
XX-03-020	Conny the Night Watchman	G. Skrobek	Closed	Unkn.	42-50.00
XX-03-021	Ed the Wine Cellar Steward	G. Skrobek	Closed	Unkn.	42-50.00
XX-03-022	Toni the Skier	G. Skrobek	Closed	Unkn.	72.00
XX-03-023	Candy the Baker's Delight	G. Skrobek	Closed	Unkn.	78.00
XX-03-024	Mark-Safety First	G. Skrobek	Closed	Unkn.	78.00
XX-03-025	Bert the Soccer Star	G. Skrobek	Closed	Unkn.	50.00
XX-03-026	Jim the Bowler	G. Skrobek	Closed	Unkn.	50.00
XX-03-027	Max the Boxing Champ	G. Skrobek	Closed	Unkn.	50.00
78-03-028	Gil the Goalie	G. Skrobek	Closed	34.00	50.00
78-03-029	Pat the Pitcher	G. Skrobek	Closed	34.00	50.00
78-03-030	Tommy Touchdown	G. Skrobek	Closed	34.00	50.00
80-03-031	Ted the Tennis Player	G. Skrobek	Closed	49.00	50.00
80-03-032	Herb the Horseman	G. Skrobek	Closed	49.00	90.00
80-03-033	Monty the Mountain Climber	G. Skrobek	Closed	49.00	72.00
80-03-034	Carl the Chef	G. Skrobek	Closed	49.00	72-80.00
80-03-035	Doc the Doctor	G. Skrobek	Closed	49.00	72.00
80-03-036	Gerd the Diver	G. Skrobek	Closed	49.00	125-175.
81-03-037	George the Gourmand	G. Skrobek	Closed	45.00	72.00
81-03-038	Greg the Gourmet	G. Skrobek	Closed	45.00	50.00
81-03-039	Ben the Blacksmith	G. Skrobek	Closed	45.00	50.00
81-03-040	Al the Trumpet Player	G. Skrobek	Closed	45.00	50.00
81-03-041	Peter the Accordionist	G. Skrobek	Closed	45.00	50.00
81-03-042	Niels the Strummer	G. Skrobek	Closed	45.00	50.00
81-03-043	Greta the Happy Housewife	G. Skrobek	Closed	45.00	50.00
81-03-044	Nick the Nightclub Singer	G. Skrobek	Closed	45.00	50.00
81-08-045	Walter the Jogger	G. Skrobek	Closed	45.00	50.00
84-03-046	Rudy the World Traveler	G. Skrobek	Closed	45.00	100.00
84-03-047	Sid the Vintner	G. Skrobek	Closed	45.00	50.00
84-03-048	Herman the Butcher	G. Skrobek	Closed	45.00	50.00

		ARTIST	EDITION	ISSUE	QUOTE
84-03-049	Rick the Fireman	G. Skrobek	Closed	45.00	50-80.00
84-03-050	Chuck the Chimney Sweep	G. Skrobek	Closed	45.00	50.00
84-03-051	Chris the Shoemaker	G. Skrobek	Closed	45.00	50.00
84-03-052	Felix the Baker	G. Skrobek	Closed	45.00	85.00
84-03-053	Marthe the Nurse	G. Skrobek	Closed	45.00	50.00
84-03-054	Paul the Dentist	G. Skrobek	Closed	45.00	80.00
84-03-055	Homer the Driver	G. Skrobek	Closed	45.00	50-80.00
84-03-056	Brad the Clockmaker	G. Skrobek	Closed	75.00	125.00
87-03-057	Clock-Cony the Watchman	G. Skrobek	Closed	125.00	125.00
87-03-058	Clock-Sepp and the Beer Keg	G. Skrobek	Closed	125.00	125.00
87-03-059	Bank-Pete the Pirate	G. Skrobek	Closed	80.00	80.00
87-03-060	Bank-Utz the Money Bags	G. Skrobek	Closed	80.00	80.00
87-03-061	Chuck on His Pig	G. Skrobek	Closed	75.00	75.00
Goebel	**Co-Boys-Culinary**				
94-04-001	Mike the Jam Maker 301050	Welling/Skrobek	Open	30.00	30.00
94-04-002	Sepp the Drunkard 301051	Welling/Skrobek	Open	30.00	30.00
94-04-003	Plum the Sweets Maker 301052	Welling/Skrobek	Open	30.00	30.00
94-04-004	Tom the Sweet Tooth 301053	Welling/Skrobek	Open	30.00	30.00
94-04-005	Robby the Vegetarian 301054	Welling/Skrobek	Open	30.00	30.00
Goebel	**Co-Boys-Sports**				
94-05-001	Petri the Fisherman 301055	Welling/Skrobek	Open	30.00	30.00
94-05-002	Toni the Skier 301056	Welling/Skrobek	Open	30.00	30.00
94-05-003	Jim the Bowler 301057	Welling/Skrobek	Open	30.00	30.00
94-05-004	Ted the Tennis Player 301058	Welling/Skrobek	Open	30.00	30.00
94-05-005	Bert the Soccer Player 301059	Welling/Skrobek	Open	30.00	30.00
Goebel	**Co-Boys-Professionals**				
94-06-001	Brum the Lawyer 301060	Welling/Skrobek	Open	30.00	30.00
94-06-002	Utz the Banker 301061	Welling/Skrobek	Open	30.00	30.00
94-06-003	Conny the Nightwatchman 301062	Welling/Skrobek	Open	30.00	30.00
94-06-004	John the Hunter 301063	Welling/Skrobek	Open	30.00	30.00
94-06-005	Doc the Doctor 301064	Welling/Skrobek	Open	30.00	30.00
Goebel/M.I. Hummel	**M.I. Hummel Collectibles Figurines**				
88-01-001	A Budding Maestro 477	M.I. Hummel	Open	Unkn.	95.00
XX-01-002	A Fair Measure 345	M.I. Hummel	Open	Unkn.	165-260.
93-01-003	A Free Flight 569	M.I. Hummel	Open	Unkn.	185.00
XX-01-004	A Gentle Glow 439	M.I. Hummel	Open	Unkn.	190.00
91-01-005	A Nap 534	M.I. Hummel	Open	Unkn.	70-110.
XX-01-006	Accordion Boy 185	M.I. Hummel	12/94	Unkn.	180.00
XX-01-007	Adoration 23/I	M.I. Hummel	Open	Unkn.	215-325.
XX-01-008	Adoration 23/III	M.I. Hummel	Open	Unkn.	510.00
XX-01-009	Adventure Bound 347	M.I. Hummel	Open	Unkn.	3500.00
89-01-010	An Apple A Day 403	M.I. Hummel	Open	Unkn.	260.00
XX-01-011	Angel Duet 261	M.I. Hummel	Open	Unkn.	195.00
XX-01-012	Angel Serenade 214/0	M.I. Hummel	Open	Unkn.	80.00
XX-01-013	Angel Serenade with Lamb 83	M.I. Hummel	Open	Unkn.	170-175.
XX-01-014	Angel with Accordion 238/B	M.I. Hummel	Open	Unkn.	40-50.00
XX-01-015	Angel with Lute 238/A	M.I. Hummel	Open	Unkn.	32-50.00
XX-01-016	Angel With Trumpet 238/C	M.I. Hummel	Open	Unkn.	40-50.00
XX-01-017	Angelic Song 144	M.I. Hummel	Open	Unkn.	135.00
XX-01-018	Apple Tree Boy 142/3/0	M.I. Hummel	Open	Unkn.	90-130.
XX-01-019	Apple Tree Boy 142/I	M.I. Hummel	Open	Unkn.	250.00
XX-01-020	Apple Tree Boy 142/V	M.I. Hummel	Open	Unkn.	1080.00
XX-01-021	Apple Tree Girl 141/3/0	M.I. Hummel	Open	Unkn.	174.00
XX-01-022	Apple Tree Girl 141/I	M.I. Hummel	Open	Unkn.	245.00
XX-01-023	Apple Tree Girl 141/V	M.I. Hummel	Open	Unkn.	1080.00
91-01-024	Art Critic 318	M.I. Hummel	Open	Unkn.	260.00
XX-01-025	Artist, The 304	M.I. Hummel	Open	Unkn.	220.00
XX-01-026	Auf Wiedersehen 153/0	M.I. Hummel	Open	Unkn.	220.00
XX-01-027	Auf Wiedersehen 153/I	M.I. Hummel	Open	Unkn.	270.00
XX-01-028	Autumn Harvest 355	M.I. Hummel	Open	Unkn.	195.00
XX-01-029	Baker 128	M.I. Hummel	Open	Unkn.	175.00
XX-01-030	Baking Day 330	M.I. Hummel	Open	Unkn.	240.00
XX-01-031	Band Leader 129	M.I. Hummel	Open	Unkn.	180.00
XX-01-032	Band Leader 129/4/0	M.I. Hummel	Open	Unkn.	90.00
XX-01-033	Barnyard Hero 195/2/0	M.I. Hummel	Open	Unkn.	150.00
XX-01-034	Barnyard Hero 195/I	M.I. Hummel	Open	Unkn.	290.00
XX-01-035	Bashful 377	M.I. Hummel	Open	Unkn.	180.00
90-01-036	Bath Time 412	M.I. Hummel	Open	Unkn.	350.00
XX-01-037	Begging His Share 9	M.I. Hummel	Open	Unkn.	220.00
XX-01-038	Be Patient 197/2/0	M.I. Hummel	Open	Unkn.	175-182.
XX-01-039	Be Patient 197/I	M.I. Hummel	Open	Unkn.	260.00
XX-01-040	Big Housecleaning 363	M.I. Hummel	Open	Unkn.	260.00
XX-01-041	Bird Duet 169	M.I. Hummel	Open	Unkn.	90-130.
XX-01-042	Bird Watcher 300	M.I. Hummel	Open	Unkn.	205.00
89-01-043	Birthday Cake 338	M.I. Hummel	Open	Unkn.	130.00
94-01-044	Birthday Present (Special Event)	M.I. Hummel	Open	140.00	140.00
XX-01-045	Birthday Serenade 218/2/0	M.I. Hummel	Open	Unkn.	160.00
XX-01-046	Birthday Serenade 218/0	M.I. Hummel	Open	Unkn.	270.00
XX-01-047	Blessed Event 333	M.I. Hummel	Open	Unkn.	300.00
XX-01-048	Bookworm 8	M.I. Hummel	Open	Unkn.	195.00
XX-01-049	Bookworm 3/I	M.I. Hummel	Open	Unkn.	270.00
XX-01-050	Boots 143/0	M.I. Hummel	Open	Unkn.	180.00
XX-01-051	Boots 143/I	M.I. Hummel	Open	Unkn.	300.00
XX-01-052	Botanist, The 351	M.I. Hummel	Open	Unkn.	195.00
XX-01-053	Boy with Accordion 390	M.I. Hummel	Open	Unkn.	75.00
XX-01-054	Boy with Horse 239C	M.I. Hummel	Open	Unkn.	50.00
XX-01-055	Boy with Toothache 217	M.I. Hummel	Open	Unkn.	200.00
XX-01-056	Brother 95	M.I. Hummel	Open	Unkn.	180.00
XX-01-057	Builder, The 305	M.I. Hummel	Open	Unkn.	220.00
XX-01-058	Busy Student 367	M.I. Hummel	Open	Unkn.	150.00
XX-01-059	Call to Glory 739	M.I. Hummel	Open	250.00	250.00
XX-01-060	Carnival 328	M.I. Hummel	Open	Unkn.	205.00
XX-01-061	Celestial Musician 188/0	M.I. Hummel	Open	Unkn.	195.00
93-01-062	Celestial Musician (mini) 188/4/0	M.I. Hummel	Open	Unkn.	90.00
XX-01-063	Chick Girl 57/2/0	M.I. Hummel	Open	Unkn.	135.00
XX-01-064	Chick Girl 57/0	M.I. Hummel	Open	Unkn.	155-164.
XX-01-065	Chick Girl 57/I	M.I. Hummel	Open	Unkn.	250.00
XX-01-066	Chicken-Licken 385	M.I. Hummel	Open	Unkn.	260.00
XX-01-067	Chicken-Licken 385/4	M.I. Hummel	Open	Unkn.	90.00
XX-01-068	Chimney Sweep 12/2/0	M.I. Hummel	Open	Unkn.	110.00
XX-01-069	Chimney Sweep 12/I	M.I. Hummel	Open	Unkn.	195-218.
89-01-070	Christmas Angel 301	M.I. Hummel	Open	Unkn.	230.00
XX-01-071	Christmas Song 343	M.I. Hummel	Open	Unkn.	195.00
XX-01-072	Cinderella 337	M.I. Hummel	Open	Unkn.	260.00
XX-01-073	Close Harmony 336	M.I. Hummel	Open	Unkn.	260.00
XX-01-074	Confidentially 314	M.I. Hummel	Open	Unkn.	260.00
XX-01-075	Congratulations 17/0	M.I. Hummel	Open	Unkn.	165-180.
XX-01-076	Coquettes 179	M.I. Hummel	Open	Unkn.	260.00

		ARTIST	EDITION	ISSUE	QUOTE
XX-01-077	Crossroads (Original) 331	M.I. Hummel	Open	Unkn.	255-468.
XX-01-078	Crossroads (Commemorative) 331	M.I. Hummel	10,000	Unkn.	470-500.
XX-01-079	Culprits 56/A	M.I. Hummel	Open	Unkn.	265.00
89-01-080	Daddy's Girls 371	M.I. Hummel	Open	Unkn.	150-220.
XX-01-081	Doctor 127	M.I. Hummel	Open	Unkn.	100-145.
XX-01-082	Doll Bath 319	M.I. Hummel	Open	Unkn.	260.00
XX-01-083	Doll Mother 67	M.I. Hummel	Open	Unkn.	190.00
XX-01-084	Duet 130	M.I. Hummel	Open	Unkn.	250.00
XX-01-085	Easter Greetings 378	M.I. Hummel	Open	Unkn.	195.00
XX-01-086	Easter Time 384	M.I. Hummel	Open	Unkn.	240.00
92-01-087	Evening Prayer 495	M.I. Hummel	Open	Unkn.	67-105.
XX-01-088	Eventide 99	M.I. Hummel	Open	Unkn.	240-315.
XX-01-089	Farm Boy 66	M.I. Hummel	Open	Unkn.	205.00
XX-01-090	Favorite Pet 361	M.I. Hummel	Open	Unkn.	260.00
XX-01-091	Feathered Friends 344	M.I. Hummel	Open	Unkn.	240.00
XX-01-092	Feeding Time 199/0	M.I. Hummel	Open	Unkn.	175.00
XX-01-093	Feeding Time 199/I	M.I. Hummel	Open	Unkn.	240.00
XX-01-094	Festival Harmony, with Mandolin 172/0	M.I. Hummel	Open	Unkn.	280.00
94-01-095	Festival Harmony w/Mandolin 172	M.I. Hummel	Open	95.00	95.00
XX-01-096	Festival Harmony, with Flute 173/0	M.I. Hummel	Open	Unkn.	245-280.
XX-01-097	Flower Vendor 381	M.I. Hummel	Open	Unkn.	220.00
XX-01-098	Follow the Leader 369	M.I. Hummel	Open	Unkn.	1100.00
XX-01-099	For Father 87	M.I. Hummel	Open	Unkn.	195.00
XX-01-100	For Mother 257/2/0	M.I. Hummel	Open	Unkn.	110.00
XX-01-101	For Mother 257	M.I. Hummel	Open	Unkn.	130-185.
XX-01-102	Forest Shrine 183	M.I. Hummel	Open	Unkn.	495.00
91-01-103	Friend Or Foe 434	M.I. Hummel	Open	Unkn.	195.00
XX-01-104	Friends 136/I	M.I. Hummel	Open	Unkn.	195.00
XX-01-105	Friends 136/V	M.I. Hummel	Open	Unkn.	1080.00
93-01-106	Friends Together 662/I	M.I. Hummel	25,000	475.00	475.00
93-01-107	Friends Together 662/0	M.I. Hummel	Open	260.00	260.00
XX-01-108	Gay Adventure 356	M.I. Hummel	Open	Unkn.	175.00
XX-01-109	Girl with Doll 239/B	M.I. Hummel	Open	Unkn.	50.00
XX-01-110	Girl with Nosegay 239/A	M.I. Hummel	Open	Unkn.	50.00
XX-01-111	Girl with Sheet Music 389	M.I. Hummel	Open	Unkn.	75-174.
XX-01-112	Girl with Trumpet 391	M.I. Hummel	Open	Unkn.	75.00
XX-01-113	Going Home 383	M.I. Hummel	Open	Unkn.	280.00
XX-01-114	Going to Grandma's 52/0	M.I. Hummel	Open	Unkn.	250.00
XX-01-115	Good Friends 182	M.I. Hummel	Open	Unkn.	120-175.
XX-01-116	Good Hunting 307	M.I. Hummel	Open	Unkn.	220.00
XX-01-117	Good Night 214/C	M.I. Hummel	Open	Unkn.	80.00
XX-01-118	Good Shepherd 42/0	M.I. Hummel	Open	Unkn.	220.00
XX-01-119	Goose Girl 47/3/0	M.I. Hummel	Open	Unkn.	145-160.
XX-01-120	Goose Girl 47/0	M.I. Hummel	Open	Unkn.	205.00
XX-01-121	Grandma's Girl 561	M.I. Hummel	Open	Unkn.	135.00
XX-01-122	Grandpa's Boy 562	M.I. Hummel	Open	Unkn.	135.00
XX-01-123	Guiding Angel 357	M.I. Hummel	Open	Unkn.	80.00
XX-01-124	Happiness 86	M.I. Hummel	Open	Unkn.	120.00
XX-01-125	Happy Birthday 176/0	M.I. Hummel	Open	Unkn.	195.00
XX-01-126	Happy Birthday 176/I	M.I. Hummel	Open	Unkn.	270.00
XX-01-127	Happy Days 150/2/0	M.I. Hummel	Open	Unkn.	160.00
XX-01-128	Happy Days 150/0	M.I. Hummel	Open	Unkn.	270.00
XX-01-129	Happy Days 150/I	M.I. Hummel	Open	Unkn.	430.00
XX-01-130	Happy Pastime 69	M.I. Hummel	Open	Unkn.	145.00
XX-01-131	Happy Traveller 109/0	M.I. Hummel	Open	Unkn.	130.00
XX-01-132	Hear Ye! Hear Ye! 15/0	M.I. Hummel	Open	Unkn.	180-280.
XX-01-133	Hear Ye! Hear Ye! 15/I	M.I. Hummel	Open	Unkn.	225.00
XX-01-134	Hear Ye! Hear Ye! 15/2/0	M.I. Hummel	Open	Unkn.	135.00
XX-01-135	Heavenly Angel 21/0	M.I. Hummel	Open	Unkn.	110.00
XX-01-136	Heavenly Angel 21/0/1/2	M.I. Hummel	Open	Unkn.	160-190.
XX-01-137	Heavenly Angel 21/I	M.I. Hummel	Open	Unkn.	230.00
XX-01-138	Heavenly Lullaby 262	M.I. Hummel	Open	Unkn.	170.00
XX-01-139	Heavenly Protection 88/I	M.I. Hummel	Open	Unkn.	350-395.
XX-01-140	Hello 124/0	M.I. Hummel	Open	Unkn.	195-210.
XX-01-141	Home from Market 198/2/0	M.I. Hummel	Open	Unkn.	130.00
XX-01-142	Home from Market 198/I	M.I. Hummel	Open	Unkn.	195.00
XX-01-143	Homeward Bound 334	M.I. Hummel	Open	Unkn.	320.00
90-01-144	Horse Trainer 423	M.I. Hummel	Open	Unkn.	200.00
89-01-145	Hosanna 480	M.I. Hummel	Open	Unkn.	90.00
89-01-146	I'll Protect Him 483	M.I. Hummel	Open	Unkn.	75.00
94-01-147	I'm Carefree 633	M.I. Hummel	Open	365.00	365.00
89-01-148	I'm Here 478	M.I. Hummel	Open	Unkn.	95.00
89-01-149	In D Major 430	M.I. Hummel	Open	Unkn.	180.00
XX-01-150	In The Meadow 459	M.I. Hummel	Open	Unkn.	180.00
XX-01-151	In Tune 414	M.I. Hummel	Open	Unkn.	250.00
XX-01-152	Is It Raining? 420	M.I. Hummel	Open	Unkn.	240.00
XX-01-153	Joyful 53	M.I. Hummel	Open	Unkn.	110-130.
XX-01-154	Joyous News 27/III	M.I. Hummel	Open	Unkn.	158-195.
XX-01-155	Just Fishing 373	M.I. Hummel	Open	Unkn.	140-205.
XX-01-156	Just Resting 112/3/0	M.I. Hummel	Open	Unkn.	135.00
XX-01-157	Just Resting 112/I	M.I. Hummel	Open	Unkn.	250.00
XX-01-158	Kindergartner 467	M.I. Hummel	Open	Unkn.	180.00
XX-01-159	Kiss Me 311	M.I. Hummel	Open	Unkn.	168-260.
XX-01-160	Knitting Lesson 256	M.I. Hummel	Open	Unkn.	475.00
XX-01-161	Knit One, Purl One 432	M.I. Hummel	Open	Unkn.	105.00
92-01-162	Land in Sight 530	M.I. Hummel	30,000	Unkn.	1-1600.
XX-01-163	Latest News 184/0	M.I. Hummel	Open	Unkn.	195-260.
XX-01-164	Let's Sing 110/0	M.I. Hummel	Open	Unkn.	115.00
XX-01-165	Let's Sing 110/I	M.I. Hummel	Open	Unkn.	155.00
XX-01-166	Letter to Santa Claus 340	M.I. Hummel	Open	Unkn.	225-300.
93-01-166	Little Architect 410/I	M.I. Hummel	Open	Unkn.	290.00
XX-01-167	Little Bookkeeper 306	M.I. Hummel	Open	Unkn.	220-260.
XX-01-168	Little Cellist 89/I	M.I. Hummel	Open	Unkn.	195.00
XX-01-169	Little Drummer 240	M.I. Hummel	Open	Unkn.	135.00
XX-01-170	Little Fiddler 2/4/0	M.I. Hummel	Open	Unkn.	90.00
XX-01-171	Little Fiddler 4	M.I. Hummel	Open	Unkn.	185.00
XX-01-172	Little Fiddler 2/0	M.I. Hummel	Open	Unkn.	205.00
XX-01-173	Little Gabriel 32	M.I. Hummel	Open	Unkn.	125.00
XX-01-174	Little Gardener 74	M.I. Hummel	Open	Unkn.	110.00
XX-01-175	Little Goat Herder 200/0	M.I. Hummel	Open	Unkn.	175-180.
XX-01-176	Little Goat Herder 200/I	M.I. Hummel	Open	Unkn.	220.00
XX-01-177	Little Guardian 145	M.I. Hummel	Open	Unkn.	135.00
XX-01-178	Little Helper 73	M.I. Hummel	Open	Unkn.	110-130.
XX-01-179	Little Hiker 16/2/0	M.I. Hummel	Open	Unkn.	110.00
XX-01-180	Little Hiker 16/I	M.I. Hummel	Open	Unkn.	200.00
XX-01-181	Little Nurse 376	M.I. Hummel	Open	Unkn.	108-225.
XX-01-182	Little Pharmacist 322	M.I. Hummel	Open	Unkn.	185-220.
XX-01-183	Little Scholar 80	M.I. Hummel	Open	Unkn.	195.00
XX-01-184	Little Shopper 96	M.I. Hummel	Open	Unkn.	130.00
XX-01-185	Little Sweeper 171/4/0	M.I. Hummel	Open	Unkn.	60-90.00
88-01-186	Little Sweeper 171	M.I. Hummel	Open	Unkn.	126.00
XX-01-187	Little Tailor 308	M.I. Hummel	Open	Unkn.	220.00

		ARTIST	EDITION	ISSUE	QUOTE
XX-01-188	Little Thrifty 118	M.I. Hummel	Open	Unkn.	130.00
XX-01-189	Little Tooter 214/H	M.I. Hummel	Open	Unkn.	95.00
XX-01-190	Little Tooter 214/H	M.I. Hummel	Open	Unkn.	110.00
XX-01-191	Lost Stocking 374	M.I. Hummel	Open	Unkn.	130.00
XX-01-192	Mail is Here 226	M.I. Hummel	Open	Unkn.	505.00
89-01-193	Make A Wish 475	M.I. Hummel	Open	Unkn.	175.00
XX-01-194	March Winds 43	M.I. Hummel	Open	Unkn.	145-180.
XX-01-195	Max and Moritz 123	M.I. Hummel	Open	Unkn.	205.00
XX-01-196	Meditation 13/2/0	M.I. Hummel	Open	Unkn.	130.00
XX-01-197	Meditation 13/0	M.I. Hummel	Open	Unkn.	205.00
XX-01-198	Merry Wanderer 11/2/0	M.I. Hummel	Open	Unkn.	125.00
XX-01-199	Merry Wanderer 11/0	M.I. Hummel	Open	Unkn.	175.00
XX-01-200	Merry Wanderer 7/0	M.I. Hummel	Open	Unkn.	245.00
XX-01-201	Mischief Maker 342	M.I. Hummel	Open	Unkn.	240.00
94-01-202	Morning Stroll 375	M.I. Hummel	Open	170.00	170.00
XX-01-203	Mother's Darling 175	M.I. Hummel	Open	Unkn.	195.00
XX-01-204	Mother's Helper 133	M.I. Hummel	Open	Unkn.	165-175.
XX-01-205	Mountaineer 315	M.I. Hummel	Open	Unkn.	145-195.
XX-01-206	Not For You 317	M.I. Hummel	Open	Unkn.	220.00
89-01-207	One For You, One For Me 482	M.I. Hummel	Open	Unkn.	95.00
93-01-208	One Plus One 556	M.I. Hummel	Open	Unkn.	115.00
XX-01-209	On Holiday 350	M.I. Hummel	Open	Unkn.	160.00
XX-01-210	On Secret Path 386	M.I. Hummel	Open	Unkn.	160-225.
XX-01-211	Out of Danger 56/B	M.I. Hummel	Open	Unkn.	265.00
93-01-212	Parade Of Lights 616	M.I. Hummel	Open	Unkn.	235.00
XX-01-213	Photographer 178	M.I. Hummel	Open	Unkn.	260.00
XX-01-214	Playmates 58/2/0	M.I. Hummel	Open	Unkn.	135.00
XX-01-215	Playmates 58/0	M.I. Hummel	Open	Unkn.	110-150.
XX-01-216	Playmates 58/I	M.I. Hummel	Open	Unkn.	250.00
XX-01-217	Postman 119	M.I. Hummel	Open	Unkn.	180.00
89-01-218	Postman 119/2/0	M.I. Hummel	Open	Unkn.	90-125.
XX-01-219	Prayer Before Battle 20	M.I. Hummel	Open	Unkn.	155.00
XX-01-220	Retreat to Safety 201/2/0	M.I. Hummel	Open	Unkn.	150.00
XX-01-221	Retreat to Safety 201/I	M.I. Hummel	Open	Unkn.	275.00
XX-01-222	Ride into Christmas 396/2/0	M.I. Hummel	Open	Unkn.	220.00
XX-01-223	Ride into Christmas 396/I	M.I. Hummel	Open	Unkn.	280-390.
XX-01-224	Ring Around the Rosie 348	M.I. Hummel	Open	Unkn.	2500.00
XX-01-225	Run-A-Way 327	M.I. Hummel	Open	Unkn.	225.00
XX-01-226	St. George 55	M.I. Hummel	Open	Unkn.	300.00
92-01-227	Scamp 553	M.I. Hummel	Open	Unkn.	105.00
XX-01-228	School Boy 82/2/0	M.I. Hummel	Open	Unkn.	130.00
XX-01-229	School Boy 82/0	M.I. Hummel	Open	Unkn.	175.00
XX-01-230	School Boy 82/II	M.I. Hummel	Open	Unkn.	415.00
XX-01-231	School Boys 170/I	M.I. Hummel	Open	Unkn.	1100.00
XX-01-232	School Girl 81/2/0	M.I. Hummel	Open	Unkn.	130.00
XX-01-233	School Girl 81/0	M.I. Hummel	Open	Unkn.	175.00
XX-01-234	School Girls 177/I	M.I. Hummel	Open	Unkn.	1100.00
XX-01-235	Sensitive Hunter 6/0	M.I. Hummel	Open	Unkn.	175.00
XX-01-236	Sensitive Hunter 6/I	M.I. Hummel	Open	Unkn.	230.00
XX-01-237	Sensitive Hunter 6/2/0	M.I. Hummel	Open	Unkn.	135.00
XX-01-238	Serenade 85/0	M.I. Hummel	Open	Unkn.	120.00
XX-01-239	Serenade 85/4/0	M.I. Hummel	Open	Unkn.	90.00
XX-01-240	Serenade 85/II	M.I. Hummel	Open	Unkn.	410.00
XX-01-241	She Loves Me, She Loves Me Not 174	M.I. Hummel	Open	Unkn.	170.00
XX-01-242	Shepherd's Boy 214/G/II	M.I. Hummel	Open	Unkn.	120.00
XX-01-243	Shepherd's Boy 64	M.I. Hummel	Open	Unkn.	200.00
XX-01-244	Shining Light 358	M.I. Hummel	Open	Unkn.	80.00
XX-01-245	Sing Along 433	M.I. Hummel	Open	Unkn.	260.00
XX-01-246	Singing Lesson 63	M.I. Hummel	Open	Unkn.	80-110.
XX-01-247	Sing With Me 405	M.I. Hummel	Open	Unkn.	100-280.
XX-01-248	Sister 98/2/0	M.I. Hummel	Open	Unkn.	130.00
XX-01-249	Sister 98/0	M.I. Hummel	Open	Unkn.	180.00
XX-01-250	Skier 59	M.I. Hummel	Open	Unkn.	195.00
90-01-251	Sleep Tight 424	M.I. Hummel	Open	Unkn.	200.00
XX-01-252	Smart Little Sister 346	M.I. Hummel	Open	Unkn.	225.00
XX-01-253	Soldier Boy 332	M.I. Hummel	Open	Unkn.	195.00
XX-01-254	Soloist 135/4/0	M.I. Hummel	Open	Unkn.	90.00
XX-01-255	Soloist 135	M.I. Hummel	Open	Unkn.	120.00
88-01-256	Song of Praise 454	M.I. Hummel	Open	Unkn.	90.00
88-01-257	Sound the Trumpet 457	M.I. Hummel	Open	Unkn.	90.00
88-01-258	Sounds of the Mandolin 438	M.I. Hummel	Open	Unkn.	110.00
XX-01-259	Spring Dance 353/0	M.I. Hummel	Open	Unkn.	280.00
XX-01-260	Star Gazer 132	M.I. Hummel	Open	Unkn.	195.00
XX-01-261	Stitch in Time 255	M.I. Hummel	Open	Unkn.	260.00
XX-01-262	Stitch in Time 255	M.I. Hummel	Open	Unkn.	85.00
XX-01-263	Stormy Weather 71/I	M.I. Hummel	Open	Unkn.	415.00
XX-01-264	Stormy Weather 71/2/0	M.I. Hummel	Open	Unkn.	190-275.
92-01-265	Storybook Time 458	M.I. Hummel	Open	Unkn.	230-360.
XX-01-266	Street Singer 131	M.I. Hummel	Open	Unkn.	170.00
XX-01-267	Surprise 94/3/0	M.I. Hummel	Open	Unkn.	140.00
XX-01-268	Surprise 94/I	M.I. Hummel	Open	Unkn.	260.00
XX-01-269	Sweet Greetings 352	M.I. Hummel	Open	Unkn.	195.00
XX-01-270	Sweet Music 186	M.I. Hummel	Open	Unkn.	180.00
XX-01-271	Telling Her Secret 196/0	M.I. Hummel	Open	Unkn.	270.00
88-01-272	The Accompanist 453	M.I. Hummel	Open	Unkn.	90.00
91-01-273	The Guardian 455	M.I. Hummel	Open	Unkn.	115-155.
94-01-274	The Poet 397	M.I. Hummel	Open	220.00	220.00
92-01-275	The Professor 320/0	M.I. Hummel	Open	Unkn.	195.00
XX-01-276	Thoughtful 415	M.I. Hummel	Open	Unkn.	205.00
XX-01-277	Timid Little Sister 394	M.I. Hummel	Open	Unkn.	390.00
XX-01-278	To Market 49/3/0	M.I. Hummel	Open	Unkn.	150.00
XX-01-279	To Market 49/0	M.I. Hummel	Open	Unkn.	250.00
XX-01-280	Trumpet Boy 97	M.I. Hummel	Open	Unkn.	120-130.
89-01-281	Tuba Player 437	M.I. Hummel	Open	Unkn.	240.00
XX-01-282	Tuneful Angel 359	M.I. Hummel	Open	Unkn.	80.00
XX-01-283	Umbrella Boy 152/0/A	M.I. Hummel	Open	Unkn.	330-530.
XX-01-284	Umbrella Boy 152/II/A	M.I. Hummel	Open	Unkn.	1300.00
XX-01-285	Umbrella Girl 152/0/B	M.I. Hummel	Open	Unkn.	530.00
XX-01-286	Umbrella Girl 152/II/B	M.I. Hummel	Open	Unkn.	1300.00
XX-01-287	Village Boy 51/3/0	M.I. Hummel	Open	Unkn.	110.00
XX-01-288	Village Boy 51/2/0	M.I. Hummel	Open	Unkn.	125.00
XX-01-289	Village Boy 51/0	M.I. Hummel	Open	Unkn.	220.00
XX-01-290	Visiting an Invalid 382	M.I. Hummel	Open	Unkn.	195.00
XX-01-291	Volunteers 50/2/0	M.I. Hummel	Open	Unkn.	205.00
XX-01-292	Volunteers 50/0	M.I. Hummel	Open	Unkn.	270.00
XX-01-293	Waiter 154/0	M.I. Hummel	Open	Unkn.	195.00
XX-01-294	Waiter 154/I	M.I. Hummel	Open	Unkn.	260.00
XX-01-295	Wash Day 321	M.I. Hummel	Open	Unkn.	260.00
89-01-296	Wash Day 321/4/0	M.I. Hummel	Open	Unkn.	90.00
XX-01-297	Watchful Angel 194	M.I. Hummel	Open	Unkn.	290.00
XX-01-298	Wayside Devotion 28/II	M.I. Hummel	Open	Unkn.	395.00
XX-01-299	Wayside Devotion 28/III	M.I. Hummel	Open	Unkn.	520.00

		ARTIST	EDITION	ISSUE	QUOTE
XX-01-300	Wayside Harmony 111/3/0	M.I. Hummel	Open	Unkn.	135.00
XX-01-301	Wayside Harmony 111/I	M.I. Hummel	Open	Unkn.	245.00
XX-01-302	Weary Wanderer 204	M.I. Hummel	Open	Unkn.	225.00
XX-01-303	We Congratulate 214/E/II	M.I. Hummel	Open	Unkn.	150.00
XX-01-304	We Congratulate 220	M.I. Hummel	Open	Unkn.	145.00
90-01-305	What's New? 418	M.I. Hummel	Open	Unkn.	260.00
XX-01-306	Which Hand? 258	M.I. Hummel	Open	Unkn.	180.00
92-01-307	Whistler's Duet 413	M.I. Hummel	Open	Unkn.	250.00
XX-01-308	Whitsuntide 163	M.I. Hummel	Open	Unkn.	290.00
88-01-309	Winter Song 476	M.I. Hummel	Open	Unkn.	100.00
XX-01-310	With Loving Greetings 309	M.I. Hummel	Open	Unkn.	175.00
XX-01-311	Worship 84/0	M.I. Hummel	Open	Unkn.	145.00

Goebel/M.I. Hummel — **M.I. Hummel's Temp. Out of Production**

		ARTIST	EDITION	ISSUE	QUOTE
XX-02-001	Angel Serenade 260/E	M.I. Hummel	Suspd.	Unkn.	345.00
XX-02-002	Apple Tree Boy 142/X	M.I. Hummel	Suspd.	Unkn.	17000.00
XX-02-003	Apple Tree Girl 141/X	M.I. Hummel	Suspd.	Unkn.	17000.00
XX-02-004	Blessed Child 78/I/83	M.I. Hummel	Suspd.	Unkn.	35.00
XX-02-005	Blessed Child 78/II/83	M.I. Hummel	Suspd.	Unkn.	40.00
XX-02-006	Blessed Child 78/III/83	M.I. Hummel	Suspd.	Unkn.	50.00
XX-02-007	Bookworm 3/II	M.I. Hummel	Suspd.	Unkn.	900-1200
XX-02-008	Bookworm 3/III	M.I. Hummel	Suspd.	Unkn.	975-1300
XX-02-009	Celestial Musician 188/I	M.I. Hummel	Suspd.	Unkn.	230.00
XX-02-010	Christ Child 18	M.I. Hummel	Suspd.	Unkn.	120-300.
XX-02-011	Donkey 260/L	M.I. Hummel	Suspd.	Unkn.	115.00
XX-02-012	Festival Harmony, with Mandolin 172/II	M.I. Hummel	Suspd.	Unkn.	325-400.
XX-02-013	Festival Harmony ,with Flute 173/II	M.I. Hummel	Suspd.	Unkn.	325-400.
XX-02-014	Flower Madonna, color 10/III/II	M.I. Hummel	Suspd.	Unkn.	375-475.
XX-02-015	Flower Madonna, white 10/III/W	M.I. Hummel	Suspd.	Unkn.	250-310.
XX-02-016	Going to Grandma's 52/I	M.I. Hummel	Suspd.	Unkn.	180-390.
XX-02-017	Good Night 260/D	M.I. Hummel	Suspd.	Unkn.	120.00
XX-02-018	Goose Girl 47/II	M.I. Hummel	Suspd.	Unkn.	380.00
XX-02-019	Happy Traveler 109/II	M.I. Hummel	Suspd.	Unkn.	350-750.
XX-02-020	Hear Ye! Hear Ye! 15/II	M.I. Hummel	Suspd.	Unkn.	400.00
XX-02-021	Heavenly Angel 21/II	M.I. Hummel	Suspd.	Unkn.	390.00
XX-02-022	Heavenly Protection 88/II	M.I. Hummel	Suspd.	Unkn.	590.00
XX-02-023	Hello 124/I	M.I. Hummel	Suspd.	Unkn.	160-230.
XX-02-024	Holy Child 70	M.I. Hummel	Suspd.	Unkn.	135-160.
XX-02-025	Hummel Display Plaque 187	M.I. Hummel	Suspd.	Unkn.	150-200.
XX-02-026	King, Kneeling 260/P	M.I. Hummel	Suspd.	Unkn.	430.00
XX-02-027	King, Moorish 260/N	M.I. Hummel	Suspd.	Unkn.	450.00
XX-02-028	King, Standing 260/O	M.I. Hummel	Suspd.	Unkn.	450.00
XX-02-029	Little Band 392	M.I. Hummel	Suspd.	Unkn.	132-225.
XX-02-030	Little Cellist 89/II	M.I. Hummel	Suspd.	Unkn.	380.00
XX-02-031	Little Fiddler 2/I	M.I. Hummel	Suspd.	Unkn.	370.00
XX-02-032	Little Fiddler 2/II	M.I. Hummel	Suspd.	Unkn.	975-1200
XX-02-033	Little Fiddler 2/III	M.I. Hummel	Suspd.	Unkn.	975-1300
XX-02-034	Little Tooter 260/K	M.I. Hummel	Suspd.	Unkn.	140.00
XX-02-035	Lullaby 24/III	M.I. Hummel	Suspd.	Unkn.	285-450.
XX-02-036	Madonna w/o Halo, color 46/I/6	M.I. Hummel	Suspd.	Unkn.	N/A
XX-02-037	Madonna w/o Halo,white 46/I/W	M.I. Hummel	Suspd.	Unkn.	N/A
XX-02-038	Madonna Praying, color 46/III/6	M.I. Hummel	Suspd.	Unkn.	155.00
XX-02-039	Madonna Praying, white 46/0/W	M.I. Hummel	Suspd.	Unkn.	45.00
XX-02-040	Madonna Praying, white 46/I/W	M.I. Hummel	Suspd.	Unkn.	75-95.00
XX-02-041	Meditation 13/II	M.I. Hummel	Suspd.	Unkn.	275-310.
XX-02-042	Meditation 13/V	M.I. Hummel	Suspd.	Unkn.	975-1250
XX-02-043	Merry Wanderer 7/I	M.I. Hummel	Suspd.	Unkn.	360.00
XX-02-044	Merry Wanderer 7/II	M.I. Hummel	Suspd.	Unkn.	1100.00
XX-02-045	Merry Wanderer 7/III	M.I. Hummel	Suspd.	Unkn.	875-1200
XX-02-046	Merry Wanderer 7/X	M.I. Hummel	Suspd.	Unkn.	17000.00
XX-02-047	Ox 260/M	M.I. Hummel	Suspd.	Unkn.	130.00
XX-02-048	School Boys 170/III	M.I. Hummel	Suspd.	Unkn.	18-5000.
XX-02-049	School Girls 177/III	M.I. Hummel	Suspd.	Unkn.	18-5000.
XX-02-050	Sensitive Hunter 6/II	M.I. Hummel	Suspd.	Unkn.	300-400.
XX-02-051	Sheep (Lying) 260/R	M.I. Hummel	Suspd.	Unkn.	40.00
XX-02-052	Sheep (Standing) w/ Lamb 260/H	M.I. Hummel	Suspd.	Unkn.	80.00
XX-02-053	Shepherd, Standing 260/G	M.I. Hummel	Suspd.	Unkn.	475.00
XX-02-054	Shepherd Boy, Kneeling 260/J	M.I. Hummel	Suspd.	Unkn.	270.00
XX-02-055	Spring Cheer 72	M.I. Hummel	Suspd.	Unkn.	150-200.
XX-02-056	Spring Dance 353/I	M.I. Hummel	Suspd.	Unkn.	265-500.
XX-02-057	Telling Her Secret 196/I	M.I. Hummel	Suspd.	Unkn.	225-375.
XX-02-058	To Market 49/I	M.I. Hummel	Suspd.	Unkn.	100-420.
XX-02-059	Volunteers 50/I	M.I. Hummel	Suspd.	Unkn.	240-425.
XX-02-060	Village Boy 51/I	M.I. Hummel	Suspd.	Unkn.	110-250.
XX-02-061	We Congratulate 260/F	M.I. Hummel	Suspd.	Unkn.	220-330.
XX-02-062	Worship 84/V	M.I. Hummel	Suspd.	Unkn.	925-1050

Goebel/M.I. Hummel — **M.I. Hummel Collectibles Figurines Retired**

		ARTIST	EDITION	ISSUE	QUOTE
XX-03-001	Farewell 65	M.I. Hummel	Closed	Unkn.	240.00
XX-03-002	Globe Trotter 79	M.I. Hummel	Closed	Unkn.	150-200.
XX-03-003	Jubilee 416	M.I. Hummel	Closed	200.00	325-400.
37-03-004	Lost Sheep 68/2/0	M.I. Hummel	Closed	Unkn.	125.00
37-03-005	Lost Sheep 68/0	M.I. Hummel	Closed	Unkn.	180.00
XX-03-006	Puppy Love I	M.I. Hummel	Closed	125.00	230-400.
XX-03-007	Signs Of Spring 203/I	M.I. Hummel	Closed	155.00	225-500.
XX-03-008	Signs Of Spring 203/2/0	M.I. Hummel	Closed	120.00	190.00
XX-03-009	Strolling Along 5	M.I. Hummel	Closed	115.00	200.00
XX-03-010	Supreme Protection 364	M.I. Hummel	Closed	150.00	200-250.

Goebel/M.I. Hummel — **M.I. Hummel Collectibles-Century Collection**

		ARTIST	EDITION	ISSUE	QUOTE
86-04-001	Chapel Time 442	M.I. Hummel	Closed	500.00	1-1200.
87-04-002	Pleasant Journey 406	M.I. Hummel	Closed	500.00	12-1800.
88-04-003	Call to Worship 441	M.I. Hummel	Closed	600.00	660-950.
89-04-004	Harmony in Four Parts 471	M.I. Hummel	Closed	850.00	1-1400.
90-04-005	Let's Tell the World 487	M.I. Hummel	Closed	875.00	600-1100
91-04-006	We Wish You The Best 600	M.I. Hummel	Closed	1300.00	13-1500.
92-04-007	On Our Way 472	M.I. Hummel	Closed	950.00	950.00
93-04-008	Welcome Spring 635	M.I. Hummel	Closed	1085.00	1085.00
94-04-009	Rock-A-Bye 111	M.I. Hummel	12/94	1150.00	1150.00

Goebel/M.I. Hummel — **M.I. Hummel Collectibles Nativity Components**

		ARTIST	EDITION	ISSUE	QUOTE
XX-05-001	Madonna 214/A/M/0	M.I. Hummel	Open	Unkn.	120.00
XX-05-002	Infant Jesus 214/A/K/0	M.I. Hummel	Open	Unkn.	40.00
XX-05-003	St. Joseph 214/B/0	M.I. Hummel	Open	Unkn.	120.00
XX-05-004	Shepherd Standing 214/F/0	M.I. Hummel	Open	Unkn.	145.00
XX-05-005	Shepherd Kneeling 214/G/0	M.I. Hummel	Open	Unkn.	110.00
XX-05-006	Donkey 214/J/0	M.I. Hummel	Open	Unkn.	50.00
XX-05-007	Ox,214/K/0	M.I. Hummel	Open	Unkn.	50.00
XX-05-008	King, Moorish 214/L/0	M.I. Hummel	Open	Unkn.	140.00
XX-05-009	King, Kneeling 214M/0	M.I. Hummel	Open	Unkn.	130.00
XX-05-010	King, Kneeling w/ Box 214/N/0	M.I. Hummel	Open	Unkn.	131.00
XX-05-011	Lamb 214/O/0	M.I. Hummel	Open	Unkn.	17.00

		ARTIST	EDITION	ISSUE	QUOTE
XX-05-012	Flying Angel 366/0	M.I. Hummel	Open	Unkn.	85.00
XX-05-013	Little Tooter 214/14/0	M.I. Hummel	Open	Unkn.	95.00
XX-05-014	Small Camel Standing	Goebel	Open	Unkn.	160.00
XX-05-015	Small Camel Lying	Goebel	Open	Unkn.	160.00
XX-05-016	Small Camel Kneeling	Goebel	Open	Unkn.	160.00
XX-05-017	Madonna 214/A/M/I	M.I. Hummel	Open	Unkn.	160.00
XX-05-018	Infant Jesus 214/A/K/I	M.I. Hummel	Open	Unkn.	60.00
XX-05-019	St. Joseph color 214/B/I	M.I. Hummel	Open	Unkn.	160.00
XX-05-020	Good Night 214/C/I	M.I. Hummel	Open	Unkn.	80.00
XX-05-021	Angel Serenade 214/D/I	M.I. Hummel	Open	Unkn.	80.00
XX-05-022	We Congratulate 214/E/I	M.I. Hummel	Open	Unkn.	150.00
XX-05-023	Shepherd with Sheep-1 piece 214/F/I	M.I. Hummel	Open	Unkn.	165.00
XX-05-024	Shepherd Boy 214/G/I	M.I. Hummel	Open	Unkn.	120.00
XX-05-025	Little Tooter 214/H/I	M.I. Hummel	Open	Unkn.	110.00
XX-05-026	Donkey 214/J/I	M.I. Hummel	Open	Unkn.	65.00
XX-05-027	Ox 214/K/I	M.I. Hummel	Open	Unkn.	65.00
XX-05-028	King, Moorish 214/L/I	M.I. Hummel	Open	Unkn.	170.00
XX-05-029	King, Kneeling 214/M/I	M.I. Hummel	Open	Unkn.	160.00
XX-05-030	King, Kneeling w/Box 214/N/I	M.I. Hummel	Open	Unkn.	150.00
XX-05-031	Lamb 214/O/I	M.I. Hummel	Open	Unkn.	20.00
XX-05-032	Flying Angel/color 366/I	M.I. Hummel	Open	Unkn.	115.00
XX-05-033	Camel Standing	Goebel	Open	Unkn.	205.00
XX-05-034	Camel Lying	Goebel	Open	Unkn.	205.00
XX-05-035	Camel Kneeling	Goebel	Open	Unkn.	205.00
XX-05-036	Madonna-260/A	M.I. Hummel	Suspd.	Unkn.	590.00
XX-05-037	St. Joseph 260/B	M.I. Hummel	Suspd.	Unkn.	590.00
XX-05-038	Infant Jesus 260/C	M.I. Hummel	Suspd.	Unkn.	120.00
XX-05-039	Good Night 260/D	M.I. Hummel	Suspd.	Unkn.	120.00
XX-05-040	Angel Serenade 260/E	M.I. Hummel	Suspd.	Unkn.	115.00
XX-05-041	We Congratulate 260/F	M.I. Hummel	Suspd.	Unkn.	330.00
XX-05-042	Shepherd, Standing 260/G	M.I. Hummel	Suspd.	Unkn.	475.00
XX-05-043	Sheep (Standing) w/ Lamb 260/H	M.I. Hummel	Suspd.	Unkn.	80.00
XX-05-044	Shepherd Boy, Kneeling 260/J	M.I. Hummel	Suspd.	Unkn.	270.00
XX-05-045	Little Tooter 260/K	M.I. Hummel	Suspd.	Unkn.	140.00
XX-05-046	Donkey 260/L	M.I. Hummel	Suspd.	Unkn.	115.00
XX-05-047	Ox 260/M	M.I. Hummel	Suspd.	Unkn.	130.00
XX-05-048	King, Moorish 260/N	M.I. Hummel	Suspd.	Unkn.	450.00
XX-05-049	King, Standing 260/O	M.I. Hummel	Suspd.	Unkn.	450.00
XX-05-050	King, Kneeling 260/P	M.I. Hummel	Suspd.	Unkn.	430.00
XX-05-051	Sheep (Lying) 260/R	M.I. Hummel	Suspd.	Unkn.	40.00
XX-05-052	Holy Family,3 Pcs., Color 214/A/M/0, B/0, A/K/0	M.I. Hummel	Open	Unkn.	270.00
XX-05-053	Holy Family 3 Pcs.,Color 214/A/M/I, B/I, A/K/I	M.I. Hummel	Open	Unkn.	380.00
XX-05-054	12-Pc. Set Figs. only, Color, 214/A/M/I, B/I, A/K/I, F/I,G/I,J/I K/I, L/I, M/I, N/I, O/I, 366/I	M.I. Hummel	Open	Unkn.	1350.00
XX-05-055	16-Pc. Set Figs. only, Color, 214/A/M/I, B/I, A/K/I, C/I, D/I, E/I, F/I, G/I, H/I, J/I, K/I, L/I, M/I, N/I, O/I, 366/I	M.I. Hummel	Suspd.	Unkn.	1820.00
XX-05-056	17-Pc. Set Large Color 16 Figs.& Wooden Stable 260 A-R	M.I. Hummel	Suspd.	Unkn.	4540.00
XX-05-057	Stable only, fits 3-pc. HUM214 Set	M.I. Hummel	Open	Unkn.	45.00
XX-05-058	Stable only fits12 or 16-pc. HUM214/II Set	M.I. Hummel	Open	Unkn.	100.00
XX-05-059	Stable only, fits 16-piece HUM260 Set	M.I. Hummel	Open	Unkn.	400.00

Goebel/M.I. Hummel — M.I. Hummel Collectibles-Madonna Figurines

		ARTIST	EDITION	ISSUE	QUOTE
XX-06-001	Flower Madonna, color 10/I/II	M.I. Hummel	Open	Unkn.	390.00
XX-06-002	Flower Madonna, white 10/I/W	M.I. Hummel	Open	Unkn.	165.00
XX-06-003	Madonna Holding Child, color 151/II	M.I. Hummel	Suspd.	Unkn.	115.00
XX-06-004	Madonna Holding Child, white 151/W	M.I. Hummel	Suspd.	Unkn.	320.00
XX-06-005	Madonna with Halo, color 45/I/6	M.I. Hummel	Open	Unkn.	115.00
XX-06-006	Madonna with Halo, white 45/I/W	M.I. Hummel	Open	Unkn.	70.00
XX-06-007	Madonna without Halo, color 46/I/6	M.I. Hummel	Suspd.	Unkn.	75.00
XX-06-008	Madonna without Halo, white 46/I/W	M.I. Hummel	Suspd.	Unkn.	50.00

Goebel/M.I. Hummel — M.I. Hummel Collectibles-Christmas Angels

		ARTIST	EDITION	ISSUE	QUOTE
93-07-001	Angel in Cloud 585	M.I. Hummel	Open	25.00	25.00
93-07-002	Angel with Lute 580	M.I. Hummel	Open	25.00	25.00
93-07-003	Angel with Trumpet 586	M.I. Hummel	Open	25.00	25.00
93-07-004	Celestial Musician 578	M.I. Hummel	Open	25.00	25.00
93-07-005	Festival Harmony with Flute 577	M.I. Hummel	Open	25.00	25.00
93-07-006	Festival Harmony with Mandolin 576	M.I. Hummel	Open	25.00	25.00
93-07-007	Gentle Song 582	M.I. Hummel	Open	25.00	25.00
93-07-008	Heavenly Angel 575	M.I. Hummel	Open	25.00	25.00
93-07-009	Prayer of Thanks 581	M.I. Hummel	Open	25.00	25.00
93-07-010	Song of Praise 579	M.I. Hummel	Open	25.00	25.00

Goebel/M.I. Hummel — First Edition M.I. Hummel Miniatures

		ARTIST	EDITION	ISSUE	QUOTE
91-08-001	Accordion Boy -37225	M.I. Hummel	Suspd.	105.00	105.00
89-08-002	Apple Tree Boy -37219	M.I. Hummel	Suspd.	115.00	250-300.
90-08-003	Baker -37222	M.I. Hummel	Suspd.	100.00	125-280.
92-08-004	Bavarian Church (Display) -37370	M.I. Hummel	Retrd.	60.00	60.00
88-08-005	Bavarian Cottage (Display) -37355	M.I. Hummel	Retrd.	60.00	64.00
90-08-006	Bavarian Marketsquare Bridge(Display) -37358	M.I. Hummel	Retrd.	110.00	250.00
88-08-007	Bavarian Village (Display) -37356	M.I. Hummel	Retrd.	100.00	100.00
91-08-008	Busy Student -37226	M.I. Hummel	Suspd.	105.00	105.00
91-08-009	Countryside School (Display) -37365	M.I. Hummel	Retrd.	100.00	100.00
90-08-010	Cinderella -37223	M.I. Hummel	Suspd.	115.00	115-175.
89-08-011	Doll Bath -37214	M.I. Hummel	Suspd.	95.00	115-175.
92-08-012	Goose Girl -37238	M.I. Hummel	Suspd.	130.00	150-168.
89-08-013	Little Fiddler -37211	M.I. Hummel	Suspd.	90.00	120-200.
89-08-014	Little Sweeper -37212	M.I. Hummel	Suspd.	90.00	125-200.
90-08-015	Marketsquare Hotel (Display)-37359	M.I. Hummel	Retrd.	70.00	100.00
90-08-016	Marketsquare Flower Stand (Display) -37360	M.I. Hummel	Retrd.	35.00	45-200.
89-08-017	Merry Wanderer -37213	M.I. Hummel	Suspd.	95.00	120-200.
91-08-018	Merry Wanderer Dealer Plaque -37229	M.I. Hummel	Retrd.	130.00	130.00
89-08-019	Postman -37217	M.I. Hummel	Suspd.	95.00	100-200.
91-08-020	Roadside Shrine (Display)-37366	M.I. Hummel	Retrd.	60.00	60.00
92-08-021	School Boy -37236	M.I. Hummel	Suspd.	120.00	150-170.
91-08-022	Serenade -37228	M.I. Hummel	Suspd.	105.00	105.00
92-08-023	Snow-Covered Mountain (Display)-37371	M.I. Hummel	Retrd.	100.00	100.00
89-08-024	Stormy Weather -37215	M.I. Hummel	Suspd.	115.00	180-250.
92-08-025	Trees (Display)-37369	M.I. Hummel	Retrd.	40.00	40.00
89-08-026	Visiting an Invalid -37218	M.I. Hummel	Suspd.	105.00	115-140.
90-08-027	Waiter -37221	M.I. Hummel	Suspd.	100.00	125-250.
92-08-028	Wayside Harmony -37237	M.I. Hummel	Suspd.	140.00	140.00
91-08-029	We Congratulate -37227	M.I. Hummel	Suspd.	130.00	130.00

Goebel/M.I. Hummel — M.I. Hummel Collectors Club Exclusives

		ARTIST	EDITION	ISSUE	QUOTE
77-09-001	Valentine Gift 387	M.I. Hummel	Closed	45.00	360-400.
78-09-002	Smiling Through Plaque 690	M.I. Hummel	Closed	50.00	240-275.
79-09-003	Bust of Sister-M.I.Hummel HU-3	G. Skrobek	Closed	75.00	180-240.
80-09-004	Valentine Joy 399	M.I. Hummel	Closed	95.00	150-200.
81-09-005	Daisies Don't Tell 380	M.I. Hummel	Closed	80.00	200.00
82-09-005	It's Cold 421	M.I. Hummel	Closed	80.00	150-193.
83-09-007	What Now? 422	M.I. Hummel	Closed	90.00	150-180.
83-09-008	Valentine Gift Mini Pendant	R. Olszewski	Closed	85.00	180-250.
84-09-009	Coffee Break 409	M.I. Hummel	Closed	90.00	145-150.
85-09-010	Smiling Through 408/0	M.I. Hummel	Closed	125.00	200.00
86-09-011	Birthday Candle 440	M.I. Hummel	Closed	95.00	150-165.
86-09-012	What Now? Mini Pendant	R. Olszewski	Closed	125.00	275.00
87-09-013	Morning Concert 447	M.I. Hummel	Closed	98.00	135-155.
87-09-014	Little Cocopah Indian Girl	T. DeGrazia	Closed	140.00	175-300.
88-09-015	The Surprise 431	M.I. Hummel	Closed	125.00	125-295.
89-09-016	Mickey and Minnie	H. Fischer	Closed	275.00	350-500.
89-09-017	Hello World 429	M.I. Hummel	Closed	130.00	160-250.
90-09-018	I Wonder 486	M.I. Hummel	Closed	140.00	170-250.
91-09-019	Gift From A Friend 485	M.I. Hummel	Closed	160.00	185.00
91-09-020	Miniature Morning Concert w/ Display	R. Olszewski	Closed	175.00	190.00
92-09-021	My Wish Is Small 463/0	M.I. Hummel	Closed	170.00	170.00
92-09-022	Cheeky Fellow 554	M.I. Hummel	Closed	120.00	120.00
93-09-023	I Didn't Do It 623	M.I. Hummel	5/95	175.00	175.00
93-09-024	Sweet As Can Be 541	M.I. Hummel	5/95	125.00	125.00
94-09-025	Little Visitor 563	M.I. Hummel	5/96	180.00	180.00
94-09-026	Little Troubadour 558	M.I. Hummel	5/96	130.00	130.00
94-09-027	Miniature Honey Lover Pendant	M.I. Hummel	5/96	165.00	165.00

Goebel/M.I. Hummel — Sp. Ed. Anniversary Fig. For 5/10/15 Year Membership

		ARTIST	EDITION	ISSUE	QUOTE
90-10-001	Flower Girl 548 (5 year)	M.I. Hummel	Open	105.00	130.00
90-10-002	The Little Pair 449 (10 year)	M.I. Hummel	Open	170.00	200.00
91-10-003	Honey Lover 312 (15 year)	M.I. Hummel	Open	190.00	210-325.

Goebel/M.I. Hummel — M.I. Hummel Tree Toppers

		ARTIST	EDITION	ISSUE	QUOTE
94-11-001	Heavenly Angel 755	M.I. Hummel	Open	450.00	450.00

Goebel Miniatures — Children's Series

		ARTIST	EDITION	ISSUE	QUOTE
80-01-001	Blumenkinder-Courting 630-P	R. Olszewski	Closed	55.00	250.00
81-01-002	Summer Days 631-P	R. Olszewski	Closed	65.00	290.00
82-01-003	Out and About 632-P	R. Olszewski	Closed	85.00	300.00
83-01-004	Backyard Frolic 633-P	R. Olszewski	Closed	65.00	100-250.
85-01-005	Snow Holiday 635-P	R. Olszewski	Closed	75.00	100-125.
86-01-006	Clowning Around 636-P	R. Olszewski	Closed	85.00	100-195.
87-01-007	Carrousel Days 637-P	R. Olszewski	Closed	85.00	165-245.
88-01-008	Little Ballerina 638-P	R. Olszewski	Closed	85.00	100-150.
88-01-009	Children's Display (small)	R. Olszewski	Closed	45.00	60.00
84-01-010	Grandpa 634-P	R. Olszewski	Closed	75.00	125-165.
90-01-011	Building Blocks Castle (large) 968-D	R. Olszewski	Closed	75.00	100.00

Goebel Miniatures — Wildlife Series

		ARTIST	EDITION	ISSUE	QUOTE
80-02-001	Chipping Sparrow 620-P	R. Olszewski	Open	55.00	85.00
81-02-002	Owl-Daylight Encounter 621-P	R. Olszewski	Closed	65.00	230-340.
82-02-003	Western Bluebird 622-P	R. Olszewski	Closed	65.00	195.00
83-02-004	Red-Winged Blackbird 623-P	R. Olszewski	Closed	65.00	150-245.
84-02-005	Winter Cardinal 624-P	R. Olszewski	Closed	65.00	200.00
85-02-006	American Goldfinch 625-P	R. Olszewski	Open	65.00	90-120.
86-02-007	Autumn Blue Jay 626-P	R. Olszewski	Open	65.00	135-205.
87-02-008	Mallard Duck 627-P	R. Olszewski	Open	75.00	185.00
88-02-009	Spring Robin 628-P	R. Olszewski	Closed	75.00	165-195.
87-02-010	Country Display (small) 940-D	R. Olszewski	Open	45.00	65.00
90-02-011	Wildlife Display (large) 957-D	R. Olszewski	Open	85.00	110.00
89-02-012	Hooded Oriole 629-P	R. Olszewski	Open	80.00	115-175.
90-02-013	Hummingbird 696-P	R. Olszewski	Closed	85.00	125.00

Goebel Miniatures — Women's Series

		ARTIST	EDITION	ISSUE	QUOTE
80-03-001	Dresden Dancer 610-P	R. Olszewski	Closed	55.00	520.00
81-03-002	The Hunt With Hounds 611-P	R. Olszewski	Closed	75.00	385.00
82-03-003	Precious Years 612-P	R. Olszewski	Closed	65.00	250.00
83-03-004	On The Avenue 613-P	R. Olszewski	Closed	65.00	95-150.
84-03-005	Roses 614-P	R. Olszewski	Closed	65.00	95-150.
86-03-006	I Do 615-P	R. Olszewski	Closed	85.00	200.00
89-03-007	Women's Display (small) 950-D	R. Olszewski	Closed	40.00	65.00

Goebel Miniatures — Historical Series

		ARTIST	EDITION	ISSUE	QUOTE
80-04-001	Capodimonte 600-P	R. Olszewski	Closed	90.00	535.00
81-04-002	Masquerade-St. Petersburg 601-P	R. Olszewski	Closed	65.00	210-260.
83-04-003	The Cherry Pickers 602-P	R. Olszewski	Closed	85.00	290.00
84-04-004	Moor With Spanish Horse 603-P	R. Olszewski	Open	85.00	110-200.
85-04-005	Floral Bouquet Pompadour 604-P	R. Olszewski	Open	85.00	115-130.
87-04-006	Meissen Parrot 605-P	R. Olszewski	Open	85.00	110-150.
88-04-007	Minton Rooster 606-P	R. Olszewski	7,500	85.00	110-195.
89-04-008	Farmer w/Doves 607-P	R. Olszewski	Open	85.00	110-150.
90-04-009	Gentleman Fox Hunt 616-P	R. Olszewski	Open	145.00	180.00
88-04-010	Historical Display 943-D	R. Olszewski	Suspd.	45.00	60.00
90-04-011	English Country Garden 970-D	R. Olszewski	Open	85.00	105.00
92-04-012	Poultry Seller 608-G	R. Olszewski	Open	200.00	230.00

Goebel Miniatures — Oriental Series

		ARTIST	EDITION	ISSUE	QUOTE
80-05-001	Kuan Yin 640-W	R. Olszewski	Closed	40.00	245.00
82-05-002	The Geisha 641-P	R. Olszewski	Closed	65.00	150-250.
85-05-003	Tang Horse 642-P	R. Olszewski	Open	65.00	95-175.
86-05-004	The Blind Men and the Elephant 643-P	R. Olszewski	Open	70.00	100-175.
87-05-005	Chinese Water Dragon 644-P	R. Olszewski	Closed	70.00	165-175.
87-05-006	Oriental Display (small) 945-D	R. Olszewski	Suspd.	45.00	65.00
89-05-007	Tiger Hunt 645-P	R. Olszewski	Open	85.00	100-105.
90-05-008	Chinese Temple Lion 646-P	R. Olszewski	Open	90.00	110-125.
90-05-009	Empress' Garden Display 967-D	R. Olszewski	Open	95.00	130.00

Goebel Miniatures — Americana Series

		ARTIST	EDITION	ISSUE	QUOTE
81-06-001	The Plainsman 660-B	R. Olszewski	Closed	45.00	250.00
82-06-002	American Bald Eagle 661-B	R. Olszewski	Closed	45.00	335.00
83-06-003	She Sounds the Deep 662-B	R. Olszewski	Closed	45.00	65.00
84-06-004	Eyes on the Horizon 663-B	R. Olszewski	Closed	45.00	70.00
85-06-005	Central Park Sunday 664-B	R. Olszewski	Closed	45.00	70.00
86-06-006	Carrousel Ride 665-B	R. Olszewski	Closed	45.00	70-115.
87-06-007	To The Bandstand 666-B	R. Olszewski	Closed	45.00	70-110.
89-06-008	Blacksmith 676-B	R. Olszewski	Closed	55.00	145-165.
86-06-009	Americana Display 951-D	R. Olszewski	Suspd.	80.00	105.00

Goebel Miniatures — The American Frontier Collection

		ARTIST	EDITION	ISSUE	QUOTE
87-07-001	The End of the Trail 340-B	Frazier	Closed	80.00	80-125.
87-07-002	The First Ride 330-B	Rogers	Open	85.00	100.00
87-07-003	Eight Count 310-B	Pounder	Open	75.00	90.00
87-07-004	Grizzly's Last Stand 320-B	Jonas	Open	65.00	65-85.00
87-07-005	Indian Scout and Buffalo 300-B	Bonheur	Closed	95.00	95-135.
87-07-006	The Bronco Buster 350-B	Remington	Closed	80.00	80.00

		ARTIST	EDITION	ISSUE	QUOTE
87-07-007	American Frontier Museum Display 947-D	R. Olszewski	Open	80.00	110.00
Goebel Miniatures	**Portrait of America/Saturday Evening Post (Pewter)**				
88-08-001	The Doctor and the Doll 361-P	N. Rockwell	Suspd.	85.00	100.00
88-08-002	No Swimming 360-P	N. Rockwell	Open	85.00	85.00
88-08-003	Marbles Champion 362-P	N. Rockwell	Open	85.00	85.00
88-08-004	Check-Up 363-P	N. Rockwell	Open	85.00	85.00
88-08-005	Triple Self-Portrait 364-P	N. Rockwell	Suspd.	85.00	100.00
88-08-006	Bottom of the Sixth 365-P	N. Rockwell	Suspd.	85.00	100.00
89-08-007	Bottom Drawer 366-P	N. Rockwell	7,500	85.00	85.00
88-08-008	Rockwell Display-952-D	N. Rockwell	Open	80.00	100.00
91-08-009	Soldier 368-P	N. Rockwell	Open	85.00	100.00
91-08-010	Mother 369-P	N. Rockwell	Open	85.00	100.00
91-08-011	Home Coming Vignette-Soldier/Mother 990-D	N. Rockwell	Closed	200.00	300.00
Goebel Miniatures	**Disney-Snow White**				
87-09-001	Sneezy 161-P	R. Olszewski	Closed	60.00	85.00
87-09-002	Doc 162-P	R. Olszewski	Closed	60.00	85-200.
87-09-003	Sleepy 163-P	R. Olszewski	Closed	60.00	85.00
87-09-004	Happy 164-P	R. Olszewski	Closed	60.00	85.00
87-09-005	Bashful 165-P	R. Olszewski	Closed	60.00	85.00
87-09-006	Grumpy 166-P	R. Olszewski	Closed	60.00	85.00
87-09-007	Dopey 167-P	R. Olszewski	Closed	60.00	250-300.
87-09-008	Snow White 168-P	R. Olszewski	Closed	60.00	95-120.
90-09-009	Snow White's Prince 170-P	R. Olszewski	19,500	80.00	115.00
87-09-010	Cozy Cottage Display 941-D	R. Olszewski	Closed	35.00	320.00
88-09-011	House In The Woods Display 944-D	R. Olszewski	Open	60.00	110.00
90-09-012	The Wishing Well Display 969-D	R. Olszewski	Open	65.00	85.00
91-09-013	Castle Courtyard Display 981-D	R. Olszewski	Open	105.00	125.00
92-09-014	Snow White's Witch 183-P	R. Olszewski	Open	100.00	115.00
92-09-015	Snow White's Queen 182-P	R. Olszewski	Open	100.00	115.00
92-09-016	Path In The Woods 996-D	R. Olszewski	Open	140.00	150.00
92-09-017	Complete set of 16	R. Olszewski	Open	1165.00	1800.00
Goebel Miniatures	**Disney-Pinocchio**				
90-10-001	Geppetto/Figaro 682-P	R. Olszewski	Open	90.00	110.00
90-10-002	Gideon 683-P	R. Olszewski	Open	75.00	100.00
90-10-003	J. Worthington Foulfellow 684-P	R. Olszewski	Open	95.00	115.00
90-10-004	Jiminy Cricket 685-P	R. Olszewski	Open	75.00	100.00
90-10-005	Pinocchio 686-P	R. Olszewski	Open	75.00	110.00
91-10-006	Little Street Lamp Display 964-D	R. Olszewski	Open	65.00	80.00
90-10-007	Geppetto's Toy Shop Display 965-D	R. Olszewski	Open	95.00	120.00
91-10-008	Stromboli 694-P	R. Olszewski	Open	95.00	120.00
91-10-009	Blue Fairy 693-P	R. Olszewski	Open	95.00	120.00
91-10-010	Stromboli's Street Wagon 979-D	R. Olszewski	Open	105.00	125.00
92-10-011	Monstro The Whale 985-D	R. Olszewski	Open	120.00	130.00
Goebel Miniatures	**Disney-Cinderella**				
91-11-001	Anastasia 172-P	R.Olszewski	Open	85.00	100.00
91-11-002	Jaq 173-P	R.Olszewski	Open	80.00	90.00
91-11-003	Drizella 174-P	R.Olszewski	Open	85.00	100.00
91-11-004	Lucifer 175-P	R.Olszewski	Open	80.00	90.00
91-11-005	Cinderella 176-P	R.Olszewski	Open	85.00	105.00
91-11-006	Gus 177-P	R.Olszewski	Open	80.00	90.00
91-11-007	Stepmother 178-P	R.Olszewski	Open	85.00	100.00
91-11-008	Prince Charming 179-P	R.Olszewski	Open	85.00	100.00
91-11-009	Fairy Godmother 180-P	R.Olszewski	Open	85.00	100.00
91-11-010	Footman 181-P	R.Olszewski	Open	85.00	100.00
91-11-011	Cinderella's Dream Castle 976-D	R.Olszewski	Open	95.00	115.00
91-11-012	Cinderella's Coach Display 978-D	R.Olszewski	Open	95.00	120.00
91-11-013	Set of 12	R.Olszewski	Open	1025.00	1152.00
Goebel Miniatures	**Mickey Mouse**				
90-12-001	The Sorcerer's Apprentice 171-P	R. Olszewski	Suspd.	80.00	165-200.
90-12-002	Fantasia Living Brooms 972-D	R. Olszewski	Suspd.	85.00	165.00
90-12-003	Set	R. Olszweski	Suspd.	165.00	350.00
Goebel Miniatures	**Night Before Christmas (1st Edition)**				
90-13-001	Sugar Plum Boy 687-P	R. Olszewski	5,000	70.00	95.00
90-13-002	Yule Tree 688-P	R. Olszewski	5,000	90.00	105.00
90-13-003	Sugar Plum Girl 689-P	R. Olszewski	5,000	70.00	95.00
90-13-004	St. Nicholas 690-P	R. Olszewski	5,000	95.00	120.00
90-13-005	Eight Tiny Reindeer 691-P	R. Olszewski	5,000	110.00	130.00
90-13-006	Mama & Papa 692-P	R. Olszewski	5,000	110.00	125.00
91-13-007	Up To The Housetop 966-D	R. Olszewski	5,000	95.00	105.00
Goebel Miniatures	**Special Release-Alice in Wonderland**				
82-14-001	Alice In the Garden 670-P	R. Olszewski	Closed	60.00	835.00
83-14-002	Down the Rabbit Hole 671-P	R. Olszewski	Closed	75.00	540.00
84-14-003	The Cheshire Cat 672-P	R. Olszewski	Closed	75.00	520.00
Goebel Miniatures	**Special Release-Wizard of Oz**				
84-15-001	Scarecrow 673-P	R. Olszewski	Closed	75.00	300-455.
85-15-002	Tinman 674-P	R. Olszewski	Closed	80.00	355.00
86-15-003	The Cowardly Lion 675-P	R. Olszewski	Closed	85.00	160-325.
87-15-004	The Wicked Witch 676-P	R. Olszewski	Closed	85.00	105.00
88-15-005	The Munchkins 677-P	R. Olszewski	Closed	85.00	100.00
87-15-006	Oz Display 942-D	R. Olszewski	Closed	45.00	45.00
XX-15-007	Oz Display Set	R. Olszewski	Closed	410.00	19-2000.
92-15-008	Dorothy/Glinda 695-P	R. Olszewski	Closed	135.00	155.00
92-15-009	Good-Bye to Oz Display 980-D	R. Olszewski	Closed	110.00	160.00
Goebel Miniatures	**Three Little Pigs**				
89-16-001	Little Sticks Pig 678-P	R. Olszewski	7,500	75.00	105.00
90-16-002	Little Straw Pig 679-P	R. Olszewski	7,500	75.00	105.00
91-16-003	Little Bricks Pig 680-P	R. Olszewski	Closed	75.00	105.00
91-16-004	The Hungry Wolf 681-P	R. Olszewski	Closed	80.00	105.00
91-16-005	Three Little Pigs House 956-D	R. Olszewski	7,500	50.00	125.00
89-16-006	Set of 5	R. Olszewski	Closed	355.00	516.00
Goebel Miniatures	**Pendants**				
90-17-001	Hummingbird 697-P	R. Olszewski	Open	125.00	150.00
91-17-002	Rose Pendant 220-P	R. Olszewski	Open	135.00	150.00
91-17-003	Daffodil Pendant 221-P	R. Olszewski	Open	135.00	150.00
91-17-004	Chrysanthemum Pendant 222-P	R. Olszewski	Open	135.00	150.00
91-17-005	Poinsettia Pendant 223-P	R. Olszewski	Open	135.00	150.00
Goebel Miniatures	**Nativity Collection**				
91-18-001	Mother/Child 440-P	R. Olszewski	10,000	120.00	150.00
91-18-002	Joseph 401-P	R. Olszewski	10,000	95.00	125.00
91-18-003	Joyful Cherubs 403-P	R. Olszewski	10,000	130.00	175.00
91-18-004	The Stable Donkey 402-P	R. Olszewski	10,000	95.00	125.00
91-18-005	Holy Family Display 982-D	R. Olszewski	10,000	85.00	90.00
92-18-006	Balthazar 405-P	R. Olszewski	10,000	135.00	195.00
92-18-007	Melchoir 404-P	R. Olszewski	10,000	135.00	195.00

		ARTIST	EDITION	ISSUE	QUOTE
92-18-008	Gaspar 406-P	R. Olszewski	10,000	135.00	195.00
92-18-009	3 Kings Display 987-D	R. Olszewski	10,000	85.00	100.00
94-18-010	Guardian Angel 407-P	R. Olszewski	10,000	200.00	200.00
94-18-011	Final Nativity Display 991-D	R. Olszewski	10,000	260.00	260.00
94-18-012	Camel & Tender 819292	R. Olszewski	10,000	380.00	380.00
94-18-013	Sheep & Shepherd 819290	R. Olszewski	10,000	N/A	N/A
Goebel Miniatures	**Special Releases**				
91-19-001	Portrait Of The Artist 658-P	R. Olszewski	Open	195.00	210.00
92-19-002	Summer Days Collector Plaque 659-P	R. Olszewski	Open	130.00	155.00
94-19-003	Dresden Timepiece 450-P	R. Olszewski	750	1250.00	1250.00
Goebel Miniatures	**Disney-Peter Pan**				
92-20-001	Peter Pan 184-P	R. Olszewski	Open	90.00	125.00
92-20-002	Wendy 185-P	R. Olszewski	Open	90.00	110.00
92-20-003	John 186-P	R. Olszewski	Open	90.00	110.00
92-20-004	Michael 187-P	R. Olszewski	Open	90.00	110.00
92-20-005	Nana 189-P	R. Olszewski	Open	95.00	110.00
92-20-006	Peter Pan's London 986-D	R. Olszewski	Open	125.00	135.00
94-20-007	Neverland Display 997-D	R. Olszewski	Open	150.00	150.00
94-20-008	Captain Hook 188-P	R. Olszewski	Open	160.00	160.00
94-20-009	Smee 190-P	R. Olszewski	Open	140.00	140.00
94-20-010	Lost Boy-Fox 191-P	R. Olszewski	Open	130.00	130.00
94-20-011	Lost Boy-Rabbit 192-P	R. Olszewski	Open	130.00	130.00
Goebel Miniatures	**Archive Releases**				
92-21-001	Autumn Blue Jay 626-P	R. Olszewski	Open	125.00	125.00
93-21-002	Cherry Pickers 602-P	R. Olszewski	Open	175.00	175.00
93-21-003	Kuan Yin 640-W	R. Olszewski	Open	100.00	100.00
Goebel Miniatures	**Jack & The Beanstalk**				
94-22-001	Jack & The Beanstalk Display 999-D	R. Olszewski	2,500	225.00	250.00
94-22-002	Jack's Mom 741-P	R. Olszewski	2,500	145.00	175.00
94-22-003	Jack and the Cow 819270	R. Olszewski	2,500	180.00	180.00
Gorham	**A Boy And His Dog (Four Seasons)**				
72-01-001	A Boy Meets His Dog	N. Rockwell	2,500	200.00	1300.
72-01-002	Adventurers Between Adventures	N. Rockwell	2,500	Set	Set
72-01-003	The Mysterious Malady	N. Rockwell	2,500	Set	Set
72-01-004	Pride of Parenthood	N. Rockwell	2,500	Set	Set
Gorham	**Young Love (Four Seasons)**				
73-02-001	Downhill Daring	N. Rockwell	2,500	250.00	1100.
73-02-002	Beguiling Buttercup	N. Rockwell	2,500	Set	Set
73-02-003	Flying High	N. Rockwell	2,500	Set	Set
73-02-004	A Scholarly Pace	N. Rockwell	2,500	Set	Set
Gorham	**Four Ages of Love (Four Seasons)**				
74-03-001	Gaily Sharing Vintage Times	N. Rockwell	2,500	300.00	600-1250
74-03-002	Sweet Song So Young	N. Rockwell	2,500	Set	Set
74-03-003	Flowers In Tender Bloom	N. Rockwell	2,500	Set	Set
74-03-004	Fondly Do We Remember	N. Rockwell	2,500	Set	Set
Gorham	**Grandpa and Me (Four Seasons)**				
75-04-001	Gay Blades	N. Rockwell	2,500	300.00	700.00
75-04-002	Day Dreamers	N. Rockwell	2,500	Set	Set
75-04-003	Goin' Fishing	N. Rockwell	2,500	Set	Set
75-04-004	Pensive Pals	N. Rockwell	2500	Set	Set
Gorham	**Me and My Pal (Four Seasons)**				
76-05-001	A Licking Good Bath	N. Rockwell	2500	300.00	750-800.
76-05-002	Young Man's Fancy	N. Rockwell	2500	Set	Set
76-05-003	Fisherman's Paradise	N. Rockwell	2500	Set	Set
76-05-004	Disastrous Daring	N. Rockwell	2500	Set	Set
Gorham	**Grand Pals (Four Seasons)**				
77-06-001	Snow Sculpturing	N. Rockwell	2500	350.00	650-675.
77-06-002	Soaring Spirits	N. Rockwell	2500	Set	Set
77-06-003	Fish Finders	N. Rockwell	2500	Set	Set
77-06-004	Ghostly Gourds	N. Rockwell	2500	Set	Set
Gorham	**Going On Sixteen (Four Seasons)**				
78-07-001	Chilling Chore	N. Rockwell	2500	400.00	650-675.
78-07-002	Sweet Serenade	N. Rockwell	2500	Set	Set
78-07-003	Shear Agony	N. Rockwell	2500	Set	Set
78-07-004	Pilgrimage	N. Rockwell	2500	Set	Set
Gorham	**Tender Years (Four Seasons)**				
79-08-001	New Year Look	N. Rockwell	2500	500.00	700.00
79-08-002	Spring Tonic	N. Rockwell	2500	Set	Set
79-08-003	Cool Aid	N. Rockwell	2500	Set	Set
79-08-004	Chilly Reception	N. Rockwell	2500	Set	Set
Gorham	**A Helping Hand (Four Seasons)**				
80-09-001	Year End Court	N. Rockwell	2500	650.00	650-700.
80-09-002	Closed For Business	N. Rockwell	2500	Set	Set
80-09-003	Swatter's Right	N. Rockwell	2500	Set	Set
80-09-004	Coal Seasons Coming	N. Rockwell	2500	Set	Set
Gorham	**Dad's Boy (Four Seasons)**				
81-10-001	Ski Skills	N. Rockwell	2500	750.00	750-800.
81-10-002	In His Spirit	N. Rockwell	2500	Set	Set
81-10-003	Trout Dinner	N. Rockwell	2500	Set	Set
81-10-004	Careful Aim	N. Rockwell	2500	Set	Set
Gorham	**Rockwell**				
74-11-001	Weighing In	N. Rockwell	Closed	40.00	80-90.00
74-11-002	Missing Tooth	N. Rockwell	Closed	30.00	90.00
74-11-003	Tiny Tim	N. Rockwell	Closed	30.00	50.00
74-11-004	At The Vets	N. Rockwell	Closed	25.00	65.00
74-11-005	Fishing	N. Rockwell	Closed	50.00	100-125.
74-11-006	Batter Up	N. Rockwell	Closed	40.00	90-235.
74-11-007	Skating	N. Rockwell	Closed	37.50	85.00
74-11-008	Captain	N. Rockwell	Closed	45.00	95.00
75-11-009	Boy And His Dog	N. Rockwell	Closed	38.00	95.00
75-11-010	No Swimming	N. Rockwell	Closed	35.00	95-200.
75-11-011	Old Mill Pond	N. Rockwell	Closed	45.00	95.00
76-11-012	Saying Grace	N. Rockwell	Closed	75.00	150.00
76-11-013	God Rest Ye Merry Gentlemen	N. Rockwell	Closed	50.00	1500.00
76-11-014	Tackled (Ad Stand)	N. Rockwell	Closed	35.00	100.00
76-11-015	Independence	N. Rockwell	Closed	40.00	120.00
76-11-016	Marriage License	N. Rockwell	Closed	50.00	125.00
76-11-017	The Occultist	N. Rockwell	Closed	50.00	125-180.
81-11-018	Day in the Life Boy II	N. Rockwell	Closed	75.00	100.00
81-11-019	Wet Sport	N. Rockwell	Closed	85.00	100.00
82-11-020	April Fool's (At The Curiosity Shop)	N. Rockwell	Closed	55.00	100-110.

	ARTIST	EDITION	ISSUE	QUOTE
82-11-021 Tackled (Rockwell Name Signed)	N. Rockwell	Closed	45.00	100.00
82-11-022 A Day in the Life Boy III	N. Rockwell	Closed	85.00	125-150.
82-11-023 A Day in the Life Girl III	N. Rockwell	Closed	85.00	150.00
81-11-024 Christmas Dancers	N. Rockwell	7,500	130.00	195.00
82-11-025 Marriage License	N. Rockwell	5,000	110.00	400-500.
82-11-026 Saying Grace	N. Rockwell	5,000	110.00	500-600.
82-11-027 Triple Self Portrait	N. Rockwell	5,000	300.00	600-650.
80-11-028 Jolly Coachman	N. Rockwell	7,500	75.00	145.00
82-11-029 Merrie Christmas	N. Rockwell	7,500	75.00	150.00
83-11-030 Facts of Life	N. Rockwell	7,500	110.00	180.00
83-11-031 Antique Dealer	N. Rockwell	7,500	130.00	200.00
84-11-032 Serenade	N. Rockwell	7,500	95.00	165.00
84-11-033 Card Tricks	N. Rockwell	7,500	110.00	180.00
84-11-034 Santa's Friend	N. Rockwell	7,500	75.00	160.00
85-11-035 Puppet Maker	N. Rockwell	7,500	130.00	130-200.
85-11-036 The Old Sign Painter	N. Rockwell	7,500	130.00	210.00
86-11-037 Drum For Tommy	N. Rockwell	Annual	90.00	N/A
87-11-038 Santa Planning His Annual Visit	N. Rockwell	7,500	95.00	95.00
88-11-039 Home for the Holidays	N. Rockwell	7,500	100.00	100.00
88-11-040 Gary Cooper in Hollywood	N. Rockwell	15,000	90.00	90.00
88-11-041 Cramming	N. Rockwell	15,000	80.00	80.00
88-11-042 Dolores & Eddie	N. Rockwell	15,000	75.00	75.00
88-11-043 Confrontation	N. Rockwell	15,000	75.00	75.00
88-11-044 The Diary	N. Rockwell	15,000	80.00	80.00
Gorham	**Miniature Christmas Figurines**			
79-12-001 Tiny Tim	N. Rockwell	Yr.Iss.	15.00	20.00
80-12-002 Santa Plans His Trip	N. Rockwell	Yr.Iss.	15.00	15.00
81-12-003 Yuletide Reckoning	N. Rockwell	Yr.Iss.	20.00	20.00
82-12-004 Checking Good Deeds	N. Rockwell	Yr.Iss.	20.00	20.00
83-12-005 Santa's Friend	N. Rockwell	Yr.Iss.	20.00	20.00
84-12-006 Downhill Daring	N. Rockwell	Yr.Iss.	20.00	20.00
85-12-007 Christmas Santa	T. Nast	Yr.Iss.	20.00	20.00
86-12-008 Christmas Santa	T. Nast	Yr.Iss.	25.00	25.00
87-12-009 Annual Thomas Nast Santa	T. Nast	Yr.Iss.	25.00	25.00
Gorham	**Miniatures**			
81-13-001 Young Man's Fancy	N. Rockwell	Closed	55.00	55.00
81-13-002 Beguiling Buttercup	N. Rockwell	Closed	45.00	45.00
81-13-003 Gay Blades	N. Rockwell	Closed	45.00	70.00
81-13-004 Sweet Song So Young	N. Rockwell	Closed	55.00	55.00
81-13-005 Snow Sculpture	N. Rockwell	Closed	45.00	70.00
81-13-006 Sweet Serenade	N. Rockwell	Closed	45.00	45.00
81-13-007 At the Vets	N. Rockwell	Closed	27.50	39.50
81-13-008 Boy Meets His Dog	N. Rockwell	Closed	37.50	37.50
81-13-009 Downhill Daring	N. Rockwell	Closed	45.00	70.00
81-13-010 Flowers in Tender Bloom	N. Rockwell	Closed	60.00	60.00
82-13-011 Triple Self Portrait	N. Rockwell	Closed	60.00	75-95.00
82-13-012 Marriage License	N. Rockwell	Closed	60.00	75.00
82-13-013 The Runaway	N. Rockwell	Closed	50.00	50.00
82-13-014 Vintage Times	N. Rockwell	Closed	50.00	50.00
82-13-015 The Annual Visit	N. Rockwell	Closed	50.00	75.00
83-13-016 Trout Dinner	N. Rockwell	15,000	60.00	60.00
84-13-017 Ghostly Gourds	N. Rockwell	Closed	60.00	60.00
84-13-018 Years End Court	N. Rockwell	Closed	60.00	60.00
84-13-019 Shear Agony	N. Rockwell	Closed	60.00	60.00
84-13-020 Pride of Parenthood	N. Rockwell	Closed	50.00	50.00
84-13-021 Goin Fishing	N. Rockwell	Closed	60.00	60.00
84-13-022 Careful Aims	N. Rockwell	Closed	55.00	55.00
84-13-023 In His Spirit	N. Rockwell	Closed	60.00	60.00
85-13-024 To Love & Cherish	N. Rockwell	Closed	32.50	35.00
85-13-025 Spring Checkup	N. Rockwell	Closed	60.00	60.00
85-13-026 Engineer	N. Rockwell	Closed	55.00	55.00
85-13-027 Best Friends	N. Rockwell	Closed	27.50	27.50
85-13-028 Muscle Bound	N. Rockwell	Closed	30.00	30.00
85-13-029 New Arrival	N. Rockwell	Closed	32.50	35.00
85-13-030 Little Red Truck	N. Rockwell	Closed	25.00	25.00
86-13-031 The Old Sign Painter	N. Rockwell	Closed	70.00	75.00
86-13-032 The Graduate	N. Rockwell	Closed	30.00	30.00
86-13-033 Football Season	N. Rockwell	Closed	60.00	60.00
86-13-034 Lemonade Stand	N. Rockwell	Closed	60.00	60.00
86-13-035 Welcome Mat	N. Rockwell	Closed	70.00	75.00
86-13-036 Shoulder Ride	N. Rockwell	Closed	50.00	60.00
86-13-037 Morning Walk	N. Rockwell	Closed	60.00	60.00
86-13-038 Little Angel	N. Rockwell	Closed	50.00	60.00
87-13-039 Starstruck	N. Rockwell	15,000	75.00	75.00
87-13-040 The Prom Dress	N. Rockwell	15,000	75.00	75.00
87-13-041 The Milkmaid	N. Rockwell	15,000	80.00	85.00
87-13-042 Cinderella	N. Rockwell	15,000	70.00	75.00
87-13-043 Springtime	N. Rockwell	15,000	65.00	75.00
87-13-044 Babysitter	N. Rockwell	15,000	75.00	75.00
87-13-045 Between The Acts	N. Rockwell	15,000	60.00	60.00
Gorham	**Old Timers (Four Seasons)**			
82-14-001 Canine Solo	N. Rockwell	2,500	250.00	250.00
82-14-002 Sweet Surprise	N. Rockwell	2,500	Set	Set
82-14-003 Lazy Days	N. Rockwell	2,500	Set	Set
82-14-004 Fancy Footwork	N. Rockwell	2,500	Set	Set
Gorham	**Life With Father (Four Seasons)**			
83-15-001 Big Decision	N. Rockwell	2,500	250.00	250.00
83-15-002 Blasting Out	N. Rockwell	2,500	Set	Set
83-15-003 Cheering The Champs	N. Rockwell	2,500	Set	Set
83-15-004 A Tough One	N. Rockwell	2,500	Set	Set
Gorham	**Old Buddies (Four Seasons)**			
84-16-001 Shared Success	N. Rockwell	2,500	250.00	250.00
84-16-002 Hasty Retreat	N. Rockwell	2,500	Set	Set
84-16-003 Final Speech	N. Rockwell	2,500	Set	Set
Gorham	**Traveling Salesman (Four Seasons)**			
85-17-001 Horse Trader	N. Rockwell	2500	275.00	250-275.
85-17-002 Expert Salesman	N. Rockwell	2500	Set	Set
85-17-003 Traveling Salesman	N. Rockwell	2500	Set	Set
85-17-004 Country Pedlar	N. Rockwell	2500	Set	Set
Gorham	**Parasol Lady**			
91-18-001 On the Boardwalk	Unknown	Open	95.00	95.00
94-18-002 Sunday Promenade	Unknown	Open	95.00	95.00
Great American Taylor Collectibles	**Old World Santas**			
88-01-001 Jangle Claus-Ireland 335s	L. Smith	Retrd.	20.00	75-125.
88-01-002 Hans Von Claus-Germany 337s	L. Smith	Retrd.	20.00	75-125.
88-01-003 Ching Chang Claus-China 338s	L. Smith	Retrd.	20.00	75-125.
88-01-004 Kris Kringle Claus-Switzerland 339s	L. Smith	Retrd.	20.00	75-125.
88-01-005 Jingle Claus-England 336s	L. Smith	Retrd.	20.00	75-125.
89-01-006 Rudy Claus-Austria 410s	L. Smith	Retrd.	20.00	75-100.
89-01-007 Noel Claus-Belguim 412s	L. Smith	Retrd.	20.00	60-90.00
89-01-008 Pierre Claus-France 414s	L. Smith	Retrd.	20.00	60-90.00
89-01-009 Nicholai Claus-Russia 413s	L. Smith	Retrd.	20.00	60-90.00
89-01-010 Yule Claus-Germany 411s	L. Smith	Retrd.	20.00	75-100.
90-01-011 Matts Claus-Sweden 430s	L. Smith	Retrd.	20.00	55-70.00
90-01-012 Vander Claus-Holland 433s	L. Smith	Retrd.	20.00	55-70.00
90-01-013 Sven Claus-Norway 432s	L. Smith	Retrd.	20.00	55-70.00
90-01-014 Cedric Claus-England 434s	L. Smith	Retrd.	20.00	55-70.00
90-01-015 Mario Claus-Italy 431s	L. Smith	Retrd.	20.00	55-70.00
91-01-016 Mitch Claus-England 437s	L. Smith	Retrd.	25.00	50-55.00
91-01-017 Samuel Claus-USA 436s	L. Smith	Retrd.	25.00	50-55.00
91-01-018 Duncan Claus-Scotland 439s	L. Smith	Retrd.	25.00	50-55.00
91-01-019 Benjamin Claus-Israel 438s	L. Smith	Retrd.	25.00	50-55.00
91-01-020 Boris Claus-Russia 435s	L. Smith	Retrd.	25.00	50-55.00
92-01-021 Mickey Claus-Ireland 701s	L. Smith	12/94	25.00	25.00
92-01-022 Jacques Claus-France 702s	L. Smith	12/94	25.00	25.00
92-01-023 Terry Claus-Denmark 703s	L. Smith	12/94	25.00	25.00
92-01-024 JosÅ Claus-Spain 704s	L. Smith	12/94	25.00	25.00
92-01-025 Stu Claus-Poland 705s	L. Smith	12/94	25.00	25.00
93-01-026 Otto Claus-Germany 707s	L. Smith	12/94	27.50	27.50
93-01-027 Franz Claus-Switzerland 706s	L. Smith	12/94	27.50	27.50
93-01-028 Bjorn Claus-Sweden 709s	L. Smith	12/94	27.50	27.50
93-01-029 Ryan Claus-Canada 710s	L. Smith	12/94	27.50	27.50
93-01-030 Vito Claus-Italy 708s	L. Smith	12/94	27.50	27.50
94-01-031 Angus Claus-Scotland 713s	L. Smith	12/94	29.00	29.00
94-01-032 Ivan Claus-Russia 712s	L. Smith	12/94	29.00	29.00
94-01-033 Desmond Claus-England 715s	L. Smith	12/94	29.00	29.00
94-01-034 Gord Claus-Canada 714s	L. Smith	12/94	29.00	29.00
94-01-035 Wilhelm Claus-Holland 711s	L. Smith	12/94	29.00	29.00
Great American Taylor Collectibles	**Jim Clement's Santas**			
94-02-001 Mrs. Clement's Santa 808	J. Clement	12/94	17.00	17.00
94-02-002 Bearded Shorty Santa 812	J. Clement	12/94	13.50	13.50
94-02-003 Santa High Hat 815	J. Clement	12/94	30.00	30.00
94-02-004 Patriotic Santa 807	J. Clement	12/94	20.00	20.00
94-02-005 Santa w/Tree 804	J. Clement	12/94	15.00	15.00
94-02-006 Down the Chimny Santa 814	J. Clement	12/95	28.00	28.00
94-02-007 Day After Christmas 809	J. Clement	12/95	16.50	16.50
94-02-008 Mr. Egg Santa 802	J. Clement	12/95	19.50	19.50
94-02-009 Sm. Hobby Horse Santa 803	J. Clement	12/95	28.00	28.00
94-02-010 Golfer Santa 806	J. Clement	12/95	28.00	28.00
94-02-011 Tennis Santa 816	J. Clement	12/96	28.00	28.00
94-02-012 Night After Christmas 810	J. Clement	12/96	16.50	16.50
94-02-013 Noah Santa 805	J. Clement	12/96	28.00	28.00
94-02-014 Santa w/Rover 811	J. Clement	12/96	20.00	20.00
94-02-015 Big Santa w/Toys 813	J. Clement	12/96	70.00	70.00
Great American Taylor Collectibles	**Great American Collectors' Club**			
93-03-001 William Claus-USA 700s	L. Smith	12/94	35.00	35.00
94-03-002 Winston-England	L. Smith	12/95	35.00	35.00
Dave Grossman Creations	**Saturday Evening Post**			
90-01-001 No Swimming NRP-901	Rockwell-Inspired	Retrd.	50.00	50.00
90-01-002 Daydreamer NRP-902	Rockwell-Inspired	Open	55.00	55.00
90-01-003 Prom Dress NRP-903	Rockwell-Inspired	Retrd.	60.00	60.00
90-01-004 Bedside Manner NRP-904	Rockwell-Inspired	Open	65.00	65.00
90-01-005 Runaway NRP-905	Rockwell-Inspired	Open	130.00	130.00
90-01-006 Big Moment NRP-906	Rockwell-Inspired	Retrd.	100.00	135.00
90-01-007 Doctor and Doll NRP-907	Rockwell-Inspired	Retrd.	110.00	150.00
90-01-008 Bottom of the Sixth NRP-908	Rockwell-Inspired	Open	165.00	165.00
91-01-009 Catching The Big One NRP-909	Rockwell-Inspired	Open	75.00	75.00
91-01-010 Gramps NRP-910	Rockwell-Inspired	Open	85.00	85.00
91-01-011 The Pharmacist NRP-911	Rockwell-Inspired	Open	70.00	70.00
92-01-012 Choosin Up NRP-912	Rockwell-Inspired	Retrd.	110.00	140-150.
92-01-013 Missed NRP-914	Rockwell-Inspired	Open	110.00	110.00
92-01-014 Gone Fishing NRP-915	Rockwell-Inspired	Open	65.00	65.00
92-01-015 After the Prom NRP-916	Rockwell-Inspired	Open	75.00	75.00
92-01-016 Locomotive NRC-603	Rockwell-Inspired	Open	110.00	110.00
93-01-017 Baby's First Step NRC-604	Rockwell-Inspired	Open	100.00	100.00
93-01-018 Bride & Groom NRC-605	Rockwell-Inspired	Open	100.00	100.00
93-01-019 Bed Time NRC-606	Rockwell-Inspired	Open	100.00	100.00
94-01-020 Little Mother NRC-607	Rockwell-Inspired	Open	75.00	75.00
94-01-021 For A Good Boy NRC-608	Rockwell-Inspired	Open	100.00	100.00
94-01-022 Almost Grown Up NRC-609	Rockwell-Inspired	Open	75.00	75.00
94-01-023 A Visit with Rockwell (100th Aniversary)- NRP-100	Rockwell-Inspired	1,994	100.00	100.00
Dave Grossman Creations	**Saturday Evening Post-Miniatures**			
91-02-001 A Boy Meets His Dog BMR-01	Rockwell-Inspired	Retrd.	35.00	35.00
91-02-002 Downhill Daring BMR-02	Rockwell-Inspired	Retrd.	40.00	40.00
91-02-003 Flowers in Tender Bloom BMR-03	Rockwell-Inspired	Retrd.	32.00	32.00
91-02-004 Fondly Do We Remember BMR-04	Rockwell-Inspired	Retrd.	30.00	30.00
91-02-005 In His Spirit BMR-05	Rockwell-Inspired	Retrd.	30.00	30.00
91-02-006 Pride of Parenthood BMR-06	Rockwell-Inspired	Retrd.	35.00	35.00
91-02-007 Sweet Serenade BMR-07	Rockwell-Inspired	Retrd.	32.00	32.00
91-02-008 Sweet Song So Young BMR-08	Rockwell-Inspired	Retrd.	30.00	30.00
Dave Grossman Creations	**Norman Rockwell America Collection-Large Limited Edition**			
89-03-001 Doctor and Doll NRP-300	Rockwell-Inspired	Retrd.	150.00	150.00
89-03-002 Bottom of the Sixth NRP-307	Rockwell-Inspired	Retrd.	190.00	190.00
89-03-003 Runaway NRP-310	Rockwell-Inspired	Retrd.	190.00	190.00
89-03-004 Weigh-In NRP-311	Rockwell-Inspired	Retrd.	160.00	175.00
Dave Grossman Creations	**Norman Rockwell America Collection**			
89-04-001 Doctor and Doll NRP-600	Rockwell-Inspired	Retrd.	90.00	90.00
89-04-002 Locomotive NRC-603	Rockwell-Inspired	Retrd.	110.00	110.00
89-04-003 First Haircut NRC-604	Rockwell-Inspired	Retrd.	75.00	75.00
89-04-004 First Visit NRC-605	Rockwell-Inspired	Retrd.	110.00	110.00
89-04-005 First Day Home NRC-606	Rockwell-Inspired	Retrd.	80.00	80.00
89-04-006 Bottom of the Sixth NRC-607	Rockwell-Inspired	Retrd.	140.00	140.00
89-04-007 Runaway NRC-610	Rockwell-Inspired	Retrd.	140.00	140.00
89-04-008 Weigh-In NRC-611	Rockwell-Inspired	Retrd.	120.00	120.00
93-04-009 Missed NRP-914	Rockwell-Inspired	7,500	110.00	110.00
93-04-010 Gone Fishing NRP-915	Rockwell-Inspired	7,500	65.00	65.00
93-04-011 After The Prom NRP-916	Rockwell-Inspired	7,500	75.00	75.00
Dave Grossman Creations	**Norman Rockwell America Collection-Miniatures**			
89-05-001 First Haircut MRC-904	Rockwell-Inspired	Retrd.	45.00	45.00
89-05-002 First Day Home MRC-906	Rockwell-Inspired	Retrd.	45.00	45.00
Dave Grossman Creations	**Gone With The Wind Series**			
87-06-001 Tara GWW-5	Unknown	Retrd.	70.00	70.00

		ARTIST	EDITION	ISSUE	QUOTE
88-06-002	Mammy GWW-6	Unknown	Retrd.	70.00	70.00
91-06-003	Prissy GWW-8	Unknown	Open	50.00	50.00
92-06-004	Scarlett in Green Dress GWW-9	Unknown	Open	70.00	70.00
93-06-005	Belle Waiting GWW-10	Unknown	Open	70.00	70.00
93-06-006	Rhett & Bonnie GWW-11	Unknown	Open	80.00	80.00
93-06-007	Rhett in White Suit GWW-12	Unknown	Open	70.00	70.00
94-06-008	Scarlett in Bar B Que Dress GWW-14	Unknown	Open	70.00	70.00
94-06-009	Gerald O'Hara GWW-15	Unknown	Open	70.00	70.00
Dave Grossman Creations		**6" Gone With The Wind Series**			
94-07-001	Scarlett GWW-101	Unknown	Open	40.00	40.00
94-07-002	Ashley GWW-102	Unknown	Open	40.00	40.00
94-07-003	Rhett GW-104	Unknown	Open	40.00	40.00
Dave Grossman Designs		**Norman Rockwell Collection**			
73-01-001	Redhead NR-01	Rockwell-Inspired	Retrd.	20.00	200-225.
73-01-002	Back To School NR-02	Rockwell-Inspired	Retrd.	20.00	40-45.00
73-01-003	Caroller NR-03	Rockwell-Inspired	Retrd.	22.50	40-45.00
73-01-004	Daydreamer NR-04	Rockwell-Inspired	Retrd.	22.50	60.00
73-01-005	No Swimming NR-05	Rockwell-Inspired	Retrd.	25.00	65-145.
73-01-006	Love Letter NR-06	Rockwell-Inspired	Retrd.	25.00	60.00
73-01-007	Lovers NR-07	Rockwell-Inspired	Retrd.	45.00	65-160.
73-01-008	Lazybones NR-08	Rockwell-Inspired	Retrd.	30.00	250.00
73-01-009	Leapfrog NR-09	Rockwell-Inspired	Retrd.	50.00	600-700.
73-01-010	Schoolmaster NR-10	Rockwell-Inspired	Retrd.	55.00	250.00
73-01-011	Marble Players NR-11	Rockwell-Inspired	Retrd.	60.00	400-450.
73-01-012	Doctor & Doll NR-12	Rockwell-Inspired	Retrd.	65.00	150-285.
74-01-013	Friends In Need NR-13	Rockwell-Inspired	Retrd.	45.00	100.00
74-01-014	Springtime '33 NR-14	Rockwell-Inspired	Retrd.	30.00	90-100
74-01-015	Summertime '33 NR-15	Rockwell-Inspired	Retrd.	45.00	50-60.00
74-01-016	Baseball NR-16	Rockwell-Inspired	Retrd.	45.00	100.00
74-01-017	See America First NR-17	Rockwell-Inspired	Retrd.	50.00	95.00
74-01-018	Take Your Medicine NR-18	Rockwell-Inspired	Retrd.	50.00	100.00
75-01-019	Discovery NR-20	Rockwell-Inspired	Retrd.	55.00	160-170.
75-01-020	Big Moment NR-21	Rockwell-Inspired	Retrd.	60.00	125.00
75-01-021	Circus NR-22	Rockwell-Inspired	Retrd.	55.00	100.00
75-01-022	Barbershop Quartet NR-23	Rockwell-Inspired	Retrd.	100.00	15-1700.
76-01-023	Drum For Tommy NRC-24	Rockwell-Inspired	Retrd.	40.00	95.00
77-01-024	Springtime '35 NR-19	Rockwell-Inspired	Retrd.	50.00	55.00
77-01-025	Pals NR-25	Rockwell-Inspired	Retrd.	60.00	95.00
78-01-026	Young Doctor NRD-26	Rockwell-Inspired	Retrd.	100.00	120.00
78-01-027	First Day of School NR-27	Rockwell-Inspired	Retrd.	100.00	150.00
78-01-028	Magic Potion NR-28	Rockwell-Inspired	Retrd.	84.00	125.00
78-01-029	At the Doctor NR-29	Rockwell-Inspired	Retrd.	108.00	150-275.
79-01-030	Teacher's Pet NRA-30	Rockwell-Inspired	Retrd.	35.00	50.00
79-01-031	Dreams of Long Ago NR-31	Rockwell-Inspired	Retrd.	100.00	125.00
79-01-032	Grandpa's Ballerina NR-32	Rockwell-Inspired	Retrd.	100.00	110.00
79-01-033	Back From Camp NR-33	Rockwell-Inspired	Retrd.	96.00	100.00
80-01-034	The Toss NR-34	Rockwell-Inspired	Retrd.	110.00	150-225.
80-01-035	Exasperated Nanny NR-35	Rockwell-Inspired	Retrd.	96.00	100.00
80-01-036	Hankerchief NR-36	Rockwell-Inspired	Retrd.	110.00	100-110.
80-01-037	Santa's Good Boys NR-37	Rockwell-Inspired	Retrd.	90.00	100.00
81-01-038	Spirit of Education NR-38	Rockwell-Inspired	Retrd.	96.00	110.00
82-01-039	A Visit With Rockwell NR-40	Rockwell-Inspired	Retrd.	120.00	100-120.
82-01-040	Croquet NR-41	Rockwell-Inspired	Retrd.	100.00	135.00
82-01-041	American Mother NRG-42	Rockwell-Inspired	Retrd.	100.00	125.00
83-01-042	Country Critic NR-43	Rockwell-Inspired	Retrd.	75.00	125.00
83-01-043	Graduate NR-44	Rockwell-Inspired	Retrd.	30.00	60.00
83-01-044	Scotty's Surprise NRS-20	Rockwell-Inspired	Retrd.	25.00	50-60.00
84-01-045	Scotty's Home Plate NR-46	Rockwell-Inspired	Retrd.	30.00	60.00
86-01-046	Red Cross NR-47	Rockwell-Inspired	Retrd.	67.00	100.00
87-01-047	Young Love NR-48	Rockwell-Inspired	Retrd.	70.00	100.00
88-01-048	Wedding March NR-49	Rockwell-Inspired	Retrd.	110.00	150.00
Dave Grossman Designs		**Norman Rockwell Collection Miniatures**			
79-02-001	Redhead NR-201	Rockwell-Inspired	Retrd.	18.00	50.00
79-02-002	Back To School NR-202	Rockwell-Inspired	Retrd.	18.00	25.00
79-02-003	Caroller NR-203	Rockwell-Inspired	Retrd.	20.00	25.00
79-02-004	Daydreamer NR-204	Rockwell-Inspired	Retrd.	20.00	30.00
79-02-005	No Swimming NR-205	Rockwell-Inspired	Retrd.	22.00	30.00
79-02-006	Love Letter NR-206	Rockwell-Inspired	Retrd.	26.00	30.00
79-02-007	Lovers NR-207	Rockwell-Inspired	Retrd.	28.00	30.00
79-02-008	Lazybones NR-208	Rockwell-Inspired	Retrd.	22.00	30.00
79-02-009	Leapfrog NR-209	Rockwell-Inspired	Retrd.	32.00	32.00
79-02-010	Schoolmaster NR-210	Rockwell-Inspired	Retrd.	34.00	40.00
79-02-011	Marble Players NR-211	Rockwell-Inspired	Retrd.	36.00	38.00
79-02-012	Doctor and Doll NR-212	Rockwell-Inspired	Retrd.	40.00	40.00
80-02-013	Friends In Need NR-213	Rockwell-Inspired	Retrd.	30.00	40.00
80-02-014	Springtime '33 NR-214	Rockwell-Inspired	Retrd.	24.00	80.00
80-02-015	Summertime '33 NR-215	Rockwell-Inspired	Retrd.	22.00	25.00
80-02-016	Baseball NR-216	Rockwell-Inspired	Retrd.	40.00	50.00
80-02-017	See America First NR-217	Rockwell-Inspired	Retrd.	28.00	40.00
80-02-018	Take Your Medicine NR-218	Rockwell-Inspired	Retrd.	36.00	40.00
82-02-019	Springtime '35 NR-219	Rockwell-Inspired	Retrd.	24.00	30.00
82-02-020	Discovery NR-220	Rockwell-Inspired	Retrd.	35.00	45.00
82-02-021	Big Moment NR-221	Rockwell-Inspired	Retrd.	36.00	40.00
82-02-022	Circus NR-222	Rockwell-Inspired	Retrd.	35.00	40.00
82-02-023	Barbershop Quartet NR-223	Rockwell-Inspired	Retrd.	40.00	50.00
82-02-024	Drum For Tommy NRC-224	Rockwell-Inspired	Retrd.	25.00	30.00
83-02-025	Santa On the Train NR-245	Rockwell-Inspired	Retrd.	35.00	55.00
84-02-026	Pals NR-225	Rockwell-Inspired	Retrd.	25.00	25.00
84-02-027	Young Doctor NRD-226	Rockwell-Inspired	Retrd.	30.00	50.00
84-02-028	First Day of School NR-227	Rockwell-Inspired	Retrd.	35.00	35.00
84-02-029	Magic Potion NR-228	Rockwell-Inspired	Retrd.	30.00	40.00
84-02-030	At the Doctor's NR-229	Rockwell-Inspired	Retrd.	35.00	35.00
84-02-031	Dreams of Long Ago NR-231	Rockwell-Inspired	Retrd.	30.00	30.00
Dave Grossman Designs		**Norman Rockwell Collection-Large Limited Editions**			
74-03-001	Doctor and Doll NR-100	Rockwell-Inspired	Retrd.	300.00	1400.00
74-03-002	See America First NR-103	Rockwell-Inspired	Retrd.	100.00	500-550.
75-03-003	No Swimming NR-101	Rockwell-Inspired	Retrd.	150.00	550-600.
75-03-004	Baseball NR-102	Rockwell-Inspired	Retrd.	125.00	600.00
79-03-005	Leapfrog NR-104	Rockwell-Inspired	Retrd.	440.00	700.00
81-03-006	Dreams of Long Ago NR-105	Rockwell-Inspired	Retrd.	500.00	500.00
82-03-007	Circus NR-106	Rockwell-Inspired	Retrd.	500.00	500.00
84-03-008	Marble Players NR-107	Rockwell-Inspired	Retrd.	500.00	500.00
Dave Grossman Designs		**Norman Rockwell Collection-American Rockwell Series**			
81-04-001	Breaking Home Ties NRV-300	Rockwell-Inspired	Retrd.	2000.00	2300.00
82-04-002	Lincoln NRV-301	Rockwell-Inspired	Retrd.	300.00	375.00
82-04-003	Thanksgiving NRV-302	Rockwell-Inspired	Retrd.	2500.00	2650.00
Dave Grossman Designs		**Norman Rockwell Collection-Lladro Series**			
82-05-001	Lladro Love Letter RL-400	Rockwell-Inspired	Retrd.	650.00	700-800.
82-05-002	Summer Stock RL-401	Rockwell-Inspired	Retrd.	750.00	700-800.
82-05-003	Practice Makes Perfect RL-402	Rockwell-Inspired	Retrd.	725.00	700-800.
82-05-004	Young Love RL-403	Rockwell-Inspired	Retrd.	450.00	700-800.
82-05-005	Daydreamer RL-404	Rockwell-Inspired	Retrd.	450.00	1200.00
82-05-006	Court Jester RL-405	Rockwell-Inspired	Retrd.	600.00	15-1600.
82-05-007	Springtime RL-406	Rockwell-Inspired	Retrd.	450.00	1600.00
Dave Grossman Designs		**Norman Rockwell Collection-Rockwell Club Series**			
81-06-001	Young Artist RCC-01	Rockwell-Inspired	Retrd.	96.00	105.00
82-06-002	Diary RCC-02	Rockwell-Inspired	Retrd.	35.00	50.00
83-06-003	Runaway Pants RCC-03	Rockwell-Inspired	Retrd.	65.00	75.00
84-06-004	Gone Fishing RCC-04	Rockwell-Inspired	Retrd.	30.00	55.00
Dave Grossman Designs		**Norman Rockwell Collection-Tom Sawyer Series**			
75-07-001	Whitewashing the Fence TS-01	Rockwell-Inspired	Retrd.	60.00	200-250.
76-07-002	First Smoke TS-02	Rockwell-Inspired	Retrd.	60.00	200-250.
77-07-003	Take Your Medicine TS-03	Rockwell-Inspired	Retrd.	63.00	175.00
78-07-004	Lost In Cave TS-04	Rockwell-Inspired	Retrd.	70.00	175.00
Dave Grossman Designs		**Norman Rockwell Collection-Tom Sawyer Miniatures**			
83-08-001	Whitewashing the Fence TSM-01	Rockwell-Inspired	Retrd.	40.00	50.00
83-08-002	First Smoke TSM-02	Rockwell-Inspired	Retrd.	40.00	45.00
83-08-003	Take Your Medicine TSM-04	Rockwell-Inspired	Retrd.	40.00	45.00
83-08-004	Lost In Cave TSM-05	Rockwell-Inspired	Retrd.	40.00	45.00
Dave Grossman Designs		**Norman Rockwell Collection-Huck Finn Series**			
79-09-001	The Secret HF-01	Rockwell-Inspired	Retrd.	110.00	130.00
80-09-002	Listening HF-02	Rockwell-Inspired	Retrd.	110.00	120.00
80-09-003	No Kings HF-03	Rockwell-Inspired	Retrd.	110.00	110.00
80-09-004	Snake Escapes HF-04	Rockwell-Inspired	Retrd.	110.00	120.00
Dave Grossman Designs		**Norman Rockwell Collection-Boy Scout Series**			
81-10-001	Can't Wait BSA-01	Rockwell-Inspired	Retrd.	30.00	50.00
81-10-002	Scout Is Helpful BSA-02	Rockwell-Inspired	Retrd.	38.00	45.00
81-10-003	Physically Strong BSA-03	Rockwell-Inspired	Retrd.	56.00	60.00
81-10-004	Good Friends BSA-04	Rockwell-Inspired	Retrd.	58.00	65.00
81-10-005	Good Turn BSA-05	Rockwell-Inspired	Retrd.	65.00	100.00
81-10-006	Scout Memories BSA-06	Rockwell-Inspired	Retrd.	65.00	70.00
82-10-007	Guiding Hand BSA-07	Rockwell-Inspired	Retrd.	58.00	60.00
83-10-008	Tomorrow's Leader BSA-08	Rockwell-Inspired	Retrd.	45.00	55.00
Dave Grossman Designs		**Norman Rockwell Collection-Country Gentlemen Series**			
82-11-001	Turkey Dinner CG-01	Rockwell-Inspired	Retrd.	85.00	90.00
82-11-002	Bringing Home the Tree CG-02	Rockwell-Inspired	Retrd.	60.00	75.00
82-11-003	Pals CG-03	Rockwell-Inspired	Retrd.	36.00	45.00
82-11-004	The Catch CG-04	Rockwell-Inspired	Retrd.	50.00	60.00
82-11-005	On the Ice CG-05	Rockwell-Inspired	Retrd.	50.00	60.00
82-11-006	Thin Ice CG-06	Rockwell-Inspired	Retrd.	50.00	60.00
Dave Grossman Designs		**Norman Rockwell Collection-Select Collection, Ltd.**			
82-12-001	Boy & Mother With Puppies SC-1001	Rockwell-Inspired	Retrd.	27.50	27.50
82-12-002	Girl With Dolls In Crib SC-1002	Rockwell-Inspired	Retrd.	26.50	26.50
82-12-003	Young Couple SC-1003	Rockwell-Inspired	Retrd.	27.50	27.50
82-12-004	Football Player SC-1004	Rockwell-Inspired	Retrd.	22.00	22.00
82-12-005	Father With Child SC-1005	Rockwell-Inspired	Retrd.	22.00	22.00
82-12-006	Girl Bathing Dog SC-1006	Rockwell-Inspired	Retrd.	26.50	26.50
82-12-007	Helping Hand SC-1007	Rockwell-Inspired	Retrd.	32.00	32.00
82-12-008	Lemonade Stand SC-1008	Rockwell-Inspired	Retrd.	32.00	32.00
82-12-009	Shaving Lesson SC-1009	Rockwell-Inspired	Retrd.	30.00	30.00
82-12-010	Save Me SC-1010	Rockwell-Inspired	Retrd.	35.00	35.00
Dave Grossman Designs		**Norman Rockwell Collection-Pewter Figurines**			
80-13-001	Back to School FP-02	Rockwell-Inspired	Retrd.	25.00	25.00
80-13-002	Caroller FP-03	Rockwell-Inspired	Retrd.	25.00	25.00
80-13-003	No Swimming FP-05	Rockwell-Inspired	Retrd.	25.00	25.00
80-13-004	Lovers FP-07	Rockwell-Inspired	Retrd.	25.00	25.00
80-13-005	Doctor and Doll FP-12	Rockwell-Inspired	Retrd.	25.00	25.00
80-13-006	See America First FP-17	Rockwell-Inspired	Retrd.	25.00	25.00
80-13-007	Take Your Medicine FP-18	Rockwell-Inspired	Retrd.	25.00	25.00
80-13-008	Big Moment FP-21	Rockwell-Inspired	Retrd.	25.00	25.00
80-13-009	Circus FP-22	Rockwell-Inspired	Retrd.	25.00	25.00
80-13-010	Barbershop Quartet FP-23	Rockwell-Inspired	Retrd.	25.00	25.00
80-13-011	Magic Potion FP-28	Rockwell-Inspired	Retrd.	25.00	25.00
80-13-012	Grandpa's Ballerina FP-32	Rockwell-Inspired	Retrd.	25.00	25.00
80-13-013	Figurine Display Rack FDR-01	Rockwell-Inspired	Retrd.	60.00	60.00
Hallmark Galleries		**Moustershire**			
92-01-001	Andrew Allsgood- Honorable Citizen 1000QHG8001	D. Rhodus	Open	10.00	10.00
92-01-002	Chelsea Goforth- Ingenue 1000QHG8002	D. Rhodus	Open	10.00	10.00
92-01-003	Miles Fielding- Farmer 1000QHG8003	D. Rhodus	Open	10.00	10.00
92-01-004	Colin Tuneman- Musician of Note 1000QHG8004	D. Rhodus	Open	10.00	10.00
92-01-005	Olivia Puddingsby- Baker 1000QHG8005	D. Rhodus	Retrd.	10.00	10.00
92-01-006	Hillary Hemstitch- Seamstress 1000QHG8006	D. Rhodus	Open	10.00	10.00
92-01-007	L.E. Hosten- Innkeeper 1000QHG8007	D. Rhodus	Open	10.00	10.00
92-01-008	Malcolm Cramwell- Mouserly Scholar 1000QHG8008	D. Rhodus	Open	10.00	10.00
92-01-009	Acorn Inn/Timothy Duzmuch 6500QHG8009	D. Rhodus	9,500	65.00	65.00
92-01-010	Bakery/Dunne Eaton 5500QHG8010	D. Rhodus	Retrd.	55.00	55.00
92-01-011	Bandstand/Cyrus & Cecilia Sunnyside 5000QHG8011	D. Rhodus	9,500	50.00	50.00
92-01-012	Nigel Puffmore- Talented Tubist 1000QHG8012	D. Rhodus	19,500	10.00	10.00
92-01-013	Robin Ripengood- Grocer 2800QHG8013	D. Rhodus	19,500	28.00	28.00
92-01-014	Claire Lovencare- Nanny 1800QHG8014	D. Rhodus	19,500	18.00	18.00
92-01-015	Hattie Chapeau- Milliner 1500QHG8015	D. Rhodus	19,500	15.00	15.00
92-01-016	Trio 2300QHG8016	D. Rhodus	19,500	23.00	23.00
92-01-017	The Picnic/Tree 5000QHG8017	D. Rhodus	9,500	50.00	50.00
92-01-018	The Park Gate 6000QHG8019	D. Rhodus	9,500	60.00	60.00
92-01-019	Acorn Inn Customers 2800QHG8020	D. Rhodus	9,500	28.00	28.00
92-01-020	Hyacinth House 6500QHG8021	D. Rhodus	9,500	65.00	65.00
92-01-021	Peter Philpott- Gardener 1200QHG8022	D. Rhodus	19,500	12.00	12.00
92-01-022	Village/Bay Crossroads Sign 1000QHG8023	D. Rhodus	19,500	10.00	10.00
92-01-023	Tess Tellingtale/Well 2800QHG8024	D. Rhodus	19,500	28.00	28.00
93-01-024	Michael McFogg At Lighthouse 5500QHG8025	D. Rhodus	9,500	55.00	55.00
92-01-025	Henrietta Seaworthy 1500QHG8026	D. Rhodus	19,500	15.00	15.00
Hallmark Galleries		**Times to Cherish**			
92-02-001	The Joys of Fatherhood 6000QHG6001	T. Andrews	Retrd.	60.00	60.00
92-02-002	The Embrace 6000QHG6002	T. Andrews	Retrd.	60.00	60.00
92-02-003	Sister Time 5500QHG6003	T. Andrews	Retrd.	55.00	55.00

		ARTIST	EDITION	ISSUE	QUOTE
92-02-004	Daily Devotion 4000QHG6005	T. Andrews	Retrd.	40.00	40.00
92-02-005	A Child's Prayer 3500QHG6006	T. Andrews	Retrd.	35.00	35.00
92-02-006	A Mother's Touch 6000QHG6007	T. Andrews	Retrd.	60.00	60.00
92-02-007	Mother's Blessing 6500QHG6008	T. Andrews	Retrd.	65.00	65.00
92-02-008	Dancer's Dream 5000QHG6009	T. Andrews	Retrd.	50.00	50.00
92-02-009	Beautiful Dreamer 6500QHG6010	T. Andrews	Retrd.	65.00	65.00
93-02-010	Showing The Way 4500QHG6011	P. Andrews	Retrd.	45.00	45.00
93-02-011	Spring Tulip Lidded Box 2500QHG6012	P. Andrews	Retrd.	25.00	25.00

Hallmark Galleries — Birds of North America

		ARTIST	EDITION	ISSUE	QUOTE
92-03-001	House Wren 5500QHG9801	G.&G. Dooly	Retrd.	85.00	85.00
92-03-002	Red-breasted Nuthatch 5500QHG9802	G.&G. Dooly	Retrd.	95.00	95.00
92-03-003	Ovenbird 6500QHG9837	G.&G. Dooly	Retrd.	95.00	95.00
92-03-004	American Robins 2QHG9878	G.&G. Dooly	Retrd.	175.00	175.00
92-03-005	American Goldfinch 5500QHG9887	G.&G. Dooly	Retrd.	85.00	85.00
92-03-006	Cedar Waxwing 8000QHG9889	G.&G. Dooly	Retrd.	120.00	120.00
92-03-007	Cardinal 7500QHG9897	G.&G. Dooly	Retrd.	110.00	110.00
92-03-008	Dark-eyed Junco 5500QHG9899	G.&G. Dooly	Retrd.	85.00	85.00

Hallmark Galleries — Lou Rankin's Creations

		ARTIST	EDITION	ISSUE	QUOTE
92-04-001	Reclining Bear 3500QHG9901	L. Rankin	19,500	35.00	35.00
92-04-002	Pair of Pigs -Pork & Beans 3800QHG9902	L. Rankin	19,500	38.00	38.00
92-04-003	Pig with Head Raised - Fair Lady 3500QHG9903	L. Rankin	19,500	35.00	35.00
92-04-004	Seated Bear 3000QHG9905	L. Rankin	19,500	30.00	30.00
92-04-005	Bulldog and Beagle -Best Buddies 4800QHG9906	L. Rankin	9,500	48.00	48.00
92-04-006	Shih Tzu -The Sophisticate 3000QHG9907	L. Rankin	19,500	30.00	30.00
92-04-007	Basset Hound -Faithful Friend 3800QHG9908	L. Rankin	19,500	38.00	38.00
92-04-008	Squirrel I -Satisfied 2500QHG9909	L. Rankin	19,500	25.00	25.00
92-04-009	Squirrel II -Sassy 2500QHG9910	L. Rankin	19,500	25.00	25.00
92-04-010	Seated Rabbit 3000QHG9911	L. Rankin	19,500	30.00	30.00
92-04-011	Reclining Cat -Birdwatcher 3000QHG9912	L. Rankin	19,500	30.00	30.00
92-04-012	Two Otters -Two's Company 4500QHG9914	L. Rankin	9,500	45.00	45.00
92-04-013	Orangutan -The Thinker 3800QHG9915	L. Rankin	19,500	38.00	38.00
93-04-014	Fairbanks Polar Bear 7000QHG9916	L. Rankin	19,500	70.00	70.00
93-04-015	Slowpoke Turtle 3000QHG9917	L. Rankin	19,500	30.00	30.00
93-04-016	Happy Frog -Feelin' Fine 3500QHG9918	L. Rankin	19,500	35.00	35.00
93-04-017	Backyard Bandit Raccoon 3000QHG9920	L. Rankin	19,500	30.00	30.00
93-04-018	Seal Winsome 3200QHG9921	L. Rankin	19,500	32.00	32.00
93-04-019	Mini Paws Happy-Looking Cat 2500QHG9922	L. Rankin	19,500	25.00	25.00
94-04-020	Frog Pucker Up Baby 3500QHG9923	L. Rankin	19,500	35.00	35.00
94-04-021	Cocker Spaniel Pal 3500QHG9924	L. Rankin	19,500	35.00	35.00
94-04-022	Two Pigs 4500QHG9925	L. Rankin	19,500	45.00	45.00
94-04-023	Bulldog 3800QHG9926	L. Rankin	19,500	38.00	38.00

Hallmark Galleries — Eileen's Richardson's Enchanted Garden

		ARTIST	EDITION	ISSUE	QUOTE
92-05-001	Promenade (bowl) 6500QHG3002	E. Richardson	Retrd.	65.00	65.00
92-05-002	Baby Bunny Hop (bowl) 8500QHG3004	E. Richardson	Retrd.	85.00	85.00
92-05-003	Bunny Abundance (vase) 7500QHG3005	E. Richardson	Retrd.	75.00	75.00
92-05-004	Enchanted Garden (vase) 1QHG3006	E. Richardson	Retrd.	115.00	115.00
92-05-005	Everybunny Can Fly (vase) 7000QHG3007	E. Richardson	Retrd.	70.00	70.00
92-05-006	Milk Bath (vase) 8000QHG3009	E. Richardson	Retrd.	80.00	80.00
92-05-007	Let Them Eat Carrots (pitcher) 7000QHG3013	E. Richardson	Retrd.	70.00	70.00
93-05-008	Peaceable Kingdom Lidded Box 3800QHG3017	E. Richardson	Retrd.	38.00	38.00

Hallmark Galleries — Days to Remember-The Art of Norman Rockwell

		ARTIST	EDITION	ISSUE	QUOTE
92-06-001	Santa and His Helpers 9500QHG9702	D. Unruh	7,500	95.00	95.00
92-06-002	Sleeping Children 1QHG9703	D. Unruh	7,500	105.00	105.00
92-06-003	Marbles Champion 7500QHG9704	D. Unruh	4,500	75.00	75.00
92-06-004	Little Spooners 7000QHG9705	D. Unruh	4,500	70.00	70.00
92-06-005	Springtime 1927 9500QHG9706	D. Unruh	4,500	95.00	95.00
92-06-006	The Fiddler 9500QHG9708	D. Unruh	4,500	95.00	95.00
92-06-007	The Fiddler-Musical Jewelry Box 4800QHG9711	D. Unruh	Retrd.	48.00	48.00
92-06-008	Little Spooner-Musical Jewelry Box 4800QHG9712	D. Unruh	Retrd.	48.00	48.00
92-06-009	Springtime, 1927-Musical Jewelry Box 4800QHG9713	D. Unruh	Retrd.	48.00	48.00
92-06-010	Low and Outside 9500QHG9714	D. Unruh	4,500	95.00	95.00
92-06-011	Saying Grace 1QHG9719	D. Unruh	1,500	375.00	375.00
92-06-012	The Truth About Santa 8500QHG9720	D. Unruh	7,500	85.00	85.00
93-06-013	Secrets 7000QHG9721	D. Unruh	7,500	70.00	70.00
93-06-014	A Child's Prayer 7500QHG9722	D. Unruh	7,500	75.00	75.00
94-06-015	No Swimming 7000QHG9725	D. Unruh	4,500	70.00	70.00

Hallmark Galleries — Innocent Wonders

		ARTIST	EDITION	ISSUE	QUOTE
92-07-001	Waggletag 1QHG4001	T. Blackshear	Retrd.	125.00	125.00
92-07-002	Pinkie Poo 1QHG4002	T. Blackshear	2,500	135.00	135.00
92-07-003	Dinky Toot 1QHG4004	T. Blackshear	4,500	125.00	125.00
92-07-004	Bobo Bipps 1QHG4005	T. Blackshear	2,500	150.00	150.00
92-07-005	Pippy Lou 1QHG4006	T. Blackshear	4,500	150.00	150.00
92-07-006	Square Music Box 4500QHG4008	T. Blackshear	9,500	45.00	45.00
92-07-007	Rectangular Music Box 6000QHG4009	T. Blackshear	9,500	60.00	60.00
92-07-008	Zip Doodle 1QHG4010	T. Blackshear	4,500	125.00	125.00
92-07-009	Wood Base 2000QHG4011	T. Blackshear	Open	20.00	20.00
92-07-010	Pockets 1QHG4018	T. Blackshear	4,500	125.00	125.00
92-07-011	Waterdome-Dinky Toot 3500QHG4020	T. Blackshear	Retrd.	35.00	35.00
93-07-012	Twinky Wink 1QHG4021	T. Blackshear	4,500	115.00	115.00

Hallmark Galleries — Tobin Fraley Carousels

		ARTIST	EDITION	ISSUE	QUOTE
92-08-001	Charles Looff/1915 5000QHG1	T. Fraley	4,500	50.00	50.00
92-08-002	Philadelphia Toboggan Co/1928 5000QHG2	T. Fraley	4,500	50.00	50.00
92-08-003	M.C. Illions & Sons/1910 5000QHG3	T. Fraley	4,500	50.00	50.00
92-08-004	Stein & Goldstein/1914 5000QHG4	T. Fraley	4,500	50.00	50.00
92-08-005	C.W. Parker/1922 3000QHG5	T. Fraley	4,500	30.00	30.00
92-08-006	M.C. Illions & Sons/1910 3000QHG6	T. Fraley	4,500	30.00	30.00
92-08-007	Philadelphia Toboggan Co/1910 3000QHG7	T. Fraley	4,500	30.00	30.00
92-08-008	Charles Carmel/1914 3000QHG8	T. Fraley	4,500	30.00	30.00
92-08-009	Charles Looff/1915/musical 6000QHG09	T. Fraley	2,500	60.00	60.00
92-08-010	Philadelphia Toboggan Co/1928/musical 6000QHG10	T. Fraley	Retrd.	60.00	60.00
92-08-011	M.C. Illions & Sons/1910/musical 6000QHG11	T. Fraley	2,500	60.00	60.00
92-08-012	Stein & Goldstein/1914/musical 6000QHG12	T. Fraley	2,500	60.00	60.00
92-08-013	C.W. Parker/1922/musical 4000QHG13	T. Fraley	4,500	40.00	40.00
92-08-014	M.C. Illions & Sons/1910/musical 4000QHG14	T. Fraley	4,500	40.00	40.00
92-08-015	Philadelphia Toboggan Co/1910/musical 4000QHG15	T. Fraley	4,500	40.00	40.00
92-08-016	Charles Carmel, circa 1914/musical 4000QHG16	T. Fraley	4,500	40.00	40.00
92-08-017	Playland Carousel/musical 1QHG17	T. Fraley	Retrd.	195.00	195.00
92-08-018	Revolving Brass/Wood Display 4000QHG19	T. Fraley	4,500	40.00	40.00
92-08-019	Musical Premier Horse 1QHG21	T. Fraley	1,200	275.00	275.00
94-08-020	Armour 6000QHG25	T. Fraley	4,500	60.00	60.00
94-08-021	Patriot 6000QHG26	T. Fraley	4,500	60.00	60.00
94-08-022	Floral 6000QHG27	T. Fraley	4,500	60.00	60.00
94-08-023	Indian 6000QHG28	T. Fraley	4,500	60.00	60.00

Hallmark Galleries — Majestic Wilderness

		ARTIST	EDITION	ISSUE	QUOTE
92-09-001	Male Grizzly 1QHG2001	M. Newman	2,500	145.00	145.00
92-09-002	White-tailed Doe with Fawn 1QHG2002	M. Newman	2,500	135.00	135.00
92-09-003	Timber Wolves 1QHG2003	M. Newman	2,500	135.00	135.00
92-09-004	Grizzly Mother with Cub 1QHG2004	M. Newman	2,500	135.00	135.00
92-09-005	Bighorn Sheep 1QHG2005	M. Newman	4,500	125.00	125.00
92-09-006	Mountain Lion 7500QHG2006	M. Newman	4,500	75.00	75.00
92-09-007	Snowshoe Rabbit 7000QHG2007	M. Newman	4,500	70.00	70.00
92-09-008	White-tailed Buck 1QHG2008	M. Newman	2,500	135.00	135.00
92-09-009	American Bald Eagle 1QHG2009	M. Newman	Retrd.	195.00	195.00
92-09-010	Lidded Box/Deer 4000QHG2010	M. Newman	9,500	40.00	40.00
92-09-011	Lidded Box/Wolves 4000QHG2011	M. Newman	9,500	40.00	40.00
92-09-012	Bison 1QHG2016	M. Newman	4,500	120.00	120.00
92-09-013	Red Fox 7500QHG2017	M. Newman	4,500	75.00	75.00
92-09-014	American Wilderness Mini Environment With Dome 8000QHG2019	M. Newman	Open	80.00	80.00
92-09-015	Mini Black Bear 2800QHG2020	M. Newman	14,500	28.00	28.00
92-09-016	Mini Cottontail Rabbits 2000QHG2021	M. Newman	14,500	20.00	20.00
92-09-017	Mini Raccoons 2000QHG2022	M. Newman	14,500	20.00	20.00
92-09-018	Mini Red Fox 2000QHG2023	M. Newman	14,500	20.00	20.00
92-09-019	Mini Mule Deer 2800QHG2024	M. Newman	14,500	28.00	28.00
92-09-020	The Launch 1QHG2025	M. Newman	2,500	165.00	165.00
92-09-021	Mini Eagle 2800QHG2026	M. Newman	14,500	28.00	28.00
92-09-022	Large Base 3500QHG2028	M. Newman	Open	3.50	3.50
92-09-023	Small Base 2500QHG2027	M. Newman	Open	2.50	2.50
93-09-024	American Wilderness Mini Environment Set 1QHG2029	M. Newman	2,500	225.00	225.00
94-09-025	Arctic Wolves 13000QHG2031	M. Newman	4,500	130.00	130.00
94-09-026	Elk in Water 12000QHG2032	M. Newman	4,500	120.00	120.00
94-09-027	Winter Environment 7000QHG2033	M. Newman	Open	70.00	70.00
94-09-028	Mini Snow Owl 1800QHG2034	M. Newman	14,500	18.00	18.00
94-09-029	Mini White Tailed Buck 2500QHG2035	M. Newman	14,500	25.00	25.00
94-09-030	Mini Deer 2500QHG2036	M. Newman	14,500	25.00	25.00
94-09-031	Mini Snowshoe Rabbits 2000QHG2037	M. Newman	14,500	20.00	20.00
94-09-032	Winter Environment Set 1QHG2038	M. Newman	2,500	160.00	160.00

Hallmark Galleries — Tender Touches

		ARTIST	EDITION	ISSUE	QUOTE
92-10-001	Tender Touches Tree House 5500QHG7001	E. Seale	9,500	55.00	55.00
92-10-002	Bear Family Christmas 4500QHG7002	E. Seale	9,500	45.00	45.00
92-10-003	Chatting Mice 2300QHG7003	E. Seale	19,500	23.00	23.00
92-10-004	Raccoons on Bridge 2500QHG7004	E. Seale	19,500	25.00	25.00
92-10-005	Soapbox Racer 2300QHG7005	E. Seale	19,500	23.00	23.00
92-10-006	Bunny with Kite 1900QHG7006	E. Seale	19,500	19.00	19.00
92-10-007	Beaver Growth Chart 2000QHG7007	E. Seale	19,500	20.00	20.00
90-10-008	Bunny Pulling Wagon 2300QHG7008	E. Seale	Retrd.	23.00	23.00
89-10-009	Bride & Groom 2000QHG7009	E. Seale	Retrd.	20.00	20.00
89-10-010	Birthday Mouse 1600QHG7010	E. Seale	Retrd.	16.00	16.00
90-10-011	Tucking Baby in Bed 1800QHG7011	E. Seale	Retrd.	18.00	18.00
89-10-012	Bunny in Flowers 1600QHG7012	E. Seale	Retrd.	16.00	26.00
90-10-013	Raccoon Mail Carrier 1600QHG7013	E. Seale	Open	16.00	16.00
90-10-014	Raccoons with Wagon 2300QHG7014	E. Seale	Retrd.	23.00	23.00
90-10-015	Dad and Son Bears 2300QHG7015	E. Seale	Retrd.	23.00	33.00
90-10-016	Bunnies with Slide 2000QHG7016	E. Seale	Retrd.	20.00	20.00
90-10-017	Mice with Quilt 2000QHG7017	E. Seale	Retrd.	20.00	20.00
90-10-018	Bunny Cheerleader 1600QHG7018	E. Seale	Retrd.	16.00	16.00
90-10-019	Teacher and Student Chipmunks 2000QHG7019	E. Seale	Retrd.	20.00	30.00
90-10-020	Bunny with Ice Cream 1500QHG7020	E. Seale	Open	15.00	15.00
90-10-021	Bunny in Boat 1800QHG7021	E. Seale	Retrd.	18.00	18.00
89-10-027	Rabbit Painting Egg 1800QHG7022	E. Seale	Retrd.	18.00	18.00
89-10-028	Chipmunk With Roses 1600QHG7023	E. Seale	Retrd.	16.00	26.00
88-10-029	Mouse with Heart 1800QHG7024	E. Seale	Retrd.	18.00	18.00
88-10-030	Rabbits with Cake 2000QHG7025	E. Seale	Retrd.	20.00	40.00
88-10-031	Teacher with Student 1800QHG7026	E. Seale	Open	18.00	18.00
88-10-032	Rabbit with Ribbon 1500QHG7027	E. Seale	Retrd.	15.00	15.00
88-10-033	Mice at Tea Party 2300QHG7028	E. Seale	Retrd.	23.00	23.00
88-10-034	Bear with Umbrella 1600QHG7029	E. Seale	Retrd.	16.00	16.00
88-10-035	Mice in Rocking Chair 1800QHG7030	E. Seale	Retrd.	18.00	18.00
88-10-036	Baby Raccoon 2000QHG7031	E. Seale	Retrd.	20.00	40.00
88-10-037	Squirrels with Bandage 1800QHG7032	E. Seale	Retrd.	18.00	18.00
88-10-038	Rabbits at Juice Stand 2300QHG7033	E. Seale	Retrd.	23.00	23.00
88-10-039	Raccoons Fishing 1800QHG7034	E. Seale	Retrd.	18.00	18.00
90-10-040	Bunny Hiding Valentine 1600QHG7035	E. Seale	Open	16.00	16.00
90-10-041	Raccoon Watering Roses 2000QHG7036	E. Seale	Retrd.	20.00	20.00
90-10-042	Mouse Nurse 1500QHG7037	E. Seale	Open	15.00	15.00
90-10-043	Bunnies Eating Ice Cream 2000QHG7038	E. Seale	Retrd.	20.00	20.00
90-10-044	Bears Playing Baseball 2000QHG7039	E. Seale	Retrd.	20.00	20.00
90-10-045	Bear's Easter Parade 2300QHG7040	E. Seale	Open	23.00	23.00
91-10-046	Father Bear Barbequing 2300QHG7041	E. Seale	Open	23.00	23.00
91-10-047	Mother Raccoon Reading Bible Stories 2000QHG7042	E. Seale	Retrd.	20.00	20.00
90-10-048	Bear Graduate 1500QHG7043	E. Seale	Open	15.00	15.00
90-10-049	Raccoons with Flag 2300QHG7044	E. Seale	Retrd.	23.00	23.00
91-10-050	Raccoon Witch 1600QHG7045	E. Seale	Retrd.	16.00	16.00
91-10-051	Christmas Bunny Skiing 1800QHG7046	E. Seale	Open	18.00	18.00
91-10-052	Love-American Gothic-Farmer Raccoons 2000QHG7047	E. Seale	Open	20.00	20.00
92-10-053	Thanksgiving Family Around Table 2500QHG7048	E. Seale	Open	25.00	25.00
89-10-054	Mouse with Violin 1600QHG7049	E. Seale	Retrd.	16.00	28.00
89-10-055	Bear Decorating Tree 1800QHG7050	E. Seale	Retrd.	18.00	18.00
90-10-056	Santa in Chimney 1800QHG7051	E. Seale	Open	18.00	18.00
90-10-057	Beavers with Tree 2300QHG7052	E. Seale	Open	23.00	23.00
91-10-058	Foxes in Rowboat 2300QHG7053	E. Seale	Open	23.00	23.00
91-10-059	Bunny in High Chair 1600QHG7054	E. Seale	Retrd.	16.00	16.00
91-10-060	Mouse Couple Sharing Soda 2300QHG7055	E. Seale	Retrd.	23.00	23.00
91-10-061	Bunny with Large Eggs 1600QHG7056	E. Seale	Retrd.	16.00	16.00

		ARTIST	EDITION	ISSUE	QUOTE
92-10-062	Chipmunks with Album 2300QHG7057	E. Seale	Open	23.00	23.00
92-10-063	Beaver with Double Bass 1800QHG7058	E. Seale	Open	18.00	18.00
92-10-064	Breakfast in Bed 1800QHG7059	E. Seale	Open	18.00	18.00
92-10-065	Newsboy Bear 1600QHG7060	E. Seale	Open	16.00	16.00
92-10-066	Building a Pumpkin Man 1800QHG7061	E. Seale	Open	18.00	18.00
92-10-067	Sweet Sharing 2000QHG7062	E. Seale	Open	20.00	20.00
92-10-068	Bunny Clarinet 1600QHG7063	E. Seale	Retrd.	16.00	16.00
92-10-069	Waiting for Santa 2000QHG7064	E. Seale	Open	20.00	20.00
92-10-070	Fitting Gift 2300QHG7065	E. Seale	Open	23.00	23.00
92-10-071	Stealing a Kiss 2300QHG7066	E. Seale	19,500	23.00	23.00
92-10-072	Delightful Fright 2300QHG7067	E. Seale	19,500	23.00	23.00
92-10-073	New World, Ahoy! 2500QHG7068	E. Seale	Open	25.00	25.00
92-10-074	Raccoon in Bath 1800QHG7069	E. Seale	Retrd.	18.00	18.00
92-10-075	Swingtime Love 2100QHG7070	E. Seale	Retrd.	21.00	21.00
92-10-076	From Your Valentine 2000QHG7071	E. Seale	Open	20.00	20.00
92-10-077	Mom's Easter Bonnet 1800QHG7072	E. Seale	Open	18.00	18.00
92-10-078	Mouse Matinee 2200QHG7073	E. Seale	Open	22.00	22.00
92-10-079	Younger Than Springtime 3500QHG7074	E. Seale	19,500	35.00	35.00
93-10-080	Mr. Repair Bear 1800QHG7075	E. Seale	Open	18.00	18.00
93-10-081	Handling a Big Thirst 2100QHG7076	E. Seale	Open	21.00	21.00
93-10-082	Teeter For Two 2300QHG7077	E. Seale	Open	23.00	23.00
93-10-083	Garden Capers 2000QHG7078	E. Seale	Open	20.00	20.00
93-10-084	Woodland Americana-Stitching the Stars and Stripes 2100QHG7079	E. Seale	Open	21.00	21.00
93-10-085	Downhill Dash 2300QHG7080	E. Seale	Open	23.00	23.00
93-10-086	Woodland Americana-Liberty Mouse 2100QHG7081	E. Seale	Open	21.00	21.00
93-10-087	Woodland Americana-Patriot George 2500QHG7082	E. Seale	Open	25.00	25.00
93-10-088	Sculpting Santa 2000QHG7083	E. Seale	Open	20.00	20.00
93-10-089	Easter Stroll 2100QHG7084	E. Seale	Open	21.00	21.00
93-10-090	Love at First Sight 2300QHG7085	E. Seale	Open	23.00	23.00
93-10-091	The Old Swimming Hole 6000QHG7086	E. Seale	9,500	45.00	60.00
93-10-092	Ensemble Chipmunk Kettledrum 1800QHG7087	E. Seale	Open	18.00	18.00
93-10-093	Making A Splash 2000QHG7088	E. Seale	Open	20.00	20.00
93-10-094	Playground Go-Round 2300QHG7089	E. Seale	Open	23.00	23.00
94-10-095	Fireman 2300QHG7090	E. Seale	Open	23.00	23.00
94-10-096	Golfing 2300QHG7091	E. Seale	Open	23.00	23.00
94-10-097	"Happy Campers" 2500QHG7092	E. Seale	Open	25.00	25.00
94-10-098	Halloween 2300QHG7093	E. Seale	Open	23.00	23.00
94-10-099	Jesus, Mary, Joseph 2300QHG7094	E. Seale	Open	23.00	23.00
91-10-100	Baby's 1st Bear Riding Rocking Bear 1600QEC9349	E. Seale	Retrd.	16.00	16.00
91-10-101	First Christmas Mice @ Piano 2300QEC9357	E. Seale	Retrd.	23.00	23.00
89-10-102	Rabbits Ice Skating 1800QEC9391	E. Seale	Retrd.	18.00	28.00
89-10-103	Santa Mouse in Chair 2000QEC9394	E. Seale	Retrd.	20.00	28.00
89-10-104	Chipmunk Praying 1800QEC9431	E. Seale	Retrd.	18.00	28.00
90-10-105	Bunny With Stocking 1500QEC9416	E. Seale	Retrd.	15.00	25.00
90-10-106	Mice With Mistletoe 2000QEC9423	E. Seale	Retrd.	20.00	30.00
89-10-107	Mouse at Desk 1800QEC9434	E. Seale	Retrd.	18.00	28.00
91-10-108	Mice Couple Slow Waltzing 2000QEC9437	E. Seale	Retrd.	20.00	20.00
90-10-109	Bears With Gift 1800QEC9461	E. Seale	Retrd.	18.00	28.00
90-10-110	Pilgrim Bear Praying 1800QEC9466	E. Seale	Retrd.	18.00	28.00
90-10-111	Mouse in Pumpkin 1800QEC9473	E. Seale	Retrd.	18.00	28.00
89-10-112	Halloween Trio 1800QEC9714	E. Seale	Retrd.	18.00	26.00
89-10-113	Pilgrim Mouse 1600QEC9721	E. Seale	Retrd.	16.00	30.00
88-10-114	Raccoon with Cake 1800QEC9724	E. Seale	Retrd.	18.00	36.00
88-10-115	Raccoons Playing Ball 1800QEC9771	E. Seale	Retrd.	18.00	36.00
90-10-116	Baby Bear in Backpack 1600QEC9863	E. Seale	Retrd.	16.00	26.00
90-10-117	Easter Egg Hunt 1800QEC9866	E. Seale	Retrd.	18.00	28.00
90-10-118	Mice in Red Car 2100QEC9886	E. Seale	Retrd.	20.00	30.00
90-10-119	Romeo and Juliet Mice 2500QEC9903	E. Seale	Retrd.	25.00	35.00

Hallmark Galleries — Kiddie Car Classics

92-11-001	Murray Fire Truck 5000QHG9001	E. Weirick	Retrd.	48.00	100.00
92-11-002	1955 Red Champion 4500QHG9002	E. Weirick	19,500	45.00	45.00
92-11-003	Murray Airplane 5000QHG9003	E. Weirick	Retrd.	50.00	100.00
92-11-004	Murray Tractor and Trailer 5500QHG9004	E. Weirick	Retrd.	55.00	55.00
93-11-005	Murray Boat Jolly Roger 5000QHG9005	E. Weirick	19,500	50.00	50.00
93-11-006	Murray Fire Chief 4500QHG9006	E. Weirick	19,500	45.00	45.00
93-11-007	Murray Ranch Wagon 4800QHG9007	E. Weirick	24,500	48.00	48.00
92-11-008	Murray Champion 4500QHG9008	E. Weirick	Retrd.	45.00	100.00
92-11-009	1941 Spitfire Airplane 5000QHG9009	E. Weirick	19,500	50.00	50.00
92-11-010	1955 Murray Fire Truck 5000QHG9010	E. Weirick	19,500	50.00	50.00
92-11-011	1955 Murray Dump Truck 4800QHG9011	E. Weirick	Retrd.	48.00	48.00
92-11-012	Murray Dump Truck 4800QHG9012	E. Weirick	Retrd.	48.00	100.00
94-11-013	1961 Speedway Pace Car 4500QHG9013	E. Weirick	24,500	45.00	45.00
94-11-014	1961 Circus Car 4800QHG9014	E. Weirick	24,500	48.00	48.00
94-11-015	1936 Lincoln Zephyr 5000QHG9015	E. Weirick	19,500	50.00	50.00
94-11-016	1956 Dragnet Police Car 5000QHG9016	E. Weirick	24,500	50.00	50.00
94-11-017	1956 Garton Kiddilac (Special Edition) 5500QHX9094	E. Weirick	24,500	55.00	55.00

Hallmark Galleries — Victorian Memories

92-12-001	Lillian-cold cast 5500QHG1001	J. Lyle	Retrd.	55.00	55.00
92-12-002	Sarah-cold cast 6000QHG1003	J. Lyle	Retrd.	60.00	60.00
92-12-003	Doll Trunk IQHG1015	J. Greene	7,500	125.00	125.00
92-12-004	Rabbit (on wheels) 6500QHG1022	J. Greene	4,500	65.00	65.00
92-12-005	Rebecca-cold cast 6000QHG1024	J. Lyle	Retrd.	60.00	60.00
92-12-006	Music Box 5000QHG1025	J. Greene	9,500	50.00	50.00
92-12-007	Tea Set 3500QHG1026	J. Greene	9,500	35.00	35.00
93-12-008	Toy Cradle 2000QHG1027	J. Greene	9,500	20.00	20.00
93-12-009	Hobby Horse 1800QHG1028	J. Greene	Retrd.	18.00	18.00
93-12-010	Mini Snow Globe 1800QHG1031	J. Greene	9,500	18.00	18.00
93-12-011	Gloria Summer Figurine 6000QHG1032	Greene/Lyle	Retrd.	60.00	60.00
93-12-012	Shoo-Fly Rocking Horse 1800QHG1036	J. Greene	9,500	18.00	18.00
93-12-013	Victorian Toy Cupboard 7500QHG1038	J. Greene	7,500	75.00	75.00
92-12-014	Wooden Train-miniature 2200QHG9501	J. Greene	9,500	15.00	15.00
92-12-015	Musical Jack-in-the Box 2000QHG9502	J. Greene	9,500	20.00	20.00
92-12-016	Wooden Noah's Ark-miniature 1500QHG9503	J. Greene	9,500	15.00	15.00
92-12-017	Wooden Horse Pull Toy-miniature 2000QHG9504	J. Greene	9,500	18.00	18.00
92-12-018	Wooden Jewelry Box 1800QHG9505	J. Greene	9,500	18.00	18.00
92-12-019	Wooden Doll Carriage-miniature 2000QHG9506	J. Greene	9,500	20.00	20.00
92-12-020	Wicker Rocker 4500QHG9510	J. Greene	Retrd.	45.00	45.00
92-12-021	Wooden Rocking Horse 7500QHG9511	J. Greene	4,500	75.00	75.00

Hallmark Galleries — Mary Engelbreit Friendship Garden

93-12-001	Blue Teapot 5000QHG5004	M. Engelbreit	9,500	50.00	50.00
93-12-002	Cherry Teapot 5000QHG5005	M. Engelbreit	9,500	50.00	50.00
93-12-003	Yellow Teapot 5000QHG5006	M. Engelbreit	9,500	50.00	50.00
93-12-004	Mini Tea Set 4500QHG5007	M. Engelbreit	9,500	45.00	45.00
93-12-005	Watering Can 3000QHG5008	M. Engelbreit	Retrd.	30.00	30.00
93-12-006	Cookie Jar 5000QHG5009	M. Engelbreit	9,500	50.00	50.00
93-12-007	Birdhouse 4500QHG5013	M. Engelbreit	9,500	45.00	45.00
93-12-008	Teatime Table and Chairs 7500QHG5014	M. Engelbreit	12,500	75.00	75.00

Hallmark Galleries — Little Creations

93-13-001	Squirrel-Cheeky 750QEC1223	L. Rankin	Open	7.50	7.50
94-13-002	Sitting Pig Li'l Piggy 1000QEC1224	L. Rankin	Open	10.00	10.00
93-13-003	Turtle-Tenderfoot 1200QEC1225	L. Rankin	Open	12.00	12.00
94-13-004	Polar Bear McKinley 1800QEC1226	L. Rankin	Open	18.00	18.00
93-13-005	Cat Lookin' for Trouble 1000QEC1227	L. Rankin	Open	10.00	10.00
94-13-006	Orangutan Peace & Quiet 1200QEC1228	L. Rankin	Open	12.00	12.00
93-13-007	White Seal Sea Baby 1000QEC1235	L. Rankin	Open	10.00	10.00
93-13-008	Bear Honey 1200QEC1243	L. Rankin	Open	12.00	12.00
93-13-009	Otter-Water Sport 1200QEC1245	L. Rankin	Open	12.00	12.00
93-13-010	Seated Rabbit Bashful 1000QEC1253	L. Rankin	Open	10.00	10.00
93-13-011	Pig-Pee Wee Porker 750QEC1263	L. Rankin	Open	7.50	7.50
93-13-012	Reclining Terrier Dreamer 750QEC1265	L. Rankin	Open	7.50	7.50
93-13-013	Bulldog-Bone Tired 8500QEC1273	L. Rankin	Open	8.50	8.50
93-13-014	Beagle Daydreamin 8500QEC1275	L. Rankin	Open	8.50	8.50
93-13-015	Spaniel & Beagle 1500QEC1283	L. Rankin	Open	12.00	12.00
93-13-016	Frog Ribbett 1000QEC1285	L. Rankin	Open	10.00	10.00
93-13-017	Shih Tzu-Daddy's Girl 750QEC1293	L. Rankin	Open	7.50	7.50
93-13-018	Basset Hound-Happy Hound 1000QEC1294	L. Rankin	Open	10.00	10.00

Hallmark Galleries — 1994 Heartland Merry Miniatures

94-14-001	Chipmunk With Kite 375QSM8003	Hallmark	Open	3.75	3.75
94-14-002	Bear Mail Man 375QSM8006	Hallmark	Open	3.75	3.75
94-14-003	Beaver With Card 375QSM8013	Hallmark	Open	3.75	3.75
94-14-004	Rabbit With Heart Cutouts 325QSM8016	Hallmark	Open	3.25	3.25
94-14-005	Mailbox 675QSM8023	Hallmark	Open	6.75	6.75
94-14-006	Raccoon With Cutout Heart 350QSM8062	Hallmark	Open	3.50	3.50
94-14-007	Tree Stump and Paint Can 300QSM8075	Hallmark	Open	3.00	3.00
94-14-008	Owl in Stump 275QSM8085	Hallmark	Open	2.75	2.75
94-14-009	Dog With Balloon Heart 250QSM8092	Hallmark	Open	2.50	2.50

Hallmark Galleries — 1994 Easter Egg Hunt Merry Miniatures

94-15-001	Egg Wishing Well 675QSM8033	Hallmark	Open	6.75	6.75
94-15-002	Rabbit with Egg-Shaped Watering Can 325QSM8083	Hallmark	Open	3.25	3.25
94-15-003	Rabbit with Croquet 375QSM8113	Hallmark	Open	3.75	3.75
94-15-004	Birds in Nest 375QSM8116	Hallmark	Open	3.75	3.75
94-15-005	Chick in Wagon 375QSM8123	Hallmark	Open	3.75	3.75
94-15-006	Bunny with Cracked Egg 300QSM8125	Hallmark	Open	3.00	3.00
94-15-007	Lamb in Flower Patch 325QSM8132	Hallmark	Open	3.25	3.25
94-15-008	Duck with Egg on Spoon 300QSM8135	Hallmark	Open	3.00	3.00
94-15-009	Easter Basket 250QSM8145	Hallmark	Open	2.50	2.50
94-15-010	Mouse with Flower 275QSM8243	Hallmark	Open	2.75	2.75

Hallmark Galleries — 1994 Patriotic Merry Miniatures

94-16-001	Eagle with Hat 375QSM8036	Hallmark	Open	3.75	3.75
94-16-002	Bear with Flag 375QSM8043	Hallmark	Open	3.75	3.75
94-16-003	Document 275QSM8053	Hallmark	Open	2.75	2.75
94-16-004	Flag 675QSM8056	Hallmark	Open	6.75	6.75
94-16-005	Goat Uncle Sam 300QSM8472	Hallmark	Open	3.00	3.00
94-16-006	Mouse Statue of Liberty 300QSM8475	Hallmark	Open	3.00	3.00
94-16-007	Lamb Betsy Ross with Flag 350QSM8482	Hallmark	Open	3.50	3.50
94-16-008	Hedgehog with Fife 350QSM8492	Hallmark	Open	3.50	3.50

Hallmark Galleries — 1994 At The Beach Merry Miniatures

94-17-001	Chipmunk on Inflated Horse 350QSM8002	Hallmark	Open	3.50	3.50
94-17-002	Bear with Surfboard 350QSM8015	Hallmark	Open	3.50	3.50
94-17-003	Hedgehog Eating Hot Dog 300QSM8026	Hallmark	Open	3.00	3.00
94-17-004	Hippo in Inner Tube 300QSM8032	Hallmark	Open	3.00	3.00
94-17-005	Mouse with Sunglasses 250QSM8035	Hallmark	Open	2.50	2.50
94-17-006	Pail of Seashells 275QSM8052	Hallmark	Open	2.75	2.75
94-17-007	Raccoon with Scuba Gear 375QSM8063	Hallmark	Open	3.75	3.75
94-17-008	Rabbit with Ice Cream Cone 275QSM8066	Hallmark	Open	2.75	2.75
94-17-009	Dock 675QSM8076	Hallmark	Open	6.75	6.75

Hallmark Galleries — 1994 Thanksgiving Feast Merry Miniatures

94-18-001	Indian Bear with Honey 350QFM8162	Hallmark	Open	3.50	3.50
94-18-002	Pilgrim Mouse Praying 300QFM8175	Hallmark	Open	3.00	3.00
94-18-003	Indian Squirrel with Pie 300QFM8182	Hallmark	Open	3.00	3.00
94-18-004	Beaver with Apple 375QFM8336	Hallmark	Open	3.75	3.75
94-18-005	Pilgrim Girl Bunny 375QFM8343	Hallmark	Open	3.75	3.75
94-18-006	Indian Chickadee with Corn 325QFM8346	Hallmark	Open	3.25	3.25
94-18-007	Cute Indian Bunny 275QFM8353	Hallmark	Open	2.75	2.75
94-18-008	Basket of Apples 275QFM8356	Hallmark	Open	2.75	2.75
94-18-009	Corn Stalk 675QFM8363	Hallmark	Open	6.75	6.75

Hallmark Galleries — 1994 Haunted House Party Merry Miniatures

94-19-001	Squirrel Dressed as Clown 375QFM8263	Hallmark	Open	3.75	3.75
94-19-002	Bunny Alien 375QFM8266	Hallmark	Open	3.75	3.75
94-19-003	Cute Black Kitten 325QFM8273	Hallmark	Open	3.25	3.25
94-19-004	Pumpkin with Hat 275QFM8276	Hallmark	Open	2.75	2.75
94-19-005	Ghost on Tombstone 250QFM8282	Hallmark	Open	2.50	2.50
94-19-006	Fence with Lantern 675QFM8283	Hallmark	Open	6.75	6.75
94-19-007	Bear Dressed as Bat 300QFM8285	Hallmark	Open	3.00	3.00
94-19-008	Mouse Dressed as Witch 300QFM8292	Hallmark	Open	3.00	3.00
94-19-009	Bunny Super Hero 300QFM8422	Hallmark	Open	3.00	3.00

Hallmark Galleries — 1994 A North Pole Christmas Merry Miniatures

94-20-001	Baby Whale with Hat 350QFM8222	Hallmark	Open	3.50	3.50
94-20-002	Walrus in Hat with Gifts 300QFM8232	Hallmark	Open	3.00	3.00
94-20-003	Seal with Earmuffs 250QFM8272	Hallmark	Open	2.50	2.50
94-20-004	Mrs. Claus 375QFM8286	Hallmark	Open	3.75	3.75
94-20-005	Polar Bear on Skates 375QFM8293	Hallmark	Open	3.75	3.75
94-20-006	White Arctic Fox on Skates 375QFM8303	Hallmark	Open	3.75	3.75
94-20-007	Sled Dog with Candy Cane 325QFM8306	Hallmark	Open	3.25	3.25
94-20-008	Penguin Throwing Snowball 275QFM8313	Hallmark	Open	2.75	2.75
94-20-009	Snowman 275QFM8316	Hallmark	Open	2.75	2.75
94-20-010	Polar Snuggle Bears 325QFM8323	Hallmark	Open	3.25	3.25
94-20-011	Tree 275QFM8326	Hallmark	Open	2.75	2.75
94-20-012	North Pole Sign 675QFM8333	Hallmark	Open	6.75	6.75

Hamilton Collection — American Wildlife Bronze Collection

79-01-001	Cougar	H./N. Deaton	7,500	60.00	125.00
79-01-002	White-Tailed Deer	H./N. Deaton	7,500	60.00	105.00
79-01-003	Bobcat	H./N. Deaton	7,500	60.00	75.00
80-01-004	Beaver	H./N. Deaton	7,500	60.00	65.00

	ARTIST	EDITION	ISSUE	QUOTE
80-01-005 Polar Bear	H./N. Deaton	7,500	60.00	65.00
80-01-006 Sea Otter	H./N. Deaton	7,500	60.00	65.00
Hamilton Collection	**Rockwell Home of The Brave**			
82-02-001 Reminiscing	N. Rockwell	7,500	75.00	52-75.00
82-02-002 Hero's Welcome	N. Rockwell	7,500	75.00	52-75.00
82-02-003 Uncle Sam Takes Wings	N. Rockwell	7,500	75.00	75.00
82-02-004 Back to His Old Job	N. Rockwell	7,500	75.00	52-75.00
82-02-005 Willie Gillis in Church	N. Rockwell	7,500	75.00	52-75.00
82-02-006 Taking Mother over the Top	N. Rockwell	7,500	75.00	52-75.00
Hamilton Collection	**Ringling Bros. Circus Animals**			
83-03-001 Miniature Show Horse	P. Cozzolino	9,800	49.50	68.00
83-03-002 Baby Elephant	P. Cozzolino	9,800	49.50	55.00
83-03-003 Acrobatic Seal	P. Cozzolino	9,800	49.50	49.50
83-03-004 Skating Bear	P. Cozzolino	9,800	49.50	49.50
83-03-005 Mr. Chimpanzee	P. Cozzolino	9,800	49.50	49.50
83-03-006 Performing Poodles	P. Cozzolino	9,800	49.50	49.50
84-03-007 Roaring Lion	P. Cozzolino	9,800	49.50	49.60
84-03-008 Parade Camel	P. Cozzolino	9,800	49.50	49.50
Hamilton Collection	**Great Animals of the American Wilderness**			
83-04-001 Mountain Lion	H. Deaton	7,500	75.00	75.00
83-04-002 Grizzly Bear	H. Deaton	7,500	75.00	75.00
83-04-003 Timber Wolf	H. Deaton	7,500	75.00	75.00
83-04-004 Pronghorn Antelope	H. Deaton	7,500	75.00	75.00
83-04-005 Plains Bison	H. Deaton	7,500	75.00	75.00
83-04-006 Elk	H. Deaton	7,500	75.00	75.00
83-04-007 Mustang	H. Deaton	7,500	75.00	75.00
83-04-008 Bighorn Sheep	H. Deaton	7,500	75.00	75.00
Hamilton Collection	**American Garden Flowers**			
87-05-001 Camelia	D. Fryer	9,800	55.00	75.00
87-05-002 Gardenia	D. Fryer	15,000	75.00	75.00
87-05-003 Azalea	D. Fryer	15,000	75.00	75.00
87-05-004 Rose	D. Fryer	15,000	75.00	75.00
88-05-005 Day Lily	D. Fryer	15,000	75.00	75.00
88-05-006 Petunia	D. Fryer	15,000	75.00	75.00
88-05-007 Calla Lilly	D. Fryer	15,000	75.00	75.00
89-05-008 Pansy	D. Fryer	15,000	75.00	75.00
Hamilton Collection	**Celebration of Opera**			
86-06-001 Cio-Cio-San	J. Villena	7,500	95.00	95.00
86-06-002 Carmen	J. Villena	7,500	95.00	95.00
87-06-003 Figaro	J. Villena	7,500	95.00	95.00
88-06-004 Mimi	J. Villena	7,500	95.00	95.00
88-06-005 Aida	J. Villena	7,500	95.00	95.00
88-06-006 Canio	J. Villena	7,500	95.00	95.00
Hamilton Collection	**Exotic Birds of the World**			
84-07-001 The Cockatoo	Francesco	7,500	75.00	115.00
84-07-002 The Budgerigar	Francesco	7,500	75.00	105.00
84-07-003 The Rubenio Parakeet	Francesco	7,500	75.00	95.00
84-07-004 The Quetzal	Francesco	7,500	75.00	95.00
84-07-005 The Red Lorg	Francesco	7,500	75.00	95.00
84-07-006 The FisherOs Whydah	Francesco	7,500	75.00	95.00
84-07-007 The Diamond Dove	Francesco	7,500	75.00	95.00
84-07-008 The Peach-faced Lovebird	Francesco	7,500	75.00	95.00
Hamilton Collection	**Majestic Wildlife of North America**			
85-08-001 White-tailed Deer	H. Deaton	7,500	75.00	75.00
85-08-002 Ocelot	H. Deaton	7,500	75.00	75.00
85-08-003 Alaskan Moose	H. Deaton	7,500	75.00	75.00
85-08-004 Black Bear	H. Deaton	7,500	75.00	75.00
85-08-005 Mountain Goat	H. Deaton	7,500	75.00	75.00
85-08-006 Coyote	H. Deaton	7,500	75.00	75.00
85-08-007 Barren Ground Caribou	H. Deaton	7,500	75.00	75.00
85-08-008 Harbour Seal	H. Deaton	7,500	75.00	75.00
Hamilton Collection	**Magnificent Birds of Paradise**			
85-09-001 Emperor of Germany	Francesco	12,500	75.00	95.00
85-09-002 Greater Bird of Paradise	Francesco	12,500	75.00	95.00
85-09-003 Magnificent Bird of Paradise	Francesco	12,500	75.00	95.00
85-09-004 Raggiana Bird of Paradise	Francesco	12,500	75.00	95.00
85-09-005 Princess Stephanie Bird of Paradise	Francesco	12,500	75.00	95.00
85-09-006 GoldieOs Bird of Paradise	Francesco	12,500	75.00	95.00
85-09-007 Blue Bird of Paradise	Francesco	12,500	75.00	95.00
85-09-008 Black Sickle-Billed Bird of Paradise	Francesco	12,500	75.00	95.00
Hamilton Collection	**Legendary Flowers of the Orient**			
85-10-001 Iris	Ito	15,000	55.00	55.00
85-10-002 Lotus	Ito	15,000	55.00	55.00
85-10-003 Chinese Peony	Ito	15,000	55.00	55.00
85-10-004 Gold Band Lily	Ito	15,000	55.00	55.00
85-10-005 Chrysanthemum	Ito	15,000	55.00	55.00
85-10-006 Cherry Blossom	Ito	15,000	55.00	55.00
85-10-007 Japanese Orchid	Ito	15,000	55.00	55.00
85-10-008 Wisteria	Ito	15,000	55.00	55.00
Hamilton Collection	**The Splendor of Ballet**			
87-11-001 Juliet	E. Daub	15,000	95.00	95.00
87-11-002 Odette	E. Daub	15,000	95.00	95.00
87-11-003 Giselle	E. Daub	15,000	95.00	95.00
87-11-004 Kitri	E. Daub	15,000	95.00	95.00
88-11-005 Aurora	E. Daub	15,000	95.00	95.00
89-11-006 Swanilda	E. Daub	15,000	95.00	95.00
89-11-007 Firebird	E. Daub	15,000	95.00	95.00
89-11-008 Clara	E. Daub	15,000	95.00	95.00
Hamilton Collection	**The Noble Swan**			
85-12-001 The Noble Swan	G. Granget	5,000	295.00	295.00
Hamilton Collection	**The Gibson Girls**			
86-13-001 The Actress	Unknown	Open	75.00	75.00
87-13-002 The Career Girl	Unknown	Open	75.00	75.00
87-13-003 The College Girl	Unknown	Open	75.00	75.00
87-13-004 The Bride	Unknown	Open	75.00	75.00
87-13-005 The Sportswoman	Unknown	Open	75.00	75.00
88-13-006 The Debutante	Unknown	Open	75.00	75.00
88-13-007 The Artist	Unknown	Open	75.00	75.00
88-13-008 The Society Girl	Unknown	Open	75.00	75.00
Hamilton Collection	**The Romance of Flowers**			
87-14-001 Springtime Bouquet	Maruri	15,000	95.00	95.00
87-14-002 Summer Bouquet	Maruri	15,000	95.00	95.00
88-14-003 Autumn Bouquet	Maruri	15,000	95.00	95.00
88-14-004 Winter Bouquet	Maruri	15,000	95.00	95.00
Hamilton Collection	**Wild Ducks of North America**			
87-15-001 Common Mallard	C. Burgess	15,000	95.00	95.00
87-15-002 Wood Duck	C. Burgess	15,000	95.00	95.00
87-15-003 Green Winged Teal	C. Burgess	15,000	95.00	95.00
87-15-004 Hooded Merganser	C. Burgess	15,000	95.00	95.00
88-15-005 Northern Pintail	C. Burgess	15,000	95.00	95.00
88-15-006 Ruddy Duck Drake	C. Burgess	15,000	95.00	95.00
88-15-007 Bufflehead	C. Burgess	15,000	95.00	95.00
88-15-008 American Widgeon	C. Burgess	15,000	95.00	95.00
Hamilton Collection	**Snuggle Babies**			
88-16-001 Baby Bunnies	Jacqueline B.	Open	35.00	35.00
88-16-002 Baby Bears	Jacqueline B.	Open	35.00	35.00
88-16-003 Baby Skunks	Jacqueline B.	Open	35.00	35.00
88-16-004 Baby Foxes	Jacqueline B.	Open	35.00	35.00
89-16-005 Baby Chipmunks	Jacqueline B.	Open	35.00	35.00
89-16-006 Baby Raccoons	Jacqueline B.	Open	35.00	35.00
89-16-007 Baby Squirrels	Jacqueline B.	Open	35.00	35.00
89-16-008 Baby Fawns	Jacqueline B.	Open	35.00	35.00
Hamilton Collection	**Tropical Treasures**			
89-17-001 Sail-finned Surgeonfish	M. Wald	Open	37.50	37.50
89-17-002 Flag-tail Surgeonfish	M. Wald	Open	37.50	37.50
89-17-003 Pennant Butterfly Fish	M. Wald	Open	37.50	37.50
89-17-004 Sea Horse	M. Wald	Open	37.50	37.50
90-17-005 Zebra Turkey Fish	M. Wald	Open	37.50	37.50
90-17-006 Spotted Angel Fish	M. Wald	Open	37.50	37.50
90-17-007 Blue Girdled Angel Fish	M. Wald	Open	37.50	37.50
90-17-008 Beaked Coral Butterfly Fish	M. Wald	Open	37.50	37.50
Hamilton Collection	**A Celebration of Roses**			
89-18-001 Tiffany	N/A	Open	55.00	55.00
89-18-002 Color Magic	N/A	Open	55.00	55.00
89-18-003 Honor	N/A	Open	55.00	55.00
89-18-004 Brandy	N/A	Open	55.00	55.00
89-18-005 Miss All-American Beauty	N/A	Open	55.00	55.00
90-18-006 Oregold	N/A	Open	55.00	55.00
91-18-007 Paradise	N/A	Open	55.00	55.00
91-18-008 Ole'	N/A	Open	55.00	55.00
Hamilton Collection	**Heroes of Baseball-Porcelain Baseball Cards**			
90-19-001 Brooks Robinson	N/A	Open	19.50	19.50
90-19-002 Roberto Clemente	N/A	Open	19.50	19.50
90-19-003 Willie Mays	N/A	Open	19.50	19.50
90-19-004 Duke Snider	N/A	Open	19.50	19.50
91-19-005 Whitey Ford	N/A	Open	19.50	19.50
91-19-006 Gil Hodges	N/A	Open	19.50	19.50
91-19-007 Mickey Mantle	N/A	Open	19.50	19.50
91-19-008 Casey Stengel	N/A	Open	19.50	19.50
91-19-009 Jackie Robinson	N/A	Open	19.50	19.50
91-19-010 Ernie Banks	N/A	Open	19.50	19.50
91-19-011 Yogi Berra	N/A	Open	19.50	19.50
91-19-012 Satchel Page	N/A	Open	19.50	19.50
Hamilton Collection	**Little Night Owls**			
90-20-001 Tawny Owl	D.T. Lyttleton	Open	45.00	45.00
90-20-002 Barn Owl	D.T. Lyttleton	Open	45.00	45.00
90-20-003 Snowy Owl	D.T. Lyttleton	Open	45.00	45.00
91-20-004 Barred Owl	D.T. Lyttleton	Open	45.00	45.00
91-20-005 Great Horned Owl	D.T. Lyttleton	Open	45.00	45.00
91-20-006 White-Faced Owl	D.T. Lyttleton	Open	45.00	45.00
91-20-007 Great Grey Owl	D.T. Lyttleton	Open	45.00	45.00
91-20-008 Short-Eared Owl	D.T. Lyttleton	Open	45.00	45.00
Hamilton Collection	**Puppy Playtime Sculpture Collection**			
90-21-001 Double Take	J. Lamb	Open	29.50	29.50
91-21-002 Catch of the Day	J. Lamb	Open	29.50	29.50
91-21-003 Cabin Fever	J. Lamb	Open	29.50	29.50
91-21-004 Weekend Gardner	J. Lamb	Open	29.50	29.50
91-21-005 Hanging Out	J. Lamb	Open	29.50	29.50
91-21-006 Getting Acquainted	J. Lamb	Open	29.50	29.50
91-21-007 A New Leash on Life	J. Lamb	Open	29.50	29.50
91-21-008 Fun and Games	J. Lamb	Open	29.50	29.50
Hamilton Collection	**Freshwater Challenge**			
91-22-001 The Strike	M. Wald	Open	75.00	75.00
91-22-002 Rainbow Lure	M. Wald	Open	75.00	75.00
91-22-003 Sun Catcher	M. Wald	Open	75.00	75.00
92-22-004 Prized Catch	M. Wald	Open	75.00	75.00
Hamilton Collection	**Puss in Boots**			
92-23-001 Caught Napping	P. Cooper	Open	35.00	35.00
92-23-002 Sweet Dreams	P. Cooper	Open	35.00	35.00
93-23-003 Hide'n Go Seek	P. Cooper	Open	35.00	35.00
93-23-004 All Dressed Up	P. Cooper	Open	35.00	35.00
Hamilton Collection	**International Santa**			
92-24-001 Father Christmas	N/A	Open	55.00	55.00
92-24-002 Santa Claus	N/A	Open	55.00	55.00
92-24-003 Grandfather Frost	N/A	Open	55.00	55.00
93-24-004 Belsnickel	N/A	Open	55.00	55.00
93-24-005 Kris Kringle	N/A	Open	55.00	55.00
93-24-006 Jolly Old St. Nick	N/A	Open	55.00	55.00
94-24-007 Yuletide Santa	N/A	Open	55.00	55.00
94-24-008 Pére Nöel	N/A	Open	55.00	55.00
Hamilton Collection	**Noble American Indian Women**			
93-25-001 Sacajawea	N/A	Open	55.00	55.00
93-25-002 White Rose	N/A	Open	55.00	55.00
94-25-003 Falling Star	N/A	Open	55.00	55.00
94-25-004 Minnehaha	N/A	Open	55.00	55.00
94-25-005 Pine Leaf	N/A	Open	55.00	55.00
Hamilton Collection	**Noble Warriors**			
93-26-001 Deliverance	N/A	Open	135.00	135.00
94-26-002 Spirit of the Plains	N/A	Open	135.00	135.00
Hamilton Collection	**Visions of Christmas**			
93-27-001 Santa's Delivery	M. Griffin	Open	135.00	135.00
93-27-002 Toys in Progress	M. Griffin	Open	135.00	135.00
94-27-003 Mrs. Claus' Kitchen	M. Griffin	Open	135.00	135.00
Hamilton Collection	**Santa Clothtique**			
92-28-001 Checking His List	Possible Dreams	Open	95.00	95.00
93-28-002 Twas the Nap Before Christmas	Possible Dreams	Open	95.00	95.00

		ARTIST	EDITION	ISSUE	QUOTE
93-28-003	Last Minute Details	Possible Dreams	Open	95.00	95.00
94-28-004	O Tannenbaum!	Possible Dreams	Open	95.00	95.00
94-28-005	Upon the Rooftop	Possible Dreams	Open	95.00	95.00
Hamilton Collection		**The Nolan Ryan Collectors Edition-Porcelain Baseball Cards**			
93-29-001	Mets 1968-C #177	N/A	Open	19.50	19.50
93-29-002	Rangers 1990-C #1	N/A	Open	19.50	19.50
93-29-003	Mets 1969-C #533	N/A	Open	19.50	19.50
93-29-004	Angels 1972-C #595	N/A	Open	19.50	19.50
93-29-005	Rangers 1992-C #1	N/A	Open	19.50	19.50
93-29-006	Astros 1985-C #7	N/A	Open	19.50	19.50
Hamilton Collection		**Princess of the Plains**			
94-30-001	Snow Princess	D. Wright	Open	55.00	55.00
94-30-002	Wild Flower	D. Wright	Open	55.00	55.00
94-30-003	Noble Guardian	D. Wright	Open	55.00	55.00
Hamilton Collection		**Unbridled Spirits**			
94-31-001	Wild Fury	C. DeHaan	Open	135.00	135.00
Hamilton Collection		**Monthly Friends to Cherish**			
93-32-001	January-Jack-A New Year With Old Friends 914754	P. Hillman	Open	19.50	19.50
93-32-002	February-Phoebe-Be Mine 914762	P. Hillman	Open	19.50	19.50
93-32-003	March-Mark-Friendship is in the Air 914770	P. Hillman	Open	19.50	19.50
93-32-004	April-Alan-Showers of Friendship 914789	P. Hillman	Open	19.50	19.50
93-32-005	May-May-Friendship is in Bloom 914797	P. Hillman	Open	19.50	19.50
93-32-006	June-June-Planting the Seed of Friendship 914800	P. Hillman	Open	19.50	19.50
93-32-007	July-Julie-A Day in the Park 914819	P. Hillman	Open	19.50	19.50
93-32-008	August-Arthur-Smooth Sailing 914827	P. Hillman	Open	19.50	19.50
93-32-009	September-Seth-School Days 914835	P. Hillman	Open	19.50	19.50
93-32-010	October-Oscar-Sweet Treats 914843	P. Hillman	Open	19.50	19.50
93-32-011	November-Nichole-Thanks For Friends 914851	P. Hillman	Open	19.50	19.50
93-32-012	December-Denise-Happy Holidays, Friend 914878	P. Hillman	Open	19.50	19.50
Harbour Lights		**Original Collection**			
91-01-001	Admiralty Head 101	Harbour Lights	5,500	60.00	60.00
91-01-002	Cape Hatteras 102 (with house)	Harbour Lights	Retrd.	60.00	900.00
92-01-003	Cape Hatteras 102R	Harbour Lights	Retrd.	60.00	100-150.
91-01-004	West Quoddy Head 103	Harbour Lights	5,500	60.00	60.00
91-01-005	Sandy Hook 104	Harbour Lights	Retrd.	60.00	90-95.00
91-01-006	Point Loma 105	Harbour Lights	5,500	60.00	60.00
91-01-007	North Head 106	Harbour Lights	5,500	60.00	60.00
91-01-008	Umpqua River 107	Harbour Lights	5,500	60.00	60.00
91-01-009	Burrows Island 108	Harbour Lights	Retrd.	60.00	60.00
91-01-010	Cape Blanco 109	Harbour Lights	5,500	60.00	60.00
91-01-011	Yaquina Head 110	Harbour Lights	5,500	60.00	60.00
91-01-012	Coquille River 111	Harbour Lights	Retrd.	60.00	100.00
91-01-013	Sand Island 112	Harbour Lights	5,500	60.00	60.00
91-01-014	Port Niagara 113	Harbour Lights	5,500	60.00	60.00
91-01-015	Gt. Captain's Island 114	Harbour Lights	5,500	60.00	60.00
91-01-016	St. George's Reef 115	Harbour Lights	5,500	60.00	60.00
91-01-017	Castle Hill 116	Harbour Lights	5,500	60.00	60.00
91-01-018	Boston Harbor 117	Harbour Lights	5,500	60.00	60.00
Harbour Lights		**Great Lakes Series**			
92-02-001	Old Mackinac Point 118	Harbour Lights	5,500	65.00	65.00
92-02-002	Cana Island 119	Harbour Lights	5,500	60.00	60.00
92-02-003	Grosse Point 120	Harbour Lights	5,500	60.00	60.00
92-02-004	Marblehead 121	Harbour Lights	5,500	50.00	50.00
92-02-005	Buffalo 122	Harbour Lights	5,500	60.00	60.00
92-02-006	Michigan City123	Harbour Lights	5,500	60.00	60.00
92-02-007	Split Rock 124	Harbour Lights	5,500	60.00	60.00
Harbour Lights		**New England Series**			
92-03-001	Portland Head 125	Harbour Lights	5,500	65.00	65.00
92-03-002	Nauset 126	Harbour Lights	5,500	65.00	65.00
92-03-003	Whaleback127	Harbour Lights	5,500	60.00	60.00
92-03-004	Southeast Block Island128	Harbour Lights	5,500	70.00	70.00
92-03-005	New London Ledge 129	Harbour Lights	5,500	65.00	65.00
92-03-006	Portland Breakwater 130	Harbour Lights	5,500	60.00	60.00
92-03-007	Minot's Ledge131	Harbour Lights	5,500	60.00	60.00
Harbour Lights		**Southern Belles**			
93-04-001	Ponce de Leon, FL 132	Harbour Lights	5,500	60.00	60.00
93-04-002	Tybee, GA 133	Harbour Lights	5,500	60.00	60.00
93-04-003	Key West, FL 134	Harbour Lights	5,500	60.00	60.00
93-04-004	Ocracoke, NC 135	Harbour Lights	5,500	60.00	60.00
93-04-005	Hilton Head, SC 136	Harbour Lights	5,500	60.00	60.00
93-04-006	St. Simons, GA 137	Harbour Lights	5,500	65.00	65.00
93-04-007	St. Augustine, FL 138	Harbour Lights	5,500	70.00	70.00
Harbour Lights		**1993 Releases**			
93-05-001	Barnegat, NJ 139	Harbour Lights	5,500	60.00	60.00
93-05-002	Diamond Head, HI 140	Harbour Lights	5,500	60.00	60.00
93-05-003	Cape Neddick (Nubble), ME 141	Harbour Lights	5,500	65.00	70.00
93-05-004	Holland (Big Red), MI 142	Harbour Lights	5,500	60.00	60.00
Harbour Lights		**1994 Releases**			
94-06-001	Montauk 143	Harbour Lights	5,500	85.00	85.00
94-06-002	Heceta Head 144	Harbour Lights	5,500	65.00	65.00
94-06-003	Assateague 145	Harbour Lights	5,500	69.00	69.00
94-06-004	Cape Hatteras (2nd Edition) 146	Harbour Lights	Open	N/A	N/A
Hawthorne Architectural Register		**Concord: The Hometown of American Literature**			
92-01-001	Hawthorne's Wayside Retreat	K.&H. LeVan	Closed	39.90	39.90
92-01-002	Emerson's Old Manse	K.&H. LeVan	Closed	39.90	39.90
93-01-003	Alcott's Orchard House	K.&H. LeVan	Closed	39.90	39.90
Hawthorne Architectural Register		**Victorian Grove Collection**			
92-02-001	Lilac Cottage	K.&H. LeVan	Closed	34.90	34.90
92-02-002	Rose Haven	K.&H. LeVan	Closed	34.90	34.90
93-02-003	Cherry Blossom	K.&H. LeVan	Closed	34.90	34.90
Hawthorne Architectural Register		**Stonefield Valley**			
92-03-001	Springbridge Cottage	K.&H. LeVan	Closed	34.90	34.90
92-03-002	Meadowbrook School	K.&H. LeVan	Closed	34.90	34.90
92-03-003	Weaver's Cottage	K.&H. LeVan	Closed	37.90	37.90
92-03-004	Church in the Glen	K.&H. LeVan	Closed	37.90	37.90
93-03-005	Parson's Cottage	K.&H. LeVan	1/95	37.90	37.90
93-03-006	Hillside Country Store	K.&H. LeVan	Open	37.90	37.90
93-03-007	Ferryman's Cottage	K.&H. LeVan	Open	39.90	39.90
94-03-008	Valley View Farm	K.&H. LeVan	Open	39.90	39.90

		ARTIST	EDITION	ISSUE	QUOTE
Hawthorne Architectural Register		**Strolling Through Colonial America**			
91-04-001	Jefferson's Ordinance	K.&H. LeVan	Closed	34.90	34.90
92-04-002	Millrace Store	K.&H. LeVan	Closed	34.90	34.90
92-04-003	Higgins' Grist Mill	K.&H. LeVan	Closed	37.90	37.90
92-04-004	Eastbrook Church	K.&H. LeVan	Closed	37.90	37.90
92-04-005	Court House on the Green	K.&H. LeVan	Closed	37.90	37.90
92-04-006	Captain Lee's Grammar School	K.&H. LeVan	Closed	37.90	37.90
92-04-007	The Village Smithy	K.&H. LeVan	Closed	39.90	39.90
93-04-008	Everette's Joiner Shop	K.&H. LeVan	Closed	39.90	39.90
Hawthorne Architectural Register		**Lost Victorians of Old San Francisco**			
92-05-001	The Grande Dame of Nob Hill	R. Brouillette	Closed	34.90	34.90
92-05-002	The Empress of Russian Hill	R. Brouillette	Closed	34.90	34.90
93-05-003	The Princess of Pacific Heights	R. Brouillette	Closed	34.90	34.90
Hawthorne Architectural Register		**Rockwell's Home for the Holidays**			
92-06-001	Christmas Eve at the Studio	Unkn.	Closed	34.90	34.90
92-06-002	Bringing Home the Tree	Unkn.	Closed	34.90	34.90
92-06-003	Carolers In The Church Yard	Unkn.	12/94	37.90	37.90
93-06-004	Three-Day Pass	Unkn.	Closed	37.90	37.90
93-06-005	Over the River	Unkn.	9/95	37.90	37.90
93-06-006	School's Out	Unkn.	11/95	39.90	39.90
93-06-007	A Room at the Inn	Unkn.	12/95	39.90	39.90
Hawthorne Architectural Register		**Gone With theWInd Collection**			
92-07-001	Tara . . .Scarlett's Pride	K.&H. LeVan	12/94	39.90	39.90
92-07-002	Twelve Oaks: The Romance Begins	K.&H. LeVan	3/95	39.90	39.90
93-07-003	Rhett Returns	K.&H. LeVan	6/95	39.90	39.90
93-07-004	Against Her Will	K.&H. LeVan	3/95	42.90	42.90
93-07-005	A Message for Captain Butler	K.&H. LeVan	12/95	42.90	42.90
94-07-006	Hope for a New Tomorrow	K.&H. LeVan	3/96	42.90	42.90
94-07-007	Swept Away	K.&H. LeVan	6/96	45.90	45.90
Hawthorne Architectural Register		**Chestnut Hill Station**			
93-08-001	Wishing Well Cottage	K.&H. LeVan	Open	29.90	29.90
93-08-002	Parkside Cafe	K.&H. LeVan	Open	29.90	29.90
94-08-003	Chestnut Hill Depot	K.&H. LeVan	Open	29.90	29.90
Hawthorne Architectural Register		**Thatcher's Crossing**			
93-09-001	Rose Arbour Cottage	Unkn.	Open	29.90	29.90
93-09-002	Midsummer's Cottage	Unkn.	Open	29.90	29.90
94-09-003	Chapel Crossing	Unkn.	Open	29.90	29.90
94-09-004	Woodcutter's Cottage	Unkn.	Open	29.90	29.90
Hawthorne Architectural Register		**Kinkade's Candlelight Cottages**			
93-10-001	Olde Porterfield Tea Room	Kinkade-Inspired	Open	24.90	24.90
93-10-002	Swanbrooke Cottage	Kinkade-Inspired	Open	24.90	24.90
93-10-003	Chandler's Cottage	Kinkade-Inspired	Open	24.90	24.90
94-10-003	Merritt's Cottage	Kinkade-Inspired	Open	27.90	27.90
94-10-004	Seaside Cottage	Kinkade-Inspired	Open	27.90	27.90
Hawthorne Architectural Register		**Kinkade's Candlelight Cottages (Illuminated)**			
93-11-001	Olde Porterfield Tea Room	Kinkade-Inspired	Open	29.90	29.90
93-11-002	Chandler's Cottage	Kinkade-Inspired	Open	29.90	29.90
Hawthorne Architectural Register		**Rockwell's Christmas in Stockbridge (Illuminated)**			
93-12-001	Rockwell's Studio	Rockwell-Inspired	Open	29.90	29.90
93-12-002	Country Store	Rockwell-Inspired	Open	29.90	29.90
93-12-003	Antique Shop	Rockwell-Inspired	Open	29.90	29.90
93-12-004	Town Offices	Rockwell-Inspired	Open	29.90	29.90
93-12-005	Bank	Rockwell-Inspired	Open	29.90	29.90
93-12-006	Library	Rockwell-Inspired	Open	29.90	29.90
93-12-007	Red Lion Inn	Rockwell-Inspired	Open	29.90	29.90
Hawthorne Architectural Register		**Gone With the Wind (Illuminated)**			
93-13-001	Tara	Unkn.	Open	39.90	39.90
94-13-002	Twelve Oaks	Unkn.	Open	39.90	39.90
Hawthorne Architectural Register		**Rockwell's Neighborhood Collection**			
94-14-001	The Lemonade Stand	Rockwell-Inspired	Open	29.90	29.90
94-14-002	Fido's New Home	Rockwell-Inspired	Open	29.90	29.90
Hawthorne Architectural Register		**Peaceable Kingdom**			
93-15-001	Squire Boone's Homestead	K.&H. LeVan	Open	34.90	34.90
94-15-002	White Horse Inn	K.&H. LeVan	Open	34.90	34.90
Hawthorne Architectural Register		**Tara: The Only Thing Worth Fighting For**			
94-16-001	A Dream Remembered	K.&H. LeVan	Open	29.90	29.90
94-16-002	Spring House & Hideaway	K.&H. LeVan	Open	29.90	29.90
94-16-003	Carriage House	K.&H. LeVan	Open	29.90	29.90
Hawthorne Architectural Register		**Best of England**			
94-17-001	Mayfair Hill	R. Dowling	Open	59.90	59.90
Hawthorne Architectural Register		**P.O. #1, North Pole Collection (Illuminated)**			
94-18-001	Santa's Toy Shoppe	G. Hoover	Open	39.90	39.90
Hawthorne Architectural Register		**St. Nicholas Circle (Illuminated)**			
94-19-001	Town Hall	Kinkade-Inspired	Open	39.90	39.90
John Hine N.A. Ltd.		**David Winter Cottages**			
80-01-001	Rose Cottage	D. Winter	Open	28.90	55.00
80-01-002	Market Street	D. Winter	Open	48.80	90.00
81-01-003	Stratford House	D. Winter	Open	74.80	130.00
81-01-004	The Village	D. Winter	Open	362.00	580.00
81-01-005	Drover's Cottage	D. Winter	Open	22.00	35.00
81-01-006	Sussex Cottage	D. Winter	Open	22.00	50.00
81-01-007	The Village Shop	D. Winter	Open	22.00	35.00
81-01-008	Cotswold Cottage	D. Winter	Open	22.00	35.00
83-01-009	The Bakehouse	D. Winter	Open	31.40	60.00
83-01-010	The Bothy	D. Winter	Open	31.40	60.00
83-01-011	Fisherman's Wharf	D. Winter	Open	31.40	60.00
83-01-012	The Green Dragon Inn	D. Winter	Open	31.40	60.00
84-01-013	The Parsonage	D. Winter	Open	390.00	560.00
85-01-014	Kent Cottage	D. Winter	Open	48.80	110.00
85-01-015	The Schoolhouse	D. Winter	Open	24.10	45.00
85-01-016	Craftsmen's Cottages	D. Winter	Open	24.10	40.00
85-01-017	The Vicarage	D. Winter	Open	24.10	45.00
85-01-018	The Hogs Head Tavern	D. Winter	Open	24.10	50.00
85-01-019	Blackfriars Grange	D. Winter	Open	24.10	45.00
85-01-020	Shirehall	D. Winter	Open	24.10	50.00
85-01-021	The Apothecary Shop	D. Winter	Open	24.10	50.00
85-01-022	Yeoman's Farmhouse	D. Winter	Open	24.10	40.00
85-01-023	Meadowbank Cottages	D. Winter	Open	24.10	40.00
85-01-024	St. George's Church	D. Winter	Open	24.10	45.00
87-01-025	Smuggler's Creek	D. Winter	Open	390.00	520.00
87-01-026	Devoncombe	D. Winter	Open	73.00	110.00

		ARTIST	EDITION	ISSUE	QUOTE
87-01-027	Tamar Cottage	D. Winter	Open	45.30	75.00
87-01-028	There was a Crooked House	D. Winter	Open	96.90	155.00
87-01-029	Devon Creamery	D. Winter	Open	62.90	110.00
88-01-030	Windmill	D. Winter	Open	37.50	50.00
88-01-031	Lock-keepers Cottage	D. Winter	Open	65.00	85.00
88-01-032	Gunsmiths	D. Winter	Open	78.00	100.00
88-01-033	Coal Miner's Row	D. Winter	Open	90.00	120.00
88-01-034	Lacemaker's Cottage	D. Winter	Open	120.00	155.00
88-01-035	Cornish Harbour	D. Winter	Open	120.00	155.00
88-01-036	Cornish Engine House	D. Winter	Open	120.00	155.00
91-01-037	Inglenook Cottage	D. Winter	Open	60.00	75.00
91-01-038	The Weaver's Lodgings	D. Winter	Open	65.00	75.00
91-01-039	Moonlight Haven	D. Winter	Open	120.00	155.00
91-01-040	Castle in the Air	D. Winter	Open	675.00	710.00
94-01-041	Quindene Manor	D. Winter	3,000	695.00	695.00
94-01-042	Premier Quindene Manor	D. Winter	1,500	850.00	850.00
94-01-043	Scrooge's Family Home (Xmas '94)	D. Winter	12/94	175.00	175.00
94-01-044	Premier Scrooge's Family Home (Xmas '94)	D. Winter	12/94	230.00	230.00
94-01-045	Plaque, Scrooge's Family Home	D. Winter	3,500	125.00	125.00
94-01-046	Toymaker	D. Winter	Yr.Iss.	135.00	135.00
94-01-047	Premier Toymaker	D. Winter	Yr.Iss.	175.00	175.00
94-01-048	Clockhouse	D. Winter	Yr.Iss.	165.00	165.00
94-01-049	Premier Clockhouse	D. Winter	Yr.Iss.	215.00	215.00
John Hine N.A. Ltd.		**David Winter Retired Cottages**			
89-02-001	A Christmas Carol (Xmas '89)	D. Winter	Closed	135.00	125-200.
83-02-002	The Alms Houses	D. Winter	Closed	59.90	400-425.
92-02-003	Audrey's Tea Room	D. Winter	Closed	90.00	110-225.
92-02-004	Audrey's Tea Shop	D. Winter	Closed	90.00	125-300.
82-02-005	Blacksmith's Cottage	D. Winter	Closed	22.00	300-500.
88-02-006	Bottle Kilns	D. Winter	Closed	78.00	50-150.
82-02-007	Brookside Hamlet	D. Winter	Closed	74.80	100-150.
84-02-008	Castle Gate	D. Winter	Closed	155.00	150-320.
81-02-009	Castle Keep	D. Winter	Closed	30.00	1500.00
84-02-010	The Chapel	D. Winter	Closed	48.80	80.00
81-02-011	Chichester Cross	D. Winter	Closed	50.00	4000.00
80-02-012	The Coaching Inn	D. Winter	Closed	165.00	25-2800.
85-02-013	The Cooper's Cottage	D. Winter	Closed	57.90	70-80.00
82-02-014	Cornish Cottage	D. Winter	Closed	30.00	400-975.
83-02-015	Cornish Tin Mine	D. Winter	Closed	22.00	60-150.
82-02-016	Cotswold Village	D. Winter	Closed	59.90	65-125.
83-02-017	The Cotton Mill	D. Winter	Closed	41.30	500-575.
86-02-018	Crofter's Cottage	D. Winter	Closed	51.00	51-90.00
88-02-019	Derbyshire Cotton Mill	D. Winter	Closed	65.00	75-90.00
81-02-020	Double Oast	D. Winter	Closed	60.00	3300.00
80-02-021	Dove Cottage	D. Winter	Closed	60.00	1400.00
82-02-022	The Dower House	D. Winter	Closed	22.00	60.00
87-02-023	Ebenezer Scrooge's Counting House (Xmas '87)	D. Winter	Closed	96.90	110-225.
82-02-024	Fairytale Castle	D. Winter	Closed	115.00	240-500.
86-02-025	Falstaff's Manor	D. Winter	Closed	242.00	300-500.
92-02-026	Fogartys	D. Winter	Closed	75.00	85.00
80-02-027	The Forge	D. Winter	Closed	60.00	1700.00
91-02-028	Fred's Home: "A Merry Christmas, Uncle Ebenezer," saids Scrooge's Nephew Fred, "and a Happy New Year. (Xmas '91)	D. Winter	Closed	145.00	125-200.
88-02-029	The Grange	D. Winter	Closed	120.00	600-1000
82-02-030	The Haybarn	D. Winter	Closed	22.00	325-400.
85-02-031	Hermit's Humble Home	D. Winter	Closed	87.00	200-300.
83-02-032	Hertford Court	D. Winter	Closed	87.00	90-175.
88-02-033	Hogmanay (Xmas '88)	D. Winter	Closed	100.00	95-150.
93-02-034	Horatio Pernickety's Amorous Intent	D. Winter	Closed	375.00	375.00
84-02-034	House of the Master Mason	D. Winter	Closed	74.80	250-325.
89-02-035	House on the Loch	D. Winter	Closed	65.00	85-100.
82-02-036	The House on Top	D. Winter	Closed	92.30	250-350.
82-02-037	Ivy Cottage	D. Winter	Closed	22.00	40-100.
88-02-038	Jim'll Fixit	D. Winter	Closed	350.00	35-4000.
88-02-039	John Benbow's Farmhouse	D. Winter	Closed	78.00	95-150.
80-02-040	Little Forge	D. Winter	Closed	40.00	15-2000.
80-02-041	Little Market	D. Winter	Closed	28.90	35-95.00
80-02-042	Little Mill	D. Winter	Closed	40.00	15-1700.
80-02-043	Little Mill-remodeled	D. Winter	Closed	Unkn.	1600.00
92-02-044	Mad Baron Fourthrite's Folly	D. Winter	Closed	275.00	200-400.
80-02-045	Mill House	D. Winter	Closed	50.00	1-2000.
80-02-046	Mill House-remodeled	D. Winter	Closed	Unkn.	1600.00
82-02-047	Miner's Cottage	D. Winter	Closed	22.00	200-250.
82-02-048	Moorland Cottage	D. Winter	Closed	22.00	200-250.
90-02-049	Mr. Fezziwig's Emporium (Xmas '90)	D. Winter	Closed	135.00	125-265.
81-02-050	The Old Curiosity Shop	D. Winter	Closed	40.00	1-1600.
82-02-051	The Old Distillery	D. Winter	Closed	312.00	312-500.
91-02-052	Old Joe's Beetling Shop A Veritable Den of Iniquity! (Xmas '93)	D. Winter	Closed	175.00	175-195.
92-02-053	Only A Span Apart	D. Winter	Closed	80.00	75-85.00
87-02-054	Orchard Cottage	D. Winter	Closed	91.30	110-150.
83-02-055	Pilgrim's Rest	D. Winter	Closed	48.80	70-80.00
91-02-056	The Printers and The Bookbinders	D. Winter	Closed	120.00	138.00
80-02-057	Quayside	D. Winter	Closed	60.00	750-1300
82-02-058	Sabrina's Cottage	D. Winter	Closed	30.00	16-2300.
92-02-059	Scrooge's School (Xmas '92)	D. Winter	Closed	160.00	160.00
92-06-060	Secret Shebeen	D. Winter	Closed	70.00	70-100.
81-02-061	Single Oast	D. Winter	Closed	22.00	50.00
84-02-062	Snow Cottage	D. Winter	Closed	74.80	100-125.
84-02-063	Spinner's Cottage	D. Winter	Closed	28.90	40-95.00
85-02-064	Squires Hall	D. Winter	Closed	92.30	85-120.
81-02-065	St. Paul's Cathedral	D. Winter	Closed	40.00	18-2000.
85-02-066	Suffolk House	D. Winter	Closed	48.80	60-130.
80-02-067	Three Ducks Inn	D. Winter	Closed	60.00	16-2000.
84-02-068	Tollkeeper's Cottage	D. Winter	Closed	87.00	110-145.
81-02-069	Triple Oast	D. Winter	Closed	59.90	112-135.
81-02-070	Tudor Manor House	D. Winter	Closed	48.80	65-200.
81-02-071	Tythe Barn	D. Winter	Closed	39.30	14-1950.
82-02-072	William Shakespeare's Birthplace (large)	D. Winter	Closed	60.00	500-1200
80-02-073	The Wine Merchant	D. Winter	Closed	28.90	50-100.
83-02-074	Woodcutter's Cottage	D. Winter	Closed	87.00	260-495.
John Hine N.A. Ltd.		**David Winter Retired Cottages-Tiny Series**			
80-03-001	William Shakespeare's Birthplace	D. Winter	Closed	Unkn.	500-700.
80-03-002	Ann Hathaway's Cottage	D. Winter	Closed	Unkn.	400-600.
80-03-003	Sulgrave Manor	D. Winter	Closed	Unkn.	400-700.
80-03-004	Cotswold Farmhouse	D. Winter	Closed	Unkn.	400-700.
80-03-005	Crown Inn	D. Winter	Closed	Unkn.	400-700.
80-03-006	St. Nicholas' Church	D. Winter	Closed	Unkn.	500-700.
John Hine N.A. Ltd.		**Collectors Guild Exclusives**			
87-04-001	The Village Scene	D. Winter	Closed	Gift	180-400.
87-04-002	Robin Hood's Hideaway	D. Winter	Closed	54.00	300-600.
88-04-003	Queen Elizabeth Slept Here	D. Winter	Closed	183.00	250-475.
88-04-004	Black Bess Inn	D. Winter	Closed	60.00	100-125.
88-04-005	The Pavillion	D. Winter	Closed	52.00	100-160.
89-04-006	Street Scene	D. Winter	Closed	Gift	120-200.
89-04-007	Homeguard	D. Winter	Closed	105.00	120-300.
89-04-008	Coal Shed	D. Winter	Closed	112.00	125-300.
90-04-009	Plucked Duck	D. Winter	Closed	Gift	60-145.
90-04-010	The Cobblers	D. Winter	Closed	40.00	65-150.
90-04-011	The Pottery	D. Winter	Closed	40.00	60-150.
90-04-012	Cartwrights Cottage	D. Winter	Closed	45.00	60-150.
91-04-013	Pershore Mill	D. Winter	Closed	Gift	55-125.
91-04-014	Tomfool's Cottage	D. Winter	Closed	100.00	80-150.
91-04-015	Will O' The Wisp	D. Winter	Closed	120.00	85-150.
92-04-016	Irish Water Mill	D. Winter	Closed	Gift	50-80.00
92-04-017	Patrick's Water Mill	D. Winter	Closed	Gift	100-200.
92-04-018	Candle Maker's	D. Winter	Closed	65.00	65-100.
92-04-019	Bee Keeper's	D. Winter	Closed	65.00	65-100.
93-04-020	On The River Bank	D. Winter	Closed	Gift	50-100.
93-04-021	Thameside	D. Winter	Closed	79.00	79.00
93-04-022	Swan Upping Cottage	D. Winter	Closed	69.00	69.00
94-04-023	15 Lawnside Road	D. Winter	Yr.Iss.	Gift	Gift
94-04-024	While Away Cottage	D. Winter	Yr.Iss.	70.00	70.00
94-04-025	Ashe Cottage	D. Winter	Yr.Iss.	62.00	62.00
John Hine N.A. Ltd.		**Scottish Collection**			
89-05-001	Scottish Crofter	D. Winter	Open	42.00	65.00
89-05-002	Gillie's Cottage	D. Winter	Open	65.00	85.00
89-05-003	Gatekeeper's	D. Winter	Open	65.00	85.00
89-05-004	MacBeth's Castle	D. Winter	Open	200.00	260.00
John Hine N.A. Ltd.		**Irish Collection**			
92-06-001	Irish Round Tower	D. Winter	Open	65.00	70.00
92-06-002	Murphys	D. Winter	Open	100.00	110.00
92-06-003	O'Donovan's Castle	D. Winter	Open	145.00	170.00
John Hine N.A. Ltd.		**British Traditions**			
90-07-001	Burns' Reading Room	D. Winter	Open	31.00	50.00
90-07-002	Stonecutters Cottage	D. Winter	Open	48.00	65.00
90-07-003	The Boat House	D. Winter	Open	37.50	65.00
90-07-004	Pudding Cottage	D. Winter	Open	78.00	90.00
90-07-005	Blossom Cottage	D. Winter	Open	59.00	65.00
90-07-006	Knight's Castle	D. Winter	Open	59.00	85.00
90-07-007	St. Anne's Well	D. Winter	Open	48.00	70.00
90-07-008	Grouse Moor Lodge	D. Winter	Open	48.00	70.00
90-07-009	Staffordshire Vicarage	D. Winter	Open	48.00	70.00
90-07-010	Harvest Barn	D. Winter	Open	31.00	50.00
90-07-011	Guy Fawkes	D. Winter	Open	31.00	50.00
90-07-012	Bull & Bush	D. Winter	Open	37.50	50.00
John Hine N.A. Ltd.		**David Winter Cameos**			
92-08-001	Brooklet Bridge	D. Winter	Open	12.50	15.00
92-08-002	Poultry Ark	D. Winter	Open	12.50	15.00
92-08-003	The Potting Shed	D. Winter	Open	12.50	15.00
92-08-004	Lych Gate	D. Winter	Open	12.50	15.00
92-08-005	One Man Jail	D. Winter	Open	12.50	15.00
92-08-006	Market Day	D. Winter	Open	12.50	15.00
92-08-007	Welsh Pig Pen	D. Winter	Open	12.50	15.00
92-08-008	The Privy	D. Winter	Open	12.50	15.00
92-08-009	Greenwood Wagon	D. Winter	Open	12.50	15.00
92-08-010	Saddle Steps	D. Winter	Open	12.50	15.00
92-08-011	Barley Malt Kilns	D. Winter	Open	12.50	15.00
92-08-012	Penny Wishing Well	D. Winter	Open	12.50	15.00
92-08-013	Diorama-Light	D. Winter	Closed	30.00	60-100.
92-08-014	Diorama-Bright	D. Winter	Open	50.00	50.00
John Hine N.A. Ltd.		**David Winter Scenes**			
92-09-001	At The Bothy Vignette Base	D. Winter	5,000	39.00	39.00
92-09-002	Farmer And Plough	Cameo Guild	5,000	60.00	60.00
92-09-003	Farm Hand And Spade	Cameo Guild	5,000	40.00	40.00
92-09-004	Farmer's Wife	Cameo Guild	5,000	45.00	45.00
92-09-005	Goose Girl	Cameo Guild	5,000	45.00	45.00
92-09-006	At The Bake House Vignette	D. Winter	5,000	35.00	35.00
92-09-007	Hot Cross Bun Seller	Cameo Guild	5,000	60.00	60.00
92-09-008	Woman At Pump	Cameo Guild	5,000	45.00	45.00
92-09-009	Lady Customer	Cameo Guild	5,000	45.00	45.00
92-09-010	Small Boy And Dog	Cameo Guild	5,000	45.00	45.00
92-09-011	Girl Selling Eggs	Cameo Guild	5,000	30.00	30.00
92-09-012	At Rose cottage Vignette	D. Winter	5,000	39.00	39.00
92-09-013	Mother	Cameo Guild	5,000	50.00	50.00
92-09-014	Father	Cameo Guild	5,000	45.00	45.00
92-09-015	Son	Cameo Guild	5,000	30.00	30.00
92-09-016	Daughter	D. Winter	5,000	30.00	30.00
93-09-017	Miss Belle	Cameo Guild	5,000	35.00	35.00
93-09-018	Bob Cratchit And Tiny Tim	Cameo Guild	5,000	50.00	50.00
93-09-019	Fred	Cameo Guild	5,000	35.00	35.00
93-09-020	Mrs. Fezziwig	Cameo Guild	5,000	35.00	35.00
93-09-021	Tom The Street Shoveler	Cameo Guild	5,000	60.00	60.00
93-09-022	Ebenezer Scrooge	Cameo Guild	5,000	45.00	45.00
93-09-023	Christmas Snow Vignette	D. Winter	5,000	50.00	50.00
John Hine N.A. Ltd.		**Shires Collection**			
93-10-001	Oxfordshire Goat Yard	D. Winter	Open	32.00	40.00
93-10-002	Shropshire Pig Shelter	D. Winter	Open	32.00	40.00
93-10-003	Hampshire Hutches	D. Winter	Open	34.00	40.00
93-10-004	Wiltshire Waterwheel	D. Winter	Open	34.00	40.00
93-10-005	Cheshire Kennels	D. Winter	Open	36.00	40.00
93-10-006	Derbyshire Dovecote	D. Winter	Open	36.00	40.00
93-10-007	Staffordshire Stable	D. Winter	Open	36.00	40.00
93-10-008	Berkshire Milking Byre	D. Winter	Open	38.00	40.00
93-10-009	Buckinghamshire Bull Pen	D. Winter	Open	38.00	40.00
93-10-010	Lancashire Donkey Shed	D. Winter	Open	38.00	40.00
93-10-011	Yorkshire Sheep Fold	D. Winter	Open	38.00	40.00
93-10-012	Gloucestershire Greenhouse	D. Winter	Open	40.00	40.00
John Hine N.A. Ltd.		**Welsh Collection**			
93-11-001	Pen Y Graig	D. Winter	Open	88.00	90.00
93-11-002	Tyddyn Siriol	D. Winter	Open	88.00	90.00
93-11-003	Y Ddraig Goch	D. Winter	Open	88.00	90.00
93-11-004	A Bit of Nonsense	D. Winter	Open	50.00	50.00

		ARTIST	EDITION	ISSUE	QUOTE
John Hine N.A. Ltd.		**The English Village**			
94-12-001	Post Office	D. Winter	Open	53.00	53.00
94-12-002	Rectory	D. Winter	Open	55.00	55.00
94-12-003	Smithy	D. Winter	Open	50.00	50.00
94-12-004	Tannery	D. Winter	Open	50.00	50.00
94-12-005	Hall	D. Winter	Open	55.00	55.00
94-12-006	One Acre Cottage	D. Winter	Open	55.00	55.00
94-12-007	Cat & Pipe	D. Winter	Open	53.00	53.00
94-12-008	Quack's Cottage	D. Winter	Open	57.00	57.00
94-12-009	Constabulatory	D. Winter	Open	60.00	60.00
94-12-010	Crystal Cottage	D. Winter	Open	53.00	53.00
94-12-011	Chandlery	D. Winter	Open	53.00	53.00
94-12-012	Seminary	D. Winter	Open	57.00	57.00
94-12-013	Church & Vestry	D. Winter	Open	57.00	57.00
94-12-014	Glebe Cottage	D. Winter	Open	53.00	53.00
94-12-015	The Engine House	D. Winter	Open	55.00	55.00
94-12-016	Guardian Castle	D. Winter	8,490	275.00	350-650.
94-12-017	Premier Guardian Castle	D. Winter	1,500	350.00	350.00
John Hine N.A. Ltd.		**David Winter Special Event Pieces**			
93-13-001	Birthstone Wishing Well	D. Winter	Closed	40.00	50-75.00
93-13-002	Birthday Cottage	D. Winter	Closed	55.00	55.00
94-13-003	Wishing Falls Cottage	D. Winter	6/95	65.00	65.00
John Hine N.A. Ltd.		**David Winter Tour Special Event Piece**			
93-14-001	Arches Thrice	D. Winter	Closed	150.00	130-250.
John Hine N.A. Ltd.		**American Collection**			
89-15-001	The Out House	M. Wideman	Closed	15.00	12-16.00
89-15-002	Colonial Wellhouse	M. Wideman	Closed	15.00	16.00
89-15-003	Wisteria	M. Wideman	Closed	15.00	12.00
89-15-004	The Blockhouse	M. Wideman	Closed	25.00	25.00
89-15-005	Garconniere	M. Wideman	Closed	25.00	70.00
89-15-006	The Log Cabin	M. Wideman	Closed	45.00	40.00
89-15-007	Cherry Hill School	M. Wideman	Closed	45.00	56.00
89-15-008	The Maple Sugar Shack	M. Wideman	Closed	50.00	56.00
89-15-009	The Kissing Bridge	M. Wideman	Closed	50.00	56.00
89-15-010	The Gingerbread House	M. Wideman	Closed	60.00	72.00
89-15-011	The New England Church	M. Wideman	Closed	79.00	115.00
89-15-012	The Opera House	M. Wideman	Closed	89.00	100.00
89-15-013	The Pacific Lighthouse	M. Wideman	Closed	89.00	80-155.
89-15-014	King William Tavern	M. Wideman	Closed	99.00	75-100.
89-15-015	The Mission	M. Wideman	Closed	99.00	110.00
89-15-016	New England Lighthouse	M. Wideman	Closed	99.00	115.00
89-15-017	The River Bell	M. Wideman	Closed	99.00	120.00
89-15-018	Plantation House	M. Wideman	Closed	119.00	185.00
89-15-019	Town Hall	M. Wideman	Closed	129.00	85-95.00
89-15-020	Dog House	M. Wideman	Closed	10.00	10.00
89-15-021	Star Cottage	M. Wideman	Closed	30.00	34.00
89-15-022	Sod House	M. Wideman	Closed	40.00	62.00
89-15-023	Barber Shop	M. Wideman	Closed	40.00	44.00
89-15-024	Octagonal House	M. Wideman	Closed	40.00	44.00
89-15-025	Cajun Cottage	M. Wideman	Closed	50.00	56.00
89-15-026	Prairie Forge	M. Wideman	Closed	65.00	72.00
89-15-027	Oxbow Saloon	M. Wideman	Closed	90.00	100.00
89-15-028	Sierra Mine	M. Wideman	Closed	120.00	149.00
89-15-029	California Winery	M. Wideman	Closed	180.00	198.00
89-15-030	Railhead Inn	M. Wideman	Closed	250.00	165-276.
89-15-031	Haunted House	M. Wideman	Closed	100.00	80-110.
89-15-032	Tobacconist	M. Wideman	Closed	45.00	50.00
89-15-033	Hawaiian Grass Hut	M. Wideman	Closed	45.00	50.00
89-15-034	The Old Mill	M. Wideman	Closed	100.00	110.00
89-15-035	Band Stand	M. Wideman	Closed	90.00	90-100.
89-15-036	Seaside Cottage	M. Wideman	Closed	225.00	248.00
89-15-037	Tree House	M. Wideman	Closed	45.00	30-45.00
89-15-038	Hacienda	M. Wideman	Closed	51.00	52-56.00
89-15-039	Sweetheart Cottage	M. Wideman	Closed	45.00	50.00
89-15-040	Forty-Niner Cabin	M. Wideman	Closed	50.00	40-56.00
91-15-041	Desert Storm Tent	M. Wideman	Closed	75.00	125-150.
91-15-042	Paul Revere's House	M. Wideman	Closed	90.00	100.00
91-15-043	Mo At Work	M. Wideman	Closed	35.00	28-36.00
91-15-044	Church in the Dale	M. Wideman	Closed	130.00	75-130.
91-15-045	Milk House	M. Wideman	Closed	20.00	20-24.00
91-15-046	Moe's Diner	M. Wideman	Closed	100.00	300.00
91-15-047	Fire Station	M. Wideman	Closed	160.00	100.00
91-15-048	Joe's Service Station	M. Wideman	Closed	90.00	68-75.00
92-15-049	News Stand	M. Wideman	Closed	30.00	36-45.00
92-15-050	Village Mercantile	M. Wideman	Closed	60.00	60.00
92-15-051	Grain Elevator	M. Wideman	Closed	110.00	110.00
92-15-052	Telephone Booth	M. Wideman	Closed	15.00	30.00
92-15-053	Topper's Drive-In	M. Wideman	Closed	120.00	110.00
John Hine N.A. Ltd.		**First Nation Collection**			
93-16-001	The First Nation Collection, set of 8	M. Wideman	Closed	500.00	1000.00
93-16-002	Elm Bark Longhouse	M. Wideman	Closed	56.00	56.00
93-16-003	Igloo	M. Wideman	Closed	60.00	90.00
93-16-004	Mandan Earth Lodge	M. Wideman	Closed	56.00	300.00
93-16-005	Plains Teepee	M. Wideman	Closed	68.00	300.00
93-16-006	Stilt House	M. Wideman	Closed	60.00	60-90.00
93-16-007	Sweat Lodge	M. Wideman	Closed	34.00	100.00
93-16-008	West Coast Longhouse	M. Wideman	Closed	100.00	100.00
93-16-009	Wigwam	M. Wideman	Closed	65.00	300.00
John Hine N.A. Ltd.		**Wideman**			
92-17-001	Moe's Clubhouse	M. Wideman	Closed	40.00	200.00
John Hine N.A. Ltd.		**Mushrooms**			
89-18-001	Royal Bank of Mushland	C. Lawrence	Closed	235.00	235.00
89-18-002	The Elders Mushroom	C. Lawrence	Closed	175.00	175.00
89-18-003	The Cobblers	C. Lawrence	Closed	265.00	265.00
89-18-004	The Mush Hospital for Malingerers	C. Lawrence	Closed	250.00	250.00
89-18-005	The Ministry	C. Lawrence	Closed	185.00	185.00
89-18-006	The Gift Shop	C. Lawrence	Closed	350.00	420.00
89-18-007	The Constables	C. Lawrence	Closed	200.00	200.00
89-18-008	The Princess Palace	C. Lawrence	Closed	600.00	730.00
John Hine N.A. Ltd.		**Bugaboos**			
89-19-001	Arnold	John Hine Studio	Closed	45.00	45.00
89-19-002	Edna	John Hine Studio	Closed	45.00	45.00
89-19-003	Wilbur	John Hine Studio	Closed	45.00	45.00
89-19-004	Beryl	John Hine Studio	Closed	45.00	45.00
89-19-005	Gerald	John Hine Studio	Closed	45.00	45.00
89-19-006	Wesley	John Hine Studio	Closed	45.00	45.00
89-19-007	Oscar	John Hine Studio	Closed	45.00	45.00

		ARTIST	EDITION	ISSUE	QUOTE
89-19-008	Lizzie	John Hine Studio	Closed	45.00	45.00
89-19-009	Enid	John Hine Studio	Closed	45.00	45.00
John Hine N.A. Ltd.		**Great British Pubs**			
89-20-001	Smith's Arms	M. Cooper	Closed	28.00	28.00
89-20-002	The Plough	M. Cooper	Closed	28.00	28.00
89-20-003	King's Arms	M. Cooper	Closed	28.00	28.00
89-20-004	White Tower	M. Cooper	Closed	35.00	35.00
89-20-005	Old Bridge House	M. Cooper	Closed	37.50	37.50
89-20-006	White Horse	M. Cooper	Closed	39.50	39.50
89-20-007	Jamaica Inn	M. Cooper	Closed	39.50	39.50
89-20-008	The George	M. Cooper	Closed	57.50	57.50
89-20-009	Montague Arms	M. Cooper	Closed	57.50	57.50
89-20-010	Blue Bell	M. Cooper	Closed	57.50	57.50
89-20-011	The Lion	M. Cooper	Closed	57.50	57.50
89-20-012	Coach & Horses	M. Cooper	Closed	79.50	79.50
89-20-013	Ye Olde Spotted Horse	M. Cooper	Closed	79.50	79.50
89-20-014	The Crown Inn	M. Cooper	Closed	79.50	79.50
89-20-015	The Bell	M. Cooper	Closed	79.50	100-350.
89-20-016	Black Swan	M. Cooper	Closed	79.50	100-350.
89-20-017	Ye Grapes	M. Cooper	Closed	87.50	87.50
89-20-018	Old Bull Inn	M. Cooper	Closed	87.50	87.50
89-20-019	Dickens Inn	M. Cooper	Closed	100.00	100.00
89-20-020	Sherlock Holmes	M. Cooper	Closed	100.00	200.00
89-20-021	George Somerset	M. Cooper	Closed	100.00	100.00
89-20-022	The Feathers	M. Cooper	Closed	200.00	200.00
89-20-023	Hawkeshead	M. Cooper	Closed	Unkn.	900.00
John Hine N.A. Ltd.		**Great British Pubs-Yard of Pubs**			
89-21-001	Grenadier	M. Cooper	Closed	25.00	25.00
89-21-002	Black Friars	M. Cooper	Closed	25.00	25.00
89-21-003	Falkland Arms	M. Cooper	Closed	25.00	25.00
89-21-004	George & Pilgrims	M. Cooper	Closed	25.00	25.00
89-21-005	Dirty Duck	M. Cooper	Closed	25.00	25.00
89-21-006	Wheatsheaf	M. Cooper	Closed	35.00	35.00
89-21-007	Lygon Arms	M. Cooper	Closed	35.00	35.00
89-21-008	Suffolk Bull	M. Cooper	Closed	35.00	35.00
89-21-009	The Swan	M. Cooper	Closed	35.00	35.00
89-21-010	The Falstaff	M. Cooper	Closed	35.00	35.00
89-21-011	The Eagle	M. Cooper	Closed	35.00	35.00
89-21-012	The Green Man	M. Cooper	Closed	Unkn.	75.00
John Hine N.A. Ltd.		**The Shoemaker's Dream**			
91-22-001	The Jester Boot	J. Herbert	Open	29.00	29.00
91-22-002	The Crooked Boot	J. Herbert	Open	35.00	35.00
91-22-003	Rosie's Cottage	J. Herbert	Open	40.00	40.00
91-22-004	Baby Booty (pink)	J. Herbert	Open	45.00	45.00
91-22-005	Baby Booty (blue)	J. Herbert	Open	45.00	45.00
91-22-006	Shoemaker's Palace	J. Herbert	Open	50.00	50.00
91-22-007	Tavern Boot	J. Herbert	Open	55.00	55.00
91-22-008	River Shoe Cottage	J. Herbert	Open	55.00	55.00
91-22-009	The Chapel	J. Herbert	Open	55.00	55.00
91-22-010	Castle Boot	J. Herbert	Open	55.00	55.00
91-22-011	The Clocktower Boot	J. Herbert	Open	60.00	60.00
91-22-012	Watermill Boot	J. Herbert	Open	60.00	60.00
91-22-013	Windmill Boot	J. Herbert	Open	65.00	65.00
91-22-014	The Gate Lodge	J. Herbert	Open	65.00	65.00
92-22-015	Wishing Well Shoe	J. Herbert	Open	32.00	35.00
92-22-016	The Golf Shoe	J. Herbert	Open	35.00	40.00
92-22-017	The Sports Shoe	J. Herbert	Open	35.00	40.00
92-22-018	Clown Boot	J. Herbert	Open	45.00	45.00
92-22-019	Upside Down Boot	J. Herbert	Open	45.00	45.00
92-22-020	Christmas Boot	J. Herbert	Open	55.00	55.00
93-22-021	Wedding Bells	J. Herbert	Open	45.00	50.00
93-22-022	Shiver me Timbers	J. Herbert	Open	45.00	55.00
93-22-023	The Woodcutter's Shoe	J. Herbert	Open	40.00	40.00
John Hine N.A. Ltd.		**Animal Antics**			
93-23-001	Sir Mouse	J. Herbert	Open	20.00	20.00
93-23-002	Lady Mouse	J. Herbert	Open	20.00	20.00
93-23-003	You're Bone Idle	J. Herbert	Open	30.00	30.00
93-23-004	Real Cool Carrot	J. Herbert	Open	30.00	30.00
93-23-005	Tabby Tabitha	J. Herbert	Open	37.00	37.00
93-23-006	Lucky Dragon	J. Herbert	Open	40.00	40.00
93-23-007	Slow Progress	J. Herbert	Open	40.00	40.00
93-23-008	Bird Brain	J. Herbert	Open	32.00	32.00
93-23-009	Snail Place	J. Herbert	Open	37.00	37.00
John Hine N.A. Ltd.		**Heartstrings**			
92-24-001	Hush, It's Sleepytime	S. Kuck	Closed	97.50	97.50
92-24-002	Taking Tea	S. Kuck	Closed	92.50	92.50
92-24-003	Day Dreaming	S. Kuck	Closed	92.50	92.50
92-24-004	Watch Me Waltz	S. Kuck	Closed	97.50	97.50
John Hine N.A. Ltd.		**Santa's Big Day**			
92-25-001	Booting Up	J. King	Closed	40.00	40.00
92-25-002	Home Rudolph	J. King	Closed	50.00	50.00
92-25-003	Reindeer Breakfast	J. King	Closed	50.00	50.00
92-25-004	Feet First	J. King	Closed	55.00	55.00
92-25-005	Santa's Night Ride	J. King	Closed	55.00	55.00
92-25-006	Tight Fit!	J. King	Closed	55.00	55.00
92-25-007	Wakey, Wakey!	J. King	Closed	55.00	55.00
92-25-008	Rest-a-while	J. King	Closed	60.00	60.00
92-25-009	Whoops!	J. King	Closed	60.00	60.00
92-25-010	Heave Ho!	J. King	Closed	70.00	70.00
92-25-011	Ready Boys?	J. King	Closed	80.00	80.00
92-25-012	Zzzzz...	J. King	Closed	85.00	85.00
John Hine N.A. Ltd.		**Father Christmas**			
88-26-001	Standing	J. King	Closed	70.00	70.00
88-26-002	Feet	J. King	Closed	70.00	70.00
88-26-003	Falling	J. King	Closed	70.00	70.00
John Hine N.A. Ltd.		**Father Time Clocks**			
92-27-001	Little Thatched	J. Herbert	Open	78.00	78.00
92-27-002	The Manor	J. Herbert	Open	90.00	90.00
92-27-003	Treehouse	J. Herbert	Open	99.00	99.00
92-27-004	Watermill	J. Herbert	Open	99.00	99.00
92-27-005	Farmhouse	J. Herbert	Open	99.00	99.00
92-27-006	Castle	J. Herbert	Open	110.00	110.00
92-27-007	Windmill	J. Herbert	Open	120.00	120.00
93-27-008	Tudor Ruin	J. Herbert	Open	94.00	94.00
93-27-009	Riverside Haven	J. Herbert	Open	99.00	99.00
93-27-010	Marshland Castle	J. Herbert	Open	99.00	99.00

	ARTIST	EDITION	ISSUE	QUOTE
Historical Miniatures	**American Heritage:Charleston**			
94-01-001 Rutledge House	M. Weisser	Open	50.00	50.00
94-01-002 The Pink House	M. Weisser	Open	36.00	36.00
94-01-003 Rainbow Row:Blue #1	M. Weisser	Open	36.00	36.00
94-01-004 Rainbow Row:Green #1	M. Weisser	Open	36.00	36.00
94-01-005 Rainbow Row:Pink #1	M. Weisser	Open	36.00	36.00
94-01-006 The City Market	M. Weisser	Open	39.00	39.00
94-01-007 Citadel's Summerall Chapel	M. Weisser	Open	36.00	36.00
Historical Miniatures	**American Heritage: New Orleans**			
94-02-001 Royal Cafe	M. Weisser	Open	39.00	39.00
94-02-002 Chart House	M. Weisser	Open	34.00	34.00
Historical Miniatures	**American Heritage:Miami Beach: Deco District**			
94-03-001 Hotel Taft	M. Weisser	Open	29.90	29.90
94-03-002 Hotel Carlyle	M. Weisser	Open	36.00	36.00
94-03-003 Hotel Century	M. Weisser	Open	31.00	31.00
Historical Miniatures	**American Heritage:Cape May, N.J.**			
94-04-001 The Linda Lee	M. Weisser	Open	39.80	39.80
94-04-002 The Abbey	M. Weisser	Open	39.00	39.00
Historical Miniatures	**Doors & Gates of America:Charleston**			
94-05-001 The Harp Gate	M. Weisser	Open	15.00	15.00
94-05-002 Bull Street Door:Blue/Beige	M. Weisser	Open	15.00	15.00
94-05-003 The Pineapple Gate	M. Weisser	Open	16.00	16.00
94-05-004 The Charleston College Gate	M. Weisser	Open	16.00	16.00
Historical Miniatures	**Doors & Gates of America:Miami Beach: Deco District**			
94-06-001 Key West Door	M. Weisser	Open	15.00	15.00
94-06-002 The Moon Gate	M. Weisser	Open	16.00	16.00
94-06-003 The Flamingo Door	M. Weisser	Open	15.00	15.00
94-06-004 Residential Door #1	M. Weisser	Open	16.00	16.00
94-06-005 Residential Door #2	M. Weisser	Open	15.00	15.00
Iris Arc Crystal	**1981 Introductions**			
81-01-001 Octopus	P. Hale	Open	32.00	50.00
81-01-002 Kitten	T. Holliman	Retrd.	40.00	48.00
81-01-003 Dachshund	P. Hale	Retrd.	48.00	58.00
81-01-004 Mushrooms	T. Holliman	Retrd.	50.00	60.00
81-01-005 Miniature Snail (Silver)	P. Hale	Retrd.	20.00	24.00
81-01-006 Miniature Snail (Rainbow)	P. Hale	Open	20.00	27.00
81-01-007 Miniature Koala	T. Holliman	Retrd.	24.00	29.00
81-01-008 Miniature Dragonfly	T. Holliman	Retrd.	20.00	24.00
81-01-009 Miniature Bunny	T. Holliman	Retrd.	28.00	33.75
81-01-010 Miniature Frog	P. Hale	Retrd.	20.00	24.00
81-01-011 Miniature Firefly (Silver)	T. Holliman	Retrd.	20.00	24.00
81-01-012 Miniature Firefly (Rainbow)	T. Holliman	Retrd.	20.00	24.00
81-01-013 Miniature Angel	T. Holliman	Retrd.	24.00	29.00
Iris Arc Crystal	**1982 Introductions**			
82-02-001 Seal (Silver)	P. Hale	Retrd.	32.00	38.00
82-02-002 Seal (Rainbow)	P. Hale	Open	32.00	35.00
82-02-003 Hippo	P. Hale	Retrd.	64.00	77.00
82-02-004 Small Teddy Bear w/Heart (Silver)	P. Hale	Retrd.	36.00	43.00
82-02-005 Small Teddy Bear w/Heart (Rose)	P. Hale	Open	36.00	45.00
82-02-006 Polar Bear	P. Hale	Retrd.	32.00	39.00
82-02-007 Koala	T. Holliman	Retrd.	44.00	53.00
82-02-008 Squirrel	P. Hale	Retrd.	36.00	43.00
82-02-009 Small Mouse	Iris Arc	Retrd.	38.00	46.00
82-02-010 Large Mouse	Iris Arc	Retrd.	48.00	58.00
82-02-011 Swan Lake	P. Hale	Retrd.	40.00	48.00
82-02-012 Small Elephant	P. Hale	Retrd.	70.00	84.00
82-02-013 Arc Angel	Iris Arc	Retrd.	40.00	48.00
82-02-014 Birdbath	T. Holliman	Retrd.	60.00	90.00
82-02-015 Snowman	P. Hale	Retrd.	42.00	51.00
82-02-016 Siamese Cat	T. Holliman	Retrd.	48.00	58.00
82-02-017 Unicorn	P. Hale	Retrd.	76.00	91.00
82-02-018 Small Butterfly	T. Holliman	Retrd.	44.00	53.00
82-02-019 Large Butterfly	T. Holliman	Retrd.	56.00	67.00
82-02-020 Miniature Swan	T. Holliman	Retrd.	20.00	27.00
Iris Arc Crystal	**1983 Introductions**			
83-03-001 Panda	P. Hale	Retrd.	56.00	67.00
83-03-002 Kangaroo	P. Hale	Retrd.	36.00	43.00
83-03-003 Otter (Silver)	P. Hale	Retrd.	36.00	43.00
83-03-004 Otter (Rainbow)	P. Hale	Retrd.	36.00	43.00
83-03-005 Turtle	Iris Arc	Retrd.	48.00	58.00
83-03-006 Crab	P. Hale	Retrd.	32.00	38.00
83-03-007 Camel	T. Holliman	Retrd.	136.00	163.00
83-03-008 Miniature Turtle	P. Hale	Open	20.00	27.00
83-03-009 Miniature Dove	P. Hale	Retrd.	20.00	24.00
83-03-010 Miniature Owl	P. Patruno	Retrd.	24.00	29.00
83-03-011 Miniature Frog	P. Hale	Retrd.	20.00	24.00
Iris Arc Crystal	**1984 Introductions**			
84-04-001 Enchanted Castle	T. Holliman	Retrd.	1200.00	1440.00
84-04-002 Dragon Slayer	P. Hale	Retrd.	120.00	144.00
84-04-003 Dragon	P. Hale	Retrd.	190.00	228.00
84-04-004 Pegasus	P. Hale	Retrd.	100.00	120.00
84-04-005 Knight	P. Hale	Retrd.	56.00	67.00
84-04-006 Jester	P. Hale	Retrd.	50.00	60.00
84-04-007 Fairy	P. Hale	Retrd.	32.00	39.00
84-04-008 Maiden	P. Hale	Retrd.	56.00	67.00
84-04-009 Wizard	P. Hale	Retrd.	64.00	77.00
84-04-010 Med. Teddy Bear w/Heart (Silver)	P. Hale	Retrd.	56.00	67.00
84-04-011 Med. Teddy Bear w/Heart (Rose)	P. Hale	Retrd.	56.00	70.00
84-04-012 Mini Teddy Bear w/Heart (Silver)	P. Hale	Retrd.	18.00	22.00
84-04-013 Mini Teddy Bear w/Heart (Rose)	P. Hale	Open	18.00	25.00
84-04-014 Panda w/Heart	P. Hale	Retrd.	58.00	70.00
84-04-015 Miniature Panda	P. Hale	Retrd.	18.00	22.00
84-04-016 Mini Panda w/Heart	P. Hale	Open	20.00	27.00
84-04-017 Koala w/Heart	P. Hale	Retrd.	46.00	55.00
84-04-018 Mini Koala w/Heart	P. Hale	Retrd.	13.00	16.00
84-04-019 Large Giraffe	P. Hale	Retrd.	240.00	288.00
84-04-020 Small Giraffe	P. Hale	Retrd.	100.00	120.00
84-04-021 Medium Elephant	P. Hale	Retrd.	150.00	180.00
84-04-022 Kangaroo	P. Hale	Retrd.	48.00	58.00
84-04-023 Rhino	P. Hale	Retrd.	56.00	67.00
84-04-024 Lion w/Heart	P. Hale	Retrd.	70.00	84.00
84-04-025 Peacock	P. Hale	Retrd.	140.00	168.00
84-04-026 Dog w/Bone	P. Hale	Retrd.	50.00	60.00
84-04-027 Kitten w/Ball	P. Hale	Retrd.	50.00	60.00
84-04-028 Dolphin	P. Hale	Retrd.	48.00	58.00
84-04-029 Whale	P. Hale	Retrd.	44.00	53.00
84-04-030 Penguin	P. Hale	Retrd.	32.00	39.00
84-04-031 Miniature Rabbit	P. Hale	Retrd.	18.00	22.00
84-04-032 Miniature Kitten	P. Hale	Open	18.00	27.00
84-04-033 Miniature Puppy	P. Hale	Retrd.	18.00	22.00
84-04-034 Miniature Robin	P. Hale	Retrd.	18.00	21.00
Iris Arc Crystal	**1985 Introductions**			
85-05-001 Rainbow Juggler	P. Hale	Retrd.	100.00	120.00
85-05-002 Small Rainbow Juggler	P. Hale	Retrd.	50.00	60.00
85-05-003 Nativity Scene	P. Hale	Retrd.	130.00	156.00
85-05-004 Baby Bunny with Carrot	P. Hale	Open	45.00	60.00
85-05-005 Small Unicorn	P. Hale	Retrd.	45.00	54.00
85-05-006 Ballerina	P. Hale	Retrd.	70.00	84.00
85-05-007 Rudolph the Rednose Reindeer*	P. Hale	Retrd.	100.00	120.00
85-05-008 Christmas Tree	P. Hale	Retrd.	150.00	180.00
85-05-009 Small Camel	P. Hale	Retrd.	88.00	106.00
85-05-010 Small Lion with Heart	P. Hale	Retrd.	45.00	54.00
85-05-011 Small Peacock	P. Hale	Retrd.	50.00	60.00
85-05-012 Small AB Peacock	P. Hale	Open	60.00	120.00
85-05-013 Medium AB Peacock	P. Hale	Retrd.	160.00	200.00
85-05-014 Large Peacock	P. Hale	Retrd.	700.00	840.00
85-05-015 Large Swan Lake	P. Hale	Retrd.	170.00	204.00
85-05-016 Poodle	P. Hale	Retrd.	150.00	180.00
85-05-017 Bunny with Carrot	P. Hale	Retrd.	65.00	78.00
85-05-018 Medium Turtle	P. Hale	Retrd.	55.00	66.00
85-05-019 Medium Swan	P. Hale	Retrd.	60.00	72.00
85-05-020 Large Swan	P. Hale	Retrd.	350.00	420.00
85-05-021 Feeding Time	P. Hale	Retrd.	120.00	144.00
85-05-022 Wildflower with Hummingbird	P. Hale	Open	240.00	390.00
85-05-023 Wildflower	P. Hale	Retrd.	190.00	228.00
85-05-024 Large Owl	P. Hale	Retrd.	140.00	168.00
85-05-025 Small Owl	P. Hale	Retrd.	55.00	66.00
Iris Arc Crystal	**1986 Introductions**			
86-06-001 Rainbow Cloud Castle	P. Hale	Open	350.00	400.00
86-06-002 Lovebirds	P. Hale	Retrd.	150.00	180.00
86-06-003 Caprice Carousel Horse	P. Hale	Retrd.	100.00	130.00
86-06-004 Angel with Cymbals	P. Hale	Open	30.00	35.00
86-06-005 Angel with Flute	P. Hale	Open	30.00	35.00
86-06-006 Angel with Guitar	P. Hale	Open	30.00	35.00
86-06-007 Angel with Harp	P. Hale	Open	30.00	35.00
86-06-008 Angel Singing	P. Hale	Open	30.00	35.00
86-06-009 Angel Gabriel	P. Hale	Open	30.00	35.00
86-06-010 Santa	P. Hale	Retrd.	90.00	108.00
86-06-011 Small Snowman	P. Hale	Open	36.00	45.00
86-06-012 Large Snowman	J. Mulroy	Retrd.	56.00	67.25
86-06-013 Guardian Angel	P. Hale	Retrd.	50.00	65.00
86-06-014 Moose	P. Hale	Open	60.00	90.00
86-06-015 Large Parrot	P. Hale	Retrd.	350.00	420.00
86-06-016 Parrot	P. Hale	Retrd.	120.00	144.00
86-06-017 Baby Elephant	P. Hale	Open	52.00	65.00
86-06-018 Beaver	P. Hale	Retrd.	48.00	58.00
86-06-019 Small Swan	P. Hale	Open	30.00	40.00
86-06-020 U.S. Space Shuttle	P. Hale	Retrd.	250.00	300.00
86-06-021 Pig	P. Hale	Retrd.	65.00	78.00
86-06-022 Baby Butterfly	P. Hale	Retrd.	40.00	48.00
86-06-023 Small Butterfly	P. Hale	Retrd.	90.00	108.00
86-06-024 Medium Butterfly	P. Hale	Retrd.	130.00	156.00
86-06-025 Large Butterfly	P. Hale	Retrd.	170.00	204.00
86-06-026 Small Sailboat	P. Hale	Retrd.	65.00	85.00
86-06-027 Medium Sailboat	P. Hale	Retrd.	170.00	204.00
86-06-028 Large Sailboat	P. Hale	Retrd.	230.00	276.00
Iris Arc Crystal	**1987 Introductions**			
87-07-001 Calliope Carousel Horse	P. Hale	Retrd.	110.00	132.00
87-07-002 Cleanup Clown	P. Hale	Retrd.	72.00	87.00
87-07-003 Happy Birthday Clown	P. Hale	Retrd.	50.00	60.00
87-07-004 Have a Happy Day Clown	P. Hale	Retrd.	50.00	60.00
87-07-005 Congratulations Clown	P. Hale	Retrd.	50.00	60.00
87-07-006 I Love You Clown	P. Hale	Retrd.	50.00	60.00
87-07-007 Merry Christmas Clown	P. Hale	Retrd.	50.00	60.00
87-07-008 Flower Clown	M. Goena	Retrd.	80.00	96.00
87-07-009 Airplane	P. Hale	Open	48.00	55.00
87-07-010 Horse and Rider	P. Hale	Retrd.	130.00	156.00
87-07-011 Bison/Buffalo	M. Goena	Retrd.	50.00	60.00
87-07-012 Mother and Baby Bear	P. Hale	Retrd.	60.00	72.00
87-07-013 Small Santa	P. Hale	Retrd.	30.00	36.00
87-07-014 Sweetie Bear Couple	T. Holliman	Retrd.	140.00	168.00
87-07-015 Sweetie Bear Dancer	T. Holliman	Retrd.	72.00	87.00
87-07-016 Medium AB Swan	P. Hale	Retrd.	100.00	100.00
87-07-017 Carousel Reindeer	P. Hale	Retrd.	120.00	144.00
87-07-018 Grand Duckling	P. Hale	Retrd.	300.00	360.00
87-07-019 Ram	M. Goena	Retrd.	60.00	72.00
87-07-020 Gazelle	M. Goena	Retrd.	130.00	156.00
87-07-021 Allegro Caousel Horse	P. Hale	Retrd.	170.00	204.00
87-07-022 Golf Cart	P. Hale	Retrd.	75.00	90.00
87-07-023 Roadster	P. Hale	Retrd.	60.00	72.00
87-07-024 Pickup Truck	P. Hale	Retrd.	60.00	72.00
87-07-025 Locomotive	P. Hale	Retrd.	90.00	108.00
87-07-026 Passenger Car	P. Hale	Retrd.	80.00	96.00
87-07-027 Coal Car	P. Hale	Retrd.	80.00	96.00
87-07-028 Semi Truck	P. Hale	Retrd.	100.00	120.00
87-07-029 Miniature Duckling	P. Hale	Retrd.	20.00	24.00
Iris Arc Crystal	**1988 Introductions**			
88-08-001 Bullfrog	M. Goena	Retrd.	30.00	36.00
88-08-002 Tambourine Gator	M. Goena	Retrd.	120.00	144.00
88-08-003 Drummer Gator	M. Goena	Retrd.	140.00	168.00
88-08-004 Banjo Gator	M. Goena	Retrd.	120.00	144.00
88-08-005 Lighthouse	P. Hale	Retrd.	150.00	150.00
88-08-006 Rocking Horse	P. Hale	Retrd.	120.00	135.00
88-08-007 Bunny with Flowers	P. Hale	Open	55.00	60.00
88-08-008 Basket of Violets	M. Goena	Open	50.00	60.00
88-08-009 Bear with Honey	M. Goena	Retrd.	80.00	96.00
88-08-010 Bear with Milk and Cookies	M. Goena	Retrd.	80.00	96.00
88-08-011 Bear with Candle	M. Goena	Retrd.	80.00	96.00
88-08-012 Miniature Frog	M. Goena	Open	23.00	27.00
88-08-013 Small Enchanted Castle*	P. Hale	Open	50.00	75.00
88-08-014 Medium Enchanted Castle*	P. Hale	Open	100.00	150.00
88-08-015 Large Enchanted Castle*	P. Hale	Open	180.00	250.00
88-08-016 Clown with Dog	M. Goena	Retrd.	90.00	108.00
88-08-017 Computer Bear	M. Goena	Retrd.	80.00	95.00

		ARTIST	EDITION	ISSUE	QUOTE
88-08-018	Angel Bear	M. Goena	Retrd.	60.00	72.00
88-08-019	Golf Bag	M. Goena/P. Hale	Open	100.00	130.00
88-08-020	Cable Car	M. Goena/P. Hale	Retrd.	70.00	84.00
Iris Arc Crystal		**1989 Introductions**			
89-09-001	Small Mouse	P. Hale	Retrd.	45.00	50.00
89-09-002	Blue Whale	M. Goena	Retrd.	32.00	39.00
89-09-003	Magic Bunny	P. Hale	Retrd.	48.00	58.00
89-09-004	Flower Cart	P. Hale	Open	90.00	95.00
89-09-005	Big Hearted Bunny	M. Goena	Open	55.00	60.00
89-09-006	Golfing Bear	P. Hale	Open	70.00	75.00
89-09-007	Basket of Bunnies	P. Hale	Retrd.	100.00	120.00
89-09-008	Gingerbread Cottage	M. Goena	Open	130.00	170.00
89-09-009	Miniature Clown	M. Goena	Retrd.	23.00	27.00
89-09-010	Miniature Lion	M. Goena	Retrd.	23.00	27.00
89-09-011	Miniature Mouse	M. Goena	Open	23.00	27.00
89-09-012	Miniature Angel	M. Goena	Open	23.00	27.00
89-09-013	Miniature Sailboat	M. Goena	Retrd.	23.00	27.00
89-09-014	Miniature Bunny with Carrot	P. Hale	Open	23.00	27.00
89-09-015	Rudolph the Red Nosed Reindeer"	M. Goena	Retrd.	80.00	96.00
89-09-016	Santa Claus	M. Goena	Open	55.00	60.00
89-09-017	Ski Bunny	M. Goena	Open	55.00	70.00
89-09-018	Train Set	M. Goena	Open	100.00	120.00
89-09-019	Dragon	M. Goena	Retrd.	70.00	95.00
89-09-020	Wizard	M. Goena	Retrd.	80.00	96.00
89-09-021	Miniature Dog	M. Goena	Retrd.	23.00	27.00
89-09-022	Miniature Pig	M. Goena	Open	23.00	27.00
89-09-023	Miniature Moose	M. Goena	Open	23.00	27.00
89-09-024	Miniature Butterfly AB	M. Goena	Retrd.	23.00	27.00
89-09-025	Miniature Butterfly MV	M. Goena	Retrd.	23.00	27.00
89-09-026	Miniature Oyster with Pearl	M. Goena	Open	23.00	27.00
Iris Arc Crystal		**1990 Introductions**			
90-10-001	Snuggle Bunnies	M. Goena	Open	40.00	45.00
90-10-002	Lovebirds	M. Goena	Open	90.00	100.00
90-10-003	Wishing Well	M. Goena	Open	130.00	150.00
90-10-004	Toy Chest	P. Hale	Open	60.00	60.00
90-10-005	Tennis Bear	P. Hale	Open	70.00	75.00
90-10-006	Large Rainbow Butterfly	M. Goena	Retrd.	80.00	96.00
90-10-007	Legendary Castle	P. Hale	Open	200.00	220.00
90-10-008	American Beauty Rose	P. Hale	Retrd.	90.00	95.00
90-10-009	Baby Carriage	M. Goena	Open	50.00	50.00
90-10-010	Miniature Koala with Heart	M. Goena	Open	23.00	27.00
90-10-011	Miniature Castle	M. Goena	Open	23.00	27.00
90-10-012	Vase of Red Roses	M. Goena	Open	20.00	25.00
90-10-013	Small Flower Cart	P. Hale	Open	40.00	45.00
90-10-014	Lotus	P. Hale	Retrd.	60.00	60.00
90-10-015	Crab	P. Hale	Open	40.00	45.00
90-10-016	Dog	M. Goena	Retrd.	70.00	75.00
90-10-017	Cat	M. Goena	Open	70.00	75.00
90-10-018	Hummingbird	M. Goena	Open	85.00	90.00
90-10-019	Loveboat	P. Hale	Retrd.	55.00	60.00
90-10-020	Carousel	C. Hughes	Retrd.	100.00	120.00
90-10-021	Medium Legendary Castle	P. Hale	Open	140.00	150.00
90-10-022	Mushroom Cottage	C. Hughes	Retrd.	130.00	156.00
90-10-023	Space Shuttle	M. Goena	Retrd.	140.00	168.00
90-10-024	Jazz Piano	C. Hughes	Retrd.	150.00	160.00
90-10-025	Miniature Vase of Flowers	P. Hale	Retrd.	25.00	27.00
Iris Arc Crystal		**1991 Introductions**			
91-11-001	Snuggle Bears	M. Goena	Open	40.00	45.00
91-11-002	Bride and Groom	P. Hale	Retrd.	130.00	150.00
91-11-003	Honeymoon Cottage	P. Hale	Open	120.00	130.00
91-11-004	Courting Bears	M. Goena	Open	90.00	90.00
91-11-005	Mouse Mobile	M. Goena	Retrd.	120.00	144.00
91-11-006	Beach Bunnies	M. Goena	Open	120.00	125.00
91-11-007	Red Wagon	P. Hale	Open	70.00	75.00
91-11-008	Jack in the Box	C. Hughes	Open	40.00	40.00
91-11-009	Mother and Baby Bunny	C. Hughes	Retrd.	65.00	78.00
91-11-010	Oyster with Pearl RB	M. Goena	Open	40.00	40.00
91-11-011	Pelican	P. Hale	Retrd.	75.00	90.00
91-11-012	Otter	P. Hale	Open	35.00	40.00
91-11-013	Small Legendary Castle	P. Hale	Open	90.00	95.00
91-11-014	Baseball Bear	M. Goena	Open	75.00	75.00
91-11-015	Speedboat Bunnies	P. Hale	Retrd.	90.00	100.00
91-11-016	Miniature Whale	M. Goena	Open	25.00	27.00
91-11-017	Miniature Mushrooms	C. Hughes	Retrd.	25.00	27.00
91-11-018	Miniature Bunny with Heart	M. Goena	Open	25.00	27.00
91-11-019	Miniature Elephant	M. Goena	Open	25.00	27.00
91-11-020	Miniature Bud Vase	M. Goena	Retrd.	25.00	27.00
91-11-021	Miniature Penguin	M. Goena	Open	25.00	27.00
91-11-022	Miniature Bluebird	M. Goena	Open	25.00	27.00
91-11-023	Miniature Chistmas Tree	C. Hughes	Open	25.00	27.00
91-11-024	Miniature School of Fish	M. Goena	Open	125.00	135.00
91-11-025	Storybook Cottage	P. Hale	Retrd.	80.00	80.00
91-11-026	Teeter Totter	C. Hughes	Retrd.	80.00	96.00
91-11-027	Cat and Fishbowl	P. Hale	Open	70.00	70.00
91-11-028	Mice and Cheese	P. Hale	Retrd.	70.00	75.00
91-11-029	Turtle Grotto	C. Hughes	Retrd.	130.00	135.00
91-11-030	Happy Campers	C. Hughes	Retrd.	110.00	120.00
91-11-031	Country Church	M. Goena	Open	150.00	170.00
91-11-032	Small Mushroom Cottage	C. Hughes	Retrd.	80.00	85.00
91-11-033	Tea for Two	C. Hughes	Retrd.	85.00	90.00
91-11-034	Christmas Morning	C. Hughes	Retrd.	80.00	90.00
91-11-035	Small Gingerbread Cottage	M. Goena	Open	55.00	55.00
91-11-036	Basket of Roses	P. Hale	Open	60.00	60.00
91-11-037	Bouquet Basket	P. Hale	Retrd.	80.00	85.00
91-11-038	Fishing Bear	C. Hughes	Retrd.	50.00	50.00
Iris Arc Crystal		**1992 Introductions**			
92-12-001	Tunnel of Love	C. Hughes	Open	150.00	150.00
92-12-002	Love Doves	M. Goena	Open	40.00	45.00
92-12-003	Video Bear	C. Hughes	Retrd.	75.00	80.00
92-12-004	Bible Bear	C. Hughes	Retrd.	100.00	100.00
92-12-005	Rainbow Apple	M. Goena	Open	45.00	50.00
92-12-006	School House	M. Goena	Open	180.00	180.00
92-12-007	Windmill	C. Hughes	Open	100.00	100.00
92-12-008	Guitar with Stand	C. Hughes	Open	100.00	100.00
92-12-009	Grand Piano	C. Hughes	Open	150.00	150.00
92-12-010	Baby Grand Piano	C. Hughes	Open	50.00	50.00
92-12-011	Small Bouquet Basket	M. Goena	Open	50.00	50.00
92-12-012	Kitty in a Basket	M. Goena	Open	60.00	60.00
92-12-013	Birdhouse	M. Goena	Open	180.00	180.00

		ARTIST	EDITION	ISSUE	QUOTE
92-12-014	Kitten with Ball	M. Goena	Open	55.00	55.00
92-12-015	Treasure Chest	C. Hughes	Open	55.00	55.00
92-12-016	Golf Cart	M. Goena	Open	80.00	85.00
92-12-017	Basketball Bears	C. Hughes	Retrd.	100.00	100.00
92-12-018	Teddy Bear with Blocks	C. Hughes	Retrd.	55.00	60.00
92-12-019	Miniature Baby Carriage	M. Goena	Open	25.00	27.00
92-12-020	Miniature Vase of Pink Flowers	M. Goena	Open	25.00	27.00
92-12-021	Miniature Vase of Violets	M. Goena	Open	25.00	27.00
92-12-022	Miniature Oyster with Pearl AB	M. Goena	Open	25.00	27.00
92-12-023	Snuggle Kittens	M. Goena	Open	40.00	45.00
92-12-024	Romeo and Juliet	C. Hughes	Retrd.	130.00	130.00
92-12-025	Home Sweet Home	C. Hughes	Retrd.	150.00	150.00
92-12-026	Mouse House	C. Hughes	Retrd.	170.00	170.00
92-12-027	Billiards Bunny	C. Hughes	Open	75.00	75.00
92-12-028	Surfin' USA	M. Goena	Retrd.	100.00	100.00
92-12-029	Cruise Ship	M. Goena	Open	100.00	100.00
92-12-030	Cluster of Butterflies	M. Goena	Open	125.00	135.00
92-12-031	Miniature Owl	M. Goena	Open	25.00	27.00
92-12-032	Miniature Bumblebee	M. Goena	Open	25.00	27.00
92-12-033	Nativity Scene	C. Hughes	Open	130.00	130.00
Iris Arc Crystal		**1993 Introductions**			
93-13-001	Balloon Bears	M. Goena	Open	130.00	130.00
93-13-002	Mountain Chapel	C. Hughes	Open	135.00	135.00
93-13-003	Business Bear	C. Hughes	Open	75.00	75.00
93-13-004	Antique Telephone	C. Hughes	Open	40.00	40.00
93-13-005	Dice	M. Goena	Open	45.00	45.00
93-13-006	Slot Machine	M. Goena	Open	100.00	100.00
93-13-007	Basket of Mice	C. Hughes	Open	55.00	55.00
93-13-008	Hide-N-Seek	C. Hughes	Open	70.00	70.00
93-13-009	Hockey Bear	C. Hughes	Open	90.00	90.00
93-13-010	Pacifier	M. Goena	Open	45.00	45.00
93-13-011	Kitty Carriage	C. Hughes	Open	70.00	70.00
93-13-012	Baby Seal	C. Hughes	Open	35.00	35.00
93-13-013	Miniature Rainbow Apple	M. Goena	Open	27.00	27.00
93-13-014	Table for Two	M. Goena	Open	75.00	75.00
93-13-015	Sunday Drive	M. Goena	Open	65.00	65.00
93-13-016	Small Lovebirds	R. Barrera	Open	65.00	65.00
93-13-017	I Love You Hearts	M. Goena	Open	75.00	75.00
93-13-018	Empire State Building	M. Goena	Retrd.	90.00	90.00
93-13-019	Cactus	C. Hughes	Open	55.00	55.00
93-13-020	Pineapple	M. Goena	Open	30.00	30.00
93-13-021	Blue Bird Nest	C. Hughes	Open	50.00	50.00
93-13-022	Cat and Bird	C. Hughes	Open	55.00	55.00
93-13-023	Small Cloud Castle	M. Goena	Open	150.00	150.00
93-13-024	Ping Pong Bears	C. Hughes	Open	75.00	75.00
93-13-025	Birthday Cake	M. Goena	Open	75.00	75.00
93-13-026	Dolphin	C. Hughes	Open	90.00	90.00
93-13-027	Kissing Fish	M. Goena	Open	55.00	55.00
93-13-028	T-Rex	C. Hughes	Open	130.00	130.00
93-13-029	Miniature Rainbow Apple	M. Goena	Open	25.00	25.00
93-13-030	Rainbow Church	M. Goena	Open	50.00	50.00
93-13-031	Small Red Dice	M. Goena	Open	40.00	40.00
93-13-032	Black Dice	M. Goena	Open	45.00	45.00
93-13-033	Small Slot Machine	M. Goena	Open	55.00	55.00
93-13-034	Choir Bears	C. Hughes	Open	90.00	90.00
93-13-035	Charmer Jack in the Box	C. Hughes	Open	14.00	14.00
93-13-036	Charmer Basket of Flowers	C. Hughes	Open	14.00	14.00
93-13-037	Charmer AB Hearts	C. Hughes	Open	14.00	14.00
93-13-038	Charmer Turtle	C. Hughes	Open	14.00	14.00
93-13-039	Charmer Cactus	C. Hughes	Open	14.00	14.00
93-13-040	Charmer Angel	C. Hughes	Open	14.00	14.00
93-13-041	Charmer Flower Vase	M. Goena	Open	14.00	14.00
93-13-042	Charmer Aladdin's Lamp	M. Goena	Open	14.00	14.00
93-13-043	Charmer Oyster w/ Pearl AB	M. Goena	Open	14.00	14.00
93-13-044	Charmer Oyster w/ Pearl Pink Ice	M. Goena	Open	14.00	14.00
93-13-045	Charmer Pacifer	C. Hughes	Open	14.00	14.00
93-13-046	Charmer Kitten	C. Hughes	Open	19.00	19.00
93-13-047	Charmer Telephone	M. Goena	Open	19.00	19.00
93-13-048	Charmer Teddy Bear with Heart	M. Goena	Open	19.00	19.00
93-13-049	Charmer Bunny with Heart	M. Goena	Open	19.00	19.00
93-13-050	Charmer Seal with Ball	M. Goena	Open	19.00	19.00
93-13-051	Charmer Snail RB	M. Goena	Open	19.00	19.00
93-13-052	Charmer Sailboat	C. Hughes	Open	19.00	19.00
93-13-053	Charmer Bluebird	M. Goena	Open	19.00	19.00
93-13-054	Charmer Butterfly	M. Goena	Open	19.00	19.00
Iris Arc Crystal		**1994 Introductions**			
94-14-001	Blue Dolphin	C. Hughes	Retrd.	40.00	40.00
94-14-002	Kitty Jack in the Box	C. Hughes	Open	45.00	45.00
94-14-003	Baby Cradle	C. Hughes	Open	90.00	90.00
94-14-004	Catamaran	C. Hughes	Open	70.00	70.00
94-14-005	Wedding Bears	C. Hughes	Open	80.00	80.00
94-14-006	Skyscraper	M. Goena	Open	90.00	90.00
94-14-007	Charmer Oyster w/ Pearl RB	M. Goena	Open	14.95	14.95
94-14-008	Charmer Mushrooms	M. Goena	Open	19.95	19.95
94-14-009	Charmer Candle	M. Goena	Open	19.95	19.95
94-14-010	Charmer Rainbow Apple	M. Goena	Open	19.95	19.95
94-14-011	Aladdin's Lamp	M. Goena	Open	55.00	55.00
94-14-012	Bluebird Basket, Small	C. Hughes	Open	60.00	60.00
94-14-013	Fairy Tale Castle	M. Goena	Open	140.00	140.00
94-14-014	Hummingbird, Small	M. Goena	Open	55.00	55.00
94-14-015	Princess Carriage	C. Hughes	Open	150.00	150.00
94-14-016	Princess Palace	M. Goena	Open	100.00	100.00
94-14-017	Rose Vase	C. Hughes	Open	90.00	90.00
94-14-018	Roulette Bear	C. Hughes	Open	85.00	85.00
94-14-019	Birdbath	M. Goena	Open	90.00	90.00
94-14-020	Owls, Pink Ice	C. Hughes	Open	75.00	75.00
94-14-021	Double Dophins, Blue	M. Goena	Open	60.00	60.00
94-14-022	Swimming Fish	C. Hughes	Open	30.00	30.00
94-14-023	Waltzing Kitties	M. Goena	Open	90.00	90.00
94-14-024	T.V. Bear	M. Goena	Open	100.00	100.00
94-14-025	Mini Bunny w/Teddy Bear	M. Goena	Open	25.00	25.00
Iris Arc Crystal		**Limited Editions**			
83-15-001	Teddy Bear with Heart (Silver)	P. Hale	Retrd.	170.00	204.00
83-15-002	Teddy Bear with Heart (Rose)	P. Hale	Retrd.	170.00	204.00
83-15-003	Elephant	P. Hale	Retrd.	190.00	228.00
83-15-004	Peacock	P. Hale	Retrd.	140.00	168.00
86-15-005	Classic Car	T. Holliman	Retrd.	500.00	600.00
87-15-006	Carousel	T. Holliman	Retrd.	600.00	720.00
87-15-007	Eagle	P. Hale	Retrd.	700.00	840.00

		ARTIST	EDITION	ISSUE	QUOTE
88-15-008	Horse and Foal	M. Goena	Retrd.	1000.00	1200.00
89-15-009	Angel	M. Goena	Retrd.	180.00	240.00
90-15-010	Rainbow Enchanted Castle"	C. Hughes	500	1500.00	1500.00
91-15-011	Vase of Flowers	P. Hale	750	250.00	250.00
91-15-012	Country Cottage	M. Goena	300	1500.00	1500.00
91-15-013	Basket of Flowers	M. Goena	Retrd.	250.00	300.00
92-15-014	Victorian House	C. Hughes	750	270.00	290.00
92-15-015	Water Mill	M. Goena	350	900.00	950.00
92-15-016	Rainbow Cathedral	M. Goena	150	2500.00	2500.00
93-15-017	Country Church	M. Goena	350	590.00	590.00
93-15-018	Basket of Violets	M. Goena	750	190.00	190.00
93-15-019	Birdbath	M. Goena	Retrd.	190.00	190.00
93-15-020	Nob Hill Victorian	C. Hughes	250	1000.00	1000.00
94-15-021	Bluebird Basket	M. Goena	1,000	190.00	190.00
94-15-022	Mystic Star Castle	M. Goena	500	390.00	390.00
94-15-023	Garden Cottage	C. Hughes	500	390.00	390.00
94-15-024	Hummingbirds	M. Goena	750	290.00	290.00
Iris Arc Crystal	**Collector's Society Edition**				
92-16-001	Gramophone	C. Hughes	Retrd.	100.00	180.00
93-16-002	Classic Telephone	C. Hughes	Retrd.	150.00	150.00
94-16-003	Antique Clock	C. Hughes	Open	150.00	150.00
Kaiser	**Birds of America Collection**				
72-01-001	Blue Bird-496, color/base	W. Gawantka	2,500	120.00	480.00
73-01-002	Blue Jay-503, color/base	W. Gawantka	1,500	475.00	1198.00
76-01-003	Baltimore Oriole-536, color/base	G. Tagliariol	1,000	280.00	746.00
73-01-004	Cardinal-504, color/base	W. Gawantka	1,500	60.00	600.00
75-01-005	Sparrow-516, color/base	G. Tagliariol	1,500	300.00	596.00
70-01-006	Scarlet Tanager, color/base	Kaiser	Closed	60.00	90.00
XX-01-007	Sparrow Hawk-749, color/base	Kaiser	3,000	575.00	906.00
82-01-008	Hummingbird Group-660, color/base	G. Tagliariol	3,000	650.00	1232.00
81-01-009	Kingfisher-639, color/base	G. Tagliariol	Closed	45.00	60.00
73-01-010	Robin-502, color/base	W. Gawantka	1,500	340.00	718.00
XX-01-011	Robin II-537, color/base	Kaiser	1,000	260.00	888.00
XX-01-012	Robin & Worm, color/base	Kaiser	Closed	60.00	90.00
XX-01-013	Baby Titmice-501, white/base	W. Gawantka	1,200	200.00	754.00
XX-01-014	Baby Titmice-501, color/base	W. Gawantka	Closed	400.00	500.00
78-01-015	Baby Titmice-601, color/base	G. Tagliariol	2,000	Unkn.	956.00
78-01-016	Baby Titmice-601, white/base	G. Tagliariol	2,000	Unkn.	562.00
68-01-017	Pidgeon Group-475, white/base	U. Netzsch	2,000	60.00	412.00
68-01-018	Pidgeon Group-475, color/base	U. Netzsch	1,500	150.00	812.00
76-01-019	Pheasant-556, color/base	G. Tagliariol	1,500	3200.00	6020.00
84-01-020	Pheasant-715, color/base	G. Tagliariol	1,500	1000.00	1962.00
76-01-021	Pelican-534, color/base	G. Tagliariol	1,200	925.00	1768.00
XX-01-022	Pelican-534, white/base	G. Tagliariol	Closed	Unkn.	625.00
84-01-023	Peregrine Falcon-723, color/base	M. Tandy	1,500	850.00	4946.00
72-01-024	Goshawk-491, white/base	W. Gawantka	1,500	850.00	1992.00
72-01-025	Goshawk-491, color/base	W. Gawantka	1,500	2400.00	4326.00
XX-01-026	Roadrunner-492, color/base	Kaiser	Closed	350.00	900.00
72-01-027	Seagull-498, white/base	W. Gawantka	700	550.00	1586.00
72-01-028	Seagull-498, color/base	W. Gawantka	Closed	850.00	1150.00
73-01-028	Seagull-498, color bisque	W. Gawantka	Closed	Unkn.	1150.00
75-01-029	Woodpeckers-515, color/base	G. Tagliariol	800	900.00	1762.00
76-01-030	Screech Owl-532, white/base	W. Gawantka	Closed	175.00	199.00
76-01-031	Screech Owl-532, color bisque	W. Gawantka	Closed	Unkn.	175.00
XX-01-032	Horned Owl II-524, white/base	G. Tagliariol	1,000	Unkn.	918.00
XX-01-033	Horned Owl II- 524, color/base	G. Tagliariol	1,000	650.00	2170.00
69-01-034	Owl-476, color bisque	W. Gawantka	Closed	Unkn.	550.00
69-01-035	Owl -476, white bisque	W. Gawantka	Closed	Unkn.	180.00
77-01-036	Owl IV-559, color/base	G. Tagliariol	1,000	Unkn.	1270.00
XX-01-037	Snowy Owl -776, white/base	Kaiser	1,500	Unkn.	668.00
XX-01-038	Snowy Owl -776, color/base	Kaiser	1,500	Unkn.	1146.00
68-01-039	Pair of Mallards-456, white/base	U. Netzsch	2,000	75.00	518.00
68-01-040	Pair of Mallards-456, color/base	U. Netzsch	Closed	150.00	500.00
78-01-041	Pair of Mallards II-572, color/base	G. Tagliariol	1,500	Unkn.	1156.00
78-01-042	Pair of Mallards II-572, white/base	G. Tagliariol	1,500	Unkn.	2366.00
75-01-043	Wood Ducks-514, color/base	G. Tagliariol	800	Unkn.	2804.00
85-01-044	Pintails-747, white/base	Kaiser	1,500	Unkn.	364.00
85-01-045	Pintails-747, color/base	Kaiser	1,500	Unkn.	838.00
76-01-046	Canadian Geese-550, white/base	G. Tagliariol	1,500	1500.00	3490.00
81-01-047	Quails-640, color/base	G. Tagliariol	1,500	Unkn.	2366.00
79-01-048	Swan-602, color/base	G. Tagliariol	2,000	Unkn.	1370.00
69-01-049	Bald Eagle I -464, color	U. Netzsch	Closed	Unkn.	650.00
69-01-050	Bald Eagle I -464, white	U. Netzsch	Closed	Unkn.	250.00
73-01-051	Bald Eagle II -497, color bisque	G. Tagliariol	Closed	Unkn.	1300.00
74-01-052	Bald Eagle III -513, color bisque	W. Gawantka	Closed	Unkn.	850.00
74-01-053	Bald Eagle III -513,white bisque	W. Gawantka	Closed	Unkn.	378.00
76-01-054	Bald Eagle IV-552, white/base	W. Gawantka	1,500	210.00	572.00
76-01-055	Bald Eagle IV-552, color/base	W. Gawantka	1,500	450.00	998.00
78-01-056	Bald Eagle V-600, color/base	G. Tagliariol	1,500	Unkn.	3848.00
80-01-057	Bald Eagle VI-634, white/base	W. Gawantka	3,000	Unkn.	622.00
XX-01-058	Bald Eagle VII-637, color/base	G. Tagliariol	200	Unkn.	20694.00
82-01-059	Bald Eagle VIII-656, color/base	G. Tagliariol	Closed	800.00	880.00
82-01-060	Bald Eagle VIII-656, white/base	G. Tagliariol	1,000	400.00	904.00
84-01-061	Bald Eagle IX-714, white/base	W. Gawantka	4,000	190.00	374.00
84-01-062	Bald Eagle IX-714, color/base	W. Gawantka	3,500	500.00	850.00
85-01-063	Bald Eagle X-746, white/base	W. Gawantka	1,500	375.00	672.00
85-01-064	Bald Eagle X-746, color/base	W. Gawantka	1,500	Unkn.	1198.00
85-01-065	Bald Eagle XI-751, white/base	W. Gawantka	1,000	Unkn.	902.00
85-01-066	Bald Eagle XI-751, color/base	W. Gawantka	1,000	880.00	1422.00
81-01-067	Rooster-642, white/base	G. Tagliariol	1,500	380.00	688.00
81-01-068	Rooster-642, color/base	G. Tagliariol	1,500	860.00	1304.00
74-01-069	Falcon-507, color/base	W. Gawantka	1,500	820.00	1928.00
86-01-070	Sparrow Hawk-777, white bisque	M. Tandy	1,000	440.00	716.00
86-01-071	Sparrow Hawk-777, colored bisque	M. Tandy	10,000	950.00	1336.00
XX-01-072	Bald Eagle II-497, Colored	Kaiser	Closed	Unkn.	1300.00
XX-01-073	Paradise Bird-318, white bisque	Kaiser	Closed	Unkn.	135.00
XX-01-074	Fighting Peacocks -337, color glaze	G. Bochman	Closed	Unkn.	340.00
XX-01-075	Wild Ducks-456, color bisque	Kaiser	Closed	Unkn.	500.00
68-01-076	Wild Ducks-456, white bisque	Kaiser	2,000	Unkn.	175.00
72-01-077	Roadrunner-492, color bisque	W. Gawantka	1,000	175.00	199.00
Kaiser	**Horse Sculpture**				
69-02-001	Arabian Stallion-Comet, color/bisque	W. Gawantka	Closed	Unkn.	850.00
76-02-002	Hassan/Arabian-553, white/base	W. Gawantka	Closed	250.00	600.00
76-02-003	Hassan/Arabian-553, color/base	W. Gawantka	1,500	600.00	11-1200.
80-02-004	Orion/Arabian-629, color/base	W. Gawantka	2,000	600.00	1038.00
80-02-005	Orion/Arabian-629, white/base	W. Gawantka	2,000	250.00	442.00
78-02-006	Capitano/Lipizzaner- 597, white	W. Gawantka	Closed	275.00	574.00
78-02-007	Capitano/Lipizzaner- 597, color	W. Gawantka	1,500	625.00	1496.00
75-02-008	Mare & Foal II-510, color/base	W. Gawantka	Closed	650.00	775.00

		ARTIST	EDITION	ISSUE	QUOTE
75-02-009	Mare & Foal II-510, white/bisque	W. Gawantka	Closed	Unkn.	775.00
80-02-010	Mare & Foal III-636, white/base	W. Gawantka	1,500	300.00	646.00
80-02-011	Mare & Foal III-636, color/base	W. Gawantka	1,500	950.00	1632.00
71-02-012	Pony Group-488, white/base	W. Gawantka	2,500	50.00	418.00
71-02-013	Pony Group-488, color/base	W. Gawantka	Closed	Unkn.	350.00
71-02-014	Pony Group-488, color bisque	W. Gawantka	Closed	Unkn.	350.00
87-02-015	Trotter-780, white/base	W. Gawantka	1,500	574.00	652.00
87-02-016	Trotter-780, color/base	W. Gawantka	1,500	1217.00	1350.00
87-02-017	Pacer-792, white/base	W. Gawantka	1,500	574.00	652.00
87-02-018	Pacer-792, color/base	W. Gawantka	1,500	1217.00	1350.00
90-02-019	Argos-633101/wht. bisq./base	W. Gawantka	1,000	578.00	672.00
90-02-020	Argos-633103/lt. color/base	W. Gawantka	1,000	1194.00	1388.00
90-02-021	Argos-633143/color/base	W. Gawantka	1,000	1194.00	1388.00
75-02-022	Lipizzaner/Maestoso-517/color bisque	W. Gawantka	Closed	Unkn.	1150.00
75-02-023	Lipizzaner/Maestoso-517white bisque	W. Gawantka	Closed	Unkn.	750.00
Kaiser	**Animals**				
75-03-001	German Shepherd-528, white bisque	W. Gawantka	Closed	185.00	420.00
75-03-002	German Shepherd-528, color bisque	W. Gawantka	Closed	250.00	652.00
76-03-003	Irish Setter-535, color bisque	W. Gawantka	1,000	290.00	652.00
76-03-004	Irish Setter-535, white/base	W. Gawantka	1,500	Unkn.	424.00
79-03-005	Bear & Cub-521, white bisque	W. Gawantka	Closed	125.00	378.00
79-03-006	Bear & Cub-521, color bisque	W. Gawantka	900	400.00	1072.00
85-03-007	Trout-739, color bisque	W. Gawantka	Open	95.00	488.00
85-03-008	Rainbow Trout-739, color bisque	W. Gawantka	Open	250.00	488.00
85-03-009	Brook Trout-739, color bisque	W. Gawantka	Open	250.00	488.00
85-03-010	Pike-737, color bisque	W. Gawantka	Open	350.00	682.00
69-03-011	Porpoise Group (3)-478, white bisque	W. Gawantka	Closed	85.00	375.00
78-03-012	Dolphin Group (4)-596/4, white bisque	W. Gawantka	4,500	75.00	956.00
75-03-013	Dolphin Group (4)-508, white bisque	W. Gawantka	Closed	Unkn.	575.00
75-03-014	Dolphin Group (5)-520/5, white bisque	W. Gawantka	800	850.00	3002.00
78-03-015	Killer Whale-579, color/bisque	W. Gawantka	2,000	420.00	798.00
78-03-016	Killer Whale-579, white/bisque	W. Gawantka	2,000	85.00	404.00
78-03-017	Killer Whales (2)-594, color	W. Gawantka	2,000	925.00	2008.00
78-03-018	Killer Whales (2)-594, white	W. Gawantka	2,000	425.00	1024.00
82-03-019	Two wild Boars-664, color bisque	H. Liederly	1,000	650.00	890.00
80-03-020	Bison-630, color bisque	G. Tagliariol	2,000	620.00	1044.00
80-03-021	Bison-690, white bisque	G. Tagliariol	2,000	350.00	488.00
91-03-022	Lion-701203, color bisque	W. Gawantka	1,500	1300.00	1300.00
91-03-023	Lion-701201, white bisque	W. Gawantka	1,500	650.00	650.00
Kaiser	**Human Figures**				
82-04-001	Father & Son-659, white/base	W. Gawantka	2,500	100.00	384.00
82-04-002	Father & Son-659, color/base	W. Gawantka	2,500	400.00	712.00
83-04-003	Mother & Child/bust-696, white	W. Gawantka	4,000	225.00	428.00
83-04-004	Mother & Child/bust-696, color	W. Gawantka	3,500	500.00	1066.00
XX-04-005	Father & Daughter-752, white	Kaiser	2,500	175.00	362.00
XX-04-006	Father & Daughter-752, color	Kaiser	2,500	390.00	710.00
82-04-007	Swan Lake Ballet-641, white	W. Gawantka	2,500	200.00	974.00
82-04-008	Swan Lake Ballet-641, color	W. Gawantka	2,500	650.00	1276.00
82-04-009	Ice Princess-667, white	W. Gawantka	5,000	200.00	416.00
82-04-010	Ice Princess-667, color	W. Gawantka	5,000	375.00	732.00
XX-04-011	Mother & Child-757, white	Kaiser	4,000	300.00	430.00
XX-04-012	Mother & Child-757, color	Kaiser	3,500	600.00	864.00
XX-04-013	Mother & Child-775, white	Kaiser	4,000	300.00	430.00
XX-04-014	Mother & Child-775, color	Kaiser	3,500	600.00	864.00
60-04-015	Mother & Child-398, white bisque	G. Bochmann	Open	Unkn.	312.00
Lalique Society of America	**Lalique Society Annual Series**				
89-01-001	Degas Box 10585	R. Lalique	Yr.Iss.	295.00	725.00
90-01-002	Hestia Medallion 61051	M.C. Lalique	Yr.Iss.	295.00	700.00
91-01-003	Lily of Valley (perfume bottle) 61053	R. Lalique	Yr.Iss.	275.00	450.00
92-01-004	La Patineuse (paperweight) 61054	M.C. Lalique	Yr.Iss.	325.00	375.00
93-01-005	Enchantment (figurine) 61055	M.C. Lalique	Yr.Iss.	395.00	395.00
94-01-006	Eclipse (perfume bottle)	M.C. Lalique	Yr.Iss.	395.00	395.00
Lance Corporation	**Chilmark Pewter American West**				
74-01-001	Cheyenne	D. Polland	S/O	200.00	27-3000.
74-01-002	Counting Coup	D. Polland	S/O	225.00	16-2000.
74-01-003	Crow Scout	D. Polland	S/O	250.00	1-1700.
75-01-004	Maverick Calf	D. Polland	S/O	250.00	13-1700.
76-01-005	Cold Saddles, Mean Horses	D. Polland	S/O	200.00	800-1100
75-01-006	The Outlaws	D. Polland	S/O	450.00	900-1180
76-01-007	Buffalo Hunt	D. Polland	S/O	300.00	1625.00
76-01-008	Rescue	D. Polland	S/O	275.00	1150.00
76-01-009	Painting the Town	D. Polland	S/O	300.00	15-1700.
76-01-010	Monday Morning Wash	D. Polland	S/O	200.00	13-1800.
78-01-011	Dangerous Encounter	B. Rodden	Retrd.	475.00	600-950.
79-01-012	Border Rustlers	D. Polland	S/O	1295.00	1500.00
79-01-013	Mandan Hunter	D. Polland	S/O	65.00	780-900.
79-01-014	Getting Acquainted	D. Polland	S/O	215.00	800-1100
79-01-015	Cavalry Officer	D. LaRocca	S/O	125.00	400-650.
79-01-016	Cowboy	D. LaRocca	S/O	125.00	500-750.
79-01-017	Mountain Man	D. LaRocca	Retrd.	95.00	500-650.
79-01-018	Indian Warrior	D. LaRocca	Retrd.	95.00	400.00
79-01-019	Running Battle	B. Rodden	Retrd.	400.00	750-900.
81-01-020	Buffalo Robe	D. Polland	2,500	235.00	335.00
81-01-021	When War Chiefs Meet	D. Polland	S/O	300.00	800.00
81-01-022	War Party	D. Polland	Retrd.	550.00	975-1150
81-01-023	Dog Soldier	D. Polland	2,500	235.00	315.00
81-01-024	Enemy Tracks	D. Polland	S/O	225.00	700-725.
81-01-025	Ambushed	D. Polland	Retrd.	2370.00	2700.00
81-01-026	U.S. Marshal	D. Polland	S/O	95.00	450-600.
81-01-027	Plight of the Huntsman	M. Boyett	S/O	495.00	850.00
82-01-028	Last Arrow	D. Polland	S/O	95.00	300-400.
82-01-029	Sioux War Chief	D. Polland	S/O	95.00	240-480.
82-01-030	Navajo Kachina Dancer	D. Polland	2,500	95.00	115.00
82-01-031	Arapaho Drummer	D. Polland	2,500	95.00	115.00
82-01-032	Apache Hostile	D. Polland	2,500	95.00	115.00
82-01-033	Buffalo Prayer	D. Polland	S/O	95.00	225-400.
82-01-034	Jemez Eagle Dancer	D. Polland	S/O	95.00	250-450.
82-01-035	Flathead War Dancer	D. Polland	2,500	95.00	115.00
82-01-036	Hopi Kachina Dancer	D. Polland	2,500	95.00	115.00
82-01-037	Apache Gan Dancer	D. Polland	2,500	95.00	115.00
82-01-038	Crow Medicine Dancer	D. Polland	2,500	95.00	115.00
82-01-039	Comanche Plaines Drummer	D. Polland	2,500	95.00	115.00
82-01-040	Yakima Salmon Fisherman	D. Polland	S/O	200.00	700.00
82-01-041	Mustanger	D. Polland	2,500	425.00	580.00
82-01-042	Blood Brothers	M. Boyett	Retrd.	250.00	610-995.
83-01-043	Line Rider	D. Polland	S/O	195.00	975.00
83-01-044	Bounty Hunter	D. Polland	S/O	250.00	300-600.
83-01-045	The Wild Bunch	D. Polland	S/O	200.00	225-400.
83-01-046	Too Many Aces	D. Polland	Retrd.	400.00	495.00

		ARTIST	EDITION	ISSUE	QUOTE
83-01-047	Eye to Eye	D. Polland	2,500	350.00	500.00
83-01-048	Now or Never	D. Polland	Retrd.	265.00	800.00
84-01-049	Flat Out for Red River Station	M. Boyett	S/O	3000.00	45-7200.
85-01-050	Postal Exchange	S. York	Retrd.	300.00	400-600.
85-01-051	Bear Meet	S. York	Retrd.	500.00	600-800.
85-01-052	Horse of A Different Color	S. York	Retrd.	500.00	600-800.
87-01-053	Cool Waters	F. Barnum	Suspd.	350.00	395.00
87-01-054	Treed	F. Barnum	Suspd.	300.00	345.00
88-01-055	Custer's Last Stand	F. Barnum	Suspd.	350.00	395.00
88-01-056	A Father's Farewell	F. Barnum	S/O	150.00	225.00
90-01-057	Pequot Wars	D. Polland	S/O	395.00	450-800.
90-01-058	Tecumseh's Rebellion	D. Polland	S/O	350.00	700.00
90-01-059	Red River Wars	D. Polland	S/O	425.00	700-850.
90-01-060	Buffalo Spirit	D. Polland	S/O	110.00	110.00
90-01-061	Eagle Dancer (deNatura)	D. Polland	Retrd.	300.00	300.00
90-01-062	Running Wolf (deNatura)	D. Polland	Retrd.	350.00	350.00
91-01-063	Kiowa Princess (deNatura)	D. Polland	Retrd.	300.00	300.00
91-01-064	Yellow Boy (deNatura)	D. Polland	Retrd.	350.00	350.00

Lance Corporation — **Chilmark Pewter American West Redemption Specials**

83-02-001	The Chief	D. Polland	Yr.Iss.	275.00	16-2700.
84-02-002	Unit Colors	D. Polland	Yr.Iss.	250.00	12-1700.
85-02-003	Oh Great Spirit	D. Polland	Yr.Iss.	300.00	1-1300.
86-02-004	Eagle Catcher	M. Boyett	Yr.Iss.	300.00	850-1200
87-02-005	Surprise Encounter	F. Barnum	Yr.Iss.	250.00	600-800.
88-02-006	I Will Fight No More Forever (Chief Joseph)	D. Polland	Yr.Iss.	350.00	700-750.
89-02-007	Geronimo	D. Polland	Yr.Iss.	375.00	700-875.
90-02-008	Cochise	D. Polland	Yr.Iss.	400.00	600.00
91-02-009	Crazy Horse	D. Polland	Yr.Iss.	295.00	600-750.
92-02-010	Strong Hearts to the Front	D. Polland	Yr.Iss.	425.00	600.00
93-02-011	Sacred Ground Reclaimed	D. Polland	Yr.Iss.	495.00	495.00

Lance Corporation — **Chilmark Pewter American West Christmas Special**

91-03-001	Merry Christmas Neighbor	D. Polland	Annual	395.00	625.00
92-03-002	Merry Christmas My Love	D. Polland	Annual	350.00	350-450.
93-03-003	Almost Home	D. Polland	Annual	375.00	375.00

Lance Corporation — **Chilmark Pewter American West Event Specials**

91-04-001	Uneasy Truce	D. Polland	Annual	125.00	175-195.
92-04-002	Irons In The Fire	D. Polland	Annual	125.00	125.00
94-04-003	Bacon 'N' Beans Again?	D. Polland	Annual	150.00	150.00

Lance Corporation — **Chilmark Pewter Civil War Redemption Specials**

89-05-001	Lee To The Rear	F. Barnum	Yr.Iss.	300.00	600-900.
90-05-002	Lee And Jackson	F. Barnum	Yr.Iss.	375.00	500-800.
91-05-003	Stonewall Jackson	F. Barnum	Yr.Iss.	295.00	500.00
92-05-004	Zouaves 1st Manassas	F. Barnum	Yr.Iss.	375.00	375.00
93-05-005	Letter to Sarah	F. Barnum	Yr.Iss.	395.00	395.00

Lance Corporation — **Chilmark Pewter Civil War Event Specials**

91-06-001	Boots and Saddles	F. Barnum	Annual	95.00	200.00
92-06-002	140th NY Zouave	F. Barnum	Annual	95.00	150.00
93-06-003	Johnny Reb	F. Barnum	Annual	95.00	125.00
94-06-004	Billy Yank	F. Barnum	Annual	95.00	95.00

Lance Corporation — **Chilmark Pewter Civil War Christmas Specials**

92-07-001	Merry Christmas Yank	F. Barnum	Annual	350.00	400.00
93-07-002	Silent Night	F. Barnum	Annual	350.00	475.00

Lance Corporation — **Chilmark Pewter Wildlife**

78-08-001	Buffalo	B. Rodden	S/O	170.00	375-400.
79-08-002	Elephant	D. Polland	S/O	315.00	450-550.
79-08-003	Giraffe	D. Polland	S/O	145.00	145.00
79-08-004	Kudu	D. Polland	S/O	160.00	160.00
79-08-005	Rhino	D. Polland	S/O	135.00	135-550.
80-08-006	Ruby-Throated Hummingbird	V. Hayton	S/O	275.00	350.00
80-08-007	Prairie Sovereign	M. Boyett	Retrd.	550.00	800.00
80-08-008	Duel of the Bighorns	M. Boyett	Retrd.	650.00	1200.00
80-08-009	Lead Can't Catch Him	M. Boyett	Retrd.	645.00	845.00
80-08-010	Voice of Experience	M. Boyett	Retrd.	645.00	850.00
88-08-011	The Patriarch	F. Barnum	Suspd.	350.00	395.00
88-08-012	Fishing Lesson	F. Barnum	Suspd.	325.00	365.00
89-08-013	Summit	F. Barnum	Suspd.	250.00	265.00

Lance Corporation — **Chilmark Pewter Horses**

76-09-001	Stallion	B. Rodden	S/O	75.00	260.00
76-09-002	Running Free	B. Rodden	S/O	75.00	300.00
77-09-003	Rise and Shine	B. Rodden	S/O	135.00	200.00
77-09-004	The Challenge	B. Rodden	S/O	175.00	250-300.
78-09-005	Paddock Walk	A. Petitto	Retrd.	85.00	215.00
80-09-006	Born Free	B. Rodden	S/O	250.00	500-680.
80-09-007	Affirmed	M. Jovine	Retrd.	850.00	1275.00
81-09-008	Clydesdale Wheel Horse	C. Keim	Retrd.	120.00	430.00
82-09-009	Tender Persuasion	J. Mootry	Retrd.	950.00	1250.00
85-09-010	Fighting Stallions	D. Polland	2,500	225.00	300.00
85-09-011	Wild Stallion	D. Polland	Retrd.	145.00	350.00

Lance Corporation — **Chilmark Pewter Rodeo**

85-10-001	Saddle Bronc Rider	D. Polland	2,500	250.00	315.00
85-10-002	Bareback Rider	D. Polland	2,500	225.00	315.00
85-10-003	Bull Rider	D. Polland	2,500	265.00	350.00
85-10-004	Steer Wrestling	D. Polland	2,500	500.00	635.00
85-10-005	Team Roping	D. Polland	2,500	500.00	660.00
85-10-006	Calf Roper	D. Polland	2,500	300.00	395.00
85-10-007	Barrel Racer	D. Polland	2,500	275.00	345.00

Lance Corporation — **Chilmark Pewter Legacy of Courage**

81-11-001	Apache Signals	M. Boyett	Retrd.	175.00	550-575.
81-11-002	Iroquois Warfare	M. Boyett	Retrd.	125.00	600.00
81-11-003	Victor Cheyenne	M. Boyett	Retrd.	175.00	500.00
81-11-004	Buffalo Stalker	M. Boyett	Retrd.	175.00	560.00
81-11-005	Comanche	M. Boyett	Retrd.	175.00	530-670.
81-11-006	Unconquered Seminole	M. Boyett	Retrd.	175.00	540.00
81-11-007	Blackfoot Snow Hunter	M. Boyett	Retrd.	175.00	650.00
82-11-008	Shoshone Eagle Catcher	M. Boyett	S/O	225.00	16-2000.
82-11-009	Plains Talk-Pawnee	M. Boyett	Retrd.	195.00	625.00
82-11-010	Kiowa Scout	M. Boyett	Retrd.	195.00	525.00
82-11-011	Mandan Buffalo Dancer	M. Boyett	Retrd.	195.00	450-600.
82-11-012	Listening For Hooves	M. Boyett	Retrd.	150.00	400.00
82-11-013	Arapaho Sentinel	M. Boyett	Retrd.	195.00	500.00
82-11-014	Dance of the Eagles	M. Boyett	Retrd.	150.00	215.00
82-11-015	The Tracker Nez Perce	M. Boyett	Retrd.	150.00	575.00
83-11-016	Moment of Truth	M. Boyett	Retrd.	295.00	550-620.
83-11-017	Winter Hunt	M. Boyett	Retrd.	295.00	400.00
83-11-018	Along the Cherokee Trace	M. Boyett	Retrd.	295.00	720.00
83-11-019	Forest Watcher	M. Boyett	Retrd.	215.00	540.00
83-11-020	Rite of the Whitetail	M. Boyett	Retrd.	295.00	400.00
83-11-021	Circling the Enemy	M. Boyett	Retrd.	295.00	395.00
83-11-022	A Warrior's Tribute	M. Boyett	Retrd.	335.00	635.00

Lance Corporation — **Chilmark Pewter OffCanvas™**

90-12-001	Smoke Signal	A. T. McGrory	S/O	345.00	550-700.
90-12-002	Vigil	A. T. McGrory	S/O	345.00	500-700.
90-12-003	Warrior	A. T. McGrory	S/O	300.00	350-600.
91-12-004	Blanket Signal	A. T. McGrory	S/O	750.00	850.00

Lance Corporation — **Chilmark Pewter Sculptures**

79-13-001	Unicorn	R. Sylvan	S/O	115.00	550.00
79-13-002	Carousel	R. Sylvan	S/O	115.00	115.00
79-13-003	Moses	B. Rodden	S/O	140.00	235.00
79-13-004	Pegasus	R. Sylvan	Retrd.	95.00	175.00
80-13-005	Charge of the 7th Cavalry	B. Rodden	Retrd.	600.00	950.00
81-13-006	Budweiser Wagon	C. Keim	Retrd.	2000.00	3000.00
83-13-007	Dragon Slayer	D. LaRocca	Retrd.	385.00	500.00
84-13-008	Garden Unicorn	J. Royce	Retrd.	160.00	200.00
86-13-009	Camelot Chess Set	P. Jackson	Retrd.	2250.00	2250.00
92-13-010	Christopher Columbus	D. LaRocca	Retrd.	295.00	295.00

Lance Corporation — **Chilmark Pewter The Sorcerer's Apprentice Collectors Series**

90-14-001	The Sorcerer's Apprentice	Staff	2,500	225.00	240.00
90-14-002	The Incantation	Staff	2,500	150.00	160.00
90-14-003	The Dream	Staff	2,500	225.00	240.00
90-14-004	The Whirlpool	Staff	2,500	225.00	250.00
90-14-005	The Repentant Apprentice	Staff	Retrd.	195.00	205.00

Lance Corporation — **Chilmark Pewter Mickey & Co.**

89-15-001	Hollywood Mickey	Staff	Suspd.	165.00	225-350.
89-15-002	"Gold Edition" Hollywood Mickey	Staff	Retrd.	200.00	N/A
91-15-003	Mickey's Carousel Ride	Staff	2,500	150.00	160.00
92-15-004	Minnie's Carousel Ride	Staff	2,500	150.00	160.00
94-15-005	Mouse in a Million (Bronze)	Staff	S/O	1250.00	N/A
94-15-006	Mouse in a Million (MetalART))	Staff	S/O	650.00	850.00
94-15-007	Mouse in a Million (Pewter)	Staff	S/O	500.00	600.00
94-15-008	Mickey on Parade (Bronze)	Staff	S/O	950.00	950.00
94-15-009	Mickey on Parade (MetalART))	Staff	S/O	500.00	500.00
94-15-010	Mickey on Parade (Pewter)	Staff	S/O	375.00	375.00
94-15-011	Lights, Camera, Action (Bronze)	Staff	50	3250.00	3250.00
94-15-012	Lights, Camera, Action (Pewter)	Staff	500	1500.00	1500.00
94-15-013	Puttin' on the Ritz (Bronze)	Staff	50	2000.00	2000.00
94-15-014	Puttin' on the Ritz (MetalART))	Staff	250	1000.00	1000.00
94-15-015	Puttin' on the Ritz (Pewter)	Staff	350	750.00	750.00

Lance Corporation — **Chilmark Pewter Mickey & Co. Sweethearts**

94-16-001	Jitterbugging	Staff	S/O	450.00	450.00
94-16-002	Rowboat Serenade	Staff	S/O	495.00	495.00

Lance Corporation — **Chilmark Pewter Mickey & Co. Comic Capers**

94-17-001	Foursome Follies (Bronze)	Staff	S/O	2000.00	2000.00
94-17-002	Foursome Follies (Pewter)	Staff	S/O	750.00	750.00

Lance Corporation — **Chilmark Pewter Mickey & Co. Two Wheeling**

94-18-001	Get Your Motor Runnin' (Bronze)	Staff	S/O	1200.00	1200.00
94-18-002	Get Your Motor Runnin' (Pewter)	Staff	S/O	475.00	750.00

Lance Corporation — **Chilmark Pewter Mickey & Co. Invitation-Only Special**

94-19-001	Bicycle Built For Two	Staff	Yr.Iss.	195.00	195.00

Lance Corporation — **Chilmark Pewter Mickey & Co. Christmas**

93-20-001	Checking it Twice	Staff	Yr.Iss.	195.00	250.00
93-20-002	Hanging the Stockings	Staff	Yr.Iss.	295.00	350-450.

Lance Corporation — **Chilmark Pewter Generations of Mickey**

87-21-001	Antique Mickey	Staff	S/O	95.00	475-650.
89-21-002	Steamboat Willie	Staff	S/O	165.00	200-350.
89-21-003	Sorcerer's Apprentice	Staff	S/O	150.00	225.00
89-21-004	Mickey's Gala Premiere	Staff	2,500	150.00	160.00
90-21-005	Disneyland Mickey	Staff	2,500	150.00	160.00
90-21-006	The Band Concert	Staff	2,500	185.00	195.00
90-21-007	The Band Concert (Painted)	Staff	S/O	215.00	250-500.
91-21-008	Plane Crazy-1928	Staff	2,500	175.00	185.00
91-21-009	The Mouse-1935	Staff	1,200	185.00	195.00

Lance Corporation — **Chilmark Pewter The Adversaries**

91-22-001	Robert E. Lee	F. Barnum	S/O	350.00	12-1300.
92-22-002	Ulysses S. Grant	F. Barnum	S/O	350.00	600-750.
92-22-003	Stonewall Jackson	F. Barnum	S/O	375.00	375-850.
93-22-004	Wm. Tecumseh Sherman	F. Barnum	S/O	375.00	375-750.

Lance Corporation — **Chilmark Pewter Civil War**

87-23-001	Saving The Colors	F. Barnum	Retrd.	350.00	700.00
88-23-002	Johnny Shiloh	F. Barnum	S/O	100.00	220.00
92-23-003	Kennesaw Mountain	F. Barnum	S/O	650.00	765-1300
92-23-004	Parson's Battery	F. Barnum	S/O	495.00	500-575.
93-23-005	Abraham Lincoln Bust (Bronze)	F. Barnum	S/O	2000.00	2250.00
94-23-006	Gentleman Soldier (Bronze)	F. Barnum	S/O	1500.00	1500.00

Lance Corporation — **Chilmark Pewter Eagles**

81-24-001	Freedom Eagle	G. deLodzia	S/O	195.00	750-900.
82-24-002	Wings of Liberty	M. Boyett	S/O	625.00	1200.00
87-24-003	Winged Victory	J. Mullican	Suspd.	275.00	315.00
89-24-004	High and Mighty	A. McGrory	Suspd.	185.00	200.00
91-24-005	Cry of Freedom	S. Knight	Suspd.	395.00	395.00

Lance Corporation — **Chilmark Pewter Masters of the American West**

84-25-001	Cheyenne (Remington)	C. Rousell	Retrd.	400.00	600.00
85-25-002	Bronco Buster (Large)	C. Rousell	Retrd.	400.00	400.00
86-25-003	Buffalo Hunt	A. McGrory	Retrd.	550.00	800.00
88-25-004	End of the Trail (Mini)	A. McGrory	S/O	225.00	325.00
89-25-005	Trooper of the Plains	A. McGrory	Suspd.	250.00	265.00
89-25-006	The Triumph	A. McGrory	Suspd.	275.00	290.00
90-25-007	Remington Self Portrait	A. McGrory	Suspd.	275.00	275.00

Lance Corporation — **Chilmark Pewter The Cavalry Generals**

92-26-001	J.E.B. Stuart	F. Barnum	S/O	375.00	375.00
93-26-002	George Armstrong Custer	F. Barnum	950	375.00	375.00
93-26-003	Nathan Bedford Forrest	F. Barnum	950	375.00	375.00
94-26-004	Philip Sheridan	F. Barnum	950	375.00	375.00

Lance Corporation — **Chilmark Pewter World War II**

90-27-001	Navy Pearl Harbor	D. LaRocca	Suspd.	425.00	450.00
90-27-002	Army Corregidor	D. LaRocca	Suspd.	315.00	325.00

	ARTIST	EDITION	ISSUE	QUOTE
90-27-003 Air Corps Hickam Field	D. LaRocca	Suspd.	200.00	210.00
90-27-004 Marines Wake Island	D. LaRocca	Suspd.	200.00	210.00
91-27-005 Marines In Solomons	D. LaRocca	Suspd.	275.00	275.00
91-27-006 Army North Africa	D. LaRocca	Suspd.	375.00	375.00
91-27-007 Navy North Atlantic	D. LaRocca	Suspd.	375.00	375.00
91-27-008 Air Corps Tokyo Raid	D. LaRocca	Suspd.	350.00	350.00
Lance Corporation	**Chilmark Pewter Beautiful Women**			
84-28-001 Sibyl	A. Kann	Suspd.	150.00	165-375.
84-28-002 Adrienne	A. Kann	Suspd.	175.00	195.00
84-28-003 Clarisse	A. Kann	Suspd.	195.00	200.00
84-28-004 Desiree	A. Kann	Suspd.	195.00	200.00
85-28-005 Giselle	A. Kann	Suspd.	225.00	225.00
89-28-006 Michelle	A. Kann	Suspd.	350.00	365.00
Lance Corporation	**Chilmark Pewter The Ballet**			
89-29-001 Nadia	S. Feldman	Suspd.	250.00	275.00
89-29-002 The Pair	S. Feldman	Suspd.	300.00	315.00
89-29-003 Anna	S. Feldman	Suspd.	350.00	375.00
Lance Corporation	**Chilmark MetalART™ The Great Chiefs**			
92-30-001 Chief Joseph	J. Slockbower	S/O	975.00	15-1900.
92-30-002 Geronimo	J. Slockbower	S/O	975.00	975.00
93-30-003 Sitting Bull	J. Slockbower	750	1075.00	1075.00
93-30-004 Crazy Horse	J. Slockbower	750	975.00	975.00
Lance Corporation	**Chilmark Pewter/MetalART™ The Warriors**			
92-31-001 Spirit of the Wolf (pewter)	D. Polland	S/O	350.00	850.00
93-31-002 Son of the Morning Star (pewter)	D. Polland	S/O	375.00	460.00
92-31-003 Spirit of the Wolf (MetalART)	D. Polland	1,000	500.00	500.00
93-31-004 Son of the Morning Star (MetalART)	D. Polland	1,000	495.00	495.00
Lance Corporation	**Chilmark Pewter/MetalART™ The Medicine Men**			
92-32-001 False Face (pewter)	D. Polland	S/O	375.00	375.00
92-32-002 False Face (MetalART)	D. Polland	1,000	550.00	550.00
Lance Corporation	**Chilmark MetalART™ To The Great Spirit**			
92-33-001 Shooting Star	T. Sullivan	S/O	775.00	775.00
93-33-002 Two Eagles	T. Sullivan	950	775.00	775.00
93-33-003 Gray Elk	T. Sullivan	950	775.00	775.00
94-33-004 Thunder Cloud	T. Sullivan	950	775.00	775.00
Lance Corporation	**Chilmark MetalART™ Mickey & Co. On the Road**			
92-34-001 Cruising	Staff	S/O	275.00	1500.00
93-34-002 Sunday Drive	Staff	S/O	325.00	800-1250
94-34-003 Beach Bound	Staff	S/O	350.00	600-950.
Lance Corporation	**Chilmark MetalART™ The Seekers**			
92-35-001 Buffalo Vision	A. McGrory	S/O	1075.00	1075.00
93-35-002 Eagle Vision	A. McGrory	500	1250.00	1250.00
93-35-003 Bear Vision	A. McGrory	500	1375.00	1375.00
Lance Corporation	**Chilmark Pewter Turning Points**			
93-36-001 The High Tide	F. Barnum	S/O	600.00	900.00
94-36-002 Clashing Sabers	F. Barnum	500	600.00	600.00
Lance Corporation	**cp smithshire™ Annual Santa**			
93-37-001 St. Nicholai	C. Smith	Yr.Iss.	75.00	75.00
94-37-002 Santa and Nicky	C. Smith	Yr.Iss.	90.00	90.00
Lance Corporation	**cp smithshire™ Event Figurine**			
93-38-001 Sap	C. Smith	Yr.Iss.	60.00	60.00
Lance Corporation	**cp smithshire™-Gone Home to the Forest**			
93-39-001 Florence and Lila	C. Smith	Retrd.	80.00	80.00
93-39-002 Chipper	C. Smith	Retrd.	70.00	70.00
93-39-003 Hyde N' Seek	C. Smith	Retrd.	70.00	70.00
Lance Corporation	**Pere Noel Collection**			
94-40-001 Father Christmas	C. Smith	750	150.00	150.00
94-40-002 Christ Kindle	C. Smith	3,500	95.00	95.00
94-40-003 Checking His List	C. Smith	3,500	75.00	75.00
94-40-004 Grandfather Frost	C. Smith	3,500	75.00	75.00
94-40-005 Sinter Klaas	C. Smith	3,500	75.00	75.00
94-40-006 Pere Noel	C. Smith	3,500	75.00	75.00
94-40-007 Santa Claus	C. Smith	3,500	75.00	75.00
Lance Corporation	**Pangaean Society Member Only Redemption Specials**			
93-41-001 Dentzel	C. Smith	12/94	90.00	90.00
Lance Corporation	**Pangaean Society Membership Figurines**			
93-42-001 Fellowship Inn	C. Smith	12/94	Gift	N/A
Lance Corporation	**Sebastian Miniature Figurines**			
83-43-001 Harry Hood	P.W. Baston, Jr.	S/O	Unkn.	200-250.
85-43-002 It's Hoods (Wagon)	P.W. Baston, Jr.	S/O	Unkn.	150-175.
86-43-003 Statue of Liberty (AT & T)	P.W. Baston, Jr.	S/O	Unkn.	175-200.
87-43-004 White House (Gold, Oval Base)	P.W. Baston, Jr.	S/O	17.00	75-100.
90-43-005 America's Hometown	P.W. Baston, Jr.	4,750	34.00	34.00
91-43-006 America Salutes Desert Storm-painted	P.W. Baston, Jr.	S/O	49.50	200-325.
91-43-007 America Salutes Desert Storm-bronze	P.W. Baston, Jr.	Retrd.	26.50	100.00
91-43-008 Happy Hood Holidays	P.W. Baston, Jr.	2,000	32.50	85.00
92-43-009 Firefighter	P.W. Baston, Jr.	S/O	28.00	50.00
92-43-010 I Know I Left It Here Somewhere	P.W. Baston, Jr.	1,000	28.50	28.50
93-43-011 Soap Box Derby	P.W. Baston, Jr.	500	45.00	45.00
93-43-012 The Lamplighter	P.W. Baston, Jr.	1,000	28.00	28.00
93-43-013 Pumpkin Island Light	P.W. Baston, Jr.	3,500	55.00	55.00
94-43-014 A Job Well Done	P.W. Baston, Jr.	1,000	27.50	27.50
94-43-015 Boston Light	P.W. Baston, Jr.	3,500	45.00	45.00
94-43-016 Nubble Light	P.W. Baston, Jr.	3,500	45.00	45.00
94-43-017 Egg Rock Light	P.W. Baston, Jr.	3,500	55.00	55.00
Lance Corporation	**Sebastian Miniatures Children At Play**			
78-44-001 Sidewalk Days Boy	P.W. Baston	S/O	19.50	35-50.00
78-44-002 Sidewalk Days Girl	P.W. Baston	S/O	19.50	30-50.00
79-44-003 Building Days Boy	P.W. Baston	S/O	19.50	20-40.00
79-44-004 Building Days Girl	P.W. Baston	S/O	19.50	20-40.00
80-44-005 Snow Days Boy	P.W. Baston	S/O	19.50	20-40.00
80-44-006 Snow Days Girl	P.W. Baston	S/O	19.50	20-40.00
81-44-007 Sailing Days Boy	P.W. Baston	S/O	19.50	20-30.00
81-44-008 Sailing Days Girl	P.W. Baston	S/O	19.50	20-30.00
82-44-009 School Days Boy	P.W. Baston	S/O	19.50	20-30.00
82-44-010 School Days Girl	P.W. Baston	S/O	19.50	20-30.00
Lance Corporation	**Sebastian Miniatures America Remembers**			
79-45-001 Family Sing	P.W. Baston	Yr.Iss.	29.50	125-150.
80-45-002 Family Picnic	P.W. Baston	Yr.Iss.	29.50	30-60.00
81-45-003 Family Reads Aloud	P.W. Baston	Yr.Iss.	34.50	34.50

	ARTIST	EDITION	ISSUE	QUOTE
82-45-004 Family Fishing	P.W. Baston	Yr.Iss.	34.50	34.50
83-45-005 Family Feast	P.W. Baston	Yr.Iss.	37.50	100-150.
Lance Corporation	**Sebastian Miniatures Jimmy Fund**			
83-46-001 Schoolboy	P.W. Baston	Yr.Iss.	24.50	35-75.00
84-46-002 Catcher	P.W. Baston	Yr.Iss.	24.50	35-75.00
85-46-003 Hockey Player	P.W. Baston,Jr.	Yr.Iss.	24.50	35-50.00
86-46-004 Soccer Player	P.W. Baston,Jr.	Yr.Iss.	25.00	25.00
87-46-005 Football Player	P.W. Baston,Jr.	Yr.Iss.	26.50	26.50
88-46-006 Santa	P.W. Baston,Jr.	Closed	32.50	32.50
93-46-007 Boy With Ducks	P.W. Baston,Jr.	500	27.50	27.50
94-46-008 Girl on Bench	P.W. Baston,Jr.	500	28.00	28.00
Lance Corporation	**Sebastian Miniatures Exchange Figurines**			
83-47-001 Newspaper Boy	P.W. Baston	Yr.Iss.	28.50	60-95.00
84-47-002 First Things First	P.W. Baston,Jr.	Yr.Iss.	30.00	45.00
85-47-003 Newstand	P.W. Baston,Jr.	Yr.Iss.	30.00	45.00
86-47-004 News Wagon	P.W. Baston,Jr.	Yr.Iss.	35.00	45.00
87-47-005 It's About Time	P.W. Baston,Jr.	Yr.Iss.	25.00	40.00
Lance Corporation	**Sebastian Miniatures Washington Irving-Member Only**			
80-48-001 Rip Van Winkle	P.W. Baston	Closed	19.50	19.50
81-48-002 Dame Van Winkle	P.W. Baston	Closed	19.50	19.50
81-48-003 Ichabod Crane	P.W. Baston	Closed	19.50	19.50
82-48-004 Katrina Van Tassel	P.W. Baston	Closed	19.50	19.50
82-48-005 Brom Bones(Headless Horseman)	P.W. Baston	Closed	22.50	22.50
83-48-006 Diedrich Knickerbocker	P.W. Baston	Closed	22.50	22.50
Lance Corporation	**Sebastian Miniatures Shakespearean-Member Only**			
84-49-001 Henry VIII	P.W. Baston	Yr.Iss.	19.50	19.50
84-49-002 Anne Boyeln	P.W. Baston	6-mo.	17.50	17.50
85-49-003 Falstaff	P.W. Baston	Yr.Iss.	19.50	19.50
85-49-004 Mistress Ford	P.W. Baston	6-mo.	17.50	17.50
86-49-005 Romeo	P.W. Baston	Yr.Iss.	19.50	19.50
86-49-006 Juliet	P.W. Baston	6-mo.	17.50	17.50
87-49-007 Malvolio	P.W. Baston	Yr.Iss.	21.50	21.50
87-49-008 Countess Olivia	P.W. Baston	6-mo.	19.50	19.50
88-49-009 Touchstone	P.W. Baston	Yr.Iss.	22.50	22.50
88-49-010 Audrey	P.W. Baston	6-mo.	22.50	22.50
89-49-011 Mark Anthony	P.W. Baston	Yr.Iss.	27.00	27.00
89-49-012 Cleopatra	P.W. Baston	6-mo.	27.00	27.00
88-49-013 Shakespeare	P.W. Baston,Jr.	Yr.Iss.	23.50	23.50
Lance Corporation	**Sebastian Miniatures Member Only**			
89-50-001 The Collectors	P.W. Baston,Jr.	Yr.Iss.	39.50	39.50
92-50-002 Christopher Columbus	P.W. Baston,Jr.	Yr.Iss.	28.50	28.50
Lance Corporation	**Sebastian Miniatures Holiday Memories-Member Only**			
90-51-001 Thanksgiving Helper	P.W. Baston,Jr.	Yr.Iss.	39.50	39.50
90-51-002 Leprechaun	P.W. Baston,Jr.	Yr.Iss.	27.50	27.50
91-51-003 Trick or Treat	P.W. Baston,Jr.	Yr.Iss.	25.50	25.50
93-51-004 Father Time	P.W. Baston,Jr.	Yr.Iss.	27.50	27.50
93-51-005 New Year Baby	P.W. Baston,Jr.	Yr.Iss.	27.50	27.50
Lance Corporation	**Sebastian Miniatures Collectors Society**			
80-52-001 S.M.C. Society Plaque ('80 Charter)	P.W. Baston	Yr.Iss.	Unkn.	50-75.00
81-52-002 S.M.C. Society Plaque	P.W. Baston	Yr.Iss.	Unkn.	20-30.00
82-52-003 S.M.C. Society Plaque	P.W. Baston	Yr.Iss.	Unkn.	20-30.00
83-52-004 S.M.C. Society Plaque	P.W. Baston	Yr.Iss.	Unkn.	20-30.00
84-52-005 S.M.C. Society Plaque	P.W. Baston	Yr.Iss.	Unkn.	20-30.00
84-52-006 Self Portrait	P.W. Baston	Open	34.50	45.00
Lance Corporation	**Sebastian Miniatures Christmas**			
93-53-001 Caroling With Santa	P.W. Baston,Jr.	1,000	29.00	29.00
93-53-002 Harmonizing With Santa	P.W. Baston,Jr.	1,000	27.00	27.00
94-53-003 Victorian Christmas Skaters	P.W. Baston,Jr.	1,000	32.50	32.50
Lance Corporation	**Sebastian Miniatures Firefighter Collection**			
93-54-001 Firefighter No. 1	P.W. Baston,Jr.	950	48.00	48.00
94-54-002 Firefighter No. 2	P.W. Baston,Jr.	950	48.00	48.00
Lance Corporation	**Hudson Pewter Figures**			
69-55-001 George Washington (Cannon)	P.W. Baston	Closed	35.00	75-100.
69-55-002 John Hancock	P.W. Baston	Closed	15.00	100-125.
69-55-003 Colonial Blacksmith	P.W. Baston	Closed	30.00	100-125.
69-55-004 Betsy Ross	P.W. Baston	Closed	30.00	100-125.
72-55-005 Benjamin Franklin	P.W. Baston	Closed	15.00	75-100.
72-55-006 Thomas Jefferson	P.W. Baston	Closed	15.00	75-100.
72-55-007 George Washington	P.W. Baston	Closed	15.00	75-100.
72-55-008 John Adams	P.W. Baston	Closed	15.00	75-100.
72-55-009 James Madison	P.W. Baston	Closed	15.00	50-75.00
75-55-010 Declaration Wall Plaque	P.W. Baston	Closed	Unkn.	300-500.
75-55-011 Washington's Letter of Acceptance	P.W. Baston	Closed	Unkn.	300-400.
75-55-012 Lincoln's Gettysburg Address	P.W. Baston	Closed	Unkn.	300-400.
75-55-013 Lee's Ninth General Order	P.W. Baston	Closed	Unkn.	300-400.
75-55-014 The Favored Scholar	P.W. Baston	Closed	Unkn.	600-1000
75-55-015 Neighboring Pews	P.W. Baston	Closed	Unkn.	600-1000
75-55-016 Weighing the Baby	P.W. Baston	Closed	Unkn.	600-1000
75-55-017 Spirit of '76	P.W. Baston	Closed	Unkn.	750-1500
76-55-018 Great Horned Owl	H. Wilson	Closed	Unkn.	41.50
76-55-019 Bald Eagle	H. Wilson	Closed	100.00	112.50
Lance Corporation	**Hudson Pewter Crystals of Zorn**			
88-56-001 Guarding the Crystal	D. Liberty	950	450.00	460.00
88-56-002 Charging the Stone	D. Liberty	950	375.00	395.00
88-56-003 USS Strikes Back	D. Liberty	500	650.00	675.00
88-56-004 Response of Ornic Force	D. Liberty	950	275.00	285.00
88-56-005 Battle on the Plains of Xenon	D. Liberty	950	250.00	265.00
88-56-006 Restoration	D. Liberty	950	425.00	435.00
90-56-007 Struggle For Supremacy	D. Liberty	950	395.00	400.00
90-56-008 Asmund's Workshop	D. Liberty	950	275.00	275.00
90-56-009 Vesting The Grail	D. Liberty	950	200.00	200.00
Lance Corporation	**Military Commemoratives**			
91-57-001 Desert Liberator (Pewter)	D. LaRocca	Retrd.	295.00	295.00
91-57-002 Desert Liberator (Painted Porcelain)	D. LaRocca	Retrd.	125.00	125.00
Lance Corporation	**Hudson Pewter The Villagers-Retired**			
87-58-001 Mr. Bosworth	Hudson Studios	Retrd.	35.00	35.00
87-58-002 Emily	Hudson Studios	Retrd.	23.00	23.00
87-58-003 Reginald	Hudson Studios	Retrd.	23.00	23.00
87-58-004 Oliver	Hudson Studios	Retrd.	20.00	20.00
87-58-005 Jenny	Hudson Studios	Retrd.	20.00	20.00
87-58-006 Thomas	Hudson Studios	Retrd.	20.00	20.00
87-58-007 Mr. Hazen	Hudson Studios	Retrd.	24.00	24.00
88-58-008 Melissa	Hudson Studios	Retrd.	18.00	18.00

		ARTIST	EDITION	ISSUE	QUOTE
88-58-009	Tully's Pond	Hudson Studios	Retrd.	49.00	49.00
88-58-010	Main Street	Hudson Studios	Retrd.	47.00	47.00
88-58-011	Bosworth Manor	Hudson Studios	Retrd.	57.00	57.00
88-58-012	Santa	Hudson Studios	Retrd.	28.00	28.00
88-58-013	Nellie	Hudson Studios	Retrd.	41.00	41.00
89-58-014	Grandpa Todd	Hudson Studios	Retrd.	23.00	23.00
89-58-015	Grandma Todd & Sarah	Hudson Studios	Retrd.	29.00	29.00
89-58-016	Rascal	Hudson Studios	Retrd.	25.00	25.00
89-58-017	Creche	Hudson Studios	Retrd.	15.00	15.00
89-58-018	Ben Torpey	Hudson Studios	Retrd.	28.00	28.00
89-58-019	Villagers Plaque	Hudson Studios	Retrd.	27.00	27.00
89-58-020	Danny	Hudson Studios	Retrd.	19.00	19.00
89-58-021	Mrs. Dillman and Amanda	Hudson Studios	Retrd.	42.00	42.00
90-58-022	Toy Shop	Hudson Studios	Retrd.	60.00	60.00
90-58-023	Sweet Shop	Hudson Studios	Retrd.	50.00	50.00
90-58-024	Cliff	Hudson Studios	Retrd.	37.00	37.00
90-58-025	Johnny Hart	Hudson Studios	Retrd.	24.00	24.00
90-58-026	Mrs. Bosworth	Hudson Studios	Retrd.	29.00	29.00
90-58-027	Mrs. Fearnley	Hudson Studios	Retrd.	24.00	24.00
90-58-028	Mr. Whiteaker	Hudson Studios	Retrd.	24.00	24.00
90-58-029	Bakery	Hudson Studios	Retrd.	95.00	95.00
90-58-030	Mr. Morgan	Hudson Studios	Retrd.	37.00	37.00
91-58-031	Hudson Depot	Hudson Studios	Retrd.	58.00	58.00
91-58-032	"Skip" Mc Keever	Hudson Studios	Retrd.	24.00	24.00
91-58-033	Mr. LeClair	Hudson Studios	Retrd.	24.00	24.00
91-58-034	Mr. and Mrs. Howard	Hudson Studios	Retrd.	37.00	37.00
91-58-035	Billy Mitchell	Hudson Studios	Retrd.	41.00	41.00
91-58-036	Peeble's Market	Hudson Studios	Retrd.	72.00	72.00
91-58-037	Ed Peeble	Hudson Studios	Retrd.	24.00	24.00
91-58-038	Jeff	Hudson Studios	Retrd.	25.00	25.00
91-58-039	Hudson Town Hall	Hudson Studios	Retrd.	72.00	72.00
91-58-040	Alderman Petersen	Hudson Studios	Retrd.	27.00	27.00
91-58-041	Mayor Bower	Hudson Studios	Retrd.	27.00	27.00
91-58-042	Claff	Hudson Studios	Retrd.	29.00	29.00
91-58-043	Mrs. McNally	Hudson Studios	Retrd.	27.00	27.00
91-58-044	Delivery Wagon	Hudson Studios	Retrd.	39.00	39.00
91-58-045	"Doc" Walker	Hudson Studios	Retrd.	37.00	37.00
91-58-046	Andrew	Hudson Studios	Retrd.	15.00	15.00
91-58-047	Cannon	Hudson Studios	Retrd.	20.00	20.00
Lance Corporation		**Hudson Pewter The Villagers-Limited Editions**			
92-59-001	Crack the Whip	Hudson Studios	S/O	95.00	95.00
93-59-002	Toboggan Ride	Hudson Studios	1,500	110.00	110.00
93-59-003	Family Caroling	Hudson Studios	1,500	95.00	95.00
94-59-004	John and Julie	Hudson Studios	1,500	75.00	75.00
94-59-005	Building a Snowman	Hudson Studios	1,500	150.00	150.00
Lance Corporation		**Hudson Pewter Summer Villagers-Limited Editions**			
94-60-001	Ring Around the Rosie	Hudson Studios	1,500	110.00	110.00
94-60-002	Woody and Marge	Hudson Studios	1,500	95.00	95.00
Lance Corporation		**Hudson Pewter The Villagers-Annual Santa**			
89-61-001	Seated Santa	Hudson Studios	Yr.Iss.	25.00	25.00
90-61-002	Santa & Holly	Hudson Studios	Yr.Iss.	32.00	32.00
91-61-003	Santa and Matthew	Hudson Studios	Yr.Iss.	35.00	35.00
92-61-004	Santa with Teddy	Hudson Studios	Yr.Iss.	32.00	32.00
93-61-005	Special Delivery Santa	Hudson Studios	Yr.Iss.	32.00	32.00
94-61-006	Skating Santa	Hudson Studios	Yr.Iss.	34.00	34.00
Lance Corporation		**Hudson Pewter Noah's Ark-Retired**			
81-62-001	Monkey Pair	Hudson Studios	Retrd.	16.50	16.50
81-62-002	Pelican Pair	Hudson Studios	Retrd.	16.50	16.50
81-62-003	Female Hippo	Hudson Studios	Retrd.	12.00	12.00
81-62-004	Male Hippo	Hudson Studios	Retrd.	12.00	12.00
81-62-005	Male Turtle	Hudson Studios	Retrd.	12.00	12.00
81-62-006	Female Turtle	Hudson Studios	Retrd.	12.00	12.00
81-62-007	Lion Pair	Hudson Studios	Retrd.	18.00	18.00
81-62-008	Kangaroo Pair	Hudson Studios	Retrd.	19.00	19.00
82-62-009	Toucan Pair	Hudson Studios	Retrd.	18.00	18.00
82-62-010	Male Horse	Hudson Studios	Retrd.	12.00	12.00
82-62-011	Female Horse	Hudson Studios	Retrd.	12.00	12.00
83-62-012	Male Rhino	Hudson Studios	Retrd.	13.00	13.00
83-62-013	Female Rhino	Hudson Studios	Retrd.	13.00	13.00
83-62-014	Panda Pair	Hudson Studios	Retrd.	18.00	18.00
84-62-015	Male Tiger	Hudson Studios	Retrd.	13.00	13.00
84-62-016	Female Tiger	Hudson Studios	Retrd.	13.00	13.00
84-62-017	Male Deer	Hudson Studios	Retrd.	13.00	13.00
84-62-018	Female Deer	Hudson Studios	Retrd.	13.00	13.00
84-62-019	Mice Pair	Hudson Studios	Retrd.	14.00	14.00
84-62-020	Raccoon Pair	Hudson Studios	Retrd.	14.00	14.00
87-62-021	Cat Pair	Hudson Studios	Retrd.	18.00	18.00
87-62-022	Female Dog	Hudson Studios	Retrd.	13.00	13.00
87-62-023	Male Dog	Hudson Studios	Retrd.	16.00	16.00
87-62-024	Ram	Hudson Studios	Retrd.	16.00	16.00
87-62-025	Ewe	Hudson Studios	Retrd.	16.00	16.00
87-62-026	Bull	Hudson Studios	Retrd.	16.00	16.00
87-62-027	Fox Pair	Hudson Studios	Retrd.	18.00	18.00
87-62-028	Cow	Hudson Studios	Retrd.	16.00	16.00
88-62-029	Geese Pair	Hudson Studios	Retrd.	18.00	18.00
88-62-030	Skunk Pair	Hudson Studios	Retrd.	18.00	18.00
89-62-031	Male Bear	Hudson Studios	Retrd.	16.00	16.00
89-62-032	Female Bear	Hudson Studios	Retrd.	16.00	16.00
91-62-033	Male Unicorn	Hudson Studios	Retrd.	18.00	18.00
91-62-034	Female Unicorn	Hudson Studios	Retrd.	18.00	18.00
91-62-035	Male Eagle	Hudson Studios	Retrd.	16.00	16.00
91-62-036	Female Eagle	Hudson Studios	Retrd.	16.00	16.00
91-62-037	Chipmunk Pair	Hudson Studios	Retrd.	18.00	18.00
91-62-038	Aardvark Pair	Hudson Studios	Retrd.	18.00	18.00
Lance Corporation		**Hudson Pewter Mickey & Co.**			
88-63-001	Happy Birthday Mickey	Staff	Yr. Iss.	60.00	125.00
Lance Corporation		**Hudson Pewter Registered Mickey & Co.**			
94-64-001	Be My Valentine	Staff	Closed	65.00	65-100.
94-64-002	Christmas Waltz	Staff	Closed	65.00	65.00
Lance Corporation		**Hudson Pewter World of Mickey**			
88-65-001	Sweethearts	Staff	Retrd.	45.00	45.00
91-65-002	Mouse Waltz	Staff	Retrd.	41.00	41.00
Ron Lee's World of Clowns		**The Original Ron Lee Collection-1976**			
76-01-001	Pinky Upside Down 111	R. Lee	Closed	25.00	150.00
76-01-002	Pinky Lying Down 112	R. Lee	Closed	25.00	150.00
76-01-003	Hobo Joe Hitchiking 116	R. Lee	Closed	55.00	65.00
76-01-004	Hobo Joe with Umbrella 117	R. Lee	Closed	58.00	65-160.

		ARTIST	EDITION	ISSUE	QUOTE
76-01-005	Pinky Sitting 119	R. Lee	Closed	25.00	150.00
76-01-006	Hobo Joe with Balloons 120	R. Lee	Closed	63.00	90.00
76-01-007	Hobo Joe with Pal 115	R. Lee	Closed	63.00	85-170.
76-01-008	Clown and Dog Act 101	R. Lee	Closed	48.00	78-140.
76-01-009	Clown Tightrope Walker 104	R. Lee	Closed	50.00	82-155.
76-01-010	Clown and Elephant Act 107	R. Lee	Closed	56.00	85-140.
76-01-011	Pinky Standing 118	R. Lee	Closed	25.00	45-130.
76-01-012	Owl With Guitar 500	R. Lee	Closed	15.00	35-78.00
76-01-013	Turtle On Skateboard 501	R. Lee	Closed	15.00	35-78.00
76-01-014	Frog Surfing 502	R. Lee	Closed	15.00	35-78.00
76-01-015	Penguin on Snowskis 503	R. Lee	Closed	15.00	35-78.00
76-01-016	Alligator Bowling 504	R. Lee	Closed	15.00	35-78.00
76-01-017	Hippo on Scooter 505	R. Lee	Closed	15.00	35-78.00
76-01-018	Rabbit Playing Tennis 507	R. Lee	Closed	15.00	35-78.00
76-01-019	Kangaroos Boxing 508	R. Lee	Closed	15.00	35-78.00
76-01-020	Pig Playing Violin 510	R. Lee	Closed	15.00	35-78.00
76-01-021	Bear Fishing 511	R. Lee	Closed	15.00	35-78.00
76-01-022	Dog Fishing 512	R. Lee	Closed	15.00	35-78.00
Ron Lee's World of Clowns		**The Original Ron Lee Collection-1977**			
77-02-001	Koala Bear In Tree 514	R. Lee	Closed	15.00	35-78.00
77-02-002	Koala Bear With Baby 515	R. Lee	Closed	15.00	35-78.00
77-02-003	Koala Bear On Log 516	R. Lee	Closed	15.00	35-78.00
77-02-004	Mr. Penguin 518	R. Lee	Closed	18.00	39-85.00
77-02-005	Owl Graduate 519	R. Lee	Closed	22.00	44-90.00
77-02-006	Mouse and Cheese 520	R. Lee	Closed	18.00	30-80.00
77-02-007	Monkey With Banana 521	R. Lee	Closed	18.00	30-80.00
77-02-008	Pelican and Python 522	R. Lee	Closed	18.00	30-80.00
77-02-009	Bear On Rock 523	R. Lee	Closed	18.00	30-80.00
Ron Lee's World of Clowns		**The Original Ron Lee Collection-1978**			
78-03-001	Polly, the Parrot & Crackers 201	R. Lee	Closed	63.00	100-170.
78-03-002	Corky, the Drummer Boy 202	R. Lee	Closed	53.00	85-130.
78-03-003	Tinker Bowing 203	R. Lee	Closed	37.00	55-110.
78-03-004	Bobbi on Unicyle 204	R. Lee	Closed	45.00	65-98.00
78-03-005	Clara-Bow 205	R. Lee	Closed	52.00	70-120.
78-03-006	Sparky Skating 206	R. Lee	Closed	55.00	72-260.
78-03-007	Pierrot Painting 207	R. Lee	Closed	50.00	80-170.
78-03-008	Cuddles 208	R. Lee	Closed	37.00	55-110.
78-03-009	Poppy with Puppet 209	R. Lee	Closed	60.00	75-140.
78-03-010	Clancy, the Cop 210	R. Lee	Closed	55.00	72-130.
78-03-011	Driver the Golfer 211	R. Lee	Closed	55.00	200-225.
78-03-012	Sad Sack 212	R. Lee	Closed	48.00	62-210.
78-03-013	Elephant on Stand 213	R. Lee	Closed	26.00	42-80.00
78-03-014	Elephant on Ball 214	R. Lee	Closed	26.00	42-80.00
78-03-015	Elephant Sitting 215	R. Lee	Closed	26.00	42-80.00
78-03-016	Fireman with Hose 216	R. Lee	Closed	62.00	85-170.
78-03-017	Tobi-Hands Outstretched 217	R. Lee	Closed	70.00	98-260.
78-03-018	Coco-Hands on Hips 218	R. Lee	Closed	70.00	85-250.
78-03-019	Jeri In a Barrel 219	R. Lee	Closed	75.00	110-180.
78-03-020	Hey Rube 220	R. Lee	Closed	35.00	53-92.00
78-03-021	Jocko with Lollipop 221	R. Lee	Closed	67.50	93-215.
78-03-022	Bow Tie 222	R. Lee	Closed	67.50	93-215.
78-03-023	Oscar On Stilts 223	R. Lee	Closed	55.00	90-120.
78-03-024	Fancy Pants 224	R. Lee	Closed	55.00	90-120.
78-03-025	Skippy Swinging 239	R. Lee	Closed	52.00	65-85.00
78-03-026	Sailfish 524	R. Lee	Closed	18.00	40-95.00
78-03-027	Dolphins 525	R. Lee	Closed	22.00	40-85.00
78-03-028	Prince Frog 526	R. Lee	Closed	22.00	40-85.00
78-03-029	Seagull 527	R. Lee	Closed	22.00	40-85.00
78-03-030	Hummingbird 528	R. Lee	Closed	22.00	40-85.00
78-03-031	Butterfly and Flower 529	R. Lee	Closed	22.00	40-85.00
78-03-032	Turtle on Rock 530	R. Lee	Closed	22.00	40-85.00
78-03-033	Sea Otter on Back 531	R. Lee	Closed	22.00	40-85.00
78-03-034	Sea Otter on Rock 532	R. Lee	Closed	22.00	40-85.00
Ron Lee's World of Clowns		**The Original Ron Lee Collection-1979**			
79-04-001	Timmy Tooting 225	R. Lee	Closed	35.00	52-85.00
79-04-002	Tubby Tuba 226	R. Lee	Closed	35.00	55-90.00
79-04-003	Lilli 227	R. Lee	Closed	75.00	105-145.
79-04-004	Doctor Sawbones 228	R. Lee	Closed	75.00	110-150.
79-04-005	Buttons Bicycling 229	R. Lee	Closed	75.00	110-150.
79-04-006	Kelly in Kar 230	R. Lee	Closed	164.00	210-380.
79-04-007	Kelly's Kar 231	R. Lee	Closed	75.00	90-280.
79-04-008	Carousel Horse 232	R. Lee	Closed	119.00	130-195.
79-04-009	Harry and the Hare 233	R. Lee	Closed	69.00	102-180.
79-04-010	Fearless Fred in Cannon 234	R. Lee	Closed	80.00	105-300.
79-04-011	Darby with Flower 235	R. Lee	Closed	35.00	60-140.
79-04-012	Darby with Umbrella 236	R. Lee	Closed	35.00	60-140.
79-04-013	Darby With Violin 237	R. Lee	Closed	35.00	60-140.
79-04-014	Darby Tipping Hat 238	R. Lee	Closed	35.00	60-140.
79-04-015	Kelly at the Piano 241	R. Lee	Closed	185.00	285-510.
Ron Lee's World of Clowns		**The Original Ron Lee Collection-1980**			
80-05-001	Cubby Holding Balloon 240	R. Lee	Closed	50.00	65-70.00
80-05-002	Jingles Telling Time 242	R. Lee	Closed	75.00	90-190.
80-05-003	Donkey What 243	R. Lee	Closed	60.00	92-250.
80-05-004	Chuckles Juggling 244	R. Lee	Closed	98.00	105-150.
80-05-005	P. T. Dinghy 245	R. Lee	Closed	65.00	80-190.
80-05-006	Roni Riding Horse 246	R. Lee	Closed	115.00	180-290.
80-05-007	Peanuts Playing Concertina 247	R. Lee	Closed	65.00	150-285.
80-05-008	Carousel Horse 248	R. Lee	Closed	88.00	115-285.
80-05-009	Carousel Horse 249	R. Lee	Closed	88.00	115-285.
80-05-010	Jo-Jo at Make-up Mirror 250	R. Lee	Closed	86.00	125-185.
80-05-011	Monkey 251	R. Lee	Closed	60.00	85-210.
80-05-012	Dennis Playing Tennis 252	R. Lee	Closed	74.00	95-185.
80-05-013	Jaque Downhill Racer 253	R. Lee	Closed	74.00	90-210.
80-05-014	Ruford 254	R. Lee	Closed	43.00	80-190.
80-05-015	Happy Waving 255	R. Lee	Closed	43.00	82-190.
80-05-016	Zach 256	R. Lee	Closed	43.00	82-190.
80-05-017	Emile 257	R. Lee	Closed	43.00	82-190.
80-05-018	Banjo Willie 258	R. Lee	Closed	68.00	85-195.
80-05-019	Hobo Joe in Tub 259	R. Lee	Closed	96.00	105-125.
80-05-020	Doctor Jawbones 260	R. Lee	Closed	85.00	110-305.
80-05-021	Alexander's One Man Band 261	R. Lee	Closed	N/A	N/A
80-05-022	The Menagerie 262	R. Lee	Closed	N/A	N/A
80-05-023	Horse Drawn Chariot 263	R. Lee	Closed	N/A	N/A
Ron Lee's World of Clowns		**The Original Ron Lee Collection-1981**			
81-06-001	Executive Reading 264	R. Lee	Closed	23.00	45-110.
81-06-002	Executive with Umbrella 265	R. Lee	Closed	23.00	45-110.
81-06-003	Executive Resting 266	R. Lee	Closed	23.00	45-110.
81-06-004	Executive Hitchiking 267	R. Lee	Closed	23.00	45-110.

	ARTIST	EDITION	ISSUE	QUOTE
81-06-005 Louie on Park Bench 268	R. Lee	Closed	56.00	85-160.
81-06-006 Louie Hitching A Ride 269	R. Lee	Closed	47.00	58-135.
81-06-007 Louie On Railroad Car 270	R. Lee	Closed	77.00	95-180.
81-06-008 Elephant Reading 271	R. Lee	Closed	N/A	N/A
81-06-009 Pistol Pete 272	R. Lee	Closed	76.00	85-180.
81-06-010 Barbella 273	R. Lee	Closed	N/A	N/A
81-06-011 Larry and His Hotdogs 274	R. Lee	Closed	76.00	90-200.
81-06-012 Cashew On One Knee 275	R. Lee	Closed	N/A	N/A
81-06-013 Bojangles 276	R. Lee	Closed	N/A	N/A
81-06-014 Bozo Playing Cymbols 277	R. Lee	Closed	28.00	99-185.
81-06-015 Bozo Riding Car 278	R. Lee	Closed	28.00	99-185.
81-06-016 Bozo On Unicycle 279	R. Lee	Closed	28.00	99-185.
81-06-017 Carousel Horse 280	R. Lee	Closed	88.00	125-290.
81-06-018 Carousel Horse 281	R. Lee	Closed	88.00	125-290.
81-06-019 Ron Lee Trio 282	R. Lee	Closed	144.00	280-435.
81-06-020 Kevin at the Drums 283	R. Lee	Closed	50.00	92-150.
81-06-021 Al at the Bass 284	R. Lee	Closed	48.00	52-112.
81-06-022 Ron at the Piano 285	R. Lee	Closed	46.00	55-110.
81-06-023 Timothy In Big Shoes 286	R. Lee	Closed	37.00	50-95.00
81-06-024 Perry Sitting With Balloon 287	R. Lee	Closed	37.00	50-95.00
81-06-025 Perry Standing With Balloon 288	R. Lee	Closed	37.00	50-95.00
81-06-026 Nicky Sitting on Ball 289	R. Lee	Closed	39.00	48-92.00
81-06-027 Nicky Standing on Ball 290	R. Lee	Closed	39.00	48-92.00
81-06-028 Mickey With Umbrella 291	R. Lee	Closed	50.00	75-140.
81-06-029 Mickey Tightrope Walker 292	R. Lee	Closed	50.00	75-140.
81-06-030 Mickey Upside Down 293	R. Lee	Closed	50.00	75-140.
81-06-031 Rocketman 294	R. Lee	Closed	77.00	92-150.
81-06-032 My Son Darren 295	R. Lee	Closed	57.00	72-140.
81-06-033 Harpo 296	R. Lee	Closed	120.00	190-350.
81-06-034 Pickles and Pooch 297	R. Lee	Closed	90.00	200-240.
81-06-035 Hobo Joe Praying 298	R. Lee	Closed	57.00	65-85.00
81-06-036 Bosom Buddies 299	R. Lee	Closed	135.00	90-280.
81-06-037 Carney and Seal Act 300	R. Lee	Closed	63.00	75-290.
Ron Lee's World of Clowns	**The Original Ron Lee Collection-1982**			
82-07-001 Ron Lee Carousel	R. Lee	Closed	1000.00	12500.00
82-07-002 Carney and Dog Act 301	R. Lee	Closed	63.00	75-149.
82-07-003 Georgie Going Anywhere 302	R. Lee	Closed	95.00	125-256.
82-07-004 Fireman Watering House 303	R. Lee	Closed	99.00	99-180.
82-07-005 Quincy Lying Down 304	R. Lee	Closed	80.00	92-210.
82-07-006 Denny Eating Ice Cream 305	R. Lee	Closed	39.00	50-170.
82-07-007 Denny Holding Gift Box 306	R. Lee	Closed	39.00	50-170.
82-07-008 Denny Juggling Ball 307	R. Lee	Closed	39.00	50-170.
82-07-009 Buster in Barrel 308	R. Lee	Closed	85.00	90-120.
82-07-010 Sammy Riding Elephant 309	R. Lee	Closed	90.00	125-250.
82-07-011 Benny Pulling Car 310	R. Lee	Closed	190.00	235-360.
82-07-012 Dr. Painless and Patient 311	R. Lee	Closed	195.00	240-385.
82-07-013 Too Loose-L'Artiste 312	R. Lee	Closed	150.00	180-290.
82-07-014 Slim Charging Bull 313	R. Lee	Closed	195.00	265-410.
82-07-015 Norman Painting Dumbo 314	R. Lee	Closed	126.00	150-210.
82-07-016 Barnum Feeding Bacon 315	R. Lee	Closed	120.00	160-270.
82-07-017 Kukla and Friend 316	R. Lee	Closed	100.00	140-210.
82-07-018 Marion With Marrionette 317	R. Lee	Closed	105.00	135-225.
82-07-019 Two Man Valentinos 318	R. Lee	Closed	45.00	60-130.
82-07-020 Three Man Valentinos 319	R. Lee	Closed	55.00	70-120.
82-07-021 Captain Cranberry 320	R. Lee	Closed	115.00	145-180.
82-07-022 Charlie in the Rain 321	R. Lee	Closed	80.00	90-160.
82-07-023 Hobo Joe on Cycle 322	R. Lee	Closed	125.00	170-280.
82-07-024 Tou Tou 323	R. Lee	Closed	70.00	90-190.
82-07-025 Toy Soldier 324	R. Lee	Closed	95.00	140-270.
82-07-026 Herbie Dancing 325	R. Lee	Closed	26.00	40-110.
82-07-027 Herbie Hands Outstretched 326	R. Lee	Closed	26.00	40-110.
82-07-028 Herbie Balancing Hat 327	R. Lee	Closed	26.00	40-110.
82-07-029 Herbie Lying Down 328	R. Lee	Closed	26.00	40-110.
82-07-030 Herbie Legs in Air 329	R. Lee	Closed	26.00	40-110.
82-07-031 Herbie Touching Ground 330	R. Lee	Closed	26.00	40-110.
82-07-032 Clarence - The Lawyer 331	R. Lee	Closed	100.00	140-230.
82-07-033 Pinball Pal 332	R. Lee	Closed	150.00	195-287.
82-07-034 Clancy, the Cop and Dog 333	R. Lee	Closed	115.00	140-250.
82-07-035 Burrito Bandito 334	R. Lee	Closed	150.00	190-260.
82-07-036 Ali on His Magic Carpet 335	R. Lee	Closed	105.00	150-210.
82-07-037 Chico Playing Guitar 336	R. Lee	Closed	70.00	95-180.
82-07-038 Murphy On Unicycle 337	R. Lee	Closed	115.00	160-288.
82-07-039 Robin Resting 338	R. Lee	Closed	110.00	125-210.
82-07-040 Nappy Snoozing 346	R. Lee	Closed	110.00	125-210.
82-07-041 Laurel & Hardy 700	R. Lee	Closed	225.00	290-500.
82-07-042 Charlie Chaplain 701	R. Lee	Closed	230.00	285-650.
82-07-044 Self Portrait 702	R. Lee	Closed	355.00	550-816.
82-07-045 Captain Mis-Adventure 703	R. Lee	Closed	250.00	300-550.
82-07-046 Steppin' Out 704	R. Lee	Closed	325.00	390-700.
82-07-047 Limousine Service 705	R. Lee	Closed	330.00	375-750.
82-07-048 Pig Brick Layer 800	R. Lee	Closed	23.00	35-92.00
82-07-049 Rabbit With Egg 801	R. Lee	Closed	23.00	35-92.00
82-07-050 Smokey, the Bear 802	R. Lee	Closed	23.00	35-92.00
82-07-051 Fish With Shoe 803	R. Lee	Closed	23.00	35-92.00
82-07-052 Seal Blowing His Horns 804	R. Lee	Closed	23.00	35-92.00
82-07-053 Dog Playing Guitar 805	R. Lee	Closed	23.00	35-92.00
82-07-054 Fox In An Airplane 806	R. Lee	Closed	23.00	35-92.00
82-07-055 Beaver Playing Accordian 807	R. Lee	Closed	23.00	35-92.00
82-07-056 Rooster With Barbell 808	R. Lee	Closed	23.00	35-92.00
82-07-057 Parrot Rollerskating 809	R. Lee	Closed	23.00	35-92.00
82-07-058 Walrus With Umbrella 810	R. Lee	Closed	23.00	35-92.00
82-07-059 Turtle With Gun 811	R. Lee	Closed	57.00	75-150.
82-07-060 Reindeer 812	R. Lee	Closed	57.00	75-150.
82-07-061 Ostrich 813	R. Lee	Closed	57.00	75-150.
82-07-062 Tiger 814	R. Lee	Closed	57.00	75-150.
82-07-063 Rooster 815	R. Lee	Closed	57.00	75-150.
82-07-064 Giraffe 816	R. Lee	Closed	57.00	75-150.
82-07-065 Lion 817	R. Lee	Closed	57.00	75-150.
82-07-066 Camel 818	R. Lee	Closed	57.00	75-150.
82-07-067 Horse 819	R. Lee	Closed	57.00	75-150.
Ron Lee's World of Clowns	**The Original Ron Lee Collection-1983**			
83-08-001 Clyde Juggling 339	R. Lee	Closed	39.00	100-115.
83-08-002 Clyde Upside Down 340	R. Lee	Closed	39.00	100-115.
83-08-003 Little Horse - Head Up 341	R. Lee	Closed	29.00	72.00
83-08-004 Little Horse - Head Down 342	R. Lee	Closed	29.00	72.00
83-08-005 Rufus and His Refuse 343	R. Lee	Closed	65.00	160.00
83-08-006 Hobi in His Hammock 344	R. Lee	Closed	85.00	175-250.
83-08-007 Flipper Diving 345	R. Lee	Closed	115.00	200-350.
83-08-008 Ride 'em Roni 347	R. Lee	Closed	125.00	200-375.
83-08-009 Little Saturday Night 348	R. Lee	Closed	53.00	200.00
83-08-010 Tottie Scottie 349	R. Lee	Closed	39.00	75-115.
83-08-011 Teeter Tottie Scottie 350	R. Lee	Closed	55.00	105-165.
83-08-012 Casey Cruising 351	R. Lee	Closed	57.00	95-170.
83-08-013 Tatters and Balloons 352	R. Lee	Closed	65.00	125-200.
83-08-014 Bumbles Selling Balloons 353	R. Lee	Closed	80.00	170-240.
83-08-015 Cecil and Sausage 354	R. Lee	Closed	90.00	200-270.
83-08-016 On The Road Again 355	R. Lee	Closed	220.00	300-650.
83-08-017 Engineer Billie 356	R. Lee	Closed	190.00	275-550.
83-08-018 My Daughter Deborah 357	R. Lee	Closed	63.00	125-185.
83-08-019 Beethoven's Fourth Paws 358	R. Lee	Closed	59.00	110-165.
83-08-020 Say It With Flowers 359	R. Lee	Closed	35.00	95-110.
83-08-021 I Love You From My Heart 360	R. Lee	Closed	35.00	95-105.
83-08-022 Chef's Cuisine 361	R. Lee	Closed	57.00	100-110.
83-08-023 Singin' In The Rain 362	R. Lee	Closed	105.00	225-300.
83-08-024 Buster and His Balloons 363	R. Lee	Closed	47.00	90-125.
83-08-025 Up, Up and Away 364	R. Lee	Closed	50.00	100-150.
83-08-026 Lou Proposing 365	R. Lee	Closed	57.00	120-170.
83-08-027 Knickers Balancing Feather 366	R. Lee	Closed	47.00	120-135.
83-08-028 Daring Dudley 367	R. Lee	Closed	65.00	100-200.
83-08-029 Wilt the Stilt 368	R. Lee	Closed	49.00	100-155.
83-08-030 Coco and His Compact 369	R. Lee	Closed	55.00	145-175.
83-08-031 Josephine 370	R. Lee	Closed	55.00	145-175.
83-08-032 The Jogger 372	R. Lee	Closed	75.00	120-220.
83-08-033 Door to Door Dabney 373	R. Lee	Closed	100.00	200-285.
83-08-034 Riches to Rags 374	R. Lee	Closed	55.00	200-265.
83-08-035 Captain Freddy 375	R. Lee	Closed	85.00	200-425.
83-08-036 Gilbert Tee'd Off 376	R. Lee	Closed	60.00	100-200.
83-08-037 Cotton Candy 377	R. Lee	Closed	150.00	200-400.
83-08-038 Matinee Jitters 378	R. Lee	Closed	175.00	200-450.
83-08-039 The Last Scoop 379	R. Lee	Closed	175.00	300-475.
83-08-040 Cimba the Elephant 706	R. Lee	Closed	225.00	300-550.
83-08-041 The Bandwagon 707	R. Lee	Closed	900.00	1527.00
83-08-042 Catch the Brass Ring 708	R. Lee	Closed	510.00	900-1350
83-08-043 The Last Scoop 900	R. Lee	Closed	325.00	300-725.
83-08-044 Matinee Jitters 901	R. Lee	Closed	325.00	350-500.
83-08-045 No Camping or Fishing 902	R. Lee	Closed	325.00	350-600.
83-08-046 Black Carousel Horse 1001	R. Lee	Closed	450.00	450-600.
83-08-047 Chestnut Carousel Horse 1002	R. Lee	Closed	450.00	700-1100
83-08-048 White Carousel Horse 1003	R. Lee	Closed	450.00	700-1100
83-08-049 Gazebo 1004	R. Lee	Closed	750.00	13-1750.
Ron Lee's World of Clowns	**The Original Ron Lee Collection-1984**			
84-09-001 No Camping or Fishing 380	R. Lee	Closed	175.00	275-450.
84-09-002 Wheeler Sheila 381	R. Lee	Closed	75.00	175-225.
84-09-003 Mortimer Fishing 382	R. Lee	Closed	N/A	N/A
84-09-004 Give a Dog a Bone 383	R. Lee	Closed	95.00	95-182.
84-09-005 The Peppermints 384	R. Lee	Closed	150.00	180-250.
84-09-006 T.K. and OH!! 385	R. Lee	Closed	85.00	200-325.
84-09-007 Just For You 386	R. Lee	Closed	110.00	150-250.
84-09-008 Baggy Pants 387	R. Lee	Closed	98.00	250-300.
84-09-009 Look at the Birdy 388	R. Lee	Closed	138.00	200-300.
84-09-010 Bozo's Seal of Approval 389	R. Lee	Closed	138.00	200-350.
84-09-011 A Bozo Lunch 390	R. Lee	Closed	148.00	250-400.
84-09-012 My Fellow Americans 391	R. Lee	Closed	138.00	250-425.
84-09-013 No Loitering 392	R. Lee	Closed	113.00	150-250.
84-09-014 Tisket and Tasket 393	R. Lee	Closed	93.00	150-250.
84-09-015 White Circus Horse 709	R. Lee	Closed	305.00	350-520.
84-09-016 Chestnut Circus Horse 710A	R. Lee	Closed	305.00	350-520.
84-09-017 Black Circus Horse 711A	R. Lee	Closed	305.00	350-520.
84-09-018 Rudy Holding Balloons 713	R. Lee	Closed	230.00	300-550.
84-09-019 Saturday Night 714	R. Lee	Closed	250.00	600-825.
Ron Lee's World of Clowns	**The Original Ron Lee Collection-1985**			
85-10-001 From Riches to Rags 374	R. Lee	Closed	108.00	250.00
85-10-002 Gilbert TeeOd OFF 376	R. Lee	Closed	63.00	55-63.00
85-10-003 Twas the Night Before 408	R. Lee	Closed	235.00	405.00
85-10-004 The Finishing Touch 409	R. Lee	Closed	178.00	305.00
85-10-005 Bull-Can-Rear-You 422	R. Lee	Closed	120.00	206.00
85-10-006 Giraffe Getting a Bath 428	R. Lee	Closed	160.00	235-450.
85-10-007 Rosebuds 433	R. Lee	Closed	155.00	315.00
85-10-008 Pee Wee With Umbrella 434	R. Lee	Closed	50.00	100.00
85-10-009 Pee Wee With Balloons 435	R. Lee	Closed	50.00	100.00
85-10-010 Catch of the Day 441	R. Lee	Closed	170.00	305.00
85-10-011 Ham Track 451	R. Lee	Closed	240.00	430.00
85-10-012 Get the Picture 456	R. Lee	Closed	70.00	140.00
85-10-013 Dr. Sigmund Fraud 457	R. Lee	Closed	98.00	190.00
85-10-014 Yo Yo Stravinsky-Attoney at Law 458	R. Lee	Closed	98.00	185.00
85-10-015 Dr. Timothy DeCay 459	R. Lee	Closed	98.00	185.00
85-10-016 Duster Buster 461	R. Lee	Closed	43.00	90.00
85-10-017 Hi Ho Blinky 462	R. Lee	Closed	53.00	105.00
85-10-018 One Wheel Winky 464	R. Lee	Closed	43.00	83.00
85-10-019 Cannonball 466	R. Lee	Closed	43.00	83.00
85-10-020 Whiskers Sweeping 744	R. Lee	Closed	240.00	500-800.
85-10-021 Whiskers Hitchhiking 745	R. Lee	Closed	240.00	800.00
85-10-022 Whiskers Holding Balloons 746	R. Lee	Closed	265.00	500-800.
85-10-023 Whiskers Holding Umbrella 747	R. Lee	Closed	265.00	500-800.
85-10-024 Whiskers Bathing 749	R. Lee	Closed	305.00	500-800.
85-10-025 Whiskers On The Beach 750	R. Lee	Closed	230.00	500.00
85-10-026 Clowns of the Caribbean PS101	R. Lee	Closed	1250.00	2-2800.
85-10-027 Fred Figures 903	R. Lee	Closed	175.00	340.00
85-10-028 Policy Paul 904	R. Lee	Closed	175.00	310.00
Ron Lee's World of Clowns	**The Original Ron Lee Collection-1986**			
86-11-001 Wet Paint 436	R. Lee	Closed	80.00	100-200.
86-11-002 Bathing Buddies 450	R. Lee	Closed	145.00	250-375.
86-11-003 Hari and Hare 454	R. Lee	Closed	57.00	85-135.
86-11-004 Ride 'Em Peanuts 463	R. Lee	Closed	55.00	70-135.
86-11-005 Captain Cranberry 469	R. Lee	Closed	140.00	175-335.
86-11-006 Getting Even 485	R. Lee	Closed	85.00	125-225.
86-11-007 Bums Day at the Beach L105	R. Lee	Closed	97.00	N/A
86-11-008 The Last Stop L106	R. Lee	Closed	99.00	N/A
86-11-009 Christmas Morning Magic L107	R. Lee	Closed	99.00	N/A
86-11-010 Most Requested Toy L108	R. Lee	Closed	264.00	N/A
86-11-011 High Above the Big Top L112	R. Lee	Closed	162.00	N/A
86-11-012 Puppy Love's Portrait L113	R. Lee	Closed	168.00	N/A
Ron Lee's World of Clowns	**The Original Ron Lee Collection-1987**			
87-12-001 Heartbroken Harry L101	R. Lee	Closed	63.00	125-225.
87-12-002 Lovable Luke L102	R. Lee	Closed	70.00	70.00
87-12-003 Puppy Love L103	R. Lee	Closed	71.00	71.00
87-12-004 Would You Like To Ride? L104	R. Lee	Closed	246.00	300-475.
87-12-005 Sugarland Express L109	R. Lee	Closed	342.00	400-600.
87-12-006 First & Main L110	R. Lee	Closed	368.00	500-775.

	ARTIST	EDITION	ISSUE	QUOTE
87-12-007 Show of Shows L115	R. Lee	Closed	175.00	N/A
87-12-008 Happines Is L116	R. Lee	Closed	155.00	N/A

Ron Lee's World of Clowns — The Original Ron Lee Collection-1988

	ARTIST	EDITION	ISSUE	QUOTE
88-13-001 New Ron Lee Carousel	R. Lee	Closed	7000.00	9500.00
88-13-002 The Fifth Wheel L117	R. Lee	Closed	250.00	375.00
88-13-003 Bozorina L118	R. Lee	Closed	95.00	N/A
88-13-004 Dinner for Two L119	R. Lee	Closed	140.00	N/A
88-13-005 Anchors-A-Way L120	R. Lee	Closed	195.00	N/A
88-13-006 Pumpkuns Galore L121	R. Lee	Closed	135.00	N/A
88-13-007 Fore! L122	R. Lee	Closed	135.00	N/A
88-13-008 Tunnel of Love L123	R. Lee	Closed	490.00	600-800.
88-13-009 Boulder Bay L124	R. Lee	Closed	700.00	N/A
88-13-010 Cactus Pete L125	R. Lee	Closed	495.00	N/A
88-13-011 Together Again L126	R. Lee	Closed	130.00	N/A
88-13-012 To The Rescue L127	R. Lee	Closed	130.00	160-550.
88-13-013 When You're Hot, You're Hot! L128	R. Lee	Closed	221.00	250-800.

Ron Lee's World of Clowns — The Original Ron Lee Collection-1989

	ARTIST	EDITION	ISSUE	QUOTE
89-14-001 Be It Ever So Humble L111	R. Lee	Closed	900.00	950-1250
89-14-002 Wishful Thinking L114	R. Lee	Closed	230.00	250-500.
89-14-003 No Fishing L130	R. Lee	Closed	247.00	N/A
89-14-004 Get Well L131	R. Lee	Closed	79.00	N/A
89-14-005 Maestro L132	R. Lee	Closed	173.00	N/A
89-14-006 If I Were A Rich Man L133	R. Lee	Closed	315.00	400-600.
89-14-007 I Pledge Allegiance L134	R. Lee	Closed	131.00	150-250.
89-14-008 In Over My Head L135	R. Lee	Closed	95.00	125-190.
89-14-009 Eye Love You L136	R. Lee	Closed	68.00	N/A
89-14-010 My Heart Beats For You L137	R. Lee	Closed	74.00	N/A
89-14-011 Just Carried Away L138	R. Lee	Closed	135.00	N/A
89-14-012 O' Solo Mia L139	R. Lee	Closed	85.00	90-150.
89-14-013 Beauty Is In The Eye Of L140	R. Lee	Closed	190.00	N/A
89-14-014 Tee for Two L141	R. Lee	Closed	125.00	150.00
89-14-015 My Money's OnThe Bull L142	R. Lee	Closed	187.00	160-187.
89-14-016 Circus Little L143	R. Lee	Closed	990.00	1250.00
89-14-017 Hughie Mungus L144	R. Lee	Closed	250.00	300-825.
89-14-018 Not A Ghost Of A Chance L145	R. Lee	Closed	195.00	245.00
89-14-019 Sh-h-h-h! L146	R. Lee	Closed	210.00	400-1000
89-14-020 Today's Catch L147	R. Lee	Closed	230.00	245-325.
89-14-021 Catch A Falling Star L148	R. Lee	Closed	57.00	48-57.00
89-14-022 Rest Stop L149	R. Lee	Closed	47.00	N/A
89-14-023 Marcelle L150	R. Lee	Closed	47.00	N/A
89-14-024 Butt-R-Fly L151	R. Lee	Closed	47.00	N/A
89-14-025 Stormy Weathers L152	R. Lee	Closed	47.00	N/A
89-14-026 I Just Called! L153	R. Lee	Closed	47.00	N/A
89-14-027 Sunflower L154	R. Lee	Closed	47.00	N/A
89-14-028 Candy Apple L155	R. Lee	Closed	47.00	N/A
89-14-029 Just Go! L156	R. Lee	Closed	47.00	N/A
89-14-030 My Affections L157	R. Lee	Closed	47.00	N/A
89-14-031 Wintertime Pals L158	R. Lee	Closed	90.00	N/A
89-14-032 Merry Xmas L159	R. Lee	Closed	94.00	N/A
89-14-033 Santa's Dilemma L160	R. Lee	Closed	97.00	N/A
89-14-034 My First Tree L161	R. Lee	Closed	92.00	N/A
89-14-035 Happy Chanakah L162	R. Lee	Closed	106.00	N/A
89-14-036 Snowdrifter L163	R. Lee	Closed	230.00	275-450.
89-14-037 If That's Your Drive How's Your Putts L164	R. Lee	Closed	260.00	N/A
89-14-038 The Policeman L165	R. Lee	Closed	68.00	100-200.
89-14-039 The Pharmacist L166	R. Lee	Closed	65.00	N/A
89-14-040 The Salesman L167	R. Lee	Closed	68.00	N/A
89-14-041 The Nurse L168	R. Lee	Closed	65.00	N/A
89-14-042 The Fireman L169	R. Lee	Closed	68.00	150-200.
89-14-043 The Doctor L170	R. Lee	Closed	65.00	150-200.
89-14-044 The Lawyer 171	R. Lee	Closed	68.00	150-200.
89-14-045 The Photographer L172	R. Lee	Closed	68.00	150-200.
89-14-046 The Accountant L173	R. Lee	Closed	68.00	150-200.
89-14-047 The Optometrist L174	R. Lee	Closed	65.00	150-200.
89-14-048 The Dentist L175	R. Lee	Closed	65.00	150-200.
89-14-049 The Plumber L176	R. Lee	Closed	65.00	150-200.
89-14-050 The Real Estate Man L177	R. Lee	Closed	65.00	150-200.
89-14-051 The Chef L178	R. Lee	Closed	65.00	150-200.
89-14-052 The Secretary L179	R. Lee	Closed	65.00	150-200.
89-14-053 The Chiropractor L180	R. Lee	Closed	68.00	150-200.
89-14-054 The Housewife L181	R. Lee	Closed	75.00	150-200.
89-14-055 The Veterinarian L182	R. Lee	Closed	72.00	150-200.
89-14-056 The Beautician L183	R. Lee	Closed	68.00	150-200.
89-14-057 The Mechanic L184	R. Lee	Closed	68.00	150-200.
89-14-058 The Real Estate Lady L185	R. Lee	Closed	70.00	150-200.
89-14-059 The Football Player L186	R. Lee	Closed	65.00	150-200.
89-14-060 The Basketball Player L187	R. Lee	Closed	68.00	150-200.
89-14-061 The Golfer L188	R. Lee	Closed	72.00	150-200.
89-14-062 The Baseball Player L189	R. Lee	Closed	72.00	150-200.
89-14-063 The Tennis Player L190	R. Lee	Closed	72.00	150-200.
89-14-064 The Bowler L191	R. Lee	Closed	68.00	150-200.
89-14-065 The Surfer L192	R. Lee	Closed	72.00	150-200.
89-14-066 The Skier L193	R. Lee	Closed	75.00	150-200.
89-14-067 The Fisherman L194	R. Lee	Closed	72.00	150-200.
89-14-068 I Ain't Got No Money L195	R. Lee	Closed	325.00	N/A
89-14-069 I Should've When I Could've L196	R. Lee	Closed	325.00	340.00
89-14-070 Memories L197	R. Lee	Closed	325.00	N/A
89-14-071 Be Happy L198	R. Lee	Closed	160.00	N/A
89-14-072 Two a.m. Blues L199	R. Lee	Closed	125.00	N/A
89-14-073 Dang It L200	R. Lee	Closed	47.00	N/A
89-14-074 Hot Diggity Dog L201	R. Lee	Closed	47.00	N/A
89-14-075 The Serenade L202	R. Lee	Closed	47.00	N/A
89-14-076 Rain Bugs Me L203	R. Lee	Closed	225.00	N/A
89-14-077 Butterflies Are Free L204	R. Lee	Closed	225.00	N/A
89-14-078 She Loves Me Not L205	R. Lee	Closed	225.00	N/A
89-14-079 Birdbrain L206	R. Lee	Closed	110.00	N/A
89-14-080 Jingles With Umbrella L207	R. Lee	Closed	90.00	200.00
89-14-081 Jingles Holding Balloon L208	R. Lee	Closed	90.00	N/A
89-14-082 Jingles Hitchhiking L209	R. Lee	Closed	90.00	N/A
89-14-083 The Greatest Little Shoe On Earth L210	R. Lee	Closed	165.00	200-300.
89-14-084 Slots Of Luck L211	R. Lee	Closed	90.00	N/A
89-14-085 Craps L212	R. Lee	Closed	530.00	N/A
89-14-086 My Last Chip L213	R. Lee	Closed	550.00	N/A
89-14-087 Over 21 L214	R. Lee	Closed	550.00	N/A
89-14-088 I-D-D-D-Do! L215	R. Lee	Closed	180.00	N/A
89-14-089 You Must Be Kidding L216	R. Lee	Closed	N/A	800.00
89-14-090 Candy Man L217	R. Lee	Closed	350.00	360.00
89-14-091 The New Self Portrait L218	R. Lee	Closed	800.00	950.00

Ron Lee's World of Clowns — The Original Ron Lee Collection-1990

	ARTIST	EDITION	ISSUE	QUOTE
90-15-001 Carousel Horse L219	R. Lee	Closed	150.00	N/A
90-15-002 Carousel Horse L220	R. Lee	Closed	150.00	N/A
90-15-003 Carousel Horse L221	R. Lee	Closed	150.00	N/A
90-15-004 Carousel Horse L222	R. Lee	Closed	150.00	N/A
90-15-005 Flapper Riding Carousel L223	R. Lee	Closed	190.00	N/A
90-15-006 Peaches Riding Carousel L224	R. Lee	Closed	190.00	N/A
90-15-007 Rascal Riding Carousel L225	R. Lee	Closed	190.00	N/A
90-15-008 Jo-Jo Riding Carousel L226	R. Lee	Closed	190.00	N/A
90-15-009 New Pinky Upside Down L227	R. Lee	8,500	42.00	42.00
90-15-010 New Pinky Lying Down L228	R. Lee	8,500	42.00	42.00
90-15-011 New Pinky Standing L229	R. Lee	8,500	42.00	42.00
90-15-012 New Pinky Sitting L230	R. Lee	8,500	42.00	42.00
90-15-013 Me Too!! L231	R. Lee	Closed	70.00	70-80.00
90-15-014 Par Three L232	R. Lee	2,750	144.00	144.00
90-15-015 Heartbroken Hobo L233	R. Lee	Closed	116.00	160.00
90-15-016 Scooter L234	R. Lee	Closed	240.00	275.00
90-15-017 Tandem Mania L235	R. Lee	Closed	360.00	360.00
90-15-018 The Big Wheel L236	R. Lee	Closed	240.00	240.00
90-15-019 Uni-Cycle L237	R. Lee	Closed	240.00	240.00
90-15-020 All Show No Go L238	R. Lee	1,500	285.00	285.00
90-15-021 Skiing My Way L239	R. Lee	2,500	400.00	400.00
90-15-022 My Heart's on for You L240	R. Lee	5,500	55.00	55.00
90-15-023 Swinging on a Star L241	R. Lee	5,500	55.00	55.00
90-15-024 I Love You L242	R. Lee	5,500	55.00	55.00
90-15-025 Stuck on Me L243	R. Lee	5,500	55.00	55.00
90-15-026 Loving You L244	R. Lee	5,500	55.00	55.00
90-15-027 L-O-V-E L245	R. Lee	5,500	55.00	55.00
90-15-028 Heart of My Heart L246	R. Lee	5,500	55.00	55.00
90-15-029 Watch Your Step L247	R. Lee	2,500	78.00	78.00
90-15-030 Fill'er Up L248	R. Lee	Closed	280.00	300.00
90-15-031 Push and Pull L249	R. Lee	Closed	260.00	280.00
90-15-032 Snowdrifter II L250	R. Lee	Closed	340.00	280.00
90-15-033 Kiss! Kiss! L251	R. Lee	Closed	37.00	37.00
90-15-034 Na! Na! L252	R. Lee	Closed	33.00	33.00
90-15-035 I.Q. Two L253	R. Lee	2,750	33.00	33.00
90-15-036 Your Heaviness L254	R. Lee	2,750	37.00	37.00
90-15-037 Same To "U" L255	R. Lee	2,750	37.00	37.00
90-15-038 Yo Mama L256	R. Lee	2,750	35.00	35.00
90-15-039 Q.T. Pie L257	R. Lee	2,750	37.00	37.00
90-15-040 Squirt L258	R. Lee	2,750	37.00	37.00
90-15-041 Paddle L259	R. Lee	2,750	33.00	33.00
90-15-042 Henry 8-3/4 L260	R. Lee	Closed	37.00	50.00
90-15-043 Pitch L261	R. Lee	2,750	35.00	35.00
90-15-044 Horsin' Around L262	R. Lee	Closed	37.00	37-50.00

Ron Lee's World of Clowns — The Original Ron Lee Collection-1991

	ARTIST	EDITION	ISSUE	QUOTE
91-16-001 The Visit L263	R. Lee	1,750	100.00	100.00
91-16-002 Tender-Lee L264	R. Lee	1,750	96.00	96.00
91-16-003 Cruising L265	R. Lee	Closed	170.00	170-175.
91-16-004 Business is Business L266	R. Lee	Closed	110.00	110.00
91-16-005 Refugee L267	R. Lee	1,750	88.00	88.00
91-16-006 I'm Singin' In The Rain L268	R. Lee	Closed	135.00	150.00
91-16-007 Anywhere? L269	R. Lee	Closed	125.00	125-145.
91-16-008 Gilbert's Dilemma L270	R. Lee	Closed	90.00	125.00
91-16-009 Marcelle I L271	R. Lee	2,250	50.00	50.00
91-16-010 Marcelle II L272	R. Lee	2,250	50.00	50.00
91-16-011 Marcelle III L273	R. Lee	2,250	50.00	50.00
91-16-012 Marcelle IV L274	R. Lee	2,250	50.00	50.00
91-16-013 Puppy Love Scootin' L275	R. Lee	Closed	73.00	73-80.00
91-16-014 Puppy Love's Free Ride L276	R. Lee	Closed	73.00	73-80.00
91-16-015 Puppy Love's Treat L277	R. Lee	Closed	73.00	73-80.00
91-16-016 Happy Birthday Puppy Love L278	R. Lee	Closed	73.00	85.00
91-16-017 Winter L279	R. Lee	1,500	115.00	115-125.
91-16-018 Spring L280	R. Lee	1,500	95.00	95-110.
91-16-019 Summer L281	R. Lee	1,500	95.00	95-110.
91-16-020 Fall L282	R. Lee	1,500	120.00	120-125.
91-16-021 Makin Tracks L283	R. Lee	1,500	142.00	142.00
91-16-022 Soap Suds Serenade L284	R. Lee	1,750	85.00	85.00
91-16-023 IRS or Bust L285	R. Lee	1,500	122.00	122.00
91-16-024 Tootie Tuba L286	R. Lee	1,750	42.00	42.00
91-16-025 Truly Trumpet L287	R. Lee	1,750	42.00	42.00
91-16-026 Trusty Trombone L288	R. Lee	1,750	42.00	42.00
91-16-027 Clarence Clarinet L289	R. Lee	1,750	42.00	42.00
91-16-028 Droopy Drummer L290	R. Lee	1,750	42.00	42.00
91-16-029 Harley Horn L291	R. Lee	1,750	42.00	42.00
91-16-030 Banjo Willie L293	R. Lee	1,750	90.00	90.00
91-16-031 TA DA L294	R. Lee	Closed	220.00	220-225.
91-16-032 Trash Can Sam L295	R. Lee	1,750	118.00	118.00
91-16-033 This Won't Hurt L296	R. Lee	1,750	110.00	110.00
91-16-034 Two For Fore L297	R. Lee	1,750	120.00	120.00
91-16-035 Lit'l Snowdrifter L298	R. Lee	1,750	70.00	85-115.
91-16-036 Hobi Daydreaming L299	R. Lee	1,750	112.00	112.00
91-16-037 Surf's Up L300	R. Lee	1,750	80.00	80.00
91-16-038 Sand Trap L301	R. Lee	1,750	100.00	100.00
91-16-039 Strike!!! L302	R. Lee	1,750	76.00	76.00
91-16-040 Hook, Line and Sinker L303	R. Lee	1,750	100.00	60-100.
91-16-041 Geronimo L304	R. Lee	1,750	127.00	127.00
91-16-042 New Harpo L305	R. Lee	1,250	130.00	130.00
91-16-043 New Toy Soldier L306	R. Lee	1,250	115.00	115.00
91-16-044 New Darby with Flower L307	R. Lee	1,250	57.00	57.00
91-16-045 New Darby with Umbrella L308	R. Lee	1,250	57.00	57.00
91-16-046 New Darby with Violin L309	R. Lee	1,250	57.00	57.00
91-16-047 New Darby Tipping Hat L310	R. Lee	1,250	57.00	57.00
91-16-048 Eight Ball-Corner Pocket L311	R. Lee	1,750	224.00	180-224.
91-16-049 Our Nation's Pride L312	R. Lee	Closed	150.00	150.00
91-16-050 Give Me Liberty L313	R. Lee	Closed	155.00	155-165.
91-16-051 United We Stand L314	R. Lee	Closed	150.00	150.00
91-16-052 Ain't No Havana L315	R. Lee	500	230.00	230.00
91-16-053 Hot Dawg! L316	R. Lee	500	255.00	255.00

Ron Lee's World of Clowns — The Original Ron Lee Collection-1992

	ARTIST	EDITION	ISSUE	QUOTE
92-17-001 Snowdrifter Blowin' In Wind L317	R. Lee	1,750	77.50	77.50
92-17-002 Snowdrifter's Special Delivery L318	R. Lee	1,750	136.00	136.00
92-17-003 Scrub-A- Dub-Dub L319	R. Lee	Closed	185.00	195.00
92-17-004 Hippolong Cassidy L320	R. Lee	Closed	166.00	140.00
92-17-005 Handy Standy L321	R. Lee	2,500	26.00	27.00
92-17-006 Cyclin' Around L322	R. Lee	2,500	26.00	27.00
92-17-007 Strike Out L323	R. Lee	2,500	26.00	27.00
92-17-008 Shake Jake L324	R. Lee	2,500	26.00	27.00
92-17-009 Howdy L325	R. Lee	2,500	26.00	27.00
92-17-010 Lolly L326	R. Lee	2,500	26.00	27.00

	ARTIST	EDITION	ISSUE	QUOTE
92-17-011 To-Tee L327	R. Lee	2,500	26.00	27.00
92-17-012 Dunkin' L328	R. Lee	2,500	26.00	27.00
92-17-013 Heel's Up L329	R. Lee	2,500	26.00	27.00
92-17-014 Twirp Chirp L330	R. Lee	2,500	26.00	27.00
92-17-015 Stop Cop L331	R. Lee	2,500	26.00	27.00
92-17-016 Dreams L332	R. Lee	2,500	26.00	27.00
92-17-017 Penny Saver L333	R. Lee	2,500	26.00	27.00
92-17-018 My Pal L334	R. Lee	2,500	26.00	27.00
92-17-019 Break Point L335	R. Lee	2,500	26.00	27.00
92-17-020 Clar-A-Bow L336	R. Lee	2,500	26.00	27.00
92-17-021 Myak Kyak L337	R. Lee	2,500	26.00	27.00
92-17-022 Steamer L338	R. Lee	2,500	26.00	27.00
92-17-023 Hi-Five L339	R. Lee	2,500	26.00	27.00
92-17-024 Flyin' High L340	R. Lee	2,500	26.00	27.00
92-17-025 Forget Me Not L341	R. Lee	2,500	26.00	27.00
92-17-026 Beau Regards L342	R. Lee	2,500	26.00	27.00
92-17-027 Shufflin' L343	R. Lee	2,500	26.00	27.00
92-17-028 Go Man Go L344	R. Lee	2,500	26.00	27.00
92-17-029 Ship Ahoy L345	R. Lee	2,500	26.00	27.00
92-17-030 Struttin' L346	R. Lee	2,500	26.00	27.00
92-17-031 Juggles L347	R. Lee	2,500	26.00	27.00
92-17-032 On My Way L348	R. Lee	2,500	26.00	27.00
92-17-033 Little Pard L349	R. Lee	2,500	26.00	27.00
92-17-034 Baloony L350	R. Lee	2,500	26.00	27.00
92-17-035 Wrong Hole Clown L351	R. Lee	1,750	125.00	125.00
92-17-036 Birdy The Hard Way L352	R. Lee	1,750	85.00	85.00
92-17-037 Vincent Van Clown L353	R. Lee	Closed	160.00	160.00
92-17-038 My Portrait L354	R. Lee	Closed	315.00	315.00
92-17-039 Love Ya' Baby L355	R. Lee	1,250	190.00	190.00
92-17-040 Seven's Up L356	R. Lee	1,250	165.00	165.00
92-17-041 Beats Nothin' L357	R. Lee	1,500	145.00	145.00
92-17-042 Fish in Pail L358	R. Lee	1,500	130.00	130.00
92-17-043 Buster Too PC100	R. Lee	1,500	65.00	65.00
92-17-044 Miles PC105	R. Lee	1,500	65.00	65.00
92-17-045 Topper PC110	R. Lee	1,500	65.00	65.00
92-17-046 Webb-ster PC115	R. Lee	1,500	65.00	65.00
92-17-047 Popcorn & Cotton Candy RLC1001	R. Lee	1,750	70.00	70.00
92-17-048 Jo-Jo Juggling RLC1002	R. Lee	1,750	70.00	70.00
92-17-049 Bo-Bo Balancing RLC1003	R. Lee	1,750	75.00	75.00
92-17-050 Gassing Up RLC1004	R. Lee	1,750	70.00	70.00
92-17-051 Big Wheel Kop RLC1005	R. Lee	1,750	65.00	65.00
92-17-052 Brokenhearted Huey RLC1006	R. Lee	1,750	65.00	65.00
92-17-053 Sure-Footed Freddie RLC1007	R. Lee	1,750	80.00	80.00
92-17-054 Cannonball RLC1009	R. Lee	1,750	95.00	95.00
92-17-055 Dudley's Dog Act RLC1010	R. Lee	1,750	75.00	75.00
92-17-056 Walking A Fine Line RMB7000	R. Lee	1,750	65.00	65.00

Ron Lee's World of Clowns — **The Original Ron Lee Collection-1993**

	ARTIST	EDITION	ISSUE	QUOTE
93-18-001 Tinker And Toy L359	R. Lee	950	95.00	95.00
93-18-002 Dave Bomber L360	R. Lee	950	90.00	90.00
93-18-003 Scrubs L361	R. Lee	950	87.00	87.00
93-18-004 Yo-Yo L362	R. Lee	950	87.00	87.00
93-18-005 Lollipop L363	R. Lee	950	87.00	87.00
93-18-006 Andy Jackson L364	R. Lee	950	87.00	87.00
93-18-007 Bo-Bo L365	R. Lee	950	95.00	95.00
93-18-008 Sailin' L366	R. Lee	950	95.00	95.00
93-18-009 Skittles L367	R. Lee	950	95.00	95.00
93-18-010 Buster L368	R. Lee	950	87.00	87.00
93-18-011 Happy Trails L369	R. Lee	950	90.00	90.00
93-18-012 Honk Honk L370	R. Lee	950	90.00	90.00
93-18-013 Wagone Hes L371	R. Lee	750	210.00	210.00
93-18-014 Pretzels L372	R. Lee	750	195.00	195.00
93-18-015 Sho-Sho L373	R. Lee	750	115.00	115.00
93-18-016 Chattanooga Choo-Choo L374	R. Lee	750	420.00	420.00
93-18-017 Sole-Full L375	R. Lee	750	250.00	250.00
93-18-018 Hot Buns L376	R. Lee	750	175.00	175.00
93-18-019 Britches L377	R. Lee	750	205.00	205.00
93-18-020 Taxi L378	R. Lee	750	470.00	470.00
93-18-021 Piggy Backin' L379	R. Lee	750	205.00	205.00
93-18-022 Moto Kris L380	R. Lee	750	255.00	255.00
93-18-023 Charkles L381	R. Lee	750	220.00	220.00
93-18-024 Blinky Standing L382	R. Lee	1,200	45.00	45.00
93-18-025 Blinky Sitting L383	R. Lee	1,200	45.00	45.00
93-18-026 Blinky Lying Down L384	R. Lee	1,200	45.00	45.00
93-18-027 Blinky Upside Down L385	R. Lee	1,200	45.00	45.00
93-18-028 Bellboy L390	R. Lee	950	80.00	80.00
93-18-029 North Pole L396	R. Lee	950	75.00	75.00
93-18-030 Anywhere Warm L398	R. Lee	950	90.00	90.00
93-18-031 Snoozin' L399	R. Lee	950	90.00	90.00
93-18-032 Soft Shoe L400	R. Lee	750	275.00	275.00
93-18-033 Wanderer L401	R. Lee	750	255.00	255.00
93-18-034 Special Occasion L402	R. Lee	750	280.00	280.00
93-18-035 Bumper Fun L403	R. Lee	750	330.00	330.00
93-18-036 Shriner Cop L404	R. Lee	750	175.00	175.00
93-18-037 Merry Go Clown L405	R. Lee	750	375.00	375.00

Ron Lee's World of Clowns — **The Ron Lee Disney Collection Exclusives**

	ARTIST	EDITION	ISSUE	QUOTE
90-19-001 The Bandleader MM100	R. Lee	Closed	75.00	75.00
90-19-002 The Sorcerer MM200	R. Lee	Closed	85.00	120.00
90-19-003 Steamboat Willie MM300	R. Lee	2,750	95.00	95.00
90-19-004 Mickey's Christmas MM400	R. Lee	2,750	95.00	95.00
90-19-005 Pinocchio MM500	R. Lee	2,750	85.00	85.00
90-19-006 Dumbo MM600	R. Lee	2,750	110.00	110.00
90-19-007 Uncle Scrooge MM700	R. Lee	2,750	110.00	110.00
90-19-008 Snow White & Grumpy MM800	R. Lee	2,750	140.00	140.00
91-19-009 Goofy MM110	R. Lee	2,750	115.00	115.00
91-19-010 Dopey MM120	R. Lee	2,750	80.00	80.00
91-19-011 The Witch MM130	R. Lee	2,750	115.00	115.00
91-19-012 Two Gun Mickey MM140	R. Lee	2,750	115.00	115.00
91-19-013 Mickey's Adventure MM150	R. Lee	2,750	195.00	195.00
91-19-014 Mt. Mickey MM900	R. Lee	2,750	175.00	175.00
91-19-015 Tugboat Mickey MM160	R. Lee	2,750	180.00	180.00
91-19-016 Minnie Mouse MM170	R. Lee	2,750	80.00	80.00
91-19-017 Mickey & Minnie at the Piano MM180	R. Lee	2,750	195.00	195.00
91-19-018 Decorating Donald MM210	R. Lee	2,750	60.00	60.00
91-19-019 Mickey's Delivery MM220	R. Lee	2,750	70.00	70.00
91-19-020 Goofy's Gift MM230	R. Lee	2,750	70.00	70.00
91-19-021 Pluto's Treat MM240	R. Lee	2,750	60.00	60.00
91-19-022 Jiminy's List MM250	R. Lee	2,750	60.00	60.00
91-19-023 Lady and the Tramp MM280	R. Lee	1,500	295.00	295.00
91-19-024 Lion Around MM270	R. Lee	2,750	140.00	140.00
91-19-025 The Tea Cup Ride (Disneyland Exclusive) MM260	R. Lee	1,250	225.00	225.00
92-19-026 Sorcerer's Apprentice MM290	R. Lee	2,750	125.00	125.00
92-19-027 Little Mermaid MM310	R. Lee	2,750	230.00	230.00
92-19-028 Captain Hook MM320	R. Lee	2,750	175.00	175.00
92-19-029 Bambi MM330	R. Lee	2,750	195.00	195.00
92-19-030 Litt'l Sorcerer MM340	R. Lee	2,750	57.00	57.00
92-19-031 Lumiere & Cogsworth MM350	R. Lee	2,750	145.00	145.00
92-19-032 Mrs. Potts & Chip MM360	R. Lee	2,750	125.00	125.00
92-19-033 The Dinosaurs MM370	R. Lee	2,750	195.00	195.00
92-19-034 Workin' Out MM380	R. Lee	2,750	95.00	95.00
92-19-035 Winnie The Pooh & Tigger MM390	R. Lee	2,750	105.00	105.00
92-19-036 Stocking Stuffer MM410	R. Lee	1,500	63.00	63.00
92-19-037 Christmas '92 MM420	R. Lee	1,500	145.00	145.00
92-19-038 Wish Upon A Star MM430	R. Lee	1,500	80.00	80.00
92-19-039 Finishing Touch MM440	R. Lee	1,500	85.00	85.00
92-19-040 Genie MM450	R. Lee	2,750	110.00	110.00
92-19-041 Big Thunder Mountain MM460	R. Lee	250	1650.00	3000.00
93-19-042 Darkwing Duck MM470	R. Lee	1,750	105.00	105.00
93-19-043 Winnie The Pooh MM480	R. Lee	1,750	125.00	125.00
93-19-044 Tinker Bell MM490	R. Lee	1,750	85.00	85.00
93-19-045 Cinderella's Slipper MM510	R. Lee	1,750	115.00	115.00
93-19-046 Mickey's Dream MM520	R. Lee	250	400.00	600-800.
93-19-047 Flying With Dumbo MM530	R. Lee	1,000	330.00	330.00
93-19-048 Santa's Workshop MM540	R. Lee	1,500	170.00	170.00
93-19-049 Letters to Santa MM550	R. Lee	1,500	170.00	170.00
93-19-050 Aladdin MM560	R. Lee	500	550.00	550.00
92-19-051 Beauty & The Beast (shadow box) DIS100	R. Lee	500	1650.00	1650.00
93-19-052 Snow White & The Seven Dwarfs (shadow box) DIS200	R. Lee	250	1800.00	1800.00

Ron Lee's World of Clowns — **The Ron Lee Emmett Kelly, Sr. Collection**

	ARTIST	EDITION	ISSUE	QUOTE
91-20-001 That-A-Way EK201	R. Lee	Closed	125.00	125.00
91-20-002 Help Yourself EK202	R. Lee	Closed	145.00	145.00
91-20-003 Spike's Uninvited Guest EK203	R. Lee	Closed	165.00	165.00
91-20-004 Love at First Sight EK204	R. Lee	Closed	197.00	197.00
91-20-005 Time for a Change EK205	R. Lee	Closed	190.00	400.00
91-20-006 God Bless America EK206	R. Lee	Closed	130.00	130.00
91-20-007 My Protege EK207	R. Lee	Closed	160.00	160.00
91-20-008 Emmett Kelly, Sr. Sign E208	R. Lee	Closed	110.00	110.00

Ron Lee's World of Clowns — **The Ron Lee Warner Bros. Collection**

	ARTIST	EDITION	ISSUE	QUOTE
91-21-001 The Maltese Falcon WB100	R. Lee	Closed	175.00	175.00
91-21-002 Robin Hood Bugs WB200	R. Lee	1,000	190.00	190.00
92-21-003 Yankee Doodle Bugs WB300	R. Lee	850	195.00	195.00
92-21-004 Dickens' Christmas WB400	R. Lee	850	198.00	198.00
93-21-005 Hare Under Par WB001	R. Lee	1,000	102.00	102.00
93-21-006 Gridiron Glory WB002	R. Lee	1,000	102.00	102.00
93-21-007 Courtly Gent WB003	R. Lee	1,000	102.00	102.00
93-21-008 Home Plate Heroes WB004	R. Lee	1,000	102.00	102.00
93-21-009 Duck Dodgers WB005	R. Lee	1,000	300.00	300.00
93-21-010 Hair-Raising Hare WB006	R. Lee	1,000	300.00	300.00

Ron Lee's World of Clowns — **The Flintstones**

	ARTIST	EDITION	ISSUE	QUOTE
91-22-001 The Flinstones HB100	R. Lee	2,750	410.00	410.00
91-22-002 Yabba-Dabba-Doo HB110	R. Lee	2,750	230.00	230.00
91-22-003 Saturday Blues HB120	R. Lee	2,750	105.00	105.00
91-22-004 Bedrock Serenade HB130	R. Lee	2,750	250.00	250.00
91-22-005 Joyride-A-Saurus HB140	R. Lee	2,750	107.00	107.00
91-22-006 Bogey Buddies HB150	R. Lee	2,750	143.00	143.00
91-22-007 Vac-A-Saurus HB160	R. Lee	2,750	105.00	110.00
91-22-008 Buffalo Brothers HB170	R. Lee	2,750	134.00	134.00

Ron Lee's World of Clowns — **The Jetsons**

	ARTIST	EDITION	ISSUE	QUOTE
91-23-001 The Jetsons HB500	R. Lee	2,750	500.00	500.00
91-23-002 The Cosmic Couple HB510	R. Lee	2,750	105.00	105.00
91-23-003 Astro: Cosmic Canine HB520	R. Lee	2,750	275.00	275.00
91-23-004 I Rove Roo HB530	R. Lee	2,750	105.00	105.00
91-23-005 Scare-D-Dog HB540	R. Lee	2,750	160.00	160.00
91-23-006 4 O'Clock Tea HB550	R. Lee	2,750	203.00	203.00

Ron Lee's World of Clowns — **The Classics**

	ARTIST	EDITION	ISSUE	QUOTE
91-24-001 Yogi Bear & Boo Boo HB800	R. Lee	2,750	95.00	95.00
91-24-002 Quick Draw McGraw HB805	R. Lee	2,750	90.00	90.00
91-24-003 Scooby Doo & Shaggy HB810	R. Lee	2,750	114.00	114.00
91-24-004 Huckleberry Hound HB815	R. Lee	2,750	90.00	90.00

Ron Lee's World of Clowns — **Rocky & Bullwinkle And Friends Collection**

	ARTIST	EDITION	ISSUE	QUOTE
92-25-001 Rocky & Bullwinkle RB600	R. Lee	1,750	120.00	120.00
92-25-002 The Swami RB605	R. Lee	1,750	175.00	175.00
92-25-003 Dudley Do-Right RB610	R. Lee	1,750	175.00	175.00
92-25-004 My Hero RB615	R. Lee	1,750	275.00	275.00
92-25-005 KA-BOOM! RB620	R. Lee	1,750	175.00	175.00

Ron Lee's World of Clowns — **The Wizard of Oz Collection**

	ARTIST	EDITION	ISSUE	QUOTE
92-26-001 Kansas WZ400	R. Lee	750	550.00	550.00
92-26-002 The Munchkins WZ405	R. Lee	750	620.00	620.00
92-26-003 The Ruby Slippers WZ410	R. Lee	750	620.00	620.00
92-26-004 The Scarecrow WZ415	R. Lee	750	510.00	510.00
92-26-005 The Tin Man WZ420	R. Lee	750	530.00	530.00
92-26-006 The Cowardly Lion WZ425	R. Lee	750	620.00	620.00

Ron Lee's World of Clowns — **Wizard of Oz II**

	ARTIST	EDITION	ISSUE	QUOTE
94-27-001 Dorothy WZ430	R. Lee	500	150.00	150.00
94-27-002 The Scarecrow WZ435	R. Lee	500	130.00	130.00
94-27-003 The Tinman WZ440	R. Lee	500	110.00	110.00
94-27-004 The Cowardly Lion WZ445	R. Lee	500	130.00	130.00
94-27-005 The Wicked Witch WZ450	R. Lee	500	125.00	125.00
94-27-006 Glinda WZ455	R. Lee	500	225.00	225.00

Ron Lee's World of Clowns — **The Woody Woodpecker And Friends Collection**

	ARTIST	EDITION	ISSUE	QUOTE
92-28-001 Birdy for Woody WL005	R. Lee	1,750	117.00	117.00
92-28-002 Peck of My Heart WL010	R. Lee	1,750	370.00	370.00
92-28-003 Woody Woodpecker WL015	R. Lee	1,750	73.00	73.00
92-28-004 1940 Woody Woodpecker WL020	R. Lee	1,750	73.00	73.00
92-28-005 Andy and Miranda Panda WL025	R. Lee	1,750	140.00	140.00
92-28-006 Pals WL030	R. Lee	1,750	179.00	179.00

Ron Lee's World of Clowns — **The Popeye Collection**

	ARTIST	EDITION	ISSUE	QUOTE
92-29-001 Liberty P001	R. Lee	1,750	184.00	184.00
92-29-002 Men!!! P002	R. Lee	1,750	230.00	230.00
92-29-003 Strong to The Finish P003	R. Lee	1,750	95.00	95.00
92-29-004 That's My Boy P004	R. Lee	1,750	145.00	145.00
92-29-005 Oh Popeye P005	R. Lee	1,750	230.00	230.00
92-29-006 Par Excellence P006	R. Lee	1,750	220.00	220.00

	ARTIST	EDITION	ISSUE	QUOTE
Ron Lee's World of Clowns	**The Ron Lee Looney Tunes Collection**			
91-30-001 Western Daffy Duck LT105	R. Lee	Closed	87.00	87-90.00
91-30-002 Michigan J. Frog LT110	R. Lee	Closed	115.00	115.00
91-30-003 Porky Pig LT115	R. Lee	Closed	97.00	97-100.
91-30-004 Tasmanian Devil LT120	R. Lee	Closed	105.00	105.00
91-30-005 Elmer Fudd LT125	R. Lee	Closed	87.00	87-90.00
91-30-006 Yosemite Sam LT130	R. Lee	Closed	110.00	110.00
91-30-007 Sylvester & Tweety LT135	R. Lee	Closed	110.00	110-115.
91-30-008 Daffy Duck LT140	R. Lee	Closed	80.00	80-85.00
91-30-009 Pepe LePew & Penelope LT145	R. Lee	Closed	115.00	115.00
91-30-010 Bugs Bunny LT150	R. Lee	Closed	123.00	125.00
91-30-011 Tweety LT155	R. Lee	Closed	110.00	110-115.
91-30-012 Foghorn Leghorn & Henry Hawk LT160	R. Lee	Closed	115.00	115.00
91-30-013 1940 Bugs Bunny LT165	R. Lee	Closed	85.00	85.00
91-30-014 Marvin the Martian LT170	R. Lee	Closed	75.00	75.00
91-30-015 Wile E. Coyote & Roadrunner LT175	R. Lee	Closed	165.00	165-175.
91-30-016 Mt. Yosemite LT180	R. Lee	850	160.00	160-300.
Ron Lee's World of Clowns	**The Ron Lee Looney Tunes II Collection**			
92-31-001 Speedy Gonzales LT185	R. Lee	2,750	73.00	73.00
92-31-002 For Better or Worse LT190	R. Lee	1,500	285.00	285.00
92-31-003 What The ...? LT195	R. Lee	1,500	240.00	240.00
92-31-004 Ditty Up LT200	R. Lee	2,750	110.00	110.00
92-31-005 Leopold & Giovanni LT205	R. Lee	1,500	225.00	225.00
92-31-006 No Pain No Gain LT210	R. Lee	950	270.00	270.00
92-31-007 What's up Doc? LT215	R. Lee	950	270.00	270.00
92-31-008 Beep Beep LT220	R. Lee	1,500	115.00	115.00
92-31-009 Rackin' Frackin' Varmint LT225	R. Lee	950	260.00	260.00
92-31-010 Van Duck LT230	R. Lee	950	335.00	335.00
92-31-011 The Virtuosos LT235	R. Lee	950	350.00	350.00
Ron Lee's World of Clowns	**The Ron Lee Looney Tunes III Collection**			
92-32-001 Bugs Bunny w/ Horse LT245	R. Lee	1,500	105.00	105.00
92-32-002 Sylvester w/ Horse LT250	R. Lee	1,500	105.00	105.00
92-32-003 Tasmanian Devil w/ Horse LT255	R. Lee	1,500	105.00	105.00
92-32-004 Porky Pig w/ Horse LT260	R. Lee	1,500	105.00	105.00
92-32-005 Yosemite Sam w/ Horse LT265	R. Lee	1,500	105.00	105.00
92-32-006 Elmer Fudd w/ Horse LT270	R. Lee	1,500	105.00	105.00
92-32-007 Daffy Duck w/ Horse LT275	R. Lee	1,500	105.00	105.00
92-32-008 Wile E. Coyote w/ Horse LT280	R. Lee	1,500	105.00	105.00
92-32-009 Pepe Le Pew w/ Horse LT285	R. Lee	1,500	105.00	105.00
92-32-010 Cowboy Bugs LT290	R. Lee	1,500	70.00	70.00
Ron Lee's World of Clowns	**The Ron Lee Looney Tunes IV Collection**			
93-33-001 Me Deliver LT295	R. Lee	1,200	110.00	110.00
93-33-002 Yo-Ho-Ho- LT300	R. Lee	1,200	105.00	105.00
93-33-003 Martian's Best Friend LT305	R. Lee	1,200	140.00	140.00
93-33-004 The Essence of Love LT310	R. Lee	1,200	145.00	145.00
93-33-005 The Rookie LT315	R. Lee	1,200	75.00	75.00
93-33-006 A Christmas Carrot LT320	R. Lee	1,200	175.00	175.00
93-33-007 Puttin' on the Glitz LT325	R. Lee	1,200	79.00	79.00
93-33-008 Bugs LT330	R. Lee	1,200	79.00	79.00
Ron Lee's World of Clowns	**The Ron Lee Looney Tunes V Collection**			
94-34-001 Smashing LT335	R. Lee	1,200	80.00	80.00
94-34-002 Ma Cherie LT340	R. Lee	1,200	185.00	185.00
94-34-003 Guilty LT345	R. Lee	1,200	80.00	80.00
94-34-004 A Carrot a Day LT350	R. Lee	1,200	85.00	85.00
94-34-005 No H20 LT355	R. Lee	1,200	160.00	160.00
94-34-006 Taz On Ice LT360	R. Lee	1,200	115.00	115.00
94-34-007 Puttin' on the Glitz LT325	R. Lee	1,200	79.00	79.00
94-34-008 Bugs LT330	R. Lee	1,200	79.00	79.00
Ron Lee's World of Clowns	**The Ron Lee Looney Tunes VI Collection**			
94-35-001 Tweety Pharoah LT365	R. Lee	500	110.00	110.00
94-35-002 Bugs Pharoah LT370	R. Lee	500	130.00	130.00
94-35-003 Warrior Taz LT375	R. Lee	500	140.00	140.00
94-35-004 Ramases & Son LT380	R. Lee	500	230.00	230.00
94-35-005 Cruising Down the Nile LT385	R. Lee	500	295.00	295.00
94-35-006 Yosemite's Chariot LT390	R. Lee	500	310.00	310.00
94-35-007 King Bugs and Friends LT395	R. Lee	500	480.00	480.00
94-35-008 Cleopatra's Barge LT400	R. Lee	500	550.00	550.00
Ron Lee's World of Clowns	**The Betty Boop Collection**			
92-36-001 Harvest Moon BB700	R. Lee	1,500	93.00	93.00
92-36-002 Boop Oop A Doop BB705	R. Lee	1,500	97.00	97.00
92-36-003 Spicy Dish BB710	R. Lee	1,500	215.00	215.00
92-36-004 Bamboo Isle BB715	R. Lee	1,500	240.00	240.00
92-36-005 Max's Cafe BB720	R. Lee	1,500	99.00	99.00
Ron Lee's World of Clowns	**The E.T. Collection**			
92-37-001 E.T. ET100	R. Lee	1,500	94.00	94.00
92-37-002 It's Mee...E.T. ET105	R. Lee	1,500	94.00	94.00
93-37-003 Friends ET110	R. Lee	1,500	125.00	125.00
93-37-004 Flight ET115	R. Lee	1,500	325.00	325.00
Ron Lee's World of Clowns	**Superman I**			
93-38-001 Help Is On The Way SP100	R. Lee	750	280.00	280.00
93-38-002 Proudly We Wave SP105	R. Lee	750	185.00	185.00
93-38-003 Metropolis SP110	R. Lee	750	320.00	320.00
93-38-004 Meteor Moment SP115	R. Lee	750	314.00	314.00
Ron Lee's World of Clowns	**Superman II**			
94-39-001 Quick Change SP120	R. Lee	750	125.00	125.00
94-39-002 To The Rescue SP125	R. Lee	750	195.00	195.00
94-39-003 More Powerful SP130	R. Lee	750	420.00	420.00
94-39-004 Good and Evil SP135	R. Lee	750	190.00	190.00
Ron Lee's World of Clowns	**Around the World With Hobo Joe**			
94-40-001 Hobo Joe in Italy L406	R. Lee	750	110.00	110.00
94-40-002 Hobo Joe in France L407	R. Lee	750	110.00	110.00
94-40-003 Hobo Joe in Japan L408	R. Lee	750	110.00	110.00
94-40-004 Hobo Joe in the U.S.A L409	R. Lee	750	110.00	110.00
94-40-005 Hobo Joe in Tahiti L410	R. Lee	750	110.00	110.00
94-40-006 Hobo Joe in England L411	R. Lee	750	110.00	110.00
94-40-007 Hobo Joe in Caribbean L412	R. Lee	750	110.00	110.00
94-40-008 Hobo Joe in Norway L413	R. Lee	750	110.00	110.00
94-40-009 Hobo Joe in Spain L414	R. Lee	750	110.00	110.00
94-40-010 Hobo Joe in Egypt L415	R. Lee	750	110.00	110.00
Ron Lee's World of Clowns	**Musical Clowns in Harmony**			
94-41-001 Puddles L-416	R. Lee	750	175.00	175.00
94-41-002 Daisy L-417	R. Lee	750	175.00	175.00
94-41-003 Hot Dog L-418	R. Lee	750	175.00	175.00
94-41-004 Kandy L-419	R. Lee	750	175.00	175.00
94-41-005 Poodles L-420	R. Lee	750	175.00	175.00
94-41-006 Carpet Bagger L-421	R. Lee	750	175.00	175.00
94-41-007 Bubbles L-422	R. Lee	750	175.00	175.00
94-41-008 Barella L-423	R. Lee	750	175.00	175.00
94-41-009 Aristocrat L-424	R. Lee	750	175.00	175.00
94-41-010 Snacks L-425	R. Lee	750	175.00	175.00
Ron Lee's World of Clowns	**Premier Dealer Collection**			
92-42-001 Framed Again PD001	R. Lee	Closed	110.00	110.00
92-42-002 Dream On PD002	R. Lee	Closed	125.00	125.00
92-42-003 Nest to Nothing PD003	R. Lee	Closed	110.00	115.00
92-42-004 Moonlighting PD004	R. Lee	Closed	125.00	125.00
93-42-005 Pockets PD005	R. Lee	500	175.00	175.00
93-42-006 Jake-A-Juggling Cylinder PD006	R. Lee	500	85.00	85.00
93-42-007 Jake-A-Juggling Clubs PD007	R. Lee	500	85.00	85.00
93-42-008 Jake-A-Juggling Balls PD008	R. Lee	500	85.00	85.00
Ron Lee's World of Clowns	**Center Ring**			
94-43-001 Puddles L-416SE	R. Lee	750	125.00	125.00
94-43-002 Daisy L-417SE	R. Lee	750	125.00	125.00
94-43-003 Hot Dog L-418SE	R. Lee	750	125.00	125.00
94-43-004 Kandy L-419SE	R. Lee	750	125.00	125.00
94-43-005 Poodles L-420SE	R. Lee	750	125.00	125.00
94-43-006 Carpetbagger L-421SE	R. Lee	750	125.00	125.00
94-43-007 Bubbles L-422SE	R. Lee	750	125.00	125.00
94-43-008 Barella L-423SE	R. Lee	750	125.00	125.00
94-43-009 Aristocrat L-424SE	R. Lee	750	125.00	125.00
94-43-010 Snacks L-425SE	R. Lee	750	125.00	125.00
94-43-011 Mal-Lett L-426SE	R. Lee	750	125.00	125.00
94-43-012 Belt-a-Loon L-427SE	R. Lee	750	125.00	125.00
94-43-013 Forget-Me-Not L-428SE	R. Lee	750	125.00	125.00
94-43-014 Rabbit's Foot L-429SE	R. Lee	750	125.00	125.00
94-43-015 Boo-Boo L-430SE	R. Lee	750	125.00	125.00
94-43-016 According To L-431SE	R. Lee	750	125.00	125.00
94-43-017 Maid in the USA L-432SE	R. Lee	750	125.00	125.00
94-43-018 Glamour Boy L-433SE	R. Lee	750	125.00	125.00
94-43-019 Hoop-De-Doo L-434SE	R. Lee	750	125.00	125.00
94-43-020 Ruffles L-435SE	R. Lee	750	125.00	125.00
Ron Lee's World of Clowns	**The Ron Lee Collector's Club Gifts**			
87-44-001 Hooping It Up CCG1	R. Lee	Closed	Gift	N/A
88-44-002 Pudge CCG2	R. Lee	Closed	Gift	N/A
89-44-003 Pals CCG3	R. Lee	Closed	Gift	N/A
90-44-004 Potsie CCG4	R. Lee	Closed	Gift	N/A
91-44-005 Hi! Ya! CCG5	R. Lee	Closed	Gift	N/A
92-44-006 Bashful Beau CCG6	R. Lee	Closed	Gift	N/A
93-44-007 Lit'l Mate CCG7	R. Lee	Closed	Gift	N/A
94-44-008 Chip Off the Old Block CCG8	R. Lee	Yr.Iss.	Gift	N/A
Ron Lee's World of Clowns	**The Ron Lee Collector's Club Renewal Sculptures**			
87-45-001 Doggin' Along CC1	R. Lee	Yr.Iss.	75.00	115.00
88-45-002 Midsummer's Dream CC2	R. Lee	Yr.Iss.	97.00	140.00
89-45-003 Peek-A-Boo Charlie CC3	R. Lee	Yr.Iss.	65.00	100.00
90-45-004 Get The Message CC4	R. Lee	Yr.Iss.	65.00	65.00
91-45-005 I'm So Pretty CC5	R. Lee	Yr.Iss.	65.00	65.00
92-45-006 It's For You CC6	R. Lee	Yr.Iss.	65.00	65.00
93-45-007 My Son Keven CC7	R. Lee	Yr.Iss.	70.00	70.00
Geo. Zoltan Lefton Company	**Colonial Village**			
86-01-001 Original Set of 6	Lefton	Unkn.	210.00	N/A
86-01-002 Nelson House 05891	Lefton	Closed	35.00	150-390.
86-01-003 McCauley House 05892	Lefton	Closed	35.00	150-450.
86-01-004 Old Stone Church 05825	Lefton	Open	35.00	47.00
86-01-005 Charity Chapel 05895	Lefton	Closed	35.00	150-325.
86-01-006 King's Cottage 05890	Lefton	Open	35.00	50.00
86-01-007 The Welcome Home 05824	Lefton	Open	35.00	47.00
86-01-008 Original Set of 6	Lefton	Unkn.	210.00	N/A
86-01-009 General Store 05823	Lefton	Closed	35.00	390-600.
86-01-010 Lil Red School House 05821	Lefton	Closed	35.00	110-130.
86-01-011 Penny House 05893	Lefton	Closed	35.00	175-485.
86-01-012 Church of the Golden Rule 05820	Lefton	Open	35.00	50.00
86-01-013 Train Station 05822	Lefton	Closed	35.00	150-400.
86-01-014 Ritter House 05894	Lefton	Closed	35.00	150-350.
86-01-015 Village Express 05826	Lefton	Closed	27.00	120.00
88-01-016 Faith Church 06333	Lefton	Closed	40.00	100-300.
88-01-017 Friendship Chapel 06334	Lefton	Closed	40.00	65-150.
88-01-018 Old Time Station 06335	Lefton	Open	40.00	50.00
88-01-019 Trader Tom's Gen'l Store 06336	Lefton	Open	40.00	47.00
88-01-020 House of Blue Gables 06337	Lefton	Open	40.00	47.00
88-01-021 The Stone House 06338	Lefton	Open	40.00	47.00
88-01-022 Greystone House 06339	Lefton	Open	40.00	47.00
88-01-023 City Hall 06340	Lefton	Suspd.	40.00	75-300.
88-01-024 The Ritz Hotel 06341	Lefton	Suspd.	40.00	75-120.
88-01-025 Engine Co. No. 5 Firehouse 06342	Lefton	Open	40.00	50.00
88-01-026 First Post Office 06343	Lefton	Open	40.00	50.00
88-01-027 Village Police Station 06344	Lefton	Open	40.00	50.00
88-01-028 The State Bank 06345	Lefton	Open	40.00	50.00
88-01-029 Johnson's Antiques 06346	Lefton	Closed	40.00	75-200.
88-01-030 New Hope Church (Musical) 06470	Lefton	Closed	40.00	75-88.00
89-01-031 Gull's Nest Lighthouse 06747	Lefton	Open	40.00	47.00
89-01-032 Maple St. Church 06748	Lefton	Closed	40.00	75-250.
89-01-033 Village School 06749	Lefton	Closed	40.00	50-100.
89-01-034 Cole's Barn 06750	Lefton	Closed	40.00	65-150.
89-01-035 Sweetheart's Bridge 06751	Lefton	Open	40.00	47.00
89-01-036 Village Library 06752	Lefton	Open	40.00	47.00
89-01-037 Bijou Theatre 06897	Lefton	Closed	40.00	120-440.
89-01-038 The Village Bakery 06898	Lefton	Open	40.00	47.00
89-01-039 Quincy's Clock Shop 06899	Lefton	Open	40.00	47.00
89-01-040 Victorian Apothecary 06900	Lefton	Closed	40.00	100-300.
89-01-041 Village Barber Shop 06901	Lefton	Open	40.00	47.00
89-01-042 The Major's Manor 06902	Lefton	Open	40.00	47.00
89-01-043 Cobb's Bootery 06903	Lefton	Suspd.	40.00	75-130.
89-01-044 Capper's Millinery 06904	Lefton	Suspd.	40.00	75-130.
89-01-045 Miller Bros. Silversmiths 06905	Lefton	Suspd.	40.00	75-125.
90-01-046 The First Church 07333	Lefton	Open	45.00	47.00
90-01-047 Fellowship Church 07334	Lefton	Open	45.00	47.00
90-01-048 The Victorian House 07335	Lefton	Closed	45.00	100-150.
90-01-049 Hampshire House 07336	Lefton	Open	45.00	50.00
90-01-050 The Nob Hill 07337	Lefton	Open	45.00	47.00
90-01-051 The Ardmore House 07338	Lefton	Open	45.00	47.00
90-01-052 Ship's Chandler's Shop 07339	Lefton	Suspd.	45.00	47.00
90-01-053 Village Hardware 07340	Lefton	Open	45.00	50.00
90-01-054 Country Post Office 07341	Lefton	Closed	45.00	65-150.
90-01-055 Coffee & Tea Shoppe 07342	Lefton	Open	45.00	47.00

		ARTIST	EDITION	ISSUE	QUOTE
90-01-056	Pierpont-Smithe's Curios 07343	Lefton	Closed	45.00	75-200.
90-01-057	Mulberry Station 07344	Lefton	Open	50.00	65.00
90-01-058	Ryman Auditorium-Special Edition 08010	Lefton	Open	50.00	55.00
90-01-059	Hillside Church 11991	Lefton	Closed	60.00	205-400.
91-01-060	Smith's Smithy 07476	Lefton	Closed	45.00	100-300.
91-01-061	The Toy Maker's Shop 07477	Lefton	Open	45.00	47.00
91-01-062	Daisy's Flower Shop 07478	Lefton	Open	45.00	47.00
91-01-063	Watt's Candle Shop 07479	Lefton	Closed	45.00	65-150.
91-01-064	Wig Shop 07480	Lefton	Suspd.	45.00	75-90.00
91-01-065	Sweet Shop 07481	Lefton	Open	45.00	47.00
91-01-066	Belle-Union Saloon 07482	Lefton	Closed	45.00	68-150.
91-01-067	Victorian Gazebo 07925	Lefton	Open	45.00	45.00
91-01-068	Sanderson's Mill 07927	Lefton	Open	45.00	47.00
92-01-069	Northpoint School 07960	Lefton	Open	45.00	50.00
92-01-070	Brenner's Apothecary 07961	Lefton	Open	45.00	50.00
92-01-071	The Village Inn 07962	Lefton	Open	45.00	50.00
92-01-072	Village Green Gazebo 00227	Lefton	Open	22.00	22.00
92-01-073	Stearn's Stable 00228	Lefton	Open	45.00	50.00
92-01-074	Windmilll 00229	Lefton	Open	45.00	47.00
92-01-075	Main St. Church 00230	Lefton	Open	45.00	50.00
92-01-076	San Sebastian Mission 00231	Lefton	Open	45.00	50.00
92-01-077	Elegant Lady Dress Shop 00232	Lefton	Open	45.00	50.00
92-01-078	County Courthouse 00233	Lefton	Open	45.00	50.00
92-01-079	Lakehurst House 11992	Lefton	Closed	55.00	150-300.
93-01-080	St. Peter's Church w/Speaker 00715	Lefton	Open	60.00	60.00
93-01-081	Kirby House-CVRA Exclusive 00716	Lefton	Closed	50.00	200.00
93-01-082	Burnside 00717	Lefton	Open	50.00	50.00
93-01-083	Joseph House 00718	Lefton	Open	50.00	50.00
93-01-084	Mark Hall 00719	Lefton	Open	50.00	50.00
93-01-085	Blacksmith 00720	Lefton	Open	47.00	47.00
93-01-086	Doctor's Office 00721	Lefton	Open	50.00	50.00
93-01-087	Baldwin's Fine Jewelry 00722	Lefton	Open	50.00	50.00
93-01-088	Antiques & Curiosities 00723	Lefton	Open	50.00	50.00
93-01-089	Dentist's Office 00724	Lefton	Open	50.00	50.00
93-01-090	Green's Grocery 00725	Lefton	Open	50.00	50.00
93-01-091	St. James Cathedral 11993	Lefton	Closed	75.00	150-235.
94-01-092	Mt. Zion Church 11994	Lefton	Closed	70.00	70.00
94-01-093	Rosamond 00988	Lefton	Open	50.00	50.00
94-01-094	Springfield 00989	Lefton	Open	50.00	50.00
94-01-095	Brown's Book Shop 01001	Lefton	Open	50.00	50.00
94-01-096	Black Sheep Tavern 01003	Lefton	Open	50.00	50.00
94-01-097	Village Hospital 01004	Lefton	Open	50.00	50.00
94-01-098	White's Butcher Shop 01005	Lefton	Open	50.00	50.00
94-01-099	Smith and Jones Drug Store 01007	Lefton	Open	50.00	50.00
94-01-100	Real Estate Office -CVRA Exclusive 01006	Lefton	Open	50.00	50.00
94-01-101	Notfel Cabin 01320	Lefton	Open	50.00	50.00
95-01-102	Zachary Peters Cabinet Maker 01322	Lefton	Open	50.00	50.00
95-01-103	O'Doul's Ice House 01324	Lefton	Open	50.00	50.00
95-01-104	Colonial Savings and Loan 01321	Lefton	Open	50.00	50.00
95-01-104	Patriot Bridge 01325	Lefton	Open	50.00	50.00
95-01-106	Rainy Days Barn 01323	Lefton	Open	50.00	50.00
95-01-107	Colonial Village News 01002	Lefton	Open	50.00	50.00
Legends		**The Legendary West Premier Edition**			
88-01-001	Red Cloud's Coup	C. Pardell	S/O	480.00	36-7000.
89-01-002	Pursued	C. Pardell	S/O	750.00	2-4000.
89-01-003	Songs of Glory	C. Pardell	S/O	850.00	2900.00
90-01-004	Crow Warrior	C. Pardell	S/O	1225.00	16-2000.
91-01-005	Triumphant	C. Pardell	S/O	1150.00	14-2600.
92-01-006	The Final Charge	C. Pardell	S/O	1250.00	15-2000.
Legends		**The Legacies Of The West Premier Edition**			
90-02-001	Mystic Vision	C. Pardell	S/O	990.00	2-4000.
90-02-002	Victorious	C. Pardell	S/O	1275.00	23-4200.
91-02-003	Defiant Comanche	C. Pardell	S/O	1300.00	13-2800.
91-02-004	No More, Forever	C. Pardell	S/O	1500.00	16-2850.
92-02-005	Esteemed Warrior	C. Pardell	S/O	1750.00	4000.00
92-02-006	Rebellious	C. Pardell	950	1500.00	15-1800.
93-02-007	Eminent Crow	C. Pardell	950	1500.00	1500.00
94-02-008	Enduring	C. Pardell	950	1250.00	1250.00
Legends		**The Legendary West Collection**			
87-03-001	Pony Express (Bronze)	C. Pardell	S/O	320.00	320-450.
87-03-002	Pony Express (Pewter)	C. Pardell	S/O	320.00	320-450.
89-03-003	White Feather's Vision	C. Pardell	S/O	390.00	560.00
89-03-004	Johnson's Last Fight	C. Pardell	S/O	590.00	850-2000
89-03-005	Tables Turned	C. Pardell	2,500	680.00	680.00
89-03-006	Bustin' A Herd Quitter	C. Pardell	2,500	590.00	590.00
89-03-007	Eagle Dancer	C. Pardell	2,500	370.00	370.00
89-03-008	Pony Express (Mixed Media)	C. Pardell	2,500	390.00	390.00
89-03-009	Sacajawea	C. Pardell	2,500	380.00	380.00
90-03-010	Unbridled	C. Pardell	2,500	290.00	290.00
90-03-011	Shhh	C. Pardell	2,500	390.00	390.00
90-03-012	Stand of the Sash Wearer	C. Pardell	2,500	390.00	390.00
90-03-013	Keeper of Eagles	C. Pardell	2,500	370.00	370.00
91-03-014	Warning	C. Pardell	2,500	390.00	390.00
92-03-015	Crazy Horse	C. Pardell	S/O	390.00	550-950.
92-03-016	Beating Bad Odds	C. Pardell	2,500	390.00	390.00
93-03-017	Cliff Hanger	C. Pardell	2,500	990.00	990.00
93-03-018	Hunter's Brothers	C. Pardell	2,500	590.00	590.00
Legends		**American West Premier Edition**			
91-04-001	Unexpected Rescuer	C. Pardell	S/O	990.00	13-2000.
91-04-002	First Coup	C. Pardell	S/O	1150.00	1150.00
92-04-003	American Horse	C. Pardell	950	1300.00	1300.00
92-04-004	Defending the People	C. Pardell	950	1350.00	1350.00
93-04-005	Four Bears' Challenge	C. Pardell	950	990.00	990.00
94-04-006	Season of Victory	C. Pardell	950	1500.00	1500.00
Legends		**The Endangered Wildlife Collection**			
90-05-001	Forest Spirit	K. Cantrell	S/O	290.00	600-1600
90-05-002	Savannah Prince	K. Cantrell	950	290.00	290.00
91-05-003	Mountain Majesty	K. Cantrell	950	350.00	350.00
91-05-004	Old Tusker	K. Cantrell	950	390.00	390.00
92-05-005	Plains Monarch	K. Cantrell	950	350.00	350.00
92-05-006	Spirit Song	K. Cantrell	S/O	350.00	450-600.
92-05-007	Unchallenged	K. Cantrell	950	350.00	350.00
92-05-008	Songs of Autumn	K. Cantrell	950	390.00	390.00
93-05-009	Big Pine Survivor	K. Cantrell	950	390.00	390.00
93-05-010	Silvertip	K. Cantrell	950	370.00	370.00
XX-05-011	Prairie Phantom	K. Cantrell	950	N/A	N/A
XX-05-012	Twilight	K. Cantrell	950	N/A	N/A

		ARTIST	EDITION	ISSUE	QUOTE
Legends		**Endangered Wildlife Eagle Series**			
89-06-001	Sentinel	K. Cantrell	S/O	280.00	360-650.
89-06-002	Unbounded	K. Cantrell	2,500	280.00	280.00
89-06-003	Outpost	K. Cantrell	2,500	280.00	280.00
89-06-004	Aquila Libre	K. Cantrell	2,500	280.00	280.00
92-06-005	Food Fight	K. Cantrell	2,500	650.00	650.00
92-06-006	Sunday Brunch	K. Cantrell	2,500	550.00	550.00
93-06-007	Defiance	K. Cantrell	2,500	350.00	350.00
93-06-008	Spiral Flight	K. Cantrell	2,500	290.00	290.00
Legends		**Annual Collectors Edition**			
90-07-001	The Night Before	C. Pardell	S/O	990.00	12-1500.
91-07-002	Medicine Gift of Manhood	C. Pardell	S/O	990.00	12-1900.
92-07-003	Spirit of the Wolf	C. Pardell	S/O	950.00	11-2100.
93-07-004	Tomorrow's Warrior	C. Pardell	S/O	590.00	690-850.
94-07-005	Guiding Hand	C. Pardell	S/O	590.00	590.00
Legends		**The Great Outdoorsman**			
88-08-001	Both Are Hooked (Bronze)	C. Pardell	Retrd.	320.00	320.00
88-08-002	Both Are Hooked (Pewter)	C. Pardell	Retrd.	320.00	320.00
Legends		**Classic Equestrian Collection**			
88-09-001	Lippizzaner (Bronze)	C. Pardell	Retrd.	200.00	200.00
Legends		**Wild Realm Collection**			
88-10-001	Fly Fisher (Bronze)	C. Pardell	Retrd.	330.00	330.00
88-10-002	Fly Fisher (Pewter)	C. Pardell	Retrd.	330.00	330.00
Legends		**Wild Realm Premier Edition**			
89-11-001	High Spirit	C. Pardell	1,600	870.00	870.00
91-11-002	Speed Incarnate	C. Pardell	Retrd.	790.00	790.00
Legends		**Indian Arts Collection**			
90-12-001	Chief's Blanket	C. Pardell	S/O	350.00	450.00
90-12-002	Kachina Carver	C. Pardell	S/O	270.00	325-450.
90-12-003	Story Teller	C. Pardell	S/O	290.00	350-550.
90-12-004	Indian Maiden	C. Pardell	1,500	240.00	240.00
90-12-005	Indian Potter	C. Pardell	1,500	260.00	260.00
Legends		**Gallery Editions**			
92-13-001	Resolute	C. Pardell	S/O	7950.00	8-1400.
93-13-002	Visionary	C. Pardell	350	7500.00	7500.00
93-13-003	Over the Rainbow	K. Cantrell	600	2900.00	2900.00
93-13-004	The Wanderer	K. Cantrell	350	3500.00	3500.00
94-13-005	Center Fire	W. Whitten	350	2500.00	2500.00
94-13-006	Mountain Family	D. Lemon	150	8000.00	8000.00
Legends		**Oceanic World**			
89-14-001	Freedom's Beauty (Bronze)	D. Medina	Retrd.	330.00	330.00
89-14-002	Freedom's Beauty (Pewter)	D. Medina	Retrd.	130.00	130.00
89-14-003	Together (Bronze)	D. Medina	Retrd.	140.00	140.00
89-14-004	Together (Pewter)	D. Medina	Retrd.	130.00	130.00
Legends		**North American Wildlife**			
88-15-001	Double Trouble (Bronze)	D. Edwards	Retrd.	300.00	300.00
88-15-002	Double Trouble (Pewter)	D. Edwards	Retrd.	320.00	320.00
88-15-003	Grizzly Solitude (Bronze)	D. Edwards	Retrd.	310.00	310.00
88-15-004	Grizzly Solitude (Pewter)	D. Edwards	Retrd.	330.00	330.00
88-15-005	Defenders of Freedom (Bronze)	D. Edwards	Retrd.	340.00	340.00
88-15-006	Defenders of Freedom (Pewter)	D. Edwards	Retrd.	370.00	370.00
88-15-007	The Proud American (Bronze)	D. Edwards	Retrd.	330.00	330.00
88-15-008	The Proud American (Pewter)	D. Edwards	Retrd.	340.00	340.00
88-15-009	Downhill Run (Bronze)	D. Edwards	Retrd.	330.00	330.00
88-15-010	Downhill Run (Pewter)	D. Edwards	Retrd.	340.00	340.00
88-15-011	Sudden Alert (Bronze)	D. Edwards	Retrd.	300.00	300.00
88-15-012	Sudden Alert (Pewter)	D. Edwards	Retrd.	320.00	320.00
88-15-013	Ridge Runners (Bronze)	D. Edwards	Retrd.	300.00	300.00
88-15-014	Ridge Runners (Pewter)	D. Edwards	Retrd.	310.00	310.00
88-15-015	Last Glance (Bronze)	D. Edwards	Retrd.	300.00	300.00
88-15-016	Last Glance (Pewter)	D. Edwards	Retrd.	320.00	320.00
Legends		**American Heritage**			
87-16-001	Grizz Country (Bronze)	D. Edwards	Retrd.	350.00	350.00
87-16-002	Grizz Country (Pewter)	D. Edwards	Retrd.	370.00	370.00
87-16-003	Winter Provisions (Bronze)	D. Edwards	Retrd.	340.00	340.00
87-16-004	Winter Provisions (Pewter)	D. Edwards	Retrd.	370.00	370.00
87-16-005	Wrangler's Dare (Bronze)	D. Edwards	Retrd.	630.00	630.00
87-16-006	Wrangler's Dare (Pewter)	D. Edwards	Retrd.	660.00	660.00
Legends		**Special Commissions**			
87-17-001	Mama's Joy (Bronze)	D. Edwards	Retrd.	200.00	200.00
87-17-002	Mama's Joy (Pewter)	D. Edwards	Retrd.	250.00	250.00
87-17-003	Wild Freedom (Bronze)	D. Edwards	Retrd.	320.00	320.00
87-17-004	Wild Freedom (Pewter)	D. Edwards	Retrd.	330.00	330.00
88-17-005	Alpha Pair (Bronze)	C. Pardell	Retrd.	330.00	330.00
88-17-006	Alpha Pair (Pewter)	C. Pardell	Retrd.	330.00	330.00
88-17-007	Alpha Pair (Mixed Media)	C. Pardell	S/O	390.00	600.00
91-17-008	Symbols of Freedom	K. Cantrell	2,500	490.00	490.00
92-17-009	Yellowstone Bound	K. Cantrell	S/O	2500.00	2500.00
Legends		**American Indian Dance Premier Edition**			
93-18-001	Drum Song	C. Pardell	750	2800.00	2800.00
94-18-002	Image of the Eagle	C. Pardell	750	1900.00	1900.00
94-18-003	Footprints of the Butterfly	C. Pardell	750	N/A	N/A
Legends		**Kachina Dancers Collection**			
91-19-001	Angakchina	C. Pardell	2,500	370.00	370.00
91-19-002	Ahote	C. Pardell	2,500	370.00	370.00
91-19-003	Koyemsi	C. Pardell	2,500	370.00	370.00
91-19-004	Hilili	C. Pardell	2,500	390.00	390.00
92-19-005	Tawa	C. Pardell	2,500	390.00	390.00
92-19-006	Kwahu	C. Pardell	2,500	390.00	390.00
93-19-007	Koshari	C. Pardell	2,500	370.00	370.00
93-19-008	Mongwa	C. Pardell	2,500	390.00	390.00
94-19-009	Palhik Mana	C. Pardell	2,500	390.00	390.00
94-19-010	Eototo	C. Pardell	2,500	390.00	390.00
Legends		**Way of the Warrior Collection**			
91-20-001	Rite of Manhood	C. Pardell	1,600	170.00	170.00
91-20-002	Seeker of Visions	C. Pardell	1,600	170.00	170.00
91-20-003	Tribal Defender	C. Pardell	1,600	170.00	170.00
91-20-004	Medicine Dancer	C. Pardell	1,600	170.00	170.00
91-20-005	Clan Leader	C. Pardell	1,600	170.00	170.00
91-20-006	Elder Chief	C. Pardell	1,600	170.00	170.00
Legends		**Way of the Wolf Collection**			
93-21-001	Courtship	K. Cantrell	S/O	590.00	650-900.

Left Column

		ARTIST	EDITION	ISSUE	QUOTE
94-21-002	Renewal	K. Cantrell	S/O	700.00	700-900.
Legends		**Warriors of the Sacred Circle**			
92-22-001	Dog Soldier	K. Cantrell	950	450.00	450.00
92-22-002	Peace Offering	K. Cantrell	950	550.00	550.00
93-22-003	Coup Feather	K. Cantrell	950	450.00	450.00
93-22-004	Yellow Boy	K. Cantrell	950	450.00	450.00
94-22-005	Traditional Weapons	W. Whitten	950	550.00	550.00
Legends		**Relics of the Americas**			
93-23-001	Dream Medicine	W. Whitten	950	1150.00	1150.00
94-23-002	Flared Glory	W. Whitten	950	N/A	N/A
Legends		**The North & South Collection**			
92-24-001	Victory at Hand	W. Whitten	950	390.00	390.00
93-24-002	The Noble Heart	W. Whitten	950	450.00	450.00
93-24-003	Brother Against Brother	W. Whitten	950	550.00	550.00
94-24-004	Stonewall	W. Whitten	950	450.00	450.00
Legends		**Mystical Quest Collection**			
92-25-001	Vision Quest	D. Medina	950	990.00	990.00
93-25-002	Hunter's Quest	D. Medina	950	990.00	990.00
94-25-003	Peace Quest	D. Medina	950	1150.00	1150.00
Legends		**Clear Visions**			
93-26-001	Salmon Falls	W. Whitten	950	950.00	950.00
94-26-002	Saving Their Skins	C. Pardell	950	1590.00	1590.00
Legends		**Collectors Only**			
93-27-001	Give Us Peace	C. Pardell	Retrd.	270.00	350-600.
94-27-002	First Born	C. Pardell	1,250	350.00	350.00
94-27-003	River Bandits	K. Cantrell	1,250	350.00	350.00
Legends		**Happy Trails Collection**			
94-28-001	Cowboy Soul	W. Whitten	750	450.00	450.00
Legends		**The North American Collection**			
94-29-001	Spirit of the Wolf	K. Cantrell	2,500	150.00	150.00
94-29-002	Eagles Realm	K. Cantrell	2,500	150.00	150.00
94-29-003	Buffalo Spirit	K. Cantrell	2,500	150.00	150.00
94-29-004	Elusive	K. Cantrell	2,500	150.00	150.00
94-29-005	Northern Express	K. Cantrell	2,500	150.00	150.00
94-29-006	Wild Music	K. Cantrell	2,500	150.00	150.00
Legends		**Hidden Images Collection**			
94-30-001	In Search of Bear Rock	D. Lemon	350	1300.00	1300.00
Legends		**Western Memories Premier Edition**			
94-31-001	Vacant Thunder	D. Lemon	500	1900.00	1900.00
Lenox Collections		**American Fashion**			
83-01-001	Springtime Promenade	Unknown	Open	95.00	95.00
84-01-002	Tea at the Ritz	Unknown	Open	95.00	95.00
84-01-003	First Waltz	Unknown	Open	95.00	95.00
85-01-004	Governor's Garden Party	Unknown	Open	95.00	95.00
86-01-005	Grand Tour	Unknown	Open	95.00	95.00
86-01-006	Belle of the Ball	Unknown	Open	95.00	95.00
87-01-007	Centennial Bride	Unknown	Open	95.00	95.00
87-01-008	Gala at the Whitehouse	Unknown	Open	95.00	95.00
92-01-009	Royal Reception	Unknown	Open	95.00	95.00
Lenox Collections		**Wildlife of the Seven Continents**			
84-02-001	North American Bighorn Sheep	Unknown	Open	120.00	120.00
85-02-002	Australian Koala	Unknown	Open	120.00	120.00
85-02-003	Asian Elephant	Unknown	Open	120.00	120.00
86-02-004	South American Puma	Unknown	Open	120.00	120.00
87-02-005	European Red Deer	Unknown	Open	136.00	136.00
87-02-006	Antarctic Seals	Unknown	Open	136.00	136.00
88-02-007	African Lion	Unknown	Open	136.00	136.00
Lenox Collections		**Legendary Princesses**			
85-03-001	Rapunzel	Unknown	Open	119.00	136.00
86-03-002	Sleeping Beauty	Unknown	Open	119.00	136.00
87-03-003	Snow Queen	Unknown	Open	119.00	136.00
88-03-004	Cinderella	Unknown	Open	136.00	136.00
89-03-005	Swan Princess	Unknown	Open	136.00	136.00
89-03-006	Snow White	Unknown	Open	136.00	136.00
90-03-007	Juliet	Unknown	Open	136.00	136.00
90-03-008	Guinevere	Unknown	Open	136.00	136.00
90-03-009	Cleopatra	Unknown	Open	136.00	136.00
91-03-010	Peacock Maiden	Unknown	Open	136.00	136.00
91-03-011	Pocohontas	Unknown	9,500	136.00	136.00
92-03-012	Firebird	Unknown	Open	156.00	156.00
92-03-013	Sheherezade	Unknown	Open	156.00	156.00
93-03-014	Little Mermaid, Princess of the Sea	Unknown	Open	156.00	156.00
93-03-015	Princess and the Pea	Unknown	Open	156.00	156.00
93-03-016	Princes Beauty	Unknown	Open	156.00	156.00
94-03-017	Maid Marion	Unknown	Open	156.00	156.00
94-03-018	Frog Princess	Unknown	Open	156.00	156.00
94-03-019	Fairy Godmother	Unknown	9,500	156.00	156.00
Lenox Collections		**Carousel Animals**			
87-04-001	Carousel Horse	Unknown	Open	136.00	152.00
88-04-002	Carousel Unicorn	Unknown	Open	136.00	152.00
89-04-003	Carousel Circus Horse	Unknown	Open	136.00	152.00
89-04-004	Carousel Reindeer	Unknown	Open	136.00	152.00
90-04-005	Carousel Elephant	Unknown	Open	136.00	152.00
90-04-006	Carousel Lion	Unknown	Open	136.00	152.00
90-04-007	Carousel Charger	Unknown	Open	136.00	152.00
91-04-008	Carousel Polar Bear	Unknown	Open	152.00	152.00
91-04-009	Pride of America	Unknown	Closed	152.00	152.00
91-04-010	Western Horse	Unknown	Open	152.00	152.00
92-04-011	Camelot Horse	Unknown	Open	152.00	152.00
92-04-012	Statement Piece	Unknown	Open	395.00	395.00
92-04-013	Victorian Romance Horse	Unknown	Open	156.00	156.00
92-04-014	Tropical Horse	Unknown	Open	156.00	156.00
92-04-015	1992 Christmas Horse	Unknown	Yr.Iss.	156.00	156.00
93-04-016	Nautical Horse	Unknown	Open	156.00	156.00
93-04-017	1993 Christmas Horse	Unknown	Yr.Iss.	156.00	156.00
93-04-018	Rose Prancer	Unknown	9,500	156.00	156.00
93-04-019	Statement Horse #1 Victorian Romance	Unknown	2,500	395.00	395.00
94-04-020	Statement Horse #2 Ribbons & Roses	Unknown	2,500	395.00	395.00
94-04-021	Midnight Charger	Unknown	9,500	156.00	156.00
94-04-022	1994 Christmas Horse	Unknown	Yr.Iss.	156.00	156.00
Lenox Collections		**Nativity**			
86-05-001	Holy Family	Unknown	Open	119.00	136.00

Right Column

		ARTIST	EDITION	ISSUE	QUOTE
87-05-002	Three Kings	Unknown	Open	119.00	152.00
88-05-003	Shepherds	Unknown	Open	119.00	152.00
88-05-004	Animals of the Nativity	Unknown	Open	119.00	152.00
89-05-005	Angels of Adoration	Unknown	Open	136.00	152.00
90-05-006	Children of Bethlehem	Unknown	Open	136.00	152.00
91-05-007	Townspeople of Bethlehem	Unknown	Open	136.00	152.00
91-05-008	Standing Camel & Driver	Unknown	9,500	152.00	152.00
Lenox Collections		**Garden Birds**			
85-06-001	Chickadee	Unknown	Open	39.00	45.00
86-06-002	Blue Jay	Unknown	Open	39.00	45.00
86-06-003	Eastern Bluebird	Unknown	Open	39.00	45.00
86-06-004	Tufted Titmouse	Unknown	Open	39.00	45.00
87-06-005	Red-Breasted Nuthatch	Unknown	Open	39.00	45.00
87-06-006	Cardinal	Unknown	Open	39.00	45.00
87-06-007	Turtle Dove	Unknown	Open	39.00	45.00
87-06-008	American Goldfinch	Unknown	Open	39.00	45.00
88-06-009	Hummingbird	Unknown	Open	39.00	45.00
88-06-010	Cedar Waxwing	Unknown	Open	39.00	45.00
89-06-011	Robin	Unknown	Open	39.00	45.00
89-06-012	Downy Woodpecker	Unknown	Open	39.00	45.00
89-06-013	Saw Whet Owl	Unknown	Open	45.00	45.00
90-06-014	Baltimore Oriole	Unknown	Open	45.00	45.00
90-06-015	Marsh Wren	Unknown	Open	45.00	45.00
90-06-016	Chipping Sparrow	Unknown	Open	45.00	45.00
90-06-017	Wood Duck	Unknown	Open	45.00	45.00
91-06-018	Purple Finch	Unknown	Open	45.00	45.00
91-06-019	Golden Crowned Kinglet	Unknown	Open	45.00	45.00
91-06-020	Dark Eyed Junco	Unknown	Open	45.00	45.00
91-06-021	Broadbilled Hummingbird	Unknown	Open	45.00	45.00
91-06-022	Rose Grosbeak	Unknown	Open	45.00	45.00
92-06-023	Scarlet Tanger	Unknown	Open	45.00	45.00
92-06-024	Magnificent Hummingbird	Unknown	Open	45.00	45.00
92-06-025	Western Meadowlark	Unknown	Open	45.00	45.00
93-06-026	Statement Piece	Unknown	Open	45.00	45.00
93-06-027	Mockingbird	Unknown	Open	45.00	45.00
93-06-028	Barn Swallow	Unknown	Open	45.00	45.00
93-06-029	Indigo Bunting	Unknown	Open	45.00	45.00
93-06-030	Chipping Sparrow	Unknown	Open	45.00	45.00
93-06-031	Red Winged Blackbird	Unknown	Open	45.00	45.00
93-06-032	Female Cardinal	Unknown	Open	45.00	45.00
93-06-033	Female Kinglet	Unknown	Open	45.00	45.00
93-06-034	Yellow Warbler	Unknown	Open	45.00	45.00
93-06-035	Mountain Bluebird	Unknown	Open	45.00	45.00
94-06-036	Christmas Dove	Unknown	Yr.Iss.	45.00	45.00
94-06-037	Vermillion Flycatcher	Unknown	Open	45.00	45.00
94-06-038	Female BlueJay	Unknown	Open	45.00	45.00
94-06-039	Western Tanager	Unknown	Open	45.00	45.00
94-06-040	Female Chickadee	Unknown	Open	45.00	45.00
94-06-041	Purple Martin	Unknown	Open	45.00	45.00
Lenox Collections		**Floral Sculptures**			
86-07-001	Rubrum Lily	Unknown	Open	119.00	136.00
87-07-002	Iris	Unknown	Open	119.00	136.00
88-07-003	Magnolia	Unknown	Open	119.00	136.00
88-07-004	Peace Rose	Unknown	Open	119.00	136.00
Lenox Collections		**Garden Flowers**			
88-08-001	Tea Rose	Unknown	Open	39.00	45.00
88-08-002	Cattleya Orchid	Unknown	Open	39.00	45.00
88-08-003	Parrot Tulip	Unknown	Open	39.00	39.00
89-08-004	Iris	Unknown	Open	45.00	45.00
90-08-005	Day Lily	Unknown	Open	45.00	45.00
90-08-006	Carnation	Unknown	Open	45.00	45.00
90-08-007	Daffodil	Unknown	Open	45.00	45.00
91-08-008	Morning Glory	Unknown	Open	45.00	45.00
91-08-009	Magnolia	Unknown	Open	45.00	45.00
91-08-010	Calla Lily	Unknown	Open	45.00	45.00
91-08-011	Camelia	Unknown	Open	45.00	45.00
91-08-012	Poinsettia	Unknown	Open	39.00	39.00
93-08-013	Red Rose	Unknown	Open	45.00	45.00
Lenox Collections		**Mother & Child**			
86-09-001	Cherished Moment	Unknown	Open	119.00	119.00
86-09-002	Sunday in the Park	Unknown	Open	119.00	119.00
87-09-003	Storytime	Unknown	Open	119.00	119.00
88-09-004	The Present	Unknown	Open	119.00	119.00
89-09-005	Christening	Unknown	Open	119.00	119.00
90-09-006	Bedtime Prayers	Unknown	Open	119.00	119.00
91-09-007	Afternoon Stroll	Unknown	7,500	136.00	136.00
91-09-008	Evening Lullaby	Unknown	7,500	136.00	136.00
92-09-009	Morning Playtime	Unknown	Open	136.00	136.00
Lenox Collections		**Owls of America**			
88-10-001	Snowy Owl	Unknown	Open	136.00	136.00
89-10-002	Barn Owl	Unknown	Open	136.00	136.00
90-10-003	Screech Owl	Unknown	Open	136.00	136.00
91-10-004	Great Horned Owl	Unknown	9,500	136.00	136.00
Lenox Collections		**International Horse Sculptures**			
88-11-001	Arabian Knight	Unknown	Open	136.00	136.00
89-11-002	Thoroughbred	Unknown	Open	136.00	136.00
90-11-003	Lippizan	Unknown	Open	136.00	136.00
90-11-004	Appaloosa	Unknown	Open	136.00	136.00
Lenox Collections		**Nature's Beautiful Butterflies**			
89-12-001	Blue Temora	Unknown	Open	39.00	45.00
90-12-002	Yellow Swallowtail	Unknown	Open	39.00	45.00
90-12-003	Monarch	Unknown	Open	39.00	45.00
90-12-004	Purple Emperor	Unknown	Open	45.00	45.00
91-12-005	Malachite	Unknown	Open	45.00	45.00
91-12-006	Adonis	Unknown	Open	45.00	45.00
93-12-007	Black Swallowtail	Unknown	Open	45.00	45.00
93-12-008	Great Orange Wingtip	Unknown	Open	45.00	45.00
93-12-009	American Painted Lady	Unknown	Open	45.00	45.00
94-12-010	Rainforest Dazzler	Unknown	Open	45.00	45.00
Lenox Collections		**Kings of the Sky**			
89-13-001	Lord of Skies, American Bald Eagle	Unknown	Open	195.00	195.00
91-13-002	Eagle of Glory, Golden Eagle	Unknown	Open	234.00	234.00
91-13-003	Defender of Freedom, American Bald Eagle	Unknown	Closed	234.00	234.00
92-13-004	Wings of Majesty, American Bald Eagle	Unknown	Open	252.00	252.00
93-13-004	Wings of Power, Golden Eagle	Unknown	Open	252.00	252.00
93-13-005	Foundation of Freedom	Unknown	Open	252.00	252.00

		ARTIST	EDITION	ISSUE	QUOTE
94-13-006	Eagle of Splendor, American Bald Eagle	Unknown	Open	252.00	252.00
94-13-007	Wings of Pride, Golden Eagle	Unknown	Open	252.00	252.00
Lenox Collections		**Endangered Baby Animals**			
90-14-001	Panda	Unknown	Open	39.00	39.00
91-14-002	Elephant	Unknown	Open	57.00	57.00
91-14-003	Baby Florida Panther	Unknown	Open	57.00	57.00
91-14-004	Baby Grey Wolf	Unknown	Open	57.00	57.00
92-14-005	Baby Rhinocerous	Unknown	Open	57.00	57.00
93-14-006	Indian Elephant Calf	Unknown	Open	57.00	57.00
94-14-007	Pigmy Hippo	Unknown	Open	58.00	58.00
94-14-008	Baby Orangatan	Unknown	Open	58.00	58.00
94-14-009	Sumatra Tiger Cub	Unknown	Open	58.00	58.00
94-14-010	Bridled Nail-Tailed Wallaby Joey	Unknown	Open	58.00	58.00
Lenox Collections		**Lenox Baby Book**			
90-15-001	Baby's First Shoes	Unknown	Open	57.00	57.00
91-15-002	Baby's First Steps	Unknown	Open	57.00	57.00
91-15-003	Baby's First Christmas	Unknown	Open	57.00	57.00
92-15-004	Baby's First Portrait	Unknown	Open	57.00	57.00
Lenox Collections		**Lenox Puppy Collection**			
90-16-001	Beagle	Unknown	Open	76.00	76.00
91-16-002	Cocker Spaniel	Unknown	Open	76.00	76.00
92-16-003	Poodle	Unknown	Open	76.00	76.00
94-16-004	German Shepherd	Unknown	Open	75.00	75.00
Lenox Collections		**International Brides**			
90-17-001	Russian Bride	Unknown	Open	136.00	136.00
92-17-002	Japanese Bride, Kiyoshi	Unknown	Open	136.00	136.00
Lenox Collections		**Life of Christ**			
90-18-001	The Children's Blessing	Unknown	Open	95.00	95.00
90-18-002	Madonna And Child	Unknown	Open	95.00	95.00
90-18-003	The Good Shepherd	Unknown	Open	95.00	95.00
91-18-004	The Savior	Unknown	Open	95.00	95.00
91-18-005	Jesus, The Teacher	Unknown	9,500	95.00	95.00
92-18-006	A Child's Prayer	Unknown	Open	95.00	95.00
92-18-007	Childrens's Devotion (Painted)	Unknown	Open	195.00	195.00
92-18-008	Mary & Christ Child (Painted)	Unknown	Open	195.00	195.00
92-18-009	A Child's Comfort	Unknown	Open	95.00	95.00
93-18-010	Jesus, The Carpenter	Unknown	Open	95.00	95.00
93-18-011	Children's Adoration	Unknown	Open	95.00	95.00
Lenox Collections		**North American Bird Pairs**			
90-19-001	Hummingbirds	Unknown	Open	119.00	119.00
91-19-002	Chickadees	Unknown	Open	119.00	119.00
91-19-003	Blue Jay Pairs	Unknown	Open	119.00	119.00
92-19-004	Cardinal	Unknown	Open	119.00	119.00
Lenox Collections		**Santa Claus Collection**			
90-20-001	Father Christmas	Unknown	Open	136.00	136.00
91-20-002	Americana Santa	Unknown	Open	136.00	136.00
91-20-003	Kris Kringle	Unknown	Open	136.00	136.00
92-20-004	Grandfather Frost	Unknown	Open	136.00	136.00
92-20-005	Pere Noel	Unknown	Open	136.00	136.00
93-20-006	St. Nick	Unknown	Open	136.00	136.00
94-20-007	Bavarian Santa	Unknown	Open	136.00	136.00
94-20-008	Victorian Santa	Unknown	Open	136.00	136.00
Lenox Collections		**Miniature Santas Around the World-8"**			
93-21-001	Father Christmas	Unknown	Open	19.50	19.50
93-21-002	Americana Santa	Unknown	Open	19.50	19.50
93-21-003	Kris Kringle	Unknown	Open	19.50	19.50
93-21-004	Grandfather Frost	Unknown	Open	19.50	19.50
93-21-005	Pere Noel	Unknown	Open	19.50	19.50
93-21-006	St. Nick	Unknown	Open	19.50	19.50
93-21-007	Bavarian Santa	Unknown	Open	19.50	19.50
94-21-008	Victorian Santa	Unknown	Open	19.50	19.50
94-21-009	Patriotic Santa	Unknown	Open	19.50	19.50
94-21-010	Santa Lucia	Unknown	Open	19.50	19.50
94-21-011	Befona	Unknown	Open	19.50	19.50
94-21-012	Christkindle	Unknown	Open	19.50	19.50
94-21-013	Sinterklaus	Unknown	Open	19.50	19.50
94-21-014	St. Mikulase	Unknown	Open	19.50	19.50
94-21-015	Sanct Herr Nikolaus	Unknown	Open	19.50	19.50
Lenox Collections		**Woodland Animals**			
90-22-001	Red Squirrel	Unknown	Open	39.00	39.00
90-22-002	Raccoon	Unknown	Open	39.00	39.00
91-22-003	Chipmunk	Unknown	Open	39.00	39.00
92-22-004	Rabbit	Unknown	Open	39.00	39.00
93-22-005	Fawn	Unknown	Open	39.00	39.00
93-22-006	Deer	Unknown	Open	45.00	45.00
93-22-007	Skunk	Unknown	Open	45.00	45.00
94-22-008	Mouse	Unknown	Open	45.00	45.00
94-22-009	Beaver	Unknown	Open	45.00	45.00
Lenox Collections		**Gentle Majesty**			
90-23-001	Bear Hug Polar Bear	Unknown	Open	76.00	76.00
90-23-002	Penguins	Unknown	Open	76.00	76.00
91-23-003	Keeping Warm (Foxes)	Unknown	Open	76.00	76.00
Lenox Collections		**Street Crier Collection**			
90-24-001	French Flower Maiden	Unknown	Open	136.00	136.00
91-24-002	Belgian Lace Maker	Unknown	Open	136.00	136.00
Lenox Collections		**Doves & Roses**			
91-26-001	Love's Promise	Unknown	Open	95.00	95.00
91-26-002	Doves of Peace	Unknown	Open	95.00	95.00
92-26-003	Doves of Honor	Unknown	Open	119.00	119.00
93-26-004	Doves of Love	Unknown	Open	119.00	119.00
Lenox Collections		**Exotic Birds**			
91-27-001	Cockatoo	Unknown	Open	45.00	45.00
93-27-002	"Plum Headed" Parakeet	Unknown	Open	49.50	49.50
Lenox Collections		**Jessie Willcox Smith**			
91-28-001	Rosebuds	J.W.Smith	Open	60.00	60.00
91-28-002	Feeding Kitty	J.W.Smith	Open	60.00	60.00
Lenox Collections		**Baby Bears**			
91-29-001	Polar Bear	Unknown	Open	45.00	45.00
Lenox Collections		**Baby Bird Pairs**			
91-30-001	Robins	Unknown	Open	64.00	64.00
92-30-002	Orioles	Unknown	Open	64.00	64.00
92-30-003	Chickadee	Unknown	Open	64.00	64.00
Lenox Collections		**Lenox Sea Animals**			
91-31-001	Dance of the Dolphins	Unknown	Open	119.00	119.00
92-31-002	Song of the Whales	Unknown	Open	136.00	136.00
93-31-003	Flight of the Dolphins	Unknown	Open	119.00	119.00
93-31-004	Journey of the Whales	Unknown	Open	136.00	136.00
93-31-005	Otter Escapade	Unknown	Open	136.00	136.00
94-31-006	Adventure of Fur Seals	Unknown	Open	136.00	136.00
94-31-007	Voyage of the Sea Turtles	Unknown	Open	136.00	136.00
94-31-008	Penguins at Play	Unknown	Open	136.00	136.00
Lenox Collections		**North American Wildlife**			
91-32-001	White Tailed Deer	Unknown	Open	195.00	195.00
Lenox Collections		**Porcelain Duck Collection**			
91-33-001	Wood Duck	Unknown	Open	45.00	45.00
91-33-002	Mallard Duck	Unknown	Open	45.00	45.00
92-33-003	Blue Winged Teal Duck	Unknown	Open	45.00	45.00
93-33-004	Pintail Duck	Unknown	Open	45.00	45.00
Lenox Collections		**Religious Sculptures**			
92-34-001	Moses	Unknown	Open	95.00	95.00
93-34-002	Last Supper	Unknown	Open	152.00	152.00
94-34-003	Pieta	Unknown	Open	152.00	152.00
Lenox Collections		**Parent & Child Bird Pairs**			
92-35-001	Blue Jay Pairs	Unknown	Open	119.00	119.00
Lenox Collections		**Renaissance Nativity**			
91-36-001	Holy Family	Unknown	Open	195.00	195.00
91-36-002	Shepherds of Bethlehem	Unknown	Open	195.00	195.00
91-36-003	Three Kings	Unknown	Open	195.00	195.00
91-36-004	Animals of the Nativity	Unknown	Open	195.00	195.00
91-36-005	Angels	Unknown	Open	195.00	195.00
93-36-006	Camel & Driver	Unknown	9,500	195.00	195.00
94-36-007	Children of Bethlehem	Unknown	9,500	195.00	195.00
Lenox Collections		**International Songbirds**			
92-37-001	European Goldfinch	Unknown	Open	152.00	152.00
92-37-002	American Goldfinch	Unknown	Open	152.00	152.00
Lenox Collections		**Classical Goddesses**			
92-39-001	Aphrodite, Painted	Unknown	Open	136.00	136.00
92-39-002	Aphrodite	Unknown	Open	95.00	95.00
Lenox Collections		**Crystal Animal Pairs**			
93-40-001	Prim & Proper, Cats	Unknown	Open	76.00	76.00
93-40-002	Silk & Satin, Rabbits	Unknown	Open	76.00	76.00
94-40-003	Preen & Serene, Cats	Unknown	Open	76.00	76.00
Lenox Collections		**Hunters of the Sky**			
93-41-001	Challenge of the Eagles, Double Eagles	Unknown	Open	275.00	275.00
94-41-002	Challenge of the Red Tailed Hawks	Unknown	Open	295.00	295.00
94-41-003	Golden Conquerors	Unknown	Open	295.00	295.00
94-41-004	Masters of the Wind, Peregian Falcons	Unknown	Open	295.00	295.00
Lenox Collections		**Crystal Eagles**			
94-42-001	Soaring Majesty	Unknown	Open	195.00	195.00
Lilliput Lane Ltd.		**Collectors Club Specials**			
86-01-001	Packhorse Bridge	D. Tate	Retrd.	Gift	500-1000
86-01-002	Crendon Manor	D. Tate	Retrd.	285.00	650-1000
86-01-003	Gulliver	Unknown	Retrd.	65.00	200-240.
87-01-004	Little Lost Dog	D. Tate	Retrd.	Gift	275-290.
87-01-005	Yew Tree Farm	D. Tate	Retrd.	160.00	155-260.
88-01-006	Wishing Well	D. Tate	Retrd.	Gift	65-100.
89-01-007	Dovecot	D. Tate	Retrd.	Gift	60-100.
89-01-008	Wenlock Rise	D. Tate	Retrd.	175.00	165-225.
90-01-009	Cosy Corner	D. Tate	Retrd.	Gift	50-100.
90-01-010	Lavender Cottage	D. Tate	Retrd.	50.00	60-100.
90-01-011	Bridle Way	D. Tate	Retrd.	100.00	100-160.
91-01-012	Puddlebrook	D. Tate	Retrd.	Gift	45-60.00
91-01-013	Gardeners Cottage	D. Tate	Retrd.	120.00	90-120.
91-01-014	Wren Cottage	D. Tate	Retrd.	13.95	65-125.
92-01-015	Pussy Willow	D. Tate	Retrd.	Gift	36-60.00
92-01-016	Forget-Me-Not	D. Tate	Retrd.	130.00	83-160.
93-01-017	The Spinney	Lilliput Lane	Retrd.	Gift	N/A
93-01-018	Heaven Lea Cottage	Lilliput Lane	Retrd.	150.00	150.00
93-01-019	Curlew Cottage	Lilliput Lane	Retrd.	18.95	18.95
94-01-020	Petticoat Cottage	Lilliput Lane	4/95	Gift	N/A
94-01-021	Woodman's Retreat	Lilliput Lane	4/95	135.00	135.00
Lilliput Lane Ltd.		**Lilliput Lane Cottage Collection-English Cottages**			
82-02-001	Old Mine	D. Tate	Retrd.	15.95	6500.00
82-02-002	Drapers	D. Tate	Retrd.	15.95	4025.00
82-02-003	Dale House	D. Tate	Retrd.	25.00	840.00
82-02-004	Sussex Mill	D. Tate	Retrd.	25.00	325-500.
82-02-005	Lakeside House-Mold 1	D. Tate	Retrd.	40.00	1500.00
82-02-006	Lakeside House-Mold 2	D. Tate	Retrd.	40.00	810-940.
82-02-007	Stone Cottage-Mold 1	D. Tate	Retrd.	40.00	1500.00
82-02-008	Stone Cottage-Mold 2	D. Tate	Retrd.	40.00	260-275.
82-02-009	Acorn Cottage-Mold 1	D. Tate	Retrd.	30.00	125-400.
83-02-010	Acorn Cottage-Mold 2	D. Tate	Retrd.	30.00	55-80.00
82-02-011	Bridge House-Mold 1	D. Tate	Retrd.	15.95	450.00
82-02-012	Bridge House-Mold 2	D. Tate	Retrd.	15.95	50-200.
82-02-013	April Cottage-Mold 1	D. Tate	Retrd.	Unkn.	300.00
82-02-014	April Cottage-Mold 2	D. Tate	Retrd.	Unkn.	40-80.00
82-02-015	Honeysuckle	D. Tate	Retrd.	45.00	70-230.
82-02-016	Oak Lodge	D. Tate	Retrd.	40.00	100-170.
82-02-017	Dale Farm	D. Tate	Retrd.	30.00	875.00
82-02-018	The Old Post Office	D. Tate	Retrd.	35.00	475-670.
82-02-019	Coach House	D. Tate	Retrd.	100.00	11-1895.
82-02-020	Castle Street	D. Tate	Retrd.	130.00	240-350.
82-02-021	Holly Cottage	D. Tate	Retrd.	42.50	55-95.00
82-02-022	Burnside	D. Tate	Retrd.	30.00	550.00
83-02-023	Coopers	D. Tate	Retrd.	15.00	440-825.
83-02-024	Millers	D. Tate	Retrd.	15.00	120-200.
83-02-025	Miners	D. Tate	Retrd.	15.00	375-455.
83-02-026	Toll House	D. Tate	Retrd.	15.00	125-200.
83-02-027	Woodcutters	D. Tate	Retrd.	15.00	125.00
83-02-028	Tuck Shop	D. Tate	Retrd.	35.00	625-875.
83-02-029	Warwick Hall-Mold 1	D. Tate	Retrd.	185.00	3-4000.
83-02-030	Warwick Hall-Mold 2	D. Tate	Retrd.	185.00	13-1800.
82-02-031	Anne Hathaway's-Mold 1	D. Tate	Retrd.	40.00	14-2650.
83-02-032	Anne Hathaway's-Mold 2	D. Tate	Retrd.	40.00	400-600.

		ARTIST	EDITION	ISSUE	QUOTE
84-02-033	Anne Hathaway's-Mold 3	D. Tate	Retrd.	40.00	375.00
89-02-034	Anne HathawayOs-Mold 4	D. Tate	Open	130.00	150.00
82-02-035	William Shakespeare-Mold 1	D. Tate	Retrd.	55.00	3000.00
83-02-036	William Shakespeare-Mold 2	D. Tate	Retrd.	55.00	200.00
86-02-037	William Shakespeare-Mold 3	D. Tate	Retrd.	55.00	215.00
89-02-038	William Shakespeare-Mold 4	D. Tate	Retrd.	130.00	150.00
83-02-039	Red Lion	D. Tate	Retrd.	125.00	264-400.
83-02-040	Thatcher's Rest	D. Tate	Retrd.	185.00	180-260.
83-02-041	Troutbeck Farm	D. Tate	Retrd.	125.00	225-275.
83-02-042	Dove Cottage-Mold 1	D. Tate	Retrd.	35.00	725-1800
84-02-043	Dove Cottage-Mold 2	D. Tate	Retrd.	35.00	55-85.00
84-02-044	Old School House	D. Tate	Retrd.	Unkn.	1-1400.
84-02-045	Tintagel	D. Tate	Retrd.	39.50	110-170.
85-02-046	Old Curiosity Shop	D. Tate	Retrd.	62.50	75-100.
85-02-047	St. Mary's Church	D. Tate	Retrd.	40.00	60-85.00
85-02-048	Clare Cottage	D. Tate	Retrd.	30.00	63.00
85-02-049	Fisherman's Cottage	D. Tate	Retrd.	30.00	55-95.00
85-02-050	Sawrey Gill	D. Tate	Retrd.	30.00	175-230.
85-02-051	Ostlers Keep	D. Tate	Retrd.	55.00	66-150.
85-02-052	Moreton Manor	D. Tate	Retrd.	55.00	60-150.
85-02-053	Kentish Oast	D. Tate	Retrd.	55.00	70-175.
85-02-054	Watermill	D. Tate	Retrd.	40.00	85.00
85-02-055	Bronte Parsonage	D. Tate	Retrd.	72.00	80-225.
85-02-056	Farriers	D. Tate	Retrd.	40.00	75-110.
86-02-057	Dale Head	D. Tate	Retrd.	75.00	85-200.
86-02-058	Bay View	D. Tate	Retrd.	39.50	90-125.
86-02-059	Cobblers Cottage	D. Hall	Retrd.	42.00	65.00
86-02-060	Three Feathers	D. Tate	Retrd.	115.00	200-250.
86-02-061	Spring Bank	D. Tate	Retrd.	42.00	50-70.00
86-02-062	Scroll on the Wall	D. Tate	Retrd.	55.00	120-175.
86-02-063	Tudor Court	Lilliput Lane	Retrd.	260.00	260-350.
87-02-064	Beacon Heights	Lilliput Lane	Retrd.	125.00	150-235.
87-02-065	Wealden House	D. Tate	Retrd.	125.00	100-165.
87-02-066	The Gables	Lilliput Lane	Retrd.	145.00	135-200.
87-02-067	Secret Garden	M. Adkinson	Retrd.	145.00	220.00
87-02-068	Rydal View	D. Tate	Retrd.	220.00	205-300.
87-02-069	Stoneybeck	D. Tate	Retrd.	45.00	60-75.00
87-02-070	Riverview	D. Tate	Retrd.	27.50	40.00
87-02-071	Clover Cottage	D. Tate	Retrd.	27.50	58.00
87-02-072	Inglewood	D. Tate	Retrd.	27.50	40.00
87-02-073	Tanners Cottage	D. Tate	Retrd.	27.50	65.00
87-02-074	Holme Dyke	D. Tate	Retrd.	50.00	50-100.
87-02-075	Saddlers Inn	M. Adkinson	Retrd.	50.00	50-70.00
87-02-076	Four Seasons	M. Adkinson	Retrd.	70.00	100-140.
87-02-077	Magpie Cottage	D. Tate	Retrd.	70.00	85-250.
87-02-078	Izaak Waltons Cottage	D. Tate	Retrd.	75.00	80-200.
87-02-079	Keepers Lodge	D. Tate	Retrd.	75.00	75-130.
87-02-080	Summer Haze	D. Tate	Retrd.	90.00	105-130.
87-02-081	Street Scene No. 1	Unknown	Retrd.	40.00	120-240.
87-02-082	Street Scene No. 2	Unknown	Retrd.	45.00	120-240.
87-02-083	Street Scene No. 3	Unknown	Retrd.	45.00	120-240.
87-02-084	Street Scene No. 4	Unknown	Retrd.	45.00	120-240.
87-02-085	Street Scene No. 5	Unknown	Retrd.	40.00	120-240.
87-02-086	Street Scene No. 6	Unknown	Retrd.	40.00	120-240.
87-02-087	Street Scene No. 7	Unknown	Retrd.	40.00	120-240.
87-02-088	Street Scene No. 8	Unknown	Retrd.	40.00	120-240.
87-02-089	Street Scene No. 9	Unknown	Retrd.	45.00	120-240.
87-02-090	Street Scene No. 10	Unknown	Retrd.	45.00	120-240.
88-02-091	Brockbank	D. Tate	Retrd.	58.00	80.00
88-02-092	St. Marks	D. Tate	Retrd.	75.00	125-180.
88-02-093	Swift Hollow	D. Tate	Retrd.	75.00	60-150.
88-02-094	Pargetters Retreat	D. Tate	Retrd.	75.00	70-300.
88-02-095	Swan Inn	D. Tate	Retrd.	120.00	170-225.
88-02-096	Ship Inn	Lilliput Lane	Retrd.	210.00	228-325.
88-02-097	Saxon Cottage	D. Tate	Retrd.	245.00	175-450.
88-02-098	Smallest Inn	D. Tate	Retrd.	42.50	65-150.
88-02-099	Rising Sun	D. Tate	Retrd.	58.00	84-105.
88-02-100	Crown Inn	D. Tate	Retrd.	120.00	120-215.
88-02-101	Royal Oak	D. Tate	Retrd.	145.00	100-325.
88-02-102	Bredon House	D. Tate	Retrd.	145.00	100-150.
89-02-103	Chine Cot	D. Tate	Open	36.00	50.00
89-02-104	Fiveways	D. Tate	Open	42.50	55.00
89-02-105	Ash Nook	D. Tate	Open	47.50	60.00
89-02-106	The Briary	D. Tate	Open	47.50	60.00
89-02-107	Victoria Cottage	D. Tate	Retrd.	52.50	65.00
89-02-108	Butterwick	D. Tate	Open	52.50	70.00
89-02-109	Greensted Church	D. Tate	Open	72.50	95.00
89-02-110	Beehive Cottage	D. Tate	Open	72.50	95.00
89-02-111	Tanglewood Lodge	D. Tate	Retrd.	97.00	145-185.
89-02-112	St. Peter's Cove	D. Tate	Retrd.	1375.00	14-2200.
89-02-113	Wight Cottage	D. Tate	Retrd.	52.50	65.00
89-02-114	Helmere	D. Tate	Open	65.00	80.00
89-02-115	Titmouse Cottage	D. Tate	Open	92.50	120.00
89-02-116	St. Lawrence Church	D. Tate	Open	110.00	140.00
89-02-117	Olde York Toll	D. Tate	Retrd.	82.50	83-110.
89-02-118	Chiltern Mill	D. Tate	Open	87.50	110.00
90-02-119	Strawberry Cottage	D. Tate	Open	36.00	45.00
90-02-120	Buttercup Cottage	D. Tate	Retrd.	40.00	46.50
90-02-121	Bramble Cottage	D. Tate	Open	55.00	70.00
90-02-122	Mrs. Pinkerton's Post Office	D. Tate	Open	72.50	85.00
90-02-123	Sulgrave Manor	D. Tate	Retrd.	120.00	130-280.
90-02-124	Periwinkle Cottage	D. Tate	Open	165.00	220.00
90-02-125	Robin's Gate	D. Tate	Open	33.50	45.00
90-02-126	Cherry Cottage	D. Tate	Open	33.50	45.00
90-02-127	Otter Reach	D. Tate	Open	33.50	45.00
90-02-128	Runswick House	D. Tate	Open	62.50	80.00
90-02-129	The King's Arms	D. Tate	Open	450.00	550.00
90-02-130	Convent in The Woods	D. Tate	Open	175.00	220.00
91-02-131	Armada House	D. Tate	Open	175.00	185.00
91-02-132	Moonlight Cove	D. Tate	Open	82.50	85.00
91-02-133	Pear Tree House	D. Tate	Open	82.50	85.00
91-02-134	Lapworth Lock	D. Tate	Retrd.	82.50	85.00
91-02-135	Micklegate Antiques	D. Tate	Open	90.00	95.00
91-02-136	Bridge House 1991	D. Tate	Open	25.00	30.00
91-02-137	Tillers Green	D. Tate	Open	60.00	65.00
91-02-138	Wellington Lodge	D. Tate	Open	55.00	60.00
91-02-139	Primrose Hill	D. Tate	Open	46.50	50.00
91-02-140	Daisy Cottage	D. Tate	Open	37.50	40.00
91-02-141	Farthing Lodge	D. Tate	Open	37.50	40.00
91-02-142	Dovetails	D. Tate	Open	90.00	95.00
91-02-143	Lace Lane	D. Tate	Open	90.00	95.00
91-02-144	The Flower Sellers	D. Tate	Open	110.00	120.00

		ARTIST	EDITION	ISSUE	QUOTE
91-02-145	Witham Delph	D. Tate	Retrd.	110.00	120.00
91-02-146	Village School	D. Tate	Open	120.00	130.00
91-02-147	Hopcroft Cottage	D. Tate	Open	120.00	130.00
91-02-148	John Barleycorn Cottage	D. Tate	Open	130.00	140.00
91-02-149	Paradise Lodge	D. Tate	Open	130.00	140.00
91-02-150	The Priest's House	D. Tate	Open	180.00	195.00
91-02-151	Old Shop at Bignor	D. Tate	Open	215.00	220.00
91-02-152	Chatsworth View	D. Tate	Open	250.00	275.00
91-02-153	Anne of Cleves	D. Tate	Open	360.00	395.00
91-02-154	Saxham St. Edmunds	D. Tate	4,500	1550.00	1650.00
92-02-155	Bow Cottage	D. Tate	Open	128.00	135.00
92-02-156	Granny Smiths	D. Tate	Open	60.00	65.00
92-02-157	Oakwood Smithy	D. Tate	Open	450.00	475.00
92-02-158	Pixie House	D. Tate	Open	55.00	60.00
92-02-159	Puffin Row	D. Tate	Open	128.00	135.00
92-02-160	Rustic Root House	D. Tate	Open	110.00	120.00
92-02-161	Wheyside Cottage	Lilliput Lane	Open	46.50	50.00
92-02-162	Wedding Bells	Lilliput Lane	Open	75.00	80.00
92-02-163	Derwent-le-Dale	Lilliput Lane	Open	75.00	80.00
92-02-164	The Nutshell	Lilliput Lane	Open	75.00	80.00
92-02-165	Finchingfields	Lilliput Lane	Open	82.50	95.00
92-02-166	The Chocolate House	Lilliput Lane	Open	130.00	140.00
92-02-167	Grantchester Meadows	Lilliput Lane	Open	275.00	275.00
92-02-168	High Ghyll Farm	Lilliput Lane	Open	360.00	395.00
93-02-169	Cat's Coombe Cottage	Lilliput Lane	Open	95.00	95.00
93-02-170	Cley-next-the-sea	Lilliput Lane	2,500	725.00	725.00
93-02-171	Foxglove Fields	Lilliput Lane	Open	130.00	130.00
93-02-172	Junk and Disorderly	Lilliput Lane	Open	150.00	150.00
93-02-173	Purbeck Stores	Lilliput Lane	Open	55.00	55.00
93-02-174	Stocklebeck Mill	Lilliput Lane	Open	325.00	325.00
93-02-175	Stradling Priory	Lilliput Lane	Open	130.00	130.00
93-02-176	Birdlip Bottom	Lilliput Lane	Open	80.00	80.00
93-02-177	Marigold Meadow	Lilliput Lane	Open	120.00	120.00
93-02-178	Old Mother Hubbard's	Lilliput Lane	Open	185.00	185.00
93-02-179	Titwillow Cottage	Lilliput Lane	Open	70.00	70.00
94-02-180	Applejack Cottage	Lilliput Lane	Open	45.00	45.00
94-02-181	Camomile Lawn	Lilliput Lane	Open	125.00	125.00
94-02-182	Gulliver's Gate	Lilliput Lane	Open	45.00	45.00
94-02-183	Orchard Farm Cottage	Lilliput Lane	Open	145.00	145.00
94-02-184	Saffron House	Lilliput Lane	Open	220.00	220.00
94-02-185	Teacaddy Cottage	Lilliput Lane	Open	79.00	79.00
94-02-186	Waterside Mill	Lilliput Lane	Open	65.00	65.00
94-02-187	Creel Cottage	Lilliput Lane	Open	40.00	40.00
94-02-188	Elm Cottage	Lilliput Lane	Open	65.00	65.00
94-02-189	Lenora's Secret	Lilliput Lane	2,500	350.00	350.00
94-02-190	Spring Gate Cottage	Lilliput Lane	Open	130.00	130.00
94-02-191	Sunnyside	Lilliput Lane	Open	40.00	40.00
94-02-192	Sweet Pea Cottage	Lilliput Lane	Open	40.00	40.00
94-02-193	Tired Timbers	Lilliput Lane	Open	80.00	80.00
94-02-194	Two Hoots	Lilliput Lane	Open	75.00	75.00

Lilliput Lane Ltd. **German Collection**

87-03-001	Meersburger Weinstube	D. Tate	Open	82.50	95.00
87-03-002	Jaghutte	D. Tate	Open	82.50	95.00
87-03-003	Das Gebirgskirchlein	D. Tate	Open	120.00	140.00
87-03-004	Nurnberger Burgerhaus	D. Tate	Open	140.00	160.00
87-03-005	Schwarzwaldhaus	D. Tate	Open	140.00	160.00
87-03-006	Moselhaus	D. Tate	Open	140.00	160.00
87-03-007	Haus Im Rheinland	D. Tate	Open	220.00	250.00
88-03-008	Der Familienschrein	D. Tate	Retrd.	52.50	100.00
88-03-009	Das Rathaus	D. Tate	Open	140.00	160.00
88-03-010	Die Kleine Backerei	D. Tate	Retrd.	68.00	80.00
92-03-011	Alte Schmiede	D. Tate	Open	175.00	185.00
92-03-012	Der Bücherwurm	D. Tate	Open	140.00	160.00
92-03-013	Rosengartenhaus	D. Tate	Open	120.00	130.00
92-03-014	Strandvogthaus	D. Tate	Open	120.00	130.00

Lilliput Lane Ltd. **Christmas Collection**

88-04-001	Deer Park Hall	D. Tate	Retrd.	120.00	176-500.
89-04-002	St. Nicholas Church	D. Tate	Retrd.	130.00	130-165.
90-04-003	Yuletide Inn	D. Tate	Retrd.	145.00	145-175.
91-04-004	The Old Vicarage at Christmas	D. Tate	Retrd.	180.00	170-200.
92-04-005	Chestnut Cottage	Lilliput Lane	Open	46.50	50.00
92-04-006	Cranberry Cottage	Lilliput Lane	Open	46.50	50.00
92-04-007	Hollytree House	Lilliput Lane	Open	46.50	50.00
93-04-008	The Gingerbread Shop	Lilliput Lane	Open	50.00	50.00
93-04-009	Partridge Cottage	Lilliput Lane	Open	50.00	50.00
93-04-010	St. Joseph's Church	Lilliput Lane	Open	70.00	70.00
94-04-011	Ring O' Bells	Lilliput Lane	Open	50.00	50.00
94-04-012	St. Joseph's School	Lilliput Lane	Open	50.00	50.00
94-04-013	The Vicarage	Lilliput Lane	Open	50.00	50.00

Lilliput Lane Ltd. **Christmas Lodge Collection**

92-05-001	Highland Lodge	Lilliput Lane	Retrd.	180.00	120-300.
93-05-002	Eamont Lodge	Lilliput Lane	Retrd.	185.00	250.00
94-05-003	Snowdon Lodge	Lilliput Lane	Yr.Iss.	175.00	175.00

Lilliput Lane Ltd. **Blaise Hamlet Collection**

89-06-001	Diamond Cottage	D. Tate	Retrd.	110.00	135.00
89-06-002	Oak Cottage	D. Tate	Retrd.	110.00	135.00
89-06-003	Circular Cottage	D. Tate	Retrd.	110.00	135.00
90-06-004	Dial Cottage	D. Tate	Open	110.00	135.00
90-06-005	Vine Cottage	D. Tate	Open	110.00	135.00
90-06-006	Sweetbriar Cottage	D. Tate	Open	110.00	135.00
91-06-007	Double Cottage	D. Tate	Open	200.00	220.00
91-06-008	Jasmine Cottage	D. Tate	Open	140.00	150.00
91-06-009	Rose Cottage	D. Tate	Open	140.00	150.00

Lilliput Lane Ltd. **Irish Cottages**

87-07-001	Donegal Cottage	D. Tate	Retrd.	29.00	80.00
89-07-002	Kennedy Homestead	D. Tate	Open	33.50	45.00
89-07-003	Magilligans	D. Tate	Open	33.50	45.00
89-07-004	St. Columba's School	D. Tate	Open	47.50	60.00
89-07-005	St. Kevin's Church	D. Tate	Open	55.00	70.00
89-07-006	O'Lacey's Store	D. Tate	Open	68.00	85.00
89-07-007	Hegarty's Home	D. Tate	Retrd.	68.00	70-110.
89-07-008	Kilmore Quay	D. Tate	Retrd.	68.00	200.00
89-07-009	Quiet Cottage	D. Tate	Retrd.	72.50	220.00
89-07-010	Thoor Ballylee	D. Tate	Retrd.	105.00	160-170.
89-07-011	Pat Cohan's Bar	D. Tate	Open	110.00	140.00
89-07-012	Limerick House	D. Tate	Retrd.	110.00	160-170.
89-07-013	St. Patrick's Church	D. Tate	Retrd.	185.00	220.00
89-07-014	Ballykerne Croft	D. Tate	Open	75.00	95.00

		ARTIST	EDITION	ISSUE	QUOTE
Lilliput Lane Ltd.		**Scottish Collection**			
82-08-001	The Croft (without sheep)	D. Tate	Retrd.	29.00	800-1250
84-08-002	The Croft (renovated)	D. Tate	Retrd.	36.00	75-200.
85-08-003	Preston Mill	D. Tate	Retrd.	45.00	175-200.
85-08-004	Burns Cottage	D. Tate	Retrd.	35.00	100-250.
85-08-005	7 St. Andrews Square	A. Yarrington	Retrd.	15.95	110-150.
87-08-006	East Neuk	D. Tate	Retrd.	29.00	60-75.00
87-08-007	Preston Mill (renovated)	D. Tate	Retrd.	62.50	78.00
89-08-008	Culloden Cottage	D. Tate	Open	36.00	45.00
89-08-009	Inverlochie Hame	D. Tate	Open	47.50	60.00
89-08-010	Carrick House	D. Tate	Open	47.50	60.00
89-08-011	Stockwell Tenement	D. Tate	Open	62.50	80.00
89-08-012	John Knox House	D. Tate	Retrd.	68.00	250.00
89-08-013	Claypotts Castle	D. Tate	Open	72.50	95.00
89-08-014	Kenmore Cottage	D. Tate	Retrd.	87.00	110.00
89-08-015	Craigievar Castle	D. Tate	Retrd.	185.00	300-525.
89-08-016	Blair Atholl	D. Tate	Retrd.	275.00	300-600.
90-08-017	Fishermans Bothy	D. Tate	Open	36.00	45.00
90-08-018	Hebridean Hame	D. Tate	Retrd.	55.00	65-120.
90-08-019	Kirkbrae Cottage	D. Tate	Retrd.	55.00	70-95.00
90-08-020	Kinlochness	D. Tate	Retrd.	79.00	85-125.
90-08-021	Glenlochie Lodge	D. Tate	Retrd.	110.00	120.00
90-08-022	Eilean Donan	D. Tate	Open	145.00	185.00
90-08-023	Cawdor Castle	D. Tate	Retrd.	295.00	425-725.
92-08-024	Culross House	D. Tate	Open	90.00	95.00
92-08-025	Duart Castle	D. Tate	3,000	450.00	475.00
92-08-026	Eriskay Croft	D. Tate	Open	50.00	55.00
92-08-027	Mair Haven	D. Tate	Open	46.50	50.00
93-08-028	Edzell Summer House	Lilliput Lane	Open	110.00	110.00
94-08-029	Ladybank Lodge	Lilliput Lane	Open	80.00	80.00
Lilliput Lane Ltd.		**Lakeland Bridge Plaques**			
89-09-001	Aira Force	D. Simpson	Retrd.	35.00	35.00
89-09-002	Birks Bridge	D. Simpson	Retrd.	35.00	35.00
89-09-003	Stockley Bridge	D. Simpson	Retrd.	35.00	35.00
89-09-004	Hartsop Packhorse	D. Simpson	Retrd.	35.00	35.00
89-09-005	Bridge House	D. Simpson	Retrd.	35.00	105-120.
89-09-006	Ashness Bridge	D. Simpson	Retrd.	35.00	35.00
Lilliput Lane Ltd.		**Countryside Scene Plaques**			
89-10-001	Country Inn	D. Simpson	Retrd.	49.50	49.50
89-10-002	Norfolk Windmill	D. Simpson	Retrd.	49.50	49.50
89-10-003	Watermill	D. Simpson	Retrd.	49.50	49.50
89-10-004	Parish Church	D. Simpson	Retrd.	49.50	49.50
89-10-005	Bottle Kiln	D. Simpson	Retrd.	49.50	49.50
89-10-006	Cornish Tin Mine	D. Simpson	Retrd.	49.50	49.50
89-10-007	Lighthouse	D. Simpson	Retrd.	49.50	49.50
89-10-008	Cumbrian Farmhouse	D. Simpson	Retrd.	49.50	49.50
89-10-009	Post Office	D. Simpson	Retrd.	49.50	49.50
89-10-010	Village School	D. Simpson	Retrd.	49.50	49.50
89-10-011	Old Smithy	D. Simpson	Retrd.	49.50	49.50
89-10-012	Oasthouse	D. Simpson	Retrd.	49.50	49.50
Lilliput Lane		**Framed Scottish Plaques**			
90-11-001	Preston Oat Mill	D. Tate	Retrd.	59.50	59.50
90-11-002	Barra Black House	D. Tate	Retrd.	59.50	59.50
90-11-003	Kyle Point	D. Tate	Retrd.	59.50	59.50
90-11-004	Fife Ness	D. Tate	Retrd.	59.50	59.50
Lilliput Lane Ltd.		**Unframed Plaques**			
89-12-001	Small Stoney Wall Lea	D. Tate	Retrd.	47.50	47.50
89-12-002	Small Woodside Farm	D. Tate	Retrd.	47.50	47.50
89-12-003	Medium Cobble Combe Cottage	D. Tate	Retrd.	68.00	68.00
89-12-004	Medium Wishing Well	D. Tate	Retrd.	75.00	75.00
89-12-005	Large Lower Brockhampton	D. Tate	Retrd.	120.00	120.00
89-12-006	Large Somerset Springtime	D. Tate	Retrd.	130.00	130.00
Lilliput Lane Ltd.		**London Plaques**			
89-13-001	Buckingham Palace	D. Simpson	Retrd.	39.50	39.50
89-13-002	Trafalgar Square	D. Simpson	Retrd.	39.50	39.50
89-13-003	Tower Bridge	D. Simpson	Retrd.	39.50	39.50
89-13-004	Tower of London	D. Simpson	Retrd.	39.50	39.50
89-13-005	Big Ben	D. Simpson	Retrd.	39.50	39.50
89-13-006	Piccadilly Circus	D. Simpson	Retrd.	39.50	39.50
Lilliput Lane Ltd.		**Framed Irish Plaques**			
90-14-001	Ballyteag House	D. Tate	Retrd.	59.50	59.50
90-14-002	Shannons Bank	D. Tate	Retrd.	59.50	59.50
90-14-003	Pearses Cottages	D. Tate	Retrd.	59.50	59.50
90-14-004	Crockuna Croft	D. Tate	Retrd.	59.50	59.50
Lilliput Lane Ltd.		**Framed English Plaques**			
90-15-001	Huntingdon House	D. Tate	Retrd.	59.50	59.50
90-15-002	Coombe Cot	D. Tate	Retrd.	59.50	59.50
90-15-003	Ashdown Hall	D. Tate	Retrd.	59.50	59.50
90-15-004	Flint Fields	D. Tate	Retrd.	59.50	59.50
90-15-005	Fell View	D. Tate	Retrd.	59.50	59.50
90-15-006	Cat Slide Cottage	D. Tate	Retrd.	59.50	59.50
90-15-007	Battleview	D. Tate	Retrd.	59.50	59.50
90-15-008	Stowside	D. Tate	Retrd.	59.50	59.50
90-15-009	Jubilee Lodge	D. Tate	Retrd.	59.50	59.50
90-15-010	Trevan Cove	D. Tate	Retrd.	59.50	59.50
Lilliput Lane Ltd.		**American Landmark Series**			
89-16-001	Countryside Barn	R. Day	Retrd.	75.00	115-180.
89-16-002	Mail Pouch Barn	R. Day	Retrd.	75.00	110-240.
89-16-003	Falls Mill	R. Day	Retrd.	130.00	175-225.
90-16-004	Sign Of The Times	R. Day	Open	27.50	35.00
90-16-005	Pioneer Barn	R. Day	Retrd.	30.00	55-100.
90-16-006	Great Point Light	R. Day	Open	39.50	55.00
90-16-007	Hometown Depot	R. Day	Retrd.	68.00	95.00
90-16-008	Country Church	R. Day	Retrd.	82.50	120-160.
90-16-009	Riverside Chapel	R. Day	Retrd.	82.50	130.00
90-16-010	Pepsi Cola Barn	R. Day	Retrd.	87.00	100-200.
90-16-011	Roadside Coolers	R. Day	Retrd.	75.00	110-190.
90-16-012	Covered Memories	R. Day	Retrd.	110.00	160-250.
91-16-013	Rambling Rose	R. Day	Open	60.00	65.00
91-16-014	School Days	R. Day	Open	60.00	80.00
91-16-015	Fire House 1	R. Day	Open	87.50	110.00
91-16-016	Victoriana	R. Day	Retrd.	295.00	450.00
92-16-017	Home Sweet Home	R. Day	Open	120.00	130.00
92-16-018	Small Town Library	R. Day	Open	130.00	140.00
92-16-019	16.9 Cents Per Gallon	R. Day	Open	150.00	160.00
92-16-020	Gold Miners' Claim	R. Day	Open	110.00	120.00

		ARTIST	EDITION	ISSUE	QUOTE
92-16-021	Winnie's Place	R. Day	Closed	395.00	600-1000
93-16-022	Simply Amish	R. Day	Open	160.00	160.00
93-16-023	See Rock City	R. Day	N/A	60.00	60.00
93-16-024	Shave and A Haircut	R. Day	N/A	160.00	160.00
94-16-025	Birdsong	R. Day	Open	120.00	120.00
94-16-026	Harvest Mill	R. Day	3,500	395.00	395.00
94-16-027	Fresh Bread	R. Day	Open	150.00	150.00
94-16-028	Holy Night	R. Day	Open	225.00	225.00
94-16-029	Spring Victorian	R. Day	Open	250.00	250.00
Lilliput Lane Ltd.		**American Collection**			
84-17-001	Adobe Church	D. Tate	Retrd.	22.50	525.00
84-17-002	Adobe Village	D. Tate	Retrd.	60.00	1-1500.
84-17-003	Cape Cod	D. Tate	Retrd.	22.50	570-910.
84-17-004	Covered Bridge	D. Tate	Retrd.	22.50	3200.00
84-17-005	Country Church	D. Tate	Retrd.	22.50	500-800.
84-17-006	Forge Barn	D. Tate	Retrd.	22.50	550-660.
84-17-007	Grist Mill	D. Tate	Retrd.	22.50	500-785.
84-17-008	Log Cabin	D. Tate	Retrd.	22.50	500-1000
84-17-009	General Store	D. Tate	Retrd.	22.50	600-1000
84-17-010	Light House	D. Tate	Retrd.	22.50	800-1000
84-17-011	Midwest Barn	D. Tate	Retrd.	22.50	250-450.
84-17-012	Wallace Station	D. Tate	Retrd.	22.50	350-1000
84-17-013	San Francisco House	D. Tate	Retrd.	22.50	400-650.
Lilliput Lane Ltd.		**Welsh Collection**			
85-18-001	Hermitage	D. Tate	Retrd.	30.00	250.00
87-18-002	Hermitage Renovated	D. Tate	Retrd.	42.50	43-85.00
86-18-003	Brecon Bach	D. Tate	Retrd.	42.00	65.00
91-18-004	Tudor Merchant	D. Tate	Open	90.00	95.00
91-18-005	Ugly House	D. Tate	Open	55.00	60.00
91-18-006	Bro Dawel	D. Tate	Open	37.50	40.00
92-18-007	St. Govan's Chapel	Lilliput Lane	Open	75.00	80.00
Lilliput Lane Ltd.		**Dutch Collection**			
91-19-001	Aan de Amstel	D. Tate	Open	79.00	85.00
91-19-002	Begijnhof	D. Tate	Open	55.00	60.00
91-19-003	Bloemenmarkt	D. Tate	Open	79.00	85.00
91-19-004	De Branderij	D. Tate	Open	72.50	80.00
91-19-005	De Diamantair	D. Tate	Open	79.00	85.00
91-19-006	De Pepermolen	D. Tate	Open	55.00	60.00
91-19-007	De Wolhandelaar	D. Tate	Open	72.50	80.00
91-19-008	De Zijdewever	D. Tate	Open	79.00	85.00
91-19-009	Rembrant van Rijn	D. Tate	Open	120.00	130.00
91-19-010	Rozengracht	D. Tate	Open	72.50	80.00
Lilliput Lane Ltd.		**French Collection**			
91-20-001	L' Auberge d'Armorique	D. Tate	Open	220.00	250.00
91-20-002	La Bergerie du Perigord	D. Tate	Open	230.00	250.00
91-20-003	La Cabane du Gardian	D. Tate	Open	55.00	60.00
91-20-004	La Chaumiere du Verger	D. Tate	Open	120.00	130.00
91-20-005	La Maselle de Nadaillac	D. Tate	Open	130.00	140.00
91-20-006	La Porte Schoenenberg	D. Tate	Open	75.00	85.00
91-20-007	Le Manoir de Champfleuri	D. Tate	Open	265.00	295.00
91-20-008	Le Mas du Vigneron	D. Tate	Open	120.00	130.00
91-20-009	Le Petite Montmartre	D. Tate	Open	130.00	140.00
91-20-010	Locmaria	D. Tate	Open	65.00	80.00
Lilliput Lane Ltd.		**Village Shop Collection**			
92-21-001	The Greengrocers	D. Tate	Open	120.00	130.00
92-21-002	Penny Sweets	Lilliput Lane	Open	130.00	130.00
93-21-003	Jones The Butcher	Lilliput Lane	Open	120.00	120.00
93-21-004	Toy Shop	Lilliput Lane	Open	120.00	120.00
Lilliput Lane Ltd.		**Blaise Hamlet Classics**			
93-22-001	Jasmine Cottage	Lilliput Lane	Open	95.00	95.00
93-22-002	Double Cottage	Lilliput Lane	Open	95.00	95.00
93-22-003	Vine Cottage	Lilliput Lane	Open	95.00	95.00
93-22-004	Circular Cottage	Lilliput Lane	Open	95.00	95.00
93-22-005	Diamond Cottage	Lilliput Lane	Open	95.00	95.00
93-22-006	Dial Cottage	Lilliput Lane	Open	95.00	95.00
93-22-007	Rose Cottage	Lilliput Lane	Open	95.00	95.00
93-22-008	Sweet Briar Cottage	Lilliput Lane	Open	95.00	95.00
93-22-009	Oak Cottage	Lilliput Lane	Open	95.00	95.00
Lilliput Lane Ltd.		**Studley Royal Collection**			
94-23-001	Temple of Piety	Lilliput Lane	5,000	95.00	95.00
94-23-002	Octagon Tower	Lilliput Lane	5,000	85.00	85.00
94-23-003	St. Mary's Church	Lilliput Lane	5,000	115.00	115.00
94-23-004	Banqueting House	Lilliput Lane	5,000	65.00	65.00
Lilliput Lane Ltd.		**A Year In An English Garden**			
94-24-001	Autumn Hues	Lilliput Lane	Open	120.00	120.00
94-24-002	Winter's Wonder	Lilliput Lane	Open	120.00	120.00
Lilliput Lane Ltd.		**Historic Castles of England**			
94-25-001	Bodiam Castle	Lilliput Lane	Open	129.00	129.00
94-25-002	Castell Coch	Lilliput Lane	Open	149.00	149.00
94-25-003	Stokesay Castle	Lilliput Lane	Open	99.00	99.00
Lilliput Lane Ltd.		**Anniversary Special**			
92-26-001	Honeysuckle Cottage	Lilliput Lane	Yr.Iss.	195.00	250-350.
93-26-002	Cotman Cottage	Lilliput Lane	Yr.Iss.	220.00	265-350.
94-26-003	Watermeadows	Lilliput Lane	Yr.Iss.	189.00	189.00
Lilliput Lane Ltd.		**Special Event Collection**			
89-27-001	Commemorative Medallion-1989 South Bend	D. Tate	Retrd.	N/A	130-200.
90-27-002	Rowan Lodge-1990 South Bend	D. Tate	Retrd.	N/A	370.00
91-27-003	Gamekeepers Cottage-1991 South Bend	D. Tate	Retrd.	N/A	150-200.
92-27-004	Ashberry Cottage-1992 South Bend	D. Tate	Retrd.	N/A	275-300.
93-27-005	Magnifying Glass-1993 South Bend	Lilliput Lane	Retrd.	N/A	N/A
Lilliput Lane Ltd.		**Specials**			
83-28-001	Cliburn School	D. Tate	Retrd.	22.50	6-7000.
83-28-002	Bridge House Dealer Sign	D. Tate	Retrd.	N/A	345.00
85-28-003	Bermuda Cottage (3 Colors)	D. Tate	Retrd.	29.00	40-50.00
85-28-004	Bermuda Cottage (3 Colors)-set	D. Tate	Retrd.	87.00	175-345.
86-28-005	Seven Dwarf's Cottage	D. Tate	Retrd.	N/A	330.00
87-28-006	Clockmaker's Cottage	D. Tate	Retrd.	40.00	240-275.
87-28-007	Guildhall	D. Tate	Retrd.	N/A	210-225.
88-28-008	Chantry Chapel	D. Tate	Retrd.	N/A	200-325.
89-28-009	Mayflower House	D. Tate	Retrd.	79.50	150-240.
90-28-010	Rowan Lodge	D. Tate	Retrd.	50.00	120-200.
91-28-011	Gamekeeper's Cottage	Lilliput Lane	Retrd.	75.00	100-140.
92-28-012	Ploughman's Cottage	Lilliput Lane	Retrd.	75.00	75.00

		ARTIST	EDITION	ISSUE	QUOTE
93-28-013	Aberford Gate	Lilliput Lane	Retrd.	95.00	95.00
94-28-014	Leagrave Cottage	Lilliput Lane	Open	75.00	75.00
Lladro	**Capricho**				
87-01-001	Orchid Arrangement C1541	Lladro	Closed	500.00	17-2100.
87-01-002	Iris Arrangement C1542	Lladro	Closed	800.00	1-1200.
87-01-003	Fan C1546	Lladro	Closed	650.00	900-1600
87-01-004	Fan C1546.3	Lladro	Closed	650.00	900-1600
87-01-005	Iris with Vase C1551	Lladro	Closed	110.00	375.00
88-01-006	Bust w/ Black Veil & base C1538	Lladro	Open	650.00	835.00
88-01-007	Small Bust w/ Veil & base C1539	Lladro	Open	225.00	357.00
87-01-008	Flowers Chest C1572	Lladro	Open	550.00	750.00
87-01-009	Flat Basket with Flowers C1575	Lladro	Closed	450.00	750.00
89-01-010	Romantic Lady / Black Veil w/base C1666	Lladro	Closed	420.00	520.00
XX-01-011	White Bust w/ Veil & base C5927	Lladro	Open	550.00	790.00
XX-01-012	Special Museum Flower Basket C7606	Lladro	Closed	N/A	300.00
Lladro	**Lladro**				
66-02-001	Poodle 325.13	Lladro	Closed	N/A	2300.00
69-02-002	Shepherdess with Goats L1001M	Lladro	Closed	80.00	460.00
69-02-003	Girl's Head L1003M	Lladro	Closed	150.00	700-900.
69-02-004	Girl With Lamb L1010G	Lladro	Open	26.00	180.00
69-02-005	Girl With Pig L1011G	Lladro	Open	13.00	85.00
69-02-006	Centaur Girl L1012M	Lladro	Closed	45.00	350-400.
69-02-007	Centaur Boy L1013M	Lladro	Closed	425.00	400-450.
69-02-008	Dove L1015 G	Lladro	Open	21.00	105.00
69-02-009	Dove L1016 G	Lladro	Open	36.00	180.00
69-02-010	Idyl L1017G	Lladro	Closed	115.00	615.00
69-02-011	Idyl L1017M	Lladro	Closed	115.00	550-615.
69-02-012	King Gaspar L1018M	Lladro	Open	345.00	1895.00
69-02-013	King Melchior L1019M	Lladro	Open	345.00	1850.00
69-02-014	King Baltasar L1020M	Lladro	Open	345.00	1850.00
69-02-015	Horse Group L1021G	Lladro	Closed	950.00	16-1950.
69-02-016	Horse Group/All White L1022M	Lladro	Open	465.00	2100.00
69-02-017	Flute Player L1025G	Lladro	Closed	73.00	700.00
69-02-018	Clown with Concertina L1027G	Lladro	Closed	95.00	735.00
69-02-019	Don Quixote w/Stand L1030G	Lladro	Open	225.00	1450.00
69-02-020	Sancho Panza L1031G	Lladro	Closed	65.00	450-525.
69-02-021	Old Folks L1033G	Lladro	Closed	140.00	14-1600.
69-02-022	Girl with Basket L1034	Lladro	Closed	30.00	275.00
69-02-023	Girl with Geese L1035G	Lladro	Open	37.50	180.00
69-02-024	Girl With Geese L1035M	Lladro	Closed	37.50	165.00
69-02-025	Girl with Turkeys L1038G	Lladro	Closed	95.00	650.00
69-02-026	Violinist and Girl L1039G	Lladro	Closed	120.00	1-1200.
69-02-027	Violinist and Girl L1039M	Lladro	Closed	120.00	825.00
69-02-028	Hunters L1048	Lladro	Closed	115.00	11-2000.
69-02-029	Del Monte (Boy) L1050	Lladro	Closed	65.00	N/A
69-02-030	Girl with Duck L1052G	Lladro	Open	30.00	205.00
69-02-031	Girl with Duck L1052M	Lladro	Closed	30.00	190.00
69-02-032	Girl with Pheasant L1055G	Lladro	Closed	105.00	N/A
69-02-033	Panchito L1059	Lladro	Closed	28.00	N/A
69-02-034	Deer L1064	Lladro	Closed	27.50	400.00
69-02-035	Fox and Cub L1065	Lladro	Closed	17.50	300-500.
69-02-036	Basset L1066G	Lladro	Closed	23.50	400.00
69-02-037	Old dog L1067G	Lladro	Closed	40.00	450.00
69-02-038	Afghan (sitting) L1069G	Lladro	Closed	36.00	450-550.
69-02-039	Beagle Puppy L1070	Lladro	Closed	16.50	180-225.
69-02-040	Beagle Puppy L1071G	Lladro	Closed	16.50	225.00
69-02-041	Beagle Puppy L1071M	Lladro	Closed	16.50	225.00
69-02-042	Beagle Puppy L1072G	Lladro	Closed	16.50	250.00
69-02-043	Dutch Girl L1077	Lladro	Closed	57.50	135.00
69-02-044	Herald 1078	Lladro	Closed	110.00	1100.00
69-02-045	Girl With Brush L1081	Lladro	Closed	14.50	300.00
69-02-046	Girl Manicuring L1082	Lladro	Closed	14.50	300.00
69-02-047	Girl With Doll L1083	Lladro	Closed	14.50	300.00
69-02-048	Girl with Mother's Shoe L1084	Lladro	Closed	14.50	300.00
69-02-049	Girl Seated with Flowers L1088G	Lladro	Closed	45.00	650.00
71-02-050	Lawyer (Face) L1089G	Lladro	Closed	35.00	N/A
71-02-051	Girl and Gazelle 1091	Lladro	Closed	225.00	1200.00
69-02-052	Beggar L1094	Lladro	Closed	65.00	650.00
71-02-053	Pelusa Clown L1125	Lladro	Closed	70.00	875-1150
71-02-054	Clown with Violin L1126	Lladro	Closed	71.00	1200.00
71-02-055	Puppy Love L1127G	Lladro	Open	50.00	285.00
71-02-056	Dog in the Basket L1128G	Lladro	Closed	17.50	450.00
71-02-057	Faun L1131G	Lladro	Closed	155.00	1200.00
71-02-058	Bull L1134G	Lladro	Closed	130.00	1000.00
71-02-059	Dog and Snail L1139G	Lladro	Closed	40.00	270.00
71-02-060	Dog's Head L1149G	Lladro	Closed	27.50	N/A
71-02-061	Elephants (3) L1150G	Lladro	Open	100.00	795.00
71-02-062	Elephants (2) L1151G	Lladro	Open	45.00	390.00
71-02-063	Dog Playing Guitar L1152	Lladro	Closed	32.50	600.00
71-02-064	Dog Playing Guitar L1153	Lladro	Closed	32.50	400.00
71-02-065	Dog Playing Bass Fiddle L1154G	Lladro	Closed	36.50	400.00
71-02-066	Dog w/Microphone L1155G	Lladro	Closed	35.00	400-475.
71-02-067	Dog Playing Bongos L1156	Lladro	Closed	32.50	600.00
71-02-068	Seated Torero L1162	Lladro	Closed	35.00	700.00
71-02-069	Kissing Doves L1169G	Lladro	Open	32.00	140.00
71-02-070	Kissing Doves L1169M	Lladro	Closed	32.00	150.00
71-02-071	Kissing Doves L1170G	Lladro	Closed	25.00	250.00
71-02-072	Girl With Flowers L1172G	Lladro	Closed	27.00	295.00
71-02-073	Girl With Domino L1175G	Lladro	Closed	34.00	350.00
71-02-074	Girl With Dice L1176	Lladro	Closed	25.00	350.00
71-02-075	Clown on Domino L1179G	Lladro	Closed	34.00	350.00
71-02-076	Platero and Marcelino L1181G	Lladro	Closed	50.00	400.00
72-02-077	Little Girl with Cat L1187G	Lladro	Closed	37.00	375.00
72-02-078	Boy Meets Girl L1188	Lladro	Closed	310.00	400.00
72-02-079	Eskimo L1195G	Lladro	Open	30.00	135.00
72-02-080	Attentive Bear, brown L1204G	Lladro	Closed	16.00	100-125.
72-02-081	Good Bear, brown L1205G	Lladro	Closed	16.00	100-125.
72-02-082	Bear Seated, brown L1206G	Lladro	Closed	16.00	100-125.
72-02-083	Attentive Polar Bear, white L1207G	Lladro	Open	16.00	75.00
72-02-084	Bear, White L1208G	Lladro	Open	16.00	75.00
72-02-085	Bear, White L1209G	Lladro	Open	16.00	75.00
72-02-086	Round Fish L1210G	Lladro	Closed	35.00	N/A
72-02-087	Girl With Doll L1211G	Lladro	Closed	72.00	440.00
72-02-088	Woman Carrying Water L1212	Lladro	Closed	100.00	400.00
72-02-089	Little Jug Magno L1222.3	Lladro	Closed	35.00	275.00
72-02-090	Young Harlequin L1229G	Lladro	Open	70.00	520.00
72-02-091	Friendship L1230G	Lladro	Closed	68.00	325.00
72-02-092	Friendship L1230M	Lladro	Closed	68.00	325.00
72-02-093	Angel with Lute L1231	Lladro	Closed	60.00	450.00
72-02-094	Angel with Clarinet L1232	Lladro	Closed	60.00	450.00
72-02-095	Angel with Flute L1233	Lladro	Closed	60.00	450.00
72-02-096	Little Jesus of Prag L1234	Lladro	Closed	70.00	725.00
73-02-097	Christmas Carols L1239G	Lladro	Closed	125.00	800-900.
73-02-098	Girl with Wheelbarrow L1245	Lladro	Closed	75.00	500-600.
72-02-099	Caress and Rest L1246	Lladro	Closed	50.00	300.00
74-02-100	Honey Lickers L1248G	Lladro	Closed	100.00	475.00
74-02-101	The Race L1249G	Lladro	Closed	450.00	18-2250.
74-02-102	Lovers from Verona L 1250G	Lladro	Closed	330.00	900.00
74-02-103	Pony Ride L1251	Lladro	Closed	220.00	1200.00
74-02-104	Shepherd L1252	Lladro	Closed	100.00	N/A
74-02-105	Sad Chimney Sweep L1253G	Lladro	Closed	180.00	1200.00
74-02-106	Hamlet and Yorick L1254G	Lladro	Closed	325.00	11-1200.
74-02-107	Seesaw L1255G	Lladro	Closed	110.00	550.00
74-02-108	Mother with Pups L1257	Lladro	Closed	50.00	700.00
74-02-109	Playing Poodles L1258	Lladro	Closed	47.50	650-850.
74-02-110	Poodle L1259G	Lladro	Closed	27.50	450.00
74-02-111	Flying Duck L1263G	Lladro	Open	20.00	90.00
74-02-112	Flying Duck L1264G	Lladro	Open	20.00	90.00
74-02-113	Flying Duck L1265G	Lladro	Open	20.00	90.00
74-02-114	Girl with Ducks L1267G	Lladro	Closed	55.00	260.00
74-02-115	Reminiscing L1270G	Lladro	Closed	975.00	1375.00
74-02-116	Thoughts L1272G	Lladro	Open	87.50	3200.00
74-02-117	Lovers in the Park L1274G	Lladro	Closed	450.00	1365.00
74-02-118	Christmas Seller L1276G	Lladro	Closed	120.00	750.00
74-02-119	Feeding Time L1277G	Lladro	Closed	120.00	415.00
74-02-120	Devotion L1278G	Lladro	Closed	140.00	475.00
74-02-121	The Wind L1279M	Lladro	Open	250.00	795.00
74-02-122	Playtime L1280G	Lladro	Closed	160.00	475-725.
74-02-123	Afghan Standing L1282G	Lladro	Closed	45.00	400-475.
74-02-124	Little Gardener L1283G	Lladro	Open	250.00	785.00
74-02-125	"My Flowers"L1284G	Lladro	Open	200.00	550.00
74-02-126	"My Goodness" L1285G	Lladro	Open	190.00	415.00
74-02-127	Flower Harvest L1286G	Lladro	Open	200.00	495.00
74-02-128	Picking Flowers L1287G	Lladro	Open	170.00	440.00
74-02-129	Aggressive Duck L1288G	Lladro	Open	170.00	475.00
74-02-130	Victorian Girl on Swing L1297G	Lladro	Closed	520.00	16-2100.
74-02-131	Valencian Lady with Flowers L1304G	Lladro	Open	200.00	625.00
74-02-132	"On the Farm" L1306	Lladro	Closed	130.00	240.00
74-02-133	Ducklings L1307G	Lladro	Open	47.50	150.00
74-02-134	Girl with Cats L1309G	Lladro	Open	120.00	310.00
74-02-135	Girl with Puppies in Basket L1311G	Lladro	Open	120.00	345.00
74-02-136	Schoolgirl L1313G	Lladro	Closed	201.00	575-650.
76-02-137	Collie L1316G	Lladro	Closed	45.00	400.00
76-02-138	IBIS L1319G	Lladro	Open	1550.00	2625.00
77-02-139	Angel with Tamborine L1320G	Lladro	Closed	125.00	450-500.
77-02-140	Angel with Lyre L1321G	Lladro	Closed	125.00	450-500.
77-02-141	Angel with Song L1322G	Lladro	Closed	125.00	450-500.
77-02-142	Angel with Accordian L1323	Lladro	Closed	125.00	370-450.
77-02-143	Angel with Mandolin L1324G	Lladro	Closed	125.00	375-500.
76-02-144	The Helmsman L1325M	Lladro	Closed	600.00	900-1200
76-02-145	Playing Cards L1327 M, numbered series	Lladro	Open	3800.00	6600.00
77-02-146	Dove Group L1335G	Lladro	Closed	950.00	1700.00
77-02-147	Blooming Roses L1339G	Lladro	Closed	325.00	425.00
77-02-148	Male Jockey L1341G	Lladro	Closed	120.00	450.00
77-02-149	Wrath of Don Quixote L1343G	Lladro	Closed	250.00	850.00
77-02-150	Derby L1344G	Lladro	Closed	1125.00	2500.00
78-02-151	Sacristan L1345G	Lladro	Closed	385.00	2200.00
78-02-152	Under the Willow L1346G	Lladro	Closed	1600.00	2000.00
78-02-153	Mermaid on Wave L1347G	Lladro	Closed	425.00	16-3000.
78-02-154	Nautical Vision L1349G	Lladro	Closed	Unkn.	3000.00
78-02-155	In the Gondola L1350G, numberedáseries	Lladro	Open	1850.00	3250.00
78-02-155	Lady with Girl L1353G	Lladro	Closed	175.00	600.00
78-02-156	Growing Roses L1354G	Lladro	Closed	485.00	635.00
78-02-157	Phyllis L1356G	Lladro	Closed	75.00	175.00
78-02-158	Shelley L1357G	Lladro	Closed	75.00	175.00
78-02-159	Beth L1358G	Lladro	Closed	75.00	175.00
78-02-160	Heather L1359G	Lladro	Closed	75.00	175.00
78-02-161	Laura L1360G	Lladro	Closed	75.00	175.00
78-02-162	Julia L1361G	Lladro	Closed	75.00	175.00
78-02-163	Swinging L1366G	Lladro	Closed	825.00	1375.00
78-02-164	Playful Dogs L1367	Lladro	Closed	160.00	650.00
78-02-165	Spring Birds L1368G	Lladro	Closed	1600.00	2500.00
78-02-166	Anniversary Waltz L1372G	Lladro	Open	260.00	545.00
78-02-167	Chestnut Seller L1373G	Lladro	Closed	800.00	N/A
78-02-168	Waiting in the Park L1374G	Lladro	Closed	235.00	450.00
78-02-169	Watering Flowers L1376G	Lladro	Closed	400.00	700-1000
78-02-170	Suzy and Her Doll L1378G	Lladro	Closed	215.00	600-800.
78-02-171	Debbie and Her Doll L1379G	Lladro	Closed	215.00	600-825.
78-02-172	Cathy and Her Doll L1380G	Lladro	Closed	215.00	570-950.
78-02-173	Princess Sitting L1381G	Lladro	Closed	11.80	400-600.
78-02-174	Medieval Girl L1381G	Lladro	Closed	11.80	600.00
78-02-175	Medieval Boy L1382G	Lladro	Closed	235.00	650-700.
78-02-176	A Rickshaw Ride L1383G	Lladro	Open	1500.00	2150.00
78-02-177	The Brave Knight L1385G	Lladro	Closed	350.00	750.00
81-02-179	St. Joseph L1386G	Lladro	Open	250.00	385.00
81-02-180	Mary L1387G	Lladro	Open	240.00	385.00
81-02-181	Baby Jesus L1388G	Lladro	Open	85.00	140.00
81-02-182	Donkey L1389G	Lladro	Open	95.00	180.00
81-02-183	Cow L1390G	Lladro	Open	95.00	180.00
82-02-184	Holy Mary, L1394G, numbered series	Lladro	Open	1000.00	1450.00
82-02-185	Full of Mischief L1395G	Lladro	Open	420.00	765.00
82-02-186	Appreciation L1396G	Lladro	Open	420.00	765.00
82-02-187	Second Thoughts L1397G	Lladro	Open	420.00	750.00
82-02-188	Reverie L1398G	Lladro	Open	490.00	895.00
82-02-189	Dutch Woman with Tulips L1399G	Lladro	Closed	750.00	750.00
82-02-190	Valencian Boy L1400G	Lladro	Closed	298.00	400.00
82-02-191	Sleeping Nymph L1401G	Lladro	Closed	210.00	600-875.
82-02-192	Daydreaming Nymph L1402G	Lladro	Closed	210.00	525-625.
82-02-193	Butterfly Girl L1403G	Lladro	Closed	210.00	550.00
82-02-194	Matrimony L1404G	Lladro	Open	320.00	585.00
82-02-195	Illusion L1413G	Lladro	Open	115.00	245.00
82-02-196	Fantasy L1414G	Lladro	Open	115.00	240.00
82-02-197	Mirage L1415G	Lladro	Open	115.00	240.00
82-02-198	From My Garden L1416G	Lladro	Open	140.00	275.00
82-02-199	Nature's Bounty L1417G	Lladro	Open	160.00	310.00
82-02-200	Flower Harmony L1418G	Lladro	Open	130.00	245.00
82-02-201	A Barrow of Blossoms L1419G	Lladro	Open	390.00	675.00
82-02-202	Born Free w/base L1420G	Lladro	Open	1520.00	2880.00
82-02-203	Mariko w/base L1421G	Lladro	Open	860.00	1575.00
82-02-204	Miss Valencia L1422G	Lladro	Open	175.00	350.00
82-02-205	King Melchor L1423G	Lladro	Open	225.00	440.00

		ARTIST	EDITION	ISSUE	QUOTE
82-02-206	King Gaspar L1424G	Lladro	Open	265.00	475.00
82-02-207	King Baltasar L1425G	Lladro	Open	315.00	585.00
82-02-208	Male Tennis Player L1426M	Lladro	Closed	200.00	350-375.
82-02-209	Female Tennis Player L1427M	Lladro	Closed	200.00	350-425.
82-02-210	Afternoon Tea L1428G	Lladro	Open	115.00	250.00
82-02-211	Afternoon Tea L1428M	Lladro	Open	115.00	250.00
82-02-212	Winter Wonderland w/base L1429G	Lladro	Open	1025.00	1950.00
82-02-213	High Society L1430G	Lladro	Closed	305.00	595.00
82-02-214	The Debutante L1431G	Lladro	Open	115.00	250.00
82-02-215	The Debutante L1431M	Lladro	Open	115.00	250.00
83-02-216	Vows L1434G	Lladro	Closed	600.00	950.00
83-02-217	Blue Moon L1435G	Lladro	Closed	98.00	450.00
83-02-218	Moon Glow L1436	Lladro	Closed	98.00	425.00
83-02-219	Moon Light L1437	Lladro	Closed	98.00	425.00
83-02-220	Full Moon L1438	Lladro	Closed	115.00	550.00
83-02-221	"How Do You Do!" L1439G	Lladro	Open	185.00	295.00
83-02-222	Pleasantries L1440G	Lladro	Closed	960.00	1900.00
83-02-223	A Litter of Love L1441G	Lladro	Open	385.00	645.00
83-02-224	Kitty Confrontation L1442G	Lladro	Open	155.00	285.00
83-02-225	Bearly Love L1443G	Lladro	Open	55.00	100.00
83-02-226	Purr-Fect L1444G	Lladro	Open	350.00	615.00
83-02-227	Springtime in Japan L1445G	Lladro	Open	965.00	1800.00
83-02-228	"Here Comes the Bride" L1446G	Lladro	Open	518.00	965.00
83-02-229	Michiko L1447G	Lladro	Open	235.00	460.00
83-02-230	Yuki L1448G	Lladro	Open	285.00	550.00
83-02-231	Mayumi L1449G	Lladro	Open	235.00	460.00
83-02-232	Kiyoko L1450G	Lladro	Open	235.00	460.00
83-02-233	Teruko L1451G	Lladro	Open	235.00	460.00
83-02-234	On the Town L1452G	Lladro	Closed	220.00	440.00
83-02-235	Golfing Couple L1453G	Lladro	Open	248.00	485.00
83-02-236	Flowers of the Season L1454G	Lladro	Open	1460.00	2550.00
83-02-237	Reflections of Hamlet L1455G	Lladro	Closed	1000.00	1260.00
83-02-238	Cranes w/base L1456G	Lladro	Open	1000.00	1950.00
85-02-239	A Boy and His Pony L1460G	Lladro	Closed	285.00	800.00
85-02-240	Carefree Angel with Flute L1463G	Lladro	Closed	220.00	575-650.
85-02-241	Carefree Angel with Lyre L1464G	Lladro	Closed	220.00	575.00
85-02-242	Girl on Carousel Horse L1469G	Lladro	Open	470.00	860.00
85-02-243	Boy on Carousel Horse L1470G	Lladro	Open	470.00	860.00
85-02-244	Wishing On A Star L1475G	Lladro	Closed	130.00	600.00
85-02-245	Star Light Star Bright L1476G	Lladro	Closed	130.00	350.00
85-02-246	Star Gazing L1477G	Lladro	Closed	130.00	375.00
85-02-247	Hawaiian Dancer/Aloha! L1478G	Lladro	Open	230.00	440.00
85-02-248	In a Tropical Garden L1479G	Lladro	Open	230.00	440.00
85-02-249	Aroma of the Islands L1480G	Lladro	Open	260.00	480.00
85-02-250	Sunning L1481G	Lladro	Closed	145.00	525.00
85-02-251	Eve L1482	Lladro	Closed	145.00	650.00
85-02-252	Free As a Butterfly L1483G	Lladro	Closed	145.00	450.00
86-02-253	Lady of the East w/base L1488G	Lladro	Closed	625.00	1100.00
86-02-254	Valencian Children L1489G	Lladro	Open	700.00	1225.00
86-02-255	My Wedding Day L1494G	Lladro	Open	800.00	1450.00
86-02-256	A Lady of Taste L1495G	Lladro	Open	575.00	1025.00
86-02-257	Don Quixote & The Windmill L1497G	Lladro	Open	1100.00	2050.00
86-02-258	Tahitian Dancing Girls L1498G	Lladro	Open	750.00	1325.00
86-02-259	Blessed Family L1499G	Lladro	Open	200.00	360.00
86-02-260	Ragamuffin L1500G	Lladro	Closed	125.00	300.00
86-02-261	Ragamuffin L1500M	Lladro	Closed	125.00	300.00
86-02-262	Rag Doll L1501G	Lladro	Closed	125.00	300.00
86-02-263	Rag Doll L1501M	Lladro	Closed	125.00	300.00
86-02-264	Forgotten L1502G	Lladro	Closed	125.00	200.00
86-02-265	Forgotten L1502M	Lladro	Closed	125.00	300.00
86-02-266	Neglected L1503G	Lladro	Closed	125.00	300.00
86-02-267	Neglected L1503M	Lladro	Closed	125.00	300.00
86-02-268	The Reception L1504G	Lladro	Closed	625.00	1050.00
86-02-269	Nature Boy L1505G	Lladro	Closed	100.00	250.00
86-02-270	Nature Boy L1505M	Lladro	Closed	100.00	N/A
86-02-271	A New Friend L1506G	Lladro	Closed	110.00	180.00
86-02-272	A New Friend L1506M	Lladro	Closed	110.00	N/A
86-02-273	Boy & His Bunny L1507G	Lladro	Closed	90.00	200-225.
86-02-274	Boy & His Bunny L1507M	Lladro	Closed	90.00	N/A
86-02-275	In the Meadow L1508G	Lladro	Closed	100.00	225.00
86-02-276	In the Meadow L1508M	Lladro	Closed	100.00	N/A
86-02-277	Spring Flowers L1509G	Lladro	Closed	100.00	248.00
86-02-278	Spring Flowers L1509M	Lladro	Closed	100.00	N/A
87-02-279	Cafe De Paris L1511G	Lladro	Open	1900.00	2950.00
87-02-280	Hawaiian Beauty L1512G	Lladro	Closed	575.00	1000.00
87-02-281	A Flower for My Lady L1513G	Lladro	Closed	1150.00	1375.00
87-02-282	Gaspar 's Page L1514G	Lladro	Closed	275.00	450.00
87-02-283	Melchior's Page L1515G	Lladro	Closed	290.00	400-500.
87-02-284	Balthasar's Page L1516G	Lladro	Closed	275.00	700-1100
87-02-285	Circus Train L1517G	Lladro	Open	2900.00	4350.00
87-02-286	Valencian Garden L1518G	Lladro	Closed	1100.00	1650.00
87-02-287	Stroll in the Park L1519G	Lladro	Open	1600.00	2600.00
87-02-288	The Landau Carriage L1521G	Lladro	Open	2500.00	3850.00
87-02-289	I am Don Quixote! L1522G	Lladro	Open	2600.00	3950.00
87-02-290	Valencian Bouquet L1524G	Lladro	Closed	250.00	400.00
87-02-291	Valencian Dreams L1525G	Lladro	Closed	240.00	450.00
87-02-292	Valencian Flowers L1526G	Lladro	Closed	375.00	550.00
87-02-293	Tenderness L1527G	Lladro	Open	260.00	415.00
87-02-294	I Love You Truly L1528G	Lladro	Open	375.00	575.00
87-02-295	Momi L1529G	Lladro	Closed	275.00	450.00
87-02-296	Leilani L1530G	Lladro	Closed	275.00	500.00
87-02-297	Malia L1531G	Lladro	Closed	275.00	500.00
87-02-298	Lehua L1532G	Lladro	Closed	275.00	575.00
87-02-299	Not So Fast! L1533G	Lladro	Open	175.00	245.00
88-02-300	Little Sister L1534G	Lladro	Open	180.00	240.00
88-02-301	Sweet Dreams L1535G	Lladro	Open	150.00	200.00
88-02-302	Stepping Out L1537G	Lladro	Open	230.00	310.00
88-02-303	Pink Ballet Slippers L1540	Lladro	Closed	275.00	450.00
87-02-304	Wild Stallions w/base L1566G	Lladro	Closed	1100.00	1465.00
87-02-305	Running Free w/base L1567G	Lladro	Open	1500.00	1525.00
87-02-306	Grand Dame L1568G	Lladro	Open	290.00	395.00
89-02-307	Fluttering Crane L1598G	Lladro	Open	115.00	145.00
89-02-308	Nesting Crane L1599G	Lladro	Open	95.00	115.00
89-02-309	Landing Crane L1600G	Lladro	Open	115.00	145.00
89-02-310	Rock Nymph L1601G	Lladro	Open	665.00	795.00
89-02-311	Spring Nymph L1602G	Lladro	Open	665.00	825.00
89-02-312	Latest Addition L1606G	Lladro	Open	385.00	480.00
89-02-313	Flight Into Egypt w/base L1610G	Lladro	Open	885.00	1150.00
89-02-314	Courting Cranes L1611G	Lladro	Open	565.00	695.00
89-02-315	Preening Crane L1612G	Lladro	Open	385.00	485.00
89-02-316	Bowing Crane L1613G	Lladro	Open	385.00	485.00
89-02-317	Dancing Crane L1614G	Lladro	Open	385.00	485.00
88-02-318	Cellist L1700M	Lladro	Closed	1200.00	1200.00
88-02-319	Saxophone Player L1701M	Lladro	Closed	835.00	835.00
88-02-320	Boy at the Fair (Decorated) L1708M	Lladro	Closed	650.00	650.00
88-02-321	Exodus L1709M	Lladro	Closed	875.00	875.00
88-02-322	School Boy L1710M	Lladro	Closed	750.00	750.00
88-02-323	School Girl L1711M	Lladro	Closed	950.00	950.00
88-02-324	On Our Way Home (decorated) L1715M	Lladro	Closed	2000.00	2000.00
88-02-325	Nanny L1714M	Lladro	Closed	700.00	700.00
88-02-326	Harlequin with Puppy L1716M	Lladro	Closed	825.00	825.00
88-02-327	Harlequin with Dove L1717M	Lladro	Closed	900.00	900.00
88-02-328	Dress Rehearsal L1718M	Lladro	Closed	1150.00	1150.00
89-02-329	Back From the Fair L1719M	Lladro	Closed	1825.00	1825.00
90-02-330	Sprite w/base L1720G, numbered series	Lladro	Open	1200.00	1400.00
90-02-331	Leprechaun w/base L1721G, numrd series	Lladro	Open	1200.00	1395.00
89-02-332	Group Discussion L1722M	Lladro	Closed	1500.00	1500.00
89-02-333	Hopeful Group L1723M	Lladro	Closed	1825.00	1825.00
89-02-334	Belle Epoque L1724M	Lladro	Closed	700.00	700.00
89-02-335	Young Lady with Parasol L1725M	Lladro	Closed	950.00	950.00
89-02-336	Young Lady with Fan L1726M	Lladro	Closed	750.00	750.00
89-02-337	Pose L1727M	Lladro	Closed	725.00	725.00
91-02-338	Nativity L1730M	Lladro	Open	725.00	725.00
70-02-338	Gothic King L2002G	Lladro	Closed	25.00	450.00
70-02-339	Gothic Queen L2003G	Lladro	Closed	25.00	450.00
70-02-339	Shepherdess with Lamb L2005M	Lladro	Closed	100.00	710.00
70-02-340	Water Carrier Girl Lamp L2006	Lladro	Closed	30.00	600.00
71-02-341	Girl with Dog L2013M	Lladro	Closed	300.00	N/A
71-02-342	Little Eagle Owl L2020	Lladro	Closed	15.00	425.00
71-02-343	Boy/Girl Eskimo L2038.3M	Lladro	Closed	100.00	275-455.
74-02-344	Setter's Head L2045M	Lladro	Closed	42.50	550.00
74-02-345	Magistrates L2052M	Lladro	Closed	135.00	1200.00
74-02-346	Oriental L2056M	Lladro	Open	35.00	100.00
74-02-347	Oriental L2057M	Lladro	Open	30.00	100.00
74-02-348	Thailandia L2058M	Lladro	Open	650.00	1725.00
74-02-349	Muskateer L2059M	Lladro	Closed	900.00	2000-3.
77-02-350	Monk L2060M	Lladro	Open	60.00	130.00
77-02-351	Dogs-Bust L2067M	Lladro	Closed	280.00	800.00
77-02-352	Thai Dancers L2069M	Lladro	Open	300.00	725.00
77-02-353	A New Hairdo L2070M	Lladro	Closed	1060.00	1430.00
77-02-354	Graceful Duo L2073M	Lladro	Open	775.00	1650.00
77-02-355	Nuns L2075M	Lladro	Open	90.00	230.00
78-02-356	Lonely L2076M	Lladro	Open	72.50	185.00
78-02-357	Rain in Spain L2077M	Lladro	Closed	190.00	550.00
78-02-358	Don Quixote Dreaming L2084M	Lladro	Closed	550.00	1800.00
78-02-359	The Little Kiss L2086M	Lladro	Closed	180.00	475.00
78-02-360	Saint Francis L2090	Lladro	Closed	565.00	N/A
78-02-361	Holy Virgin L2092M	Lladro	Closed	200.00	N/A
78-02-362	Girl Waiting L2093M	Lladro	Open	90.00	185.00
78-02-363	Tenderness L2094M	Lladro	Open	100.00	205.00
78-02-364	Duck Pulling Pigtail L2095M	Lladro	Open	110.00	275.00
78-02-365	Nosy Puppy L2096M	Lladro	Closed	190.00	410.00
78-02-366	Laundress L2109M	Lladro	Closed	325.00	325-650.
80-02-367	Marujita with Two Ducks L2113M	Lladro	Closed	240.00	295.00
80-02-368	Kissing Father L2114M	Lladro	Closed	575.00	450.00
80-02-369	Mother's Kiss L2115M	Lladro	Closed	575.00	450.00
80-02-370	The Whaler L2121M	Lladro	Closed	820.00	1050.00
81-02-371	Lost in Thought L2125M	Lladro	Closed	210.00	250.00
83-02-372	American Heritage L2127M	Lladro	Closed	525.00	650-950.
83-02-373	Venus L2128M	Lladro	Closed	650.00	1150.00
83-02-374	Egyptian Cat L2130M	Lladro	Closed	75.00	500.00
83-02-375	Mother & Son L2131M, numbered series	Lladro	Open	850.00	1425.00
83-02-376	Spring Sheperdess L2132M	Lladro	Closed	450.00	N/A
83-02-377	Autumn Sheperdess L2133M	Lladro	Closed	285.00	N/A
84-02-378	Nautical Watch L2134M	Lladro	Closed	450.00	750.00
84-02-379	Mystical Joseph L2135M	Lladro	Closed	428.00	700.00
84-02-380	The King L2136M	Lladro	Closed	510.00	710.00
84-02-381	Fairy Ballerina L2137M	Lladro	Closed	500.00	625.00
84-02-382	Friar Juniper L2138M	Lladro	Closed	160.00	275.00
84-02-383	Aztec Indian L2139M	Lladro	Closed	553.00	600.00
84-02-384	Pepita wth Sombrero L2140M	Lladro	Open	97.50	185.00
84-02-385	Pedro with Jug L2141M	Lladro	Open	100.00	185.00
84-02-386	Sea Harvest L2142M	Lladro	Closed	535.00	700.00
84-02-387	Aztec Dancer L2143M	Lladro	Closed	463.00	650.00
84-02-388	Leticia L2144M	Lladro	Open	100.00	170.00
84-02-389	Gabriela L2145M	Lladro	Open	100.00	170.00
84-02-390	Desiree L2146M	Lladro	Open	100.00	170.00
84-02-391	Alida L2147M	Lladro	Open	100.00	170.00
84-02-392	Head of Congolese Woman L2148M	Lladro	Closed	55.00	300-500.
85-02-393	Young Madonna L2149M	Lladro	Closed	400.00	675.00
85-02-394	A Tribute to Peace w/base L2150M	Lladro	Open	470.00	850.00
85-02-395	A Bird on Hand L2151M	Lladro	Open	118.00	230.00
85-02-396	Chinese Girl L2152M	Lladro	Closed	90.00	200-250.
85-02-397	Chinese Boy L2153	Lladro	Closed	90.00	200-250.
85-02-398	Hawaiian Flower Vendor L2154M	Lladro	Open	245.00	420.00
85-02-399	Arctic inter L2156M	Lladro	Open	75.00	140.00
85-02-400	Eskimo Girl with Cold Feet L2157M	Lladro	Open	140.00	260.00
85-02-401	Pensive Eskimo Girl L2158M	Lladro	Open	100.00	190.00
85-02-402	Pensive Eskimo Boy L2159M	Lladro	Open	100.00	190.00
85-02-403	Flower Vendor L2160M	Lladro	Open	110.00	200.00
85-02-404	Fruit Vendor L2161M	Lladro	Open	120.00	230.00
85-02-405	Fish Vendor L2162M	Lladro	Open	110.00	205.00
87-02-406	Mountain Shepherd L2163M	Lladro	Open	120.00	190.00
87-02-407	My Lost Lamb L2164M	Lladro	Open	100.00	165.00
87-02-408	Chiquita L2165M	Lladro	Closed	100.00	170.00
87-02-409	Paco L2166M	Lladro	Closed	100.00	170.00
87-02-410	Fernando L2167M	Lladro	Closed	100.00	170.00
87-02-411	Julio L2168M	Lladro	Closed	100.00	170.00
87-02-412	Repose L2169M	Lladro	Open	120.00	175.00
87-02-413	Spanish Dancer L2170M	Lladro	Open	190.00	315.00
87-02-414	Ahoy Tere L2173M	Lladro	Open	190.00	295.00
87-02-415	Andean Flute Player L2174M	Lladro	Closed	250.00	350.00
88-02-416	Harvest Helpers L2178M	Lladro	Open	190.00	250.00
88-02-417	Sharing the Harvest L2179M	Lladro	Open	190.00	250.00
88-02-418	Dreams of Peace w/base L2180M	Lladro	Open	880.00	1025.00
88-02-419	Bathing Nymph w/base L2181M	Lladro	Open	560.00	760.00
88-02-420	Daydreamer w/base L2182M	Lladro	Open	560.00	760.00
89-02-421	Wakeup Kitty L2183M	Lladro	Closed	225.00	300.00
89-02-422	Angel and Friend L2184M	Lladro	Open	150.00	185.00
89-02-423	Devoted Reader L2185M	Lladro	Open	125.00	160.00
89-02-424	The Greatest Love L2186M	Lladro	Open	235.00	290.00
89-02-425	Jealous Friend L2187M	Lladro	Open	275.00	340.00
90-02-426	Mother's Pride L2189M	Lladro	Open	300.00	350.00

		ARTIST	EDITION	ISSUE	QUOTE
80-02-427	To The Well L2190M	Lladro	Open	250.00	295.00
90-02-428	Forest Born L2191M	Lladro	Closed	230.00	400.00
80-02-429	King Of The Forest L2192M	Lladro	Closed	290.00	310.00
80-02-430	Heavenly Strings L2194M	Lladro	Closed	170.00	195.00
90-02-431	Heavenly Sounds L2195M	Lladro	Closed	170.00	195.00
90-02-432	Heavenly Solo L2196M	Lladro	Closed	170.00	195.00
90-02-433	Heavenly Song L2197M	Lladro	Closed	175.00	185.00
90-02-434	A King is Born w/base L2198M	Lladro	Open	750.00	880.00
90-02-435	Devoted Friends w/base L2199M	Lladro	Open	700.00	825.00
90-02-436	A Big Hug! L2200M	Lladro	Open	250.00	295.00
90-02-437	Our Daily Bread L2201M	Lladro	Open	150.00	185.00
90-02-438	A Helping Hand L2202M	Lladro	Closed	150.00	185.00
90-02-439	Afternoon Chores L2203M	Lladro	Open	150.00	185.00
90-02-440	Farmyard Grace L2204M	Lladro	Closed	180.00	210.00
90-02-441	Prayerful Stitch L2205M	Lladro	Open	160.00	190.00
90-02-442	Sisterly Love L2206M	Lladro	Open	300.00	350.00
90-02-443	What A Day! L2207M	Lladro	Open	550.00	630.00
90-02-444	Let's Rest L2208M	Lladro	Open	550.00	630.00
91-02-445	Long Dy L2209M	Lladro	Open	295.00	315.00
91-02-446	Lazy Day L2210M	Lladro	Open	240.00	260.00
91-02-447	Patrol Leader L2212M	Lladro	Closed	390.00	420.00
91-02-448	Nature's Friend L2213M	Lladro	Closed	390.00	420.00
91-02-449	Seaside Angel L2214M	Lladro	Open	150.00	165.00
91-02-450	Friends in Flight L2215M	Lladro	Open	165.00	180.00
91-02-451	Laundry Day L2216M	Lladro	Open	350.00	385.00
91-02-452	Gentle Play L2217M	Lladro	Closed	380.00	415.00
91-02-453	Costumed Couple L2218M	Lladro	Closed	680.00	750.00
92-02-454	Underfoot L2219M	Lladro	Open	360.00	375.00
92-02-455	Free Spirit L2220M	Lladro	Open	235.00	245.00
92-02-456	Spring Beauty L2221M	Lladro	Open	285.00	295.00
92-02-457	Tender Moment L2222M	Lladro	Open	400.00	420.00
92-02-458	New Lamb L2223M	Lladro	Open	365.00	385.00
92-02-459	Cherish L2224M	Lladro	Open	1750.00	1850.00
92-02-460	FriendlySparrow L2225M	Lladro	Open	295.00	310.00
92-02-461	Boy's Best Friend L2226M	Lladro	Open	390.00	410.00
92-02-462	Artic Allies L2227M	Lladro	Open	585.00	615.00
92-02-463	Snowy Sunday L2228M	Lladro	Open	550.00	575.00
92-02-464	Seasonal Gifts L2229M	Lladro	Open	450.00	475.00
92-02-465	Mary's Child L2230M	Lladro	Open	525.00	550.00
92-02-466	Afternoon Verse L2231M	Lladro	Open	580.00	595.00
92-02-467	Poor Little Bear L2232M	Lladro	Open	250.00	265.00
92-02-468	Guess What I Have L2233M	Lladro	Open	340.00	360.00
92-02-469	Playful Push L2234M	Lladro	Open	850.00	875.00
93-02-470	Adoring Mother L2235M	Lladro	Open	405.00	405.00
93-02-471	Frosty Outing L2236M	Lladro	Open	375.00	375.00
93-02-472	The Old Fishing Hole L2237M	Lladro	Open	625.00	625.00
93-02-473	Learning Together L2238M	Lladro	Open	500.00	500.00
93-02-474	Valencian Courtship L2239M	Lladro	Open	880.00	880.00
93-02-475	WingedLove L2240M	Lladro	Open	285.00	285.00
93-02-476	Winged Harmony L2241M	Lladro	Open	285.00	285.00
93-02-477	Away to School L2242M	Lladro	Open	465.00	465.00
93-02-478	Lion Tamer L2246M	Lladro	Open	375.00	375.00
93-02-479	Just Us L2247M	Lladro	Open	650.00	650.00
93-02-480	Noella L2251M	Lladro	Open	405.00	405.00
93-02-481	Waiting For Father L2252M	Lladro	Open	660.00	660.00
93-02-482	Noisy Friend L2253M	Lladro	Open	280.00	280.00
93-02-483	Step Aside L2254M	Lladro	Open	280.00	280.00
94-02-484	Solitude L2256M	Lladro	Open	398.00	398.00
94-02-485	Constant Companions L2257M	Lladro	Open	575.00	575.00
94-02-486	Family Love L2258M	Lladro	Open	450.00	450.00
94-02-487	Little Fisherman L2259M	Lladro	Open	298.00	298.00
94-02-488	Artic Friends L2260M	Lladro	Open	345.00	345.00
78-02-489	Native L3502M	Lladro	Open	700.00	2450.00
78-02-490	Letters to Dulcinea L3509M, numbered series	Lladro	Open	875.00	2050.00
78-02-491	Horse Heads L3511M	Lladro	Closed	260.00	700.00
78-02-492	Girl With Pails L3512M	Lladro	Open	140.00	285.00
78-02-493	A Wintry Day L3513M	Lladro	Closed	525.00	750.00
78-02-494	Pensive w/ base L3514M	Lladro	Open	500.00	1050.00
78-02-495	Jesus Christ L3516M	Lladro	Closed	1050.00	1450.00
78-02-496	Nude with Rose w/ base L3517M	Lladro	Open	225.00	760.00
80-02-497	Lady Macbeth L3518M	Lladro	Closed	385.00	425-1000
80-02-498	Mother's Love L3521M	Lladro	Closed	1000.00	1100.00
81-02-499	Weary w/ base L3525M	Lladro	Open	360.00	625.00
82-02-500	Contemplation w/ base L3526M	Lladro	Open	265.00	540.00
82-02-501	Stormy Sea w/base L3554M	Lladro	Open	675.00	1325.00
84-02-502	Innocence w/base/green L3558M	Lladro	Closed	960.00	1650.00
84-02-503	Innocence w/base/red L3558.3M	Lladro	Closed	960.00	1200.00
85-02-504	Peace Offering w/base L3559M	Lladro	Open	397.00	665.00
69-02-505	Marketing Day L4502G	Lladro	Closed	40.00	300.00
69-02-506	Girl with Lamb L4505G	Lladro	Open	20.00	110.00
69-02-507	Boy with Kid L4506M	Lladro	Closed	22.50	300-400.
69-02-508	Girl with Parasol and Geese L4510G	Lladro	Closed	40.00	245.00
69-02-509	Nude L4511M	Lladro	Closed	45.00	750-800.
69-02-510	Man on Horse L4515G	Lladro	Closed	180.00	N/A
69-02-511	Female Equestrian L4516G	Lladro	Open	170.00	710.00
69-02-512	Flamenco Dancers L4519G	Lladro	Closed	150.00	1100.00
70-02-513	Boy With Dog L4522M	Lladro	Closed	25.00	155.00
69-02-514	Girl With Slippers L4523G	Lladro	Closed	17.00	100.00
69-02-515	Girl With Slippers L4523M	Lladro	Closed	17.00	100.00
69-02-516	Donkey in Love L4524G	Lladro	Closed	15.00	450.00
69-02-517	Donkey in Love L4524M	Lladro	Closed	15.00	350.00
69-02-518	Violinist L4527G	Lladro	Closed	75.00	500.00
69-02-519	Joseph L4533G	Lladro	Open	60.00	100.00
69-02-520	Joseph L4533M	Lladro	Open	60.00	100.00
69-02-521	Mary L4534G	Lladro	Open	60.00	85.00
69-02-522	Mary L4534M	Lladro	Open	60.00	85.00
71-02-523	Baby Jesus L4535.3G	Lladro	Open	60.00	70.00
69-02-524	Baby Jesus L4535.3M	Lladro	Open	60.00	70.00
69-02-525	Angel, Chinese L4536G	Lladro	Open	45.00	90.00
69-02-526	Angel, Chinese L4536M	Lladro	Open	45.00	90.00
69-02-527	Angel, Black L4537G	Lladro	Open	13.00	90.00
69-02-528	Angel, Black L4537M	Lladro	Open	13.00	90.00
69-02-529	Angel, Praying L4538G	Lladro	Open	13.00	90.00
69-02-530	Angel, Praying L4538M	Lladro	Open	13.00	90.00
69-02-531	Angel, Thinking L4539G	Lladro	Open	13.00	90.00
69-02-532	Angel, Thinking L4539M	Lladro	Open	13.00	90.00
69-02-533	Angel with Horn L4540G	Lladro	Open	13.00	90.00
69-02-534	Angel with Horn L4540M	Lladro	Open	13.00	90.00
69-02-535	Angel Reclining L4541G	Lladro	Open	13.00	90.00
69-02-536	Angel Reclining L4541M	Lladro	Open	13.00	90.00
69-02-537	Group of Angels L4542G	Lladro	Open	31.00	185.00

		ARTIST	EDITION	ISSUE	QUOTE
69-02-538	Group of Angels L4542M	Lladro	Open	31.00	185.00
69-02-539	Geese Group L4549G	Lladro	Open	28.50	210.00
69-02-540	Geese Group L4549M	Lladro	Closed	28.50	200.00
69-02-541	Flying Dove L4550G	Lladro	Open	47.50	245.00
69-02-542	Flying Dove L4550M	Lladro	Closed	47.50	225.00
69-02-543	Ducks,set of 3 asst. L4551-3G	Lladro	Open	18.00	140.00
69-02-544	Shepherd L4554	Lladro	Closed	69.00	N/A
69-02-545	Sad Harlequin L4558G	Lladro	Closed	110.00	550.00
69-02-546	Waiting Backstage L4559G	Lladro	Closed	110.00	440.00
69-02-547	Couple with Parasol L4563G	Lladro	Closed	180.00	625.00
69-02-548	Girl with Geese L4568G	Lladro	Closed	45.00	220.00
69-02-549	Girl With Turkey L4569G	Lladro	Closed	28.50	375.00
69-02-550	Shepherd Resting L4571G	Lladro	Closed	60.00	475.00
69-02-551	Girl with Piglets L4572G	Lladro	Closed	70.00	400.00
69-02-552	Girl with Piglets L4572M	Lladro	Closed	70.00	400.00
69-02-553	Mother & Child L4575G	Lladro	Open	50.00	265.00
69-02-554	New Shepherdess L4576G	Lladro	Closed	37.50	275-300.
69-02-555	Girl with Sheep L4584G	Lladro	Open	27.00	170.00
69-02-556	Holy Family L4585G	Lladro	Closed	18.00	135.00
69-02-557	Holy Family L4585M	Lladro	Closed	18.00	125.00
69-02-558	Madonna L4586G	Lladro	Closed	32.50	350.00
69-02-559	White Cockeral L4588G	Lladro	Closed	17.50	300.00
69-02-560	Girl with Pitcher L4590	Lladro	Closed	47.50	425.00
69-02-561	Shepherdess with Basket L4591G	Lladro	Closed	20.00	140.00
69-02-562	Lady with Greyhound L4594	Lladro	Closed	60.00	750.00
69-02-563	Fairy L4595G	Lladro	Open	27.50	140.00
69-02-564	Playfull Horses L4597	Lladro	Closed	240.00	925-1000
69-02-565	Doctor L4602.3G	Lladro	Open	33.00	185.00
69-02-566	Nurse-L4603.3G	Lladro	Open	35.00	190.00
69-02-567	Clown with Girl L4605	Lladro	Closed	160.00	1-1200.
69-02-568	Accordian Player L4606	Lladro	Closed	60.00	550.00
69-02-569	Cupid L4607G	Lladro	Closed	15.00	150.00
69-02-570	Cook in Trouble L4608	Lladro	Closed	27.50	480-600.
69-02-571	Nuns L4611G	Lladro	Open	37.50	155.00
69-02-572	Nuns L4611M	Lladro	Open	37.50	155.00
69-02-573	Girl Singer L4612G	Lladro	Closed	14.00	450.00
69-02-574	Boy With Cymbals L4613G	Lladro	Closed	14.00	400.00
69-02-575	Boy With Guitar L4614G	Lladro	Closed	19.50	400.00
69-02-576	Boy With Drum L4616G	Lladro	Closed	16.50	400.00
69-02-577	Group of Musicians L4617G	Lladro	Closed	33.00	500.00
69-02-578	Clown L4618G	Lladro	Open	70.00	415.00
69-02-579	Sea Captain L4621G	Lladro	Closed	45.00	265.00
69-02-580	Sea Captain L4621M	Lladro	Closed	42.50	255.00
69-02-581	Angel with Child L4635G	Lladro	Open	15.00	95.00
69-02-582	Honey Peddler L4638G	Lladro	Closed	60.00	575.00
69-02-583	Cow With Pig L4640	Lladro	Closed	42.50	540.00
69-02-584	Pekinese L4641G	Lladro	Closed	20.00	575.00
69-02-585	Dog L4642	Lladro	Closed	22.50	400.00
69-02-586	Skye Terrier L4643	Lladro	Closed	15.00	375-650.
69-02-587	Andalucians Group L4647G	Lladro	Closed	412.00	1400.00
69-02-588	Valencian Couple on Horseback L4648	Lladro	Closed	900.00	950.00
69-02-589	Madonna Head L4649G	Lladro	Open	25.00	145.00
69-02-590	Madonna Head L4649M	Lladro	Open	25.00	145.00
69-02-591	Girl with Calla Lillies L4650G	Lladro	Open	18.00	135.00
69-02-592	Cellist L4651G	Lladro	Closed	70.00	650.00
69-02-593	Happy Travelers L4652	Lladro	Closed	115.00	650.00
69-02-594	Orchestra Conductor L4653G	Lladro	Closed	95.00	850.00
69-02-595	Horses L4655G	Lladro	Open	110.00	760.00
69-02-596	Shepherdess L4660G	Lladro	Closed	21.00	175.00
69-02-597	Girl with Basket L4665G	Lladro	Closed	50.00	450.00
69-02-598	Maja Head L4668G	Lladro	Closed	50.00	550.00
69-02-599	Baby Jesus L4670BG	Lladro	Open	18.00	50.00
69-02-600	Mary L4671G	Lladro	Open	33.00	75.00
69-02-601	St. Joseph L4672G	Lladro	Open	33.00	90.00
69-02-602	King Melchior L4673G	Lladro	Open	35.00	95.00
69-02-603	King Gaspar L4674G	Lladro	Open	35.00	95.00
69-02-604	King Balthasar L4675G	Lladro	Open	35.00	95.00
69-02-605	Shepherd with Lamb L4676G	Lladro	Open	14.00	95.00
69-02-606	Girl with Rooster L4677G	Lladro	Open	14.00	90.00
69-02-607	Shepherdess with Basket L4678G	Lladro	Open	13.00	90.00
69-02-608	Donkey L4679G	Lladro	Open	36.50	100.00
69-02-609	Cow L4680G	Lladro	Open	36.50	90.00
70-02-610	Girl with Milkpail L4682	Lladro	Closed	28.00	350.00
70-02-611	Hebrew Student L4684G	Lladro	Closed	33.00	575-700.
70-02-612	Troubadour in Love L4699	Lladro	Closed	60.00	1000.00
70-02-613	Dressmaker L4700G	Lladro	Closed	45.00	360.00
70-02-614	Mother & Child L4701G	Lladro	Open	45.00	295.00
70-02-615	Bird Watcher L4730	Lladro	Closed	35.00	375.00
71-02-616	Small dog L4749	Lladro	Closed	5.50	150.00
71-02-617	Romeo and Juliet L4750G	Lladro	Open	150.00	1250.00
71-02-618	Doncel With Roses L4757G	Lladro	Closed	35.00	500.00
74-02-619	Lady with Dog L4761G	Lladro	Closed	60.00	260.00
71-02-620	Dentist L4762	Lladro	Closed	36.00	500.00
71-02-621	Dentist (Reduced) L4762. 3G	Lladro	Closed	30.00	500-600.
71-02-622	Obstetrician L4763.3G	Lladro	Open	40.00	235.00
71-02-623	Rabbit L4772G	Lladro	Open	17.50	135.00
71-02-624	Rabbit L4773G	Lladro	Open	17.50	130.00
71-02-625	Dormouse L4774	Lladro	Closed	30.00	375.00
72-02-626	Girl Tennis Player L4778	Lladro	Closed	50.00	400.00
71-02-627	Children, Praying L4779G	Lladro	Open	36.00	180.00
71-02-628	Children, Praying L4779M	Lladro	Closed	36.00	N/A
71-02-629	Boy with Goat L4780	Lladro	Closed	80.00	475.00
72-02-630	Gypsy with Brother L4800G	Lladro	Closed	36.00	400.00
72-02-631	Girl with Dog L4806G	Lladro	Closed	80.00	N/A
72-02-632	Geisha L4807G	Lladro	Closed	190.00	475.00
72-02-633	Wedding L4808G	Lladro	Open	50.00	175.00
72-02-634	Wedding L4808M	Lladro	Open	50.00	175.00
72-02-635	Going Fishing L4809G	Lladro	Open	33.00	160.00
72-02-636	Young Sailor L4810G	Lladro	Open	33.00	165.00
72-02-637	Boy with Pails L4811	Lladro	Closed	30.00	350-425.
72-02-638	Getting Her Goat L4812G	Lladro	Closed	55.00	450.00
72-02-639	Girl with Geese L4815G	Lladro	Closed	72.00	275-295.
72-02-640	Girl with Geese L4815M	Lladro	Closed	72.00	295.00
74-02-641	Pery Girl with Baby L4822	Lladro	Closed	65.00	775.00
74-02-642	Legionary L4823	Lladro	Closed	55.00	400-500.
72-02-643	Male Golfer L4824G	Lladro	Open	66.00	285.00
72-02-644	Veterinarian L4825	Lladro	Closed	48.00	400-500.
72-02-645	Girl Feeding Rabbit L4826G	Lladro	Closed	40.00	185.00
72-02-646	Caressing Calf L4827G	Lladro	Closed	55.00	475.00
72-02-647	Cinderella L4828G	Lladro	Open	47.00	225.00
75-02-648	Swan L4829G	Lladro	Closed	16.00	275-500.

		ARTIST	EDITION	ISSUE	QUOTE
73-02-649	Clean Up Time L4838G	Lladro	Closed	36.00	170.00
73-02-650	Clean Up Time L4838M	Lladro	Closed	36.00	155.00
72-02-651	Shepherdess L4835G	Lladro	Closed	42.00	225.00
72-02-652	Oriental Flower Arranger/Girl L4840G	Lladro	Open	90.00	515.00
72-02-653	Oriental Flower Arranger/Girl L4840M	Lladro	Open	90.00	515.00
74-02-654	Girl from Valencia L4841G	Lladro	Open	35.00	205.00
73-02-655	Pharmacist L4844	Lladro	Closed	70.00	13-2500.
73-02-656	Classic Dance L4847G	Lladro	Closed	80.00	600.00
73-02-657	Feeding The Ducks L4849G	Lladro	Open	60.00	250.00
73-02-658	Feeding The Ducks L4849M	Lladro	Closed	60.00	250.00
73-02-659	Aesthetic Pose L4850G	Lladro	Closed	110.00	650.00
73-02-660	Lady Golfer L4851M	Lladro	Closed	70.00	250.00
73-02-661	Gardner in Trouble L4852	Lladro	Closed	65.00	500.00
74-02-662	Cobbler L4853G	Lladro	Closed	100.00	500-600.
73-02-663	Don Quixote L4854G	Lladro	Open	40.00	205.00
73-02-664	Ballerina L4855G	Lladro	Open	45.00	330.00
83-02-665	Ballerina, white L4855.3	Lladro	Closed	110.00	250.00
74-02-666	Waltz Time L4856G	Lladro	Closed	65.00	550.00
74-02-667	Dog L4857G	Lladro	Closed	40.00	450.00
74-02-668	Peddler L4859G	Lladro	Closed	180.00	750-1000
74-02-669	Dutch Girl L4860G	Lladro	Closed	45.00	300.00
74-02-670	Horse L4861	Lladro	Closed	55.00	400.00
74-02-671	Horse L4862	Lladro	Closed	55.00	400.00
74-02-672	Horse L4863	Lladro	Closed	55.00	400.00
74-02-673	Embroiderer L4865G	Lladro	Open	115.00	645.00
74-02-674	Girl with Swan and Dog L4866G	Lladro	Closed	26.00	205.00
74-02-675	Seesaw L4867G	Lladro	Open	55.00	350.00
74-02-676	Girl with Candle L4868G	Lladro	Open	13.00	90.00
74-02-677	Girl with Candle L4868M	Lladro	Closed	13.00	80.00
74-02-678	Boy Kissing L4869G	Lladro	Open	13.00	90.00
74-02-679	Boy Kissing L4869M	Lladro	Closed	13.00	175.00
74-02-680	Boy Yawning L4870G	Lladro	Open	13.00	90.00
74-02-681	Boy Yawning L4870M	Lladro	Closed	13.00	175.00
74-02-682	Girl with Guitar L4871G	Lladro	Open	13.00	90.00
74-02-683	Girl with Guitar L4871M	Lladro	Closed	13.00	80.00
74-02-684	Girl Stretching L4872G	Lladro	Open	13.00	90.00
74-02-685	Girl Stretching L4872M	Lladro	Closed	13.00	80.00
74-02-686	Girl Kissing L4873G	Lladro	Open	13.00	90.00
74-02-687	Girl Kissing L4873M	Lladro	Closed	13.00	80.00
74-02-688	Boy & Girl L4874G	Lladro	Open	25.00	150.00
74-02-689	Boy & Girl L4874M	Lladro	Closed	25.00	135.00
74-02-690	Girl with Jugs L4875	Lladro	Closed	40.00	N/A
74-02-691	Boy Thinking L4876G	Lladro	Closed	20.00	135.00
74-02-692	Boy Thinking L4876M	Lladro	Closed	20.00	120.00
74-02-693	Lady with Parasol L4879G	Lladro	Open	48.00	300.00
74-02-694	Carnival Couple L4882G	Lladro	Open	60.00	300.00
74-02-695	Seraph's Head No.1 L4884	Lladro	Closed	10.00	100.00
74-02-696	Seraph's Head No.2 L4885	Lladro	Closed	10.00	100.00
74-02-697	Seraph's Head No.3 L4886	Lladro	Closed	10.00	100.00
74-02-698	The Kiss L4888G	Lladro	Closed	150.00	700.00
79-02-699	Spanish Policeman L4889	Lladro	Closed	55.00	295.00
76-02-700	"My Dog" L4893G	Lladro	Open	85.00	210.00
74-02-701	Tennis Player Boy L4894	Lladro	Closed	75.00	450.00
74-02-702	Ducks L4895G	Lladro	Open	45.00	90.00
74-02-703	Ducks L4895M	Lladro	Closed	45.00	85.00
74-02-704	Boy with Snails L4896G	Lladro	Closed	50.00	400.00
74-02-705	Boy From Madrid L4898G	Lladro	Open	55.00	145.00
74-02-706	Boy From Madrid L4898M	Lladro	Closed	55.00	130.00
74-02-707	Boy with Smoking Jacket L4900	Lladro	Closed	45.00	N/A
74-02-708	Barrister L4908G	Lladro	Closed	100.00	450-650.
74-02-709	Girl With Dove L4909G	Lladro	Closed	70.00	450.00
74-02-710	Young Lady in Trouble L4912G	Lladro	Closed	110.00	450.00
75-02-711	Lady with Shawl L4914G	Lladro	Open	220.00	685.00
75-02-712	Girl with Pigeons L4915	Lladro	Closed	110.00	215.00
76-02-713	Chinese Noblewoman L4916G	Lladro	Closed	300.00	2000.00
76-02-714	Gypsy Woman L4919G	Lladro	Closed	165.00	975-1200
74-02-715	Country Lass with Dog L4920G	Lladro	Open	185.00	495.00
74-02-716	Country Lass with Dog L4920M	Lladro	Closed	185.00	450.00
74-02-717	Windblown Girl L4922G	Lladro	Open	150.00	375.00
74-02-718	Lanquid Clown L4924G	Lladro	Closed	200.00	13-1750.
74-02-719	Sisters L4930	Lladro	Closed	250.00	625.00
74-02-720	Children with Fruits L4931G	Lladro	Closed	210.00	500.00
74-02-721	Dainty Lady L4934G	Lladro	Closed	60.00	400.00
74-02-722	"Closing Scene" L4935G	Lladro	Open	180.00	520.00
83-02-723	"Closing Scene"/white L4935.3M	Lladro	Closed	213.00	265.00
74-02-724	Spring Breeze L4936G	Lladro	Open	145.00	410.00
76-02-725	Baby's Outing L4938G	Lladro	Open	250.00	725.00
77-02-726	Missy L4951M	Lladro	Closed	300.00	600-850.
77-02-727	Meditation L4952M	Lladro	Closed	200.00	N/A
77-02-728	Tavern Drinkers L4956G	Lladro	Closed	1125.00	3500.00
77-02-729	Attentive Dogs L4957G	Lladro	Closed	350.00	15-2200.
77-02-730	Cherub, Puzzled L4959G	Lladro	Open	40.00	100.00
77-02-731	Cherub, Smiling L4960G	Lladro	Open	40.00	100.00
77-02-732	Cherub, Dreaming L4961G	Lladro	Open	40.00	100.00
77-02-733	Cherub, Wondering L4962G	Lladro	Open	40.00	100.00
77-02-734	Cherub, Wondering L4962M	Lladro	Closed	40.00	100.00
77-02-735	Infantile Candour L4963G	Lladro	Closed	285.00	675.00
77-02-736	Little Red Riding Hood L4965G	Lladro	Closed	210.00	600-825.
77-02-737	Tennis Player Puppet L4966G	Lladro	Closed	60.00	500.00
77-02-738	Soccer Puppet L4967G	Lladro	Closed	65.00	550.00
77-02-739	Oympic Puppet L4968	Lladro	Closed	65.00	800.00
77-02-740	Cowboy & Sherriff Puppet L4969G	Lladro	Closed	85.00	550.00
77-02-741	Skier Puppet L4970G	Lladro	Closed	85.00	500-900.
77-02-742	Hunter Puppet L4971G	Lladro	Closed	95.00	500.00
77-02-743	Girl with Calla Lillies sitting L4972G	Lladro	Open	65.00	170.00
77-02-744	Choir Lesson L4973G	Lladro	Closed	350.00	1450.00
77-02-745	Augustina of Aragon L4976G	Lladro	Closed	475.00	15-1800.
77-02-746	Harlequin Serenade L4977	Lladro	Closed	185.00	675.00
78-02-747	Naughty Dog L4982G	Lladro	Open	130.00	250.00
78-02-748	Gossip L4984G	Lladro	Closed	260.00	800-900.
78-02-749	Oriental Spring L4988G	Lladro	Open	125.00	325.00
78-02-750	Sayonara L4989G	Lladro	Open	125.00	300.00
78-02-751	Chrysanthemum L4990G	Lladro	Open	125.00	310.00
78-02-752	Butterfly L4991G	Lladro	Open	125.00	295.00
78-02-753	Dancers Resting L4992G	Lladro	Closed	350.00	850.00
78-02-754	Gypsy Venders L4993G	Lladro	Closed	165.00	475.00
78-02-755	Don Quixote & Sancho L4998G	Lladro	Closed	875.00	3300.00
78-02-756	Reading L5000G	Lladro	Open	150.00	255.00
78-02-757	Elk Family L5001G	Lladro	Closed	550.00	700.00
78-02-758	Sunny Day L5003G	Lladro	Closed	193.00	360.00
78-02-759	Naughty L5006G	Lladro	Open	55.00	140.00
78-02-760	Bashful L5007G	Lladro	Open	55.00	140.00
78-02-761	Static-Girl w/Straw Hat L5008G	Lladro	Open	55.00	140.00
78-02-762	Curious-Girl w/Straw Hat L5009G	Lladro	Open	55.00	140.00
78-02-763	Coiffure-Girl w/Straw Hat L5010G	Lladro	Open	55.00	140.00
78-02-764	Trying on a Straw Hat L5011G	Lladro	Open	55.00	140.00
78-02-765	Daughters L5013G	Lladro	Closed	425.00	900.00
78-02-766	Painful Giraffe L5019	Lladro	Closed	115.00	750.00
78-02-767	Woman With Scarf L5024G	Lladro	Closed	141.00	450.00
80-02-768	A Clean Sweep L5025G	Lladro	Open	100.00	275.00
80-02-769	Planning the Day L5026G	Lladro	Open	90.00	275.00
79-02-770	Flower Curtsy L5027G	Lladro	Open	230.00	470.00
80-02-771	Boy with Tricycle & Flowers L5029G	Lladro	Closed	675.00	12-1350.
80-02-772	Wildflower L5030G	Lladro	Open	360.00	695.00
79-02-773	Little Friskies L5032G	Lladro	Open	108.00	220.00
79-02-774	Avoiding the Goose L5033G	Lladro	Closed	160.00	350.00
79-02-775	Goose Trying To Eat L5034G	Lladro	Open	135.00	290.00
80-02-776	Act II w/base L5035G	Lladro	Open	700.00	1425.00
79-02-777	Jockey with Lass L5036G	Lladro	Open	950.00	2050.00
80-02-778	Sleighride w/base L5037G	Lladro	Open	585.00	1045.00
80-02-779	Candid L5039G	Lladro	Closed	145.00	475.00
79-02-780	Girl Walking L5040G	Lladro	Closed	150.00	420-450.
80-02-781	Ladies Talking L5042G	Lladro	Closed	385.00	575-1000
80-02-782	Hind and Baby Deer L5043G	Lladro	Closed	650.00	3600.00
80-02-783	Girl with Toy Wagon L5044G	Lladro	Open	115.00	220.00
80-02-784	Belinda with Doll L5045G	Lladro	Open	115.00	205.00
80-02-785	Organ Grinder L5046G	Lladro	Closed	328.00	1250.00
79-02-786	Dancer L5050G	Lladro	Open	85.00	190.00
80-02-787	Samson and Delilah L5051G	Lladro	Closed	350.00	1600.00
80-02-788	Clown and Girl/ At the Circus L5052G	Lladro	Closed	525.00	1200.00
80-02-789	Festival Time L5053G	Lladro	Closed	250.00	400.00
80-02-790	Little Senorita L5054G	Lladro	Closed	235.00	600.00
80-02-791	Ship-Boy with Baskets L5055G	Lladro	Closed	140.00	400.00
80-02-792	Clown with Clock L5056G	Lladro	Closed	290.00	750-950.
80-02-793	Clown with Violin and Top Hat L5057G	Lladro	Closed	270.00	690.00
80-02-794	Clown with Concertina L5058G	Lladro	Closed	290.00	690.00
80-02-795	Clown with Saxaphone L5059G	Lladro	Closed	320.00	690.00
80-02-796	Girl Clown with Trumpet L5060G	Lladro	Closed	290.00	500-600.
80-02-797	Girl Bending/March Wind L5061G	Lladro	Closed	370.00	325-400.
80-02-798	Kristina L5062G	Lladro	Closed	225.00	400.00
80-02-799	Dutch Girl With Braids L5063G	Lladro	Closed	265.00	425-450.
80-02-800	Dutch Girl, Hands Akimbo L5064G	Lladro	Closed	255.00	650.00
80-02-801	Ingrid L5065G	Lladro	Closed	370.00	700.00
80-02-802	Ilsa L5066G	Lladro	Closed	275.00	300.00
81-02-803	Halloween L5067G	Lladro	Closed	450.00	1300.00
80-02-804	Fairy Queen L5068G	Lladro	Closed	625.00	1200.00
80-02-805	Choir Boy L5070G	Lladro	Closed	240.00	400-600.
80-02-806	Nostalgia L5071G	Lladro	Closed	185.00	310.00
80-02-807	Courtship L5072	Lladro	Closed	327.00	525.00
80-02-808	My Hungry Brood L5074G	Lladro	Open	295.00	415.00
80-02-809	Harlequin L5076G	Lladro	Closed	185.00	400.00
80-02-810	Harlequin C L5077G	Lladro	Closed	185.00	400.00
80-02-811	Teasing the Dog L5078G	Lladro	Closed	300.00	750.00
80-02-812	Woman Painting Vase L5079G	Lladro	Closed	300.00	600-750.
80-02-813	Boy Pottery Seller L5080G	Lladro	Closed	320.00	650-700.
80-02-814	Girl Pottery Seller L5081G	Lladro	Closed	300.00	550-600.
80-02-815	Flower Vendor L5082G	Lladro	Closed	750.00	1850.00
80-02-816	A Good Book L5084G	Lladro	Closed	175.00	350-525.
80-02-817	Mother Amabilis L5086G	Lladro	Closed	275.00	400.00
80-02-818	Roses for My Mom L5088G	Lladro	Closed	645.00	1150.00
80-02-819	Scare-Dy Cat/Playful Cat L5091G	Lladro	Open	65.00	95.00
80-02-820	After the Dance L5092G	Lladro	Closed	165.00	350.00
80-02-821	A Dancing Partner L5093G	Lladro	Closed	165.00	500.00
80-02-822	Ballet First Step L5094G	Lladro	Closed	165.00	300-375.
80-02-823	Ballet Bowing L5095G	Lladro	Closed	165.00	375.00
89-02-824	Her Ladyship, L5097G, numbered series	Lladro	Closed	5900.00	6700.00
82-02-825	Playful Tot L5099G	Lladro	Closed	58.00	N/A
82-02-826	Cry Baby L5100G	Lladro	Closed	58.00	N/A
82-02-827	Learning to Crawl L5101G	Lladro	Closed	58.00	275.00
82-02-828	Teething L5102G	Lladro	Closed	58.00	275.00
82-02-829	Time for a Nap L5103G	Lladro	Closed	58.00	275.00
82-02-830	Natalia L5106G	Lladro	Closed	85.00	350.00
82-02-831	Little Ballet Girl L5108G	Lladro	Closed	85.00	400.00
82-02-832	Little Ballet Girl L5109G	Lladro	Closed	85.00	400.00
82-02-833	Dog Sniffing L5110G	Lladro	Closed	50.00	425.00
82-02-834	Timid Dog L5111	Lladro	Closed	44.00	425.00
82-02-835	Play with Me L5112G	Lladro	Open	40.00	80.00
82-02-836	Feed Me L5113G	Lladro	Open	40.00	80.00
82-02-837	Pet Me L5114G	Lladro	Open	40.00	80.00
82-02-838	Little Boy Bullfighter L5115G	Lladro	Closed	123.00	400.00
82-02-839	A Victory L5116G	Lladro	Closed	123.00	400-500.
82-02-840	Proud Matador L5117G	Lladro	Closed	123.00	425-500.
82-02-841	Girl in Green Dress L5118G	Lladro	Closed	170.00	475.00
82-02-842	Lilly (Bluish Dress w/ Flowers) L5119G	Lladro	Closed	170.00	540.00
82-02-843	August Moon L5122G	Lladro	Closed	185.00	310.00
82-02-844	My Precious Bundle L5123G	Lladro	Open	150.00	230.00
82-02-845	Dutch Couple with Tulips L5124G	Lladro	Closed	310.00	900.00
82-02-846	Amparo L5125G	Lladro	Closed	130.00	330-350.
82-02-847	Sewing A Trousseau L5126G	Lladro	Closed	185.00	300.00
82-02-848	Marcelina L5127G	Lladro	Closed	255.00	N/A
82-02-849	Lost Love L5128G	Lladro	Closed	400.00	650-750.
82-02-850	Jester w/base L5129G	Lladro	Open	220.00	405.00
82-02-851	Pensive Clown w/base L5130G	Lladro	Open	250.00	415.00
82-02-852	Cervantes L5132G	Lladro	Closed	925.00	1175.00
82-02-853	Trophy with Base L5133G	Lladro	Closed	250.00	650.00
82-02-854	Girl Soccer Player L5134G	Lladro	Closed	140.00	500-590.
82-02-855	Billy Football Player L5135G	Lladro	Closed	140.00	500-590.
82-02-856	Billy Skier L5136G	Lladro	Closed	140.00	500.00
82-02-857	Billy Baseball Player L5137G	Lladro	Closed	140.00	800-900.
82-02-858	A New Doll House L5139G	Lladro	Closed	185.00	750.00
82-02-859	Feed Her Son L5140G	Lladro	Closed	170.00	375.00
82-02-860	Balloons for Sale L5141G	Lladro	Open	145.00	250.00
82-02-861	Comforting Daughter L5142G	Lladro	Closed	195.00	325.00
82-02-862	Scooting L5143G	Lladro	Closed	575.00	850-1000
82-02-863	Amy L5145G	Lladro	Closed	110.00	1250.00
82-02-864	Ellen L5146G	Lladro	Closed	110.00	1200.00
82-02-865	Ivy L5147G	Lladro	Closed	100.00	600.00
82-02-866	Olivia L5148G	Lladro	Closed	100.00	450-500.
82-02-867	Ursula L5149G	Lladro	Closed	100.00	450-500.
82-02-868	Girl's Head L5151G	Lladro	Closed	380.00	575.00
82-02-869	Girl's Head L5153G	Lladro	Closed	475.00	575.00
82-02-870	First Prize L5154G	Lladro	Closed	90.00	N/A
82-02-871	Monks at Prayer L5155M	Lladro	Open	130.00	250.00

		ARTIST	EDITION	ISSUE	QUOTE
82-02-872	Susan and the Doves L5156G	Lladro	Closed	203.00	325-360.
82-02-873	Bongo Beat L5157G	Lladro	Open	135.00	230.00
82-02-874	A Step In Time L5158G	Lladro	Open	90.00	180.00
82-02-875	Harmony L5159G	Lladro	Open	270.00	495.00
82-02-876	Rhumba L5160G	Lladro	Open	113.00	185.00
82-02-877	Cycling To A Picnic L5161G	Lladro	Closed	2000.00	2800.00
82-02-878	Mouse Girl/Mindy L5162G	Lladro	Closed	125.00	425-450.
82-02-879	Bunny Girl/Bunny L5163G	Lladro	Closed	125.00	425-450.
82-02-880	Cat Girl/Kitty L5164G	Lladro	Closed	125.00	400-450.
82-02-881	A Toast by Sancho L5165	Lladro	Closed	100.00	325.00
82-02-882	Sea Fever L5166M	Lladro	Closed	130.00	235.00
82-02-883	Jesus L5167G	Lladro	Open	130.00	265.00
82-02-884	King Solomon L5168G	Lladro	Closed	205.00	750.00
82-02-885	Abraham L5169G	Lladro	Closed	155.00	700-750.
82-02-886	Moses L5170G	Lladro	Open	175.00	360.00
82-02-887	Madonna with Flowers L5171G	Lladro	Open	173.00	310.00
82-02-888	Fish A'Plenty L5172G	Lladro	Open	190.00	385.00
82-02-889	Pondering L5173G	Lladro	Closed	300.00	495.00
82-02-890	Roaring 20's L5174G	Lladro	Closed	173.00	295.00
82-02-891	Flapper L5175G	Lladro	Open	185.00	365.00
82-02-892	Rhapsody in Blue L5176G	Lladro	Closed	325.00	1350.00
82-02-893	Dante L5177G	Lladro	Closed	263.00	600.00
82-02-894	Stubborn Mule L5178G	Lladro	Closed	250.00	420.00
83-02-895	Three Pink Roses w/base L5179M	Lladro	Closed	70.00	110.00
83-02-896	Dahlia L5180M	Lladro	Closed	65.00	140.00
83-02-897	Japanese Camelia w/base L5181M	Lladro	Closed	60.00	90.00
83-02-898	White Peony L5182M	Lladro	Closed	85.00	125.00
83-02-899	Two Yellow Roses L5183M	Lladro	Closed	57.50	85.00
83-02-900	White Carnation L5184M	Lladro	Closed	65.00	100.00
83-02-901	Lactiflora Peony L5185M	Lladro	Closed	65.00	100.00
83-02-902	Begonia L5186M	Lladro	Closed	67.50	100.00
83-02-903	Rhododendrom L5187M	Lladro	Closed	67.50	100.00
83-02-904	Miniature Begonia L5188M	Lladro	Closed	80.00	120.00
83-02-905	Chrysanthemum L5189M	Lladro	Closed	100.00	150.00
83-02-906	California Poppy L5190M	Lladro	Closed	97.50	180.00
85-02-907	Predicting the Future L5191G	Lladro	Closed	135.00	400.00
84-02-908	Lolita L5192G	Lladro	Open	80.00	155.00
84-02-909	Juanita L5193G	Lladro	Open	80.00	155.00
84-02-910	Roving Photographer L5194G	Lladro	Closed	145.00	750.00
83-02-911	Say "Cheese!" L5195G	Lladro	Closed	170.00	450.00
83-02-912	"Maestro, Music Please!" L5196G	Lladro	Closed	135.00	450.00
83-02-913	Female Physician L5197	Lladro	Open	120.00	240.00
84-02-914	Boy Graduate L5198G	Lladro	Open	160.00	275.00
84-02-915	Girl Graduate L5199G	Lladro	Open	160.00	260.00
84-02-916	Male Soccer Player L5200G	Lladro	Closed	155.00	475.00
84-02-917	Special Male Soccer Player L5200.3G	Lladro	Closed	150.00	450.00
83-02-918	Josefa Feeding Duck L5201G	Lladro	Closed	125.00	250.00
83-02-919	Aracely with Ducks L5202G	Lladro	Closed	125.00	250-300.
84-02-920	Little Jester L5203G	Lladro	Closed	75.00	140.00
84-02-921	Little Jester L5203M	Lladro	Closed	75.00	125.00
83-02-922	Sharpening the Cutlery L5204	Lladro	Closed	210.00	700.00
83-02-923	Lamplighter L5205G	Lladro	Open	170.00	360.00
83-02-924	Yachtsman L5206G	Lladro	Open	110.00	210.00
83-02-925	A Tall Yarn L5207G	Lladro	Open	260.00	515.00
83-02-926	Professor L5208G	Lladro	Closed	205.00	450-750.
83-02-927	School Marm L5209G	Lladro	Closed	205.00	775-834.
84-02-928	Jolie L5210G	Lladro	Open	105.00	200.00
84-02-929	Angela L5211G	Lladro	Open	105.00	200.00
84-02-930	Evita L5212G	Lladro	Open	105.00	195.00
83-02-931	Lawyer L5213G	Lladro	Open	250.00	520.00
83-02-932	Architect L5214G	Lladro	Closed	140.00	400.00
83-02-933	Fishing with Gramps w/base L5215G	Lladro	Open	410.00	780.00
83-02-934	On the Lake L5216G	Lladro	Closed	660.00	900.00
83-02-935	Spring L5217G	Lladro	Open	90.00	170.00
83-02-936	Spring L5217M	Lladro	Open	90.00	170.00
83-02-937	Autumn L5218G	Lladro	Open	90.00	170.00
83-02-938	Autumn L5218M	Lladro	Open	90.00	170.00
83-02-939	Summer L5219G	Lladro	Open	90.00	170.00
83-02-940	Summer L5219M	Lladro	Open	90.00	170.00
83-02-941	Winter L5220G	Lladro	Open	90.00	170.00
83-02-942	Winter L5220M	Lladro	Open	90.00	170.00
83-02-943	Sweet Scent L5221G	Lladro	Open	80.00	130.00
83-02-944	Sweet Scent L5221M	Lladro	Open	80.00	130.00
83-02-945	Pretty Pickings L5222G	Lladro	Open	80.00	130.00
83-02-946	Pretty Pickings L5222M	Lladro	Open	80.00	130.00
83-02-947	Spring is Here L5223G	Lladro	Open	80.00	130.00
83-02-948	Spring is Here L5223M	Lladro	Open	80.00	130.00
84-02-949	The Quest L5224G	Lladro	Open	125.00	275.00
84-02-950	Male Candleholder L5226	Lladro	Closed	660.00	660-1000
84-02-951	Playful Piglets L5228G	Lladro	Open	80.00	135.00
83-02-952	Storytime L5229G	Lladro	Closed	245.00	800.00
84-02-953	Graceful Swan L5230G	Lladro	Open	35.00	80.00
84-02-954	Swan with Wings Spread L5231G	Lladro	Open	50.00	115.00
83-02-955	Playful Kittens L5232G	Lladro	Open	130.00	255.00
84-02-956	Charlie the Tramp L5233G	Lladro	Closed	150.00	750.00
84-02-957	Artistic Endeavor L5234G	Lladro	Closed	225.00	750.00
84-02-958	Ballet Trio L5235G	Lladro	Open	785.00	1525.00
84-02-959	Cat and Mouse L5236G	Lladro	Open	55.00	98.00
84-02-960	Cat and Mouse L5236M	Lladro	Closed	55.00	95.00
84-02-961	School Chums L5237G	Lladro	Open	225.00	440.00
84-02-962	Eskimo Boy with Pet L5238G	Lladro	Open	55.00	105.00
84-02-963	Eskimo Boy with Pet L5238M	Lladro	Closed	55.00	95.00
84-02-964	Wine Taster L5239G	Lladro	Open	190.00	360.00
84-02-965	Lady from Majorca L5240G	Lladro	Closed	120.00	400.00
84-02-966	Best Wishes L5244G	Lladro	Closed	185.00	275.00
84-02-967	A Thought for Today L5245	Lladro	Closed	180.00	300.00
84-02-968	St. Christopher L5246	Lladro	Closed	265.00	600.00
84-02-969	Penguin L5247G	Lladro	Closed	70.00	200.00
84-02-970	Penguin L5248G	Lladro	Open	70.00	200.00
84-02-971	Penguin L5249G	Lladro	Open	70.00	200.00
84-02-972	Exam Day L5250G	Lladro	Open	115.00	210.00
84-02-973	Torch Bearer L5251G	Lladro	Closed	100.00	550.00
84-02-974	Dancing the Polka L5252G	Lladro	Closed	205.00	395.00
84-02-975	Cadet L5253G	Lladro	Closed	150.00	750.00
84-02-976	Making Paella L5254G	Lladro	Closed	215.00	400.00
84-02-977	Spanish Soldier L5255G	Lladro	Closed	185.00	650.00
84-02-978	Folk Dancing L5256	Lladro	Closed	205.00	300.00
85-02-979	Bust of Lady from Elche L5269M	Lladro	Closed	432.00	750.00
85-02-980	Racing Motor Cyclist L5270G	Lladro	Closed	360.00	550-800.
85-02-981	Gazelle L5271G	Lladro	Closed	205.00	425.00
85-02-982	Biking in the Country L5272G	Lladro	Closed	295.00	775.00
85-02-983	Civil Guard at Attention L5273G	Lladro	Open	170.00	450.00

		ARTIST	EDITION	ISSUE	QUOTE
85-02-984	Wedding Day L5274G	Lladro	Open	240.00	415.00
85-02-985	Weary Ballerina L5275G	Lladro	Open	175.00	295.00
85-02-986	Weary Ballerina L5275M	Lladro	Closed	175.00	275.00
85-02-987	Sailor Serenades His Girl L5276G	Lladro	Closed	315.00	475.00
85-02-988	Pierrot with Puppy L5277G	Lladro	Open	95.00	160.00
85-02-989	Pierrot with Puppy and Ball L5278G	Lladro	Open	95.00	160.00
85-02-990	Pierrot with Concertina L5279G	Lladro	Open	95.00	160.00
85-02-991	Hiker L5280G	Lladro	Closed	195.00	425.00
85-02-992	Nativity Scene "Haute Relief" L5281M	Lladro	Closed	210.00	450.00
85-02-993	Over the Threshold L5282G	Lladro	Open	150.00	270.00
85-02-994	Socialite of the Twenties L5283G	Lladro	Open	175.00	340.00
85-02-995	Glorious Spring L5284G	Lladro	Open	355.00	650.00
85-02-996	Summer on the Farm L5285G	Lladro	Open	235.00	440.00
85-02-997	Fall Clean-up L5286G	Lladro	Open	295.00	550.00
85-02-998	Winter Frost L5287G	Lladro	Open	270.00	520.00
85-02-999	Mallard Duck L5288G	Lladro	Open	310.00	520.00
85-02-1000	Ltl. Leaguer, Catcher L5290	Lladro	Closed	150.00	450.00
85-02-1001	Love in Bloom L5292G	Lladro	Open	225.00	415.00
85-02-1002	Mother and Child and Lamb L5299G	Lladro	Closed	180.00	450.00
85-02-1003	Medieval Courtship L5300G	Lladro	Closed	735.00	850.00
85-02-1004	Waiting to Tee Off L5301G	Lladro	Open	145.00	285.00
85-02-1005	Playing with Ducks at the Pond L5303	Lladro	Closed	425.00	700.00
85-02-1006	Children at Play L5304	Lladro	Closed	220.00	450-550.
85-02-1007	A Visit with Granny L5305G	Lladro	Closed	275.00	515.00
85-02-1008	Young Street Musicians L5306	Lladro	Closed	300.00	950.00
85-02-1009	Mini Kitten L5307G	Lladro	Closed	35.00	100-150.
85-02-1010	Mini Cat L5308G	Lladro	Closed	35.00	100.00
85-02-1011	Mini Cocker Spaniel Pup L5309G	Lladro	Closed	35.00	100.00
85-02-1012	Mini Cocker Spaniel L5310G	Lladro	Closed	35.00	100.00
85-02-1013	Mini Puppies L5311G	Lladro	Closed	65.00	200.00
85-02-1014	Mini Bison Resting L5312G	Lladro	Closed	50.00	162.50
85-02-1015	Mini Bison Attacking L5313G	Lladro	Closed	57.50	162.50
85-02-1016	Mini Seal Family L5318G	Lladro	Closed	77.50	275.00
85-02-1017	Wistful Centaur Girl L5319	Lladro	Closed	157.00	340.00
85-02-1018	Demure Centaur Girl L5320	Lladro	Closed	157.00	300.00
85-02-1019	Parisian Lady L5321G	Lladro	Open	193.00	325.00
85-02-1020	Viennese Lady L5322G	Lladro	Open	160.00	295.00
85-02-1021	Milanese Lady L5323G	Lladro	Open	180.00	340.00
85-02-1022	English Lady L5324G	Lladro	Open	225.00	410.00
85-02-1023	Ice Cream Vendor L5325G	Lladro	Open	380.00	650.00
85-02-1024	The Tailor L5326G	Lladro	Closed	335.00	850.00
85-02-1025	Nippon Lady L5327G	Lladro	Open	325.00	545.00
85-02-1026	Lady Equestrian L5328G	Lladro	Closed	160.00	400-425.
85-02-1027	Gentleman Equestrian L5329G	Lladro	Closed	160.00	525.00
85-02-1028	Concert Violinist L5330G	Lladro	Closed	220.00	425-500.
85-02-1029	Gymnast with Ring L5331	Lladro	Closed	95.00	295.00
85-02-1030	Aerobics Push-Up L5334G	Lladro	Closed	110.00	850.00
85-02-1031	Aerobics Floor Exercies L5335G	Lladro	Closed	110.00	295.00
85-02-1032	"La Giaconda" L5337	Lladro	Closed	110.00	400.00
86-02-1033	A Stitch in Time L5344G	Lladro	Open	425.00	745.00
86-02-1034	A New Hat L5345G	Lladro	Closed	200.00	375.00
86-02-1035	Nature Girl L5346G	Lladro	Closed	450.00	950.00
86-02-1036	Bedtime L5347G	Lladro	Open	300.00	545.00
86-02-1037	On Guard L5350G	Lladro	Closed	50.00	200.00
86-02-1038	Woe is Me L5351G	Lladro	Closed	45.00	200.00
86-02-1039	Hindu Children L5352G	Lladro	Open	250.00	410.00
86-02-1040	Eskimo Riders L5353G	Lladro	Open	150.00	250.00
86-02-1041	Eskimo Riders L5353M	Lladro	Open	150.00	250.00
86-02-1042	A Ride in the Country L5354G	Lladro	Closed	225.00	415.00
86-02-1043	Consideration L5355M	Lladro	Closed	100.00	225.00
86-02-1044	Wolf Hound L5356G	Lladro	Closed	45.00	55.00
86-02-1045	Oration L5357G	Lladro	Open	170.00	275.00
86-02-1046	Little Sculptor L5358	Lladro	Closed	160.00	300.00
86-02-1047	El Greco L5359G	Lladro	Closed	300.00	800.00
86-02-1048	Sewing Circle L5360G	Lladro	Closed	600.00	1200.00
86-02-1049	Try This One L5361G	Lladro	Open	225.00	385.00
86-02-1050	Still Life L5363G	Lladro	Open	180.00	365.00
86-02-1051	Litter of Fun L5364G	Lladro	Open	275.00	465.00
86-02-1052	Sunday in the Park L5365G	Lladro	Open	375.00	625.00
86-02-1053	Can Can L5370G	Lladro	Closed	700.00	11-1400.
86-02-1054	Family Roots L5371G	Lladro	Open	575.00	895.00
86-02-1055	Lolita L5372G	Lladro	Closed	120.00	200.00
86-02-1056	Carmencita L5373G	Lladro	Closed	120.00	200.00
86-02-1057	Pepita L5374G	Lladro	Closed	120.00	200.00
86-02-1058	Teresita L5375G	Lladro	Closed	120.00	200.00
86-02-1059	This One's Mine L5376G	Lladro	Open	300.00	520.00
86-02-1060	A Touch of Class L5377G	Lladro	Open	475.00	795.00
86-02-1061	Time for Reflection L5378G	Lladro	Open	425.00	745.00
86-02-1062	Children's Games L5379G	Lladro	Closed	325.00	650.00
86-02-1063	Sweet Harvest L5380G	Lladro	Closed	450.00	900.00
86-02-1064	Serenade L5381	Lladro	Closed	450.00	625.00
86-02-1065	Lovers Serenade L5382G	Lladro	Closed	350.00	850.00
86-02-1066	Petite Maiden L5383	Lladro	Closed	110.00	350.00
86-02-1067	Petite Pair L5384	Lladro	Closed	225.00	400.00
86-02-1068	Scarecrow & the Lady L5385G	Lladro	Open	350.00	625.00
86-02-1069	St. Vincent L5387	Lladro	Closed	190.00	350.00
86-02-1070	Sidewalk Serenade L5388G	Lladro	Closed	750.00	11-1300.
86-02-1071	Deep in Thought L5389G	Lladro	Closed	170.00	325.00
86-02-1072	Spanish Dancer L5390	Lladro	Closed	170.00	340.00
86-02-1073	A Time to Rest L5391G	Lladro	Closed	170.00	300-350.
86-02-1074	Balancing Act L5392G	Lladro	Closed	35.00	150.00
86-02-1075	Curiosity L5393G	Lladro	Closed	25.00	175.00
86-02-1076	Poor Puppy L5394G	Lladro	Closed	25.00	40.00
86-02-1077	Valencian Boy L5395G	Lladro	Closed	200.00	325.00
86-02-1078	The Puppet Painter L5396G	Lladro	Open	500.00	850.00
86-02-1079	The Poet L5397G	Lladro	Closed	425.00	550.00
86-02-1080	At the Ball L5398G	Lladro	Closed	375.00	700.00
87-02-1081	Time To Rest L5399G	Lladro	Closed	175.00	295.00
87-02-1082	The Wanderer L5400G	Lladro	Open	150.00	245.00
87-02-1083	My Best Friend L5401G	Lladro	Open	150.00	240.00
87-02-1084	Desert Tour L5402G	Lladro	Closed	950.00	1050.00
87-02-1085	The Drummer Boy L5403G	Lladro	Closed	225.00	320-550.
87-02-1086	Cadet Captain L5404G	Lladro	Closed	175.00	360.00
87-02-1087	The Flag Bearer L5405G	Lladro	Closed	200.00	450.00
87-02-1088	The Bugler L5406G	Lladro	Closed	175.00	300-400.
87-02-1089	At Attention L5407G	Lladro	Closed	175.00	325.00
87-02-1090	Sunday Stroll L5408G	Lladro	Closed	250.00	600.00
87-02-1091	Courting Time L5409	Lladro	Closed	425.00	550.00
87-02-1092	Pilar L5410G	Lladro	Closed	200.00	375.00
87-02-1093	Teresa L5411G	Lladro	Closed	225.00	430.00
87-02-1094	Isabel L5412G	Lladro	Closed	225.00	450.00

	ARTIST	EDITION	ISSUE	QUOTE
87-02-1095 Mexican Dancers L5415G	Lladro	Open	800.00	1150.00
87-02-1096 In the Garden L5416G	Lladro	Open	200.00	325.00
87-02-1097 Artist's Model L5417	Lladro	Closed	425.00	475.00
87-02-1098 Short Eared Owl L5418G	Lladro	Closed	200.00	360.00
87-02-1099 Great Gray Owl L5419G	Lladro	Closed	190.00	195-225.
87-02-1100 Horned Owl L5420G	Lladro	Closed	150.00	300.00
87-02-1101 Barn Owl L5421G	Lladro	Closed	120.00	275.00
87-02-1102 Hawk Owl L5422G	Lladro	Closed	120.00	145.00
87-02-1103 Intermezzo L5424	Lladro	Closed	325.00	550.00
87-02-1104 Studying in the Park L5425G	Lladro	Closed	675.00	950.00
87-02-1105 Studying in the Park L5425M	Lladro	Closed	675.00	950.00
87-02-1106 One, Two, Three L5426G	Lladro	Open	240.00	365.00
87-02-1107 Saint Nicholas L5427G	Lladro	Closed	425.00	600.00
87-02-1108 Feeding the Pigeons L5428	Lladro	Closed	490.00	700.00
87-02-1109 Happy Birthday L5429G	Lladro	Open	100.00	155.00
87-02-1110 Music Time L5430G	Lladro	Closed	500.00	700.00
87-02-1111 Midwife L5431	Lladro	Closed	175.00	380-525.
87-02-1112 Monkey L5432G	Lladro	Closed	60.00	100-150.
87-02-1113 Kangaroo L5433G	Lladro	Closed	65.00	150.00
87-02-1114 Miniature Polar Bear L5434G	Lladro	Open	65.00	100.00
87-02-1115 Cougar L5435G	Lladro	Closed	65.00	300.00
87-02-1116 Lion L5436G	Lladro	Closed	50.00	150.00
87-02-1117 Rhino L5437G	Lladro	Closed	50.00	150.00
87-02-1118 Elephant L5438G	Lladro	Closed	50.00	100-150.
87-02-1119 The Bride L5439G	Lladro	Open	250.00	385.00
87-02-1120 Poetry of Love L5442G	Lladro	Open	500.00	825.00
87-02-1121 Sleepy Trio L5443G	Lladro	Open	190.00	305.00
87-02-1122 Will You Marry Me? L5447G	Lladro	Open	750.00	1250.00
87-02-1123 Naptime L5448G	Lladro	Open	135.00	230.00
87-02-1124 Naptime L5448M	Lladro	Open	135.00	230.00
87-02-1125 Goodnight L5449	Lladro	Open	225.00	350.00
87-02-1126 I Hope She Does L5450G	Lladro	Open	190.00	315.00
88-02-1127 Study Buddies L5451G	Lladro	Open	225.00	295.00
88-02-1128 Masquerade Ball L5452G	Lladro	Closed	220.00	290.00
88-02-1129 Masquerade Ball L5452M	Lladro	Closed	220.00	265.00
88-02-1130 For You L5453G	Lladro	Open	450.00	595.00
88-02-1131 For Me? L5454G	Lladro	Open	290.00	380.00
88-02-1132 Bashful Bather L5455G	Lladro	Open	150.00	190.00
88-02-1133 Bashful Bather L5455M	Lladro	Closed	150.00	180.00
88-02-1134 New Playmates L5456G	Lladro	Open	160.00	210.00
88-02-1135 New Playmates L5456M	Lladro	Closed	160.00	190.00
88-02-1136 Bedtime Story L5457G	Lladro	Open	275.00	355.00
88-02-1137 Bedtime Story L5457M	Lladro	Closed	275.00	330.00
88-02-1138 A Barrow of Fun L5460G	Lladro	Open	370.00	485.00
88-02-1139 A Barrow of Fun L5460M	Lladro	Closed	370.00	450.00
88-02-1140 Koala Love L5461G	Lladro	Closed	115.00	150.00
88-02-1141 Practice Makes Perfect L5462G	Lladro	Open	375.00	495.00
88-02-1142 Look At Me! L5465G	Lladro	Open	375.00	475.00
88-02-1143 Look At Me! L5465M	Lladro	Closed	375.00	435.00
88-02-1144 "Chit-Chat" L5466G	Lladro	Open	150.00	190.00
88-02-1145 "Chit-Chat" L5466M	Lladro	Closed	150.00	180.00
88-02-1146 May Flowers L5467G	Lladro	Open	160.00	195.00
88-02-1147 May Flowers L5467M	Lladro	Closed	160.00	190.00
88-02-1148 "Who's The Fairest?" L5468G	Lladro	Open	150.00	195.00
88-02-1149 "Who's The Fairest?" L5468M	Lladro	Closed	150.00	180.00
88-02-1150 Lambkins L5469G	Lladro	Closed	150.00	210.00
88-02-1151 Lambkins L5469M	Lladro	Closed	150.00	195.00
88-02-1152 Tea Time L5470G	Lladro	Open	280.00	360.00
88-02-1153 Sad Sax L5471G	Lladro	Open	175.00	205.00
88-02-1154 Circus Sam L5472G	Lladro	Open	175.00	205.00
88-02-1155 How You've Grown! L5474G	Lladro	Open	180.00	235.00
88-02-1156 How You've Grown! L5474M	Lladro	Closed	180.00	215.00
88-02-1157 A Lesson Shared L5475G	Lladro	Open	150.00	180.00
88-02-1158 A Lesson Shared L5475M	Lladro	Closed	150.00	170.00
88-02-1159 St. Joseph L5476G	Lladro	Open	210.00	270.00
88-02-1160 Mary L5477G	Lladro	Open	130.00	165.00
88-02-1161 Baby Jesus L5478G	Lladro	Open	55.00	75.00
88-02-1162 King Melchior L5479G	Lladro	Open	210.00	265.00
88-02-1163 King Gaspar L5480G	Lladro	Open	210.00	265.00
88-02-1164 King Balthasar L5481G	Lladro	Open	210.00	265.00
88-02-1165 Ox L5482G	Lladro	Open	125.00	165.00
88-02-1166 Donkey L5483G	Lladro	Open	125.00	165.00
88-02-1167 Lost Lamb L5484G	Lladro	Open	100.00	140.00
88-02-1168 Shepherd Boy L5485G	Lladro	Open	140.00	180.00
88-02-1169 Debutantes L5486G	Lladro	Open	490.00	695.00
88-02-1170 Debutantes L5486M	Lladro	Closed	490.00	635.00
88-02-1171 Ingenue L5487G	Lladro	Open	110.00	140.00
88-02-1172 Ingenue L5487M	Lladro	Closed	110.00	130.00
88-02-1173 Sandcastles L5488G	Lladro	Closed	160.00	220.00
88-02-1174 Sandcastles L5488M	Lladro	Closed	160.00	200.00
88-02-1175 Justice L5489G	Lladro	Closed	675.00	825.00
88-02-1176 Flor Maria L5490G	Lladro	Open	500.00	635.00
88-02-1177 Heavenly Strings L5491G	Lladro	Closed	140.00	185.00
88-02-1178 Heavenly Cellist L5492G	Lladro	Closed	240.00	315.00
88-02-1179 Angel with Lute L5493G	Lladro	Closed	140.00	185.00
88-02-1180 Angel with Clarinet L5494G	Lladro	Closed	140.00	185.00
88-02-1181 Angelic Choir L5495G	Lladro	Closed	300.00	395.00
88-02-1182 Recital L5496G	Lladro	Open	190.00	265.00
88-02-1183 Dress Rehearsal L5497G	Lladro	Open	290.00	385.00
88-02-1184 Opening Night L5498G	Lladro	Open	190.00	260.00
88-02-1185 Pretty Ballerina L5499G	Lladro	Open	190.00	260.00
88-02-1186 Prayerful Moment (blue) L5500G	Lladro	Open	90.00	110.00
88-02-1187 Time to Sew (blue) L5501G	Lladro	Open	90.00	110.00
88-02-1188 Meditation (blue) L5502G	Lladro	Open	90.00	110.00
88-02-1189 Hurry Now L5503G	Lladro	Open	180.00	240.00
88-02-1190 Hurry Now L5503M	Lladro	Closed	180.00	240.00
89-02-1191 Flowers for Sale L5537G	Lladro	Open	1200.00	1550.00
89-02-1192 Puppy Dog Tails L5539G	Lladro	Open	1200.00	1550.00
89-02-1193 An Evening Out L5540G	Lladro	Closed	350.00	400.00
89-02-1194 Melancholy w/base L5542G	Lladro	Open	375.00	440.00
89-02-1195 "Hello, Flowers" L5543G	Lladro	Closed	385.00	485.00
89-02-1196 Reaching the Goal L5546G	Lladro	Open	215.00	275.00
89-02-1197 Only the Beginning L5547G	Lladro	Open	215.00	275.00
89-02-1198 Pretty Posies L5548G	Lladro	Open	425.00	530.00
89-02-1199 My New Pet L5549G	Lladro	Open	150.00	185.00
89-02-1200 Serene Moment (blue) L5550G	Lladro	Closed	115.00	150.00
89-02-1201 Serene Moment (white) L5550.3G	Lladro	Closed	115.00	135.00
89-02-1202 Serene Moment (white) L5550.3M	Lladro	Closed	115.00	135.00
89-02-1203 Call to Prayer (blue) L5551G	Lladro	Closed	100.00	135.00
89-02-1204 Call to Prayer (white) L5551.3G	Lladro	Closed	100.00	120.00
89-02-1205 Call to Prayer (white) L5551.3M	Lladro	Closed	100.00	120.00
89-02-1206 Morning Chores (blue) L5552G	Lladro	Closed	115.00	140.00
89-02-1207 Wild Goose Chase L5553G	Lladro	Open	175.00	230.00
89-02-1208 Pretty and Prim L5554G	Lladro	Open	215.00	270.00
89-02-1209 "Let's Make Up" L5555G	Lladro	Open	215.00	265.00
89-02-1210 Sad Parting L5583G	Lladro	Closed	375.00	525.00
89-02-1211 Daddy's Girl/Father's Day L5584G	Lladro	Open	315.00	395.00
89-02-1212 Fine Melody w/base L5585G	Lladro	Closed	225.00	295.00
89-02-1213 Sad Note w/base L5586G	Lladro	Closed	185.00	275.00
89-02-1214 Wedding Cake L5587G	Lladro	Open	595.00	750.00
89-02-1215 Blustery Day L5588G	Lladro	Closed	185.00	230.00
89-02-1216 Pretty Pose L5589G	Lladro	Closed	185.00	230.00
89-02-1217 Spring Breeze L5590G	Lladro	Closed	185.00	230.00
89-02-1218 Garden Treasures L5591G	Lladro	Closed	185.00	230.00
89-02-1219 Male Siamese Dancer L5592G	Lladro	Closed	345.00	420.00
89-02-1220 Siamese Dancer L5593G	Lladro	Closed	345.00	420.00
89-02-1221 Playful Romp L5594G	Lladro	Open	215.00	270.00
89-02-1222 Joy in a Basket L5595G	Lladro	Open	215.00	270.00
89-02-1223 A Gift of Love L5596G	Lladro	Open	400.00	495.00
89-02-1224 Summer Soiree L5597G	Lladro	Open	150.00	180.00
89-02-1225 Bridesmaid L5598G	Lladro	Open	150.00	180.00
89-02-1226 Coquette L5599G	Lladro	Open	150.00	180.00
89-02-1227 The Blues w/base L5600G	Lladro	Closed	265.00	340.00
89-02-1228 "Ole" L5601G	Lladro	Open	365.00	450.00
89-02-1229 Close To My Heart L5603G	Lladro	Open	125.00	165.00
89-02-1230 Spring Token L5604G	Lladro	Open	175.00	230.00
89-02-1231 Floral Treasures L5605G	Lladro	Open	195.00	250.00
89-02-1232 Quiet Evening L5606G	Lladro	Closed	125.00	165.00
89-02-1233 Calling A Friend L5607G	Lladro	Open	125.00	165.00
89-02-1234 Baby Doll L5608G	Lladro	Open	150.00	180.00
89-02-1235 Playful Friends L5609G	Lladro	Open	135.00	170.00
89-02-1236 Star Struck w/base L5610G	Lladro	Open	335.00	420.00
89-02-1237 Sad Clown w/base L5611G	Lladro	Open	335.00	420.00
89-02-1238 Reflecting w/base L5612G	Lladro	Open	335.00	420.00
90-02-1239 Cat Nap L5640G	Lladro	Open	125.00	145.00
90-02-1240 The King's Guard w/base L5642G	Lladro	Closed	950.00	1100.00
90-02-1241 Cathy L5643G	Lladro	Open	200.00	235.00
90-02-1242 Susan L5644G	Lladro	Open	190.00	215.00
90-02-1243 Elizabeth L5645G	Lladro	Open	190.00	215.00
90-02-1244 Cindy L5646G	Lladro	Open	190.00	215.00
90-02-1245 Sara L5647G	Lladro	Open	200.00	230.00
90-02-1246 Courtney L5648G	Lladro	Open	200.00	230.00
90-02-1247 Nothing To Do L5649G	Lladro	Open	190.00	220.00
90-02-1248 Anticipation L5650G	Lladro	Closed	300.00	340.00
90-02-1249 Musical Muse L5651G	Lladro	Open	375.00	440.00
90-02-1250 Venetian Carnival L5658G	Lladro	Closed	500.00	575.00
90-02-1251 Barnyard Scene L5659G	Lladro	Open	200.00	235.00
90-02-1252 Sunning In Ipanema L5660G	Lladro	Closed	370.00	420.00
90-02-1253 Traveling Artist L5661G	Lladro	Open	250.00	290.00
90-02-1254 May Dance L5662G	Lladro	Open	170.00	190.00
90-02-1255 Spring Dance L5663G	Lladro	Open	170.00	195.00
90-02-1256 Giddy Up L5664G	Lladro	Open	190.00	230.00
90-02-1257 Hang On! L5665G	Lladro	Open	225.00	260.00
90-02-1258 Trino At The Beach L5666G	Lladro	Open	390.00	460.00
90-02-1259 Valencian Harvest L5668G	Lladro	Closed	175.00	205.00
90-02-1260 Valencian FLowers L5669G	Lladro	Closed	370.00	420.00
90-02-1261 Valencian Beauty L5670G	Lladro	Closed	175.00	205.00
90-02-1262 Little Dutch Gardener L5671G	Lladro	Closed	400.00	475.00
90-02-1263 Hi There! L5672G	Lladro	Open	450.00	520.00
90-02-1264 A Quiet Moment L5673G	Lladro	Open	450.00	520.00
90-02-1265 A Faun And A Friend L5674G	Lladro	Open	450.00	520.00
90-02-1266 Tee Time L5675G	Lladro	Closed	280.00	315.00
90-02-1267 Wandering Minstrel L5676G	Lladro	Closed	270.00	310.00
90-02-1268 Twilight Years L5677G	Lladro	Open	370.00	420.00
90-02-1269 I Feel Pretty L5678G	Lladro	Open	190.00	230.00
90-02-1270 In No Hurry L5679G	Lladro	Open	550.00	640.00
90-02-1271 Traveling In Style L5680G	Lladro	Open	425.00	495.00
90-02-1272 On The Road L5681G	Lladro	Closed	320.00	500.00
90-02-1273 Breezy Afternoon L5682G	Lladro	Open	180.00	195.00
90-02-1274 Breezy Afternoon L5682M	Lladro	Open	180.00	195.00
90-02-1275 Beautiful Burro L5683G	Lladro	Closed	280.00	396.00
90-02-1276 Barnyard Reflections L5684G	Lladro	Closed	460.00	525.00
90-02-1277 Promenade L5685G	Lladro	Open	275.00	325.00
90-02-1278 On The Avenue L5686G	Lladro	Open	275.00	325.00
90-02-1279 Afternoon Stroll L5687G	Lladro	Open	275.00	325.00
90-02-1280 Dog's Best Friend L5688G	Lladro	Open	250.00	295.00
90-02-1281 Can I Help? L5689G	Lladro	Open	250.00	295.00
90-02-1282 Marshland Mates w/base L5691G	Lladro	Open	950.00	1200.00
90-02-1283 Street Harmonies w/base L5692G	Lladro	Closed	3200.00	3750.00
90-02-1284 Circus Serenade L5694G	Lladro	Open	300.00	360.00
90-02-1285 Concertina L5695G	Lladro	Open	300.00	360.00
90-02-1286 Mandolin Serenade L5696G	Lladro	Open	300.00	360.00
90-02-1287 Over The Clouds L5697G	Lladro	Open	275.00	310.00
90-02-1288 Don't Look Down L5698G	Lladro	Open	330.00	375.00
90-02-1289 Sitting Pretty L5699G	Lladro	Open	300.00	340.00
90-02-1290 Southern Charm L5700G	Lladro	Open	675.00	1025.00
90-02-1291 Just A Little Kiss L5701G	Lladro	Open	320.00	375.00
90-02-1292 Back To School L5702G	Lladro	Closed	350.00	405.00
90-02-1293 Behave! L5703G	Lladro	Open	230.00	265.00
90-02-1294 Swan Song L5704G	Lladro	Open	350.00	410.00
90-02-1295 The Swan And The Princess L5705G	Lladro	Open	350.00	410.00
90-02-1296 We Can't Play L5706G	Lladro	Open	200.00	235.00
90-02-1297 After School L5707G	Lladro	Closed	280.00	315.00
90-02-1298 My First Class L5708G	Lladro	Closed	280.00	315.00
90-02-1299 Between Classes L5709G	Lladro	Closed	280.00	315.00
90-02-1300 Fantasy Friend L5710G	Lladro	Closed	420.00	495.00
90-02-1301 A Christmas Wish L5711G	Lladro	Open	350.00	410.00
90-02-1302 Sleepy Kitten L5712G	Lladro	Open	110.00	130.00
90-02-1303 The Snow Man L5713G	Lladro	Open	300.00	350.00
90-02-1304 First Ballet L5714G	Lladro	Open	370.00	420.00
90-02-1305 Mommy, it's Cold! L5715G	Lladro	Open	360.00	415.00
90-02-1306 Land of The Giants L5716G	Lladro	Open	275.00	315.00
90-02-1307 Rock A Bye Baby L5717G	Lladro	Open	300.00	350.00
90-02-1308 Sharing Secrets L5720G	Lladro	Open	290.00	335.00
90-02-1309 Once Upon A Time L5721G	Lladro	Open	550.00	615.00
90-02-1310 Follow Me L5722G	Lladro	Open	140.00	160.00
90-02-1311 Heavenly Chimes L5723G	Lladro	Open	100.00	120.00
90-02-1312 Angelic Voice L5724G	Lladro	Open	125.00	145.00
90-02-1313 Making A Wish L5725G	Lladro	Open	125.00	145.00
90-02-1314 Sweep Away The Clouds L5726G	Lladro	Open	125.00	145.00
90-02-1315 Angel Care L5727G	Lladro	Open	190.00	210.00
90-02-1316 Heavenly Dreamer L5728G	Lladro	Open	100.00	120.00
91-02-1317 Carousel Charm L5731G	Lladro	Open	1700.00	1850.00

	ARTIST	EDITION	ISSUE	QUOTE
91-02-1318 Carousel Canter L5732G	Lladro	Open	1700.00	1850.00
91-02-1319 Horticulturist L5733G	Lladro	Closed	450.00	495.00
91-02-1320 Pilgrim Couple L5734G	Lladro	Closed	490.00	525.00
91-02-1321 Big Sister L5735G	Lladro	Open	650.00	685.00
91-02-1322 Puppet Show L5736G	Lladro	Open	280.00	295.00
91-02-1323 Little Prince L5737G	Lladro	Closed	295.00	315.00
91-02-1324 Best Foot Forward L5738G	Lladro	Open	280.00	305.00
91-02-1325 Lap Full Of Love L5739G	Lladro	Open	275.00	295.00
91-02-1326 Alice In Wonderland L5740G	Lladro	Open	440.00	485.00
91-02-1327 Dancing Class L5741G	Lladro	Open	340.00	365.00
91-02-1328 Bridal Portrait L5742G	Lladro	Open	480.00	525.00
91-02-1329 Don't Forget Me L5743G	Lladro	Open	150.00	160.00
91-02-1330 Bull & Donkey L5744G	Lladro	Open	250.00	275.00
91-02-1331 Baby Jesus L5745G	Lladro	Open	170.00	185.00
91-02-1332 St. Joseph L5746G	Lladro	Open	350.00	375.00
91-02-1333 Mary L5747G	Lladro	Open	275.00	295.00
91-02-1334 Shepherd Girl L5748G	Lladro	Open	150.00	165.00
91-02-1335 Shepherd Boy L5749G	Lladro	Open	225.00	245.00
91-02-1336 Little Lamb L5750G	Lladro	Open	40.00	42.00
91-02-1337 Walk With Father L5751G	Lladro	Open	375.00	410.00
91-02-1338 Little Virgin L5752G	Lladro	Open	295.00	325.00
91-02-1339 Hold Her Still L5753G	Lladro	Closed	650.00	695.00
91-02-1340 Singapore Dancers L5754G	Lladro	Closed	950.00	1025.00
91-02-1341 Claudette L5755G	Lladro	Closed	265.00	285.00
91-02-1342 Ashley L5756G	Lladro	Closed	265.00	290.00
91-02-1343 Beautiful Tresses L5757G	Lladro	Closed	725.00	785.00
91-02-1344 Sunday Best L5758G	Lladro	Open	725.00	785.00
91-02-1345 Presto! L5759G	Lladro	Closed	275.00	295.00
91-02-1346 Interrupted Nap L5760G	Lladro	Open	325.00	350.00
91-02-1347 Out For A Romp L5761G	Lladro	Open	375.00	410.00
91-02-1348 Checking The Time L5762G	Lladro	Open	560.00	595.00
91-02-1349 Musical Partners L5763G	Lladro	Open	625.00	675.00
91-02-1350 Seeds Of Laughter L5764G	Lladro	Open	525.00	575.00
91-02-1351 Hats Off To Fun L5765G	Lladro	Open	475.00	510.00
91-02-1352 Charming Duet L5766G	Lladro	Open	575.00	625.00
91-02-1353 First Sampler L5767G	Lladro	Open	625.00	680.00
91-02-1354 Academy Days L5768G	Lladro	Closed	280.00	310.00
91-02-1355 Faithful Steed L5769G	Lladro	Open	370.00	395.00
91-02-1356 Out For A Spin L5770G	Lladro	Open	390.00	420.00
91-02-1357 The Magic Of Laughter L5771G	Lladro	Open	950.00	995.00
91-02-1358 Little Dreamers L5772G	Lladro	Open	230.00	240.00
91-02-1359 Little Dreamers L5772M	Lladro	Open	230.00	240.00
91-02-1360 Graceful Offering L5773G	Lladro	Open	850.00	895.00
91-02-1361 Nature's Gifts L5774G	Lladro	Open	900.00	975.00
91-02-1362 Gift Of Beauty L5775G	Lladro	Open	850.00	895.00
91-02-1363 Lover's Paradise L5779G	Lladro	Open	2250.00	2450.00
91-02-1364 Walking The Fields L5780G	Lladro	Closed	725.00	795.00
91-02-1365 Not Too Close L5781G	Lladro	Open	365.00	395.00
91-02-1366 My Chores L5782G	Lladro	Open	325.00	355.00
91-02-1367 Special Delivery L5783G	Lladro	Open	525.00	550.00
91-02-1368 A Cradle Of Kittens L5784G	Lladro	Open	360.00	385.00
91-02-1369 Ocean Beauty L5785G	Lladro	Open	625.00	665.00
91-02-1370 Story Hour L5786G	Lladro	Open	550.00	585.00
91-02-1371 Sophisticate L5787G	Lladro	Open	185.00	195.00
91-02-1372 Talk Of The Town L5788G	Lladro	Open	185.00	195.00
91-02-1373 The Flirt L5789G	Lladro	Open	185.00	195.00
91-02-1374 Carefree L5790G	Lladro	Open	300.00	325.00
91-02-1375 Fairy Godmother L5791G	Lladro	Open	375.00	410.00
91-02-1376 Reverent Moment L5792G	Lladro	Open	295.00	320.00
91-02-1377 Precocious Ballerina L5793G	Lladro	Open	575.00	625.00
91-02-1378 Precious Cargo L5794G	Lladro	Open	460.00	495.00
91-02-1379 Floral Getaway L5795G	Lladro	Closed	625.00	685.00
91-02-1380 Holy Night L5796G	Lladro	Open	330.00	360.00
91-02-1381 Come Out And Play L5797G	Lladro	Open	275.00	295.00
91-02-1382 Milkmaid L5798G	Lladro	Closed	450.00	495.00
91-02-1383 Shall We Dance? L5799G	Lladro	Closed	600.00	650.00
91-02-1384 Elegant Promenade L5802G	Lladro	Open	775.00	825.00
91-02-1385 Playing Tag L5804G	Lladro	Closed	170.00	190.00
91-02-1386 Tumbling L5805G	Lladro	Closed	130.00	140.00
91-02-1387 Tumbling L5805M	Lladro	Open	130.00	130.00
91-02-1388 Tickling L5806G	Lladro	Closed	130.00	145.00
91-02-1389 Tickling L5806M	Lladro	Open	130.00	130.00
91-02-1390 My Puppies L5807G	Lladro	Closed	325.00	360.00
91-02-1391 Musically Inclined L5810G	Lladro	Closed	235.00	250.00
91-02-1392 Littlest Clown L5811G	Lladro	Open	225.00	240.00
91-02-1393 Tired Friend L5812G	Lladro	Open	225.00	245.00
91-02-1394 Having A Ball L5813G	Lladro	Open	225.00	240.00
91-02-1395 Curtain Call L5814G	Lladro	Open	490.00	520.00
91-02-1396 Curtain Call L5814M	Lladro	Open	490.00	520.00
91-02-1397 In Full Relave L5815G	Lladro	Open	490.00	520.00
91-02-1398 In Full Relave L5815M	Lladro	Open	490.00	520.00
91-02-1399 Prima Ballerina L5816G	Lladro	Open	490.00	520.00
91-02-1400 Prima Ballerina L5816M	Lladro	Open	490.00	520.00
91-02-1401 Backstage Preparation L5817G	Lladro	Open	490.00	520.00
91-02-1402 Backstage Preparation L5817M	Lladro	Open	490.00	520.00
91-02-1403 On Her Toes L5818G	Lladro	Open	490.00	520.00
91-02-1404 On Her Toes L5818M	Lladro	Open	490.00	520.00
91-02-1405 Allegory Of Liberty L5819G	Lladro	Open	1950.00	2100.00
91-02-1406 Dance Of Love L5820G	Lladro	Closed	575.00	625.00
91-02-1407 Minstrel's Love L5821G	Lladro	Closed	525.00	575.00
91-02-1408 Little Unicorn L5826G	Lladro	Open	275.00	295.00
91-02-1409 Little Unicorn L5826M	Lladro	Open	275.00	295.00
91-02-1410 I've Got It L5827G	Lladro	Open	170.00	180.00
91-02-1411 Next At Bat L5828G	Lladro	Open	170.00	180.00
91-02-1412 Jazz Horn L5832G	Lladro	Open	295.00	295.00
91-02-1413 Jazz Sax L5833G	Lladro	Open	295.00	295.00
91-02-1414 Jazz Bass L5834G	Lladro	Open	395.00	405.00
91-02-1415 I Do L5835G	Lladro	Open	165.00	175.00
91-02-1416 Sharing Sweets L5836G	Lladro	Open	220.00	245.00
91-02-1417 Sing With Me L5837G	Lladro	Open	240.00	250.00
91-02-1418 On The Move L5838G	Lladro	Open	340.00	365.00
92-02-1419 A Quiet Afternoon L5843G	Lladro	Open	1050.00	1100.00
92-02-1420 Flirtatious Jester L5844G	Lladro	Open	890.00	925.00
92-02-1421 Dressing The Baby L5845G	Lladro	Open	295.00	295.00
92-02-1422 All Tuckered Out L5846G	Lladro	Open	220.00	235.00
92-02-1423 All Tuckered Out L5846M	Lladro	Open	220.00	235.00
92-02-1424 The Loving Family L5848G	Lladro	Open	950.00	985.00
92-02-1425 Inspiring Muse L5850G	Lladro	Open	1200.00	1250.00
92-02-1426 Feathered Fantasy L5851G	Lladro	Open	1200.00	1250.00
92-02-1427 Easter Bonnets L5852G	Lladro	Closed	265.00	275.00
92-02-1428 Floral Admiration L5853G	Lladro	Open	690.00	725.00
92-02-1429 Floral Fantasy L5854G	Lladro	Open	690.00	710.00

	ARTIST	EDITION	ISSUE	QUOTE
92-02-1430 Afternoon Jaunt L5855G	Lladro	Closed	420.00	440.00
92-02-1431 Circus Concert L5856G	Lladro	Open	570.00	585.00
92-02-1432 Grand Entrance L5857G	Lladro	Open	265.00	275.00
92-02-1433 Waiting to Dance L5858G	Lladro	Open	295.00	310.00
92-02-1434 At The Ball L5859G	Lladro	Open	295.00	300.00
92-02-1435 Fairy Garland L5860G	Lladro	Open	630.00	650.00
92-02-1436 Fairy Flowers L5861G	Lladro	Open	630.00	655.00
92-02-1437 Fragrant Bouquet L5862G	Lladro	Open	350.00	360.00
92-02-1438 Dressing For The Ballet L5865G	Lladro	Open	395.00	415.00
92-02-1439 Final Touches L5866G	Lladro	Open	395.00	415.00
92-02-1440 Serene Valenciana L5867G	Lladro	Open	365.00	385.00
92-02-1441 Loving Valenciana L5868G	Lladro	Open	365.00	385.00
92-02-1442 Fallas Queen L5869G	Lladro	Open	420.00	440.00
92-02-1443 Olympic Torch w/Fantasy Logo L5870G	Lladro	Open	165.00	145.00
92-02-1444 Olympic Champion w/Fantasy Logo L5871G	Lladro	Open	165.00	145.00
92-02-1445 Olympic Pride w/Fantasy Logo L5872G	Lladro	Open	165.00	495.00
92-02-1446 Modern Mother L5873G	Lladro	Open	325.00	335.00
92-02-1447 Off We Go L5874G	Lladro	Open	365.00	385.00
92-02-1448 Guest Of Honor L5877G	Lladro	Open	195.00	200.00
92-02-1449 Sister's Pride L5878G	Lladro	Open	595.00	615.00
92-02-1450 Shot On Goal L5879G	Lladro	Open	1100.00	1150.00
92-02-1451 Playful Unicorn L5880G	Lladro	Open	295.00	310.00
92-02-1452 Playful Unicorn L5880M	Lladro	Open	295.00	310.00
92-02-1453 Mischievous Mouse L5881G	Lladro	Open	285.00	295.00
92-02-1454 Restful Mouse L5882G	Lladro	Open	285.00	295.00
92-02-1455 Loving Mouse L5883G	Lladro	Open	285.00	295.00
92-02-1456 From This Day Forward L5885G	Lladro	Open	265.00	265.00
92-02-1457 Hippity Hop L5886G	Lladro	Open	95.00	95.00
92-02-1458 Washing Up L5887G	Lladro	Open	95.00	95.00
92-02-1459 That Tickles! L5888G	Lladro	Open	95.00	100.00
92-02-1460 Snack Time L5889G	Lladro	Open	95.00	100.00
92-02-1461 The Aviator L5891G	Lladro	Open	375.00	380.00
92-02-1462 Circus Magic L5892G	Lladro	Open	470.00	495.00
92-02-1463 Friendship In Bloom L5893G	Lladro	Open	650.00	685.00
92-02-1464 Precious Petals L5894G	Lladro	Open	395.00	415.00
92-02-1465 Bouquet of Blossoms L5895G	Lladro	Open	295.00	295.00
92-02-1466 The Loaves & Fishes L5896G	Lladro	Open	695.00	710.00
92-02-1467 Trimming The Tree L5897G	Lladro	Open	900.00	925.00
92-02-1468 Spring Splendor L5898G	Lladro	Open	440.00	450.00
92-02-1469 Just One More L5899G	Lladro	Open	450.00	460.00
92-02-1470 Sleep Tight L5900G	Lladro	Open	450.00	465.00
92-02-1471 Surprise L5901G	Lladro	Open	325.00	335.00
92-02-1472 Easter Bunnies L5902G	Lladro	Open	240.00	250.00
92-02-1473 Down The Aisle L5903G	Lladro	Open	295.00	295.00
92-02-1474 Sleeping Bunny L5904G	Lladro	Open	75.00	75.00
92-02-1475 Attentive Bunny L5905G	Lladro	Open	75.00	75.00
92-02-1476 Preening Bunny L5906G	Lladro	Open	75.00	75.00
92-02-1477 Sitting Bunny L5907G	Lladro	Open	75.00	75.00
92-02-1478 Just A Little More L5908G	Lladro	Open	370.00	380.00
92-02-1479 All Dressed Up L5909G	Lladro	Open	440.00	450.00
92-02-1480 Making A Wish L5910G	Lladro	Open	790.00	825.00
92-02-1481 Swans Take Flight L5912G	Lladro	Open	2850.00	2950.00
92-02-1482 Rose Ballet L5919G	Lladro	Open	210.00	215.00
92-02-1483 Swan Ballet L5920G	Lladro	Open	210.00	215.00
92-02-1484 Take Your Medicine L5921G	Lladro	Open	360.00	370.00
92-02-1485 Jazz Clarinet L5928G	Lladro	Open	295.00	295.00
92-02-1486 Jazz Drums L5929G	Lladro	Open	595.00	610.00
92-02-1487 Jazz Duo L5930G	Lladro	Open	795.00	810.00
93-02-1488 The Ten Commandments w/Base L5933G	Lladro	Open	930.00	930.00
93-02-1489 The Holy Teacher L5934G	Lladro	Open	375.00	375.00
93-02-1490 Nutcracker Suite L5935G	Lladro	Open	620.00	620.00
93-02-1491 Little Skipper L5936G	Lladro	Open	320.00	320.00
93-02-1492 Riding The Waves L5941G	Lladro	Open	405.00	405.00
93-02-1493 World of Fantasy L5943G	Lladro	Open	295.00	295.00
93-02-1494 The Great Adventure L5944G	Lladro	Open	325.00	325.00
93-02-1495 A Mother's Way L5946G	Lladro	Open	1350.00	1350.00
93-02-1496 General Practitioner L5947G	Lladro	Open	360.00	360.00
93-02-1497 Physician L5948G	Lladro	Open	360.00	360.00
93-02-1498 Angel Candleholder w/Lyre L5949G	Lladro	Open	295.00	295.00
93-02-1499 Angel Candleholder w/Tambourine L5950G	Lladro	Open	295.00	295.00
93-02-1500 Sounds of Summer L5953G	Lladro	Open	125.00	129.00
93-02-1501 Sounds of Winter L5954G	Lladro	Open	125.00	129.00
93-02-1502 Sounds of Fall L5955G	Lladro	Open	125.00	129.00
93-02-1503 Sounds of Spring L5956G	Lladro	Open	125.00	129.00
93-02-1504 The Glass Slipper L5957G	Lladro	Open	475.00	475.00
93-02-1505 Country Ride w/base L5958G	Lladro	Open	2850.00	2850.00
93-02-1506 It's Your Turn L5959G	Lladro	Open	365.00	365.00
93-02-1507 On Patrol L5960G	Lladro	Open	395.00	410.00
93-02-1508 The Great Teacher w/base L5961G	Lladro	Open	850.00	850.00
93-02-1509 The Clipper Ship w/base L5965M	Lladro	Open	240.00	240.00
93-02-1510 Flowers Forever w/base L5966G	Lladro	Open	4150.00	4150.00
93-02-1511 Honeymoon Ride w/base L5968G	Lladro	Open	2750.00	2750.00
93-02-1512 A Special Toy L5971G	Lladro	Open	815.00	815.00
93-02-1513 Before the Dance w/base L5972G	Lladro	Open	3550.00	3550.00
93-02-1514 Before the Dance w/base L5972M	Lladro	Open	3550.00	3550.00
93-02-1515 Family Outing w/base L5974G	Lladro	Open	4275.00	4275.00
93-02-1516 Up and Away w/base L5975G	Lladro	Open	2850.00	2850.00
93-02-1517 The Fireman L5976G	Lladro	Open	395.00	410.00
93-02-1518 Revelation w/base (white) L5977G	Lladro	Open	310.00	310.00
93-02-1519 Revelation w/base (black) L5978M	Lladro	Open	310.00	310.00
93-02-1520 Revelation w/base (sand) L5979M	Lladro	Open	310.00	310.00
93-02-1521 The Past w/base (white) L5980G	Lladro	Open	310.00	310.00
93-02-1522 The Past w/base (black) L5981M	Lladro	Open	310.00	310.00
93-02-1523 The Past w/base (sand) L5982M	Lladro	Open	310.00	310.00
93-02-1524 Beauty w/base (white) L5983G	Lladro	Open	310.00	310.00
93-02-1525 Beauty w/base (black) L5984M	Lladro	Open	310.00	310.00
93-02-1526 Beauty w/base (sand) L5985M	Lladro	Open	310.00	310.00
93-02-1527 Sunday Sermon L5986G	Lladro	Open	425.00	425.00
93-02-1528 Talk to Me L5987G	Lladro	Open	145.00	150.00
93-02-1529 Taking Time L5988G	Lladro	Open	145.00	150.00
93-02-1530 A Mother's Touch L5989G	Lladro	Open	470.00	470.00
93-02-1531 Thoughtful Caress L5990G	Lladro	Open	225.00	225.00
93-02-1532 Love Story L5991G	Lladro	Open	2800.00	2800.00
93-02-1533 Unicorn and Friend L5993G	Lladro	Open	355.00	355.00
93-02-1534 Unicorn and Friend L5993M	Lladro	Open	355.00	355.00
93-02-1535 Meet My Friend L5994G	Lladro	Open	695.00	695.00
93-02-1536 Soft Meow L5995G	Lladro	Open	480.00	490.00
93-02-1537 Bless the Child L5996G	Lladro	Open	465.00	465.00
93-02-1538 One More Try L5997G	Lladro	Open	715.00	715.00
93-02-1539 My Dad L6001G	Lladro	Open	550.00	550.00

	ARTIST	EDITION	ISSUE	QUOTE
93-02-1540 Down You Go L6002G	Lladro	Open	815.00	815.00
93-02-1541 Ready To Learn L6003G	Lladro	Open	650.00	650.00
93-02-1542 Bar Mitzvah Day L6004G	Lladro	Open	395.00	395.00
93-02-1543 Christening Day w/base L6005G	Lladro	Open	1425.00	1425.00
93-02-1544 Oriental Colonade w/base L6006G	Lladro	Open	1875.00	1875.00
93-02-1545 The Goddess & Unicorn w/base L6007G	Lladro	Open	1675.00	1675.00
93-02-1546 Joyful Event L6008G	Lladro	Open	825.00	825.00
93-02-1547 Monday's Child (Boy) L6011G	Lladro	Open	245.00	250.00
93-02-1548 Monday's Child (Girl) L6012G	Lladro	Open	260.00	260.00
93-02-1549 Tuesday's Child (Boy) L6013G	Lladro	Open	225.00	250.00
93-02-1550 Tuesday's Child (Girl) L6014G	Lladro	Open	245.00	250.00
93-02-1551 Wednesday's Child (Boy) L6015G	Lladro	Open	245.00	250.00
93-02-1552 Wednesday's Child (Girl) L6016G	Lladro	Open	245.00	250.00
93-02-1553 Thursday's Child (Boy) L6017G	Lladro	Open	225.00	250.00
93-02-1554 Thursday's Child (Girl) L6018G	Lladro	Open	245.00	250.00
93-02-1555 Friday's Child (Boy) L6019G	Lladro	Open	225.00	250.00
93-02-1556 Friday's Child (Girl) L6020G	Lladro	Open	225.00	250.00
93-02-1557 Saturday's Child (Boy) L6021G	Lladro	Open	245.00	250.00
93-02-1558 Saturday's Child (Girl) L6022G	Lladro	Open	245.00	250.00
93-02-1559 Sunday's Child (Boy) L6023G	Lladro	Open	225.00	250.00
93-02-1560 Sunday's Child (Girl) L6024G	Lladro	Open	225.00	250.00
93-02-1561 Barnyard See Saw L6025G	Lladro	Open	500.00	500.00
93-02-1562 My Turn L6026G	Lladro	Open	515.00	515.00
93-02-1563 Hanukah Lights L6027G	Lladro	Open	345.00	360.00
93-02-1564 Mazel Tov! L6028G	Lladro	Open	380.00	395.00
93-02-1565 Hebrew Scholar L6029G	Lladro	Open	225.00	235.00
93-02-1566 On The Go L6031G	Lladro	Open	475.00	475.00
93-02-1567 On The Green L6032G	Lladro	Open	645.00	645.00
93-02-1568 Monkey Business L6034G	Lladro	Open	745.00	745.00
93-02-1569 Young Princess L6036G	Lladro	Open	240.00	240.00
94-02-1570 Saint James L6084G	Lladro	Open	310.00	310.00
94-02-1571 Angelic Harmony L6085G	Lladro	Open	495.00	495.00
94-02-1572 Allow Me L6086G	Lladro	Open	1625.00	1625.00
94-02-1573 Loving Care L6087G	Lladro	Open	250.00	250.00
94-02-1574 Communion Prayer (Boy) L6088G	Lladro	Open	194.00	194.00
94-02-1575 Communion Prayer (Girl) L6089G	Lladro	Open	198.00	198.00
94-02-1576 Baseball Player L6090G	Lladro	Open	295.00	295.00
94-02-1577 Basketball Player L6091G	Lladro	Open	295.00	295.00
94-02-1578 The Prince L6092G	Lladro	Open	325.00	325.00
94-02-1579 Songbird L6093G	Lladro	Open	395.00	395.00
94-02-1580 The Sportsman L6096G	Lladro	Open	495.00	495.00
94-02-1581 Sleeping Bunny With Flowers L6097G	Lladro	Open	110.00	110.00
94-02-1582 Attentive Bunny With Flowers L6098G	Lladro	Open	140.00	140.00
94-02-1583 Preening Bunny With Flowers L6099G	Lladro	Open	140.00	140.00
94-02-1584 Sitting Bunny With Flowers L6100G	Lladro	Open	110.00	110.00
94-02-1585 Follow Us L6101G	Lladro	Open	198.00	198.00
94-02-1586 Mother's Little Helper L6102G	Lladro	Open	275.00	275.00
94-02-1587 Beautiful Ballerina L6103G	Lladro	Open	250.00	250.00
94-02-1588 Finishing Touches L6104	Lladro	Open	240.00	240.00
94-02-1589 Spring Joy L6106G	Lladro	Open	795.00	795.00
94-02-1590 Football Player L6107	Lladro	Open	295.00	295.00
94-02-1591 Hockey Player L6108G	Lladro	Open	295.00	295.00
94-02-1592 Meal Time L6109G	Lladro	Open	495.00	495.00
94-02-1593 Medieval Maiden L6110G	Lladro	Open	150.00	150.00
94-02-1594 Medieval Soldier L6111G	Lladro	Open	225.00	225.00
94-02-1595 Medieval Lord L6112G	Lladro	Open	285.00	285.00
94-02-1596 Medieval Lady L6113G	Lladro	Open	225.00	225.00
94-02-1597 Medieval Princess L6114G	Lladro	Open	245.00	245.00
94-02-1598 Medieval Prince L6115G	Lladro	Open	295.00	295.00
94-02-1599 Medieval Majesty L6116G	Lladro	Open	315.00	315.00
94-02-1600 Constance L6117G	Lladro	Open	195.00	195.00
94-02-1601 Musketeer Portos L6118G	Lladro	Open	220.00	220.00
94-02-1602 Musketeer Aramis L6119G	Lladro	Open	275.00	275.00
94-02-1603 Musketeer Dartagnan L6120G	Lladro	Open	245.00	245.00
94-02-1604 Musketeer Athos L6121G	Lladro	Open	245.00	245.00
94-02-1605 A Great Adventure L6122	Lladro	Open	198.00	198.00
94-02-1606 Out For a Stroll L6123G	Lladro	Open	198.00	198.00
94-02-1607 Travelers Rest L6124G	Lladro	Open	275.00	275.00
94-02-1608 Sweet Dreamers L6127G	Lladro	Open	280.00	280.00
94-02-1609 Christmas Melodies L6128G	Lladro	Open	375.00	375.00
94-02-1610 Little Friends L6129G	Lladro	Open	225.00	225.00
94-02-1611 Angel of Peace L6131G	Lladro	Open	345.00	345.00
94-02-1612 Angel with Garland L6133G	Lladro	Open	345.00	345.00
94-02-1613 Birthday Party L6134G	Lladro	Open	395.00	395.00
94-02-1614 Football Star L6135	Lladro	Open	295.00	295.00
94-02-1615 Basketball Star L6136G	Lladro	Open	295.00	295.00
94-02-1616 Baseball Star L6137G	Lladro	Open	295.00	295.00
94-02-1617 Globe Paperweight L6138M	Lladro	Open	95.00	95.00
94-02-1618 Springtime Friends L6140G	Lladro	Open	485.00	485.00
94-02-1619 Kitty Cart L6141G	Lladro	Open	750.00	750.00
94-02-1620 Indian Pose L6142G	Lladro	Open	475.00	475.00
94-02-1621 Indian Dancer L6143G	Lladro	Open	475.00	475.00
94-02-1622 Heavenly Prayer L6145	Lladro	Open	675.00	675.00
94-02-1623 Spring Angel L6146G	Lladro	Open	250.00	250.00
94-02-1624 Fall Angel L6147G	Lladro	Open	250.00	250.00
94-02-1625 Summer Angel L6148G	Lladro	Open	220.00	220.00
94-02-1626 Winter Angel L6149G	Lladro	Open	250.00	250.00
94-02-1627 Playing The Flute L6150G	Lladro	Open	175.00	175.00
94-02-1628 Bearing Flowers L6151G	Lladro	Open	175.00	175.00
94-02-1629 Flower Gazer L6152G	Lladro	Open	175.00	175.00
94-02-1630 American Love L6153G	Lladro	Open	225.00	225.00
94-02-1631 African Love L6154G	Lladro	Open	225.00	225.00
94-02-1632 European Love L6155G	Lladro	Open	225.00	225.00
94-02-1633 Asian Love L6156G	Lladro	Open	225.00	225.00
94-02-1634 Polynesian Love L6157G	Lladro	Open	225.00	225.00
94-02-1635 Wedding Bells L6164G	Lladro	Open	175.00	175.00
94-02-1636 The Apollo Landing L6168G	Lladro	Open	450.00	450.00
85-02-1637 Lladro Plaque L7116	Lladro	Open	17.50	18.00
85-02-1638 Lladro Plaque L7118	Lladro	Closed	17.00	18.00
92-02-1639 Special Torch L7513G	Lladro	Open	165.00	165.00
92-02-1640 Special Champion L7514G	Lladro	Open	165.00	165.00
92-02-1641 Special Pride L7515G	Lladro	Open	165.00	165.00
93-02-1642 Courage L7522G	Lladro	Open	195.00	200.00
94-02-1643 Dr. Martin Luther King, Jr. L7528G	Lladro	Open	345.00	345.00
94-02-1644 Spike L7543G	Lladro	Open	95.00	95.00
94-02-1645 Brutus L7544G	Lladro	Open	125.00	125.00
94-02-1646 Rocky L7545G	Lladro	Open	110.00	110.00
94-02-1647 Stretch L7546G	Lladro	Open	125.00	125.00
94-02-1648 Rex L7547G	Lladro	Open	125.00	125.00
85-02-1649 Lladro Plaque w/ Blue Writing L7601G	Lladro	Closed	35.00	35-75.00
89-02-1650 Starting Forward/Lolo L7605G	Lladro	Closed	125.00	350.00

Lladro — **Limited Edition**

		ARTIST	EDITION	ISSUE	QUOTE
71-03-001	Hamlet LL1144	Lladro	Closed	250.00	2500.00
71-03-002	Othello and Desdemona LL1145	Lladro	Closed	275.00	25-3300
71-03-003	Antique Auto LL1146	Lladro	Closed	1000.00	16000.00
71-03-004	Floral LL1184	Lladro	Closed	400.00	2200.00
71-03-005	Floral LL1185	Lladro	Closed	475.00	1800.00
71-03-006	Floral LL1186	Lladro	Closed	575.00	2200.00
72-03-007	Eagles LL1189	Lladro	Closed	900.00	3200.00
72-03-008	Sea Birds with Nest LL1194	Lladro	Closed	600.00	2750.00
72-03-009	Turkey Group LL1196	Lladro	Closed	650.00	1800.00
72-03-010	Peace LL1202	Lladro	Closed	550.00	7500.00
72-03-011	Eagle Owl LL1223	Lladro	Closed	450.00	1050.00
72-03-012	Hansom Carriage LL1225	Lladro	Closed	1250.00	10-12000
73-03-013	Hunting Scene LL1238	Lladro	Closed	800.00	2000.00
73-03-014	Turtle Doves LL1240	Lladro	Closed	500.00	23-2500.
73-03-015	The Forest LL1243	Lladro	Closed	1250.00	3300.00
74-03-016	Soccer Players LL1266	Lladro	Closed	2000.00	7500.00
74-03-017	Man From LaMancha LL1269	Lladro	Closed	700.00	4-5000.
74-03-018	Queen Elizabeth II LL1275	Lladro	Closed	3650.00	5000.00
74-03-019	Judge LL1281	Lladro	Closed	325.00	12-1400.
74-03-020	The Hunt LL1308	Lladro	Closed	4750.00	6900.00
74-03-021	Ducks at Pond LL1317	Lladro	Closed	4250.00	5700.00
76-03-022	Impossible Dream LL1318	Lladro	Closed	2400.00	6200.00
76-03-023	Comforting Baby LL1329	Lladro	Closed	700.00	1050.00
76-03-024	Mountain Country Lady LL1330	Lladro	Closed	900.00	1850.00
76-03-025	My Baby LL1331	Lladro	Closed	550.00	775.00
78-03-026	Flight of Gazelles LL1352	Lladro	Closed	2450.00	3100.00
78-03-027	Car in Trouble LL1375	Lladro	Closed	3000.00	7600.00
78-03-028	Fearful Flight LL1377	Lladro	750	7000.00	14200.00
78-03-029	Henry VIII LL 1384	Lladro	Closed	650.00	995.00
81-03-030	Venus and Cupid LL1392	Lladro	Closed	1100.00	2000.00
82-03-031	First Date w/base LL1393	Lladro	1,500	3800.00	5900.00
82-03-032	Columbus LL1432	Lladro	Closed	535.00	2-2500.
83-03-033	Venetian Serenade LL1433	Lladro	Closed	2600.00	3750.00
85-03-034	Festival in Valencia w/base LL1457	Lladro	3,000	1475.00	2350.00
85-03-035	Camelot LL1458	Lladro	3,000	1000.00	1650.00
85-03-036	Napoleon Planning Battle w/base LL1459	Lladro	1,500	875.00	1450.00
85-03-037	Youthful Beauty w/base LL1461	Lladro	5,000	800.00	1200.00
85-03-038	Flock of Birds w/base LL1462	Lladro	1,500	1125.00	1750.00
85-03-039	Classic Spring LL1465	Lladro	Closed	650.00	11-1400.
85-03-040	Classic Fall LL1466	Lladro	Closed	650.00	1000.00
85-03-041	Valencian Couple on Horse LL1472	Lladro	3,000	1175.00	1550.00
85-03-042	Coach XVIII Century w/base LL1485	Lladro	500	14000.00	25500.00
86-03-043	The New World w/base LL1486	Lladro	4,000	700.00	1350.00
86-03-044	Fantasia w/base LL1487	Lladro	5,000	1500.00	2700.00
86-03-045	Floral Offering w/base LL1490	Lladro	3,000	2500.00	4450.00
86-03-046	Oriental Music w/base LL1491	Lladro	5,000	1350.00	2400.00
86-03-047	Three Sisters w/base LL1492	Lladro	3,000	1850.00	3250.00
86-03-048	At the Stroke of Twelve w/base LL1493	Lladro	1,500	4250.00	7500.00
86-03-049	Hawaiian Festival w/base LL1496	Lladro	4,000	1850.00	3150.00
87-03-050	A Sunday Drive w/base LL1510	Lladro	1,000	2600.00	5250.00
87-03-051	Listen to Don Quixote w/base LL1520	Lladro	750	1800.00	2900.00
87-03-052	A Happy Encounter LL1523	Lladro	1,500	2900.00	4900.00
88-03-053	Garden Party w/base LL1578	Lladro	500	5500.00	7250.00
88-03-054	Blessed Lady w/base LL1579	Lladro	Closed	1150.00	1500.00
88-03-055	Return to La Mancha w/base LL1580	Lladro	500	6400.00	8350.00
89-03-056	Southern Tea LL1597	Lladro	1,000	1775.00	2300.00
89-03-057	Kitakami Cruise w/base LL1605	Lladro	500	5800.00	7350.00
89-03-058	Mounted Warriors w/base LL1608	Lladro	500	2850.00	3450.00
89-03-059	Circus Parade w/base LL1609	Lladro	1,000	5200.00	6550.00
89-03-060	"Jesus the Rock" w/baseLL1615	Lladro	1,000	1175.00	1550.00
88-02-061	On Our Way Home (Decorated) LL1715	Lladro	Closed	2000.00	2000.00
89-02-062	Hopeful Group LL1723	Lladro	Closed	1825.00	1825.00
91-03-063	Valencian Cruise LL1731	Lladro	1,000	2700.00	2950.00
91-03-064	Venice Vows LL1732	Lladro	1,500	3750.00	4100.00
91-03-065	Liberty Eagle LL1738	Lladro	1,500	1000.00	1100.00
91-03-066	Heavenly Swing LL1739	Lladro	1,000	1900.00	2050.00
91-03-067	Columbus, Two Routes LL1740	Lladro	1,000	1500.00	1650.00
91-03-068	Columbus Reflecting LL1741	Lladro	1,000	1850.00	1995.00
91-03-069	Onward! LL1742	Lladro	1,000	2500.00	2700.00
91-03-070	The Prophet LL1743	Lladro	300	800.00	875.00
90-03-071	My Only Friend LL1744	Lladro	Closed	2950.00	2400.00
91-03-072	Dawn LL1745	Lladro	Closed	1200.00	1260.00
91-03-073	Champion LL1746	Lladro	300	1800.00	1950.00
91-03-074	Nesting Doves LL1747	Lladro	300	800.00	875.00
91-03-075	Comforting News LL1748	Lladro	300	1200.00	1325.00
91-03-076	Baggy Pants LL1749	Lladro	300	1500.00	1650.00
91-03-077	Circus Show LL1750	Lladro	300	1400.00	1525.00
91-03-078	Maggie LL1751	Lladro	300	900.00	990.00
91-03-079	Apple Seller LL1752	Lladro	300	900.00	990.00
91-03-080	The Student LL1753	Lladro	300	1300.00	1425.00
91-03-081	Tree Climbers LL1754	Lladro	300	1500.00	1650.00
91-03-082	The Princess And The Unicorn LL1755	Lladro	Closed	1750.00	1880.00
91-03-083	Outing In Seville LL1756	Lladro	500	23000.00	24500.00
92-03-084	Hawaiian Ceremony LL1757	Lladro	1,000	9800.00	10250.00
92-03-085	Circus Time LL1758	Lladro	2,500	9200.00	9650.00
92-03-086	Tea In The Garden LL1759	Lladro	2,000	9500.00	9750.00
93-03-087	Paella Valenciano w/base LL1762	Lladro	500	10000.00	10000.00
93-03-088	Trusting Friends w/base LL1763	Lladro	350	1200.00	1200.00
93-03-089	He's My Brother w/base LL1764	Lladro	350	1500.00	1500.00
93-03-090	The Course of Adventure LL1765	Lladro	250	1625.00	1625.00
93-03-091	Ties That Bind LL1766	Lladro	250	1700.00	1700.00
93-03-092	Motherly Love LL1767	Lladro	250	1330.00	1330.00
93-03-093	Travellers' Respite w/base LL1768	Lladro	250	1825.00	1825.00
93-03-094	Fruitful Harvest LL1769	Lladro	350	1300.00	1300.00
93-03-095	Gypsy Dancers LL1770	Lladro	250	2250.00	2250.00
93-03-096	Country Doctor w/base LL1771	Lladro	250	1475.00	1475.00
93-03-097	Back To Back LL1772	Lladro	350	1450.00	1450.00
93-03-098	Mischevous Musician LL1773	Lladro	350	975.00	975.00
93-03-099	A Treasured Moment w/base LL1774	Lladro	350	950.00	950.00
93-03-100	Oriental Garden w/base LL1775	Lladro	750	22500.00	22500.00
94-03-101	Conquered by Love w/base LL1776	Lladro	2,500	2850.00	2850.00
94-03-102	Farewell Of The Samurai w/base LL1777	Lladro	2,500	3950.00	3950.00
94-03-103	Pegasus w/base LL1778	Lladro	1,500	1950.00	1950.00
94-03-104	High Speed w/base LL1779	Lladro	1,500	3830.00	3830.00
94-03-105	Indian Princess w/base LL1780	Lladro	3,000	1630.00	1630.00
94-03-106	Allegory of Time LL1781	Lladro	5,000	1290.00	1290.00
94-03-107	Circus Fanfare w/base LL1783	Lladro	1,500	14240.00	14240.00
94-03-108	Flower Wagon w/base LL1784	Lladro	3,000	3290.00	3290.00
94-03-109	Cinderella's Arrival w/base LL1785	Lladro	1,500	25950.00	25950.00
94-03-110	Floral Figure w/base LL1788	Lladro	300	2198.00	2198.00
94-03-111	Natural Beauty LL1795	Lladro	500	650.00	650.00

		ARTIST	EDITION	ISSUE	QUOTE
94-03-112	Floral Enchantment w/base LL1796	Lladro	300	2990.00	2990.00
70-03-113	Girl with Guitar LL2016	Lladro	Closed	650.00	1800.00
70-03-114	Madonna with Child LL2018	Lladro	Closed	450.00	1750.00
71-03-115	Oriental Man LL2021	Lladro	Closed	500.00	1850.00
71-03-116	Three Girls LL2028	Lladro	Closed	950.00	3500.00
71-03-117	Eve at Tree LL2029	Lladro	Closed	450.00	3000.00
71-03-118	Oriental Horse LL2030	Lladro	Closed	1100.00	35-5000.
71-03-119	Lyric Muse LL2031	Lladro	Closed	750.00	2100.00
71-03-120	Madonna and Child LL2043	Lladro	Closed	400.00	1500.00
73-03-121	Peasant Woman LL2049	Lladro	Closed	400.00	1300.00
73-03-122	Passionate Dance LL2051	Lladro	Closed	450.00	2750.00
77-03-123	St. Theresa LL2061	Lladro	Closed	775.00	1600.00
77-03-124	Concerto LL2063	Lladro	Closed	1000.00	1235.00
77-03-125	Flying Partridges LL2064	Lladro	Closed	3500.00	4300.00
87-03-126	Christopher Columbus w/base LL2176	Lladro	1,000	1000.00	1350.00
90-03-127	Invincible w/base LL2188	Lladro	300	1100.00	1250.00
93-03-128	Flight of Fancy w/base LL2243	Lladro	300	1400.00	1400.00
93-03-129	The Awakening w/base LL2244	Lladro	300	1200.00	1200.00
93-03-130	Inspired Voyage w/base LL2245	Lladro	1,000	4800.00	4800.00
93-03-131	Days of Yore w/base LL2248	Lladro	1,000	2050.00	2050.00
93-03-132	Holiday Glow w/base LL2249	Lladro	1,500	750.00	750.00
93-03-133	Autumn Glow w/base LL2250	Lladro	1,500	750.00	750.00
93-03-134	Humble Grace w/base LL2255	Lladro	2,000	2150.00	2150.00
83-03-135	Dawn w/base LL3000	Lladro	300	325.00	550.00
83-03-136	Monks w/base LL3001	Lladro	Closed	1675.00	2550.00
83-03-137	Waiting w/base LL3002	Lladro	Closed	1550.00	1900.00
83-03-138	Indolence LL3003	Lladro	Closed	1465.00	2100.00
83-03-139	Venus in the Bath LL3005	Lladro	Closed	1175.00	1450.00
87-03-140	Classic Beauty w/base LL3012	Lladro	500	1300.00	1750.00
87-03-141	Youthful Innocence w/base LL3013	Lladro	500	1300.00	1750.00
87-03-142	The Nymph w/base LL3014	Lladro	250	1000.00	1450.00
87-03-143	Dignity w/base LL3015	Lladro	150	1400.00	1900.00
88-03-144	Passion w/base LL3016	Lladro	750	865.00	1100.00
88-03-145	Muse w/base LL3017	Lladro	Closed	650.00	875.00
88-03-146	Cellist w/base LL3018	Lladro	Closed	650.00	875.00
88-03-147	True Affection w/base LL3019	Lladro	300	750.00	975.00
89-03-148	Demureness w/base LL3020	Lladro	Closed	400.00	700.00
90-03-149	Daydreaming w/base LL3022	Lladro	500	550.00	775.00
90-03-150	After The Bath w/base LL3023	Lladro	Closed	350.00	750-1000
90-03-151	Discoveries w/Base LL3024	Lladro	Closed	1500.00	1750.00
91-03-152	Resting Nude LL3025	Lladro	Closed	650.00	725.00
91-03-153	Unadorned Beauty LL3026	Lladro	200	1700.00	1850.00
94-03-154	Ebony w/base LL3027	Lladro	300	1295.00	1295.00
94-03-155	Modesty w/base LL3028	Lladro	300	1295.00	1295.00
94-03-156	Danae LL3029	Lladro	300	2880.00	2880.00
82-03-157	Elk LL3501	Lladro	Closed	950.00	1200.00
78-03-158	Nude with Dove LL3503	Lladro	Closed	500.00	1400.00
81-03-159	The Rescue LL3504	Lladro	Closed	3500.00	4450.00
78-03-160	St. Michael w/base LL3515	Lladro	1,500	2200.00	4300.00
80-03-161	Turtle Dove Nest w/base LL3519	Lladro	1,200	3600.00	6050.00
80-03-162	Turtle Dove Group w/base LL3520	Lladro	750	6800.00	11500.00
81-03-163	Philippine Folklore LL3522	Lladro	1,500	1450.00	2400.00
81-03-164	Nest of Eagles w/base LL3523	Lladro	300	6900.00	11500.00
81-03-165	Drum Beats/Watusi Queen w/base LL3524	Lladro	1,500	1875.00	3050.00
82-03-166	Togetherness LL3527	Lladro	Closed	750.00	975.00
82-03-167	Wrestling LL3528	Lladro	Closed	950.00	1125.00
83-03-168	Companionship w/base LL3529	Lladro	Closed	1000.00	1790.00
83-03-169	Anxiety w/base LL3530	Lladro	Closed	1075.00	1875.00
83-03-170	Victory LL3531	Lladro	Closed	1500.00	1800.00
83-03-171	Plentitude LL3532	Lladro	Closed	1000.00	1375.00
83-03-172	The Observe w/baser LL3533	Lladro	Closed	900.00	1650.00
83-03-173	In the Distance LL3534	Lladro	Closed	525.00	1275.00
83-03-174	Slave LL3535	Lladro	Closed	950.00	1150.00
83-03-175	Relaxation LL3536	Lladro	Closed	525.00	1000.00
83-03-176	Dreaming w/base LL3537	Lladro	Closed	950.00	1475.00
83-03-177	Youth LL3538	Lladro	Closed	525.00	1120.00
83-03-178	Dantiness LL3539	Lladro	Closed	1000.00	1400.00
83-03-179	Pose LL3540	Lladro	Closed	1250.00	1450.00
83-03-180	Tranquility LL3541	Lladro	Closed	1000.00	1400.00
83-03-181	Yoga LL3542	Lladro	Closed	650.00	900.00
83-03-182	Demure LL3543	Lladro	Closed	1250.00	1700.00
83-03-183	Reflections w/base LL3544	Lladro	Closed	650.00	1050.00
83-03-184	Adoration LL3545	Lladro	Closed	1050.00	1600.00
83-03-185	African Woman LL3546	Lladro	Closed	1300.00	2000.00
83-03-186	Reclining Nude LL3547	Lladro	Closed	650.00	875.00
83-03-187	Serenity w/base LL3548	Lladro	Closed	925.00	1550.00
83-03-188	Reposing LL3549	Lladro	Closed	425.00	575.00
83-03-189	Boxer w/base LL3550	Lladro	Closed	850.00	1450.00
83-03-190	Bather LL3551	Lladro	Closed	975.00	1300.00
82-03-191	Blue God LL3552	Lladro	1,500	900.00	1575.00
82-03-192	Fire Bird LL3553	Lladro	1,500	800.00	1350.00
82-03-193	Desert People w/base LL3555	Lladro	Closed	1680.00	3000.00
82-03-194	Road to Mandalay LL3556	Lladro	Closed	1390.00	2500.00
82-03-195	Jesus in Tiberias w/base LL3557	Lladro	1,200	2600.00	4500.00
92-03-196	The Reader LL3560	Lladro	200	2650.00	2750.00
93-02-197	Trail Boss LL3561M	Lladro	1,500	2450.00	2495.00
93-02-198	Indian Brave LL3562M	Lladro	1,500	2250.00	2250.00
94-03-199	Saint James The Apostle w/base LL3563	Lladro	1,000	950.00	950.00
94-03-200	Gentle Moment w/base LL3564	Lladro	1,000	1795.00	1795.00
94-03-201	At Peace w/base LL3565	Lladro	1,000	1650.00	1650.00
94-03-202	Indian Chief w/base LL3566	Lladro	3,000	1095.00	1095.00
94-03-203	Trapper w/base LL3567	Lladro	3,000	950.00	950.00
94-03-204	American Cowboy w/base LL3568	Lladro	3,000	950.00	950.00
94-03-205	A Moment's Pause w/base LL3569	Lladro	3,500	1495.00	1495.00
94-03-206	Ethereal Music w/base LL3570	Lladro	1,000	2450.00	2450.00
94-03-207	At The Helm w/base LL3571	Lladro	3,500	1495.00	1495.00
80-03-208	Successful Hunt LL5098	Lladro	Closed	5200.00	8150.00
85-03-209	Napoleon Bonaparte LL 5338	Lladro	5,000	275.00	495.00
85-03-210	Beethoven w/base LL 5339	Lladro	Closed	800.00	1300.00
85-03-211	Thoroughbred Horse w/base LL5340	Lladro	1,000	625.00	1050.00
85-03-212	I Have Found Thee, Dulcinea LL5341	Lladro	Closed	1850.00	2000-3.
85-03-213	Pack of Hunting Dogs w/base LL5342	Lladro	3,000	925.00	1650.00
85-03-214	Love Boat w/base LL5343	Lladro	3,000	825.00	1350.00
86-03-214	Fox Hunt w/base LL5362	Lladro	1,000	5200.00	8750.00
86-03-215	Rey De Copas w/base LL5366	Lladro	Closed	325.00	600.00
86-03-216	Rey De Oros w/base LL5367	Lladro	Closed	325.00	600.00
86-03-217	Rey De Espadas w/base LL5368	Lladro	Closed	325.00	600.00
86-03-218	Rey De Bastos w/base LL5369	Lladro	Closed	325.00	600.00
86-03-219	Pastoral Scene w/base LL5386	Lladro	750	1100.00	2100.00
87-03-220	Inspiration LL5413	Lladro	Closed	1200.00	2100.00
87-03-221	Carnival Time w/base LL5423	Lladro	Closed	2400.00	3900.00
89-03-222	"Pious" LL5541	Lladro	Closed	1075.00	2000.00

		ARTIST	EDITION	ISSUE	QUOTE
89-03-223	Freedom LL5602	Lladro	Closed	875.00	950.00
90-03-224	A Ride In The Park LL5718	Lladro	Closed	3200.00	3500.00
91-03-225	Youth LL5800	Lladro	Closed	650.00	725.00
91-03-226	Charm LL5801	Lladro	Closed	650.00	725.00
91-03-227	New World Medallion LL5808	Lladro	5,000	200.00	215.00
92-03-228	The Voyage of Columbus LL5847	Lladro	Closed	1450.00	13-2200.
92-03-229	Sorrowful Mother LL5849	Lladro	1,500	1750.00	1850.00
92-03-230	Justice Eagle LL5863	Lladro	1,500	1700.00	1800.00
92-03-231	Maternal Joy LL5864	Lladro	1,500	1600.00	1700.00
92-03-232	Motoring In Style LL5884	Lladro	1,500	3700.00	3850.00
92-03-233	The Way Of The Cross LL5890	Lladro	2,000	975.00	1050.00
92-03-234	Presenting Credentials LL5911	Lladro	1,500	19500.00	20500.00
92-03-235	Young Mozart LL5915	Lladro	Closed	500.00	900-1800
93-03-236	Jester's Serenade w/base LL5932	Lladro	3,000	1995.00	1995.00
93-03-237	The Blessing w/base LL5942	Lladro	2,000	1345.00	1345.00
93-03-238	Our Lady of Rocio w/base LL5951	Lladro	2,000	3500.00	3500.00
93-03-239	Where to Sir w/base LL5952	Lladro	1,500	5250.00	5250.00
93-03-240	Discovery Mug LL5967	Lladro	1,992	90.00	90.00
93-03-241	Graceful Moment w/base LL6033	Lladro	3,000	1475.00	1475.00
93-03-242	The Hand of Justice w/base LL6033	Lladro	1,000	1250.00	1250.00
92-03-243	Tinkerbell LL7518	Lladro	1,000	350.00	19-2800.
93-03-244	Peter Pan LL7529	Lladro	3,000	400.00	1-1500.

Lladro — **Lladro Collectors Society**

85-04-001	Little Pals S7600G	Lladro	Closed	95.00	22-3500.
86-04-002	Little Traveler S7602G	Lladro	Closed	95.00	11-1825.
87-04-003	Spring Bouquets S7603G	Lladro	Closed	125.00	600-825.
88-04-004	School Days S7604G	Lladro	Closed	125.00	400-700.
88-04-005	Flower Song S7607G	Lladro	Closed	175.00	460-850.
89-04-006	My Buddy S7609G	Lladro	Closed	145.00	210-500.
90-04-007	Can I Play? S7610G	Lladro	Closed	150.00	300-425.
91-04-008	Summer Stroll S7611G	Lladro	Closed	195.00	225-350.
91-04-009	Picture Perfect S7612G	Lladro	Closed	350.00	300-450.
92-04-010	All Aboard S7619G	Lladro	Closed	165.00	200-300.
93-04-011	Best Friend S7620G	Lladro	Closed	195.00	195.00
94-04-012	Basket of Love S7622G	Lladro	Yr.Iss.	225.00	225.00

Lladro — **Lladro Event Figurines**

91-05-001	Garden Classic L7617G	Lladro	Closed	295.00	335-500.
92-05-002	Garden Song L7618G	Lladro	Closed	295.00	400-675.
93-05-003	Pick of the Litter L7621G	Lladro	Closed	350.00	420-550.
94-05-004	Little Riders L7623P	Lladro	Yr.Iss.	250.00	250.00

Lladro — **Lladro Limited Edition Egg Series**

93-06-001	1993 Limited Edition Egg L6083M	Lladro	Yr.Iss.	145.00	170-350.
94-06-002	1994 Limited Edition Egg L7532M	Lladro	Yr.Iss.	150.00	195.00

Also see Dave Grossman: Series 05 for Lladro Norman Rockwell

Seymour Mann, Inc. — **Wizard Of Oz - 40th Anniversary**

79-01-001	Dorothy, Scarecrow, Lion, Tinman	E. Mann	Closed	7.50	45.00
79-01-002	Dorothy, Scarecrow, Lion, Tinman, Musical	E. Mann	Closed	12.50	75.00

Seymour Mann, Inc. — **Christmas In America**

88-02-001	Doctor's Office Lite Up	E. Mann	Closed	27.50	27.50
88-02-002	Set Of 3, Capitol, White House, Mt. Vernon	E. Mann	Closed	75.00	150.00
89-02-003	Santa in Sleigh	E. Mann	Closed	25.00	45.00
90-02-004	Cart With People	E. Mann	Closed	25.00	35.00
91-02-005	New England Church Lite Up House MER-375	J. White	Closed	27.50	27.50
91-02-006	New England General Store Lite Up House MER-377	J. White	Closed	27.50	27.50

Seymour Mann, Inc. — **Christmas Village**

91-03-001	Away, Away	L. Sciola	Closed	30.00	30.00
91-03-002	The Fire Station	L. Sciola	Closed	60.00	60.00
91-03-003	Curiosity Shop	L. Sciola	Closed	45.00	45.00
91-03-004	Scrooge/Marley's Counting House	L. Sciola	Closed	45.00	45.00
91-03-005	The Playhouse	L. Sciola	Closed	60.00	60.00
91-03-006	Ye Old Gift Shoppe	L. Sciola	Closed	50.00	50.00
91-03-007	Emily's Toys	L. Sciola	Closed	45.00	45.00
91-03-008	Counsil House	L. Sciola	Closed	60.00	60.00
91-03-009	Public Library	L. Sciola	Closed	50.00	50.00
91-03-010	On Thin Ice	L. Sciola	Closed	30.00	30.00
91-03-011	Story Teller	L. Sciola	Closed	20.00	20.00

Seymour Mann, Inc. — **Christmas Collection**

85-04-001	Trumpeting Angel w/Jesus XMAS-527	J. White	Closed	40.00	40.00
85-04-002	Virgin w/Christ Musical XMAS-528	J. White	Closed	33.50	33.50
86-04-003	Antique Santa Musical XMAS-364	J. White	Closed	20.00	20.00
86-04-004	Jumbo Santa/Toys XMAS-38	J. White	Closed	45.00	45.00
89-04-005	Cat in Teacup Musical XMAS-600	J. White	Closed	30.00	30.00
89-04-006	Santa in Sled w/Reindeer CJ-3	Jaimy	Closed	25.00	25.00
89-04-007	Santa Musicals CJ-1/4	Jaimy	Closed	27.50	27.50
89-04-008	Santa on Horse CJ-33A	Jaimy	Closed	33.50	33.50
89-04-009	Santa w/List CJ-23	Jaimy	Closed	27.50	27.50
90-04-010	Antique Shop Lite Up House MER-376	J. White	Closed	27.50	27.50
90-04-011	Bakery Lite Up House MER-373	J. White	Closed	27.50	27.50
90-04-012	Bethlehem Lite Up Set 3 CP-59893	J. White	Closed	120.00	120.00
90-04-013	Brick Church Lite Up House MER-360C	J. White	Closed	35.00	35.00
90-04-014	Cathedral Lite Up House MER-362	J. White	Closed	37.50	37.50
90-04-015	Church Lite Up House MER-310	J. White	Closed	27.50	27.50
90-04-016	Deep Gold Church Lite Up House MER-360D	J. White	Closed	35.00	35.00
90-04-017	Double Store Lite Up House MER-311	J. White	Closed	27.50	27.50
90-04-018	Fire Station Lite Up House XMS-1550C	E.Mann	Closed	25.00	25.00
90-04-019	Grist Mill Lite Up House MER-372	J. White	Closed	27.50	27.50
90-04-020	Inn Lite Up House MER-316	J. White	Closed	27.50	27.50
90-04-021	Leatherworks Lite Up House MER-371	J. White	Closed	27.50	27.50
90-04-022	Library Lite Up House MER-317	J. White	Closed	27.50	27.50
90-04-023	Light House Lite Up House MER-370	J. White	Closed	27.50	27.50
90-04-024	Mansion Lite Up House MER-319	J. White	Closed	27.50	27.50
90-04-025	Mr/Mrs Santa Musical CJ-281	Jaimy	Closed	37.50	37.50
90-04-026	New England Church Lite Up House MER-375	J. White	Closed	27.50	27.50
90-04-027	New England General Store Lite Up House MER-377	J. White	Closed	27.50	27.50
90-04-028	Railroad Station Lite Up House MER-374	J. White	Closed	27.50	27.50
90-04-029	Roly Poly Santa 3 Asst. CJ-253/4/7	Jaimy	Closed	17.50	17.50
90-04-030	Santa on Chimney Musical CJ-212	Jaimy	Closed	33.50	33.50
90-04-031	Santa on See Saw TR-14	E. Mann	Closed	30.00	30.00
90-04-032	Santa Packing Bag CJ-210	Jaimy	Closed	33.50	33.50
90-04-033	Santa w/List CJ-23	Jaimy	Closed	27.50	27.50

	ARTIST	EDITION	ISSUE	QUOTE
90-04-034 School Lite Up House MER-320	J. White	Closed	27.50	27.50
90-04-035 Town Hall Lite Up House MER-315	J. White	Closed	27.50	27.50
91-04-036 Apothecary Lite Up CJ-128	Jaimy	Closed	33.50	33.50
91-04-037 Beige Church Lite Up House MER-360A	Jaimy	Closed	35.00	35.00
91-04-038 Boy and Girl on Bell CJ-132	Jaimy	Closed	13.50	13.50
91-04-039 Boy on Horse CJ-457	Jaimy	Closed	6.00	6.00
91-04-040 Carolers Under Lamppost CJ-114A	Jaimy	Closed	7.50	7.50
91-04-041 Church Lite Up MER-410	J. White	Closed	17.50	17.50
91-04-042 Church w/Blue Roof Lite Up House MER-360E	J. White	Closed	35.00	35.00
91-04-043 Covered Bridge CJ-101	Jaimy	Closed	27.50	27.50
91-04-044 Elf w/Doll House CB-14	E. Mann	Closed	30.00	30.00
91-04-045 Elf w/Hammer CB-11	E. Mann	Closed	30.00	30.00
91-04-046 Elf w/Reindeer CJ-422	Jaimy	Closed	9.00	9.00
91-04-047 Elf w/Rocking Horse CB-10	E. Mann	Closed	30.00	30.00
91-04-048 Elf w/Teddy Bear CB-12	E. Mann	Closed	30.00	30.00
91-04-049 Emily's Toys CJ-127	Jaimy	Closed	35.00	35.00
91-04-050 Father and Mother w/Daughter CJ-133	Jaimy	Closed	13.50	13.50
91-04-051 Father Christmas CJ-233	Jaimy	Closed	33.50	33.50
91-04-052 Father Christmas w/Holly CJ-239	Jaimy	Closed	35.00	35.00
91-04-053 Fire Station CJ-129	Jaimy	Closed	50.00	50.00
91-04-054 Four Men Talking CJ-138	Jaimy	Closed	27.50	27.50
91-04-055 Gift Shop Lite Up CJ-125	Jaimy	Closed	33.50	33.50
91-04-056 Girls w/Instruments CJ-131	Jaimy	Closed	13.50	13.50
91-04-057 Horse and Coach CJ-207	Jaimy	Closed	25.00	25.00
91-04-058 Kids Building Igloo CJ-137	Jaimy	Closed	13.50	13.50
91-04-059 Lady w/Dogs CJ-208	Jaimy	Closed	13.50	13.50
91-04-060 Man w/Wheelbarrow CJ-134	Jaimy	Closed	13.50	13.50
91-04-061 Newsboy Under Lamppost CJ-144B	Jaimy	Closed	15.00	15.00
91-04-062 Old Curiosity Lite Up CJ-201	Jaimy	Closed	37.50	37.50
91-04-063 Playhouse Lite Up CJ-122	Jaimy	Closed	50.00	50.00
91-04-064 Public Library Lite Up CJ-121	Jaimy	Closed	45.00	45.00
91-04-065 Reindeer Barn Lite Up CJ-421	Jaimy	Closed	55.00	55.00
91-04-066 Restaurant Lite Up House MER-354	J. White	Closed	27.50	27.50
91-04-067 Santa Cat Roly Poly CJ-252	Jaimy	Closed	17.50	17.50
91-04-068 Santa Fixing Sled CJ-237	Jaimy	Closed	35.00	35.00
91-04-069 Santa In Barrel Waterball CJ-243	Jaimy	Closed	33.50	33.50
91-04-070 Santa In Toy Shop CJ-441	Jaimy	Closed	33.50	33.50
91-04-071 Santa On Train CJ-458	Jaimy	Closed	6.00	6.00
91-04-072 Santa On White Horse CJ-338	E. Mann	Closed	33.50	33.50
91-04-073 Santa Packing Bag CJ-210	Jaimy	Closed	33.50	33.50
91-04-074 Santa Packing Bag CJ-236	Jaimy	Closed	35.00	35.00
91-04-075 Santa Sleeping Musical CJ-214	Jaimy	Closed	30.00	30.00
91-04-076 Santa w/Bag and List CJ-431	Jaimy	Closed	33.50	33.50
91-04-077 Santa w/Deer Musical CJ-21R	Jaimy	Closed	33.50	33.50
91-04-078 Santa w/Girl Waterball CJ-241	Jaimy	Closed	33.50	33.50
91-04-079 Santa w/Lantern Musical CJ-211	Jaimy	Closed	33.50	33.50
91-04-080 Santa w/List CJ-23R	Jaimy	Closed	27.50	27.50
91-04-081 Snowball Fight CJ-124B	Jaimy	Closed	25.00	25.00
91-04-082 Soup Seller Waterball CJ-209	Jaimy	Closed	25.00	25.00
91-04-083 Stone Cottage Lite Up CJ-100	Jaimy	Closed	37.50	37.50
91-04-084 Stone House Lite Up CJ-102	Jaimy	Closed	45.00	45.00
91-04-085 Teddy Bear On Wheels CB-42	E. Mann	Closed	25.00	25.00
91-04-086 The Skaters CJ-205	Jaimy	Closed	25.00	25.00
91-04-087 The Story Teller CJ-204	Jaimy	Closed	20.00	20.00
91-04-088 The Toy Seller CJ-206	Jaimy	Closed	13.50	13.50
91-04-089 Three Ladies w/Food CJ-136	Jaimy	Closed	13.50	13.50
91-04-090 Trader Santa Musical CJ-442	Jaimy	Closed	30.00	30.00
91-04-091 Train Set MER-378	J. White	Closed	25.00	25.00
91-04-092 2 Tone Stone Church MER-360B	J. White	Closed	35.00	35.00
91-04-093 Toy Store Lite Up House MER-355	J. White	Closed	27.50	27.50
91-04-094 Two Old Men Talking CJ-107	Jaimy	Closed	13.50	13.50
91-04-095 Village Mill Lite Up CJ-104	Jaimy	Closed	30.00	30.00
91-04-096 Village People CJ-116A	Jaimy	Closed	60.00	60.00
91-04-097 Woman w/Cow CJ-135	Jaimy	Closed	15.00	15.00
91-04-098 Ye Olde Town Tavern CJ-130	Jaimy	Closed	45.00	45.00

Seymour Mann, Inc. — Dickens Collection

	ARTIST	EDITION	ISSUE	QUOTE
89-05-001 Cratchits Lite Up XMS-7000A	J. White	Closed	30.00	30.00
89-05-002 Fezziwigs Lite Up XMS-7000C	J. White	Closed	30.00	30.00
89-05-003 Gift Shoppe Lite Up XMS-7000D	J. White	Closed	30.00	30.00
89-05-004 Scrooge/Marley Lite Up XMS-7000B	J. White	Closed	30.00	30.00
90-05-005 Black Swan Inn Lite Up XMS-7000E	J. White	Closed	30.00	30.00
90-05-006 Cratchit Family MER-121	J. White	Closed	37.50	37.50
90-05-007 Hen Poultry Lite Up XMS-7000H	J. White	Closed	30.00	30.00
90-05-008 Tea and Spice Lite Up XMS-7000F	J. White	Closed	30.00	30.00
90-05-009 Waite Fish Store Lite Up XMS-7000G	J. White	Closed	30.00	30.00
90-05-010 Cratchit/Tiny Tim Musical MER-105	J. White	Closed	33.50	33.50
91-05-011 Cratchit/Tiny Tim Musical CJ-117	Jaimy	Closed	33.50	33.50
91-05-012 Cratchit's Lite Up House CJ-200	Jaimy	Closed	37.50	37.50
91-05-013 Scrooge/Marley Counting House CJ-202	Jaimy	Closed	37.50	37.50
91-05-014 Scrooge Musical CJ-118	Jaimy	Closed	30.00	30.00

Seymour Mann, Inc. — Gingerbread Christmas Collection

	ARTIST	EDITION	ISSUE	QUOTE
91-06-001 Gingerbread Angel CJ-411	J. Sauerbrey	Closed	7.50	7.50
91-06-002 Gingerbread Church Lite Up House CJ-403	J. Sauerbrey	Closed	65.00	65.00
91-06-003 Gingerbread House CJ-416	J. Sauerbrey	Closed	7.50	7.50
91-06-004 Gingerbread House Lite Up CJ-404	J. Sauerbrey	Closed	65.00	65.00
91-06-005 Gingerbread Man CJ-415	J. Sauerbrey	Closed	7.50	7.50
91-06-006 Gingerbread Mansion Lite Up CJ-405	J. Sauerbrey	Closed	70.00	70.00
91-06-007 Gingerbread Mouse/Boot CJ-409	J. Sauerbrey	Closed	7.50	7.50
91-06-008 Gingerbread Mrs. Claus CJ-414	J. Sauerbrey	Closed	7.50	7.50
91-06-009 Gingerbread Reindeer CJ-410	J. Sauerbrey	Closed	7.50	7.50
91-06-010 Gingerbread Rocking Horse Music CJ-460	J. Sauerbrey	Closed	33.50	33.50
91-06-011 Gingerbread Santa CJ-408	J. Sauerbrey	Closed	7.50	7.50
91-06-012 Gingerbread Sleigh CJ-406	J. Sauerbrey	Closed	7.50	7.50
91-06-013 Gingerbread Snowman CJ-412	J. Sauerbrey	Closed	7.50	7.50
91-06-014 Gingerbread Swan Musical CJ-462	J. Sauerbrey	Closed	33.50	33.50
91-06-015 Gingerbread Sweet Shop Lite Up House	J. Sauerbrey	Closed	60.00	60.00
91-06-016 Gingerbread Teddy Bear Music CJ-461	J. Sauerbrey	Closed	33.50	33.50
91-06-017 Gingerbread Toy Shop Lite Up House CJ-402	J. Sauerbrey	Closed	60.00	60.00
91-06-018 Gingerbread Tree CJ-407	J. Sauerbrey	Closed	7.50	7.50
91-06-019 Gingerbread Village Lite Up House CJ-400	J. Sauerbrey	Closed	60.00	60.00

Seymour Mann, Inc. — Victorian Christmas Collection

	ARTIST	EDITION	ISSUE	QUOTE
90-07-001 Toy/Doll House Lite Up MER-314	J. White	Closed	27.50	27.50
90-07-002 Victorian House Lite Up House MER-312	J. White	Closed	27.50	27.50
90-07-003 Yarn Shop Lite Up House MER-313	J. White	Closed	27.50	27.50
91-07-004 Antique Shop Lite Up House MER-353	J. White	Closed	27.50	27.50
91-07-005 Beige Church Lite Up House MER-351	J. White	Closed	35.00	35.00
91-07-006 Book Store Lite Up House MER-351	J. White	Closed	27.50	27.50
91-07-007 Church Lite Up House MER-350	J. White	Closed	37.50	37.50
91-07-008 Country Store Lite Up House MER-356	J. White	Closed	27.50	27.50
91-07-009 Inn Lite Up House MER-352	J. White	Closed	27.50	27.50
91-07-010 Little Match Girl CJ-419	Jaimy	Closed	9.00	9.00
90-07-011 Two Boys w/Snowman CJ-106	Jaimy	Closed	12.00	12.00
93-07-012 Couple Against Wind CJ-420	Jaimy	Closed	15.00	15.00

Seymour Mann, Inc. — Cat Musical Figurines

	ARTIST	EDITION	ISSUE	QUOTE
85-08-001 Cats Ball Shape MH-303A/G	Kenji	Closed	25.00	25.00
86-08-002 Cats w/Ribbon MH-481A/C	Kenji	Open	30.00	30.00
87-08-003 Brown Cat in Teacup MH-600VGB16	Kenji	Open	30.00	30.00
87-08-004 Cat in Garbage Can MH-490	Kenji	Open	35.00	35.00
87-08-005 Cat on Tipped Garbage Can MH-498	Kenji	Open	35.00	35.00
87-08-006 Cat in Rose Teacup MH-600VG	Kenji	Open	30.00	30.00
87-08-007 Cat in Teapot Brown MH-600VGB	Kenji	Open	30.00	30.00
87-08-008 Cat in Teacup MH-600VGG	Kenji	Open	30.00	30.00
87-08-009 Valentine Cat in Teacup MH-600VLT	Kenji	Open	33.50	33.50
87-08-010 Musical Bear MH-602	Kenji	Closed	27.50	27.50
87-08-011 Kittens w/Balls of Yarn MH-612	Kenji	Open	30.00	30.00
87-08-012 Cat in Bag MH-614	Kenji	Open	30.00	30.00
87-08-013 Cat in Bag MH-617	Kenji	Open	30.00	30.00
87-08-014 Brown Cat in Bag MH-617B/6	Kenji	Open	30.00	30.00
87-08-015 Valentine Cat in Bag Musical MH-600	Kenji	Open	33.50	33.50
87-08-016 Teapot Cat MH-631	Kenji	Open	30.00	30.00
88-08-017 Cat in Hat Box MH-634	Kenji	Open	35.00	35.00
88-08-018 Cat in Hat MH-634B	Kenji	Open	35.00	35.00
88-08-019 Brown Cat in Hat MH-634B/6	Kenji	Open	35.00	35.00
89-08-020 Cat w/Coffee Cup Musical MH-706	Kenji	Open	35.00	35.00
89-08-021 Cat in Flower MH-709	Kenji	Open	35.00	35.00
89-08-022 Cat w/Swing Musical MH-710	Kenji	Open	35.00	35.00
89-08-023 Cat in Water Can Musical MH-712	Kenji	Closed	35.00	35.00
89-08-024 Cat on Basket MH-713	Kenji	Closed	35.00	35.00
89-08-025 Cat in Basinet MH-714	Kenji	Closed	35.00	35.00
89-08-026 Cat in Basket MH-713B	Kenji	Open	35.00	35.00
89-08-027 Cat in Gift Box Musical MH-732	Kenji	Open	40.00	40.00
89-08-028 Cat in Shoe MH-718	Kenji	Open	30.00	30.00
89-08-029 Cats in Basket XMAS-664	E. Mann	Closed	7.50	7.50
90-08-030 Bride/Groom Cat MH-738	Kenji	Open	37.50	37.50
90-08-031 Cat in Bootie MH-728	Kenji	Open	35.00	35.00
90-08-032 Grey Cat in Bootie MH-728G/6	Kenji	Open	35.00	35.00
90-08-033 Cat Sailor in Rocking Boat MH-734	Kenji	Open	45.00	45.00
90-08-034 Cat Asleep MH-735	Kenji	Open	17.50	17.50
90-08-035 Cat on Gift Box Music MH-740	Kenji	Open	40.00	40.00
90-08-036 Cat on Pillow MH-731	Kenji	Open	17.50	17.50
90-08-037 Cat w/Bow on Pink Pillow MH-741P	Kenji	Open	33.50	33.50
90-08-038 Cat w/Parrot MH-730	Kenji	Open	37.50	37.50
90-08-039 Kitten Trio in Carriage MH-742	Kenji	Open	37.50	37.50
90-08-040 Cat Calico in Easy Chair MH-743VG	Kenji	Open	27.50	27.50
90-08-041 Cats Graduation MH-745	Kenji	Open	27.50	27.50
90-08-042 Cat in Dress MH-751VG	Kenji	Open	37.50	37.50
91-08-043 Brown Cat in Bag	Kenji	Open	30.00	30.00
91-08-044 Brown Cat in Hat	Kenji	Open	35.00	35.00
91-08-045 Brown Cat in Teacup	Kenji	Open	30.00	30.00
91-08-046 Cat in Bag	Kenji	Open	30.00	30.00
91-08-047 Cat in Bag	Kenji	Open	30.00	30.00
91-08-048 Cat in Bootie	Kenji	Open	35.00	35.00
91-08-049 Cat in Garbage Can	Kenji	Open	35.00	35.00
91-08-050 Cat in Hat	Kenji	Open	35.00	35.00
91-08-051 Cat in Hat Box	Kenji	Open	35.00	35.00
91-08-052 Cat in Rose Teacup	Kenji	Open	30.00	30.00
91-08-053 Cat in Teacup	Kenji	Open	30.00	30.00
91-08-054 Cat in Teapot Brown	Kenji	Open	30.00	30.00
91-08-055 Cat Momma MH-758	Kenji	Open	35.00	35.00
91-08-056 Cat on Tipped Garbage Can	Kenji	Open	35.00	35.00
91-08-057 Cats Ball Shape	Kenji	Open	25.00	25.00
91-08-058 Cats w/Ribbon	Kenji	Open	30.00	30.00
91-08-059 Grey Cat in Bootie	Kenji	Open	35.00	35.00
91-08-060 Kittens w/Balls of Yarn	Kenji	Open	30.00	30.00
91-08-061 Musical Bear	Kenji	Open	27.50	27.50
91-08-062 Teapot Cat	Kenji	Open	30.00	30.00
91-08-063 Cat in Basket MH-768	Kenji	Open	35.00	35.00
91-08-064 Cat Watching Butterfly MH-784	Kenji	Open	17.50	17.50
91-08-065 Cat Watching Canary MH-783	Kenji	Open	25.00	25.00
91-08-066 Cat With Bow on Pink Pillow MH-741P	Kenji	Open	33.50	33.50
91-08-067 Family Cat MH-770	Kenji	Open	35.00	35.00
91-08-068 Kitten Picking Tulips MH-756	Kenji	Open	40.00	40.00
91-08-069 Revolving Cat with Butterfly MH-759	Kenji	Open	40.00	40.00

Seymour Mann, Inc. — Bunny Musical Figurines

	ARTIST	EDITION	ISSUE	QUOTE
91-09-001 Bunny In Teacup MH-781	Kenji	Open	25.00	25.00
91-09-002 Bunny In Teapot MH-780	Kenji	Open	25.00	25.00

Maruri USA — Birds of Prey

	ARTIST	EDITION	ISSUE	QUOTE
81-01-001 Screech Owl	W. Gaither	300	960.00	960.00
81-01-002 American Bald Eagle I	W. Gaither	Closed	165.00	1750.00
82-01-003 American Bald Eagle II	W. Gaither	Closed	245.00	2750.00
83-01-004 American Bald Eagle III	W. Gaither	Closed	445.00	1750.00
84-01-005 American Bald Eagle IV	W. Gaither	Closed	360.00	1750.00
86-01-006 American Bald Eagle V	W. Gaither	Closed	325.00	1250.00

Maruri USA — North American Waterfowl I

	ARTIST	EDITION	ISSUE	QUOTE
81-02-001 Blue Winged Teal	W. Gaither	200	980.00	980.00
81-02-002 Wood Duck, decoy	W. Gaither	950	480.00	480.00
81-02-003 Flying Wood Ducks	W. Gaither	Closed	880.00	880.00
81-02-004 Canvasback Ducks	W. Gaither	Closed	780.00	780.00
81-02-005 Mallard Drake	W. Gaither	Closed	2380.00	2380.00

Maruri USA — North American Waterfowl II

	ARTIST	EDITION	ISSUE	QUOTE
81-03-001 Mallard Ducks Pair	W. Gaither	1,500	225.00	225.00
82-03-002 Goldeneye Ducks Pair	W. Gaither	Closed	225.00	225.00
82-03-003 Bufflehead Ducks Pair	W. Gaither	1,500	225.00	225.00
82-03-004 Widgeon, male	W. Gaither	Closed	225.00	225.00
82-03-005 Widgeon, female	W. Gaither	Closed	225.00	225.00
82-03-006 Pintail Ducks Pair	W. Gaither	Closed	225.00	225.00
83-03-007 Loon	W. Gaither	Closed	245.00	245.00

Maruri USA — North American Songbirds

	ARTIST	EDITION	ISSUE	QUOTE
82-04-001 Cardinal, male	W. Gaither	Closed	95.00	95.00
82-04-002 Chickadee	W. Gaither	Closed	95.00	95.00
82-04-003 Bluebird	W. Gaither	Closed	95.00	95.00
82-04-004 Mockingbird	W. Gaither	Closed	95.00	95.00
82-04-005 Carolina Wren	W. Gaither	Closed	95.00	95.00
83-04-006 Cardinal, female	W. Gaither	Closed	95.00	95.00
83-04-007 Robin	W. Gaither	Closed	95.00	95.00

		ARTIST	EDITION	ISSUE	QUOTE
Maruri USA	**North American Game Birds**				
81-05-001	Canadian Geese, pair	W. Gaither	Closed	2000.00	2000.00
81-05-002	Eastern Wild Turkey	W. Gaither	Closed	300.00	300.00
82-05-003	Ruffed Grouse	W. Gaither	Closed	1745.00	1745.00
83-05-004	Bobtail Quail, male	W. Gaither	Closed	375.00	375.00
83-05-005	Bobtail Quail, female	W. Gaither	Closed	375.00	375.00
83-05-006	Wild Turkey Hen with Chicks	W. Gaither	Closed	300.00	300.00
Maruri USA	**Baby Animals**				
81-06-001	African Lion Cubs	W. Gaither	1,500	195.00	195.00
81-06-002	Wolf Cubs	W. Gaither	Closed	195.00	195.00
81-06-003	Black Bear Cubs	W. Gaither	Closed	195.00	195.00
Maruri USA	**Upland Birds**				
81-07-001	Mourning Doves	W. Gaither	Closed	780.00	780.00
Maruri USA	**Americana**				
81-08-001	Grizzley Bear and Indian	W. Gaither	Closed	650.00	650.00
82-08-002	Sioux Brave and Bison	W. Gaither	Closed	985.00	985.00
Maruri USA	**Stump Animals**				
82-09-001	Red Fox	W. Gaither	Closed	175.00	175.00
83-09-002	Raccoon	W. Gaither	Closed	175.00	175.00
83-09-003	Owl	W. Gaither	Closed	175.00	175.00
84-09-004	Gray Squirrel	W. Gaither	1,200	175.00	175.00
84-09-005	Chipmunk	W. Gaither	Closed	175.00	175.00
84-09-006	Bobcat	W. Gaither	Closed	175.00	175.00
Maruri USA	**Shore Birds**				
84-10-001	Pelican	W. Gaither	Closed	260.00	260.00
84-10-002	Sand Piper	W. Gaither	Closed	285.00	285.00
Maruri USA	**North American Game Animals**				
84-11-001	White Tail Deer	W. Gaither	950	285.00	285.00
Maruri USA	**African Safari Animals**				
83-12-001	African Elephant	W. Gaither	Closed	3500.00	3500.00
83-12-002	Southern White Rhino	W. Gaither	150	3200.00	3200.00
83-12-003	Cape Buffalo	W. Gaither	Closed	2200.00	2200.00
83-12-004	Black Maned Lion	W. Gaither	Closed	1450.00	1450.00
83-12-005	Southern Leopard	W. Gaither	Closed	1450.00	1450.00
83-12-006	Southern Greater Kudu	W. Gaither	Closed	1800.00	1800.00
83-12-007	Southern Impala	W. Gaither	Closed	1200.00	1200.00
81-12-008	Nyala	W. Gaither	300	1450.00	1450.00
83-12-009	Sable	W. Gaither	Closed	1200.00	1200.00
83-12-010	Grant's Zebras, pair	W. Gaither	500	1200.00	1200.00
Maruri USA	**Special Commissions**				
81-13-001	White Bengal Tiger	W. Gaither	240	340.00	340.00
82-13-002	Cheetah	W. Gaither	Closed	995.00	995.00
83-13-003	Orange Bengal Tiger	W. Gaither	240	340.00	340.00
Maruri USA	**Signature Collection**				
85-14-001	American Bald Eagle	W. Gaither	Closed	60.00	60.00
85-14-002	Canada Goose	W. Gaither	Closed	60.00	60.00
85-14-003	Hawk	W. Gaither	Closed	60.00	60.00
85-14-004	Snow Goose	W. Gaither	Closed	60.00	60.00
85-14-005	Pintail Duck	W. Gaither	Closed	60.00	60.00
85-14-006	Swallow	W. Gaither	Closed	60.00	60.00
Maruri USA	**Legendary Flowers of the Orient**				
85-15-001	Iris	Ito	15,000	45.00	55.00
85-15-002	Lotus	Ito	15,000	45.00	45.00
85-15-003	Chinese Peony	Ito	15,000	45.00	55.00
85-15-004	Lily	Ito	15,000	45.00	55.00
85-15-005	Chrysanthemum	Ito	15,000	45.00	55.00
85-15-006	Cherry Blossom	Ito	15,000	45.00	55.00
85-15-007	Orchid	Ito	15,000	45.00	55.00
85-15-008	Wisteria	Ito	15,000	45.00	55.00
Maruri USA	**American Eagle Gallery**				
85-16-001	E-8501	Maruri Studios	Closed	45.00	75.00
85-16-002	E-8502	Maruri Studios	Open	55.00	65.00
85-16-003	E-8503	Maruri Studios	Open	60.00	65.00
85-16-004	E-8504	Maruri Studios	Open	65.00	75.00
85-16-005	E-8505	Maruri Studios	Closed	65.00	150.00
85-16-006	E-8506	Maruri Studios	Open	75.00	90.00
85-16-007	E-8507	Maruri Studios	Open	75.00	90.00
85-16-008	E-8508	Maruri Studios	Closed	75.00	85.00
85-16-009	E-8509	Maruri Studios	Closed	85.00	125.00
85-16-010	E-8510	Maruri Studios	Open	85.00	95.00
85-16-011	E-8511	Maruri Studios	Closed	85.00	125.00
85-16-012	E-8512	Maruri Studios	Open	295.00	325.00
87-16-013	E-8721	Maruri Studios	Open	40.00	50.00
87-16-014	E-8722	Maruri Studios	Open	45.00	55.00
87-16-015	E-8723	Maruri Studios	Closed	55.00	60.00
87-16-016	E-8724	Maruri Studios	Open	175.00	195.00
89-16-017	E-8931	Maruri Studios	Open	55.00	60.00
89-16-018	E-8932	Maruri Studios	Open	75.00	80.00
89-16-019	E-8933	Maruri Studios	Open	95.00	95.00
89-16-020	E-8934	Maruri Studios	Open	135.00	140.00
89-16-021	E-8935	Maruri Studios	Open	175.00	185.00
89-16-022	E-8936	Maruri Studios	Open	185.00	195.00
91-16-023	E-9141 Eagle Landing	Maruri Studios	Open	60.00	60.00
91-16-024	E-9142 Eagle w/ Totem Pole	Maruri Studios	Open	75.00	75.00
91-16-025	E-9143 Pair in Flight	Maruri Studios	Open	95.00	95.00
91-16-026	E-9144 Eagle w/Salmon	Maruri Studios	Open	110.00	110.00
91-16-027	E-9145 Eagle w/Snow	Maruri Studios	Open	135.00	135.00
91-16-028	E-9146 Eagle w/Babies	Maruri Studios	Open	145.00	145.00
Maruri USA	**Wings of Love Doves**				
87-17-001	D-8701 Single Dove w/ Forget-Me-Not	Maruri Studios	Closed	45.00	55.00
87-17-002	D-8702 Double Dove w/ Primrose	Maruri Studios	Open	55.00	65.00
87-17-003	D-8703 Single Dove w/Buttercup	Maruri Studios	Closed	65.00	70.00
87-17-004	D-8704 Double Dove w/Daisy	Maruri Studios	Open	75.00	85.00
87-17-005	D-8705 Single Dove w/Blue Flax	Maruri Studios	Closed	95.00	95.00
87-17-006	D-8706 Double Dove w/Cherry Blossom	Maruri Studios	Open	175.00	195.00
90-17-007	D-9021 Double Dove w/Gentian	Maruri Studios	Open	50.00	55.00
90-17-008	D-9022 Double Dove w/Azalea	Maruri Studios	Open	75.00	75.00
90-17-009	D-9023 Double Dove w/Apple Blossom	Maruri Studios	Open	115.00	120.00
90-17-010	D-9024 Double Dove w/Morning Glory	Maruri Studios	Open	150.00	160.00
Maruri USA	**Majestic Owls of the Night**				
87-18-001	Burrowing Owl	D. Littleton	15,000	55.00	55.00
88-18-002	Barred Owl	D. Littleton	15,000	55.00	55.00
88-18-003	Elf Owl	D. Littleton	15,000	55.00	55.00

		ARTIST	EDITION	ISSUE	QUOTE
Maruri USA	**Studio Collection**				
90-19-001	Majestic Eagles-MS-100	Maruri Studios	Closed	350.00	800.00
91-19-002	Delicate Motion-MS-200	Maruri Studios	3,500	325.00	325.00
92-19-003	Imperial Panda-MS-300	Maruri Studios	3,500	350.00	350.00
93-19-004	Wild Wings-MS-400	Maruri Studios	3,500	395.00	450.00
94-19-005	Waltz of the Dolphins-MS-500	Maruri Studios	3,500	300.00	300.00
Maruri USA	**Polar Expedition**				
90-20-001	Baby Emperor Penguin-P-9001	Maruri Studios	Open	45.00	50.00
90-20-002	Baby Arctic Fox-P-9002	Maruri Studios	Open	50.00	55.00
90-20-003	Polar Bear Cub Sliding-P-9003	Maruri Studios	Open	50.00	55.00
90-20-004	Polar Bear Cubs Playing-P-9004	Maruri Studios	Open	60.00	65.00
90-20-005	Baby Harp Seals-P-9005	Maruri Studios	Open	65.00	70.00
90-20-006	Mother & Baby Emperor Penguins-P-9006	Maruri Studios	Open	80.00	85.00
90-20-007	Mother & Baby Harp Seals-P-9007	Maruri Studios	Open	90.00	95.00
90-20-008	Mother & Baby Polar Bears-P-9008	Maruri Studios	Open	125.00	130.00
90-20-009	Polar Expedition Sign-PES-001	Maruri Studios	Open	18.00	18.00
92-20-010	Baby Harp Seal-P-9221	Maruri Studios	Open	55.00	55.00
92-20-011	Emperor Penguins-P-9222	Maruri Studios	Open	60.00	60.00
92-20-012	Arctic Fox Cubs Playing-P-9223	Maruri Studios	Open	65.00	65.00
92-20-013	Polar Bear Family-P-9224	Maruri Studios	Open	90.00	90.00
Maruri USA	**Eyes Of The Night**				
90-21-001	Single Screech Owl-O-8801	Maruri Studios	Closed	50.00	55.00
90-21-002	Single Snowy Owl-O-8802	Maruri Studios	Closed	50.00	55.00
90-21-003	Single Great Horned Owl-O-8803	Maruri Studios	Closed	60.00	65.00
90-21-004	Single Tawny Owl-O-8804	Maruri Studios	Closed	60.00	65.00
90-21-005	Single Snowy Owl-O-8805	Maruri Studios	Closed	80.00	85.00
90-21-006	Single Screech Owl-O-8806	Maruri Studios	Closed	90.00	95.00
90-21-007	Double Barn Owl 0-8807	Maruri Studios	Closed	125.00	130.00
90-21-008	Single Great Horned Owl-O-8808	Mauurl Studios	Closed	145.00	150.00
90-21-009	Double Snowy Owl-O-8809	Maruri Studios	Closed	245.00	250.00
Maruri USA	**Songbirds Of Beauty**				
91-22-001	Chickadee w/ Roses SB-9101	Maruri Studios	Closed	85.00	85.00
91-22-002	Goldfinch w/ Hawthorne SB-9102	Maruri Studios	Closed	85.00	85.00
91-22-003	Cardinal w/ Cherry Blossom SB-9103	Maruri Studios	Closed	85.00	85.00
91-22-004	Robin w/ Lilies SB-9104	Maruri Studios	Closed	85.00	85.00
91-22-005	Bluebird w/ Apple Blossom SB-9105	Maruri Studios	Closed	85.00	85.00
91-22-006	Robin & Baby w/ Azalea SB-9106	Maruri Studios	Closed	115.00	115.00
91-22-007	Dbl. Bluebird w/ Peach Blossom SB-9107	Maruri Studios	Closed	145.00	145.00
91-22-008	Dbl. Cardinal w/ Dogwood SB-9108	Maruri Studios	Closed	145.00	145.00
Maruri USA	**Hummingbirds**				
91-23-001	Rufous w/Trumpet Creeper H-8901	Maruri Studios	Open	70.00	75.00
89-23-002	White-eared w/Morning Glory H-8902	Maruri Studios	Open	85.00	85.00
89-23-003	Violet-crowned w/Gentian H-8903	Maruri Studios	Open	90.00	90.00
89-23-004	Calliope w/Azalea H-8904	Maruri Studios	Open	120.00	120.00
91-23-005	Anna's w/Lily H-8905	Maruri Studios	Open	160.00	160.00
91-23-006	Allew's w/Hibiscus H-8906	Maruri Studios	Open	195.00	195.00
91-23-007	Ruby-Throated w/Azalea H-8911	Maruri Studios	Open	75.00	75.00
91-23-008	White-Eared w/Morning Glory H-8912	Maruri Studios	Open	75.00	75.00
91-23-009	Violet-Crowned w/Gentian H-8913	Maruri Studios	Open	75.00	75.00
91-23-010	Ruby-Throated w/Orchid H-8914	Maruri Studios	Open	150.00	150.00
Maruri USA	**Graceful Reflections**				
91-24-001	Single Mute Swan SW-9151	Maruri Studios	Closed	85.00	85.00
91-24-002	Mute Swan w/Baby SW-9152	Maruri Studios	Closed	95.00	95.00
91-24-003	Pair-Mute Swan SW-9153	Maruri Studios	Closed	145.00	145.00
91-24-004	Pair-Mute Swan SW-9154	Maruri Studios	Closed	195.00	195.00
Maruri USA	**Precious Panda**				
92-25-001	Snack Time PP-9201	Maruri Studios	Open	60.00	60.00
92-25-002	Lazy Lunch PP-9202	Maruri Studios	Open	60.00	60.00
92-25-003	Tug Of War PP-9203	Maruri Studios	Open	70.00	70.00
92-25-004	Mother's Cuddle-PP-9204	Maruri Studios	Open	120.00	120.00
Maruri USA	**Gentle Giants**				
92-26-001	Baby Elephant Standing GG-9251	Maruri Studios	Open	50.00	50.00
92-26-002	Baby Elephant Sitting GG-9252	Maruri Studios	Open	65.00	65.00
92-26-003	Elephant Pair Playing GG-9253	Maruri Studios	Open	80.00	80.00
92-26-004	Mother & Baby Elephant GG-9254	Maruri Studios	Open	160.00	160.00
92-26-005	Elephant Pair GG-9255	Maruri Studios	Open	220.00	220.00
Maruri USA	**Horses Of The World**				
93-27-001	Clydesdale HW-9351	Maruri Studios	Open	145.00	145.00
93-27-002	Thoroughbred HW-9352	Maruri Studios	Open	145.00	145.00
93-27-003	Quarter Horse HW-9353	Maruri Studios	Open	145.00	145.00
93-27-004	Camargue HW-9354	Maruri Studios	Open	150.00	150.00
93-27-005	Paint Horse HW-9355	Maruri Studios	Open	160.00	160.00
93-27-006	Arabian HW-9356	Maruri Studios	Open	175.00	175.00
Maruri USA	**National Parks**				
93-28-001	Baby Bear NP-9301	Maruri Studios	Open	60.00	60.00
93-28-002	Cougar Cubs NP-9302	Maruri Studios	Open	70.00	70.00
93-28-003	Deer Family NP-9303	Maruri Studios	Open	120.00	120.00
93-28-004	Bear Family NP-9304	Maruri Studios	Open	160.00	160.00
93-28-005	Howling Wolves NP-9305	Maruri Studios	Open	165.00	165.00
93-28-006	Buffalo NP-9306	Maruri Studios	Open	170.00	170.00
93-28-007	Eagle NP-9307	Maruri Studios	Open	180.00	180.00
93-28-008	Falcon NP-9308	Maruri Studios	Open	195.00	195.00
Maruri USA	**Wonders of the Sea**				
94-29-001	Dolphin WS-9401	Maruri Studios	Open	70.00	70.00
94-29-002	Sea Otter & Baby WS-9402	Maruri Studios	Open	75.00	75.00
94-29-003	Manatee & Baby WS-9403	Maruri Studios	Open	75.00	75.00
94-29-004	Manta Ray WS-9404	Maruri Studios	Open	80.00	80.00
94-29-005	Green Sea Turtle WS-9405	Maruri Studios	Open	85.00	85.00
94-29-006	Great White Shark WS-9406	Maruri Studios	Open	90.00	90.00
94-29-007	Two Dolphins WS-9407	Maruri Studios	Open	120.00	120.00
94-29-008	Three Dolphins WS-9408	Maruri Studios	Open	135.00	135.00
94-29-009	Humpback Mother & Baby WS-9409	Maruri Studios	Open	150.00	150.00
94-29-010	Orca Mother & Baby WS-9410	Maruri Studios	Open	150.00	150.00
June McKenna Collectibles, Inc.	**Limited Edition**				
83-01-001	Father Christmas	J. McKenna	Closed	90.00	27-3100.
84-01-002	Old Saint Nick	J. McKenna	Closed	100.00	650-1800
85-01-003	Woodland	J. McKenna	Closed	140.00	750-1500
86-01-004	Victorian	J. McKenna	Closed	150.00	500-1400
87-01-005	Christmas Eve	J. McKenna	Closed	170.00	350-750.
87-01-006	Kris Kringle	J. McKenna	Closed	350.00	500-1100
88-01-007	Bringing Home Christmas	J. McKenna	Closed	170.00	250-950.
88-01-008	Remembrance of Christmas Past	J. McKenna	4,000	400.00	400-450.
89-01-009	Seasons Greetings	J. McKenna	Closed	200.00	300-350.

		ARTIST	EDITION	ISSUE	QUOTE
89-01-010	Santa's Wardrobe	J. McKenna	Closed	750.00	800-1000
90-01-011	Wilderness	J. McKenna	Closed	200.00	240-300.
90-01-012	Night Before Christmas	J. McKenna	Closed	750.00	750.00
91-01-013	Coming to Town	J. McKenna	4,000	220.00	220.00
91-01-014	Santa's Hot Air Balloon	J. McKenna	Closed	800.00	800.00
92-01-015	Christmas Gathering	J. McKenna	4,000	220.00	220.00
93-01-016	The Patriot	J. McKenna	4,000	250.00	250.00
94-01-017	St. Nicholas	J. McKenna	4,000	240.00	240.00

June McKenna Collectibles, Inc. — **Registered Edition**

86-02-001	Colonial	J. McKenna	Closed	150.00	350-450.
87-02-002	White Christmas	J. McKenna	Closed	170.00	12-2200.
88-02-003	Jolly Ole St. Nick	J. McKenna	Closed	170.00	300-350.
89-02-004	Traditional	J. McKenna	Closed	180.00	300.00
90-02-005	Toy Maker	J. McKenna	Closed	200.00	250.00
91-02-006	Checking His List	J. McKenna	Open	230.00	240.00
92-02-007	Forty Winks	J. McKenna	Open	250.00	250.00
93-02-008	Tomorrow's Christmas	J. McKenna	Open	250.00	250.00
94-02-009	Say Cheese, Please	J. McKenna	Open	250.00	250.00

June McKenna Collectibles, Inc. — **Special Limited Edition**

89-03-001	Santa & His Magic Sleigh	J. McKenna	Closed	280.00	400-450.
89-03-002	Last Gentle Nudge	J. McKenna	Closed	280.00	400-500.
90-03-003	Up On The Rooftop	J. McKenna	Closed	280.00	425.00
90-03-004	Santa's Reindeer	J. McKenna	Closed	400.00	400-600.
90-03-005	Christmas Dreams	J. McKenna	Closed	280.00	350.00
90-03-006	Christmas Dreams (Hassock)	J. McKenna	Closed	280.00	14-2500.
91-03-006	Bedtime Stories	J. McKenna	2,000	500.00	500.00
92-03-007	Santa's Arrival	J. McKenna	2,000	300.00	300.00
93-03-008	Baking Cookies	J. McKenna	2,000	450.00	450.00
94-03-009	Welcome to the World	J. McKenna	2,000	400.00	400.00
94-03-010	All Aboard-North Pole Express	J. McKenna	Open	500.00	500.00

June McKenna Collectibles, Inc. — **June McKenna Figurines**

84-04-001	Tree Topper	J. McKenna	Closed	70.00	300-425.
85-04-002	Bride-3D	J. McKenna	Closed	25.00	200.00
85-04-003	Bride w/o base-3D	J. McKenna	Closed	25.00	100.00
85-04-004	Groom-3D	J. McKenna	Closed	25.00	200.00
85-04-005	Groom w/o base-3D	J. McKenna	Closed	25.00	105.00
85-04-006	Soldier	J. McKenna	Closed	40.00	100-275.
85-04-007	Father Times - 3D	J. McKenna	Closed	40.00	100-165.
86-04-008	Male Angel	J. McKenna	Closed	44.00	11-3500.
86-04-009	Little St. Nick	J. McKenna	Closed	50.00	165.00
87-04-010	Patriotic Santa	J. McKenna	Closed	50.00	250-500.
87-04-011	Name Plaque	J. McKenna	Closed	50.00	135-165.
87-04-012	Country Rag Boy	J. McKenna	Closed	40.00	150-187.
87-04-013	Country Rag Girl	J. McKenna	Closed	40.00	150-187.
88-04-014	Mrs. Santa	J. McKenna	Closed	50.00	100-125.
88-04-015	Mr. Santa - 3D	J. McKenna	Closed	44.00	125.00
89-04-016	16th Century Santa - 3D	J. McKenna	Closed	60.00	145-290.
89-04-017	17th Century Santa - 3D	J. McKenna	Closed	70.00	95-120.
89-04-018	Jolly Ole Santa - 3D	J. McKenna	Closed	44.00	90-150.
90-04-019	Noel - 3D	J. McKenna	Closed	50.00	70.00
92-04-020	Taking A Break	J. McKenna	Open	60.00	70.00
92-04-021	Christmas Santa	J. McKenna	Closed	60.00	70.00
92-04-022	Choir of Angels	J. McKenna	Closed	60.00	60.00
92-04-023	Let It Snow	J. McKenna	Open	60.00	60.00
93-04-024	A Good Night's Sleep	J. McKenna	Open	70.00	70.00
93-04-025	Santa and Friends	J. McKenna	Open	70.00	70.00
93-04-026	Mr. Snowman	J. McKenna	Open	40.00	40.00
93-04-027	The Snow Family	J. McKenna	Open	40.00	40.00
93-04-028	Santa Name Plaque	J. McKenna	Open	70.00	70.00
93-04-029	Angel Name Plaque	J. McKenna	Open	70.00	70.00
93-04-030	Children Ice Skaters	J. McKenna	Open	60.00	60.00
94-04-031	Snowman and Child	J. McKenna	Open	70.00	70.00
94-04-032	Star of Bethlehem-Angel	J. McKenna	Open	40.00	40.00

June McKenna Collectibles, Inc. — **Carolers**

85-05-001	Man Caroler	J. McKenna	Closed	36.00	80-100.
85-05-002	Woman Caroler	J. McKenna	Closed	36.00	60-100.
85-05-003	Girl Caroler	J. McKenna	Closed	36.00	70-125.
85-05-004	Boy Caroler	J. McKenna	Closed	36.00	50-100.
91-05-005	Carolers, Man With Girl	J. McKenna	Open	50.00	50.00
91-05-006	Carolers, Woman With Boy	J. McKenna	Open	50.00	50.00
92-05-007	Carolers, Grandparents	J. McKenna	Open	70.00	70.00
94-05-008	Children Carolers	J. McKenna	Open	90.00	90.00

June McKenna Collectibles, Inc. — **Limited Edition Flatback**

88-06-001	Toys of Joy	J. McKenna	Closed	30.00	60-70.00
88-06-002	Mystical Santa	J. McKenna	Closed	30.00	75.00
89-06-003	Blue Christmas	J. McKenna	Closed	32.00	100.00
89-06-004	Victorian	J. McKenna	Closed	32.00	60-85.00
90-06-006	Old Time Santa	J. McKenna	Closed	34.00	60.00
90-06-007	Medieval Santa	J. McKenna	Closed	34.00	60.00
91-06-008	Farewell Santa	J. McKenna	Closed	34.00	40.00
91-06-009	Bag of Stars	J. McKenna	Closed	34.00	40.00
92-06-010	Good Tidings	J. McKenna	10,000	34.00	40.00
92-06-011	Deck The Halls	J. McKenna	10,000	34.00	40.00
93-06-012	Bells of Christmas	J. McKenna	10,000	40.00	40.00
93-06-013	Santa's Love	J. McKenna	10,000	40.00	40.00
94-06-014	Not Once But Twice	J. McKenna	10,000	40.00	40.00
94-06-015	Post Marked North Pole	J. McKenna	10,000	40.00	40.00

June McKenna Collectibles, Inc. — **7" Limited Edition**

88-07-001	Joyful Christmas	J. McKenna	Closed	90.00	150-175.
88-07-002	Christmas Memories	J. McKenna	Closed	90.00	110-175.
89-07-003	Old Fashioned Santa	J. McKenna	Closed	100.00	150-175.
89-07-004	Santa's Bag of Surprises	J. McKenna	Closed	100.00	110-200.
90-07-005	Christmas Delight	J. McKenna	Closed	100.00	100.00
90-07-006	Ethnic Santa	J. McKenna	Closed	100.00	110-150.
91-07-007	Christmas Bishop	J. McKenna	Closed	110.00	110-120.
92-07-008	Christmas Wizard	J. McKenna	7,500	110.00	120.00
93-07-009	Christmas Cheer 1st ed.	J. McKenna	Closed	120.00	300-450.
93-07-010	Christmas Cheer 2nd. ed.	J. McKenna	7,500	120.00	120.00
94-07-011	Santa's One Man Band	J. McKenna	7,500	120.00	120.00
94-07-012	Mrs. Claus, Dancing to the Tune	J. McKenna	7,500	120.00	120.00

June McKenna Collectibles, Inc. — **Nativity Set**

88-08-001	Nativity - 6 Pieces	J. McKenna	Open	130.00	150.00
89-08-002	Three Wise Men	J. McKenna	Open	60.00	90.00
91-08-003	Sheep With Shepherds - 2 Pieces	J. McKenna	Open	60.00	60.00
93-08-004	Donkey	J. McKenna	Open	30.00	30.00
93-08-005	Ram & Ewe	J. McKenna	Open	30.00	30.00
93-08-006	Cow	J. McKenna	Open	30.00	30.00

June McKenna Collectibles, Inc. — **Black Folk Art**

		ARTIST	EDITION	ISSUE	QUOTE
85-09-001	Mammie With Kids - 3D	J. McKenna	Closed	90.00	105.00
85-09-002	Kids in a Tub - 3D	J. McKenna	Closed	30.00	75-90.00
85-09-003	Toaster Cover	J. McKenna	Closed	50.00	425.00
85-09-004	Kissing Cousins - sill sitter	J. McKenna	Closed	36.00	85-110.
83-09-005	Black Boy With Watermelon	J. McKenna	Closed	12.00	100.00
83-09-006	Black Girl With Watermelon	J. McKenna	Closed	12.00	95-100.
84-09-007	Black Man With Pig	J. McKenna	Closed	13.00	80.00
84-09-008	Black Woman With Broom	J. McKenna	Closed	13.00	60-110.
84-09-009	Mammie Cloth Doll	J. McKenna	Closed	90.00	510.00
84-09-010	Remus Cloth Doll	J. McKenna	Closed	90.00	540.00
85-09-011	Watermelon Patch Kids	J. McKenna	Closed	24.00	75.00
85-09-012	Mammie With Spoon	J. McKenna	Closed	13.00	N/A
86-09-013	Black Butler	J. McKenna	Closed	13.00	40.00
87-09-014	Aunt Bertha - 3D	J. McKenna	Closed	36.00	80.00
87-09-015	Uncle Jacob- 3D	J. McKenna	Closed	36.00	55-70.00
87-09-016	Lil' Willie -3D	J. McKenna	Closed	36.00	40-70.00
87-09-017	Sweet Prissy -3D	J. McKenna	Closed	36.00	70.00
88-09-018	Renty	J. McKenna	Closed	16.00	40.00
88-09-019	Netty	J. McKenna	Closed	16.00	40.00
89-09-020	Jake	J. McKenna	Closed	16.00	40.00
89-09-021	Delia	J. McKenna	Closed	16.00	N/A
90-09-022	Tasha	J. McKenna	Closed	17.00	40.00
90-09-023	Tyree	J. McKenna	Closed	17.00	40.00
90-09-024	Let's Play Ball -3D	J. McKenna	Closed	45.00	N/A
90-09-025	Sunday's Best -3D	J. McKenna	Closed	45.00	N/A
92-09-026	Fishing John -3D	J. McKenna	1,000	160.00	160.00
92-09-027	Sweet Sister Sue -3D	J. McKenna	1,000	160.00	160.00

June McKenna Collectibles, Inc. — **Victorian Limited Edition**

90-10-001	Edward - 3D	J. McKenna	Closed	180.00	450.00
90-10-002	Elizabeth - 3D	J. McKenna	Closed	180.00	450.00
90-10-003	Joseph - 3D	J. McKenna	Closed	50.00	50-250.
90-10-004	Victoria - 3D	J. McKenna	Closed	50.00	50-250.

June McKenna Collectibles, Inc. — **Personal Appearance Figurines**

89-11-001	Father Christmas	J. McKenna	Closed	30.00	105.00
90-11-002	Old Saint Nick	J. McKenna	Closed	30.00	30.00

Michael's Limited — **Brian Baker's Deja Vu Collection**

87-01-001	Hotel Couronne (original)wh./br. 1000	B. Baker	Retrd.	49.00	49.00
87-01-002	Parisian Apartment-golden brown 1001	B. Baker	Retrd.	53.00	60.00
87-01-003	The Bernese Guesthouse-golden br. 1010	B. Baker	Retrd.	49.00	49.00
87-01-004	Bavarian Church-yellow 1020	B. Baker	Retrd.	38.00	38.00
87-01-005	Bavarian Church-white 1021	B. Baker	Retrd.	38.00	38.00
87-01-006	Japanese House-white/brown 1100	B. Baker	Retrd.	47.00	47.00
87-01-007	Snow Cabin-brown/white 1500	B. Baker	Retrd.	51.00	70.00
87-01-008	Colonial House-blue 1510	B. Baker	Retrd.	49.00	49.00
87-01-009	Colonial House-wine 1511	B. Baker	Retrd.	40.00	40.00
87-01-010	Colonial Store-brick 1512	B. Baker	Retrd.	53.00	60.00
87-01-011	Old West General Store-white/grey 1520	B. Baker	Retrd.	50.00	68.00
87-01-012	Old West General Store-yellow 1521	B. Baker	Retrd.	50.00	50.00
87-01-013	The Farm House-beige/blue 1525	B. Baker	Retrd.	49.00	49.00
87-01-014	The Farm House-spiced tan 1526	B. Baker	Retrd.	49.00	49.00
87-01-015	The Cottage House-white 1530	B. Baker	Retrd.	47.00	53.00
87-01-016	The Cottage House-blue 1531	B. Baker	Retrd.	42.00	42.00
87-01-017	The Lighthouse-white 1535	B. Baker	Retrd.	53.00	60.00
87-01-018	Queen Ann Victorian-peach/green 1540	B. Baker	Retrd.	53.00	53.00
87-01-019	Queen Ann Victorian-rose 1541	B. Baker	Retrd.	53.00	60.00
87-01-020	Queen Ann Victorian-rust/green 1542	B. Baker	Retrd.	49.00	49.00
87-01-021	Italianate Victorian-brown 1543	B. Baker	Retrd.	51.00	51.00
87-01-022	Italianate Victorian-rust/blue 1544	B. Baker	Retrd.	49.00	49.00
87-01-023	Italianate Victorian-mauve/blue 1545	B. Baker	Retrd.	49.00	49.00
87-01-024	Turreted Victorian-beige/blue 1546	B. Baker	Retrd.	55.00	55.00
87-01-025	Turreted Victorian-peach 1547	B. Baker	Retrd.	55.00	55.00
87-01-026	Ultimate Victorian-maroon/slate 1548	B. Baker	Retrd.	60.00	65.00
87-01-027	Ultimate Victorian-lt. blue/rose 1549	B. Baker	Retrd.	60.00	65.00
87-01-028	Italianate Victorian-lavendar 1550	B. Baker	Retrd.	45.00	45.00
88-01-029	Roeder Gate, Rothenburg-brown 1022	B. Baker	Retrd.	49.00	49.00
88-01-030	Hampshire House-brick 1040	B. Baker	Retrd.	49.00	49.00
88-01-031	Andulusian Village-white 1060	B. Baker	Retrd.	53.00	63.00
88-01-032	Fairy Tale Cottage-white/brown 1200	B. Baker	Retrd.	46.00	46.00
88-01-033	Christmas House-blue 1225	B. Baker	Retrd.	51.00	51.00
88-01-034	Casa Chiquita-natural 1400	B. Baker	Retrd.	53.00	60.00
88-01-035	Georgian Colonial House-white/blue 1514	B. Baker	Retrd.	53.00	53.00
88-01-036	Adam Colonial Cottage-blue/white 1515	B. Baker	Retrd.	53.00	53.00
88-01-037	French Colonial Cottage-beige 1516	B. Baker	Retrd.	42.00	42.00
88-01-038	Antebellum Mansion-peach 1517	B. Baker	Retrd.	49.00	49.00
88-01-039	Antebellum Mansion-white/green 1518	B. Baker	Retrd.	49.00	49.00
88-01-040	Antebellum Mansion-blue/white 1519	B. Baker	Retrd.	49.00	49.00
88-01-041	Country Church-white/blue 1522	B. Baker	Retrd.	49.00	49.00
88-01-042	One Room School House-red 1524	B. Baker	Retrd.	53.00	60-70.00
88-01-043	Gothic Victorian-peach 1536	B. Baker	Retrd.	51.00	60.00
88-01-044	Gothic Victorian-sea green 1537	B. Baker	Retrd.	47.00	47.00
88-01-045	Second Empire House-white/blue 1538	B. Baker	Retrd.	54.00	54.00
88-01-046	Second Empire House-sea grn./desert 1539	B. Baker	Retrd.	50.00	50.00
88-01-047	Stone Victorians-browns 1554	B. Baker	Retrd.	56.00	56.00
89-01-048	Parisian Apartment-beige/blue 1002	B. Baker	Retrd.	53.00	60.00
89-01-049	Hotel Couronne-white/brown 1003	B. Baker	Retrd.	55.00	55.00
89-01-050	Blumen Shop-white/brown 1023	B. Baker	Retrd.	53.00	60.00
89-01-051	Windmill on the Dike-beige/green 1034	B. Baker	Retrd.	60.00	75.00
89-01-052	Hampshire House-brick 1041	B. Baker	Retrd.	49.00	56.00
89-01-053	Henry VIII Pub-white/brown 1043	B. Baker	Retrd.	56.00	65.00
89-01-054	Swedish House-Swed.red 1050	B. Baker	Retrd.	51.00	58.00
89-01-055	Norwegian House-brown 1051	B. Baker	Retrd.	51.00	58.00
89-01-056	Antebellum Mansion-blue/rose 1505	B. Baker	Retrd.	53.00	61.00
89-01-057	Antebellum Mansion-peach 1506	B. Baker	Retrd.	49.00	56.00
89-01-058	Country Barn-red 1527	B. Baker	Retrd.	53.00	60-63.00
89-01-059	Country Barn-blue 1528	B. Baker	Retrd.	49.00	63.00
89-01-060	Italianate Victorian-rose/blue 1551	B. Baker	Retrd.	51.00	55-58.00
89-01-061	Italianate Victorian-peach/teal 1552	B. Baker	Retrd.	51.00	62.00
89-01-062	Ultimate Victorian-peach/green 1553	B. Baker	Retrd.	60.00	65-69.00
89-01-063	Deja Vu Sign-ivory/brown 1600	B. Baker	Retrd.	21.00	24-29.00
90-01-064	Palm Villa-white/blue 1420	B. Baker	Open	54.00	61.00
90-01-065	Palm Villa-desert/green 1421	B. Baker	Open	54.00	61.00
90-01-066	Old Country Cottage-blue 1502	B. Baker	Retrd.	51.00	58.00
90-01-067	Old Country Cottage-red 1503	B. Baker	Retrd.	51.00	58.00
90-01-068	Old Country Cottage-peach 1504	B. Baker	Retrd.	47.00	54.00
90-01-069	Gothic Victorian-blue/mauve 1534	B. Baker	Retrd.	47.00	52-54.00
90-01-070	Classic Victorian-blue/white 1555	B. Baker	Retrd.	60.00	60.00
90-01-071	Classic Victorian-rose/blue 1556	B. Baker	Retrd.	60.00	60.00
90-01-072	Classic Victorian-peach 1557	B. Baker	Retrd.	60.00	60.00

		ARTIST	EDITION	ISSUE	QUOTE
90-01-073	Victorian Country Estate-desert/br. 1560	B. Baker	Retrd.	62.00	62.00
90-01-074	Victorian Country Estate-rose/blue 1561	B. Baker	Retrd.	62.00	62.00
90-01-075	Victorian Country Estate-peach/blue 1562	B. Baker	Retrd.	62.00	62.00
91-01-076	Wind and Roses-brick 1470	B. Baker	Open	63.00	63.00
91-01-077	Log Cabin-brown 1501	B. Baker	Retrd.	55.00	55.00
91-01-078	Colonial Color-brown 1508	B. Baker	Retrd.	62.00	65-71.00
91-01-079	Colonial Cottage-white/bue 1509	B. Baker	Retrd.	59.00	59.00
91-01-080	Victorian Farmhouse-goldenbrown 1565	B. Baker	Retrd.	59.00	59.00
91-01-081	Teddy's Place-teal/rose 1570	B. Baker	Open	61.00	61.00
91-01-082	Mayor's Mansion-blue/peach 1585	B. Baker	Retrd.	57.00	57.00
92-01-083	Alpine Ski Lodge-brown/white 1012	B. Baker	Retrd.	62.00	71.00
92-01-084	Firehouse-brick 1140	B. Baker	Open	60.00	60.00
92-01-085	Flower Store-tan/green 1145	B. Baker	Open	67.00	67.00
92-01-086	Country Station-blue/rust 1156	B. Baker	Open	64.00	64.00
92-01-087	Tropical Fantasy-blue/coral 1410	B. Baker	Open	67.00	67.00
92-01-088	Tropical Fantasy-rose/blue 1411	B. Baker	Open	67.00	67.00
92-01-089	Tropical Fantasy-yellowl/teal 1412	B. Baker	Open	67.00	67.00
92-01-090	Rose Cottage-grey 1443	B. Baker	Open	59.00	59.00
92-01-091	Looks Like Nantucket-grey 1451	B. Baker	Open	62.00	62.00
92-01-092	Victorian Tower House-blue/maroon 1558	B. Baker	Open	63.00	63.00
92-01-093	Victorian Tower House-peach/blue 1559	B. Baker	Open	63.00	63.00
92-01-094	Victorian Bay View-rose/blue 1563	B. Baker	Open	63.00	63.00
92-01-095	Victorian Bay View-cream/teal 1564	B. Baker	Open	63.00	63.00
92-01-096	Angel of the Sea-mauve/white 1586	B. Baker	Open	67.00	67.00
92-01-097	Angel of the Sea-blue/white 1587	B. Baker	Open	67.00	67.00
92-01-098	Victorian Charm-cream 1588	B. Baker	Open	61.00	61.00
92-01-099	Victorian Charm-mauve 1589	B. Baker	Open	61.00	61.00
92-01-100	Deja Vu Sign-ivory/brown 1999	B. Baker	Open	21.00	21.00
93-01-101	Dinard Mansion-beige/brick 1005	B. Baker	Open	67.00	67.00
93-01-102	Old West Hotel-cream 1120	B. Baker	Open	62.00	62.00
93-01-103	Corner Grocery-brick 1141	B. Baker	Open	67.00	67.00
93-01-104	Post Office-light green 1146	B. Baker	Open	60.00	60.00
93-01-105	Enchanted Cottage-natural 1205	B. Baker	Open	63.00	63.00
93-01-106	Homestead Christmas-red 1224	B. Baker	Open	57.00	57.00
93-01-107	Monday's Wash-white/blue 1449	B. Baker	Open	62.00	62.00
93-01-108	Monday's Wash-cream/blue 1450	B. Baker	Open	62.00	62.00
93-01-109	The Stone House-stone/blue 1453	B. Baker	Open	63.00	63.00
93-01-110	Grandpa's Barn-brown 1498	B. Baker	Open	63.00	63.00
93-01-111	Sunday Afternoon-brick 1523	B. Baker	Open	62.00	62.00
93-01-112	Smuggler's Cove-grey/brown 1529	B. Baker	Open	72.00	72.00
93-01-113	Admiralty Head Lighthouse-white 1532	B. Baker	Open	62.00	62.00
93-01-114	Charleston Single House-blue/white 1583	B. Baker	Open	60.00	60.00
93-01-115	Charleston Single House-peach/white 1584	B. Baker	Open	60.00	60.00
93-01-116	Mansard Lady-blue/rose 1606	B. Baker	Open	64.00	64.00
93-01-117	Mansard Lady-tan/green 1607	B. Baker	Open	64.00	64.00
93-01-118	Steiner Street-peach/green 1674	B. Baker	Open	63.00	63.00
93-01-119	Steiner Street-rose/blue 1675	B. Baker	Open	63.00	63.00
94-01-120	Craftsman Cottage-grey 1477	B. Baker	Open	56.00	56.00
94-01-121	Craftsman Cottage-cream 1478	B. Baker	Open	56.00	56.00
94-01-122	Riverside Mill 1507	B. Baker	Open	65.00	65.00
94-01-123	Mukilteo Lighthouse 1569	B. Baker	Open	55.00	55.00
94-01-124	Paris by the Bay 1004	B. Baker	Open	55.00	55.00
94-01-125	Police Station 1147	B. Baker	Open	55.00	55.00
94-01-126	Towered Lady-blue/rose 1688	B. Baker	Open	65.00	65.00
94-01-127	Towered Lady-rose 1689	B. Baker	Open	65.00	65.00
94-01-128	Barber Shop 1164	B. Baker	Open	53.00	53.00
94-01-129	Ellis Island 1250	B. Baker	Open	62.00	62.00
94-01-130	Covered Bridge 1513	B. Baker	Open	69.00	69.00
94-01-131	Cabbagetown 1704	B. Baker	Open	65.00	65.00
94-01-132	Christmas at Church 1223	B. Baker	Open	63.00	63.00
94-01-133	Orleans Cottage-white/blue 1447	B. Baker	Open	63.00	63.00
94-01-134	Orleans Cottage-white/red 1448	B. Baker	Open	63.00	63.00
94-01-135	San Francisco Stick-cream/blue 1624	B. Baker	Open	61.00	61.00
94-01-136	San Francisco Stick-brick/teal 1625	B. Baker	Open	61.00	61.00
94-01-137	Castle in the Clouds 1090	B. Baker	Open	75.00	75.00
94-01-138	Country Store 1435	B. Baker	Open	61.00	61.00
94-01-139	Mission Dolores 1435	B. Baker	Open	47.00	47.00
94-01-140	The Old School House 1439	B. Baker	Open	61.00	61.00
95-01-141	River Belle-white 1092	B. Baker	Open	N/A	N/A
95-01-142	Old West Sheriff-red 1125	B. Baker	Open	N/A	N/A
95-01-143	Main Street Cafe-blue 1142	B. Baker	Open	N/A	N/A
95-01-144	Tudor Christmas-red brick 1221	B. Baker	Open	N/A	N/A
95-01-145	Tudor Christmas-tan brick 1222	B. Baker	Open	N/A	N/A
95-01-146	Mountain Homestead-brown 1401	B. Baker	Open	N/A	N/A
95-01-147	St. Nicholas Church-white/blue 1409	B. Baker	Open	N/A	N/A
95-01-148	Old White Church-white 1424	B. Baker	Open	N/A	N/A
95-01-149	Peggy's Cove Light-white 1533	B. Baker	Open	N/A	N/A
95-01-150	Southern Exposure-tan/green 1581	B. Baker	Open	N/A	N/A
95-01-151	Southern Exposure-cream/rose 1582	B. Baker	Open	N/A	N/A
95-01-152	Quiet Neighborhood-rose/blue 1622	B. Baker	Open	N/A	N/A
95-01-153	Quiet Neighborhood-cream/green 1623	B. Baker	Open	N/A	N/A
95-01-154	Southern Mansion-brick 1744	B. Baker	Open	N/A	N/A
95-01-155	Maple Lane-blue/white 1904	B. Baker	Open	N/A	N/A
95-01-156	Maple Lane-desert/white 1905	B. Baker	Open	N/A	N/A
95-01-157	Victorian Living-teal/tan 1926	B. Baker	Open	N/A	N/A
95-01-158	Victorian Living-clay/white 1927	B. Baker	Open	N/A	N/A

Michael's Limited — **Limited Editions From Brian Baker**

87-02-001	Amsterdam Canal-brown, S/N 1030	B. Baker	Retrd.	79.00	100.00
93-02-002	James River Plantation-brick, Numbrd.1454	B. Baker	Retrd.	108.00	175-300.
93-02-003	American Classic-rose, Numbrd.1566	B. Baker	Retrd.	99.00	600.00
94-02-004	Painted Ladies 1190	B. Baker	Retrd.	125.00	125.00
94-02-005	White Point 1596	B. Baker	Retrd.	100.00	100.00
94-02-006	Hill Top Mansion 1598	B. Baker	Retrd.	97.00	97.00
95-02-007	Philadelphia-brick 1441	B. Baker	1,500	N/A	N/A

Michael's Limited — **Collectors' Corner**

93-03-001	City Cottage (Membership House)-rose/grn.1682	B. Baker	Retrd.	35.00	45.00
93-03-002	Brian's House (Redemption House)-red1496	B. Baker	Retrd.	71.00	71.00
94-03-003	Gothic Cottage (Membership Sculpture) 1571	B. Baker	Retrd.	35.00	35.00
94-03-004	Duke of Gloucester Street (Redemption House) 1459	B. Baker	Retrd.	69.00	69.00
95-03-005	Marie's Cottage-grey (Membership Sculpture) 1942	B. Baker	Yr.Iss.	35.00	35.00
95-03-006	Welcome Home-brick (Redemption House) 1599	B. Baker	Yr.Iss.	35.00	35.00

Midwest of Cannon Falls — **Christian Ulbricht Nutcracker Collection**

		ARTIST	EDITION	ISSUE	QUOTE
86-01-001	Pilgrim Nutcracker, 16 1/2" 00393-0	C. Ulbricht	Open	145.00	155.00
93-01-002	Mrs. Claus Nutcracker 09587-4	C. Ulbricht	5,000	180.00	185.00
93-01-003	Mr. Claus Nutcracker 09588-1	C. Ulbricht	5,000	180.00	185.00
93-01-004	Leprechaun Nutcracker 09110-4	C. Ulbricht	Open	170.00	170.00
94-01-005	Prince on Rocking Horse Nutcracker 12964-7	C. Ulbricht	Open	160.00	160.00

Midwest of Cannon Falls — **Christian Ulbricht "Traditional Santa Series" Nutcracker Collec**

92-02-001	Father Christmas Nutcracker 07094-9	C. Ulbricht	Retrd.	190.00	300.00
93-02-002	Toymaker Nutcracker 09531-7	C. Ulbricht	2,500	220.00	250.00
94-02-003	Victorian Santa Nutcracker 12961-1	C. Ulbricht	2,500	220.00	220.00

Midwest of Cannon Falls — **Christian Ulbricht "A Christmas Carol" Nutcrackers**

93-03-001	Bob Cratchit &Tiny Tim Nutcracker 09577-5	C. Ulbricht	6,000	240.00	240.00
93-03-002	Scrooge Nutcracker 09584-3	C. Ulbricht	6,000	210.00	220.00
94-03-003	Ghost of Christmas Present Nutcracker 12041-5	C. Ulbricht	5,000	190.00	190.00

Midwest of Cannon Falls — **Christian Ulbricht "Nutcracker Fantasy" Nutcrackers**

91-04-001	Herr Drosselmeyer Nutcracker, 16 1/4" 03656-3	C. Ulbricht	Open	170.00	187.00
91-04-002	Clara Nutcracker, 11 1/2" 03657-0	C. Ulbricht	Open	125.00	145.00
91-04-003	Prince Nutcracker, 17" 03665-5	C. Ulbricht	Open	160.00	177.00
91-04-004	Toy Soldier, 14" 03666-2	C. Ulbricht	Open	160.00	177.00
91-04-005	Mouse King Nutcracker, 13 1/2" 04510-7	C. Ulbricht	Open	170.00	184.00

Midwest of Cannon Falls — **Christian Ulbricht "American Folk Hero" Nutcracker Collection**

94-05-001	Johnny Appleseed Nutcracker 12959-3	C. Ulbricht	2500	196.00	196.00
94-05-002	Davy Crockett Nutcracker 12960-9	C. Ulbricht	2500	185.00	185.00

Midwest of Cannon Falls — **Ore Mountain Nutcracker Collection**

92-06-001	Christopher Columbus Nutcracker 00152-3	Midwest	Closed	80.00	80.00
84-06-002	Pinocchio Nutcracker 00160-8	Midwest	Open	60.00	65.00
92-06-003	Victorian Santa Nutcracker 00187-5	Midwest	Open	130.00	140.00
92-06-004	Pilgrim Nutcracker 00188-2	Midwest	Open	96.00	100.00
92-06-005	Indian Nutcracker 00195-0	Midwest	Open	96.00	100.00
92-06-006	Ringmaster Nutcracker 00196-7	Midwest	Closed	135.00	137.00
92-06-007	Cowboy Nutcracker 00298-8	Midwest	Open	97.00	133.00
92-06-008	Farmer Nutcracker 01109-6	Midwest	Open	65.00	77.00
92-06-009	Santa with Skis Nutcracker 01305-2	Midwest	Open	100.00	110.00
91-06-010	Clown Nutcracker 03561-0	Midwest	Open	115.00	118.00
91-06-011	Nutcracker-Maker Nutcracker 03601-3	Midwest	Closed	62.00	65.00
90-06-012	Elf Nutcracker 04154-3	Midwest	Closed	70.00	73.00
90-06-013	Sea Captain Nutcracker 04157-4	Midwest	Open	86.00	95.00
90-06-014	Witch Nutcracker 04159-8	Midwest	Open	75.00	76.00
90-06-015	Windsor Club Nutcracker 04160-4	Midwest	Open	85.00	86.50
90-06-016	Woodland Santa Nutcracker 04191-8	Midwest	Open	105.00	132.00
90-06-017	Uncle Sam Nutcracker 04206-9	Midwest	Closed	50.00	61.50
90-06-018	Merlin the Magician Nutcracker 04207-6	Midwest	Open	67.00	70.00
88-06-019	Santa w/ Tree & Toys Nutcracker 07666-8	Midwest	Closed	76.00	87.00
88-06-020	Nordic Santa Nutcracker 08872-2	Midwest	Open	84.00	110.00
89-06-021	Golfer Nutcracker 09325-2	Midwest	Open	85.00	90.00
89-06-022	Country Santa Nutcracker 09326-9	Midwest	Open	95.00	132.00
89-06-023	Fisherman Nutcracker 09327-6	Midwest	Open	90.00	100.00
93-06-024	Fireman with Dog Nutcracker 06592-1	Midwest	Open	134.00	134.00
93-06-025	Gepetto Santa Nutcracker 09417-4	Midwest	Open	115.00	115.00
93-06-026	Santa with Animals Nutcracker 09424-2	Midwest	Open	117.00	117.00
93-06-027	Cat Witch Nutcracker 09426-6	Midwest	Open	93.00	93.00
93-06-028	White Santa Nutcracker 09533-1	Midwest	Open	100.00	100.00
94-06-029	Miner Nutcracker 10493-4	Midwest	Open	110.00	110.00
94-06-030	Cavalier Nutcracker 12953-1	Midwest	Open	65.00	65.00
94-06-031	Cavalier Nutcracker 12952-4	Midwest	Open	80.00	80.00
94-06-032	Cavalier Nutcracker 12958-6	Midwest	Open	57.00	57.00
94-06-033	Regal Prince Nutcracker 10452-1	Midwest	Open	140.00	140.00
94-06-034	Prince Charming Nutcracker 10457-6	Midwest	Open	125.00	125.00
94-06-035	Santa with Basket Nutcracker 10472-9	Midwest	Open	80.00	80.00
94-06-036	Pinecone Santa Nutcracker 10461-3	Midwest	Open	92.00	92.00
94-06-037	Black Santa Nutcracker 10460-6	Midwest	Open	74.00	74.00
94-06-038	Santa in Nightshirt Nutcracker 10462-0	Midwest	Open	108.00	108.00
94-06-039	Sorcerer Nutcracker 10471-2	Midwest	Open	100.00	100.00
94-06-040	Snow King Nutcracker 10470-5	Midwest	Open	108.00	108.00
94-06-041	Sultan King Nutcracker 10455-2	Midwest	Open	130.00	130.00
94-06-042	Toy Vendor Nutcracker 11987-7	Midwest	Open	124.00	124.00
94-06-043	Engineer Nutcracker 10454-5	Midwest	Open	108.00	108.00
94-06-044	Gardening Lady Nutcracker 10450-7	Midwest	Open	104.00	104.00
94-06-045	Nature Lover Nutcracker 10446-0	Midwest	Open	112.00	112.00
94-06-046	Baseball Player Nutcracker 10459-0	Midwest	Open	111.00	111.00
94-06-047	Soccer Player Nutcracker 10494-1	Midwest	Open	97.00	97.00
94-06-048	Union Soldier Nutcracker 12836-7	Midwest	Open	93.00	93.00
94-06-049	Confederate Soldier Nutcracker 12837-4	Midwest	Open	93.00	93.00
94-06-050	Pumpkin Head Scarecrow Nutcracker 10451-1	Midwest	Open	127.00	127.00
94-06-051	Annie Oakley Nutcracker 10464-4	Midwest	Open	128.00	128.00

Midwest of Cannon Falls — **Ore Mountain Easter Nutcrackers**

91-07-001	Bunny with Egg Nutcracker 00145-5	Midwest	Closed	77.00	80.00
84-07-002	March Hare Nutcracker 00312-1	Midwest	Closed	77.00	80.00
92-07-003	Bunny Painter Nutcracker 06480-1	Midwest	Closed	77.00	80.00

Midwest of Cannon Falls — **Ore Mountain "Nutcracker Fantasy" Nutcrackers**

91-08-001	Clara Nutcracker, 8" 01254-3	Midwest	Open	77.00	85.00
88-08-002	Herr Drosselmeyer Nutcracker, 14 1/2" 07506-7	Midwest	Open	75.00	100.00
88-08-003	The Prince Nutcracker, 12 3/4" 07507-4	Midwest	Open	75.00	90.00
88-08-004	The Toy Soldier Nutcracker, 11" 07508-1	Midwest	Open	70.00	80.00
88-08-005	The Mouse King Nutcracker, 10" 07509-8	Midwest	Open	60.00	70.00
93-08-006	The Mouse King Nutcracker 05350-8	Midwest	5,000	100.00	110.00
94-08-007	Herr Drosselmeyer Nutcracker 10456-9	Midwest	5,000	110.00	110.00
94-08-008	Nutcracker Prince Nutcracker 11001-0	Midwest	5,000	104.00	104.00

Midwest of Cannon Falls — **Ore Mountain "A Christmas Carol" Nutcrackers**

93-09-001	Ghost of Christmas Present	Midwest Importers	5,000	116.00	120.00
93-09-002	Scrooge Nutcracker 05522-9	Midwest Importers	5,000	104.00	110.00
93-09-003	Bob Cratchit Nutcracker 09421-1	Midwest Importers	5,000	120.00	130.00
94-09-004	Ghost of Christmas Past Nutcracker 10447-7	Midwest Importers	4,000	116.00	116.00
94-09-005	Marley's Ghost Nutcracker 10448-4	Midwest Importers	4,000	116.00	116.00
94-09-006	Ghost of Christmas Future Nutcracker 10449-1	Midwest Importers	4,000	116.00	116.00

Midwest of Cannon Falls — **Wendt and Kuhn Collection**

79-10-001	Angel Playing Violin 00403-6	Wendt/Kuhn	Closed	34.00	35.00
83-10-002	Angel Percussion Musicians set/6 00443-2	Wendt/Kuhn	Open	110.00	120.00
84-10-003	Angels Bearing Toys, set/6 00451-7	Wendt/Kuhn	Open	97.00	100.00

		ARTIST	EDITION	ISSUE	QUOTE
83-10-004	Angel String Musicians, set/6 00455-5	Wendt/Kuhn	Open	105.00	112.00
83-10-005	Angel String & Woodwind Musicians, set/6	Wendt/Kuhn	Open	108.00	115.00
83-10-006	Angel Conductor on Stand 00469-2	Wendt/Kuhn	Open	21.00	23.00
83-10-007	Angel Brass Musicians, set/6 00470-8	Wendt/Kuhn	Open	92.00	100.00
79-10-008	Angel Trio, set/3 00471-5	Wendt/Kuhn	Open	140.00	150.00
76-10-009	Santa with Angel 00473-9	Wendt/Kuhn	Open	50.00	52.00
83-10-010	Margarita Birthday Angels, set/3 00480-7	Wendt/Kuhn	Open	44.00	50.00
80-10-011	Angel Pulling Wagon 00553-8	Wendt/Kuhn	Open	43.00	46.00
81-10-012	Angel w/Tree & Basket 11908	Wendt/Kuhn	Closed	24.00	25.00
81-10-013	Santa w/Angel in Sleigh 01192-8	Wendt/Kuhn	Open	52.00	55.00
81-10-014	Angels at Cradle, set/4 01193-5	Wendt/Kuhn	Open	73.00	76.00
83-10-015	Girl w/Wagon 01196-6	Wendt/Kuhn	Closed	27.00	29.00
79-10-016	Girl w/Scissors 01197-3	Wendt/Kuhn	Open	25.00	32.00
79-10-017	Girl w/Porridge Bowl 01198-0	Wendt/Kuhn	Open	29.00	32.00
91-10-018	Girl with Doll 01200-0	Wendt/Kuhn	Open	31.50	32.00
91-10-019	Boy on Rocking Horse, 2 asst. 01202-4	Wendt/Kuhn	Open	35.00	36.00
79-10-020	Girl w/Cradle, set/2 01203-1	Wendt/Kuhn	Open	37.50	40.00
91-10-021	White Angel with Violin 01205-5	Wendt/Kuhn	Closed	25.50	26.50
78-10-022	Madonna w/Child 01207-9	Wendt/Kuhn	Open	120.00	125.00
91-10-023	Birdhouse 01209-3	Wendt/Kuhn	Closed	22.50	23.00
91-10-024	Flower Children, set/6 01213-0	Wendt/Kuhn	Open	130.00	137.00
91-10-025	Display Base for Wendt und Kuhn Figures, 12 1/2 x 2" 01214-7	Wendt/Kuhn	Open	32.00	35.00
79-10-026	Pied Piper and Children, set/7 02843-8	Wendt/Kuhn	Open	120.00	130.00
79-10-027	Bavarian Moving Van 02854-4	Wendt/Kuhn	Open	134.00	140.00
79-10-028	Magarita Angels, set/6 02938-1	Wendt/Kuhn	Open	94.00	100.00
76-10-029	Angel with Sled 02940-4	Wendt/Kuhn	Closed	36.50	38.00
80-10-030	Little People Napkin Rings 6 asst. 03504-7	Wendt/Kuhn	Open	21.00	23.00
90-10-031	Angel Duet in Celestial Stars 04158-1	Wendt/Kuhn	Open	60.00	63.00
87-10-032	Child on Skis, 2 asst. 06083-4	Wendt/Kuhn	Open	28.00	29.00
87-10-033	Child on Sled 06085-8	Wendt/Kuhn	Open	25.50	26.50
92-10-034	Wendt und Kuhn Display Sign w/ Sitting Angel 07535-7	Wendt/Kuhn	Open	20.00	23.00
88-10-035	Lucia Parade Figures, set/3 07667-5	Wendt/Kuhn	Open	75.00	80.00
88-10-036	Children Carrying Lanterns Procession, set/6	Wendt/Kuhn	Open	117.00	127.00
89-10-037	Angel at Piano 09403-7	Wendt/Kuhn	Open	31.00	35.00
94-10-038	Busy Elf, 3 asst. 12856-5	Wendt/Kuhn	Open	22.00	22.00
94-10-039	Santa with Tree 12942-5	Wendt/Kuhn	Open	29.00	29.00
94-10-040	Sun, Moon, Star Set 12943-2	Wendt/Kuhn	Open	69.00	69.00
94-10-041	Child with Flowers Set 12947-0	Wendt/Kuhn	Open	45.00	45.00

Midwest of Cannon Falls — **Wendt and Kuhn Figurines Candleholders**

		ARTIST	EDITION	ISSUE	QUOTE
76-11-001	Angel Candleholder Pair 00472-2	Wendt/Kuhn	Open	70.00	75.00
91-11-002	Angel with Friend Candleholder 01191-1	Wendt/Kuhn	Open	33.30	34.00
91-11-003	Small Angel Candleholder Pair 01195-9	Wendt/Kuhn	Closed	60.00	63.00
80-11-004	Large Angel Candleholder Pair 01201-7	Wendt/Kuhn	Closed	270.00	277.00
86-11-005	Pair of Angels Candleholder 01204-8	Wendt/Kuhn	Closed	30.00	32.00
91-11-006	White Angel Candleholder 01206-2	Wendt/Kuhn	Closed	28.00	29.00
87-11-007	Santa Candleholder 06082-7	Wendt/Kuhn	Closed	53.00	54.00
94-11-008	Angel with Wagon Candleholder 12860-2	Wendt/Kuhn	Open	35.00	35.00

Midwest of Cannon Falls — **Wendt and Kuhn Collection Music Boxes**

		ARTIST	EDITION	ISSUE	QUOTE
91-12-001	Angels & Santa Around Tree 01211-6	Wendt/Kuhn	Open	300.00	300.00
78-12-002	Rotating Angels 'Round Cradle 01911-5	Wendt/Kuhn	Open	270.00	270.00
78-12-003	Angel at Pipe Organ 01929-0	Wendt/Kuhn	Open	176.00	190.00
76-12-004	Girl Rocking Cradle 09215-6	Wendt/Kuhn	Open	180.00	190.00
94-12-005	Angel Under Stars Crank Music Box 12974-6	Wendt/Kuhn	Closed	150.00	190.00

Midwest of Cannon Falls — **Belenes Puig Nativity Collection**

		ARTIST	EDITION	ISSUE	QUOTE
85-13-001	Nativity, set/6: Holy Family, Angel, Animals 6 3/4" 00205-6	J.P. Llobera	Open	250.00	250.00
85-13-002	Shepherd, set/2 00458-6	J.P. Llobera	Open	110.00	110.00
85-13-003	Wise Men, set/3 00459-3	J.P. Llobera	Open	185.00	185.00
86-13-004	Sheep, set/3 00475-3	J.P. Llobera	Open	28.00	28.00
89-13-005	Wise Man with Gold on Camel 02075-3	J.P. Llobera	Open	155.00	155.00
89-13-006	Wise Man with Myrrh on Camel 02076-0	J.P. Llobera	Open	155.00	155.00
89-13-007	Wise Man with Frankincense on Camel 02077-7	J.P. Llobera	Open	155.00	155.00
89-13-008	Donkey 02082-1	J.P. Llobera	Open	26.00	26.00
89-13-009	Ox 02083-8	J.P. Llobera	Open	26.00	26.00
89-13-010	Mother Mary 02084-5	J.P. Llobera	Open	62.00	62.00
89-13-011	Baby Jesus 02085-2	J.P. Llobera	Open	62.00	62.00
89-13-012	Joseph 02086-9	J.P. Llobera	Open	62.00	62.00
89-13-013	Angel 02087-6	J.P. Llobera	Open	50.00	50.00
89-13-014	Wise Man with Frankincense 02088-3	J.P. Llobera	Open	66.00	66.00
89-13-015	Wise Man with Gold 02089-0	J.P. Llobera	Open	66.00	66.00
89-13-016	Wise Man with Myrrh 02090-6	J.P. Llobera	Open	66.00	66.00
89-13-017	Shepherd with Staff 02091-3	J.P. Llobera	Open	56.00	56.00
89-13-018	Shepherd Carrying Lamb 02092-0	J.P. Llobera	Open	56.00	56.00
90-13-019	Resting Camel 04025-6	J.P. Llobera	Open	115.00	115.00
87-13-020	Shepherd & Angel Scene, set/7 06084-1	J.P. Llobera	Open	305.00	305.00
88-13-021	Standing Camel 08792-3	J.P. Llobera	Open	115.00	115.00

Midwest of Cannon Falls — **Leo R. Smith III Collection**

		ARTIST	EDITION	ISSUE	QUOTE
91-14-001	Stars and Stripes Santa 01743-2	L.R. Smith	5,000	190.00	200.00
91-14-002	Woodsman Santa 03310-4	L.R. Smith	5,000	230.00	250.00
91-14-003	Pilgrim Riding Turkey 03312-8	L.R. Smith	5,000	230.00	250.00
91-14-004	Milkmaker 03541-2	L.R. Smith	5,000	170.00	184.00
91-14-005	'Tis a Witching Time 03544-3	L.R. Smith	Retrd.	140.00	850.00
91-14-006	Toymaker 03540-5	L.R. Smith	5,000	120.00	130.00
91-14-007	Cossack Santa 01092-1	L.R. Smith	Retrd.	95.00	129.00
91-14-008	Pilgrim Man 03313-5	L.R. Smith	5,000	78.00	84.00
91-14-009	Pilgrim Woman 03315-9	L.R. Smith	5,000	78.00	84.00
91-14-010	Fisherman Santa 03311-1	L.R. Smith	5,000	270.00	290.00
92-14-011	Dreams of Night Buffalo 07999-7	L.R. Smith	5,000	250.00	270.00
92-14-012	Santa of Peace 07328-5	L.R. Smith	5,000	250.00	270.00
92-14-013	Great Plains Santa 08049-8	L.R. Smith	5,000	270.00	293.00
92-14-014	Ms. Liberty 07866-2	L.R. Smith	5,000	190.00	210.00
92-14-015	Woodland Brave 07867-9	L.R. Smith	Retrd.	87.00	94.00
92-14-016	Leo Smith Name Plaque 07881-5	Midwest	Open	12.00	12.00
93-14-017	Gnome Santa on Deer 05206-8	L.R. Smith	5,000	270.00	270.00
93-14-018	Folk Angel 05444-4	L.R. Smith	5,000	145.00	150.00
93-14-019	Santa Fisherman 08979-8	L.R. Smith	5,000	250.00	250.00
93-14-020	Dancing Santa 09042-8	L.R. Smith	5,000	170.00	170.00
93-14-021	Voyageur 09043-5	L.R. Smith	5,000	170.00	170.00
94-14-022	Santa Skier 12054-5	L.R. Smith	1,500	190.00	190.00
94-14-023	Gift Giver Santa 12056-9	L.R. Smith	1,500	180.00	180.00
94-14-024	Old-World Santa 12053-8	L.R. Smith	Retrd.	75.00	75.00
94-14-025	Star of the Roundup Cowboy 11966-1	L.R. Smith	1,500	100.00	100.00
94-14-026	Weatherwise Angel 12055-2	L.R. Smith	1,500	150.00	150.00

Midwest of Cannon Falls — **Heritage Santa Collection**

		ARTIST	EDITION	ISSUE	QUOTE
90-15-001	Scanda Klaus 00536-1	Midwest	Retrd.	26.50	27.50
90-15-002	Herr Kristmas 00537-8	Midwest	Retrd.	26.50	27.50
90-15-003	MacNicholas 00538-5	Midwest	Retrd.	26.50	27.50
90-15-004	Papa Frost 00539-2	Midwest	Open	26.50	27.50
91-15-005	Father Christmas 01798-2	Midwest	Retrd.	26.50	27.50
91-15-006	Santa Niccolo 01792-5	Midwest	Retrd.	26.50	27.50
92-15-007	Santa Nykolai 06772-7	Midwest	Retrd.	26.50	26.50
92-15-008	Pere Noel 06771-0	Midwest	Retrd.	26.50	26.50
93-15-009	Santa España 07368-1	Midwest	Retrd.	25.00	26.50
93-15-010	Santa O'Nicholas 07370-4	Midwest	Retrd.	25.00	26.50
94-15-011	American Santa 11622-7	Midwest	Retrd.	20.00	20.00

Midwest of Cannon Falls — **Heritage Santa Roly-Polys**

		ARTIST	EDITION	ISSUE	QUOTE
90-16-001	Scanda Klaus Roly-Poly 00528-6	Midwest	Retrd.	24.00	25.00
90-16-002	Herr Kristmas Roly-Poly 00529-3	Midwest	Retrd.	24.00	25.00
90-16-003	MacNicholas Roly-Poly 00530-9	Midwest	Retrd.	24.00	25.00
90-16-004	Papa Frost Roly-Poly 00531-6	Midwest	Open	24.00	25.00
91-16-005	Father Christmas Roly-Poly 01796-8	Midwest	Retrd.	24.00	25.00
91-16-006	Santa Niccolo Roly-Poly 01795-1	Midwest	Retrd.	24.00	25.00
92-16-007	Santa Nykolai Roly-Poly 06769-7	Midwest	Open	24.00	24.00
92-16-008	Pere Noel Roly-Poly 06768-0	Midwest	Retrd.	24.00	24.00
93-16-009	Santa España Roly-Poly 07373-5	Midwest	Open	20.00	24.00
93-16-010	Santa O'Nicholas Roly-Poly 07375-9	Midwest	Retrd.	20.00	24.00
94-16-011	American Santa Roly-Poly 11620-3	Midwest	Retrd.	17.00	17.00

Midwest of Cannon Falls — **Heritage Santa Collection Fabric Mache**

		ARTIST	EDITION	ISSUE	QUOTE
90-17-001	Scanda Klaus Fabric Mache set 00514-9	Midwest	Retrd.	160.00	170.00
90-17-002	Herr Kristmas Fabric Mache set 00515-6	Midwest	Retrd.	160.00	170.00
90-17-003	MacNicholas Fabric Mache set 00516-3	Midwest	Open	160.00	180.00
90-17-004	Papa Frost Fabric Mache set 00517-0	Midwest	Retrd.	160.00	170.00
91-17-005	Father Christmas Fabric Mache set 01800-2	Midwest	Open	160.00	180.00
91-17-006	Santa Niccolo Fabric Mache set 01799-9	Midwest	Retrd.	160.00	180.00
92-17-007	Santa Nykolai Fabric Mache set 06767-3	Midwest	Open	160.00	180.00
92-17-008	Pere Noel Fabric Mache set 06766-6	Midwest	Open	160.00	180.00
93-17-009	Santa España Fabric Mache set 07357-5	Midwest	Open	170.00	180.00
93-17-010	Santa O'Nicholas Fabric Mache set 07365-0	Midwest	Open	170.00	180.00
94-17-011	American Santa Fabric Mache Set 11944-0	Midwest	Retrd.	180.00	180.00

Midwest of Cannon Falls — **Heritage Santa Collection Music Boxes**

		ARTIST	EDITION	ISSUE	QUOTE
90-18-001	Scanda Klaus Music Box 00532-3	Midwest	Open	53.00	59.00
90-18-002	Herr Kristmas Music Box 00533-1	Midwest	Retrd.	53.00	56.00
90-18-003	MacNicholas Music Box 00534-7	Midwest	Retrd.	53.00	59.00
90-18-004	Papa Frost Music Box 00535-4	Midwest	Open	53.00	59.00
91-18-005	Father Christmas Music Box 01802-6	Midwest	Retrd.	53.00	59.00
91-18-006	Santa Niccolo Music Box 01801-9	Midwest	Retrd.	53.00	56.00
92-18-007	Santa Nykolai Music Box 06790-1	Midwest	Retrd.	53.00	59.00
92-18-008	Pere Noel Music Box 06789-5	Midwest	Retrd.	53.00	59.00
93-18-009	Santa España Music Box 07366-7	Midwest	Open	56.00	59.00
93-18-010	Santa O'Nicholas Music Box 07367-4	Midwest	Retrd.	56.00	59.00
94-18-011	American Santa Music Box 11618-0	Midwest	Retrd.	59.00	59.00

Midwest of Cannon Falls — **Heritage Santa Collection Snowglobes**

		ARTIST	EDITION	ISSUE	QUOTE
90-19-001	Scanda Klaus Snowglobe 00524-8	Midwest	Retrd.	40.00	45.00
90-19-002	Herr Kristmas Snowglobe 00525-5	Midwest	Retrd.	40.00	43.00
90-19-003	MacNicholas Snowglobe 00526-2	Midwest	Retrd.	40.00	45.00
90-19-004	Papa Frost Snowglobe 00527-9	Midwest	Retrd.	40.00	43.00
91-19-005	Father Christmas Snowglobe 01794-4	Midwest	Open	40.00	45.00
91-19-006	Santa Niccolo Snowglobe 01793-7	Midwest	Retrd.	40.00	43.00
92-19-007	Santa Nykolai Snowglobe 06783-3	Midwest	Retrd.	40.00	43.00
92-19-008	Pere Noel Snowglobe 06778-9	Midwest	Open	40.00	45.00
93-19-009	Santa España Snowglobe 07371-1	Midwest	Open	43.00	45.00
93-19-010	Santa O'Nicholas Snowglobe 07372-8	Midwest	Retrd.	43.00	45.00
94-19-011	American Santa Snowglobe 11623-4	Midwest	Retrd.	45.00	45.00

Midwest of Cannon Falls — **Creepy Hollow Houses**

		ARTIST	EDITION	ISSUE	QUOTE
93-20-001	Witches Cove (lighted) 01665-7	Midwest	Open	40.00	40.00
93-20-002	Mummy's Mortuary (lighted) 01641-1	Midwest	Open	40.00	40.00
93-20-003	Dracula's Castle (lighted) 01627-5	Midwest	Open	40.00	40.00
93-20-004	Dr. Frankenstein's House (lighted) 01621-3	Midwest	Open	40.00	40.00
93-20-005	Haunted Hotel (lighted) 08549-3	Midwest	Open	40.00	40.00
93-20-006	Blood Bank (lighted) 08548-6	Midwest	Open	40.00	40.00
93-20-007	Shoppe of Horrors (lighted) 08850-9	Midwest	Open	40.00	40.00
94-20-008	Phantom's Opera (lighted) 10650-1	Midwest	Open	40.00	40.00
94-20-009	Cauldron Cafe (lighted) 10649-5	Midwest	Open	40.00	40.00
94-20-010	Medical Ghoul School (lighted) 10651-8	Midwest	Open	40.00	40.00

Midwest of Cannon Falls — **Creepy Hollow Figurines and Accessories**

		ARTIST	EDITION	ISSUE	QUOTE
93-21-001	Witch 06706-2	Midwest	Open	6.00	6.00
93-21-002	Pumpkin Patch Sign, 2 asst. 05898-5	Midwest	Open	6.50	6.50
93-21-003	Hinged Dracula's Coffin 08545-5	Midwest	Open	11.00	11.00
93-21-004	Trick or Treater, 3 asst. 08591-2	Midwest	Open	5.50	5.50
93-21-005	Halloween Sign, 2 asst. 06709-3	Midwest	Open	6.00	6.00
93-21-006	Resin Skeleton 06651-5	Midwest	Open	5.50	5.50
93-21-007	Pumpkin Head Ghost 06661-4	Midwest	Open	5.50	5.50
93-21-008	Haunted Tree, 2 asst. 05892-3	Midwest	Open	7.00	7.00
94-21-009	Mad Scientist 10646-4	Midwest	Open	6.00	6.00
94-21-010	Phantom of the Opera 10645-7	Midwest	Open	6.00	6.00
94-21-011	Werewolf 10643-4	Midwest	Open	6.00	6.00
94-21-012	Street Sign, 2 asst. 10644-0	Midwest	Open	5.70	5.70
94-21-013	Outhouse 10648-8	Midwest	Open	7.00	7.00
94-21-014	Creepy Hollow Sign 10647-1	Midwest	Open	5.50	5.50
94-21-015	Tombstone Sign, 3 asst. 10642-6	Midwest	Open	3.50	3.50
94-21-016	Black Picket Fence 10685-3	Midwest	Open	13.50	13.50
94-21-017	Ghost, 3 asst. 10652-5	Midwest	Open	6.00	6.00

Midwest of Cannon Falls — **Cottontail Lane Houses**

		ARTIST	EDITION	ISSUE	QUOTE
93-22-001	Church (lighted) 01385-4	Midwest	Retrd.	42.00	42.00
93-22-002	Cottontail Inn (lighted) 01394-6	Midwest	Open	43.00	45.00
93-22-003	Schoolhouse (lighted) 01378-6	Midwest	Open	43.00	45.00
93-22-004	Painting Studio (lighted) 01395-5	Midwest	Open	43.00	45.00
93-22-005	Rose Cottage (lighted) 01386-1	Midwest	Open	43.00	45.00
93-22-006	Bakery (lighted) 01396-0	Midwest	Open	43.00	45.00
93-22-007	Confectionary Shop (lighted) 06335-5	Midwest	Open	43.00	45.00
93-22-008	Springtime Cottage (lighted) 06329-8	Midwest	Retrd.	43.00	45.00
93-22-009	Flower Shop (lighted) 06333-9	Midwest	Retrd.	43.00	45.00
93-22-010	Victorian House (lighted) 06332-1	Midwest	Open	43.00	45.00
93-22-011	Chapel (lighted) 00331-2	Midwest	Retrd.	43.00	45.00
93-22-012	Bed & Breakfast House (lighted) 00337-4	Midwest	Open	43.00	45.00
93-22-013	General Store (lighted) 00340-4	Midwest	Open	43.00	45.00
93-22-014	Train Station (lighted) 00330-5	Midwest	Open	43.00	45.00

Midwest of Cannon Falls — **Cottontail Lane Figurines and Accessories**

		ARTIST	EDITION	ISSUE	QUOTE
94-23-001	Wedding Bunny Couple, 2 asst. 00347-3	Midwest	Open	4.20	4.20
94-23-002	Cobblestone Road 10072-1	Midwest	Open	9.00	9.00
94-23-003	Bunny Shopping Couple, 2 asst. 10362-3	Midwest	Open	4.20	4.20
94-23-004	Easter Bunny Figure, 2 asst. 00356-5	Midwest	Open	4.20	4.20
94-23-005	Tree & Shrub, 2 asst. 00382-4	Midwest	Open	5.00	5.00
94-23-006	Bunny Couple on Bicycle 02978-7	Midwest	Open	5.30	5.30
94-23-007	Train Station Couple, 2 asst. 00357-2	Midwest	Open	4.20	4.20
94-23-008	Policeman, Conductor Bunny, 2 asst.00367-1	Midwest	Open	4.20	4.20
94-23-009	Trees, 3 asst. 02194-1	Midwest	Open	6.20	6.20
94-23-010	Strolling Bunny, 2 asst. 02976-3	Midwest	Open	4.20	4.20
94-23-011	Bunny Child Collecting Eggs, 2 asst. 02880-3	Midwest	Open	4.20	4.20
94-23-012	Bunny Marching Band, 6 asst. 00355-8	Midwest	Open	4.20	4.20
94-23-013	Cone-Shaped Tree Set 10369-2	Midwest	Open	7.50	7.50
94-23-014	Topiary Trees, 3 asst. 00346-6	Midwest	Open	2.50	2.50
94-23-015	Bunny Preparing for Easter, 3 asst. 02971-8	Midwest	Open	4.20	4.20
94-23-016	Egg Stand & Flower Cart, 2 asst. 10354-8	Midwest	Open	6.00	6.00
94-23-017	Birdhouse, Sundial & Fountain, 3 asst. 00371-8	Midwest	Open	4.50	4.50
94-23-018	Birdbath, Bench & Mailbox, 02184-2	Midwest	Open	4.00	4.00
94-23-019	Bridge & Gazebo, 2 asst. 02182-9	Midwest	Open	11.50	11.50
94-23-020	Cottontail Lane Sign 10063-9	Midwest	Open	5.00	5.00
94-23-021	Arbor w/ Fence Set 02188-0	Midwest	Open	14.00	14.00
94-23-022	Lamppost, Birdhouse & Mailbox, 3 asst. 02187-3	Midwest	Open	4.50	4.50
94-23-023	Sweeper & Flower Peddler Bunny Couple, 2 asst. 00359-6	Midwest	Open	4.20	4.20

Midwest of Cannon Falls — **Cannon Valley Houses**

		ARTIST	EDITION	ISSUE	QUOTE
94-24-001	Family Farmhouse (lighted) 11292-2	Midwest	Open	43.00	43.00
94-24-002	Red Barn (lighted) 11296-0	Midwest	Open	43.00	43.00
94-24-003	Hen House (lighted) 11294-6	Midwest	Open	33.00	33.00
94-24-004	General Store (lighted) 11295-3	Midwest	Open	43.00	43.00
94-24-005	Little Red Schoolhouse (lighted) 11293-9	Midwest	Yr. Iss.	43.00	43.00

Midwest of Cannon Falls — **Cannon Valley Figurines and Accessories**

		ARTIST	EDITION	ISSUE	QUOTE
94-25-001	Cannon Valley Sign 11297-7	Midwest	Open	5.50	5.50
94-25-002	Hay Wagon and Horse Set 11303-5	Midwest	Open	19.00	19.00
94-25-003	Farm Tractor 11305-9	Midwest	Open	9.50	9.50
94-25-004	Farm Couple, 2 asst. 11458-2	Midwest	Open	5.50	5.50
94-25-005	Children, 2 asst. 11461-2	Midwest	Open	5.50	5.50
94-25-006	Pig and Piglets 11302-8	Midwest	Open	5.30	5.30
94-25-007	Cow, 3 asst. 11309-7	Midwest	Open	5.50	5.50
94-25-008	Horse, 2 asst. 11485-8	Midwest	Open	10.00	10.00
94-25-009	Chicken, 3 asst. 11299-1	Midwest	Open	2.00	2.00
94-25-010	Mailbox and Water Pump, 2 asst. 11301-1	Midwest	Open	4.00	4.00
94-25-011	Farm Town Windmill 11306-6	Midwest	Open	9.50	9.50
94-25-012	Apple Tree 2 asst. 11484-1	Midwest	Open	10.00	10.00
94-25-013	Pickup Truck 11304-2	Midwest	Open	12.00	12.00
94-25-014	Teacher and Children, 3 asst. 11460-5	Midwest	Open	5.50	5.50
94-25-015	Storekeeper 11459-9	Midwest	Open	5.50	5.50
94-25-016	Flagpole 11300-4	Midwest	Open	5.30	5.30

Museum Collections, Inc. — **American Family I**

		ARTIST	EDITION	ISSUE	QUOTE
79-01-001	Baby's First Step	N. Rockwell	22,500	90.00	175-200.
80-01-002	Happy Birthday, Dear Mother	N. Rockwell	22,500	90.00	135.00
80-01-003	Sweet Sixteen	N. Rockwell	22,500	90.00	125.00
80-01-004	First Haircut	N. Rockwell	22,500	90.00	150.00
80-01-005	First Prom	N. Rockwell	22,500	90.00	125.00
80-01-006	Wrapping Christmas Presents	N. Rockwell	22,500	90.00	125.00
80-01-007	The Student	N. Rockwell	22,500	110.00	140.00
80-01-008	Birthday Party	N. Rockwell	22,500	110.00	140.00
80-01-009	Little Mother	N. Rockwell	22,500	110.00	125.00
80-01-010	Washing Our Dog	N. Rockwell	22,500	110.00	125.00
81-01-011	Mother's Little Helpers	N. Rockwell	22,500	110.00	125.00
81-01-012	Bride and Groom	N. Rockwell	22,500	110.00	200.00

Museum Collections, Inc. — **Christmas**

		ARTIST	EDITION	ISSUE	QUOTE
80-02-001	Checking His List	N. Rockwell	Yr.Iss.	65.00	110.00
81-02-002	Ringing in Good Cheer	N. Rockwell	Yr.Iss.	95.00	100.00
82-02-003	Waiting for Santa	N. Rockwell	Yr.Iss.	95.00	110.00
83-02-004	High Hopes	N. Rockwell	Yr.Iss.	95.00	175.00
84-02-005	Space Age Santa	N. Rockwell	Yr.Iss.	65.00	100.00

Museum Collections, Inc. — **Classic**

		ARTIST	EDITION	ISSUE	QUOTE
80-03-001	Lighthouse Keeper's Daughter	N. Rockwell	Closed	65.00	95-100.
80-03-002	The Cobbler	N. Rockwell	Closed	65.00	95.00
80-03-003	The Toymaker	N. Rockwell	Closed	65.00	90-95.00
80-03-004	Bedtime	N. Rockwell	Closed	65.00	90-95.00
80-03-005	Memories	N. Rockwell	Closed	65.00	90-95.00
80-03-006	For A Good Boy	N. Rockwell	Closed	65.00	90-95.00
81-03-007	A Dollhouse for Sis	N. Rockwell	Closed	65.00	90-95.00
81-03-008	Music Master	N. Rockwell	Closed	65.00	90-95.00
81-03-009	The Music Lesson	N. Rockwell	Closed	65.00	90-95.00
81-03-010	Puppy Love	N. Rockwell	Closed	65.00	90-95.00
81-03-011	While The Audience Waits	N. Rockwell	Closed	65.00	90-95.00
81-03-012	Off to School	N. Rockwell	Closed	65.00	90-95.00
82-03-013	The Country Doctor	N. Rockwell	Closed	65.00	90-95.00
82-03-014	Spring Fever	N. Rockwell	Closed	65.00	90-95.00
82-03-015	Words of Wisdom	N. Rockwell	Closed	65.00	90-95.00
82-03-016	The Kite Maker	N. Rockwell	Closed	65.00	90-100.
82-03-017	Dreams in the Antique Shop	N. Rockwell	Closed	65.00	90-95.00
83-03-018	Winter Fun	N. Rockwell	Closed	65.00	90-95.00
83-03-019	A Special Treat	N. Rockwell	Closed	65.00	90-95.00
83-03-020	High Stepping	N. Rockwell	Closed	65.00	90-95.00
83-03-021	Bored of Education	N. Rockwell	Closed	65.00	90-95.00
83-03-022	A Final Touch	N. Rockwell	Closed	65.00	90-95.00
83-03-023	Braving the Storm	N. Rockwell	Closed	65.00	90-95.00
84-03-024	Goin' Fishin'	N. Rockwell	Closed	65.00	90-95.00
84-03-025	The Big Race	N. Rockwell	Closed	65.00	90-95.00
84-03-026	Saturday's Hero	N. Rockwell	Closed	65.00	90-95.00
84-03-027	All Wrapped Up	N. Rockwell	Closed	65.00	90-95.00

Museum Collections, Inc. — **Commemorative**

		ARTIST	EDITION	ISSUE	QUOTE
81-04-001	Norman Rockwell Display	N. Rockwell	5,000	125.00	200-250.
82-04-002	Spirit of America	N. Rockwell	5,000	125.00	200-250.
83-04-003	Norman Rockwell, America's Artist	N. Rockwell	5,000	125.00	200-250.
84-04-004	Outward Bound	N. Rockwell	5,000	125.00	200-250.
85-04-005	Another Masterpiece by Norman Rockwell	N. Rockwell	5,000	125.00	200-250.
86-04-006	The Painter and the Pups	N. Rockwell	5,000	125.00	250.00

Old World Christmas — **Night Lights**

		ARTIST	EDITION	ISSUE	QUOTE
85-01-001	Santa 529701	E.M. Merck	Retrd.	37.00	175.00
86-01-002	Angel 529703	E.M. Merck	Retrd.	18.00	65.00
86-01-003	Santa in Chimney 529707	E.M. Merck	Retrd.	37.00	135.00
86-01-004	Snowman 529709	E.M. Merck	Retrd.	37.00	55.00
86-01-005	Teddy Bear 529711	E.M. Merck	Retrd.	37.00	75.00
86-01-006	ABC Block 529713	E.M. Merck	Open	37.00	37.00
87-01-007	Santa with Tree 529715	E.M. Merck	Retrd.	39.50	110.00
88-01-008	Santa Hugging Tree 529717	E.M. Merck	Retrd.	42.00	110.00
89-01-009	Santa on Locomotive 529719	E.M. Merck	Retrd.	42.00	95.00
90-01-010	Father Christmas 529721	E.M. Merck	Retrd.	45.00	85.00
91-01-011	Santa with Stocking 529723	E.M. Merck	Retrd.	45.00	85.00
92-01-012	Santa with Nutcracker 529725	E.M. Merck	Retrd.	45.00	110.00
93-01-013	Father Christmas with Toys 529727	E.M. Merck	Open	48.50	48.50

Old World Christmas — **Smoking Men**

		ARTIST	EDITION	ISSUE	QUOTE
85-02-001	Toy Peddler Smoker 70020	K.W.O.	Open	55.00	55.00
85-02-002	Large Toy Peddler Smoker 70020-9	K.W.O.	Open	280.00	280.00
85-02-003	Woodsman Smoker 70021	K.W.O.	Open	50.00	50.00
85-02-004	Large Hunter 70021-9	K.W.O.	Open	250.00	250.00
85-02-005	Nightwatchman Smoker 70022	K.W.O.	Open	48.50	48.50
85-02-006	Hunter 70023	K.W.O.	Open	49.50	49.50
85-02-007	Chimney Sweep 70024	K.W.O.	Open	47.50	47.50
85-02-008	Gardener 70040	K.W.O.	Open	57.00	57.00
87-02-009	Blacksmith 70041	K.W.O.	Open	50.00	50.00
87-02-010	Fisherman 70042	K.W.O.	Open	49.50	49.50
87-02-011	Woodcarver 70043	K.W.O.	Retrd.	40.00	40.00
87-02-012	Tailor 70044	K.W.O.	Open	50.00	50.00
87-02-013	Shepherd 70045	K.W.O.	Open	49.00	49.00
88-02-014	Bird Seller 70046	K.W.O.	Open	56.00	56.00
88-02-015	Artist 70047	K.W.O.	Open	50.00	50.00
88-02-016	Postman 70048	K.W.O.	Open	48.50	48.50
88-02-017	Antique Style Cook 70052	K.W.O.	Retrd.	27.50	27.50
88-02-018	Antique Style Coachman 70053	K.W.O.	Retrd.	28.00	28.00
91-02-019	Santa with Toys 70060	K.W.O.	Open	57.00	57.00
91-02-020	Cook 70061	K.W.O.	Open	49.00	49.00
92-02-021	Coachman 70062	K.W.O.	Open	50.00	50.00
92-02-022	White Santa 70063	K.W.O.	Open	60.00	60.00
92-02-023	Red Santa 70064	K.W.O.	Open	60.00	60.00
94-02-024	Large Red Santa 70064-9	K.W.O.	Open	270.00	270.00
92-02-025	Teal Santa 70065	K.W.O.	Open	60.00	60.00
92-02-026	Peddler 70066	K.W.O.	Open	59.50	59.50
93-02-027	Large Peddler 70066-9	K.W.O.	Open	295.00	295.00
93-02-028	Poacher 70068	K.W.O.	Open	47.50	47.50
93-02-029	Basket Peddler 70069	K.W.O.	Open	58.50	58.50
93-02-030	Highwayman 70070	K.W.O.	Open	50.00	50.00
94-02-031	Mushroom Collector 70071	K.W.O.	Open	50.00	50.00
94-02-032	Grandpa at Oven 70073	K.W.O.	Open	72.00	72.00
94-02-033	Grandpa with Accordion 70076	K.W.O.	Open	59.50	59.50
94-02-034	Grandma 70077	K.W.O.	Open	59.50	59.50
94-02-035	Sitting Hunter 70082	K.W.O.	Open	60.00	60.00
94-02-036	Zither Player 70083	K.W.O.	Open	63.00	63.00
86-02-037	Hunter 701	O.W.C.	Retrd.	30.00	30.00
86-02-038	Father Christmas with Toys 7010	O.W.C.	Retrd.	60.00	60.00
86-02-039	Carved Hunter 70100	O.W.C.	Retrd.	90.00	90.00
93-02-040	Large Clock Peddler 70101	K.W.O.	Open	120.00	120.00
93-02-041	Large Flower Peddler 70103	K.W.O.	Open	120.00	120.00
93-02-042	Large Pottery Peddler 70104	K.W.O.	Open	120.00	120.00
92-02-043	Small Santa 7011	O.W.C.	Open	37.50	37.50
92-02-044	Father Christmas 70113-1	O.W.C.	Retrd.	45.00	45.00
91-02-045	Natural Father Christmas 7012	O.W.C.	Retrd.	60.00	60.00
91-02-046	Woodsman 7013	O.W.C..	Retrd.	60.00	60.00
91-02-047	Bird Seller 7014	O.W.C..	Retrd.	50.00	50.00
92-02-048	Carved Woodsman 7015	O.W.C.	Open	67.50	67.50
94-02-049	Father Christmas 70150	K.W.O.	Open	110.00	110.00
91-02-050	Gardner 7016	E.M. Merck	Retrd.	55.00	55.00
89-02-051	Chimney Sweep 7017	E.M. Merck	Retrd.	55.00	55.00
91-02-052	Hunter 7018	E.M. Merck	Retrd.	55.00	55.00
91-02-053	Woodsman 7019	E.M. Merck	Retrd.	55.00	55.00
86-02-054	Father Christmas 702	O.W.C.	Open	60.00	60.00
86-02-055	Artist 7020	E.M. Merck	Retrd.	55.00	55.00
86-02-056	Small Old World Santa 70202	O.W.C.	Retrd.	37.50	37.50
86-02-057	Large Old World Santa 70203	O.W.C.	Retrd.	77.50	77.50
86-02-058	Old World Santa 70204	O.W.C.	Retrd.	42.50	42.50
92-02-059	Hunter with Crate 7021	O.W.C.	Open	150.00	150.00
92-02-060	Robber with Crate 7022	O.W.C.	Open	150.00	150.00
92-02-061	St. Peter 70228	O.W.C.	Retrd.	95.00	95.00
92-02-062	King 70229	E.M. Merck	Retrd.	95.00	95.00
92-02-063	Farmer with Crate 7023	O.W.C.	Open	150.00	150.00
91-02-064	Cook 7025	O.W.C.	Retrd.	55.00	55.00
92-02-065	Farmer 7026	O.W.C.	Retrd.	55.00	55.00
92-02-066	Tyrolian 702613	O.W.C.	Retrd.	45.00	45.00
85-02-067	Grandpa 702615	O.W.C.	Open	42.50	42.50
86-02-068	Skier 702616	O.W.C.	Retrd.	54.00	54.00
85-02-069	Snowman 702621	O.W.C.	Retrd.	30.00	30.00
92-02-070	Grandma 702622	O.W.C.	Retrd.	42.50	42.50
92-02-071	Innkeeper 70268	O.W.C.	Retrd.	54.00	54.00
91-02-072	Nightwatchman 7027	O.W.C.	Retrd.	55.00	55.00
91-02-073	Postman 7028	O.W.C.	Retrd.	55.00	55.00
91-02-074	Fisherman 7029	O.W.C.	Retrd.	55.00	55.00
91-02-075	Frosty Snowman 703	O.W.C.	Retrd.	22.50	22.50
91-02-076	Toy Peddler 7030	O.W.C.	Retrd.	60.00	60.00
91-02-077	Wood Worker 7031	O.W.C.	Open	79.50	79.50
91-02-078	Bavarian Hunter 7032	O.W.C.	Open	79.50	79.50
91-02-079	Beer Drinker 7033	O.W.C.	Open	67.50	67.50
85-02-080	Nightwatchman 7034	O.W.C.	Retrd.	32.50	32.50
92-02-081	Carved Santa 7035	O.W.C.	Open	67.50	67.50
91-02-082	Mountain Climber 7036	O.W.C.	Open	67.50	67.50
91-02-083	Innkeeper 7037	O.W.C.	Open	60.00	60.00
91-02-084	Ice Skater 7038	E.M. Merck.	Retrd.	60.00	60.00
92-02-085	Clock Salesman 7039	O.W.C.	Retrd.	275.00	275.00
86-02-086	Santa Smoker/Candleholder 704	O.W.C.	Open	55.00	55.00
92-02-087	Basket Peddler 7040	O.W.C.	Retrd.	130.00	130.00
91-02-088	Champion Archer 7041	O.W.C.	Open	67.50	67.50
91-02-089	Butcher 7043	O.W.C.	Retrd.	49.50	49.50
91-02-090	Baker 7044	O.W.C.	Retrd.	49.50	49.50
91-02-091	Gardener 7045	O.W.C.	Retrd.	49.50	49.50
91-02-092	Santa Claus 705	O.W.C.	Retrd.	45.00	45.00
91-02-093	Father Christmas 7051	O.W.C.	Open	80.00	79.95
92-02-094	Captain 7052	O.W.C.	Open	80.00	79.95
92-02-095	Carved Shepherd 7053	O.W.C.	Retrd.	150.00	150.00

		ARTIST	EDITION	ISSUE	QUOTE
92-02-096	Carved Hunter 7054	O.W.C.	Retrd.	200.00	200.00
92-02-097	Witch 70543	E.M. Merck	Retrd.	49.50	49.50
91-02-098	Toy Peddler 7055	O.W.C.	Retrd.	60.00	60.00
91-02-099	Prussian Soldier 7056	O.W.C.	Retrd.	60.00	60.00
91-02-100	Coachman 7057	O.W.C.	Retrd.	60.00	60.00
92-02-101	Alpenhorn Player 7058	O.W.C.	Open	70.00	70.00
92-02-102	Skier 7059	O.W.C.	Open	59.50	59.50
91-02-103	Natural Santa 706	O.W.C.	Retrd.	40.00	40.00
92-02-104	Toy Peddler 7060	O.W.C.	Open	110.00	110.00
92-02-105	Minstrel 7061	O.W.C.	Open	85.00	85.00
92-02-106	Angler with Crate 7062	O.W.C.	Open	150.00	150.00
93-02-107	Father Christmas 7063	O.W.C.	Retrd.	45.00	45.00
92-02-108	Santa in Crate 707	O.W.C.	Open	165.00	165.00
92-02-109	Carved King 7072	O.W.C.	Open	68.50	68.50
88-02-110	Snowman with Bird 708	O.W.C.	Open	26.00	26.00
89-02-111	Santa 7086	O.W.C.	Retrd.	55.00	55.00
92-02-112	Christmas Tree Vendor 709	O.W.C.	Open	150.00	150.00
91-02-113	Snowman on Skis 7092	O.W.C.	Retrd.	30.00	30.00
87-02-114	Chimney Sweep 72014	K.W.O.	Open	48.50	48.50
87-02-115	Guard Nutcracker 72015	K.W.O.	Open	52.50	52.50
94-02-116	Small Cook Nutcracker 72020	E.M. Merck	Open	42.00	42.00
94-02-117	Small Skier Nutcracker 72021	E.M. Merck	Open	44.00	44.00
94-02-118	Small Toy Peddler Nutcracker 72022	E.M. Merck	Open	44.00	44.00
94-02-119	Small Gardener Nutcracker 72023	E.M. Merck	Open	44.00	44.00
94-02-120	Small Santa Nutcracker 72024	E.M. Merck	Open	42.00	42.00
94-02-121	Small Chimney Sweep Nutcracker 72025	E.M. Merck	Open	42.00	42.00
87-02-122	Small King Nutcracker 72030	K.W.O.	Open	40.00	39.95
87-02-123	King Nutcracker 72031	K.W.O.	Open	50.00	50.00
93-02-124	Large King Nutcracker 72033	K.W.O.	Open	80.00	79.95
93-02-125	Stained King with Crown Nutcracker 72034	K.W.O.	Open	65.00	65.00
87-02-126	Dutch Guard Nutcracker 72040	K.W.O.	Open	55.00	55.00
87-02-127	British Guard Nutcracker 72041	K.W.O.	Open	60.00	60.00
87-02-128	British General Nutcracker 72042	K.W.O.	Open	55.00	55.00
87-02-129	Austrian General Nutcracker 72043	K.W.O.	Open	57.50	57.50
87-02-130	Prussian Hussar Nutcracker 72044	K.W.O.	Open	60.00	60.00
87-02-131	Prussian Sergeant Nutcracker 72045	K.W.O.	Open	60.00	60.00
87-02-132	Spanish Guard Nutcracker 72046	K.W.O.	Open	65.00	65.00
87-02-133	Austrian Musketeer Nutcracker 72048	K.W.O.	Open	57.50	57.50
87-02-134	Saxon Guard Nutcracker 72049	K.W.O.	Open	65.00	65.00
89-02-135	British Major Nutcracker 72050	K.W.O.	Open	65.00	65.00
92-02-136	Saxonian Officer Nutcracker 72051	K.W.O.	Open	65.00	65.00
92-02-137	Prussian Officer Nutcracker 72052	K.W.O.	Open	65.00	65.00
92-02-138	French Officer Nutcracker 72053	K.W.O.	Open	67.50	67.50
92-02-139	Portuguese Guard Nutcracker 72055	K.W.O.	Open	65.00	65.00
92-02-140	Swedish Officer Nutcracker 72056	K.W.O.	Open	67.50	67.50
92-02-141	Austrian Hussar Nutcracker 72058	K.W.O.	Open	62.50	62.50
92-02-142	Hungarian Hussar Nutcracker 72059	K.W.O.	Open	62.50	62.50
92-02-143	Farmer Nutcracker 72064	K.W.O.	Open	62.50	62.50
93-02-144	Traditional Erzgebirge Nutcracker 72067	K.W.O.	Open	62.50	62.50
93-02-145	Hunter Nutcracker 72070	K.W.O.	Open	59.50	59.50
91-02-146	Large Carved Hunter Nutcracker 721	K.W.O.	Open	175.00	175.00
91-02-147	Inlaid Natural King Nutcracker 7214	O.W.C.	Retrd.	150.00	150.00
92-02-148	Large Dutch Guard Nutcracker 72140	K.W.O.	Open	90.00	90.00
92-02-149	Large British Guard 72141	K.W.O.	Open	90.00	90.00
92-02-150	Large Prussian Hussar Nutcracker 72144	K.W.O.	Open	90.00	90.00
92-02-151	Large Prussian Sargeant 72145	K.W.O.	Open	90.00	90.00
92-02-152	Large Austrian Musketeer Nutcracker 72148	K.W.O.	Open	87.50	87.50
92-02-153	Carved Hunter Nutcracker 72213	O.W.C.	Retrd.	150.00	150.00
92-02-154	Large Carved Santa Nutcracker 7223	K.W.O.	Open	175.00	175.00
92-02-155	Large Fireman Nutcracker 72240	K.W.O.	Open	99.50	99.50
92-02-156	Large Saxon Duke Nutcracker 72241	K.W.O.	Open	130.00	129.50
92-02-157	Large Bavarian Duke Nutcracker 72242	K.W.O.	Open	130.00	129.50
92-02-158	Large Austrian King Nutcracker 72243	K.W.O..	Open	130.00	129.50
92-02-159	Large Prussian King Nutcracker 72244	K.W.O.	Open	130.00	129.50
91-02-160	Inlaid Natural Muskateer 7225	O.W.C.	Retrd.	150.00	150.00
91-02-161	Large Hunter Nutcracker 7228	K.W.O.	Open	97.50	97.50
92-02-162	Exceptional King Nutcracker 7230	E.M. Merck	50	950.00	950.00
93-02-163	Exceptional Guard Nutcracker 7231	K.W.O.	50	995.00	995.00
92-02-164	Large Traditional Red King Nutcracker 7237	K.W.O.	Open	115.00	115.00
93-02-165	Brandenburger Guard Nutcracker 7250	E.M. Merck	Retrd.	110.00	110.00
93-02-166	Prussian King Nutcracker 7251	E.M. Merck	Open	110.00	110.00
93-02-167	Rostocker Pirate Nutcracker 7252	E.M. Merck	Open	110.00	110.00
93-02-168	Berliner Baker Nutcracker 7253	E.M. Merck	Open	110.00	110.00
93-02-169	Waldheimer Hunter Nutcracker 7254	E.M. Merck	Open	110.00	110.00
93-02-170	Chemnitzer Clown 7255	E.M. Merck	Open	110.00	110.00
93-02-171	Sonnenberger Toy Peddler Nutcracker 7256	E.M. Merck	Open	110.00	110.00
93-02-172	Seiffener Santa Nutcracker 7257	E.M. Merck	Retrd.	110.00	110.00
93-02-173	Tegernsee Golfer Nutcracker 7259	E.M. Merck	Open	135.00	135.00
93-02-174	Freitaler Fisherman Nutcracker 7260	E.M. Merck	Open	110.00	110.00
93-02-175	Falkensteiner Wizard 7261	E.M. Merck	Open	110.00	110.00
93-02-176	Saalfelder Shepherd Nutcracker 7263	E.M. Merck	Open	110.00	110.00
93-02-177	Bohemian Beekeeper Nutcracker 7264	E.M. Merck	Open	110.00	110.00
93-02-178	Coburger Chimney Sweep Nutcracker 7265	E.M. Merck	Open	110.00	110.00
93-02-179	Altenburger Grandma Nutcracker 7266	E.M. Merck	Open	135.00	135.00
93-02-180	Altenburger Grandpa Nutcracker 7267	E.M. Merck	Open	135.00	135.00
93-02-181	Wittlicher Witch Nutcracker 7268	E.M. Merck	Open	135.00	135.00
93-02-182	Bremer Sea Captain Nutcracker 7269	E.M. Merck	Open	110.00	110.00
93-02-183	Kulmbacher Beer Drinker Nutcracker 7270	E.M. Merck	Open	110.00	110.00
93-02-184	Schneeberger Skier Nutcracker 7271	E.M. Merck	Open	135.00	135.00
93-02-185	Neustadter Nurse Nutcracker 7272	E.M. Merck	Open	135.00	135.00
93-02-186	Berchtesgaden Doctor Nutcracker 7273	E.M. Merck	Open	110.00	110.00
93-02-187	Fuessen Father Christmas Nutcracker 7274	E.M. Merck	Open	135.00	135.00
94-02-188	Salzburger St. Nicholas Nutcracker 7275	E.M. Merck	Open	140.00	140.00
94-02-189	Waldkirchen Father Christmas 7276	E.M. Merck	Open	140.00	140.00
92-02-190	Large Snow Prince Nutcracker 7277	E.M. Merck	Retrd.	100.00	100.00
94-02-184	Giessener Gardener Nutcracker 7278	E.M. Merck	Open	110.00	110.00
94-02-191	Partinkirchen Bride 7279	E.M. Merck	Open	140.00	140.00
94-02-192	Garmish Groom Nutcracker 7280	E.M. Merck	Open	110.00	110.00
94-02-193	Neuschwanstein Knight 7281	E.M. Merck	Open	110.00	110.00
94-02-194	Nuremberger Nightwatchman 7282	E.M. Merck	Open	110.00	110.00
94-02-195	Wyker Viking Nutcracker 7283	E.M. Merck	Open	110.00	110.00
92-02-196	Natural Guard Nutcracker 72915	K.W.O.	Open	52.50	52.50
92-02-197	Skier Nutcracker 7294	E.M. Merck	Retrd.	82.50	82.50
93-02-198	Snowman Nutcracker 7295	E.M. Merck	Open	110.00	110.00
93-02-199	Teddy Bear Nutcracker 7296	E.M. Merck	Open	135.00	135.00
94-02-200	Easter Bunny Nutcracker 7297	E.M. Merck	Open	140.00	140.00

		ARTIST	EDITION	ISSUE	QUOTE
94-02-201	Black Cat Nutcracker 7298	E.M. Merck	Open	140.00	140.00
Old World Christmas		**Collectibles**			
91-03-001	Noah's Ark 861	O.W.C.	Open	250.00	250.00
92-03-002	Weather House 86109	O.W.C.	Open	31.50	31.50
92-03-003	Large Seiffener Candle Arch 8616	O.W.C.	Open	450.00	450.00
92-03-004	Candle Arch with Church 862	O.W.C.	Retrd.	28.50	28.50
Old World Christmas		**Pyramids**			
86-04-001	Angel Musicians Pyramid 88001	K.W.O.	Open	58.50	58.50
91-04-002	Deer in Forest Pyramid 8810	O.W.C.	Open	97.50	97.50
91-04-003	Camel Caravan Pyramid 8812	O.W.C.	Open	92.50	92.50
91-04-004	Musical 4-Tier Pyramid 8815	O.W.C.	Retrd.	775.00	775.00
91-04-005	White 3-Tier Pyramid 8816	O.W.C.	Retrd.	225.00	225.00
91-04-006	Santa with Train 8817	O.W.C.	Retrd.	62.50	62.50
91-04-007	3-Tier Painted Nativity Pyramid 8818	O.W.C.	Retrd.	225.00	225.00
92-04-008	Mini Natural Angel 8819	O.W.C.	Open	42.50	42.50
92-04-009	3-Tier Forest Pyramid 882	O.W.C.	Open	225.00	225.00
92-04-010	Mini-Pyramid, Santa 8820	O.W.C.	Open	32.50	32.50
92-04-011	Natural Pyramid with Deer 8821	O.W.C.	Open	65.00	65.00
92-04-012	Small Nativity 8822	O.W.C.	Open	110.00	110.00
92-04-013	Mini Painted Angel 8823	O.W.C.	Open	47.50	47.50
92-04-014	White Pyramid with Angels 8824	O.W.C.	Retrd.	55.00	55.00
92-04-015	Traditional 3-Tier Pyramid 8826	K.W.O.	Open	175.00	175.00
92-04-016	3 Tier Nativity Pyramid 883	O.W.C.	Open	250.00	250.00
92-04-017	Traditional 4-Tier Pyramid 8836	K.W.O.	Open	225.00	225.00
92-04-018	4-Tier White Pyramid with Music 8837	K.W.O.	Open	550.00	550.00
92-04-019	Miniature Forest Pyramid 884	O.W.C.	Open	35.00	35.00
92-04-020	6ft Hand-Carved Pyramid 884006	O.W.C.	Retrd.	4000.00	4000.00
92-04-021	5ft Hand-Carved Pyramid 884007	O.W.C.	Retrd.	1295.00	1295.00
92-04-022	Miniature Choir Pyramid 885	O.W.C.	Open	35.00	35.00
92-04-023	Detailed Nativity Pyramid 8851	O.W.C.	Retrd.	175.00	175.00
92-04-024	Miniature Music Band Pyramid 886	O.W.C.	Retrd.	30.00	30.00
92-04-025	Santa with Angels Pyramid 887	O.W.C.	Retrd.	175.00	175.00
92-04-026	Small Choir Pyramid 8879	O.W.C.	Retrd.	68.50	68.50
92-04-027	Fairytale Pyramid 888	O.W.C.	Open	175.00	175.00
92-04-028	Small Nativity Pyramid 889	O.W.C.	Retrd.	82.00	82.00
Old World Christmas		**Candleholders**			
89-05-001	Rocking Horse 9011	E.M. Merck	Open	7.50	7.50
89-05-002	Santa 9012	E.M. Merck	Retrd.	7.55	7.55
89-05-003	Hummingbird 9013	E.M. Merck	Open	7.50	7.50
89-05-004	Teddy Bear 9014	E.M. Merck	Open	7.50	7.50
89-05-005	Angel 9015	E.M. Merck	Open	7.50	7.50
89-05-006	Nutcracker 9016	E.M. Merck	Open	7.50	7.50
Old World Christmas		**Halloween**			
87-06-001	Pumpkin Light with Ghosts 9201	E.M. Merck	Open	39.50	39.50
87-06-002	Pumpkin Light with Scarecrow 9202	E.M. Merck	Retrd.	37.00	37.00
87-06-003	Haunted House with Lights 9203	E.M. Merck	Open	99.50	99.50
87-06-004	Lighted Ghost Dish 9204	E.M. Merck	Open	45.00	45.00
87-06-005	Ghost Light 9205	E.M. Merck	Retrd.	37.00	43.00
88-06-006	Haunted House Waterglobe 9206	E.M. Merck	Retrd.	22.50	22.50
88-06-007	Pumpkin Head on Wire 9207	E.M. Merck	Retrd.	7.35	7.35
88-06-008	Black Cat on Wire 9208	E.M. Merck	Retrd.	8.35	8.35
89-06-009	Ghost Votive 9211	E.M. Merck	Open	8.50	8.50
89-06-010	Witch on Moon Night Light 9212	E.M. Merck	Open	37.50	37.50
89-06-011	Cast Iron Scarecrow 9218	E.M. Merck	Open	32.50	32.50
89-06-012	Black Cat/Witch with Cart (A) 9251	E.M. Merck	Open	10.00	10.00
88-06-013	Pumpkin Votive 9271	E.M. Merck	Retrd.	8.90	8.90
88-06-014	Pumpkin Taper Holder 9272	E.M. Merck	Retrd.	5.65	5.65
88-06-015	Large Pumpkin Bowl 9273	E.M. Merck	Open	18.50	18.50
88-06-016	Witch Votive Holder 9281	E.M. Merck	Open	29.50	29.50
88-06-017	Witch Taper Holder 9282	E.M. Merck	Retrd.	11.00	11.00
Old World Christmas		**Porcelain Christmas**			
87-07-001	Santa Head Votive 9411	E.M. Merck	Retrd.	10.00	10.00
87-07-002	Santa Head Night Light 9412	E.M. Merck	Retrd.	19.00	19.00
87-07-003	Santa in Chimney Music Box 9413	E.M. Merck	Retrd.	44.00	44.00
87-07-004	Santa Head Stocking Holder 9414	E.M. Merck	Retrd.	18.00	18.00
87-07-005	Cast Iron Santa on Horse 9418	E.M. Merck	Retrd.	37.50	37.50
87-07-006	Cast Iron Santa 9419	E.M. Merck	Retrd.	35.00	35.00
87-07-007	Angels, set of 3 9421	E.M. Merck	Retrd.	15.50	15.45
87-07-008	Roly-Poly Santa 9440	E.M. Merck	Retrd.	27.00	27.00
87-07-009	Four Castles of Germany 9450	E.M. Merck	Retrd.	31.00	31.00
88-07-010	Santa on Polar Bear 9471	E.M. Merck	Retrd.	6.25	6.25
88-07-011	Santa Visiting Lighthouse 9472	E.M. Merck	Retrd.	6.25	6.25
88-07-012	Santa in Swing 9473	E.M. Merck	Retrd.	6.25	6.25
88-07-013	Santa with Angel 9474	E.M. Merck	Retrd.	6.25	6.25
88-07-014	Santa on Teeter-Totter 9475	E.M. Merck	Retrd.	6.25	6.25
88-07-015	Santa Visiting Igloo 9476	E.M. Merck	Retrd.	6.25	6.25
88-07-016	Bunny on Skies Music Box 9491	E.M. Merck	Retrd.	44.00	44.00
88-07-017	Bear on Skates Music Box 9492	E.M. Merck	Retrd.	44.00	44.00
88-07-018	Penguin with Gifts Music Box 9493	E.M. Merck	Retrd.	44.00	44.00
Old World Christmas		**Paper Mache**			
88-08-001	Father Christmas (A) 9600	E.M. Merck	Retrd.	19.50	19.50
88-08-002	Red Father Christmas 9601	E.M. Merck	Retrd.	19.50	19.50
88-08-003	Blue Father Christmas 9602	E.M. Merck	Retrd.	19.50	19.50
88-08-004	White Father Christmas 9603	E.M. Merck	Retrd.	19.50	19.50
88-08-005	Father Christmas with Gifts 9610	E.M. Merck	Retrd.	32.50	32.50
89-08-006	Father Christmas 9612	E.M. Merck	Retrd.	38.50	38.50
88-08-007	Assorted Father Christmas 9615	E.M. Merck	Retrd.	44.00	44.00
88-08-008	White Father Christmas 9616	E.M. Merck	Retrd.	50.00	50.00
89-08-009	Father Christmas with Pack 9638	E.M. Merck	Retrd.	40.00	40.00
88-08-010	52 cm. Father Christmas 9652	E.M. Merck	Retrd.	175.00	175.00
88-08-011	Traditional Belznickel 9661	E.M. Merck	Open	40.00	40.00
88-08-012	Small Traditional Belznickel 9662	E.M. Merck	Open	35.00	35.00
89-08-013	Santa in Sleigh 9672	E.M. Merck	Retrd.	39.50	39.50
89-08-014	Assorted Santas 9691	E.M. Merck	Retrd.	35.00	35.00
Pacific Rim Import Corp.		**Bristol Township**			
90-01-001	Bristol Township Sign	P. Sebern	Open	10.00	10.00
90-01-002	Maps & Charts	P. Sebern	Open	25.00	25.00
90-01-003	Iron Horse Livery	P. Sebern	Retrd.	30.00	30.00
90-01-004	Southwick Church	P. Sebern	Open	30.00	30.00
90-01-005	Wexford Manor	P. Sebern	Open	25.00	25.00
90-01-006	Coventry House	P. Sebern	Open	30.00	30.00
90-01-007	Bedford Manor	P. Sebern	Open	30.00	30.00
90-01-008	Geo. Straith Grocer	R. S. Benson	Open	25.00	25.00
90-01-009	Bristol Books	P. Sebern	Open	35.00	35.00
90-01-010	Black Swan Millinery	P. Sebern	Open	30.00	30.00
90-01-011	Violin Shop	P. Sebern	Open	30.00	30.00
90-01-012	Trinity Church	P. Sebern	Retrd.	30.00	30.00

		ARTIST	EDITION	ISSUE	QUOTE
90-01-013	Silversmith	P. Sebern	Open	30.00	30.00
90-01-014	High Gate Mill	P. Sebern	Open	40.00	40.00
90-01-015	Queen's Road Church	P. Sebern	Open	40.00	40.00
91-01-016	Hardwicke House	P. Sebern	Retrd.	30.00	45.00
91-01-017	Elmstone House	P. Sebern	Retrd.	30.00	45.00
91-01-018	Pegglesworth Inn	P. Sebern	Open	40.00	40.00
91-01-019	Flower Shop	P. Sebern	Open	30.00	30.00
91-01-020	Kilby Cottage	P. Sebern	Retrd.	30.00	45.00
91-01-021	Bridgestone Church	P. Sebern	Retrd.	30.00	30.00
93-01-022	Foxdown Manor	P. Sebern	Open	30.00	30.00
93-01-023	Chesterfield House	P. Sebern	Open	30.00	30.00
94-01-024	Surrey Road Church	P. Sebern	Open	40.00	40.00
94-01-025	Shotwick Inn/Surgery	P. Sebern	Open	35.00	35.00
Pacific Rim Import Corp.		**Bristol Waterfront**			
92-02-001	Admiralty Shipping	P. Sebern	Open	30.00	30.00
92-02-002	Avon Fish Co.	P. Sebern	Open	30.00	30.00
92-02-003	Chandler	P. Sebern	Retrd.	30.00	30.00
92-02-004	Customs House	P. Sebern	Open	40.00	40.00
92-02-005	Hawke Exports	P. Sebern	Open	40.00	40.00
92-02-006	Quarter Deck Inn	P. Sebern	Open	40.00	40.00
92-02-007	Regent Warehouse	P. Sebern	Open	40.00	40.00
93-02-008	Bristol Point Lighthouse	P. Sebern	Open	45.00	45.00
93-02-009	Lower Quay Chapel	P. Sebern	Open	40.00	40.00
93-02-010	Rusty Knight Inn	P. Sebern	Open	35.00	35.00
94-02-011	Bristol Tattler	P. Sebern	Open	40.00	40.00
94-02-012	Portshead Lighthouse	P. Sebern	Open	30.00	30.00
Pacific Rim Import Corp.		**Bunny Toes**			
94-03-001	Bunny Toes Sign	P. Sebern	Open	20.00	20.00
94-03-002	Timothy With Flower Cart	Pacific Rim Team	Open	17.00	17.00
94-03-003	Willis & Skeeter	Pacific Rim Team	Open	17.00	17.00
94-03-004	Wendell at the Mail Box	Pacific Rim Team	Open	17.00	17.00
94-03-005	Wendell With Eggs in Hat	Pacific Rim Team	Open	13.00	13.00
94-03-006	Timothy With Tulips	Pacific Rim Team	Open	13.00	13.00
94-03-007	Winifred With Blooms	Pacific Rim Team	Open	13.00	13.00
94-03-008	Tillie Making a Wreath	Pacific Rim Team	Open	13.00	13.00
94-03-009	Mazie at Play	Pacific Rim Team	Open	13.00	13.00
94-03-010	Phoebe Goes Ballooning	Pacific Rim Team	Open	7.00	7.00
94-03-011	Sophie Pops Out	Pacific Rim Team	Open	7.00	7.00
94-03-012	Sweethearts (lighted)	Pacific Rim Team	Open	50.00	50.00
94-03-013	Hannah With Maximillian	Pacific Rim Team	Open	13.00	13.00
94-03-014	Timothy With Eggs	Pacific Rim Team	Open	13.00	13.00
94-03-015	Winifred Paints Eggs	Pacific Rim Team	Open	15.00	15.00
94-03-016	Willis & Skeeter Gardening	Pacific Rim Team	Open	15.00	15.00
94-03-017	Wendell With Flowers	Pacific Rim Team	Open	13.00	13.00
94-03-018	Tillie With Her Bike	Pacific Rim Team	Open	15.00	15.00
94-03-019	Garden Gate	Pacific Rim Team	Open	30.00	30.00
Pemberton & Oakes		**Zolan's Children**			
82-01-001	Erik and the Dandelion	D. Zolan	17,000	48.00	48.00
83-01-002	Sabina in the Grass	D. Zolan	6,800	48.00	48.00
84-01-003	Winter Angel	D. Zolan	8,000	28.00	28.00
85-01-004	Tender Moment	D. Zolan	10,000	29.00	75.00
PenDelfin		**Nursery Rhymes**			
85-01-001	Apple Barrel	J. Heap	Retrd.	N/A	N/A
63-01-002	Aunt Agatha	J. Heap	Retrd.	N/A	N/A
55-01-003	Balloon Woman	J. Heap	Retrd.	1.00	N/A
55-01-004	Bell Man	J. Heap	Retrd.	1.00	N/A
84-01-005	Blossom	D. Roberts	Retrd.	16.50	35.00
56-01-006	Bobbin Woman	J. Heap	Retrd.	N/A	N/A
64-01-007	Bongo	D. Roberts	Retrd.	31.00	N/A
66-01-008	Cakestand	J. Heap	Retrd.	2.00	200.00
53-01-009	Cauldron Witch	J. Heap	Retrd.	3.50	N/A
59-01-010	Cha Cha	J. Heap	Retrd.	N/A	N/A
62-01-011	Cornish Prayer (Corny)	J. Heap	Retrd.	N/A	N/A
80-01-012	Crocker	D. Roberts	Retrd.	20.00	42.00
63-01-013	Cyril Squirrel	J. Heap	Retrd.	N/A	N/A
56-01-014	Desmond Duck	J. Heap	Retrd.	2.50	N/A
55-01-015	Elf	J. Heap	Retrd.	1.00	N/A
61-01-016	Father Mouse	J. Heap	Retrd.	N/A	N/A
55-01-017	Flying Witch	J. Heap	Retrd.	1.00	N/A
60-01-018	Gussie	J. Heap	Retrd.	N/A	N/A
56-01-019	Little Bo Peep	J. Heap	Retrd.	2.00	N/A
56-01-020	Little Jack Horner	J. Heap	Retrd.	2.00	N/A
61-01-021	Lollipop (Mouse)	J. Heap	Retrd.	N/A	N/A
60-01-022	Lucy Pocket	J. Heap	Retrd.	4.20	350.00
56-01-023	Manx Kitten	J. Heap	Retrd.	2.00	N/A
55-01-024	Margot	J. Heap	Retrd.	2.00	N/A
56-01-025	Mary Mary Quite Contrary	J. Heap	Retrd.	2.00	N/A
67-01-026	Maud	J. Heap	Retrd.	N/A	300.00
61-01-027	Megan	J. Heap	Retrd.	3.00	N/A
56-01-028	Midge (Replaced by Picnic Midge)	J. Heap	Retrd.	2.00	N/A
66-01-029	Milk Jug Stand	J. Heap	Retrd.	2.00	N/A
56-01-030	Miss Muffet	J. Heap	Retrd.	2.00	N/A
60-01-031	Model Stand	J. Heap	Retrd.	4.00	N/A
61-01-032	Mother Mouse	J. Heap	Retrd.	N/A	N/A
65-01-033	Mouse House	J. Heap	Retrd.	N/A	N/A
65-01-034	Muncher	D. Roberts	Retrd.	26.00	N/A
81-01-035	Nipper	D. Roberts	Retrd.	20.50	35.00
55-01-036	Old Adam	J. Heap	Retrd.	4.00	N/A
55-01-037	Old Father	J. Heap	Retrd.	6.25	900.00
57-01-038	Old Mother	J. Heap	Retrd.	6.25	N/A
56-01-039	Original Robert	J. Heap	Retrd.	2.50	N/A
53-01-040	Pendle Witch	J. Heap	Retrd.	4.00	N/A
67-01-041	Phumf	J. Heap	Retrd.	24.00	N/A
55-01-042	Phynnodderee (Commissioned-Exclusive)	J. Heap	Retrd.	1.00	N/A
66-01-043	Picnic Basket	J. Heap	Retrd.	2.00	N/A
65-01-044	Picnic Stand	J. Heap	Retrd.	62.50	N/A
67-01-045	Picnic Table	J. Heap	Retrd.	N/A	N/A
66-01-046	Pieface	D. Roberts	Retrd.	31.00	95.00
65-01-047	Pixie Bods	J. Heap	Retrd.	N/A	N/A
53-01-048	Pixie House	J. Heap	Retrd.	N/A	N/A
62-01-049	Pooch	D. Roberts	Retrd.	24.50	N/A
58-01-050	Rabbit Book Ends	J. Heap	Retrd.	10.00	N/A
54-01-051	Rhinegold Lamp	J. Heap	Retrd.	21.00	N/A
67-01-052	Robert	D. Roberts	Retrd.	12.00	100.00
57-01-053	Romeo & Juliet	J. Heap	Retrd.	11.00	N/A
60-01-054	Shiner	J. Heap	Retrd.	2.50	N/A
60-01-055	Squeezy	J. Heap	Retrd.	2.50	N/A
57-01-056	Tammy	D. Roberts	Retrd.	24.50	N/A
67-01-057	The Bath Tub	J. Heap	Retrd.	4.50	N/A

		ARTIST	EDITION	ISSUE	QUOTE
69-01-058	The Gallery Series: Wakey, Pieface, Poppet, Robert, Dodger	J. Heap	Retrd.	N/A	N/A
56-01-059	Timber Stand	J. Heap	Retrd.	35.00	N/A
53-01-060	Tipsy Witch	J. Heap	Retrd.	3.50	N/A
56-01-061	Tom Tom the Piper's Son	J. Heap	Retrd.	2.00	N/A
55-01-062	Toper	J. Heap	Retrd.	1.00	N/A
71-01-063	Totty	J. Heap	Retrd.	21.00	250.00
59-01-064	Uncle Soames	J. Heap	Retrd.	105.00	300.00
56-01-065	Wee Willie Winkie	J. Heap	Retrd.	2.00	N/A
PenDelfin		**Bed Series**			
XX-02-001	Dodger	J. Heap	Open	24.00	24.00
XX-02-002	Peeps	J. Heap	Open	21.00	21.00
XX-02-003	Poppet	D. Roberts	Open	23.00	23.00
XX-02-004	Snuggles	J. Heap	Open	20.00	20.00
XX-02-005	Twins	J. Heap	Open	25.00	25.00
XX-02-006	Wakey	J. Heap	Open	24.00	24.00
XX-02-007	Victoria	J. Heap	Open	47.50	47.50
XX-02-008	Parsley	D. Roberts	Open	25.00	25.00
XX-02-009	Chirpy	D. Roberts	Retrd.	31.50	60.00
XX-02-010	Snuggles Awake	J. Heap	Open	60.00	60.00
92-02-011	Sunny	D. Roberts	Open	40.00	40.00
93-02-012	Forty Winks	D. Roberts	Open	57.00	57.00
PenDelfin		**Band Series**			
XX-03-001	Rocky	J. Heap	Open	32.00	32.00
XX-03-002	Rolly	J. Heap	Open	17.50	17.50
XX-03-003	Thumper	J. Heap	Open	25.00	25.00
XX-03-004	Piano	D. Roberts	Open	25.00	25.00
XX-03-005	Casanova	J. Heap	Open	35.00	35.00
XX-03-006	Clanger	J. Heap	Open	35.00	35.00
XX-03-007	Rosa	J. Heap	Open	40.00	40.00
XX-03-008	Solo	D. Roberts	Retrd.	40.00	40.00
XX-03-009	Jingles	D. Roberts	Retrd.	11.25	22.50
XX-03-010	Bandstand	J. Heap	Open	70.00	70.00
94-03-011	Mike	D. Roberts	Open	55.00	55.00
PenDelfin		**Picnic Series**			
XX-04-001	Picnic Midge	J. Heap	Open	25.00	25.00
XX-04-002	Barrow Boy	J. Heap	Open	35.00	35.00
XX-04-003	Oliver	D. Roberts	Open	25.00	25.00
XX-04-004	Apple Barrel	D. Roberts	Retrd.	7.50	15.00
XX-04-005	Scrumpy	J. Heap	Open	35.00	35.00
XX-04-006	Picnic Island	J. Heap	Open	85.00	85.00
93-04-007	Vanilla	D. Roberts	Open	41.00	41.00
94-04-008	Pipkin	J. Heap	Open	50.00	50.00
PenDelfin		**Toy Shop Series**			
XX-05-001	Jacky	D. Roberts	Open	45.00	45.00
XX-05-002	The Toy Shop	D. Roberts	Open	325.00	325.00
PenDelfin		**Fisherman Series**			
XX-06-001	Whopper	D. Roberts	Open	35.00	35.00
XX-06-002	Jim-Lad	D. Roberts	Retrd.	22.50	45.00
XX-06-003	Little Mo	D. Roberts	Open	35.00	35.00
XX-06-004	The Raft	J. Heap	Open	70.00	70.00
XX-06-005	Shrimp Stand	D. Roberts	Open	70.00	70.00
XX-06-006	The Jetty	J. Heap	Open	180.00	180.00
PenDelfin		**Sport Series**			
XX-07-001	Birdie	J. Heap	Open	47.50	47.50
XX-07-002	Tennyson	D. Roberts	Open	35.00	35.00
XX-07-003	Humphrey Go-Kart	J. Heap	Open	70.00	70.00
XX-07-004	Rambler	D. Roberts	Open	65.00	65.00
XX-07-005	Scout	D. Roberts	Open	N/A	N/A
93-07-006	Campfire	D. Roberts	Open	30.00	30.00
PenDelfin		**School Series**			
XX-08-001	Boswell	J. Heap	Open	37.50	37.50
XX-08-002	Euclid	J. Heap	Open	35.00	35.00
XX-08-003	Digit	D. Roberts	Open	35.00	35.00
XX-08-004	Duffy	J. Heap	Open	50.00	50.00
XX-08-005	Old School House	J. Heap	Open	250.00	250.00
XX-08-006	Angelo	J. Heap	Open	90.00	90.00
XX-08-007	New Boy	D. Roberts	Open	50.00	50.00
XX-08-008	Wordsworth	D. Roberts	Retrd.	60.00	60.00
PenDelfin		**Various**			
XX-09-001	Dandy	D. Roberts	Open	50.00	50.00
XX-09-002	Barney	J. Heap	Open	18.00	18.00
XX-09-003	Honey	D. Roberts	Retrd.	40.00	40.00
XX-09-004	Charlotte	D. Roberts	Retrd.	25.00	50.00
XX-09-005	Butterfingers	D. Roberts	Open	55.00	55.00
XX-09-006	Scoffer	D. Roberts	Open	55.00	55.00
XX-09-007	Mother with baby	J. Heap	Open	150.00	150.00
55-09-008	Original Father	J. Heap	Retrd.	150.00	150.00
93-09-009	Cousin Beau	D. Roberts	Open	55.00	55.00
85-09-010	Christmas Set	D. Roberts	Retrd.	N/A	N/A
55-09-011	Daisy Duck	J. Leap	Retrd.	N/A	N/A
54-09-012	Fairy Jardiniere	N/A	Retrd.	N/A	N/A
PenDelfin		**Village Series**			
XX-10-001	Fruit Shop	J. Heap	Open	125.00	125.00
XX-10-002	Castle Tavern	D. Roberts	Open	120.00	120.00
XX-10-003	Caravan	D. Roberts	Open	350.00	350.00
XX-10-004	Large House	J. Heap	Open	275.00	275.00
XX-10-005	Cobble Cottage	D. Roberts	Open	80.00	80.00
XX-10-006	Curiosity Shop	J. Heap	Open	350.00	350.00
XX-10-007	Balcony Scene	D. Roberts	Open	175.00	175.00
XX-10-008	Grand Stand	J. Heap	Retrd.	150.00	150.00
53-10-009	The Fairy Shop	J. Heap	Retrd.	N/A	N/A
PenDelfin		**PenDelfin Family Circle Collectors' Club**			
93-11-001	Herald	J. Heap	Closed	30.00	30.00
94-11-002	Buttons	J. Heap	Yr.Iss.	Gift	N/A
94-11-003	Puffer	J. Heap	Yr.Iss.	85.00	85.00
PenDelfin		**Event Piece**			
94-12-001	Event Piece	J. Heap	3-Yr.	75.00	75.00
Polland Studios		**Collectible Bronzes**			
67-01-001	Bull Session	D. Polland	11	200.00	1200.00
69-01-002	Blowin' Cold	D. Polland	30	375.00	1250.00
69-01-003	The Breed	D. Polland	30	350.00	975.00
68-01-004	Buffalo Hunt	D. Polland	30	450.00	1250.00

		ARTIST	EDITION	ISSUE	QUOTE
69-01-005	Comanchero	D. Polland	30	350.00	750.00
69-01-006	Dancing Indian with Lance	D. Polland	50	250.00	775.00
69-01-007	Dancing Indian with Tomahawk	D. Polland	50	250.00	775.00
69-01-008	Dancing Medicine Man	D. Polland	50	250.00	775.00
69-01-009	Drawn Sabers	D. Polland	50	2000.00	5650.00
69-01-010	Lookouts	D. Polland	30	375.00	1300.00
69-01-011	Top Money	D. Polland	30	275.00	800.00
69-01-012	Trail Hazzard	D. Polland	30	700.00	1750.00
69-01-013	War Cry	D. Polland	30	350.00	975.00
69-01-014	When Enemies Meet	D. Polland	30	700.00	2350.00
70-01-015	Coffee Time	D. Polland	50	1200.00	2900.00
70-01-016	The Lost Dispatch	D. Polland	50	1200.00	2950.00
70-01-017	Wanted	D. Polland	50	500.00	1150.00
70-01-018	Dusted	D. Polland	50	400.00	1175.00
71-01-019	Ambush at Rock Canyon	D. Polland	5	20000.00	45000.00
71-01-020	Oh Sugar!	D. Polland	40	700.00	1525.00
71-01-021	Shakin' Out a Loop	D. Polland	40	500.00	1075.00
72-01-022	Buffalo Robe	D. Polland	50	1000.00	2350.00
73-01-023	Bunch Quitter	D. Polland	60	750.00	1975.00
73-01-024	Challenge	D. Polland	60	750.00	1800.00
73-01-025	War Party	D. Polland	60	1500.00	5500.00
73-01-026	Tracking	D. Polland	60	500.00	1150.00
75-01-027	Cheyenne	D. Polland	6	1300.00	1800.00
75-01-028	Counting Coup	D. Polland	6	1450.00	1950.00
75-01-029	Crow Scout	D. Polland	6	1300.00	1800.00
75-01-030	Buffalo Hunt	D. Polland	6	2200.00	3500.00
76-01-031	Rescue	D. Polland	6	2400.00	3000.00
76-01-032	Painting the Town	D. Polland	6	3000.00	4200.00
76-01-033	Monday Morning Wash	D. Polland	6	2800.00	2800.00
76-01-034	Mandan Hunter	D. Polland	12	775.00	775.00
80-01-035	Buffalo Prayer	D. Polland	25	375.00	675.00

Polland Studios — **Collector Society**

87-02-001	I Come In Peace	D. Polland	Closed	35.00	400-600.
87-02-002	Silent Trail	D. Polland	Closed	300.00	1300.00
87-02-003	I Come In Peace, Silent Trail-Matched Numbered Set	D. Polland	Closed	335.00	15-1895.
88-02-004	The Hunter	D. Polland	Closed	35.00	545.00
88-02-005	Disputed Trail	D. Polland	Closed	300.00	700-1045
88-02-006	The Hunter, Disputed Trail-Matched Numbered Set	D. Polland	Closed	335.00	11-1450.
89-02-007	Crazy Horse	D. Polland	Closed	35.00	300-470.
89-02-008	Apache Birdman	D. Polland	Closed	300.00	700-970.
89-02-009	Crazy Horse, Apache Birdman-Matched Numbered Set	D. Polland	Closed	335.00	13-1700.
90-02-010	Chief Pontiac	D. Polland	Closed	35.00	420.00
90-02-011	Buffalo Pony	D. Polland	Closed	300.00	600-800.
90-02-012	Chief Pontiac, Buffalo Pony-Matched Numbered Set	D. Polland	Closed	335.00	900-1350
91-02-013	War Drummer	D. Polland	Closed	35.00	330.00
91-02-014	The Signal	D. Polland	Closed	350.00	730.00
91-02-015	War Drummer, The Signal-Matched Numbered Set	D. Polland	Closed	385.00	900-1150
92-02-016	Cabinet Sign	D. Polland	Closed	35.00	125.00
92-02-017	Warrior's Farewell	D. Polland	Closed	350.00	400.00
92-02-018	Cabinet Sign, Warrior's Farewell-Matched Numbered Set	D. Polland	Closed	385.00	465.00
93-02-019	Mountain Man	D. Polland	Closed	35.00	125.00
93-02-020	Blue Bonnets & Yellow Ribbon	D. Polland	Closed	350.00	350-400.
93-02-021	Mountain Man, Blue Bonnets & Yellow Ribbon-Matched Numbered Set	D. Polland	Closed	385.00	385.00
94-02-022	The Wedding Robe	D. Polland	Yr.Iss.	45.00	45.00
94-02-023	The Courtship Race	D. Polland	Yr.Iss.	375.00	375.00
94-02-024	The Wedding Robe, The Courtside Race-Matched Numbered Set	D. Polland	Yr.Iss.	385.00	420.00

Possible Dreams® — **Clothtique® The Saturday Evening Post Norman Rockwell**

89-01-001	Dear Santa-3050	N. Rockwell	Closed	160.00	180.00
89-01-002	Santa with Globe-3051	N. Rockwell	Closed	154.00	175.00
90-01-003	Hobo-3052	N. Rockwell	Open	159.00	167.00
90-01-004	Love Letters-3053	N. Rockwell	Open	172.00	180.00
91-01-005	Gone Fishing-3054	N. Rockwell	Closed	250.00	263.00
91-01-006	Doctor and Doll-3055	N. Rockwell	Open	196.00	206.00
91-01-007	Springtime-3056	N. Rockwell	Open	130.00	137.00
91-01-008	The Gift-3057	N. Rockwell	Open	160.00	168.00
91-01-009	Gramps at the Reins-3058	N. Rockwell	Open	290.00	305.00
91-01-010	Man with Geese-3059	N. Rockwell	Open	120.00	126.00
91-01-011	Plotting His Course-3060	N. Rockwell	Open	160.00	168.00
92-01-012	Triple Self Portrait-3061	N. Rockwell	Open	230.00	242.00
92-01-013	Marriage License-3062	N. Rockwell	Open	195.00	205.00
92-01-014	Santa's Helpers-3063	N. Rockwell	Closed	170.00	179.00
92-01-015	Balancing the Budget-3064	N. Rockwell	Open	120.00	126.00

Possible Dreams® — **Clothtique® The Saturday Evening Post J.C. Leyendecker**

90-02-001	Traditional Santa-3600	J. Leyendecker	Closed	100.00	175.00
91-02-002	Hugging Santa-3599	J. Leyendecker	Closed	129.00	150.00
92-02-003	Santa on Ladder-3598	J. Leyendecker	Open	135.00	142.00

Possible Dreams® — **Clothtique® The American Artist Collection™**

91-03-001	Magic of Christmas-15001	L. Bywaters	Closed	132.00	139.00
91-03-002	A Peaceful Eve-15002	L. Bywaters	Closed	99.50	105.00
91-03-003	Alpine Christmas-15003	J. Brett	Closed	129.00	135.00
91-03-004	Traditions-15004	T. Blackshear	Closed	50.00	53.00
91-03-005	A Friendly Visit-15005	T. Browning	Closed	99.50	105.00
91-03-006	Santa's Cuisine-15006	T. Browning	Closed	138.00	145.50
91-03-007	Father Christmas-15007	J. Vaillancourt	Closed	59.50	63.00
92-03-008	An Angel's Kiss-15008	J. Griffith	Open	85.00	89.00
92-03-009	Peace on Earth-15009	M. Alvin	Open	87.50	92.00
92-03-010	Lighting the Way-15012	L. Bywaters	Open	85.00	89.00
92-03-011	Out of the Forest-15013	J. Vaillancourt	Open	60.00	63.00
92-03-012	Heralding the Way-15014	J. Griffith	Open	72.00	75.00
92-03-013	Music Makers-15010	T. Browning	Open	135.00	142.00
92-03-014	Santa in Rocking Chair-713090	M. Monteiro	Open	85.00	89.00
92-03-015	Christmas Company-15011	T. Browning	Open	77.00	77.00
93-03-016	Strumming the Lute-15015	M. Alvin	Open	79.00	83.00
93-03-017	Nature's Love-15016	M. Alvin	Open	75.00	79.00
93-03-018	Father Earth-15017	M. Monteiro	Open	77.00	80.00
93-03-019	Easy Putt-15018	T. Browning	Open	110.00	115.00
93-03-020	The Workshop-15019	T. Browning	Open	140.00	147.00
93-03-021	The Tree Planter-15020	J. Griffith	Open	79.50	84.00
93-03-022	A Beacon of Light-15022	J. Vaillancourt	Open	60.00	63.00
93-03-023	Just Scooting Along-15023	J. Vaillancourt	Open	79.50	83.00
93-03-024	A Brighter Day-15024	J. St. Denis	Open	67.50	70.00
93-03-025	Ice Capers-15025	T. Browning	Open	99.50	105.00
94-03-026	And Feathered Friend-15026	D. Wenzel	Open	84.00	84.00
94-03-027	A Touch of Magic-15027	T. Browning	Open	95.00	95.00
94-03-028	Spirit of Santa-15028	T. Browning	Open	68.00	68.00
94-03-029	Captain Claus-15030	M. Monteiro	Open	77.00	77.00
94-03-030	The Gentle Craftsman-15031	J. Griffith	Open	81.00	81.00
94-03-031	Gifts from the Garden-15032	J. Griffith	Open	77.00	77.00
94-03-032	Chrstmas Surprise-15033	M. Alvin	Open	88.00	88.00
94-03-033	Tea Time-15034	M. Alvin	Open	90.00	90.00
94-03-034	Spirit of Christmas Past-15036	J. Vaillancourt	Open	79.00	79.00
94-03-035	Teddy Love-15037	J. Griffith	Open	89.00	89.00

Possible Dreams® — **Clothtique® Limited Edition Santas**

88-04-001	Patriotic Santa-3000	Unknown	Closed	240.00	240.00
88-04-002	Father Christmas-3001	Unknown	Closed	240.00	240.00
88-04-003	Kris Kringle-3002	Unknown	Closed	240.00	240.00
89-04-004	Traditional Santa 40's-3003	Unknown	Closed	240.00	252.00

Possible Dreams® — **Clothtique® Pepsi® Santa Collection**

90-05-001	Pepsi Cola Santa 1940's-3601	Unknown	Open	68.00	74.00
91-05-002	Rockwell Pepsi Santa 1952-3602	N. Rockwell	Closed	75.00	82.00
92-05-003	Pepsi Santa Sitting-3603	Unknown	Closed	84.00	88.00
94-05-004	Pepsi Holiday Host-3605	Unknown	Open	62.00	62.00

Possible Dreams® — **Clothtique® Santas Collection**

87-06-001	Traditional Santa-713028	Unknown	Closed	34.50	34.50
87-06-002	Ukko-713031	Unknown	Closed	38.00	38.00
87-06-003	Colonial Santa-713032	Unknown	Closed	38.00	39.50
87-06-004	Christmas Man-713027	Unknown	Closed	34.50	34.50
87-06-005	Santa with Pack-713026	Unknown	Closed	34.50	34.50
87-06-006	Traditional Deluxe Santa-713030	Unknown	Closed	38.00	38.00
88-06-007	Frontier Santa-713034	Unknown	Closed	40.00	42.00
88-06-008	St. Nicholas-713035	Unknown	Closed	40.00	42.00
88-06-009	Weihnachtsman-713037	Unknown	Closed	40.00	43.00
88-06-010	Carpenter Santa-713033	Unknown	Closed	38.00	44.00
88-06-011	Russian St. Nicholas-713036	Unknown	Open	40.00	43.00
89-06-012	Traditional Santa-713038	Unknown	Closed	42.00	43.00
89-06-013	Pelze Nichol-713039	Unknown	Closed	40.00	47.00
89-06-014	Mrs. Claus w/doll-713041	Unknown	Closed	42.00	43.00
89-06-015	Baby's First Christmas-713042	Unknown	Closed	42.00	46.00
89-06-016	Exhausted Santa-713043	Unknown	Closed	60.00	65.00
89-06-017	Santa with Embroidered Coat-713040	Unknown	Closed	43.00	43.00
90-06-018	Workbench Santa-713044	Unknown	Closed	72.00	75.50
90-06-019	Santa "Please Stop Here"-713045	Unknown	Closed	63.00	66.00
90-06-020	Harlem Santa-713046	Unknown	Closed	46.00	55.00
90-06-021	Santa Skiing-713047	Unknown	Closed	62.00	65.00
90-06-022	Santa With Blue Robe-713048	Unknown	Closed	46.00	50.00
91-06-023	The True Spirit of Christmas-713075	Unknown	Closed	97.00	97.00
91-06-024	Santa in Bed-713076	Unknown	Closed	76.00	83.00
91-06-025	Siberian Santa-713077	Unknown	Closed	49.00	51.50
91-06-026	Mrs. Claus in Coat -713078	Unknown	Open	47.00	52.00
91-06-027	Decorating the Tree-713079	Unknown	Closed	60.00	60.00
91-06-028	Father Christmas-713087	Unknown	Open	43.00	47.00
91-06-029	Kris Kringle-713088	Unknown	Closed	43.00	45.20
91-06-030	Santa Shelf Sitter-713089	Unknown	Open	55.50	60.00
92-06-031	1940's Traditional Santa-713049	Unknown	Closed	44.00	46.00
92-06-032	Santa on Sled-713050	Unknown	Closed	75.00	79.00
92-06-033	Nicholas-713052	Unknown	Open	57.50	60.00
92-06-034	Fireman Santa-713053	Unknown	Open	60.00	63.00
92-06-035	African American Santa-713056	Unknown	Open	65.00	68.00
92-06-036	Engineer Santa-713057	Unknown	Open	130.00	137.00
92-06-037	Santa on Reindeer-713058	Unknown	Open	75.00	83.00
92-06-038	Santa on Sleigh-713091	Unknown	Open	79.00	83.00
92-06-039	Santa on Motorbike-713054	Unknown	Closed	115.00	120.00
93-06-040	European Santa-713095	Unknown	Open	53.00	55.00
93-06-041	May Your Wishes Come True-713096	Unknown	Open	59.00	62.00
93-06-042	Victorian Santa-713097	Unknown	Open	55.50	58.00
93-06-043	His Favorite Color-713098	Unknown	Open	48.00	50.00
93-06-044	Santa w/Groceries-713099	Unknown	Open	47.50	50.00
93-06-045	Afro Santa & Doll-713102	Unknown	Open	40.00	42.00
93-06-046	The Modern Shopper-713103	Unknown	Open	40.00	42.00
93-06-047	Nigel as Santa-713427	Unknown	Open	53.50	56.00
93-06-048	A Long Trip-713105	A. Gilberts	Open	95.00	100.00
93-06-049	Fireman & Child-713106	Unknown	Open	55.00	58.00
94-06-050	Good Tidings-713107	Unknown	Open	51.00	51.00
94-06-051	Yuletide Journey-713108	Unknown	Open	58.00	58.00
94-06-052	Christmas Cheer-713109	Unknown	Open	58.00	58.00
94-06-053	Holiday Friend-713110	Unknown	Open	104.00	104.00
94-06-054	Playmates-713111	Unknown	Open	104.00	104.00
94-06-055	A Christmas Guest-713112	Unknown	Open	79.00	79.00
94-06-056	Welcome Visitor-713113	Unknown	Open	63.00	63.00
94-06-057	A Welcome Visit-713114	Unknown	Open	62.00	62.00
94-06-058	Christmas is for Children-713115	Unknown	Open	62.00	62.00
94-06-059	Our Hero-713116	Unknown	Open	62.00	62.00
94-06-060	Puppy Love-713117	Unknown	Open	62.00	62.00
94-06-061	Mrs. Claus-713118	Unknown	Open	58.00	58.00

Possible Dreams® — **The Citizens of Londonshire®**

92-07-001	Beth-713417	Unknown	Open	35.00	37.00
92-07-002	Albert-713426	Unknown	Open	65.00	68.00
89-07-003	Lady Ashley-713405	Unknown	Open	65.00	68.00
89-07-004	Lord Winston of Riverside-713403	Unknown	Open	65.00	68.00
89-07-005	Sir Robert-713401	Unknown	Open	65.00	68.00
89-07-006	Rodney-713404	Unknown	Open	65.00	68.00
90-07-007	Dr. Isaac-713409	Unknown	Closed	65.00	68.00
90-07-008	Admiral Waldo-713407	Unknown	Open	65.00	68.00
91-07-009	Sir Red-713415	Unknown	Open	72.00	76.00
91-07-010	Bernie-713414	Unknown	Open	68.00	71.00
92-07-011	Tiffany Sorbet-713416	Unknown	Open	65.00	68.00
90-07-012	Margaret of Foxcroft-713408	Unknown	Open	65.00	68.00
90-07-013	Officer Kevin-713406	Unknown	Open	65.00	68.00
89-07-014	Lord Nicholas-713402	Unknown	Open	72.00	76.00
92-07-015	Countess of Hamlett-713419	Unknown	Open	65.00	68.00
89-07-016	Earl of Hamlett-713400	Unknown	Closed	65.00	68.00
92-07-017	Rebecca-713424	Unknown	Open	35.00	37.00
90-07-018	Dianne-713413	Unknown	Open	33.00	35.00
90-07-019	Phillip-713412	Unknown	Open	33.00	35.00
90-07-020	Walter-713410	Unknown	Closed	33.00	35.00
90-07-021	Wendy-713411	Unknown	Open	33.00	35.00
92-07-022	Jean Claude-713421	Unknown	Open	35.00	37.00
92-07-023	Nicole-713420	Unknown	Open	35.00	37.00
92-07-024	David-713423	Unknown	Open	37.50	39.00
92-07-025	Debbie-713422	Unknown	Open	37.50	39.00

	ARTIST	EDITION	ISSUE	QUOTE
92-07-026 Christopher-713418	Unknown	Open	35.00	37.00
92-07-027 Richard-713425	Unknown	Open	35.00	37.00
93-07-028 Nigel As Santa-713427	Unknown	Open	53.50	56.00
94-07-029 Maggie-713428	Unknown	Open	60.00	60.00
Possible Dreams®	**Santa Claus Network® Collectors Club**			
92-08-001 The Gift Giver-805001	Unknown	Closed	Gift	40.00
92-08-002 Santa's Special Friend-805050	Unknown	Closed	59.00	59.00
93-08-003 Special Delivery-805002	Unknown	Closed	Gift	N/A
94-08-004 On a Winter's Eve-805051	Unknown	Yr. Iss.	65.00	65.00
94-08-005 Jolly St. Nick-805003	Unknown	7/95	Gift	N/A
Possible Dreams®	**The Thickets at Sweetbriar™**			
93-09-001 Maude Tweedy-350100	B. Ross	Open	26.25	26.25
93-09-002 Clovis Buttons-350101	B. Ross	Open	24.15	24.15
93-09-003 Peablossom Thorndike-350102	B. Ross	Open	26.25	26.25
93-09-004 Orchid Beasley-350103	B. Ross	Open	26.25	26.25
93-09-005 Morning Glory-350104	B. Ross	Open	30.45	30.45
93-09-006 Lily Blossom-350105	B. Ross	Open	36.75	36.75
93-09-007 Jewel Blossom-350106	B. Ross	Open	36.75	36.75
93-09-008 Rose Blossom-350107	B. Ross	Open	36.75	36.75
93-09-009 Raindrop-350108	B. Ross	Open	47.25	47.25
93-09-010 Mr. Claws-350109	B. Ross	Open	34.00	34.00
93-09-011 Mrs. Claws-350110	B. Ross	Open	34.00	34.00
93-09-012 The Groom-Oliver Doone-350111	B. Ross	Open	30.00	30.00
93-09-013 The Bride-Emily Feathers-350112	B. Ross	Open	30.00	30.00
94-09-014 Morning Dew-350113	B. Ross	Open	30.00	30.00
94-09-015 Sweetie Flowers-350114	B. Ross	Open	33.00	33.00
94-09-016 Precious Petals-350115	B. Ross	Open	34.00	34.00
94-09-017 Lady Slipper-350116	B. Ross	Open	20.00	20.00
94-09-018 Sunshine-350118	B. Ross	Open	33.00	33.00
Precious Art/Panton	**World of Krystonia**			
80-01-001 Gateway to Kystonia-3301	Panton	Retrd.	35.00	45.00
87-01-002 Small Graffyn/Grunch -1012	Panton	Retrd.	45.00	110-250.
87-01-003 Owhey -1071	Panton	Retrd.	32.00	100-176.
87-01-004 Small N'Borg -1091	Panton	Retrd.	50.00	375.00
87-01-005 Large N'Borg -1092	Panton	Retrd.	98.00	98.00
87-01-006 Large Rueggan -1701	Panton	Retrd.	55.00	200-400.
87-01-007 Medium Stoope -1101	Panton	Retrd.	52.00	250.00
87-01-008 Small Shepf -1152	Panton	Retrd.	40.00	200.00
87-01-009 Large Wodema -1301	Panton	Retrd.	50.00	100-350.
87-01-010 Large Krak N'Borg -3001	Panton	Retrd.	240.00	735.00
87-01-011 Large Moplos -1021	Panton	Retrd.	90.00	205-400.
87-01-012 Large Myzer -1201	Panton	Retrd.	50.00	66-250.
87-01-013 Large Turfen -1601	Panton	Retrd.	50.00	100-250.
87-01-014 Large Haapf -1901	Panton	Retrd.	38.00	100-200.
87-01-015 Small Groc -1042B	Panton	Retrd.	24.00	4600.00
87-01-016 Large Graffyn on Grumblypeg Grunch -1011	Panton	Retrd.	52.00	165.00
87-01-017 Grumblypeg Grunch -1081	Panton	Retrd.	52.00	200.00
87-01-018 Spyke -1061	Panton	Retrd.	50.00	72.00
87-01-019 Medium Wodema -1302	Panton	Retrd.	44.00	66.00
87-01-020 Small N' Tormett -2602	Panton	Retrd.	44.00	50.00
87-01-021 Small Krak N' Borg -3003	Panton	Retrd.	60.00	140.00
88-01-022 Medium Rueggan -1702	Panton	Retrd.	48.00	66.00
88-01-023 Large N'Grall -2201	Panton	Retrd.	108.00	400.00
88-01-024 Medium N'Grall -2202	Panton	Retrd.	70.00	70.00
88-01-025 Small Tulan Captain -2502	Panton	Retrd.	44.00	100-175.
88-01-026 Tarnhold-Med. -3202	Panton	Retrd.	120.00	280.00
89-01-027 Kephren -2702	Panton	Retrd.	56.00	65.00
89-01-028 Caught At Last! -1107	Panton	Retrd.	150.00	225-350.
89-01-029 Stoope (waterglobe) -9003	Panton	Retrd.	40.00	156.00
89-01-030 Graffyn on Grunch (waterglobe) -9006	Panton	Retrd.	42.00	78.00
89-01-031 Krystonia Sign -701	Panton	Retrd.	N/A	25.00
90-01-032 N'Chakk-Mini -607	Panton	Retrd.	29.00	29.00
90-01-033 Shadra -3411	Panton	Retrd.	30.00	30.00
90-01-034 Owhey (waterglobe) -9004	Panton	Retrd.	42.00	42.00
91-01-035 Maj-Dron Migration -1108	Panton	Retrd.	145.00	145.00
91-01-036 N'Borg-Mini -609	Panton	Retrd.	29.00	29.00
91-01-037 Large Grunch's Toothache -1082	Panton	Retrd.	76.00	76.00
92-01-038 Zanzibar -3431	Panton	Retrd.	45.00	45.00
92-01-039 N' Leila-3801	Panton	Retrd.	60.00	65.00
Precious Art/Panton	**Krystonia Collector's Club**			
89-02-001 Pultzr	Panton	Retrd.	55.00	225.00
89-02-002 Key	Panton	Retrd.	Gift	100-130.
91-02-003 Dragons Play	Panton	Retrd.	65.00	170-200.
91-02-004 Kephrens Chest	Panton	Retrd.	Gift	130.00
92-02-005 Vaaston	Panton	Retrd.	65.00	155-200.
92-02-006 Lantern	Panton	Retrd.	Gift	80-100.
93-02-007 Sneaking A Peek	Panton	Retrd.	Gift	N/A
93-02-008 Spreading His Wings	Panton	Retrd.	60.00	100-105
94-02-009 All Tuckered Out	Panton	Yr.Iss.	65.00	65.00
94-02-010 Fill-Er-Up	Panton	Yr.Iss.	Gift	N/A
Princeton Gallery	**Unicorn Collection**			
90-01-001 Love's Delight	Unknown	Open	75.00	75.00
90-01-002 Love's Sweetness	Unknown	Open	75.00	75.00
91-01-003 Love's Devotion	Unknown	Open	119.00	119.00
91-01-004 Love's Purity	Unknown	Open	95.00	95.00
91-01-005 Love's Majesty	Unknown	Open	95.00	95.00
91-01-006 Christmas Unicorn	Unknown	Yr.Iss.	85.00	85.00
92-01-007 Love's Fancy	Unknown	Open	95.00	95.00
93-01-008 Love's Courtship	Unknown	Open	95.00	95.00
Princeton Gallery	**Playful Pups**			
90-02-001 Dalmation-Where's The Fire	Unknown	Open	19.50	19.50
90-02-002 Beagle	Unknown	Open	19.50	19.50
91-02-003 St. Bernard	Unknown	Open	19.50	19.50
91-02-004 Labrador Retriever	Unknown	Open	19.50	19.50
91-02-005 Wrinkles (Shar Pei)	Unknown	Open	19.50	19.50
Princeton Gallery	**Garden Capers**			
90-03-001 Any Mail?	Unknown	Open	29.50	29.50
91-03-002 Blue Jays	Unknown	Open	29.50	29.50
91-03-003 Robin	Unknown	Open	29.50	29.50
92-03-004 Goldfinch, Home Sweet Home	Unknown	Open	29.50	29.50
92-03-005 Bluebird, Spring Planting	Unknown	Open	29.50	29.50
Princeton Gallery	**Baby bird Trios**			
91-04-001 Woodland Symphony (Bluebirds)	Unknown	Open	45.00	45.00
91-04-002 Cardinals	Unknown	Open	45.00	45.00

	ARTIST	EDITION	ISSUE	QUOTE
Princeton Gallery	**Pegasus**			
92-05-001 Wings of Magic	Unknown	Open	95.00	95.00
Princeton Gallery	**Enchanted Nursery**			
92-06-001 Caprice	Unknown	Open	57.00	57.00
93-06-002 Pegasus	Unknown	Open	57.00	57.00
Princeton Gallery	**Lady And The Unicorn**			
92-07-001 Love's Innocence	Unknown	Open	119.00	119.00
Rawcliffe Corporation	**Garden Fairies™**			
93-01-001 The Fairy Slipper	J. deStefano	4,500	115.00	115.00
93-01-002 The Dream Fairy	J. deStefano	4,500	115.00	115.00
93-01-003 The Dew Fairy	J. deStefano	4,500	115.00	115.00
93-01-004 The Illusive Fairy	J. deStefano	4,500	115.00	115.00
Rawcliffe Corporation	**Baby Bubble Fairies™**			
92-02-001 Turquoise-January	J. deStefano	6,700	70.00	70.00
92-02-002 Magenta-February	J. deStefano	6,700	70.00	70.00
92-02-003 Blush-March	J. deStefano	6,700	70.00	70.00
92-02-004 Chartreuse-April	J. deStefano	6,700	70.00	70.00
92-02-005 Violet-May	J. deStefano	6,700	70.00	70.00
92-02-006 Coral-June	J. deStefano	6,700	70.00	70.00
92-02-007 Saffron-July	J. deStefano	6,700	70.00	70.00
92-02-008 Azure-August	J. deStefano	6,700	70.00	70.00
92-02-009 Lavender-September	J. deStefano	6,700	70.00	70.00
92-02-010 Amber-October	J. deStefano	6,700	70.00	70.00
92-02-011 Vermilion-November	J. deStefano	6,700	70.00	70.00
92-02-012 Emerald-December	J. deStefano	6,700	70.00	70.00
Rawcliffe Corporation	**Four Seasons Fairies™**			
91-03-001 Snow-Winter	J. deStefano	9,500	95.00	95.00
91-03-002 Petal-Spring	J. deStefano	9,500	95.00	95.00
91-03-003 Aria-Summer	J. deStefano	9,500	95.00	95.00
91-03-004 Harvest-Fall	J. deStefano	9,500	95.00	95.00
Rawcliffe Corporation	**Original Bubble Fairy™ Collection**			
88-04-001 Luna	J. deStefano	Open	145.00	145.00
88-04-002 Meadow	J. deStefano	Retrd.	145.00	145.00
88-04-003 Mist	J. deStefano	Retrd.	145.00	145.00
88-04-004 Sky	J. deStefano	Open	145.00	145.00
88-04-005 Bliss	J. deStefano	Open	85.00	85.00
88-04-006 Breeze	J. deStefano	Retrd.	85.00	85.00
88-04-007 Echo	J. deStefano	Open	85.00	85.00
88-04-008 Twilight	J. deStefano	Open	85.00	85.00
88-04-009 Whisper	J. deStefano	Open	85.00	85.00
88-04-010 Wishes	J. deStefano	Retrd.	85.00	85.00
88-04-011 Nimbus	J. deStefano	Retrd.	85.00	85.00
88-04-012 Sunbeam	J. deStefano	Retrd.	85.00	85.00
Rawcliffe Corporation	**Wish Fairy™ Collection**			
94-05-001 Fun	J. deStefano	Open	30.00	30.00
94-05-002 Dreams	J. deStefano	Open	30.00	30.00
94-05-003 Happiness	J. deStefano	Open	30.00	30.00
94-05-004 Rainbows	J. deStefano	Open	30.00	30.00
94-05-005 Love	J. deStefano	Open	30.00	30.00
94-05-006 Good Fortune	J. deStefano	Open	30.00	30.00
94-05-007 Health	J. deStefano	Open	30.00	30.00
94-05-008 Good Luck	J. deStefano	Open	30.00	30.00
94-05-009 Friendship	J. deStefano	Open	30.00	30.00
94-05-010 Success	J. deStefano	Open	30.00	30.00
94-05-011 Sunshine	J. deStefano	Open	30.00	30.00
94-05-012 Laughter	J. deStefano	Open	30.00	30.00
Rawcliffe Corporation	**Star Trek™ Starships**			
93-06-001 USS Enterprise RF797 (The Next Generation)	M. Schwabe	15,000	100.00	100.00
Rawcliffe Corporation	**Star Wars™ Starships**			
93-07-001 Darth Vader Tie Fighter Ship RF950	M. Schwabe	15,000	135.00	135.00
93-07-002 Millenium Falcon RF951	M. Schwabe	15,000	115.00	115.00
93-07-003 X-Wing Fighter RF952	M. Schwabe	15,000	95.00	95.00
Reco International	**Grangét Crystal Sculpture**			
73-01-001 Long Earred Owl, Asio Otus	G. Granget	Retrd.	2250.00	2250.00
XX-01-002 Ruffed Grouse	G. Granget	Retrd.	1000.00	1000.00
Reco International	**Porcelains in Miniature by John McClelland**			
XX-02-001 John	J. McClelland	10,000	34.50	34.50
XX-02-002 Alice	J. McClelland	10,000	34.50	34.50
XX-02-003 Chimney Sweep	J. McClelland	10,000	34.50	34.50
XX-02-004 Dressing Up	J. McClelland	10,000	34.50	34.50
XX-02-005 Autumn Dreams	J. McClelland	Open	29.50	29.50
XX-02-006 Tuck-Me-In	J. McClelland	Open	29.50	29.50
XX-02-007 Country Lass	J. McClelland	Open	29.50	29.50
XX-02-008 Sudsie Suzie	J. McClelland	Open	29.50	29.50
XX-02-009 Smooth Smailing	J. McClelland	Open	29.50	29.50
XX-02-010 The Clown	J. McClelland	Open	29.50	29.50
XX-02-011 The Baker	J. McClelland	Open	29.50	29.50
XX-02-012 Quiet Moments	J. McClelland	Open	29.50	29.50
XX-02-013 The Farmer	J. McClelland	Open	29.50	29.50
XX-02-014 The Nurse	J. McClelland	Open	29.50	29.50
XX-02-015 The Policeman	J. McClelland	Open	29.50	29.50
XX-02-016 The Fireman	J. McClelland	Open	29.50	29.50
XX-02-017 Winter Fun	J. McClelland	Open	29.50	29.50
XX-02-018 Cowgirl	J. McClelland	Open	29.50	29.50
XX-02-019 Cowboy	J. McClelland	Open	29.50	29.50
XX-02-020 Doc	J. McClelland	Open	29.50	29.50
XX-02-021 Lawyer	J. McClelland	Open	29.50	29.50
XX-02-022 Farmer's Wife	J. McClelland	Open	29.50	29.50
XX-02-023 First Outing	J. McClelland	Open	29.50	29.50
XX-02-024 Club Pro	J. McClelland	Open	29.50	29.50
XX-02-025 Batter Up	J. McClelland	Retrd.	29.50	29.50
XX-02-026 Love 40	J. McClelland	Open	29.50	29.50
XX-02-027 The Painter	J. McClelland	Open	29.50	29.50
XX-02-028 Special Delivery	J. McClelland	Open	29.50	29.50
XX-02-029 Center Ice	J. McClelland	Open	29.50	29.50
XX-02-030 First Solo	J. McClelland	Open	29.50	29.50
XX-02-031 Highland Fling	J. McClelland	7,500	34.50	34.50
XX-02-032 Cheerleader	J. McClelland	Open	29.50	29.50
Reco International	**The Reco Clown Collection**			
85-03-001 Whoopie	J. McClelland	Open	12.00	13.00
85-03-002 The Professor	J. McClelland	Open	12.00	13.00
85-03-003 Top Hat	J. McClelland	Open	12.00	13.00

		ARTIST	EDITION	ISSUE	QUOTE
85-03-004	Winkie	J. McClelland	Retrd.	12.00	13.00
85-03-005	Scamp	J. McClelland	Open	12.00	13.00
85-03-006	Curly	J. McClelland	Open	12.00	13.00
85-03-007	Bow Jangles	J. McClelland	Open	12.00	13.00
85-03-008	Sparkles	J. McClelland	Open	12.00	13.00
85-03-009	Ruffles	J. McClelland	Open	12.00	13.00
85-03-010	Arabesque	J. McClelland	Open	12.00	13.00
85-03-011	Hobo	J. McClelland	Open	12.00	13.00
85-03-012	Sad Eyes	J. McClelland	Open	12.00	13.00
87-03-013	Love	J. McClelland	Open	12.00	13.00
87-03-014	Mr. Big	J. McClelland	Open	12.00	13.00
87-03-015	Twinkle	J. McClelland	Open	12.00	13.00
87-03-016	Disco Dan	J. McClelland	Open	12.00	13.00
87-03-017	Smiley	J. McClelland	Open	12.00	13.00
87-03-018	The Joker	J. McClelland	Open	12.00	13.00
87-03-019	Jolly Joe	J. McClelland	Open	12.00	13.00
87-03-020	Zany Jack	J. McClelland	Open	12.00	13.00
87-03-021	Domino	J. McClelland	Open	12.00	13.00
87-03-022	Happy George	J. McClelland	Open	12.00	13.00
87-03-023	Tramp	J. McClelland	Open	12.00	13.00
87-03-024	Wistful	J. McClelland	Open	12.00	13.00
Reco International		**The Reco Angel Collection**			
86-04-001	Innocence	J. McClelland	Open	12.00	12.00
86-04-002	Harmony	J. McClelland	Open	12.00	12.00
86-04-003	Love	J. McClelland	Open	12.00	12.00
86-04-004	Gloria	J. McClelland	Open	12.00	12.00
86-04-005	Praise	J. McClelland	Open	20.00	20.00
86-04-006	Devotion	J. McClelland	Open	15.00	15.00
86-04-007	Faith	J. McClelland	Open	24.00	24.00
86-04-008	Joy	J. McClelland	Open	15.00	15.00
86-04-009	Adoration	J. McClelland	Open	24.00	24.00
86-04-010	Peace	J. McClelland	Open	24.00	24.00
86-04-011	Serenity	J. McClelland	Open	24.00	24.00
86-04-012	Hope	J. McClelland	Open	24.00	24.00
88-04-013	Reverence	J. McClelland	Open	12.00	12.00
88-04-014	Minstral	J. McClelland	Open	12.00	12.00
Reco International		**Sophisticated Ladies Figurines**			
87-05-001	Felicia	A. Fazio	Retrd.	29.50	32.50
87-05-002	Samantha	A. Fazio	Retrd.	29.50	32.50
87-05-003	Phoebe	A. Fazio	Retrd.	29.50	32.50
87-05-004	Cleo	A. Fazio	Retrd.	29.50	32.50
87-05-005	Cerissa	A. Fazio	Retrd.	29.50	32.50
87-05-006	Natasha	A. Fazio	Retrd.	29.50	32.50
87-05-007	Bianka	A. Fazio	Retrd.	29.50	32.50
87-05-008	Chelsea	A. Fazio	Retrd.	29.50	32.50
Reco International		**Clown Figurines by John McClelland**			
87-06-001	Mr. Tip	J. McClelland	9,500	35.00	35.00
87-06-002	Mr. Cure-All	J. McClelland	9,500	35.00	35.00
87-06-003	Mr. One-Note	J. McClelland	9,500	35.00	35.00
87-06-004	Mr. Lovable	J. McClelland	9,500	35.00	35.00
88-06-005	Mr. Magic	J. McClelland	9,500	35.00	35.00
88-06-006	Mr. Cool	J. McClelland	9,500	35.00	35.00
88-06-007	Mr. Heart-Throb	J. McClelland	9,500	35.00	35.00
Reco International		**The Reco Angel Collection Miniatures**			
87-07-001	Innocence	J. McClelland	Retrd.	7.50	7.50
87-07-002	Harmony	J. McClelland	Retrd.	7.50	7.50
87-07-003	Love	J. McClelland	Retrd.	7.50	7.50
87-07-004	Gloria	J. McClelland	Open	7.50	7.50
87-07-005	Devotion	J. McClelland	Open	7.50	7.50
87-07-006	Joy	J. McClelland	Open	7.50	7.50
87-07-007	Adoration	J. McClelland	Open	10.00	10.00
87-07-008	Peace	J. McClelland	Retrd.	10.00	10.00
87-07-009	Serenity	J. McClelland	Retrd.	10.00	10.00
87-07-010	Hope	J. McClelland	Open	10.00	10.00
87-07-011	Praise	J. McClelland	Retrd.	10.00	10.00
87-07-012	Faith	J. McClelland	Open	10.00	10.00
Reco International		**Faces of Love**			
88-08-001	Cuddles	J. McClelland	Open	29.50	32.50
88-08-002	Sunshine	J. McClelland	Open	29.50	32.50
Reco International		**Reco Creche Collection**			
87-09-001	Holy Family (3 Pieces)	J. McClelland	Open	49.00	49.00
87-09-002	Lamb	J. McClelland	Open	9.50	9.50
87-09-003	Shepherd-Kneeling	J. McClelland	Open	22.50	22.50
87-09-004	Shepherd-Standing	J. McClelland	Open	22.50	22.50
88-09-005	King/Frankincense	J. McClelland	Open	22.50	22.50
88-09-006	King/Myrrh	J. McClelland	Open	22.50	22.50
88-09-007	King/Gold	J. McClelland	Open	22.50	22.50
88-09-008	Donkey	J. McClelland	Open	16.50	16.50
88-09-009	Cow	J. McClelland	Open	15.00	15.00
Reco International		**The Reco Collection Clown Busts**			
88-10-001	Hobo	J. McClelland	5,000	40.00	40.00
88-10-002	Love	J. McClelland	5,000	40.00	40.00
88-10-003	Sparkles	J. McClelland	5,000	40.00	40.00
88-10-004	Bow Jangles	J. McClelland	5,000	40.00	40.00
88-10-005	Domino	J. McClelland	5,000	40.00	40.00
Reco International		**Wedding Gifts**			
91-11-001	Cake Topper Bride & Groom	J. McClelland	Open	35.00	35.00
91-11-002	Bride & Groom- Musical	J. McClelland	Open	90.00	90.00
91-11-003	Bride-Blond-Musical	J. McClelland	Open	80.00	80.00
91-11-004	Bride-Brunette-Musical	J. McClelland	Open	80.00	80.00
91-11-005	Bride & Groom	J. McClelland	Open	85.00	85.00
91-11-006	Bride-Blond	J. McClelland	Open	60.00	60.00
91-11-007	Bride-Brunette	J. McClelland	Open	60.00	60.00
Rhodes Studio		**Rockwell's Main Street**			
90-01-001	Rockwell's Studio	Rockwell-Inspired	150-day	28.00	85.00
90-01-002	The Antique Shop	Rockwell-Inspired	150-day	28.00	150.00
90-01-003	The Town Offices	Rockwell-Inspired	150-day	32.00	36.00
90-01-004	The Country Store	Rockwell-Inspired	150-day	32.00	36.00
91-01-005	The Library	Rockwell-Inspired	150-day	36.00	36.00
91-01-006	The Bank	Rockwell-Inspired	150-day	36.00	36.00
91-01-007	Red Lion Inn	Rockwell-Inspired	150-day	39.00	39.00
Rhodes Studio		**Rockwell's Hometown**			
91-02-001	Rockwell's Residence	Rhodes	Closed	34.95	34.95
91-02-002	Greystone Church	Rhodes	Closed	34.95	34.95
91-02-003	Bell Tower	Rockwell-Inspired	Closed	36.95	36.95
91-02-004	Firehouse	Rockwell-Inspired	Closed	36.95	36.95
91-02-005	Church On The Green	Rockwell-Inspired	Closed	39.95	39.95
92-02-006	Town Hall	Rockwell-Inspired	Closed	39.95	39.95
92-02-007	Citizen's Hall	Rockwell-Inspired	Closed	42.95	42.95
92-02-008	The Berkshire Playhouse	Rockwell-Inspired	Closed	42.95	42.95
92-02-009	Mission House	Rockwell-Inspired	Closed	42.95	42.95
92-02-010	Old Corner House	Rockwell-Inspired	12/94	42.95	42.95
Rhodes Studio		**Rockwell's Heirloom Santa Collection**			
90-03-001	Santa's Workshop	Rockwell-Inspired	150-day	49.95	49.95
91-03-002	Christmas Dream	Rockwell-Inspired	150-day	49.95	49.95
92-03-003	Making His List	Rockwell-Inspired	Closed	49.95	49.95
Rhodes Studio		**Rockwell's Age of Wonder**			
91-04-001	Splish Splash	Rockwell-Inspired	Closed	34.95	34.95
91-04-002	Hush-A-Bye	Rockwell-Inspired	Closed	34.95	34.95
91-04-003	Stand by Me	Rockwell-Inspired	Closed	36.95	36.95
91-04-004	School Days	Rockwell-Inspired	Closed	36.95	36.95
91-04-005	Summertime	Rockwell-Inspired	Closed	39.95	39.95
92-04-006	The Birthday Party	Rockwell-Inspired	Closed	39.95	39.95
Rhodes Studio		**Rockwell's Beautiful Dreamers**			
91-05-001	Sitting Pretty	Rockwell-Inspired	Closed	37.95	37.95
91-05-002	Dear Diary	Rockwell-Inspired	Closed	37.95	37.95
91-05-003	Secret Sonnets	Rockwell-Inspired	Closed	39.95	39.95
91-05-004	Springtime Serenade	Rockwell-Inspired	Closed	39.95	39.95
92-05-005	Debutante's Dance	Rockwell-Inspired	Closed	42.95	42.95
92-05-006	Walk in the Park	Rockwell-Inspired	Closed	42.95	42.95
Rhodes Studio		**Rockwell's Gems of Wisdom**			
91-06-001	Love Cures All	Rockwell-Inspired	Closed	39.95	39.95
91-06-002	Practice Makes Perfect	Rockwell-Inspired	Closed	39.95	39.95
91-06-003	A Stitch In Time	Rockwell-Inspired	Closed	42.95	42.95
River Shore		**Rockwell Single Issues**			
81-01-001	Looking Out To Sea	N. Rockwell	9,500	85.00	225.00
82-01-002	Grandpa's Guardian	N. Rockwell	9,500	125.00	125.00
Roman, Inc.		**Fontanini, The Collectible Creche**			
73-01-001	10cm., (15 piece Set)	E. Simonetti	Closed	63.60	88.50
73-01-002	12cm., (15 piece Set)	E. Simonetti	Closed	76.50	102.00
79-01-003	16cm., (15 piece Set)	E. Simonetti	Closed	178.50	285.00
82-01-004	17cm., (15 piece Set)	E. Simonetti	Closed	189.00	305.00
73-01-005	19cm., (15 piece Set)	E. Simonetti	Closed	175.50	280.00
80-01-006	30cm., (15 piece Set)	E. Simonetti	Closed	670.00	758.50
Roman, Inc.		**A Child's World 1st Edition**			
80-02-001	Nighttime Thoughts	F. Hook	Closed	25.00	65.00
80-02-002	Kiss Me Good Night	F. Hook	15,000	29.00	40.00
80-02-003	Sounds of the Sea	F. Hook	15,000	45.00	140.00
80-02-004	Beach Buddies, signed	F. Hook	15,000	29.00	600.00
80-02-005	My Big Brother	F. Hook	Closed	39.00	200.00
80-02-006	Helping Hands	F. Hook	Closed	45.00	75.00
80-02-007	Beach Buddies, unsigned	F. Hook	15,000	29.00	450.00
Roman, Inc.		**A Child's World 2nd Edition**			
81-03-001	Making Friends	F. Hook	15,000	42.00	46.00
81-03-002	Cat Nap	F. Hook	15,000	42.00	100.00
81-03-003	The Sea and Me	F. Hook	15,000	39.00	43.00
81-03-004	Sunday School	F. Hook	15,000	39.00	70.00
81-03-005	I'll Be Good	F. Hook	15,000	36.00	70.00
81-03-006	All Dressed Up	F. Hook	15,000	36.00	70.00
Roman, Inc.		**A Child's World 3rd Edition**			
81-04-001	Pathway to Dreams	F. Hook	15,000	47.00	50.00
81-04-002	Road to Adventure	F. Hook	15,000	47.00	50.00
81-04-003	Sisters	F. Hook	15,000	64.00	69.00
81-04-004	Bear Hug	F. Hook	15,000	42.00	45.00
81-04-005	Spring Breeze	F. Hook	15,000	37.50	40.00
81-04-006	Youth	F. Hook	15,000	37.50	40.00
Roman, Inc.		**A Child's World 4th Edition**			
82-05-001	All Bundled Up	F. Hook	15,000	37.50	40.00
82-05-002	Bedtime	F. Hook	15,000	35.00	38.00
82-05-003	Birdie	F. Hook	15,000	37.50	40.00
82-05-004	My Dolly!	F. Hook	15,000	39.00	40.00
82-05-005	Ring Bearer	F. Hook	15,000	39.00	40.00
82-05-006	Flower Girl	F. Hook	15,000	42.00	45.00
Roman, Inc.		**A Child's World 5th Edition**			
83-06-001	Ring Around the Rosie	F. Hook	15,000	99.00	105.00
83-06-002	Handful of Happiness	F. Hook	15,000	36.00	40.00
83-06-003	He Loves Me...	F. Hook	15,000	49.00	55.00
83-06-004	Finish Line	F. Hook	15,000	39.00	42.00
83-06-005	Brothers	F. Hook	15,000	64.00	70.00
83-06-006	Puppy's Pal	F. Hook	15,000	39.00	42.00
Roman, Inc.		**A Child's World 6th Edition**			
84-07-001	Good Doggie	F. Hook	15,000	47.00	50.00
84-07-002	Sand Castles	F. Hook	15,000	37.50	40.00
84-07-003	Nature's Wonders	F. Hook	15,000	29.00	31.00
84-07-004	Let's Play Catch	F. Hook	15,000	33.00	35.00
84-07-005	Can I Help?	F. Hook	15,000	37.50	40.00
84-07-006	Future Artist	F. Hook	15,000	42.00	45.00
Roman, Inc.		**A Child's World 7th Edition**			
85-08-001	Art Class	F. Hook	15,000	99.00	105.00
85-08-002	Please Hear Me	F. Hook	15,000	29.00	30.00
85-08-003	Don't Tell Anyone	F. Hook	15,000	49.00	50.00
85-08-004	Mother's Helper	F. Hook	15,000	45.00	50.00
85-08-005	Yummm!	F. Hook	15,000	36.00	39.00
85-08-006	Look at Me!	F. Hook	15,000	42.00	45.00
Roman, Inc.		**A Child's World 8th Edition**			
85-09-001	Private Ocean	F. Hook	15,000	29.00	31.00
85-09-002	Just Stopped By	F. Hook	15,000	36.00	40.00
85-09-003	Dress Rehearsal	F. Hook	15,000	33.00	35.00
85-09-004	Chance of Showers	F. Hook	15,000	33.00	35.00
85-09-005	Engine	F. Hook	15,000	36.00	40.00
85-09-006	Puzzling	F. Hook	15,000	36.00	40.00
Roman, Inc.		**A Child's World 9th Edition**			
87-10-001	Li'l Brother	F. Hook	15,000	60.00	65.00
87-10-002	Hopscotch	F. Hook	15,000	67.50	70.00
Roman, Inc.		**Rohn's Clowns**			
84-11-001	White Face	E. Rohn	7,500	95.00	95.00

	ARTIST	EDITION	ISSUE	QUOTE
84-11-002 Auguste	E. Rohn	7,500	95.00	95.00
84-11-003 Hobo	E. Rohn	7,500	95.00	95.00
Roman, Inc.	**The Masterpiece Collection**			
79-12-001 Adoration	F. Lippe	5,000	73.00	73.00
80-12-002 Madonna with Grapes	P. Mignard	5,000	85.00	85.00
81-12-003 The Holy Family	G. delle Notti	5,000	98.00	98.00
82-12-004 Madonna of the Streets	R. Ferruzzi	5,000	65.00	65.00
Roman, Inc.	**Ceramica Excelsis**			
77-13-001 Madonna and Child with Angels	Unknown	5,000	60.00	60.00
77-13-002 What Happened to Your Hand?	Unknown	5,000	60.00	60.00
77-13-003 Madonna with Child	Unknown	5,000	65.00	65.00
77-13-004 St. Francis	Unknown	5,000	60.00	60.00
77-13-005 Christ Knocking at the Door	Unknown	5,000	60.00	60.00
78-13-006 Infant of Prague	Unknown	5,000	37.50	60.00
78-13-007 Christ in the Garden of Gethsemane	Unknown	5,000	40.00	60.00
78-13-008 Flight into Egypt	Unknown	5,000	59.00	90.00
78-13-009 Christ Entering Jerusalem	Unknown	5,000	96.00	96.00
78-13-010 Holy Family at Work	Unknown	5,000	96.00	96.00
78-13-011 Assumption Madonna	Unknown	5,000	56.00	56.00
78-13-012 Guardian Angel with Girl	Unknown	5,000	69.00	69.00
78-13-013 Guardian Angel with Boy	Unknown	5,000	69.00	69.00
79-13-014 Moses	Unknown	5,000	77.00	77.00
79-13-015 Noah	Unknown	5,000	77.00	77.00
79-13-016 Jesus Speaks in Parables	Unknown	5,000	90.00	90.00
80-13-017 Way to Emmaus	Unknown	5,000	155.00	155.00
80-13-018 Daniel in the Lion's Den	Unknown	5,000	80.00	80.00
80-13-019 David	Unknown	5,000	77.00	77.00
81-13-020 Innocence	Unknown	5,000	95.00	95.00
81-13-021 Journey to Bethlehem	Unknown	5,000	89.00	89.00
81-13-022 Way of the Cross	Unknown	5,000	59.00	59.00
81-13-023 Sermon on the Mount	Unknown	5,000	56.00	56.00
83-13-024 Good Shepherd	Unknown	5,000	49.00	49.00
83-13-025 Holy Family	Unknown	5,000	72.00	72.00
83-13-026 St. Francis	Unknown	5,000	59.50	59.50
83-13-027 St. Anne	Unknown	5,000	49.00	49.00
83-13-028 Jesus with Children	Unknown	5,000	74.00	74.00
83-13-029 Kneeling Santa	Unknown	5,000	95.00	95.00
Roman, Inc.	**Hook**			
82-14-001 Sailor Mates	F. Hook	2,000	290.00	315.00
82-14-002 Sun Shy	F. Hook	2,000	290.00	315.00
Roman, Inc.	**Frances Hook's Four Seasons**			
84-15-001 Winter	F. Hook	12,500	95.00	100.00
85-15-002 Spring	F. Hook	12,500	95.00	100.00
85-15-003 Summer	F. Hook	12,500	95.00	100.00
85-15-004 Fall	F. Hook	12,500	95.00	100.00
Roman, Inc.	**Jam Session**			
85-16-001 Trombone Player	E. Rohn	7,500	145.00	145.00
85-16-002 Bass Player	E. Rohn	7,500	145.00	145.00
85-16-003 Banjo Player	E. Rohn	7,500	145.00	145.00
85-16-004 Coronet Player	E. Rohn	7,500	145.00	145.00
85-16-005 Clarinet Player	E. Rohn	7,500	145.00	145.00
85-16-006 Drummer	E. Rohn	7,500	145.00	145.00
Roman, Inc.	**Spencer**			
85-17-001 Moon Goddess	I. Spencer	5,000	195.00	195.00
85-17-002 Flower Princess	I. Spencer	5,000	195.00	195.00
Roman, Inc.	**Hook**			
86-18-001 Carpenter Bust	F. Hook	Yr.Iss.	95.00	95.00
86-18-002 Carpenter Bust-Heirloom Edition	F. Hook	Yr.Iss.	95.00	95.00
87-18-003 Madonna and Child	F. Hook	15,000	39.50	39.50
87-18-004 Little Children, Come to Me	F. Hook	15,000	45.00	45.00
Roman, Inc.	**Catnippers**			
85-19-001 The Paw that Refreshes	I. Spencer	15,000	45.00	45.00
85-19-002 A Christmas Mourning	I. Spencer	15,000	45.00	49.50
85-19-003 A Tail of Two Kitties	I. Spencer	15,000	45.00	45.00
85-19-004 Sandy Claws	I. Spencer	15,000	45.00	45.00
85-19-005 Can't We Be Friends	I. Spencer	15,000	45.00	45.00
85-19-006 A Baffling Yarn	I. Spencer	15,000	45.00	45.00
85-19-007 Flying Tiger-Retired	I. Spencer	15,000	45.00	45.00
85-19-008 Flora and Felina	I. Spencer	15,000	45.00	49.50
Roman, Inc.	**Heartbeats**			
86-20-001 Miracle	I. Spencer	5,000	145.00	145.00
87-20-002 Storytime	I. Spencer	5,000	145.00	145.00
Roman, Inc.	**Classic Brides of the Century**			
89-21-001 1900-Flora	E. Williams	5,000	175.00	175.00
89-21-002 1910-Elizabeth Grace	E. Williams	5,000	175.00	175.00
89-21-003 1920-Mary Claire	E. Williams	5,000	175.00	175.00
89-21-004 1930-Kathleen	E. Williams	5,000	175.00	175.00
89-21-005 1940-Margaret	E. Williams	5,000	175.00	175.00
89-21-006 1950-Barbara Ann	E. Williams	5,000	175.00	175.00
89-21-007 1960-Dianne	E. Williams	5,000	175.00	175.00
89-21-008 1970-Heather	E. Williams	5,000	175.00	175.00
89-21-009 1980-Jennifer	E. Williams	5,000	175.00	175.00
92-21-010 1990-Stephanie Helen	E. Williams	5,000	175.00	175.00
Roman, Inc.	**Dolfi Original-5" Wood**			
89-22-001 My First Kitten	L. Martin	5,000	230.00	230.00
89-22-002 Flower Child	L. Martin	5,000	230.00	230.00
89-22-003 Pampered Puppies	L. Martin	5,000	230.00	230.00
89-22-004 Wrapped In Love	L. Martin	5,000	230.00	230.00
89-22-005 Garden Secrets	L. Martin	5,000	230.00	230.00
89-22-006 Puppy Express	L. Martin	5,000	230.00	230.00
89-22-007 Sleepyhead	L. Martln	5,000	230.00	230.00
89-22-008 Mother Hen	L. Martln	5,000	230.00	230.00
89-22-009 Holiday Herald	L. Martln	5,000	230.00	230.00
89-22-010 Birdland Cafe	L. Martin	5,000	230.00	230.00
89-22-011 My First Cake	L. Martin	5,000	230.00	230.00
89-22-012 Mud Puddles	L. Martin	5,000	230.00	230.00
89-22-013 Study Break	L. Martin	5,000	250.00	250.00
89-22-014 Dress Rehearsal	L. Martin	5,000	375.00	375.00
89-22-015 Friends & Flowers	L. Martin	5,000	300.00	300.00
89-22-016 Merry Little Light	L. Martin	5,000	250.00	250.00
89-22-017 Mary & Joey	L. Martin	5,000	375.00	375.00
89-22-018 Little Santa	L. Martin	5,000	250.00	250.00
89-22-019 Sing a Song of Joy	L. Martin	5,000	300.00	300.00
89-22-020 Barefoot In Spring	L. Martin	5,000	300.00	300.00
89-22-021 My Favorite Things	L. Martin	5,000	300.00	300.00
89-22-022 Have I Been That Good	L. Martin	5,000	375.00	375.00
89-22-023 A Shoulder to Lean On	L. Martin	5,000	300.00	300.00
89-22-024 Big Chief Sitting Dog	L. Martin	5,000	250.00	250.00
Roman, Inc.	**Dolfi Original-7" Stoneart**			
89-23-001 My First Kitten	L. Martin	Open	110.00	110.00
89-23-002 Flower Child	L. Martin	Open	110.00	110.00
89-23-003 Pampered Puppies	L. Martin	Open	110.00	110.00
89-23-004 Wrapped In Love	L. Martin	Open	110.00	110.00
89-23-005 Garden Secrets	L. Martin	Open	110.00	110.00
89-23-006 Puppy Express	L. Martin	Open	110.00	110.00
89-23-007 Sleepyhead	L. Martln	Open	110.00	110.00
89-23-008 Mother Hen	L. Martin	Open	110.00	110.00
89-23-009 Holiday Herald	L. Martin	Open	110.00	110.00
89-23-010 Birdland Cafe	L. Martin	Open	110.00	110.00
89-23-011 My First Cake	L. Martin	Open	110.00	110.00
89-23-012 Mud Puddles	L. Martin	Open	110.00	110.00
89-23-013 Study Break	L. Martin	Open	120.00	120.00
89-23-014 Dress Rehearsal	L. Martin	Open	185.00	185.00
89-23-015 Friends & Flowers	L. Martin	Open	150.00	150.00
89-23-016 Merry Little Light	L. Martin	Open	120.00	120.00
89-23-017 Mary & Joey	L. Martin	Open	185.00	185.00
89-23-018 Little Santa	L. Martin	Open	120.00	120.00
89-23-019 Sing a Song of Joy	L. Martin	Open	150.00	150.00
89-23-020 Barefoot In Spring	L. Martin	Open	150.00	150.00
89-23-021 My Favorite Things	L. Martin	Open	150.00	150.00
89-23-022 Have I Been That Good	L. Martin	Open	185.00	185.00
89-23-023 A Shoulder to Lean On	L. Martin	Open	150.00	150.00
89-23-024 Big Chief Sitting Dog	L. Martin	Open	120.00	120.00
Roman, Inc.	**Dolfi Original-10" Stoneart**			
89-24-001 My First Kitten	L. Martin	Open	300.00	300.00
89-24-002 Flower Child	L. Martin	Open	300.00	300.00
89-24-003 Pampered Puppies	L. Martin	Open	300.00	300.00
89-24-004 Wrapped in Love	L. Martin	Open	300.00	300.00
89-24-005 Garden Secrets	L. Martin	Open	300.00	300.00
89-24-006 Puppy Express	L. Martin	Open	300.00	300.00
89-24-007 Sleepyhead	L. Martin	Open	300.00	300.00
89-24-008 Mother Hen	L. Martin	Open	300.00	300.00
89-24-009 Holiday Herald	L. Martin	Open	300.00	300.00
89-24-010 Birdland Cafe	L. Martin	Open	300.00	300.00
89-24-011 My First Cake	L. Martin	Open	300.00	300.00
89-24-012 Mud Puddles	L. Martin	Open	300.00	300.00
89-24-013 Study Break	L. Martin	Open	325.00	325.00
89-24-014 Dress Rehearsal	L. Martin	Open	495.00	495.00
89-24-015 Friends & Flowers	L. Martin	Open	400.00	400.00
89-24-016 Merry Little Light	L. Martin	Open	325.00	325.00
89-24-017 Mary & Joey	L. Martin	Open	495.00	495.00
89-24-018 Little Santa	L. Martin	Open	325.00	325.00
89-24-019 Sing a Song of Joy	L. Martin	Open	400.00	400.00
89-24-020 Barefoot In Spring	L. Martin	Open	400.00	400.00
89-24-021 My Favorite Things	L. Martin	Open	400.00	400.00
89-24-022 Have I Been That Good	L. Martin	Open	495.00	495.00
89-24-023 A Shoulder to Lean On	L. Martin	Open	400.00	400.00
89-24-024 Big Chief Sitting Dog	L. Martin	Open	325.00	325.00
Roman, Inc.	**Dolfi Original-10" Wood**			
89-25-001 My First Kitten	L. Martin	2,000	750.00	750.00
89-25-002 Flower Child	L. Martin	2,000	750.00	750.00
89-25-003 Pampered Puppies	L. Martin	2,000	750.00	750.00
89-25-004 Wrapped in Love	L. Martin	2,000	750.00	750.00
89-25-005 Garden Secrets	L. Martin	2,000	750.00	750.00
89-25-006 Puppy Express	L. Martin	2,000	750.00	750.00
89-25-007 Sleepyhead	L. Martin	2,000	750.00	750.00
89-25-008 Mother Hen	L. Martin	2,000	750.00	750.00
89-25-009 Holiday Herald	L. Martin	2,000	750.00	750.00
89-25-010 Birdland Cafe	L. Martin	2,000	750.00	750.00
89-25-011 My First Cake	L. Martin	2,000	750.00	750.00
89-25-012 Mud Puddles	L. Martin	2,000	750.00	750.00
89-25-013 Study Break	L. Martin	2,000	825.00	825.00
89-25-014 Dress Rehearsal	L. Martin	2,000	1250.00	1250.00
89-25-015 Friends & Flowers	L. Martin	2,000	1000.00	1000.00
89-25-016 Merry Little Light	L. Martin	2,000	825.00	825.00
89-25-017 Mary & Joey	L. Martin	2,000	1250.00	1250.00
89-26-018 Little Santa	L. Martin	2,000	825.00	825.00
89-25-019 Sing a Song of Joy	L. Martin	2,000	1000.00	1000.00
89-25-020 Barefoot In Spring	L. Mariin	2,000	1000.00	1000.00
89-25-021 My Favorite Things	L. Martin	2,000	1000.00	1000.00
89-25-022 Have I Been That Good	L. Martin	2,000	1250.00	1250.00
89-25-023 A Shoulder to Lean On	L. Martin	2,000	1000.00	1000.00
89-25-024 Big Chief Sitting Dog	L. Martin	2,000	825.00	825.00
Roman, Inc.	**The Museum Collection by Angela Tripi**			
90-26-001 The Mentor	A. Tripi	1,000	290.00	290.27
91-26-002 The Fiddler	A. Tripi	1,000	175.00	175.27
91-26-003 Christopher Columbus	A. Tripi	1,000	250.00	250.00
91-26-004 St. Francis of Assisi	A. Tripi	1,000	175.00	175.00
91-26-005 The Caddie	A. Tripi	1,000	135.00	135.00
91-26-006 A Gentleman's Game	A. Tripi	1,000	175.00	175.00
91-26-007 Tee Time at St. Andrew's	A. Tripi	1,000	175.00	175.00
92-26-008 Prince of the Plains	A. Tripi	1,000	175.00	175.00
92-26-009 The Fur Trapper	A. Tripi	1,000	175.00	175.00
92-26-010 Justice for All	A. Tripi	1,000	95.00	95.00
92-26-011 Flying Ace	A. Tripi	1,000	95.00	95.00
92-26-012 Our Family Doctor	A. Tripi	1,000	95.00	95.00
92-26-013 To Serve and Protect	A. Tripi	1,000	95.00	95.00
92-26-014 Ladies' Day	A. Tripi	1,000	175.00	175.00
92-26-015 Ladies' Tee	A. Tripi	1,000	250.00	250.00
92-26-016 The Tap In	A. Tripi	1,000	175.00	175.00
92-26-017 Fore!	A. Tripi	1,000	175.00	175.00
92-26-018 Checking It Twice	A. Tripi	2,500	95.00	95.00
92-26-019 The Tannenbaum Santa	A. Tripi	2,500	95.00	95.00
92-26-020 This Way, Santa	A. Tripi	2,500	95.00	95.00
92-26-021 The Gift Giver	A. Tripi	2,500	95.00	95.00
92-26-022 8-pc. Nativity Set	A. Tripi	2,500	425.00	425.00
93-26-023 Small Tripi Crucifix	A. Tripi	Open	27.50	27.50
93-26-024 Medium Tripi Crucifix	A. Tripi	Open	35.00	35.00
93-26-025 Large Tripi Crucifix	A. Tripi	Open	59.00	59.00
93-26-026 Jesus, The Good Shepherd	A. Tripi	1,000	95.00	95.00
93-26-027 Preacher of Peace	A. Tripi	1,000	175.00	175.00
93-26-028 Public Protector	A. Tripi	1,000	95.00	95.00
93-26-029 Right on Schedule	A. Tripi	1,000	95.00	95.00

		ARTIST	EDITION	ISSUE	QUOTE
93-26-030	Be a Clown	A. Tripi	1,000	95.00	95.00
93-26-031	Road Show	A. Tripi	1,000	95.00	95.00
93-26-032	One Man Band Clown	A. Tripi	1,000	95.00	95.00
93-26-033	For My Next Trick	A. Tripi	1,000	95.00	95.00
94-26-034	Rhapsody	A. Tripi	1,000	95.00	95.00
94-26-035	Serenade	A. Tripi	1,000	95.00	95.00
94-26-036	Sonata	A. Tripi	1,000	95.00	95.00
94-26-037	Native American Woman-Cherokee Maiden	A. Tripi	1,000	95.00	95.00
94-26-038	Native American Chief	A. Tripi	1,000	95.00	95.00
94-26-039	Iroquois Warrior	A. Tripi	1,000	95.00	95.00
94-26-040	Blackfoot Woman with Baby	A. Tripi	1,000	95.00	95.00
94-26-041	Crow Warrior	A. Tripi	1,000	195.00	195.00

Roman, Inc. — Bristol Falls Carolers Society

93-27-001	Catherine Lucy Lancaster	E. Simonetti	Open	23.50	24.50
93-27-002	Timothy Palmer	E. Simonetti	Open	27.50	29.50
93-27-003	Elizabeth Anne Abbot & Stephen	E. Simonetti	Open	23.50	24.50
93-27-004	James Fisk Cushing	E. Simonetti	Open	27.50	29.50
93-27-005	Chester Adams	E. Simonetti	Open	23.50	24.50
93-27-006	Amos Eleazor Whipple	E. Simonetti	Open	23.50	24.50
94-27-007	Mayor Jeremiah Bradshaw Smith	E. Simonetti	Open	23.50	24.50
94-27-008	Margaret Louise Winslow Smith	E. Simonetti	Open	23.50	24.50
94-27-009	Mary Beth Lancaster	E. Simonetti	Open	23.50	24.50
94-27-010	Albert Sinclair	E. Simonetti	Open	23.50	24.50
94-27-011	Jack O'Halloran	E. Simonetti	Open	23.50	24.50
94-27-012	Caroline Williams	E. Simonetti	Open	23.50	29.50
95-27-013	Priscilla and Baby Susanna	E. Simonetti	Open	N/A	N/A
95-27-014	Charity	E. Simonetti	Open	N/A	N/A
95-27-015	Emily Adams	E. Simonetti	Open	N/A	N/A
95-27-016	Charles	E. Simonetti	Open	N/A	N/A

Roman, Inc. — Fontanini Heirloom Nativity

74-28-001	5" Mary (5")	E. Simonetti	Closed	2.50	9.50
74-28-002	Jesus (5")	E. Simonetti	Closed	2.50	9.50
74-28-003	Joseph (5")	E. Simonetti	Closed	2.50	9.50
79-28-004	Gabriel (5")	E. Simonetti	Retrd.	11.50	11.50
79-28-005	Melchior (5")	E. Simonetti	Retrd.	11.50	11.50
79-28-006	Gaspar (5")	E. Simonetti	Retrd.	11.50	11.50
79-28-007	Balthazar (5")	E. Simonetti	Retrd.	11.50	11.50
91-28-008	New (5") Joseph	E. Simonetti	Open	11.50	11.50
91-28-009	New (5") Mary	E. Simonetti	Open	11.50	11.50
91-28-010	New (5") Jesus	E. Simonetti	Open	11.50	11.50
93-28-011	New Gabriel (5")	E. Simonetti	Open	11.50	11.50
93-28-012	New Melchior (5")	E. Simonetti	Open	11.50	11.50
93-28-013	New Gaspar (5")	E. Simonetti	Open	11.50	11.50
93-28-014	New Balthazar (5")	E. Simonetti	Open	11.50	11.50

Roman, Inc. — Fontanini Heirloom Nativity Limited Edition Figurines

92-29-001	Ariel	E. Simonetti	Yr.Iss.	29.50	29.50
93-29-002	Jeshua & Adin	E. Simonetti	Yr.Iss.	29.50	29.50
93-29-003	Abigail & Peter	E. Simonetti	25,000	29.50	29.50
95-29-004	Gabriella	E. Simonetti	25,000	15.00	15.00

Roman, Inc. — Fontanini Collectors' Club Member's Only

91-30-001	The Pilgrimage	E. Simonetti	Yr.Iss.	24.95	24.95
92-30-002	She Rescued Me	E. Simonetti	Yr.Iss.	23.50	23.50
93-30-003	Christmas Symphony	E. Simonetti	Yr.Iss.	13.50	13.50
94-30-004	Sweet Harmony	E. Simonetti	Yr.Iss.	13.50	13.50

Roman, Inc. — First Year Fontanini Collectors' Club Welcome Gift

90-31-001	I Found Him	E. Simonetti	Open	Gift	N/A

Roman, Inc. — Fontanini Collectors' Club Special Event Piece

90-32-001	Gideon	E. Simonetti	Open	15.00	15.00

Roman, Inc. — Fontanini Collector Club Renewal Gift

93-33-001	He Comforts Me	E. Simonetti	Yr.Iss.	12.50	12.50
94-33-002	I'm Heaven Bound	E. Simonetti	Yr.Iss.	12.50	12.50

Roman, Inc. — Fontanini 5" Collection

94-34-001	Aaron (Resculptured)	E. Simonetti	Open	11.50	11.50
94-34-002	Len (Resculptured)	E. Simonetti	Open	11.50	11.50
94-34-003	Miriam (Resculptured)	E. Simonetti	Open	11.50	11.50
94-34-004	Josiah (Resculptured)	E. Simonetti	Open	11.50	11.50
94-34-005	Jeremiah	E. Simonetti	Open	11.50	11.50
94-34-006	Rachel (Resculptured)	E. Simonetti	Open	11.50	11.50
95-34-007	Kneeling Angel (Resculptured)	E. Simonetti	Open	11.50	11.50
95-34-008	Standing Angel (Resculptured)	E. Simonetti	Open	11.50	11.50

Roman, Inc. — Fontanini 7.5" Collection

94-35-001	Gariel (Resculptured)	E. Simonetti	Open	24.50	24.50
94-35-002	Mary (Resculptured)	E. Simonetti	Open	24.50	24.50
94-35-003	Joseph (Resculptured)	E. Simonetti	Open	24.50	24.50
94-35-004	Jesus (Resculptured)	E. Simonetti	Open	24.50	24.50
94-35-005	Miriam	E. Simonetti	Open	24.50	24.50
94-35-006	Deborah	E. Simonetti	Open	24.50	24.50
94-35-007	Michael	E. Simonetti	Open	24.50	24.50
94-35-008	Eli	E. Simonetti	Open	24.50	24.50
94-35-009	Rachel	E. Simonetti	Open	24.50	24.50
95-35-010	King Melchior (Resculptured)	E. Simonetti	Open	24.50	24.50
95-35-011	King Gaspar (Resculptured)	E. Simonetti	Open	24.50	24.50
95-35-012	King Balthazar (Resculptured)	E. Simonetti	Open	24.50	24.50

Roman, Inc. — The Richard Judson Zolan Collection

92-36-001	Summer at the Seashore	R.J. Zolan	1,200	125.00	125.00
94-36-002	Terrace Dancing	R.J. Zolan	1,200	175.00	175.00

Roman, Inc. — Tender Expressions

92-37-001	You Are Always in the Thoughts That Fill My Day	B. Sargent	Open	27.50	27.50
92-37-002	I Even Love the Rain When You Share My Umbrella	B. Sargent	Open	27.50	27.50
92-37-003	I Tell Everyone How Special You Are	B. Sargent	Open	27.50	27.50
92-37-004	The Greatest Love Shines From A Mother's Face	B. Sargent	Open	27.50	27.50
92-37-005	I Count My Blessings...And There You Are!	B. Sargent	Open	27.50	27.50
92-37-006	Thoughts Of You Are In My Heart	B. Sargent	Open	27.50	27.50
94-37-007	Life Gives Us Precious Moments To Fill Our Hearts With Joy	B. Sargent	Open	39.50	39.50
94-37-008	Each Day is Special...And So Are You	B. Sargent	Open	29.50	29.50
94-37-009	Tender Moments Last Forever	B. Sargent	Open	29.50	29.50
94-37-010	The Tiniest Flower Blossoms With Love	B. Sargent	Open	29.50	29.50
94-37-011	Know What's Special About You?...Everything	B. Sargent	Open	29.50	29.50
94-37-012	I'm On Top of the World When I'm With You	B. Sargent	Open	29.50	29.50
94-37-013	Magic Happens When You Smile	B. Sargent	Open	29.50	29.50
94-37-014	I Saved A Place For You In My Heart	B. Sargent	Open	29.50	29.50
94-37-015	You're In Every Little Prayer (Boy)	B. Sargent	Open	29.50	29.50
94-37-016	You're In Every Little Prayer (Girl)	B. Sargent	Open	29.50	29.50
94-37-017	You Fill My Days With Tiny Blessings	B. Sargent	Open	39.50	39.50
94-37-018	Safely Rest, By Angels Blessed	B. Sargent	Open	32.50	32.50
94-37-019	Home Is In Mother's Heart	B. Sargent	Open	32.50	32.50

Roman, Inc. — Bill Jauquet Americana Collection

93-38-001	Sunday Driver	B. Jauquet	Open	395.00	395.00
93-38-002	Sunrise Ride	B. Jauquet	Open	175.00	175.00
93-38-003	Last Train Out	B. Jauquet	Open	125.00	125.00

Roman, Inc. — Divine Servant

93-39-001	Divine Servant, porcelain sculpture	M. Greiner Jr.	Open	59.50	59.50
93-39-002	Divine Servant, resin sculpture	M. Greiner Jr.	Open	250.00	250.00
93-39-003	Divine Servant, pewter sculpture	M. Greiner Jr.	Open	200.00	200.00

Royal Doulton — Royal Doulton Figurines

24-01-001	Tony Weller HN684	C. Noke	Closed	N/A	1800.00
33-01-002	Beethoven	R. Garbe	25	N/A	6500.00
75-01-003	The Milkmaid HN2057A	L. Harradine	Closed	N/A	225.00
87-01-004	Life Boatman HN2764	W. Harper	Closed	N/A	300.00

Royal Doulton — Royalty

73-02-001	Queen Elizabeth II HN2502	P. Davis	750	N/A	1800.00
80-02-002	Queen Mother HN2882	P. Davies	1,500	650.00	1250.00
81-02-003	Duke Of Edinburgh HN2386	P. Davies	750	395.00	450.00
81-02-004	Prince Of Wales HN2883	E. Griffiths	1,500	395.00	750.00
81-02-005	Prince Of Wales HN2884	E. Griffiths	1,500	750.00	1000.00
82-02-006	Queen Elizabeth II HN2878	E. Griffiths	2,500	N/A	N/A
82-02-007	Lady Diana Spencer HN2885	E. Griffiths	1,500	395.00	600.00
82-02-008	Princess Of Wales HN2887	E. Griffiths	1,500	750.00	1200.00
86-02-009	Duchess Of York HN3086	E. Griffiths	1,500	495.00	750.00
89-02-010	Queen Elizabeth, the Queen Mother as the Duchess of York HN3230	P. Parsons	9,500	N/A	N/A
90-02-011	Queen Elizabeth, the Queen Mother HN3189	E. Griffiths	2,500	N/A	N/A
92-02-012	Queen Elizabeth II, 2nd. Version HN3440	P. Gee	3,500	460.00	460.00

Royal Doulton — Lady Musicians

70-03-001	Cello HN2331	P. Davies	750	250.00	1000.00
71-03-002	Virginals HN2427	P. Davies	750	250.00	12-1500.
72-03-003	Lute HN2431	P. Davies	750	250.00	950.00
72-03-004	Violin HN2432	P. Davies	750	250.00	900-950.
73-03-005	Harp HN2482	P. Davies	750	250.00	15-1800.
73-03-006	Flute HN2483	P. Davies	750	250.00	950-1100
74-03-007	Chitarrone HN2700	P. Davies	750	250.00	700.00
74-03-008	Cymbals HN2699	P. Davies	750	325.00	700.00
75-03-009	Dulcimer HN2798	P. Davies	750	375.00	700.00
75-03-010	Hurdy Gurdy HN2796	P. Davies	750	375.00	700.00
76-03-011	French Horn HN2795	P. Davies	750	400.00	650.00
76-03-012	Viola d'Amore HN2797	P. Davies	750	400.00	650.00

Royal Doulton — Dancers Of The World

77-04-001	Dancers, Indian Temple HN2830	M. Davies	750	400.00	1-1200.
77-04-002	Dancers, Flamenco HN2831	M. Davies	750	400.00	12-1500.
78-04-003	Dancers, Philippine HN2439	M. Davies	750	450.00	750-900.
78-04-004	Dancers, Scottish HN2436	M. Davies	750	450.00	850-1200
79-04-005	Dancers, Kurdish HN2867	M. Davies	750	550.00	550-650.
79-04-006	Dancers, Mexican HN2866	M. Davies	750	550.00	550-650.
80-04-007	Dancers, Polish HN2836	M. Davies	750	750.00	850-950.
80-04-008	Dancers, Chinese HN2840	M. Davies	750	750.00	750-800.
81-04-009	Dancers, Breton HN2383	M. Davies	750	850.00	650-750.
81-04-010	Dancers, West Indian HN2384	M. Davies	750	850.00	600.00
82-04-011	Dancers, Balinese HN2808	M. Davies	750	950.00	600.00
82-04-012	Dancers, No. American Indian HN2809	M. Davies	750	950.00	600.00

Royal Doulton — Soldiers of The Revolution

75-05-001	Soldiers, Georgia HN2779	E. Griffiths	350	750.00	850.00
75-05-002	Soldiers, New Hampshire HN2780	E. Griffiths	350	750.00	750.00
75-05-003	Soldiers, New Jersey HN2752	E. Griffiths	350	750.00	2000.00
75-05-004	Soldiers, South Carolina HN2717	E. Griffiths	350	750.00	850.00
76-05-005	Soldiers, New York HN2260	E. Griffiths	350	750.00	750.00
76-05-006	Soldiers, North Carolina HN2754	E. Griffiths	350	750.00	750.00
76-05-007	Soldiers, Maryland HN2815	E. Griffiths	350	750.00	750.00
77-05-008	Soldiers, Delaware HN2761	E. Griffiths	350	750.00	750.00
77-05-009	Soldiers, Massachusetts HN2760	E. Griffiths	350	750.00	750.00
77-05-010	Soldiers, Rhode Island HN2759	E. Griffiths	350	750.00	750.00
78-05-011	Soldiers, Connecticut HN2845	E. Griffiths	350	750.00	750.00
78-05-012	Soldiers, Pennsylvania HN2846	E. Griffiths	350	750.00	750.00
78-05-013	Soldiers, Virginia HN2844	E. Griffiths	350	1500.00	2700.00

Royal Doulton — Femmes Fatales

79-06-001	Cleopatra HN2868	P. Davies	750	750.00	1350.00
81-06-002	Helen of Troy HN2387	P. Davies	750	1250.00	13-1400.
82-06-003	Queen of Sheba HN2328	P. Davies	750	1250.00	13-1400.
83-06-004	Tz'u-Hsi HN2391	P. Davies	750	1250.00	1250.00
84-06-005	Eve HN2466	P. Davies	750	1250.00	1250.00
85-06-006	Lucrezia Borgia HN2342	P. Davies	750	1250.00	1250.00

Royal Doulton — Myths & Maidens

82-07-001	Lady & Unicorn HN2825	R. Jefferson	S/O	2500.00	25-3500.
83-07-002	Leda & Swan HN2826	R. Jefferson	300	2950.00	29-3200.
84-07-003	Juno & Peacock HN2827	R. Jefferson	300	2950.00	29-3200.
85-07-004	Europa & Bull HN2828	R. Jefferson	300	2950.00	29-3200.
86-07-005	Diana The Huntress HN2829	R. Jefferson	300	2950.00	29-3200.

Royal Doulton — Gentle Arts

84-08-001	Spinning HN2390	P. Davies	750	1250.00	12-1400.
85-08-002	Tapestry Weaving HN3048	P. Parsons	750	1250.00	1250.00
86-08-003	Writing HN3049	P. Parsons	750	1350.00	1350.00
87-08-004	Painting HN3012	P. Parsons	750	1350.00	1350.00
88-08-006	Flower Arranging HN3040	P. Parsons	750	1350.00	1350.00
89-08-005	Adornment HN3015	P. Parsons	750	1350.00	1350.00

Royal Doulton — Ships Figureheads

80-09-001	Ajax HN2908	S. Keenan	950	N/A	550-700.
80-09-002	Benmore HN2909	S. Keenan	950	N/A	550-700.
81-09-003	Lalla Rookh HN2910	S. Keenan	950	N/A	750.00
81-09-004	Lord Nelson HN2928	S. Keenan	950	N/A	850.00
82-09-005	Pocahontas HN2930	S. Keenan	950	N/A	950.00
82-09-006	Chieftain HN2929	S. Keenan	950	N/A	850.00
83-09-007	Hibernia HN2932	S. Keenan	950	N/A	950.00
83-09-008	Mary, Queen of Scots HN2931	S. Keenan	950	N/A	1200.00

	ARTIST	EDITION	ISSUE	QUOTE
Royal Doulton	Les Saisons			
86-10-001 Automne HN3068	R. Jefferson	300	850.00	950.00
87-10-002 Printemps HN3061	R. Jefferson	300	850.00	850.00
88-10-003 L'Hiver HN3069	R. Jefferson	300	850.00	850.00
89-10-004 L'Ete HN3067	R. Jefferson	300	850.00	895.00
Royal Doulton	Queens of Realm			
86-11-001 Queen Elizabeth I HN3099	P. Parsons	S/O	495.00	495-650.
87-11-002 Queen Victoria HN3125	P Parsons	S/O	495.00	850-1000.
88-11-003 Queen Anne HN3141	P. Parsons	Retrd.	525.00	550.00
89-11-004 Mary, Queen of Scots HN3142	P. Parsons	S/O	550.00	850-950.
Royal Doulton	Gainsborough Ladies			
90-12-001 Mary, Countess Howe HN3007	P. Gee	5,000	650.00	650-700.
91-12-002 Lady Sheffield HN3008	P. Gee	5,000	650.00	650-700.
91-12-003 Hon Frances Duncombe HN3009	P. Gee	5,000	650.00	650-700.
91-12-004 Countess of Sefton HN3010	P. Gee	5,000	650.00	650-700.
Royal Doulton	Reynolds Collection			
91-13-001 Lady Worsley HN3318	P. Gee	5,000	550.00	595.00
92-13-002 Countess Harrington HN3317	P. Gee	5,000	550.00	595.00
92-13-003 Mrs. Hugh Bonfoy HN3319	P. Gee	5,000	550.00	595.00
93-13-004 Countess Spencer HN3320	P. Gee	5,000	595.00	595.00
Royal Doulton	Age of Innocence			
91-14-001 Feeding Time HN3373	N. Pedley	9,500	245.00	290.00
91-14-002 Making Friends HN3372	N. Pedley	9,500	270.00	310.00
91-14-003 Puppy Love HN3371	N. Pedley	9,500	270.00	310.00
92-14-004 First Outing HN3377	N. Pedley	9,500	275.00	310.00
Royal Doulton	Prestige Figures			
50-15-001 King Charles HN2084	C.J. Noke	N/A	2500.00	2500.00
52-15-002 Jack Point HN2080	C.J. Noke	N/A	2900.00	3100.00
52-15-003 Princess Badoura HN2081	N/A	N/A	28000.00	30000.00
52-15-004 The Moor HN2082	C.J. Noke	N/A	2500.00	2700.00
64-15-005 Matador and Bull HN2324	M. Davis	N/A	21500.00	23000.00
64-15-006 Indian Brave HN2376	M. Davis	500	2500.00	5700.00
64-15-007 The Palio HN2428	M. Davis	500	2500.00	6500.00
78-15-008 St George and Dragon HN2856	W.K. Harper	N/A	13600.00	14500.00
82-15-009 Columbine HN2738	D. Tootle	N/A	1250.00	1350.00
82-15-010 Harlequin HN2737	D. Tootle	N/A	1250.00	1350.00
Royal Doulton	Figure of the Year			
91-16-001 Amy HN3316	P. Gee	Closed	195.00	295.00
92-16-002 Mary HN3375	P. Gee	Closed	225.00	300.00
93-16-003 Patricia HN3365	V. Annand	Closed	250.00	250.00
94-16-004 Jennifer HN3447	P. Gee	Yr.Iss.	250.00	250.00
Royal Doulton	British Sporting Heritage			
93-17-001 Henley HN3367	V. Annand	5,000	475.00	475.00
94-17-002 Ascot HN3471	V. Annand	5,000	475.00	475.00
Royal Doulton	Williamsburg			
60-18-001 Blacksmith HN2240	M. Davies	Closed	N/A	200.00
60-18-002 Hostess HN2209	M. Davies	Closed	N/A	200.00
60-18-003 Silversmith HN2208	M. Davies	Closed	N/A	200.00
60-18-004 Boy HN2183	M. Davies	Closed	N/A	165.00
60-18-005 Gentleman From Williamsburg HN2227	M. Davies	Closed	N/A	185.00
60-18-006 Lady From Williamsburg HN2228	M. Davies	Closed	N/A	185.00
60-18-007 Royal Govenor's Cook HN2233	M. Davies	Closed	N/A	350.00
60-18-008 Wigmaker of Williamsburg HN2239	M. Davies	Closed	N/A	185.00
64-18-009 Child of Williamsburg HN2154	M. Davies	Closed	N/A	165.00
Royal Doulton	Limited Editions			
92-19-001 Christopher Columbus HN3392	A. Maslankowski	1,492	1950.00	1950.00
92-19-002 Napoleon at Waterloo HN3429	A. Maslankowski	1,500	1900.00	1900.00
93-19-003 Lt. General Ulysses S. Grant HN3403	R. Tabbenor	5,000	1175.00	1175.00
93-19-004 General Robert E. Lee HN3404	R. Tabbenor	5,000	1175.00	1175.00
93-19-005 Duke of Wellington HN3432	A. Maslankowski	1,500	1750.00	1750.00
93-19-006 Winston S. Churchill HN3433	A. Maslankowski	5,000	595.00	595.00
93-19-007 Vice Admiral Lord Nelson HN3489	A. Maslankowski	950	1750.00	1750.00
94-19-008 Field Marshal Montgomery HN3405	N/A	1,944	1100.00	1100.00
Royal Doulton	Great Lovers			
93-20-001 Romeo and Juliet HN3113	R. Jefferson	150	5250.00	5250.00
94-20-002 Robin Hood and Maid Marian HN3111	R. Jefferson	150	5250.00	5250.00
Royal Doulton	Classic Heroes			
93-21-001 Long John Silver	A. Maslankowski	N/A	250.00	250.00
93-21-002 Captain Hook	R. Tabbenor	N/A	250.00	250.00
93-21-003 Robin Hood	A. Maslankowski	N/A	250.00	250.00
93-21-004 Dick Turpin	R. Tabbenor	N/A	250.00	250.00
94-21-005 D'Artagnan	R. Tabbenor	N/A	260.00	260.00
94-21-006 Pied Piper	A. Maslankowski	N/A	260.00	260.00
Royal Doulton	Images			
91-22-001 Bride & Groom HN3281	R. Tabbenor	Open	85.00	85.00
91-22-002 Bridesmaid HN3280	R. Tabbenor	Open	90.00	90.00
91-22-003 Brothers HN3191	E. Griffiths	Open	90.00	90.00
93-22-004 Brother & Sister HN3460	A. Hughes	Retrd.	52.50	52.50
81-22-005 Family HN2720	E. Griffiths	Open	210.00	210.00
88-22-006 First Love HN2747	D. Tootle	Open	170.00	170.00
91-22-007 First Steps HN3282	R. Tabbenor	Open	142.00	142.00
XX-22-008 Gift of Freedom HN3443	N/A	Retrd.	90.00	90.00
89-22-009 Happy Anniversary HN3254	D. Tootle	Open	315.00	315.00
81-22-010 Lovers HN2762	D. Tootle	Retrd.	205.00	205.00
80-22-011 Mothers & Daughters HN2841	E. Griffiths	Open	210.00	210.00
XX-22-012 Our First Christmas HN3452	N/A	Open	185.00	185.00
89-22-013 Over the Threshold HN3274	R. Tabbenor	Open	310.00	310.00
83-22-014 Sisters HN3018	P. Parson	Open	90.00	90.00
87-22-015 Wedding Day HN2748	D. Tootle	Open	205.00	205.00
Royal Doulton	The Four Seasons			
93-23-001 Springtime HN3477	V. Annand	Open	340.00	340.00
94-23-001 Summertime HN3478	V. Annand	Open	325.00	325.00
93-23-001 Autumntime HN3621	V. Annand	Open	325.00	325.00
Royal Doulton	Limited Edition Character Jugs			
88-23-001 Sir Francis Drake D6805	P .Gee	Closed	N/A	100.00
90-23-002 Henry VIII	N/A	Open	150.00	150.00
91-23-003 Henry VIII	W. Harper	1,991	395.00	950.00
91-23-004 Santa Claus Miniature D6900	N/A	5,000	50.00	55.00
91-23-005 Jester	S. Taylor	2,500	125.00	150.00
92-23-006 Mrs. Claus Miniature D6922	N/A	2,500	50.00	55.00
92-23-007 King Charles I D6917	W. Harper	2,500	450.00	450.00
92-23-008 Town Crier D6895	S. Taylor	2,500	175.00	175.00
92-23-009 William Shakespeare D6933	W. Harper	2,500	625.00	625.00

	ARTIST	EDITION	ISSUE	QUOTE
92-23-010 Abraham Lincoln D6936	S. Taylor	2,500	190.00	190.00
93-23-011 Napoleon (Large size) D6941	S. Taylor	2,000	225.00	225.00
94-23-012 Thomas Jefferson	N/A	2,500	200.00	200.00
93-23-013 Clown Toby	N/A	3,000	175.00	175.00
XX-23-014 Father Christmas Toby	N/A	3,500	125.00	125.00
94-23-015 Leprechaun Toby	N/A	2,500	150.00	150.00
XX-23-016 Snake Charmer	N/A	2,500	210.00	210.00
93-23-017 Elf Miniature D6942	N/A	2,500	55.00	55.00
94-23-018 Oliver Cromwell D6968	W. Harper	2,500	475.00	475.00
94-23-019 King & Queen of Diamonds D6969	J. Taylor	2,500	260.00	260.00
94-23-020 Aladdin's Genie D6971	D. Biggs	1,500	335.00	335.00
Royal Doulton	Character Jug of the Year			
91-24-001 Fortune Teller D6824	S. Taylor	Closed	130.00	225.00
92-24-002 Winston Churchill D6907	S. Taylor	Closed	195.00	195.00
93-24-003 Vice-Admiral Lord Nelson D6932	S. Taylor	Closed	225.00	225.00
94-24-004 Captain Hook	N/A	Yr.Iss.	235.00	235.00
Royal Doulton	Star Crossed Lovers Character Jugs			
85-25-001 Anthony & Cleopatra D6728	M. Abberley	S/O	195.00	195.00
86-25-002 Napoleon & Josephine D6750	M. Abberley	S/O	195.00	195.00
88-25-003 Samson & Delilah D6787	S. Taylor	9,500	195.00	195.00
89-25-004 King Arthur & Guinevere D6836	S. Taylor	9,500	195.00	195.00
Royal Doulton	Antagonists Character Jugs			
83-26-001 Ulysses S. Grant & Robert E. Lee D6698	M. Abberley	9,500	N/A	295.00
84-26-002 Chief Sitting Bull & George Armstrong Custer-10000	M. Abberley	9,500	N/A	150.00
85-26-003 Davey Crockett & Santa Anna D6729	M. Abberley	9,500	N/A	145.00
86-26-004 George Washington & George III D6749	M. Abberley	9,500	195.00	150-195.
Royal Doulton	Character Jugs			
XX-27-001 Airman, sm.	N/A	Open	82.50	82.50
XX-27-002 Angler, sm.	N/A	Open	82.50	82.50
XX-27-003 Beefeater, lg.	N/A	Open	150.00	150.00
XX-27-004 Beefeater, sm.	N/A	Open	82.50	82.50
XX-27-005 Columbus, lg.	N/A	Open	160.00	160.00
XX-27-006 Clown, lg.	N/A	Open	205.00	205.00
XX-27-007 D'Artagnan, lg.	N/A	Open	150.00	150.00
XX-27-008 D'Artagnan, sm.	N/A	Open	82.50	82.50
XX-27-009 Equestrian, sm.	N/A	Open	82.50	82.50
XX-27-010 George Washington, lg.	N/A	Open	150.00	150.00
XX-27-011 Golfer, lg.	N/A	Open	150.00	150.00
XX-27-012 Graduate-Male, sm.	N/A	Open	85.00	85.00
XX-27-013 Guardsman, lg.	N/A	Open	150.00	150.00
XX-27-014 Gurardsman, sm.	N/A	Open	82.50	82.50
XX-27-015 Guy Fawkes, lg.	N/A	Open	150.00	150.00
XX-27-016 Henry VIII, lg.	N/A	Open	150.00	150.00
XX-27-017 Henry VIII, sm.	N/A	Open	82.50	82.50
XX-27-018 Jockey, sm.	N/A	Open	82.50	82.50
XX-27-019 Lawyer, lg.	N/A	Open	150.00	150.00
XX-27-020 Lawyer, sm.	N/A	Open	82.50	82.50
XX-27-021 Leprechaun, lg	N/A	Open	205.00	205.00
XX-27-022 Leprechaun, sm.	N/A	Open	85.00	85.00
XX-27-023 London Bobby, lg.	N/A	Open	150.00	150.00
XX-27-024 London Bobby, sm.	N/A	Open	82.50	82.50
XX-27-025 Long John Silver, lg.	N/A	Open	150.00	150.00
XX-27-026 Long John Silver, sm.	N/A	Open	82.50	82.50
XX-27-027 Merlin, lg.	N/A	Open	150.00	150.00
XX-27-028 Merlin, sm.	N/A	Open	82.50	82.50
XX-27-029 Modern Golfer, sm.	N/A	Open	82.50	82.50
XX-27-030 Rip Van Winkle, lg.	N/A	Open	150.00	150.00
XX-27-031 Rip Van Winkle, sm.	N/A	Open	82.50	82.50
XX-27-032 Sailor, sm.	N/A	Open	82.50	82.50
XX-27-033 Santa Claus, lg.	N/A	Open	150.00	150.00
XX-27-034 Santa Claus, sm.	N/A	Open	82.50	82.50
XX-27-034 Shakespeare, sm.	N/A	Open	99.00	99.00
XX-27-035 The Sleuth, lg.	N/A	Open	150.00	150.00
XX-27-036 The Sleuth, sm.	N/A	Open	82.50	82.50
XX-27-037 Snooker Player, sm.	N/A	Open	82.50	82.50
XX-27-038 Soldier, sm.	N/A	Open	82.50	82.50
XX-27-039 Town Crier, lg.	N/A	Open	170.00	170.00
XX-27-040 Winston Churchill, sm.	N/A	Open	99.00	99.00
XX-27-041 Wizard, lg.	N/A	Open	175.00	175.00
XX-27-042 Wizard, sm.	N/A	Open	85.00	85.00
XX-27-043 Yeoman of the Guard, lg.	N/A	Open	150.00	150.00
Royal Doulton	Diamond Anniversary Tinies			
XX-28-001 John Barleycorn	N/A	2,500	350.00	350.00
XX-28-002 Dick Turpin	N/A	2,500	set	set
XX-28-003 Jester	N/A	2,500	set	set
XX-28-004 Granny	N/A	2,500	set	set
XX-28-005 Parson Brown	N/A	2,500	set	set
XX-28-006 The Cellarer	N/A	2,500	set	set
Royal Doulton	Bunnykins			
XX-29-001 Be Prepared	N/A	Open	40.00	40.00
XX-29-002 Bed Time	N/A	Open	40.00	40.00
XX-29-003 Bride	N/A	Open	40.00	40.00
XX-29-004 Brownie	N/A	Retrd.	39.00	45.00
XX-29-005 Cook	N/A	Open	35.00	35.00
XX-29-006 Father, Mother, Victoria	N/A	Open	40.00	40.00
XX-29-007 Fireman	N/A	Open	40.00	40.00
XX-29-008 Fisherman	N/A	Retrd.	39.00	50.00
XX-29-009 Groom	N/A	Open	40.00	40.00
XX-29-010 Halloween Bunnykin	N/A	Open	50.00	50.00
XX-29-011 Happy Birthday	N/A	Open	40.00	40.00
XX-29-012 Harry	N/A	Retrd.	34.00	45.00
XX-29-013 Helping Mother	N/A	Retrd.	34.00	50.00
XX-29-014 Home Run	N/A	Retrd.	39.00	60.00
XX-29-015 Ice Cream	N/A	Retrd.	39.00	60.00
XX-29-016 Mr. Bunnykin Easter Parade	N/A	Retrd.	39.00	45.00
XX-29-017 Mrs. Bunnykin Easter Parade	N/A	Open	40.00	40.00
XX-29-018 Nurse	N/A	Open	35.00	35.00
XX-29-019 Paper Boy	N/A	Retrd.	39.00	45.00
XX-29-020 Playtime	N/A	Retrd.	34.00	45.00
XX-29-021 Policeman	N/A	Open	40.00	40.00
XX-29-022 Polly	N/A	Retrd.	34.00	45.00
XX-29-023 Santa Bunnykins	N/A	Open	40.00	40.00
XX-29-024 School Days	N/A	Open	40.00	40.00
XX-29-025 School Master	N/A	Open	40.00	40.00
XX-29-026 Sleigh Ride	N/A	Open	40.00	40.00
XX-29-027 Sleepytime	N/A	Retrd.	39.00	50.00

		ARTIST	EDITION	ISSUE	QUOTE
XX-29-028	Story Time	N/A	Open	35.00	35.00
XX-29-029	Susan	N/A	Retrd.	34.00	45.00
XX-29-030	Sweetheart Bunnykin	N/A	Open	40.00	40.00
XX-29-031	Tom	N/A	Retrd.	34.00	45.00
XX-29-032	Uncle Sam	N/A	Open	40.00	40.00
XX-29-033	William	N/A	Retrd.	340.00	50.00

Royal Doulton — Beatrix Potter Figures

		ARTIST	EDITION	ISSUE	QUOTE
XX-30-001	And This Pig Had None P3319	N/A	Open	29.95	29.95
XX-30-002	Appley Dapply P2333	N/A	Open	29.95	29.95
XX-30-003	Aunt Pettitoes P2276	N/A	Retrd.	29.95	75.00
XX-30-004	Babbity Bumble P2971	N/A	Retrd.	29.95	50.00
XX-30-005	Benjamin Bunny P1105	N/A	Open	29.95	29.95
XX-30-006	Benjamin Ate a Lettuce Leaf P3317	N/A	Open	29.95	29.95
XX-30-007	Benjamin Bunny Sat on a Bank P2803	N/A	Open	29.95	29.95
XX-30-008	Benjamin Wakes Up P3234	N/A	Open	29.95	29.95
XX-30-009	Cecily Parsley P1941	N/A	Retrd.	29.95	85.00
XX-30-010	Chippy Hackee P2627	N/A	Retrd.	29.95	45.00
XX-30-011	Cottontail at Lunchtime P2878	N/A	Open	29.95	29.95
XX-30-012	Cousin Ribby P2284	N/A	Retrd.	29.95	45.00
XX-30-013	Diggory Diggory Delvet P2713	N/A	Open	29.95	29.95
XX-30-014	Fierce Bad Rabbit P2586	N/A	Open	29.95	29.95
XX-30-015	Flopsy Mopsy and Cottontail P1274	N/A	Open	29.95	29.95
XX-30-016	Foxy Whiskered Gentleman P1277	N/A	Open	29.95	29.95
XX-30-017	Gentleman Mouse Made a Bow P3200	N/A	Open	29.95	29.95
XX-30-018	Goody Tiptoes P1675	N/A	Open	29.95	29.95
XX-30-019	Hunca Munca P1198	N/A	Open	29.95	29.95
XX-30-020	Hunca Munca Spills the Beas P3288	N/A	Open	29.95	29.95
XX-30-021	Hunca Munca Sweeping P2584	N/A	Open	29.95	29.95
XX-30-022	Jemima Puddleduck P1092	N/A	Open	29.95	29.95
XX-30-023	Jemima Puddleduck Made a Feather Nest-P2823	N/A	Open	29.95	29.95
XX-30-024	Jeremy Fisher P1157	N/A	Open	29.95	29.95
XX-30-025	John Joiner P2965	N/A	Open	29.95	29.95
XX-30-026	Johnny Townmouse P1276	N/A	Retrd.	29.95	45.00
XX-30-027	Lady Mouse P1183	N/A	Open	29.95	29.95
XX-30-028	Lady Mouse Made a Curtsy P3220	N/A	Open	29.95	29.95
XX-30-029	Little Black Rabbit P2585	N/A	Open	29.95	29.95
XX-30-030	Little Pig Robinson Spying P3031	N/A	Retrd.	29.95	60.00
XX-30-031	Mother Ladybird P2966	N/A	Open	29.95	29.95
XX-30-032	Mr. Alderman Ptolemy P2424	N/A	Open	29.95	29.95
XX-30-033	Mr. Benjamin Bunny P1940	N/A	Open	29.95	29.95
XX-30-034	Mr. Drake Puddleduck P2628	N/A	Open	29.95	29.95
XX-30-035	Mr. Jackson P2453	N/A	Open	29.95	29.95
XX-30-036	Mr. Tod P3091	N/A	Retrd.	29.95	40.00
XX-30-037	Mrs. Flopsy Bunny P1942	N/A	Open	29.95	29.95
XX-30-038	Mrs. Rabbit P1200	N/A	Open	29.95	29.95
XX-30-039	Mrs. Rabbit Cooking P3278	N/A	Open	29.95	29.95
XX-30-040	Mrs. Rabbit with Bunnies P2543	N/A	Open	29.95	29.95
XX-30-041	Mrs. Ribby P1199	N/A	Open	29.95	29.95
XX-30-042	Mrs. Tittlemouse P1103	N/A	Retrd.	29.95	75.00
XX-30-043	No More Twist P3325	N/A	Open	29.95	29.95
XX-30-044	Old Mr. Bouncer P2956	N/A	Open	29.95	29.95
XX-30-045	Old Mr. Brown P1796	N/A	Open	29.95	29.95
XX-30-046	Old Woman Who Lived in a Shoe P1545	N/A	Open	29.95	29.95
XX-30-047	Old Woman Who Lived in a Shoe, Knitting P2804	N/A	Open	29.95	29.95
XX-30-048	Peter Rabbit P1098	N/A	Open	29.95	29.95
XX-30-049	Pig Robinson P1104	N/A	Open	29.95	29.95
XX-30-050	Pigling Bland P1365	N/A	Open	29.95	29.95
XX-30-051	Poorly Peter Rabbit P2560	N/A	Open	29.95	29.95
XX-30-052	Rebeccah Puddleduck P2647	N/A	Open	29.95	29.95
XX-30-053	Ribby and the Patty Pan P3280	N/A	Open	29.95	29.95
XX-30-054	Sally Henry Penney P2452	N/A	Retrd.	29.95	45.00
XX-30-055	Samuel Whiskers P1106	N/A	Open	29.95	29.95
XX-30-056	Squirrel Nutkin P1102	N/A	Open	29.95	29.95
XX-30-057	Tabitha Twitchitt P1678	N/A	Open	29.95	29.95
XX-30-058	Tabitha Twitchitt with Miss Moppett P2544	N/A	Retrd.	29.95	60.00
XX-30-059	Tailor Gloucester P1108	N/A	Open	29.95	29.95
XX-30-060	Tiggy Windle P1107	N/A	Open	29.95	29.95
XX-30-061	Tiggy Winkle Takes Tea P2877	N/A	Open	29.95	29.95
XX-30-062	Timmy Tiptoes P1101	N/A	Open	29.95	29.95
XX-30-063	Timmie Willie P1109	N/A	Retrd.	29.95	40.00
XX-30-064	Timmie Willie Sleeping P2996	N/A	Open	29.95	29.95
XX-30-065	Tom Kitten P1100	N/A	Open	29.95	29.95
XX-30-066	Tom Thumb P2989	N/A	Open	29.95	29.95
XX-30-067	Tommy Brock P1348	N/A	Open	29.95	29.95
XX-30-068	Benjamin Bunny with Peter Rabbit P2509	N/A	Open	50.00	50.00
XX-30-069	Christmas Stocking P3257	N/A	Open	65.00	65.00
XX-30-070	Cottontail at Lunchtime P2878	N/A	Open	34.00	34.00
XX-30-071	Foxy Reading Country News P3219	N/A	Open	55.00	55.00
XX-30-072	Goody and Timmy Tiptoes P2957	N/A	Open	55.00	55.00
XX-30-073	Hunca Munca Spills the Beads P3288	N/A	Open	34.00	34.00
XX-30-074	Jemema Puddleduck-Foxy Whiskered Gentleman P3193	N/A	Open	80.00	80.00
XX-30-075	Jemima Puddleduck-Large size P3373	N/A	Open	65.00	65.00
XX-30-076	Jeremy Fisher Digging P3090	N/A	Open	50.00	50.00
XX-30-077	Johnny Townmouse with Bag P3094	N/A	Open	50.00	50.00
XX-30-078	Miss Dormouse P3251	N/A	Open	65.00	65.00
XX-30-079	Mittens & Moppet P3197	N/A	Open	50.00	50.00
XX-30-080	Mother Ladybird P2966	N/A	Open	34.00	34.00
XX-30-081	Old Mr. Bouncer P2956	N/A	Open	34.00	34.00
XX-30-082	Peter Rabbit-Large size P3356	N/A	Open	65.00	65.00
XX-30-083	Peter & The Red Handkerchief P3242	N/A	Open	45.00	45.00
XX-30-084	Peter Rabbit in the Gooseberry Net P3157	N/A	Open	50.00	50.00
XX-30-085	Pigling Eats Porridge P3252	N/A	Open	50.00	50.00
XX-30-086	Tom Kittten and Butterfly P3030	N/A	Open	50.00	50.00

Royal Doulton — Royal Doulton Collectors' Club

		ARTIST	EDITION	ISSUE	QUOTE
80-32-001	John Doulton Jug (8 O'Clock) D6656	N/A	Yr.Iss.	70.00	125-150.
81-32-002	Sleepy Darling Figure HN2953	N/A	Yr.Iss.	100.00	250.00
82-32-003	Dog of Fo-Flambe	N/A	Yr.Iss.	50.00	150.00
82-32-004	Prized Possessions Figure HN2942	N/A	Yr.Iss.	125.00	600.00
83-32-005	Loving Cup	N/A	Yr.Iss.	75.00	225.00
83-32-006	Springtime HN3033	N/A	Yr.Iss.	125.00	325.00
84-32-007	Sir Henry Doulton Jug D6703	N/A	Yr.Iss.	50.00	150.00
84-32-008	Pride & Joy Figure HN2945	N/A	Yr.Iss.	125.00	275.00
85-32-009	Top of the Hill Plate HN2126	N/A	Yr.Iss.	35.00	100.00
85-32-010	Wintertime Figure HN3060	N/A	Yr.Iss.	125.00	225.00
86-32-011	Albert Sagger Toby Jug	N/A	Yr.Iss.	35.00	85.00
86-32-012	Auctioneer Figure HN2988	N/A	Yr.Iss.	150.00	250.00
87-32-013	Collector Bunnykins	N/A	Yr.Iss.	40.00	350.00
87-32-014	Summertime Figurine HN3137	N/A	Yr.Iss.	140.00	225.00
88-32-015	Top of the Hill Miniature Figurine HN2126	N/A	Yr.Iss.	95.00	125.00
88-32-016	Beefeater Tiny Jug	N/A	Yr.Iss.	25.00	125.00
88-32-017	Old Salt Tea Pot	N/A	Yr.Iss.	135.00	250.00
89-32-018	Geisha Flambe Figure HN3229	N/A	Yr.Iss.	195.00	200-250.
89-32-019	Flower Sellers Children Plate	N/A	Yr.Iss.	65.00	125.00
90-32-020	Autumntime Figure HN3231	N/A	Yr.Iss.	190.00	225.00
90-32-021	Jester Mini Figure HN3196	N/A	Yr.Iss.	115.00	125-150.
90-32-022	Old King Cole Tiny Jug	N/A	Yr.Iss.	35.00	140.00
91-32-023	Bunny's Bedtime Figure HN3370	N/A	Yr.Iss.	195.00	195.00
91-32-024	Charles Dickens Jug D6901	N/A	Yr.Iss.	100.00	100.00
91-32-025	L'Ambiteuse Figure (Tissot Lady)	N/A	Yr.Iss.	295.00	300.00
91-32-026	Christopher Columbus Jug D6911	N/A	Yr.Iss.	95.00	95.00
92-32-027	Discovery Figure HN3428	N/A	Yr.Iss.	160.00	160.00
92-32-028	King Edward Jug D6923	N/A	Yr.Iss.	250.00	250.00
92-32-029	Master Potter Bunnykins DB131	N/A	Yr.Iss.	50.00	95.00
92-32-030	Eliza Farren Prestige Figure HN3442	N/A	Yr.Iss.	335.00	335.00
93-32-031	Barbara Figure	N/A	Yr.Iss.	285.00	285.00
93-32-032	Lord Mountbatten L/S Jug	N/A	N/A	225.00	225.00
93-32-033	Punch & Judy Double Sided Jug	N/A	2,500	400.00	400.00
93-32-034	Flambe Dragon HN3552	R. Tabbenor	N/A	260.00	260.00
94-32-035	Diane HN3604	N/A	N/A	250.00	250.00

Royal Worcester — Dorothy Doughty Porcelains

		ARTIST	EDITION	ISSUE	QUOTE
35-01-001	American Redstarts and Hemlock	D. Doughty	66	Unkn.	5500.00
41-01-002	Apple Blossoms	D. Doughty	250	400.00	14-3750.
63-01-003	Audubon Warblers	D. Doughty	500	1350.00	21-4200.
38-01-004	Baltimore Orioles	D. Doughty	250	350.00	Unkn.
56-01-005	Bewick's Wrens & Yellow Jasmine	D. Doughty	500	600.00	21-3800.
36-01-006	Bluebirds	D. Doughty	350	500.00	85-9000.
64-01-007	Blue Tits & Pussy Willow	D. Doughty	500	250.00	3000.00
40-01-008	Bobwhite Quail	D. Doughty	22	275.00	11000.00
59-01-009	Cactus Wrens	D. Doughty	500	1250.00	17-4500.
60-01-010	Canyon Wrens	D. Doughty	500	750.00	2-4000.
37-01-011	Cardinals	D. Doughty	500	500.00	2-9000.
68-01-012	Carolina Paroquet, Color	D. Doughty	350	1200.00	19-2200.
68-01-013	Carolina Paroquet, White	D. Doughty	75	600.00	Unkn.
65-01-014	Cerulean Warblers & Red Maple	D. Doughty	500	1350.00	14-3000.
38-01-015	Chickadees & Larch	D. Doughty	300	350.00	85-8900.
65-01-016	Chuffchaff	D. Doughty	500	1500.00	13-2900.
42-01-017	Crabapple Blossom Sprays And A Butterfly	D. Doughty	250	Unkn.	800.00
40-01-018	Crabapples	D. Doughty	250	400.00	37-4250.
67-01-019	Downy Woodpecker & Pecan, Color	D. Doughty	400	1500.00	1-2400.
67-01-020	Downy Woodpecker & Pecan, White	D. Doughty	75	1000.00	1900.00
59-01-021	Elf Owl	D. Doughty	500	875.00	Unkn.
55-01-022	Gnatcatchers	D. Doughty	500	600.00	27-4900.
72-01-023	Goldcrests, Pair	D. Doughty	500	4200.00	Unkn.
36-01-024	Goldfinches & Thistle	D. Doughty	250	350.00	4300.00
68-01-025	Gray Wagtail	D. Doughty	500	600.00	Unkn.
61-01-026	Hooded Warblers	D. Doughty	500	950.00	4300.00
50-01-027	Hummingbirds And Fuchsia	D. Doughty	500	Unkn.	2800.00
42-01-028	Indigo Bunting And Plum Twig	D. Doughty	5,000	Unkn.	Unkn.
42-01-029	Indigo Buntings, Blackberry Sprays	D. Doughty	500	375.00	17-3500.
65-01-030	Kingfisher Cock & Autumn Beech	D. Doughty	500	1250.00	19-2300.
52-01-031	Kinglets & Noble Pine	D. Doughty	500	450.00	13-4800.
66-01-032	Lark Sparrow	D. Doughty	500	750.00	Unkn.
62-01-033	Lazuli Bunting & Chokecherries, Color	D. Doughty	500	1350.00	30-4500.
62-01-034	Lazuli Bunting & Chokecherries, White	D. Doughty	100	1350.00	26-3000.
64-01-035	Lesser Whitethroats	D. Doughty	500	350.00	12-4000.
50-01-036	Magnolia Warbler	D. Doughty	150	1100.00	19-3600.
77-01-037	Meadow Pipit	D. Doughty	500	1800.00	1800.00
50-01-038	Mexican Feijoa	D. Doughty	250	600.00	26-4900.
40-01-039	Mockingbirds	D. Doughty	500	450.00	72-7750.
42-01-040	Mockingbirds and Peach Blossom	D. Doughty	500	Unkn.	Unkn.
64-01-041	Moorhen Chick	D. Doughty	500	1000.00	Unkn.
64-01-042	Mountain Bluebirds	D. Doughty	500	950.00	17-2300.
55-01-043	Myrtle Warblers	D. Doughty	500	550.00	13-4000.
71-01-044	Nightingale & Honeysuckle	D. Doughty	500	2500.00	25-2750.
47-01-045	Orange Blossoms & Butterfly	D. Doughty	250	500.00	42-4500.
57-01-046	Ovenbirds	D. Doughty	250	650.00	4500.00
57-01-047	Parula Warblers	D. Doughty	500	600.00	17-3600.
58-01-048	Phoebes On Flame Vine	D. Doughty	500	750.00	22-3500.
52-01-049	Red-Eyed Vireos	D. Doughty	500	450.00	2000.00
68-01-050	Redstarts & Gorse	D. Doughty	500	1900.00	2300.00
64-01-051	Robin	D. Doughty	500	750.00	Unkn.
56-01-052	Scarlet Tanagers	D. Doughty	500	675.00	3-4200.
62-01-053	Scissor-Tailed Flycatcher, Color	D. Doughty	250	950.00	Unkn.
62-01-054	Scissor-Tailed Flycatcher, White	D. Doughty	75	950.00	13-1600.
63-01-055	Vermillion Flycatchers	D. Doughty	500	250.00	11-3400.
64-01-056	Wrens & Burnet Rose	D. Doughty	500	650.00	1000.00
52-01-057	Yellow-Headed Blackbirds	D. Doughty	350	650.00	2-2400.
58-01-058	Yellowthroats on Water Hyacinth	D. Doughty	350	750.00	17-4000.

Royal Worcester — Ronald Van Ruyckevelt Porcelains

		ARTIST	EDITION	ISSUE	QUOTE
XX-02-001	Alice	R. Van Ruyckevelt	500	1875.00	1875.00
70-02-002	American Pintail, Pair	R. Van Ruyckevelt	500	Unkn.	3000.00
69-02-003	Argenteuil A-108	R. Van Ruyckevelt	338	Unkn.	Unkn.
68-02-004	Blue Angel Fish	R. Van Ruyckevelt	500	375.00	900.00
67-02-005	Bluefin Tuna	R. Van Ruyckevelt	500	500.00	Unkn.
65-02-006	Blue Marlin	R. Van Ruyckevelt	500	500.00	1000.00
69-02-007	Bobwhite Quail, Pair	R. Van Ruyckevelt	500	Unkn.	2000.00
67-02-008	Butterfly Fish	R. Van Ruyckevelt	500	375.00	1600.00
69-02-009	Castelneau Pink	R. Van Ruyckevelt	429	Unkn.	825-875.
69-02-010	Castelneau Yellow	R. Van Ruyckevelt	163	Unkn.	825-875.
XX-02-011	Cecilia	R. Van Ruyckevelt	500	1875.00	1875.00
68-02-012	Dolphin	R. Van Ruyckevelt	500	500.00	900.00
71-02-013	Elaine	R. Van Ruyckevelt	750	600.00	600-650.
62-02-014	Flying Fish	R. Van Ruyckevelt	300	400.00	450.00
71-02-015	Green-Winged Teal	R. Van Ruyckevelt	500	1450.00	1450.00
62-02-016	Hibiscus	R. Van Ruyckevelt	500	300.00	350.00
56-02-017	Hogfish & Sergeant Major	R. Van Ruyckevelt	500	375.00	650.00
68-02-018	Honfleur A-105	R. Van Ruyckevelt	290	Unkn.	600.00
68-02-019	Honfleur A-106	R. Van Ruyckevelt	290	Unkn.	600.00
71-02-020	Languedoc	R. Van Ruyckevelt	216	Unkn.	1150.00
68-02-021	Mallards	R. Van Ruyckevelt	500	Unkn.	2000.00
68-02-022	Mennecy A-101	R. Van Ruyckevelt	338	Unkn.	675-725.
68-02-023	Mennecy A-102	R. Van Ruyckevelt	334	Unkn.	675-725.
61-02-024	Passionflower	R. Van Ruyckevelt	500	300.00	400.00
76-02-025	Picnic	R. Van Ruyckevelt	250	2850.00	2850.00
76-02-026	Queen Elizabeth I	R. Van Ruyckevelt	250	3850.00	3850.00
77-02-027	Queen Elizabeth II	R. Van Ruyckevelt	250	Unkn.	Unkn.
76-02-028	Queen Mary I	R. Van Ruyckevelt	250	4850.00	4850.00

		ARTIST	EDITION	ISSUE	QUOTE
68-02-029	Rainbow Parrot Fish	R. Van Ruyckevelt	500	1500.00	1500.00
58-02-030	Red Hind	R. Van Ruyckevelt	500	375.00	900.00
68-02-031	Ring-Necked Pheasants	R. Van Ruyckevelt	500	Unkn.	32-3400.
64-02-032	Rock Beauty	R. Van Ruyckevelt	500	425.00	850.00
62-02-033	Sailfish	R. Van Ruyckevelt	500	400.00	550.00
69-02-034	Saint Denis A-109	R. Van Ruyckevelt	500	Unkn.	925-950.
61-02-035	Squirrelfish	R. Van Ruyckevelt	500	400.00	9000.00
66-02-036	Swordfish	R. Van Ruyckevelt	500	575.00	650.00
64-02-037	Tarpon	R. Van Ruyckevelt	500	500.00	975.00
72-02-038	White Doves	R. Van Ruyckevelt	25	3600.00	27850.00
Royal Worcester		**Ruth Van Ruyckevelt Porcelains**			
60-03-001	Beatrice	R. Van Ruyckevelt	500	125.00	Unkn.
69-03-002	Bridget	R. Van Ruyckevelt	500	300.00	600-700.
60-03-003	Caroline	R. Van Ruyckevelt	500	125.00	Unkn.
68-03-004	Charlotte and Jane	R. Van Ruyckevelt	500	1,000.00	15-1650.
67-03-005	Elizabeth	R. Van Ruyckevelt	750	300.00	750-800.
69-03-006	Emily	R. Van Ruyckevelt	500	300.00	600.00
78-03-007	Esther	R. Van Ruyckevelt	500	Unkn.	Unkn.
71-03-008	Felicity	R. Van Ruyckevelt	750	600.00	600.00
59-03-009	Lisette	R. Van Ruyckevelt	500	100.00	Unkn.
62-03-010	Louisa	R. Van Ruyckevelt	500	400.00	975.00
68-03-011	Madeline	R. Van Ruyckevelt	500	300.00	750-800.
68-03-012	Marion	R. Van Ruyckevelt	500	275.00	575-625.
64-03-013	Melanie	R. Van Ruyckevelt	500	150.00	Unkn.
59-03-014	Penelope	R. Van Ruyckevelt	500	100.00	Unkn.
64-03-015	Rosalind	R. Van Ruyckevelt	500	150.00	Unkn.
63-03-016	Sister of London Hospital	R. Van Ruyckevelt	500	Unkn.	475-500.
63-03-017	Sister of St. Thomas Hospital	R. Van Ruyckevelt	500	Unkn.	475-500.
70-03-018	Sister of the Red Cross	R. Van Ruyckevelt	750	Unkn.	525-1500
66-03-019	Sister of University College Hospital	R. Van Ruyckevelt	500	Unkn.	475-500.
64-03-020	Tea Party	R. Van Ruyckevelt	250	400.00	7000.00
Royal Worcester		**Equestrians**			
XX-04-001	Winner Brown/Bay	D. Linder	Closed	1721.00	1721.00
XX-04-002	Winner Grey/Bay	D. Linder	Closed	1721.00	1721.00
36-04-003	At The Meet	D. Linder	Closed	944.00	944.00
36-04-004	Cantering to the Post	D. Linder	Closed	944.00	944.00
36-04-005	Hog Hunting	D. Linder	Closed	1277.00	1277.00
36-04-006	Huntsman and Hounds	D. Linder	Closed	1110.00	1110.00
36-04-007	Over the Sticks	D. Linder	Closed	944.00	944.00
36-04-008	Polo Player	D. Linder	Closed	1055.00	1055.00
36-04-009	Three Circus Horses Rearing	D. Linder	Closed	4440.00	4440.00
50-04-010	Two Galloping Horses	D. Linder	Closed	2553.00	2553.00
60-04-011	Foxhunter	D. Linder	Closed	1200.00	1200.00
61-04-012	Officer Royal Horse Guards	D. Linder	Closed	1400.00	1400.00
62-04-013	Quarter Horse	D. Linder	Closed	900.00	900.00
63-04-014	Merand	D. Linder	Closed	1550.00	1550.00
64-04-015	Shire Stallion	D. Linder	Closed	1500.00	1500.00
65-04-016	Hyperion	D. Linder	Closed	1000.00	1000.00
66-04-017	Percheron	D. Linder	Closed	1450.00	1450.00
66-04-018	Royal Canadian Policeman	D. Linder	Closed	1700.00	1700.00
68-04-019	Duke of Edinburgh	D. Linder	Closed	2400.00	2400.00
69-04-020	Appaloosa	D. Linder	Closed	1350.00	1350.00
69-04-021	Suffolk Punch	D. Linder	Closed	1350.00	1350.00
71-04-022	Palomino	D. Linder	Closed	1350.00	1350.00
71-04-023	Prince's Grace & Foal (colored)	D. Linder	Closed	2700.00	2700.00
71-04-024	Prince's Grace & Foal (white)	D. Linder	Closed	2600.00	2600.00
72-04-025	Nijinsky	D. Linder	Closed	2300.00	2300.00
72-04-026	M Coakes Mould on Stroller	D. Linder	Closed	1600.00	1600.00
73-04-027	American Saddle Horse	D. Linder	Closed	1525.00	1525.00
73-04-028	Princess Anne on Doublet	D. Linder	Closed	8000.00	8000.00
74-04-029	Galloping in Winter	D. Linder	Closed	8500.00	8500.00
74-04-030	Galloping Ponies (colored)	D. Linder	Closed	4600.00	4600.00
74-04-031	Galloping Ponies (white)	D. Linder	Closed	2900.00	2900.00
75-04-032	Meade on Laurieston	D. Linder	Closed	3600.00	3600.00
75-04-033	Mill Reef	D. Linder	Closed	2300.00	2300.00
76-04-034	Hackney Pony	D. Linder	Closed	2000.00	2000.00
76-04-035	New Born (colored)	D. Linder	Closed	2700.00	2700.00
76-04-036	New Born (white)	D. Linder	Closed	1600.00	1600.00
76-04-037	Red Rum	D. Linder	Closed	2000.00	2000.00
77-04-038	Clydesdale	D. Linder	Closed	2300.00	2300.00
77-04-039	Grundy	D. Linder	Closed	3400.00	3400.00
Royal Worcester		**Bicentennial L.E. Commemoratives**			
73-05-001	Potter	P.W. Baston	500	Unkn.	300-400.
73-05-002	Cabinetmaker	P.W. Baston	500	Unkn.	300-400.
73-05-003	Blacksmith	P.W. Baston	500	Unkn.	500.00
75-05-004	Clockmaker	P.W. Baston	Unkn.	Unkn.	500.00
R.R. Creations, Inc.		**Pre-Open Window Series**			
90-01-001	Stone House 9002	D. Ross	Retrd.	8.50	8.50
90-01-002	Stone Barn 9003	D. Ross	Retrd.	8.50	8.50
90-01-003	Mission 9004	D. Ross	Retrd.	8.50	8.50
90-01-004	Adobe House 9005	D. Ross	Retrd.	8.50	8.50
90-01-005	Strater Hotel 9008	D. Ross	Retrd.	8.50	8.50
90-01-006	Fox Theater 9009	D. Ross	Retrd.	8.50	8.50
91-01-007	Faulkner House 9108	D. Ross	Retrd.	8.50	8.50
91-01-008	John Hayes House 9109	D. Ross	Retrd.	11.95	11.95
91-01-009	Memphis Mansion 9110	D. Ross	Retrd.	8.50	8.50
R.R. Creations, Inc.		**Colonial Collection Series I**			
89-02-001	Colonial Inn 8903	D. Ross	Retrd.	8.95	8.95
89-02-002	Tavern 8908	D. Ross	Retrd.	8.95	8.95
89-02-003	Silversmith 8909	D. Ross	Retrd.	8.95	8.95
89-02-004	Boot & Shoemaker 8910	D. Ross	Retrd.	8.95	8.95
89-02-005	Large Lampost 8911	D. Ross	Open	2.75	2.75
89-02-006	Easton House 8918	D. Ross	Retrd.	8.95	8.95
92-02-007	Pine Tree 9250	D. Ross	Open	3.50	3.50
R.R. Creations, Inc.		**Colonial Collection Series II**			
89-03-001	C.L. Edwards 8901	D. Ross	12/94	8.95	8.95
89-03-002	Kiistner 8902	D. Ross	12/94	8.95	8.95
89-03-003	Dry Good 8904	D. Ross	12/94	8.95	8.95
89-03-004	Town Hall 8906	D. Ross	12/94	8.95	8.95
89-03-005	G. Dressmaker 8920	D. Ross	12/94	8.95	8.95
91-03-006	4" Fence w/Tree 9124	D. Ross	Open	7.25	7.25
92-03-007	Pine Tree 9250	D. Ross	Open	3.50	3.50
92-03-008	Small Lamp Post 9254	D. Ross	Open	2.95	2.95
R.R. Creations, Inc.		**Court House Collection**			
89-04-001	Chase Country 8924	D. Ross	Retrd.	8.95	8.95
90-04-002	Mount Holly 9010	D. Ross	Retrd.	8.95	8.95
90-04-003	Franklin County 9011	D. Ross	Retrd.	8.95	8.95

		ARTIST	EDITION	ISSUE	QUOTE
90-04-004	Large Flag Pole 9017	D. Ross	Open	2.95	2.95
92-04-005	Pine Tree 9250	D. Ross	Open	3.50	3.50
R.R. Creations, Inc.		**In The Country Series I**			
89-05-001	Church 8905	D. Ross	Retrd.	8.95	8.95
89-05-002	School 8907	D. Ross	Retrd.	8.95	8.95
90-05-003	Grist Mill 9001	D. Ross	Retrd.	8.95	8.95
90-05-004	Large Flag Pole 9017	D. Ross	Open	2.95	2.95
91-05-005	Oak Tree 9123	D. Ross	Open	3.50	3.50
91-05-006	4" Fence w/ Tree 9124	D. Ross	Open	3.65	3.65
92-05-007	Pine Tree 9250	D. Ross	Open	3.50	3.50
R.R. Creations, Inc.		**In The Country Series II**			
93-06-001	Toll House 9301	D. Ross	12/95	8.95	8.95
93-06-002	Country Livin' Shop 9307	D. Ross	12/95	8.95	8.95
93-06-003	Country Church 9322	D. Ross	12/95	8.95	8.95
90-06-004	Sunflower 9016	D. Ross	Open	2.80	2.80
91-06-005	4" Fence w/ Tree 9124	D. Ross	Open	7.25	7.25
92-06-006	Pine Tree 9250	D. Ross	Open	3.50	3.50
R.R. Creations, Inc.		**Main Street Collection Series I**			
89-07-001	Kingman Firehouse 8919	D. Ross	Retrd.	8.95	8.95
89-07-002	Myerstown Depot 8921	D. Ross	Retrd.	8.95	8.95
89-07-003	Barron Theatre 8922	D. Ross	Retrd.	8.95	8.95
89-07-004	Gas Station 8923	D. Ross	Retrd.	8.95	8.95
90-07-005	Santa Fe Depot 9006	D. Ross	Retrd.	8.95	8.95
90-07-006	Library 9007	D. Ross	Retrd.	8.95	8.95
90-07-007	Main Street Sign 9018	D. Ross	Open	2.75	2.75
90-07-008	Large Flag Pole 9017	D. Ross	Open	2.95	2.95
91-07-009	Telephone Company 9107	D. Ross	Retrd.	8.95	8.95
91-07-010	Oak Tree 9123	D. Ross	Open	3.50	3.50
91-07-011	4" Fence w/ Tree 9124	D. Ross	Open	3.65	3.65
92-07-012	Pine Tree 9250	D. Ross	Open	3.50	3.50
R.R. Creations, Inc.		**Main Street Collection Series II**			
89-08-001	Harold's Hardware 8925	D. Ross	12/94	8.95	8.95
91-08-002	Chautaqua Hills Jelly 9105	D. Ross	12/94	8.95	8.95
92-08-003	Beauty Shop 9209	D. Ross	12/94	8.95	8.95
92-08-004	Bank 9211	D. Ross	12/94	8.95	8.95
92-08-005	Bakery 9212	D. Ross	12/94	8.95	8.95
92-08-006	Oak Brook Fire Co. 9207	D. Ross	12/94	8.95	8.95
R.R. Creations, Inc.		**Historical Collection Series I**			
92-09-001	Smith-Bly 9201	D. Ross	12/94	8.95	8.95
92-09-002	Canfield 9205	D. Ross	12/94	8.95	8.95
92-09-003	Hexagon 9208	D. Ross	12/94	8.95	8.95
92-09-004	Lincoln 9217	D. Ross	12/94	8.95	8.95
92-09-005	Susan B. Anthony 9222	D. Ross	12/94	8.95	8.95
90-09-006	Main Street Sign 9018	D. Ross	Open	2.75	2.75
91-09-007	4" Fence w/ Tree 9124	D. Ross	Open	7.25	7.25
R.R. Creations, Inc.		**Historical Collection Series II**			
93-10-001	Betsy Ross 9305	D. Ross	12/95	8.95	8.95
93-10-002	Kennedy Home 9308	D. Ross	12/95	8.95	8.95
93-10-003	Stone House 9319	D. Ross	12/95	8.95	8.95
89-10-004	Lamp Post 8911	D. Ross	Open	2.75	2.75
91-10-005	Oak Tree 9123	D. Ross	Open	3.50	3.50
92-10-006	Pine Tree 9250	D. Ross	Open	3.50	3.50
R.R. Creations, Inc.		**Williamsburg Collection Series I**			
92-11-001	Davidson Shop 9213	D. Ross	12/94	8.95	8.95
92-11-002	Orrell House 9214	D. Ross	12/94	8.95	8.95
92-11-003	Tarpley's Shop 9215	D. Ross	12/94	8.95	8.95
92-11-004	Small Lamp Post 9254	D. Ross	Open	2.95	2.95
91-11-005	Oak Tree 9123	D. Ross	Open	3.50	3.50
92-11-006	Pine Tree 9250	D. Ross	Open	3.50	3.50
R.R. Creations, Inc.		**Williamsburg Collection Series II**			
93-12-001	Court House 9302	D. Ross	12/95	8.95	8.95
93-12-002	Capitol 9303	D. Ross	12/95	8.95	8.95
93-12-003	Governors Palace 9304	D. Ross	12/95	8.95	8.95
91-12-004	4" Fence w/ Tree 9124	D. Ross	Open	7.25	7.25
92-12-005	Pine Tree 9250	D. Ross	Open	3.50	3.50
R.R. Creations, Inc.		**Victorian Collection**			
91-13-001	Victorian Michigan 9106	D. Ross	12/94	8.95	8.95
92-13-002	Queen Anne 9203	D. Ross	12/94	8.95	8.95
92-13-003	Chapline 9206	D. Ross	12/94	8.95	8.95
92-13-004	Trolley 9255	D. Ross	Open	5.95	5.95
90-13-005	Main Street Sign 9018	D. Ross	Open	2.75	2.75
91-13-006	4" Fence w/ Tree 9124	D. Ross	Open	7.25	7.25
91-13-007	Oak Tree 9123	D. Ross	Open	3.50	3.50
R.R. Creations, Inc.		**Christmas Memories Series I**			
92-14-001	Christmas Chapel 9216	D. Ross	12/94	8.95	8.95
92-14-002	Christmas F Douglass 9218	D. Ross	12/94	8.95	8.95
92-14-003	Daniel Boone 9219	D. Ross	12/94	8.95	8.95
89-14-004	Lamp Post 8911	D. Ross	Open	2.75	2.75
92-14-005	Pine Tree 9250	D. Ross	Open	3.50	3.50
92-14-006	Sister Sled 9252	D. Ross	Open	5.95	5.95
R.R. Creations, Inc.		**Christmas Memories Series II**			
93-15-001	Christmas Church 9318	D. Ross	12/95	8.95	8.95
93-15-002	Boscobel 9320	D. Ross	12/95	8.95	8.95
93-15-003	Dell House 9321	D. Ross	12/95	8.95	8.95
89-15-004	4" Picket Fence 8917	D. Ross	Open	3.65	3.65
92-15-005	Sister Sled 9252	D. Ross	Open	5.95	5.95
89-15-006	Lamp Post 8911	D. Ross	Open	2.75	2.75
92-15-007	Pine Tree 9250	D. Ross	Open	3.50	3.50
R.R. Creations, Inc.		**Amish Collection Series I**			
87-16-001	Windmill 8725	D. Ross	Open	3.60	3.60
90-16-002	Amish Buggy 9013	D. Ross	Open	4.40	6.50
90-16-003	Wheat 9015	D. Ross	Open	2.80	3.60
90-16-004	Sunflower 9016	D. Ross	Open	2.80	2.80
91-16-005	Amish House 9101	D. Ross	12/94	8.95	8.95
91-16-006	Amish Barn 9102	D. Ross	12/94	8.95	8.95
91-16-007	Amish School 9103	D. Ross	12/94	8.95	8.95
91-16-008	Amish Outhouse 9104	D. Ross	Open	4.25	4.25
91-16-009	Amish Family 9120	D. Ross	Open	4.40	6.50
91-16-010	Slow Vehicle 9121	D. Ross	Open	2.95	2.95
92-16-011	Quilt Shop 9204	D. Ross	12/94	8.95	8.95
92-16-012	Barn Raising 9220	D. Ross	12/94	8.95	8.95
92-16-013	Clothesline 9253	D. Ross	Open	2.95	6.50

		ARTIST	EDITION	ISSUE	QUOTE
R.R. Creations, Inc.		**Amish Collection Series II**			
93-17-001	Troyer Bakery 9328	D. Ross	12/95	8.95	8.95
93-17-002	Blacksmith 9329	D. Ross	12/95	8.95	8.95
93-17-003	Amish Garden 9330	D. Ross	Open	5.95	5.95
93-17-004	Harness & Buggy 9331	D. Ross	12/95	8.95	8.95
91-17-005	Amish Family 9120	D. Ross	Open	4.40	6.50
91-17-006	4" Fence w/ Tree 9124	D. Ross	Open	7.25	7.25
92-17-007	Pine Tree 9250	D. Ross	Open	3.50	3.50
R.R. Creations, Inc.		**Grandpa's Farm Coll. Series I (No Open Wind./Prtd. Both Sides)**			
87-18-001	Farm House 8720	D. Ross	Retrd.	8.95	8.95
87-18-002	Barn 8721	D. Ross	Retrd.	8.95	8.95
87-18-003	Chicken Coop 8722	D. Ross	Retrd.	6.50	6.50
87-18-004	Wash House 8723	D. Ross	Retrd.	6.00	6.00
87-18-005	Outhouse 8724	D. Ross	Retrd.	4.25	4.25
R.R. Creations, Inc.		**Grandpa's Farm Collection Series II**			
93-19-001	Hofacre House 9323	D. Ross	12/95	8.95	8.95
93-19-002	New Barn 9324	D. Ross	12/95	8.95	10.50
93-19-003	Wash House 9325	D. Ross	12/95	6.50	10.50
93-19-004	Chicken Coop 9326	D. Ross	12/95	6.50	10.50
87-19-005	Windmill 8725	D. Ross	Open	3.60	3.60
90-19-006	Wheat 9015	D. Ross	Open	2.80	2.80
92-19-007	Pine Tree 9250	D. Ross	Open	3.50	3.50
92-19-008	Outhouse 9327	D. Ross	Open	4.25	4.25
R.R. Creations, Inc.		**On the Square I (No Open Window/Printed Both Sides)**			
87-20-001	Antique Shop 8708	D. Ross	Retrd.	8.95	8.95
87-20-002	Book Store 8709	D. Ross	Retrd.	8.95	8.95
87-20-003	Bakery 8710	D. Ross	Retrd.	8.95	8.95
87-20-004	Craft Shop 8711	D. Ross	Retrd.	8.95	8.95
87-20-005	Candle Shop 8712	D. Ross	Retrd.	8.95	8.95
88-20-006	Ice Cream Parlor 8806	D. Ross	Retrd.	8.95	8.95
88-20-007	Flower Shop 8807	D. Ross	Retrd.	8.95	8.95
88-20-008	Hardesty House 8808	D. Ross	Retrd.	8.95	8.95
R.R. Creations, Inc.		**On the Square II**			
93-21-001	Book Store 9309	D. Ross	12/95	8.95	8.95
93-21-002	Ice Cream Shop 9310	D. Ross	12/95	9.95	9.95
93-21-003	Flower Shop 9311	D. Ross	12/95	9.95	9.95
93-21-004	Candle Shop 9312	D. Ross	12/95	8.95	8.95
93-21-005	Craft Shop 9313	D. Ross	12/95	8.95	8.95
93-21-006	Antique Shop 9314	D. Ross	12/95	8.95	8.95
90-21-007	Flag Pole 9017	D. Ross	Open	2.95	2.95
91-21-008	Oak Tree 9123	D. Ross	Open	3.50	3.50
92-21-009	Small Lamp Pole 9254	D. Ross	Open	2.95	2.95
R.R. Creations, Inc.		**Author Collection Series I**			
94-22-001	Mark Twain 9401	D. Ross	2,500	11.00	11.00
94-22-002	Edgar Allan Poe 9403	D. Ross	2,500	11.00	11.00
94-22-003	Harriet Beecher Stowe 9404	D. Ross	2,500	11.00	11.00
R.R. Creations, Inc.		**Lighthouse Collection Series I**			
94-23-001	Old Point Betsie 9402	D. Ross	2,500	11.00	11.00
94-23-002	Mystic Sea Port 9406	D. Ross	2,500	11.00	11.00
94-23-003	Quoddy Head 9407	D. Ross	2,500	11.00	11.00
R.R. Creations, Inc.		**Landmark Collection Series I**			
94-24-001	Locust Grove 9405	D. Ross	2,500	11.00	11.00
94-24-002	Longfellow 9408	D. Ross	2,500	11.00	11.00
94-24-003	Melrose 9409	D. Ross	2,500	11.00	11.00
R.R. Creations, Inc.		**Inn Collection Series I**			
94-25-001	Nathaniel Porter Inn 9410	D. Ross	2,500	11.00	11.00
94-25-002	Black Horse Inn 9411	D. Ross	2,500	11.00	11.00
94-25-003	Herlong Mansion 9412	D. Ross	2,500	11.00	11.00
R.R. Creations, Inc.		**Accessories**			
87-26-001	Welcome Mat 8717	D. Ross	Open	1.80	1.80
87-26-002	Windmill 8725	D. Ross	Open	3.60	3.60
87-26-003	4" Corral Fence 8726	D. Ross	Retrd.	3.60	3.60
89-26-004	Large Lamp Post 8911	D. Ross	Open	2.75	2.75
89-26-005	4" Fence 8912	D. Ross	Retrd.	3.25	3.25
89-26-006	Pine Tree w/Bow other side 8915	D. Ross	Retrd.	3.25	3.25
89-26-007	Trees 8914	D. Ross	Retrd.	3.25	3.25
90-26-008	Sunflower 9016	D. Ross	Open	2.80	2.80
90-26-009	Large Flag Pole 9017	D. Ross	Open	2.95	2.95
90-26-010	Mainstreet Sign 9018	D. Ross	Open	2.75	2.75
90-26-011	Natural Windmill 9019	D. Ross	Retrd.	3.60	3.60
90-26-012	Cactus Set/12 9014	D. Ross	Retrd.	2.80	2.80
91-26-013	Oak Tree 9123	D. Ross	Open	3.50	3.50
91-26-014	4" Fence w/ Tree 9124	D. Ross	Open	7.25	7.25
92-26-015	Small Flag Pole 9251	D. Ross	Retrd.	2.95	2.95
92-26-016	Pine Tree 9250	D. Ross	Open	3.50	3.50
92-26-017	Sisters Sled 9252	D. Ross	Open	5.95	5.95
92-26-018	Small Lamp Post 9254	D. Ross	Open	2.95	2.95
92-26-019	Trolley 9255	D. Ross	Retrd.	5.95	5.95
93-26-020	Welcome R.R. Sign 9332	D. Ross	Retrd.	4.50	4.50
93-26-021	Honey Pine Shelf 9333	D. Ross	Open	9.95	9.95
R.R. Creations, Inc.		**Collectors' Club**			
94-27-001	Cape Cod 9400	D. Ross	12/94	9.95	9.95
Salvino Inc.		**Brooklyn Dodger**			
89-01-001	Sandy Koufax	Salvino	S/O	195.00	225.00
89-01-002	Sandy Koufax AP	Salvino	500	250.00	250-325.
89-01-003	Don Drysdale	Salvino	S/O	185.00	250-275.
89-01-004	Don Drysdale AP	Salvino	300	200.00	350.00
90-01-005	Roy Campanella	Salvino	2,000	395.00	450-600.
90-01-006	Roy Campanella (Special Edition)	Salvino	S/O	550.00	650.00
93-01-007	Duke Snider	Salvino	1,000	275.00	275.00
Salvino Inc.		**Heroes of the Diamond**			
91-02-001	Rickey Henderson (Home)	Salvino	S/O	275.00	275.00
91-02-002	Rickey Henderson (Away)	Salvino	600	275.00	275.00
91-02-003	Rickey Henderson (Special Edition)	Salvino	550	375.00	375.00
92-02-004	Mickey Mantle Fielding	Salvino	S/O	395.00	450-600.
92-02-005	Mickey Mantle Batting	Salvino	S/O	395.00	450-600.
92-02-006	Willie Mays New York	Salvino	750	395.00	395.00
92-02-007	Willie Mays San Francisco	Salvino	750	395.00	395.00
93-02-008	Brooks Robinson	Salvino	1,000	275.00	275.00
Salvino Inc.		**Boxing Greats**			
90-03-001	Muhammed Ali	Salvino	S/O	250.00	350.00
90-03-002	Muhammed Ali (Special Edition)	Salvino	S/O	375.00	395-575.

		ARTIST	EDITION	ISSUE	QUOTE
Salvino Inc.		**NFL Superstar**			
90-04-001	Jim Brown	Salvino	S/O	275.00	275-550.
90-04-002	Jim Brown (Special Edition)	Salvino	S/O	525.00	525-750.
90-04-003	Joe Montana	Salvino	S/O	275.00	275-325.
90-04-004	Joe Montana (Special Edition)	Salvino	S/O	395.00	375-475.
90-04-005	Joe Namath	Salvino	2,500	275.00	275.00
90-04-006	Joe Namath (Special Edition)	Salvino	500	375.00	375-475.
90-04-007	OJ Simpson	Salvino	1,000	250.00	300-350.
93-04-008	Joe Montana 49'er	Salvino	1,000	275.00	275.00
93-04-009	Joe Montana Chiefs	Salvino	450	275.00	400.00
Salvino Inc.		**Pittsburgh Stealer Greats**			
92-05-001	Terry Bradshaw	Salvino	S/O	275.00	275.00
Salvino Inc.		**Chicago Bears Greats**			
92-06-001	Gale Sayers	Salvino	1,000	275.00	275.00
Salvino Inc.		**Green Bay Packer Legends**			
92-07-001	Bart Starr	Salvino	500	250.00	250.00
92-07-002	Paul Hornung	Salvino	500	250.00	250.00
92-07-003	Jim Taylor	Salvino	500	250.00	250.00
Salvino Inc.		**NBA Laker Legends**			
91-08-001	Elgin Baylor	Salvino	700	250.00	250.00
91-08-002	Elgin Baylor (Special Edition)	Salvino	300	350.00	350.00
91-08-003	Jerry West	Salvino	700	250.00	250.00
91-08-004	Jerry West (Special Edition)	Salvino	300	350.00	350.00
Salvino Inc.		**Boston Celtic Greats**			
91-09-001	Larry Bird	Salvino	S/O	285.00	350-425.
93-09-002	Larry Bird (Special Edition)	Salvino	S/O	375.00	450.00
Salvino Inc.		**Hockey Greats**			
91-10-001	Mario Lemieux	Salvino	S/O	275.00	375-600.
92-10-002	Mario Lemieux (Special Editon)	Salvino	S/O	285.00	385-600.
94-10-003	Wayne Gretzky	Salvino	S/O	395.00	400-550.
Salvino Inc.		**Racing Legends**			
91-11-001	Richard Petty	Salvino	S/O	250.00	250.00
91-11-002	Richard Petty (Special Edition)	Salvino	S/O	279.00	350-400.
91-11-003	AJ Foyt	Salvino	S/O	250.00	250.00
91-11-004	Darrell Waltrip	Salvino	S/O	250.00	250.00
93-11-005	Richard Petty Farewell Tour	Salvino	2,500	275.00	275.00
Salvino Inc.		**Dealer Special Series**			
92-12-001	Joe Namath	Salvino	S/O	700.00	700.00
92-12-002	Mickey Mantle #6	Salvino	S/O	700.00	700.00
92-12-003	Mickey Mantle #7	Salvino	S/O	700.00	700.00
93-12-004	Willie Mays	Salvino	S/O	700.00	700.00
Salvino Inc.		**Collegiate Series**			
92-13-001	OJ Simpson	Salvino	1,000	275.00	400.00
92-13-002	Joe Montana	Salvino	S/O	275.00	325.00
Salvino Inc.		**Tennis Greats**			
93-14-001	Bjorn Borg	Salvino	500	275.00	275.00
Salvino Inc.		**Unsigned Collection**			
93-15-001	Richard Petty 6" hand-painted	Salvino	2,500	69.95	69.95
93-15-002	Mario Lemieux 6" hand-painted	Salvino	S/O	69.95	69.95
93-15-003	Richard Petty 8" cold-cast pewter	Salvino	2,500	99.95	99.95
93-15-004	Mario Lemieux 8" cold-cast pewter	Salvino	S/O	99.95	99.95
93-15-005	Richard Petty 6" cold-cast pewter	Salvino	5,000	43.95	43.95
93-15-006	Mario Lemieux 6" cold-cast pewter	Salvino	S/O	43.95	43.95
93-15-007	Richard Petty cold-cast pewter plaque	Salvino	5,000	24.95	24.95
93-15-008	Mario Lemieux cold-cast pewter plaque	Salvino	S/O	24.95	24.95
94-15-009	Roberto Clemente	Salvino	1,750	125.00	125.00
Salvino Inc.		**Collector Club Figurines**			
93-16-001	6" Mario Lemieux-Painted Away Uniform (Unsigned)	Salvino	Closed	70.00	90.00
93-16-002	Joe Montana-"KC" Away Uniform (Hand Signed)	Salvino	Closed	275.00	275.00
Sarah's Attic, Inc.		**Angels In The Attic**			
88-01-001	Small Angel Resin Candle 3071	Sarah's Attic	Closed	9.00	9.00
89-01-002	St. Gabbe 2322	Sarah's Attic	Closed	30.00	33.00
89-01-003	St. Anne 2323	Sarah's Attic	Closed	29.00	32.00
89-01-004	Wendall-Angel 2324	Sarah's Attic	Closed	10.00	14.00
89-01-005	Winnie-Angel 2325	Sarah's Attic	Closed	10.00	14.00
89-01-006	Wendy-Angel 2326	Sarah's Attic	Closed	10.00	14.00
89-01-007	Wilbur-Angel 2327	Sarah's Attic	Closed	10.00	21.50
89-01-008	Bonnie-Angel 2328	Sarah's Attic	Closed	17.00	20.00
89-01-009	Clyde-Angel 2329	Sarah's Attic	Closed	17.00	20.00
89-01-010	Floppy-Angel 2330	Sarah's Attic	Closed	10.00	20.00
89-01-011	Eddie-Angel 2331	Sarah's Attic	Closed	10.00	10.00
89-01-012	Jessica-Angel 2332	Sarah's Attic	Closed	14.00	14.00
89-01-013	Jeffrey-Angel 2333	Sarah's Attic	Closed	14.00	14.00
89-01-014	Amelia-Angel 2334	Sarah's Attic	Closed	10.00	14.00
89-01-015	Alex-Angel 2335	Sarah's Attic	Closed	10.00	14.00
89-01-016	Abbee-Angel-2336	Sarah's Attic	Closed	10.00	13.00
89-01-017	Ashbee-Angel 2337	Sarah's Attic	Closed	10.00	13.00
89-01-018	Rayburn-Angel 2338	Sarah's Attic	Closed	12.00	19.00
89-01-019	Reggie-Angel 2339	Sarah's Attic	Closed	12.00	15.00
89-01-020	Reba-Angel 2340	Sarah's Attic	Closed	12.00	12.00
89-01-021	Ruthie-Angel 2341	Sarah's Attic	Closed	12.00	12.00
89-01-022	Daisy Angel 2352	Sarah's Attic	Closed	14.00	14.00
89-01-023	Patsy Angel 2353	Sarah's Attic	Closed	13.00	13.00
89-01-024	Ashlee Angel 2354	Sarah's Attic	Closed	14.00	14.00
89-01-025	Shooter Angel 2355	Sarah's Attic	Closed	12.00	18.00
89-01-026	Grams Angel 2356	Sarah's Attic	Closed	17.00	35.00
89-01-027	Gramps Angel 2357	Sarah's Attic	Closed	17.00	95.00
89-01-028	Dusty Angel 2358	Sarah's Attic	Closed	12.00	95.00
89-01-029	Emmy Lou Angel 2359	Sarah's Attic	Closed	12.00	12.00
89-01-030	Saint Willie Bill 2360	Sarah's Attic	Closed	30.00	40.00
89-01-031	Bevie-Angel 2361	Sarah's Attic	Closed	10.00	10.00
89-01-032	Angelica Angel 3201	Sarah's Attic	Closed	25.00	25.00
89-01-033	Regina 3208	Sarah's Attic	Closed	24.00	24.00
89-01-034	St. George 3211	Sarah's Attic	Closed	60.00	65.00
89-01-035	Heavenly Guardian 3213	Sarah's Attic	Closed	40.00	40.00
90-01-036	Adair-Victorian Boy 3230	Sarah's Attic	Closed	29.00	29.00
90-01-037	Enos Boy Angel Sitting 3275	Sarah's Attic	Closed	33.00	100.00
90-01-038	Adora Girl Angel Standing 3276	Sarah's Attic	Closed	35.00	100-165.
90-01-039	Angel Rabbit in Basket 3293	Sarah's Attic	Closed	25.00	25.00
90-01-040	Angel Bear in Basket 3294	Sarah's Attic	Closed	23.00	23.00
90-01-041	Billi-Angel 3295	Sarah's Attic	Closed	18.00	22.00
90-01-042	Cindi-Angel 3296	Sarah's Attic	Closed	18.00	22.00

	ARTIST	EDITION	ISSUE	QUOTE
90-01-043 Lena-Angel 3297	Sarah's Attic	Closed	36.00	40.00
90-01-044 Trudy-Angel 3298	Sarah's Attic	Closed	36.00	36.00
90-01-045 Trapper-Angel 3299	Sarah's Attic	Closed	17.00	20.00
90-01-046 Louise-Angel 3300	Sarah's Attic	Closed	17.00	20.00
90-01-047 Flossy-Angel 3301	Sarah's Attic	Closed	15.00	15.00
90-01-048 Buster-Angel 3302	Sarah's Attic	Closed	15.00	15.00
91-01-049 Crate of Love-White 2403	Sarah's Attic	Closed	40.00	40.00
91-01-050 Angel Adora With Bunny 3390	Sarah's Attic	Closed	50.00	50.00
91-01-051 Angel Enos With Frog 3391	Sarah's Attic	Closed	50.00	50.00
91-01-052 Donald Angel 3415	Sarah's Attic	Closed	50.00	50.00
91-01-053 Bert Angel 3416	Sarah's Attic	Closed	60.00	60.00
91-01-054 Crate of Love-Black 3496	Sarah's Attic	Closed	40.00	40.00
92-01-055 Contentment 3500	Sarah's Attic	Closed	100.00	100.00
92-01-056 Love 3501	Sarah's Attic	Closed	80.00	80.00
92-01-057 Priscilla-Angel 3511	Sarah's Attic	Closed	46.00	46.00
92-01-058 Angel Pup 3519	Sarah's Attic	Closed	14.00	14.00
92-01-059 Hope Angel 3659	Sarah's Attic	12/94	40.00	40.00
92-01-060 Heavenly Caring 3661	Sarah's Attic	Closed	70.00	70.00
92-01-061 Heavenly Sharing 3662	Sarah's Attic	Closed	70.00	70.00
92-01-062 Heavenly Giving 3663	Sarah's Attic	Closed	70.00	70.00
92-01-063 Heavenly Loving 3664	Sarah's Attic	Closed	70.00	70.00
92-01-064 Enos & Adora-Small 3671	Sarah's Attic	Closed	35.00	35.00
92-01-065 Harmony Angel 3710	Sarah's Attic	3,500	26.00	26.00
92-01-066 Joy Angel 3711	Sarah's Attic	3,500	26.00	26.00
92-01-067 Noble Angel 3712	Sarah's Attic	3,500	24.00	24.00
92-01-068 Sincerity Angel 3713	Sarah's Attic	3,500	24.00	24.00
93-01-069 Heavenly Uniting 3794	Sarah's Attic	2,500	45.00	45.00
93-01-070 Heavenly Protecting 3795	Sarah's Attic	2,500	40.00	40.00
93-01-071 Heavenly Peace 3833	Sarah's Attic	2,500	47.00	47.00
93-01-072 Risen Christ 3931	Sarah's Attic	1,994	48.00	48.00
93-01-073 Blessed is He 3952	Sarah's Attic	Closed	48.00	48.00
93-01-074 Faith-Black Angel 3953	Sarah's Attic	1,994	40.00	40.00
93-01-075 Grace-White Angel 3954	Sarah's Attic	1,994	40.00	40.00
93-01-076 Mr. Ward-Happy Me 3971	Sarah's Attic	Closed	40.00	40.00
94-01-077 Adora w/Harp 4137	Sarah's Attic	4,000	26.00	26.00
94-01-078 Enos w/Horn 4138	Sarah's Attic	4,000	26.00	26.00
94-01-079 Blessed is He II 4189	Sarah's Attic	2,500	66.00	66.00
94-01-080 Black Girl-Wings of Love 4202	Sarah's Attic	1,000	36.00	36.00
94-01-081 Black Boy-Wings of Love 4203	Sarah's Attic	1,000	36.00	36.00
94-01-082 White Girl-Wings of Love 4204	Sarah's Attic	1,000	36.00	36.00
94-01-083 White Boy-Wings of Love 4205	Sarah's Attic	1,000	36.00	36.00
94-01-084 Asian Girl-Wings of Love 4206	Sarah's Attic	1,000	36.00	36.00
94-01-085 Asian Boy-Wings of Love 4207	Sarah's Attic	1,000	36.00	36.00
94-01-086 Hispanic Girl-Wings of Love 4208	Sarah's Attic	1,000	36.00	36.00
94-01-087 Hispanic Boy-Wings of Love 4209	Sarah's Attic	1,000	36.00	36.00
94-01-088 Angel Kitty with Basket 4240	Sarah's Attic	2,050	20.00	20.00
94-01-089 Angel Bunny with Cage 4241	Sarah's Attic	2,050	20.00	20.00
94-01-090 Angel Pup with Victrola 4242	Sarah's Attic	2,050	20.00	20.00
94-01-091 Angel Bear with Horse 4243	Sarah's Attic	2,050	26.00	26.00
94-01-092 Lacy Angel 4244	Sarah's Attic	2,050	32.00	32.00
94-01-093 Casey Angel 4245	Sarah's Attic	2,050	32.00	32.00
94-01-094 Jovae Angel 4252	Sarah's Attic	2,050	32.00	32.00
94-01-095 Jonathon Angel 4253	Sarah's Attic	2,050	32.00	32.00
Sarah's Attic, Inc.	**Spirit of America**			
88-02-001 Betsy Ross 3024	Sarah's Attic	Closed	40.00	40.00
88-02-002 Indian Brave 4007	Sarah's Attic	Closed	10.00	10.00
88-02-003 Indian Girl 4008	Sarah's Attic	Closed	10.00	10.00
88-02-004 Pilgrim Boy 4009	Sarah's Attic	Closed	12.00	12.00
88-02-005 Pilgrim Girl 4010	Sarah's Attic	Closed	12.00	12.00
91-02-006 Iron Hawk Father Indian 3344	Sarah's Attic	Closed	70.00	100-140.
91-02-007 Bright Sky Mother Indian 3345	Sarah's Attic	Closed	70.00	140.00
91-02-008 Little Dove Girl Indian 3346	Sarah's Attic	Closed	40.00	80.00
91-02-009 Spotted Eagle Boy Indian 3347	Sarah's Attic	Closed	30.00	60.00
91-02-010 Forever in Our Hearts 3413	Sarah's Attic	Closed	90.00	90.00
92-02-011 Gray Wolf Father Indian 3692	Sarah's Attic	2,000	46.00	46.00
92-02-012 Morning Flower Indian 3693	Sarah's Attic	2,000	46.00	46.00
92-02-013 Red Feather Boy Indian 3694	Sarah's Attic	2,000	30.00	30.00
92-02-014 Moon Dance Girl Indian 3695	Sarah's Attic	2,000	30.00	30.00
93-02-015 Abraham Lincoln 3876	Sarah's Attic	1,863	60.00	60.00
93-02-016 Lincoln's Birth House 3877	Sarah's Attic	Closed	34.00	34.00
93-02-017 George Washington 3878	Sarah's Attic	1,789	60.00	60.00
93-02-018 George Washington's Birth House 3879	Sarah's Attic	Closed	45.00	45.00
93-02-019 Tallman House 3900	Sarah's Attic	Closed	50.00	50.00
93-02-020 Democrat Donkey 3955	Sarah's Attic	1,840	40.00	40.00
93-02-021 Republican Elephant 3956	Sarah's Attic	1,854	40.00	40.00
94-02-022 Asthon-Mother Indian 3977	Sarah's Attic	1,000	40.00	40.00
94-02-023 Hosteen-Father Indian 3978	Sarah's Attic	1,000	40.00	40.00
94-02-024 Siyah-Girl Indian 3979	Sarah's Attic	1,000	25.00	25.00
94-02-025 Shine-Boy Indian 3980	Sarah's Attic	1,000	25.00	50.00
94-02-026 Hogan-Indian House 3981	Sarah's Attic	1,000	40.00	40.00
94-02-027 Daniel Boone 4109	Sarah's Attic	1,769	60.00	60.00
94-02-028 Benjamin Franklin 4124	Sarah's Attic	1,776	70.00	70.00
Sarah's Attic, Inc.	**Beary Adorables Collection**			
86-03-001 Bear Resin Candle 2022	Sarah's Attic	Closed	12.00	12.00
86-03-002 Collectible Bear 2035	Sarah's Attic	Closed	14.00	14.00
87-03-003 Alex Bear 2003	Sarah's Attic	Closed	10.00	11.50
87-03-004 Amelia Bear 2004	Sarah's Attic	Closed	8.00	11.50
87-03-005 Abbee Bear 2005	Sarah's Attic	Closed	6.00	10.00
87-03-006 Ashbee Bear 2006	Sarah's Attic	Closed	6.00	10.00
87-03-007 Double Bear on Swing 5114	Sarah's Attic	Closed	20.00	20.00
87-03-008 Bear on Trunk 5126	Sarah's Attic	Closed	16.00	20.00
87-03-009 Bear with Bow 5130	Sarah's Attic	Closed	8.00	8.00
87-03-010 Bear on Cart 5148	Sarah's Attic	Closed	6.00	6.00
87-03-011 Bear on Heart 5154	Sarah's Attic	Closed	6.00	6.00
87-03-012 Double Bears w/Wood Heart 5400	Sarah's Attic	Closed	10.00	10.00
88-03-013 Americana Bear w/Bow 2072	Sarah's Attic	Closed	10.00	10.00
88-03-014 Americana Bear w/Jacket 2073	Sarah's Attic	Closed	10.00	10.00
88-03-015 Americana Collectible Bear 2074	Sarah's Attic	Closed	18.00	18.00
88-03-016 Girl Bear Resin Candle 3027	Sarah's Attic	Closed	11.00	11.00
88-03-017 Ghost Bear 3028	Sarah's Attic	Closed	9.00	12.00
88-03-018 Americana Bear 3047	Sarah's Attic	Closed	50.00	50.00
88-03-019 Lefty Bear in Stocking 3049	Sarah's Attic	Closed	70.00	70.00
88-03-020 Bear in Basket 4022	Sarah's Attic	Closed	48.00	48.00
88-03-021 Einstein Bear 6266	Sarah's Attic	Closed	8.00	8.50
88-03-022 Benni Bear 6267	Sarah's Attic	Closed	7.00	7.00
88-03-023 Bear Clown 6276	Sarah's Attic	Closed	12.00	12.50
88-03-024 Honey Ma Bear 6316	Sarah's Attic	Closed	16.00	20.00
88-03-025 Rufus Pa Bear 6317	Sarah's Attic	Closed	15.00	20.00
88-03-026 Marti Girl Bear 6318	Sarah's Attic	Closed	12.00	20.00
88-03-027 Arti Boy Bear 6319	Sarah's Attic	Closed	7.00	15.00

	ARTIST	EDITION	ISSUE	QUOTE
88-03-028 Boy Bear Resin Candle 3070	Sarah's Attic	Closed	12.00	12.00
89-03-029 Mini Girl Bear 2315	Sarah's Attic	Closed	5.00	5.00
89-03-030 Mini Boy Bear 2316	Sarah's Attic	Closed	5.00	5.00
89-03-031 Mini Sleeping Bear 2317	Sarah's Attic	Closed	5.00	5.00
89-03-032 Sid Papa Bear 3092	Sarah's Attic	Closed	18.00	25.00
89-03-033 Sophie Mama Bear 3093	Sarah's Attic	Closed	18.00	25.00
89-03-034 Sarah's Bear 3096	Sarah's Attic	Closed	7.25	7.25
89-03-035 Betsy Bear w/Flag 3097	Sarah's Attic	Closed	22.00	22.00
89-03-036 Colonial Bear w/Hat 3098	Sarah's Attic	Closed	22.00	22.00
89-03-037 Daisy Bear 3101	Sarah's Attic	Closed	48.00	55.00
89-03-038 Griswald Bear 3102	Sarah's Attic	Closed	48.00	55.00
89-03-039 Missy Bear 3103	Sarah's Attic	Closed	26.00	30.00
89-03-040 Mikey Bear 3104	Sarah's Attic	Closed	26.00	30.00
89-03-041 Angel Bear 3105	Sarah's Attic	Closed	24.00	24.50
89-03-042 Spice Bear Crawling 3109	Sarah's Attic	Closed	12.00	15.00
89-03-043 Mini Teddy Bear 3110	Sarah's Attic	Closed	5.00	5.00
89-03-044 Sammy Boy Bear 3111	Sarah's Attic	Closed	12.00	15.00
89-03-045 Sugar Bear Sitting 3112	Sarah's Attic	Closed	12.00	12.00
90-03-046 Bailey 50's Papa Bear 3250	Sarah's Attic	Closed	30.00	30.00
90-03-047 Beulah 50's Mama Bear 3251	Sarah's Attic	Closed	30.00	30.00
90-03-048 Birkey 50's Boy Bear Teddy 3252	Sarah's Attic	Closed	25.00	25.00
90-03-049 Belinda 50's Girl Bear 3253	Sarah's Attic	Closed	25.00	25.00
91-03-050 Miss Love Bear 3354	Sarah's Attic	Closed	42.00	42.00
91-03-051 Dudley Bear 3355	Sarah's Attic	Closed	32.00	32.00
91-03-052 Margie Bear 3356	Sarah's Attic	Closed	32.00	32.00
91-03-053 Joey Bear 3357	Sarah's Attic	Closed	32.00	32.00
91-03-054 Franny Bear 3358	Sarah's Attic	Closed	32.00	32.00
91-03-055 Oliver Bear 3359	Sarah's Attic	Closed	32.00	32.00
92-03-056 Mandy-Mother Bear 3726	Sarah's Attic	3,500	20.00	20.00
92-03-057 Andy-Father Bear 3727	Sarah's Attic	3,500	20.00	20.00
92-03-058 Brandy-Baby Bear 3728	Sarah's Attic	3,500	14.00	14.00
92-03-059 Beary Huggable Bear 3760	Sarah's Attic	Open	18.00	18.00
92-03-060 Miss You Beary Much Bear 3761	Sarah's Attic	Open	18.00	18.00
92-03-061 You're Beary Special Bear 3762	Sarah's Attic	Open	18.00	18.00
92-03-062 I'm Beary Sorry Bear 3763	Sarah's Attic	Open	18.00	18.00
92-03-063 I Love You Bears 3812	Sarah's Attic	Open	22.00	22.00
92-03-064 Beary Happy Halloween 3830	Sarah's Attic	Open	18.00	18.00
92-03-065 Beary Merry Christmas 3831	Sarah's Attic	Open	20.00	20.00
92-03-066 Beary Special Sister Bear 3872	Sarah's Attic	Open	18.00	18.00
92-03-067 Beary Special Brother Bear 3873	Sarah's Attic	Open	18.00	18.00
92-03-068 Beary Special Mother Bear 3874	Sarah's Attic	Open	18.00	18.00
92-03-069 Beary Special Father Bear 3875	Sarah's Attic	Open	22.00	22.00
92-03-070 Professor Bear 3906	Sarah's Attic	Open	24.00	24.00
92-03-071 Tommy's Bear 3907	Sarah's Attic	Open	24.00	24.00
92-03-072 Irish Bear 3908	Sarah's Attic	Open	24.00	24.00
92-03-073 Just Ted Bear 3909	Sarah's Attic	Open	24.00	24.00
92-03-074 Dowager Twins Bear 3910	Sarah's Attic	Open	24.00	24.00
92-03-075 Me and My Shadow Bear 3911	Sarah's Attic	Open	26.00	26.00
92-03-076 Second Hand-Rose Bear 3912	Sarah's Attic	Open	24.00	24.00
92-03-077 Witchie Bear 3913	Sarah's Attic	Open	24.00	24.00
92-03-078 Bellhop Bear 3914	Sarah's Attic	Open	24.00	24.00
92-03-079 Eddie Bear 3915	Sarah's Attic	Open	24.00	24.00
92-03-080 Librarian Bear 3916	Sarah's Attic	Open	24.00	24.00
92-03-081 Aunt Eunice Bear 3917	Sarah's Attic	Open	24.00	24.00
92-03-082 Eddie w/Trunk 3918	Sarah's Attic	Open	40.00	40.00
92-03-083 Librarian w/Desk 3919	Sarah's Attic	Open	40.00	40.00
92-03-084 Bellhop & Second-Hand Rose 3920	Sarah's Attic	Open	40.00	40.00
92-03-085 Witchie w/Pot 3921	Sarah's Attic	Open	40.00	40.00
92-03-086 Tommy w/Dog 3922	Sarah's Attic	Open	40.00	40.00
92-03-087 Just Ted w/Mirror 3923	Sarah's Attic	Open	40.00	40.00
92-03-088 Aunt Eunice Bathtime 3924	Sarah's Attic	Open	40.00	40.00
92-03-089 Professor w/Board 3925	Sarah's Attic	Open	40.00	40.00
92-03-090 Me and My Shadow w/Chair 3926	Sarah's Attic	Open	45.00	45.00
92-03-091 Dowager Twins on Couch 3927	Sarah's Attic	Open	60.00	60.00
92-03-092 Irish Bear at Pub 3928	Sarah's Attic	Open	40.00	40.00
92-03-093 Michaud Bear Sign 3929	Sarah's Attic	Open	35.00	35.00
94-03-094 Beary Special Friend Bear 3961	Sarah's Attic	Open	20.00	20.00
94-03-095 Beary Special Birthday Bear 3962	Sarah's Attic	Open	20.00	20.00
94-03-096 Get Well Soon Bear 3992	Sarah's Attic	Open	20.00	20.00
Sarah's Attic, Inc.	**Black Heritage Collection**			
87-04-001 Gramps 5104	Sarah's Attic	Closed	16.00	16.00
87-04-002 Grams 5105	Sarah's Attic	Closed	16.00	16.00
89-04-003 Quilting Ladies 3099	Sarah's Attic	Closed	90.00	275.00
89-04-004 Pappy Jake 3100	Sarah's Attic	Closed	40.00	100-150.
90-04-005 Susie Mae 3231	Sarah's Attic	Open	22.00	22.00
90-04-006 Caleb-Lying Down 3232	Sarah's Attic	Open	23.00	23.00
90-04-007 Hattie-Knitting 3233	Sarah's Attic	Closed	40.00	100-135.
90-04-008 Whoopie & Wooster 3255	Sarah's Attic	Closed	50.00	275-300.
90-04-009 Portia Reading Book 3256	Sarah's Attic	Closed	30.00	65-85.00
90-04-010 Harpster W/Banjo 3257	Sarah's Attic	Closed	60.00	275-310.
90-04-011 Libby w/Overalls 3259	Sarah's Attic	Closed	36.00	125-150.
90-04-012 Lucas w/Overalls 3260	Sarah's Attic	Closed	36.00	125-150.
90-04-013 Praise the Lord I (Preacher I) 3277	Sarah's Attic	Closed	55.00	100.00
90-04-014 Pearl-Black Girl Dancing 3291	Sarah's Attic	Closed	45.00	75.00
90-04-015 Percy-Black Boy Dancing 3292	Sarah's Attic	Closed	45.00	75.00
90-04-016 Brotherly Love 3336	Sarah's Attic	Closed	80.00	80-120.
91-04-017 Nighttime Pearl 3362	Sarah's Attic	Closed	50.00	55.00
91-04-018 Nighttime Percy 3363	Sarah's Attic	Closed	50.00	50.00
91-04-019 Sadie & Osie Mae 3365	Sarah's Attic	Closed	70.00	70.00
91-04-020 Corporal Pervis 3366	Sarah's Attic	Closed	60.00	60.00
91-04-021 Portia-Victorian Dress 3373	Sarah's Attic	Closed	35.00	35.00
91-04-022 Webster-Victorian Suit 3374	Sarah's Attic	Closed	35.00	35.00
91-04-023 Caleb W/Vegetables 3375	Sarah's Attic	Closed	50.00	50.00
91-04-024 Praise the Lord II w/Kids 3376	Sarah's Attic	5,000	100.00	100.00
91-04-025 Harpster W/Harmonica II 3384	Sarah's Attic	Closed	60.00	60.00
91-04-026 Whoopie & Wooster II 3385	Sarah's Attic	Closed	70.00	70.00
91-04-027 Libby W/Puppy 3386	Sarah's Attic	Closed	50.00	65.00
91-04-028 Lucas W/Dog 3387	Sarah's Attic	Closed	50.00	65.00
91-04-029 Black Baby Tansy 3388	Sarah's Attic	Closed	40.00	50.00
91-04-030 Uncle Reuben 3389	Sarah's Attic	Closed	70.00	110.00
91-04-031 Pappy Jake & Susie Mae 3482	Sarah's Attic	Closed	60.00	60.00
91-04-032 Hattie Quilting 3483	Sarah's Attic	Closed	60.00	60.00
91-04-033 Portia Quilting 3484	Sarah's Attic	Closed	40.00	40.00
91-04-034 Caleb With Football 3485	Sarah's Attic	Closed	40.00	40.00
92-04-035 Muffy-Prayer Time 3509	Sarah's Attic	Closed	46.00	46.00
92-04-036 Calvin Prayer Time 3510	Sarah's Attic	Closed	46.00	46.00
92-04-037 Miss Lettie-Teacher 3513	Sarah's Attic	Closed	50.00	50.00
92-04-038 Buffalo Soldier 3524	Sarah's Attic	Closed	80.00	80.00
92-04-039 Porter 3525	Sarah's Attic	Closed	80.00	80.00
92-04-040 Music Masters 3533	Sarah's Attic	Closed	300.00	300.00

		ARTIST	EDITION	ISSUE	QUOTE
92-04-041	Granny Wynne & Olivia 3535	Sarah's Attic	Closed	85.00	85.00
92-04-042	Esther w/Butter Churn 3536	Sarah's Attic	Closed	70.00	70.00
92-04-043	Rhythm & Blues 3620	Sarah's Attic	Closed	80.00	80.00
92-04-044	Music Masters II 3621	Sarah's Attic	Closed	250.00	250.00
92-04-045	Sojourner Truth 3629	Sarah's Attic	Closed	80.00	80.00
92-04-046	Ida B. Wells & Frederick Douglass 3642	Sarah's Attic	Closed	160.00	160.00
92-04-047	Booker T. Washington 3648	Sarah's Attic	Closed	80.00	80.00
92-04-048	Jomo-African Boy 3652	Sarah's Attic	4,000	27.00	27.00
92-04-049	Boys Night Out 3660	Sarah's Attic	Closed	350.00	350.00
92-04-050	Kaminda-African Woman 3679	Sarah's Attic	4,000	50.00	50.00
92-04-051	Shamba-African Man 3680	Sarah's Attic	4,000	50.00	50.00
92-04-052	Nurturing with Love-3686	Sarah's Attic	Closed	60.00	60.00
92-04-053	Harriet Tubman 3687	Sarah's Attic	Closed	60.00	60.00
93-04-054	Miles Boy Angel 3752	Sarah's Attic	2,500	27.00	27.00
93-04-055	Praise the Lord III 3753	Sarah's Attic	2,500	44.00	44.00
93-04-056	Bessie Gospel Singer 3754	Sarah's Attic	2,500	40.00	40.00
93-04-057	Jesse Gospel Singer 3755	Sarah's Attic	2,500	40.00	40.00
93-04-058	Vanessa Gospel Singer 3756	Sarah's Attic	2,500	40.00	40.00
93-04-059	Claudia w/Tamborine Singer 3757	Sarah's Attic	2,500	27.00	27.00
93-04-060	Brewster Clapping Singer 3758	Sarah's Attic	2,500	27.00	27.00
93-04-061	Moriah Girl Angel 3759	Sarah's Attic	2,500	27.00	27.00
93-04-062	Nat Love Cowboy (Isom Dart) 3792	Sarah's Attic	Closed	45.00	45.00
93-04-063	Otis Redding 3793	Sarah's Attic	Closed	70.00	150.00
93-04-064	Carter Woodson 3845	Sarah's Attic	3,000	45.00	45.00
93-04-065	Phillis Wheatley 3846	Sarah's Attic	3,000	45.00	45.00
93-04-066	Mary McLeod Bethune 3847	Sarah's Attic	3,000	45.00	45.00
93-04-067	George Washington Carver 3848	Sarah's Attic	3,000	45.00	45.00
93-04-068	Madame CJ Walker 3849	Sarah's Attic	3,000	45.00	45.00
94-04-069	Harriet Tubman 4110	Sarah's Attic	2,500	50.00	50.00
94-04-070	Nat Love w/Saddle 4121	Sarah's Attic	2,500	60.00	60.00
94-04-071	Mary Church Terrell 4122	Sarah's Attic	2,500	50.00	50.00
94-04-072	W.E.B. DuBois 4123	Sarah's Attic	2,500	60.00	60.00
94-04-073	Peaches-Clown 4135	Sarah's Attic	4,000	29.00	29.00
94-04-074	Pug-Clown 4136	Sarah's Attic	4,000	29.00	29.00
94-04-075	Libby w/Jacks 4139	Sarah's Attic	4,000	26.00	26.00
94-04-076	Lucas w/Papers 4140	Sarah's Attic	4,000	26.00	26.00
94-04-077	Kitty w/Microphone 4141	Sarah's Attic	2,000	50.00	50.00
94-04-078	Music Master III 4142	Sarah's Attic	2,000	80.00	80.00
94-04-079	Coretta Scott King 4178	Sarah's Attic	12/96	60.00	60.00
94-04-080	Martin Luther King, Jr. 4179	Sarah's Attic	12/96	65.00	65.00

Sarah's Attic, Inc. — **Cuddly Critters Collection**

		ARTIST	EDITION	ISSUE	QUOTE
86-05-001	Goose Resin Candle 2021	Sarah's Attic	Closed	12.00	12.00
87-05-002	Small Duck 0062	Sarah's Attic	Closed	2.00	2.00
87-05-003	Small Long Neck Goose 2007	Sarah's Attic	Closed	5.00	5.00
87-05-004	Large Long Neck Goose 2008	Sarah's Attic	Closed	8.00	8.00
87-05-005	Small Sitting Goose 2009	Sarah's Attic	Closed	3.00	3.00
87-05-006	Medium Sitting Goose 2010	Sarah's Attic	Closed	4.00	4.00
87-05-007	Large Sitting Goose 2011	Sarah's Attic	Closed	7.00	7.00
87-05-008	Sparky 2012	Sarah's Attic	Closed	10.00	10.00
87-05-009	Goose 2037	Sarah's Attic	Closed	14.00	14.00
87-05-010	Snapper-Turtle 5109	Sarah's Attic	Closed	8.00	8.00
87-05-011	Sheep Sitting 5132	Sarah's Attic	Closed	6.00	6.00
87-05-012	Sheep Standing 5133	Sarah's Attic	Closed	6.00	6.00
87-05-013	Cat on Heart 5138	Sarah's Attic	Closed	6.00	6.00
87-05-014	Goose on Heart 5147	Sarah's Attic	Closed	6.00	6.00
87-05-015	Pig on Heart 5161	Sarah's Attic	Closed	6.00	6.00
88-05-016	Americana Sparky 2075	Sarah's Attic	Closed	12.00	12.00
88-05-017	Ox-Nativity 2105	Sarah's Attic	Closed	16.00	16.00
88-05-018	Sheep-Nativity 2106	Sarah's Attic	Closed	8.00	8.00
88-05-019	Cow w/Bell 3023	Sarah's Attic	Closed	28.00	28.00
88-05-020	Rocking Horse 6150	Sarah's Attic	Closed	44.00	44.00
88-05-021	Mini Duck 6218	Sarah's Attic	Closed	5.00	5.00
88-05-022	Mini Pig 6219	Sarah's Attic	Closed	5.00	5.00
88-05-023	Mini Sheep 6220	Sarah's Attic	Closed	6.00	6.00
88-05-024	Mini Chicken 6221	Sarah's Attic	Closed	5.00	5.00
88-05-025	Mini Rabbit 6222	Sarah's Attic	Closed	5.00	5.00
88-05-026	Mini Cow 6223	Sarah's Attic	Closed	8.00	8.00
88-05-027	Lazy-cat On Back 6265	Sarah's Attic	Closed	13.00	13.00
88-05-028	Clown Puppy 6273	Sarah's Attic	Closed	8.00	8.00
88-05-029	Buster Boy Cat 6275	Sarah's Attic	Closed	14.00	14.00
88-05-030	Flossy Girl Cat 6277	Sarah's Attic	Closed	10.00	10.00
88-05-031	Trapper Papa Cat 6278	Sarah's Attic	Closed	20.00	25.00
88-05-032	Louise Mama Cat 6279	Sarah's Attic	Closed	20.00	25.00
88-05-033	Sheep on Wheels 6280	Sarah's Attic	Closed	16.00	16.00
88-05-034	Pig on Wheels 6281	Sarah's Attic	Closed	16.00	16.00
88-05-035	Ox 6310	Sarah's Attic	Closed	13.00	13.00
88-05-036	Sheep 6311	Sarah's Attic	Closed	10.00	10.00
88-05-037	Sleeping Cat 6315	Sarah's Attic	Closed	6.00	6.00
88-05-038	Carousel Horse 6332	Sarah's Attic	Closed	31.00	31.00
88-05-039	Cocker with Pup-white 2277	Sarah's Attic	Closed	8.00	8.00
88-05-040	Cocker with Pup-brown 2278	Sarah's Attic	Closed	8.00	8.00
88-05-041	Kitten Diaper-white 2279	Sarah's Attic	Closed	8.00	8.00
88-05-042	Kitten Diaper-brown 2280	Sarah's Attic	Closed	8.00	8.00
88-05-043	Kitty Cat w/Bonnet 2283	Sarah's Attic	Closed	10.00	10.00
88-05-044	Santa Mouse 3062	Sarah's Attic	Closed	10.00	10.00
88-05-045	Grady Pa Mouse 3075	Sarah's Attic	Closed	13.00	13.00
88-05-046	Lila Mom Mouse 4000	Sarah's Attic	Closed	18.00	27.00
88-05-047	Lucky Boy Mouse 4001	Sarah's Attic	Closed	13.00	20.00
88-05-048	Lucy Girl Mouse 4002	Sarah's Attic	Closed	12.00	20.00
88-05-049	Old Reindeer 4012	Sarah's Attic	Closed	6.00	6.00
88-05-050	Young Reindeer 4013	Sarah's Attic	Closed	6.00	6.00
88-05-051	Red Reindeer 4014	Sarah's Attic	Closed	6.00	6.00
88-05-052	Myrtle The Pig 6504	Sarah's Attic	Closed	38.00	45.00
89-05-053	Brown Cow 2113	Sarah's Attic	Closed	18.00	18.00
89-05-054	Madam Donna 2321	Sarah's Attic	Closed	36.00	45.00
89-05-055	Maggie's Puppy 3091	Sarah's Attic	Closed	8.00	8.00
89-05-056	Whiskers Boy Cat 3106	Sarah's Attic	Closed	10.00	10.00
89-05-057	Puddin Girl Cat 3107	Sarah's Attic	Closed	10.00	10.00
89-05-058	Otis Pa Cat 3108	Sarah's Attic	Closed	13.00	13.00
89-05-059	Messieur Pierre 2346	Sarah's Attic	Closed	36.00	45.00
89-05-060	Wiggley Pig 3205	Sarah's Attic	Closed	17.00	17.00
90-05-061	Sherman Pa Squirrel 3221	Sarah's Attic	Closed	19.00	29.00
90-05-062	Sasha Ma Squirrel 3222	Sarah's Attic	Closed	19.00	29.00
90-05-063	Sonny Boy Squirrel 3223	Sarah's Attic	Closed	18.00	28.00
90-05-064	Sis Girl Squirrel 3224	Sarah's Attic	Closed	18.00	18.00
90-05-065	Waldo Dog 3274	Sarah's Attic	Closed	11.00	11.00
90-05-066	Horace & Sissy Dogs 3330	Sarah's Attic	Closed	50.00	50.00
90-05-067	Rebecca Mom Dog 3331	Sarah's Attic	Closed	40.00	40.00
90-05-068	Penny Girl Dog 3332	Sarah's Attic	Closed	35.00	35.00
90-05-069	Scooter Boy Dog 3333	Sarah's Attic	Closed	30.00	30.00
90-05-070	Jasper Dad Cat 3337	Sarah's Attic	Closed	36.00	36.00
90-05-071	Winnie Mom Cat 3338	Sarah's Attic	Closed	36.00	36.00
90-05-072	Scuffy Boy Cat 3339	Sarah's Attic	Closed	26.00	26.00
90-05-073	Lulu Girl Cat 3340	Sarah's Attic	Closed	26.00	26.00
91-05-074	Waldo with Flower 3379	Sarah's Attic	Closed	14.00	14.00
91-05-075	Kit-Nativity 3421	Sarah's Attic	12/94	15.00	15.00
91-05-076	Waldo-Nativity 3426	Sarah's Attic	12/94	15.00	15.00
91-05-077	Cracker-Dog 3434	Sarah's Attic	12/94	9.00	9.00
92-05-078	Jiggs Sleeping Cat 3537	Sarah's Attic	Closed	10.00	10.00
92-05-079	Banjo Dog 3622	Sarah's Attic	Closed	100.00	100.00
92-05-080	Donkey 3656	Sarah's Attic	Closed	26.00	26.00
92-05-081	Cow 3657	Sarah's Attic	Closed	30.00	30.00
92-05-082	Sheep 3658	Sarah's Attic	Closed	20.00	20.00
93-05-083	Waldo Dog-Gospel 3751	Sarah's Attic	2,500	10.00	10.00
93-05-084	Squeaks-Dog 3787	Sarah's Attic	Closed	7.00	7.00
93-05-085	Sparky-Winter 3824	Sarah's Attic	2,500	8.00	8.00
93-05-086	Ducks on Base 3944	Sarah's Attic	1,994	12.00	12.00
93-05-087	Chicks in Crate 3945	Sarah's Attic	1,994	10.00	10.00
93-05-088	Lambs on Base 3947	Sarah's Attic	1,994	16.00	16.00
94-05-089	Cheri-Mom Cat 3964	Sarah's Attic	12/94	30.00	30.00
94-05-090	Chester-Dad Cat 3965	Sarah's Attic	12/94	30.00	30.00
94-05-091	Stinky-Boy Cat 3966	Sarah's Attic	12/94	22.00	22.00
94-05-092	Sweetie-Girl Cat 3967	Sarah's Attic	12/94	16.00	16.00
94-05-093	Dottie-Mom Dog 3973	Sarah's Attic	12/94	30.00	30.00
94-05-094	Duke-Dad Dog 3974	Sarah's Attic	12/94	30.00	30.00
94-05-095	Dixie-Girl Dog 3975	Sarah's Attic	12/94	20.00	20.00
94-05-096	Dusty-Boy Dog 3976	Sarah's Attic	12/94	18.00	18.00
94-05-097	Lamb-lying down 3982	Sarah's Attic	Open	4.00	4.00
94-05-098	Meadow-Horses 3991	Sarah's Attic	500	40.00	40.00
94-05-099	Blaze-Fire Dog 3993	Sarah's Attic	Open	24.00	24.00
94-05-100	Bumbers-Cat Sleeping 3994	Sarah's Attic	Open	18.00	18.00
94-05-101	Gizmo-Cat w/Bow 3995	Sarah's Attic	Open	22.00	22.00
94-05-102	Popper-Dog 3996	Sarah's Attic	Open	14.00	14.00
94-05-103	Winkie-Cat 3997	Sarah's Attic	Open	14.00	14.00
94-05-104	Look at Me Cat 4134	Sarah's Attic	Open	25.00	25.00
94-05-105	Spot-Fire Dog 4231	Sarah's Attic	Open	10.00	10.00

Sarah's Attic, Inc. — **Classroom Memories**

		ARTIST	EDITION	ISSUE	QUOTE
88-06-001	Miss Pritchett	Sarah's Attic	Open	28.00	35.00
91-06-002	Achieving Our Goals	Sarah's Attic	10,000	80.00	80.00

Sarah's Attic, Inc. — **Cotton Tale Collection**

		ARTIST	EDITION	ISSUE	QUOTE
86-07-001	Winnie Rabbit 2036	Sarah's Attic	Closed	14.00	14.00
87-07-002	Wendall Rabbit 5285	Sarah's Attic	Closed	14.00	25.00
87-07-003	Wendy Rabbit 5286	Sarah's Attic	Closed	15.00	25.00
87-07-004	Wilbur Rabbit 5287	Sarah's Attic	Closed	13.00	25.00
87-07-005	Bonnie 5727	Sarah's Attic	Closed	30.00	30.00
87-07-006	Clyde 5728	Sarah's Attic	Closed	30.00	30.00
87-07-007	Floppy 5729	Sarah's Attic	Closed	19.00	19.00
88-07-008	Girl Rabbit Resin candle 3025	Sarah's Attic	Closed	9.00	9.00
88-07-009	Boy Rabbit Resin Candle 3026	Sarah's Attic	Closed	9.00	9.00
88-07-010	Lizzy Hare 3037	Sarah's Attic	Closed	8.00	8.00
88-07-011	Izzy Hare 3038	Sarah's Attic	Closed	8.00	8.00
88-07-012	Maddy Hare 3039	Sarah's Attic	Closed	11.00	11.00
88-07-013	Amos Hare 3040	Sarah's Attic	Closed	11.00	11.00
88-07-014	Americana Bunny 3048	Sarah's Attic	Closed	58.00	58.00
88-07-015	Bunny in Basket 4021	Sarah's Attic	Closed	48.00	55.00
88-07-016	Wendall Mini Rabbit 6268	Sarah's Attic	Closed	8.00	8.00
88-07-017	Wilbur Mini Rabbit 6269	Sarah's Attic	Closed	8.00	8.00
88-07-018	Wendy Mini Rabbit 6270	Sarah's Attic	Closed	8.00	8.00
88-07-019	Winnie Mini Rabbit 6271	Sarah's Attic	Closed	8.00	8.00
88-07-020	Cindi Rabbit 6282	Sarah's Attic	Closed	27.00	35.00
88-07-021	Billi Rabbit 6283	Sarah's Attic	Closed	27.00	35.00
89-07-022	Crumb Rabbit 3077	Sarah's Attic	Closed	29.00	35-43.00
89-07-023	Cookie Rabbit 3078	Sarah's Attic	Closed	29.00	35-43.00
89-07-024	Papa Rabbit 3079	Sarah's Attic	Closed	50.00	60-75.00
89-07-025	Nana Rabbit 3080	Sarah's Attic	Closed	50.00	60-75.00
89-07-026	Thelma Rabbit 3084	Sarah's Attic	Closed	33.00	40.00
89-07-027	Thomas Rabbit 3085	Sarah's Attic	Closed	33.00	40.00
89-07-028	Tessy Rabbit 3086	Sarah's Attic	Closed	15.00	20.00
89-07-029	Toby Rabbit 3087	Sarah's Attic	Closed	17.00	20.00
89-07-030	Sleepy Rabbit 3088	Sarah's Attic	Closed	16.00	16.00
90-07-031	Zeb Pa Rabbit w/Carrots 3217	Sarah's Attic	Closed	18.00	32.00
90-07-032	Zelda Ma Rabbit w/Carrots 3218	Sarah's Attic	Closed	18.00	32.00
90-07-033	Zeke Boy Rabbit w/Carrots 3219	Sarah's Attic	Closed	17.00	32.00
87-07-034	Zoe Girl Rabbit w/Carrots 3220	Sarah's Attic	Closed	17.00	32.00
90-07-035	Ollie Rabbit w/Vest 3239	Sarah's Attic	Closed	75.00	96.00
90-07-036	Molly Rabbit w/Vest 3240	Sarah's Attic	Closed	75.00	75.00
90-07-037	Henry Dad Rabbit w/Pipe 3263	Sarah's Attic	Closed	32.00	32.00
90-07-038	Hannah Mom Rabbit 3264	Sarah's Attic	Closed	32.00	32.00
90-07-039	Herbie Boy Rabbit 3265	Sarah's Attic	Closed	22.00	22.00
90-07-040	Hether Girl Rabbit 3266	Sarah's Attic	Closed	22.00	22.00
90-07-041	Zeb Sailor Dad 3319	Sarah's Attic	Closed	28.00	28.00
90-07-042	Zelda Sailor Mom 3320	Sarah's Attic	Closed	28.00	28.00
90-07-043	Zeke Sailor Boy 3321	Sarah's Attic	Closed	26.00	26.00
90-07-044	Zoe Sailor Girl 3322	Sarah's Attic	Closed	26.00	26.00
90-07-045	Snowball Rabbit 3329	Sarah's Attic	Closed	8.00	8.00
91-07-046	Papa Rabbit w/Hat 3348	Sarah's Attic	Closed	80.00	80.00
91-07-047	Nana Rabbit w/Washboard 3349	Sarah's Attic	Closed	100.00	100.00
91-07-048	Chuckles Rabbit 3350	Sarah's Attic	Closed	53.00	53.00
91-07-049	Cookie Rabbit 3351	Sarah's Attic	Closed	47.00	47.00
91-07-050	Crumb Rabbit 3352	Sarah's Attic	Closed	53.00	53.00
91-07-051	Sleepy Rabbit 3353	Sarah's Attic	Closed	35.00	35.00
91-07-052	Thomas Victorian Rabbit 3367	Sarah's Attic	Closed	60.00	60.00
91-07-053	Thelma Victorian Rabbit 3368	Sarah's Attic	Closed	60.00	60.00
91-07-054	Toby Victorian Rabbit 3369	Sarah's Attic	Closed	40.00	40.00
91-07-055	Tessy Victorian Rabbit 3370	Sarah's Attic	Closed	20.00	20.00
91-07-056	Tabitha Victorian Rabbit 3371	Sarah's Attic	Closed	30.00	30.00
91-07-057	Tucker Victorian Rabbit 3372	Sarah's Attic	Closed	37.00	37.00
92-07-058	Toby w/Train-Small 3673	Sarah's Attic	Closed	35.00	35.00
92-07-059	Tabitha Christmas 3688	Sarah's Attic	2500	24.00	24.00
92-07-060	Toby w/Hobby Horse 3689	Sarah's Attic	2500	32.00	32.00
92-07-061	Flower Girl Rabbit 3699	Sarah's Attic	Closed	32.00	32.00
92-07-062	Dustin Boy Rabbit 3700	Sarah's Attic	Closed	32.00	32.00
92-07-063	Petals Girl Rabbit 3701	Sarah's Attic	Closed	30.00	30.00
92-07-064	Pockets Boy Rabbit 3702	Sarah's Attic	Closed	30.00	30.00
92-07-065	Higgins Dad Rabbit 3703	Sarah's Attic	Closed	40.00	40.00
92-07-066	Annabelle Mom Rabbit 3704	Sarah's Attic	Closed	40.00	40.00
93-07-067	Hannah w/Muff 3733	Sarah's Attic	Closed	30.00	30.00
93-07-068	Henry w/Wreath 3734	Sarah's Attic	Closed	30.00	30.00
93-07-069	Hether in Sled 3735	Sarah's Attic	Closed	30.00	30.00
93-07-070	Herbie Sitting 3736	Sarah's Attic	Closed	25.00	25.00

		ARTIST	EDITION	ISSUE	QUOTE
93-07-071	Toby with Book/Christmas 3737	Sarah's Attic	2500	20.00	20.00
93-07-072	Tabitha Cowgirl 3738	Sarah's Attic	2500	30.00	30.00
93-07-073	Bunny Love Rabbit 3799	Sarah's Attic	12/94	18.00	18.00
93-07-074	Bunnies w/Eggs 3946	Sarah's Attic	1994	15.00	15.00
93-07-075	Thelma-Easter 3948	Sarah's Attic	1994	26.00	26.00
93-07-076	Thomas-Easter 3949	Sarah's Attic	1994	26.00	26.00
93-07-077	Tessy-Easter 3950	Sarah's Attic	1994	24.00	24.00
93-07-078	Toby-Easter 3951	Sarah's Attic	1994	24.00	24.00
94-07-079	Tabitha-Valentine 4117	Sarah's Attic	12/94	24.00	24.00
94-07-080	Toby-Valentine 4118	Sarah's Attic	12/94	24.00	24.00
94-07-081	Nana-Rabbit w/Book 4193	Sarah's Attic	6/96	55.00	55.00
94-07-082	Papa-Rabbit w/Paper 4194	Sarah's Attic	6/96	55.00	55.00
94-07-083	Crumb-Rabbit w/Book 4195	Sarah's Attic	6/96	40.00	40.00
94-07-084	Cookie-Rabbit Quilting 4196	Sarah's Attic	6/96	40.00	40.00
94-07-085	Corkey-Rabbit Chair 4197	Sarah's Attic	6/96	30.00	30.00
94-07-086	Sleepy-Bunny 4198	Sarah's Attic	6/96	23.00	23.00
94-07-087	Fluff-Angel Bunny 4199	Sarah's Attic	6/96	19.00	19.00
Sarah's Attic, Inc.		**Daisy Collection**			
89-08-001	Sally Booba 2344	Sarah's Attic	Closed	40.00	40.00
90-08-002	Jack Boy Ball & Glove 3249	Sarah's Attic	Closed	40.00	40.00
90-08-003	Sparky-Mark 3307	Sarah's Attic	Closed	55.00	55.00
90-08-004	Spike-Tim 3308	Sarah's Attic	Closed	46.00	46.00
90-08-005	Bomber-Tom 3309	Sarah's Attic	Closed	52.00	52.00
90-08-006	Jewel-Julie 3310	Sarah's Attic	Closed	62.00	62.00
90-08-007	Stretch-Mike 3311	Sarah's Attic	Closed	52.00	52.00
93-08-008	Jack Boy w/Broken Arm 3970	Sarah's Attic	2,000	30.00	30.00
Sarah's Attic, Inc.		**Ginger Babies Collection**			
89-09-001	Ginger 3202	Sarah's Attic	Closed	17.00	17.00
89-09-002	Molasses 3203	Sarah's Attic	Closed	17.00	17.00
89-09-003	Ginger Basket 3204	Sarah's Attic	Closed	6.00	6.00
90-09-004	Cinnamon 3226	Sarah's Attic	Closed	16.00	16.00
90-09-005	Nutmeg 3227	Sarah's Attic	Closed	16.00	16.00
92-09-006	Home Sweet Home 3608	Sarah's Attic	Closed	100.00	100.00
92-09-007	Ginger Cookie 3909	Sarah's Attic	Closed	50.00	50.00
92-09-008	Ginger Bench 3910	Sarah's Attic	Closed	10.00	10.00
92-09-009	Ginger Fence 3611	Sarah's Attic	Closed	13.00	13.00
92-09-010	Vanilla 3612	Sarah's Attic	Closed	18.00	18.00
92-09-011	Almond 3613	Sarah's Attic	Closed	18.00	18.00
92-09-012	Cinnamon & Nutmeg 3614	Sarah's Attic	Closed	36.00	36.00
92-09-013	Ginger Tree 3615	Sarah's Attic	Closed	20.00	20.00
Sarah's Attic, Inc.		**Happy Collection**			
87-10-001	Large Happy Clown 5113	Sarah's Attic	Closed	20.00	20.00
87-10-002	Mini. Happy Clown 5139	Sarah's Attic	Closed	8.00	8.00
87-10-003	Sitting Happy 3008	Sarah's Attic	Closed	19.00	19.00
87-10-004	Happy w/Balloons 3009	Sarah's Attic	Closed	14.00	14.00
87-10-005	Clown Necklace 5407	Sarah's Attic	Closed	10.00	10.00
88-10-006	Americana Clown 4025	Sarah's Attic	Closed	80.00	80.00
88-10-007	Christmas Clown 4026	Sarah's Attic	Closed	88.00	88.00
88-10-008	Clown Handstand X 6243	Sarah's Attic	Closed	10.00	10.00
88-10-009	Clown Sitting Y 6244	Sarah's Attic	Closed	10.00	10.00
88-10-010	Sitting Clown Z 6259	Sarah's Attic	Closed	10.00	10.00
88-10-011	Lady Clown 6313	Sarah's Attic	Closed	20.00	20.00
89-10-012	Curly Circus Clown 3148	Sarah's Attic	Closed	23.00	23.00
90-10-013	Encore Clown w/Dog 3306	Sarah's Attic	Closed	100.00	100.00
Sarah's Attic, Inc.		**Matt & Maggie**			
86-11-001	Matt Candle Holder	Sarah's Attic	Closed	12.00	12.00
86-11-002	Maggie Candle Holder	Sarah's Attic	Closed	12.00	12.00
86-11-003	Maggie	Sarah's Attic	Closed	14.00	14.00
86-11-004	Matt	Sarah's Attic	Closed	14.00	14.00
87-11-005	Standing Matt	Sarah's Attic	Closed	11.00	11.00
87-11-006	Standing Maggie	Sarah's Attic	Closed	11.00	11.00
87-11-007	Matt on Heart	Sarah's Attic	Closed	9.00	9.00
87-11-008	Maggie on Heart	Sarah's Attic	Closed	9.00	9.00
87-11-009	Matt & Maggie w/ Bear	Sarah's Attic	Closed	100.00	100.00
88-11-010	Large Matt	Sarah's Attic	Closed	48.00	48.00
88-11-011	Small Sitting Matt	Sarah's Attic	Closed	11.50	11.50
88-11-012	Small Sitting Maggie	Sarah's Attic	Closed	11.50	11.50
89-11-013	Mini Matt	Sarah's Attic	Closed	6.00	6.00
89-11-014	Mini Maggie	Sarah's Attic	Closed	6.00	6.00
89-11-015	Matt Bench Sitter	Sarah's Attic	Closed	32.00	32.00
89-11-016	Maggie Bench Sitter	Sarah's Attic	Closed	32.00	32.00
Sarah's Attic, Inc.		**Sarah's Neighborhood Friends**			
87-12-001	Bevie 5103	Sarah's Attic	Closed	14.00	14.00
87-12-002	Gramps-white 5104	Sarah's Attic	Closed	16.00	98.00
87-12-003	Grams-white 5105	Sarah's Attic	Closed	16.00	98.00
87-12-004	Dusty 5106	Sarah's Attic	Closed	19.00	19.00
87-12-005	Willie Bill 5108	Sarah's Attic	Closed	20.00	20.00
87-12-006	Shooter 5110	Sarah's Attic	Closed	20.00	20.00
87-12-007	Emmy Lou 5112	Sarah's Attic	Closed	14.00	14.00
87-12-008	Patsy-Cheerleader 5120	Sarah's Attic	Closed	19.00	19.00
87-12-009	Eddie 5337	Sarah's Attic	Closed	14.00	14.00
87-12-010	Daisy 3002	Sarah's Attic	Closed	24.00	24.00
87-12-011	Ashlee 5726	Sarah's Attic	Closed	44.00	44.00
87-12-012	Corky-Boy Sailor Suit 5793	Sarah's Attic	Closed	12.00	12.00
87-12-013	Clementine-Girl Sailor Suit 5794	Sarah's Attic	Closed	12.00	12.00
87-12-014	Butch-Boy Book sitting 5795	Sarah's Attic	Closed	14.00	14.00
87-12-015	Blondie-Girl doll sitting 5796	Sarah's Attic	Closed	14.00	14.00
87-12-016	Amber-Small Girl standing 5797	Sarah's Attic	Closed	14.00	14.00
87-12-017	Archie-Small Boy standing 5798	Sarah's Attic	Closed	14.00	14.00
87-12-018	Bare Bottom Baby 5799	Sarah's Attic	Closed	8.00	8.00
87-12-019	Beau-Cupie Boy 5861	Sarah's Attic	Closed	20.00	20.00
87-12-020	Buttons-Cupie Girl 5862	Sarah's Attic	Closed	20.00	20.00
88-12-021	Americana Beau 2076	Sarah's Attic	Closed	25.00	25.00
88-12-022	Americana Buttons 2077	Sarah's Attic	Closed	25.00	25.00
88-12-023	Trudy-W/Teacup 3042	Sarah's Attic	Closed	34.00	34.00
88-12-024	Lena-w/Doll 3043	Sarah's Attic	Closed	40.00	40.00
88-12-025	Jeffrey Boy w/Clown 6151	Sarah's Attic	Closed	26.00	26.00
88-12-026	Jessica 4033	Sarah's Attic	Closed	30.00	30.00
89-12-027	Baby Doll-mini 2318	Sarah's Attic	Closed	5.00	5.00
89-12-028	Jennifer & Max 2319	Sarah's Attic	Closed	57.00	57.00
89-12-029	Sweet Rose 3214	Sarah's Attic	Closed	50.00	50.00
89-12-030	Moose Boy Sitting 3215	Sarah's Attic	Closed	20.00	20.00
90-12-031	Cody-Victorian Boy 3229	Sarah's Attic	Closed	46.00	46.00
90-12-032	Bubba w/Lantern 3268	Sarah's Attic	Closed	40.00	40.00
90-12-033	Pansy w/Sled 3269	Sarah's Attic	Closed	35.00	35.00
90-12-034	Bud w/Book 3270	Sarah's Attic	Closed	40.00	40.00
90-12-035	Weasel w/Cap 3271	Sarah's Attic	Closed	40.00	40.00
90-12-036	Annie w/Violin 3272	Sarah's Attic	Closed	40.00	40.00

		ARTIST	EDITION	ISSUE	QUOTE
90-12-037	Hewett w/Drum 3273	Sarah's Attic	Closed	40.00	40.00
90-12-038	Tyler Victorian Boy 3327	Sarah's Attic	Closed	40.00	40.00
90-12-039	Tiffany Victorian Girl 3328	Sarah's Attic	Closed	40.00	40.00
91-12-040	Baby Tansy-white 2402	Sarah's Attic	Closed	40.00	40.00
91-12-041	Hewett w/Apples 3377	Sarah's Attic	Closed	40.00	40.00
91-12-042	Bud w/Newspaper 3378	Sarah's Attic	Closed	40.00	40.00
91-12-043	Annie w/Flower Basket 3380	Sarah's Attic	Closed	56.00	56.00
91-12-044	Pansy Pushing Carriage 3381	Sarah's Attic	Closed	50.00	50.00
91-12-045	Bubba w/Lemonade Stand 3382	Sarah's Attic	Closed	54.00	54.00
91-12-046	Weasel w/Newspaper 3383	Sarah's Attic	Closed	40.00	40.00
91-12-047	Dolly Nativity (Jesus) 3418	Sarah's Attic	12/94	20.00	20.00
91-12-048	Annie Nativity (Mary) 3419	Sarah's Attic	12/94	30.00	30.00
91-12-049	Bud Nativity (Joseph) 3420	Sarah's Attic	12/94	34.00	34.00
91-12-050	Bubba-Nativity King 3422	Sarah's Attic	12/94	40.00	40.00
91-12-051	Weasel-Nativity King 3423	Sarah's Attic	12/94	40.00	40.00
91-12-052	Hewitt-Nativity King 3424	Sarah's Attic	12/94	40.00	40.00
91-12-053	Pansy-Nativity Angel 3425	Sarah's Attic	12/94	30.00	30.00
91-12-054	Babes-Nativity Jesus 3427	Sarah's Attic	12/94	20.00	20.00
91-12-055	Noah-Nativity Jesus 3428	Sarah's Attic	12/94	36.00	36.00
91-12-056	Shelby-Nativity Mary 3429	Sarah's Attic	12/94	30.00	30.00
92-12-057	Misty 3616	Sarah's Attic	Closed	60.00	60.00
93-12-058	Grams w/Rolling Pin 3782	Sarah's Attic	Closed	50.00	50.00
93-12-059	Rosie on Crate 3783	Sarah's Attic	Closed	50.00	50.00
93-12-060	Ellie-Girl w/Book 3784	Sarah's Attic	Closed	28.00	28.00
93-12-061	Evan-Boy w/Bowl 3785	Sarah's Attic	Closed	28.00	28.00
93-12-062	Emily & Gideon-Small 3670	Sarah's Attic	Closed	40.00	40.00
Sarah's Attic, Inc.		**Memory Lane Collection**			
87-13-001	House W/Dormers 5731	Sarah's Attic	Closed	15.00	15.00
87-13-002	Barn 5732	Sarah's Attic	Closed	16.50	16.50
87-13-003	Mill 5733	Sarah's Attic	Closed	16.50	16.50
87-13-004	Cottage 5734	Sarah's Attic	Closed	13.00	13.00
87-13-005	Barber Shop 5735	Sarah's Attic	Closed	13.00	13.00
87-13-006	Grandma's House 5736	Sarah's Attic	Closed	13.00	13.00
87-13-007	Church 5737	Sarah's Attic	Closed	19.00	19.00
87-13-008	School 5738	Sarah's Attic	Closed	14.00	14.00
87-13-009	General Store 5739	Sarah's Attic	Closed	13.00	13.00
87-13-010	Drug Store 5740	Sarah's Attic	Closed	13.00	13.00
88-13-011	Mini Barber Shop 6210	Sarah's Attic	Closed	6.50	6.50
88-13-012	Mini Drug Store 6211	Sarah's Attic	Closed	6.00	6.00
88-13-013	Mini General Store 6212	Sarah's Attic	Closed	6.00	6.00
88-13-014	Mini Salt Box 6213	Sarah's Attic	Closed	6.00	6.00
88-13-015	Mini Church 6214	Sarah's Attic	Closed	6.50	6.50
88-13-016	Mini School 6215	Sarah's Attic	Closed	6.50	6.50
88-13-017	Mini Barn 6224	Sarah's Attic	Closed	6.00	6.00
88-13-018	Mini Grandma's House 6225	Sarah's Attic	Closed	7.00	7.00
88-13-019	Mini Mill 6227	Sarah's Attic	Closed	6.50	6.50
88-13-020	Bank 6237	Sarah's Attic	Closed	13.00	13.00
88-13-021	Train Depot 6256	Sarah's Attic	Closed	13.50	13.50
89-13-022	Fire Station 3196	Sarah's Attic	Closed	20.00	20.00
89-13-023	Post Office 3197	Sarah's Attic	Closed	25.00	25.00
89-13-024	Mini Depot 3198	Sarah's Attic	Closed	7.00	7.00
89-13-025	Mini Bank 3199	Sarah's Att!c	Closed	6.00	6.00
89-13-026	Briton Church 3216	Sarah's Attic	Closed	25.00	25.00
94-13-027	USA Victorian House 4263	Sarah's Attic	1,000	64.00	64.00
94-13-028	USA Barn 4264	Sarah's Attic	1,000	70.00	70.00
94-13-029	USA Out House 4265	Sarah's Attic	1,000	27.00	27.00
94-13-030	USA General Store 4266	Sarah's Attic	1,000	60.00	60.00
94-13-031	USA Church 4267	Sarah's Attic	1,000	60.00	60.00
94-13-032	USA School 4268	Sarah's Attic	1,000	56.00	56.00
94-13-033	USA Sarah's Home 4269	Sarah's Attic	1,000	70.00	70.00
Sarah's Attic, Inc.		**Dreams of Tomorrow**			
87-14-001	Baseball Player 5802	Sarah's Attic	Closed	24.00	24.00
87-14-002	Football Player 5803	Sarah's Attic	Closed	24.00	24.00
87-14-003	Woman Golfer 5804	Sarah's Attic	Closed	24.00	24.00
87-14-004	Man Golfer 5805	Sarah's Attic	Closed	24.00	24.00
88-14-005	Bowler 6152	Sarah's Attic	Closed	24.00	24.00
88-14-006	Basketball Player 6314	Sarah's Attic	Closed	24.00	24.00
91-14-007	Charity Sewing Flags 3486	Sarah's Attic	Closed	46.00	46.00
91-14-008	Benjamin w/Drums 3487	Sarah's Attic	Closed	46.00	46.00
91-14-009	Susie Painting Train 3488	Sarah's Attic	Closed	46.00	46.00
91-14-010	Skip Building Houses 3489	Sarah's Attic	Closed	50.00	50.00
92-14-011	Blossom 3502	Sarah's Attic	Closed	50.00	50.00
92-14-012	Madge-Farmer 3503	Sarah's Attic	Closed	50.00	50.00
92-14-013	Marty-Farmer 3504	Sarah's Attic	Closed	50.00	50.00
92-14-014	Pansy-Nurse 3505	Sarah's Attic	Closed	46.00	46.00
92-14-015	Bubba-Doctor 3506	Sarah's Attic	Closed	60.00	60.00
92-14-016	Annie-Teacher 3507	Sarah's Attic	Closed	55.00	55.00
92-14-017	Noah-Executive 3508	Sarah's Attic	Closed	46.00	46.00
92-14-018	Cupcake-Nurse 3514	Sarah's Attic	Closed	46.00	46.00
92-14-019	Twinkie-Doctor 3515	Sarah's Attic	Closed	50.00	50.00
92-14-020	Tillie-Teacher 3520	Sarah's Attic	Closed	50.00	50.00
92-14-021	Whimpy-Executive 3521	Sarah's Attic	Closed	46.00	46.00
92-14-022	Cricket-Graduate 3531	Sarah's Attic	Closed	46.00	46.00
92-14-023	Chips-Graduate 3532	Sarah's Attic	Closed	46.00	46.00
92-14-024	Katie-Executive 3665	Sarah's Attic	Closed	46.00	46.00
92-14-025	Shelby-Executive 3666	Sarah's Attic	Closed	46.00	46.00
92-14-026	Willie-Fireman 3667	Sarah's Attic	Closed	46.00	46.00
92-14-027	Bud-Fireman 3668	Sarah's Attic	Closed	50.00	50.00
92-14-028	Pansy-Ballerina 3682	Sarah's Attic	Closed	46.00	46.00
92-14-029	Cupcake-Ballerina 3683	Sarah's Attic	Closed	46.00	46.00
92-14-030	Twinkie-Policeman 3684	Sarah's Attic	Closed	46.00	46.00
92-14-031	Bubba-Policeman 3685	Sarah's Attic	Closed	46.00	46.00
93-14-032	Lottie-White Girl Graduate 3739	Sarah's Attic	Closed	35.00	35.00
93-14-033	Logan-White Boy Graduate 3740	Sarah's Attic	Closed	35.00	35.00
93-14-034	Tillie-Girl Basketball 3774	Sarah's Attic	Open	32.00	32.00
93-14-035	Willie-Boy Baseball 3775	Sarah's Attic	Open	32.00	32.00
93-14-036	Champ-White Boy Baseball 3776	Sarah's Attic	Open	32.00	32.00
93-14-037	Jojo-White Girl Basketball 3777	Sarah's Attic	Open	32.00	32.00
93-14-038	Pansy-Black Waitress 3778	Sarah's Attic	2,000	40.00	40.00
93-14-039	Dana-White Waitress 3779	Sarah's Attic	2,000	34.00	34.00
93-14-040	Noah-Black Pharmacist 3780	Sarah's Attic	2,000	34.00	34.00
93-14-041	Jack-Boy White Pharmacist 3781	Sarah's Attic	2,000	34.00	34.00
93-14-042	Willie-Pilot 3868	Sarah's Attic	2,000	27.00	27.00
93-14-043	Twinkie-Pilot 3869	Sarah's Attic	2,000	27.00	35.00
93-14-044	Tillie-Photographer 3870	Sarah's Attic	2,000	27.00	32.00
93-14-045	Rachel-Photographer 3871	Sarah's Attic	2,000	27.00	32.00
93-14-046	Cody-Cowboy 3886	Sarah's Attic	2,000	30.00	30.00
93-14-047	Josh-Jogger 3887	Sarah's Attic	2,000	25.00	25.00
93-14-048	Katie-Pharmacist 3898	Sarah's Attic	2,000	32.00	32.00
93-14-049	Pansy-Pharmacist 3899	Sarah's Attic	2,000	32.00	32.00

		ARTIST	EDITION	ISSUE	QUOTE
94-14-050	Sally Booba-Graduate 3983	Sarah's Attic	3,000	30.00	30.00
94-14-051	Jack Boy-Graduate 3984	Sarah's Attic	3,000	30.00	30.00
94-14-052	Tillie-Graduate 3985	Sarah's Attic	3,000	30.00	30.00
94-14-053	Willie-Graduate 3986	Sarah's Attic	3,000	30.00	30.00
94-14-054	Katie-Nurse 3987	Sarah's Attic	3,000	33.00	33.00
94-14-055	Whimpy-Doctor 3988	Sarah's Attic	3,000	33.00	33.00
94-14-056	Tillie-Nurse 3989	Sarah's Attic	3,000	33.00	33.00
94-14-057	Willie-Doctor 3990	Sarah's Attic	3,000	33.00	33.00
94-14-058	Dedication-White Doctor 4111	Sarah's Attic	3,000	38.00	38.00
94-14-059	Devotion-Black Doctor 4112	Sarah's Attic	3,000	33.00	33.00
94-14-060	Peaches-Dentist 4113	Sarah's Attic	3,000	33.00	33.00
94-14-061	Pug-Dentist 4114	Sarah's Attic	3,000	33.00	33.00
94-14-062	Twinkie-White Dentist 4115	Sarah's Attic	3,000	33.00	33.00
94-14-063	Cupcake-Dentist 4116	Sarah's Attic	12/94	33.00	33.00
94-14-064	John-Farmer w/Tractor 4119	Sarah's Attic	3,000	36.00	36.00
94-14-065	Joe-Farmer w/Basket 4120	Sarah's Attic	3,000	33.00	33.00
94-14-066	Shelby-Nurse 4127	Sarah's Attic	3,000	33.00	33.00
94-14-067	Annie-Nurse 4128	Sarah's Attic	3,000	33.00	33.00
94-14-068	Juliana-Teacher 4129	Sarah's Attic	3,000	34.00	34.00
94-14-069	Boyd-Teacher 4130	Sarah's Attic	3,000	34.00	34.00
94-14-070	Judy-Teacher 4131	Sarah's Attic	3,000	38.00	38.00
94-14-071	Bernie-Teacher 4132	Sarah's Attic	3,000	38.00	38.00
94-14-072	Calvin-Black Golfer 4161	Sarah's Attic	3,000	35.00	35.00
94-14-073	Spike-White Golfer 4162	Sarah's Attic	3,000	35.00	35.00
94-14-074	R. C. Mounted Police 4228	Sarah's Attic	2,000	32.00	32.00
94-14-075	Bubba-Fireman 4229	Sarah's Attic	2,000	37.00	37.00
94-14-076	Whimpy-Fireman 4230	Sarah's Attic	2,000	37.00	37.00
94-14-077	Willie-Police (blue) 4256	Sarah's Attic	2,000	32.00	32.00
94-14-078	Willie-Police (brown) 4257	Sarah's Attic	2,000	32.00	32.00
94-14-079	Hewett-Police (blue) 4258	Sarah's Attic	2,000	45.00	45.00
94-14-080	Hewett-Police (brown) 4259	Sarah's Attic	2,000	45.00	45.00
94-14-081	Bud-Police (blue) 4260	Sarah's Attic	2,000	45.00	45.00
94-14-082	Bud-Police (brown) 4261	Sarah's Attic	2,000	45.00	45.00
94-14-083	Josh-Hockey 4270	Sarah's Attic	2,000	38.00	38.00
94-14-084	Cody-Hockey 4271	Sarah's Attic	2,000	38.00	38.00
94-14-085	Bubba-Football 4272	Sarah's Attic	2,000	36.00	36.00
94-14-086	Moose-Football 4273	Sarah's Attic	2,000	36.00	36.00
94-14-087	Tillie-Soccer 4274	Sarah's Attic	2,000	36.00	36.00
94-14-088	Calvin-Soccer 4275	Sarah's Attic	2,000	36.00	36.00
94-14-089	Cupcake-Soccer 4276	Sarah's Attic	2,000	36.00	36.00
94-14-090	Champ-Soccer 4277	Sarah's Attic	2,000	36.00	36.00
94-14-091	Spike-Basketball 4278	Sarah's Attic	2,000	36.00	36.00
94-14-092	Boyd-Basketball 4279	Sarah's Attic	2,000	36.00	36.00

Sarah's Attic, Inc. **Snowflake Collection**

89-15-001	Flurry 2342	Sarah's Attic	Closed	12.00	12.00
89-15-002	Boo Mini Snowman 3200	Sarah's Attic	Closed	6.00	6.00
89-15-003	Winter Frolic 3209	Sarah's Attic	Closed	70.00	70.00
90-15-004	Old Glory Snowman 3225	Sarah's Attic	Closed	26.00	26.00
92-15-005	Christmas Love-Small 3674	Sarah's Attic	Closed	30.00	30.00
92-15-006	Crystal Mother Snowman 3721	Sarah's Attic	3,500	20.00	20.00
92-15-007	Topper Father Snowman 3722	Sarah's Attic	3,500	20.00	20.00
92-15-008	Sparkles Baby Snowman 3723	Sarah's Attic	3,500	14.00	14.00
93-15-009	Sparkles & Topper on Log 3840	Sarah's Attic	4,000	28.00	28.00
93-15-010	Cruiser Snowwman on Bike 3865	Sarah's Attic	4,000	23.00	23.00
93-15-011	Blizzard Snowman News 3866	Sarah's Attic	4,000	20.00	20.00
93-15-012	Bottles Snowman Milkman 3867	Sarah's Attic	4,000	20.00	20.00

Sarah's Attic, Inc. **Sarah's Gang Collection**

86-16-001	Willie Resin Candle 2023	Sarah's Attic	Closed	12.00	12.00
86-16-002	Tillie Resin Candle 2024	Sarah's Attic	Closed	12.00	12.00
86-16-003	Tillie-Original 2027	Sarah's Attic	Closed	14.00	20.00
86-16-004	Willie-Original 2028	Sarah's Attic	Closed	14.00	20-75.00
86-16-005	Whimpy-Original 2031	Sarah's Attic	Closed	14.00	20.00
86-16-006	Katie-Original 2032	Sarah's Attic	Closed	14.00	20.00
86-16-007	Twinkie-Original 2033	Sarah's Attic	Closed	14.00	20.00
86-16-008	Cupcake-Original 2034	Sarah's Attic	Closed	14.00	20-75.00
87-16-009	Whimpy Sitting 2001	Sarah's Attic	Closed	14.00	20.00
87-16-010	Katie Sitting 2002	Sarah's Attic	Closed	14.00	20.00
87-16-011	Twinkie w/Pole 5107	Sarah's Attic	Closed	20.00	20.00
87-16-012	Cupcake w/Rope 5119	Sarah's Attic	Closed	16.00	16.00
87-16-013	Cupcake On Heart 5140	Sarah's Attic	Closed	9.00	20.00
87-16-014	Katie On Heart 5141	Sarah's Attic	Closed	9.00	20.00
87-16-015	Whimpy on Heart 5142	Sarah's Attic	Closed	9.00	20.00
87-16-016	Twinkie On Heart 5143	Sarah's Attic	Closed	9.00	20.00
87-16-017	Tillie On Heart 5150	Sarah's Attic	Closed	9.00	20.00
87-16-018	Willie On Heart 5151	Sarah's Attic	Closed	9.00	20.00
88-16-019	Cupcake 4027	Sarah's Attic	Open	20.00	20.00
88-16-020	Twinkie 4028	Sarah's Attic	Open	20.00	20.00
88-16-021	Katie 4029	Sarah's Attic	Open	20.00	20.00
88-16-022	Whimpy 4030	Sarah's Attic	Open	20.00	20.00
88-16-023	Willie 4031	Sarah's Attic	Open	20.00	20.00
88-16-024	Tillie 4032	Sarah's Attic	Open	20.00	20.00
89-16-025	Willie-Americana 2300	Sarah's Attic	Closed	21.00	21.00
89-16-026	Tillie-Americana 2301	Sarah's Attic	Closed	21.00	21.00
89-16-027	Katie-Americana 2302	Sarah's Attic	Closed	21.00	21.00
89-16-028	Whimpy-Americana 2303	Sarah's Attic	Closed	21.00	21.00
89-16-029	Cupcake-Americana 2304	Sarah's Attic	Closed	21.00	21.00
89-16-030	Twinkie-Americana 2305	Sarah's Attic	Closed	21.00	21.00
89-16-031	Baby Rachel 2306	Sarah's Attic	Open	20.00	20.00
89-16-032	Katie-Small Sailor 2307	Sarah's Attic	Closed	14.00	20.00
89-16-033	Whimpy-Small Sailor 2308	Sarah's Attic	Closed	14.00	20.00
89-16-034	Cupcake-Small School 2309	Sarah's Attic	Closed	11.00	20.00
89-16-035	Twinkie-Small School 2310	Sarah's Attic	Closed	11.00	20.00
89-16-036	Willie-Small Country 2311	Sarah's Attic	Closed	18.00	18.00
89-16-037	Tillie-Small Country 2312	Sarah's Attic	Closed	18.00	18.00
89-16-038	Cupcake Clown 3144	Sarah's Attic	Closed	21.00	21.00
89-16-039	Twinkie Clown 3145	Sarah's Attic	Closed	19.00	19.00
90-16-040	Katie & Whimpy-Beachtime 3243	Sarah's Attic	Closed	60.00	60-75.00
90-16-041	Cupcake-Beachtime 3244	Sarah's Attic	Closed	35.00	35.00
90-16-042	Twinkie-Beachtime 3245	Sarah's Attic	Closed	35.00	35.00
90-16-043	Willie-Beachtime 3246	Sarah's Attic	Closed	35.00	35.00
90-16-044	Tillie-Beachtime 3247	Sarah's Attic	Closed	35.00	35.00
90-16-045	Baby Rachel-Beachtime 3248	Sarah's Attic	Closed	35.00	35.00
90-16-046	Katie-Witch 3312	Sarah's Attic	Closed	40.00	40.00
90-16-047	Whimpy-Scarecrow 3313	Sarah's Attic	Closed	40.00	40.00
90-16-048	Cupcake-Devil 3314	Sarah's Attic	Closed	40.00	40.00
90-16-049	Twinkie-Devil 3315	Sarah's Attic	Closed	40.00	40.00
90-16-050	Tillie-Clown 3316	Sarah's Attic	Closed	40.00	40.00
90-16-051	Willie-Clown 3317	Sarah's Attic	Closed	40.00	40.00
90-16-052	Rachel-Pumpkin 3318	Sarah's Attic	Closed	40.00	40.00
91-16-053	Rachel-Americana 3364	Sarah's Attic	Closed	30.00	30.00
91-16-054	Tillie Masquerade 3412	Sarah's Attic	Closed	45.00	45.00
91-16-055	Whimpy-Groom 3430	Sarah's Attic	12/94	47.00	47.00
91-16-056	Katie-Bride 3431	Sarah's Attic	12/94	47.00	47.00
91-16-057	Rachel-Flower Girl 3432	Sarah's Attic	12/94	40.00	40.00
91-16-058	Tyler-Ring Bearer 3433	Sarah's Attic	12/94	40.00	40.00
91-16-059	Twinkie-Minister 3435	Sarah's Attic	12/94	50.00	50.00
91-16-060	Tillie-Bride 3436	Sarah's Attic	12/94	47.00	47.00
91-16-061	Willie-Groom 3437	Sarah's Attic	12/94	47.00	47.00
91-16-062	Peaches-Flower Girl 3438	Sarah's Attic	12/94	40.00	40.00
91-16-063	Pug-Ringbearer 3439	Sarah's Attic	12/94	40.00	40.00
91-16-064	Percy-Minister 3440	Sarah's Attic	12/94	50.00	50.00
91-16-065	Katie-Thanksgiving 3468	Sarah's Attic	Closed	32.00	32.00
91-16-066	Whimpy-Thanksgiving 3469	Sarah's Attic	Closed	32.00	32.00
91-16-067	Tillie-Thanksgiving 3472	Sarah's Attic	Closed	32.00	32.00
91-16-068	Willie-Thanksgiving 3473	Sarah's Attic	Closed	32.00	32.00
91-16-069	Rachel-Thanksgiving 3474	Sarah's Attic	Closed	32.00	32.00
92-16-070	Tillie On Log 3705	Sarah's Attic	2,500	35.00	35.00
92-16-071	Willie w/Skates 3706	Sarah's Attic	2,500	35.00	35.00
92-16-072	Katie On Sled 3707	Sarah's Attic	2,500	35.00	35.00
92-16-073	Whimpy w/Book 3708	Sarah's Attic	2,,500	35.00	35.00
93-16-074	Katie & Rachel in Chair 3764	Sarah's Attic	12/94	60.00	60.00
93-16-075	Twinkie w/Football 3765	Sarah's Attic	12/94	28.00	28.00
93-16-076	Cupcake on Bench 3766	Sarah's Attic	12/94	28.00	28.00
93-16-077	Whimpy w/Train 3767	Sarah's Attic	12/94	28.00	28.00
93-16-078	Willie Lying w/Pillow 3768	Sarah's Attic	12/94	28.00	28.00
93-16-079	Tillie w/Bear 3769	Sarah's Attic	12/94	28.00	28.00
93-16-080	Twinkie w/Snowballs 3821	Sarah's Attic	2,500	35.00	35.00
93-16-081	Cupcake w/Snowman 3822	Sarah's Attic	2,500	35.00	35.00
93-16-082	Rachel in Snowsuit 3823	Sarah's Attic	2,500	25.00	25.00
93-16-083	Whimpy-Spring 3934	Sarah's Attic	1,994	28.00	28.00
93-16-084	Katie-Spring 3935	Sarah's Attic	1,994	28.00	28.00
93-16-085	Twinkie-Spring 3936	Sarah's Attic	1,994	28.00	28.00
93-16-086	Cupcake-Spring 3937	Sarah's Attic	1,994	30.00	30.00
93-16-087	Tillie-Spring 3938	Sarah's Attic	1,994	30.00	30.00
93-16-088	Willie-Spring 3939	Sarah's Attic	1,994	28.00	28.00
93-16-089	Rachel-Spring 3940	Sarah's Attic	1,994	30.00	30.00

Sarah's Attic, Inc. **Santas Of The Month-Series A**

88-17-001	January White Santa	Sarah's Attic	Closed	50.00	135-150.
88-17-002	January Black Santa	Sarah's Attic	Closed	50.00	200-300.
88-17-003	February White Santa	Sarah's Attic	Closed	50.00	135-150.
88-17-004	February Black Santa	Sarah's Attic	Closed	50.00	200-300.
88-17-005	March White Santa	Sarah's Attic	Closed	50.00	135-150.
88-17-006	March Black Santa	Sarah's Attic	Closed	50.00	200-300.
88-17-007	April White Santa	Sarah's Attic	Closed	50.00	135-150.
88-17-008	April Black Santa	Sarah's Attic	Closed	50.00	200-300.
88-17-009	May White Santa	Sarah's Attic	Closed	50.00	135-150.
88-17-010	May Black Santa	Sarah's Attic	Closed	50.00	200-300.
88-17-011	June White Santa	Sarah's Attic	Closed	50.00	135-150.
88-17-012	June Black Santa	Sarah's Attic	Closed	50.00	200-300.
88-17-013	July White Santa	Sarah's Attic	Closed	50.00	175.00
88-17-014	July Black Santa	Sarah's Attic	Closed	50.00	200-300.
88-17-015	August White Santa	Sarah's Attic	Closed	50.00	135-150.
88-17-016	August Black Santa	Sarah's Attic	Closed	50.00	200-300.
88-17-017	September White Santa	Sarah's Attic	Closed	50.00	135-150.
88-17-018	September Black Santa	Sarah's Attic	Closed	50.00	200-300.
88-17-019	October White Santa	Sarah's Attic	Closed	50.00	135-150.
88-17-020	October Black Santa	Sarah's Attic	Closed	50.00	200-300.
88-17-021	November White Santa	Sarah's Attic	Closed	50.00	135-150.
88-17-022	November Black Santa	Sarah's Attic	Closed	50.00	200-300.
88-17-023	December White Santa	Sarah's Attic	Closed	50.00	135-150.
88-17-024	December Black Santa	Sarah's Attic	Closed	50.00	225-375.
88-17-025	Mini January White Santa	Sarah's Attic	Closed	14.00	33-35.00
88-17-026	Mini January Black Santa	Sarah's Attic	Closed	14.00	35.00
88-17-027	Mini February White Santa	Sarah's Attic	Closed	14.00	33-35.00
88-17-028	Mini February Black Santa	Sarah's Attic	Closed	14.00	35.00
88-17-029	Mini March White Santa	Sarah's Attic	Closed	14.00	33-35.00
88-17-030	Mini March Black Santa	Sarah's Attic	Closed	14.00	35.00
88-17-031	Mini April White Santa	Sarah's Attic	Closed	14.00	33-35.00
88-17-032	Mini April Black Santa	Sarah's Attic	Closed	14.00	35.00
88-17-033	Mini May White Santa	Sarah's Attic	Closed	14.00	33-35.00
88-17-034	Mini May Black Santa	Sarah's Attic	Closed	14.00	35.00
88-17-035	Mini June White Santa	Sarah's Attic	Closed	14.00	33-35.00
88-17-036	Mini June Black Santa	Sarah's Attic	Closed	14.00	35.00
88-17-037	Mini July White Santa	Sarah's Attic	Closed	14.00	33-35.00
88-17-038	Mini July Black Santa	Sarah's Attic	Closed	14.00	35.00
88-17-039	Mini August White Santa	Sarah's Attic	Closed	14.00	33-35.00
88-17-040	Mini August Black Santa	Sarah's Attic	Closed	14.00	35.00
88-17-041	Mini September White Santa	Sarah's Attic	Closed	14.00	33-35.00
88-17-042	Mini September Black Santa	Sarah's Attic	Closed	14.00	35.00
88-17-043	Mini October White Santa	Sarah's Attic	Closed	14.00	33-35.00
88-17-044	Mini October Black Santa	Sarah's Attic	Closed	14.00	35.00
88-17-045	Mini November White Santa	Sarah's Attic	Closed	14.00	33-35.00
88-17-046	Mini November Black Santa	Sarah's Attic	Closed	14.00	35.00
88-17-047	Mini December White Santa	Sarah's Attic	Closed	14.00	33-35.00
88-17-048	Mini December Black Santa	Sarah's Attic	Closed	14.00	35.00

Sarah's Attic, Inc. **Santas Of The Month-Series B**

90-18-001	Jan. Santa Winter Fun 7135	Sarah's Attic	Closed	80.00	80.00
90-18-002	Feb. Santa Cupids Help 7136	Sarah's Attic	Closed	120.00	120.00
90-18-003	Mar. Santa Irish Delight 7137	Sarah's Attic	Closed	120.00	120.00
90-18-004	Apr. Santa Spring/Joy 7138	Sarah's Attic	Closed	150.00	150.00
90-18-005	May Santa Par For Course 7139	Sarah's Attic	Closed	100.00	100.00
90-18-006	June Santa Graduation 7140	Sarah's Attic	Closed	70.00	70.00
90-18-007	July Santa God Bless 7141	Sarah's Attic	Closed	100.00	100.00
90-18-008	Aug. Santa Summers Tranquility 7142	Sarah's Attic	Closed	110.00	110.00
90-18-009	Sep. Santa Touchdown 7143	Sarah's Attic	Closed	90.00	90.00
90-18-010	Oct. Santa Seasons Plenty 7144	Sarah's Attic	Closed	120.00	120.00
90-18-011	Nov. Santa Give Thanks 7145	Sarah's Attic	Closed	100.00	100.00
90-18-012	Dec. Santa Peace 7146	Sarah's Attic	Closed	120.00	120.00
90-18-013	Mrs. January 7147	Sarah's Attic	Closed	80.00	80.00
90-18-014	Mrs. February 7148	Sarah's Attic	Closed	110.00	110.00
90-18-015	Mrs. March 7149	Sarah's Attic	Closed	80.00	80.00
90-18-016	Mrs. April 7150	Sarah's Attic	Closed	110.00	110.00
90-18-017	Mrs. May 7151	Sarah's Attic	Closed	80.00	80.00
90-18-018	Mrs. June 7152	Sarah's Attic	Closed	70.00	70.00
90-18-019	Mrs. July 7153	Sarah's Attic	Closed	100.00	100.00
90-18-020	Mrs. August 7154	Sarah's Attic	Closed	90.00	90.00
90-18-021	Mrs. September 7155	Sarah's Attic	Closed	90.00	90.00
90-18-022	Mrs. October 7156	Sarah's Attic	Closed	90.00	90.00
90-18-023	Mrs. November 7157	Sarah's Attic	Closed	90.00	90.00
90-18-024	Mrs. December 7158	Sarah's Attic	Closed	110.00	110.00

		ARTIST	EDITION	ISSUE	QUOTE
Sarah's Attic, Inc.	**Santas Of The Month-Series C**				
90-19-001	Jan. Fruits of Love 3400	Sarah's Attic	Closed	90.00	90.00
90-19-002	Feb. From The Heart 3401	Sarah's Attic	Closed	90.00	90.00
90-19-003	Mar. Irish Love 3402	Sarah's Attic	Closed	100.00	100.00
90-19-004	Apr. Spring Time 3403	Sarah's Attic	Closed	90.00	90.00
90-19-005	May Caddy Chatter 3404	Sarah's Attic	Closed	100.00	100.00
90-19-006	June Homerun 3405	Sarah's Attic	Closed	90.00	90.00
90-19-007	July Celebrate America 3406	Sarah's Attic	Closed	90.00	90.00
90-19-008	Aug. Fun In The Sun 3407	Sarah's Attic	Closed	90.00	90.00
90-19-009	Sept. Lessons In Love 3408	Sarah's Attic	Closed	90.00	90.00
90-19-010	Oct. Masquerade 3409	Sarah's Attic	Closed	120.00	120.00
90-19-011	Nov. Harvest Of Love 3410	Sarah's Attic	Closed	120.00	120.00
90-19-012	Dec. A Gift Of Peace 3411	Sarah's Attic	Closed	90.00	90.00
Sarah's Attic, Inc.	**Santas Of The Month-Series D**				
93-20-001	January White Wintertime Santa 3881	Sarah's Attic	12/94	35.00	35.00
93-20-002	February White Valentine Santa 3882	Sarah's Attic	12/94	35.00	35.00
93-20-003	March White St. Patrick's Santa 3885	Sarah's Attic	12/94	35.00	35.00
93-20-004	April White Easter Santa 3741	Sarah's Attic	12/94	35.00	35.00
93-20-005	May White Springtime Santa 3742	Sarah's Attic	12/94	35.00	35.00
93-20-006	June White Summertime Santa 3743	Sarah's Attic	12/94	35.00	35.00
93-20-007	July White Americana Santa 3815	Sarah's Attic	12/94	35.00	35.00
93-20-008	August White Beachtime Santa 3816	Sarah's Attic	12/94	35.00	35.00
93-20-009	September White Classroom Santa 3817	Sarah's Attic	12/94	35.00	35.00
92-20-010	Oct. White Halloween Santa 3696	Sarah's Attic	12/94	35.00	35.00
92-20-011	Nov. White Harvest Santa 3697	Sarah's Attic	12/94	35.00	35.00
92-20-012	Dec. White Father X-Mas Santa 3698	Sarah's Attic	12/94	35.00	35.00
Sarah's Attic, Inc.	**Santas Of The Month-Series E**				
93-21-001	January Black Wintertime Santa 3880	Sarah's Attic	12/94	35.00	35.00
93-21-002	February Black Valentine Santa 3883	Sarah's Attic	12/94	35.00	35.00
93-21-003	March Black St. Patrick's Santa 3884	Sarah's Attic	12/94	35.00	35.00
93-21-004	April Black Easter Santa 3746	Sarah's Attic	12/94	35.00	35.00
93-21-005	May Black Springtime Santa 3747	Sarah's Attic	12/94	35.00	35.00
93-21-006	June Black Summertime Santa 3748	Sarah's Attic	12/94	35.00	35.00
93-21-007	July Black Americana Santa 3818	Sarah's Attic	12/94	35.00	35.00
93-21-008	August Black Beachtime Santa 3819	Sarah's Attic	12/94	35.00	35.00
93-21-009	September Black Classroom Santa 3820	Sarah's Attic	12/94	35.00	35.00
92-21-010	Oct. Black Halloween Santa 3729	Sarah's Attic	12/94	35.00	35.00
92-21-011	Nov. Black Harvest Santa 3730	Sarah's Attic	12/94	35.00	35.00
92-21-012	Dec. Black Father X-Mas Santa 3731	Sarah's Attic	12/94	35.00	35.00
Sarah's Attic, Inc.	**Tender Moments**				
92-22-001	Black Baby Boy Birth 3516	Sarah's Attic	Closed	50.00	50.00
92-22-002	Black Baby Girl 1-2 3517	Sarah's Attic	Closed	50.00	50.00
92-22-003	Black Baby Boy 1-2 3518	Sarah's Attic	Closed	50.00	50.00
92-22-004	Black Baby Girl Birth 3526	Sarah's Attic	Closed	50.00	50.00
92-22-005	White Baby Boy 1 3527	Sarah's Attic	Closed	60.00	60.00
92-22-006	White Baby Girl 1 3528	Sarah's Attic	Closed	60.00	60.00
92-22-007	White Girl 1-2 3529	Sarah's Attic	Closed	60.00	60.00
92-22-008	White Boy 1-2 3530	Sarah's Attic	Closed	60.00	60.00
92-22-009	Misty 3616	Sarah's Attic	Closed	60.00	60.00
92-22-010	White Girl 2-3 3623	Sarah's Attic	Closed	60.00	60.00
92-22-011	White Boy 2-3 3624	Sarah's Attic	Closed	60.00	60.00
92-22-012	Small Black Girl 2-3 3675	Sarah's Attic	Closed	50.00	50.00
92-22-013	Small Black Boy 2-3 3676	Sarah's Attic	Closed	50.00	50.00
92-22-014	White Girl 3-4 3690	Sarah's Attic	Closed	50.00	50.00
92-22-015	White Boy 3-4 3691	Sarah's Attic	Closed	50.00	50.00
93-22-016	Black Girl 3-4/Tricycle 3744	Sarah's Attic	Open	40.00	60.00
93-22-017	Black Boy 3-4/In Wagon 3745	Sarah's Attic	Open	40.00	40.00
93-22-018	Love of Life-Black Couple 3788	Sarah's Attic	Closed	70.00	85.00
93-22-019	True Love-White Couple 3789	Sarah's Attic	1,000	70.00	70.00
93-22-020	New Beginning White Pregnant Woman 3790	Sarah's Attic	1,000	55.00	55.00
93-22-021	Joy of Motherhood Black Pregnant Woman 3791	Sarah's Attic	1,000	55.00	55.00
93-22-022	Gentle Touch Black Girls 3825	Sarah's Attic	2,500	40.00	40.00
93-22-023	Special Times White Girls 3826	Sarah's Attic	2,500	40.00	40.00
93-22-024	Catch of Love White Men Fishing 3827	Sarah's Attic	4,000	50.00	50.00
93-22-025	Days to Remember Black Men Fishing 3828	Sarah's Attic	4,000	50.00	50.00
93-22-026	Always & Forever White Wedding 3834	Sarah's Attic	4,000	60.00	60.00
93-22-027	Promise of Love Black Wedding 3835	Sarah's Attic	4,000	60.00	60.00
93-22-028	Bless This Child White Couple 3838	Sarah's Attic	2,500	60.00	60.00
93-22-029	Little Blessing Black Couple 3839	Sarah's Attic	2,500	75.00	75.00
93-22-030	Special White Girl in Wheelchair 3968	Sarah's Attic	Open	38.00	38.00
93-22-031	Special Black Boy in Wheelchair 3969	Sarah's Attic	Open	38.00	38.00
94-22-032	Black Girl on Horse 4-5 3957	Sarah's Attic	Open	37.00	37.00
94-22-033	Black Boy w/Hobby Horse 4-5 3958	Sarah's Attic	Open	33.00	33.00
94-22-034	White Girl w/Trunk 4-5 3959	Sarah's Attic	Open	40.00	40.00
94-22-035	White Boy w/Fire Truck 4-5 3960	Sarah's Attic	Open	40.00	40.00
94-22-036	Special White Boy 4125	Sarah's Attic	Open	38.00	38.00
94-22-037	Special Black Girl 4126	Sarah's Attic	Open	38.00	38.00
94-22-038	I Love You-Sign 4216	Sarah's Attic	Open	16.00	16.00
94-22-039	Thinking of You-Sign 4217	Sarah's Attic	Open	16.00	16.00
94-22-040	White Special Angel-Sign 4218	Sarah's Attic	Open	16.00	16.00
94-22-041	Thank You-Sign 4219	Sarah's Attic	Open	16.00	16.00
94-22-042	Get Well Soon-Sign 4220	Sarah's Attic	Open	16.00	16.00
94-22-043	Special Father-Sign 4221	Sarah's Attic	Open	16.00	16.00
94-22-044	Special Mother-Sign 4222	Sarah's Attic	Open	16.00	16.00
94-22-045	I'm Sorry-Sign 4223	Sarah's Attic	Open	16.00	16.00
94-22-046	Black Special Angel-Sign 4224	Sarah's Attic	Open	16.00	16.00
94-22-047	Love & Hugs Girl 4255	Sarah's Attic	Open	38.00	38.00
Sarah's Attic, Inc.	**Tattered n' Torn Collection**				
90-23-001	Opie Boy Rag Doll 3241	Sarah's Attic	Closed	50.00	50.00
90-23-002	Polly Girl Rag Daoll 3242	Sarah's Attic	Closed	50.00	50.00
90-23-003	Muffin Rag Doll 3335	Sarah's Attic	Closed	30.00	30.00
90-23-004	Puffin Rag Doll 3343	Sarah's Attic	Closed	30.00	30.00
91-23-005	Prissy & Peanut-White 2400	Sarah's Attic	Closed	120.00	120.00
91-23-006	Muffin & Puffin-White 2401	Sarah's Attic	Closed	55.00	55.00
91-23-007	Prissy & Peanut 3360	Sarah's Attic	Closed	120.00	120.00
91-23-008	Muffin & Puffin w/Trunk 3361	Sarah's Attic	Closed	55.00	55.00
94-23-009	Jellie-Girl Rag Doll 4163	Sarah's Attic	2,500	30.00	30.00
94-23-010	Beanie-Boy Rag Doll 4164	Sarah's Attic	2,500	30.00	30.00
94-23-011	Belle-Girl Rag Doll 4180	Sarah's Attic	2,500	30.00	30.00
94-23-012	Britches-Boy Rag Doll 4181	Sarah's Attic	2,500	30.00	30.00
Sarah's Attic, Inc.	**Spirit of Christmas Collection**				
87-24-001	Santa Sitting 5122	Sarah's Attic	Closed	18.00	18.00
87-24-002	Mini Santa w/Cane 5123	Sarah's Attic	Closed	8.00	8.00
87-24-003	Large Santa w/Cane 5124	Sarah's Attic	Closed	27.00	27.00
87-24-004	Small Santa w/Tree 5125	Sarah's Attic	Closed	14.00	14.00
87-24-005	Mary 5134	Sarah's Attic	Closed	12.00	12.00

		ARTIST	EDITION	ISSUE	QUOTE
87-24-006	Joseph 5135	Sarah's Attic	Closed	12.00	12.00
87-24-007	Jesus 5136	Sarah's Attic	Closed	11.00	11.00
87-24-008	Mrs. Claus 5289	Sarah's Attic	Closed	26.00	26.00
87-24-009	Naughty or Nice 2048	Sarah's Attic	Closed	100.00	100.00
87-24-010	Father Snow 2049	Sarah's Attic	Closed	42.00	42.00
87-24-011	Jingle Bells 2050	Sarah's Attic	Closed	20.00	20.00
87-24-012	Long Journey 2051	Sarah's Attic	Closed	19.00	19.00
87-24-013	St. Nick 3005	Sarah's Attic	Closed	28.00	28.00
87-24-014	Santa's Workshop 3006	Sarah's Attic	Closed	50.00	50.00
87-24-015	Colonel Santa 3007	Sarah's Attic	Closed	30.00	30.00
87-24-016	Santa Head-3/4 3018	Sarah's Attic	Closed	8.00	8.00
87-24-017	Santa Head-Full 3019	Sarah's Attic	Closed	8.00	8.00
87-24-018	Santa /wBasket 3020	Sarah's Attic	Closed	9.00	9.00
87-24-019	Santa-Necklace 5408	Sarah's Attic	Closed	10.00	10.00
87-24-020	Kris Kringle 5860	Sarah's Attic	Closed	100.00	100.00
88-24-021	Mary-Natural 2080	Sarah's Attic	Closed	11.00	11.00
88-24-022	Joseph-Natural 2081	Sarah's Attic	Closed	11.00	11.00
88-24-023	Baby Jesus-Natural 2082	Sarah's Attic	Closed	7.00	7.00
88-24-024	Mini Mary-Natural 2087	Sarah's Attic	Closed	5.00	5.00
88-24-025	Mini Joseph-Natural 2088	Sarah's Attic	Closed	5.00	5.00
88-24-026	Mini-Jesus 2089	Sarah's Attic	Closed	4.00	4.00
88-24-027	Mary-Mini 3034	Sarah's Attic	Closed	6.00	6.00
88-24-028	Mini Joseph-Natural 3035	Sarah's Attic	Closed	6.00	6.00
88-24-029	Mini Jesus 3036	Sarah's Attic	Closed	4.00	4.00
88-24-030	Elf Grabbing Hat 3041	Sarah's Attic	Closed	8.00	8.00
88-24-031	Ho Ho Santa w/Elf 3053	Sarah's Attic	Closed	84.00	84.00
88-24-032	Santa in Chimney 4020	Sarah's Attic	Closed	110.00	110.00
88-24-033	Sitting Elf 6238	Sarah's Attic	Closed	7.00	7.00
88-24-034	Elf w/Gift 6239	Sarah's Attic	Closed	8.00	8.00
88-24-035	Small sitting Santa 6258	Sarah's Attic	Closed	11.00	11.00
88-24-036	Mrs. Claus Small 6272	Sarah's Attic	Closed	11.00	11.00
88-24-037	Mary 6307	Sarah's Attic	Closed	19.00	19.00
88-24-038	Joseph 6308	Sarah's Attic	Closed	19.00	19.00
88-24-039	Jesus 6309	Sarah's Attic	Closed	11.00	11.00
88-24-040	Large Santa Resin Candle 3068	Sarah's Attic	Closed	11.00	11.00
88-24-041	Large Mrs. Claus Resin Candle 3069	Sarah's Attic	Closed	11.00	11.00
88-24-042	Small Santa Resin Candle 3072	Sarah's Attic	Closed	10.00	10.00
88-24-043	Small Mrs. Claus Resin Candle 3073	Sarah's Attic	Closed	10.00	10.00
88-24-044	Mini Santa Resin Candle 3074	Sarah's Attic	Closed	7.00	7.00
88-24-045	Santa Kneeling 4011	Sarah's Attic	Closed	22.00	22.00
89-24-046	Spirit of Christmas Santa 2320	Sarah's Attic	Closed	80.00	80.00
89-24-047	Silent Night 2343	Sarah's Attic	Closed	33.00	33.00
89-24-048	Woodland Santa 2345	Sarah's Attic	Closed	100.00	100.00
89-24-049	Jolly II 2347	Sarah's Attic	Closed	17.00	17.00
89-24-050	Yule Tiding II 2348	Sarah's Attic	Closed	23.00	23.00
89-24-051	St. Nick II 2349	Sarah's Attic	Closed	43.00	43.00
89-24-052	Blessed Christmas 2350	Sarah's Attic	Closed	100.00	100.00
89-24-053	Father Snow II 2351	Sarah's Attic	Closed	36.00	36.00
89-24-054	Christmas Joy 3177	Sarah's Attic	Closed	32.00	32.00
89-24-055	Jingle Bells II 3178	Sarah's Attic	Closed	26.00	26.00
89-24-056	Colonel Santa II 3179	Sarah's Attic	Closed	35.00	35.00
89-24-057	Papa Santa Sitting 3180	Sarah's Attic	Closed	30.00	30.00
89-24-058	Mama Santa sitting 3181	Sarah's Attic	Closed	30.00	30.00
89-24-059	Papa Santa Stocking 3182	Sarah's Attic	Closed	50.00	50.00
89-24-060	Mama Santa Stocking 3183	Sarah's Attic	Closed	50.00	50.00
89-24-061	Long Journey II 3184	Sarah's Attic	Closed	35.00	35.00
89-24-062	Stinky Elf sitting 3185	Sarah's Attic	Closed	16.00	16.00
89-24-063	Winky Elf Letter 3186	Sarah's Attic	Closed	16.00	16.00
89-24-064	Blinkey Elf Ball 3187	Sarah's Attic	Closed	16.00	16.00
89-24-065	Colonel Santa-Mini 3188	Sarah's Attic	Closed	14.00	14.00
89-24-066	St. Nick-Mini 3189	Sarah's Attic	Closed	14.00	14.00
89-24-067	Jingle Bells-Mini 3190	Sarah's Attic	Closed	16.00	16.00
89-24-068	Father Snow-Mini 3191	Sarah's Attic	Closed	16.00	16.00
89-24-069	Long Journey-Mini 3192	Sarah's Attic	Closed	11.00	11.00
89-24-070	Jolly-Mini 3193	Sarah's Attic	Closed	10.00	10.00
89-24-071	Naughty or Nice-Mini 3210	Sarah's Attic	Closed	20.00	20.00
90-24-072	Christmas Wonder Santa 3278	Sarah's Attic	Closed	50.00	50.00
90-24-073	Santa Claus Express 3304	Sarah's Attic	Closed	150.00	150.00
90-24-074	Christmas Music 3305	Sarah's Attic	Closed	60.00	60.00
90-24-075	Love the Children 3324	Sarah's Attic	5000	75.00	75.00
90-24-076	Christmas Wishes 3325	Sarah's Attic	5000	50.00	50.00
90-24-077	Bells of Christmas 3326	Sarah's Attic	Closed	35.00	35.00
91-24-078	Santa Tex 3392	Sarah's Attic	Closed	30.00	30.00
91-24-079	Treasures of Love Santa 3490	Sarah's Attic	Closed	140.00	140.00
91-24-080	Sharing Love Santa 3491	Sarah's Attic	Closed	120.00	120.00
92-24-081	Blessed Christmas-Small 3669	Sarah's Attic	Closed	40.00	40.00
92-24-082	Love the Children-Small 3672	Sarah's Attic	Closed	35.00	35.00
92-24-083	Gifts of Christmas Santa 3677	Sarah's Attic	Closed	90.00	90.00
92-24-084	Gifts of Love Santa 3678	Sarah's Attic	Closed	90.00	90.00
93-24-085	Let There Be Love Santa 3796	Sarah's Attic	2,000	70.00	70.00
93-24-086	Let The Be Peace Santa 3797	Sarah's Attic	2,000	70.00	70.00
93-24-087	Been Good Santa/Boy 3813	Sarah's Attic	2,500	60.00	60.00
93-24-088	Oh My! Santa/Girl 3814	Sarah's Attic	2,500	55.00	55.00
93-24-089	Christmas Rabbit 3852	Sarah's Attic	Closed	23.00	23.00
93-24-090	Christmas Bear 3853	Sarah's Attic	Closed	23.00	23.00
93-24-091	Christmas Jeb 3854	Sarah's Attic	Closed	25.00	25.00
93-24-092	Christmas Christine 3855	Sarah's Attic	Closed	30.00	30.00
93-24-093	Christmas Jaleesa 3856	Sarah's Attic	Closed	25.00	25.00
93-24-094	Christmas Justin 3857	Sarah's Attic	Closed	25.00	25.00
93-24-095	Christmas Jessica 3858	Sarah's Attic	Closed	25.00	25.00
93-24-096	Christmas Holly Santa 3859	Sarah's Attic	Closed	50.00	50.00
93-24-097	Christmas Proclaim. Love Santa 3860	Sarah's Attic	Closed	50.00	50.00
94-24-098	Gift of Love-Black Santa 4145	Sarah's Attic	2,000	60.00	60.00
94-24-099	Gift of Christmas-White Santa 4146	Sarah's Attic	2,000	60.00	60.00
94-24-100	Jessica-Christmas 4147	Sarah's Attic	12/94	28.00	28.00
94-24-101	Justin-Christmas 4148	Sarah's Attic	12/94	30.00	30.00
94-24-102	Christine-Christmas 4149	Sarah's Attic	12/94	24.00	24.00
94-24-103	Sarah Elizabeth Christmas 4150	Sarah's Attic	12/94	27.00	27.00
94-24-104	Labor of Love-Christmas 4151	Sarah's Attic	12/94	30.00	30.00
94-24-105	Jalessa-Christmas 4154	Sarah's Attic	12/94	28.00	28.00
94-24-106	Jeb-Christmas 4155	Sarah's Attic	12/94	28.00	28.00
94-24-107	Teapot-Christmas 4156	Sarah's Attic	12/94	4.00	4.00
94-24-108	Christmas Bear 4157	Sarah's Attic	12/94	23.00	23.00
94-24-109	Christmas Rabbit 4158	Sarah's Attic	12/94	23.00	23.00
94-24-110	Deck the Halls-Black Santa 4159	Sarah's Attic	3,000	30.00	30.00
94-24-111	Rejoice-White Santa 4160	Sarah's Attic	3,000	34.00	34.00
94-24-112	Golden Memories Santa 4254	Sarah's Attic	1,000	70.00	70.00
Sarah's Attic, Inc.	**United Hearts Collection**				
91-25-001	Tillie-January 3441	Sarah's Attic	Closed	32.00	32.00
91-25-002	Willie-January 3442	Sarah's Attic	Closed	32.00	32.00

FIGURINES/COTTAGES

	ARTIST	EDITION	ISSUE	QUOTE
91-25-003 Chilly Snowman-January 3443	Sarah's Attic	Closed	33.00	33.00
91-25-004 Prissy w/Shaggy-February 3444	Sarah's Attic	Closed	36.00	36.00
91-25-005 Peanut-February 3445	Sarah's Attic	Closed	32.00	32.00
91-25-006 Shelby w/Shamrock-March 3446	Sarah's Attic	Closed	36.00	36.00
91-25-007 Noah w/Pot of Gold-March 3447	Sarah's Attic	Closed	36.00	36.00
91-25-008 Hewett w/Leprechaun-March 3448	Sarah's Attic	Closed	56.00	56.00
91-25-009 Tabitha April 3449	Sarah's Attic	Closed	32.00	32.00
91-25-010 Toby & Tessie-April 3450	Sarah's Attic	Closed	44.00	44.00
91-25-011 Wooly Lamb-April 3451	Sarah's Attic	Closed	16.00	16.00
91-25-012 Emily-Springtime May 3452	Sarah's Attic	Closed	53.00	53.00
91-25-013 Gideon-Springtime May 3453	Sarah's Attic	Closed	40.00	40.00
91-25-014 Sally Booba Graduation-June 3454	Sarah's Attic	Closed	45.00	45.00
91-25-015 Jack Boy Graduation-June 3455	Sarah's Attic	Closed	40.00	40.00
91-25-016 Sparky Dog Graduation-June 3456	Sarah's Attic	Closed	16.00	16.00
91-25-017 Bibi-Miss Liberty Bear-July 3457	Sarah's Attic	Closed	30.00	30.00
91-25-018 Papa Barney & Biff-July 3458	Sarah's Attic	Closed	64.00	64.00
91-25-019 Pansy Beach-August 3459	Sarah's Attic	Closed	34.00	34.00
91-25-020 Annie & Waldo Beach-August 3460	Sarah's Attic	Closed	40.00	40.00
91-25-021 Bubba Beach-August 3461	Sarah's Attic	Closed	34.00	34.00
91-25-022 Cookie w/Kitten-September 3462	Sarah's Attic	Closed	28.00	28.00
91-25-023 Crumb on Stool-September 3463	Sarah's Attic	Closed	32.00	32.00
91-25-024 Chuckles-September 3464	Sarah's Attic	Closed	26.00	26.00
91-25-025 School Desk w/Book 3465	Sarah's Attic	Closed	15.00	15.00
91-25-026 Barney the Great-October 3466	Sarah's Attic	Closed	40.00	40.00
91-25-027 Bibi & Biff Clowns-October 3467	Sarah's Attic	Closed	35.00	35.00
91-25-028 Cupcake-Thanksgiving 3470	Sarah's Attic	Closed	36.00	36.00
91-25-029 Twinkie-Thanksgiving 3471	Sarah's Attic	Closed	32.00	32.00
91-25-030 Adora Christmas-December 3479	Sarah's Attic	Closed	36.00	36.00
91-25-031 Enos Christmas-December 3480	Sarah's Attic	Closed	36.00	36.00
91-25-032 Christmas Tree-December 3481	Sarah's Attic	Closed	40.00	40.00
92-25-034 Hether-January 3617	Sarah's Attic	Closed	26.00	26.00
92-25-035 Herbie-January 3618	Sarah's Attic	Closed	26.00	26.00
92-25-036 Carrotman-January 3619	Sarah's Attic	Closed	30.00	30.00
92-25-037 Fluffy Bear-February 3625	Sarah's Attic	Closed	35.00	35.00
92-25-038 Puffy Bear-Febuary 3626	Sarah's Attic	Closed	35.00	35.00
92-25-039 Young Kim-March 3627	Sarah's Attic	Closed	40.00	40.00
92-25-040 Kyu Lee-March 3628	Sarah's Attic	Closed	40.00	40.00
92-25-041 Jewels-April 3630	Sarah's Attic	Closed	60.00	60.00
92-25-042 Stretch-April 3631	Sarah's Attic	Closed	50.00	50.00
92-25-043 Adora Angel-May 3632	Sarah's Attic	Closed	50.00	50.00
92-25-044 Enos Angel-May 3633	Sarah's Attic	Closed	50.00	50.00
92-25-045 May Pole 3634	Sarah's Attic	Closed	35.00	35.00
92-25-046 Toby w/Bat-June 3635	Sarah's Attic	Closed	34.00	34.00
92-25-047 Tabitha w/Glove-June 3636	Sarah's Attic	Closed	34.00	34.00
92-25-048 Tessie w/Ball-June 3637	Sarah's Attic	Closed	34.00	34.00
92-25-049 Cookie-July 3638	Sarah's Attic	Closed	34.00	34.00
92-25-050 Crumb-July 3639	Sarah's Attic	Closed	34.00	34.00
92-25-051 Zena Angel-August 3640	Sarah's Attic	Closed	46.00	46.00
92-25-052 Ethan Angel-August 3641	Sarah's Attic	Closed	46.00	46.00
92-25-053 Katie-September 3643	Sarah's Attic	Closed	35.00	35.00
92-25-054 Willie-September 3644	Sarah's Attic	Closed	35.00	35.00
92-25-055 September Desk 3645	Sarah's Attic	Closed	36.00	36.00
92-25-056 Pug-October 3646	Sarah's Attic	Closed	47.00	47.00
92-25-057 Peaches-October 3647	Sarah's Attic	Closed	30.00	30.00
92-25-058 Cupcake-November 3649	Sarah's Attic	Closed	35.00	35.00
92-25-059 Twinkie-November 3650	Sarah's Attic	Closed	35.00	35.00
92-25-060 Haystack-November 3651	Sarah's Attic	Closed	23.00	23.00
92-25-061 Mrs. Claus December 3653	Sarah's Attic	Closed	45.00	45.00
92-25-062 Santa-December 3654	Sarah's Attic	Closed	45.00	45.00
92-25-063 December Tree 3655	Sarah's Attic	Closed	40.00	40.00
Sarah's Attic, Inc.	**Collector's Club Promotion**			
91-26-001 Diamond 3497	Sarah's Attic	Closed	36.00	100-120.
91-26-002 Ruby 3498	Sarah's Attic	Closed	42.00	100.00
92-26-003 Christmas Love Santa 3522	Sarah's Attic	Closed	45.00	45.00
92-26-004 Forever Frolicking Friends 3523	Sarah's Attic	Closed	Gift	50-80.00
92-26-005 Love One Another 3561	Sarah's Attic	Closed	60.00	60.00
92-26-006 Sharing Dreams 3562	Sarah's Attic	Closed	75.00	150.00
92-26-007 Life Time Friends 3563	Sarah's Attic	Closed	75.00	75.00
92-26-008 Love Starts With Children 3607	Sarah's Attic	Closed	Gift	70.00
93-26-009 First Forever Friend Celebration 3903	Sarah's Attic	Closed	50.00	50.00
93-26-010 Pledge of Allegiance 3749	Sarah's Attic	Closed	45.00	55.00
93-26-011 I Love America Heart 3832	Sarah's Attic	Closed	Gift	N/A
93-26-012 Love Starts With Children II 3837	Sarah's Attic	Closed	Gift	60.00
93-26-013 Gem White Girl w/Basket 3842	Sarah's Attic	Closed	33.00	33.00
93-26-014 Rocky Black Boy w/Marbles 3843	Sarah's Attic	Closed	25.00	25.00
94-26-015 America Boy 4191	Sarah's Attic	12/94	25.00	25.00
94-26-016 America Girl 4192	Sarah's Attic	12/94	25.00	25.00
94-26-017 Saturday Night Round Up 4232	Sarah's Attic	5/95	Gift	N/A
94-26-018 Billy Bob 4233	Sarah's Attic	7/95	38.00	38.00
94-26-019 Jimmy Dean 4234	Sarah's Attic	7/95	38.00	38.00
94-26-020 Sally/Jack 4235	Sarah's Attic	7/95	55.00	55.00
94-26-021 Ellie/T.J. 4236	Sarah's Attic	7/95	55.00	55.00
Schmid/B.F.A.	**Don Polland Figurines I**			
83-01-001 Young Bull	D. Polland	2,750	125.00	250.00
83-01-002 Escape	D. Polland	2,500	175.00	650.00
83-01-003 Fighting Bulls	D. Polland	2,500	200.00	600.00
83-01-004 Hot Pursuit	D. Polland	2,500	225.00	550.00
83-01-005 The Hunter	D. Polland	2,500	225.00	500.00
83-01-006 Downed	D. Polland	2,500	250.00	600.00
83-01-007 Challenge	D. Polland	2,000	275.00	600.00
83-01-008 A Second Chance	D. Polland	2,000	350.00	650.00
83-01-009 Dangerous Moment	D. Polland	2,000	250.00	350.00
83-01-010 The Great Hunt	D. Polland	350	3750.00	3750.00
86-01-011 Running Wolf-War Chief	D. Polland	2,500	170.00	295.00
86-01-012 Eagle Dancer	D. Polland	2,500	170.00	295.00
86-01-013 Plains Warrior	D. Polland	1,250	350.00	550.00
86-01-014 Second Chance	D. Polland	2,000	125.00	650.00
86-01-015 Shooting the Rapids	D. Polland	2,500	195.00	495.00
86-01-016 Down From The High Country	D. Polland	2,250	225.00	295.00
86-01-017 War Trophy	D. Polland	2,250	225.00	500.00
Schmid/B.F.A.	**RFD America**			
79-02-001 Country Road 25030	L. Davis	Closed	100.00	700-750.
79-02-002 Ignorance is Bliss 25031	L. Davis	Closed	165.00	1250-13.
79-02-003 Blossom 25032	L. Davis	Closed	180.00	1800.00
79-02-004 Fowl Play 25033	L. Davis	Closed	100.00	275-325.
79-02-005 Slim Pickins 25034	L. Davis	Closed	165.00	825-850.
79-02-006 Broken Dreams 25035	L. Davis	Closed	165.00	10-1300.
80-02-007 Good, Clean Fun 25020	L. Davis	Closed	40.00	125-160.
80-02-008 Strawberry Patch 25021	L. Davis	Closed	25.00	59-95.00

	ARTIST	EDITION	ISSUE	QUOTE
80-02-009 Forbidden Fruit 25022	L. Davis	Closed	25.00	120-175.
80-02-010 Milking Time 25023	L. Davis	Closed	20.00	200-240.
80-02-011 Sunday Afternoon 25024	L. Davis	Closed	22.50	225-250.
80-02-012 New Day 25025	L. Davis	Closed	20.00	165.00
80-02-013 Wilbur 25029	L. Davis	Closed	100.00	600-750.
80-02-014 Itching Post 25037	L. Davis	Closed	30.00	75-115.
80-02-015 Creek Bank Bandit 25038	L. Davis	Closed	37.50	400.00
81-02-016 Split Decision 25210	L. Davis	Closed	45.00	175-325.
81-02-017 Double Trouble 25211	L. Davis	Closed	35.00	475.00
81-02-018 Under the Weather 25212	L. Davis	Closed	25.00	85.00
81-02-019 Country Boy 25213	L. Davis	Closed	37.50	250-375.
81-02-020 Hightailing It 25214	L. Davis	Closed	50.00	375-500.
81-02-021 Studio Mouse 25215	L. Davis	Closed	60.00	360.00
81-02-022 Dry as a Bone 25216	L. Davis	Closed	45.00	275-325.
81-02-023 Rooted Out 25217	L. Davis	Closed	45.00	85-115.
81-02-024 Up To No Good 25218	L. Davis	Closed	200.00	850-950.
81-02-025 Punkin' Seeds 25219	L. Davis	Closed	225.00	12-1750.
81-02-026 Scallawags 25221	L. Davis	Closed	65.00	125-200.
82-02-027 Baby Bobs 25222	L. Davis	Closed	47.50	200-250.
82-02-028 Stray Dog 25223	L. Davis	Closed	35.00	60-75.00
82-02-029 Two's Company 25224	L. Davis	Closed	43.50	200-250.
82-02-030 Moving Day 25225	L. Davis	Closed	43.50	225-300.
82-02-031 Brand New Day 25226	L. Davis	Closed	23.50	150-175.
82-02-032 Baby Blossom 25227	L. Davis	Closed	40.00	175-300.
82-02-033 When Mama Gets Mad 25228	L. Davis	Closed	37.50	300-375.
82-02-034 A Shoe to Fill 25229	L. Davis	Closed	37.50	150-175.
82-02-035 Idle Hours 25230	L. Davis	Closed	37.50	225-300.
82-02-036 Thinking Big 25231	L. Davis	Closed	35.00	68.00
82-02-037 Country Crook 25280	L. Davis	Closed	37.50	300-400.
82-02-038 Waiting for His Master 25281	L. Davis	Closed	50.00	225-300.
82-02-039 Moon Raider 25325	L. Davis	Closed	190.00	325-400.
82-02-040 Blossom and Calf 25326	L. Davis	Closed	250.00	700-1000
82-02-041 Treed 25327	L. Davis	Closed	155.00	250-300.
83-02-042 Woman's Work 25232	L. Davis	Closed	35.00	90-95.00
83-02-043 Counting the Days 25233	L. Davis	Closed	40.00	60.00
83-02-044 Licking Good 25234	L. Davis	Closed	35.00	200-250.
83-02-045 Mama's Prize Leghorn 25235	L. Davis	Closed	55.00	100-135.
83-02-046 Fair Weather Friend 25236	L. Davis	Closed	25.00	75.00
83-02-047 False Alarm 25237	L. Davis	Closed	65.00	150-185.
83-02-048 Makin' Tracks 25238	L. Davis	Closed	70.00	125-185.
83-02-049 Hi Girls, The Name's Big Jack 25328	L. Davis	Closed	200.00	354.00
83-02-050 City Slicker 25329	L. Davis	Closed	150.00	300-375.
83-02-051 Happy Hunting Ground 25330	L. Davis	Closed	160.00	240.00
83-02-052 Stirring Up Trouble 25331	L. Davis	Closed	160.00	250.00
83-02-053 His Eyes Are Bigger Than His Stomach 25332	L. Davis	Closed	235.00	325-350.
84-02-054 Courtin' 25220	L. Davis	Closed	45.00	120-135.
84-02-055 Anybody Home 25239	L. Davis	Closed	35.00	90-130.
84-02-056 Headed Home 25240	L. Davis	Closed	25.00	50.00
84-02-057 One for the Road 25241	L. Davis	Open	37.50	60-70.00
84-02-058 Huh? 25242	L. Davis	Closed	40.00	60-95.00
84-02-059 Gonna Pay for His Sins 25243	L. Davis	Open	27.50	90.00
84-02-060 His Master's Dog 25244	L. Davis	Closed	45.00	90-120.
84-02-061 Pasture Pals 25245	L. Davis	Closed	52.00	75.00
84-02-062 Country Kitty 25246	L. Davis	Closed	52.00	115-125.
84-02-063 Catnapping Too? 25247	L. Davis	Closed	70.00	100-125.
84-02-064 Gossips 25248	L. Davis	Closed	110.00	250.00
84-02-066 Prairie Chorus 25333	L. Davis	Closed	135.00	10-1500.
84-02-067 Mad As A Wet Hen 25334	L. Davis	Closed	185.00	700-800.
85-02-068 Country Crooner 25256	L. Davis	Open	25.00	35-65.00
85-02-069 Barn Cats 25257	L. Davis	Open	39.50	80.00
85-02-070 Don't Play with Your Food 25258	L. Davis	Open	28.50	80.00
85-02-071 Out-of-Step 25259	L. Davis	Open	45.00	90.00
85-02-072 Renoir 25261	L. Davis	Closed	45.00	80.00
85-02-073 Too Good to Waste on Kids 25262	L. Davis	Open	70.00	130.00
85-02-074 Ozark Belle 25264	L. Davis	Closed	35.00	80.00
85-02-075 Will You Still Respect Me in the Morning 25265	L. Davis	Open	35.00	70.00
85-02-076 Country Cousins 25266	L. Davis	Open	42.50	80.00
85-02-077 Love at First Sight 25267	L. Davis	Open	70.00	90-105.
85-02-078 Feelin' His Oats 25275	L. Davis	1,500	150.00	275-300.
85-02-079 Furs Gonna Fly 25335	L. Davis	1,500	145.00	220-225.
85-02-080 Hog Heaven 25336	L. Davis	1,500	165.00	260-450.
86-02-081 Comfy? 25273	L. Davis	Open	40.00	80.00
86-02-082 Mama? 25277	L. Davis	Closed	15.00	40.00
86-02-083 Bit Off More Than He Could Chew 25279	L. Davis	Open	15.00	60.00
87-02-084 Mail Order Bride 25263	L. Davis	Closed	150.00	163.00
87-02-085 Glutton for Punishment 25268	L. Davis	Closed	95.00	150.00
87-02-086 Easy Pickins 25269	L. Davis	Closed	45.00	85.00
87-02-087 Bottoms Up 25270	L. Davis	Open	80.00	90-105.
87-02-088 The Orphans 25271	L. Davis	Open	50.00	85.00
87-02-089 When the Cat's Away 25276	L. Davis	Open	40.00	60.00
87-02-090 Two in the Bush 25337	L. Davis	Closed	150.00	205-245.
87-02-091 Chicken Thief 25338	L. Davis	Closed	200.00	300.00
88-02-092 Sawin' Logs 25260	L. Davis	Open	85.00	105.00
88-02-093 Fleas 25272	L. Davis	Open	20.00	24.00
88-02-094 Making a Bee Line 25274	L. Davis	Closed	75.00	125.00
88-02-095 Missouri Spring 25278	L. Davis	Open	115.00	130.00
88-02-096 Perfect Ten 25282	L. Davis	Closed	95.00	105-177.
88-02-097 Goldie and Her Peeps 25283	L. Davis	Open	25.00	36.50
88-02-098 In a Pickle 25284	L. Davis	Open	40.00	50.00
88-02-099 Wishful Thinking 25285	L. Davis	Open	55.00	70.00
88-02-100 Brothers 25286	L. Davis	Closed	55.00	85.00
88-02-101 Happy Hour 25287	L. Davis	Open	57.50	65-80.00
88-02-102 When Three Foot's a Mile 25315	L. Davis	Closed	230.00	200-286.
88-02-103 No Private Time 25316	L. Davis	Closed	200.00	250-325.
88-02-104 Wintering Lamb 25317	L. Davis	Closed	200.00	225.00
89-02-105 New Friend 25288	L. Davis	Open	45.00	60.00
89-02-106 Family Outing 25289	L. Davis	Open	45.00	60.00
89-02-107 Left Overs 25290	L. Davis	Open	90.00	100.00
89-02-108 Coon Capers 25291	L. Davis	Open	67.50	90.00
89-02-109 Mother Hen 25292	L. Davis	Open	37.50	50.00
89-02-110 Meeting of Sheldon 25293	L. Davis	Open	120.00	150.00
89-02-111 Boy's Night Out 25339	L. Davis	1,500	190.00	225.00
89-02-112 A Tribute to Hooker 25340	L. Davis	Closed	180.00	200-300.
89-02-113 Woodscolt 25342	L. Davis	Closed	300.00	350-500.
90-02-114 Corn Crib Mouse 25295	L. Davis	Closed	35.00	45.00
90-02-115 Seein' Red (Gus w/shoes) 25296	L. Davis	Open	35.00	47.00
90-02-116 Little Black Lamb (Baba) 25297	L. Davis	Closed	30.00	37.50
90-02-117 Hanky Panky 25298	L. Davis	Closed	65.00	100.00
90-02-118 Finder's Keepers 25299	L. Davis	Open	39.50	45.00
90-02-119 Foreplay 25300	L. Davis	Closed	59.50	80.00

		ARTIST	EDITION	ISSUE	QUOTE
90-02-120	The Last Straw 25301	L. Davis	Open	125.00	147-163.
90-02-121	Long Days, Cold Nights 25344	L. Davis	Closed	175.00	190.00
90-02-122	Piggin' Out 25345	L. Davis	Closed	190.00	250.00
90-02-123	Tricks Of The Trade 25346	L. Davis	Closed	300.00	300-375.
91-02-124	First Offense 25304	L. Davis	Closed	70.00	70.00
91-02-125	Gun Shy 25305	L. Davis	Closed	70.00	70.00
91-02-126	Heading For The Persimmon Grove 25306	L. Davis	Closed	80.00	80.00
91-02-127	Kissin' Cousins 25307	L. Davis	Closed	80.00	80.00
91-02-128	Washed Ashore 25308	L. Davis	Closed	70.00	70.00
91-02-129	Long, Hot Summer 25343	L. Davis	1,950	250.00	250.00
91-02-130	Cock Of The Walk 25347	L. Davis	2,500	300.00	300.00
91-02-131	Sooieee 25360	L. Davis	1,500	350.00	350.00
92-02-132	Ozark's Vittles 25318	L. Davis	Open	60.00	60.00
92-02-133	Don't Play With Fire 25319	L. Davis	Open	120.00	120.00
92-02-134	Safe Haven 25320	L. Davis	Open	95.00	95.00
92-02-135	Free Lunch 25321	L. Davis	Open	85.00	85.00
92-02-136	Headed South 25327	L. Davis	Open	45.00	45.00
92-02-137	My Favorite Chores 25362	L. Davis	1,500	750.00	750.00
92-02-138	OH Sheeeit . . . 25363	L. Davis	Open	120.00	120.00
92-02-139	She Lay Low 25364	L. Davis	Open	120.00	120.00
92-02-140	Snake Doctor 25365	L. Davis	Open	70.00	70.00
92-02-141	The Grass is Always Greener 25367	L. Davis	Open	195.00	195.00
92-02-142	School Yard Dogs 25369	L. Davis	Open	100.00	100.00
92-02-143	The Honeymoon's Over 25370	L. Davis	1,950	300.00	300.00
93-02-144	Sweet Tooth 25373	L. Davis	Open	60.00	60.00
93-02-145	Dry Hole 25374	L. Davis	Open	30.00	30.00
93-02-146	No Hunting 25375	L. Davis	1,000	95.00	95.00
93-02-147	Peep Show 25376	L. Davis	Open	35.00	35.00
93-02-148	If You Can't Beat Em Join Em 25379	L. Davis	1,750	250.00	250.00
93-02-149	King of The Mountain 25380	L. Davis	750	500.00	500.00
93-02-150	Sheep Sheerin Time 25388	L. Davis	1,200	500.00	500.00
93-02-151	Happy Birthday My Sweet 27560	L. Davis	Open	35.00	35.00
93-02-152	Be My Valentine 27561	L. Davis	Open	35.00	35.00
93-02-153	Don't Open Till Christmas 27562	L. Davis	Open	35.00	35.00
93-02-154	I'm Thankful For You 27563	L. Davis	Open	35.00	35.00
93-02-155	You're a Basket Full of Fun 27564	L. Davis	Open	35.00	35.00
93-02-156	Trick or Treat 27565	L. Davis	Open	35.00	35.00
93-02-157	Oh Where is He Now 95041	L. Davis	1,250	250.00	250.00
93-02-158	The Freeloaders 95042	L. Davis	1,250	230.00	230.00

Schmid/B.F.A. — Farm Set

85-03-001	Privy 25348	L. Davis	Closed	12.50	40.00
85-03-002	Windmill 25349	L. Davs	Closed	25.00	50.00
85-03-003	Remus' Cabin 25350	L. Davis	Closed	42.50	45-65.00
85-03-004	Main House 25351	L. Davis	Closed	42.50	65-125.
85-03-005	Barn 25352	L. Davis	Closed	47.50	350-400.
85-03-006	Goat Yard and Studio 25353	L. Davis	Closed	32.50	45-75.00
85-03-007	Corn Crib and Sheep Pen 25354	L. Davis	Closed	25.00	50-85.00
85-03-008	Hog House 25355	L. Davis	Closed	27.50	60-85.00
85-03-009	Hen House 25356	L. Davis	Closed	32.50	50-85.00
85-03-010	Smoke House 25357	L. Davis	Closed	12.50	30-65.00
85-03-011	Chicken House 25358	L. Davis	Closed	19.00	65.00
85-03-012	Garden and Wood Shed 25359	L. Davis	Closed	25.00	65.00

Schmid/B.F.A. — Davis Cat Tales Figurines

82-04-001	Right Church, Wrong Pew 25204	L. Davis	Closed	70.00	288-350.
82-04-002	Company's Coming 25205	L. Davis	Closed	60.00	170-225.
82-04-003	On the Move 25206	L. Davis	Closed	70.00	550-650.
82-04-004	Flew the Coop 25207	L. Davis	Closed	60.00	275-325.

Schmid/B.F.A. — Davis Special Edition Figurines

83-05-001	The Critics 23600	L. Davis	Closed	400.00	13-1650.
85-05-002	Home from Market 23601	L. Davis	Closed	400.00	1500.00
89-05-003	From A Friend To A Friend 23602	L. Davis	1,200	750.00	15-1600.
90-05-004	What Rat Race? 23603	L. Davis	1,200	800.00	950.00
92-05-005	Last Laff 23604	L. Davis	1,200	900.00	900.00

Schmid/B.F.A. — Davis Country Christmas Figurines

83-06-001	Hooker at Mailbox with Presents 23550	L. Davis	Closed	80.00	750.00
84-06-002	Country Christmas 23551	L. Davis	Closed	80.00	450.00
85-06-003	Christmas at Fox Fire Farm 23552	L. Davis	Closed	80.00	200-350.
86-06-004	Christmas at Red Oak 23553	L. Davis	Closed	80.00	150-225.
87-06-005	Blossom's Gift 23554	L. Davis	Closed	150.00	350-500.
88-06-006	Cutting the Family Christmas Tree 23555	L. Davis	Closed	80.00	300-350.
89-06-007	Peter and the Wren 23556	L. Davis	Closed	165.00	300-450.
90-06-008	Wintering Deer 23557	L. Davis	Closed	165.00	250.00
91-06-009	Christmas At Red Oak II 23558	L. Davis	Closed	250.00	250.00
92-06-010	Born on a Starry Night 23559	L. Davis	2,500	225.00	225.00
93-06-011	Waiting For Mr. Lowell 23606	L. Davis	2,500	250.00	250.00

Schmid/B.F.A. — Little Critters

89-07-001	Gittin' a Nibble 25294	L. Davis	Open	50.00	57.00
90-07-002	Outing With Grandpa 25502	L. Davis	Closed	200.00	250.00
90-07-003	Home Squeezins 25504	L. Davis	Closed	90.00	90.00
90-07-004	Punkin' Pig 25505	L. Davis	2,500	250.00	350.00
90-07-005	Private Time 25506	L. Davis	Closed	18.00	40.00
91-07-006	Great American Chicken Race 25500	L. Davis	2,500	225.00	275.00
91-07-007	Punkin' Wine 25501	L. Davis	Closed	100.00	150.00
91-07-008	Milk Mouse 25503	L. Davis	2,500	175.00	228.00
91-07-009	When Coffee Never Tasted So Good 25507	L. Davis	1,250	800.00	800.00
91-07-010	Toad Strangler 25509	L. Davis	Open	57.00	57.00
91-07-011	Hittin' The Sack 25510	L. Davis	Open	70.00	70.00
91-07-012	Itiskit, Itasket 25511	L. Davis	Open	45.00	45.00
91-07-013	Christopher Critter 25514	L. Davis	Closed	150.00	150.00
92-07-014	Double Yolker 25516	L. Davis	Yr.Iss.	70.00	70.00
92-07-015	Miss Private Time 25517	L. Davis	Yr.Iss.	35.00	35.00
92-07-016	A Wolf in Sheep's Clothing 25518	L. Davis	Yr.Iss.	110.00	110.00
92-07-017	Charivari 25707	L. Davis	950	250.00	250.00

Schmid/B.F.A. — Lowell Davis Farm Club

85-08-001	The Bride 221001 / 20993	L. Davis	Closed	45.00	250-375.
87-08-002	The Party's Over 221002 / 20994	L. Davis	Closed	50.00	100-190.
88-08-003	Chow Time 221003 / 20995	L. Davis	Closed	55.00	125-150.
89-08-004	Can't Wait 221004 / 20996	L. Davis	Closed	75.00	125.00
90-08-005	Pit Stop 221005 / 20997	L. Davis	Closed	75.00	125-150.
91-08-006	Arrival Of Stanley 221006 / 20998	L. Davis	Yr.Iss.	100.00	100.00
91-08-007	Don't Pick The Flowers 221007 / 21007	L. Davis	Yr.Iss.	100.00	143.00
92-08-008	Hog Wild	L. Davis	Yr.Iss.	100.00	100.00
92-08-009	Check's in the Mail	L. Davis	Yr.Iss.	100.00	100.00
93-08-010	The Survivor 25371	L. Davis	Yr.Iss.	70.00	70.00

Schmid/B.F.A. — Lowell Davis Farm Club Renewal Figurine

85-09-001	Thirsty? 892050 / 92050	L. Davis	Yr.Iss.	Gift	N/A
87-09-002	Cackle Berries 892051 / 92051	L. Davis	Yr.Iss.	Gift	N/A
88-09-003	Ice Cream Churn 892052 / 92052	L. Davis	Yr.Iss.	Gift	50.00
90-09-004	Not A Sharing Soul 892053 / 92053	L. Davis	Yr.Iss.	Gift	40.00
91-09-005	New Arrival 892054 / 92054	L. Davis	Yr.Iss.	Gift	40.00
92-09-006	Garden Toad 92055	L. Davis	Yr.Iss.	Gift	N/A
93-09-007	Luke 12:6 25372	L. Davis	Yr.Iss.	Gift	N/A

Schmid/B.F.A. — Country Pride

81-10-001	Surprise in the Cellar 25200	L. Davis	Closed	100.00	930-1000
81-10-002	Plum Tuckered Out 25201	L. Davis	Closed	100.00	600-950.
81-10-003	Bustin' with Pride 25202	L. Davis	Closed	100.00	225-250.
81-10-004	Duke's Mixture 25203	L. Davis	Closed	100.00	160-300.

Schmid/B.F.A. — Uncle Remus

81-11-001	Brer Fox 25250	L. Davis	Closed	70.00	900-950.
81-11-002	Brer Bear 25251	L. Davis	Closed	80.00	900-1200
81-11-003	Brer Rabbit 25252	L. Davis	Closed	85.00	15-2000.
81-11-004	Brer Wolf 25253	L. Davis	Closed	85.00	425-475.
81-11-005	Brer Weasel 25254	L. Davis	Closed	80.00	475-700.
81-11-006	Brer Coyote 25255	L. Davis	Closed	80.00	425-475.

Schmid/B.F.A. — Promotional Figurine

91-12-001	Leavin' The Rat Race 225512	L. Davis	N/A	125.00	120-125.
92-12-002	Hen Scratch Prom 225968	L. Davis	N/A	95.00	95.00

Schmid/B.F.A. — Route 66

91-13-001	Just Check The Air 25600	L. Davis	350	700.00	900-1400
91-13-002	Nel's Diner 25601	L. Davis	350	700.00	1600.00
91-13-003	Little Bit Of Shade 25602	L. Davis	Open	100.00	100.00
91-13-004	Just Check The Air 25603	L. Davis	2,500	550.00	550.00
91-13-005	Nel's Diner 25604	L. Davis	2,500	550.00	550.00
92-13-006	Relief 25605	L. Davis	Open	80.00	80.00
92-13-007	Welcome Mat (w/ wooden base)25606	L. Davis	1,500	400.00	400-500.
92-13-008	Fresh Squeezed? 25608	L. Davis	2,500	450.00	450.00
92-13-009	Fresh Squeezed? (w/ wooden base) 25609	L. Davis	350	600.00	600.00
92-13-010	Quiet Day at Maple Grove 25618	L. Davis	Open	130.00	130.00
92-13-011	Going To Grandma's 25619	L. Davis	Open	80.00	80.00
92-13-012	What Are Pals For? 25620	L. Davis	Open	100.00	100.00
93-13-013	Home For Christmas 25621	L. Davis	Open	80.00	80.00
93-13-014	Kickin' Himself 25622	L. Davis	Open	80.00	80.00
93-13-015	Summer Days 25607	L. Davis	Yr.Iss.	100.00	100.00

Schmid/B.F.A. — Friends of Mine

89-14-001	Sun Worshippers 23620	L. Davis	Closed	120.00	134.00
89-14-002	Sun Worshippers Mini Figurine 23621	L. Davis	Closed	32.50	32.50
90-14-003	Sunday Afternoon Treat 23625	L. Davis	Closed	120.00	130-170.
90-14-004	Sunday Afternoon Treat Mini Figurine 23626	L. Davis	Closed	32.50	37.50
91-14-005	Warm Milk 23629	L. Davis	Closed	120.00	200.00
91-14-006	Warm Milk Mini Figurine 23630	L. Davis	Closed	32.50	37.50
92-14-007	Cat and Jenny Wren 23633	L. Davis	5,000	170.00	175.00
92-14-008	Cat and Jenny Wren Mini Figurine 23634	L. Davis	Open	35.00	35.00

Schmid/B.F.A. — Pen Pals

93-15-001	The Old Home Place Mini Figurine 25801	L. Davis	Open	30.00	30.00
93-15-002	The Old Home Place 25802	L. Davis	1,200	200.00	200.00

Schmid/B.F.A. — Dealer Counter Signs

80-16-001	RFD America 888902	L. Davis	Closed	40.00	175-275.
81-16-002	Uncle Remus 888904	L. Davis	Closed	30.00	300.00
85-16-003	Fox Fire Farm 888907	L. Davis	Closed	30.00	150-275.
90-16-004	Mr. Lowell's Farm 25302	L. Davis	Open	50.00	55-70.00
92-16-005	Little Critters 25515	L. Davis	Open	50.00	50.00

Schmid/B.F.A. — Tour Figurines

92-17-001	Leapin Lizard 25969	L. Davis	Open	80.00	80.00

Schmid/B.F.A. — Kitty Cucumber Musical Figurine

92-18-001	Dance 'Round the Maypole 30215	M. Lillemoe	5,000	55.00	55.00
92-18-002	Butterfly 30221	M. Lillemoe	5,000	50.00	50.00

Sebastian Studios — Large Ceramastone Figures

39-01-001	Paul Revere Plaque	P.W. Baston	Closed	Unkn.	400-500.
40-01-002	Jesus	P.W. Baston	Closed	Unkn.	300-400.
40-01-003	Mary	P.W. Baston	Closed	Unkn.	600-1000.
40-01-004	Caroler	P.W. Baston	Closed	Unkn.	300-400.
40-01-005	Candle Holder	P.W. Baston	Closed	Unkn.	300-400.
40-01-006	Lamb	P.W. Baston	Closed	Unkn.	300-400.
40-01-007	Basket	P.W. Baston	Closed	Unkn.	300-400.
40-01-008	Horn of Plenty	P.W. Baston	Closed	Unkn.	300-400.
40-01-009	Breton Man	P.W. Baston	Closed	Unkn.	10-1500.
40-01-010	Breton Woman	P.W. Baston	Closed	Unkn.	10-1500.
47-01-011	Large Victorian Couple	P.W. Baston	Closed	Unkn.	600-1000.
48-01-012	Woody at Three	P.W. Baston	Closed	Unkn.	600-1000.
56-01-013	Jell-O Cow Milk Pitcher	P.W. Baston	Closed	Unkn.	175-225.
58-01-014	Swift Instrument Girl	P.W. Baston	Closed	Unkn.	500-750.
59-01-015	Wasp Plaque	P.W. Baston	Closed	Unkn.	500-750.
63-01-016	Henry VIII	P.W. Baston	Closed	Unkn.	600-1000.
63-01-017	Anne Boleyn	P.W. Baston	Closed	Unkn.	600-1000.
63-01-018	Tom Sawyer	P.W. Baston	Closed	Unkn.	600-1000.
63-01-019	Mending Time	P.W. Baston	Closed	Unkn.	600-1000.
63-01-020	David Copperfield	P.W. Baston	Closed	Unkn.	600-1000.
63-01-021	Dora	P.W. Baston	Closed	Unkn.	600-1000.
63-01-022	George Washington Toby Jug	P.W. Baston	Closed	Unkn.	600-1000.
63-01-023	Abraham Lincoln Toby Jug	P.W. Baston	Closed	Unkn.	600-1000.
63-01-024	John F. Kennedy Toby Jug	P.W. Baston	Closed	Unkn.	600-1000.
64-01-025	Colonial Boy	P.W. Baston	Closed	Unkn.	600-1000.
64-01-026	Colonial Man	P.W. Baston	Closed	Unkn.	600-1000.
64-01-027	Colonial Woman	P.W. Baston	Closed	Unkn.	600-1000.
64-01-028	Colonial Girl	P.W. Baston	Closed	Unkn.	600-1000.
64-01-029	IBM Mother	P.W. Baston	Closed	Unkn.	600-1000.
64-01-030	IBM Father	P.W. Baston	Closed	Unkn.	600-1000.
64-01-031	IBM Son	P.W. Baston	Closed	Unkn.	600-1000.
64-01-032	IBM Woman	P.W. Baston	Closed	Unkn.	600-1000.
64-01-033	IBM Photographer	P.W. Baston	Closed	Unkn.	600-1000.
65-01-034	N.E. Home For Little Wanderers	P.W. Baston	Closed	Unkn.	600-1000.
65-01-035	Stanley Music Box	P.W. Baston	Closed	Unkn.	300-500.
65-01-036	The Dentist	P.W. Baston	Closed	Unkn.	600-1000.
66-01-037	Guitarist	P.W. Baston	Closed	Unkn.	600-1000.
67-01-038	Infant of Prague	P.W. Baston	Closed	Unkn.	600-1000.
73-01-039	Potter	P.W. Baston	Closed	Unkn.	300-400.
73-01-040	Cabinetmaker	P.W. Baston	Closed	Unkn.	300-400.
73-01-041	Blacksmith	P.W. Baston	Closed	Unkn.	300-400.
73-01-042	Clockmaker	P.W. Baston	Closed	Unkn.	600-1000.
75-01-043	Minuteman	P.W. Baston	Closed	Unkn.	600-1000.
78-01-044	Mt. Rushmore	P.W. Baston	Closed	Unkn.	400-500.

		ARTIST	EDITION	ISSUE	QUOTE
XX-01-045	Santa Fe...All The Way	P.W. Baston	Closed	Unkn.	600-1000.
XX-01-046	St. Francis (Plaque)	P.W. Baston	Closed	Unkn.	600-1000.
Sebastian Studios		**Sebastian Miniatures**			
38-02-001	Shaker Man	P.W. Baston	Closed	Unkn.	50-100.
38-02-002	Shaker Lady	P.W. Baston	Closed	Unkn.	50-100.
39-02-003	George Washington	P.W. Baston	Closed	Unkn.	35-75.00
39-02-004	Martha Washington	P.W. Baston	Closed	Unkn.	35-75.00
39-02-005	John Alden	P.W. Baston	Closed	Unkn.	35-50.00
39-02-006	Priscilla	P.W. Baston	Closed	Unkn.	35-50.00
39-02-007	Williamsburg Governor	P.W. Baston	Closed	Unkn.	75-100.
39-02-008	Williamsburg Lady	P.W. Baston	Closed	Unkn.	75-100.
39-02-009	Benjamin Franklin	P.W. Baston	Closed	Unkn.	75-100.
39-02-010	Deborah Franklin	P.W. Baston	Closed	Unkn.	75-100.
39-02-011	Gabriel	P.W. Baston	Closed	Unkn.	100-125.
39-02-012	Evangeline	P.W. Baston	Closed	Unkn.	100-125.
39-02-013	Coronado	P.W. Baston	Closed	Unkn.	75-100.
39-02-014	Coronado's Senora	P.W. Baston	Closed	Unkn.	75-100.
39-02-015	Sam Houston	P.W. Baston	Closed	Unkn.	75-100.
39-02-016	Margaret Houston	P.W. Baston	Closed	Unkn.	75-100.
39-02-017	Indian Warrior	P.W. Baston	Closed	Unkn.	100-125.
39-02-018	Indian Maiden	P.W. Baston	Closed	Unkn.	100-125.
40-02-019	Jean LaFitte	P.W. Baston	Closed	Unkn.	75-100.
40-02-020	Catherine LaFitte	P.W. Baston	Closed	Unkn.	75-100.
40-02-021	Dan'l Boone	P.W. Baston	Closed	Unkn.	75-100.
40-02-022	Mrs. Dan'l Boone	P.W. Baston	Closed	Unkn.	75-100.
40-02-023	Peter Stvyvesant	P.W. Baston	Closed	Unkn.	75-100.
40-02-024	Ann Stvyvesant	P.W. Baston	Closed	Unkn.	75-100.
40-02-025	John Harvard	P.W. Baston	Closed	Unkn.	125-150.
40-02-026	Mrs. Harvard	P.W. Baston	Closed	Unkn.	125-150.
40-02-027	John Smith	P.W. Baston	Closed	Unkn.	75-150.
40-02-028	Pocohontas	P.W. Baston	Closed	Unkn.	75-150.
40-02-029	William Penn	P.W. Baston	Closed	Unkn.	100-150.
40-02-030	Hannah Penn	P.W. Baston	Closed	Unkn.	100-150.
40-02-031	Buffalo Bill	P.W. Baston	Closed	Unkn.	75-100.
40-02-032	Annie Oakley	P.W. Baston	Closed	Unkn.	75-100.
40-02-033	James Monroe	P.W. Baston	Closed	Unkn.	150-175.
40-02-034	Elizabeth Monroe	P.W. Baston	Closed	Unkn.	150-175.
41-02-035	Rooster	P.W. Baston	Closed	Unkn.	600-1000.
41-02-036	Ducklings	P.W. Baston	Closed	Unkn.	600-1000.
41-02-037	Peacock	P.W Baston	Closed	Unkn.	600-1000.
41-02-038	Doves	P.W. Baston	Closed	Unkn.	600-1000.
41-02-039	Pheasant	P.W. Baston	Closed	Unkn.	600-1000.
41-02-040	Swan	P.W. Baston	Closed	Unkn.	600-1000.
41-02-041	Secrets	P.W. Baston	Closed	Unkn.	600-1000.
41-02-042	Kitten (Sleeping)	P.W. Baston	Closed	Unkn.	600-1000.
41-02-043	Kitten (Sitting)	P.W. Baston	Closed	Unkn.	600-1000.
42-02-044	Majorette	P.W. Baston	Closed	Unkn.	325-375.
42-02-045	Cymbals	P.W. Baston	Closed	Unkn.	325-375.
42-02-046	Horn	P.W. Baston	Closed	Unkn.	325-375.
42-02-047	Tuba	P.W. Baston	Closed	Unkn.	325-375.
42-02-048	Drum	P.W. Baston	Closed	Unkn.	325-375.
42-02-049	Accordion	P.W. Baston	Closed	Unkn.	325-375.
46-02-050	Puritan Spinner	P.W. Baston	Closed	Unkn.	500-1000.
46-02-051	Satchel-Eye Dyer	P.W. Baston	Closed	Unkn.	125-150.
47-02-052	Down East	P.W. Baston	Closed	Unkn.	125-150.
47-02-053	First Cookbook Author	P.W. Baston	Closed	Unkn.	125-150.
47-02-054	Fisher Pair PS	P.W. Baston	Closed	Unkn.	400-1000.
47-02-055	Mr. Beacon Hill	P.W. Baston	Closed	Unkn.	50-75.00
47-02-056	Mrs. Beacon Hill	P.W. Baston	Closed	Unkn.	50-75.00
47-02-057	Dahl's Fisherman	P.W. Baston	Closed	Unkn.	150-175.
47-02-058	Dilemma	P.W. Baston	Closed	Unkn.	275-300.
47-02-059	Princess Elizabeth	P.W. Baston	Closed	Unkn.	200-300.
47-02-060	Prince Philip	P.W. Baston	Closed	Unkn.	200-300.
47-02-061	Howard Johnson Pieman	P.W. Baston	Closed	Unkn.	300-450.
47-02-062	Tollhouse Town Crier	P.W. Baston	Closed	Unkn.	125-175.
48-02-063	Slalom	P.W. Baston	Closed	Unkn.	175-200.
48-02-064	Sitzmark	P.W. Baston	Closed	Unkn.	175-200.
48-02-065	Mr. Rittenhouse Square	P.W. Baston	Closed	Unkn.	150-175.
48-02-066	Mrs. Rittenhouse Square	P.W. Baston	Closed	Unkn.	150-175.
48-02-067	Swedish Boy	P.W. Baston	Closed	Unkn.	250-500.
48-02-068	Swedish Girl	P.W. Baston	Closed	Unkn.	250-500.
48-02-069	Democratic Victory	P.W. Baston	Closed	Unkn.	350-500.
48-02-070	Republican Victory	P.W. Baston	Closed	Unkn.	600-1000.
48-02-071	Nathaniel Hawthorne	P.W. Baston	Closed	Unkn.	175-200.
48-02-072	Jordan Marsh Observer	P.W. Baston	Closed	Unkn.	150-175.
48-02-073	Mr. Sheraton	P.W. Baston	Closed	Unkn.	400-500.
48-02-074	A Harvey Girl	P.W. Baston	Closed	Unkn.	250-300.
48-02-075	Mary Lyon	P.W. Baston	Closed	Unkn.	250-300.
49-02-076	Uncle Mistletoe	P.W. Baston	Closed	Unkn.	250-300.
49-02-077	Eustace Tilly	P.W. Baston	Closed	Unkn.	750-1500.
49-02-078	Menotomy Indian	P.W. Baston	Closed	Unkn.	175-250.
49-02-079	Boy Scout Plaque	P.W. Baston	Closed	Unkn.	300-350.
49-02-080	Patrick Henry	P.W. Baston	Closed	Unkn.	100-125.
49-02-081	Sarah Henry	P.W. Baston	Closed	Unkn.	100-125.
49-02-082	Paul Bunyan	P.W. Baston	Closed	Unkn.	150-250.
49-02-083	Emmett Kelly	P.W. Baston	Closed	Unkn.	200-300.
49-02-084	Giant Royal Bengal Tiger	P.W. Baston	Closed	Unkn.	1-1500.
49-02-085	The Thinker	P.W. Baston	Closed	Unkn.	175-250.
49-02-086	The Mark Twain Home in Hannibal, MO	P.W. Baston	Closed	Unkn.	600-1000.
49-02-087	Dutchman's Pipe	P.W. Baston	Closed	Unkn.	175-225.
49-02-088	Gathering Tulips	P.W. Baston	Closed	Unkn.	225-250.
50-02-089	Phoebe, House of 7 Gables	P.W. Baston	Closed	Unkn.	150-175.
50-02-090	Mr. Obocell	P.W. Baston	Closed	Unkn.	75-125.
50-02-091	National Diaper Service	P.W. Baston	Closed	Unkn.	250-300.
51-02-092	Judge Pyncheon	P.W. Baston	Closed	Unkn.	175-225.
51-02-093	Seb. Dealer Plaque (Marblehead)	P.W. Baston	Closed	Unkn.	300-350.
51-02-094	Great Stone Face	P.W. Baston	Closed	Unkn.	600-1000.
51-02-095	Christopher Columbus	P.W. Baston	Closed	Unkn.	250-300.
51-02-096	Sir Frances Drake	P.W. Baston	Closed	Unkn.	250-300.
51-02-097	Jesse Buffman (WEEI)	P.W. Baston	Closed	Unkn.	200-350.
51-02-098	Carl Moore (WEEI)	P.W. Baston	Closed	Unkn.	200-300.
51-02-099	Caroline Cabot (WEEI)	P.W. Baston	Closed	Unkn.	200-350.
51-02-100	Mother Parker (WEEI)	P.W. Baston	Closed	Unkn.	200-350.
51-02-101	Charles Ashley (WEEI)	P.W. Baston	Closed	Unkn.	200-350.
51-02-102	E. B. Rideout (WEEI)	P.W. Baston	Closed	Unkn.	200-350.
51-02-103	Priscilla Fortesue (WEEI)	P.W. Baston	Closed	Unkn.	200-350.
51-02-104	Chiquita Banana	P.W. Baston	Closed	Unkn.	350-400.
51-02-105	Mit Seal	P.W. Baston	Closed	Unkn.	350-425.
51-02-106	The Observer & Dame New England.	P.W. Baston	Closed	Unkn.	325-375.
51-02-107	Jordon Marsh Observer Rides the A.W. Horse	P.W. Baston	Closed	Unkn.	300-325.
51-02-108	The Iron Master's House	P.W. Baston	Closed	Unkn.	350-500.
51-02-109	Chief Pontiac	P.W. Baston	Closed	Unkn.	400-700.
52-02-110	The Favored Scholar	P.W. Baston	Closed	Unkn.	200-300.
52-02-111	Neighboring Pews	P.W. Baston	Closed	Unkn.	200-300.
52-02-112	Weighing the Baby	P.W. Baston	Closed	Unkn.	200-300.
52-02-113	The First House, Plimoth Plantation	P.W. Baston	Closed	Unkn.	150-195.
52-02-114	Scottish Girl (Jell-O)	P.W. Baston	Closed	Unkn.	350-375.
52-02-115	Lost in the Kitchen (Jell-O)	P.W. Baston	Closed	Unkn.	350-375.
52-02-116	The Fat Man (Jell-O)	P.W. Baston	Closed	Unkn.	525-600.
52-02-117	Baby (Jell-O)	P.W. Baston	Closed	Unkn.	525-600.
52-02-118	Stork (Jell-O)	P.W. Baston	Closed	Unkn.	425-525.
52-02-119	Tabasco Sauce	P.W. Baston	Closed	Unkn.	400-500.
52-02-120	Aerial Tramway	P.W. Baston	Closed	Unkn.	300-600.
52-02-121	Marblehead High School Plaque	P.W. Baston	Closed	Unkn.	200-300.
52-02-122	St. Joan d'Arc	P.W. Baston	Closed	Unkn.	300-350.
52-02-123	St. Sebastian	P.W. Baston	Closed	Unkn.	300-350.
52-02-124	Our Lady of Good Voyage	P.W. Baston	Closed	Unkn.	200-250.
52-02-125	Old Powder House	P.W. Baston	Closed	Unkn.	250-300.
53-02-126	Holgrave the Daguerrotypist	P.W. Baston	Closed	Unkn.	200-250.
53-02-127	St. Teresa of Lisieux	P.W. Baston	Closed	Unkn.	225-275.
53-02-128	Darned Well He Can	P.W. Baston	Closed	Unkn.	300-350.
53-02-129	R.H. Stearns Chestnut Hill Mall	P.W. Baston	Closed	Unkn.	225-275.
53-02-130	Boy Jesus in the Temple	P.W. Baston	Closed	Unkn.	350-400.
53-02-131	Blessed Julie Billart	P.W. Baston	Closed	Unkn.	400-500.
53-02-132	Old Put Enjoys a Licking	P.W. Baston	Closed	Unkn.	300-350.
53-02-133	Lion (Jell-O)	P.W. Baston	Closed	Unkn.	350-375.
53-02-134	The Schoolboy of 1850	P.W. Baston	Closed	Unkn.	350-400.
54-02-135	Whale (Jell-O)	P.W. Baston	Closed	Unkn.	350-375.
54-02-136	Rabbit (Jell-O)	P.W. Baston	Closed	Unkn.	350-375.
54-02-137	Moose (Jell-O)	P.W. Baston	Closed	Unkn.	350-375.
54-02-138	Scuba Diver	P.W. Baston	Closed	Unkn.	400-450.
54-02-139	Stimalose (Woman)	P.W. Baston	Closed	Unkn.	175-200.
54-02-140	Stimalose (Men)	P.W. Baston	Closed	Unkn.	600-1000.
54-02-141	Bluebird Girl	P.W. Baston	Closed	Unkn.	400-450.
54-02-142	Campfire Girl	P.W. Baston	Closed	Unkn.	400-450.
54-02-143	Horizon Girl	P.W. Baston	Closed	Unkn.	400-450.
54-02-144	Kernel-Fresh Ashtray	P.W. Baston	Closed	Unkn.	400-450.
54-02-145	William Penn	P.W. Baston	Closed	Unkn.	175-225.
54-02-146	St. Pius X	P.W. Baston	Closed	Unkn.	400-475.
54-02-147	Resolute Ins. Co. Clipper PS	P.W. Baston	Closed	Unkn.	300-325.
54-02-148	Dachshund (Audiovox)	P.W. Baston	Closed	Unkn.	300-350.
54-02-149	Our Lady of Laleche	P.W. Baston	Closed	Unkn.	300-350.
54-02-150	Swan Boat Brooch-Enpty Seats	P.W. Baston	Closed	Unkn.	600-1000.
54-02-151	Swan Boat Brooch-Full Seats	P.W. Baston	Closed	Unkn.	600-1000.
55-02-152	Davy Crockett	P.W. Baston	Closed	Unkn.	225-275.
55-02-153	Giraffe (Jell-O)	P.W. Baston	Closed	Unkn.	350-375.
55-02-154	Old Woman in the Shoe (Jell-O)	P.W. Baston	Closed	Unkn.	500-600.
55-02-155	Santa (Jell-O)	P.W. Baston	Closed	Unkn.	500-600.
55-02-156	Captain Doliber	P.W. Baston	Closed	Unkn.	300-350.
55-02-157	Second Bank-State St. Trust PS	P.W. Baston	Closed	Unkn.	300-325.
55-02-158	Horse Head PS	P.W. Baston	Closed	Unkn.	350-375.
56-02-159	Robin Hood & Little John	P.W. Baston	Closed	Unkn.	400-500.
56-02-160	Robin Hood & Friar Tuck	P.W. Baston	Closed	Unkn.	400-500.
56-02-161	77th Bengal Lancer (Jell-O)	P.W. Baston	Closed	Unkn.	600-1000.
56-02-162	Three Little Kittens (Jell-O)	P.W. Baston	Closed	Unkn.	375-400.
56-02-163	Texcel Tape Boy	P.W. Baston	Closed	Unkn.	350-425.
56-02-164	Permacel Tower of Tape Ashtray	P.W. Baston	Closed	Unkn.	600-1000.
56-02-165	Arthritic Hands (J & J)	P.W. Baston	Closed	Unkn.	600-1000.
56-02-166	Rarical Blacksmith	P.W. Baston	Closed	Unkn.	300-500.
56-02-167	Praying Hands	P.W. Baston	Closed	Unkn.	250-300.
56-02-168	Eastern Paper Plaque	P.W. Baston	Closed	Unkn.	350-400.
56-02-169	Girl on Diving Board	P.W. Baston	Closed	Unkn.	400-450.
56-02-170	Elsie the Cow Billboard	P.W. Baston	Closed	Unkn.	600-1000.
56-02-171	Mrs. Obocell	P.W. Baston	Closed	Unkn.	400-450.
56-02-172	Alike, But Oh So Different	P.W. Baston	Closed	Unkn.	300-350.
56-02-173	NYU Grad School of Bus. Admin. Bldg.	P.W. Baston	Closed	Unkn.	300-350.
56-02-174	The Green Giant	P.W. Baston	Closed	Unkn.	400-500.
56-02-175	Michigan Millers PS	P.W. Baston	Closed	Unkn.	200-275.
57-02-176	Mayflower PS	P.W. Baston	Closed	Unkn.	300-325.
57-02-177	Jamestown Church	P.W. Baston	Closed	Unkn.	400-450.
57-02-178	Olde James Fort	P.W. Baston	Closed	Unkn.	250-300.
57-02-179	Jamestown Ships	P.W. Baston	Closed	Unkn.	350-475.
57-02-180	IBM 305 Ramac	P.W. Baston	Closed	Unkn.	400-450.
57-02-181	Colonial Fund Doorway PS	P.W. Baston	Closed	Unkn.	600-1000.
57-02-182	Speedy Alka Seltzer	P.W. Baston	Closed	Unkn.	600-1000.
57-02-183	Nabisco Spoonmen	P.W. Baston	Closed	Unkn.	600-1000.
57-02-184	Nabisco Buffalo Bee	P.W. Baston	Closed	Unkn.	600-1000.
57-02-185	Borden's Centennial (Elsie the Cow)	P.W. Baston	Closed	Unkn.	600-1000.
57-02-186	Along the Albany Road PS	P.W. Baston	Closed	Unkn.	600-1000.
58-02-187	Romeo & Juliet	P.W. Baston	Closed	Unkn.	400-500.
58-02-188	Mt. Vernon	P.W. Baston	Closed	Unkn.	400-500.
58-02-189	Hannah Duston PS	P.W. Baston	Closed	Unkn.	250-325.
58-02-190	Salem Savings Bank	P.W. Baston	Closed	Unkn.	250-300.
58-02-191	CBS Miss Columbia PS	P.W. Baston	Closed	Unkn.	600-1000.
58-02-192	Connecticut Bank & Trust	P.W. Baston	Closed	Unkn.	225-275.
58-02-193	Jackie Gleason	P.W. Baston	Closed	Unkn.	600-1000.
58-02-194	Harvard Trust Colonial Man	P.W. Baston	Closed	Unkn.	275-325.
58-02-195	Jordan Marsh Observer	P.W. Baston	Closed	Unkn.	175-275.
58-02-196	Cliquot Club Eskimo PS	P.W. Baston	Closed	Unkn.	10-2300.
58-02-197	Commodore Stephen Decatur	P.W. Baston	Closed	Unkn.	125-175.
59-02-198	Siesta Coffee PS	P.W. Baston	Closed	Unkn.	600-1000.
59-02-199	Harvard Trust Co. Town Crier	P.W. Baston	Closed	Unkn.	350-400.
59-02-200	Mrs. S.O.S.	P.W. Baston	Closed	Unkn.	300-350.
59-02-201	H.P. Hood Co. Cigar Store Indian	P.W. Baston	Closed	Unkn.	600-1000.
59-02-202	Alexander Smith Weaver	P.W. Baston	Closed	Unkn.	350-425.
59-02-203	Fleischman's Margarine PS	P.W. Baston	Closed	Unkn.	225-325.
59-02-204	Alcoa Wrap PS	P.W. Baston	Closed	Unkn.	350-400.
59-02-205	Fiorello LaGuardia	P.W. Baston	Closed	Unkn.	125-175.
59-02-206	Henry Hudson	P.W. Baston	Closed	Unkn.	125-175.
59-02-207	Giovanni Verrazzano	P.W. Baston	Closed	Unkn.	125-175.
60-02-208	Peter Stvyvesant	P.W. Baston	Closed	Unkn.	125-175.
60-02-209	Masonic Bible	P.W. Baston	Closed	Unkn.	300-400.
60-02-210	Son of the Desert	P.W. Baston	Closed	Unkn.	200-275.
60-02-211	Metropolitan Life Tower PS	P.W. Baston	Closed	Unkn.	350-400.
60-02-212	Supp-Hose Lady	P.W. Baston	Closed	Unkn.	300-500.
60-02-213	Marine Memorial	P.W. Baston	Closed	Unkn.	300-400.
60-02-214	The Infantryman	P.W. Baston	Closed	Unkn.	600-1000.
61-02-215	Tony Piet	P.W. Baston	Closed	Unkn.	600-1000.
61-02-216	Bunky Knudsen	P.W. Baston	Closed	Unkn.	600-1000.
61-02-217	Merchant's Warren Sea Capt.	P.W. Baston	Closed	Unkn.	200-250.
61-02-218	Pope John 23rd	P.W. Baston	Closed	Unkn.	400-450.
61-02-219	St. Jude Thaddeus	P.W. Baston	Closed	Unkn.	400-500.

		ARTIST	EDITION	ISSUE	QUOTE
62-02-220	Seaman's Bank for Savings	P.W. Baston	Closed	Unkn.	300-350.
62-02-221	Yankee Clipper Sulfide	P.W. Baston	Closed	Unkn.	600-1000.
62-02-222	Big Brother Bob Emery	P.W. Baston	Closed	Unkn.	600-1000.
62-02-223	Blue Belle Highlander	P.W. Baston	Closed	Unkn.	200-250.
63-02-224	John F. Kennedy Toby Jug	P.W. Baston	Closed	Unkn.	600-1000.
63-02-225	Jackie Kennedy Toby Jug	P.W. Baston	Closed	Unkn.	600-1000.
63-02-226	Naumkeag Indian	P.W. Baston	Closed	Unkn.	225-275.
63-02-227	Dia-Mel Fat Man	P.W. Baston	Closed	Unkn.	375-400.
65-02-228	Pope Paul VI	P.W. Baston	Closed	Unkn.	400-500.
65-02-229	Henry Wadsworth Longfellow	P.W. Baston	Closed	Unkn.	275-325.
65-02-230	State Street Bank Globe	P.W. Baston	Closed	Unkn.	250-300.
65-02-231	Panti-Legs Girl PS	P.W. Baston	Closed	Unkn.	250-300.
66-02-232	Paul Revere Plaque (W.T. Grant)	P.W. Baston	Closed	Unkn.	300-350.
66-02-233	Massachusetts SPCA	P.W. Baston	Closed	Unkn.	250-350.
66-02-234	Little George	P.W. Baston	Closed	Unkn.	350-450.
66-02-235	Gardeners (Thermometer)	P.W. Baston	Closed	Unkn.	300-400.
66-02-236	Gardener Man	P.W. Baston	Closed	Unkn.	250-300.
66-02-237	Gardener Women	P.W. Baston	Closed	Unkn.	250-300.
66-02-238	Town Lyne Indian	P.W. Baston	Closed	Unkn.	600-1000.
67-02-239	Doc Berry of Berwick (yellow shirt)	P.W. Baston	Closed	Unkn.	300-350.
67-02-240	Ortho-Novum	P.W. Baston	Closed	Unkn.	600-1000.
68-02-241	Captain John Parker	P.W. Baston	Closed	Unkn.	300-350.
68-02-242	Watermill Candy Plaque	P.W. Baston	Closed	Unkn.	600-1000.
70-02-243	Uncle Sam in Orbit	P.W. Baston	Closed	Unkn.	350-400.
71-02-244	Town Meeting Plaque	P.W. Baston	Closed	Unkn.	350-400.
71-02-245	Boston Gas Tank	P.W. Baston	Closed	Unkn.	300-500.
72-02-246	George & Hatchet	P.W. Baston	Closed	Unkn.	400-450.
72-02-247	Martha & the Cherry Pie	P.W. Baston	Closed	Unkn.	350-400.
XX-02-248	The King	P.W. Baston	Closed	Unkn.	600-1000.
XX-02-249	Bob Hope	P.W. Baston	Closed	Unkn.	600-1000.
XX-02-250	Coronation Crown	P.W. Baston	Closed	Unkn.	600-1000.
XX-02-251	Babe Ruth	P.W. Baston	Closed	Unkn.	600-1000.
XX-02-252	Sylvania Electric-Bulb Display	P.W. Baston	Closed	Unkn.	600-1000.
XX-02-252	Ortho Gynecic	P.W. Baston	Closed	Unkn.	600-1000.
XX-02-254	Eagle Plaque	P.W. Baston	Closed	Unkn.	1000-15.

Shelia's Collectibles — Painted Ladies I

90-01-001	San Francisco Stick House-yellow LAD01	S.Thompson	Retrd.	10.00	50-100.
90-01-002	San Francisco Stick House-blue LAD02	S.Thompson	Retrd.	10.00	50-100.
90-01-003	San Francisco Italianate-yellow LAD03	S.Thompson	Retrd.	10.00	50-100.
90-01-004	Colorado Queen Anne LAD04	S.Thompson	Retrd.	10.00	50-100.
90-01-005	Cincinnati Gothic LAD05	S.Thompson	Retrd.	10.00	50-100.
90-01-006	Illinois Queen Anne LAD06	S.Thompson	Retrd.	10.00	125-200.
90-01-007	Atlanta Queen Anne LAD07	S.Thompson	Retrd.	10.00	50-100.
90-01-008	The Abbey LAD08	S.Thompson	Retrd.	10.00	50-100.

Shelia's Collectibles — Painted Ladies II

92-02-001	The Gingerbread Mansion LAD09	S.Thompson	Retrd.	15.00	15.00
94-02-002	The Gingerbread Mansion (renovated) LAD09II	S.Thompson	Retrd.	16.00	16.00
92-02-003	Pitkin House LAD10	S.Thompson	Open	15.00	15.00
94-02-004	Pitkin House (renovated) LAD10II	S.Thompson	Open	16.00	16.00
92-02-005	The Young-Larson House LAD11	S.Thompson	Open	15.00	15.00
94-02-006	The Young-Larson House (renovated) LAD11II	S.Thompson	Open	16.00	16.00
92-02-007	Queen Anne Townhouse LAD12	S.Thompson	Retrd.	15.00	15.00
94-02-008	Queen Anne Townhouse (renovated) LAD12II	S.Thompson	Retrd.	16.00	16.00
92-02-009	Cape May Gothic LAD13	S.Thompson	Open	15.00	15.00
94-02-010	Cape May Gothic (renovated) LAD13II	S.Thompson	Open	16.00	16.00
92-02-011	The Victorian Blue Rose LAD14	S.Thompson	Open	15.00	15.00
94-02-012	The Victorian Blue Rose (renovated) LAD14II	S.Thompson	Open	16.00	16.00
92-02-013	Morningstar Inn LAD15	S.Thompson	Retrd.	15.00	15.00
94-02-014	Morningstar Inn (renovated) LAD15II	S.Thompson	Retrd.	16.00	16.00
92-02-015	Cape May Victorian Pink House LAD16	S.Thompson	Open	15.00	15.00
94-02-016	Cape May Victorian Pink House (renovated) LAD16II	S.Thompson	Open	16.00	16.00

Shelia's Collectibles — Painted Ladies III

93-03-001	Cape May Linda Lee LAD17	S.Thompson	Open	16.00	16.00
94-03-002	Cape May Linda Lee (renovated) LAD17II	S.Thompson	Open	16.00	16.00
93-03-003	Cape May Tan Stockton Row LAD18	S.Thompson	Open	16.00	16.00
94-03-004	Cape May Tan Stockton Row (renovated)LAD18II	S.Thompson	Open	16.00	16.00
93-03-005	Cape May Pink Stockton Row LAD19	S.Thompson	Open	16.00	16.00
94-03-006	Cape May Pink Stockton Row (renovated)LAD19II	S.Thompson	Open	16.00	16.00
93-03-007	Cape May Green Stockton Row LAD20	S.Thompson	Open	16.00	16.00
94-03-008	Cape May Green Stockton Row (renovated) LAD20II	S.Thompson	Open	16.00	16.00

Shelia's Collectibles — Dicken's Village

91-04-001	Scrooge & Marley's Shop XMS01	S.Thompson	Retrd.	15.00	20-25.00
91-04-002	Victorian Apartment Building XMS02	S.Thompson	Retrd.	15.00	20-25.00
91-04-003	Butcher Shop XMS03	S.Thompson	Retrd.	15.00	20-25.00
91-04-004	Toy Shoppe XMS04	S.Thompson	Retrd.	15.00	20-25.00
91-04-005	Scrooge's Home XMS05	S.Thompson	Retrd.	15.00	20-25.00
91-04-006	Gazebo & Carolers XMS06	S.Thompson	Retrd.	12.00	20-25.00
91-04-007	Victorian Skaters XMS07	S.Thompson	Retrd.	12.00	20-25.00
91-04-008	Evergreen Tree XMS08	S.Thompson	Retrd.	11.00	20-25.00
92-04-009	Victorian Church XMS09	S.Thompson	Retrd.	15.00	20-25.00
92-04-010	Set	S.Thompson	Retrd.	125.00	160-185.

Shelia's Collectibles — Charleston

90-06-001	Rainbow Row-rust CHS31	S.Thompson	Retrd.	9.00	16-30.00
90-06-002	Rainbow Row-cream CHS32	S.Thompson	Retrd.	9.00	16-30.00
90-06-003	Rainbow Row-tan CHS33	S.Thompson	Retrd.	9.00	16-30.00
90-06-004	Rainbow Row-green CHS34	S.Thompson	Retrd.	9.00	16-30.00
90-06-005	Rainbow Row-lavender CHS35	S.Thompson	Retrd.	9.00	16-35.00
90-06-006	Rainbow Row-pink CHS36	S.Thompson	Retrd.	9.00	16-40.00
90-06-007	Rainbow Row-blue CHS37	S.Thompson	Retrd.	9.00	16-30.00
90-06-008	Rainbow Row-lt. yellow CHS38	S.Thompson	Retrd.	9.00	16-30.00
90-06-009	Rainbow Row-lt. pink CHS39	S.Thompson	Retrd.	9.00	75-100.
90-06-010	Powder Magazine CHS16	S.Thompson	Retrd.	9.00	125-130.
90-06-011	Middleton Plantation CHS19	S.Thompson	Retrd.	9.00	20-25.00
90-06-012	Manigault House CHS01	S.Thompson	Retrd.	15.00	20-25.00
90-06-013	Heyward-Washington House CHS02	S.Thompson	Retrd.	15.00	23.00
91-06-014	Magnolia Plantation House (beige curtains)CHS03	S.Thompson	Open	16.00	16.00
91-06-015	Magnolia Plantation House (white curtains)CHS03	S.Thompson	Open	16.00	16.00
94-06-016	Magnolia Plantation House (renovated) CHS03II	S.Thompson	Open	16.00	16.00
91-06-017	Edmonston-Alston CHS04	S.Thompson	Open	15.00	15.00
94-06-018	Edmonston-Alston (renovated) CHS04II	S.Thompson	Open	16.00	16.00
91-06-019	St. Phillip's Church (misspelling Phillips) CHS05	S.Thompson	Open	15.00	15.00
91-06-020	St. Philip's Church CHS05	S.Thompson	Open	15.00	15.00
94-06-021	St. Philip's Church (renovated) CHS05II	S.Thompson	Open	15.00	15.00
91-06-022	#2 Meeting Street CHS06	S.Thompson	Open	15.00	15.00
94-06-023	#2 Meeting Street (renovated) CHS06II	S.Thompson	Open	16.00	16.00
91-06-024	City Market (closed gates) CHS07	S.Thompson	Retrd.	15.00	20.00
91-06-025	City Market (open gates) CHS07	S.Thompson	Open	15.00	15.00
94-06-026	City Market (renovated) CHS07II	S.Thompson	Open	15.00	15.00
91-06-027	Dock Street Theater (no chimney) CHS08	S.Thompson	Retrd.	15.00	15.00
92-06-028	Dock Street Theater (chimney) CHS08	S.Thompson	Retrd.	15.00	20-25.00
90-06-029	St. Michael's Church CHS14	S.Thompson	Retrd.	15.00	15.00
90-06-030	Exchange Building CHS15	S.Thompson	Retrd.	15.00	15.00
90-06-031	90 Church St. CHS17	S.Thompson	Retrd.	12.00	15-22.00
90-06-032	Pink House CHS18	S.Thompson	Retrd.	12.00	15-22.00
91-06-033	Beth Elohim Temple CHS20	S.Thompson	Retrd.	15.00	20-30.00
93-06-034	City Hall CHS21	S.Thompson	Retrd.	15.00	30-50.00
93-06-035	The Citadel CHS22	S.Thompson	Open	16.00	16.00
94-06-036	The Citadel (renovated) CHS22II	S.Thompson	Open	16.00	16.00
93-06-037	Single Side Porch CHS30	S.Thompson	Open	16.00	16.00
93-06-038	Single Side Porch, AP CHS30	S.Thompson	102	20.00	20.00
94-06-039	Single Side Porch (renovated) CHS30II	S.Thompson	Open	16.00	16.00
93-06-040	College of Charleston CHS40	S.Thompson	Open	16.00	16.00
93-06-041	College of Charleston, AP CHS40	S.Thompson	54	20.00	20.00
94-06-042	College of Charleston (renovated) CHS40II	S.Thompson	Open	16.00	16.00
93-06-043	Rainbow Row-aurora CHS41	S.Thompson	Open	13.00	13.00
94-06-044	Rainbow Row-aurora (renovated) CHS41II	S.Thompson	Open	13.00	13.00
93-06-045	Rainbow Row-off-white CHS42	S.Thompson	Open	13.00	13.00
94-06-046	Rainbow Row-off-white (renovated) CHS42II	S.Thompson	Open	13.00	13.00
93-06-047	Rainbow Row-cream CHS43	S.Thompson	Open	13.00	13.00
94-06-048	Rainbow Row-cream (renovated) CHS43II	S.Thompson	Open	13.00	13.00
93-06-049	Rainbow Row-green CHS44	S.Thompson	Open	13.00	13.00
94-06-050	Rainbow Row-green (renovated) CHS44II	S.Thompson	Open	13.00	13.00
93-06-051	Rainbow Row-lavender CHS45	S.Thompson	Open	13.00	13.00
94-06-052	Rainbow Row-lavender (renovated) CHS45II	S.Thompson	Open	13.00	13.00
93-06-053	Rainbow Row-pink CHS46	S.Thompson	Open	13.00	13.00
94-06-054	Rainbow Row-pink (renovated) CHS46II	S.Thompson	Open	13.00	13.00
93-06-055	Rainbow Row-blue CHS47	S.Thompson	Open	13.00	13.00
94-06-056	Rainbow Row-blue (renovated) CHS47II	S.Thompson	Open	13.00	13.00
93-06-057	Rainbow Row-yellow CHS48	S.Thompson	Open	13.00	13.00
94-06-058	Rainbow Row-yellow (renovated) CHS48	S.Thompson	Open	13.00	13.00
93-06-059	Rainbow Row-gray CHS49	S.Thompson	Open	13.00	13.00
94-06-060	Rainbow Row-gray (renovated) CHS49II	S.Thompson	Open	13.00	13.00
93-06-061	John Rutledge House Inn CHS50	S.Thompson	Open	16.00	16.00
94-06-062	John Rutledge House Inn (renovated) CHS50II	S.Thompson	Open	16.00	16.00
93-06-063	Ashe House CHS51	S.Thompson	Open	16.00	16.00
94-06-064	Ashe House (renovated) CHS51II	S.Thompson	Open	16.00	16.00
94-06-065	Drayton House CHS52	S.Thompson	Open	18.00	18.00

Shelia's Collectibles — Charleston Gold Seal

88-07-001	Rainbow Row-rust (gold seal) CHS31	S.Thompson	Retrd.	9.00	N/A
88-07-002	Rainbow Row-tan (gold seal) CHS32	S.Thompson	Retrd.	9.00	N/A
88-07-003	Rainbow Row-cream (gold seal) CHS33	S.Thompson	Retrd.	9.00	N/A
88-07-004	Rainbow Row-green (gold seal) CHS34	S.Thompson	Retrd.	9.00	N/A
88-07-005	Rainbow Row-lavender (gold seal) CHS35	S.Thompson	Retrd.	9.00	N/A
88-07-006	Rainbow Row-pink (gold seal) CHS36	S.Thompson	Retrd.	9.00	N/A
88-07-007	Rainbow Row-blue (gold seal) CHS37	S.Thompson	Retrd.	9.00	N/A
88-07-008	Rainbow Row-lt. yellow (gold seal) CHS38	S.Thompson	Retrd.	9.00	N/A
88-07-009	Rainbow Row-lt. pink (gold seal) CHS39	S.Thompson	Retrd.	9.00	N/A
88-07-010	90 Church St. (gold seal) CHS17	S.Thompson	Retrd.	9.00	N/A
88-07-011	Pink House (gold seal) CHS18	S.Thompson	Retrd.	9.00	N/A
88-07-012	St. Michael's Church (gold seal) CHS14	S.Thompson	Retrd.	9.00	N/A
88-07-013	Exchange Building (gold seal) CHS15	S.Thompson	Retrd.	9.00	N/A
88-07-014	Powder Magazine (gold seal) CHS16	S.Thompson	Retrd.	9.00	65-85.00
88-07-015	Middleton Plantation (gold seal) CHS19	S.Thompson	Retrd.	9.00	100.00

Shelia's Collectibles — Texas

90-08-001	The Alamo TEX01	S.Thompson	Retrd.	15.00	40.00
90-08-002	Mission San Jose' TEX02	S.Thompson	Retrd.	15.00	40.00
90-08-003	Mission San Francisco TEX03	S.Thompson	Retrd.	15.00	30-40.00
90-08-004	Mission Concepcion TEX04	S.Thompson	Retrd.	15.00	30-40.00

Shelia's Collectibles — New England

90-09-001	Longfellow's House NEW01	S.Thompson	Retrd.	15.00	25-30.00
90-09-002	Motif #1 Boathouse NEW02	S.Thompson	Retrd.	15.00	25-54.00
90-09-003	Paul Revere's Home MEW03	S.Thompson	Retrd.	15.00	25-54.00
90-09-004	Old North Church NEW04	S.Thompson	Retrd.	15.00	25-30.00
90-09-005	Malden Mass. Victorian Inn NEW05	S.Thompson	Retrd.	10.00	50-100.
91-09-006	President Bush's Home NEW07	S.Thompson	Retrd.	15.00	50.00
91-09-007	Wedding Cake House NEW08	S.Thompson	Retrd.	15.00	30.00
91-09-008	Faneuil Hall NEW09	S.Thompson	Retrd.	15.00	25-65.00
90-09-009	Martha's Vineyard Cottage-blue/mauve MAR06	S.Thompson	Retrd.	15.00	20-65.00
90-09-010	Martha's Vineyard Cottage-blue/orange MAR05	S.Thompson	Retrd.	15.00	20-65.00

Shelia's Collectibles — Williamsburg

90-10-001	Governor's Palace WIL04	S.Thompson	Open	15.00	15.00
94-10-002	Governor's Palace (renovated) WIL04II	S.Thompson	Open	15.00	15.00
90-10-003	The Printing Offices WIL05	S.Thompson	Retrd.	12.00	20-25.00
90-10-004	Milliner WIL06	S.Thompson	Retrd.	12.00	18-25.00
90-10-005	The Golden Ball Jeweler WIL07	S.Thompson	Retrd.	12.00	18-25.00
90-10-006	Nicolson Shop WIL08	S.Thompson	Retrd.	12.00	18-25.00
90-10-007	Apothecary WIL09	S.Thompson	Retrd.	12.00	18-25.00
90-10-008	KIng's Arm Tavern WIL10	S.Thompson	Open	15.00	15.00
94-10-009	KIng's Arm Tavern (renovated) WIL10II	S.Thompson	Open	15.00	15.00
90-10-010	Courthouse WIL11	S.Thompson	Open	15.00	15.00
94-10-011	Courthouse (renovated) WIL11II	S.Thompson	Open	15.00	15.00
90-10-012	Homesite WIL12	S.Thompson	Open	15.00	15.00
94-10-013	Homesite (renovated) WIL12II	S.Thompson	Open	15.00	15.00
92-10-014	Bruton Parish Church WIL13	S.Thompson	Open	15.00	15.00
94-10-015	Bruton Parish Church (renovated) WIL13II	S.Thompson	Open	15.00	15.00

Shelia's Collectibles — Philadelphia

90-11-001	Carpenter's Hall PHI01	S.Thompson	Retrd.	15.00	20-45.00
90-11-002	Market St. Post Office PHI02	S.Thompson	Retrd.	15.00	20-45.00
90-11-003	Betsy Ross House PHI03	S.Thompson	Retrd.	15.00	20-45.00
90-11-004	"Besty" Ross House (misspelling) PHI03	S.Thompson	Retrd.	15.00	20-45.00
90-11-005	Independence Hall PHI04	S.Thompson	Retrd.	15.00	20-45.00

		ARTIST	EDITION	ISSUE	QUOTE
90-11-006	Elphreth's Alley PHI05	S.Thompson	Retrd.	15.00	20-45.00
90-11-007	Old Tavern PHI06	S.Thompson	Retrd.	15.00	20-45.00
90-11-008	Graff House PHI07	S.Thompson	Retrd.	15.00	20-45.00
90-11-009	Old City Hall PHI08	S.Thompson	Retrd.	15.00	20-45.00
Shelia's Collectibles	**Washington D.C.**				
91-12-001	National Archives DC001	S.Thompson	Retrd.	16.00	20-45.00
92-12-002	Library of Congress DC002	S.Thompson	Retrd.	16.00	25-40.00
92-12-003	White House DC003	S.Thompson	Retrd.	16.00	25-50.00
91-12-004	Washington Monument DC004	S.Thompson	Retrd.	16.00	20-46.00
92-12-005	Cherry Trees DC005	S.Thompson	Retrd.	12.00	20.00
Shelia's Collectibles	**North Carolina**				
90-13-001	Josephus Hall House NC101	S.Thompson	Retrd.	15.00	20-30.00
90-13-002	Presbyterian Bell Tower NC102	S.Thompson	Retrd.	15.00	20-30.00
91-13-003	The Tryon Palace NC104	S.Thompson	Retrd.	15.00	25-30.00
Shelia's Collectibles	**South Carolina**				
90-14-001	The Hermitage SC101	S.Thompson	Open	15.00	25.00
94-14-002	The Hermitage (renovated) SC101II	S.Thompson	Open	15.00	25.00
90-14-003	The Governor's Mansion SC102	S.Thompson	Open	15.00	25-30.00
90-14-004	The Governer's Mansion (misspelling) SC102	S.Thompson	Retrd.	15.00	15.00
94-14-005	The Governor's Mansion (renovated) SC102II	S.Thompson	Open	15.00	15.00
90-14-006	The Lace House SC103	S.Thompson	Open	15.00	15.00
94-14-007	The Lace House (renovated) SC103II	S.Thompson	Open	15.00	15.00
91-14-008	The State Capitol SC104	S.Thompson	Retrd.	15.00	25.00
94-14-009	The State Capitol (renovated) SC104II	S.Thompson	Retrd.	15.00	15.00
91-14-010	All Saints' Church SC105	S.Thompson	Retrd.	15.00	20-30.00
Shelia's Collectibles	**St. Augustine**				
91-15-001	The "Oldest House" FL101	S.Thompson	Retrd.	15.00	20-45.00
91-15-002	Old City Gates FL102	S.Thompson	Retrd.	15.00	20-45.00
91-15-003	Anastasia Lighthousekeeper's House FL104	S.Thompson	Retrd.	15.00	20-45.00
91-15-004	Mission Nombre deDios FL105	S.Thompson	Retrd.	15.00	20-45.00
Shelia's Collectibles	**Savannah**				
90-16-001	Olde Pink House SAV01	S.Thompson	Open	15.00	15.00
94-16-002	Olde Pink House (renovated) SAV01II	S.Thompson	Open	15.00	15.00
90-16-003	Andrew Low Mansion SAV02	S.Thompson	Retrd.	15.00	20.00
90-16-004	Davenport House SAV03	S.Thompson	Retrd.	15.00	20.00
90-16-005	Juliette Low House (w/o logo) SAV04	S.Thompson	Open	15.00	15.00
90-16-006	Juliette Low House (w/logo) SAV04	S.Thompson	Open	15.00	15.00
94-16-007	Juliette Low House (renovated) SAV04II	S.Thompson	Open	15.00	15.00
90-16-008	Herb House SAV05	S.Thompson	Retrd.	15.00	20.00
90-16-009	Mikve Israel Temple SAV06	S.Thompson	Retrd.	15.00	20-23.00
90-16-010	Savannah Gingerbread House I SAV08	S.Thompson	Retrd.	15.00	200.00
90-16-011	Savannah Gingerbread House II SAV08	S.Thompson	Retrd.	15.00	50.00
92-16-012	Catherdral of St. John SAV09	S.Thompson	Open	16.00	16.00
94-16-013	Catherdral of St. John (renovated) SAV09II	S.Thompson	Open	16.00	16.00
93-16-014	Owens Thomas House SAV10	S.Thompson	Open	16.00	16.00
93-16-015	Owens Thomas House AP SAV10	S.Thompson	Retrd.	20.00	20.00
94-16-016	Owens Thomas House (renovated) SAV10II	S.Thompson	Open	16.00	16.00
94-16-017	Chestnut House SAV11	S.Thompson	Open	18.00	18.00
Shelia's Collectibles	**Lighthouse Series**				
90-17-001	Tybee Lighthouse SAV07	S.Thompson	Retrd.	15.00	20-25.00
90-17-002	Stage Harbor Lighthouse NEW06	S.Thompson	Retrd.	15.00	30-70.00
91-17-003	Cape Hatteras Lighthouse NC103	S.Thompson	Retrd.	15.00	20-25.00
91-17-004	Anastasia Lighthouse (burgundy) FL103	S.Thompson	Retrd.	15.00	25.00
91-17-005	Anastasia Lighthouse (red) FL103	S.Thompson	Retrd.	15.00	15.00
93-17-006	Charleston Light LTS01	S.Thompson	Open	15.00	15.00
94-17-007	Charleston Light (renovated) LTS01	S.Thompson	Open	15.00	15.00
93-17-008	Thomas Point Light LTS05	S.Thompson	Open	17.00	17.00
94-17-009	Thomas Point Light, AP LTS05	S.Thompson	Retrd.	20.00	20.00
93-17-010	Round Island Light LTS06	S.Thompson	Open	17.00	17.00
94-17-011	Round Island Light, AP LTS06	S.Thompson	Retrd.	20.00	20.00
93-17-012	Assateague Island Light LTS07	S.Thompson	Open	17.00	17.00
94-17-013	Assateague Island Light, AP LTS07	S.Thompson	Retrd.	20.00	20.00
93-17-014	New London Ledge Light LTS08	S.Thompson	Open	17.00	17.00
94-17-015	New London Ledge Light, AP LTS08	S.Thompson	Retrd.	20.00	20.00
Shelia's Collectibles	**Martha's Vineyard**				
93-18-001	Campground Cottage MAR07	S.Thompson	Open	16.00	16.00
93-18-002	Campground Cottage, AP MAR07	S.Thompson	Retrd.	20.00	20.00
94-18-003	Campground Cottage (renovated) MAR07II	S.Thompson	Open	16.00	16.00
93-18-004	Alice's Wonderland MAR08	S.Thompson	Open	16.00	16.00
93-18-005	Alice's Wonderland, AP MAR08	S.Thompson	Retrd.	20.00	20.00
94-18-006	Alice's Wonderland (renovated) MAR08II	S.Thompson	Open	16.00	16.00
93-18-007	Gingerbread Cottage-grey MAR09	S.Thompson	Open	16.00	16.00
93-18-008	Gingerbread Cottage-grey AP MAR09	S.Thompson	Retrd.	20.00	20.00
94-18-009	Gingerbread Cottage-grey (renovated) MAR09II	S.Thompson	Open	16.00	16.00
93-18-010	Wood Valentine MAR10	S.Thompson	Open	16.00	16.00
93-18-011	Wood Valentine, AP MAR10	S.Thompson	Retrd.	20.00	20.00
94-18-012	Wood Valentine (renovated) MAR10II	S.Thompson	Open	16.00	16.00
Shelia's Collectibles	**Amish Village**				
93-19-001	Amish Home AMS01	S.Thompson	Open	17.00	17.00
93-19-002	Amish Home, AP AMS101	S.Thompson	Retrd.	20.00	20.00
94-19-003	Amish Home (renovated) AMS01II	S.Thompson	Open	17.00	17.00
93-19-004	Amish School AMS102	S.Thompson	Open	15.00	15.00
93-19-005	Amish School, AP AMS02	S.Thompson	Retrd.	20.00	20.00
94-19-006	Amish School (renovated) AMS102II	S.Thompson	Open	15.00	15.00
93-19-007	Covered Bridge AMS03	S.Thompson	Open	16.00	16.00
93-19-008	Covered Bridge, AP AMS03	S.Thompson	Retrd.	20.00	20.00
94-19-009	Covered Bridge (renovated) AMS03II	S.Thompson	Open	16.00	16.00
93-19-010	Amish Barn AMS04	S.Thompson	Open	17.00	17.00
93-19-011	Amish Barn, AP AMS04	S.Thompson	Retrd.	20.00	20.00
94-19-012	Amish Barn (renovated) AMS04II	S.Thompson	Open	17.00	17.00
93-19-013	Amish Buggy AMS05	S.Thompson	Open	12.00	12.00
93-19-014	Amish Buggy, AP AMS05	S.Thompson	Retrd.	16.00	16.00
94-19-015	Amish Buggy (renovated) AMS05II	S.Thompson	Open	12.00	12.00
Shelia's Collectibles	**Collectible Accessories**				
92-20-001	Wrought Iron Gate With Magnolias COL01	S.Thompson	Retrd.	11.00	13-22.00
92-20-002	Gazebo With Victorian Lady COL02	S.Thompson	Open	11.00	11.00
92-20-003	Oak Bower COL03	S.Thompson	Retrd.	11.00	13-18.00
92-20-004	Fence 5" COL04	S.Thompson	Retrd.	9.00	11-15.00
92-20-005	Fence 7" COL05	S.Thompson	Open	10.00	10.00
92-20-006	Lake With Swan COL06	S.Thompson	Retrd.	11.00	13-25.00
92-20-007	Tree With Bush COL07	S.Thompson	Open	10.00	10.00

		ARTIST	EDITION	ISSUE	QUOTE
93-20-008	Dogwood Tree COL08	S.Thompson	Open	12.00	12.00
93-20-009	Apple Tree COL09	S.Thompson	Open	12.00	12.00
94-20-010	Sunrise At 80 Meeting COL10	S.Thompson	Retrd.	18.00	30.00
94-20-011	Victorian Arbor COL11	S.Thompson	Retrd.	18.00	35.00
94-20-012	Amish Quilt Line COL12	S.Thompson	Retrd.	18.00	25-35.00
94-20-013	Formal Garden COL13	S.Thompson	Retrd.	18.00	30.00
Shelia's Collectibles	**Victorian Springtime**				
93-21-001	Ralston House VST01	S.Thompson	Open	17.00	17.00
93-21-002	Ralston House, AP VST01	S.Thompson	Retrd.	20.00	20.00
93-21-003	Sessions House VST02	S.Thompson	Open	17.00	17.00
93-21-004	Sessions House ,AP VST02	S.Thompson	Retrd.	20.00	20.00
93-21-005	Heffron House VST03	S.Thompson	Open	17.00	17.00
93-21-006	Heffron House, AP VST03	S.Thompson	Retrd.	20.00	20.00
93-21-007	Jacobsen House VST04	S.Thompson	Open	17.00	17.00
93-21-008	Jacobsen House, AP VST04	S.Thompson	Retrd.	20.00	20.00
93-21-009	Set of 4, AP	S.Thompson	Closed	100.00	100-140.
Shelia's Collectibles	**Inventor Series**				
93-22-001	Ford Motor Company (green) INV01	S.Thompson	Retrd.	17.00	17.00
93-22-002	Ford Motor Company (grey) INV01	S.Thompson	Open	17.00	17.00
93-22-003	Ford Motor Company, AP INV01	S.Thompson	Retrd.	20.00	20.00
93-22-004	Menlo Park Laboratory (cream) INV02	S.Thompson	Retrd.	16.00	16.00
93-22-005	Menlo Park Laboratory (grey) INV02	S.Thompson	Open	16.00	16.00
93-22-006	Menlo Park Laboratory, AP INV02	S.Thompson	Retrd.	20.00	20.00
93-22-007	Noah Webster House INV03	S.Thompson	Open	15.00	15.00
93-22-008	Noah Webster House, AP INV03	S.Thompson	Retrd.	20.00	20.00
93-22-009	Wright Cycle Shop INV04	S.Thompson	Open	17.00	17.00
93-22-010	Wright Cycle Shop, AP INV04	S.Thompson	Retrd.	20.00	20.00
Shelia's Collectibles	**Limited Edition American Gothic**				
93-23-001	Gothic Revival Cottage ACL01	S.Thompson	Retrd.	20.00	20.00
93-23-002	Perkins House ACL02	S.Thompson	Retrd.	20.00	20.00
93-23-003	Roseland Cottage ACL03	S.Thompson	Retrd.	20.00	20.00
93-23-004	Mele House ACL04	S.Thompson	Retrd.	20.00	20.00
93-23-005	Rose Arbor ACL05	S.Thompson	Retrd.	14.00	14.00
93-23-006	Set of 5	S.Thompson	Retrd.	94.00	105-150.
Shelia's Collectibles	**Jazzy New Orleans Series**				
94-24-001	La Branche Building JNO01	S.Thompson	Open	18.00	18.00
94-24-002	La Branche Building, AP JNO01	S.Thompson	N/A	20.00	20.00
94-24-003	Gallier House JNO02	S.Thompson	Open	18.00	18.00
94-24-004	Gallier House, AP JNO02	S.Thompson	N/A	20.00	20.00
94-24-005	LePretre House JNO03	S.Thompson	Open	18.00	18.00
94-24-006	LePretre House, AP JNO03	S.Thompson	N/A	20.00	20.00
94-24-007	Beauregard-Keys House JNO04	S.Thompson	Open	18.00	18.00
94-24-008	Beauregard-Keys House, AP JNO04	S.Thompson	N/A	20.00	20.00
Shelia's Collectibles	**Old-Fashioned Christmas**				
94-25-001	Old First Church OFC01	S.Thompson	Open	18.00	18.00
94-25-002	Old First Church, AP OFC01	S.Thompson	N/A	20.00	20.00
94-25-003	Dwight House OFC02	S.Thompson	Open	18.00	18.00
94-25-004	Dwight House, AP OFC02	S.Thompson	N/A	20.00	20.00
94-25-005	General Merchandise OFC03	S.Thompson	Open	18.00	18.00
94-25-006	General Merchandise, AP OFC03	S.Thompson	N/A	20.00	20.00
94-25-007	Conway Scenic Railroad Station OFC04	S.Thompson	Open	18.00	18.00
94-25-008	Conway Scenic Railroad Station, AP OFC04	S.Thompson	N/A	20.00	20.00
Shelia's Collectibles	**Ghost House Series**				
94-26-001	Inside-Outside House GHO01	S.Thompson	Open	18.00	18.00
94-26-002	Inside-Outside House, AP GHO01	S.Thompson	Retrd.	20.00	20.00
94-26-003	Pirates' House GHO02	S.Thompson	Open	18.00	18.00
94-26-004	Pirates' House, AP GHO02	S.Thompson	Retrd.	20.00	20.00
Shelia's Collectibles	**American Barns**				
94-27-001	Rock City Barn BAR01	S.Thompson	Open	18.00	18.00
94-27-002	Pennsylvania Dutch Barn BAR02	S.Thompson	Open	18.00	18.00
Shelia's Collectibles	**Limited Edition Mail-Order Victorians**				
94-28-001	Titman House ACL06	S.Thompson	Retrd.	24.00	24.00
94-28-002	Henderson House ACL07	S.Thompson	Retrd.	24.00	24.00
94-28-003	Goeller House ACL08	S.Thompson	Retrd.	24.00	24.00
94-28-004	Brehaut House ACL09	S.Thompson	Retrd.	24.00	24.00
Shelia's Collectibles	**Shelia's Collectors' Society**				
93-29-001	Susan B. Anthony CGA93	S.Thompson	Retrd.	Gift	N/A
93-29-002	Anne Peacock House SOC01	S.Thompson	Retrd.	16.00	16.00
94-29-003	Helen Keller's Birthplace-Ivy Green CGA94	S.Thompson	5/95	Gift	N/A
94-29-004	Seaview Cottage SOC02	S.Thompson	5/95	17.00	17.00
Sports Impressions/Enesco	**Baseball Superstar Figurines**				
87-01-001	Wade Boggs	S. Impressions	Closed	90-125.	150-225.
88-01-002	Jose Canseco	S. Impressions	Closed	90-125.	125-200.
89-01-003	Will Clark	S. Impressions	Closed	90-125.	125-250.
88-01-004	Andre Dawson	S. Impressions	2,500	90-125.	125-200.
88-01-005	Bob Feller	S. Impressions	2,500	90-125.	125-200.
89-01-006	Kirk Gibson	S. Impressions	Closed	90-125.	125-200.
87-01-007	Keith Hernandez	S. Impressions	2,500	90-125.	125-200.
88-01-008	Reg Jackson (Yankees)	S. Impressions	Closed	90-125.	125-200.
89-01-009	Reg Jackson (Angels)	S. Impressions	Closed	90-125.	125-250.
88-01-010	Al Kaline	S. Impressions	2,500	90-125.	125-250.
87-01-011	Mickey Mantle	S. Impressions	Closed	90-125.	175-295.
87-01-012	Don Mattingly	S. Impressions	Closed	90-125.	250.00
87-01-013	Don Mattingly (Franklin glove variation)	S. Impressions	Closed	90-125.	750.00
88-01-014	Paul Molitor	S. Impressions	2,500	90-125.	125.00
89-01-015	Duke Snider	S. Impressions	2,500	90-125.	125.00
89-01-016	Alan Trammell	S. Impressions	2,500	90-125.	125.00
89-01-017	Frank Viola	S. Impressions	2,500	90-125.	125.00
90-01-018	Ted Williams	S. Impressions	Closed	90-125.	200-375.
90-01-019	Abbott/Costello Double	S. Impressions	Closed	100.00	100.00
90-01-020	Babe Ruth	S. Impressions	Closed	100.00	100.00
90-01-021	Twins Kirby Puckett	S. Impressions	Closed	100.00	100.00
90-01-022	Ted Williams Supersize	S. Impressions	Closed	250.00	250.00
90-01-023	Mark McGwire	S. Impressions	Closed	90.00	90.00
90-01-024	Angels Rod Carew	S. Impressions	Closed	100.00	100.00
90-01-025	Yankees Thurman Munson	S. Impressions	Closed	100.00	100.00
90-01-026	Lenny Dykstra	S. Impressions	Closed	100.00	100.00
90-01-027	Twins Harmon Killebrew	S. Impressions	Closed	100.00	100.00
90-01-028	Giants Willie McCovey	S. Impressions	Closed	100.00	100.00
90-01-029	Jimmie Foxx	S. Impressions	Closed	100.00	100.00
90-01-030	Rockwell Yer Out	N. Rockwell	Closed	125.00	125.00
90-01-031	Jose Canseco Super	S. Impressions	Closed	250.00	250.00
90-01-032	Nolan Ryan Supersize	S. Impressions	Closed	250.00	250.00
90-01-033	Nolan Ryan Kings of K	S. Impressions	Closed	125.00	125.00

		ARTIST	EDITION	ISSUE	QUOTE
90-01-034	Rickey Henderson	S. Impressions	Closed	125.00	125.00
90-01-035	Nolan Ryan	S. Impressions	Closed	50.00	50.00
90-01-036	Nolan Ryan Mini	S. Impressions	Closed	50.00	50.00
92-01-037	Ryne Sandberg Home	S. Impressions	Closed	150.00	150.00
Sports Impressions/Enesco	**Collectors' Club Members Only**				
90-02-001	The Mick-Mickey Mantle 5000-1	S. Impressions	Yr.Iss.	75.00	95.00
91-02-002	Rickey Henderson-Born to Run 5001-11	S. Impressions	Yr.Iss.	49.95	49.95
91-02-003	Nolan Ryan-300 Wins 5002-01	S. Impressions	Yr.Iss.	125.00	125.00
91-02-004	Willie, Mickey & Duke plate 5003-04	S. Impressions	Yr.Iss.	39.95	39.95
92-02-005	Babe Ruth 5006-11	S. Impressions	Yr.Iss.	40.00	40.00
92-02-006	Walter Payton 5015-01	S. Impressions	Yr.Iss.	50.00	50.00
93-02-007	The 1927 Yankees plate	R.Tanenbaum	Yr.Iss.	60.00	60.00
Sports Impressions/Enesco	**Collectors' Club Symbol of Membership**				
91-03-001	Mick/7 plate 5001-02	S. Impressions	Yr.Iss.	Gift	N/A
92-03-002	USA Basketball team plate 5008-30	S. Impressions	Yr.Iss.	Gift	N/A
93-03-003	Nolan Ryan porcelain card	S. Impressions	Yr.Iss.	Gift	N/A
Summerhill Crystal	**Disney Collection**				
92-01-001	Mickey Mouse, Lg. A671S	Summerhill	Retrd.	295.00	425.00
92-01-002	Mickey Mouse, Med. A672S	Summerhill	Retrd.	165.00	165.00
92-01-003	Minnie Mouse, Lg. A673S	Summerhill	Retrd.	295.00	425.00
92-01-004	Minnie Mouse, Med. A674S	Summerhill	Retrd.	165.00	165.00
92-01-005	Epcot Center, Lg. A687S	Summerhill	Open	245.00	245.00
92-01-006	Epcot Center, Med. A686S	Summerhill	Open	110.00	110.00
92-01-007	Epcot Center, Sm. A685S	Summerhill	Open	75.00	75.00
93-01-008	Aladdin's Lamp A684S	Summerhill	2,500	70.00	75.00
93-01-009	Classic Mickey A676S	Summerhill	Open	325.00	325.00
93-01-010	Medium Classic Mickey A677S	Summerhill	Open	185.00	185.00
93-01-011	Classic Minnie A678S	Summerhill	Open	325.00	325.00
93-01-012	Medium Classic Minnie A679S	Summerhill	Open	185.00	185.00
93-01-013	Pinocchio A675S	Summerhill	Open	180.00	180.00
94-01-014	The Sorcerer A668S	Summerhill	N/A	N/A	N/A
93-01-015	Winnie the Pooh A682S	Summerhill	2,500	145.00	145.00
93-01-016	Small Cinderella Coach A759S	Summerhill	Open	65.00	65.00
93-01-017	Cinderella Coach A764S	Summerhill	Open	125.00	125.00
Summerhill Crystal	**Warner Brothers Collection**				
92-02-001	Tasmanian Devil A634S	Summerhill	2,750	220.00	220.00
92-02-002	Speedy Gonzales A633S	Summerhill	2,750	164.00	164.00
92-02-003	Tweety Bird A631S	Summerhill	Retrd.	120.00	120.00
92-02-004	Bugs Bunny A652S	Summerhill	Retrd.	203.00	203.00
92-02-005	Large Porky Pig A635S	Summerhill	Open	273.00	273.00
92-02-006	Small Yosemite Sam A641S	Summerhill	Open	123.00	123.00
92-02-007	Small Tasmanian Devil A639S	Summerhill	Open	125.00	125.00
92-02-008	Small Porky Pig A649S	Summerhill	Open	165.00	165.00
92-02-009	Small Speedy Gonzales A638S	Summerhill	Open	813.00	81.00
92-02-010	Bugs Bunny "What's Up Doc?" A654S	Summerhill	Open	150.00	150.00
92-02-011	Tweety on a Perch A653S	Summerhill	Open	90.00	90.00
Summerhill Crystal	**United Media Collection**				
93-03-001	Garfieldc 3" A690S	Summerhill	Open	300.00	300.00
93-03-002	Odiec A691S	Summerhill	Open	224.00	224.00
93-03-003	Pookiec 1 1/4" A692S	Summerhill	Open	80.00	80.00
93-03-004	Pookiec1 5/8" A694S	Summerhill	Open	115.00	115.00
93-03-005	Pookiec 2 1/2" A693S	Summerhill	Open	190.00	190.00
93-03-006	Garfieldc 2 1/4" A689S	Summerhill	Open	120.00	120.00
93-03-007	Pookiec Standing 1 1/2" A695S	Summerhill	Open	90.00	90.00
93-03-008	Pookiec Standing Med.2 1/4" A696S	Summerhill	Open	120.00	120.00
93-03-009	Odiec Med. 2 3/4" A703S	Summerhill	Open	160.00	160.00
Summerhill Crystal	**Turner Inc.**				
93-04-001	Tomc 4 1/4" A272S	Summerhill	Open	308.00	308.00
93-04-002	Jerryc 2 3/4" A272S	Summerhill	Open	154.00	154.00
93-04-003	Tom med.c 2 3/4" A273S	Summerhill	Open	140.00	140.00
Summerhill Crystal	**Collector Society**				
92-05-001	Robbie Rabbit A183S	Summerhill	Retrd.	125.00	125.00
Swarovski America	**Our Woodland Friends**				
79-01-001	Mini Owl	M. Schreck	Open	16.00	29.50
79-01-002	Small Owl	M. Schreck	Open	59.00	85.00
79-01-003	Large Owl	M. Schreck	Open	90.00	120.00
83-01-004	Giant Owl	M. Schreck	Open	1200.00	2000.00
85-01-005	Mini Bear	M. Schreck	Open	16.00	55.00
82-01-006	Small Bear	M. Schreck	Open	44.00	75.00
81-01-007	Large Bear	M. Schreck	Open	75.00	95.00
87-01-008	Fox	A. Stocker	Open	50.00	75.00
88-01-009	Mini Sitting Fox	A. Stocker	Open	35.00	42.50
88-01-010	Mini Running Fox	A. Stocker	Open	35.00	42.50
85-01-011	Squirrel	M. Schreck	Open	35.00	55.00
89-01-012	Mushrooms	A. Stocker	Open	35.00	42.50
94-01-013	Roe Deer Fawn	E. Mair	Open	75.00	75.00
Swarovski America	**African Wildlife**				
89-02-001	Small Elephant	A. Stocker	Open	50.00	65.00
88-02-002	Large Elephant	A. Stocker	Open	70.00	95.00
89-02-003	Small Hippopotamus	A. Stocker	Open	70.00	75.00
90-02-004	Small Rhinoceros	A. Stocker	Open	70.00	75.00
94-02-005	Cheetah	M. Stamey	Open	275.00	275.00
Swarovski America	**Kingdom Of Ice And Snow**				
86-03-001	Mini Baby Seal	A. Stocker	Open	30.00	42.50
85-03-002	Large Seal	M. Schreck	Open	44.00	85.00
84-03-003	Mini Penguin	M. Schreck	Open	16.00	37.50
84-03-004	Large Penguin	M. Schreck	Open	44.00	95.00
86-03-005	Large Polar Bear	A. Stocker	Open	140.00	195.00
Swarovski America	**In A Summer Meadow**				
87-04-001	Small Hedgehog	M. Schreck	Open	50.00	55.00
85-04-002	Medium Hedgehog	M. Schreck	Open	70.00	85.00
85-04-003	Large Hedgehog	M. Schreck	Open	120.00	135.00
88-04-004	Mini Lying Rabbit	A. Stocker	Open	35.00	42.50
88-04-005	Mini Sitting Rabbit	A. Stocker	Open	35.00	42.50
88-04-006	Mother Rabbit	A. Stocker	Open	60.00	75.00
76-04-007	Medium Mouse	M. Schreck	Open	48.00	85.00
86-04-008	Mini Butterfly	Team	Open	16.00	42.50
82-04-009	Butterfly	Team	Open	44.00	85.00
86-04-010	Snail	M. Stamey	Open	35.00	55.00
91-04-011	Field Mouse	A. Stocker	Open	47.50	49.50
92-04-012	Sparrow	Schneiderbauer	Open	29.50	29.50
94-04-013	Field Mice (set of 3)	A. Stocker	Open	42.50	42.50
Swarovski America	**Beauties of the Lake**				
89-05-001	Small Swan	M. Schreck	Open	35.00	49.50

		ARTIST	EDITION	ISSUE	QUOTE
77-05-002	Medium Swan	M. Schreck	Open	44.00	75.00
77-05-003	Large Swan	M. Schreck	Open	55.00	95.00
86-05-004	Mini Standing Duck	A. Stocker	Open	22.00	37.50
86-05-005	Mini Swimming Duck	M. Schreck	Open	16.00	37.50
83-05-006	Mini Drake	M. Schreck	Open	20.00	42.50
89-05-007	Giant Mallard	M. Stamey	Open	2000.00	4500.00
94-05-008	Frog	G. Stamey	Open	49.50	49.50
Swarovski America	**When We Were Young**				
88-06-001	Locomotive	G. Stamey	Open	150.00	150.00
88-06-002	Tender	G. Stamey	Open	55.00	55.00
88-06-003	Wagon	G. Stamey	Open	85.00	85.00
90-06-004	Petrol Wagon	G. Stamey	Open	75.00	85.00
89-06-005	Old Timer Automobile	G. Stamey	Open	130.00	150.00
90-06-006	Airplane	A. Stocker	Open	135.00	150.00
91-06-007	Santa Maria	G. Stamey	Open	375.00	375.00
93-06-008	Tipping Wagon	G. Stamey	Open	95.00	95.00
94-06-009	Sailboat	G. Stamey	Open	195.00	195.00
Swarovski America	**Exquisite Accents**				
80-07-001	Birdbath	M. Schreck	Open	150.00	195.00
87-07-002	Birds' Nest	Team	Open	90.00	120.00
87-07-003	Small Dinner Bell	M. Schreck	Open	60.00	65.00
87-07-004	Medium Dinner Bell	M. Schreck	Open	80.00	95.00
Swarovski America	**Sparkling Fruit**				
86-08-001	Small Pineapple/Gold	M. Schreck	Open	55.00	85.00
81-08-002	Large Pineapple/Gold	M. Schreck	Open	150.00	250.00
81-08-003	Giant Pineapple/Gold	M. Schreck	Open	1750.00	3250.00
85-08-004	Small Grapes	Team	Open	200.00	250.00
85-08-005	Medium Grapes	Team	Open	300.00	375.00
91-08-006	Apple	M. Stamey	Open	175.00	175.00
91-08-007	Pear	M. Stamey	Open	175.00	175.00
Swarovski America	**Pets' Corner**				
90-09-001	Beagle Puppy	A. Stocker	Open	40.00	49.50
90-09-002	Scotch Terrier	A. Stocker	Open	60.00	75.00
87-09-003	Mini Dachshund	A. Stocker	Open	20.00	49.50
91-09-004	Sitting Cat	M. Stamey	Open	75.00	75.00
91-09-005	Kitten	M. Stamey	Open	47.50	49.50
92-09-006	Poodle	A. Stocker	Open	125.00	135.00
93-09-007	Beagle Playing	A. Stocker	Open	49.50	49.50
93-09-008	Sitting Poodle	A. Stocker	Open	85.00	85.00
Swarovski America	**South Sea**				
88-10-001	Open Shell With Pearl	M. Stamey	Open	120.00	165.00
87-10-002	Mini Blowfish	Team	Open	22.00	29.50
86-10-003	Small Blowfish	Team	Open	35.00	55.00
91-10-004	Butterfly Fish	M. Stamey	Open	150.00	165.00
93-10-005	Three South Sea Fish	M. Stamey	Open	135.00	135.00
93-10-006	Sea Horse	M. Stamey	Open	85.00	85.00
Swarovski America	**Endangered Species**				
91-11-001	Kiwi	M. Stamey	Open	37.50	37.50
89-11-002	Mini Koala	A. Stocker	Open	35.00	42.50
87-11-003	Koala	A. Stocker	Open	50.00	65.00
77-11-004	Small Turtle	M. Schreck	Open	35.00	49.50
77-11-005	Large Turtle	M. Schreck	Open	48.00	75.00
81-11-006	Giant Turtle	M. Schreck	Open	2500.00	4500.00
92-11-007	Mother Beaver	A. Stocker	Open	110.00	120.00
92-11-008	Sitting Baby Beaver	A. Stocker	Open	47.50	49.50
92-11-009	Lying Baby Beaver	A. Stocker	Open	47.50	49.50
93-11-010	Baby Panda	A. Stocker	Open	24.50	24.50
93-11-011	Mother Panda	A. Stocker	Open	120.00	120.00
93-11-012	Mother Kangaroo with Baby	G. Stamey	Open	95.00	95.00
Swarovski America	**Barnyard Friends**				
82-12-001	Mini Pig	M. Schreck	Open	16.00	29.50
84-12-002	Medium Pig	M. Schreck	Open	35.00	55.00
88-12-003	Mini Chicks (Set of 3)	G. Stamey	Open	35.00	37.50
87-12-004	Mini Rooster	G. Stamey	Open	35.00	55.00
87-12-005	Mini Hen	G. Stamey	Open	35.00	42.50
Swarovski America	**Game of Kings**				
84-13-001	Chess Set	M. Schreck	Open	950.00	1375.00
Swarovski America	**Among Flowers And Foliage**				
92-14-001	Hummingbird	Schneiderbauer	Open	195.00	195.00
92-14-002	Bumblebee	Schneiderbauer	Open	85.00	85.00
94-14-003	Butterfly in Leaf	Schneiderbauer	Open	75.00	75.00
Swarovski America	**Our Candleholders**				
85-15-001	Small Water Lily 7600NR124	M. Schreck	Open	100.00	165.00
83-15-002	Medium Water Lily 7600NR123	M. Schreck	Open	150.00	250.00
85-15-003	Large Water Lily 7600NR125	M. Schreck	Open	200.00	375.00
89-15-004	Medium Star 7600NR143001	Team	Open	200.00	250.00
87-15-005	Large Star 7600NR143	Team	Open	250.00	375.00
Swarovski America	**Decorative Items For The Desk (Paperweights)**				
87-16-001	Small Chaton 7433NR50	M. Schreck	Open	50.00	65.00
87-16-002	Large Chaton 7433NR80	M. Schreck	Open	190.00	250.00
90-16-003	Giant Chaton 7433NR180000	M. Schreck	Open	4500.00	4500.00
87-16-004	Small Pyramid Crystal Cal.7450NR40	M. Schreck	Open	100.00	120.00
87-16-005	Small Pyramid Vitrail Med.7450NR40	M. Schreck	Open	100.00	120.00
Swarovski America	**Crystal Melodies**				
92-17-001	Lute	M. Zendron	Open	125.00	135.00
92-17-002	Harp	M. Zendron	Open	175.00	195.00
93-17-003	Grand Piano w/ Stool	M. Zendron	Open	250.00	250.00
Swarovski America	**Feathered Friends**				
93-18-001	Pelican	A. Hirzinger	Open	37.50	37.50
Swarovski America	**Collectors Society Editions**				
87-19-001	Togetherness-The Lovebirds	Schreck/Stocker	Retrd.	150.00	3-4000.
88-19-002	Sharing-The Woodpeckers	A. Stocker	Retrd.	165.00	1-1900.
89-19-003	Amour-The Turtledoves	A. Stocker	Retrd.	195.00	600-1400
90-19-004	Lead Me-The Dolphins	M. Stamey	Retrd.	225.00	900-1400
91-19-005	Save Me-The Seals	M. Stamey	Retrd.	225.00	380-600.
92-19-006	Care For Me - The Whales	M. Stamey	Retrd.	265.00	360-600.
91-19-008	Dolphin Brooch	Team	Retrd.	75.00	115-150.
92-19-007	5th Anniversary Edition-The Birthday Cake	G. Stamey	Retrd.	85.00	130-300.
93-19-009	Inspiration Africa-The Elephant	M. Zendron	Retrd.	325.00	450-600.
93-19-010	Elephant Brooch	Team	12/94	85.00	85.00
94-19-011	Inspiration Africa-The Kudu	M. Stamey	12/94	295.00	295.00

		ARTIST	EDITION	ISSUE	QUOTE
Swarovski America	**Retired**				
XX-20-001	Giant Size Bear 7637NR112	M. Schreck	Retrd.	125.00	1000-15.
XX-20-002	King Size Bear7637NR92	M. Schreck	Retrd.	95.00	750-1200
84-20-003	Mini Bear 7670NR32	M. Schreck	Retrd.	16.00	100-125.
84-20-004	Large Blowfish 7644NR41	Team	Retrd.	40.00	100-125.
XX-20-005	Mini Butterfly 7671NR30	Team	Retrd.	16.00	50-120.
77-20-006	Large Cat 7634NR70	M. Schreck	Retrd.	44.00	55-95.00
XX-20-007	Medium Cat 7634NR52	Team	Retrd.	38.00	300-360.
82-20-008	Mini Cat 7659NR31	M. Schreck	Retrd.	16.00	35-100.
XX-20-009	Mini Chicken 7651NR20	Team	Retrd.	16.00	30-100.
84-20-010	Dachshund 7641NR75	M. Schreck	Retrd.	48.00	45-95.00
XX-20-011	Mini Dachshund 7672NR42	A. Stocker	Retrd.	20.00	90-125.
XX-20-012	Dog 7635NR70	Team	Retrd.	44.00	50-90.00
XX-20-013	Large Duck 7653NR75	Team	Retrd.	44.00	120-250.
XX-20-014	Medium Duck 7653NR55	Team	Retrd.	38.00	80-125.
XX-20-015	Mini Duck 7653NR45	Team	Retrd.	16.00	50-105.
XX-20-016	Elephant 7640NR55	Team	Retrd.	90.00	180-250.
84-20-017	Large Falcon Head 7645NR100	M. Schreck	Retrd.	600.00	600-1000
86-20-018	Small Falcon Head 7645NR45	M. Schreck	Retrd.	60.00	100-125.
84-20-019	Frog 7642NR48	M. Schreck	Retrd.	30.00	55-105.
XX-20-020	King Size Hedgehog 7630NR60	M. Schreck	Retrd.	98.00	250-500.
XX-20-021	Large Hedgehog 7630NR50	M. Schreck	Retrd.	65.00	140-300.
XX-20-022	Medium Hedgehog 7630NR40	M. Schreck	Retrd.	44.00	100-200.
XX-20-023	Small Hedgehog 7630NR30	M. Schreck	Retrd.	38.00	300-450.
88-20-024	Hippopotamus 7626NR65	A. Stocker	Retrd.	70.00	75-125.
90-20-025	Kingfisher 7621NR000001	M. Stamey	Retrd.	75.00	80-120.
XX-20-026	King Size Mouse 7631NR60	M. Schreck	Retrd.	95.00	400-600.
XX-20-027	Large Mouse 7631NR50	M. Schreck	Retrd.	69.00	130-250.
XX-20-028	Small Mouse 7631NR30	M. Schreck	Retrd.	35.00	48-60.00
XX-20-029	Mini Mouse 7655NR23	Team	Retrd.	16.00	50-125.
89-20-030	Parrot 7621NR000004	M. Stamey	Retrd.	70.00	88-120.
87-20-031	Partridge 7625NR50	A. Stocker	Retrd.	85.00	130-200.
XX-20-032	Large Pig 7638NR65	M. Schreck	Retrd.	50.00	200-370.
89-20-033	Owl 7621NR000003	M. Stamey	Retrd.	70.00	75-120.
XX-20-034	Large Rabbit 7652NR45	Team	Retrd.	38.00	170-180.
XX-20-035	Mini Rabbit 7652NR20	Team	Retrd.	16.00	50-100.
88-20-036	Rhinoceros 7622NR70	A. Stocker	Retrd.	70.00	90-125.
XX-20-037	Large Sparrow 7650NR32	Team	Retrd.	38.00	70-125.
79-20-038	Mini Sparrow7650NR20	M. Schreck	Retrd.	16.00	30-60.00
XX-20-039	Mini Swan 7658NR27	M. Schreck	Retrd.	16.00	60-125.
89-20-040	Toucan 7621NR000002	M. Stamey	Retrd.	70.00	75-120.
XX-20-041	King Size Turtle 7632NR75	M. Schreck	Retrd.	58.00	170-215.
89-20-042	Walrus 7620NR100000	M. Stamey	Retrd.	120.00	135-150.
88-20-043	Whale 7628NR80	M. Stamey	Retrd.	70.00	85-125.
XX-20-044	Sm. Apple Photo Stand(Gold) 7504NR030G	Team	Retrd.	40.00	250.00
XX-20-045	Sm. Apple Photo Stand 7504NR030R	Team	Retrd.	40.00	110-250.
XX-20-046	Lg. Apple Photo Stand(Gold) 7504NR050G	Team	Retrd.	80.00	375.00
XX-20-047	Lg. Apple Photo Stand 7504NR050R	Team	Retrd.	80.00	375-450.
XX-20-048	Kg Sz Apple Photo Stand(Gold) 7504NR060G	Team	Retrd.	120.00	355-475.
XX-20-049	Large Grapes 7550NR30015	Team	Retrd.	250.00	550-960.
85-20-050	Butterfly (Gold) 7551NR100	Team	Retrd.	200.00	550-900.
85-20-051	Butterfly (Rhodium) 7551NR200	Team	Retrd.	200.00	1500.00
85-20-052	Hummingbird (Gold) 7552NR100	Team	Retrd.	200.00	800-1200
85-20-053	Hummingbird (Rhodium) 7552NR200	Team	Retrd.	200.00	1800.00
85-20-054	Bee (Gold) 7553NR100	Team	Retrd.	200.00	1-1200.
85-20-055	Bee (Rhodium) 7553NR200	Team	Retrd.	200.00	960-1500
87-20-056	Sm. Pineapple/Rhodium 7507NR060002	M. Schreck	Retrd.	55.00	100-200.
82-20-057	Lg. Pineapple/Rhodium 7507NR105002	M. Schreck	Retrd.	150.00	420-450.
85-20-058	Giant Pineapple/Rhodium 7507NR26002	M. Schreck	Retrd.	1750.00	3500.00
81-20-059	Large Dinner Bell 7467NR071000	M. Schreck	Retrd.	80.00	120-165.
XX-20-060	Rd. Pprwgt-Green 7404NR40	Team	Retrd.	20.00	N/A
XX-20-061	Rd. Pprwgt-Sahara 7404NR40	Team	Retrd.	20.00	N/A
XX-20-062	Rd. Pprwgt-Berm Blue 7404NR40	Team	Retrd.	20.00	N/A
XX-20-063	Rd. Pprwgt-Green 7404NR30	Team	Retrd.	15.00	N/A
XX-20-064	Rd. Pprwgt-Sahara 7404NR30	Team	Retrd.	15.00	N/A
XX-20-065	Rd. Pprwgt-Berm. Blue 7404NR30	Team	Retrd.	15.00	N/A
XX-20-066	Rd. Pprwgt-Green 7404NR50	Team	Retrd.	40.00	N/A
XX-20-067	Rd. Pprwgt-Sahara 7404NR50	Team	Retrd.	40.00	N/A
XX-20-068	Rd. Pprwgt-Berm. Blue 7404NR50	Team	Retrd.	40.00	N/A
XX-20-069	Carousel Pprwgt-Vitrl Med 7451NR60087	Team	Retrd.	80.00	12-1600.
XX-20-070	Carousel Pprwgt-Crystal Cal 7451NR60095	Team	Retrd.	80.00	12-1600.
XX-20-071	Atomic Pprwgt-Vitrl Med 7454NR60087	Team	Retrd.	80.00	750-1650
XX-20-072	Atomic Pprwgt-Crystal Cal 7454NR60095	Team	Retrd.	80.00	12-1650.
XX-20-073	Barrel Pprwgt 7453NR60087 Vitrl Med	Team	Retrd.	80.00	240-400.
XX-20-074	Barrel Pprwgt 7453NR60095 Crystal Cal	Team	Retrd.	80.00	400.00
XX-20-075	Rd. Pprwgt-Crystal Cal 7404NR30095	Team	Retrd.	15.00	75.00
XX-20-076	Rd. Pprwgt-Vitrl Med 7404NR30087	Team	Retrd.	15.00	75.00
XX-20-077	Rd. Pprwgt-Crystal Cal 7404NR40095	Team	Retrd.	20.00	95.00
XX-20-078	Rd. Pprwgt-Vitrl Med 7404NR40087	Team	Retrd.	20.00	95.00
XX-20-079	Rd. Pprwgt-Crystal Cal 7404NR50095	Team	Retrd.	40.00	200.00
XX-20-080	Rd. Pprwgt-Vitrl Med 7404NR50087	Team	Retrd.	40.00	200.00
XX-20-081	Rd. Pprwgt-Crystal Cal 7404NR60095	Team	Retrd.	50.00	250.00
XX-20-082	Rd. Pprwgt-Vitrl Med 7404NR60087	Team	Retrd.	50.00	250.00
XX-20-083	Geometric Pprwgt 7432NR57002n	Team	Retrd.	75.00	300.00
XX-20-084	One Ton Pprwgt 7495NR65	Team	Retrd.	75.00	115-175.
XX-20-085	Octron Pprwgt 7456NR41	Team	Retrd.	75.00	150.00
XX-20-086	Octron Pprwgt 7456NR1087	Team	Retrd.	90.00	150.00
XX-20-087	Candleholder 7600NR101	Team	Retrd.	23.00	350.00
XX-20-088	Candleholder 7600NR102	Team	Retrd.	35.00	100-125.
XX-20-089	Candleholder 7600NR103	Team	Retrd.	40.00	110-175.
XX-20-090	Candleholder European Style 7600NR103	Team	Retrd.	N/A	750.00
XX-20-091	Candleholder 7600NR104	Team	Retrd.	95.00	200-300.
XX-20-092	Candleholder 7600NR106	Team	Retrd.	85.00	265-400.
XX-20-093	Candleholder 7600NR107	Team	Retrd.	100.00	270-400.
XX-20-094	Candleholder European Style 7600NR108	Team	Retrd.	N/A	850.00
XX-20-095	Candleholder 7600NR109	Team	Retrd.	37.00	110-200.
XX-20-096	Candleholder 7600NR110	Team	Retrd.	40.00	120-160.
XX-20-097	Candleholder 7600NR111	Team	Retrd.	100.00	275-400.
XX-20-098	Candleholder 7600NR112	Team	Retrd.	75.00	300.00
XX-20-099	Candleholder 7600NR114	Team	Retrd.	37.00	190-300.
XX-20-100	Candleholder 7600NR115	Team	Retrd.	185.00	400-455.
XX-20-101	Candleholder 7600NR116	Team	Retrd.	350.00	1500.00
XX-20-102	Candleholder 7600NR119	Team	Retrd.	N/A	500.00
XX-20-103	Sm.Candleholder w/ Flowers 7600NR120	Team	Retrd.	60.00	240-270.
XX-20-104	Baroque Candleholder 7600NR121	Team	Retrd.	150.00	245-450.
XX-20-105	Candleholder 7600NR122	Team	Retrd.	85.00	160-200.
XX-20-106	Sm.Candleholder w/ Leaves 7600NR126	Team	Retrd.	100.00	200-330.
XX-20-107	Candleholder 7600NR127	Team	Retrd.	65.00	165-200.
XX-20-108	Candleholder 7600NR128	Team	Retrd.	100.00	180-275.
XX-20-109	Candleholder 7600NR129	Team	Retrd.	120.00	265-300.
XX-20-110	Candleholder 7600NR130	Team	Retrd.	275.00	950-1500
XX-20-111	Candleholder 7600NR131(Set of 6)	Team	Retrd.	43.00	605-900.
XX-20-112	Small Global Candleholder (4) 7600NR132	Team	Retrd.	60.00	115-250.
XX-20-113	Med. Global Candleholder (2) 7600NR133	Team	Retrd.	40.00	75-100.
XX-20-114	Large Global Candleholder 7600NR134	Team	Retrd.	40.00	75-80.00
XX-20-115	Kingsize Global Candleholder 7600NR135	Team	Retrd.	50.00	200.00
XX-20-116	Pineapple Candleholder 7600NR136	Team	Retrd.	150.00	450.00
XX-20-117	Large Candleholderw/Flowers 7600NR137	Team	Retrd.	150.00	300.00
XX-20-118	Candleholder 7600NR138	Team	Retrd.	160.00	480-500.
XX-20-119	Candleholder 7600NR139	Team	Retrd.	140.00	245-500.
XX-20-120	Candleholder 7600NR140	Team	Retrd.	120.00	355-500.
XX-20-120	Candleholder European Style 7600NR141	Team	Retrd.	N/A	750.00
XX-20-122	Candleholder European Style 7600NR142	Team	Retrd.	N/A	500.00
90-20-123	Sm. Neo-Classic Candleholder 7600NR144070	A. Stocker	Retrd.	170.00	200.00
90-20-124	Med. Neo-Classic Candleholder 600NR144080	A. Stocker	Retrd.	190.00	225.00
90-20-125	Large Neo-Classic Candleholder 7600NR144090	A. Stocker	Retrd.	220.00	250.00
XX-20-126	Beetle Bottle Opener (Rodium) 7505NR76	Team	Retrd.	80.00	600-1650
XX-20-127	Beetle Bottle Opener (Gold) 7505NR76	Team	Retrd.	80.00	13-2000.
XX-20-128	Table Magnifyer 7510NR01	Team	Retrd.	80.00	12-1650.
XX-20-129	Treasure Box (Round/Butterfly) 7464NR50/10	Team	Retrd.	80.00	210-250.
XX-20-130	Treasure Box (Heart/Flower)7465NR52	Team	Retrd.	80.00	250.00
XX-20-131	Treasure Box (Oval/Butterfly)7466NR063100	Team	Retrd.	80.00	250-300.
XX-20-132	Salt and Pepper Shakers 7508NR068034	Team	Retrd.	80.00	260-350.
XX-20-133	Picture Frame/Oval 7505NR75G	Team	Retrd.	90.00	200-235.
XX-20-134	Picture Frame/Square 7506NR60G	Team	Retrd.	100.00	230-250.
XX-20-135	Treasure Box (Round/Flower) 7464NR50	Team	Retrd.	80.00	155-250.
XX-20-136	Treasure Box (Heart/Butterfly)7465NR52/100	Team	Retrd.	80.00	155-250.
XX-20-137	Treasure Box (Oval/Flower) 7466NR063000	Team	Retrd.	80.00	250.00
XX-20-138	Vase 7511NR70	Team	Retrd.	50.00	70-125.
XX-20-139	Schnapps Glasses, Set of 6- 7468NR039000	Team	Retrd.	150.00	235-350.
XX-20-140	Ashtray 7461NR100	Team	Retrd.	45.00	240-250.
XX-20-141	Lighter 7462NR062	Team	Retrd.	160.00	250-273.
XX-20-142	Cigarette Holder 7463NR062	Team	Retrd.	85.00	150-175.
XX-20-143	Small Cardholders, Set of 4 - 7403NR20095	Team	Retrd.	25.00	120-200.
XX-20-144	Large Cardholders, Set of 4 - 7403NR30095	Team	Retrd.	45.00	180-400.
82-20-145	Cone Vitrail Medium 7452NR60087	M. Schreck	Retrd.	80.00	225.00
82-20-146	Cone Crystal Cal 7452NR60095	M. Schreck	Retrd.	80.00	225.00
81-20-147	Egg 7458NR63069	M. Schreck	Retrd.	60.00	125-150.
81-20-148	Chess Set/Wooden Board	Team	Retrd.	950.00	3000.00
87-20-149	Large Pyramid Crystal Cal 7450NR50095	M. Schreck	Retrd.	90.00	200-250.
87-20-150	Large Pyramid Vitrail Medium 7450NR50087	M. Schreck	Retrd.	90.00	200-250.
91-20-151	Holy Family With Arch 7475NR001	Team	Retrd.	250.00	275-350.
92-20-152	Wise Men (Set of 3) 7475NR200000	Team	Retrd.	175.00	285-295.
92-20-153	Shepherd 7475NR000007	Team	Retrd.	65.00	80-125.
92-20-154	Angel 6475NR000009	Team	Retrd.	65.00	65.00
90-20-155	Silver Crystal City-Cathedral 7474NR000021	G. Stamey	Retrd.	95.00	120.00
90-20-156	Silver Crystal City-Houses I& II(Set of 2) 7474NR100000	G. Stamey	Retrd.	75.00	75.00
90-20-157	Silver Crystal City-Houses III & IV (Set of 2) 7474NR200000	G. Stamey	Retrd.	75.00	75.00
90-20-158	Silver Crystal City-Poplars (Set of 3) 7474NR020003	G. Stamey	Retrd.	40.00	49.50
91-20-159	City Tower 7474NR000022	G. Stamey	Retrd.	37.50	42.50
91-20-160	City Gates 7474NR000023	G. Stamey	Retrd.	95.00	95.00
93-20-161	Town Hall 7474NR000027	G. Stamey	Retrd.	135.00	135.00
91-20-162	South Sea Shell 7624NR72000	M. Stamey	Retrd.	110.00	120.00
86-20-163	Mallard 7647NR80	M. Schreck	Retrd.	80.00	135.00
Swarovski America	**Commemorative Single Issues**				
90-21-001	Elephant*(Introduced by Swarovski America as a commemorative item test during Design Celebration/January '90 in Walt Disney World)	Team	Closed	125.00	900-2400
93-21-002	Elephant*(Introduced by Swarovski America as a commemorative item during Design Celebration/January '93 in Walt Disney World)	Team	Open	150.00	150.00
Todays' Creations Inc.	**Times to Remember**				
95-01-001	Bride with Bouquet	A. Gordon	5,000	85.00	85.00
95-01-002	First Dance	A. Gordon	5,000	95.00	95.00
95-01-003	With This Ring	A. Gordon	5,000	95.00	95.00
95-01-004	Mother and Bride	A. Gordon	5,000	95.00	95.00
95-01-005	Daddy's Little Girl	A. Gordon	5,000	95.00	95.00
95-01-006	Slice of Life	A. Gordon	5,000	100.00	100.00
95-01-007	Bride with Bouquet-white	A. Gordon	5,000	70.00	70.00
95-01-008	First Dance-white	A. Gordon	5,000	75.00	75.00
95-01-009	With This Ring-white	A. Gordon	5,000	75.00	75.00
95-01-010	Mother and Bride-white	A. Gordon	5,000	75.00	75.00
95-01-011	Daddy's Little Girl-white	A. Gordon	5,000	75.00	75.00
95-01-012	Slice of Life-white	A. Gordon	5,000	80.00	80.00
95-01-013	First Dance-musical	A. Gordon	5,000	125.00	125.00
95-01-014	Daddy's Little Girl-musical	A. Gordon	5,000	125.00	125.00
95-01-015	First Dance-white-musical	A. Gordon	5,000	115.00	115.00
95-01-016	Daddy's Little Girl-white-musical	A. Gordon	5,000	115.00	115.00
United Design Corp.	**Legend of Santa Claus**				
86-01-001	Santa At Rest CF-001	L. Miller	Retrd.	70.00	500-1000
86-01-002	Kris Kringle CF-002	L. Miller	Retrd.	60.00	175.00
86-01-003	Santa With Pups CF-003	S. Bradford	Retrd.	65.00	570.00
86-01-004	Rooftop Santa CF-004	S. Bradford	Retrd.	65.00	170.00
86-01-005	Elf Pair CF-005	L. Miller	Retrd.	60.00	125.00
87-01-006	Mrs. Santa CF-006	S. Bradford	Retrd.	60.00	195.00
87-01-007	On Santa's Knee-CF007	S. Bradford	Retrd.	65.00	90.00
87-01-008	Dreaming Of Santa CF-008	S. Bradford	Retrd.	65.00	325.00
87-01-009	Checking His List CF-009	L. Miller	Retrd.	75.00	100.00
87-01-010	Loading Santa's Sleigh CF-010	L. Miller	Retrd.	100.00	110.00
87-01-011	Santa On Horseback CF-011	S. Bradford	Retrd.	75.00	270.00
88-01-012	St. Nicholas CF-015	L. Miller	Retrd.	75.00	135.00
88-01-013	Load 'Em Up CF-016	S. Bradford	Retrd.	79.00	350.00

		ARTIST	EDITION	ISSUE	QUOTE
88-01-014	Assembly Required CF-017	L. Miller	Retrd.	79.00	110.00
88-01-015	Father Christmas CF-018	S. Bradford	Retrd.	75.00	100.00
89-01-016	A Purrr-Fect Christmas CF-019	S. Bradford	Retrd.	95.00	110.00
89-01-017	Christmas Harmony CF-020	S. Bradford	Retrd.	85.00	140.00
89-01-018	Hitching Up CF-021	L. Miller	Retrd.	90.00	100.00
90-01-019	Puppy Love CF-024	L. Miller	Retrd.	100.00	130.00
90-01-020	Forest Friends CF-025	L. Miller	Retrd.	90.00	110.00
90-01-021	Waiting For Santa CF-026	S. Bradford	7,500	100.00	130.00
90-01-022	Safe Arrival CF-027	Memoli/Jonas	7,500	150.00	175.00
90-01-023	Victorian Santa CF-028	S. Bradford	Retrd.	125.00	350.00
91-01-024	For Santa CF-029	L. Miller	7,500	99.00	135.00
91-01-025	Santa At Work CF-030	L. Miller	7,500	99.00	110.00
91-01-026	Reindeer Walk CF-031	K. Memoli	7,500	150.00	165.00
91-01-027	Blessed Flight CF-032	K. Memoli	7,500	159.00	185.00
91-01-028	Victorian Santa w/ Teddy CF-033	S. Bradford	7,500	150.00	160.00
92-01-029	Arctic Santa CF-035	S. Bradford	7,500	90.00	100.00
92-01-030	Letters to Santa CF-036	L. Miller	7,500	125.00	130.00
92-01-031	Santa and Comet CF-037	L. Miller	7,500	110.00	110.00
92-01-032	The Christmas Tree CF-038	L. Miller	7,500	90.00	90.00
92-01-031	Santa and Mrs. Claus CF-039	K. Memoli	7,500	150.00	150.00
92-01-032	Earth Home Santa CF-040	S. Bradford	7,500	135.00	140.00
92-01-033	Loads of Happiness CF-041	K. Memoli	7,500	100.00	110.00
92-01-034	Santa and Mrs. Claus, Victorian CF-042	K. Memoli	7,500	135.00	140.00
93-01-035	The Night Before Christmas CF-043	L. Miller	Retrd.	75.00	100.00
93-01-036	Santa's Friends CF-044	L. Miller	Retrd.	85.00	100.00
93-01-037	Jolly St. Nick CF-045	K. Memoli	Retrd.	100.00	130.00
93-01-038	Dear Santa CF-046	K. Memoli	Retrd.	159.00	170.00
93-01-039	Northwoods Santa CF-047	S. Bradford	Retrd.	85.00	100.00
93-01-040	Victorian Lion & Lamb Santa CF-048	S. Bradford	Retrd.	64.00	100.00
93-01-041	Jolly St. Nick, Victorian CF-050	K. Memoli	Retrd.	100.00	120.00
94-01-042	The Story of Christmas CF-051	K. Memoli	Retrd.	90.00	180.00
94-01-043	Longstocking Dilemma CF-052	K. Memoli	Retrd.	85.00	170.00
94-01-044	Santa Riding Dove CF-053	L. Miller	Retrd.	60.00	120.00
94-01-045	Star Santa w/ Polar Bear CF-054	S. Bradford	Retrd.	65.00	130.00
94-01-046	Long Stocking Dilemma, Victorian CF-055	K. Memoli	Retrd.	85.00	170.00

United Design Corp. — Legend Of The Little People

		ARTIST	EDITION	ISSUE	QUOTE
89-02-001	Woodland Cache LL-001	L. Miller	Retrd.	35.00	50.00
89-02-002	Adventure Bound LL-002	L. Miller	Retrd.	35.00	50.00
89-02-003	A Friendly Toast LL-003	L. Miller	Retrd.	35.00	50.00
89-02-004	Treasure Hunt LL-004	L. Miller	Retrd.	45.00	50.00
89-02-005	Magical Discovery LL-005	L. Miller	Retrd.	45.00	50.00
89-02-006	Spring Water Scrub LL-006	L. Miller	Retrd.	35.00	50.00
89-02-007	Caddy's Helper LL-007	L. Miller	Retrd.	35.00	50.00
90-02-008	Husking Acorns LL-008	L. Miller	Retrd.	60.00	65.00
90-02-009	Traveling Fast LL-009	L. Miller	Retrd.	45.00	50.00
90-02-010	Hedgehog In Harness LL-010	L. Miller	Retrd.	45.00	50.00
90-02-011	Woodland Scout LL-011	L. MIller	Retrd.	40.00	50.00
90-02-012	Fishin' Hole LL-012	L. Miller	Retrd.	35.00	50.00
90-02-013	A Proclamation LL-013	L. Miller	Retrd.	45.00	55.00
90-02-014	Gathering Acorns LL-014	L. Miller	Retrd.	100.00	100.00
90-02-015	A Look Through The Spyglass LL-015	L. Miller	Retrd.	40.00	50.00
90-02-016	Writing The Legend LL-016	L. Miller	Retrd.	35.00	65.00
90-02-017	Ministral Magic LL-017	L. Miller	Retrd.	45.00	50.00
90-02-018	A Little Jig LL-018	L. Miller	Retrd.	45.00	50.00
91-02-019	Viking LL-019	L. Miller	Retrd.	45.00	50.00
91-02-020	The Easter Bunny's Cart LL-020	L. Miller	Retrd.	45.00	50.00
91-02-021	Got It LL-021	L. Miller	Retrd.	45.00	50.00
91-02-022	It's About Time LL-022	L. Miller	Retrd.	55.00	60.00
91-02-023	Fire it Up LL-023	L. Miller	Retrd.	50.00	55.00

United Design Corp. — Music Makers

		ARTIST	EDITION	ISSUE	QUOTE
89-03-001	Santa's Sleigh MM-004	L. Miller	Retrd.	69.00	69.00
89-03-002	Evening Carolers MM-005	D. Kennicutt	Retrd.	69.00	69.00
89-03-003	Teddy Drummers MM-009	D. Kennicutt	Retrd.	69.00	69.00
89-03-004	Herald Angel MM-011	S. Bradford	Retrd.	79.00	79.00
89-03-005	Teddy Bear Band MM-012	S. Bradford	Retrd.	99.00	100.00
91-03-006	Dashing Through The Snow MM-013	D. Kennicutt	Retrd.	59.00	59.00
91-03-007	A Christmas Gift MM-015	D. Kennicutt	Retrd.	59.00	59.00
91-03-008	Crystal Angel MM-017	D. Kennicutt	Retrd.	59.00	59.00
91-03-009	Teddy Soldiers MM-018	D. Kennicutt	Open	69.00	84.00
91-03-010	Teddy Bear Band #2 MM-023	D. Kennicutt	Open	90.00	90.00
91-03-011	Nutcracker MM-024	P.J. Jonas	Retrd.	69.00	69.00
91-03-012	Peace Descending MM-025	P.J. Jonas	Retrd.	69.00	69.00
91-03-013	Victorian Santa MM-026	L. Miller	Retrd.	69.00	69.00
91-03-014	Renaissance Angel MM-028	P.J. Jonas	Retrd.	69.00	69.00

United Design Corp. — Easter Bunny Family

		ARTIST	EDITION	ISSUE	QUOTE
88-04-001	Bunnies, Basket Of SEC-001	D. Kennicutt	Retrd.	13.00	17.50
88-04-002	Bunny Boy w/Duck SEC-002	D. Kennicutt	Retrd.	13.00	17.50
88-04-003	Bunny, Easter SEC-003	D. Kennicutt	Retrd.	15.00	17.50
88-04-004	Bunny Girl w/Hen SEC-004	D. Kennicutt	Retrd.	13.00	17.50
88-04-005	Rabbit, Grandma SEC-005	D. Kennicutt	Retrd.	15.00	20.00
88-04-006	Rabbit, Grandpa SEC-006	D. Kennicutt	Retrd.	15.00	20.00
88-04-007	Rabbit, Momma w/Bonnet SEC-007	D. Kennicutt	Retrd.	15.00	20.00
89-04-008	Auntie Bunny SEC-008	D. Kennicutt	Retrd.	20.00	23.00
89-04-009	Little Sis w/Lolly SEC-009	D. Kennicutt	Retrd.	14.50	17.50
89-04-010	Bunny w/Prize Egg SEC-010	D. Kennicutt	Retrd.	19.50	20.00
89-04-011	Sis & Bubba Sharing SEC-011	D. Kennicutt	Open	22.50	24.50
89-04-012	Easter Egg Hunt SEC-012	D. Kennicutt	Open	16.50	22.00
89-04-013	Rock-A-Bye Bunny SEC-013	D. Kennicutt	Open	20.00	24.50
89-04-014	Ducky w/Bonnet, Pink SEC-014	D. Kennicutt	Retrd.	10.00	12.00
89-04-015	Ducky w/Bonnet,Blue SEC-015	D. Kennicutt	Retrd.	10.00	12.00
90-04-016	Bubba w/Wagon SEC-016	D. Kennicutt	Retrd.	16.50	17.50
90-04-017	Easter Bunny w/Crystal SEC-017	D. Kennicutt	Open	23.00	24.50
90-04-018	Hen w/Chick SEC-018	D. Kennicutt	Retrd.	23.00	23.00
90-04-019	Momma Making Basket SEC-019	D. Kennicutt	Retrd.	23.00	23.00
90-04-020	Mother Goose SEC-020	D. Kennicutt	Retrd.	16.50	20.00
91-04-021	Bubba In Wheelbarrow SEC-021	D. Kennicutt	Retrd.	20.00	20.00
91-04-022	Lop-Ear w/Crystal SEC-022	D. Kennicutt	Open	23.00	24.50
91-04-023	Nest of Bunny Eggs SEC-023	D. Kennicutt	Open	17.50	22.00
91-04-024	Victorian Momma SEC-024	D. Kennicutt	Retrd.	20.00	20.00
91-04-025	Bunny Boy w/Basket SEC-025	D. Kennicutt	Retrd.	20.00	20.00
91-04-026	Victorian Auntie Bunny SEC-026	D. Kennicutt	Retrd.	20.00	20.00
91-04-027	Baby in Buggy, Boy SEC-027R	D. Kennicutt	Retrd.	20.00	22.00
91-04-028	Fancy Find SEC-028	D. Kennicutt	Open	20.00	22.00
91-04-029	Baby in Buggy, Girl SEC-029R	D. Kennicutt	Retrd.	20.00	22.00
92-04-030	Easter Bunny w/Back Pack SEC-030	D. Kennicutt	Open	20.00	22.00
92-04-031	Grandma w/ Bible SEC-031	D. Kennicutt	Open	20.00	22.00
92-04-032	Grandpa w/Carrots SEC-032R	D. Kennicutt	Retrd.	20.00	22.00
92-04-033	Auntie Bunny w/Cake SEC-033R	D. Kennicutt	Retrd.	20.00	22.00
92-04-034	Boy Bunny w/Large Egg SEC-034R	D. Kennicutt	Retrd.	20.00	22.00
92-04-035	Girl Bunny w/Large Egg SEC-035R	D. Kennicutt	Retrd.	20.00	22.00
93-04-036	Egg Roll SEC-036	D. Kennicutt	Open	23.00	24.50
93-04-037	Grandma & Quilt SEC-037	D. Kennicutt	Open	23.00	24.50
93-04-038	Rocking Horse SEC-038	D. Kennicutt	Open	20.00	22.00
93-04-039	Girl Bunny w/Basket SEC-039	D. Kennicutt	Open	20.00	22.00
93-04-040	Christening Day SEC-040	D. Kennicutt	Open	20.00	22.00
93-04-041	Easter Bunny, Chocolate Egg SEC-041	D. Kennicutt	Open	23.00	24.50
93-04-042	Lop Ear Dying Eggs SEC-042	D. Kennicutt	Open	23.00	24.50
93-04-043	Mom Storytime SEC-043	D. Kennicutt	Open	20.00	22.00
94-04-044	Bath Time SEC-044	D. Kennicutt	Open	24.50	24.50
94-04-045	All Hidden SEC-045	D. Kennicutt	Open	24.50	24.50
94-04-046	Gift Carrot SEC-046	D. Kennicutt	Open	22.00	22.00
94-04-047	Large Prize Egg SEC-047	D. Kennicutt	Open	22.00	22.00
94-04-048	First Steps SEC-048	D. Kennicutt	Open	24.50	24.50
94-04-049	Babysitter SEC-049	D. Kennicutt	Open	24.50	24.50
94-04-050	Wheelbarrow SEC-050	D. Kennicutt	Open	24.50	24.50

United Design Corp. — Easter Bunny Family Miniatures

		ARTIST	EDITION	ISSUE	QUOTE
93-05-001	Bunny under Bonnet SEC-500	P.J. Jonas	Open	7.50	7.50
93-05-002	Girl Bunny with Carrots SEC-501	P.J. Jonas	Open	8.50	8.50
93-05-003	Girl Bunny with Hen mini SEC-502	P.J. Jonas	Open	7.50	7.50
93-05-004	Lop Ear and Paint Bucket SEC-503	D. Newburn	Open	8.50	8.50
93-05-005	Basket of Bunnies mini SEC-504	P.J. Jonas	Open	7.50	7.50
93-05-006	Bubba with Goose mini SEC-505	D. Newburn	Open	7.50	7.50
93-05-007	Boy Bunny with Blocks SEC-506	P.J. Jonas	Open	8.50	8.50
93-05-008	Grandma Rabbit mini SEC-507	P.J. Jonas	Open	8.50	8.50
93-05-009	Grandpa Rabbit mini SEC-508	P.J. Jonas	Open	8.50	8.50
93-05-010	Lop Ear Girl with Egg SEC-509	D. Newburn	Open	7.50	7.50
93-05-011	Easter Bunny mini SEC-510	D. Newburn	Open	8.50	8.50
93-05-012	Momma Rabbit mini SEC-511	D. Newburn	Open	8.50	8.50
93-05-013	Baby Boy with Pail SEC-512	D. Newburn	Open	8.50	8.50
93-05-014	Baby Girl with Bunny SEC-513	D. Newburn	Open	7.50	7.50
93-05-015	Lilly mini SEC-514	D. Newburn	Open	7.50	7.50
93-05-016	Baby in Cradle SEC-515	P.J. Jonas	Open	7.50	7.50
94-05-017	Bunny and Goose Reading SEC-516	P.J. Jonas	Open	8.50	8.50
94-05-018	Mini Momma with Basket SEC-517	P.J. Jonas	Open	8.50	8.50
94-05-019	Victorian Momma Bunny mini SEC-518	D. Newburn	Open	8.50	8.50
94-05-020	Little Sis with Lolly mini SEC-519	D. Newburn	Open	8.50	8.50
94-05-021	Little Lop Artist SEC-520	D. Newburn	Open	8.50	8.50
94-05-022	Victorian Auntie Bunny mini SEC-521	P.J. Jonas	Open	7.50	7.50
94-05-023	Spring Showers SEC-522	P.J. Jonas	Open	8.50	8.50
94-05-024	Easter Bonnet (Lop Ear) SEC-523	D. Newburn	Open	7.50	7.50
94-05-025	Mini Prize Egg SEC-524	P.J. Jonas	Open	7.50	7.50
94-05-026	Auntie Bunny mini SEC-525	D. Newburn	Open	8.50	8.50
94-05-027	Lop Ear Boy with Wagon SEC-526	D. Newburn	Open	7.50	7.50
94-05-028	Bunny with Toy Cow SEC-527	P.J. Jonas	Open	7.50	7.50

United Design Corp. — Easter Bunny Family Babies

		ARTIST	EDITION	ISSUE	QUOTE
94-06-001	Girl with Blanket SEC-800	D. Kennicutt	Open	6.50	6.50
94-06-002	Boy with Baseball Bat SEC-801	D. Kennicutt	Open	6.50	6.50
94-06-003	Boy with Basket and Egg SEC-802	D. Kennicutt	Open	6.50	6.50
94-06-004	Boy with Stick Horse SEC-803	D. Kennicutt	Open	6.50	6.50
94-06-005	Girl with Toy Rabbit SEC-804	D. Kennicutt	Open	6.50	6.50
94-06-006	Boy Baby with Blocks SEC-805	D. Kennicutt	Open	6.50	6.50
94-06-007	Girl with Big Egg SEC-806	D. Kennicutt	Open	6.50	6.50
94-06-008	Baby on Blanket, Naptime SEC-807	D. Kennicutt	Open	6.50	6.50

United Design Corp. — Backyard Birds

		ARTIST	EDITION	ISSUE	QUOTE
88-07-001	Bluebird, Small BB-001	S. Bradford	Open	10.00	10.50
88-07-002	Cardinal, Small BB-002	S. Bradford	Open	10.00	10.50
88-07-003	Chickadee, Small BB-003	S. Bradford	Open	10.00	10.50
88-07-004	Hummingbird Flying, Small BB-004	S. Bradford	Open	10.00	10.50
88-07-005	Hummingbird Female, Small BB-005	S. Bradford	Retrd.	10.00	10.00
88-07-006	Robin Baby, Small BB-006	S. Bradford	Open	10.00	10.50
88-07-007	Sparrow, Small BB-007	S. Bradford	Open	10.00	10.50
88-07-008	Robin Babies BB-008	S. Bradford	Open	15.00	19.00
88-07-009	Bluebird BB-009	S. Bradford	Open	15.00	21.00
88-07-010	Chickadee BB-010	S. Bradford	Open	15.00	18.00
88-07-011	Cardinal, Female BB-011	S. Bradford	Open	15.00	17.00
88-07-012	Humingbird BB-012	S. Bradford	Open	15.00	18.00
88-07-013	Cardinal, Male BB-013	S. Bradford	Open	15.00	18.00
88-07-014	Red-winged Blackbird BB-014	S. Bradford	Retrd.	15.00	16.50
88-07-015	Robin BB-015	S. Bradford	Open	15.00	21.00
88-07-016	Sparrow BB-016	S. Bradford	Open	15.00	17.00
88-07-017	Bluebird Hanging BB-017	S. Bradford	Retrd.	11.00	16.50
88-07-018	Cardinal Hanging BB-018	S. Bradford	Retrd.	11.00	11.00
88-07-019	Chickadee Hanging BB-019	S. Bradford	Retrd.	11.00	11.00
88-07-020	Robin Hanging BB-020	S. Bradford	Retrd.	11.00	11.00
88-07-021	Sparrow Hanging BB-021	S. Bradford	Retrd.	11.00	11.00
88-07-022	Hummingbird Sm., Hanging BB-022	S. Bradford	Retrd.	11.00	11.00
88-07-023	Hummingbird, Lg., Hanging BB-023	S. Bradford	Retrd.	15.00	15.00
89-07-024	Baltimore Oriole BB-024	S. Bradford	Open	19.50	22.00
89-07-025	Hoot Owl BB-025	S. Bradford	Open	15.00	20.00
89-07-026	Blue Jay BB-026	S. Bradford	Open	19.50	22.00
89-07-027	Blue Jay, Baby BB-027	S. Bradford	Open	15.00	15.00
89-07-028	Goldfinch BB-028	S. Bradford	Open	16.50	20.00
89-07-029	Saw-Whet Owl BB-029	S. Bradford	Open	15.00	18.00
89-07-030	Woodpecker BB-030	S. Bradford	Open	16.50	20.00
90-07-031	Bluebird (Upright) BB-031	S. Bradford	Open	20.00	20.00
90-07-032	Cedar Waxwing BB-032	S. Bradford	Open	20.00	20.00
90-07-033	Cedar Waxwing Babies BB-033	S. Bradford	Open	22.00	22.00
90-07-034	Indigo Bunting BB-036	S. Bradford	Open	20.00	20.00
90-07-035	Indigo Bunting, Female BB-039	S. Bradford	Open	20.00	20.00
90-07-036	Nuthatch, White-throated BB-037	S. Bradford	Open	20.00	20.00
90-07-037	Painted Bunting BB-040	S. Bradford	Open	20.00	20.00
90-07-038	Painted Bunting, Female BB-041	S. Bradford	Open	20.00	20.00
90-07-039	Purple Finch BB-038	S. Bradford	Open	20.00	20.00
90-07-040	Rose Breasted Grosbeak BB-042	S. Bradford	Open	20.00	20.00
90-07-041	Evening Grosbeak BB-034	S. Bradford	Open	22.00	22.00
94-07-042	Broadbill on Trumpet Vine BB-043	P.J. Jonas	Open	22.00	22.00
94-07-043	Allen's on Pink Flowers BB-044	P.J. Jonas	Open	22.00	22.00
94-07-044	Rubythroat on Yellow Flowers BB-045	P.J. Jonas	Open	22.00	22.00
94-07-045	Magnificent Pair on Trumpet Vine BB-046	P.J. Jonas	Open	30.00	30.00
94-07-046	Rubythroat Pair on Pink Flowers BB-047	P.J. Jonas	Open	30.00	30.00
94-07-047	Broadbill Pair on Yellow Flowers BB-048	P.J. Jonas	Open	30.00	30.00
94-07-048	Rubythroat on Thistle BB-049	P.J. Jonas	Open	16.50	16.50
94-07-049	Allen's on Purple Morning Glory BB-051	P.J. Jonas	Open	22.00	22.00
94-07-050	Rubythroat on Red Morning Glory BB-052	P.J. Jonas	Open	22.00	22.00
94-07-051	Broadbill on Blue Morning Glory BB-053	P.J. Jonas	Open	22.00	22.00
94-07-052	Rubythroat on Pink Fuscia BB-054	P.J. Jonas	Open	22.00	22.00
94-07-053	Broadbill on Yellow Fuscia BB-055	P.J. Jonas	Open	22.00	22.00

United Design Corp. — **PenniBear™**

		ARTIST	EDITION	ISSUE	QUOTE
89-08-001	Bouquet Girl PB-001	P.J. Jonas	Retrd.	20.00	45-50.00
89-08-002	Honey Bear PB-002	P.J. Jonas	Retrd.	20.00	45-50.00
89-08-003	Bouquet Boy PB-003	P.J. Jonas	Retrd.	20.00	45-50.00
89-08-004	Beautiful Bride PB-004	P.J. Jonas	Retrd.	20.00	45-50.00
89-08-005	Butterfly Bear PB-005	P.J. Jonas	Retrd.	20.00	45-50.00
89-08-006	Cookie Bandit PB-006	P.J. Jonas	Retrd.	20.00	22.00
89-08-007	Baby Hugs PB-007	P.J. Jonas	Retrd.	20.00	35.00
89-08-008	Doctor Bear PB-008	P.J. Jonas	Retrd.	20.00	22.00
89-08-009	Lazy Days PB-009	P.J. Jonas	Retrd.	20.00	22.00
89-08-010	Petite Mademoiselle PB-010	P.J. Jonas	Retrd.	20.00	45.00
90-08-011	Giddiap Teddy PB-011	P.J. Jonas	Retrd.	20.00	35-50.00
90-08-012	Buttons & Bows PB-012	P.J. Jonas	Retrd.	20.00	45-50.00
90-08-013	Country Spring PB-013	P.J. Jonas	Retrd.	20.00	45-50.00
90-08-014	Garden Path PB-014	P.J. Jonas	Retrd.	20.00	45-50.00
89-08-015	Handsome Groom PB-015	P.J. Jonas	Retrd.	20.00	45.00
89-08-016	Nap Time PB-016	P.J. Jonas	Retrd.	20.00	22.00
89-08-017	Nurse Bear PB-017	P.J. Jonas	Retrd.	20.00	22.00
89-08-018	Birthday Bear PB-018	P.J. Jonas	Retrd.	20.00	40.00
89-08-019	Attic Fun PB-019	P.J. Jonas	Retrd.	20.00	30.00
89-08-020	Puppy Bath PB-020	P.J. Jonas	Retrd.	20.00	22.00
89-08-021	Puppy Love PB-021	P.J. Jonas	Retrd.	20.00	22.00
89-08-022	Tubby Teddy PB-022	P.J. Jonas	Retrd.	20.00	22.00
89-08-023	Bathtime Buddies PB-023	P.J. Jonas	Retrd.	20.00	22.00
89-08-024	Southern Belle PB-024	P.J. Jonas	Retrd.	20.00	45-50.00
90-08-025	Boooo Bear PB-025	P.J. Jonas	Retrd.	20.00	22.00
90-08-026	Sneaky Snowball PB-026	P.J. Jonas	Retrd.	20.00	22.00
90-08-027	Count Bearacula PB-027	P.J. Jonas	Retrd.	22.00	24.00
90-08-028	Dress Up Fun PB-028	P.J. Jonas	Retrd.	22.00	24.00
90-08-029	Scarecrow Teddy PB-029	P.J. Jonas	Retrd.	24.00	24.00
90-08-030	Country Quilter PB-030	P.J. Jonas	Retrd.	22.00	26.00
90-08-031	Santa Bear-ing Gifts PB-031	P.J. Jonas	Retrd.	24.00	26.00
90-08-032	Stocking Surprise PB-032	P.J. Jonas	Retrd.	22.00	26.00
91-08-033	Bearly Awake PB-033	P.J. Jonas	Retrd.	22.00	22.00
91-08-034	Lil' Mer-teddy PB-034	P.J. Jonas	Retrd.	24.00	24.00
91-08-035	Bump-bear-Crop PB-035	P.J. Jonas	Retrd.	26.00	26.00
91-08-036	Country Lullabye PB-036	P.J. Jonas	Retrd.	24.00	24.00
91-08-037	Bear Footin' it PB-037	P.J. Jonas	Retrd.	24.00	24.00
91-08-038	Windy Day PB-038	P.J. Jonas	Retrd.	24.00	24.00
91-08-039	Summer Sailing PB-039	P.J. Jonas	Retrd.	26.00	26.00
91-08-040	Goodnight Sweet Princess PB-040	P.J. Jonas	Retrd.	26.00	26.00
91-08-041	Goodnight Little Prince PB-041	P.J. Jonas	Retrd.	26.00	26.00
91-08-042	Bunny Buddies PB-042	P.J. Jonas	Retrd.	22.00	22.00
91-08-043	Baking Goodies PB-043	P.J. Jonas	Retrd.	26.00	26.00
91-08-044	Sweetheart Bears PB-044	P.J. Jonas	Retrd.	28.00	28.00
91-08-045	Bountiful Harvest PB-045	P.J. Jonas	Retrd.	24.00	24.00
91-08-046	Christmas Reinbear PB-046	P.J. Jonas	Retrd.	28.00	28.00
91-08-047	Pilgrim Provider PB-047	P.J. Jonas	Retrd.	32.00	32.00
91-08-048	Sweet Lil 'Sis PB-048	P.J. Jonas	Retrd.	22.00	22.00
91-08-049	Curtain Call PB-049	P.J. Jonas	Retrd.	24.00	24.00
91-08-050	Boo Hoo Bear PB-050	P.J. Jonas	Retrd.	22.00	22.00
91-08-051	Happy Hobo PB-051	P.J. Jonas	Retrd.	26.00	26.00
91-08-052	A Wild Ride PB-052	P.J. Jonas	Retrd.	26.00	26.00
92-08-053	Spanish Rose PB-053	P.J. Jonas	12/94	24.00	24.00
92-08-054	Tally Ho! PB-054	P.J. Jonas	12/94	22.00	22.00
92-08-055	Smokey's Nephew PB-055	P.J. Jonas	12/94	22.00	22.00
92-08-056	Cinderella PB-056	P.J. Jonas	12/94	22.00	22.00
92-08-057	Puddle Jumper PB-057	P.J. Jonas	12/94	24.00	24.00
92-08-058	After Every Meal PB-058	P.J. Jonas	12/94	22.00	22.00
92-08-059	Pot O' Gold PB-059	P.J. Jonas	12/94	22.00	22.00
92-08-050	I Made It Girl PB-060	P.J. Jonas	12/94	22.00	22.00
92-08-061	I Made It Boy PB-061	P.J. Jonas	12/94	22.00	22.00
92-08-062	Dust Bunny Roundup PB-062	P.J. Jonas	12/94	22.00	22.00
92-08-063	Sandbox Fun PB-063	P.J. Jonas	12/94	22.00	22.00
92-08-064	First Prom PB-064	P.J. Jonas	12/94	22.00	22.00
92-08-065	Clowning Around PB-065	P.J. Jonas	12/94	22.00	22.00
92-08-066	Batter Up PB-066	P.J. Jonas	12/94	22.00	22.00
92-08-067	Will You Be Mine? PB-067	P.J. Jonas	12/94	22.00	22.00
92-08-068	On Your Toes PB-068	P.J. Jonas	12/94	24.00	24.00
92-08-069	Apple For Teacher PB-069	P.J. Jonas	12/94	24.00	24.00
92-08-070	Downhill Thrills PB-070	P.J. Jonas	12/94	24.00	24.00
92-08-071	Lil' Devil PB-071	P.J. Jonas	12/94	24.00	24.00
92-08-072	Touchdown PB-072	P.J. Jonas	12/94	22.00	22.00
92-08-073	Bear-Capade PB-073	P.J. Jonas	12/94	22.00	22.00
92-08-074	Lil' Sis Makes Up PB-074	P.J. Jonas	12/94	22.00	22.00
92-08-075	Christmas Cookies PB-075	P.J. Jonas	12/94	22.00	22.00
92-08-076	Decorating The Wreath PB-076	P.J. Jonas	12/94	22.00	22.00
93-08-077	A Happy Camper PB-077	P.J. Jonas	12/95	28.00	28.00
93-08-078	My Forever Love PB-078	P.J. Jonas	12/95	28.00	28.00
93-08-079	Rest Stop PB-079	P.J. Jonas	12/95	24.00	24.00
93-08-080	May Joy Be Yours PB-080	P.J. Jonas	12/95	24.00	24.00
93-08-081	Santa's Helper PB-081	P.J. Jonas	12/95	28.00	28.00
93-08-082	Gotta Try Again PB-082	P.J. Jonas	12/95	24.00	24.00
93-08-083	Little Bear Peep PB-083	P.J. Jonas	12/95	24.00	24.00
93-08-084	Happy Birthday PB-084	P.J. Jonas	12/95	26.00	26.00
93-08-085	Getting 'Round On My Own PB-085	P.J. Jonas	12/95	26.00	26.00
93-08-086	Summer Belle PB-086	P.J. Jonas	12/95	24.00	24.00
93-08-087	Making It Better PB-087	P.J. Jonas	12/95	24.00	24.00
93-08-088	Big Chief Little Bear PB-088	P.J. Jonas	12/95	28.00	28.00

United Design Corp. — **PenniBear™ Collector's Club Members Only Editions**

91-09-001	First Collection PB-C90	P.J. Jonas	Retrd.	26.00	100-125.
92-09-002	Collecting Makes Cents PB-C91	P.J. Jonas	Retrd.	26.00	75-150.
92-09-003	Today's Pleasures, Tomorrow's Treasures	P.J. Jonas	Retrd.	26.00	100.00
93-09-004	Chalkin Up Another Year PBC-93	P.J. Jones	Retrd.	26.00	26.00
94-09-005	Artist's Touch-Collector's Treasure PBC-94	P.J. Jones	Yr.Iss.	26.00	26.00

United Design Corp. — **Party Animal™**

84-10-001	Democratic Donkey ('84)	D. Kennicutt	Retrd.	14.50	16.00
84-10-002	GOP Elephant ('84)	L. Miller	Retrd.	14.50	16.00
86-10-003	Democratic Donkey ('86)	L. Miller	Retrd.	14.50	14.50
86-10-004	GOP Elephant ('86)	L. Miller	Retrd.	14.50	14.50
88-10-005	Democratic Donkey ('88)	L. Miller	Retrd.	14.50	16.00
88-10-006	GOP Elephant ('88)	L. Miller	Retrd.	14.50	16.00
90-10-007	Democratic Donkey ('90)	D. Kennicutt	Open	16.00	16.00
90-10-008	GOP Elephant ('90)	D. Kennicutt	Retrd.	16.00	16.00
92-10-009	Democratic Donkey ('92)	K. Memoli	Open	20.00	20.00
92-10-010	GOP Elephant ('92)	K. Memol	Open	20.00	20.00

United Design Corp. — **Angels Collection**

91-11-001	Christmas Angel AA-003	S. Bradford	Retrd.	125.00	125.00
91-11-002	Trumpeter Angel AA-004	S. Bradford	10,000	99.00	99.00
91-11-003	Classical Angel AA-005	S. Bradford	10,000	79.00	79.00
91-11-004	Messenger of Peace AA-006	S. Bradford	10,000	75.00	79.00
91-11-005	Winter Rose Angel AA-007	S. Bradford	Retrd.	65.00	65.00
91-11-006	Heavenly Shepherdess AA-008	S. Bradford	10,000	99.00	99.00
91-11-007	The Gift AA-009	S. Bradford	Retrd.	135.00	350-475.
91-11-008	Peace Descending Angel AA-013	P.J. Jonas	Open	20.00	20.00
92-11-009	Joy To The World AA-016	D. Newburn	10,000	90.00	95.00
92-11-010	Peaceful Encounter AA-017	D. Newburn	10,000	100.00	100.00
92-11-011	The Gift '92 AA-018	S. Bradford	Retrd.	140.00	180-200.
92-11-012	Winter Angel AA-019	D. Newburn	10,000	75.00	75.00
92-11-013	Angel, Lion & Lamb AA-020	K. Memoli	10,000	135.00	135.00
92-11-014	Angel, Lamb & Critters AA-021	S. Bradford	10,000	90.00	95.00
92-11-015	Crystal Angel AA-022	P.J. Jonas	Open	20.00	20.00
92-11-016	Rose Of Sharon AA-023	P.J. Jonas	Open	20.00	20.00
92-11-017	Victorian Angel AA-024	P.J. Jonas	Open	20.00	20.00
92-11-018	Star Glory AA-025	P.J. Jonas	Open	20.00	20.00
93-11-019	Madonna AA-031	K. Memoli	Retrd.	65.00	100.00
93-11-020	Angel of Flight AA-032	K. Memoli	Retrd.	79.00	100.00
93-11-021	Angel w/ Lillies-033	D. Newburn	Retrd.	55.00	80.00
93-11-022	Angel w/ Birds AA-034	D. Newburn	Retrd.	55.00	75.00
93-11-023	Angel w/ Leaves AA-035	D. Newburn	Retrd.	55.00	70.00
93-11-024	The Gift '93 AA-037	S. Bradford	Retrd.	100.00	120.00
93-11-026	Angel w/Lillies, Crimson AA-040	D. Newburn	Retrd.	80.00	80.00
93-11-025	Angel w/ Leaves, Emerald AA-041	D. Newburn	Retrd.	55.00	70.00
94-11-027	Angel, Roses and Bluebirds AA-054	D. Newburn	Retrd.	65.00	65.00
94-11-028	The Gift '94 AA-057	D. Newburn	Retrd.	140.00	140.00
94-11-029	Angel w/Book AA-058	D. Newburn	Retrd.	84.00	84.00
94-11-030	Earth Angel AA-059	S. Bradford	Retrd.	84.00	84.00
94-11-031	Dreaming of Angels AA-060	K. Memoli	Retrd.	120.00	120.00
94-11-032	Angel w/Christ Child AA-061	K. Memoli	Retrd.	84.00	84.00
94-11-033	Harvest Angel AA-063	S. Bradford	Retrd.	84.00	84.00

United Design Corp. — **Lil' Dolls**

91-12-001	The Nutcracker LD-006	P.J. Jonas	Retrd.	35.00	35.00
92-12-002	Clara & The Nutcracker LD-017	D. Newburn	Retrd.	35.00	35.00

United Design Corp. — **Storytime Rhymes & Tales**

91-13-001	Mother Goose SL-001	H. Henriksen	Retrd.	64.00	64.00
91-13-002	Mistress Mary SL-002	H. Henriksen	Retrd.	64.00	64.00
91-13-003	Simple Simon SL-003	H. Henriksen	Retrd.	90.00	90.00
91-13-004	Owl & Pussy Cat SL-004	H. Henriksen	Retrd.	100.00	100.00
91-13-005	Three Little Pigs SL-005	H. Henriksen	Retrd.	100.00	100.00
91-13-006	Little Miss Muffet SL-006	H. Henriksen	Retrd.	64.00	64.00
91-13-007	Little Jack Horner SL-007	H. Henriksen	Retrd.	50.00	50.00
91-13-008	Humpty Dumpty SL-008	H. Henriksen	Retrd.	64.00	64.00

VickiLane — **Sweet Thumpins**

86-01-001	Bunnies in Frilly Dress with Pillows	V. Anderson	Retrd.	22.00	22.00
87-01-002	Bunny Sleeping in a Basket	V. Anderson	Retrd.	18.00	18.00
88-01-003	Girl Bunny with a Hat and Doll	V. Anderson	Retrd.	18.00	18.00
88-01-004	Farmer Bunny with Carrots	V. Anderson	Retrd.	18.00	18.00
88-01-005	Bunny With Christmas Wreath	V. Anderson	Retrd.	19.00	19.00
90-01-006	Venture into Sweet Thumpins	V. Anderson	Retrd.	60.00	73.00
90-01-007	Tea Time	V. Anderson	1,000	79.00	82.00
90-01-008	Making Memories	V. Anderson	1,000	70.00	73.00
90-01-009	Just For You, Girl Bunny With Carrot	V. Anderson	Retrd.	29.00	29.00
92-01-010	Cookie Peddler	V. Anderson	750	90.00	90.00
93-01-011	Bunny Throwing Snowball	V. Anderson	Retrd.	31.00	31.00

VickiLane — **Mice Memories**

90-02-001	Happiness Together	V. Anderson	1,000	65.00	73.00
90-02-002	Mouse on the Beach	V. Anderson	Retrd.	28.00	28.00

VickiLane — **Time For Teddy**

83-03-001	Bear Holding His Foot	V. Anderson	Retrd.	14.00	14.00
84-03-002	Teddy Bear With Bow & Heart	V. Anderson	Retrd.	13.50	13.50
84-03-003	Sailor Bear	V. Anderson	Retrd.	17.00	17.00
85-03-004	Teddy Bear with a Bow	V. Anderson	Retrd.	14.00	14.00
86-03-005	Sailor Bear With Duck	V. Anderson	Retrd.	16.00	16.00
86-03-006	Wedding Pair Bears	V. Anderson	Retrd.	19.00	19.00
86-03-007	Teddy Riding Goose	V. Anderson	Retrd.	20.50	20.50
89-03-008	Boy Teddy Building Sandcastles	V. Anderson	Retrd.	17.00	17.00
89-03-009	Girl Teddy Sunbathing	V. Anderson	Retrd.	18.00	18.00
90-03-010	Teddy With Antique Radio	V. Anderson	Retrd.	18.00	18.00

VickiLane — **Collector Club Series**

93-04-001	Sweet Secrets	V. Anderson	Retrd.	30.00	30.00
94-04-002	Take Me Home-Little Miss April	V. Anderson	Retrd.	28.00	28.00

WACO Products Corp. — **Melody In Motion/Willie**

85-01-001	Willie The Trumpeter	S. Nakane	Open	130.00	148.00
85-01-002	Willie The Hobo	S. Nakane	Open	130.00	148.00
85-01-003	Willie The Whistler	S. Nakane	Open	130.00	148.00
87-01-004	Lamppost Willie	S. Nakane	Open	110.00	135.00
91-01-005	Willie The Fisherman	S. Nakane	Open	150.00	170.00
92-01-006	Dockside Willie	S. Nakane	Open	160.00	170.00
92-01-007	Wild West Willie	S. Nakane	Open	175.00	190.00
93-01-008	Lamp Light Willie	S. Nakane	Open	240.00	240.00
93-01-009	Willie The Golfer	S. Nakane	Open	240.00	240.00
93-01-010	The Artist	S. Nakane	Open	240.00	240.00
93-01-011	Heartbreak Willie	S. Nakane	Open	180.00	180.00
94-01-012	Willie the Golfer	S. Nakane	Open	240.00	240.00
94-01-013	Smooth Sailing	S. Nakane	Open	200.00	200.00
94-01-014	Longest Drive	S. Nakane	Open	150.00	150.00
94-01-015	Chatanooga Choo Choo	S. Nakane	Open	180.00	180.00

WACO Products Corp. — **Melody In Motion/Vendor**

87-02-001	Organ Grinder	S. Nakane	Retrd.	130.00	160.00
89-02-002	Peanut Vendor	S. Nakane	Open	140.00	170.00
89-02-003	Ice Cream Vendor	S. Nakane	Retrd.	140.00	170.00

WACO Products Corp. — **Melody In Motion/Santa**

86-03-001	Santa Claus-1986	S. Nakane	Retrd.	100.00	2500.00
87-03-002	Santa Claus-1987	S. Nakane	Retrd.	130.00	700-2000
88-03-003	Santa Claus-1988	S. Nakane	Retrd.	130.00	1000.00
89-03-004	Willie The Santa-1989	S. Nakane	Retrd.	130.00	N/A
90-03-005	Santa Claus-1990	S. Nakane	Retrd.	150.00	200-225.
91-03-006	Santa Claus-1991	S. Nakane	Retrd.	150.00	160.00
92-03-007	Santa Claus -1992	S. Nakane	11,000	160.00	160.00
93-03-008	Coca-Cola Santa Claus-1993	S. Nakane	Retrd.	180.00	180.00
94-03-009	Coca-Cola Santa Claus-1994	S. Nakane	9,000	190.00	190.00

WACO Products Corp. — **Melody In Motion/Madame**

88-04-001	Madame Violin Player	S. Nakane	Retrd.	130.00	130.00
88-04-002	Madame Mandolin Player	S. Nakane	Retrd.	130.00	130.00

		ARTIST	EDITION	ISSUE	QUOTE
88-04-003	Madame Cello Player	S. Nakane	Retrd.	130.00	130.00
88-04-004	Madame Flute Player	S. Nakane	Retrd.	130.00	130.00
88-04-005	Madame Harp Player	S. Nakane	Open	130.00	170.00
88-04-006	Madame Harpsichord Player	S. Nakane	Retrd.	130.00	130.00
88-04-007	Madame Lyre Player	S. Nakane	Retrd.	130.00	130.00
88-04-008	Madame Cello Player (glazed)	S. Nakane	Retrd.	170.00	170.00
88-04-009	Madame Flute Player (glazed)	S. Nakane	Retrd.	170.00	170.00
88-04-010	Madame Harp Player (glazed)	S. Nakane	Retrd.	190.00	190.00
88-04-011	Madame Harpsichord Player (glazed)	S. Nakane	Retrd.	170.00	170.00

WACO Products Corp. **Melody In Motion/Spotlight Clown**

89-05-001	Spotlight Clown Cornet	S. Nakane	Retrd.	85.00	125.00
89-05-002	Spotlight Clown Banjo	S. Nakane	Retrd.	85.00	85.00
89-05-003	Spotlight Clown Trombone	S. Nakane	Retrd.	85.00	125.00
89-05-004	Spotlight Clown With Bingo The Dog	S. Nakane	Retrd.	85.00	125.00
89-05-005	Spotlight Clown Tuba	S. Nakane	Retrd.	85.00	85.00
89-05-006	Spotlight Clown With Upright Bass	S. Nakane	Retrd.	85.00	90.00

WACO Products Corp. **Melody In Motion/Various**

85-06-001	Salty 'N' Pepper	S. Nakane	Retrd.	88.00	275.00
86-06-002	The Cellist	S. Nakane	Retrd.	130.00	152.00
86-06-003	The Guitarist	S. Nakane	Retrd.	130.00	152.00
86-06-004	The Fiddler	S. Nakane	Open	130.00	152.00
87-06-005	Violin Clown	S. Nakane	Retrd.	84.00	84.00
87-06-006	Clarinet Clown	S. Nakane	Retrd.	110.00	110.00
87-06-007	Saxophone Clown	S. Nakane	Retrd.	110.00	110.00
87-06-008	Accordion Clown	S. Nakane	Retrd.	110.00	110.00
87-06-009	Balloon Clown	S. Nakane	Open	110.00	135.00
87-06-010	The Carousel	S. Nakane	Open	240.00	260.00
89-06-011	The Grand Carousel	S. Nakane	Open	3000.00	3000.00
90-06-012	Shoemaker	S. Nakane	Retrd.	110.00	120.00
90-06-013	Blacksmith	S. Nakane	Retrd.	110.00	120.00
90-06-014	Woodchopper	S. Nakane	Retrd.	110.00	120.00
90-06-015	Accordion Boy	S. Nakane	Retrd.	120.00	125.00
90-06-016	Hunter	S. Nakane	Open	110.00	150.00
91-06-017	Robin Hood	C. Johnson	Retrd.	180.00	280.00
91-06-018	Little John	C. Johnson	Retrd.	180.00	180.00
91-06-019	Victoria Park Carousel	S. Nakane	Open	300.00	330.00
92-06-020	King of Clown Carousel	S. Nakane	Open	740.00	800.00
91-06-021	The Carousel (2nd Edition)	S. Nakane	Retrd.	240.00	260.00
92-06-022	King of Clowns	S. Nakane	Open	700.00	800.00
93-06-023	South of the Border	S. Nakane	Open	180.00	180.00
94-06-024	Low Pressure Job	S. Nakane	Open	240.00	240.00
94-06-025	Day's End	S. Nakane	Open	240.00	240.00
94-06-026	When I Grow Up	S. Nakane	Open	200.00	200.00
94-06-027	Campfire Cowboy	S. Nakane	Open	180.00	180.00
94-06-028	Blue Danube Carousel	S. Nakane	Open	280.00	280.00
94-06-029	Christmas Caroler Boy	S. Nakane	10,000	172.00	172.00
94-06-030	Christmas Caroler Girl	S. Nakane	10,000	172.00	172.00

WACO Products Corp. **Melody In Motion/Timepiece**

89-07-001	Clockpost Willie	S. Nakane	Open	150.00	190.00
89-07-002	Lull'aby Willie	S. Nakane	Retrd.	170.00	170.00
90-07-003	Grandfather's Clock	S. Nakane	Retrd.	200.00	250.00
91-07-004	Hunter Timepiece	S. Nakane	Retrd.	250.00	320.00
92-07-005	Wall Street Willie	S. Nakane	Open	180.00	185-210.
92-07-006	Golden Mountain Clock	S. Nakane	Open	250.00	300.00

WACO Products Corp. **The Herman Collection**

90-08-001	Tennis/Wife	J. Unger	Open	20.00	20.00
90-08-002	Doctor/High Cost	J. Unger	Retrd.	20.00	20.00
90-08-003	Bowling/Wife	J. Unger	Open	20.00	20.00
90-08-004	Husband/Check	J. Unger	Open	20.00	20.00
90-08-005	Birthday Cake	J. Unger	Open	20.00	20.00
90-08-006	Doctor/Fat Man	J. Unger	Open	20.00	20.00
90-08-007	Fry Pan/Fisherman	J. Unger	Retrd.	20.00	20.00
90-08-008	Stop Smoking	J. Unger	Open	20.00	20.00
90-08-009	Husband/Newspaper	J. Unger	Open	20.00	20.00
90-08-010	Wedding Ring	J. Unger	Retrd.	20.00	20.00
90-08-011	Golf/Camel	J. Unger	Retrd.	20.00	20.00
90-08-012	Lawyer/Cabinet	J. Unger	Retrd.	20.00	20.00

WACO Products Corp. **Whimsicals**

92-09-001	Just For You	S. Nakane	Open	60.00	60.00
92-09-002	The Entertainer	S. Nakane	Open	60.00	60.00
92-09-003	Cheers	S. Nakane	Open	60.00	60.00
92-09-004	Happy Endings	S. Nakane	Open	60.00	60.00
92-09-005	Pals	S. Nakane	Open	60.00	60.00
92-09-006	The Merrymakers	S. Nakane	Open	60.00	60.00
92-09-007	Showtime	S. Nakane	Open	60.00	60.00
92-09-008	Pampered Pets	S. Nakane	Open	60.00	60.00
92-09-009	Apple Pickin' Time	S. Nakane	Retrd.	60.00	60.00
92-09-010	Special Delivery	S. Nakane	Retrd.	60.00	60.00
92-09-011	Tea Time	S. Nakane	Retrd.	60.00	60.00
92-09-012	Bon Voyage	S. Nakane	Retrd.	60.00	60.00
92-09-013	Storytime	S. Nakane	Retrd.	60.00	60.00

Wee Forest Folk **Animals**

73-01-001	Miss Ducky D-1	A. Petersen	Closed	6.00	N/A
74-01-002	Miss Hippo H-1	A. Petersen	Closed	8.00	N/A
74-01-003	Baby Hippo H-2	A. Petersen	Closed	7.00	N/A
74-01-004	Miss and Baby Hippo H-3	A. Petersen	Closed	15.00	800-1000
77-01-005	Nutsy Squirrel SQ-1	W. Petersen	Closed	3.00	400-500.
78-01-006	Beaver Wood Cutter BV-1	W. Petersen	Closed	8.00	250-475.
79-01-007	Turtle Jogger TS-1	A. Petersen	Closed	4.00	300-400.

Wee Forest

78-02-001	Mole Scout MO-1	A. Petersen	Closed	4.25	225-400.
94-02-002	Bell Ringer Mole MO-2	A. Petersen	Open	44.00	44.00

Wee Forest Folk **Bears**

77-03-001	Blueberry Bears BR-1	A. Petersen	Closed	8.75	500-700.
77-03-002	Girl Blueberry Bear BR-2	A. Petersen	Closed	4.25	250-400.
77-03-003	Boy Blueberry Bear BR-3	A. Petersen	Closed	4.50	250-700.
78-03-004	Big Lady Bear BR-4	A. Petersen	Closed	7.50	N/A
78-03-005	Traveling Bear BR-5	A. Petersen	Closed	8.00	250-375.

Wee Forest Folk **Rats**

75-04-001	Seedy Rat R-1	A. Petersen	Closed	5.25	200-400.
75-04-002	Doc Rat R-2	W. Petersen	Closed	5.25	200-400.

Wee Forest Folk **Book / Figurine**

88-05-001	Tom & Eon BK-1	W. Petersen	Suspd.	45.00	175-250.

Wee Forest Folk **Bunnies**

		ARTIST	EDITION	ISSUE	QUOTE
72-06-001	Double Bunnies B-1	A. Petersen	Closed	4.25	400.00
72-06-002	Housekeeping Bunny B-2	A. Petersen	Closed	4.50	400.00
73-06-003	Sir Rabbit B-3	W. Petersen	Closed	4.50	300-400.
73-06-004	The Professor B-4	A. Petersen	Closed	4.75	350-400.
73-06-005	Sunday Bunny B-5	A. Petersen	Closed	4.75	N/A
73-06-006	Broom Bunny B-6	A. Petersen	Closed	9.50	N/A
73-06-007	Muff Bunny B-7	A. Petersen	Closed	9.00	N/A
73-06-008	Market Bunny B-8	A. Petersen	Closed	9.00	N/A
77-06-009	Batter Bunny B-9	A. Petersen	Closed	4.50	275.00
78-06-010	Wedding Bunnies B-10	W. Petersen	Closed	12.50	450-600.
80-06-011	Professor Rabbit B-11	W. Petersen	Closed	14.00	400-500.
85-06-012	Tiny Easter Bunny B-12	D. Petersen	Closed	25.00	60-80.00
92-06-013	Windy Day! B-13	D. Petersen	Open	37.00	38.00
77-06-014	Tennis Bunny BS-1	A. Petersen	Closed	3.75	250-350.

Wee Forest Folk **Christmas Carol Series**

87-07-001	Scrooge CC-1	A. Petersen	Open	23.00	30.00
87-07-002	Bob Cratchit and Tiny Tim CC-2	A. Petersen	Open	36.00	45.00
87-07-003	Marley's Ghost CC-3	A. Petersen	Open	24.00	31.00
87-07-004	Ghost of Christmas Past CC-4	A. Petersen	Open	24.00	31.00
87-07-006	Ghost of Christmas Present CC-5	A. Petersen	Open	54.00	61.00
87-07-006	Ghost of Christmas Yet to Come CC-6	A. Petersen	Open	24.00	30.00
88-07-007	The Fezziwigs CC-7	A. Petersen	Open	65.00	82.00

Wee Forest Folk **Cinderella Series**

88-08-001	Cinderella's Slipper (with Prince) C-1	A. Petersen	Closed	62.00	230-235.
89-08-002	Cinderella's Slipper C-1a	A. Petersen	Closed	32.00	75.00
88-08-003	The Ugly Stepsisters C-2	A. Petersen	Closed	62.00	75-100.
88-08-004	The Mean Stepmother C-3	A. Petersen	Closed	32.00	75.00
88-08-005	The Flower Girls C-4	A. Petersen	Closed	42.00	80.00
88-08-006	Cinderella's Wedding C-5	A. Petersen	Closed	62.00	140-155.
88-08-007	Flower Girl C-6	A. Petersen	Closed	22.00	28.00
89-08-008	The Fairy Godmother C-7	A. Petersen	Closed	69.00	83.00

Wee Forest Folk **Fairy Tale Series**

80-09-001	Red Riding Hood & Wolf FT-1	A. Petersen	Closed	29.00	1200.00
80-09-002	Red Riding Hood FT-2	A. Petersen	Closed	13.00	500-610.

Wee Forest Folk **Forest Scene**

88-10-001	Woodland Serenade FS-1	W. Petersen	Open	125.00	132.00
89-10-002	Hearts and Flowers FS-2	W. Petersen	Open	110.00	112.00
90-10-003	Mousie Comes A-Calling FS-3	W. Petersen	Open	128.00	132.00
91-10-004	Mountain Stream FS-4	W. Petersen	Open	128.00	130.00
92-10-005	Love Letter FS-5	W. Petersen	Open	98.00	98.00
93-10-006	Picnic on the Riverbank FS-6	A. Petersen	Open	150.00	150.00
94-10-007	Wayside Chat FS-7	A. Petersen	Open	170.00	170.00

Wee Forest Folk **Foxes**

77-11-001	Fancy Fox FX-1	A. Petersen	Closed	4.75	350-475.
77-11-002	Dandy Fox FX-2	A. Petersen	Closed	6.00	450-500.
78-11-003	Barrister Fox FX-3	A. Petersen	Closed	7.50	450-500.

Wee Forest Folk **Frogs**

74-12-001	Prince Charming F-1	W. Petersen	Closed	7.50	400-500.
74-12-002	Frog on Rock F-2	A. Petersen	Closed	6.00	N/A
77-12-003	Frog Friends F-3	W. Petersen	Closed	5.75	350-450.
77-12-004	Spring Peepers F-4	A. Petersen	Closed	3.50	N/A
77-12-005	Grampa Frog F-5	W. Petersen	Closed	6.00	350-450.
78-12-006	Singing Frog F-6	A. Petersen	Closed	5.50	250-300.

Wee Forest Folk **Limited Edition**

81-13-001	Beauty and the Beast BB-1	W. Petersen	Closed	89.00	15-2000.
84-13-002	Postmouster LTD-1	W. Petersen	Closed	46.00	600-755.
85-13-002	Helping Hand LTD-2	A. Petersen	Closed	62.00	650.00
87-13-003	Statue in the Park LTD-3	W. Petersen	Closed	93.00	750-830.
88-13-004	Uncle Sammy LTD-4	A. Petersen	Closed	85.00	240-300.

Wee Forest Folk **Mice**

77-14-001	King "Tut" Mouse TM-1	A. Petersen	Closed	4.50	N/A
77-14-002	Queen "Tut" Mouse TM-2	A. Petersen	Closed	4.50	N/A
72-14-003	Miss Mouse M-1	A. Petersen	Closed	4.25	300-350.
72-14-004	Market Mouse M-1a	A. Petersen	Closed	4.25	175-350.
72-14-005	Miss Mousey M-2	A. Petersen	Closed	4.00	250-350.
72-14-006	Miss Mousey w/ Straw Hat M-2a	A. Petersen	Closed	4.25	250-350.
72-14-007	Miss Mousey w/ Bow Hat M-2b	A. Petersen	Closed	4.25	250-350.
73-14-008	Miss Nursey Mouse M-3	A. Petersen	Closed	4.00	275-400.
74-14-009	Good Knight Mouse M-4	W. Petersen	Closed	7.50	350-500.
74-14-010	Farmer Mouse M-5	A. Petersen	Closed	3.75	350-450.
74-14-011	Wood Sprite M-6a	A. Petersen	Closed	4.00	350-500.
74-14-012	Wood Sprite M-6b	A. Petersen	Closed	4.00	350-500.
74-14-013	Wood Sprite M-6c	A. Petersen	Closed	4.00	350-500.
75-14-014	Two Mice with Candle M-7	A. Petersen	Closed	4.50	350-450.
75-14-015	Two Tiny Mice M-8	A. Petersen	Closed	4.50	350-500.
75-14-016	Bride Mouse M-9	A. Petersen	Closed	4.00	400-500.
76-14-017	Fan Mouse M-10	A. Petersen	Closed	5.75	450-500.
76-14-018	Tea Mouse M-11	A. Petersen	Closed	5.75	450-500.
76-14-019	May Belle M-12	A. Petersen	Closed	4.25	225-375.
76-14-020	June Belle M-13	A. Petersen	Closed	4.25	350-400.
76-14-021	Nightie Mouse M-14	A. Petersen	Closed	4.75	350-500.
76-14-022	Mrs. Mousey M-15	A. Petersen	Closed	4.00	N/A
76-14-023	Mrs. Mousey w/ Hat M-15a	A. Petersen	Closed	4.25	N/A
76-14-024	Mouse with Muff M-16	A. Petersen	Closed	9.00	N/A
76-14-025	Shawl Mouse M-17	A. Petersen	Closed	9.00	N/A
76-14-026	Mama Mouse with Baby M-18	A. Petersen	Closed	6.00	350-450.
77-14-027	Baby Sitter M-19	A. Petersen	Closed	5.75	300.00
78-14-028	Bridge Club Mouse M-20	A. Petersen	Closed	6.00	300.00
78-14-029	Bridge Club Mouse Partner M-21	A. Petersen	Closed	6.00	300.00
78-14-030	Secretary, Miss Spell/Miss Pell M-22	A. Petersen	Closed	4.50	375-500.
78-14-031	Picnic Mice M-23	W. Petersen	Closed	7.25	375-500.
78-14-032	Wedding Mice M-24	W. Petersen	Closed	7.50	375-750.
78-14-033	Cowboy Mouse M-25	A. Petersen	Closed	6.00	300-600.
78-14-034	Chief Nip-a-Way Mouse M-26	A. Petersen	Closed	7.00	300-600.
78-14-035	Pirate Mouse M-27	A. Petersen	Closed	6.50	400.00
78-14-036	Town Crier Mouse M-28	A. Petersen	Closed	10.50	500.00
79-14-037	Mouse Duet M-29	A. Petersen	Closed	25.00	550-700.
79-14-038	Mouse Pianist M-30	A. Petersen	Closed	17.00	400-475.
79-14-039	Mouse Violinist M-31	A. Petersen	Closed	9.00	300.00
79-14-040	Chris-Miss M-32	A. Petersen	Closed	9.00	175-225.
79-14-041	Chris-Mouse M-33	A. Petersen	Closed	9.00	230.00
79-14-042	Mousey Baby, heart book M-34	A. Petersen	Closed	9.50	250-450.
79-14-043	Rock-a-bye Baby Mouse M-35	A. Petersen	Closed	17.00	350-450.
79-14-044	Raggedy and Mouse M-36	A. Petersen	Closed	12.00	350-410.
79-14-045	Gardener Mouse M-37	A. Petersen	Closed	12.00	400.00
79-14-046	Mouse Ballerina M-38	A. Petersen	Closed	12.50	400-450.
79-14-047	Mouse Artiste M-39	A. Petersen	Closed	12.50	300-450.

		ARTIST	EDITION	ISSUE	QUOTE
80-14-048	Miss Bobbin M-40	A. Petersen	Open	22.00	56.00
80-14-049	Fishermouse M-41	A. Petersen	Closed	16.00	500-700.
80-14-050	Commo-Dormouse M-42	W. Petersen	Closed	14.00	500-900.
80-14-051	Santa Mouse M-43	A. Petersen	Closed	12.00	225-250.
80-14-052	Witch Mouse M-44	A. Petersen	Closed	12.00	150-200.
80-14-053	Miss Teach M-45	A. Petersen	Closed	18.00	400-500.
80-14-054	Miss Polly Mouse M-46	A. Petersen	Closed	23.00	300-400.
80-14-055	Pirate Mouse M-47	W. Petersen	Closed	16.00	1350.00
80-14-056	Photographer Mouse M-48	W. Petersen	Closed	23.00	400-700.
80-14-057	Carpenter Mouse M-49	A. Petersen	Closed	15.00	400.00
80-14-058	Mrs. Tidy and Helper M-50	A. Petersen	Closed	24.00	500-700.
80-14-059	Mrs. Tidy M-51	A. Petersen	Closed	19.50	350-500.
81-14-060	Mother's Helper M-52	A. Petersen	Closed	11.00	200-300.
81-14-061	Flower Girl M-53	A. Petersen	Closed	15.00	350.00
81-14-062	Nurse Mousey M-54	A. Petersen	Closed	14.00	410.00
81-14-063	Doc Mouse & Patient M-55	W. Petersen	Closed	14.00	400-475.
81-14-064	School Marm Mouse M-56	A. Petersen	Closed	19.50	500.00
81-14-065	Barrister Mouse M-57	A. Petersen	Closed	16.00	400.00
81-14-066	Graduate Mouse M-58	A. Petersen	Closed	15.00	110-130.
81-14-067	Pearl Knit Mouse M-59	A. Petersen	Closed	20.00	250-260.
81-14-068	Mom and Squeaky Clean M-60	A. Petersen	Open	27.00	52.00
81-14-069	Little Devil M-61	A. Petersen	Open	12.50	28.00
81-14-070	Blue Devil M-61	A. Petersen	Closed	12.50	125.00
81-14-071	Little Ghost M-62	A. Petersen	Open	8.50	19.00
81-14-072	The Carolers M-63	A. Petersen	Closed	29.00	400-600.
81-14-073	Lone Caroler M-64	A. Petersen	Closed	15.50	375-575.
81-14-074	Mousey Express M-65	A. Petersen	Closed	22.00	85-120.
82-14-075	Baby Sitter M-66	A. Petersen	Closed	23.50	75-130.
82-14-076	Wedding Mice M-67	W. Petersen	Closed	29.50	100-140.
82-14-077	Office Mousey M-68	A. Petersen	Closed	23.00	400-475.
82-14-078	Beddy-bye Mousey M-69	A. Petersen	Open	29.00	49.00
82-14-079	Me and Raggedy Ann M-70	A. Petersen	Open	18.50	33.00
82-14-080	Arty Mouse M-71	A. Petersen	Closed	19.00	105-125.
82-14-081	Say "Cheese" M-72	W. Petersen	Closed	15.50	500.00
82-14-082	Miss Teach & Pupil M-73	A. Petersen	Closed	29.50	275-475.
82-14-083	Tea for Two M-74	A. Petersen	Closed	26.00	300-410.
82-14-084	Mousey's Teddy M-75	A. Petersen	Closed	29.00	300-350.
82-14-085	Beach Mousey M-76	A. Petersen	Closed	19.00	65-95.00
82-14-086	Little Fire Chief M-77	W. Petersen	Closed	29.00	500-530.
82-14-087	Moon Mouse M-78	A. Petersen	Closed	15.50	400-450.
82-14-088	Sweethearts M-79	A. Petersen	Closed	26.00	375-500.
82-14-089	Girl Sweetheart M-80	A. Petersen	Open	13.50	22.00
82-14-090	Boy Sweetheart M-81	A. Petersen	Closed	13.50	500.00
82-14-091	Easter Bunny Mouse M-82	A. Petersen	Open	18.00	33.00
82-14-092	Happy Birthday! M-83	A. Petersen	Open	17.50	31.00
82-14-093	Snowmouse & Friend M-84	A. Petersen	Closed	23.50	300-350.
82-14-094	Little Sledders M-85	A. Petersen	Closed	24.00	250-310.
82-14-095	Lamplight Carolers M-86	A. Petersen	Closed	35.00	180-310.
82-14-096	Holly Mouse M-87	A. Petersen	Open	13.50	28.00
82-14-097	Littlest Angel M-88	A. Petersen	Closed	15.00	127-133.
82-14-098	Poorest Angel M-89	A. Petersen	Closed	15.00	127-133.
83-14-099	Merry Chris-Miss M-90	A. Petersen	Closed	17.00	250-310.
83-14-100	Merry Chris-Mouse M-91	A. Petersen	Closed	16.00	250-310.
83-14-101	Christmas Morning M-92	A. Petersen	Closed	35.00	225.00
83-14-102	First Christmas M-93	A. Petersen	Closed	16.00	200-250.
83-14-103	Cupid Mouse M-94	W. Petersen	Open	22.00	38.00
83-14-104	Mousey Nurse M-95	A. Petersen	Open	15.00	27.00
83-14-105	Get Well Soon! M-96	A. Petersen	Closed	15.00	350-390.
83-14-106	Mouse Call M-97	W. Petersen	Closed	24.00	250-400.
83-14-107	Clown Mouse M-98	A. Petersen	Closed	22.00	350-450.
83-14-108	Birthday Girl M-99	A. Petersen	Open	18.50	30.00
83-14-109	Mousey's Cone M-100	A. Petersen	Closed	22.00	60-80.00
83-14-110	Mousey's Tricycle M-101	A. Petersen	Open	24.00	44.00
83-14-111	Mousey's Dollhouse M-102	A. Petersen	Closed	30.00	275-400.
83-14-112	Rocking Tot M-103	A. Petersen	Closed	19.00	55-80.00
83-14-113	Harvest Mouse M-104	W. Petersen	Closed	23.00	250-395.
83-14-114	Wash Day M-105	A. Petersen	Closed	23.00	375-425.
83-14-115	Pack Mouse M-106	W. Petersen	Closed	19.00	300-375.
83-14-116	Chief Geronimouse M-107a	A. Petersen	Open	21.00	38.00
83-14-117	Running Doe/Little Deer M-107b	A. Petersen	Open	35.00	40.00
83-14-118	Rope 'em Mousey M-108	A. Petersen	Closed	19.00	350-435.
84-14-119	Campfire Mouse M-109	W. Petersen	Closed	26.00	350-425.
84-14-120	Traveling Mouse M-110	A. Petersen	Closed	28.00	250-320.
84-14-121	Spring Gardener M-111	A. Petersen	Open	26.00	39.00
84-14-122	First Day of School M-112	A. Petersen	Closed	27.00	300-450.
84-14-123	Tidy Mouse M-113	A. Petersen	Closed	38.00	300-400.
84-14-124	Pen Pal Mousey M-114	A. Petersen	Closed	26.00	300-400.
84-14-125	Mom & Ginger Baker M-115	W. Petersen	Open	38.00	59.00
84-14-126	Santa's Trainee M-116	W. Petersen	Closed	36.50	400-550.
84-14-127	Chris-Mouse Pageant M-117	A. Petersen	Open	38.00	54.00
84-14-128	Peter's Pumpkin M-118	A. Petersen	Closed	19.00	75-100.
84-14-129	Prudence Pie Maker M-119	A. Petersen	Closed	18.50	60-100.
84-14-130	Witchy Boo! M-120	A. Petersen	Open	21.00	34.00
85-14-131	Pageant Wiseman M-121	A. Petersen	Closed	58.00	125-200.
85-14-132	Wise Man with Turban M-121a	A. Petersen	Open	28.00	34.00
85-14-133	Wise Man in Robe M-121b	A. Petersen	Open	26.00	32.00
85-14-134	Wise Man Kneeling M-121c	A. Petersen	Open	29.00	35.00
85-14-135	Pageant Shepherds M-122	A. Petersen	Closed	35.00	100-200.
85-14-136	Shepherd Kneeling M-122a	A. Petersen	Open	20.00	27.00
85-14-137	Shepherd Standing M-122b	A. Petersen	Open	20.00	27.00
85-14-138	Under the Chris-Mouse Tree M-123	A. Petersen	Open	48.00	74.00
85-14-139	Chris-Mouse Tree M-124	A. Petersen	Open	28.00	43.00
85-14-140	Quilting Bee M-125	W. Petersen	Open	30.00	40.00
85-14-141	Attic Treasure M-126	A. Petersen	Open	42.00	55.00
85-14-142	Family Portrait M-127	A. Petersen	Closed	54.00	250-300.
85-14-143	Strolling with Baby M-128	A. Petersen	Open	42.00	55.00
85-14-144	Piggy-Back Mousey M-129	W. Petersen	Closed	28.00	300-465.
85-14-145	Mouse Talk M-130	A. Petersen	Closed	44.00	110-195.
85-14-146	Come Play! M-131	A. Petersen	Closed	18.00	70-85.00
85-14-147	Sunday Drivers M-132	W. Petersen	Closed	58.00	190-205.
85-14-148	Field Mouse M-133	W. Petersen	Open	46.00	82.00
86-14-149	First Date M-134	W. Petersen	Open	60.00	65.00
86-14-150	Waltzing Matilda M-135	W. Petersen	Closed	48.00	80-100.
86-14-151	Sweet Dreams M-136	A. Petersen	Closed	58.00	165-200.
92-14-152	Tuckered Out! M-136a	A. Petersen	Closed	46.00	46.00
86-14-153	First Haircut M-137	W. Petersen	Closed	58.00	110-155.
86-14-154	Fun Float M-138	W. Petersen	Open	34.00	36.00
86-14-155	Mouse on Campus M-139	W. Petersen	Closed	25.00	90-110.
86-14-156	Just Checking M-140	A. Petersen	Open	34.00	39.00
86-14-157	Come & Get It! M-141	A. Petersen	Closed	34.00	165-180.
86-14-158	Christ-Mouse Stocking M-142	A. Petersen	Open	34.00	39.00

		ARTIST	EDITION	ISSUE	QUOTE
86-14-159	Down the Chimney M-143	A. Petersen	Closed	48.00	175-250.
87-14-160	Pageant Stable M-144	A. Petersen	Open	56.00	66.00
87-14-161	Pageant Angel M-145	A. Petersen	Open	19.00	23.00
87-14-162	Miss Noel M-146	A. Petersen	Open	32.00	38.00
87-14-163	Choir Mouse M-147	W. Petersen	Closed	23.00	70-80.00
87-14-164	Tooth Fairy M-148	A. Petersen	Open	32.00	37.00
87-14-165	Don't Cry! M-149	A. Petersen	Closed	33.00	50-120.
87-14-166	Market Mouse M-150	W. Petersen	Closed	49.00	105-120.
87-14-167	The Red Wagon M-151	W. Petersen	Closed	54.00	160.00
87-14-168	Scooter Mouse M-152	W. Petersen	Open	34.00	39.00
87-14-169	Trumpeter M-153a	W. Petersen	Closed	29.00	50-90.00
87-14-170	Drummer M-153b	W. Petersen	Closed	29.00	50-90.00
87-14-171	Tuba Player M-153c	W. Petersen	Closed	29.00	50-90.00
87-14-172	Bat Mouse M-154	A. Petersen	Closed	25.00	30-45.00
87-14-173	Littlest Witch and Skeleton M-155	A. Petersen	Open	49.00	57.00
87-14-174	Littlest Witch M-156	A. Petersen	Closed	24.00	70-120.
87-14-175	Skeleton Mousey M-157	A. Petersen	Closed	27.00	50-72.00
88-14-176	Aloha! M-158	A. Petersen	Closed	32.00	64.00
88-14-177	Forty Winks M-159	W. Petersen	Open	36.00	42.00
88-14-178	Mousey's Easter Basket M-160	A. Petersen	Open	32.00	90-150.
89-14-179	Commencement Day M-161	W. Petersen	Open	28.00	32.00
89-14-180	Prima Ballerina M-162	A. Petersen	Open	35.00	39.00
89-14-181	Elf Tales M-163	A. Petersen	Open	48.00	49.00
89-14-182	Father Chris-Mouse M-164	A. Petersen	Open	34.00	37.00
89-14-183	Haunted Mouse House M-165	D. Petersen	Open	125.00	168.00
90-14-184	Chris-Mouse Slipper M-166	A. Petersen	Open	35.00	38.00
90-14-185	Colleen O'Green M-167	A. Petersen	Open	40.00	44.00
90-14-186	Stars & Stripes M-168	A. Petersen	Open	34.00	37.00
90-14-187	Hans & Greta M-169	A. Petersen	Closed	64.00	100-160.
92-14-188	Hans M-169a	A. Petersen	Closed	35.00	75-80.00
92-14-189	Greta M-169b	A. Petersen	Closed	35.00	65-85.00
90-14-190	Polly's Parasol M-170	A. Petersen	Closed	39.00	75-100.
90-14-191	Zelda M-171	A. Petersen	Open	37.00	42.00
91-14-192	Red Riding Hood at Grandmother's House	D. Petersen	Open	295.00	295.00
91-14-193	Silent Night M-173	A. Petersen	Open	64.00	69.00
91-14-194	The Nutcracker M-174	D. Petersen	Open	49.00	53.00
91-14-195	Mousie's Egg Factory M-175	A. Petersen	Open	73.00	82.00
91-14-196	Grammy-Phone M-176	A. Petersen	Open	75.00	80.00
91-14-197	Tea For Three M-177	D. Petersen	Open	135.00	148.00
91-14-198	Night Prayer M-178	A. Petersen	Open	52.00	57.00
91-14-199	Sea Sounds M-179	A. Petersen	Open	34.00	37.00
91-14-200	April Showers M-180	A. Petersen	Open	27.00	31.00
91-14-201	Little Squirt M-181	W. Petersen	Open	49.00	52.00
92-14-202	Miss Daisy M-182	A. Petersen	Open	42.00	43.00
92-14-203	Peekaboo! M-183	D. Petersen	Open	52.00	52.00
92-14-204	Mrs. Mousey's Studio M-184	W. Petersen	Open	150.00	150.00
92-14-205	The Old Black Stove M-185	D. Petersen	Open	130.00	132.00
92-14-206	High on the Hog M-186	A. Petersen	Open	52.00	53.00
92-14-207	Adam's Apples M-187	A. Petersen	Open	148.00	148.00
92-14-208	Snow Buddies M-188	D. Petersen	Open	58.00	59.00
93-14-209	Little Mice Who Lived in a Shoe M-189	D. Petersen	Open	395.00	395.00
93-14-210	Peter Pumpkin Eater M-190	A. Petersen	Open	98.00	98.00
93-14-211	Christmas Eve M-191	A. Petersen	Open	145.00	145.00
93-14-212	First Kiss! M-192	A. Petersen	Open	65.00	65.00
93-14-213	Welcome Chick! M-193	A. Petersen	Open	64.00	64.00
93-14-214	The Mummy M-194	A. Petersen	Open	34.00	34.00
93-14-215	Lord & Lady Mousebatten M-195	A. Petersen	Open	85.00	85.00
93-14-216	One-Mouse Band M-196	A. Petersen	Open	95.00	95.00
94-14-217	Chief Mouse-asoit M-197	A. Petersen	Open	90.00	90.00
94-14-218	Pilgrim's Welcome M-198	A. Petersen	Open	55.00	55.00
94-14-219	We Gather Together M-199	A. Petersen	Open	90.00	90.00
94-14-220	The Wedding Pair M-200	A. Petersen	Open	98.00	98.00
94-14-221	Midnight Snack M-201	A. Petersen	Open	230.00	230.00
94-14-222	The Yard Sale M-202	A. Petersen	Open	325.00	325.00

Wee Forest Folk — **Minutemice**

74-15-001	Mouse on Drum with Fife MM-1	A. Petersen	Closed	9.00	N/A
74-15-002	Mouse on Drum with Fife Wood Base MM-1a	A. Petersen	Closed	9.00	N/A
74-15-003	Mouse on Drum with Black Hat MM-2	A. Petersen	Closed	9.00	N/A
74-15-004	Mouse Carrying Large Drum MM-3	A. Petersen	Closed	8.00	N/A
74-15-005	Concordian On Drum with Glasses MM-4	A. Petersen	Closed	9.00	N/A
74-15-006	Concordian Wood Base w/Tan Coat MM-4a	A. Petersen	Closed	7.50	N/A
74-15-007	Concordian Wood Base w/Hat MM-4b	A. Petersen	Closed	8.00	N/A
74-15-008	Little Fifer on Drum with Fife MM-5	A. Petersen	Closed	8.00	N/A
74-15-009	Little Fifer on Wood Base MM-5a	A. Petersen	Closed	8.00	N/A
74-15-010	Little Fifer on Drum MM-5b	A. Petersen	Closed	8.00	N/A
79-15-011	Minute Mouse and Red Coat MM-9	W. Petersen	Open	28.00	28.00
79-15-012	Concord Minute Mouse MM-10	W. Petersen	Open	14.00	14.00
79-15-013	Red Coat Mouse MM-11	W. Petersen	Open	14.00	14.00

Wee Forest Folk — **Mouse Sports**

75-16-001	Bobsled Three MS-1	A. Petersen	Closed	12.00	400-500.
75-16-002	Skater Mouse MS-2	A. Petersen	Closed	4.50	300-400.
76-16-003	Mouse Skier MS-3	A. Petersen	Closed	4.25	300-400.
76-16-004	Tennis Star MS-4	A. Petersen	Closed	3.75	150-300.
76-16-005	Tennis Star MS-5	A. Petersen	Closed	3.75	150-300.
77-16-006	Skating Star Mouse MS-6	A. Petersen	Closed	3.75	250-400.
77-16-007	Golfer Mouse MS-7	A. Petersen	Closed	5.25	356.00
80-16-008	Skater Mouse MS-8	A. Petersen	Closed	16.50	400-450.
80-16-009	Skier Mouse MS-9	A. Petersen	Open	13.00	40.00
80-16-010	Skier Mouse (Red/Yellow, Red/Green) MS-9	A. Petersen	N/A	13.00	225-400.
81-16-011	Golfer Mouse MS-10	A. Petersen	Closed	15.50	335-465.
82-16-012	Two in a Canoe MS-11	W. Petersen	Open	29.00	62.00
84-16-013	Land Ho! MS-12	A. Petersen	Closed	36.50	235-300.
84-16-014	Tennis Anyone? MS-13	A. Petersen	Closed	18.00	120-145.
85-16-015	Fishin' Chip MS-14	W. Petersen	Closed	46.00	270-290.
89-16-016	Joe Di'Mousio MS-15	A. Petersen	Open	39.00	50.00
94-16-017	Camping Out MS-16	A. Petersen	Open	75.00	75.00

Wee Forest Folk — **Owls**

74-17-001	Mr. and Mrs. Owl O-1	A. Petersen	Closed	6.00	300-400.
74-17-002	Mrs. Owl O-2	A. Petersen	Closed	3.00	150-300.
74-17-003	Mr. Owl O-3	A. Petersen	Closed	3.25	150-300.
75-17-004	Colonial Owls O-4	A. Petersen	Closed	11.50	350-500.
79-17-005	Grad Owl O-5	W. Petersen	Closed	4.25	350-550.
80-17-006	Graduate Owl (On Books) O-6	W. Petersen	Closed	12.00	330-500.

Wee Forest Folk — **Piggies**

78-18-001	Miss Piggy School Marm P-1	A. Petersen	Closed	4.50	225-325.
78-18-002	Piggy Baker P-2	A. Petersen	Closed	4.50	225-425.
78-18-003	Jolly Tar Piggy P-3	A. Petersen	Closed	4.50	200-250.

		ARTIST	EDITION	ISSUE	QUOTE
78-18-004	Picnic Piggies P-4	A. Petersen	Closed	7.75	200-300.
78-18-005	Girl Piglet/Picnic Piggy P-5	A. Petersen	Closed	4.00	100-150.
78-18-006	Boy Piglet/ Picnic Piggy P-6	A. Petersen	Closed	4.00	100-150.
80-18-007	Piggy Ballerina P-7	A. Petersen	Closed	15.50	200-275.
80-18-008	Piggy Policeman P-8	A. Petersen	Closed	17.50	200-350.
80-18-009	Pig O' My Heart P-9	A. Petersen	Closed	12.00	200-275.
80-18-010	Nurse Piggy P-10	A. Petersen	Closed	15.50	200-225.
81-18-011	Holly Hog P-11	A. Petersen	Closed	25.00	350-425.
78-18-012	Piggy Jogger PS-1	A. Petersen	Closed	4.50	125-200.
Wee Forest Folk		**Raccoons**			
77-19-001	Mother Raccoon RC-1	A. Petersen	Closed	4.50	300-475.
77-19-002	Hiker Raccoon RC-2	A. Petersen	Closed	4.50	300-475.
78-19-003	Bird Watcher Raccoon RC-3	A. Petersen	Closed	6.50	410.00
78-19-004	Raccoon Skater RCS-1	A. Petersen	Closed	4.75	250-400.
78-19-005	Raccoon Skier RCS-2	A. Petersen	Closed	6.00	350-450.
Wee Forest Folk		**Robin Hood Series**			
90-20-001	Robin Hood RH-1	A. Petersen	Closed	37.00	40.00
90-20-002	Maid Marion RH-2	A. Petersen	Closed	32.00	85.00
90-20-003	Friar Tuck RH-3	A. Petersen	Closed	32.00	35.00
Wee Forest Folk		**Single Issues**			
72-21-001	Party Mouse in Sailor Suit	A. Petersen	Closed	N/A	N/A
72-21-002	Party Mouse with Bow Tie	A. Petersen	Closed	N/A	N/A
72-21-003	Party Mouse in Plain Dress	A. Petersen	Closed	N/A	N/A
72-21-004	Party Mouse in Polka-Dot Dress	A. Petersen	Closed	N/A	N/A
79-21-005	Ezra Ripley	A. Petersen	Open	40.00	40-95.00
79-21-006	Sarah Ripley	A. Petersen	Open	48.00	48-110.
80-21-007	Cave Mouse	W. Petersen	Closed	N/A	500-600.
80-21-008	Cave Mouse with Baby	W. Petersen	Closed	26.00	N/A
83-21-009	Wee Forest Folk Display Piece	A. Petersen	Open	70.00	70.00
80-21-010	Screech Owl	W. Petersen	Closed	N/A	N/A
Wee Forest Folk		**Tiny Teddies**			
83-22-001	Tiny Teddy TT-1	D. Petersen	Closed	16.00	100.00
84-22-002	Little Teddy T-1	D. Petersen	Closed	20.00	100.00
84-22-003	Sailor Teddy T-2	D. Petersen	Suspd.	20.00	60-95.00
84-22-004	Boo Bear T-3	D. Petersen	Suspd.	20.00	100-155.
84-22-005	Drummer Bear T-4	D. Petersen	Suspd.	22.00	80.00
84-22-006	Santa Bear T-5	D. Petersen	Suspd.	27.00	100-150.
85-22-007	Ride 'em Teddy! T-6	D. Petersen	Suspd.	32.00	85-95.00
85-22-008	Seaside Teddy T-7	D. Petersen	Suspd.	28.00	95-100.
86-22-009	Huggy Bear T-8	D. Petersen	Suspd.	26.00	60-95.00
87-22-010	Wedding Bears T-9	D. Petersen	Suspd.	54.00	125-150.
87-22-011	Christmas Teddy T-10	D. Petersen	Suspd.	26.00	90.00
88-22-012	Hansel & Gretel Bears @ Witch's House T-11	D. Petersen	Suspd.	175.00	245.00
89-22-013	Momma Bear T-12	D. Petersen	Suspd.	27.00	100-150.
Wee Forest Folk		**Wind in the Willows**			
82-23-001	Mole WW-1	A. Petersen	Closed	18.00	200-400.
82-23-002	Badger WW-2	A. Petersen	Closed	18.00	200-400.
82-23-003	Toad WW-3	W. Petersen	Closed	18.00	200-400.
82-23-004	Ratty WW-4	A. Petersen	Closed	18.00	200-400.

GRAPHICS

		ARTIST	EDITION	ISSUE	QUOTE
American Artists		**Fred Stone**			
79-01-001	Affirmed, Steve Cauthen Up	F. Stone	750	100.00	600.00
88-01-002	Alysheba	F. Stone	950	195.00	650.00
92-01-003	The American Triple Crown I, 1948-1978	F. Stone	1,500	325.00	325.00
93-01-004	The American Triple Crown II, 1937-1946	F. Stone	1,500	325.00	325.00
93-01-005	The American Triple Crown III, 1919-1935	F. Stone	1,500	225.00	225.00
83-01-006	Andalusian, The	F. Stone	750	150.00	350.00
81-01-007	Arabians, The	F. Stone	750	115.00	525.00
89-01-008	Battle For The Triple Crown	F. Stone	950	225.00	650.00
80-01-009	Belmont-Bold Forbes, The	F. Stone	500	100.00	375.00
91-01-010	Black Stallion	F. Stone	1,500	225.00	250.00
88-01-011	Cam-Fella	F. Stone	950	175.00	350.00
81-01-012	Contentment	F. Stone	750	115.00	525.00
92-01-013	Dance Smartly-Pat Day Up	F. Stone	950	225.00	325.00
83-01-014	Duel, The	F. Stone	750	150.00	400.00
85-01-015	Eternal Legacy	F. Stone	950	175.00	950.00
80-01-016	Exceller-Bill Shoemaker	F. Stone	500	90.00	800.00
90-01-017	Final Tribute- Secretariat	F. Stone	1,150	265.00	1300.00
87-01-018	First Day, The	F. Stone	950	175.00	225.00
91-01-019	Forego	F. Stone	1,150	225.00	250.00
86-01-020	Forever Friends	F. Stone	950	175.00	725.00
85-01-021	Fred Stone Paints the Sport of Kings (Book)	F. Stone	750	265.00	750.00
80-01-022	Genuine Risk	F. Stone	500	100.00	700.00
91-01-023	Go For Wand-A Candle in the Wind	F. Stone	1,150	225.00	225.00
86-01-024	Great Match Race-Ruffian & Foolish Pleasure	F. Stone	950	175.00	375.00
81-01-025	John Henry-Bill Shoemaker Up	F. Stone	595	160.00	1500.00
85-01-026	John Henry-McCarron Up	F. Stone	750	175.00	500-750.
85-01-027	Kelso	F. Stone	950	175.00	750.00
80-01-028	Kentucky Derby, The	F. Stone	750	100.00	650.00
80-01-029	Kidnapped Mare-Franfreluche	F. Stone	750	115.00	575.00
87-01-030	Lady's Secret	F. Stone	950	175.00	425.00
82-01-031	Man O'War "Final Thunder"	F. Stone	750	175.00	25-3100.
79-01-032	Mare and Foal	F. Stone	500	90.00	500.00
79-01-033	Moment After, The	F. Stone	500	90.00	350.00
86-01-034	Nijinski II	F. Stone	950	175.00	275.00
84-01-035	Northern Dancer	F. Stone	950	175.00	625.00
82-01-036	Off and Running	F. Stone	750	125.00	250-350.
90-01-037	Old Warriors Shoemaker-John Henry	F. Stone	1,950	265.00	595.00
79-01-038	One, Two, Three	F. Stone	500	100.00	1000.00
80-01-039	Pasture Pest, The	F. Stone	500	100.00	875.00
79-01-040	Patience	F. Stone	1,000	90.00	1200.00
89-01-041	Phar Lap	F. Stone	950	195.00	275.00
82-01-042	Power Horses, The	F. Stone	750	125.00	250.00
87-01-043	Rivalry-Alysheba and Bet Twice, The	F. Stone	950	195.00	550.00
79-01-044	Rivals-Affirmed & Alydar, The	F. Stone	500	90.00	500.00
83-01-045	Ruffian-For Only a Moment	F. Stone	750	175.00	1100.00
83-01-046	Secretariat	F. Stone	950	175.00	995-1200
89-01-047	Shoe Bald Eagle	F. Stone	950	195.00	675.00
81-01-048	Shoe-8,000 Wins, The	F. Stone	395	200.00	7000.00
80-01-049	Spectacular Bid	F. Stone	500	65.00	350-400.
XX-01-050	Sunday Silence	F. Stone	950	195.00	425.00
81-01-051	Thoroughbreds, The	F. Stone	750	115.00	425.00
83-01-052	Tranquility	F. Stone	750	150.00	525.00
84-01-053	Turning For Home	F. Stone	750	150.00	425.00
82-01-054	Water Trough, The	F. Stone	750	125.00	575.00
Anheuser-Busch		**Anheuser-Busch**			
94-01-001	Gray Wolf Mirror N4570	H. Droog	2,500	135.00	135.00
Armani		**Wall Art**			
94-01-001	Lady w/Peacock 100A	G. Armani	675	475.00	475.00
94-01-002	Lady w/Mirror 101A	G. Armani	675	475.00	475.00
94-01-003	La Pieta 102A	G. Armani	675	475.00	475.00
94-01-004	The Embrace 103A	G. Armani	675	475.00	475.00
94-01-005	Wind Song 104A	G. Armani	675	475.00	475.00
94-01-006	Abiding Love 105A	G. Armani	675	475.00	475.00
94-01-007	Lady w/Peacock A/P 106A	G. Armani	25	675.00	675.00
94-01-008	Lady w/Mirror A/P 107A	G. Armani	25	675.00	675.00
94-01-009	La Pieta A/P 108A	G. Armani	25	675.00	675.00
94-01-010	The Embrace A/P 109A	G. Armani	25	675.00	675.00
94-01-011	Wind Song A/P 110A	G. Armani	25	675.00	675.00
94-01-012	Abiding Love A/P 111A	G. Armani	25	675.00	675.00
Artaffects		**Perillo**			
77-01-001	Madre, S/N	G. Perillo	500	125.00	250-950.
78-01-002	Madonna of the Plains, S/N	G. Perillo	500	125.00	200-600.
78-01-003	Snow Pals, S/N	G. Perillo	500	125.00	150-550.
79-01-004	Sioux Scout and Buffalo Hunt, matched set	G. Perillo	500	150.00	250-850.
80-01-005	Babysitter, S/N	G. Perillo	3,000	45.00	125-350.
80-01-006	Puppies, S/N	G. Perillo	3,000	45.00	200-450.
81-01-007	Peaceable Kingdom, S/N	G. Perillo	950	100.00	375-800.
82-01-008	Tinker, S/N	G. Perillo	3,000	45.00	100-350.
82-01-009	Tender Love, S/N	G. Perillo	950	75.00	125-450.
82-01-010	Lonesome Cowboy, S/N	G. Perillo	950	75.00	100-450.
82-01-011	Chief Pontiac, S/N	G. Perillo	950	75.00	100.00
82-01-012	Hoofbeats, S/N	G. Perillo	950	100.00	150.00
82-01-013	Indian Style, S/N	G. Perillo	950	75.00	100.00
82-01-014	Maria, S/N	G. Perillo	550	150.00	350.00
82-01-015	Papoose, S/N	G. Perillo	950	125.00	125.00
83-01-016	The Moment Poster, S/N	G. Perillo	495	20.00	60.00
84-01-017	Out of the Forest, S/N	G. Perillo	Unkn.	Unkn.	450.00
84-01-018	Navajo Love, S/N	G. Perillo	300	125.00	700.00
85-01-019	Chief Crazy Horse, S/N	G. Perillo	950	125.00	450.00
85-01-020	Chief Sitting Bull, S/N	G. Perillo	500	125.00	350.00
85-01-021	Marigold, S/N	G. Perillo	500	125.00	150-450.
85-01-022	Whirlaway, S/N	G. Perillo	950	125.00	150.00
85-01-023	Secretariat, S/N	G. Perillo	950	125.00	150.00
86-01-024	The Rescue, S/N	G. Perillo	325	150.00	200-550.
86-01-025	War Pony, S/N	G. Perillo	325	150.00	250.00
86-01-026	Learning His Ways, S/N	G. Perillo	325	150.00	250.00
86-01-027	The Pout, S/N	G. Perillo	325	150.00	200-450.
88-01-028	Magnificent Seven, S/N	G. Perillo	950	125.00	125.00
88-01-029	By the Stream, S/N	G. Perillo	950	100.00	150.00
90-01-030	The Pack, S/N	G. Perillo	950	150.00	250.00
Artaffects		**Grand Gallery Collection (Framed)**			
88-02-001	Tender Love	G. Perillo	2,500	75.00	90.00
88-02-002	Brave & Free	G. Perillo	2,500	75.00	175.00
88-02-003	Noble Heritage	G. Perillo	2,500	75.00	90.00
88-02-004	Chief Crazy Horse	G. Perillo	2,500	75.00	90.00
88-02-005	The Cheyenne Nation	G. Perillo	2,500	75.00	90.00
88-02-006	Late Mail	G. Perillo	2,500	75.00	90.00
88-02-007	The Peaceable Kingdom	G. Perillo	2,500	75.00	100.00
88-02-008	Chief Red Cloud	G. Perillo	2,500	75.00	90.00
88-02-009	The Last Frontier	G. Perillo	2,500	75.00	95.00
88-02-010	Native American	G. Perillo	2,500	75.00	90.00
88-02-011	Blackfoot Hunter	G. Perillo	2,500	75.00	90.00
88-02-012	Lily of the Mohawks	G. Perillo	2,500	75.00	90.00
88-02-013	Amy	MaGo	2,500	75.00	90.00
88-02-014	Mischief	MaGo	2,500	75.00	90.00
88-02-015	Tomorrows	MaGo	2,500	75.00	90.00
88-02-016	Lauren	MaGo	2,500	75.00	90.00
88-02-017	Visiting the Doctor	R. Sauber	2,500	75.00	90.00
88-02-018	Home Sweet Home	R. Sauber	2,500	75.00	90.00
88-02-019	God Bless America	R. Sauber	2,500	75.00	90.00
88-02-020	The Wedding	R. Sauber	2,500	75.00	90.00
88-02-021	Motherhood	R. Sauber	2,500	75.00	90.00
88-02-022	Venice	L. Marchetti	2,500	75.00	90.00
88-02-023	Paris	L. Marchetti	2,500	75.00	90.00
Artaffects		**Captured On Canvas**			
91-03-001	Brave and Free	G. Perillo	Open	195.00	195.00
Artaffects		**Members Only Limited Edition Redemption Offerings**			
84-04-001	Out of the Forest (Litho)	G. Perillo	Yr.Iss.	50.00	50.00
Artaffects		**Limited Edition Free Gifts to Members**			
83-05-001	Perillo/Cougar (Poster)	G. Perillo	Yr.Iss.	Gift	N/A
85-05-002	Litte Plum Blossom (Poster)	G. Perillo	Yr.Iss.	Gift	N/A
Artaffects		**Sauber**			
82-06-001	Butterfly	R. Sauber	3,000	45.00	100.00
Artaffects		**Mago**			
88-07-001	Serenity	Mago	950	95.00	200.00
88-07-002	Beth	Mago	950	95.00	200.00
88-07-003	Jessica	Mago	550	225.00	325.00
88-07-004	Sebastian	Mago	Pair	Pair	Pair
Artaffects		**Deneen**			
88-08-001	Twentieth Century Limited	J. Deneen	950	75.00	75.00
88-08-002	Santa Fe	J. Deneen	950	75.00	75.00
88-08-003	Empire Builder	J. Deneen	950	75.00	75.00
Marty Bell		**Limited Edition Lithographs**			
87-01-001	Alderton Village	M. Bell	S/O	235.00	750-899.
88-01-002	Allington Castle, Kent	M. Bell	1,800	540.00	540.00
92-01-003	Antiques of Rye	M. Bell	1,100	220.00	220.00
90-01-004	Arbor Cottage	M. Bell	S/O	130.00	150-250.
93-01-005	Arundel Row	M. Bell	750	130.00	130.00
91-01-006	Bay Tree Cottage, Rye	M. Bell	S/O	230.00	230-520.
81-01-007	Bibury Cottage	M. Bell	S/O	280.00	800-1000
81-01-008	Big Daddy's Shoe	M. Bell	S/O	64.00	150-300.
88-01-009	Bishop's Roses, The	M. Bell	S/O	220.00	300-500.
89-01-010	Blush of Spring	M. Bell	S/O	96.00	120-160.
88-01-011	Bodiam Twilight	M. Bell	S/O	520.00	900-1100
88-01-012	Brendon Hills Lane	M. Bell	900	304.00	304.00
92-01-013	Briarwood	M. Bell	S/O	220.00	220.00
93-01-014	Broadway Cottage	M. Bell	750	330.00	330.00

		ARTIST	EDITION	ISSUE	QUOTE
87-01-015	Broughton Village	M. Bell	S/O	128.00	400-500.
84-01-016	Brown Eyes	M. Bell	S/O	296.00	296.00
90-01-017	Bryants Puddle Thatch	M. Bell	S/O	130.00	150-295.
86-01-018	Burford Village Store	M. Bell	S/O	106.00	500-1500
93-01-019	Byfleet	M. Bell	900	180.00	180.00
94-01-020	Canterbury Roses	M. Bell	750	180.00	180.00
81-01-021	Castle Combe Cottage	M. Bell	S/O	230.00	795.00
93-01-022	Castle Tearoom, The	M. Bell	S/O	88.00	88.00
87-01-023	Chaplains Garden, The	M. Bell	S/O	235.00	1-2000.
92-01-024	Chelsea Roses	M. Bell	750	298.00	298.00
89-01-025	Cherry Tree Thatch	M. Bell	2,400	88.00	88.00
91-01-026	Childswickham Morning	M. Bell	S/O	396.00	396.00
87-01-027	Chippenham Farm	M. Bell	S/O	120.00	300-900.
88-01-028	Clove Cottage	M. Bell	S/O	128.00	225-600.
88-01-029	Clover Lane Cottage	M. Bell	S/O	272.00	750-1400
91-01-030	Cobblestone	M. Bell	1,200	374.00	374.00
93-01-031	Coln St. Aldwyn's	M. Bell	1,000	730.00	730.00
86-01-032	Cotswold Parish Church	M. Bell	S/O	98.00	500-1500
88-01-033	Cotswold Twilight	M. Bell	S/O	128.00	200-495.
93-01-034	Cottontail Lodge	M. Bell	700	375.00	375.00
91-01-035	Cozy Cottage	M. Bell	S/O	130.00	130.00
93-01-036	Craigton Cottage	M. Bell	500	130.00	130.00
82-01-037	Crossroads Cottage	M. Bell	S/O	38.00	200.00
92-01-038	Devon Cottage	M. Bell	900	374.00	374.00
91-01-039	Devon Roses	M. Bell	S/O	78.00	195-500.
91-01-040	Dorset Roses	M. Bell	S/O	96.00	195.00
87-01-041	Dove Cottage Garden	M. Bell	S/O	260.00	304-495.
87-01-042	Driftstone Manor	M. Bell	S/O	440.00	2500.00
87-01-043	Ducksbridge Cottage	M. Bell	S/O	400.00	2-2400.
87-01-044	Eashing Cottage	M. Bell	S/O	120.00	200-400.
92-01-045	East Sussex Roses (Archival)	M. Bell	S/O	184.00	184.00
89-01-046	Elegance of Spring	M. Bell	1,800	396.00	396.00
89-01-047	Fernbank Cottage	M. Bell	2,400	96.00	88.00
85-01-048	Fiddleford Cottage	M. Bell	S/O	78.00	1950.00
89-01-049	Fireside Christmas	M. Bell	S/O	136.00	750.00
93-01-050	Flower Box, The	M. Bell	900	300.00	300.00
88-01-051	Friday Street Lane	M. Bell	S/O	280.00	450.00
89-01-052	The Game Keeper's Cottage	M. Bell	S/O	560.00	18-2000.
92-01-053	Garlands Flower Shop	M. Bell	S/O	220.00	220.00
88-01-054	Ginger Cottage	M. Bell	S/O	320.00	550-800.
89-01-055	Glory Cottage	M. Bell	S/O	96.00	96.00
89-01-056	Goater's Cottage	M. Bell	S/O	368.00	400-560.
90-01-057	Gomshall Flower Shop	M. Bell	S/O	396.00	12-2000.
93-01-058	Graffam House	M. Bell	900	180.00	180.00
87-01-059	Halfway Cottage	M. Bell	S/O	260.00	300-500.
92-01-060	Happy Heart Cottage	M. Bell	1,200	368.00	368.00
89-01-061	Hideaway Cottage	M. Bell	2,400	88.00	88.00
92-01-062	Hollybush	M. Bell	1,200	560.00	560.00
91-01-063	Horsham Farmhouse	M. Bell	1,200	180.00	180.00
86-01-064	Housewives Choice	M. Bell	S/O	98.00	750-1000
88-01-065	Icomb Village Garden	M. Bell	S/O	620.00	13-1500.
88-01-066	Jasmine Thatch	M. Bell	S/O	272.00	495.00
89-01-067	Larkspur Cottage	M. Bell	S/O	220.00	495.00
85-01-068	Little Boxford	M. Bell	S/O	78.00	300-900.
91-01-069	Little Bromley Lodge	M. Bell	1,200	456.00	456.00
91-01-070	Little Timbers	M. Bell	S/O	130.00	130.00
87-01-071	Little Tulip Thatch	M. Bell	S/O	120.00	400-700.
90-01-072	Little Well Thatch	M. Bell	S/O	130.00	150-250.
90-01-073	Longparish Cottage	M. Bell	S/O	368.00	300-550.
90-01-074	Longstock Lane	M. Bell	S/O	130.00	150-250.
86-01-075	Lorna Doone Cottage	M. Bell	S/O	380.00	8-9000.
90-01-076	Lower Brockhampton Manor	M. Bell	S/O	640.00	1800.00
88-01-077	Lullabye Cottage	M. Bell	S/O	220.00	300-400.
90-01-078	Martin's Market, Rye	M. Bell	1,100	304.00	304.00
87-01-079	May Cottage	M. Bell	S/O	120.00	200-699.
88-01-080	Meadow School	M. Bell	S/O	220.00	350.00
85-01-081	Meadowlark Cottage	M. Bell	S/O	78.00	450-699.
90-01-082	Mermaid Inn, Rye, The	M. Bell	1,100	560.00	560.00
87-01-083	Millpond, Stockbridge, The	M. Bell	S/O	120.00	999-1600
92-01-084	Miss Hathaway's Garden	M. Bell	1,800	694.00	694.00
87-01-085	Morning Glory Cottage	M. Bell	S/O	120.00	450-599.
88-01-086	Morning's Glow	M. Bell	S/O	280.00	320-650.
94-01-087	Mother Hubbard's Garden	M. Bell	2-Yr.	230.00	230.00
88-01-088	Murrle Cottage	M. Bell	S/O	320.00	450-650.
83-01-089	Nestlewood	M. Bell	S/O	300.00	2500.00
89-01-090	Northcote Lane	M. Bell	S/O	88.00	88.00
89-01-091	Old Beams Cottage	M. Bell	S/O	368.00	650.00
88-01-092	Old Bridge, Grasmere	M. Bell	S/O	640.00	640.00
90-01-093	Old Hertfordshire Thatch	M. Bell	S/O	396.00	700-1500
93-01-094	Old Mother Hubbard's Cottage	M. Bell	2-Yr.	230.00	230.00
89-01-095	Overbrook	M. Bell	S/O	220.00	220.00
92-01-096	Pangbourne on Thames	M. Bell	900	304.00	304.00
84-01-097	Penshurst Tea Rooms (Archival)	M. Bell	S/O	335.00	950.00
84-01-098	Penshurst Tea Rooms (Canvas)	M. Bell	S/O	335.00	15-3600.
89-01-099	Periwinkle Tea Rooms, The	M. Bell	2,400	694.00	694.00
89-01-100	Pride of Spring	M. Bell	S/O	96.00	200-400.
89-01-101	Primrose Cottage	M. Bell	2,400	88.00	88.00
88-01-102	Rodway Cottage	M. Bell	S/O	694.00	700-1500
89-01-103	Rose Bedroom, The	M. Bell	S/O	388.00	388.00
90-01-104	Sanctuary	M. Bell	S/O	220.00	350.00
82-01-105	Sandhills Cottage	M. Bell	S/O	38.00	38.00
88-01-106	Sandy Lane Thatch	M. Bell	S/O	380.00	500.00
82-01-107	School Lane Cottage	M. Bell	S/O	38.00	38.00
93-01-108	Selborne Cottage	M. Bell	750	300.00	300.00
92-01-109	Sheffield Roses	M. Bell	750	298.00	298.00
88-01-110	Shere Village Antiques	M. Bell	S/O	272.00	304-699.
93-01-111	Simon the Pieman, Rye	M. Bell	1,100	240.00	240.00
91-01-112	Somerset Inn	M. Bell	1,200	180.00	180.00
93-01-113	Speldhurst Farm	M. Bell	1,200	248.00	248.00
81-01-114	Spring in the Santa Ynez	M. Bell	S/O	400.00	950.00
91-01-115	Springtime at Scotney	M. Bell	S/O	730.00	950-1200
89-01-116	St. Martin's Ashurst	M. Bell	S/O	344.00	344.00
92-01-117	Strand Quay, Rye, The	M. Bell	1,100	248.00	248.00
90-01-118	Summer's Garden	M. Bell	S/O	78.00	400-800.
85-01-119	Summers Glow	M. Bell	S/O	98.00	600-1000
94-01-120	Summer's Song, Scotney	M. Bell	1,200	730.00	730.00
87-01-121	Sunrise Thatch	M. Bell	S/O	120.00	200-300.
85-01-122	Surrey Garden House	M. Bell	S/O	98.00	850-1499
91-01-123	Swan Cottage Tea Room, Rye	M. Bell	1,100	176.00	176.00
89-01-124	Sweet Blue	M. Bell	1,800	396.00	396.00
90-01-125	Sweetheart Thatch	M. Bell	S/O	220.00	220.00

		ARTIST	EDITION	ISSUE	QUOTE
85-01-126	Sweet Pine Cottage	M. Bell	S/O	78.00	350-1499
88-01-127	Sweet Twilight	M. Bell	S/O	220.00	350-600.
91-01-128	Tea Time	M. Bell	S/O	130.00	130-350.
82-01-129	Thatchcolm Cottage	M. Bell	S/O	38.00	38.00
89-01-130	Thimble Pub, The	M. Bell	S/O	344.00	344.00
93-01-131	Tithe Barn Cottage	M. Bell	900	368.00	368.00
93-01-132	Umbrella Cottage	M. Bell	900	176.00	176.00
91-01-133	Upper Chute	M. Bell	S/O	496.00	850-1500
92-01-134	Valentine Cottage	M. Bell	900	304.00	304.00
87-01-135	The Vicar's Gate	M. Bell	S/O	110.00	600-1500
87-01-136	Wakehurst Place	M. Bell	S/O	480.00	2-2500.
87-01-137	Well Cottage, Sandy Lane	M. Bell	S/O	440.00	650-1500
91-01-138	Wepham Cottage	M. Bell	S/O	396.00	1200.00
84-01-139	West Kington Dell	M. Bell	S/O	215.00	480-999.
94-01-140	Westminster Roses	M. Bell	750	180.00	180.00
90-01-141	Weston Manor	M. Bell	900	694.00	694.00
92-01-142	West Sussex Roses (Archival)	M. Bell	S/O	184.00	184.00
87-01-143	White Lilac Thatch	M. Bell	S/O	260.00	400-700.
92-01-144	Wild Rose Cottage	M. Bell	S/O	248.00	248.00
85-01-145	Windsong Cottage	M. Bell	S/O	156.00	350-799.
91-01-146	Windward Cottage, Rye	M. Bell	S/O	228.00	550-635.
91-01-147	Ye Olde Bell, Rye	M. Bell	1,100	196.00	196.00
86-01-148	York Garden Shop	M. Bell	S/O	98.00	250-999.
Marty Bell		**Members Only Collectors Club**			
91-02-001	Little Thatch Twilight	M. Bell	Closed	288.00	320-380.
91-02-002	Charter Rose, The	M. Bell	Closed	Gift	N/A
92-02-003	Candle At Eventide	M. Bell	Closed	Gift	N/A
92-02-004	Blossom Lane	M. Bell	Closed	288.00	288.00
93-02-005	Laverstoke Lodge	M. Bell	Closed	328.00	328.00
93-02-006	Chideock Gate	M. Bell	Closed	Gift	N/A
94-02-007	Hummingbird Hill	M. Bell	Yr.Iss.	320.00	320.00
94-02-008	The Hummingbird	M. Bell	Yr.Iss.	Gift	N/A
Marty Bell		**America the Beautiful**			
93-03-001	Abbey, The	M. Bell	750	400.00	400.00
94-03-002	Bayside Morning	M. Bell	750	400.00	400.00
93-03-003	Idaho Hideaway	M. Bell	750	400.00	400.00
93-03-004	Jones Victorian	M. Bell	S/O	400.00	400.00
94-03-005	Love Tide	M. Bell	750	400.00	400.00
94-03-006	My Garden	M. Bell	750	430.00	430.00
93-03-007	Turlock Spring	M. Bell	500	700.00	700.00
94-03-008	Woodland Garden	M. Bell	750	460.00	460.00
Marty Bell		**Christmas**			
90-04-001	Ready For Christmas	M. Bell	S/O	148.00	495.00
91-04-002	Christmas in Rochester	M. Bell	S/O	148.00	275-350.
92-04-003	McCoy's Toy Shoppe	M. Bell	S/O	148.00	350.00
93-04-004	Christmas Treasures	M. Bell	900	200.00	200.00
94-04-005	Rocky Mountain Christmas	M. Bell	750	400.00	400.00
Circle Fine Art		**Rockwell**			
XX-01-001	American Family Folio	N. Rockwell	200	Unkn.	17500.00
XX-01-002	The Artist at Work	N. Rockwell	130	Unkn.	3500.00
XX-01-003	At the Barber	N. Rockwell	200	Unkn.	4900.00
XX-01-004	Autumn	N. Rockwell	200	Unkn.	3500.00
XX-01-005	Autumn/Japon	N. Rockwell	25	Unkn.	3600.00
XX-01-006	Aviary	N. Rockwell	200	Unkn.	4200.00
XX-01-007	Barbershop Quartet	N. Rockwell	200	Unkn.	4200.00
XX-01-008	Baseball	N. Rockwell	200	Unkn.	3600.00
XX-01-009	Ben Franklin's Philadelphia	N. Rockwell	200	Unkn.	3600.00
XX-01-010	Ben's Belles	N. Rockwell	200	Unkn.	3500.00
XX-01-011	The Big Day	N. Rockwell	200	Unkn.	3400.00
XX-01-012	The Big Top	N. Rockwell	148	Unkn.	2800.00
XX-01-013	Blacksmith Shop	N. Rockwell	200	Unkn.	6300.00
XX-01-014	Bookseller	N. Rockwell	200	Unkn.	2700.00
XX-01-015	Bookseller/Japon	N. Rockwell	25	Unkn.	2750.00
XX-01-016	The Bridge	N. Rockwell	200	Unkn.	3100.00
XX-01-017	Cat	N. Rockwell	200	Unkn.	3400.00
XX-01-018	Cat/Collotype	N. Rockwell	200	Unkn.	4000.00
XX-01-019	Cheering	N. Rockwell	200	Unkn.	3600.00
XX-01-020	Children at Window	N. Rockwell	200	Unkn.	3600.00
XX-01-021	Church	N. Rockwell	200	Unkn.	3400.00
XX-01-022	Church/Collotype	N. Rockwell	200	Unkn.	4000.00
XX-01-023	Circus	N. Rockwell	200	Unkn.	2650.00
XX-01-024	County Agricultural Agent	N. Rockwell	200	Unkn.	3900.00
XX-01-025	The Critic	N. Rockwell	200	Unkn.	4650.00
XX-01-026	Day in the Life of a Boy	N. Rockwell	200	Unkn.	6200.00
XX-01-027	Day in the Life of a Boy/Japon	N. Rockwell	25	Unkn.	6500.00
XX-01-028	Debut	N. Rockwell	200	Unkn.	3600.00
XX-01-029	Discovery	N. Rockwell	200	Unkn.	5900.00
XX-01-030	Doctor and Boy	N. Rockwell	200	Unkn.	9400.00
XX-01-031	Doctor and Doll-Signed	N. Rockwell	200	Unkn.	11900.00
XX-01-032	Dressing Up/Pencil	N. Rockwell	200	Unkn.	3700.00
XX-01-033	Dressing Up/Ink	N. Rockwell	60	Unkn.	4400.00
XX-01-034	The Drunkard	N. Rockwell	200	Unkn.	3600.00
XX-01-035	The Expected and Unexpected	N. Rockwell	200	Unkn.	3700.00
XX-01-036	Family Tree	N. Rockwell	200	Unkn.	5900.00
XX-01-037	Fido's House	N. Rockwell	200	Unkn.	3600.00
XX-01-038	Football Mascot	N. Rockwell	200	Unkn.	3700.00
XX-01-039	Four Seasons Folio	N. Rockwell	200	Unkn.	13500.00
XX-01-040	Four Seasons Folio/Japon	N. Rockwell	25	Unkn.	14000.00
XX-01-041	Freedom from Fear-Signed	N. Rockwell	200	Unkn.	6400.00
XX-01-042	Freedom from Want-Signed	N. Rockwell	200	Unkn.	6400.00
XX-01-043	Freedom of Speech-Signed	N. Rockwell	200	Unkn.	6400.00
XX-01-044	Freedom of Religion-Signed	N. Rockwell	200	Unkn.	6400.00
XX-01-045	Gaiety Dance Team	N. Rockwell	200	Unkn.	4300.00
XX-01-046	Girl at Mirror-Signed	N. Rockwell	200	Unkn.	8400.00
XX-01-047	The Golden Age	N. Rockwell	200	Unkn.	3500.00
XX-01-048	Golden Rule-Signed	N. Rockwell	200	Unkn.	4400.00
XX-01-049	Golf	N. Rockwell	200	Unkn.	3600.00
XX-01-050	Gossips	N. Rockwell	200	Unkn.	5000.00
XX-01-051	Gossips/Japon	N. Rockwell	25	Unkn.	5100.00
XX-01-052	Grotto	N. Rockwell	200	Unkn.	3400.00
XX-01-053	Grotto/Collotype	N. Rockwell	200	Unkn.	4000.00
XX-01-054	High Dive	N. Rockwell	200	Unkn.	3400.00
XX-01-055	The Homecoming	N. Rockwell	200	Unkn.	3700.00
XX-01-056	The House	N. Rockwell	200	Unkn.	3700.00
XX-01-057	Huck Finn Folio	N. Rockwell	200	Unkn.	35000.00
XX-01-058	Ichabod Crane	N. Rockwell	200	Unkn.	6700.00
XX-01-059	The Inventor	N. Rockwell	200	Unkn.	4100.00
XX-01-060	Jerry	N. Rockwell	200	Unkn.	4700.00
XX-01-061	Jim Got Down on His Knees	N. Rockwell	200	Unkn.	4500.00

		ARTIST	EDITION	ISSUE	QUOTE
XX-01-062	Lincoln	N. Rockwell	200	Unkn.	11400.00
XX-01-063	Lobsterman	N. Rockwell	200	Unkn.	5500.00
XX-01-064	Lobsterman/Japon	N. Rockwell	25	Unkn.	5750.00
XX-01-065	Marriage License	N. Rockwell	200	Unkn.	6900.00
XX-01-066	Medicine	N. Rockwell	200	Unkn.	3400.00
XX-01-067	Medicine/Color Litho	N. Rockwell	200	Unkn.	4000.00
XX-01-068	Miss Mary Jane	N. Rockwell	200	Unkn.	4500.00
XX-01-069	Moving Day	N. Rockwell	200	Unkn.	3900.00
XX-01-070	My Hand Shook	N. Rockwell	200	Unkn.	4500.00
XX-01-071	Music Hath Charms	N. Rockwell	200	Unkn.	4200.00
XX-01-072	Out the Window	N. Rockwell	200	Unkn.	3400.00
XX-01-073	Out the Window/ Collotype	N. Rockwell	200	Unkn.	4000.00
XX-01-074	Outward Bound-Signed	N. Rockwell	200	Unkn.	7900.00
XX-01-075	Poor Richard's Almanac	N. Rockwell	200	Unkn.	24000.00
XX-01-076	Prescription	N. Rockwell	200	Unkn.	4900.00
XX-01-077	Prescription/Japon	N. Rockwell	25	Unkn.	5000.00
XX-01-078	The Problem We All Live With	N. Rockwell	200	Unkn.	4500.00
XX-01-079	Puppies	N. Rockwell	200	Unkn.	3700.00
XX-01-080	Raliegh the Dog	N. Rockwell	200	Unkn.	3900.00
XX-01-081	Rocket Ship	N. Rockwell	200	Unkn.	3650.00
XX-01-082	The Royal Crown	N. Rockwell	200	Unkn.	3500.00
XX-01-083	Runaway	N. Rockwell	200	Unkn.	3800.00
XX-01-084	Runaway/Japon	N. Rockwell	200	Unkn.	5700.00
XX-01-085	Safe and Sound	N. Rockwell	200	Unkn.	3800.00
XX-01-086	Saturday People	N. Rockwell	200	Unkn.	3300.00
XX-01-087	Save Me	N. Rockwell	200	Unkn.	3600.00
XX-01-088	Saying Grace-Signed	N. Rockwell	200	Unkn.	7400.00
XX-01-089	School Days Folio	N. Rockwell	200	Unkn.	14000.00
XX-01-090	Schoolhouse	N. Rockwell	200	Unkn.	4500.00
XX-01-091	Schoolhouse/Japon	N. Rockwell	25	Unkn.	4650.00
XX-01-092	See America First	N. Rockwell	200	Unkn.	5650.00
XX-01-093	See America First/Japon	N. Rockwell	25	Unkn.	6100.00
XX-01-094	Settling In	N. Rockwell	200	Unkn.	3600.00
XX-01-095	Shuffelton's Barbershop	N. Rockwell	200	Unkn.	7400.00
XX-01-096	Smoking	N. Rockwell	200	Unkn.	3400.00
XX-01-097	Smoking/Collotype	N. Rockwell	200	Unkn.	4000.00
XX-01-098	Spanking	N. Rockwell	200	Unkn.	3400.00
XX-01-099	Spanking/ Collotype	N. Rockwell	200	Unkn.	4000.00
XX-01-100	Spelling Bee	N. Rockwell	200	Unkn.	6500.00
XX-01-101	Spring	N. Rockwell	200	Unkn.	3500.00
XX-01-102	Spring/Japon	N. Rockwell	25	Unkn.	3600.00
XX-01-103	Spring Flowers	N. Rockwell	200	Unkn.	5200.00
XX-01-104	Study for the Doctor's Office	N. Rockwell	200	Unkn.	6000.00
XX-01-105	Studying	N. Rockwell	200	Unkn.	3600.00
XX-01-106	Summer	N. Rockwell	200	Unkn.	3500.00
XX-01-107	Summer/Japon	N. Rockwell	25	Unkn.	3600.00
XX-01-108	Summer Stock	N. Rockwell	200	Unkn.	4900.00
XX-01-109	Summer Stock/Japon	N. Rockwell	25	Unkn.	5000.00
XX-01-110	The Teacher	N. Rockwell	200	Unkn.	3400.00
XX-01-111	The Teacher/Japon	N. Rockwell	25	Unkn.	3500.00
XX-01-112	Teacher's Pet	N. Rockwell	200	Unkn.	3600.00
XX-01-113	The Texan	N. Rockwell	200	Unkn.	3700.00
XX-01-114	Then For Three Minutes	N. Rockwell	200	Unkn.	4500.00
XX-01-115	Then Miss Watson	N. Rockwell	200	Unkn.	4500.00
XX-01-116	There Warn't No Harm	N. Rockwell	200	Unkn.	4500.00
XX-01-117	Three Farmers	N. Rockwell	200	Unkn.	3600.00
XX-01-118	Ticketseller	N. Rockwell	200	Unkn.	4200.00
XX-01-119	Ticketseller/Japon	N. Rockwell	25	Unkn.	4400.00
XX-01-120	Tom Sawyer Color Suite	N. Rockwell	200	Unkn.	30000.00
XX-01-121	Tom Sawyer Folio	N. Rockwell	200	Unkn.	26500.00
XX-01-122	Top of the World	N. Rockwell	200	Unkn.	4200.00
XX-01-123	Trumpeter	N. Rockwell	200	Unkn.	3900.00
XX-01-124	Trumpeter/Japon	N. Rockwell	25	Unkn.	4100.00
XX-01-125	Two O'Clock Feeding	N. Rockwell	200	Unkn.	3600.00
XX-01-126	The Village Smithy	N. Rockwell	200	Unkn.	3500.00
XX-01-127	Welcome	N. Rockwell	200	Unkn.	3500.00
XX-01-128	Wet Paint	N. Rockwell	200	Unkn.	3800.00
XX-01-129	When I Lit My Candle	N. Rockwell	200	Unkn.	4500.00
XX-01-130	White Washing	N. Rockwell	200	Unkn.	3400.00
XX-01-131	Whitewashing the Fence/Collotype	N. Rockwell	200	Unkn.	4000.00
XX-01-132	Window Washer	N. Rockwell	200	Unkn.	4800.00
XX-01-133	Winter	N. Rockwell	200	Unkn.	3500.00
XX-01-134	Winter/Japon	N. Rockwell	25	Unkn.	3600.00
XX-01-135	Ye Old Print Shoppe	N. Rockwell	200	Unkn.	3500.00
XX-01-136	Your Eyes is Lookin'	N. Rockwell	200	Unkn.	4500.00
Cross Gallery, Inc.	**Limited Edition Prints**				
83-01-001	Isbaaloo Eetshiileehcheek(Sorting Her Beads)	P.A. Cross	S/O	150.00	1750.00
83-01-002	Ayla-Sah-Xuh-Xah (Pretty Colours, Many Designs)	P.A. Cross	S/O	150.00	450.00
84-01-003	Blue Beaded Hair Ties	P.A. Cross	S/O	85.00	330.00
84-01-004	Profile of Caroline	P.A. Cross	S/O	85.00	185.00
84-01-005	Whistling Water Clan Girl: Crow Indian	P.A. Cross	S/O	85.00	85.00
84-01-006	Thick Lodge Clan Boy: Crow Indian	P.A. Cross	475	85.00	85.00
85-01-007	The Water Vision	P.A. Cross	S/O	150.00	325.00
86-01-008	The Winter Shawl	P.A. Cross	S/O	150.00	1600.00
86-01-009	The Red Capote	P.A. Cross	S/O	150.00	850.00
86-01-010	Grand Entry	P.A. Cross	S/O	85.00	85.00
84-01-011	Winter Morning	P.A. Cross	S/O	185.00	1450.00
84-01-012	Dii-tah-shteh Ee-wihza-ahook (A Coat of much Value)	P.A. Cross	S/O	90.00	740.00
87-01-013	Caroline	P.A. Cross	S/O	45.00	145.00
87-01-014	Tina	P.A. Cross	S/O	45.00	110.00
87-01-015	The Red Necklace	P.A. Cross	S/O	90.00	210.00
87-01-016	The Elkskin Robe	P.A. Cross	S/O	190.00	640.00
88-01-017	Ma-a-luppis-she-La-dus (She is above everything, nothing can touch her)	P.A. Cross	S/O	190.00	525.00
88-01-018	Dance Apache	P.A. Cross	S/O	190.00	360.00
89-01-019	The Dreamer	P.A. Cross	S/O	190.00	600.00
89-01-020	Chey-ayjeh: Prey	P.A. Cross	S/O	190.00	325-600.
89-01-021	Teesa Waits To Dance	P.A. Cross	S/O	135.00	180.00
89-01-022	Biaachee-itah Bah-achbeh	P.A. Cross	S/O	225.00	525.00
90-01-023	Baape Ochia (Night Wind, Turquoise)	P.A. Cross	S/O	185.00	370.00
90-01-024	Ishia-Kahda #1 (Quiet One)	P.A. Cross	S/O	185.00	400.00
90-01-025	Eshte	P.A. Cross	S/O	185.00	200.00
91-01-026	The Blue Shawl	P.A. Cross	S/O	185.00	275.00
91-01-027	Ashpahdua Hagay Ashae-Gyoke (My Home & Heart Is Crow)	P.A. Cross	S/O	225.00	225-350.
94-01-028	Winter Girl Bride	P.A. Cross	1,730	225.00	225.00
Cross Gallery, Inc.	**Star Quilt Series**				
85-02-001	Winter Warmth	P.A. Cross	S/O	150.00	900-1215

		ARTIST	EDITION	ISSUE	QUOTE
86-02-002	Reflections	P.A. Cross	S/O	185.00	865.00
88-02-003	The Quilt Makers	P.A. Cross	S/O	190.00	1200.00
Cross Gallery, Inc.	**Wolf Series**				
85-03-001	Dii-tah-shteh Bii-wik; Chedah-bah liidah	P.A. Cross	S/O	185.00	3275.00
87-03-002	The Morning Star Gives Long Otter His Hoop Medicine Power	P.A. Cross	S/O	190.00	18-2500.
89-03-003	Biagoht Eecuebeh Hehsheesh-Checah: (Red Ridinghood and Her Wolves), Gift I	P.A. Cross	S/O	225.00	15-2500.
90-03-004	Agninaug Amaguut;Inupiag (Women With Her Wolves)	P.A. Cross	S/O	325.00	350-750.
93-03-005	Ahmah-ghut, Tuhtu-loo; Eelahn-nuht Kah-auhk (Wolves and Caribou; My Furs and My Friends)	P.A. Cross	1,050	255.00	255.00
Cross Gallery, Inc.	**Half Breed Series**				
89-04-001	Ach-hua Dlubh: (Body Two), Half Breed	P.A. Cross	S/O	190.00	1450.00
89-04-002	Ach-hua Dlubh: (Body Two), Half Breed II	P.A. Cross	S/O	225.00	800-1100
90-04-003	Ach-hua Dlubh: (Body Two), Half Breed III	P.A. Cross	S/O	225.00	850.00
Cross Gallery, Inc.	**Limited Edition Original Graphics**				
87-05-001	Caroline, Stone Lithograph	P.A. Cross	S/O	300.00	600.00
88-05-002	Maidenhood Hopi, Stone Lithograph	P.A. Cross	S/O	950.00	1150.00
89-05-003	The Red Capote, Serigraph	P.A. Cross	S/O	750.00	1150.00
89-05-004	Rosapina, Etching	P.A. Cross	74	1200.00	1200.00
90-05-005	Nighteyes, I, Serigraph	P.A. Cross	S/O	225.00	425.00
91-05-006	Bia-A-Hoosh (A Very Special Woman), Stone Lithograph	P.A. Cross	S/O	500.00	500.00
91-05-007	Wooltalkers, Serigraph	P.A. Cross	275	750.00	750.00
Cross Gallery, Inc.	**Miniature Line**				
91-06-001	BJ	P.A. Cross	447	80.00	80.00
91-06-002	Watercolour Study #2 For Half Breed	P.A. Cross	447	80.00	80.00
91-06-003	The Floral Shawl	P.A. Cross	447	80.00	80.00
91-06-004	Kendra	P.A. Cross	447	80.00	80.00
93-06-005	Sundown	P.A. Cross	447	80.00	80.00
93-06-006	Daybreak	P.A. Cross	447	80.00	80.00
93-06-007	Ponytails	P.A. Cross	447	80.00	80.00
93-06-008	Braids	P.A. Cross	447	80.00	80.00
Cross Gallery, Inc.	**The Painted Ladies' Suite**				
92-07-001	The Painted Ladies	P.A. Cross	S/O	225.00	1200.00
92-07-002	Avisola	P.A. Cross	475	185.00	185.00
92-07-003	Itza-chu (Apache; The Eagle)	P.A. Cross	475	185.00	185.00
92-07-004	Kel'hoya (Hopi; Little Sparrow Hawk)	P.A. Cross	475	185.00	185.00
92-07-005	Dah-say (Crow; Heart)	P.A. Cross	475	185.00	185.00
92-07-006	Tze-go-juni (Chiricahua Apache)	P.A. Cross	447	80.00	80.00
92-07-007	Sus(h)gah-daydus(h) (Crow; Quick)	P.A. Cross	447	80.00	80.00
92-07-008	Acoria (Crow; Seat of Honor)	P.A. Cross	475	185.00	185.00
Cross Gallery, Inc.	**The Gift**				
89-08-001	B' Achua Dlubh-bia Bii Noskiiyahi The Gift, Part II	P.A. Cross	S/O	225.00	650.00
93-08-002	The Gift, Part III	P.A. Cross	S/O	225.00	350-1000
Cross Gallery, Inc.	**Bandits & Bounty Hunters**				
94-09-001	Bandits	P.A. Cross	865	225.00	225.00
94-09-002	Bounty Hunters	P.A. Cross	865	225.00	225.00
Gartlan USA	**Lithograph**				
86-01-001	George Brett-"The Swing"	J. Martin	2,000	85.00	150.00
87-01-002	Roger Staubach	C. Soileau	1,979	85.00	125.00
89-01-003	Kareem Abdul Jabbar-The Record Setter	M. Taylor	1,989	85.00	175-225.
90-01-004	Darryl Strawberry	M. Taylor	500	295.00	295.00
91-01-005	Darryl Strawberry, signed Artist Proof	M. Taylor	50	395.00	395.00
91-01-006	Joe Montana	M. Taylor	500	495.00	495.00
91-01-007	Negro League 1st World Series (print)	Unknown	1,924	109.00	109.00
Gartlan USA	**Gallery Series I**				
92-02-001	Wayne Gretzky (16x20) Tri-Cut	M. Taylor	500	195.00	195.00
92-02-002	Ken Griffey Jr. (16x20) Tri-Cut	M. Taylor	500	195.00	195.00
92-02-003	Joe Montana (16x20) Tri-Cut	M. Taylor	500	195.00	195.00
92-02-004	Brett Hull (16x20) Tri-Cut	M. Taylor	500	195.00	195.00
Gartlan USA	**Gallery Series 2**				
92-03-001	Yogi Berra (12x20 w/8 1/2" plate)	M. Taylor	950	89.00	89.00
92-03-002	Rod Carew (12x20 w/8 1/2" plate)	M. Taylor	950	89.00	89.00
92-03-003	Carlton Fisk (12x20 w/8 1/2" plate)	M. Taylor	950	89.00	89.00
92-03-004	Whitey Ford (12x20 w/8 1/2" plate)	M. Taylor	950	89.00	89.00
92-03-005	Wayne Gretzky (12x20 w/8 1/2" plate)	M. Taylor	950	89.00	89.00
92-03-006	Ken Griffey Jr. (12x20 w/8 1/2" plate)	M. Taylor	950	89.00	89.00
92-03-007	Gordy Howe (12x20 w/8 1/2" plate)	M. Taylor	950	89.00	89.00
92-03-008	Joe Montana (12x20 w/8 1/2" plate)	M. Taylor	950	89.00	89.00
92-03-009	Tom Seaver (12x20 w/8 1/2" plate)	M. Taylor	950	89.00	89.00
92-03-010	John Wooden (12x20 w/8 1/2" plate)	M. Taylor	950	89.00	89.00
92-03-011	Carl Yastrzemski (12x20 w/8 1/2" plate)	M. Taylor	950	89.00	89.00
92-03-012	Brett & Bobby Hull (12x20 w/8 1/2" plate)	M. Taylor	950	89.00	89.00
Gartlan USA	**Gallery Series 3**				
92-04-001	Wayne Gretzky (12x16 w/photo)	M. Taylor	Open	79.00	79.00
92-04-002	Ken Griffey, Jr. (12x16 w/photo)	M. Taylor	Open	79.00	79.00
92-04-003	Joe Montana (12x16 w/photo)	M. Taylor	Open	79.00	79.00
92-04-004	Brett Hull (12x16 w/photo)	M. Taylor	Open	79.00	79.00
Gartlan USA	**Gallery Series 4**				
92-05-001	Wayne Gretzky (8x10 w/mini fig.)	M. Taylor	950	89.00	89.00
92-05-002	Carlton Fisk (8x10 w/mini fig.)	M. Taylor	950	89.00	89.00
92-05-003	Ken Griffey, Jr. (8x10 w/mini fig.)	M. Taylor	950	89.00	89.00
92-05-004	Brett Hull (8x10 w/mini fig.)	M. Taylor	950	89.00	89.00
92-05-005	Gordie Howe (8x10 w/mini fig.)	M. Taylor	950	89.00	89.00
92-05-006	Joe Montana (8x10 w/mini fig.)	M. Taylor	950	89.00	89.00
92-05-007	Tom Seaver (8x10 w/mini fig.)	M. Taylor	950	89.00	89.00
92-05-008	Carl Yastrzemski (8x10 w/mini fig.)	M. Taylor	950	89.00	89.00
92-05-009	George Brett (8x10 w/mini fig. & signed rounder)	J. Martin	300	125.00	125.00
Gartlan USA	**Gallery Series 5**				
92-06-001	Carlton Fisk (8x10)	M. Taylor	950	69.00	69.00
92-06-002	Wayne Gretzky (8x10)	M. Taylor	950	69.00	69.00
92-06-003	Ken Griffey, Jr. (8x10)	M. Taylor	950	69.00	69.00
92-06-004	Brett Hull (8x10)	M. Taylor	950	69.00	69.00
92-06-005	Gordie Howe (8x10)	M. Taylor	950	69.00	69.00
92-06-006	Joe Montana (8x10)	M. Taylor	950	69.00	69.00
92-06-007	Tom Seaver (8x10)	M. Taylor	950	69.00	69.00
92-06-008	Carl Yastrzemski (8x10)	M. Taylor	950	69.00	69.00
92-06-009	George Brett (8x10)	J. Martin	3,000	59.00	59.00
94-06-010	Wayne Gretzky & Gordie Howe (8x10)	M. Taylor	999	69.00	69.00

Greenwich Workshop — Bama

		ARTIST	EDITION	ISSUE	QUOTE
74-01-001	Ken Hunder, Working Cowboy	J. Bama	1,000	55.00	55.00
74-01-002	Shoshone Chief	J. Bama	1,000	65.00	65.00
75-01-003	Chuck Wagon in the Snow	J. Bama	1,000	50.00	50.00
76-01-004	Sage Grinder	J. Bama	1,000	65.00	65.00
77-01-005	Timber Jack Joe	J. Bama	1,000	65.00	65.00
77-01-006	A Crow Indian	J. Bama	1,000	65.00	65.00
78-01-007	A Mountain Ute	J. Bama	1,000	75.00	75.00
78-01-008	Contemporary Sioux Indian	J. Bama	1,000	75.00	75.00
78-01-009	Rookie Bronc Rider	J. Bama	1,000	75.00	75.00
78-01-010	Mountain Man	J. Bama	1,000	75.00	75.00
78-01-011	Indian at Crow Fair	J. Bama	1,500	75.00	75.00
79-01-012	Pre-Columbian Indian with Atlatl	J. Bama	1,500	75.00	75.00
79-01-013	Heritage	J. Bama	1,500	75.00	75.00
79-01-014	Little Star	J. Bama	1,500	80.00	80.00
79-01-015	Mountain Man and His Fox	J. Bama	1,500	90.00	90.00
80-01-016	Ken Blackbird	J. Bama	1,500	95.00	95.00
80-01-017	Old Sod House	J. Bama	1,500	80.00	80.00
80-01-018	Mountain Man 1820-1840 Period	J. Bama	1,500	115.00	115.00
80-01-019	Old Saddle in the Snow	J. Bama	1,500	75.00	75.00
80-01-020	Young Plains Indian	J. Bama	1,500	125.00	125.00
80-01-021	Sheep Skull in Drift	J. Bama	1,500	75.00	75.00
81-01-022	Portrait of a Sioux	J. Bama	1,500	135.00	135.00
81-01-023	At a Mountain Man Wedding	J. Bama	1,500	145.00	145.00
81-01-024	At Burial Gallager and Blind Bill	J. Bama	1,500	135.00	135.00
81-01-025	Old Arapaho Story-Teller	J. Bama	1,500	135.00	135.00
81-01-026	Winter Trapping	J. Bama	1,500	150.00	150.00
81-01-027	Oldest Living Crow Indian	J. Bama	1,500	135.00	135.00
82-01-028	Sioux Indian with Eagle Feather	J. Bama	1,250	150.00	150.00
82-01-029	Crow Indian Dancer	J. Bama	1,250	150.00	150.00
82-01-030	Mountain Man with Rifle	J. Bama	1,250	135.00	135.00
83-01-031	Don Walker-Bareback Rider	J. Bama	1,250	85.00	85.00
83-01-032	The Davilla Brothers-Bronc Riders	J. Bama	1,250	145.00	145.00
83-01-033	Southwest Indian Father and Son	J. Bama	1,250	145.00	145.00
87-01-034	Winter on Trout Creek	J. Bama	1,000	150.00	150.00
87-01-035	Buck Norris-Crossed Sabres Ranch	J. Bama	1,000	195.00	195.00
88-01-036	Indian Wearing War Medicine Bonnet	J. Bama	1,000	225.00	225.00
88-01-037	Dan-Mountain Man	J. Bama	1,250	195.00	195.00
88-01-038	Crow Indian From Lodge Grass	J. Bama	1,250	225.00	225.00
88-01-039	The Volunteer	J. Bama	1,500	225.00	225.00
88-01-040	Bittin' Up-Rimrock Ranch	J. Bama	1,250	195.00	195.00
89-01-041	Little Fawn-Cree Indian Girl	J. Bama	1,250	195.00	195.00
90-01-042	Ridin' the Rims	J. Bama	1,250	210.00	210.00
90-01-043	Buffalo Bill	J. Bama	1,250	210.00	210.00
90-01-044	Newman/Butch Cassidy & Video	J. Bama	1,000	375.00	500.00
90-01-045	Young Sheepherder	J. Bama	1,500	225.00	225.00
90-01-046	Paul Newman as Butch Cassidy & Video	J. Bama	2,000	250.00	250.00
91-01-047	The Drift on Skull Creek Pass	J. Bama	1,500	225.00	225.00
91-01-048	Ceremonial Lance	J. Bama	1,250	225.00	225.00
91-01-049	Chuck Wagon	J. Bama	1,000	225.00	225.00
91-01-050	Ready to Rendezvous	J. Bama	1,000	225.00	225.00
91-01-051	Riding the High Country	J. Bama	1,250	225.00	225.00
92-01-052	Coming' Round the Bend	J. Bama	1,000	195.00	195.00
92-01-053	Northern Cheyene Wolf Scout	J. Bama	1,000	195.00	195.00
92-01-054	Crow Cavalry Scout	J. Bama	1,000	195.00	195.00
92-01-055	Blackfeet War Robe	J. Bama	1,000	195.00	195.00
92-01-056	Sioux Subchief	J. Bama	1,000	195.00	195.00
93-01-057	Making Horse Medicine	J. Bama	1,000	225.00	225.00
93-01-058	Magua-"The Last of the Mohicans"	J. Bama	1,000	225.00	225.00
93-01-059	Art of James Bama Book with Chester Medicine Crow Fathers Flag Print	J. Bama	2,500	345.00	345.00
93-01-060	The Buffalo Dance	J. Bama	1,000	195.00	195.00
93-01-061	On the North Fork of the Shoshoni	J. Bama	1,000	195.00	195.00
94-01-062	Slim Warren, The Old Cowboy	J. Bama	1,000	125.00	125.00
94-01-063	Cheyene Dog Soldier	J. Bama	1,000	225.00	225.00

Greenwich Workshop — Bean

		ARTIST	EDITION	ISSUE	QUOTE
87-02-001	Helping Hands	A. Bean	850	150.00	150.00
88-02-002	How It Felt to Walk on the Moon	A. Bean	850	150.00	150.00
92-02-003	In Flight	A. Bean	850	385.00	385.00
93-02-004	Conrad Gordon and Bean:The Fantasy	A. Bean	1,000	385.00	385.00
94-02-005	In The Beginning Apollo 25 C/S	A. Bean	1,000	600.00	600.00

Greenwich Workshop — Blackshear

		ARTIST	EDITION	ISSUE	QUOTE
93-03-001	Hero Harriet Tubman	T. Blackshear	753	20.00	20.00
93-03-002	Hero Martin Luther King, Jr.	T. Blackshear	762	20.00	20.00
93-03-003	Hero Frederick Douglass	T. Blackshear	746	20.00	20.00
93-03-004	Heroes of Our Heritage Portfolio	T. Blackshear	5,000	35.00	35.00
94-03-005	Swansong	T. Blackshear	1,000	175.00	175.00
94-03-006	Beauty and the Beast	T. Blackshear	1,000	225.00	225.00

Greenwich Workshop — Blossom

		ARTIST	EDITION	ISSUE	QUOTE
88-04-001	Heading Home	C. Blossom	950	150.00	150.00
89-04-002	Harbor Light	C. Blossom	950	165.00	165.00
90-04-003	Ebb Tide	C. Blossom	950	175.00	175.00
92-04-004	Port of Call	C. Blossom	850	175.00	175.00
92-04-005	Windward	C. Blossom	950	175.00	175.00
92-04-006	Silhouette	C. Blossom	850	175.00	175.00
94-04-007	Traveling in Company	C. Blossom	850	175.00	175.00
94-04-008	Traveling in Company, Remarque	C. Blossom	100	415.00	415.00

Greenwich Workshop — Bullas

		ARTIST	EDITION	ISSUE	QUOTE
93-05-001	Wine-Oceros	W. Bullas	850	95.00	95.00
93-05-002	Billy the Pig	W. Bullas	850	95.00	95.00
93-05-003	Some Set of Buns	W. Bullas	850	95.00	95.00
93-05-004	Our Ladies of the Front Lawn	W. Bullas	850	95.00	95.00
93-05-005	You Rang, Madam?	W. Bullas	850	95.00	95.00
93-05-006	Mr. Harry Buns	W. Bullas	850	95.00	95.00
93-05-007	The Pale Prince	W. Bullas	850	110.00	110.00
93-05-008	Sand Trap Pro	W. Bullas	850	95.00	95.00
94-05-009	Clucks Unlimited	W. Bullas	850	95.00	95.00
94-05-010	Court of Appeals	W. Bullas	850	95.00	95.00
94-05-011	Ductor	W. Bullas	850	95.00	95.00
94-05-012	Fridays After Five	W. Bullas	850	95.00	95.00

Greenwich Workshop — Christensen

		ARTIST	EDITION	ISSUE	QUOTE
85-06-001	The Gift For Mrs. Claus	J. Christensen	3,500	80.00	700.00
86-06-002	Olde World Santa	J. Christensen	3,500	80.00	600.00
86-06-003	Your Plaice, or Mine?	J. Christensen	850	125.00	125.00
86-06-004	Jonah	J. Christensen	850	95.00	400.00
87-06-005	Old Man with a Lot on His Mind	J. Christensen	850	85.00	600.00
87-06-006	Voyage of the Basset w/Journal	J. Christensen	850	225.00	2000.00
87-06-007	Low Tech	J. Christensen	2,000	35.00	35.00
88-06-008	The Widows Mite	J. Christensen	850	145.00	1500.00
88-06-009	The Man Who Minds the Moon	J. Christensen	850	145.00	950.00
89-06-010	The Fish Walker (Bronze)	J. Christensen	100	711.00	711.00
89-06-011	The Annunciation	J. Christensen	850	175.00	175.00
90-06-012	The Burden of the Responsible Man	J. Christensen	850	145.00	1500.00
90-06-013	Two Sisters	J. Christensen	650	325.00	325.00
90-06-014	Rhymes & Reasons w/Booklet, remarque	J. Christensen	500	208.00	600.00
90-06-015	Rhymes & Reasons w/Booklet	J. Christensen	3,000	150.00	150.00
90-06-016	The Candleman, AP (Bronze)	J. Christensen	100	737.00	737.00
91-06-017	The Candleman	J. Christensen	850	160.00	250.00
91-06-018	Pelican King	J. Christensen	850	115.00	350-435.
91-06-019	Once Upon a Time	J. Christensen	1,500	175.00	1600.00
91-06-020	Once Upon a Time, remarque	J. Christensen	500	220.00	2000.00
91-06-021	Lawrence and a Bear	J. Christensen	850	145.00	310-400.
91-06-022	Three Blind Mice-Etching	J. Christensen	75	210.00	210.00
91-06-023	Three Wise Men of Gotham-Etching	J. Christensen	75	210.00	210.00
91-06-024	Man in the Moon-Etching	J. Christensen	75	210.00	210.00
91-06-025	Diggery Diggery Dar- Etching	J. Christensen	75	210.00	210.00
91-06-026	Jack Be Nimble-Etching	J. Christensen	75	210.00	210.00
91-06-027	Peter Peter Pumpkin Eater-Etching	J. Christensen	75	210.00	210.00
91-06-028	Tweedle Dee & Tweedle Dum-Etching	J. Christensen	75	210.00	210.00
91-06-029	Mother Goose-Etching	J. Christensen	75	210.00	210.00
92-06-030	The Reponsible Woman	J. Christensen	2,500	175.00	190.00
92-06-031	The Royal Processional	J. Christensen	1,500	185.00	500-550.
92-06-032	The Royal Processional, remarque	J. Christensen	500	252.50	650.00
92-06-033	The Oldest Angel	J. Christensen	850	125.00	650.00
93-06-034	Waiting for the Tide	J. Christensen	2,250	150.00	150.00
93-06-035	College of Magical Knowledge	J. Christensen	4,500	185.00	300-325.
93-06-036	College of Magical Knowledge, remarque	J. Christensen	500	252.50	450.00
93-06-037	The Scholar	J. Christensen	3,250	125.00	125.00
93-06-038	Getting it Right	J. Christensen	4,000	185.00	185.00
93-06-039	The Royal Music Barque	J. Christensen	2,750	375.00	375.00
94-06-040	Six Bird Hunters-Full Camouflage 3	J. Christensen	4,662	165.00	165.00
94-06-041	Bird Hunters (Bronze)	J. Christensen	50	4500.00	4500.00
94-06-042	Two Angels Discussing Botticelli	J. Christensen	2,950	145.00	145.00
94-06-043	Sometimes the Spirit Touches w/book	J. Christensen	3,600	195.00	195.00
94-06-044	Evening Angels	J. Christensen	4,000	195.00	195.00
94-06-044	Framed Evening Angels	J. Christensen	200	800.00	800.00

Greenwich Workshop — Combes

		ARTIST	EDITION	ISSUE	QUOTE
80-07-001	Facing the Wind	S. Combes	1,500	75.00	75.00
80-07-002	Solitary Hunter	S. Combes	1,500	75.00	75.00
80-07-003	Interlude	S. Combes	1,500	85.00	85.00
80-07-004	Manyara Afternoon	S. Combes	1,500	75.00	75.00
80-07-005	Serengeti Monarch	S. Combes	1,500	85.00	85.00
81-07-006	Leopard Cubs	S. Combes	1,000	95.00	95.00
81-07-007	Alert	S. Combes	1,000	95.00	95.00
83-07-008	Chui	S. Combes	275	250.00	250.00
85-07-009	Tension at Dawn	S. Combes	825	145.00	145.00
85-07-010	Tension at Dawn, remarque	S. Combes	25	275.00	275.00
86-07-011	The Wildebeest Migration	S. Combes	450	350.00	350.00
87-07-012	The Angry One	S. Combes	850	95.00	95.00
87-07-013	Tall Shadows	S. Combes	850	150.00	150.00
88-07-014	Confrontation	S. Combes	850	145.00	145.00
88-07-015	Bushwhacker	S. Combes	850	145.00	145.00
88-07-016	Simba	S. Combes	850	125.00	125.00
88-07-017	The Crossing	S. Combes	1,250	245.00	245.00
89-07-018	Masai-Longonot, Kenya	S. Combes	850	145.00	145.00
89-07-019	Mountain Gorillas	S. Combes	550	135.00	135.00
89-07-020	The Watering Hole	S. Combes	850	225.00	225.00
90-07-021	The Guardian (Silverback)	S. Combes	1,000	185.00	185.00
90-07-022	Standoff	S. Combes	850	375.00	375.00
91-07-023	Kilimanjaro Morning	S. Combes	850	185.00	185.00
91-07-024	Study in Concentration	S. Combes	850	185.00	185.00
92-07-025	Midday Sun (Lioness & Cubs)	S. Combes	850	125.00	125.00
92-07-026	African Oasis	S. Combes	650	375.00	375.00
92-07-027	The Hypnotist	S. Combes	1,250	145.00	145.00
92-07-028	Lookout	S. Combes	1,250	95.00	95.00
93-07-029	Fearful Symmetry	S. Combes	850	110.00	110.00
94-07-030	Disdain	S. Combes	850	110.00	110.00

Greenwich Workshop — Crowley

		ARTIST	EDITION	ISSUE	QUOTE
78-08-001	The Starquilt	D. Crowley	1,000	65.00	65.00
78-08-002	Hudson's Bay Blanket	D. Crowley	1,000	75.00	75.00
78-08-003	Dorena	D. Crowley	1,000	75.00	75.00
79-08-004	Desert Sunset	D. Crowley	1,500	75.00	75.00
79-08-005	Security Blanket	D. Crowley	1,500	65.00	65.00
79-08-006	Arizona Mountain Man	D. Crowley	1,500	85.00	85.00
80-08-007	Apache in White	D. Crowley	1,500	85.00	85.00
80-08-008	Beauty and the Beast	D. Crowley	1,500	85.00	85.00
80-08-009	The Littlest Apache	D. Crowley	275	325.00	325.00
81-08-010	Eagle Feathers	D. Crowley	1,500	95.00	95.00
81-08-011	Afterglow	D. Crowley	1,500	110.00	110.00
81-08-012	Shannandoah	D. Crowley	275	325.00	325.00
81-08-013	The Heirloom	D. Crowley	1,000	125.00	125.00
82-08-014	Hopi Butterfly	D. Crowley	275	350.00	350.00
86-08-015	The Trapper	D. Crowley	550	75.00	75.00
88-08-016	Ermine and Beads	D. Crowley	550	85.00	85.00
89-08-017	The Gunfighters	D. Crowley	3,000	35.00	35.00
92-08-018	Colors of the Sunset	D. Crowley	650	175.00	175.00
92-08-019	Anna Thorne	D. Crowley	650	160.00	160.00
94-08-020	Plumes and Ribbons	D. Crowley	650	160.00	160.00

Greenwich Workshop — Dawson

		ARTIST	EDITION	ISSUE	QUOTE
92-09-001	The Attack (Cougars)	J. Dawson	850	690.00	690.00
92-09-002	Taking a Break	J. Dawson	850	690.00	690.00
93-09-003	Ready for the Attack	J. Dawson	850	690.00	690.00
93-09-004	Berry Contented	J. Dawson	850	690.00	690.00
93-09-005	Berry Contented (Remarque)	J. Dawson	850	690.00	690.00
93-09-006	Looking Back	J. Dawson	850	690.00	690.00
93-09-007	Otter Wise	J. Dawson	850	690.00	690.00
94-09-008	The Face Off (Right & Left Panel)	J. Dawson	850	690.00	690.00

Greenwich Workshop — Doolittle

		ARTIST	EDITION	ISSUE	QUOTE
79-10-001	Pintos	B. Doolittle	1,000	65.00	9000.00
80-10-002	Good Omen, The	B. Doolittle	1,000	85.00	6000.00
80-10-003	Bugged Bear	B. Doolittle	1,000	85.00	2500.00
80-10-004	Whoo !?	B. Doolittle	1,000	75.00	2000.00
81-10-005	Woodland Encounter	B. Doolittle	1,500	145.00	9000.00
81-10-006	Unknown Presence	B. Doolittle	1,500	150.00	2500.00
81-10-007	Spirit of the Grizzly	B. Doolittle	1,500	150.00	3500.00
82-10-008	Eagle's Flight	B. Doolittle	1,500	185.00	3500.00
83-10-009	Escape by a Hare	B. Doolittle	1,500	80.00	900.00

		ARTIST	EDITION	ISSUE	QUOTE
83-10-010	Rushing War Eagle	B. Doolittle	1,500	150.00	1200.00
83-10-011	Art of Camouflage, signed	B. Doolittle	2,000	55.00	600.00
83-10-012	Runs With Thunder	B. Doolittle	1,500	150.00	2000.00
83-10-013	Christmas Day, Give or Take a Week	B. Doolittle	4,581	80.00	2000.00
84-10-014	Let My Spirit Soar	B. Doolittle	1,500	195.00	3500.00
84-10-015	Forest Has Eyes, The	B. Doolittle	8,544	175.00	4000.00
85-10-016	Wolves of the Crow	B. Doolittle	2,650	225.00	1700.00
85-10-017	Two Indian Horses	B. Doolittle	12,253	225.00	28-3500.
86-10-018	Where Silence Speaks, Doolittle The Art of Bev Doolittle	B. Doolittle	3,500	650.00	3300.00
86-10-019	Two Bears of the Blackfeet	B. Doolittle	2,650	225.00	1500.00
87-10-020	Guardian Spirits	B. Doolittle	13,238	295.00	1200.00
87-10-021	Calling the Buffalo	B. Doolittle	8,500	245.00	1500.00
87-10-022	Season of the Eagle	B. Doolittle	36,548	245.00	700.00
88-10-023	Doubled Back	B. Doolittle	15,000	245.00	12-1500.
89-10-024	Sacred Ground	B. Doolittle	69,996	265.00	600-700.
90-10-025	Hide and Seek Suite	B. Doolittle	25,000	1200.00	1200.00
90-10-025	Hide and Seek (Composite & Video)	B. Doolittle	25,000	300.00	300.00
91-10-026	The Sentinel	B. Doolittle	35,000	275.00	750.00
91-10-027	Sacred Circle (Print & Video)	B. Doolittle	40,192	325.00	325.00
92-10-028	Walk Softly (Chapbook)	B. Doolittle	40,192	225.00	225.00
92-10-029	Eagle Heart	B. Doolittle	48,000	285.00	285.00
93-10-030	Wilderness? Wilderness!	B. Doolittle	50,000	65.00	65.00
93-10-031	Prayer for the Wild Things	B. Doolittle	65,000	325.00	350-375.
94-10-032	When The Wind Had Wings	B. Doolittle	57,500	325.00	325.00

Greenwich Workshop — Ferris

82-11-001	Sunrise Encounter	K. Ferris	1,000	145.00	145.00
83-11-002	Little Willie Coming Home	K. Ferris	1,000	145.00	145.00
90-11-003	The Circus Outbound	K. Ferris	1,000	225.00	225.00
91-11-004	Linebacker in the Buff	K. Ferris	1,000	225.00	225.00
91-11-005	Farmer's Nightmare	K. Ferris	850	185.00	185.00
91-11-006	Too Little, Too Late w/Video	K. Ferris	1,000	245.00	245.00
93-11-007	A Test of Courage	K. Ferris	850	185.00	185.00

Greenwich Workshop — Frederick

84-12-001	From Timber's Edge	R. Frederick	850	125.00	125.00
84-12-002	Misty Morning Sentinel	R. Frederick	850	125.00	125.00
84-12-003	First Moments of Gold	R. Frederick	825	145.00	145.00
84-12-004	First Moments of Gold, remarque	R. Frederick	25	172.50	172.50
85-12-005	High Society	R. Frederick	950	115.00	115.00
85-12-006	Early Evening Gathering	R. Frederick	475	325.00	325.00
85-12-007	Los Colores De Chiapas	R. Frederick	950	85.00	85.00
85-12-008	Misty Morning Lookout	R. Frederick	950	145.00	145.00
86-12-009	Winter's Call	R. Frederick	1,250	165.00	165.00
86-12-010	Winter's Call Raptor, AP	R. Frederick	100	165.00	165.00
86-12-011	Out on a Limb	R. Frederick	1,250	145.00	145.00
86-12-012	Great Horned Owl	R. Frederick	1,250	115.00	115.00
86-12-013	Sounds of Twilight	R. Frederick	1,500	135.00	135.00
87-12-014	Northern Light	R. Frederick	1,500	165.00	165.00
87-12-015	Evening Shadows (White-Tail Deer)	R. Frederick	1,500	125.00	125.00
87-12-016	Tundra Watch (Snowy Owl)	R. Frederick	1,500	145.00	145.00
87-12-017	Woodland Crossing (Caribou)	R. Frederick	1,500	145.00	145.00
87-12-018	Before the Storm (Diptych)	R. Frederick	550	350.00	350.00
87-12-019	Winter's Brilliance (Cardinal)	R. Frederick	1,500	135.00	135.00
88-12-020	The Nesting Call	R. Frederick	2,500	150.00	150.00
88-12-021	The Nesting Call, remarque	R. Frederick	1,000	165.00	165.00
88-12-022	World of White	R. Frederick	2,500	150.00	150.00
88-12-023	Rim Walk	R. Frederick	1,500	90.00	90.00
88-12-024	Shadows of Dusk	R. Frederick	1,500	165.00	165.00
88-12-025	Glimmer of Solitude	R. Frederick	1,500	145.00	145.00
88-12-026	Timber Ghost w/Mini Wine Label	R. Frederick	3,000	150.00	150.00
88-12-027	Gifts of the Land w/Wine & Wine Label	R. Frederick	500	150.00	150.00
89-12-028	Colors of Home	R. Frederick	1,500	165.00	165.00
89-12-029	Monarch of the North	R. Frederick	2,000	150.00	150.00
89-12-030	Gifts of the Land #2	R. Frederick	500	150.00	150.00
89-12-031	Barely Spring	R. Frederick	1,500	165.00	165.00
90-12-032	Autumn Leaves	R. Frederick	1,250	175.00	175.00
90-12-033	Echoes of Sunset	R. Frederick	1,750	235.00	235.00
90-12-034	Silent Watch (High Desert Museum)	R. Frederick	2,000	35.00	35.00
90-12-035	Morning Surprise	R. Frederick	1,750	165.00	165.00
90-12-036	Snowy Reflections (Snowy Egret)	R. Frederick	1,500	150.00	150.00
91-12-037	Morning Thunder	R. Frederick	1,750	185.00	185.00
91-12-038	The Long Run	R. Frederick	1,750	235.00	235.00
91-12-039	The Long Run, AP	R. Frederick	200	167.50	167.50
91-12-040	Summer's Song (Triptych)	R. Frederick	2,500	225.00	225.00
91-12-041	Breaking the Ice	R. Frederick	2,750	235.00	235.00
92-12-042	Fire and Ice (Suite of 2)	R. Frederick	1,750	175.00	175.00
92-12-043	Fast Break	R. Frederick	2,250	235.00	235.00
92-12-044	Rain Forest Rendezvous	R. Frederick	1,500	225.00	225.00
92-12-045	Snowstorm	R. Frederick	1,750	195.00	195.00
92-12-046	An Early Light Breakfast	R. Frederick	1,750	235.00	235.00
93-12-047	Glory Days	R. Frederick	1,750	115.00	115.00
93-12-048	New Heights	R. Frederick	1,950	195.00	195.00
93-12-049	Temple of the Jaguar	R. Frederick	1,500	225.00	225.00
93-12-050	Point of View	R. Frederick	1,000	235.00	235.00
94-12-051	Tropic Moon	R. Frederick	850	165.00	165.00
94-12-052	Way of the Caribou	R. Frederick	1,235	235.00	235.00
94-12-053	Beeline (C)	R. Frederick	1,000	195.00	195.00
94-12-054	Snow Park	R. Frederick	1,000	175.00	175.00

Greenwich Workshop — Gurney

90-13-001	Dinosaur Parade, remarque	J. Gurney	150	130.00	2500.00
90-13-002	Morning in Treetown	J. Gurney	1,500	175.00	400.00
90-13-003	Seaside Romp	J. Gurney	1,000	175.00	400.00
91-13-004	Waterfall City	J. Gurney	3,000	125.00	125.00
91-13-005	Waterfall City, remarque	J. Gurney	250	186.00	700.00
91-13-006	Dinosaur Boulevard	J. Gurney	2,000	125.00	125.00
91-13-007	Dinosaur Boulevard, remarque	J. Gurney	250	196.00	700.00
92-13-008	Dream Canyon	J. Gurney	N/A	125.00	125.00
92-13-009	Dream Canyon, remarque	J. Gurney	150	196.00	400.00
92-13-010	Skyback Print w/Dinotopia Book	J. Gurney	3,500	295.00	295.00
92-13-011	Birthday Pageant	J. Gurney	2,500	60.00	60.00
92-13-012	Birthday Pageant, remarque	J. Gurney	300	275.00	500.00
93-13-013	Ring Riders	J. Gurney	2,500	175.00	175.00
93-13-014	Palace in the Clouds	J. Gurney	3,500	175.00	175.00
93-13-015	The Excursion	J. Gurney	3,500	175.00	175.00
93-13-016	Garden of Hope	J. Gurney	3,500	175.00	175.00
94-13-017	Steep Street	J. Gurney	3,500	95.00	95.00
94-13-018	Small Wonder	J. Gurney	Open	75.00	75.00

Greenwich Workshop — Gustafson

		ARTIST	EDITION	ISSUE	QUOTE
93-14-001	Humpty Dumpty	S. Gustafson	3,500	125.00	125.00
93-14-002	Goldilocks and the Three Bears	S. Gustafson	3,500	125.00	150-300.
93-14-003	Little Red Riding Hood	S. Gustafson	3,500	125.00	125-175.
93-14-004	Snow White and the Seven Dwarfs	S. Gustafson	3,500	165.00	400-500.
94-14-005	Frog Prince	S. Gustafson	3,500	125.00	125.00
94-14-006	Pat-A-Cake	S. Gustafson	4,000	125.00	125.00

Greenwich Workshop — Johnson

93-15-001	Wolf Creek	J. Johnson	550	165.00	165.00
94-15-002	Winter Thaw	J. Johnson	650	150.00	150.00
94-15-003	Moose River	J. Johnson	650	175.00	175.00

Greenwich Workshop — Kennedy

88-16-001	Distant Relations	S. Kennedy	950	200.00	600.00
88-16-002	Eager to Run	S. Kennedy	950	200.00	1500.00
88-16-003	After Dinner Music	S. Kennedy	2,500	175.00	400.00
89-16-004	Up a Creek	S. Kennedy	2,500	185.00	285.00
89-16-005	Snowshoes	S. Kennedy	4,000	185.00	185.00
90-16-006	Fish Tales	S. Kennedy	5,500	225.00	225.00
90-16-007	On the Edge	S. Kennedy	4,000	225.00	225.00
91-16-008	In Training	S. Kennedy	3,350	165.00	165.00
91-16-009	In Training, remarque	S. Kennedy	150	215.50	215.50
91-16-010	A Breed Apart	S. Kennedy	2,750	225.00	225.00
92-16-011	Cabin Fever	S. Kennedy	2,250	175.00	175.00
92-16-012	Aurora	S. Kennedy	2,250	195.00	195.00
93-16-013	Never Alone	S. Kennedy	2,250	225.00	225.00
93-16-014	Never Alone, remarque	S. Kennedy	250	272.50	600.00
93-16-015	Midnight Eyes	S. Kennedy	1,750	125.00	125.00
93-16-016	The Touch	S. Kennedy	1,500	115.00	115.00
94-16-017	Spruce and Fur	S. Kennedy	1,500	165.00	165.00
94-16-018	Quiet Time Companions-Samoyed	S. Kennedy	1,000	125.00	125.00
94-16-019	Quiet Time Companions-Siberian Husky	S. Kennedy	1,000	125.00	125.00
94-16-020	Silent Observers	S. Kennedy	1,250	165.00	165.00

Greenwich Workshop — Kodera

86-17-001	The A Team (K10)	C. Kodera	850	145.00	145.00
87-17-002	Fifty Years a Lady	C. Kodera	550	150.00	150.00
87-17-003	Voyager: The Skies Yield	C. Kodera	1,500	225.00	225.00
88-17-004	Moonlight Intruders	C. Kodera	1,000	125.00	125.00
88-17-005	The Great Greenwich Balloon Race	C. Kodera	1,000	145.00	145.00
89-17-006	Springtime Flying in the Rockies	C. Kodera	550	95.00	95.00
90-17-007	Green Light-Jump!	C. Kodera	650	145.00	145.00
90-17-008	A Moment's Peace	C. Kodera	1,250	150.00	150.00
91-17-009	Darkness Visible (Stealth)	C. Kodera	2,671	40.00	40.00
91-17-010	This is No Drill w/Video	C. Kodera	1,000	225.00	225.00
92-17-011	Thirty Seconds Over Tokyo	C. Kodera	1,000	275.00	275.00
92-17-012	Looking For Nagumo	C. Kodera	1,000	225.00	225.00
92-17-013	Memphis Belle/Dauntless Dotty	C. Kodera	1,250	245.00	245.00
92-17-014	Halsey's Surprise	C. Kodera	850	95.00	95.00
94-17-015	Tiger's Bite	C. Kodera	850	150.00	150.00
94-17-016	This is No Time to Lose an Engine	C. Kodera	850	150.00	150.00

Greenwich Workshop — Landry

84-18-001	Regatta	P. Landry	500	75.00	75.00
84-18-002	Regatta, remarque	P. Landry	50	97.50	97.50
85-18-003	The Skaters	P. Landry	500	75.00	75.00
85-18-004	The Skaters, remarque	P. Landry	50	97.50	97.50
86-18-005	Seaside Mist	P. Landry	450	85.00	400.00
87-18-006	Bluenose Country	P. Landry	550	115.00	115.00
88-18-007	Flower Boxes	P. Landry	550	75.00	75.00
88-18-008	Seaside Cottage	P. Landry	550	125.00	125.00
89-18-009	Summer Garden	P. Landry	850	125.00	700.00
89-18-010	Cape Cod Welcome	P. Landry	850	75.00	700.00
89-18-011	A Canadian Christmas	P. Landry	1,250	125.00	125.00
90-18-012	The Captain's Garden	P. Landry	1,000	165.00	500.00
90-18-013	Morning Papers	P. Landry	1,250	135.00	135.00
90-18-014	Seaside Carousel	P. Landry	1,500	165.00	165.00
90-18-015	Christmas Treasures	P. Landry	2,500	165.00	165.00
90-18-016	Flower Wagon	P. Landry	1,500	165.00	165.00
91-18-017	Flower Market	P. Landry	1,500	185.00	735-1000
91-18-018	Victorian Memories	P. Landry	1,500	150.00	150.00
91-18-019	Summer Concert	P. Landry	1,500	195.00	195.00
91-18-020	Nantucket Colors	P. Landry	1,500	150.00	150.00
91-18-021	The Toymaker	P. Landry	1,500	165.00	165.00
92-18-022	Apple Orchard	P. Landry	1,250	150.00	150.00
92-18-023	Boardwalk Promenade	P. Landry	1,250	175.00	175.00
92-18-024	Cottage Garden	P. Landry	1,250	160.00	160.00
92-18-025	Sunflowers	P. Landry	1,250	125.00	125.00
92-18-026	Christmas at the Flower Market	P. Landry	2,500	125.00	125.00
92-18-027	Aunt Martha's Country Farm	P. Landry	1,500	185.00	185.00
93-18-028	The Antique Shop	P. Landry	1,250	125.00	125.00
93-18-029	Hometown Parade	P. Landry	1,250	165.00	165.00
93-18-030	A Place in the Park	P. Landry	1,500	185.00	185.00
93-18-031	Christmas at Mystic Seaport	P. Landry	2,000	125.00	125.00
93-18-032	Paper Boy	P. Landry	1,500	150.00	150.00
94-18-033	An English Cottage	P. Landry	850	150.00	150.00
94-18-034	Morning Walk	P. Landry	850	135.00	135.00
94-18-035	Flower Barn	P. Landry	1,500	175.00	175.00
94-18-036	Flowers For Mary Hope	P. Landry	1,250	165.00	165.00
94-18-037	Christmas Carousel Pony	P. Landry	2,000	125.00	125.00

Greenwich Workshop — Lyman

83-19-001	End Of The Ridge	S. Lyman	850	95.00	900.00
83-19-002	The Pass	S. Lyman	850	95.00	400-575.
83-19-003	Early Winter In The Mountains	S. Lyman	850	95.00	400.00
84-19-004	Free Flight	S. Lyman	850	70.00	70-120.
84-19-005	Noisy Neighbors	S. Lyman	650	95.00	1000.00
84-19-006	Noisy Neighbors, remarque	S. Lyman	25	215.00	520-1800
85-19-007	Autumn Gathering	S. Lyman	850	115.00	250.00
85-19-008	Bear & Blossoms (C)	S. Lyman	850	75.00	75-220.
86-19-009	Colors of Twilight	S. Lyman	850	N/A	N/A
86-19-010	Morning Solitude	S. Lyman	850	115.00	150-250.
86-19-011	Snowy Throne (C)	S. Lyman	850	85.00	85-295.
86-19-012	High Trail At Sunset	S. Lyman	1,000	125.00	700.00
87-19-013	Twilight Snow (C)	S. Lyman	950	85.00	85-225.
87-19-014	High Creek Crossing	S. Lyman	1,000	165.00	800.00
87-19-015	New Territory (Grizzly & Cubs)	S. Lyman	1,000	135.00	210-235.
87-19-016	An Elegant Couple (Wood Ducks)	S. Lyman	1,000	125.00	150-235.
87-19-017	Canadian Autumn	S. Lyman	1,500	165.00	175.00
87-19-018	Moon Shadows	S. Lyman	1,500	135.00	135.00
88-19-019	Snow Hunter	S. Lyman	1,500	135.00	135.00
88-19-020	Return Of The Falcon	S. Lyman	1,500	150.00	500.00
88-19-021	Uzumati: Great Bear of Yosemite	S. Lyman	1,750	150.00	500.00
88-19-022	The Intruder	S. Lyman	1,500	150.00	150.00

		ARTIST	EDITION	ISSUE	QUOTE
88-19-023	The Raptor's Watch	S. Lyman	1,500	150.00	600.00
89-19-024	Quiet Rain	S. Lyman	1,500	165.00	475-600.
89-19-025	High Light	S. Lyman	1,250	165.00	200-350.
89-19-026	Last Light of Winter	S. Lyman	1,500	175.00	1400.00
89-19-027	Color In The Snow (Pheasant)	S. Lyman	1,500	165.00	1700.00
90-19-028	A Mountain Campfire	S. Lyman	1,500	195.00	2400.00
90-19-029	Among The Wild Brambles	S. Lyman	1,750	185.00	180-275.
90-19-030	Silent Snows	S. Lyman	1,750	210.00	400.00
90-19-031	Evening Light	S. Lyman	2,500	225.00	1700.00
91-19-032	Dance of Cloud and Cliff	S. Lyman	1,500	225.00	500.00
91-19-033	Embers at Dawn	S. Lyman	3,500	225.00	1100.00
91-19-034	Secret Watch (Lynx)	S. Lyman	2,250	150.00	150.00
91-19-035	Dance of Water and Light	S. Lyman	3,000	225.00	225.00
92-19-036	River of Light (Geese)	S. Lyman	2,950	225.00	225.00
92-19-037	Warmed by the View	S. Lyman	8,500	235.00	400.00
92-19-038	Wildflower Suite (Hummingbird)	S. Lyman	2,250	175.00	175.00
92-19-039	Wilderness Welcome	S. Lyman	8,500	235.00	400-550.
92-19-040	Lantern Light Print w Firelight Chapbook	S. Lyman	10,000	195.00	195.00
92-19-041	Woodland Haven	S. Lyman	2,500	195.00	195.00
93-19-042	Lake of the Shining Rocks	S. Lyman	2,250	235.00	325.00
93-19-043	Riparian Riches	S. Lyman	2,500	235.00	235.00
93-19-044	Fire Dance	S. Lyman	8,500	235.00	235.00
93-19-045	The Spirit of Christmas	S. Lyman	2,750	165.00	165.00
94-19-046	New Kid on the Rock	S. Lyman	2,250	185.00	185.00
94-19-047	Moon Fire	S. Lyman	7,500	245.00	245.00
94-19-048	North Country Shores	S. Lyman	3,000	225.00	225.00
94-19-049	Moonlit Flight on Christmas Night	S. Lyman	2,750	165.00	165.00

Greenwich Workshop **Marris**

		ARTIST	EDITION	ISSUE	QUOTE
85-20-001	The Fishing Lesson	B. Marris	1,000	145.00	145.00
85-20-002	Kenai Dusk	B. Marris	1,000	145.00	145.00
86-20-003	Best Friends	B. Marris	850	85.00	85.00
86-20-004	Other Footsteps	B. Marris	950	75.00	75.00
87-20-005	Desperados	B. Marris	850	135.00	135.00
87-20-006	Honey Creek Whitetales	B. Marris	850	145.00	145.00
87-20-007	Above the Glacier	B. Marris	850	145.00	145.00
88-20-008	Courtship	B. Marris	850	145.00	145.00
88-20-009	Waiting For the Freeze	B. Marris	1,000	125.00	125.00
89-20-010	Bittersweet	B. Marris	1,000	135.00	135.00
89-20-011	The Playgroud Showoff	B. Marris	850	165.00	165.00
89-20-012	New Beginnings	B. Marris	1,000	175.00	175.00
90-20-013	Bugles and Trumpets!	B. Marris	1,000	175.00	175.00
90-20-014	Mom's Shadow	B. Marris	1,000	165.00	165.00
90-20-015	Of Myth and Magic	B. Marris	1,500	175.00	175.00
91-20-016	Cops & Robbers	B. Marris	1,000	165.00	165.00
91-20-017	The Stillness (Grizzly & Cubs)	B. Marris	1,000	165.00	165.00
91-20-018	Under the Morning Star	B. Marris	1,500	175.00	175.00
91-20-019	End of the Season	B. Marris	1,000	165.00	165.00
92-20-020	The Comeback	B. Marris	1,250	175.00	175.00
92-20-021	Security Blanket	B. Marris	1,250	175.00	175.00
92-20-022	To Stand and Endure	B. Marris	1,000	195.00	195.00
92-20-023	Sun Bath	B. Marris	1,000	95.00	95.00
93-20-024	Spring Fever	B. Marris	1,000	165.00	165.00
94-20-025	Lady Marmalade's Bed & Breakfast	B. Marris	1,000	125.00	125.00
94-20-026	Moonshine	B. Marris	1,000	95.00	95.00
94-20-027	Big Gray's Barn and Bistro	B. Marris	1,000	125.00	125.00

Greenwich Workshop **F. McCarthy**

		ARTIST	EDITION	ISSUE	QUOTE
74-21-001	Lone Sentinel	F. McCarthy	1,000	55.00	14-1800.
74-21-002	Long Column	F. McCarthy	1,000	75.00	450.00
74-21-003	The Hunt	F. McCarthy	1,000	75.00	620-930.
74-21-004	The Night They Needed a Good Ribbon Man	F. McCarthy	1,000	65.00	350-475.
75-21-005	The Survivor	F. McCarthy	1,000	65.00	350.00
75-21-006	Waiting for the Escort	F. McCarthy	1,000	75.00	225-250.
75-21-007	Smoke Was Their Ally	F. McCarthy	1,000	75.00	425-550.
75-21-008	Returning Raiders	F. McCarthy	1,000	75.00	450.00
76-21-009	Packing In	F. McCarthy	1,000	65.00	500.00
76-21-010	Sioux Warriors	F. McCarthy	650	55.00	375-450.
76-21-011	The Warrior	F. McCarthy	650	50.00	450-600.
76-21-012	The Hostiles	F. McCarthy	1,000	75.00	600.00
77-21-013	The Beaver Men	F. McCarthy	1,000	75.00	500-710.
77-21-014	Distant Thunder	F. McCarthy	1,500	75.00	650-900.
77-21-015	Comanche Moon	F. McCarthy	1,000	75.00	300.00
77-21-016	Robe Signal	F. McCarthy	850	60.00	420-500.
77-21-017	Dust Stained Posse	F. McCarthy	1,000	75.00	600.00
77-21-018	An Old Time Mountain Man	F. McCarthy	1,000	65.00	275.00
78-21-019	The Fording	F. McCarthy	1,000	75.00	300-360.
78-21-020	To Battle	F. McCarthy	1,000	75.00	370.00
78-21-021	Single File	F. McCarthy	1,000	75.00	300-490.
78-21-022	Before the Norther	F. McCarthy	1,000	90.00	400-525.
78-21-023	Night Crossing	F. McCarthy	1,000	75.00	200-250.
78-21-024	In The Pass	F. McCarthy	1,500	90.00	200.00
78-21-025	Ambush, The	F. McCarthy	1,000	125.00	300-345.
79-21-026	The Loner	F. McCarthy	1,000	75.00	350.00
79-21-027	The Prayer	F. McCarthy	1,500	90.00	550-600.
79-21-028	Retreat to Higher Ground	F. McCarthy	2,000	90.00	350-500.
79-21-029	On the Warpath	F. McCarthy	1,000	75.00	195-250.
80-21-030	Snow Moon	F. McCarthy	1,000	115.00	250-300.
80-21-031	Before the Charge	F. McCarthy	1,000	115.00	200-400.
80-21-032	Burning the Way Station	F. McCarthy	1,000	175.00	375-500.
80-21-033	The Trooper	F. McCarthy	1,000	90.00	295.00
80-21-034	Forbidden Land	F. McCarthy	1,000	125.00	225.00
80-21-035	Roar of the Norther	F. McCarthy	1,000	90.00	250-450.
80-21-036	A Time Of Decision	F. McCarthy	1,150	125.00	250.00
81-21-037	Under Hostile Fire	F. McCarthy	1,000	150.00	210-250.
81-21-038	The Coup	F. McCarthy	1,000	125.00	375-450.
81-21-039	Headed North	F. McCarthy	1,000	150.00	225-275.
81-21-040	Surrounded	F. McCarthy	1,000	150.00	195-275.
81-21-041	Race with the Hostiles	F. McCarthy	1,000	135.00	170-225.
81-21-042	Crossing the Divide (The Old West)	F. McCarthy	1,500	850.00	1100.00
82-21-043	Alert	F. McCarthy	1,000	135.00	160.00
82-21-044	The Warriors	F. McCarthy	1,000	150.00	200.00
82-21-045	Attack on the Wagon Train	F. McCarthy	1,400	150.00	220-395.
82-21-046	Apache Scout	F. McCarthy	1,000	165.00	175-190.
82-21-047	The Challenge	F. McCarthy	1,000	175.00	425.00
82-21-048	Whirling He Raced to Meet the Challenge	F. McCarthy	1,000	175.00	275-340.
83-21-049	Out Of The Mist They Came	F. McCarthy	1,000	165.00	225-325.
83-21-050	Moonlit Trail	F. McCarthy	1,000	90.00	210.00
83-21-051	Blackfeet Raiders	F. McCarthy	1,000	90.00	250.00
83-21-052	Under Attack	F. McCarthy	5,676	125.00	295-350.
83-21-053	In The Land Of The Sparrow Hawk People	F. McCarthy	1,000	165.00	180.00
84-21-054	Along the West Fork	F. McCarthy	1,000	175.00	225-285.
84-21-055	Hostiles, signed	F. McCarthy	1,000	55.00	55.00
84-21-056	Leading the Charge, signed	F. McCarthy	1,000	55.00	55.00
84-21-057	Watching the Wagons	F. McCarthy	1,400	175.00	440.00
84-21-058	The Decoys	F. McCarthy	450	325.00	500.00
84-21-059	The Savage Taunt	F. McCarthy	1,000	225.00	250-375.
84-21-060	After the Dust Storm	F. McCarthy	1,000	145.00	165.00
85-21-061	The Long Knives	F. McCarthy	1,000	175.00	300.00
85-21-062	The Fireboat	F. McCarthy	1,000	175.00	200.00
85-21-063	Charging the Challenger	F. McCarthy	1,000	150.00	200-300.
85-21-064	Scouting The Long Knives	F. McCarthy	1,400	195.00	250-300.
85-21-065	The Last Crossing	F. McCarthy	550	350.00	450-500.
85-21-066	The Traders	F. McCarthy	1,000	195.00	195-275.
86-21-067	Comanche War Trail	F. McCarthy	1,000	165.00	165-250.
86-21-068	The Buffalo Runners	F. McCarthy	1,000	195.00	195-250.
86-21-069	The Drive (C)	F. McCarthy	1,000	95.00	95-175.
86-21-070	Children of the Raven	F. McCarthy	1,000	185.00	550.00
86-21-071	Where Tracks Will Be Lost	F. McCarthy	550	350.00	350-375.
86-21-072	Spooked	F. McCarthy	1,400	195.00	200.00
86-21-073	Red Bull's War Party	F. McCarthy	1,000	165.00	225-275.
87-21-074	Following the Herds	F. McCarthy	1,000	195.00	250-300.
87-21-075	When Omens Turn Bad	F. McCarthy	1,000	165.00	400.00
87-21-076	Chiricahua Raiders	F. McCarthy	1,000	165.00	165-275.
87-21-077	In The Land Of The Winter Hawk	F. McCarthy	1,000	225.00	350-525.
87-21-078	From the Rim	F. McCarthy	1,000	225.00	225-310.
88-21-079	The Hostile Land	F. McCarthy	1,000	225.00	235.00
88-21-080	Saber Charge	F. McCarthy	2,250	225.00	225-250.
88-21-081	In Pursuit of the White Buffalo	F. McCarthy	1,500	225.00	900.00
88-21-082	Turning The Leaders	F. McCarthy	1,500	225.00	240.00
88-21-083	Apache Trackers (C)	F. McCarthy	1,000	95.00	135-150.
89-21-084	The Coming Of The Iron Horse	F. McCarthy	1,500	225.00	225-375.
89-21-085	The Coming Of The Iron Horse (Print/Pewter Train Special Publ. Ed.)	F. McCarthy	100	1500.00	16-2150.
89-21-086	The Last Stand: Little Big Horn	F. McCarthy	2,250	225.00	225-250.
89-21-087	Big Medicine	F. McCarthy	1,000	225.00	500.00
89-21-088	Los Diablos	F. McCarthy	1,250	225.00	225-275.
89-21-089	Down From The Mountains	F. McCarthy	1,500	245.00	245-290.
89-21-090	Canyon Lands	F. McCarthy	1,250	225.00	235.00
89-21-091	Winter Trail	F. McCarthy	1,500	235.00	235-300.
90-21-092	On The Old North Trail (Triptych)	F. McCarthy	650	550.00	550.00
90-21-093	Below The Breaking Dawn	F. McCarthy	1,250	225.00	185-225.
90-21-094	Hoka Hey: Sioux War Cry	F. McCarthy	1,250	225.00	225.00
90-21-095	Out Of The Windswept Ramparts	F. McCarthy	1,250	225.00	225.00
91-21-096	Pony Express	F. McCarthy	1,000	225.00	225.00
91-21-097	The Pursuit	F. McCarthy	650	550.00	550.00
91-21-098	The Wild Ones	F. McCarthy	1,000	225.00	225.00
91-21-099	The Chase	F. McCarthy	1,000	225.00	225.00
92-21-100	Where Others Has Passed	F. McCarthy	1,000	245.00	300.00
92-21-101	Where Ancient Ones Had Hunted	F. McCarthy	1,000	245.00	300.00
92-21-102	When the Land Was Theirs	F. McCarthy	1,000	225.00	225.00
92-21-103	Navajo Ponies Comanchie Warriors	F. McCarthy	1,000	225.00	225.00
92-21-104	The Art of Frank McCarthy	F. McCarthy	10,418	60.00	60.00
92-21-105	Breaking the Moonlit Silence	F. McCarthy	650	375.00	300-375.
92-21-106	Heading Back	F. McCarthy	1,000	225.00	200-225.
92-21-107	In the Land of the Ancient Ones	F. McCarthy	1,250	245.00	300.00
93-21-108	Sighting the Intruders	F. McCarthy	1,000	225.00	225.00
93-21-109	By the Ancient Trails They Passed	F. McCarthy	1,000	245.00	245.00
93-21-110	With Pistols Drawn	F. McCarthy	1,000	195.00	195.00
93-21-111	Shadows of Warriors (3 Print Suite)	F. McCarthy	1,000	225.00	225.00
94-21-112	Show of Defiance	F. McCarthy	1,000	195.00	195.00
94-21-113	Flashes of Lighting (3 Panels)	F. McCarthy	550	435.00	435.00
94-21-114	Beneath the Cliff (Petraglyphs)	F. McCarthy	1,500	295.00	295.00

Greenwich Workshop **K. McCarthy**

		ARTIST	EDITION	ISSUE	QUOTE
91-22-001	Pony Express-Bronze	K. McCarthy	10	934.00	934.00
92-22-002	Comanche Raider-Bronze	K. McCarthy	100	812.50	812.50
94-22-003	Thunder of Hooves-Bronze	K. McCarthy	10	7000.00	7000.00

Greenwich Workshop **Mitchell**

		ARTIST	EDITION	ISSUE	QUOTE
92-23-001	Rowena	D. Mitchell	550	195.00	195.00
93-23-002	Psalms 4:1	D. Mitchell	550	195.00	195.00
93-23-003	Country Church	D. Mitchell	550	175.00	175.00
94-23-004	Bonding Years	D. Mitchell	550	175.00	175.00

Greenwich Workshop **Parker**

		ARTIST	EDITION	ISSUE	QUOTE
94-24-001	Grizzlies at the Falls	R. Parker	850	225.00	225.00
94-24-002	Forest Flight	R. Parker	850	195.00	195.00

Greenwich Workshop **Phillips**

		ARTIST	EDITION	ISSUE	QUOTE
82-25-001	Advantage Eagle	W. Phillips	1,000	135.00	400.00
82-25-002	Welcome Home Yank	W. Phillips	1,000	135.00	1100.00
83-25-003	Two Down, One to Go	W. Phillips	3,000	15.00	15.00
83-25-004	Those Clouds Won't Help You Now	W. Phillips	625	135.00	135.00
83-25-005	Those Clouds Won't Help You Now, remarque	W. Phillips	25	275.00	275.00
83-25-006	The Giant Begins to Stir	W. Phillips	1,250	185.00	2500.00
84-25-007	Into the Teeth of the Tiger	W. Phillips	975	135.00	1200.00
84-25-008	Into the Teeth of the Tiger, remarque	W. Phillips	25	167.50	2000.00
84-25-009	Hellfire Corner	W. Phillips	1,225	185.00	1000.00
84-25-010	Hellfire Corner, remarque	W. Phillips	25	225.80	225.80
85-25-011	The Phantoms and the Wizard	W. Phillips	850	145.00	850.00
85-25-012	Lest We Forget	W. Phillips	1,250	195.00	195.00
85-25-013	Heading For Trouble	W. Phillips	1,000	125.00	500.00
86-25-014	Thunder in the Canyon	W. Phillips	1,000	165.00	1000.00
86-25-015	Changing of the Guard	W. Phillips	500	100.00	100.00
86-25-016	Top Cover for the Straggler	W. Phillips	1,000	145.00	145.00
86-25-017	Confrontation at Beachy Head	W. Phillips	1,000	150.00	150.00
86-25-018	Next Time Get 'Em All	W. Phillips	1,500	225.00	550.00
87-25-019	Range Wars	W. Phillips	1,000	160.00	160.00
87-25-020	Sunward We Climb	W. Phillips	1,000	175.00	175.00
87-25-021	Shore Birds at Point Lobos	W. Phillips	1,250	175.00	175.00
87-25-022	Those Last Critical Moments	W. Phillips	1,250	185.00	550.00
88-25-023	America on the Move	W. Phillips	1,500	185.00	210.00
88-25-024	The Long Green Line	W. Phillips	3,500	185.00	185.00
89-25-025	Sierra Hotel	W. Phillips	1,250	175.00	175.00
89-25-026	Over the Top	W. Phillips	1,000	165.00	165.00
89-25-027	No Flying Today	W. Phillips	1,500	185.00	185.00
89-25-028	Time to Head Home	W. Phillips	1,500	165.00	165.00
89-25-029	No Empty Bunks Tonight	W. Phillips	1,500	165.00	165.00
90-25-030	Going in Hot w/Book	W. Phillips	1,500	250.00	250.00
90-25-031	Hunter Becomes the Hunted	W. Phillips	1,500	265.00	265.00
90-25-032	A Time of Eagles	W. Phillips	1,250	245.00	245.00
91-25-033	Fifty Miles Out	W. Phillips	1,000	175.00	175.00

		ARTIST	EDITION	ISSUE	QUOTE
91-25-034	When You See Zeros, Fight Em'	W. Phillips	1,000	245.00	245.00
91-25-035	Low Pass For the Home Folks, BP	W. Phillips	1,000	175.00	175.00
91-25-036	Last Chance	W. Phillips	1,000	165.00	245.00
91-25-037	Dauntless Against a Rising Sun	W. Phillips	850	195.00	195.00
91-25-038	Intruder Outbound	W. Phillips	1,000	225.00	225.00
92-25-039	I Could Never Be So Lucky Again	W. Phillips	850	295.00	800.00
92-25-040	The Long Ride Home (P-51D)	W. Phillips	850	195.00	195.00
92-25-041	Ploesti: Into the Fire and Fury	W. Phillips	850	195.00	195.00
92-25-042	Alone No More	W. Phillips	850	195.00	195.00
93-25-043	And Now the Trap	W. Phillips	850	175.00	175.00
93-25-044	Chasing the Daylight	W. Phillips	850	185.00	185.00
93-25-045	When Prayers are Answered	W. Phillips	850	245.00	400.00
93-25-046	If Only in My Dreams	W. Phillips	1,000	175.00	260.00
93-25-047	Threading the Eye of the Needle	W. Phillips	1,000	195.00	195.00
94-25-048	Lethal Encounter	W. Phillips	1,000	225.00	225.00
94-25-049	Into the Throne Room of God w/book "The Glory of Flight"	W. Phillips	750	195.00	195.00
94-25-050	Christmas Leave When Dreams Come True	W. Phillips	1,500	185.00	185.00
Greenwich Workshop		**Reynolds**			
94-26-001	Arizona Cowboys	J. Reynolds	850	195.00	195.00
94-26-002	The Henry	J. Reynolds	850	195.00	195.00
94-26-003	Quiet Place	J. Reynolds	1,000	185.00	185.00
Greenwich Workshop		**Simpkins**			
93-27-001	Angels	J. Simpkins	850	225.00	225.00
94-27-002	All My Love	J. Simpkins	850	125.00	125.00
94-27-003	Reverence For Life w/border & card	J. Simpkins	750	175.00	175.00
94-27-004	Reverence For Life w/frame	J. Simpkins	100	600.00	600.00
94-27-005	Gold Falls	J. Simpkins	1,750	195.00	195.00
Greenwich Workshop		**Terpning**			
81-28-001	Stones that Speak	H. Terpning	1,000	150.00	1400.00
81-28-002	Small Comfort	H. Terpning	1,000	135.00	135.00
81-28-003	The Spectators	H. Terpning	1,000	135.00	1400.00
81-28-004	The Victors	H. Terpning	1,000	150.00	700.00
81-28-005	Sioux Flag Carrier	H. Terpning	1,000	125.00	125.00
82-28-006	Search For the Renegades	H. Terpning	1,000	150.00	150.00
82-28-007	Chief Joseph Rides to Surrender	H. Terpning	1,000	150.00	3500.00
82-28-008	CA Set Pony Soldiers/Warriors	H. Terpning	1,000	200.00	200.00
82-28-009	Shield of Her Husband	H. Terpning	1,000	150.00	1400.00
83-28-010	Shoshonis	H. Terpning	1,250	85.00	85.00
83-28-011	Crossing Medicine Lodge Creek	H. Terpning	1,000	150.00	1000.00
83-28-012	Staff Carrier	H. Terpning	1,250	90.00	90.00
83-28-013	Paints	H. Terpning	1,000	140.00	140.00
84-28-014	The Long Shot, signed	H. Terpning	1,000	55.00	55.00
84-28-015	Woman of the Sioux	H. Terpning	1,000	165.00	165.00
84-28-016	Crow Pipe Holder	H. Terpning	1,000	150.00	150.00
84-28-017	Medicine Man of the Cheyene	H. Terpning	450	350.00	4000.00
85-28-018	One Man's Castle	H. Terpning	1,000	150.00	150.00
85-28-019	The Scouts of General Crook	H. Terpning	1,000	175.00	175.00
85-28-020	The Warning	H. Terpning	1,650	175.00	175.00
85-28-021	The Signal	H. Terpning	1,250	90.00	625-800.
85-28-022	The Cache	H. Terpning	1,000	175.00	175.00
85-28-023	Blackfeet Spectators	H. Terpning	475	350.00	350.00
86-28-024	Status Symbols	H. Terpning	1,000	185.00	12-1450.
86-28-025	Thunderpipe and the Holy Man	H. Terpning	550	350.00	350.00
86-28-026	Watching the Column	H. Terpning	1,250	90.00	90.00
86-28-027	Comanche Spoilers	H. Terpning	1,000	195.00	195.00
87-28-028	The Ploy	H. Terpning	1,000	195.00	1100.00
87-28-029	Preparing for the Sun Dance	H. Terpning	1,000	175.00	175.00
87-28-030	Winter Coat	H. Terpning	1,250	95.00	95.00
87-28-031	Blackfeet Among the Aspen	H. Terpning	1,000	225.00	225.00
88-28-032	Search For the Pass	H. Terpning	1,000	225.00	225.00
88-28-033	Hope Springs Eternal-Ghost Dance	H. Terpning	2,250	225.00	225.00
88-28-034	Blood Man	H. Terpning	1,250	95.00	95.00
88-28-035	Sunday Best	H. Terpning	1,250	195.00	195.00
88-28-036	Pride of the Cheyene	H. Terpning	1,250	195.00	195.00
89-28-037	Scout's Report	H. Terpning	1,250	225.00	225.00
89-28-038	Shepherd of the Plains	H. Terpning	1,250	125.00	125.00
89-28-039	The Storyteller w/Video & Book	H. Terpning	1,500	950.00	950.00
90-28-040	When Careless Spelled Disaster	H. Terpning	1,000	225.00	225.00
90-28-041	Cree Finery	H. Terpning	1,000	225.00	225.00
90-28-042	Telling of the Legends	H. Terpning	1,250	225.00	1200.00
91-28-043	The Last Buffalo	H. Terpning	1,000	225.00	225.00
91-28-044	Transferring the Medicine Shield	H. Terpning	850	375.00	1800.00
91-28-045	Leader of Men	H. Terpning	1,250	235.00	235.00
91-28-046	Digging in at Sappa Creek MW	H. Terpning	650	375.00	375.00
92-28-047	Prairie Knights	H. Terpning	1,000	225.00	225.00
92-28-048	Four Sacred Drummers	H. Terpning	1,000	225.00	225.00
92-28-049	The Strength of Eagles	H. Terpning	1,250	235.00	235.00
92-28-050	Passing Into Womanhood	H. Terpning	650	375.00	400.00
92-28-051	Against the Coldmaker	H. Terpning	1,000	195.00	195.00
92-28-052	Capture of the Horse Bundle	H. Terpning	1,250	235.00	235.00
93-28-053	Army Regulations	H. Terpning	1,000	235.00	235.00
93-28-054	Medicine Pipe	H. Terpning	1,000	150.00	150.00
93-28-055	Profile of Wisdom	H. Terpning	1,000	175.00	175.00
93-28-056	The Apache Fire Makers	H. Terpning	1,000	235.00	235.00
93-28-057	Soldier Hat	H. Terpning	1,000	235.00	235.00
94-28-058	Crow Camp, 1864	H. Terpning	1,000	235.00	235.00
94-28-059	Isdzan-Apache Woman	H. Terpning	1,000	175.00	175.00
94-28-060	The Feast	H. Terpning	1,850	245.00	245.00
Greenwich Workshop		**Townsend**			
92-29-001	Riverbend	B. Townsend	1,000	185.00	185.00
92-29-002	Open Ridge	B. Townsend	1,500	225.00	225.00
93-29-003	Out of the Shadows	B. Townsend	1,500	195.00	195.00
93-29-004	Hailstorm Creek	B. Townsend	1,250	195.00	195.00
93-29-005	Dusk	B. Townsend	1,250	195.00	195.00
94-29-006	Autumn Hillside	B. Townsend	1,000	175.00	175.00
94-29-007	Mountain Light	B. Townsend	1,000	195.00	195.00
Greenwich Workshop		**Weiss**			
82-30-001	Lab Puppies	J. Weiss	1,000	65.00	65.00
82-30-002	Rebel & Soda	J. Weiss	1,000	45.00	45.00
83-30-003	Golden Retriever Puppies	J. Weiss	1,000	65.00	65.00
84-30-004	Basset Hound Puppies	J. Weiss	1,000	65.00	65.00
84-30-005	Cocker Spaniel Puppies	J. Weiss	1,000	75.00	75.00
84-30-006	Old English Sheepdog Puppies	J. Weiss	1,000	65.00	65.00
85-30-007	Persian Kitten	J. Weiss	1,000	65.00	65.00
86-30-008	One Morning in October	J. Weiss	850	125.00	125.00
88-30-009	Goldens at the Shore	J. Weiss	850	145.00	145.00
88-30-010	Yellow Labrador Head Study	J. Weiss	1,000	90.00	90.00
88-30-011	Black Labrador Head Study	J. Weiss	1,000	90.00	90.00

		ARTIST	EDITION	ISSUE	QUOTE
91-30-012	Wake Up Call	J. Weiss	850	165.00	165.00
92-30-013	No Swimming Lessons Today	J. Weiss	1,000	140.00	140.00
92-30-014	Cuddle Time	J. Weiss	850	95.00	95.00
93-30-015	A Feeling of Warmth	J. Weiss	1,000	165.00	165.00
93-30-016	Old Friends	J. Weiss	1,000	95.00	95.00
94-30-017	Forever Friends	J. Weiss	1,000	95.00	95.00
Greenwich Workshop		**Williams**			
93-31-001	Avant Garde S&N	B.D. Williams	500	60.00	60.00
93-31-002	Avant Garde unsigned	B.D. Williams	2,603	30.00	30.00
94-31-003	The Savoy (Greenwich Platinum Series)	B.D. Williams	100	1250.00	1250.00
Greenwich Workshop		**Wootton**			
82-32-001	Knights of the Sky	F. Wootton	850	165.00	165.00
83-32-002	The Battle of Britain	F. Wootton	850	150.00	150.00
85-32-003	Huntsmen and Hounds	F. Wootton	650	115.00	115.00
86-32-004	The Spitfire Legend	F. Wootton	850	195.00	195.00
88-32-005	Encounter with the Red Baron	F. Wootton	850	165.00	165.00
90-32-006	Adlertag, 15 August 1940 & Video	F. Wootton	1,500	245.00	245.00
92-32-007	The Last of the First F. Wooten	F. Wootton	850	235.00	235.00
93-32-008	April Morning:France, 1918	F. Wootton	850	245.00	245.00
93-32-009	Last Combat of the Red Baron	F. Wootton	850	185.00	185.00
94-32-010	Peenemunde	F. Wootton	850	245.00	245.00
Greenwich Workshop		**Wysocki**			
79-33-001	Fox Run	C. Wysocki	1,000	75.00	1700.00
79-33-002	Butternut Farms	C. Wysocki	1,000	75.00	1000.00
79-33-003	Shall We?	C. Wysocki	1,000	75.00	500.00
79-33-004	Fairhaven by the Sea	C. Wysocki	1,000	75.00	700.00
80-33-005	Derby Square	C. Wysocki	1,000	90.00	1100.00
80-33-006	Jolly Hill Farms	C. Wysocki	1,000	75.00	850.00
80-33-007	Caleb's Buggy Barn	C. Wysocki	1,000	80.00	300.00
84-33-008	Yankee Wink Hollow	C. Wysocki	1,000	95.00	1300.00
81-33-009	Page's Bake Shoppe	C. Wysocki	1,000	115.00	500.00
81-33-010	Prairie Wind Flowers	C. Wysocki	1,000	125.00	1800.00
81-33-011	Olde America	C. Wysocki	1,500	125.00	700.00
81-33-012	Carver Coggins	C. Wysocki	1,000	145.00	900.00
82-33-013	Sunset Hills, Texas Wildcatters	C. Wysocki	1,000	125.00	150.00
82-33-014	Sleepy Town West	C. Wysocki	1,500	150.00	500.00
82-33-015	The Nantucket	C. Wysocki	1,000	145.00	400.00
82-33-016	Christmas Print, 1982	C. Wysocki	2,000	80.00	700.00
83-33-017	Amish Neighbors	C. Wysocki	1,000	150.00	500.00
83-33-018	Commemorative Print, 1983	C. Wysocki	2,000	55.00	55.00
83-33-019	Tea by the Sea	C. Wysocki	1,000	145.00	1500.00
83-33-020	Plum Island Sound, signed	C. Wysocki	1,000	55.00	55.00
83-33-021	Plum Island Sound, unsigned	C. Wysocki	Open	40.00	40.00
83-33-022	Applebutter Makers	C. Wysocki	1,000	135.00	500.00
83-33-023	Country Race	C. Wysocki	1,000	150.00	400.00
83-33-024	Commemorative Print, 1984	C. Wysocki	2,000	55.00	55.00
84-33-025	Sweetheart Chessmate	C. Wysocki	1,000	95.00	350.00
84-33-026	Cape Cod Cold Fish Party	C. Wysocki	1,000	150.00	150.00
84-33-027	Cotton Country	C. Wysocki	1,000	150.00	200.00
84-33-028	Chumbuddies, signed	C. Wysocki	1,000	55.00	55.00
84-33-029	The Gang's All Here	C. Wysocki	Open	65.00	65.00
84-33-030	The Gang's All Here, remarque	C. Wysocki	250	90.00	90.00
84-33-031	Storin' Up	C. Wysocki	450	325.00	1000.00
84-33-032	Bird House (C)	C. Wysocki	1,000	85.00	450.00
84-33-033	The Foxy Fox Outfoxes the Fox Hunters	C. Wysocki	1,500	150.00	600.00
84-33-034	Commemorative Print, 1985	C. Wysocki	2,000	55.00	55.00
84-33-035	A Warm Christmas Love	C. Wysocki	3,951	80.00	350.00
85-33-036	Salty Witch Bay	C. Wysocki	475	350.00	2400.00
85-33-037	Clammers at Hodge's Horn	C. Wysocki	1,000	150.00	1500.00
85-33-038	I Love America	C. Wysocki	2,000	20.00	20.00
85-33-039	Birds of a Feather	C. Wysocki	1,250	145.00	400.00
85-33-040	Merrymakers Serenade	C. Wysocki	1,250	135.00	135.00
85-33-041	Commemorative Print, 1986	C. Wysocki	2,000	55.00	55.00
86-33-042	Carnival Capers	C. Wysocki	620	200.00	200.00
86-33-043	Devilstone Harbor/An American Celebration (Print & Book)	C. Wysocki	3,500	195.00	400.00
86-33-044	Hickory Haven Canal	C. Wysocki	1,500	165.00	800.00
86-33-045	Devilbelly Bay	C. Wysocki	1,000	145.00	300.00
86-33-046	Daddy's Coming Home	C. Wysocki	1,250	150.00	1100.00
86-33-047	Lady Liberty's Independence Day Enterprising Immigrants	C. Wysocki	1,500	140.00	200-300.
86-33-048	Mr. Swallobark	C. Wysocki	2,000	145.00	1500.00
86-33-049	Dancing Pheasant Farms	C. Wysocki	1,750	165.00	350.00
87-33-050	Yearning For My Captain	C. Wysocki	2,000	150.00	285-300.
87-33-051	Dahalia Dinalhaven Makes a Dory Deal	C. Wysocki	2,250	150.00	250.00
87-33-052	Bach's Magnificat in D Minor	C. Wysocki	2,250	150.00	500.00
87-33-053	You've Been So Long at Sea, Horatio	C. Wysocki	2,500	150.00	200.00
87-33-054	'Twas the Twilight Before Christmas	C. Wysocki	7,500	95.00	150.00
88-33-055	Home Is My Sailor	C. Wysocki	2,500	150.00	150.00
88-33-056	Feathered Critics	C. Wysocki	2,500	150.00	150.00
88-33-057	The Americana Bowl	C. Wysocki	3,500	295.00	295.00
89-33-058	Bostonians And Beans (PC)	C. Wysocki	6,711	225.00	565-600.
89-33-059	The Memory Maker	C. Wysocki	2,500	165.00	165.00
89-33-060	Dreamers	C. Wysocki	3,000	175.00	350.00
89-33-061	Another Year At Sea	C. Wysocki	2,500	175.00	250-410.
89-33-062	Christmas Greeting	C. Wysocki	11,000	125.00	100.00
89-33-063	Fun Lovin' Silly Folks	C. Wysocki	3,000	185.00	300-400.
90-33-064	Belly Warmers	C. Wysocki	2,500	150.00	195-200.
90-33-065	Wednesday Night Checkers	C. Wysocki	2,500	175.00	175.00
90-33-066	Robin Hood	C. Wysocki	2,000	165.00	165.00
90-33-067	Where The Bouys Are	C. Wysocki	2,750	175.00	200.00
90-33-068	Jingle Bell Teddy and Friends	C. Wysocki	5,000	125.00	125.00
91-33-069	Rockland Breakwater Light	C. Wysocki	2,500	165.00	280.00
91-33-070	Beauty And The Beast	C. Wysocki	2,000	125.00	125.00
91-33-071	Sea Captain's Wife Abiding	C. Wysocki	1,500	150.00	150.00
91-33-072	West Quoddy Head Light, Maine	C. Wysocki	2,500	165.00	165.00
91-33-073	Whistle Stop Christmas	C. Wysocki	5,000	125.00	125.00
92-33-074	Frederick the Literate	C. Wysocki	6,500	150.00	2000.00
92-33-075	Gay Head Light	C. Wysocki	2,500	165.00	165.00
92-33-076	Proud Little Angler	C. Wysocki	2,750	150.00	150.00
92-33-077	Ethel the Gourmet	C. Wysocki	10,179	150.00	350.00
92-33-078	Love Letter From Laramie	C. Wysocki	1,500	150.00	150.00
93-33-079	The Three Sisters of Nauset, 1880	C. Wysocki	2,500	165.00	200.00
94-33-080	Remington w/Book-Heartland	C. Wysocki	15,000	195.00	195.00
Guildhall, Inc.		**DeHaan**			
79-01-001	Foggy Mornin' Wait	C. DeHaan	650	75.00	2525.00
80-01-002	Texas Panhandle	C. DeHaan	650	75.00	1525.00
81-01-003	MacTavish	C. DeHaan	650	75.00	1000.00
81-01-004	Forgin' The Keechi	C. DeHaan	650	85.00	725.00

		ARTIST	EDITION	ISSUE	QUOTE
81-01-005	Surprise Encounter	C. DeHaan	750	85.00	475.00
82-01-006	O' That Strawberry Roan	C. DeHaan	750	85.00	125.00
83-01-007	Ridin' Ol' Paint	C. DeHaan	750	85.00	625.00
83-01-008	Crossin' Horse Creek	C. DeHaan	650	100.00	625.00
83-01-009	Keep A Movin' Dan	C. DeHaan	750	85.00	125.00
84-01-010	Jake	C. DeHaan	650	100.00	600.00
84-01-011	Spooked	C. DeHaan	650	95.00	1825.00
85-01-012	Up the Chisholm	C. DeHaan	750	85.00	125.00
85-01-013	Keechi Country	C. DeHaan	750	100.00	375.00
85-01-014	Oklahoma Paints	C. DeHaan	750	100.00	425.00
85-01-015	Horsemen of the West (Suite of 3)	C. DeHaan	650	145.00	975.00
86-01-016	The Mustangers	C. DeHaan	750	100.00	400.00
86-01-017	The Searchers	C. DeHaan	650	100.00	375.00
86-01-018	Moon Dancers	C. DeHaan	750	100.00	165.00
86-01-019	The Loner (with matching buckle)	C. DeHaan	750	145.00	425.00
87-01-020	Snow Birds	C. DeHaan	750	100.00	350.00
87-01-021	Murphy's Law	C. DeHaan	750	100.00	225.00
87-01-022	Crow Ceremonial Dress	C. DeHaan	750	100.00	175.00
87-01-023	Supremacy	C. DeHaan	750	100.00	175.00
88-01-024	Mornin' Gather	C. DeHaan	750	100.00	350.00
88-01-025	Stage To Deadwood	C. DeHaan	750	100.00	275.00
88-01-026	Water Breakin'	C. DeHaan	750	125.00	600.00
89-01-027	Kentucky Blue	C. DeHaan	750	125.00	575.00
89-01-028	Village Markers	C. DeHaan	750	125.00	525.00
89-01-029	The Quarter Horse	C. DeHaan	800	125.00	325.00
89-01-030	Crows	C. DeHaan	800	135.00	525.00
90-01-031	War Cry	C. DeHaan	925	135.00	275.00
90-01-032	Crow Autumn	C. DeHaan	925	135.00	250.00
90-01-033	Escape	C. DeHaan	925	135.00	200.00
90-01-034	High Plains Drifters	C. DeHaan	925	140.00	200.00
90-01-035	The Pipe Carrier	C. DeHaan	925	140.00	175.00
91-01-036	The Encounter	C. DeHaan	925	140.00	300.00
91-01-037	Sundance	C. DeHaan	925	140.00	175.00
91-01-038	The Prideful Ones (Set of 2)	C. DeHaan	925	150.00	200.00
92-01-039	Crossing At The Big Trees	C. DeHaan	925	140.00	200.00
92-01-040	Silent Trail Talk	C. DeHaan	925	140.00	175.00
92-01-041	73o In Amarillo...Yesterday	C. DeHaan	925	140.00	140.00
93-01-042	The Return	C. DeHaan	925	150.00	150.00
93-01-043	Appeasing The Water People	C. DeHaan	925	150.00	150.00
93-01-044	As The Buffalo Leave	C. DeHaan	925	150.00	150.00
93-01-045	Goosed	C. DeHaan	925	150.00	150.00

Hadley House **Franca**

		ARTIST	EDITION	ISSUE	QUOTE
88-01-001	Sitting Bull	O. Franca	950	70.00	250.00
88-01-002	The Apache	O. Franca	950	70.00	175.00
88-01-003	Slow Bull	O. Franca	950	70.00	250.00
88-01-004	Cacique	O. Franca	950	70.00	175.00
88-01-005	The Red Shawl	O. Franca	600	80.00	300.00
88-01-006	Feathered Hair Ties	O. Franca	600	80.00	300.00
89-01-007	Young Warrior	O. Franca	999	80.00	425.00
89-01-008	Navajo Fantasy	O. Franca	999	80.00	150.00
89-01-009	Winter	O. Franca	999	80.00	220.00
89-01-010	Pink Navajo	O. Franca	999	80.00	250.00
90-01-011	Cecy	O. Franca	1,500	125.00	225.00
90-01-012	Santa Fe	O. Franca	1,500	125.00	300.00
90-01-013	Blue Navajo	O. Franca	1,500	125.00	125.00
90-01-014	Destiny	O. Franca	999	100.00	100.00
90-01-015	Blue Tranquility	O. Franca	999	100.00	100.00
90-01-016	Wind Song	O. Franca	999	100.00	425.00
90-01-017	Navajo Summer	O. Franca	999	100.00	240.00
90-01-018	Feathered Hair Ties II	O. Franca	999	100.00	300.00
90-01-019	Turqoise Necklace	O. Franca	999	100.00	450.00
91-01-020	Early Morning	O. Franca	3,600	125.00	225.00
91-01-021	Red Wolf	O. Franca	1,500	125.00	225.00
91-01-022	Olympia	O. Franca	1,500	125.00	250.00
91-01-023	The Lovers	O. Franca	2,400	125.00	800.00
91-01-024	The Model	O. Franca	1,500	125.00	400.00
92-01-025	Navajo Reflection	O. Franca	4,000	80.00	225.00
92-01-026	Wind Song II	O. Franca	4,000	80.00	150.00
92-01-027	Navajo Daydream	O. Franca	3,600	175.00	360.00
92-01-028	Navajo Meditating	O. Franca	4,000	80.00	125.00
93-01-029	Evening In Taos	O. Franca	4,000	80.00	80.00

Hadley House **Hanks**

		ARTIST	EDITION	ISSUE	QUOTE
90-02-001	Contemplation	S. Hanks	999	100.00	150.00
90-02-002	Quiet Rapport	S. Hanks	999	150.00	300.00
90-02-003	Emotional Appeal	S. Hanks	999	150.00	200.00
91-02-004	Duet	S. Hanks	999	150.00	250.00
91-02-005	A World For Our Children	S. Hanks	999	125.00	475.00
91-02-006	Sunday Afternoon	S. Hanks	Open	40.00	40.00
92-02-007	Stepping Stones	S. Hanks	999	150.00	250.00
92-02-008	An Innocent View	S. Hanks	999	150.00	350.00
92-02-009	Sometimes It's the Little Things	S. Hanks	999	125.00	225.00
92-02-010	Things Worth Keeping	S. Hanks	999	125.00	1500.00
92-02-011	Conferring With the Sea	S. Hanks	999	125.00	250.00
93-02-012	Gathering Thoughts	S. Hanks	1,500	150.00	150.00
93-02-013	The Thinkers	S. Hanks	1,500	150.00	150.00
93-02-014	The New Arrival	S. Hanks	1,500	150.00	300.00
93-02-015	Places I Remember	S. Hanks	1,500	150.00	150.00
93-02-016	Catching The Sun	S. Hanks	999	150.00	250.00

Hadley House **Redlin**

		ARTIST	EDITION	ISSUE	QUOTE
77-03-001	Apple River Mallards	T. Redlin	Open	10.00	150.00
77-03-002	Over the Blowdown	T. Redlin	Open	20.00	70.00
77-03-003	Winter Snows	T. Redlin	Open	20.00	100.00
78-03-004	Back from the Fields	T. Redlin	720	40.00	325.00
78-03-005	Backwater Mallards	T. Redlin	720	40.00	900.00
78-03-006	Old Loggers Trail	T. Redlin	720	40.00	550.00
78-03-007	Over the Rushes	T. Redlin	720	40.00	400.00
78-03-008	Quiet Afternoon	T. Redlin	720	40.00	400.00
78-03-009	Startled	T. Redlin	720	30.00	400.00
79-03-010	Ageing Shoreline	T. Redlin	960	40.00	250.00
79-03-011	Colorful Trio	T. Redlin	960	40.00	400.00
79-03-012	Fighting a Headwind	T. Redlin	960	30.00	250.00
79-03-013	Morning Chores	T. Redlin	960	40.00	1100.00
79-03-014	The Loner	T. Redlin	960	40.00	200.00
79-03-015	Whitecaps	T. Redlin	960	40.00	375.00
80-03-016	Autumn Run	T. Redlin	960	60.00	450.00
80-03-017	Breaking Away	T. Redlin	960	60.00	300.00
80-03-018	Clearing the Rail	T. Redlin	960	60.00	350.00
80-03-019	Country Road	T. Redlin	960	60.00	375.00
80-03-020	Drifting	T. Redlin	960	60.00	300.00

		ARTIST	EDITION	ISSUE	QUOTE
80-03-021	The Homestead	T. Redlin	960	60.00	375.00
80-03-022	Intruders	T. Redlin	960	60.00	200.00
80-03-023	Night Watch	T. Redlin	2,400	60.00	700.00
80-03-024	Rusty Refuge	T. Redlin	960	60.00	475.00
80-03-025	Secluded Pond	T. Redlin	960	60.00	250.00
80-03-026	Silent Sunset	T. Redlin	960	60.00	850.00
80-03-027	Spring Thaw	T. Redlin	960	60.00	350.00
80-03-028	Squall Line	T. Redlin	960	60.00	300.00
81-03-029	1981 Mn Duck Stamp Print	T. Redlin	7,800	125.00	200.00
81-03-030	All Clear	T. Redlin	960	150.00	350.00
81-03-031	April Snow	T. Redlin	960	100.00	450.00
81-03-032	Broken Covey	T. Redlin	960	100.00	325.00
81-03-033	High Country	T. Redlin	960	100.00	450.00
81-03-034	Hightailing	T. Redlin	960	75.00	200.00
81-03-035	The Landmark	T. Redlin	960	100.00	400.00
81-03-036	Morning Retreat (AP)	T. Redlin	240	400.00	2700.00
81-03-037	Passing Through	T. Redlin	960	100.00	225.00
81-03-038	Rusty Refuge II	T. Redlin	960	100.00	375.00
81-03-039	Sharing the Bounty	T. Redlin	960	100.00	550.00
81-03-040	Soft Shadows	T. Redlin	960	100.00	225.00
81-03-041	Spring Run-Off	T. Redlin	1,700	125.00	350.00
82-03-042	1982 Mn Trout Stamp Print	T. Redlin	960	125.00	600.00
82-03-043	Evening Retreat (AP)	T. Redlin	300	400.00	2500.00
82-03-044	October Evening	T. Redlin	960	100.00	450.00
82-03-045	Reflections	T. Redlin	960	100.00	400.00
82-03-046	Seed Hunters	T. Redlin	960	100.00	450.00
82-03-047	Spring Mapling	T. Redlin	960	100.00	450.00
82-03-048	The Birch Line	T. Redlin	960	100.00	500.00
82-03-049	The Landing	T. Redlin	Open	30.00	80.00
82-03-050	Whitewater	T. Redlin	960	100.00	400.00
82-03-051	Winter Haven	T. Redlin	500	85.00	800.00
83-03-052	1983 ND Duck Stamp Print	T. Redlin	3,438	135.00	135.00
83-03-053	Autumn Shoreline	T. Redlin	Open	50.00	200.00
83-03-054	Backwoods Cabin	T. Redlin	960	150.00	675.00
83-03-055	Evening Glow	T. Redlin	960	150.00	1400.00
83-03-056	Evening Surprise	T. Redlin	960	150.00	900.00
83-03-057	Hidden Point	T. Redlin	960	150.00	350.00
83-03-058	On the Alert	T. Redlin	960	125.00	400.00
83-03-059	Peaceful Evening	T. Redlin	960	100.00	350.00
83-03-060	Prairie Springs	T. Redlin	960	150.00	325.00
83-03-061	Rushing Rapids	T. Redlin	960	125.00	400.00
84-03-062	1984 Quail Conservation	T. Redlin	1,500	135.00	135.00
84-03-063	Bluebill Point (AP)	T. Redlin	240	300.00	400.00
84-03-064	Changing Seasons-Summer	T. Redlin	960	150.00	800.00
84-03-065	Closed for the Season	T. Redlin	960	150.00	300.00
84-03-066	Leaving the Sanctuary	T. Redlin	960	150.00	475.00
84-03-067	Morning Glow	T. Redlin	960	150.00	1200.00
84-03-068	Night Harvest	T. Redlin	960	150.00	575.00
84-03-069	Nightflight (AP)	T. Redlin	360	600.00	22-2800.
84-03-070	Prairie Skyline	T. Redlin	960	150.00	550.00
84-03-071	Rural Route	T. Redlin	960	150.00	350.00
84-03-072	Rusty Refuge III	T. Redlin	960	150.00	400.00
84-03-073	Silent Wings Suite (set of 4)	T. Redlin	960	200.00	450.00
84-03-074	Sundown	T. Redlin	960	300.00	575.00
84-03-075	Sunny Afternoon	T. Redlin	960	150.00	375.00
84-03-076	Winter Windbreak	T. Redlin	960	150.00	450.00
85-03-077	1985 MN Duck Stamp	T. Redlin	4,385	135.00	135.00
85-03-078	Afternoon Glow	T. Redlin	960	150.00	1000.00
85-03-079	Breaking Cover	T. Redlin	960	150.00	325.00
85-03-080	Brousing	T. Redlin	960	150.00	350.00
85-03-081	Clear View	T. Redlin	1,500	300.00	450.00
85-03-082	Delayed Departure	T. Redlin	1,500	150.00	450.00
85-03-083	Evening Company	T. Redlin	960	150.00	450.00
85-03-084	Night Light	T. Redlin	1,500	300.00	600.00
85-03-085	Riverside Pond	T. Redlin	960	150.00	525.00
85-03-086	Rusty Refuge IV	T. Redlin	960	150.00	500.00
85-03-087	The Sharing Season	T. Redlin	Open	60.00	150.00
85-03-088	Whistle Stop	T. Redlin	960	150.00	550.00
85-03-089	Back to the Sanctuary	T. Redlin	960	150.00	450.00
86-03-090	Changing Seasons-Autumn	T. Redlin	960	150.00	400.00
86-03-091	Changing Seasons-Winter	T. Redlin	960	200.00	400.00
86-03-092	Coming Home	T. Redlin	2,400	100.00	1200.00
86-03-093	Hazy Afternoon	T. Redlin	2,560	200.00	650.00
86-03-094	Night Mapling	T. Redlin	960	200.00	550.00
86-03-095	Prairie Monuments	T. Redlin	960	200.00	400.00
86-03-096	Sharing Season II	T. Redlin	Open	60.00	150.00
86-03-097	Silent Flight	T. Redlin	960	150.00	250.00
86-03-098	Stormy Weather	T. Redlin	1,500	200.00	550.00
86-03-099	Sunlit Trail	T. Redlin	960	150.00	325.00
86-03-100	Twilight Glow	T. Redlin	960	200.00	700.00
87-03-101	Autumn Afternoon	T. Redlin	4,800	100.00	750.00
87-03-102	Changing Seasons-Spring	T. Redlin	960	200.00	450.00
87-03-103	Deer Crossing	T. Redlin	2,400	200.00	450.00
87-03-104	Evening Chores (print & book)	T. Redlin	2,400	400.00	500.00
87-03-105	Evening Harvest	T. Redlin	960	200.00	475.00
87-03-106	Golden Retreat (AP)	T. Redlin	500	800.00	1600.00
87-03-107	Prepared for the Season	T. Redlin	Open	70.00	100.00
87-03-108	Sharing the Solitude	T. Redlin	2,400	125.00	700.00
87-03-109	That Special Time	T. Redlin	2,400	125.00	650.00
87-03-110	Together for the Season	T. Redlin	Open	70.00	150.00
88-03-111	Boulder Ridge	T. Redlin	4,800	150.00	150-200.
88-03-112	Catching the Scent	T. Redlin	2,400	200.00	150-250.
88-03-113	Country Neighbors	T. Redlin	4,800	150.00	350.00
88-03-114	Homeward Bound	T. Redlin	Open	70.00	125.00
88-03-115	Lights of Home	T. Redlin	9,500	125.00	275-750.
88-03-116	Moonlight Retreat (A/P)	T. Redlin	530	1000.00	1000.00
88-03-117	Prairie Morning	T. Redlin	4,800	150.00	250.00
88-03-118	Quiet of the Evening	T. Redlin	4,800	150.00	850.00
88-03-119	The Master's Domain	T. Redlin	2,400	225.00	700.00
88-03-120	Wednesday Afternoon	T. Redlin	6,800	175.00	400.00
88-03-121	House Call	T. Redlin	6,800	175.00	450.00
89-03-122	Office Hours	T. Redlin	6,800	175.00	450.00
89-03-123	Morning Rounds	T. Redlin	6,800	175.00	175-350.
89-03-124	Indian Summer	T. Redlin	4,800	200.00	300.00
89-03-125	Aroma of Fall	T. Redlin	6,800	200.00	1300.00
89-03-126	Homeward Bound	T. Redlin	Open	80.00	100.00
89-03-127	Special Memories (AP Only)	T. Redlin	570	1000.00	1000.00
90-03-128	Family Traditions	T. Redlin	Open	80.00	100.00
90-03-129	Pure Contentment	T. Redlin	9,500	150.00	475.00
90-03-130	Master of the Valley	T. Redlin	6,800	200.00	200.00
90-03-131	Evening Solitude	T. Redlin	9,500	200.00	500-650.
90-03-132	Best Friends (AP Only)	T. Redlin	570	1000.00	1000.00

		ARTIST	EDITION	ISSUE	QUOTE
90-03-133	Heading Home	T. Redlin	Open	80.00	100.00
90-03-134	Welcome to Paradise	T. Redlin	14,500	150.00	400.00
90-03-135	Evening With Friends	T. Redlin	19,500	225.00	475-975.
91-03-136	Morning Solitude	T. Redlin	12,107	250.00	450-475.
91-03-137	Flying Free	T. Redlin	14,500	200.00	200.00
91-03-138	Hunter's Haven (A/P Only)	T. Redlin	N/A	175.00	175.00
91-03-140	Pleasures of Winter	T. Redlin	24,500	150.00	200-275.
91-03-141	Comforts of Home	T. Redlin	22,900	175.00	350.00
92-03-142	Summertime	T. Redlin	24,900	225.00	225.00
92-03-143	Oh Beautiful for Spacious Skies	T. Redlin	29,500	250.00	250.00
92-03-144	Winter Wonderland	T. Redlin	29,500	150.00	150-200.
92-03-145	The Conservationists	T. Redlin	29,500	175.00	175.00
93-03-146	For Amber Waves of Grain	T. Redlin	29,500	250.00	250.00
93-03-147	For Purple Mountains Majesty	T. Redlin	29,500	250.00	250.00
93-03-148	Autumn Evening	T. Redlin	29,500	250.00	250.00
Hadley House	**Casper**				
92-04-001	Comes the Dawn	M. Casper	600	100.00	100.00
92-04-002	Silence Unbroken	M. Casper	600	100.00	100.00
92-04-003	The Watch	M. Casper	600	100.00	350.00
92-04-004	Reflections	M. Casper	600	100.00	100.00
93-04-005	Skyline Serenade	M. Casper	600	100.00	100.00
93-04-006	Pickets & Vines	M. Casper	999	100.00	100.00
93-04-007	Whispering Wings	M. Casper	1,500	100.00	100.00
Hadley House	**Daniel**				
92-05-001	Puppy Love	K. Daniel	850	75.00	75.00
92-05-002	Nightwatch	K. Daniel	999	150.00	225.00
92-05-003	Forever Friends	K. Daniel	850	185.00	185.00
92-05-004	Lone Drifter	K. Daniel	999	150.00	200.00
93-05-005	Mystic Point	K. Daniel	999	150.00	150.00
Hadley House	**Hulings**				
88-06-001	Ile de la Cite-Paris	C. Hulings	580	150.00	300.00
88-06-002	Onteniente	C. Hulings	580	150.00	425.00
88-06-003	Three Cats on a Grapevine	C. Hulings	580	65.00	225.00
89-06-004	Chechaquene-Morocco Market Square	C. Hulings	999	150.00	150.00
89-06-005	Portuguese Vegetable Woman	C. Hulings	999	85.00	85.00
90-06-006	The Lonely Man	C. Hulings	999	150.00	150.00
90-06-007	Spanish Shawl	C. Hulings	999	125.00	175.00
90-06-008	Ancient French Farmhouse	C. Hulings	999	150.00	240.00
91-06-009	Place des Ternes	C. Hulings	580	195.00	700.00
92-06-010	Cuernavaca Flower Market	C. Hulings	580	225.00	325.00
92-06-011	Sunday Afternoon	C. Hulings	580	195.00	300.00
93-06-012	Spring Flowers	C. Hulings	580	225.00	300.00
93-06-013	Washday In Provence	C. Hulings	580	225.00	225.00
Hallmark Galleries	**Innocent Wonders**				
92-01-001	Pinkie Poo 7500QHG4016	T. Blackshear	9,500	75.00	75.00
Hallmark Galleries	**Majestic Wilderness**				
92-02-001	Timber Wolves 7500QHG2013	M. Newman	9,500	75.00	75.00
92-02-002	White-tailed Deer 7500QHG2014	M. Newman	9,500	75.00	75.00
Hallmark Galleries	**Tobin Fraley Carousel Collection**				
93-03-001	Magical Ride 8000QHG22	Fraley/ Taylor Bruce	9,500	80.00	80.00
John Hine	**Rambles**				
89-01-001	Two for Joy	A. Wyatt	Closed	59.90	59.90
89-01-002	Riverbank	A. Wyatt	Closed	59.90	59.90
89-01-003	Waters Edge	A. Wyatt	Closed	59.90	59.90
89-01-004	Summer Harvest	A. Wyatt	Closed	59.90	59.90
89-01-005	Garden Gate	A. Wyatt	Closed	59.90	59.90
89-01-006	Hedgerow	A. Wyatt	Closed	59.90	59.90
89-01-007	Frog	A. Wyatt	Closed	33.00	33.00
89-01-008	Wren	A. Wyatt	Closed	33.00	33.00
89-01-009	Kingfisher	A. Wyatt	Closed	33.00	33.00
89-01-010	Blue Tit	A. Wyatt	Closed	33.00	33.00
89-01-011	Lobster Pot	A. Wyatt	Closed	50.00	50.00
89-01-012	Puffin Rock	A. Wyatt	Closed	50.00	50.00
89-01-013	Otter's Holt	A. Wyatt	Closed	50.00	50.00
89-01-014	Bluebell Cottage	A. Wyatt	Closed	50.00	50.00
89-01-015	Shirelarm	A. Wyatt	Closed	42.00	42.00
89-01-016	St. Mary's Church	A. Wyatt	Closed	42.00	42.00
89-01-017	The Swan	A. Wyatt	Closed	42.00	42.00
89-01-018	Castle Street	A. Wyatt	Closed	42.00	42.00
Lightpost Group Inc./ Lightpost Publishing	**Canvas Editions-Framed**				
91-01-001	Afternoon Light, Dogwood S/N	T. Kinkade	Closed	495.00	995-1495
91-01-002	Afternoon Light, Dogwood A/P	T. Kinkade	Closed	595.00	1050.00
92-01-003	Amber Afternoon S/N	T. Kinkade	Closed	595.00	815-950.
92-01-004	Amber Afternoon A/P	T. Kinkade	Closed	695.00	1700.00
91-01-005	The Autumn Gate S/N	T. Kinkade	Closed	595.00	16-2300.
91-01-006	The Autumn Gate A/P	T. Kinkade	Closed	695.00	1700.00
94-01-007	Beacon of Hope S/N	T. Kinkade	Closed	615.00	765-865.
94-01-008	Beacon of Hope A/P	T. Kinkade	Closed	765.00	915.00
93-01-009	Beside Still Waters S/N	T. Kinkade	Closed	495.00	995-1095
93-01-010	Beside Still Waters A/P	T. Kinkade	Closed	695.00	995-1150
93-01-011	Beside Still Waters G/P	T. Kinkade	Closed	645.00	895.00
93-01-012	Beyond Autumn Gate S/N	T. Kinkade	Closed	815.00	17-2600.
93-01-013	Beyond Autumn Gate A/P	T. Kinkade	Closed	915.00	16-2200.
93-01-014	The Blessings of Autumn S/N	T. Kinkade	1,250	615.00	615.00
93-01-015	The Blessings of Autumn A/P	T. Kinkade	300	715.00	715.00
94-01-016	The Blessings of Spring S/N	T. Kinkade	Closed	515.00	515-665.
94-01-017	The Blessings of Spring A/P	T. Kinkade	Closed	665.00	665-815.
92-01-018	Blossom Hill Church S/N	T. Kinkade	980	595.00	615.00
92-01-018	Blossom Hill Church A/P	T. Kinkade	200	695.00	715.00
91-01-020	Boston S/N	T. Kinkade	Closed	495.00	1595.00
91-01-021	Boston A/P	T. Kinkade	Closed	595.00	1050.00
92-01-022	Broadwater Bridge S/N	T. Kinkade	Closed	495.00	995-1395
92-01-023	Broadwater BridgeA/P	T. Kinkade	Closed	595.00	1450.00
92-01-024	Broadwater Bridge G/P	T. Kinkade	Closed	645.00	1400.00
89-01-025	Carmel, Ocean Avenue S/N	T. Kinkade	Closed	645.00	37-4000.
89-01-026	Carmel, Ocean Avenue A/P	T. Kinkade	Closed	745.00	5200.00
91-01-027	Carmel, Delores Street and the Tuck Box Tea Room S/N	T. Kinkade	Closed	645.00	16-2400.
91-01-028	Carmel, Delores Street and the Tuck Box Tea Room A/P	T. Kinkade	Closed	745.00	1400.00
91-01-029	Cedar Nook Cottage S/N	T. Kinkade	Closed	195.00	315-700.
90-01-030	Chandler's Cottage S/N	T. Kinkade	Closed	495.00	15-3000.
90-01-031	Christmas At the Ahwahnee S/N	T. Kinkade	980	495.00	515.00
90-01-032	Christmas At the Ahwahnee A/P	T. Kinkade	200	595.00	615.00
90-01-033	Christmas Cottage 1990 S/N	T. Kinkade	Closed	295.00	900-1595
90-01-034	Christmas Cottage 1990 A/P	T. Kinkade	Closed	295.00	1600.00
90-01-035	Christmas Eve S/N	T. Kinkade	Closed	395.00	595-1195

		ARTIST	EDITION	ISSUE	QUOTE
90-01-036	Christmas Eve A/P	T. Kinkade	Closed	495.00	1900.00
92-01-036	Cottage-By-The-Sea S/N	T. Kinkade	Closed	595.00	12-2000.
92-01-037	Cottage-By-The-Sea A/P	T. Kinkade	Closed	695.00	1150.00
92-01-038	Cottage-By-The-Sea G/P	T. Kinkade	Closed	745.00	1250.00
92-01-039	Country Memories S/N	T. Kinkade	Closed	395.00	595-695.
92-01-040	Country Memories A/P	T. Kinkade	Closed	495.00	1550.00
94-01-041	Emerald Isle Cottage S/N	T. Kinkade	2,750	515.00	515.00
94-01-042	Emerald Isle Cottage A/P	T. Kinkade	Closed	665.00	665.00
93-01-043	The End of a Perfect Day S/N	T. Kinkade	Closed	515.00	995-1495
93-01-044	The End of a Perfect Day A/P	T. Kinkade	Closed	615.00	1150.00
93-01-045	The End of a Perfect Day G/P	T. Kinkade	Closed	665.00	1295.00
94-01-046	The End of a Perfect Day II S/N	T. Kinkade	Closed	815.00	995-1995
94-01-047	The End of a Perfect Day II A/P	T. Kinkade	Closed	965.00	965.00
89-01-048	Entrance to the Manor House S/N	T. Kinkade	Closed	495.00	13-2200.
89-01-049	Entrance to the Manor House A/P	T. Kinkade	Closed	595.00	1200.00
89-01-050	Evening at Merritt's Cottage S/N	T. Kinkade	Closed	495.00	2200.00
89-01-051	Evening at Merritt's Cottage A/P	T. Kinkade	Closed	595.00	2200.00
92-01-052	Evening at Swanbrooke Cottage Thomashire S/N	T. Kinkade	Closed	495.00	12-1900.
92-01-053	Evening at Swanbrooke Cottage Thomashire A/P	T. Kinkade	Closed	595.00	1900.00
92-01-054	Evening at Swanbrooke Cottage Thomashire G/P	T. Kinkade	Closed	645.00	1700.00
92-01-055	Evening Carolers S/N	T. Kinkade	1,960	295.00	315.00
92-01-056	Evening Carolers A/P	T. Kinkade	200	395.00	415.00
93-01-057	Fisherman's Wharf; San Francisco S/N	T. Kinkade	Closed	965.00	965-1750
93-01-058	Fisherman's Wharf; San Francisco A/P	T. Kinkade	Closed	1065.00	1950.00
91-01-059	Flags Over The Capitol S/N	T. Kinkade	980	595.00	615.00
91-01-060	Flags Over The Capitol A/P	T. Kinkade	200	695.00	715.00
93-01-061	The Garden of Promise S/N	T. Kinkade	Closed	615.00	615.00
93-01-062	The Garden of Promise A/P	T. Kinkade	Closed	715.00	715.00
92-01-063	The Garden Party S/N	T. Kinkade	980	495.00	515.00
92-01-064	The Garden Party A/P	T. Kinkade	200	595.00	615.00
93-01-065	Glory of Morning S/N	T. Kinkade	Closed	315.00	315.00
93-01-066	Glory of Morning A/P	T. Kinkade	400	415.00	415.00
93-01-067	Glory of Evening S/N	T. Kinkade	Closed	315.00	315.00
93-01-068	Glory of Evening A/P	T. Kinkade	400	415.00	415.00
93-01-069	Glory of Winter S/N	T. Kinkade	1,250	615.00	615.00
93-01-070	Glory of Winter A/P	T. Kinkade	300	715.00	715.00
94-01-071	Guardian Castle S/N	T. Kinkade	4,750	865.00	865.00
94-01-072	Guardian Castle A/P	T. Kinkade	475	1015.00	1015.00
93-01-073	Heather's Hutch S/N	T. Kinkade	Closed	415.00	415.00
93-01-074	Heather's Hutch A/P	T. Kinkade	400	515.00	515.00
94-01-075	Hidden Arbor S/N	T. Kinkade	2,750	515.00	515.00
94-01-076	Hidden Arbor A/P	T. Kinkade	275	615.00	615.00
90-01-077	Hidden Cottage S/N	T. Kinkade	Closed	495.00	15-4000.
90-01-078	Hidden Cottage A/P	T. Kinkade	Closed	595.00	4700.00
93-01-079	Hidden Cottage II S/N	T. Kinkade	Closed	515.00	515.00
93-01-080	Hidden Cottage II A/P	T. Kinkade	400	615.00	615.00
94-01-081	Hidden Gazebo S/N	T. Kinkade	Closed	515.00	995-1195
94-01-082	Hidden Gazebo A/P	T. Kinkade	Closed	615.00	1395.00
92-01-083	Home is Where the Heart Is S/N	T. Kinkade	Closed	595.00	13-1500.
92-01-084	Home is Where the Heart Is A/P	T. Kinkade	Closed	695.00	2700.00
91-01-085	Home For The Evening S/N	T. Kinkade	Closed	195.00	315-395.
91-01-086	Home For The Evening A/P	T. Kinkade	Closed	295.00	N/A
91-01-087	Home For The Holidays S/N	T. Kinkade	Closed	595.00	12-1900.
91-01-088	Home For The Holidays A/P	T. Kinkade	Closed	695.00	2200.00
93-01-089	Homestead House S/N	T. Kinkade	1,250	615.00	615.00
93-01-090	Homestead House A/P	T. Kinkade	300	715.00	715.00
92-01-091	Julianne's Cottage S/N	T. Kinkade	Closed	395.00	995-1195
92-01-092	Julianne's Cottage A/P	T. Kinkade	Closed	495.00	N/A
92-01-093	Julianne's Cottage G/P	T. Kinkade	Closed	565.00	1400.00
93-01-094	Lamplight Brooke S/N	T. Kinkade	Closed	615.00	895-1595
93-01-095	Lamplight Brooke A/P	T. Kinkade	Closed	715.00	995-1550
93-01-096	Lamplight Brooke G/P	T. Kinkade	Closed	765.00	N/A
94-01-097	Lamplight Inn S/N	T. Kinkade	Closed	615.00	615-895.
94-01-098	Lamplight Inn A/P	T. Kinkade	Closed	765.00	765-915.
93-01-099	Lamplight Lane S/N	T. Kinkade	Closed	595.00	22-4000.
93-01-100	Lamplight Lane A/P	T. Kinkade	Closed	695.00	N/A
91-01-101	The Lit Path S/N	T. Kinkade	1,960	195.00	215.00
91-01-102	The Lit Path A/P	T. Kinkade	200	295.00	315.00
91-01-103	McKenna's Cottage S/N	T. Kinkade	980	495.00	515.00
91-01-104	McKenna's Cottage A/P	T. Kinkade	100	595.00	615.00
92-01-105	Miller's Cottage,Thomashire S/N	T. Kinkade	Closed	495.00	12-2200.
92-01-106	Miller's Cottage, Thomashire A/P	T. Kinkade	Closed	595.00	N/A
94-01-107	Moonlight Lane I S/N	T. Kinkade	2,400	515.00	515.00
94-01-108	Moonlight Lane I A/P	T. Kinkade	240	665.00	665.00
92-01-109	Moonlit Sleigh Ride S/N	T. Kinkade	1,960	295.00	315.00
92-01-110	Moonlit Sleigh Ride A/P	T. Kinkade	200	395.00	415.00
90-01-111	Morning Light A/P	T. Kinkade	Closed	695.00	12-1600.
92-01-112	Olde Porterfield Gift Shoppe S/N	T. Kinkade	980	495.00	515.00
92-01-113	Olde Porterfield Gift Shoppe A/P	T. Kinkade	200	595.00	615.00
91-01-114	Olde Porterfield Tea Room S/N	T. Kinkade	Closed	495.00	795-1495
91-01-115	Olde Porterfield Tea Room A/P	T. Kinkade	Closed	595.00	N/A
91-01-116	Open Gate, Sussex S/N	T. Kinkade	Closed	195.00	215.00
91-01-117	Open Gate, Sussex A/P	T. Kinkade	100	295.00	315.00
93-01-118	Paris, City of Lights S/N	T. Kinkade	Closed	715.00	995-1495
93-01-119	Paris, City of Lights A/P	T. Kinkade	Closed	815.00	N/A
93-01-120	Paris, City of Lights G/P	T. Kinkade	Closed	865.00	1150.00
94-01-121	Paris, Eiffel Tower S/N	T. Kinkade	Closed	795.00	795-1095
94-01-122	Paris, Eiffel Tower A/P	T. Kinkade	Closed	945.00	945-1095
94-01-123	The Power & The Majesty S/N	T. Kinkade	2,750	615.00	615.00
94-01-124	The Power & The Majesty A/P	T. Kinkade	275	765.00	765.00
91-01-125	Pye Corner Cottage S/N	T. Kinkade	1,960	195.00	215.00
91-01-126	Pye Corner Cottage A/P	T. Kinkade	200	295.00	315.00
90-01-127	Rose Arbor S/N	T. Kinkade	Closed	495.00	1200.00
90-01-128	Rose Arbor A/P	T. Kinkade	Closed	595.00	1100.00
92-01-129	San Francisco, Nob Hill (California St.) S/N	T. Kinkade	Closed	645.00	32-4000.
92-01-130	San Francisco, Nob Hill (California St.) A/P	T. Kinkade	Closed	715.00	3700.00
92-01-131	San Francisco, Nob Hill (California St.) P/P	T. Kinkade	Closed	815.00	2900.00
89-01-132	San Francisco, Union Square S/N	T. Kinkade	Closed	595.00	4500.00
89-01-133	San Francisco, Union Square A/P	T. Kinkade	Closed	595.00	5200.00
92-01-134	Silent Night S/N	T. Kinkade	Closed	395.00	595-695.
92-01-135	Silent Night A/P	T. Kinkade	Closed	495.00	950.00
90-01-136	Spring At Stonegate S/N	T. Kinkade	550	295.00	415.00
90-01-137	Spring At Stonegate A/P	T. Kinkade	Closed	395.00	515.00
93-01-138	Stonehearth Hutch S/N	T. Kinkade	Closed	415.00	500-750.
93-01-139	Stonehearth Hutch A/P	T. Kinkade	Closed	515.00	515-950.
93-01-140	St. Nicholas Circle S/N	T. Kinkade	Closed	615.00	615.00

GRAPHICS

		ARTIST	EDITION	ISSUE	QUOTE
93-01-141	St. Nicholas Circle A/P	T. Kinkade	420	715.00	715.00
93-01-142	Studio in the Garden S/N	T. Kinkade	1,480	415.00	415.00
93-01-143	Studio in the GardenA/P	T. Kinkade	400	515.00	515.00
92-01-144	Sunday at Apple Hill S/N	T. Kinkade	Closed	495.00	795-1250
92-01-145	Sunday at Apple Hill A/P	T. Kinkade	Closed	595.00	N/A
93-01-146	Sunday Outing S/N	T. Kinkade	Closed	495.00	795-1000
93-01-147	Sunday Outing A/P	T. Kinkade	Closed	595.00	1000.00
92-01-148	Sweetheart Cottage S/N	T. Kinkade	Closed	495.00	750-995.
92-01-149	Sweetheart Cottage A/P	T. Kinkade	Closed	595.00	795.00
93-01-150	Sweetheart Cottage II S/N	T. Kinkade	Closed	595.00	895-1195
93-01-151	Sweetheart Cottage II A/P	T. Kinkade	Closed	695.00	N/A
93-01-152	Sweetheart Cottage II G/P	T. Kinkade	Closed	745.00	1000.00
94-01-153	Sweetheart Cottage III S/N	T. Kinkade	Closed	515.00	515-895.
94-01-154	Sweetheart Cottage III A/P	T. Kinkade	Closed	615.00	615.00
92-01-155	Victorian Christmas S/N	T. Kinkade	Closed	595.00	12-1800.
92-01-156	Victorian Christmas A/P	T. Kinkade	Closed	695.00	1700.00
92-01-157	Victorian Christmas II S/N	T. Kinkade	Closed	615.00	815-1395.
92-01-158	Victorian Christmas II A/P	T. Kinkade	Closed	715.00	1400.00
91-01-159	Victorian Evening	T. Kinkade	Closed	495.00	495-1200
92-01-160	Victorian Garden S/N	T. Kinkade	Closed	795.00	18-2500.
92-01-161	Victorian Garden A/P	T. Kinkade	Closed	895.00	2200.00
93-01-162	Village Inn S/N	T. Kinkade	1,200	515.00	515.00
93-01-163	Village Inn A/P	T. Kinkade	400	615.00	615.00
92-01-164	Weathervane Hutch S/N	T. Kinkade	1,960	295.00	315.00
92-01-165	Weathervane Hutch A/P	T. Kinkade	200	395.00	415.00
93-01-166	Winter's End S/N	T. Kinkade	1,450	615.00	615.00
93-01-167	Winter's End A/P	T. Kinkade	400	715.00	715.00
91-01-168	Woodman's Thatch S/N	T. Kinkade	1,960	195.00	215.00
91-01-169	Woodman's Thatch A/P	T. Kinkade	200	295.00	315.00
92-01-170	Yosemite S/N	T. Kinkade	980	595.00	615.00
92-01-171	Yosemite A/P	T. Kinkade	200	695.00	715.00

Lightpost Group Inc./ Lightpost Publishing Archival Paper-UnFramed

		ARTIST	EDITION	ISSUE	QUOTE
91-02-001	Afternoon Light, Dogwood	T. Kinkade	Closed	185.00	195.00
92-02-002	Amber Afternoon	T. Kinkade	980	225.00	235.00
91-02-003	The Autumn Gate	T. Kinkade	Closed	225.00	425-500.
94-02-004	Beacon of Hope S/N	T. Kinkade	2,750	235.00	235.00
93-02-005	Beside Still Waters S/N	T. Kinkade	Closed	185.00	240.00
93-02-006	Beyond Autumn Gate	T. Kinkade	1,750	285.00	285.00
85-02-007	Birth of a City	T. Kinkade	Closed	150.00	595.00
93-02-008	The Blessings of Autumn	T. Kinkade	1,250	235.00	235.00
94-02-009	The Blessings of Spring S/N	T. Kinkade	2,750	195.00	195.00
92-02-010	Blossom Hill Church	T. Kinkade	980	225.00	235.00
91-02-011	Boston S/N	T. Kinkade	Closed	175.00	195.00
92-02-012	Broadwater Bridge S/N	T. Kinkade	Closed	225.00	420.00
89-02-013	Carmel, Ocean Avenue	T. Kinkade	Closed	225.00	12-1350.
91-02-014	Carmel, Delores Street and the Tuck Box Tea Room S/N	T. Kinkade	Closed	275.00	375.00
90-02-015	Chandler's Cottage	T. Kinkade	Closed	125.00	595.00
92-02-016	Christmas At the Ahwahnee	T. Kinkade	980	175.00	175.00
90-02-017	Christmas Cottage 1990	T. Kinkade	Closed	95.00	595.00
91-02-018	Christmas Eve	T. Kinkade	980	125.00	175.00
92-02-019	Cottage-By-The-Sea	T. Kinkade	Closed	250.00	250.00
92-02-020	Country Memories	T. Kinkade	980	185.00	185.00
84-02-021	Dawson	T. Kinkade	Closed	150.00	300-595.
94-02-022	Emerald Isle Cottage S/N	T. Kinkade	2,750	195.00	195.00
93-02-023	The End of a Perfect Day I S/N	T. Kinkade	Closed	195.00	195.00
94-02-024	The End of a Perfect Day II, S/N	T. Kinkade	2,750	285.00	285.00
89-02-025	Entrance to the Manor House	T. Kinkade	Closed	125.00	600-800.
89-02-026	Evening at Merritt's Cottage	T. Kinkade	Closed	125.00	675.00
92-02-027	Evening at Swanbrooke Cottage, S/N	T. Kinkade	Closed	250.00	250.00
85-02-028	Evening Service	T. Kinkade	Closed	90.00	495.00
91-02-029	Flags Over The Capitol	T. Kinkade	1,991	195.00	235.00
93-02-030	The Garden of Promise	T. Kinkade	1,250	235.00	235.00
92-02-031	The Garden Party	T. Kinkade	980	175.00	195.00
93-02-032	Glory of Winter	T. Kinkade	1,250	235.00	235.00
94-02-033	Guardian Castle S/N	T. Kinkade	2,750	580.00	580.00
93-02-034	Heather's Hutch	T. Kinkade	1,250	175.00	195.00
94-02-035	Hidden Arbor S/N	T. Kinkade	Closed	195.00	195.00
90-02-036	Hidden Cottage	T. Kinkade	Closed	125.00	650.00
94-02-037	Hidden Gazebo, S/N	T. Kinkade	2,400	195.00	195.00
91-02-038	Home For The Evening	T. Kinkade	Closed	100.00	110.00
91-02-039	Home For The Holidays	T. Kinkade	980	225.00	235.00
92-02-040	Home is Where the Heart Is, S/N	T. Kinkade	Closed	225.00	235.00
93-02-041	Homestead House	T. Kinkade	1,250	235.00	235.00
92-02-042	Julianne's Cottage	T. Kinkade	Closed	185.00	395.00
93-02-043	Lamplight Brook	T. Kinkade	1,650	235.00	235.00
93-02-044	Lamplight Lane	T. Kinkade	Closed	225.00	235.00
94-02-045	Lamplight Inn S/N	T. Kinkade	2,750	235.00	235.00
91-02-046	McKenna's Cottage	T. Kinkade	Closed	150.00	195.00
92-02-047	Miller's Cottage	T. Kinkade	980	175.00	195.00
94-02-048	Moonlight Lane I S/N	T. Kinkade	2,400	195.00	195.00
85-02-049	Moonlight on the Waterfront	T. Kinkade	Closed	150.00	495.00
86-02-050	New York, 6th Avenue	T. Kinkade	Closed	150.00	995.00
92-02-051	Olde Porterfield Gift Shoppe	T. Kinkade	980	175.00	195.00
91-02-052	Olde Porterfield Tea Room	T. Kinkade	980	150.00	195.00
91-02-053	Open Gate, Sussex	T. Kinkade	980	100.00	110.00
93-02-054	Paris, City of Lights	T. Kinkade	1,980	285.00	285.00
94-02-055	Paris, Eiffel Tower S/N	T. Kinkade	2,750	235.00	235.00
84-02-056	Placerville, 1916	T. Kinkade	Closed	90.00	1200.00
94-02-057	The Power & The Majesty S/N	T. Kinkade	2,750	235.00	235.00
88-02-058	Room with a View	T. Kinkade	Closed	150.00	650-950.
90-02-059	Rose Arbor	T. Kinkade	Closed	125.00	300.00
86-02-060	San Francisco, 1909	T. Kinkade	Closed	150.00	16-1900.
93-02-061	San Francisco, Fisherman's Wharf	T. Kinkade	2,750	305.00	305.00
92-02-062	San Francisco, Nob Hill (California St.)	T. Kinkade	Closed	285.00	895-1500
89-02-063	San Francisco, Union Square	T. Kinkade	Closed	225.00	14-1800.
92-02-064	Silent Night	T. Kinkade	980	185.00	185.00
90-02-065	Spring At Stonegate	T. Kinkade	550	95.00	95.00
93-02-066	St. Nicholas Circle	T. Kinkade	1,750	235.00	235.00
93-02-067	Stonehearth Hutch	T. Kinkade	1,650	175.00	175.00
93-02-068	Studio in the Garden	T. Kinkade	980	175.00	175.00
92-02-069	Sunday At Apple Hill, S/N	T. Kinkade	Closed	175.00	195.00
93-02-070	Sunday Outing	T. Kinkade	980	175.00	195.00
92-02-071	Sweetheart Cottage	T. Kinkade	980	150.00	150.00
93-02-072	Sweetheart Cottage II S/N	T. Kinkade	Closed	150.00	150.00
93-02-073	Sweetheart Cottage III S/N	T. Kinkade	1,650	235.00	235.00
92-02-074	Victorian Christmas	T. Kinkade	Closed	250.00	250.00
93-02-075	Victorian Christmas II	T. Kinkade	1,650	235.00	235.00
91-02-076	Victorian Evening, S/N	T. Kinkade	Closed	150.00	150.00
92-02-077	Victorian Garden, S/N	T. Kinkade	Closed	275.00	285.00
93-02-078	Village Inn	T. Kinkade	1,200	195.00	195.00
93-02-079	Winter's End	T. Kinkade	875	235.00	235.00
92-02-080	Yosemite	T. Kinkade	980	225.00	235.00

Lightpost Group Inc./ Lightpost Publishing Archival Paper/Canvas-Combined Edition-Framed

		ARTIST	EDITION	ISSUE	QUOTE
90-03-001	Blue Cottage(Paper)	T. Kinkade	Closed	125.00	125.00
90-03-002	Blue Cottage(Canvas)	T. Kinkade	Closed	495.00	495.00
90-03-003	Moonlit Village(Paper)	T. Kinkade	Closed	225.00	995-1500
90-03-004	Moonlit Village(Canvas)	T. Kinkade	Closed	595.00	2-3000.
90-03-005	New York, 1932(Paper)	T. Kinkade	Closed	225.00	650-1200
90-03-006	New York, 1932(Canvas)	T. Kinkade	Closed	595.00	2900.00
90-03-007	Skating in the Park(Paper)	T. Kinkade	Closed	275.00	275.00
90-03-008	Skating in the Park(Canvas)	T. Kinkade	Closed	645.00	950-1150

Lightpost Group Inc./ Lightpost Publishing Member's Only Collectors' Society

		ARTIST	EDITION	ISSUE	QUOTE
92-04-001	Skater's Pond	T. Kinkade	Closed	295.00	295.00
92-04-002	Morning Lane	T. Kinkade	Closed	Gift	N/A
94-04-003	Collector's Cottage I	T. Kinkade	Yr.Iss.	315.00	315.00
94-04-004	Painter of Light Book	T. Kinkade	Yr.Iss.	Gift	N/A

Lightpost Group Inc./ Lightpost Publishing Cinema Classics Collection-Framed

		ARTIST	EDITION	ISSUE	QUOTE
93-05-001	Over The Rainbow	Recollections	7,500	240.00	249.00
93-05-002	Not A Marrying Man	Recollections	12,500	240.00	249.00
93-05-003	You Do Waltz Divinely	Recollections	12,500	299.00	299.00
93-05-004	Scarlett & Her Beaux	Recollections	12,500	240.00	249.00
93-05-005	You Need Kissing	Recollections	12,500	299.00	299.00
94-05-006	Frankly My Dear	Recollections	Open	40.00	40.00
94-05-007	As God As My Witness	Recollections	Open	40.00	40.00
94-05-008	The Kiss	Recollections	Open	40.00	40.00
94-05-009	A Dream Remembered	Recollections	Open	40.00	40.00
94-05-010	Gone With the Wind-Movie Ticket	Recollections	2,000	40.00	40.00
94-05-011	We're Off to See the Wizard	Recollections	Open	40.00	40.00
94-05-012	Follow the Yellow Brick Road	Recollections	Open	40.00	40.00
94-05-013	The Ruby Slippers	Recollections	Open	40.00	40.00
94-05-014	The Emerald City	Recollections	Open	40.00	40.00
94-05-015	There's No Place Like Home	Recollections	Open	40.00	40.00
94-05-016	If Only I Had a Brain	Recollections	Open	40.00	40.00
94-05-017	If Only I Had a Heart	Recollections	Open	40.00	40.00
94-05-018	If Only I Had the Nerve	Recollections	Open	40.00	40.00
94-05-019	The Gift	Recollections	Open	40.00	40.00
94-05-020	Attempted Deception	Recollections	Open	40.00	40.00
94-05-021	The Proposal	Recollections	Open	40.00	40.00
94-05-022	A Chance Meeting	Recollections	Open	40.00	40.00

Lightpost Group Inc./ Recollections by Lightpost American Heroes Collection-Framed

		ARTIST	EDITION	ISSUE	QUOTE
93-06-001	Babe Ruth	Recollections	2,250	136.00	139.00
93-06-002	A Nation United	Recollections	1,000	149.00	149.00
93-06-003	Ben Franklin	Recollections	1,000	136.00	139.00
93-06-004	Mark Twain	Recollections	7,500	190.00	195.00
93-06-005	Abraham Lincoln	Recollections	7,500	190.00	195.00
93-06-006	George Washington	Recollections	7,500	190.00	195.00
93-06-007	John F. Kennedy	Recollections	7,500	190.00	195.00
94-06-008	Eternal Love (Civil War)	Recollections	1,861	195.00	195.00
94-06-009	A Nation Divided	Recollections	1,000	149.00	149.00
94-06-010	George Washington	Recollections	Open	40.00	40.00
94-06-011	Dwight D. Eisenhower	Recollections	Open	40.00	40.00
94-06-012	Franklin D. Roosevelt	Recollections	Open	40.00	40.00
94-06-013	John F. Kennedy	Recollections	Open	40.00	40.00

Lightpost Group Inc./ Recollections by Lightpost The Elvis Collection

		ARTIST	EDITION	ISSUE	QUOTE
94-07-001	Public Image/Private Man	Recollections	Open	40.00	40.00
94-07-002	Vulgar Shoman/Serious Musician	Recollections	Open	40.00	40.00
94-07-003	Dreams Remembered/Dreams Realized	Recollections	Open	40.00	40.00
94-07-004	Celebrity Soldier/Regular G.I.	Recollections	Open	40.00	40.00
94-07-005	Elvis the Pelvis	Recollections	2,750	295.00	295.00
94-07-006	Elvis the Pelvis, PP	Recollections	250	495.00	495.00
94-07-007	Elvis the King	Recollections	2,750	295.00	295.00
94-07-008	Elvis the King, PP	Recollections	250	495.00	495.00
94-07-009	To Elvis with Love	Recollections	2,750	295.00	295.00
94-07-010	The King/The Servant	Recollections	Open	40.00	40.00
94-07-011	Professional Artist/Practical Joker	Recollections	Open	40.00	40.00
94-07-012	Sex Symbol/Boy Next Door	Recollections	Open	40.00	40.00
94-07-013	Lavish Spender/Generous Giver	Recollections	Open	40.00	40.00

Mill Pond Press Bateman

		ARTIST	EDITION	ISSUE	QUOTE
86-01-001	A Resting Place-Cape Buffalo	R. Bateman	950	265.00	265.00
82-01-002	Above the River-Trumpeter Swans	R. Bateman	950	200.00	850-925.
84-01-003	Across the Sky-Snow Geese	R. Bateman	950	220.00	650-750.
80-01-004	African Amber-Lioness Pair	R. Bateman	950	175.00	525-900.
79-01-005	Afternoon Glow-Snowy Owl	R. Bateman	950	125.00	550-625.
90-01-006	Air, The Forest and The Watch	R. Bateman	42,558	325.00	425.00
84-01-007	Along the Ridge-Grizzly Bears	R. Bateman	950	200.00	700-950.
84-01-008	American Goldfinch-Winter Dress	R. Bateman	950	75.00	200-300.
79-01-009	Among the Leaves-Cottontail Rabbit	R. Bateman	950	75.00	1200.00
80-01-010	Antarctic Elements	R. Bateman	950	125.00	150.00
91-01-011	Arctic Cliff-White Wolves	R. Bateman	13,000	325.00	600-800.
82-01-012	Arctic Evening-White Wolf	R. Bateman	950	185.00	950-1200
80-01-013	Arctic Family-Polar Bears	R. Bateman	950	150.00	1400.00
92-01-014	Arctic Landscape-Polar Bear	R. Bateman	5,000	345.00	345.00
92-01-014	Arctic Landscape-Polar Bear-Premier Ed.	R. Bateman	450	800.00	800.00
82-01-014	Arctic Portrait-White Gyrfalcon	R. Bateman	950	175.00	250.00
85-01-015	Arctic Tern Pair	R. Bateman	950	175.00	200.00
81-01-016	Artist and His Dog	R. Bateman	950	150.00	550.00
80-01-017	Asleep on the Hemlock-Screech Owl	R. Bateman	950	125.00	600.00
91-01-018	At the Cliff-Bobcat	R. Bateman	12,500	325.00	325.00
92-01-019	At the Feeder-Cardinal	R. Bateman	950	125.00	225.00
87-01-020	At the Nest-Secretary Birds	R. Bateman	950	290.00	290.00
82-01-021	At the Roadside-Red-Tailed Hawk	R. Bateman	950	185.00	550.00
80-01-022	Autumn Overture-Moose	R. Bateman	950	245.00	1450.00
80-01-023	Awesome Land-American Elk	R. Bateman	950	245.00	1450.00
89-01-024	Backlight-Mute Swan	R. Bateman	950	275.00	600.00
83-01-025	Bald Eagle Portrait	R. Bateman	950	185.00	350.00
82-01-026	Baobab Tree and Impala	R. Bateman	950	245.00	350.00
80-01-027	Barn Owl in the Churchyard	R. Bateman	950	125.00	950.00
89-01-028	Barn Swallow and Horse Collar	R. Bateman	950	225.00	225.00
82-01-029	Barn Swallows in August	R. Bateman	950	245.00	425.00
92-01-030	Beach Grass and Tree Frog	R. Bateman	1,250	345.00	350.00
85-01-031	Beaver Pond Reflections	R. Bateman	950	185.00	225.00
84-01-032	Big Country, Pronghorn Antelope	R. Bateman	950	185.00	200.00
86-01-033	Black Eagle	R. Bateman	950	200.00	200.00
93-01-034	Black Jaguar-Premier Edition	R. Bateman	450	850.00	850.00
86-01-035	Black-Tailed Deer in the Olympics	R. Bateman	950	245.00	300.00
86-01-036	Blacksmith Plover	R. Bateman	950	185.00	185.00
91-01-037	Bluebird and Blossoms	R. Bateman	4,500	235.00	235.00

		ARTIST	EDITION	ISSUE	QUOTE
91-01-038	Bluebird and Blossoms-Prestige Ed.	R. Bateman	450	625.00	625.00
80-01-039	Bluffing Bull-African Elephant	R. Bateman	950	135.00	1125.00
81-01-040	Bright Day-Atlantic Puffins	R. Bateman	950	175.00	875.00
89-01-041	Broad-Tailed Hummingbird Pair	R. Bateman	950	225.00	225.00
80-01-042	Brown Pelican and Pilings	R. Bateman	950	165.00	950.00
79-01-043	Bull Moose	R. Bateman	950	125.00	1275.00
78-01-044	By the Tracks-Killdeer	R. Bateman	950	75.00	1200.00
83-01-045	Call of the Wild-Bald Eagle	R. Bateman	950	200.00	250.00
81-01-046	Canada Geese-Nesting	R. Bateman	950	295.00	2950.00
85-01-047	Canada Geese Family(stone lithograph)	R. Bateman	260	350.00	1000.00
85-01-048	Canada Geese Over the Escarpment	R. Bateman	950	135.00	175.00
86-01-049	Canada Geese With Young	R. Bateman	950	195.00	325.00
93-01-050	Cardinal and Sumac	R. Bateman	2,510	235.00	235.00
88-01-051	Cardinal and Wild Apples	R. Bateman	950	235.00	235.00
89-01-052	Catching The Light-Barn Owl	R. Bateman	2,000	295.00	295.00
88-01-053	Cattails, Fireweed and Yellowthroat	R. Bateman	950	235.00	275.00
89-01-054	Centennial Farm	R. Bateman	950	295.00	450.00
80-01-055	Chapel Doors	R. Bateman	950	135.00	375.00
86-01-056	Charging Rhino	R. Bateman	950	325.00	500.00
88-01-057	Cherrywood with Juncos	R. Bateman	950	245.00	245-345.
82-01-058	Cheetah Profile	R. Bateman	950	245.00	500.00
78-01-059	Cheetah With Cubs	R. Bateman	950	95.00	450.00
90-01-060	Chinstrap Penguin	R. Bateman	810	150.00	150.00
92-01-061	Clan of the Raven	R. Bateman	950	235.00	600.00
81-01-062	Clear Night-Wolves	R. Bateman	950	245.00	65-8100.
88-01-063	Colonial Garden	R. Bateman	950	245.00	245.00
87-01-064	Continuing Generations-Spotted Owls	R. Bateman	950	525.00	1150.00
91-01-065	Cottage Lane-Red Fox	R. Bateman	950	285.00	285.00
84-01-066	Cougar Portrait	R. Bateman	950	95.00	200.00
79-01-067	Country Lane-Pheasants	R. Bateman	950	85.00	300.00
81-01-068	Courting Pair-Whistling Swans	R. Bateman	950	245.00	550.00
81-01-069	Courtship Display-Wild Turkey	R. Bateman	950	175.00	175.00
80-01-070	Coyote in Winter Sage	R. Bateman	950	245.00	3600.00
92-01-071	Cries of Courtship-Red Crowned Cranes	R. Bateman	950	350.00	350.00
80-01-072	Curious Glance-Red Fox	R. Bateman	950	135.00	1200.00
86-01-073	Dark Gyrfalcon	R. Bateman	950	225.00	325.00
93-01-074	Day Lilies and Dragonflies	R. Bateman	1,250	345.00	345.00
82-01-075	Dipper By the Waterfall	R. Bateman	950	165.00	225.00
89-01-076	Dispute Over Prey	R. Bateman	950	325.00	325.00
89-01-077	Distant Danger-Raccoon	R. Bateman	1,600	225.00	225.00
84-01-078	Down for a Drink-Morning Dove	R. Bateman	950	135.00	200.00
78-01-079	Downy Woodpecker on Goldenrod Gall	R. Bateman	950	50.00	1425.00
88-01-080	Dozing Lynx	R. Bateman	950	335.00	1900.00
86-01-081	Driftwood Perch-Striped Swallows	R. Bateman	950	195.00	250.00
83-01-082	Early Snowfall-Ruffed Grouse	R. Bateman	950	195.00	225.00
83-01-083	Early Spring-Bluebird	R. Bateman	950	185.00	450.00
81-01-084	Edge of the Ice-Ermine	R. Bateman	950	175.00	475.00
82-01-085	Edge of the Woods-Whitetail Deer, w/Book	R. Bateman	950	745.00	1400.00
91-01-086	Elephant Cow and Calf	R. Bateman	950	300.00	300.00
86-01-087	Elephant Herd and Sandgrouse	R. Bateman	950	235.00	235.00
91-01-088	Encounter in the Bush-African Lions	R. Bateman	950	295.00	325.00
87-01-089	End of Season-Grizzly	R. Bateman	950	325.00	500.00
91-01-090	Endangered Spaces-Grizzly	R. Bateman	4,008	325.00	425.00
85-01-091	Entering the Water-Common Gulls	R. Bateman	950	195.00	200.00
86-01-092	European Robin and Hydrangeas	R. Bateman	950	130.00	225.00
89-01-093	Evening Call-Common Loon	R. Bateman	950	235.00	525.00
80-01-094	Evening Grosbeak	R. Bateman	950	125.00	1175.00
83-01-095	Evening Idyll-Mute Swans	R. Bateman	950	245.00	450-525.
81-01-096	Evening Light-White Gyrfalcon	R. Bateman	950	245.00	1100.00
79-01-097	Evening Snowfall-American Elk	R. Bateman	950	150.00	1900.00
87-01-098	Everglades	R. Bateman	950	360.00	360.00
80-01-099	Fallen Willow-Snowy Owl	R. Bateman	950	200.00	950.00
87-01-100	Farm Lane and Blue Jays	R. Bateman	950	225.00	450.00
86-01-101	Fence Post and Burdock	R. Bateman	950	130.00	130.00
91-01-102	Fluid Power-Orca	R. Bateman	290	2500.00	2500.00
80-01-103	Flying High-Golden Eagle	R. Bateman	950	150.00	975.00
82-01-104	Fox at the Granary	R. Bateman	950	165.00	225.00
82-01-105	Frosty Morning-Blue Jay	R. Bateman	950	185.00	1000.00
82-01-106	Gallinule Family	R. Bateman	950	135.00	135.00
81-01-107	Galloping Herd-Giraffes	R. Bateman	950	175.00	1200.00
85-01-108	Gambel's Quail Pair	R. Bateman	950	95.00	350.00
82-01-109	Gentoo Penguins and Whale Bones	R. Bateman	950	205.00	300.00
83-01-110	Ghost of the North-Great Gray Owl	R. Bateman	950	200.00	2675.00
82-01-111	Golden Crowned Kinglet and Rhododendron	R. Bateman	950	150.00	2575.00
79-01-112	Golden Eagle	R. Bateman	950	150.00	250.00
85-01-113	Golden Eagle Portrait	R. Bateman	950	115.00	175.00
89-01-114	Goldfinch In the Meadow	R. Bateman	1,600	150.00	200.00
83-01-115	Goshawk and Ruffed Grouse	R. Bateman	950	185.00	400-700.
88-01-116	Grassy Bank-Great Blue Heron	R. Bateman	950	285.00	285.00
81-01-117	Gray Squirrel	R. Bateman	950	180.00	1250.00
79-01-118	Great Blue Heron	R. Bateman	950	125.00	1300.00
87-01-119	Great Blue Heron in Flight	R. Bateman	950	295.00	550.00
88-01-120	Great Crested Grebe	R. Bateman	950	135.00	135.00
87-01-121	Great Egret Preening	R. Bateman	950	315.00	500.00
83-01-122	Great Horned Owl in the White Pine	R. Bateman	950	225.00	575.00
87-01-123	Greater Kudu Bull	R. Bateman	950	145.00	145.00
93-01-124	Grizzly and Cubs	R. Bateman	2,250	335.00	400.00
91-01-125	Gulls on Pilings	R. Bateman	1,950	265.00	265.00
88-01-126	Hardwood Forest-White-Tailed Buck	R. Bateman	950	345.00	2100.00
88-01-127	Harlequin Duck-Bull Kelp-Executive Ed.	R. Bateman	950	550.00	550.00
88-01-128	Harlequin Duck-Bull Kelp-Gold Plated	R. Bateman	950	300.00	300.00
80-01-129	Heron on the Rocks	R. Bateman	950	75.00	300.00
81-01-130	High Camp at Dusk	R. Bateman	950	245.00	300.00
79-01-131	High Country-Stone Sheep	R. Bateman	950	125.00	325.00
87-01-132	High Kingdom-Snow Leopard	R. Bateman	950	325.00	675-850.
90-01-133	Homage to Ahmed	R. Bateman	290	3300.00	3300.00
84-01-134	Hooded Mergansers in Winter	R. Bateman	950	210.00	650-700.
84-01-135	House Finch and Yucca	R. Bateman	950	95.00	175.00
86-01-136	House Sparrow	R. Bateman	950	125.00	350.00
87-01-137	House Sparrows and Bittersweet	R. Bateman	950	220.00	400.00
86-01-138	Hummingbird Pair Diptych	R. Bateman	950	330.00	475.00
87-01-139	Hurricane Lake-Wood Ducks	R. Bateman	950	135.00	200.00
81-01-140	In for the Evening	R. Bateman	950	150.00	1500.00
94-01-141	In His Prime-Mallard	R. Bateman	950	195.00	295-350.
84-01-142	In the Brier Patch-Cottontail	R. Bateman	950	165.00	350.00
86-01-143	In the Grass-Lioness	R. Bateman	950	245.00	245.00
85-01-144	In the Highlands-Golden Eagle	R. Bateman	950	235.00	425.00
85-01-145	In the Mountains-Osprey	R. Bateman	950	95.00	125.00
92-01-146	Intrusion-Mountain Gorilla	R. Bateman	2,250	325.00	325.00
90-01-147	Ireland House	R. Bateman	950	265.00	318.00
85-01-148	Irish Cottage and Wagtail	R. Bateman	950	175.00	175.00

		ARTIST	EDITION	ISSUE	QUOTE
92-01-149	Junco in Winter	R. Bateman	1,250	185.00	185.00
90-01-150	Keeper of the Land	R. Bateman	290	3300.00	3300.00
93-01-151	Kestrel and Grasshopper	R. Bateman	1,250	335.00	335.00
79-01-152	King of the Realm	R. Bateman	950	125.00	675.00
87-01-153	King Penguins	R. Bateman	950	130.00	135.00
81-01-154	Kingfisher and Aspen	R. Bateman	950	225.00	600.00
80-01-155	Kingfisher in Winter	R. Bateman	950	175.00	825.00
80-01-156	Kittiwake Greeting	R. Bateman	950	75.00	550.00
81-01-157	Last Look-Bighorn Sheep	R. Bateman	950	195.00	225.00
87-01-158	Late Winter-Black Squirrel	R. Bateman	950	165.00	165.00
81-01-159	Laughing Gull and Horseshoe Crab	R. Bateman	950	125.00	125.00
82-01-160	Leopard Ambush	R. Bateman	950	245.00	600.00
88-01-161	Leopard and Thomson Gazelle Kill	R. Bateman	950	275.00	275.00
85-01-162	Leopard at Seronera	R. Bateman	950	175.00	280.00
80-01-163	Leopard in a Sausage Tree	R. Bateman	950	150.00	1250.00
84-01-164	Lily Pads and Loon	R. Bateman	950	200.00	1875.00
87-01-165	Lion and Wildebeest	R. Bateman	950	265.00	265.00
80-01-166	Lion at Tsavo	R. Bateman	950	150.00	275.00
78-01-167	Lion Cubs	R. Bateman	950	125.00	800.00
87-01-168	Lioness at Serengeti	R. Bateman	950	325.00	325.00
85-01-169	Lions in the Grass	R. Bateman	950	265.00	1250.00
81-01-170	Little Blue Heron	R. Bateman	950	95.00	275.00
82-01-171	Lively Pair-Chickadees	R. Bateman	950	160.00	450.00
83-01-172	Loon Family	R. Bateman	950	200.00	750.00
90-01-173	Lunging Heron	R. Bateman	1,250	225.00	225.00
78-01-174	Majesty on the Wing-Bald Eagle	R. Bateman	950	150.00	2650.00
88-01-175	Mallard Family at Sunset	R. Bateman	950	235.00	235.00
86-01-176	Mallard Family-Misty Marsh	R. Bateman	950	130.00	175.00
86-01-177	Mallard Pair-Early Winter	R. Bateman	41,740	135.00	200.00
86-01-178	Mallard Pair-Early Winter Gold Plated	R. Bateman	7,691	250.00	375.00
85-01-179	Mallard Pair-Early Winter 24K Gold	R. Bateman	950	1650.00	2000.00
89-01-180	Mangrove Morning-Roseate Spoonbills	R. Bateman	2,000	325.00	325.00
91-01-181	Mangrove Shadow-Common Egret	R. Bateman	1,250	285.00	285.00
93-01-182	Marbled Murrelet	R. Bateman	55	1200.00	1200.00
86-01-183	Marginal Meadow	R. Bateman	950	220.00	350.00
79-01-184	Master of the Herd-African Buffalo	R. Bateman	950	150.00	2250.00
84-01-185	May Maple-Scarlet Tanager	R. Bateman	950	175.00	825.00
82-01-186	Meadow's Edge-Mallard	R. Bateman	950	175.00	900.00
82-01-187	Merganser Family in Hiding	R. Bateman	950	200.00	525.00
94-01-188	Meru Dusk-Lesser Kudu	R. Bateman	950	135.00	135.00
89-01-189	Midnight-Black Wolf	R. Bateman	25,352	325.00	2300.00
80-01-190	Mischief on the Prowl-Raccoon	R. Bateman	950	85.00	350.00
80-01-191	Misty Coast-Gulls	R. Bateman	950	135.00	600.00
84-01-192	Misty Lake-Osprey	R. Bateman	950	95.00	300.00
81-01-193	Misty Morning-Loons	R. Bateman	950	150.00	3000.00
86-01-194	Moose at Water's Edge	R. Bateman	950	130.00	225.00
90-01-195	Morning Cove-Common Loon	R. Bateman	950	165.00	165.00
85-01-196	Morning Dew-Roe Deer	R. Bateman	950	175.00	175.00
83-01-197	Morning on the Flats-Bison	R. Bateman	950	200.00	300.00
84-01-198	Morning on the River-Trumpeter Swans	R. Bateman	950	185.00	300.00
90-01-199	Mossy Branches-Spotted Owl	R. Bateman	4,500	300.00	525.00
90-01-200	Mowed Meadow	R. Bateman	950	190.00	190.00
86-01-201	Mule Deer in Aspen	R. Bateman	950	175.00	175.00
83-01-202	Mule Deer in Winter	R. Bateman	950	200.00	275-350.
88-01-203	Muskoka Lake-Common Loons	R. Bateman	950	265.00	450.00
89-01-204	Near Glenburnie	R. Bateman	950	265.00	265.00
83-01-205	New Season-American Robin	R. Bateman	950	200.00	450.00
86-01-206	Northern Reflections-Loon Family	R. Bateman	8,631	255.00	2100.00
85-01-207	Old Whaling Base and Fur Seals	R. Bateman	950	195.00	550.00
87-01-208	Old Willow and Mallards	R. Bateman	950	325.00	390.00
80-01-209	On the Alert-Chipmunk	R. Bateman	950	60.00	500.00
93-01-210	On the Brink-River Otters	R. Bateman	1,250	345.00	345.00
85-01-211	On the Garden Wall	R. Bateman	950	115.00	300.00
85-01-212	Orca Procession	R. Bateman	950	245.00	2525.00
81-01-213	Osprey Family	R. Bateman	950	245.00	325.00
83-01-214	Osprey in the Rain	R. Bateman	950	110.00	650.00
87-01-215	Otter Study	R. Bateman	950	235.00	375.00
81-01-216	Pair of Skimmers	R. Bateman	950	150.00	150.00
88-01-217	Panda's At Play (stone lithograph)	R. Bateman	160	400.00	1650.00
94-01-218	Path of the Panther	R. Bateman	1,950	295.00	295.00
84-01-219	Peregrine and Ruddy Turnstones	R. Bateman	950	200.00	350.00
85-01-220	Peregrine Falcon and White-Throated Swifts	R. Bateman	950	245.00	550.00
87-01-221	Peregrine Falcon on the Cliff-Stone Litho	R. Bateman	525	350.00	625.00
83-01-222	Pheasant in Cornfield	R. Bateman	950	200.00	375.00
88-01-223	Pheasants at Dusk	R. Bateman	950	325.00	525.00
82-01-224	Pileated Woodpecker on Beech Tree	R. Bateman	950	175.00	525.00
90-01-225	Pintails in Spring	R. Bateman	9,651	135.00	135.00
82-01-226	Pioneer Memories-Magpie Pair	R. Bateman	950	175.00	250.00
87-01-227	Plowed Field-Snowy Owl	R. Bateman	950	145.00	400.00
90-01-228	Polar Bear	R. Bateman	290	3300.00	3300.00
82-01-229	Polar Bear Profile	R. Bateman	950	210.00	2350.00
82-01-230	Polar Bears at Bafin Island	R. Bateman	950	245.00	875.00
90-01-231	Power Play-Rhinoceros	R. Bateman	950	320.00	320.00
80-01-232	Prairie Evening-Short-Eared Owl	R. Bateman	950	150.00	200.00
94-01-233	Predator Portfolio/Black Bear	R. Bateman	950	475.00	475.00
92-01-234	Predator Portfolio/Cougar	R. Bateman	950	465.00	465.00
93-01-235	Predator Portfolio/Grizzly	R. Bateman	950	475.00	475.00
93-01-236	Predator Portfolio/Polar Bear	R. Bateman	950	485.00	485.00
93-01-237	Predator Portfolio/Wolf	R. Bateman	950	475.00	475.00
88-01-238	Preening Pair-Canada Geese	R. Bateman	950	235.00	300.00
87-01-239	Pride of Autumn-Canada Goose	R. Bateman	950	135.00	245.00
86-01-240	Proud Swimmer-Snow Goose	R. Bateman	950	185.00	185.00
89-01-241	Pumpkin Time	R. Bateman	950	195.00	195.00
82-01-242	Queen Anne's Lace and American Goldfinch	R. Bateman	950	150.00	1000.00
84-01-243	Ready for Flight-Peregrine Falcon	R. Bateman	950	185.00	500.00
82-01-244	Ready for the Hunt-Snowy Owl	R. Bateman	950	245.00	550.00
93-01-245	Reclining Snow Leopard	R. Bateman	1,250	335.00	335.00
88-01-246	Red Crossbills	R. Bateman	950	125.00	125.00
84-01-247	Red Fox on the Prowl	R. Bateman	950	245.00	1500.00
82-01-248	Red Squirrel	R. Bateman	950	175.00	700.00
86-01-249	Red Wolf	R. Bateman	950	250.00	525.00
81-01-250	Red-Tailed Hawk by the Cliff	R. Bateman	950	245.00	550.00
81-01-251	Red-Winged Blackbird and Rail Fence	R. Bateman	950	195.00	225.00
84-01-252	Reeds	R. Bateman	950	185.00	575.00
86-01-253	Resting Place-Cape Buffalo	R. Bateman	950	265.00	265.00
87-01-254	Rhino at Ngoro Ngoro	R. Bateman	950	325.00	325.00
93-01-255	River Otter-North American Wilderness	R. Bateman	350	325.00	500.00
93-01-256	River Otters	R. Bateman	290	1500.00	1500.00
86-01-257	Robins at the Nest	R. Bateman	950	185.00	225.00

		ARTIST	EDITION	ISSUE	QUOTE
87-01-258	Rocky Point-October	R. Bateman	950	195.00	275.00
80-01-258	Rocky Wilderness-Cougar	R. Bateman	950	175.00	1425.00
90-01-259	Rolling Waves-Lesser Scaup	R. Bateman	3,330	125.00	125.00
93-01-260	Rose-breasted Grosbeak	R. Bateman	290	450.00	450.00
81-01-261	Rough-Legged Hawk in the Elm	R. Bateman	950	175.00	250.00
81-01-262	Royal Family-Mute Swans	R. Bateman	950	245.00	1100.00
83-01-263	Ruby Throat and Columbine	R. Bateman	950	150.00	2200.00
87-01-264	Ruddy Turnstones	R. Bateman	950	175.00	175.00
94-01-265	Salt Spring Sheep	R. Bateman	1,250	235.00	235.00
81-01-266	Sarah E. with Gulls	R. Bateman	950	245.00	2625.00
93-01-267	Saw Whet Owl and Wild Grapes	R. Bateman	950	185.00	185.00
91-01-268	Sea Otter Study	R. Bateman	950	150.00	150.00
81-01-269	Sheer Drop-Mountain Goats	R. Bateman	950	245.00	2800.00
93-01-270	Shadow of the Rain Forest	R. Bateman	9,000	345.00	500.00
88-01-271	Shelter	R. Bateman	950	325.00	1000.00
92-01-272	Siberian Tiger	R. Bateman	4,500	325.00	325.00
84-01-273	Smallwood	R. Bateman	950	200.00	500.00
90-01-274	Snow Leopard	R. Bateman	290	2500.00	3500.00
85-01-275	Snowy Hemlock-Barred Owl	R. Bateman	950	245.00	400.00
94-01-276	Snowy Nap-Tiger	R. Bateman	950	185.00	185.00
94-01-277	Snowy Owl	R. Bateman	150	265.00	1000.00
87-01-278	Snowy Owl and Milkweed	R. Bateman	950	235.00	950.00
83-01-279	Snowy Owl on Driftwood	R. Bateman	950	245.00	1450.00
83-01-280	Spirits of the Forest	R. Bateman	950	170.00	1750.00
86-01-281	Split Rails-Snow Buntings	R. Bateman	950	220.00	220.00
80-01-282	Spring Cardinal	R. Bateman	950	125.00	600.00
82-01-283	Spring Marsh-Pintail Pair	R. Bateman	950	200.00	275.00
80-01-284	Spring Thaw-Killdeer	R. Bateman	950	85.00	150.00
82-01-285	Still Morning-Herring Gulls	R. Bateman	950	200.00	250.00
87-01-286	Stone Sheep Ram	R. Bateman	950	175.00	175.00
85-01-287	Stream Bank June	R. Bateman	950	160.00	175.00
84-01-288	Stretching-Canada Goose	R. Bateman	950	225.00	36-3900.
85-01-289	Strutting-Ring-Necked Pheasant	R. Bateman	950	225.00	325.00
85-01-290	Sudden Blizzard-Red-Tailed Hawk	R. Bateman	950	245.00	600.00
84-01-291	Summer Morning-Loon	R. Bateman	950	185.00	1250.00
90-01-292	Summer Morning Pasture	R. Bateman	950	175.00	175.00
86-01-293	Summertime-Polar Bears	R. Bateman	950	225.00	475.00
79-01-294	Surf and Sanderlings	R. Bateman	950	65.00	450.00
81-01-295	Swift Fox	R. Bateman	950	175.00	350.00
86-01-296	Swift Fox Study	R. Bateman	950	115.00	150.00
87-01-297	Sylvan Stream-Mute Swans	R. Bateman	950	125.00	125.00
84-01-298	Tadpole Time	R. Bateman	950	135.00	475.00
88-01-299	Tawny Owl In Beech	R. Bateman	950	325.00	600.00
92-01-300	Tembo (African Elephant)	R. Bateman	1,550	350.00	350.00
88-01-301	The Challenge-Bull Moose	R. Bateman	10,671	325.00	325.00
91-01-302	The Scolding-Chickadees & Screech Owl	R. Bateman	12,500	235.00	235.00
84-01-303	Tiger at Dawn	R. Bateman	950	225.00	2500.00
83-01-304	Tiger Portrait	R. Bateman	950	130.00	400.00
88-01-305	Tree Swallow over Pond	R. Bateman	950	290.00	290.00
91-01-306	Trumpeter Swan Family	R. Bateman	290	2500.00	2500.00
85-01-307	Trumpeter Swans and Aspen	R. Bateman	950	245.00	550.00
79-01-308	Up in the Pine-Great Horned Owl	R. Bateman	950	150.00	550.00
80-01-309	Vantage Point	R. Bateman	950	245.00	1300.00
93-01-310	Vigilance	R. Bateman	9,500	330.00	330.00
89-01-311	Vulture And Wildebeest	R. Bateman	550	295.00	295.00
81-01-312	Watchful Repose-Black Bear	R. Bateman	950	245.00	700.00
85-01-313	Weathered Branch-Bald Eagle	R. Bateman	950	115.00	300.00
91-01-314	Whistling Swan-Lake Erie	R. Bateman	1,950	325.00	325.00
85-01-315	White-Breasted Nuthatch on a Beech Tree	R. Bateman	950	175.00	300.00
80-01-316	White Encounter-Polar Bear	R. Bateman	950	245.00	42-4800.
80-01-317	White-Footed Mouse in Wintergreen	R. Bateman	950	60.00	650.00
82-01-318	White-Footed Mouse on Aspen	R. Bateman	950	90.00	180.00
92-01-319	White-Tailed Deer Through the Birches	R. Bateman	10,000	335.00	335.00
84-01-320	White-Throated Sparrow and Pussy Willow	R. Bateman	950	150.00	580.00
90-01-321	White on White-Snowshoe Hare	R. Bateman	950	195.00	590.00
82-01-322	White World-Dall Sheep	R. Bateman	950	200.00	450.00
91-01-323	Wide Horizon-Tundra Swans	R. Bateman	2,862	325.00	350-450.
91-01-324	Wide Horizon-Tundra Swans Companion	R. Bateman	2,862	325.00	325.00
86-01-325	Wildbeest	R. Bateman	950	185.00	185.00
82-01-326	Willet on the Shore	R. Bateman	950	125.00	225.00
79-01-327	Wily and Wary-Red Fox	R. Bateman	950	125.00	1500.00
84-01-328	Window into Ontario	R. Bateman	950	265.00	1500.00
83-01-329	Winter Barn	R. Bateman	950	170.00	400.00
79-01-330	Winter Cardinal	R. Bateman	950	75.00	3550.00
92-01-331	Winter Coat	R. Bateman	1,250	245.00	245.00
85-01-332	Winter Companion	R. Bateman	950	175.00	500.00
80-01-333	Winter Elm-American Kestrel	R. Bateman	950	135.00	600.00
86-01-334	Winter in the Mountains-Raven	R. Bateman	950	200.00	200.00
83-01-335	Winter-Lady Cardinal	R. Bateman	950	200.00	1500.00
81-01-336	Winter Mist-Great Horned Owl	R. Bateman	950	245.00	900.00
79-01-337	Winter-Snowshoe Hare	R. Bateman	950	95.00	1200.00
80-01-338	Winter Song-Chickadees	R. Bateman	950	95.00	900.00
84-01-339	Winter Sunset-Moose	R. Bateman	950	245.00	2700.00
92-01-340	Winter Trackers	R. Bateman	4,500	335.00	375.00
81-01-341	Winter Wren	R. Bateman	950	135.00	250.00
87-01-342	Wise One, The	R. Bateman	950	325.00	800.00
79-01-343	Wolf Pack in Moonlight	R. Bateman	950	95.00	3000.00
94-01-344	Wolf Pair in the Snow	R. Bateman	290	795.00	795.00
94-01-345	Wolverine Porfolio	R. Bateman	950	275.00	275.00
83-01-346	Wolves on the Trail	R. Bateman	950	225.00	700.00
85-01-347	Wood Bison Portrait	R. Bateman	950	165.00	200.00
83-01-348	Woodland Drummer-Ruffed Grouse	R. Bateman	950	185.00	250.00
81-01-349	Wrangler's Campsite-Gray Jay	R. Bateman	950	195.00	550.00
79-01-350	Yellow-Rumped Warbler	R. Bateman	950	50.00	575.00
78-01-351	Young Barn Swallow	R. Bateman	950	75.00	700.00
83-01-352	Young Elf Owl-Old Saguaro	R. Bateman	950	95.00	250.00
91-01-353	Young Giraffe	R. Bateman	290	850.00	850.00
89-01-354	Young Kittiwake	R. Bateman	950	195.00	195.00
88-01-355	Young Sandhill-Cranes	R. Bateman	950	325.00	325.00
89-01-356	Young Snowy Owl	R. Bateman	950	195.00	195.00
Mill Pond Press		**Brenders**			
88-02-001	A Hunter's Dream	C. Brenders	950	165.00	850.00
90-02-002	A Threatened Symbol	C. Brenders	1,950	145.00	300.00
89-02-003	A Young Generation	C. Brenders	1,250	165.00	375-425.
86-02-004	The Acrobat's Meal-Red Squirrel	C. Brenders	950	65.00	275.00
88-02-005	Apple Harvest	C. Brenders	950	115.00	295.00
89-02-006	The Apple Lover	C. Brenders	1,500	125.00	275.00
87-02-007	Autumn Lady	C. Brenders	950	150.00	375.00
91-02-008	The Balance of Nature	C. Brenders	1,950	225.00	225.00

		ARTIST	EDITION	ISSUE	QUOTE
86-02-009	Black-Capped Chickadees	C. Brenders	950	40.00	450.00
93-02-010	Black Sphinx	C. Brenders	950	235.00	235.00
90-02-011	Blond Beauty	C. Brenders	1,950	185.00	185.00
86-02-012	Bluebirds	C. Brenders	950	40.00	200-300.
88-02-013	California Quail	C. Brenders	950	95.00	350-400.
91-02-014	Calm Before the Challenge-Moose	C. Brenders	1,950	225.00	225.00
87-02-015	Close to Mom	C. Brenders	950	150.00	1500.00
93-02-016	Collectors Group (Butterfly Collections)	C. Brenders	290	375.00	375.00
86-02-017	Colorful Playground-Cottontails	C. Brenders	950	75.00	475.00
89-02-018	The Companions	C. Brenders	18,036	200.00	900-1250
94-02-019	Dall Sheep Portrait	C. Brenders	950	115.00	115.00
92-02-020	Den Mother-Pencil Sketch	C. Brenders	2,500	135.00	135.00
92-02-021	Den Mother-Wolf Family	C. Brenders	25,000	250.00	400.00
86-02-022	Disturbed Daydreams	C. Brenders	950	95.00	425.00
87-02-023	Double Trouble-Raccoons	C. Brenders	950	120.00	500-750.
93-02-024	Exotic Group (Butterfly Collections)	C. Brenders	290	375.00	375.00
93-02-025	European Group (Butterfly Collections)	C. Brenders	290	375.00	375.00
89-02-026	Forager's Reward-Red Squirrel	C. Brenders	1,250	135.00	135.00
88-02-027	Forest Sentinel-Bobcat	C. Brenders	950	135.00	500.00
90-02-028	Full House-Fox Family	C. Brenders	20,106	235.00	400.00
90-02-029	Ghostly Quiet-Spanish Lynx	C. Brenders	1,950	200.00	200.00
86-02-030	Golden Season-Gray Squirrel	C. Brenders	950	85.00	450-525.
86-02-031	Harvest Time-Chipmunk	C. Brenders	950	65.00	150-250.
88-02-032	Hidden In the Pines-Immature Great Hor	C. Brenders	950	175.00	1500.00
88-02-033	High Adventure-Black Bear Cubs	C. Brenders	950	105.00	375.00
93-02-034	In Northern Hunting Grounds	C. Brenders	1,750	375.00	375.00
92-02-035	Island Shores-Snowy Egret	C. Brenders	2,500	250.00	250.00
87-02-036	Ivory-Billed Woodpecker	C. Brenders	950	95.00	500.00
88-02-037	Long Distance Hunters	C. Brenders	950	175.00	2250.00
89-02-038	Lord of the Marshes	C. Brenders	1,250	135.00	175.00
86-02-039	Meadowlark	C. Brenders	950	40.00	150.00
89-02-040	Merlins at the Nest	C. Brenders	1,250	165.00	300-375.
85-02-041	Mighty Intruder	C. Brenders	950	95.00	275.00
87-02-042	Migration Fever-Barn Swallows	C. Brenders	950	150.00	295.00
90-02-043	The Monarch is Alive	C. Brenders	4,071	265.00	400.00
93-02-044	Mother of Pearls	C. Brenders	5,000	275.00	275.00
90-02-045	Mountain Baby-Bighorn Sheep	C. Brenders	1,950	165.00	165.00
87-02-046	Mysterious Visitor-Barn Owl	C. Brenders	950	150.00	250.00
93-02-047	Narrow Escape-Chipmunk	C. Brenders	1,750	150.00	150.00
91-02-048	The Nesting Season-House Sparrow	C. Brenders	1,950	195.00	200-250.
89-02-049	Northern Cousins-Black Squirrels	C. Brenders	950	150.00	250.00
84-02-050	On the Alert-Red Fox	C. Brenders	950	95.00	475.00
90-02-051	On the Old Farm Door	C. Brenders	1,500	225.00	450.00
91-02-052	One to One-Gray Wolf	C. Brenders	10,000	245.00	375.00
92-02-053	Pathfinder-Red Fox	C. Brenders	5,000	245.00	37500
84-02-054	Playful Pair-Chipmunks	C. Brenders	950	60.00	400.00
94-02-055	Power and Grace	C. Brenders	2,500	265.00	265.00
89-02-056	The Predator's Walk	C. Brenders	1,250	150.00	375.00
92-02-057	Red Fox Study	C. Brenders	1,250	125.00	125.00
94-02-058	Riverbank Kestrel	C. Brenders	2,500	225.00	225.00
88-02-059	Roaming the Plains-Pronghorns	C. Brenders	950	150.00	150.00
86-02-060	Robins	C. Brenders	950	40.00	125.00
93-02-061	Rocky Camp-Cougar Family	C. Brenders	5,000	275.00	275.00
93-02-062	Rocky Camp-Cubs	C. Brenders	950	225.00	225.00
92-02-063	Rocky Kingdom-Bighorn Sheep	C. Brenders	1,750	255.00	255.00
91-02-064	Shadows in the Grass-Young Cougars	C. Brenders	1,950	235.00	235.00
90-02-065	Shoreline Quartet-White Ibis	C. Brenders	1,950	265.00	265.00
84-02-066	Silent Hunter-Great Horned Owl	C. Brenders	950	95.00	450.00
84-02-067	Silent Passage	C. Brenders	950	150.00	495.00
90-02-068	Small Talk	C. Brenders	1,500	125.00	150-250.
92-02-069	Snow Leopard Portrait	C. Brenders	1,750	150.00	150.00
90-02-070	Spring Fawn	C. Brenders	1,500	125.00	300.00
90-02-071	Squirrel's Dish	C. Brenders	1,950	110.00	110.00
89-02-072	Steller's Jay	C. Brenders	1,250	135.00	175.00
91-02-073	Study for One to One	C. Brenders	1,950	120.00	200.00
93-02-074	Summer Roses-Winter Wren	C. Brenders	1,500	250.00	350.00
89-02-075	The Survivors-Canada Geese	C. Brenders	1,500	225.00	850-950.
94-02-076	Take Five-Canadian Lynx	C. Brenders	1,500	245.00	245.00
88-02-077	Talk on the Old Fence	C. Brenders	950	165.00	550.00
94-02-078	Tundra Summit-Arctic Wolves	C. Brenders	6,061	265.00	325.00
84-02-079	Waterside Encounter	C. Brenders	950	95.00	1000.00
87-02-080	White Elegance-Trumpeter Swans	C. Brenders	950	115.00	390.00
93-02-081	White Wolves-North American Wilderness Portfolio	C. Brenders	350	325.00	475.00
88-02-082	Witness of a Past-Bison	C. Brenders	950	110.00	110.00
92-02-083	Wolf Scout #1	C. Brenders	2,500	105.00	105.00
92-02-084	Wolf Scout #2	C. Brenders	2,500	105.00	105.00
91-02-085	Wolf Study	C. Brenders	950	125.00	125.00
87-02-086	Yellow-Bellied Marmot	C. Brenders	950	95.00	425.00
Mill Pond Press		**Calle**			
84-03-001	A Brace for the Spit	P. Calle	950	110.00	275.00
88-03-002	A New Day	P. Calle	950	150.00	150.00
89-03-003	A Winter Feast	P. Calle	1,250	265.00	265.00
89-03-004	A Winter Feast-Prestige Ed.	P. Calle	290	465.00	465.00
83-03-005	A Winter Surprise	P. Calle	950	195.00	800.00
81-03-006	Almost Home	P. Calle	950	150.00	150.00
91-03-007	Almost There	P. Calle	950	165.00	165.00
89-03-008	And A Good Book For Company	P. Calle	950	135.00	190.00
93-03-009	And A Grizzly Claw Necklace	P. Calle	750	150.00	150.00
81-03-010	And Still Miles to Go	P. Calle	950	245.00	300.00
81-03-011	Andrew At The Falls	P. Calle	950	150.00	175.00
89-03-012	The Beaver Men	P. Calle	950	125.00	125.00
80-03-013	Caring for the Herd	P. Calle	950	110.00	110.00
85-03-014	The Carrying Place	P. Calle	950	195.00	195.00
84-03-015	Chance Encounter	P. Calle	950	225.00	300.00
81-03-016	Chief High Pipe (Color)	P. Calle	950	265.00	275.00
80-03-017	Chief High Pipe (Pencil)	P. Calle	950	75.00	165.00
80-03-018	Chief Joseph-Man of Peace	P. Calle	950	135.00	150.00
90-03-019	Children of Walpi	P. Calle	350	160.00	160.00
90-03-020	The Doll Maker	P. Calle	950	95.00	95.00
82-03-021	Emerging from the Woods	P. Calle	950	110.00	110-160.
81-03-022	End of a Long Day	P. Calle	950	150.00	150-190.
84-03-023	Fate of the Late Migrant	P. Calle	950	110.00	300.00
83-03-024	Free Spirits	P. Calle	950	195.00	325.00
83-03-025	Free Trapper Study	P. Calle	550	75.00	125-300.
81-03-026	Fresh Tracks	P. Calle	950	150.00	165.00
81-03-027	Friend of Foe	P. Calle	950	125.00	125.00
81-03-028	Friends	P. Calle	950	150.00	150.00
85-03-029	The Frontier Blacksmith	P. Calle	950	245.00	245.00
89-03-030	The Fur Trapper	P. Calle	550	75.00	175.00
82-03-031	Generations in the Valley	P. Calle	950	245.00	245.00

		ARTIST	EDITION	ISSUE	QUOTE
85-03-032	The Grandmother	P. Calle	950	400.00	400.00
89-03-033	The Great Moment	P. Calle	950	350.00	350.00
92-03-034	Hunter of Geese	P. Calle	950	125.00	125.00
93-03-035	I Call Him Friend	P. Calle	950	235.00	235.00
83-03-036	In Search of Beaver	P. Calle	950	225.00	600.00
91-03-037	In the Beginning . . . Friends	P. Calle	1,250	250.00	250.00
87-03-038	In the Land of the Giants	P. Calle	950	245.00	780.00
90-03-039	Interrupted Journey	P. Calle	1,750	265.00	265.00
90-03-040	Interrupted Journey-Prestige Ed.	P. Calle	290	465.00	465.00
87-03-041	Into the Great Alone	P. Calle	950	245.00	600.00
81-03-042	Just Over the Ridge	P. Calle	950	245.00	325.00
80-03-043	Landmark Tree	P. Calle	950	125.00	225.00
91-03-044	Man of the Fur Trade	P. Calle	550	110.00	110.00
93-03-045	Mountain Man-North American Wilderness Portfolio	P. Calle	350	325.00	N/A
84-03-046	Mountain Man	P. Calle	550	95.00	250-550.
89-03-047	The Mountain Men	P. Calle	300	400.00	400.00
89-03-048	Navajo Madonna	P. Calle	650	95.00	95.00
81-03-049	One With The Land	P. Calle	950	245.00	325.00
92-03-050	Out of the Silence	P. Calle	2,500	265.00	265.00
92-03-051	Out of the Silence-Prestige	P. Calle	290	465.00	465.00
81-03-052	Pause at the Lower Falls	P. Calle	950	110.00	125.00
80-03-053	Prayer to the Great Mystery	P. Calle	950	245.00	400.00
82-03-054	Return to Camp	P. Calle	950	245.00	400.00
80-03-055	Sioux Chief	P. Calle	950	85.00	85-140.
90-03-056	Son of Sitting Bull	P. Calle	950	95.00	95.00
86-03-057	Snow Hunter	P. Calle	950	150.00	250-410.
80-03-058	Something for the Pot	P. Calle	950	175.00	1000.00
85-03-059	Storyteller of the Mountains	P. Calle	950	225.00	575.00
83-03-060	Strays From the Flyway	P. Calle	950	195.00	250-340.
81-03-061	Teton Friends	P. Calle	950	150.00	200.00
91-03-0622	The Silenced Honkers	P. Calle	1,250	250.00	250.00
91-03-063	They Call Me Matthew	P. Calle	950	125.00	125.00
92-03-064	Through the Tall Grass	P. Calle	950	175.00	175.00
88-03-065	Trapper at Rest	P. Calle	550	95.00	95.00
82-03-066	Two from the Flock	P. Calle	950	245.00	400.00
80-03-067	View from the Heights	P. Calle	950	245.00	350.00
88-03-068	Voyageurs and Waterfowl...Constant	P. Calle	950	265.00	265.00
80-03-069	When Snow Came Early	P. Calle	950	85.00	250-340.
84-03-070	When Trails Cross	P. Calle	950	245.00	750.00
91-03-071	When Trails Grow Cold	P. Calle	2,500	265.00	265.00
91-03-072	When Trails Grow Cold-Prestige Ed.	P. Calle	290	465.00	465-600.
94-03-073	When Trappers Meet	P. Calle	750	165.00	165.00
89-03-074	Where Eagles Fly	P. Calle	1,250	265.00	265.00
81-03-075	Winter Hunter (Color)	P. Calle	950	245.00	725.00
80-03-076	Winter Hunter (Pencil)	P. Calle	950	65.00	450.00

Mill Pond Press — Cross

		ARTIST	EDITION	ISSUE	QUOTE
94-04-001	April	T. Cross	750	55.00	55.00
94-04-002	August	T. Cross	750	55.00	55.00
93-04-003	Ever Green	T. Cross	750	135.00	135.00
93-04-004	Flame Catcher	T. Cross	750	185.00	185.00
93-04-005	Flicker, Flash and Twirl	T. Cross	525	165.00	165.00
94-04-006	July	T. Cross	750	55.00	55.00
94-04-007	June	T. Cross	750	55.00	55.00
94-04-008	May	T. Cross	750	55.00	55.00
94-04-009	March	T. Cross	750	55.00	55.00
92-04-010	Shell Caster	T. Cross	750	150.00	150.00
93-04-011	Shepards of Magic	T. Cross	750	135.00	135.00
93-04-012	Spellbound	T. Cross	750	85.00	85.00
94-04-013	Spring Forth	T. Cross	750	145.00	145.00
92-04-014	Star Weaver	T. Cross	750	150.00	150.00
94-04-015	Summer Musings	T. Cross	750	145.00	145.00
93-04-016	The Summons...And Then They Are One	T. Cross	750	195.00	195.00
94-04-017	When Water Takes to Air	T. Cross	750	135.00	135.00
93-04-018	Wind Sifter	T. Cross	750	150.00	150.00

Mill Pond Press — Daly

		ARTIST	EDITION	ISSUE	QUOTE
91-05-001	A New Beginning	J. Daly	5,000	125.00	125.00
90-05-002	The Big Moment	J. Daly	1,500	125.00	125.00
94-05-003	Catch of My Dreams	J. Daly	4,500	45.00	45.00
91-05-004	Cat's Cradle-Prestige Edition	J. Daly	950	450.00	450.00
94-05-005	Childhood Friends	J. Daly	950	110.00	110.00
90-05-006	Confrontation	J. Daly	1,500	85.00	85.00
90-05-007	Contentment	J. Daly	1,500	95.00	275.00
92-05-008	Dominoes	J. Daly	1,500	155.00	155.00
92-05-009	Favorite Gift	J. Daly	2,500	175.00	175.00
87-05-010	Favorite Reader	J. Daly	950	85.00	85.00
86-05-011	Flying High	J. Daly	950	50.00	350.00
92-05-012	The Flying Horse	J. Daly	950	325.00	325.00
93-05-013	Good Company	J. Daly	1,500	155.00	155.00
92-05-014	Her Secret Place	J. Daly	1,500	135.00	250.00
91-05-015	Home Team: Zero	J. Daly	1,500	150.00	150.00
91-05-016	Homemade	J. Daly	1,500	125.00	125.00
90-05-017	Honor and Allegiance	J. Daly	1,500	110.00	110.00
90-05-018	The Ice Man	J. Daly	1,500	125.00	125.00
92-05-019	The Immigrant Spirit	J. Daly	5,000	125.00	125.00
92-05-020	The Immigrant Spirit-Prestige Edition	J. Daly	950	125.00	125.00
89-05-021	In the Doghouse	J. Daly	1,500	75.00	250.00
90-05-022	It's That Time Again	J. Daly	1,500	120.00	120.00
92-05-023	Left Out	J. Daly	1,500	110.00	110.00
89-05-024	Let's Play Ball	J. Daly	1,500	75.00	150.00
90-05-025	Make Believe	J. Daly	1,500	75.00	125.00
94-05-026	Mud Mates	J. Daly	950	150.00	150.00
94-05-027	My Best Friends	J. Daly	950	85.00	85.00
93-05-028	The New Citizen	J. Daly	5,000	125.00	125.00
93-05-029	The New Citizen-Prestige Edition	J. Daly	950	125.00	125.00
87-05-030	Odd Man Out	J. Daly	950	85.00	85.00
88-05-031	On Thin Ice	J. Daly	950	95.00	95.00
91-05-032	Pillars of a Nation-Charter Edition	J. Daly	20,000	175.00	175.00
92-05-033	Playmates	J. Daly	1,500	155.00	350.00
90-05-034	Radio Daze	J. Daly	1,500	150.00	150.00
83-05-035	Saturday Night	J. Daly	950	85.00	1125.00
90-05-036	The Scholar	J. Daly	1,500	110.00	110.00
93-05-037	Secret Admirer	J. Daly	1,500	150.00	150.00
94-05-038	Slugger	J. Daly	950	75.00	75.00
82-05-039	Spring Fever	J. Daly	950	85.00	750.00
93-05-040	Sunday Afternoon	J. Daly	1,500	150.00	150.00
88-05-041	Territorial Rights	J. Daly	950	85.00	85.00
89-05-042	The Thief	J. Daly	1,500	95.00	175.00
89-05-043	The Thorn	J. Daly	1,500	125.00	125.00
88-05-044	Tie Breaker	J. Daly	950	95.00	95.00
91-05-045	Time-Out	J. Daly	1,500	125.00	125.00
93-05-046	To All a Good Night	J. Daly	1,500	160.00	160.00
92-05-047	Walking the Rails	J. Daly	1,500	175.00	175.00
93-05-048	When I Grow Up	J. Daly	1,500	175.00	175.00
94-05-049	Wind-Up, The	J. Daly	950	75.00	75.00
88-05-050	Wiped Out	J. Daly	1,250	125.00	125.00

Mill Pond Press — Morrissey

		ARTIST	EDITION	ISSUE	QUOTE
94-06-001	The Amazing Time Elevator	D. Morrissey	950	195.00	195.00
93-06-002	Charting the Skies	D. Morrissey	1,250	195.00	195.00
93-06-003	Charting the Skies-Caprice Edition	D. Morrissey	550	375.00	375.00
93-06-004	Draft of Dream	D. Morrissey	175	250.00	250.00
94-06-005	The Dreamer's Trunk	D. Morrissey	1,500	195.00	195.00
93-06-006	Draft of a Dream	D. Morrissey	175	250.00	250.00
93-06-007	Drifting Closer	D. Morrissey	1,250	175.00	175.00
93-06-008	The Mystic Mariner	D. Morrissey	750	150.00	250.00
93-06-009	The Redd Rocket	D. Morrissey	1,250	175.00	375.00
94-06-010	The Redd Rocket-Pre-Flight	D. Morrissey	950	110.00	110.00
92-06-011	The Sandman's Ship of Dreams	D. Morrissey	750	150.00	150.00
94-06-012	Sighting off the Stern	D. Morrissey	950	135.00	135.00
93-06-013	Sleeper Flight	D. Morrissey	1,250	195.00	195.00
93-06-014	The Telescope of Time	D. Morrissey	5,000	195.00	195.00

Mill Pond Press — Olsen

		ARTIST	EDITION	ISSUE	QUOTE
93-07-001	Airship Adventures	G. Olsen	750	150.00	150.00
93-07-002	Angels of Christmas	G. Olsen	750	135.00	135.00
93-07-003	Dress Rehearseal	G. Olsen	750	165.00	750.00
93-07-004	The Fraternity Tree	G. Olsen	750	195.00	195.00
94-07-005	Little Girls Will Mothers Be	G. Olsen	750	135.00	175.00
94-07-006	Mother's Love	G. Olsen	750	165.00	165.00
94-07-007	Summerhouse	G. Olsen	750	165.00	165.00

Mill Pond Press — Seerey-Lester

		ARTIST	EDITION	ISSUE	QUOTE
94-08-001	Abandoned	J. Seerey-Lester	950	175.00	175.00
86-08-002	Above the Treeline-Cougar	J. Seerey-Lester	950	130.00	175.00
86-08-003	After the Fire-Grizzly	J. Seerey-Lester	950	95.00	95.00
86-08-004	Along the Ice Floe-Polar Bears	J. Seerey-Lester	950	200.00	200.00
87-08-005	Alpenglow-Artic Wolf	J. Seerey-Lester	950	200.00	275.00
87-08-006	Amboseli Child-African Elephant	J. Seerey-Lester	950	160.00	160.00
84-08-007	Among the Cattails-Canada Geese	J. Seerey-Lester	950	130.00	425.00
84-08-008	Artic Procession-Willow Ptarmigan	J. Seerey-Lester	950	220.00	600.00
90-08-009	Artic Wolf Pups	J. Seerey-Lester	290	500.00	500.00
87-08-010	Autumn Mist-Barred Owl	J. Seerey-Lester	950	160.00	225.00
87-08-011	Autumn Thunder-Muskoxen	J. Seerey-Lester	950	150.00	150.00
85-08-012	Awakening Meadow-Cottontail	J. Seerey-Lester	950	50.00	50.00
92-08-013	Banyan Ambush- Black Panther	J. Seerey-Lester	950	235.00	400.00
84-08-014	Basking-Brown Pelicans	J. Seerey-Lester	950	115.00	125.00
88-08-015	Bathing-Blue Jay	J. Seerey-Lester	950	95.00	95.00
87-08-016	Bathing-Mute Swan	J. Seerey-Lester	950	175.00	175.00
89-08-017	Before The Freeze-Beaver	J. Seerey-Lester	950	165.00	165.00
90-08-018	Bittersweet Winter-Cardinal	J. Seerey-Lester	1,250	150.00	275.00
92-08-019	Black Jade	J. Seerey-Lester	1,950	275.00	275.00
92-08-020	Black Magic-Panther	J. Seerey-Lester	750	195.00	195.00
93-08-021	Black Wolf-North American Wilderness	J. Seerey-Lester	350	325.00	N/A
84-08-022	Breaking Cover-Black Bear	J. Seerey-Lester	950	130.00	130.00
87-08-023	Canyon Creek-Cougar	J. Seerey-Lester	950	195.00	450.00
92-08-024	The Chase-Snow Leopard	J. Seerey-Lester	950	200.00	200.00
94-08-025	Child of the Outback	J. Seerey-Lester	950	175.00	175.00
85-08-026	Children of the Forest-Red Fox Kits	J. Seerey-Lester	950	110.00	150.00
85-08-027	Children of the Tundra-Artic Wolf Pup	J. Seerey-Lester	950	110.00	225.00
88-08-028	Cliff Hanger-Bobcat	J. Seerey-Lester	950	200.00	200.00
84-08-029	Close Encounter-Bobcat	J. Seerey-Lester	950	130.00	190.00
88-08-030	Coastal Clique-Harbor Seals	J. Seerey-Lester	950	160.00	160.00
86-08-031	Conflict at Dawn-Heron and Osprey	J. Seerey-Lester	950	130.00	130.00
83-08-032	Cool Retreat-Lynx	J. Seerey-Lester	950	85.00	100.00
86-08-033	Cottonwood Gold-Baltimore Oriole	J. Seerey-Lester	950	85.00	85.00
85-08-034	Cougar Head Study	J. Seerey-Lester	950	60.00	60.00
89-08-035	Cougar Run	J. Seerey-Lester	950	185.00	350-450.
94-08-036	The Courtship	J. Seerey-Lester	950	175.00	175.00
90-08-037	Dawn Majesty	J. Seerey-Lester	1,250	185.00	185.00
93-08-038	Dark Encounter	J. Seerey-Lester	3,500	200.00	200.00
87-08-039	Dawn on the Marsh-Coyote	J. Seerey-Lester	950	200.00	200.00
85-08-040	Daybreak-Moose	J. Seerey-Lester	950	135.00	135.00
91-08-041	Denali Family-Grizzly Bear	J. Seerey-Lester	950	195.00	195.00
86-08-042	Early Arrivals-Snow Buntings	J. Seerey-Lester	950	75.00	75.00
83-08-043	Early Windfall-Gray Squirrels	J. Seerey-Lester	950	85.00	85.00
88-08-044	Edge of the Forest-Timber Wolves	J. Seerey-Lester	950	500.00	700.00
89-08-045	Evening Duet-Snowy Egrets	J. Seerey-Lester	1,250	185.00	185.00
91-08-046	Evening Encounter-Grizzly & Wolf	J. Seerey-Lester	1,250	185.00	185.00
88-08-047	Evening Meadow-American Goldfinch	J. Seerey-Lester	950	150.00	150.00
91-08-048	Face to Face	J. Seerey-Lester	1,250	200.00	200.00
85-08-049	Fallen Birch-Chipmunk	J. Seerey-Lester	950	60.00	250.00
85-08-050	First Light-Gray Jays	J. Seerey-Lester	950	130.00	200.00
83-08-051	First Snow-Grizzly Bears	J. Seerey-Lester	950	95.00	250.00
87-08-052	First Tracks-Cougar	J. Seerey-Lester	950	150.00	150.00
89-08-053	Fluke Sighting-Humback Whales	J. Seerey-Lester	950	185.00	185.00
93-08-054	Freedom I	J. Seerey-Lester	350	500.00	500.00
93-08-055	Frozen Moonlight	J. Seerey-Lester	2,500	225.00	225.00
85-08-056	Gathering-Gray Wolves, The	J. Seerey-Lester	950	165.00	350.00
89-08-057	Gorilla	J. Seerey-Lester	290	400.00	600.00
93-08-058	Grizzly Impact	J. Seerey-Lester	950	225.00	225.00
90-08-059	Grizzly Litho	J. Seerey-Lester	290	400.00	600.00
89-08-060	Heavy Going-Grizzly	J. Seerey-Lester	950	175.00	300.00
86-08-061	Hidden Admirer-Moose	J. Seerey-Lester	950	165.00	275.00
88-08-062	Hiding Place-Saw-Whet Owl	J. Seerey-Lester	950	95.00	95.00
89-08-063	High and Mighty-Gorilla	J. Seerey-Lester	950	185.00	225.00
86-08-064	High Country Champion-Grizzly	J. Seerey-Lester	950	175.00	275.00
84-08-065	High Ground-Wolves	J. Seerey-Lester	950	130.00	325.00
87-08-066	High Refuge-Red Squirrel	J. Seerey-Lester	950	120.00	120.00
84-08-067	Icy Outcrop-White Gyrfalcon	J. Seerey-Lester	950	115.00	200.00
87-08-068	In Deep-Black Bear Cub	J. Seerey-Lester	950	135.00	135.00
90-08-069	In Their Presence	J. Seerey-Lester	1,250	200.00	200.00
85-08-070	Island Sanctuary-Mallards	J. Seerey-Lester	950	95.00	175.00
86-08-071	Kenyan Family-Cheetahs	J. Seerey-Lester	950	130.00	130.00
86-08-072	Lakeside Family-Canada Geese	J. Seerey-Lester	950	75.00	75.00
88-08-073	Last Sanctuary-Florida Panther	J. Seerey-Lester	950	175.00	175.00
83-08-074	Lone Fisherman-Great Blue Heron	J. Seerey-Lester	950	85.00	300.00
93-08-075	Loonlight	J. Seerey-Lester	1,500	225.00	225.00
86-08-076	Low Tide-Bald Eagles	J. Seerey-Lester	950	130.00	130.00
87-08-077	Lying in Wait-Arctic Fox	J. Seerey-Lester	950	175.00	175.00
84-08-078	Lying Low-Cougar	J. Seerey-Lester	950	85.00	450.00
91-08-079	Monsoon-White Tiger	J. Seerey-Lester	950	195.00	195.00

		ARTIST	EDITION	ISSUE	QUOTE
91-08-080	Moonlight Chase-Cougar	J. Seerey-Lester	1,250	195.00	195-220.
88-08-081	Moonlight Fishermen-Raccoons	J. Seerey-Lester	950	175.00	175.00
88-08-082	Moose Hair	J. Seerey-Lester	950	165.00	165.00
88-08-083	Morning Display-Common Loons	J. Seerey-Lester	950	135.00	300.00
86-08-084	Morning Forage-Ground Squirrel	J. Seerey-Lester	950	75.00	75.00
93-08-085	Morning Glory	J. Seerey-Lester	1,250	225.00	225.00
84-08-086	Morning Mist-Snowy Owl	J. Seerey-Lester	950	95.00	95-180.
90-08-087	Mountain Cradle	J. Seerey-Lester	1,250	200.00	300.00
88-08-088	Night Moves-African Elephants	J. Seerey-Lester	950	150.00	150.00
90-08-089	Night Run-Artic Wolves	J. Seerey-Lester	1,250	200.00	250.00
93-08-090	Night Specter	J. Seerey-Lester	1,250	195.00	195.00
86-08-091	Northwoods Family-Moose	J. Seerey-Lester	950	75.00	75.00
87-08-092	Out of the Blizzard-Timber Wolves	J. Seerey-Lester	950	215.00	350.00
92-08-093	Out of the Darkness	J. Seerey-Lester	290	200.00	200.00
87-08-094	Out of the Mist-Grizzly	J. Seerey-Lester	950	200.00	200.00
91-08-095	Out on a Limb-Young Barred Owl	J. Seerey-Lester	950	185.00	185.00
91-08-096	Panda Trilogy	J. Seerey-Lester	950	375.00	375.00
93-08-097	Phantoms of the Tundra	J. Seerey-Lester	950	235.00	235.00
84-08-098	Plains Hunter-Prairie Falcon	J. Seerey-Lester	950	95.00	95.00
90-08-099	The Plunge-Northern Sea Lions	J. Seerey-Lester	1,250	200.00	200.00
86-08-0100	Racing the Storm-Artic Wolves	J. Seerey-Lester	950	200.00	350.00
87-08-101	Rain Watch-Belted Kingfisher	J. Seerey-Lester	950	125.00	125.00
93-08-102	The Rains-Tiger	J. Seerey-Lester	950	225.00	225.00
92-08-103	Ranthambhore Rush	J. Seerey-Lester	950	225.00	225.00
83-08-104	The Refuge-Raccoon	J. Seerey-Lester	950	85.00	300.00
92-08-105	Regal Majesty	J. Seerey-Lester	290	200.00	200.00
85-08-106	Return to Winter-Pintails	J. Seerey-Lester	950	135.00	135.00
83-08-107	River Watch-Peregrine Falcon	J. Seerey-Lester	950	85.00	85.00
88-08-108	Savana Siesta-African Lions	J. Seerey-Lester	950	165.00	165.00
90-08-109	Seasonal Greeting-Cardinal	J. Seerey-Lester	1,250	150.00	150.00
93-08-110	Seeking Attention	J. Seerey-Lester	950	200.00	200.00
91-08-111	Sisters-Artic Wolves	J. Seerey-Lester	1,250	185.00	185.00
89-08-112	Sneak Peak	J. Seerey-Lester	950	185.00	185.00
86-08-113	Snowy Excursion-Red Squirrel	J. Seerey-Lester	950	75.00	75.00
88-08-114	Snowy Watch-Great Gray Owl	J. Seerey-Lester	950	175.00	175.00
89-08-115	Softly, Softly-White Tiger	J. Seerey-Lester	950	220.00	490.00
91-08-116	Something Stirred (Bengal Tiger)	J. Seerey-Lester	950	195.00	195.00
88-08-117	Spanish Mist-Young Barred-Owl	J. Seerey-Lester	950	175.00	175.00
84-08-118	Spirit of the North-White Wolf	J. Seerey-Lester	950	130.00	185.00
90-08-119	Spout	J. Seerey-Lester	290	500.00	500.00
86-08-120	Spring Mist-Chickadees	J. Seerey-Lester	950	105.00	150.00
89-08-121	Spring Flurry-Adelie Penguins	J. Seerey-Lester	950	185.00	185.00
90-08-122	Suitors-Wood Ducks	J. Seerey-Lester	3,313	135.00	135.00
90-08-123	Summer Rain-Common Loons	J. Seerey-Lester	4,500	200.00	200.00
90-08-124	Summer Rain-Common Loons (Prestige)	J. Seerey-Lester	450	425.00	425.00
87-08-125	Sundown Alert-Bobcat	J. Seerey-Lester	950	150.00	150.00
85-08-126	Sundown Reflections-Wood Ducks	J. Seerey-Lester	950	85.00	85.00
90-08-127	Their First Season	J. Seerey-Lester	1,250	200.00	200.00
90-08-128	Togetherness	J. Seerey-Lester	1,250	125.00	185.00
86-08-129	Treading Thin Ice-Chipmunk	J. Seerey-Lester	950	75.00	75.00
88-08-130	Tundra Family-Arctic Wolves	J. Seerey-Lester	950	200.00	200.00
85-08-131	Under the Pines-Bobcat	J. Seerey-Lester	950	95.00	275.00
89-08-132	Water Sport-Bobcat	J. Seerey-Lester	950	185.00	185.00
90-08-133	Whitetail Spring	J. Seerey-Lester	1,250	185.00	185.00
88-08-134	Winter Grazing-Bison	J. Seerey-Lester	950	185.00	185.00
86-08-135	Winter Hiding-Cottontail	J. Seerey-Lester	950	75.00	75.00
83-08-136	Winter Lookout-Cougar	J. Seerey-Lester	950	85.00	500.00
86-08-137	Winter Perch-Cardinal	J. Seerey-Lester	950	85.00	175.00
85-08-138	Winter Rendezvous-Coyotes	J. Seerey-Lester	950	140.00	225.00
88-08-139	Winter Spirit-Gray Wolf	J. Seerey-Lester	950	200.00	200.00
87-08-140	Winter Vigil-Great Horned Owl	J. Seerey-Lester	950	175.00	175.00
93-08-141	Wolong Whiteout	J. Seerey-Lester	950	225.00	225.00
86-08-142	The Young Explorer-Red Fox Kit	J. Seerey-Lester	950	75.00	75.00
Mill Pond Press		**Smith**			
93-09-001	African Ebony-Black Leopard	D. Smith	1,250	195.00	195.00
92-09-002	Armada	D. Smith	950	195.00	195.00
93-09-003	Catching the Scent-Polar Bear	D. Smith	950	175.00	175.00
94-09-004	Curious Presence-Whitetail Deer	D. Smith	950	195.00	195.00
91-09-005	Dawn's Early Light-Bald Eagles	D. Smith	950	185.00	185.00
93-09-006	Echo Bay-Loon Family	D. Smith	1,150	185.00	250.00
92-09-007	Eyes of the North	D. Smith	2,500	225.00	225.00
93-09-008	Guardians of the Den	D. Smith	1,500	195.00	350.00
91-09-009	Icy Reflections-Pintails	D. Smith	500	250.00	250.00
92-09-010	Night Moves-Cougar	D. Smith	950	185.00	185.00
94-09-011	Parting Reflections	D. Smith	950	185.00	185.00
93-09-012	Shrouded Forest-Bald Eagle	D. Smith	950	150.00	950.00
91-09-013	Twilight's Calling-Common Loons	D. Smith	950	175.00	300.00
93-09-014	What's Bruin	D. Smith	1,750	185.00	275.00
New Masters Publishing		**Bannister**			
78-01-001	Bandstand	P. Bannister	S/O	75.00	450.00
80-01-002	Dust of Autumn	P. Bannister	S/O	200.00	1225.00
80-01-003	Faded Glory	P. Bannister	S/O	200.00	1225.00
80-01-004	Gift of Happiness	P. Bannister	S/O	200.00	2000.00
80-01-005	Girl on the Beach	P. Bannister	S/O	200.00	1200.00
80-01-006	The Silver Bell	P. Bannister	S/O	200.00	2000.00
81-01-007	April	P. Bannister	S/O	200.00	1100.00
81-01-008	Easter	P. Bannister	S/O	260.00	950.00
81-01-009	Juliet	P. Bannister	S/O	260.00	5000.00
81-01-010	My Special Place	P. Bannister	S/O	260.00	1850.00
81-01-011	Porcelain Rose	P. Bannister	S/O	260.00	2000.00
81-01-012	Rehearsal	P. Bannister	S/O	260.00	1850.00
81-01-013	Sea Haven	P. Bannister	S/O	260.00	1100.00
81-01-014	Titania	P. Bannister	S/O	260.00	900.00
82-01-015	Amaryllis	P. Bannister	S/O	285.00	1900.00
82-01-016	Emily	P. Bannister	S/O	285.00	800.00
82-01-017	Ivy	P. Bannister	S/O	285.00	700.00
82-01-018	Jasmine	P. Bannister	S/O	285.00	650.00
82-01-019	Mail Order Brides	P. Bannister	S/O	325.00	2300.00
82-01-020	Memories	P. Bannister	S/O	235.00	500.00
82-01-021	Nuance	P. Bannister	S/O	235.00	470.00
82-01-022	The Present	P. Bannister	S/O	260.00	800.00
83-01-023	The Duchess	P. Bannister	S/O	250.00	1800.00
84-01-024	The Fan Window	P. Bannister	S/O	195.00	450.00
84-01-025	Window Seat	P. Bannister	S/O	150.00	600.00
83-01-026	Ophelia	P. Bannister	S/O	150.00	675.00
84-01-027	Scarlet Ribbons	P. Bannister	S/O	150.00	325.00
83-01-028	Mementos	P. Bannister	S/O	150.00	1400.00
84-01-029	April Light	P. Bannister	S/O	150.00	600.00
84-01-030	Make Believe	P. Bannister	S/O	150.00	600.00
88-01-031	Summer Choices	P. Bannister	S/O	250.00	800.00

		ARTIST	EDITION	ISSUE	QUOTE
88-01-032	Guinevere	P. Bannister	S/O	265.00	1000.00
88-01-033	Love Seat	P. Bannister	S/O	230.00	500.00
88-01-034	Apples and Oranges	P. Bannister	S/O	265.00	600.00
89-01-035	Daydreams	P. Bannister	S/O	265.00	530.00
86-01-036	Pride & Joy	P. Bannister	S/O	150.00	300.00
87-01-037	September Harvest	P. Bannister	S/O	150.00	300.00
87-01-038	Quiet Corner	P. Bannister	S/O	115.00	300.00
87-01-039	First Prize	P. Bannister	S/O	115.00	175.00
88-01-040	Floribunda	P. Bannister	S/O	265.00	550.00
89-01-041	March Winds	P. Bannister	S/O	265.00	530.00
89-01-042	Peace	P. Bannister	S/O	265.00	1100.00
89-01-043	The Quilt	P. Bannister	S/O	265.00	900.00
89-01-044	Low Tide	P. Bannister	S/O	265.00	550.00
89-01-045	Chapter One	P. Bannister	S/O	265.00	1300.00
90-01-046	Lavender Hill	P. Bannister	S/O	265.00	625.00
90-01-047	Rendezvous	P. Bannister	S/O	265.00	650.00
90-01-048	Sisters	P. Bannister	S/O	265.00	950.00
90-01-049	Seascapes	P. Bannister	S/O	265.00	550.00
90-01-050	Songbird	P. Bannister	S/O	265.00	550.00
90-01-051	Good Friends	P. Bannister	S/O	265.00	750.00
91-01-052	String of Pearls	P. Bannister	S/O	265.00	850.00
91-01-053	Wildflowers	P. Bannister	S/O	295.00	590.00
91-01-054	Crossroads	P. Bannister	S/O	295.00	590.00
91-01-055	Teatime	P. Bannister	S/O	295.00	600.00
91-01-056	Celebration	P. Bannister	S/O	350.00	700.00
91-01-057	Pudding & Pies	P. Bannister	S/O	265.00	265.00
92-01-058	Morning Mist	P. Bannister	S/O	265.00	265.00
92-01-059	Love Letters	P. Bannister	S/O	265.00	265.00
92-01-060	Crystal Bowl	P. Bannister	S/O	265.00	265.00
93-01-061	Deja Vu	P. Bannister	S/O	265.00	265.00
93-01-062	Crowning Glory	P. Bannister	S/O	265.00	265.00
Past Impressions		**Maley**			
84-01-001	Secluded Garden	A. Maley	Closed	150.00	970.00
84-01-002	Glorious Summer	A. Maley	Closed	150.00	725.00
85-01-003	Secret Thoughts	A. Maley	Closed	150.00	850.00
85-01-004	Passing Elegance	A. Maley	Closed	150.00	750.00
86-01-005	Winter Romance	A. Maley	Closed	150.00	650.00
86-01-006	Tell Me	A. Maley	Closed	150.00	850.00
88-01-007	Opening Night	A. Maley	Closed	250.00	2000.00
67-01-008	Love Letter	A. Maley	Closed	200.00	300-550.
87-01-009	The Promise	A. Maley	Closed	200.00	315.00
88-01-010	Day Dreams	A. Maley	Closed	200.00	350-450.
88-01-011	The Boardwalk	A. Maley	Closed	250.00	340.00
88-01-012	Tranquil Moment	A. Maley	Closed	250.00	315.00
88-01-013	Joys of Childhood	A. Maley	Closed	250.00	250.00
88-01-014	Victorian Trio	A. Maley	Closed	250.00	340.00
89-01-015	English Rose	A. Maley	Closed	250.00	285.00
89-01-016	Winter Impressions	A. Maley	750	250.00	315.00
89-01-017	In Harmony	A. Maley	750	250.00	250.00
89-01-018	Victoria	A. Maley	750	125.00	125.00
89-01-019	Alexandria	A. Maley	750	125.00	125.00
89-01-020	Catherine	A. Maley	750	125.00	125.00
89-01-021	Beth	A. Maley	750	125.00	125.00
90-01-022	Festive Occasion	A. Maley	Closed	250.00	250.00
90-01-023	Summer Pastime	A. Maley	Closed	250.00	250.00
90-01-024	Cafe Royale	A. Maley	750	275.00	275.00
90-01-025	Romantic Engagement	A. Maley	750	275.00	275.00
90-01-026	Gracious Era	A. Maley	750	275.00	275.00
90-01-027	Evening Performance	A. Maley	750	150.00	150.00
91-01-028	Between Friends	A. Maley	750	275.00	275.00
91-01-029	Summer Carousel	A. Maley	750	200.00	200.00
91-01-030	Sunday Afternoon	A. Maley	750	275.00	275.00
91-01-031	Winter Carousel	A. Maley	750	200.00	200.00
92-01-032	Intimate Moment	A. Maley	750	250.00	250.00
92-01-033	A Walk in the Park	A. Maley	500	260.00	260.00
92-01-034	An Elegant Affair	A. Maley	500	260.00	260.00
92-01-035	Circle of Love	A. Maley	500	250.00	250.00
93-01-036	Rags and Riches	A. Maley	500	250.00	250.00
93-01-037	Sleigh Bells	A. Maley	500	260.00	260.00
94-01-038	Summer Elegance	A. Maley	500	275.00	275.00
94-01-039	Parisian Beauties	A. Maley	500	275.00	275.00
94-01-040	The Recital	A. Maley	500	275.00	275.00
94-01-041	Visiting The Nursery	A. Maley	500	250.00	250.00
Pemberton & Oakes		**Zolan's Children-Lithographs**			
82-01-001	By Myself	D. Zolan	Retrd.	98.00	280.00
82-01-002	Erik and the Dandelion	D. Zolan	Retrd.	98.00	400.00
84-01-003	Sabina in the Grass	D. Zolan	Retrd.	98.00	150-600.
86-01-004	Tender Moment	D. Zolan	Retrd.	98.00	300.00
87-01-005	Touching the Sky	D. Zolan	Retrd.	98.00	270.00
88-01-006	Tiny Treasures	D. Zolan	Retrd.	150.00	150-215.
88-01-007	Winter Angel	D. Zolan	Retrd.	98.00	250-400.
88-01-009	Small Wonder	D. Zolan	Retrd.	98.00	285.00
88-01-010	Day Dreamer	D. Zolan	Retrd.	35.00	130.00
88-01-011	Waiting to Play	D. Zolan	Retrd.	35.00	140.00
89-01-012	Christmas Prayer	D. Zolan	Retrd.	98.00	225-245.
89-01-013	Almost Home	D. Zolan	Retrd.	98.00	265-310.
89-01-014	Brotherly Love	D. Zolan	Retrd.	98.00	360.00
89-01-015	Daddy's Home	D. Zolan	Retrd.	98.00	300.00
89-01-016	Grandma's Mirror	D. Zolan	Retrd.	98.00	155.00
89-01-017	Mother's Angels	D. Zolan	Retrd.	98.00	265-370.
89-01-018	Rodeo Girl	D. Zolan	Retrd.	98.00	170.00
89-01-019	Snowy Adventure	D. Zolan	Retrd.	98.00	240.00
89-01-020	Summer's Child	D. Zolan	Retrd.	98.00	234.00
90-01-021	Colors of Spring	D. Zolan	Retrd.	98.00	200-325.
90-01-022	Crystal's Creek	D. Zolan	Retrd.	98.00	170.00
90-01-023	First Kiss	D. Zolan	Retrd.	98.00	250.00
90-01-024	Laurie and the Creche	D. Zolan	Retrd.	98.00	114.00
91-01-025	Autumn Leaves	D. Zolan	Retrd.	98.00	120.00
91-01-026	Flowers for Mother	D. Zolan	Retrd.	98.00	165.00
91-01-027	Summer Suds	D. Zolan	Retrd.	98.00	130.00
92-01-028	Enchanted Forest	D. Zolan	Retrd.	98.00	130.00
92-01-029	New Shoes	D. Zolan	Retrd.	98.00	115.00
93-01-030	The Big Catch	D. Zolan	Retrd.	98.00	125.00
93-01-031	Grandma's Garden	D. Zolan	Retrd.	98.00	115.00
Pemberton & Oakes		**Zolan's Children-Miniature Lithographs**			
91-02-001	Morning Discovery	D. Zolan	Retrd.	35.00	48.00
92-02-002	The Little Fisherman	D. Zolan	Retrd.	35.00	36-45.00
92-02-003	Colors of Spring	D. Zolan	Retrd.	35.00	35.00
92-02-004	Forest & Fairytales	D. Zolan	Retrd.	22.00	35-45.00

		ARTIST	EDITION	ISSUE	QUOTE
Pemberton & Oakes	**Grandparents Day-Miniature Lithographs**				
92-03-001	Letter to Grandma	D. Zolan	Retrd.	35.00	35.00
Pemberton & Oakes	**Single Issues-Miniature Lithographs**				
91-04-001	Tender Moment	D. Zolan	Retrd.	35.00	64.00
93-04-002	1993 A Christmas Prayer	D. Zolan	Retrd.	35.00	35.00
93-04-003	Daddy's Home	D. Zolan	Retrd.	22.00	40-45.00
93-04-004	Letter To Grandma	D. Zolan	Retrd.	22.00	34.00
93-04-005	First Kiss	D. Zolan	Retrd.	22.00	30-40.00
94-04-006	Rodeo Girl	D. Zolan	Retrd.	35.00	35.00
94-04-007	A Gift for Laurie	D. Zolan	Yr.Iss.	22.00	22.00
Pemberton & Oakes	**Miniature Replicas of Oils**				
90-05-001	Brotherly Love	D. Zolan	Retrd.	24.40	75.00
90-05-002	Daddy's Home	D. Zolan	Retrd.	24.40	65-70.00
91-05-003	Crystal's Creek	D. Zolan	Retrd.	24.40	42.00
92-05-004	It's Grandma & Grandpa	D. Zolan	Retrd.	24.40	37.00
92-05-005	Mother's Angels	D. Zolan	Retrd.	24.40	36.00
92-05-006	Touching the Sky	D. Zolan	Retrd.	24.40	35.00
Pemberton & Oakes	**Canvas Replicas**				
92-06-001	Quiet Time	D. Zolan	Retrd.	18.80	35-45.00
92-06-002	September Girl	D. Zolan	Retrd.	18.80	24-36.00
92-06-003	Summer Garden	D. Zolan	Retrd.	18.80	35-45.00
Pemberton & Oakes	**Quiet Moments-Miniature Lithographs**				
92-07-001	92 One Summer Day	D. Zolan	Retrd.	22.00	35.00
93-07-002	Crystal's Creek	D. Zolan	Retrd.	22.00	30-40.00
93-07-003	Birthday Greetings	D. Zolan	Retrd.	22.00	36-45.00
93-07-004	Country Kitten	D. Zolan	Retrd.	22.00	27-36.00
Pemberton & Oakes	**Membership-Miniature Lithographs**				
92-08-001	Brotherly Love	D. Zolan	Retrd.	18.00	60.00
93-08-002	New Shoes	D. Zolan	Retrd.	18.00	40.00
93-08-003	Country Walk	D. Zolan	Retrd.	22.00	35.00
94-08-004	Enchanted Forest	D. Zolan	Yr.Iss.	22.00	22.00
Pemberton & Oakes	**Canvas Transfer**				
92-09-001	Daisy Days	D. Zolan	Retrd.	24.20	38-45.00
93-09-002	It's Grandma & Grandpa	D. Zolan	Retrd.	24.20	30-38.00
93-09-003	Spring Duet	D. Zolan	Retrd.	24.40	36.00
Reco International	**Limited Edition Print**				
84-01-001	Jessica	S. Kuck	Retrd.	60.00	400.00
85-01-002	Heather	S. Kuck	Retrd.	75.00	150.00
86-01-003	Ashley	S. Kuck	500	85.00	150.00
Reco International	**McClelland**				
XX-02-001	Olivia	J. McClelland	300	175.00	175.00
XX-02-002	Sweet Dreams	J. McClelland	300	145.00	145.00
XX-02-003	Just for You	J. McClelland	300	155.00	155.00
XX-02-004	Reverie	J. McClelland	300	110.00	110.00
XX-02-005	I Love Tammy	J. McClelland	500	75.00	100.00
Reco International	**Fine Art Canvas Reproduction**				
90-03-001	Beach Play	J. McClelland	350	80.00	80.00
91-03-002	Flower Swing	J. McClelland	350	100.00	100.00
91-03-003	Summer Conversation	J. McClelland	350	80.00	80.00
Roman, Inc.	**Hook**				
81-01-001	The Carpenter	F. Hook	Yr.Iss	100.00	1000.00
81-01-002	The Carpenter (remarque)	F. Hook	Yr.Iss	100.00	3000.00
82-01-003	Frolicking	F. Hook	1,200	60.00	350.00
82-01-004	Gathering	F. Hook	1,200	60.00	350-450.
82-01-005	Poulets	F. Hook	1,200	60.00	350.00
82-01-006	Bouquet	F. Hook	1,200	70.00	350.00
82-01-007	Surprise	F. Hook	1,200	50.00	350.00
82-01-008	Posing	F. Hook	1,200	70.00	350.00
82-01-009	Little Children, Come to Me	F. Hook	1,950	50.00	500.00
82-01-010	Little Children, Come to Me, remarque	F. Hook	50	100.00	500.00
Roman, Inc.	**Portraits of Love**				
88-02-001	Sharing	F. Hook	2,500	25.00	25.00
88-02-002	Expectation	F. Hook	2,500	25.00	25.00
88-02-003	Remember When...	F. Hook	2,500	25.00	25.00
88-02-004	My Kitty	F. Hook	2,500	25.00	25.00
88-02-005	In Mother's Arms	F. Hook	2,500	25.00	25.00
88-02-006	Sunkissed Afternoon	F. Hook	2,500	25.00	25.00
Roman, Inc.	**Abble Williams**				
88-03-001	Mary, Mother of the Carpenter	A. Williams	Closed	100.00	100.00
Roman, Inc.	**The Discovery of America Miniature Art Print**				
91-04-001	The Discovery of America	I. Spencer	Open	2.00	2.00
Roman, Inc.	**Divine Servant**				
93-05-001	Divine Servant, print of drawing	M. Greiner Jr.	Open	35.00	35.00
94-05-002	Divine Servant, print of painting	M. Greiner Jr.	Yr.Iss.	75.00	75.00
94-05-003	Divine Servant, print of painting w/remarque	M. Greiner Jr.	Yr.Iss.	75.00	75.00
94-05-004	Divine Servant, print of painting	M. Greiner Jr.	Yr.Iss.	150.00	150.00
94-05-005	Divine Servant, print of painting w/remarque	M. Greiner Jr.	Yr.Iss.	150.00	150.00
Schmid	**Lowell Davis Lithographs**				
81-01-001	Surprise in the Cellar, remarque	L. Davis	101	100.00	400.00
81-01-002	Surprise in the Cellar, regular edition	L. Davis	899	75.00	375.00
81-01-003	Plum Tuckered Out, remarque	L. Davis	101	100.00	350.00
81-01-004	Plum Tuckered Out, regular edition	L. Davis	899	75.00	400.00
81-01-005	Duke's Mixture, remarque	L. Davis	101	150.00	350.00
81-01-006	Duke's Mixture, regular edition	L. Davis	899	75.00	125.00
82-01-007	Bustin' with Pride, remarque	L. Davis	101	150.00	250.00
82-01-008	Bustin' with Pride, regular edition	L. Davis	899	75.00	125.00
82-01-009	Birth of a Blossom, remarque	L. Davis	50	200.00	450.00
82-01-010	Birth of a Blossom, regular edition	L. Davis	400	125.00	300.00
82-01-011	Suppertime, remarque	L. Davis	50	200.00	450.00
82-01-012	Suppertime, regular edition	L. Davis	400	125.00	300.00
82-01-013	Foxfire Farm, remarque	L. Davis	100	200.00	250.00
82-01-014	Foxfire Farm, regular edition	L. Davis	800	125.00	125.00
85-01-015	Self Portrait	L. Davis	450	75.00	192.00
87-01-016	Blossom's Gift	L. Davis	450	75.00	300.00
89-01-017	Sun Worshippers	L. Davis	750	100.00	100.00
90-01-018	Sunday Afternoon Treat	L. Davis	750	100.00	100.00
91-01-019	Warm Milk	L. Davis	750	100.00	179.00
92-01-020	Cat and Jenny Wren	L. Davis	750	100.00	100.00
93-01-021	The Old Home Place	L. Davis	750	130.00	130.00

		ARTIST	EDITION	ISSUE	QUOTE
Schmid	**Berta Hummel Lithographs**				
80-02-001	Moonlight Return	B. Hummel	900	150.00	850.00
80-02-002	1984 American Visit	B. Hummel	5	550.00	1000.00
81-02-003	A Time to Remember	B. Hummel	720	150.00	300.00
81-02-004	1984 American Visit	B. Hummel	5	550.00	1100.00
81-02-005	Remarqued	B. Hummel	180	250.00	1250.00
81-02-006	1984 American Visit	B. Hummel	2	1100.00	1700.00
82-02-007	Poppies	B. Hummel	450	150.00	650.00
82-02-008	1984 American Visit	B. Hummel	3	250.00	850.00
83-02-009	Angelic Messenger, 75th Anniversary	B. Hummel	195	375.00	700.00
83-02-010	Angelic Messenger, Christmas Message	B. Hummel	400	275.00	450.00
83-02-011	1984 American Visit	B. Hummel	10	275.00	600.00
83-02-012	Regular	B. Hummel	100	175.00	350.00
83-02-013	1984 American Visit	B. Hummel	10	175.00	400.00
85-02-014	Birthday Bouquet, Edition 1	B. Hummel	195	450.00	550.00
85-02-015	Birthday Bouquet, Edition 2	B. Hummel	225	375.00	375.00
85-02-016	Birthday Bouquet, Edition 3	B. Hummel	100	195.00	395.00
Schmid	**Ferrandiz Lithographs**				
80-03-001	Most Precious Gift, remarque	J. Ferrandiz	50	225.00	2800.00
80-03-002	Most Precious Gift, regular edition	J. Ferrandiz	425	125.00	1200.00
80-03-003	My Star, remarque	J. Ferrandiz	75	175.00	1800.00
80-03-004	My Star, regular edition	J. Ferrandiz	675	100.00	650.00
81-03-005	Heart of Seven Colors, remarque	J. Ferrandiz	75	175.00	1300.00
81-03-006	Heart of Seven Colors, regular edition	J. Ferrandiz	600	100.00	395.00
82-03-007	Oh Small Child, remarque	J. Ferrandiz	50	225.00	1450.00
82-03-008	Oh Small Child, regular edition	J. Ferrandiz	450	125.00	495.00
82-03-009	Spreading the Word, remarque	J. Ferrandiz	75	225.00	1075.00
82-03-010	Spreading the Word, regular edition	J. Ferrandiz	675	125.00	190-250.
82-03-011	On the Threshold of Life, remarque	J. Ferrandiz	50	275.00	1350.00
82-03-012	On the Threshold of Life, regular edition	J. Ferrandiz	425	150.00	450.00
82-03-013	Riding Through the Rain, remarque	J. Ferrandiz	100	300.00	950.00
82-03-014	Riding Through the Rain, regular edition	J. Ferrandiz	900	165.00	350.00
82-03-015	Mirror of the Soul, regular edition	J. Ferrandiz	225	150.00	425.00
82-03-016	Mirror of the Soul, remarque	J. Ferrandiz	35	250.00	2400.00
82-03-017	He Seems to Sleep, regular edition	J. Ferrandiz	450	150.00	700.00
82-03-018	He Seems to Sleep, remarque	J. Ferrandiz	25	300.00	3200.00
83-03-019	Friendship, remarque	J. Ferrandiz	15	1200.00	2300.00
83-03-020	Friendship, regular edition	J. Ferrandiz	460	165.00	450.00
84-03-021	Star in the Teapot; regular edition	J. Ferrandiz	410	165.00	165.00
84-03-022	Star in the Teapot; remarque	J. Ferrandiz	15	1200.00	2100.00
V.F. Fine Arts	**Kuck**				
86-01-001	Tender Moments, proof	S. Kuck	50	80.00	295.00
86-01-002	Tender Moments, S/N	S. Kuck	500	70.00	250.00
86-01-003	Summer Reflections, proof	S. Kuck	90	70.00	300.00
86-01-004	Summer Reflections, S/N	S. Kuck	900	60.00	250.00
86-01-005	Silhouette, proof	S. Kuck	25	90.00	250.00
86-01-006	Silhouette, S/N	S. Kuck	250	80.00	220.00
87-01-007	Le Papillion, remarque	S. Kuck	7	150.00	250.00
87-01-008	Le Papillion, proof	S. Kuck	35	110.00	175.00
87-01-009	Le Papillion, S/N	S. Kuck	350	90.00	150.00
87-01-010	The Reading Lesson, proof	S. Kuck	90	70.00	190-250.
87-01-011	The Reading Lesson, S/N	S. Kuck	900	60.00	200.00
87-01-012	The Daisy, proof	S. Kuck	90	40.00	200.00
87-01-013	The Daisy, S/N	S. Kuck	900	30.00	75.00
87-01-014	The Loveseat, proof	S. Kuck	90	40.00	50-75.00
87-01-015	The Loveseat, S/N	S. Kuck	900	30.00	50.00
87-01-016	A Quiet Time, proof	S. Kuck	90	50.00	75.00
87-01-017	A Quiet Time, S/N	S. Kuck	900	40.00	50.00
87-01-018	The Flower Girl, proof	S. Kuck	90	50.00	75.00
87-01-019	The Flower Girl, S/N	S. Kuck	900	40.00	50-60.00
87-01-020	Mother's Love, proof	S. Kuck	12	225.00	1800.00
87-01-021	Mother's Love, S/N	S. Kuck	150	195.00	1200.00
88-01-022	My Dearest, S/N	S. Kuck	350	160.00	775.00
88-01-023	My Dearest, proof	S. Kuck	50	200.00	900.00
88-01-024	My Dearest, remarque	S. Kuck	25	325.00	1100.00
88-01-025	The Kitten, S/N	S. Kuck	350	120.00	1200.00
88-01-026	The Kitten, proof	S. Kuck	50	150.00	1300.00
88-01-027	The Kitten, remarque	S. Kuck	25	250.00	950-1450
88-01-028	Wild Flowers, S/N	S. Kuck	350	160.00	250.00
88-01-029	Wild Flowers, proof	S. Kuck	50	175.00	300.00
88-01-030	Wild Flowers, remarque	S. Kuck	25	250.00	350.00
88-01-031	Little Ballerina, S/N	S. Kuck	150	110.00	300.00
88-01-032	Little Ballerina, proof	S. Kuck	25	150.00	350.00
88-01-033	Little Ballerina, remarque	S. Kuck	25	225.00	450.00
88-01-034	First Recital, S/N	S. Kuck	150	200.00	900.00
88-01-035	First Recital, proof	S. Kuck	25	250.00	1000.00
88-01-036	First Recital, remarque	S. Kuck	25	400.00	1200.00
89-01-037	Sisters, S/N	S. Kuck	900	95.00	190.00
89-01-038	Sisters, proof	S. Kuck	90	150.00	395.00
89-01-039	Sisters, remarque	S. Kuck	50	200.00	375.00
89-01-040	Rose Garden, S/N	S. Kuck	500	95.00	400.00
89-01-041	Rose Garden, proof	S. Kuck	50	150.00	450.00
89-01-042	Rose Garden, remarque	S. Kuck	50	200.00	600.00
89-01-043	Sonatina, S/N	S. Kuck	900	150.00	350.00
89-01-044	Sonatina, proof	S. Kuck	90	225.00	450.00
89-01-045	Sonatina, remarque	S. Kuck	50	300.00	600.00
89-01-046	Puppy, S/N	S. Kuck	500	120.00	600.00
89-01-047	Puppy, proof	S. Kuck	50	180.00	650.00
89-01-048	Puppy, remarque	S. Kuck	50	240.00	750-950.
89-01-049	Innocence, S/N	S. Kuck	900	150.00	200.00
89-01-050	Innocence, proof	S. Kuck	90	225.00	250.00
89-01-051	Innocence, remarque	S. Kuck	50	300.00	350.00
89-01-052	Bundle of Joy, S/N	S. Kuck	1,000	125.00	250.00
89-01-053	Day Dreaming, S/N	S. Kuck	900	150.00	200.00
89-01-054	Day Dreaming, proof	S. Kuck	90	225.00	225.00
89-01-055	Day Dreaming, remarque	S. Kuck	50	300.00	300.00
90-01-056	Lilly Pond, S/N	S. Kuck	750	150.00	150.00
90-01-057	Lilly Pond, proof	S. Kuck	75	200.00	200.00
90-01-058	Lilly Pond, color remarque	S. Kuck	125	500.00	500.00
90-01-059	First Snow, S/N	S. Kuck	500	95.00	225.00
90-01-060	First Snow, proof	S. Kuck	50	150.00	275.00
90-01-061	First Snow, remarque	S. Kuck	25	200.00	325.00
90-01-062	Le Beau, S/N	S. Kuck	1,500	80.00	160.00
90-01-063	Le Beau, proof	S. Kuck	150	120.00	200.00
90-01-064	Le Beau, remarque	S. Kuck	25	160.00	250.00
90-01-065	Chopsticks, S/N	S. Kuck	1,500	80.00	80.00
90-01-066	Chopsticks, proof	S. Kuck	150	120.00	120.00
90-01-067	Chopsticks, remarque	S. Kuck	25	160.00	160.00
91-01-068	Memories, S/N	S. Kuck	5,000	195.00	195.00
91-01-069	God's Gift, proof	S. Kuck	150	150.00	150.00

	ARTIST	EDITION	ISSUE	QUOTE
91-01-070 God's Gift, S/N	S. Kuck	1,500	95.00	95.00
92-01-071 Joyous Day, S/N	S. Kuck	1,200	125.00	125.00
92-01-072 Joyous Day, proof	S. Kuck	120	175.00	175.00
92-01-073 Joyous Day, Canvas Transfer	S. Kuck	250	250.00	250.00
92-01-074 Yesterday, S/N	S. Kuck	950	95.00	95.00
92-01-075 Yesterday, proof	S. Kuck	95	150.00	150.00
92-01-076 Yesterday, Canvas Framed	S. Kuck	550	195.00	195.00
92-01-077 Duet, S/N	S. Kuck	950	125.00	125.00
92-01-078 Duet, proof	S. Kuck	95	175.00	175.00
92-01-079 Duet, Canvas Framed	S. Kuck	500	255.00	255.00
93-01-080 Good Morning, S/N	S. Kuck	2,500	145.00	145.00
93-01-081 Good Morning, proof	S. Kuck	50	175.00	175.00
93-01-082 Good Morning, Canvas	S. Kuck	250	500.00	500.00
93-01-083 Best Friends, S/N	S. Kuck	2,500	145.00	145.00
93-01-084 Best Friend, proof	S. Kuck	250	175.00	175.00
93-01-085 Best Friends, Cansvas Transfer	S. Kuck	250	500.00	500.00
93-01-086 Thinking of You, S/N	S. Kuck	2,500	145.00	145.00
93-01-087 Thinking of You, Canvas Transfer	S. Kuck	250	500.00	500.00
93-01-088 Buttons & Bows, S/N	S. Kuck	950	95.00	95.00
93-01-089 Buttons & Bows, proof	S. Kuck	95	125.00	125.00
93-01-090 Good Morning, S/N	S. Kuck	2,500	145.00	145.00
93-01-091 Good Morning, proof	S. Kuck	250	175.00	175.00
93-01-092 Good Morning, Canvas Transfer	S. Kuck	250	500.00	500.00
94-01-093 Garden Memories, S/N	S. Kuck	2,500	145.00	145.00
94-01-094 Garden Memories, Canvas Transfer	S. Kuck	250	500.00	500.00
94-01-095 Dear Santa, S/N	S. Kuck	950	95.00	95.00
94-01-096 Best of Days, S/N	S. Kuck	750	160.00	160.00

PLATES

	ARTIST	EDITION	ISSUE	QUOTE
American Artists	**The Horses of Fred Stone**			
82-01-001 Patience	F. Stone	9,500	55.00	145.00
82-01-002 Arabian Mare and Foal	F. Stone	9,500	55.00	125.00
82-01-003 Safe and Sound	F. Stone	9,500	55.00	80-120.
83-01-004 Contentment	F. Stone	9,500	55.00	70-120.
American Artists	**The Stallion Series**			
83-02-001 Black Stallion	F. Stone	19,500	49.50	100.00
83-02-002 Andalusian	F. Stone	19,500	49.50	80.00
American Artists	**Sport of Kings Series**			
84-03-001 Man O'War	F. Stone	9,500	65.00	200-275.
84-03-002 Secretariat	F. Stone	9,500	65.00	295.00
85-03-003 John Henry	F. Stone	9,500	65.00	100.00
86-03-004 Seattle Slew	F. Stone	9,500	65.00	65.00
American Artists	**Mare and Foal Series**			
86-04-001 Water Trough	F. Stone	12,500	49.50	125.00
86-04-002 Tranquility	F. Stone	12,500	49.50	65.00
86-04-003 Pasture Pest	F. Stone	12,500	49.50	100.00
87-04-004 The Arabians	F. Stone	12,500	49.50	49.50
American Artists	**Mare and Foal Series II**			
89-05-001 The First Day	F. Stone	Open	35.00	35.00
89-05-002 Diamond in the Rough	F. Stone	Retrd.	35.00	35.00
American Artists	**Fred Stone Classic Series**			
86-06-001 The Shoe-8,000 Wins	F. Stone	9,500	75.00	95.00
86-06-002 The Eternal Legacy	F. Stone	9,500	75.00	95.00
88-06-003 Forever Friends	F. Stone	9,500	75.00	85.00
89-06-004 Alysheba	F. Stone	9,500	75.00	85.00
American Artists	**Famous Fillies Series**			
87-07-001 Lady's Secret	F. Stone	9,500	65.00	85.00
88-07-002 Ruffian	F. Stone	9,500	65.00	85.00
88-07-003 Genuine Risk	F. Stone	9,500	65.00	85.00
92-07-004 Go For The Wand	F. Stone	9,500	65.00	85.00
American Artists	**Racing Legends**			
89-08-001 Phar Lap	F. Stone	9,500	75.00	75.00
89-08-002 Sunday Silence	F. Stone	9,500	75.00	75.00
90-08-003 John Henry-Shoemaker	F. Stone	9,500	75.00	75.00
American Artists	**Gold Signature Series**			
90-09-001 Secretariat Final Tribute, signed	F. Stone	4,500	150.00	150.00
90-09-002 Secretariat Final Tribute, unsigned	F. Stone	7,500	75.00	75.00
91-09-003 Old Warriors, signed	F. Stone	4,500	150.00	150.00
91-09-004 Old Warriors, unsigned	F. Stone	7,500	75.00	75.00
American Artists	**Gold Signature Series II**			
91-10-001 Northern Dancer, double signature	F. Stone	1,500	175.00	175.00
91-10-002 Northern Dancer, single signature	F. Stone	3,000	150.00	150.00
91-10-003 Northern Dancer, unsigned	F. Stone	7,500	75.00	75.00
91-10-004 Kelso, double signature	F. Stone	1,500	175.00	175.00
91-10-005 Kelso, single signature	F. Stone	3,000	150.00	150.00
91-10-006 Kelso, unsigned	F. Stone	7,500	75.00	75.00
American Artists	**Gold Signature Series III**			
92-11-001 Dance Smartly-Pat Day, Up, double signature	F. Stone	1,500	175.00	175.00
92-11-002 Dance Smartly-Pat Day, Up, single signature	F. Stone	3,000	150.00	150.00
92-11-003 Dance Smartly-Pat Day, Up, unsigned	F. Stone	7,500	75.00	75.00
93-11-004 American Triple Crown-1937-1946, signed	F. Stone	2,500	195.00	195.00
93-11-005 American Triple Crown-1937-1946, unsigned	F. Stone	7,500	75.00	75.00
93-11-006 American Triple Crown-1948-1978, signed	F. Stone	2,500	195.00	195.00
93-11-007 American Triple Crown-1948-1978, unsigned	F. Stone	7,500	75.00	75.00
94-11-008 American Triple Crown-1919-1935, signed	F. Stone	2,500	95.00	95.00
94-11-009 American Triple Crown-1919-1935, unsigned	F. Stone	7,500	75.00	75.00
American Artists	**The Best of Fred Stone-Mares & Foals Series (6 1/2 ")**			
91-12-001 Patience	F. Stone	19,500	25.00	25.00
92-12-002 Water Trough	F. Stone	19,500	25.00	25.00
92-12-003 Pasture Pest	F. Stone	19,500	25.00	25.00
92-12-004 Kidnapped Mare	F. Stone	19,500	25.00	25.00
93-12-005 Contentment	F. Stone	19,500	25.00	25.00
93-12-006 Arabian Mare & Foal	F. Stone	19,500	25.00	25.00
Anheuser-Busch, Inc.	**Holiday Plate Series**			
89-01-001 Winters Day N2295	B. Kemper	Retrd.	30.00	75.00
90-01-002 An American Tradition N2767	S. Sampson	Retrd.	30.00	50.00
91-01-003 The Season's Best N3034	S. Sampson	25-day	30.00	30.00
92-01-004 A Perfect Christmas N3440	S. Sampson	25-day	27.50	27.50

	ARTIST	EDITION	ISSUE	QUOTE
93-01-005 Special Delivery N4002	N. Koerber	Retrd.	27.50	27.50
94-01-006 Hometown Holiday N4572	B. Kemper	25-day	27.50	27.50
Anheuser-Busch, Inc.	**Man's Best Friend Series**			
90-02-001 Buddies N2615	M. Urdahl	Retrd.	30.00	60-75.00
90-02-002 Six Pack N3005	M. Urdahl	Retrd.	30.00	40.00
92-02-003 Something's Brewing N3147	M. Urdahl	25-day	30.00	30.00
93-02-004 Outstanding in Their Field N4003	M. Urdahl	25-day	27.50	27.50
Anheuser-Busch, Inc.	**1992 Olympic Team Series**			
91-03-001 1992 Olympic Team Winter Plate N3180	A-Busch, Inc.	25-day	35.00	35.00
92-03-002 1992 Olympic Team Summer Plate N3122	A-Busch, Inc.	25-day	35.00	35.00
Anheuser-Busch, Inc.	**Civil War Series**			
92-04-001 General Grant N3478	D. Langeneckert	25-day	45.00	45.00
93-04-002 General Robert E. Lee N3590	D. Langeneckert	25-day	45.00	45.00
93-04-003 President Abraham Lincoln N3591	D. Langeneckert	25-day	45.00	45.00
Anheuser-Busch, Inc.	**Archives Plate Series**			
92-05-001 1893 Columbian Exposition N3477	D. Langeneckert	25-day	27.50	27.50
92-05-002 Ganymede N4004	D. Langeneckert	25-day	45.00	45.00
Anna-Perenna Porcelain	**Uncle Tad's Cats**			
79-01-001 Oliver's Birthday	T. Krumeich	5,000	75.00	225.00
80-01-002 Peaches & Cream	T. Krumeich	5,000	75.00	95.00
81-01-003 Princess Aurora	T. Krumeich	5,000	80.00	95.00
81-01-004 Walter's Window	T. Krumeich	5,000	80.00	120.00
Anna-Perenna Porcelain	**Annual Christmas Plate**			
84-02-001 Noel, Noel	P. Buckley Moss	5,000	67.50	325.00
85-02-002 Helping Hands	P. Buckley Moss	5,000	67.50	225.00
86-02-003 Night Before Christmas	P. Buckley Moss	5,000	67.50	150.00
87-02-004 Christmas Sleigh	P. Buckley Moss	5,000	75.00	95.00
88-02-005 Christmas Joy	P. Buckley Moss	7,500	75.00	75.00
89-02-006 Christmas Carol	P. Buckley Moss	7,500	80.00	95.00
90-02-007 Christmas Eve	P. Buckley Moss	7,500	80.00	80.00
91-02-008 The Snowman	P. Buckley Moss	7,500	80.00	80.00
92-02-009 Christmas Warmth	P. Buckley Moss	7,500	85.00	85.00
Anna-Perenna Porcelain	**American Silhouettes-Childrens Series**			
81-03-001 Fiddlers Two	P. Buckley Moss	5,000	75.00	95.00
83-03-002 Mary With The Lambs	P. Buckley Moss	5,000	75.00	85.00
84-03-003 Ring-Around-the-Rosie	P. Buckley Moss	5,000	75.00	200.00
84-03-004 Waiting For Tom	P. Buckley Moss	5,000	75.00	175.00
Anna-Perenna Porcelain	**The Celebration Series**			
86-04-001 Wedding Joy	P. Buckley Moss	5,000	100.00	200-350.
87-04-002 The Christening	P. Buckley Moss	5,000	100.00	175.00
88-04-003 The Anniversary	P. Buckley Moss	5,000	100.00	120-190.
89-04-004 Family Reunion	P. Buckley Moss	5,000	100.00	150.00
Anna-Perenna Porcelain	**American Silhouettes Family Series**			
81-05-001 Family Outing	P. Buckley Moss	5,000	75.00	95.00
82-05-002 John and Mary	P. Buckley Moss	5,000	75.00	95.00
82-05-003 Homemakers Quilting	P. Buckley Moss	5,000	75.00	85-195.
84-05-004 Leisure Time	P. Buckley Moss	5,000	75.00	85.00
Anna-Perenna Porcelain	**American Silhouettes Valley Series**			
81-06-001 Frosty Frolic	P. Buckley Moss	5,000	75.00	85-95.00
82-06-002 Hay Ride	P. Buckley Moss	5,000	75.00	85.00
83-06-003 Sunday Ride	P. Buckley Moss	5,000	75.00	85-100.
84-06-004 Market Day	P. Buckley Moss	5,000	75.00	120.00
ANRI	**Ferrandiz Christmas**			
72-01-001 Christ In The Manger	J. Ferrandiz	Closed	35.00	230.00
73-01-002 Christmas	J. Ferrandiz	Unkn.	40.00	225.00
74-01-003 Holy Night	J. Ferrandiz	Unkn.	50.00	100.00
75-01-004 Flight into Egypt	J. Ferrandiz	Unkn.	60.00	95.00
76-01-005 Tree of Life	J. Ferrandiz	Unkn.	60.00	85.00
76-01-006 Girl with Flowers	J. Ferrandiz	Closed	65.00	185.00
78-01-007 Leading the Way	J. Ferrandiz	Closed	77.50	180.00
79-01-008 The Drummer	J. Ferrandiz	Closed	120.00	175.00
80-01-009 Rejoice	J. Ferrandiz	Closed	150.00	160.00
81-01-010 Spreading the Word	J. Ferrandiz	Closed	150.00	150.00
82-01-011 The Shepherd Family	J. Ferrandiz	Closed	150.00	150.00
83-01-012 Peace Attend Thee	J. Ferrandiz	Closed	150.00	150.00
ANRI	**Ferrandiz Mother's Day Series**			
72-02-001 Mother Sewing	J. Ferrandiz	Closed	35.00	200.00
73-02-002 Alpine Mother & Child	J. Ferrandiz	Closed	40.00	150.00
74-02-003 Mother Holding Child	J. Ferrandiz	Closed	50.00	150.00
75-02-004 Dove Girl	J. Ferrandiz	Closed	60.00	150.00
76-02-005 Mother Knitting	J. Ferrandiz	Closed	60.00	200.00
77-02-006 Alpine Stroll	J. Ferrandiz	Closed	65.00	125.00
78-02-007 The Beginning	J. Ferrandiz	Closed	75.00	150.00
79-02-008 All Hearts	J. Ferrandiz	Closed	120.00	170.00
80-02-009 Spring Arrivals	J. Ferrandiz	Closed	150.00	165.00
81-02-010 Harmony	J. Ferrandiz	Closed	150.00	150.00
82-02-011 With Love	J. Ferrandiz	Closed	150.00	150.00
ANRI	**Ferrandiz Wooden Wedding Plates**			
72-03-001 Boy and Girl Embracing	J. Ferrandiz	Unkn.	40.00	150.00
73-03-002 Wedding Scene	J. Ferrandiz	Unkn.	40.00	150.00
74-03-003 Wedding	J. Ferrandiz	Unkn.	48.00	150.00
75-03-004 Wedding	J. Ferrandiz	Unkn.	60.00	150.00
76-03-005 Wedding	J. Ferrandiz	Unkn.	60.00	90-150.
ANRI	**Christmas**			
71-04-001 St. Jakob in Groden	J. Malfertheiner	Closed	37.50	65.00
72-04-002 Pipers at Alberobello	J. Malfertheiner	Closed	45.00	75.00
73-04-003 Alpine Horn	J. Malfertheiner	Closed	45.00	390.00
74-04-004 Young Man and Girl	J. Malfertheiner	Closed	50.00	95.00
75-04-005 Christmas in Ireland	J. Malfertheiner	Closed	60.00	60.00
76-04-006 Alpine Christmas	J. Malfertheiner	Closed	65.00	190.00
77-04-007 Legend of Heiligenblut	J. Malfertheiner	Closed	65.00	91.00
78-04-008 Klockler Singers	J. Malfertheiner	Closed	80.00	80.00
79-04-009 Moss Gatherers	Unknown	Closed	135.00	177.00
80-04-010 Wintry Churchgoing	Unknown	Closed	165.00	165.00
81-04-011 Santa Claus in Tyrol	Unknown	Closed	165.00	200.00
82-04-012 The Star Singers	Unknown	Closed	165.00	165.00
83-04-013 Unto Us a Child is Born	Unknown	Closed	165.00	310.00
84-04-014 Yuletide in the Valley	Unknown	Closed	165.00	170.00
85-04-015 Good Morning, Good Cheer	J. Malfertheiner	Closed	165.00	165.00
86-04-016 A Groden Christmas	J. Malfertheiner	Closed	165.00	200.00
87-04-017 Down From the Alps	J. Malfertheiner	Closed	195.00	250.00
88-04-018 Christkindl Markt	J. Malfertheiner	Closed	220.00	230.00
88-04-019 Flight Into Egypt	J. Malfertheiner	Closed	275.00	275.00

	ARTIST	EDITION	ISSUE	QUOTE
90-04-020 Holy Night	J. Malfertheiner	Closed	300.00	300.00
ANRI	**ANRI Mother's Day**			
72-05-001 Alpine Mother & Children	Unknown.	Closed	35.00	50.00
73-05-002 Alpine Mother & Children	Unknown	Closed	40.00	50.00
74-05-003 Alpine Mother & Children	Unknown	Closed	50.00	55.00
75-05-004 Alpine Stroll	Unknown	Closed	60.00	65.00
76-05-005 Knitting	Unknown	Closed	60.00	65.00
ANRI	**ANRI Father's Day**			
72-06-001 Alpine Father & Children	Unknown	Closed	35.00	100.00
73-06-002 Alpine Father & Children	Unknown	Closed	40.00	95.00
74-06-003 Cliff Gazing	Unknown	Closed	50.00	100.00
76-06-004 Sailing	Unknown	Closed	60.00	90.00
ANRI	**Disney Four Star Collection**			
89-07-001 Mickey Mini Plate	Disney Studios	Closed	40.00	45.00
90-07-002 Minnie Mini Plate	Disney Studios	Closed	40.00	45.00
91-07-003 Donald Mini Plate	Disney Studios	Closed	50.00	50.00
Armstrong's	**Commemorative Issues**			
83-01-001 70 Years Young (10 1/2")	R. Skelton	15,000	85.00	90.00
84-01-002 Freddie the Torchbearer (8 1/2")	R. Skelton	15,000	62.50	85.00
Armstrong's	**The Signature Collection**			
86-02-001 Anyone for Tennis?	R. Skelton	9,000	62.50	62.50
86-02-002 Anyone for Tennis? (signed)	R. Skelton	1,000	125.00	295.00
87-02-003 Ironing the Waves	R. Skelton	9,000	62.50	75.00
87-02-004 Ironing the Waves (signed)	R. Skelton	1,000	125.00	265.00
88-02-005 The Cliffhanger	R. Skelton	9,000	62.50	65.00
88-02-006 The Cliffhanger (signed)	R. Skelton	1,000	150.00	275.00
88-02-007 Hooked on Freddie	R. Skelton	9,000	62.50	62.50
88-02-008 Hooked on Freddie (signed)	R. Skelton	1,000	175.00	175.00
Armstrong's	**Happy Art Series**			
81-03-001 Woody's Triple Self-Portrait, Signed	W. Lantz	1,000	100.00	100.00
81-03-002 Woody's Triple Self-Portrait	W. Lantz	9,000	39.50	39.50
83-03-003 Gothic Woody, Signed	W. Lantz	1,000	100.00	100.00
83-03-004 Gothic Woody	W. Lantz	9,000	39.50	39.50
84-03-005 Blue Boy Woody, Signed	W. Lantz	1,000	100.00	100.00
84-03-006 Blue Boy Woody	W. Lantz	9,000	39.50	39.50
Armstrong's	**Freedom Collection of Red Skelton**			
90-04-001 The All American, (signed)	R. Skelton	1,000	195.00	375.00
90-04-002 The All American	R. Skelton	9,000	62.50	85.00
91-04-003 Independence Day? (signed)	R. Skelton	1,000	195.00	225-275.
91-04-004 Independence Day?	R. Skelton	9,000	62.50	62.50
92-04-005 Let Freedom Ring, (signed)	R. Skelton	1,000	195.00	275.00
92-04-006 Let Freedom Ring	R. Skelton	9,000	62.50	62.50
93-04-007 Freddie's Gift of Life, (signed)	R. Skelton	1,000	195.00	275.00
93-04-008 Freddie's Gift of Life	R. Skelton	9,000	62.50	62.50
Armstrong's	**Sports**			
XX-05-001 Pete Rose h/s (10 1/4")	Schenken	1,000	100.00	595.00
XX-05-002 Pete Rose u/s (10 1/4")	Schenken	10,000	45.00	55.00
Armstrong's/Crown Parlan	**Freddie The Freeloader**			
79-01-001 Freddie in the Bathtub	R. Skelton	10,000	60.00	195-225.
80-01-002 Freddie's Shack	R. Skelton	10,000	60.00	90.00
81-01-003 Freddie on the Green	R. Skelton	10,000	60.00	60-75.00
82-01-004 Love that Freddie	R. Skelton	10,000	60.00	60-65.00
Armstrong's/Crown Parlan	**Freddie's Adventures**			
82-02-001 Captain Freddie	R. Skelton	15,000	60.00	85.00
82-02-002 Bronco Freddie	R. Skelton	15,000	60.00	30-39.00
83-02-003 Sir Freddie	R. Skelton	15,000	62.50	65.00
84-02-004 Gertrude and Heathcliffe	R. Skelton	15,000	62.50	63-75.00
Artaffects	**Portraits of American Brides**			
86-01-001 Caroline	R. Sauber	10-day	29.50	75-85.00
86-01-002 Jacqueline	R. Sauber	10-day	29.50	30-45.00
87-01-003 Elizabeth	R. Sauber	10-day	29.50	37-45.00
87-01-004 Emily	R. Sauber	10-day	29.50	45.00
87-01-005 Meredith	R. Sauber	10-day	29.50	45-55.00
87-01-006 Laura	R. Sauber	10-day	29.50	45.00
87-01-007 Sarah	R. Sauber	10-day	29.50	46.00
87-01-008 Rebecca	R. Sauber	10-day	29.50	64.00
Artaffects	**How Do I Love Thee?**			
82-02-001 Alaina	R. Sauber	19,500	39.95	60.00
82-02-002 Taylor	R. Sauber	19,500	39.95	60.00
83-02-003 Rendezvouse	R. Sauber	19,500	39.95	60.00
83-02-004 Embrace	R. Sauber	19,500	39.95	60.00
Artaffects	**Childhood Delights**			
83-03-001 Amanda	R. Sauber	7,500	45.00	75.00
Artaffects	**Songs of Stephen Foster**			
84-04-001 Oh! Susannah	R. Sauber	3,500	60.00	80.00
84-04-002 Jeanie with the Light Brown Hair	R. Sauber	3,500	60.00	80.00
84-04-003 Beautiful Dreamer	R. Sauber	3,500	60.00	80.00
Artaffects	**Times of Our Lives Collection**			
84-05-001 Happy Birthday-(10 1/4")	R. Sauber	Open	37.50	39.50
88-05-002 Happy Birthday-(6 1/2")	R. Sauber	Open	19.50	22.50
85-05-003 Home Sweet Home-(10 1/4")	R. Sauber	Open	37.50	39.50
88-05-004 Home Sweet Home-(6 1/2")	R. Sauber	Open	19.50	22.50
82-05-005 The Wedding-(10 1/4")	R. Sauber	Open	37.50	39.50
88-05-006 The Wedding-(6 1/2")	R. Sauber	Open	19.50	22.50
86-05-007 The Anniversary-(10 1/4")	R. Sauber	Open	37.50	39.50
88-05-008 The Anniversary-(6 1/2")	R. Sauber	Open	19.50	22.50
86-05-009 Sweethearts-(10 1/4")	R. Sauber	Open	37.50	49.00
88-05-010 Sweethearts-(6 1/2")	R. Sauber	Open	19.50	22.50
86-05-011 The Christening-(10 1/4")	R. Sauber	Open	37.50	39.50
88-05-012 The Christening-(6 1/2")	R. Sauber	Open	19.50	22.50
85-05-013 All Adore Him-(10 1/4")	R. Sauber	Open	37.50	39.50
88-05-014 All Adore Him-(6 1/2")	R. Sauber	Open	19.50	22.50
87-05-015 Motherhood-(10 1/4")	R. Sauber	Open	37.50	39.50
88-05-016 Motherhood-(6 1/2")	R. Sauber	Open	19.50	22.50
87-05-017 Fatherhood-(10 1/4")	R. Sauber	Open	37.50	39.50
88-05-018 Fatherhood-(6 1/2")	R. Sauber	Open	19.50	22.50
87-05-019 Sweet Sixteen-(10 1/4")	R. Sauber	Open	37.50	39.50
89-05-020 God Bless America-(10 1/4")	R. Sauber	14-day	39.50	39.50
89-05-021 God Bless America-(6 1/4")	R. Sauber	14-day	21.50	22.50
89-05-022 Visiting the Doctor (10 1/4")	R. Sauber	14-day	39.50	39.50
90-05-023 Mother's Joy-(6 1/2")	R. Sauber	Open	22.50	22.50
90-05-024 Mother's Joy-(10 1/4")	R. Sauber	Open	39.50	39.50

	ARTIST	EDITION	ISSUE	QUOTE
Artaffects	**Timeless Love**			
89-06-001 The Proposal	R. Sauber	14-day	35.00	38.00
89-06-002 Sweet Embrace	R. Sauber	14-day	35.00	35.00
90-06-003 Afternoon Light	R. Sauber	14-day	35.00	35.00
90-06-004 Quiet Moments	R. Sauber	14-day	35.00	35.00
Artaffects	**Winter Mindscape**			
89-07-001 Peaceful Village	R. Sauber	14-day	29.50	65.00
89-07-002 Snowbound	R. Sauber	14-day	29.50	40.00
90-07-003 Papa's Surprise	R. Sauber	14-day	29.50	40.00
90-07-004 Well Traveled Road	R. Sauber	14-day	29.50	40.00
90-07-005 First Freeze	R. Sauber	14-day	29.50	40.00
90-07-006 Country Morning	R. Sauber	14-day	29.50	40.00
90-07-007 Sleigh Ride	R. Sauber	14-day	29.50	40.00
90-07-008 January Thaw	R. Sauber	14-day	29.50	40.00
Artaffects	**Baby's Firsts**			
89-08-001 Visiting the Doctor (6 1/2")	R. Sauber	14-day	21.50	22.50
89-08-002 Baby's First Step (6 1/2")	R. Sauber	14-day	21.50	22.50
89-08-003 First Birthday (6 1/2")	R. Sauber	14-day	21.50	22.50
89-08-004 Christmas Morn (6 1/2")	R. Sauber	14-day	21.50	22.50
89-08-005 Picture Perfect (6 1/2")	R. Sauber	14-day	21.50	22.50
Artaffects	**American Blues Special Occasions**			
92-09-001 Happily Ever After (Wedding)	R. Sauber	N/A	35.00	35.00
92-09-002 The Perfect Tree (Christmas)	R. Sauber	N/A	35.00	35.00
92-09-003 My Sunshine (Motherhood)	R. Sauber	N/A	35.00	35.00
Artaffects	**An Old Fashioned Christmas**			
93-10-001 Up On The Roof Top	R. Sauber	N/A	29.50	29.50
94-10-002 The Toy Shoppe	R. Sauber	N/A	29.50	29.50
94-10-003 Christmas Delight	R. Sauber	N/A	29.50	29.50
94-10-004 Christmas Eve	R. Sauber	N/A	29.50	29.50
Artaffects	**Masterpieces of Rockwell**			
80-11-001 After the Prom	N. Rockwell	17,500	42.50	150.00
80-11-002 The Challenger	N. Rockwell	17,500	50.00	75.00
82-11-003 Girl at the Mirror	N. Rockwell	17,500	50.00	100.00
82-11-004 Missing Tooth	N. Rockwell	17,500	50.00	75.00
Artaffects	**Rockwell Americana**			
81-12-001 Shuffleton's Barbershop	N. Rockwell	17,500	75.00	150.00
82-12-002 Breaking Home Ties	N. Rockwell	17,500	75.00	125.00
83-12-003 Walking to Church	N. Rockwell	17,500	75.00	125.00
Artaffects	**Rockwell Trilogy**			
81-13-001 Stockbridge in Winter 1	N. Rockwell	Open	35.00	50-65.00
82-13-002 Stockbridge in Winter 2	N. Rockwell	Open	35.00	50-65.00
82-13-003 Stockbridge in Winter 3	N. Rockwell	Open	35.00	50-75.00
Artaffects	**Simpler Times Series**			
84-14-001 Lazy Daze	N. Rockwell	7,500	35.00	75.00
84-14-002 One for the Road	N. Rockwell	7,500	35.00	75.00
Artaffects	**On the Road Series**			
84-15-001 Pride of Stockbridge	N. Rockwell	Open	35.00	75.00
84-15-002 City Pride	N. Rockwell	Open	35.00	75.00
84-15-003 Country Pride	N. Rockwell	Open	35.00	75.00
Artaffects	**Special Occasions**			
82-16-001 Bubbles	F. Tipton Hunter	Open	29.95	50.00
82-16-002 Butterflies	F. Tipton Hunter	Open	29.95	50.00
Artaffects	**Masterpieces of Impressionism**			
80-17-001 Woman with Parasol	Monet/Cassat	17,500	35.00	75.00
81-17-002 Young Mother Sewing	Monet/Cassat	17,500	35.00	60.00
82-17-003 Sara in Green Bonnet	Monet/Cassat	17,500	35.00	60.00
83-17-004 Margot in Blue	Monet/Cassat	17,500	35.00	50.00
Artaffects	**Magical Moment**			
81-18-001 Happy Dreams	B. P. Gutmann	Open	29.95	100.00
81-18-002 Harmony	B. P. Gutmann	Open	29.95	90.00
82-18-003 His Majesty	B. P. Gutmann	Open	29.95	60.00
83-18-003 The Lullaby	B. P. Gutmann	Open	29.95	50.00
82-18-004 Waiting for Daddy	B. P. Gutmann	Open	29.95	50.00
82-18-005 Thank You God	B. P. Gutmann	Open	29.95	50.00
Artaffects	**Mother's Love**			
84-19-001 Daddy's Here	B. P. Gutmann	Open	29.95	60.00
Artaffects	**Bessie's Best**			
84-20-001 Oh! Oh! A Bunny	B. P. Gutmann	Open	29.95	65.00
84-20-002 The New Love	B. P. Gutmann	Open	29.95	65.00
84-20-003 My Baby	B. P. Gutmann	Open	29.95	65.00
84-20-004 Looking for Trouble	B. P. Gutmann	Open	29.95	65.00
84-20-005 Taps	B. P. Gutmann	Open	29.95	65.00
Artaffects	**Masterpieces of the West**			
80-21-001 Texas Night Herder	Johnson	17,500	35.00	75.00
80-21-002 Indian Trapper	Remington	17,500	35.00	100.00
82-21-003 Cowboy Style	Leigh	17,500	35.00	75.00
82-21-004 Indian Style	Perillo	17,500	35.00	150.00
Artaffects	**Playful Pets**			
82-22-001 Curiosity	J. H. Dolph	7,500	45.00	75.00
82-22-002 Master's Hat	J. H. Dolph	7,500	45.00	75.00
Artaffects	**The Tribute Series**			
82-23-001 I Want You	J. M. Flagg	Open	29.95	50.00
82-23-002 Gee, I Wish	H. C. Christy	Open	29.95	50.00
83-23-003 Soldier's Farewell	N. Rockwell	Open	29.95	50.00
Artaffects	**The Carnival Series**			
82-24-001 Knock em' Down	T. Newsom	19,500	35.00	50.00
82-24-002 Carousel	T. Newsom	19,500	35.00	50.00
Artaffects	**The Adventures of Peter Pan**			
90-25-001 Flying Over London	T. Newsom	14-day	29.50	40.00
90-25-002 Look At Me	T. Newsom	14-day	29.50	40.00
90-25-003 The Encounter	T. Newsom	14-day	29.50	40.00
90-25-004 Never land	T. Newsom	14-day	29.50	40.00
Artaffects	**Nursery Pair**			
83-26-001 In Slumberland	C. Becker	Open	25.00	60.00
83-26-002 The Awakening	C. Becker	Open	25.00	60.00
Artaffects	**Becker Babies**			
83-27-001 Snow Puff	C. Becker	Open	29.95	60.00
84-27-002 Smiling Through	C. Becker	Open	29.95	60.00

		ARTIST	EDITION	ISSUE	QUOTE
84-27-003	Pals	C. Becker	Open	29.95	60.00
Artaffects		**Melodies of Childhood**			
83-28-001	Twinkle, Twinkle Little Star	H. Garrido	19,500	35.00	50.00
83-28-002	Row, Row, Row Your Boat	H. Garrido	19,500	35.00	50.00
83-28-003	Mary had a Little Lamb	H. Garrido	19,500	35.00	50.00
Artaffects		**Unicorn Magic**			
83-29-001	Morning Encounter	J. Terreson	7,500	50.00	60.00
83-29-002	Afternoon Offering	J. Terreson	7,500	50.00	60.00
Artaffects		**Baker Street**			
83-30-001	Sherlock Holmes	M. Hooks	9,800	55.00	55-95.00
83-30-002	Watson	M. Hooks	9,800	55.00	55-75.00
Artaffects		**Angler's Dream**			
83-31-001	Brook Trout	J. Eggert	9,800	55.00	75.00
83-31-002	Striped Bass	J. Eggert	9,800	55.00	75.00
83-31-003	Largemouth Bass	J. Eggert	9,800	55.00	75.00
83-31-004	Chinook Salmon	J. Eggert	9,800	55.00	75.00
Artaffects		**Portrait Series**			
86-32-001	Chantilly	J. Eggert	14-day	24.50	40.00
86-32-002	Dynasty	J. Eggert	14-day	24.50	40.00
86-32-003	Velvet	J. Eggert	14-day	24.50	40.00
86-32-004	Jambalaya	J. Eggert	14-day	24.50	40.00
Artaffects		**The Great Trains**			
85-33-001	Santa Fe	J. Deneen	7,500	35.00	100.00
85-33-002	Twentieth Century Ltd.	J. Deneen	7,500	35.00	100.00
86-33-003	Empire Builder	J. Deneen	7,500	35.00	100.00
Artaffects		**Classic American Trains**			
88-34-001	Homeward Bound	J. Deneen	14-day	35.00	53.00
88-34-002	A Race Against Time	J. Deneen	14-day	35.00	63.00
88-34-003	Midday Stop	J. Deneen	14-day	35.00	55.00
88-34-004	The Silver Bullet	J. Deneen	14-day	35.00	65.00
88-34-005	Traveling in Style	J. Deneen	14-day	35.00	50-66.00
88-34-006	Round the Bend	J. Deneen	14-day	35.00	56.00
88-34-007	Taking the High Road	J. Deneen	14-day	35.00	45-56.00
88-34-008	Competition	J. Deneen	14-day	35.00	40-55.00
Artaffects		**Classic American Cars**			
89-35-001	Duesenberg	J. Deneen	14-day	35.00	40.00
89-35-002	Cadillac	J. Deneen	14-day	35.00	35.00
89-35-003	Cord	J. Deneen	14-day	35.00	35.00
89-35-004	Ruxton	J. Deneen	14-day	35.00	35.00
90-35-005	Lincoln	J. Deneen	14-day	35.00	35.00
90-35-006	Packard	J. Deneen	14-day	35.00	35.00
90-35-007	Hudson	J. Deneen	14-day	35.00	35.00
90-35-008	Pierce-Arrow	J. Deneen	14-day	35.00	35.00
Artaffects		**Great American Trains**			
92-36-001	The Alton Limited	J. Deneen	75-day	27.00	27.00
92-36-002	The Capitol Limited	J. Deneen	75-day	27.00	27.00
92-36-003	The Merchants Limited	J. Deneen	75-day	27.00	27.00
92-36-004	The Broadway Limited	J. Deneen	75-day	27.00	27.00
92-36-005	The Southwestern Limited	J. Deneen	75-day	27.00	27.00
92-36-006	The Blackhawk Limited	J. Deneen	75-day	27.00	27.00
92-36-007	The Sunshine Special Limited	J. Deneen	75-day	27.00	27.00
92-36-008	The Panama Special Limited	J. Deneen	75-day	27.00	27.00
Artaffects		**Sailing Through History**			
86-37-001	Flying Cloud	K. Soldwedel	14-day	29.50	60.00
86-37-002	Santa Maria	K. Soldwedel	14-day	29.50	60.00
86-37-003	Mayflower	K. Soldwedel	14-day	29.50	60.00
Artaffects		**American Maritime Heritage**			
87-38-001	U.S.S. Constitution	K. Soldwedel	14 Day	35.00	35.00
Artaffects		**Christian Collection**			
87-39-001	Bring to Me the Children	A. Tobey	Unkn.	35.00	35.00
87-39-002	Wedding Feast at Cana	A. Tobey	Unkn.	35.00	35.00
87-39-003	The Healer	A. Tobey	Unkn.	35.00	35.00
Artaffects		**Reflections of Youth**			
88-40-001	Julia	Mago	14-day	29.50	45-55.00
88-40-002	Jessica	Mago	14-day	29.50	35.00
88-40-003	Sebastian	Mago	14-day	29.50	35.00
88-40-004	Michelle	Mago	14-day	29.50	55.00
88-40-005	Andrew	Mago	14-day	29.50	35.00
88-40-006	Beth	Mago	14-day	29.50	39.00
88-40-007	Amy	Mago	14-day	29.50	39.00
88-40-008	Lauren	Mago	14-day	29.50	39.00
Artaffects		**MaGo's Motherhood**			
90-41-001	Serenity	MaGo	14-day	50.00	50.00
Artaffects		**Studies of Early Childhood**			
90-42-001	Christopher & Kate	MaGo	150-day	34.90	35.00
90-42-002	Peek-A-Boo	MaGo	150-day	34.90	35.00
90-42-003	Anybody Home?	MaGo	150-day	34.90	32.00
90-42-004	Three-Part Harmony	MaGo	150-day	34.90	53.00
Artaffects		**Heavenly Angels**			
92-43-001	Hush-A-Bye	MaGo	75-day	27.00	27.00
92-43-002	Heavenly Helper	MaGo	75-day	27.00	27.00
92-43-003	Heavenly Light	MaGo	75-day	27.00	27.00
92-43-004	The Angel's Kiss	MaGo	75-day	27.00	27.00
92-43-005	Caught In The Act	MaGo	75-day	27.00	27.00
92-43-006	My Angel	MaGo	75-day	27.00	27.00
92-43-007	Angel Cake	MaGo	75-day	27.00	27.00
92-43-008	Sleepy Sentinel	MaGo	75-day	27.00	27.00
Artaffects		**Bring Unto Me the Children**			
94-44-001	Love's Blessing	MaGo	75-day	29.50	29.50
94-44-002	Heavenly Embrace	MaGo	75-day	29.50	29.50
94-44-003	Sweet Serenity	MaGo	75-day	29.50	29.50
94-44-004	The Lord's Prayer	MaGo	75-day	29.50	29.50
94-44-005	Communion	MaGo	75-day	29.50	29.50
94-44-006	The Baptism	MaGo	75-day	29.50	29.50
94-44-007	A Little Love Song	MaGo	75-day	29.50	29.50
94-44-008	Sweet Dreams	MaGo	75-day	29.50	29.50
Artaffects		**Special Issue**			
94-45-001	Divine Intervention	MaGo	75-day	35.00	35.00

		ARTIST	EDITION	ISSUE	QUOTE
Artaffects		**Good Sports**			
89-46-001	Purrfect Game (6 1/2")	S. Miller-Maxwell	14-day	22.50	25.00
89-46-002	Alley Cats (6 1/2")	S. Miller-Maxwell	14-day	22.50	25.00
89-46-003	Tee Time (6 1/2")	S. Miller-Maxwell	14-day	22.50	25.00
89-46-004	Two/Love (6 1/2")	S. Miller-Maxwell	14-day	22.50	25.00
89-46-005	What's the Catch (6 1/2")	S. Miller-Maxwell	14-day	22.50	25.00
89-46-006	Quaterback Sneak (6 1/2")	S. Miller-Maxwell	14-day	22.50	25.00
Artaffects		**Romantic Cities of Europe**			
89-47-001	Venice	L. Marchetti	14-day	35.00	65.00
89-47-002	Paris	L. Marchetti	14-day	35.00	50.00
90-47-003	London	L. Marchetti	14-day	35.00	50.00
90-47-004	Moscow	L. Marchetti	14-day	35.00	35.00
Artaffects		**The Life of Jesus**			
92-48-001	The Last Supper	L. Marchetti	25-day	27.00	27.00
92-48-002	The Sermon on the Mount	L. Marchetti	25-day	27.00	27.00
92-48-003	The Agony in the Garden	L. Marchetti	25-day	27.00	27.00
92-48-004	The Entry Into Jerusalem	L. Marchetti	25-day	27.00	27.00
92-48-005	The Blessing of the Children	L. Marchetti	25-day	27.00	27.00
92-48-006	The Resurrection	L. Marchetti	25-day	27.00	27.00
92-48-007	The Healing of the Sick	L. Marchetti	25-day	27.00	27.00
92-48-008	The Descent from the Cross	L. Marchetti	25-day	27.00	27.00
Artaffects		**Backstage**			
90-49-001	The Runaway	B. Leighton-Jones	14-day	29.50	29.50
90-49-002	The Letter	B. Leighton-Jones	14-day	29.50	29.50
90-49-003	Bubbling Over	B. Leighton-Jones	14-day	29.50	29.50
Artaffects		**Rose Wreaths**			
93-50-001	Summer's Bounty	Knox/Robertson	N/A	27.00	27.00
93-50-002	Victorian Fantasy	Knox/Robertson	N/A	27.00	27.00
93-50-003	Gentle Persuasion	Knox/Robertson	N/A	27.00	27.00
93-50-004	Sunset Splendor	Knox/Robertson	N/A	27.00	27.00
94-50-005	Sweethearts Delight	Knox/Robertson	N/A	27.00	27.00
94-50-006	Sweet Sunshine	Knox/Robertson	N/A	27.00	27.00
94-50-007	Floral Fascination	Knox/Robertson	N/A	27.00	27.00
94-50-008	Love's Embrace	Knox/Robertson	N/A	27.00	27.00
Artaffects		**Christmas Celebrations Of Yesterday**			
93-51-001	Christmas On Main Street	M. Leone	N/A	27.00	27.00
93-51-002	Christmas On The Farm	M. Leone	N/A	27.00	27.00
93-51-003	Christmas Eve	M. Leone	N/A	27.00	27.00
93-51-004	Wreath Maker	M. Leone	N/A	27.00	27.00
93-51-005	Christmas Party	M. Leone	N/A	27.00	27.00
93-51-006	Trimming The Tree	M. Leone	N/A	27.00	27.00
93-51-007	Christmas Blessings	M. Leone	N/A	27.00	27.00
93-51-008	Home For Christmas	M. Leone	N/A	27.00	27.00
Artaffects		**Lands Before Time**			
94-52-001	Pharoah's Return	A. Chesterman	75-day	29.50	29.50
94-52-002	Roman Holiday	A. Chesterman	75-day	29.50	29.50
94-52-003	Imperial Dynasty	A. Chesterman	75-day	29.50	29.50
94-52-004	Knights in Shining Armour	A. Chesterman	75-day	29.50	29.50
Artaffects		**Chieftains I**			
79-53-001	Chief Sitting Bull	G. Perillo	7,500	65.00	400.00
79-53-002	Chief Joseph	G. Perillo	7,500	65.00	110.00
80-53-003	Chief Red Cloud	G. Perillo	7,500	65.00	120.00.
80-53-004	Chief Geronimo	G. Perillo	7,500	65.00	85.00
81-53-005	Chief Crazy Horse	G. Perillo	7,500	65.00	150.00
Artaffects		**The Plainsmen**			
78-54-001	Buffalo Hunt (Bronze)	G. Perillo	2,500	350.00	500.00
79-54-002	The Proud One (Bronze)	G. Perillo	2,500	350.00	800.00
Artaffects		**The Professionals**			
79-55-001	The Big Leaguer	G. Perillo	15,000	29.95	33-55.00
80-55-002	Ballerina's Dilemma	G. Perillo	15,000	32.50	33-55.00
81-55-003	Quarterback	G. Perillo	15,000	32.50	40-55.00
81-55-004	Rodeo Joe	G. Perillo	15,000	35.00	40.00
82-55-005	Major Leaguer	G. Perillo	15,000	35.00	40-55.00
83-55-006	The Hockey Player	G. Perillo	15,000	35.00	40-55.00
Artaffects		**Pride of America's Indians**			
86-56-001	Brave and Free	G. Perillo	10-day	24.50	50-65.00
86-56-002	Dark-Eyed Friends	G. Perillo	10-day	24.50	20-50.00
86-56-003	Noble Companions	G. Perillo	10-day	24.50	20-50.00
87-56-004	Kindred Spirits	G. Perillo	10-day	24.50	27-50.00
87-56-005	Loyal Alliance	G. Perillo	10-day	24.50	60-85.00
87-56-006	Small and Wise	G. Perillo	10-day	24.50	35.00
87-56-007	Winter Scouts	G. Perillo	10-day	24.50	25-40.00
87-56-008	Peaceful Comrades	G. Perillo	10-day	24.50	37-50.00
Artaffects		**Legends of the West**			
82-57-001	Daniel Boone	G. Perillo	10,000	65.00	80.00
83-57-002	Davy Crockett	G. Perillo	10,000	65.00	80.00
83-57-003	Kit Carson	G. Perillo	10,000	65.00	80.00
83-57-004	Buffalo Bill	G. Perillo	10,000	65.00	80.00
Artaffects		**Chieftains II**			
83-58-001	Chief Pontiac	G. Perillo	7,500	70.00	85.00
83-58-002	Chief Victorio	G. Perillo	7,500	70.00	85.00
84-58-003	Chief Tecumseh	G. Perillo	7,500	70.00	85.00
84-58-004	Chief Cochise	G. Perillo	7,500	70.00	85.00
84-58-005	Chief Black Kettle	G. Perillo	7,500	70.00	110.00
Artaffects		**Child's Life**			
83-59-001	Siesta	G. Perillo	10,000	45.00	50.00
84-59-002	Sweet Dreams	G. Perillo	10,000	45.00	50.00
Artaffects		**Indian Nations**			
83-60-001	Blackfoot	G. Perillo	7,500	140.00	350-500.
83-60-002	Cheyenne	G. Perillo	7,500	set	set
83-60-003	Apache	G. Perillo	7,500	set	set
83-60-004	Sioux	G. Perillo	7,500	set	set
Artaffects		**Storybook Collection**			
80-61-001	Little Red Riding Hood	G. Perillo	18-day	29.95	30-52.00
81-61-002	Cinderella	G. Perillo	18-day	29.95	30-60.00
81-61-003	Hansel & Gretel	G. Perillo	18-day	29.95	30-52.00
82-61-004	Goldilocks & 3 Bears	G. Perillo	18-day	29.95	30-60.00
Artaffects		**Perillo Santas**			
80-62-001	Santa's Joy	G. Perillo	Open	29.95	50.00
81-62-002	Santa's Bundle	G. Perillo	Open	29.95	48.00

		ARTIST	EDITION	ISSUE	QUOTE
Artaffects		**The Princesses**			
82-63-001	Lily of the Mohawks	G. Perillo	7,500	50.00	85.00
82-63-002	Pocahontas	G. Perillo	7,500	50.00	50-65.00
82-63-003	Minnehaha	G. Perillo	7,500	50.00	65.00
82-63-004	Sacajawea	G. Perillo	7,500	50.00	85.00
Artaffects		**Nature's Harmony**			
82-64-001	The Peaceable Kingdom	G. Perillo	12,500	100.00	200-250.
82-64-002	Zebra	G. Perillo	12,500	50.00	60.00
82-64-003	Bengal Tiger	G. Perillo	12,500	50.00	60.00
83-64-004	Black Panther	G. Perillo	12,500	50.00	70.00
83-64-005	Elephant	G. Perillo	12,500	50.00	80.00
Artaffects		**Arctic Friends**			
82-65-001	Siberian Love	G. Perillo	7,500	100.00	100.00
82-65-002	Snow Pals	G. Perillo	7,500	set	set
Artaffects		**Motherhood Series**			
83-66-001	Madre	G. Perillo	10,000	50.00	75.00
84-66-002	Madonna of the Plains	G. Perillo	3,500	50.00	75-100.
85-66-003	Abuela	G. Perillo	3,500	50.00	75.00
86-66-004	Nap Time	G. Perillo	3,500	50.00	75.00
Artaffects		**The War Ponies**			
83-67-001	Sioux War Pony	G. Perillo	7,500	60.00	95-125.
83-67-002	Nez Perce War Pony	G. Perillo	7,500	60.00	149-195.
83-67-003	Apache War Pony	G. Perillo	7,500	60.00	95-125.
Artaffects		**The Tribal Ponies**			
84-68-001	Arapaho Tribal Pony	G. Perillo	3,500	65.00	150.00
84-68-002	Comanche Tribal Pony	G. Perillo	3,500	65.00	150.00
84-68-003	Crow Tribal Pony	G. Perillo	3,500	65.00	200.00
Artaffects		**The Thoroughbreds**			
84-69-001	Whirlaway	G. Perillo	9,500	50.00	250.00
84-69-002	Secretariat	G. Perillo	9,500	50.00	350.00
84-69-003	Man o' War	G. Perillo	9,500	50.00	150.00
84-69-004	Seabiscuit	G. Perillo	9,500	50.00	150.00
Artaffects		**Special Issue**			
81-70-001	Apache Boy	G. Perillo	5,000	95.00	175.00
83-70-002	Papoose	G. Perillo	3,000	100.00	125.00
83-70-003	Indian Style	G. Perillo	17,500	50.00	50.00
84-70-004	The Lovers	G. Perillo	Open	50.00	100.00
84-70-005	Navajo Girl	G. Perillo	3,500	95.00	350.00
86-70-006	Navajo Boy	G. Perillo	3,500	95.00	150-250.
87-70-007	We The People	H.C. Christy	Open	35.00	35.00
Artaffects		**The Arabians**			
86-71-001	Silver Streak	G. Perillo	3,500	95.00	150.00
Artaffects		**The Colts**			
85-72-001	Appaloosa	G. Perillo	5,000	40.00	100.00
85-72-002	Pinto	G. Perillo	5,000	40.00	110.00
85-72-003	Arabian	G. Perillo	5,000	40.00	100.00
85-72-004	Thoroughbred	G. Perillo	5,000	40.00	100.00
Artaffects		**Tender Moments**			
85-73-001	Sunset	G. Perillo	2,000	150.00	250.00
85-73-002	Winter Romance	G. Perillo	2,000	set	set
Artaffects		**Young Emotions**			
86-74-001	Tears	G. Perillo	5,000	75.00	250.00
86-74-002	Smiles	G. Perillo	5,000	set	set
Artaffects		**The Maidens**			
85-75-001	Shimmering Waters	G. Perillo	5,000	60.00	150.00
85-75-002	Snow Blanket	G. Perillo	5,000	60.00	150.00
85-75-003	Song Bird	G. Perillo	5,000	60.00	150.00
Artaffects		**The Young Chieftains**			
85-76-001	Young Sitting Bull	G. Perillo	5,000	50.00	75-150.
85-76-002	Young Joseph	G. Perillo	5,000	50.00	100.00
86-76-003	Young Red Cloud	G. Perillo	5,000	50.00	100.00
86-76-004	Young Geronimo	G. Perillo	5,000	50.00	100.00
86-76-005	Young Crazy Horse	G. Perillo	5,000	50.00	100.00
Artaffects		**Perillo Christmas**			
87-77-001	Shining Star	G. Perillo	Yr.Iss.	29.50	125-300.
88-77-002	Silent Light	G. Perillo	Yr.Iss.	35.00	50-200.
89-77-003	Snow Flake	G. Perillo	Yr.Iss.	35.00	50.00
90-77-004	Bundle Up	G. Perillo	Yr.Iss.	39.50	75.00
91-77-005	Christmas Journey	G. Perillo	Yr.Iss.	39.50	50.00
Artaffects		**America's Indian Heritage**			
87-78-001	Cheyenne Nation	G. Perillo	10-day	24.50	45-85.00
88-78-002	Arapaho Nation	G. Perillo	10-day	24.50	45.00
88-78-003	Kiowa Nation	G. Perillo	10-day	24.50	45.00
88-78-004	Sioux Nation	G. Perillo	10-day	24.50	55-80.00
88-78-005	Chippewa Nation	G. Perillo	10-day	24.50	50.00
88-78-006	Crow Nation	G. Perillo	10-day	24.50	60.00
88-78-007	Nez Perce Nation	G. Perillo	10-day	24.50	55.00
88-78-008	Blackfoot Nation	G. Perillo	10-day	24.50	95.00
Artaffects		**Mother's Love**			
88-79-001	Feelings	G. Perillo	Yr.Iss.	35.00	90.00
89-79-002	Moonlight	G. Perillo	Yr.Iss.	35.00	65.00
90-79-003	Pride & Joy	G. Perillo	Yr.Iss.	39.50	50.00
91-79-004	Little Shadow	G. Perillo	Yr.Iss.	39.50	45.00
Artaffects		**North American Wildlife**			
89-80-001	Mustang	G. Perillo	14-day	29.50	45.00
89-80-002	White-Tailed Deer	G. Perillo	14-day	29.50	35.00
89-80-003	Mountain Lion	G. Perillo	14-day	29.50	45.00
90-80-004	American Bald Eagle	G. Perillo	14-day	29.50	29.50
90-80-005	Timber Wolf	G. Perillo	14-day	29.50	35.00
90-80-006	Polar Bear	G. Perillo	14-day	29.50	39.00
90-80-007	Buffalo	G. Perillo	14-day	29.50	39.00
90-80-008	Bighorn Sheep	G. Perillo	14-day	29.50	39.00
Artaffects		**Portraits By Perillo-Mini Plates**			
89-81-001	Smiling Eyes-(4 1/4")	G. Perillo	9,500	19.50	19.50
89-81-002	Bright Sky-(4 1/4")	G. Perillo	9,500	19.50	19.50
89-81-003	Running Bear-(4 1/4")	G. Perillo	9,500	19.50	19.50
89-81-004	Little Feather-(4 1/4")	G. Perillo	9,500	19.50	19.50
90-81-005	Proud Eagle-(4 1/4")	G. Perillo	9,500	19.50	19.50
90-81-006	Blue Bird-(4 1/4")	G. Perillo	9,500	19.50	19.50
90-81-007	Wildflower-(4 1/4")	G. Perillo	9,500	19.50	19.50
90-81-008	Spring Breeze-(4 1/4")	G. Perillo	9,500	19.50	19.50
Artaffects		**March of Dimes: Our Children, Our Future**			
89-82-001	A Time to Be Born	G. Perillo	150-day	29.00	30.00
Artaffects		**Indian Bridal**			
90-83-001	Yellow Bird (6 1/2")	G. Perillo	14-day	25.00	25.00
90-83-002	Autumn Blossom (6 1/2")	G. Perillo	14-day	25.00	25.00
90-83-003	Misty Waters (6 1/2")	G. Perillo	14-day	25.00	25.00
90-83-004	Sunny Skies (6 1/2")	G. Perillo	14-day	25.00	25.00
Artaffects		**Proud Young Spirits**			
90-84-001	Protector of the Plains	G. Perillo	14-day	29.50	45-65.00
90-84-002	Watchful Eyes	G. Perillo	14-day	29.50	55.00
90-84-003	Freedom's Watch	G. Perillo	14-day	29.50	35-45.00
90-84-004	Woodland Scouts	G. Perillo	14-day	29.50	35-45.00
90-84-005	Fast Friends	G. Perillo	14-day	29.50	35-45.00
90-84-006	Birds of a Feather	G. Perillo	14-day	29.50	35-45.00
90-84-007	Prairie Pals	G. Perillo	14-day	29.50	35-45.00
90-84-008	Loyal Guardian	G. Perillo	14-day	29.50	35-45.00
Artaffects		**Perillo's Four Seasons**			
91-85-001	Summer (6 1/2")	G. Perillo	14-day	25.00	25.00
91-85-002	Autumn (6 1/2")	G. Perillo	14-day	25.00	25.00
91-85-003	Winter (6 1/2")	G. Perillo	14-day	25.00	25.00
91-85-004	Spring (6 1/2")	G. Perillo	14-day	25.00	25.00
Artaffects		**Council of Nations**			
92-86-001	Strength of the Sioux	G. Perillo	14-day	29.50	45.00
92-86-002	Pride of the Cheyenne	G. Perillo	14-day	29.50	29.50
92-86-003	Dignity of the Nez Perce	G. Perillo	14-day	29.50	29.50
92-86-004	Courage of the Arapaho	G. Perillo	14-day	29.50	29.50
92-86-005	Power of the Blackfoot	G. Perillo	14-day	29.50	29.50
92-86-006	Nobility of the Algonquin	G. Perillo	14-day	29.50	29.50
92-86-007	Wisdom of the Cherokee	G. Perillo	14-day	29.50	29.50
92-86-008	Boldness of the Seneca	G. Perillo	14-day	29.50	29.50
Artaffects		**War Ponies of the Plains**			
92-87-001	Nightshadow	G. Perillo	75-day	27.00	27.00
92-87-002	Windcatcher	G. Perillo	75-day	27.00	27.00
92-87-003	Prairie Prancer	G. Perillo	75-day	27.00	27.00
92-87-004	Thunderfoot	G. Perillo	75-day	27.00	27.00
92-87-005	Proud Companion	G. Perillo	75-day	27.00	27.00
92-87-006	Sun Dancer	G. Perillo	75-day	27.00	27.00
92-87-007	Free Spirit	G. Perillo	75-day	27.00	27.00
92-87-008	Gentle Warrior	G. Perillo	75-day	27.00	27.00
Artaffects		**Living In Harmony**			
91-88-001	Peaceable Kingdom	G. Perillo	75-day	29.50	29.50
Artaffects		**Studies in Black and White-Collector's Club Only (Miniatures)**			
92-89-001	Dignity	G. Perillo	Yr. Iss.	75.00	75.00
92-89-002	Determination	G. Perillo	Yr. Iss.	set	set
92-89-003	Diligence	G. Perillo	Yr. Iss.	set	set
92-89-004	Devotion	G. Perillo	Yr. Iss.	set	set
Artaffects		**Club Member Limited Edition Redemption Offerings**			
92-90-001	The Pencil	G. Perillo	Yr. Iss.	35.00	75.00
92-90-002	Studies in Black and White (Set of 4)	G. Perillo	Yr. Iss.	75.00	75.00
93-90-003	Watcher of the Wilderness	G. Perillo	Yr. Iss.	60.00	60.00
Artaffects		**Spirits of Nature**			
93-91-001	Protector of the Nations	G. Perillo	3,500	60.00	60.00
93-91-002	Defender of the Mountain	G. Perillo	3,500	60.00	60.00
93-91-003	Spirit of the Plains	G. Perillo	3,500	60.00	60.00
93-91-004	Guardian of Safe Passage	G. Perillo	3,500	60.00	60.00
93-91-005	Keeper of the Forest	G. Perillo	3,500	60.00	60.00
Artaffects		**Children Of The Prairie**			
93-92-001	Tender Loving Care	G. Perillo	N/A	29.50	29.50
93-92-002	Daydreamers	G. Perillo	N/A	29.50	29.50
93-92-003	Play Time	G. Perillo	N/A	29.50	29.50
93-92-004	The Sentinal	G. Perillo	N/A	29.50	29.50
93-92-005	Beach Comber	G. Perillo	N/A	29.50	29.50
93-92-006	Watchful Waiting	G. Perillo	N/A	29.50	29.50
93-92-007	Patience	G. Perillo	N/A	29.50	29.50
93-92-008	Sisters	G. Perillo	N/A	29.50	29.50
Artaffects		**Native American Christmas**			
93-93-001	The Little Shepherd (Single Issue '93)	G. Perillo	Annual	35.00	35.00
94-93-002	Joy to the World (Single Issue '94)	G. Perillo	Annual	45.00	45.00
Artaffects		**Tribal Images**			
94-94-001	Sioux Cheiftans	G. Perillo	75-day	35.00	35.00
94-94-002	Crow Cheiftans	G. Perillo	75-day	35.00	35.00
94-94-003	Cheyenne Cheiftans	G. Perillo	75-day	35.00	35.00
94-94-004	Blackfoot Cheiftans	G. Perillo	75-day	35.00	35.00
Artaffects		**Perillo's Favorites**			
94-95-001	Buffalo and the Brave	G. Perillo	75-day	45.00	45.00
94-96-001	Home of the Brave and Free	G. Perillo	75-day	35.00	35.00
Artists of the World		**Holiday**			
76-01-001	Festival of Lights	T. DeGrazia	9,500	45.00	80-108.
77-01-002	Bell of Hope	T. DeGrazia	9,500	45.00	48-75.00
78-01-003	Little Madonna	T. DeGrazia	9,500	45.00	50-59.00
79-01-004	The Nativity	T. DeGrazia	9,500	50.00	68-90.00
80-01-005	Little Pima Drummer	T. DeGrazia	9,500	50.00	62.00
81-01-006	A Little Prayer	T. DeGrazia	9,500	55.00	35-65.00
82-01-007	Blue Boy	T. DeGrazia	10,000	60.00	36-65.00
83-01-008	Heavenly Blessings	T. DeGrazia	10,000	65.00	24-30.00
84-01-009	Navajo Madonna	T. DeGrazia	10,000	65.00	28-65.00
85-01-010	Saguaro Dance	T. DeGrazia	10,000	65.00	40-65.00
Artists of the World		**Holiday (Signed)**			
76-02-001	Festival of Lights, signed	T. DeGrazia	500	100.00	350.00
77-02-002	Bell of Hope, signed	T. DeGrazia	500	100.00	200.00
78-02-003	Little Madonna, signed	T. DeGrazia	500	100.00	350.00
79-02-004	The Nativity, signed	T. DeGrazia	500	100.00	200.00
80-02-005	Little Pima Drummer, signed	T. DeGrazia	500	100.00	200.00
81-02-006	A Little Prayer, signed	T. DeGrazia	500	100.00	200.00
82-02-007	Blue Boy, signed	T. DeGrazia	96	100.00	200.00
Artists of the World		**Holiday Mini-Plates**			
80-03-001	Festival of Lights	T. DeGrazia	5,000	15.00	250.00
81-03-002	Bell of Hope	T. DeGrazia	5,000	15.00	95.00
82-03-003	Little Madonna	T. DeGrazia	5,000	15.00	95.00

		ARTIST	EDITION	ISSUE	QUOTE
82-03-004	The Nativity	T. DeGrazia	5,000	15.00	95.00
83-03-005	Little Pima Drummer	T. DeGrazia	5,000	15.00	25.00
83-03-006	Little Prayer	T. DeGrazia	5,000	20.00	25.00
84-03-007	Blue Boy	T. DeGrazia	5,000	20.00	25.00
84-03-008	Heavenly Blessings	T. DeGrazia	5,000	20.00	25.00
85-03-009	Navajo Madonna	T. DeGrazia	5,000	20.00	25.00
85-03-010	Saguaro Dance	T. DeGrazia	5,000	20.00	25.00
Artists of the World		**Children**			
76-04-001	Los Ninos	T. DeGrazia	5,000	35.00	675-900.
77-04-002	White Dove	T. DeGrazia	5,000	40.00	75-100.
78-04-003	Flower Girl	T. DeGrazia	9,500	45.00	50-85.00
79-04-004	Flower Boy	T. DeGrazia	9,500	45.00	62.00
80-04-005	Little Cocopah	T. DeGrazia	9,500	50.00	65.00
81-04-006	Beautiful Burden	T. DeGrazia	9,500	50.00	50.00
82-04-007	Merry Little Indian	T. DeGrazia	9,500	55.00	50.00
83-04-008	Wondering	T. DeGrazia	10,000	60.00	33-60.00
84-04-009	Pink Papoose	T. DeGrazia	10,000	65.00	26-65.00
85-04-010	Sunflower Boy	T. DeGrazia	10,000	65.00	50-65.00
Artists of the World		**Children (Signed)**			
78-05-001	Los Ninos, signed	T. DeGrazia	500	100.00	900.00
78-05-002	White Dove, signed	T. DeGrazia	500	100.00	450.00
78-05-003	Flower Girl, signed	T. DeGrazia	500	100.00	450.00
79-05-004	Flower Boy, signed	T. DeGrazia	500	100.00	450.00
80-05-005	Little Cocopah Girl, signed	T. DeGrazia	500	100.00	320.00
81-05-006	Beautiful Burden, signed	T. DeGrazia	500	100.00	320.00
81-05-007	Merry Little Indian, signed	T. DeGrazia	500	100.00	450.00
Artists of the World		**Children Mini-Plates**			
80-06-001	Los Ninos	T. DeGrazia	5,000	15.00	300.00
81-06-002	White Dove	T. DeGrazia	5,000	15.00	35.00
82-06-003	Flower Girl	T. DeGrazia	5,000	15.00	35.00
82-06-004	Flower Boy	T. DeGrazia	5,000	15.00	35.00
83-06-005	Little Cocopah Indian Girl	T. DeGrazia	5,000	15.00	25.00
83-06-006	Beautiful Burden	T. DeGrazia	5,000	20.00	53.00
84-06-007	Merry Little Indian	T. DeGrazia	5,000	20.00	25.00
84-06-008	Wondering	T. DeGrazia	5,000	20.00	25.00
85-06-009	Pink Papoose	T. DeGrazia	5,000	20.00	25.00
85-06-010	Sunflower Boy	T. DeGrazia	5,000	20.00	25.00
Artists of the World		**Children at Play**			
85-07-001	My First Horse	T. DeGrazia	15,000	65.00	65.00
86-07-002	Girl With Sewing Machine	T. DeGrazia	15,000	65.00	65.00
87-07-003	Love Me	T. DeGrazia	15,000	65.00	65.00
88-07-004	Merrily, Merrily, Merrily	T. DeGrazia	15,000	65.00	65.00
89-07-005	My First Arrow	T. DeGrazia	15,000	65.00	85.00
90-07-006	Away With My Kite	T. DeGrazia	15,000	65.00	75.00
Artists of the World		**Western**			
86-08-001	Morning Ride	T. DeGrazia	5,000	65.00	85.00
87-08-002	Bronco	T. DeGrazia	5,000	65.00	85.00
88-08-003	Apache Scout	T. DeGrazia	5,000	65.00	85.00
89-08-004	Alone	T. DeGrazia	5,000	65.00	85.00
Artists of the World		**Children of the Sun**			
87-09-001	Spring Blossoms	T. DeGrazia	150-day	34.50	45.00
87-09-002	My Little Pink Bird	T. DeGrazia	150-day	34.50	45.00
87-09-003	Bright Flowers of the Desert	T. DeGrazia	150-day	37.90	45.00
88-09-004	Gifts from the Sun	T. DeGrazia	150-day	37.90	45.00
88-09-005	Growing Glory	T. DeGrazia	150-day	37.90	45.00
88-09-006	The Gentle White Dove	T. DeGrazia	150-day	37.90	45.00
88-09-007	Sunflower Maiden	T. DeGrazia	150-day	39.90	45.00
89-09-008	Sun Showers	T. DeGrazia	150-day	39.90	45.00
Artists of the World		**Fiesta of the Children**			
90-10-001	Welcome to the Fiesta	T. DeGrazia	150-day	34.50	38.00
90-10-002	Castanets in Bloom	T. DeGrazia	150-day	34.50	45.00
91-10-003	Fiesta Flowers	T. DeGrazia	150-day	34.50	45.00
91-10-004	Fiesta Angels	T. DeGrazia	150-day	34.50	40.00
Artists of the World		**Celebration Series**			
93-11-001	The Lord's Candle	T. DeGrazia	5,000	39.50	39.50
93-11-002	Pinata Party	T. DeGrazia	5,000	39.50	39.50
93-11-003	Holiday lullaby	T. DeGrazia	5,000	39.50	39.50
93-11-004	Caroling	T. DeGrazia	5,000	39.50	39.50
Bareuther		**Christmas**			
67-01-001	Stiftskirche	H. Mueller	10,000	12.00	85.00
68-01-002	Kapplkirche	H. Mueller	10,000	12.00	25.00
69-01-003	Christkindlesmarkt	H. Mueller	10,000	12.00	18.00
70-01-004	Chapel in Oberndorf	H. Mueller	10,000	12.50	22.00
71-01-005	Toys for Sale	From Drawing By L. Richter	10,000	12.75	27.00
72-01-006	Christmas in Munich	H. Mueller	10,000	14.50	25.00
73-01-007	Sleigh Ride	H. Mueller	10,000	15.00	35.00
74-01-008	Black Forest Church	H. Mueller	10,000	19.00	19.00
75-01-009	Snowman	H. Mueller	10,000	21.50	30.00
76-01-010	Chapel in the Hills	H. Mueller	10,000	23.50	26.00
77-01-011	Story Time	H. Mueller	10,000	24.50	40.00
78-01-012	Mittenwald	H. Mueller	10,000	27.50	31.00
79-01-013	Winter Day	H. Mueller	10,000	35.00	35.00
80-01-014	Mittenberg	H. Mueller	10,000	37.50	39.00
81-01-015	Walk in the Forest	H. Mueller	10,000	39.50	39.50
82-01-016	Bad Wimpfen	H. Mueller	10,000	39.50	43.00
83-01-017	The Night before Christmas	H. Mueller	10,000	39.50	39.50
84-01-018	Zeil on the River Main	H. Mueller	10,000	42.50	45.00
85-01-019	Winter Wonderland	H. Mueller	10,000	42.50	57.00
86-01-020	Christmas in Forchheim	H. Mueller	10,000	42.50	70.00
87-01-021	Decorating the Tree	H. Mueller	10,000	42.50	85.00
88-01-022	St. Coloman Church	H. Mueller	10,000	52.50	65.00
89-01-023	Sleigh Ride	H. Mueller	10,000	52.50	80-90.00
90-01-024	The Old Forge in Rothenburg	H. Mueller	10,000	52.50	52.50
91-01-025	Christmas Joy	H. Mueller	10,000	56.50	56.50
92-01-026	Market Place in Heppenheim	H. Mueller	10,000	59.50	59.50
93-01-027	Winter Fun	H. Mueller	10,000	59.50	59.50
94-01-028	Coming Home For Christmas	H. Mueller	10,000	59.50	59.50
Belleek		**Christmas**			
70-01-001	Castle Caldwell	Unknown	7,500	25.00	70-85.00
71-01-002	Celtic Cross	Unknown	7,500	25.00	60.00
72-01-003	Flight of the Earls	Unknown	7,500	30.00	35.00
73-01-004	Tribute To Yeats	Unknown	7,500	38.50	40.00
74-01-005	Devenish Island	Unknown	7,500	45.00	190.00
75-01-006	The Celtic Cross	Unknown	7,500	48.00	80.00
76-01-007	Dove of Peace	Unknown	7,500	55.00	55.00

		ARTIST	EDITION	ISSUE	QUOTE
77-01-008	Wren	Unknown	7,500	55.00	55.00
Belleek		**Holiday Scenes in Ireland**			
91-02-001	Traveling Home	Unknown	7,500	75.00	75.00
92-02-002	Bearing Gifts	Unknown	7,500	75.00	75.00
Berlin Design		**Christmas**			
70-01-001	Christmas in Bernkastel	Unknown	4,000	14.50	125.00
71-01-002	Christmas in Rothenburg	Unknown	20,000	14.50	45.00
72-01-003	Christmas in Michelstadt	Unknown	20,000	15.00	55.00
73-01-004	Christmas in Wendlestein	Unknown	20,000	20.00	55.00
74-01-005	Christmas in Bremen	Unknown	20,000	25.00	53.00
75-01-006	Christmas in Dortland	Unknown	20,000	30.00	35.00
76-01-007	Christmas in Augsburg	Unknown	20,000	32.00	75.00
77-01-008	Christmas in Hamburg	Unknown	20,000	32.00	32.00
78-01-009	Christmas in Berlin	Unknown	20,000	36.00	85.00
79-01-010	Christmas in Greetsiel	Unknown	20,000	47.50	60.00
80-01-011	Christmas in Mittenberg	Unknown	20,000	50.00	55.00
81-01-012	Christmas Eve In Hahnenklee	Unknown	20,000	55.00	55.00
82-01-013	Christmas Eve In Wasserberg	Unknown	20,000	55.00	50.00
83-01-014	Christmas in Oberndorf	Unknown	20,000	55.00	65.00
84-01-015	Christmas in Ramsau	Unknown	20,000	55.00	55.00
85-01-016	Christmas in Bad Wimpfen	Unknown	20,000	55.00	59.00
86-01-017	Christmas Eve in Gelnhaus	Unknown	20,000	65.00	65.00
87-01-018	Christmas Eve in Goslar	Unknown	20,000	65.00	65.00
88-01-019	Christmas Eve in Ruhpolding	Unknown	20,000	65.00	90.00
89-01-020	Christmas Eve in Friedechsdadt	Unknown	20,000	80.00	80.00
90-01-021	Christmas Eve in Partenkirchen	Unknown	20,000	80.00	80.00
91-01-022	Christmas Eve in Allendorf	Unknown	20,000	80.00	80.00
Bing & Grondahl		**Christmas**			
95-01-001	Behind The Frozen Window	F.A. Hallin	Annual	.50	5700.00
96-01-002	New Moon	F.A. Hallin	Annual	.50	12-1760.
97-01-003	Sparrows	F.A. Hallin	Annual	.75	11-1700.
98-01-004	Roses and Star	F. Garde	Annual	.75	600-900.
99-01-005	Crows	F. Garde	Annual	.75	1265.00
00-01-006	Church Bells	F. Garde	Annual	.75	800-1100
00-01-006	Three Wise Men	S. Sabra	Annual	1.00	410-495.
00-01-008	Gothic Church Interior	D. Jensen	Annual	1.00	300-350.
00-01-009	Expectant Children	M. Hyldahl	Annual	1.00	250-330.
00-01-010	Fredericksberg Hill	C. Olsen	Annual	1.00	135-150.
00-01-011	Christmas Night	D. Jensen	Annual	1.00	135-170.
00-01-012	Sleighing to Church	D. Jensen	Annual	1.00	80-105.
00-01-013	Little Match Girl	E. Plockross	Annual	1.00	100-150.
00-01-014	St. Petri Church	P. Jorgensen	Annual	1.00	65-90.00
00-01-015	Yule Tree	Aarestrup	Annual	1.50	80-105.
00-01-016	The Old Organist	C. Ersgaard	Annual	1.50	75.00
00-01-017	Angels and Shepherds	H. Moltke	Annual	1.50	60-90.00
00-01-018	Going to Church	E. Hansen	Annual	1.50	65-90.00
13-01-019	Bringing Home the Tree	T. Larsen	Annual	1.50	70-90.00
14-01-020	Amalienborg Castle	T. Larsen	Annual	1.50	65-77.00
15-01-021	Dog Outside Window	D. Jensen	Annual	1.50	105-155.
16-01-022	Sparrows at Christmas	P. Jorgensen	Annual	1.50	60-70.00
17-01-023	Christmas Boat	A. Friis	Annual	1.50	60-80.00
18-01-024	Fishing Boat	A. Friis	Annual	1.50	58-82.00
19-01-025	Outside Lighted Window	A. Friis	Annual	2.00	53-80.00
20-01-026	Hare in the Snow	A. Friis	Annual	2.00	53-100.
21-01-027	Pigeons	A. Friis	Annual	2.00	46-67.00
22-01-028	Star of Bethlehem	A. Friis	Annual	2.00	48-64.00
23-01-029	The Ermitage	A. Friis	Annual	2.00	48-65.00
24-01-030	Lighthouse	A. Friis	Annual	2.50	48-80.00
25-01-031	Child's Christmas	A. Friis	Annual	2.50	48-80.00
26-01-032	Churchgoers	A. Friis	Annual	2.50	48-89.00
27-01-033	Skating Couple	A. Friis	Annual	2.50	57-100.
28-01-034	Eskimos	A. Friis	Annual	2.50	43-61.00
29-01-035	Fox Outside Farm	A. Friis	Annual	2.50	55-105.
30-01-036	Town Hall Square	H. Flugenring	Annual	2.50	70-95.00
31-01-037	Christmas Train	A. Friis	Annual	2.50	62-105.
32-01-038	Life Boat	H. Flugenring	Annual	2.50	65.00
33-01-039	Korsor-Nyborg Ferry	H. Flugenring	Annual	3.00	48-80.00
34-01-040	Church Bell in Tower	H. Flugenring	Annual	3.00	48-86.00
35-01-041	Lillebelt Bridge	O. Larson	Annual	3.00	48-78.00
36-01-042	Royal Guard	O. Larson	Annual	3.00	48-84.00
37-01-043	Arrival of Christmas Guests	O. Larson	Annual	3.00	66-96.00
38-01-044	Lighting the Candles	I. Tjerne	Annual	3.00	120-143.
39-01-045	Old Lock-Eye, The Sandman	I. Tjerne	Annual	3.00	120-238.
40-01-046	Christmas Letters	O. Larson	Annual	4.00	130-295.
41-01-047	Horses Enjoying Meal	O. Larson	Annual	4.00	175-255.
42-01-048	Danish Farm	O. Larson	Annual	4.00	140-244.
43-01-049	Ribe Cathedral	O. Larson	Annual	5.00	137-238.
44-01-050	Sorgenfri Castle	O. Larson	Annual	5.00	69-123.
45-01-051	The Old Water Mill	O. Larson	Annual	5.00	87-141.
46-01-052	Commemoration Cross	M. Hyldahl	Annual	5.00	48-83.00
47-01-053	Dybbol Mill	M. Hyldahl	Annual	5.00	70-120.
48-01-054	Watchman	M. Hyldahl	Annual	5.50	50-80.00
49-01-055	Landsoldaten	M. Hyldahl	Annual	5.50	50-85.00
50-01-056	Kronborg Castle	M. Hyldahl	Annual	5.50	80-128.
51-01-057	Jens Bang	M. Hyldahl	Annual	6.00	90.00
52-01-058	Thorsvaldsen Museum	B. Pramvig	Annual	6.00	50-85.00
53-01-059	Snowman	B. Pramvig	Annual	7.50	80-128.
54-01-060	Royal Boat	K. Bonfils	Annual	7.00	90.00
55-01-061	Kaulundorg Church	K. Bonfils	Annual	8.00	67-111.
56-01-062	Christmas in Copenhagen	K. Bonfils	Annual	8.50	90-145.
57-01-063	Christmas Candles	K. Bonfils	Annual	9.00	105-125.
58-01-064	Santa Claus	K. Bonfils	Annual	9.50	78-148.
59-01-065	Christmas Eve	K. Bonfils	Annual	10.00	100-145.
60-01-066	Village Church	K. Bonfils	Annual	10.00	135-200.
61-01-067	Winter Harmony	K. Bonfils	Annual	10.50	75-90.00
62-01-068	Winter Night	K. Bonfils	Annual	11.00	55.00
63-01-069	The Christmas Elf	H. Thelander	Annual	11.00	80-89.00
64-01-070	The Fir Tree and Hare	H. Thelander	Annual	11.50	39.00
65-01-071	Bringing Home the Tree	H. Thelander	Annual	12.00	32-39.00
66-01-072	Home for Christmas	H. Thelander	Annual	12.00	24-33.00
67-01-073	Sharing the Joy	H. Thelander	Annual	13.00	24-33.00
68-01-074	Christmas in Church	H. Thelander	Annual	14.00	18-30.00
69-01-075	Arrival of Guests	H. Thelander	Annual	14.00	12-21.00
70-01-076	Pheasants in Snow	H. Thelander	Annual	14.50	10-16.00
71-01-077	Christmas at Home	H. Thelander	Annual	15.00	9-15.00
72-01-078	Christmas in Greenland	H. Thelander	Annual	16.50	8-15.00
73-01-079	Country Christmas	H. Thelander	Annual	19.50	16.00
74-01-080	Christmas in the Village	H. Thelander	Annual	22.00	15.00
75-01-081	Old Water Mill	H. Thelander	Annual	27.50	13-15.00
76-01-082	Christmas Welcome	H. Thelander	Annual	27.50	17.00

		ARTIST	EDITION	ISSUE	QUOTE
77-01-083	Copenhagen Christmas	H. Thelander	Annual	29.50	18.00
78-01-084	Christmas Tale	H. Thelander	Annual	32.00	14-26.00
79-01-085	White Christmas	H. Thelander	Annual	36.50	16-21.00
80-01-086	Christmas in Woods	H. Thelander	Annual	42.50	22.00
81-01-087	Christmas Peace	H. Thelander	Annual	49.50	22.00
82-01-088	Christmas Tree	H. Thelander	Annual	54.50	30.00
83-01-089	Christmas in Old Town	H. Thelander	Annual	54.50	30-38.00
84-01-090	The Christmas Letter	E. Jensen	Annual	54.50	25-29.00
85-01-091	Christmas Eve at the Farmhouse	E. Jensen	Annual	54.50	29-34.00
86-01-092	Silent Night, Holy Night	E. Jensen	Annual	54.50	30.00
87-01-093	The Snowman's Christmas Eve	E. Jensen	Annual	59.50	44-48.00
88-01-094	In the Kings Garden	E. Jensen	Annual	64.50	26-46.00
89-01-095	Christmas Anchorage	E. Jensen	Annual	59.50	50.00
90-01-096	Changing of the Guards	E. Jensen	Annual	64.50	49-62.00
91-01-097	Copenhagen Stock Exchange	E. Jensen	Annual	69.50	50-60.00
92-01-098	Christmas At the Rectory	J. Steensen	Annual	69.50	54-85.00
93-01-099	Father Christmas in Copenhagen	J. Nielson	Annual	69.50	54-72.00
94-01-100	A Day At The Deer Park	J. Nielson	Annual	72.50	72.50
95-01-101	The Towers of Copenhagen	J. Nielson	Annual	72.50	72.50

Bing & Grondahl — **Jubilee-5 Year Cycle**

15-02-001	Frozen Window	F.A. Hallin	Annual	Unkn.	120.00
20-02-002	Church Bells	F. Garde	Annual	Unkn.	45.00
25-02-003	Dog Outside Window	D. Jensen	Annual	Unkn.	100.00
30-02-004	The Old Organist	C. Ersgaard	Annual	Unkn.	125.00
35-02-005	Little Match Girl	E. Plockross	Annual	Unkn.	570.00
40-02-006	Three Wise Men	S. Sabra	Annual	Unkn.	1225.00
45-02-007	Amalienborg Castle	T. Larsen	Annual	Unkn.	130.00
50-02-008	Eskimos	A. Friis	Annual	Unkn.	140.00
55-02-009	Dybbol Mill	M. Hyldahl	Annual	Unkn.	120.00
60-02-010	Kronborg Castle	M. Hyldahl	Annual	25.00	100-129.
65-02-011	Chruchgoers	A. Friis	Annual	25.00	30-69.00
70-02-012	Amalienborg Castle	T. Larsen	Annual	30.00	16-30.00
75-02-013	Horses Enjoying Meal	O. Larson	Annual	40.00	20-50.00
80-02-014	Yule Tree	Aarestrup	Annual	60.00	40-60.00
85-02-015	Lifeboat at Work	H. Flugenring	Annual	65.00	50-93.00
90-02-016	The Royal Yacht Dannebrog	J. Bonfils	Annual	95.00	60-95.00

Bing & Grondahl — **Mother's Day**

69-03-001	Dogs and Puppies	H. Thelander	Annual	9.75	300-450.
70-03-002	Bird and Chicks	H. Thelander	Annual	10.00	19-35.00
71-03-003	Cat and Kitten	H. Thelander	Annual	11.00	12-25.00
72-03-004	Mare and Foal	H. Thelander	Annual	12.00	12-20.00
73-03-005	Duck and Ducklings	H. Thelander	Annual	13.00	12-20.00
74-03-006	Bear and Cubs	H. Thelander	Annual	16.50	9-20.00
75-03-007	Doe and Fawns	H. Thelander	Annual	19.50	9-20.00
76-03-008	Swan Family	H. Thelander	Annual	22.50	10-25.00
77-03-009	Squirrel and Young	H. Thelander	Annual	23.50	17-25.00
78-03-010	Heron	H. Thelander	Annual	24.50	11-25.00
79-03-011	Fox and Cubs	H. Thelander	Annual	27.50	18-43.00
80-03-012	Woodpecker and Young	H. Thelander	Annual	29.50	18-30.00
81-03-013	Hare and Young	H. Thelander	Annual	36.50	18-29.00
82-03-014	Lioness and Cubs	H. Thelander	Annual	39.50	20-42.00
83-03-015	Raccoon and Young	H. Thelander	Annual	39.50	27-30.00
84-03-016	Stork and Nestlings	H. Thelander	Annual	39.50	22-44.00
85-03-017	Bear and Cubs	H. Thelander	Annual	39.50	25-32.00
86-03-018	Elephant with Calf	H. Thelander	Annual	39.50	28-35.00
87-03-019	Sheep with Lambs	H. Thelander	Annual	42.50	90-120.
88-03-020	Crested Ployer & Young	H. Thelander	Annual	47.50	55-62.00
88-03-021	Lapwing Mother with Chicks	H. Thelander	Annual	49.50	45-80.00
89-03-022	Cow With Calf	H. Thelander	Annual	49.50	40-60.00
90-03-023	Hen with Chicks	L. Jensen	Annual	52.50	50-67.00
91-03-024	The Nanny Goat and her Two Frisky Kids	L. Jensen	Annual	54.50	45-75.00
92-03-025	Panda With Cubs	L. Jensen	Annual	59.50	50-67.00
93-03-026	St. Bernard Dog and Puppies	A. Therkelsen	Annual	59.50	45-78.00
94-03-027	Cat with Kittens	A. Therkelsen	Annual	59.50	59.50

Bing & Grondahl — **Children's Day Plate Series**

85-04-001	The Magical Tea Party	C. Roller	Annual	24.50	25-35.00
86-04-002	A Joyful Flight	C. Roller	Annual	26.50	30-35.00
86-04-003	The Little Gardeners	C. Roller	Annual	29.50	65-85.00
88-04-004	Wash Day	C. Roller	Annual	34.50	35-50.00
89-04-005	Bedtime	C. Roller	Annual	37.00	38-55.00
90-04-006	My Favorite Dress	S. Vestergaard	Annual	37.00	39-45.00
91-04-007	Fun on the Beach	S. Vestergaard	Annual	45.00	35-40.00
92-04-008	A Summer Day in the Meadow	S. Vestergaard	Annual	45.00	40-50.00
93-04-009	The Carousel	S. Vestergaard	Annual	45.00	45-50.00
94-04-010	The Little Fisherman	S. Vestergaard	Annual	45.00	45.00

Bing & Grondahl — **Statue of Liberty**

85-05-001	Statue of Liberty	Unknown	10,000	60.00	85-100.

Bing & Grondahl — **Christmas In America**

86-06-001	Christmas Eve in Williamsburg	J. Woodson	Annual	29.50	150.00
87-06-002	Christmas Eve at the White House	J. Woodson	Annual	34.50	35.00
88-06-003	Christmas Eve at Rockefeller Center	J. Woodson	Annual	34.50	49.00
89-06-004	Christmas In New England	J. Woodson	Annual	37.00	49.00
90-06-005	Christmas Eve at the Capitol	J. Woodson	Annual	39.50	40.00
91-06-006	Christmas Eve at Independence Hall	J. Woodson	Annual	45.00	45.00
92-06-007	Christmas in San Francisco	J. Woodson	Annual	47.50	40.00
93-06-008	Coming Home For Christmas	J. Woodson	Annual	47.50	47.50
94-06-009	Christmas Eve In Alaska	J. Woodson	Annual	47.50	47.50

Bing & Grondahl — **Santa Claus Collection**

89-07-001	Santa's Workshop	H. Hansen	Annual	59.50	70-90.00
90-07-002	Santa's Sleigh	H. Hansen	Annual	59.50	59.50
91-07-003	Santa's Journey	H. Hansen	Annual	69.50	60-69.50
92-07-004	Santa's Arrival	H. Hansen	Annual	74.50	74.50
93-07-005	Santa's Gifts	H. Hansen	Annual	74.50	74.50
94-07-006	Christmas Stories	H. Hansen	Annual	74.50	74.50

Bing & Grondahl — **Young Adventurer Plate**

90-08-001	The Little Viking	S. Vestergaard	Annual	52.50	65.00

Bing & Grondahl — **Christmas in America Anniversary Plate**

91-09-001	Christmas Eve in Williamsburg	J. Woodson	Annual	69.50	69.50

Bing & Grondahl — **Centennial Collection**

91-10-001	Crows Enjoying Christmas	D. Jensen	Annual	59.50	47.50
92-10-002	Copenhagen Christmas	H. Vlugenring	Annual	59.50	47.50
93-10-003	Christmas Elf	H. Thelander	Annual	59.50	59.50
94-10-004	Christmas in Church	H. Thelander	Annual	59.50	59.50
95-10-005	Behind The Frozen Window	A. Hallin	Annual	59.50	59.50

Bing & Grondahl — **Olympic**

		ARTIST	EDITION	ISSUE	QUOTE
72-11-001	Munich, Germany	Unknown	Closed	20.00	15-25.00
76-11-002	Montreal, Canada	Unknown	Closed	29.50	30-59.00
80-11-003	Moscow, Russia	Unknown	Closed	43.00	89.00
84-11-004	Los Angeles, USA	Unknown	Closed	45.00	259.00
88-11-005	Seoul, Korea	Unknown	Closed	60.00	90.00
92-11-006	Barcelona, Spain	Unknown	Closed	74.50	79.00

Boehm Studios — **Panda**

82-01-001	Panda, Harmony	Boehm	5,000	65.00	65.00
82-01-002	Panda, Peace	Boehm	5,000	65.00	65.00

The Bradford Exchange/Russia — **The Nutcracker**

93-01-001	Marie's Magical Gift	N. Zaitseva	95-day	39.87	39.87
93-01-002	Dance of Sugar Plum Fairy	N. Zaitseva	95-day	39.87	39.87
93-01-003	Waltz of the Flowers	N. Zaitseva	95-day	39.87	39.87
93-01-004	Battle With the Mice King	N. Zaitseva	95-day	39.87	39.87

The Bradford Exchange/United States — **Lincoln's Portraits of Valor**

93-02-001	The Gettysburg Address	B. Maguire	95-day	29.90	29.90
93-02-002	Emancipation Proclamation	B. Maguire	95-day	29.90	29.90
93-02-003	The Lincoln-Douglas Debates	B. Maguire	95-day	29.90	29.90
93-02-004	The Second Inaugural Address	B. Maguire	95-day	29.90	29.90

The Bradford Exchange/United States — **Superstars of Country Music**

93-03-001	Dolly Parton: I Will Always Love You	N. Giorgro	95-day	29.90	29.90
93-03-002	Kenny Rogers: Sweet Music Man	N. Giorgro	95-day	29.90	29.90

The Bradford Exchange/United States — **Elvis: Young & Wild**

93-04-001	The King of Creole	B. Emmett	95-day	29.90	29.90
93-04-002	King of the Road	B. Emmett	95-day	29.90	29.90
94-04-003	Tough But Tender	B. Emmett	95-day	32.90	32.90
94-04-004	With Love, Elvis	B. Emmett	95-day	32.90	32.90
94-04-005	The Picture of Cool	B. Emmett	95-day	32.90	32.90

The Bradford Exchange/United States — **Great Moments in Baseball**

93-05-001	Joe DiMaggio: The Streak	S. Gardner	95-day	29.90	29.90
93-05-002	Stan Musial: 5 Homer Double Header	S. Gardner	95-day	29.90	29.90
94-05-003	Bobby Thomson: Shot Heard Round the World	S. Gardner	95-day	32.90	32.90
94-05-004	Bill Mazeroski: Winning Home Run	S. Gardner	95-day	32.90	32.90
94-05-005	Don Larsen: Perfect Series Game	S. Gardner	95-day	32.90	32.90

The Bradford Exchange/United States — **America's Triumph in Space**

93-06-001	The Eagle Has Landed	R. Schaar	95-day	29.90	29.90
93-06-002	The March Toward Destiny	R. Schaar	95-day	29.90	29.90
94-06-003	Flight of Glory	R. Schaar	95-day	32.90	32.90

The Bradford Exchange/United States — **New Horizons**

93-07-001	Building For a New Generation	R. Copple	95-day	29.90	29.90
93-07-002	The Power of Gold	R. Copple	95-day	29.90	29.90

The Bradford Exchange/United States — **Mystic Guardians**

93-08-001	Soul Mates	S. Hill	95-day	29.90	29.90
93-08-002	Majestic Messenger	S. Hill	95-day	29.90	29.90
93-08-003	Companion Spirits	S. Hill	95-day	32.90	32.90
94-08-004	Faithful Fellowship	S. Hill	95-day	32.90	32.90

The Bradford Exchange/United States — **When All Hearts Come Home**

93-09-001	Oh Christmas Tree	J. Barnes	95-day	29.90	29.90
93-09-002	Night Before Christmas	J. Barnes	95-day	29.90	29.90
93-09-003	Comfort and Joy	J. Barnes	95-day	29.90	29.90
93-09-004	Grandpa's Farm	J. Barnes	95-day	29.90	29.90
93-09-005	Peace on Earth	J. Barnes	95-day	29.90	29.90
93-09-006	Night Departure	J. Barnes	95-day	29.90	29.90
93-09-007	Supper and Small Talk	J. Barnes	95-day	29.90	29.90
93-09-008	Christmas Wish	J. Barnes	95-day	29.90	29.90

The Bradford Exchange/United States — **Promise of a Savior**

93-10-001	An Angel's Message	Various	95-day	29.90	29.90
93-10-002	Gifts to Jesus	Various	95-day	29.90	29.90
93-10-003	The Heavenly King	Various	95-day	29.90	29.90
93-10-004	Angels Were Watching	Various	95-day	29.90	29.90
93-10-005	Holy Mother and Child	Various	95-day	29.90	29.90
94-10-006	A Child is Born	Various	95-day	29.90	29.90

The Bradford Exchange/United States — **Footsteps of the Brave**

93-11-001	Noble Quest	H. Schaare	95-day	24.90	24.90
93-11-002	At Storm's Passage	H. Schaare	95-day	24.90	24.90
93-11-003	With Boundless Vision	H. Schaare	95-day	27.90	27.90
93-11-004	Horizons of Destiny	H. Schaare	95-day	27.90	27.90
93-11-005	Path of His Forefathers	H. Schaare	95-day	27.90	27.90
93-11-006	Soulful Reflection	H. Schaare	95-day	29.90	29.90
93-11-007	The Reverent Trail	H. Schaare	95-day	29.90	29.90

The Bradford Exchange/United States — **Old Fashioned Christmas with Thomas Kinkade**

93-12-001	All Friends Are Welcome	T. Kinkade	95-day	29.90	29.90
93-12-002	Winters Memories	T. Kinkade	95-day	29.90	29.90
93-12-003	A Holiday Gathering	T. Kinkade	95-day	32.90	32.90

The Bradford Exchange/United States — **Alice in Wonderland**

93-13-001	The Mad Tea Party	S. Gustafson	95-day	29.90	29.90
93-13-002	The Cheshire Cat	S. Gustafson	95-day	29.90	29.90
94-13-003	Croquet with the Queen	S. Gustafson	95-day	29.90	29.90

The Bradford Exchange/United States — **Notorious Disney Villains**

93-14-001	The Wicked Queen	Disney-Studios	95-day	29.90	29.90

The Bradford Exchange/United States — **Hideaway Lake**

93-15-001	Rusty's Retreat	R. Rust	95-day	34.90	34.90
93-15-002	Fishing For Dreams	R. Rust	95-day	34.90	34.90
93-15-003	Sunset Cabin	R. Rust	95-day	34.90	34.90
93-15-004	Echoes of Morning	R. Rust	95-day	34.90	34.90

The Bradford Exchange/United States — **Vanishing Paradises**

93-16-001	The Rainforest	G. Dieckhoner	95-day	29.90	29.90
93-16-002	The Panda's World	G. Dieckhoner	95-day	29.90	29.90
93-16-003	Splendors of India	G. Dieckhoner	95-day	29.90	29.90
93-16-004	An African Safari	G. Dieckhoner	95-day	29.90	29.90

The Bradford Exchange/United States — **A Hidden World**

93-17-001	Two by Night, Two by Light	R. Rust	95-day	29.90	29.90
93-17-002	Two by Steam, Two in Dream	R. Rust	95-day	29.90	29.90
93-17-003	Two on Sly, Two Watch Nearby	R. Rust	95-day	32.90	32.90
93-17-004	Hunter Growls, Spirits Prowl	R. Rust	95-day	32.90	32.90
93-17-005	In Moonglow One Drinks	R. Rust	95-day	32.90	32.90
93-17-006	Sings at the Moon, Spirits Sing in Tune	R. Rust	95-day	34.90	34.90

	ARTIST	EDITION	ISSUE	QUOTE
The Bradford Exchange/United States	**Dog Days**			
93-18-001 Sweet Dreams	J. Gadmus	95-day	29.90	29.90
93-18-002 Pier Group	J. Gadmus	95-day	29.90	29.90
93-18-003 Wagon Train	J. Gadmus	95-day	32.90	32.90
93-18-004 First Flush	J. Gadmus	95-day	32.90	32.90
93-18-005 Little Rascals	J. Gadmus	95-day	32.90	32.90
93-18-006 Where'd He Go	J. Gadmus	95-day	32.90	32.90
The Bradford Exchange/United States	**Baskets of Love**			
93-19-001 Andrew and Abbey	A. Isakov	95-day	29.90	29.90
93-19-002 Cody and Courtney	A. Isakov	95-day	29.90	29.90
93-19-003 Emily and Elliott	A. Isakov	95-day	32.90	32.90
93-19-004 Heather and Hannah	A. Isakov	95-day	32.90	32.90
93-19-005 Justin and Jessica	A. Isakov	95-day	32.90	32.90
93-19-006 Katie and Kelly	A. Isakov	95-day	34.90	34.90
The Bradford Exchange/United States	**Keepsakes of the Heart**			
93-20-001 Forever Friends	C. Layton	95-day	29.90	29.90
93-20-002 Afternoon Tea	C. Layton	95-day	29.90	29.90
93-20-003 Riding Companions	C. Layton	95-day	29.90	29.90
93-20-004 Sentimental Sweethearts	C. Layton	95-day	29.90	29.90
The Bradford Exchange/United States	**Charles Wysocki's Peppercricket Grove**			
93-21-001 Peppercricket Farms	C. Wysocki	95-day	24.90	24.90
93-21-002 Gingermut Valley Inn	C. Wysocki	95-day	24.90	24.90
93-21-003 Budzen's Fruits and Vegetables	C. Wysocki	95-day	24.90	24.90
93-21-004 Virginia's Market	C. Wysocki	95-day	24.90	24.90
93-21-005 Pumpkin Hollow Emporium	C. Wysocki	95-day	24.90	24.90
93-21-006 Liberty Star Farms	C. Wysocki	95-day	24.90	24.90
93-21-007 Overflow Antique Market	C. Wysocki	95-day	24.90	24.90
93-21-008 Black Crow Antique Shoppe	C. Wysocki	95-day	24.90	24.90
The Bradford Exchange/United States	**Trains of the Great West**			
93-22-001 Moonlit Journey	K. Randle	95-day	29.90	29.90
93-22-002 Mountain Hideaway	K. Randle	95-day	29.90	29.90
93-22-003 Early Morning Arrival	K. Randle	95-day	29.90	29.90
94-22-004 The Snowy Pass	K. Randle	95-day	29.90	29.90
The Bradford Exchange/United States	**Kingdom of the Unicorn**			
93-23-001 The Magic Begins	M. Ferraro	95-day	29.90	29.90
93-23-002 In Crystal Waters	M. Ferraro	95-day	29.90	29.90
93-23-003 Chasing a Dream	M. Ferraro	95-day	29.90	29.90
93-23-004 The Fountain of Youth	M. Ferraro	95-day	29.90	29.90
The Bradford Exchange/United States	**Christmas Memories**			
93-24-001 A Winter's Tale	J. Tanton	95-day	29.90	29.90
93-24-002 Finishing Touches	J. Tanton	95-day	29.90	29.90
93-24-003 Welcome to Our Home	J. Tanton	95-day	29.90	29.90
93-24-004 Christmas Celebration	J. Tanton	95-day	29.90	29.90
The Bradford Exchange/United States	**Little Bandits**			
93-25-001 Handle With Care	C. Jagodits	95-day	29.90	29.90
93-25-002 All Tied Up	C. Jagodits	95-day	29.90	29.90
93-25-003 Everything's Coming Up Daisies	C. Jagodits	95-day	32.90	32.90
93-25-004 Out of Hand	C. Jagodits	95-day	32.90	32.90
93-25-005 Pupsicles	C. Jagodits	95-day	32.90	32.90
93-25-006 Unexpected Guests	C. Jagodits	95-day	32.90	32.90
The Bradford Exchange/United States	**Pathways of the Heart**			
93-26-001 October Radiance	J. Barnes	95-day	29.90	29.90
93-26-002 Daybreak	J. Barnes	95-day	29.90	29.90
94-26-003 Harmony with Nature	J. Barnes	95-day	29.90	29.90
94-26-004 Distant Lights	J. Barnes	95-day	29.90	29.90
94-26-005 A Night to Remember	J. Barnes	95-day	29.90	29.90
94-26-006 Peaceful Evening	J. Barnes	95-day	29.90	29.90
The Bradford Exchange/United States	**Panda Bear Hugs**			
93-27-001 Rock-a-Bye	W. Nelson	3/95	39.00	39.00
94-27-002 Loving Advice	W. Nelson	5/95	39.00	39.00
94-27-003 A Playful Interlude	W. Nelson	7/95	39.00	39.00
94-27-004 A Taste of Life	W. Nelson	9/95	39.00	39.00
The Bradford Exchange/United States	**Aladdin**			
93-28-001 Magic Carpet Ride	Disney-Studios	95-day	29.90	29.90
93-28-001 A Friend Like Me	Disney-Studios	95-day	29.90	29.90
94-28-003 Aladdin in Love	Disney-Studios	95-day	29.90	29.90
94-28-004 Traveling Companions	Disney-Studios	95-day	29.90	29.90
The Bradford Exchange/United States	**Family Circles**			
93-29-001 Great Gray Owl Family	R. Rust	95-day	29.90	29.90
94-29-002 Great Horned Owl Family	R. Rust	95-day	29.90	29.90
94-29-003 Barred Owl Family	R. Rust	95-day	29.90	29.90
94-29-004 Spotted Owl Family	R. Rust	95-day	29.90	29.90
The Bradford Exchange/United States	**Peace on Earth**			
93-30-001 Winter Lullaby	D. Geisness	95-day	29.90	29.90
94-30-002 Heavenly Slumber	D. Geisness	95-day	29.90	29.90
94-30-003 Sweet Embrace	D. Geisness	95-day	32.90	32.90
The Bradford Exchange/United States	**A Christmas Carol**			
93-31-001 God Bless Us Everyone	L. Garrison	95-day	29.90	29.90
93-31-002 Ghost of Christmas Present	L. Garrison	95-day	29.90	29.90
94-31-003 A Merry Christmas to All	L. Garrison	95-day	29.90	29.90
94-31-004 A Visit From Marley's Ghost	L. Garrison	95-day	29.90	29.90
94-31-005 Remembereing Christmas Past	L. Garrison	95-day	29.90	29.90
94-31-006 A Spirit's Warning	L. Garrison	95-day	29.90	29.90
94-31-007 The True Spirit of Christmas	L. Garrison	95-day	29.90	29.90
The Bradford Exchange/United States	**Windows on a World of Song**			
93-32-001 The Library: Cardinals	K. Daniel	95-day	34.90	34.90
93-32-002 The Den: Black-Capped Chickadees	K. Daniel	95-day	34.90	34.90
93-32-003 The Bedroom: Bluebirds	K. Daniel	95-day	34.90	34.90
94-32-004 The Kitchen: Goldfinches	K. Daniel	95-day	34.90	34.90
The Bradford Exchange/United States	**America's Favorite Classic Cars**			
93-33-001 1957 Corvette	D. Everhart	3/95	54.00	54.00
93-33-002 1956 Thunderbird	D. Everhart	5/95	54.00	54.00
94-33-003 1957 Bel Air	D. Everhart	7/95	54.00	54.00
94-33-004 1965 Mustang	D. Everhart	9/95	54.00	54.00
The Bradford Exchange/United States	**Untamed Spirits**			
93-34-001 Wild Hearts	P. Weirs	95-day	29.90	29.90
94-34-002 Breakaway	P. Weirs	95-day	29.90	29.90
94-34-003 Forever Free	P. Weirs	95-day	29.90	29.90
94-34-004 Distant Thunder	P. Weirs	95-day	29.90	29.90

	ARTIST	EDITION	ISSUE	QUOTE
The Bradford Exchange/United States	**Sacred Circle**			
93-35-001 Before the Hunt	K. Randle	95-day	29.90	29.90
93-35-002 Spiritual Guardian	K. Randle	95-day	29.90	29.90
93-35-003 Ghost Dance	K. Randle	95-day	32.90	32.90
94-35-004 Deer Dance	K. Randle	95-day	32.90	32.90
94-35-005 The Wolf Dance	K. Randle	95-day	32.90	32.90
94-35-006 The Painted Hourse	K. Randle	95-day	34.90	34.90
The Bradford Exchange/United States	**American Frontier**			
93-36-001 Timberline Jack's Trading Post	C. Wysocki	95-day	29.90	29.90
94-36-002 Dr. Livingwell's Medicine Show	C. Wysocki	95-day	29.90	29.90
94-36-003 Bustling Boomtown	C. Wysocki	95-day	29.90	29.90
94-36-004 Kirbyville	C. Wysocki	95-day	29.90	29.90
94-36-005 Hearty Homesteaders	C. Wysocki	95-day	29.90	29.90
94-36-006 Oklahoma or Bust	C. Wysocki	95-day	29.90	29.90
The Bradford Exchange/United States	**Sovereigns of the Wild**			
93-37-001 The Snow Queen	D. Grant	95-day	29.90	29.90
94-37-001 Let Us Survive	D. Grant	95-day	29.90	29.90
94-37-002 Cool Cats	D. Grant	95-day	29.90	29.90
94-37-003 Siberian Snow Tigers	D. Grant	95-day	29.90	29.90
94-37-004 African Evening	D. Grant	95-day	29.90	29.90
The Bradford Exchange/United States	**101 Dalmations**			
93-38-001 Watch Dogs	Disney-Studios	95-day	29.90	29.90
94-38-002 A Happy Reunion	Disney-Studios	95-day	29.90	29.90
94-38-003 Hello Darlings	Disney-Studios	95-day	32.90	32.90
The Bradford Exchange/United States	**In A Hidden Garden**			
93-39-001 Curious Kittens	T. Clausnitzer	95-day	29.90	29.90
94-39-002 Through Eyes of Blue	T. Clausnitzer	95-day	29.90	29.90
94-39-003 Amber Gaze	T. Clausnitzer	95-day	29.90	29.90
94-39-004 Fascinating Find	T. Clausnitzer	95-day	29.90	29.90
The Bradford Exchange/United States	**Field Pup Follies**			
94-40-001 Sleeping on the Job	L. Kaatz	7/95	29.90	29.90
The Bradford Exchange/United States	**Thundering Waters**			
94-41-001 Niagara Falls	F. Miller	95-day	34.90	34.90
94-41-002 Lower Falls, Yellowstone	F. Miller	95-day	34.90	34.90
The Bradford Exchange/United States	**Nightwatch: The Wolf**			
94-42-001 Moonlight Serenade	D. Ningewance	95-day	29.90	29.90
94-42-002 Midnight Guard	D. Ningewance	95-day	29.90	29.90
94-42-003 Snowy Lookout	D. Ningewance	95-day	29.90	29.90
The Bradford Exchange/United States	**The World of the Eagle**			
94-43-001 Sentinel of the Night	J. Hansel	95-day	29.90	29.90
The Bradford Exchange/United States	**Nightsong: The Loon**			
94-44-001 Moonlight Echoes	J. Hansel	95-day	29.90	29.90
94-44-002 Evening Mist	J. Hansel	95-day	29.90	29.90
94-44-003 Nocturnal Glow	J. Hansel	95-day	32.90	32.90
94-44-004 Tranquil Reflections	J. Hansel	95-day	32.90	32.90
The Bradford Exchange/United States	**Woodland Wings**			
94-45-001 Twilight Flight	J. Hansel	95-day	34.90	34.90
The Bradford Exchange/United States	**Nature's Little Treasures**			
94-46-001 Garden Whispers	L. Martin	95-day	29.90	29.90
94-46-002 Wings of Grace	L. Martin	95-day	29.90	29.90
94-46-003 Delicate Splendor	L. Martin	95-day	32.90	32.90
94-46-004 Perfect Jewels	L. Martin	95-day	32.90	32.90
94-46-005 Miniature Glory	L. Martin	95-day	32.90	32.90
The Bradford Exchange/United States	**Chosen Messangers**			
94-47-001 The Pathfinders	G. Running Wolf	95-day	29.90	29.90
94-47-002 The Overseers	G. Running Wolf	95-day	29.90	29.90
94-47-003 The Providers	G. Running Wolf	95-day	32.90	32.90
The Bradford Exchange/United States	**Heirloom Memories**			
94-48-001 Porcelain Treasure	A. Pech	95-day	29.90	29.90
94-48-002 Rhythms in Lace	A. Pech	95-day	29.90	29.90
94-48-003 Pink Lemonade Roses	A. Pech	95-day	29.90	29.90
94-48-004 Victorian Romance	A. Pech	95-day	29.90	29.90
94-48-005 Teatime Tulips	A. Pech	95-day	29.90	29.90
The Bradford Exchange/United States	**The Life of Christ**			
94-49-001 The Passion in the Garden	R. Barrett	95-day	29.90	29.90
94-49-002 Jesus Enters Jerusalem	R. Barrett	95-day	29.90	29.90
94-49-003 Jesus Calms the Waters	R. Barrett	95-day	32.90	32.90
The Bradford Exchange/United States	**Sovereigns of the Sky**			
94-50-001 Spirit of Freedom	G. Dieckhoner	8/95	39.00	39.00
94-50-002 Spirit of Pride	G. Dieckhoner	10/95	39.00	39.00
The Bradford Exchange/United States	**Kingdom of Great Cats: Signature Collection**			
94-51-001 Mystic Realm	C. Frace	95-day	39.90	39.90
The Bradford Exchange/United States	**A Visit to Brambly Hedge**			
94-52-001 Summer Story	J. Barklem	6/95	39.90	39.90
The Bradford Exchange/United States	**Tale of Peter Rabbit and Benjamin Bunny**			
94-53-001 A Pocket Full of Onions	Inspired by B. Potter	3/96	39.00	39.00
The Bradford Exchange/United States	**Lena Liu's Beautiful Gardens**			
94-54-001 Iris Garden	Inspired by L. Liu	12/95	34.00	34.00
The Bradford Exchange/United States	**When Dreams Blossom**			
94-55-001 Dreams to Gather	R. McGinnis	95-day	29.90	29.90
The Bradford Exchange/United States	**Heaven Sent**			
94-56-001 Sweet Dreams	L. Bogle	95-day	29.90	29.90
The Bradford Exchange/United States	**Radiant Messengers**			
94-57-001 Peace	L. Martin	95-day	29.90	29.90
The Bradford Exchange/United States	**Visions of Our Lady**			
94-58-001 Our Lady of Lourdes	H. Garrido	95-day	29.90	29.90
94-58-002 Our Lady of Medjugorje	H. Garrido	95-day	29.90	29.90
The Bradford Exchange/United States	**Mysterious Case of Fowl Play**			
94-59-001 Inspector Clawseau	B.H. Bond	95-day	29.90	29.90
94-59-002 Glamourpuss	B.H. Bond	95-day	29.90	29.90
94-59-003 Sophisicat	B.H. Bond	95-day	29.90	29.90
The Bradford Exchange/United States	**Practice Makes Perfect**			
94-60-001 What's a Mother to Do?	L. Kaatz	95-day	29.90	29.90
94-60-002 The Ones That Got Away	L. Kaatz	95-day	29.90	29.90

		ARTIST	EDITION	ISSUE	QUOTE
The Bradford Exchange/United States		**Warm County Moments**			
94-61-001	Mabel's Sunny Retreat	M.A. Lasher	95-day	29.90	29.90
The Bradford Exchange/United States		**Visions of the Sacred**			
94-63-001	Snow Rider	L. Medaris	95-day	29.90	29.90
The Bradford Exchange/United States		**Night Fairies**			
94-64-001	Trails of Starlight	M. Jobe	95-day	29.90	29.90
The Bradford Exchange/United States		**WWII: A Rememberance**			
94-65-001	D-Day	J. Griffin	95-day	29.90	29.90
The Bradford Exchange/United States		**Reflections of Marilyn**			
94-66-001	All That Glitters	C. Notarile	95-day	29.90	29.90
Curator Collections:See Artaffects					
CUI/Carolina Collection/Dram Tree		**Native American Series**			
91-01-001	Hunt for the Buffalo Edition I	P. Kethley	Retrd.	39.50	39.50
CUI/Carolina Collection/Dram Tree		**Christmas Series**			
91-02-001	Checkin' it Twice Edition I	CUI	Retrd.	39.50	39.50
CUI/Carolina Collection/Dram Tree		**Environmental Series**			
91-03-001	Rainforest Magic Edition I	C. L. Bragg	Retrd.	39.50	39.50
92-03-002	First Breath	M. Hoffman	Retrd.	40.00	40.00
CUI/Carolina Collection/Dram Tree		**Girl In The Moon**			
91-04-001	Miller Girl in the Moon Edition I	CUI	9,950	39.50	39.50
CUI/Carolina Collection/Dram Tree		**DU Great American Sporting Dogs**			
92-05-001	Black Lab Edition I	J. Killen	20,000	40.00	40.00
93-05-002	Golden Retriever Edition II	J. Killen	28-day	40.00	40.00
93-05-003	Springer Spaniel Edition III	J. Killen	28-day	40.00	40.00
93-05-004	Yellow Labrador Edition IV	J. Killen	28-day	40.00	40.00
93-05-005	English Setter Edition V	J. Killen	28-day	40.00	40.00
93-05-006	Brittany Spaniel Edition VI	J. Killen	28-day	40.00	40.00
CUI/Carolina Collection/Dram Tree		**Classic Car Series**			
92-06-001	1957 Chevy	G. Geivette	Retrd.	40.00	40.00
CUI/Carolina Collection/Dram Tree		**Corvette Series**			
92-07-001	1953 Corvette	G. Geivette	28-day	40.00	40.00
CUI/Carolina Collection/Dram Tree		**Coors Winterfest**			
92-08-001	Skating Party	T. Stortz	Retrd.	29.50	29.50
CUI/Carolina Collection/Dram Tree		**Coors Factory Plate**			
92-09-001	First Edition	Unknown	45-day	29.50	29.50
93-09-002	Second Edition	Unknown	45-day	29.50	29.50
CUI/Carolina Collection/Dram Tree		**First Encounter**			
93-10-001	Stand Off	R. Cruwys	45-day	29.50	29.50
94-10-002	Class Clown	R. Cruwys	45-day	29.50	29.50
Delphi		**Elvis Presley: Looking At A Legend**			
88-01-001	Elvis at/Gates of Graceland	B. Emmett	150-day	24.75	100-175.
89-01-002	Jailhouse Rock	B. Emmett	150-day	24.75	100-149.
89-01-003	The Memphis Flash	B. Emmett	150-day	27.75	68-75.00
89-01-004	Homecoming	B. Emmett	150-day	27.75	75.00
90-01-005	Elvis and Gladys	B. Emmett	150-day	27.75	55-65.00
90-01-006	A Studio Session	B. Emmett	150-day	27.75	35-49.00
90-01-007	Elvis in Hollywood	B. Emmett	150-day	29.75	45-49.00
90-01-008	Elvis on His Harley	B. Emmett	150-day	29.75	45-75.00
90-01-009	Stage Door Autographs	B. Emmett	150-day	29.75	45-65.00
91-01-010	Christmas at Graceland	B. Emmett	150-day	32.75	95-100.
91-01-011	Entering Sun Studio	B. Emmett	150-day	32.75	70.00
91-01-012	Going for the Black Belt	B. Emmett	150-day	32.75	60-65.00
91-01-013	His Hand in Mine	B. Emmett	150-day	32.75	45-65.00
91-01-014	Letters From Fans	B. Emmett	150-day	32.75	50-75.00
91-01-015	Closing the Deal	B. Emmett	150-day	34.75	59.00
92-01-016	Elvis Returns to the Stage	B. Emmett	150-day	34.75	49-59.00
Delphi		**Elvis Presley: In Performance**			
90-02-001	'68 Comeback Special	B. Emmett	150-day	24.75	69-89.00
91-02-002	King of Las Vegas	B. Emmett	150-day	24.75	60-89.00
91-02-003	Aloha From Hawaii	B. Emmett	150-day	27.75	57-85.00
91-02-004	Back in Tupelo, 1956	B. Emmett	150-day	27.75	50-59.00
91-02-005	If I Can Dream	B. Emmett	150-day	27.75	40-69.00
91-02-006	Benefit for the USS Arizona	B. Emmett	150-day	29.75	40-59.00
91-02-007	Madison Square Garden, 1972	B. Emmett	150-day	29.75	40-49.00
91-02-008	Tampa, 1955	B. Emmett	150-day	29.75	30-49.00
91-02-009	Concert in Baton Rouge, 1974	B. Emmett	150-day	29.75	30-49.00
92-02-010	On Stage in Wichita, 1974	B. Emmett	150-day	31.75	31.75
92-02-011	In the Spotlight: Hawaii, '72	B. Emmett	150-day	31.75	31.75
92-02-012	Tour Finale: Indianapolis 1977	B. Emmett	150-day	31.75	31.75
Delphi		**Portraits of the King**			
91-03-001	Love Me Tender	D. Zwierz	150-day	27.75	45-49.00
91-03-002	Are You Lonesome Tonight?	D. Zwierz	150-day	27.75	45.00
91-03-003	I'm Yours	D. Zwierz	150-day	30.75	45.00
91-03-004	Treat Me Nice	D. Zwierz	150-day	30.75	30.75
92-03-005	The Wonder of You	D. Zwierz	150-day	30.75	30.75
92-03-006	You're a Heartbreaker	D. Zwierz	150-day	32.75	32.75
92-03-007	Just Because	D. Zwierz	150-day	32.75	32.75
92-03-008	Follow That Dream	D. Zwierz	150-day	32.75	32.75
Delphi		**The Elvis Presley Hit Parade**			
92-04-001	Heartbreak Hotel	N. Giorgio	150-day	29.75	29.75
92-04-002	Blue Suede Shoes	N. Giorgio	150-day	29.75	29.75
92-04-003	Hound Dog	N. Giorgio	150-day	32.75	32.75
92-04-004	Blue Christmas	N. Giorgio	150-day	32.75	32.75
92-04-005	Return to Sender	N. Giorgio	150-day	32.75	32.75
93-04-006	Teddy Bear	N. Giorgio	150-day	34.75	34.75
93-04-007	Always on My Mind	N. Giorgio	150-day	34.75	34.75
93-04-008	Mystery Train	N. Giorgio	150-day	34.75	34.75
93-04-009	Blue Moon of Kentucky	N. Giorgio	150-day	34.75	34.75
93-04-010	Wear My Ring Around Your Neck	N. Giorgio	150-day	36.75	36.75
93-04-011	Suspicious Minds	N. Giorgio	150-day	36.75	36.75
93-04-012	Peace in the Valley	N. Giorgio	150-day	36.75	36.75
Delphi		**Elvis on the Big Screen**			
92-05-001	Elvis in Loving You	B. Emmett	150-day	29.75	52.00
92-05-002	Elvis in G.I. Blues	B. Emmett	150-day	29.75	29.75
92-05-003	Viva Las Vegas	B. Emmett	150-day	32.75	32.75
93-05-004	Elvis in Blue Hawaii	B. Emmett	150-day	32.75	32.75
93-05-005	Elvis in Jailhouse Rock	B. Emmett	150-day	32.75	32.75
93-05-006	Elvis in Spinout	B. Emmett	150-day	34.75	34.75
93-05-007	Elvis in Speedway	B. Emmett	150-day	34.75	34.75

		ARTIST	EDITION	ISSUE	QUOTE
93-05-008	Elvis in Harum Scarum	B. Emmett	150-day	34.75	34.75
Delphi		**Dream Machines**			
88-06-001	'56 T-Bird	P. Palma	150-day	24.75	42-49.00
88-06-002	'57 'Vette	P. Palma	150-day	24.75	30.00
89-06-003	'58 Biarritz	P. Palma	150-day	27.75	28.00
89-06-004	'56 Continental	P. Palma	150-day	27.75	28.00
89-06-005	'57 Bel Air	P. Palma	150-day	27.75	29-49.00
89-06-006	'57 Chrysler 300C	P. Palma	150-day	27.75	28-35.00
Delphi		**Indiana Jones**			
89-07-001	Indiana Jones	V. Gadino	150-day	24.75	25-35.00
89-07-002	Indiana Jones and His Dad	V. Gadino	150-day	24.75	45.00
90-07-003	Indiana Jones/Dr. Schneider	V. Gadino	150-day	27.75	40-45.00
90-07-004	A Family Discussion	V. Gadino	150-day	27.75	55-65.00
90-07-005	Young Indiana Jones	V. Gadino	150-day	27.75	60-65.00
91-07-006	Indiana Jones/The Holy Grail	V. Gadino	150-day	27.75	60-65.00
Delphi		**The Marilyn Monroe Collection**			
89-08-001	Marilyn Monroe/7 Year Itch	C. Notarile	150-day	24.75	80-99.00
90-08-002	Diamonds/Girls Best Friend	C. Notarile	150-day	24.75	91-99.00
91-08-003	Marilyn Monroe/River of No Return	C. Notarile	150-day	27.75	54-75.00
92-08-004	How to Marry a Millionaire	C. Notarile	150-day	27.75	50-75.00
92-08-005	There's No Business/Show Business	C. Notarile	150-day	27.75	65-125.
92-08-006	Marilyn Monroe in Niagra	C. Notarile	150-day	29.75	60-75.00
92-08-007	My Heart Belongs to Daddy	C. Notarile	150-day	29.75	45-59.00
92-08-008	Marilyn Monroe as Cherie in Bus Stop	C. Notarile	150-day	29.75	40-59.00
92-08-009	Marilyn Monroe in All About Eve	C. Notarile	150-day	29.75	39-59.00
92-08-010	Marilyn Monroe in Monkey Business	C. Notarile	150-day	31.75	54-59.00
92-08-011	Marilyn Monroe in Don't Bother to Knock	C. Notarile	150-day	31.75	40-55.00
92-08-012	Marilyn Monroe in We're Not Married	C. Notarile	150-day	31.75	69.00
Delphi		**The Magic of Marilyn**			
92-09-001	For Our Boys in Korea, 1954	C. Notarile	150-day	24.75	24.75
92-09-002	Opening Night	C. Notarile	150-day	24.75	24.75
93-09-003	Rising Star	C. Notarile	150-day	27.75	27.75
92-09-004	Stopping Traffic	C. Notarile	150-day	27.75	27.75
92-09-005	Strasberg's Class	C. Notarile	150-day	27.75	27.75
93-09-006	Photo Opportunity	C. Notarile	150-day	29.75	29.75
93-09-007	Shining Star	C. Notarile	150-day	29.75	29.75
93-09-008	Curtain Call	C. Notarile	150-day	29.75	29.75
Delphi		**The Beatles Collection**			
91-10-001	The Beatles, Live In Concert	N. Giorgio	150-day	24.75	55.00
91-10-002	Hello America	N. Giorgio	150-day	24.75	49.00
91-10-003	A Hard Day's Night	N. Giorgio	150-day	27.75	45.00
92-10-004	Beatles '65	N. Giorgio	150-day	27.75	27.75
92-10-005	Help	N. Giorgio	150-day	27.75	27.75
92-10-006	The Beatles at Shea Stadium	N. Giorgio	150-day	29.75	29.75
92-10-007	Rubber Soul	N. Giorgio	150-day	29.75	29.75
92-10-008	Yesterday and Today	N. Giorgio	150-day	29.75	29.75
Delphi		**The Beatles '67-'70**			
92-11-001	Sgt. Pepper the 25th Anniversary	D. Sivavec	150-day	27.75	27.75
92-11-002	All You Need is Love	D. Sivavec	150-day	27.75	27.75
93-11-003	Magical Mystery Tour	D. Sivavec	150-day	30.75	30.75
93-11-004	Hey Jude	D. Sivavec	150-day	30.75	30.75
93-11-005	Abbey Road	D. Sivavec	150-day	30.75	30.75
93-11-006	Let It Be	D. Sivavec	150-day	30.75	30.75
Delphi		**Legends of Baseball**			
92-12-001	Babe Ruth: The Called Shot	B. Benger	150-day	24.95	24.95
92-12-002	Lou Gehrig: The Luckiest Man	J. Barson	150-day	24.75	24.75
93-12-003	Ty Cobb: The Georgia Peach	J. Barson	150-day	27.95	27.95
93-12-004	Cy Young: The Perfect Game	J. Barson	150-day	27.75	27.75
93-12-005	Roger Hornsby: .424 Season	J. Barson	150-day	27.75	27.75
93-12-006	Honus Wagner: Flying Dutchman	J. Barson	150-day	29.75	29.75
93-12-007	Jimmie Fox: The Beast	J. Barson	150-day	29.75	29.75
93-12-008	Walter Johnson: The Shutout	J. Barson	150-day	29.75	29.75
93-12-009	Tris Speaker: The Gray Eagle	J. Barson	150-day	29.75	29.75
Delphi		**Commemorating The King**			
93-13-001	The Rock and Roll Legend	M. Stutzman	95-day	29.75	69.00
93-13-002	Las Vegas, Live	M. Stutzman	95-day	29.75	29.75
93-13-003	Blues and Black Leather	M. Stutzman	95-day	29.75	29.75
93-13-004	Private Presley	M. Stutzman	95-day	29.75	29.75
93-13-005	Golden Boy	M. Stutzman	95-day	29.75	29.75
93-13-006	Screen Idol	M. Stutzman	95-day	29.75	29.75
Delphi		**Take Me Out To The Ballgame**			
93-14-001	Wrigley Field: The Friendly Confines	D. Henderson	95-day	29.75	29.75
93-14-002	Yankee Stadium: House that Ruth Built	D. Henderson	95-day	29.75	29.75
93-14-003	Fenway Park: Home of the Green Monster	D. Henderson	95-day	32.75	32.75
93-14-004	Briggs Stadium: Home of the Tigers	D. Henderson	95-day	32.75	32.75
93-14-005	Comiskey Park: Home of the White Sox	D. Henderson	95-day	32.75	32.75
94-14-006	Cleveland Stadium: Home of the Indians	D. Henderson	95-day	34.75	34.75
Delphi		**Fabulous Cars of the '50's**			
93-15-001	'57 Red Corvette	G. Angelini	95-day	24.75	24.75
93-15-002	'57 White T-Bird	G. Angelini	95-day	24.75	24.75
93-15-003	'57 Blue Belair	G. Angelini	95-day	27.75	27.75
93-15-004	'59 Cadillac	G. Angelini	95-day	27.75	27.75
93-15-005	'56 Lincoln Premier	G. Angelini	95-day	27.75	27.75
Delphi		**In the Footsteps of the King**			
93-16-001	Graceland: Memphis, Tenn.	D. Sivavec	95-day	27.75	27.75
Department 56		**Dickens' Village**			
87-01-001	Dickens' Village Porcelain Plates, 5917-0 Set of 4	Department 56	Closed	140.00	220.00
Department 56		**A Christmas Carol**			
91-02-001	The Cratchit's Christmas Pudding, 5706-1	R. Innocenti	18,000	60.00	71-82.00
92-02-002	Marley's Ghost Appears To Scrooge, 5721-5	R. Innocenti	18,000	60.00	60.00
93-02-003	The Spirit of Christmas Present, 5722-3	R. Innocenti	18,000	60.00	60.00
94-02-004	Visions of Christmas Past 5723-1	R. Innocenti	18,000	60.00	60.00
Duncan Royale		**History of Santa Claus I**			
85-01-001	Medieval	S. Morton	Retrd.	40.00	50.00
85-01-002	Kris Kringle	S. Morton	Retrd.	40.00	65.00
85-01-003	Pioneer	S. Morton	10,000	40.00	40.00
86-01-004	Russian	S. Morton	Retrd.	40.00	40.00
86-01-005	Soda Pop	S. Morton	Retrd.	40.00	65.00
86-01-006	Civil War	S. Morton	10,000	40.00	40.00
86-01-007	Nast	S. Morton	Retrd.	40.00	75.00

	ARTIST	EDITION	ISSUE	QUOTE
87-01-008 St. Nicholas	S. Morton	Retrd.	40.00	75.00
87-01-009 Dedt Moroz	S. Morton	10,000	40.00	40.00
87-01-010 Black Peter	S. Morton	10,000	40.00	40.00
87-01-011 Victorian	S. Morton	Retrd.	40.00	40.00
87-01-012 Wassail	S. Morton	Retrd.	40.00	40.00
XX-01-013 Collection of 12 Plates	S. Morton	Retrd.	480.00	480.00
Enchantica	**Retired Enchantica Collection**			
92-01-001 Winter Dragon-Grawlfang-2200	J. Woodward	Retrd.	50.00	60.00
92-01-002 Spring Dragon-Gorgoyle-2201	J. Woodward	Retrd.	50.00	60.00
93-01-003 Summer Dragon-Arangast-2202	J. Woodward	Retrd.	50.00	60.00
93-01-004 Autumn Dragon-Snarlgard-2203	J. Woodward	Retrd.	50.00	60.00
Enesco Corporation	**Precious Moments Inspired Thoughts**			
85-01-001 Love One Another-E-5215	S. Butcher	15,000	40.00	66.00
82-01-002 Make a Joyful Noise-E-7174	S. Butcher	15,000	40.00	40-55.00
83-01-003 I Believe In Miracles-E-9257	S. Butcher	15,000	40.00	45.00
84-01-004 Love is Kind-E-2847	S. Butcher	15,000	40.00	48.00
Enesco Corporation	**Precious Moments Mother's Love**			
81-02-001 Mother Sew Dear-E-5217	S. Butcher	15,000	40.00	72.00
82-02-002 The Purr-fect Grandma-E-7173	S. Butcher	15,000	40.00	48.00
83-02-003 The Hand that Rocks the Future-E-9256	S. Butcher	15,000	40.00	48.00
84-02-004 Loving Thy Neighbor-E-2848	S. Butcher	15,000	40.00	40-48.00
Enesco Corporation	**Precious Moments Christmas Collection**			
81-03-001 Come Let Us Adore Him-E-5646	S. Butcher	15,000	40.00	48-65.00
82-03-002 Let Heaven and Nature Sing-E-2347	S. Butcher	15,000	40.00	45-49.00
83-03-003 Wee Three Kings-E-0538	S. Butcher	15,000	40.00	50.00
84-03-004 Unto Us a Child Is Born-E-5395	S. Butcher	15,000	40.00	40-45.00
Enesco Corporation	**Precious Moments Joy of Christmas**			
82-04-001 I'll Play My Drum For Him-E-2357	S. Butcher	Yr.Iss.	40.00	90-93.00
83-04-002 Christmastime is for Sharing-E-0505	S. Butcher	Yr.Iss.	40.00	95-110.
84-04-003 The Wonder of Christmas-E-5396	S. Butcher	Yr.Iss.	40.00	84.00
85-04-004 Tell Me the Story of Jesus-15237	S. Butcher	Yr.Iss.	40.00	90-105.
Enesco Corporation	**Precious Moments The Four Seasons**			
85-05-001 The Voice of Spring-12106	S. Butcher	Yr.Iss.	40.00	87.00
85-05-002 Summer's Joy-12114	S. Butcher	Yr.Iss.	40.00	80.00
86-05-003 Autumn's Praise-12122	S. Butcher	Yr.Iss.	40.00	53.00
86-05-004 Winter's Song-12130	S. Butcher	Yr.Iss.	40.00	58.00
Enesco Corporation	**Precious Moments Open Editions**			
82-06-001 Our First Christmas Together-E-2378	S. Butcher	Suspd.	30.00	45-55.00
81-06-002 The Lord Bless You and Keep You-E-5216	S. Butcher	Suspd.	30.00	40-45.00
82-06-003 Rejoicing with You-E-7172	S. Butcher	Suspd.	30.00	40.00
83-06-004 Jesus Loves Me-E-9275	S. Butcher	Suspd.	30.00	45-48.00
83-06-005 Jesus Loves Me-E-9276	S. Butcher	Suspd.	30.00	45-48.00
94-06-006 Bring The Little Ones To Jesus-531359	S. Butcher	Yr.Iss.	50.00	50.00
Enesco Corporation	**Precious Moments Christmas Love**			
86-07-001 I'm Sending You a White Christmas-101834	S. Butcher	Yr.Iss.	45.00	48-76.50
87-07-002 My Peace I Give Unto Thee-102954	S. Butcher	Yr.Iss.	45.00	90.00
88-07-003 Merry Christmas Deer-520284	S. Butcher	Yr.Iss.	50.00	80.00
89-07-004 May Your Christmas Be A Happy Home-523003	S. Butcher	Yr.Iss.	50.00	50-75.00
Enesco Corporation	**Precious Moments Christmas Blessings**			
90-08-001 Wishing You A Yummy Christmas-523801	S. Butcher	Yr.Iss.	50.00	70.00
91-08-002 Blessings From Me To Thee-523860	S. Butcher	Yr.Iss.	50.00	60.00
92-08-003 But The Greatest of These Is Love-527742	S. Butcher	Yr.Iss.	50.00	50.00
93-08-004 Wishing You the Sweetest Christmas-530204	S. Butcher	Yr.Iss.	50.00	50.00
Enesco Corporation	**Precious Moments Mother's Day**			
93-09-001 Thinking of You is What I Really Like to Do-531766	S. Butcher	Yr.Iss.	50.00	50.00
Enesco Corporation	**Memories of Yesterday Dated Plate Series**			
93-10-001 Look Out-Something Good Is Coming Your Way!-530298	S. Butcher	Yr.Iss.	50.00	50.00
94-10-002 Pleasant Dreams and Sweet Repose-528102	M. Atwell	Yr.Iss.	50.00	50.00
Ernst Enterprises/Porter & Price, Inc.	**Women of the West**			
79-01-001 Expectations	D. Putnam	Retrd.	39.50	39.50
81-01-002 Silver Dollar Sal	D. Putnam	Retrd.	39.50	45.00
82-01-003 School Marm	D. Putnam	Retrd.	39.50	39.50
83-01-004 Dolly	D. Putnam	Retrd.	39.50	39.50
Ernst Enterprises/Porter & Price, Inc.	**A Beautiful World**			
81-02-001 Tahitian Dreamer	S. Morton	Retrd.	27.50	30.00
82-02-002 Flirtation	S. Morton	Retrd.	27.50	27.50
84-02-003 Elke of Oslo	S. Morton	Retrd.	27.50	27.50
Ernst Enterprises/Porter & Price, Inc.	**Seems Like Yesterday**			
81-03-001 Stop & Smell the Roses	R. Money	Retrd.	24.50	24.50
82-03-002 Home by Lunch	R. Money	Retrd.	24.50	24.50
82-03-003 Lisa's Creek	R. Money	Retrd.	24.50	24.50
83-03-004 It's Got My Name on It	R. Money	Retrd.	24.50	24.50
83-03-005 My Magic Hat	R. Money	Retrd.	24.50	24.50
84-03-006 Little Prince	R. Money	Retrd.	24.50	24.50
Ernst Enterprises/Porter & Price, Inc.	**Turn of The Century**			
81-04-001 Riverboat Honeymoon	R. Money	Retrd.	35.00	35.00
82-04-002 Children's Carousel	R. Money	Retrd.	35.00	37.50
84-04-003 Flower Market	R. Money	Retrd.	35.00	35.00
85-04-004 Balloon Race	R. Money	Retrd.	35.00	35.00
Ernst Enterprises/Porter & Price, Inc.	**Hollywood Greats**			
81-05-001 John Wayne	S. Morton	Retrd.	29.95	50-165.
81-05-002 Gary Cooper	S. Morton	Retrd.	29.95	32.50
82-05-003 Clark Gable	S. Morton	Retrd.	29.95	65-85.00
84-05-004 Alan Ladd	S. Morton	Retrd.	29.95	95.00
Ernst Enterprises/Porter & Price, Inc.	**Commemoratives**			
81-06-001 John Lennon	S. Morton	Retrd.	39.50	155.00
82-06-002 Elvis Presley	S. Morton	Retrd.	39.50	148-150.
82-06-003 Marilyn Monroe	S. Morton	Retrd.	39.50	75.00
83-06-004 Judy Garland	S. Morton	Retrd.	39.50	95.00
84-06-005 John Wayne	S. Morton	Retrd.	39.50	75.00
Ernst Enterprises/Porter & Price, Inc.	**Classy Cars**			
82-07-001 The 26T	S. Kuhnly	Retrd.	24.50	32.00
82-07-002 The 31A	S. Kuhnly	Retrd.	24.50	30.00
83-07-003 The Pickup	S. Kuhnly	Retrd.	24.50	27.50
84-07-004 Panel Van	S. Kuhnly	Retrd.	24.50	35.00
Ernst Enterprises/Porter & Price, Inc.	**Star Trek**			
84-08-001 Mr. Spock	S. Morton	Retrd.	29.50	150-199.
85-08-002 Dr. McCoy	S. Morton	Retrd.	29.50	45-99.00
85-08-003 Sulu	S. Morton	Retrd.	29.50	54-80.00
85-08-004 Scotty	S. Morton	Retrd.	29.50	54-80.00
85-08-005 Uhura	S. Morton	Retrd.	29.50	50.00
85-08-006 Chekov	S. Morton	Retrd.	29.50	50.00
85-08-007 Captain Kirk	S. Morton	Retrd.	29.50	50-150.
85-08-008 Beam Us Down Scotty	S. Morton	Retrd.	29.50	75-100.
85-08-009 The Enterprise	S. Morton	Retrd.	39.50	60-150.
Ernst Enterprises/Porter & Price, Inc.	**Star Trek: Commemorative Collection**			
87-09-001 The Trouble With Tribbles	S. Morton	Retrd.	29.50	75-150.
87-09-002 Mirror, Mirror	S. Morton	Retrd.	29.50	175.00
87-09-003 A Piece of the Action	S. Morton	Retrd.	29.50	75-149.
87-09-004 The Devil in the Dark	S. Morton	Retrd.	29.50	75-135.
87-09-005 Amok Time	S. Morton	Retrd.	29.50	75-135.
87-09-006 The City on the Edge of Forever	S. Morton	Retrd.	29.50	165-250.
87-09-007 Journey to Babel	S. Morton	Retrd.	29.50	112-175.
87-09-008 The Menagerie	S. Morton	Retrd.	29.50	75-179.
Ernst Enterprises/Porter & Price, Inc.	**Elvira**			
88-10-001 Night Rose	S. Morton	90-day	29.50	29.50
88-10-002 Red Velvet	S. Morton	90-day	29.50	29.50
88-10-003 Mistress of the Dark	S. Morton	90-day	29.50	29.50
Ernst Enterprises/Porter & Price, Inc.	**The Republic Pictures Library**			
91-11-001 Showdown With Laredo	S. Morton	28-day	37.50	37.50
91-11-002 The Ride Home	S. Morton	28-day	37.50	37.50
91-11-003 Attack at Tarawa	S. Morton	28-day	37.50	37.50
91-11-003 Thoughts of Angelique	S. Morton	28-day	37.50	37.50
92-11-004 War of the Wildcats	S. Morton	28-day	37.50	37.50
92-11-005 The Fighting Seabees	S. Morton	28-day	37.50	37.50
92-11-006 The Quiet Man	S. Morton	28-day	37.50	37.50
92-11-007 Angel and the Badman	S. Morton	28-day	37.50	37.50
93-11-008 Sands of Iwo Jima	S. Morton	28-day	37.50	37.50
93-11-009 Flying Tigers	S. Morton	28-day	37.50	37.50
93-11-010 The Tribute (12")	S. Morton	28-day	97.50	97.50
94-11-011 The Tribute (8¼")	S. Morton	9,500	29.50	29.50
Ernst Enterprises/Porter & Price, Inc.	**Hollywood, Walk of Fame**			
89-12-001 Jimmy Stewart	S. Morton	Retrd.	39.50	39.50
89-12-002 Elizabeth Taylor	S. Morton	Retrd.	39.50	39.50
89-12-003 Tom Selleck	S. Morton	Retrd.	39.50	39.50
89-12-004 Joan Collins	S. Morton	Retrd.	39.50	39.50
90-12-005 Burt Reynolds	S. Morton	Retrd.	39.50	39.50
90-12-006 Sylvester Stallone	S. Morton	Retrd.	39.50	39.50
Ernst Enterprises/Porter & Price, Inc.	**Elvis Presley**			
87-13-001 The King	S. Morton	Retrd.	39.50	39.50
87-13-002 Loving You	S. Morton	Retrd.	39.50	39.50
87-13-003 Early Years	S. Morton	Retrd.	39.50	39.50
87-13-004 Tenderly	S. Morton	Retrd.	39.50	39.50
88-13-005 Forever Yours	S. Morton	Retrd.	39.50	39.50
88-13-006 Rockin in the Moonlight	S. Morton	Retrd.	39.50	39.50
88-13-007 Moody Blues	S. Morton	Retrd.	39.50	39.50
88-13-008 Elvis Presley	S. Morton	Retrd.	39.50	39.50
89-13-009 Elvis Presley-Special Request	S. Morton	Retrd.	150.00	150.00
Fairmont	**Spencer Special**			
78-01-001 Hug Me	I. Spencer	10,000	55.00	150.00
78-01-002 Sleep Little Baby	I. Spencer	10,000	65.00	125.00
Fairmont	**Famous Clowns**			
76-02-001 Freddie the Freeloader	R. Skelton	10,000	55.00	475-525.
77-02-002 W. C. Fields	R. Skelton	10,000	55.00	85-95.00
78-02-003 Happy	R. Skelton	10,000	55.00	80-95.00
79-02-004 The Pledge	R. Skelton	10,000	55.00	80.00
Fenton Art Glass	**American Craftsman Carnival**			
70-01-001 Glassmaker	Unknown	600	10.00	140.00
70-01-002 Glassmaker	Unknown	200	10.00	220.00
70-01-003 Glassmaker	Unknown	Annual	10.00	68.00
71-01-004 Printer	Unknown	Annual	10.00	80.00
72-01-005 Blacksmith	Unknown	Annual	10.00	150.00
73-01-006 Shoemaker	Unknown	Annual	12.50	70.00
74-01-007 Cooper	Unknown	Annual	12.50	55.00
75-01-008 Silversmith Revere	Unknown	Annual	12.50	60.00
76-01-009 Gunsmith	Unknown	Annual	15.00	45.00
77-01-010 Potter	Unknown	Annual	15.00	35.00
78-01-011 Wheelwright	Unknown	Annual	15.00	25.00
79-01-012 Cabinetmaker	Unknown	Annual	15.00	23.00
80-01-013 Tanner	Unknown	Annual	16.50	20.00
81-01-014 Housewright	Unknown	Annual	17.50	17.50
Fenton Art Glass	**Christmas Star**			
94-02-001 Silent Night	F. Burton	1,500	65.00	65.00
Fenton Art Glass	**Handpainted Mother's Day Series**			
80-03-001 New Born	Fenton	Closed	28.50	28.50
81-03-002 Gentle Fawn	Fenton	Closed	32.50	32.50
82-03-003 Natures Awakening	Fenton	Closed	35.00	35.00
83-03-004 Where's Mom	Fenton	Closed	35.00	35.00
84-03-005 Precious Panda	Fenton	Closed	35.00	35.00
85-03-006 Mother's Little Lamb	Fenton	Closed	35.00	35.00
90-03-007 White Swan	M. Reynolds	Closed	45.00	45.00
91-03-008 Mother's Watchful Eye	M. Reynolds	Closed	45.00	45.00
92-03-009 Let's Play With Mom	M. Reynolds	Closed	49.50	49.50
93-03-010 Mother Deer	M. Reynolds	Closed	49.50	49.50
94-03-011 Loving Puppy	M. Reynolds	Closed	49.50	49.50
Fitz and Floyd, Inc.	**Annual Christmas Plate**			
92-01-001 Nutcracker Sweets "The Magic of the Nutcracker"	R. Havins	Closed	65.00	65.00
93-01-002 A Dickens Christmas	T. Kerr	5,000	75.00	75.00
94-01-003 Night Before Christmas	T. Kerr	7,500	75.00	75.00
Fitz and Floyd, Inc.	**Wonderland**			
93-02-001 A Mad Tea Party	R. Havins	5,000	70.00	70.00
Fitz and Floyd, Inc.	**The Twelve Days of Christmas**			
93-03-001 Twelve Days of Christmas	R. Havins	5,000	75.00	75.00
Fitz and Floyd, Inc.	**The Myth of Santa Claus**			
93-04-001 Father Frost	R. Havins	5,000	70.00	70.00

	ARTIST	EDITION	ISSUE	QUOTE
94-04-002 Candyland Santa	R. Havins	5,000	75.00	75.00
Flambro Imports	**Emmett Kelly, Jr. Plates**			
83-01-001 Why Me? Plate I	C. Kelly	10,000	40.00	450.00
84-01-002 Balloons For Sale Plate II	C. Kelly	10,000	40.00	350.00
85-01-003 Big Business Plate III	C. Kelly	10,000	40.00	350.00
86-01-004 And God Bless America IV	C. Kelly	10,000	40.00	325.00
88-01-005 Tis the Season	D. Rust	10,000	50.00	75.00
89-01-006 Looking Back- 65th Birthday	D. Rust	6,500	50.00	125.00
91-01-007 Winter	D. Rust	10,000	60.00	45-60.00
92-01-008 Spring	D. Rust	10,000	60.00	45-60.00
92-01-009 Summer	D. Rust	10,000	60.00	45-60.00
92-01-010 Autumn	D. Rust	10,000	60.00	45-60.00
93-01-011 Santa's Stowaway	D. Rust	10,000	30.00	30.00
94-01-012 70th Birthday Commemorative	D. Rust	5,000	30.00	30.00
Fountainhead	**The Wings of Freedom**			
85-01-001 Courtship Flight	M. Fernandez	2,500	250.00	2400.00
86-01-002 Wings of Freedom	M. Fernandez	2,500	250.00	1100.00
Fountainhead	**As Free As The Wind**			
89-02-001 As Free As The Wind	M. Fernandez	Unkn.	295.00	300-600.
Gartlan USA	**Pete Rose Platinum Edition**			
85-01-001 Pete Rose "The Best of Baseball"(3 1/4")	T. Sizemore	Open	12.95	15-20.00
85-01-002 Pete Rose "The Best of Baseball"(10 1/4")	T. Sizemore	4,192	100.00	325-450.
85-01-003 Pete Rose "The Best of Baseball"(10 1/4"), (signed & dated)	T. Sizemore	50	100.00	675.00
Gartlan USA	**The Round Tripper**			
86-02-001 Reggie Jackson (3 1/4" diameter)	J. Martin	Open	12.95	15-20.00
Gartlan USA	**George Brett Gold Crown Collection**			
86-03-001 George Brett "Baseball's All Star" (3 1/4")	J. Martin	Open	12.95	15-20.00
86-03-002 George Brett "Baseball's All Star" (10 1/4"),signed	J. Martin	2,000	100.00	200.00
Gartlan USA	**Roger Staubach Sterling Collection**			
87-04-001 Roger Staubach (3 1/4" diameter)	C. Soileau	Open	12.95	15-20.00
87-04-002 Roger Staubach (10 1/4" diameter) signed	C. Soileau	1,979	100.00	125-195.
Gartlan USA	**Magic Johnson Gold Rim Collection**			
87-05-001 Magic Johnson "The Magic Show" (10 1/4"), signed	R. Winslow	1,987	100.00	400-500.
87-05-002 Magic Johnson "The Magic Show" (3 1/4")	R. Winslow	Closed	14.50	25-35.00
Gartlan USA	**Mike Schmidt "500th" Home Run Edition**			
87-06-001 Mike Schmidt "Power at the Plate" (10 1/4"), signed	C. Paluso	1,987	100.00	395.00
87-06-002 Mike Schmidt "Power at the Plate" (3 1/4")	C. Paluso	Open	14.50	19.00
87-06-003 Mike Schmidt Artist Proof	C. Paluso	56	150.00	150.00
87-06-004 Mike Schmidt (signed & dated)	C. Paluso	50	100.00	595.00
Gartlan USA	**Pete Rose Diamond Collection**			
88-07-001 Pete Rose "The Reigning Legend" (10 1/4"), signed	Forbes	950	195.00	275-295.
88-07-002 Pete Rose "The Reigning Legend" (10 1/4"), signed Artist Proof	Forbes	50	300.00	395.00
88-07-003 Pete Rose "The Reigning Legend"(3 1/4")	Forbes	Open	14.50	15-19.00
Gartlan USA	**Kareem Abdul-Jabbar Sky-Hook Collection**			
89-08-001 Kareem Abdul-Jabbar "Path of Glory" (10 1/4"), signed	M. Taylor	1,989	100.00	195-225.
89-08-002 Collector plate (3 1/4")	M. Taylor	Closed	16.00	30.00
Gartlan USA	**Johnny Bench**			
89-09-001 Collector Plate (10 1/4") signed	M. Taylor	1,989	100.00	200.00
89-09-002 Collector Plate (3 1/4")	M. Taylor	Open	15-16.00	15-19.00
Gartlan USA	**Coaching Classics-John Wooden**			
89-10-001 Collector Plate (10 1/4") signed	M. Taylor	1,975	100.00	100.00
89-10-002 Collector Plate (8 1/2")	M. Taylor	10,000	30-45.00	30-45.00
89-10-003 Collector Plate (3 1/4")	M. Taylor	Open	15-16.00	15-19.00
Gartlan USA	**Wayne Gretzky**			
89-11-001 Collector Plate (10 1/4"), signed by Gretzky and Howe	M. Taylor	1,851	225.00	275-300.
89-11-002 Collector Plate (10 1/4") Artist Proof, signed by Gretzky and Howe	M. Taylor	300	300.00	425.00
89-11-003 Collector Plate (8 1/2")	M. Taylor	10,000	45.00	45-50.00
89-11-004 Collector Plate (3 1/4")	M. Taylor	Open	15-16.00	15-20.00
Gartlan USA	**Yogi Berra**			
89-12-001 Collector Plate (10 1/4") signed	M. Taylor	2,150	100-125.	100-150.
89-12-002 Collector Plate (10 1/4") signed Artist Proof	M. Taylor	250	175.00	175.00
89-12-003 Collector Plate (3 1/4")	M. Taylor	Open	15-16.00	20.00
89-12-004 Collector Plate (8 1/2")	M. Taylor	10,000	30-45.00	30-45.00
Gartlan USA	**Whitey Ford**			
90-13-001 Signed Plate (10 1/4")	M. Taylor	2,360	70-125.	70-150.
90-13-002 Signed Plate (10 1/4") Artist Proof	M. Taylor	250	175.00	175.00
90-13-003 Plate (8 1/2")	M. Taylor	10,000	30-45.00	30-45.00
90-13-004 Plate (3 1/4")	M. Taylor	Open	15-16.00	15-20.00
Gartlan USA	**Darryl Strawberry**			
90-14-001 Signed Plate (10 1/4")	M. Taylor	2,500	70-125.	70-125.
90-14-002 Plate (8 1/2")	M. Taylor	10,000	30-45.00	30-45.00
90-14-003 Plate (3 1/4")	M. Taylor	Open	15-16.00	15-20.00
Gartlan USA	**Luis Aparicio**			
90-15-001 Signed Plate (10 1/4")	M. Taylor	1,984	70-125.	70-125.
90-15-002 Signed Plate (10 1/4") Artist Proof	M. Taylor	250	150.00	150.00
90-15-003 Plate (8 1/2")	M. Taylor	10,000	30-45.00	30-45.00
90-15-004 Plate (3 1/4")	M. Taylor	Open	15-16.00	15-20.00
Gartlan USA	**Rod Carew**			
91-16-001 Hitting For The Hall(10 1/4") signed	M. Taylor	950	70-150.	70-150
91-16-002 Hitting For The Hall(8 1/2")	M. Taylor	10,000	30-45.00	30-45.00
91-16-003 Hitting For The Hall(3 1/4")	M. Taylor	Open	15-16.00	15-20.00
Gartlan USA	**Brett & Bobby Hull**			
91-17-001 Hockey's Golden Boys (10 1/4") signed	M. Taylor	950	250.00	250.00
92-17-002 Plate Artist Proof	M. Taylor	300	350.00	350.00
91-17-003 Hockey's Golden Boys (8 1/2")	M. Taylor	10,000	30-45.00	30-45.00
91-17-004 Hockey's Golden Boys (3 1/4")	M. Taylor	Open	15-16.00	15-20.00
Gartlan USA	**Joe Montana**			
91-18-001 Signed Plate (10 1/4")	M. Taylor	2,250	125.00	125.00
91-18-002 Signed Plate (10 1/4") Artist Proof	M. Taylor	250	195.00	195.00

	ARTIST	EDITION	ISSUE	QUOTE
91-18-003 Plate (8 1/2")	M. Taylor	10,000	30-45.00	30-45.00
91-18-004 Plate (3 1/4")	M. Taylor	Open	15-16.00	15-20.00
Gartlan USA	**Al Barlick**			
91-19-001 Plate (3 1/4")	M. Taylor	Open	15-16.00	15-19.00
Gartlan USA	**Carlton Fisk**			
92-20-001 Signed Plate (10 1/4")	M. Taylor	950	70-150.	70-150.
92-20-002 Signed Plate (10 1/4") Artist Proof	M. Taylor	300	175.00	225.00
92-20-003 Plate (8 1/2")	M. Taylor	10,000	30-45.00	30-45.00
92-20-004 Plate (3 1/4")	M. Taylor	Open	15-19.00	15-19.00
Gartlan USA	**Ken Griffey Jr.**			
92-21-001 Signed Plate (10 1/4")	M. Taylor	1,989	100-125.	100-125.
92-21-002 Signed Plate (10 1/2") Artist Proof	M. Taylor	300	195.00	195.00
92-21-003 Plate (8 1/2")	M. Taylor	10,000	30-45.00	30-45.00
92-21-004 Plate (3 1/4")	M. Taylor	Open	15-19.00	15-19.00
Gartlan USA	**Phil Esposito**			
92-22-001 Signed Plate (10 1/4")	M. Taylor	1,984	150.00	150.00
92-22-002 Signed Plate (10 1/2") Artist Proof	M. Taylor	300	195.00	195.00
92-22-003 Plate (8 1/2")	M. Taylor	10,000	30-45.00	30-45.00
92-22-004 Plate (3 1/4")	M. Taylor	Open	15-19.00	15-19.00
Gartlan USA	**Tom Seaver**			
92-23-001 Signed Plate (10 1/4")	M. Taylor	1,992	90-150.	90-150.
92-23-002 Signed Plate (10 1/4") Artist Proof	M. Taylor	250	195.00	195.00
92-23-003 Signed Plate (8 1/2")	M. Taylor	10,000	30-45.00	30-45.00
92-23-004 Signed Plate (3 1/4")	M. Taylor	Open	15-19.00	15-19.00
Gartlan USA	**Gordie Howe**			
92-24-001 Signed Plate (10 1/4")	M. Taylor	2,358	90-150.	90-150.
92-24-002 Signed Plate (10 1/4") Artist Proof	M. Taylor	250	150-195.	150-195.
92-24-003 Signed Plate (8 1/2")	M. Taylor	10,000	30-45.00	30-45.00
92-24-004 Signed Plate (3 1/4")	M. Taylor	Open	15-19.00	15-19.00
Gartlan USA	**Carl Yastrzemski-The Impossible Dream**			
93-25-001 Signed Plate (10 1/4")	M. Taylor	950	150-175.	150-175.
93-25-002 Plate (8 1/2")	M. Taylor	10,000	30-49.00	30-49.00
93-25-003 Plate (3 1/4")	M. Taylor	Open	15-19.00	15-19.00
Gartlan USA	**Bob Cousy**			
93-26-001 Signed Plate (10 1/4")	M. Taylor	950	100-150.	100-150.
93-26-002 Plate (8 1/2")	M. Taylor	5,000	30-49.00	30-49.00
93-26-003 Plate (3 1/4")	M. Taylor	Open	15-19.00	15-19.00
Gartlan USA	**Sam Sneed**			
93-27-001 Signed Plate (10 1/4")	M. Taylor	950	100-175.	100-175.
93-27-002 Plate (8 1/2")	M. Taylor	5,000	30-49.00	30-49.00
93-27-003 Plate (3 1/4")	M. Taylor	Open	15-19.00	15-19.00
Gartlan USA	**Kristi Yamaguchi**			
93-28-001 Signed Plate (10 1/4")	M. Taylor	950	100-150.	100-150.
93-28-002 Plate (8 1/2")	M. Taylor	5,000	30-49.00	30-49.00
93-28-003 Plate (3 1/4")	M. Taylor	Open	15-19.00	15-19.00
Gartlan USA	**Shaquille O'Neal**			
94-29-001 Signed Plate (10 1/4")	M. Taylor	1,993	195.00	195.00
94-29-002 Plate (8 1/2")	M. Taylor	10,000	30-49.00	30-49.00
94-29-003 Plate (3 1/4")	M. Taylor	Open	14.95	14.95
Gartlan USA	**Troy Aikman**			
94-30-001 Signed Plate (10 1/4")	M. Taylor	1,993	150.00	150.00
94-30-002 Plate (8 1/2")	M. Taylor	10,000	30-49.00	30-49.00
94-30-003 Plate (3 1/4")	M. Taylor	Open	14.95	14.95
Gartlan USA	**Frank Thomas**			
94-31-001 Signed Plate (10 1/4")	M. Taylor	1,994	150.00	150.00
94-31-002 Plate (8 1/2")	M. Taylor	10,000	29.95	29.95
94-31-003 Plate (3 1/4")	M. Taylor	Open	14.95	14.95
Gartlan USA	**Patrick Ewing**			
95-32-001 Signed Plate (10 1/4")	M. Taylor	950	150.00	150.00
95-32-002 Plate (8 1/2")	M. Taylor	10,000	29.95	29.95
95-32-003 Plate (3 1/4")	M. Taylor	Open	14.95	14.95
Gartlan USA	**Dale Earnhardt**			
95-33-001 Signed Plate (10 1/4")	M. Taylor	1,994	150.00	150.00
95-33-002 Plate (8 1/2")	M. Taylor	10,000	29.95	29.95
95-33-003 Plate (3 1/4")	M. Taylor	Open	14.95	14.95
Gartlan USA	**Joe Montana**			
94-34-001 Plate (8 1/2") (K.C. Chiefs)	M. Taylor	10,000	29.95	29.95
94-34-002 Plate (3 1/4") (K.C. Chiefs)	M. Taylor	Open	14.95	14.95
W.S. George	**Gone With the Wind: Golden Anniversary**			
88-01-001 Scarlett and Her Suitors	H. Rogers	150-day	24.50	60-89.00
88-01-002 The Burning of Atlanta	H. Rogers	150-day	24.50	55-85.00
88-01-003 Scarlett and Ashley After the War	H. Rogers	150-day	27.50	68-95.00
88-01-004 The Proposal	H. Rogers	150-day	27.50	80-115.
89-01-005 Home to Tara	H. Rogers	150-day	27.50	48-55.00
89-01-006 Strolling in Atlanta	H. Rogers	150-day	27.50	47-65.00
89-01-007 A Question of Honor	H. Rogers	150-day	29.50	35-55.00
89-01-008 Scarlett's Resolve	H. Rogers	150-day	29.50	46-59.00
89-01-009 Frankly My Dear	H. Rogers	150-day	29.50	63-69.00
89-01-010 Melane and Ashley	H. Rogers	150-day	32.50	40-55.00
90-01-011 A Toast to Bonnie Blue	H. Rogers	150-day	32.50	50-59.00
90-01-012 Scarlett and Rhett's Honeymoon	H. Rogers	150-day	32.50	50-69.00
W.S. George	**Scenes of Christmas Past**			
87-02-001 Holiday Skaters	L. Garrison	150-day	27.50	50.00
88-02-002 Christmas Eve	L. Garrison	150-day	27.50	35.00
89-02-003 The Homecoming	L. Garrison	150-day	30.50	31.00
90-02-004 The Toy Store	L. Garrison	150-day	30.50	31.00
91-02-005 The Carollers	L. Garrison	150-day	30.50	31.00
92-02-006 Family Traditions	L. Garrison	150-day	32.50	35-55.00
93-02-007 Holiday Past	L. Garrison	150-day	32.50	32.50
W.S. George	**On Gossamer Wings**			
88-03-001 Monarch Butterflies	L. Liu	150-day	24.50	25-50.00
88-03-002 Western Tiger Swallowtails	L. Liu	150-day	24.50	32-47.00
88-03-003 Red-Spotted Purple	L. Liu	150-day	27.50	30.00
88-03-004 Malachites	L. Liu	150-day	27.50	29.00
88-03-005 White Peacocks	L. Liu	150-day	27.50	40-45.00
89-03-006 Eastern Tailed Blues	L. Liu	150-day	27.50	28.00
89-03-007 Zebra Swallowtails	L. Liu	150-day	29.50	30.00
89-03-008 Red Admirals	L. Liu	150-day	29.50	30-35.00

	ARTIST	EDITION	ISSUE	QUOTE
W.S. George	**Flowers of Your Garden**			
88-04-001 Roses	V. Morley	150-day	24.50	60-75.00
88-04-002 Lilacs	V. Morley	150-day	24.50	48.00
88-04-003 Daisies	V. Morley	150-day	27.50	40.00
88-04-004 Peonies	V. Morley	150-day	27.50	28.00
88-04-005 Chrysanthemums	V. Morley	150-day	27.50	28.00
89-04-006 Daffodils	V. Morley	150-day	27.50	28.00
89-04-007 Tulips	V. Morley	150-day	29.50	30.00
89-04-008 Irises	V. Morley	150-day	29.50	34.00
W.S. George	**Beloved Hymns of Childhood**			
88-05-001 The Lord's My Shepherd	C. Barker	150-day	29.50	47.00
88-05-002 Away In a Manger	C. Barker	150-day	29.50	30.00
89-05-003 Now Thank We All Our God	C. Barker	150-day	32.50	33.00
89-05-004 Love Divine	C. Barker	150-day	32.50	33.00
89-05-005 I Love to Hear the Story	C. Barker	150-day	32.50	33.00
89-05-006 All Glory, Laud and Honour	C. Barker	150-day	32.50	33.00
90-05-007 All People on Earth Do Dwell	C. Barker	150-day	34.50	35.00
90-05-008 Loving Shepherd of Thy Sheep	C. Barker	150-day	34.50	35.00
W.S. George	**Classic Waterfowl: The Ducks Unlimited**			
88-06-001 Mallards at Sunrise	L. Kaatz	150-day	36.50	40.00
88-06-002 Geese in the Autumn Fields	L. Kaatz	150-day	36.50	37.00
89-06-003 Green Wings/Morning Marsh	L. Kaatz	150-day	39.50	40.00
89-06-004 Canvasbacks, Breaking Away	L. Kaatz	150-day	39.50	40.00
89-06-005 Pintails in Indian Summer	L. Kaatz	150-day	39.50	40.00
90-06-006 Wood Ducks Taking Flight	L. Kaatz	150-day	39.50	40.00
90-06-007 Snow Geese Against November Skies	L. Kaatz	150-day	41.50	42.00
90-06-008 Bluebills Coming In	L. Kaatz	150-day	41.50	42.00
W.S. George	**The Elegant Birds**			
88-07-001 The Swan	J. Faulkner	150-day	32.50	33.00
88-07-002 Great Blue Heron	J. Faulkner	150-day	32.50	33.00
89-07-003 Snowy Egret	J. Faulkner	150-day	32.50	36.00
89-07-004 The Anhinga	J. Faulkner	150-day	35.50	36.00
89-07-005 The Flamingo	J. Faulkner	150-day	35.50	38.00
90-07-006 Sandhill and Whooping Crane	J. Faulkner	150-day	35.50	36.00
W.S. George	**Last of Their Kind: The Endangered Species**			
88-08-001 The Panda	W. Nelson	150-day	27.50	45.00
89-08-002 The Snow Leopard	W. Nelson	150-day	27.50	45-50.00
89-08-003 The Red Wolf	W. Nelson	150-day	30.50	31.00
89-08-004 The Asian Elephant	W. Nelson	150-day	30.50	31.00
90-08-005 The Slender-Horned Gazelle	W. Nelson	150-day	30.50	31.00
90-08-006 The Bridled Wallaby	W. Nelson	150-day	30.50	31.00
90-08-007 The Black-Footed Ferret	W. Nelson	150-day	33.50	34.00
90-08-008 The Siberian Tiger	W. Nelson	150-day	33.50	35.00
91-08-009 The Vicuna	W. Nelson	150-day	33.50	34.00
91-08-010 Przewalski's Horse	W. Nelson	150-day	33.50	34.00
W.S. George	**America the Beautiful**			
88-09-001 Yosemite Falls	H. Johnson	150-day	34.50	35.00
89-09-002 The Grand Canyon	H. Johnson	150-day	34.50	35.00
89-09-003 Yellowstone River	H. Johnson	150-day	37.50	38.00
89-09-004 The Great Smokey Mountains	H. Johnson	150-day	37.50	38.00
90-09-005 The Everglades	H. Johnson	150-day	37.50	38.00
90-09-006 Acadia	H. Johnson	150-day	37.50	40.00
90-09-007 The Grand Tetons	H. Johnson	150-day	39.50	39.50
90-09-008 Crater Lake	H. Johnson	150-day	39.50	40.00
W.S. George	**Bonds of Love**			
89-10-001 Precious Embrace	B. Burke	150-day	29.50	35.00
90-10-002 Cherished Moment	B. Burke	150-day	29.50	30.00
91-10-003 Tender Caress	B. Burke	150-day	32.50	35.00
92-10-004 Loving Touch	B. Burke	150-day	32.50	40.00
92-10-005 Treasured Kisses	B. Burke	150-day	32.50	48.00
94-10-006 Endearing Whispers	B. Burke	150-day	32.50	32.50
W.S. George	**The Golden Age of the Clipper Ships**			
89-11-001 The Twilight Under Full Sail	C. Vickery	150-day	29.50	30.00
89-11-002 The Blue Jacket at Sunset	C. Vickery	150-day	29.50	30.00
89-11-003 Young America, Homeward	C. Vickery	150-day	32.50	33.00
90-11-004 Flying Cloud	C. Vickery	150-day	32.50	45.00
90-11-005 Davy Crocket at Daybreak	C. Vickery	150-day	32.50	35.00
90-11-006 Golden Eagle Conquers Wind	C. Vickery	150-day	32.50	35.00
90-11-007 The Lightning in Lifting Fog	C. Vickery	150-day	34.50	35.00
90-11-008 Sea Witch, Mistress/Oceans	C. Vickery	150-day	34.50	45.00
W.S. George	**Romantic Gardens**			
89-12-001 The Woodland Garden	C. Smith	150-day	29.50	30.00
89-12-002 The Plantation Garden	C. Smith	150-day	29.50	30.00
90-12-003 The Cottage Garden	C. Smith	150-day	32.50	40.00
90-12-004 The Colonial Garden	C. Smith	150-day	32.50	33.00
W.S. George	**Country Nostalgia**			
89-13-001 The Spring Buggy	M. Harvey	150-day	29.50	30.00
89-13-002 The Apple Cider Press	M. Harvey	150-day	29.50	40.00
89-13-003 The Vintage Seed Planter	M. Harvey	150-day	29.50	40.00
89-13-004 The Old Hand Pump	M. Harvey	150-day	32.50	40-50.00
90-13-005 The Wooden Butter Churn	M. Harvey	150-day	32.50	47.00
90-13-006 The Dairy Cans	M. Harvey	150-day	32.50	35-45.00
90-13-007 The Forgotten Plow	M. Harvey	150-day	34.50	38.00
90-13-008 The Antique Spinning Wheel	M. Harvey	150-day	34.50	37.00
W.S. George	**Hollywood's Glamour Girls**			
89-14-001 Jean Harlow-Dinner at Eight	E. Dzenis	150-day	24.50	40.00
90-14-002 Lana Turner-Postman Ring Twice	E. Dzenis	150-day	29.50	30.00
90-14-003 Carol Lombard-The Gay Bride	E. Dzenis	150-day	29.50	30.00
90-14-004 Greta Garbo-In Grand Hotel	E. Dzenis	150-day	29.50	30.00
W.S. George	**Purebred Horses of the Americas**			
89-15-001 The Appalosa	D. Schwartz	150-day	34.50	35.00
89-15-002 The Tenessee Walker	D. Schwartz	150-day	34.50	35.00
90-15-003 The Quarterhorse	D. Schwartz	150-day	37.50	38.00
90-15-004 The Saddlebred	D. Schwartz	150-day	37.50	45.00
90-15-005 The Mustang	D. Schwartz	150-day	37.50	39.00
90-15-006 The Morgan	D. Schwartz	150-day	37.50	70.00
W.S. George	**Nature's Poetry**			
89-16-001 Morning Serenade	L. Liu	150-day	24.50	37.00
89-16-002 Song of Promise	L. Liu	150-day	24.50	43.00
90-16-003 Tender Lullaby	L. Liu	150-day	27.50	28.00
90-16-004 Nature's Harmony	L. Liu	150-day	27.50	50.00
90-16-005 Gentle Refrain	L. Liu	150-day	27.50	30.00
90-16-006 Morning Chorus	L. Liu	150-day	27.50	35.00
90-16-007 Melody at Daybreak	L. Liu	150-day	29.50	30.00
91-16-008 Delicate Accord	L. Liu	150-day	29.50	35.00
91-16-009 Lyrical Beginnings	L. Liu	150-day	29.50	37.00
91-16-010 Song of Spring	L. Liu	150-day	32.50	40.00
91-16-011 Mother's Melody	L. Liu	150-day	32.50	40.00
91-16-012 Cherub Chorale	L. Liu	150-day	32.50	45.00
W.S. George	**Art Deco**			
89-17-001 A Flapper With Greyhounds	M. McDonald	150-day	39.50	50.00
90-17-002 Tango Dancers	M. McDonald	150-day	39.50	60.00
90-17-003 Arriving in Style	M. McDonald	150-day	39.50	75.00
90-17-004 On the Town	M. McDonald	150-day	39.50	75.00
W.S. George	**Our Woodland Friends**			
90-18-002 Beneath the Pines	C. Brenders	150-day	29.50	32.00
90-18-003 High Adventure	C. Brenders	150-day	32.50	33.00
90-18-004 Shy Explorers	C. Brenders	150-day	32.50	37.00
91-18-005 Golden Season:Gray Squirrel	C. Brenders	150-day	32.50	35.00
91-18-006 Full House Fox Family	C. Brenders	150-day	32.50	60.00
91-18-007 A Jump Into Life: Spring Fawn	C. Brenders	150-day	34.50	40.00
91-18-008 Forest Sentinel:Bobcat	C. Brenders	150-day	34.50	40.00
W.S. George	**The Federal Duck Stamp Plate Collection**			
90-19-001 The Lesser Scaup	N. Anderson	150-day	27.50	40.00
90-19-002 Mallard	N. Anderson	150-day	27.50	55.00
90-19-003 The Ruddy Ducks	N. Anderson	150-day	30.50	31.00
90-19-004 Canvasbacks	N. Anderson	150-day	30.50	42.00
91-19-005 Pintails	N. Anderson	150-day	30.50	31.00
91-19-006 Wigeons	N. Anderson	150-day	30.50	35.00
91-19-007 Cinnamon Teal	N. Anderson	150-day	32.50	34.00
91-19-008 Fulvous Wistling Duck	N. Anderson	150-day	32.50	45.00
91-19-009 The Redheads	N. Anderson	150-day	32.50	45.00
91-19-010 Snow Goose	N. Anderson	150-day	32.50	32.50
W.S. George	**Dr. Zhivago**			
90-20-001 Zhivago and Lara	G. Bush	150-day	39.50	40.00
91-20-002 Love Poems For Lara	G. Bush	150-day	39.50	40.00
91-20-003 Zhivago Says Farewell	G. Bush	150-day	39.50	40.00
91-20-004 Lara's Love	G. Bush	150-day	39.50	45.00
W.S. George	**Blessed Are The Children**			
90-21-001 Let the/Children Come To Me	W. Rane	150-day	29.50	35.00
90-21-002 I Am the Good Shepherd	W. Rane	150-day	29.50	50.00
91-21-003 Whoever Welcomes/Child	W. Rane	150-day	32.50	45-50.00
91-21-004 Hosanna in the Highest	W. Rane	150-day	32.50	40.00
91-21-005 Jesus Had Compassion on Them	W. Rane	150-day	32.50	35.00
91-21-006 Blessed are the Peacemakers	W. Rane	150-day	34.50	46.00
91-21-007 I am the Vine, You are the Branches	W. Rane	150-day	34.50	60.00
91-21-008 Seek and You Will Find	W. Rane	150-day	34.50	40.00
W.S. George	**The Vanishing Gentle Giants**			
91-22-001 Jumping For Joy	A. Casay	150-day	32.50	35-44.00
91-22-002 Song of the Humpback	A. Casay	150-day	32.50	34-45.00
91-22-003 Monarch of the Deep	A. Casay	150-day	35.50	45.00
91-22-004 Travelers of the Sea	A. Casay	150-day	35.50	50-60.00
91-22-005 White Whale of the North	A. Casay	150-day	35.50	54-58.00
91-22-006 Unicorn of the Sea	A. Casay	150-day	35.50	55.00
W.S. George	**Spirit of Christmas**			
90-23-001 Silent Night	J. Sias	150-day	29.50	40.00
91-23-002 Jingle Bells	J. Sias	150-day	29.50	25-30.00
91-23-003 Deck The Halls	J. Sias	150-day	32.50	45.00
91-23-004 I'll Be Home For Christmas	J. Sias	150-day	32.50	50.00
91-23-005 Winter Wonderland	J. Sias	150-day	32.50	40.00
91-23-006 O Christmas Tree	J. Sias	150-day	32.50	35.00
W.S. George	**Flowers From Grandma's Garden**			
90-24-001 Country Cuttings	G. Kurz	150-day	24.50	45-58.00
90-24-002 The Morning Bouquet	G. Kurz	150-day	24.50	41-49.00
91-24-003 Homespun Beauty	G. Kurz	150-day	27.50	35.00
91-24-004 Harvest in the Meadow	G. Kurz	150-day	27.50	30.00
91-24-005 Gardener's Delight	G. Kurz	150-day	27.50	60-65.00
91-24-006 Nature's Bounty	G. Kurz	150-day	27.50	50.00
91-24-007 A Country Welcome	G. Kurz	150-day	29.50	55.00
91-24-008 The Springtime Arrangement	G. Kurz	150-day	29.50	50.00
W.S. George	**The Secret World Of The Panda**			
90-25-001 A Mother's Care	J. Bridgett	150-day	27.50	32.00
91-25-002 A Frolic in the Snow	J. Bridgett	150-day	27.50	28.00
91-25-003 Lazy Afternoon	J. Bridgett	150-day	30.50	31.00
91-25-004 A Day of Exploring	J. Bridgett	150-day	30.50	31-37.00
91-25-005 A Gentle Hug	J. Bridgett	150-day	32.50	33-38.00
91-25-006 A Bamboo Feast	J. Bridgett	150-day	32.50	75.00
W.S. George	**Wonders Of The Sea**			
91-26-001 Stand By Me	R.Harm	150-day	34.50	35.00
91-26-002 Heart to Heart	R.Harm	150-day	34.50	35.00
91-26-003 Warm Embrace	R.Harm	150-day	34.50	44.00
91-26-004 A Family Affair	R.Harm	150-day	34.50	34.50
W.S. George	**Critic's Choice: Gone With The Wind**			
91-27-001 Marry Me, Scarlett	P. Jennis	150-day	27.50	45-55.00
91-27-002 Waiting for Rhett	P. Jennis	150-day	27.50	46-59.00
91-27-003 A Declaration of Love	P. Jennis	150-day	30.50	46-75.00
91-27-004 The Paris Hat	P. Jennis	150-day	30.50	50-85.00
91-27-005 Scarlett Asks a Favor	P. Jennis	150-day	30.50	47-55.00
92-27-006 Scarlett Gets Her Way	P. Jennis	150-day	32.50	50-59.00
92-27-007 The Smitten Suitor	P. Jennis	150-day	32.50	32.50
92-27-008 Scarlett's Shopping Spree	P. Jennis	150-day	32.50	32.50
92-27-009 The Buggy Ride	P. Jennis	150-day	32.50	32.50
92-27-010 Scarlett Gets Down to Business	P. Jennis	150-day	34.50	34.50
93-27-011 Scarlett's Heart is with Tara	P. Jennis	150-day	34.50	34.50
93-27-012 At Cross Purposes	P. Jennis	150-day	34.50	34.50
W.S. George	**Victorian Cat**			
90-29-001 Mischief With The Hatbox	H. Bonner	150-day	24.50	44-54.00
91-29-002 String Quartet	H. Bonner	150-day	24.50	55.00
91-29-003 Daydreams	H. Bonner	150-day	27.50	45.00
91-29-004 Frisky Felines	H. Bonner	150-day	27.50	53.00
91-29-005 Kittens at Play	H. Bonner	150-day	27.50	45-54.00
91-29-006 Playing in the Parlor	H. Bonner	150-day	29.50	50-68.00
91-29-007 Perfectly Poised	H. Bonner	150-day	29.50	40-75.00
92-29-008 Midday Repose	H. Bonner	150-day	29.50	30.00
W.S. George	**Victorian Cat Capers**			
92-30-001 Who's the Fairest of Them All?	F. Paton	150-day	24.50	24.50

		ARTIST	EDITION	ISSUE	QUOTE
92-30-002	Puss in Boots	Unknown	150-day	24.50	24.50
92-30-003	My Bowl is Empty	W. Hepple	150-day	27.50	27.50
92-30-004	A Curious Kitty	W. Hepple	150-day	27.50	27.50
92-30-005	Vanity Fair	W. Hepple	150-day	27.50	27.50
92-30-006	Forbidden Fruit	W. Hepple	150-day	29.50	29.50
93-30-007	The Purr-fect Pen Pal	W. Hepple	150-day	29.50	29.50
93-30-008	The Kitten Express	W. Hepple	150-day	29.50	29.50
W.S. George		**Glorious Songbirds**			
91-31-001	Cardinals on a Snowy Branch	R. Cobane	150-day	29.50	35.00
91-31-002	Indigo Buntings and/Blossoms	R. Cobane	150-day	29.50	32.00
91-31-003	Chickadees Among The Lilacs	R. Cobane	150-day	32.50	32.50
91-31-004	Goldfinches in/Thistle	R. Cobane	150-day	32.50	32.50
91-31-005	Cedar Waxwing/Winter Berries	R. Cobane	150-day	32.50	34.00
91-31-006	Bluebirds in a Blueberry Bush	R. Cobane	150-day	34.50	35.00
91-31-007	Baltimore Orioles/Autumn Leaves	R. Cobane	150-day	34.50	38.00
91-31-008	Robins with Dogwood in Bloom	R. Cobane	150-day	34.50	35.00
W.S. George		**Nature's Lovables**			
90-32-001	The Koala	C. Frace	150-day	27.50	40-50.00
91-32-002	New Arrival	C. Frace	150-day	27.50	45.00
91-32-003	Chinese Treasure	C. Frace	150-day	27.50	28.00
91-32-004	Baby Harp Seal	C. Frace	150-day	30.50	60-70.00
91-32-005	Bobcat: Nature's Dawn	C. Frace	150-day	30.50	31.00
91-32-006	Clouded Leopard	C. Frace	150-day	32.50	35.00
91-32-007	Zebra Foal	C. Frace	150-day	32.50	60.00
91-32-008	Bandit	C. Frace	150-day	32.50	42.00
W.S. George		**Soaring Majesty**			
91-33-001	Freedom	C. Frace	150-day	29.50	48-54.00
91-33-002	The Northern Goshhawk	C. Frace	150-day	29.50	40-45.00
91-33-003	Peregrine Falcon	C. Frace	150-day	32.50	32.50
91-33-004	Red-Tailed Hawk	C. Frace	150-day	32.50	32.50
91-33-005	The Osprey	C. Frace	150-day	32.50	35.00
91-33-006	The Gyrfalcon	C. Frace	150-day	34.50	48.00
91-33-007	The Golden Eagle	C. Frace	150-day	34.50	62.00
92-33-008	Red-Shouldered Hawk	C. Frace	150-day	34.50	34.50
W.S. George		**The World's Most Magnificent Cats**			
91-34-001	Fleeting Encounter	C. Frace	150-day	24.50	55-85.00
91-34-002	Cougar	C. Frace	150-day	24.50	65-90.00
91-34-003	Royal Bengal	C. Frace	150-day	27.50	40-53.00
91-34-004	Powerful Presence	C. Frace	150-day	27.50	60.00
91-34-005	Jaguar	C. Frace	150-day	27.50	75.00
91-34-006	The Clouded Leopard	C. Frace	150-day	29.50	80-139.
91-34-007	The African Leopard	C. Frace	150-day	29.50	50-75.00
91-34-008	Mighty Warrior	C. Frace	150-day	29.50	50-95.00
92-34-009	The Cheetah	C. Frace	150-day	31.50	65.00
92-34-010	Siberian Tiger	C. Frace	150-day	31.50	66.00
W.S. George		**A Loving Look: Duck Families**			
90-35-001	Family Outing	B. Langton	150-day	34.50	34.50
91-35-002	Sleepy Start	B. Langton	150-day	34.50	34.50
91-35-003	Quiet Moment	B. Langton	150-day	37.50	37.50
91-35-004	Safe and Sound	B. Langton	150-day	37.50	37.50
91-35-005	Spring Arrivals	B. Langton	150-day	37.50	73.00
91-35-006	The Family Tree	B. Langton	150-day	37.50	50-60.00
W.S. George		**Nature's Legacy**			
90-36-001	Blue Snow at Half Dome	J. Sias	150-day	24.50	30.00
91-36-002	Misty Morning/Mt. McKinley	J. Sias	150-day	24.50	25-53.00
91-36-003	Mount Ranier	J. Sias	150-day	27.50	28-55.00
91-36-004	Havasu Canyon	J. Sias	150-day	27.50	28.00
91-36-005	Autumn Splendor in the Smoky Mts.	J. Sias	150-day	27.50	28.00
91-36-006	Winter Peace in Yellowstone Park	J. Sias	150-day	29.50	30.00
91-36-007	Golden Majesty/Rocky Mountains	J. Sias	150-day	29.50	30.00
91-36-008	Radiant Sunset Over the Everglades	J. Sias	150-day	29.50	30.00
W.S. George		**Symphony of Shimmering Beauties**			
91-37-001	Iris Quartet	L. Liu	150-day	29.50	54.00
91-37-002	Tulip Ensemble	L. Liu	150-day	29.50	35.00
91-37-003	Poppy Pastorale	L. Liu	150-day	32.50	35.00
91-37-004	Lily Concerto	L. Liu	150-day	32.50	50.00
91-37-005	Peony Prelude	L. Liu	150-day	32.50	32.50
91-37-006	Rose Fantasy	L. Liu	150-day	34.50	34.50
91-37-007	Hibiscus Medley	L. Liu	150-day	34.50	34.50
92-37-008	Dahlia Melody	L. Liu	150-day	34.50	34.50
92-37-009	Hollyhock March	L. Liu	150-day	34.50	34.50
92-37-010	Carnation Serenade	L. Liu	150-day	36.50	36.50
92-37-011	Gladiolus Romance	L. Liu	150-day	36.50	36.50
92-37-012	Zinnia Finale	L. Liu	150-day	36.50	36.50
W.S. George		**Portraits of Christ**			
91-38-001	Father, Forgive Them	J. Salamanca	150-day	29.50	90.00
91-38-002	Thy Will Be Done	J. Salamanca	150-day	29.50	50.00
91-38-003	This is My Beloved Son	J. Salamanca	150-day	32.50	50.00
91-38-004	Lo, I Am With You	J. Salamanca	150-day	32.50	60.00
91-38-005	Become as Little Children	J. Salamanca	150-day	32.50	60.00
91-38-006	Peace I Leave With You	J. Salamanca	150-day	34.50	65.00
92-38-007	For God So Loved the World	J. Salamanca	150-day	34.50	63.00
92-38-008	I Am the Way, the Truth and the Life	J. Salamanca	150-day	34.50	80.00
92-38-009	Weep Not For Me	J. Salamanca	150-day	34.50	50.00
92-38-010	Follow Me	J. Salamanca	150-day	34.50	35.00
W.S. George		**Portraits of Exquisite Birds**			
90-39-001	Backyard Treasure/Chickadee	C. Brenders	150-day	29.50	35.00
90-39-002	The Beautiful Bluebird	C. Brenders	150-day	29.50	35.00
91-39-003	Summer Gold: The Robin	C. Brenders	150-day	32.50	35.00
91-39-004	The Meadowlark's Song	C. Brenders	150-day	32.50	33.00
91-39-005	Ivory-Billed Woodpecker	C. Brenders	150-day	32.50	33.00
91-39-006	Red-Winged Blackbird	C. Brenders	150-day	32.50	33.00
W.S. George		**Alaska: The Last Frontier**			
91-40-001	Icy Majesty	H. Lambson	150-day	34.50	34.50
91-40-002	Autumn Grandeur	H. Lambson	150-day	34.50	34.50
92-40-003	Mountain Monarch	H. Lambson	150-day	37.50	37.50
92-40-004	Down the Trail	H. Lambson	150-day	37.50	37.50
92-40-005	Moonlight Lookout	H. Lambson	150-day	37.50	37.50
92-40-006	Graceful Passage	H. Lambson	150-day	39.50	39.50
92-40-007	Arctic Journey	H. Lambson	150-day	39.50	39.50
92-40-008	Summit Domain	H. Lambson	150-day	39.50	39.50
W.S. George		**On Wings of Snow**			
91-41-001	The Swans	L. Liu	150-day	34.50	34.50
91-41-002	The Doves	L. Liu	150-day	34.50	34.50
91-41-003	The Peacocks	L. Liu	150-day	37.50	37.50

		ARTIST	EDITION	ISSUE	QUOTE
91-41-004	The Egrets	L. Liu	150-day	37.50	37.50
91-41-005	The Cockatoos	L. Liu	150-day	37.50	37.50
92-41-006	The Herons	L. Liu	150-day	37.50	37.50
W.S. George		**Nature's Playmates**			
91-42-001	Partners	C. Frace	150-day	29.50	45.00
91-42-002	Secret Heights	C. Frace	150-day	29.50	35.00
91-42-003	Recess	C. Frace	150-day	32.50	45.00
91-42-004	Double Trouble	C. Frace	150-day	32.50	45.00
91-42-005	Pals	C. Frace	150-day	32.50	45.00
92-42-006	Curious Trio	C. Frace	150-day	34.50	35.00
92-42-007	Playmates	C. Frace	150-day	34.50	35.00
92-42-008	Surprise	C. Frace	150-day	34.50	34.50
92-42-009	Peace On Ice	C. Frace	150-day	36.50	36.50
92-42-010	Ambassadors	C. Frace	150-day	36.50	36.50
W.S. George		**Field Birds of North America**			
91-43-001	Winter Colors: Ring-Necked Pheasant	D. Bush	150-day	39.50	50.00
91-43-002	In Display: Ruffed Goose	D. Bush	150-day	39.50	40-60.00
91-43-003	Morning Light: Bobwhite Quail	D. Bush	150-day	42.50	62.00
91-43-004	Misty Clearing: Wild Turkey	D. Bush	150-day	42.50	55.00
92-43-005	Autumn Moment: American Woodcock	D. Bush	150-day	42.50	70.00
92-43-006	Season's End: Willow Ptarmigan	D. Bush	150-day	42.50	42.50
W.S. George		**Country Bouquets**			
91-44-001	Morning Sunshine	G. Kurz	150-day	29.50	40-50.00
91-44-002	Summer Perfume	G. Kurz	150-day	29.50	50.00
91-44-003	Warm Welcome	G. Kurz	150-day	32.50	50.00
91-44-004	Garden's Bounty	G. Kurz	150-day	32.50	35.00
W.S. George		**Gentle Beginnings**			
91-45-001	Tender Loving Care	W. Nelson	150-day	34.50	55.00
91-45-002	A Touch of Love	W. Nelson	150-day	34.50	65.00
91-45-003	Under Watchful Eyes	W. Nelson	150-day	37.50	60.00
91-45-004	Lap of Love	W. Nelson	150-day	37.50	40.00
92-45-005	Happy Together	W. Nelson	150-day	37.50	45.00
92-45-006	First Steps	W. Nelson	150-day	37.50	45.00
W.S. George		**Garden of the Lord**			
92-46-001	Love One Another	C. Gillies	150-day	29.50	29.50
92-46-002	Perfect Peace	C. Gillies	150-day	29.50	29.50
92-46-003	Trust In the Lord	C. Gillies	150-day	32.50	32.50
92-46-004	The Lord's Love	C. Gillies	150-day	32.50	32.50
92-46-005	The Lord Bless You	C. Gillies	150-day	32.50	32.50
92-46-006	Ask In Prayer	C. Gillies	150-day	34.50	34.50
93-46-007	Peace Be With You	C. Gillies	150-day	34.50	34.50
93-46-008	Give Thanks To The Lord	C. Gillies	150-day	34.50	34.50
W.S. George		**The Majestic Horse**			
92-47-001	Classic Beauty: Thoroughbred	P. Wildermuth	150-day	34.50	45-50.00
92-47-002	American Gold: The Quarterhorse	P. Wildermuth	150-day	34.50	40.00
92-47-003	Regal Spirit: The Arabian	P. Wildermuth	150-day	34.50	50.00
92-47-004	Western Favorite: American Paint Horse	P. Wildermuth	150-day	34.50	55.00
W.S. George		**Columbus Discovers America: The 500th Anniversary**			
92-48-001	Under Full Sail	J. Penalva	150-day	29.50	30.00
92-48-002	Ashore at Dawn	J. Penalva	150-day	29.50	47.00
92-48-003	Columbus Raises the Flag	J. Penalva	150-day	32.50	54.00
92-48-004	Bringing Together Two Cultures	J. Penalva	150-day	32.50	60.00
92-48-005	The Queen's Approval	J. Penalva	150-day	32.50	53.00
92-48-006	Treasures From The New World	J. Penalva	150-day	32.50	50.00
W.S. George		**Lena Liu's Basket Bouquets**			
92-49-001	Roses	L. Liu	150-day	29.50	29.50
92-49-002	Pansies	L. Liu	150-day	29.50	29.50
92-49-003	Tulips and Lilacs	L. Liu	150-day	32.50	32.50
92-49-004	Irises	L. Liu	150-day	32.50	50.00
92-49-005	Lilies	L. Liu	150-day	32.50	60.00
92-49-006	Parrot Tulips	L. Liu	150-day	32.50	45.00
92-49-007	Peonies	L. Liu	150-day	32.50	45.00
93-49-008	Begonias	L. Liu	150-day	32.50	32.50
93-49-009	Magnolias	L. Liu	150-day	32.50	32.50
93-49-010	Calla Lilies	L. Liu	150-day	32.50	32.50
93-49-011	Orchids	L. Liu	150-day	32.50	32.50
93-49-012	Hydrangeas	L. Liu	150-day	32.50	32.50
W.S. George		**Tomorrow's Promise**			
92-50-001	Curiosity: Asian Elephants	W. Nelson	150-day	29.50	50.00
92-50-002	Playtime Pandas	W. Nelson	150-day	29.50	29.50
92-50-003	Innocence: Rhinos	W. Nelson	150-day	32.50	62.00
92-50-004	Friskiness: Kit Foxes	W. Nelson	150-day	32.50	45.00
W.S. George		**Sonnets in Flowers**			
92-51-001	Sonnet of Beauty	G. Kurz	150-day	29.50	40.00
92-51-002	Sonnet of Happiness	G. Kurz	150-day	34.50	35.00
92-51-003	Sonnet of Love	G. Kurz	150-day	34.50	34.50
92-51-004	Sonnet of Peace	G. Kurz	150-day	34.50	36.00
W.S. George		**The Sound of Music: Silver Anniversary**			
91-52-001	The Hills are Alive	V. Gadino	150-day	29.50	29.50
92-52-002	Let's Start at the Very Beginning	V. Gadino	150-day	29.50	29.50
92-52-003	Something Good	V. Gadino	150-day	32.50	32.50
92-52-004	Maria's Wedding Day	V. Gadino	150-day	32.50	32.50
W.S. George		**On the Wing**			
92-53-001	Winged Splendor	T. Humphrey	150-day	29.50	29.50
92-53-002	Rising Mallard	T. Humphrey	150-day	29.50	29.50
92-53-003	Glorious Ascent	T. Humphrey	150-day	32.50	32.50
92-53-004	Taking Wing	T. Humphrey	150-day	32.50	32.50
92-53-005	Upward Bound	T. Humphrey	150-day	32.50	32.50
93-53-006	Wondrous Motion	T. Humphrey	150-day	34.50	34.50
93-53-007	Springing Forth	T. Humphrey	150-day	34.50	34.50
93-53-008	On the Wing	T. Humphrey	150-day	34.50	34.50
W.S. George		**Grand Safari: Images of Africa**			
92-54-001	A Moment's Rest	C. Frace	150-day	34.50	34.50
92-54-002	Elephant's of Kilimanjaro	C. Frace	150-day	34.50	34.50
92-54-003	Undivided Attention	C. Frace	150-day	37.50	37.50
93-54-004	Quiet Time in Samburu	C. Frace	150-day	37.50	37.50
93-54-005	Lone Hunter	C. Frace	150-day	37.50	37.50
93-54-006	The Greater Kudo	C. Frace	150-day	37.50	37.50
W.S. George		**A Treasury of Songbirds**			
92-55-001	Springtime Splendor	R. Stine	150-day	29.50	29.50
92-55-002	Morning's Glory	R. Stine	150-day	29.50	29.50
92-55-003	Golden Daybreak	R. Stine	150-day	32.50	32.50

	ARTIST	EDITION	ISSUE	QUOTE
92-55-004 Afternoon Calm	R. Stine	150-day	32.50	32.50
92-55-005 Dawn's Radiance	R. Stine	150-day	32.50	32.50
93-55-006 Scarlet Sunrise	R. Stine	150-day	34.50	34.50
93-55-007 Sapphire Dawn	R. Stine	150-day	34.50	34.50
93-55-008 Alluring Daylight	R. Stine	150-day	34.50	34.50
W.S. George	**Heart of the Wild**			
91-56-001 A Gentle Touch	G. Beecham	150-day	29.50	50.00
92-56-002 Mother's Pride	G. Beecham	150-day	29.50	100.00
92-56-003 An Afternoon Together	G. Beecham	150-day	32.50	45.00
92-56-004 Quiet Time?	G. Beecham	150-day	32.50	33.00
W.S. George	**Spirits of the Sky**			
92-57-001 Twilight Glow	C. Fisher	150-day	29.50	29.50
92-57-002 First Light	C. Fisher	150-day	29.50	29.50
92-57-003 Evening Glimmer	C. Fisher	150-day	32.50	32.50
92-57-004 Golden Dusk	C. Fisher	150-day	32.50	32.50
93-57-005 Sunset Splendor	C. Fisher	150-day	32.50	32.50
93-57-006 Amber Flight	C. Fisher	150-day	34.50	34.50
93-57-007 Winged Radiance	C. Fisher	150-day	34.50	34.50
93-57-008 Day's End	C. Fisher	150-day	34.50	34.50
W.S. George	**Poetic Cottages**			
92-58-001 Garden Paths of Oxfordshire	C. Valente	150-day	29.50	29.50
92-58-002 Twilight at Woodgreen Pond	C. Valente	150-day	29.50	29.50
92-58-003 Stonewall Brook Blossoms	C. Valente	150-day	32.50	32.50
92-58-004 Bedfordshire Evening Sky	C. Valente	150-day	32.50	32.50
93-58-005 Wisteria Summer	C. Valente	150-day	32.50	32.50
93-58-006 Wiltshire Rose Arbor	C. Valente	150-day	32.50	32.50
93-58-007 Alderbury Gardens	C. Valente	150-day	32.50	32.50
93-58-008 Hampshire Spring Splendor	C. Valente	150-day	32.50	32.50
W.S. George	**Memories of a Victorian Childhood**			
92-59-001 You'd Better Not Pout	Unknown	150-day	29.50	30-35.00
92-59-002 Sweet Slumber	Unknown	150-day	29.50	55.00
92-59-003 Through Thick and Thin	Unknown	150-day	32.50	52.00
92-59-004 An Armful of Treasures	Unknown	150-day	32.50	45.00
93-59-005 A Trio of Bookworms	Unknown	150-day	32.50	60.00
93-59-006 Pugnacious Playmate	Unknown	150-day	32.50	60.00
W.S. George	**Petal Pals**			
92-60-001 Garden Discovery	L. Chang	150-day	24.50	24.50
92-60-002 Flowering Fascination	L. Chang	150-day	24.50	24.50
93-60-003 Alluring Lilies	L. Chang	150-day	24.50	24.50
93-60-004 Springtime Oasis	L. Chang	150-day	24.50	24.50
93-60-005 Blossoming Adventure	L. Chang	150-day	24.50	24.50
93-60-006 Dancing Daffodils	L. Chang	150-day	24.50	24.50
93-60-007 Summer Surprise	L. Chang	150-day	24.50	24.50
93-60-008 Morning Melody	L. Chang	150-day	24.50	24.50
W.S. George	**Lena Liu's Hummingbird Treasury**			
92-61-001 The Ruby-Throated Hummingbird	L. Liu	150-day	29.50	29.50
92-61-002 Anna's Hummingbird	L. Liu	150-day	29.50	29.50
92-61-003 Violet-Crowned Hummingbird	L. Liu	150-day	32.50	32.50
92-61-004 The Rufous Hummingbird	L. Liu	150-day	32.50	32.50
93-61-005 White-Eared Hummingbird	L. Liu	150-day	32.50	32.50
93-61-006 Broad-Billed Hummingbird	L. Liu	150-day	34.50	34.50
93-61-007 Calliope Hummingbird	L. Liu	150-day	34.50	34.50
93-61-008 The Allen's Hummingbird	L. Liu	150-day	34.50	34.50
W.S. George	**The Christmas Story**			
92-62-001 Gifts of the Magi	H. Garrido	150-day	29.50	29.50
93-62-002 Rest on the Flight into Egypt	H. Garrido	150-day	29.50	29.50
93-62-003 Journey of the Magi	H. Garrido	150-day	29.50	29.50
93-62-004 The Nativity	H. Garrido	150-day	29.50	29.50
93-62-005 The Annunciation	H. Garrido	150-day	29.50	29.50
93-62-006 Adoration of the Shepherds	H. Garrido	150-day	29.50	29.50
W.S. George	**Winter's Majesty**			
92-63-001 The Quest	C. Frace	150-day	34.50	34.50
92-63-002 The Chase	C. Frace	150-day	34.50	34.50
93-63-003 Alaskan Friend	C. Frace	150-day	34.50	34.50
93-63-004 American Cougar	C. Frace	150-day	34.50	34.50
93-63-005 On Watch	C. Frace	150-day	34.50	34.50
93-63-006 Solitude	C. Frace	150-day	34.50	34.50
W.S. George	**America's Pride**			
92-64-001 Misty Fjords	R. Richert	150-day	29.50	65.00
92-64-002 Rugged Shores	R. Richert	150-day	29.50	50.00
92-64-003 Mighty Summit	R. Richert	150-day	32.50	65.00
93-64-004 Lofty Reflections	R. Richert	150-day	32.50	32.50
93-64-005 Tranquil Waters	R. Richert	150-day	32.50	32.50
93-64-006 Mountain Majesty	R. Richert	150-day	34.50	34.50
93-64-007 Canyon Climb	R. Richert	150-day	34.50	34.50
93-64-008 Golden Vista	R. Richert	150-day	34.50	34.50
W.S. George	**A Black Tie Affair: The Penguin**			
92-65-001 Little Explorer	C. Jagodits	150-day	29.50	29.50
92-65-002 Penguin Parade	C. Jagodits	150-day	29.50	29.50
92-65-003 Baby-Sitters	C. Jagodits	150-day	29.50	29.50
93-65-004 Belly Flopping	C. Jagodits	150-day	29.50	29.50
W.S. George	**The Faces of Nature**			
92-66-001 Canyon of the Cat	J. Kramer Cole	150-day	29.50	29.50
92-66-002 Wolf Ridge	J. Kramer Cole	150-day	29.50	29.50
93-66-003 Trail of the Talisman	J. Kramer Cole	150-day	29.50	29.50
93-66-004 Wolfpack of the Ancients	J. Kramer Cole	150-day	29.50	29.50
93-66-005 Two Bears Camp	J. Kramer Cole	150-day	29.50	29.50
93-66-006 Wintering With the Wapiti	J. Kramer Cole	150-day	29.50	29.50
93-66-007 Within Sunrise	J. Kramer Cole	150-day	29.50	29.50
93-66-008 Wambli Okiye	J. Kramer Cole	150-day	29.50	29.50
W.S. George	**Wings of Winter**			
92-67-001 Moonlight Retreat	D. Rust	150-day	29.50	29.50
93-67-002 Twilight Serenade	D. Rust	150-day	29.50	29.50
93-67-003 Silent Sunset	D. Rust	150-day	29.50	29.50
93-67-004 Night Lights	D. Rust	150-day	29.50	29.50
93-67-005 Winter Haven	D. Rust	150-day	29.50	29.50
93-67-006 Full Moon Companions	D. Rust	150-day	29.50	29.50
93-67-007 White Night	D. Rust	150-day	29.50	29.50
93-67-008 Winter Reflections	D. Rust	150-day	29.50	29.50
W.S. George	**Gardens of Paradise**			
92-68-001 Tranquility	L. Chang	150-day	29.50	29.50
92-68-002 Serenity	L. Chang	150-day	29.50	29.50
93-68-003 Splendor	L. Chang	150-day	32.50	32.50

	ARTIST	EDITION	ISSUE	QUOTE
93-68-004 Harmony	L. Chang	150-day	32.50	32.50
93-68-005 Beauty	L. Chang	150-day	32.50	32.50
93-68-006 Elegance	L. Chang	150-day	32.50	32.50
93-68-007 Grandeur	L. Chang	150-day	32.50	32.50
93-68-008 Majesty	L. Chang	150-day	32.50	32.50
W.S. George	**The Passions of Scarlett O'Hara**			
92-69-001 Fiery Embrace	P. Jennis	150-day	29.50	60-75.00
92-69-002 Pride and Passion	P. Jennis	150-day	29.50	50-85.00
92-69-003 Dreams of Ashley	P. Jennis	150-day	32.50	70-80.00
92-69-004 The Fond Farewell	P. Jennis	150-day	32.50	50-60.00
92-69-005 The Waltz	P. Jennis	150-day	32.50	70-75.00
92-69-006 As God Is My Witness	P. Jennis	150-day	34.50	34.50
93-69-007 Brave Scarlett	P. Jennis	150-day	34.50	34.50
93-69-008 Nightmare	P. Jennis	150-day	34.50	34.50
93-69-009 Evening Prayers	P. Jennis	150-day	34.50	34.50
93-69-010 Naptime	P. Jennis	150-day	36.50	36.50
93-69-011 Dangerous Attraction	P. Jennis	150-day	36.50	36.50
94-69-012 The End of An Era	P. Jennis	150-day	36.50	36.50
W.S. George	**Little Angels**			
92-70-001 Angels We Have Heard on High	B. Burke	150-day	29.50	29.50
92-70-002 O Tannenbaum	B. Burke	150-day	29.50	29.50
93-70-003 Joy to the World	B. Burke	150-day	32.50	32.50
93-70-004 Hark the Herald Angels Sing	B. Burke	150-day	32.50	32.50
93-70-005 It Came Upon a Midnight Clear	B. Burke	150-day	32.50	32.50
93-70-006 The First Noel	B. Burke	150-day	32.50	32.50
W.S. George	**Wild Spirits**			
92-71-001 Solitary Watch	T. Hirata	150-day	29.50	29.50
92-71-002 Timber Ghost	T. Hirata	150-day	29.50	29.50
92-71-003 Mountain Magic	T. Hirata	150-day	32.50	32.50
93-71-004 Silent Guard	T. Hirata	150-day	32.50	32.50
93-71-005 Sly Eyes	T. Hirata	150-day	32.50	32.50
93-71-006 Mighty Presence	T. Hirata	150-day	34.50	34.50
93-71-007 Quiet Vigil	T. Hirata	150-day	34.50	34.50
93-71-008 Lone Vanguard	T. Hirata	150-day	34.50	34.50
W.S. George	**Paw Prints: Baby Cats of the Wild**			
92-72-001 Morning Mischief	C. Frace	95-day	29.50	29.50
93-72-002 Togetherness	C. Frace	95-day	29.50	29.50
93-72-003 The Buddy System	C. Frace	95-day	32.50	32.50
93-72-004 Nap Time	C. Frace	95-day	32.50	32.50
W.S. George	**A Delicate Balance: Vanishing Wildlife**			
92-73-001 Tomorrow's Hope	G. Beecham	95-day	29.50	29.50
93-73-002 Today's Future	G. Beecham	95-day	29.50	29.50
93-73-003 Present Dreams	G. Beecham	95-day	32.50	32.50
93-73-004 Eyes on the New Day	G. Beecham	95-day	32.50	32.50
W.S. George	**Bear Tracks**			
92-74-001 Denali Family	J. Seerey-Lester	150-day	29.50	29.50
93-74-002 Their First Season	J. Seerey-Lester	150-day	29.50	29.50
93-74-003 High Country Champion	J. Seerey-Lester	150-day	29.50	29.50
93-74-004 Heavy Going	J. Seerey-Lester	150-day	29.50	29.50
93-74-005 Breaking Cover	J. Seerey-Lester	150-day	29.50	29.50
93-74-006 Along the Ice Flow	J. Seerey-Lester	150-day	29.50	29.50
W.S. George	**Hometown Memories**			
93-75-001 Moonlight Skaters	H.T. Becker	150-day	29.50	29.50
93-75-002 Mountain Sleigh Ride	H.T. Becker	150-day	29.50	29.50
93-75-003 Heading Home	H.T. Becker	150-day	29.50	29.50
93-75-004 A Winter Ride	H.T. Becker	150-day	29.50	29.50
W.S. George	**Wild Innocents**			
93-76-001 Reflections	C. Frace	95-day	29.50	29.50
93-76-002 Spiritual Heir	C. Frace	95-day	29.50	29.50
93-76-003 Lion Cub	C. Frace	95-day	29.50	29.50
93-76-004 Sunny Spot	C. Frace	95-day	29.50	29.50
W.S. George	**Rare Encounters**			
93-77-001 Softly, Softly	J. Seerey-Lester	95-day	29.50	29.50
93-77-002 Black Magic	J. Seerey-Lester	95-day	29.50	29.50
93-77-003 Future Song	J. Seerey-Lester	95-day	32.50	32.50
93-77-004 High and Mighty	J. Seerey-Lester	95-day	32.50	32.50
93-77-005 Last Sanctuary	J. Seerey-Lester	95-day	32.50	32.50
93-77-006 Something Stirred	J. Seerey-Lester	95-day	34.50	34.50
W.S. George	**Along an English Lane**			
93-78-001 Summer's Bright Welcome	M. Harvey	95-day	29.50	29.50
93-78-002 Greeting the Day	M. Harvey	95-day	29.50	29.50
93-78-003 Friends and Flowers	M. Harvey	95-day	29.50	29.50
93-78-004 Cottage Around the Bend	M. Harvey	95-day	29.50	29.50
W.S. George	**Romantic Harbors**			
93-79-001 Advent of the Golden Bough	C. Vickery	95-day	34.50	34.50
93-79-002 Christmas Tree Schooner	C. Vickery	95-day	34.50	34.50
93-79-003 Prelude to the Journey	C. Vickery	95-day	37.50	37.50
93-79-004 Shimmering Light of Dusk	C. Vickery	95-day	37.50	37.50
W.S. George	**Lena Liu's Flower Fairies**			
93-80-001 Magic Makers	L. Liu	95-day	29.50	29.50
93-80-002 Petal Playmates	L. Liu	95-day	29.50	29.50
93-80-003 Delicate Dancers	L. Liu	95-day	32.50	32.50
93-80-003 Mischief Masters	L. Liu	95-day	32.50	32.50
93-80-003 Amorous Angels	L. Liu	95-day	32.50	32.50
93-80-003 Winged Wonders	L. Liu	95-day	34.50	34.50
W.S. George	**Touching the Spirit**			
93-81-001 Running With the Wind	J. Kramer Cole	95-day	29.50	29.50
93-81-002 Kindred Spirits	J. Kramer Cole	95-day	29.50	29.50
93-81-003 The Marking Tree	J. Kramer Cole	95-day	29.50	29.50
93-81-004 Wakan Tanka	J. Kramer Cole	95-day	29.50	29.50
93-81-005 He Who Watches	J. Kramer Cole	95-day	29.50	29.50
93-81-006 Twice Traveled Trail	J. Kramer Cole	95-day	29.50	29.50
93-81-007 Keeper of the Secret	J. Kramer Cole	95-day	29.50	29.50
93-81-008 Camp of the Sacred Dogs	J. Kramer Cole	95-day	29.50	29.50
W.S. George	**Eyes of the Wild**			
93-82-001 Eyes in the Mist	D. Pierce	95-day	29.50	29.50
93-82-002 Eyes in the Pines	D. Pierce	95-day	29.50	29.50
93-82-003 Eyes on the Sly	D. Pierce	95-day	29.50	29.50
93-82-004 Eyes of Gold	D. Pierce	95-day	29.50	29.50
93-82-005 Eyes of Silence	D. Pierce	95-day	29.50	29.50
93-82-006 Eyes in the Snow	D. Pierce	95-day	29.50	29.50
93-82-007 Eyes of Wonder	D. Pierce	95-day	29.50	29.50
94-82-008 Eyes of Strength	D. Pierce	95-day	29.50	29.50

		ARTIST	EDITION	ISSUE	QUOTE
W.S. George		**Enchanted Garden**			
93-83-001	A Peaceful Retreat	E. Antonaccio	95-day	24.50	24.50
93-83-002	Pleasant Pathways	E. Antonaccio	95-day	24.50	24.50
93-83-003	A Place to Dream	E. Antonaccio	95-day	24.50	24.50
93-83-004	Tranquil Hideaway	E. Antonaccio	95-day	24.50	24.50
W.S. George		**Feline Fancy**			
93-84-001	Globetrotters	H. Ronner	95-day	34.50	34.50
93-84-002	Little Athletes	H. Ronner	95-day	34.50	34.50
93-84-003	Young Adventurers	H. Ronner	95-day	34.50	34.50
93-84-004	The Geographers	H. Ronner	95-day	34.50	34.50
W.S. George		**'Tis the Season**			
93-85-001	A World Dressed in Snow	J. Sias	95-day	29.50	29.50
93-85-002	A Time for Tradition	J. Sias	95-day	29.50	29.50
93-85-003	We Shall Come Rejoining	J. Sias	95-day	29.50	29.50
93-85-004	Our Family Tree	J. Sias	95-day	29.50	29.50
W.S. George		**Floral Fancies**			
93-86-001	Sitting Softly	C. Callog	95-day	34.50	34.50
93-86-002	Sitting Pretty	C. Callog	95-day	34.50	34.50
93-86-003	Sitting Sunny	C. Callog	95-day	34.50	34.50
93-86-004	Sitting Pink	C. Callog	95-day	34.50	34.50
W.S. George		**Melodies in the Mist**			
93-87-001	Early Morning Rain	A. Sakhavarz	95-day	34.50	34.50
93-87-002	Among the Dewdrops	A. Sakhavarz	95-day	34.50	34.50
93-87-003	Feeding Time	A. Sakhavarz	95-day	37.50	37.50
93-87-004	The Garden Party	A. Sakhavarz	95-day	37.50	37.50
93-87-005	Unpleasant Surprise	A. Sakhavarz	95-day	37.50	37.50
93-87-006	Spring Rain	A. Sakhavarz	95-day	37.50	37.50
W.S. George		**On Golden Wings**			
93-88-001	Morning Light	W. Goebel	95-day	29.50	29.50
93-88-002	Early Risers	W. Goebel	95-day	29.50	29.50
93-88-003	As Day Breaks	W. Goebel	95-day	32.50	32.50
93-88-004	Daylight Flight	W. Goebel	95-day	32.50	32.50
93-88-005	Winter Dawn	W. Goebel	95-day	32.50	32.50
94-88-006	First Light	W. Goebel	95-day	34.50	34.50
W.S. George		**Romantic Roses**			
93-89-001	Victorian Beauty	V. Morley	95-day	29.50	29.50
93-89-002	Old-Fashioned Grace	V. Morley	95-day	29.50	29.50
93-89-003	Country Charm	V. Morley	95-day	32.50	32.50
93-89-004	Summer Romance	V. Morley	95-day	32.50	32.50
93-89-005	Pastoral Delight	V. Morley	95-day	32.50	32.50
93-89-006	Springtime Elegance	V. Morley	95-day	34.50	34.50
93-89-007	Vintage Splendor	V. Morley	95-day	34.50	34.50
94-89-008	Heavenly Perfection	V. Morley	95-day	34.50	34.50
Georgetown		**Children of the Great Spirit**			
93-01-001	Buffalo Child	C. Theroux	35-day	29.95	29.95
93-01-002	Winter Baby	C. Theroux	35-day	29.95	29.95
Goebel/M.I. Hummel		**M.I. Hummel Collectibles-Annual Plates**			
71-01-001	Heavenly Angel 264	M.I. Hummel	Closed	25.00	600-900.
72-01-002	Hear Ye, Hear Ye 265	M.I. Hummel	Closed	30.00	40-66.00
73-01-003	Glober Trotter 266	M.I. Hummel	Closed	32.50	75-120.
74-01-004	Goose Girl 267	M.I. Hummel	Closed	40.00	45-70.00
75-01-005	Ride into Christmas 268	M.I. Hummel	Closed	50.00	40-60.00
76-01-006	Apple Tree Girl 269	M.I. Hummel	Closed	50.00	45-75.00
77-01-007	Apple Tree Boy 270	M.I. Hummel	Closed	52.50	50-75.00
78-01-008	Happy Pastime 271	M.I. Hummel	Closed	65.00	40-55.00
79-01-009	Singing Lesson 272	M.I. Hummel	Closed	90.00	25-45.00
80-01-010	School Girl 273	M.I. Hummel	Closed	100.00	45-70.00
81-01-011	Umbrella Boy 274	M.I. Hummel	Closed	100.00	30-55.00
82-01-012	Umbrella Girl 275	M.I. Hummel	Closed	100.00	118-135.
83-01-013	The Postman 276	M.I. Hummel	Closed	108.00	180-230.
84-01-014	Little Helper 277	M.I. Hummel	Closed	108.00	58.00
85-01-015	Chick Girl 278	M.I. Hummel	Closed	110.00	65-100.
86-01-016	Playmates 279	M.I. Hummel	Closed	125.00	85-190.
87-01-017	Feeding Time 283	M.I. Hummel	Closed	135.00	300-375.
88-01-018	Little Goat Herder 284	M.I. Hummel	Closed	145.00	96-102.
89-01-019	Farm Boy 285	M.I. Hummel	Closed	160.00	117-124.
90-01-020	Shepherd's Boy 286	M.I. Hummel	Closed	170.00	176-230.
91-01-021	Just Resting 287	M.I. Hummel	Closed	196.00	120-190.
92-01-022	Wayside Harmony 288	M.I. Hummel	Closed	210.00	240.00
93-01-023	Doll Bath 289	M.I. Hummel	Yr.Iss.	210.00	190-215.
94-01-024	Doctor 290	M.I. Hummel	Yr.Iss.	225.00	225.00
Goebel/M.I. Hummel		**M.I. Hummel Collectibles Anniversary Plates**			
75-02-001	Stormy Weather 280	M.I. Hummel	Closed	100.00	65-115.
80-02-002	Spring Dance 281	M.I. Hummel	Closed	225.00	54.00
85-02-003	Auf Wiedersehen 282	M.I. Hummel	Closed	225.00	230-375.
Goebel/M.I. Hummel		**M.I. Hummel-Little Music Makers**			
84-03-001	Little Fiddler 744	M.I. Hummel	Closed	30.00	70-125.
85-03-002	Serenade 741	M.I. Hummel	Closed	30.00	70-125.
86-03-003	Soloist 743	M.I. Hummel	Closed	35.00	70-125.
87-03-004	Band Leader 742	M.I. Hummel	Closed	40.00	70-125.
Goebel/M.I. Hummel		**M.I. Hummel Club Exclusive-Celebration**			
86-04-001	Valentine Gift (Hum 738)	M.I. Hummel	Closed	90.00	100-150.
87-04-002	Valentine Joy (Hum 737)	M.I. Hummel	Closed	98.00	130-150.
88-04-003	Daisies Don't Tell (Hum 736)	M.I. Hummel	Closed	115.00	120-150.
89-04-004	It's Cold (Hum 735)	M.I. Hummel	Closed	120.00	130-150.
Goebel/M.I. Hummel		**M.I. Hummel-The Little Homemakers**			
88-05-001	Little Sweeper (Hum 745)	M.I. Hummel	Closed	45.00	28-35.00
89-05-002	Wash Day (Hum 746)	M.I. Hummel	Closed	50.00	24-35.00
90-05-003	A Stitch in Time (Hum 747)	M.I. Hummel	Closed	50.00	70-90.00
91-05-004	Chicken Licken (Hum 748)	M.I. Hummel	Closed	70.00	35-70.00
Goebel/M.I. Hummel		**M.I. Hummel-Friends Forever**			
92-06-001	Meditation 292	M.I. Hummel	Open	180.00	180.00
93-06-002	For Father 293	M.I. Hummel	Open	195.00	195.00
94-06-003	Sweet Greetings 294	M.I. Hummel	Open	205.00	205.00
Gorham		**Christmas**			
74-01-001	Tiny Tim	N. Rockwell	Annual	12.50	35.00
75-01-002	Good Deeds	N. Rockwell	Annual	17.50	35.00
76-01-003	Christmas Trio	N. Rockwell	Annual	19.50	20.00
77-01-004	Yuletide Reckoning	N. Rockwell	Annual	19.50	30.00
78-01-005	Planning Christmas Visit	N. Rockwell	Annual	24.50	24.50
79-01-006	Santa's Helpers	N. Rockwell	Annual	24.50	24.50
80-01-007	Letter to Santa	N. Rockwell	Annual	27.50	32.00
81-01-008	Santa Plans His Visit	N. Rockwell	Annual	29.50	50.00
82-01-009	Jolly Coachman	N. Rockwell	Annual	29.50	30.00
83-01-010	Christmas Dancers	N. Rockwell	Annual	29.50	35.00
84-01-011	Christmas Medley	N. Rockwell	17,500	29.95	29.95
85-01-012	Home For The Holidays	N. Rockwell	17,500	29.95	30.00
86-01-013	Merry Christmas Grandma	N. Rockwell	17,500	29.95	65.00
87-01-014	The Homecoming	N. Rockwell	17,500	35.00	52.00
88-01-015	Discovery	N. Rockwell	17,500	37.50	37.50
Gorham		**A Boy and His Dog Four Seasons Plates**			
71-02-001	Boy Meets His Dog	N. Rockwell	Annual	50.00	140.00
71-02-002	Adventures Between Adventures	N. Rockwell	Annual	Set	Set
71-02-003	The Mysterious Malady	N. Rockwell	Annual	Set	Set
71-02-004	Pride of Parenthood	N. Rockwell	Annual	Set	Set
Gorham		**Young Love Four Seasons Plates**			
72-03-001	Downhill Daring	N. Rockwell	Annual	60.00	125.00
72-03-002	Beguiling Buttercup	N. Rockwell	Annual	Set	Set
72-03-003	Flying High	N. Rockwell	Annual	Set	Set
72-03-004	A Scholarly Pace	N. Rockwell	Annual	Set	Set
Gorham		**Four Ages of Love**			
73-04-001	Gaily Sharing Vintage Time	N. Rockwell	Annual	60.00	165.00
73-04-002	Flowers in Tender Bloom	N. Rockwell	Annual	Set	Set
73-04-003	Sweet Song So Young	N. Rockwell	Annual	Set	Set
73-04-004	Fondly We Do Remember	N. Rockwell	Annual	Set	Set
Gorham		**Grandpa and Me Four Seasons Plates**			
74-05-001	Gay Blades	N. Rockwell	Annual	60.00	90.00
74-05-002	Day Dreamers	N. Rockwell	Annual	Set	Set
74-05-003	Goin' Fishing	N. Rockwell	Annual	Set	Set
74-05-004	Pensive Pals	N. Rockwell	Annual	Set	Set
Gorham		**Me and My Pals Four Seasons Plates**			
75-06-001	A Lickin' Good Bath	N. Rockwell	Annual	70.00	115.00
75-06-002	Young Man's Fancy	N. Rockwell	Annual	Set	Set
75-06-003	Fisherman's Paradise	N. Rockwell	Annual	Set	Set
75-06-004	Disastrous Daring	N. Rockwell	Annual	Set	Set
Gorham		**Grand Pals Four Seasons Plates**			
76-07-001	Snow Sculpturing	N. Rockwell	Annual	70.00	118.00
76-07-002	Soaring Spirits	N. Rockwell	Annual	Set	Set
76-07-003	Fish Finders	N. Rockwell	Annual	Set	Set
76-07-004	Ghostly Gourds	N. Rockwell	Annual	Set	Set
Gorham		**Going on Sixteen Four Seasons Plates**			
77-08-001	Chilling Chore	N. Rockwell	Annual	75.00	95.00
77-08-002	Sweet Serenade	N. Rockwell	Annual	Set	Set
77-08-003	Shear Agony	N. Rockwell	Annual	Set	Set
77-08-004	Pilgrimage	N. Rockwell	Annual	Set	Set
Gorham		**Tender Years Four Seasons Plates**			
78-09-001	New Year Look	N. Rockwell	Annual	100.00	70.00
78-09-002	Spring Tonic	N. Rockwell	Annual	Set	Set
78-09-003	Cool Aid	N. Rockwell	Annual	Set	Set
78-09-004	Chilly Reception	N. Rockwell	Annual	Set	Set
Gorham		**A Helping Hand Four Seasons Plates**			
79-10-001	Year End Court	N. Rockwell	Annual	100.00	44.00
79-10-002	Closed for Business	N. Rockwell	Annual	Set	Set
79-10-003	Swatter's Rights	N. Rockwell	Annual	Set	Set
79-10-004	Coal Season's Coming	N. Rockwell	Annual	Set	Set
Gorham		**Dad's Boys Four Seasons Plates**			
80-11-001	Ski Skills	N. Rockwell	Annual	135.00	98.00
80-11-002	In His Spirits	N. Rockwell	Annual	Set	Set
80-11-003	Trout Dinner	N. Rockwell	Annual	Set	Set
80-11-004	Careful Aim	N. Rockwell	Annual	Set	Set
Gorham		**Old Timers Four Seasons Plates**			
81-12-001	Canine Solo	N. Rockwell	Annual	100.00	100.00
81-12-002	Sweet Surprise	N. Rockwell	Annual	Set	Set
81-12-003	Lazy Days	N. Rockwell	Annual	Set	Set
81-12-004	Fancy Footwork	N. Rockwell	Annual	Set	Set
Gorham		**Life with Father Four Seasons Plates**			
82-13-001	Big Decision	N. Rockwell	Annual	100.00	200-300
82-13-002	Blasting Out	N. Rockwell	Annual	Set	Set
82-13-003	Cheering the Champs	N. Rockwell	Annual	Set	Set
82-13-004	A Tough One	N. Rockwell	Annual	Set	Set
Gorham		**Old Buddies Four Seasons Plates**			
83-14-001	Shared Success	N. Rockwell	Annual	115.00	115.00
83-14-002	Endless Debate	N. Rockwell	Annual	Set	Set
83-14-003	Hasty Retreat	N. Rockwell	Annual	Set	Set
83-14-004	Final Speech	N. Rockwell	Annual	Set	Set
Gorham		**Bas Relief**			
81-15-001	Sweet Song So Young	N. Rockwell	Undis.	100.00	100.00
81-15-002	Beguiling Buttercup	N. Rockwell	Undis.	62.50	70.00
82-15-003	Flowers in Tender Bloom	N. Rockwell	Undis.	100.00	100.00
82-15-004	Flying High	N. Rockwell	Undis.	62.50	65.00
Gorham		**Single Release**			
74-16-001	Weighing In	N. Rockwell	Annual	12.50	80-99.00
Gorham		**Single Release**			
74-17-001	The Golden Rule	N. Rockwell	Annual	12.50	30.00
Gorham		**Single Release**			
75-18-001	Ben Franklin	N. Rockwell	Annual	19.50	35.00
Gorham		**Boy Scout Plates**			
75-19-001	Our Heritage	N. Rockwell	18,500	19.50	40.00
76-19-002	A Scout is Loyal	N. Rockwell	18,500	19.50	55.00
77-19-003	The Scoutmaster	N. Rockwell	18,500	19.50	60.00
77-19-004	A Good Sign	N. Rockwell	18,500	19.50	50.00
78-19-005	Pointing the Way	N. Rockwell	18,500	19.50	50.00
78-19-006	Campfire Story	N. Rockwell	18,500	19.50	25.00
80-19-007	Beyond the Easel	N. Rockwell	18,500	45.00	45.00
Gorham		**Single Release**			
76-20-001	The Marriage License	N. Rockwell	Numbrd	37.50	52-75.00
Gorham		**Presidential**			
76-21-001	John F. Kennedy	N. Rockwell	9,800	30.00	65.00
76-21-002	Dwight D. Eisenhower	N. Rockwell	9,800	30.00	35.00
Gorham		**Single Release**			
78-22-001	Triple Self Portrait Memorial Plate	N. Rockwell	Annual	37.50	60.00

		ARTIST	EDITION	ISSUE	QUOTE
Gorham	**Four Seasons Landscapes**				
80-23-001	Summer Respite	N. Rockwell	Annual	45.00	80.00
81-23-002	Autumn Reflection	N. Rockwell	Annual	45.00	65.00
82-23-003	Winter Delight	N. Rockwell	Annual	50.00	62.50
83-23-004	Spring Recess	N. Rockwell	Annual	60.00	60.00
Gorham	**Single Release**				
80-24-001	The Annual Visit	N. Rockwell	Annual	32.50	70.00
81-25-002	Day in Life of Boy	N. Rockwell	Annual	50.00	80.00
81-25-003	Day in Life of Girl	N. Rockwell	Annual	50.00	80-108.
Gorham	**Gallery of Masters**				
71-26-001	Man with a Gilt Helmet	Rembrandt	10,000	50.00	50.00
72-26-002	Self Portrait with Saskia	Rembrandt	10,000	50.00	50.00
73-26-003	The Honorable Mrs. Graham	Gainsborough	7,500	50.00	50.00
Gorham	**Barrymore**				
71-27-001	Quiet Waters	Barrymore	15,000	25.00	25.00
72-27-002	San Pedro Harbor	Barrymore	15,000	25.00	25.00
72-27-003	Nantucket, Sterling	Barrymore	1,000	100.00	100.00
72-27-004	Little Boatyard, Sterling	Barrymore	1,000	100.00	145.00
Gorham	**Pewter Bicentennial**				
71-29-001	Burning of the Gaspee	R. Pailthorpe	5,000	35.00	35.00
72-29-002	Boston Tea Party	R. Pailthorpe	5,000	35.00	35.00
Gorham	**Vermeil Bicentennial**				
72-30-001	1776 Plate	Gorham	250	750.00	800.00
Gorham	**Silver Bicentennial**				
72-31-001	1776 Plate	Gorham	500	500.00	500.00
72-31-002	Burning of the Gaspee	R. Pailthorpe	750	500.00	500.00
73-31-003	Boston Tea Party	R. Pailthorpe	750	550.00	575.00
Gorham	**China Bicentennial**				
72-32-001	1776 Plate	Gorham	18,500	17.50	35.00
76-32-002	1776 Bicentennial	Gorham	8,000	17.50	35.00
Gorham	**Remington Western**				
73-33-001	A New Year on the Cimarron	F. Remington	Annual	25.00	35-50.00
73-33-002	Aiding a Comrade	F. Remington	Annual	25.00	30-125.
73-33-003	The Flight	F. Remington	Annual	25.00	30-95.00
73-33-004	The Fight for the Water Hole	F. Remington	Annual	25.00	30-125.
75-33-005	Old Ramond	F. Remington	Annual	20.00	35-60.00
75-33-006	A Breed	F. Remington	Annual	20.00	35-65.00
76-33-007	Cavalry Officer	F. Remington	5,000	37.50	60-75.00
76-33-008	A Trapper	F. Remington	5,000	37.50	60-75.00
Gorham	**Moppet Plates-Christmas**				
73-34-001	M. Plate Christmas	Unknown	Annual	10.00	35.00
74-34-002	M. Plate Christmas	Unknown	Annual	12.00	12.00
75-34-003	M. Plate Christmas	Unknown	Annual	13.00	13.00
76-34-004	M. Plate Christmas	Unknown	Annual	13.00	15.00
77-34-005	M. Plate Christmas	Unknown	Annual	13.00	14.00
78-34-006	M. Plate Christmas	Unknown	Annual	10.00	10.00
79-34-007	M. Plate Christmas	Unknown	Annual	12.00	12.00
80-34-008	M. Plate Christmas	Unknown	Annual	12.00	12.00
81-34-009	M. Plate Christmas	Unknown	Annual	12.00	12.00
82-34-010	M. Plate Christmas	Unknown	Annual	12.00	12.00
83-34-011	M. Plate Christmas	Unknown	Annual	12.00	12.00
Gorham	**Moppet Plates-Mother's Day**				
73-35-001	M. Plate Mother's Day	Unknown	Annual	10.00	30.00
74-35-002	M. Plate Mother's Day	Unknown	Annual	12.00	20.00
75-35-003	M. Plate Mother's Day	Unknown	Annual	13.00	15.00
76-35-004	M. Plate Mother's Day	Unknown	Annual	13.00	15.00
77-35-005	M. Plate Mother's Day	Unknown	Annual	13.00	15.00
78-35-006	M. Plate Mother's Day	Unknown	Annual	10.00	10.00
Gorham	**Moppet Plates-Anniversary**				
76-36-001	M. Plate Anniversary	Unknown	20,000	13.00	13.00
Gorham	**Julian Ritter, Fall In Love**				
77-37-001	Enchantment	J. Ritter	5,000	100.00	100.00
77-37-002	Frolic	J. Ritter	5,000	set	set
77-37-003	Gutsy Gal	J. Ritter	5,000	set	set
77-37-004	Lonely Chill	J. Ritter	5,000	set	set
Gorham	**Julian Ritter**				
77-38-001	Christmas Visit	J. Ritter	9,800	24.50	29.00
Gorham	**Julian Ritter, To Love a Clown**				
78-39-001	Awaited Reunion	J. Ritter	5,000	120.00	120.00
78-39-002	Twosome Time	J. Ritter	5,000	120.00	120.00
78-39-003	Showtime Beckons	J. Ritter	5,000	120.00	120.00
78-39-004	Together in Memories	J. Ritter	5,000	120.00	120.00
Gorham	**Julian Ritter**				
78-40-001	Valentine, Fluttering Heart	J. Ritter	7,500	45.00	45.00
Gorham	**Christmas/Children's Television Workshop**				
81-41-001	Sesame Street Christmas	Unknown	Annual	17.50	17.50
82-41-002	Sesame Street Christmas	Unknown	Annual	17.50	17.50
83-41-003	Sesame Street Christmas	Unknown	Annual	19.50	19.50
Gorham	**Pastoral Symphony**				
82-42-001	When I Was a Child	B. Felder	7,500	42.50	50.00
82-42-002	Gather the Children	B. Felder	7,500	42.50	50.00
84-42-003	Sugar and Spice	B. Felder	7,500	42.50	50.00
XX-42-004	He Loves Me	B. Felder	7,500	42.50	50.00
Gorham	**Encounters, Survival and Celebrations**				
82-43-001	A Fine Welcome	J. Clymer	7,500	50.00	75.00
83-43-002	Winter Trail	J. Clymer	7,500	50.00	125.00
83-43-003	Alouette	J. Clymer	7,500	62.50	62.50
83-43-004	The Trader	J. Clymer	7,500	62.50	62.50
83-43-005	Winter Camp	J. Clymer	7,500	62.50	75.00
83-43-006	The Trapper Takes a Wife	J. Clymer	7,500	62.50	62.50
Gorham	**Charles Russell**				
80-44-001	In Without Knocking	C. Russell	9,800	38.00	75.00
81-44-002	Bronc to Breakfast	C. Russell	9,800	38.00	75-115.
82-44-003	When Ignorance is Bliss	C. Russell	9,800	45.00	75-115.
83-44-004	Cowboy Life	C. Russell	9,800	45.00	100.00
Gorham	**Gorham Museum Doll Plates**				
84-45-001	Lydia	Gorham	5,000	29.00	125.00
84-45-002	Belton Bebe	Gorham	5,000	29.00	55.00

		ARTIST	EDITION	ISSUE	QUOTE
84-45-003	Christmas Lady	Gorham	7,500	32.50	32.50
85-45-004	Lucille	Gorham	5,000	29.00	35.00
85-45-005	Jumeau	Gorham	5,000	29.00	35.00
Gorham	**Time Machine Teddies Plates**				
86-46-001	Miss Emily, Bearing Up	B. Port	5,000	32.50	32.50
87-46-002	Big Bear, The Toy Collector	B. Port	5,000	32.50	45.00
88-46-003	Hunny Munny	B. Port	5,000	37.50	37.50
Gorham	**Leyendecker Annual Christmas Plates**				
88-47-001	Christmas Hug	J. C. Leyendecker	10,000	37.50	50.00
Gorham	**Single Release**				
76-48-001	The Black Regiment 1778	F. Quagon	7,500	25.00	58.00
Gorham	**American Artist**				
76-49-001	Apache Mother & Child	R. Donnelly	9,800	25.00	56.00
Dave Grossman Creations	**Emmett Kelly Plates**				
86-01-001	Christmas Carol	B. Leighton-Jones	Yr.Iss.	20.00	20.00
87-01-002	Christmas Wreath	B. Leighton-Jones	Yr.Iss.	20.00	20.00
88-01-003	Christmas Dinner	B. Leighton-Jones	Yr.Iss.	20.00	49.00
89-01-004	Christmas Feast	B. Leighton-Jones	Yr.Iss.	20.00	39.00
90-01-005	Just What I Needed	B. Leighton-Jones	Yr.Iss.	24.00	39.00
91-01-006	Emmett The Snowman	B. Leighton-Jones	Yr.Iss.	25.00	45.00
92-01-007	Christmas Tunes	B. Leighton-Jones	Yr.Iss.	25.00	25.00
93-01-008	Downhill-Christmas Plate	B. Leighton-Jones	Yr.Iss.	30.00	30.00
94-01-009	Holiday Skater EKP-94	B. Leighton-Jones	Yr.Iss.	30.00	30.00
Dave Grossman Creations	**Saturday Evening Post Collection**				
91-02-001	Downhill Daring BRP-91	Rockwell-Inspired	Yr.Iss.	25.00	25.00
91-02-002	Missed BRP-101	Rockwell-Inspired	Yr.Iss.	25.00	25.00
92-02-003	Choosin Up BRP-102	Rockwell-Inspired	Yr.Iss.	25.00	25.00
Dave Grossman Designs	**Norman Rockwell Collection**				
79-01-001	Leapfrog NRP-79	Rockwell-Inspired	Retrd.	50.00	50.00
80-01-002	Lovers NRP-80	Rockwell-Inspired	Retrd.	60.00	60.00
81-01-003	Dreams of Long Ago NRP-81	Rockwell-Inspired	Retrd.	60.00	60.00
82-01-004	Doctor and Doll NRP-82	Rockwell-Inspired	Retrd.	65.00	95.00
83-01-005	Circus NRP-83	Rockwell-Inspired	Retrd.	65.00	65.00
84-01-006	Visit With Rockwell NRP-84	Rockwell-Inspired	Retrd.	65.00	65.00
80-01-007	Christmas Trio RXP-80	Rockwell-Inspired	Retrd.	75.00	75.00
81-01-008	Santa's Good Boys RXP-81	Rockwell-Inspired	Retrd.	75.00	75.00
82-01-009	Faces of Christmas RXP-82	Rockwell-Inspired	Retrd.	75.00	75.00
83-01-010	Christmas Chores RXP-83	Rockwell-Inspired	Retrd.	75.00	75.00
84-01-011	Tiny Tim RXP-84	Rockwell-Inspired	Retrd.	75.00	75.00
80-01-012	Back To School RMP-80	Rockwell-Inspired	Retrd.	24.00	24.00
81-01-013	No Swimming RMP-81	Rockwell-Inspired	Retrd.	25.00	25.00
82-01-014	Love Letter RMP-82	Rockwell-Inspired	Retrd.	27.00	30.00
83-01-015	Doctor and Doll RMP-83	Rockwell-Inspired	Retrd.	27.00	27.00
84-01-016	Big Moment RMP-84	Rockwell-Inspired	Retrd.	27.00	27.00
79-01-017	Butterboy RP-01	Rockwell-Inspired	Retrd.	40.00	40.00
82-01-018	American Mother RGP-42	Rockwell-Inspired	Retrd.	45.00	45.00
83-01-019	Dreamboat RGP-83	Rockwell-Inspired	Retrd.	24.00	30.00
78-01-020	Young Doctor RDP-26	Rockwell-Inspired	Retrd.	50.00	65.00
Dave Grossman Designs	**Norman Rockwell Collection-Tom Sawyer Plates**				
75-02-001	Whitewashing the Fence TSP-01	Rockwell-Inspired	Retrd.	26.00	35.00
76-02-002	First Smoke TSP-02	Rockwell-Inspired	Retrd.	26.00	35.00
77-02-003	Take Your Medicine TSP-03	Rockwell-Inspired	Retrd.	26.00	40.00
78-02-004	Lost in Cave TSP-04	Rockwell-Inspired	Retrd.	26.00	40.00
Dave Grossman Designs	**Norman Rockwell Collection-Huck Finn Plates**				
79-03-001	Secret HFP-01	Rockwell-Inspired	Retrd.	40.00	40.00
80-03-002	Listening HFP-02	Rockwell-Inspired	Retrd.	40.00	40.00
80-03-003	No Kings HFP-03	Rockwell-Inspired	Retrd.	40.00	40.00
81-03-004	Snake Escapes HFP-04	Rockwell-Inspired	Retrd.	40.00	40.00
Dave Grossman Designs	**Norman Rockwell Collection-Boy Scout Plates**				
81-04-001	Can't Wait BSP-01	Rockwell-Inspired	Retrd.	30.00	45.00
82-04-002	Guiding Hand BSP-02	Rockwell-Inspired	Retrd.	30.00	35.00
83-04-003	Tomorrow's Leader BSP-03	Rockwell-Inspired	Retrd.	30.00	45.00
Hackett American	**Sports**				
81-01-001	Reggie Jackson h/s	Paluso	Retrd.	100.00	895.00
82-01-002	Steve Garvey h/s	Paluso	Retrd.	100.00	225.00
83-01-003	Nolan Ryan h/s	Paluso	Retrd.	100.00	795.00
XX-01-004	Tom Seaver h/s	Paluso	Retrd.	100.00	325.00
XX-01-005	Steve Carlton h/s	Paluso	Retrd.	100.00	350.00
XX-01-006	Willie Mays h/s	Paluso	Retrd.	125.00	275-395.
XX-01-007	Whitey Ford h/s	Paluso	Retrd.	125.00	295.00
XX-01-008	Hank Aaron h/s	Paluso	Retrd.	125.00	275-350.
XX-01-009	Sandy Koufax h/s	Paluso	Retrd.	125.00	275-495.
XX-01-010	H. Killebrew d/s	Paluso	Retrd.	125.00	325.00
XX-01-011	E. Mathews d/s	Paluso	Retrd.	125.00	225.00
86-01-012	T. Seaver 300 d/s	Paluso	Retrd.	125.00	250.00
XX-01-013	Roger Clemens d/s	Paluso	Retrd.	125.00	595.00
86-01-014	Reggie Jackson d/s	Paluso	Retrd.	125.00	395.00
XX-01-015	Wally Joyner d/s	Paluso	Retrd.	125.00	295.00
XX-01-016	Don Sutton d/s	Paluso	Retrd.	125.00	325.00
XX-01-017	Gary Carter d/s	Simon	Retrd.	125.00	175.00
XX-01-018	Dwight Gooden u/s	Simon	Retrd.	55.00	100.00
XX-01-019	Arnold Palmer h/s	Alexander	Retrd.	125.00	225.00
XX-01-020	Gary Player h/s	Alexander	Retrd.	125.00	395.00
XX-01-021	Reggie Jackson h/s	Alexander	Retrd.	125.00	695.00
XX-01-022	Reggie Jackson, proof	Alexander	Retrd.	250.00	N/A
86-01-023	Joe Montana d/s	Alexander	Retrd.	125.00	795.00
Hadley House	**Glow Series**				
85-01-001	Evening Glow	T. Redlin	5,000	55.00	450-500.
85-01-002	Morning Glow	T. Redlin	5,000	55.00	200-250.
85-01-003	Twilight Glow	T. Redlin	5,000	55.00	90-125.
88-01-004	Afternoon Glow	T. Redlin	5,000	55.00	55.00
Hadley House	**Retreat Series**				
87-02-001	Morning Retreat	T. Redlin	9,500	65.00	90-125.
87-02-002	Evening Retreat	T. Redlin	9,500	65.00	65-75.00
88-02-003	Golden Retreat	T. Redlin	9,500	65.00	95.00
89-02-004	Moonlight Retreat	T. Redlin	9,500	65.00	65.00
Hadley House	**American Memories Series**				
87-03-001	Coming Home	T. Redlin	9,500	85.00	85.00
88-03-002	Lights of Home	T. Redlin	9,500	85.00	85.00
89-03-003	Homeward Bound	T. Redlin	9,500	85.00	85.00
91-03-004	Family Traditions	T. Redlin	9,500	85.00	85.00

		ARTIST	EDITION	ISSUE	QUOTE
Hadley House		**Annual Christmas Series**			
91-04-001	Heading Home	T. Redlin	9,500	65.00	65.00
92-04-002	Pleasures Of Winter	T. Redlin	19,500	65.00	65.00
93-04-003	Winter Wonderland	T. Redlin	19,500	65.00	65.00
Hadley House		**Windows to the Wild**			
90-05-001	Master's Domain	T. Redlin	9,500	65.00	65.00
91-05-002	Winter Windbreak	T. Redlin	9,500	65.00	65.00
92-05-003	Evening Company	T. Redlin	9,500	65.00	65.00
94-05-004	Night Mapling	T. Redlin	9,500	65.00	65.00
Hadley House		**That Special Time**			
91-06-001	Evening Solitude	T. Redlin	9,500	65.00	65.00
92-06-002	Aroma of Fall	T. Redlin	9,500	65.00	65.00
93-06-003	Welcome To Paradise	T. Redlin	9,500	65.00	65.00
Hadley House		**Lovers Collection**			
92-07-001	Lovers	O. Franca	9,500	50.00	50.00
Hadley House		**Navajo Woman Series**			
90-08-001	Feathered Hair Ties	O. Franca	5,000	50.00	50.00
91-08-002	Navajo Summer	O. Franca	5,000	50.00	50.00
92-08-003	Turquoise Necklace	O. Franca	5,000	50.00	50.00
93-08-004	Pink Navajo	O. Franca	5,000	50.00	50.00
Hadley House		**Navajo Visions Suite**			
93-09-001	Navajo Fantasy	O. Franca	5,000	50.00	50.00
93-09-002	Young Warrior	O. Franca	5,000	50.00	50.00
Hallmark Galleries		**Enchanted Garden**			
92-01-001	Neighborhood Dreamer 4500QHG3001	E. Richardson	Retrd.	45.00	45.00
92-01-002	Swan Lake (tile) 3500QHG3010	E. Richardson	Retrd.	35.00	35.00
92-01-003	Fairy Bunny Tale: The Beginning (tile) 2500QHG3011	E. Richardson	Retrd.	25.00	25.00
92-01-004	Fairy Bunny Tale: Beginning II (tile) 3500QHG3015	E. Richardson	Retrd.	35.00	35.00
Hallmark Galleries		**Days to Remember-The Art of Norman Rockwell**			
92-02-001	A Boy Meets His Dog (pewter medallion) 4500QHG9715	Rockwell-Inspired	Retrd.	45.00	45.00
92-02-002	Sweet Song So Young (pewter medallion) 4500QHG9716	Rockwell-Inspired	Retrd.	45.00	45.00
92-02-003	Fisherman's Paradise (pewter medallion) 4500QHG9717	Rockwell-Inspired	Retrd.	45.00	45.00
92-02-004	Sleeping Children (pewter medallion) 4500QHG9718	Rockwell-Inspired	Retrd.	45.00	45.00
93-02-005	Breaking Home Ties 3500QHG9723	Rockwell-Inspired	9,500	35.00	35.00
94-02-006	Growing Years 3500QHG9724	Rockwell-Inspired	9,500	35.00	35.00
Hallmark Galleries		**Innocent Wonders**			
92-03-001	Pinkie Poo 3500QHG4017	T. Blackshear	9,500	35.00	35.00
92-03-002	Dinky Toot 3500QHG4019	T. Blackshear	9,500	35.00	35.00
93-03-003	Pockets 3500QHG4022	T. Blackshear	9,500	35.00	35.00
94-03-004	Twinky Wink 3500QHG4023	T. Blackshear	9,500	35.00	35.00
Hallmark Galleries		**Tobin Fraley Carousels**			
92-04-001	Philadelphia Toboggan Co/1920 (pewter medallion) 4500QHG20	T. Fraley	Retrd.	45.00	45.00
93-04-002	Magical Ride 3500QHG30	T. Fraley	9,500	35.00	35.00
94-04-003	Riding to Adventure 3500QHG23	T. Fraley	9,500	35.00	35.00
Hallmark Galleries		**Majestic Wilderness**			
92-05-001	Timber Wolves (porcelain) 3500QHG2012	M. Newman	9,500	35.00	35.00
92-05-002	Vixen & Kits 3500QHG2018	M. Newman	9,500	35.00	35.00
94-05-003	White Tail Buck 3500QHG2030	M. Newman	9,500	35.00	35.00
Hallmark Galleries		**Easter Plate**			
94-06-001	Collector's Plate-First Ed. 775QE08233	L. Votruba	Yr.Iss.	7.75	7.75
Hallmark Galleries		**Majestic Wilderness**			
94-07-001	Golden Rule (tile) 3000QHG5010	M. Englebreit	14,500	30.00	30.00
94-07-002	Recipe for Happiness (tile) 3000QHG5011	M. Englebreit	14500	30.00	30.00
Hamilton/Boehm		**Award Winning Roses**			
79-01-001	Peace Rose	Boehm	15,000	45.00	62.50
79-01-002	White Masterpiece Rose	Boehm	15,000	45.00	62.50
79-01-003	Tropicana Rose	Boehm	15,000	45.00	62.50
79-01-004	Elegance Rose	Boehm	15,000	45.00	62.50
79-01-005	Queen Elizabeth Rose	Boehm	15,000	45.00	62.50
79-01-006	Royal Highness Rose	Boehm	15,000	45.00	62.50
79-01-007	Angel Face Rose	Boehm	15,000	45.00	62.50
79-01-008	Mr. Lincoln Rose	Boehm	15,000	45.00	62.50
Hamilton/Boehm		**Owl Collection**			
80-02-001	Boreal Owl	Boehm	15,000	45.00	75.00
80-02-002	Snowy Owl	Boehm	15,000	45.00	62.50
80-02-003	Barn Owl	Boehm	15,000	45.00	62.50
80-02-004	Saw Whet Owl	Boehm	15,000	45.00	62.50
80-02-005	Great Horned Owl	Boehm	15,000	45.00	62.50
80-02-006	Screech Owl	Boehm	15,000	45.00	62.50
80-02-007	Short Eared Owl	Boehm	15,000	45.00	62.50
80-02-008	Barred Owl	Boehm	15,000	45.00	62.50
Hamilton/Boehm		**Hummingbird Collection**			
80-03-001	Calliope	Boehm	15,000	62.50	80.00
80-03-002	Broadbilled	Boehm	15,000	62.50	62.50
80-03-003	Rufous Flame Bearer	Boehm	15,000	62.50	80.00
80-03-004	Broadtail	Boehm	15,000	62.50	62.50
80-03-005	Streamertail	Boehm	15,000	62.50	80.00
80-03-006	Blue Throated	Boehm	15,000	62.50	80.00
80-03-007	Crimson Topaz	Boehm	15,000	62.50	62.50
80-03-008	Brazilian Ruby	Boehm	15,000	62.50	80.00
Hamilton/Boehm		**Water Birds**			
81-04-001	Canada Geese	Boehm	15,000	62.50	75.00
81-04-002	Wood Ducks	Boehm	15,000	62.50	62.50
81-04-003	Hooded Merganser	Boehm	15,000	62.50	87.00
81-04-004	Ross's Geese	Boehm	15,000	62.50	62.50
81-04-005	Common Mallard	Boehm	15,000	62.50	62.50
81-04-006	Canvas Back	Boehm	15,000	62.50	62.50
81-04-007	Green Winged Teal	Boehm	15,000	62.50	62.50
81-04-008	American Pintail	Boehm	15,000	62.50	62.50
Hamilton/Boehm		**Gamebirds of North America**			
84-05-001	Ring-Necked Pheasant	Boehm	15,000	62.50	62.50
84-05-002	Bob White Quail	Boehm	15,000	62.50	62.50
84-05-003	American Woodcock	Boehm	15,000	62.50	62.50
84-05-004	California Quail	Boehm	15,000	62.50	62.50
84-05-005	Ruffed Grouse	Boehm	15,000	62.50	62.50

		ARTIST	EDITION	ISSUE	QUOTE
84-05-006	Wild Turkey	Boehm	15,000	62.50	62.50
84-05-007	Willow Partridge	Boehm	15,000	62.50	62.50
84-05-008	Prairie Grouse	Boehm	15,000	62.50	62.50
Hamilton Collection		**Precious Portraits**			
87-01-001	Sunbeam	B. P. Gutmann	14-day	24.50	36.00
87-01-002	Mischief	B. P. Gutmann	14-day	24.50	30.00
87-01-003	Peach Blossom	B. P. Gutmann	14-day	24.50	36.00
87-01-004	Goldilocks	B. P. Gutmann	14-day	24.50	30.00
87-01-005	Fairy Gold	B. P. Gutmann	14-day	24.50	36.00
87-01-006	Bunny	B. P. Gutmann	14-day	24.50	30.00
Hamilton Collection		**Bundles of Joy**			
88-02-001	Awakening	B. P. Gutmann	14-day	24.50	75.00
88-02-002	Happy Dreams	B. P. Gutmann	14-day	24.50	60-99.00
88-02-003	Tasting	B. P. Gutmann	14-day	24.50	36-59.00
88-02-004	Sweet Innocence	B. P. Gutmann	14-day	24.50	30.00
88-02-005	Tommy	B. P. Gutmann	14-day	24.50	30.00
88-02-006	A Little Bit of Heaven	B. P. Gutmann	14-day	24.50	75.00
88-02-007	Billy	B. P. Gutmann	14-day	24.50	30-35.00
88-02-008	Sun Kissed	B. P. Gutmann	14-day	24.50	30-35.00
Hamilton Collection		**The Nutcracker Ballet**			
78-03-001	Clara	S. Fisher	28-day	19.50	36.00
79-03-002	Godfather	S. Fisher	28-day	19.50	15-19.50
79-03-003	Sugar Plum Fairy	S. Fisher	28-day	19.50	45.00
79-03-004	Snow Queen and King	S. Fisher	28-day	19.50	40.00
80-03-005	Waltz of the Flowers	S. Fisher	28-day	19.50	19.50
80-03-006	Clara and the Prince	S. Fisher	28-day	19.50	45.00
Hamilton Collection		**Precious Moments Plates**			
79-04-001	Friend in the Sky	T. Utz	28-day	21.50	50.00
80-04-002	Sand in her Shoe	T. Utz	28-day	21.50	27.00
80-04-003	Snow Bunny	T. Utz	28-day	21.50	18.00
80-04-004	Seashells	T. Utz	28-day	21.50	37.50
81-04-005	Dawn	T. Utz	28-day	21.50	27.00
82-04-006	My Kitty	T. Utz	28-day	21.50	36.00
Hamilton Collection		**The Greatest Show on Earth**			
81-05-001	Clowns	F. Moody	10-day	30.00	45.00
81-05-002	Elephants	F. Moody	10-day	30.00	30.00
81-05-003	Aerialists	F. Moody	10-day	30.00	30.00
81-05-004	Great Parade	F. Moody	10-day	30.00	30.00
81-05-005	Midway	F. Moody	10-day	30.00	30.00
81-05-006	Equestrians	F. Moody	10-day	30.00	30.00
82-05-007	Lion Tamer	F. Moody	10-day	30.00	30.00
82-05-008	Grande Finale	F. Moody	10-day	30.00	30.00
Hamilton Collection		**Rockwell Home of the Brave**			
81-06-001	Reminiscing	N. Rockwell	18,000	35.00	52.50
81-06-002	Hero's Welcome	N. Rockwell	18,000	35.00	52.50
81-06-003	Back to his Old Job	N. Rockwell	18,000	35.00	52.50
81-06-004	War Hero	N. Rockwell	18,000	35.00	35.00
82-06-005	Willie Gillis in Church	N. Rockwell	18,000	35.00	52.50
82-06-006	War Bond	N. Rockwell	18,000	35.00	35.00
82-06-007	Uncle Sam Takes Wings	N. Rockwell	18,000	35.00	75.00
82-06-008	Taking Mother over the Top	N. Rockwell	18,000	35.00	35.00
Hamilton Collection		**Japanese Floral Calendar**			
81-07-001	New Year's Day	Shuho/Kage	10-day	32.50	32.50
82-07-002	Early Spring	Shuho/Kage	10-day	32.50	32.50
82-07-003	Spring	Shuho/Kage	10-day	32.50	32.50
82-07-004	Girl's Doll Day Festival	Shuho/Kage	10-day	32.50	32.50
82-07-005	Buddha's Birthday	Shuho/Kage	10-day	32.50	32.50
82-07-006	Early Summer	Shuho/Kage	10-day	32.50	32.50
82-07-007	Boy's Doll Day Festival	Shuho/Kage	10-day	32.50	32.50
82-07-008	Summer	Shuho/Kage	10-day	32.50	32.50
82-07-009	Autumn	Shuho/Kage	10-day	32.50	32.50
83-07-010	Festival of the Full Moon	Shuho/Kage	10-day	32.50	32.50
83-07-011	Late Autumn	Shuho/Kage	10-day	32.50	32.50
83-07-012	Winter	Shuho/Kage	10-day	32.50	32.50
Hamilton Collection		**Portraits of Childhood**			
81-08-001	Butterfly Magic	T. Utz	28-day	24.95	24.95
82-08-002	Sweet Dreams	T. Utz	28-day	24.95	24.95
83-08-003	Turtle Talk	T. Utz	28-day	24.95	24.95
84-08-004	Friends Forever	T. Utz	28-day	24.95	24.95
Hamilton Collection		**Carefree Days**			
82-09-001	Autumn Wanderer	T. Utz	10-day	24.50	18-24.50
82-09-002	Best Friends	T. Utz	10-day	24.50	30.00
82-09-003	Feeding Time	T. Utz	10-day	24.50	24.50
82-09-004	Bathtime Visitor	T. Utz	10-day	24.50	30.00
82-09-005	First Catch	T. Utz	10-day	24.50	30.00
82-09-006	Monkey Business	T. Utz	10-day	24.50	30.00
82-09-007	Touchdown	T. Utz	10-day	24.50	24.50
82-09-008	Nature Hunt	T. Utz	10-day	24.50	24.50
Hamilton Collection		**Utz Mother's Day**			
83-10-001	A Gift of Love	T. Utz	N/A	27.50	37.50
83-10-002	Mother's Helping Hand	T. Utz	N/A	27.50	27.50
83-10-003	Mother's Angel	T. Utz	N/A	27.50	27.50
Hamilton Collection		**Single Issues**			
83-11-001	Princess Grace	T. Utz	21-day	39.50	60.00
Hamilton Collection		**Summer Days of Childhood**			
83-12-001	Mountain Friends	T. Utz	10-day	29.50	29.50
83-12-002	Garden Magic	T. Utz	10-day	29.50	29.50
83-12-003	Little Beachcomber	T. Utz	10-day	29.50	29.50
83-12-004	Blowing Bubbles	T. Utz	10-day	29.50	29.50
83-12-005	The Birthday Party	T. Utz	10-day	29.50	29.50
83-12-006	Playing Doctor	T. Utz	10-day	29.50	29.50
83-12-007	A Stolen Kiss	T. Utz	10-day	29.50	29.50
83-12-008	Kitty's Bathtime	T. Utz	10-day	29.50	29.50
83-12-009	Cooling Off	T. Utz	10-day	29.50	29.50
83-12-010	First Customer	T. Utz	10-day	29.50	29.50
83-12-011	A Jumping Contest	T. Utz	10-day	29.50	29.50
83-12-012	Balloon Carnival	T. Utz	10-day	29.50	29.50
Hamilton Collection		**Passage to China**			
83-13-001	Empress of China	R. Massey	15,000	55.00	55.00
83-13-002	Alliance	R. Massey	15,000	55.00	55.00
85-13-003	Grand Turk	R. Massey	15,000	55.00	55.00
85-13-004	Sea Witch	R. Massey	15,000	55.00	55.00
85-13-005	Flying Cloud	R. Massey	15,000	55.00	55.00

		ARTIST	EDITION	ISSUE	QUOTE
85-13-006	Romance of the Seas	R. Massey	15,000	55.00	55.00
85-13-007	Sea Serpent	R. Massey	15,000	55.00	55.00
85-13-008	Challenge	R. Massey	15,000	55.00	55.00
Hamilton Collection		**Springtime of Life**			
85-14-001	Teddy's Bathtime	T. Utz	14-day	29.50	29.50
85-14-002	Just Like Mommy	T. Utz	14-day	29.50	29.50
85-14-003	Among the Daffodils	T. Utz	14-day	29.50	29.50
85-14-004	My Favorite Dolls	T. Utz	14-day	29.50	29.50
85-14-005	Aunt Tillie's Hats	T. Utz	14-day	29.50	29.50
85-14-006	Little Emily	T. Utz	14-day	29.50	29.50
85-14-007	Granny's Boots	T. Utz	14-day	29.50	29.50
85-14-008	My Masterpiece	T. Utz	14-day	29.50	29.50
Hamilton Collection		**A Child's Best Friend**			
85-15-001	In Disgrace	B. P. Gutmann	14-day	24.50	90.00
85-15-002	The Reward	B. P. Gutmann	14-day	24.50	60.00
85-15-003	Who's Sleepy	B. P. Gutmann	14-day	24.50	90-99.00
85-15-004	Good Morning	B. P. Gutmann	14-day	24.50	75.00
85-15-005	Sympathy	B. P. Gutmann	14-day	24.50	54.00
85-15-006	On the Up and Up	B. P. Gutmann	14-day	24.50	75-99.00
85-15-007	Mine	B. P. Gutmann	14-day	24.50	90.00
85-15-008	Going to Town	B. P. Gutmann	14-day	24.50	66-95.00
Hamilton Collection		**A Country Summer**			
85-16-001	Butterfly Beauty	N. Noel	10-day	29.50	36.00
85-16-002	The Golden Puppy	N. Noel	10-day	29.50	29.50
86-16-003	The Rocking Chair	N. Noel	10-day	29.50	36.00
86-16-004	My Bunny	N. Noel	10-day	29.50	33.00
88-16-005	The Piglet	N. Noel	10-day	29.50	29.50
88-16-006	Teammates	N. Noel	10-day	29.50	29.50
Hamilton Collection		**The Little Rascals**			
85-17-001	Three for the Show	Unknown	10-day	24.50	30-50.00
85-17-002	My Gal	Unknown	10-day	24.50	45.00
85-17-003	Skeleton Crew	Unknown	10-day	24.50	24.50
85-17-004	Roughin' It	Unknown	10-day	24.50	45.00
85-17-005	Spanky's Pranks	Unknown	10-day	24.50	24.50
85-17-006	Butch's Challenge	Unknown	10-day	24.50	24.50
85-17-007	Darla's Debut	Unknown	10-day	24.50	24.50
85-17-008	Pete's Pal	Unknown	10-day	24.50	24.50
Hamilton Collection		**The Japanese Blossoms of Autumn**			
85-18-001	Bellflower	Koseki/Ebihara	10-day	45.00	45.00
85-18-002	Arrowroot	Koseki/Ebihara	10-day	45.00	45.00
85-18-003	Wild Carnation	Koseki/Ebihara	10-day	45.00	45.00
85-18-004	Maiden Flower	Koseki/Ebihara	10-day	45.00	45.00
85-18-005	Pampas Grass	Koseki/Ebihara	10-day	45.00	45.00
85-18-006	Bush Clover	Koseki/Ebihara	10-day	45.00	45.00
85-18-007	Purple Trousers	Koseki/Ebihara	10-day	45.00	45.00
Hamilton Collection		**Kitten Classics**			
85-18-001	Cat Nap	P. Cooper	14-day	29.50	36.00
85-18-002	Purrfect Treasure	P. Cooper	14-day	29.50	29.50
85-18-003	Wild Flower	P. Cooper	14-day	29.50	29.50
85-18-004	Birdwatcher	P. Cooper	14-day	29.50	29.50
85-18-005	Tiger's Fancy	P. Cooper	14-day	29.50	33.00
85-18-006	Country Kitty	P. Cooper	14-day	29.50	33.00
85-18-007	Little Rascal	P. Cooper	14-day	29.50	29.50
85-18-008	First Prize	P. Cooper	14-day	29.50	29.50
Hamilton Collection		**America's Greatest Sailing Ships**			
88-19-001	USS Constitution	T. Freeman	14-day	29.50	36.00
88-19-002	Great Republic	T. Freeman	14-day	29.50	36.00
88-19-003	America	T. Freeman	14-day	29.50	45.00
88-19-004	Charles W. Morgan	T. Freeman	14-day	29.50	36.00
88-19-005	Eagle	T. Freeman	14-day	29.50	48.00
88-19-006	Bonhomme Richard	T. Freeman	14-day	29.50	36.00
88-19-007	Gertrude L. Thebaud	T. Freeman	14-day	29.50	45.00
88-19-008	Enterprise	T. Freeman	14-day	29.50	36.00
Hamilton Collection		**Noble Owls of America**			
86-20-001	Morning Mist	J. Seerey-Lester	15,000	55.00	55.00
87-20-002	Prairie Sundown	J. Seerey-Lester	15,000	55.00	55.00
87-20-003	Winter Vigil	J. Seerey-Lester	15,000	55.00	55.00
87-20-004	Autumn Mist	J. Seerey-Lester	15,000	75.00	55.00
87-20-005	Dawn in the Willows	J. Seerey-Lester	15,000	55.00	55.00
87-20-006	Snowy Watch	J. Seerey-Lester	15,000	60.00	55.00
88-20-007	Hiding Place	J. Seerey-Lester	15,000	55.00	55.00
88-20-008	Waiting for Dusk	J. Seerey-Lester	15,000	55.00	55.00
Hamilton Collection		**Treasured Days**			
87-21-001	Ashley	H. Bond	14-day	29.50	60.00
87-21-002	Christopher	H. Bond	14-day	24.50	45.00
87-21-003	Sara	H. Bond	14-day	24.50	30.00
87-21-004	Jeremy	H. Bond	14-day	24.50	45.00
87-21-005	Amanda	H. Bond	14-day	24.50	45.00
88-21-006	Nicholas	H. Bond	14-day	24.50	45.00
88-21-007	Lindsay	H. Bond	14-day	24.50	45.00
88-21-008	Justin	H. Bond	14-day	24.50	45.00
Hamilton Collection		**Butterfly Garden**			
87-22-001	Spicebush Swallowtail	P. Sweany	14-day	29.50	45.00
87-22-002	Common Blue	P. Sweany	14-day	29.50	37.50
87-22-003	Orange Sulphur	P. Sweany	14-day	29.50	30.00
87-22-004	Monarch	P. Sweany	14-day	29.50	37.50
87-22-005	Tiger Swallowtail	P. Sweany	14-day	29.50	30.00
87-22-006	Crimson Patched Longwing	P. Sweany	14-day	29.50	37.50
88-22-007	Morning Cloak	P. Sweany	14-day	29.50	29.50
88-22-008	Red Admiral	P. Sweany	14-day	29.50	37.50
Hamilton Collection		**The Golden Classics**			
87-23-001	Sleeping Beauty	C. Lawson	10-day	37.50	37.50
87-23-002	Rumpelstiltskin	C. Lawson	10-day	37.50	37.50
87-23-003	Jack and the Beanstalk	C. Lawson	10-day	37.50	37.50
87-23-004	Snow White and Rose Red	C. Lawson	10-day	37.50	37.50
87-23-005	Hansel and Gretel	C. Lawson	10-day	37.50	37.50
88-23-006	Cinderella	C. Lawson	10-day	37.50	37.50
88-23-007	The Golden Goose	C. Lawson	10-day	37.50	37.50
88-23-008	The Snow Queen	C. Lawson	10-day	37.50	37.50
Hamilton Collection		**Children of the American Frontier**			
86-24-001	In Trouble Again	D. Crook	10-day	24.50	35.00
86-24-002	Tubs and Suds	D. Crook	10-day	24.50	27.00
86-24-003	A Lady Needs a Little Privacy	D. Crook	10-day	24.50	38.00

		ARTIST	EDITION	ISSUE	QUOTE
86-24-004	The Desperadoes	D. Crook	10-day	24.50	27.00
86-24-005	Riders Wanted	D. Crook	10-day	24.50	30.00
87-24-006	A Cowboy's Downfall	D. Crook	10-day	24.50	24.50
87-24-007	Runaway Blues	D. Crook	10-day	24.50	24.50
87-24-008	A Special Patient	D. Crook	10-day	24.50	38.00
Hamilton Collection		**Puppy Playtime**			
87-25-001	Double Take-Cocker Spaniels	J. Lamb	14-day	24.50	75.00
87-25-002	Catch of the Day-Golden Retrievers	J. Lamb	14-day	24.50	45.00
87-25-003	Cabin Fever-Black Labradors	J. Lamb	14-day	24.50	45.00
87-25-004	Weekend Gardener-Lhasa Apsos	J. Lamb	14-day	24.50	36.00
87-25-005	Getting Acquainted-Beagles	J. Lamb	14-day	24.50	36.00
87-25-006	Hanging Out-German Shepherd	J. Lamb	14-day	24.50	45.00
87-25-007	New Leash on Life-Mini Schnauzer	J. Lamb	14-day	24.50	45.00
87-25-008	Fun and Games-Poodle	J. Lamb	14-day	24.50	36.00
Hamilton Collection		**The Official Honeymooners Plate Collection**			
87-26-001	The Honeymooners	D. Kilmer	14-day	24.50	110-160.
87-26-002	The Hucklebuck	D. Kilmer	14-day	24.50	110-160.
87-26-003	Baby, You're the Greatest	D. Kilmer	14-day	24.50	110-180.
88-26-004	The Golfer	D. Kilmer	14-day	24.50	110-160.
88-26-005	The TV Chefs	D. Kilmer	14-day	24.50	120-160.
88-26-006	Bang! Zoom!	D. Kilmer	14-day	24.50	110-160 .
88-26-007	The Only Way to Travel	D. Kilmer	14-day	24.50	120-160.
88-26-008	The Honeymoon Express	D. Kilmer	14-day	24.50	150-299.
Hamilton Collection		**North American Waterbirds**			
88-27-001	Wood Ducks	R. Lawrence	14-day	37.50	54.00
88-27-002	Hooded Mergansers	R. Lawrence	14-day	37.50	54.00
88-27-003	Pintails	R. Lawrence	14-day	37.50	45.00
88-27-004	Canada Geese	R. Lawrence	14-day	37.50	45.00
89-27-005	American Widgeons	R. Lawrence	14-day	37.50	54.00
89-27-006	Canvasbacks	R. Lawrence	14-day	37.50	55.00
89-27-007	Mallard Pair	R. Lawrence	14-day	37.50	60.00
89-27-008	Snow Geese	R. Lawrence	14-day	37.50	45.00
Hamilton Collection		**Nature's Quiet Moments**			
88-28-001	A Curious Pair	R. Parker	14-day	37.50	37.50
88-28-002	Northern Morning	R. Parker	14-day	37.50	37.50
88-28-003	Just Resting	R. Parker	14-day	37.50	37.50
89-28-004	Waiting Out the Storm	R. Parker	14-day	37.50	37.50
89-28-005	Creekside	R. Parker	14-day	37.50	37.50
89-28-006	Autumn Foraging	R. Parker	14-day	37.50	37.50
89-28-007	Old Man of the Mountain	R. Parker	14-day	37.50	37.50
89-28-008	Mountain Blooms	R. Parker	14-day	37.50	37.50
Hamilton Collection		**Wizard of Oz Commemorative**			
88-29-001	We're Off to See the Wizard	T. Blackshear	14-day	24.50	180-250.
88-29-002	Dorothy Meets the Scarecrow	T. Blackshear	14-day	24.50	90-140.
89-29-003	The Tin Man Speaks	T. Blackshear	14-day	24.50	105-150.
89-29-004	A Glimpse of the Munchkins	T. Blackshear	14-day	24.50	90-150.
89-29-005	The Witch Casts A Spell	T. Blackshear	14-day	24.50	113-180.
89-29-006	If I Were King Of The Forest	T. Blackshear	14-day	24.50	120-180.
89-29-007	The Great and Powerful Oz	T. Blackshear	14-day	24.50	120-180.
89-29-008	There's No Place Like Home	T. Blackshear	14-day	24.50	120-190.
Hamilton Collection		**Petals and Purrs**			
88-30-001	Blushing Beauties	B. Harrison	14-day	24.50	55.00
88-30-002	Spring Fever	B. Harrison	14-day	24.50	37.50
88-30-003	Morning Glories	B. Harrison	14-day	24.50	36.00
88-30-004	Forget-Me-Not	B. Harrison	14-day	24.50	36.00
89-30-005	Golden Fancy	B. Harrison	14-day	24.50	30.00
89-30-006	Pink Lillies	B. Harrison	14-day	24.50	30.00
89-30-007	Summer Sunshine	B. Harrison	14-day	24.50	30.00
89-30-008	Siamese Summer	B. Harrison	14-day	24.50	30.00
Hamilton Collection		**The Jeweled Hummingbirds Plate Collection**			
89-31-001	Ruby-throated Hummingbirds	J. Landenberger	14-day	37.50	37.50
89-31-002	Great Sapphire Wing Hummingbirds	J. Landenberger	14-day	37.50	37.50
89-31-003	Ruby-Topaz Hummingbirds	J. Landenberger	14-day	37.50	37.50
89-31-004	Andean Emerald Hummingbirds	J. Landenberger	14-day	37.50	37.50
89-31-005	Garnet-throated Hummingbirds	J. Landenberger	14-day	37.50	37.50
89-31-006	Blue-Headed Sapphire Hummingbirds	J. Landenberger	14-day	37.50	37.50
89-31-007	Pearl Coronet Hummingbirds	J. Landenberger	14-day	37.50	37.50
89-31-008	Amethyst-throated Sunangels	J. Landenberger	14-day	37.50	37.50
Hamilton Collection		**Stained Glass Gardens**			
89-32-001	Peacock and Wisteria	Unknown	15,000	55.00	55.00
89-32-002	Garden Sunset	Unknown	15,000	55.00	55.00
89-32-003	The Cockatoo's Garden	Unknown	15,000	55.00	55.00
89-32-004	Waterfall and Iris	Unknown	15,000	55.00	55.00
90-32-005	Roses and Magnolias	Unknown	15,000	55.00	55.00
90-32-006	A Hollyhock Sunrise	Unknown	15,000	55.00	55.00
90-32-007	Peaceful Waters	Unknown	15,000	55.00	55.00
90-32-008	Springtime in the Valley	Unknown	15,000	55.00	55.00
Hamilton Collection		**The I Love Lucy Plate Collection**			
89-33-001	California, Here We Come	J. Kritz	14-day	29.50	85-150.
89-33-002	It's Just Like Candy	J. Kritz	14-day	29.50	60-140.
90-33-003	The Big Squeeze	J. Kritz	14-day	29.50	75-140.
90-33-004	Eating the Evidence	J. Kritz	14-day	29.50	75-150.
90-33-005	Two of a Kind	J. Kritz	14-day	29.50	45-99.00
91-33-006	Queen of the Gypsies	J. Kritz	14-day	29.50	54-90.00
92-33-007	Night at the Copa	J. Kritz	14-day	29.50	75-105.
92-33-008	A Rising Problem	J. Kritz	14-day	29.50	90-129.
Hamilton Collection		**Great Fighter Planes Of World War II**			
92-34-001	Old Crow	R. Waddey	14-day	29.50	29.50
92-34-002	Big Hog	R. Waddey	14-day	29.50	29.50
92-34-003	P-47 Thunderbolt	R. Waddey	14-day	29.50	29.50
92-34-004	P-40 Flying Tiger	R. Waddey	14-day	29.50	29.50
92-34-005	F4F Wildcat	R. Waddey	14-day	29.50	29.50
92-34-006	P-38F Lightning	R. Waddey	14-day	29.50	29.50
93-34-007	F6F Hellcat	R. Waddey	14-day	29.50	29.50
93-34-008	P-39M Airacobra	R. Waddey	14-day	29.50	29.50
Hamilton Collection		**Birds of the Temple Gardens**			
89-35-001	Doves of Fidelity	J. Cheng	14-day	29.50	29.50
89-35-002	Cranes of Eternal Life	J. Cheng	14-day	29.50	29.50
89-35-003	Honorable Swallows	J. Cheng	14-day	29.50	29.50
89-35-004	Oriental White Eyes of Beauty	J. Cheng	14-day	29.50	29.50
89-35-005	Pheasants of Good Fortune	J. Cheng	14-day	29.50	29.50
89-35-006	Imperial Goldcrest	J. Cheng	14-day	29.50	29.50
89-35-007	Goldfinches of Virtue	J. Cheng	14-day	29.50	29.50
89-35-008	Magpies: Birds of Good Omen	J. Cheng	14-day	29.50	29.50

	ARTIST	EDITION	ISSUE	QUOTE
Hamilton Collection	**Winter Wildlife**			
89-36-001 Close Encounters	J. Seerey-Lester	15,000	55.00	55.00
89-36-002 Among the Cattails	J. Seerey-Lester	15,000	55.00	55.00
89-36-003 The Refuge	J. Seerey-Lester	15,000	55.00	55.00
89-36-004 Out of the Blizzard	J. Seerey-Lester	15,000	55.00	55.00
89-36-005 First Snow	J. Seerey-Lester	15,000	55.00	55.00
89-36-006 Lying In Wait	J. Seerey-Lester	15,000	55.00	55.00
89-36-007 Winter Hiding	J. Seerey-Lester	15,000	55.00	55.00
89-36-008 Early Snow	J. Seerey-Lester	15,000	55.00	55.00
Hamilton Collection	**Big Cats of the World**			
89-37-001 African Shade	D. Manning	14-day	29.50	29.50
89-37-002 View from Above	D. Manning	14-day	29.50	29.50
90-37-003 On The Prowl	D. Manning	14-day	29.50	29.50
90-37-004 Deep In The Jungle	D. Manning	14-day	29.50	29.50
90-37-005 Spirit Of The Mountain	D. Manning	14-day	29.50	29.50
90-37-006 Spotted Sentinel	D. Manning	14-day	29.50	29.50
90-37-007 Above the Treetops	D. Manning	14-day	29.50	29.50
90-37-008 Mountain Dweller	D. Manning	14-day	29.50	29.50
92-37-009 Jungle Habitat	D. Manning	14-day	29.50	29.50
92-37-010 Solitary Sentry	D. Manning	14-day	29.50	29.50
Hamilton Collection	**Mixed Company**			
90-38-001 Two Against One	P. Cooper	14-day	29.50	36.00
90-38-002 A Sticky Situation	P. Cooper	14-day	29.50	36.00
90-38-003 What's Up	P. Cooper	14-day	29.50	29.50
90-38-004 All Wrapped Up	P. Cooper	14-day	29.50	36.00
90-38-005 Picture Perfect	P. Cooper	14-day	29.50	29.50
91-38-006 A Moment to Unwind	P. Cooper	14-day	29.50	33.00
91-38-007 Ole	P. Cooper	14-day	29.50	33.00
91-38-008 Picnic Prowlers	P. Cooper	14-day	29.50	29.50
Hamilton Collection	**Portraits From Oz**			
89-39-001 Dorothy	T. Blackshear	14-day	29.50	120-199.
89-39-002 Scarecrow	T. Blackshear	14-day	29.50	100-139.
89-39-003 Tin Man	T. Blackshear	14-day	29.50	105-149.
90-39-004 Cowardly Lion	T. Blackshear	14-day	29.50	120-149.
90-39-005 Glinda	T. Blackshear	14-day	29.50	75-139.
90-39-006 Wizard	T. Blackshear	14-day	29.50	75-139.
90-39-007 Wicked Witch	T. Blackshear	14-day	29.50	100-299.
90-39-008 Toto	T. Blackshear	14-day	29.50	150-299.
Hamilton Collection	**Delights of Childhood**			
89-40-001 Crayon Creations	J. Lamb	14-day	29.50	29.50
89-40-002 Little Mother	J. Lamb	14-day	29.50	29.50
90-40-003 Bathing Beauty	J. Lamb	14-day	29.50	29.50
90-40-004 Is That You, Granny?	J. Lamb	14-day	29.50	36.00
90-40-005 Nature's Little Helper	J. Lamb	14-day	29.50	29.50
90-40-006 So Sorry	J. Lamb	14-day	29.50	33.00
90-40-007 Shower Time	J. Lamb	14-day	29.50	33.00
90-40-008 Storytime Friends	J. Lamb	14-day	29.50	29.50
Hamilton Collection	**Classic Sporting Dogs**			
89-41-001 Golden Retrievers	B. Christie	14-day	24.50	54.00
89-41-002 Labrador Retrievers	B. Christie	14-day	24.50	60.00
89-41-003 Beagles	B. Christie	14-day	24.50	36.00
89-41-004 Pointers	B. Christie	14-day	24.50	30.00
89-41-005 Springer Spaniels	B. Christie	14-day	24.50	39.00
90-41-006 German Short-Haired Pointers	B. Christie	14-day	24.50	54.00
90-41-007 Irish Setters	B. Christie	14-day	24.50	36.00
90-41-008 Brittany Spaniels	B. Christie	14-day	24.50	48.00
Hamilton Collection	**Majesty of Flight**			
89-42-001 The Eagle Soars	T. Hirata	14-day	37.50	48.00
89-42-002 Realm of the Red-Tail	T. Hirata	14-day	37.50	39.00
89-42-003 Coastal Journey	T. Hirata	14-day	37.50	45.00
89-42-004 Sentry of the North	T. Hirata	14-day	37.50	48.00
89-42-005 Commanding the Marsh	T. Hirata	14-day	37.50	37.50-45.
90-42-006 The Vantage Point	T. Hirata	14-day	29.50	45.00
90-42-007 Silent Watch	T. Hirata	14-day	29.50	48.00
90-42-008 Fierce and Free	T. Hirata	14-day	29.50	45.00
Hamilton Collection	**The Proud Nation**			
89-43-001 Navajo Little One	R. Swanson	14-day	24.50	45.00
89-43-002 In a Big Land	R. Swanson	14-day	24.50	24.50
89-43-003 Out with Mama's Flock	R. Swanson	14-day	24.50	24.50
89-43-004 Newest Little Sheepherder	R. Swanson	14-day	24.50	30.00
89-43-005 Dressed Up for the Powwow	R. Swanson	14-day	24.50	30.00
89-43-006 Just a Few Days Old	R. Swanson	14-day	24.50	30.00
89-43-007 Autumn Treat	R. Swanson	14-day	24.50	30.00
89-43-008 Up in the Red Rocks	R. Swanson	14-day	24.50	24.50
Hamilton Collection	**Thornton Utz 10th Anniversary Commemorative Plate Collection**			
89-44-001 Dawn	T. Utz	14-day	29.50	29.50
89-44-002 Just Like Mommy	T. Utz	14-day	29.50	29.50
89-44-003 Playing Doctor	T. Utz	14-day	29.50	29.50
89-44-004 My Kitty	T. Utz	14-day	29.50	29.50
89-44-005 Turtle Talk	T. Utz	14-day	29.50	29.50
89-44-006 Best Friends	T. Utz	14-day	29.50	29.50
89-44-007 Among the Daffodils	T. Utz	14-day	29.50	39.00
89-44-008 Friends in the Sky	T. Utz	14-day	29.50	29.50
89-44-009 Teddy's Bathtime	T. Utz	14-day	29.50	29.50
89-44-010 Little Emily	T. Utz	14-day	29.50	29.50
Hamilton Collection	**Country Kitties**			
89-45-001 Mischief Makers	G. Gerardi	14-day	24.50	45.00
89-45-002 Table Manners	G. Gerardi	14-day	24.50	36.00
89-45-003 Attic Attack	G. Gerardi	14-day	24.50	45.00
89-45-004 Rock and Rollers	G. Gerardi	14-day	24.50	30-40.00
89-45-005 Just For the Fern of It	G. Gerardi	14-day	24.50	30-40.00
89-45-006 All Washed Up	G. Gerardi	14-day	24.50	39.00
89-45-007 Stroller Derby	G. Gerardi	14-day	24.50	39.00
89-45-008 Captive Audience	G. Gerardi	14-day	24.50	39.00
Hamilton Collection	**Winged Reflections**			
89-46-001 Following Mama	R. Parker	14-day	37.50	37.50
89-46-002 Above the Breakers	R. Parker	14-day	37.50	37.50
89-46-003 Among the Reeds	R. Parker	14-day	37.50	37.50
89-46-004 Freeze Up	R. Parker	14-day	37.50	37.50
89-46-005 Wings Above the Water	R. Parker	14-day	37.50	37.50
90-46-006 Summer Loon	R. Parker	14-day	29.50	29.50
90-46-007 Early Spring	R. Parker	14-day	29.50	29.50
90-46-008 At The Water's Edge	R. Parker	14-day	29.50	29.50
Hamilton Collection	**Elvis Remembered**			
89-47-001 Loving You	S. Morton	90-day	37.50	75-99.00
89-47-002 Early Years	S. Morton	90-day	37.50	75-99.00
89-47-003 Tenderly	S. Morton	90-day	37.50	75-99.00
89-47-004 The King	S. Morton	90-day	37.50	75-129.
89-47-005 Forever Yours	S. Morton	90-day	37.50	75-99.00
89-47-006 Rockin in the Moonlight	S. Morton	90-day	37.50	75-99.00
89-47-007 Moody Blues	S. Morton	90-day	37.50	75-99.00
89-47-008 Elvis Presley	S. Morton	90-day	37.50	125-129.
Hamilton Collection	**Fifty Years of Oz**			
89-48-001 Fifty Years of Oz	T. Blackshear	14-day	37.50	135-199.
Hamilton Collection	**Small Wonders of the Wild**			
89-49-001 Hideaway	C. Frace	14-day	29.50	45.00
90-49-002 Young Explorers	C. Frace	14-day	29.50	36.00
90-49-003 Three of a Kind	C. Frace	14-day	29.50	75.00
90-49-004 Quiet Morning	C. Frace	14-day	29.50	29.50
90-49-005 Eyes of Wonder	C. Frace	14-day	29.50	29.50
90-49-006 Ready for Adventure	C. Frace	14-day	29.50	29.50
90-49-007 Uno	C. Frace	14-day	29.50	29.50
90-49-008 Exploring a New World	C. Frace	14-day	29.50	29.50
Hamilton Collection	**Dear to My Heart**			
90-50-001 Cathy	J. Hagara	14-day	29.50	29.50
90-50-002 Addie	J. Hagara	14-day	29.50	29.50
90-50-003 Jimmy	J. Hagara	14-day	29.50	29.50
90-50-004 Dacy	J. Hagara	14-day	29.50	29.50
90-50-005 Paul	J. Hagara	14-day	29.50	29.50
91-50-006 Shelly	J. Hagara	14-day	29.50	29.50
91-50-007 Jenny	J. Hagara	14-day	29.50	29.50
91-50-008 Joy	J. Hagara	14-day	29.50	29.50
Hamilton Collection	**North American Gamebirds**			
90-51-001 Ring-necked Pheasant	J. Killen	14-day	37.50	37.50
90-51-002 Bobwhite Quail	J. Killen	14-day	37.50	45.00
90-51-003 Ruffed Grouse	J. Killen	14-day	37.50	37.50
90-51-004 Gambel Quail	J. Killen	14-day	37.50	42.00
90-51-005 Mourning Dove	J. Killen	14-day	37.50	45.00
90-51-006 Woodcock	J. Killen	14-day	37.50	45.00
91-51-007 Chukar Partridge	J. Killen	14-day	37.50	45.00
91-51-008 Wild Turkey	J. Killen	14-day	37.50	45.00
Hamilton Collection	**The Saturday Evening Post Plate Collection**			
89-52-001 The Wonders of Radio	N. Rockwell	14-day	35.00	35.00
89-52-002 Easter Morning	N. Rockwell	14-day	35.00	60.00
89-52-003 The Facts of Life	N. Rockwell	14-day	35.00	35.00
90-52-004 The Window Washer	N. Rockwell	14-day	35.00	45.00
90-52-005 First Flight	N. Rockwell	14-day	35.00	54.00
90-52-006 Traveling Companion	N. Rockwell	14-day	35.00	35.00
90-52-007 Jury Room	N. Rockwell	14-day	35.00	35.00
90-52-008 Furlough	N. Rockwell	14-day	35.00	35.00
Hamilton Collection	**Favorite American Songbirds**			
89-53-001 Blue Jays of Spring	D. O'Driscoll	14-day	29.50	36.00
89-53-002 Red Cardinals of Winter	D. O'Driscoll	14-day	29.50	36.00
89-53-003 Robins & Apple Blossoms	D. O'Driscoll	14-day	29.50	36.00
89-53-004 Goldfinches of Summer	D. O'Driscoll	14-day	29.50	36.00
90-53-005 Autumn Chickadees	D. O'Driscoll	14-day	29.50	36.00
90-53-006 Bluebirds and Morning Glories	D. O'Driscoll	14-day	29.50	36.00
90-53-007 Tufted Titmouse and Holly	D. O'Driscoll	14-day	29.50	29.50
91-53-008 Carolina Wrens of Spring	D. O'Driscoll	14-day	29.50	29.50
Hamilton Collection	**Coral Paradise**			
89-54-001 The Living Oasis	H. Bond	14-day	29.50	29.50
90-54-002 Riches of the Coral Sea	H. Bond	14-day	29.50	29.50
90-54-003 Tropical Pageantry	H. Bond	14-day	29.50	36.00
90-54-004 Caribbean Spectacle	H. Bond	14-day	29.50	33.00
90-54-005 Undersea Village	H. Bond	14-day	29.50	36.00
90-54-006 Shimmering Reef Dwellers	H. Bond	14-day	29.50	36.00
90-54-007 Mysteries of the Galapagos	H. Bond	14-day	29.50	33.00
90-54-008 Forest Beneath the Sea	H. Bond	14-day	29.50	29.50
Hamilton Collection	**Noble American Indian Women**			
89-55-001 Sacajawea	D. Wright	14-day	29.50	45.00
90-55-002 Pocahontas	D. Wright	14-day	29.50	45.00
90-55-003 Minnehaha	D. Wright	14-day	29.50	36.00
90-55-004 Pine Leaf	D. Wright	14-day	29.50	45.00
90-55-005 Lily of the Mohawk	D. Wright	14-day	29.50	36.00
90-55-006 White Rose	D. Wright	14-day	29.50	45.00
91-55-007 Lozen	D. Wright	14-day	29.50	33.00
91-55-008 Falling Star	D. Wright	14-day	29.50	45.00
Hamilton Collection	**Little Ladies**			
89-56-001 Playing Bridesmaid	M.H. Bogart	14-day	29.50	75-100.
90-56-002 The Seamstress	M.H. Bogart	14-day	29.50	60.00
90-56-003 Little Captive	M.H. Bogart	14-day	29.50	45.00
90-56-004 Playing Mama	M.H. Bogart	14-day	29.50	60.00
90-56-005 Susanna	M.H. Bogart	14-day	29.50	45-60.00
90-56-006 Kitty's Bath	M.H. Bogart	14-day	29.50	54-65.00
90-56-007 A Day in the Country	M.H. Bogart	14-day	29.50	45-60.00
91-56-008 Sarah	M.H. Bogart	14-day	29.50	45.00
91-56-009 First Party	M.H. Bogart	14-day	29.50	29.50
91-56-010 The Magic Kitten	M.H. Bogart	14-day	29.50	29.50
Hamilton Collection	**A Country Season of Horses**			
90-57-001 First Day of Spring	J.M. Vass	14-day	29.50	36.00
90-57-002 Summer Splendor	J.M. Vass	14-day	29.50	33.00
90-57-003 A Winter's Walk	J.M. Vass	14-day	29.50	33.00
90-57-004 Autumn Grandeur	J.M. Vass	14-day	29.50	30.00
90-57-005 Cliffside Beauty	J.M. Vass	14-day	29.50	29.50
90-57-006 Frosty Morning	J.M. Vass	14-day	29.50	29.50
90-57-007 Crisp Country Morning	J.M. Vass	14-day	29.50	29.50
90-57-008 River Retreat	J.M. Vass	14-day	29.50	29.50
Hamilton Collection	**Good Sports**			
90-58-001 Wide Retriever	J. Lamb	14-day	29.50	45.00
90-58-002 Double Play	J. Lamb	14-day	29.50	36.00
90-58-003 Hole in One	J. Lamb	14-day	29.50	60.00
90-58-004 The Bass Masters	J. Lamb	14-day	29.50	36.00
90-58-005 Spotted on the Sideline	J. Lamb	14-day	29.50	36.00
90-58-006 Slap Shot	J. Lamb	14-day	29.50	45.00
91-58-007 Net Play	J. Lamb	14-day	29.50	45.00
91-58-008 Bassetball	J. Lamb	14-day	29.50	36.00
92-58-009 Boxer Rebellion	J. Lamb	14-day	29.50	33.00
92-58-010 Great Try	J. Lamb	14-day	29.50	39.00

		ARTIST	EDITION	ISSUE	QUOTE
Hamilton Collection		**Curious Kittens**			
90-59-001	Rainy Day Friends	B. Harrison	14-day	29.50	36.00
90-59-002	Keeping in Step	B. Harrison	14-day	29.50	36.00
91-59-003	Delightful Discovery	B. Harrison	14-day	29.50	36.00
91-59-004	Chance Meeting	B. Harrison	14-day	29.50	36.00
91-59-005	All Wound Up	B. Harrison	14-day	29.50	36.00
91-59-006	Making Tracks	B. Harrison	14-day	29.50	36.00
91-59-007	Playing Cat and Mouse	B. Harrison	14-day	29.50	36.00
91-59-008	A Paw's in the Action	B. Harrison	14-day	29.50	36.00
92-59-009	Little Scholar	B. Harrison	14-day	29.50	36.00
92-59-010	Cat Burglar	B. Harrison	14-day	29.50	36.00
Hamilton Collection		**The American Civil War**			
90-60-001	General Robert E. Lee	D. Prechtel	14-day	37.50	75.00
90-60-002	Generals Grant and Lee At Appomattox	D. Prechtel	14-day	37.50	48.00
90-60-003	General Thomas "Stonewall" Jackson	D. Prechtel	14-day	37.50	54.00
90-60-004	Abraham Lincoln	D. Prechtel	14-day	37.50	60.00
91-60-005	General J.E.B. Stuart	D. Prechtel	14-day	37.50	45.00
91-60-006	General Philip Sheridan	D. Prechtel	14-day	37.50	60.00
91-60-007	A Letter from Home	D. Prechtel	14-day	37.50	60.00
91-60-008	Going Home	D. Prechtel	14-day	37.50	45.00
92-60-009	Assembling The Troop	D. Prechtel	14-day	37.50	75.00
92-60-010	Standing Watch	D. Prechtel	14-day	37.50	75.00
Hamilton Collection		**Growing Up Together**			
90-61-001	My Very Best Friends	P. Brooks	14-day	29.50	36.00
90-61-002	Tea for Two	P. Brooks	14-day	29.50	29.50
90-61-003	Tender Loving Care	P. Brooks	14-day	29.50	29.50
90-61-004	Picnic Pals	P. Brooks	14-day	29.50	29.50
91-61-005	Newfound Friends	P. Brooks	14-day	29.50	29.50
91-61-006	Kitten Caboodle	P. Brooks	14-day	29.50	29.50
91-61-007	Fishing Buddies	P. Brooks	14-day	29.50	29.50
91-61-008	Bedtime Blessings	P. Brooks	14-day	29.50	29.50
Hamilton Collection		**Classic TV Westerns**			
90-62-001	The Lone Ranger and Tonto	K. Milnazik	14-day	29.50	68-75.00
90-62-002	Bonanza ™	K. Milnazik	14-day	29.50	60-65.00
90-62-003	Roy Rogers and Dale Evans	K. Milnazik	14-day	29.50	60-69.00
91-62-004	Rawhide	K. Milnazik	14-day	29.50	36-69.00
91-62-005	Wild Wild West	K. Milnazik	14-day	29.50	60-69.00
91-62-006	Have Gun, Will Travel	K. Milnazik	14-day	29.50	36-69.00
91-62-007	The Virginian	K. Milnazik	14-day	29.50	69.00
91-62-008	Hopalong Cassidy	K. Milnazik	14-day	29.50	60.00
Hamilton Collection		**Timeless Expressions of the Orient**			
90-63-001	Fidelity	M. Tsang	15,000	75.00	95.00
91-63-002	Femininity	M. Tsang	15,000	75.00	75.00
91-63-003	Longevity	M. Tsang	15,000	75.00	75.00
91-63-004	Beauty	M. Tsang	15,000	55.00	55.00
92-63-005	Courage	M. Tsang	15,000	55.00	55.00
Hamilton Collection		**The Star Wars Plate Collection**			
87-64-001	Hans Solo	T. Blackshear	14-day	29.50	90-95.00
87-64-002	R2-D2 and Wicket	T. Blackshear	14-day	29.50	45-79.00
87-64-003	Luke Skywalker and Darth Vader	T. Blackshear	14-day	29.50	60-79.00
87-64-004	Princess Leia	T. Blackshear	14-day	29.50	60-150.
87-64-005	The Imperial Walkers	T. Blackshear	14-day	29.50	60-150.
87-64-006	Luke and Yoda	T. Blackshear	14-day	29.50	60-79.00
88-64-007	Space Battle	T. Blackshear	14-day	29.50	299.00
88-64-008	Crew in Cockpit	T. Blackshear	14-day	29.50	150-200.
Hamilton Collection		**Star Wars 10th Anniversary Commemorative**			
90-65-001	Star Wars 10th Anniversary Commemorative Plates	T. Blackshear	14-day	39.50	89-95.00
Hamilton Collection		**Star Wars Trilogy**			
93-66-001	Star Wars	M. Weistling	28-day	37.50	37.50
93-66-002	The Empire Strikes Back	M. Weistling	28-day	37.50	37.50
93-66-003	Return Of The Jedi	M. Weistling	28-day	37.50	37.50
Hamilton Collection		**Romantic Castles of Europe**			
90-67-001	Ludwig's Castle	D. Sweet	19,500	55.00	55.00
91-67-002	Palace of the Moors	D. Sweet	19,500	55.00	55.00
91-67-003	Swiss Isle Fortress	D. Sweet	19,500	55.00	55.00
91-67-004	The Legendary Castle of Leeds	D. Sweet	19,500	55.00	55.00
91-67-005	Davinci's Chambord	D. Sweet	19,500	55.00	55.00
91-67-006	Eilean Donan	D. Sweet	19,500	55.00	55.00
92-67-007	Eltz Castle	D. Sweet	19,500	55.00	55.00
92-67-008	Kylemore Abbey	D. Sweet	19,500	55.00	55.00
Hamilton Collection		**The American Rose Garden**			
88-68-001	American Spirit	P.J. Sweany	14-day	29.50	29.50
88-68-002	Peace Rose	P.J. Sweany	14-day	29.50	29.50
89-68-003	White Knight	P.J. Sweany	14-day	29.50	36.00
89-68-004	American Heritage	P.J. Sweany	14-day	29.50	36.00
89-68-005	Eclipse	P.J. Sweany	14-day	29.50	33.00
89-68-006	Blue Moon	P.J. Sweany	14-day	29.50	36.00
89-68-007	Coral Cluster	P.J. Sweany	14-day	29.50	33.00
89-68-008	President Herbert Hoover	P.J. Sweany	14-day	29.50	29.50
Hamilton Collection		**English Country Cottages**			
90-69-001	Periwinkle Tea Room	M. Bell	14-day	29.50	45.00
91-69-002	Gamekeeper's Cottage	M. Bell	14-day	29.50	75.00
91-69-003	Ginger Cottage	M. Bell	14-day	29.50	60.00
91-69-004	Larkspur Cottage	M. Bell	14-day	29.50	45.00
91-69-005	The Chaplain's Garden	M. Bell	14-day	29.50	35.00
91-69-006	Lorna Doone Cottage	M. Bell	14-day	29.50	45.00
91-69-007	Murrle Cottage	M. Bell	14-day	29.50	35.00
91-69-008	Lullabye Cottage	M. Bell	14-day	29.50	35.00
Hamilton Collection		**The Angler's Prize**			
91-70-001	Trophy Bass	M. Susinno	14-day	29.50	36.00
91-70-002	Blue Ribbon Trout	M. Susinno	14-day	29.50	33.00
91-70-003	Sun Dancers	M. Susinno	14-day	29.50	36.00
91-70-004	Freshwater Barracuda	M. Susinno	14-day	29.50	36.00
91-70-005	Bronzeback Fighter	M. Susinno	14-day	29.50	36.00
91-70-006	Autumn Beauty	M. Susinno	14-day	29.50	36.00
92-70-007	Old Mooneyes	M. Susinno	14-day	29.50	36.00
92-70-008	Silver King	M. Susinno	14-day	29.50	33.00
Hamilton Collection		**Woodland Encounters**			
91-71-001	Want to Play?	G. Giordano	14-day	29.50	29.50
91-71-002	Peek-a-boo!	G. Giordano	14-day	29.50	29.50
91-71-003	Lunchtime Visitor	G. Giordano	14-day	29.50	33.00
91-71-004	Anyone for a Swim?	G. Giordano	14-day	29.50	36.00

		ARTIST	EDITION	ISSUE	QUOTE
91-71-005	Nature Scouts	G. Giordano	14-day	29.50	36.00
91-71-006	Meadow Meeting	G. Giordano	14-day	29.50	33.00
91-71-007	Hi Neighbor	G. Giordano	14-day	29.50	29.50
92-71-008	Field Day	G. Giordano	14-day	29.50	36.00
Hamilton Collection		**Childhood Reflections**			
91-72-001	Harmony	B.P. Gutmann	14-day	29.50	60-100.
91-72-002	Kitty's Breakfast	B.P. Gutmann	14-day	29.50	36.00
91-72-003	Friendly Enemies	B.P. Gutmann	14-day	29.50	36.00
91-72-004	Smile, Smile, Smile	B.P. Gutmann	14-day	29.50	36.00
91-72-005	Lullaby	B.P. Gutmann	14-day	29.50	36.00
91-72-006	Oh! Oh! A Bunny	B.P. Gutmann	14-day	29.50	29.50
91-72-007	Little Mother	B.P. Gutmann	14-day	29.50	33.00
91-72-008	Thank You, God	B.P. Gutmann	14-day	29.50	36.00
Hamilton Collection		**Great Mammals of the Sea**			
91-73-001	Orca Trio	Wyland	14-day	35.00	45.00
91-73-002	Hawaii Dolphins	Wyland	14-day	35.00	37.50
91-73-003	Orca Journey	Wyland	14-day	35.00	43.00
91-73-004	Dolphin Paradise	Wyland	14-day	35.00	45.00
91-73-005	Children of the Sea	Wyland	14-day	35.00	60.00
91-73-006	Kissing Dolphins	Wyland	14-day	35.00	39.00
91-73-007	Islands	Wyland	14-day	35.00	60.00
91-73-008	Orcas	Wyland	14-day	35.00	45.00
Hamilton Collection		**The West of Frank McCarthy**			
91-74-001	Attacking the Iron Horse	F. McCarthy	14-day	37.50	60.00
91-74-002	Attempt on the Stage	F. McCarthy	14-day	37.50	45.00
91-74-003	The Prayer	F. McCarthy	14-day	37.50	54.00
91-74-004	On the Old North Trail	F. McCarthy	14-day	37.50	48.00
91-74-005	The Hostile Threat	F. McCarthy	14-day	37.50	45.00
91-74-006	Bringing Out the Furs	F. McCarthy	14-day	37.50	45.00
91-74-007	Kiowa Raider	F. McCarthy	14-day	37.50	45.00
91-74-008	Headed North	F. McCarthy	14-day	37.50	37.50
Hamilton Collection		**The Quilted Countryside: A Signature Collection by Mel Steele**			
91-75-001	The Old Country Store	M. Steele	14-day	29.50	54.00
91-75-002	Winter's End	M. Steele	14-day	29.50	29.50
91-75-003	The Quilter's Cabin	M. Steele	14-day	29.50	45.00
91-75-004	Spring Cleaning	M. Steele	14-day	29.50	36.00
91-75-005	Summer Harvest	M. Steele	14-day	29.50	29.50
91-75-006	The Country Merchant	M. Steele	14-day	29.50	36.00
92-75-007	Wash Day	M. Steele	14-day	29.50	29.50
92-75-008	The Antiques Store	M. Steele	14-day	29.50	33.00
Hamilton Collection		**Sporting Generation**			
91-76-001	Like Father, Like Son	J. Lamb	14-day	29.50	36.00
91-76-002	Golden Moments	J. Lamb	14-day	29.50	29.50
91-76-003	The Lookout	J. Lamb	14-day	29.50	29.50
92-76-004	Picking Up The Scent	J. Lamb	14-day	29.50	29.50
92-76-005	First Time Out	J. Lamb	14-day	29.50	29.50
92-76-006	Who's Tracking Who	J. Lamb	14-day	29.50	29.50
92-76-007	Springing Into Action	J. Lamb	14-day	29.50	29.50
92-76-008	Point of Interest	J. Lamb	14-day	29.50	29.50
Hamilton Collection		**Seasons of the Bald Eagle**			
91-77-001	Autumn in the Mountains	J. Pitcher	14-day	37.50	37.50
91-77-002	Winter in the Valley	J. Pitcher	14-day	37.50	37.50
91-77-003	Spring on the River	J. Pitcher	14-day	37.50	37.50
91-77-004	Summer on the Seacoast	J. Pitcher	14-day	37.50	37.50
Hamilton Collection		**Vanishing Rural America**			
91-78-001	Quiet Reflections	J. Harrison	14-day	29.50	45.00
91-78-002	Autumn's Passage	J. Harrison	14-day	29.50	45.00
91-78-003	Storefront Memories	J. Harrison	14-day	29.50	45.00
91-78-004	Country Path	J. Harrison	14-day	29.50	36.00
91-78-005	When the Circus Came To Town	J. Harrison	14-day	29.50	36.00
91-78-006	Covered in Fall	J. Harrison	14-day	29.50	45.00
91-78-007	America's Heartland	J. Harrison	14-day	29.50	33.00
91-78-008	Rural Delivery	J. Harrison	14-day	29.50	33.00
Hamilton Collection		**North American Ducks**			
91-79-001	Autumn Flight	R. Lawrence	14-day	29.50	36.00
91-79-002	The Resting Place	R. Lawrence	14-day	29.50	29.50
91-79-003	Twin Flight	R. Lawrence	14-day	29.50	29.50
92-79-004	Misty Morning	R. Lawrence	14-day	29.50	29.50
92-79-005	Springtime Thaw	R. Lawrence	14-day	29.50	29.50
92-79-006	Summer Retreat	R. Lawrence	14-day	29.50	29.50
92-79-007	Overcast	R. Lawrence	14-day	29.50	29.50
92-79-008	Perfect Pintails	R. Lawrence	14-day	29.50	29.50
Hamilton Collection		**Proud Indian Families**			
91-80-001	The Storyteller	K. Freeman	14-day	29.50	29.50
91-80-002	The Power of the Basket	K. Freeman	14-day	29.50	29.50
91-80-003	The Naming Ceremony	K. Freeman	14-day	29.50	29.50
92-80-004	Playing With Tradition	K. Freeman	14-day	29.50	29.50
92-80-005	Preparing the Berry Harvest	K. Freeman	14-day	29.50	29.50
92-80-006	Ceremonial Dress	K. Freeman	14-day	29.50	29.50
92-80-007	Sounds of the Forest	K. Freeman	14-day	29.50	29.50
92-80-008	The Marriage Ceremony	K. Freeman	14-day	29.50	29.50
93-80-009	The Jewelry Maker	K. Freeman	14-day	29.50	29.50
93-80-010	Beautiful Creations	K. Freeman	14-day	29.50	29.50
Hamilton Collection		**Little Shopkeepers**			
90-81-001	Sew Tired	G. Gerardi	14-day	29.50	29.50
91-81-002	Break Time	G. Gerardi	14-day	29.50	29.50
91-81-003	Purrfect Fit	G. Gerardi	14-day	29.50	29.50
91-81-004	Toying Around	G. Gerardi	14-day	29.50	36.00
91-81-005	Chain Reaction	G. Gerardi	14-day	29.50	45.00
91-81-006	Inferior Decorators	G. Gerardi	14-day	29.50	36.00
91-81-007	Tulip Tag	G. Gerardi	14-day	29.50	36.00
91-81-008	Candy Capers	G. Gerardi	14-day	29.50	36.00
Hamilton Collection		**Our Cherished Seas**			
92-82-001	Whale Song	S. Barlowe	48-day	37.50	37.50
92-82-002	Lions of the Sea	S. Barlowe	48-day	37.50	37.50
92-82-003	Flight of the Dolphins	S. Barlowe	48-day	37.50	37.50
92-82-004	Palace of the Seals	S. Barlowe	48-day	37.50	37.50
93-82-005	Orca Ballet	S. Barlowe	48-day	37.50	37.50
93-82-006	Emporers of the Ice	S. Barlowe	48-day	37.50	37.50
93-82-007	Sea Turtles	S. Barlowe	48-day	37.50	37.50
93-82-008	Splendor of the Sea	S. Barlowe	48-day	37.50	37.50
Hamilton Collection		**Republic Pictures Film Library Collection**			
92-83-001	Showdown With Laredo	S. Morton	28-day	37.50	37.50
92-83-002	The Ride Home	S. Morton	28-day	37.50	37.50

	ARTIST	EDITION	ISSUE	QUOTE
92-83-003 Attack at Tarawa	S. Morton	28-day	37.50	37.50
92-83-004 Thoughts of Angelique	S. Morton	28-day	37.50	37.50
92-83-005 War of the Wildcats	S. Morton	28-day	37.50	37.50
92-83-006 The Fighting Seabees	S. Morton	28-day	37.50	37.50
92-83-007 The Quiet Man	S. Morton	28-day	37.50	37.50
93-83-008 Angel & The Badman	S. Morton	28-day	37.50	37.50
93-83-009 Sands of Iwo Jima	S. Morton	28-day	37.50	37.50
93-83-010 Flying Tigers	S. Morton	28-day	39.50	39.50
Hamilton Collection	**Unbridled Spirit**			
92-84-001 Surf Dancer	C. DeHaan	28-day	29.50	29.50
92-84-002 Winter Renegade	C. DeHaan	28-day	29.50	29.50
92-84-003 Desert Shadows	C. DeHaan	28-day	29.50	29.50
93-84-004 Painted Sunrise	C. DeHaan	28-day	29.50	29.50
93-84-005 Desert Duel	C. DeHaan	28-day	29.50	29.50
93-84-006 Midnight Run	C. DeHaan	28-day	29.50	29.50
93-84-007 Moonlight Majesty	C. DeHaan	28-day	29.50	29.50
93-84-008 Autumn Reverie	C. DeHaan	28-day	29.50	29.50
93-84-009 Blizzard's Peril	C. DeHaan	28-day	29.50	29.50
93-84-010 Sunrise Surprise	C. DeHaan	28-day	29.50	29.50
Hamilton Collection	**Victorian Playtime**			
91-85-001 A Busy Day	M. H. Bogart	14-day	29.50	29.50
92-85-002 Little Masterpiece	M. H. Bogart	14-day	29.50	29.50
92-85-003 Playing Bride	M. H. Bogart	14-day	29.50	29.50
92-85-004 Waiting for a Nibble	M. H. Bogart	14-day	29.50	29.50
92-85-005 Tea and Gossip	M. H. Bogart	14-day	29.50	29.50
92-85-006 Cleaning House	M. H. Bogart	14-day	29.50	29.50
92-85-007 A Little Persuasion	M. H. Bogart	14-day	29.50	29.50
92-85-008 Peek-a-Boo	M. H. Bogart	14-day	29.50	29.50
Hamilton Collection	**Winter Rails**			
92-86-001 Winter Crossing	T. Xaras	28-day	29.50	29.50
93-86-002 Coal Country	T. Xaras	28-day	29.50	29.50
93-86-003 Daylight Run	T. Xaras	28-day	29.50	29.50
93-86-004 By Sea or Rail	T. Xaras	28-day	29.50	29.50
93-86-005 Country Crossroads	T. Xaras	28-day	29.50	29.50
93-86-006 Timber Line	T. Xaras	28-day	29.50	29.50
93-86-007 The Long Haul	T. Xaras	28-day	29.50	29.50
93-86-008 Darby Crossing	T. Xaras	28-day	29.50	29.50
Hamilton Collection	**Farmyard Friends**			
92-87-001 Mistaken Identity	J. Lamb	28-day	29.50	29.50
92-87-002 Little Cowhands	J. Lamb	28-day	29.50	29.50
93-87-003 Shreading the Evidence	J. Lamb	28-day	29.50	29.50
93-87-004 Partners in Crime	J. Lamb	28-day	29.50	29.50
93-87-005 Fowl Play	J. Lamb	28-day	29.50	29.50
93-87-006 Follow The Leader	J. Lamb	28-day	29.50	29.50
93-87-007 Pony Tales	J. Lamb	28-day	29.50	29.50
93-87-008 An Apple A Day	J. Lamb	28-day	29.50	29.50
Hamilton Collection	**Man's Best Friend**			
92-88-001 Special Delivery	L. Picken	28-day	29.50	29.50
92-88-002 Making Waves	L. Picken	28-day	29.50	29.50
92-88-003 Good Catch	L. Picken	28-day	29.50	29.50
93-88-004 Time For a Walk	L. Picken	28-day	29.50	29.50
93-88-005 Faithful Friend	L. Picken	28-day	29.50	29.50
93-88-006 Let's Play Ball	L. Picken	28-day	29.50	29.50
93-88-007 Sitting Pretty	L. Picken	28-day	29.50	29.50
93-88-008 Bedtime Story	L. Picken	28-day	29.50	29.50
93-88-009 Trusted Companion	L. Picken	28-day	29.50	29.50
Hamilton Collection	**Nature's Nighttime Realm**			
92-89-001 Bobcat	G. Murray	28-day	29.50	29.50
92-89-002 Cougar	G. Murray	28-day	29.50	29.50
93-89-003 Jaguar	G. Murray	28-day	29.50	29.50
93-89-004 White Tiger	G. Murray	28-day	29.50	29.50
93-89-005 Lynx	G. Murray	28-day	29.50	29.50
93-89-006 Lion	G. Murray	28-day	29.50	29.50
93-89-007 Snow Leopard	G. Murray	28-day	29.50	29.50
93-89-008 Cheetah	G. Murray	28-day	29.50	29.50
Hamilton Collection	**Precious Moments Bible Story**			
90-90-001 Come Let Us Adore Him	S. Butcher	28-day	29.50	29.50
92-90-002 They Followed The Star	S. Butcher	28-day	29.50	29.50
92-90-003 The Flight Into Egypt	S. Butcher	28-day	29.50	29.50
92-90-004 The Carpenter Shop	S. Butcher	28-day	29.50	29.50
92-90-005 Jesus In The Temple	S. Butcher	28-day	29.50	29.50
92-90-006 The Crucifixion	S. Butcher	28-day	29.50	29.50
93-90-007 He Is Not Here	S. Butcher	28-day	29.50	29.50
Hamilton Collection	**The Wonder Of Christmas**			
91-91-001 Santa's Secret	J. McClelland	28-day	29.50	29.50
91-91-002 My Favorite Ornament	J. McClelland	28-day	29.50	29.50
91-91-003 Waiting For Santa	J. McClelland	28-day	29.50	29.50
93-91-004 The Caroler	J. McClelland	28-day	29.50	29.50
Hamilton Collection	**Romantic Victorian Keepsake**			
92-92-001 Dearest Kiss	J. Grossman	28-day	35.00	35.00
92-92-002 First Love	J. Grossman	28-day	35.00	35.00
92-92-003 As Fair as a Rose	J. Grossman	28-day	35.00	35.00
92-92-004 Springtime Beauty	J. Grossman	28-day	35.00	35.00
92-92-005 Summertime Fancy	J. Grossman	28-day	35.00	35.00
92-92-006 Bonnie Blue Eyes	J. Grossman	28-day	35.00	35.00
92-92-007 Precious Friends	J. Grossman	28-day	35.00	35.00
94-92-008 Bonnets and Bouquets	J. Grossman	28-day	35.00	35.00
Hamilton Collection	**The World Of Zolan**			
92-93-001 First Kiss	D. Zolan	28-day	29.50	29.50
92-93-002 Morning Discovery	D. Zolan	28-day	29.50	29.50
93-93-003 The Little Fisherman	D. Zolan	28-day	29.50	29.50
93-93-004 Letter to Grandma	D. Zolan	28-day	29.50	29.50
93-93-005 Twilight Prayer	D. Zolan	28-day	29.50	29.50
93-93-006 Flowers for Mother	D. Zolan	28-day	29.50	29.50
Hamilton Collection	**Mystic Warriors**			
92-94-001 Deliverance	C. Ren	28-day	29.50	29.50
92-94-002 Mystic Warrior	C. Ren	28-day	29.50	29.50
92-94-003 Sun Seeker	C. Ren	28-day	29.50	29.50
92-94-004 Top Gun	C. Ren	28-day	29.50	29.50
92-94-005 Man Who Walks Alone	C. Ren	28-day	29.50	29.50
92-94-006 Windrider	C. Ren	28-day	29.50	29.50
92-94-007 Spirit of the Plains	C. Ren	28-day	29.50	29.50
93-94-008 Blue Thunder	C. Ren	28-day	29.50	29.50
93-94-009 Sun Glow	C. Ren	28-day	29.50	29.50
93-94-010 Peace Maker	C. Ren	28-day	29.50	29.50

	ARTIST	EDITION	ISSUE	QUOTE
Hamilton Collection	**Andy Griffith**			
92-95-001 Sheriff Andy Taylor	R. Tanenbaum	28-day	29.50	29.50
92-95-002 A Startling Conclusion	R. Tanenbaum	28-day	29.50	29.50
93-95-003 Mayberry Sing-a-long	R. Tanenbaum	28-day	29.50	29.50
93-95-004 Aunt Bee's Kitchen	R. Tanenbaum	28-day	29.50	29.50
93-95-005 Surprise! Surprise!	R. Tanenbaum	28-day	29.50	29.50
93-95-006 An Explosive Situation	R. Tanenbaum	28-day	29.50	29.50
93-95-007 Meeting Aunt Bee	R. Tanenbaum	28-day	29.50	29.50
93-95-008 Opie's Big Catch	R. Tanenbaum	28-day	29.50	29.50
Hamilton Collection	**Madonna And Child**			
92-96-001 Madonna Della Sedia	R. Sanzio	28-day	37.50	37.50
92-96-002 Virgin of the Rocks	L. DaVinci	28-day	37.50	37.50
93-96-003 Madonna of Rosary	B. E. Murillo	28-day	37.50	37.50
93-96-004 Sistine Madonna	R. Sanzio	28-day	37.50	37.50
93-96-005 Virgin Adoring Christ Child	A. Correggio	28-day	37.50	37.50
93-96-006 Virgin of the Grape	P. Mignard	28-day	37.50	37.50
93-96-007 Madonna del Magnificat	S. Botticelli	28-day	37.50	37.50
93-96-008 Madonna col Bambino	S. Botticelli	28-day	37.50	37.50
Hamilton Collection	**Council Of Nations**			
91-97-001 Strength of the Sioux	G. Perillo	28-day	29.50	29.50
92-97-002 Pride of the Cheyenne	G. Perillo	28-day	29.50	29.50
92-97-003 Dignity of the Nez Parce	G. Perillo	28-day	29.50	29.50
92-97-004 Courage of the Arapaho	G. Perillo	28-day	29.50	29.50
92-97-005 Power of the Blackfoot	G. Perillo	28-day	29.50	29.50
92-97-006 Nobility of the Algonqui	G. Perillo	28-day	29.50	29.50
92-97-007 Wisdom of the Cherokee	G. Perillo	28-day	29.50	29.50
92-97-008 Boldness of the Seneca	G. Perillo	28-day	29.50	29.50
Hamilton Collection	**Beauty Of Winter**			
92-98-001 Silent Night	N/A	28-day	29.50	29.50
93-98-002 Moonlight Sleighride	N/A	28-day	29.50	29.50
Hamilton Collection	**Bialosky® & Friends**			
92-99-001 Family Addition	P./A.Bialosky	28-day	29.50	29.50
93-99-002 Sweetheart	P./A.Bialosky	28-day	29.50	29.50
93-99-003 Let's Go Fishing	P./A.Bialosky	28-day	29.50	29.50
93-99-004 U.S. Mail	P./A.Bialosky	28-day	29.50	29.50
93-99-005 Sleigh Ride	P./A.Bialosky	28-day	29.50	29.50
93-99-006 Honey For Sale	P./A.Bialosky	28-day	29.50	29.50
93-99-007 Breakfast In Bed	P./A.Bialosky	28-day	29.50	29.50
93-99-008 My First Two-Wheeler	P./A.Bialosky	28-day	29.50	29.50
Hamilton Collection	**Country Garden Cottages**			
92-101-001 Riverbank Cottage	E. Dertner	28-day	29.50	29.50
92-101-002 Sunday Outing	E. Dertner	28-day	29.50	29.50
92-101-003 Shepherd's Cottage	E. Dertner	28-day	29.50	29.50
93-101-004 Daydream Cottage	E. Dertner	28-day	29.50	29.50
93-101-005 Garden Glorious	E. Dertner	28-day	29.50	29.50
93-101-006 This Side of Heaven	E. Dertner	28-day	29.50	29.50
93-101-007 Summer Symphony	E. Dertner	28-day	29.50	29.50
93-101-008 April Cottage	E. Dertner	28-day	29.50	29.50
Hamilton Collection	**Quiet Moments Of Childhood**			
91-102-001 Elizabeth's Afternoon Tea	D. Green	14-day	29.50	45.00
91-102-002 Christina's Secret Garden	D. Green	14-day	29.50	36.00
91-102-003 Eric & Erin's Storytime	D. Green	14-day	29.50	29.50
92-102-004 Jessica's Tea Party	D. Green	14-day	29.50	33.00
92-102-005 Megan & Monique's Bakery	D. Green	14-day	29.50	36.00
92-102-006 Children's Day By The Sea	D. Green	14-day	29.50	29.50
92-102-007 Jordan's Playful Pups	D. Green	14-day	29.50	33.00
92-102-008 Daniel's Morning Playtime	D. Green	14-day	29.50	29.50
Hamilton Collection	**The STAR TREK 25th Anniversary Commemorative Collection**			
91-103-001 SPOCK	T. Blackshear	14-day	35.00	99-130.
91-103-002 Kirk	T. Blackshear	14-day	35.00	75-120.
92-103-003 McCoy	T. Blackshear	14-day	35.00	35.00
92-103-004 Uhura	T. Blackshear	14-day	35.00	35.00
92-103-005 Scotty	T. Blackshear	14-day	35.00	35.00
93-103-006 Sulu	T. Blackshear	14-day	35.00	35.00
93-103-007 Chekov	T. Blackshear	14-day	35.00	35.00
94-103-008 U.S.S. Enterprise NCC-1701	T. Blackshear	14-day	35.00	35.00
Hamilton Collection	**The Spock® Commemorative Wall Plaque**			
93-104-001 Spock®/STAR TREK VI The Undiscovered Country	N/A	2,500	195.00	195.00
Hamilton Collection	**First Officer Spock® Autographed Wall Plaque**			
94-105-001 First Officer Spockr	N/A	2,500	195.00	195.00
Hamilton Collection	**Captain Jean-Luc Picard Autographed Wall Plaque**			
94-106-001 Captain Jean-Luc Picard	N/A	5,000	195.00	195.00
Hamilton Collection	**STAR TREK 25th Anniversary Commemorative Plate**			
91-107-001 STAR TREK 25th Anniversary Commemorative Plate	T. Blackshear	14-day	37.50	120-149.
Hamilton Collection	**STAR TREK: The Next Generation**			
98-108-001 Captain Jean-Luc Picard	T. Blackshear	28-day	35.00	128.00
98-108-002 Commander William T. Riker	T. Blackshear	28-day	35.00	35.00
94-108-003 Lieutenant Commander Data	T. Blackshear	28-day	35.00	90.00
94-108-004 Lieutenant Worf	T. Blackshear	28-day	35.00	35.00
Hamilton Collection	**STAR TREK®:THE NEXT GENERATION™The Episodes**			
94-109-001 The Best of Both Worlds	K. Birdsong	28-day	35.00	35.00
94-109-002 Encounter at Far Point	K. Birdsong	28-day	35.00	35.00
Hamilton Collection	**STAR TREK® The Movies**			
94-110-001 STAR TREK IV: The Voyage Home	M. Weistling	28-day	35.00	35.00
94-110-002 STAR TREK II: The Wrath of Khan	M. Weistling	28-day	35.00	35.00
Hamilton Collection	**STAR TREK®: The Voyagers**			
94-111-001 U.S.S. Enterprise NCC-1701	K. Birdsong	28-day	35.00	35.00
94-111-002 U.S.S. Enterprise NCC-1701-D	K. Birdsong	28-day	35.00	35.00
94-111-003 Klingon Battlecruiser	K. Birdsong	28-day	35.00	35.00
94-111-004 Romulan Warbird	K. Birdsong	28-day	35.00	35.00
Hamilton Collection	**Portraits of the Bald Eagle**			
93-112-001 Ruler of the Sky	J. Pitcher	28-day	37.50	37.50
93-112-002 In Bold Defiance	J. Pitcher	28-day	37.50	37.50
93-112-003 Master Of The Summer Skies	J. Pitcher	28-day	37.50	37.50
93-112-004 Spring's Sentinel	J. Pitcher	28-day	37.50	37.50
Hamilton Collection	**A Lisi Martin Christmas**			
92-113-001 Santa's Littlest Reindeer	L. Martin	28-day	29.50	29.50
93-113-002 Not A Creature Was Stirring	L. Martin	28-day	29.50	29.50

	ARTIST	EDITION	ISSUE	QUOTE
93-113-003 Christmas Dreams	L. Martin	28-day	29.50	29.50
93-113-004 The Christmas Story	L. Martin	28-day	29.50	29.50
93-113-005 Trimming The Tree	L. Martin	28-day	29.50	29.50
93-113-006 A Taste Of The Holidays	L. Martin	28-day	29.50	29.50
93-113-007 The Night Before Christmas	L. Martin	28-day	29.50	29.50
93-113-008 Christmas Watch	L. Martin	28-day	29.50	29.50
Hamilton Collection	**Glory of Christ**			
92-114-001 The Ascension	C. Micarelli	48-day	29.50	29.50
92-114-002 Jesus Teaching	C. Micarelli	48-day	29.50	29.50
93-114-003 Last Supper	C. Micarelli	48-day	29.50	29.50
93-114-004 The Nativity	C. Micarelli	48-day	29.50	29.50
93-114-005 The Baptism of Christ	C. Micarelli	48-day	29.50	29.50
93-114-006 Jesus Heals the Sick	C. Micarelli	48-day	29.50	29.50
94-114-007 Jesus Walks on Water	C. Micarelli	48-day	29.50	29.50
94-114-008 Descent From the Cross	C. Micarelli	48-day	29.50	29.50
Hamilton Collection	**Norman Rockwell's Saturday Evening Post Baseball Plate Collection**			
92-115-001 100th Year of Baseball	N. Rockwell	Open	19.50	19.50
93-115-002 The Rookie	N. Rockwell	Open	19.50	19.50
93-115-003 The Dugout	N. Rockwell	Open	19.50	19.50
93-115-004 Bottom of the Sixth	N. Rockwell	Open	19.50	19.50
Hamilton Collection	**Cameo Kittens**			
93-116-001 Ginger Snap	Q. Lemonds	28-day	29.50	29.50
93-116-002 Cat Tails	Q. Lemonds	28-day	29.50	29.50
93-116-003 Lady Blue	Q. Lemonds	28-day	29.50	29.50
93-116-004 Tiny Heart Stealer	Q. Lemonds	28-day	29.50	29.50
93-116-005 Blossom	Q. Lemonds	28-day	29.50	29.50
94-116-006 Whisker Antics	Q. Lemonds	28-day	29.50	29.50
94-116-007 Tiger's Temptation	Q. Lemonds	28-day	29.50	29.50
94-116-008 Scout	Q. Lemonds	28-day	29.50	29.50
Hamilton Collection	**Princesses of the Plains**			
93-117-001 Prairie Flower	D. Wright	28-day	29.50	29.50
93-117-002 Snow Princess	D. Wright	28-day	29.50	29.50
93-117-003 Wild Flower	D. Wright	28-day	29.50	29.50
93-117-004 Noble Beauty	D. Wright	28-day	29.50	29.50
93-117-005 Winter's Rose	D. Wright	28-day	29.50	29.50
93-117-006 Gentle Beauty	D. Wright	28-day	29.50	29.50
94-117-007 Nature's Guardian	D. Wright	28-day	29.50	29.50
94-117-008 Mountain Princess	D. Wright	28-day	29.50	29.50
Hamilton Collection	**Victorian Christmas Memories**			
92-118-001 A Visit from St. Nicholas	J. Grossman	28-day	29.50	29.50
93-118-002 Christmas Delivery	J. Grossman	28-day	29.50	29.50
93-118-003 Christmas Angels	J. Grossman	28-day	29.50	29.50
92-118-004 With Visions of Sugar Plums	J. Grossman	28-day	29.50	29.50
93-118-005 Merry Olde Kris Kringle	J. Grossman	28-day	29.50	29.50
93-118-006 Grandfather Frost	J. Grossman	28-day	29.50	29.50
93-118-007 Joyous Noel	J. Grossman	28-day	29.50	29.50
93-118-008 Christmas Innocence	J. Grossman	28-day	29.50	29.50
Hamilton Collection	**Daughters Of The Sun**			
93-119-001 Sun Dancer	K. Thayer	28-day	29.50	29.50
93-119-002 Shining Feather	K. Thayer	28-day	29.50	29.50
93-119-003 Delighted Dancer	K. Thayer	28-day	29.50	29.50
93-119-004 Evening Dancer	K. Thayer	28-day	29.50	29.50
93-119-005 A Secret Glance	K. Thayer	28-day	29.50	29.50
93-119-006 Chippewa Charmer	K. Thayer	28-day	29.50	29.50
94-119-007 Pride of the Yakima	K. Thayer	28-day	29.50	29.50
94-119-008 Radiant Beauty	K. Thayer	28-day	29.50	29.50
Hamilton Collection	**The Best Of Baseball**			
93-120-001 The Legendary Mickey Mantle	R. Tanenbaum	28-day	29.50	29.50
93-120-002 The Immortal Babe Ruth	R. Tanenbaum	28-day	29.50	29.50
93-120-003 The Great Willie Mays	R. Tanenbaum	28-day	29.50	29.50
93-120-004 The Unbeatable Duke Snider	R. Tanenbaum	28-day	29.50	29.50
93-120-005 The Extraordinary Lou Gehrig	R. Tanenbaum	28-day	29.50	29.50
93-120-006 The Phenomenal Roberto Clemente	R. Tanenbaum	28-day	29.50	29.50
93-120-007 The Remarkable Johnny Bench	R. Tanenbaum	28-day	29.50	29.50
93-120-008 The Incredible Nolan Ryan	R. Tanenbaum	28-day	29.50	29.50
93-120-009 The Exceptional Brooks Robinson	R. Tanenbaum	28-day	29.50	29.50
93-120-010 The Unforgettable Phil Rizzuto	R. Tanenbaum	28-day	29.50	29.50
Hamilton Collection	**Lore Of The West**			
93-121-001 A Mile In His Mocassins	L. Danielle	28-day	29.50	29.50
93-121-002 Path of Honor	L. Danielle	28-day	29.50	29.50
93-121-003 A Chief's Pride	L. Danielle	28-day	29.50	29.50
94-121-004 Pathways of the Pueblo	L. Danielle	28-day	29.50	29.50
94-121-005 In Her Seps	L. Danielle	28-day	29.50	29.50
94-121-006 Growing Up Brave	L. Danielle	28-day	29.50	29.50
94-121-007 Nomads of the Southwest	L. Danielle	28-day	29.50	29.50
94-121-008 Sacred Spirit of the Plains	L. Danielle	28-day	29.50	29.50
Hamilton Collection	**The Fierce And The Free**			
92-122-001 Big Medicine	F. McCarthy	28-day	29.50	29.50
93-122-002 Land of the Winter Hawk	F. McCarthy	28-day	29.50	29.50
93-122-003 Warrior of Savage Splendor	F. McCarthy	28-day	29.50	29.50
94-122-004 War Party	F. McCarthy	28-day	29.50	29.50
94-122-005 The Challenge	F. McCarthy	28-day	29.50	29.50
Hamilton Collection	**Year Of The Wolf**			
93-123-001 Broken Silence	A. Agnew	28-day	29.50	29.50
93-123-002 Leader of the Pack	A. Agnew	28-day	29.50	29.50
93-123-003 Solitude	A. Agnew	28-day	29.50	29.50
94-123-004 Tundra Light	A. Agnew	28-day	29.50	29.50
94-123-005 Guardians of the High Country	A. Agnew	28-day	29.50	29.50
94-123-006 A Second Glance	A. Agnew	28-day	29.50	29.50
94-123-007 Free as the Wind	A. Agnew	28-day	29.50	29.50
94-123-008 Song of the Wolf	A. Agnew	28-day	29.50	29.50
Hamilton Collection	**Precious Moments Classics**			
93-124-001 God Loveth A Cheerful Giver	S. Butcher	28-day	35.00	35.00
93-124-002 Make A Joyful Noise	S. Butcher	28-day	35.00	35.00
Hamilton Collection	**The Golden Age of American Railroads**			
91-125-001 The Blue Comet	T. Xaras	14-day	29.50	45.00
91-125-002 The Morning Local	T. Xaras	14-day	29.50	60.00
91-125-003 The Pennsylvania K-4	T. Xaras	14-day	29.50	90.00
91-125-004 Above the Canyon	T. Xaras	14-day	29.50	90.00
91-125-005 Portrait in Steam	T. Xaras	14-day	29.50	75.00
91-125-006 The Santa Fe Super Chief	T. Xaras	14-day	29.50	105.00
91-125-007 The Big Boy	T. Xaras	14-day	29.50	60.00
91-125-008 The Empire Builder	T. Xaras	14-day	29.50	60.00

	ARTIST	EDITION	ISSUE	QUOTE
92-125-009 An American Classic	T. Xaras	14-day	29.50	33.00
92-125-010 Final Destination	T. Xaras	14-day	29.50	36.00
Hamilton Collection	**Lucy Collage**			
93-126-001 Lucy	M. Weistling	28-day	37.50	60-100.
Hamilton Collection	**The Last Warriors**			
93-127-001 Winter of '41	C. Ren	28-day	29.50	29.50
93-127-002 Morning of Reckoning	C. Ren	28-day	29.50	29.50
93-127-003 Twilights Last Gleaming	C. Ren	28-day	29.50	29.50
93-127-004 Lone Winter Journey	C. Ren	28-day	29.50	29.50
94-127-005 Victory's Reward	C. Ren	28-day	29.50	29.50
94-127-006 Solitary Hunter	C. Ren	28-day	29.50	29.50
94-127-007 Solemn Reflection	C. Ren	28-day	29.50	29.50
94-127-008 Confronting Danger	C. Ren	28-day	29.50	29.50
Hamilton Collection	**Classic American Santas**			
93-128-001 A Christmas Eve Visitor	G. Hinke	28-day	29.50	29.50
94-128-002 Up on the Rooftop	G. Hinke	28-day	29.50	29.50
94-128-003 Santa's Candy Kitchen	G. Hinke	28-day	29.50	29.50
94-128-004 A Christmas Chorus	G. Hinke	28-day	29.50	29.50
94-128-005 An Exciting Christmas Eve	G. Hinke	28-day	29.50	29.50
94-128-006 Rest Ye Merry Gentlemen	G. Hinke	28-day	29.50	29.50
94-128-007 Preparing the Sleigh	G. Hinke	28-day	29.50	29.50
94-128-008 The Reindeer's Stable	G. Hinke	28-day	29.50	29.50
Hamilton Collection	**Nature's Majestic Cats**			
93-129-001 Siberian Tiger	M. Richter	28-day	29.50	29.50
93-129-002 Himalayan Snow Leopard	M. Richter	28-day	29.50	29.50
93-129-003 African Lion	M. Richter	28-day	29.50	29.50
94-129-004 Asian Clouded Leopard	M. Richter	28-day	29.50	29.50
94-129-005 American Cougar	M. Richter	28-day	29.50	29.50
94-129-006 East African Leopard	M. Richter	28-day	29.50	29.50
94-129-007 African Cheetah	M. Richter	28-day	29.50	29.50
94-129-008 Canadian Lynx	M. Richter	28-day	29.50	29.50
Hamilton Collection	**Enchanted Seascapes**			
93-130-001 Sanctuary of the Dolphin	J. Enright	28-day	29.50	29.50
94-130-002 Rhapsody of Hope	J. Enright	28-day	29.50	29.50
94-130-003 Oasis of the Gods	J. Enright	28-day	29.50	29.50
94-130-004 Sphere of Life	J. Enright	28-day	29.50	29.50
94-130-005 Edge of Time	J. Enright	28-day	29.50	29.50
94-130-006 Sea of Light	J. Enright	28-day	29.50	29.50
94-130-007 Lost Beneath the Blue	J. Enright	28-day	29.50	29.50
94-130-008 Blue Paradise	J. Enright	28-day	29.50	29.50
Hamilton Collection	**Call to Adventure**			
93-131-001 USS Constitution	R. Cross	28-day	29.50	29.50
93-131-002 The Bounty	R. Cross	28-day	29.50	29.50
94-131-003 Bonhomme Richard	R. Cross	28-day	29.50	29.50
94-131-004 Old Nantucket	R. Cross	28-day	29.50	29.50
94-131-005 Golden West	R. Cross	28-day	29.50	29.50
94-131-006 Boston	R. Cross	28-day	29.50	29.50
94-131-007 Hannah	R. Cross	28-day	29.50	29.50
94-131-008 Improvement	R. Cross	28-day	29.50	29.50
Hamilton Collection	**Official Honeymooner's Commemorative Plate**			
93-132-001 The Official Honeymooner's Commemorative Plate	D. Bobnick	28-day	37.50	37.50
Hamilton Collection	**All in a Day's Work**			
94-133-001 Where's the Fire?	J. Lamb	28-day	29.50	29.50
94-133-002 Lunch Break	J. Lamb	28-day	29.50	29.50
94-133-003 Puppy Patrol	J. Lamb	28-day	29.50	29.50
94-133-004 Decoy Delivery	J. Lamb	28-day	29.50	29.50
Hamilton Collection	**Forging New Frontiers**			
94-134-001 The Race is On	J. Deneen	28-day	29.50	29.50
94-134-002 Big Boy	J. Deneen	28-day	29.50	29.50
94-134-003 Cresting the Summit	J. Deneen	28-day	29.50	29.50
94-134-004 Spring Roundup	J. Deneen	28-day	29.50	29.50
94-134-005 Winter in the Rockies	J. Deneen	28-day	29.50	29.50
94-134-006 High Country Logging	J. Deneen	28-day	29.50	29.50
Hamilton Collection	**Romance of the Rails**			
94-135-001 Starlight Limited	D. Tutwiler	28-day	29.50	29.50
94-135-002 Portland Rose	D. Tutwiler	28-day	29.50	29.50
94-135-003 Orange Blossom Special	D. Tutwiler	28-day	29.50	29.50
94-135-004 Morning Star	D. Tutwiler	28-day	29.50	29.50
94-135-005 Crescent Limited	D. Tutwiler	28-day	29.50	29.50
94-135-006 Sunset Limited	D. Tutwiler	28-day	29.50	29.50
94-135-007 Western Star	D. Tutwiler	28-day	29.50	29.50
94-135-008 Sunrise Limited	D. Tutwiler	28-day	29.50	29.50
Hamilton Collection	**Warrior's Pride**			
94-136-001 Crow War Pony	C. DeHaan	28-day	29.50	29.50
94-136-002 Running Free	C. DeHaan	28-day	29.50	29.50
94-136-003 Blackfoot War Pony	C. DeHaan	28-day	29.50	29.50
94-136-004 Southern Cheyenne	C. DeHaan	28-day	29.50	29.50
Hamilton Collection	**Classic Corvettes**			
94-137-001 1957 Corvette	M. Lacourciere	28-day	29.50	29.50
94-137-002 1963 Corvette	M. Lacourciere	28-day	29.50	29.50
94-137-003 1968 Corvette	M. Lacourciere	28-day	29.50	29.50
94-137-004 1986 Corvette	M. Lacourciere	28-day	29.50	29.50
Hamilton Collection	**Dreamsicles**			
94-138-001 The Flying Lesson	K. Haynes	28-day	19.50	19.50
Hamilton Collection	**A Garden Song**			
94-139-001 Winter's Splendor	M. Hanson	28-day	29.50	29.50
94-139-002 In Full Bloom	M. Hanson	28-day	29.50	29.50
94-139-003 Golden Glories	M. Hanson	28-day	29.50	29.50
Hamilton Collection	**Proud Innocence**			
94-140-001 Desert Bloom	J. Schmidt	28-day	29.50	29.50
Hamilton Collection	**The Legend of Father Christmas**			
94-141-001 The Return of Father Christmas	V. Dezerin	28-day	29.50	29.50
94-141-002 Gifts From Father Christmas	V. Dezerin	28-day	29.50	29.50
94-141-003 The Feast of the Holiday	V. Dezerin	28-day	29.50	29.50
Hamilton Collection	**Drivers of Victory Lane**			
94-142-001 Bill Elliott	R. Tanenbaum	28-day	29.50	29.50
94-142-002 Jeff Gordon	R. Tanenbaum	28-day	29.50	29.50
Hamilton Collection	**The Renaissance Angels**			
94-143-001 Doves of Peace	L. Bywaters	28-day	29.50	29.50

	ARTIST	EDITION	ISSUE	QUOTE
94-143-002 Angelic Innocence	L. Bywaters	28-day	29.50	29.50
Hamilton Collection	**Portraits of the Wild**			
94-144-001 Interlude	J. Meger	28-day	29.50	29.50
94-144-002 Winter Solitude	J. Meger	28-day	29.50	29.50
94-144-003 Devoted Protector	J. Meger	28-day	29.50	29.50
94-144-004 Call of Autumn	J. Meger	28-day	29.50	29.50
94-144-005 Watchful Eyes	J. Meger	28-day	29.50	29.50
Hamilton Collection	**The Call of the North**			
93-145-001 Winter's Dawn	J. Tift	28-day	29.50	29.50
94-145-002 Evening Silence	J. Tift	28-day	29.50	29.50
94-145-003 Moonlit Wilderness	J. Tift	28-day	29.50	29.50
94-145-004 Silent Snowfall	J. Tift	28-day	29.50	29.50
94-145-005 Snowy Watch	J. Tift	28-day	29.50	29.50
94-145-006 Sentinels of the Summit	J. Tift	28-day	29.50	29.50
94-145-007 Arctic Seclusion	J. Tift	28-day	29.50	29.50
94-145-008 Forest Twilight	J. Tift	28-day	29.50	29.50
Hamilton Collection	**Mike Schmidt**			
94-146-001 The Ultimate Competitor: Mike Schmidt	R. Tanenbaum	28-day	29.50	29.50
Hamilton Collection	**Nolan Ryan**			
94-147-001 The Strikeout Express	R. Tanenbaum	28-day	29.50	29.50
94-147-002 Birth of a Legend	R. Tanenbaum	28-day	29.50	29.50
94-147-003 Mr. Fastball	R. Tanenbaum	28-day	29.50	29.50
94-147-004 Million-Dollar Player	R. Tanenbaum	28-day	29.50	29.50
94-147-005 27 Seasons	R. Tanenbaum	28-day	29.50	29.50
94-147-006 Farewell	R. Tanenbaum	28-day	29.50	29.50
Hamilton Collection	**On Wings of Eagles**			
94-148-001 "By Dawn's Early Light"	J. Pitcher	28-day	29.50	29.50
Hamilton Collection	**Scenes of An American Christmas**			
94-149-001 I'll Be Home for Christmas	B. Perry	28-day	29.50	29.50
94-149-002 Christmas Eve Worship	B. Perry	28-day	29.50	29.50
Hamilton Collection	**Glory of the Game**			
94-150-001 "Hank Aaron's Record-Breaking Home Run"	T. Fogerhty	28-day	29.50	29.50
94-150-002 "Bobby Thompson's Shot Heard 'Round the World"	T. Fogerhty	28-day	29.50	29.50
Hamilton Collection	**Civil War Generals**			
94-151-001 Robert E. Lee	M. Gnatek	28-day	29.50	29.50
94-151-002 J.E.B. Stewart	M. Gnatek	28-day	29.50	29.50
94-151-003 Joshua L. Chamberlain	M. Gnatek	28-day	29.50	29.50
94-151-004 George Armstrong Custer	M. Gnatek	28-day	29.50	29.50
94-151-005 Nathan Bedford Forrest	M. Gnatek	28-day	29.50	29.50
94-151-006 James Longstreet	M. Gnatek	28-day	29.50	29.50
Hamilton Collection	**Romantic Flights of Fancy**			
94-152-001 Sunlit Waltz	Q. Lemonds	28-day	29.50	29.50
94-152-002 Morning Minuet	Q. Lemonds	28-day	29.50	29.50
Hamilton Collection	**Cottage Puppies**			
93-153-001 Little Gardeners	K. George	28-day	29.50	29.50
93-153-002 Springtime Fancy	K. George	28-day	29.50	29.50
93-153-003 Endearing Innocence	K. George	28-day	29.50	29.50
94-153-004 Picnic Playtime	K. George	28-day	29.50	29.50
94-153-005 Lazy Afternoon	K. George	28-day	29.50	29.50
94-153-006 Summertime Pals	K. George	28-day	29.50	29.50
94-153-007 A Gardening Trio	K. George	28-day	29.50	29.50
94-153-008 Taking a Break	K. George	28-day	29.50	29.50
Haviland	**Twelve Days of Christmas**			
70-01-001 Partridge	R. Hetreau	30,000	25.00	54.00
71-01-002 Two Turtle Doves	R. Hetreau	30,000	25.00	25.00
72-01-003 Three French Hens	R. Hetreau	30,000	27.50	27.50
73-01-004 Four Calling Birds	R. Hetreau	30,000	28.50	30.00
74-01-005 Five Golden Rings	R. Hetreau	30,000	30.00	30.00
75-01-006 Six Geese a'laying	R. Hetreau	30,000	32.50	32.50
76-01-007 Seven Swans	R. Hetreau	30,000	38.00	38.00
77-01-008 Eight Maids	R. Hetreau	30,000	40.00	40.00
78-01-009 Nine Ladies Dancing	R. Hetreau	30,000	45.00	67.00
79-01-010 Ten Lord's a'leaping	R. Hetreau	30,000	50.00	50.00
80-01-011 Eleven Pipers Piping	R. Hetreau	30,000	55.00	65.00
81-01-012 Twelve Drummers	R. Hetreau	30,000	60.00	60.00
Haviland & Parlon	**Christmas Madonnas**			
72-01-001 By Raphael	Raphael	5,000	35.00	42.00
73-01-002 By Feruzzi	Feruzzi	5,000	40.00	78.00
74-01-003 By Raphael	Raphael	5,000	42.50	42.50
75-01-004 By Murillo	Murillo	7,500	42.50	42.50
76-01-005 By Botticelli	Botticelli	7,500	45.00	45.00
77-01-006 By Bellini	Bellini	7,500	48.00	48.00
78-01-007 By Lippi	Lippi	7,500	48.00	53.00
79-01-008 Madonna of The Eucharist	Botticelli	7,500	49.50	112.00
Edna Hibel Studios	**Mother and Child**			
73-01-001 Colette & Child	E. Hibel	15,000	40.00	725.00
74-01-002 Sayuri & Child	E. Hibel	15,000	40.00	425.00
75-01-003 Kristina & Child	E. Hibel	15,000	50.00	400.00
76-01-004 Marilyn & Child	E. Hibel	15,000	55.00	400.00
77-01-005 Lucia & Child	E. Hibel	15,000	60.00	350.00
81-01-006 Kathleen & Child	E. Hibel	15,000	85.00	275.00
Edna Hibel Studios	**Oriental Gold**			
75-02-001 Yasuko	E. Hibel	2,000	275.00	3000.00
76-02-002 Mr. Obata	E. Hibel	2,000	275.00	2100.00
78-02-003 Sakura	E. Hibel	2,000	295.00	1800.00
79-02-004 Michio	E. Hibel	2,000	325.00	1500.00
Edna Hibel Studios	**Nobility Of Children**			
76-03-001 La Contessa Isabella	E. Hibel	12,750	120.00	425.00
77-03-002 Le Marquis Maurice Pierre	E. Hibel	12,750	120.00	225.00
78-03-003 Baronesse Johanna-Maryke Van Vollendam Tot Marken	E. Hibel	12,750	130.00	225.00
79-03-004 Chief Red Feather	E. Hibel	12,750	140.00	200.00
Edna Hibel Studios	**Museum Commemorative**			
77-04-001 Flower Girl of Provence	E. Hibel	12,750	175.00	425.00
80-04-002 Diana	E. Hibel	3,000	350.00	395.00
Edna Hibel Studios	**David Series**			
79-05-001 Wedding of David & Bathsheba	E. Hibel	5,000	250.00	650.00
80-05-002 David, Bathsheba & Solomon	E. Hibel	5,000	275.00	425.00
82-05-003 David the King	E. Hibel	5,000	275.00	295.00

	ARTIST	EDITION	ISSUE	QUOTE
82-05-004 David the King, cobalt A/P	E. Hibel	25	275.00	1200.00
84-05-005 Bathsheba	E. Hibel	5,000	275.00	295.00
84-05-006 Bathsheba, cobalt A/P	E. Hibel	100	275.00	1200.00
Edna Hibel Studios	**Allegro**			
78-06-001 Plate & Book	E. Hibel	7,500	120.00	135.00
Edna Hibel Studios	**Arte Ovale**			
80-07-001 Takara, gold	E. Hibel	300	1000.00	4200.00
80-07-002 Takara, blanco	E. Hibel	700	450.00	1200.00
80-07-003 Takara, cobalt blue	E. Hibel	1,000	595.00	2350.00
84-07-004 Taro-kun, gold	E. Hibel	300	1000.00	2700.00
84-07-005 Taro-kun, blanco	E. Hibel	700	450.00	825.00
84-07-006 Taro-kun, cobalt blue	E. Hibel	1,000	995.00	1050.00
Edna Hibel Studios	**The World I Love**			
81-08-001 Leah's Family	E. Hibel	17,500	85.00	225.00
82-08-002 Kaylin	E. Hibel	17,500	85.00	375.00
83-08-003 Edna's Music	E. Hibel	17,500	85.00	195.00
83-08-004 O' Hana	E. Hibel	17,500	85.00	195.00
Edna Hibel Studios	**Famous Women & Children**			
80-09-001 Pharaoh's Daughter & Moses, gold	E. Hibel	2,500	350.00	625.00
80-09-002 Pharaoh's Daughter & Moses, cobalt blue	E. Hibel	500	350.00	1350.00
82-09-003 Cornelia & Her Jewels, gold	E. Hibel	2,500	350.00	495.00
82-09-004 Cornelia & Her Jewels, cobalt blue	E. Hibel	500	350.00	1350.00
82-09-005 Anna & The Children of the King of Siam, gold	E. Hibel	2,500	350.00	495.00
82-09-006 Anna & The Children of the King of Siam, colbalt blue	E. Hibel	500	350.00	1350.00
84-09-007 Mozart & The Empress Marie Theresa, gold	E. Hibel	2,500	350.00	395.00
84-09-008 Mozart & The Empress Marie Theresa, cobalt blue	E. Hibel	500	350.00	975.00
Edna Hibel Studios	**Tribute To All Children**			
84-10-001 Giselle	E. Hibel	19,500	55.00	95.00
84-10-002 Gerard	E. Hibel	19,500	55.00	95.00
85-10-003 Wendy	E. Hibel	19,500	55.00	125.00
86-10-004 Todd	E. Hibel	19,500	55.00	125.00
Edna Hibel Studios	**International Mother Love German**			
82-11-001 Gesa Und Kinder	E. Hibel	5,000	195.00	195.00
83-11-002 Alexandra Und Kinder	E. Hibel	5,000	195.00	195.00
Edna Hibel Studios	**International Mother Love French**			
85-12-001 Yvette Avec Ses Enfants	E. Hibel	5,000	125.00	225.00
91-12-002 Liberte, Egalite, Fraternite	E. Hibel	5,000	95.00	95.00
Edna Hibel Studios	**Mother's Day Annual**			
84-13-001 Abby & Lisa	E. Hibel	Yr.Iss.	29.50	400.00
85-13-002 Erica & Jamie	E. Hibel	Yr.Iss.	29.50	250.00
86-13-003 Emily & Jennifer	E. Hibel	Yr.Iss.	29.50	325.00
87-13-004 Catherine & Heather	E. Hibel	Yr.Iss.	34.50	275.00
88-13-005 Sarah & Tess	E. Hibel	Yr.Iss.	34.90	175-225.
89-13-006 Jessica & Kate	E. Hibel	Yr.Iss.	34.90	125.00
90-13-007 Elizabeth, Jorday & Janie	E. Hibel	Yr.Iss.	36.90	95.00
91-13-008 Michele & Anna	E. Hibel	Yr.Iss.	36.90	55.00
92-13-009 Olivia & Hildy	E. Hibel	Yr.Iss.	39.90	59.95
Edna Hibel Studios	**Flower Girl Annual**			
85-14-001 Lily	E. Hibel	15,000	79.00	300.00
86-14-002 Iris	E. Hibel	15,000	79.00	225.00
87-14-003 Rose	E. Hibel	15,000	79.00	175.00
88-14-004 Camellia	E. Hibel	15,000	79.00	165.00
89-14-005 Peony	E. Hibel	15,000	79.00	95.00
92-14-006 Wisteria	E. Hibel	15,000	79.00	79.00
Edna Hibel Studios	**Christmas Annual**			
85-15-001 The Angels' Message	E. Hibel	Yr.Iss.	45.00	225.00
86-15-002 Gift of the Magi	E. Hibel	Yr.Iss.	45.00	275.00
87-15-003 Flight Into Egypt	E. Hibel	Yr.Iss.	49.00	250.00
88-15-004 Adoration of the Shepherds	E. Hibel	Yr.Iss.	49.00	175.00
89-15-005 Peaceful Kingdom	E. Hibel	Yr.Iss.	49.00	165.00
90-15-006 The Nativity	E. Hibel	Yr.Iss.	49.00	150.00
Edna Hibel Studios	**To Life Annual**			
86-16-001 Golden's Child	E. Hibel	5,000	99.00	275.00
87-16-002 Triumph! Everyone A Winner	E. Hibel	19,500	55.00	55-75.00
88-16-003 The Whole Earth Bloomed as a Sacred Place	E. Hibel	15,000	85.00	90.00
89-16-004 Lovers of the Summer Palace	E. Hibel	5,000	65.00	75.00
92-16-005 People of the Fields	E. Hibel	5,000	49.00	49.00
Edna Hibel Studios	**Scandinavian Mother & Child**			
87-17-001 Pearl & Flowers	E. Hibel	7,500	55.00	225.00
89-17-002 Anemone & Violet	E. Hibel	7,500	75.00	90.00
90-17-003 Holly & Talia	E. Hibel	7,500	75.00	85.00
Edna Hibel Studios	**Nordic Families**			
87-18-001 A Tender Moment	E. Hibel	7,500	79.00	95.00
Edna Hibel Studios	**March of Dimes: Our Children, Our Future**			
90-19-001 A Time To Embrace	E. Hibel	150-day	29.00	29.00
Edna Hibel Studios	**Eroica**			
90-20-001 Compassion	E. Hibel	10,000	49.50	65.00
92-20-002 Darya	E. Hibel	10,000	49.50	49.50
Edna Hibel Studios	**Edna Hibel Holiday**			
91-21-001 The First Holiday	E. Hibel	Yr.Iss.	49.00	80-90.00
91-21-002 The First Holiday, gold	E. Hibel	1,000	99.00	150.00
92-21-003 The Christmas Rose	E. Hibel	Yr.Iss.	49.00	49.00
92-21-004 The Christmas Rose, gold	E. Hibel	1,000	99.00	99.00
Edna Hibel Studios	**Mother's Day**			
92-22-001 Molly & Annie	E. Hibel	Yr.Iss.	39.00	70.00
92-22-002 Molly & Annie, gold	E. Hibel	2,500	95.00	150.00
92-22-003 Molly & Annie, platinum	E. Hibel	500	275.00	275.00
John Hine N.A. Ltd.	**David Winter Plate Collection**			
91-01-001 A Christmas Carol	M. Fisher	10,000	30.00	30-35.00
91-01-002 Cotswold Village Plate	M. Fisher	10,000	30.00	30-35.00
92-01-003 Chichester Cross Plate	M. Fisher	10,000	30.00	30-35.00
92-01-004 Little Mill Plate	M. Fisher	10,000	30.00	30-35.00
92-01-005 Old Curiosity Shop	M. Fisher	10,000	30.00	30-35.00
92-01-006 Scrooge's Counting House	M. Fisher	10,000	30.00	30-35.00
93-01-007 Dove Cottage	M. Fisher	10,000	30.00	30-35.00

		ARTIST	EDITION	ISSUE	QUOTE
93-01-008	Little Forge	M. Fisher	10,000	30.00	30-35.00
Hutschenreuther		**Gunther Granget**			
72-01-001	American Sparrows	G. Granget	5,000	50.00	150.00
72-01-002	European Sparrows	G. Granget	5,000	30.00	65.00
73-01-003	American Kildeer	G. Granget	2,250	75.00	90.00
73-01-004	American Squirrel	G. Granget	2,500	75.00	75.00
73-01-005	European Squirrel	G. Granget	2,500	35.00	50.00
74-01-006	American Partridge	G. Granget	2,500	75.00	90.00
75-01-007	American Rabbits	G. Granget	2,500	90.00	90.00
76-01-008	Freedom in Flight	G. Granget	5,000	100.00	100.00
76-01-009	Wrens	G. Granget	2,500	100.00	110.00
76-01-010	Freedom in Flight, Gold	G. Granget	200	200.00	200.00
77-01-011	Bears	G. Granget	2,500	100.00	100.00
78-01-012	Foxes' Spring Journey	G. Granget	1,000	125.00	200.00
Hutschenreuther		**The Glory of Christmas**			
82-02-001	The Nativity	W./C. Hallett	25,000	80.00	125.00
83-02-002	The Annunciation	W./C. Hallett	25,000	80.00	115.00
84-02-003	The Shepherds	W./C. Hallett	25,000	80.00	100.00
85-02-004	The Wiseman	W./C. Hallett	25,000	80.00	100.00
Imperial Ching-te Chen		**Beauties of the Red Mansion**			
86-01-001	Pao-chai	Z. HuiMin	115-day	27.92	30.00
86-01-002	Yuan-chun	Z. HuiMin	115-day	27.92	30.00
87-01-003	Hsi-feng	Z. HuiMin	115-day	30.92	31.00
87-01-004	Hsi-chun	Z. HuiMin	115-day	30.92	31-35.00
88-01-005	Miao-yu	Z. HuiMin	115-day	30.92	31.00
88-01-006	Ying-chun	Z. HuiMin	115-day	30.92	35.00
88-01-007	Tai-yu	Z. HuiMin	115-day	32.92	35.00
88-01-008	Li-wan	Z. HuiMin	115-day	32.92	35.00
88-01-009	Ko-Ching	Z. HuiMin	115-day	32.92	40.00
88-01-010	Hsiang-yun	Z. HuiMin	115-day	34.92	40.00
89-01-011	Tan-Chun	Z. HuiMin	115-day	34.92	46-55.00
89-01-012	Chiao-chieh	Z. HuiMin	115-day	34.92	35.00
Imperial Ching-te Chen		**Scenes from the Summer Palace**			
88-02-001	The Marble Boat	Z. Song Mao	175-day	29.92	30.00
88-02-002	Jade Belt Bridge	Z. Song Mao	175-day	29.92	30.00
89-02-003	Hall that Dispels the Clouds	Z. Song Mao	175-day	32.92	33.00
89-02-004	The Long Promenade	Z. Song Mao	175-day	32.92	33.00
89-02-005	Garden/Harmonious Pleasure	Z. Song Mao	175-day	32.92	33.00
89-02-006	The Great Stage	Z. Song Mao	175-day	32.92	33.00
89-02-007	Seventeen Arch Bridge	Z. Song Mao	175-day	34.92	35.00
89-02-008	Boaters on Kumming Lake	Z. Song Mao	175-day	34.92	35.00
Imperial Ching-te Chen		**Blessings From a Chinese Garden**			
88-03-001	The Gift of Purity	Z. Song Mao	175-day	39.92	40.00
89-03-002	The Gift of Grace	Z. Song Mao	175-day	39.92	40.00
89-03-003	The Gift of Beauty	Z. Song Mao	175-day	42.92	43.00
89-03-004	The Gift of Happiness	Z. Song Mao	175-day	42.92	43.00
90-03-005	The Gift of Truth	Z. Song Mao	175-day	42.92	43.00
90-03-006	The Gift of Joy	Z. Song Mao	175-day	42.92	43.00
Imperial Ching-te Chen		**Legends of West Lake**			
89-04-001	Lady White	J. Xue-Bing	175-day	29.92	35.00
90-04-002	Lady Silkworm	J. Xue-Bing	175-day	29.92	32.00
90-04-003	Laurel Peak	J. Xue-Bing	175-day	29.92	33.00
90-04-004	Rising Sun Terrace	J. Xue-Bing	175-day	32.92	33.00
90-04-005	The Apricot Fairy	J. Xue-Bing	175-day	32.92	33.00
90-04-006	Bright Pearl	J. Xue-Bing	175-day	32.92	33.00
90-04-007	Thread of Sky	J. Xue-Bing	175-day	34.92	35.00
91-04-008	Phoenix Mountain	J. Xue-Bing	175-day	34.92	35-40.00
91-04-009	Ancestors of Tea	J. Xue-Bing	175-day	34.92	55-62.00
91-04-010	Three Pools Mirroring/Moon	J. Xue-Bing	175-day	36.92	70-75.00
91-04-011	Fly-In Peak	J. Xue-Bing	175-day	36.92	45-50.00
91-04-012	The Case of the Folding Fans	J. Xue-Bing	175-day	36.92	45-50.00
Imperial Ching-te Chen		**Flower Goddesses of China**			
91-05-001	The Lotus Goddess	Z. HuiMin	175-day	34.92	35-40.00
91-05-002	The Chrysanthemum Goddess	Z. HuiMin	175-day	34.92	35.00
91-05-003	The Plum Blossom Goddess	Z. HuiMin	175-day	37.92	40.00
91-05-004	The Peony Goddess	Z. HuiMin	175-day	37.92	35-52.00
91-05-005	The Narcissus Goddess	Z. HuiMin	175-day	37.92	60.00
91-05-006	The Camellia Goddess	Z. HuiMin	175-day	37.92	50.00
Imperial Ching-te Chen		**The Forbidden City**			
90-06-001	Pavilion of 10,000 Springs	S. Fu	150-day	39.92	40.00
90-06-002	Flying Kites/Spring Day	S. Fu	150-day	39.92	40.00
90-06-003	Pavilion/Floating Jade Green	S. Fu	150-day	42.92	44.00
91-06-004	The Lantern Festival	S. Fu	150-day	42.92	45.00
91-06-005	Nine Dragon Screen	S. Fu	150-day	42.92	60.00
91-06-006	The Hall of the Cultivating Mind	S. Fu	150-day	42.92	45.00
91-06-007	Dressing the Empress	S. Fu	150-day	45.92	42-50.00
91-06-008	Pavilion of Floating Cups	S. Fu	150-day	45.92	46-50.00
Imperial Ching-te Chen		**Maidens of the Folding Sky**			
92-07-001	Lady Lu	J. Xue-Bing	175-day	29.92	32.00
92-07-002	Mistress Yang	J. Xue-Bing	175-day	29.92	30.00
92-07-003	Bride Yen Chun	J. Xue-Bing	175-day	32.92	32.92
93-07-004	Parrot Maiden	J. Xue-Bing	175-day	32.92	32.92
Imperial Ching-te Chen		**Garden of Satin Wings**			
92-08-001	A Morning Dream	J. Xue-Bing	115-day	29.92	29.92
93-08-002	An Evening Mist	J. Xue-Bing	115-day	29.92	29.92
93-08-003	A Garden Whisper	J. Xue-Bing	115-day	29.92	29.92
International Silver		**Bicentennial**			
72-01-001	Signing Declaration	M. Deoliveira	7,500	40.00	310.00
73-01-002	Paul Revere	M. Deoliveira	7,500	40.00	160.00
74-01-003	Concord Bridge	M. Deoliveira	7,500	40.00	115.00
75-01-004	Crossing Delaware	M. Deoliveira	7,500	50.00	80.00
76-01-005	Valley Forge	M. Deoliveira	7,500	50.00	65.00
77-01-006	Surrender at Yorktown	M. Deoliveira	7,500	50.00	60.00
Kaiser		**Christmas Plates**			
70-01-001	Waiting for Santa Claus	T. Schoener	Closed	12.50	25.00
71-01-002	Silent Night	K. Bauer	Closed	13.50	23.00
72-01-003	Welcome Home	K. Bauer	Closed	16.50	43.00
73-01-004	Holy Night	T. Schoener	Closed	18.00	44.00
74-01-005	Christmas Carolers	K. Bauer	Closed	25.00	30.00
75-01-006	Bringing Home the Tree	J. Northcott	Closed	25.00	30.00
76-01-007	Christ/Saviour Born	C. Maratti	Closed	25.00	35.00
77-01-008	The Three Kings	T. Schoener	Closed	25.00	25.00
78-01-009	Shepherds in The Field	T. Schoener	Closed	30.00	30.00
79-01-010	Christmas Eve	H. Blum	Closed	32.00	45.00
80-01-011	Joys of Winter	H. Blum	Closed	40.00	43.00
81-01-012	Adoration by Three Kings	K. Bauer	Closed	40.00	41.00
82-01-013	Bringing Home the Tree	K. Bauer	Closed	40.00	45.00
Kaiser		**Mother's Day**			
71-02-001	Mare and Foal	T. Schoener	Closed	13.00	25.00
72-02-002	Flowers for Mother	T. Schoener	Closed	16.50	20.00
73-02-003	Cats	T. Schoener	Closed	17.00	40.00
74-02-004	Fox	T. Schoener	Closed	20.00	40.00
75-02-005	German Shepherd	T. Schoener	Closed	25.00	100.00
76-02-006	Swan and Cygnets	T. Schoener	Closed	25.00	27.50
77-02-007	Mother Rabbit and Young	T. Schoener	Closed	25.00	30.00
78-02-008	Hen and Chicks	T. Schoener	Closed	30.00	50.00
79-02-009	A Mother's Devotion	N. Peterner	Closed	32.00	40.00
80-02-010	Raccoon Family	J. Northcott	Closed	40.00	45.00
81-02-011	Safe Near Mother	H. Blum	Closed	40.00	40.00
82-02-012	Pheasant Family	K. Bauer	Closed	40.00	44.00
83-02-013	Tender Care	K. Bauer	Closed	40.00	65.00
Kaiser		**King Tut**			
78-03-001	King Tut	Unknown	Closed	65.00	100.00
Kaiser		**Egyptian**			
80-04-001	Nefertiti	Unknown	10,000	275.00	458.00
80-04-002	Tutankhamen	Unknown	10,000	275.00	458.00
Kaiser		**Bicentennial Plate**			
76-05-001	Signing Declaration	J. Trumball	Closed	75.00	150.00
Edwin M. Knowles		**Wizard of Oz**			
77-01-001	Over the Rainbow	J. Auckland	100-day	19.00	53.00
78-01-002	If I Only Had a Brain	J. Auckland	100-day	19.00	65.00
78-01-003	If I Only Had a Heart	J. Auckland	100-day	19.00	57.00
78-01-004	If I Were King of the Forest	J. Auckland	100-day	19.00	55.00
79-01-005	Wicked Witch of the West	J. Auckland	100-day	19.00	45-50.00
79-01-006	Follow the Yellow Brick Road	J. Auckland	100-day	19.00	40.00
79-01-007	Wonderful Wizard of Oz	J. Auckland	100-day	19.00	40-44.00
80-01-008	The Grand Finale	J. Auckland	100-day	24.00	45.00
Edwin M. Knowles		**Gone with the Wind**			
78-02-001	Scarlett	R. Kursar	100-day	21.50	220-250.
79-02-002	Ashley	R. Kursar	100-day	21.50	120.00
80-02-003	Melanie	R. Kursar	100-day	21.50	50-59.00
81-02-004	Rhett	R. Kursar	100-day	23.50	40-45.00
82-02-005	Mammy Lacing Scarlett	R. Kursar	100-day	23.50	60-75.00
83-02-006	Melanie Gives Birth	R. Kursar	100-day	23.50	65-94.00
84-02-007	Scarlet's Green Dress	R. Kursar	100-day	25.50	68-75.00
85-02-008	Rhett and Bonnie	R. Kursar	100-day	25.50	70-94.00
85-02-009	Scarlett and Rhett: The Finale	R. Kursar	100-day	29.50	55-81.00
Edwin M. Knowles		**Csatari Grandparent**			
80-03-001	Bedtime Story	J. Csatari	100-day	18.00	18.00
81-03-002	The Skating Lesson	J. Csatari	100-day	20.00	20.00
82-03-003	The Cookie Tasting	J. Csatari	100-day	20.00	20.00
83-03-004	The Swinger	J. Csatari	100-day	20.00	20.00
84-03-005	The Skating Queen	J. Csatari	100-day	22.00	22-25.00
85-03-006	The Patriot's Parade	J. Csatari	100-day	22.00	22.00
86-03-007	The Home Run	J. Csatari	100-day	22.00	22.00
87-03-008	The Sneak Preview	J. Csatari	100-day	22.00	22.00
Edwin M. Knowles		**Americana Holidays**			
78-04-001	Fourth of July	D. Spaulding	Yr.Iss.	26.00	26.00
79-04-002	Thanksgiving	D. Spaulding	Yr.Iss.	26.00	26.00
80-04-003	Easter	D. Spaulding	Yr.Iss.	26.00	26.00
81-04-004	Valentine's Day	D. Spaulding	Yr.Iss.	26.00	26.00
82-04-005	Father's Day	D. Spaulding	Yr.Iss.	26.00	26.00
83-04-006	Christmas	D. Spaulding	Yr.Iss.	26.00	26.00
84-04-007	Mother's Day	D. Spaulding	Yr.Iss.	26.00	27.00
Edwin M. Knowles		**Annie**			
83-05-001	Annie and Sandy	W. Chambers	100-day	19.00	19.00
83-05-002	Daddy Warbucks	W. Chambers	100-day	19.00	19.00
83-05-003	Annie and Grace	W. Chambers	100-day	19.00	19.00
84-05-004	Annie and the Orphans	W. Chambers	100-day	21.00	21.00
85-05-005	Tomorrow	W. Chambers	100-day	21.00	21.00
86-05-006	Annie and Miss Hannigan	W. Chambers	100-day	21.00	21.00
86-05-007	Annie, Lily and Rooster	W. Chambers	100-day	24.00	24.00
86-05-008	Grand Finale	W. Chambers	100-day	24.00	24.00
Edwin M. Knowles		**The Four Ancient Elements**			
84-06-001	Earth	G. Lambert	75-day	27.50	28.00
84-06-002	Water	G. Lambert	75-day	27.50	28.00
85-06-003	Air	G. Lambert	75-day	29.50	30.00
85-06-004	Fire	G. Lambert	75-day	29.50	50.00
Edwin M. Knowles		**Biblical Mothers**			
83-07-001	Bathsheba and Solomon	E. Licea	Yr.Iss.	39.50	40.00
84-07-002	Judgment of Solomon	E. Licea	Yr.Iss.	39.50	30.00
84-07-003	Pharaoh's Daughter and Moses	E. Licea	Yr.Iss.	39.50	40.00
85-07-004	Mary and Jesus	E. Licea	Yr.Iss.	39.50	40.00
85-07-005	Sarah and Isaac	E. Licea	Yr.Iss.	44.50	45.00
86-07-006	Rebekah, Jacob and Esau	E. Licea	Yr.Iss.	44.50	45.00
Edwin M. Knowles		**Hibel Mother's Day**			
84-08-001	Abby and Lisa	E. Hibel	Yr.Iss.	29.50	32.00
85-08-002	Erica and Jamie	E. Hibel	Yr.Iss.	29.50	30.00
86-08-003	Emily and Jennifer	E. Hibel	Yr.Iss.	29.50	45-50.00
87-08-004	Catherine and Heather	E. Hibel	Yr.Iss.	34.50	49-59.00
88-08-005	Sarah and Tess	E. Hibel	Yr.Iss.	34.90	35.00
89-08-006	Jessica and Kate	E. Hibel	Yr.Iss.	34.90	35.00
90-08-007	Elizabeth, Jordan & Janie	E. Hibel	Yr.Iss.	36.90	45.00
91-08-008	Michele and Anna	E. Hibel	Yr.Iss.	36.90	37.00
Edwin M. Knowles		**Friends I Remember**			
83-09-001	Fish Story	J. Down	97-day	17.50	18.00
84-09-002	Office Hours	J. Down	97-day	17.50	18.00
85-09-003	A Coat of Paint	J. Down	97-day	17.50	18.00
85-09-004	Here Comes the Bride	J. Down	97-day	19.50	20.00
85-09-005	Fringe Benefits	J. Down	97-day	19.50	20.00
86-09-006	High Society	J. Down	97-day	19.50	20.00
86-09-007	Flower Arrangement	J. Down	97-day	21.50	22-29.00
86-09-008	Taste Test	J. Down	97-day	21.50	22.00
Edwin M. Knowles		**Father's Love**			
84-10-001	Open Wide	B. Bradley	100-day	19.50	20.00
84-10-002	Batter Up	B. Bradley	100-day	19.50	20.00

		ARTIST	EDITION	ISSUE	QUOTE
85-10-003	Little Shaver	B. Bradley	100-day	19.50	20.00
85-10-004	Swing Time	B. Bradley	100-day	22.50	23.00
Edwin M. Knowles		**The King and I**			
84-11-001	A Puzzlement	W. Chambers	150-day	19.50	20-25.00
85-11-002	Shall We Dance?	W. Chambers	150-day	19.50	30.00
85-11-003	Getting to Know You	W. Chambers	150-day	19.50	20.00
85-11-004	We Kiss in a Shadow	W. Chambers	150-day	19.50	20-25.00
Edwin M. Knowles		**Ency. Brit. Birds of Your Garden**			
85-12-001	Cardinal	K. Daniel	100-day	19.50	35.00
85-12-002	Blue Jay	K. Daniel	100-day	19.50	28.00
85-12-003	Oriole	K. Daniel	100-day	22.50	33.00
86-12-004	Chickadees	K. Daniel	100-day	22.50	37.00
86-12-005	Bluebird	K. Daniel	100-day	22.50	30.00
86-12-006	Robin	K. Daniel	100-day	22.50	30.00
86-12-007	Hummingbird	K. Daniel	100-day	24.50	25.00
87-12-008	Goldfinch	K. Daniel	100-day	24.50	30.00
87-12-009	Downy Woodpecker	K. Daniel	100-day	24.50	34.00
87-12-010	Cedar Waxwing	K. Daniel	100-day	24.90	30.00
Edwin M. Knowles		**Frances Hook Legacy**			
85-13-001	Fascination	F. Hook	100-day	19.50	19.50
85-13-002	Daydreaming	F. Hook	100-day	19.50	19.50
86-13-003	Discovery	F. Hook	100-day	22.50	22.50
86-13-004	Disappointment	F. Hook	100-day	22.50	22.50
86-13-005	Wonderment	F. Hook	100-day	22.50	22.50
87-13-006	Expectation	F. Hook	100-day	22.50	22.50
Edwin M. Knowles		**Hibel Christmas**			
85-14-001	The Angel's Message	E. Hibel	Yr.Iss.	45.00	45.00
86-14-002	The Gifts of the Magi	E. Hibel	Yr.Iss.	45.00	45.00
87-14-003	The Flight Into Egypt	E. Hibel	Yr.Iss.	49.00	49.00
88-14-004	Adoration of the Shepherd	E. Hibel	Yr.Iss.	49.00	49.00
89-14-005	Peaceful Kingdom	E. Hibel	Yr.Iss.	49.00	49.00
90-14-006	Nativity	E. Hibel	Yr.Iss.	49.00	59.00
Edwin M. Knowles		**Upland Birds of North America**			
86-15-001	The Pheasant	W. Anderson	150-day	24.50	25.00
86-15-002	The Grouse	W. Anderson	150-day	24.50	25.00
87-15-003	The Quail	W. Anderson	150-day	27.50	28.00
87-15-004	The Wild Turkey	W. Anderson	150-day	27.50	28.00
87-15-005	The Gray Partridge	W. Anderson	150-day	27.50	28.00
87-15-006	The Woodcock	W. Anderson	150-day	27.90	28.00
Edwin M. Knowles		**Oklahoma!**			
85-16-001	Oh, What a Beautiful Mornin'	M. Kunstler	150-day	19.50	19.50
86-16-002	Surrey with the Fringe on Top'	M. Kunstler	150-day	19.50	19.50
86-16-003	I Cain't Say No	M. Kunstler	150-day	19.50	19.50
86-16-004	Oklahoma	M. Kunstler	150-day	19.50	21.00
Edwin M. Knowles		**Sound of Music**			
86-17-001	Sound of Music	T. Crnkovich	150-day	19.50	20.00
86-17-002	Do-Re-Mi	T. Crnkovich	150-day	19.50	20.00
86-17-003	My Favorite Things	T. Crnkovich	150-day	22.50	23.00
86-17-004	Laendler Waltz	T. Crnkovich	150-day	22.50	26-36.00
87-17-005	Edelweiss	T. Crnkovich	150-day	22.50	30-48.00
87-17-006	I Have Confidence	T. Crnkovich	150-day	22.50	36.00
87-17-007	Maria	T. Crnkovich	150-day	24.90	40.00
87-17-008	Climb Ev'ry Mountain	T. Crnkovich	150-day	24.90	42.00
Edwin M. Knowles		**American Innocents**			
86-18-001	Abigail in the Rose Garden	Marsten/Mandrajji	100-day	19.50	19.50
86-18-002	Ann by the Terrace	Marsten/Mandrajji	100-day	19.50	19.50
86-18-003	Ellen and John in the Parlor	Marsten/Mandrajji	100-day	19.50	19.50
86-18-004	William on the Rocking Horse	Marsten/Mandrajji	100-day	19.50	48.00
Edwin M. Knowles		**J. W. Smith Childhood Holidays**			
86-19-001	Easter	J. W. Smith	97-day	19.50	21.00
86-19-002	Thanksgiving	J. W. Smith	97-day	19.50	25.00
86-19-003	Christmas	J. W. Smith	97-day	19.50	24.00
86-19-004	Valentine's Day	J. W. Smith	97-day	22.50	25.00
87-19-005	Mother's Day	J. W. Smith	97-day	22.50	25.00
87-19-006	Fourth of July	J. W. Smith	97-day	22.50	25-30.00
Edwin M. Knowles		**Living with Nature-Jerner's Ducks**			
86-20-001	The Pintail	B. Jerner	150-day	19.50	26-34.00
86-20-002	The Mallard	B. Jerner	150-day	19.50	35.00
87-20-003	The Wood Duck	B. Jerner	150-day	22.50	36.00
87-20-004	The Green-Winged Teal	B. Jerner	150-day	22.50	40.00
87-20-005	The Northern Shoveler	B. Jerner	150-day	22.90	35.00
87-20-006	The American Widgeon	B. Jerner	150-day	22.90	40.00
87-20-007	The Gadwall	B. Jerner	150-day	24.90	40.00
88-20-008	The Blue-Winged Teal	B. Jerner	150-day	24.90	35.00
Edwin M. Knowles		**Lincoln Man of America**			
86-21-001	The Gettysburg Address	M. Kunstler	150-day	24.50	24.50
87-21-002	The Inauguration	M. Kunstler	150-day	24.50	24.50
87-21-003	The Lincoln-Douglas Debates	M. Kunstler	150-day	27.50	27.50
87-21-004	Beginnings in New Salem	M. Kunstler	150-day	27.90	27.90
88-21-005	The Family Man	M. Kunstler	150-day	27.90	27.90
88-21-006	Emancipation Proclamation	M. Kunstler	150-day	27.90	27.90
Edwin M. Knowles		**Portraits of Motherhood**			
87-22-001	Mother's Here	W. Chambers	150-day	29.50	35.00
88-22-002	First Touch	W. Chambers	150-day	29.50	32.00
Edwin M. Knowles		**A Swan is Born**			
87-23-001	Hopes and Dreams	L. Roberts	150-day	24.50	24.50
87-23-002	At the Barre	L. Roberts	150-day	24.50	25.00
87-23-003	In Position	L. Roberts	150-day	24.50	27.00
88-23-004	Just For Size	L. Roberts	150-day	24.50	45.00
Edwin M. Knowles		**South Pacific**			
87-24-001	Some Enchanted Evening	E. Gignilliat	150-day	24.50	24.50
87-24-002	Happy Talk	E. Gignilliat	150-day	24.50	24.50
87-24-003	Dites Moi	E. Gignilliat	150-day	24.90	24.50
88-24-004	Honey Bun	E. Gignilliat	150-day	24.90	24.90
Edwin M. Knowles		**Tom Sawyer**			
87-25-001	Whitewashing the Fence	W. Chambers	150-day	27.50	27.50
87-25-002	Tom and Becky	W. Chambers	150-day	27.90	27.90
87-25-003	Tom Sawyer the Pirate	W. Chambers	150-day	27.90	27.90
88-25-004	First Pipes	W. Chambers	150-day	27.90	30.00
Edwin M. Knowles		**Friends of the Forest**			
87-26-001	The Rabbit	K. Daniel	150-day	24.50	26.00

		ARTIST	EDITION	ISSUE	QUOTE
87-26-002	The Raccoon	K. Daniel	150-day	24.50	35.00
87-26-003	The Squirrel	K. Daniel	150-day	27.90	28.00
88-26-004	The Chipmunk	K. Daniel	150-day	27.90	28.00
88-26-005	The Fox	K. Daniel	150-day	27.90	28.00
88-26-006	The Otter	K. Daniel	150-day	27.90	28.00
Edwin M. Knowles		**Amy Brackenbury's Cat Tales**			
87-27-001	A Chance Meeting: White American Shorthairs	A. Brackenbury	150-day	21.50	31-50.00
87-27-002	Gone Fishing: Maine Coons	A. Brackenbury	150-day	21.50	60-75.00
88-27-003	Strawberries and Cream: Cream Persians	A. Brackenbury	150-day	24.90	70.00
88-27-004	Flower Bed: British Shorthairs	A. Brackenbury	150-day	24.90	25.00
88-27-005	Kittens and Mittens: Silver Tabbies	A. Brackenbury	150-day	24.90	29.00
88-27-006	All Wrapped Up: Himalayans	A. Brackenbury	150-day	24.90	48.00
Edwin M. Knowles		**The Story of Christmas by Eve Licea**			
87-28-001	The Annunciation	E. Licea	Yr.Iss.	44.90	45.00
88-28-002	The Nativity	E. Licea	Yr.Iss.	44.90	45.00
89-28-003	Adoration Of The Shepherds	E. Licea	Yr.Iss.	49.90	50.00
90-28-004	Journey Of The Magi	E. Licea	Yr.Iss.	49.90	56.00
91-28-005	Gifts Of The Magi	E. Licea	Yr.Iss.	49.90	65.00
92-28-006	Rest on the Flight into Egypt	E. Licea	Yr.Iss.	49.90	58.00
Edwin M. Knowles		**Carousel**			
87-29-001	If I Loved You	D. Brown	150-day	24.90	25.00
88-29-002	Mr. Snow	D. Brown	150-day	24.90	25.00
88-29-003	The Carousel Waltz	D. Brown	150-day	24.90	35-45.00
88-29-004	You'll Never Walk Alone	D. Brown	150-day	24.90	35.00
Edwin M. Knowles		**Field Puppies**			
87-30-001	Dog Tired-The Springer Spaniel	L. Kaatz	150-day	24.90	45-58.00
87-30-002	Caught in the Act-The Golden Retriever	L. Kaatz	150-day	24.90	50-60.00
88-30-003	Missing/Point/Irish Setter	L. Kaatz	150-day	27.90	28.00
88-30-004	A Perfect Set-Labrador	L. Kaatz	150-day	27.90	42-48.00
88-30-005	Fritz's Folly-German Shorthaired Pointer	L. Kaatz	150-day	27.90	42.00
88-30-006	Shirt Tales: Cocker Spaniel	L. Kaatz	150-day	27.90	57.00
89-30-007	Fine Feathered Friends-English Setter	L. Kaatz	150-day	29.90	30-32.00
89-30-008	Command Performance/ Wiemaraner	L. Kaatz	150-day	29.90	35.00
Edwin M. Knowles		**The American Journey**			
87-31-001	Westward Ho	M. Kunstler	150-day	29.90	30.00
88-31-002	Kitchen With a View	M. Kunstler	150-day	29.90	32.00
88-31-003	Crossing the River	M. Kunstler	150-day	29.90	30.00
88-31-004	Christmas at the New Cabin	M. Kunstler	150-day	29.90	30.00
Edwin M. Knowles		**Precious Little Ones**			
88-32-001	Little Red Robins	M. T. Fangel	150-day	29.90	29.90
88-32-002	Little Fledglings	M. T. Fangel	150-day	29.90	29.90
88-32-003	Saturday Night Bath	M. T. Fangel	150-day	29.90	33.00
88-32-004	Peek-A-Boo	M. T. Fangel	150-day	29.90	38.00
Edwin M. Knowles		**Aesop's Fables**			
88-33-001	The Goose That Laid the Golden Egg	M. Hampshire	150-day	27.90	28.00
88-33-002	The Hare and the Tortoise	M. Hampshire	150-day	27.90	28.00
88-33-003	The Fox and the Grapes	M. Hampshire	150-day	30.90	31.00
89-33-004	The Lion And The Mouse	M. Hampshire	150-day	30.90	40.00
89-33-005	The Milk Maid And Her Pail	M. Hampshire	150-day	30.90	48.00
89-33-006	The Jay And The Peacock	M. Hampshire	150-day	30.90	33.00
Edwin M. Knowles		**Not So Long Ago**			
88-34-001	Story Time	J. W. Smith	150-day	24.90	24.90
88-34-002	Wash Day for Dolly	J. W. Smith	150-day	24.90	24.90
88-34-003	Suppertime for Kitty	J. W. Smith	150-day	24.90	30-35.00
88-34-004	Mother's Little Helper	J. W. Smith	150-day	24.90	26-30.00
Edwin M. Knowles		**Jerner's Less Travelled Road**			
88-35-001	The Weathered Barn	B. Jerner	150-day	29.90	29.90
88-35-002	The Murmuring Stream	B. Jerner	150-day	29.90	29.90
88-35-003	The Covered Bridge	B. Jerner	150-day	32.90	33-36.00
89-35-004	Winter's Peace	B. Jerner	150-day	32.90	33-40.00
89-35-005	The Flowering Meadow	B. Jerner	150-day	32.90	33-35.00
89-35-006	The Hidden Waterfall	B. Jerner	150-day	32.90	33.00
Edwin M. Knowles		**Once Upon a Time**			
88-36-001	Little Red Riding Hood	K. Pritchett	150-day	24.90	24.90
88-36-002	Rapunzel	K. Pritchett	150-day	24.90	24.90
88-36-003	Three Little Pigs	K. Pritchett	150-day	27.90	31.00
89-36-004	The Princess and the Pea	K. Pritchett	150-day	27.90	28.00
89-36-005	Goldilocks and the Three Bears	K. Pritchett	150-day	27.90	29.00
89-36-006	Beauty and the Beast	K. Pritchett	150-day	27.90	50.00
Edwin M. Knowles		**Majestic Birds of North America**			
88-37-001	The Bald Eagle	D. Smith	150-day	29.90	45.00
88-37-002	Peregrine Falcon	D. Smith	150-day	29.90	37.00
88-37-003	The Great Horned Owl	D. Smith	150-day	32.90	33.00
89-37-004	The Red-Tailed Hawk	D. Smith	150-day	32.90	33.00
89-37-005	The White Gyrfalcon	D. Smith	150-day	32.90	33.00
89-37-006	The American Kestral	D. Smith	150-day	32.90	33.00
90-37-007	The Osprey	D. Smith	150-day	34.90	35.00
90-37-008	The Golden Eagle	D. Smith	150-day	34.90	35.00
Edwin M. Knowles		**Cinderella**			
88-38-001	Bibbidi, Bobbidi, Boo	Disney Studios	150-day	29.90	60-74.00
88-38-002	A Dream Is A Wish Your Heart Makes	Disney Studios	150-day	29.90	75-80.00
89-38-003	Oh Sing Sweet Nightingale	Disney Studios	150-day	32.90	40-45.00
89-38-004	A Dress For Cinderelly	Disney Studios	150-day	32.90	71-89.00
89-38-005	So This Is Love	Disney Studios	150-day	32.90	50-52.00
90-38-006	At The Stroke Of Midnight	Disney Studios	150-day	32.90	51-54.00
90-38-007	If The Shoe Fits	Disney Studios	150-day	34.90	52.00
90-38-008	Happily Ever After	Disney Studios	150-day	34.90	35.00
Edwin M. Knowles		**Mary Poppins**			
89-40-001	Mary Poppins	M. Hampshire	150-day	29.90	30-35.00
89-40-002	A Spoonful of Sugar	M. Hampshire	150-day	29.90	30.00
90-40-003	A Jolly Holiday With Mary	M. Hampshire	150-day	32.90	35-39.00
90-40-004	We Love To Laugh	M. Hampshire	150-day	32.90	50.00
91-40-005	Chim Chim Cher-ee	M. Hampshire	150-day	32.90	39.00
91-40-006	Tuppence a Bag	M. Hampshire	150-day	32.90	55.00
Edwin M. Knowles		**Home Sweet Home**			
89-41-001	The Victorian	R. McGinnis	150-day	39.90	39.90
89-41-002	The Greek Revival	R. McGinnis	150-day	39.90	30-39.90
89-41-003	The Georgian	R. McGinnis	150-day	39.90	39.90
90-41-004	The Mission	R. McGinnis	150-day	39.90	39.90
Edwin M. Knowles		**My Fair Lady**			
89-42-001	Opening Day at Ascot	W. Chambers	150-day	24.90	25.00

	ARTIST	EDITION	ISSUE	QUOTE
89-42-002 I Could Have Danced All Night	W. Chambers	150-day	24.90	25.00
89-42-003 The Rain in Spain	W. Chambers	150-day	27.90	28.00
89-42-004 Show Me	W. Chambers	150-day	27.90	28.00
90-42-005 Get Me To/Church On Time	W. Chambers	150-day	27.90	28.00
90-42-006 I've Grown Accustomed/Face	W. Chambers	150-day	27.90	41.00
Edwin M. Knowles	**Sundblom Santas**			
89-43-001 Santa By The Fire	H. Sundblom	Closed	27.90	40-45.00
90-43-002 Christmas Vigil	H. Sundblom	Closed	27.90	42-47.00
91-43-003 To All A Good Night	H. Sundblom	Closed	32.90	30-45.00
92-43-004 Santa's on His Way	H. Sundblom	Closed	32.90	63-68.00
Edwin M. Knowles	**Great Cats Of The Americas**			
89-44-001 The Jaguar	L. Cable	150-day	29.90	50-70.00
89-44-002 The Cougar	L. Cable	150-day	29.90	40-50.00
89-44-003 The Lynx	L. Cable	150-day	32.90	33.00
90-44-004 The Ocelot	L. Cable	150-day	32.90	33.00
90-44-005 The Bobcat	L. Cable	150-day	32.90	33.00
90-44-006 The Jaguarundi	L. Cable	150-day	32.90	35.00
90-44-007 The Margay	L. Cable	150-day	34.90	35.00
91-44-008 The Pampas Cat	L. Cable	150-day	34.90	35.00
Edwin M. Knowles	**Heirlooms And Lace**			
89-45-001 Anna	C. Layton	150-day	34.90	55.00
89-45-002 Victoria	C. Layton	150-day	34.90	54-64.00
90-45-003 Tess	C. Layton	150-day	37.90	84.00
90-45-004 Olivia	C. Layton	150-day	37.90	125.00
91-45-005 Bridget	C. Layton	150-day	37.90	110-120.
91-45-006 Rebecca	C. Layton	150-day	37.90	90.00
Edwin M. Knowles	**Stately Owls**			
89-46-001 The Snowy Owl	J. Beaudoin	150-day	29.90	47.00
89-46-002 The Great Horned Owl	J. Beaudoin	150-day	29.90	30-35.00
90-46-003 The Barn Owl	J. Beaudoin	150-day	32.90	33.00
90-46-004 The Screech Owl	J. Beaudoin	150-day	32.90	34.00
90-46-005 The Short-Eared Owl	J. Beaudoin	150-day	32.90	33.00
90-46-006 The Barred Owl	J. Beaudoin	150-day	32.90	50.00
90-46-007 The Great Grey Owl	J. Beaudoin	150-day	34.90	34.90
91-46-008 The Saw-Whet Owl	J. Beaudoin	150-day	34.90	35.00
Edwin M. Knowles	**Singin' In The Rain**			
90-47-001 Singin' In The Rain	M. Skolsky	150-day	32.90	35.00
90-47-002 Good Morning	M. Skolsky	150-day	32.90	34.00
91-47-003 Broadway Melody	M. Skolsky	150-day	32.90	40.00
91-47-004 We're Happy Again	M. Skolsky	150-day	32.90	36-40.00
Edwin M. Knowles	**Pinocchio**			
89-48-001 Gepetto Creates Pinocchio	Disney Studios	150-day	29.90	55-80.00
90-48-002 Pinocchio And The Blue Fairy	Disney Studios	150-day	29.90	75.00
90-48-003 It's an Actor's Life For Me	Disney Studios	150-day	32.90	47.00
90-48-004 I've Got No Strings On Me	Disney Studios	150-day	32.90	48.00
91-48-005 Pleasure Island	Disney Studios	150-day	32.90	45.00
91-48-006 A Real Boy	Disney Studios	150-day	32.90	60-80.00
Edwin M. Knowles	**Nature's Child**			
90-49-001 Sharing	M. Jobe	150-day	29.90	31.00
90-49-002 The Lost Lamb	M. Jobe	150-day	29.90	30.00
90-49-003 Seems Like Yesterday	M. Jobe	150-day	32.90	35.00
90-49-004 Faithful Friends	M. Jobe	150-day	32.90	33.00
90-49-005 Trusted Companion	M. Jobe	150-day	32.90	48-55.00
91-49-006 Hand in Hand	M. Jobe	150-day	32.90	45.00
Edwin M. Knowles	**Fantasia: (The Sorcerer's Apprentice) Golden Anniversary**			
90-50-001 The Apprentice's Dream	Disney Studios	150-day	29.90	70.00
90-50-002 Mischievous Apprentice	Disney Studios	150-day	29.90	70.00
91-50-003 Dreams of Power	Disney Studios	150-day	32.90	60-68.00
91-50-004 Mickey's Magical Whirlpool	Disney Studios	150-day	32.90	48.00
91-50-005 Wizardry Gone Wild	Disney Studios	150-day	32.90	56.00
91-50-006 Mickey Makes Magic	Disney Studios	150-day	34.90	34.90
91-50-007 The Penitent Apprentice	Disney Studios	150-day	34.90	34.90
92-50-008 An Apprentice Again	Disney Studios	150-day	34.90	34.90
Edwin M. Knowles	**Casablanca**			
90-51-001 Here's Looking At You, Kid	J. Griffin	150-day	34.90	40-47.00
90-51-002 We'll Always Have Paris	J. Griffin	150-day	34.90	42.00
91-51-003 We Loved Each Other Once	J. Griffin	150-day	37.90	39.00
91-51-004 Rick's Cafe Americain	J. Griffin	150-day	37.90	42.00
91-51-005 A Franc For Your Thoughts	J. Griffin	150-day	37.90	58.00
91-51-006 Play it Sam	J. Griffin	150-day	37.90	60.00
Edwin M. Knowles	**Field Trips**			
90-52-001 Gone Fishing	L. Kaatz	150-day	24.90	24.90
91-52-002 Ducking Duty	L. Kaatz	150-day	24.90	26.00
91-52-003 Boxed In	L. Kaatz	150-day	27.90	32.00
91-52-004 Pups 'N Boots	L. Kaatz	150-day	27.90	35.00
91-52-005 Puppy Tales	L. Kaatz	150-day	27.90	37.00
91-52-006 Pail Pals	L. Kaatz	150-day	29.90	29.90
91-52-007 Chesapeake Bay Retrievers	L. Kaatz	150-day	29.90	29.90
91-52-008 Hat Trick	L. Kaatz	150-day	29.90	29.90
Edwin M. Knowles	**The Old Mill Stream**			
90-53-001 New London Grist Mill	C. Tennant	150-day	39.90	40.00
91-53-002 Wayside Inn Grist Mill	C. Tennant	150-day	39.90	40-49.00
91-53-003 Old Red Mill	C. Tennant	150-day	39.90	40-54.00
91-53-004 Glade Creek Grist Mill	C. Tennant	150-day	39.90	45-58.00
Edwin M. Knowles	**Birds of the Seasons**			
90-54-001 Cardinals In Winter	S. Timm	150-day	24.90	47-50.00
90-54-002 Bluebirds In Spring	S. Timm	150-day	24.90	35-40.00
91-54-003 Nuthatches In Fall	S. Timm	150-day	27.90	28.00
91-54-004 Baltimore Orioles In Summer	S. Timm	150-day	27.90	27-32.00
91-54-005 Blue Jays In Early Fall	S. Timm	150-day	27.90	45.00
91-54-006 Robins In Early Spring	S. Timm	150-day	27.90	30.00
91-54-007 Cedar Waxwings in Fall	S. Timm	150-day	29.90	50.00
91-54-008 Chickadees in Winter	S. Timm	150-day	29.90	40.00
Edwin M. Knowles	**Cozy Country Corners**			
90-55-001 Lazy Morning	H. H. Ingmire	150-day	24.90	50-58.00
90-55-002 Warm Retreat	H. H. Ingmire	150-day	24.90	55.00
91-55-003 A Sunny Spot	H. H. Ingmire	150-day	27.90	44.00
91-55-004 Attic Afternoon	H. H. Ingmire	150-day	27.90	50.00
91-55-005 Mirror Mischief	H. H. Ingmire	150-day	27.90	60.00
91-55-006 Hide and Seek	H. H. Ingmire	150-day	29.90	50-60.00
91-55-007 Apple Antics	H. H. Ingmire	150-day	29.90	60.00
91-55-008 Table Trouble	H. H. Ingmire	150-day	29.90	70.00

	ARTIST	EDITION	ISSUE	QUOTE
Edwin M. Knowles	**Jewels of the Flowers**			
91-56-001 Sapphire Wings	T.C. Chiu	150-day	29.90	34-37.00
91-56-002 Topaz Beauties	T.C. Chiu	150-day	29.90	38-44.00
91-56-003 Amethyst Flight	T.C. Chiu	150-day	32.90	45.00
91-56-004 Ruby Elegance	T.C. Chiu	150-day	32.90	55.00
91-56-005 Emerald Pair	T.C. Chiu	150-day	32.90	45.00
91-56-006 Opal Splendor	T.C. Chiu	150-day	34.90	38.00
92-56-007 Pearl Luster	T.C. Chiu	150-day	34.90	69.00
92-56-008 Aquamarine Glimmer	T.C. Chiu	150-day	34.90	34.90
Edwin M. Knowles	**Pussyfooting Around**			
91-57-001 Fish Tales	C. Wilson	150-day	24.90	25.00
91-57-002 Teatime Tabbies	C. Wilson	150-day	24.90	25.00
91-57-003 Yarn Spinners	C. Wilson	150-day	24.90	30.00
91-57-004 Two Maestros	C. Wilson	150-day	24.90	24.90
Edwin M. Knowles	**Baby Owls of North America**			
91-58-001 Peek-A-Whoo:Screech Owls	J. Thornbrugh	150-day	27.90	40-45.00
91-58-002 Forty Winks: Saw-Whet Owls	J. Thornbrugh	150-day	29.90	44.00
91-58-003 The Tree House: Northern Pygmy Owls	J. Thornbrugh	150-day	30.90	47.00
91-58-004 Three of a Kind: Great Horned Owls	J. Thornbrugh	150-day	30.90	50.00
91-58-005 Out on a Limb: Great Gray Owls	J. Thornbrugh	150-day	30.90	50.00
91-58-006 Beginning to Explore: Boreal Owls	J. Thornbrugh	150-day	32.90	33.00
92-58-007 Three's Company: Long Eared Owls	J. Thornbrugh	150-day	32.90	32.90
92-58-008 Whoo's There: Barred Owl	J. Thornbrugh	150-day	32.90	32.90
Edwin M. Knowles	**Season For Song**			
91-59-001 Winter Concert	M. Jobe	150-day	34.90	45-58.00
91-59-002 Snowy Symphony	M. Jobe	150-day	34.90	58.00
91-59-003 Frosty Chorus	M. Jobe	150-day	34.90	38.00
91-59-004 Silver Serenade	M. Jobe	150-day	34.90	40.00
Edwin M. Knowles	**Garden Cottages of England**			
91-60-001 Chandler's Cottage	T. Kinkade	150-day	27.90	60.00
91-60-002 Cedar Nook Cottage	T. Kinkade	150-day	27.90	50.00
91-60-003 Candlelit Cottage	T. Kinkade	150-day	30.90	60.00
91-60-004 Open Gate Cottage	T. Kinkade	150-day	30.90	31.00
91-60-005 McKenna's Cottage	T. Kinkade	150-day	30.90	31.00
91-60-006 Woodsman's Thatch Cottage	T. Kinkade	150-day	32.90	32.90
92-60-007 Merritt's Cottage	T. Kinkade	150-day	32.90	32.90
92-60-008 Stonegate Cottage	T. Kinkade	150-day	32.90	32.90
Edwin M. Knowles	**Sleeping Beauty**			
91-61-001 Once Upon A Dream	Disney Studios	150-day	39.90	50.00
91-61-002 Awakened by a Kiss	Disney Studios	150-day	39.90	45.00
91-61-003 Happy Birthday Briar Rose	Disney Studios	150-day	42.90	60.00
92-61-004 Together At Last	Disney Studios	150-day	42.90	43.00
Edwin M. Knowles	**Snow White and the Seven Dwarfs**			
91-62-001 The Dance of Snow White/Seven Dwarfs	Disney Studios	150-day	29.90	60.00
91-62-002 With a Smile and a Song	Disney Studios	150-day	29.90	30.00
91-62-003 A Special Treat	Disney Studios	150-day	32.90	50.00
92-62-004 A Kiss for Dopey	Disney Studios	150-day	32.90	32.90
92-62-005 The Poison Apple	Disney Studios	150-day	32.90	32.90
92-62-006 Fireside Love Story	Disney Studios	150-day	34.90	34.90
92-62-007 Stubborn Grumpy	Disney Studios	150-day	34.90	34.90
92-62-008 A Wish Come True	Disney Studios	150-day	34.90	34.90
92-62-009 Time To Tidy Up	Disney Studios	150-day	34.50	34.50
93-62-010 May I Have This Dance?	Disney Studios	150-day	36.90	36.90
93-62-011 A Surprise in the Clearing	Disney Studios	150-day	36.50	36.50
93-62-012 Happy Ending	Disney Studios	150-day	36.90	36.90
Edwin M. Knowles	**Classic Fairy Tales**			
91-63-001 Goldilocks and the Three Bears	S. Gustafson	150-day	29.90	55-60.00
91-63-002 Little Red Riding Hood	S. Gustafson	150-day	29.90	52.00
91-63-003 The Three Little Pigs	S. Gustafson	150-day	32.90	50.00
91-63-004 The Frog Prince	S. Gustafson	150-day	32.90	60.00
92-63-005 Jack and the Beanstalk	S. Gustafson	150-day	32.90	35.00
92-63-006 Hansel and Gretel	S. Gustafson	150-day	34.90	34.90
92-63-007 Puss in Boots	S. Gustafson	150-day	34.90	34.90
92-63-008 Tom Thumb	S. Gustafson	150-day	34.90	34.90
Edwin M. Knowles	**Wizard of Oz: A National Treasure**			
91-64-001 Yellow Brick Road	R. Laslo	150-day	29.90	29.90
92-64-002 I Haven't Got a Brain	R. Laslo	150-day	29.90	29.90
92-64-003 I'm a Little Rusty Yet	R. Laslo	150-day	32.90	32.90
92-64-004 I Even Scare Myself	R. Laslo	150-day	32.90	32.90
92-64-005 We're Off To See the Wizard	R. Laslo	150-day	32.90	32.90
92-64-006 I'll Never Get Home	R. Laslo	150-day	34.90	34.90
92-64-007 I'm Melting	R. Laslo	150-day	34.90	34.90
92-64-008 There's No Place Like Home	R. Laslo	150-day	34.90	34.90
Edwin M. Knowles	**First Impressions**			
91-65-001 Taking a Gander	J. Giordano	150-day	29.90	40.00
91-65-002 Two's Company	J. Giordano	150-day	29.90	25.00
91-65-003 Fine Feathered Friends	J. Giordano	150-day	32.90	40.00
91-65-004 What's Up?	J. Giordano	150-day	32.90	35.00
91-65-005 All Ears	J. Giordano	150-day	32.90	65.00
92-65-006 Between Friends	J. Giordano	150-day	32.90	40.00
Edwin M. Knowles	**Santa's Christmas**			
91-66-001 Santa's Love	T. Browning	150-day	29.90	50.00
91-66-002 Santa's Cheer	T. Browning	150-day	29.90	65.00
91-66-003 Santa's Promise	T. Browning	150-day	32.90	59-65.00
91-66-004 Santa's Gift	T. Browning	150-day	32.90	35-63.00
92-66-005 Santa's Surprise	T. Browning	150-day	32.90	65.00
92-66-006 Santa's Magic	T. Browning	150-day	32.90	95.00
Edwin M. Knowles	**Home for the Holidays**			
91-67-001 Sleigh Ride Home	T. Kinkade	150-day	29.90	40-63.00
91-67-002 Home to Grandma's	T. Kinkade	150-day	29.90	47-55.00
91-67-003 Home Before Christmas	T. Kinkade	150-day	32.90	55-65.00
91-67-004 The Warmth of Home	T. Kinkade	150-day	32.90	50.00
92-67-005 Homespun Holiday	T. Kinkade	150-day	32.90	45.00
92-67-006 Hometime Yuletide	T. Kinkade	150-day	34.90	60.00
92-67-007 Home Away From Home	T. Kinkade	150-day	34.90	55.00
92-67-008 The Journey Home	T. Kinkade	150-day	34.90	35.00
Edwin M. Knowles	**Call of the Wilderness**			
91-68-001 First Outing	K. Daniel	150-day	29.90	29.90
91-68-002 Howling Lesson	K. Daniel	150-day	29.90	29.90
91-68-003 Silent Watch	K. Daniel	150-day	32.90	32.90
91-68-004 Winter Travelers	K. Daniel	150-day	32.90	32.90
92-68-005 Ahead of the Pack	K. Daniel	150-day	32.90	32.90
92-68-006 Northern Spirits	K. Daniel	150-day	34.90	34.90
92-68-007 Twilight Friends	K. Daniel	150-day	34.90	34.90

	ARTIST	EDITION	ISSUE	QUOTE
92-68-008 A New Future	K. Daniel	150-day	34.90	34.90
92-68-009 Morning Mist	K. Daniel	150-day	36.90	36.90
92-68-010 The Silent One	K. Daniel	150-day	36.90	36.90
Edwin M. Knowles	**Old-Fashioned Favorites**			
91-69-001 Apple Crisp	M. Weber	150-day	29.90	75.00
91-69-002 Blueberry Muffins	M. Weber	150-day	29.90	55.00
91-69-003 Peach Cobbler	M. Weber	150-day	29.90	60.00
91-69-004 Chocolate Chip Oatmeal Cookies	M. Weber	150-day	29.90	80.00
Edwin M. Knowles	**Songs of the American Spirit**			
91-70-001 The Star Spangled Banner	H. Bond	150-day	29.90	30.00
91-70-002 Battle Hymn of the Republic	H. Bond	150-day	29.90	60.00
91-70-003 America the Beautiful	H. Bond	150-day	29.90	35.00
91-70-004 My Country 'Tis of Thee	H. Bond	150-day	29.90	40.00
Edwin M. Knowles	**Backyard Harmony**			
91-71-001 The Singing Lesson	J. Thornbrugh	150-day	27.90	35.00
91-71-002 Welcoming a New Day	J. Thornbrugh	150-day	27.90	45.00
91-71-003 Announcing Spring	J. Thornbrugh	150-day	30.90	31.00
92-71-004 The Morning Harvest	J. Thornbrugh	150-day	30.90	30.90
92-71-005 Spring Time Pride	J. Thornbrugh	150-day	30.90	30.90
92-71-006 Treetop Serenade	J. Thornbrugh	150-day	32.90	32.90
92-71-007 At The Peep Of Day	J. Thornbrugh	150-day	32.90	32.90
92-71-008 Today's Discoveries	J. Thornbrugh	150-day	32.90	32.90
Edwin M. Knowles	**Bambi**			
92-72-001 Bashful Bambi	Disney Studios	150-day	34.90	34.90
92-72-002 Bambi's New Friends	Disney Studios	150-day	34.90	34.90
92-72-003 Hello Little Prince	Disney Studios	150-day	37.90	37.90
92-72-004 Bambi's Morning Greetings	Disney Studios	150-day	37.90	37.90
92-72-005 Bambi's Skating Lesson	Disney Studios	150-day	37.90	37.90
93-72-006 What's Up Possums?	Disney Studios	150-day	37.90	37.90
Edwin M. Knowles	**Purrfect Point of View**			
92-73-001 Unexpected Visitors	J. Giordano	150-day	29.90	30.00
92-73-002 Wistful Morning	J. Giordano	150-day	29.90	31.00
92-73-003 Afternoon Catnap	J. Giordano	150-day	29.90	32.00
92-73-004 Cozy Company	J. Giordano	150-day	29.90	29.90
Edwin M. Knowles	**China's Natural Treasures**			
92-74-001 The Siberian Tiger	T.C. Chiu	150-day	29.90	45.00
92-74-002 The Snow Leopard	T.C. Chiu	150-day	29.90	30.00
92-74-003 The Giant Panda	T.C. Chiu	150-day	32.90	45.00
92-74-004 The Tibetan Brown Bear	T.C. Chiu	150-day	32.90	45.00
92-74-005 The Asian Elephant	T.C. Chiu	150-day	32.90	45.00
92-74-006 The Golden Monkey	T.C. Chiu	150-day	34.90	35.00
Edwin M. Knowles	**Under Mother's Wing**			
92-75-001 Arctic Spring: Snowy Owls	J. Beaudoin	150-day	29.90	39.00
92-75-002 Forest's Edge: Great Gray Owls	J. Beaudoin	150-day	29.90	47.00
92-75-003 Treetop Trio: Long-Eared Owls	J. Beaudoin	150-day	32.90	45.00
92-75-004 Woodland Watch: Spotted Owls	J. Beaudoin	150-day	32.90	35.00
92-75-005 Vast View: Saw Whet Owls	J. Beaudoin	150-day	32.90	55.00
92-75-006 Lofty-Limb: Great Horned Owl	J. Beaudoin	150-day	34.90	35.00
93-75-007 Perfect Perch: Barred Owls	J. Beaudoin	150-day	34.90	34.90
93-75-008 Happy Home: Short-Eared Owl	J. Beaudoin	150-day	34.90	34.90
Edwin M. Knowles	**Classic Mother Goose**			
92-76-001 Little Miss Muffet	S. Gustafson	150-day	29.90	30.00
92-76-002 Mary had a Little Lamb	S. Gustafson	150-day	29.90	69.00
92-76-003 Mary, Mary, Quite Contrary	S. Gustafson	150-day	29.90	69.00
92-76-004 Little Bo Peep	S. Gustafson	150-day	29.90	29.90
Edwin M. Knowles	**Keepsake Rhymes**			
92-77-001 Humpty Dumpty	S. Gustafson	150-day	29.90	50.00
93-77-002 Peter Pumpkin Eater	S. Gustafson	150-day	29.90	40.00
93-77-003 Pat-a-Cake	S. Gustafson	150-day	29.90	29.90
93-77-004 Old King Cole	S. Gustafson	150-day	29.90	29.90
Edwin M. Knowles	**Thomas Kinkade's Thomashire**			
92-78-001 Olde Porterfield Tea Room	T. Kinkade	150-day	29.90	29.90
92-78-002 Olde Thomashire Mill	T. Kinkade	150-day	29.90	29.90
92-78-003 Swanbrook Cottage	T. Kinkade	150-day	32.90	32.90
92-78-004 Pye Corner Cottage	T. Kinkade	150-day	32.90	32.90
93-78-005 Blossom Hill Church	T. Kinkade	150-day	32.90	32.90
93-78-006 Olde Garden Cottage	T. Kinkade	150-day	32.90	32.90
Edwin M. Knowles	**Small Blessings**			
92-79-001 Now I Lay Me Down to Sleep	C. Layton	150-day	29.90	29.90
92-79-002 Bless Us O Lord For These, Thy Gifts	C. Layton	150-day	29.90	29.90
92-79-003 Jesus Loves Me, This I Know	C. Layton	150-day	32.90	32.90
92-79-004 This Little Light of Mine	C. Layton	150-day	32.90	32.90
92-79-005 Blessed Are The Pure In Heart	C. Layton	150-day	32.90	32.90
93-79-006 Bless Our Home	C. Layton	150-day	32.90	32.90
Edwin M. Knowles	**Seasons of Splendor**			
92-80-001 Autumn's Grandeur	K. Randle	150-day	29.90	49.00
92-80-002 School Days	K. Randle	150-day	29.90	40-50.00
92-80-003 Woodland Mill Stream	K. Randle	150-day	32.90	65.00
92-80-004 Harvest Memories	K. Randle	150-day	32.90	50.00
92-80-005 A Country Weekend	K. Randle	150-day	32.90	45.00
93-80-006 Indian Summer	K. Randle	150-day	32.90	40.00
Edwin M. Knowles	**Lady and the Tramp**			
92-81-001 First Date	Disney Studios	150-day	34.90	34.90
92-81-002 Puppy Love	Disney Studios	150-day	34.90	34.90
92-81-003 Dog Pound Blues	Disney Studios	150-day	37.90	37.90
92-81-004 Merry Christmas To All	Disney Studios	150-day	37.90	37.90
93-81-005 Double Siamese Trouble	Disney Studios	150-day	37.90	37.90
93-81-006 Ruff House	Disney Studios	150-day	39.90	39.90
93-81-007 Telling Tails	Disney Studios	150-day	39.90	39.90
93-81-008 Moonlight Romance	Disney Studios	150-day	39.90	39.90
Edwin M. Knowles	**Sweetness and Grace**			
92-82-001 God Bless Teddy	J. Welty	150-day	34.90	38.00
92-82-002 Sunshine and Smiles	J. Welty	150-day	34.90	34.90
92-82-003 Favorite Buddy	J. Welty	150-day	34.90	34.90
92-82-004 Sweet Dreams	J. Welty	150-day	34.90	34.90
Edwin M. Knowles	**Thomas Kinkade's Yuletide Memories**			
92-83-001 The Magic of Christmas	T. Kinkade	150-day	29.90	29.90
92-83-002 A Beacon of Faith	T. Kinkade	150-day	29.90	29.90
93-83-003 Moonlit Sleighride	T. Kinkade	150-day	29.90	29.90
93-83-004 Silent Night	T. Kinkade	150-day	29.90	29.90
93-83-005 Olde Porterfield Gift Shoppe	T. Kinkade	150-day	29.90	29.90
93-83-006 The Wonder of the Season	T. Kinkade	150-day	29.90	29.90

	ARTIST	EDITION	ISSUE	QUOTE
93-83-007 A Winter's Walk	T. Kinkade	150-day	29.90	29.90
93-83-008 Skater's Delight	T. Kinkade	150-day	32.90	32.90
Edwin M. Knowles	**It's a Dog's Life**			
92-84-001 We've Been Spotted	L. Kaatz	150-day	29.90	29.90
92-84-002 Literary Labs	L. Kaatz	150-day	29.90	29.90
93-84-003 Retrieving Our Dignity	L. Kaatz	150-day	32.90	32.90
93-84-004 Lodging a Complaint	L. Kaatz	150-day	32.90	32.90
93-84-005 Barreling Along	L. Kaatz	150-day	32.90	32.90
93-84-006 Play Ball	L. Kaatz	150-day	34.90	34.90
93-84-007 Dogs and Suds	L. Kaatz	150-day	34.90	34.90
93-84-008 Paws for a Picnic	L. Kaatz	150-day	34.90	34.90
Edwin M. Knowles	**Mickey's Christmas Carol**			
92-85-001 Bah Humbug	Disney Studios	150-day	29.90	29.90
92-85-002 What's So Merry About Christmas?	Disney Studios	150-day	29.90	29.90
93-85-003 God Bless Us Every One	Disney Studios	150-day	32.90	32.90
93-85-004 A Christmas Surprise	Disney Studios	150-day	32.90	32.90
93-85-005 Yuletide Greetings	Disney Studios	150-day	32.90	32.90
93-85-006 Marley's Warning	Disney Studios	150-day	34.90	34.90
93-85-007 A Cozy Christmas	Disney Studios	150-day	34.90	34.90
93-85-008 A Christmas Feast	Disney Studios	150-day	34.90	34.90
Edwin M. Knowles	**The Disney Treasured Moments Collection**			
92-86-001 Cinderella	Disney Studios	150-day	29.90	29.90
92-86-002 Snow White and the Seven Dwarves	Disney Studios	150-day	29.90	29.90
93-86-003 Alice in Wonderland	Disney Studios	150-day	32.90	32.90
93-86-004 Sleeping Beauty	Disney Studios	150-day	32.90	32.90
93-86-005 Peter Pan	Disney Studios	150-day	32.90	32.90
93-86-006 Pinocchio	Disney Studios	150-day	34.90	34.90
93-86-007 The Jungle Book	Disney Studios	150-day	34.90	34.90
Edwin M. Knowles	**Christmas in the City**			
92-87-001 A Christmas Snowfall	A. Leimanis	150-day	34.90	50.00
92-87-002 Yuletide Celebration	A. Leimanis	150-day	34.90	60.00
93-87-003 Holiday Cheer	A. Leimanis	150-day	34.90	34.90
93-87-004 The Magic of Christmas	A. Leimanis	150-day	34.90	35.00
Edwin M. Knowles	**Romantic Age of Steam**			
92-88-001 The Empire Builder	R.B. Pierce	150-day	29.90	29.90
92-88-002 The Broadway Limited	R.B. Pierce	150-day	29.90	29.90
92-88-003 Twentieth Century Limited	R.B. Pierce	150-day	32.90	32.90
92-88-004 The Chief	R.B. Pierce	150-day	32.90	32.90
92-88-005 The Crescent Limited	R.B. Pierce	150-day	32.90	32.90
93-88-006 The Overland Limited	R.B. Pierce	150-day	34.90	34.90
93-88-007 The Jupiter	R.B. Pierce	150-day	34.90	34.90
93-88-008 The Daylight	R.B. Pierce	150-day	34.90	34.90
Edwin M. Knowles	**The Comforts of Home**			
92-89-001 Sleepyheads	H. Hollister Ingmire	150-day	24.90	24.90
92-89-002 Curious Pair	H. Hollister Ingmire	150-day	24.90	24.90
93-89-003 Mother's Retreat	H. Hollister Ingmire	150-day	27.90	27.90
93-89-004 Welcome Friends	H. Hollister Ingmire	150-day	27.90	27.90
93-89-005 Playtime	H. Hollister Ingmire	150-day	27.90	27.90
93-89-006 Feline Frolic	H. Hollister Ingmire	150-day	29.90	29.90
93-89-007 Washday Helpers	H. Hollister Ingmire	150-day	29.90	29.90
93-89-008 A Cozy Fireside	H. Hollister Ingmire	150-day	29.90	29.90
Edwin M. Knowles	**Free as the Wind**			
92-90-001 Skyward	M. Budden	150-day	29.90	29.90
92-90-002 Aloft	M. Budden	150-day	29.90	29.90
92-90-003 Airborne	M. Budden	150-day	32.90	32.90
93-90-004 Flight	M. Budden	150-day	32.90	32.90
93-90-005 Ascent	M. Budden	150-day	32.90	32.90
93-90-006 Heavenward	M. Budden	150-day	32.90	32.90
Edwin M. Knowles	**Yesterday's Innocents**			
92-91-001 My First Book	J. Wilcox Smith	150-day	29.90	30.00
92-91-002 Time to Smell the Roses	J. Wilcox Smith	150-day	29.90	40.00
93-91-003 Hush, Baby's Sleeping	J. Wilcox Smith	150-day	32.90	38.00
93-91-004 Ready and Waiting	J. Wilcox Smith	150-day	32.90	50.00
Edwin M. Knowles	**Home is Where the Heart Is**			
92-92-001 Home Sweet Home	T. Kinkade	150-day	29.90	29.90
92-92-002 A Warm Welcome Home	T. Kinkade	150-day	29.90	29.90
92-92-003 A Carriage Ride Home	T. Kinkade	150-day	32.90	32.90
92-92-004 Amber Afternoon	T. Kinkade	150-day	32.90	32.90
93-92-005 Country Memories	T. Kinkade	150-day	32.90	32.90
93-92-006 The Twilight Cafe	T. Kinkade	150-day	34.90	34.90
93-92-007 Our Summer Home	T. Kinkade	150-day	34.90	34.90
93-92-008 Hometown Hospitality	T. Kinkade	150-day	34.90	34.90
Edwin M. Knowles	**Shadows and Light: Winter's Wildlife**			
93-93-001 Winter's Children	N. Glazier	150-day	29.90	55.00
93-93-002 Cub Scouts	N. Glazier	150-day	29.90	65.00
93-93-003 Little Snowman	N. Glazier	150-day	29.90	50.00
93-93-004 The Snow Cave	N. Glazier	150-day	29.90	30.00
Edwin M. Knowles	**Beauty and the Beast**			
93-94-001 Love's First Dance	Disney Studios	150-day	29.90	29.90
93-94-002 A Blossoming Romance	Disney Studios	150-day	29.90	29.90
93-94-003 Warming Up	Disney Studios	150-day	32.90	32.90
93-94-004 Learning to Love	Disney Studios	150-day	32.90	32.90
93-94-005 Papa's Workshop	Disney Studios	150-day	32.90	32.90
93-94-006 Be Our Guest	Disney Studios	150-day	34.90	34.90
93-94-007 Belle's Favorite Story	Disney Studios	150-day	34.90	34.90
93-94-008 A Mismatch	Disney Studios	150-day	34.90	34.90
Edwin M. Knowles	**Nature's Nursery**			
92-95-001 Testing the Waters	J. Thornbrugh	150-day	29.90	29.90
93-95-002 Taking the Plunge	J. Thornbrugh	150-day	29.90	29.90
93-95-003 Race Ya Mom	J. Thornbrugh	150-day	29.90	29.90
93-95-004 Time to Wake Up	J. Thornbrugh	150-day	29.90	29.90
93-95-005 Hide and Seek	J. Thornbrugh	150-day	29.90	29.90
93-95-006 Piggyback Ride	J. Thornbrugh	150-day	29.90	29.90
Edwin M. Knowles	**Proud Sentinels of the American West**			
93-96-001 Youngblood	N. Glazier	150-day	29.90	29.90
93-96-002 Cat Nap	N. Glazier	150-day	29.90	29.90
93-96-003 Desert Bighorn-Mormon Ridge	N. Glazier	150-day	32.90	32.90
93-96-004 Crown Prince	N. Glazier	150-day	32.90	32.90
Edwin M. Knowles	**Garden Secrets**			
93-97-001 Nine Lives	B. Higgins Bond	150-day	24.90	24.90
93-97-002 Floral Purr-fume	B. Higgins Bond	150-day	24.90	24.90
93-97-003 Bloomin' Kitties	B. Higgins Bond	150-day	24.90	24.90

Number	Name	ARTIST	EDITION	ISSUE	QUOTE
93-97-004	Kitty Corner	B. Higgins Bond	150-day	24.90	24.90
93-97-005	Flower Fanciers	B. Higgins Bond	150-day	24.90	24.90
93-97-006	Meadow Mischief	B. Higgins Bond	150-day	24.90	24.90
93-97-007	Pussycat Potpourri	B. Higgins Bond	150-day	24.90	24.90
93-97-008	Frisky Business	B. Higgins Bond	150-day	24.90	24.90
Edwin M. Knowles		**Windows of Glory**			
93-98-001	King of Kings	J. Welty	95-day	29.90	29.90
93-98-002	Prince of Peace	J. Welty	95-day	29.90	29.90
93-98-003	The Messiah	J. Welty	95-day	32.90	32.90
93-98-004	The Good Shepherd	J. Welty	95-day	32.90	32.90
93-98-005	The Light of the World	J. Welty	95-day	32.90	32.90
93-98-006	The Everlasting Father	J. Welty	95-day	32.90	32.90
Edwin M. Knowles		**Nature's Garden**			
93-99-001	Springtime Friends	C. Decker	95-day	29.90	29.90
93-99-002	A Morning Splash	C. Decker	95-day	29.90	29.90
93-99-003	Flury of Activity	C. Decker	95-day	32.90	32.90
93-99-004	Hanging Around	C. Decker	95-day	32.90	32.90
93-99-005	Tiny Twirling Treasures	C. Decker	95-day	32.90	32.90
Edwin M. Knowles		**The Little Mermaid**			
93-100-001	A Song From the Sea	Disney Studios	95-day	29.90	29.90
93-100-002	A Visit to the Surface	Disney Studios	95-day	29.90	29.90
93-100-003	Daddy's Girl	Disney Studios	95-day	32.90	32.90
93-100-004	Underwater Buddies	Disney Studios	95-day	32.90	32.90
93-100-005	Ariel's Treasured Collection	Disney Studios	95-day	32.90	32.90
93-100-006	Kiss the Girl	Disney Studios	95-day	32.90	32.90
Edwin M. Knowles		**Enchanted Cottages**			
93-101-001	Fallbrooke Cottage	T. Kinkade	95-day	29.90	29.90
93-101-002	Julianne's Cottage	T. Kinkade	95-day	29.90	29.90
93-101-003	Seaside Cottage	T. Kinkade	95-day	29.90	29.90
93-101-004	Sweetheart Cottage	T. Kinkade	95-day	29.90	29.90
93-101-005	Weathervane Cottage	T. Kinkade	95-day	29.90	29.90
93-101-006	Rose Garden Cottage	T. Kinkade	95-day	29.90	29.90
Edwin M. Knowles		**Musical Moments From the Wizard of Oz**			
93-102-001	Over the Rainbow	K. Milnazik	95-day	29.90	29.90
93-102-002	We're Off to See the Wizard	K. Milnazik	95-day	29.90	29.90
93-102-003	Munchkin Land	K. Milnazik	95-day	29.90	29.90
93-102-004	If I Only Had a Brain	K. Milnazik	95-day	29.90	29.90
93-102-005	Ding Dong The Witch is Dead	K. Milnazik	95-day	29.90	29.90
93-102-006	The Lullabye League	K. Milnazik	95-day	29.90	29.90
KPM-Royal Berlin		**Christmas**			
69-01-001	Christmas Star	Unknown	5,000	28.00	380.00
70-01-002	Three Kings	Unknown	5,000	28.00	300.00
71-01-003	Christmas Tree	Unknown	5,000	28.00	290.00
72-01-004	Christmas Angel	Unknown	5,000	31.00	300.00
73-01-005	Christ Child on Sled	Unknown	5,000	33.00	280.00
74-01-006	Angel and Horn	Unknown	5,000	35.00	180.00
75-01-007	Shepherds	Unknown	5,000	40.00	165.00
76-01-008	Star of Bethlehem	Unknown	5,000	43.00	140.00
77-01-009	Mary at Crib	Unknown	5,000	46.00	100.00
78-01-010	Three Wise Men	Unknown	5,000	49.00	54.00
79-01-011	The Manger	Unknown	5,000	55.00	55.00
80-01-012	Shepherds in Fields	Unknown	5,000	55.00	55.00
Lalique		**Annual**			
65-01-001	Deux Oiseaux (Two Birds)	M. Lalique	2,000	25.00	13-1400.
66-01-002	Rose de Songerie (Dream Rose)	M. Lalique	5,000	25.00	120.00
67-01-003	Ballet de Poisson (Fish Ballet)	M. Lalique	5,000	25.00	104.00
68-01-004	Gazelle Fantaisie (Gazelle Fantasy)	M. Lalique	5,000	25.00	75.00
69-01-005	Papillon (Butterfly)	M. Lalique	5,000	30.00	34-48.00
70-01-006	Paon (Peacock)	M. Lalique	5,000	30.00	59.00
71-01-007	Hibou (Owl)	M. Lalique	5,000	35.00	69.00
72-01-008	Coquillage (Shell)	M. Lalique	5,000	40.00	70-74.00
73-01-009	Petit Geai (Jayling)	M. Lalique	5,000	42.50	104.00
74-01-010	Sous d'Argent (Silver Pennies)	M. Lalique	5,000	47.50	99.00
75-01-011	Duo de Poisson (Fish Duet)	M. Lalique	5,000	50.00	145.00
76-01-012	Aigle (Eagle)	M. Lalique	5,000	60.00	90.00
Lance Corporation		**Sebastian Plates**			
78-01-001	Motif No. 1	P.W. Baston	Closed	75.00	50-75.00
79-01-002	Grand Canyon	P.W. Baston	Closed	75.00	50-75.00
80-01-003	Lone Cypress	P.W. Baston	Closed	75.00	150-175.
80-01-004	In The Candy Store	P.W. Baston	Closed	39.50	39.50
81-01-005	The Doctor	P.W. Baston	Closed	39.50	39.50
83-01-006	Little Mother	P.W. Baston	Closed	39.50	39.50
84-01-007	Switching The Freight	P.W. Baston	Closed	42.50	80-100.
Lance Corporation		**Miscellaneous (Hudson Pewter)**			
74-02-001	Spirit of '76 9"	P.W. Baston	Retrd.	27.50	75.00
76-02-002	Declaration of Independence 8 1/2"	Unknown	Retrd.	25.00	50.00
78-02-003	Zodiac 8"	Unknown	Retrd.	60.00	75.00
Lance Corporation		**The American Expansion (Hudson Pewter)**			
75-03-001	Spirit of '76 (6" Plate)	P.W. Baston	Closed	Unkn.	100-120.
75-03-002	American Independence	P.W. Baston	Closed	Unkn.	100-125.
75-03-003	American Expansion	P.W. Baston	Closed	Unkn.	50-75.00
75-03-004	The American War Between the States	P.W. Baston	Closed	Unkn.	150-200.
Lance Corporation		**American Commemoratives (Hudson Pewter)**			
75-04-001	Mt. Vernon 6"	R. Lamb	Retrd.	N/A	55.00
75-04-002	Monticello 6"	R. Lamb	Retrd.	N/A	55.00
75-04-003	Log Cabin 6"	R. Lamb	Retrd.	N/A	55.00
75-04-004	Hyde Park 6"	R. Lamb	Retrd.	N/A	55.00
75-04-005	Spirit of '76 6"	R. Lamb	Retrd.	N/A	55.00
Lance Corporation		**Sailing Ships (Hudson Pewter)**			
78-05-001	Flying Cloud 6"	A. Petito	Retrd.	35.00	55.00
78-05-002	America 6"	A. Petito	Retrd.	35.00	55.00
78-05-003	Morgan 6"	A. Petito	Retrd.	35.00	55.00
78-05-004	Constitution 6"	A. Petito	Retrd.	35.00	55.00
Lance Corporation		**Songbirds of the Four Seasons (Hudson Pewter)**			
78-06-001	Cardinal (Winter) 6"	Hollis/Yourdon	Retrd.	35.00	55.00
78-06-002	Hummingbird (Summer) 6"	Hollis/Yourdon	Retrd.	35.00	55.00
78-06-003	Sparrow (Autumn) 6"	Hollis/Yourdon	Retrd.	35.00	55.00
78-06-004	Wood Thrush (Spring) 6"	Hollis/Yourdon	Retrd.	35.00	55.00
Lance Corporation		**America's Favorite Birds (Hudson Pewter/Crystal)**			
78-07-001	Crystal Wren 8"	C. Terris	Retrd.	79.50	79.50

Number	Name	ARTIST	EDITION	ISSUE	QUOTE
Lance Corporation		**A Child's Christmas (Hudson Pewter)**			
78-08-001	Bedtime Story	A. Petitto	Suspd.	35.00	60.00
79-08-002	Littlest Angels	A. Petitto	Suspd.	35.00	60.00
80-08-003	Heaven's Christmas Tree	A. Petitto	Suspd.	42.50	60.00
81-08-004	Filling The Sky	A. Petitto	Suspd.	47.50	60.00
Lance Corporation		**Mother's Day (Hudson Pewter)**			
79-09-001	Cherished 6"	A. Petito	Retrd.	42.50	55.00
80-09-002	1980 Mother's Day 6"	A. Petito	Retrd.	42.50	55.00
Lance Corporation		**Twas The Night Before Christmas (Hudson Pewter)**			
82-10-001	Not A Creature Was Stirring	A. Hollis	Suspd.	47.50	60.00
83-10-002	Visions Of Sugar Plums	A. Hollis	Suspd.	47.50	60.00
84-10-003	His Eyes How They Twinkled	A. Hollis	Suspd.	47.50	60.00
85-10-004	Happy Christmas To All	A. Hollis	Suspd.	47.50	60.00
Lance Corporation		**Mickey's Christmas (Hudson Pewter)**			
86-11-001	God Bless Us, Every One	Staff	Suspd.	47.50	60.00
87-11-002	Jolly Old Saint Mick	Staff	Suspd.	55.00	60.00
88-11-003	He's Checking It Twice	Staff	Suspd.	50.00	60.00
Lance Corporation		**The Songs of Christmas (Hudson Pewter)**			
88-12-001	Silent Night	A. McGrory	Suspd.	55.00	60.00
89-12-002	Hark! The Herald Angels Sing	A. McGrory	Suspd.	60.00	60.00
90-12-003	The First Noel	A. McGrory	Suspd.	60.00	60.00
91-12-004	We Three Kings	A. McGrory	Suspd.	60.00	60.00
Lance Corporation		**Christmas (Hudson Pewter)**			
86-13-001	Bringing Home The Tree	J. Wanat	Suspd.	47.50	60.00
87-13-002	The Caroling Angels	A. Petitto	Suspd.	47.50	60.00
93-13-003	Crack the Whip	A. McGrory	950	55.00	55.00
94-13-004	Home For Christmas	A. McGrory	950	50.00	50.00
Lance Corporation		**Mother's Day (Chilmark Pewter)**			
74-14-001	Flowers of the Field 8"	Unknown	Retrd.	65.00	75.00
80-14-002	1980 Mother's Day	Unknown	Retrd.	90.00	90.00
Lance Corporation		**Christmas (Chilmark Pewter)**			
77-15-001	Currier & Ives Christmas 8"	Unknown	Retrd.	60.00	75.00
78-15-002	Trimming the Tree 8"	Unknown	Retrd.	65.00	75.00
79-15-003	Three Wisemen 8"	Unknown	Retrd.	75.00	75.00
Lance Corporation		**Twelve Days of Christmas (Chilmark Pewter/Stained Glass)**			
79-16-001	Partridge in a Pear Tree 8"	Unknown	Retrd.	99.50	99.50
80-16-002	Two Turtle Doves 8"	Unknown	Retrd.	99.50	99.50
LCS Products		**Early Innings**			
93-01-001	Ebbets Field	LCS	25-day	29.95	29.95
94-01-002	Tiger Stadium	C. Wilkinson	25-day	29.95	29.95
Lenox China		**Colonial Christmas Wreath**			
81-01-001	Colonial Virginia	Unknown	Yr.Iss.	65.00	76.00
82-01-002	Massachusetts	Unknown	Yr.Iss.	70.00	93.00
83-01-003	Maryland	Unknown	Yr.Iss.	70.00	79.00
84-01-004	Rhode Island	Unknown	Yr.Iss.	70.00	82.00
85-01-005	Connecticut	Unknown	Yr.Iss.	70.00	75.00
86-01-006	New Hampshire	Unknown	Yr.Iss.	70.00	75.00
87-01-007	Pennsylvania	Unknown	Yr.Iss.	70.00	75.00
88-01-008	Delaware	Unknown	Yr.Iss.	70.00	70.00
89-01-009	New York	Unknown	Yr.Iss.	75.00	82.00
90-01-010	New Jersey	Unknown	Yr.Iss.	75.00	78.00
91-01-011	South Carolina	Unknown	Yr.Iss.	75.00	75.00
92-01-012	North Carolina	Unknown	Yr.Iss.	75.00	75.00
93-01-013	Georgia	Unknown	Yr.Iss.	75.00	75.00
Lenox China		**Christmas Trees Around the World**			
91-02-001	Germany	Unknown	Yr.Iss.	75.00	75.00
92-02-002	France	Unknown	Yr.Iss.	75.00	75.00
93-02-003	England	Unknown	Yr.Iss.	75.00	75.00
94-02-004	Poland	Unknown	Yr.Iss.	75.00	75.00
Lenox China		**Annual Holiday**			
91-03-001	1991 Holiday Plate-Sleigh	Unknown	Yr.Iss.	75.00	75.00
92-03-002	1992 Holiday Plate-Rock Horse	Unknown	Yr.Iss.	75.00	75.00
93-03-003	1993 Holiday Plate-Fireplace	Unknown	Yr.Iss.	75.00	75.00
94-03-004	1994 Annual Holiday	Unknown	Yr.Iss.	75.00	75.00
Lenox China		**Nativity Vignettes**			
93-04-001	The Holy Family	Unknown	Yr.Iss.	57.00	57.00
94-04-002	The Wisemen	Unknown	Yr.Iss.	59.00	59.00
Lenox Collections		**Boehm Birds**			
70-01-001	Wood Thrush	E. Boehm	Yr.Iss.	35.00	100.00
71-01-002	Goldfinch	E. Boehm	Yr.Iss.	35.00	53.00
72-01-003	Mountain Bluebird	E. Boehm	Yr.Iss.	37.50	50.00
73-01-004	Meadowlark	E. Boehm	Yr.Iss.	50.00	30.00
74-01-005	Rufous Hummingbird	E. Boehm	Yr.Iss.	45.00	49.00
75-01-006	American Redstart	E. Boehm	Yr.Iss.	50.00	30.00
76-01-007	Cardinals	E. Boehm	Yr.Iss.	53.00	70-80.00
77-01-008	Robins	E. Boehm	Yr.Iss.	55.00	45.00
78-01-009	Mockingbirds	E. Boehm	Yr.Iss.	58.00	52-59.00
79-01-010	Golden-Crowned Kinglets	E. Boehm	Yr.Iss.	65.00	95.00
80-01-011	Black-Throated Blue Warblers	E. Boehm	Yr.Iss.	80.00	112.00
81-01-012	Eastern Phoebes	E. Boehm	Yr.Iss.	92.50	100.00
Lenox Collections		**Boehm Woodland Wildlife**			
73-02-001	Racoons	E. Boehm	Yr.Iss.	50.00	50.00
74-02-002	Red Foxes	E. Boehm	Yr.Iss.	52.50	52.50
75-02-003	Cottontail Rabbits	E. Boehm	Yr.Iss.	58.50	58.50
76-02-004	Eastern Chipmunks	E. Boehm	Yr.Iss.	62.50	62.50
77-02-005	Beaver	E. Boehm	Yr.Iss.	67.50	67.50
78-02-006	Whitetail Deer	E. Boehm	Yr.Iss.	70.00	70.00
79-02-007	Squirrels	E. Boehm	Yr.Iss.	76.00	76.00
80-02-008	Bobcats	E. Boehm	Yr.Iss.	82.50	82.50
81-02-009	Martens	E. Boehm	Yr.Iss.	100.00	150.00
82-02-010	River Otters	E. Boehm	Yr.Iss.	100.00	180.00
Lenox Collections		**American Wildlife**			
82-03-001	Red Foxes	N. Adams	9,500	65.00	65.00
82-03-002	Ocelots	N. Adams	9,500	65.00	65.00
82-03-003	Sea Lions	N. Adams	9,500	65.00	65.00
82-03-004	Raccoons	N. Adams	9,500	65.00	65.00
82-03-005	Dall Sheep	N. Adams	9,500	65.00	65.00
82-03-006	Black Bears	N. Adams	9,500	65.00	65.00
82-03-007	Mountain Lions	N. Adams	9,500	65.00	65.00
82-03-008	Polar Bears	N. Adams	9,500	65.00	65.00
82-03-009	Otters	N. Adams	9,500	65.00	65.00

		ARTIST	EDITION	ISSUE	QUOTE
82-03-010	White Tailed Deer	N. Adams	9,500	65.00	65.00
82-03-011	Buffalo	N. Adams	9,500	65.00	65.00
82-03-012	Jack Rabbits	N. Adams	9,500	65.00	65.00
Lenox Collections		**Garden Bird Plate Collection**			
88-04-001	Chickadee	Unknown	Open	48.00	48.00
88-04-002	Bluejay	Unknown	Open	48.00	48.00
89-04-003	Hummingbird	Unknown	Open	48.00	48.00
91-04-004	Dove	Unknown	Open	48.00	48.00
91-04-005	Cardinal	Unknown	Open	48.00	48.00
92-04-006	Goldfinch	Unknown	Open	48.00	48.00
Lenox Collections		**Annual Christmas Plates**			
92-05-001	Sleigh	Unknown	Yr.Iss.	75.00	75.00
93-05-002	Midnight Sleighride	L. Bywater	90-day	119.00	119.00
Lenox Collections		**Nature's Collage**			
92-06-001	Cedar Waxwing, Among The Berries	C. McClung	Open	34.50	34.50
92-06-002	Gold Finches, Golden Splendor	C. McClung	Open	34.50	34.50
93-06-003	Bluebirds, Summer Interlude	C. McClung	90-day	39.50	39.50
93-06-004	Chickadees, Rose Morning	C. McClung	90-day	39.50	39.50
93-06-005	Bluejays, Winter Song	C. McClung	90-day	39.50	39.50
93-06-006	Cardinals, Spring Courtship	C. McClung	90-day	39.50	39.50
93-06-007	Hummingbirds, Jeweled Glory	C. McClung	90-day	39.50	39.50
93-06-008	Indigo Buntings, Indigo Evening	C. McClung	90-day	39.50	39.50
Lenox Collections		**Children of the Sun & Moon**			
93-07-001	Desert Blossom	D. Crowley	Open	39.50	39.50
93-07-002	Shy One	D. Crowley	Open	39.50	39.50
93-07-003	Feathers & Furs	D. Crowley	Open	39.50	39.50
94-07-004	Little Flower	D. Crowley	Open	39.90	39.90
94-07-005	Daughter of the Sun	D. Crowley	Open	39.90	39.90
94-07-006	Red Feathers	D. Crowley	Open	39.90	39.90
94-07-007	Stars in Her Eyes	D. Crowley	Open	39.90	39.90
94-07-008	Indigo Girl	D. Crowley	Open	39.90	39.90
Lenox Collections		**Dolphins of the Seven Seas**			
93-08-001	Bottlenose Dolphins	J. Holderby	Open	39.50	39.50
Lenox Collections		**Whale Conservation**			
93-09-001	Orca	J. Holderby	Open	39.50	39.50
Lenox Collections		**Pierced Nativity**			
93-10-001	Holy Family	Unknown	Open	45.00	45.00
94-10-002	Three Kings	Unknown	Open	45.00	45.00
94-10-003	Heralding Angels	Unknown	Open	45.00	45.00
94-10-004	Shepherds	Unknown	Open	45.00	45.00
Lenox Collections		**International Victorian Santas**			
92-11-001	Kris Kringle	R. Hoover	90-day	39.50	39.50
93-11-002	Father Christmas	R. Hoover	90-day	39.50	39.50
94-11-003	Grandfather Frost	R. Hoover	90-day	39.50	39.50
95-11-004	American Santa Claus	R. Hoover	90-day	39.50	39.50
Lenox Collections		**Owls of North America**			
93-12-001	Spirit of the Arctic, Snowy Owl	L. Laffin	Open	39.50	39.50
Lenox Collections		**Magic of Christmas**			
93-13-001	Santa of the Northen Forest	L. Bywaters	Open	39.50	39.50
93-13-002	Santa's Gift of Peace	L. Bywaters	Open	39.50	39.50
93-13-003	Gifts For All	L. Bywaters	Open	39.50	39.50
94-13-004	Coming Home	L. Bywaters	Open	39.50	39.50
94-13-005	Santa's Sentinels	L. Bywaters	Open	39.50	39.50
94-13-006	Wonder of Wonders	L. Bywaters	Open	39.50	39.50
94-13-007	A Berry Merry Christmas	L. Bywaters	Open	39.50	39.50
Lenox Collections		**Big Cats of the World**			
93-14-001	Black Panther	Q. Lemonds	Open	39.50	39.50
93-14-002	Chinese Leopard	Q. Lemonds	Open	39.50	39.50
93-14-003	Cougar	Q. Lemonds	Open	39.50	39.50
93-14-004	Bobcat	Q. Lemonds	Open	39.50	39.50
93-14-005	White Tiger	Q. Lemonds	Open	39.50	39.50
93-14-006	Tiger	Q. Lemonds	Open	39.50	39.50
93-14-007	Lion	Q. Lemonds	Open	39.50	39.50
93-14-008	Snow Leopard	Q. Lemonds	Open	39.50	39.50
Lenox Collections		**Eagle Conservation**			
93-15-001	Soaring the Peaks	R. Kelley	Open	39.50	39.50
93-15-002	Solo Flight	R. Kelley	Open	39.50	39.50
93-15-003	Northern Heritage	R. Kelley	Open	39.50	39.50
93-15-004	Lone Sentinel	R. Kelley	Open	39.50	39.50
93-15-005	River Scout	R. Kelley	Open	39.50	39.50
93-15-006	Eagles on Mt. McKinley	R. Kelley	Open	39.50	39.50
93-15-007	Daybreak on River's Edge	R. Kelley	Open	39.50	39.50
93-15-008	Northwood's Legend	R. Kelley	Open	39.50	39.50
Lenox Collections		**Great Cats of the World**			
93-16-001	Siberian Tiger	G. Coheleach	Open	39.50	39.50
93-16-002	Lion	G. Coheleach	Open	39.50	39.50
93-16-003	Lioness	G. Coheleach	Open	39.50	39.50
93-16-004	Snow Leopard	G. Coheleach	Open	39.50	39.50
93-16-005	White Tiger	G. Coheleach	Open	39.50	39.50
93-16-006	Jaquar	G. Coheleach	Open	39.50	39.50
93-16-007	Cougar	G. Coheleach	Open	39.50	39.50
93-16-008	Chinese Leopard	G. Coheleach	Open	39.50	39.50
Lenox Collections		**Royal Cats of Guy Coheleach**			
94-17-001	Afternoon Shade	G. Coheleach	Open	39.50	39.50
94-17-002	Jungle Jaquar	G. Coheleach	Open	39.50	39.50
94-17-003	Rocky Mountain Puma	G. Coheleach	Open	39.50	39.50
94-17-004	Rocky Refuge	G. Coheleach	Open	39.50	39.50
94-17-005	Siesta	G. Coheleach	Open	39.50	39.50
94-17-006	Ambush in the Snow	G. Coheleach	Open	39.50	39.50
94-17-007	Lion in Wait	G. Coheleach	Open	39.50	39.50
94-17-008	Cat Nap	G. Coheleach	Open	39.50	39.50
Lenox Collections		**Cubs of the Big Cats**			
93-18-001	Jaquar Cub	Q. Lemonds	90-day	29.90	29.90
Lenox Collections		**Darling Dalmations**			
93-19-001	Three Alarm Fire	L. Picken	90-day	29.90	29.90
93-19-002	All Fired Up	L. Picken	90-day	29.90	29.90
93-19-003	Fire Brigade	L. Picken	90-day	29.90	29.90
93-19-004	Pup in Boots	L. Picken	90-day	29.90	29.90
93-19-005	Caught in the Act	L. Picken	90-day	29.90	29.90
93-19-006	Please Don't Pick the Flowers	L. Picken	90-day	29.90	29.90

		ARTIST	EDITION	ISSUE	QUOTE
Lenox Collections		**Arctic Wolves**			
93-20-001	Far Country Crossing	J. VanZyle	90-day	29.90	29.90
93-20-002	Cry of the Wild	J. VanZyle	90-day	29.90	29.90
93-20-003	Nightwatch	J. VanZyle	90-day	29.90	29.90
93-20-004	Midnight Renegade	J. VanZyle	90-day	29.90	29.90
93-20-005	On the Edge	J. VanZyle	90-day	29.90	29.90
93-20-006	Picking Up the Trail	J. VanZyle	90-day	29.90	29.90
Lenox Collections		**Enchanted World of the Unicorn**			
92-21-001	Hidden Glade of Unicorn	R. Sanderson	90-day	29.90	29.90
92-21-002	Secret Garden of Unicorn	R. Sanderson	90-day	29.90	29.90
93-21-003	Joyful Meadow of Unicorn	R. Sanderson	90-day	29.90	29.90
93-21-004	Misty Hills of Unicorn	R. Sanderson	90-day	29.90	29.90
93-21-005	Tropical Paradise of Unicorn	R. Sanderson	90-day	29.90	29.90
93-21-006	Springtime Pasture of Unicorn	R. Sanderson	90-day	29.90	29.90
Lenox Collections		**Birds of the Garden**			
92-22-001	Spring Glory, Cardinals	W. Mumm	Open	39.50	39.50
93-22-002	Sunbright Songbirds, Goldfinch	W. Mumm	Open	39.50	39.50
93-22-003	Bluebirds Haven, Bluebirds	W. Mumm	Open	39.50	39.50
93-22-004	Blossoming Bough, Chickadees	W. Mumm	Open	39.50	39.50
93-22-005	Jewels of the Garden, Hummingbirds	W. Mumm	Open	39.50	39.50
93-22-006	Indigo Meadow, Indigo Buntings	W. Mumm	Open	39.50	39.50
93-22-007	Scarlet Tanagers	W. Mumm	Open	39.50	39.50
Lenox Collections		**King of the Plains**			
94-23-001	Tsava Elephant	S. Combes	Open	39.90	39.90
94-23-002	Guardian	S. Combes	Open	39.90	39.90
94-23-003	Rainbow Trail	S. Combes	Open	39.90	39.90
94-23-004	African Ancients	S. Combes	Open	39.90	39.90
94-23-005	Protecting the Flanks	S. Combes	Open	39.90	39.90
94-23-006	The Last Elephant	S. Combes	Open	39.90	39.90
94-23-007	End of the Line	S. Combes	Open	39.90	39.90
94-23-008	Sparring Bulls	S. Combes	Open	39.90	39.90
Lightpost Publishing		**Thomas Kinkade Signature Collection**			
91-01-001	Chandler's Cottage	T. Kinkade	2,500	49.95	49.95
91-01-002	Cedar Nook	T. Kinkade	2,500	49.95	49.95
91-01-003	Sleigh Ride Home	T. Kinkade	2,500	49.95	49.95
91-01-004	Home To Grandma's	T. Kinkade	2,500	49.95	49.95
Lilliput Lane, Ltd.		**American Landmarks Collection**			
90-01-001	Country Church	R. Day	5,000	35.00	35.00
90-01-002	Riverside Chapel	R. Day	5,000	35.00	35.00
90-01-003	Mail Barn	R. Day	5,000	35.00	125.00
Lladro		**Lladro Plate Collection**			
93-01-001	The Great Voyage L5964G	Lladro	Open	50.00	50.00
93-01-002	Looking Out L5998G	Lladro	Open	38.00	38.00
93-01-003	Swinging L5999G	Lladro	Open	38.00	38.00
93-01-004	Duck Plate L6000G	Lladro	Open	38.00	38.00
94-01-005	Friends L6158	Lladro	Open	32.00	32.00
94-01-006	Apple Picking L6159M	Lladro	Open	32.00	32.00
94-01-007	Turtledove L6160	Lladro	Open	32.00	32.00
94-01-008	Flamingo L6161M	Lladro	Open	32.00	32.00
94-01-009	Resting L6162M	Lladro	Open	32.00	32.00
March of Dimes		**Our Children, Our Future**			
89-01-001	A Time for Peace	D. Zolan	150-day	29.00	30.00
89-01-002	A Time To Love	S. Kuck	150-day	29.00	50.00
89-01-003	A Time To Plant	J. McClelland	150-day	29.00	30.00
89-01-004	A Time To Be Born	G. Perillo	150-day	29.00	30.00
90-01-005	A Time To Embrace	E. Hibel	150-day	29.00	30.00
90-01-006	A Time To Laugh	A. Williams	150-day	29.00	30.00
Marigold		**Sport**			
89-01-001	Mickey Mantle h/s	Carreno	Retrd.	100.00	650.00
89-01-002	Mickey Mantle u/s	Carreno	Retrd.	60.00	100.00
89-01-003	Joe DiMaggio h/s	Carreno	Retrd.	100.00	1400.00
89-01-004	Joe DiMaggio f/s (blue sig.)	Carreno	Retrd.	60.00	125.00
90-01-005	Joe DiMaggio AP h/s	Carreno	Retrd.	N/A	2250.00
Maruri USA		**Eagle Plate Series**			
84-01-001	Free Flight	W. Gaither	Closed	150.00	150-198.
Museum Collections, Inc.		**American Family I**			
79-01-001	Baby's First Step	N. Rockwell	9,900	28.50	48.00
79-01-002	Happy Birthday Dear Mother	N. Rockwell	9,900	28.50	45.00
79-01-003	Sweet Sixteen	N. Rockwell	9,900	28.50	35.00
79-01-004	First Haircut	N. Rockwell	9,900	28.50	60.00
79-01-005	First Prom	N. Rockwell	9,900	28.50	35.00
79-01-006	Wrapping Christmas Presents	N. Rockwell	9,900	28.50	35.00
79-01-007	The Student	N. Rockwell	9,900	28.50	35.00
79-01-008	Birthday Party	N. Rockwell	9,900	28.50	35.00
79-01-009	Little Mother	N. Rockwell	9,900	28.50	35.00
79-01-010	Washing Our Dog	N. Rockwell	9,900	28.50	35.00
79-01-011	Mother's Little Helpers	N. Rockwell	9,900	28.50	35.00
79-01-012	Bride and Groom	N. Rockwell	9,900	28.50	35.00
Museum Collections, Inc.		**American Family II**			
80-02-001	New Arrival	N. Rockwell	22,500	35.00	55.00
80-02-002	Sweet Dreams	N. Rockwell	22,500	35.00	37.50
80-02-003	Little Shaver	N. Rockwell	22,500	35.00	40.00
80-02-004	We Missed You Daddy	N. Rockwell	22,500	35.00	37.50
80-02-005	Home Run Slugger	N. Rockwell	22,500	35.00	37.50
80-02-006	Giving Thanks	N. Rockwell	22,500	35.00	37.50
80-02-007	Space Pioneers	N. Rockwell	22,500	35.00	37.50
80-02-008	Little Salesman	N. Rockwell	22,500	35.00	37.50
80-02-009	Almost Grown up	N. Rockwell	22,500	35.00	37.50
80-02-010	Courageous Hero	N. Rockwell	22,500	35.00	37.50
81-02-011	At the Circus	N. Rockwell	22,500	35.00	37.50
81-02-012	Good Food, Good Friends	N. Rockwell	22,500	35.00	37.50
Museum Collections, Inc.		**Christmas**			
79-03-001	Day After Christmas	N. Rockwell	Yr.Iss	75.00	75.00
80-03-002	Checking His List	N. Rockwell	Yr.Iss	75.00	75.00
81-03-003	Ringing in Good Cheer	N. Rockwell	Yr.Iss	75.00	75.00
82-03-004	Waiting for Santa	N. Rockwell	Yr.Iss	75.00	75.00
83-03-005	High Hopes	N. Rockwell	Yr.Iss	75.00	75.00
84-03-006	Space Age Santa	N. Rockwell	Yr.Iss	55.00	55.00
Pemberton & Oakes		**Zolan's Children**			
78-01-001	Erik and Dandelion	D. Zolan	Retrd.	19.00	240-267.
79-01-002	Sabina in the Grass	D. Zolan	Retrd.	22.00	180-250.
80-01-003	By Myself	D. Zolan	Retrd.	24.00	30-59.00
81-01-004	For You	D. Zolan	Retrd.	24.00	23-37.00

	ARTIST	EDITION	ISSUE	QUOTE
Pemberton & Oakes	**Wonder of Childhood**			
82-02-001 Touching the Sky	D. Zolan	Retrd.	19.00	25-39.00
83-02-002 Spring Innocence	D. Zolan	Retrd.	19.00	26-45.00
84-02-003 Winter Angel	D. Zolan	Retrd.	22.00	38-60.00
85-02-004 Small Wonder	D. Zolan	Retrd.	22.00	32-45.00
86-02-005 Grandma's Garden	D. Zolan	Retrd.	22.00	38-48.00
87-02-006 Day Dreamer	D. Zolan	Retrd.	22.00	36-50.00
Pemberton & Oakes	**Children and Pets**			
84-03-001 Tender Moment	D. Zolan	Retrd.	19.00	40-63.00
84-03-002 Golden Moment	D. Zolan	Retrd.	19.00	25-45.00
85-03-003 Making Friends	D. Zolan	Retrd.	19.00	30-45.00
85-03-004 Tender Beginning	D. Zolan	Retrd.	19.00	35-45.00
86-03-005 Backyard Discovery	D. Zolan	Retrd.	19.00	30-40.00
86-03-006 Waiting to Play	D. Zolan	Retrd.	19.00	35-45.00
Pemberton & Oakes	**Children at Christmas**			
81-04-001 A Gift for Laurie	D. Zolan	Retrd.	48.00	70-95.00
82-04-002 Christmas Prayer	D. Zolan	Retrd.	48.00	75-90.00
83-04-003 Erik's Delight	D. Zolan	Retrd.	48.00	56-66.00
84-04-004 Christmas Secret	D. Zolan	Retrd.	48.00	50-66.00
85-04-005 Christmas Kitten	D. Zolan	Retrd.	48.00	62-75.00
86-04-006 Laurie and the Creche	D. Zolan	Retrd.	48.00	75-78.00
Pemberton & Oakes	**Special Moments of Childhood Collection**			
88-05-001 Brotherly Love	D. Zolan	Retrd.	19.00	60-75.00
88-05-002 Sunny Surprise	D. Zolan	Retrd.	19.00	35-51.00
89-05-003 Summer's Child	D. Zolan	Retrd.	22.00	38-50.00
90-05-004 Meadow Magic	D. Zolan	Retrd.	22.00	29-36.00
90-05-005 Cone For Two	D. Zolan	Retrd.	24.60	25-30.00
90-05-006 Rodeo Girl	D. Zolan	Retrd.	24.60	25-31.00
Pemberton & Oakes	**Childhood Friendship Collection**			
86-06-001 Beach Break	D. Zolan	Retrd.	19.00	55.00
87-06-002 Little Engineers	D. Zolan	Retrd.	19.00	62-66.00
88-06-003 Tiny Treasures	D. Zolan	Retrd.	19.00	48-52.00
88-06-004 Sharing Secrets	D. Zolan	Retrd.	19.00	43-60.00
88-06-005 Dozens of Daisies	D. Zolan	Retrd.	19.00	34-40.00
90-06-006 Country Walk	D. Zolan	Retrd.	19.00	31-36.00
Pemberton & Oakes	**Tenth Anniversary**			
88-07-001 Ribbons and Roses	D. Zolan	Retrd.	24.40	42-54.00
Pemberton & Oakes	**Father's Day**			
86-08-001 Daddy's Home	D. Zolan	Retrd.	19.00	105-120.
Pemberton & Oakes	**Mother's Day**			
88-09-001 Mother's Angels	D. Zolan	Retrd.	19.00	58-75.00
Pemberton & Oakes	**Grandparent's Day**			
90-10-001 It's Grandma & Grandpa	D. Zolan	Retrd.	24.40	37.00
93-10-002 Grandpa's Fence	D. Zolan	Retrd.	24.40	31-45.00
Pemberton & Oakes	**Adventures of Childhood Collection**			
89-11-001 Almost Home	D. Zolan	Retrd.	19.60	56-60.00
89-11-002 Crystal's Creek	D. Zolan	Retrd.	19.60	45-50.00
89-11-003 Summer Suds	D. Zolan	Retrd.	22.00	27-35.00
90-11-004 Snowy Adventure	D. Zolan	Retrd.	22.00	24-40.00
91-11-005 Forests & Fairy Tales	D. Zolan	Retrd.	24.40	25-33.00
Pemberton & Oakes	**Thanksgiving**			
81-12-001 I'm Thankful Too	D. Zolan	Retrd.	19.00	70-100.
Pemberton & Oakes	**Nutcracker II**			
81-13-001 Grand Finale	S. Fisher	Retrd.	24.40	36.00
82-13-002 Arabian Dancers	S. Fisher	Retrd.	24.40	67.50
83-13-003 Dew Drop Fairy	S. Fisher	Retrd.	24.40	40-70.00
84-13-004 Clara's Delight	S. Fisher	Retrd.	24.40	45.00
85-13-005 Bedtime for Nutcracker	S. Fisher	Retrd.	24.40	45.00
86-13-006 The Crowning of Clara	S. Fisher	Retrd.	24.40	36.00
87-13-007 Dance of the Snowflakes	D. Zolan	Retrd.	24.40	50-68.00
88-13-008 The Royal Welcome	R. Anderson	Retrd.	24.40	47.00
89-13-009 The Spanish Dancer	M. Vickers	Retrd.	24.40	24.40
Pemberton & Oakes	**March of Dimes: Our Children, Our Future**			
89-14-001 A Time for Peace	D. Zolan	Retrd.	29.00	50.00
Pemberton & Oakes	**Christmas**			
91-15-001 Candlelight Magic	D. Zolan	Retrd.	24.80	30-80.00
Pemberton & Oakes	**Companion to Brotherly Love**			
89-16-001 Sisterly Love	D. Zolan	Retrd.	22.00	42-47.00
Pemberton & Oakes	**Single Issue Day to Day Spode**			
91-17-001 Daisy Days	D. Zolan	Retrd.	48.00	48.00
Pemberton & Oakes	**Plaques-Single Issues**			
91-18-001 Flowers for Mother	D. Zolan	Retrd.	16.80	21-45.00
Pemberton & Oakes	**Heirloom Ovals**			
92-19-001 My Kitty	D. Zolan	Retrd.	18.80	40.00
Pemberton & Oakes	**Single Issue**			
93-20-001 Winter Friends	D. Zolan	Retrd.	18.80	30-45.00
Pemberton & Oakes	**The Best of Zolan in Miniature**			
85-21-001 Sabina	D. Zolan	Retrd.	12.50	114.00
86-21-002 Erik and Dandelion	D. Zolan	Retrd.	12.50	120.00
86-21-003 Tender Moment	D. Zolan	Retrd.	12.50	86.00
86-21-004 Touching the Sky	D. Zolan	Retrd.	12.50	80.00
87-21-005 A Gift for Laurie	D. Zolan	Retrd.	12.50	80.00
87-21-006 Small Wonder	D. Zolan	Retrd.	12.50	77.00
Pemberton & Oakes	**Childhood Discoveries (Miniature)**			
90-22-001 Colors of Spring	D. Zolan	Retrd.	14.40	41-49.00
90-22-002 Autumn Leaves	D. Zolan	Retrd.	14.40	35-45.00
91-22-003 Enchanted Forest	D. Zolan	Retrd.	16.60	35-45.00
91-22-004 Just Ducky	D. Zolan	Retrd.	16.60	34-37.00
91-22-005 Rainy Day Pals	D. Zolan	Retrd.	16.60	35.00
92-22-006 Double Trouble	D. Zolan	Retrd.	16.60	28-45.00
90-23-001 First Kiss	D. Zolan	Retrd.	14.40	60.00
93-23-002 Peppermint Kiss	D. Zolan	Retrd.	16.60	24-36.00
95-23-003 Tender Hearts	D. Zolan	19-day	16.60	16.60
Pemberton & Oakes	**Easter (Miniature)**			
91-24-001 Easter Morning	D. Zolan	Retrd.	16.60	30-37.00
Pemberton & Oakes	**Mother's Day (Miniature)**			
90-25-001 Flowers for Mother	D. Zolan	Retrd.	14.40	45-50.00

	ARTIST	EDITION	ISSUE	QUOTE
92-25-002 Twilight Prayer	D. Zolan	Retrd.	16.60	30-38.00
93-25-003 Jessica's Field	D. Zolan	Retrd.	16.60	30-40.00
94-25-004 One Summer Day	D. Zolan	Retrd.	16.60	24-32.00
Pemberton & Oakes	**Moments To Remember (Miniature)**			
92-26-001 Just We Two	D. Zolan	Retrd.	16.60	27-48.00
92-26-002 Almost Home	D. Zolan	Retrd.	16.60	24-32.00
93-26-003 Tiny Treasures	D. Zolan	Retrd.	16.60	21-28.00
93-26-004 Forest Friends	D. Zolan	Retrd.	16.60	21-28.00
Pemberton & Oakes	**Single Issues (Miniature)**			
86-27-001 Backyard Discovery	D. Zolan	Retrd.	12.50	96.00
86-27-002 Daddy's Home	D. Zolan	Retrd.	12.50	815.00
89-27-003 Sunny Surprise	D. Zolan	Retrd.	12.50	65.00
89-27-004 My Pumpkin	D. Zolan	Retrd.	14.40	55-70.00
91-27-005 Backyard Buddies	D. Zolan	Retrd.	16.60	35-40.00
91-27-006 The Thinker	D. Zolan	Retrd.	16.60	36-39.00
93-27-007 Quiet Time	D. Zolan	Retrd.	16.60	25-60.00
94-27-008 Little Fisherman	D. Zolan	19-day	16.60	16.60
Pemberton & Oakes	**Plaques**			
91-28-001 New Shoes	D. Zolan	Retrd.	18.80	34-36.00
92-28-002 Grandma's Garden	D. Zolan	Retrd.	18.80	24-31.00
92-28-003 Small Wonder	D. Zolan	Retrd.	18.80	20-33.00
92-28-004 Easter Morning	D. Zolan	Retrd.	18.80	24-32.00
Pemberton & Oakes	**Membership (Miniature)**			
87-29-001 For You	D. Zolan	Retrd.	12.50	100.00
88-29-002 Making Friends	D. Zolan	Retrd.	12.50	75.00
89-29-003 Grandma's Garden	D. Zolan	Retrd.	12.50	65-71.00
90-29-004 A Christmas Prayer	D. Zolan	Retrd.	14.40	55.00
91-29-005 Golden Moment	D. Zolan	Retrd.	15.00	44.00
92-29-006 Brotherly Love	D. Zolan	Retrd.	15.00	53.00
93-29-007 New Shoes	D. Zolan	Retrd.	17.00	35.00
94-29-008 My Kitty	D. Zolan	19-day	Gift	32.00
Pemberton & Oakes	**Single Issue Bone China (Miniature)**			
92-30-001 Window of Dreams	D. Zolan	Retrd.	18.80	30-32.00
Pemberton & Oakes	**Times To Treasure Bone China (Miniature)**			
93-31-001 Little Traveler	D. Zolan	Retrd.	16.60	16.60-37.
93-31-002 Garden Swing	D. Zolan	Retrd.	16.60	16.60
94-31-003 Summer Garden	D. Zolan	19-day	16.60	16.60
94-31-004 September Girl	D. Zolan	19-day	16.60	16.60
Pemberton & Oakes	**Members Only Single Issue (Miniature)**			
90-32-001 By Myself	D. Zolan	Retrd.	14.40	61.00
93-32-002 Summer's Child	D. Zolan	Retrd.	16.60	33.00
94-32-003 Little Slugger	D. Zolan	10-day	16.60	16.60
Pemberton & Oakes	**Christmas (Miniature)**			
93-33-001 Snowy Adventure	D. Zolan	Retrd.	16.60	21-28.00
94-33-002 Candlelight Magic	D. Zolan	19-day	16.60	16.60
Pemberton & Oakes	**Thanksgiving (Miniature)**			
93-34-001 I'm Thankful Too	D. Zolan	Retrd.	16.60	21-29.00
Pemberton & Oakes	**Father's Day (Miniature)**			
94-35-001 Two of a Kind	D. Zolan	Retrd.	16.60	24-36.00
Pemberton & Oakes	**Yesterday's Children (Miniature)**			
94-36-001 Little Friends	D. Zolan	19-day	16.60	16.60
94-36-002 Seaside Treasures	D. Zolan	19-day	16.60	16.60
PenDelfin	**Plate Series**			
XX-01-001 Mother With Baby	J. Heap	Retrd.	40.00	200.00
XX-01-002 Father	J. Heap	7,500	40.00	40.00
XX-01-003 Whopper	D. Roberts	7,500	50.00	50.00
XX-01-004 Gingerbread Day	J. Heap	7,500	55.00	55.00
XX-01-005 Caravan	D. Roberts	7,500	60.00	60.00
XX-01-006 Old Schoolhouse	J. Heap	7,500	60.00	60.00
Pickard	**Mother's Love**			
80-01-001 Miracle	I. Spencer	7,500	95.00	95.00
81-01-002 Story Time	I. Spencer	7,500	110.00	110.00
82-01-003 First Edition	I. Spencer	7,500	115.00	115.00
83-01-004 Precious Moment	I. Spencer	7,500	120.00	145.00
Pickard	**Symphony of Roses**			
82-02-001 Wild Irish Rose	I. Spencer	10,000	85.00	95.00
83-02-002 Yellow Rose of Texas	I. Spencer	10,000	90.00	100-110.
84-02-003 Honeysuckle Rose	I. Spencer	10,000	95.00	135.00
85-02-004 Rose of Washington Square	I. Spencer	10,000	100.00	175.00
Princeton Gallery	**Circus Friends Collection**			
89-01-001 Don't Be Shy	R. Sanderson	Unkn.	29.50	29.50
90-01-002 Make Me A Clown	R. Sanderson	Unkn.	29.50	29.50
90-01-003 Looks Like Rain	R. Sanderson	Unkn.	29.50	29.50
90-01-004 Cheer Up Mr. Clown	R. Sanderson	Unkn.	29.50	29.50
Princeton Gallery	**Cubs Of The Big Cats**			
90-02-001 Cougar Cub	Q. Lemond	Unkn.	29.50	29.50
91-02-002 Lion Cub	Q. Lemond	90-day	29.50	29.50
91-02-003 Snow Leopard	Q. Lemond	90-day	29.50	29.50
91-02-004 Cheetah	Q. Lemond	90-day	29.50	29.50
91-02-005 Tiger	Q. Lemond	90-day	29.50	29.50
92-02-006 Lynx Cub	Q. Lemond	90-day	29.50	29.50
92-02-007 White Tiger Cub	Q. Lemond	90-day	29.50	29.50
Princeton Gallery	**Arctic Wolves**			
91-03-001 Song of the Wilderness	J. Van Zyle	90-day	29.50	29.50
92-03-002 In The Eye of the Moon	J. Van Zyle	90-day	29.50	29.50
Princeton Gallery	**Enchanted World of the Unicorn**			
91-04-001 Rainbow Valley	R. Sanderson	90-day	29.50	29.50
92-04-002 Golden Shore	R. Sanderson	90-day	29.50	29.50
Princeton Gallery	**Darling Dalmations**			
91-05-001 Dalmatian	L. Picken	90-day	29.50	29.50
92-05-002 Firehouse Frolic	L. Picken	90-day	29.50	29.50
Reco International	**Bohemian Annuals**			
74-01-001 1974	Unknown	Retrd.	130.00	155.00
75-01-002 1975	Unknown	Retrd.	140.00	160.00
76-01-003 1976	Unknown	Retrd.	150.00	160.00
Reco International	**Americana**			
72-02-001 Gaspee Incident	S. Devlin	Retrd.	200.00	325.00

	ARTIST	EDITION	ISSUE	QUOTE
Reco International	**Dresden Christmas**			
71-03-001 Shepherd Scene	Unknown	Retrd.	15.00	50.00
72-03-002 Niklas Church	Unknown	Retrd.	15.00	25.00
73-03-003 Schwanstein Church	Unknown	Retrd.	18.00	35.00
74-03-004 Village Scene	Unknown	Retrd.	20.00	30.00
75-03-005 Rothenburg Scene	Unknown	Retrd.	24.00	30.00
76-03-006 Village Church	Unknown	Retrd.	26.00	35.00
77-03-007 Old Mill (Issue Closed)	Unknown	Retrd.	28.00	30.00
Reco International	**Dresden Mother's Day**			
72-04-001 Doe and Fawn	Unknown	Retrd.	15.00	20.00
73-04-002 Mare and Colt	Unknown	Retrd.	16.00	25.00
74-04-003 Tiger and Cub	Unknown	Retrd.	20.00	23.00
75-04-004 Dachshunds	Unknown	Retrd.	24.00	28.00
76-04-005 Owl and Offspring	Unknown	Retrd.	26.00	30.00
77-04-006 Chamois (Issue Closed)	Unknown	Retrd.	28.00	30.00
Reco International	**Furstenberg Christmas**			
71-05-001 Rabbits	Unknown	Retrd.	15.00	30.00
72-05-002 Snowy Village	Unknown	Retrd.	15.00	20.00
73-05-003 Christmas Eve	Unknown	Retrd.	18.00	35.00
74-05-004 Sparrows	Unknown	Retrd.	20.00	30.00
75-05-005 Deer Family	Unknown	Retrd.	22.00	30.00
76-05-006 Winter Birds	Unknown	Retrd.	25.00	25.00
Reco International	**Furstenberg Deluxe Christmas**			
71-06-001 Wise Men	E. Grossberg	Retrd.	45.00	45.00
72-06-002 Holy Family	E. Grossberg	Retrd.	45.00	45.00
73-06-003 Christmas Eve	E. Grossberg	Retrd.	60.00	65.00
Reco International	**Furstenberg Easter**			
71-07-001 Sheep	Unknown	Retrd.	15.00	150.00
72-07-002 Chicks	Unknown	Retrd.	15.00	60.00
73-07-003 Bunnies	Unknown	Retrd.	16.00	80.00
74-07-004 Pussywillow	Unknown	Retrd.	20.00	32.50
75-07-005 Easter Window	Unknown	Retrd.	22.00	30.00
76-07-006 Flower Collecting	Unknown	Retrd.	25.00	25.00
Reco International	**Furstenberg Mother's Day**			
72-08-001 Hummingbirds, Fe	Unknown	Retrd.	15.00	45.00
73-08-002 Hedgehogs	Unknown	Retrd.	16.00	40.00
74-08-003 Doe and Fawn	Unknown	Retrd.	20.00	30.00
75-08-004 Swans	Unknown	Retrd.	22.00	23.00
76-08-005 Koala Bears	Unknown	Retrd.	25.00	30.00
Reco International	**Furstenberg Olympic**			
72-09-001 Munich	J. Poluszynski	Retrd.	20.00	75.00
76-09-002 Montreal	J. Poluszynski	Retrd.	37.50	37.50
Reco International	**Grafburg Christmas**			
75-10-001 Black-Capped Chickadee	Unknown	Retrd.	20.00	60.00
76-10-002 Squirrels	Unknown	Retrd.	22.00	22.00
Reco International	**King's Christmas**			
73-11-001 Adoration	Merli	Retrd.	100.00	265.00
74-11-002 Madonna	Merli	Retrd.	150.00	250.00
75-11-003 Heavenly Choir	Merli	Retrd.	160.00	235.00
76-11-004 Siblings	Merli	Retrd.	200.00	225.00
Reco International	**King's Flowers**			
73-12-001 Carnation	A. Falchi	Retrd.	85.00	130.00
74-12-002 Red Rose	A. Falchi	Retrd.	100.00	145.00
75-12-003 Yellow Dahlia	A. Falchi	Retrd.	110.00	162.00
76-12-004 Bluebells	A. Falchi	Retrd.	130.00	165.00
77-12-005 Anemones	A. Falchi	Retrd.	130.00	175.00
Reco International	**King's Mother's Day**			
73-13-001 Dancing Girl	Merli	Retrd.	100.00	225.00
74-13-002 Dancing Boy	Merli	Retrd.	115.00	250.00
75-13-003 Motherly Love	Merli	Retrd.	140.00	225.00
76-13-004 Maiden	Merli	Retrd.	180.00	200.00
Reco International	**Four Seasons**			
73-14-001 Spring	J. Poluszynski	Retrd.	50.00	75.00
73-14-002 Summer	J. Poluszynski	Retrd.	50.00	75.00
73-14-003 Fall	J. Poluszynski	Retrd.	50.00	75.00
73-14-004 Winter	J. Poluszynski	Retrd.	50.00	75.00
Reco International	**Marmot Father's Day**			
70-15-001 Stag	Unknown	Retrd.	12.00	100.00
71-15-002 Horse	Unknown	Retrd.	12.50	40.00
Reco International	**Marmot Christmas**			
70-16-001 Polar Bear, Fe	Unknown	Retrd.	13.00	60.00
71-16-002 Buffalo Bill	Unknown	Retrd.	16.00	55.00
72-16-003 Boy and Grandfather	Unknown	Retrd.	20.00	50.00
71-16-004 American Buffalo	Unknown	Retrd.	14.50	35.00
73-16-005 Snowman	Unknown	Retrd.	22.00	45.00
74-16-006 Dancing	Unknown	Retrd.	24.00	30.00
75-16-007 Quail	Unknown	Retrd.	30.00	40.00
76-16-008 Windmill	Unknown	Retrd.	40.00	40.00
Reco International	**Marmot Mother's Day**			
72-17-001 Seal	Unknown	Retrd.	16.00	60.00
73-17-002 Bear with Cub	Unknown	Retrd.	20.00	140.00
74-17-003 Penguins	Unknown	Retrd.	24.00	50.00
75-17-004 Raccoons	Unknown	Retrd.	30.00	45.00
76-17-005 Ducks	Unknown	Retrd.	40.00	40.00
Reco International	**Moser Christmas**			
70-18-001 Hradcany Castle	Unknown	Retrd.	75.00	170.00
71-18-002 Karlstein Castle	Unknown	Retrd.	75.00	80.00
72-18-003 Old Town Hall	Unknown	Retrd.	85.00	85.00
73-18-004 Karlovy Vary Castle	Unknown	Retrd.	90.00	100.00
Reco International	**Moser Mother's Day**			
71-19-001 Peacocks	Unknown	Retrd.	75.00	100.00
72-19-002 Butterflies	Unknown	Retrd.	85.00	90.00
73-19-003 Squirrels	Unknown	Retrd.	90.00	95.00
Reco International	**Royale**			
69-20-001 Apollo Moon Landing	Unknown	Retrd.	30.00	80.00
Reco International	**Royale Christmas**			
69-21-001 Christmas Fair	Unknown	Retrd.	12.00	125.00
70-21-002 Vigil Mass	Unknown	Retrd.	13.00	110.00
71-21-003 Christmas Night	Unknown	Retrd.	16.00	50.00
72-21-004 Elks	Unknown	Retrd.	16.00	45.00

	ARTIST	EDITION	ISSUE	QUOTE
73-21-005 Christmas Down	Unknown	Retrd.	20.00	37.50
74-21-006 Village Christmas	Unknown	Retrd.	22.00	60.00
75-21-007 Feeding Time	Unknown	Retrd.	26.00	35.00
76-21-008 Seaport Christmas	Unknown	Retrd.	27.50	30.00
77-21-009 Sledding	Unknown	Retrd.	30.00	30.00
Reco International	**Royal Mother's Day**			
70-22-001 Swan and Young	Unknown	Retrd.	12.00	80.00
71-22-002 Doe and Fawn	Unknown	Retrd.	13.00	55.00
72-22-003 Rabbits	Unknown	Retrd.	16.00	40.00
73-22-004 Owl Family	Unknown	Retrd.	18.00	40.00
74-22-005 Duck and Young	Unknown	Retrd.	22.00	40.00
75-22-006 Lynx and Cubs	Unknown	Retrd.	26.00	40.00
76-22-007 Woodcock and Young	Unknown	Retrd.	27.50	32.50
77-22-008 Koala Bear	Unknown	Retrd.	30.00	30.00
Reco International	**Royale Father's Day**			
70-23-001 Frigate Constitution	Unknown	Retrd.	13.00	80.00
71-23-002 Man Fishing	Unknown	Retrd.	13.00	35.00
72-23-003 Mountaineer	Unknown	Retrd.	16.00	55.00
73-23-004 Camping	Unknown	Retrd.	18.00	45.00
74-23-005 Eagle	Unknown	Retrd.	22.00	35.00
75-23-006 Regatta	Unknown	Retrd.	26.00	35.00
76-23-007 Hunting	Unknown	Retrd.	27.50	32.50
77-23-008 Fishing	Unknown	Retrd.	30.00	30.00
Reco International	**Royale Game Plates**			
72-24-001 Setters	J. Poluszynski	Retrd.	180.00	200.00
73-24-002 Fox	J. Poluszynski	Retrd.	200.00	250.00
74-24-003 Osprey	W. Schiener	Retrd.	250.00	250.00
75-24-004 California Quail	W. Schiener	Retrd.	265.00	265.00
Reco International	**Royale Germania Christmas Annual**			
70-25-001 Orchid	Unknown	Retrd.	200.00	650.00
71-25-002 Cyclamen	Unknown	Retrd.	200.00	325.00
72-25-003 Silver Thistle	Unknown	Retrd.	250.00	290.00
73-25-004 Tulips	Unknown	Retrd.	275.00	310.00
74-25-005 Sunflowers	Unknown	Retrd.	300.00	320.00
75-25-006 Snowdrops	Unknown	Retrd.	450.00	500.00
Reco International	**Royale Germania Crystal Mother's Day**			
71-26-001 Roses	Unknown	Retrd.	135.00	650.00
72-26-002 Elephant and Youngster	Unknown	Retrd.	180.00	250.00
73-26-003 Koala Bear and Cub	Unknown	Retrd.	200.00	225.00
74-26-004 Squirrels	Unknown	Retrd.	240.00	250.00
75-26-005 Swan and Young	Unknown	Retrd.	350.00	360.00
Reco International	**Western**			
74-27-001 Mountain Man	E. Berke	Retrd.	165.00	165.00
Reco International	**The World of Children**			
77-28-001 Rainy Day Fun	J. McClelland	10,000	50.00	32.00
78-28-002 When I Grow Up	J. McClelland	15,000	50.00	29.00
79-28-003 You're Invited	J. McClelland	15,000	50.00	30.00
80-28-004 Kittens for Sale	J. McClelland	15,000	50.00	17.00
Reco International	**Mother Goose**			
79-29-001 Mary, Mary	J. McClelland	Retrd.	22.50	99.00
80-29-002 Little Boy Blue	J. McClelland	Retrd.	22.50	30.00
81-29-003 Little Miss Muffet	J. McClelland	Yr.Iss.	24.50	25.00
82-29-004 Little Jack Horner	J. McClelland	Retrd.	24.50	25.00
83-29-005 Little Bo Peep	J. McClelland	Yr.Iss.	24.50	24.50
84-29-006 Diddle, Diddle Dumpling	J. McClelland	Yr.Iss.	24.50	24.50
85-29-007 Mary Had a Little Lamb	J. McClelland	Yr.Iss.	27.50	28.00
86-29-008 Jack and Jill	J. McClelland	Retrd.	27.50	30.00
Reco International	**The McClelland Children's Circus Collection**			
82-30-001 Tommy the Clown	J. McClelland	Retrd.	29.50	49.00
82-30-002 Katie, the Tightrope Walker	J. McClelland	Retrd.	29.50	49.00
83-30-003 Johnny the Strongman	J. McClelland	Retrd.	29.50	39.00
84-30-004 Maggie the Animal Trainer	J. McClelland	100-day	29.50	30.00
Reco International	**Becky's Day**			
85-31-001 Awakening	J. McClelland	90-day	24.50	29.00
85-31-002 Getting Dressed	J. McClelland	Retrd.	24.50	29.00
86-31-003 Breakfast	J. McClelland	Retrd.	27.50	35.00
86-31-004 Learning is Fun	J. McClelland	Retrd.	27.50	27.50
86-31-005 Muffin Making	J. McClelland	Retrd.	27.50	27.50
86-31-006 Tub Time	J. McClelland	Retrd.	27.50	35.00
86-31-007 Evening Prayer	J. McClelland	Retrd.	27.50	27.50
Reco International	**Treasured Songs of Childhood**			
87-32-001 Twinkle, Twinkle, Little Star	J. McClelland	Retrd.	29.50	30.00
88-32-002 A Tisket, A Tasket	J. McClelland	150-day	29.50	30.00
88-32-003 Baa, Baa, Black Sheep	J. McClelland	Retrd.	32.90	33.00
89-32-004 Round The Mulberry Bush	J. McClelland	150-day	32.90	33.00
89-32-005 Rain, Rain Go Away	J. McClelland	Retrd.	32.90	33.00
89-32-006 I'm A Little Teapot	J. McClelland	Retrd.	32.90	33.00
89-32-007 Pat-A-Cake	J. McClelland	150-day	34.90	35.00
90-32-008 Hush Little Baby	J. McClelland	150-day	34.90	35.00
Reco International	**The Wonder of Christmas**			
91-33-001 Santa's Secret	J. McClelland	48-day	29.50	29.50
92-33-002 My Favorite Ornament	J. McClelland	48-day	29.50	29.50
92-33-003 Waiting For Santa	J. McClelland	48-day	29.50	29.50
93-33-004 Candlelight Christmas	J. McClelland	48-day	29.50	29.50
Reco International	**The Premier Collection**			
91-34-001 Love	J. McClelland	7,500	75.00	75.00
Reco International	**Golf Collection**			
92-35-001 Par Excellence	J. McClelland	180-day	35.00	35.00
Reco International	**The Children's Garden**			
93-36-001 Garden Friends	J. McClelland	120-day	29.50	29.50
93-36-002 Tea for Three	J. McClelland	120-day	29.50	29.50
93-36-003 Puppy Love	J. McClelland	120-day	29.50	29.50
Reco International	**March of Dimes: Our Children, Our Future**			
89-37-001 A Time to Love (2nd in Series)	S. Kuck	Retrd.	29.00	45.00
89-37-002 A Time to Plant (3rd in Series)	J. McClelland	150-day	29.00	50.00
Reco International	**Games Children Play**			
79-38-001 Me First	S. Kuck	Retrd.	45.00	50.00
80-38-002 Forever Bubbles	S. Kuck	Retrd.	45.00	48.00
81-38-003 Skating Pals	S. Kuck	Retrd.	45.00	47.50
82-38-004 Join Me	S. Kuck	10,000	45.00	45.00

	ARTIST	EDITION	ISSUE	QUOTE
Reco International	**The Grandparent Collector's Plates**			
81-39-001 Grandma's Cookie Jar	S. Kuck	Yr.Iss.	37.50	37.50
81-39-002 Grandpa and the Dollhouse	S. Kuck	Yr.Iss.	37.50	37.50
Reco International	**Little Professionals**			
82-40-001 All is Well	S. Kuck	Retrd.	39.50	43-65.00
83-40-002 Tender Loving Care	S. Kuck	Retrd.	39.50	50-75.00
84-40-003 Lost and Found	S. Kuck	10,000	39.50	45.00
85-40-004 Reading, Writing and...	S. Kuck	Retrd.	39.50	45.00
Reco International	**Days Gone By**			
83-41-001 Sunday Best	S. Kuck	Retrd.	29.50	39.00
83-41-002 Amy's Magic Horse	S. Kuck	Retrd.	29.50	36.00
84-41-003 Little Anglers	S. Kuck	Retrd.	29.50	22-30.00
84-41-004 Afternoon Recital	S. Kuck	Retrd.	29.50	42-74.00
84-41-005 Little Tutor	S. Kuck	Retrd.	29.50	18-24.00
85-41-006 Easter at Grandma's	S. Kuck	Retrd.	29.50	24.00
85-41-007 Morning Song	S. Kuck	Retrd.	29.50	14.00
85-41-008 The Surrey Ride	S. Kuck	Retrd.	29.50	30-40.00
Reco International	**A Childhood Almanac**			
85-42-001 Fireside Dreams-January	S. Kuck	Retrd.	29.50	45-49.00
85-42-002 Be Mine-February	S. Kuck	Retrd.	29.50	45.00
86-42-003 Winds of March-March	S. Kuck	Retrd.	29.50	45-49.00
85-42-004 Easter Morning-April	S. Kuck	Retrd.	29.50	55.00
85-42-005 For Mom-May	S. Kuck	Retrd.	29.50	45.00
85-42-006 Just Dreaming-June	S. Kuck	Retrd.	29.50	55.00
85-42-007 Star Spangled Sky-July	S. Kuck	14-day	29.50	45.00
85-42-008 Summer Secrets-August	S. Kuck	Retrd.	29.50	49-55.00
85-42-009 School Days-September	S. Kuck	Retrd.	29.50	55-60.00
86-42-010 Indian Summer-October	S. Kuck	Retrd.	29.50	45.00
86-42-011 Giving Thanks-November	S. Kuck	14-day	29.50	45-49.00
85-42-012 Christmas Magic-December	S. Kuck	14-day	35.00	45-55.00
Reco International	**Mother's Day Collection**			
85-43-001 Once Upon a Time	S. Kuck	Retrd.	29.50	55-75.00
86-43-002 Times Remembered	S. Kuck	Yr.Iss.	29.50	50-75.00
87-43-003 A Cherished Time	S. Kuck	Yr.Iss.	29.50	55.00
88-43-004 A Time Together	S. Kuck	Yr.Iss.	29.50	59.00
Reco International	**A Children's Christmas Pageant**			
86-44-001 Silent Night	S. Kuck	Retrd.	32.50	35-55.00
87-44-002 Hark the Herald Angels Sing	S. Kuck	Retrd.	32.50	35.00
88-44-003 While Shepherds Watched...	S. Kuck	Retrd.	32.50	32.50
89-44-004 We Three Kings	S. Kuck	Yr.Iss.	32.50	32.50
Reco International	**Barefoot Children**			
87-45-001 Night-Time Story	S. Kuck	Retrd.	29.50	40.00
87-45-002 Golden Afternoon	S. Kuck	14-day	29.50	40.00
88-45-003 Little Sweethearts	S. Kuck	14-day	29.50	40.00
88-45-004 Carousel Magic	S. Kuck	14-day	29.50	49.00
88-45-005 Under the Apple Tree	S. Kuck	14-day	29.50	40.00
88-45-006 The Rehearsal	S. Kuck	14-day	29.50	45-55.00
88-45-007 Pretty as a Picture	S. Kuck	Retrd.	29.50	45.00
88-45-008 Grandma's Trunk	S. Kuck	Retrd.	29.50	45.00
Reco International	**Special Occasions by Reco**			
88-46-001 The Wedding	S. Kuck	Open	35.00	35.00
89-46-002 Wedding Day (6 1/2")	S. Kuck	Open	25.00	25.00
90-46-003 The Special Day	S. Kuck	Open	25.00	25.00
Reco International	**Victorian Mother's Day**			
89-47-001 Mother's Sunshine	S. Kuck	Retrd.	35.00	45-85.00
90-47-002 Reflection Of Love	S. Kuck	Retrd.	35.00	50-80.00
91-47-003 A Precious Time	S. Kuck	Retrd.	35.00	45-75.00
92-47-004 Loving Touch	S. Kuck	Retrd.	35.00	45-49.00
Reco International	**Plate Of The Month Collection**			
90-48-001 January	S. Kuck	28-day	25.00	25.00
90-48-002 February	S. Kuck	28-day	25.00	25.00
90-48-003 March	S. Kuck	28-day	25.00	25.00
90-48-004 April	S. Kuck	28-day	25.00	25.00
90-48-005 May	S. Kuck	28-day	25.00	25.00
90-48-006 June	S. Kuck	28-day	25.00	25.00
90-48-007 July	S. Kuck	28-day	25.00	25.00
90-48-008 August	S. Kuck	28-day	25.00	25.00
90-48-009 September	S. Kuck	28-day	25.00	25.00
90-48-010 October	S. Kuck	28-day	25.00	25.00
90-48-011 November	S. Kuck	28-day	25.00	25.00
90-48-012 December	S. Kuck	28-day	25.00	25.00
Reco International	**Premier Collection**			
91-49-001 Puppy	S. Kuck	Retrd.	95.00	125-150.
91-49-002 Kitten	S. Kuck	Retrd.	95.00	150-200.
92-49-003 La Belle	S. Kuck	7,500	95.00	95.00
92-49-004 Le Beau	S. Kuck	7,500	95.00	95.00
Reco International	**Hearts And Flowers**			
91-50-001 Patience	S. Kuck	120-day	29.50	50.00
91-50-002 Tea Party	S. Kuck	120-day	29.50	29.50
92-50-003 Cat's In The Cradle	S. Kuck	120-day	32.50	32.50
92-50-004 Carousel of Dreams	S. Kuck	120-day	32.50	32.50
92-50-005 Storybook Memories	S. Kuck	120-day	32.50	32.50
93-50-006 Delightful Bundle	S. Kuck	120-day	34.50	34.50
93-50-007 Easter Morning Visitor	S. Kuck	120-day	34.50	34.50
93-50-008 Me and My Pony	S. Kuck	120-day	34.50	34.50
Reco International	**Gift of Love Mother's Day Collection**			
93-51-001 Morning Glory	S. Kuck	Retrd.	65.00	65.00
94-51-002 Memories From The Heart	S. Kuck	Retrd.	65.00	65.00
Reco International	**Tidings Of Joy**			
92-52-001 Peace on Earth	S. Kuck	N/A	35.00	50.00
93-52-002 Rejoice	S. Kuck	N/A	35.00	45.00
94-52-003 Noel	S. Kuck	75-day	35.00	35.00
Reco International	**Little Angel Plate Collection**			
94-53-001 Angel of Charity	S. Kuck	95-day	29.50	29.50
94-53-002 Angel of Joy	S. Kuck	95-day	29.50	29.50
94-53-003 Angel of Grace	S. Kuck	95-day	29.50	29.50
94-53-004 Angel of Hope	S. Kuck	95-day	29.50	29.50
Reco International	**Sugar and Spice**			
93-54-001 Best Friends	S. Kuck	95-day	29.90	29.90
93-54-002 Sisters	S. Kuck	95-day	29.90	29.90
94-54-003 Little One	S. Kuck	95-day	32.90	32.90
94-54-004 Teddy Bear Tales	S. Kuck	95-day	32.90	32.90
94-54-005 Morning Prayers	S. Kuck	95-day	32.90	32.90
Reco International	**The Sophisticated Ladies Collection**			
85-55-001 Felicia	A. Fazio	21-day	29.50	32.50
85-55-002 Samantha	A. Fazio	21-day	29.50	32.50
85-55-003 Phoebe	A. Fazio	21-day	29.50	32.50
85-55-004 Cleo	A. Fazio	21-day	29.50	32.50
86-55-005 Cerissa	A. Fazio	21-day	29.50	32.50
86-55-006 Natasha	A. Fazio	21-day	29.50	32.50
86-55-007 Bianka	A. Fazio	21-day	29.50	32.50
86-55-008 Chelsea	A. Fazio	21-day	29.50	32.50
Reco International	**Gardens of Beauty**			
88-56-001 English Country Garden	D. Barlowe	14-day	29.50	29.50
88-56-002 Dutch Country Garden	D. Barlowe	14-day	29.50	29.50
88-56-003 New England Garden	D. Barlowe	14-day	29.50	29.50
88-56-004 Japanese Garden	D. Barlowe	14-day	29.50	29.50
89-56-005 Italian Garden	D. Barlowe	14-day	29.50	29.50
89-56-006 Hawaiian Garden	D. Barlowe	14-day	29.50	29.50
89-56-007 German Country Garden	D. Barlowe	14-day	29.50	29.50
89-56-008 Mexican Garden	D. Barlowe	14-day	29.50	29.50
Reco International	**Gardens of America**			
92-57-001 Colonial Splendor	D. Barlowe	48-day	29.50	29.50
Reco International	**Vanishing Animal Kingdoms**			
86-58-001 Rama the Tiger	S. Barlowe	21,500	35.00	35.00
86-58-002 Olepi the Buffalo	S. Barlowe	21,500	35.00	35.00
87-58-003 Coolibah the Koala	S. Barlowe	21,500	35.00	42.00
87-58-004 Ortwin the Deer	S. Barlowe	21,500	35.00	39.00
87-58-005 Yen-Poh the Panda	S. Barlowe	21,500	35.00	40.00
88-58-006 Mamakuu the Elephant	S. Barlowe	21,500	35.00	59.00
Reco International	**Town And Country Dogs**			
90-59-001 Fox Hunt	S. Barlowe	36-day	35.00	35.00
91-59-002 The Retrieval	S. Barlowe	36-day	35.00	35.00
91-59-003 Golden Fields (Golden Retriever)	S. Barlowe	36-day	35.00	35.00
93-59-004 Faithful Companions (Cocker Spaniel)	S. Barlowe	36-day	35.00	35.00
Reco International	**Our Cherished Seas**			
91-60-001 Whale Song	S. Barlowe	48-day	37.50	37.50
91-60-002 Lions of the Sea	S. Barlowe	48-day	37.50	37.50
91-60-003 Flight of the Dolphins	S. Barlowe	48-day	37.50	37.50
92-60-004 Palace of the Seals	S. Barlowe	48-day	37.50	37.50
92-60-005 Orca Ballet	S. Barlowe	48-day	37.50	37.50
93-60-006 Emperors of the Ice	S. Barlowe	48-day	37.50	37.50
93-60-007 Turtle Treasure	S. Barlowe	48-day	37.50	37.50
93-60-008 Splendor of the Sea	S. Barlowe	48-day	37.50	37.50
Reco International	**Great Stories from the Bible**			
87-61-001 Moses in the Bulrushes	G. Katz	14-day	29.50	35.00
87-61-002 King Saul & David	G. Katz	14-day	29.50	35.00
87-61-003 Moses and the Ten Commandments	G. Katz	14-day	29.50	38.00
87-61-004 Joseph's Coat of Many Colors	G. Katz	14-day	29.50	35.00
88-61-005 Rebekah at the Well	G. Katz	14-day	29.50	35.00
88-61-006 Daniel Reads the Writing on the Wall	G. Katz	14-day	29.50	35.00
88-61-007 The Story of Ruth	G. Katz	14-day	29.50	35.00
88-61-008 King Solomon	G. Katz	14-day	29.50	35.00
Reco International	**The Nutcracker Ballet**			
89-62-001 Christmas Eve Party	C. Micarelli	14-day	35.00	35.00
90-62-002 Clara And Her Prince	C. Micarelli	14-day	35.00	37.00
90-62-003 The Dream Begins	C. Micarelli	14-day	35.00	35.00
91-62-004 Dance of the Snow Fairies	C. Micarelli	14-day	35.00	35.00
92-62-005 The Land of Sweets	C. Micarelli	14-day	35.00	35.00
92-62-006 The Sugar Plum Fairy	C. Micarelli	14-day	35.00	35.00
Reco International	**Special Occasions-Wedding**			
91-63-001 From This Day Forward (9 1/2")	C. Micarelli	Open	35.00	35.00
91-63-002 From This Day Forward (6 1/2")	C. Micarelli	Open	25.00	25.00
91-63-003 To Have And To Hold (9 1/2")	C. Micarelli	Open	35.00	35.00
91-63-004 To Have And To Hold (6 1/2")	C. Micarelli	Open	25.00	25.00
Reco International	**The Glory Of Christ**			
92-64-001 The Ascension	C. Micarelli	48-day	29.50	29.50
93-64-002 Jesus Teaching	C. Micarelli	48-day	29.50	29.50
93-64-003 The Last Supper	C. Micarelli	48-day	29.50	29.50
93-64-004 The Nativity	C. Micarelli	48-day	29.50	29.50
93-64-005 The Baptism Of Christ	C. Micarelli	48-day	29.50	29.50
93-64-006 Jesus Heals The Sick	C. Micarelli	48-day	29.50	29.50
94-64-007 Jesus Walks On Water	C. Micarelli	48-day	29.50	29.50
94-64-008 Descent From The Cross	C. Micarelli	48-day	29.50	29.50
Reco International	**J. Bergsma Mother's Day Series**			
90-65-001 The Beauty Of Life	J. Bergsma	14-day	35.00	35.00
92-65-002 Life's Blessing	J. Bergsma	14-day	35.00	35.00
93-65-003 My Greatest Treasures	J. Bergsma	14-day	35.00	35.00
94-65-004 Forever In My Heart	J. Bergsma	14-day	35.00	35.00
Reco International	**Guardians Of The Kingdom**			
90-66-001 Rainbow To Ride On	J. Bergsma	Retrd.	35.00	37.00
90-66-002 Special Friends Are Few	J. Bergsma	17,500	35.00	35.00
90-66-003 Guardians Of The Innocent Children	J. Bergsma	17,500	35.00	38.00
90-66-004 The Miracle Of Love	J. Bergsma	17,500	35.00	37.00
91-66-005 The Magic Of Love	J. Bergsma	17,500	35.00	35.00
91-66-006 Only With The Heart	J. Bergsma	17,500	35.00	35.00
91-66-007 To Fly Without Wings	J. Bergsma	17,500	35.00	35.00
91-66-008 In Faith I Am Free	J. Bergsma	17,500	35.00	35.00
Reco International	**Castles & Dreams**			
92-67-001 The Birth of a Dream	J. Bergsma	48-day	29.50	29.50
92-67-002 Dreams Come True	J. Bergsma	48-day	29.50	29.50
93-67-003 Believe In Your Dreams	J. Bergsma	48-day	29.50	29.50
94-67-004 Follow Your Dreams	J. Bergsma	48-day	29.50	29.50
Reco International	**The Christmas Series**			
90-68-001 Down The Glistening Lane	J. Bergsma	14-day	35.00	39.00
91-68-002 A Child Is Born	J. Bergsma	14-day	35.00	35.00
92-68-003 Christmas Day	J. Bergsma	14-day	35.00	35.00
93-68-004 I Wish You An Angel	J. Bergsma	14-day	35.00	35.00
Reco International	**Magic Companions**			
94-69-001 Believe in Love	J. Bergsma	48-day	29.50	29.50
94-69-002 Imagine Peace	J. Bergsma	48-day	29.50	29.50

		ARTIST	EDITION	ISSUE	QUOTE
Reco International		**Christmas Wishes**			
94-70-001	I Wish You Love	J. Bergsma	75-day	29.50	29.50
Reco International		**Totems of the West**			
94-71-001	The Watchmen	J. Bergsma	96-day	29.50	29.50
Reco International		**God's Own Country**			
90-72-001	Daybreak	I. Drechsler	14-day	30.00	30.00
90-72-002	Coming Home	I. Drechsler	14-day	30.00	30.00
90-72-003	Peaceful Gathering	I. Drechsler	14-day	30.00	30.00
90-72-004	Quiet Waters	I. Drechsler	14-day	30.00	30.00
Reco International		**The Flower Fairies Year Collection**			
90-73-001	The Red Clover Fairy	C.M. Barker	14-day	29.50	29.50
90-73-002	The Wild Cherry Blossom Fairy	C.M. Barker	14-day	29.50	29.50
90-73-003	The Pine Tree Fairy	C.M. Barker	14-day	29.50	29.50
90-73-004	The Rose Hip Fairy	C.M. Barker	14-day	29.50	29.50
Reco International		**Oscar & Bertie's Edwardian Holiday**			
91-74-001	Snapshot	P.D. Jackson	48-day	29.50	29.50
92-74-002	Early Rise	P.D. Jackson	48-day	29.50	29.50
92-74-003	All Aboard	P.D. Jackson	48-day	29.50	29.50
92-74-004	Learning To Swim	P.D. Jackson	48-day	29.50	29.50
Reco International		**In The Eye of The Storm**			
91-75-001	First Strike	W. Lowe	120-day	29.50	29.50
92-75-002	Night Force	W. Lowe	120-day	29.50	29.50
92-75-003	Tracks Across The Sand	W. Lowe	120-day	29.50	29.50
92-75-004	The Storm Has Landed	W. Lowe	120-day	29.50	29.50
Reco International		**Celebration of Love**			
92-76-001	Happy Anniversary (9 1/4")	J. Hall	Open	35.00	35.00
92-76-002	10th (9 1/4")	J. Hall	Open	35.00	35.00
92-76-003	25th (9 1/4")	J. Hall	Open	35.00	35.00
92-76-004	50th (9 1/4")	J. Hall	Open	35.00	35.00
92-76-005	Happy Anniversary (6 1/2")	J. Hall	Open	25.00	35.00
92-76-006	10th (6 1/2")	J. Hall	Open	25.00	35.00
92-76-007	25th (6 1/2")	J. Hall	Open	25.00	35.00
92-76-008	50th (6 1/2")	J. Hall	Open	25.00	35.00
Reco International		**The Heart of the Family**			
92-77-001	Sharing Secrets	J. York	48-day	29.50	29.50
93-77-002	Spinning Dreams	J. York	48-day	29.50	29.50
Reco International		**The Enchanted Norfin Trolls**			
93-78-001	Troll Maiden	C. Hopkins	75-day	19.50	19.50
93-78-002	The Wizard Troll	C. Hopkins	75-day	19.50	19.50
93-78-003	The Troll and His Dragon	C. Hopkins	75-day	19.50	19.50
94-78-004	Troll in Shinning Armor	C. Hopkins	75-day	19.50	19.50
94-78-005	Minstrel Troll	C. Hopkins	75-day	19.50	19.50
94-78-006	If Trolls Could Fly	C. Hopkins	75-day	19.50	19.50
94-78-007	Chef le Troll	C. Hopkins	75-day	19.50	19.50
94-78-008	Queen of Trolls	C. Hopkins	75-day	19.50	19.50
Reco International		**Noble and Free**			
94-79-001	Gathering Storm	Kelly	95-day	29.50	29.50
94-79-002	Protected Journey	Kelly	95-day	29.50	29.50
94-79-003	Moonlight Run	Kelly	95-day	29.50	29.50
Reco International		**Memories Of Yesterday**			
93-80-001	Hush	M. Attwell	Open	29.50	29.50
93-80-002	Time For Bed	M. Attwell	Open	29.50	29.50
93-80-003	I'se Been Painting	M. Attwell	Open	29.50	29.50
93-80-004	Just Looking Pretty	M. Attwell	Open	29.50	29.50
94-80-005	Give it Your Best Shot	M. Attwell	Open	29.50	29.50
94-80-006	I Pray The Lord My Soul to Keep	M. Attwell	Open	29.50	29.50
94-80-007	Just Thinking About You	M. Attwell	Open	29.50	29.50
94-80-008	What Will I Grow Up To Be	M. Attwell	Open	29.50	29.50
Reco International		**Trains of the Orient**			
93-81-001	The Golden Arrow-England	R. Johnson	N/A	29.50	29.50
94-81-002	Austria	R. Johnson	N/A	29.50	29.50
94-81-003	Bavaria	R. Johnson	N/A	29.50	29.50
94-81-004	Rumania	R. Johnson	N/A	29.50	29.50
94-81-005	Greece	R. Johnson	N/A	29.50	29.50
94-81-006	Frankonia	R. Johnson	N/A	29.50	29.50
94-81-007	Turkey	R. Johnson	N/A	29.50	29.50
94-81-008	France	R. Johnson	N/A	29.50	29.50
Reco International		**Kittens 'N Hats**			
94-82-001	Opening Night	S. Somerville	48-day	29.50	29.50
94-82-002	Sitting Pretty	S. Somerville	48-day	29.50	29.50
Reco International		**Birds of the Hidden Forest**			
94-83-001	Macaw Waterfall	G. Ratnavira	96-day	29.50	29.50
94-83-002	Paradise Valley	G. Ratnavira	96-day	29.50	29.50
Reco International		**Haven of the Hunters**			
94-84-001	Eagle's Castle	H. Roe	96-day	29.50	29.50
94-84-002	Sanctuary of the Hawk	H. Roe	96-day	29.50	29.50
Reco International		**Women of the Plains**			
94-85-001	Pride of a Maiden	C. Corcilius	36-day	29.50	29.50
Reco International		**Amish Traditions**			
94-86-001	Golden Harvest	B. Farnsworth	95-day	29.50	29.50
94-86-002	Family Outing	B. Farnsworth	95-day	29.50	29.50
94-86-003	The Quilting Bee	B. Farnsworth	95-day	29.50	29.50
River Shore		**Famous Americans**			
76-01-001	Brown's Lincoln	Rockwell-Brown	9,500	40.00	40.00
77-01-002	Rockwell's Triple Self-Portrait	Rockwell-Brown	9,500	45.00	45.00
78-01-003	Peace Corps	Rockwell-Brown	9,500	45.00	45.00
79-01-004	Spirit of Lindbergh	Rockwell-Brown	9,500	50.00	50.00
River Shore		**Norman Rockwell Single Issue**			
79-02-001	Spring Flowers	N. Rockwell	17,000	75.00	145.00
80-02-002	Looking Out to Sea	N. Rockwell	17,000	75.00	195.00
82-02-003	Grandpa's Guardian	N. Rockwell	17,000	80.00	80.00
82-02-004	Grandpa's Treasures	N. Rockwell	17,000	80.00	80.00
River Shore		**Baby Animals**			
79-03-001	Akiku	R. Brown	20,000	50.00	80.00
80-03-002	Roosevelt	R. Brown	20,000	50.00	90.00
81-03-003	Clover	R. Brown	20,000	50.00	65.00
82-03-004	Zuela	R. Brown	20,000	50.00	65.00
River Shore		**Rockwell Four Freedoms**			
81-04-001	Freedom of Speech	N. Rockwell	17,000	65.00	80-99.00

		ARTIST	EDITION	ISSUE	QUOTE
82-04-002	Freedom of Worship	N. Rockwell	17,000	65.00	80.00
82-04-003	Freedom from Fear	N. Rockwell	17,000	65.00	65.00
82-04-004	Freedom from Want	N. Rockwell	17,000	65.00	65.00
River Shore		**Puppy Playtime**			
87-05-001	Double Take	J. Lamb	14-day	24.50	32-35.00
88-05-002	Catch of the Day	J. Lamb	14-day	24.50	24.50
88-05-003	Cabin Fever	J. Lamb	14-day	24.50	24.50
88-05-004	Weekend Gardener	J. Lamb	14-day	24.50	24.50
88-05-005	Getting Acquainted	J. Lamb	14-day	24.50	24.50
88-05-006	Hanging Out	J. Lamb	14-day	24.50	24.50
88-05-007	A New Leash On Life	J. Lamb	14-day	24.50	29.50
87-05-008	Fun and Games	J. Lamb	14-day	24.50	29.50
River Shore		**Little House on the Prairie**			
85-06-001	Founder's Day Picnic	E. Christopherson	10-day	29.50	50.00
85-06-002	Women's Harvest	E. Christopherson	10-day	29.50	45.00
85-06-003	Medicine Show	E. Christopherson	10-day	29.50	45.00
85-06-004	Caroline's Eggs	E. Christopherson	10-day	29.50	45.00
85-06-005	Mary's Gift	E. Christopherson	10-day	29.50	45.00
85-06-006	A Bell for Walnut Grove	E. Christopherson	10-day	29.50	45.00
85-06-007	Ingall's Family	E. Christopherson	10-day	29.50	45.00
85-06-008	The Sweetheart Tree	E. Christopherson	10-day	29.50	45.00
Norman Rockwell Gallery		**Rockwell's Christmas Legacy**			
92-01-001	Santa's Workshop	Rockwell Inspired	Closed	49.90	49.90
93-01-002	Making a List	Rockwell Inspired	Closed	49.90	49.90
93-01-003	While Santa Slumbers	Rockwell Inspired	Closed	54.90	54.90
93-01-004	Visions of Santa	Rockwell Inspired	Closed	54.90	54.90
Norman Rockwell Gallery		**Norman Rockwell Centennial**			
93-02-001	The Toymaker	Rockwell Inspired	Closed	39.90	39.90
93-02-002	The Cobbler	Rockwell Inspired	Closed	39.90	39.90
Rockwell Society		**Christmas**			
74-01-001	Scotty Gets His Tree	N. Rockwell	Yr.Iss.	24.50	100.00
75-01-002	Angel with Black Eye	N. Rockwell	Yr.Iss.	24.50	35-75.00
76-01-003	Golden Christmas	N. Rockwell	Yr.Iss.	24.50	35-49.00
77-01-004	Toy Shop Window	N. Rockwell	Yr.Iss.	24.50	25.00
78-01-005	Christmas Dream	N. Rockwell	Yr.Iss.	24.50	25.00
79-01-006	Somebody's Up There	N. Rockwell	Yr.Iss.	24.50	25.00
80-01-007	Scotty Plays Santa	N. Rockwell	Yr.Iss.	24.50	24.50
81-01-008	Wrapped Up in Christmas	N. Rockwell	Yr.Iss.	25.50	26.50
82-01-009	Christmas Courtship	N. Rockwell	Yr.Iss.	25.50	25.50
83-01-010	Santa in the Subway	N. Rockwell	Yr.Iss.	25.50	26-35.00
84-01-011	Santa in the Workshop	N. Rockwell	Yr.Iss.	27.50	27.50
85-01-012	Grandpa Plays Santa	N. Rockwell	Yr.Iss.	27.90	28-35.00
86-01-013	Dear Santy Claus	N. Rockwell	Yr.Iss.	27.90	27.90
87-01-014	Santa's Golden Gift	N. Rockwell	Yr.Iss.	27.90	30.00
88-01-015	Santa Claus	N. Rockwell	Yr.Iss.	29.90	29.90
89-01-016	Jolly Old St. Nick	N. Rockwell	Yr.Iss.	29.90	29.90
90-01-017	A Christmas Prayer	N. Rockwell	Yr.Iss.	29.90	29.90
91-01-018	Santa's Helpers	N. Rockwell	Yr.Iss.	32.90	32.90
92-01-019	The Christmas Surprise	N. Rockwell	Yr.Iss.	32.90	34-40.00
93-01-020	The Tree Brigade	N. Rockwell	Yr.Iss.	32.90	53.00
Rockwell Society		**Mother's Day**			
76-02-001	A Mother's Love	N. Rockwell	Yr.Iss.	24.50	90.00
77-02-002	Faith	N. Rockwell	Yr.Iss.	24.50	47-50.00
78-02-003	Bedtime	N. Rockwell	Yr.Iss.	24.50	30-34.00
79-02-004	Reflections	N. Rockwell	Yr.Iss.	24.50	24.50
80-02-005	A Mother's Pride	N. Rockwell	Yr.Iss.	24.50	32.00
81-02-006	After the Party	N. Rockwell	Yr.Iss.	24.50	24.50
82-02-007	The Cooking Lesson	N. Rockwell	Yr.Iss.	24.50	30.00
83-02-008	Add Two Cups and Love	N. Rockwell	Yr.Iss.	25.50	26.00
84-02-009	Grandma's Courting Dress	N. Rockwell	Yr.Iss.	25.50	26.00
85-02-010	Mending Time	N. Rockwell	Yr.Iss.	27.50	28.00
86-02-011	Pantry Raid	N. Rockwell	Yr.Iss.	27.90	28.00
87-02-012	Grandma's Surprise	N. Rockwell	Yr.Iss.	29.90	30.00
88-02-013	My Mother	N. Rockwell	Yr.Iss.	29.90	29.90
89-02-014	Sunday Dinner	N. Rockwell	Yr.Iss.	29.90	30.00
90-02-015	Evening Prayers	N. Rockwell	Yr.Iss.	29.90	30.00
91-02-016	Building Our Future	N. Rockwell	Yr.Iss.	32.90	33.00
91-02-017	Gentle Reassurance	N. Rockwell	Yr.Iss.	32.90	34.00
92-02-018	A Special Delivery	N. Rockwell	Yr.Iss.	32.90	44-48.00
Rockwell Society		**Heritage**			
77-03-001	Toy Maker	N. Rockwell	Yr.Iss.	14.50	90-97.00
78-03-002	Cobbler	N. Rockwell	Yr.Iss.	19.50	46-54.00
79-03-003	Lighthouse Keeper's Daughter	N. Rockwell	Yr.Iss.	19.50	20-30.00
80-03-004	Ship Builder	N. Rockwell	Yr.Iss.	19.50	20.00
81-03-005	Music maker	N. Rockwell	Yr.Iss.	19.50	19.50
82-03-006	Tycoon	N. Rockwell	Yr.Iss.	19.50	19.50
83-03-007	Painter	N. Rockwell	Yr.Iss.	19.50	19.50
84-03-008	Storyteller	N. Rockwell	Yr.Iss.	19.50	19.50
85-03-009	Gourmet	N. Rockwell	Yr.Iss.	19.50	19.50
86-03-010	Professor	N. Rockwell	Yr.Iss.	22.90	22.90
87-03-011	Shadow Artist	N. Rockwell	Yr.Iss.	22.90	32.00
88-03-012	The Veteran	N. Rockwell	Yr.Iss.	22.90	23.00
88-03-013	The Banjo Player	N. Rockwell	Yr.Iss.	22.90	22-31.00
90-03-014	The Old Scout	N. Rockwell	Yr.Iss.	24.90	35.00
91-03-015	The Young Scholar	N. Rockwell	Yr.Iss.	24.90	33.00
91-03-016	The Family Doctor	N. Rockwell	Yr.Iss.	27.90	49.00
92-03-017	The Jeweler	N. Rockwell	Yr.Iss.	27.90	40.00
93-03-018	Halloween Frolic	N. Rockwell	Yr.Iss.	27.90	27.90
Rockwell Society		**Rockwell's Rediscovered Women**			
84-04-001	Dreaming in the Attic	N. Rockwell	100-day	19.50	20.00
84-04-002	Waiting on the Shore	N. Rockwell	100-day	22.50	23.00
84-04-003	Pondering on the Porch	N. Rockwell	100-day	22.50	23.00
84-04-004	Making Believe at the Mirror	N. Rockwell	100-day	22.50	23-30.00
84-04-005	Waiting at the Dance	N. Rockwell	100-day	22.50	23.00
84-04-006	Gossiping in the Alcove	N. Rockwell	100-day	22.50	23.00
84-04-007	Standing in the Doorway	N. Rockwell	100-day	22.50	20-35.00
84-04-008	Flirting in the Parlor	N. Rockwell	100-day	22.50	23-35.00
84-04-009	Working in the Kitchen	N. Rockwell	100-day	22.50	23.00
84-04-010	Meeting on the Path	N. Rockwell	100-day	22.50	23.00
84-04-011	Confiding in the Den	N. Rockwell	100-day	22.50	23.00
84-04-012	Reminiscing in the Quiet	N. Rockwell	100-day	22.50	22.50
XX-04-013	Complete Collection	N. Rockwell	100-day	267.00	267.00
Rockwell Society		**Rockwell on Tour**			
83-05-001	Walking Through Merrie Englande	N. Rockwell	150-day	16.00	16.00
83-05-002	Promenade a Paris	N. Rockwell	150-day	16.00	16.00

		ARTIST	EDITION	ISSUE	QUOTE
83-05-003	When in Rome	N. Rockwell	150-day	16.00	16.00
84-05-004	Die Walk am Rhein	N. Rockwell	150-day	16.00	16.00
Rockwell Society		**Rockwell's Light Compaign**			
83-06-001	This is the Room that Light Made	N. Rockwell	150-day	19.50	20.00
84-06-002	Grandpa's Treasure Chest	N. Rockwell	150-day	19.50	20.00
84-06-003	Father's Help	N. Rockwell	150-day	19.50	19.50
84-06-004	Evening's Ease	N. Rockwell	150-day	19.50	19.50
84-06-005	Close Harmony	N. Rockwell	150-day	21.50	21.50
84-06-006	The Birthday Wish	N. Rockwell	150-day	21.50	21.50
Rockwell Society		**Rockwell's American Dream**			
85-07-001	A Young Girl's Dream	N. Rockwell	150-day	19.90	20.00
85-07-002	A Couple's Commitment	N. Rockwell	150-day	19.90	25.00
85-07-003	A Family's Full Measure	N. Rockwell	150-day	22.90	22.90
86-07-004	A Mother's Welcome	N. Rockwell	150-day	22.90	23-28.00
86-07-005	A Young Man's Dream	N. Rockwell	150-day	22.90	39.00
86-07-006	The Musician's Magic	N. Rockwell	150-day	22.90	24.00
87-07-007	An Orphan's Hope	N. Rockwell	150-day	24.90	26.00
87-07-008	Love's Reward	N. Rockwell	150-day	24.90	41.00
Rockwell Society		**Colonials-The Rarest Rockwells**			
85-08-001	Unexpected Proposal	N. Rockwell	150-day	27.90	27.90
86-08-002	Words of Comfort	N. Rockwell	150-day	27.90	27.90
86-08-003	Light for the Winter	N. Rockwell	150-day	30.90	30.90
87-08-004	Portrait for a Bridegroom	N. Rockwell	150-day	30.90	30.90
87-08-005	The Journey Home	N. Rockwell	150-day	30.90	30.90
87-08-006	Clinching the Deal	N. Rockwell	150-day	30.90	30.90
88-08-007	Sign of the Times	N. Rockwell	150-day	32.90	32.90
88-08-008	Ye Glutton	N. Rockwell	150-day	32.90	32.90
Rockwell Society		**A Mind of Her Own**			
86-09-001	Sitting Pretty	N. Rockwell	150-day	24.90	22-25.00
87-09-002	Serious Business	N. Rockwell	150-day	24.90	25.00
87-09-003	Breaking the Rules	N. Rockwell	150-day	24.90	32.00
87-09-004	Good Intentions	N. Rockwell	150-day	27.90	28.00
88-09-005	Second Thoughts	N. Rockwell	150-day	27.90	27.90
88-09-006	World's Away	N. Rockwell	150-day	27.90	28.00
88-09-007	Kiss and Tell	N. Rockwell	150-day	29.90	29.90
88-09-008	On My Honor	N. Rockwell	150-day	29.90	30.00
Rockwell Society		**Rockwell's Golden Moments**			
87-10-001	Grandpa's Gift	N. Rockwell	150-day	19.90	25.00
87-10-002	Grandma's Love	N. Rockwell	150-day	19.90	30.00
88-10-003	End of day	N. Rockwell	150-day	22.90	23.00
88-10-004	Best Friends	N. Rockwell	150-day	22.90	23.00
89-10-005	Love Letters	N. Rockwell	150-day	22.90	23.00
89-10-006	Newfound Worlds	N. Rockwell	150-day	22.90	23.00
89-10-007	Keeping Company	N. Rockwell	150-day	24.90	24.90
89-10-008	Evening's Repose	N. Rockwell	150-day	24.90	24.90
Rockwell Society		**Rockwell's The Ones We Love**			
88-11-001	Tender Loving Care	N. Rockwell	150-day	19.90	38.00
89-11-002	A Time to Keep	N. Rockwell	150-day	19.90	25.00
89-11-003	The Inventor And The Judge	N. Rockwell	150-day	22.90	35.00
89-11-004	Ready For The World	N. Rockwell	150-day	22.90	22.90
89-11-005	Growing Strong	N. Rockwell	150-day	22.90	25.00
90-11-006	The Story Hour	N. Rockwell	150-day	22.90	25.00
90-11-007	The Country Doctor	N. Rockwell	150-day	24.90	24.90
90-11-008	Our Love of Country	N. Rockwell	150-day	24.90	24.90
90-11-009	The Homecoming	N. Rockwell	150-day	24.90	24.90
91-11-010	A Helping Hand	N. Rockwell	150-day	24.90	24.90
Rockwell Society		**Coming Of Age**			
90-12-001	Back To School	N. Rockwell	150-day	29.90	33.00
90-12-002	Home From Camp	N. Rockwell	150-day	29.90	29.90
90-12-003	Her First Formal	N. Rockwell	150-day	32.90	44.00
90-12-004	The Muscleman	N. Rockwell	150-day	32.90	33-44.00
90-12-005	A New Look	N. Rockwell	150-day	32.90	40.00
91-12-006	A Balcony Seat	N. Rockwell	150-day	32.90	32.90
91-12-007	Men About Town	N. Rockwell	150-day	34.90	35.00
91-12-008	Paths of Glory	N. Rockwell	150-day	34.90	35.00
91-12-009	Doorway to the Past	N. Rockwell	150-day	34.90	45-55.00
91-12-010	School's Out!	N. Rockwell	150-day	34.90	60-90.00
Rockwell Society		**Innocence and Experience**			
91-13-001	The Sea Captain	N. Rockwell	150-day	29.90	35.00
91-13-002	The Radio Operator	N. Rockwell	150-day	29.90	30-32.00
91-13-003	The Magician	N. Rockwell	150-day	32.90	32-38.00
92-13-004	The American Heroes	N. Rockwell	150-day	32.90	39-46.00
Rockwell Society		**Rockwell's Treasured Memories**			
91-14-001	Quiet Reflections	N. Rockwell	150-day	29.90	29.90
91-14-002	Romantic Reverie	N. Rockwell	150-day	29.90	29.90
91-14-003	Tender Romance	N. Rockwell	150-day	32.90	32.90
91-14-004	Evening Passage	N. Rockwell	150-day	32.90	32.90
91-14-005	Heavenly Dreams	N. Rockwell	150-day	32.90	34.00
91-14-006	Sentimental Shores	N. Rockwell	150-day	32.90	32.90
Roman, Inc.		**The Masterpiece Collection**			
79-01-001	Adoration	F. Lippe	5,000	65.00	65.00
80-01-002	Madonna with Grapes	P. Mignard	5,000	87.50	87.50
81-01-003	The Holy Family	G. Delle Notti	5,000	95.00	95.00
82-01-004	Madonna of the Streets	R. Ferruzzi	5,000	85.00	85.00
Roman, Inc.		**A Child's World**			
80-02-001	Little Children, Come to Me	F. Hook	15,000	45.00	49.00
Roman, Inc.		**A Child's Play**			
82-03-001	Breezy Day	F. Hook	30-day	29.95	39.00
82-03-002	Kite Flying	F. Hook	30-day	29.95	39.00
84-03-003	Bathtub Sailor	F. Hook	30-day	29.95	35.00
84-03-004	The First Snow	F. Hook	30-day	29.95	35.00
Roman, Inc.		**Frances Hook Collection-Set I**			
82-04-001	I Wish, I Wish	F. Hook	15,000	24.95	35-39.00
82-04-002	Baby Blossoms	F. Hook	15,000	24.95	35-39.00
82-04-003	Daisy Dreamer	F. Hook	15,000	24.95	35-39.00
82-04-004	Trees So Tall	F. Hook	15,000	24.95	35-39.00
Roman, Inc.		**Frances Hook Collection-Set II**			
83-05-001	Caught It Myself	F. Hook	15,000	24.95	25.00
83-05-002	Winter Wrappings	F. Hook	15,000	24.95	25.00
83-05-003	So Cuddly	F. Hook	15,000	24.95	25.00
83-05-004	Can I Keep Him?	F. Hook	15,000	24.95	25.00

		ARTIST	EDITION	ISSUE	QUOTE
Roman, Inc.		**Pretty Girls of the Ice Capades**			
83-06-001	Ice Princess	G. Petty	30-day	24.50	24.50
Roman, Inc.		**The Ice Capades Clown**			
83-07-001	Presenting Freddie Trenkler	G. Petty	30-day	24.50	24.50
Roman, Inc.		**Roman Memorial**			
84-08-001	The Carpenter	F. Hook	Yr.Iss.	100.00	135.00
Roman, Inc.		**Roman Cats**			
84-09-001	Grizabella	Unknown	30-day	29.50	29.50
84-09-002	Mr. Mistoffelees	Unknown	30-day	29.50	29.50
84-09-003	Rum Rum Tugger	Unknown	30-day	29.50	29.50
Roman, Inc.		**The Magic of Childhood**			
85-10-001	Special Friends	A. Williams	10-day	24.50	35.00
85-10-002	Feeding Time	A. Williams	10-day	24.50	35.00
85-10-003	Best Buddies	A. Williams	10-day	24.50	35.00
85-10-004	Getting Acquainted	A. Williams	10-day	24.50	35.00
86-10-005	Last One In	A. Williams	10-day	24.50	35.00
86-10-006	A Handful Of Love	A. Williams	10-day	24.50	35.00
86-10-007	Look Alikes	A. Williams	10-day	24.50	35.00
86-10-008	No Fair Peeking	A. Williams	10-day	24.50	35.00
Roman, Inc.		**Frances Hook Legacy**			
85-11-001	Fascination	F. Hook	100-day	19.50	35-39.00
85-11-002	Daydreaming	F. Hook	100-day	19.50	35-39.00
85-11-003	Discovery	F. Hook	100-day	22.50	35-39.00
85-11-004	Disappointment	F. Hook	100-day	22.50	35-39.00
85-11-005	Wonderment	F. Hook	100-day	22.50	35-39.00
85-11-006	Expectation	F. Hook	100-day	22.50	35-39.00
Roman, Inc.		**The Lord's Prayer**			
86-12-001	Our Father	A. Williams	10-day	24.50	24.50
86-12-002	Thy Kingdom Come	A. Williams	10-day	24.50	24.50
86-12-003	Give Us This Day	A. Williams	10-day	24.50	24.50
86-12-004	Forgive Our Trespasses	A. Williams	10-day	24.50	34.00
86-12-005	As We Forgive	A. Williams	10-day	24.50	24.50
86-12-006	Lead Us Not	A. Williams	10-day	24.50	24.50
86-12-007	Deliver Us From Evil	A. Williams	10-day	24.50	24.50
86-12-008	Thine Is The Kingdom	A. Williams	10-day	24.50	24.50
Roman, Inc.		**The Sweetest Songs**			
86-13-001	A Baby's Prayer	I. Spencer	30-day	39.50	45.00
86-13-002	This Little Piggie	I. Spencer	30-day	39.50	39.50
88-13-003	Long, Long Ago	I. Spencer	30-day	39.50	39.50
89-13-004	Rockabye	I. Spencer	30-day	39.50	39.50
Roman, Inc.		**Fontanini Annual Christmas Plate**			
86-14-001	A King Is Born	E. Simonetti	Yr.Iss.	60.00	60.00
87-14-002	O Come, Let Us Adore Him	E. Simonetti	Yr.Iss.	60.00	65.00
88-14-003	Adoration of the Magi	E. Simonetti	Yr.Iss.	70.00	75.00
89-14-004	Flight Into Egypt	E. Simonetti	Yr.Iss.	75.00	85.00
Roman, Inc.		**The Love's Prayer**			
88-15-001	Love Is Patient and Kind	A. Williams	14-day	29.50	29.50
88-15-002	Love Is Never Jealous or Boastful	A. Williams	14-day	29.50	29.50
88-15-003	Love Is Never Arrogant or Rude	A. Williams	14-day	29.50	29.50
88-15-004	Love Does Not Insist on Its Own Way	A. Williams	14-day	29.50	29.50
88-15-005	Love Is Never Irritable or Resentful	A. Williams	14-day	29.50	29.50
88-15-006	Love Rejoices In the Right	A. Williams	14-day	29.50	29.50
88-15-007	Love Believes All Things	A. Williams	14-day	29.50	29.50
88-15-008	Love Never Ends	A. Williams	14-day	29.50	29.50
Roman, Inc.		**March of Dimes: Our Children, Our Future**			
90-16-001	A Time To Laugh	A. Williams	150-day	29.00	39-49.00
Roman, Inc.		**Abbie Williams Collection**			
91-17-001	Legacy of Love	A. Williams	Open	29.50	29.50
91-17-002	Bless This Child	A. Williams	Open	29.50	29.50
Roman, Inc.		**Catnippers**			
86-18-001	Christmas Mourning	I. Spencer	9,500	34.50	34.50
92-18-002	Happy Holidaze	I. Spencer	9,500	34.50	34.50
Roman, Inc.		**God Bless You, Little One**			
91-19-001	Baby's First Birthday (Girl)	A. Williams	Open	29.50	29.50
91-19-002	Baby's First Birthday (Boy)	A. Williams	Open	29.50	29.50
91-19-003	Baby's First Smile	A. Williams	Open	19.50	19.50
91-19-004	Baby's First Word	A. Williams	Open	19.50	19.50
91-19-005	Baby's First Step	A. Williams	Open	19.50	19.50
91-19-006	Baby's First Tooth	A. Williams	Open	19.50	19.50
Roman, Inc.		**Millenium Series**			
92-20-001	Silent Night	Morcaldo/Lucchesi	Closed	49.50	49.50
93-20-002	The Annunciation	Morcaldo/Lucchesi	5,000	49.50	49.50
94-20-003	Peace On Earth	Morcaldo/Lucchesi	5,000	49.50	49.50
95-20-004	Cause of Our Joy	M. Lucchesi	5,000	49.50	49.50
Roman, Inc.		**Tender Expressions**			
92-21-001	Thoughts of You Are In My Heart	B. Sargent	100-day	29.50	29.50
Roman, Inc.		**The Richard Judson Zolan Collection**			
92-22-001	The Butterfly Net	R.J. Zolan	100-day	29.50	29.50
94-22-002	The Ring	R.J. Zolan	100-day	29.50	29.50
94-22-003	Terrace Dancing	R.J. Zolan	100-day	29.50	29.50
Roman, Inc.		**Precious Children**			
93-23-001	Bless Baby Brother	A. Williams	N/A	29.50	29.50
93-23-002	Blowing Bubbles	A. Williams	N/A	29.50	29.50
93-23-003	Don't Worry, Mother Duck	A. Williams	N/A	29.50	29.50
93-23-004	Treetop Discovery	A. Williams	N/A	29.50	29.50
93-23-005	The Tea Party	A. Williams	N/A	29.50	29.50
93-23-006	Mother's Little Angel	A. Williams	N/A	29.50	29.50
93-23-007	Picking Daisies	A. Williams	N/A	29.50	29.50
93-23-008	Let's Say Grace	A. Williams	N/A	29.50	29.50
Roman, Inc.		**Promise of a Savior**			
93-24-001	An Angel's Message	Unknown	95-day	29.90	29.90
93-24-002	Gifts to Jesus	Unknown	95-day	29.90	29.90
93-24-003	The Heavenly King	Unknown	95-day	29.90	29.90
93-24-004	Angels Were Watching	Unknown	95-day	29.90	29.90
93-24-005	Holy Mother & Child	Unknown	95-day	29.90	29.90
93-24-006	A Child is Born	Unknown	95-day	29.90	29.90
Roman, Inc.		**Single Releases**			
87-25-001	The Christening	A. Williams	Open	29.50	29.50
90-25-002	The Dedication	A. Williams	Open	29.50	29.50

		ARTIST	EDITION	ISSUE	QUOTE
90-25-003	The Baptism	A. Williams	Open	29.50	29.50
Rorstrand		**Christmas**			
68-01-001	Bringing Home the Tree	G. Nylund	Annual	12.00	500.00
69-01-002	Fisherman Sailing Home	G. Nylund	Annual	13.50	45.00
70-01-003	Nils with His Geese	G. Nylund	Annual	13.50	45.00
71-01-004	Nils in Lapland	G. Nylund	Annual	15.00	15.00
72-01-005	Dalecarlian Fiddler	G. Nylund	Annual	15.00	20-22.00
73-01-006	Farm in Smaland	G. Nylund	Annual	16.00	60.00
74-01-007	Vadslena	G. Nylund	Annual	19.00	43.00
75-01-008	Nils in Vastmanland	G. Nylund	Annual	20.00	35.00
76-01-009	Nils in Uapland	G. Nylund	Annual	20.00	43-49.00
77-01-010	Nils in Varmland	G. Nylund	Annual	29.50	29.50
78-01-011	Nils in Fjallbacka	G. Nylund	Annual	32.50	49.00
79-01-012	Nils in Vaestergoetland	G. Nylund	Annual	38.50	38.50
80-01-013	Nils in Halland	G. Nylund	Annual	55.00	60.00
81-01-014	Nils in Gotland	G. Nylund	Annual	55.00	45.00
82-01-015	Nils at Skansen	G. Nylund	Annual	47.50	40.00
83-01-016	Nils in Oland	G. Nylund	Annual	42.50	55.00
84-01-017	Angerman land	G. Nylund	Annual	42.50	35.00
85-01-018	Nils in Jamtland	G. Nylund	Annual	42.50	70.00
86-01-019	Nils in Karlskr	G. Nylund	Annual	42.50	50.00
87-01-020	Dalsland, Forget-Me-Not	G. Nylund	Annual	47.50	150.00
88-01-021	Nils in Halsingland	G. Nylund	Annual	55.00	60.00
89-01-022	Nils Visits Gothenborg	G. Nylund	Annual	60.00	61.00
90-01-023	Nils in Kvikkjokk	G. Nylund	Annual	75.00	75.00
91-01-024	Nils in Medelpad	G. Nylund	Annual	85.00	85.00
92-01-025	Gastrikland, Lily of the Valley	G. Nylund	Annual	92.50	92.50
93-01-026	Narke's Castle	G. Nylund	Annual	92.50	92.50
Rosenthal		**Christmas**			
10-01-001	Winter Peace	Unknown	Annual	Unkn.	550.00
11-01-002	Three Wise Men	Unknown	Annual	Unkn.	325.00
12-01-003	Stardust	Unknown	Annual	Unkn.	255.00
13-01-004	Christmas Lights	Unknown	Annual	Unkn.	235.00
14-01-005	Christmas Song	Unknown	Annual	Unkn.	350.00
15-01-006	Walking to Church	Unknown	Annual	Unkn.	180.00
16-01-007	Christmas During War	Unknown	Annual	Unkn.	240.00
17-01-008	Angel of Peace	Unknown	Annual	Unkn.	200.00
18-01-009	Peace on Earth	Unknown	Annual	Unkn.	200.00
19-01-010	St. Christopher with Christ Child	Unknown	Annual	Unkn.	225.00
20-01-011	Manger in Bethlehem	Unknown	Annual	Unkn.	325.00
21-01-012	Christmas in Mountains	Unknown	Annual	Unkn.	200.00
22-01-013	Advent Branch	Unknown	Annual	Unkn.	200.00
23-01-014	Children in Winter Woods	Unknown	Annual	Unkn.	200.00
24-01-015	Deer in the Woods	Unknown	Annual	Unkn.	200.00
25-01-016	Three Wise Men	Unknown	Annual	Unkn.	200.00
26-01-017	Christmas in Mountains	Unknown	Annual	Unkn.	195.00
27-01-018	Station on the Way	Unknown	Annual	Unkn.	200.00
28-01-019	Chalet Christmas	Unknown	Annual	Unkn.	185.00
29-01-020	Christmas in Alps	Unknown	Annual	Unkn.	225.00
30-01-021	Group of Deer Under Pines	Unknown	Annual	Unkn.	225.00
31-01-022	Path of the Magi	Unknown	Annual	Unkn.	225.00
32-01-023	Christ Child	Unknown	Annual	Unkn.	185.00
33-01-024	Thru the Night to Light	Unknown	Annual	Unkn.	190.00
34-01-025	Christmas Peace	Unknown	Annual	Unkn.	190.00
35-01-026	Christmas by the Sea	Unknown	Annual	Unkn.	190.00
36-01-027	Nurnberg Angel	Unknown	Annual	Unkn.	195.00
37-01-028	Berchtesgaden	Unknown	Annual	Unkn.	195.00
38-01-029	Christmas in the Alps	Unknown	Annual	Unkn.	195.00
39-01-030	Schneekoppe Mountain	Unknown	Annual	Unkn.	195.00
40-01-031	Marien Chruch in Danzig	Unknown	Annual	Unkn.	250.00
41-01-032	Strassburg Cathedral	Unknown	Annual	Unkn.	250.00
42-01-033	Marianburg Castle	Unknown	Annual	Unkn.	300.00
43-01-034	Winter Idyll	Unknown	Annual	Unkn.	300.00
44-01-035	Wood Scape	Unknown	Annual	Unkn.	300.00
45-01-036	Christmas Peace	Unknown	Annual	Unkn.	400.00
46-01-037	Christmas in an Alpine Valley	Unknown	Annual	Unkn.	240.00
47-01-038	Dillingen Madonna	Unknown	Annual	Unkn.	985.00
48-01-039	Message to the Shepherds	Unknown	Annual	Unkn.	875.00
49-01-040	The Holy Family	Unknown	Annual	Unkn.	185.00
50-01-041	Christmas in the Forest	Unknown	Annual	Unkn.	185.00
51-01-042	Star of Bethlehem	Unknown	Annual	Unkn.	450.00
52-01-043	Christmas in the Alps	Unknown	Annual	Unkn.	195.00
53-01-044	The Holy Light	Unknown	Annual	Unkn.	195.00
54-01-045	Christmas Eve	Unknown	Annual	Unkn.	195.00
55-01-046	Christmas in a Village	Unknown	Annual	Unkn.	195.00
56-01-047	Christmas in the Alps	Unknown	Annual	Unkn.	195.00
57-01-048	Christmas by the Sea	Unknown	Annual	Unkn.	195.00
58-01-049	Christmas Eve	Unknown	Annual	Unkn.	195.00
59-01-050	Midnight Mass	Unknown	Annual	Unkn.	195.00
60-01-051	Christmas in a Small Village	Unknown	Annual	Unkn.	195.00
61-01-052	Solitary Christmas	Unknown	Annual	Unkn.	225.00
62-01-053	Christmas Eve	Unknown	Annual	Unkn.	195.00
63-01-054	Silent Night	Unknown	Annual	Unkn.	195.00
64-01-055	Christmas Market in Nurnberg	Unknown	Annual	Unkn.	225.00
65-01-056	Christmas Munich	Unknown	Annual	Unkn.	185.00
66-01-057	Christmas in Ulm	Unknown	Annual	Unkn.	275.00
67-01-058	Christmas in Reginburg	Unknown	Annual	Unkn.	185.00
68-01-059	Christmas in Bremen	Unknown	Annual	Unkn.	195.00
69-01-060	Christmas in Rothenburg	Unknown	Annual	Unkn.	220.00
70-01-061	Christmas in Cologne	Unknown	Annual	Unkn.	175.00
71-01-062	Christmas in Garmisch	Unknown	Annual	42.00	100.00
72-01-063	Christmas in Franconia	Unknown	Annual	50.00	95.00
73-01-064	Lubeck-Holstein	Unknown	Annual	77.00	105.00
74-01-065	Christmas in Wurzburg	Unknown	Annual	85.00	100.00
Rosenthal		**Wiinblad Christmas**			
71-02-001	Maria & Child	B. Wiinblad	Undis.	100.00	700.00
72-02-002	Caspar	B. Wiinblad	Undis.	100.00	290.00
73-02-003	Melchior	B. Wiinblad	Undis.	125.00	335.00
74-02-004	Balthazar	B. Wiinblad	Undis.	125.00	300.00
75-02-005	The Annunciation	B. Wiinblad	Undis.	195.00	195.00
76-02-006	Angel with Trumpet	B. Wiinblad	Undis.	195.00	195.00
77-02-007	Adoration of Shepherds	B. Wiinblad	Undis.	225.00	225.00
78-02-008	Angel with Harp	B. Wiinblad	Undis.	275.00	295.00
79-02-009	Exodus from Egypt	B. Wiinblad	Undis.	310.00	310.00
80-02-010	Angel with Glockenspiel	B. Wiinblad	Undis.	360.00	360.00
81-02-011	Christ Child Visits Temple	B. Wiinblad	Undis.	375.00	375.00
82-02-012	Christening of Christ	B. Wiinblad	Undis.	375.00	375.00
Rosenthal		**Nobility of Children**			
76-03-001	La Contessa Isabella	E. Hibel	12,750	120.00	120.00

		ARTIST	EDITION	ISSUE	QUOTE
77-03-002	La Marquis Maurice-Pierre	E. Hibel	12,750	120.00	120.00
78-03-003	Baronesse Johanna	E. Hibel	12,750	130.00	140.00
79-03-004	Chief Red Feather	E. Hibel	12,750	140.00	180.00
Rosenthal		**Oriental Gold**			
76-04-001	Yasuko	E. Hibel	2,000	275.00	650.00
77-04-002	Mr. Obata	E. Hibel	2,000	275.00	500.00
78-04-003	Sakura	E. Hibel	2,000	295.00	400.00
79-04-004	Michio	E. Hibel	2,000	325.00	375.00
Royal Copenhagen		**Christmas**			
08-01-001	Madonna and Child	C. Thomsen	Annual	1.00	32-3500.
09-01-002	Danish Landscape	S. Ussing	Annual	1.00	140-199.
10-01-003	The Magi	C. Thomsen	Annual	1.00	135-159.
11-01-004	Danish Landscape	O. Jensen	Annual	1.00	130-185.
12-01-005	Christmas Tree	C. Thomsen	Annual	1.00	135-180.
13-01-006	Frederik Church Spire	A. Boesen	Annual	1.50	110-160.
14-01-007	Holy Spirit Church	A. Boesen	Annual	1.50	120-195.
15-01-008	Danish Landscape	A. Krog	Annual	1.50	120-199.
16-01-009	Shepherd at Christmas	R. Bocher	Annual	1.50	80-125.
17-01-010	Our Savior Church	O. Jensen	Annual	2.00	78-96.00
18-01-011	Sheep and Shepherds	O. Jensen	Annual	2.00	76-96.00
19-01-012	In the Park	O. Jensen	Annual	2.00	76-115.
20-01-013	Mary and Child Jesus	G. Rode	Annual	2.00	76-96.00
21-01-014	Aabenraa Marketplace	O. Jensen	Annual	2.00	65-81.00
22-01-015	Three Singing Angels	E. Selschau	Annual	2.00	62-97.00
23-01-016	Danish Landscape	O. Jensen	Annual	2.00	62-74.00
24-01-017	Sailing Ship	B. Olsen	Annual	2.00	89-110.
25-01-018	Christianshavn	O. Jensen	Annual	2.00	76-88.00
26-01-019	Christianshavn Canal	R. Bocher	Annual	2.00	68-88.00
27-01-020	Ship's Boy at Tiller	B. Olsen	Annual	2.00	126.00
28-01-021	Vicar's Family	G. Rode	Annual	2.00	75-90.00
29-01-022	Grundtvig Church	O. Jensen	Annual	2.00	75-90.00
30-01-023	Fishing Boats	B. Olsen	Annual	2.50	93-100.
31-01-024	Mother and Child	G. Rode	Annual	2.50	93-100.
32-01-025	Frederiksberg Gardens	O. Jensen	Annual	2.50	80-100.
33-01-026	Ferry and the Great Belt	B. Olsen	Annual	2.50	165.00
34-01-027	The Hermitage Castle	O. Jensen	Annual	2.50	165.00
35-01-028	Kronborg Castle	B. Olsen	Annual	2.50	205.00
36-01-029	Roskilde Cathedral	R. Bocher	Annual	2.50	175.00
37-01-030	Main Street Copenhagen	N. Thorsson	Annual	2.50	190.00
38-01-031	Round Church in Osterlars	H. Nielsen	Annual	3.00	145-295.
39-01-032	Greenland Pack-Ice	S. Nielsen	Annual	3.00	345.00
40-01-033	The Good Shepherd	K. Lange	Annual	3.00	190-415.
41-01-034	Danish Village Church	T. Kjolner	Annual	3.00	175-345.
42-01-035	Bell Tower	N. Thorsson	Annual	4.00	245-365.
43-01-036	Flight into Egypt	N. Thorsson	Annual	4.00	200-475.
44-01-037	Danish Village Scene	V. Olson	Annual	4.00	225-259.
45-01-038	A Peaceful Motif	R. Bocher	Annual	4.00	339-400.
46-01-039	Zealand Village Church	N. Thorsson	Annual	4.00	165.00
47-01-040	The Good Shepherd	K. Lange	Annual	4.50	225-465.
48-01-041	Nodebo Church	T. Kjolner	Annual	4.50	190-389.
49-01-042	Our Lady's Cathedral	H. Hansen	Annual	5.00	218.00
50-01-043	Boeslunde Church	V. Olson	Annual	5.00	200-500.
51-01-044	Christmas Angel	R. Bocher	Annual	5.00	299.00
52-01-045	Christmas in the Forest	K. Lange	Annual	5.00	110-300.
53-01-046	Frederiksberg Castle	T. Kjolner	Annual	6.00	110-219.
54-01-047	Amalienborg Palace	K. Lange	Annual	6.00	120-279.
55-01-048	Fano Girl	K. Lange	Annual	7.00	165-239.
56-01-049	Rosenborg Castle	K. Lange	Annual	7.00	147-167.
57-01-050	The Good Shepherd	H. Hansen	Annual	8.00	105-299.
58-01-051	Sunshine over Greenland	H. Hansen	Annual	9.00	112-389.
59-01-052	Christmas Night	H. Hansen	Annual	9.00	112-120.
60-01-053	The Stag	H. Hansen	Annual	10.00	123-160.
61-01-054	Training Ship	K. Lange	Annual	10.00	141-152.
62-01-055	The Little Mermaid	Unknown	Annual	11.00	228.00
63-01-056	Hojsager Mill	K. Lange	Annual	11.00	70-199.
64-01-057	Fetching the Tree	K. Lange	Annual	11.00	60-120.
65-01-058	Little Skaters	K. Lange	Annual	12.00	60-145.
66-01-059	Blackbird	K. Lange	Annual	12.00	50-180.
67-01-060	The Royal Oak	K. Lange	Annual	13.00	42.00
68-01-061	The Last Umiak	K. Lange	Annual	13.00	25-35.00
69-01-062	The Old Farmyard	K. Lange	Annual	14.00	27-48.00
70-01-063	Christmas Rose and Cat	K. Lange	Annual	14.00	27-45.00
71-01-064	Hare In Winter	K. Lange	Annual	15.00	13-30.00
72-01-065	In the Desert	K. Lange	Annual	16.00	13-30.00
73-01-066	Train Homeward Bound	K. Lange	Annual	22.00	13-40.00
74-01-067	Winter Twilight	K. Lange	Annual	22.00	21-35.00
75-01-068	Queen's Palace	K. Lange	Annual	27.50	13-38.00
76-01-069	Danish Watermill	S. Vestergaard	Annual	27.50	18-30.00
77-01-070	Immervad Bridge	K. Lange	Annual	32.00	13-38.00
78-01-071	Greenland Scenery	K. Lange	Annual	35.00	13-25.00
79-01-072	Choosing Christmas Tree	K. Lange	Annual	42.50	27-61.00
80-01-073	Bringing Home the Tree	K. Lange	Annual	49.50	19-27.00
81-01-074	Admiring Christmas Tree	K. Lange	Annual	52.50	29-55.00
82-01-075	Waiting for Christmas	K. Lange	Annual	54.50	45-60.00
83-01-076	Merry Christmas	K. Lange	Annual	54.50	30-35.00
84-01-077	Jingle Bells	K. Lange	Annual	54.50	35-45.00
85-01-078	Snowman	K. Lange	Annual	54.50	27-53.00
86-01-079	Christmas Vacation	K. Lange	Annual	54.50	48-60.00
87-01-080	Winter Birds	S. Vestergaard	Annual	59.50	35-56.00
88-01-081	Christmas Eve in Copenhagen	S. Vestergaard	Annual	59.50	67.00
89-01-082	The Old Skating Pond	S. Vestergaard	Annual	59.50	79.00
90-01-083	Christmas at Tivoli	S. Vestergaard	Annual	64.50	69-115.
91-01-084	The Festival of Santa Lucia	S. Vestergaard	Annual	69.50	65.00
92-01-085	The Queen's Carriage	S. Vestergaard	Annual	69.50	55-80.00
93-01-086	Christmas Guests	S. Vestergaard	Annual	69.50	55.00
94-01-087	Christmas Shopping	S. Vestergaard	Annual	72.50	72.50
95-01-088	Christmas at the Manor House	S. Vestergaard	Annual	72.50	72.50
Royal Copenhagen		**Nature's Children**			
93-02-001	The Robins	J. Nielsen	Annual	39.50	39.50
94-02-002	The Fawn	J. Nielsen	Annual	39.50	39.50
Royal Copenhagen		**Christmas in Denmark**			
91-03-001	Bringing Home the Tree	H. Hansen	Annual	72.50	55-72.50
92-03-002	Christmas Shopping	H. Hansen	Annual	72.50	55-72.50
93-03-003	The Skating Party	H. Hansen	Annual	74.50	58-74.50
94-03-004	The Sleigh Ride	H. Hansen	Annual	74.50	60-74.50
Royal Copenhagen		**American Mother's Day**			
88-04-001	Western Trail	S. Vestergaard	Annual	34.50	34.50
89-04-002	Indian Love Call	S. Vestergaard	Annual	37.00	35-37.00

		ARTIST	EDITION	ISSUE	QUOTE
90-04-003	Southern Belle	S. Vestergaard	Annual	39.50	35-39.50
91-04-004	Mother's Day at the Mission	S. Vestergaard	Annual	42.50	35-42.50
92-04-005	Turn of the Century Boston	S. Vestergaard	Annual	45.00	40-45.00
94-04-006	Tropical Paradise	S. Vestergaard	Annual	47.50	35-47.50
Royal Devon		**Rockwell Christmas**			
75-01-001	Downhill Daring	N. Rockwell	Yr.Iss.	24.50	30.00
76-01-002	The Christmas Gift	N. Rockwell	Yr.Iss.	24.50	35.00
77-01-003	The Big Moment	N. Rockwell	Yr.Iss.	27.50	50.00
78-01-004	Puppets for Christmas	N. Rockwell	Yr.Iss.	27.50	27.50
79-01-005	One Present Too Many	N. Rockwell	Yr.Iss.	31.50	31.50
80-01-006	Gramps Meets Gramps	N. Rockwell	Yr.Iss.	33.00	33.00
Royal Devon		**Rockwell Mother's Day**			
75-02-001	Doctor and Doll	N. Rockwell	Yr.Iss.	23.50	50.00
76-02-002	Puppy Love	N. Rockwell	Yr.Iss.	24.50	104.00
77-02-003	The Family	N. Rockwell	Yr.Iss.	24.50	85.00
78-02-004	Mother's Day Off	N. Rockwell	Yr.Iss.	27.00	35.00
79-02-005	Mother's Evening Out	N. Rockwell	Yr.Iss.	30.00	32.00
80-02-006	Mother's Treat	N. Rockwell	Yr.Iss.	32.50	35.00
Royal Doulton		**Family Christmas Plates**			
91-01-001	Dad Plays Santa	N/A	Yr.Iss.	60.00	60.00
Royal Doulton		**Christmas Plates**			
93-02-001	Royal Doulton-Together For Christmas	N/A	N/A	45.00	45.00
93-02-002	Royal Albert-Sleighride	N/A	N/A	45.00	45.00
Royal Worcester		**Birth Of A Nation**			
72-01-001	Boston Tea Party	P.W. Baston	10,000	45.00	140-275.
73-01-002	Paul Revere	P.W. Baston	10,000	45.00	140-250.
74-01-003	Concord Bridge	P.W. Baston	10,000	50.00	140.00
75-01-004	Signing Declaration	P.W. Baston	10,000	65.00	140.00
76-01-005	Crossing Delaware	P.W. Baston	10,000	65.00	140.00
77-01-006	Washington's Inauguration	P.W. Baston	1,250	65.00	140.00
Royal Worcester		**Currier and Ives Plates**			
74-02-001	Road in Winter	P.W. Baston	5,570	59.50	55-100.
75-02-002	Old Grist Mill	P.W. Baston	3,200	59.50	55-100.
76-02-003	Winter Pastime	P.W. Baston	1,500	59.50	55-125.
77-02-004	Home to Thanksgiving	P.W. Baston	546	59.50	200-250.
Royal Worcester		**Water Birds of North America**			
85-03-001	Mallards	J. Cooke	15,000	55.00	55.00
85-03-002	Canvas Backs	J. Cooke	15,000	55.00	55.00
85-03-003	Wood Ducks	J. Cooke	15,000	55.00	55.00
85-03-004	Snow Geese	J. Cooke	15,000	55.00	55.00
85-03-005	American Pintails	J. Cooke	15,000	55.00	55.00
85-03-006	Green Winged Teals	J. Cooke	15,000	55.00	55.00
85-03-007	Hooded Mergansers	J. Cooke	15,000	55.00	55.00
85-03-008	Canada Geese	J. Cooke	15,000	55.00	55.00
Royal Worcester		**Kitten Encounters**			
87-04-001	Fishful Thinking	P. Cooper	14-day	29.50	30-54.00
87-04-002	Puppy Pal	P. Cooper	14-day	29.50	36.00
87-04-003	Just Ducky	P. Cooper	14-day	29.50	36.00
87-04-004	Bunny Chase	P. Cooper	14-day	29.50	30.00
87-04-005	Flutter By	P. Cooper	14-day	29.50	30.00
87-04-006	Bedtime Buddies	P. Cooper	14-day	29.50	30.00
88-04-007	Cat and Mouse	P. Cooper	14-day	29.50	33.00
88-04-008	Stablemates	P. Cooper	14-day	29.50	48.00
Royal Worcester		**Kitten Classics**			
85-05-001	Cat Nap	P. Cooper	14-day	29.50	36.00
85-05-002	Purrfect Treasure	P. Cooper	14-day	29.50	29.50
85-05-003	Wild Flower	P. Cooper	14-day	29.50	29.50
85-05-004	Birdwatcher	P. Cooper	14-day	29.50	29.50
85-05-005	Tiger's Fancy	P. Cooper	14-day	29.50	33.00
85-05-006	Country Kitty	P. Cooper	14-day	29.50	33.00
85-05-007	Little Rascal	P. Cooper	14-day	29.50	29.50
86-05-008	First Prize	P. Cooper	14-day	29.50	29.50
Sarah's Attic		**Classroom Memories**			
91-01-001	Classroom Memories	Sarah's Attic	Closed	80.00	80.00
Schmid		**Davis Red Oak Sampler**			
86-01-001	General Store	L. Davis	5,000	45.00	55-150.
87-01-002	Country Wedding	L. Davis	5,000	45.00	110.00
89-01-003	Country School	L. Davis	5,000	45.00	75.00
90-01-004	Blacksmith Shop	L. Davis	5,000	52.50	60.00
Schmid		**Davis Country Pride Plates**			
81-02-001	Surprise in the Cellar	L. Davis	7,500	35.00	80-200.
81-02-002	Plum Tuckered Out	L. Davis	7,500	35.00	200.00
81-02-003	Duke's Mixture	L. Davis	7,500	35.00	190.00
82-02-004	Bustin' with Pride	L. Davis	7,500	35.00	100-125.
Schmid		**Davis Cat Tales Plates.**			
82-03-001	Right Church, Wrong Pew	L. Davis	12,500	37.50	190.00
82-03-002	Company's Coming	L. Davis	12,500	37.50	180.00
82-03-003	On the Move	L. Davis	12,500	37.50	145.00
82-03-004	Flew the Coop	L. Davis	12,500	37.50	145.00
Schmid		**Davis Special Edition Plates**			
83-04-001	The Critics	L. Davis	12,500	45.00	60-145.
84-04-002	Good Ole Days Privy Set 2	L. Davis	5,000	60.00	185.00
86-04-003	Home From Market	L. Davis	7,500	55.00	145.00
Schmid		**Davis Christmas Plates**			
83-05-001	Hooker at Mailbox With Present	L. Davis	7,500	45.00	125.00
84-05-002	Country Christmas	L. Davis	7,500	45.00	125.00
85-05-003	Christmas at Foxfire Farm	L. Davis	7,500	45.00	135.00
86-05-004	Christmas at Red Oak	L. Davis	7,500	45.00	125.00
87-05-005	Blossom's Gift	L. Davis	7,500	47.50	100.00
88-05-006	Cutting the Family Christmas Tree	L. Davis	7,500	47.50	100.00
89-05-007	Peter and the Wren	L. Davis	7,500	47.50	75.00
90-05-008	Wintering Deer	L. Davis	7,500	47.50	47.50
91-05-009	Christmas at Red Oak II	L. Davis	7,500	55.00	75.00
92-05-010	Born On A Starry Night	L. Davis	7,500	55.00	55.00
93-05-011	Waiting For Mr. Lowell	L. Davis	5,000	55.00	55.00
Schmid		**Friends of Mine**			
89-06-001	Sun Worshippers	L. Davis	7,500	53.00	53.00
90-06-002	Sunday Afternoon Treat	L. Davis	7,500	53.00	53.00
91-06-003	Warm Milk	L. Davis	7,500	55.00	55.00
92-06-004	Cat and Jenny Wren	L. Davis	7,500	55.00	55.00

		ARTIST	EDITION	ISSUE	QUOTE
Schmid		**Pen Pals**			
93-07-001	The Old Home Place	L. Davis	5,000	50.00	50.00
Schmid		**Disney Annual**			
83-08-001	Sneak Preview	Disney Studios	20,000	22.50	22.50
84-08-002	Command Performance	Disney Studios	20,000	22.50	22.50
85-08-003	Snow Biz	Disney Studios	20,000	22.50	22.50
86-08-004	Tree For Two	Disney Studios	20,000	22.50	22.50
87-08-005	Merry Mouse Medley	Disney Studios	20,000	25.00	25.00
88-08-006	Warm Winter Ride	Disney Studios	20,000	25.00	25.00
89-08-007	Merry Mickey Claus	Disney Studios	20,000	32.50	60.00
90-08-008	Holly Jolly Christmas	Disney Studios	20,000	32.50	32.50
91-08-009	Mickey and Minnie's Rockin' Christmas	Disney Studios	20000	37.00	37.00
Schmid		**Disney Christmas**			
73-09-001	Sleigh Ride	Disney Studio	Annual	10.00	300-325.
74-09-002	Decorating The Tree	Disney Studio	Annual	10.00	80-84.00
75-09-003	Caroling	Disney Studio	Annual	12.50	14.00
76-09-004	Building A Snowman	Disney Studio	Annual	13.00	15.00
77-09-005	Down The Chimney	Disney Studio	Annual	13.00	14.00
78-09-006	Night Before Christmas	Disney Studio	Annual	15.00	31.00
79-09-007	Santa's Suprise	Disney Studio	15,000	17.50	27.00
80-09-008	Sleigh Ride	Disney Studio	15,000	17.50	33.00
81-09-009	Happy Holidays	Disney Studio	15,000	17.50	20.00
82-09-010	Winter Games	Disney Studio	15,000	18.50	25.00
Schmid		**Disney Mother's Day**			
74-10-001	Flowers For Mother	Disney Studio	Annual	10.00	45.00
75-10-002	Snow White & Dwarfs	Disney Studio	Annual	12.50	50.00
76-10-003	Minnie Mouse	Disney Studio	Annual	13.00	25.00
77-10-004	Pluto's Pals	Disney Studio	Annual	13.00	18.00
78-10-005	Flowers For Bambi	Disney Studio	Annual	15.00	40.00
79-10-006	Happy Feet	Disney Studio	10,000	17.50	20.00
80-10-007	Minnie's Surprise	Disney Studio	10,000	17.50	30.00
81-10-008	Playmates	Disney Studio	10,000	17.50	35.00
82-10-009	A Dream Come True	Disney Studio	10,000	18.50	40.00
Schmid		**Disney Special Edition Plates**			
78-11-001	Mickey Mouse At Fifty	Disney Studios	15,000	25.00	65-100.
80-11-002	Happy Birthday Pinocchio	Disney Studios	7,500	17.50	25-60.00
81-11-003	Alice in Wonderland	Disney Studios	7,500	17.50	17.50
82-11-004	Happy Birthday Pluto	Disney Studios	7,500	17.50	39.00
82-11-005	Goofy's Golden Jubilee	Disney Studios	7,500	18.50	29.00
87-11-006	Snow White Golden Anniversary	Disney Studios	5,000	47.50	47.50
88-11-007	Mickey Mouse & Minnie Mouse 60th	Disney Studios	10,000	50.00	95-125.
89-11-008	Sleeping Beauty 30th Anniversary	Disney Studios	5,000	80.00	95.00
90-11-009	Fantasia-Sorcerer's Apprentice	Disney Studios	5,000	59.00	59-99.00
90-11-010	Pinocchio's Friend	Disney Studios	Annual	25.00	25.00
90-11-011	Fantasia Relief Plate	Disney Studios	20,000	25.00	39.00
Schmid		**Ferrandiz Music Makers Porcelain Plates**			
81-12-001	The Flutist	J. Ferrandiz	10,000	25.00	29.00
81-12-002	The Entertainer	J. Ferrandiz	10,000	25.00	29.00
82-12-003	Magical Medley	J. Ferrandiz	10,000	25.00	29.00
82-12-004	Sweet Serenade	J. Ferrandiz	10,000	25.00	32.00
Schmid		**Ferrandiz Beautiful Bounty Porcelain Plates**			
82-13-001	Summer's Golden Harvest	J. Ferrandiz	10,000	40.00	40.00
82-13-002	Autumn's Blessing	J. Ferrandiz	10,000	40.00	40.00
82-13-003	A Mid-Winter's Dream	J. Ferrandiz	10,000	40.00	42.50
82-13-004	Spring Blossoms	J. Ferrandiz	10,000	40.00	40.00
Schmid		**Ferrandiz Wooden Birthday Plates**			
72-14-001	Boy	J. Ferrandiz	Unkn.	15.00	150.00
72-14-002	Girl	J. Ferrandiz	Unkn.	15.00	160.00
73-14-003	Boy	J. Ferrandiz	Unkn.	20.00	200.00
73-14-004	Girl	J. Ferrandiz	Unkn.	20.00	150.00
74-14-005	Boy	J. Ferrandiz	Unkn.	22.00	160.00
74-14-006	Girl	J. Ferrandiz	Unkn.	22.00	160.00
Schmid		**Juan Ferrandiz Porcelain Christmas Plates**			
72-15-001	Christ in the Manger	J. Ferrandiz	Unkn.	30.00	179.00
73-15-002	Christmas	J. Ferrandiz	Unkn.	30.00	229.00
Schmid		**Christmas**			
71-16-001	Angel	B. Hummel	Annual	15.00	19-39.00
72-16-002	Angel With Flute	B. Hummel	Annual	15.00	15.00
73-16-003	The Nativity	B. Hummel	Annual	15.00	73.00
74-16-004	The Guardian Angel	B. Hummel	Annual	18.50	18.50
75-16-005	Christmas Child	B. Hummel	Annual	25.00	25.00
76-16-006	Sacred Journey	B. Hummel	Annual	27.50	32.00
77-16-007	Herald Angel	B. Hummel	Annual	27.50	32.00
78-16-008	Heavenly Trio	B. Hummel	Annual	32.50	32.50
79-16-009	Starlight Angel	B. Hummel	Annual	38.00	38.00
80-16-010	Parade Into Toyland	B. Hummel	Annual	45.00	45.00
81-16-011	A Time To Remember	B. Hummel	Annual	45.00	45.00
82-16-012	Angelic Procession	B. Hummel	Annual	45.00	49.00
83-16-013	Angelic Messenger	B. Hummel	Annual	45.00	45.00
84-16-014	A Gift from Heaven	B. Hummel	Annual	45.00	48.00
85-16-015	Heavenly Light	B. Hummel	Annual	45.00	46.50
86-16-016	Tell The Heavens	B. Hummel	Annual	45.00	45.00
87-16-017	Angelic Gifts	B. Hummel	Annual	47.50	47.50
88-16-018	Cheerful Cherubs	B. Hummel	Annual	53.00	60.00
89-16-019	Angelic Musician	B. Hummel	Annual	53.00	53.00
90-16-020	Angel's Light	B. Hummel	Annual	53.00	57.00
91-16-021	Message From Above	B. Hummel	Annual	60.00	60.00
92-16-022	Sweet Blessings	B. Hummel	Annual	65.00	65.00
Schmid		**Mother's Day**			
72-17-001	Playing Hooky	B. Hummel	Annual	15.00	15.00
73-17-002	Little Fisherman	B. Hummel	Annual	15.00	33.00
74-17-003	Bumblebee	B. Hummel	Annual	18.50	20.00
75-17-004	Message of Love	B. Hummel	Annual	25.00	29.00
76-17-005	Devotion For Mother	B. Hummel	Annual	27.50	30.00
77-17-006	Moonlight Return	B. Hummel	Annual	27.50	29.00
78-17-007	Afternoon Stroll	B. Hummel	Annual	32.50	32.50
79-17-008	Cherub's Gift	B. Hummel	Annual	38.00	38.00
80-17-009	Mother's Little Helpers	B. Hummel	Annual	45.00	52.00
81-17-010	Playtime	B. Hummel	Annual	45.00	52.00
82-17-011	The Flower Basket	B. Hummel	Annual	45.00	47.50
83-17-012	Spring Bouquet	B. Hummel	Annual	45.00	54.00
84-17-013	A Joy to Share	B. Hummel	Annual	45.00	45.00
85-17-014	A Mother's Journey	B. Hummel	Annual	45.00	45.00
86-17-015	Home From School	B. Hummel	Annual	45.00	55.00
88-17-016	Young Reader	B. Hummel	Annual	52.50	81.00

		ARTIST	EDITION	ISSUE	QUOTE
89-17-017	Pretty as a Picture	B. Hummel	Annual	53.00	75.00
90-17-018	Mother's Little Athlete	B. Hummel	Annual	53.00	53.00
91-17-019	Soft & Gentle	B. Hummel	Annual	55.00	55.00
Schmid		**The Littlest Night**			
93-18-001	The Littlest Night	B. Hummel	Annual	25.00	25.00
Schmid		**Peanuts Mother's Day Plates**			
72-19-001	Linus	C. Schulz	Unkn.	10.00	10.00
73-19-002	Mom?	C. Schulz	Unkn.	10.00	10.00
74-19-003	Snoopy/Woodstock/Parade	C. Schulz	Unkn.	10.00	10.00
75-19-004	A Kiss for Lucy	C. Schulz	Unkn.	12.50	10.00
76-19-005	Linus and Snoopy	C. Schulz	Unkn.	13.00	35.00
77-19-006	Dear Mom	C. Schulz	Unkn.	13.00	30.00
78-19-007	Thoughts That Count	C. Schulz	Unkn.	15.00	25.00
79-19-008	A Special Letter	C. Schulz	Unkn.	17.50	22.50
80-19-009	A Tribute to Mom	C. Schulz	Unkn.	17.50	22.50
81-19-010	Mission for Mom	C. Schulz	Unkn.	17.50	20.00
82-19-011	Which Way to Mother	C. Schulz	Unkn.	18.50	18.50
Schmid		**Peanuts Valentine's Day Plates**			
77-20-001	Home Is Where the Heart is	C. Schulz	Unkn.	13.00	32.50
78-20-002	Heavenly Bliss	C. Schulz	Unkn.	13.00	30.00
79-20-003	Love Match	C. Schulz	Unkn.	17.50	27.50
80-20-004	From Snoopy, With Love	C. Schulz	Unkn.	17.50	25.00
81-20-005	Hearts-A-Flutter	C. Schulz	Unkn.	17.50	20.00
82-20-006	Love Patch	C. Schulz	Unkn.	17.50	17.50
Schmid		**Peanuts World's Greatest Athlete**			
82-21-001	Go Deep	C. Schulz	10,000	17.50	25.00
82-21-002	The Puck Stops Here	C. Schulz	10,000	17.50	22.50
82-21-003	The Way You Play The Game	C. Schulz	10,000	17.50	20.00
82-21-004	The Crowd Went Wild	C. Schulz	10,000	17.50	17.50
Schmid		**Peanuts Special Edition Plate**			
76-22-001	Bi-Centennial	C. Schulz	Unkn.	13.00	30.00
Schmid		**Peanuts Christmas**			
72-23-001	Snoopy Guides the Sleigh	C. Schulz	Annual	10.00	40.00
73-23-002	Christmas Eve at Doghouse	C. Schulz	Annual	10.00	88.00
74-23-003	Christmas At Fireplace	C. Schulz	Annual	10.00	48.00
75-23-004	Woodstock and Santa Claus	C. Schulz	Annual	12.50	19.00
76-23-005	Woodstock's Christmas	C. Schulz	Annual	13.00	20.00
77-23-006	Deck The Doghouse	C. Schulz	Annual	13.00	19.00
78-23-007	Filling the Stocking	C. Schulz	Annual	15.00	40.00
79-23-008	Christmas at Hand	C. Schulz	15,000	17.50	24.00
80-23-009	Waiting for Santa	C. Schulz	15,000	17.50	30.00
81-23-010	A Christmas Wish	C. Schulz	15,000	17.50	28.00
82-23-011	Perfect Performance	C. Schulz	15,000	18.50	50.00
Schmid		**Raggedy Ann Annual Plates**			
80-24-001	The Sunshine Wagon	Unknown	10,000	17.50	80-100.
81-24-002	The Raggedy Shuffle	Unknown	10,000	17.50	28-75.00
82-24-003	Flying High	Unknown	10,000	18.50	18.50
83-24-004	Winning Streak	Unknown	10,000	22.50	22.50
84-24-005	Rocking Rodeo	Unknown	10,000	22.50	22.50
Schmid		**Raggedy Ann Bicentennial Plate**			
76-25-001	Bicentennial Plate	Unknown	Unkn.	13.00	30-60.00
Schmid		**Raggedy Ann Christmas Plates**			
75-26-001	Gifts of Love	Unknown	Unkn.	12.50	45.00
76-26-002	Merry Blades	Unknown	Unkn.	13.00	37.50
77-26-003	Christmas Morning	Unknown	Unkn.	13.00	22.50
78-26-004	Checking the List	Unknown	Unkn.	15.00	20.00
79-26-005	Little Helper	Unknown	Unkn.	17.50	19.50
Schmid		**Raggedy Ann Valentine's Day Plates**			
78-27-001	As Time Goes By	Unknown	Unkn.	13.00	25.00
79-27-002	Daisies Do Tell	Unknown	Unkn.	17.50	20.00
Sports Impressions/Enesco		**Gold Edition Plates**			
86-01-001	Larry Bird	R. Simon	Closed	125.00	150.00
86-01-002	Wade Boggs	B. Johnson	Closed	125.00	150.00
86-01-003	Mickey Mantle At Night	R. Simon	Closed	125.00	250.00
86-01-004	Keith Hernandez	R. Simon	Closed	125.00	175.00
86-01-005	Don Mattingly	B. Johnson	Closed	125.00	175.00
87-01-006	Darryl Strawberry #1	R. Simon	Closed	125.00	125.00
87-01-007	Ted Williams	R. Simon	Closed	125.00	495.00
87-01-008	Carl Yastrzemski	R. Simon	Closed	125.00	175.00
87-01-009	Mickey, Willie, & Duke	R. Simon	Closed	150.00	225.00
88-01-010	Brooks Robinson	R. Simon	Closed	125.00	225.00
88-01-011	Larry Bird	R. Simon	Closed	125.00	275.00
88-01-012	Magic Johnson	R. Simon	Closed	125.00	350.00
88-01-013	Yankee Tradition	J. Catalano	Closed	150.00	150.00
89-01-014	Mantle Switch Hitter	J. Catalano	Closed	150.00	150.00
89-01-015	Will Clark	J. Catalano	Closed	125.00	150.00
89-01-016	Darryl Strawberry #2	T. Fogerty	Closed	125.00	125.00
90-01-017	Living Triple Crown	R. Lewis	Closed	150.00	150.00
90-01-018	Tom Seaver	R. Lewis	Closed	150.00	150.00
90-01-019	Andre Dawson	R. Lewis	Closed	150.00	150.00
90-01-020	Rickey Henderson	R. Lewis	Closed	150.00	150.00
90-01-021	Nolan Ryan 300	J. Catalano	Closed	150.00	150.00
90-01-022	Joe Montana 49ers	J. Catalano	Closed	150.00	150.00
90-01-023	Michael Jordan	J. Catalano	Closed	150.00	150.00
91-01-024	Larry Bird	J. Catalano	Closed	150.00	195.00
91-01-025	Mickey Mantle 7	B. Simon	Closed	150.00	195.00
91-01-026	Hawks Dominique Wilkins	J. Catalano	Closed	150.00	195.00
91-01-027	Lakers Magic Johnson	W.C. Mundy	Closed	150.00	225.00
91-01-028	Michael Jordan	J. Catalano	Closed	150.00	275.00
91-01-029	Dream Team (1st Ten Chosen)	L. Salk	Closed	150.00	275.00
92-01-030	Dream Team	R.Tanenbaum	Closed	150.00	150-175.
92-01-031	Michael Jordan	R.Tanenbaum	Closed	150.00	200.00
92-01-032	Chicago Bulls '92 World Champions	C. Hayes	Closed	150.00	150.00
93-01-033	Magic Johnson	T. Fogerty	Closed	150.00	175.00
93-01-034	Magic Johnson (4042-04)	R.Tanenbaum	Closed	150.00	200.00
93-01-035	Michael Jordan	T. Fogerty	Closed	150.00	200.00
V-Palekh Art Studios		**Russian Legends**			
88-01-001	Ruslan and Ludmilla	G. Lubimov	195-day	29.87	33-40.00
88-01-002	The Princess/Seven Bogatyrs	A. Kovalev	195-day	29.87	35-38.00
88-01-003	The Golden Cockerel	V. Vleshko	195-day	32.87	33.00
88-01-004	Lukomorya	R. Belousov	195-day	32.87	35.00
89-01-005	Fisherman and the Magic Fish	N. Lopatin	195-day	32.87	30-38.00
89-01-006	Tsar Saltan	G. Zhiryakova	195-day	32.87	33-47.00
89-01-007	The Priest and His Servant	O. An	195-day	34.87	36-42.00

		ARTIST	EDITION	ISSUE	QUOTE
90-01-008	Stone Flower	V. Bolshakova	195-day	34.87	40.00
90-01-009	Sadko	E. Populor	195-day	34.87	45.00
90-01-010	The Twelve Months	N. Lopatin	195-day	36.87	36.87
90-01-011	Silver Hoof	S. Adeyanor	195-day	36.87	38.00
90-01-012	Morozko	N. Lopatin	195-day	36.87	37.00
Villeroy & Boch		**Villeroy & Boch**			
80-01-001	The Snow Maiden	B. Zvorykin	27,500	70.00	110-130.
81-01-002	Snegurochka at the Court of Tsar Berendei	B. Zvorykin	27,500	70.00	65-70.00
81-01-003	Snegurochka and Lei, the Shepherd Boy	B. Zvorykin	27,500	70.00	67-73.00
Villeroy & Boch		**Russian Fairytales The Red Knight**			
81-02-001	The Red Knight	B. Zvorykin	27,500	70.00	40-70.00
81-02-002	Vassilissa and Her Stepsisters	B. Zvorykin	27,500	70.00	45-77.00
81-02-003	Vassilissa is Presented to the Tsar	B. Zvorykin	27,500	70.00	56-75.00
Villeroy & Boch		**Russian Fairytales The Firebird**			
81-03-001	In Search of the Firebird	B. Zvorykin	27,500	70.00	95-120.
81-03-002	Ivan and Tsarevna on the Grey Wolf	B. Zvorykin	27,500	70.00	70-78.00
81-03-003	The Wedding of Tsarevna Elena the Fair	B. Zvorykin	27,500	70.00	100-118.
Villeroy & Boch		**Russian Fairytales Maria Morevna**			
82-04-001	Maria Morevna and Tsarevich Ivan	B. Zvorykin	27,500	70.00	90.00
82-04-002	Koshchey Carries Off Maria Morevna	B. Zvorykin	27,500	70.00	70.00
82-04-003	Tsarevich Ivan and the Beautiful Castle	B. Zvorykin	27,500	70.00	95-115.
Villeroy & Boch		**Flower Fairy**			
79-05-001	Lavender	C. Barker	21-day	35.00	125.00
80-05-002	Sweet Pea	C. Barker	21-day	35.00	125.00
80-05-003	Candytuft	C. Barker	21-day	35.00	89.00
81-05-004	Heliotrope	C. Barker	21-day	35.00	75.00
81-05-005	Blackthorn	C. Barker	21-day	35.00	75.00
81-05-006	Appleblossom	C. Barker	21-day	35.00	95.00
Waterford Wedgwood USA		**Wedgwood Christmas**			
69-01-001	Windsor Castle	T. Harper	Annual	25.00	200.00
70-01-002	Trafalgar Square	T. Harper	Annual	30.00	60.00
71-01-003	Picadilly Circus	T. Harper	Annual	30.00	50.00
72-01-004	St. Paul's Cathedral	T. Harper	Annual	35.00	50.00
73-01-005	Tower of London	T. Harper	Annual	40.00	90.00
74-01-006	Houses of Parliament	T. Harper	Annual	40.00	40.00
75-01-007	Tower Bridge	T. Harper	Annual	45.00	45.00
76-01-008	Hampton Court	T. Harper	Annual	50.00	50.00
77-01-009	Westminister Abbey	T. Harper	Annual	55.00	60.00
78-01-010	Horse Guards	T. Harper	Annual	60.00	60.00
79-01-011	Buckingham Palace	Unknown	Annual	65.00	65.00
80-01-012	St. James Palace	Unknown	Annual	70.00	70.00
81-01-013	Marble Arch	Unknown	Annual	75.00	75.00
82-01-014	Lambeth Palace	Unknown	Annual	80.00	90.00
83-01-015	All Souls, Langham Palace	Unknown	Annual	80.00	80.00
84-01-016	Constitution Hill	Unknown	Annual	80.00	80.00
85-01-017	The Tate Gallery	Unknown	Annual	80.00	80.00
86-01-018	The Albert Memorial	Unknown	Annual	80.00	150.00
87-01-019	Guildhall	Unknown	Annual	80.00	85.00
88-01-020	The Observatory/Greenwich	Unknown	Annual	80.00	90.00
89-01-021	Winchester Cathedral	Unknown	Annual	88.00	88.00
Waterford Wedgwood USA		**Bicentennial**			
72-03-001	Boston Tea Party	Unknown	Annual	40.00	40.00
73-03-002	Paul Revere's Ride	Unknown	Annual	40.00	115.00
74-03-003	Battle of Concord	Unknown	Annual	40.00	55.00
75-03-004	Across the Delaware	Unknown	Annual	40.00	105.00
75-03-005	Victory at Yorktown	Unknown	Annual	45.00	53.00
76-03-006	Declaration Signed	Unknown	Annual	45.00	45.00

STEINS

Anheuser-Busch, Inc.		**Specialty Steins**			
75-01-001	Bud Man CS1	A-Busch,Inc.	Retrd.	N/A	350-450.
75-01-002	A&Eagle CS2	A-Busch,Inc.	Retrd.	N/A	150-275.
75-01-003	A&Eagle Lidded CSL2 (Reference CS28)	A-Busch,Inc.	Retrd.	N/A	250-350.
75-01-004	Katakombe CS3	A-Busch,Inc.	Retrd.	N/A	175-300.
75-01-005	Katakombe Lidded CSL3	A-Busch,Inc.	Retrd.	N/A	350-450.
75-01-006	German Olympia CS4	A-Busch,Inc.	Retrd.	N/A	50-150.
75-01-007	Senior Grande Lidded CSL4	A-Busch,Inc.	Retrd.	N/A	475-650.
75-01-008	German Pilique CS5	A-Busch,Inc.	Retrd.	N/A	375-500.
75-01-009	German Pilique Lidded CSL5	A-Busch,Inc.	Retrd.	N/A	450-550.
75-01-010	Senior Grande CS6	A-Busch,Inc.	Retrd.	N/A	700-800.
75-01-011	German Olympia Lidded CSL6	A-Busch,Inc.	Retrd.	N/A	150-300.
75-01-012	Miniature Bavarian CS7	A-Busch,Inc.	Retrd.	N/A	225-300.
76-01-013	Budweiser Centennial Lidded CSL7	A-Busch,Inc.	Retrd.	N/A	425-500.
76-01-014	U.S. Bicentennial Lidded CSL8	A-Busch,Inc.	Retrd.	N/A	425-500.
76-01-015	Natural Light CS9	A-Busch,Inc.	Retrd.	N/A	170-250.
76-01-016	Clydesdales Hofbrau Lidded CSL9	A-Busch,Inc.	Retrd.	N/A	225-325.
76-01-017	Blue Delft CS11	A-Busch,Inc.	Retrd.	N/A	18-2400.
76-01-018	Clydesdales CS12	A-Busch,Inc.	Retrd.	N/A	200-350.
76-01-019	Budweiser Centennial CS13	A-Busch,Inc.	Retrd.	N/A	325-450
76-01-020	U.S. Bicentennial CS14	A-Busch,Inc.	Retrd.	N/A	325-450.
76-01-021	Clydesdales Grants Farm CS15	A-Busch,Inc.	Retrd.	N/A	250-300.
76-01-022	German Cities (6 assorted) CS16	A-Busch,Inc.	Retrd.	N/A	15-1800.
76-01-023	Americana CS17	A-Busch,Inc.	Retrd.	N/A	350-550.
76-01-024	Budweiser Label CS18	A-Busch,Inc.	Retrd.	N/A	350-450.
80-01-025	Budweiser Ladies (4 assorted) CS20	A-Busch,Inc.	Retrd.	N/A	2-2500.
77-01-026	Budweiser Girl CS21	A-Busch,Inc.	Retrd.	N/A	500.00
76-01-027	Budweiser Centennial CS22	A-Busch,Inc.	Retrd.	N/A	325-475.
77-01-028	A&Eagle CS24	A-Busch,Inc.	Retrd.	N/A	450.00
76-01-029	A&Eagle Barrel CS26	A-Busch,Inc.	Retrd.	N/A	85-175.
76-01-030	Michelob CS27	A-Busch,Inc.	Retrd.	N/A	175-250.
76-01-031	A&Eagle Lidded CS28 (Reference CSL2)	A-Busch,Inc.	Retrd.	N/A	265-350.
76-01-032	Clydesdales Lidded CS29	A-Busch,Inc.	Retrd.	N/A	245-350.
76-01-033	Coracao Decanter Set (7 piece) CS31	A-Busch,Inc.	Retrd.	N/A	560-750.
76-01-034	Geraman Wine Set (7 piece) CS32	A-Busch,Inc.	Retrd.	N/A	400-500.
76-01-035	Clydesdales Decanter CS33	A-Busch,Inc.	Retrd.	N/A	1-1200.
76-01-036	Holanda Brown Decanter Set (7 piece) CS34	A-Busch,Inc.	Retrd.	N/A	275.00
76-01-037	Holanda Blue Decanter Set (7 piece) CS35	A-Busch,Inc.	Retrd.	N/A	750.00
76-01-038	Canteen Decanter Set (7 piece) CS36	A-Busch,Inc.	Retrd.	N/A	N/A
76-01-039	St. Louis Decanter CS37	A-Busch,Inc.	Retrd.	N/A	400.00
76-01-040	St. Louis Decanter Set (7 piece) CS38	A-Busch,Inc.	Retrd.	N/A	1-1200.
80-01-041	Wurzburger Hofbrau CS39	A-Busch,Inc.	Retrd.	N/A	350-450.
80-01-042	Budweiser Chicago Skyline CS40	A-Busch,Inc.	Retrd.	N/A	100-225.
78-01-043	Busch Gardens CS41	A-Busch,Inc.	Retrd.	N/A	350.00
80-01-044	Oktoberfest-- "The Old Country" CS42	A-Busch,Inc.	Retrd.	N/A	275-350.
80-01-045	Natural Light Label CS43	A-Busch,Inc.	Retrd.	N/A	125-175.

		ARTIST	EDITION	ISSUE	QUOTE
80-01-046	Busch Label CS44	A-Busch,Inc.	Retrd.	N/A	150-175.
80-01-047	Michelob Label CS45	A-Busch,Inc.	Retrd.	N/A	75-125.
80-01-048	Budweiser Label CS46	A-Busch,Inc.	Retrd.	N/A	75-150.
81-01-049	Budweiser Chicagoland CS51	A-Busch,Inc.	Retrd.	N/A	40-50.00
81-01-050	Budweiser Texas CS52	A-Busch,Inc.	Retrd.	N/A	40-55.00
81-01-051	Budweiser California CS56	A-Busch,Inc.	Retrd.	N/A	45-50.00
83-01-052	Budweiser San Francisco CS59	A-Busch,Inc.	Retrd.	N/A	170-175.
84-01-053	Budweiser Olympic Games CS60	A-Busch,Inc.	Retrd.	N/A	15-50.00
83-01-054	Bud Light Baron CS61	A-Busch,Inc.	Retrd.	N/A	30-50.00
87-01-055	Santa Claus CS79	A-Busch,Inc.	Retrd.	N/A	75-80.00
87-01-056	King Cobra CS80	A-Busch,Inc.	Retrd.	N/A	N/A
87-01-057	Winter Olympic Games, Lidded CS81	A-Busch,Inc.	Retrd.	49.95	65-90.00
88-01-058	Budweiser Winter Olympic Games CS85	A-Busch,Inc.	Retrd.	24.95	20-27.00
88-01-059	Summer Olympic Games, Lidded CS91	A-Busch,Inc.	Retrd.	54.95	50-60.00
88-01-060	Budweiser Summer Olympic Games CS92	A-Busch,Inc.	Retrd.	54.95	20.00
88-01-061	Budweiser/ Field&Stream Set (4 piece) CS95	A-Busch,Inc.	Retrd.	69.95	200-300.
89-01-062	Bud Man CS100	A-Busch,Inc.	Retrd.	29.95	30-45.00
90-01-063	Baseball Cardinal Stein CS125	A-Busch,Inc.	Retrd.	30.00	25-30.00
91-01-064	Bevo Fox Stein CS160	A-Busch,Inc.	Retrd.	250.00	175-250.
Anheuser-Busch, Inc.	**Clydesdales Holiday Series**				
80-02-001	1st Holiday CS19	A-Busch,Inc.	Retrd.	9.95	95-125.
76-02-002	Budweiser Champion Clydesdales CS19A	A-Busch,Inc.	Retrd.	N/A	135-300.
81-02-003	2nd Holiday CS50	A-Busch,Inc.	Retrd.	9.95	190-250.
82-02-004	3rd Holiday CS57 50th Anniversary	A-Busch,Inc.	Retrd.	9.95	65-95.00
83-02-005	4th Holiday CS58	A-Busch,Inc.	Retrd.	9.95	30-40.00
84-02-006	5th Holiday CS62	A-Busch,Inc.	Retrd.	9.95	15-20.00
85-02-007	6th Holiday CS63	A-Busch,Inc.	Retrd.	9.95	15-20.00
86-02-008	7th Holiday CS66	A-Busch,Inc.	Retrd.	9.95	25-40.00
87-02-009	8th Holiday CS70	A-Busch,Inc.	Retrd.	9.95	13-25.00
88-02-010	9th Holiday CS88	A-Busch,Inc.	Retrd.	9.95	13-20.00
89-02-011	10th Holiday CS89	A-Busch,Inc.	Retrd.	12.95	13-20.00
Anheuser-Busch, Inc.	**Horseshoe Series**				
86-03-001	Horseshoe CS68	A-Busch,Inc.	Retrd.	14.95	40-75.00
87-03-002	Horsehead CS76	A-Busch,Inc.	Retrd.	16.00	30-50.00
86-03-003	Horseshoe CS77	A-Busch,Inc.	Retrd.	16.00	40-75.00
87-03-004	Horsehead CS78	A-Busch,Inc.	Retrd.	14.95	60-75.00
88-03-005	Harness CS94	A-Busch,Inc.	Retrd.	16.00	50-80.00
Anheuser-Busch, Inc.	**Limited Edition Series**				
85-04-001	Ltd. Ed. I Brewing & Fermenting CS64	A-Busch,Inc.	Retrd.	29.95	175-200.
86-04-002	Ltd. Ed. II Aging & Cooperage CS65	A-Busch,Inc.	Retrd.	29.95	45-75.00
87-04-003	Ltd. Ed. III Transportation CS71	A-Busch,Inc.	Retrd.	29.95	30-50.00
88-04-004	Ltd. Ed. IV Taverns & Public Houses CS75	A-Busch,Inc.	Retrd.	29.95	25-35.00
89-04-005	Ltd. Ed.V Festival Scene CS98	A-Busch,Inc.	Retrd.	34.95	25-35.00
Anheuser-Busch, Inc.	**Historical Landmark Series**				
86-05-001	Brew House CS67 (First)	A-Busch,Inc.	Retrd.	19.95	30-45.00
87-05-002	Stables CS73 (Second)	A-Busch,Inc.	Retrd.	19.95	25-35.00
88-05-003	Grant Cabin CS83 (Third)	A-Busch,Inc.	Retrd.	19.95	25-40.00
88-05-004	Old School House CS84 (Fourth)	A-Busch,Inc.	Retrd.	19.95	25-35.00
Anheuser-Busch, Inc.	**Classic Series**				
88-06-001	1st Edition CS93	A-Busch,Inc.	Retrd.	34.95	135-175.
89-06-002	2nd Edition CS104	A-Busch,Inc.	Retrd.	54.95	95-110.
90-06-003	3rd Edition CS113	A-Busch,Inc.	Retrd.	65.00	40-100.
91-06-004	4th Edition CS130	A-Busch,Inc.	Retrd.	75.00	40-75.00
Anheuser-Busch, Inc.	**Wholesaler Holiday Series**				
90-07-001	An American Tradition, CS112, 1990	S. Sampson	Retrd.	13.50	13-15.00
90-07-002	An American Tradition, CS112-SE	S. Sampson	Retrd.	50.00	50-80.00
91-07-003	The Season's Best, CS133, 1991	S. Sampson	Retrd.	14.50	13-15.00
91-07-004	The Season's Best, CS133-SE Signature Edition, 1991	S. Sampson	Retrd.	50.00	25-50.00
92-07-005	The Perfect Christmas, CS167, 1992	S. Sampson	Open	14.50	14.50
92-07-006	The Perfect Christmas, CS167-SE Signature Edition, 1992	S. Sampson	Open	50.00	25.00
93-07-007	Special Delivery, CS192, 1993	N. Koerber	Retrd.	15.00	20-25.00
93-07-008	Special Delivery, CS192-SE Signature Edition, 1993	N. Koerber	Retrd.	60.00	100-125.
94-07-009	Hometown Holiday, CS211, 1994	B. Kemper	Open	14.00	14.00
94-07-010	Hometown Holiday, CS211-SE Signature Edition, 1994	B. Kemper	10,000	65.00	65.00
Anheuser-Busch, Inc.	**Giftware Edition**				
92-08-001	1992 Rodeo CS184	A-Busch,Inc.	Open	18.00	25.00
93-08-002	Bud Man Character Stein CS213	A-Busch,Inc.	Open	45.00	45.00
94-08-003	Budweiser Golf Bag Stein CS225	A-Busch,Inc.	Open	16.00	16.00
94-08-004	"Walking Tall" Budweiser Cowboy Boot Stein CS251	A-Busch,Inc.	Open	17.50	17.50
Anheuser-Busch, Inc.	**Clydesdales Series-Giftware Edition**				
87-09-001	Eight Horse Hitch CS74	A-Busch,Inc.	Retrd.	9.95	20-25.00
88-09-002	Mare & Foal CS90	A-Busch,Inc.	Retrd.	11.50	20-25.00
89-09-003	Parade Dress CS99	A-Busch,Inc.	Retrd.	11.50	40-50.00
91-09-004	Training Hitch CS131	A-Busch,Inc.	Retrd.	13.00	11-25.00
92-09-005	Clydesdales on Parade CS161	A-Busch,Inc.	Retrd.	16.00	16-25.00
94-09-006	Proud and Free CS223	A-Busch,Inc.	Open	17.00	17.00
Anheuser-Busch, Inc.	**Sports History Series-Giftware Edition**				
90-10-001	Baseball, America's Favorite Pastime CS124	A-Busch,Inc.	Retrd.	20.00	20-25.00
90-10-002	Football, Gridiron Legacy CS128	A-Busch,Inc.	Retrd.	20.00	20-22.00
91-10-003	Auto Racing, Chasing The Checkered Flag CS432	A-Busch,Inc.	100,000	22.00	22.00
91-10-004	Basketball, Heroes of the Hardwood CS134	A-Busch,Inc.	100,000	22.00	22.00
92-10-005	Golf, Par For The Course CS165	A-Busch,Inc.	100,000	22.00	22.00
93-10-006	Hockey, Center Ice CS209	A-Busch,Inc.	100,000	22.00	22.00
Anheuser-Busch, Inc.	**Bud Label Series-Giftware Edition**				
89-11-001	Budweiser Label CS101	A-Busch,Inc.	Open	14.00	14.00
90-11-002	Antique Label II CS127	A-Busch,Inc.	Retrd.	14.00	16.00
90-11-003	Bottled Beer III CS136	A-Busch,Inc.	Open	15.00	15.00
Anheuser-Busch, Inc.	**St. Patrick's Day Series-Giftware Edition**				
91-12-001	1991 St. Patrick's Day CS109	A-Busch,Inc.	Retrd.	15.00	40-45.00
92-12-002	1992 St. Patrick's Day CS166	A-Busch,Inc.	100,000	15.00	15.00
93-12-003	1993 St. Patrick's Day CS193	A-Busch,Inc.	Retrd.	15.30	20-25.00
94-12-004	Luck O' The Irish CS210	A-Busch,Inc.	Open	18.00	18.00
Anheuser-Busch, Inc.	**Logo Series Steins-Giftware Edition**				
91-13-001	Budweiser CS143	A-Busch,Inc.	Open	16.00	16.00
91-13-002	Bud Light CS144	A-Busch,Inc.	Open	16.00	16.00

		ARTIST	EDITION	ISSUE	QUOTE
91-13-003	Michelob CS145	A-Busch,Inc.	Retrd.	16.00	16.00
91-13-004	Michelob Dry CS146	A-Busch,Inc.	Open	16.00	16.00
91-13-005	Busch CS147	A-Busch,Inc.	Open	16.00	16.00
91-13-006	A&Eagle CS148	A-Busch,Inc.	Open	16.00	16.00
91-13-007	Bud Dry Draft CS156	A-Busch,Inc.	Open	16.00	16.00
Anheuser-Busch, Inc.	**A & Eagle Historical Trademark Series-Giftware Edition**				
93-14-001	The 1872 Edition CS191, boxed	D. Langeneckert	Retrd.	22.00	30-45.00
93-14-002	The 1872 Edition CS201, tin	D. Langeneckert	Retrd.	31.00	30-45.00
93-14-003	The 1890 Edition CS218, tin	A-Busch,Inc.	Retrd.	24.00	24.00
94-14-004	The 1890 Edition CS219, boxed	A-Busch,Inc.	Retrd.	24.00	24-40.00
94-14-005	The 1900 Edition CS238, tin	A-Busch,Inc.	20,000	28.00	28.00
Anheuser-Busch, Inc.	**Octoberfest Series-Giftware Edition**				
92-15-001	1992 Octoberfest CS185	A-Busch,Inc.	35,000	16.00	16.00
93-15-002	1993 Octoberfest CS202	A-Busch,Inc.	35,000	18.00	18.00
Anheuser-Busch, Inc.	**Budweiser Racing Series-Giftware Edition**				
92-16-001	Budweiser Racing-Elliot/Johnson N3553	T. Watts	Retrd.	19.00	30-45.00
93-16-002	Budweiser RacingTeam CS194	H. Droog	Open	19.00	19.00
Anheuser-Busch, Inc.	**Budweiser Military Series-Giftware Edition**				
94-17-001	Army CS224	H. Droog	Open	19.00	19.00
94-17-002	Air Force CS228	M. Watts	Open	19.00	19.00
Anheuser-Busch, Inc.	**Marine Conservation Series-Collector Edition**				
94-18-001	Manatee Stein CS203	B. Kemper	25,000	33.50	33.50
Anheuser-Busch, Inc.	**Endangered Species Series-Collector Edition**				
89-19-001	Bald Eagle CS106(First)	A-Busch,Inc.	Retrd.	24.95	250-275.
90-19-002	Asian Tiger CS126 (Second)	A-Busch,Inc.	Retrd.	27.50	35-60.00
91-19-003	African Elephant CS135 (Third)	A-Busch,Inc.	100,000	29.00	29.00
92-19-004	Giant Panda CS173(Fourth)	B. Kemper	100,000	29.00	29.00
92-19-005	Grizzly CS199(Fifth)	B. Kemper	100,000	29.50	29.50
94-19-006	Gray Wolf Stein CS226	B. Kemper	100,000	29.50	29.50
Anheuser-Busch, Inc.	**Discover America Series-Collector Edition**				
90-20-001	Nina CS107	A-Busch,Inc.	100,000	40.00	40.00
91-20-002	Pinta CS129	A-Busch,Inc.	100,000	40.00	40.00
92-20-003	Santa Maria CS138	A-Busch,Inc.	100,000	40.00	40.00
Anheuser-Busch, Inc.	**Sports Legend Series-Collector Edition**				
91-21-001	Babe Ruth CS142	A-Busch,Inc.	50,000	85.00	85.00
92-21-002	Jim Thorpe CS171	M. Caito	50,000	85.00	85.00
93-21-003	Joe Louis CS206	M. Caito	50,000	85.00	85.00
Anheuser-Busch, Inc.	**1992 Olympic Team Series-Collector Edition**				
91-22-001	1992 Winter Olympic Stein CS162	A-Busch,Inc.	25,000	85.00	85.00
92-22-002	1992 Summer Olympic Stein CS163	A-Busch,Inc.	25,000	85.00	85.00
92-22-003	1992 U.S.Olympic Stein CS168	A-Busch,Inc.	50,000	16.00	19.00
Anheuser-Busch, Inc.	**Archives Series-Collector Edition**				
92-23-001	1893 Columbian Exposition CS169	A-Busch,Inc.	75,000	35.00	35.00
92-23-002	Ganymede CS190	D. Langeneckert	75,000	35.00	35.00
94-23-003	Budweiser's Greatest Triumph CS222	D. Langeneckert	75,000	35.00	35.00
Anheuser-Busch, Inc.	**Sea World Series-Collector Edition**				
92-24-001	Killer Whale CS186	A-Busch, Inc.	25,000	100.00	100.00
92-24-002	Dolphin CS187	A-Busch, Inc.	22,500	90.00	90.00
Anheuser-Busch, Inc.	**Hunter's Companion Series-Collector Edition**				
93-25-001	Labrador Retriever CS195	L. Freeman	50,000	32.50	32.50
94-25-002	The Setter Stein CS205	S. Ryan	50,000	32.50	32.50
Anheuser-Busch, Inc.	**Collector Edition**				
94-26-001	Budweiser World Cup Stein CS230	J. Tull	25,000	40.00	40.00
Anheuser-Busch, Inc.	**Porcelain Heritage Series-Premier Edition**				
90-27-001	Berninghaus CS105	Berninghaus	Retrd.	75.00	40-75.00
91-27-002	After The Hunt CS155	A-Busch,Inc.	25,000	100.00	100.00
92-27-003	Cherub CS182	D. Langeneckert	25,000	100.00	100.00
Anheuser-Busch, Inc.	**Birds of Prey Series-Premier Edition**				
91-28-001	American Bald Eagle CS164	P. Ford	25,000	125.00	125.00
92-28-002	Peregrine Falcon CS183	P. Ford	25,000	125.00	125.00
94-28-003	Osprey CS212	P. Ford	25,000	135.00	135.00
Anheuser-Busch, Inc.	**Civil War Series-Premier Edition**				
92-29-001	General Grant CS181	D. Langeneckert	25,000	150.00	150.00
93-29-002	General Robert E. Lee CS188	D. Langeneckert	25,000	150.00	150.00
93-29-003	President Abraham Lincoln CS189	D. Langeneckert	25,000	150.00	150.00
Anheuser-Busch, Inc.	**Anheuser-Busch Founder Series-Premier Collection**				
93-30-001	Adophus Busch CS216	A-Busch,Inc.	10,000	180.00	180.00
94-30-002	August A. Busch, Sr. CS229	A-Busch,Inc.	10,000	220.00	220.00
Anheuser-Busch, Inc.	**Premier Collection**				
93-31-001	Bill Elliott CS196	H. Droog	25,000	150.00	150.00
93-31-002	Bill Elliott, Signature Edition, CS196SE	H. Droog	1,500	295.00	295.00
Anheuser-Busch, Inc./Gerz Meisterwerke Collection	**First Hunt Series**				
92-32-001	Golden Retriever GM-2	P. Ford	10,000	150.00	150.00
94-32-002	Springer Spaniel GM-5	P. Ford	10,000	170.00	170.00
Anheuser-Busch, Inc./Gerz Meisterwerke Collection	**Saturday Evening Post Collection**				
93-33-001	Santa's Mailbag GM-1	Gerz	Retrd.	195.00	250-300.
93-33-002	Santa's Helper GM-3	Gerz	7,500	200.00	200.00
94-33-003	"All I Want For Christmas" GM-13	J.C. Leyendecker	5,000	220.00	220.00
Anheuser-Busch, Inc./Gerz Meisterwerke Collection	**American Heritage Collection**				
93-34-001	John F. Kennedy Stein-GM-4	Gerz	10,000	220.00	220.00
Anheuser-Busch, Inc.	**Gerz Meisterwerke Collection**				
94-35-001	Norman Rockwell-Triple Self Portrait GM6	A-Busch,Inc.	5,000	250.00	250.00
94-35-002	Mallard Stein GM7	A-Busch,Inc.	5,000	220.00	220.00
94-35-003	Winchester "Model 94" Centennial Stein GM10	A-Busch,Inc.	5,000	150.00	150.00
Anheuser-Busch, Inc./Gerz Meisterwerke Collection	**Favorite Past Times Collection**				
93-36-001	The Dugout-GL1	Gerz	10,000	110.00	110.00
94-36-002	Winchester Stein-GL2	A-Busch,Inc.	10,000	120.00	120.00
Artaffects	**Perillo Steins**				
89-01-001	Buffalo Hunt	G. Perillo	5,000	125.00	125.00
91-01-002	Hoofbeats	G. Perillo	5,000	125.00	125.00
CUI/Carolina Collection/Dram Tree	**Ducks Unlimited**				
87-01-001	Wood Duck Edition I	K. Bloom	Retrd.	80.00	200.00
88-01-002	Mallard Edition II	M. Bradford	Retrd.	80.00	125.00
89-01-003	Canvasbacks Edition III	L. Barnicle	Retrd.	80.00	100.00
90-01-004	Pintails Edition IV	R. Plasschaert	Retrd.	80.00	90.00

		ARTIST	EDITION	ISSUE	QUOTE
91-01-005	Canada Geese Edition V	J. Meger	20,000	80.00	80.00
CUI/Carolina Collection/Dram Tree	**Federal Duck Stamp**				
90-02-001	Lesser Scaup Edition I	N. Anderson	6,950	80.00	80.00
91-02-002	Black Bellied Whistling Duck Edition II	J. Hautman	6,950	80.00	80.00
92-02-003	King Eiders Edition III	N. Howe	Retrd.	80.00	80.00
93-02-004	Spectacled Eiders	J. Hautman	6,950	80.00	80.00
93-02-005	50th Anniversary Commemorative	W.C. Morris	6,950	85.00	85.00
94-02-006	Canvasbacks	B. Miller	6,950	80.00	80.00
CUI/Carolina Collection/Dram Tree	**National Wild Turkey Federation**				
90-03-001	The Apprentice Edition I	M.T. Noe	9,950	125.00	125.00
91-03-002	Sultan's Sunrise Edition II	A. Agnew	6,950	100.00	100.00
92-03-003	Double Gobble Edition III	J.S. Eberhardt	6,950	100.00	100.00
93-02-004	Tempting Trio	J. Kasper	6,950	100.00	105.50
CUI/Carolina Collection/Dram Tree	**North American Hunting Club**				
90-04-001	Deer Crossing Edition I	R. McGovern	Retrd.	85.00	85.00
92-04-002	Yukon Grizzly Edition II	L. Anderson	6,950	74.00	74.00
93-04-003	Interrupted Crossing	J. Kasper	6,950	74.00	74.00
94-04-004	Untouchables	H. Lambson	2,950	74.00	74.00
CUI/Carolina Collection/Dram Tree	**Nat'l. Foundation to Protect America's Eagles**				
91-05-001	Great American Patriots Edition I	R.J. McDonald	Retrd.	80.00	80.00
CUI/Carolina Collection/Dram Tree	**American Angler Series Limited Edition**				
90-06-001	Large Mouth Bass	J.R. Hook	Retrd.	25.00	25.00
CUI/Carolina Collection/Dram Tree	**Pheasants Forever**				
91-07-001	Jumping Ringnecks Edition I	J. Killen	Retrd.	100.00	100.00
92-07-002	Foggy Morning Magic Edition II	P. Crowe	Retrd.	100.00	100.00
CUI/Carolina Collection/Dram Tree	**Trout Unlimited**				
91-08-001	Rainbow Edition I	M. Stidham	6,950	90.00	90.00
92-08-002	Downstream & Across Edition II	E. Hardle	6,950	90.00	90.00
94-08-003	Williams Fork River	CUI	6,950	85.00	85.00
CUI/Carolina Collection/Dram Tree	**Quail Unlimited**				
91-09-001	Hedgerow Bobs Edition I	D. Chapple	Retrd.	90.00	90.00
92-09-002	California Trio Edition II	J. Garcia	Retrd.	90.00	90.00
CUI/Carolina Collection/Dram Tree	**Whitetails Unlimited**				
91-10-001	Last Glance at Trails End	J. Paluh	Retrd.	90.00	90.00
92-10-002	Indian Summer Flight Edition II	B. Miller	Retrd.	90.00	90.00
CUI/Carolina Collection/Dram Tree	**Jack Russell Terrier**				
91-11-001	Jack Russell Terrier Edition I	B.B. Atwater	Retrd.	90.00	90.00
CUI/Carolina Collection/Dram Tree	**Statue of Liberty**				
91-12-001	Lady Liberty	CUI	Retrd.	50.00	50.00
86-12-002	Statue of Liberty	CUI	Retrd.	42.50	42.50
93-12-003	Ellis Island	CUI	Open	25.00	25.00
CUI/Carolina Collection/Dram Tree	**Civil War**				
91-13-001	Firing on Fort Sumter Edition I	CUI	4,950	125.00	125.00
92-13-002	Stonewall Jackson Edition II	CUI	4,950	125.00	125.00
92-13-003	J.E.B. Stuart Edition III	CUI	4,950	128.00	128.00
93-13-004	Robert E. Lee Edition IV	CUI	4,950	128.00	128.00
CUI/Carolina Collection/Dram Tree	**Native American Series**				
91-14-001	Hunt for the Buffalo Edition I	P. Kethley	Retrd.	100.00	100.00
92-14-002	Story Teller	P. Kethley	Retrd.	50.00	50.00
CUI/Carolina Collection/Dram Tree	**Christmas Series**				
91-15-001	Checkin' It Twice Edition I	CUI	Retrd.	125.00	125.00
92-15-002	With A Finger Aside His Nose	CUI	Retrd.	125.00	128.00
93-15-003	Mrs. Claus	CUI	Retrd.	128.00	128.00
CUI/Carolina Collection/Dram Tree	**Environmental Series**				
91-16-001	Rain Forest Magic Edition I	C.L. Bragg	4,950	90.00	90.00
92-16-002	First Breath Edition II	M. Hoffman	4,950	90.00	90.00
93-16-003	Humpback Whale	CUI	4,950	95.00	95.00
CUI/Carolina Collection/Dram Tree	**Miller Girl in the Moon**				
90-17-001	Miller Girl in the Moon	CUI	Open	50.00	50.00
CUI/Carolina Collection/Dram Tree	**Miller Girl in the Moon (Miniatures)**				
94-18-001	The Original Toast	CUI	Open	25.00	25.00
94-18-002	Twilight Gazebo	CUI	Open	25.00	25.00
94-18-003	Moonbeam Girl Over the Water	CUI	Open	25.00	25.00
94-18-004	Celestial Beer Garden Escape	CUI	Open	25.00	25.00
94-18-005	Moontime Relaxation	CUI	Open	25.00	25.00
94-18-006	Moonlight Picnic	CUI	Open	25.00	25.00
CUI/Carolina Collection/Dram Tree	**Wild Life Series**				
94-19-001	Timber Wolf	A. Agnew	Open	30.00	30.00
94-19-002	Eagle	R. McGovern	Open	30.00	30.00
94-19-003	Mallards	R. Cruwys	Open	30.00	30.00
94-19-004	Whitetail Deer	R. Cruwys	Open	30.00	30.00
CUI/Carolina Collection/Dram Tree	**Great American Achievements**				
86-20-001	First Successful Flight Edition I	CUI	Retrd.	10.95	75-95.00
87-20-002	The Model T Edition II	CUI	Retrd.	12.95	30-55.00
88-20-003	First Transcontinental Railway Edition III	CUI	Retrd.	15.95	28-55.00
89-20-004	The First River Steamer Edition IV	CUI	Retrd.	25.00	25.00
90-20-005	Man's First Walk on the Moon Edition V	CUI	Retrd.	25.00	25.00
CUI/Carolina Collection/Dram Tree	**Birth of a Nation**				
91-21-001	Paul Revere's Ride Edition I	CUI	Retrd.	25.00	25.00
91-21-002	Paul Revere's Ride Lidded Edition I	CUI	Retrd.	70.00	70.00
92-21-003	Signing Of The Declaration Of Independence-Edition II	CUI	Retrd.	25.00	25.00
92-21-004	Signing Of The Declaration Of Independence-Special Pewter Lidded Edition II	CUI	Retrd.	70.00	70.00
93-21-005	George Washington Crossing the Delaware-Edition III	CUI	Retrd.	25.00	25.00
93-21-006	George Washington Crossing the Delaware-Special Lidded Edition III	CUI	Retrd.	70.00	70.00
94-21-007	Lewis & Clark Edition IV	CUI	Open	25.00	25.00
94-21-008	Lewis & Clark-Special Lidded Edition IV	CUI	10,000	70.00	70.00
CUI/Carolina Collection/Dram Tree	**Miller Plank Road**				
91-22-001	Miller Plank Road Edition I	CUI	Retrd.	90.00	90.00
CUI/Carolina Collection/Dram Tree	**Miller Historical Collection**				
90-23-001	Frederic Miller Edition I	CUI	Retrd.	136.00	136.00
91-23-002	Miller's Delivery Wagon Edition II	CUI	Retrd.	130.00	130.00
92-23-003	Coopersmith Edition III	CUI	9,950	130.00	130.00
CUI/Carolina Collection/Dram Tree	**Miller Holiday Series**				
91-24-001	Milwaukee Waterfront Edition I	CUI	9,950	50.00	50.00
92-24-002	Christmas on Old World Third St. Edition II	CUI	9,950	50.00	50.00
92-24-003	Miller Inn Edition III	CUI	9,950	50.00	50.00
93-24-004	Plank Road Christmas	CUI	9,950	50.00	50.00
94-24-005	Girl in the Moon Holiday	CUI	9,950	50.00	50.00
CUI/Carolina Collection/Dram Tree	**Coors Historical Collection**				
88-25-001	Rocky Mountain Brewry Edition I	CUI	Retrd.	15.95	15.95
89-25-002	Old Time Delivery Wagon Edition II	CUI	Retrd.	16.95	16.95
90-25-003	Waterfall Edition III	CUI	Retrd.	25.00	25.00
CUI/Carolina Collection/Dram Tree	**Coors Rocky Mountain Legends**				
91-26-001	Skier Edition I	CUI	Open	25.00	25.00
91-26-002	Skier Lidded Edition I	CUI	10,000	70.00	70.00
92-26-003	White Water Rafting Edition II	CUI	Retrd.	25.00	25.00
92-26-004	White Water Rafting Special Lidded Edition II	CUI	Retrd.	70.00	70.00
93-26-005	Fly Fishing Edition III	CUI	Open	25.00	25.00
93-26-006	Fly Fishing Special Lidded Edition III	CUI	10,000	70.00	70.00
94-26-007	Mountain Climber Edition IV	T. Stortz	Open	25.00	25.00
94-26-008	Mountain Climber Special Lidded Edition IV	T. Stortz	10,000	70.00	70.00
CUI/Carolina Collection/Dram Tree	**Coors Rodeo Collection**				
91-27-001	Jack Hammer Edition I	M.H. Scott	20,000	90.00	90.00
92-27-002	Born To Buck Edition II	M.H. Scott	20,000	90.00	90.00
93-27-003	Bulldogger Edition III	M.H. Scott	20,000	90.00	90.00
93-27-004	Ride on the Wild Side Edition IV	M.H. Scott	20,000	90.00	90.00
93-27-005	Teamwork Edition V	M.H. Scott	20,000	90.00	90.00
93-27-006	Turning Tight Edition VI	M.H. Scott	20,000	90.00	90.00
CUI/Carolina Collection/Dram Tree	**Winterfest**				
89-28-001	Outdoor Skating Edition I	T. Stortz	9,950	50.00	50.00
90-28-002	Christmas Square Edition II	T. Stortz	9,950	50.00	50.00
91-28-003	Horsedrawn Sleighs Edition III	T. Stortz	9,950	50.00	50.00
92-28-004	Skating Party Edition IV	T. Stortz	9,950	50.00	50.00
93-28-005	Awaiting the Train Edition V	T. Stortz	9,950	50.00	50.00
CUI/Carolina Collection/Dram Tree	**Coors Legacy Series**				
91-29-001	Coors Rams Head Edition I	CUI	Retrd.	130.00	130.00
92-29-002	Bock Beer Edition II	CUI	6,950	120.00	120.00
93-29-003	Bock Beer Edition III	CUI	6,950	120.00	120.00
CUI/Carolina Collection/Dram Tree	**Miller Racing Team**				
91-30-001	Penske/Wallace	CUI	Retrd.	50.00	50.00
92-30-002	Bobby Rahal	CUI	6,950	53.00	53.00
CUI/Carolina Collection/Dram Tree	**Ruffed Grouse Society**				
90-31-001	Northwoods Grouse Edition I	G. Moss	Retrd.	50.00	50.00
91-31-002	Edition II	Z. Jones	Retrd.	50.00	50.00
CUI/Carolina Collection/Dram Tree	**Phillip Morris**				
91-32-001	London's Bond St. Edition I	D. Hilburn	9,950	50.00	50.00
CUI/Carolina Collection/Dram Tree	**The Fleet Reserve**				
91-33-001	The Arizona Edition I	T. Freeman	6,950	60.00	60.00
92-33-002	Old Salts Edition II	F. Collinyswood	6,950	63.50	63.50
CUI/Carolina Collection/Dram Tree	**Experimental Aircraft Association**				
91-34-001	Into the Teeth of a Tiger Edition I	W.S. Phillips	Retrd.	80.00	80.00
92-34-002	Tokyo Raiders Ready For Launch Edition II	J. Dietz	Retrd.	80.00	80.00
93-34-003	305th Schweinfurt Bound	J. Dietz	Retrd.	80.00	80.00
CUI/Carolina Collection/Dram Tree	**National Football League**				
91-35-001	First NFL Championship Game Edition I-Pewter Edition	CUI	Retrd.	80.00	80.00
CUI/Carolina Collection/Dram Tree	**N.F.L. National Football League**				
91-36-001	Historically Speaking Pewter Edition I	CUI	Retrd.	80.00	80.00
CUI/Carolina Collection/Dram Tree	**N.B.A. National Basketball Association**				
91-37-001	100 Years of Basketball-Pewter Edition I	CUI	Retrd.	80.00	80.00
CUI/Carolina Collection/Dram Tree	**Stroh Heritage Collection**				
84-38-001	Horsedrawn Wagon - Heritage I	CUI	Retrd.	11.95	15-25.00
85-38-002	Kirn Inn Germany - Heritage II	CUI	Retrd.	12.95	15-22.00
86-38-003	Lion Brewing Company - Heritage III	CUI	Retrd.	13.95	25-35.00
87-38-004	Bohemian Beer - Heritage IV	CUI	Retrd.	14.95	19-22.00
88-38-005	Delivery Vehicles - Heritage V	CUI	Retrd.	25.00	25.00
89-38-006	Fire Brewed - Heritage V I	CUI	Retrd.	16.95	19.00
CUI/Carolina Collection/Dram Tree	**Stroh Bavaria Collection**				
90-39-001	Dancers Edition I - Bavaria I	CUI	Retrd.	45.00	45.00
90-39-002	Dancers Pewter Figure Edition I - Bavaria I	CUI	Retrd.	70.00	70.00
91-39-003	Barrel Pusher Edition II - Bavaria II	CUI	Retrd.	45.00	45.00
91-39-004	Barrel Pusher Pewter Edition II - Bavaria II	CUI	Retrd.	70.00	70.00
92-39-005	The Aging Cellar-Edition III	CUI	Retrd.	45.00	45.00
92-39-006	The Aging Cellar-Pewter Edition III	CUI	Retrd.	70.00	70.00
93-39-007	Bandwagon Street Party-Pewter Edition II	CUI	Retrd.	70.00	70.00
93-39-008	Bandwagon Street Party-Edition IV	CUI	Retrd.	45.00	45.00
CUI/Carolina Collection/Dram Tree	**Beck's**				
90-40-001	Beck's Purity Law Edition I	CUI	Retrd.	115.00	115.00
CUI/Carolina Collection/Dram Tree	**Northern Solitude**				
90-41-001	Moosehead Northern Solitude	N. Anderson	Retrd.	72.00	72.00
CUI/Carolina Collection/Dram Tree	**Big Game Series**				
90-42-001	Wind Blown-Big Horn Sheep	J. Antolik	Retrd.	70.00	70.00
92-42-002	Heat of the Kalahari-Lions	J. Antolik	Retrd.	70.00	70.00
93-42-003	Spring Back-Polar Bears	J. Morgan	Retrd.	70.00	70.00
CUI/Carolina Collection/Dram Tree	**Team of the Decade - NFL**				
90-43-001	NFL 49ers	CUI	Retrd.	60.00	60.00
CUI/Carolina Collection/Dram Tree	**SuperBowl XXV - NFL**				
91-44-001	NFL	CUI	Retrd.	60.00	60.00
CUI/Carolina Collection/Dram Tree	**SuperBowl Champions - NFL**				
91-45-001	NY Giants - NFL	CUI	Retrd.	60.00	60.00
92-45-002	Washington Redskins - NFL	CUI	Retrd.	60.00	60.00
CUI/Carolina Collection/Dram Tree	**World Series Champions - MLB**				
90-46-001	Cincinnati Reds - MLB	CUI	Retrd.	60.00	60.00
91-46-002	Minnesota Twins - MLB	CUI	Retrd.	60.00	60.00
92-46-003	Toronto Blue Jays-MLB	CUI	Retrd.	60.00	60.00
CUI/Carolina Collection/Dram Tree	**Stanley Cup Champions - NHL**				
91-47-001	Pittsburgh Penguins - NHL	CUI	Retrd.	60.00	60.00

	ARTIST	EDITION	ISSUE	QUOTE
92-47-002 Pittsburgh Penguins - NHL	CUI	Retrd.	60.00	60.00
93-47-003 Montreal Canadians-NHL	CUI	Retrd.	60.00	60.00
CUI/Carolina Collection/Dram Tree **World Champions - NBA**				
91-48-001 Chicago Bulls - NBA	CUI	Retrd.	60.00	60.00
92-48-002 Chicago Bulls - NBA	CUI	Retrd.	60.00	60.00
93-48-003 Chicago Bulls - NBA	CUI	Retrd.	60.00	60.00
CUI/Carolina Collection/Dram Tree **Anniversary Series**				
91-49-001 Chicago Bulls 25th Anniversary	CUI	Retrd.	60.00	60.00
92-49-002 Philadelphia Eagles 60th Anniversary	CUI	Retrd.	60.00	60.00
92-49-003 Cincinnati Bengals 25th Anniversary	CUI	Retrd.	60.00	60.00
92-49-004 Pittsburgh Steelers 60th Anniversary	CUI	Open	60.00	60.00
93-49-005 Greenbay Packers-75th Anniversary	CUI	4,950	60.00	60.00
CUI/Carolina Collection/Dram Tree **Ducks Unlimited Classic Decoy Series**				
92-50-001 1930's Bert Graves Mallard Decoys Edition I	D. Boncela	Retrd.	100.00	100.00
CUI/Carolina Collection/Dram Tree **North American Fishing Club**				
92-51-001 Jumpin' Hog	V. Beck	6,950	90.00	90.00
93-51-002 Rainbow Trout	R. Cruwys	6,950	90.00	90.00
93-51-003 On the Take	R. Cruwys	6,950	91.00	91.00
94-51-003 Crappie	R. Cruwys	6,950	90.00	90.00
CUI/Carolina Collection/Dram Tree **Historical Lighthouse Collectors Series**				
92-52-001 Boston Light Edition I	CUI	4,950	100.00	100.00
92-52-002 Cape Hatteras Lighthouse Edition II	CUI	4,950	100.00	100.00
93-52-003 Split Rock Edition III	CUI	4,950	100.00	100.00
94-52-004 Old Point Loma Lighthouse IV	CUI	4,950	100.00	100.00
94-52-005 Portland Head Lighthouse	B. Blythe	4,950	100.00	100.00
94-52-006 Ponce de Leon Lighthouse	B. Blythe	4,950	100.00	100.00
CUI/Carolina Collection/Dram Tree **American Conference Champion - NFL**				
92-53-001 Buffalo Bills-91 ACC	CUI	Retrd.	60.00	60.00
CUI/Carolina Collection/Dram Tree **National League Champion - MLB**				
92-54-001 Atlanta Braves-91 NLC	CUI	Retrd.	60.00	60.00
CUI/Carolina Collection/Dram Tree **Ducks Unlimited Waterfowl of North America**				
93-55-001 Into the Wind	T. Burleson	45-day	60.00	60.00
93-55-002 Early Flight Canvasbacks	R. Plasschaert	45-day	69.00	69.00
93-55-003 Pintail Trio	R. Leslie	45-day	69.00	69.00
94-55-004 Lesser Scaup	L. Chandler	45-day	69.00	69.00
94-55-005 Wood Duck	T. Doughty	45-day	69.00	69.00
CUI/Carolina Collection/Dram Tree **Classic Car Series**				
92-56-001 1957 Chevy	G. Geivette	Retrd.	100.00	100.00
93-56-002 Classic T-Birds	K. Eberts	6,950	100.00	100.00
CUI/Carolina Collection/Dram Tree **The Corvette Series**				
92-57-001 1953 Corvette	G. Geivette	6,950	100.00	100.00
93-57-002 1963 Corvette	K. Eberts	6,950	100.00	100.00
CUI/Carolina Collection/Dram Tree **Moosehead**				
92-58-001 Moosehead 125th Anniversary	CUI	Retrd.	100.00	100.00
CUI/Carolina Collection/Dram Tree **Quarterback Legends**				
92-59-001 Hall of Fame - John Unitas Edition I	CUI	4,950	175.00	175.00
92-59-002 Hall of Fame - Y.A. Tittle Edition II	CUI	4,950	175.00	175.00
92-59-003 Hall of Fame - Bart Starr	CUI	4,950	175.00	175.00
92-59-004 Hall of Fame - Otto Graham	CUI	Retrd.	175.00	175.00
CUI/Carolina Collection/Dram Tree **Cooperstown Collection**				
92-60-001 St. Louis Cardinals 100th Anniversary	CUI	Retrd.	70.00	70.00
93-60-002 Ebbets Field	CUI	Open	75.00	75.00
94-60-003 Polo Grounds	CUI	Open	75.00	75.00
CUI/Carolina Collection/Dram Tree **Cooperstown Team Collection**				
92-61-001 Brooklyn Dodgers	CUI	Retrd.	60.00	60.00
92-61-002 Boston Braves	CUI	Retrd.	60.00	60.00
92-61-003 Washington Senators	CUI	Retrd.	60.00	60.00
CUI/Carolina Collection/Dram Tree **The History of Billiards**				
93-62-001 1694 Louis XIV	Trouvian	Retrd.	39.50	39.50
93-62-002 1745 Ich Mache Nur Colle	Unknown	Retrd.	39.50	39.50
93-62-003 1823 Indifference	D. Egerton	Retrd.	39.50	39.50
93-62-004 1859 First Major Stake Match	Unknown	Retrd.	39.50	39.50
93-62-005 1875 Grand Union Hotel, Saratoga NY	Unknown	Retrd.	39.50	39.50
93-62-006 1905 Untitled Print	M. Neuman	Retrd.	39.50	39.50
CUI/Carolina Collection/Dram Tree **Coors Racing**				
92-63-001 Keystone/Wally Dallenbach, Jr.	CUI	Retrd.	53.00	53.00
CUI/Carolina Collection/Dram Tree **Still the King**				
92-64-001 Elvis Presley Postage Stamp	Unknown	Retrd.	60.00	60.00
93-64-002 '68 Comeback Special	CUI	45-day	60.00	60.00
94-64-003 Gates of Graceland	Unknown	45-day	60.00	60.00
94-64-004 Elvis in the Army	Unknown	45-day	65.00	65.00
94-64-005 Elvis:Aloha from Hawaii	Unknown	45-day	65.00	65.00
94-64-006 Elvis in Las Vegas	Unknown	45-day	65.00	65.00
CUI/Carolina Collection/Dram Tree **Texaco Heritage Collection**				
92-65-001 Return From a Holiday	Unknown	Retrd.	90.00	90.00
93-65-002 Companions on a Winter Journey-Edition II	Unknown	Retrd.	100.00	100.00
CUI/Carolina Collection/Dram Tree **West End Brewing**				
92-66-001 Baseball	Unknown	Retrd.	95.00	95.00
93-66-002 Picnic	Unknown	Retrd.	95.00	95.00
CUI/Carolina Collection/Dram Tree **David Mann Easy Riders**				
93-67-001 Limited Edition Holiday	D. Mann	Retrd.	70.00	70.00
94-67-002 Pony Express	D. Mann	2,000	90.00	90.00
94-67-003 The Viking	D. Mann	950	35.00	35.00
CUI/Carolina Collection/Dram Tree **Sheffield Pewter**				
93-68-001 Robin Hood	Unknown	Open	95.00	95.00
CUI/Carolina Collection/Dram Tree **Special Edition Series**				
93-69-001 Killer Whale	CUI	Open	70.00	70.00
93-69-002 Pintails in the Shallows	CUI	499	58.50	58.50
94-69-003 Great Locomotive Chase: The General	CUI	Open	70.00	70.00
94-69-004 Mallard Decoy	R. Cruwys	Open	50.00	50.00
94-69-005 First Man on the Moon Anniversary	CUI	1,969	70.00	70.00
94-69-006 California Quail "Desert Edge"	CUI	500	70.00	70.00
94-69-007 Hunting Dog "Point of Pride"	R. Cruwys	Open	90.00	90.00
94-69-008 Golden Retriever Puppies "Stand-Off!"	R. Cruwys	Open	50.00	50.00
94-69-009 Cardinals in the Snow	B. Blythe	Open	20.00	20.00

	ARTIST	EDITION	ISSUE	QUOTE
CUI/Carolina Collection/Dram Tree **Sportsteins**				
94-70-001 Carolina Panthers Sports Hoffbrau	Licensed	Open	20.00	20.00
94-70-002 Jacksonville Jaquars Sports Hoffbrau	Licensed	Open	20.00	20.00
94-70-003 New York Rangers Championship	Licensed	25,000	50.00	50.00
CUI/Carolina Collection/Dram Tree **Life of Elvis Hoffbrau**				
93-71-001 Elvis Presley-Postage Stamp	Unknown	Retrd.	39.50	39.50
93-71-002 Elvis Presley '68 Comeback Special	Unknown	45-day	39.50	39.50
94-71-003 Elvis Presley-Army Days	Unknown	45-day	39.50	39.50
94-71-004 Elvis Presley-Gates of Graceland	Unknown	45-day	39.50	39.50
94-71-005 Elvis Presley -Young Elvis	Unknown	45-day	39.50	39.50
94-71-006 Elvis Presley-Las Vegas	Unknown	45-day	39.50	39.50
CUI/Carolina Collection/Dram Tree **Elvis Presley Deluxe Series**				
93-72-001 Comeback Special-25th Anniversary	Unknown	1,968	130.00	130.00
94-72-002 Life of Elvis Deluxe	Unknown	1,977	130.00	130.00
94-72-003 Elvis:Aloha from Hawaii Deluxe	Unknown	1,973	130.00	130.00
CUI/Carolina Collection/Dram Tree **Oktoberfest**				
93-73-001 Dancing Pair	CUI	Open	39.95	39.95
CUI/Carolina Collection/Dram Tree **Nostalgic Golf Series**				
93-74-001 Down the Middle	CUI	6,950	65.00	65.00
94-74-002 Follow Through	Unknown	6,950	65.00	65.00
CUI/Carolina Collection/Dram Tree **Sailing Series**				
93-75-001 Blythe Spirit	CUI	Open	25.00	25.00
CUI/Carolina Collection/Dram Tree **First Encounter**				
94-76-001 Stand Off	R. Cruwys	Open	50.00	50.00
CUI/Carolina Collection/Dram Tree **NASCAR Relief Hoffbrau**				
94-77-001 Rusty Wallace/Miller Genuine Draft	Unknown	Open	25.00	25.00
Hamilton Collection **Warriors of the Plains Tankards**				
92-01-001 Thundering Hooves	G. Stewart	Open	125.00	125.00
Hamilton Collection **The STAR TREK Tankard Collection**				
94-02-001 SPOCK	T. Blackshear	Open	49.50	49.50
LCS Products **Early Innings**				
93-01-001 Ebbets Field	LCS	25,000	59.95	59.95
Sports Impressions **Baseball Steins**				
90-01-001 Nolan Ryan Rangers	R. Lewis	Closed	30.00	30.00
90-01-002 Life Of A Legend Mickey Mantle	T. Fogarty	Closed	30.00	30.00
90-01-003 Kings of K	J. Catalano	Closed	30.00	30.00
90-01-004 Rangers Nolan Ryan 300th Win	J. Catalano	Closed	30.00	30.00
Sports Impressions **Football Steins**				
90-02-001 Dan Marino	J. Catalano	Closed	30.00	30.00
91-02-002 Jim Kelly	J. Catalano	Closed	30.00	30.00

Index

COLLECTORS' INFORMATION BUREAU:
Your Complete Source for Information on Limited Edition Collectibles

NATIONAL DEALER DIRECTORY

Directory to Limited Edition Collectible Stores

- Features over 1,000 stores coast-to-coast and in Canada.
- For collectors who wish to purchase collectibles nationwide by phone, mail and in person. A handy guide for travelers!
- Listings include location, phone, store hours, collectible lines and more!
- $14.95 plus shipping and handling.

SECOND EDITION

Directory to Secondary Market Retailers
Buying and Selling Limited Edition Artwork

- For collectors who want to buy or sell retired collectibles (plates, figurines, cottages, dolls, bells, Christmas ornaments, steins and graphics).
- Featuring 150 of today's most respected secondary market dealers and exchanges nationwide!
- Full page business histories provide valuable insight into the companies and their methods of buying and selling collectibles.
- Offers an inside track on locating hard-to-find collectibles.
- $11.95 plus shipping and handling.

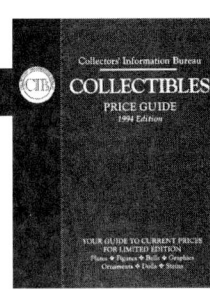

COMPREHENSIVE VALUE GUIDE

AVAILABLE APRIL 1995

Collectibles Price Guide

- 200 plus-page Price Index published annually each spring.
- Over 35,000 values for Limited Edition plates, figurines, cottages, bells, graphics, Christmas ornaments, dolls and steins.
- Secondary Market Buy-Sell Information.
- Listings for over 175 companies including Department 56, Swarovski, David Winter Cottages, Hallmark Ornaments, Lladro, Precious Moments, Hummel and Lilliput Lane.

AVAILABLE BY SUBSCRIPTION!

"C.I.B. Report & Showcase" Newsletter

- Latest news from over 80 leading collectibles manufacturers.
- Featuring new products, artists, club information, awards and more!
- 40 plus-page, easy-to-read format. Product photos and color throughout.
- Published quarterly — January, April, July and October.
- Introductory subscription rate — $15.00 plus shipping and handling.

PLEASE USE ORDER FORM ON REVERSE SIDE

Use This Form For Easy Ordering!

Quantity	Description	Price Each	Total
_____	**Directory to Limited Edition Collectible Stores**	$14.95	_____
_____	**Directory to Secondary Market Retailers**	$11.95	_____
_____	**Collectibles Price Guide**	$10.95	_____
_____	**"C.I.B. Report & Showcase"**	$15.00	_____

Shipping (see chart)		_____
Handling charge (per order)		$1.00
Illinois residents add 7.75% sales tax		_____

SHIPPING CHARGES:
Up to $14.95	$1.50
$15.00 - $22.95	$2.50
$23.00 - $61.00	$4.00
$62.00 and up	10% of total order

All orders must be prepaid.
Please allow 2 weeks for delivery.

GRAND TOTAL _____

SEND TO:

Name_____

Address_____

City_____ State_____ Zip _____

Telephone Number (_____) _____

METHOD OF PAYMENT:

❑ My check or money order, payable to the Collectors' Information Bureau, is enclosed.

❑ Please charge my credit card:
  ❑ VISA   ❑ MasterCard

Account Number_____

Expiration Date_____

Signature_____

Prices subject to change without notice. Please write us for our Canadian price list.

MAIL ORDERS TO: Order Dept., Collectors' Information Bureau
5065 Shoreline Road, Suite 200, Barrington, IL 60010

MG95

Notes

Notes